To Ewan from Mum
Last day of school 27/5/05

THE TIMES

Book of English Verse

THE TIMES

Book of English Verse

Compiled by Edward Leeson

TED SMART

This edition produced for The Book People Ltd, Hall Wood Avenue, Haydock, St Helens WA11 9UL

HarperCollins*Publishers*
Westerhill Road, Glasgow G64 2QT

The Collins website is www.collins.co.uk

This compilation © HarperCollins*Publishers* 2004
Introduction © 2004 Harold Bloom

The Times is a registered trademark of Times Newspapers Ltd

First published 2004

Reprint 10 9 8 7 6 5 4 3 2 1 0

ISBN 0-00-770845-9

This anthology was compiled by Edward Leeson who also produced most of the annotations;
the publishers would also like to thank Mike Munro and John Gardner for their contributions
to the annotations.

A catalogue record for this book is available from the British Library.

Typeset by Davidson Pre-Press Graphics Ltd, Glasgow

Printed in Italy by Legoprint

CONTENTS

CONTENTS

CONTENTS

INTRODUCTION

The full range of English poetry is extraordinary, both in its diversity and in its splendour. This anthology remarkably is able to suggest something of both that variety and that magnificence.

The greatest English poets certainly include the sequence of Chaucer, Spenser, Shakespeare, Milton, Blake and Wordsworth. And yet these six do not, in themselves, encompass the full nature of English poetic achievement. Drayton, Marlowe, Ralegh, Donne, Ben Jonson comprise an extraordinary company of Elizabethan poets. When one moves on to George Herbert, Andrew Marvell, Dryden, Pope and Dr Johnson the level of eloquence and of wisdom maintains itself.

With nineteenth-century Romanticism, in the wake of Wordsworth, the wealth of English poetry augments almost beyond limit. Coleridge, Byron, Shelley, John Clare, Keats, the Brownings and Tennyson maintain the distinction of the tradition. What particularly delights me about nineteenth-century English poetry is its grand eccentrics: Beddoes, Edward Lear, Patmore, the Rossettis and Lewis Carroll. If one adds to these the posthumously published poetry of Gerard Manley Hopkins and the enduring (though now unfashionable) work of Swinburne, one wonders if even the English Renaissance fostered so idiosyncratic an array of genius.

Twentieth-century poetry finds its great figures in Hardy, Housman, Kipling, Yeats (surely the strongest in his age), Wilfred Owen, T. S. Eliot (if, indeed, he was English), D. H. Lawrence, W. H. Auden, Seamus Heaney and Geoffrey Hill.

The English language itself is a unique blend of Germanic and Latin strains. One way of demonstrating the superiority of Chaucer and Shakespeare even to the greatest of those who came after them is the exuberance with which initially Chaucer and, following his example, Shakespeare exploited the double origins of the language. Though there are other major European traditions of poetry – Italian, French, Spanish, Russian, German – none of them had anything quite like the linguistic resources that English afforded Chaucer and Shakespeare.

And yet one might assert that the special excellence of the English tradition in poetry transcends the linguistic instrument. Whatever the theology or the metaphysics or the aesthetics of individual poets, there is an enduring capacity in most of the major figures for what Blake termed Vision. Vision, in this sense, is the gift of seeing the objects of sense perception charged with a higher degree of spiritual intensity than normally is available to our sensibilities. Because, in their very different ways, the English poets have had this impulse towards Vision, they have inspired generation after generation of readers to at least approach the threshold of transcendental possibilities.

Harold Bloom

FAVOURITE POEMS
(selected by *Times* Journalists)

Westron Wynde – *Anonymous* (page 1)

ONE of the great strengths of that miraculous author we call 'Anon' is his – or her – directness and simplicity. This poem, or song, has only four lines, yet its images are absolutely alive. The wind will bring the rain; the rain – the small rain, not a storm, a rain like tears – brings longing for the lover, who may be male or female, alive or dead. The poem's power inheres in this ambiguity, because it allows every reader into the desire expressed. It is particular, it is universal: there are few better expressions of possibility and loss.

ERICA WAGNER

The Nun's Priest's Tale – *Geoffrey Chaucer* (page 14)

IF the Nun's Priest himself is among the most shadowy of Chaucer's pilgrims, the chief character of his tale, the cockerel Chauntecleer, is one of the poet's most vivid and all too human creations. Schoolchildren may best remember this hero for his sexual athleticism (described in lines sometimes missing from educational selections); but for six hundred years readers have laughed at many different reflections of themselves and their leaders in this flawed sage of the farmyard.

Since this is a *Times* anthology, it can be admitted that even editors may occasionally lose touch with common sense, become a bit pompous, perhaps credulous, prone to flattery and to the use of more classical quotations than are good for us. Whoever feels or sees such symptoms coming on should immediately turn to England's greatest literary bird and his cautionary tale.

PETER STOTHARD (Editor of *The Times* 1992–2002)

Lycidas – *John Milton* (page 140)

BECAUSE it is deeply unfashionable. Because it is also deeply classical, but is nevertheless stiff with romantic, metaphysical and surrealist undertones. Because references to Alpheus, Hippotades, Bellerus and such are unintelligible to many today, making the elegy irritating and unreadable. Because its change of gear for the hungry sheep is as astonishing as Donne's in 'At the round earth's imagined corners'. Because its catalogue of spring flowers is almost up to two in Shakespeare. Because it talks sense about our contemporary idol, Celebrity, and our contemporary bogy, Death. Because it deals with a modern world in which the good die young, and false priests and poets prevail. Because it contains the most famous crux in English literature, 'that two-handed engine at the door'. Because it contains the most common misquotation in English literature: 'Tomorrow to fresh woods, and pastures new'. (Not *fields.*) Because it is beautiful.

PHILIP HOWARD

To His Coy Mistress – *Andrew Marvell* (page 252)

THIS poem is perfection, and has perfectly measured my life. How we pubescent schoolboys sniggered at the necrophilic imagery ('then worms shall try/That long-preserved virginity') without understanding it; how, when at art college in the liberated sixties, we regarded it as just about the classiest chat-up line for having it away in all literature; and how, in middle age with Time's wingèd chariot practically at the door, is its timeless message even stronger, though chance would be a fine thing.

I love it for its morbid, mordant humour ('The grave's a fine and private place,/But none, I think, do there embrace') and for an urgent tumescent climax which cries out loud.

It's just a crying shame that it was written by a politician (Marvell was a Humberside MP after the Restoration of 1660). Which goes to show that nothing, not even this, is perfect.

PETER BROOKES

Sally in Our Alley – *Henry Carey* (page 289)

HENRY CAREY wrote 'Sally in Our Alley' after he had seen a young courting couple walking through London. It was written from life, and its directness and vitality are what charm me.

Carey himself was one of the outer members of the Pope circle – Pope subscribed to an edition of his poems; a composer as well as a songwriter – Handel was another subscriber. He wrote comic plays, like early Fielding. He lived a life of poverty, but was known as Merry Harry Carey; he died by his own hand.

As a minor poet he has his own voice. He probably also wrote the words, but not the music, of 'God Save the King'.

WILLIAM REES-MOGG

An Essay on Criticism – *Alexander Pope* (page 291)

IT is easy to criticise, and so Alexander Pope's An Essay on Criticism provides critical lessons on the art of criticism itself. If I were to criticise, in the harsh, inexact sense of the word, I would say that the work is a little too long and a few of the rhymes are forced to fit, but the elegance and grace of the writing and delicacy of the thought make clear that the words are talking about more than writing. It has moments of overbearing pretentiousness and is reverential in its references, but, in its most enlightening moments, the poem captures the essence of its own thought: 'True wit is nature to advantage dressed, What oft was thought but ne'er so well expressed'.

ROBERT THOMSON (Editor of *The Times* from 2002)

I Remember, I Remember – *Thomas Hood* (page 512)

'STRANGE,' wrote Noel Coward, 'the potency of cheap music.' This potent poem by an otherwise forgotten Victorian poet is uncomplicated and perhaps self-pitying – cheap would not be quite the right word – yet intense. It was the first serious poem which meant anything to me as a teenager – for older children as well as adults think sadly of when they were younger and things seemed simpler. In *The Mill on the Floss* George Eliot reflects on the same feelings less despairingly. 'We could never have loved the earth so well if we had no childhood in it,' she writes, 'what novelty is worth that sweet monotony where everything is known and loved because it is known?' But she reflects too on the darker side: 'Those bitter sorrows of childhood! – when sorrow is all new and strange, when hope has not yet got wings to fly beyond the days and weeks, and the space from summer to summer seems measureless'.

MATTHEW PARRIS

Maud – *Alfred, Lord Tennyson* (page 537)

LIKE most Eng. Lit. students of the 1970s, I was quite defeated by Alfred Tennyson when I first read him. I wept over *In Memoriam* for the wrong reasons. Twenty years later, however, researching the novel that became *Tennyson's Gift*, I started to read him seriously and became obsessed with *Maud* – his strange 1400-line experimental 'monodrama' of 1855. In a series of detached, self-contained lyrics ('See what a lovely shell', 'Dead, long dead', 'Come into the garden, Maud') Tennyson lays out a disjointed story of a disordered consciousness, a mind turned mad by fear of love. Tennyson himself was obsessed with *Maud*, partly because it met with hostile reactions on publication. He called it his 'bantling abused', and read it aloud in its entirety (to guests, to hosts) whenever he got the chance. For my own part, I try to shoe-horn the words 'Come into the garden, Maud' into every novel and play I write. It makes me feel I am doing my bit.

LYNNE TRUSS

Dover Beach – *Matthew Arnold* (page 568)

THIS poem is so achingly poignant. Arnold sets up a 'calm', 'fair', 'tranquil' and 'sweet' seascape and landscape, underpinned by the permanence of the 'vast' cliffs and the predictability of the tides. His picture represents the solidity of Victorian society, buttressed by Christianity.

It was Darwin's theory of evolution that brought Arnold's structure crashing down. The permanence and predictability of Christian faith were exploded by the notion that human beings were descended from primates. The 'Sea of Faith' had once been 'at the full', but now Arnold can hear only its 'melancholy, long, withdrawing roar'.

His recourse is to appeal to the love of his sweetheart, but even that seems scant solace in a world that has 'neither joy, nor love, nor light/Nor certitude, nor peace, nor help for pain'. My heart bleeds for him.

I learned this poem one night at a party conference in Bournemouth. The next day was gloriously sunny, and I walked barefoot along the 'long line of spray' as I recited it to myself. Whenever I read it, I think of the melancholy beauty of the south coast, with its cliffs 'Glimmering and vast', its 'high strand' and its 'tranquil bay'.

The 'eternal note of sadness' haunts me still.

MARY ANN SIEGHART

The Darkling Thrush – *Thomas Hardy* (page 595)

IN the end, I suppose, the favourite has to be the one which runs most often through your head. This one is deceptively simple: rhyming, metrical, easy to grasp. Yet the more you contemplate the moment the more powerful it becomes.

Here is the bitter English winter dusk, the desolate spirit of a depressed farming world in times of fearful change, the time of Jude and Tess. The pastoral lyres are broken, and Hardy confronts the grimmest face of the countryside. Whereon the old half-starved thrush breaks into a song so joyful that no crude mechanistic explanation can belittle it. This is the Hardy who said he would go to the Christmas stable at midnight to see the oxen kneel, 'Hoping it might be so'; he perfectly expresses the common human moment when the only hope possible is the hope you cannot fully believe or express.

LIBBY PURVES

The Convergence of the Twain – *Thomas Hardy*
(page 597)

THIS is Hardy at his pessimistic best. It is said that Beethoven, on his deathbed, raised himself up and shook a fist at the heavens. Hardy shakes a fist at malevolent Fate all the time in his poetry and novels, but here he balances his anger by acknowledgement of man's 'vaingloriousness' (what a quintessential Hardy word) in building the 'unsinkable' *Titanic*.

He conjures up incredible images of hubris shattered: the 'sea-worm', for instance, crawling over mirrors 'meant/To glass the opulent'. What it all adds up to is an unforgettable picture of mankind – for all our ingenuity and ambition – hurtling inexorably towards extinction, our dreams turned to dust by the 'Spinner of the Years'.

It's not a happy poem, but it is the stuff of great tragedy. And, on a technical note, note how each stanza is shaped like an ocean liner. Masterly.

RICHARD MORRISON

The Windhover – *Gerard Manley Hopkins*
(page 605)

'MY heart in hiding/Stirred for a bird. . . .' Well, my heart does that on a more or less daily basis. The most gorgeous and attractive thing about the poem is its sudden rejoicing: the heart-stirring that, as a birder and country person, I have as a routine companion. The bouncing, baffling sprung rhythms catch the moment as the bird breaks from his hover and whizzes down the wind: the simple, complex joy of it.

Unending complexities. The poem is explicitly religious, and yet, for me, the true religion is the bird itself – in the symbol, not in what it symbolises for Hopkins. The religiosity of the poem is none the less important to me: conservation has become for man a form of secular religion, a matter of shared and individual duty, shared and individual joy. There is a profound joy in a morning sighting; but it is the Darwinian wonders of life, and our human duties to it, that are a billion times lovelier – and more dangerous.

SIMON BARNES

Anthem for Doomed Youth – *Wilfrid Owen*
(page 646)

THIS is at once the most lyrical and the most savage of Owen's First World War poems, a furious denunciation of the slaughter set to the cadence of a service in a country church: prayers, bells, choirs, candles alongside the monstrous anger of the guns and demented noise of shells meting out pointless death. There is nothing beautiful or noble about the death he depicts, of cattle bred for slaughter, nor in the girls left to mourn dead lovers in the sad shires of home. The poem is a direct antithesis to the 'Keep the home fires burning' mentality that Owen despised, the 'old lie' of *dulce et decorum est*. The light comes not from merry home fires, but the candle of a pallid, grieving girl, bringing down the blinds on an idyllic England that also perished in the trenches. This is the anthem that, for me, most powerfully evokes Owen's doomed youth: within a year of writing it, the poet was killed in a German machine gun attack at the Sambre Canal. He was twenty-five years old.

BEN MCINTYRE

Snow – *Louis MacNeice* (page 661)

LOUIS MACNEICE takes small things, everyday things, and makes them extraordinary. It is his particular magic. I love the way his poems tell little stories, and his descriptions always surprise because the imagery is so accurate, almost journalistic, but also very emotional. This poem is about how, in an instant, the world can seem a different place. It is about infinite possibilities and about that moment when something that you think you've seen 100 times transforms and becomes 'suddenly rich'. Anyone who loves to observe knows that the world IS exactly like this, as crazy and as haphazard as he says, though MacNeice is particularly good at seeing the beautiful.

ANN TRENEMAN

How To Get On In Society – *Sir John Betjeman*
(page 656)

PHILIP LARKIN said that the quickest way to start a punch-up between two British literary critics was to ask them what they think of the poems of Sir John Betjeman. Betjeman's 'How To Get On In Society' is just the sort of poem that might divide readers. It is easy enough to see it as a sniggering sneer at the solecisms of the over-striving middle classes, with all their talk of fish-knives and toilets, and of couches and cruets. But if you tilt your angle of vision just a little, as if peering at an Escher drawing, you can just as easily see this verse as a cosy, rather endearing paean to the suburbs of which Betjeman was so fond. The joke, in such a reading, falls on the would-be toffs who took all Nancy Mitford's 'U' and 'non-U' stuff seriously, without ever twigging that straining so zealously to be 'U' was, of course, very 'non-U'. Anyway, Betjeman himself was hardly in a position to be hoity-toity. Lady Chetwode grandly looked down her nose at Betjeman, saying, 'We invite people like that to tea, but we don't marry them'; which must have been sobering, since she later became his mother-in-law.

JOE JOSEPH

Poem in October – *Dylan Thomas*
(page 667)

DURING the eighties, me and my seven brothers and sisters lived in a broke-roofed caravan in Wales; and when we weren't trying to dig a tunnel through the hill, or make a swing using a cow's thighbone and a length of rope, we were sent, barefoot and poncho'd, down to the village to do 'little shops'. It was while we were waiting for two pounds of back to go in the slicer that Stompy Jim came in the shop. Jim stomped because a tractor had gone over his leg, and it was now parcelled up in polythene and string against the rain. While he waited for it to heal he was village-bound and inclined to quote. He leaned against the counter and personally told us 'Poem in October', like it was a message sent down the hill that morning from Thomas. The shop-lady imperturbably sliced. We walked home on hot tarmac singing 'Heron-priested shore' to each other, so we wouldn't forget. Then Eddie cut his foot open on a broken bottle, and we did.

CAITLIN MORAN

ANONYMOUS

'SUMER IS ICUMEN IN . . .'

SUMER is icumen in –
Lhude sing, cuccu!
Groweth sed and bloweth med
And springth the wude nu.
Sing, cuccu!   5

Awe bleteth after lomb,
Lhouth after calve cu,
Bulluc sterteth, bucke verteth.
Murie sing, cuccu!
Cuccu, cuccu,   10
Wel singes thu, cuccu!
Ne swik thu naver nu!

Sing, cuccu, nu! Sing, cuccu!
Sing, cuccu! Sing, cuccu, nu!

Thirteenth century

'SUMER IS ICUMEN IN': 2 **Lhude:** loud **cuccu:** cuckoo 3 **sed:** seed
med: meadow 4 **springth the wude nu:** leaves are on the trees now
6 **Awe:** ewe **lomb:** lamb 7 **Lhouth after calve cu:** cow lows after calf
8 **sterteth:** leapeth **verteth:** farteth 9 **Murie:** merry 11 **thu:** thou
12 **Ne:** not **swik:** stop **naver:** never

'MAIDEN IN THE MOR LAY'

MAIDEN in the mor lay,
    In the mor lay,
Sevenyst fulle, sevenist fulle,
Maiden in the mor lay,
    In the mor lay,   5
Sevenistes fulle ant a day.

Welle was hire mete;
    Wat was hire mete?
    The primerole ant the –
    The primerole ant the –   10
Welle was hire mete;
Wat was hire mete? –
    The primerole ant the violet.

Welle was hire dryng;
    Wat was hire dryng?   15
The chelde water of the welle-spring.
Welle was hire bour;
    Wat was hire bour?
The rede rose an te lilie flour.

Fourteenth century

'MAIDEN IN THE MOR LAY': 1 **mor:** moor **lay:** dwelt 3 **Sevenyst:** seven
nights 6 **ant:** and 7 **Welle:** plentiful **mete:** food 9 **primerole:**
primrose 14 **dryng:** drink 16 **chelde:** cold **welle-spring:** spring
17 **bour:** dwelling 19 **an te:** and the

'I SYNG OF A MAYDEN . . .'

I SYNG of a mayden that is makeles,
King of alle kynges to here sone che ches.

He cam also stylle ther his moder was
As dew in Aprylle that fallyt on the gras.

He cam also stylle to his moderes bowr   5
As dew in Aprille that fallyt on the flour.

He cam also stylle ther his moder lay
As dew in Aprille that fallyt on the spray.

Moder and maydyn was never non but che –
Wel may swych a lady Godes moder be!   10

Fifteenth century

'I SYNG OF A MAYDEN': 1 **makeles:** mateless, i.e. without equal 2 **to
here sone che ches:** she chose for her son 3 **also stylle:** as silently
there: where **moder:** mother 4 **fallyt:** falleth 5 **bowr:** dwelling
6 **flour:** flower 8 **spray:** leaf 10 **swych:** such

'ADAM LAY IBOWNDYN . . .'

ADAM lay ibowndyn, bowndyn in a bond,
Fowre thowsand wynter thowt he not to long.

And al was for an appil, an appil that he tok,
As clerkes fyndyn wretyn in here book.

Ne hadde the appil take ben, the appil take ben,   5
Ne hadde never our Lady a ben hevene qwen.

Blyssid be the tyme that appil take was,
Therfore we mown syngyn *'Deo gracias'*.

Fifteenth century

'ADAM LAY IBOWNDYN': 1 **ibowndyn:** bound 2 **thowt:** thought
4 **clerkes:** scholars **here:** their 5 **Ne hadde:** had not 6 **our Lady:**
Virgin Mary **a ben:** have been 8 **mown:** may ***Deo gracias':** 'Thanks
be to God'

'WESTRON WYNDE . . .'

WESTRON wynde when wyll thou blow,
The smalle rayne downe can rayne –
Cryst, yf my love wer in my armys
And I yn my bed agayne!

Fifteenth century

'WESTRON WYNDE': 2 **smalle:** gentle

1

JOHN GOWER

From CONFESSIO AMANTIS

THANNE is noght al mi weie in vein,
Somdeil I mai the betre fare,
Whan I, that mai noght fiele hir bare,
Mai lede hire clothed in myn arm:
Bot afterward it doth me harm   5
Of pure ymaginacioun;
For thanne this collacioun
I make unto miselven ofte,
And seie, 'Ha lord, hou sche is softe,
How sche is round, hou sche is smal!   10
Now wolde god I hadde hire al
Withoute danger at mi wille!'
And thanne I sike and sitte stille,
Of that I se mi besi thoght
Is torned ydel into noght.   15
Bot for al that lete I ne mai,
Whanne I se time an other dai,
That I ne do my besinesse
Unto mi ladi worthinesse.
For I therto mi wit afaite   20
To se the times and awaite
What is to done and what to leve:
And so, whan time is, be hir leve,
What thing sche bit me don, I do,
And wher sche bit me gon, I go,   25
And whanne hir liste to clepe, I come.
                              [Lines 1138–63]

CONFESSIO AMANTIS: 1 **weie:** way, road 2 **Somdeil:** somewhat 3 **fiele:** know 5–6 **doth me harm . . . ymaginacioun:** i.e. I am tormented by thinking about her constantly 7 **collacioun:** reflection 11 **wolde god:** would to God 11–12 **al/Withoute danger:** without (the lady's) disdain, i.e. lovingly 12 **wille:** desire 13 **sike:** sigh 14 **Of that:** because **se:** see **mi besi thoght:** my devotion 15 **Is . . . noght:** is pointless 16 **lete I ne mai:** I cannot help myself 18 **besinesse:** devotion 19 **mi ladi:** my lady's 20 **afaite:** prepare 22 **done:** do **leve:** let go 23 **be hir leve:** by her leave 24 **bit:** bids **don:** do 25 **gon:** go 26 **liste to clepe:** cares to call

WILLIAM LANGLAND

From PIERS PLOWMAN

[BELLING THE CAT]

THAN ran ther a route of ratones as hit were
And smale muys with hem, mo then a thousand
Comen til a conseyl for here comune profyt.
For a cat of a court cam whan hym likede
And overlep hem lightliche and laghte hem alle at
     wille   5
And playde with somme perilously and potte hem ther
     hym lykede.

'And yf we groche of his game a wol greve us sore,
To his clees clawe us and in his cloches us halde
That us lotheth the lyf ar he lette us passe.
Myghte we with eny wyt his wille withsytte   10
We myhte be lordes a-lofte and lyve as us luste.'
   A ratoun of renown moste resonable of tonge
Sayde, 'Y have seyen grete syres in cytees and in
     townes
Bere beyus of bryghte gold al aboute here nekkes
And colers of crafty werk, bothe knyghtes and
     squieres.   15
Wer ther a belle on here beygh, by Iesu, as me
     thynketh,
Men myghte ywete where thei wente and here way
     roume.
Ryght so,' quath the raton, 'reison me shewith
A belle to byggen of bras other of bryghte sylver
And knytten hit on a coler for oure comune profyt
And hongen hit aboute the cattes halse, thanne here
     we mowe   21
Wher he riht othere reste or rometh to pleye;
And yf hym lust for to layke than loke we mowe
And apere in his presence the while hym pleye lyketh
And yf hym wratheth ben we war and his way roume.'
   Alle thise route of ratones to this resoun thei
     assentide,   26
Ac tho the belle was ybroughte and on the beygh
     hangid
Ther ne was non of al the route for al the reame of
     Fraunce
That derste have ybounde the belle aboute the kattes
     nekke
Ne have hanged it aboute his hals al Yngelond to
     wynne;   30
And leten here labour ylost and al here longe study.
   A mous that moche good couthe, as me tho
     thoughte,
Strok forth sturnely and stod byfore hem alle
And to the route of ratones rehersede thise wordes:
'Thow we hadde ykuld the cat yut shulde ther come
     another   35
To crache us and alle oure kynde thogh we crope
     under benches.
Forthy y conseile for oure comune profit lat the cat
     yworthe
And be nevere so bold the belle hym to shewe.
For y herde my syre sayn, sevene yer ypassed,
Ther the cat is but a kytoun the court is ful elynge.   40
Wyttenesse at holy wryt, who-so kan rede:
Ve terre ubi puer est Rex.
Y seye it for me,' quod the mous, 'y se so muche aftur,
Shal never the cat ne kytoun be my conseil be greved
Ne carpen of here colers that costede me nevere.   45
And thow hit costed my catel, byknowen y ne wolde
But soffre and sey nought and that is the beste
Til that meschief amende hem that many man
     chasteth.

For many mannys malt we muys wolde distruye
And the route of ratones of reste men awake 50
Ne were the cat of the court and yonge kitones
   toward;
For hadde ye ratones youre reik, ye couthe nat reule
   yow-selven.'
   What this meteles bymeneth, ye men that ben
   merye,
Devyne ye, for y ne dar, by dere god almyhten.

[C text: Prologue, lines 165–218]

PIERS PLOWMAN: 1 **Than:** then **route:** crowd **ratones:** rats **hit:** it 2 **smale muys:** little mice **mo then:** more than 3 **Comen til:** come to **conseyl:** meeting **here:** their **comune profyt:** common good 4 **cat of a court:** probably refers to John of Gaunt, who came to wield great power during the minority of Richard II (see line 42), although Parliament attempted to curb his authority. (Later Archibald, 5th Earl of Angus, father of the poet Gavin Douglas, was nicknamed 'Bell-the-Cat' because, unlike the rats and mice in the fable, he *was* prepared to make a stand against authority) 5 **overlep hem lightliche:** pounced on them easily **laghte hem alle at wille:** grabbed them as he pleased 6 **potte hem ther hym lykede:** put them where he chose 7 **groche:** grumble, complain **a wol greve us sore:** he will make us suffer for it badly 8 **clees:** claws **cloches:** clutches **halde:** hold 9 **us lotheth the lyf:** we wish we were dead **ar:** ere, before 10 **with eny wyt:** by any means **withsytte:** oppose 11 **a-lofte:** on high **as us luste:** as we please 12 **resonable of tonge:** eloquent, persuasive 13 **seyen:** seen **grete syres:** important gentlemen 14 **Bere:** wear **beyus:** necklaces **here:** their 15 **colers of crafty werk:** finely fashioned collars 16 **here beygh:** their collars 17 **ywete:** know **here way roume:** avoid them 18 **quath:** quoth, said 19 **byggen:** bought **other:** or 21 **halse:** neck **thanne here we mowe:** then we might hear 22 **riht:** rides, i.e. is on the prowl **othere reste:** or rest 23 **lust for to layke:** desires to play **loke we mowe:** we can look 25 **hym wratheth:** he is angry **ben we war and his way roume:** let us be wary and keep out of his way 26 **assentide:** assented 27 **Ac:** but 28 **reame:** realm 29 **derste:** dared to 31 **leten:** reckoned **study:** deliberation 32 **moche good couthe:** knew a thing or two 33 **Strok forth sturnely:** came forward boldly 34 **rehersede:** repeated 35 **Thow . . . cat:** even if we killed the cat **yut:** yet 36 **crache:** scratch **crope:** crept 37 **Forthy y conseile:** therefore I suggest **lat the cat yworthe:** leave the cat alone 40 **Ther:** where **elynge:** miserable 42 *Ve terre ubi puer est Rex:* 'Ill fares the land where a child is king' (Richard II was only 9 years old when he came to the throne in 1377) 43 **Y seye it for me:** for myself 44 **be my conseil be greved:** be harmed by any advice I gave 45 **Ne carpen . . . nevere:** Nor complain of any collars that I helped pay for 46 **thow hit costed my catel:** though it cost me everything I possessed **byknowen y ne wolde:** know that I would not 48 **amende hem:** teaches them better **chasteth:** chastens 49 **many mannys malt:** many men's malt **distruye:** destroy 50 **of reste men awake:** disturb men's rest 51 **Ne were:** if there were not **toward:** at hand 52 **hadde . . . yow-selven:** if you rats had your own way, you would not know how to govern yourselves 53 **meteles:** dream **bymeneth:** means **ben:** are 54 **Devyne:** divine **y ne dar:** I dare not **dere god almyhten:** dear God Almighty

GEOFFREY CHAUCER

From THE CANTERBURY TALES

THE GENERAL PROLOGUE

WHAN that Aprill with his shoures soote
The droghte of March hath perced to the roote,
And bathed every veyne in swich licour
Of which vertu engendred is the flour;
Whan Zephirus eek with his sweete breeth 5
Inspired hath in every holt and heeth
The tendre croppes, and the yonge sonne
Hath in the Ram his halve cours yronne,
And smale foweles maken melodye,
That slepen al the nyght with open ye 10
(So priketh hem nature in hir corages);
Thanne longen folk to goon on pilgrimages,
And palmeres for to seken straunge strondes,
To ferne halwes, kowthe in sondry londes;
And specially from every shires ende 15
Of Engelond to Caunterbury they wende,
The hooly blisful martir for to seke,
That hem hath holpen whan that they were seeke.
   Bifil that in that seson on a day,
In Southwerk at the Tabard as I lay 20
Redy to wenden on my pilgrymage
To Caunterbury with ful devout corage,
At nyght was come into that holstelrye
Wel nyne and twenty in a compaignye,
Of sondry folk, by aventure yfalle 25
In felaweshipe, and pilgrimes were they alle,
That toward Caunterbury wolden ryde.
The chambres and the stables weren wyde,
And wel we weren esed atte beste.
And shortly, whan the sonne was to reste, 30
So hadde I spoken with hem everichon
That I was of hir felaweshipe anon,
And made forward erly for to ryse,
To take oure wey ther as I yow devyse.
   But nathelees, whil I have tyme and space, 35
Er that I ferther in this tale pace,
Me thynketh it acordaunt to resoun
To telle yow al the condicioun
Of ech of hem, so as it semed me,
And whiche they weren, and of what degree, 40
And eek in what array that they were inne;
And at a knyght than wol I first bigynne.
   A KNYGHT ther was, and that a worthy man,
That fro the tyme that he first bigan
To riden out, he loved chivalrie, 45

GENERAL PROLOGUE: 1 **his showres soote:** its sweet showers 2 **droghte:** dryness **perced:** pierced 3 **veyne:** vein of a leaf **swich licour:** such moisture 4 **vertu:** life-giving power **flour:** flower 5 **Zephirus:** the west wind 6 **Inspired:** breathed life **holt and heeth:** wood and field 7 **croppes:** new shoots **yonge sonne:** i.e., following the vernal equinox, the sun is at the beginning of its annual cycle 8 **Ram:** Aries (sign of the Zodiac) 10 **ye:** eye 11 **priketh:** spurs, urges **corages:** hearts 13 **palmeres:** pilgrims **straunge strondes:** foreign shores 14 **ferne halwes:** distant shrines **kowthe:** known **sondry londes:** various countries 17 **hooly blisful martir:** holy blessed martyr (Thomas Becket (murdered in 1170) 18 **That hem hath holpen:** who helped them 19 **Bifil:** it happened 25 **by aventure yfalle:** by chance fallen 28 **wyde:** spacious 29 **esed atte beste:** given the best accommodation 31 **everichon:** every one 33 **made forward:** agreed 34 **devyse:** describe 37 **accordaunt to resoun:** sensible 38 **condicioun:** circumstances 40 **degree:** social rank 41 **eek:** also **in what array . . . inne:** how they were dressed 42 **wol:** will 45 **chivalrie:** knightly deeds

Trouthe and honour, fredom and curteisie.
Ful worthy was he in his lordes werre,
And therto hadde he riden, no man ferre,
As wel in cristendom as in hethenesse,
And evere honoured for his worthynesse. 50
At Alisaundre he was whan it was wonne.
Ful ofte tyme he hadde the bord bigonne
Aboven alle nacions in Pruce;
In Lettow hadde he reysed and in Ruce,
No Cristen man so ofte of his degree. 55
In Gernade at the seege eek hadde he be
Of Algezir, and riden in Belmarye.
At Lyeys was he and at Satalye,
Whan they were wonne; and in the Grete See
At many a noble armee hadde he be. 60
At mortal batailles hadde he been fiftene,
And foughten for oure feith at Tramyssene
In lystes thries, and ay slayn his foo.
This ilke worthy knyght hadde been also
Somtyme with the lord of Palatye 65
Agayn another hethen in Turkye.
And everemoore he hadde a sovereyn prys;
And though that he were worthy, he was wys,
And of his port as meeke as is a mayde.
He nevere yet no vileynye ne sayde 70
In al his lyf unto no maner wight.
He was a verray, parfit gentil knyght.
But, for to tellen yow of his array,
His hors were goode, but he was nat gay.
Of fustian he wered a gypon 75
Al bismotered with his habergeon,
For he was late ycome from his viage,
And wente for to doon his pilgrymage.
    With hym there was his sone, a yong SQUIER,
A lovere and a lusty bacheler, 80
With lokkes crulle as they were leyd in presse.
Of twenty yeer of age he was, I gesse.
Of his stature he was of evene lengthe,
And wonderly delyvere, and of greet strengthe.
And he hadde been somtyme in chyvachie 85

In Flaundres, in Artoys, and Pycardie,
And born hym weel, as of so litel space,
In hope to stonden in his lady grace.
Embrouded was he, as it were a meede
Al ful of fresshe floures, whyte and reede. 90
Syngynge he was, or floytynge, al the day;
He was as fressh as is the month of May.
Short was his gowne, with sleves longe and wyde.
Wel koude he sitte on hors and faire ryde.
He koude songes make and wel endite, 95
Juste and eek daunce, and weel purtreye and write.
So hoote he lovede that by nyghtertale
He sleep namoore than dooth a nyghtyngale.
Curteis he was, lowely, and servysable,
And carf biforn his fader at the table. 100
    A YEMAN hadde he and servantz namo
At that tyme, for hym liste ride so,
And he was clad in cote and hood of grene.
A sheef of pecock arwes, bright and kene,
Under his belt he bar ful thriftily 105
(Wel koude he dresse his takel yemanly:
His arwes drouped noght with fetheres lowe),
And in his hand he bar a myghty bowe.
A not heed hadde he, with a broun visage.
Of wodecraft wel koude he al the usage. 110
Upon his arm he bar a gay bracer,
And by his syde a swerd and a bokeler,
And on that oother syde a gay daggere
Harneised wel and sharp as point of spere;
A Cristopher on his brest of silver sheene. 115
An horn he bar, the bawdryk was of grene;
A forster was he, soothly, as I gesse.
    There was also a Nonne, a PRIORESSE,
That of hir smylyng was ful symple and coy;
Hire gretteste ooth was but by Seinte Loy; 120
And she was cleped madame Eglentyne.
Ful weel she soong the service dyvyne,
Entuned in hir nose ful semely,
And Frenssh she spak ful faire and fetisly,
After the scole of Stratford atte Bowe, 125

---

46 **Trouthe:** fidelity **fredom:** generosity **curteisie:** good manners 47 **werre:** war 48 **ferre:** further 49 **hethenesse:** heathen lands 51 **Alisaundre:** Alexandria 52 **hadde the bord bigonne:** had sat at the head of the table 53 **Pruce:** Prussia 54 **Lettow:** Lithuania **reysed:** gone on expeditions **Ruce:** Russia 56 **Gernade:** Granada **Algezir:** Algeciras 57 **Belmarye:** Benmarin (Morocco) 58 **Lycys:** Ayash, Turkey **Satalye:** Atalia, Turkey 59 **the Grete See:** the Mediterranean 60 **armee:** expedition 62 **Tramyssene:** Tlemcen, western Algeria 63 **lystes:** single combats **thries:** three 64 **ilke:** same 65 **Palatye:** Balat, Turkey 66 **Agayn:** against 67 **everemoore:** always **sovereyn prys:** high reputation 68 **And though . . . wys:** And though he was brave he was prudent 69 **port:** bearing 70 **no vileynye ne sayde:** never spoke rudely 71 **unto no maner wight:** to anyone 72 **verray:** true **parfit:** perfect **gentil:** noble 75 **fustian:** coarse cotton fabric **gypon:** tunic 76 **bismotered with:** soiled by **habergeon:** coat of mail 77 **viage:** a military expedition 80 **bacheler:** knight probationer 81 **lokkes crulle:** curly hair **presse:** curling iron 83 **evene:** moderate 84 **wonderly delyvere:** wonderfully agile 85 **chyvachie:** cavalry expedition

86 **Flaundres:** Flanders **Artoys:** Artois **Pycardie:** Picardy 87 **born hym:** acquitted himself **of so litel space:** in such a short time 88 **stonden in his lady grace:** win his lady's favour 89 **Embrouded:** embroidered **meede:** meadow 91 **floytynge:** playing the flute 95 **endite:** compose verses 96 **Juste:** joust **purtreye:** draw 97 **hoote:** passionately **namoore:** no more **nyghtertale:** night-time 99 **lowely:** modest **servysable:** willing to serve 100 **carf:** carved 101 **Yeman:** yeoman, gentleman servant **namo:** no more 102 **hym liste:** it pleased him 105 **ful thriftily:** very smartly 106 **Wel koude . . . lowe:** He knew well how to take proper care of his equipment; his arrows never fell short because they were badly balanced 109 **not:** close-cropped **broun:** swarthy 111 **gay bracer:** brightly coloured arm-guard, used by archers 112 **bokeler:** buckler, small shield 114 **Harneised:** mounted 115 **Cristopher:** small image of St Christopher, patron saint of travellers **sheene:** bright 116 **bawdryk:** baldric, shoulder strap 117 **forster:** forester 119 **ful symple and coy:** very modest and quiet 120 **Seinte Loy:** St Eligius (any joke Chaucer may have intended by this reference is now lost) 121 **cleped:** called 122 **soong the service dyvyne:** sung the liturgy 123 **Entuned:** intoned **ful semely:** very pleasingly 124 **fetisly:** elegantly 125 **the scole of Stratford atte Bowe:** i.e. not courtly French

For Frenssh of Parys was to hire unknowe.
At mete wel ytaught was she with alle:
She leet no morsel from hir lippes falle,
Ne wette hir fyngres in hir sauce depe;
Wel koude she carie a morsel and wel kepe   130
That no drope ne fille upon hire brest.
In curteisie was set ful muchel hir lest.
Hir over-lippe wyped she so clene
That in hir coppe ther was no ferthyng sene
Of grece, whan she dronken hadde hir draughte.   135
Ful semely after hir mete she raughte.
And sikerly she was of greet desport,
And ful plesaunt, and amyable of port,
And peyned hire to countrefete cheere
Of court, and to been estatlich of manere,   140
And to ben holden digne of reverence.
But, for to speken of hire conscience,
She was so charitable and so pitous
She wolde wepe, if that she saugh a mous
Kaught in a trappe, if it were deed or bledde.   145
Of smale houndes hadde she that she fedde
With rosted flessh, or milk and wastel-breed.
But soore wepte she if oon of hem were deed,
Or if men smoot it with a yerde smerte;
And al was conscience and tendre herte.   150
Ful semyly hir wympul pynched was,
Hir nose tretys, hir eyen greye as glas,
Hir mouth ful smal, and therto softe and reed;
But sikerly she hadde a fair forheed;
It was almoost a spanne brood, I trowe;   155
For, hardily, she was nat undergrowe.
Ful fetis was hir cloke, as I was war.
Of smal coral aboute hire arm she bar
A peire of bedes, gauded al with grene,
And theron heng a brooch of gold ful sheene,   160
On which ther was first write a crowned A,
And after *Amor vincit omnia.*
   Another NONNE with hire hadde she,
That was hir chapeleyne, and preestes thre.
   A MONK there was, a fair for the maistrie,   165

An outridere, that lovede venerie,
A manly man, to been an abbot able.
Ful many a deyntee hors hadde he in stable,
And whan he rood, men myghte his brydel heere
Gynglen in a whistlynge wynd als cleere   170
And eek as loude as dooth the chapel belle.
Ther as this lord was kepere of the celle,
The reule of seint Maure or of seint Beneit,
By cause that it was old and somdel streit
This ilke Monk leet olde thynges pace,   175
And heeld after the newe world the space.
He yaf nat of that text a pulled hen,
That seith that hunters ben nat hooly men,
Ne that a monk, whan he is recchelees,
Is likned til a fissh that is waterlees –   180
This is to seyn, a monk out of his cloystre.
But thilke text heeld he nat worth an oystre;
And I seyde his opinion was good.
What sholde he studie and make hymselven wood,
Upon a book in cloystre alwey to poure,   185
Or swynken with his handes, and laboure,
As Austyn bit? How shal the world be served?
Lat Austyn have his swynk to hym reserved!
Therfore he was a prikasour aright:
Grehoundes he hadde as swift as fowel in flight;   190
Of prikyng and of huntyng for the hare
Was al his lust, for no cost wolde he spare.
I seigh his sleves purfiled at the hond
With grys, and that the fyneste of a lond;
And, for to festne his hood under his chyn,   195
He hadde of gold ywroght a ful curious pyn;
A love-knotte in the gretter ende ther was.
His heed was balled, that shoon as any glas,
And eek his face, as he hadde been enoynt.
He was a lord ful fat and in good poynt;   200
His eyen stepe, and rollynge in his heed,
That stemed as a forneys of a leed;
His bootes souple, his hors in greet estaat.
Now certeinly he was a fair prelaat;
He was nat pale as a forpyned goost.   205

127 **At mete:** at dinner **with alle:** indeed 128 **leet:** let 130 **kepe:** take care 132 **lest:** desire 133 **over-lippe:** upper lip 134 **coppe:** cup **ferthyng:** spot (the size of a farthing, the smallest coin) 135 **grece:** grease 136 **Ful semely . . . raughte:** she reached for her food very politely 137 **sikerly:** certainly **of greet desport:** very good-humoured 138 **amyable of port:** of a friendly disposition 139–40 **peyned hire . . . Of Court:** took pains to imitate the manners of the Court 140 **estatlich of manere:** dignified 141 **ben holden:** be considered **digne of reverence:** worthy of respect 142 **conscience:** tender feeling 143 **pitous:** kind-hearted 144 **saugh:** saw 147 **rosted flesh:** roasted meat **wastel-breed:** fine white bread 148 **soore:** bitterly 149 **yerde:** stick **smerte:** soundly, brutally 151 **Ful semyly . . . was:** Her head-dress was very becomingly pleated 152 **tretys:** graceful 153 **therto:** moreover **reed:** red 154 **sikerly:** truly 155 **a spanne brood:** a span (about nine inches) broad **trowe:** believe 156 **hardily:** unquestionably 157 **fetis:** elegant 159 **peire of bedes:** a rosary 160 **sheene:** bright 161 **crowned A:** letter A topped with a crown 162 *Amor vincit omnia:* 'Love conquers all' 164 **chapelyne:** probably a secretary rather than a spiritual adviser 165 **a fair for the maistrie:** very fine

166 **outridere:** a monk who looked after monastic estates **venerie:** hunting 167 **manly:** virile, but perhaps suggesting great presence or force of personality 168 **deyntee:** valuable, fine 170 **Gynglen:** jingling **als cleere:** as clear 172 **celle:** subordinate monastery 173 **reule of Seint Maure . . . Seint Beneit:** the Rule of St Benedict, introduced into France by St Maure 174 **somdel streit:** somewhat strict 175–6 **This ilke . . . the space:** This same monk let old things pass and adopted the new ways 177 **yaf:** gave **pulled:** plucked 179 **recchelees:** neglectful of duty 180 **til:** to **waterlees:** out of water 182 **thilke:** that **nat worth an oystre:** i.e. worthless 184 **what:** why **wood:** mad 185 **alwey:** always **poure:** pore over 186 **swynken:** labour 187 **Austyn:** Augustine **bit:** bids, commands 189 **prikasour:** hunter on horseback **aright:** certainly 190 **Grehoundes:** greyhounds 191 **prikyng:** hunting on horseback 192 **lust:** great pleasure 193 **seigh:** saw **purfiled:** trimmed at the wrists 194 **grys:** costly grey fur **fyneste of a lond:** very best 196 **curious:** distinctive 197 **love-knotte:** intricate knot **gretter:** larger 198 **balled:** bald 199 **enoynt:** anointed with oil 200 **in good poynt:** in good condition 201 **stepe:** prominent 202 **stemed . . . leed:** gleamed like a fire under a cauldron 203 **souple:** supple, of the finest leather **in greet estaat:** in superb condition 204 **prelaat:** church dignitary 205 **forpyned goost:** tormented spirit

A fat swan loved he best of any roost.
His palfrey was as broun as is a berye.
  A FRERE ther was, a wantowne and a merye,
A lymytour, a ful solempne man.
In alle the ordres foure is noon that kan   210
So muchel of daliaunce and fair langage.
He hadde maad ful many a mariage
Of yonge wommen at his owene cost.
Unto his ordre he was a noble post.
Ful wel biloved and famulier was he   215
With frankeleyns over al in his contree,
And eek with worthy wommen of the toun;
For he hadde power of confessioun,
As seyde hymself, moore than a curat,
For of his ordre he was licenciat.   220
Ful swetely herde he confessioun,
And pleasaunt was his absolucioun:
He was an esy man to yeve penaunce,
Ther as he wiste to have a good pitaunce.
For unto a povre ordre for to yive   225
Is signe that a man is wel yshryve;
For if he yaf, he dorste make avaunt,
He wiste that a man was repentaunt;
For many a man so hard is of his herte,
He may nat wepe, althogh hym soore smerte.   230
Therfore in stede of wepynge and preyeres
Men moote yeve silver to the povre freres.
His typet was ay farsed ful of knyves
And pynnes, for to yeven faire wyves.
And certeinly he hadde a murye note: 235
Wel koude he synge and pleyen on a rote;
Of yeddynges he bar outrely the pris.
His nekke whit was as the flour-de-lys;
Therto he strong was as a champioun.
He knew the tavernes wel in every toun   240
And everich hostiler and tappestere
Bet than a lazar or a beggestere;
For unto swich a worthy man as he
Acorded nat, as by his facultee,
To have with sike lazars aqueyntaunce.   245

It is nat honest, it may nat avaunce,
For to deelen with no swich poraille,
But al with riche and selleres of vitaille.
And over al, ther as profit sholde arise,
Curteis he was and lowely of servyse.   250
Ther nas no man nowher so vertuous.
He was the beste beggere in his hous;
[And yaf a certeyn ferme for the graunt;   252a
Noon of his bretheren cam ther in his haunt;]   252b
For thogh a wydwe hadde noght a sho,
So pleasaunt was his 'In principio,'
Yet wolde he have a ferthyng er he wente.   255
His purchas was wel bettre than his rente.
And rage he koude, as it were right a whelp.
In love-dayes ther koude he muchel help,
For ther he was nat lyk a cloysterer
With a thredbare cope, as is a povre scoler,   260
But he was lyk a maister or a pope.
Of double worstede was his semycope,
That rounded as a belle out of the presse.
Somwhat he lipsed, for his wantownesse,
To make his Englissh sweete upon his tonge;   265
And in his harpyng, whan that he hadde songe,
His eyen twynkled in his heed aryght,
As doon the sterres in the frosty nyght.
This worthy lymytour was cleped Huberd.
  A MARCHANT was ther with a forked berd,   270
In mottelee, and hye on horse he sat;
Upon his heed a Flaundryssh bever hat,
His bootes clasped faire and fetisly.
His resons he spak ful solempnely,
Sownynge alwey th'encrees of his wynnyng.   275
He wolde the see were kept for any thyng
Bitwixe Middelburgh and Orewelle.
Wel koude he in eschaunge sheeldes selle.
This worthy man ful wel his wit bisette:
Ther wiste no wight that he was in dette,   280

208 **wantowne:** gay 209 **lymytour:** one with the right to beg within prescribed limits **solempne:** dignified 210 **ordres foure:** i.e. Dominicans, Franciscans, Carmelites, Augustinians **kan:** knows 211 **muchel:** much **daliaunce:** the social graces, the ways of the world **fair langage:** fine words 212–13 **He hadde . . . owene cost:** He found husbands for women whom he had seduced (and perhaps made pregnant) and provided dowries 214 **post:** pillar 216 **frankeleyns:** franklins, freeholders **over al:** everywhere **eek:** also 220 **licenciat:** a friar licensed to hear confessions 223 **esy:** lenient **yeve:** give 224 **wiste:** expected **pitaunce:** gift, donation 225 **povre:** poor 226 **yshryve:** penitent 227 **For . . . avaunt:** For, if a man gave, the Friar would dare to assert 228 **wiste:** knew 230 **may nat:** cannot **hym soore smerte:** he suffers terribly 232 **moote yeve:** must give 233 **typet:** the pointed end of the Friar's long hood **farsed:** stuffed 234 **yeven:** give 235 **murye:** merry **note:** voice 236 **rote:** stringed instrument 237 **yeddynges:** singing contests **baar outrely the pris:** won the prize outright **flour-de-lys:** lily 239 **champioun:** champion, perhaps a wrestler 241 **everich:** every **hostiler:** innkeeper **tappestere:** female tapster, barmaid 242 **Bet:** better **lazar:** leper **beggestere:** female beggar 243 **swich:** such 244 **Acorded . . . facultee:** It was not appropriate, because of his official position 245 **sike:** sick

246 **honest:** honourable **it may nat avaunce:** there is no profit in it 247 **poraille:** poor people 248 **vitaille:** provisions 249 **ther as:** where 250 **lowely of servyse:** graciously humble 251 **nas:** was not **vertuous:** capable [252a–252b **And yaf . . . his haunt:** And gave a certain fee for the right to beg; none of his brothers encroached on his territory. (These lines are found in only a few manuscripts of the poem. Their authenticity is generally accepted, but their omission from some texts remains a mystery.)] 253 **sho:** shoe 254 **In principio:** the opening words of Genesis and of St John's gospel 255 **ferthyng:** farthing 256 **His purchas . . . rente:** He earned more this way than from his proper income 257 **rage . . . whelp:** play just like a puppy 258 **love-dayes:** days appointed for the settlement of disputes 260 **cope:** cloak **povre scoler:** poor scholar 262 **double worstede:** generous (and, of course, expensive) width of cloth **semycope:** short cloak 263 **rounded:** was round **presse:** mould 264 **lipsed:** lisped **for his wantownesse:** in an affected manner 266 **songe:** sung 267 **aryght:** exactly 268 **sterres:** stars 269 **cleped:** called 271 **mottelee:** motley, cloth of mixed colours 272 **Flaundryssh:** Flemish **fetisly:** elegantly 274 **resons:** opinions **ful solempnely:** very ponderously 275 **Sownynge:** tending towards **wynnyng:** profit 276 **He wolde . . . thyng:** He wished the sea to be protected at all costs 277 **Middelburgh:** a Dutch port **Orewelle:** Orwell 278 **sheeldes:** French *écus*, which he exchanged at a profit 279 **his wyt bisette:** used his wits

So estatly was he of his governaunce
With his bargaynes and with his chevyssaunce.
For sothe he was a worthy man with alle,
But, sooth to seyn, I noot how men hym calle.

    A CLERK ther was of Oxenford also,   285
That unto logyk hadde longe ygo.
As leene was his hors as is a rake,
And he nas nat right fat, I undertake,
But looked holwe, and therto sobrely.
Ful thredbare was his overeste courtepy;   290
For he hadde geten hym yet no benefice,
Ne was so worldly for to have office.
For hym was levere have at his beddes heed
Twenty bookes, clad in blak or reed,
Of Aristotle and his philosophie,   295
Than robes riche, or fithele, or gay sautrie.
But al be that he was a philosophre,
Yet hadde he but litel gold in cofre;
But al that he myghte of his freendes hente,
On bookes and on lernynge he it spente,   300
And bisily gan for the soules preye
Of hem that yaf hym wherwith to scoleye.
Of studie took he moost cure and moost heede.
Noght o word spak he moore than was neede,
And that was seyd in forme and reverence,   305
And short and quyk and ful of hy sentence;
Sownynge in moral vertu was his speche,
And gladly wolde he lerne and gladly teche.

    A SERGEANT OF THE LAWE, war and wys,
That often hadde been at the Parvys,   310
Ther was also, ful riche of excellence.
Discreet he was and of greet reverence –
He semed swich, his wordes weren so wise.
Justice he was ful often in assise,
By patente and by pleyn commissioun.   315
For his science and for his heigh renoun,
Of fees and robes hadde he many oon.

So greet a purchasour was nowher noon:
Al was fee symple to hym in effect;
His purchasyng myghte nat been infect.   320
Nowher so bisy a man as he ther nas,
And yet he semed bisier than he was.
In termes hadde he caas and doomes alle
That from the tyme of kyng William were falle.
Therto he koude endite, and make a thyng,   325
Ther koude no wight pynche at his writyng;
And every statut koude he pleyn by rote.
He rood but hoomly in a medlee cote,
Girt with a ceint of silk, with barres smale;
Of his array telle I no lenger tale.   330

    A FRANKELEYN was in his compaignye.
Whit was his berd as is the dayesye;
Of his complexioun he was sangwyn.
Wel loved he by the morwe a sop in wyn;
To lyven in delit was evere his wone,   335
For he was Epicurus owene sone,
That heeld opinioun that pleyn delit
Was verray felicitee parfit.
An housholdere, and that a greet, was he;
Seint Julian he was in his contree.   340
His breed, his ale, was alweys after oon;
A bettre envyned man was nowher noon.
Withoute bake mete was nevere his hous
Of fissh and flessh, and that so plentevous,
It snewed in his hous of mete and drynke, 345
Of alle deyntees that men koude thynke.
After the sondry sesons of the yeer,
So chaunged he his mete and his soper.
Ful many a fat partrich hadde he in muwe,
And many a breem and many a luce in stuwe. 350

281 **estatly:** dignified **governaunce:** management, conduct 282 **bargaynes:** trading **chevyssaunce:** financial dealings 283 **For sothe:** truly **with alle:** indeed 284 **noot:** do not know 285 **Clerk:** student 286 **unto logyk hadde longe ygo:** had studied logic for a long time 288 **right:** very **undertake:** avow 289 **holwe:** emaciated **sobrely:** earnest 290 **overeste courtepy:** outer short coat 291 **benefice:** ecclesiastical living **office:** a secular job 293 **hym was levere:** he would rather **his beddes heed:** the head of his bed 296 **fithele:** fiddle **gay sautrie:** psaltery, small stringed instrument plucked like a harp 297 **al be that:** even though **philosophre:** philosopher, but with a clear allusion to the alternative meaning: an alchemist 299 **myghte of his freendes hente:** might get from his friends 301 **gan . . . preye:** prayed 302 **yaf hym wherwith to scoleye:** provided the means for him to go to university 303 **cure:** care 304 **o:** one **neede:** necessary 305 **in forme:** politely, correctly **reverence:** with respect 306 **quyk:** lively **hy sentence:** the finest sentiments 307 **Sownynge in:** tending towards 309 **Sergeant of the Lawe:** a senior member of the legal profession **war:** knowing 310 **Parvys:** the porch of St Paul's Cathedral 311 **ful riche of excellence:** possessing many fine qualities 312 **Discreet:** judicious **of greet reverence:** a man of authority 314 **Justice:** judge **in assise:** at the assizes 315 **patente:** royal warrant **pleyn commissioun:** full jurisdiction 316 **science:** learning 317 **fees and robes:** i.e. sources of income **many oon:** many a one

318 **purchasour:** buyer of land 319 **fee symple:** unrestricted possession 320 **infect:** declared invalid 323 **In termes . . . falle:** He knew accurately all the cases and judgements from the time of William the Conqueror 325 **endite and make a thyng:** compose and draw up a legal document 326 **pynche at:** find fault with 327 **And every . . . by rote:** And he knew every statute by heart 328 **hoomly:** simply **medlee:** multi-coloured 329 **Girt:** encircled **ceint:** belt **barres:** stripes 330 **array:** dress 331 **Frankeleyn:** franklin, freeholder 332 **dayesye:** daisy 333 **Of his complexioun . . . sangwyn:** He was of a sanguine disposition. According to medieval physiology, a person's temperament, or *complexion*, was determined by the dominance of one of four fluids, or *humours*: blood, phlegm, bile and black bile. Blood dominates the Franklin's makeup, so he is of a *sanguine* humour, the others being the *phlegmatic*, the *bilious* (or *choleric*) and the *melancholic* 334 **sop in wyn:** piece of bread in wine 335 **evere his wone:** his only aim, i.e. he lived only for pleasure 336 **Epicurus owene sone:** an Epicurean (Epicurus, *c.*341–270 BC, taught that pleasure was the highest good, although pleasure lay in right living; but his philosophy was corrupted into a pursuit of luxury and self-indulgence) 337 **That:** who **pleyn delit:** sheer pleasure **verray felicitee parfit:** true perfect happiness 340 **Seint Julian:** patron saint of hospitality **in his contree:** in his neighbourhood 341 **breed:** bread **after oon:** uniformly good 342 **envyned:** stocked with wine 343 **bake mete . . . flessh:** meat or fish pie 344 **plentevous:** plenteous 345 **snewed:** snowed 346 **deyntees:** finest food and drink 347 **After the sondry sesons:** according to the different seasons 349 **partrich:** partridge **muwe:** bird-pen 350 **breem:** bream **luce:** pike **stuwe:** fish-pond

Wo was his cook but if his sauce were
Poynaunt and sharp, and redy al his geere.
His table dormant in his halle alway
Stood redy covered al the longe day.
At sessiouns ther was he lord and sire; 355
Ful ofte tyme he was knyght of the shire.
An anlaas and a gipser al of silk
Heeng at his girdel, whit as morne milk.
A shirreve hadde he been, and a contour.
Was nowher swich a worthy vavasour. 360

An HABERDASSHERE and a CARPENTER,
A WEBBE, a DYERE, and a TAPYCER –
And they were clothed alle in o lyveree
Of a solempne and a greet fraternitee.
Ful fressh and newe hir geere apiked was; 365
Hir knyves were chaped noght with bras
But al with silver; wroght ful clene and weel
Hire girdles and hire pouches everydeel.
Wel semed ech of hem a fair burgeys
To sitten in a yeldehalle on a deys. 370
Everich, for the wisdom that he kan,
Was shaply for to been an alderman.
For catel hadde they ynogh and rente,
And eek hir wyves wolde it wel assente;
And elles certeyn were they to blame. 375
It is ful fair to been ycleped 'madame',
And goon to vigilies al before,
And have a mantel roialliche ybore.

A COOK they hadde with hem for the nones
To boille the chiknes with the marybones, 380
And poudre-marchant tart and galyngale.
Wel koude he knowe a draughte of Londoun ale.
He koude rooste, and sethe, and broille, and frye,
Maken mortreux, and wel bake a pye.
But greet harm was it, as it thoughte me, 385
That on his shyne a mormal hadde he.
For blankmanger, that made he with the beste.

A SHIPMAN was ther, wonynge fer by weste;
For aught I woot, he was of Dertemouthe.
He rood upon a rouncy, as he kouthe, 390
In a gowne of faldyng to the knee.
A daggere hangynge on a laas hadde he
Aboute his nekke, under his arm adoun.
The hoote somer hadde maad his hewe al broun;
And certeinly he was a good felawe. 395
Ful many a draughte of wyn had he ydrawe
Fro Burdeux-ward, whil that the chapman sleep.
Of nyce conscience took he no keep.
If that he faught, and hadde the hyer hond,
By water he sente hem hoom to every lond. 400
But of his craft to rekene wel his tydes,
His stremes, and his daungers hym bisides,
His herberwe, and his moone, his lodemenage,
Ther nas noon swich from Hulle to Cartage.
Hardy he was and wys to undertake; 405
With many a tempest hadde his berd been shake.
He knew alle the havenes, as they were,
Fro Gootland to the cape of Fynystere,
And every cryke in Britaigne and in Spayne.
His barge ycleped was the Maudelayne. 410

With us ther was a DOCTOUR OF PHISIK;
In al this world ne was ther noon hym lik,
To speke of phisik and of surgerye,
For he was grounded in astronomye.
He kepte his pacient a ful greet deel 415
In houres by his magyk natureel.
Wel koude he fortunen the ascendent
Of his ymages for his pacient.
He knew the cause of everich maladye,
Were it of hoot, or coold, or moyste, or drye, 420
And where they engendred, and of what humour.
He was a verray, parfit praktisour:
The cause yknowe, and of his harm the roote,
Anon he yaf the sike man his boote.

Ful redy hadde he his apothecaries 425
To send hym drogges and his letuaries,
For ech of hem made oother for to wynne –
Hir frendshipe nas nat newe to bigynne.
Wel knew he the olde Esculapius,
And Deyscorides, and eek Rufus, 430
Olde Ypocras, Haly, and Galyen,
Serapion, Razis, and Avycen,
Averrois, Damascien, and Constantyn,
Bernard, and Gatesden, and Gilbertyn.
Of his diete mesurable was he, 435
For it was of no superfluitee,
But of greet norissyng and digestible.
His studie was but litel on the Bible.
In sangwyn and in pers he clad was al,
Lyned with taffata and with sendal; 440
And yet he was but esy of dispence;
He kepte that he wan in pestilence.
For gold in phisik is a cordial,
Therefore he lovede gold in special.
   A good WIF was ther of biside BATHE, 445
But she was somdel deef, and that was scathe.
Of clooth-makyng she hadde swich an haunt,
She passed hem of Ypres and of Gaunt.
In al the parisshe wife ne was ther noon
That to the offrynge bifore hire sholde goon; 450
And if ther dide, certeyn so wrooth was she,
That she was out of alle charitee.
Hir coverchiefs ful fyne weren of ground;
I dorste swere they weyeden ten pound
That on a Sonday weren upon hir heed. 455
Hir hosen weren of fyn scarlet reed,
Ful streit yteyd, and shoes ful moyste and newe.
Boold was hire face, and fair, and reed of hewe.
She was a worthy womman al hire lyve:
Housbondes at chirche dore she hadde fyve, 460
Withouten oother compaignye in youthe –
But thereof nedeth nat to speke as nowthe.

And thries hadde she been at Jerusalem;
She hadde passed many a straunge strem;
At Rome she hadde been, and at Boloigne, 465
In Galice at Seint-Jame, and at Coloigne.
She koude muchel of wandrynge by the weye.
Gat-tothed was she, soothly for to seye.
Upon an amblere esily she sat,
Ywympled wel, and on hir heed an hat 470
As brood as is a bokeler or a targe;
A foot-mantel avoute her hipes large,
And on hir feet a paire of spores sharpe.
In felaweshipe wel koude she laughe and carpe.
Of remedies of love she knew per chaunce, 475
For she koude of that art the olde daunce.
   A good man was ther of religioun,
And was a povre PERSOUN OF A TOUN,
But riche he was of hooly thoght and werk.
He was also a lerned man, a clerk, 480
That Cristes gospel trewely wolde preche;
His parisshens devoutly wolde he teche.
Benygne he was, and wonder diligent,
And in adversitee ful pacient,
And swich he was ypreved ofte sithes. 485
Ful looth were hym to cursen for his tithes,
But rather wolde he yeven, out of doute,
Unto his povre parisshens aboute
Of his offryng and eek of his substaunce.
He koude in litel thyng have suffisaunce. 490
Wyd was his parisshe, and houses fer asonder,
But he ne lefte nat, for reyn ne thonder,
In siknesse nor in meschief to visite
The ferreste in his parisshe, muche and lite,
Upon his feet, and in his hand a staf. 495
This noble ensample to his sheep he yaf,
That first he wroghte, and afterward he taughte.
Out of the gospel he tho wordes caughte,
And this figure he added eek therto,
That if gold ruste, what shall iren do? 500
For if a preest be foul, on whom we truste,
No wonder is a lewed man to ruste;
And shame it is, if a prest take keep,
A shiten shepherde and a clene sheep.

426 **drogges:** drugs **letuaries:** electuaries, medicines 427 **ech of hem:** each of them **wynne:** profit 428 **His frendshipe . . . bigynne:** They were old friends 429–34 **Wel knew . . . Gilbertyn:** standard medical authorities of Chaucer's time, respectively: Aesculapius, the legendary Greek founder of medicine; Dioscorides (*fl.*AD 50–70); Rufus (*fl.c.*25 BC–AD 50); Hippocrates (b.*c.*460 BC); Ali ibn el Abbas (d.994); Galen (*c.*AD 129–99); Serapion (not definitely identified); Rhazes (*c.*854–930); Avicenna (980–1037); Averroës (1126–98); Damascien (not definitely identified); Constantinus Afer, or Constantine the African (*fl.*1065–85); Bernard of Gordon (*fl.*1283–1309); John of Gaddesden (d.*c.*1349); Gilbertus Anglicus (*fl.*1250) 435 **mesurable:** moderate 439 **in sangwyn and in pers:** in red and blue-grey cloth 440 **taffata . . . sendal:** fine silk cloth 441 **esy of dispence:** slow to spend money 442 **wan:** gained 443 **a cordial:** a medicine for the heart, to lift the spirits 446 **somdel deef:** slightly deaf **scathe:** a pity 447 **haunt:** skill 448 **Ypres and Gaunt:** Ypres and Ghent: clothmaking centres 450 **offrynge:** offering at Mass 451 **wrooth:** angry 452 **out of alle charitee:** unforgiving 453 **coverchiefs:** head-coverings **ground:** texture 454 **dorste swere:** dare swear **weyeden:** weighed 456 **hosen:** stockings 457 **streit yteyd:** tied tightly **moyste:** supple, i.e. of the finest leather 460 **at chirche dore:** i.e. she had buried five husbands 461 **Withouten:** as well as 462 **as nowthe:** just now

463–6 **And thries . . . at Coloigne:** places of pilgrimage in the Middle Ages; 'Seint-Jame' is the shrine of St James of Compostella in Spain 464 **straunge strem:** foreign sea 468 **Gat-tothed:** with teeth wide apart 469 **amblere:** an ambling horse **esily:** comfortably 470 **Ywympled wel:** i.e. her head was well covered by a wimple that showed only her face 471 **bokeler . . . targe:** small round shields 472 **foot-mantel:** overskirt 473 **spores:** spurs 474 **carpe:** talk 475–6 **Of remedies . . . daunce:** She happened to know cures for love-sickness because she knew all the rules of the game 478 **povre Persoun:** poor Parson 482 **parisshens:** parishioners 483 **Benygne:** kind, considerate 485 **swich . . . sithes:** such was he often proved to be 486 **Ful looth . . . tithes:** He was very reluctant to excommunicate those who did not pay their tithes, i.e. one-tenth of their income to be paid to the priest 489 **offryng:** offering made at Mass **substaunce:** regular income 490 **suffisaunce:** sufficiency 491 **fer asonder:** set far apart 492 **ne lefte nat:** did not neglect 493 **meschief:** times of trouble 494 **ferreste:** most distant **muche and lite:** great and small 496 **ensample:** example **sheep:** flock 498 **tho:** those 499 **figure:** proverb, saying 501 **foul:** corrupt 502 **lewed:** ignorant, uneducated 503 **if a prest take keep:** where a priest is concerned 504 **shiten:** defiled

Wel oghte a preest ensample for to yive,   505
By his clennesse, how that his sheep sholde lyve.
He sette nat his benefice to hyre
And leet his sheep encombred in the myre
And ran to Londoun unto Seinte Poules
To seken hym a chaunterie for soules,   510
Or with a bretherhed to been withholde;
But dwelte at hoom, and kepte wel his folde,
So that the wolf ne made it nat myscarie;
He was a shepherde and noght a mercenarie.
And though he hooly were and vertuous,   515
He was to synful men nat despitous,
Ne of his speche daungerous ne digne,
But in his techyng discreet and benygne.
To drawen folk to hevene by fairnesse,
By good ensample, this was his bisynesse.   520
But it were any persone obstinat,
What so he were, of heigh or lough estat,
Hym wolde he snybben sharply for the nonys.
A bettre preest I trowe that nowher noon ys.
He waited after no pompe and reverence,   525
Ne maked him a spiced conscience,
But Cristes loore and his apostles twelve
He taughte, but first he folwed it hymselve.
    With hym ther was a PLOWMAN, was his brother,
That hadde ylad of dong ful many a fother;   530
A trewe swynkere and a good was he,
Lyvynge in pees and parfit charitee.
God loved he best with al his hoole herte
At alle tymes, thogh him gamed or smerte,
And thanne his neighebor right as hymselve.   535
He wolde thresshe, and therto dyke and delve,
For Cristes sake, for every povre wight,
Withouten hire, if it lay in his myght.
His tithes payde he ful faire and wel,
Bothe of his propre swynk and his catel.   540
In a tabard he rood upon a mere.
    There was also a REVE, and a MILLERE,
A SOMNOUR, and a PARDONER also,
A MAUNCIPLE, and myself – ther were namo.

The MILLERE was a stout carl for the nones;   545
Ful byg he was of brawn, and eek of bones.
That proved wel, for over al ther he cam,
At wrastlynge he wolde have alwey the ram.
He was short-sholdred, brood, a thikke knarre;
Ther was no dore that he nolde heve of harre,   550
Or breke it at a rennyng with his heed.
His berd as any sowe or fox was reed,
And therto brood, as though it were a spade.
Upon the cop right of his nose he hade
A werte, and theron stood a toft of herys,   555
Reed as the brustles of a sowes erys;
His nosethirles blake were and wyde.
A swerd and bokeler bar he by his syde.
His mouth as greet was as a greet forneys.
He was a janglere and a goliardeys,   560
And that was moost of synne and harlotries.
Wel koude he stelen corn and tollen thries;
And yet he hadde a thombe of gold, pardee.
A whit cote and a blew hood wered he.
A baggepipe wel koude he blowe and sowne,   565
And therwithal he broughte us out of towne.
    A gentil MAUNCIPLE was ther of a temple,
Of which achatours myghte take exemple
For to be wise in byynge of vitaille;
For wheither that he payde or took by taille,   570
Algate he wayted so in his achaat
That he was ay biforn and in good staat.
Now is nat that of God a ful fair grace
That swich a lewed mannes wit shal pace
The wisdom of an heep of lerned men?   575
Of maistres hadde he mo than thries ten,
That weren of lawe expert and curious,
Of which ther were a duszeyne in that hous
Worthy to been stywardes of rente and lond
Of any lord that is in Engelond,   580
To make hym lyve by his propre good

---

506 **clennesse:** purity 507 **sette . . . to hyre:** did not rent out his living 508 **leet:** left **encombred:** stuck, wallowing 510 **chaunterie:** chantry, a chapel endowed for a priest to say prayers for a departed soul 511 **Or with . . . withholde:** Or to be retained by a guild as a chaplain 513 **the wolf . . . myscarie:** i.e. so that no harm came to them 516 **despitous:** scornful 517 **daungerous ne digne:** overbearing or haughty 518 **discreet:** courteous 519 **fairness:** kindness 522 **of heigh or lough estat:** no matter what his social position 523 **snybben:** rebuke **for the nonys:** on that occasion 524 **trowe:** believe 525 **He . . . reverence:** He expected no pomp and ceremony 526 **spiced:** overscrupulous 530 **ylad:** carried **dong:** dung **fother:** load 531 **swynkere:** worker 534 **thogh him gamed or smerte:** in pleasure or in pain, in good times and bad 535 **thanne:** then **right as:** the same as 536 **therto:** moreover **dyke and delve:** make ditches and dig 537–8 **for every . . . myght:** for every poor person, without payment, if it lay in his power 540 **Bothe . . . catel:** Both by his own labours and out of his property 541 **tabard:** labourer's loose coat **mere:** mare 542 **Reve:** bailiff 543–44 **Somnour:** see note at line 623 **Pardoner:** see note at line 669 **Maunciple:** see note at line 567 544 **namo:** no others

545 **a stout carl for the nones:** a big man indeed 546 **Ful byg . . . bones:** muscular as well as having a large frame 547 **over al ther:** everywhere 548 **At wrastlynge . . . ram:** At wrestling he would always win the ram offered as the prize 549 **short-sholdred:** thickset **brood:** broad **thikke knarre:** brawny fellow 550 **nolde heve of harre:** would not lift off its hinges 551 **at a rennyng:** by running at it 554 **cop right:** very tip 555 **werte:** wart **toft of herys:** tuft of hairs 556 **brustles:** bristles **sowes erys:** sow's ears 557 **nosethirles:** nostrils 559 **greet forneys:** large cauldron 560 **janglere:** chatterer **goliardeys:** coarse buffoon 561 **harlotries:** dirty jokes 562 **stelen corn:** steal corn **tollen thries:** take three times the amount of corn he was entitled to keep as his fee 563 **a thombe of gold:** proverbially 'An honest miller hath a golden thumb', i.e. there are no honest millers 565 **sowne:** play 567 **Maunciple:** buyer of provisions **temple:** one of the Inns of Court 568 **achatours:** purchasers 569 **byynge of vitaille:** buying provisions 570 **by taille:** on credit 571 **Algate:** in any case **wayted so in his achaat:** waited for the right moment to buy 572 **ay biforn:** always ahead **in good staat:** did very well for himself 574 **lewed:** uneducated **pace:** surpass 576 **mo:** more **thries:** thrice 577 **curious:** erudite 578 **duszeyne:** dozen 579 **Worthy . . . and lond:** fit to be stewards of both income and property 581 **To make . . . propre good:** to make him live within his means

In honour dettelees (but if he were wood),
Or lyve as scarsly as hym list desire;
And able for to helpen al a shire
In any caas that myghte falle or happe; 585
And yet this Manciple sette hir alle cappe.
    The REVE was a sclendre colerik man.
His berd was shave as ny as ever he kan;
His heer was by his erys ful round yshorn;
His top was dokked lyk a preest biforn 590
Ful longe were his legges and ful lene,
Ylyk a staf, ther was no calf ysene.
Wel koude he kepe a gerner and a bynne;
Ther was noon auditour koude on him wynne.
Wel wiste he by the droghte and by the reyn 595
The yeldynge of his seed and of his greyn.
His lordes sheep, his neet, his dayerye,
His swyn, his hors, his stoor, and his pultrye
Was hoolly in this Reves governynge,
And by his covenant yaf the rekenynge, 600
Syn that his lord was twenty yeer of age.
Ther koude no man brynge him in arrerage.
Ther nas baillif, ne hierde, nor oother hyne,
That he ne knew his sleighte and his covyne;
They were adrad of hym as of the deeth. 605
His wonyng was ful faire upon an heeth;
With grene trees yshadwed was his place.
He koude bettre than his lord purchace.
Ful riche he was astored pryvely:
His lord wel koude he plesen subtilly, 610
To yeve and lene hym of his owene good,
And have a thank, and yet a cote and hood.
In youthe he hadde lerned a good myster;
He was a wel good wrighte, a carpenter.
This Reve sat upon a ful good stot, 615
That was al pomely grey and highte Scot.
A long surcote of pers upon he hade,
And by his syde he bar a rusty blade.

Of Northfolk was this Reve of which I telle,
Biside a toun men clepen Baldeswelle. 620
Tukked he was as is a frere aboute,
And evere he rood the hyndreste of oure route.
    A SOMNOUR was ther with us in that place,
That hadde a fyr-reed cherubynnes face,
For saucefleem he was, with eyen narwe. 625
As hoot he was and lecherous as a sparwe,
With scalled browes blake and piled berd.
Of his visage children were aferd.
Ther nas quyk-silver, lytarge, ne brymstoon,
Boras, ceruce, ne oille of tartre noon; 630
Ne oynement that wolde clense and byte,
That hym myghte helpen of his whelkes white,
Nor of the knobbes sittynge on his chekes.
Wel loved he garleek, oynons, and eek lekes,
And for to drynken strong wyn, reed as blood; 635
Thanne wolde he speke and crie as he were wood.
And whan that he wel dronken hadde the wyn,
Thanne wolde he speke no word but Latyn.
A fewe termes hadde he, two or thre,
That he had lerned out of som decree – 640
No wonder is, he herde it al the day;
And eek ye knowen wel how that a jay
Kan clepen 'Watte' as well as kan the pope.
But whoso koude in oother thyng hym grope,
Thanne hadde he spent al his philosophie; 645
Ay '*Questio quid iuris*' wolde he crie.
He was a gentil harlot and a kynde;
A bettre felawe sholde men noght fynde.
He wolde suffre for a quart of wyn
A good felawe to have his concubyn 650
A twelf month, and excuse him atte fulle;
Ful prively a fynch eek koude he pulle.
And if he foond owher a good felawe,
He wolde techen him to have noon awe
In swich caas of the ercedekenes curs, 655

---

582 **dettelees**: free of debt **but if he were wood**: unless he was mad 583 **Or lyve . . . desire**: Or live as frugally as he desired 585 **In any caas . . . happe**: In any situation that might arise 586 **sette hir aller cappe**: made fools of them all 587 **Reve**: reeve, steward, farm manager **sclendre**: slender **colerik**: see earlier note (line 333) 588 **as ny as ever he kan**: as closely as he could 589 **erys**: ears **round yshorn**: closely cropped 590 **His top . . . biforn**: The hair on the top of his head was cut short at the front like a priest's 592 **Ylyk a staf**: like a stick 593 **gerner**: granary **bynne**: grain-bin 594 **There was . . . him wynne**: No auditor was clever enough to earn anything by catching him out 597 **neet**: cattle **dayerye**: dairy cattle (not the dairy itself) 598 **hors**: horses **stoor**: livestock **pultrye**: poultry 600 **covenant**: contract **yaf the reckenynge**: took care of the accounts 601 **Syn that**: because 602 **arrerage**: arrears 603 **Ther nas**: there was not **bailliff**: farm manager **hierde**: herdsman **hyne**: labourer 604 **sleighte**: trickery **covyne**: deceitfulness 605 **adrad**: afraid **the deeth**: the plague 606 **wonyng**: dwelling 608 **purchace**: buy property 609 **Ful riche . . . pryvely**: He had acquired his own private fortune 610–12 **His lord . . . cote and hood**: He was able to please his lord by lending him money that was actually his own (but which the Reeve had stolen) and even receive thanks and gifts 613 **myster**: trade, craft 615 **stot**: stallion 616 **pomely**: dappled **highte**: called 617 **surcote of pers**: blue topcoat

620 **clepen**: call **Baldeswelle**: Bawdeswell, Norfolk 621 **Tukked . . . aboute**: He had his long coat hitched up like a friar 622 **hyndreste**: last **route**: company 623 **Somnour**: server of summonses for an ecclesiastical court 624 **fyr-reed**: fire-red **cherubynnes**: cherub's 625 **saucefleem**: covered with pimples **eyen narwe**: swollen eyelids 627 **scalled**: scabby **piled berd**: beard that was falling out 629–30 **Ther nas . . . noon**: medieval remedies for skin diseases: mercury (*quyk-silver*), lead monoxide (*lytarge*), sulphur (*brymstoon*), borax (*boras*), white lead (*ceruce*) and cream of tartar (*tartre*) 631 **oynement byte**: burn or cleanse 632 **whelkes**: pimples 633 **knobbes**: swellings 634 **garleek, oynons . . . lekes**: garlic, onions, leeks 636 **wood**: mad 639 **termes**: legal terms 643 **Kan clepen 'Watte'**: can say 'Walter' 644–5 **But whoso . . . philosophie**: But anyone who could examine him further discovered that to be the full extent of his learning 646 **Ay**: always **Questio quid iuris**: 'The question is, what point of law [applies in this case]?' 647 **gentil harlot**: agreeable rogue 649 **suffre**: allow 650 **concubyn**: mistress 652 **Ful prively . . . pulle**: The meaning here depends on how we interpret 'fynch'. It could mean that the Summoner is adept at fleecing gullible victims or (perhaps more likely) it could be a reference to his sexual promiscuity. (The previous lines suggest that he was both promiscuous and a pimp.) 653 **owher**: anywhere 654 **noon awe**: no fear 655 **ercedekenes curs**: archdeacon's curse, i.e. excommunication

But if a mannes soule were in his purs;
For in his purs he sholde ypunysshed be.
'Purs is the ercedekenes helle,' seyde he.
But wel I woot he lyed right in dede;
Of cursyng oghte ech gilty man him drede, 660
For curs wol slee right as assoillyng savith,
And also war hym of a *Significavit*.
In daunger hadde he at his owene gise
The yonge girles of the diocise,
And knew hir conseil, and was al hir reed. 665
A gerland hadde he set upon his heed
As greet as it were for an ale-stake.
A bokeleer hadde he maad hym of a cake.
  With hym ther rood a gentil PARDONER
Of Rouncivale, his freend and his compeer, 670
That streight was comen fro the court of Rome.
Ful loude he soong 'Com hider, love, to me!'
This Somonour bar to hym a stif burdoun;
Was nevere trompe of half so greet a soun.
This Pardoner hadde heer as yelow as wex, 675
But smothe it heeng as dooth a strike of flex;
By ounces henge his lokkes that he hadde,
And therwith he his shuldres overspradde;
But thynne it lay, by colpons oon and oon.
But hood, for jolitee, wered he noon, 680
For it was trussed up in his walet.
Hym thoughte he rood al of the newe jet;
Dischevelee, save his cappe, he rood al bare.
Swiche glarynge eyen hadd he as an hare.
A vernycle hadde he sowed upon his cappe. 685
His walet lay biforn hym in his lappe,
Bretful of pardoun, comen from Rome al hoot.
A voys he hadde as smal as hath a goot.
No berd hadde he, ne nevere sholde have;
As smothe it was as it were late shave. 690
I trowe he were a geldyng or a mare.
But of his craft, from Berwyk into Ware,
Ne was ther swich another pardoner.

For in his male he hadde a pilwe-beer,
Which that he seyde was Oure Lady veyl: 695
He seyd he hadde a gobet of the seyl
That Seint Peter hadde, whan that he wente
Upon the see, til Jhesu Crist hym hente.
He hadde a croys of latoun ful of stones,
And in a glas he hadde pigges bones. 700
But with thise relikes, whan that he fond
A povre person dwellynge upon lond,
Upon a day he gat hym moore moneye
Than that the person gat in monthes tweye;
And thus, with feyned flaterye and japes, 705
He made the person and the peple his apes.
But trewely to tellen atte laste,
He was in chirche a noble ecclesiaste.
Wel koude he rede a lessoun or a storie,
But alderbest he song an offertorie; 710
For wel he wiste, whan that song was songe,
He moste preche and wel affile his tonge
To wynne silver, as he ful wel koude;
Therefore he song the murierly and loude.
  Now have I toold you soothly, in a clause, 715
Th'estaat, th'array, the nombre, and eek the cause
Why that assembled was this compaignye
In Southwerk at this gentil hostelrye
That highte the Tabard, faste by the Belle.
But now is tyme to yow for to telle 720
How that we baren us that ilke nyght,
Whan we were in that hostelrye alyght;
And after wol I telle of our viage
And al the remenaunt of oure pilgrimage.
But first I pray yow, of youre curteisye, 725
That ye n'arette it nat my vileynye,
Thogh that I pleynly speke in this mateere,
To telle yow hir wordes and hir cheere,
Ne thogh I speke hir wordes proprely.
For this ye knowen al so wel as I, 730
Whoso shal telle a tale after a man,
He moot reherce as ny as evere he kan
Everich a word, if it be in his charge,
Al speke he never so rudeliche and large,
Or ellis he moot telle his tale untrewe, 735
Or feyne thyng, or fynde wordes newe.

656 **But if:** unless 659 **woot:** know 660 **Of cursyng . . . drede:** Every guilty man should be afraid of excommunication 661 **wol slee:** will slay **assoillyng:** absolution 662 **war him:** let him beware *Significavit:* the first word of a writ remanding to prison 663 **In daunger:** in his power **at his owene gise:** whenever he wished 664 **girles:** young people of either sex 665 **conseil:** secrets **al hir reed:** advised them all 666 **gerland:** garland 667 **ale-stake:** bush hung up as the sign of a tavern 668 **cake:** loaf of bread 669 **Pardoner:** seller of papal indulgences 670 **Rouncivale:** hospital of the Blessed Mary of Rouncivalle, Charing Cross **compeer:** companion 671 **court of Rome:** papal court 672 **'Com hider, love, to me!':** possibly a popular love-song **styf burdoun:** strong bass voice 674 **trompe:** trumpet **soun:** sound 675 **heer as yelow as wex:** hair as yellow as wax 676 **heeng:** hung **strike of flex:** hank of flax 677 **ounces:** small strands 679 **colpons oon and oon:** separate strands 680 **for jolitee:** to cut a dashing figure 681 **trussed:** packed **walet:** pouch 682 **Hym thoughte:** he believed **al of the newe jet:** in the latest fashion 683 **Dischevelee:** with his hair hanging freely 684 **glarynge eyen:** staring eyes 685 **vernycle:** small copy of the handkerchief lent by St Veronica to Christ on his way to the Cross **sowed:** sewn 687 **Bretful:** brimful **pardoun:** indulgences 688 **voys:** voice **smal:** high **goot:** goat 691 **I trowe . . . mare:** I believe he was either a eunuch or a homosexual 692 **from Berwyk into Ware:** i.e. throughout the country

694 **male:** bag **pilwe-beer:** pillow-case 695 **Oure Lady veil:** the Virgin Mary's veil 696 **gobet of the seyl:** piece of the sail 698 **see:** i.e. Sea of Galilee **hente:** caught 699 **croys:** cross **latoun:** alloy 702 **person:** parson **upon lond:** in the country 703 **gat hym:** got himself 704 **tweye:** two 705 **japes:** tricks 706 **He made . . . apes:** He fooled the parson and the people 707 **atte laste:** finally 709 **lessoun:** scriptural text read during a church service 710 **alderbest:** best of all **offertorie:** offertory, sung while gifts are offered at Mass 712 **affile:** make smooth 714 **song the murierly:** sang the more merrily 715 **in a clause:** briefly 719 **highte:** is called **faste by:** close to **Belle:** another tavern 721 **baren us:** behaved **ilke:** same 722 **alyght:** arrived 723 **wol:** will **viage:** journey 726 **That ye . . . vileynye:** That you do not attribute it to my rudeness 728 **cheere:** disposition 730 **al so wel as:** as well as 731 **Whoso:** whoever 732 **moot reherce:** must repeat **as ny as evere he kan:** as accurately as he can 733 **Everich a:** every **in his charge:** his responsibility 734 **Al speke . . . large:** Even though he speak never so crudely or so freely 735 **moot:** must **untrewe:** inaccurately 736 **feyne:** invent things

He may nat spare, althogh he were his brother;
He moot as wel seye o word as another.
Crist spak hymself ful brode in hooly writ,
And wel ye woot no vileynye is it.   740
Eek Plato seith, whoso that kan hym rede,
The wordes moote be cosyn to the dede.
Also I preye yow to foryeve it me,
Al have I nat set folk in hir degree
Heere in this tale, as that they sholde stonde.   745
My wit is short, ye may wel understonde.

   Greet chiere made oure Hoost us everichon,
And to the soper sette he us anon.
He served us with vitaille at the beste;
Strong was the wyn, and wel to drynke us leste.   750
A semely man OURE HOOSTE was withalle
For to han been a marchal in an halle.
A large man he was with eyen stepe –
A fairer burgeys is ther noon in Chepe –
Boold of his speche, and wys, and wel ytaught,   755
And of manhod hym lakkede right naught.
Eek therto he was right a myrie man,
And after soper pleyen he bigan,
And spak of myrthe amonges othere thynges,
Whan that we hadde maad oure rekenynges,   760
And seyde thus: 'Now, lordynges, trewely,
Ye been to me right welcome, hertely;
For by my trouthe, if that I shall nat lye,
I saugh nat this yeer so myrie a compaignye
Atones in this herberwe as is now.   765
Fayn wolde I doon yow myrthe, wiste I how.
And of a myrthe I am right now bythoght,
To doon yow ese, and it shal coste noght.

   'Ye goon to Caunterbury – God yow speede,
The blisful martir quite yow youre meede!   770
And wel I woot, as ye goon by the weye,
Ye shapen yow to talen and to pleye;
For trewely, comfort ne myrthe is noon
To ride by the weye doumb as a stoon;
And therfore wol I maken yow disport,   775
As I seyde erst, and doon yow som confort.

And if yow liketh alle by oon assent
For to stonden at my juggement,
And for to werken as I shal yow seye,
To-morwe, whan ye riden by the weye,   780
Now, by my fader soule that is deed,
But ye be myrie, I wol yeve yow myn heed!
Hoold up youre hondes withouten moore speche.'

   Oure conseil was nat longe for to seche.
Us thoughte it was noght worth to make it wys,   785
And graunted hym withouten moore avys,
And bade him seye his voirdit as hym leste.
'Lordynges,' quod he, 'now herkneth for the beste;
But taak it nought, I prey yow, in desdeyn.
This is the poynt, to speken short and pleyn,   790
That ech of yow, to shorte with oure weye,
In this viage shal telle tales tweye
To Caunterbury-ward, I mene it so,
And homward he shal tellen othere two,
Of aventures that whilom han bifalle.   795
And which of yow that bereth hym best of alle,
That is to seyn, that telleth in this caas
Tales of best sentence and moost solaas,
Shal have a soper at oure aller cost
Heere in this place, sittynge by this post,   800
Whan that we come agayn fro Caunterbury.
And for to make yow the moore mury,
I wol myselven goodly with yow ryde,
Right at myn owene cost, and be youre gyde;
And whoso wole my juggement withseye   805
Shal paye al that we spenden by the weye
And if ye vouche sauf that it be so,
Tel me anon, withouten wordes mo,
And I wol erly shape me therfore.'

   This thyng was graunted, and oure othes swore   810
With ful glad herte, and preyden hym also
That he wolde vouche sauf for to do so,
And that he wolde been oure governour,
And of oure tales juge and reportour,
And sette a soper at a certeyn pris,   815

---

738 **He moot . . . another:** He must take equal care over every word 739 **brode:** plainly 740 **And wel . . . is it:** And you know well that there is no rudeness in it 741 **kan hym rede:** are able to read him 742 **cosyn:** fellow 744 **Al have I . . . degree:** Although I have not presented people according to their social rank 747 **Greet chiere . . . everichon:** Our host showed the utmost hospitality to every one of us 749 **vitaille at the beste:** the finest food and drink 750 **us leste:** it pleased us 751 **semely:** impressive **withalle:** indeed 752 **marchal in an halle:** marshall in a great hall 753 **eyen stepe:** large eyes 754 **burgeys:** citizen **Chepe:** Cheapside, in the City of London 756 **manhod:** manliness **lakkede right naught:** lacked absolutely nothing 758 **pleyen:** to amuse us 760 **maad oure rekenynges:** paid our bills 763 **trouthe:** faith 764 **saugh:** saw 765 **Atones:** at one time **herberwe:** inn 766 **Fayn . . . I how:** I would gladly entertain you if I knew how 767–8 **And of a . . . noght:** And I have just thought of an entertainment that will give you pleasure and cost nothing 770 **The blisful martir . . . meede:** May the blessed martyr give you your reward! 772 **Ye shapen yow:** you intend **talen:** tell stories **pleye:** entertain yourselves 776 **erst:** before

777 **you liketh alle:** you all agree **by oon assent:** unanimously 779 **werken:** do 781 **by my fader soule that is deed:** by the soul of my dead father 782 **But ye . . . heed!:** If you are not entertained, you can have my head! 784 **Oure . . . to seche:** We did not take long to decide 785–6 **Us thoughte . . . avys:** We did not even need to discuss it, and accepted his suggestion without any further consideration 787 **voirdit:** verdict, i.e. proposal 788 **quod:** said **for the beste:** for the best way to proceed 789 **But taak . . . desdeyn:** But don't, I pray you, dismiss it out of hand 790 **short and pleyn:** clearly and to the point 791 **to shorte with our weye:** to make our journey pass more quickly 794 **othere two:** another two 795 **whilom han bifalle:** have happened in former times 796 **bereth hym best of alle:** does best of all 798 **Tales of best sentence:** most instructive stories **solaas:** entertaining 799 **at oure aller cost:** at the expense of all of us 803 **goodly:** gladly 804 **gyde:** guide 805 **withseye:** question 806 **Shal . . . the weye:** Must pay all our travelling expenses 807 **vouche saufe:** agree 808 **anon:** straight away **mo:** more 809 **shape me:** make my arrangements 811 **preyden:** we prayed 814 **juge:** judge **reportour:** recorder 815 **pris:** price

And we wol reuled been at his devys
In heigh and lough; and thus by oon assent
We been acorded to his juggement.
And therupon the wyn was fet anon;
We dronken, and to reste wente echon,   820
Withouten any lenger taryynge.

    Amorwe, whan that day bigan to sprynge,
Up roos oure Hoost, and was oure aller cok,
And gadrede us togidre alle in a flok,
And forth we riden a litel moore than paas   825
Unto the wateryng of Seint Thomas;
And there oure Hoost bigan his hors areste
And seyde, 'Lordynges, herkneth, if yow leste.
Ye woot youre foreward, and I it yow recorde.
If even-song and morwe-song accorde,   830
Lat se now who shal telle the firste tale.
As evere mote I drynke wyn or ale,
Whoso be rebel to my juggement
Shal paye for al that by the wey is spent.
Now draweth cut, er that we ferrer twynne;   835
He which that hath the shorteste shal bigynne.
Sire Knyght,' quod he, 'my mayster and my lord,
Now draweth cut, for that is myn accord.
Cometh neer,' quod he, 'my lady Prioresse.
And ye, sire Clerk, lat be youre shamefastnesse,   840
Ne studieth noght; ley hond to, every man!'
Anon to drawen every wight bigan,
And shortly for to tellen as it was,
Were it by aventure, or sort, or cas,
The sothe is this, the cut fil to the Knyght,   845
Of which ful blithe and glad was every wyght,
And telle he moste his tale, as was resoun,
By foreward and by composicioun,
As ye han herd; what nedeth wordes mo?
And whan this goode man saugh that it was so,   850
As he that wys was and obedient
To kepe his foreward by his free assent,
He seyde, 'Syn I shal bigynne the game,
What, welcome be the cut, a Goddes name!
Now lat us ryde, and herkneth what I seye.'   855
And with that word we ryden forth oure weye,
And he bigan with right a myrie cheere
His tale anon, and seyde as ye may heere.

THE NUN'S PRIEST'S TALE

A POVRE WYDWE, somdeel stape in age
Was whilom dwellyng in a narwe cotage,
Biside a grove, stondynge in a dale.
This wydwe, of which I telle yow my tale,
Syn thilke day that she was last a wyf,   5
In pacience ladde a ful symple lyf,
For litel was hir catel and hir rente.
By housbondrie of swich as God hire sente
She foond hirself and eek hir doghtren two.
Thre large sowes hadde she, and namo,   10
Three keen, and eek a sheep that highte Malle.
Ful sooty was hire bour and eek hir halle,
In which she eet ful many a sklendre meel.
Of poynaunt sauce hir neded never a deel.
No deyntee morsel passed thurgh hir throte;   15
Hir diete was accordant to hir cote.
Repleccioun ne made hire nevere sik;
Attempree diete was al hir phisik,
And exercise, and hertes suffisaunce.
The goute lette hire nothyng for to daunce,   20
N'apoplexie shente nat hir heed.
No wyn ne drank she, neither whit ne reed;
Hir bord was served moost with whit and blak –
Milk and broun breed, in which she foond no lak,
Seynd bacoun, and somtyme an ey or tweye;   25
For she was, as it were, a maner deye.
    A yeerd she hadde, enclosed al aboute
With stikkes, and a drye dych withoute,
In which she hadde a cok, hight Chauntecleer.
In al the land, of crowyng nas his peer.   30
His voys was murier than the murie orgon
On messe-dayes that in the chirche gon.
Wel sikerer was his crowyng in his logge
Than is a clokke or an abbey orlogge.
By nature he knew ech ascencioun   35
Of the equynoxial in thilke toun;
For whan degrees fiftene were ascended,
Thanne crew he, that it myghte nat been amended.

---

816 **And we wol . . . his devys:** And we agreed to abide by his
decision 817 **in heigh and lough:** in all respects 819 **fet:** fetched
820 **echon:** each one 822 **Amorwe:** in the morning 823 **was oure
aller coke:** woke us all 825 **paas:** walking pace 826 **wateryng of Seint
Thomas:** brook by the second milestone on the road from
London to Canterbury 827 **areste:** stop 828 **if you leste:** if you
please 829 **woot youre foreward:** know your agreement **I it yow
recorde:** I remind you of it 830 **If even-song . . . accorde:** If you feel
the same way this morning as you did last night 831 **Lat se:** let us
see 832 **mote:** may 835 **draweth cut:** draw lots **er that we ferrer
twynne:** before we go any further 838 **accord:** decision 840 **lat be:**
put aside **shamefastnesse:** shyness, modesty 844 **Were it . . . or cas:**
Whether it was by chance, or luck, or destiny 845 **sothe:** truth
847–8 **resoun, By . . . composicioun:** right, by our agreement and
according to the arrangement (i.e. the draw) 853 **Syn:** since

NUN'S PRIEST'S TALE: 1 **somdeel stape in age:** somewhat advanced in
years 2 **whilom:** at one time 5 **Syn:** since **thilke:** the very 7 **catel:**
property **rente:** income 8 **housbondrie:** careful management
9 **foond hirself:** provided for herself **eek:** also **doghtren:** daughters
10 **namo:** no more 11 **keen:** cows **highte Malle:** was called Malle
(pet-name for Mary) 12 **sooty:** coated in soot **bour:** private room
halle: common living-room 13 **sklendre:** scanty 14 **Of poynaunt . . .
deel:** She had no need of spicy sauces 15 **deyntee:** delicate
16 **diete:** food **cote:** small farm (i.e. she lived off her own produce)
17 **Repleccioun:** over-eating 18 **Attempree:** moderate **al hir phisik:**
her only medicine 19 **hertes suffisaunce:** a contented heart 20 **The
goute . . . daunce:** Gout didn't stop her from dancing at all
21 **shente:** injured 24 **foond no lak:** had no shortage 25 **Seynd:**
grilled **ey or tweye:** egg or two 26 **a maner deye:** a kind of
dairywoman 27 **yeerd:** garden 28 **stikkes:** a wooden fence 30 **nas
his peer:** he had no equal 31 **murie:** merry **orgon:** organ 33 **sikerer:**
more reliable **logge:** house 34 **orlogge:** clock 35–8 **Be nature . . .
were amended:** astrological references indicating that the cock
crew on time and in a way that could not be improved on

His coomb was redder than the fyn coral,
And batailled as it were a castel wal; 40
His byle was blak, and as the jeet it shoon;
Lyk asure were his legges and his toon;
His nayles whitter than the lylye flour,
And lyk the burned gold was his colour.
This gentil cok hadde in his governaunce 45
Sevene hennes for to doon al his plesaunce,
Whiche were his sustres and his paramours,
And wonder lyk to hym, as of colours;
Of whiche the faireste hewed on hir throte
Was cleped faire damoysele Pertelote. 50
Curteys she was, discreet, and debonaire,
And compaignable, and bar hyrself so faire,
Syn thilke day that she was seven nyght oold,
That trewely she hath the herte in hoold
Of Chauntecleer, loken in every lith; 55
He loved hire so that wel was hym therwith.
But swich a joye was it to here hem synge,
Whan that the brighte sonne gan to sprynge,
In sweete accord, 'My lief is faren in londe!'
For thilke tyme, as I have understonde, 60
Beestes and briddes koude speke and synge.
    And so bifel that in a dawenynge,
As Chauntecleer among his wyves alle
Sat on his perche, that was in the halle,
And next hym sat this faire Pertelote, 65
This Chauntecleer gan gronen in his throte,
As man that in his dreem is drecched soore.
And whan that Pertelote thus herde hym roore,
She was agast, and seyde, 'Herte deere,
What eyleth yow, to grone in this manere? 70
Ye been a verray sleper; fy, for shame!'
And he answerde, and seyde thus: 'Madame,
I pray yow that ye take it nat agrief.
By God, me mette I was in swich meschief
Right now, that yet myn herte is soore afright. 75
Now God,' quod he, 'my swevene recche aright,
And kepe my body out of foul prisoun!

Me mette how that I romed up and doun
Withinne our yeerd, wheer as I saugh a beest
Was lyk an hound, and wolde han maad areest 80
Upon my body, and wolde han had me deed.
His colour was bitwixe yelow and reed,
And tipped was his tayl and both his eeris
With blak, unlyk the remenant of his heeris;
His snowte smal, with glowynge eyen tweye. 85
Yet of his look for feere almoost I deye;
This caused me my gronyng, doutelees.'
    'Avoy!' quod she, 'fy on yow, hertelees!
Allas!' quod she, 'for, by that God above,
Now han ye lost myn herte and al my love. 90
I kan nat love a coward, by my feith!
For certes, what so any womman seith,
We alle desiren, if it myghte bee,
To han housbondes hardy, wise, and free,
And secree, and no nygard, ne no fool, 95
Ne hym that is agast of every tool,
Ne noon avauntour, by that God above!
How dorste ye seyn, for shame, unto youre love
That any thyng myghte make yow aferd?
Have ye no mannes herte, and han a berd? 100
Allas! and konne ye been agast of swevenys?
Nothyng, Good woot, but vanitee in sweven is.
Swevenes engendren of repleccsiouns,
And ofte of fume and of compleccsiouns,
Whan humours been to habundant in a wight. 105
Certes this dreem, which ye han met to-nyght,
Cometh of greete superfluytee
Of youre rede colera, pardee,
Which causeth folk to dreden in hir dremes
Of arwes, and of fyr with rede lemes, 110
Of rede beestes, that they wol hem byte,
Of contek, and of whelpes, gret and lyte;
Right as the humour of malencolie
Causeth ful many a man in sleep to crie
For feere of blake beres, or boles blake, 115
Or elles blake develes wole hem take.
Of othere humours koude I telle also
That werken many a man sleep ful wo;
But I wol passe as lightly as I kan.

---

39 **fyn coral:** finest red coral 40 **batailled:** crenellated 41 **byle:** beak
jeet: jet 42 **asure:** azure **toon:** toes 44 **burned:** burnished 45 **gentil:**
high-born 46 **plesaunce:** pleasure 47 **sustres:** sisters **paramours:**
concubines 49 **faireste hewed:** most beautifully coloured 50 **cleped:**
called **faire damoysele:** beautiful mistress 51 **curteys:** courteous
debonaire: charming 52 **compaignable:** friendly 53 **syn thilke day:**
since that day 54 **in hoold:** in bondage 55 **loken in every lith:**
bound fast in every limb 56 **He loved hire . . . therwith:** He found
complete contentment in his love for her 58 **sprynge:** rise 59 **my
lief is faren in londe:** my love has gone away (a popular love-
song?) 61 **briddes:** birds **koude:** knew how to 62 **bifel:** it happened
in a dawenynge: one day at dawn 66 **gan gronen:** groaned 67 **man:**
somebody **drecched soore:** badly disturbed 68 **roore:** roar 70 **what
eyleth yow?:** what is wrong with you? 71 **ye been a verray sleper:**
you're a fine sleeper! 73 **agrief:** amiss 74 **me mette:** I dreamed
swich meschief: such trouble 76 **my swevene recche aright:** make
my dream turn out all right

79 **saugh:** saw 80–1 **wolde han maad areest Upon:** would have laid
hold of 81 **deed:** dead 84 **heeris:** hairs 85 **snowte smal:** narrow
muzzle 86 **Yet:** even now 88 **Avoy!:** away! **fy:** shame **hertelees:**
faintheart 92 **certes:** certainly 94 **hardy:** bold **free:** generous
95 **secree:** discreet **nygard:** miser 96 **agast of every tool:** afraid of
every weapon 97 **avauntour:** boaster 100 **berd:** beard 101 **swevenys:**
dreams 102 **vanitee:** illusion 103 **Swevenes . . . repleccsiouns:**
Dreams are caused by going to sleep on a full stomach 104 **fume:**
i.e. indigestion 104–5 **compleccsiouns . . . wight:** see note on
humours in 'General Prologue' (line 333) 106 **met:** dreamed
108 **rede colera:** red bile **pardee:** assuredly 109 **dreden:** be afraid
110 **arwes:** arrows **lemes:** flames 111 **that they:** which 112 **contek:**
strife **whelpes, grete and lyte:** big and little dogs 113 **humour of
malencolie:** melancholy humour 115 **For feere . . . blake:** For fear
of black bears or black bulls 118 **That werken . . . wo:** That give
many people a bad night's sleep

'Lo Catoun, which that was so wys a man, 120
Seyde he nat thus, "Ne do no fors of dremes?"
'Now sire,' quod she, 'whan we flee fro the bemes,
For Goddes love, as taak som laxatyf.
Up peril of my soule and of my lyf,
I conseille yow the beste, I wol nat lye, 125
That bothe of colere and of malencolye
Ye purge yow; and for ye shal nat tarie,
Though in this toun is noon apothecarie,
I shal myself to herbes techen yow
That shul been for youre hele and for youre prow; 130
And in oure yeerd tho herbes shal I fynde 131
The whiche han of hire propretee by kynde
To purge yow bynethe and eek above.
Foryet nat this, for Goddes owene love!
Ye been ful coleryk of compleccioun; 135
Ware the sonne in his ascencioun
Ne fynde yow nat repleet of humours hoote.
And if it do, I dar wel leye a grote,
That ye shul have a fevere terciane,
Or an agu, that may be youre bane. 140
A day or two ye shul have digestyves
Of wormes, er ye take youre laxatyves
Of lawriol, centaure, and fumetere,
Or elles of ellebor, that groweth there,
Of katapuce, or of gaitrys beryis, 145
Of herbe yve, growyng in oure yeerd, ther mery is;
Pekke hem up right as they growe and ete hem yn.
Be myrie, housbonde, for youre fader kyn!
Dredeth no dreem, I kan sey yow namoore.'
'Madame,' quod he, 'graunt mercy of youre loore. 150
But nathelees, as touchyng daun Catoun, 151
That hath of wysdom swich a greet renoun,
Though that he bad no dremes for to drede,
By God, men may in olde bookes rede
Of many a man moore of auctorite 155
Than evere Caton was, so moot I thee,
That al the revers seyn of this sentence,

And han wel founden by experience
That dremes been significaciouns
As wel of joye as of tribulaciouns 160
That folk enduren in this lif present.
Ther nedeth make of this noon argument;
The verray preeve sheweth it in dede.
'Oon of the gretteste auctour that men rede
Seith thus: that whilom two felawes wente 165
On pilgrimage, in a ful good entente;
And happed so, they coomen in a toun
Wher as ther was swich congregacioun
Of peple, and eek so streit of herbergage,
That they ne founde as muche as o cotage 170
In which they bothe myghte ylogged bee.
Wherfore they mosten of necessitee,
As for that nyght, departen compaignye;
And ech of hem gooth to his holstelrye,
And took his loggyng as it wolde falle. 175
That oon of hem was logged in a stalle,
Fer in a yeerd, with oxen of the plough;
That oother man was logged wel ynough,
As was his aventure or his fortune,
That us governeth alle as in commune. 180
'And so bifel that, longe er it were day,
This man mette in his bed, ther as he lay,
How that his felawe gan upon hym calle,
And seyde, "Allas! for in an oxes stalle
This nyght I shal be mordred ther I lye. 185
Now help me, deere brother, or I dye.
In alle haste come to me!" he sayde.
This man out of his sleep for feere abrayde;
But whan that he was wakened of his sleep,
He turned hym, and took of this no keep. 190
Hym thoughte his dreem nas but a vanitee.
Thus twies in his slepyng dremed hee;
And atte thridde tyme yet his felawe
Cam, as hym thoughte, and seide, "I am now slawe.
Bihoold my bloody woundes depe and wyde! 195
Arys up erly in the morwe tyde,
And at the west gate of the toun," quod he,
"A carte ful of dong ther shaltow se,
In which my body is hid ful prively;
Do thilke carte arresten boldely. 200
My gold caused my mordre, sooth to sayn."

---

120 **Catoun:** Marcus Porcius Cato, author of Latin maxims (3rd–4th century AD) 121 **ne do no fors of dremes:** take no notice of dreams 122 **flee fro the bemes:** fly from the perches 123 **as taak:** please take 124 **Up:** on 127 **for ye shal nat tarie:** so that you need not wait 129 **techen:** direct 130 **that shul been for youre hele:** to make you better **prow:** profit, benefit 132 **The whiche . . . kynde:** Each of which has its own special quality 134 **foryet:** forget 135 **Ye been . . . compleccioun:** You have too much bile in your constitution 136–7 **Ware . . . humours hoote:** Take care that the sun, as it gets higher in the sky, doesn't find you full of hot humours 138 **leye a grote:** wager a groat (silver coin worth four pennies) 139 **fevere terciane:** tertian fever (one that recurs every third day) 140 **agu:** ague (acute fever) **bane:** death 141 **digestyves:** aids to digestion 143 **lawriol:** spurge laurel **centaure:** centaury **fumetere:** fumitory 144 **ellebor:** hellebore 145 **katapuce:** caper spurge **gaitrys beryis:** dogwood berries 146 **herbe yve:** probably buck's horn plantain **ther mery is:** where it's pleasant 148 **for youre fader kyn:** for the sake of your father's lineage 150 **graunt mercy:** many thanks 151 **daun:** master (title of respect) 153 **Though . . . to drede:** Though he told us not to fear any dreams 156 **so moot I thee:** as I may prosper 157 **al the revers syne:** say the complete opposite **sentence:** opinion

158 **han:** have 159 **significaciouns:** indicators 162 **noon argument:** no argument 163 **The verray preeve . . . dede:** The true proof is shown by experience 164 **Oon of the gretteste auctour:** one of the greatest authors 165 **felawes:** companions 166 **in a ful good entente:** with the very best intentions 168 **congregacioun:** crowd 169 **streit of herbergage:** short of accommodation 171 **ylogged:** lodged 173 **departen compaignye:** part company 175 **as it wolde falle:** as luck would have it 176 **that oon:** the one 177 **fer:** far away 179 **aventure:** luck **fortune:** destiny 180 **as in commune:** universally 182 **ther as:** where 185 **ther:** where 188 **abrayde:** started awake 190 **keep:** notice 191 **Hym thoughte . . . vanitee:** It seemed to him that his dream was nothing but an illusion 193 **thirdde:** third 194 **slawe:** slain 196 **in the morwe tyde:** in the morning 198 **dong:** dung 200 **Do thilke carte arresten:** have the cart stopped 201 **sooth to sayn:** to tell the truth

And tolde hym every point how he was slayn,
With a ful pitous face, pale of hewe.
And truste wel, his dreem he foond ful trewe,
For on the morwe, as soone as it was day,   205
To his felawes in he took the way;
And whan that he cam to this oxes stalle,
After his felawe he bigan to calle.
    'The hostiler answerede hym anon,
And seyde, "Sire, your felawe is agon.   210
As soone as day he wente out of the toun."
    'This man gan fallen in suspecioun,
Remembrynge on his dremes that he mette,
And forth he gooth – no lenger wolde he lette –
Unto the west gate of the toun, and fond   215
A donge-carte, went as it were to donge lond,
That was arrayed in that same wise
As ye han herd the dede man devyse.
And with an hardy herte he gan to crye
Vengeance and justice of this felonye.   220
"My felawe mordred is this same nyght,
And in this carte he lith gapyng upright.
I crye out on the ministres," quod he,
"That sholden kepe and reulen this citee.
Harrow! allas! heere lith my felawe slayn!"   225
What sholde I moore unto this tale sayn?
The peple out sterte and caste the cart to grounde,
And in the myddel of the dong they founde
The dede man, that mordred was al newe.
    'O blisful God, that art so just and trewe,   230
Lo, how that thou biwreyest mordre alway!
Mordre wol out, that se we day by day.
Mordre is so wlatsom and abhomynable
To God, that is so just and resonable,
That he ne wol nat suffre it heled be,   235
Though it abyde a yeer, or two, or thre.
Mordre wol out, this my conclusioun.
And right anon, ministres of that toun
Han hent the carter and so soore hym pyned,
And eek the hostiler so soore engyned,   240
That they biknewe hire wikkednesse anon,
And were anhanged by the nekke-bon.
    'Heere may men seen that dremes been to drede.
And certes in the same book I rede,
Right in the nexte chapitre after this –   245
I gabbe nat, so have I joye or blis –

Two men that wolde han passed over see,
For certeyn cause, into a fer contree,
If that the wynd ne hadde been contrarie,
That made hem in a citee for to tarie   250
That stood ful myrie upon an haven-syde;
But on a day, agayn the even-tyde,
The wynd gan chaunge, and blew right as hem leste.
Jolif and glad they wente unto hir reste,
And casten hem ful erly for to saille.   255
But to that o man fil a greet mervaille:
That oon of hem, in slepyng as he lay,
Hym mette a wonder dreem agayn the day.
Hym thoughte a man stood by his beddes syde,
And hym comanded that he sholde abyde,   260
And seyde hym thus: "If thou tomorwe wende,
Thow shalt be dreynt; my tale is at an ende."
He wook, and tolde his felawe what he mette,
And preyde hym his viage for to lette;
As for that day, he preyde hym to byde.   265
His felawe, that lay by his beddes syde,
Gan for to laughe, and scorned him ful faste.
"No dreem," quod he, "may so myn herte agaste
That I wol lette for to do my thynges.
I sette nat a straw by thy dremynges,   270
For swevenes been but vanytees and japes.
Men dreme alday of owles and of apes,
And eek of many a maze therwithal;
Men dreme of thyng that nevere was ne shal.
But sith I see that thou wolt heere abyde,   275
And thus forslewthen wilfully thy tyde,
God woot, it reweth me; and have good day!"
And thus he took his leve, and wente his way.
But er that he hadde half his cours yseyled,
Noot I nat why, ne what myschaunce it eyled,   280
But casuelly the shippes botme rente,
And ship and man under the water wente
In sighte of othere shippes it bisyde,
That with hem seyled at the same tyde.
And therfore, faire Pertelote so deere,   285
By swich ensamples olde maistow leere
That no man sholde been to recchelees
Of dremes; for I seye thee, doutelees,
That many a dreem ful soore is for to drede.

---

206 **in:** inn 209 **hostiler:** innkeeper 214 **And forth . . . lette:** And off he went – he would delay no longer 216 **wente as it were to donge lond:** looking as if it were on its way to manure the land 217 **arrayed:** arranged **wise:** manner 218 **devyse:** describe 219 **with an hardy herte:** courageously 222 **lith gapyng upright:** lies flat on his back, staring upwards 223 **crye out on:** call upon **ministres:** officers of the law **quod he:** he cried 225 **Harrow!:** Help! 226 **What sholde . . . sayn?:** What more is there to say? 229 **al newe:** very recently 231 **biwreyest:** reveal 233 **wlatsom:** loathsome 235 **heled:** hidden 237 **this:** this is 239 **hent:** seized **pyned:** tortured 240 **engyned:** tortured him on the rack 241 **biknewe:** confessed **anon:** at once 243 **been to drede:** are to be feared 246 **gabbe:** tell a lie

251 **haven-syde:** quayside 252 **agayn:** shortly before 253 **right as hem leste:** just as they wished 255 **casten hem:** made up their minds 256 **that o man:** one of the two men 258 **agayn the day:** shortly before dawn 259 **hym thoughte:** it seemed to him 261 **wende:** go 262 **dreynt:** drowned 264 **his viage for to lette:** to give up his journey 267 **Gan for laughe . . . faste:** Began to laugh and heaped scorn upon him 268 **agaste:** terrify 271 **japes:** tricks 272 **alday:** every day 273 **maze:** mystery, puzzle, conundrum 276 **forslewthen:** slothfully waste **tyde:** time 277 **God woot, it reweth me:** God knows, I'm very sorry 280 **Noot I nat why, ne what myschaunce it eyled:** I know not why, nor what mischance brought it about 281 **casuelly:** by accident **rente:** was torn 286 **maistow leere:** you may learn 287–8 **recchelees Of dremes:** dismissive of dreams

Lo, in the lyf of Seint Kenelm I rede, 290
That was Kenulphus sone, the noble kyng
Of Mercenrike, how Kenelm mette a thyng.
A lite er he was mordred, on a day,
His mordre in his avysioun he say.
His norice hym expowned every deel 295
His sweven, and bad hym for to kepe hym weel
For traisoun; but he nas but seven yeer oold,
And therfore litel tale hath he toold
Of any dreem, so hooly was his herte.
By God! I hadde levere than my sherte 300
That ye hadde rad his legende, as have I.
    'Dame Pertelote, I sey yow trewely,
Macrobeus, that writ the avisioun
In Affrike of the worthy Cipioun,
Affermeth dremes, and seith that they been 305
Warnynge of thynges that men after seen.
And forthermoore, I pray yow, looketh wel
In the olde testament, of Daniel,
If he heeld dremes any vanitee.
Reed eek of Joseph, and ther shul ye see 310
Wher dremes be somtyme – I sey nat alle –
Warnynge of thynges that shul after falle.
Looke of Egipte the kyng, daun Pharao,
His bakere and his butiller also,
Wher they ne felte noon effect in dremes. 315
Whoso wol seken actes of sondry remes
May rede of dremes many a wonder thyng.
Lo Cresus, which that was of Lyde kyng,
Mette he nat that he sat upon a tree,
Which signified he sholde anhanged bee? 320
Lo heere Andromacha, Ectores wyf,
That day that Ector sholde lese his lyf,
She dremed on the same nyght biforn
How that the lyf of Ector sholde be lorn,
If thilke day he wente into bataille. 325
She warned hym, but it myghte nat availle;
He wente for to fighte natheles,
But he was slayn anon of Achilles.
But thilke tale is al to longe to telle,
And eek it is ny day, I may nat dwelle. 330

290 **Seint Kenelm:** St Cenhelm 291 **Kenulphus:** Cenwulf, king of
Mercia (d. 821), father of Cenhelm 292 **Mercenrike:** Mercia 293 **lite:**
little 294 **His mordre . . . say:** He saw his murder foretold in a
dream 295–7 **His norice . . . traisoun:** His nurse explained every
detail of his dream, and urged him to beware of treachery
297–9 **but he nas . . . his herte:** but he was only seven years old and
therefore he took little account of any dream, so pure was his
heart 300–1 **I hadde levere . . . as have I:** I would give my shirt for
you to have read his story as I have 303 **Macrobeus:** Macrobius
(*fl.*AD 40), author of *The Dream of Scipio* 304 **Cipioun:** Scipio
Africanus Minor 305 **affermeth:** asserts the truth of 308 **of Daniel:**
the book of Daniel 310 **Joseph:** famous as the interpreter of
Pharaoh's dreams (Genesis 41) 311 **Wher:** whether 313 **daun:**
master **Pharao:** Pharaoh **butiller:** steward 315 **effect:** significance
316 **Whoso . . . remes:** Anybody who consults the records
of different kingdoms 318 **Cresus:** Croesus, king of Lydia
321 **Andromacha, Ectores wyf:** Andromache, wife of Hector of Troy
322 **sholde lese:** was destined to lose 324 **lorn:** lost 327 **natheles:**
nevertheless 330 **dwelle:** linger

Shortly I seye, as for conclusioun,
That I shal han of this avisioun
Adversitee; and I seye forthermoor,
That I ne telle of laxatyves no stoor,
For they been venymous, I woot it weel; 335
I hem diffye, I love hem never a deel!
    'Now let us speke of myrthe, and stynte al this.
Madame Pertelote, so have I blis,
Of o thyng God hath sent me large grace;
For whan I se the beautee of youre face, 340
Ye been so scarlet reed aboute youre eyen,
It maketh al my drede for to dyen;
For al so siker as *In principio*,
Mulier est hominis confusio –
Madame, the sentence of this Latyn is, 345
"Womman is mannes joye and al his blis."
For whan I feel a-nyght your softe syde,
Al be it that I may nat on yow ryde,
For that oure perche is maad so narwe, allas!
I am so ful of joye and of solas, 350
That I diffye both sweven and dreem.'
And with that word he fley doun fro the beem,
For it was day, and eke his hennes alle,
And with a chuk he gan hem for to calle,
For he hadde founde a corn, lay in the yerd. 355
Real he was, he was namoore aferd.
He fethered Pertelote twenty tyme,
And trad hire eke as ofte, er it was pryme.
He looketh as it were a grym leoun,
And on his toos he rometh up and doun; 360
Hym deigned nat to sette his foot to grounde.
He chukketh whan he hath a corn yfounde,
And to hym rennen thanne his wyves alle.
Thus roial, as a prince is in his halle,
Leve I this Chauntecleer in his pasture, 365
And after wol I telle his aventure.
    Whan that the month in which the world bigan,
That highte March, whan God first maked man,
Was compleet, and passed were also,
Syn March bigan, thritty dayes and two, 370
Bifel that Chauntecleer in al his pryde,
His sevene wyves walkynge by his syde,
Caste up his eyen to the brighte sonne,

334 **That I . . . no stoor:** That I set no store by laxatives 336 **diffye:**
defy **never a deel:** not at all 337 **stynte:** cut short 339 **Of o thyng .
. . grace:** In one thing God has sent me abundant favour 342 **It
maketh . . . dyen:** It puts an end to all my fear 343 **al so siker as
In principio:** the gospel truth ('In principio' are the opening words
of Genesis 1 and St John's gospel) 344 *Mulier est hominis confusio:*
'Woman is man's ruin' 350 **solas:** delight 352 **fley doun fro the
beem:** flew down from the perch 354 **chuk:** cluck 355 **a corn:**
a grain of corn 356 **Real:** royal, princely (i.e. ruling the roost)
357 **fethered:** wrapped in his feathers 358 **trad:** copulated with
pryme: 9 a.m. (the end of the period beginning at 6 a.m., the first
hour of the day appointed for prayer) 359 **leoun:** lion 362 **chukketh:**
clucks 364 **roial:** see note to 'real' (line 356) 365 **pasture:** feeding-
place 367–70 **Whan that . . . thritty dayes and two:** i.e. it was 3 May

That in the signe of Taurus hadde yronne
Twenty degrees and oon, and somwhat moore, 375
And knew by kynde, and by noon oother loore,
That it was pryme, and crew with blisful stevene.
'The sonne', he seyde, 'is clomben up on hevene
Fourty degrees and oon, and moore ywis.
Madame Pertelote, my worldes blis, 380
Herkneth thise blisful briddes how they synge,
And se the fresshe floures how they sprynge;
Ful is myn herte of revel and solas!'
But sodeynly hym fil a sorweful cas,
For evere the latter ende of joye is wo. 385
God woot that worldly joye is soone ago;
And if a rethor koude faire endite,
He in a cronycle saufly myghte it write
As for a sovereyn notabilitee.
Now every wys man, lat him herkne me; 390
This storie is also trewe, I undertake,
As is the book of Launcelot de Lake,
That wommen holde in ful greet reverence.
Now wol I torne agayn to my sentence.
  A col-fox, ful of sly iniquitee, 395
That in the grove hadde woned yeres three,
By heigh ymaginacioun forncast,
The same nyght thurghout the hegges brast
Into the yerd ther Chauntecleer the faire
Was wont, and eek his wyves, to repaire; 400
And in a bed of wortes stille he lay,
Til it was passed undren of the day,
Waitynge his tyme on Chauntecleer to falle,
As gladly doon thise homycides alle
That in await liggen to mordre men. 405
O false mordrour, lurkynge in thy den!
O newe Scariot, newe Genylon,
False dissymulour o Greek Synon,
That broghtest Troye al outrely to sorwe!
O Chauntecleer, acursed be that morwe 410
That thou into that yerd flaugh fro the bemes!
Thou were ful wel ywarned by thy dremes
That thilke day was perilous to thee;

But what that God forwoot moot nedes bee,
After the opinioun of certein clerkis. 415
Witnesse on hym that any parfit clerk is,
That in scole is greet altercacioun
In this mateere, and greet disputisoun,
And hath been of an hundred thousand men.
But I ne kan nat bulte it to the bren 420
As kan the hooly doctour Augustyn,
Or Boece, or the Bisshop Bradwardyn,
Wheither that Goddes worthy forwityng
Streyneth me nedely for to doon a thyng –
'Nedely' clepe I symple necessitee; 425
Or elles, if free choys be graunted me
To do that same thyng, or do it noght,
Though God forwoot it er that I was wroght;
Or if his wityng streyneth never a deel
But by necessitee condicioneel. 430
I wol nat han to do of swich mateere;
My tale is of a cok, as ye may heere,
That tok his conseil of his wyf, with sorwe,
To walken in the yerd upon that morwe
That he hadde met that dreem that I yow tolde. 435
Wommennes conseils been ful ofte colde;
Wommannes conseil broghte us first to wo,
And made Adam fro Paradys to go,
Ther as he was ful myrie and wel at ese.
But for I noot to whom it myght displese, 440
If I conseil of wommen wolde blame,
Passe over, for I seyde it in my game.
Rede auctours, where they trete of swich mateere,
And what they seyn of wommen ye may heere.
Thise been the cokkes wordes, and nat myne; 445
I kan noon harm of no womman divyne.
  Faire in the soond, to bathe hire myrily,
Lith Pertelote, and all hire sustres by,
Agayn the sonne, and Chauntecleer so free
Soong murier than the mermayde in the see; 450
For Phisiologus seith sikerly
How that they syngen wel and myrily.

374–9 **That in the signe of Taurus . . . moore ywis:** i.e. it was 9 a.m. 376 **kynde:** instinct 377 **stevene:** voice 379 **ywis:** indeed 383 **revel:** enjoyment 384 **fil:** happened **sorweful cas:** sad event 386 **ago:** gone 387 **rethor:** rhetorician **faire endite:** write elegantly 389 **sovereyn notabilitee:** very remarkable thing 392 **Launcelot de Lake:** Sir Lancelot of the Lake, knight of the Round Table in the Arthurian legends 394 **sentence:** theme 395 **col-fox:** coal-fox, a fox with black markings 396 **woned:** dwelt 397 **By heigh ymaginacioun forncast:** foreordained by high imagination (probably refers to divine foreknowledge) 398 **thurghout the hegges brast:** broke right through the fences 401 **wortes:** cabbages 402 **undren:** the morning 403 **waitynge:** watching out for 404 **gladly:** customarily 405 **liggen:** lie 407 **Scariot:** Judas Iscariot, the disciple who betrayed Jesus **Genylon:** Ganelon, who betrayed the rearguard of Charlemagne at Roncesvalles 408 **dissymulour:** deceiver **Synon:** Sinon, the Greek who persuaded the Trojans to drag the wooden horse into Troy 409 **outrely:** utterly 410 **morwe:** morning 411 **flaugh:** flew

414 **what that:** that which **forewoot:** has foreknowledge of 416 **Witnesse . . . clerk is:** Take as witness any accomplished scholar 417 **That in . . . altercacioun:** In the schools of philosophy there is much argument 420 **But I ne kan . . . bren:** But I can't sift it down to the bran, i.e. get to the bottom of it 421 **doctour:** teacher **Augustyn:** St Augustine, Bishop of Hippo 422 **Boece:** Boethius, whose *Consolation of Philosophy* was translated by Chaucer **Bradwardyn:** Thomas Bradwardine, Archbishop of Canterbury (d.1349), a theologian who held the Augustinian view of Grace 423 **forwityng:** foreknowledge 424–5 **Streyneth . . . necessitee:** Constrains me of necessity to do a certain thing; by 'necessity' I mean simple necessity (Boethius distinguished between simple necessity and conditional necessity: see 'necessitee condicionel' in line 430) 428 **forwoot:** foreknew 433 **with sorwe:** with unhappy results 436 **Wommennes . . . colde:** Women's advice is often ruinous 440–2 **But for I noot . . . my game:** But, as I don't know whom it would displease if I were to find fault with women's advice, ignore my remarks, for I meant them in fun 446 **I kan . . . divyne:** I can conceive of no fault in woman 447 **soond:** sand 448 **lith:** lies 449 **Agayn:** in 451 **Phisiologus:** a famous bestiary, or allegorical natural history of animals

And so bifel that, as he caste his ye
Among the wortes on a boterflye,
He was war of this fox, that lay ful lowe. 455
Nothyng ne liste hym thanne for to crowe,
But cride anon, 'Cok! cok!' and up he sterte
As man that was affrayed in his herte.
For natureelly a beest desireth flee
Fro his contrarie, if he may it see, 460
Though he never erst hadde seyn it with his ye.
    This Chauntecleer, whan he gan hym espye,
He wolde han fled, but that the fox anon
Seyde, 'Gentil sire, allas! wher wol ye gon?
Be ye affrayed of me that am youre freend? 465
Now, certes, I were worse than a feend,
If I to yow wolde harm or vileynye!
I am nat come youre conseil for t'espye,
But trewely, the cause of my comynge
Was oonly for to herkne how that ye synge. 470
For trewely, ye have as myrie a stevene
As any aungel hath that is in hevene.
Therwith ye han in musyk moore feelynge
Than hadde Boece, or any that kan synge.
My lord your fader – God his soule blesse! – 475
And eek youre mooder, of hire gentillesse,
Han in myn hous ybeen to me greet ese;
And certes, sire, ful fayn wolde I yow plese.
But, for men speke of syngyng, I wol seye –
So moote I brouke wel myne eyen tweye – 480
Save yow, I herde nevere man so synge
As dide youre fader in the morwenynge.
Certes, it was of herte, al that he song.
And for to make his voys the moore strong,
He wolde so peyne hym that with bothe his eyen 485
He moste wynke, so loude he wolde cryen,
And stonden on his tiptoon therwithal,
And strecche forth his nekke long and smal.
And eek he was of swich discrecioun
That ther nas no man in no regioun 490
That hym in song or wisedom myghte passe.
I have wel rad in 'Daun Burnel the Asse',
Among his vers, how that ther was a cok,
For that a preestes sone yaf hym a knok
Upon his leg whil he was yong and nyce, 495
He made hym for to lese his benefice.

But certeyn, ther nys no comparisoun
Bitwixe the wisedom and discrecioun
Of youre fader and of his subtiltee.
Now syngeth, sire, for seinte charitee; 500
Lat se, konne ye youre fader countrefete?'
    This Chauntecleer his wynges gan to bete,
As man that koude his traysoun nat espie,
So was he ravysshed with his flaterie.
    Allas! ye lordes, many a fals flatour 505
Is in youre courtes, and many a losengeour,
That plesen yow wel moore, by my feith,
Than he that soothfastnesse unto yow seith.
Redeth Ecclesiaste of flaterye;
Beth war, ye lordes, of hir trecherye. 510
    This Chauntecleer stood hye upon his toos,
Strecchynge his nekke, and heeld his eyen cloos,
And gan to crowe loude for the nones.
And daun Russell the foxe stirte up atones,
And by the gargat hente Chauntecleer, 515
And on his bak toward the wode hym beer,
For yet ne was ther no man that hym sewed.
    O destinee, that mayst nat been eschewed!
Allas, that Chauntecleer fleigh from the bemes!
Allas, his wyf ne roghte nat of dremes! 520
And on a Friday fil al this meschaunce.
    O Venus, that art goddesse of plesaunce,
Syn that thy servant was this Chauntecleer,
And in thy servyce dide al his poweer,
Moore for delit than world to multiplye, 525
Why woldestow suffre hym on thy day to dye?
    O Gaufred, deere maister soverayn,
That whan thy worthy kyng Richard was slayn
With shot, compleynedest his deeth so soore,
Why ne hadde I now thy sentence and thy loore, 530
The Friday for to chide, as diden ye?
For on a Friday, soothly, slayn was he.
Thanne wolde I shewe yow how that I koude pleyne
For Chauntecleres drede and for his peyne.
    Certes, swich cry ne lamentacioun, 535
Was nevere of ladyes maad when Ylion
Was wonne, and Pirrus with his streite swerd,
Whan he hadde hent kyng Priam by the berd,
And slayn hym, as seith us *Eneydos*,
As maden alle the hennes in the clos, 540

---

454 **wortes:** cabbages **boterflye:** butterfly 455 **war:** aware
456 **Nothyng . . . to crowe:** He didn't want to crow now 458 **affrayed:**
terrified 460 **if he may it see:** if he should see it 461 **erst:** previously
464 **gentil:** noble, well bred 467 **vileynye:** ill-treatment 468 **youre
conseil for t'espye:** to find out your secrets 471 **stevene:** voice
474 **Boece:** Boethius wrote a treatise on music 476 **hire gentillesse:**
their courtesy 477 **to my greet ese:** much to my satisfaction
478 **fayn:** gladly 479–80 **But, for men . . . eyen tweye:** But on the
subject of singing I'd like to say – so may I enjoy the use of both
my eyes – 483 **of herte:** from the heart 485 **so peyne hym:** go to
such pains 486 **moste wynke:** had to keep his eyes shut 488 **smal:**
slender 489 **discrecioun:** sound judgement 492 **'Daun Burnel the
Asse':** a tale about the adventures of a donkey in a satirical poem,
Speculum Stultorum (*Mirror of Fools*) 493 **vers:** verses 495 **nyce:** foolish
496 **lese:** lose

499 **subtiltee:** ingenuity 500 **seinte:** holy 501 **countrefete:** match
505 **flatour:** flatterer 506 **losengeour:** deceiver, smooth talker
508 **soothfastnesse:** the truth 509 **Ecclesiaste:** Ecclesiasticus,
Ecclesiastes or Proverbs 510 **beth war:** beware 513 **for the nones:**
for that occasion 514 **Russell:** meaning 'the red one' 515 **gargat:**
throat **hente:** seized 517 **sewed:** chased 518 **eschewed:** evaded
520 **ne roghte nat of:** paid no attention to 526 **Why woldestow . . .
to dye:** Why would you let him die on your day? (Roman name for
the sixth day of the week: *Veneris dies*) 527 **Gaufred:** Geoffrey de
Vinsauf, a famous rhetorician 528 **Richard:** Richard I, Richard
Coeur de Lion 529 **With shot:** by an arrow **compleynedest:**
lamented 530 **thy sentence and thy loore:** your depth of meaning
and your learning 536 **Ylion:** Ilium, or Troy, especially the Trojan
citadel 537 **Pirrus:** Pyrrhus **streite swerd:** drawn sword 539 *Eneydos:*
the *Aeneid* of Virgil 540 **clos:** yard

Whan they had seyn of Chauntecleer the sighte.
But sovereynly dame Pertelote shrighte
Ful louder than dide Hasdrubales wyf,
Whan that hir housbonde hadde lost his lyf,
And that the Romayns hadde brend Cartage.   545
She was so ful of torment and of rage
That wilfully into the fyr she sterte,
And brende hirselven with a stedefast herte.
   O woful hennes, right so criden ye,
As, whan that Nero brende the citee   550
Of Rome, cryden senatoures wyves
For that hir husbondes losten alle hir lyves –
Withouten gilt this Nero hath hem slayn.
Now wole I turne to my tale agayn.
   This sely wydwe and eek hir doghtres two   555
Herden thise hennes crie and maken wo,
And out at dores stirten they anon,
And syen the fox toward the grove gon,
And bar upon his bak the cok away,
And cryden, 'Out! harrow! and weyl-away!   560
Ha! ha! the fox!' and after hym they ran,
And eek with staves many another man,
Ran Colle oure dogge, and Talbot and Gerland,
And Malkyn, with a dystaf in hir hand;
Ran cow and calf, and eek the verray hogges,   565
So fered for the berkyng of the dogges
And shoutyng of the men and wommen eke,
They ronne so hem thoughte hir herte breeke.
They yolleden as feendes doon in helle;
The dokes cryden as men wolde hem quelle;   570
The gees for feere flowen over the trees;
Out of the hyve cam the swarm of bees.
So hydous was the noyse, a, *benedicitee!*
Certes, he Jakke Straw and his meynee
Ne made nevere shoutes half so shrille   575
Whan that they wolden any Flemyng kille,
As thilke day was maad upon the fox.
Of bras they broghten bemes, and of box,
Of horn, of boon, in whiche they blewe and powped,
And therwithal they skriked and they howped.   580
It semed as that hevene sholde falle.

   Now, goode men, I prey yow herkneth alle:
Lo, how Fortune turneth sodeynly
The hope and pryde eek of hir enemy!
This cok, that lay upon the foxes bak,   585
In al his drede unto the fox he spak,
And seyde, 'Sire, if that I were as ye,
Yet sholde I seyn, as wys God helpe me,
"Turneth agayn, ye proude cherles alle!
A verray pestilence upon yow falle!   590
Now am I come unto the wodes syde;
Maugree your heed, the cok shal herre abyde.
I wol hym ete, in feith, and that anon!" '
   The fox answerde, 'In feith, it shal be don.'
And as he spak that word, al sodeynly   595
This cok brak from his mouth delyverly,
And heighe upon a tree he fleigh anon.
And whan the fox saugh that the cok was gon,
'Allas!' quod he, 'O Chauntecleer, allas!
I have to yow,' quod he, 'ydoon trespas,   600
In as muche as I maked yow aferd
Whan I yow hente and broghte out of the yerd.
But, sire, I dide it in no wikke entente.
Com doun, and I shal telle yow what I mente;
I shal seye sooth to yow, God help me so!'   605
'Nay thanne,' quod he, 'I shrewe us bothe two.
And first I shrewe myself, bothe blood and bones,
If thou bigyle me ofter than ones.
Thou shalt namoore, thurgh thy flaterye,
Do me to synge and wynke with myn ye;   610
For he that wynketh, whan he sholde see,
Al wilfully, God lat him nevere thee!'
   'Nay,' quod the fox, 'but God yeve hym meschaunce,
That is so undiscreet of governaunce
That jangleth whan he sholde holde his pees.'   615
   Lo, swich it is for to be recchelees
And necligent, and truste on flaterye.
   But ye that holden this tale a folye,
As of a fox, or of a cok and hen,
Taketh the moralite, goode men.   620
For seint Paul seith that al that writen is,
To oure doctrine it is ywrite, ywis;
Taketh the fruyt, and lat the chaf be stille.
Now, goode God, if that it be thy wille,
As seith my lord, so make us alle goode men,   625
And brynge us to his heighe blisse! Amen.

---

542 **sovereynly:** above all the rest   **shrighte:** shrieked
543 **Hasdrubales wyf:** the wife of Hasdrubal 545 **Romayns:** Romans
brend: burned   **Cartage:** Carthage 546 **rage:** frenzy 547 **wilfully:**
by her own choice   **sterte:** rushed 555 **sely wydwe:** simple widow
556 **wo:** lament 558 **syen:** saw 560 **harrow:** help   **weyl-away:** an
exclamation of woe 562 **staves:** sticks 563 **Talbot and Gerland:** two
further dogs 564 **Malkyn:** a common name for a serving-maid
dystaf: distaff (for spinning wool) 565 **verray:** very 566 **fered for:**
frightened by   **berkyng:** barking 568 **They ronne . . . herte breeke:**
They ran so that they thought their hearts would burst
569 **yolleden:** yelled 570 **The dokes . . . quelle:** The ducks cried out
as if men were trying to kill them 573 **a:** ah!   *benedicitee!*: bless us!
574 **Jakke Straw:** a leader of the Peasants' Revolt (1381), in which
Flemings were murdered   **meynee:** mob 578 **bemes:** trumpets
box: boxwood 579 **powped:** tooted 580 **skriked:** shrieked **howped:**
whooped

588 **as wys God helpe me:** as surely as God may help me 589 **turneth**
agayn: turn back   **cherles:** peasants 592 **maugree youre heed:**
despite anything you may do 596 **delyverly:** nimbly 600 **ydoon**
trespas: done wrong 603 **wikke:** evil 606 **shrewe:** curse 608 **bigyle:**
beguile, trick 610 **wynke with myn ye:** shut my eyes 612 **thee:** thrive
613 **meschaunce:** ill luck 614 **That is . . . governaunce:** That so lacks
self-control 615 **jangleth:** chatters 618 **a folye:** a silly trifle 622 **To**
oure doctrine: for our instruction 623 **lat the chaf be stille:** leave
the husks alone 625 **if that it be thy wille, As seith my lord:** i.e. 'Thy
will be done' (Lord's Prayer)

JOHN LYDGATE

From THE TEMPLE OF GLAS

WITHIN my bed for sore I gan me shroude,
Al desolate for constreint of my wo,
The longe nyght waloing to and fro,
Til atte last, er I gan taken kepe,
Me did oppresse a sodein dedeli slepe,   5
Within the which me thoughte that I was
Ravysshid in spirit in a temple of glas –
I nyste how, ful fer in wildirnes –
That foundid was, as bi liklynesse,
Not opon stele, but on a craggy roche,   10
Like ise ifrore. And as I did approche,
Again the sonne that shone, me thought, so clere
As eny cristal, and ever nere and nere
As I gan neigh this grisli dredful place,
I wex astonyed: the light so in my face   15
Bigan to smyte, so persing ever in one
On evere part, where that I gan gone,
That I ne myght nothing, as I would,
Abouten me considre and bihold
The wondre hestres, for brightnes of the sonne;   20
Til atte last certein skyes donne,
With wind ichaced, have her cours iwent
Tofore the stremes of Titan and iblent,
So that I myght, within and withoute,
Whereso I walk, biholden me aboute,   25
Forto report the fasoun and manere
Of al this place, that was circulere
In compaswise, round b'entaile wrought.
And when that I hade long gone and sought,
I fond a wiket, and entrid in as fast   30
Into the temple, and myn eighen cast
On evere side, now lowe and eft aloft.
And right anone, as I gan walken soft,
If I the soth aright reporte shal,
I saughe depeynt opon evere wal,   35
From est to west, ful many a faire image
Of sondri lovers, lich as thei were of age
Isette in ordre, aftir thei were trwe,
With lifli colours wondir fressh of hwe.

[Lines 10–48]

TEMPLE OF GLAS: 1 **sore**: sorrow **gan me shroude**: went to hide myself 2 **constreint**: agony 3 **waloing**: tossing and turning 4 **er I gan taken kepe**: before I knew it 5 **Me did oppresse**: I was overcome by **dedeli**: deep 7 **Ravysshid**: transported 8 **nyste**: knew not **ful fer in wildirnes**: lost in amazement 9 **as bi liklynesse**: seemingly 10 **stele**: steel (i.e. solid ground, a firm foundation) **roche**: rock 11 **ise ifrore**: frozen ice 14 **neigh**: nigh 15 **wex**: became 16 **smyte**: beat **persing**: piercing, penetrating 17 **gan gone**: went 20 **wondre hestres**: wondrous apartments 21 **skyes donne**: dark clouds 23 **Tofore . . . iblent**: Across the sun and obscured its rays 26 **fasoun**: style 28 **round b'entaile wrought**: of a round construction 30 **wiket**: wicket-gate 31 **eighen**: eyes 32 **eft**: then 34 **soth**: truth 35 **saughe depeynt**: saw depicted 37 **lich**: like 38 **Isette**: set, arranged **trwe**: true 39 **lifli**: lifelike **hwe**: hue

ROBERT HENRYSON

From THE TESTAMENT OF CRESSEID

[THE COMPLAINT OF CRESSEID]

'O SOP of sorrow, sonkin into cair!
O cative Creisseid, now and ever mair
Gane is thy joy and all thy mirth in eird;
Of all thy blyithnes now art thou blaiknit bair;
Thair is na salve may saif or sound thy sair: 5
Fell is thy fortoun, wickit is thy weird;
Thy blys is baneist, and thy baill on breird:
Under the eirth, God, gif I gravin wer,
Quhair nane of Grece nor yit of Troy micht heird!

'Quhair is thy chalmer wantounlie besene,   10
With burely bed and bankouris browderit bene;
Spycis and wyne to thy collatioun,
The cowpis all of gold and silver schene,
Thy sweit meitis servit in plaittis clene
With saipheron sals of ane gud sessoun;   15
Thy gay garmentis with mony gudely goun,
Thy plesand lawn pinnit with goldin prene?
All is areir, thy greit royall renoun!

'Quhair is thy garding with thir greissis gay
And fresche flowris quhilk the quene Floray   20
Had paintit plesandly in everie pane,
Quhair thou was wont full merilye in May
To walk and tak the dew be it was day,
And heir the merle and mavis mony ane;
With ladyis fair in carrolling to gane,   25
And se the royall rinkis in thair array,
In garmentis gay garnischit on everie grane?

'Thy greit triumphand fame and hie honour,
Quhair thou was callit of eirdlye wichtis flour,
All is decayit, thy weird is welterit so;   30
Thy hei estait is turnit in darknes dour;
This lipper ludge tak for thy burelie bour,
And for thy bed tak now ane bunche of stro,
For waillit wyne and meitis thou had tho
Tak mowlit breid, peirrie and ceder sour;   35
Bot cop and clapper now is all ago.

'My cleir voice and courtlie carrolling,
Quhair I was wont with ladyis for to sing,
Is rawk as ruik, full hiddeous, hoir and hace;
My plesand port, all utheris precelling,   40
Of lustines I was hald maist conding;
Now is deformit the figour of my face –
To luik on it na leid now lyking hes.
Sowpit in syte, I say with sair siching,
Ludgeit amang the lipper leid: "Allace!"   45

'O ladyis fair of Troy and Grece, attend
My miserie, quhilk nane may comprehend,
My frivoll fortoun, my infelicitie,
My greit mischief quhilk na man can amend!
Be war in tyme – approchis neir the end –   50
And in your mynd ane mirrour make of me
As I am now; peradventure that ye,
For all your micht, may cum to that same end
Or ellis war, gif ony war may be.

'Nocht is your fairnes bot ane faiding flour;   55
Nocht is your famous laud and hie honour
Bot wind inflat in uther mennis eiris;
Your roising reid to rotting sall retour.
Exempill mak of me in your memour,
Quhilk of sic thingis wofull witnes beiris.   60
All welth in eird away as wind it weiris;
Be war thairfoir – approchis neir your hour;
Fortoun is fikkill quhen scho beginnis and steiris.'

[Stanzas 59–65]

WILLIAM DUNBAR

'I THAT IN HEILL WES AND GLADNES'

I THAT in heill wes and gladnes
Am trublit now with gret seiknes
And feblit with infermite:
Timor mortis conturbat me.

Our plesance heir is all vane glory,   5
This fals warld is bot transitory,
The flesch is brukle, the Fend is sle:
Timor mortis conturbat me.

The stait of man dois change and vary,
Now sound, now seik, now blith, now sary,   10
Now dansand mery, now like to dee:
Timor mortis conturbat me.

No stait in erd heir standis sickir;
As with the wynd wavis the wickir
Wavis this warldis vanite: 15
Timor mortis conturbat me.

On to the ded gois all estatis,
Princis, prelotis and potestatis,
Baith riche and pur of al degre:
Timor mortis conturbat me.   20

He takis the knychtis in to feild
Anarmyt undir helme and scheild,
Victour he is at all melle:
Timor mortis conturbat me.

That strang unmercifull tyrand   25
Takis on the moderis breist sowkand
The bab full of benignite:
Timor mortis conturbat me.

He takis the campioun in the stour,
The capitane closit in the tour,   30
The lady in bour full of bewte:
Timor mortis conturbat me.

TESTAMENT OF CRESSEID: 1 **sop:** bread dipped in wine, sauce, etc. (see Chaucer's 'General Prologue', line 334) **sonkin:** sunk, dipped **cair:** grief 2 **cative:** wretched 3 **in eird:** on earth 4 **blyithnes:** joy **blaiknit bair:** stripped clean 5 **na salve may saif:** no cure may relieve **sound:** heal **sair:** suffering 6 **Fell:** cruel **wickit:** wicked **weird:** fate 7 **baneist:** banished **baill on breird:** misery bursting forth 8 **gif I gravin wer:** if (only) I were buried 9 **heird:** hear, learn (of it) 10 **Quhair:** where **chalmer:** chamber **wantounlie besene:** luxuriously appointed 11 **burely:** fine **bankouris browderit bene:** finely embroidered seat-covers 12 **collatioun:** late-night refreshment 13 **cowpis:** goblets **schene:** bright 14 **meitis:** dainties 15 **saipheron sals:** saffron sauce **sessoun:** flavour 16 **mony gudely goun:** many (a) handsome gown 17 **lawn:** fine linen **prene:** pin 18 **areir:** past **renoun:** renown 19 **garding:** garden **greissis:** plants 20 **quhilk:** which **Floray:** Flora (flower goddess) 21 **pane:** part 23 **be it was:** as soon as it was 24 **merle:** blackbird **mavis:** thrush 25 **carrolling:** dancing and singing carols 26 **rinkis:** warriors 27 **garnischit:** decorated **on everie grane:** in every particular 28 **triumphand fame:** triumphant renown 29 **eirdlye wichtis:** earthly creatures 30 **decayit:** decayed **weird:** lot **welterit:** turned about 31 **dour:** harsh 32 **lipper:** leper **ludge:** lodging **burelie bour:** fine boudoir 33 **bunche of stro:** bundle of straw 34 **waillit:** choice **tho:** then 35 **mowlit:** mouldy **peirrie:** perry **ceder:** cider 36 **Bot:** except for **ago:** gone 39 **rawk:** raucous **ruik:** (a) rook **hoir:** rough **hace:** hoarse 40 **port:** bearing **all utheris precelling:** surpassing all others 41 **lustines:** youthful beauty **hald:** held **conding:** worthy 42 **figour:** appearance 43 **leid:** nobody 44 **Sowpit:** immersed **syte:** sorrow **sair siching:** agonised sighing 45 **Ludgeit:** lodged **lipper leid:** leper folk **Allace:** alas 46 **attend:** pay heed to 48 **frivoll fortoun:** fickle fortune **infelicitie:** unhappiness 49 **mischeif:** sin, misfortune 50 **Be war in tyme:** learn before it is too late 51 **mynd:** memory 54 **Or ellis war:** or else worse **gif ony war:** if any worse (fate) may be 55 **Nocht . . . flour:** Your beauty is merely a flower that fades 56 **famous laud:** much-praised fame 57 **inflat in:** puffed into **uther mennis eiris:** other men's ears 58 **roising reid:** rosy red complexion **sall retour:** shall turn 59 **memour:** memory 60 **sic:** such **wofull witnes beiris:** offers a lamentable proof 61 **welth in eird:** earthly prosperity **weiris:** fades 63 **fikill:** fickle **quhen:** when **steirs:** bestirs herself

'I THAT IN HEILL WES' (also known as 'Lament for the Makaris [poets]'): 1 **that:** who **heill:** health **gladnes:** joy 2 **trublit:** troubled **gret seiknes:** serious illness 3 **feblit:** weakened **infermite:** infirmity 4 *Timor mortis conturbat me:* the fear of death troubles me 5 **pleasance:** joyful time **vane:** empty 7 **brukle:** frail **Fend:** Fiend (Satan) **sle:** sly, devious 10 **seik:** sick **sary:** wretched 11 **dansand:** dancing **like to dee:** likely to die 13 **erd:** earth **standis sickir:** stands secure 14 **As with:** just as with **wavis:** sways **wickir:** willow 15 **Wavis:** (just as) fragile is **vanite:** hollow pride 17 **One to the ded:** onwards to death **estatis:** social ranks 18 **prelotis:** prelates **potestatis:** potentates 19 **pur:** poor **al degre:** at every level of society 21 **He:** i.e. Death **in to feild:** on the battlefield 22 **Anarmyt:** armed **helme:** helmet 23 **at all melle:** in every joust (mêlée) 25 **strang:** strong **tyrand:** tyrant 26-7 **on the moderis breist . . . benignite:** the blessed babe sucking his mother's breast 29 **campioun:** champion **stour:** strife 30 **closit:** enclosed **tour:** stronghold 31 **bour:** either a chamber or an enclosed garden **bewte:** beauty

He sparis no lord for his piscence,
Na clerk for his intelligence;
His awfull strak may no man fle: 35
Timor mortis conturbat me.

Art magicianis and astrologgis,
Rethoris, logicianis and theologgis –
Thame helpis no conclusionis sle:
Timor mortis conturbat me.   40

In medicyne the most practicianis,
Leichis, surrigianis and phisicianis,
Thame self fra ded may not supple:
Timor mortis conturbat me.

I se that makaris amang the laif   45
Playis heir ther pageant, syne gois to graif;
Sparit is nought ther faculte:
Timor mortis conturbat me.

He has done petuously devour
The noble Chaucer of makaris flour,   50
The monk of Bery, and Gower, all thre:
Timor mortis conturbat me.

The gud Syr Hew of Eglintoun
And eik Heryot and Wyntoun
He has tane out of this cuntre: 55
Timor mortis conturbat me.

That scorpion fell hes done infek
Maister Johne Clerk and James Afflek
Fra balat making and trigide:
Timor mortis conturbat me.   60

Holland and Barbour he hes berevit;
Allace that he nought with us levit
Schir Mungo Lokert of the Le:
Timor mortis conturbat me.

Clerk of Tranent eik he has tane   65
That maid the anteris of Gawane;
Schir Gilbert Hay endit has he:
Timor mortis conturbat me.

He has Blind Hary and Sandy Traill
Slane with his schour or mortall haill   70
Quhilk Patrik Johnestoun mycht nought fle:
Timor mortis conturbat me.

He has reft Merseir his endite
That did in luf so lifly write,
So schort, so quyk, of sentence hie: 75
Timor mortis conturbat me.

He hes tane Roull of Aberdene
And gentill Roull of Corstorphin –
Two bettir fallowis did no man se:
Timor mortis conturbat me.   80

In Dunfermelyne he has done roune
With Maister Robert Henrisoun;
Schir Johne the Ros enbrast has he:
Timor mortis conturbat me.

And he has now tane last of aw   85
Gud gentill Stobo and Quintyne Schaw
Of quham all wichtis has pete:
Timor mortis conturbat me.

Gud Maister Walter Kennedy
In poynt of dede lyis varaly –   90
Gret reuth it wer that so suld be:
Timor mortis conturbat me.

Sen he has all my brether tane
He will naught lat me lif alane;
On forse I man his nyxt pray be: 95
Timor mortis conturbat me.

Sen for the deid remeid is none
Best is that we for dede dispone
Eftir our deid that lif may we:
Timor mortis conturbat me.   100

33 **for his piscence**: because of his power 34 **clerk**: scholar 35 **awfull strak**: terrible stroke **fle**: escape 37 **Art magicianis**: magicians **astrologgis**: astrologers 38 **Rethoris**: rhetoricians **theologgis**: theologians 39 **sle**: subtle 41 **most practicianis**: greatest practitioners 42 **Leichis**: doctors **surrigianis**: surgeons 43 **ded**: death **may not supple**: may not deliver themselves 45 **makaris**: poets; not all the writers mentioned by Dunbar can be identified with certainty, while the identity of others will be immediately obvious **laif**: rest 46 **Playis**: play out **syne**: then **graif**: the grave 47 **faculte**: profession, discipline 49 **petuously devour**: piteously devoured 50 **flour**: flower 51 **The monk of Bery**: John Lydgate **Wyntoun**: Andrew of Wyntoun (1350?–1420?) 57 **fell**: cruel **infek**: poisoned 59 **Fra balat making and trigide**: From composing lyrical and tragic verse 61 **Holland**: Richard Holland (*fl.c.*1450) **Barbour**: John Barbour (1316?–1395) **berevit**: snatched away 62 **Allace**: Alas **nought with us levit**: did not leave with us 63 **Schir Mungo Lokert of the Le**: Mungo Lockhart (d.1489)

65 **eik**: also **tane**: taken 66 **maid the anteris**: composed the adventures **Gawane**: nephew of King Arthur and one of the foremost characters in the Arthurian legends 67 **Schir Gilbert Hay**: Sir Gilbert Hay (*fl.*1450) **endit**: terminated 69 **Blind Hary**: Blind Harry or Harry the Minstrel (*c.*1440?–1492?) 70 **schour**: shower **mortall haill**: lethal hail 73 **reft**: torn away (from) **endite**: writing 74 **luf**: life **lifly**: vividly 75 **quyk**: lively **sentence hie**: noble theme 78 **gentill**: courteous, noble 79 **fallowis**: companions 81 **done roune**: whispered 83 **enbrast**: embraced 85 **of aw**: of all 86 **Stobo**: John Reid of Stobo **Quintyne Schaw**: Quentin Shaw 87 **quham**: whom **all wichtis**: everyone **pete**: regret 89 **Walter Kennedy**: Kennedy (1460?–1508?) engaged in a celebrated 'flyting', or formal trading of poetical abuse, with Dunbar, although this reference suggests that the two men remained good friends 90 **In poynt of dede lyis varaly**: on the point of death lies truly 91 **reuth**: pity 93 **Sen**: since 94 **lat me lif alane**: let me alone live 95 **On forse**: inevitably **man**: must **pray**: prey, victim 97 **for the deid**: against death **remeid**: remedy 98 **dispone**: prepare for 99 **Eftir**: (so that) after

JOHN SKELTON

'WOFFULLY ARAID'

WOFFULLY araid,
　My blode, man,
　For the ran,
It may not be naid;
　My body bloo and wan,　　　　　5
Woffully araid.

Beholde me, I pray the, with all thi hole reson,
And be not so hard hartid, and ffor this encheson,
Sith I for thi sowle sake was slayne in good seson,
Begylde and betraide by Judas fals treson;　　　10
　Unkyndly entretid,
　With sharpe corde sore fretid,
　The Jewis me thretid
They mowid, they grynnèd, they scornyd
　　me,
Condempynyd to deth, as thou maist se,　　　15
Woffully araid.

Thus nakyd am I nailid, O man, for thy sake!
I love the, then love me; why slepist thou? awake!
Remembir my tendir hart-rote for the brake,
With panys my vaynys constreynèd to crake;　　　20
　Thus toggid to and fro,
　Thus wrappid all in woo
　Whereas never man was so,
Entretid thus in most cruel wyse,
Was like a lombe offerd in sacrifice,　　　25
Woffully araid.

Off sharpe thorne I have worne a crowne on my hede,
So paynyd, so straynyd, so rufull, so red;
Thus bobbid, thus robbid, thus for thy love ded,
Onfaynyd not deynyd my blod for to shed;　　　30
　My fete and handes sore
　The sturdy nailis bore;
　What myght I suffir more
Than I have don, O man, for the?
Cum when thou list, wellcum to me,　　　35
Woffully araid.

Off record thy good Lord I have beyn and schal bee;
I am thyn, thou artt myne, my brother I call thee;
The love I enterly; see whatt ys befall me!　　　39
Sore bettyng, sore thretyng, to make thee, man, all fre
　Why art thou unkynde?
　Why hast nott mee yn mynde?
　Cum yitt, and thou schalt fynde
Myne endlys mercy and grace;
See how a spere my hert dyd race,　　　45
Woffully arayd.

Deyr brother, noo other thyng I off thee desyre
Butt gyve me thyne hert fre to rewarde myn hyre:
I wrought the, I bowght the frome eternal fyre;
I pray the aray the tooward my hyght empyre,　　　50
　Above the oryent,
　Wheroff I am regent,
　Lord God omnypotent,
Wyth me to reyn yn endlys welthe;
Remember, man, thy sawlys helthe.　　　55

　Woffully arayd,
　　My blode, man,
　　For the ran,
　Hytt may nott be nayd;
　　My body blow and wan,　　　60
　Woffully arayde.

'WOFFULLY ARAID': 1 **araid**: treated 3 **the**: thee 4 **naid**: denied 5 **bloo and wan**: blue and pale 8 **encheson**: reason 10 **Begylde**: deceived 11 **entretid**: treated 12 **fretid**: chafed 13 **thretid**: threatened 14 **mowid**: grimaced, made mocking faces 15 **Condempynyd**: condemned **se**: see 19 **hart-rote**: heart's root 20 **panys**: pains **vaynys**: veins 21 **toggid**: tugged 23 **Whereas**: such as 24 **wyse**: manner 28 **rufull**: wretched **red**: bloody 29 **bobbid**: cheated 30 **Onfaynyd not deynyd ... shed**: Freely I shed my blood 35 **list**: wish 39 **The love I enterly**: I love thee entirely **ys befall me**: what has befallen me 40 **bettyng**: beating **thretyng**: threatening **fre**: free 45 **spere**: spear **race**: cut 48 **myn hire**: my labour 50 **aray the**: direct yourself **hyght**: high 51 **oryent**: east 55 **sawlys helthe**: soul's health

From THE GARLANDE OF LAURELL

TO MASTRES MARGERY WENTWORTHE

WITH margerain jentyll,
　The flowre of goodlyhede,
Enbrowdred the mantill
　Is of your maydenhede.
Plainly, I can not glose,　　　　5
　Ye be, as I devyne,
The praty primrose,
　The goodly columbyne.
With margerain jantill,
　The flowre of goodlyhede,　　　10
Enbrawderyd the mantyll
　Is of yowre maydenhede.
Benynge, corteise, and meke,
　With wordes well devysid,
In you, who list to seke,　　　15
　Be vertus well comprysid.
With margerain jantill,
　The flowre of goodlyhede,
Enbrawderid the mantill
　Is of yowr maydenhede.　　　20

TO MASTRES MARGERY WENTWORTHE: 1 **margerain**: marjoram **jentyll**: delicate 2 **goodlyhede**: goodness 3 **Enbrowdred**: embroidered **mantill**: mantle 5 **glose**: flatter 7 **praty**: pretty 13 **Benynge**: benign, kind **corteise**: courteous **meke**: meek 14 **well devysid**: well spoken 15 **who list to seke**: for those who care to seek 16 **comprysid**: contained

TO MAYSTRES MARGARET HUSSEY

MIRRY Margaret,
  As mydsomer flowre,
Jentill as fawcoun
Or hawke of the towre;
With solace and gladnes,   5
Moche mirthe and no madnes,
All good and no badnes;
    So joyously,
    So maydenly,
    So womanly   10
    Her demenyng;
    In every thynge
    Far, far passynge
    That I can endyght,
    Or suffyce to wryght   15
Of mirry Margarete,
  As mydsomer flowre,
Jentyll as fawcoun
Or hawke of the towre.
    As pacient and as styll   20
And as full of good wyll
As fayre Isaphill;
Colyaunder,
Swete pomaunder,
Good Cassaunder;   25
Stedfast of thought,
Wele made, wele wrought;
Far may be sought
Erst that ye can fynde
So corteise, so kynde   30
As mirry Margarete,
  This midsomer flowre,
Jentyll as fawcoun
Or hawke of the towre.

TO MAYSTRES MARGARET HUSSEY: 3 **Jentill:** delicate **fawcoun:** falcon
4 **of the towre:** towering on high 11 **demenyng:** conduct 14 **endyght:**
compose verses 22 **Isaphill:** Hypsipyle, a queen of Lemnos; when
all the other men on the island were slain by the women, she
spared her father and helped him escape 23 **Colyaunder:** coriander
24 **pomaunder:** pomander 25 **Cassaunder:** Cassandra, beautiful
daughter of Priam and Hecuba, with the gift of prophecy 27 **Wele:**
well 29 **Erst:** before 30 **corteise:** courteous

GAVIN DOUGLAS

From THE AENEID

[THE TROJAN HORSE]

THE Grekis chiftanys, irkit of the weir
Bypast or than samony langsum yeir,
And oft rebutyt by fatale destany,
Ane huge hors, lyke ane gret hil, in hy
Craftely thai wrocht in wirschip of Pallas   5

(Of sawyn beche the ribbis forgyt was)
Fenyeand ane oblacioune, as it had be
For prosper returnyng hame in thar cuntre –
The voce this wys throu owt the cite woyk.
Of choys men syne, walit by cut, thai tuke   10
A gret numbyr, and hyd in bylgis dern
Within that best, in mony huge cavern;
Schortly, the belly was stuffit every deill
Ful of knychtis armyt in plait of steill.
Thair standis into the sycht of Troy ane ile   15
Weil knawin by name, hecht Tenedos, umquhile
Myghty of gudis quhil Priamus ryng sa stude;
Now it is bot a fyrth in the sey flude,
A raid onsikkyr for schip or ballyngare.
In desert costis of this iland thar   20
The Grekis thame ful secretly withdrew,
We wenyng thame hame passit and adew,
And, with gude wynd, of Myce the realm had socht.
Quharfor al thai of Troy, blyth as thai mocht,
Thair langsum duyl and murnyng dyd away,   25
Kest up the portis and yschit furth to play,
The Grekis tentis desyrus forto se
And voyd placis quhar thai war wont to be,
The cost and strandis left desert al cleyn.
'Heir stude the army of Dolopeis,' sum wald meyn,   30
'Cruel Achil heir stentit his pailyeon;
Quhar stude the navy, lo the place yonder down;
Heir the ostis war wont to joyn in feild.'
And sum wondring the scaithfull gyft beheld
Suldbe offerit to the onweddit Pallas;   35
Thai mervellit fast the hors samekill was.
Bot Tymetes exortis first of all
It forto leid and draw within the wall
And forto set it in the cheif palyce –
Quhidder for dissait I not, or for malyce,   40
Or destany of Troy wald sa suldbe.
Bot Capis than, with ane othir menye
Quhilk bettir avys thar myndis set apon,
Bad cast or drown into the sey onone
That suspek presand of the Grekis dissait,   45
Or kyndill tharunder flambe of fyris hait,
Or forto rype that holkit hug belly,
And the hyd hyrnys to sers and weil espy.
Quhat nedis mair? The onstabill common voce
Dividit was in mony seir purpos,   50
Quhen thidder come befor thame al onone,
Followand a gret rowt, the prest Laocon
From the cheif tempil rynnand in ful gret hy.
On far, 'O wrachit pepil,' gan he cry,
'Quhou gret wodnes is this at ye now meyn,   55
Your ennymyis away salit gif ye weyn,
Or gif ye traist ony Grekis gyftis be
Withowt dissait, falshed and subtelte.
Knaw ye na bettir the quent Ulixes slycht?
Owder in this tre ar Grekis closit ful rycht,   60
Or this engyne is byggit to our skaith,
To wach our wallis and our byggyngys bath,

Or to confound and ourquhelm our cite.
Thar lurkis sum falshed tharin, trastis me.
Lippyn nocht, Trojanys, I pray you, in this hors: 65
Quhow ever it be, I dreid the Grekis fors,
And thame that sendis this gyft always I feir.'
Thus sayand, with al his strenth a gret speir
At the syde of that bysnyng best threw he,
And in jonyngis of the thrawyn wame of tre   70
Festynnyt the lance, that trymlyng gan to schaik;
The braid belly schudderit, and with the straik
The boys cavys sowndit and maid a dyn.
And had nocht beyn that owder his wit was thyn,
Or than the fatis of goddis war contrary,   75
He had assayt, but ony langar tary,
Hyd Grekis covert with irne to have rent owt;
Than suld thou, Troy, have standyn yit, but dowt,
And the prowd palyce of Kyng Priamus
Suld have remanyt yit ful gloryus.   80

[Book 2, chapter 1, lines 1–80]

AENEID: 1 **Grekis chiftanys:** Greek chieftains **irkit:** weary **weir:** war 2 **Bypast . . . yeir:** That had lasted so many tedious years 3 **rebutyt:** repulsed 4 **in hy:** in haste 5 **Craftely thai wrought:** skilfully they wrought **wirschip:** worship **Pallas:** Pallas Athena, Greek goddess of arts and crafts 6 **sawyn beche:** sawn beech **ribbis:** timbers **forgyt:** forged 7 **Fenyeand:** feigning **oblacioune:** sacrifice **as it had be:** as if it had been 8 **prosper:** safe 9 **The voce . . . woyk:** A rumour to this effect spread through the city 10 **choys:** selected **syne:** afterwards **walit by cut:** chosen by lot 11 **bylgis:** the depths **dern:** secretly 12 **best:** beast 13 **every deill:** in every part **plait of steill:** steel plate-armour 14 **Thair:** there **into the sycht:** within sight **ane ile:** an island 16 **knawin:** known **hecht:** called **umquhile:** once 17 **Myghty:** rich **Priamus ryng:** Priam's kingdom (Troy) **stude:** stood 18 **fyrth:** bay 19 **raid onsikkyr:** road (i.e. channel) unsafe **ballyngare:** ship 20 **In desert costis:** to a hidden cost (i.e. out of sight of the mainland) 22 **wenyng:** believing **adew:** departed 23 **Myce:** Mycenae **socht:** sought 24 **Quharfor:** wherefore **blyth:** cheerfully **mocht:** might 25 **duyl:** lamentation **murnying:** mourning 26 **Kest:** cast **portis:** gates **yschit:** issued 28 **And voyd . . . al clene:** And the empty places where they used to be,/The coast and beach left completely deserted 30 **Dolopeis:** Dolopians **meyn:** think 31 **Achil:** Achilles **stentit his pailyeon:** pitched his tent 33 **ostis war:** hosts (i.e. armies) were 34 **scaithfull:** harmful 35 **onweddit:** chaste 36 **fast:** greatly **samekill:** huge 37 **Tymetes:** Thymoetes 40 **Quhidder:** whether **dissait:** deceit, treason **I not:** I know not 41 **Or destany . . . suldbe:** Or because it was already ordained that such should be Troy's fate 42 **Capis:** Capys **menye:** group 43 **Quhilk . . . set apon:** Who were of sounder judgement 44 **onone:** anon 45 **presand:** present **Grekis dissait:** deceitful Greeks 46 **kyndill tharunder:** kindle beneath it **flambe:** flame **fyris hait:** hot fires 47 **rype:** open up **holkit:** hollowed **hug:** huge 48 **hyd hyrnys:** hidden chambers **sers:** search 49 **Quhat nedis mair?:** What more is there to say? 49–50 **The onstabill . . . purpos:** The crowd was divided between many different proposals 52 **Followand:** followed by **rowt:** crowd **prest:** priest **Laocon:** Laocoon; after his warning to the Trojans, Lacoon and his two young sons were killed by two giant sea-serpents that swam across from Tenedos 53 **rynnand:** running **in ful gret hy:** very excited 54 **On far:** afar off **wrachit pepil:** wretched people 55 **Quhou:** what **wodnes:** madness **meyn:** intend 56 **salit:** sailed **gif ye weyn:** if you believe 57 **traist:** trust **be:** to be 58 **falshed:** falsehood **subtelte:** cunning 59 **quent:** crafty **Ulixes:** Ulysses **slycht:** tricks 60 **Owder:** either **tre:** timber **closit ful rycht:** concealed 61 **byggit:** built **skaith:** harm 62 **wach:** overlook **byggyngis bath:** batter down our buildings 63 **ourquhelm:** overwhelm 64 **trastis:** trust 65 **Lippyn:** trust 66 **Grekis fors:** Greeks' force 68 **sayand:** saying 69 **bysnyng best:** monstrous beast 70 **jonyngis:** joints **thrawyn wame of tre:** sinister wooden womb 71 **Festynnyt:** fastened **trymlyng:** trembling 72 **braid:** broad **schudderit:** shuddered **straik:** blow 73 **boys cavys:** hollow caves 74 **had nocht beyn:** had it not been 76 **assayt:** attempted **but:** without **tary:** delay 77 **Hyd Grekis . . . owt:** Secretly hidden Greeks with spears to have rooted out 78 **standyn:** stood **but dowt:** without doubt 80 **remanyt:** remained

SIR THOMAS WYATT

'WHOSO LIST TO HUNT, I KNOW WHERE IS AN HIND'

WHOSO list to hunt, I know where is an hind,
But as for me, hélas, I may no more.
The vain travail hath wearied me so sore,
I am of them that farthest cometh behind.
Yet may I by no means my wearied mind   5
Draw from the deer, but as she fleeth afore
Fainting I follow. I leave off therefore
Sithens in a net I seek to hold the wind.
Who list her hunt, I put him out of doubt,
As well as I may spend his time in vain.   10
And graven with diamonds in letters plain
There is written her fair neck round about:
'*Noli me tangere* for Caesar's I am,
And wild for to hold though I seem tame.'

'WHOSO LIST TO HUNT': This sonnet is widely believed to refer to Wyatt's relationship with Ann Boleyn before Henry VIII laid claim to her. 'Caesar' in line 13 would therefore be the king: 1 **Who so list:** Who wishes 2 **hélas:** alas 3 **vain travail:** futile labour 6 **deer:** with a play on 'dear' 8 **Sithens:** since 10 **As well as I:** i.e. better men than I 13 *Noli me tangere:* 'Touch me not'

'FAREWELL, LOVE, AND ALL THY LAWS FOR EVER'

FAREWELL, Love, and all thy laws for ever.
Thy baited hooks shall tangle me no more.
Senec and Plato call me from thy lore
To perfect wealth my wit for to endeavour.
In blind error when I did perséver,   5
Thy sharp repulse that pricketh ay so sore
Hath taught me to set in trifles no store
And 'scape forth since liberty is lever.
Therefore farewell. Go trouble younger hearts
And in me claim no more authority.   10
With idle youth go use thy property
And thereon spend thy many brittle darts:
For hitherto though I have lost all my time,
Me lusteth no longer rotten boughs to climb.

'FAREWELL, LOVE': 1 **Love:** lines 9–12 confirm that the poem is a direct address to Cupid 3 **Senec:** Seneca (*c.*4 BC–AD 65), Roman philosopher, statesman and dramatist 4 **To perfect . . . endeavour:** I shall dedicate my talents to finer endeavours than sexual love 6 **ay:** always 8 **lever:** preferable 11 **property:** attributes 14 **me lusteth:** I desire

'MY GALLEY CHARGÈD WITH FORGETFULNESS'

My galley chargèd with forgetfulness
   Thorough sharp seas in winter nights doth pass
   'Tween rock and rock; and eke mine enemy, alas,
   That is my lord, steereth with cruelness;
And every oar a thought in readiness   5
   As though that death were light in such a case.
   And endless wind doth tear the sail apace
   Of forcèd sighs and trusty fearfulness.
A rain of tears, a cloud of dark disdain
   Hath done the wearied cords great hinderance,   10
   Wreathèd with error and eke with ignorance.
The stars be hid that led me to this pain.
   Drownèd is reason that should me comfórt
   And I remain despairing of the port.

'MY GALLEY CHARGÈD': 1 **chargèd**: laden 2 **Thorough**: through **sharp**: icy 3 **eke**: also **mine enemy**: Love 12 **The stars**: stars by which to navigate; but also his lady's eyes

'THEY FLEE FROM ME THAT SOMETIME DID ME SEEK'

They flee from me that sometime did me seek
With naked foot stalking in my chamber.
I have seen them gentle, tame, and meek,
That now are wild, and do not remember
That sometime they have put themselves in danger   5
To take bread at my hand; and now they range,
Busily seeking with a continual change.

Thankèd be Fortune, it hath been otherwise
Twenty times better; but once in special:
In thin array, after a pleasant guise,   10
When her loose gown from her shoulders did fall,
And she me caught in her arms long and small,
Therewithal sweetly did me kiss
And softly said, 'Dear heart, how like you this?'

It was no dream, – I lay broad waking.   15
But all is turned, thorough my gentleness,
Into a strange fashion of forsaking:
And I have leave to go of her goodness,
And she also to use newfangleness.
But since that I so kindly am servèd,   20
I would fain know what she hath deservèd.

'THEY FLEE FROM ME': 2 **stalking**: treading softly 5 **in danger**: in my power 6 **range**: roam 7 **seeking with**: searching for 10 **In thin array . . . guise**: Wearing a thin gown of a pleasing design 13 **Therewithal**: and then 16 **thorough**: through **gentleness**: tenderness, devotion (implying that he has loved too much) 18 **of her goodness**: (ironic) i.e. she has been so gracious as to let me go 19 **newfangleness**: inconstancy 20 **kindly**: (ironic) considerately

'MY LUTE, AWAKE! . . .'

My lute, awake! perform the last
Labour that thou and I shall waste,
And end that I have now begun;
For when this song is sung and past,
My lute, be still, for I have done.   5

As to be heard where ear is none,
As lead to grave in marble stone,
My song may pierce her heart as soon:
Should we then sigh, or sing, or moan?
No! no! my lute, for I have done.   10

The rocks do not so cruelly
Repulse the waves continually
As she my suit and áffection:
So that I am past remedy,
Whereby my lute and I have done.   15

Proud of the spoil that thou hast got
Of simple hearts thorough Love's shot,
By whom, unkind, thou hast them won,
Think not he hath his bow forgot,
Although my lute and I have done.   20

Vengeance shall fall on thy disdain
That mak'st but game on earnest pain;
Think not alone under the sun
Unquit to cause thy lovers plain,
Although my lute and I have done.   25

Perchance thee lie withered and old
The winter nights that are so cold,
Plaining in vain unto the moon;
Thy wishes then dare not be told:
Care then who list, for I have done.   30

And then may chance thee to repent
The time that thou hast lost and spent
To cause thy lovers sigh and swoon:
Then shalt thou know beauty but lent,
And wish and want as I have done.   35

Now cease, my lute! this is the last
Labour that thou and I shall waste,
And ended is that we begun;
Now is this song both sung and past:
My lute, be still, for I have done.   40

'MY LUTE, AWAKE!': 3 **that I**: that which I 7 **grave**: engrave (indicating the futility of trying to engrave in marble with a soft metal like lead) 8 **may . . . soon**: may sooner pierce her heart 17 **thorough**: through **Love's**: Cupid's 22 **game on**: light of 24 **Unquit**: unpunished **plain**: complain 30 **list**: cares 38 **that we begun**: i.e. my song

'MINE OWN JOHN POYNTZ . . .'

MINE own John Poyntz, since ye delight to know
    The cause why that homeward I me draw,
    And flee the press of courts whereso they go
Rather than to live thrall under the awe
    Of lordly looks, wrappèd within my cloak,   5
    To will and lust learning to set a law,
It is not for because I scorn or mock
    The power of them to whom Fortune hath lent
    Charge over us, of right to strike the stroke;
But true it is that I have always meant   10
    Less to esteem them than the common sort,
    Of outward things that judge in their intent
Without regard what doth inward resort.
    I grant sometime that of glory the fire
    Doth touch my heart: me list not to report   15
Blame by honour and honour to desire.
    But how may I this honour now attain
    That cannot dye the colour black a liar?
My Poyntz, I cannot frame my tongue to feign,
    To cloak the truth for praise, without desert,   20
    Of them that list all vice for to retain.
I cannot honour them that sets their part
    With Venus and Bacchus all their life long,
    Nor hold my peace of them although I smart.
I cannot crouch nor kneel, nor do so great a wrong
    To worship them like God on earth alone,   26
    That are as wolves these silly lambs among.
I cannot with my words complain and moan
    And suffer nought; nor smart without complaint,
    Nor turn the word that from my mouth is gone.
I cannot speak and look like a saint,   31
    Use wiles for wit and make deceit a pleasure,
    And call craft counsel, for profit still to paint.
I cannot wrest the law to fill the coffer,
    With innocent blood to feed myself fat,   35
    And do most hurt where most help I offer.
I am not he that can allow the state
    Of high Caesar and damn Cato to die,
    That with his death did 'scape out of the gate
From Caesar's hands, if Livy do not lie,   40
    And would not live where liberty was lost:
    So did his heart the common weal apply.
I am not he such eloquence to boast,
    To make the crow singing as the swan,
    Nor call the lion of coward beasts the most,   45
That cannot take a mouse as the cat can:
    And he that dieth for hunger of the gold
    Call him Alexander, and say that Pan
Passeth Apollo in music many fold;
    Praise Sir Thopas for a noble tale,   50
    And scorn the story that the Knight told;
Praise him for counsel that is drunk of ale;
    Grin when he laugheth, that beareth all the sway,
    Frown when he frowneth and groan when he is
        pale;

On others' lust to hang both night and day: 55
    None of these, Poyntz, would ever frame in me.
    My wit is naught, I cannot learn the way;
And much the less of things that greater be,
    That asken help of colours of device
    To join the mean with each extremity,   60
With the near'st virtue to cloak always the vice;
    And, as to purpose likewise it shall fall,
    To press the virtue that it may not rise;
As drunkenness good fellowship to call;
    The friendly foe with his double face   65
    Say he is gentle and courteous therewithal;
And say that Favel hath a goodly grace
    In eloquence; and cruelty to name
    Zeal of justice and change in time and place;
And he that suffereth offence without blame   70
    Call him pitiful, and him true and plain
    That raileth wreckless to every man's shame;
Say he is rude that cannot lie and feign,
    The lecher a lover, and tyranny
    To be the right of a prince's reign.   75
I cannot, I! No, no, it will not be!
    This is the cause that I could never yet
    Hang on their sleeves that weigh, as thou may'st
        see,
A chip of chance more than a pound of wit.
    This maketh me at home to hunt and hawk   80
    And in foul weather at my book to sit;
In frost and snow then with my bow to stalk.
    No man doth mark where so I ride or go;
    In lusty leas at liberty I walk,
And of these news I feel nor weal nor woe,   85
    Save that a clog doth hang yet at my heel:
    No force for that for it is ordered so,
That I may leap both hedge and dyke full well.
    I am not now in France to judge the wine,
    With saffron sauce the delicates to feel;   90
Nor yet in Spain where one must him incline,
    Rather than to be, outwardly to seem.
    I meddle not with wits that be so fine,
Nor Flanders cheer letteth not my sight to deem
    Of black and white, nor taketh my wit away   95
    With beastliness they, beasts, do so esteem;
Nor I am not where Christ is given in prey
    For money, poison, and treason at Rome,
    A common practice usèd night and day.
But here I am in Kent and Christendom   100
    Among the Muses where I read and rhyme;
    Where if thou list, my Poyntz, for to come,
Thou shalt be judge how I do spend my time.

'MINE OWN JOHN POYNTZ': Although Wyatt gives the impression in
the poem that he had chosen to 'flee the press of courts' (line 3)
for life in the country, this is misleading. In 1536, after a period of
imprisonment in the Tower, Wyatt was ordered to remain at his
home in Kent and, under his father's supervision, to learn 'to
address him better'. Little is known of Wyatt's friend John Poyntz,
a fellow courtier: 4 **to live thrall under:** to be enslaved to or at the
command of 5 **wrappèd within my cloak:** either (a) that the poet

had learned to know his place and to be discreet, or (*b*) that he had tried to remain aloof from the attitudes and practices of the Court, and to keep his own counsel 6 **will:** pleasure (with a suggestion of excess) **law:** limit 67 **Favel:** the word derives from a 'fallow' (pale brown) horse; to 'curry favel' (literally, to rub down a horse so that the soothing sensation would make it more amenable) came to mean flattering a person to gain a favour, and a 'curry-favel' was someone who indulged in this practice – although Wyatt has here shortened the term and personified it 69 **Zeal of justice:** the zealous pursuit of justice **change in time and place:** i.e. things have changed since the law was originally enacted 71 **plain:** straight-talking 72 **raileth:** talks loudly and abusively **wreckless:** unchastised 79 **A chip . . . wit:** (proverbial) 'An ounce of luck is worth a pound of wit' 84 **lusty leas:** lush pastures 85 **these news:** possibly either (*a*) this new situation in which I find myself or (*b*) news of events at court **I feel nor weal nor woe:** i.e. they do not affect me one way or the other 86 **clog:** weight attached to an animal's leg to restrict movement 88 **dyke:** ditch 90 **the delicates to feel:** to taste delicious dishes 94 **cheer:** i.e. eating and drinking **letteth:** prevents **deem:** judge 95 **wit:** reason 96 **beastliness:** depravity **they:** i.e. the Flemish **do so esteem:** rate so highly 97 **in prey:** literally 'as plunder' (*OED*), perhaps indicating how, in the Catholic church, greed and corruption have supplanted the love of Christ

'IS IT POSSIBLE'

Is it possible
That so high debate,
So sharp, so sore, and of such rate,
Should end so soon and was begun so late?
Is it possible?   5

Is it possible
So cruel intent,
So hasty heat and so soon spent,
From love to hate, and thence for to relent?
Is it possible?   10

Is it possible
That any may find
Within one heart so díverse mind,
To change or turn as weather and wind?
Is it possible?   15

Is it possible
To spy it in an eye
That turns as oft as chance on die?
The truth whereof can any try?
Is it possible?   20

It is possible
For to turn so oft,
To bring that lowest that was most aloft,
And to fall highest yet to light soft.
It is possible.   25

All is possible,
Whoso list believe.
Trust therefore first and after preve,
As men wed ladies by licence and leave,
All is possible.   30

'IS IT POSSIBLE': 13 **so diverse mind:** such a wide range of emotions 23 **most aloft:** highest 27 **Whoso list believe:** For whoever chooses to believe 28 **preve:** prove

'AND WILT THOU LEAVE ME THUS?'

AND wilt thou leave me thus?
Say nay, say nay, for shame,
To save thee from the blame
Of all my grief and grame.
And wilt thou leave me thus?   5
   Say nay! Say nay!

And wilt thou leave me thus,
That hath lovèd thee so long
In wealth and woe among?
And is thy heart so strong   10
As for to leave me thus?
   Say nay! Say nay!

And wilt thou leave me thus,
That hath given thee my heart
Never for to depart   15
Neither for pain nor smart;
And wilt thou leave me thus?
   Say nay! Say nay!

And wilt thou leave me thus,
And have no more pity   20
Of him that loveth thee?
Hélas! thy cruelty!
And wilt thou leave me thus?
   Say nay! Say nay!

'AND WILT THOU LEAVE ME THUS?': 4 **Of:** for **grame:** sorrow 9 **In wealth and woe among:** In good times and bad 10–11 **is thy heart so strong As for to:** are you so hard-hearted as to 16 **Neither for:** for neither **smart:** sorrow 22 **Hélas:** (French) alas

'FORGET NOT YET THE TRIED INTENT'

FORGET not yet the tried intent
Of such a truth as I have meant;
My great travail so gladly spent
   Forget not yet!

Forget not yet when first began   5
The weary life ye know, since whan
The suit, the service, none tell can;
   Forget not yet!

Forget not yet the great assays,
The cruel wrong, the scornful ways,   10
The painful patience in denays,
   Forget not yet!

Forget not yet, forget not this,
How long ago hath been, and is,
The mind that never meant amiss,   15
        Forget not yet!

Forget not then thine own approvèd,
The which so long hath thee so lovèd,
Whose steadfast faith yet never movèd,
        Forget not this!   20

'FORGET NOT YET THE TRIED INTENT': 1–2 **the tried intent Of such a truth as I have meant:** the proven sincerity of my devotion to you 3 **travail:** labour 7 **tell:** calculate, quantify 9 **assays:** attempts 11 **denays:** denials

'WHAT SHOULD I SAY'

WHAT should I say
Since faith is dead
And truth away
From you is fled?
Should I be led   5
With doubleness?
Nay, nay, mistress!

I promised you
And you promised me
To be as true   10
As I would be,
But since I see
Your double heart
Farewell, my part!

Thought for to take   15
It is not my mind
But to forsake
One so unkind
And as I find
So will I trust,   20
Farewell, unjust!

Can ye say nay
But you said
That I alway
Should be obeyed?   25
And thus betrayed
Or that I wist,
Farewell, unkissed!

'WHAT SHOULD I SAY': 5–6 **led With:** guided by 6 **doubleness:** deceitfulness (also line 13) 14 **my part:** my half of the bargain 16 **mind:** intention 22 **say nay:** deny 23 **But:** that 27 **Ere:** before **wist:** knew

HENRY HOWARD, EARL OF SURREY

'WHEN RAGING LOVE WITH EXTREME PAIN'

WHEN raging love with éxtreme pain
    Most cruelly distrains my heart,
When that my tears, as floods of rain,
    Bear witness of my woeful smart;
        When sighs have wasted so my breath   5
        That I lie at the point of death:

I call to mind the navy great
    That the Greeks brought to Troyë town,
And how the boisteous winds did beat
    Their ships, and rent their sails adown,   10
        Till Agamemnon's daughter's blood
        Appeased the gods that them withstood.

And how that in those ten years' war
    Full many a bloody deed was done,
And many a lord that came full far   15
    There caught his bane, alas, too soon,
        And many a good knight overrun,
        Before the Greeks had Helen won.

Then think I thus: sith such repair,
    So long time war of valiant men,   20
Was all to win a lady fair,
    Shall I not learn to suffer then,
        And think my life well spent to be
        Serving a worthier wight than she?

Therefore I never will repent,   25
    But pains contented still endure;
For like as when, rough winter spent,
    The pleasant spring straight draweth in ure,
        So, after raging storms of care,
        Joyful at length may be my fare.   30

'WHEN RAGING LOVE WITH EXTREME PAIN': 2 **distrains:** seizes 4 **smart:** pain 9 **boisteous:** rough 11 **Agamemnon's daughter:** Iphigenia, sacrificed by her father to gain a satisfactory wind for his fleet to sail from Aulis to Troy 16 **bane:** death 19 **sith:** since **repair:** resort 24 **wight:** person 26 **contented:** contentedly, with resignation 28 **draweth in ure:** comes in 30 **fare:** course, journey

'THE SOOTË SEASON, THAT BUD AND BLOOM FORTH BRINGS'

THE sootë season, that bud and bloom forth brings,
    With green hath clad the hill and eke the vale;
The nightingale with feathers new she sings;
    The turtle to her make hath told her tale.

Summer is come, for every spray now springs; 5
 The hart hath hung his old head on the pale;
The buck in brake his winter coat he flings;
 The fishes float with new-repairèd scale;
The adder all her slough away she slings;
 The swift swallow pursueth the fliës small; 10
The busy bee her honey now she mings;
 Winter is worn that was the flowers' bale.
  And thus I see among these pleasant things
  Each care decays, and yet my sorrow springs.

'THE SOOTË SEASON': 1 **sootë**: sweet 2 **eke**: also 4 **turtle**: turtle dove
make: mate 5 **spray**: branch **springs**: blossoms 6 **hart**: deer **head**:
i.e. antlers **pale**: fence or stake 7 **brake**: thicket 9 **slough**: old skin
11 **mings**: remembers 12 **bale**: woe

'ALAS, SO ALL THINGS NOW DO HOLD THEIR PEACE'

ALAS, so all things now do hold their peace,
 Heaven and earth disturbed in nothing;
The beasts, the air, the birds their song do cease;
 The nightës chare the stars about doth bring.
Calm is the sea, the waves work less and less; 5
 So am not I, whom love, alas, doth wring,
Bringing before my face the great increase
 Of my desires, whereat I weep and sing
In joy and woe as in a doubtful ease.
 For my sweet thoughts sometime do pleasure bring,
But by and by the cause of my disease 11
 Gives me a pang that inwardly doth sting,
  When that I think what grief it is again
  To live and lack the thing should rid my pain.

'ALAS, SO ALL THINGS NOW DO HOLD THEIR PEACE': 4 **chare**: turning
6 **wring**: afflict 11 **disease**: unease 14 **should rid**: that would rid me
of

'O HAPPY DAMES, THAT MAY EMBRACE'

O HAPPY dames, that may embrace
 The fruit of your delight,
Help to bewail the woeful case
 And eke the heavy plight
Of me, that wonted to rejoice 5
The fortune of my pleasant choice:
Good ladies, help to fill my mourning voice.

In ship, freight with rememberance
 Of thoughts and pleasures past,
He sails that hath in governance 10
 My life, while it will last;
With scalding sighs, for lack of gale,
Furthering his hope, that is his sail,
Toward me, the sweetë port of his avail.

Alas, how oft in dreams I see 15
 Those eyes that were my food;
Which sometime so delighted me,
 That yet they do me good;
Wherewith I wake with his return
Whose absent flame did make me burn. 20
But when I find the lack, Lord, how I mourn!

When other lovers in arms across
 Rejoice their chief delight,
Drownèd in tears, to mourn my loss
 I stand the bitter night 25
In my window, where I may see
Before the winds how the cloudës flee.
Lo! what a mariner love hath made me!

And in green waves when the salt flood
 Doth rise by rage of wind, 30
A thousand fancies in that mood
 Assail my restless mind.
Alas! now drencheth my sweet foe,
That with the spoil of my heart did go,
And left me; but, alas! why did he so? 35

And when the seas wax calm again,
 To chase fro me annoy,
My doubtful hope doth cause me plain;
 So dread cuts off my joy.
Thus is my wealth mingled with woe, 40
And of each thought a doubt doth grow:
Now he comes! Will he come? Alas, no, no!

'O HAPPY DAMES THAT MAY EMBRACE': 4 **eke**: also 7 **help to fill**
my mourning voice: join with me in my lament 8 **freight**: laden
22 **in arms across**: embracing 33 **drencheth**: drowns 34 **spoil**:
plunder 37 **fro**: from **annoy**: all that is troubling me 38 **plain**: (to)
complain

'SO CRUEL PRISON HOW COULD BETIDE, ALAS'

So cruel prison how could betide, alas,
 As proud Windsor, where I in lust and joy
With a king's son my childish years did pass,
 In greater feast than Priam's sons of Troy;

Where each sweet place returns a taste full sour: 5
 The large green courts, where we were wont to
  hove,
With eyes cast up unto the maidens' tower,
 And easy sighs, such as folk draw in love;

The stately sales; the ladies bright of hue;
 The dances short, long tales of great delight, 10
With words and looks that tigers could but rue,
 Where each of us did plead the other's right;

The palm-play, where, despoilèd for the game,
  With dazèd eye oft we by gleams of love
Have missed the ball and got sight of our dame   15
  To bait her eyes which kept the leads above;

The gravelled ground, with sleeves tied on the helm,
  On foaming horse, with swords and friendly hearts,
With chere as though the one should overwhelm,
  Where we have fought and chasèd oft with darts;

With silver drops the meads yet spread for ruth,   21
  In active games of nimbleness and strength
Where we did strain, trailèd by swarms of youth,
  Our tender limbs, that yet shot up in length;

The secret groves, which oft we made resound   25
  Of pleasant plaint and of our ladies' praise,
Recording soft what grace each one had found,
  What hope of speed, what dread of long delays;

The wild forest, the clothèd holts with green,
  With reins availed and swift y-breathèd horse,   30
With cry of hounds and merry blasts between,
  Where we did chase the fearful hart a-force;

The void walls eke, that harboured us each night;
  Wherewith, alas, revive within my breast
The sweet accord, such sleeps as yet delight,   35
  The pleasant dreams, the quiet bed of rest,

The secret thoughts imparted with such trust,
  The wanton talk, the divers change of play,
The friendship sworn, each promise kept so just,
  Wherewith we passed the winter nights away.   40

And with this thought the blood forsakes my face,
  The tears berain my cheek of deadly hue;
The which, as soon as sobbing sighs, alas,
  Upsuppèd have, thus I my plaint renew:

'O place of bliss, renewer of my woes,   45
  Give me account where is my noble fere,
Whom in thy walls thou did'st each night enclose,
  To other lief, but unto me most dear.'

Each stone, alas, that doth my sorrow rue,
  Returns thereto a hollow sound of plaint.   50
Thus I alone, where all my freedom grew,
  In prison pine with bondage and restraint,

And with remembrance of the greater grief,
To banish the less I find my chief relief.

'SO CRUEL PRISON': In 1537, Surrey was confined to Windsor Castle for striking another courtier within the precincts of the Court: 1 **betide**: befall   3 **a king's son**: Henry Fitzroy, Duke of Richmond, bastard son of Henry VIII; he married Lady Mary Howard, Surrey's sister, in 1533 but died in 1536 when only seventeen   **childish**: youthful   4 **Priam**: king of Troy   6 **hove**: linger   7 **the maiden's**

tower: the apartments of the ladies of the Court   9 **sales**: (French *salles*) rooms   13 **palm-play**: a game like tennis in which the palm of the hand is used instead of a racket   **despoiled for**: distracted from   16 **bait**: tempt   **kept the leads**: looked from the window   17 **gravelled ground**: tiltyard   **sleeves tied on the helm**: a knight would wear his lady's sleeve or scarf, or some other favour, on his helmet, both in a tourney and on the battlefield   19 **chere**: aspect   20 **darts**: lances   21 **ruth**: sorrow   26 **plaint**: complaint   29 **clothed holts with**: woods clothed with   30 **availed**: slackened   **swift y-breathed**: panting   32 **hart**: deer   32 **chase . . . a-force**: *chasser à force*, in which the game is run down rather than shot   **fearful**: frightened   **hart**: deer   33 **void**: deserted   **eke**: also   44 **Upsupped**: consumed   46 **fere**: companion   48 **To other lief**: beloved by others   51-2 **freedom . . . restraint**: a play on freedom as knightly courtesy and as liberty   53 **the greater grief**: the death of Richmond, which affected Surrey greatly   54 **the less**: his present imprisonment

AN EXCELLENT EPITAPH OF
SIR THOMAS WYATT

WYATT resteth here, that quick could never rest,
  Whose heavenly gifts, increasèd by disdain
And virtue, sank the deeper in his breast,
  Such profit he by envy could obtain.

A head, where wisdom mysteries did frame,   5
  Whose hammers beat still in that lively brain
As on a stithy where that some work of fame
  Was daily wrought to turn to Britain's gain.

A visage stern and mild, where both did grow
  Vice to contemn, in virtue to rejoice;   10
Amid great storms whom grace assurèd so
  To live upríght and smile at fortune's choice.

A hand that taught what might be said in rhyme,
  That reft Chaucer the glory of his wit;
A mark the which, unparfited for time,   15
  Some may approach but never none shall hit.

A tongue that served in foreign realms his king;
  Whose courteous talk to virtue did inflame
Each noble heart; a worthy guide to bring
  Our English youth by trávail unto fame.   20

An eye whose judgement none affect could blind,
  Friends to allure and foes to reconcile,
Whose piercing look did represent a mind
  With virtue fraught, reposèd, void of guile.

A heart where dread was never so impressed   25
  To hide the thought that might the truth advance;
In neither fortune loft nor yet repressed
  To swell in wealth or yield unto mischance.

A valiant corps where force and beauty met;
  Happy, alas, too happy but for foes;   30
Livèd, and ran the race that Nature set,
  Of manhood's shape where she the mould did lose.

But to the heavens that simple soul is fled,
   Which left with such as covet Christ to know
Witness of faith that never shall be dead,   35
   Sent for our health, but not receivèd so.

Thus for our guilt this jewel have we lost.
The earth his bones, the heavens possess his ghost.

AN EXCELLENT EPITAPH: Sir Thomas Wyatt died in October 1542:
1 **quick:** alive 2 **disdain:** (others') contempt 4 **envy:** malice
5 **mysteries:** profound thoughts 6–7 **hammers beat . . . stithy:**
likening the brain to a blacksmith's forge 9 **both:** i.e. sternness
and mildness 10 **contemn:** despise 14 **reft Chaucer:** robbed Chaucer
of 15 **unparfited for time:** unfinished for lack of time 20 **travail:**
labour 21 **none affect:** no passion 27 **loft:** raised 29 **corps:** body

'NORFOLK SPRANG THEE, LAMBETH HOLDS THEE DEAD'

NORFOLK sprang thee, Lambeth holds thee dead,
   Clere of the County of Clerëmont though hight;
Within the womb of Ormonde's race thou bred,
   And saw'st thy cousin crownèd in thy sight.
Shelton for love, Surrey for lord thou chase: 5
   Ay me, while life did last that league was tender;
Tracing whose steps thou sawest Kelsall blaze,
   Laundersey burnt, and battered Bullen render.
At Muttrell gates, hopeless of all recure,
   Thine earl half dead gave in thy hand his will;   10
Which cause did thee this pining death procure,
   Ere summers four times seven thou could'st fulfil.
   Ah, Clere, if love had booted, care, or cost,
   Heaven had not won, nor Earth so timely lost.

'NORFOLK SPRANG THEE': Thomas Clere, the subject of the poem, died
in April 1545 and was buried at Lambeth in the Howard chapel; he
had been Surrey's companion and squire, and had saved Surrey's
life at the siege of Montreuil (1544), Clere himself receiving a
wound that would eventually kill him (lines 9–11): 1–5 **Norfolk . . .
chase:** to unravel the family history, these lines might be paraphrased
as: 'Although you were born in Norfolk of the De Cleremont line,
in death you rest in the Howard chapel in Lambeth. You have the
blood of the Ormondes (who had been united to our family by
marriage) in your veins; and, although you took Mary Shelton (a
cousin of Anne Boleyn, whom you saw crowned as queen) as your lady,
you chose Surrey for your lord 2 **hight:** called 4 **thy cousin:** Anne
Boleyn, Clere's cousin by marriage 7 **Kelsall:** a Scottish town burned
by the English in 1542 8 **Laundersey:** Landrecy **Bullen:** Boulogne
9 **Muttrell:** Montreuil **recure:** remedy 11 **pining:** tormenting 13 **if
love had . . . cost:** if (my) love, care or money had sufficed

'MARTIAL, THE THINGS FOR TO ATTAIN'

MARTIAL, the things for to attain
The happy life be these, I find:
The riches left, not got with pain;
The fruitful ground, the quiet mind;
The equal friend; no grudge nor strife;   5
No charge of rule nor governance;
Without disease the healthful life;
The household of continuance;

The mean diet, no delicate fare;
Wisdom joined with simplicity;   10
The night dischargèd of all care
Where wine may bear no sovereignty;
The chaste wife wise, without debate;
Such sleeps as may beguile the night;
Contented with thine own estate;   15
Neither wish death nor fear his might.

'MARTIAL': a translation of Martial's 'Vitam quae faciunt beatiorum'
(*Epigrams* 10.47): 8 **continuance:** long duration 9 **mean:** modest, plain

From THE AENEID

[THE TROJAN HORSE]

THE Greekës chieftains, all irked with the war
Wherein they wasted had so many years
And oft repulsed by fatal destiny,
A huge horse made, high-raisèd like a hill,
By the divine science of Minerva;   5
Of cloven fir compacted were his ribs;
For their return a feignèd sacrifice,
The fame whereof so wandered it at point.
In the dark bulk they closèd bodies of men
Chosen by lot, and did enstuff by stealth   10
The hollow womb with armèd soldïers.
   There stands in sight an isle hight Tenedon,
Rich and of fame while Priam's kingdom stood:
Now but a bay, and road unsure for ship.
Hither them secretly the Greeks withdrew,   15
Shrouding themselves under the desert shore.
And, weening we they had been fled and gone,
And with that wind had fet the land of Greece,
Troy discharged her long-continued dole.
The gates cast up, we issued out to play,   20
The Greekish camp desirous to behold,
The places void and the forsaken coasts.
Here Pyrrhus' band, there fierce Achilles pight,
Here rode their ships, there did their battles join.
Astonied some the scatheful gift beheld,   25
Behight by vow unto the chaste Minerve,
All wond'ring at the hugeness of the horse.
   And first of all Timoetes 'gan advise
Within the walls to lead and draw the same,
And place it eke amid the palace court: 30
Whether of guile, or Troyës fate it would.
Capys, with some of judgement more discreet,
Willed it to drown, or underset with flame
The suspect present of the Greeks' deceit,
Or bore and gouge the hollow caves uncouth.   35
So díverse ran the giddy people's mind.
   Lo! foremost of a rout that followed him,
Kindled Laocoön hasted from the tower,
Crying far off, 'O wretched citizens,
What so great kind of frenzy fretteth you?   40
Deem ye the Greeks our enemies to be gone?
Or any Greekish gifts can you suppose

Devoid of guile? Is so Ulysses known?
Either the Greeks are in this timber hid,
Or this an engine is t'annoy our walls,   45
To view our towers, and overwhelm our town.
Here lurks some craft. Good Troyans, give no trust
Unto this horse, for what so ever it be,
I dread the Greeks, yea, when they offer gifts.'
And with that word, with all his force a dart   50
He lancèd then into that crooked womb:
Which trembling stack, and shook within the side,
Wherewith the caves 'gan hollowly resound.
And but for fates and for our blind forecást,
The Greeks' device and guile had he descried,   55
Troy yet had stand, and Priam's towers so high.

[Book 2, lines 18–73]

'THE AENEID': Surrey's translation of Virgil owes much to that by
Gavin Douglas (see above); although the Douglas translation would
not appear in print until 1553, it was clearly being circulated in
manuscript: 1 **irked with:** weary of 5 **Minerva:** Roman goddess of
arts and crafts, identified with the Greek goddess Pallas Athena
8 **at point:** conveniently 12 **hight:** called **Tenedon:** Tenedos
13 **Priam:** king of Troy 14 **road:** channel 16 **Shrouding:** hiding
desert: distant, remote (i.e. out of sight of the mainland)
17 **weening:** believing 18 **fet:** reached 19 **discharged:** cast off **dole:**
mourning 23 **Pyrrhus:** son of Achilles **pight:** pitched (his tents)
25 **Astonied:** astonished **scatheful:** harmful 26 **Behight:** promised
28 **Timoetes:** Thymoetes 30 **eke:** also 35 **uncouth:** strange 38 **Kindled:**
excited **Laocoön:** priest of Poseidon, god of the seas; following his
warning to the Trojans, Laocoön and his two young sons were
killed by two giant sea-serpents that swam across from Tenedos
50 **dart:** spear 52 **stack:** stuck 54 **forecast:** trust 56 **stand:** stood

RICHARD EDWARDES

'IN GOING TO MY NAKED BED . . .'

IN GOING to my naked bed as one that would have
    slept,
I heard a wife sing to her child, that long before had
    wept.
She sighèd sore and sang full sweet to bring the babe
    to rest,
That would not rest, but crièd still, in sucking at her
    breast.
She was full weary of her watch and grievèd with her
    child,   5
She rockèd it and rated it until on her it smiled.
Then did she say, 'Now have I found the proverb true
    to prove:
The falling out of faithful friends renewing is of love.'

Then took I paper, pen, and ink, this proverb for to
    write,
In register for to remain of such a worthy wight.   10
As she proceeded thus in song unto her little brat,
Much matter uttered she of weight, in place whereas
    she sat;
And provèd plain there was no beast, nor creature
    bearing life,

Could well be known to live in love without discórd
    and strife.
Then kissèd she her little babe and sware by God
    above.   15
'The falling out of faithful friends renewing is of love.'

She said that neither king, ne prince, ne lord could live
    aright,
Until their puissance they did prove, their manhood,
    and their might;
When manhood shall be matchèd so that fear can take
    no place,
Then weary works makes warriors each other to
    embrace.   20
And leave their force that failèd them, which did
    consume the rout,
That might by force with love have lived the term of
    nature out.
Then did she sing as one that thought no man could
    her reprove,
'The falling out of faithful friends renewing is of love.'

She said she saw no fish, ne fowl, nor beast within her
    haunt   25
That met a stranger in their kind, but could give it a
    taunt.
Since flesh might not endure, but rest must wrath
    succeed,
And force the fight to fall to play in pasture where they
    feed,
So noble Nature can well end the works she hath
    begun,
And bridle well that will not cease her tragedy in
    some.   30
Thus in her song she oft rehearsed, as did her well
    behove,
'The falling out of faithful friends renewing is of love.'

'I marvel much, perdy!' quoth she, 'for to behold the
    rout,
To see man, woman, boy, and beast, to toss the world
    about.
Some kneel, some crouch, some beck, some check, and
    some can smoothly smile,   35
And some embrace others in arms, and there think
    many a wile.
Some stand aloof at cap and knee, some humble and
    some stout,
Yet are they never friends indeed until they once fall
    out.'
Thus ended she her song, and said, before she did
    remove,   39
'The falling out of faithful friends renewing is of love.'

'IN GOING TO MY NAKED BED . . .': 5 **watch:** period of being awake
at night 6 **rated:** scolded 10 **In register . . . wight:** in order to
record what this worthy person said 17 **ne:** not 18 **puissance:** power
25–6 **no fish . . . taunt:** no creature meets another without initial
hostility 33 **perdy:** assuredly; from Old French, meaning 'by God'
25 **beck:** to bow or curtsy

GEORGE GASCOIGNE

'AND IF I DID, WHAT THEN?'

'AND if I did, what then?
  Are you aggrieved therefore?
The sea hath fish for every man,
  And what would you have more?'

Thus did my mistress once   5
  Amaze my mind with doubt;
And popped a question for the nonce,
  To beat my brains about.

Whereto I thus replied:
  'Each fisherman can wish   10
That all the seas at every tide
  Were his alone to fish;

'And so did I, in vain;
  But since it may not be,
Let such fish there as find the gain,   15
  And leave the loss for me.

'And with such luck and loss
  I will content myself,
Till tides of turning time may toss
  Such fishers on the shelf.   20

'And when they stick on sands,
  That every man may see,
Then will I laugh and clap my hands,
  As they do now at me.'

'AND IF I DID, WHAT THEN?': 7 **for the nonce:** for once, for a moment
15 **Let such . . . gain:** let those who are lucky make the attempt

SIR HENRY LEE

'HIS GOLDEN LOCKS TIME HATH
TO SILVER TURNED'

HIS golden locks time hath to silver turned.
  Oh, time too swift! Oh, swiftness never ceasing!
His youth 'gainst time and age hath ever spurned,
  But spurned in vain; youth waneth by increasing:
    Beauty, strength, youth, are flowers but fading
      seen;   5
    Duty, faith, love, are roots, and ever green.

His helmet not shall make a hive for bees;
  And, lovers' sonnets turned to holy psalms,
A man-at-arms must now serve on his knees,

And feed on prayers, which are age's alms: 10
  But though from court to cottage he depart,
  His saint is sure of his unspotted heart.

And when he saddest sits in homely cell,
  He'll teach his swains this carol for a song:
'Blest be the hearts that wish my sovereign well,   15
  Curst be the souls that think her any wrong.'
    Goddess, allow this agèd man his right,
    To be your beadsman now, that was your knight.
              [Formerly attributed to George Peele]

'HIS GOLDEN LOCKS TIME HATH TO SILVER TURNED': 4 **youth waneth by increasing:** youth is diminished by increasing age 18 **beadsman:** a person who recites prayers for another

THOMAS SACKVILLE,
EARL OF DORSET

From THE MIRROR FOR MAGISTRATES

LASTLY, stood War, in glittering arms yclad,
  With visage grim, stern looks, and blackly hued;
In his right hand a naked sword he had,
  That to the hilts was all with blood imbrued;
  And in his left, that kings and kingdoms rued,   5
    Famine and fire he held and therewithal
    He razèd towns and threw down towers and all.

Cities he sacked and realms, that whilom flowered
  In honour, glory, and rule above the best,
He overwhelmed and all their fame devoured,   10
  Consumed, destroyed, wasted, and never ceased,
  Till he their wealth, their name, and all oppressed;
    His face forhewed with wounds, and by his side
    There hung his targe, with gashes deep and wide.

In midst of which, depainted there, we found   15
  Deadly Debate, all full of snaky hair,
That with a bloody fillet was ybound,
  Out-breathing nought but discord everywhere.
  And round about were pórtrayed, here and there,
    The hugy hosts, Darius and his power,   20
    His kings, princes, his peers, and all his flower:

Whom great Macedo vanquished there in fight
  With deep slaughter, despoiling all his pride,
Pierced through his realms and daunted all his might.
  Duke Hannibal beheld I there beside,   25
  In Canna's field victor how he did ride,
    And woeful Romans that in vain withstood,
    And consul Paulus covered all in blood.

Yet saw I more: the fight at Thrasimene,
  And Trebery field, and eke when Hannibal   30
And worthy Scipio last in arms were seen
  Before Carthago gate, to try for all
  The world's empire, to whom it should befall;
    There saw I Pompey and Caesar clad in arms,
    Their hosts allied and all their civil harms: 35

With conquerors' hands, forbathed in their own blood,
  And Caesar weeping over Pompey's head.
Yet saw I Sulla and Marius where they stood,
  Their great cruelty and the deep bloodshed
  Of friends; Cyrus I saw and his host dead,   40
    And how the queen with great despite hath flung
    His head in blood of them she overcome.

Xerxes, the Persian king, yet saw I there
  With his huge host that drank the rivers dry,
Dismounted hills, and made the vales uprear,   45
  His host and all yet saw I plain, perdy!
  Thebës I saw, all razed how it did lie
    In heaps of stones, and Tyrus put to spoil,
    With walls and towers flat evened with the soil.

But Troy, alas! methought, above them all,   50
  It made mine eyes in very tears consume,
When I beheld the woeful weird befall,
  That by the wrathful will of gods was come;
  And Jove's unmovèd sentence and foredoom
    On Priam king and on his town so bent,   55
    I could not lin, but I must there lament.

And that the more, sith destiny was so stern
  As, force perforce, there might no force avail,
But she must fall, and by her fall we learn   59
  That cities, towers, wealth, world, and all shall quail.
  No manhood, might, nor nothing mought prevail;
    All were there prest full many a prince and peer,
    And many a knight that sold his death full dear:

Not worthy Hector, worthiest of them all,
  Her hope, her joy; his force is now for nought.   65
O Troy, Troy, Troy, there is no boot but bale;
  The hugy horse within thy walls is brought;
  Thy turrets fall, thy knights, that whilom fought
    In arms amid the field, are slain in bed,
    Thy gods defiled and all thy honour dead.   70

The flames upspring and cruelly they creep
  From wall to roof till all to cinders waste;
Some fire the houses where the wretches sleep;
  Some rush in here, some run in there as fast;
  In every where or sword or fire they taste;   75
    The walls are torn, the towers whirled to the
      ground,
    There is no mischief but may there be found.

Cassandra yet there saw I how they haled
  From Pallas' house, with spercled tress undone,
Her wrists fast bound, and with Greeks' rout empaled;
  And Priam eke, in vain how did he run   81
  To arms, whom Pyrrhus with despite hath done
    To cruel death, and bathed him in the baign
    Of his son's blood, before the altar slain.

But how can I describe the doleful sight   85
  That in the shield so livelike fair did shine?
Sith in this world I think was never wight
  Could have set forth the half, not half so fine.
  I can no more but tell how there is seen
    Fair Ilium fall in burning red gledes down,   90
    And from the soil great Troy, Neptunus' town.

[Induction, stanzas 56–68]

THE MIRROR FOR MAGISTRATES: 1 **yclad:** clad, dressed 4 **imbrued:** drenched 6 **therewithal:** with those 8 **whilom:** once 13 **forhewed:** cut, slashed 14 **targe:** a small shield 17 **fillet:** band **ybound:** bound 20 **hugy:** huge **Darius:** Persian king conquered by Alexander the Great in 331 BC 22 **Macedo:** Alexander the Great, king of Macedon 25–8 **Duke Hannibal . . . blood:** the Carthaginian general Hannibal (247–182 BC), defeated the Romans under the consul Aemilius Paulus at Cannae in Italy (216 BC); 'Duke' here is an arbitrary title 29 **Thrasimene:** Lake Trasimene, site of another of Hannibal's victories over the Romans (217 BC) 30 **Trebery:** Trebia, another such victory 31 **Scipio:** Publius Cornelius Scipio (236–184 BC), Roman general who defeated Hannibal at Zama, near Carthage 32 **Carthago:** Carthage 34 **Pompey:** Gnaeus Pompeius (106–48 BC), Roman general and dictator, defeated in civil war by his former ally Julius Caesar (100–44 BC) 38 **Sulla:** Lucius Cornelius Sulla (138–78 BC), Roman soldier who took power in Rome by force **Marius:** Gaius Marius (157–86 BC), Roman general who vied with Sulla for power and massacred his enemies 40–2 **Cyrus . . . overcome:** Cyrus (559–529 BC) was king of Persia. One version of his death has him defeated by the Scythian queen Tomyris, who placed his severed head in a pot of his own blood 43 **Xerxes:** (519–465 BC), a Persian king who led a vast army against Greece 46 **perdy:** assuredly; from Old French meaning 'by God' 47 **Thebës:** Thebes, an important city of ancient Greece, destroyed by Alexander the Great when it rebelled against him 48 **Tyrus:** Tyre, a Phoenician city besieged and destroyed by Alexander the Great in 332 BC 49 **flat evened with the soil:** razed to the ground 52 **weird:** fate 56 **lin:** stop, cease 57 **sith:** since 61 **mought:** might 62 **prest:** compelled 66 **no boot but bale:** no good, only evil 75 **or . . . or:** either . . . or 78–80 **Cassandra . . . empaled:** I saw how Cassandra (prophetess daughter of Priam) was dragged from the temple of (Pallas) Athene and impaled by the Greeks in their massacre 81 **eke:** also 83 **baign:** bath 87 **wight:** person 90 **Ilium:** Troy **glede:** a burning ember 91 **Neptunus:** Neptune, the sea-god

ARTHUR GOLDING

From OVID'S METAMORPHOSES

[ICARUS]

AS SOON AS Minos came a-land in Crete, he by and
    by
Performed his vows to Jupiter in causing for to die
A hundred bulls for sacrifice. And then he did adorn
His palace with the en'my's spoils by conquest won
    beforn.
The slander of his house increased: and now appearèd
    more   5
The mother's filthy whoredom by the monster that she
    bore
Of double shape, an ugly thing. This shameful infamy,
This monster borne him by his wife he minds by policy
To put away: and in a house with many nooks and
    krinks
From all men's sights and speech of folk to shut it up
    he thinks.   10
Immediately one Daedalus renownèd in that land
For fine devise and workmanship in building, went in
    hand
To make it. He confounds his work with sudden stops
    and stays,
And with the great uncertainty of sundry winding
    ways
Leads in and out, and to and fro, at divers doors
    astray.   15
And as with trickling stream the brook Maeander
    seems to play
In Phrygia, and with doubtful race runs counter to
    and fro,
And meeting with himself doth look if all his stream
    or no
Come after, and retiring eft clean backward to his
    spring
And marching eft to open sea as straight as any string,
Indenteth with reversèd stream: even so of winding
    ways   21
Unnumerable Daedalus within his work conveys.
Yea, scarce himself could find the means to wind
    himself well out:
So busy and so intricate the house was all about.
    Within this maze did Minos shut the monster that
    did bear   25
      The shape of man and bull. And when he twice had
      fed him there
With blood of Attic princes' sons that given for tribute
    were,

The third time at the ninth year's end the lot did
    chance to light
On Theseus, King Aegeus' son, who like a valiant
    knight
Did overcome the Minotaur, and by the policy   30
Of Minos' elder daughter (who had taught him for to
    tie
A clew of linen at the door to guide himself thereby),
As busy as the turnings were, his way he out did find,
Which never man had done before. And straight he
    having wind,
With Minos' daughter sailed away to Dia, where
    (unkind   35
And cruel creature that he was) he left her post alone
Upon the shore. Thus desolate and making doleful
    moan
God Bacchus did both comfort her and take her to his
    bed.
And with an everlasting star the more her fame to
    spread,
He took the chaplet from her head, and up to heaven
    it threw.   40
The chaplet thirlèd through the air, and as it gliding
    flew,
The precious stones were turned to stars which
    blazèd clear and bright,
And took their place (continuing like a chaplet still to
    sight)
Amid between the kneeler down and him that gripes
    the snake.
    Now in this while 'gan Daedalus a weariness to take
    Of living like a banished man and prisoner such a
    time   46
In Crete, and longèd in heart to see his native clime.
But seas enclosèd him as if he had in prison be.
Then thought he: Though both sea and land King
    Minos stop fro me,
I am assured he cannot stop the air and open sky,   50
To make my passage that way, then, my cunning I will
    try.
Although that Minos like a lord held all the world
    beside,
Yet doth the air from Minos' yoke for all men free
    abide.
This said, to uncouth arts he bent the force of all his
    wits
To alter Nature's course by craft. And orderly he
    knits   55

OVID'S METAMORPHOSES: 1 **a-land:** to land 4 **beforn:** before 8 **he minds by policy:** he is wisely careful 9 **krinks:** secret or enclosed spaces 12 **devise:** invention, inventiveness 13 **confounds:** complicates 16 **Maeander:** a proverbially winding river in ancient Phrygia (Asia Minor) 17 **doubtful race:** confusing course 20 **eft:** afterwards 27 **Attic:** Greek; strictly, of Attica, the region around Athens

32 **clew of linen:** ball of thread 34 **straight he having wind:** as soon as the winds were favourable 35 **Dia:** Naxos, island in the Cyclades 36 **post:** quickly 38 **God Bacchus:** the Roman god of wine 40 **chaplet:** a garland worn on the head 41 **thirlèd:** thrilled, vibrated 44 **gripes:** clutches, grips 45 **'gan:** began 49 **stop fro me:** bars me from

A row of feathers one by one, beginning with the short,
And overmatching still each quill with one of longer sort,
That on the shoring of a hill a man would think them grow.
Even so the country organ-pipes of oaten reeds in row
Each higher than another rise. Then fast'nèd he with flax   60
The middle quills, and joinèd in the lowest sort with wax.
And when he thus had finished them, a little he them bent
In compass, that the very birds they full might represent.
There stood me by him Icarus his son, a pretty lad,
Who knowing not that he in hands his own destruction had,   65
With smiling mouth did one while blow the feathers to and fro
Which in the air on wings of birds did flask not long ago;
And with his thumbs another while he chafes the yellow wax
And lets his father's wondrous work with childish toys and knacks.
As soon as that the work was done, the workman by and by   70
Did peize his body on his wings, and in the air on high
Hung wavering: and did teach his son how he should also fly.
'I warn thee,' quoth he, 'Icarus, a middle race to keep.
For if thou hold too low a gait, the dankness of the deep
Will overlade thy wings with wet. And if thou mount too high,   75
The Sun will singe them. Therefore see between them both thou fly.
I bid thee not behold the star Boötes in the sky,
Nor look upon the bigger Bear to make thy course thereby,
Nor yet on Orion's naked sword. But ever have an eye
To keep the race that I do keep, and I will guide thee right.'   80
In giving counsel to his son to order well his flight,
He fast'nèd to his shoulders twain a pair of uncouth wings.
And as he was in doing it and warning him of things,
His agèd cheeks were wet, his hands did quake, in fine he gave
His son a kiss, the last that he alive should ever have.

And then he mounting up aloft before him took his way   86
Right fearful for his follower's sake, as is the bird the day
That first she tolleth from her nest among the branches high
Her tender young ones in the air to teach them for to fly.
So heartens he his little son to follow, teaching him   90
A hurtful art. His own two wings he waveth very trim,
And looketh backward still upon his son's. The fishermen
Then standing angling by the sea, and shepherds leaning then
On sheep-hooks, and the ploughmen on the handles of their plough,
Beholding them, amazèd were: and thought that they that through   95
The air could fly were gods. And now did on their left side stand
The isles of Paros and of Dele, and Samos, Juno's land,
And on their right, Lebinthos, and the fair Calydna fraught
With store of honey: when the boy a frolic courage caught
To fly at random. Whereupon forsaking quite his guide,   100
Of fond desire to fly to Heaven, above his bounds he stied.
And there the nearness of the Sun which burned more hot aloft
Did make the wax (with which his wings were gluèd) lithe and soft.
As soon as that the wax was molt, his naked arms he shakes,
And wanting wherewithal to wave, no help of air he takes.   105
But calling on his father loud he drownèd in the wave;
And by this chance of his, those seas his name forever have.
His wretched father (but as then no father) cried in fear
'Oh, Icarus, oh, Icarus, where art thou? Tell me where
That I may find thee, Icarus.' He saw the feathers swim
Upon the waves, and cursed his art that so had spited him.   111
At last he took his body up and laid it in a grave,
And to the isle the name of him then buried in it gave.
    And as he of his wretched son the corse in ground did hide,
    The cackling partridge from a thick and leavy thorn him spied,   115

---

58 **shoring:** side, slope 59 **country . . . reeds:** rustic pipes, Pan pipes 62–3 **bent In compass:** made in a curved shape 67 **flask:** flap, flex 71 **peize:** balance 75 **overlade:** overburden, weigh down 77–9 **I bid thee . . . sword:** Daedalus names the stars and constellations that Icarus should not use for navigation

88 **tolleth:** entices, leads 91 **hurtful art:** dangerous skill 94 **sheep-hooks:** shepherds' crooks 97 **Dele:** Delos, an island in the Cyclades 101 **stied:** mounted, climbed 104 **molt:** molten 105 **no help of air he takes:** flapping his arms in the air cannot support him 114 **corse:** corpse

And clapping with his wings for joy aloud to call
    began.
There was of that same kind of bird no mo but he as
    than:
In times forepast had none been seen. It was but late
    anew
Since he was made a bird; and that thou, Daedalus,
    may'st rue,
For while the world doth last, thy shame shall
    thereupon ensue.   120
For why thy sister, ignorant of that which after happed,
Did put him to thee to be taught full twelve years old,
    and apt
To take instruction. He did mark the middle bone that
    goes
Through fishes, and according to the pattern ta'en of
    those
He filèd teeth upon a piece of iron one by one,   125
And so devisèd first the saw where erst was never
    none.
Moreover he two iron shanks so joined in one round
    head,
That opening an indifferent space the one point down
    shall tread,
And t'other draw a circle round. The finding of these
    things,
The spiteful heart of Daedalus with such a malice
    stings,   130
That headlong from the holy tow'r of Pallas down he
    threw
His nephew, feigning him to fall by chance, which was
    not true.
But Pallas (who doth favour wits) did stay him in his
    fall,
And changing him into a bird did clad him over all
With feathers soft amid the air. The quickness of his
    wit   135
(Which erst was swift) did shed itself among his wings
    and feet.
And as he partridge hight before, so hights he
    partridge still.
Yet mounteth not this bird aloft ne seems to have a will
To build her nest in tops of trees among the boughs on
    high,
But flecketh near the ground and lays her eggs in
    hedges dry.   140
And forbecause his former fall she ay in mind doth
    bear,
She ever since all lofty things doth warely shun for
    fear.

            [Book 8, lines 201–342]

117–8 **There was . . . seen:** He (Daedalus) was the only example of
that kind of bird 126 **erst:** before 127–9 **Moreover . . . round:**
describes the invention of compasses 131 **Pallas:** the goddess
Athene 133 **stay:** halt 137 **hight:** was called 138 **ne:** nor 140 **flecketh:**
flaps, flutters 141 **ay:** always

SIR EDWARD DYER

'THE LOWEST TREES HAVE TOPS, THE ANT HER GALL'

THE lowest trees have tops, the ant her gall,
    The fly her spleen, the little spark his heat;
The slender hairs cast shadows, though but small,
    And bees have stings, although they be not great;
Seas have their source, and so have shallow springs;   5
And love is love, in beggars and in kings.

Where waters smoothest run, there deepest are the
    fords,
    The dial stirs, yet none perceives it move;
The firmest faith is found in fewest words,
    The turtles do not sing, and yet they love;   10
True hearts have ears and eyes, no tongues to speak;
They hear and see, and sigh, and then they break.

'THE LOWEST TREES HAVE TOPS, THE ANT HER GALL': 8 **dial:** sundial
10 **turtle:** turtledove

'MY MIND TO ME A KINGDOM IS'

MY MIND to me a kingdom is;
    Such perfect joy therein I find
That it excels all other bliss
    That world affords or grows by kind.
        Though much I want which most men have,   5
        Yet still my mind forbids to crave.

No princely pomp, no wealthy store,
    No force to win the victory,
No wily wit to salve a sore,
    No shape to feed each gazing eye;   10
        To none of these I yield as thrall,
        Forwhy my mind doth serve for all.

I see how plenty suffers oft,
    And hasty climbers soon do fall;
I see that those which are aloft   15
    Mishap doth threaten most of all;
        They get with toil, they keep with fear –
        Such cares my mind could never bear.

Content I live, this is my stay,
    I seek no more than may suffice;   20
I press to bear no haughty sway;
    Look, what I lack my mind supplies.
        Lo! thus I triumph like a king,
        Content with that my mind doth bring.

Some have too much, yet still do crave;   25
    I little have, and seek no more.
They are but poor, though much they have,

And I am rich with little store.
   They poor, I rich; they beg, I give;
   They lack, I leave; they pine, I live.   30

I laugh not at another's loss,
   I grudge not at another's gain;
No worldly waves my mind can toss;
   My state at one doth still remain.
     I fear no foe, I fawn no friend;   35
     I loathe not life, nor dread my end.

Some weigh their pleasure by their lust,
   Their wisdom by their rage of will;
Their treasure is their only trust,
   And cloakèd craft their store of skill;   40
     But all the pleasure that I find
     Is to maintain a quiet mind.

My wealth is health and perfect ease,
   My conscience clear my chief defence;
I neither seek by bribes to please,   45
   Nor by desert to breed offence.
     Thus do I live, thus will I die.
     Would all did so as well as I!

'MY MIND TO ME A KINGDOM IS': 11 **thrall**: slave 12 **Forwhy**: because 13 **plenty suffers oft**: wealth does not guarantee happiness 19 **stay**: support 40 **cloakèd craft**: secret or hidden ability

NICHOLAS BRETON

'IN THE MERRY MONTH OF MAY'

IN the merry month of May,
In a morn by break of day,
Forth I walked by the wood side,
Whenas May was in his pride.
There I spièd all alone   5
Phyllida and Corydon.
Much ado there was, God wot,
He would love and she would not.
She said, never man was true;
He said, none was false to you.   10
He said, he had loved her long;
She said, love should have no wrong.
Corydon would kiss her then;
She said, maids must kiss no men
Till they did for good and all.   15
Then she made the shepherd call
All the heavens to witness truth,
Never loved a truer youth.
Thus with many a pretty oath,
Yea and nay, and faith and troth,   20
Such as silly shepherds use
When they will not love abuse,
Love, which had been long deluded,

Was with kisses sweet concluded.
And Phyllida with garlands gay   25
Was made the Lady of the May.

'IN THE MERRY MONTH OF MAY': 4 **Whenas**: when, while 6 **Phyllida and Corydon**: conventional names for lovers 7 **wot**: knows

'COME, LITTLE BABE, COME, SILLY SOUL'

COME, little babe, come silly soul,
   Thy father's shame, thy mother's grief,
Born as I doubt to all our dole,
   And to thyself unhappy chief:
     Sing lullaby and lap it warm,   5
     Poor soul that thinks no creature harm.

Thou little think'st and less dost know
   The cause of this thy mother's moan;
Thou want'st the wit to wail her woe,
   And I myself am all alone;   10
     Why dost thou weep? why dost thou wail,
     And knowest not yet what thou dost ail?

Come, little wretch! Ah, silly heart!
   Mine only joy, what can I more?
If there be any wrong thy smart,   15
   That may the destinies implore,
     'Twas I, I say, against my will:
     I wail the time, but be thou still.

And dost thou smile? Oh! thy sweet face!
   Would God himself he might thee see!   20
No doubt thou wouldst soon purchase grace,
   I know right well, for thee and me:
     But come to mother, babe, and play,
     For father false is fled away.

Sweet boy, if it by fortune chance   25
   Thy father home again to send,
If death do strike me with his lance,
   Yet mayst thou me to him commend:
     If any ask thy mother's name,
     Tell how by love she purchased blame.   30

Then will his gentle heart soon yield:
   I know him of a noble mind;
Although a lion in the field,
   A lamb in town thou shalt him find.
     Ask blessing, babe, be not afraid!   35
     His sugared words hath me betrayed.

Then mayst thou joy and be right glad,
   Although in woe I seem to moan.
Thy father is no rascal lad,
   A noble youth of blood and bone;   40
     His glancing looks, if he once smile,
     Right honest women may beguile.

Come, little boy, and rock asleep!
  Sing lullaby, and be thou still!
I, that can do nought else but weep,   45
  Will sit by thee and wail my fill:
    God bless my babe, and lullaby,
    From this thy father's quality.

'COME, LITTLE BABE, COME, SILLY SOUL': 1 **silly:** simple 3 **dole:** pain, sorrow 4 **chief:** mainly 15 **smart:** pain 37 **joy:** rejoice

'SHALL WE GO DANCE THE HAY, THE HAY?'

SHALL we go dance the hay, the hay?
Never pipe could ever play
Better shepherd's roundelay.

Shall we go sing the song, the song?
Never Love did ever wrong.   5
Fair maids, hold hands all along.

Shall we go learn to woo, to woo?
Never thought came ever to,
Better deed could better do.

Shall we go learn to kiss, to kiss?   10
Never heart could ever miss
Comfort, where true meaning is.

Thus at base they run, they run,
When the sport was scarce begun.
But I waked, and all was done.   15

'SHALL WE GO DANCE THE HAY, THE HAY?': 1 **hay:** a country dance 3 **roundelay:** a song or dance 13 **base:** a game

EDMUND SPENSER

'MOST GLORIOUS LORD OF LIFE . . .'

MOST glorious Lord of life, that on this day
  Didst make thy triumph over death and sin;
  And having harrowed hell didst bring away
  Captivity thence captive us to win;
This joyous day, dear Lord, with joy begin,   5
  And grant that we for whom thou diddest die,
  Being with thy dear blood clean washed from sin,
  May live for ever in felicity.
And that thy love we weighing worthily,
  May likewise love thee for the same again;   10
  And for thy sake that all like dear didst buy,
  With love may one another entertain.
So let us love, dear love, like as we ought,
  Love is the lesson which the Lord us taught.

'MOST GLORIOUS LORD OF LIFE . . .': 4 **Captivity . . . win:** To win our freedom from captivity (in hell) 9 **weighing worthily:** valuing highly 11 **all . . . buy:** bought at great cost

'ONE DAY I WROTE HER NAME UPON THE STRAND'

ONE day I wrote her name upon the strand,
  But came the waves and washèd it away;
  Again I wrote it with a second hand,
  But came the tide and made my pains his prey.
'Vain man,' said she, 'thou dost in vain assay   5
  A mortal thing so to immortalize,
  For I myself shall like to this decay,
  And eke my name be wipèd out likewise.'
'Not so,' quoth I, 'let baser things devise
  To die in dust, but you shall live by fame: 10
  My verse your virtues rare shall éternize,
  And in the heavens write your glorious name;
Where, whenas death shall all the world subdue,
  Our love shall live, and later life renew.'

'ONE DAY I WROTE HER NAME UPON THE STRAND': 3 **with a second hand:** once again 4 **made my pains his prey:** destroyed my work 5 **assay:** attempt 7 **I myself . . . decay:** I too will die 8 **eke:** also 13 **whenas:** when

EPITHALAMION

YE LEARNED sisters, which have oftentimes
Been to me aiding, others to adorn,
Whom ye thought worthy of your graceful rhymes,
That even the greatest did not greatly scorn
To hear their names sung in your simple lays,   5
But joyèd in their praise;
And when ye list your own mishaps to mourn,
Which death, or love, or fortune's wreck did raze,
Your string could soon to sadder tenor turn,
And teach the woods and waters to lament   10
Your doleful dreariment:
Now lay those sorrowful complaints aside,
And having all your heads with garland crowned,
Help me mine own love's praises to resound;
Ne let the same of any be envied: 15
So Orpheus did for his own bride,
So I unto myself alone will sing;
The woods shall to me answer, and my echo ring.

Early, before the world's light-giving lamp
His golden beam upon the hills doth spread,   20
Having dispersed the night's uncheerful damp,
Do ye awake, and, with fresh lustihead,
Go to the bow'r of my beloved love,

EPITHALAMION: 1 **learned sisters:** the Muses 5 **lays:** songs 6 **joyed:** were joyful 7 **list:** choose 9 **string:** harp or lute string 11 **dreariment:** sorrowful state 15 **Ne let:** Do not let 19 **the world's . . . lamp** the sun 22 **lustihead:** vigour

My truest turtle dove:
Bid her awake; for Hymen is awake, 25
And long since ready forth his masque to move,
With his bright tead that flames with many a flake,
And many a bachelor to wait on him,
In their fresh garments trim.
Bid her awake therefore, and soon her dight, 30
For lo! the wishèd day is come at last,
That shall, for all the pains and sorrows past,
Pay to her usury of long delight:
And whilst she doth her dight,
Do ye to her of joy and solace sing, 35
That all the woods may answer, and your echo ring.

Bring with you all the nymphs that you can hear,
Both of the rivers and the forests green,
And of the sea that neighbours to her near,
All with gay garlands goodly well beseen. 40
And let them also with them bring in hand
Another gay garland,
For my faire love, of lilies and of roses,
Bound true-love-wise with a blue silk riband.
And let them make great store of bridal posies, 45
And let them eke bring store of other flowers,
To deck the bridal bowers.
And let the ground whereas her foot shall tread,
For fear the stones her tender foot should wrong,
Be strewed with fragrant flowers all along, 50
And diap'rèd like the discoloured mead.
Which done, do at her chamber door await,
For she will waken straight;
The whiles do ye this song unto her sing
The woods shall to you answer, and your echo ring. 55

Ye nymphs of Mulla, which with careful heed
The silver scaly trouts do tend full well,
And greedy pikes which use therein to feed
(Those trouts and pikes all others do excel),
And ye likewise which keep the rushy lake, 60
Where none do fishes take,
Bind up the locks the which hang scattered light,
And in his waters, which your mirror make,
Behold your faces as the crystal bright,
That when you come whereas my love doth lie, 65
No blemish she may spy.
And eke ye lightfoot maids which keep the deer
That on the hoary mountain use to tow'r,
And the wild wolves, which seek them to devour,

With your steel darts do chase from coming near, 70
Be also present here,
To help to deck her, and to help to sing,
That all the woods may answer, and your echo ring.

Wake now, my love, awake! for it is time:
The rosy morn long since left Tithon's bed, 75
All ready to her silver coach to climb,
And Phoebus 'gins to show his glorious head.
Hark how the cheerful birds do chant their lays,
And carol of love's praise!
The merry lark her matins sings aloft, 80
The thrush replies, the mavis descant plays,
The ousel shrills, the ruddock warbles soft,
So goodly all agree, with sweet consent,
To this day's merriment.
Ah! my dear love, why do ye sleep thus long, 85
When meeter were that ye should now awake,
T'await the coming of your joyous make,
And hearken to the birds' love-learnèd song,
The dewy leaves among?
For they of joy and pleasance to you sing, 90
That all the woods them answer, and their echo ring.

My love is now awake out of her dream,
And her fair eyes, like stars that dimmèd were
With darksome cloud, now show their goodly beams
More bright than Hesperus his head doth rear. 95
Come now, ye damsels, daughters of delight,
Help quickly her to dight.
But first come ye, fair Hours, which were begot,
In Jove's sweet paradise, of Day and Night,
Which do the seasons of the year allot, 100
And all that ever in this world is fair
Do make and still repair.
And ye three handmaids of the Cyprian queen,
The which doe still adorn her beauty's pride,
Help to adorn my beautifullest bride; 105
And as ye her array, still throw between
Some graces to be seen;
And as ye use to Venus, to her sing,
The whiles the woods shall answer, and your echo
   ring.

Now is my love all ready forth to come. 110
Let all the virgins therefore well await,
And ye fresh boys that tend upon her groom
Prepare yourselves, for he is coming straight.

---

25 **Hymen:** god of marriage 26 **forth his masque to move:** to begin his performance or ceremony 27 **tead:** torch 30 **soon her dight:** get dressed quickly 33 **Pay . . . delight:** repay her in happiness like interest on a loan 40 **beseen:** adorned 46 **eke:** also 48 **whereas:** where 51 **diap'rèd like the discoloured mead:** variegated with colours like a flowery meadow 56 **Mulla:** an Irish river, a tributary of the Blackwater, on the banks of which Spenser once lived 58 **which use therein to feed:** which habitually feed there 68 **hoary:** white with snow

70 **darts:** spears 75 **Tithon:** Tithonus, in Greek myth, a youth beloved by Eos, goddess of the dawn 77 **Phoebus:** Apollo, Greek god of the sun 82 **ruddock:** the redbreast 86 **meeter:** more fitting 87 **make:** mate 95 **Hesperus:** Venus, when regarded as the evening star 102 **still:** always 103 **Cyprian queen:** Venus (Greek Aphrodite), particularly worshipped in Cyprus 106 **array:** dress, adorn 112 **fresh:** young 113 **straight:** directly

Set all your things in seemly good array,
Fit for so joyful day,　　　　　　　　　　　　115
The joyful'st day that ever sun did see.
Faire Sun, show forth thy favourable ray,
And let thy lifeful heat not fervent be,
For fear of burning her sunshiny face,
Her beauty to disgrace.　　　　　　　　　　　120
O fairest Phoebus, father of the Muse,
If ever I did honour thee aright,
Or sing the thing that mote thy mind delight,
Do not thy servant's simple boon refuse,
But let this day, let this one day be mine,　　125
Let all the rest be thine.
Then I thy sovereign praises loud will sing,
That all the woods shall answer, and their echo ring.

Hark how the minstrels 'gin to shrill aloud
Their merry music that resounds from far,　　130
The pipe, the tabor, and the trembling croud,
That well agree withouten breach or jar,
But most of all the damsels do delight,
When they their timbrels smite,
And thereunto do dance and carol sweet,　　135
That all the senses they do ravish quite,
The whiles the boys run up and down the street,
Crying aloud with strong confusèd noise,
As if it were one voice.
'Hymen, Io Hymen, Hymen,' they do shout,　　140
That even to the heavens their shouting shrill
Doth reach, and all the firmament doth fill;
To which the people, standing all about,
As in approvance do thereto applaud,
And loud advance her laud,　　　　　　　　　145
And evermore they 'Hymen, Hymen' sing,
That all the woods them answer, and their echo ring.

Lo! where she comes along with portly pace,
Like Phoebe, from her chamber of the east,
Arising forth to run her mighty race,　　　　150
Clad all in white, that seems a virgin best.
So well it her beseems that ye would ween
Some angel she had been.
Her long loose yellow locks like golden wire,
Sprinkled with pearl, and pearling flow'rs atween,　155
Do like a golden mantle her attire,
And being crownèd with a garland green,
Seem like some maiden queen.

Her modest eyes, abashèd to behold
So many gazers as on her do stare,　　　　　160
Upon the lowly ground affixèd are;
Ne dare lift up her countenance too bold,
But blush to hear her praises sung so loud,
So far from being proud.
Nathless do ye still loud her praises sing,　　165
That all the woods may answer, and your echo ring.

Tell me, ye merchants' daughters, did ye see
So fair a creature in your town before,
So sweet, so lovely, and so mild as she,
Adorned with beauty's grace and virtue's store?　170
Her goodly eyes like sapphires shining bright,
Her forehead ivory white,
Her cheeks like apples which the sun hath ruddied,
Her lips like cherries charming men to bite,
Her breast like to a bowl of cream uncrudded,　175
Her paps like lilies budded,
Her snowy neck like to a marble tow'r,
And all her body like a palace fair,
Ascending up, with many a stately stair,
To honour's seat and chastity's sweet bow'r.　180
Why stand ye still, ye virgins, in amaze,
Upon her so to gaze,
Whiles ye forget your former lay to sing,
To which the woods did answer, and your echo ring.

But if ye saw that which no eyes can see,　　185
The inward beauty of her lively sprite,
Garnished with heavenly gifts of high degree,
Much more then would ye wonder at that sight,
And stand astonished like to those which read
Medusa's mazeful head.　　　　　　　　　　190
There dwells sweet love and constant chastity,
Unspotted faith, and comely womanhood,
Regard of honour, and mild modesty;
There virtue reigns as queen in royal throne,
And giveth laws alone,　　　　　　　　　　　195
The which the base affections do obey,
And yield their services unto her will;
Ne thought of thing uncomely ever may
Thereto approach to tempt her mind to ill.
Had ye once seen these her celestial treasures,　200
And unrevealèd pleasures,
Then would ye wonder, and her praises sing,
That all the woods should answer, and your echo ring.

---

121 **father of the Muse:** Phoebus (Apollo), god of poetry 122 **aright:** properly 123 **mote:** might 129 **'gin:** begin 131 **tabor:** a small tambourine-like drum **croud:** an old stringed instrument 132 **withouten:** without 134 **timbrel:** tambourine 140 **Io:** a Latin interjection of joy or triumph 145 **laud:** praise 148 **portly:** dignified 149 **Phoebe:** Diana, goddess of the moon 151 **seems:** becomes, is fitting for 152 **ween:** think, believe

165 **Nathless:** nevertheless 175 **uncrudded:** not curdled 186 **sprite:** spirit 189-90 **like . . . head:** like those who, in Greek myth, were turned to stone by looking at the face of Medusa the Gorgon 190 **mazeful:** bewildering 198 **uncomely:** indecent

Open the temple gates unto my love,
Open them wide that she may enter in, 205
And all the posts adorn as doth behove,
And all the pillars deck with garlands trim,
For to receive this saint with honour due,
That cometh in to you.
With trembling steps and humble reverence, 210
She cometh in before th'Almighty's view:
Of her, ye virgins, learn obedience,
When so ye come into those holy places,
To humble your proud faces.
Bring her up to th'high altar, that she may 215
The sacred ceremonies there partake,
The which do endless matrimony make;
And let the roaring organs loudly play
The praises of the Lord in lively notes,
The whiles with hollow throats 220
The choristers the joyous anthem sing,
That all the woods may answer, and their echo ring.

Behold, whiles she before the altar stands,
Hearing the holy priest that to her speaks,
And blesseth her with his two happy hands, 225
How the red roses flush up in her cheeks,
And the pure snow with goodly vermeil stain,
Like crimson dyed in grain:
That even th'angels, which continually
About the sacred altar do remain, 230
Forget their service and about her fly,
Oft peeping in her face that seems more fair
The more they on it stare.
But her sad eyes, still fastened on the ground,
Are governèd with goodly modesty, 235
That suffers not one look to glance awry,
Which may let in a little thought unsound.
Why blush ye, love, to give to me your hand,
The pledge of all our band?
Sing, ye sweet angels, Alleluya sing, 240
That all the woods may answer, and your echo ring.

Now all is done; bring home the bride again,
Bring home the triumph of our victory,
Bring home with you the glory of her gain,
With joyance bring her and with jollity. 245
Never had man more joyful day than this,
Whom heaven would heap with bliss.
Make feast therefore now all this livelong day;
This day forever to me holy is;
Pour out the wine without restraint or stay, 250
Pour not by cups but by the bellyful,
Pour out to all that wull,
And sprinkle all the posts and walls with wine,

That they may sweat, and drunken be withal.
Crown ye god Bacchus with a coronal, 255
And Hymen also crown with wreaths of vine;
And let the Graces dance unto the rest,
For they can do it best:
The whiles the maidens do their carol sing,
To which the woods shall answer, and their echo
    ring. 260

Ring ye the bells, ye young men of the town,
And leave your wonted labours for this day:
This day is holy; do ye write it down,
That ye for ever it remember may.
This day the sun is in his chiefest height, 265
With Barnaby the bright,
From whence declining daily by degrees,
He somewhat loseth of his heat and light,
When once the Crab behind his back he sees.
But for this time it ill-ordainèd was 270
To choose the longest day in all the year,
And shortest night, when longest fitter were:
Yet never day so long but late would pass.
Ring ye the bells, to make it wear away,
And bonfires make all day, 275
And dance about them, and about them sing:
That all the woods may answer, and your echo ring.

Ah! when will this long weary day have end,
And lend me leave to come unto my love?
How slowly do the hours their numbers spend! 280
How slowly does sad Time his feathers move!
Haste thee, O fairest planet, to thy home
Within the western foam:
Thy tirèd steeds long since have need of rest.
Long though it be, at last I see it gloom, 285
And the bright evening star with golden crest
Appear out of the east.
Fair child of beauty, glorious lamp of love,
That all the host of heaven in ranks dost lead,
And guidest lovers through the nightès dread, 290
How cheerfully thou lookest from above,
And seem'st to laugh atween thy twinkling light,
As joying in the sight
Of these glad many which for joy do sing, 294
That all the woods them answer, and their echo ring!

---

227 **vermeil:** vermilion, scarlet 228 **dyed in grain:** deeply dyed
236 **suffers:** permits 239 **band:** bond, agreement 245 **joyance:** gaiety
250 **stay:** halt 252 **wull:** will, want

254 **withal:** with it (the wine) 255 **Bacchus:** Roman god of wine
257 **Graces:** in classical mythology, three sister goddesses who
embodied beauty 262 **wonted:** customary 266 **Barnaby the bright:**
St Barnabas' day (11 June), proverbially the longest day of the year,
before the adoption of the Gregorian calendar in 1752 269 **the
Crab:** the constellation of Cancer, which appears when the sun
declines from its most northerly position 273 **late:** at last 281 **Time
. . . move!:** time perceived as flying on feathered wings 282 **fairest
planet:** the sun 284 **steeds:** the horses that pull the chariot of
Phoebus across the sky 285 **gloom:** grow dark

Now cease, ye damsels, your delights forepast;
Enough is it that all the day was yours.
Now day is done, and night is nighing fast.
Now bring the bride into the bridal bow'rs.
The night is come, now soon her disarray,   300
And in her bed her lay;
Lay her in lilies and in violets,
And silken curtains over her display,
And odoured sheets, and arras coverlets.
Behold how goodly my fair love does lie   305
In proud humility!
Like unto Maia whenas Jove her took
In Tempe, lying on the flow'ry grass,
'Twixt sleep and wake, after she weary was
With bathing in the Acidalian brook.   310
Now it is night, ye damsels may be gone,
And leave my love alone,
And leave likewise your former lay to sing:
The woods no more shall answer, nor your echo ring.

Now welcome, night! thou night so long expected,   315
That long day's labour dost at last defray,
And all my cares, which cruel Love collected,
Hast summed in one, and cancellèd for aye:
Spread thy broad wing over my love and me,
That no man may us see,   320
And in thy sable mantle us enwrap,
From fear of peril and foul horror free.
Let no false treason seek us to entrap,
Nor any dread disquiet once annoy
The safety of our joy;   325
But let the night be calm and quietsome,
Without tempestuous storms or sad affray:
Like as when Jove with fair Alcmena lay,
When he begot the great Tirynthian groom;
Or like as when he with thyself did lie,   330
And begot Majesty.
And let the maids and young men cease to sing:
Ne let the woods them answer, nor their echo ring.

Let no lamenting cries, nor doleful tears,
Be heard all night within, nor yet without;   335
Ne let false whispers, breeding hidden fears,
Break gentle sleep with misconceivèd doubt.
Let no deluding dreams nor dreadful sights
Make sudden sad affrights;

Ne let house-fires, nor lightning's helpless harms, 340
Ne let the Puck, nor other evil sprites,
Ne let mischievous witches with their charms,
Ne let hobgoblins, names whose sense we see not,
Fray us with things that be not.
Let not the screech owl nor the stork be heard,   345
Nor the night raven that still deadly yells,
Nor damnèd ghosts called up with mighty spells,
Nor grisly vultures make us once afeard:
Ne let th'unpleasant quire of frogs still croaking
Make us to wish their choking.   350
Let none of these their dreary accents sing;
Ne let the woods them answer, nor their echo ring.

But let still Silence true night watches keep,
That sacred Peace may in assurance reign,
And timely Sleep, when it is time to sleep,   355
May pour his limbs forth on your pleasant plain,
The whiles an hundred little wingèd loves,
Like divers feathered doves,
Shall fly and flutter round about your bed,
And in the secret dark, that none reproves,   360
Their pretty stealths shall work, and snares shall
     spread
To filch away sweet snatches of delight,
Concealed through covert night.
Ye sons of Venus, play your sports at will:
For greedy Pleasure, careless of your toys,   365
Thinks more upon her paradise of joys
Than what ye do, albeit good or ill.
All night therefore attend your merry play,
For it will soon be day:
Now none doth hinder you, that say or sing,   370
Ne will the woods now answer, nor your echo ring.

Who is the same which at my window peeps?
Or whose is that fair face that shines so bright?
Is it not Cynthia, she that never sleeps,
But walks about high heaven all the night?   375
O fairest goddess, do thou not envy
My love with me to spy:
For thou likewise didst love, though now unthought,
And for a fleece of wool, which privily
The Latmian shepherd once unto thee brought,   380
His pleasures with thee wrought.
Therefore to us be favourable now;
And sith of women's labours thou hast charge,
And generation goodly dost enlarge,
Incline thy will t'effect our wishful vow,   385
And the chaste womb inform with timely seed,

300–1 **her disarray . . . lay:** undress her and put her to bed
304 **odoured:** perfumed **arras:** tapestry 307 **Maia:** in classical
mythology, a nymph, mother (by Jupiter, Greek Zeus) of Mercury
308 **Tempe:** a beautiful valley in Greece 316 **defray:** recompense
318 **for aye:** forever, for good 328–9 **Jove with fair Alcmena . . .
groom:** Jove (Jupiter or Zeus) and Alcmena were father and
mother of Hercules, who is referred to here as 'the great
Tirynthian groom' because he carried out his famous labours for
Eurystheus, king of Tiryns in Greece

340 **helpless:** that cannot be helped 341 **Puck:** a mischievous sprite
344 **fray:** frighten 349 **quire:** choir 374 **Cynthia:** Diana, goddess
of the moon 380 **Latmian shepherd:** Endymion, a shepherd loved
by the moon, who visited him every night on Mount Latmus
384 **generation:** reproduction, procreation

That may our comfort breed:
Till which we cease our hopeful hap to sing,
Ne let the woods us answer, nor our echo ring.

And thou, great Juno, which with awful might   390
The laws of wedlock still dost patronise
And the religion of the faith first plight
With sacred rites hast taught to solemnise,
And eke for comfort often callèd art
Of women in their smart,   395
Eternally bind thou this lovely band,
And all thy blessings unto us impart.
And thou, glad Genius, in whose gentle hand
The bridal bow'r and genial bed remain,
Without blemish or stain,   400
And the sweet pleasures of their love's delight
With secret aid dost succour and supply,
Till they bring forth the fruitful progeny,
Send us the timely fruit of this same night.
And thou, fair Hebe, and thou, Hymen free,   405
Grant that it may so be.
Till which we cease your further praise to sing,
Ne any woods shall answer, nor your echo ring.

And ye high heavens, the temple of the gods,
In which a thousand torches flaming bright   410
Do burn, that to us wretched earthly clods
In dreadful darkness lend desirèd light,
And all ye powers which in the same remain,
More than we men can fain,
Pour out your blessing on us plenteously,   415
And happy influence upon us rain,
That we may raise a large posterity,
Which from the earth, which they may long possess
With lasting happiness,
Up to your haughty palaces may mount,   420
And for the guerdon of their glorious merit
May heavenly tabernacles there inherit,
Of blessed saints for to increase the count.
So let us rest, sweet love, in hope of this,
And cease till then our timely joys to sing: 425
The woods no more us answer, nor our echo ring.

Song, made in lieu of many ornaments
With which my love should duly have been decked,
Which cutting off through hasty accidents,
Ye would not stay your due time to expect,   430
But promised both to recompense,
Be unto her a goodly ornament,
And for a short time an endless monument.

388 **hap:** fortune 390 **Juno:** in Roman myth, the wife of Jupiter, protectress of women and marriage 395 **smart:** pain 398 **Genius:** in Roman myth, a spirit that presides over a man's life 405 **Hebe:** in Greek myth, the goddess of youth 414 **fain:** desire 421 **guerdon:** reward

From THE FAERIE QUEENE

[ST GEORGE AND THE DRAGON]

HIGH time now 'gan it wax for Una fair
    To think of those her captive parents dear
    And their forwasted kingdom to repair:
    Whereto whenas they now approachèd near
    With hearty words her knight she 'gan to cheer,   5
    And in her modest manner thus bespake:
    'Dear knight, as dear, as ever knight was dear,
    That all these sorrows suffer for my sake,
High heaven behold the tedious toil ye for me take.

'Now are we come unto my native soil,   10
    And to the place where all our perils dwell;
    Here haunts that fiend and does his daily spoil,
    Therefore henceforth be at your keeping well,
    And ever ready for your foeman fell.
    The spark of noble courage now awake,   15
    And strive your excellent selfë to excel;
    That shall ye evermore renownèd make
Above all knights on earth that battle undertake.'

And pointing forth, 'Lo, yonder is', said she,
    'The brazen tow'r in which my parents dear   20
    For dread of that huge fiend imprisoned be,
    Whom I from far see on the walls appear,
    Whose sight my feeble soul doth greatly cheer;
    And on the top of all I do espy
    The watchman waiting tidings glad to hear,   25
    That, oh, my parents might I happily
Unto you bring, to ease you of your misery.'

With that they heard a roaring hideous sound,
    That all the air with terror fillèd wide,
    And seemed uneath to shake the steadfast ground.
    Eftsoons that dreadful dragon they espied,   31
    Where stretched he lay upon the sunny side
    Of a great hill, himself like a great hill.
    But all so soon as he from far descried
    Those glist'ring arms, that heaven with light did
        fill,   35
He roused himself full blithe and hast'nèd them until.

Then bade the knight his lady yede aloof,
    And to an hill herself withdraw aside,
    From whence she might behold that battle's proof
    And eke be safe from danger far descried: 40
    She him obeyed, and turned a little wide.
    Now, O thou sacred Muse, most learned dame,
    Fair imp of Phoebus, and his aged bride,
    The nurse of time, and everlasting fame,
That warlike hands ennoblest with immortal name;

THE FAERIE QUEENE: 1 **'gan it wax:** it began to happen 3 **forwasted:** devastated 4 **Whereto whenas:** to which when 6 **bespake:** address 13 **be at your keeping well:** be on your guard 14 **foeman:** enemy 20 **brazen:** made of brass 30 **uneath:** almost 31 **Eftsoons:** soon afterwards 36 **them until:** towards them 37 **yede aloof:** go away 40 **eke:** also 41 **turned a little wide:** went a distance away 43 **imp of Phoebus:** child of Apollo, god of poetry

Oh, gently come into my feeble breast,   46
  Come gently, but not with that mighty rage
  Wherewith the martial troops thou dost infest,
  And hearts of great heroës dost enrage,
  That nought their kindled courage may assuage,   50
  Soon as thy dreadful trump begins to sound;
  The god of war with his fierce equipage
  Thou dost awake, sleep never he so sound,
And scarèd nations dost with horror stern astound.

Fair Goddess, lay that furious fit aside,   55
  Till I of wars and bloody Mars do sing,
  And Briton fields with Saracen blood bedyed,
  'Twixt that great fairy queen and paynim king,
  That with their horror heaven and earth did
    ring,
  A work of labour long and endless praise;   60
  But now awhile let down that haughty string,
  And to my tunes thy second tenor raise,
That I this man of God his godly arms may blaze.

By this the dreadful beast drew nigh to hand,
  Half flying and half footing in his haste,   65
  That with his largeness measurèd much land,
  And made wide shadow under his huge waist;
  As mountain doth the valley overcast.
  Approaching nigh, he rearèd high afore
  His body monstrous, horrible, and vast,   70
  Which to increase his wondrous greatness more,
Was swoln with wrath, and poison, and with bloody
  gore.

And over all with brazen scales was armed,
  Like plated coat of steel, so couchèd near
  That nought mote pierce, ne might his corse be
    harmed   75
  With dint of sword nor push of pointed spear;
  Which as an eagle, seeing prey appear,
  His airy plumes doth rouse, full rudely dight,
  So shakèd he that horror was to hear,
  For as the clashing of an armour bright,   80
Such noise his rousèd scales did send unto the knight.

His flaggy wings when forth he did display
  Were like two sails in which the hollow wind
  Is gathered full and worketh speedy way;
  And eke the pens, that did his pinions bind,   85
  Were like main-yards, with flying canvas lined,
  With which whenas him list the air to beat,
  And there by force unwonted passage find,
  The clouds before him fled for terror great,
And all the heavens stood still amazèd with his threat.

His huge long tail wound up in hundred folds   91
  Does overspread his long brass-scaly back,
  Whose wreathèd boughts whenever he unfolds,
  And thick entangled knots adown does slack,
  Bespotted as with shields of red and black,   95
  It sweepeth all the land behind him far,
  And of three furlongs does but little lack;
  And at the point two stings in-fixèd are,
Both deadly sharp, that sharpest steel exceeden far.

But stings and sharpest steel did far exceed   100
  The sharpness of his cruel rending claws;
  Dead was it sure, as sure as death indeed,
  Whatever thing does touch his ravenous paws,
  Or what within his reach he ever draws.
  But his most hideous head my tongue to tell   105
  Does tremble; for his deep devouring jaws
  Wide gapèd, like the grisly mouth of hell,
Through which into his dark abyss all ravin fell.

And that more wondrous was, in either jaw
  Three ranks of iron teeth enrangèd were,   110
  In which yet trickling blood and gobbets raw
  Of late-devourèd bodies did appear,
  That sight thereof bred cold congealèd fear:
  Which to increase, and all at once to kill,
  A cloud of smothering smoke and sulphur sear   115
  Out of his stinking gorge forth steamèd still,
That all the air about with smoke and stench did
  fill.

His blazing eyes, like two bright shining shields,
  Did burn with wrath, and sparkled living fire;
  As two broad beacons, set in open fields,   120
  Send forth their flames far off to every shire,
  And warning give that enemies conspire
  With fire and sword the region to invade;
  So flamed his eyne with rage and rancorous ire:
  But far within, as in a hollow glade,   125
Those glaring lamps were set, that made a dreadful
  shade.

So dreadfully he towards him did pass,
  Forelifting up aloft his specklèd breast,
  And often bounding on the bruisèd grass,
  As for great joyance of his new-come guest.   130
  Eftsoons he 'gan advance his haughty crest,
  As chauffèd boar his bristles doth uprear,
  And shook his scales to battle ready dressed;
  That made the red-cross knight nigh quake for
    fear,
As bidding bold defiance to his foeman near.   135

---

51 **trump:** trumpet 56 **Mars:** Roman god of war 57 **bedyed:** stained 58 **paynim:** pagan 75 **mote:** might **corse:** body 78 **dight:** dressed 82 **flaggy:** flaglike 84 **worketh speedy way:** gives the power to move fast 85 **pens:** flight-feathers **pinions:** wings 86 **main-yards:** the beams on a sailing ship's main mast, on which the sails are stretched 87 **whenas . . . beat:** when he chose to flap in the air

93 **boughts:** coils 94 **adown:** down **slack:** loosen 99 **that sharpest steel exceeden far:** that are far sharper than sharpest steel 108 **ravin:** prey 115 **sear:** burning 124 **eyne:** eyes 130 **joyance:** gaiety 132 **chauffèd:** enraged 134 **red-cross knight:** the knight represents holiness in general and the Church of England in particular

The knight 'gan fairly couch his steady spear,
　And fiercely ran at him with rigorous might.
　The pointed steel arriving rudely there,
　His harder hide would neither pierce nor bite,
　But glancing by forth passèd forward right;　140
　Yet sore amovèd with so puissant push,
　The wrathful beast about him turnèd light,
　And him so rudely passing by, did brush
With his long tail, that horse and man to ground did
　rush.

Both horse and man up lightly rose again,　145
　And fresh encounter towards him addressed;
　But th'idle stroke yet back recoiled in vain,
　And found no place his deadly point to rest.
　Exceeding rage inflamed the furious beast,
　To be avengèd of so great despite;　150
　For never felt his impierceable breast
　So wondrous force, from hand of living wight;
Yet had he proved the pow'r of many a puissant
　knight.

Then with his waving wings displayèd wide,
　Himself up high he lifted from the ground,　155
　And with strong flight did forcibly divide
　The yielding air, which nigh too feeble found
　Her flitting parts, and element unsound,
　To bear so great a weight; he cutting way
　With his broad sails, about him soarèd round;　160
　At last low stooping with unwieldy sway,
Snatched up both horse and man, to bear them quite
　away.

Long he them bore above the subject plain,
　So far as Ewghen bow a shaft may send,
　Till struggling strong did him at last constrain,　165
　To let them down before his flightès end:
　As haggard hawk presuming to contend
　With hardy fowl, above his able might,
　His weary pounces all in vain doth spend,
　To truss the prey too heavy for his flight;　170
Which coming down to ground, does free itself by
　fight.

He so disseizèd of his griping gross,
　The knight his thrillant spear again assayed
　In his brass-plated body to emboss,　174
　And three men's strength unto the stroke he laid;
　Wherewith the stiff beam quakèd, as afraid,
　And glancing from his scaly neck, did glide
　Close under his left wing, then broad displayed.
　The piercing steel there wrought a wound full wide,
That with the uncouth smart the monster loudly
　cried.　180

He cried, as raging seas are wont to roar,
　When wintry storm his wrathful wreck does threat,
　The rolling billows beat the ragged shore,
　As they the earth would shoulder from her seat,
　And greedy gulf does gape, as he would eat　185
　His neighbour element in his revenge;
　Then 'gin the blust'ring brethren boldly threat,
　To move the world from off his steadfast henge,
And boist'rous battle make, each other to avenge.

The steely head stuck fast still in his flesh,　190
　Till with his cruel claws he snatched the wood,
　And quite asunder broke. Forth flowèd fresh
　A gushing river of black gory blood,
　That drownèd all the land whereon he stood;
　The stream thereof would drive a water-mill.　195
　Trebly augmented was his furious mood
　With bitter sense of his deep-rooted ill,
That flames of fire he threw forth from his large
　nostril.

His hideous tail then hurlèd he about,
　And therewith all enwrapped the nimble thighs　200
　Of his froth-foamy steed, whose courage stout
　Striving to loose the knot that fast him ties,
　Himself in straiter bands too rash implies,
　That to the ground he is perforce constrained
　To throw his rider: who can quickly rise　205
　From off the earth, with dirty blood distained,
For that reproachful fall right foully he disdained.

And fiercely took his trenchant blade in hand,
　With which he stroke so furious and so fell,　209
　That nothing seemed the puissance could withstand.
　Upon his crest the hard'nèd iron fell,
　But his more hard'nèd crest was armed so well
　That deeper dint therein it would not make;
　Yet so extremely did the buff him quell　214
　That from thenceforth he shunned the like to take,
But when he saw them come, he did them still forsake.

The knight was wrath to see his stroke beguiled,
　And smote again with more outrageous might;
　But back again the sparkling steel recoiled,
　And left not any mark where it did light;　220
　As if in adamant rock it had been pight.
　The beast impatient of his smarting wound,
　And of so fierce and forcible despite,
　Thought with his wings to sty above the ground;
But his late wounded wing unserviceable found.　225

---

136 **couch**: to lower a lance into a horizontal position 141 **sore amovèd**:
highly annoyed **puissant**: powerful 150 **despite**: malice 152 **wight**:
person 153 **proved**: tested, experienced 164 **Ewghen**: yewen, i.e. made
of yew **shaft**: arrow 167 **haggard hawk**: untamed hawk 168 **hardy
fowl**: resolute bird 172 **He so . . . gross**: the knight thus released
from the dragon's foul grip 173 **thrillant**: piercing

187 **'gin**: begin 188 **henge**: axis, hinge 203 **Himself . . . implies**: he
gets himself entangled in an even stronger grip 206 **distained**:
stained 209 **fell**: cruel 214 **buff**: blow **quell**: daunt 221 **pight**:
pitched 224 **sty**: rise

Then full of grief and anguish vehement,
  He loudly brayed, that like was never heard,
  And from his wide devouring oven sent
  A flake of fire, that flashing in his beard,
  Him all amazed, and almost made afeard. 230
  The scorching flame sore swingèd all his face,
  And through his armour all his body seared,
  That he could not endure so cruel case,
But thought his arms to leave, and helmet to unlace.

Not that great champion of the antique world, 235
  Whom famous poets' verse so much doth vaunt,
  And hath for twelve huge labours high extolled,
  So many furies and sharp fits did haunt,
  When him the poisoned garment did enchant 239
  With centaur's blood, and bloody verses charmed,
  As did this knight twelve thousand dolours daunt,
  Whom fiery steel now burnt, that erst him armed,
That erst him goodly armed, now most of all him
    harmed.

Faint, weary, sore, emboilèd, grievèd, brent
  With heat, toil, wounds, arms, smart, and inward
    fire 245
  That never man such mischiefs did torment;
  Death better were, death did he oft desire,
  But death will never come, when needs require.
  Whom so dismayed when that his foe beheld,
  He cast to suffer him no more respire, 250
  But 'gan his sturdy stern about to weld,
And him so strongly stroke that to the ground him
    felled.

It fortunèd (as fair it then befell)
  Behind his back unweeting, where he stood,
  Of ancient time there was a springing well, 255
  From which fast tricklèd forth a silver flood,
  Full of great virtues, and for med'cine good.
  Whilom, before that cursèd dragon got
  That happy land, and all with innocent blood
  Defiled those sacred waves, it rightly hot 260
The Well of Life, ne yet his virtues had forgot.

For unto life the dead it could restore,
  And guilt of sinful crimes clean wash away,
  Those that with sickness were infected sore
  It could recure, and aged long decay 265
  Renew, as one were born that very day.
  Both Silo this, and Jordan did excel,
  And th'English Bath, and eke the German Spa,
  Ne can Cephise nor Hebrus match this well:
Into the same the knight, back overthrown, fell. 270

Now 'gan the golden Phoebus for to steep
  His fiery face in billows of the west,
  And his faint steeds wat'rèd in ocean deep,
  Whiles from their journal labours they did rest,
  When that infernal monster, having kest 275
  His weary foe into that living well,
  Can high advance his broad discoloured breast,
  Above his wonted pitch, with countenance fell,
And clapped his iron wings, as victor he did dwell.

Which when his pensive lady saw from far, 280
  Great woe and sorrow did her soul assay,
  As weening that the sad end of the war,
  And 'gan to highest God entirely pray,
  That fearèd chance from her to turn away;
  With folded hands and knees full lowly bent 285
  All night she watched, ne once adown would lay
  Her dainty limbs in her sad dreariment,
But praying still did wake, and waking did lament.

The morrow next 'gan early to appear,
  That Titan rose to run his daily race; 290
  But early ere the morrow next 'gan rear
  Out of the sea fair Titan's dewy face,
  Up rose the gentle virgin from her place,
  And lookèd all about, if she might spy
  Her lovèd knight to move his manly pace, 295
  For she had great doubt of his safèty,
Since late she saw him fall before his enemy.

At last she saw where he upstarted brave
  Out of the well, wherein he drenchèd lay;
  As eagle fresh out of the ocean wave, 300
  Where he hath left his plumes all hoary grey,
  And decked himself with feathers youthly gay,
  Like eyas hawk up mounts unto the skies,
  His newly budded pinions to assay,
  And marvels at himself, still as he flies: 305
So new this new-born knight to battle new did rise.

Whom when the damnèd fiend so fresh did spy,
  No wonder if he wond'rèd at the sight,
  And doubted whether his late enemy
  It were, or other new-supplièd knight. 310
  He, now to prove his late-renewèd might,
  High brandishing his bright dew-burning blade,
  Upon his crested scalp so sore did smite
  That to the skull a yawning wound it made:
The deadly dint his dullèd senses all dismayed. 315

---

231 **swingèd:** singed 235–40 **that great champion . . . charmed:** the
Greek hero Hercules performed twelve famous labours or tasks.
He died when he put on a shirt stained with the enchanted blood
of Nessus, a centaur he had killed 242 **erst:** formerly 244 **brent:**
burnt 250 **cast:** decide, intend 254 **unweeting:** unknown 260 **hot:**
was called 267 **Both . . . excel:** this spring excelled both of the Biblical
rivers Siloam and Jordan 268 **Spa:** spa 269 **Cephise . . . Hebrus:**
rivers of ancient Greece

271 **Phoebus:** Apollo, the sun-god 274 **journal:** daily, diurnal 275
kest: cast 279 **as victor he did dwell:** as if he remained there
victorious 282 **As weening . . . war:** believing that this was the outcome
of the fight 284 **fearèd chance:** dreaded fate 287 **dreariment:** sorrow
290 **Titan:** Helios, the Greek sun-god 303 **eyas hawk:** new-fledged
hawk

I wot not whether the revenging steel
  Were hard'nèd with that holy water dew
  Wherein he fell, or sharper edge did feel,
  Or his baptisèd hands now greater grew;
  Or other secret virtue did ensue;   320
  Else never could the force of fleshly arm,
  Ne molten metal in his blood imbrue:
For till that stound could never wight him harm,
By subtlety, nor slight, nor might, nor mighty charm.

The cruel wound enragèd him so sore   325
  That loud he yielded for exceeding pain;
  As hundred ramping lions seemed to roar,
  Whom ravenous hunger did thereto constrain:
  Then 'gan he toss aloft his stretchèd train,
  And therewith scourge the buxom air so sore   330
  That to his force to yielden it was fain;
  Ne ought his sturdy strokes might stand afore,
That high trees overthrew, and rocks in pieces tore.

The same advancing high above his head,
  With sharp intended sting so rude him smot,   335
  That to the earth him drove, as stricken dead,
  Ne living wight would have him life behot:
  The mortal sting his angry needle shot
  Quite through his shield, and in his shoulder ceased,
  Where fast it stuck, ne would there out be got: 340
  The grief thereof him wondrous sore diseased,
Ne might his rankling pain with patience be appeased.

But yet more mindful of his honour dear
  Than of the grievous smart which him did wring,
  From loathèd soil he can him lightly rear,   345
  And strove to loose the far-infixèd sting:
  Which when in vain he tried with struggèling,
  Inflamed with wrath, his raging blade he heft,
  And strook so strongly that the knotty string
  Of his huge tail he quite asunder cleft,   350
Five joints thereof he hewed, and but the stump him
    left.

Heart cannot think what outrage and what cries,
  With foul enfould'rèd smoke and flashing fire,
  The hell-bred beast threw forth unto the skies,
  That all was coverèd with darkness dire;   355
  Then fraught with rancour, and engorgèd ire,
  He cast at once him to avenge for all,
  And gathering up himself out of the mire,
  With his uneven wings did fiercely fall
Upon his sun-bright shield, and gripped it fast
    withal.   360

Much was the man encumb'rèd with his hold,
  In fear to lose his weapon in his paw,
  Ne wist yet how his talons to unfold;
  Nor harder was from Cerberus' greedy jaw
  To pluck a bone than from his cruel claw   365
  To reave by strength the gripèd gage away.
  Thrice he assayed it from his foot to draw,
  And thrice in vain to draw it did assay,
It booted nought to think, to rob him of his prey.

Tho when he saw no power might prevail,   370
  His trusty sword he called to his last aid,
  Wherewith he fiercely did his foe assail,
  And double blows about him stoutly laid,
  That glancing fire out of the iron played;
  As sparkles from the anvil use to fly,   375
  When heavy hammers on the wedge are swayed;
  Therewith at last he forced him to untie
One of his grasping feet, him to defend thereby.

The other foot, fast fixèd on his shield,
  Whenas no strength, nor strokes mote him constrain
  To loose, ne yet the warlike pledge to yield,   381
  He smote thereat with all his might and main,
  That nought so wondrous puissance might sustain;
  Upon the joint the lucky steel did light,
  And made such way that hewed it quite in twain;
  The paw yet missèd not his 'minished might,   386
But hung still on the shield, as it at first was pight.

For grief thereof, and devilish despite,
  From his infernal furnace forth he threw
  Huge flames, that dimmèd all the heavens' light,
  Enrolled in duskish smoke and brimstone blue;   391
  As burning Etna from his boiling stew
  Doth belch out flames, and rocks in pieces broke,
  And ragged ribs of mountains molten-new,
  Enwrapped in coal-black clouds and filthy smoke,
That all the land with stench, and heaven with horror
    choke.   396

The heat whereof, and harmful pestilence
  So sore him 'noyed, that forced him to retire
  A little backward for his best defence,
  To save his body from the scorching fire,   400
  Which he from hellish entrails did expire.
  It chanced (eternal God that chance did guide),
  As he recoilèd backward, in the mire
  His nigh-forwearied feeble feet did slide,
And down he fell, with dread of shame sore
    terrified.   405

316 **wot:** know 323 **stound:** stroke, shock 324 **charm:** magic 326 **yielded:** roared 329 **train:** tail 331 **yielden:** yield 332 **Ne ought . . . afore:** nothing could withstand his powerful blows 335 **smot:** struck 337 **Ne living . . . behot:** no-one would think he was alive 353 **enfould'rèd:** like a thundercloud

363 **wist:** knew 364 **Cerberus:** in Greek myth, the three-headed dog that guards the entrance to Hades 366 **reave:** pull **gripèd gage:** clenched claws 369 **booted not:** was of no use 386 **'minished:** diminished 398 **'noyed:** annoyed, disturbed 404 **nigh-forwearied:** almost exhausted

There grew a goodly tree him fair beside,
   Loaden with fruit and apples rosy red,
   As they in pure vermilion had been dyed,
   Whereof great virtues over all were red;
   For happy life to all, which thereon fed,   410
   And life eke everlasting did befall.
   Great God it planted in that blessed stead
   With his almighty hand, and did it call
The Tree of Life, the crime of our first father's fall.

In all the world like was not to be found,   415
   Save in that soil, where all good things did grow,
   And freely sprung out of the fruitful ground,
   As incorrupted Nature did them sow,
   Till that dread dragon all did overthrow.
   Another like fair tree eke grew thereby,   420
   Whereof who so did eat eftsoons did know
   Both good and ill. Oh, mournful memory!
That tree through one man's fault hath doen us all to
   die.

From that first tree forth flowed, as from a well,
   A trickling stream of balm, most sovereign   425
   And dainty dear, which on the ground still fell,
   And overflowèd all the fertile plain,
   As it had dewèd been with timely rain:
   Life and long health that gracious ointment gave,
   And deadly wounds could heal, and rear again   430
   The senseless corse appointed for the grave.
Into that same he fell: which did from death him save.

For nigh thereto the ever-damnèd beast
   Durst not approach, for he was deadly made,
   And all that life preservèd did detest: 435
   Yet he it oft adventured to invade.
   By this the drooping daylight 'gan to fade
   And yield his room to sad succeeding night,
   Who with her sable mantle 'gan to shade
   The face of earth, and ways of living wight,   440
And high her burning torch set up in heaven bright.

When gentle Una saw the second fall
   Of her dear knight, who weary of long fight,
   And faint through loss of blood, moved not at all,
   But lay as in a dream of deep delight,   445
   Besmeared with precious balm, whose virtuous
     might
   Did heal his wounds, and scorching heat allay,
   Again she stricken was with sore affright,
   And for his safety 'gan devoutly pray;
And watch the noyous night, and wait for joyous day.

The joyous day 'gan early to appear,   451
   And fair Aurora from the dewy bed
   Of agèd Tithon 'gan herself to rear,
   With rosy cheeks, for shame as blushing red;
   Her golden locks for haste were loosely shed   455
   About her ears, when Una her did mark
   Climb to her chariot, all with flowers spread,
   From heaven high to chase the cheerless dark;
With merry note her loud salutes the mounting lark.

Then freshly up arose the doughty knight,   460
   All healèd of his hurts and woundès wide,
   And did himself to battle ready dight;
   Whose early foe awaiting him beside
   To have devoured, so soon as day he spied,
   When now he saw himself so freshly rear,   465
   As if late fight had nought him damnified,
   He wax dismayed, and 'gan his fate to fear;
Nathless with wonted rage he him advancèd near.

And in his first encounter, gaping wide,
   He thought at once him to have swallowed quite,
   And rushed upon him with outrageous pride;   471
   Who him rencount'ring fierce, as hawk in flight,
   Perforce rebutted back. The weapon bright
   Taking advantage of his open jaw,
   Ran through his mouth with so impórtune
     might,   475
   That deep empierced his darksome hollow maw,
And back retired, his life-blood forth with all did draw.

So down he fell, and forth his life did breathe,
   That vanished into smoke and cloudès swift;
   So down he fell that th'earth him underneath   480
   Did groan, as feeble so great load to lift;
   So down he fell, as an huge rocky clift,
   Whose false foundation waves have washed away,
   With dreadful poise is from the mainland rift,
   And rolling down, great Neptune doth dismay;   485
So down he fell, and like an heapèd mountain lay.

The knight himself even trembled at his fall,
   So huge and horrible a mass it seemed;
   And his dear lady, that beheld it all,
   Durst not approach for dread, which she
     misdeemed,   490
   But yet at last, whenas the direful fiend
   She saw not stir, off-shaking vain affright,
   She nigher drew, and saw that joyous end:
   Then God she praised, and thanked her faithful
     knight,   494
That had achieved so great a conquest by his might.
                         [Book 1, canto 11]

452 **Aurora:** Roman goddess of dawn 453 **agèd Tithon:** in Greek myth Tithonus was a youth beloved by Eos, goddess of dawn, who was granted immortality but not eternal youth 462 **dight:** dress 466 **damnified:** hurt 468 **Nathless:** nevertheless 475 **impórtune:** importunate, irresistible 484 **rift:** cleft away 490 **Durst:** dared **misdeemed:** judged wrongly 491 **whenas:** when

412 **stead:** place 423 **That tree . . . die:** the tree of knowledge, from which Adam ate an apple and so doomed mankind to mortality and sin 438 **yield his room:** give way 450 **noyous:** injurious

EDMUND SPENSER

PROTHALAMION

CALM was the day, and through the trembling air
Sweet-breathing Zephyrus did softly play
A gentle spirit, that lightly did delay
Hot Titan's beams, which then did glister fair;
When I – whom sullen care,   5
Through discontent of my long fruitless stay
In prince's court, and expectation vain
Of idle hopes, which still do fly away
Like empty shadows, did afflict my brain –
Walked forth to ease my pain   10
Along the shore of silver streaming Thames,
Whose rutty bank, the which his river hems,
Was painted all with variable flowers,
And all the meads adorned with dainty gems,
Fit to deck maidens' bowers,   15
And crown their paramours
Against the bridal day, which is not long.
    Sweet Thames, run softly, till I end my song!

There in a meadow, by the river's side,
A flock of nymphs I chancèd to espy,   20
All lovely daughters of the flood thereby,
With goodly greenish locks all loose untied,
As each had been a bride;
And each one had a little wicker basket,
Made of fine twigs entrailèd curiously,   25
In which they gathered flowers to fill their flasket,
And with fine fingers cropped full feateously
The tender stalks on high.
Of every sort which in that meadow grew
They gathered some: the violet pallid blue,   30
The little daisy that at evening closes,
The virgin lily, and the primrose true,
With store of vermeil roses,
To deck their bridegrooms' posies,
Against the bridal day, which was not long.   35
    Sweet Thames, run softly, till I end my song!

With that, I saw two swans of goodly hue
Come softly swimming down along the lee;
Two fairer birds I yet did never see:
The snow which doth the top of Pindus strew   40
Did never whiter show,
Nor Jove himself, when he a swan would be
For love of Leda, whiter did appear;

Yet Leda was, they say, as white as he,
Yet not so white as these, nor nothing near: 45
So purely white they were
That even the gentle stream, the which them bare,
Seemed foul to them, and bade his billows spare
To wet their silken feathers, lest they might
Soil their fair plumes with water not so fair   50
And mar their beauties bright,
That shone as Heaven's light,
Against their bridal day, which was not long.
    Sweet Thames, run softly, till I end my song!

Eftsoons the nymphs, which now had flowers their fill,   55
Ran all in haste to see that silver brood
As they came floating on the crystal flood;
Whom when they saw, they stood amazèd still,
Their wond'ring eyes to fill;
Them seemed they never saw a sight so fair,   60
Of fowls so lovely, that they sure did deem
Them heavenly born, or to be that same pair
Which through the sky draw Venus' silver team,
For sure they did not seem
To be begot of any earthly seed,   65
But rather angels or of angels' breed;
Yet were they bred of summer's heat they say,
In sweetest season, when each flower and weed
The earth did fresh array;
So fresh they seemed as day,   70
Even as their bridal day, which was not long.
    Sweet Thames, run softly, till I end my song!

Then forth they all out of their baskets drew
Great store of flowers, the honour of the field,
That to the sense did fragrant odours yield,   75
All which upon those goodly birds they threw,
And all the waves did strew,
That like old Peneus' waters they did seem,
When down along by pleasant Tempe's shore,
Scatt'rèd with flow'rs, through Thessaly they stream,
That they appear, through lilies' plenteous store,   81
Like a bride's chamber floor.
Two of those nymphs meanwhile two garlands bound,
Of freshest flow'rs which in that mead they found,
The which presenting all in trim array,   85
Their snowy foreheads therewithal they crowned,
Whilst one did sing this lay,
Prepared against that day,
Against their bridal day, which was not long.
    Sweet Thames, run softly, till I end my song!   90

PROTHALAMION: 2 **Zephyrus:** in classical myth, the west wind
4 **Titan:** the sun 12 **rutty:** furrowed 13 **variable:** variously coloured
14 **meads:** meadows 17 **Against:** in preparation for 23 **As each had been:** as if each were 25 **curiously:** skilfully 26 **flasket:** basket
27 **feateously:** dexterously 33 **vermeil:** vermilion, red 40 **Pindus:** a mountain range in Greece 42-3 **Jove . . . appear:** Jupiter, supreme Roman god, took on the likeness of a swan to make love to Leda, while she was bathing

47 **bare:** bore, carried 48-9 **spare to wet:** refrain from wetting
55 **Eftsoons:** soon 78 **Peneus:** a river in Thessaly, Greece, flowing through the valley of Tempe (line 79) which classical poets considered unsurpassed in beauty 86 **therewithal:** with them
87 **lay:** song

'Ye gentle birds, the world's fair ornament,
And Heaven's glory, whom this happy hour
Doth lead unto your lovers' blissful bower,
Joy may you have and gentle heart's content
Of your love's complement;   95
And let fair Venus, that is queen of love,
With her heart-quelling son upon you smile,
Whose smile, they say, hath virtue to remove
All love's dislike, and friendship's faulty guile
Forever to assoil.   100
Let endless peace your steadfast hearts accord,
And blessed plenty wait upon your board,
And let your bed with pleasures chaste abound,
That fruitful issue may to you afford,
Which may your foes confound,   105
And make your joys redound,
Upon your bridal day, which is not long.
    Sweet Thames, run softly, till I end my song!'

So ended she; and all the rest around
To her redoubled that her undersong,   110
Which said their bridal day should not be long.
And gentle Echo from the neighbour ground
Their accents did resound.
So forth those joyous birds did pass along,
Adown the lee, that to them murmured low,   115
As he would speak but that he lacked a tongue,
Yet did by signs his glad affection show,
Making his stream run slow.
And all the fowl which in his flood did dwell
'Gan flock about these twain, that did excel   120
The rest so far as Cynthia doth shend
The lesser stars. So they, enrangèd well,
Did on those two attend,
And their best service lend,
Against their wedding day, which was not long.   125
    Sweet Thames, run softly, till I end my song!

At length they all to merry London came,
To merry London, my most kindly nurse,
That to me gave this life's first native source;
Though from another place I take my name,   130
An house of ancient fame.
There when they came, whereas those bricky towers,
The which on Thames' broad aged back do ride,
Where now the studious lawyers have their bowers,

There whilom wont the Templar Knights to bide,   135
Till they decayed through pride;
Next whereunto there stands a stately place,
Where oft I gainèd gifts and goodly grace
Of that great lord, which therein wont to dwell,
Whose want too well now feels my friendless case;   140
But, ah! here fits not well
Old woes but joys to tell
Against the bridal day, which is not long.
    Sweet Thames, run softly, till I end my song!

Yet therein now doth lodge a noble peer,   145
Great England's glory and the world's wide wonder,
Whose dreadful name late through all Spain did
        thunder,
And Hercules' two pillars standing near
Did make to quake and fear:
Fair branch of honour, flower of chivalry,   150
That fillest England with thy triumph's fame,
Joy have thou of thy noble victory,
And endless happiness of thine own name
That promiseth the same;
That through thy prowess and victorious arms   155
Thy country may be freed from foreign harms;
And great Eliza's glorious name may ring
Through all the world, filled with thy wide alarms
Which some brave Muse may sing
To ages following,   160
Upon the bridal day, which is not long.
    Sweet Thames, run softly, till I end my song!

From those high towers this noble lord issuing,
Like radiant Hesper when his golden hair
In th'ocean billows he hath bathèd fair,   165
Descended to the river's open viewing,
With a great train ensuing.
Above the rest were goodly to be seen
Two gentle knights of lovely face and feature
Beseeming well the bower of any queen,   170
With gifts of wit, and ornaments of nature,
Fit for so goodly stature;
That like the twins of Jove they seemed in sight,
Which deck the baldric of the heavens bright.
They two forth pacing to the river's side,   175
Received those two fair brides, their love's delight,
Which, at th'appointed tide,
Each one did make his bride,
Against their bridal day, which is not long.
    Sweet Thames, run softly, till I end my song!   180

97 **heart-quelling son:** Venus' son is Cupid, Roman god of love, capable of making people fall in love   **quelling:** conquering 100 **assoil:** discharge 102 **board:** table 110 **undersong:** refrain 115 **Adown:** down 121 **Cynthia:** goddess of the moon **shend:** put to shame 134–5 **Where now . . . bide:** refers to The Temple, the site in London of buildings belonging to the Knights Templar, later occupied by lawyers and law students

148 **Hercules' two pillars:** The Pillars of Hercules, two rocks, one on either side of the Straits of Gibraltar 157 **Eliza:** Queen Elizabeth I 164 **Hesper:** Hesperus, Venus considered as the evening star

ANTHONY MUNDAY

'BEAUTY SAT BATHING BY A SPRING'

BEAUTY sat bathing by a spring,
  Where fairest shades did hide her.
The winds blew calm, the birds did sing,
  The cool streams ran beside her.
My wanton thoughts enticed mine eye   5
  To see what was forbidden:
But better memory said "Fie!"
  So vain desire was chidden.
    Hey nonny, nonny O!
    Hey nonny, nonny!   10

Into a slumber then I fell,
  When fond imagination
Seemed to see, but could not tell,
  Her feature or her fashion.
But even as babes in dreams do smile,   15
  And sometimes fall a-weeping,
So I awaked, as wise this while,
  As when I fell a-sleeping.
    Hey nonny, nonny O!
    Hey nonny, nonny!   20

'BEAUTY SAT BATHING BY A SPRING': 7 **Fie!:** an interjection of disapproval, rejection, etc 8 **chidden:** reproved 17 **this while:** by this time

SIR PHILIP SIDNEY

'MY TRUE LOVE HATH MY HEART, AND I HAVE HIS'

MY TRUE LOVE hath my heart, and I have his,
By just exchange, one for the other given.
I hold his dear, and mine he cannot miss:
There never was a better bargain driven.
His heart in me, keeps me and him in one,   5
My heart in him, his thoughts and senses guides:
He loves my heart, for once it was his own:
I cherish his, because in me it bides.
His heart his wound receivèd from my sight:
My heart was wounded, with his wounded heart,   10
For as from me, on him his hurt did smart:
  Both equal hurt, in this change sought our bliss:
  My true love hath my heart and I have his.

'YE GOATHERD GODS . . .'

Strephon. Ye goatherd gods, that love the grassy
    mountains,
  Ye nymphs which haunt the springs in pleasant
    valleys,
  Ye satyrs joyed with free and quiet forests,
  Vouchsafe your silent ears to plaining music,
  Which to my woes gives still an early morning: 5
  And draws the dolour on till very evening.

Klaius. O Mercury, foregoer to the evening,
  O heavenly huntress of the savage mountains,
  O lovely star, entitled of the morning,
  While that my voice doth fill these woeful valleys,   10
  Vouchsafe your silent ears to plaining music,
  Which oft hath Echo tired in secret forests.

Strephon. I that was once free-burgess of the forests,
  Where shade from Sun, and sport I sought in
    evening,
  I that was once esteemed for pleasant music,   15
  Am banished now among the monstrous
    mountains
  Of huge despair, and foul affliction's valleys,
  Am grown a screech-owl to my self each morning.

Klaius. I that was once delighted every morning,
  Hunting the wild inhabiters of forests,   20
  I that was once the music of these valleys,
  So darkened am, that all my day is evening,
  Heart-broken so, that molehills seem high
    mountains,
  And fill the vales with cries instead of music.

Strephon. Long since, alas, my deadly swannish
    music   25
  Hath made itself a crier of the morning,
  And hath with wailing strength climbed highest
    mountains:
  Long since my thoughts more desert be than forests:
  Long since I see my joys come to their evening,
  And state thrown down to over-trodden valleys.   30

Klaius. Long since the happy dwellers of these valleys,
  Have prayed me leave my strange exclaiming music,
  Which troubles their day's work, and joys of
    evening:
  Long since I hate the night, more hate the morning:
  Long since my thoughts chase me like beasts in
    forests,   35
  And make me wish my self laid under mountains.

'YE GOATHERD GODS . . .': 3 **joyed with:** given the enjoyment of 4 **vouchsafe your silent ears to plaining music:** listen to lamenting music 5–6 **Which to . . . evening:** which begins sorrowfully early in the day and lasts painfully until evening 7 **Mercury:** in Roman myth, the messenger of the gods 8 **heavenly huntress:** Diana, goddess of the moon and hunting 9 **star of the morning:** Venus, considered as the morning star 13 **free-burgess:** freeman 24 **swannish:** the swan was believed to sing before it died (hence swansong)

Strephon. Me seems I see the high and stately
    mountains,
  Transform themselves to low dejected valleys:
  Me seems I hear in these ill-changèd forests,
  The nightingales do learn of owls their music: 40
  Me seems I feel the comfort of the morning
  Turned to the mortal sérene of an evening.

Klaius. Me seems I see a filthy cloudy evening,
  As soon as Sun begins to climb the mountains:
  Me seems I feel a noisome scent, the morning   45
  When I do smell the flowers of these valleys:
  Me seems I hear, when I do hear sweet music,
  The dreadful cries of murdered men in forests.

Strephon. I wish to fire the trees of all these forests;
  I give the Sun a last farewell each evening;   50
  I curse the fiddling finders out of music:
  With envy I do hate the lofty mountains;
  And with despite despise the humble valleys:
  I do detest night, evening, day, and morning.

Klaius. Curse to my self my prayer is, the morning: 55
  My fire is more, than can be made with forests;
  My state more base, then are the basest valleys:
  I wish no evenings more to see, each evening;
  Shamèd I hate my self in sight of mountains,
  And stop mine ears, lest I grow mad with music.   60

Strephon. For she, whose parts maintained a perfect
    music,
  Whose beauty shined more than the blushing
    morning,
  Who much did pass in state the stately mountains,
  In straightness past the cedars of the forests,
  Hath cast me, wretch, into eternal evening,   65
  By taking her two Suns from these dark valleys.

Klaius. For she, with whom compared, the Alps are
    valleys,
  She, whose least word brings from spheres their
    music,
  At whose approach the Sun rose in the evening,
  Who, where she went, bear in her forehead
    morning,   70
  Is gone, is gone from these our spoilèd forests,
  Turning to deserts our best-pastured mountains.

Strephon. These mountains witness shall, so shall these
    valleys,

Klaius. These forests eke, made wretched by our music,
  Our morning hymn this is, and song at evening.   75

37 **Me seems:** it seems to me 40 **of:** from 61 **parts:** qualities 66 **her two Suns:** her eyes 68 **from spheres their music:** Pythagoras originated the notion that planets (spheres) produced harmonious musical sounds through their spinning motion

'THOU BLIND MAN'S MARK . . .'

THOU blind man's mark, thou fool's self-chosen snare,
Fond fancy's scum, and dregs of scattered thought,
Band of all evils, cradle of causeless care,
Thou web of will, whose end is never wrought;

Desire, desire! I have too dearly bought,   5
With price of mangled mind thy worthless ware,
Too long, too long asleep thou hast me brought,
Who should my mind to higher things prepare.

But yet in vain thou hast my ruin sought,
In vain thou madest me to vain things aspire,   10
In vain thou kindlest all thy smoky fire;

For virtue hath this better lesson taught,
Within my self to seek my only hire:
Desiring nought but how to kill desire.

'THOU BLIND MAN'S MARK . . .': 1 **blind man's mark:** a target to be aimed at by a blind man, hence impossible to hit 3 **band:** pledge **causeless:** without just cause 6 **with price of mangled mind:** at the cost of a disordered brain

'LEAVE ME, O LOVE, WHICH REACHEST BUT TO DUST'

LEAVE me, O Love, which reachest but to dust,
And thou my mind aspire to higher things:
Grow rich in that which never taketh rust:
Whatever fades, but fading pleasure brings.

Draw in thy beams, and humble all thy might,   5
To that sweet yoke, where lasting freedoms be:
Which breaks the clouds and opens forth the light,
That doth both shine and give us sight to see.

Oh, take fast hold, let that light be thy guide,
In this small course which birth draws out to death, 10
And think how evil becometh him to slide,
Who seeketh heav'n, and comes of heav'nly breath.
  Then farewell world, thy uttermost I see,
  Eternal Love maintain thy life in me.

'LEAVE ME, O LOVE, WHICH REACHEST BUT TO DUST': 11 **how evil becometh him to slide:** how wrong it is to backslide

'LOVING IN TRUTH, AND FAIN IN VERSE MY LOVE TO SHOW'

LOVING in truth, and fain in verse my love to show,
That the dear She might take some pleasure of my
    pain:
Pleasure might cause her read, reading might make
  her know,

Knowledge might pity win, and pity grace obtain,
  I sought fit words to paint the blackest face of woe,
Studying inventions fine, her wits to entertain: 6
Oft turning others' leaves, to see if thence would flow
Some fresh and fruitful showers upon my sun-burned
    brain.
  But words came halting forth, wanting Invention's
    stay,
Invention, Nature's child, fled step-dame Study's
    blows,   10
And others' feet still seemed but strangers in my way.
Thus great with child to speak, and helpless in my
    throes,
  Biting my truant pen, beating my self for spite,
  'Fool,' said my Muse to me, 'look in thy heart and
    write.'

'LOVING IN TRUTH, AND FAIN IN VERSE MY LOVE TO SHOW': 1 **fain:**
willing, desiring 3 **cause:** make 9 **stay:** support 12 **great with child
to speak:** impatient to express oneself (literally, heavily pregnant)

'WITH HOW SAD STEPS, O MOON, THOU CLIMB'ST THE SKIES'

WITH how sad steps, O Moon, thou climb'st the skies,
  How silently, and with how wan a face!
  What, may it be that even in heav'nly place
That busy archer his sharp arrows tries?
Sure, if that long-with-love-acquainted eyes   5
  Can judge of love, thou feel'st a lover's case;
  I read it in thy looks, thy languished grace,
To me that feel the like, thy state descries.
  Then, ev'n of fellowship, O Moon, tell me
Is constant love deemed there but want of wit?   10
Are beauties there as proud as here they be?
Do they above love to be loved, and yet
  Those lovers scorn whom that love doth possess?
  Do they call virtue there ungratefulness?

'WITH HOW SAD STEPS, O MOON, THOU CLIMB'ST THE SKIES': 4 **That busy
archer:** Cupid

'COME, SLEEP, O SLEEP, THE CERTAIN KNOT OF PEACE'

COME, Sleep, O Sleep, the certain knot of peace,
The baiting-place of wit, the balm of woe,
The poor man's wealth, the prisoner's release,
Th' indifferent judge between the high and low;
  With shield of proof shield me from out the prease 5
Of those fierce darts, despair at me doth throw:
Oh, make in me those civil wars to cease;
I will good tribute pay if thou do so.
  Take thou of me smooth pillows, sweetest bed,
A chamber deaf to noise, and blind to light: 10
A rosy garland, and a weary head:

And if these things, as being thine by right,
  Move not thy heavy grace, thou shalt in me,
  Livelier than elsewhere, Stella's image see.

'COME, SLEEP, O SLEEP, THE CERTAIN KNOT OF PEACE': 2 **baiting-place:**
a place for refreshment 5 **prease:** press, pressure 6 **darts:** spears

'WHO WILL IN FAIREST BOOK OF NATURE KNOW'

WHO will in fairest book of Nature know
  How virtue may best-lodged in beauty be,
  Let him but learn of Love to read in thee,
Stella, those fair lines, which true goodness show.
There shall he find all vices' overthrow,   5
  Not by rude force, but sweetest sovereignty
  Of reason, from whose light those night-birds fly;
That inward sun in thine eyes shineth so.
  And not content to be Perfection's heir
Thy self, dost strive all minds that way to move,   10
Who mark in thee what is in thee most fair.
So while thy beauty draws the heart to love,
  As fast thy virtue bends that love to good:
  'But ah,' Desire still cries, 'give me some food.'

JOHN LYLY

'CUPID AND MY CAMPASPE PLAYED'

CUPID and my Campaspe played
At cards for kisses; Cupid paid:
He stakes his quiver, bow, and arrows,
His mother's doves, and team of sparrows;
Loses them too; then down he throws   5
The coral of his lip, the rose
Growing on's cheek (but none knows how);
With these, the crystal of his brow,
And then the dimple on his chin.
All these did my Campaspe win.   10
At last he set her both his eyes –
She won, and Cupid blind did rise.
  O Love! has she done this to thee?
  What shall, alas! become of me?

'CUPID AND MY CAMPASPE PLAYED': 1 **Campaspe:** a concubine of
Alexander the Great 7 **on's:** on his 11 **set:** wagered

SONG: TO THE SPRING

WHAT bird so sings, yet does not wail?
O, 'tis the ravished nightingale!
"Jug, jug, jug, jug, tereu" she cries,
And still her woes at midnight rise.
Brave prick-song! who is't now we hear?   5

None but the lark so shrill and clear;
Now at heaven's gate she claps her wings,
The morn not waking till she sings.
Hark, hark, with what a pretty throat
Poor robin-redbreast tunes his note!   10
Hark how the jolly cuckoos sing
"Cuckoo," to welcome in the spring,
"Cuckoo," to welcome in the spring!

SONG: TO THE SPRING: 2 **ravished nightingale:** in Greek myth, Philomela was raped by her sister's husband, Tereus, and was later changed by the gods into a nightingale 5 **prick-song:** descant

'OH! FOR A BOWL OF FAT CANARY'

Granichus: Oh! for a bowl of fat canary,
   Rich Palermo, sparkling sherry,
   Some nectar else, from Juno's dairy;
   Oh! these draughts would make us merry.

Psyllus: Oh! for a wench (I deal in faces,   5
   And in other daintier things);
   Tickled am I with her embraces,
   Fine dancing in such fairy rings.

Manes: Oh! for a plump fat leg of mutton,
   Veal, lamb, capon, pig, and coney;   10
   None is happy but a glutton,
   None an ass but who wants money.

Chorus: Wines (indeed) and girls are good,
   But brave victuals feast the blood;
   For wenches, wine, and lusty cheer,   15
   Jove would leap down to surfeit here.

'OH! FOR A BOWL OF FAT CANARY': 1 **fat canary:** a full-bodied wine from the Canary Islands 3 **nectar . . . Juno's dairy:** nectar was the drink of the classical gods; Juno was the wife of Jupiter 10 **capon:** a cock fattened for eating **coney:** rabbit 16 **Jove:** Jupiter

SIR FULKE GREVILLE

'I, WITH WHOSE COLOURS MYRA DRESSED HER HEAD'

I, WITH whose colours Myra dressed her head,
I, that wore posies of her own hand-making,
I, that mine own name in the chimneys read
By Myra finely wrought ere I was waking:
Must I look on, in hope time coming may   5
With change bring back my turn again to play?

I, that on Sunday at the church-stile found,
A garland sweet, with true-love knots in flowers,
Which I to wear about mine arms was bound,

That each of us might know that all was ours: 10
Must I now lead an idle life in wishes,
And follow Cupid for his loaves and fishes?

I, that did wear the ring her mother left,
I, for whose love she gloried to be blamed,
I, with whose eyes her eyes committed theft,   15
I, who did make her blush when I was named:
Must I lose ring, flowers, blush, theft, and go naked,
Watching with sighs, till dead love be awakèd?

I, that, when drowsy Argus fell asleep,
Like jealousy o'erwatchèd with desire,   20
Was even warnèd modesty to keep,
While her breath, speaking, kindled Nature's fire:
Must I look on a-cold, while others warm them?
Do Vulcan's brothers in such fine nets arm them?

Was it for this that I might Myra see   25
Washing the water with her beauties white?
Yet would she never write her love to me.
Thinks wit of change, while thoughts are in delight?
Mad girls must safely love, as they may leave;
No man can print a kiss; lines may deceive.   30

'I, WITH WHOSE COLOURS MYRA DRESSED HER HEAD': 3 **in the chimneys:** written in the soot of a fireplace 12 **loaves and fishes:** mere temporal rewards rather than any higher motive; a biblical reference (John 6.26) 15 **eyes . . . theft:** alludes to 'stolen glances' 19 **Argus:** in classical myth, a giant with 100 eyes who was given the task of watching over the priestess Io, of whom Juno was jealous. He was charmed into sleep by Mercury 23 **them:** themselves 24 **Vulcan:** Roman god of fire and metalworking

'OH, WEARISOME CONDITION OF HUMANITY!'

OH, wearisome condition of humanity!
   Born under one law, to another bound:
Vainly begot, and yet forbidden vanity,
   Created sick, commanded to be sound:
      What meaneth Nature by these diverse laws?   5
      Passion and reason self-division cause:

Is it the mark, or majesty of power
   To make offences that it may forgive?
Nature herself doth her own self deflower,
   To hate those errors she her self doth give.   10
      For how should man think that he may not do
      If Nature did not fail, and punish too?

Tyrant to others, to her self unjust,
   Only commands things difficult and hard.
Forbids us all things, which it knows is lust,   15
   Makes easy pains, unpossible reward.
      If Nature did not take delight in blood,
      She would have made more easy ways to good.

We that are bound by vows, and by promotion,
   With pomp of holy sacrifice and rites,   20
To teach belief in good and still devotion,
   To preach of Heaven's wonders and delights:
     Yet when each of us in his own heart looks,
     He finds the God there far unlike his books.

SIR WALTER RALEGH

FAREWELL TO THE COURT

LIKE truthless dreams, so are my joys expired,
   And past return, are all my dandled days:
My love misled, and fancy quite retired,
   Of all which past, the sorrow only stays.

My lost delights, now clean from sight of land,   5
   Have left me all alone in unknown ways:
My mind to woe, my life in fortune's hand,
   Of all which past, the sorrow only stays.

As in a country strange without companion,
   I only wail the wrong of death's delays,   10
Whose sweet spring spent, whose summer well-nigh
     done,
   Of all which past, the sorrow only stays.

     Whom care forewarns, ere age and winter cold,
     To haste me hence, to find my fortune's fold.

THE LIE

GO, soul, the body's guest,
   Upon a thankless arrant,
Fear not to touch the best,
   The truth shall be thy warrant:
     Go, since I needs must die,   5
     And give the world the lie.

Say to the Court it glows
   And shines like rotten wood,
Say to the Church it shows
   What's good, and doth no good.   10
     If Church and Court reply,
     Then give them both the lie.

Tell potentates they live
   Acting by others' action,
Not loved unless they give,   15
   Not strong but by affection.
     If potentates reply,
     Give potentates the lie.

Tell men of high condition,
   That manage the estate,   20
Their purpose is ambition,
   Their practice only hate:
     And if they once reply,
     Then give them all the lie.

Tell them that brave it most,   25
   They beg for more by spending,
Who in their greatest cost
   Like nothing but commending.
     And if they make reply,
     Then give them all the lie.   30

Tell zeal it wants devotion,
   Tell love it is but lust,
Tell time it meets but motion,
   Tell flesh it is but dust.
     And wish them not reply   35
     For thou must give the lie.

Tell age it daily wasteth,
   Tell honour how it alters.
Tell beauty how she blasteth
   Tell favour how it falters   40
     And as they shall reply,
     Give every one the lie.

Tell wit how much it wrangles
   In tickle points of niceness,
Tell wisdom she entangles   45
   Her self in over-wiseness.
     And when they do reply
     Straight give them both the lie.

Tell Physic of her boldness,
   Tell skill it is prevention: 50
Tell charity of coldness,
   Tell law it is contention,
     And as they do reply
     So give them still the lie.

Tell fortune of her blindness,   55
   Tell nature of decay,
Tell friendship of unkindness,
   Tell justice of delay.
     And if they will reply,
     Then give them them all the lie.   60

Tell Arts they have no soundness,
   But vary by esteeming,
Tell schools they want profoundness
   And stand so much on seeming.
     If Arts and schools reply,   65
     Gives arts and schools the lie.

THE LIE: 2 **arrant**: errand 6 **give the world the lie**: to give the lie to someone is to tell them that they are not telling the truth, they are false

20 **estate**: state 39 **blasteth**: withers 46 **tickle**: delicate, subtle **niceness**: fine distinction 49 **physic**: medicine

Tell faith it's fled the city,
  Tell how the country erreth,
Tell manhood shakes off pity,
  Tell virtue least preferreth.   70
    And if they do reply,
    Spare not to give the lie.

So when thou hast, as I
  Commanded thee, done blabbing,
Because to give the lie,   75
  Deserves no less than stabbing,
    Stab at thee he that will,
    No stab thy soul can kill.

ON THE LIFE OF MAN

WHAT is our life? a play of passion,
Our mirth the music of division,
Our mothers' wombs the tiring-houses be,
Where we are dressed for this short comedy,
Heaven the judicious sharp spectator is,   5
That sits and marks still who doth act amiss,
Our graves that hide us from the searching Sun,
Are like drawn curtains when the play is done,
Thus march we playing to our latest rest,
Only we die in earnest, that's no jest.   10

ON THE LIFE OF MAN: 3 **tiring-houses:** dressing-rooms in a theatre
9 **latest:** last

THE AUTHOR'S EPITAPH, MADE BY HIMSELF

EVEN such is Time, which takes in trust
Our youth, our joys, and all we have,
And pays us but with age and dust;
Who in the dark and silent grave,
When we have wandered all our ways,   5
Shuts up the story of our days:
And from which earth, and grave, and dust,
The Lord shall raise me up, I trust.

'AS YOU CAME FROM THE HOLY LAND'

As YOU came from the holy land
  Of Walsingham
Met you not with my true love
  By the way as you came?

'How shall I know your true love   5
  That have met many one
As I went to the holy land
  That have come, that have gone?'

She is neither white nor brown
  But as the heavens fair;   10
There is none hath a form so divine
  In the earth or the air.

'Such an one did I meet, good sir,
  Such an angelic face
Who like a queen, like a nymph did appear   15
  By her gait, by her grace.'

She hath left me here all alone
  All alone as unknown
Who sometimes did me lead with herself
  And me loved as her own.   20

'What's the cause that she leaves you alone
  And a new way doth take,
Who loved you once as her own
  And her joy did you make?'

I have loved her all my youth   25
  But now old as you see
Love likes not the falling fruit
  From the withered tree.

Know that Love is a careless child
  And forgets promise past;   30
He is blind, he is deaf when he list
  And in faith never fast.

His desire is a dureless content
  And a trustless joy;
He is won with a world of despair   35
  And is lost with a toy.

Of womenkind such indeed is the love
  Or the word 'love' abused
Under which many childish desires
  And conceits are excused.   40

But Love is a durable fire
  In the mind ever burning:
Never sick, never old, never dead,
  From itself never turning.

'AS YOU CAME FROM THE HOLY LAND': 1 **the holy land of Walsingham:**
a village in Norfolk, site of the shrine of Our Lady of Walsingham
31 **list:** chooses 32 **fast:** constant 33 **dureless:** not enduring or lasting

ANONYMOUS

THE PASSIONATE MAN'S PILGRIMAGE
SUPPOSED TO BE WRITTEN BY ONE AT THE POINT OF DEATH

GIVE me my scallop shell of quiet,
My staff of faith to walk upon,
My scrip of joy, immortal diet,
My bottle of salvation:
My gown of glory, hope's true gage,   5
And thus I'll take my pilgrimage.

Blood must be my body's balmer,
No other balm will there be given
Whilst my soul like a white palmer
Travels to the land of heaven,   10
Over the silver mountains,
Where spring the nectar fountains:
And there I'll kiss
The bowl of bliss,
And drink my eternal fill   15
On every milken hill.
My soul will be a drie before,
But after it, will ne'er thirst more.

And by the happy blissful way
More peaceful pilgrims I shall see,   20
That have shook off their gowns of clay,
And go apparelled fresh like me.
I'll bring them first
To slake their thirst,
And then to taste those nectar suckets 25
At the clear wells
Where sweetness dwells,
Drawn up by saints in crystal buckets.

And when our bottles and all we,
Are filled with immortality: 30
Then the holy paths we'll travel
Strewed with rubies thick as gravel,
Ceilings of diamonds, sapphire floors,
High walls of coral and pearl bowers.
From thence to heaven's bribeless hall 35
Where no corrupted voices brawl,
No conscience molten into gold,
Nor forged accusers bought and sold,
No cause deferred, nor vain-spent journey,
For there Christ is the king's attorney: 40
Who pleads for all without degrees,
And he hath angels, but no fees.

When the grand twelve million jury,
Of our sins with sinful fury,
'Gainst our souls black verdicts give, 45
Christ pleads his death, and then we live,
Be thou my speaker taintless pleader,
Unblotted lawyer, true proceeder,
Thou movest salvation even for alms:
Not with a bribèd lawyer's palms.   50

And this is my eternal plea,
To him that made heaven, earth and sea,
Seeing my flesh must die so soon,
And want a head to dine next noon,
Just at the stroke when my vains start and spread 55
Set on my soul an everlasting head.
hen am I ready like a palmer fit,
To tread those blest paths which before I writ.

[Formerly attributed to Sir Walter Ralegh]

THE PASSIONATE MAN'S PILGRIMAGE: 1 **scallop shell:** the emblem of a pilgrim 3 **scrip:** a pilgrim's pouch 5 **gage:** pledge 9 **palmer:** a pilgrim, originally one carrying a palm leaf to show that he had been to the Holy Land 17 **a drie:** dry 21 **gowns of clay:** earthly bodies 25 **suckets:** candied fruit 36 **bribeless:** incorruptible 42 **angels:** a play on the common meaning and the secondary sense of an old coin with an angel stamped on it 55 **vains:** veins **start:** open

GEORGE PEELE

'GENTLY DIP, BUT NOT TOO DEEP'

GENTLY dip, but not too deep,
For fear you make the golden beard to weep.
Fair maiden, white and red,
Comb me smooth, and stroke my head;
And thou shalt have some cockle bread.   5

Gently dip, but not too deep,
For fear thou make the golden beard to weep.
Fair maiden, white and red,
Comb me smooth and stroke my head;
And every hair a sheave shall be,   10
And every sheave a golden tree.

'HOT SUN, COOL FIRE,
TEMPERED WITH SWEET AIR'

HOT sun, cool fire, tempered with sweet air,
Black shade, fair nurse, shadow my white hair;
Shine, sun; burn, fire; breathe, air, and ease me;
Black shade, fair nurse, shroud me and please me:
Shadow, my sweet nurse, keep me from burning,   5
Make not my glad cause cause of mourning.
    Let not my beauty's fire
    Inflame unstaid desire,
    Nor pierce any bright eye
    That wandereth lightly.   10

'HOT SUN, COOL FIRE, TEMPERED WITH SWEET AIR': 8 **unstaid:** uncontrolled

'WHENAS THE RYE REACH TO THE CHIN'

WHENAS the rye reach to the chin,
    And chopcherry chopcherry ripe within,
Starberries swimming in the cream,
And schoolboys playing in the stream:
    Then, oh, then, oh, then, oh, my true love said, 5
    Till that time come again,
    She could not live a maid.

'WHAT THING IS LOVE? FOR SURE LOVE IS A THING'

WHAT thing is love? for sure love is a thing.
It is a prick, it is a sting,
It is a pretty, pretty thing;
It is a fire, it is a coal,
Whose flame creeps in at every hole;   5
And as my wit doth best devise,
Love's dwelling is in ladies' eyes,
From whence do glance love's piercing darts,
That make such holes into our hearts;
And all the world herein accord,   10
Love is a great and mighty lord;
And when he list to mount so high,
With Venus he in heaven doth lie,
And evermore hath been a god,
Since Mars and she played even and odd.   15

'WHAT THING IS LOVE? FOR SURE LOVE IS A THING': 8 **darts:** spears or
arrows 12 **list:** chooses

OENONE AND PARIS

Oenone: Fair and fair, and twice so fair,
    As fair as any may be;
    The fairest shepherd on our green,
    A Love for any lady.

Paris: Fair and fair, and twice so fair,   5
    As fair as any may be;
    Thy Love is fair for thee alone,
    And for no other lady.

Oenone: My Love is fair, my Love is gay,
    As fresh as bin the flowers in May;   10
    And of my Love my roundelay,
    My merry, merry, merry roundelay,
        Concludes with Cupid's curse:
    They that do change old love for new,
        Pray gods they change for worse.   15

Together: They that do change old love for new,
        Pray gods they change for worse.

Oenone: Fair and fair, and twice so fair,
    As fair as any may be;
    The fairest shepherd on our green,   20
    A Love for any lady.

Paris: Fair and fair, and twice so fair,
    As fair as any may be;
    Thy Love is fair for thee alone,
    And for no other lady.   25

Oenone: My Love can pipe, my Love can sing,
    My Love can many a pretty thing,

And of his lovely praises ring
My merry, merry, merry roundelays.
    Amen to Cupid's curse: 30
They that do change old love for new,
    Pray gods they change for worse.

Together: They that do change old love for new,
    Pray gods they change for worse.

OENONE AND PARIS: 1 **Oenone:** in Greek myth, a nymph who was the
wife of Paris, the Trojan prince whose abduction of Helen caused
the Trojan War 10 **bin:** are 11 **roundelay:** a song with a refrain

THOMAS LODGE

'LOVE IN MY BOSOM LIKE A BEE'

LOVE in my bosom like a bee
    Doth suck his sweet;
Now with his wings he plays with me,
    Now with his feet.
With mine eyes he makes his nest,   5
His bed amidst my tender breast;
My kisses are his daily feast;
And yet he robs me of my rest.
    Ah, wanton, will ye?

And if I sleep, then percheth he   10
    With pretty flight,
And makes his pillow of my knee
    The livelong night.
Strike I my lute, he tunes the string;
He music plays if so I sing;   15
He lends me every lovely thing;
Yet cruel he my heart doth sting.
    Whist, wanton, still ye!

Else I with roses every day
    Will whip you hence;   20
And bind you, when you long to play,
    For your offence.
I'll shut mine eyes to keep you in.
I'll make you fast it for your sin,
I'll count your power not worth a pin.   25
Alas! what hereby shall I win
    If he gainsay me?

What if I beat the wanton boy
    With many a rod?
He will repay me with annoy,   30
    Because a god.
Then sit thou safely on my knee,
And let thy bower my bosom be;
Lurk in mine eyes, I like of thee.
O Cupid, so thou pity me,   35
    Spare not, but play thee!

CHIDIOCK TICHBORNE

[ON THE EVE OF HIS EXECUTION]

My prime of youth is but a frost of cares,
  My feast of joy is but a dish of pain,
My crop of corn is but a field of tares,
  And all my good is but vain hope of gain;
    The day is past, and yet I saw no sun,   5
    And now I live, and now my life is done.

My tale was heard and yet it was not told,
  My fruit is fallen and yet my leaves are green,
My youth is spent and yet I am not old,
  I saw the world and yet I was not seen;   10
    My thread is cut, and yet it is not spun,
    And now I live, and now my life is done.

I sought my death and found it in my womb,
  I looked for life and saw it was a shade,
I trod the earth and knew it was my tomb,   15
  And now I die, and now I was but made;
    My glass is full, and now my glass is run,
    And now I live, and now my life is done.

ROBERT GREENE

'AH! WERE SHE PITIFUL AS SHE IS FAIR'

AH! were she pitiful as she is fair,
  Or but as mild as she is seeming so,
Then were my hopes greater than my despair;
  Then all the world were heaven, nothing woe.
Ah! were her heart relenting as her hand,   5
  That seems to melt even with the mildest touch,
Then knew I where to seat me in a land
  Under the wide heavens - but yet not such.
So as she shows, she seems the budding rose,
  Yet sweeter far than is an earthly flower;   10
Sovereign of beauty, like the spray she grows,
  Compassed she is with thorns and cankered flower;
Yet were she willing to be plucked and worn,
She would be gathered, though she grew on thorn.

Ah! when she sings, all music else be still,   15
  For none must be comparèd to her note;
Ne'er breathed such glee from Philomela's bill,
  Nor from the morning singer's swelling throat.
Ah! when she riseth from her blissful bed,
  She comforts all the world, as doth the sun;   20
And at her sight the night's foul vapour's fled;
  When she is set, the gladsome day is done.
O glorious sun! imagine me the west,
Shine in my arms, and set thou in my breast.

'WEEP NOT, MY WANTON, SMILE UPON MY KNEE'

Weep not, my wanton, smile upon my knee;
When thou art old there's grief enough for thee.
  Mother's wag, pretty boy,
  Father's sorrow, father's joy;
  When thy father first did see   5
  Such a boy by him and me,
  He was glad, I was woe;
  Fortune changed made him so,
  When he left his pretty boy,
  Last his sorrow, first his joy.   10

Weep not, my wanton, smile upon my knee;
When thou art old there's grief enough for thee.
  Streaming tears that never stint,
  Like pearl-drops from a flint,
  Fell by course from his eyes,   15
  That one another's place supplies;
  Thus he grieved in every part,
  Tears of blood fell from his heart,
  When he left his pretty boy,
  Father's sorrow, father's joy.   20

Weep not, my wanton, smile upon my knee;
When thou art old there's grief enough for thee.
  The wanton smiled, the father wept;
  Mother cried, baby leapt;
  More he crowed, more we cried,   25
  Nature could not sorrow hide.
  He must go, he must kiss
  Child and mother, baby bliss:
  For he left his pretty boy,
  Father's sorrow, father's joy.   30
Weep not, my wanton, smile upon my knee;
When thou art old, there's grief enough for thee.

GEORGE CHAPMAN

From THE ILIAD

[THE SHIELD OF ACHILLES]

AND now the silver-footed queen had her ascension made
To that incorruptible house, that starry golden court
Of fiery Vulcan, beautiful amongst th'immortal sort,
Which yet the lame god built himself. She found him in a sweat
About his bellows, and in haste had twenty tripods beat,   5
To set for stools about the sides of his well-builded hall.
To whose feet little wheels of gold he put, to go withal
And enter his rich dining room – alone, their motion free,
And back again go out alone, miraculous to see.
And thus much he had done of them, yet handles were to add,   10
For which he now was making studs. And while their fashion had
Employment of his skilful hand, bright Thetis was come near,
Whom first fair well-haired Charis saw, that was the nuptial fere
Of famous Vulcan, who the hand of Thetis took, and said:
'Why, fair-trained, loved and honoured dame, are we thus visited   15
By your kind presence? You, I think, were never here before.
Come near, that I may banquet you and make you visit more.'
She led her in, and in a chair of silver (being the fruit
Of Vulcan's hand) she made her sit, a footstool, of a suite,
Apposing to her crystal feet; and called the god of fire –   20
For Thetis was arrived, she said, and entertained desire
Of some grace that his art might grant. 'Thetis to me,' said he,
'Is mighty, and most reverend, as one that nourished me
When grief consumed me, being cast from heaven by want of shame
In my proud mother, who because she brought me forth so lame   25
Would have me made away. And then had I been much distressed

Had Thetis and Eurynome in either's silver breast
Not rescued me – Eurynome, that to her father had
Recriprocal Oceanus. Nine years with them I made
A number of well-arted things, round bracelets, buttons brave,   30
Whistles, and carcanets. My forge stood in a hollow cave,
About which (murmuring with foam) th'unmeasured Oceän
Was ever beating, my abode known nor to god nor man
But Thetis and Eurynome, and they would see me still:
They were my loving guardians. Now then the starry hill,   35
And our particular roof, thus graced with bright-haired Thetis here,
It fits me always to repay a recompense as dear
To her thoughts as my life to me. Haste, Charis, and appose
Some dainty guest-rites to our friend, while I my bellows lose
From fire and lay up all my tools.' Then from an anvil rose   40
Th'unwieldy monster, halted down, and all awry he went.
He took his bellows from the fire, and every instrument
Locked safe up in a silver chest. Then with a sponge he dressed
His face all over, neck and hands, and all his hairy breast,
Put on his coat, his sceptre took, and then went halting forth,   45
Handmaids of gold attending him – resembling in all worth
Living young damsels, filled with minds and wisdom, and were trained
In all immortal ministry, virtue and voice contained,
And moved with voluntary pow'rs. And these still waited on
Their fiery sovereign, who (not apt to walk) sate near the throne   50
Of fair-haired Thetis, took her hand, and thus he courted her:
'For what affair, O fair-trained Queen, reverend to me and dear,
Is our court honoured with thy state, that hast not heretofore
Performed this kindness? Speak thy thoughts; thy suit can be no more
Than my mind gives me charge to grant. Can my pow'r get it wrought?   55

FROM THE ILIAD: 1 **silver-footed queen**: Thetis, sea-nymph and mother of Achilles 3 **Vulcan**: in Roman myth, the lame god of fire and metalworking 13 **Charis . . . nuptial fere**: the wife of Vulcan

27 **Euronyme**: a sea-nymph 29 **Oceanus**: a Greek sea-god 31 **carcanet**: a jewelled collar 38 **appose**: set out 43 **dressed**: cleaned

Or that it have not only pow'r of only act in thought?'
She thus: 'O Vulcan, is there one, of all that are of
    heaven,
That in her never quiet mind Saturnius hath given
So much affliction as to me? – whom only he subjects
(Of all the sea-nymphs) to a man, and makes me bear
    th'affects   60
Of his frail bed, and all against the freedom of my
    will,
And he worn to his root with age. From him another
    ill
Ariseth to me. Jupiter, you know, hath given a son
(The excellent'st of men) to me, whose education,
On my part, well hath answered his own worth,
    having grown,   65
As in a fruitful soil a tree that puts not up alone
His body to a naked height but jointly gives his growth
A thousand branches. Yet to him so short a life I
    brought
That never I shall see him more returned to Peleus'
    court.
And all that short life he hath spent in most unhappy
    sort.   70
For first he won a worthy dame, and had her by the
    hands
Of all the Grecians; yet this dame Atrides
    countermands:
For which in much disdain he mourned, and almost
    pined away.
And yet for this wrong he received some honour, I
    must say,
The Greeks being shut up at their ships, not suffered to
    advance   75
A head out of their battered sterns, and mighty
    suppliance
By all their grave men hath been made, gifts, honours,
    all proposed
For his reflection; yet he still kept close, and saw
    enclosed
Their whole host in this general plague. But now his
    friend put on
His arms, being sent by him to field and many a
    Myrmidon   80
In conduct of him. All the day they fought before the
    gates
Of Scaea; and most certainly that day had seen the
    dates
Of all Troy's honours in her dust, if Phoebus (having
    done

Much mischief more) the envied life of good
    Menoetius' son
Had not with partial hands enforced, and all the
    honour given   85
To Hector, who hath prised his arms. And therefore I
    am driven
T' embrace thy knees for new defence to my loved son.
    Alas,
His life prefixed so short a date had need spend that
    with grace.
A shield then for him, and a helm, fair greaves, and
    curets such
As may renown thy workmanship and honour him as
    much,   90
I sue for at thy famous hands.' 'Be confident,' said he,
'Let these wants breed thy thoughts.no care. I would it
    lay in me
To hide him from his heavy death when Fate shall seek
    for him,
As well as with renownèd arms to fit his goodly limb –
Which thy hands shall convey to him, and all eyes shall
    admire.   95
See, and desire again to see, thy satisfied desire.'
This said, he left her there, and forth did to his bellows
    go,
Apposed them to the fire again, commanding them to
    blow.
Through twenty holes made to his hearth at once blew
    twenty pair,
That fired his coals, sometimes with soft, sometimes
    with vehement air,   100
As he willed and his work required. Amidst the flame
    he cast
Tin, silver, precious gold and brass, and in the stock he
    placed
A mighty anvil; his right hand a weighty hammer
    held,
His left his tongs. And first he forged a strong and
    spacious shield
Adorned with twenty several hues: about whose verge
    he beat   105
A ring, three-fold and radiant, and on the back he set
A silver handle; five-fold were the equal lines he drew
About the whole circumference, in which his hand did
    show
(Directed with a knowing mind) a rare variety.
For in it he presented Earth, in it the sea and sky,   110
In it the never wearied Sun, the Moon exactly round
And all those stars with which the brows of ample
    heaven are crowned –
Orion, all the Pleiades, and those seven Atlas got,

---

58 **Saturnius:** Saturn, Roman god of the underworld 59–62 **whom
. . . age:** Thetis was the only sea-nymph to have borne a child to a
mortal (Peleus), who, because mortal, grew old 71 **worthy dame:**
Briseis, who was taken from Achilles by Atrides (Agamemnon)
79 **his friend:** when Achilles declined to continue fighting against
the Trojans his friend Patroclus put on Achilles' armour and led
his followers (Myrmidons) into battle 82 **Scaea:** Troy 83 **Phoebus:**
Apollo

84 **Meoetius' son:** Patroclus 86 **prised his arms:** taken his weapons
and armour as a trophy 89 **helm:** helmet **greaves:** pieces of
armour for the shins **curets:** cuirass 104 **verge:** edge 113 **those
seven Atlas got:** the seven daughters fathered by Atlas, who were
formed into stars (the Hyades)

The close-beamed Hyades, the Bear, surnamed the
    Chariot,
That turns about heaven's axletree, holds ope a
    constant eye   115
Upon Orion; and, of all the cressets in the sky,
His golden forehead never bows to th'ocean empery.
Two cities in the spcious shield he built with goodly
    state
Of diverse-languaged men. The one did nuptials
    celebrate,
Observing at them solemn feasts; the brides from forth
    their bow'rs   120
With torches ushered through the street, a world of
    paramours
Excited by them; youths and maids in lovely circles
    danced,
To whom the merry pipe and harp in sprightly sounds
    advanced,
The matrons standing in their doors admiring.
    Otherwhere
A solemn court of law was kept, where throngs of
    people were.   125
The case in question was a fine imposed on omne that
    slew
The friend of him that followed it and for the fine did
    sue,
Which th'other pleaded he had paid. The adverse part
    denied,
And openly affirmed he had no penny satisfied.
Both put it to arbitrement. The people cried 'twas
    best   130
For both parts, and th'assistants too gave their dooms
    like the rest.
The heralds made the people peace. The seniors then
    did bear
The voiceful heralds' sceptres, sate within a sacred
    sphere
On polished stones, and gave by turns their sentence.
    In the court
Two talents gold were cast for him that judged in
    justest sort.   135
The other city other wars employed as busily.
The armies glittering in arms, of one confederacy,
Besieged it, and a parley had with those within the
    town.
Two ways they stood resolved – to see the city over
    thrown,
Or that the citizens should heap in two parts all their
    wealth   140
And give them half. They neither liked, but armed
    themselves by stealth,
Left all their old men, wives and boys behind to man
    their walls,
And stole out to their enemy's town. The queen of
    martials

And Mars himself conducted them, both which, being
    forged of gold,
Must needs have golden furniture, and men might so
    behold   145
They were presented deities. The people Vulcan
    forged
Of meaner metal. When they came where that was to
    be urged
For which they went, within a vale close to a flood,
    whose stream
Used to give all their cattle drink, they there
    enambushed them,
And sent two scouts out to descry when th'enemy's
    herds and sheep   150
Were setting out. They straight came forth, with two
    that used to keep
Their passage always; both which piped and went on
    merrily,
Nor dreamed of ambuscadoes there. The ambush
    then let fly,
Slew all their white-fleeced sheep and neat, and by
    them laid their guard.
When those in siege before the town so strange an
    uproar heard   155
Behind, amongst their flocks and herds (being then in
    council set)
They then start up, took horse, and soon their subtle
    enemy met,
Fought with them on the river's shore, where both
    gave mutual blows
With well-piled darts. Amongst them all perverse
    Contention rose,
Amongst them Tumult was enraged, amongst them
    ruinous Fate   160
Had her red finger; some they took in an unhurt
    estate,
Some hurt yet living, some quite slain – and those they
    tugged to them
By both the feet, stripped off and took their weeds,
    with all the stream
Of blood upon them that their steels had manfully let
    out.
They fared as men alive indeed, drew dead indeed
    about.   165
To these the fiery artisan did add a new-eared field,
Large and thrice ploughed, the soil being soft and of a
    wealthy yield;
And many men at plough he made that drave earth
    here and there
And turned up stitches orderly; at whose end when
    they were,
A fellow ever gave their hands full cups of luscious
    wine,   170

---

114 **ope:** open 115 **cressets:** torches 131 **dooms:** judgments 135 **talents:**
ancient units of gold or silver 143 **queen of martials:** queen of
soldiers, the goddess Minerva

148 **flood:** river 154 **neat:** cattle 159 **well-piled darts:** spears or
arrows with well-made points 163 **weeds:** garments 166 **new-eared:**
newly ploughed 169 **stitches:** furrows

Which emptied, for another stitch the earth they
    undermine,
And long till th'utmost bound be reached of all the
    ample close.
The soil turned up behind the plough, all black like
    earth arose,
Though forged of nothing else but gold, and lay in
    show as light
As if it had been ploughed indeed, miraculous to sight.
There grew by this a field of corn, high, ripe, where
    reapers wrought,   176
And let thick handfuls fall to earth, for which some
    other brought
Bands, and made sheaves. Three binders stood and
    took the handfuls reaped
From boys that gathered quickly up, and by them
    armfuls heaped.
Amongst these at a furrow's end the king stood pleased
    at heart,   180
Said no word, but his sceptre showed. And from him,
    much apart,
His harvest bailiffs underneath an oak a feast
    prepared,
And, having killed a mighty ox, stood there to see him
    shared,
Which women for their harvest folks (then come to
    sup) had dressed,
And many white wheat-cakes bestowed, to make it up
    a feast.   185
He set near this a vine of gold that cracked beneath
    the weight
Of bunches black with being ripe; to keep which, at
    the height,
A silver rail ran all along, and round about it flowed
An azure moat, to to this guard a quick-set was
    bestowed
Of tin, one only path to all, by which the pressmen
    came   190
In time of vintage: youths and maids, that bore not yet
    the flame
Of manly Hymen, baskets bore of grapes and mellow
    fruit.
A lad that sweetly touched a harp, to which his voice
    did suit,
Centred the circles of that youth, all whose skill could
    not do
The wanton's pleasure to their minds, that danced,
    sung, whistled too.   195
A herd of oxen then he carved with high-raised heads,
    forged all
Of gold and tin (for colour mixed), and bellowing
    from their stall
Rushed to their pastures at a flood, that echoed all
    their throats,

Exceeding swift and full of reeds. And all in yellow
    coats,
Four herdsmen followed; after whom nine mastiffs
    went. In head   200
Of all the herd, upon a bull, that deadly bellowèd,
Two horrid lions ramped, and seized, and tugged off
    bellowing still.
Both men and dogs came, yet they tore the hide and
    lapped their fill
Of black blood, and the entrails eat. In vain the men
    assayed
To set their dogs on: none durst pinch, but cur-like
    stood and bayed   205
In both the faces of their kings, and all their onsets
    fled.
Then in a passing pleasant vale the famous artsman
    fed
(Upon a goodly pasture ground) rich flocks of white-
    fleeced sheep,
Built stables, cottages and cotes, that did the shepherds
    keep
From wind and weather. Next to these he cut a
    dancing place   210
All full of turnings, that was like the admirable maze
For fair-haired Ariadne made by cunning Daedalus;
And in it youths and virgins danced, all young and
    beauteous,
And gluèd in another's palmes. Weeds that the wind
    did toss
The virgins wore, the youths, woven cotes that cast a
    faint dim gloss,   215
Like that of oil. Fresh garlands too the virgins' temples
    crowned;
The youths gilt swords wore at their thighs, with silver
    baldricks bound.
Sometimes all wound close in a ring, to which as fast
    they spun
As any wheel a turner makes, being tried how it will
    run
While he is set; and out again, as full of sped, they
    wound,   220
Not one left fast or breaking hands. A multitude stood
    round,
Delighted with their nimble sport: to end which, two
    begun
('Midst all) a song, and, turning, sung the sport's
    conclusion.
All this he circled in the shield, with pouring round
    about
(In all his rage) the Oceän, that it might never out.
This shield thus done, he forged for him such curets as
    outshined   226

---

202 **still:** always, continually 204 **eat:** ate 205 **durst:** dared 206 **onsets:** attacks 209 **cotes:** shelters for animals 212 **Ariadne:** the daughter of King Minos of Crete, for whom the inventor Daedalus created the labyrinth 214 **gluèd . . . palmes:** holding hands tightly 221 **left fast:** let go 225 **out:** to escape

---

172 **close:** an enclosed field 189 **quick-set:** hedge 190 **pressmen:** men who operate a wine-press 192 **Hymen:** god of marriage 195 **wanton:** an immoral person

The blaze of fire. A helmet then (through which no
   steel could find
Forced passage) he composed, whose hue a hundred
   colours took;
And in the crest a plume of gold, that each breath
   stirred, he stuck.
All done, he all to Thetis brought, and held all up to
   her.   230
She took them all, and like to the hawk (surnámed the
   osspringer),
From Vulcan to her mighty son, with that so glorious
   show,
Stooped from the steep Olympian hill, his in eternal
   snow.

[Book 18, lines 327–559]

231 **osspringer**: osprey

ROBERT SOUTHWELL

MY CHILD MY CHOICE

LET folly praise that fancy loves, I praise and love that
   Child
Whose heart no thought, whose tongue no word,
   whose hand no deed defiled.
I praise Him most, I love Him best, all praise and love
   is His;
While Him I love, in Him I live, and cannot live amiss.

Love's sweetest mark, laud's highest theme, man's most
   desired light,   5
To love Him life, to leave Him death, to live in Him
   delight.
He mine by gift, I His by debt, thus each to other due;
First friend He was, best friend He is, all times will try
   Him true.

Though young, yet wise; though small, yet strong;
   though man, yet God He is:
As wise, He knows; as strong, He can; as God, He
   loves to bless.   10
His knowledge rules, His strength defends, His love
   doth cherish all;
His birth our joy, His life our light, His death our end
   of thrall.

Alas! He weeps, He sighs, He pants, yet do His angels
   sing;
Out of His tears, His sighs and throbs, doth bud a
   joyful spring.
Almighty Babe, whose tender arms can force all foes
   to fly,   15
Correct my faults, protect my life, direct me when I
   die!

MY CHILD MY CHOICE: 1 **child**: Christ 4 **amiss**: wrongly 5 **laud**: praise
8 **try**: prove 12 **thrall**: slavery

THE BURNING BABE

As I in hoary winter's night stood shivering in the
   snow,
Surprised I was with sudden heat, which made my
   heart to glow;
And lifting up a fearful eye, to view what fire was
   near,
A pretty Babe all burning bright did in the air appear;
Who, scorchèd with excessive heat, such floods of tears
   did shed   5
As though his floods should quench his flames, which
   with his tears were bred:
'Alas!' quoth he, 'but newly born, in fiery heats I fry,
Yet none approach to warm their hearts, or feel my
   fire, but I!
My faultless breast the furnace is; the fuel, wounding
   thorns;
Love is the fire, and sighs the smoke; the ashes, shames
   and scorns;   10
The fuel Justice layeth on, and Mercy blows the coals;
The metal in this furnace wrought are men's defilèd
   souls,
For which, as now on fire I am to work them to their
   good,
So will I melt into a bath, to wash them in my blood.'
With this he vanished out of sight, and swiftly shrunk
   away,   15
And straight I callèd unto mind that it was Christmas
   Day.

THE BURNING BABE: 1 **hoary**: frosty

'COME TO YOUR HEAVEN, YOU HEAVENLY CHOIRS!'

COME to your heaven, you heavenly choirs!
Earth hath the heaven of your desires;
Remove your dwelling to your God,
A stall is now his best abode;
Sith men their homage do deny,   5
Come, angels, all their fault supply.

His chilling cold doth heat require,
Come, seraphims, in lieu of fire;
This little ark no cover hath,
Let churbs' wings his body swathe;   10
Come, Raphael, this Babe must eat,
Provide our little Toby meat.

Let Gabriel be now his groom,
That first took up his earthly room;
Let Michael stand in his defence,   15
Whom love hath linked to feeble sense;
Let graces rock when he doth cry,
And angels sing his lullaby.

The same you saw in heavenly seat,
Is he that now sucks Mary's teat;   20
Agnize your King a mortal wight,
His borrowed weed lets not your sight;
Come, kiss the manger where he lies,
That is your bliss above the skies.

This little Babe, so few days old,   25
Is come to rifle Satan's fold;
All hell doth at his presence quake,
Though he himself for cold do shake;
For in this weak unarmèd wise
The gates of hell he will surprise.   30

With tears he fights and wins the field,
His naked breast stands for a shield;
His battering shot are babish cries,
His arrows looks of weeping eyes.
His martial ensigns cold and need,   35
And feeble flesh his warrior's steed.

His camp is pitchèd in a stall,
His bulwark but a broken wall;
The crib his trench, hay-stalks his stakes,
Of shepherds he his muster makes;   40
And thus, as sure his foe to wound,
The angels' trumps alarum sound.

My soul, with Christ join thou in fight;
Stick to the tents that he hath pight;
Within his crib is surest ward,   45
This little Babe will be thy guard;
If thou wilt foil thy foes with joy,
Then flit not from this heavenly boy.

'COME TO YOUR HEAVEN, YOU HEAVENLY CHOIRS!': 4 **stall:** ie in a stable;
a reference to the Nativity 5 **sith:** since 6 **supply:** make good
10 **churbs:** cherubs 11 **Raphael:** an angel 12 **Toby:** Tobit, who in the
Book of Tobit (Apocrypha) is helped by Raphael 13 **Gabriel:** the
archangel who foretold the birth of Christ 15 **Michael:** an archangel
21 **agnize:** acknowledge **wight:** person 22 **weed:** garment **lats not:**
does not hinder or bar 26 **rifle Satan's fold:** to rob the devil of
his sheep (human souls) 42 **trumps:** trumpets **alarum:** alarm
44 **pight:** pitched 45 **ward:** protection

SAMUEL DANIEL

'CARE-CHARMER SLEEP,
SON OF THE SABLE NIGHT'

CARE-CHARMER Sleep, son of the sable night,
  Brother to Death, in silent darkness born,
Relieve my languish, and restore the light,
  With dark forgetting of my care return.
And let the day be time enough to mourn   5
  The shipwreck of my ill adventured youth;

Let waking eyes suffice to wail their scorn,
  Without the torment of the night's untruth.
Cease, dreams, the images of day-desires,
  To model forth the passions of the morrow;   10
Never let rising sun approve you liars,
  To add more grief to aggravate my sorrow.
    Still let me sleep, embracing clouds in vain,
    And never wake to feel the day's disdain.

'LET OTHERS SING OF
KNIGHTS AND PALADINS'

LET others sing of knights and paladins
  In aged accents and untimely words,
Paint shadows in imaginary lines,
  Which well the reach of their high wit records;
But I must sing of thee, and those fair eyes   5
  Authentic shall my verse in time to come,
When yet the unborn shall say, 'Lo, where she lies!
  Whose beauty made him speak, that else was
    dumb!'
These are the arks, the trophies, I erect,
  That fortify thy name against old age;   10
And these thy sacred virtues must protect
  Against the dark and Time's consuming rage.
    Though the error of my youth in them appear,
    Suffice they show I lived, and loved thee dear.

'LET OTHERS SING OF KNIGHTS AND PALADINS': 1 **paladin** knight-errant
2 **untimely:** old-fashioned

ULYSSES AND THE SIREN

Siren. Come, worthy Greek! Ulysses, come
  Possess these shores with me:
The winds and seas are troublesome,
  And here we may be free.
    Here may we sit, and view their toil   5
    That travail in the deep,
And joy the day in mirth the while,
  And spend the night in sleep.

Ulysses. Fair nymph, if fame or honour were
  To be attained with ease,   10
Then would I come and rest with thee,
  And leave such toils as these.
    But here it dwells, and here must I
    With danger seek it forth:
To spend the time luxuriously   15
  Becomes not men of worth.

ULYSSES AND THE SIREN: 6 **travail:** labour 7 **joy:** enjoy 16 **Becomes not:**
it is not becoming to

Siren. Ulysses, Oh! be not deceived
  With that unreal name:
  This honour is a thing conceived,
  And rests on others' fame;   20
    Begotten only to molest
  Our peace, and to beguile
  (The best thing of our life) our rest,
  And give us up to toil.

Ulysses. Delicious nymph, suppose there were   25
  Nor honour nor report,
  Yet manliness would scorn to wear
  The time in idle sport;
    For toil doth give a better touch,
  To make us feel our joy,   30
  And ease finds tediousness as much
  As labour yields annoy.

Siren. Then pleasure likewise seems the shore,
  Whereto tends all your toil,
  Which you forgo to make it more,   35
  And perish oft the while.
    Who may disport them diversely
  Find never tedious day,
  And ease may have variety
  As well as action may.   40

Ulysses. But natures of the noblest frame
  These toils and dangers please;
  And they take comfort in the same,
  As much as you in ease;
    And with the thought of actions past   45
  Are recreated still;
  When pleasure leaves a touch at last,
  To show that it was ill.

Siren. That doth opinion only cause,
  That's out of custom bred,   50
  Which makes us many other laws
  Than ever Nature did.
    No widows wail for our delights,
  Our sports are without blood;
  The world we see by warlike wights   55
  Receives more hurt than good.

Ulysses. But yet the state of things require
  These motions of unrest,
  And these great spirits of high desire
  Seem born to turn them best, –   60
    To purge the mischiefs that increase,
  And all good order mar;
  For oft we see a wicked peace
  To be well changed for war.

26 **Nor . . . nor:** Neither . . . nor   **report:** fame   27 **wear:** use up
32 **annoy:** trouble   55 **wights:** people

Siren. Well, well, Ulysses, then I see   65
  I shall not have thee here,
  And therefore I will come to thee,
  And take my fortunes there.
    I must be won that cannot win,
  Yet lost were I not won;   70
  For beauty hath created been
  T' undo, or be undone.

HENRY CONSTABLE

DAMELUS' SONG TO HIS DIAPHENIA

DIAPHENIA like the daffadowndilly,
  White as the sun, fair as the lily,
Heigh ho, how I do love thee?
  I do love thee as my lambs
  Are beloved of their dams;   5
How blest were I if thou wouldst prove me!

Diaphenia like the spreading roses,
  That in thy sweets all sweets encloses,
Fair sweet, how I do love thee?
  I do love thee as each flower   10
  Loves the sun's life-giving power;
For dead, thy breath to life might move me.

Diaphenia like to all things blessèd
  When all thy praises are expressèd,
Dear joy, how I do love thee?   15
  As the birds do love the spring,
  Or the bees their careful king;
Then in requite, sweet virgin, love me!

DAMELUS' SONG TO HIS DIAPHENIA: 1 **daffadowndilly:** daffodil 5 **dams:**
mothers 6 **prove:** try

MARK ALEXANDER BOYD

'FRA BANC TO BANC FRA WOD TO WOD I RIN'

FRA banc to banc fra wod to wod I rin
  Ourhailit with my feble fantasie
  Lyc til a leif that fallis from a trie
  Or til a reid ourblawin with the wind.
Twa gods gyds me, the ane of tham is blind,   5
  Ye and a bairn brocht up in vanitie.
  The nixt a wyf ingenrit of the se,
  And lichter nor a dauphin with hir fin.
Unhappie is the man for evirmaire
  That teils the sand and sawis in the aire,   10
  Bot twyse unhappier is he I lairn
That feidis in his hairt a mad desyre,
  And follows on a woman throw the fyre
  Led be a blind and teichit be a bairn.

MICHAEL DRAYTON

'SINCE THERE'S NO HELP, COME, LET US KISS AND PART'

SINCE there's no help, come, let us kiss and part.
Nay, I have done; you get no more of me;
And I am glad, yea, glad with all my heart,
That thus so cleanly I myself can free.
Shake hands for ever; cancel all our vows; 5
And when we meet at any time again,
Be it not seen in either of our brows
That we one jot of former love retain.
Now at the last gasp of Love's latest breath,
When, his pulse failing, Passion speechless lies, 10
When Faith is kneeling by his bed of death,
And Innocence is closing up his eyes;
  Now, if thou would'st, when all have given him over,
  From death to life thou might'st him yet recover.

'SOME ATHEIST OR VILE INFIDEL IN LOVE'

SOME atheist or vile infidel in love,
When I do speak of thy divinity,
May blaspheme thus, and say I flatter thee,
And only write my skill in verse to prove.
See miracles, ye unbelieving! See 5
A dumb-born Muse, made to express the mind,
A cripple hand to write, yet lame by kind,
One by thy name, the other touching thee.
Blind were mine eyes, till they were seen of thine,
And mine ears deaf by thy fame healèd be; 10
My vices cured by virtues sprung from thee,
My hopes revived, which long in grave had lain:
  All unclean thoughts, foul sprites, cast out in me
  By thy great power, and by strong faith in thee.

TO THE VIRGINIAN VOYAGE

YOU brave heroic minds,
Worthy your country's name,
  That honour still pursue,
  Go, and subdue,
Whilst loit'ring hinds 5
Lurk here at home, with shame.

Britons, you stay too long,
Quickly aboard bestow you,
  And with a merry gale
  Swell your stretched sail, 10
With vows as strong,
As the winds that blow you.

Your course securely steer,
West and by south forth keep,
  Rocks, lee shores, nor shoals, 15
  When Aeolus scowls,
You need not fear,
So absolute the deep.

And cheerfully at sea,
Success you still entice, 20
  To get the pearl and gold,
  And ours to hold,
Virginia,
Earth's only paradise.

Where nature hath in store, 25
Fowl, venison, and fish,
  And the fruitfull'st soil,
  Without your toil,
Three harvests more,
All greater than you wish. 30

And the ambitious vine
Crowns with his purple mass,
  The cedar reaching high
  To kiss the sky,
The cypress, pine 35
And useful sassafras.

To whose, the golden age
Still nature's laws doth give,
  No other cares that tend,
  But them to defend 40
From winter's age,
That long there doth not live.

When as the luscious smell
Of that delicious land,
  Above the seas that flows, 45
  The clear wind throws,
Your hearts to swell
Approaching the dear strand,

In kenning of the shore
(Thanks to God first given,) 50
  O you the happy'st men,
  Be frolic then,
Let cannons roar,
Frighting the wide heaven.

And in regions far 55
Such heroes bring ye forth,
　As those from whom we came,
　And plant our name,
Under that star
Not known unto our north. 60

And as there plenty grows
Of laurel everywhere,
　Apollo's sacred tree,
　You it may see,
A poet's brows 65
To crown, that may sing there.

Thy voyages attend,
Industrious Hakluyt,
　Whose reading shall inflame
　Men to seek fame, 70
And much commend
To after-times thy wit.

68 **Hakluyt:** Richard Hakluyt (?1552–1616), English geographer who compiled *The Principal Navigations, Voyages, and Discoveries of the English Nation* (1589), popularly known as *Hakluyt's Voyages*

NYMPHIDIA, THE COURT OF FAIRY

OLD Chaucer doth of Topas tell,
Mad Rab'lais of Pantagruel,
A latter third of Dowsabell,
　With such poor trifles playing:
Others the like have laboured at 5
Some of this thing, and some of that,
And many of they know not what,
　But that they must be saying.

Another sort there be, that will
Be talking of the fairies still, 10
Nor never can they have their fill,
　As they were wedded to them;
No tales of them their thirst can slake,
So much delight therein they take,
And some strange thing they fain would make, 15
　Knew they the way to do them.

Then since no Muse hath been so bold,
Or of the later, or the old,
Those elvish secrets to unfold,
　Which lie from others' reading, 20
My active Muse to light shall bring,
The court of that proud fairy king,
And tell there, of the revelling,
　Jove prosper my proceeding.

NYMPHIDIA, THE COURT OF FAIRY: 1 **Topas:** Sir Thopas appears in one of Chaucer's *Canterbury Tales* as a knight trying to win an elf-queen 2 **Pantagruel:** a giant in Rabelais' *Gargantua and Pantagruel* 3 **Dowsabell:** conventional name for a sweetheart in 16th-century poetry 8 **But that they must be saying:** but that they have to say something 24 **Jove:** Jupiter, chief of the Roman gods

And thou Nymphidia gentle fay, 25
Which meeting me upon the way,
These secrets didst to me bewray,
　Which now I am in telling:
My pretty light fantastic maid,
I here invoke thee to my aid, 30
That I may speak what thou hast said,
　In numbers smoothly swelling.

This palace standeth in the air,
By necromancy placèd there,
That it no tempests needs to fear, 35
　Which way so e'er it blow it.
And somewhat southward tow'rd the noon,
Whence lies a way up to the moon,
And thence the fairy can as soon
　Pass to the earth below it. 40

The walls of spiders' legs are made,
Well mortizèd and finely laid,
He was the master of his trade,
　It curiously that builded:
The windows of the eyes of cats, 45
And for the roof, instead of slats,
Is covered with the skins of bats,
　With moonshine that are gilded.

Hence Oberon him sport to make,
(Their rest when weary mortals take) 50
And none but only fairies wake,
　Descendeth for his pleasure.
And Mab his merry queen by night
Bestrids young folks that lie upright,
(In elder times the mare that hight) 55
　Which plagues them out of measure.

Hence shadows, seeming idle shapes,
Of little frisking elves and apes,
To earth do make their wanton 'scapes,
　As hope of pastime hastes them: 60
Which maids think on the hearth they see,
When fires well near consumèd be,
Their dancing hays by two and three,
　Just as their fancy casts them.

These make our girls their sluttery rue, 65
By pinching them both black and blue,
And put a penny in their shoe,
　The house for cleanly sweeping:
And in their courses make that round,
In meadows, and in marshes found, 70
Of them so called the fairies' ground,
　Of which they have the keeping.

25 **fay:** fairy 27 **bewray:** betray 32 **numbers:** verses 44 **It curiously that builded:** who skilfully built it 49 **Oberon:** king of the fairies 53 **Mab:** queen of the fairies 54 **Bestrids . . . upright:** acts as a succubus 55 **hight:** was called 63 **hays:** country dances

These when a child haps to be got,
Which after proves an idiot,
When folk perceive it thriveth not,   75
    The fault therein to smother:
Some silly doting brainless calf,
That understands things by the half,
Say that the fairy left this aulfe,
    And took away the other.   80

But listen and I shall you tell,
A chance in Fairy that befell,
Which certainly may please some well;
    In love and arms delighting:
Of Oberon that jealous grew,   85
Of one of his own fairy crew,
Too well (he feared) his queen that knew,
    His love but ill requiting.

Pigwiggin was this fairy knight,
One wondrous gracious in the sight   90
Of fair Queen Mab, which day and night,
    He amorously observed;
Which made King Oberon suspect,
His service took too good effect,
His sauciness, and often checked,   95
    And could have wished him starved.

Pigwiggin gladly would commend,
Some token to Queen Mab to send,
If sea, or land, him ought could lend,
    Were worthy of her wearing: 100
At length this lover doth devise,
A bracelet made of emmets' eyes,
A thing he thought that she would prize,
    No whit her state impairing.

And to the queen a letter writes,   105
Which he most curiously indites,
Conjuring her by all the rites
    Of love, she would be pleasèd,
To meet him her true servant, where
They might without suspect or fear,   110
Themselves to one another clear,
    And have their poor hearts easèd.

At midnight the appointed hour,
And for the queen a fitting bower,
(Quoth he) is that fair cowslip flower,   115
    On Hidcut hill that groweth,
In all your train there's not a fay,
That ever went to gather May,
But she hath made it in her way,
    The tallest there that groweth.   120

When by Tom Thumb a fairy page,
He sent it, and doth him engage,
By promise of a mighty wage,
    It secretly to carry:
Which done, the queen her maids doth call,   125
And bids them to be ready all,
She would go see her summer hall,
    She could no longer tarry.

Her chariot ready straight is made,
Each thing therein is fitting laid,   130
That she by nothing might be stayed,
    For naught must be her letting,
Four nimble gnats the horses were,
Their harnesses of gossamer,
Fly cranion her charioteer,   135
    Upon the coach-box getting.

Her chariot of a snail's fine shell,
Which for the colours did excel:
The fair Queen Mab, becoming well,
    So lively was the limning: 140
The seat the soft wool of the bee;
The cover (gallantly to see)
The wing of a pied butterflee,
    I trow 'twas simply trimming.

The wheels composed of crickets' bones,   145
And daintily made for the nonce,
For fear of rattling on the stones,
    With thistledown they shod it;
For all her maidens much did fear,
If Oberon had chanced to hear,   150
That Mab his queen should have been there,
    He would not have abode it.

She mounts her chariot with a trice,
Nor would she stay for no advice,
Until her maids that were so nice,   155
    To wait on her were fitted,
But ran herself away alone;
Which when they heard there was not one,
But hasted after to be gone,
    As she had been diswitted.   160

Hop, and Mop, and Drop so clear,
Pip, and Trip, and Skip that were,
To Mab their sovereign ever dear:
    Her special maids of honour;
Fib, and Tib, and Pink, and Pin,   165
Tick, and Quick, and Jill, and Jin,
Tit, and Nit, and Wap, and Win,
    The train that wait upon her.

73 **when a child haps to be got:** when a baby happens to be conceived
79 **aulfe:** changeling 87 **Too well . . . knew:** with whom his queen, he
feared, was too intimate 102 **emmets:** ants 104 **No whit . . . impairing:**
not demeaning her in the least 106 **indites:** writes down 111 **clear:**
reveal their feelings fully 119 **made it in her way:** made a point of
going there

131 **stayed:** delayed 132 **naught must be her letting:** nothing must
detain her 135 **fly cranion:** cranefly 140 **limning:** painting 146 **for
the nonce:** for once, for the occasion 160 **diswitted:** driven out of
her wits, made frantic

Upon a grasshopper they got,
And what with amble, and with trot,   170
For hedge nor ditch they spared not,
    But after her they hie them.
A cobweb over them they throw,
To shield the wind if it should blow,
Themselves they wisely could bestow,   175
    Lest any should espy them.

But let us leave Queen Mab a while,
Through many a gate, o'er many a stile,
That now had gotten by this wile,
    Here dear Pigwiggin kissing,   180
And tell how Oberon doth fare,
Who grew as mad as any hare,
When he had sought each place with care,
    And found his queen was missing.

By grisly Pluto he doth swear,   185
He rent his clothes, and tore his hair,
And as he runneth, here and there,
    An acorn cup he greeteth;
Which soon he taketh by the stalk
About his head he lets it walk,   190
Nor doth he any creature balk,
    But lays on all he meeteth.

The Tuscan poet doth advance,
The frantic paladin of France,
And those more ancient do inhance,   195
    Alcides in his fury;
And others Ajax Telamon,
But to this time there hath been none,
So bedlam as our Oberon,
    Of which I dare assure you.   200

And first encount'ring with a wasp,
He in his arms the fly doth clasp
As though his breath he forth would grasp,
    Him for Pigwiggin taking:
'Where is my wife, thou rogue?' quoth he.   205
'Pigwiggin, she is come to thee,
Restore her, or thou die'st by me.'
    Whereat the poor wasp quaking,

Cries: 'Oberon, great fairy king,
Content thee I am no such thing,   210
I am a wasp behold my sting.'
    At which the fairy started:
When soon away the wasp doth go,
Poor wretch was never frighted so,
He thought his wings were much too slow,   215
    O'erjoyed, they so were parted.

He next upon a glowworm light,
(You must suppose it now was night,)
For which her hinder part was bright,
    He took to be a devil.   220
And furiously doth her assail,
For carrying fire in her tail,
He thrashed her rough coat with his flail,
    The mad King feared no evil.

'Oh,' quoth the glowworm, 'hold thy hand,   225
Thou puissant king of Fairyland,
Thy mighty strokes who may withstand,
    Hold, or of life despair I.'
Together then her self doth roll,
And timbling down into a hole,   230
She seemed as black as any coal,
    Which vexed away the fairy.

From thence he ran into a hive,
Amongst the bees he letteth drive
And down their combs begins to rive,   235
    All likely to have spoiled:
Which with their wax his face besmeared,
And with their honey daubed his beard,
It would have made a man afeard,
    To see how he way moiled.   240

A new adventure him betides,
He met an ant, which he bestrides,
And post thereon away he rides,
    Which with his haste doth stumble;
And came full over on her snout,   245
Her heels so threw the dirt about,
For she by no means could get out,
    But over him doth tumble,

And being in this piteous case,
And all be-slurried head and face,   250
On runs he in his wild-goose chase,
    As here, and there, he rambles,
Half blind, against a molehill hit,
And for a mountain taking it,
For all he was out of his wit,   255
    Yet to the top he scrambles.

172 **hie them:** hurried 185 **Pluto:** Roman god of the underworld
190 **lets it walk:** swings it 191 **balk:** pass over, let escape 192 **lays on:**
beats, belabours 193 **Tuscan poet . . . France:** the Italian poet
Ludovico Ariosto (1474–1533) wrote an epic poem *Orlando Furioso*
(Orlando Mad), whose hero is a French knight driven mad by
his beloved's faithlessness 196 **Alcides:** Hercules, who killed his
wife and children in a fit of madness 197 **Ajax Telamon:** Ajax son
of Telamon, a Greek hero of the Trojan War, killed himself in fury
when the armour of the dead Achilles was not awarded to him
but to Odysseus 199 **bedlam:** insane (a corruption of Bethlehem,
from the Hospital of St Mary of Bethlehem, London, an insane
asylum) 207 **thou diest by me:** I will kill you **Content thee:** be
assured

226 **puissant:** powerful 228 **Hold . . . I:** stop, or I fear I must die
234 **letteth drive:** aims his blows 235 **rive:** tear apart 240 **way moiled:**
made his way in a disturbed manner

And being gotten to the top,
Yet there himself he could not stop,
But down on th'other side doth chop,
　　And to the foot came tumbling:　　　　260
So that the grubs therein that bred,
Hearing such turmoil overhead,
Thought surely they had all been dead,
　　So fearful was the jumbling.

And falling down into a lake,　　　　265
Which him up to the neck doth take,
His fury somewhat it doth slake,
　　He calleth for a ferry;
Where you may some recovery note,
What was his club he made his boat,　　　　270
And in his oaken cup doth float,
　　As safe as in a wherry.

Men talk of the adventures strange,
Of Don Quishott, and of their change,
Through which he armèd oft did range,　　　　275
　　Of Sancho Pancha's travel:
But should a man tell everything,
Done by this frantic fairy king,
And them in lofty numbers sing,
　　It well his wits might gravel.　　　　280

Scarce set on shore, but therewithal,
He meeteth Puck, which most men call
Hobgoblin, and on him doth fall,
　　With words from frenzy spoken;
'Ho, hop,' quoth Hob, 'God save thy grace,　　　　285
Who dressed thee in this piteous case,
He thus that spoiled my sovereign's face,
　　I would his neck were broken.'

This Puck seems but a dreaming dolt,
Still walking like a ragged colt,　　　　290
And oft out of a bush doth bolt,
　　Of purpose to deceive us.
And leading us makes us to stray,
Long winter's nights out of the way,
And when we stick in mire and clay,　　　　295
　　Hob doth with laughter leave us.

'Dear Puck,' quoth he, 'my wife is gone,
As e'er thou love'st King Oberon,
Let everything but this alone,
　　With vengeance, and pursue her;　　　　300
Bring her to me alive or dead,

Or that vild thief Pigwiggin's head,
That villain hath defiled my bed,
　　He to this folly drew her.'

Quoth Puck: 'My liege, I'll never lin,　　　　305
But I will thorough thick and thin,
Until at length I bring her in,
　　My dearest lord ne'er doubt it:
Thorough brake, thorough briar,
Thorough muck, thorough mire,　　　　310
Thorough water, thorough fire.'
　　And thus Puck goes about it.

This thing Nymphidia overheard,
That on this mad king had a guard,
Not doubting of a great reward,　　　　315
　　For first this business broaching;
And through the air away doth go
Swift as an arrow from the bow,
To let her sovereign Mab to know,
　　What peril was approaching.　　　　320

The queen bound with love's powerful'st charm
Sat with Pigwiggin arm in arm,
Her merry maids that thought no harm,
　　About the room were skipping:
A humble-bee their minstrel, played　　　　325
Upon his hautboy; ev'ry maid
Fit for this revels was arrayed,
　　The hornpipe neatly tripping.

In comes Nymphidia, and doth cry:
'My sovereign for your safety fly,　　　　330
For there is danger but too nigh,
　　I posted to forewarn you:
The king hath sent Hobgoblin out,
To seek you all the fields about,
And of your safety you may doubt,　　　　335
　　If he but once discern you.'

When like an uproar in a town,
Before them every thing went down,
Some tore a ruff, and some a gown,
　　'Gainst one another jostling:　　　　340
They flew about like chaff i' the wind,
For haste some left their masks behind;
Some could not stay their gloves to find,
　　There never was such bustling.

Forth ran they by a secret way,　　　　345
Into a brake that near them lay;
Yet much they doubted there to stay,
　　Lest Hob should hap to find them:
He had a sharp and piercing sight,
All one to him the day and night,　　　　350
And therefoe were resolved by flight,
　　To leave this place behind them.

---

259 **chop:** to arrive suddenly　263 **Thought . . . dead:** believed they were all going to die　274 **Don Quishott:** the knight-errant hero of Cervantes' *Don Quixote* (1605), who sets about ludicrous adventures accompanied by his squire Sancho Panza. The spelling here indicates the contemporary pronunciation　280 **gravel:** to perplex　282 **Puck:** a mischievous sprite　290 **still:** always **ragged:** shaggy

302 **vild:** vile　305 **lin:** stop, cease　326 **hautboy:** oboe　332 **posted:** hurried

At length one chanced to find a nut,
In th' end of which a hole was cut,
Which lay upon a hazel root,   355
   There scattered by a squirrel:
Which out the kernel gotten had;
When quoth this fay: 'Dear queen, be glad,
Let Oberon be ne'er so mad,
   I'll set you safe from peril.   360

'Come all into this nut,' quoth she,
'Come closely in, be ruled by me,
Each one may here a chooser be,
   For room ye need not wrestle:
Nor need ye be together heaped.'   365
So one by one therein they crept,
And lying down they soundly slept,
   As safe as in a castle.

Nymphidia that this while doth watch,
Perceived if Puck the queen should catch,   370
That he would be her over-match,
   Of which she well bethought her:
Found it must be some powerful charm,
The queen against him that must arm,
Or surely he would do her harm,   375
   For throughly he had sought her.

And list'ning if he ought could hear
That her might hinder, or might fear:
But finding still the coast was clear,
   Nor creature had descried her: 380
Each circumstance and having scanned,
She came thereby to understand,
Puck would be with them out of hand,
   When to her charms she hied her:

And first her fern seed doth bestow,   385
The kernel of the mistletoe:
And here and there as Puck doth go,
   With terror to affright him:
She nightshade strews to work him ill,
Therewith her vervain and her dill,   390
That hind'reth witches of their will,
   Of purpose to despite him.

Then sprinkles she the juice of rue,
That groweth underneath the yew:
With nine drops of the midnight dew,   395
   From lunary distilling:
The molewarp's brain mixed therewithal;
And with the same the pissmire's gall,
For she in nothing short would fall;
   The fairy was so willing.   400

Then thrice under a briar doth creep,
Which at both ends was rooted deep,
And over it three times she leap;
   Her magic much availing:
Then on Proserpina doth call,   405
And so upon her spell doth fall,
Which here to you repeat I shall,
   Not in one tittle failing.

'By the croaking of the frog;
By the howling of the dog;   410
By the crying of the hog,
   Against the storm arising;
By the evening curfew bell,
By the doleful dying knell,
Oh, let this my direful spell,   415
   Hob, hinder thy surprising.

'By the mandrake's dreadful groans;
By the lubrican's sad moans;
By the noise of dead men's bones,
   In charnel houses rattling: 420
By the hissing of the snake,
The rustling of the fire-drake,
I charge thee thou this place forsake,
   Nor of Queen Mab be prattling.

'By the whirlwind's hollow sound,   425
By the thunder's dreadful stound,
Yells of spirits under ground,
   I charge thee not to fear us:
By the screech-owl's dismal note,
By the black night-raven's throat,   430
I charge thee, Hob, to tear thy coat
   With thorns if thou come near us.'

Her spell thus spoke she stepped aside,
And in a chink herself doth hide,
To see thereof what would betide,   435
   For she doth only mind him:
When presently she Puck espies,
And well she marked his gloating eye,
How under every leaf he pries,
   In seeking still to find them.   440

But once the circle got within,
The charms to work do straight begin,
And he was caught as in a gin;
   For as he thus was busy,
A pain he in his headpiece feels,   445
Against a stubbard tree he reels,
And up went poor Hobgoblin's heels,
   Alas, his brain was dizzy.

371 **be her over-match:** be too strong for her 372 **bethought her:** considered 378 **fear:** frighten 396 **from lunary distilling:** distilled from moonwort (or the honesty plant) 397 **molewarp:** mole 398 **pissmire:** ant

405 **Proserpina:** in Roman myth, queen of the underworld 418 **lubrican:** leprechaun 422 **fire-drake:** fire-breathing dragon 426 **stound:** impact, blow 443 **gin:** trap 446 **stubbard tree:** tree stump

At length upon his feet he gets,
Hobgoblin fumes, Hobgoblin frets, 450
And as again he forward sets,
   And through the bushes scrambles;
A stump doth trip him in his pace,
Down comes poor Hob upon his face,
And lamentably tore his case, 455
   Amongst the briars and brambles.

'A plague upon Queen Mab,' quoth he,
And all her maids where'er they be,
I think the devil guided me,
   To seek her so provokèd.' 460
Where stumbling at a piece of wood,
He fell into a ditch of mud,
Where to the very chin he stood,
   In danger to be chokèd.

Now worse than e'er he was before; 465
Poor Puck doth yell, poor Puck doth roar;
That waked Queen Mab who doubted sore
   Some treason had been wrought her:
Until Nymphidia told the queen
What she had done, what she had seen, 470
Who then had well-near cracked her spleen
   With very extreme laughter.

But leave we Hob to clamber out:
Queen Mab and all her fairy rout,
And come again to have about 475
   With Oberon yet madding:
And with Pigwiggin now distraught,
Who much was troubled in his thought,
That he so long the queen had sought,
   And through the fields was gadding. 480

And as he runs he still doth cry,
'King Oberon, I thee defy,
And dare thee here in arms to try,
   For my dear lady's honour:
For that she is a queen right good, 485
In whose defence I'll shed my blood,
And that thou in this jealous mood
   Hast laid this slander on her.'

And quickly arms him for the field,
A little cockleshell his shield, 490
Which he could very bravely wield:
   Yet could it not be piercèd:
His spear a bent both stiff and strong,
And well-near of two inches long;
The pile was of a horse-fly's tongue, 495
   Whose sharpness naught reversèd.

And puts him on a coat of mail,
Which was of a fish's scale,
That when his foe should him assail,
   No point should be prevailing: 500
His rapier was a hornet's sting,
It was a very dangerous thing:
For if it chanced to hurt the king,
   It would be long in healing.

His helmet was a beetle's head, 505
Most horrible and full of dread,
That able was to strike one dead,
   Yet did it well become him:
And for a plume, a horse's hair,
Which being tossèd with the air, 510
Had force to strike his foe with fear,
   And turn his weapon from him.

Himself he on an earwig set,
Yet scarce he on his back could get,
So oft and high he did curvet, 515
   Ere he himself could settle:
He made his turn, and stop, and bound,
To gallop, and to trot the round,
He scarce could stand on any ground,
   He was so full of mettle. 520

When soon he met with Tomalin,
One that a valiant knight had been,
And to King Oberon of kin;
   Quoth he: 'Thou manly fairy:
Tell Oberon I come prepared, 525
Then bid him stand upon his guard;
This hand his baseness shall reward,
   Let him be ne'er so wary.

'Say to him thus, that I defy,
His slanders, and his infamy, 530
And as a mortal enemy,
   Do publicly proclaim him:
Withal, that if I had mine own,
He should not wear the fairy crown,
But with a vengeance should come down: 535
   Nor we a king should name him.'

This Tomalin could not abide,
To hear his sovereign vilified:
But to the fairy court him hied;
   Full furiously he posted, 540
With ev'ry thing Pigwiggin said:
How title to the crown he laid,
And in what arms he was arrayed,
   As how himself he boasted.

'Twist head and foot, from point to point, 545
He told th' arming of each joint,
In every piece, how neat, and quaint,
   For Tomalin could do it:
How fair he sat, how sure he rid,

455 **case:** clothing 493 **bent:** a stiff grass stalk 495 **pile:** pointed head

As of the courser he bestrid,   550
How managed, and how well he did;
   The king which listened to it,

Quoth he: 'Go, Tomalin, with speed,
Provide me arms, provide my steed,
And every thing that I shall need,   555
   By thee I will be guided:
To strait account, call thou thy wit,
See there be wanting not a whit,
In every thing see thou me fit,
   Just as my foes provided.'   560

Soon flew this news through Fairyland,
Which gave Queen Mab to understand,
The combat that was then at hand,
   Betwixt those men so mighty;
Which greatly she began to rue,   565
Perceiving that all Fairy knew,
The first occasion from her grew,
   Of these affairs so weighty.

Wherefore attended with her maids,
Through fogs, and mists, and damps she wades,   570
To Prosperpine the queen of shades
   To treat, that it would please her,
The cause into her hands to take,
For ancient love and friendship's sake,
And soon thereof an end to make,   575
   Which of much care would ease her.

A while, there let we Mab alone,
And come we to King Oberon,
Who armed to meet his foe is gone,
   For proud Pigwiggin crying: 580
Who sought the fairy king as fast,
And had so well his journeys cast,
That he arrivèd at the last,
   His puissant foe espying:

Stout Tomalin came with the king,   585
Tom Thumb doth on Pigwiggin bring,
That perfect were in every thing,
   To single fights belonging:
And therefore they themselves engage,
To see them exercise their rage,   590
With fair and comely equipage,
   Not one the other wronging.

So like in arms, these champions were,
As they had been a very pair,
So that a man would almost swear,   595
   That either had been either;
Their furious steeds began to neigh
That they were hear a mighty way,
Their staves upon their rests they lay,
   Yet ere they flew together;   600

557 **strait:** strict   598 **hear:** heard

Their seconds minister an oath,
Which was indifferent to them both,
That on their knightly faith, and troth,
   No magic them supplied;
And sought them that they had no charms,   605
Wherewith to work, each other's harms,
But came with simple open arms,
   To have their causes tried.

Together furiously they ran,
That to the ground came horse and man,   610
The blood out of their helmets span,
   So sharp were their encounters;
And though they to the earth were thrown,
Yet quickly they regained their own,
Such nimbleness was never shown,   615
   They were two gallant mounters.

When in a second course again,
They forward came with might and main,
Yet which had better of the twain,
   The seconds could not judge yet;   620
Their shields were into pieces cleft,
Their helmets from their heads were reft,
And to defend them nothing left,
   These champions would not budge yet.

Away from them their staves they threw,   625
Their cruel swords they quickly drew,
And freshly they the fight renew;
   They every stroke redoubled:
Which made Proserpina take heed,
And made to them the greater speed,   630
For fear lest they too much should bleed,
   Which wondrously her troubled.

When to th' infernal Styx she goes,
She takes the fogs from thence that rose,
And in a bag doth them enclose;   635
   When well she had them blended:
She hies her then to Lethe spring,
A bottle and thereof doth bring,
Wherewith she meant to work the thing
   Which only she intended.   640

Now Proserpine with Mab is gone
Unto the place where Oberon
And proud Pigwiggin, one to one,
   Both to be slain were likely:
And there themselves they closely hide,   645
Because they would not be espied;
For Proserpine meant to decide
   The matter very quickly.

622 **reft:** torn away, knocked off   633 **Styx:** in classical mythology, a river of the underworld   637 **Lethe:** in Greek myth, a river of the underworld whose water, when drunk, causes oblivion

And suddenly unties the poke,
Which out of it sent such a smoke, 650
Asready was them all to choke,
  So grievous was the pother;
So that the knights each other lost,
And stood as still as any post,
Tom Thumb, nor Tomalin could boast 655
  Themselves of any other.

And when the mist 'gan somewhat cease,
Proserpina commandeth peace:
And that a while they should release,
  Each other of their peril: 660
'Which here', quoth she, 'I do proclaim
To all in dreadful Pluto's name,
That as ye will eschew his blame,
  You let me hear the quarrel,

'But here your selves you must engage, 665
Somewhat to cool your spleenish rage:
Your grievous thirst and to assuage,
  That first you drink this liquor:
Which shall your understanding clear,
As plainly shall to you appear; 670
Those things from me that you shall hear,
  Conceiving much the quicker.'

This Lethe water you must know,
The memory destroyeth so,
That of our weal, or of our woe, 675
  It all remembrance blotted;
Of it nor can you ever think:
For they no sooner took this drink;
But nought into their brains could sink,
  Of what had them besotted. 680

King Oberon forgotten had,
That he for jealousy ran mad:
But of his queen was wondrous glad,
  And asked how they came thither:
Pigwiggin likewise doth forget, 685
That he Queen Mab had ever met;
Or that they were so hard beset,
  When they were found together.

Nor neither of them both had thought,
That e'er they had each other sought; 690
Much less that they a combat fought,
  But such a dream were loathing:
Tom Thumb had got a little sup,
And Tomalin scarce kissed the cup,
Yet had their brains so sure locked up, 695
  That they remembered nothing.

Queen Mab and her light maids the while,
Amongst themselves do closely smile,
To see the king caught with this wile,
  With one another jesting: 700
And to the fairy court they went,
With mickle joy and merriment,
Which thing was done with good intent,
  And thus I left them feasting.

697 **light:** flighty, light-hearted

TO THE CAMBRO-BRITONS, AND THEIR HARP, HIS BALLAD OF AGINCOURT

FAIR stood the wind for France,
When we our sails advance,
Nor now to prove our chance,
  Longer will tarry;
But putting to the main, 5
At Caux, the mouth of Seine,
With all his martial train,
  Landed King Harry.

And taking many a fort,
Furnished in warlike sort, 10
Marcheth tow'rds Agincourt,
  In happy hour;
Skirmishing day by day,
With those that stopped his way,
Where the French gen'ral lay, 15
  With all his power.

Which in his height of pride,
King Henry to deride,
His ransom to provide
  To the king sending. 20
Which he neglects the while,
As from a nation vile,
Yet with an angry smile,
  Their fall portending.

And turning to his men, 25
Quoth our brave Henry then:
'Though they to one be ten,
  Be not amazèd.
Yet have we well begun,
Battles so bravely won, 30
Have ever to the sonne,
  By fame been raisèd.

TO THE CAMBRO-BRITONS, AND THEIR HARP, HIS BALLAD OF AGINCOURT:
Cambro-Britons: the Welsh (from *Cambria*, ancient name for
Wales) 8 **King Henry:** Henry V (1387–1422), king of England, who
defeated the French at Agincourt in 1415 31 **sonne:** sun

'And for myself,' quoth he,
'This me full rest shall be,
England ne'er mourn for me,   35
   Nor more esteem me.
Victor I will remain,
Or on this earth lie slain,
Never shall she sustain,
   Loss to redeem me.   40

'Poiters and Cressy tell,
When most their pride did swell,
Under our swords they fell,
   No less our skill is,
Than when our grandsire great,   45
Claiming the regal seat,
By many a warlike feat,
   Lopped the French lilies.'

The Duke of York so dread,
The eager vaward led;   50
With the main, Henry sped,
   Amongst his henchmen.
Exeter had the rear,
A braver man not there,
Oh Lord, how hot they were,   55
   On the false Frenchmen!

They now to fight are gone,
Armour on armour shone,
Drum now to drum did groan,
   To hear, was wonder;   60
That with cries they make,
The very earth did shake,
Trumpet to trumpet spake,
   Thunder to thunder.

Well it thine age became,   65
O noble Erpingham,
Which didst the signal aim,
   To our hid forces;
When from a meadow by,
Like a storm suddenly,   70
The English archery
   Stuck the French horses,

With Spanish yew so strong,
Arrows a cloth-yard long,
That like to serpents stung,   75
   Piercing the weather;
None from his fellow starts,
But playing manly parts,
And like true English hearts,
   Stuck close together.   80

When down their bows they threw,
And forth their bilbowes drew,
And on the French they flew,
   Not one was tardy;
Arms were from shoulders sent,   85
Scalps to the teeth were rent,
Down the French peasants went,
   Our men were hardy.

This while our noble king,
His broad sword brandishing,   90
Down the French host did ding,
   As to o'erwhelm it;
And many a deep wound lent,
His arms with blood besprent,
And many a cruel dent   95
   Bruised his helmet.

Gloucester, that duke so good,
Next of the royal blood,
For famous England stood,
   With his brave brother;   100
Clarence, in steel so bright,
Though but a maiden knight,
Yet in that furious fight,
   Scarce such another.

Warwick in blood did wade,   105
Oxford the foe invade,
And cruel slaughter made,
   Still as they ran up;
Suffolk his axe did ply,
Beaumont and Willoughby   110
Bare them right doughtily,
   Ferrers and Fanhope,

Upon Saint Crispin's day
Fought was this noble fray,
Which fame did not delay,   115
   To England to carry;
Oh, when shall English men
With such acts fill a pen,
Or England breed again,
   Such a King Harry?   120

[When Brownists banished be,
Sects and disloyalty,
Schism and popery,
   Then shall we flourish;
And when the great shall aim   125
True justice to maintain,
And shall employ their brain
   Virtue to nourish.]

---

41 **Poiters and Cressy:** two battles won by the English over the French, Poitiers in 1356, Crécy in 1346   50 **vaward:** forefront

82 **bilbowes:** swords   91 **ding:** strike   94 **besprent:** sprinkled
121 **Brownists:** followers of Robert Browne (*c*.1550–1633), an English Protestant religious leader who dissented from Anglicanism

CHRISTOPHER MARLOWE

THESE VERSES WERE MADE BY MICHAEL DRAYTON, ESQUIRE, POET LAUREATE, THE NIGHT BEFORE HE DIED

SO WELL I love thee as without thee I
Love nothing; if I might choose, I'd rather die
Than be one day debarred thy company.

Since beasts and plants do grow and live and move,
Beasts are those men that such a life approve: 5
He only lives that deadly is in love.

The corn, that in the ground is sown, first dies,
And of one seed do many ears arise;
Love, this world's corn, by dying multiplies.

The seeds of love first by thy eyes were thrown   10
Into a ground untilled, a heart unknown
To bear such fruit, till by thy hands 'twas sown.

Look as your looking-glass by chance may fall,
Divide, and break in many pieces small,
And yet shows forth the self-same face in all,   15

Proportions, features, graces, just the same,
And in the smallest piece as well the name
Of fairest one deserves as in the richest frame;

So all my thoughts are pieces but of you,
Which put together make a glass so true   20
As I therein no other's face but yours can view.

CHRISTOPHER MARLOWE

From OVID'S ELEGIES

IN summer's heat and mid-time of the day
To rest my limbs upon a bed I lay,
One window shut, the other open stood,
Which gave such light as twinkles in a wood,
Like twilight glimpse at setting of the sun   5
Or night being past, and yet not day begun.
Such light to shamefast maidens must be shown,
Where they may sport, and seem to be unknown.
Then came Corinna in a long loose gown,
Her white neck hid with tresses hanging down: 10
Resembling fair Semiramis going to bed
Or Lais of a thousand wooers sped.
I snatched her gown, being thin, the harm was small,
Yet strived she to be covered there withal.
And striving thus as one that would be cast,   15
Betrayed herself, and yielded at the last.
Stark naked as she stood before mine eye,
Not one wen in her body could I spy.
What arms and shoulders did I touch and see,
How apt her breasts were to be pressed by me?   20
How smooth a belly under her waist saw I?

How large a leg, and what a lusty thigh?
To leave the rest, all liked me passing well,
I clinged her naked body, down she fell,
Judge you the rest: being tired she bade me kiss,   25
Jove send me more such afternoons as this.

FROM OVID'S ELEGIES: 7 **shamefast:** shamefaced   11 **Semiramis:** a legendary Assyrian queen 12 **Lais . . . sped:** Lais (famous Greek courtesan) who had a thousand suitors 15 **cast:** released 23 **liked me:** pleased me 26 **Jove:** Jupiter, chief of the Roman gods

THE PASSIONATE SHEPHERD TO HIS LOVE

COME live with me, and be my love,
And we will all the pleasures prove,
That valleys, groves, hills and fields,
Woods, or steepy mountain yields.

And we will sit upon the rocks,   5
Seeing the shepherds feed their flocks
By shallow rivers, to whose falls
Melodious birds sing madrigals.

And I will make thee beds of roses,
And a thousand fragrant posies,   10
A cap of flowers, and a kirtle,
Embroidered all with leaves of myrtle.

I gown made of the finest wool,
Which from our pretty lambs we pull,
Fair linèd slippers for the cold,   15
With buckles of the purest gold.

A belt of straw and ivy buds,
With coral clasps and amber studs,
And if these pleasures may thee move,
Come live with me, and be my love.   20

The shepherds swains shall dance and sing
For thy delight each May morning.
If these delights thy mind may move,
Then live with me, and be my love.

THE PASSIONATE SHEPHERD TO HIS LOVE: 2 **prove:** try   11 **kirtle:** gown 21 **swains:** young men

HERO AND LEANDER

THE FIRST SESTIAD
ON Hellespont guilty of true-love's blood,
In view and opposite two cities stood,
Sea-borderers, disjoined by Neptune's might:
The one Abydos, the other Sestos hight.

HERO AND LEANDER: 1ST SESTIAD: 1 **Hellespont:** the Dardanelles **guilty of . . . blood:** Helle was drowned here, fleeing her mother-in-law 3 **disjointed . . . might:** separated by the power of the sea, of which Neptune was god 4 **hight:** was called

At Sestos, Hero dwelt; Hero the fair, 5
Whom young Apollo courted for her hair,
And offered as a dower his burning throne,
Where she should sit for men to gaze upon.
The outside of her garments were of lawn,
The lining purple silk, with gilt stars drawn. 10
Her wide sleeves green, and bordered with a grove,
Where Venus in her naked glory strove,
To please the careless and disdainful eyes
Of proud Adonis that before her lies.
Her kirtle blue, whereon was many a stain, 15
Made with the blood of wretched lovers slain.
Upon her head she wear a myrtle wreath,
From whence her veil reached to the ground beneath.
Her vail was artificial flowers and leaves,
Whose workmanship both man and beast deceives. 20
Many would praise the sweet smell as she passed,
When 'twas the odour which her breath forth cast,
And there for honey bees have sought in vain,
And. beat from thence, have lighted there again.
About her neck hung chains of pebble stone, 25
Which, lightened by her neck, like diamonds shone.
She wear no gloves, for neither sun nor wind
Would burn or parch her hands, but to her mind,
Or warm or cool them, for they took delight
To play upon those hands, they were so white. 30
Buskins of shells all silvered usèd she,
And branched with blushing coral to the knee;
Where sparrows perched, of hollow pearl and gold,
Such as the world would wonder to behold:
Those with sweet water oft her handmaid fills, 35
Which as she went would chirrup through the bills.
Some say, for her the fairest Cupid pined,
And, looking in her face, was strooken blind.
But this is true, so like was one the other,
As he imagined Hero was his mother. 40
And oftentimes into her bosom flew,
About her naked neck his bare arms threw,
And laid his childish head upon her breast,
And, with still panting rocked, there took his rest.
So lovely fair was Hero, Venus' nun, 45
As nature wept, thinking she was undone;
Because she took more from her than she left,
And of such wondrous beauty was bereft:
Therefore in sign her treasure suffered wrack,
Since Hero's time hath half the world been black. 50
Amorous Leander, beautiful and young,
(Whose tragedy divine Musaeus sung)
Dwelt at Abydos: since him dwelt there none
For whom succeeding times make greater moan.
His dangling tresses that were never shorn, 55
Had they been cut, and unto Colchos borne,

Would have allured the vent'rous youth of Greece
To hazard more than for the Golden Fleece.
Fair Cynthia wished his arms might be her sphere,
Grief makes her pale, because she moves not there. 60
His body was as straight as Circe's wand,
Jove might have sipped out nectar from his hand.
Even as delicious meat is to the taste,
So was his neck in touching, and surpassed
The white of Pelops' shoulder. I could tell ye 65
How smooth his breast was, and how white his belly,
And whose immortal fingers did imprint
That heavenly path with many a curious dint
That runs along his back, but my rude pen
Can hardly blazon forth the loves of men, 70
Much less of powerful gods: let it suffice
That my slack muse sings of Leander's eyes,
Those orient cheeks and lips, exceeding his
That leapt into the water for a kiss
Of his own shadow, and, despising many, 75
Died ere he could enjoy the love of any.
Had wild Hippolytus Leander seen,
Enamoured of his beauty had he been,
His presence made the rudest peasant melt,
That in the vast uplandish country dwelt, 80
The barbarous Thracian soldier, moved with nought,
Was moved with him, and for his favour sought.
Some swore he was a man in maid's attire,
For in his looks were all that men desire,
A pleasant smiling cheek, a speaking eye, 85
A brow for love to banquet royally.
And such as knew he was a man would say,
'Leander, thou art made for amorous play:
Why art thou not in love, and loved of all?
Though thou be fare, yet be not thine own thrall.' 90
    The men of wealthy Sestos, every year,
(For his sake whom their goddess held so dear,
Rose-cheeked Adonis) kept a solemn feast.
Thither resorted many a wand'ring guest,
To meet their loves; such as had none at all, 95
Came lovers home from this great festival.
For every street like to a firmament
Glistered with breathing stars, who where they went
Frighted the melancholy earth, which deemed
Eternal heaven to burn, for so it seemed, 100
As if another Phaëthon had got
The guidance of the sun's rich chariot.

---

59 **Cynthia:** the moon 61 **Circe:** a sorceress who tried to enchant Odysseus 62 **Jove:** Jupiter, chief god of the Romans 65 **Pelops:** a mythical Greek king after whom the Pelopponese was named 73 **orient:** bright 73–5 **his that . . . shadow:** Narcissus, a beautiful youth who fell in love with his own reflection in a fountain 77 **Hippolytus:** son of Theseus, king of Athens 80 **uplandish:** highland 81 **Thracian:** belonging to Thrace, a region between northern Greece and the Black Sea 90 **thrall:** slave 93 **Adonis:** a beautiful youth loved by the goddess Aphrodite 98 **glistered:** glittered 101 **Phaëthon:** son of the sun-god, Phoebus, who disastrously once took charge of his father's chariot, which carried the sun across the sky

---

15 **kirtle:** gown 17 **wear:** wore 31 **buskins:** boots 45 **Venus' nun:** priestess of Venus 52 **Musaeus:** the ancient Greek poet on whose work Marlowe based this poem 56 **Colchos:** Colchis, in Greek myth, the location of the Golden Fleece

But far above the loveliest Hero shined,
And stole away th' enchanted gazer's mind,
For like sea-nymphs' inveigling harmony,   105
So was her beauty to the standers-by.
Nor that night-wand'ring pale and wat'ry star
(When yawning dragons draw her thirling car
From Latmos' mount up to the gloomy sky,
Where crowned with blazing light and majesty,   110
She proudly sits) more over-rules the flood,
Than she the hearts of those that near her stood.
Even as, when gaudy nymphs pursue the chase,
Wretched Ixion's shaggy-footed race,
Incensed with savage heat, gallop amain   115
From steep pine-bearing mountains to the plain:
So ran the people forth to gaze upon her,
And all that viewed her were enamoured on her.
And as in fury of a dreadful fight,
Their fellows being slain or put to flight,   120
Poor soldiers stand with fear of death dead strooken,
So at her presence all surprised and tooken,
Await the sentence of her scornful eyes:
He whom she favours lives, the other dies.
There might you see one sigh, another rage,   125
And some (their violent passions to assuage)
Compile sharp satires, but alas too late,
For faithful love will never turn to hate.
But many, seeing great princes were denied,
Pined as they went, and thinking on her died.   130
On this feast day – oh, cursed day and hour! –
Went Hero thorough Sestos, from her tower
To Venus' temple, where unhappily,
As after chanced, they did each other spy.
So fair a church as this had Venus none,   135
The walls were of discoloured jasper stone,
Wherein was Proteus carved, and o'erhead
A lively vine of green sea agate spread;
Where by one hand light-headed Bacchus hung,
And with the other, wine from grapes out-wrung.   140
Of crystal shining fair the pavement was,
The town of Sestos called it Venus' glass.
There might you see the gods in sundry shapes
Committing heady riots, incest, rapes:
For know that underneath this radiant floor   145
Was Danaë's statue in a brazen tower,
Jove slyly stealing from his sister's bed
To dally with Idalian Ganymed,
And for his love Europa bellowing loud,
And tumbling with the rainbow in a cloud: 150

Blood-quaffing Mars heaving the iron net,
Which limping Vulcan and his Cyclops set:
Love kindling fire, to burn such towns as Troy,
Sylvanus weeping for the lovely boy
That now is turned into a cypress tree,   155
Under whose shade the wood-gods love to be.
And in the midst a silver altar stood;
There Hero sacrificing turtles' blood,
Vailed to the ground, vailing her eyelids close,
And modestly they opened as she rose: 160
Thence flew Love's arrow with the golden head,
And thus Leander was enamourèd.
Stone still he stood, and evermore he gazed,
Till with the fire that from his count'nance blazed
Relenting Hero's gentle heart was strook,   165
Such force and virtue hath an amorous look.
    It lies not in our power to love or hate,
For will in us is overruled by fate.
When two are stripped long ere the course begin,
We wish that one should lose, the other win;   170
And one especially do we affect
Of two gold ingots like in each respect.
The reason no man knows; let it suffice
What we behold is censured by our eyes.
Where both deliberate, the love is slight.   175
Who ever loved that loved not at first sight?
    He kneeled, but unto her devoutly prayed;
Chaste Hero to herself thus softly said:
'Were I the saint he worships, I would hear him,'
And as she spake those words, came somewhat near
    him.   180
He started up, she blushed as one ashamed;
Wherewith Leander much more was inflamed.
He touched her hand, in touching it she trembled,
Love deeply grounded, hardly is dissembled.
These lovers parlied by the touche of hands,   185
True love is mute, and oft amazèd stands.
While thus dumb signs their yielding hearts entangled,
The air with sparks of living fire was spangled,
And night deep drenched in misty Acheron
Heaved up her head, and half the world upon   190
Breathed darkness forth (dark night is Cupid's day).
And now begins Leander to display
Love's holy fire, with words, with sighs and tears,
Which like sweet music entered Hero's ears,
And yet at every word she turned aside,   195
And always cut him off as he replied.
At last, like to a bold sharp sophister,
With cheerful hope thus he accosted her.

---

107 **night-wand'ring . . . star:** the moon 108 **thirling car:** vibrating chariot 114 **Ixion's shaggy-footed race:** in Greek myth Ixion was a king who was father of the Centaurs 121 **strooken:** struck 122 **tooken:** taken 137 **Proteus:** Neptune's herdsman 139 **Bacchus:** Roman god of wine 146 **Danaë:** a Greek princess whose father locked her in a tower, but to whom Zeus gained access in the form of a shower of gold **brazen:** made of brass 148 **Ganymed:** Ganymede, a beautiful Trojan youth **Idalian:** belonging to Aphrodite, to whom Idalium in Cyprus was sacred 149 **Europa:** a maiden who was carried off by Zeus in the form of a bull

151 **blood-quaffing Mars:** the Roman god of war 152 **Vulcan:** the lame Roman god of fire and metalworking **Cyclops:** a race of one-eyed giants who assisted Vulcan 154 **Sylvanus:** in classical mythology, a woodland deity 158 **turtles:** turtledoves 159 **vailed:** veiled 165 **strook:** struck 169 **When two . . . begin:** when two athletes have undressed before running a race 185 **parlied:** spoke 189 **Acheron:** in Greek myth, a river in the underworld 197 **sophister:** a sophist, a person who uses persuasive but false reasoning

'Fair creature, let me speak without offence,
I would my rude words had the influence 200
To lead thy thoughts as thy fair looks do mine,
Then shouldst thou be his prisoner who is thine.
Be not unkind and fair, misshapen stuff
Are of behaviour boisterous and rough.
Oh, shun me not, but hear me ere you go, 205
God knows I cannot force love, as you do.
My words shall be as spotless as my youth,
Full of simplicity and naked truth.
This sacrifice (whose sweet perfume descending,
From Venus' altar to your footsteps bending) 210
Doth testify that you exceed her far,
To whom you offer, and whose nun you are.
Why should you worship her? Her you surpass,
As much as sparkling diamonds flaring glass.
A diamond set in lead his worth retains, 215
A heavenly nymph, beloved of human swains,
Receives no blemish, but oft-times more grace,
Which makes me hope, although I am but base,
Base in respect of thee, divine and pure,
Dutiful service may thy love procure, 220
And I in duty will excel all other,
As thou in beauty dost exceed love's mother.
Nor heaven nor thou were made to gaze upon,
As heaven preserves all things, so save thou one.
A stately builded ship, well rigged and tall, 225
That Ocean maketh more majestical:
Why vow'st thou, then, to live in Sestos here,
Who on Love's seas more glorious wouldst appear?
Like untuned golden strings all women are,
Which long time lie untouched, will harshly jar. 230
Vessels of brass oft handled, brightly shine,
What difference betwixt the richest mine
And basest mould, but use? for both, not used,
Are of like worth. Then treasure is abused,
When misers keep it: being put to loan, 235
In time it will return us two for one.
Rich robes themselves and others do adorn,
Neither themselves nor others, if not worn.
Who builds a palace and rams up the gate,
Shall see it ruinous and desolate. 240
Ah, simple Hero, learn thy self to cherish,
Lone women like to empty houses perish.
Less sins the poor rich man that starves himself,
In heaping up a mass of drossy pelf,
Than such as you: his golden earth remains, 245
Which after his decease some other gains.
But this fair gem, sweet in the loss alone,
When you fleet hence, can be bequeathed to none.
Or if it could, down from th' enamelled sky
All heaven would come to claim this legacy, 250
And with intestine broils the world destroy,
And quite confound nature's sweet harmony.

Well, therefore, by the gods decreed it is,
We human creatures should enjoy that bliss
One is no number, maids are nothing then, 255
Without the sweet society of men.
Wilt thou live single still? One shalt thou be,
Though never-singling Hymen couple thee.
Wild savages, that drink of running springs,
Think water far excels all earthly things: 260
But they that daily taste neat wine despise it.
Virginity, albeit some highly prize it,
Compared with marriage, had you tried them both,
Differs as much as wine and water doth.
Base bullion for the stamp's sake we allow, 265
Even so for men's impression do we you,
By which alone, our reverend fathers say,
Women receive perfection every way.
This idol which you term Virginity
Is neither essence subject to the eye, 270
No, nor to any one exterior sense,
Nor hath it any place of residence,
Nor is 't of earth or mould celestial,
Or capable of any form at all.
Of that which hath no being do not boast, 275
Things that are not at all are never lost.
Men foolishly do call it virtuous,
What virtue is it that is born with us?
Much less can honour be ascribed thereto,
Honour is purchased by the deeds we do. 280
Believe me, Hero, honour is not won
Until some honourable deed be done.
Seek you for chastity, immortal fame,
And know that some have wronged Diana's name?
Whose name is it, if she be false or not, 285
So she be fair, but some vile tongues will blot?
But you are fair (aye me!), so wondrous fair,
So young, so gentle, and so debonair,
As Greec will think, if thus you live alone,
Some one or other keeps you as his own. 290
Then, Hero, hate me not, nor from me fly,
To follow swiftly blasting infamy.
Perhaps thy sacred priesthood makes thee loath,
Tell me, to whom mad'st thou that heedless oath?'
'To Venus,' answered she, and as she spake, 295
Forth from those two translucent cisterns break
A stream of liquid pearl, which down her face
Made milk-white paths, whereon the gods might trace
To Jove's high court. He thus replied: 'The rites
In which Love's beauteous empress most delights 300
Are banquets, Doric music, midnight revel,
Plays, masques, and all that stern age counteth evil.
Thee as a holy idiot doth she scorn,
For thou in vowing chastity hast sworn
To rob her name and honour, and thereby 305

---

222 **love's mother:** Venus, mother of Cupid 244 **pelf:** riches, money
248 **fleet:** to flit, go quickly 251 **intestine broils:** mutually destructive
quarrels

258 **Hymen:** god of marriage 260 **fare:** far 265 **Base bullion . . .
allow:** impure gold or silver is still accepted as money because of
what is stamped on it 296 **translucent cisterns:** eyes

Commit'st a sin far worse than perjury,
Even sacrilege against her deity,
Through regular and formal purity.
To expiate which sin, kiss and shake hands,
Such sacrifice as this Venus demands.'   310
    Thereat she smiled, and did deny him so,
As put thereby, yet might he hope for moe.
Which makes him quickly reinforce his speech,
And her in humble manner thus beseech:
    'Though neither gods nor men may thee deserve,
Yet for her sake whom you have vowed to serve   316
Abandon fruitless cold virginity,
The gentle queen of love's sole enemy.
Then shall you most resemble Venus' nun,
When Venus' sweet rites are performed and done. 320
Flint-breasted Pallas joys in single life,
But Pallas and your mistress are at strife.
Love, Hero, then, and be not tyrannous,
But heal the heart that thou hast wounded thus,
Nor stain thy youthful years with avarice,   325
Fair fools delight to be accounted nice.
The richest corn dies, if it be not reaped,
Beauty alone is lost, too warily kept.'
These arguments he used, and many more,
Wherewith she yielded that was was won before. 330
Hero's looks yielded, but her words made war,
Women are won when they begin to jar.
Thus having swallowed Cupid's golden hook,
The more she strived, the deeper was she strook.
Yet evilly faining anger, strove she still,   335
And would be thought to grant against her will.
So, having paused a while, at last she said:
'Who taught thee rhetoric to deceive a maid?
Aye me! such words as these I should abhor,
And yet I like them for the orator.'   340
    With that Leander stooped to have embraced her,
But from his spreading arms away she cast her,
And thus bespake him: 'Gentle youth, forbear
To touch the sacred garments which I wear.
Upon a rock, and underneath a hill,   345
Far from the town (where all is whist and still,
Save that the sea playing on yellow sand,
Sends forth a rattling murmur to the land,
Whose sound allures the golden Morpheus
In silence of the night to visit us.)   350
My turret stands, and there God knows I play
With Venus' swans and sparrows all the day.
A dwarfish beldame bears me company,
That hops about the chamber where I lie,
And spends the night (that might be better spent) 355
In vain discourse and apish merriment.
Come thither.' As she spake this, her tongue tripped,
For unawares 'Come thither' from her slipped,

And suddenly her former colour changed,
And here and there her eyes through anger ranged.
And like a planet mooving several ways   361
At one self instant, she poor soul assays,
Loving, not to love at all, and every part
Strove to resist the motions of her heart.
And hands so pure, so innocent, nay such   365
As might have made heaven stoop to have a touch,
Did she uphold to Venus, and again
Vowed spotless chastity, but all in vain.
Cupid beats down her prayers with his wings,
Her vows above the empty air he flings: 370
All deep enraged, his sinewy bow he bent,
And shot a shaft that burning from him went,
Wherewith she strooken looked so dolefully
As made Love sigh, to see his tyranny.
And as she wept, her tears to pearl he turned, 375
And wound them on his arm, and for her mourned.
Then towards the palace of the Destinies,
Laden with languishment and grief he flies,
And to those stern nymphs humbly made request,
Both might enjoy each other, and be blessed.   380
But with a ghastly dreadful countenance,
Threat'ning a thousand deaths at every glance,
They answered Love, nor would vouchsafe so much
As one poor word, their hate to him was such.
Harken a while, and I will tell you why: 385
Heaven's wingèd herald, Jove-born Mercury,
The self-same day that he asleep had laid
Enchanted Argus, spied a country maid,
Whose careless hair, instead of pearl t' adorn it,
Glistered with dew, as one that seemed to scorn it: 390
Her breath as fragrant as the morning rose,
Her mind pure, and her tongue untaught to glose.
Yet proud she was (for lofty pride that dwells
In towered courts is oft in shepherds' cells.)
And too too well the fair vermilion knew,   395
And silver tincture of her cheeks, that drew
The love of every swain: On her, this god
Enamoured was, and with his snaky rod
Did charm her nimble feet, and made her stay,
The while upon a hillock down he lay,   400
And sweetly on his pipe began to play,
And with smooth speech her fancy to assay,
Till in his twining arms he locked her fast,
And then we wooed with kisses, and at last,
As shepherds do, her on the ground he laid,   405
And tumbling in the grass, he often strayed
Beyond the bounds of shame, in being bold
To eye those parts which no eye should behold.
And like an insolent commanding lover,
Boasting his parentage, would needs discover   410

312 **moe:** more 321 **Pallas:** the goddess Athene 332 **jar:** to be
inconsistent 342 **she cast her:** she threw herself 346 **whist:** quiet
349 **Morpheus:** god of dreams 353 **beldame:** old woman 357 **thither:**
there

361 **planet:** in medieval astronomy, a star that is not fixed but
wanders 362 **assays:** tries 388 **Argus:** a hundred-eyed giant who was
charmed to sleep by Mercury 392 **glose:** flatter, speak insincerely
398 **snaky rod:** Mercury bore a caduceus, a white wand with two
snakes coiled around it

The way to new Elysium: but she,
Whose only dower was her chastity,
Having striv'n in vain, was now about to cry,
And crave the help of shepherds that were nigh.
Herewith he stayed his fury, and began   415
To give her leave to rise: away she ran,
After went Mercury, who used such cunning,
As she to hear his tale, left off her running.
Maids are not won by brutish force and might,
But speeches full of pleasure and delight.   420
And knowing Hermes courted her, was glad
That she such loveliness and beauty had
As could provoke his liking, yet was mute,
And neither would deny nor grant his suit.
Still vowed he love, she wanting no excuse   425
To feed him with delays, as women use,
Or thirsting after immortality, –
All women are ambitious naturally, –
Imposed upon her lover such a task
As he ought not perform, nor yet she ask.   430
A draught of flowing nectar she requested,
Wherewith the king of gods and men is feasted.
He ready to accomplish what she willed,
Stole some from Hebe (Hebe Jove's cup filled),
And gave it to his simple rustic love,   435
Which being known (as what is hid from Jove?)
He inly stormed, and waxed more furious
Than for the fire filched by Prometheus,
And thrusts him down from heaven: he wand'ring
     here,
In mournful terms, with sad and heavy cheer   440
Complained to Cupid. Cupid for his sake,
To be revenged on Jove did undertake,
And those on whom heaven, earth, and hell relies,
I mean the Adamantine Destinies,
He wounds with love, and forced them equally   445
To dote upon deceitful Mercury.
They offered him the deadly fatal knife,
That shears the slender threads of human life,
At his fair feathered feet the engines laid,
Which th' earth from ugly Chaos' den up-weighed: 450
These he regarded not, but did entreat,
That Jove, usurper of his father's seat,
Might presently be banished into hell,
And aged Saturn in Olympus dwell.
They granted what he craved, and once again   455
Saturn and Ops began their golden reign.

Murder, rape, war, lust and treachery,
Were with Jove closed in Stygian empery.
But long this blessèd time continued not:
As soon as he his wishèd purpose got,   460
He reckless of his promise did despise
The love of th' everlasting Destinies.
They seeing it, both Love and him abhorred,
And Jupiter unto his place restored.
And but that Learning, in despite of Fate,   465
Will mount aloft, and enter heaven gate,
And to the seat of Jove itself advance,
Hermes had slept in hell with Ignorance,
Yet as a punishment they added this,
That he and Poverty should always kiss.   470
And to this day is every scholar poor,
Gross gold from them runs headlong to the boor.
Likewise the angry sisters thus deluded,
To venge themselves on Hermes, have concluded
That Midas' brood shall sit in Honour's chair,   475
To which the Muses' sons are only heir:
And fruitful wits that in aspiring are,
Shall discontent run into regions far;
And few great lords in virtuous deeds shall joy,
But be surprised with every garish toy;   480
And still enrich the lofty servile clown,
Who with encroaching guile keeps learning down
Then muse not Cupid's suit no better sped,
Seeing in their loves the Fates were injurèd.

THE SECOND SESTIAD

By this, sad Hero, with love unacquainted,
Viewing Leander's face, fell down and fainted.
He kissed her, and breathed life into her lips,
Wherewith as one displeased, away she trips.
Yet as she went, full often looked behind,   5
And many poor excuses did she find
To linger by the way, and once she stayed,
And would have turned again, but was afraid,
In off'ring parley, to be counted light.
So on she goes, and in her idle flight,   10
Her painted fan of curlèd plumes let fall,
Thinking to train Leander therewithal.
He being a novice, knew not what she meant,
But stayed, and after her a letter sent,
Which joyful Hero answered in such sort,   15
As he had hope to scale the beauteous fort,
Wherein the liberal graces locked their wealth,
And therefore to her tower he got by stealth.
Wide open stood the door, he need not climb,
And she herself before the 'pointed time   20

---

411 **Elysium:** in Greek mythology, Paradise, the abode of the blessed 412 **dower:** dowry 421 **Hermes:** the Greek equivalent of Mercury 431 **nectar:** the drink of the gods 434 **Hebe:** cup-bearer to the gods 438 **Prometheus:** a Titan who stole fire from the gods to give it to humankind 440 **cheer:** frame of mind, disposition 444 **Adamantine:** immovable **Destinies:** Destinies, ie the Fates, three goddesses who, in classical myth, decide the destinies of human beings 449 **engines:** tools, devices 450 **Chaos:** in Greek myth, the first created being 452 **Jove . . . seat:** Jove (Jupiter) deposed his father, Kronus (Saturn) 456 **Ops:** wife of Saturn

458 **Stygian:** relating to the Styx, river in the underworld **empery:** empire 475–8 **That Midas' brood . . . far:** in Greek myth Midas was a king who, amongst other things, was given asses' ears as a punishment by Apollo. Therefore, his brood refers to asses, which Marlowe says occupy the throne of honour which rightfully belongs to poets (**Muses' sons**), causing those with creative minds (**fruitful wits**) to go into exile 2ND SESTIAD 7 **stayed:** stopped 9 **light:** frivolous 12 **train:** allure, draw on

Had spread the board, with roses strowed the room,
And oft looked out, and mused he did not come.
At last he came. Oh, who can tell the greeting
These greedy lovers had at their first meeting.
He asked, she gave, and nothing was denied, 25
Both to each other quickly were affied.
Look how their hands, so were their hearts united,
And what he did she willingly requited.
(Sweet are the kisses, the embracements sweet,
When like desires and affections meet, 30
For from the earth to heaven is Cupid raised,
Where fancy is in equal balance peised)
Yet she this rashness suddenly repented,
And turned aside, and to herself lamented,
As if her name and honour had been wronged, 35
By being possessed of him for whom she longed:
Ay, and she wished, albeit not from her heart,
That he would leave her turret and depart.
The mirthful god of amorous pleasure smiled,
To see how he this captive nymph beguiled. 40
For hitherto he did but fan the fire,
And kept it down that it might mount the higher.
Now waxed she jealous, lest his love abated,
Fearing her own thoughts made her to be hated.
Therefore unto him hastily she goes, 45
And like light Salmacis, her body throes
Upon his bosom, where with yielding eyes
She offers up herself in sacrifice,
To slake his anger if he were displeased.
Oh, what god would not therewith be appeased? 50
Like Aesop's cock, his jewel he enjoyed,
And as a brother with his sister toyed,
Supposing nothing else was to be done.
Now he her favour and goodwill had won.
But know you not that creatures wanting sense 55
By nature have a mutual appetence,
And wanting organs to advance a step,
Moved by Love's force, unto each other lep?
Much more in subjects having intellect,
Some hidden influence breeds like effect. 60
Albeit Leander rude in love, and raw,
Long dallying with Hero, nothing saw
That might delight him more, yet he suspected
Some amorous rites or other were neglected.
Therefore unto his body hers he clung, 65
She, fearing on the rushes to be flung,
Strived with redoubled strength: the more she strived,
The more a gentle pleasing heat revived,
Which taught him all that elder lovers know,
And now the same 'gan so to scorch and glow, 70

As in plain terms (yet cunningly) he craved it,
Love always makes those eloquent that have it.
She, with a king of granting, put him by it,
And ever as he thought himself most nigh it,
Like to the tree of Tantalus she fled, 75
And seeming lavish, saved her maidenhead.
Ne'er king more sought to keep his diadem
Than Hero this inestimable gem.
Above our life we love a steadfast friend,
Yet when a token of great worth we send, 80
We often kiss it, often look thereon,
And stay the messenger that would be gone:
No marvel, then, though Hero would not yield
So soon to part from that she dearly held.
Jewels being lost are found again, this never, 85
'Tis lost but once, and once lost, lost for ever.
    Now had the morn espied her lover's steeds,
Whereat she starts, puts on her purple weeds,
And red for anger that he stayed so long,
All headlong throws herself the clouds among, 90
And now Leander fearing to be missed,
Embraced her suddenly, took leave, and kissed.
Long was he taking leave, and loath to go,
And kissed again, as lovers use to do.
Sad Hero wrung him by the hand, and wept, 95
Saying, 'Let your vows and promises be kept.'
Then standing at the door, she turned about,
As loath to see Leander going out.
And now the sun that through th' horizon peeps,
As pitying these lovers, downward creeps, 100
So that in silence of the cloudy night,
Though it was morning, did he take his flight.
But what the secret trusty night concealed
Leander's amorous habit soon revealed,
With Cupid's myrtle was his bonnet crowned, 105
About his arms the purple riband wound,
Wherewith she wreathed her largely spreading hair,
Nor could the youth abstain, but he must wear
The sacred ring wherewith she was endowed,
When first religious chastity she vowed: 110
Which made his love through Sestos to be known,
And thence unto Abydos sooner blown
Than he could sail, for incorporeal Fame,
Whose weight consists in nothing but her name,
Is swifter than the wind, whose tardy plumes 115
Are reeking water and dull earthly fumes.
Home when he came, he seemed not to be there,
But like exilèd air thrust from his sphere,
Set in a foreign place, and straight from thence,
Alcides-like, by mighty violence 120
He would have chased away the swelling main,
That him from her unjustly did detain.
Like as the sun in a diameter,

---

21 **spread the board:** laid the table 26 **affied:** betrothed 30 **like:** similar, equal 32 **peised:** weighed 46 **Salmacis:** in Greek myth, a nymph who loved Hermaphrodite and prayed to become united with him in one body (which was granted) **throes:** throws 51 **Aesop's cock:** in one of Aesop's fables a cock finds a jewel but rejects it in favour of an ear of barley 58 **lep:** leap 61 **rude:** unskilful 66 **rushes:** ie, used as floor-coverings

75 **tree of Tantalus:** in Greek myth, a king punished by the gods by being made to stand in water that retreated when he tried to drink, under a tree whose fruit recoiled when he tried to eat 88 **weeds:** clothes 120 **Alcides:** Hercules 123 **in a diameter:** shining directly down

Fires and inflames objects removèd far,
And heateth kindly, shining lat'rally: 125
So beauty, sweetly quickens when 'tis nigh,
But being separated and removed,
Burns where it cherished, murders where it loved.
Therefore even as an index to a book,
So to his mind was young Leander's look.   130
Oh, none but gods have power their love to hide,
Affection by the count'nance is descried.
The light of hidden fire itself discovers,
And love that is concealed betrays poor lovers.
His secret flame apparently was seen,   135
Leander's father knew where he had been,
And for the same mildly rebuked his son,
Thinking to quench the sparkles new-begun.
But love resisted once, grows passionate,
And nothing more than counsel lovers hate.   140
For as a hot proud horse highly disdains
To have his head controlled, but breaks the reins,
Spits forth the ringled bit, and with his hooves
Checks the submissive ground: so he that loves,
The more he is restrained, the worse he fares.   145
What is it now, but mad Leander dares?
'Oh, Hero, Hero,' thus he cried full oft,
And then he got him to a rock aloft,
Where having spied her tower, long stared he on't,
And prayed the narrow toiling Hellespont   150
To part in twain, that he might come and go,
But still the rising billows answered no.
With that he stripped him to the iv'rie skin,
And crying, 'Love, I come,' leapt lively in.
Whereat the sapphire-visaged god grew proud,   155
And made his cap'ring Triton sound aloud,
Imagining that Ganymed displeased,
Had left the heavens; therefore on him he seized.
Leander strived, the waves about him wound,
And pulled him to the bottom, where the ground   160
Was strewed with pearl, and in low coral groves
Sweet-singing mermaids, sported with their loves
On heaps of heavy gold, and took great pleasure
To spurn in careless sort the shipwrack treasure.
For here the stately azure palace stood,   165
Where kingly Neptune and his train abode.
The lusty god embraced him, called him 'love',
And swore he never should return to Jove.
But when he knew it was not Ganymed,
For under water he was almost dead,   170
He heaved him up, and looking on his face,
Beat down the bold waves with his triple mace,
Which mounted up, intending to have kissed him,
And fell in drops like tears, because they missed him.
Leander being up, began to swim,   175
And looking back, saw Neptune follow him,
Whereat aghast, the poor soul 'gan to cry,

'Oh, let me visit Hero ere I die.'
The god put Helle's bracelet on his arm,
And swore the sea should never do him harm.   180
He clapped his plump cheeks, with his tresses played,
And smiling wantonly, his love bewrayed.
He watched his arms, and as they opened wide,
At every stroke, betwixt them would he slide,
And steal a kiss, and then run out and dance,   185
And as he turned, cast many a lustful glance,
And threw him gaudy toys to please his eye,
And dive into the water, and there pry
Upon his breast, his thighs, and every limb,
And up again, and close beside him swim,   190
And talk of love: Leander made reply,
'You are deceived, I am no woman I.'
Thereat smiled Neptune, and then told a tale,
How that a shepherd sitting in a vale
Played with a boy so fair and kind,   195
As for his love both earth and heaven pined;
That of the cooling river durst not drink,
Lest water-nymphs should pull him from the brink.
And when he sported in the fragrant lawns,
Goat-footed satyrs and up-staring fauns   200
Would steal him thence. Ere half this tale was done,
'Aye me!' Leander cried, 'th' enamoured sun,
That now should shine on Thetis' glassy bower,
Descends upon my radiant Hero's tower.
Oh, that these tardy arms of mine were wings!'   205
And as he spake, upon the waves he springs
Neptune was angry that he gave no ear,
And in his heart revenging malice bear:
He flung at him his mace, but as it went,
He called it in, for love made him repent.   210
He mace returning back his own hand hit,
As meaning to be venged for darting it.
When this fresh bleeding wound Leander viewed,
His colour went and came, as if he rued
The grief which Neptune felt. In gentle breasts,   215
Relenting thoughts, remorse and pity rests.
And who have hard hearts, and obdurate minds,
But vicious, hare-brained, and illit'rate hinds?
The god seeing him with pity to be moved,
Thereon concluded that he was beloved.   220
(Love is too full of faith, too credulous,
With folly and false hope deluding us.)
Wherefore Leander's fancy to surprise,
To the rich Ocean for gifts he flies.
'Tis wisdom to give much, a gift prevails,   225
When deep persuading oratory fails.
By this Leander being near the land,
Cast down his weary feet, and felt the sand.
Breathless albeit he were, he rested not,
Till to the solitary tower he got,   230
And knocked and called, at which celestial noise
The longing heart of Hero much more joys

144 **checks:** marks 155 **sapphire-visaged god:** green-faced god,
Neptune 156 **Triton:** a son of Neptune who blows through a shell
to make the ocean roar

182 **bewrayed:** betrayed 203 **Thetis:** a goddess of the sea 218 **hinds:**
peasants

Than nymphs and shepherds, when the timbrel rings,
Or crooked dolphin when the sailor sings;
She stayed not for her robes, but straight arose, 235
And drunk with gladness, to the door she goes,
Where seeing a naked man, she screeched for fear,
Such sights as this to tender maids are rare,
And ran into the dark herself to hide.
Rich jewels in the dark are soonest spied. 240
Unto her was he led, or rather drawn,
By those white limbs, which sparkled through the
   lawn.
The nearer that he came, the more she fled,
And seeking refuge, slipped into her bed.
Whereon Leander sitting, thus began, 245
Through numbing cold all feeble, faint and wan:
  'If not for love, yet love, for pity sake,
Me in thy bed and maiden bosom take.
At least vouchsafe these arms some little room,
Who hoping to embrace thee, cheerly swum. 250
This head was beat with many a churlish billow,
And therefore let it rest upon thy pillow.'
Herewith affrighted Hero shrunk away,
And in her lukewarm place Leander lay.
Whose lively heat like fire from heaven fet, 255
Would animate gross clay, and higher set
The drooping thoughts of base declining souls,
Than dreary Mars carousing nectar bowls.
His hands he cast upon her like a snare,
She overcome with shame and sallow fear, 260
Like chaste Diana, when Actaeon spied her,
Being suddenly betrayed, dived down to hide her.
And as her silver body downward went,
With both her hands she made the bed a tent,
And in her own mind thought herself secure, 265
O'ercast with dim and darksome coverture.
And now she lets him whisper in her ear,
Flatter, entreat, promise, protest and swear,
Yet ever as he greedily assayed
To touch those dainties, she the harpy played, 270
And every limb did as a soldier stout,
Defend the fort, and keep the foeman out.
For though the rising iv'rie mount he scaled,
Which is with azure circling lines impaled,
Much like a globe (a globe may I term this, 275
By which love sails to regions full of bliss),
Yet there with Sisyphus he toiled in vain,
Till gentle parley did the truce obtain.
Wherein Leander on her quivering breast,
Breathless spoke something, and sighèd out the rest;
Which so prevailed, as he with small ado 281
Enclosed her in his arms and kissed her too.

And every kiss to her was as a charm,
And to Leander as a fresh alarm,
So that the truce was broke, and she alas, 285
(Poor silly maiden) at his mercy was.
Love is not full of pity (as men say)
But deaf and cruel, where he means to prey.
Even as a bird, which in our hands we wring,
Forth plungeth, and oft flutters with her wing, 290
She trembling strove, this strife of hers (like that
Which made the world) another world begat
Of unknown joy. Treason was in her thought,
And cunningly to yield herself she sought.
Seeming not won, yet won she was at length, 295
In such wars women use but half their strength.
Leander now like Theban Hercules,
Entered the orchard of th' Hesperides,
Whose fruit none rightly can describe but he
That pulls or shakes it from the golden tree: 300
And now she wished this night were never done,
And sighed to think upon th' approaching sun,
For much it grieved her that the bright day-light
Should know the pleasure of this blessèd night,
And them like Mars and Ericine display, 305
Both in each other's arms chained as they lay.
Again she knew not how to frame her look,
Or speak to him who in a moment took
That which so long so charily she kept,
And fain by stealth away she would have crept, 310
And to some corner secretly have gone,
Leaving Leander in the bed alone.
But as her naked feet were whipping out,
He on the sudden clinged her so about,
That mermaid-like unto the floor she slid, 315
One half appeared, the other half was hid.
Thus near the bed she blushing stood upright,
And from her countenance behold ye might
A kind of twilight break, which through the hair,
As from an orient cloud, glimpse here and there. 320
And round about the chamber this false morn
Brought forth the day before the day was born.
So Hero's ruddy cheek Hero betrayed,
And her all naked to his sight displayed,
Whence his admiring eyes more pleasure took 325
Than Dis, on heaps of gold fixing his look.
By this Apollo's golden harp began
To sound forth music to the Oceän,
Which watchful Hesperus no sooner heard,
But he the day bright-bearing Car prepared, 330
And ran before, as harbinger of light,
And with his flaring beams mocked ugly night,
Till she o'ercome with anguish, shame, and rage,
Danged down to hell her loathsome carriage.

---

233 **timbrel:** tambourine 242 **lawn:** linen 255 **fet:** fetched 261 **Like chaste . . . her:** Actaeon was a huntsman who surprised the goddess Diana bathing 270 **harpy:** a cruel woman 277 **Sisyphus:** in the underworld, Sisyphus was condemned to continually roll a huge boulder up a hill only to have it roll down to the bottom before the top was reached

288 **pray:** prey 298 **Hesperides:** three sisters who guarded a garden in which there was a tree bearing golden apples, one of which was taken by Hercules 305 **Ericine:** Venus 326 **Dis:** another name for Pluto, god of the underworld 329 **Hesperus:** Venus, seen as the evening star 330 **Car:** chariot, ie of the sun 334 **danged:** dashed

WILLIAM SHAKESPEARE

From THE SONNETS

2

WHEN forty winters shall besiege thy brow,
And dig deep trenches in thy beauty's field,
Thy youth's proud livery, so gazed on now,
Will be a tattered weed, of small worth held:
Then being asked where all thy beauty lies,   5
Where all the treasure of thy lusty days,
To say, within thine own deep-sunken eyes,
Were an all-eating shame and thriftless praise.
How much more praise deserved thy beauty's use,
If thou couldst answer 'This fair child of mine   10
Shall sum my count and make my old excuse,'
Proving his beauty by succession thine!
    This were to be new made when thou art old,
    And see thy blood warm when thou feel'st it cold.

12

WHEN I do count the clock that tells the time,
And see the brave day sunk in hideous night;
When I behold the violet past prime,
And sable curls all silvered o'er with white;
When lofty trees I see barren of leaves   5
Which erst from heat did canopy the herd,
And summer's green all girded up in sheaves
Borne on the bier with white and bristly beard,
Then of thy beauty do I question make,
That thou among the wastes of time must go,   10
Since sweets and beauties do themselves forsake
And die as fast as they see others grow;
    And nothing 'gainst Time's scythe can make defence
    Save breed, to brave him when he takes thee hence.

15

WHEN I consider every thing that grows
Holds in perfection but a little moment,
That this huge stage presenteth nought but shows
Whereon the stars in secret influence comment;
When I perceive that men as plants increase,   5
Cheered and chequeed even by the self-same sky,
Vaunt in their youthful sap, at height decrease,
And wear their brave state out of memory;
Then the conceit of this inconstant stay
Sets you most rich in youth before my sight,   10
Where wasteful Time debateth with Decay,
To change your day of youth to sullied night;
    And all in war with Time for love of you,
    As he takes from you, I engraft you new.

17

WHO will believe my verse in time to come,
If it were filled with your most high deserts?
Though yet, heaven knows, it is but as a tomb
Which hides your life and shows not half your parts.
If I could write the beauty of your eyes   5
And in fresh numbers number all your graces,
The age to come would say 'This poet lies:
Such heavenly touches ne'er touched earthly faces.'
So should my papers yellowed with their age
Be scorned like old men of less truth than tongue,   10
And your true rights be termed a poet's rage
And stretchèd metre of an antique song:
    But were some child of yours alive that time,
    You should live twice; in it and in my rhyme.

18

SHALL I compare thee to a summer's day?
Thou art more lovely and more temperate:
Rough winds do shake the darling buds of May,
And summer's lease hath all too short a date:
Sometime too hot the eye of heaven shines,   5
And often is his gold complexion dimmed;
And every fair from fair sometime declines,
By chance or nature's changing course untrimmed;
But thy eternal summer shall not fade
Nor lose possession of that fair thou owest;   10
Nor shall Death brag thou wander'st in his shade,
When in eternal lines to time thou growest:
    So long as men can breathe or eyes can see,
    So long lives this and this gives life to thee.

19

DEVOURING Time, blunt thou the lion's paws,
And make the earth devour her own sweet brood;
Pluck the keen teeth from the fierce tiger's jaws,
And burn the long-lived phoenix in her blood;
Make glad and sorry seasons as thou fleets,   5
And do whate'er thou wilt, swift-footed Time,
To the wide world and all her fading sweets;
But I forbid thee one most heinous crime:
O, carve not with thy hours my love's fair brow,
Nor draw no lines there with thine antique pen;   10
Him in thy course untainted do allow
For beauty's pattern to succeeding men.
    Yet, do thy worst, old Time: despite thy wrong,
    My love shall in my verse ever live young.

FROM THE SONNETS: (2) 2 **trenches:** wrinkles 4 **weed:** garment 8 **thriftless:** unprofitable 9 **use:** investment 11 **sum my count:** square my account **make my old excuse:** excuse me for having grown old (12) 4 **sable:** black 6 **erst:** formerly 9 **question make:** doubt 14 **Save breed . . . hence:** except children, to defy him when you die (15) 7 **vaunt:** boast 8 **And wear . . . memory:** and wear out their beauty until it is forgotten 9 **conceit:** idea

(17) 2 **deserts:** what one deserves 4 **parts:** abilities, qualities 6 **numbers:** verses 11 **rage:** madness, inspiration 12 **stretched:** exaggerated (18) 8 **untrimmed:** stripped of decoration 10 **thou owest:** you own (19) 4 **phoenix:** a legendary bird believed to be periodically consumed by fire but rise again from the ashes

20

A WOMAN's face with Nature's own hand painted
Hast thou, the master-mistress of my passion;
A woman's gentle heart, but not acquainted
With shifting change, as is false women's fashion;
An eye more bright than theirs, less false in rolling,   5
Gilding the object whereupon it gazeth;
A man in hue, all 'hues' in his controlling,
Much steals men's eyes and women's souls amazeth.
And for a woman wert thou first created;
Till Nature, as she wrought thee, fell a-doting,   10
And by addition me of thee defeated,
By adding one thing to my purpose nothing.
   But since she pricked thee out for women's pleasure,
   Mine be thy love and thy love's use their treasure.

23

AS AN unperfect actor on the stage
Who with his fear is put besides his part,
Or some fierce thing replete with too much rage,
Whose strength's abundance weakens his own heart;
So I, for fear of trust, forget to say   5
The perfect ceremony of love's rite,
And in mine own love's strength seem to decay,
O'ercharged with burden of mine own love's
    might.
O, let my books be then the eloquence
And dumb preságers of my speaking breast,   10
Who plead for love and look for recompense
More than that tongue that more hath more
    expressed.
   O, learn to read what silent love hath writ:
   To hear with eyes belongs to love's fine wit.

27

WEARY with toil, I haste me to my bed,
The dear repose for limbs with travel tired;
But then begins a journey in my head,
To work my mind, when body's work's expired:
For then my thoughts, from far where I abide,   5
Intend a zealous pilgrimage to thee,
And keep my drooping eyelids open wide,
Looking on darkness which the blind do see;
Save that my soul's imaginary sight
Presents thy shadow to my sightless view,   10
Which, like a jewel hung in ghastly night,
Makes black night beauteous and her old face new.
   Lo! thus, by day my limbs, by night my mind,
   For thee and for myself no quiet find.

29

WHEN, in disgrace with fortune and men's eyes,
I all alone beweep my outcast state
And trouble deaf heaven with my bootless cries
And look upon myself and curse my fate,
Wishing me like to one more rich in hope,   5
Featured like him, like him with friends possessed,
Desiring this man's art and that man's scope,
With what I most enjoy contented least;
Yet in these thoughts myself almost despising,
Haply I think on thee, and then my state,   10
Like to the lark at break of day arising
From sullen earth, sings hymns at heaven's gate;
   For thy sweet love remembered such wealth brings
   That then I scorn to change my state with kings.

30

WHEN to the sessions of sweet silent thought
I summon up remembrance of things past,
I sigh the lack of many a thing I sought,
And with old woes new wail my dear time's waste:
Then can I drown an eye, unused to flow,   5
For precious friends hid in death's dateless night,
And weep afresh love's long since cancelled woe,
And moan the expense of many a vanished sight:
Then can I grieve at grievances foregone,
And heavily from woe to woe tell o'er   10
The sad account of fore-bemoanèd moan,
Which I new pay as if not paid before.
   But if the while I think on thee, dear friend,
   All losses are restored and sorrows end.

33

FULL many a glorious morning have I seen
Flatter the mountain-tops with sovereign eye,
Kissing with golden face the meadows green,
Gilding pale streams with heavenly alchemy;
Anon permit the basest clouds to ride   5
With ugly rack on his celestial face,
And from the forlorn world his visage hide,
Stealing unseen to west with this disgrace:
Even so my sun one early morn did shine
With all triumphant splendour on my brow;   10
But out, alack! he was but one hour mine;
The region cloud hath masked him from me now.
   Yet him for this my love no whit disdaineth;
   Suns of the world may stain when heaven's sun
    staineth.

(29) 3 **bootless:** unavailing 10 **Haply:** perchance (30) 1 **sessions:** period of business for a court 4 **new wail . . . waste:** lament anew time's destruction of what is dear to me 6 **dateless:** endless 7 **cancelled:** discharged (like a debt paid) 10 **tell:** count (33) 5 **Anon:** in time 6 **rack:** flying cloud 11 **out, alack!:** alas 12 **region:** the upper atmosphere 14 **stain:** darken

(20) 5 **rolling:** straying 11 **defeated:** deprived 13 **pricked thee out:** marked or assigned you, with a play on the words suggesting 'supplied with a penis' (23) 5 **for fear of trust:** through being afraid to trust

34

WHY didst thou promise such a beauteous day,
And make me travel forth without my cloak,
To let base clouds o'ertake me in my way,
Hiding thy bravery in their rotten smoke?
'Tis not enough that through the cloud thou break,   5
To dry the rain on my storm-beaten face,
For no man well of such a salve can speak
That heals the wound and cures not the disgrace:
Nor can thy shame give physic to my grief;
Though thou repent, yet I have still the loss: 10
The offender's sorrow lends but weak relief
To him that bears the strong offence's cross.
    Ah! but those tears are pearl which thy love sheds,
    And they are rich and ransom all ill deeds.

35

NO MORE be grieved at that which thou hast done:
Roses have thorns, and silver fountains mud;
Clouds and eclipses stain both moon and sun,
And loathsome canker lives in sweetest bud.
All men make faults, and even I in this,   5
Authorizing thy trespass with compare,
Myself corrupting, salving thy amiss,
Excusing thy sins more than thy sins are;
For to thy sensual fault I bring in sense –
Thy adverse party is thy advocate –   10
And 'gainst myself a lawful plea commence:
Such civil war is in my love and hate
    That I an áccessary needs must be
    To that sweet thief which sourly robs from me.

53

WHAT is your substance, whereof are you made,
That millions of strange shadows on you tend?
Since every one hath, every one, one shade,
And you, but one, can every shadow lend.
Describe Adonis, and the counterfeit   5
Is poorly imitated after you;
On Helen's cheek all art of beauty set,
And you in Grecian tires are painted new:
Speak of the spring and foison of the year;
The one doth shadow of your beauty show,   10
The other as your bounty doth appear;
And you in every blessed shape we know.
    In all external grace you have some part,
    But you like none, none you, for constant heart.

55

NOT marble, nor the gilded monuments
Of princes, shall outlive this powerful rhyme;
But you shall shine more bright in these contents
Than unswept stone besmeared with sluttish time.
When wasteful war shall statues overturn,   5
And broils root out the work of masonry,
Nor Mars his sword nor war's quick fire shall burn
The living record of your memory.
'Gainst death and all-oblivious enmity
Shall you pace forth; your praise shall still find room
Even in the eyes of all posterity   11
That wear this world out to the ending doom.
    So, till the judgement that yourself arise,
    You live in this, and dwell in lover's eyes.

56

SWEET love, renew thy force; be it not said
Thy edge should blunter be than appetite,
Which but to-day by feeding is allayed,
To-morrow sharpened in his former might:
So, love, be thou; although today thou fill   5
Thy hungry eyes even till they wink with fullness,
To-morrow see again, and do not kill
The spirit of love with a perpetual dullness.
Let this sad interim like the ocean be
Which parts the shore, where two contracted new   10
Come daily to the banks, that, when they see
Return of love, more blest may be the view;
    Else call it winter, which being full of care
    Makes summer's welcome thrice more wished, more
    rare.

57

BEING your slave, what should I do but tend
Upon the hours and times of your desire?
I have no precious time at all to spend,
Nor services to do, till you require.
Nor dare I chide the world-without-end hour   5
Whilst I, my sovereign, watch the clock for you,
Nor think the bitterness of absence sour
When you have bid your servant once adieu;
Nor dare I question with my jealous thought
Where you may be, or your affairs suppose,   10
But, like a sad slave, stay and think of nought
Save, where you are how happy you make those.
    So true a fool is love that in your will,
    Though you do any thing, he thinks no ill.

---

(34) 4 **bravery . . . smoke:** finery in their unpleasant vapour
9 **physic:** medicine (35) 3 **stain:** darken 6 **compare:** comparison
7 **amiss:** misdeed 14 **sourly:** bitterly (53) 5 **Adonis:** in Greek myth,
a beautiful youth loved by Aphrodite **counterfeit:** description
7 **Helen:** Helen of Troy 8 **tires:** garments 9 **foison:** harvest,
supply

(55) 6 **broils:** quarrels, fights 7 **Nor:** neither **Mars:** Roman god
of war 12 **wear this world out:** outlast this world 13 **till the judgement
that yourself arise:** until Judgement Day when you will rise
(56) 10 **contracted new:** newly betrothed (57) 1 **tend:** attend, wait
5 **world-without-end:** seemingly everlasting 13 **your will:** your
wishes; also a pun on the short form of Shakespeare's name

60

LIKE as the waves make towards the pebbled shore,
So do our minutes hasten to their end;
Each changing place with that which goes before,
In sequent toil all forwards do contend.
Nativity, once in the main of light,   5
Crawls to maturity, wherewith being crowned,
Crooked elipses 'gainst his glory fight,
And Time that gave doth now his gift confound.
Time doth transfix the flourish set on youth
And delves the parallels in beauty's brow,   10
Feeds on the rarities of nature's truth,
And nothing stands but for his scythe to mow:
   And yet to times in hope my verse shall stand,
   Praising thy worth, despite his cruel hand.

64

WHEN I have seen by Time's fell hand defaced
The rich proud cost of outworn buried age;
When sometime lofty towers I see down-razed
And brass eternal slave to mortal rage;
When I have seen the hungry ocean gain   5
Advantage on the kingdom of the shore,
And the firm soil win of the watery main,
Increasing store with loss and loss with store;
When I have seen such interchange of state,
Or state itself confounded to decay;   10
Ruin hath taught me thus to ruminate,
That Time will come and take my love away.
   This thought is as a death, which cannot choose
   But weep to have that which it fears to lose.

65

SINCE brass, nor stone, nor earth, nor boundless sea,
But sad mortality o'er-sways their power,
How with this rage shall beauty hold a plea,
Whose action is no stronger than a flower?
Oh, how shall summer's honey breath hold out   5
Against the wreckful siege of battering days,
When rocks impregnable are not so stout,
Nor gates of steel so strong, but Time decays?
O fearful meditation! where, alack,
Shall Time's best jewel from Time's chest lie hid?   10
Or what strong hand can hold his swift foot back?
Or who his spoil of beauty can forbid?
   O, none, unless this miracle have might,
   That in black ink my love may still shine bright.

(60) 4 **sequent:** successive 7 **crooked:** evil 9 **transfix:** kill, destroy 10 **delves the parallels:** creates the wrinkles 13 **times in hope:** future time (64) 1 **fell:** cruel 3 **sometime:** once 8 **increasing . . . store:** one gaining by the other's loss 10 **state:** greatness (65) 1–2 **Since . . . power:** as all of the named great and enduring things are in the end subject to mortality 3 **plea:** a play on the meaning of an act of pleading and a declaration made in court 4 **action:** again a play on the ordinary meaning (something done) and the legal sense (a suit or case) 6 **wrackful:** destructive 10 **from Time's chest be hid:** be concealed so as not to be taken and put away in Time's jewel box 12 **spoil:** despoiling, plundering

66

TIRED with all these, for restful death I cry,
As, to behold desert a beggar born,
And needy nothing trimmed in jollity,
And purest faith unhappily forsworn,
And gilded honour shamefully misplaced,   5
And maiden virtue rudely strumpeted,
And right perfection wrongfully disgraced,
And strength by limping sway disabled,
And art made tongue-tied by authority,
And folly doctor-like controlling skill,   10
And simple truth miscalled simplicity,
And captive good attending captain ill:
   Tired with all these, from these would I be gone,
   Save that, to die, I leave my love alone.

71

NO LONGER mourn for me when I am dead
Then you shall hear the surly sullen bell
Give warning to the world that I am fled
From this vile world, with vilest worms to dwell:
Nay, if you read this line, remember not   5
The hand that writ it; for I love you so
That I in your sweet thoughts would be forgot
If thinking on me then should make you woe.
O, if, I say, you look upon this verse
When I perhaps compounded am with clay,   10
Do not so much as my poor name rehearse.
But let your love even with my life decay,
   Lest the wise world should look into your moan
   And mock you with me after I am gone.

73

THAT time of year thou mayst in me behold
When yellow leaves, or none, or few, do hang
Upon those boughs which shake against the cold,
Bare ruined choirs, where late the sweet birds sang.
In me thou seest the twilight of such day   5
As after sunset fadeth in the west,
Which by and by black night doth take away,
Death's second self, that seals up all in rest.
In me thou see'st the glowing of such fire
That on the ashes of his youth doth lie,   10
As the death-bed whereon it must expire
Consumed with that which it was nourished by.
   This thou perceivest, which makes thy love more
     strong,
   To love that well which thou must leave ere long.

(66) 2 **desert:** a person who deserves better 3 **needy nothing:** an insignificant person who lacks any gifts or abilities 8 **limping sway:** power held by the weak or imperfect 10 **doctor-like:** in the guise of a learned person 11 **simple truth miscalled simplicity:** pure honesty falsely labelled stupidity (73) 8 **Death's second self:** night or sleep 10 **That:** as

74

BUT be contented: when that fell arrest
Without all bail shall carry me away,
My life hath in this line some interest,
Which for memorial still with thee shall stay.
When thou reviewest this, thou dost review   5
The very part was consecrate to thee:
The earth can have but earth, which is his due;
My spirit is thine, the better part of me:
So then thou hast but lost the dregs of life,
The prey of worms, my body being dead,   10
The coward conquest of a wretch's knife,
Too base of thee to be remembered.
    The worth of that is that which it contains,
    And that is this, and this with thee remains.

87

FAREWELL! thou art too dear for my possessing,
And like enough thou know'st thy estimate:
The charter of thy worth gives thee releasing;
My bonds in thee are all determinate.
For how do I hold thee but by thy granting?   5
And for that riches where is my deserving?
The cause of this fair gift in me is wanting,
And so my patent back again is swerving.
Thyself thou gavest, thy own worth then not knowing,
Or me, to whom thou gav'st it, else mistaking;   10
So thy great gift, upon misprision growing,
Comes home again, on better judgement making.
    Thus have I had thee, as a dream doth flatter,
    In sleep a king, but waking no such matter.

90

THEN hate me when thou wilt; if ever, now;
Now, while the world is bent my deeds to cross,
Join with the spite of fortune, make me bow,
And do not drop in for an after-loss:
Ah, do not, when my heart hath 'scaped this sorrow,   5
Come in the rearward of a conquered woe;
Give not a windy night a rainy morrow,
To linger out a purposed overthrow.
If thou wilt leave me, do not leave me last,
When other petty griefs have done their spite   10
But in the onset come; so shall I taste
At first the very worst of fortune's might,
    And other strains of woe, which now seem woe,
    Compared with loss of thee will not seem so.

94

THEY that have power to hurt and will do none,
That do not do the thing they most do show,
Who, moving others, are themselves as stone,
Unmovèd, cold, and to temptation slow,
They rightly do inherit heaven's graces   5
And husband nature's riches from expense;
They are the lords and owners of their faces,
Others but stewards of their excellence.
The summer's flower is to the summer sweet,
Though to itself it only live and die,   10
But if that flower with base infection meet,
The basest weed outbraves his dignity:
    For sweetest things turn sourest by their deeds;
    Lilies that fester smell far worse than weeds.

97

HOW like a winter hath my absence been
From thee, the pleasure of the fleeting year!
What freezings have I felt, what dark days seen!
What old December's bareness every where!
And yet this time removed was summer's time,   5
The teeming autumn, big with rich increase,
Bearing the wanton burden of the prime,
Like widowed wombs after their lords' decease:
Yet this abundant issue seemed to me
But hope of orphans and unfathered fruit;   10
For summer and his pleasures wait on thee,
And, thou away, the very birds are mute;
    Or, if they sing, 'tis with so dull a cheer
    That leaves look pale, dreading the winter's near.

98

FROM you have I been absent in the spring,
When proud-pied April dressed in all his trim
Hath put a spirit of youth in every thing,
That heavy Saturn laughed and leaped with him.
Yet nor the lays of birds nor the sweet smell   5
Of different flowers in odour and in hue
Could make me any summer's story tell,
Or from their proud lap pluck them where they
    grew;
Nor did I wonder at the lily's white,
Nor praise the deep vermilion in the rose;   10
They were but sweet, but figures of delight,
Drawn after you, you pattern of all those.
    Yet seemed it winter still, and, you away,
    As with your shadow I with these did play.

---

(74) 1 **fell:** cruel 2 **Without all bail:** with no possibility of release 4 **still:** always 11 **The coward . . . knife:** the easy prey to a contemptible foe (87) 8 **my patent back again is swerving:** my right to possess you is reverting to you 11 **misprision:** a mistake (90) 4 **after-loss:** a later misfortune 5 **'scaped:** escaped 8 **purposed:** intended, deliberate

(94) 2 **do show:** seem or threaten to do 12 **outbraves:** exceeds in beauty (97) 6 **teeming:** fruitful, pregnant 7 **bearing . . . prime:** carrying the child conceived in pleasure during the spring (98) 2 **proud-pied:** proudly dressed in variegated colours 4 **That:** so that **heavy Saturn:** the gloomy god of the underworld 5 **Yet nor:** yet neither **lays:** songs

104

To me, fair friend, you never can be old,
For as you were when first your eye I eyed,
Such seems your beauty still. Three winters cold
Have from the forests shook three summers' pride,
Three beauteous springs to yellow autumn
    turned   5
In process of the seasons have I seen,
Three April perfumes in three hot Junes burned,
Since first I saw you fresh, which yet are green.
Ah! yet doth beauty, like a dial-hand,
Steal from his figure and no pace perceived;   10
So your sweet hue, which methinks still doth stand,
Hath motion and mine eye may be deceived:
    For fear of which, hear this, thou age unbred;
    Ere you were born was beauty's summer dead.

106

When in the chronicle of wasted time
I see descriptions of the fairest wights,
And beauty making beautiful old rhyme
In praise of ladies dead and lovely knights,
Then, in the blazon of sweet beauty's best,   5
Of hand, of foot, of lip, of eye, of brow,
I see their antique pen would have expressed
Even such a beauty as you master now.
So all their praises are but prophecies
Of this our time, all you prefiguring;   10
And, for they looked but with divining eyes,
They had not skill enough your worth to sing:
    For we, which now behold these present days,
    Had eyes to wonder, but lack tongues to praise.

107

Not mine own fears, nor the prophetic soul
Of the wide world dreaming on things to come
Can yet the lease of my true love control,
Supposed as forfeit to a confined doom.
The mortal moon hath her eclipse endured   5
And the sad augurs mock their own presage;
Incertainties now crown themselves assured
And peace proclaims olives of endless age.
Now with the drops of this most balmy time
My love looks fresh, and Death to me subscribes,   10
Since, spite of him, I'll live in this poor rhyme,
While he insults o'er dull and speechless tribes:
    And thou in this shalt find thy monument,
    When tyrants' crests and tombs of brass are spent.

108

What's in the brain that ink may character
Which hath not figured to thee my true spirit?
What's new to speak, what new to register,
That may express my love or thy dear merit?
Nothing, sweet boy; but yet, like prayers divine,   5
I must, each day say o'er the very same,
Counting no old thing old, thou mine, I thine,
Even as when first I hallowed thy fair name.
So that eternal love in love's fresh case
Weighs not the dust and injury of age,   10
Nor gives to necessary wrinkles place,
But makes antiquity for aye his page,
    Finding the first conceit of love there bred
    Where time and outward form would show it dead.

110

Alas, 'tis true I have gone here and there
And made myself a motley to the view,
Gored mine own thoughts, sold cheap what is most
    dear,
Made old offences of affections new;
Most true it is that I have looked on truth   5
Askance and strangely: but, by all above,
These blenches gave my heart another youth,
And worse essays proved thee my best of love.
Now all is done, have what shall have no end:
Mine appetite I never more will grind   10
On newer proof, to try an older friend,
A god in love, to whom I am confined.
    Then give me welcome, next my heaven the best,
    Even to thy pure and most most loving breast.

116

Let me not to the marriage of true minds
Admit impediments. Love is not love
Which alters when it alteration finds,
Or bends with the remover to remove:
Oh no! it is an ever-fixèd mark   5
That looks on tempests and is never shaken;
It is the star to every wandering bark,
Whose worth's unknown, although his height be
    taken.
Love's not Time's fool, though rosy lips and cheeks
Within his bending sickle's compass come: 10
Love alters not with his brief hours and weeks,
But bears it out even to the edge of doom.
    If this be error and upon me proved,
    I never writ, nor no man ever loved.

(104) 13 **unbred:** not yet born (106) 1 **wasted:** past, decayed
2 **wights:** people 5 **blazon:** description 11 **for:** although
(107) 4 **Supposed . . . doom:** believed subject to a set date of expiry
6 **And . . . presage:** and those who predicted misfortune now
laugh at their own forecasts 8 **olives of endless age:** unending
peace (symbolized by the olive branch) 10 **to me subscribes:** yields
superiority to me 12 **insults:** triumphs 14 **spent:** wasted away

(108) 1 **character:** write 2 **figured:** shown 9 **fresh case:** youthful
guise 10 **Weighs not:** cares nothing for 12 **for aye:** for ever **page:**
servant 13 **conceit:** idea, conception (110) 2 **motley:** a fool or jester
3 **Gored:** wounded 6 **strangely:** as if a stranger 7 **blenches:** sideways
looks 8 **worse essays:** tests which proved others to be lesser 11 **try:**
test (116) 7 **bark:** ship 8 **Whose worth . . . taken:** whose value
is inestimable although his altitude may be estimated (for
navigation) 10 **compass:** range 12 **bears it out:** endures

121

'TIS better to be vile than vile esteemed,
When not to be receives reproach of being,
And the just pleasure lost which is so deemed
Not by our feeling but by others' seeing:
For why should others' false adulterate eyes   5
Give salutation to my sportive blood?
Or on my frailties why are frailer spies,
Which in their wills count bad what I think good?
No, I am that I am, and they that level
At my abuses reckon up their own: 10
I may be straight, though they themselves be bevel;
By their rank thoughts my deeds must not be
    shown;
  Unless this general evil they maintain,
  All men are bad, and in their badness reign.

124

IF my dear love were but the child of state,
It might for Fortune's bastard be unfathered
As subject to Time's love or to Time's hate,
Weeds among weeds, or flowers with flowers gathered.
No, it was builded far from accident;   5
It suffers not in smiling pomp, nor falls
Under the blow of thrallèd discontent,
Whereto the inviting time our fashion calls:
It fears not policy, that heretic,
Which works on leases of short-numbered hours,   10
But all alone stands hugely politic,
That it nor grows with heat nor drowns with showers.
  To this I witness call the fools of time,
  Which die for goodness, who have lived for crime.

125

WERE'T aught to me I bore the canopy,
With my extern the outward honouring,
Or laid great bases for eternity,
Which prove more short than waste or ruining?
Have I not seen dwellers on form and favour   5
Lose all, and more, by paying too much rent,
For compound sweet forgoing simple savour,
Pitiful thrivers, in their gazing spent?
No, let me be obsequious in thy heart,
And take thou my oblation, poor but free,   10
Which is not mixed with seconds, knows no art,
But mutual render, only me for thee.
  Hence, thou suborned informer! a true soul
  When most impeached stands least in thy control.

127

IN THE old age black was not counted fair,
Or if it were, it bore not beauty's name;
But now is black beauty's successive heir,
And beauty slandered with a bastard shame:
For since each hand hath put on nature's power,   5
Fairing the foul with art's false borrowed face,
Sweet beauty hath no name, no holy bower,
But is profaned, if not lives in disgrace.
Therefore my mistress' brows are raven black,
Her eyes so suited, and they mourners seem   10
At such who, not born fair, no beauty lack,
Slandering creation with a false esteem:
    Yet so they mourn, becoming of their woe,
    That every tongue says beauty should look so.

128

HOW oft, when thou, my music, music play'st,
Upon that blessed wood whose motion sounds
With thy sweet fingers, when thou gently sway'st
The wiry concord that mine ear confounds,
Do I envy those jacks that nimble leap   5
To kiss the tender inward of thy hand,
Whilst my poor lips, which should that harvest
    reap,
At the wood's boldness by thee blushing stand.
To be so tickled, they would change their state
And situation with those dancing chips,   10
O'er whom thy fingers walk with gentle gait,
Making dead wood more blest than living lips.
  Since saucy jacks so happy are in this,
  Give them thy fingers, me thy lips to kiss.

129

TH'EXPENSE of spirit in a waste of shame
Is lust in action; and till action, lust
Is perjured, murderous, bloody, full of blame,
Savage, extreme, rude, cruel, not to trust,
Enjoyed no sooner but despisèd straight,   5
Past reason hunted, and no sooner had
Past reason hated, as a swallowed bait
On purpose laid to make the taker mad;
Mad in pursuit and in possession so;
Had, having, and in quest to have, extreme;   10
A bliss in proof, and proved, a very woe;
Before, a joy proposed; behind, a dream.
  All this the world well knows; yet none knows well
  To shun the heaven that leads men to this hell.

130

My mistress' eyes are nothing like the sun;
Coral is far more red than her lips' red;
If snow be white, why then her breasts are dun;
If hairs be wires, black wires grow on her head.
I have seen roses damasked, red and white,   5
But no such roses see I in her cheeks;
And in some perfumes is there more delight
Than in the breath that from my mistress reeks.
I love to hear her speak, yet well I know
That music hath a far more pleasing sound;   10
I grant I never saw a goddess go;
My mistress, when she walks, treads on the ground:
    And yet, by heaven, I think my love as rare
    As any she belied with false compare.

135

Whoever hath her wish, thou hast thy 'Will,'
And 'Will' to boot, and 'Will' in overplus;
More than enough am I that vex thee still,
To thy sweet will making addition thus.
Wilt thou, whose will is large and spacious,   5
Not once vouchsafe to hide my will in thine?
Shall will in others seem right gracious,
And in my will no fair acceptance shine?
The sea all water, yet receives rain still
And in abundance addeth to his store;   10
So thou, being rich in 'Will,' add to thy 'Will'
One will of mine, to make thy large 'Will' more.
    Let no unkind, no fair beseechers kill;
    Think all but one, and me in that one 'Will.'

138

When my love swears that she is made of truth
I do believe her, though I know she lies,
That she might think me some untutored youth,
Unlearnèd in the world's false subtleties.
Thus vainly thinking that she thinks me young,   5
Although she knows my days are past the best,
Simply I credit her false speaking tongue:
On both sides thus is simple truth suppressed.
But wherefore says she not she is unjust?
And wherefore say not I that I am old?   10
Oh, love's best habit is in seeming trust,
And age in love loves not to have years told:
    Therefore I lie with her and she with me,
    And in our faults by lies we flattered be.

140

Be wise as thou art cruel; do not press
My tongue-tied patience with too much disdain;
Lest sorrow lend me words and words express
The manner of my pity-wanting pain.
If I might teach thee wit, better it were,   5
Though not to love, yet, love, to tell me so;
As testy sick men, when their deaths be near,
No news but health from their physicians know;
For if I should despair, I should grow mad,
And in my madness might speak ill of thee: 10
Now this ill-wresting world is grown so bad,
Mad slanderers by mad ears believèd be,
    That I may not be so, nor thou belied,
    Bear thine eyes straight, though thy proud heart go
    wide.

144

Two loves I have of comfort and despair,
Which like two spirits do suggest me still:
The better angel is a man right fair,
The worser spirit a woman coloured ill.
To win me soon to hell, my female evil   5
Tempteth my better angel from my side,
And would corrupt my saint to be a devil,
Wooing his purity with her foul pride.
And whether that my angel be turned fiend
Suspect I may, but not directly tell;   10
But being both from me, both to each friend,
I guess one angel in another's hell:
    Yet this shall I ne'er know, but live in doubt,
    Till my bad angel fire my good one out.

151

Love is too young to know what conscience is;
Yet who knows not conscience is born of love?
Then, gentle cheater, urge not my amiss,
Lest guilty of my faults thy sweet self prove:
For, thou betraying me, I do betray   5
My nobler part to my gross body's treason;
My soul doth tell my body that he may
Triumph in love; flesh stays no farther reason;
But, rising at thy name, doth point out thee
As his triumphant prize. Proud of this pride,   10
He is contented thy poor drudge to be,
To stand in thy affairs, fall by thy side.
    No want of conscience hold it that I call
    Her 'love' for whose dear love I rise and fall.

---

(130) 5 **damasked:** woven together 8 **reeks:** emanates 11 **go:** walk
14 **she:** female **compare:** comparison (135) 1 **Will:** a play on a
shortening of Shakespeare's name 6 **vouchsafe:** grant, consent
(138) 3 **That:** so that 12 **told:** counted 13 **lie with:** tell lies to, with a
pun on the meaning 'sleep with'

(140) 4 **pity-wanting:** unpitied 7 **testy:** querulous 11 **ill-wresting:**
putting the worst interpretation on things 14 **go wide:** miss the
target (144) 2 **suggest me still:** continually urge me 4 **ill:** dark
14 **fire my good one out:** expel my good angel (151) 3 **urge not my
amiss:** bring up my fault or sin

THOMAS BASTARD

DE PUERO BALBUTIENTE

METHINKS 'tis pretty sport to hear a child
Rocking a word in mouth yet undefiled.
The tender racket rudely plays the sound,
Which weakly bandied cannot back rebound,
And the soft air the softer roof doth kiss,   5
With a sweet dying and a pretty miss,
Which hears no answer yet from the white rank
Of teeth, not risen from their coral bank.
The alphabet is searched for letters soft,
To try a word before it can be wrought,   10
And when it slideth forth, it goes as nice
As when a man does walk upon the ice.

DE PUERO BALBUTIENTE: 3–4 **The tender . . . rebound:** the baby's voice propels the sound like a shuttlecock weakly struck by a racket 5 **softer roof:** roof of the mouth 8 **coral:** pink 11 **nice:** softly, gently

THOMAS NASHE

'SPRING, THE SWEET SPRING . . .'

SPRING, the sweet spring, is the year's pleasant king;
Then blooms each thing, then maids dance in a ring,
Cold doth not sting, the pretty birds do sing,
Cuckoo, jug-jug, pu-we, to-witta-woo!

The palm and may make country houses gay,   5
Lambs frisk and play, the shepherds pipe all day,
And we hear aye birds tune this merry lay,
Cuckoo, jug-jug, pu-we, to-witta-woo!

The fields breathe sweet, the daisies kiss our feet,
Young lovers meet, old wives a-sunning sit;   10
In every street these tunes our ears do greet,
Cuckoo, jug-jug, pu-we, to-witta-woo!
   Spring! the sweet Spring!

'SPRING, THE SWEET SPRING . . .': 5 **palm and may:** willow and mayflower 7 **aye:** always **tune this merry lay:** sing this happy song 9 **breathe:** smell

'ADIEU, FAREWELL EARTH'S BLISS'

ADIEU, farewell earth's bliss,
This world uncertain is:
Fond are life's lustful joys,
Death proves them all but toys,
None from his darts can fly –   5
I am sick, I must die:
   Lord, have mercy on us!

Rich men, trust not in wealth,
Gold cannot buy you health,
Physic himself must fade.   10
All things to end are made,
The plague full swift goes by –
I am sick, I must die:
   Lord, have mercy on us!

Beauty is but a flower,   15
Which wrinkles will devour;
Brightness falls from the air,
Queens have died young and fair,
Dust hath closèd Helen's eye –
I am sick, I must die: 20
   Lord, have mercy on us!

Strength stoops unto the grave,
Worms feed on Hector brave;
Swords may not fight with fate,
Earth still holds ope her gate,   25
Come, come, the bells do cry –
I am sick, I must die:
   Lord, have mercy on us!

Wit with his wantonness
Tasteth death's bitterness;   30
Hell's executioner
Hath no ears for to hear
What vain art can reply –
I am sick, I must die:
   Lord, have mercy on us!   35

Haste therefore each degree
To welcome destiny:
Heaven is our heritage,
Earth but a player's stage;
Mount we unto the sky –   40
I am sick, I must die:
   Lord, have mercy on us!

'ADIEU, FAREWELL EARTH'S BLISS': 3 **Fond . . . joys:** the pleasures of the flesh are dear 5 **darts:** spears or arrows 10 **Physic:** medicine 19 **Helen:** Helen of Troy 25 **Earth still holds ope her gate:** the grave is always waiting 36 **degree:** rank 39 **player:** stage actor

THOMAS CAMPION

'WHEN THOU MUST HOME TO SHADES OF UNDERGROUND'

WHEN thou must home to shades of underground,
   And there arrived, a new admirèd guest,
The beauteous spirits do engirt thee round,
   White Iope, blithe Helen, and the rest,
To hear the stories of thy finished love   5
From that smooth tongue whose music hell can move;

Then wilt thou speak of banqueting delights,
   Of masques and revels which sweet youth did make,
Of tourneys and great challenges of knights,
   And all these triumphs for thy beauty's sake: 10
When thou hast told these honours done to thee,
Then tell, O tell, how thou didst murder me.

'WHEN THOU MUST HOME TO SHADES OF UNDERGROUND': 1 **When . . .
underground**: when you die and go to the underworld 3 **engirt**:
encircle 4 **Iope**: Cassiopeia, in Greek myth the mother of Andromeda
Helen: Helen of Troy 6 **hell can move**: can move (affect) hell

'ROSE-CHEEKED LAURA, COME'

ROSE-CHEEKED Laura, come;
Sing thou smoothly with thy beauty's
Silent music, either other
    Sweetly gracing.

Lovely forms do flow   5
From concent divinely framed;
Heaven is music, and thy beauty's
    Birth is heavenly.

These dull notes we sing
Discords need for helps to grace them,   10
Only beauty purely loving
    Knows no discord.

But still moves delight,
Like clear springs renewed by flowing,
Ever perfect, ever in them-   15
    selves eternal.

'THERE IS A GARDEN IN HER FACE'

THERE is a garden in her face,
   Where roses and white lilies grow;
A heavenly paradise is that place,
   Wherein all pleasant fruits do flow.
There cherries grow which none may buy,   5
Till 'Cherry-ripe' themselves do cry.

Those cherries fairly do enclose
   Of orient pearls a double row,
Which when her lovely laughter shows,
   They look like rose-buds filled with snow.   10
Yet them nor peer nor prince can buy,
Till 'Cherry-ripe' themselves do cry.

Her eyes like angels watch them still,
   Her brows like bended bows do stand,
Threat'ning with piercing frowns to kill   15
   All that attempt with eye or hand
Those sacred cherries to come nigh,
Till 'Cherry-ripe' themselves do cry.

'THERE IS A GARDEN IN HER FACE': 5 **cherries**: lips 6 **Cherry-ripe**: from
the cry of a street-vendor selling cherries 8 **orient pearls**: bright
pearls, i.e. teeth 11 **nor peer nor prince**: neither peer nor prince

'THOU ART NOT FAIR, FOR ALL THY
RED AND WHITE'

THOU art not fair, for all thy red and white,
For all those rosy ornaments in thee.
Thou art not sweet, though made of mere delight,
Nor fair nor sweet, unless thou pity me.
I will not soothe thy fancies. Thou shalt prove   5
That beauty is no beauty without love.

Yet love not me, nor seek thou to allure
My thoughts with beauty, were it more divine;
Thy smiles and kisses I cannot endure,
I'll not be wrapped up in those arms of thine.   10
Now show it, if thou be a woman right,
Embrace and kiss and love me in despite.

'FOLLOW THY FAIR SUN, UNHAPPY SHADOW'

FOLLOW thy fair sun, unhappy shadow:
    Though thou be black as night
    And she made all of light,
Yet follow thy fair sun, unhappy shadow!

Follow her whose light thy light depriveth: 5
    Though here thou live disgraced
    And she in Heav'n is placed,
Yet follow her whose light the world reviveth!

Follow those pure beams, whose beauty burneth,
    That so have scorched thee   10
    As thou still black must be
Till her kind beams thy black to brightness turneth!

Follow her while yet her glory shineth!
    There comes a luckless night
    That will dim all her light,   15
And this the black unhappy shade divineth.

Follow still, since so thy fates ordained!
    The sun must have his shade,
    Till both at once do fade;
The sun still proved, the shadow still disdained!   20

'KIND ARE HER ANSWERS'

KIND are her answers;
But her performance keeps no day,
   Breaks time, as dancers
From their own music when they stray.
   All her free favours   5

And smooth words wing my hopes in vain.
  O did ever voice so sweet but only fain?
Can true love yield such delay,
  Converting joy to pain?

Lost is our freedom   10
When we submit to women so:
  Why do we need them,
When in their best they work our woe?
  There is no wisdom
Can alter ends, by Fate prefixed.   15
  O why is the good of man with evil mixed?
Never were days yet called two,
  But one night went betwixt.

'FOLLOW YOUR SAINT, FOLLOW WITH ACCENTS SWEET'

FOLLOW your saint, follow with accents sweet;
Haste you, sad notes, fall at her flying feet!
There, wrapped in cloud of sorrow, pity move,
And tell the ravisher of my soul I perish for her love;
  But if she scorns my never-ceasing pain,   5
Then burst with sighing in her sight, and ne'er return
  again.

All that I sang still to her praise did tend,
Still she was first, still she my songs did end;
Yet she my love and music both doth fly, –
The music that her echo is and beauty's sympathy: 10
  Then let my notes pursue her scornful flight:
It shall suffice that they were breathed and died for her
  delight.

'WHEN TO HER LUTE CORINNA SINGS'

WHEN to her lute Corinna sings,
Her voice revives the leaden strings,
And doth in highest notes appear,
As any challenged echo clear;
But when she doth of mourning speak,   5
E'en with her sighs the strings do break.

And as her lute doth live or die,
Led by her passion, so must I;
For when of pleasure she doth sing,
My thoughts enjoy a sudden spring;   10
But if she doth of sorrow speak,
E'en from my heart the strings do break.

'THE MAN OF LIFE UPRIGHT'

THE man of life upright,
  Whose guiltless heart is free

From all dishonest deeds
  Or thought of vanity;

The man whose silent days   5
  In harmless joys are spent,
Whom hopes cannot delude,
  Nor sorrow discontent:

That man needs neither towers
  Nor armour for defence,   10
Nor secret vaults to fly
  From thunder's violence.

He only can behold
  With unaffrighted eyes
The horrors of the deep   15
  And terrors of the skies.

Thus scorning all the cares
  That fate or fortune brings,
He makes the heaven his book,
  His wisdom heavenly things,   20

Good thoughts his only friends,
  His wealth a well-spent age,
The earth his sober inn
  And quiet pilgrimage.

'NOW WINTER NIGHTS ENLARGE'

Now winter nights enlarge
  The number of their hours,
And clouds their storms discharge
  Upon the airy towers.
Let now the chimneys blaze,   5
  And cups o'erflow with wine;
Let well-tuned words amaze
  With harmony divine.
Now yellow waxen lights
  Shall wait on honey Love,   10
While youthful revels, masques, and courtly sights
  Sleep's leaden spells remove.

This time doth well dispense
  With lovers' long discourse.
Much speech hath some defence,   15
  Though beauty no remorse.
All do not all things well:
  Some measures comely tread,
Some knotted riddles tell,
  Some poems smoothly read.   20
The summer hath his joys,
  And winter his delights.
Though Love and all his pleasures are but toys,
  They shorten tedious nights.

'HARK, ALL YOU LADIES THAT DO SLEEP!'

Hark, all you ladies that do sleep!
  The fairy queen Proserpina
Bids you awake, and pity them that weep.
  You may do in the dark
What the day doth forbid.   5
  Fear not the dogs that bark;
    Night will have all hid.

But if you let your lovers moan,
  The fairy queen Proserpina
Will send abroad her fairies every one,   10
  That shall pinch black and blue
Your white hands and fair arms,
  That did not kindly rue
    Your paramours' harms.

In myrtle arbours on the downs,   15
  The fairy queen Proserpina
This night, by moonshine, leading merry rounds,
  Holds a watch with sweet Love,
Down the dale, up the hill;
  No plaints nor griefs may move   20
    Their holy vigil.

All you that will hold watch with Love,
  The fairy queen Proserpina
Will make you fairer than Dione's dove.
  Roses red, lilies white,   25
And the clear damask hue,
  Shall on your cheeks alight.
    Love will adorn you.

All you that love, or loved before,
  The fairy queen Proserpina   30
Bids you increase that loving humour more.
  They that have not yet fed
On delights amorous,
  She vows that they shall lead
    Apes in Avernus.   35

'HARK, ALL YOU LADIES THAT DO SLEEP!': 20 **plaints:** complaints
24 **Dione:** the mother of Venus, or, sometimes, Venus herself
34–5 **lead apes in Avernus:** the traditional fate of those who died as
old maids was to lead apes in hell (Avernus)

ANONYMOUS

'WEEP YOU NO MORE, SAD FOUNTAINS'

Weep you no more, sad fountains;
  What need you flow so fast?
Look how the snowy mountains
  Heaven's sun doth gently waste.

But my sun's heavenly eyes   5
  View not your weeping,
  That now lies sleeping
Softly, now softly lies
  Sleeping.

Sleep is a reconciling,   10
  A rest that peace begets.
Doth not the sun rise smiling
  When fair at even he sets?
Rest you, then, rest, sad eyes,
  Melt not in weeping,   15
  While she lies sleeping
Softly, now softly lies
  Sleeping.

'WEEP YOU NO MORE, SAD FOUNTAINS': 2 **What need you:** why should
you 3–4 **Look . . . waste:** see how the snow on mountain-tops is
slowly melted by the sun 13 **even:** evening

'I SAW MY LADY WEEP'

I saw my lady weep,
  And Sorrow proud to be advancèd so
In those fair eyes where all perfections keep.
  Her face was full of woe;
But such a woe, believe me, as wins more hearts   5
Than Mirth can do with her enticing parts.

Sorrow was then made fair,
  And Passion wise, tears a delightful thing;
Silence beyond all speech a wisdom rare.
  She made her sighs to sing,   10
And all things with so sweet a sadness move
As made my heart at once both grieve and love.

O fairer than aught else
  The world can show, leave off in time to grieve.
Enough, enough your joyful looks excels;   15
  Tears kills the heart, believe.
Oh! strive not to be excellent in woe,
Which only breeds your beauty's overthrow.

'MY LOVE IN HER ATTIRE DOTH SHOW HER WIT'

My love in her attire doth show her wit,
  It doth so well become her:
For every season she hath dressings fit,
  For winter, spring, and summer.
No beauty she doth miss,   5
  When all her robes are on:
But Beauty's self she is,
  When all her robes are gone.

'THULE, THE PERIOD OF COSMOGRAPHY'

THULE, the period of cosmography,
   Doth vaunt of Hecla, whose sulphureous fire
Doth melt the frozen clime and thaw the sky;
   Trinacrian Etna's flames ascend not higher.
These things seem wondrous, yet more wondrous I,   5
Whose heart with fear doth freeze, with love doth fry.

The Andalusian merchant that returns
   Laden with cochineal and China dishes,
Reports in Spain how strangely Fogo burns
   Amidst an ocean full of flying fishes.   10
These things seem wondrous, yet more wondrous I,
Whose heart with fear doth freeze, with love doth fry.

'THULE, THE PERIOD OF COSMOGRAPHY': 1 **Thule:** an island believed in classical times to be the most northerly land in the world, in this poem identified with Iceland **period:** end, final point 2 **vaunt:** boast **Hecla:** a volcano in Iceland 4 **Trinacrian:** Sicilian 9 **Fogo:** a volcano in the Cape Verde Islands

'FINE KNACKS FOR LADIES . . .'

FINE knacks for ladies, cheap, choice, brave and new!
   Good pennyworths! but money cannot move.
I keep a fair but for the fair to view;
   A beggar may be liberal of love.
Though all my wares be trash, the heart is true,   5
          The heart is true.

Great gifts are guiles and look for gifts again;
   My trifles come as treasures from my mind.
It is a precious jewel to be plain;
   Sometimes in shell th'orient'st pearls we find.   10
Of others take a sheaf, of me a grain,
          Of me a grain.

Within this pack pins, points, laces, and gloves,
   And divers toys fitting a country fair,
But in my heart, where duty serves and loves,   15
   Turtles and twins, court's brood, a heavenly pair.
Happy the heart that thinks of no removes,
          Of no removes!

'FINE KNACKS FOR LADIES . . .': 1 **knacks:** ornaments or knick-knacks 3 **the Fair:** the beautiful, i.e. ladies 7 **guiles:** tricks, deceits **look for gifts again:** expect gifts to be given in return 10 **orient'st:** brightest 13 **points:** pieces of lace made with a needle 16 **Turtles:** turtledoves **court's brood:** the children of courting 17 **removes:** changes, absences

'NOW IS THE MONTH OF MAYING'

Now is the month of maying,
When merry lads are playing
Each with his bonny lass
Upon the greeny grass.

The spring, clad all in gladness,   5
Doth laugh at winter's sadness,
And to the bagpipe's sound
The nymphs tread out their ground.

Fie, then! Why sit we musing,
Youth's sweet delight refusing?   10
Say, dainty nymphs, and speak,
Shall we play barley-break?

'NOW IS THE MONTH OF MAYING': 1 **maying:** the practising of Mayday customs 12 **barley-break:** an old rustic game in which couples took turns at catching others

'FAIN WOULD I CHANGE THAT NOTE'

FAIN would I change that note
   To which fond love hath charmed me
Long, long to sing by rote,
   Fancying that that harmed me.
Yet when this thought doth come,   5
'Love is the perfect sum
   Of all delight,'
I have no other choice
Either for pen or voice
   To sing or write.   10

O Love, they wrong thee much
   That say thy sweet is bitter,
When thy ripe fruit is such
   As nothing can be sweeter.
Fair house of joy and bliss,   15
Where truest pleasure is,
   I do adore thee.
I know thee what thou art,
I serve thee with my heart
   And fall before thee.   20

'THERE IS A LADY SWEET AND KIND'

THERE is a lady sweet and kind,
Was never face so pleased my mind;
I did but see her passing by,
And yet I love her till I die.

Her gesture, motion, and her smiles,   5
Her wit, her voice, my heart beguiles;
Beguiles my heart, I know not why,
And yet I love her till I die.

Her free behaviour, winning looks,
Will make a lawyer burn his books.   10
I touched her not, alas, not I,
And yet I love her till I die.

Had I her fast betwixt mine arms,
Judge you that think such sports were harms,
Were't any harm? No, no, fie, fie!   15
For I will love her till I die.

Should I remain confinèd there
So long as Phoebus in his sphere,
I to request, she to deny,
Yet would I love her till I die.   20

Cupid is wingèd and doth range,
Her country so my love doth change;
But change she earth, or change she sky,
Yet will I love her till I die.

'THERE IS A LADY SWEET AND KIND': 2 **Was . . . mind:** no face has ever
pleased my mind as much 14 **harms:** injuries 18 **Phoebus:** the god
of the sun, hence the sun itself 22 **Her country . . . change:** the one
I love goes from place to place

'WHEN I WAS OTHERWISE THAN NOW I AM'

WHEN I was otherwise than now I am,
  I lovèd more, but skilled not so much;
Fair words and smiles could have contented then,
  My simple age and ignorance was such.
But at the length experience made me wonder   5
That hearts and tongues did lodge so far asunder.

As watermen which on the Thames do row
  Look to the east, but west keeps on their way,
My sovereign sweet her countenance settled so
  To feed my hope, while she her snares might lay.   10
And when she saw that I was in her danger,
Good God, how soon she provèd then a ranger.

I could not choose but laugh, although too late,
  To see great craft deciphered in a toy.
I love her still, but such conditions hate   15
  Which so profanes my paradise of joy.
Love whets the wits, whose pain is but a pleasure,
A toy by fits to play withal at leisure.

'WHEN I WAS OTHERWISE THAN NOW I AM': 2 **skillèd:** mattered 4 **simple:**
innocent, guileless 8 **Look . . . way:** a man rowing a boat faces
backwards 11 **danger:** power 12 **ranger:** a rover 14 **To see . . . toy:**
to see great skill shown in doing something trivial 18 **A toy . . .**
leisure: a plaything used now and then to fill idle time

SIR HENRY WOTTON

ON HIS MISTRESS, THE QUEEN OF BOHEMIA

YOU meaner beauties of the night,
  Which poorly satisfy our eyes
More by your number than your light,
  You common people of the skies;
  What are you when the moon shall rise?   5

You curious chanters of the wood,
  That warble forth Dame Nature's lays,
Thinking your passions understood
  By your weak accents; what's your praise
  When Philomel her voice shall raise?   10

You violets, that first appear,
  By your pure purple mantles known,
Like the proud virgins of the year,
  As if the spring were all your own;
  What are you when the rose is blown?   15

So, when my mistress shall be seen
  In form and beauty of her mind,
By virtue first, then choice, a queen,
  Tell me, if she were not designed
  Th' eclipse and glory of her kind?   20

ON HIS MISTRESS, THE QUEEN OF BOHEMIA: 1 **meaner . . . night:** stars
6 **curious chanters:** skilful singers 7 **lays:** songs 10 **Philomel:** the
nightingale 12 **mantles:** cloaks, clothing 15 **blown:** bloomed

ON THE SUDDEN RESTRAINT OF THE EARL OF SOMERSET

DAZZLED thus with height of place,
Whilst our hopes our wits beguile,
No man marks the narrow space
'Twixt a prison and a smile.

Then since Fortune's favours fade,   5
You that in her arms do sleep,
Learn to swim and not to wade;
For the hearts of kings are deep.

But if greatness be so blind,
As to trust in towers of air,   10
Let it be with goodness lined,
That at least the fall be fair.

Then though darkened you shall say,
When friends fail and princes frown,
Virtue is the roughest way,   15
But proves at night a bed of down.

THE CHARACTER OF A HAPPY LIFE

HOW happy is he born and taught
That serveth not another's will;
Whose armour is his honest thought,
And simple truth his utmost skill!

Whose passions not his masters are;   5
Whose soul is still prepared for death,
Untied unto the world by care
Of public fame or private breath;

Who envies none that chance doth raise,
Nor vice; who never understood   10
How deepest wounds are giv'n by praise;
Nor rules of state, but rules of good;

Who hath his life from rumours freed;
Whose conscience is his strong retreat;
Whose state can neither flatterers feed,   15
Nor ruin make oppressors great.

Who God doth late and early pray
More of His grace than gifts to lend;
And entertains the harmless day
With a religious book or friend.   20

This man is freed from servile bands
Of hope to rise, or fear to fall;
Lord of himself, though not of lands;
And having nothing, yet hath all.

THE CHARACTER OF A HAPPY LIFE: 6 **still:** always 7 **Untied:** not tied
15 **state:** wealth and rank 19 **entertains the harmless day:** fills the
day with harmless activities 21 **bands:** bonds

SIR JOHN DAVIES

From ORCHESTRA: A POEM OF DANCING

BEHOLD the world, how it is whirlèd round!
    And for it is so whirled, is namèd so;
In whose large volumes many rules are found
    Of this new art, which it doth fairly show.
      For your quick eyes in wandering to and fro,   5
      From east to west, on no one thing can glance,
        But, if you mark it well, it seems to dance.

First you see fixed in this huge mirror blue
    Of trembling lights a number numberless;
Fixed, they are named, but with a name untrue;   10
    For they all move and in a dance express
      The great long year that doth contain no less
      Than threescore hundreds of those years in all,
        Which the sun makes with his course natural.

What if to you these sparks disordered seem,   15
    As if by chance they had been scattered there?
The gods a solemn measure do it deem
    And see a just proportion everywhere,
      And know the points whence first their movings
      were,
        To which first points when all return again,   20
        The axletree of heaven shall break in twain.

ORCHESTRA: A POEM OF DANCING: 2 **for:** because **whirled:** a pun on
'world' 10-11 **Fixed . . . move:** in medieval astronomy it was
believed that certain stars were fixed and did not move; this was
later seen to be mistaken 11–20 **For they . . . again:** a reference to
the Great Year or Platonic Cycle (made up of hundreds of years) at
the end of which the stars return to the positions with respect to the
equinoxes from which they started

Under that spangled sky five wandering flames,
    Besides the king of day and queen of night,
Are wheeled around, in all their sundry frames,
    And all in sundry measures do delight;   25
      Yet altogether keep no measure right;
      For by itself each doth itself advance,
        And by itself each doth a galliard dance.

Venus, the mother of that bastard Love,
    Which doth usurp the world's great marshal's name,
Just with the sun her dainty feet doth move,   31
    And unto her doth all her gestures frame;
      Now after, now afore, the flattering dame
      With divers cunning passages doth err,
        With him respecting that respects not her.   35

For that brave sun, the father of the day,
    Doth love this earth, the mother of the night;
And, like a reveller in rich array,
    Doth dance his galliard in his leman's sight,
      Both back and forth and sideways passing light.   40
      His gallant grace doth so the gods amaze,
        That all, stand still and at his beauty gaze.

But see the earth when she approacheth near,
    How she for joy doth spring and sweetly smile;
But see again her sad and heavy cheer,   45
    When changing places he retires a while;
      But those black clouds he shortly will exíle,
      And make them all before his presence fly,
        As mists consumed before his cheerful eye.

Who doth not see the measure of the moon?   50
    Which thirteen times she danceth every year,
And ends her pavan thirteen times as soon
    As doth her brother, of whose golden hair
      She borroweth part, and proudly doth it wear.
      Then doth she coyly turn her face aside,   55
        That half her cheek is scarce sometimes descried.

Next her, the pure, subtle, and cleansing fire
    Is swiftly carried in a circle even,
Though Vulcan be pronounced by many a liar
    The only halting god that dwells in heaven;   60
      But that foul name may be more fitly given
      To your false fire, that far from heaven is fall,
        And doth consume, waste, spoil, disorder all.

23 **king of day:** the sun **queen of night:** the moon 25 **measures:**
dances 28 **galliard:** a lively dance 29 **that bastard Love:** Cupid, the
son of Venus 30 **the world's great marshal:** God, or Christ 35 **With
him . . . her:** the planet Venus moves as if in deference to the sun,
which does not repay her respect 39 **leman:** lover 45 **heavy cheer:**
gloomy disposition 52 **pavan:** a slow courtly dance 56 **descried:**
seen 59 **Vulcan:** Roman god of fire and metalworking, also the
name given to a hypothetical planet thought to lie within the orbit
of Mercury 60 **halting:** lame

And now behold your tender nurse, the air,
  And common neighbour that aye runs around; 65
How many pictures and impressions fair
  Within her empty regions are there found,
  Which to your senses dancing do propound?
    For what are breath, speech, echoes, music, winds,
    But dancing of the air, in sundry kinds? 70

For, when you breathe, the air in order moves,
  Now in, now out, in time and measure true,
And when you speak, so well she dancing loves,
  That doubling oft and often redoubling new
  With thousand forms she doth herself endue; 75
    For all the words that from your lips repair
    Are nought but tricks and turnings of the air.

Hence is her prattling daughter, Echo, born,
  That dances to all voices she can hear.
There is no sound so harsh that she doth scorn, 80
  Nor any time wherein she will forbear
  The air pavement with her feet to wear;
    And yet her hearing sense is nothing quick,
    For after time she endeth every trick.

And thou, sweet music, dancing's only life, 85
  The ear's sole happiness, the air's best speech,
Lodestone of fellowship, charming rod of strife,
  The soft mind's paradise, the sick man's leech,
  With thine own tongue thou trees and stones canst
    teach,
    That when the air doth dance her finest measure,
    Then art thou born, the gods' and men's sweet
      pleasure. 91

Lastly, where keep the winds their revelry,
  Their violent turnings and wild whirling hays,
But in the air's tralucent gallery?
  Where she herself is turned a hundred ways, 95
  While with those masquers wantonly she plays.
    Yet in this misrule they such rule embrace
    As two, at once, encumber not the place.

If then fire, air, wandering and fixèd lights,
  In every province of th' imperial sky, 100
Yield perfect forms of dancing to your sights,
  In vain I teach the ear that which the eye,
  With certain view, already doth descry;
    But for your eyes perceive not all they see,
    In this I will your senses' master be. 105

For lo! The sea that fleets about the land,
  And like a girdle clips her solid waist,
Music and measure both doth understand;
  For his great crystal eye is always cast
  Up to the moon, and on her fixèd fast; 110
    And as she danceth in her pallid sphere,
    So danceth he about the centre here.

Sometimes his proud green waves in order set,
  One after other, flow unto the shore;
Which when they have with many kisses wet, 115
  They ebb away in order, as before;
  And to make known his courtly love the more,
    He oft doth lay aside his three-forked mace,
    And with his arms the timorous earth embrace.

Only the earth doth stand forever still: 120
  Her rocks remove not, nor her mountains meet,
Although some wits enriched with learning's skill
  Say heaven stands firm and that the earth doth
    fleet,
  And swiftly turneth underneath their feet;
    Yet, though the earth is ever steadfast seen, 125
    On her broad breast hath dancing ever been.

For those blue veins that through her body spread,
  Those sapphire streams from which great hills do
    spring,
The earth's great dugs, for every wight is fed
  With sweet fresh moisture from them issuing, 130
  Observe a dance in their wild wandering;
    And still their dance begets a murmur sweet,
    And still the murmur with the dance doth meet.

Of all their ways, I love Meander's path, 134
  Which, to the tunes of dying swans, doth dance;
Such winding sleights, such turns and tricks he
    hath,
  Such creeks, such wrenches, and such dalliance,
  That, whether it be hap or heedless chance,
    In his indented course and wriggling play,
    He seems to dance a perfect cunning hay. 140

But wherefore do these streams forever run?
  To keep themselves forever sweet and clear;
For let their everlasting course be done,
  They straight corrupt and foul with mud appear.
  O ye sweet nymphs, that beauty's loss do fear, 145
    Contemn the drugs that physic doth devise,
    And learn of Love this dainty exercise.

---

107 **clips:** encircles 118 **three-forked mace:** the trident carried by Neptune, god of the sea, as symbol of his power 121 **Her . . . meet:** the earth's rocks do not move, and its mountains do not collide 123 **fleet:** move, fly 127 **blue veins:** rivers 129 **dugs:** breasts **wight:** person 132 **still:** always 134 **Meander:** a proverbially winding river in ancient Phrygia (modern-day Turkey) 141 **wherefore:** why 144 **straight:** immediately 146 **Contemn:** despise **physic:** medicine

---

65 **aye:** always 87 **charming rod:** magician's wand 88 **soft:** weak **leech:** doctor (from the medicinal use of leeches) 93 **hay:** a country dance 96 **masquer:** reveller 104 **But for . . . see:** but because your eyes don't comprehend everything they can see

See how those flowers, that have sweet beauty too,
  The only jewels that the earth doth wear,
When the young sun in bravery her doth woo,   150
  As oft as they the whistling wind do hear,
  Do wave their tender bodies here and there;
    And though their dance no perfect measure is,
    Yet oftentimes their music makes them kiss.

What makes the vine about the elm to dance   155
  With turnings, windings, and embracements round?
What makes the lodestone to the north advance
  His subtle point, as if from thence he found
  His chief attractive virtue to redound?   159
    Kind nature first doth cause all things to love;
    Love makes them dance, and in just order move.

Hark how the birds do sing, and mark then how,
  Jump with the modulation of their lays,
They lightly leap and skip from bough to bough;
  Yet do the cranes deserve a greater praise,   165
  Which keep such measure in their airy ways,
    As when they all in order rankèd are,
    They make a perfect form triangular.

In the chief angle flies the watchful guide;
  And all the followers their heads do lay   170
On their foregoers' backs, on either side;
  But, for the captain hath no rest to stay
  His head, forwearied with the windy way,
    He back retires; and then the next behind,
    As his lieutenant, leads them through the wind.

But why relate I every singular?   176
  Since the world's great fortunes and affairs
Forward and backward rapt and whirlèd are,
  According to the music of the spheres;
  And Chance herself her nimble feet upbears   180
    On a round slippery wheel, that rolleth aye,
    And turns all states with her imperious sway;

Learn then to dance, you that are princes born,
  And lawful lords of earthly creatures all;
Imitate them, and thereof take no scorn,   185
  (For this new art to them is natural)
  And imitate the stars celestial.
    For when pale death your vital twist shall sever,
    Your better parts must dance with them for ever.

159 **redound:** rebound, reflect 163 **jump:** exactly **lays:** songs
166 **airy ways:** flight 169 **In the chief angle:** at the point of the
triangle 172 **for:** because **rest to stay:** place to rest 173 **forwearied:**
exhausted 179 **music of the spheres:** refers to the ancient belief
that the planets made harmonic musical sounds by virtue of their
spinning 188 **vital twist:** the thread of life, said to be cut by the
Fates to end a person's life 189 **better parts:** soul

JOHN DONNE

THE GOOD-MORROW

I WONDER, by my troth, what thou and I
Did, till we loved? Were we not weaned till then?
But sucked on country pleasures, childishly?
Or snorted we in the seven sleepers' den?
'Twas so; but this, all pleasures fancies be.   5
If ever any beauty I did see,
Which I desired, and got, 'twas but a dream of thee.

And now good-morrow to our waking souls,
Which watch not one another out of fear;
For love, all love of other sights controls,   10
And makes one little room an everywhere.
Let sea-discoverers to new worlds have gone,
Let maps to others, worlds on worlds have shown,
Let us possess one world, each hath one, and is one.

My face in thine eye, thine in mine appears,   15
And true plain hearts do in the faces rest;
Where can we find two better hemispheres
Without sharp North, without declining West?
Whatever dies was not mixed equally;
If our two loves be one, or thou and I   20
Love so alike that none do slacken, none can die.

THE GOOD-MORROW: 1 **troth:** faith 3 **country:** simple and
unsophisticated 4 **seven sleepers' den:** refers to seven 3rd-century
Christians who were walled up alive by Roman persecutors but
slept miraculously for 187 years 5 **but . . . be:** apart from this, all
pleasures are imaginary 19 **Whatever . . . equally:** in medieval
medicine, disease was thought to be caused by an imbalance in
the body 21 **slacken:** decline

SONG

Go and catch a falling star,
  Get with child a mandrake root,
Tell me where all past years are,
  Or who cleft the Devil's foot,
Teach me to hear mermaids singing,   5
Or to keep off envy's stinging,
      And find
      What wind
Serves to advance an honest mind.

If thou be'st born to strange sights,   10
  Things invisible to see,
Ride ten thousand days and nights,
  Till age snow white hairs on thee;
Thou, when thou return'st, wilt tell me
All strange wonders that befell thee,   15
      And swear
      No where
Lives a woman true, and fair.

If thou find'st one, let me know,
   Such a pilgrimage were sweet;   20
Yet do not, I would not go,
   Though at next door we might meet:
Though she were true when you met her,
And last till you write your letter,
      Yet she   25
      Will be
False, ere I come, to two or three.

THE SUN RISING

    BUSY old fool, unruly sun,
      Why dost thou thus
Through windows and through curtains call on us?
Must to thy motions lovers' seasons run?
      Saucy pedantic wretch, go chide   5
      Late schoolboys and sour 'prentices,
   Go tell court-huntsmen that the King will ride,
   Call country ants to harvest offices;
Love, all alike, no season knows, nor clime,
Nor hours, days, months, which are the rags of
      time.   10

    Thy beams so reverend and strong
      Why shouldst thou think?
I could eclipse and cloud them with a wink
But that I would not lose her sight so long:
      If her eyes have not blinded thine,   15
      Look, and, tomorrow late, tell me
   Whether both th'Indias of spice and mine
   Be where thou left'st them, or lie here with me.
Ask for those kings whom thou saw'st yesterday,
And thou shalt hear 'All here in one bed lay'.   20

    She is all states, and all princes I;
      Nothing else is.
Princes do but play us; compared to this,
All honour's mimic, all wealth alchemy.
      Thou, sun, art half as happy as we,   25
      In that the world's contracted thus;
   Thine age asks ease, and since thy duties be
   To warm the world, that's done in warming us.
Shine here to us, and thou art everywhere;
This bed thy centre is, these walls thy sphere.   30

THE SUN RISING: 6 **'prentices:** apprentices 7 **court-huntsmen:** men who seek honours or wealth at the monarch's court 8 **Call . . . offices:** summon the slavish unintelligent rustics to gather in the harvest 17 **both . . . mine:** both East and West Indies, sources of spices and gold 24 **All . . . alchemy:** all honour is merely a copy (of this), all wealth is pretence

THE CANONIZATION

FOR God's sake hold your tongue, and let me love,
   Or chide my palsy, or my gout,
My five grey hairs, or ruined fortune flout;

With wealth your state, your mind with arts,
     improve;
   Take you a course, get you a place,   5
   Observe his honour, or his grace,
Or the King's real or his stampèd face
   Contémplate: what you will, approve,
   So you will let me love.

Alas, alas, who's injured by my love?   10
   What merchant's ships have my sighs drowned?
Who says my tears have overflowed his ground?
   When did my colds a forward spring remove?
     When did the heats which my veins fill
     Add one more to the plaguy bill?   15
Soldiers find wars, and lawyers find out still
   Litigious men, which quarrels move,
   Though she and I do love.

Call us what you will, we are made such by love;
   Call her one, me another fly;   20
We're tapers too, and at our own cost die;
   And we in us find th'eagle and the dove.
     The phoenix riddle hath more wit
     By us: we two being one, are it.
So to one neutral thing both sexes fit: 25
   We die and rise the same, and prove
   Mysterious by this love.

We can die by it, if not live by love,
   And if unfit for tombs and hearse
Our legend be, it will be fit for verse;   30
   And if no piece of chronicle we prove,
     We'll build in sonnets pretty rooms;
     As well a well-wrought urn becomes
The greatest ashes, as half-acre tombs;
   And by these hymns all shall approve   35
   Us canonized for Love:

And thus invoke us: 'You whom reverend love
   Made one another's hermitage;
You to whom love was peace, that now is rage;
   Who did the whole world's soul contract, and drove
     Into the glasses of your eyes   41
     (So made such mirrors, and such spies,
That they did all to you epitomize,)
   Countries, towns, courts: Beg from above
   A pattern of your love!'   45

THE CANONIZATION: 2–3 **chide . . . flout:** criticize me for being too old for love, or for wasting my money 5 **place:** a position in government or the court 6 **Observe . . . grace:** pay court to a lord or a bishop 7–8 **Or . . . Contémplate:** either go the royal court (and see the king's face) or seek after riches (coins stamped with the king's head) 8 **approve:** try 15 **plaguy bill:** the list of those who have died of the plague 20–1 **Call her . . . die:** she and I are simultaneously both the moths and the flame 22 **eagle:** symbol of strength **dove:** symbol of gentleness 23 **phoenix:** a mythical bird said to consume itself in fire and be reborn out of the ashes 31 **chronicle:** history 33 **becomes:** is fitting for, is becoming to

SONG

SWEETEST love, I do not go
  For weariness of thee,
Nor in hope the world can show
  A fitter love for me;
    But since that I   5
Must die at last, 'tis best
To use my self in jest
  Thus by fained deaths to die;

Yesternight the sun went hence,
  And yet is here today,   10
He hath no desire nor sense,
  Nor half so short a way:
    Then fear not me,
But believe that I shall make
Speedier journeys, since I take   15
  More wings and spurs than he.

Oh, how feeble is man's power,
  That if good fortune fall,
Cannot add another hour,
  Nor a lost hour recall!   20
    But come bad chance,
And we join to't our strength,
And we teach it art and length,
  It self o'er us t'advance.

When thou sigh'st, thou sigh'st not wind,   25
  But sigh'st my soul away,
When thou weep'st, unkindly kind,
  My life's blood doth decay.
    It cannot be
That thou lov'st me, as thou say'st,   30
If in thine my life thou waste,
  Thou art the best of me.

Let not thy divining heart
  Forethink me any ill,
Destiny may take thy part,   35
  And may thy fears fulfil;
    But think that we
Are but turned aside to sleep;
Thy who one another keep
  Alive, ne'er parted be.   40

THE ANNIVERSARY

ALL kings, and all their favourites,
  All glory of honours, beauties, wits,
The sun it self, which makes times, as they pass,
Is elder by a year, now, than it was
When thou and I first one another saw: 5
All other things, to their destruction draw,
  Only our love hath no decay;

This, no tomorrow hath, nor yesterday,
Running it never runs from us away,
But truly keeps his first, last, everlasting day.   10

  Two graves must hide thine and my corse,
  If one might, death were no divorce.
Alas, as well as other princes, we,
(Who prince enough in one another be,)
Must leave at last in death, these eyes, and ears,   15
Oft fed with true oaths, and with sweet salt tears;
  But souls where nothing dwells but love
(All other thoughts being inmates) then shall prove
This, or a love increasèd there above,
When bodies to their graves, souls from their graves
    remove.   20

  And then we shall be throughly blest,
  But weep no more, than all the rest;
Here upon earth, we're kings, and none but we
Can be such kings, nor of such subjects be.
Who is so safe as we? where none can do   25
Treason to us, except one of us two.
  True and false fears let us refrain,
Let us love nobly, and live, and add again
Years and years unto years, till we attain
To write threescore: this is the second of our reign.   30

THE ANNIVERSARY: 11 **corse:** corpse 18 **inmates:** temporary inhabitants, lodgers 21 **throughly:** thoroughly 27 **refrain:** restrain

A NOCTURNAL UPON ST LUCY'S DAY, BEING THE SHORTEST DAY

'TIS the year's midnight, and it is the day's,
Lucy's, who scarce seven hours herself unmasks,
  The sun is spent, and now his flasks
  Send forth light squibs, no constant rays;
    The world's whole sap is sunk: 5
The general balm th'hydroptic earth hath drunk,
Whither, as to the bed's feet, life is shrunk,
Dead and interred; yet all these seem to laugh,
Compared with me, who am their epitaph.

Study me then, you who shall lovers be   10
At the next world, that is, at the next spring:
  For I am every dead thing,
  In whom love wrought new alchemy.
    For his art did express
A quintessence even from nothingness,   15
From dull privations, and lean emptiness:
He ruined me, and I am re-begot
Of absence, darkness, death; things which are not.

All others, from all things, draw all that's good,
Life, soul, form, spirit, whence they being have;   20
  I, by love's limbeck, am the grave
  Of all, that's nothing. Oft a flood

Have we two wept, and so
Drowned the whole world, us two; oft did we grow
To be two chaoses, when we did show   25
Care to ought else; and often absences
Withdrew our souls, and made us carcases.

But I am by her death, (which word wrongs her)
Of the first nothing, the elixir grown;
Were I a man, that I were one,   30
I needs must know; I should prefer,
If I were any beast,
Some ends, some means; yea plants, yea stones detest,
And love; all, all some properties invest;
If I an ordinary nothing were,   35
As shadow, a light, and body must be here.

But I am none; nor will my sun renew.
You lovers, for whose sake, the lesser sun
At this time to the Goat is run
To fetch new lust, and give it you,   40
Enjoy your summer all;
Since she enjoys her long night's festival,
Let me prepare towards her, and let me call
This hour her vigil, and her eve, since this
Both the year's and the day's deep midnight is.   45

A NOCTURNAL UPON ST LUCY'S DAY: St Lucy's Day (13 December) was believed to be the shortest day of the year 3 **flasks**: the stars, seen as having stored up some of the sun's light 4 **light squibs**: feeble flashes of light 6 **hydroptic**: suffering from dropsy (unnatural accumulation of water in the body), and thus unusually thirsty 21 **limbeck**: alembic (an apparatus used in distilling) 30–1 **Were I . . . know**: as a man knows he is a man, Donne cannot be a man since he does not know this 31–3 **I should . . . means**: even animals can make choices and decisions, but Donne cannot 33–4 **yea plants . . . love**: even plants and stones are capable of hate and love 38–40 **the lesser sun . . . lust**: the weakened sun has entered the constellation of Capricorn (the Goat), seen as a source of sexual power

A VALEDICTION: FORBIDDING MOURNING

As virtuous men pass mildly away,
And whisper to their souls to go,
Whilst some of their sad friends do say,
The breath goes now, and some say, no:

So let us melt, and make no noise,   5
No tear-floods, nor sigh-tempests move,
'Twere profanation of our joys
To tell the laity our love.

Moving of th'earth brings harms and fears,
Men reckon what it did and meant,   10
But trepidation of the spheres,
Though greater far, is innocent.

Dull sublunary lovers' love
(Whose soul is sense) cannot admit

Absence, because it doth remove   15
Those things which elemented it.

But we by a love, so much refined,
That our selves know not what it is,
Inter-assurèd of the mind,
Care less, eyes, lips, and hands to miss.   20

Our two souls, therefore, which are one,
Though I must go, endure not yet
A breach, but an expansïon,
Like gold to airy thinness beat.

If they be two, they are two so   25
As stiff twin compasses are two,
Thy soul, the fixed foot, makes no show
To move, but doth if th'other do.

And though it in the centre sit,
Yet when the other far doth roam,   30
It leans, and hearkens after it,
And grows erect, as that comes home.

Such wilt thou be to me, who must
Like th'other foot, obliquely run;
They firmness makes my circle just,   35
And makes me end, where I begun.

A VALEDICTION: FORBIDDING MOURNING: 11 **trepidation of the spheres**: movement of the stars and planets 13 **sublunary**: earthly and thus ordinary (literally, beneath the moon) 16 **elemented**: comprised 35 **just**: complete

THE ECSTASY

WHERE, like a pillow on a bed,
A pregnant bank swelled up, to rest
The violet's reclining head,
Sat we two, one another's best.

Our hands were firmly cémented   5
With a fast balm, which thence did spring,
Our eye-beams twisted, and did thread
Our eyes, upon one double string;

So t'intergraft our hands, as yet
Was all our means to make us one,   10
And pictures in our eyes to get
Was all our propagatïon.

As 'twixt two equal armies, Fate
Suspends uncertain victory,
Our souls, (which to advance their state,   15
Were gone out), hung 'twixt her, and me.

THE ECSTASY: 2 **pregnant**: fertile, blooming 15 **advance their state**: improve or show their quality

And whilst our souls negotiate there,
   We like sepulchral statues lay;
All day, the same our postures were,
   And we said nothing, all the day.   20

If any, so by love refined,
   That he soul's language understood,
And by good love were grown all mind,
   Within convenient distance stood,

He (though he knew not which soul spake,   25
   Because both meant, both spake the same)
Might thence a new concoction take,
   And part far purer than he came.

This ecstasy doth unperplex
   (We said) and tell us what we love,   30
We see by this, it was not sex,
   We see, we saw not what did move:

But as all several souls contain
   Mixture of things, they know not what,
Love, these mixed souls doth mix again,   35
   And makes both one, each this and that.

A single violet transplant,
   The strength, the colour, and the size,
(All which before was poor, and scant,)
   Redoubles still, and multiplies.   40

When love, with one another so
   Interinanimates two souls,
That abler soul, which thence doth flow,
   Defécts of loneliness controls.

We then, who are this new soul, know,   45
   Of what we are composed, and made,
For, th'atomies of which we grow,
   Are souls, whom no change can invade.

But, oh, alas, so long, so far
   Our bodies why do we forbear?   50
They are ours, though they are not we, we are
   The intelligences, they the sphere.

We owe them thanks, because they thus,
   Did us, to us, at first convey,
Yielded their forces, sense, to us,   55
   Nor are dross to us, but allay.

On man heaven's influence works not so,
   But that it first imprints the air,
So soul into the soul may flow,
   Though it to body first repair.   60

As our blood labours to beget
   Spirits, as like souls as it can,
Because such fingers need to knit
   That subtle knot, which makes us man:

So must pure lovers' souls descend   65
   T'affections, and to faculties,
Which sense may reach and apprehend,
   Else a great prince in prison lies.

T'our bodies turn we then, that so
   Weak men on love revealed may look;   70
Love's mysteries in souls do grow,
   But yet the body is his book.

And if some lover, such as we,
   Have heard this dialogue of one,
Let him still mark us, he shall see   75
   Small change, when we're to bodies gone.

THE FUNERAL

WHOEVER comes to shroud me, do not harm
     Nor question much
That subtle wreath of hair which crowns my arm;
The mystery, the sign you must not touch,
     For 'tis my outward Soul,   5
Viceroy to that which then to heaven being gone
     Will leave this to control
And keep these limbs, her provinces, from dissolution.

For if the sinewy thread my brain lets fall
     Through every part   10
Can tie those parts, and make me one of all,
These hairs, which upward grew, and strength and art
     Have from a better brain,
Can better do't; except she meant that I
     By this should know my pain,   15
As prisoners then are manaclèd when they're
     condemned to die.

Whate'er she meant by't, bury it with me,
     For since I am
Love's martyr, it might breed idolatry
If into others' hands these relics came;   20
     As 'twas humility
To afford to it all that a soul can do,
     So 'tis some bravery
That since you would save none of me, I bury some of
     you.

---

32 **what did move:** the motive 33 **several:** separate 47 **atomies:**
constituent parts 56 **allay:** alloy 60 **repair:** go

THE FUNERAL: 1 **shroud:** prepare for burial 3 **subtle:** fine 12 **upward:**
i.e. towards heaven 24 **some of you:** i.e., your lock of hair

THE RELIC

WHEN my grave is broke up again
Some second guest to entertain,
(For graves have learned that woman-head
To be to more than one a bed)
 And he that digs it, spies   5
A bracelet of bright hair about the bone,
 Will he not let's alone,
And think that there a loving couple lies,
Who thought that this device might be some way
To make their souls, at the last busy day,   10
Meet at this grave, and make a little stay?

If this fall in a time, or land,
Where mis-devotion doth command,
Then, he that digs us up, will bring
Us, to the bishop, and the king,   15
 To make us relics; then
Thou shalt be a Mary Magdalen, and I
 A something else thereby;
All women shall adore us, and some men;
And since at such time, miracles are sought,   20
I would have that age by this paper taught
What miracles we harmless lovers wrought.

First, we loved well and faithfully,
Yet knew not what we loved, nor why,
Difference of sex no more we knew,   25
 Than our guardian angels do;
 Coming and going, we
Perchance might kiss, but not between those meals;
 Our hands ne'er touched the seals,
Which nature, injured by late law, sets free: 30
These miracles we did; but now alas,
All measure, and all language, I should pass,
Should I tell what a miracle she was.

THE RELIC: 1 **broke up:** opened 21 **this paper:** this poem 30 **injured by late law:** subject, in modern times, to restrictions that did not apply in earlier, more innocent, times

TO HIS MISTRESS GOING TO BED

COME, Madam, come, all rest my powers defy,
Until I labour, I in labour lie.
The foe oft-times having the foe in sight,
Is tired with standing though they never fight.
Off with that girdle, like heaven's zone glittering,   5
But a far fairer world encompassing.
Unpin that spangled breastplate which you wear,
That th'eyes of busy fools may be stopped there.
Unlace yourself, for that harmonious chime
Tells me from you, that now it is bed time.   10
Off with that happy busk, which I envy,
That still can be, and still can stand so nigh.
Your gown going off, such beauteous state reveals,
As when from flow'ry meads th'hill's shadow steals.
Off with that wiry coronet and show   15
The hairy diadem which on you doth grow;
Now off with those shoes, and then safely tread
In this love's hallowed temple, this soft bed.
In such white robes heaven's angels used to be
Received by men; thou angel bring'st with thee   20
A heaven like Mahomet's paradise; and though
Ill spirits walk in white, we eas'ly know
By this these angels from an evil sprite,
Those set our hairs, but these our flesh upright.
 License my roving hands, and let them go   25
Before, behind, between, above, below.
O my America! my new-found-land,
My kingdom, safeliest when with one man manned,
My mine of precious stones, my empery,
How blest am I in this discovering thee!   30
To enter in these bonds, is to be free;
Then where my hand is set, my seal shall be.
 Full nakedness! All joys are due to thee,
As souls unbodied, bodies unclothed must be,
To taste whole joys. Gems which you women use   35
Are like Atlanta's balls, cast in men's views,
That when a fool's eye lighteth on a gem,
His earthly soul may covet theirs, not them.
Like pictures, or like books' gay coverings made
For laymen, are all women thus arrayed;   40
Themselves are mystic books, which only we
(Whom their imputed grace will dignify)
Must see revealed. Then since I may know,
As liberally, as to a midwife, show
Thyself: cast all, yea, this white linen hence,   45
Here is no penance due to innocence.
 To teach thee, I am naked first; why then
What needst thou have more covering than a man?

TO HIS MISTRESS GOING TO BED: 1 **all rest . . . defy:** desire will not let me sleep 2 **Until . . . lie:** I am in restless anticipation until I am in action 5 **heaven's zone:** the constellation Orion's Belt 9 **harmonious chime:** i.e. she is acceding to his requests 11 **busk:** corset 21 **Mahomet's paradise:** the Muslim paradise, seen as full of sensual pleasure 22 **Ill:** evil 23 **sprite:** spirit 24 **set . . . upright:** give us an erection 29 **empery:** empire 32 **Then . . . be:** a play on the signing of a document followed by setting a seal on it 36 **Atlanta's balls:** in Greek myth, Atalanta would only marry a man who could beat her in a foot race. Hippomenes accomplished this by dropping three golden apples, which she stopped to pick up 48 **What needst thou:** why do you require

From HOLY SONNETS

AT the round earth's imagined corners blow
Your trumpets, Angels, and arise, arise
From death, you numberless infinities
Of souls, and to your scattered bodies go,

All whom the flood did, and fire shall overthrow,   5
All whom war, dearth, age, agues, tyrannies,
Despair, law, chance, hath slain, and you whose eyes
Shall behold God, and never taste death's woe.
But let them sleep, Lord, and me mourn a space,
For, if above all these, my sins abound,   10
'Tis late to ask abundance of Thy grace,
When we are there; here on this lowly ground
Teach me how to repent; for that's as good
As if Thou'dst sealed my pardon with Thy blood.

DEATH, be not proud, though some have callèd thee
Mighty and dreadful, for thou art not so:
For those whom thou think'st thou dost overthrow
Die not, poor Death; nor yet canst thou kill me.
From rest and sleep, which but thy pictures be,   5
Much pleasure, then from thee much more must flow;
And soonest our best men with thee do go,
Rest of their bones, and souls' delivery.
Thou art slave to fate, chance, kings, and desperate
  men,
And dost with poison, war, and sickness dwell;   10
And poppy or charms can make us sleep as well,
And better, than thy stroke; why swell'st thou then?
One short sleep past, we wake eternally,
And death shall be no more: Death, thou shalt die.

BATTER my heart, three-personed God; for, you
As yet but knock, breathe, shine, and seek to mend;
That I may rise, and stand, o'erthrow me, and bend
Your force, to break, blow, burn and make me new.
I, like an úsurped town, t'another due,   5
Labour t'admit you, but Oh, to no end,
Reason your vicĕroy in me, me should defend,
But is captived, and proves weak or untrue.
Yet dearly I love you, and would be lovèd fain,
But am betrothed unto your enemy: 10
Divorce me, untie, or break that knot again,
Take me to you, imprison me, for I
Except you enthrall me, never shall be free,
Nor ever chaste, except you ravish me.

HOLY SONNETS: AT THE ROUND EARTH'S IMAGINED CORNERS: 5 **fire:** the end of the world 6 **dearth:** famine **agues:** fevers, illnesses 9 **a space:** for a moment DEATH, BE NOT PROUD: 5 **rest . . . be:** rest and sleep are mildly imitative of death 8 **Rest . . . delivery:** repose for the body and liberation for the soul 11 **poppy:** extract of the opium poppy, a narcotic **charms:** magic BATTER MY HEART: 5 **t'another due:** owing allegiance to someone other than the usurper 9 **would . . . fain:** would like to be loved 13 **enthrall:** enslave

GOOD FRIDAY, 1613. RIDING WESTWARD

LET man's soul be a sphere, and then, in this,
The intelligence that moves, devotion is,
And as the other spheres, by being grown

Subject to foreign motions, lose their own,
And being by others hurried every day,   5
Scarce in a year their natural form obey:
Pleasure or business, so, our souls admit
For their first mover, and are whirled by it.
Hence is't, that I am carrièd towards the west
This day, when my soul's form bends toward the east.
There I should see a sun, by rising set,   11
And by that setting endless day beget;
But that Christ on this cross, did rise and fall,
Sin had eternally benighted all.
Yet dare I almost be glad, I do not see   15
That spectacle of too much weight for me.
Who sees God's face, that is self life, must die;
What a death were it then to see God die?
It made his own Lieutenant Nature shrink,
It made his footstool crack, and the sun wink.   20
Could I behold those hands which span the poles,
And turn all spheres at once, pierced with those holes?
Could I behold that endless height which is
Zenith to us, and t'our Antipodes,
Humbled below us? or that blood which is   25
The seat of all our souls, if not of his,
Made dirt of dust, or that flesh which was worn
By God, for His apparel, ragg'd, and torn?
If on these things I durst not look, durst I
Upon his miserable mother cast mine eye,   30
Who was God's partner here, and furnished thus
Half of that sacrifice, which ransomed us?
Though these things, as I ride, be from mine eye,
They're present yet unto my memory,
For that looks towards them; and thou look'st towards
  me,   35
O Saviour, as thou hang'st upon the tree;
I turn my back to thee, but to receive
Corrections, till thy mercies bid thee leave.
Oh, think me worth thine anger, punish me,
Burn off my rusts, and my deformity,   40
Restore thine image, so much, by thy grace,
That thou may'st know me, and I'll turn my face.

GOOD FRIDAY, 1613. RIDING WESTWARD: 1–2 **Let . . . is:** as a sphere is moved by intelligence, so is the soul moved by devotion 10 **the east:** the sunrise, i.e. Christ 13-14 **But . . . all:** if Christ had not died for mankind and risen again, everyone would be lost in sin 20 **footstool:** a biblical reference: 'Thus saith the Lord, The heaven is my throne, and the earth is my footstool' (Isaiah 66.1). The Gospels say that there was an earthquake when Christ died 29 **durst:** dare 30 **miserable:** sad 36 **tree:** the cross

A HYMN TO GOD THE FATHER

WILT thou forgive that sin where I begun,
  Which is my sin, though it were done before?
Wilt thou forgive that sin through which I run,
  And do run still, though still I do deplore?
    When thou hast done, thou hast not done,   5
      For I have more.

Wilt thou forgive that sin which I have won
  Others to sin? and made my sin their door?
Wilt thou forgive that sin which I did shun
  A year or two, but wallowèd in a score?   10
    When thou hast done, thou hast not done,
      For I have more.

I have a sin of fear, that when I have spun
  My last thread I shall perish on the shore;
But swear by thy self, that at my death thy sun   15
  Shall shine as he shines now and heretofore;
    And having done that, Thou hast done,
      I fear no more.

A HYMN TO GOD THE FATHER: 1–2 **that sin . . . before:** original sin 4 **still:** always, continually 5 **thou hast not done:** literally, you have not finished, but also a play on the poet's name (you do not have Donne) 15 **thy sun:** a play on 'thy son' i.e. Christ

THOMAS DEKKER

'GOLDEN SLUMBERS KISS YOUR EYES'

GOLDEN slumbers kiss your eyes,
Smiles awake you when you rise.
Sleep, pretty wantons, do not cry,
And I will sing a lullaby:
Rock them, rock them, lullaby.   5

Care is heavy, therefore sleep you;
You are care, and care must keep you.
Sleep, pretty wantons, do not cry,
And I will sing a lullaby:
Rock them, rock them, lullaby.   10

BEN JONSON

ON MY FIRST SON

FAREWELL, thou child of my right hand, and joy;
My sin was too much hope of thee, loved boy.
Seven years thou wert lent to me, and I thee pay,
Exacted by thy fate, on the just day.
Oh, could I lose all father now! For why   5
Will man lament the state he should envy,
To have so soon 'scaped world's and flesh's rage,
And if no other misery, yet age?
Rest in soft peace, and asked, say, 'Here doth lie
Ben Jonson his best piece of poetry.'   10
For whose sake henceforth all his vows be such,
As what he loves may never like too much.

ON MY FIRST SON: 4 **just:** due 5 **lose all father:** renounce fatherhood 10 **Ben Jonson his:** Ben Jonson's 12 **As . . . much:** may he never become too attached to what he loves

INVITING A FRIEND TO SUPPER

TONIGHT, grave sir, both my poor house, and I
Do equally desire your company:
Not that we think us worthy such a guest,
But that your worth will dignify our feast,
With those that come; whose grace may make that
  seem   5
Something, which else, could hope for no esteem.
It is the fair acceptance, sir, creates
The entertainment perfect: not the cates.
Yet you shall have, to rectify your palate,
An olive, capers, or some better salad   10
Ush'ring the mutton; with a short-legged hen,
If we can get her, full of eggs, and then,
Lemons, and wine for sauce: to these, a cony
Is not to be despaired of, for our money;
And, though fowl, now, be scarce, yet there are clerks,
The sky not falling, think we may have larks.   16
I'll tell you of more, and lie, so you will come:
Of partridge, pheasant, woodcock, of which some
May yet be there; and godwit, if we can:
Knat, rail, and ruff too. Howsoe'er, my man   20
Shall read a piece of Virgil, Tacitus,
Livy, or of some better book to us,
Of which we'll speak our minds, amidst our meat;
And I'll profess no verses to repeat:
To this, if aught appear, which I not know of,   25
That will the pastry, not my paper, show of.
Digestive cheese, and fruit there sure will be;
But that, which most doth take my muse, and me,
Is a pure cup of rich canary wine,
Which is the Mermaid's, now, but shall be mine: 30
Of which had Horace, or Anacreon tasted,
Their lives, as do their lines, till now had lasted.
Tobacco, nectar, or the Thespian spring,
Are all but Luther's beer, to this I sing.
Of this we will sup free, but moderately,   35
And we will have no Pooly, or Parrot by;
Nor shall our cups make any guilty men:
But, at our parting, we will be, as when
We innocently met. No simple word,
That shall be uttered at our mirthful board,   40
Shall make us sad next morning: or affright
The liberty, that we'll enjoy tonight.

INVITING A FRIEND TO SUPPER: 6 **else:** otherwise 8 **cates:** dainties, delicacies 13 **cony:** rabbit 15 **clerks:** scholars, educated men 20 **Knat:** knot (the bird) **man:** servant 26 **paper:** writings 30 **Mermaid:** The Mermaid Tavern in London 31 **Horace:** the Roman poet Quintus Horatius Flaccus (65-8 BC) **Anacreon:** the Greek poet (*c.*572–*c.*488 BC) 33 **nectar:** the drink of the gods **Thespian spring:** in Greek myth, a spring on Mount Helicon whose waters gave poetic inspiration 34 **Luther's beer:** poor quality German beer 36 **Pooly, Parrot:** government spies 40 **board:** table

EPITAPH ON S.P.,
A CHILD OF QUEEN ELIZABETH'S CHAPEL

WEEP with me all you that read
    This little story:
And know, for whom a tear you shed,
    Death's self is sorry.
'Twas a child, that so did thrive   5
    In grace, and feature,
As Heaven and Nature seemed to strive
    Which owned the creature.
Years he numbered scarce thirteen
    When Fates turned cruel,   10
Yet three filled zodiacs had he been
    The stage's jewel;
And did act (what now we moan)
    Old men so duly,
As, sooth, the Parcae thought him one,   15
    He played so truly.
So, by error, to his fate
    They all consented;
But viewing him since (alas, too late)
    They have repented.   20
And have sought (to give new birth)
    In baths to steep him;
But, being so much too good for earth,
    Heaven vows to keep him.

EPITAPH ON S.P.: 7–8 **As . . . creature:** that heaven and nature appeared to argue over his ownership 11 **zodiacs:** years 14 **duly:** exactly 15 **sooth:** truly **Parcae:** the Fates, in classical mythology, three goddesses who decided the destinies of humans. The suggestion is that the boy so successfully portrayed an old man that the Fates, thinking he really was old, ended his life prematurely

TO PENSHURST

THOU art not, Penshurst, built to envious show,
Of touch, or marble; nor canst boast a row
Of polished pillars, or a roof of gold:
Thou hast no lanthern, whereof tales are told;
Or stair, or courts; but stand'st an ancient pile,   5
And these grudged at, art reverenced the while.
Thou joy'st in better marks, of soil, of air,
Of wood, of water: therein thou art fair.
Thou hast thy walks for health, as well as sport:
Thy Mount, to which the dryads do resort,   10
Where Pan, and Bacchus their high feasts have made,
Beneath the broad beech, and the chestnut shade;
That taller tree, which of a nut was set,
At his great birth, where all the muses met.
There, in the writhèd bark, are cut the names   15
Of many a Sylvan, taken with his flames.
And thence, the ruddy satyrs oft provoke
The lighter fauns, to reach thy lady's oak.

Thy copse, too, named of Gamage, thou hast there,
That never fails to serve thee seasoned deer,   20
When thou would'st feast, or exercise thy friends.
The lower land, that to the river bends,
Thy sheep, thy bullocks, kine, and calves do feed:
The middle grounds thy mares, and horses breed.
Each bank doth yield thee conies; and the tops   25
Fertile of wood, Ashore, and Sidney's copse,
To crown thy open table, doth provide
The purpled pheasant, with the speckled side:
The painted partridge lies in every field,
And, for thy mess, is willing to be killed.   30
And if the high-swoll'n Medway fail thy dish,
Thou hast thy ponds, that pay thee tribute fish,
Fat, agèd carps, that run into thy net.
And pikes, now weary their own kind to eat,
As loth, the second draught, or cast to stay,   35
Officiously, at first, themselves betray.
Bright eels, that emulate them, and leap on land,
Before the fisher, or into his hand.
Then hath thy orchard fruit, thy garden flowers,
Fresh as the air, and new as are the hours.   40
The early cherry, with the later plum,
Fig, grape, and quince, each in his time doth come:
The blushing apricot, and woolly peach
Hang on thy walls, that every child may reach.
And though thy walls be of the country stone,   45
They are reared with no man's ruin, no man's groan,
There's none, that dwell about them, wish them down;
But all come in, the farmer, and the clown:
And no one empty-handed, to salute
Thy lord, and lady, though they have no suit.   50
Some bring a capon, some a rural cake,
Some nuts, some apples; some that think they make
The better cheeses, bring them; or else send
By their ripe daughters, whom they would commend
This way to husbands; and whose baskets bear   55
An emblem of themselves, in plum, or pear.
But what can this (more than express their love)
Add to thy free provisions, far above
The need of such? Whose liberal board doth flow,
With all, that hospitality doth know!   60
Where comes no guest, but is allowed to eat,
Without his fear, and of the lord's own meat:
Where the same beer, and bread, and self-same wine,
That is his lordship's, shall be also mine.
And I not fain to sit (as some, this day,   65
At great men's tables) and yet dine away.
Here no man tells my cups; nor, standing by,
A waiter, doth my gluttony envy;
But gives me what I call, and lets me eat,
He knows, below, he shall find plenty of meat,   70
Thy tables hoard not up for the next day,
Nor, when I take my lodging, need I pray
For fire, or lights, or livery: all is there;

As if thou, then, wert mine, or I reigned here:
There's nothing I can wish, for which I stay.   75
That found King James, when hunting late, this way,
With his brave son, the prince, they saw thy fires
Shine bright on every hearth as the desires
Of thy Penates had been set on flame,
To entertain them; or the country came,   80
With all their zeal, to warm their welcome here.
What (great, I will not say, but) sudden cheer
Didst thou, then, make them! And what praise was
    heaped
On thy good lady, then! Who, therein, reaped
The just reward of her high huswifery;   85
To have her linen, plate, and all things nigh,
When she was far: and not a room, but dressed,
As if it had expected such a guest!
These, Penshurst, are thy praise, and yet not all.
Thy lady's noble, fruitful, chaste withal.   90
His children thy great lord may call his own:
A fortune, in this age, but rarely known.
They are, and have been taught religion: thence
Their gentler spirits have sucked innocence.
Each morn, and even, they are taught to pray,   95
With the whole household, and may, every day,
Read, in their virtuous parents' noble parts,
The mysteries of manners, arms, and arts.
Now, Penshurst, they that will proportion thee
With other edifices, when they see   100
Those proud, ambitious heaps, and nothing else,
May say, their lords have built, but thy lord dwells.

TO PENSHURST: 1 **Penshurst:** Penshurst Place, a mansion in Kent where Sir Philip Sidney was born 10 **dryads:** in classical mythology, tree-nymphs 11 **Pan:** in Greek mythology, the god of forest, pastures, flocks, etc **Bacchus:** Roman god of wine 13 **set:** planted 14 **At his . . . met:** the birth of Sidney 15 **writhèd:** twisted 16 **Sylvan:** wood-god **taken . . . flames:** attracted by his brightness 20 **seasoned:** mature 23 **kine:** cattle 25 **conies:** rabbits 30 **mess:** meal 31 **And . . . dish:** if the River Medway fails to yield fish 48 **clown:** rustic 51 **capon:** a cock fattened for eating 59 **board:** table 65 **fain:** willing, desiring 67 **tells:** counts 70 **below:** downstairs, i.e. the servants' quarters 73 **livery:** clothes 75 **stay:** wait 79 **Penates:** household gods 90 **withal:** as well 95 **even:** evening 97 **parts:** qualities

SONG: TO CELIA

COME, my Celia, let us prove,
While we may, the sports of love;
Time will not be ours for ever:
He, at length, our good will sever.
Spend not then his gifts in vain.   5
Suns, that set, may rise again:
But if once we lose this light,
'Tis, with us, perpetual night.
Why should we defer our joys?
Fame, and rumour are but toys.   10

Cannot we delude the eyes
Of a few poor household spies?
Or his easier ears beguile,
So removèd by our wile?
'Tis no sin, love's fruits to steal,   15
But the sweet theft to reveal:
To be taken, to be seen,
These have crimes accounted been.

SONG: TO CELIA: 1 **prove:** try 2 **sports:** enjoyments 4 **our . . . sever:** will end our pleasure 10 **Fame . . . toys:** reputation and gossip are unimportant 14 **So . . . wile:** kept at a distance by our cunning

SONG: THAT WOMEN ARE BUT MEN'S SHADOWS

FOLLOW a shadow, it still flies you;
Seem to fly it, it will pursue:
So court a mistress, she denies you;
Let her alone, she will court you.
Say, are not women truly then   5
Styled but the shadows of us men?

At morn and even shades are longest,
At noon they are or short or none;
So men at weakest, they are strongest,
But grant us perfect, they're not known.   10
Say, are not women truly then
Styled but the shadows of us men?

SONG: THAT WOMEN ARE BUT MEN'S SHADOWS: 1 **still:** always, continually 2 **fly:** run away from 7 **even:** evening

SONG: TO CELIA

DRINK to me only with thine eyes,
    And I will pledge with mine;
Or leave a kiss but in the cup
    And I'll not look for wine.
The thirst that from the soul doth rise   5
    Doth ask a drink divine;
But might I of Jove's nectar sup,
    I would not change for thine.

I sent thee late a rosy wreath,
    Not so much honouring thee   10
As giving it a hope that there
    It could not wither'd be;
But thou thereon didst only breathe
    And sent'st it back to me;
Since when it grows, and smells, I swear,   15
    Not of itself but thee!

SONG: TO CELIA: 2 **pledge:** make a toast 7 **Jove:** Jupiter, chief of the Roman gods **nectar:** the drink of the gods 9 **late:** lately

BEN JONSON

TO THE MEMORY OF MY BELOVED, THE AUTHOR MR WILLIAM SHAKESPEARE, AND WHAT HE HATH LEFT US

To draw no envy, Shakespeare, on thy name,
Am I thus ample to thy book, and fame:
While I confess thy writings to be such,
As neither man, nor muse, can praise too much.
'Tis true, and all men's suffrage. But these ways   5
Were not the paths I meant unto thy praise:
For seeliest ignorance on these may light,
Which, when it sounds at best, but echoes right;
Or blind affection, which doth ne'er advance
The truth, but gropes, and urgeth all by chance;   10
Or crafty malice, might pretend this praise,
And think to ruin, where it seemed to raise.
These are, as some infamous bawd, or whore,
Should praise a matron. What could hurt her more?
But thou art proof against them, and indeed   15
Above the ill fortune of them, or the need.
I therefore will begin. Soul of the age!
The applause, delight, the wonder of the stage!
My Shakespeare, rise; I will not lodge thee by
Chaucer, or Spenser, or bid Beaumont lie   20
A little further, to make thee a room:
Thou art a monument, without a tomb,
And art alive still, while thy book doth live,
And we have wits to read, and praise to give.
That I not mix thee so, my brain excuses;   25
I mean with great, but disproportioned muses:
For, if I thought my judgement were of years,
I should commit thee surely with thy peers,
And tell, how far thou didst our Lyly outshine,
Or sporting Kyd, or Marlowe's mighty line.   30
And though thou hadst small Latin, and less Greek,
From thence to honour thee, I would not seek
For names; but call forth thundering Aeschylus,
Euripides, and Sophocles to us,
Pacuvius, Accius, him of Cordova dead,   35
To life again, to hear thy buskin tread,
And shake a stage: or, when thy socks were on,
Leave thee alone, for the comparison
Of all that insolent Greece, or haughty Rome
Sent forth, or since did from their ashes come.   40
Triumph, my Britain, thou hast one to show,
To whom all scenes of Europe homage owe.
He was not of an age, but for all time!
And all the muses still were in their prime,
When like Apollo he came forth to warm   45
Our ears, or like a Mercury to charm!
Nature herself was proud of his designs,
And joyed to wear the dressing of his lines!
Which were so richly spun, and woven so fit,
As, since, she will vouchsafe no other wit.   50
The merry Greek, tart Aristophanes,
Neat Terence, witty Plautus, now not please;
But antiquated, and deserted lie
As they were not of nature's family.

Yet must I not give nature all: thy art,   55
My gentle Shakespeare, must enjoy a part.
For though the poet's matter, nature be,
His art doth give the fashion. And, that he,
Who casts to write a living line, must sweat,
(Such as thine are), and strike the second heat   60
Upon the muses' anvil: turn the same,
(And himself with it) that he thinks to frame;
Or for the laurel, he may gain a scorn,
For a good poet's made, as well as born.
And such wert thou. Look how the father's face   65
Lives in his issue, even so, the race
Of Shakespeare's mind, and manners brightly shines
In his well-turnèd, and true-filèd lines:
In each of which, he seems to shake a lance,
As brandished at the eyes of ignorance.   70
Sweet swan of Avon, what a sight it were
To see thee in our waters yet appear,
And make those flights upon the banks of Thames,
That did so take Eliza, and our James!
But stay, I see thee in the hemisphere   75
Advanced, and made a constellation there!
Shine forth, thou star of poets, and with rage,
Or influence, chide, or cheer the drooping stage;
Which, since thy flight from hence, hath mourned like
    night.
And despairs day, but for thy volume's light.   80

TO THE MEMORY OF MY BELOVED, THE AUTHOR MR WILLIAM SHAKESPEARE:
2 **ample:** copious 5 **suffrage:** consent 7 **seeliest:** silliest, simplest
13 **as:** as if 19–21 **I will . . . room:** Chaucer, Spenser and Beaumont
were buried in Westminster Abbey, but Shakespeare was buried in
Stratford-on-Avon 23 **book:** writings 26 **disproportioned:** not truly
comparable 29–30 **Lyly:** John Lyly (?1554–1606), Thomas **Kyd** (1558–94),
Christopher **Marlowe** (1564–93), English dramatists 32 **seek:** have to
look 33 **Aeschylus:** Greek tragedian (?525–?456 BC) 34 **Euripides:** Greek
tragedian (?480–406 BC) **Sophocles:** Greek tragedian (?496–406 BC)
35 **Pacuvius:** Marcus Pacuvius, Lucius **Accius** 2nd-century BC Roman
tragedians **him of Cordova:** Lucius Annaeus Seneca (?4 BC–65 AD),
Roman tragedian born in Spain 36 **buskin:** a boot traditionally
worn by classical actors in tragedies 37 **socks:** light shoes traditionally
worn by classical actors in comedies 45 **Apollo:** god of poetry
46 **Mercury:** messenger of the gods, with the power to work charms
48 **joyed:** enjoyed 50 **vouchsafe:** grant, acknowledge 51 **Aristophanes:**
Greek comic dramatist (?448–?380 BC) 52 **Terence:** Publius Terentius
Afer (?190–159 BC), Roman comic dramatist **Plautus:** Titus Maccius
Plautus (?254–?184 BC), Roman comic dramatist 58 **fashion:** style or
form 59 **casts:** tries 63 **laurel:** a wreath of laurel awarded to a victor
69 **shake a lance:** a play on Shakespeare 74 **That did . . . James:** that
so pleased Queen Elizabeth and King James 77 **rage:** inspiration
80 **despairs . . . light:** feels that day will never come, but for the
light shed by Shakespeare's writings

'QUEEN AND HUNTRESS, CHASTE AND FAIR'

Queen and huntress, chaste and fair,
    Now the sun is laid to sleep,
Seated in thy silver chair
    State in wonted manner keep:
Hesperus entreats thy light,   5
Goddess excellently bright.

Earth, let not thy envious shade
  Dare itself to interpose;
Cynthia's shining orb was made
  Heaven to clear when day did close: 10
Bless us then with wished sight,
Goddess excellently bright.

Lay thy bow of pearl apart,
  And thy crystal-shining quiver;
Give unto the flying hart
  Space to breathe, how short soever: 15
Thou that mak'st a day of night,
Goddess excellently bright.

[From *Cynthia's Revels*]

'QUEEN AND HUNTRESS, CHASTE AND FAIR': 1 **Queen and huntress:**
Cynthia (or Diana), goddess of the moon and hunting 5 **Hesperus:**
the evening star 15 **hart:** stag

'STILL TO BE NEAT, STILL TO BE DRESSED'

STILL to be neat, still to be dressed,
As you were going to a feast;
Still to be powdered, still perfumed:
Lady, it is to be presumed,
Though art's hid causes are not found,   5
All is not sweet, all is not sound.

Give me a look, give me a face,
That makes simplicity a grace;
Robes loosely flowing, hair as free;
Such sweet neglect more taketh me   10
Than all th' adulteries of art:
They strike mine eyes, but not my heart.

[From *The Silent Woman*]

'STILL TO BE NEAT, STILL TO BE DRESSED': 1 **still:** always 2 **As:** as if
10 **taketh:** pleases, attracts

RICHARD BARNEFIELD

'AS IT FELL UPON A DAY . . .'

As it fell upon a day
In the merry month of May,
Sitting in a pleasant shade
Which a grove of myrtles made,
Beasts did leap and birds did sing,   5
Trees did grow and plants did spring;
Everything did banish moan
Save the Nightingale alone.
She, poor bird, as all forlorn,
Leaned her breast up-till a thorn,   10
And there sung the dolefull'st ditty
That to hear it was great pity.
'Fie, fie, fie' now would she cry;
'Tereu, tereu' by and by;
That to hear her so complain   15

Scarce I could from tears refrain;
For her griefs so lively shown
Made me think upon mine own.
Ah, thought I, thou mourn'st in vain,
None takes pity on thy pain: 20
Senseless trees, they cannot hear thee,
Ruthless beasts, they will not cheer thee;
King Pandion, he is dead,
All thy friends are lapped in lead:
All thy fellow birds do sing   25
Careless of thy sorrowing:
Even so, poor bird, like thee,
None alive will pity me.

'AS IT FELL UPON A DAY . . .': 1 **As it fell:** it so happened 10 **up-till:** up
against 17 **lively:** vividly 23 **Pandion:** in Greek myth, the father of
Philomela, a maiden who was turned into a nightingale 24 **lapped
in lead:** dead and buried

JOHN WEBSTER

'CALL FOR THE ROBIN-REDBREAST AND THE WREN'

CALL for the robin-redbreast and the wren,
Since o'er shady groves they hover,
And with leaves and flowers do cover
The friendless bodies of unburied men.
Call unto his funeral dole   5
The ant, the field-mouse, and the mole
To rear him hillocks that shall keep him warm,
And (when gay tombs are robbed) sustain no harm;
But keep the wolf far thence, that's foe to men,
For with his nails he'll dig them up again.   10

[From *The White Devil*, 5.4]

'HARK, NOW EVERY THING IS STILL'

HARK, now every thing is still,
The screech-owl, and the whistler shrill,
Call upon our Dame, aloud,
And bid her quickly don her shroud:
Much you had of land and rent,   5
Your length in clay's now competent.
A long war disturbed your mind,
Here your perfect peace is signed,
Of what is't, fools make such vain keeping?
Sin their conception, their birth weeping: 10
Their life a general mist of error,
Their death a hideous storm of terror.
Strew your hair with powders sweet:
Don clean linen, bathe your feet,
And (the foul fiend more to check)   15
A crucifix let bless your neck.
'Tis now full tide, 'tween night and day,
End your groan, and come away.

[From *The Duchess of Malfi*, 4.2]

RICHARD CORBET

THE FAIRIES' FAREWELL

FAREWELL, rewards and fairies,
  Good housewives now may say;
For now foul sluts in dairies
  Do fare as well as they;
And though they sweep their hearths no less   5
  Than maids were wont to do,
Yet who of late for cleanliness
  Finds sixpence in her shoe?

Lament, lament, old abbeys,
  The faeries lost command: 10
They did but change priests' babies,
  But some have changed your land;
And all your children sprung from thence
  Are now grown Puritans;
Who live as changelings ever since   15
  For love of your domains.

At morning and at evening both
  You merry were and glad,
So little care of sleep or sloth
  These pretty ladies had.   20
When Tom came home from labour,
  Or Cis to milking rose,
Then merrily, merrily went their tabor,
  And nimbly went their toes.

Witness those rings and roundelays   25
  Of theirs, which yet remain,
Were footed in Queen Mary's days
  On many a grassy plain;
But, since of late Elizabeth,
  And later James, came in,   30
They never danced on any heath
  As when the time hath been.

By which we note the faeries
  We of the old profession;
Their songs were Ave Marys,   35
  Their dances were procession.
But now, alas! they all are dead,
  Or gone beyond the seas,
Or farther for religion fled,
  Or else they take their ease.   40

A tell-tale in their company
  They never could endure,
And whoso kept not secretly
  Their mirth was punished sure.
It was a just and Christian deed   45
  To pinch such black and blue.
Oh, how the Commonwealth doth need
  Such justices as you!

Now they have left our quarters
  A register they have,   50
Who looketh to their charters,
  A man both wise and grave;
An hundred of their merry pranks
  By one that I could name
Are kept in store, con twenty thanks   55
  To William for the same.

I marvel who his cloak would turn
  When Puck had led him round,
Or where those walking fires would burn,
  Where Cureton would be found;   60
How Broker would appear to be,
  For whom this age doth mourn;
But that their spirits live in thee,
  In thee, old William Chourne.

To William Chourne of Staffordshire   65
  Give laud and praises due,
Who every meal can mend your cheer
  With tales both old and true.
To William all give audience,
  And pray ye for his noddle,   70
For all the faeries' evidence
  Were lost, if that were addle.

THE FAIRIES' FAREWELL: 15 **changeling:** a child left by the fairies in exchange for a child they take away 23 **tabor:** a small tambourine-like drum 25 **roundelay:** a dance in which dancers form a ring 34 **profession:** faith 50 **register:** registrar 55 **con:** acknowledge 56 **William:** William Chourne (see below) 58 **Puck:** a mischievous sprite 59 **walking fires:** will-o'-the-wisps 64 **William Chourne:** an expert on fairies and the supernatural 67 **mend your cheer:** cheer you up 70 **noddle:** head 72 **addle:** addled

EDWARD, LORD HERBERT OF CHERBURY

ELEGY OVER A TOMB

MUST I then see, alas, eternal night
  Sitting upon those fairest eyes,
And closing all those beams, which once did rise
  So radiant and bright,
That light and heat in them to us did prove   5
  Knowledge and love?

Oh, if you did delight no more to stay
  Upon this low and earthly stage,
But rather chose an endless heritage,
  Tell us at least, we pray,   10
Where all the beauties that those ashes owed
  Are now bestowed?

Doth the sun now his light with yours renew?
  Have waves the curling of your hair?
Did you restore unto the sky and air   15
  The red, and white, and blue?
Have you vouchsafed to flowers since your death
  That sweetest breath?

Had not heaven's lights else in their houses slept,
  Or to some private life retired?   20
Must not the sky and air have else conspired,
  And in their regions wept?
Must not each flower else the earth could breed
  Have been a weed?

But thus enriched may we not yield some cause   25
  Why they themselves lament no more?
That must have changed the course they held before,
  And broke their proper laws,
Had not your beauties given this second birth
  To heaven and earth?   30

Tell us – for oracles must still ascend,
  For those that crave them at your tomb –
Tell us, where are those beauties now become,
  And what they now intend:
Tell us, alas, that cannot tell our grief,   35
  Or hope relief.

ELEGY OVER A TOMB: 11 **owed:** owned   17 **vouchsafed:** granted
19 **heaven's lights:** the stars   36 **hope:** hope for

AN ODE UPON A QUESTION MOVED,
WHETHER LOVE SHOULD CONTINUE
FOR EVER?

HAVING interred her infant-birth,
  The wat'ry ground that late did mourn,
Was strewed with flow'rs for the return
Of the wished bridegroom of the earth.

The well-accorded birds did sing   5
  Their hymns unto the pleasant time,
  And in a sweet consorted chime
Did welcome in the cheerful spring.

To which, soft whistles of the wind,
  And warbling murmurs of a brook,   10
  And varied notes of leaves that shook,
An harmony of parts did bind.

While doubling joy unto each other,
  All in so rare consent was shown,
  No happiness that came alone,   15
Nor pleasure that was not another.

AN ODE UPON A QUESTION MOVED: 5 **well-accorded:** harmonious

When with a love none can express,
  That mutually happy pair,
  Melander and Celinda fair,
The season with their loves did bless.   20

Walking thus towards a pleasant grove,
  Which did, it seemed, in new delight
  The pleasures of the time unite,
To give a triumph to their love,

They stayed at last, and on the grass   25
  Reposèd so, as o'er his breast
  She bowed her gracious head to rest,
Such a weight as no burden was.

While over either's compassed waist
  Their folded arms were so composed,   30
  As if in straitest bonds enclosed,
They suffered for joys they did taste.

Long their fixed eyes to Heaven bent,
  Unchangèd, they did never move,
  As if so great and pure a love   35
No glass but it could represent.

When with a sweet, though troubled look,
  She first brake silence, saying, 'Dear friend,
  Oh, that our love might take no end,
Or never had beginning took!   40

'I speak not this with a false heart'
  (Wherewith his hand she gently strained)
  'Or that would change a love maintained
With so much love on either part.

'Nay, I protest, though Death with his   45
  Worst counsel should divide us here,
  His terrors could not make me fear
To come where your loved presence is.

'Only if love's fire with the breath
  Of life be kindlèd, I doubt,   50
  With our last air 'twill be breathed out,
And quenchèd with the cold of death.

That is affections be a line,
  Which is closed up in our last hour;
  Oh, how 'twould grieve me any pow'r   55
Could force so dear a love as mine!'

She scarce had done, when his shut eyes
  An inward joy did represent,
  To hear Celinda thus intent
To a love he so much did prize.   60

25 **stayed:** halted   29 **compassed:** encircled   36 **glass:** mirror   38 **brake:**
broke

Then with a look, it seemed, denied
   All earthly pow'r but hers, yet so,
   As if to her breath he did owe
This borrowed life, he thus replied:

'O you, wherein, they say, souls rest,   65
   Till they descend pure heavenly fires,
   Shall lustful and corrupt desires
With your immortal seed be blest?

'And shall our love, so far beyond
   That low and dying appetite,   70
   And which so chaste desires unite,
Not hold in an eternal bond?

'Is it, because we should decline,
   And wholly from our thoughts exclude
   Objects that may the sense delude,   75
And study only the divine?

'No, sure, for if none can ascend
   Ev'n to the visible degree
   Of things created, how should we
The invisible comprehend?   80

'Or rather since that Pow'r exprest
   His greatness in his works alone,
   Being here best in his creatures known,
Why is he not loved in them best?

'But is't not true, which you pretend,   85
   That since our love and knowledge here
   Only as parts of life appear,
So they with it should take their end.

'Oh no, Belov'd, I am most sure
   Those virtuous habits we acquire,   90
   As being with the soul entire,
Must with it evermore endure.

'For if where sins and vice reside,
   We find so foul a guilt remain,
   As never dying in his stain,   95
Still punished in the soul doth bide.

'Much more that true and real joy,
   Which in a virtuous love is found,
   Must be more solid in its ground,
Than Fate or Death can e'er destroy.   100

'Else should our souls in vain elect,
   And vainer yet were Heaven's laws,
   When to an everlasting Cause
They gave a perishing Effect.

'Nor here on earth, then, nor above,   105
   Our good affection can impair,
   For where God doth admit the fair,
Think you that he excludeth love?

'These eyes again, then, eyes shall see,
   And hands again these hands enfold,   110
   And all chaste pleasures can be told
Shall with us everlasting be.

'For if no use of sense remain
   When bodies once this life forsake,
   Or they could no delight partake,   115
Why should they ever rise again?

'And if every imperfect mind
   Make love the end of knowledge here,
   How perfect will our love be where
All imperfection is refined?   120

'Let, then, no doubt, Celinda, touch,
   Much less your fairest mind invade,
   Were not our souls immortal made,
Our equal loves can make them such.

'So when one wing can make no way,   125
   Two joinèd can themselves dilate,
   So can two persons propagate,
When singly either would decay.

'So when from hence we shall be gone,
   And be no more, nor you, nor I,   130
   Ad one another's mystery,
Each shall be both, yet both but one.'

This said, in her uplifted face,
   Her eyes which did that beauty crown,
   Were like two stars, that having fallen down,   135
Look up again to find their place:

While such a moveless silent peace
   Did seize on their becalmèd sense,
   One would have thought some influence
Their ravished spirits did possess.   140

AURELIAN TOWNSHEND

A DIALOGUE BETWIXT TIME AND A PILGRIM

Pilgrim. Agèd man that mows these fields.
Time. Pilgrim, speak. What is thy will?
Pilgrim. Whose soil is this that such pretty pasture
         yields?
Or who art thou, whose foot stands never still?
      Or where am I? *Time.* In love.   5

104 **perishing:** transitory

Pilgrim. His Lordship lies above?
Time. Yes, and below, and round about,
Wherein all sorts of flow'rs are growing,
Which as the early spring puts out,
    Time falls as fast a-mowing.   10
Pilgrim. If thou art Time, these flow'rs have lives,
    And then I fear,
Under some lily, she I love
    May now be growing there.
Time. And in some thistle or some spire of grass   15
My scythe thy stalk. before hers come, may pass.
Pilgrim. Wilt thou provide it may? *Time.* No. *Pilgrim.*
    Allege the cause.
Time. Because Time cannot alter but obey fate's laws.

Chorus. Then, happy those whom Fate, that is the
    stronger,
Together twists their threads, and yet draws hers the
    longer.   20

WILLIAM DRUMMOND OF HAWTHORNDEN

'LIKE THE IDALIAN QUEEN'

LIKE the Idalian queen,
Her hair about her eyne,
With neck and breast's ripe apples to be seen,
At first glance of the morn
In Cyprus' gardens gathering those fair flowers   5
Which of her blood were born,
I saw, but fainting saw, my paramours.
The Graces naked danced about the place,
The winds and trees amazed
With silence on her gazed,   10
The flowers did smile, like those upon her face;
And as their aspen stalks those fingers band,
That she might read my case,
A hyacinth I wished me in her hand.

'LIKE THE IDALIAN QUEEN': 1 **the Idalian queen:** Aphrodite, to whom
Idalium in Cyprus was sacred 2 **eyne:** eyes 8 **Graces:** in Greek
myth, three sister goddesses, givers of charm and beauty 12 **aspen:**
trembling **band:** bound

'MY THOUGHTS HOLD MORTAL STRIFE'

MY thoughts hold mortal strife;
I do detest my life,
And with lamenting cries
Peace to my soul to bring
Oft call that prince which here doth monarchize: 5
But he, grim grinning King,
Who caitiffs scorns, and doth the blest surprise,
    Late having decked with beauty's rose his tomb,
    Disdains to crop a weed, and will not come.

'MY THOUGHTS HOLD MORTAL STRIFE': 5 **prince:** death 7 **caitiffs:**
despicable people 8 **Late:** lately

FOR THE BAPTIST

THE last and greatest herald of heaven's king,
Girt with rough skins, hies to the deserts wild,
Among that savage brood the woods forth bring,
Which he than Man more harmless found and mild:
His food was blossoms, and what young doth spring,   5
With honey that from virgin hives distilled;
Parched body, hollow eyes, some uncouth thing
Made him appear, long since from Earth exiled.
There burst he forth: 'All ye whose hopes rely
On God, with me amidst these deserts mourn,   10
Repent, repent, and from old errors turn.'
    Who listened to his voice, obeyed his cry?
    Only the echoes which he made relent,
    Rung from their marble caves, 'Repent, repent'.

'THE WORLD A-HUNTING IS'

THE world a-hunting is:
The prey poor Man, the Nimrod fierce is Death;
His speedy greyhounds are
Lust, Sickness, Envy, Care,
Strife that ne'er falls amiss,   5
With all those ills which haunt us while we breathe.
Now if by chance we fly
Of these the eager chase,
Old Age with stealing pace
Casts up his nets, and there we panting die.   10

'THE WORLD A-HUNTING IS': 2 **Nimrod:** a great hunter in the Bible
(Genesis 10. 8–10)

'THRICE HAPPY HE, WHO BY SOME SHADY GROVE'

THRICE happy he, who by some shady grove,
Far from the clamorous world, doth live his own;
Though solitary, who is not alone,
But doth converse with that eternal love.
Oh, how more sweet is birds' harmonious moan,   5
Or the hoarse sobbings of the widowed dove,
Than those smooth whisperings near a prince's throne,
Which good make doubtful, do the evil approve!
Oh, how more sweet is zephyr's wholesome breath,
And sighs embalmed, which new-born flow'rs
    unfold,   10
That that applause vain honour doth bequeath!
How sweet are streams to poison drunk in gold!
    The world is full of horrors, troubles, slights,
    Woods' harmless shades have only true delights.

THE ANGELS FOR THE NATIVITY

RUN, shepherds, run where Bethlem blest appears,
We bring the best of news, be not dismayed,
A Saviour there is born more old than years,
Amidst heaven's rolling heights this earth who stayed.
In a poor cottage inned, a virgin maid   5
A weakling did him bear, who all upbears;
There is he, poorly swaddled, in manger laid,
To whom too narrow swaddlings are our spheres:
Run, shepherd, run, and solemnize his birth,
This is that night – no, day, grown great with bliss,   10
In which the power of Satan broken is;
In heaven be glory, peace unto the earth!
    Thus singing, through the air the angels swam,
    And cope of stars re-echoèd the same.

THE ANGELS FOR THE NATIVITY: 4 **stayed:** supported 14 **cope:** covering

FRANCIS BEAUMONT

ON THE TOMBS IN WESTMINSTER ABBEY

MORTALITY, behold and fear
What a change of flesh is here!
Think how many royal bones
Sleep within these heaps of stones;
Here they lie, had realms and lands,   5
Who now want strength to stir their hands,
Where from their pulpits sealed with dust
They preach, 'In greatness is no trust.'
Here's an acre sown indeed
With the richest royallest seed   10
That the earth did e'er suck in
Since the first man died for sin:
Here the bones of birth have cried
'Though gods they were, as men they died!'
Here are sands, ignoble things,   15
Dropped from the ruined sides of kings;
Here's a world of pomp and state
Buried in dust, once dead by fate.

GEORGE WITHER

'SHALL I, WASTING IN DESPAIR . . .'

SHALL I, wasting in despair,
Die because a woman's fair?
Or make pale my cheeks with care
'Cause another's rosy are?
Be she fairer than the day   5
Or the flow'ry meads in May,
    If she be not so to me
    What care I how fair she be?

Shall my heart be grieved or pined
'Cause I see a woman kind;   10
Or a well disposed nature
Joined with a lovely feature?
Be she meeker, kinder than
Turtle-dove or pelican,
    If she be not so to me   15
    What care I how kind she be?

Shall a woman's virtues move
Me to perish for her love?
Or her well-deserving known
Make me quite forget mine own?   20
Be she with that goodness blest
Which may gain her name of Best,
    If she be not such to me
    What care I how good she be?

'Cause her fortune seems too high,   25
Shall I play the fool and die?
Those that bear a noble mind,
Where they want of riches find,
Think what with them they would do,
That without them dare to woo;   30
    And unless that mind I see
    What care I though great she be?

Great, or good, or kind, or fair,
I will ne'er the more despair;
If she love me, this believe,   35
I will die ere she shall grieve;
If she slight me when I woo,
I can scorn and let her go;
    For if she be not for me,
    What care I for whom she be?   40

'SHALL I, WASTING IN DESPAIR . . .': 6 **meads:** meadows 14 **pelican:** the pelican was traditionally believed to be so devoted to its young that it would wound its own breast to feed them with its blood

WILLIAM BROWNE OF TAVISTOCK

THE SIRENS' SONG

STEER, hither steer your wingèd pines,
    All beaten mariners!
Here lie Love's undiscovered mined,
    A prey to passengers;
Perfumes far sweeter than the best   5
Which make the Phoenix' urn and nest.
    Fear not your ships,
Nor any to oppose you save our lips;
    But come on shore,
Where no joy dies till Love hath gotten more.   10

For swelling waves our panting breasts,
    Where never storms arise,
Exchange, and be awhile our guests:
    For stars gaze on our eyes.

The compass Love shall hourly sing,   15
And as he goes about the ring,
  We will not miss
To tell each point he nameth with a kiss.
  Then come on shore,
Where no joy dies till Love hath gotten more.   20

THE SIRENS' SONG: 1 **wingèd pines:** masts with sails spread
6 **Phoenix' urn and nest:** in traditional legend, the phoenix was a
bird that at the end of its life made a nest of spices which it then
set on fire, arising new-born out of the ashes

ROBERT HERRICK

DELIGHT IN DISORDER

A SWEET disorder in the dress
Kindles in clothes a wantonness:
A lawn about the shoulders thrown
Into a fine distraction:
An erring lace, which here and there   5
Enthralls the crimson stomacher:
A cuff neglectful, and thereby
Ribbands to flow confusedly:
A winning wave (deserving note)
In the tempestuous petticoat: 10
A careless shoe-string, in whose tie
I see a wild civility:
Do more bewitch me, than when Art
Is too precise in every part.

DELIGHT IN DISORDER: 3 **lawn:** a linen scarf 6 **stomacher:** a decorative
V-shaped piece of material worn over the bosom

CORINNA'S GOING A-MAYING

GET UP, get up for shame! the blooming morn
Upon her wings presents the god unshorn.
See how Aurora throws her fair
Fresh-quilted colours through the air!
Get up, sweet slug-a-bed, and see   5
The dew bespangled herb and tree.
Each flower has wept and bowed toward the east
Above an hour since, – yet you not dressed;
Nay! not so much as out of bed?
  When all the birds have matins said   10
  And sung their thankful hymns, 'tis sin –
  Nay, profanation – to keep in,
Whenas a thousand virgins on this day
Spring, sooner than the lark, to fetch in May.

Rise, and put on your foliage, and be seen   15
To come forth, like the springtime, fresh and green
  And sweet as Flora. Take no care
  For jewels for your gown or hair:
  Fear not, the leaves will strew
  Gems in abundance upon you: 20

CORINNA'S GOING A-MAYING: 3 **Aurora:** in Roman myth, the goddess
of the dawn 13 **Whenas:** when 17 **Flora:** in Roman myth, the goddess
of flowers and spring

Besides, the childhood of the day has kept,
Against you come, some orient pearls unwept.
  Come, and receive them while the light
  Hangs on the dew-locks of the night:
  And Titan on the eastern hill   25
  Retires himself, or else stands still
Till you come forth. Wash, dress, be brief in praying:
Few beads are best when once we go a-Maying.

Come, my Corinna, come; and coming, mark
How each field turns a street, each street a park   30
  Made green and trimmed with trees! See how
  Devotion gives each house a bough
  Or branch! Each porch, each door, ere this
  An ark, a tabernacle is,
Made up of whitethorn neatly interwove,   35
As if here were those cooler shades of love.
  Can such delights be in the street
  And open fields and we not see 't?
  Come, we'll abroad; and let's obey
  The proclamation made for May,   40
And sin no more, as we have done, by staying;
But, my Corinna, come, let's go a-Maying.

There's not a budding boy or girl this day
But is got up and gone to bring in May.
  A deal of youth, ere this, is come   45
  Back, and with whitethorn laden, home.
  Some have dispatched their cakes and cream,
  Before that we have left to dream;
And some have wept and wooed and plighted troth,
And chose their priest, ere we can cast off sloth: 50
  Many a green-gown has been given,
  Many a kiss, both odd and even;
  Many a glance too has been sent
  From out the eye, love's firmament;
Many a jest told of the key's betraying   55
This night, and locks picked: yet we're not a-Maying!

Come, let us go while we are in our prime,
And take the harmless folly of the time!
  We shall grow old apace, and die
  Before we know our liberty.   60
  Our life is short, and our days run
  As fast away as does the sun;
And, as a vapour or a drop of rain,
Once lost can ne'er be found again;
  So when or you or I are made   65
  A fable, song, or fleeting shade,
  All love, all liking, all delight
  Lies drowned with us in endless night.
Then while time serves, and we are but decaying,
Come, my Corinna, come, let's go a-Maying!   70

22 **Against you come:** in readiness for your arrival **orient pearls
unwept:** bright drops of dew 25 **Titan:** the sun 28 **beads:** prayers
(counted by beads on a rosary) **a-Maying:** the celebration of May
customs 30 **turns:** turns into 41 **staying:** delaying 45 **a deal:** a great
many 48 **Before that . . . dream:** before we have stopped dreaming
51 **green-gown:** a roll on the grass (through which a girl's gown is
stained green)

TO THE VIRGINS, TO MAKE MUCH OF TIME

GATHER ye rosebuds while ye may,
   Old Time is still a flying:
And this same flower that smiles to day,
   Tomorrow will be dying.

The glorious lamp of heaven, the sun,   5
   The higher he's a getting;
The sooner will his race be run,
   And nearer he's to setting.

That Age is best, which is the first,
   When youth and blood are warmer;   10
But being spent, the worse, and worst
   Times, still succeed the former.

Then be not coy, but use your time;
   And while ye may, goe marry:
For having lost but once your prime,   15
   You may for ever tarry.

TO ANTHEA, WHO MAY COMMAND HIM ANY THING

BID me to live, and I will live
   Thy Protestant to be;
Or bid me love, and I will give
   A loving heart to thee.

A heart as soft, a heart as kind,   5
   A heart as sound and free,
As in the whole world thou canst find,
   That heart I'll give to thee.

Bid that heart stay, and it will stay,
   To honour thy decree;   10
Or bid it languish quite away,
   And 't shall do so for thee.

Bid me to weep, and I will weep
   While I have eyes to see;
And having none, yet I will keep   15
   A heart to weep for thee.

Bid me despair, and I'll despair
   Under that cypress-tree;
Or bid me die, and I will dare
   E'en death to die for thee.   20

Thou art my life, my love, my heart,
   The very eyes of me;
And hast command of every part
   To live and die for thee.

TO ANTHEA: 2 **Protestant:** avowed lover

TO DAFFODILS

FAIR daffodils, we weep to see
   You haste away so soon:
As yet the early-rising sun
   Has not attained his noon.
      Stay, stay,   5
     Until the hasting day
      Has run
     But to the Evensong;
And, having prayed together, we
     Will go with you along.   10

We have short time to stay, as you,
   We have as short a spring;
As quick a growth to meet decay,
   As you, or any thing.
      We die,   15
     As your hours do, and dry
      Away,
     Like to the summer's rain;
Or as the pearls of morning's dew
     Ne'er to be found again.   20

THE NIGHT-PIECE, TO JULIA

HER eyes the glow-worm lend thee,
   The shooting stars attend thee;
     And the elves also,
     Whose little eyes glow,
Like the sparks of fire, befriend thee.   5

No will-o'-the-wisp mislight thee;
Nor snake, or slow-worm bite thee:
     But on, on thy way
     Not making a stay,
Since ghost there's none to affright thee.   10

Let not the dark thee cumber;
What though the moon does slumber?
     The stars of the night
     Will lend thee their light,
Like tapers clear without number.   15

Then, Julia, let me woo thee,
Thus, thus to come unto me:
     And when I shall meet
     Thy silv'ry feet,
My soul I'll pour into thee.   20

THE NIGHT-PIECE, TO JULIA: 6 **No . . . thee:** let you not be led astray
by a will-o'-the-wisp 11 **cumber:** encumber 15 **tapers:** candles

TO ELECTRA

I DARE not ask a kiss;
   I dare not beg a smile;
Lest having that, or this,
   I might grow proud the while.

No, no, the utmost share   5
   Of my desire, shall be
Only to kiss that air,
   That lately kissèd thee.

UPON JULIA'S CLOTHES

WHENAS in silks my Julia goes,
Then, then (me thinks) how sweetly flows
The liquefaction of her clothes.

Next, when I cast mine eyes and see
That brave vibration each way free;   5
O how that glittering taketh me!

FRANCIS QUARLES

JOB XIII.XXIV

Wherefore hidest thou thy face, and holdest me for thy enemy?

WHY dost thou shade thy lovely face? Oh, why
Does that eclipsing hand, so long, deny
The sunshine of thy soul-enliv'ning eye?

Without that Light, what light remains in me?
Thou art my Life, my Way, my Light; in Thee   5
I live, I move, and by thy beams I see.

Thou art my Life; if thou but turn away,
My life's a thousand deaths: thou art my Way;
Without thee, Lord, I travel not, but stray.

My Light thou art; without thy glorious sight,   10
Mine eyes are darkened with perpetual night.
My God, thou art my Way, my Life, my Light.

Thou art my Way; I wander, if thou fly:
Thou art my Light; if hid, how blind am I?
Thou art my Life; if thou withdraw, I die.   15

Mine eyes are blind and dark, I cannot see;
To whom, or whither should my darkness flee,
But to the Light? And who's that Light but Thee?

My path is lost; my wand'ring steps do stray;
I cannot safely go, nor safely stay;   20
Whom should I seek but Thee, my Path, my Way?

Oh, I am dead. To whom shall I, poor I,
Repair? To whom shall my sad ashes fly
But Life? And where is Life but in thine eye?

And yet thou turn'st away thy face, and fly'st me;   25
And yet I sue for Grace, and thou deny'st me;
Speak, art thou angry, Lord, or only try'st me?

Unscreen those heavenly lamps, or tell me why
Thou shad'st thy face; perhaps, thou think'st, no eye
Can view those flames, and not drop down and die.   30

If that be all, shine forth, and draw thee nigher;
Let me behold and die; for my desire
Is phoenix-like to perish in that Fire.

Death-conquered Laz'rus was redeemed by Thee;
If I am dead, Lord sets death's pris'ner free;   35
Am I more spent, or stink I worse than he?

If my puffed light be out, give leave to tine
My shameless snuff at that bright Lamp of thine;
Oh, what's thy Light the less for lighting mine?

If I have lost my Path, great Shepherd, say,   40
Shall I still wander in a doubtful way?
Lord, shall a Lamb of Israel's sheepfold stray?

Thou art the pilgrim's Path; the blind man's Eye;
The dead man's Life; on thee my hopes rely;
If thou remove, I err; I grope; I die.   45

Disclose thy sunbeams; close thy wings, and stay;
See, see, how I am blind, and dead, and stray,
O thou, that art my Light, my Life, my Way.

JOB XIII.XXIV: 33 **phoenix-like:** like the mythical bird, the phoenix, that dies in fire and is reborn from the ashes 37 **tine:** kindle 38 **snuff:** a burnt wick of a candle

CANTICLES II.XVI

My beloved is mine, and I am his; he feedeth among the lilies

EV'N like two little bank-dividing brooks,
   That wash the pebbles with their wanton streams,
And having ranged and searched a thousand nooks,
   Meet both at length in silver-breasted Thames,
     Where in a greater current they conjoin: 5
So I my Best-Beloved's am; so He is mine.

Ev'n so we met; and after long pursuit,
   Ev'n so we joined; we both became entire;
No need for either to renew a suit,
   For I was flux and he was flames of fire: 10
     Our firm united souls did more than twine;
So I my Best-Beloved's am; so He is mine.

If all those glitt'ring monarchs that command
  The servile quarters of this earthly ball,
Should tender, in exchange, their shares of land,   15
  I would not change my fortunes for them all:
    Their wealth is but a counter to my coin;
The world's but theirs; but my Beloved's mine.

Nay, more. If the fair thespian ladies all
  Should heap together their diviner treasure: 20
That treasure should be deemed a price too small
  To buy a minute's lease of half my pleasure;
    'Tis not the sacred wealth of all the Nine
Can buy my heart from Him; or His, from being mine.

Nor time, nor place, nor death can bow   25
  My least desires unto the least remove;
He's firmly mine by oath; I, His, by vow;
  He's mine by faith; and I am His by love;
    He's mine by water; I am His by wine;
Thus I my Best-Beloved's am; thus He is mine.   30

He is my altar; I, His holy place;
  I am His guest; and He my living food;
I'm His by penitence; He mine by grace;
  I'm His by purchase; He is mine by blood;
    He's my supporting elm; and I His vine: 35
Thus I my Best-Beloved's am; thus He is mine.

He gives me wealth; I give Him all my vows:
  I give Him songs; He gives me length of days:
With wreaths of grace He crowns my conqu'ring
    brows:
  And I His temples, with a crown of praise,   40
    Which He accepts as an everlasting sign,
That I my Best-Beloved's am; that He is mine.

CANTICLES II.XVI: 10 **flux:** a substance easily melted 11 **twine:** entwine
17 **counter:** a token, not a real coin 19 **thespian ladies:** the Muses,
who had temple at Thespis 23 **the Nine:** the Muses 29 **He's mine
. . . wine:** I am made his by being christened; he becomes mine
by transubstantiation in communion wine

HENRY KING

AN EXEQUY
To His Matchless and
Never-To-Be-Forgotten Friend

Accept, thou shrine of my dead saint,
Instead of dirges this complaint;
And, for sweet flowers to crown thy hearse,
Receive a strew of weeping verse
From thy grieved friend; whom thou might'st see   5
Quite melted into tears for thee.

AN EXEQUY: 4 **strew:** scattering

Dear loss! since thy untimely fate
My task hath been to meditate
On thee, on thee: thou art the book,
The library whereon I look   10
Though almost blind. For thee, loved clay!
I languish out, not live, the day,
Using no other exercise
But what I practise with mine eyes.
By which wet glasses I find out   15
How lazily time creeps about
To one that mourns: this, only this,
My exercise and business is;
So I compute the weary hours
With sighs dissolvèd into showers.   20
  Nor wonder if my time go thus
Backward and most preposterous:
Thou hast benighted me. Thy set
This eve of blackness did beget,
Who wast my day, though overcast   25
Before thou had'st thy noontide past,
And I remember must in tears
Thou scarce had'st seen so many years
As day tells hours. By thy clear sun
My love and fortune first did run;   30
But thou wilt never more appear
Folded within my hemisphere,
Since both thy light and motïon,
Like a fled star, is fallen and gone;
And 'twixt me and my soul's dear wish   35
The earth now interposèd is,
Which such a strange eclipse doth make
As ne'er was read in almanac.
  I could allow thee for a time
To darken me and my sad clime;   40
Were it a month, a year, or ten,
I would thy exile live till then;
And all that space my mirth adjourn,
So thou would'st promise to return
And, putting off thy ashy shroud,   45
At length disperse this sorrow's cloud.
  But woe is me! The longest date
Too narrow is to calculate
These empty hopes. Never shall I
Be so much blest as to descry   50
A glimpse of thee, till that day come
Which shall the earth to cinders doom,
And a fierce fever must calcine
The body of this world, like thine,
My little world! That fit of fire   55
Once off, our bodies shall aspire
To our souls' bliss; then we shall rise,
And view ourselves with clearer eyes
In that calm region where no night
Can hide us from each other's sight.   60

11 **clay:** flesh, earthly body 23 **set:** setting (as of the sun) 51–2 **till
that . . . doom:** till the end of the world 53 **calcine:** to heat a
substance until it is oxidized

Meantime, thou hast her, Earth; much good
May my harm do thee. Since it stood
With heaven's will I might not call
Her longer mine, I give thee all
My short-lived right and interest   65
In her, whom living I loved best:
With a most free and bounteous grief,
I give thee what I could not keep.
Be kind to her; and prithee look
Thou write into thy Doomsday book   70
Each parcel of this rarity,
Which in thy casket shrined doth lie.
See that thou make thy reck'ning straight,
And yield her back again by weight;
For thou must audit on thy trust   75
Each grain and atom of this dust,
As thou wilt answer Him that lent,
Not gave thee, my dear monument.
    So close the ground, and 'bout her shade
Black curtains draw; my bride is laid.   80
    Sleep on, my love, in thy cold bed
Never to be disquieted.
My last goodnight! Thou wilt not wake
Till I thy fate shall overtake:
Till age, or grief, or sickness must   85
Marry my body to that dust
It so much loves; and fill the room
My heart keeps empty in thy tomb.
Stay for me there: I will not fail
To meet thee in that hollow vale.   90
And think not much of my delay;
I am already on the way,
And follow thee with all the speed
Desire can make, or sorrows breed.
Each minute is a short degree   95
And ev'ry hour a step towards thee.
At night when I betake to rest,
Next morn I rise nearer my west
Of life, almost by eight hours' sail,
Than when Sleep breathed his drowsy gale.   100
    Thus from the sun my bottom steers,
And my day's compass downward bears.
Nor labour I to stem the tide
Through which to thee I swiftly glide.
'Tis true; with shame and grief I yield: 105
Thou, like the van, first took'st the field,
And gotten hast the victory
In thus adventuring to die
Before me, whose more years might crave
A just precédence in the grave.   110
But hark! my pulse, like a soft drum,
Beats my approach, tells thee I come;
And, slow howe'er my marches be,
I shall at last sit down by thee.

98 **west**: where the sun sets, hence sunset, end of life   101 **bottom**: ship (literally keel)   106 **van**: vanguard, the leading part of an army going into battle

The thought of this bids me go on,   115
And wait my dissolution
With hope and comfort. Dear! (forgive
The crime) I am content to live
Divided, with but half a heart,
Till we shall meet and never part.   120

GEORGE HERBERT

REDEMPTION

HAVING been tenant long to a rich lord,
    Not thriving, I resolvèd to be bold,
    And make a suit unto him, to afford
A new small-rented lease, and cancel th' old.
In heaven at his manor I him sought: 5
    They told me there, that he was lately gone
    About some land, which he had dearly bought
Long since on earth, to take possessïon.
I straight returned, and knowing his great birth,
    Sought him accordingly in great resorts;   10
    In cities, theatres, gardens, parks, and courts:
At length I heard a ragged noise and mirth
    Of thieves and murderers: there I him espied,
    Who straight, *Your suit is granted*, said, and died.

REDEMPTION: 3 **afford**: grant   9 **straight**: right away   10 **resorts**: places where people congregate

EASTER

I got me flowers to strew thy way;
I got me boughs off many a tree:
But thou wast up by break of day,
And brought'st thy sweets along with thee.

The sun arising in the east,   5
Though he give light, and th' east perfume;
If they should offer to contest
With thy arising, they presume.

Can there be any day but this,
Though many suns to shine endeavour?   10
We count three hundred, but we miss:
There is but one, and that one ever.

PRAYER

PRAYER the Church's banquet, angels' age,
    God's breath in man returning to his birth,
     The soul in paraphrase, heart in pilgrimage,
The Christian plummet sounding heav'n and earth;
Engine against th' Almighty, sinners tower,   5

Reversèd thunder, Christ-side-piercing spear,
The six-days world transposing in an hour,
A kind of tune, which all things hear and fear;
Softness, and peace, and joy, and love, and bliss,
　　Exalted manna, gladness of the best,　　　　　　10
　　Heaven in ordinary, man well dressed,
The Milky Way, the bird of Paradise,
Church-bells beyond the stars heard, the soul's blood,
The land of spices; something understood.

PRAYER: 4 **plummet:** a lead weight on a line, used to find the depth
of water under a ship　5 **Engine:** a piece of equipment used in
warfare, eg a catapult　11 **in ordinary:** in regular attendance

JORDAN

WHO says that fictions only and false hair
Become a verse? Is there in truth no beauty?
Is all good structure in a winding stair?
May no lines pass, except they do their duty
　　Not to a true, but painted chair?　　　　　　5

Is it no verse, except enchanted groves
And sudden arbours shadow coarse-spun lines?
Must purling streams refresh a lover's loves?
Must all be veiled, which he that reads, divines,
　　Catching the sense at two removes?　　　　　　10

Shepherds are honest people; let them sing:
Riddle who list, for me, and pull for Prime:
I envy no man's nightingale or spring;
Nor let them punish me with loss of rhyme,
　　Who plainly say, *My God, My King.*　　　　　　15

JORDAN: 12 **list:** choose　**pull for Prime:** attempt to draw a winning
card in the old game of primero

VIRTUE

SWEET day, so cool, so calm, so bright,
The bridal of the earth and sky,
The dew shall weep thy fall tonight;
　　For thou must die.

Sweet rose, whose hue angry and brave　　　　　　5
Bids the rash gazer wipe his eye,
Thy root is ever in its grave,
　　And thou must die.

Sweet spring, full of sweet days and roses,
A box where sweets compacted lie,　　　　　　10
My music shows ye have your closes,
　　And all must die.

Only a sweet and virtuous soul,
Like seasoned timber, never gives;
But though the whole world turn to coal,　　　　　　15
　　Then chiefly lives.

THE PEARL

The Kingdom of heaven is like unto a merchant man, seeking goodly
pearls; who, when he had found one, sold all that he had and bought it.
　　　　　　MATTHEW 13.45

I KNOW the ways of Learning; both the head
And pipes that feed the press, and make it run;
What reason hath from nature borrowed,
Or of itself, like a good huswife, spun
In laws and policy; what the stars conspire,　　　　　　5
What willing nature speaks, what forced by fire;
Both th' old discoveries, and the new-found seas,
The stock and surplus, cause and history:
All these stand open, or I have the keys:
　　　　Yet I love thee.　　　　　　10

I know the ways of Honour, what maintains
The quick returns of courtesy and wit:
In vies of favours whether party gains,
When glory swells the heart, and moldeth it
To all expressions both of hand and eye,　　　　　　15
Which on the world a true-love-knot may tie,
And bear the bundle, wheresoe'er it goes:
How many drams of spirit there must be
To sell my life unto my friends or foes:
　　　　Yet I love thee.　　　　　　20

I know the ways of Pleasure, the sweet strains,
The lullings and the relishes of it;
The propositions of hot blood and brains;
What mirth and music mean; what love and wit
Have done these twenty hundred years, and more:　　　　　　25
I know the projects of unbridled store:
My stuff is flesh, not brass; my senses live,
And grumble oft, that they have more in me
Than he that curbs them, being but one to five:
　　　　Yet I love thee.　　　　　　30

I know all these, and have them in my hand:
Therefore not sealed, but with open eyes
I fly to thee, and fully understand
Both the main sale, and the commodities;
And at what rate and price I have thy love;　　　　　　35
With all the circumstances that may move:
Yet through these labyrinths, not my grovelling wit,
But thy silk twist let down from heav'n to me,
Did both conduct and teach me, how by it
　　　　To climb to thee.　　　　　　40

THE PEARL: 6 **forced by fire:** compelled by torture　13 **vies:** challenges,
contests　26 **projects of unbridled store:** schemes to acquire great
wealth　29 **he that . . . five:** the five bodily senses are held in check
by the soul or conscience　38 **twist:** thread

GEORGE HERBERT

THE QUIP

THE merry world did on a day
With his train-bands and mates agree
To meet together where I lay,
And all in sport to jeer at me.

First, Beauty crept into a rose,   5
Which when I plucked not, 'Sir,' said she,
'Tell me, I pray, whose hands are those?'
But thou shalt answer, Lord, for me.

Then Money came, and chinking still,
'What tune is this, poor man?' said he,   10
'I heard in music you had skill.'
But thou shalt answer, Lord, for me.

Then came brave Glory puffing by
In silks that whistled – who but he?
He scarce allowed me half an eye.   15
But thou shalt answer, Lord, for me.

Then came quick Wit and Conversation,
And he would needs a comfort be,
And, to be short, make an oration.
But thou shalt answer, Lord, for me.   20

Yet when the hour of thy design
To answer these fine things shall come,
Speak not at large: say, I am thine;
And then they have their answer home.

THE QUIP: 2 **train-bands:** bands of citizens trained in the use of
weapons, available for use as militia 15 **He scarce . . . eye:** he was
too proud to do more than glance at me

HOPE

I GAVE to Hope a watch of mine: but he
          An anchor gave to me.
Then an old prayer-book I did present:
          And he an optic sent.
With that I gave a vial full of tears: 5
          But he a few green ears.
Ah loiterer! I'll no more, no more I'll bring:
          I did expect a ring.

HOPE: 2 **anchor:** symbol of surety and steadfastness   4 **optic:**
telescope (with which to see something which distant) 6 **green
ears:** corn which is yet to ripen 8 **a ring:** i.e. a wedding-ring,
symbol of being united with God

THE COLLAR

I STRUCK the board, and cried 'No more!
          I will abroad.

What, shall I ever sigh and pine?
My lines and life are free; free as the road,
          Loose as the wind, as large as store.   5
          Shall I be still in suit?
Have I no harvest but a thorn
To let me blood, and not restore
What I have lost with cordial fruit?
          Sure there was wine   10
Before my sighs did dry it; there was corn
          Before my tears did drown it.
     Is the year only lost to me?
          Have I no bays to crown it?
No flowers, no garlands gay? all blasted?   15
          All wasted?
Not so, my heart: but there is fruit,
          And thou hast hands.
     Recover all thy sigh-blown age
On double pleasures: leave thy cold dispute   20
Of what is fit, and not. Forsake thy cage,
          Thy rope of sands,
Which petty thoughts have made, and made to thee
     Good cable, to enforce and draw,
          And be thy law,   25
     While thou didst wink and wouldst not see.
          Away; take heed:
          I will abroad.
Call in thy death's head there: tie up thy fears.
          He that forbears   30
     To suit and serve his need,
          Deserves his load.'
But as I raved and grew more fierce and wild
          At every word,
Methoughts I heard one calling 'Child!'   35
          And I replied 'My Lord'.

THE COLLAR: The title plays on the literal meaning of a collar put
on a dog by its master, on 'caller', and 'choler' (in the old sense
of 'anger') 1 **board:** table 2 **I will abroad:** I will go out of doors, out
into the world 4 **lines:** part or lot in life 5 **store:** abundance 6 **Shall
. . . suit:** will I always have to plead 8 **let me blood:** bleed me (for
medicinal reasons) 14 **bays:** a crown of victory, especially in
poetical achievement 22 **rope of sands:** a bond which is easily
broken 26 **wink:** blink

THE PULLEY

WHEN God at first made man,
Having a glass of blessings standing by,
Let us (said He) pour on him all we can:
Let the world's riches, which dispersed lie,
          Contract into a span.   5

So strength first made a way;
Then beauty flowed, then wisdom, honour, pleasure:
When almost all was out, God made a stay,
Perceiving that alone of all His treasure
          Rest in the bottom lay.   10

For if I should (said He)
Bestow this jewel also on my creature,
He would adore My gifts instead of Me,
And rest in Nature, not the God of Nature:
    So both should losers be.   15

    Yet let him keep the rest,
But keep them with repining restlessness:
Let him be rich and weary, that, at least,
If goodness lead him not, yet weariness
    May toss him to My breast.   20

THE PULLEY: 5 **span:** a measure, extent 8 **made a stay:** halted

THE FLOWER

How fresh, O Lord, how sweet and clean
Are thy returns! ev'n as the flowers in spring;
    To which, besides their own demean,
The late-past frosts tributes of pleasure bring.
        Grief melts away   5
        Like snow in May,
    As if there were no such cold thing.

    Who would have thought my shrivelled heart
Could have recovered greenness? It was gone
    Quite under ground; as flowers depart   10
To see their mother-root, when they have blown;
        Where they together
        All the hard weather,
    Dead to the world, keep house unknown.

    These are thy wonders, Lord of power,   15
Killing and quick'ning, bringing down to hell
    And up to heaven in an hour;
Making a chiming of a passing-bell.
        We say amiss,
        This or that is: 20
    Thy word is all, if we could spell.

    O that I once past changing were,
Fast in thy Paradise, where no flower can wither!
    Many a spring I shoot up fair,
Off'ring at heav'n, growing and groaning thither: 25
        Nor doth my flower
        Want a spring shower,
    My sins and I joining together.

    But while I grow in a straight line,
Still upwards bent, as if heav'n were mine own,   30
    Thy anger comes, and I decline:
What frost to that? What pole is not the zone,
        Where all things burn,
        When thou dost turn,
    And the least frown of thine is shown?   35

    And now in age I bud again,
After so many deaths I live and write;
    I once more smell the dew and rain,
And relish versing: O my only light,
        It cannot be   40
        That I am he
    On whom thy tempests fell all night.

    These are thy wonders, Lord of love,
To make us see we are but flowers that glide;
    Which when we once can find and prove,   45
Thou hast a garden for us, where to bide.
        Who would be more,
        Swelling through store,
    Forfeit their Paradise by their pride.

THE FLOWER: 3 **demean:** appearance 11 **blown:** bloomed 16 **quick'ning:** bringing to life 18 **passing-bell:** a bell rung after someone has died 19 **amiss:** wrongly 23 **Fast:** secure

LOVE

LOVE bade me welcome; yet my soul drew back,
    Guilty of dust and sin.
But quick-eyed Love, observing me grow slack
    From my first entrance in,
Drew nearer to me, sweetly questioning   5
    If I lacked anything.

'A guest,' I answered 'worthy to be here';
    Love said 'You shall be he.'
'I, the unkind, ungrateful? Ah, my dear,
    I cannot look on Thee.'   10
Love took my hand, and smiling did reply
    'Who made the eyes but I?'

'Truth, Lord; but I have marred them: let my shame
    Go where it doth deserve.'
'And know you not,' says Love 'who bore the blame?'
    'My dear, then I will serve.'   16
'You must sit down,' says Love 'and taste my meat.'
    So I did sit and eat.

LOVE: 2 **dust:** dirt 3 **slack:** reluctant

THOMAS CAREW

'ASK ME NO MORE WHERE JOVE BESTOWS'

ASK me no more where Jove bestows,
When June is past, the fading rose;
For in your beauty's orient deep
These flowers, as in their causes, sleep.

Ask me no more whither do stray 5
The golden atoms of the day;
For in pure love heaven did prepare
Those powders to enrich your hair.

Ask me no more whither doth haste
The nightingale when May is past; 10
For in your sweet dividing throat
She winters and keeps warm her note.

Ask me no more where those stars 'light
That downwards fall in dead of night;
For in your eyes they sit, and there 15
Fixèd become as in their sphere.

Ask me no more if east or west
The Phoenix builds her spicy nest;
For unto you at last she flies,
And in your fragrant bosom dies. 20

'ASK ME NO MORE WHERE JOVE BESTOWS': 1 **Jove:** Jupiter, chief of
the Roman gods 3 **orient:** bright 11 **dividing:** singing in an
ornamented way, splitting long notes into many short ones
18 **Phoenix:** a mythical bird which, when it dies, builds a nest of
spices, is consumed by flames and then reborn from the ashes

EPITAPH ON THE LADY MARY VILLIERS

THE Lady Mary Villiers lies
Under this stone; with weeping eyes
The parents that first gave her birth,
And their sad friends, laid her in earth.
If any of them, reader, were 5
Known unto thee, shed a tear;
Or if thyself possess a gem
As dear to thee as this to them,
Though a stranger to this place,
Bewail in theirs thine own hard case, 10
For thou perhaps at thy return
Mayst find thy darling in an urn.

JAMES SHIRLEY

'YOU VIRGINS THAT DID LATE DESPAIR'

YOU virgins that did late despair
  To keep your wealth from cruel men,
Tie up in silk your careless hair:
  Soft peace is come again.

Now lovers' eyes may gently shoot 5
  A flame that will not kill;
The drum was angry, but the lute
  Shall whisper what you will.

Sing, Io, Io! for his sake
  That hath restored your drooping heads; 10
With choice of sweetest flowers make
  A garden where he treads;

Whilst we whole groves of laurel bring,
  A petty triumph to his brow,
Who is the Master of our spring 15
  And all the bloom we owe.

'YOU VIRGINS THAT DID LATE DESPAIR': 9 **Io:** a Greek cry of triumph
13 **laurel:** laurel leaves used to make wreaths to crown victors

'THE GLORIES OF OUR BLOOD AND STATE'

THE glories of our blood and state,
  Are shadows, not substantial things,
There is no armour against fate,
  Death lays his icy hand on kings,
    Sceptre and crown 5
    Must tumble down,
And in the dust be equal made,
With the poor crooked scythe and spade.

Some men with swords may reap the field,
  And plant fresh laurels where they kill, 10
But their strong nerves at last must yield,
  They tame but one another still;
    Early or late,
    They stoop to fate,
And must give up their murmuring breath, 15
When they pale captives creep to death.

The garlands wither on your brow,
  Then boast no more your mighty deeds,
Upon Death's purple altar now,
  See where the victor-victim bleeds, 20
    Your heads must come,
    To the cold tomb,
Only the actions of the just
Smell sweet, and blossom in their dust.

WILLIAM HABINGTON

NOX NOCTI INDICAT SCIENTIAM

WHEN I survey the bright
  Celestial sphere:
So rich with jewels hung, that night
Doth like an Ethiop bride appear,

My soul her wings doth spread 5
  And heavenward flies,
Th' Almighty's mysteries to read
In the large volumes of the skies.

For the bright firmament
    Shoots forth no flame   10
So silent, but is eloquent
In speaking the Creator's name.

No unregarded star
    Contracts its light
Into so small a character,   15
Removed far from our humane sight:

But if we steadfast look,
    We shall discern
In it as in some holy book,
How man may heavenly knowledge learn.   20

It tells the conqueror,
    That far-stretched pow'r
Which his proud dangers traffic for,
Is but the triumph of an hour.

That from the farthest north,   25
    Some nation may
Yet undiscoverèd issue forth,
And o'er his new-got conquest sway.

Some nation yet shut in
    With hills of ice   30
May be let out to scourge his sin
Till they shall equal him in vice.

And then they likewise shall
    Their ruin have,
For as your selves your empires fall,   35
And every kingdom hath a grave.

Thus those celestial fires,
    Though seeming mute,
The fallacy of our desires
And all the pride of life confute.   40

For they have watched since first
    The world had birth:
And found sin in itself accurst,
And nothing permanent on earth.

NOX NOCTI INDICAT SCIENTIAM: 4 **Ethiop:** Ethiopian, i.e. African or black 23 **dangers:** powers

THOMAS RANDOLPH

UPON HIS PICTURE

WHEN age hath made me what I am not now;
And every wrinkle tells me where the plough
Of time hath furrowed; when an ice shall flow
Through every vein, and all my head wear snow;
When death displays his coldness in my cheek   5

And I myself in my own picture seek,
Not finding what I am, but what I was,
In doubt which to believe, this or my glass;
Yet though I alter, this remains the same
As it was drawn, retains the primitive frame   10
And first complexion; here will still be seen
Blood on the cheek, and down upon the chin.
Here the smooth brow will stay, the lively eye,
The ruddy lip, and hair of youthful dye.
Behold what frailty we in man may see   15
Whose shadow is less given to change than he.

SIR WILLIAM D'AVENANT

'THE LARK NOW LEAVES HIS WAT'RY NEST'

THE lark now leaves his wat'ry nest
    And climbing, shakes his dewy wings;
He takes this window for the east;
    And to implore your light, he sings,
'Awake, awake, the morn will never rise,   5
Till she can dress her beauty at your eyes.

'The merchant bows unto the seaman's star,
    The ploughman from the sun his season takes;
But still the lover wonders what they are,
    Who look for day before his mistress wakes.   10
Awake, awake, break through your veils of lawn!
Then draw your curtains, and begin the dawn.'

'THE LARK NOW LEAVES HIS WAT'RY NEST': 11 **lawn:** linen

EDMUND WALLER

'GO, LOVELY ROSE'

Go, lovely Rose,
Tell her that wastes her time and me
    That now she knows,
When I resemble her to thee,
How sweet and fair she seems to be.   5

Tell her that's young
And shuns to have her graces spied,
    That had'st thou sprung
In deserts, where no men abide,
Thou must have uncommended died.   10

Small is the worth
Of beauty from the light retired;
    Bid her come forth,
Suffer herself to be desired,
And not blush so to be admired.   15

Then die! that she
The common fate of all things rare
  May read in thee:
How small a part of time they share
That are so wondrous sweet and fair!   20

'GO, LOVELY ROSE': 4 **resemble:** compare

OF THE LAST VERSES IN THE BOOK

WHEN we for age could neither read nor write,
The subject made us able to indite.
The soul with nobler resolutions decked,
The body stooping, does herself erect:
No mortal parts are requisite to raise   5
Her, that unbodied can her Maker praise.
  The seas are quiet, when the winds give o'er;
So calm are we, when passions are no more:
For then we know how vain it was to boast
Of fleeting things, so certain to be lost.   10
Clouds of affection from our younger eyes
Conceal that emptiness, which age descries.
  The soul's dark cottage, battered and decayed,
Lets in new light, thro' chinks that time has made.
Stronger by weakness, wiser men become   15
As they draw near to their eternal home:
Leaving the old, both worlds at once they view,
That stand upon the threshold of the new.

JOHN MILTON

ON THE MORNING OF CHRIST'S NATIVITY

THIS is the month, and this the happy morn
Wherein the Son of Heaven's eternal King,
Of wedded maid, and virgin mother born,
Our great redemption from above did bring;
For so the holy sages once did sing,   5
  That he our deadly forfeit should release,
And with his Father work us a perpetual peace.

That glorious form, that light unsufferable,
And that far-beaming blaze of majesty,
Wherewith He wont at heaven's high council-table,   10
To sit the midst of trinal unity,
He laid aside; and here with us to be,
  Forsook the courts of everlasting day,
And chose with us a darksome house of mortal clay.

ON THE MORNING OF CHRIST'S NATIVITY: 5 **holy sages:** the Old Testament prophets   6 **deadly forfeit:** the penalty of death imposed by God on man after the Fall of Adam   10 **wont:** was accustomed   11 **trinal unity:** the Holy Trinity

Say, heavenly Muse, shall not thy sacred vein   15
Afford a present to the infant God?
Hast thou no verse, no hymn, or solemn strain,
To welcome Him to this His new abode,
Now while the heaven by the sun's team untrod,
  Hath took no print of the approaching light,   20
And all the spangled host keep watch in squadrons
    bright?

See how from far upon the eastern road
The star-led wizards haste with odours sweet!
Oh, run, prevent them with thy humble ode,
And lay it lowly at His blessèd feet;   25
Have thou the honour first, thy Lord to greet,
  And join thy voice unto the angel choir,
From out his secret altar touched with hallowed fire.

THE HYMN

  It was the winter wild,
    While the heaven-born child,   30
All meanly wrapped in the rude manger lies;
  Nature, in awe to him,
    Had doffed her gaudy trim,
With her great Master so to sympathize:
It was no season then for her   35
To wanton with the sun, her lusty paramour.

  Only with speeches fair
    She woos the gentle air
To hide her guilty front with innocent snow,
  And on her naked shame,   40
    Pollute with sinful blame,
The saintly veil of maiden white to throw,
Confounded, that her Maker's eyes
Should look so near upon her foul deformities.

  But He, her fears to cease,   45
    Sent down the meek-eyed Peace:
She, crowned with olive green, came softly sliding
  Down through the turning sphere,
    His ready harbinger,
With turtle wing the amorous clouds dividing,   50
And waving wide her myrtle wand,
She strikes a universal peace through sea and land.

15 **heavenly Muse:** this could be a reference to Urania, the Muse of astronomy, but is more probably an attempt by Milton to Christianise a pagan reference. There were nine Muses, and all of these daughters of Zeus are associated with inspiring the arts, particularly poetry and music 21 **spangled:** bright 23 **star-led wizards:** the wise men who were led by a star to Christ's birthplace in Bethlehem 24 **prevent them:** Arrive before them 28 **touched with hallowed fire:** in Isaiah VI, 6–7 the prophet is purified by a hot coal, taken from the Altar of God, being placed on his lips 33 **doffed her gaudy trim:** Milton stretches autumn into winter as Nature sheds her leaves 47 **olive:** a symbol of peace 48 **through the turning sphere:** through the planets of the heavens 50 **turtle wing:** turtle dove, the emblem of constant devotion 51 **myrtle:** The tree of love

No war or battle's sound
  Was heard the world around,
The idle spear and shield were high up-hung;   55
  The hookèd chariot stood
  Unstained with hostile blood;
The trumpet spake not to the armèd throng;
And kings sat still with awful eye,
As if they surely knew their sovran Lord was by.   60

  But peaceful was the night
  Wherein the Prince of Light
His reign of peace upon the earth began.
  The winds with wonder whist,
  Smoothly the waters kissed,   65
Whispering new joys, the mild oceān,
Who now hath quite forgot to rave,
While birds of calm sit brooding on the charmèd wave.

  The stars with deep amaze
  Stand fixed in steadfast gaze,   70
Bending one way their precious influence,
  And will not take their flight,
  For all the morning light,
Or Lucifer that often warned them thence;
But in their glimmering orbs did glow,   75
Until their Lord himself bespake, and bid them go.

  And though the shady gloom
  Had given day her room,
The sun himself withheld his wonted speed,
  And hid his head for shame,   80
  As his inferior flame,
The new enlightened world no more should need;
He saw a greater sun appear
Then his bright throne or burning axletree could
    bear.

  The shepherds on the lawn,   85
  Or ere the point of dawn,
Sat simply chatting in a rustic row;
  Full little thought they then
  That the mighty Pan
Was kindly come to live with them below;   90
Perhaps their loves, or else their sheep,
Was all that did their silly thoughts so busy keep.

  When such music sweet
  Their hearts and ears did greet,
As never was by mortal finger strook,   95
  Divinely warbled voice
  Answering the stringèd noise,
As all their souls in blissful rapture took:
The air, such pleasure loath to lose,
With thousand echoes still prolongs each heavenly
    close.   100

  Nature that heard such sound
  Beneath the hollow round
Of Cynthia's seat, the airy region thrilling,
  Now was almost won
  To think her part was done,   105
And that her reign had here its last fulfilling;
She knew such harmony alone
Could hold all heaven and earth in happier union.

  At last surrounds their sight
  A globe of circular light,   110
That with long beams the shamefaced night
    arrayed;
  The helmèd cherubim
  And sworded seraphim
Are seen in glittering ranks with wings displayed,
Harping in loud and solemn choir,   115
With unexpressive notes to heaven's new-born heir.

  Such Music (as 'tis said)
  Before was never made,
But when of old the sons of morning sung,
  While the Creator great   120
  His constellations set,
And the well-balanced world on hinges hung,
And cast the dark foundations deep,
And bid the welt'ring waves their oozy channel keep.

  Ring out, ye crystal spheres,   125
  Once bless our human ears
(If ye have power to touch our senses so),
  And let your silver chime
  Move in melodious time;
And let the base of heaven's deep organ blow;   130
And with your ninefold harmony
Make up full consort to th'angelic symphony.

  For, if such holy song
  Enwrap our fancy long,
Time will run back and fetch the age of gold;   135
  And speckled vanity
  Will sicken soon and die,
And leprous sin will melt from earthly mould,
And hell itself will pass away,
And leave her dolorous mansions to the peering day.

  Yea, Truth, and Justice then   141
  Will down return to men,
Th'enamelled arras of the rainbow wearing,
  And Mercy set between,
  Throned in celestial sheen,   145
With radiant feet the tissued clouds down steering;
And heaven, as at some festival,
Will open wide the gates of her high palace-hall.

102–3 **hollow round/Of Cynthia's seat:** The sphere of the moon. Cynthia is the moon goddess 112 **helmèd cherubim:** helmeted angels 113 **sworded seraphim:** another class of angels, this time armed with swords 116 **unexpressive:** inexpressible 125 **Ring out, ye crystal spheres:** the theory that each of the heavenly spheres creates a musical note as it revolves, making up the 'ninefold harmony' (the tenth sphere produces no note as it is fixed) 135 **the age of gold:** the first age of the world when man was innocent 143 **arras:** tapestry

56 **hookèd chariot:** a reference to the cutting blades fixed to the axle of a war chariot 64 **whist:** hushed 68 **birds of calm:** halcyons (kingfishers), said to bring calm weather 74 **Lucifer:** Venus, the morning star 84 **burning axletree:** the chariot of the sun 89 **Pan:** God of shepherds 92 **silly:** humble, unsophisticated 95 **strook:** struck 100 **close:** musical cadence

But wisest Fate says no,
This must not yet be so; 150
The Babe lies yet in smiling infancy
That on the bitter cross
Must redeem our loss,
So both himself and us to glorify:
Yet first, to those ychained in sleep, 155
The wakeful trump of doom must thunder through
 the deep,

With such a horrid clang
As on Mount Sinai rang
While the red fire, and smould'ring clouds out
 break:
The agèd earth aghast, 160
With terror of that blast,
Shall from the surface to the centre shake,
When, at the world's last session,
The dreadful Judge in middle air shall spread His
 throne.

And then at last our bliss 165
Full and perfect is,
But now begins; for from this happy day
Th'old dragon under ground,
In straiter limits bound,
Not half so far casts his usurpèd sway, 170
And, wrath to see his kingdom fail,
Swinges the scaly horror of his folded tail.

The oracles are dumb,
No voice or hideous hum
Runs through the archèd roof in words deceiving.
Apollo from his shrine 176
Can no more divine,
With hollow shriek the steep of Delphos leaving.
No nightly trance, or breathèd spell,
Inspires the pale-eyed priest from the prophetic cell.

The lonely mountains o'er, 181
And the resounding shore,
A voice of weeping heard and loud lament;
From haunted spring, and dale
Edged with poplar pale, 185
The parting genius is with sighing sent,
With flower-inwoven tresses torn
The nymphs in twilight shade of tangled thickets
 mourn.

In consecrated earth,
And on the holy hearth, 190
The lars and lemures moan with midnight plaint,
In urns, and altars round,
A drear and dying sound
Affrights the flamens at their service quaint;
And the chill marble seems to sweat, 195
While each peculiar power forgoes his wonted seat.

Peor and Baalim
Forsake their temples dim,
With that twice-battered god of Palestine;
And moonèd Ashtaroth, 200
Heaven's queen and mother both,
Now sits not girt with tapers' holy shine:
The Libyc Hammon shrinks his horn;
In vain the Tyrian maids their wounded Thammuz
 mourn.

And sullen Moloch, fled, 205
Hath left in shadows dread
His burning idol all of blackest hue;
In vain with cymbals' ring
They call the grisly king,
In dismal dance about the furnace blue; 210
The brutish gods of Nile as fast,
Isis, and Orus, and the dog Anubis, haste.

Nor is Osiris seen
In Memphian grove, or green,
Trampling the unshow'red grass with lowings loud;
Nor can he be at rest 216
Within his sacred chest,
Nought but profoundest hell can be his shroud;
In vain, with timbrelled anthems dark,
The sable-stolèd sorcerers bear his worshipped ark.

He feels from Judah's land 221
The dreaded infant's hand;
The rays of Bethlehem blind his dusky eyn;
Nor all the gods beside
Longer dare abide, 225
Not Typhon huge ending in snaky twine:
Our Babe, to show his godhead true,
Can in his swaddling bands control the damnèd crew.

So, when the sun in bed,
Curtained with cloudy red, 230
Pillows his chin upon an orient wave,
The flocking shadows pale
Troop to th'infernal jail,
Each fettered ghost slips to his several grave,
And the yellow-skirted fays, 235
Fly after the night-steeds, leaving their moon-loved
 maze.

But see the Virgin blest,
Hath laid her Babe to rest.
Time is our tedious song should here have ending,
Heaven's youngest teemèd star 240
Hath fixed her polished car,
Her sleeping Lord with handmaid lamp attending;
And all about the courtly stable,
Bright-harnessed angels sit in order serviceable.

197 **Peor and Baalim:** Mount Peor, in Canaan, was the home of the
Phoenician god Baal-Peor 200 **Ashtaroth:** Phoenician moon goddess
203 **Hammon:** Libyan god 204 **Thammuz:** Phoenician god 205 **Moloch:**
Ammonite god whose worship is associated with fire and sacrifice
212 **Isis . . . Orus . . . Aubis:** Egyptian deities 223 **eyn:** archaic plural
of eye 226 **Typhon:** hundred-headed monster of Greek mythology
235 **fays:** faeries

168 **old dragon:** the devil 178 **Delphos:** the shrine of Apollo was at
Delphi 191 **lars and lemures:** ghosts of the dead 194 **flamen:** Roman
priests

ON SHAKESPEARE. 1630

WHAT needs my Shakespeare for his honoured bones
The labour of an age in pilèd stones,
Or that his hallowed relics should be hid
Under a star-ypointing pyramid?
Dear son of memory, great heir of fame,   5
What need'st thou such weak witness of thy name?
Thou in our wonder and astonishment
Hast built thyself a livelong monument.
For whilst, to the shame of slow-endeavouring art,
Thy easy numbers flow, and that each heart   10
Hath from the leaves of thy unvaluèd book
Those Delphic lines with deep impression took,
Then thou, our fancy of itself bereaving,
Dost make us marble with too much conceiving;
And so sepúlchred in such pomp dost lie   15
That kings for such a tomb would wish to die.

ON SHAKESPEARE: 8 **livelong:** long-lasting 11 **unvaluèd:** invaluable

L'ALLEGRO

HENCE, loathèd Melancholy
    Of Cerberus and blackest Midnight born
In Stygian cave forlorn
    'Mongst horrid shapes, and shrieks, and sights
        unholy;
Find out some uncouth cell,   5
    Where brooding Darkness spreads his jealous wings,
And the night-raven sings;
    There, under ebon shades, and low-browed rocks,
As ragged as thy locks,
    In dark Cimmerian desert ever dwell.   10
But come, thou goddess fair and free,
In heaven yclept Euphrosyne,
And by men heart-easing Mirth;
Whom lovely Venus, at a birth,
With two sister Graces more,   15
To ivy-crownèd Bacchus bore;
Or whether (as some sager sing)
The frolic wind that breathes the spring,
Zephyr, with Aurora playing,
As he met her once a-Maying,   20
There, on beds of violets blue,
And fresh-blown roses washed in dew,
Filled her with thee, a daughter fair,
So buxom, blithe, and debonair.
Haste thee, Nymph, and bring with thee   25

L'ALLEGRO: 2 **Cerberus:** three-headed hound of Greek mythology who guarded the Underworld of the dead 3 **Stygian:** on the Styx, river of the underworld 8 **ebon:** ebony 10 **Cimmerian:** the Cimmerians were thought to live in constant darkness 12 **yclept:** called **Euphrosyne:** one of the Three Graces. The name means 'mirth' 14 **Venus:** goddess of love 16 **Bacchus:** god of wine 19 **Zephyr:** the west wind **Aurora:** goddess of the dawn

Jest and youthful Jollity,
Quips and cranks and wanton wiles,
Nods and becks and wreathèd smiles,
Such as hang on Hebe's cheek,
And love to live in dimple sleek;   30
Sport that wrinkled Care derides,
And Laughter holding both his sides.
Come, and trip it as ye go,
On the light fantastic toe;
And in thy right hand lead with thee   35
The mountain nymph, sweet Liberty;
And, if I give thee honour due,
Mirth, admit me of thy crew
To live with her, and live with thee,
In unreprovèd pleasures free;   40
To hear the lark begin his flight,
And, singing, startle the dull night,
From his watch-tow'r in the skies,
Till the dappled dawn doth rise;
Then to come in spite of sorrow,   45
And at my window bid good-morrow,
Through the sweet-briar or the vine,
Or the twisted eglantine;
While the cock, with lively din,
Scatters the rear of darkness thin;   50
And to the stack, or the barn door,
Stoutly struts his dames before,
Oft list'ning how the hounds and horn
Clearly rouse the slumb'ring morn,
From the side of some hoar hill,   55
Through the high wood echoing shrill.
Sometime walking not unseen,
By hedgerow elms, on hillocks green,
Right against the eastern gate
Where the great sun begins his state,   60
Robed in flames and amber light,
The clouds in thousand liveries dight;
While the ploughman, near at hand,
Whistles o'er the furrowed land,
And the milkmaid singeth blithe,   65
And the mower whets his scythe,
And every shepherd tells his tale
Under the hawthorn in the dale.
Straight mine eye hath caught new pleasures,
Whilst the landskip round it measures: 70
Russet lawns, and fallows grey,
Where the nibbling flocks do stray;
Mountains on whose barren breast
The labouring clouds do often rest:
Meadows trim, with daisies pied,   75
Shallow brooks, and rivers wide.
Towers and battlements it sees
Bosomed high in tufted trees,
Where perhaps some beauty lies,
The cynosure of neighbouring eyes.   80

27 **cranks:** jokes 29 **Hebe's:** goddess of youth 62 **dight:** dressed 70 **landskip:** landscape 80 **cynosure:** the polestar

Hard by, a cottage chimney smokes
From betwixt two agèd oaks,
Where Corydon and Thyrsis met
Are at their savoury dinner set
Of herbs and other country messes,   85
Which the neat-handed Phyllis dresses;
And then in haste her bow'r she leaves,
With Thestylis to bind the sheaves;
Or, if the earlier season lead,
To the tanned haycock in the mead.   90
Sometimes, with secure delight,
The upland hamlets will invite,
When the merry bells ring round,
And the jocund rebecks sound
To many a youth and many a maid   95
Dancing in the chequered shade;
And young and old come forth to play
On a sunshine holiday,
Till the livelong daylight fail,
Then to the spicy nut-brown ale,   100
With stories told of many a feat,
How fairy Mab the junkets eat;
She was pinched and pulled, she said,
And he by friar's lanthorn led,
Tells how the drudging goblin sweat   105
To earn his cream-bowl duly set,
When in one night, ere glimpse of morn,
His shadowy flail hath threshed the corn
That ten day-labourers could not end;
Then lies him down, the lubber fiend,   110
And, stretched out all the chimney's length,
Basks at the fire his hairy strength;
And crop-full out of doors he flings,
Ere the first cock his matin rings.
Thus done the tales, to bed they creep,   115
By whispering winds soon lulled asleep.
Towered cities please us then,
And the busy hum of men,
Where throngs of knights and barons bold,
In weeds of peace, high triumphs hold,   120
With store of ladies, whose bright eyes
Rain influence, and judge the prize
Of wit, or arms, while both contend
To win her grace, whom all commend.
There let Hymen oft appear   125
In saffron robe, with taper clear,
And pomp, and feast, and revelry,
With mask and antique pageantry:
Such sights as youthful poets dream
On summer eaves by haunted stream.   130

83 **Corydon:** a traditional shepherds' name **Thyrsis:** a shepherdess
85 **messes:** meals 86 **Phyllis:** woman from Virgil's *Eclogues*
88 **Thestylis:** man from Virgil's *Eclogues* 102 **junkets:** sweetmeats
104 **lanthorn:** lantern 110 **lubber:** drudging 120 **weeds:** clothes
125 **Hymen:** god of marriage 128 **mask:** court entertainment
consisting of acting and dancing

Then to the well-trod stage anon,
If Jonson's learnèd sock be on,
Or sweetest Shakespeare, Fancy's child,
Warble his native wood-notes wild;
And ever, against eating cares,   135
Lap me in soft Lydian airs,
Married to immortal verse,
Such as the meeting soul may pierce,
In notes with many a winding bout
Of linkèd sweetness long drawn out   140
With wanton heed and giddy cunning,
The melting voice through mazes running,
Untwisting all the chains that tie
The hidden soul of harmony.
That Orpheus' self may heave his head   145
From golden slumber on a bed
Of heaped Elysian flow'rs, and hear
Such strains as would have won the ear
Of Pluto to have quite set free
His half-regained Eurydice.   150
These delights, if thou canst give,
Mirth, with thee I mean to live.

132 **Jonson's:** Ben Jonson (1572–1640), playwright and poet who also
created masques for James I 136 **Lydian airs:** soft music 145 **Orpheus:**
mythical Greek poet who went into the Underworld to retrieve
his wife Eurydice 147 **Elysian:** In Greek mythology Elysium is
the state of the blessed after death 149 **Pluto:** Roman god of
the Underworld

IL PENSEROSO

HENCE, vain deluding Joys,
   The brood of Folly without father bred,
How little you bestead,
   Or fill the fixèd mind with all your toys;
Dwell in some idle brain,   5
   And fancies fond with gaudy shapes possess,
As thick and numberless
   As the gay motes that people the sun beams,
Or likest hovering dreams,
   The fickle pensioners of Morpheus' train.   10
But hail, thou goddess, sage and holy,
Hail, divinest Melancholy,
Whose saintly visage is too bright
To hit the sense of human sight,
And therefore to our weaker view   15
O'erlaid with black, staid Wisdom's hue.
Black, but such as in esteem
Prince Memnon's sister might beseem,
Or that starred Ethiop queen that strove
To set her beauty's praise above   20
The sea nymphs, and their powers offended.
Yet thou art higher far descended,

IL PENSEROSO: 3 **bestead:** help 8 **gay motes:** fine dust that is visible
in beams of light 10 **Morpheus:** god of dreams 18 **Memnon:** an
Ethiopian king who fought for Troy

Thee bright-haired Vesta long of yore
To solitary Saturn bore;
His daughter she (in Saturn's reign, 25
Such mixture was not held a stain),
Oft in glimmering bow'rs, and glades
He met her, and in secret shades
Of woody Ida's inmost grove,
While yet there was no fear of Jove. 30
Come, pensive nun, devout and pure,
Sober, steadfast, and demure,
All in a robe of darkest grain,
Flowing with majestic train,
And sable stole of cypress lawn 35
Over thy decent shoulders drawn.
Come, but keep thy wonted state,
With even step, and musing gait,
And looks commércing with the skies,
Thy rapt soul sitting in thine eyes: 40
There, held in holy passion still,
Forget thyself to marble, till
With a sad leaden downward cast
Thou fix them on the earth as fast.
And join with thee calm Peace and Quiet, 45
Spare Fast, that oft with gods doth diet,
And hears the Muses in a ring,
Aye round about Jove's altar sing.
And add to these retired Leisure,
That in trim gardens takes his pleasure; 50
But first, and chiefest, with thee bring
Him that yon soars on golden wing,
Guiding the fiery-wheelèd throne,
The cherub Contemplation,
And the mute Silence hist along, 55
'Less Philomel will deign a song,
In her sweetest, saddest plight,
Smoothing the rugged brow of Night,
While Cynthia checks her dragon yoke,
Gently o'er th'accustomed oak; 60
Sweet bird, that shunn'st the noise of folly,
Most musical, most melancholy!
Thee, Chantress, oft the woods among,
I woo, to hear thy even-song;
And, missing thee, I walk unseen 65
On the dry smooth-shaven green
To behold the wand'ring moon,
Riding near her highest noon,
Like one that had been led astray
Through the heaven's wide pathless way; 70
And oft, as if her head she bowed,
Stooping through a fleecy cloud.
Oft on a plat of rising ground,

I hear the far-off curfew sound,
Over some wide-watered shore, 75
Swinging slow with sullen roar;
Or, if the air will not permit,
Some still removèd place will fit,
Where glowing embers through the room
Teach light to counterfeit a gloom, 80
Far from all resort of mirth,
Save the cricket on the hearth,
Or the bellman's drowsy charm
To bless the doors from nightly harm;
Or let my lamp, at midnight hour, 85
Be seen in some high lonely tow'r,
Where I may oft out-watch the Bear,
With thrice-great Hermes, or unsphere
The spirit of Plato, to unfold
What worlds or what vast regions hold 90
The immortal mind that hath forsook
Her mansion in this fleshly nook;
And of those demons that are found
In fire, air, flood, or under ground,
Whose power hath a true consent 95
With planet or with element.
Some time let gorgeous Tragedy
In sceptred pall come sweeping by,
Presenting Thebes, or Pelops' line,
Or the tale of Troy divine, 100
Or what (though rare) of later age
Ennobled hath the buskined stage.
But, O sad Virgin, that thy power
Might raise Musaeus from his bower,
Or bid the soul of Orpheus sing 105
Such notes as, warbled to the string,
Drew iron tears down Pluto's cheek,
And made hell grant what love did seek;
Or call up him that left half told
The story of Cambuscan bold, 110
Of Camball, and of Algarsife,
And who had Canace to wife,
That owned the virtuous ring and glass,
And of the wondrous horse of brass,
On which the Tartar king did ride; 115
And if ought else great bards beside
In sage and solemn tunes have sung,
Of tourneys and of trophies hung,
Of forests, and enchantments drear,
Where more is meant than meets the ear. 120
Thus, Night, oft see me in thy pale career,
Till civil-suited Morn appear,
Not tricked and frounced, as she was wont

83 **bellman's:** night watchman 88 **Hermes:** god of arts and sciences
89 **Plato:** (427–347 BC) philosopher 95 **consent:** harmony 98 **sacred
pall:** Royal robe 99 **Thebes:** the city of Thebes featured in many
Greek tragedies **Pelops:** legendary king of Pisa in Greece
102 **buskined stage:** tragic drama 104 **Musaeus:** mythical priest
110–115 in his unfinished *Squire's Tale,* Chaucer tells the story of the
Tartar king Cambuscan, his two sons Camball and Algarsife, and
his daughter Canace

23 **Vesta:** Roman goddess of the hearth 24 **Saturn:** Associated with
Greek god Cronos. Father of Jupiter (Zeus) 29 **Ida:** a mountain
near Troy 31 **nun:** priestess 33 **grain:** colour 55 **hist:** summon
56 **Philomel:** nightingale 59 **Cynthia:** moon goddess who drives a
chariot harnessed with a pair of dragons 73 **plat:** patch

With the Attic boy to hunt,
But kerchiefed in a comely cloud, 125
While rocking winds are piping loud,
Or ushered with a shower still,
When the gust hath blown his fill,
Ending on the rustling leaves,
With minute drops from off the eaves. 130
And, when the sun begins to fling
His flaring beams, me, Goddess, bring
To archèd walks of twilight groves
And shadows brown that Sylvan loves,
Of pine, or monumental oak, 135
Where the rude axe with heavèd stroke
Was never heard the nymphs to daunt,
Or fright them from their hallowed haunt.
There in close covert by some brook,
Where no profaner eye may look, 140
Hide me from day's garish eye,
While the bee with honeyed thigh,
That at her flow'ry work doth sing,
And the waters murmuring,
With such consort as they keep, 145
Entice the dewy-feathered Sleep;
And let some strange mysterious dream
Wave at his wings, in airy stream
Of lively portraiture displayed,
Softly on my eyelids laid; 150
And, as I wake, sweet music breathe
Above, about, or underneath,
Sent by some spirit to mortals good,
Or th'unseen genius of the wood.
But let my due feet never fail 155
To walk the studious cloister's pale,
And love the high embowèd roof,
With antique pillars massy-proof,
And storied windows richly dight,
Casting a dim religious light. 160
There let the pealing organ blow,
To the full-voiced choir below,
In service high and anthems clear,
As may with sweetness, through mine ear,
Dissolve me into ecstasies, 165
And bring all heaven before mine eyes.
And may at last my weary age
Find out the peaceful hermitage,
The hairy gown and mossy cell,
Where I may sit and rightly spell 170
Of every star that heaven doth show,
And every herb that sips the dew,
Till old experience do attain
To something like prophetic strain.
These pleasures, Melancholy, give, 175
And I with thee will choose to live.

124 **Attic boy:** the hunting prince, Cephalus of Thessaly, who
had charmed Aurora 134 **Sylvan:** Roman god of woodlands
157 **embowèd:** arched 159 **dight:** arrayed

WHEN THE ASSAULT WAS INTENDED
TO THE CITY

CAPTAIN or colonel, or knight in arms,
  Whose chance on these defenceless doors may seize,
  If deed of honour did thee ever please,
  Guard them, and him within protect from harms.
He can requite thee, for he knows the charms 5
  That call fame on such gentle acts as these,
  And he can spread thy name o'er lands and seas,
  Whatever clime the sun's bright circle warms.
Lift not thy spear against the Muses' bow'r:
  The great Emathian conqueror bid spare 10
  The house of Pindarus, when temple and tow'r
Went to the ground; and the repeated air
  Of sad Electra's poet had the pow'r
  To save th'Athenian walls from ruin bare.

WHEN THE ASSAULT WAS INTENDED TO THE CITY: **Title:** London was
being threatened by the Charles's Royalist army in November 1642
10 **Emathian conqueror:** Alexander the Great 11 **house of Pindarus:**
Alexander spared the poet Pindar's house when he conquered
Thebes 13 **Electra's poet:** Plutarch

TO THE LORD GENERAL CROMWELL
MAY 1652
ON THE PROPOSALS OF CERTAIN MINISTERS
AT THE COMMITTEE FOR PROPAGATION
OF THE GOSPEL

CROMWELL, our chief of men, who through a cloud
  Not of war only, but detractions rude,
  Guided by faith and matchless fortitude,
  To peace and truth thy glorious way hast ploughed,
And on the neck of crownèd Fortune proud 5
  Hast reared God's trophies, and His work pursued,
  While Darwen stream, with blood of Scots
    imbrued,
  And Dunbar field resounds thy praises loud,
And Worcester's laureate wreath; yet much remains
  To conquer still; Peace hath her victories 10
  No less renowned than War: new foes arise,
Threat'ning to bind our souls with secular chains:
  Help us to save free conscience from the paw
  Of hireling wolves whose gospel is their maw.

TO THE LORD GENERAL CROMWELL: 1 **Cromwell:** Oliver Cromwell
(1599–1658), soldier and politician. Lord Protector of England:
1653–1658 5 **neck of crownèd Fortune:** a reference to Charles I,
who was beheaded in 1649 7 **Darwen stream:** the Darwen in
Lancashire where Cromwell's army defeated the Scots in 1648
8 **Dunbar field:** Cromwell defeated the Scots army at Dunbar in
1650 9 **Worcester's:** Cromwell routed Charles II's Scottish army at
Worcester in 1651

ON THE LATE MASSACRE IN PIEDMONT

AVENGE, O Lord, thy slaughtered saints, whose bones
  Lie scattered on the Alpine mountains cold;
  Even them who kept thy truth so pure of old,
When all our fathers worshipped stocks and stones,
Forget not: in thy book record their groans   5
  Who were thy sheep, and in their ancient fold
  Slain by the bloody Piedmontese, that rolled
Mother with infant down the rocks. Their moans
The vales redoubled to the hills, and they
  To heaven. Their martyred blood and ashes sow   10
  O'er all th'Italian fields; where still doth sway
The triple Tyrant: that from these may grow
  A hundredfold, who, having learnt Thy way,
  Early may fly the Babylonian woe.

ON THE LATE MASSACRE IN PIEDMONT: 1–2 The Protestant community of Piedmont were massacred by the Duke of Savoy's men, in 1655, for refusing to convert to Catholicism 4 a reference to pre-Reformation English Catholicism 12 **triple Tyrant:** the Pope 14 **Babylonian woe:** Babylon here is identified with Rome, and is symbolic with tyranny

'WHEN I CONSIDER HOW MY LIGHT IS SPENT'

WHEN I consider how my light is spent
  Ere half my days in this dark world and wide,
  And that one talent which is death to hide,
  Lodged with me useless, though my soul more bent
To serve therewith my Maker, and present   5
  My true account, lest He returning chide,
  'Doth God exact day-labour, light denied?'
I fondly ask. But patience, to prevent
That murmur, soon replies, 'God doth not need
  Either man's work or his own gifts; who best   10
  Bear His mild yoke, they serve Him best: His state
Is kingly. Thousands at his bidding speed,
  And post o'er land and ocean without rest:
  They also serve who only stand and wait.'

'METHOUGHT I SAW MY LATE ESPOUSÈD SAINT'

METHOUGHT I saw my late espousèd saint
  Brought to me like Alcestis from the grave,
  Whom Jove's great son to her glad husband gave,
  Rescued from Death by force, though pale and faint.
Mine as whom washed from spot of child-bed taint   5
  Purification in the old Law did save,
  And such as yet once more I trust to have
Full sight of her in heaven without restraint,
Came vested all in white, pure as her mind.
  Her face was veiled; yet to my fancied sight   10
  Love, sweetness, goodness, in her person shined

So clear, as in no face with more delight.
  But, oh, as to embrace me she inclined
  I waked, she fled, and day brought back my night.

METHOUGHT I SAW MY LATE ESPOUSÈD SAINT: 2 **Alcestis:** in Euripides's *Alcestis*, Alcestis died in place of her husband.

LYCIDAS

In this monody the author bewails a learned friend, unfortunately drowned in his passage from Chester on the Irish Seas, 1637. And by occasion foretells the ruin of our corrupted clergy then in their height.

YET once more, O ye Laurels, and once more
Ye Myrtles brown, with ivy never sere,
I come to pluck your berries harsh and crude,
And with forced fingers rude,
Shatter your leaves before the mellowing year.   5
Bitter constraint and sad occasion dear
Compels me to disturb your season due;
For Lycidas is dead, dead ere his prime,
Young Lycidas, and hath not left his peer.
Who would not sing for Lycidas? He knew   10
Himself to sing, and build the lofty rhyme.
He must not float upon his wat'ry bier
Unwept, and welter to the parching wind,
Without the meed of some melodious tear.
  Begin, then, sisters of the sacred well   15
That from beneath the seat of Jove doth spring;
Begin, and somewhat loudly sweep the string.
Hence with denial vain, and coy excuse,
So may some gentle Muse
With lucky words favour my destined urn,   20
And as he passes turn,
And bid fair peace be to my sable shroud.
For we were nursed upon the self-same hill,
Fed the same flock, by fountain, shade, and rill.
  Together both, ere the high lawns appeared   25
Under the opening eye-lids of the morn,
We drove a-field, and both together heard
What time the grey-fly winds her sultry horn,
Batt'ning our flocks with the fresh dews of night,
Oft till the star that rose, at ev'ning, bright   30
Toward heaven's descent had sloped his westering
    wheel.
Meanwhile the rural ditties were not mute;
Tempered to th'oaten flute;
Rough satyrs danced, and fauns with cloven heel,
From the glad sound would not be absent long;   35
And old Dametas loved to hear our song.

LYCIDAS: 1–2 **laurels . . . myrtles . . . ivy:** laurels for poetry (from Apollo's crown), myrtles for love (from Venus) and Ivy for victory and learning 14 **meed:** reward 25 **high lawns:** hill pastures 28 a buzzing greyfly 33 **oaten flute:** panpipes 36 **Demetas:** a character in Virgil's *Eclogues*

But, oh, the heavy change, now thou art gone,
Now thou art gone, and never must return!
Thee, Shepherd, thee the woods and desert caves,
With wild thyme and the gadding vine o'ergrown,　40
And all their echoes, mourn.
The willows, and the hazel copses green,
Shall now no more be seen
Fanning their joyous leaves to thy soft lays.
As killing as the canker to the rose,　45
Or taint-worm to the weanling herds that graze,
Or frost to flowers, that their gay wardrobe wear,
When first the white-thorn blows;
Such, Lycidas, thy loss to shepherd's ear.

Where were ye, nymphs, when the remorseless deep
Closed o'er the head of your loved Lycidas?　51
For neither were ye playing on the steep,
Where your old bards, the famous Druids lie,
Nor on the shaggy top of Mona high,
Nor yet where Deva spreads her wizard stream.　55
Ay me! I fondly dream
'Had ye been there' – for what could that have done?
What could the Muse herself that Orpheus bore,
The Muse herself, for her enchanting son
Whom universal Nature did lament,　60
When by the rout that made the hideous roar
His gory visage down the stream was sent,
Down the swift Hebrus to the Lesbian shore?

Alas! What boots it with uncessant care
To tend the homely slighted shepherd's trade,　65
And strictly meditate the thankless Muse?
Were it not better done as others use,
To sport with Amaryllis in the shade,
Or with the tangles of Neaera's hair?
Fame is the spur that the clear spirit doth raise　70
(That last infirmity of noble mind)
To scorn delights and live laborious days;
But the fair guerdon when we hope to find,
And think to burst out into sudden blaze,
Comes the blind Fury with th'abhorrèd shears,　75
And slits the thin-spun life. 'But not the praise,'
Phoebus replied, and touched my trembling ears.
'Fame is no plant that grows on mortal soil,
Nor in the glistering foil
Set off to the world, nor in broad rumour lies,　80
But lives and spreads aloft by those pure eyes
And perfect witness of all-judging Jove;
As he pronounces lastly on each deed,
Of so much fame in heaven expect thy meed.'

O fountain Arethuse, and thou honoured flood,　85
Smooth-sliding Mincius, crowned with vocal reeds,
That strain I heard was of a higher mood:
But now my oat proceeds,
And listens to the herald of the sea,
That came in Neptune's plea.　90
He asked the waves, and asked the felon winds,
What hard mishap hath doomed this gentle swain?
And questioned every gust of rugged wings
That blows from off each beakèd promontory.
They knew not of his story;　95
And sage Hippotades their answer brings,
That not a blast was from his dungeon strayed;
The air was calm, and on the level brine
Sleek Panope with all her sisters played.
It was that fatal and perfidious bark　100
Built in th'eclipse, and rigged with curses dark,
That sunk so low that sacred head of thine.

Next Camus, reverend sire, went footing slow,
His mantle hairy, and his bonnet sedge,
Inwrought with figures dim, and on the edge　105
Like to that sanguine flower inscribed with woe.
'Ah! who hath reft', quoth he, 'my dearest pledge?'
Last came, and last did go,
The pilot of the Galilean lake;
Two massy keys he bore of metals twain　110
(The golden opes, the iron shuts amain).
He shook his mitrèd locks, and stern bespake:
'How well could I have spared for thee, young swain,
Enow of such as, for their bellies' sake,
Creep, and intrude, and climb into the fold!　115
Of other care they little reck'ning make
Than how to scramble at the shearers' feast,
And shove away the worthy bidden guest.
Blind mouths! that scarce themselves know how to hold
A sheep-hook, or have learned aught else the least　120
That to the faithful herdman's art belongs!
What recks it them? What need they? They are sped;
And when they list, their lean and flashy songs
Grate on their scrannel pipes of wretched straw;
The hungry sheep look up, and are not fed,　125
But swoll'n with wind and the rank mist they draw,
Rot inwardly, and foul contagion spread;
Besides what the grim wolf with privy paw
Daily devours apace, and nothing said.
But that two-handed engine at the door　130
Stands ready to smite once, and smite no more.'

---

48 **blows:** blossoms 52 **steep:** a mountain slope 54 **Mona:** Anglesey, where the Celtic druids are said to be buried 55 **Deva:** the river Dee 58 a reference to Calliope, the mother of the mythological poet Orpheus 63 **Hebrus . . . Lesbian shore:** the head of Orpheus (torn off by the Thracian women) floated down the Hebrus to the Island of Lesbos 68 **Amaryllis:** a shepherdess in Virgil's *Eclogues* 69 **Neaera:** another character in Virgil's *Eclogues* 73 **guerdon:** reward 75 **the blind Fury:** Atropos the Fate who cut the thread of Man's life 77 **Phoebus:** Greek god of enlightenment 79 **foil:** a leaf of metal (usually gold or silver) used to set a precious stone

85 **Arethuse:** a fountain in Sicily 86 **Mincius:** a river in Lombardy 88 **oat:** song 89 **herald of the sea:** Triton 90 **Neptune:** Roman god of the sea 96 **Hippotades:** the wind god, Aeolus 99 **Panope:** a sea nymph 103 **Camus:** the Cambridge river Cam 107 **pledge:** child 109 **pilot of the Galilean lake:** St. Peter 111 **amain:** with force 114 **Enow:** enough 122 **recks:** what has it got to do with them? 122 **sped:** satisfied 123 **list:** choose 124 **scrannel:** meagre 130 **two-handed engine:** perhaps the 'two-edged sword' that comes out of the mouth of Christ in Revelation (1:16). An instrument of retribution

Return, Alpheus, the dread voice is past
That shrunk thy streams; return, Sicilian Muse,
And call the vales, and bid them hither cast
Their bells and flow'rets of a thousand hues.   135
Ye valleys low, where the mild whispers use
Of shades, and wanton winds, and gushing brooks,
On whose fresh lap the swart star sparely looks,
Throw hither all your quaint enamelled eyes,
That on the green turf suck the honeyed show'rs,   140
And purple all the ground with vernal flow'rs.
Bring the rathe primrose that forsaken dies,
The tufted crow-toe, and pale jessamine,
The white pink, and the pansy freaked with jet,
The glowing violet,   145
The musk rose, and the well attired woodbine.
With cowslips wan that hang the pensive head,
And every flower that sad embroidery wears:
Bid amaranthus all his beauty shed,
And daffadillies fill their cups with tears,   150
To strew the laureate hearse where Lycid lies.
For so to interpose a little ease,
Let our frail thoughts dally with false surmise.
Ay me! Whilst thee the shores, and sounding seas
Wash far away, where'er thy bones are hurled;   155
Whether beyond the stormy Hebrides,
Where thou perhaps under the whelming tide
Visit'st the bottom of the monstrous world;
Or whether thou, to our moist vows denied,
Sleep'st by the fable of Bellerus old,   160
Where the great vision of the guarded mount
Looks toward Namancos and Bayona's hold;
Look homeward, Angel, now, and melt with ruth.
And, O ye Dolphins, waft the hapless youth.
  Weep no more, woeful Shepherds weep no more,
For Lycidas, your sorrow, is not dead,   166
Sunk though he be beneath the wat'ry floor.
So sinks the day-star in the ocean bed,
And yet anon repairs his drooping head,
And tricks his beams, and with new-spangled ore   170
Flames in the forehead of the morning sky:
So Lycidas sunk low, but mounted high,
Through the dear might of Him that walked the
          waves,
Where, other groves and other streams along,
With nectar pure his oozy locks he laves,   175
And hears the unexpressive nuptial song,
In the blest kingdoms meek of joy and love.
There entertain him all the saints above,
In solemn troops, and sweet societies,
That sing, and singing in their glory move,   180
And wipe the tears for ever from his eyes.

132 **Alpheus:** Arcadian river 138 **swart star:** the Dog star, Sirius
142 **rathe:** early 149 **amaranthus:** a mythological crimson flower that
will never fade 160 **Bellerus:** a monster said to be buried at
Land's End in Cornwall 162 **Namancos and Bayona's:** places on the
Spanish North West coast 168 **day-star:** the sun 176 **unexpressive:**
inexpressible

Now, Lycidas, the shepherds weep no more;
Henceforth thou art the genius of the shore,
In thy large recompense, and shalt be good
To all that wander in that perilous flood.   185

  Thus sang the uncouth swain to th'oaks and rills,
While the still morn went out with sandals grey;
He touched the tender stops of various quills,
With eager thought warbling his Doric lay:
And now the sun had stretched out all the hills,   190
And now was dropped into the western bay,
At last he rose, and twitched his mantle blue:
Tomorrow to fresh woods, and pastures new.

186 **uncouth:** unknown 189 **Doric:** rustic

From COMUS

THE star that bids the shepherd fold,
Now the top of heaven doth hold;
And the gilded car of day
His glowing axle doth allay
In the steep Atlantic stream;   5
And the slope sun his upward beam
Shoots against the dusky pole,
Pacing toward the other goal
Of his chamber in the east.
Meanwhile, welcome joy and feast,   10
Midnight shout and revelry,
Tipsy dance and jollity.
Braid your locks with rosy twine,
Dropping odours, dropping wine.
Rigour now is gone to bed;   15
And Advice with scrupulous head,
Strict Age, and sour Severity,
With their grave saws in slumber lie.
We, that are of purer fire,
Imitate the starry choir,   20
Who, in their nightly watchful spheres,
Lead in swift round the months and years.
The sounds and seas, with all their finny drove,
Now to the moon in wavering morris move;
And on the tawny sands and shelves   25
Trip the pert fairies and the dapper elves;
By dimpled brook and fountain-brim,
The wood-nymphs, decked with daisies trim,
Their merry wakes and pastimes keep:
What hath night to do with sleep?   30
Night hath better sweets to prove;
Venus now wakes, and wakens Love.
Come let us our rights begin;
'Tis only daylight that makes sin,
Which these dun shades will ne'er report.   35
Hail, goddess of nocturnal sport,
Dark-veiled Cotytto, t'whom the secret flame
Of midnight torches burns; mysterious dame
That ne'er art called but when the dragon womb

Of Stygian darkness spits her thickest gloom,　　　40
And makes one blot of all the air;
Stay thy cloudy ebon chair,
Wherein thou rid'st with Hecat, and befriend
Us thy vowed priests, till utmost end
Of all thy dues be done, and none left out;　　　45
Ere the blabbing eastern scout,
The nice Morn on th'Indian steep
From her cabined loop-hole peep,
And to the tell-tale sun descry
Our concealed solemnity.　　　50
Come, knit hands, and beat the ground,
In a light fantastic round.

[Lines 93–144]

COMUS: 2–9 Milton represents the sun 24 **wavering morris:** a dance
32 **Venus:** the morning star 37 **Cotytto:** goddess of debauchery
40 **Stygian:** pertaining to the Styx, river of the underworld 42 **ebon:**
ebony 43 **Hecat:** Greek goddess of the moon 46 **blabbing eastern
scout:** the morning star 49 **descry:** proclaim

PARADISE LOST

BOOK ONE

OF Man's first disobedience, and the fruit
Of that forbidden tree whose mortal taste
Brought death into the world, and all our woe,
With loss of Eden, till one greater Man
Restore us, and regain the blissful seat,　　　5
Sing, heavenly Muse, that on the secret top
Of Oreb, or of Sinai, didst inspire
That shepherd who first taught the chosen seed
In the beginning how the heavens and earth
Rose out of Chaos: or, if Sion hill　　　10

PARADISE LOST: BOOK ONE – THE ARGUMENT: This first Book proposes,
first in brief, the whole Subject, Man's disobedience, and the loss
thereupon of Paradise wherein he was plac't: Then touches the
prime cause of his fall, the Serpent, or rather Satan in the Serpent;
who revolting from God, and drawing to his side many Legions of
Angels, was by the command of God driven out of Heaven with all
his Crew into the great Deep. Which action past over, the Poem
hastes into the midst of things, presenting Satan with his Angels
now fallen into Hell, describ'd here, not in the Center (for
Heaven and Earth may be suppos'd as yet not made, certainly not
yet accurst) but in a place of utter darkness, fitliest call'd Chaos:
Here Satan with his Angels lying on the burning Lake, thunder-
struck and astonisht, after a certain space recovers, as from
confusion, calls up him who next in Order and Dignity lay by him;
they confer of their miserable fall. Satan awakens all his Legions,
who lay till then in the same manner confounded; They rise, their
Numbers, array of Battle, their chief Leaders nam'd, according to
the Idols known afterwards in Canaan and the Countries
adjoining. To these Satan directs his Speech, comforts them with
hope yet of regaining Heaven, but tells them lastly of a new World
and new kind of Creature to be created, according to an ancient
Prophecy or report in Heaven; for that Angels were long before
this visible Creation, was the opinion of many ancient Fathers. To
find out the truth of this Prophecy, and what to determine thereon
he refers to a full Council. What his Associates thence attempt.
Pandemonium the Palace of Satan rises, suddenly built out of the
Deep: The infernal Peers there sit in Council 2 **mortal:** deadly
7–9 'The chosen seed' are the children of Israel. Moses, the author
of Genesis, was visited by God on Mount Oreb and Mount Sinai
10 **Sion hill:** ceremonial place

Delight thee more, and Siloa's brook that flowed
Fast by the oracle of God, I thence
Invoke thy aid to my advent'rous song,
That with no middle flight intends to soar
Above th'Aonian mount, while it pursues　　　15
Things unattempted yet in prose or rhyme.
And chiefly thou, O Spirit, that dost prefer
Before all temples th'upright heart and pure,
Instruct me, for thou know'st; thou from the first
Wast present, and, with mighty wings outspread,　　　20
Dove-like sat'st brooding on the vast Abyss,
And mad'st it pregnant. What in me is dark
Illumine, what is low raise and support;
That to the height of this great argument
I may assert eternal providence,　　　25
And justify the ways of God to men.

　　Say first – for heaven hides nothing from thy view,
Nor the deep tract of hell – say first what cause
Moved our grand parents in that happy state,
Favoured of heaven so highly, to fall off　　　30
From their Creator, and transgress His will
For one restraint, lords of the world besides.
Who first seduced them to that foul revolt?
Th'infernal serpent; he it was whose guile,
Stirred up with envy and revenge, deceived　　　35
The mother of mankind, what time his pride
Had cast him out from heaven, with all his host
Of rebel angels, by whose aid aspiring
To set himself in glory above his peers,
He trusted to have equalled the Most High,　　　40
If He opposed; and with ambitious aim
Against the throne and monarchy of God
Raised impious war in heaven and battle proud,
With vain attempt. Him the Almighty Power
Hurled headlong flaming from th'ethereal sky　　　45
With hideous ruin and combustion down
To bottomless perdition, there to dwell
In adamantine chains and penal fire,
Who durst defy th'Omnipotent to arms.
Nine times the space that measures day and night
To mortal men, he, with his horrid crew　　　51
Lay vanquished, rolling in the fiery gulf
Confounded though immortal. But his doom
Reserved him to more wrath; for now the thought
Both of lost happiness and lasting pain　　　55
Torments him; round he throws his baleful eyes,
That witnessed huge affliction and dismay
Mixed with obdurate pride and steadfast hate.
At once, as far as angels ken, he views
The dismal situation waste and wild:　　　60
A dungeon horrible, on all sides round
As one great furnace flamed, yet from those flames
No light, but rather darkness visible

11 **Siloa:** a spring near Calvary 15 **Aonian mount:** Mount Helicon,
a place sacred to the Muses 17–22 here the Holy Spirit is addressed
34 **Th'infernal serpent:** Satan 48 **adamantine chains:** chains made
of the hardest rocks

Served only to discover sights of woe,
Regions of sorrow, doleful shades, where peace 65
And rest can never dwell, hope never comes
That comes to all; but torture without end
Still urges, and a fiery deluge, fed
With ever-burning sulphur unconsumed.
Such place Eternal Justice had prepared 70
For these rebellious, here their pris'n ordained
In utter darkness, and their portion set
As far removed from God and light of heaven
As from the centre thrice to th'utmost pole.
Oh, how unlike the place from whence they fell! 75
There the companions of his fall, o'erwhelmed
With floods and whirlwinds of tempestuous fire,
He soon discerns; and, welt'ring by his side,
One next himself in power, and next in crime,
Long after known in Palestine, and named 80
Beelzebub. To whom th'arch-enemy,
And thence in heaven called Satan, with bold words
Breaking the horrid silence thus began:
    'If thou beest he – but, oh, how fall'n! how changed
From him who, in the happy realms of light 85
Clothed with transcendent brightness, didst outshine
Myriads, though bright! – if he whom mutual league,
United thoughts and counsels, equal hope
And hazard in the glorious enterprise,
Joined with me once, now misery hath joined 90
In equal ruin: into what pit thou seest
From what height fallen, so much the stronger proved
He with his thunder; and till then who knew
The force of those dire arms? Yet not for those,
Nor what the potent victor in his rage 95
Can else inflict, do I repent, or change,
Though changed in outward lustre, that fixed mind
And high disdain, from sense of injured merit,
That with the mightiest raised me to contend,
And to the fierce contention brought along 100
Innumerable force of spirits armed
That durst dislike his reign, and, me preferring,
His utmost power with adverse power opposed
In dubious battle on the plains of heaven,
And shook His throne. What though the field be lost?
All is not lost – th'unconquerable will, 106
And study of revenge, immortal hate,
And courage never to submit or yield:
And what is else not to be overcome?
That glory never shall His wrath or might 110
Extort from me. To bow and sue for grace
With suppliant knee, and deify his power
Who, from the terror of this arm so late
Doubted his empire – that were low indeed;
That were an ignominy and shame beneath 115
This downfall; since by fate the strength of gods
And this empyreal substance cannot fail,

Since through experience of this great event
In arms not worse, in foresight much advanced,
We may with more successful hope resolve 120
To wage by force or guile eternal war,
Irreconcilable to our grand Foe,
Who now triumphs, and in th'excess of joy
Sole reigning holds the tyranny of heaven.'
    So spake th'apostate angel, though in pain, 125
Vaunting aloud, but racked with deep despair;
And him thus answered soon his bold compeer:
    'O Prince, O Chief of many thronèd powers
That led th'embattled seraphim to war
Under thy conduct, and in dreadful deeds 130
Fearless endangered heaven's perpetual King,
And put to proof His high supremacy,
Whether upheld by strength, or chance, or fate,
Too well I see and rue the dire event
That with sad overthrow and foul defeat 135
Hath lost us heaven, and all this mighty host
In horrible destruction laid thus low,
As far as gods and heavenly essences
Can perish: for the mind and spirit remains
Invincible, and vigour soon returns, 140
Though all our glory extinct, and happy state
Here swallowed up in endless misery.
But what if He our conqueror (whom I now
Of force believe almighty, since no less
Than such could have o'erpowered such force as ours)
Have left us this our spirit and strength entire, 146
Strongly to suffer and support our pains,
That we may so suffice his vengeful ire,
Or do him mightier service as his thralls
By right of war, whate'er his business be, 150
Here in the heart of hell to work in fire,
Or do his errands in the gloomy deep?
What can it then avail though yet we feel
Strength undiminished, or eternal being
To undergo eternal punishment?' 155
    Whereto with speedy words th'arch-fiend replied:
'Fallen Cherub, to be weak is miserable,
Doing or suffering: but of this be sure –
To do aught good never will be our task,
But ever to do ill our sole delight, 160
As being the contrary to His high will
Whom we resist. If then His providence
Out of our evil seek to bring forth good,
Our labour must be to pervert that end,
And out of good still to find means of evil; 165
Which ofttimes may succeed so as perhaps
Shall grieve Him, if I fail not, and disturb
His inmost counsels from their destined aim.
But see! the angry Victor hath recalled
His ministers of vengeance and pursuit 170
Back to the gates of heaven: the sulphurous hail,
Shot after us in storm, o'erblown hath laid

81 **Beelzebub:** Hebrew for 'Lord of the flies' as he infests the human race. Milton makes him Satan's spokesman 117 **empyreal substance:** heavenly essence

129 **seraphim:** a class of angel

The fiery surge that from the precipice
Of heaven received us falling; and the thunder,
Winged with red lightning and impetuous rage,   175
Perhaps hath spent his shafts, and ceases now
To bellow through the vast and boundless deep.
Let us not slip th'occasion, whether scorn
Or satiate fury yield it from our Foe.
Seest thou yon dreary plain, forlorn and wild,   180
The seat of desolation, void of light,
Save what the glimmering of these livid flames
Casts pale and dreadful? Thither let us tend
From off the tossing of these fiery waves;
There rest, if any rest can harbour there;   185
And, reassembling our afflicted powers,
Consult how we may henceforth most offend
Our enemy, our own loss how repair,
How overcome this dire calamity,
What reinforcement we may gain from hope,   190
If not, what resolution from despair.'
    Thus Satan, talking to his nearest mate,
With head uplift above the wave, and eyes
That sparkling blazed; his other parts besides
Prone on the flood, extended long and large,   195
Lay floating many a rood, in bulk as huge
As whom the fables name of monstrous size,
Titanian or earth-born, that warred on Jove,
Briareos or Typhon, whom the den
By ancient Tarsus held, or that sea-beast   200
Leviathan, which God of all His works
Created hugest that swim th'ocean-stream.
Him, haply slumbering on the Norway foam,
The pilot of some small night-foundered skiff,
Deeming some island, oft, as seamen tell,   205
With fixèd anchor in his scaly rind,
Moors by his side under the lee, while night
Invests the sea, and wishèd morn delays.
So stretched out huge in length the arch-fiend lay,
Chained on the burning lake; nor ever thence   210
Had risen, or heaved his head, but that the will
And high permission of all-ruling heaven
Left him at large to his own dark designs,
That with reiterated crimes he might
Heap on himself damnation, while he sought   215
Evil to others, and enraged might see
How all his malice served but to bring forth
Infinite goodness, grace, and mercy, shown
On Man by him seduced, but on himself
Treble confusion, wrath, and vengeance poured.   220
    Forthwith upright he rears from off the pool
His mighty stature; on each hand the flames
Driven backward slope their pointing spires, and,
    rolled

In billows, leave i' the midst a horrid vale.
Then with expanded wings he steers his flight   225
Aloft, incumbent on the dusky air,
That felt unusual weight; till on dry land
He lights – if it were land that ever burned
With solid, as the lake with liquid fire,
And such appeared in hue as when the force   230
Of subterranean wind transports a hill
Torn from Pelorus, or the shattered side
Of thundering Etna, whose combustible
And fuelled entrails, thence conceiving fire,
Sublimed with mineral fury, aid the winds,   235
And leave a singèd bottom all involved
With stench and smoke. Such resting found the sole
Of unblessed feet. Him followed his next mate;
Both glorying to have 'scaped the Stygian flood
As gods, and by their own recovered strength,   240
Not by the sufferance of supernal Power.
    'Is this the region, this the soil, the clime,'
Said then the lost archangel, 'this the seat
That we must change for heaven? – this mournful
    gloom
For that celestial light? Be it so, since He   245
Who now is sovereign can dispose and bid
What shall be right: farthest from Him is best
Whom reason hath equalled, force hath made
    supreme
Above his equals. Farewell, happy fields,
Where joy for ever dwells! Hail, horrors! hail,   250
Infernal world! and thou, profoundest hell,
Receive thy new possessor – one who brings
A mind not to be changed by place or time.
The mind is its own place, and in itself
Can make a heaven of hell, a hell of heaven.   255
What matter where, if I be still the same,
And what I should be, all but less than he
Whom thunder hath made greater? Here at least
We shall be free; th'Almighty hath not built
Here for his envy, will not drive us hence: 260
Here we may reign secure; and, in my choice,
To reign is worth ambition, though in hell:
Better to reign in hell than serve in heaven.
But wherefore let we then our faithful friends,
Th'associates and co-partners of our loss,   265
Lie thus astonished on th'oblivious pool,
And call them not to share with us their part
In this unhappy mansion, or once more
With rallied arms to try what may be yet
Regained in heaven, or what more lost in hell?'   270
    So Satan spake; and him Beelzebub
Thus answered: 'Leader of those armies bright
Which, but th'Omnipotent, none could have foiled!
If once they hear that voice, their liveliest pledge
Of hope in fears and dangers – heard so oft   275

198 **Titanian**: the Titans were a race of giants, the children of Uranus (Heaven) and Gæa (Earth) 199 **Briareos or Typhon**: Briareos was a Titan and Typhon was a Giant 200 **Tarsus**: the Biblical capital of Cilicia 201 **Leviathan**: a whale. But also the monster in the book of Job (41:1) 204 **skiff**: a small boat

232 **Pelorus**: in Sicily near the volcano, Mount Etna 239 **Stygian**: on the Styx, river of the underworld

In worst extremes, and on the perilous edge
Of battle, when it raged, in all assaults
Their surest signal – they will soon resume
New courage and revive, though now they lie
Grovelling and prostrate on yon lake of fire, 280
As we erewhile, astounded and amazed;
No wonder, fallen such a pernicious height!'

   He scarce had ceased when the superior fiend
Was moving toward the shore; his ponderous shield,
Ethereal temper, massy, large, and round, 285
Behind him cast. The broad circumference
Hung on his shoulders like the moon, whose orb
Through optic glass the Tuscan artist views
At evening, from the top of Fesole,
Or in Valdarno, to descry new lands, 290
Rivers, or mountains, in her spotty globe.
His spear – to equal which the tallest pine
Hewn on Norwegian hills, to be the mast
Of some great admiral, were but a wand –
He walked with, to support uneasy steps 295
Over the burning marl, not like those steps
On heaven's azure; and the torrid clime
Smote on him sore besides, vaulted with fire.
Nathless he so endured, till on the beach
Of that inflamèd sea he stood, and called 300
His legions – angel forms, who lay entranced
Thick as autumnal leaves that strow the brooks
In Vallombrosa, where th'Etrurian shades
High over-arched embower; or scattered sedge
Afloat, when with fierce winds Orion armed 305
Hath vexed the Red Sea coast, whose waves o'erthrew
Busiris and his Memphian chivalry,
While with perfidious hatred they pursued
The sojourners of Goshen, who beheld
From the safe shore their floating carcasses 310
And broken chariot-wheels. So thick bestrown,
Abject and lost, lay these, covering the flood,
Under amazement of their hideous change.
He called so loud that all the hollow deep
Of hell resounded: 'Princes, Potentates, 315
Warriors, the Flower of Heaven – once yours; now
    lost,
If such astonishment as this can seize
Eternal spirits! Or have ye chosen this place
After the toil of battle to repose
Your wearied virtue, for the ease you find 320
To slumber here, as in the vales of heaven?
Or in this abject posture have ye sworn
To adore the Conqueror, who now beholds
Cherub and seraph rolling in the flood

With scattered arms and ensigns, till anon 325
His swift pursuers from heaven-gates discern
Th'advantage, and, descending, tread us down
Thus drooping, or with linkèd thunderbolts
Transfix us to the bottom of this gulf?
Awake, arise, or be forever fallen!' 330

   They heard, and were abashed, and up they sprung
Upon the wing, as when men wont to watch
On duty, sleeping found by whom they dread,
Rouse and bestir themselves ere well awake.
Nor did they not perceive the evil plight 335
In which they were, or the fierce pains not feel;
Yet to their general's voice they soon obeyed
Innumerable. As when the potent rod
Of Amram's son, in Egypt's evil day,
Waved round the coast, up-called a pitchy cloud 340
Of locusts, warping on the eastern wind,
That o'er the realm of impious Pharaoh hung
Like night, and darkened all the land of Nile;
So numberless were those bad angels seen
Hovering on wing under the cope of hell, 345
'Twixt upper, nether, and surrounding fires;
Till, as a signal given, th'uplifted spear
Of their great sultan waving to direct
Their course, in even balance down they light
On the firm brimstone, and fill all the plain: 350
A multitude like which the populous North
Poured never from her frozen loins to pass
Rhene or the Danaw, when her barbarous sons
Came like a deluge on the south, and spread
Beneath Gibraltar to the Libyan sands. 355
Forthwith, form every squadron and each band,
The heads and leaders thither haste where stood
Their great commander – godlike shapes, and forms
Excelling human; princely dignities;
And powers that erst in heaven sat on thrones, 360
Though on their names in heavenly records now
Be no memorial, blotted out and rased
By their rebellion from the Books of Life.
Nor had they yet among the sons of Eve 364
Got them new names, till, wand'ring o'er the earth,
Through God's high sufferance for the trial of man,
By falsities and lies the greatest part
Of mankind they corrupted to forsake
God their Creator, and th'invisible
Glory of Him that made them to transform 370
Oft to the image of a brute, adorned
With gay religions full of pomp and gold,
And devils to adore for deities:
Then were they known to men by various names,
And various idols through the heathen world. 375
   Say, Muse, their names then known, who first, who
    last,
Roused from the slumber on that fiery couch,
At their great emperor's call, as next in worth

---

288 **Tuscan artist:** Galileo, who Milton had visited in 1639
289–290 Galileo had been placed under house arrest by the Spanish
Inquisition in Valdarno near the Fesole hills   296 **marl:** soil
299 **Nathless:** Nevertheless 303 **Vallombrosa . . . Etrurian:** places near
Florence 305 **Orion:** here the constellation of stars 306–311 Busiris
is the Memphian (Egyptian) Pharaoh of Exodus who had chased
the Israelites (formally his prisoners in Goshen) across the Red Sea

339 **Amram's son:** Moses 353 **Rhene:** the river Rhine **Danaw:** the
river Danube

Came singly where he stood on the bare strand,
While the promiscuous crowd stood yet aloof? 380
  The chief were those who, from the pit of hell
Roaming to seek their prey on earth, durst fix
Their seats, long after, next the seat of God,
Their altars by His altar, gods adored
Among the nations round, and durst abide 385
Jehovah thundering out of Sion, throned
Between the cherubim; yea, often placed
Within His sanctuary itself their shrines,
Abominations; and with cursèd things
His holy rites and solemn feasts profaned, 390
And with their darkness durst affront His light.
First, Moloch, horrid king, besmeared with blood
Of human sacrifice, and parents' tears;
Though, for the noise of drums and timbrels loud,
Their children's cries unheard that passed through
  fire 395
To his grim idol. Him the Ammonite
Worshipped in Rabba and her watery plain,
In Argob and in Basan, to the stream
Of utmost Arnon. Nor content with such
Audacious neighbourhood, the wisest heart 400
Of Solomon he led by fraud to build
His temple right against the temple of God
On that opprobrious hill, and made his grove
The pleasant valley of Hinnom, Tophet thence
And black Gehenna called, the type of hell. 405
Next Chemos, th'obscene dread of Moab's sons,
From Aroar to Nebo and the wild
Of southmost Abarim; in Hesebon
And Horonaim, Seon's realm, beyond
The flow'ry dale of Sibma clad with vines, 410
And Eleale to th'Asphaltic Pool:
Peor his other name, when he enticed
Israel in Sittim, on their march from Nile,
To do him wanton rites, which cost them woe.
Yet thence his lustful orgies he enlarged 415
Ev'n to that hill of scandal, by the grove
Of Moloch homicide, lust hard by hate,
Till good Josiah drove them thence to hell.
With these came they who, from the bordering flood
Of old Euphrates to the brook that parts 420
Egypt from Syrian ground, had general names
Of Baalim and Ashtaroth – those male,
These feminine. For spirits, when they please,
Can either sex assume, or both; so soft
And uncompounded is their essence pure, 425
Not tried or manacled with joint or limb,
Nor founded on the brittle strength of bones,

Like cumbrous flesh; but, in what shape they choose,
Dilated or condensed, bright or obscure,
Can execute their airy purposes, 430
And works of love or enmity fulfil.
For those the race of Israel oft forsook
Their Living Strength, and unfrequented left
His righteous altar, bowing lowly down
To bestial gods; for which their heads as low 435
Bowed down in battle, sunk before the spear
Of despicable foes. With these in troop
Came Astoreth, whom the Phoenicians called
Astarte, queen of heaven, with crescent horns;
To whose bright image nightly by the moon 440
Sidonian virgins paid their vows and songs;
In Sion also not unsung, where stood
Her temple on th'offensive mountain, built
By that uxorious king whose heart, though large,
Beguiled by fair idolatresses, fell 445
To idols foul. Thammuz came next behind,
Whose annual wound in Lebanon allured
The Syrian damsels to lament his fate
In amorous ditties all a summer's day,
While smooth Adonis from his native rock 450
Ran purple to the sea, supposed with blood
Of Thammuz yearly wounded: the love-tale
Infected Sion's daughters with like heat,
Whose wanton passions in the sacred porch
Ezekiel saw, when, by the vision led, 455
His eye surveyed the dark idolatries
Of alienated Judah. Next came one
Who mourned in earnest, when the captive ark
Maimed his brute image, head and hands lopped off,
In his own temple, on the grunsel-edge, 460
Where he fell flat and shamed his worshippers:
Dagon his name, sea-monster, upward man
And downward fish; yet had his temple high
Reared in Azotus, dreaded through the coast
Of Palestine, in Gath and Ascalon, 465
And Accaron and Gaza's frontier bounds.
Him followed Rimmon, whose delightful seat
Was fair Damascus, on the fertile banks
Of Abbana and Pharphar, lucid streams.
He also against the house of God was bold: 470
A leper once he lost, and gained a king –
Ahaz, his sottish conqueror, whom he drew
God's altar to disparage and displace
For one of Syrian mode, whereon to burn
His odious off'rings, and adore the gods 475
Whom he had vanquished. After these appeared
A crew who, under names of old renown –
Osiris, Isis, Orus, and their train –
With monstrous shapes and sorceries abused

392–490 Satan calls together twelve of his devils (mirroring Christ's twelve disciples): Moloch, Chemos, Baalim, Ashtaroth, Astoreth, Thammuz, Dagon, Rimmon, Osiris, Isis, Horus and Belial 399 **Arnon:** east Jordan 403 **opprobrious hill:** The Mount of Olives 404–405 Milton associates Hinnom, Tophet and Gehenna with hell 407–411 places found in the Old Testament 409 **Seon's:** King Sihon, Amorite ruler of Transjordan at the time of Moses

450–451 **Adonis:** a beautiful youth loved by Aphrodite, but here, the river Adonis which becomes discoloured by red mud ('supposed with blood') each year 460 **grunsel:** threshold 462 **Dagon:** half man, half fish, god of the Philistines 464–466 Philistine cities 478 Egyptian gods

Fanatic Egypt and her priests to seek 480
Their wandering gods disguised in brutish forms
Rather than human. Nor did Israel 'scape
Th'infection, when their borrowed gold composed
The calf in Oreb; and the rebel king
Doubled that sin in Bethel and in Dan, 485
Likening his Maker to the grazèd ox –
Jehovah, who, in one night, when He passed
From Egypt marching, equalled with one stroke
Both her first-born and all her bleating gods.
Belial came last; than whom a spirit more lewd 490
Fell not from heaven, or more gross to love
Vice for itself. To him no temple stood
Or altar smoked; yet who more oft than he
In temples and at altars, when the priest
Turns atheist, as did Eli's sons, who filled 495
With lust and violence the house of God?
In courts and palaces he also reigns,
And in luxurious cities, where the noise
Of riot ascends above their loftiest towers,
And injury and outrage; and, when night 500
Darkens the streets, then wander forth the sons
Of Belial, flown with insolence and wine.
Witness the streets of Sodom, and that night
In Gibeah, when the hospitable door
Exposed a matron, to avoid worse rape. 505
    These were the prime in order and in might:
The rest were long to tell; though far renowned
Th'Ionian gods – of Javan's issue held
Gods, yet confessèd later than heaven and earth,
Their boasted parents; Titan, heaven's first-born, 510
With his enormous brood, and birthright seized
By younger Saturn: he from mightier Jove,
His own and Rhea's son, like measure found;
So Jove usurping reigned. These, first in Crete
And Ida known, thence on the snowy top 515
Of cold Olympus ruled the middle air,
Their highest heaven; or on the Delphian cliff,
Or in Dodona, and through all the bounds
Of Doric land; or who with Saturn old
Fled over Adria to th'Hesperian fields, 520
And o'er the Celtic roamed the utmost isles.
    All these and more came flocking; but with looks
Downcast and damp; yet such wherein appeared
Obscure some glimpse of joy to have found their
    chief
Not in despair, to have found themselves not lost 525
In loss itself; which on his countenance cast
Like doubtful hue. But he, his wonted pride
Soon recollecting, with high words, that bore

Semblance of worth, not substance, gently raised
Their fainted courage, and dispelled their fears. 530
Then straight commands that, at the warlike sound
Of trumpets loud and clarions, be upreared
His mighty standard. That proud honour claimed
Azazel as his right, a cherub tall:
Who forthwith from the glittering staff unfurled 535
Th'imperial ensign; which, full high advanced,
Shone like a meteor streaming to the wind,
With gems and golden lustre rich emblazed,
Seraphic arms and trophies; all the while
Sonorous metal blowing martial sounds: 540
At which the universal host up-sent
A shout that tore hell's concave, and beyond
Frighted the reign of Chaos and old Night.
All in a moment through the gloom were seen
Ten thousand banners rise into the air, 545
With orient colours waving: with them rose
A forest huge of spears; and thronging helms
Appeared, and serried shields in thick array
Of depth immeasurable. Anon they move
In perfect phalanx to the Dorian mood 550
Of flutes and soft recorders – such as raised
To height of noblest temper heroes old
Arming to battle, and instead of rage
Deliberate valour breathed, firm, and unmoved
With dread of death to flight or foul retreat; 555
Nor wanting power to mitigate and 'suage
With solemn touches troubled thoughts, and chase
Anguish and doubt and fear and sorrow and pain
From mortal or immortal minds. Thus they,
Breathing united force with fixèd thought, 560
Moved on in silence to soft pipes that charmed
Their painful steps o'er the burnt soil. And now
Advanced in view they stand – a horrid front
Of dreadful length and dazzling arms, in guise
Of warriors old, with ordered spear and shield, 565
Awaiting what command their mighty chief
Had to impose. He through the armèd files
Darts his experienced eye, and soon traverse
The whole battalion views – their order due,
Their visages and stature as of gods; 570
Their number last he sums. And now his heart
Distends with pride, and, hardening in his strength,
Glories: for never, since created Man,
Met such embodied force as, named with these,
Could merit more than that small infantry 575
Warred on by cranes – though all the giant brood
Of Phlegra with th'heroic race were joined
That fought at Thebes and Ilium, on each side
Mixed with auxiliar gods; and what resounds
In fable or romance of Uther's son, 580

484–485 **the rebel king:** Jeroboam who led the Israeli revolt against Solomon's successor, Rehoboam 503–504 **Sodom . . . Gibeah:** scenes of Biblical atrocities 505 a reference to Judges (19) where a concubine is raped to death 508 **Javan:** grandson of Noah and ancestor of the Greeks 515 **Ida:** mountain in Crete and the birthplace of Jove 517 **Delphian cliff:** the site of Apollo's oracle 518 **Dodona:** the site of Zeus's oracle 519 **Doric Land:** Greece 520 **Hesperian fields:** Italy 521 **utmost isles:** Britain

534 **Azazel:** one of the fallen angels 550 **phalanx:** a line of battle 575 **small infantry:** the Pygmies who fought against the Cranes 577 **Phlegra:** this is where the Giants fought the Gods 578 **Thebes and Ilium:** sites of famous Greek battles 580 **Uther's son:** King Arthur

Begirt with British and Armoric knights;
And all who since, baptised or infidel,
Jousted in Aspramont, or Montalban,
Damasco, or Marocco, or Trebizond,
Or whom Biserta sent from Afric shore   585
When Charlemagne with all his peerage fell
By Fontarabbia. Thus far these beyond
Compare of mortal prowess, yet observed
Their dread commander. He, above the rest
In shape and gesture proudly eminent,   590
Stood like a tower. His form had yet not lost
All her original brightness, nor appeared
Less than archangel ruined, and th'excess
Of glory obscured: as when the sun new-risen
Looks through the horizontal misty air   595
Shorn of his beams, or, from behind the moon,
In dim eclipse, disastrous twilight sheds
On half the nations, and with fear of change
Perplexes monarchs. Darkened so, yet shone
Above them all th'archangel: but his face   600
Deep scars of thunder had entrenched, and care
Sat on his faded cheek, but under brows
Of dauntless courage, and considerate pride
Waiting revenge. Cruel his eye, but cast
Signs of remorse and passion, to behold   605
The fellows of his crime, the followers rather
(Far other once beheld in bliss), condemned
For ever now to have their lot in pain –
Millions of spirits for his fault amerced
Of heaven, and from eternal splendours flung   610
For his revolt – yet faithful how they stood,
Their glory withered; as, when heaven's fire
Hath scathed the forest oaks or mountain pines,
With singèd top their stately growth, though bare,
Stands on the blasted heath. He now prepared   615
To speak; whereat their doubled ranks they bend
From wing to wing, and half enclose him round
With all his peers: attention held them mute.
Thrice he assayed, and thrice, in spite of scorn,
Tears, such as angels weep, burst forth: at last   620
Words interwove with sighs found out their way:
'O myriads of immortal Spirits! O Powers
Matchless, but with th'Almighty! – and that strife
Was not inglorious, though th'event was dire,
As this place testifies, and this dire change,   625
Hateful to utter. But what power of mind,
Foreseeing or presaging, from the depth
Of knowledge past or present, could have feared
How such united force of gods, how such
As stood like these, could ever know repulse?   630
For who can yet believe, though after loss,
That all these puissant legions, whose exile
Hath emptied heaven, shall fail to reascend,

Self-raised, and repossess their native seat?
For me, be witness all the host of heaven,   635
If counsels different, or danger shunned
By me, have lost our hopes. But He who reigns
Monarch in heaven till then as one secure
Sat on His throne, upheld by old repute,
Consent or custom, and His regal state   640
Put forth at full, but still His strength concealed –
Which tempted our attempt, and wrought our fall.
Henceforth His might we know, and know our own,
So as not either to provoke, or dread
New war provoked: our better part remains   645
To work in close design, by fraud or guile,
What force effected not; that He no less
At length from us may find, who overcomes
By force hath overcome but half his foe.
Space may produce new worlds; whereof so rife   650
There went a fame in heaven that he ere long
Intended to create, and therein plant
A generation whom his choice regard
Should favour equal to the Sons of Heaven.
Thither, if but to pry, shall be perhaps   655
Our first eruption – thither, or elsewhere;
For this infernal pit shall never hold
Celestial spirits in bondage, nor th'Abyss
Long under darkness cover. But these thoughts
Full counsel must mature. Peace is despaired;   660
For who can think submission? War, then, war
Open or understood, must be resolved.'
He spake; and, to confirm his words, outflew
Millions of flaming swords, drawn from the thighs
Of mighty cherubim; the sudden blaze   665
Far round illumined hell. Highly they raged
Against the Highest, and fierce with graspèd arms
Clashed on their sounding shields the din of war,
Hurling defiance toward the vault of heaven.
There stood a hill not far, whose grisly top   670
Belched fire and rolling smoke; the rest entire
Shone with a glossy scurf – undoubted sign
That in his womb was hid metallic ore,
The work of sulphur. Thither, winged with speed,
A numerous brigade hastened: as when bands   675
Of pioneers, with spade and pickaxe armed,
Forerun the royal camp, to trench a field,
Or cast a rampart. Mammon led them on –
Mammon, the least erected spirit that fell
From heaven; for even in heaven his looks and
      thoughts   680
Were always downward bent, admiring more
The riches of heaven's pavement, trodden gold,
Than aught divine or holy else enjoyed
In vision beatific. By him first
Men also, and by his suggestion taught,   685
Ransacked the centre, and with impious hands
Rifled the bowels of their mother earth
For treasures better hid. Soon had his crew

---

583 **Aspramont:** a castle near Nice **Montalban:** the castle of
Rinaldo 585 **Biserta:** a port in Tunis 586 **Charlemagne:** King of
the Franks (768–814) 587 **Fontarabbia:** scene of a battle where
Charlemagne was defeated 609 **amerced:** paid the penalty

665 **cherubim:** a class of angel

Opened into the hill a spacious wound,
And digged out ribs of gold. Let none admire   690
That riches grow in hell; that soil may best
Deserve the precious bane. And here let those
Who boast in mortal things, and wondering tell
Of Babel, and the works of Memphian kings,
Learn how their greatest monuments of fame   695
And strength, and art, are easily outdone
By spirits reprobate, and in an hour
What in an age they, with incessant toil
And hands innumerable, scarce perform.
Nigh on the plain, in many cells prepared,   700
That underneath had veins of liquid fire
Sluiced from the lake, a second multitude
With wondrous art founded the massy ore,
Severing each kind, and scummed the bullion-dross.
A third as soon had formed within the ground   705
A various mould, and from the boiling cells
By strange conveyance filled each hollow nook;
As in an organ, from one blast of wind,
To many a row of pipes the sound-board breathes.
Anon out of the earth a fabric huge   710
Rose like an exhalation, with the sound
Of dulcet symphonies and voices sweet –
Built like a temple, where pilasters round
Were set, and Doric pillars overlaid
With golden architrave; nor did there want   715
Cornice or frieze, with bossy sculptures graven;
The roof was fretted gold. Not Babylon
Nor great Alcairo such magnificence
Equalled in all their glories, to enshrine
Belus or Serapis their gods, or seat   720
Their kings, when Egypt with Assyria strove
In wealth and luxury. Th'ascending pile
Stood fixed her stately height, and straight the doors,
Opening their brazen folds, discover, wide
Within, her ample spaces o'er the smooth   725
And level pavement: from the archèd roof,
Pendent by subtle magic, many a row
Of starry lamps and blazing cressets, fed
With naphtha and asphaltus, yielded light
As from a sky. The hasty multitude   730
Admiring entered; and the work some praise,
And some the architect. His hand was known
In heaven by many a towered structure high,
Where sceptred angels held their residence,
And sat as princes, whom the supreme King   735
Exalted to such power, and gave to rule,
Each in his hierarchy, the orders bright.
Nor was his name unheard or unadored
In ancient Greece; and in Ausonian land
Men called him Mulciber; and how he fell   740
From heaven they fabled, thrown by angry Jove
Sheer o'er the crystal battlements: from morn

To noon he fell, from noon to dewy eve,
A summer's day, and with the setting sun
Dropped from the zenith, like a falling star,   745
On Lemnos, th'Aegean isle. Thus they relate,
Erring; for he with this rebellious rout
Fell long before; nor aught availed him now
To have built in heaven high tow'rs; nor did he 'scape
By all his engines, but was headlong sent,   750
With his industrious crew, to build in hell.
    Meanwhile the wingèd heralds, by command
Of sovereign power, with awful ceremony
And trumpet's sound, throughout the host proclaim
A solemn council forthwith to be held   755
At Pandemonium, the high capital
Of Satan and his peers. Their summons called
From every band and squarèd regiment
By place or choice the worthiest: they anon
With hundreds and with thousands trooping came   760
Attended. All access was thronged; the gates
And porches wide, but chief the spacious hall
(Though like a covered field, where champions bold
Wont ride in armed, and at the soldan's chair
Defied the best of paynim chivalry   765
To mortal combat, or career with lance),
Thick swarmed, both on the ground and in the air,
Brushed with the hiss of rustling wings. As bees
In spring-time, when the sun with Taurus rides.
Pour forth their populous youth about the hive   770
In clusters; they among fresh dews and flowers
Fly to and fro, or on the smoothèd plank,
The suburb of their straw-built citadel,
New-rubbed with balm, expatiate, and confer
Their state-affairs: so thick the airy crowd   775
Swarmed and were straitened; till, the signal given,
Behold a wonder! They but now who seemed
In bigness to surpass earth's giant sons,
Now less than smallest dwarfs, in narrow room
Throng numberless – like that pygmean race   780
Beyond the Indian mount; or fairy elves,
Whose midnight revels, by a forest-side
Or fountain, some belated peasant sees,
Or dreams he sees, while overhead the moon
Sits arbitress, and nearer to the earth   785
Wheels her pale course: they, on their mirth and dance
Intent, with jocund music charm his ear;
At once with joy and fear his heart rebounds.
Thus incorporeal spirits to smallest forms
Reduced their shapes immense, and were at large,   790
Though without number still, amidst the hall
Of that infernal court. But far within,
And in their own dimensions like themselves,
The great seraphic lords and cherubim
In close recess and secret conclave sat,   795
A thousand demi-gods on golden seats,
Frequent and full. After short silence then,
And summons read, the great consult began.

---

694 **Babel:** the Biblical Tower of Babel   **Memphian:** Egyptian
718 **Alcairo:** Memphis (Cairo)   738–40 **Mulciber:** also known as
Vulcan and Hephaistos, god of metalworking. He built the palaces
of the gods

764 **soldan's:** Sultan's   765 **paynim:** pagan   769 **Taurus:** the second
sign of the zodiac

BOOK TWO

HIGH on a throne of royal state, which far
Outshone the wealth or Ormus and of Ind,
Or where the gorgeous East with richest hand
Show'rs on her kings barbaric pearl and gold,
Satan exalted sat, by merit raised   5
To that bad eminence; and, from despair
Thus high uplifted beyond hope, aspires
Beyond thus high, insatiate to pursue
Vain war with heaven; and, by success untaught,
His proud imaginations thus displayed: 10
   'Powers and Dominions, Deities of Heaven! –
For, since no deep within her gulf can hold
Immortal vigour, though oppressed and fallen,
I give not heaven for lost: from this descent
Celestial virtues rising will appear   15
More glorious and more dread than from no fall,
And trust themselves to fear no second fate! –
Me though just right, and the fixed laws of heaven,
Did first create your leader – next, free choice
With what besides in council or in fight   20
Hath been achieved of merit – yet this loss,
Thus far at least recovered, hath much more
Established in a safe, unenvied throne,
Yielded with full consent. The happier state
In heaven, which follows dignity, might draw   25
Envy from each inferior; but who here
Will envy whom the highest place exposes
Foremost to stand against the Thunderer's aim
Your bulwark, and condemns to greatest share
Of endless pain? Where there is, then, no good   30
For which to strive, no strife can grow up there
From faction: for none sure will claim in hell
Precedence; none whose portion is so small
Of present pain that with ambitious mind
Will covet more! With this advantage, then,   35
To union, and firm faith, and firm accord,
More than can be in heaven, we now return
To claim our just inheritance of old,
Surer to prosper than prosperity
Could have assured us; and by what best way,   40
Whether of open war or covert guile,
We now debate. Who can advise may speak.'

BOOK TWO – THE ARGUMENT: The Consultation begun, Satan debates whether another Battle be to be hazarded for the recovery of Heaven: some advise it, others dissuade: A third proposal is preferr'd, mention'd before by Satan, to search the truth of that Prophecy or Tradition in Heaven concerning another world, and another kind of creature equal or not much inferior to themselves, about this time to be created: Their doubt who shall be sent on this difficult search: Satan their chief undertakes alone the voyage, is honoured and applauded. The Council thus ended, the rest betake them several ways and to several employments, as their inclinations lead them, to entertain the time till Satan return. He passes on his journey to Hell Gates, finds them shut, and who sat there to guard them, by whom at length they are open'd, and discover to him the great Gulf between Hell and Heaven; with what difficulty he passes through, directed by Chaos, the Power of that place, to the sight of this new World which he sought 2 **Ormus:** town in the Persian Gulf

He ceased; and next him Moloch, sceptred king,
Stood up – the strongest and the fiercest spirit
That fought in heaven, now fiercer by despair.   45
His trust was with th'Eternal to be deemed
Equal in strength, and rather than be less
Cared not to be at all; with that care lost
Went all his fear: of God, or hell, or worse,
He recked not, and these words thereafter spake: 50
   'My sentence is for open war. Of wiles,
More unexpert, I boast not: them let those
Contrive who need, or when they need; not now.
For, while they sit contriving, shall the rest –
Millions that stand in arms, and longing wait   55
The signal to ascend – sit lingering here,
Heaven's fugitives, and for their dwelling-place
Accept this dark opprobrious den of shame,
The prison of His tyranny who reigns
By our delay? No! let us rather choose,   60
Armed with hell-flames and fury, all at once
O'er heaven's high towers to force resistless way,
Turning our tortures into horrid arms
Against the Torturer; when, to meet the noise
Of His almighty engine, he shall hear   65
Infernal thunder, and, for lightning, see
Black fire and horror shot with equal rage
Among his angels, and his throne itself
Mixed with Tartarean sulphur and strange fire,
His own invented torments. But perhaps   70
The way seems difficult, and steep to scale
With upright wing against a higher foe!
Let such bethink them, if the sleepy drench
Of that forgetful lake benumb not still,
That in our proper motion we ascend   75
Up to our native seat; descent and fall
To us is adverse. Who but felt of late,
When the fierce foe hung on our broken rear
Insulting, and pursued us through the deep,
With what compulsion and laborious flight   80
We sunk thus low? Th'ascent is easy, then;
Th'event is feared! Should we again provoke
Our stronger, some worse way His wrath may find
To our destruction, if there be in hell
Fear to be worse destroyed! What can be worse   85
Than to dwell here, driven out from bliss, condemned
In this abhorrèd deep to utter woe!
Where pain of unextinguishable fire
Must exercise us without hope of end
The vassals of his anger, when the scourge   90
Inexorably, and the torturing hour,
Calls us to penance? More destroyed than thus,
We should be quite abolished, and expire.
What fear we then? what doubt we to incense
His utmost ire? which, to the height enraged,   95
Will either quite consume us, and reduce
To nothing this essential – happier far
Than miserable to have eternal being! –
Or, if our substance be indeed divine,
And cannot cease to be, we are at worst   100

On this side nothing; and by proof we feel
Our power sufficient to disturb His heaven,
And with perpetual inroads to alarm,
Though inaccessible, His fatal throne:
Which, if not victory, is yet revenge.'   105
    He ended frowning, and his look denounced
Desperate revenge, and battle dangerous
To less than gods. On th'other side up rose
Belial, in act more graceful and humane.
A fairer person lost not heaven; he seemed   110
For dignity composed, and high exploit.
But all was false and hollow; though his tongue
Dropped manna, and could make the worse appear
The better reason, to perplex and dash
Maturest counsels: for his thoughts were low –   115
To vice industrious, but to nobler deeds
Timorous and slothful. Yet he pleased the ear,
And with persuasive accent thus began:
    'I should be much for open war, O Peers,
As not behind in hate, if what was urged   120
Main reason to persuade immediate war
Did not dissuade me most, and seem to cast
Ominous conjecture on the whole success;
When he who most excels in fact of arms,
In what he counsels and in what excels   125
Mistrustful, grounds his courage on despair
And utter dissolution, as the scope
Of all his aim, after some dire revenge.
First, what revenge? The tow'rs of heaven are filled
With armèd watch, that render all access   130
Impregnable: oft on the bordering deep
Encamp their legions, or with obscure wing
Scout far and wide into the realm of Night,
Scorning surprise. Or, could we break our way
By force, and at our heels all hell should rise   135
With blackest insurrection to confound
Heaven's purest light, yet our great Enemy,
All incorruptible, would on His throne
Sit unpolluted, and th'ethereal mould,
Incapable of stain, would soon expel   140
Her mischief, and purge off the baser fire,
Victorious. Thus repulsed, our final hope
Is flat despair: we must exasperate
Th'Almighty Victor to spend all His rage;
And that must end us; that must be our cure –   145
To be no more. Sad cure! for who would lose,
Though full of pain, this intellectual being,
Those thoughts that wander through eternity,
To perish rather, swallowed up and lost
In the wide womb of uncreated night,   150
Devoid of sense and motion? And who knows,
Let this be good, whether our angry Foe
Can give it, or will ever? How He can
Is doubtful; that He never will is sure.
Will He, so wise, let loose at once His ire,   155

Belike through impotence or unaware,
To give His enemies their wish, and end
Them in His anger whom His anger saves
To punish endless? "Wherefore cease we, then?"
Say they who counsel war. "We are decreed,   160
Reserved, and destined to eternal woe;
Whatever doing, what can we suffer more,
What can we suffer worse?" Is this, then, worst –
Thus sitting, thus consulting, thus in arms?
What when we fled amain, pursued and struck   165
With heaven's afflicting thunder, and besought
The deep to shelter us? This hell then seemed
A refuge from those wounds. Or when we lay
Chained on the burning lake? That sure was worse.
What if the breath that kindled those grim fires,   170
Awaked, should blow them into sevenfold rage,
And plunge us in the flames; or from above
Should intermitted vengeance arm again
His red right hand to plague us? What if all
Her stores were opened, and this firmament   175
Of hell should spout her cataracts of fire,
Impendent horrors, threatening hideous fall
One day upon our heads; while we perhaps,
Designing or exhorting glorious war,
Caught in a fiery tempest, shall be hurled,   180
Each on his rock transfixed, the sport and prey
Or racking whirlwinds, or forever sunk
Under yon boiling ocean, wrapped in chains,
There to converse with everlasting groans,
Unrespited, unpitied, unreprieved,   185
Ages of hopeless end? This would be worse.
War, therefore, open or concealed, alike
My voice dissuades; for what can force or guile
With Him, or who deceive His mind, whose eye
Views all things at one view? He from heaven's
      height   190
All these our motions vain sees and derides,
Not more almighty to resist our might
Than wise to frustrate all our plots and wiles.
Shall we, then, live thus vile – the race of heaven
Thus trampled, thus expelled, to suffer here   195
Chains and these torments? Better these than worse,
By my advice; since fate inevitable
Subdues us, and omnipotent decree,
The Victor's will. To suffer, as to do,
Our strength is equal; nor the law unjust   200
That so ordains. This was at first resolved,
If we were wise, against so great a foe
Contending, and so doubtful what might fall.
I laugh when those who at the spear are bold
And vent'rous, if that fail them, shrink, and fear   205
What yet they know must follow – to endure
Exile, or ignominy, or bonds, or pain,
The sentence of their Conqueror. This is now
Our doom; which if we can sustain and bear,

113 **manna:** sweetness

165 **amain:** with speed

Our Supreme Foe in time may much remit 210
His anger, and perhaps, thus far removed,
Not mind us not offending, satisfied
With what is punished; whence these raging fires
Will slacken, if His breath stir not their flames.
Our purer essence then will overcome 215
Their noxious vapour; or, inured, not feel;
Or, changed at length, and to the place conformed
In temper and in nature, will receive
Familiar the fierce heat; and, void of pain,
This horror will grow mild, this darkness light; 220
Besides what hope the never-ending flight
Of future days may bring, what chance, what change
Worth waiting – since our present lot appears
For happy though but ill, for ill not worst,
If we procure not to ourselves more woe.' 225
     Thus Belial, with words clothed in reason's garb,
Counselled ignoble ease and peaceful sloth,
Not peace; and after him thus Mammon spake:
     'Either to disenthrone the King of Heaven
We war, if war be best, or to regain 230
Our own right lost. Him to unthrone we then
May hope, when everlasting Fate shall yield
To fickle Chance, and Chaos judge the strife.
The former, vain to hope, argues as vain
The latter; for what place can be for us 235
Within heaven's bound, unless heaven's Lord
     supreme
We overpower? Suppose He should relent
And publish grace to all, on promise made
Of new subjection; with what eyes could we
Stand in His presence humble, and receive 240
Strict laws imposed, to celebrate His throne
With warbled hymns, and to His godhead sing
Forced hallelujahs, while He lordly sits
Our envied sovereign, and His altar breathes
Ambrosial odours and ambrosial flowers, 245
Our servile offerings? This must be our task
In heaven, this our delight. How wearisome
Eternity so spent in worship paid
To whom we hate! Let us not then pursue,
By force impossible, by leave obtained 250
Unacceptable, though in heaven, our state
Of splendid vassalage; but rather seek
Our own good from ourselves, and from our own
Live to ourselves, though in this vast recess,
Free and to none accountable, preferring 255
Hard liberty before the easy yoke
Of servile pomp. Our greatness will appear
Then most conspicuous when great things of small,
Useful of hurtful, prosperous of adverse,
We can create, and in what place soe'er 260
Thrive under evil, and work ease out of pain
Through labour and endurance. This deep world
Of darkness do we dread? How oft amidst

Thick clouds and dark doth heaven's all-ruling Sire
Choose to reside, His glory unobscured, 265
And with the majesty of darkness round
Covers His throne, from whence deep thunders roar.
Mustering their rage, and heaven resembles hell!
As He our darkness, cannot we His light
Imitate when we please? This desert soil 270
Wants not her hidden lustre, gems and gold;
Nor want we skill or art from whence to raise
Magnificence; and what can heaven show more?
Our torments also may, in length of time,
Become our elements, these piercing fires 275
As soft as now severe, our temper changed
Into their temper; which must needs remove
The sensible of pain. All things invite
To peaceful counsels, and the settled state
Of order, how in safety best we may 280
Compose our present evils, with regard
Of what we are and where, dismissing quite
All thoughts of war. Ye have what I advise.'
     He scarce had finished, when such murmur filled
Th'assembly as when hollow rocks retain 285
The sound of blustering winds, which all night long
Had roused the sea, now with hoarse cadence lull
Seafaring men o'erwatched, whose bark by chance
Or pinnace, anchors in a craggy bay
After the tempest. Such applause was heard 290
As Mammon ended, and his sentence pleased,
Advising peace: for such another field
They dreaded worse than hell; so much the fear
Of thunder and the sword of Michael
Wrought still within them; and no less desire 295
To found this nether empire, which might rise,
By policy and long process of time,
In emulation opposite to heaven.
Which when Beelzebub perceived – than whom,
Satan except, none higher sat – with grave 300
Aspect he rose, and in his rising seemed
A pillar of state. Deep on his front engraven
Deliberation sat, and public care;
And princely counsel in his face yet shone,
Majestic, though in ruin. Sage he stood 305
With Atlantean shoulders, fit to bear
The weight of mightiest monarchies; his look
Drew audience and attention still as night
Or summer's noontide air, while thus he spake:
     'Thrones and Imperial Powers, Offspring of
          Heaven, 310
Ethereal Virtues! or these titles now
Must we renounce, and, changing style, be called
Princes of hell? for so the popular vote
Inclines – here to continue, and build up here
A growing empire; doubtless! while we dream, 315
And know not that the King of Heaven hath doomed

289 **pinnace:** small boat 294 **sword of Michael:** Satan was injured
by the two-handed sword of Michael during the war in Heaven
306 **Atlantean:** Atlas carried the heavens on his shoulders

245 **Ambrosial:** fragrant

This place our dungeon, not our safe retreat
Beyond His potent arm, to live exempt
From heaven's high jurisdiction, in new league
Banded against His throne, but to remain   320
In strictest bondage, though thus far removed,
Under th'inevitable curb, reserved
His captive multitude. For He, to be sure,
In height or depth, still first and last will reign
Sole king, and of His kingdom lose no part   325
By our revolt, but over hell extend
His empire, and with iron sceptre rule
Us here, as with His golden those in heaven.
What sit we then projecting peace and war?
War hath determined us and foiled with loss   330
Irreparable; terms of peace yet none
Vouchsafed or sought; for what peace will be given
To us enslaved, but custody severe,
And stripes and arbitrary punishment
Inflicted? and what peace can we return,   335
But, to our power, hostility and hate,
Untamed reluctance, and revenge, though slow,
Yet ever plotting how the Conqueror least
May reap His conquest, and may least rejoice
In doing what we most in suffering feel?   340
Nor will occasion want, nor shall we need
With dangerous expedition to invade
Heaven, whose high walls fear no assault or siege,
Or ambush from the deep. What if we find
Some easier enterprise? There is a place   345
(If ancient and prophetic fame in heaven
Err not) – another world, the happy seat
Of some new race, called Man, about this time
To be created like to us, though less
In power and excellence, but favoured more   350
Of Him who rules above; so was His will
Pronounced among the Gods, and by an oath
That shook heaven's whole circumference confirmed.
Thither let us bend all our thoughts, to learn
What creatures there inhabit, of what mould   355
Or substance, how endued, and what their power
And where their weakness: how attempted best,
By force of subtlety. Though heaven be shut,
And heaven's high Arbitrator sit secure
In His own strength, this place may lie exposed,   360
The utmost border of His kingdom, left
To their defence who hold it: here, perhaps,
Some advantageous act may be achieved
By sudden onset – either with hell-fire
To waste His whole creation, or possess   365
All as our own, and drive, as we were driven,
The puny habitants; or, if not drive,
Seduce them to our party, that their God
May prove their foe, and with repenting hand
Abolish His own works. This would surpass   370
Common revenge, and interrupt His joy
In our confusion, and our joy upraise
In His disturbance; when His darling sons,
Hurled headlong to partake with us, shall curse
Their frail original, and faded bliss –   375
Faded so soon! Advise if this be worth
Attempting, or to sit in darkness here
Hatching vain empires.' Thus Beelzebub
Pleaded his devilish counsel – first devised
By Satan, and in part proposed: for whence,   380
But from the author of all ill, could spring
So deep a malice, to confound the race
Of mankind in one root, and earth with hell
To mingle and involve, done all to spite
The great Creator? But their spite still serves   385
His glory to augment. The bold design
Pleased highly those infernal states, and joy
Sparkled in all their eyes: with full assent
They vote: whereat his speech he thus renews:
'Well have ye judged, well ended long debate,   390
Synod of Gods, and, like to what ye are,
Great things resolved, which from the lowest deep
Will once more lift us up, in spite of fate,
Nearer our ancient seat – perhaps in view
Of those bright confines, whence, with neighbouring
      arms,   395
And opportune excursion, we may chance
Re-enter heaven; or else in some mild zone
Dwell, not unvisited of heaven's fair light,
Secure, and at the brightening orient beam
Purge off this gloom: the soft delicious air,   400
To heal the scar of these corrosive fires,
Shall breathe her balm. But, first, whom shall we send
In search of this new world? whom shall we find
Sufficient? who shall tempt with wandering feet
The dark, unbottomed, infinite abyss,   405
And through the palpable obscure find out
His uncouth way, or spread his airy flight,
Up-borne with indefatigable wings
Over the vast abrupt, ere he arrive
The happy isle? What strength, what art, can then
Suffice, or what evasion bear him safe,   411
Through the strict senteries and stations thick
Of angels watching round? Here he had need
All circumspection: and we now no less
Choice in our suffrage; for on whom we send   415
The weight of all, and our last hope, relies.'
   This said, he sat; and expectation held
His look suspense, awaiting who appeared
To second, or oppose, or undertake
The perilous attempt. But all sat mute,   420
Pondering the danger with deep thoughts; and each
In other's countenance read his own dismay,
Astonished. None among the choice and prime
Of those heaven-warring champions could be found
So hardy as to proffer or accept,   425
Alone, the dreadful voyage; till, at last,
Satan, whom now transcendent glory raised

383 **one root:** Adam, the father of mankind

Above his fellows, with monarchal pride
Conscious of highest worth, unmoved thus spake:
  'O Progeny of Heaven! Empyreal Thrones!   430
With reason hath deep silence and demur
Seized us, though undismayed. Long is the way
And hard, that out of hell leads up to light.
Our prison strong, this huge convex of fire,
Outrageous to devour, immures us round   435
Ninefold; and gates of burning adamant,
Barred over us, prohibit all egress.
These passed, if any pass, the void profound
Of unessential Night receives him next,
Wide-gaping, and with utter loss of being   440
Threatens him, plunged in that abortive gulf.
If thence he 'scape, into whatever world,
Or unknown region, what remains him less
Than unknown dangers, and as hard escape?
But I should ill become this throne, O Peers,   445
And this imperial sovereignty, adorned
With splendour, armed with power, if aught proposed
And judged of public moment in the shape
Of difficulty or danger, could deter
Me from attempting. Wherefore do I assume   450
These royalties, and not refuse to reign,
Refusing to accept as great a share
Of hazard as of honour, due alike
To him who reigns, and so much to him due
Of hazard more as he above the rest   455
High honoured sits? Go, therefore, mighty Powers,
Terror of heaven, though fallen; intend at home,
While here shall be our home, what best may ease
The present misery, and render hell
More tolerable; if there be cure or charm   460
To respite, or deceive, or slack the pain
Of this ill mansion: intermit no watch
Against a wakeful foe, while I abroad
Through all the coasts of dark destruction seek
Deliverance for us all. This enterprise   465
None shall partake with me.' Thus saying, rose
The monarch, and prevented all reply;
Prudent lest, from his resolution raised,
Others among the chief might offer now,
Certain to be refused, what erst they feared,   470
And, so refused, might in opinion stand
His rivals, winning cheap the high repute
Which he through hazard huge must earn. But they
Dreaded not more th'adventure than his voice
Forbidding; and at once with him they rose.   475
Their rising all at once was as the sound
Of thunder heard remote. Towards him they bend
With awful reverence prone, and as a god
Extol him equal to the highest in heaven.
Nor failed they to express how much they praised   480
That for the general safety he despised
His own: for neither do the spirits damned
Lose all their virtue; lest bad men should boast
Their specious deeds on earth, which glory excites,

Or close ambition varnished o'er with zeal.   485
  Thus they their doubtful consultations dark
Ended, rejoicing in their matchless chief:
As, when from mountain-tops the dusky clouds
Ascending, while the north wind sleeps, o'erspread
Heaven's cheerful face, the louring element   490
Scowls o'er the darkened landscape snow or shower,
If chance the radiant sun, with farewell sweet,
Extend his evening beam, the fields revive,
The birds their notes renew, and bleating herds
Attest their joy, that hill and valley rings.   495
Oh, shame to men! Devil with devil damned
Firm concord holds; men only disagree
Of creatures rational, though under hope
Of heavenly grace, and, God proclaiming peace,
Yet live in hatred, enmity, and strife   500
Among themselves, and levy cruel wars
Wasting the earth, each other to destroy:
As if (which might induce us to accord)
Man had not hellish foes enow besides,
That day and night for his destruction wait!   505
  The Stygian council thus dissolved; and forth
In order came the grand infernal peers:
'Midst came their mighty paramount, and seemed
Alone th'antagonist of heaven, nor less
Than hell's dread emperor, with pomp supreme,   510
And god-like imitated state: him round
A globe of fiery seraphim enclosed
With bright emblazonry, and horrent arms.
Then of their session ended they bid cry
With trumpet's regal sound the great result: 515
Toward the four winds four speedy cherubim
Put to their mouths the sounding alchemy,
By herald's voice explained; the hollow Abyss
Heard far and wide, and all the host of hell   519
With deaf'ning shout returned them loud acclaim.
Thence more at ease their minds, and somewhat
    raised
By false presumptuous hope, the rangèd powers
Disband; and, wandering, each his several way
Pursues, as inclination or sad choice
Leads him perplexed, where he may likeliest find   525
Truce to his restless thoughts, and entertain
The irksome hours, till his great chief return.
Part on the plain, or in the air sublime,
Upon the wing or in swift race contend,
As at th'Olympian games or Pythian fields;   530
Part curb their fiery steeds, or shun the goal
With rapid wheels, or fronted brigades form:
As when, to warn proud cities, war appears
Waged in the troubled sky, and armies rush
To battle in the clouds; before each van   535
Prick forth the airy knights, and couch their spears,
Till thickest legions close; with feats of arms
From either end of heaven the welkin burns.

530 **Pythian:** the Pythian games (second only to the Olympic games)
were held at Delphi 538 **welkin:** sky

Others, with vast Typhoean rage, more fell,
Rend up both rocks and hills, and ride the air   540
In whirlwind; hell scarce holds the wild uproar:
As when Alcides, from Oechalia crowned
With conquest, felt th'envenomed robe, and tore
Through pain up by the roots Thessalian pines,
And Lichas from the top of Oeta threw   545
Into th'Euboic sea. Others, more mild,
Retreated in a silent valley, sing
With notes angelical to many a harp
Their own heroic deeds, and hapless fall
By doom of battle, and complain that fate   550
Free virtue should enthrall to force or chance.
Their song was partial; but the harmony
(What could it less when spirits immortal sing?)
Suspended hell, and took with ravishment
The thronging audience. In discourse more sweet   555
(For eloquence the soul, song charms the sense)
Others apart sat on a hill retired,
In thoughts more elevate, and reasoned high
Of providence, foreknowledge, will, and fate
Fixed fate, free will, foreknowledge absolute,   560
And found no end, in wandering mazes lost.
Of good and evil much they argued then,
Of happiness and final misery,
Passion and apathy, and glory and shame:
Vain wisdom all, and false philosophy! –   565
Yet, with a pleasing sorcery, could charm
Pain for a while or anguish, and excite
Fallacious hope, or arm th'obdurèd breast
With stubborn patience as with triple steel.
Another part, in squadrons and gross bands,   570
On bold adventure to discover wide
That dismal world, if any clime perhaps
Might yield them easier habitation, bend
Four ways their flying march, along the banks
Of four infernal rivers, that disgorge   575
Into the burning lake their baleful streams –
Abhorrèd Styx, the flood of deadly hate;
Sad Acheron of sorrow, black and deep;
Cocytus, named of lamentation loud
Heard on the rueful stream; fierce Phlegeton,   580
Whose waves of torrent fire inflame with rage.
Far off from these, a slow and silent stream,
Lethe, the river of oblivion, rolls
Her watery labyrinth, whereof who drinks
Forthwith his former state and being forgets –   585
Forgets both joy and grief, pleasure and pain.
Beyond this flood a frozen continent
Lies dark and wild, beat with perpetual storms
Of whirlwind and dire hail, which on firm land

Thaws not, but gathers heap, and ruin seems   590
Of ancient pile; all else deep snow and ice,
A gulf profound as that Serbonian bog
Betwixt Damiata and Mount Casius old,
Where armies whole have sunk: the parching air
Burns frore, and cold performs th'effect of fire.   595
Thither, by harpy-footed furies haled,
At certain revolutions all the damned
Are brought; and feel by turns the bitter change
Of fierce extremes, extremes by change more fierce,
From beds of raging fire to starve in ice   600
Their soft ethereal warmth, and there to pine
Immovable, infixed, and frozen round
Periods of time – thence hurried back to fire.
They ferry over this Lethean sound
Both to and fro, their sorrow to augment,   605
And wish and struggle, as they pass, to reach
The tempting stream, with one small drop to lose
In sweet forgetfulness all pain and woe,
All in one moment, and so near the brink;
But Fate withstands, and, to oppose th'attempt,   610
Medusa with Gorgonian terror guards
The ford, and of itself the water flies
All taste of living wight, as once it fled
The lip of Tantalus. Thus roving on   614
In confused march forlorn, th'adventurous bands,
With shuddering horror pale, and eyes aghast,
Viewed first their lamentable lot, and found
No rest. Through many a dark and dreary vale
They passed, and many a region dolorous,
O'er many a frozen, many a fiery alp,   620
Rocks, caves, lakes, fens, bogs, dens, and shades of
     death –
A universe of death, which God by curse
Created evil, for evil only good;
Where all life dies, death lives, and Nature breeds,
Perverse, all monstrous, all prodigious things,   625
Abominable, inutterable, and worse
Than fables yet have feigned or fear conceived,
Gorgons, and hydras, and chimeras dire.
     Meanwhile the adversary of God and Man,
Satan, with thoughts inflamed of highest design,   630
Puts on swift wings, and toward the gates of hell
Explores his solitary flight: sometimes
He scours the right-hand coast, sometimes the left;
Now shaves with level wing the deep, then soars
Up to the fiery concave towering high.   635
As when far off at sea a fleet descried
Hangs in the clouds, by equinoctial winds
Close sailing from Bengala, or the isles

539 **Typhoean:** pertaining to Typhon, a Giant who warred on Jupiter
542–546 Hercules (Alcides), on his return from Oechalia, put on a
victor's robe that had been accidentally soaked in poison by his
wife. Thinking his friend Lichas (who brought the robe) was to blame,
Hercules threw him into 'th'Euboic sea' 575–581 a description of the
four rivers of hell

592 **Serbonian bog:** lake Serbonis on the Egyptian coast 595 **frore:**
frostily 604 **Lethean sound:** channel of the mythical river Lethe
611 **Medusa:** one of the Gorgons. Her glance would turn a person
to stone 614 **Tantalus:** son of Zeus and the nymph Pluto. Tantalus
is afflicted with a raging thirst that he can never quench
628 **Gorgons:** three terrifying maidens whose hair consisted of
hissing serpents **hydra:** a nine-headed serpent **chimeras:** fire-
breathing monsters

Of Ternate and Tidore, whence merchants bring
Their spicy drugs; they on the trading flood,   640
Through the wide Ethiopian to the Cape,
Ply stemming nightly toward the pole: so seemed
Far off the flying fiend. At last appear
Hell-bounds, high reaching to the horrid roof,
And thrice threefold the gates; three folds were brass,
Three iron, three of adamantine rock,   646
Impenetrable, impaled with circling fire,
Yet unconsumed. Before the gates there sat
On either side a formidable shape.
The one seemed woman to the waist, and fair,   650
But ended foul in many a scaly fold,
Voluminous and vast – a serpent armed
With mortal sting. About her middle round
A cry of hell-hounds never-ceasing barked
With wide Cerberean mouths full loud, and rung   655
A hideous peal; yet, when they list, would creep,
If aught disturbed their noise, into her womb,
And kennel there; yet there still barked and howled
Within unseen. Far less abhorred than these
Vexed Scylla, bathing in the sea that parts   660
Calabria from the hoarse Trinacrian shore;
Nor uglier follow the night-hag, when, called
In secret, riding through the air she comes,
Lured with the smell of infant blood, to dance
With Lapland witches, while the labouring moon   665
Eclipses at their charms. The other shape –
If shape it might be called that shape had none
Distinguishable in member, joint, or limb;
Or substance might be called that shadow seemed,
For each seemed either – black it stood as night,   670
Fierce as ten furies, terrible as hell,
And shook a dreadful dart: what seemed his head
The likeness of a kingly crown had on.
Satan was now at hand, and from his seat
The monster moving onward came as fast   675
With horrid strides; hell trembled as he strode.
Th'undaunted fiend what this might be admired –
Admired, not feared (God and his Son except,
Created thing naught valued he nor shunned),
And with disdainful look thus first began: 680
  'Whence and what art thou, execrable Shape,
That dar'st, though grim and terrible, advance
Thy miscreated front athwart my way
To yonder gates? Through them I mean to pass,
That be assured, without leave asked of thee.   685
Retire; or taste thy folly, and learn by proof,
Hell-born, not to contend with spirits of heaven.'
  To whom the goblin, full of wrath, replied:
'Art thou that traitor angel? art thou he,
Who first broke peace in heaven and faith, till then
Unbroken, and in proud rebellious arms   691

Drew after him the third part of heaven's sons,
Conjúred against the Highest – for which both thou
And they, out-cast from God, are here condemned
To waste eternal days in woe and pain?   695
And reckon'st thou thyself with spirits of heaven
Hell-doomed, and breath'st defiance here and scorn,
Where I reign king, and, to enrage thee more,
Thy king and lord? Back to thy punishment,
False fugitive; and to thy speed add wings,   700
Lest with a whip of scorpions I pursue
Thy lingering, or with one stroke of this dart
Strange horror seize thee, and pangs unfelt before.'
  So spake the grisly terror, and in shape,
So speaking and so threat'ning, grew tenfold,   705
More dreadful and deform. On th'other side,
Incensed with indignation, Satan stood
Unterrified, and like a comet burned,
That fires the length of Ophiuchus huge
In th'arctic sky, and from his horrid hair   710
Shakes pestilence and war. Each at the head
Levelled his deadly aim; their fatal hands
No second stroke intend; and such a frown
Each cast at th'other as when two black clouds,
With heaven's artillery fraught, come rattling on   715
Over the Caspian – then stand front to front
Hovering a space, till winds the signal blow
To join their dark encounter in mid-air.
So frowned the mighty combatants that hell
Grew darker at their frown; so matched they stood;
For never but once more was either like   721
To meet so great a foe. And now great deeds
Had been achieved, whereof all hell had rung,
Had not the snaky sorceress, that sat
Fast by hell-gate and kept the fatal key,   725
Risen, and with hideous outcry rushed between.
  'O father, what intends thy hand', she cried,
'Against thy only son? What fury, O son,
Possesses thee to bend that mortal dart
Against thy father's head? And know'st for whom?   730
For Him who sits above, and laughs the while
At thee, ordained His drudge to execute
Whate'er His wrath, which He calls justice, bids –
His wrath, which one day will destroy ye both!'
  She spake, and at her words the hellish pest   735
Forbore: then these to her Satan returned:
  'So strange thy outcry, and thy words so strange
Thou interposest, that my sudden hand,
Prevented, spares to tell thee yet by deeds
What it intends, till first I know of thee   740
What thing thou art, thus double-formed, and why,
In this infernal vale first met, thou call'st
Me father, and that phantasm call'st my son.
I know thee not, nor ever saw till now
Sight more detestable than him and thee.'   745

639–640 **famous trading centres**   655 **Cerberean:** Cerberus, the hell
hound who guarded the entrance to the underworld   660 **Scylla:**
a nymph who was changed into a rock   662 **night-hag:** Hecate,
goddess of witchcraft

709 **Ophiuchus:** a constellation in the northern sky meaning
'serpent holder'   739 **spares:** refrains from

T'whom thus the portress of hell-gate replied:
'Hast thou forgot me, then; and do I seem
Now in thine eye so foul? – once deemed so fair
In heaven, when at th'assembly, and in sight
Of all the seraphim with thee combined   750
In bold conspiracy against heaven's King,
All on a sudden miserable pain
Surprised thee, dim thine eyes and dizzy swum
In darkness, while thy head flames thick and fast
Threw forth, till on the left side op'ning wide,   755
Likest to thee in shape and countenance bright,
Then shining heavenly fair, a goddess armed,
Out of thy head I sprung. Amazement seized
All th'host of heaven; back they recoiled afraid
At first, and called me Sin, and for a sign   760
Portentous held me; but, familiar grown,
I pleased, and with attractive graces won
The most averse – thee chiefly, who, full oft
Thyself in me thy perfect image viewing,
Becam'st enamoured; and such joy thou took'st   765
With me in secret that my womb conceived
A growing burden. Meanwhile war arose,
And fields were fought in heaven: wherein remained
(For what could else?) to our Almighty Foe
Clear victory; to our part loss and rout   770
Through all the empyrean. Down they fell,
Driven headlong from the pitch of heaven, down
Into this deep; and in the general fall
I also: at which time this powerful key
Into my hand was given, with charge to keep   775
These gates forever shut, which none can pass
Without my opening. Pensive here I sat
Alone; but long I sat not, till my womb,
Pregnant by thee, and now excessive grown,
Prodigious motion felt and rueful throes.   780
At last this odious offspring whom thou seest,
Thine own begotten, breaking violent way,
Tore through my entrails, that, with fear and pain
Distorted, all my nether shape thus grew
Transformed: but he my inbred enemy   785
Forth issued, brandishing his fatal dart,
Made to destroy. I fled, and cried out 'Death!'
Hell trembled at the hideous name, and sighed
From all her caves, and back resounded 'Death!'
I fled; but he pursued (though more, it seems,   790
Inflamed with lust than rage), and, swifter far,
Me overtook, his mother, all dismayed,
And, in embraces forcible and foul
Engendering with me, of that rape begot
These yelling monsters, that with ceaseless cry   795
Surround me, as thou saw'st – hourly conceived
And hourly born, with sorrow infinite
To me; for, when they list, into the womb
That bred them they return, and howl, and gnaw
My bowels, their repast; then, bursting forth   800
Afresh, with conscious terrors vex me round,
That rest or intermission none I find.

Before mine eyes in opposition sits
Grim Death, my son and foe, who set them on,
And me, his parent, would full soon devour   805
For want of other prey, but that he knows
His end with mine involved, and knows that I
Should prove a bitter morsel, and his bane,
Whenever that shall be: so Fate pronounced.
But thou, O father, I forewarn thee, shun   810
His deadly arrow; neither vainly hope
To be invulnerable in those bright arms,
Though tempered heavenly; for that mortal dint,
Save he who reigns above, none can resist.'
    She finished; and the subtle fiend his lore   815
Soon learned, now milder, and thus answered smooth:
'Dear daughter – since thou claim'st me for thy sire,
And my fair son here show'st me, the dear pledge
Of dalliance had with thee in heaven, and joys
Then sweet, now sad to mention, through dire
    change   820
Befallen us unforeseen, unthought of – know,
I come no enemy, but to set free
From out this dark and dismal house of pain
Both him and thee, and all the heavenly host
Of spirits that, in our just pretences armed,   825
Fell with us from on high. From them I go
This uncouth errand sole, and one for all
Myself expose, with lonely steps to tread
Th'unfounded deep, and through the void immense
To search, with wand'ring quest, a place foretold   830
Should be – and, by concurring signs, ere now
Created vast and round – a place of bliss
In the purlieus of heaven; and therein placed
A race of upstart creatures, to supply
Perhaps our vacant room, though more removed,   835
Lest heaven, surcharged with potent multitude,
Might hap to move new broils. Be this, or aught
Than this more secret, now designed, I haste
To know; and, this once known, shall soon return,
And bring ye to the place where thou and Death   840
Shall dwell at ease, and up and down unseen
Wing silently the buxom air, embalmed
With odours. There ye shall be fed and filled
Immeasurably; all things shall be your prey.'
    He ceased; for both seemed highly pleased, and
    Death   845
Grinned horrible a ghastly smile, to hear
His famine should be filled, and blessed his maw
Destined to that good hour. No less rejoiced
His mother bad, and thus bespake her sire:
'The key of this infernal pit, by due   850
And by command of heaven's all-powerful King,
I keep, by him forbidden to unlock
These adamantine gates; against all force
Death ready stands to interpose his dart,
Fearless to be o'ermatched by living might.   855

829 **Th'unfounded deep**: the depth is incalculable 847 **maw**: stomach

But what owe I to his commands above,
Who hates me, and hath hither thrust me down
Into this gloom of Tartarus profound,
To sit in hateful office here confined,
Inhabitant of heaven and heavenly born – 860
Here in perpetual agony and pain,
With terrors and with clamours compassed round
Of mine own brood, that on my bowels feed?
Thou art my father, thou my author, thou
My being gav'st me; whom should I obey 865
But thee? whom follow? Thou wilt bring me soon
To that new world of light and bliss, among
The gods who live at ease, where I shall reign
At thy right hand voluptuous, as beseems
Thy daughter and thy darling, without end.' 870
   Thus saying, from her side the fatal key,
Sad instrument of all our woe, she took;
And, towards the gate rolling her bestial train,
Forthwith the huge portcullis high up-drew,
Which, but herself, not all the Stygian powers 875
Could once have moved; then in the key-hole turns
Th'intricate wards, and every bolt and bar
Of massy iron or solid rock with ease
Unfastens. On a sudden open fly,
With impetuous recoil and jarring sound, 880
Th'infernal doors, and on their hinges grate
Harsh thunder, that the lowest bottom shook
Of Erebus. She opened; but to shut
Excelled her power: the gates wide open stood,
That with extended wings a bannered host, 885
Under spread ensigns marching, might pass through
With horse and chariots ranked in loose array;
So wide they stood, and like a furnace-mouth
Cast forth redounding smoke and ruddy flame.
Before their eyes in sudden view appear 890
The secrets of the hoary deep – a dark
Illimitable ocean, without bound,
Without dimension; where length, breadth, and
   height,
And time, and place, are lost; where eldest Night
And Chaos, ancestors of Nature, hold 895
Eternal anarchy, amidst the noise
Of endless wars, and by confusion stand.
For Hot, Cold, Moist, and Dry, four champions fierce,
Strive here for mastery, and to battle bring
Their embryon atoms: they around the flag 900
Of each his faction, in their several clans,
Light-armed or heavy, sharp, smooth, swift, or slow,
Swarm populous, unnumbered as the sands
Of Barca or Cyrene's torrid soil,
Levied to side with warring winds, and poise 905
Their lighter wings. To whom these most adhere
He rules a moment: Chaos umpire sits,
And by decision more embroils the fray
By which he reigns: next him, high arbiter,

Chance governs all. Into this wild abyss, 910
The womb of Nature, and perhaps her grave,
Of neither sea, nor shore, nor air, nor fire,
But all these in their pregnant causes mixed
Confusedly, and which thus must ever fight,
Unless th'Almighty Maker them ordain 915
His dark materials to create more worlds –
Into this wild abyss the wary fiend
Stood on the brink of hell and looked a while,
Pondering his voyage; for no narrow frith
He had to cross. Nor was his ear less pealed 920
With noises loud and ruinous (to compare
Great things with small) than when Bellona storms
With all her battering engines, bent to rase
Some capital city; or less than if this frame
Of heaven were falling, and these elements 925
In mutiny had from her axle torn
The steadfast earth. At last his sail-broad vans
He spread for flight, and, in the surging smoke
Uplifted, spurns the ground; thence many a league,
As in a cloudy chair, ascending rides 930
Audacious; but, that seat soon failing, meets
A vast vacuity. All unawares,
Fluttering his pennons vain, plumb-down he drops
Ten thousand fathom deep, and to this hour
Down had been falling, had not, by ill chance, 935
The strong rebuff of some tumultuous cloud,
Instinct with fire and nitre, hurried him
As many miles aloft. That fury stayed –
Quenched in a boggy Syrtis, neither sea,
Nor good dry land – nigh foundered, on he fares, 940
Treading the crude consistence, half on foot,
Half flying; behoves him now both oar and sail.
As when a gryphon through the wilderness
With wingèd course, o'er hill or moory dale,
Pursues the Arimaspian, who by stealth 945
Had from his wakeful custody purloined
The guarded gold; so eagerly the fiend
O'er bog or steep, through strait, rough, dense, or rare,
With head, hands, wings, or feet, pursues his way,
And swims, or sinks, or wades, or creeps, or flies. 950
At length a universal hubbub wild
Of stunning sounds, and voices all confused,
Borne through the hollow dark, assaults his ear
With loudest vehemence. Thither he plies
Undaunted, to meet there whatever power 955
Or spirit of the nethermost abyss
Might in that noise reside, of whom to ask
Which way the nearest coast of darkness lies
Bordering on light; when straight behold the throne
Of Chaos, and his dark pavilion spread 960
Wide on the wasteful deep! With him enthroned
Sat sable-vested Night, eldest of things,
The consort of his reign; and by them stood

---

883 **Erebus:** hell 900 **embryon:** embryonic, unborn 904 North African cities

922 **Bellona:** Minerva, goddess of war 939 **Syrtis:** quicksand off the North African shore 943 **gryphon:** griffin. A monster that was half lion, half eagle 945 **Arimaspian:** a tribe from the north of Scythia

Orcus and Ades, and the dreaded name
Of Demogorgon; Rumour next, and Chance, 965
And Tumult, and Confusion, all embroiled,
And Discord with a thousand various mouths.
    T'whom Satan, turning boldly, thus: 'Ye Powers
And Spirits of this nethermost abyss,
Chaos and ancient Night, I come no spy 970
With purpose to explore or to disturb
The secrets of your realm; but, by constraint
Wandering this darksome desert, as my way
Lies through your spacious empire up to light,
Alone and without guide, half lost, I seek, 975
What readiest path leads where your gloomy bounds
Confine with heaven; or, if some other place,
From your dominion won, th'Ethereal King
Possesses lately, thither to arrive
I travel this profound. Direct my course: 980
Directed, no mean recompense it brings
To your behoof, if I that region lost,
All usurpation thence expelled, reduce
To her original darkness and your sway
(Which is my present journey), and once more 985
Erect the standard there of ancient Night.
Yours be th'advantage all, mine the revenge!'
    Thus Satan; and him thus the anarch old,
With faltering speech and visage incomposed,
Answered: 'I know thee, stranger, who thou art – 990
That mighty leading angel, who of late
Made head against heaven's King, though
      overthrown.
I saw and heard; for such a numerous host
Fled not in silence through the frighted deep,
With ruin upon ruin, rout on rout, 995
Confusion worse confounded; and heaven-gates
Poured out by millions her victorious bands,
Pursuing. I upon my frontiers here
Keep residence; if all I can will serve
That little which is left so to defend, 1000
Encroached on still through our intestine broils
Weakening the sceptre of old Night: first, hell,
Your dungeon, stretching far and wide beneath;
Now lately heaven and earth, another world
Hung o'er my realm, linked in a golden chain 1005
To that side heaven from whence your legions fell!
If that way be your walk, you have not far;
So much the nearer danger. Go, and speed;
Havoc, and spoil, and ruin, are my gain.'
    He ceased; and Satan stayed not to reply, 1010
But, glad that now his sea should find a shore,
With fresh alacrity and force renewed
Springs upward, like a pyramid of fire,
Into the wild expanse, and through the shock
Of fighting elements, on all sides round 1015

Environed, wins his way; harder beset
And more endangered than when Argo passed
Through Bosporus betwixt the jostling rocks,
Or when Ulysses on the larboard shunned
Charybdis, and by th'other whirlpool steered. 1020
So he with difficulty and labour hard
Moved on, with difficulty and labour he;
But, he once passed, soon after, when Man fell,
Strange alteration! Sin and Death amain,
Following his track (such was the will of heaven) 1025
Paved after him a broad and beaten way
Over the dark abyss, whose boiling gulf
Tamely endured a bridge of wondrous length,
From hell continued, reaching th'utmost orb
Of this frail world; by which the spirits perverse 1030
With easy intercourse pass to and fro
To tempt or punish mortals, except whom
God and good angels guard by special grace.
    But now at last the sacred influence
Of light appears, and from the walls of heaven 1035
Shoots far into the bosom of dim Night
A glimmering dawn. Here Nature first begins
Her farthest verge, and Chaos to retire,
As from her outmost works, a broken foe,
With tumult less and with less hostile din; 1040
That Satan with less toil, and now with ease,
Wafts on the calmer wave by dubious light,
And, like a weather-beaten vessel, holds
Gladly the port, though shrouds and tackle torn;
Or in the emptier waste, resembling air, 1045
Weighs his spread wings, at leisure to behold
Far off th'empyreal heaven, extended wide
In circuit, undetermined square or round,
With opal towers and battlements adorned
Of living sapphire, once his native seat; 1050
And, fast by, hanging in a golden chain,
This pendent world, in bigness as a star
Of smallest magnitude close by the moon.
Thither, full fraught with mischievous revenge,
Accursed, and in a cursèd hour, he hies. 1055

1017–1018 Jason and the Argonauts sailed the Bosphorus in their ship the Argo 1019 **larboard:** left 1019–1020 Ulysses avoided the Charybdis whirlpool as he made his way through the straits of Messina 1052 **pendent:** hanging

BOOK THREE

HAIL, holy Light, offspring of heaven firstborn,
Or of the Eternal coeternal beam
May I express thee unblamed? since God is light,
And never but in unapproachèd light
Dwelt from eternity, dwelt then in thee 5
Bright effluence of bright essence increate.
Or hear'st thou rather pure ethereal stream,
Whose fountain who shall tell? before the sun,
Before the heavens thou wert, and at the voice
Of God, as with a mantle, didst invest 10

964 **Orcus and Ades:** gods of hell 965 **Demogorgon:** the dreaded 'people monster' 988 **anarch:** conversely Anarch is the ruler of Anarchy 1001 **intestine:** internal

The rising world of waters dark and deep,
Won from the void and formless infinite.
Thee I revisit now with bolder wing,
Escaped the Stygian pool, though long detained
In that obscure sojourn, while in my flight   15
Through utter and through middle darkness borne,
With other notes than to the Orphean lyre
I sung of Chaos and eternal Night;
Taught by the heavenly Muse to venture down
The dark descent, and up to reascend,   20
Though hard and rare. Thee I revisit safe,
And feel thy sovran vital lamp; but thou
Revisit'st not these eyes, that roll in vain
To find thy piercing ray, and find no dawn;
So thick a drop serene hath quenched their orbs,   25
Or dim suffusion veiled. Yet not the more
Cease I to wander, where the Muses haunt,
Clear spring, or shady grove, or sunny hill,
Smit with the love of sacred song; but chief
Thee, Sion, and the flow'ry brooks beneath,   30
That wash thy hallowed feet, and warbling flow,
Nightly I visit: nor sometimes forget
So were I equalled with them in renown,
Thy sovran command, that Man should find grace;
Blind Thamyris, and blind Maeonides,   35
And Tiresias, and Phineus, prophets old:
Then feed on thoughts, that voluntary move
Harmonious numbers; as the wakeful bird

Sings darkling, and in shadiest covert hid
Tunes her nocturnal note. Thus with the year   40
Seasons return; but not to me returns
Day, or the sweet approach of even or morn,
Or sight of vernal bloom, or summer's rose,
Or flocks, or herds, or human face divine;
But cloud instead, and ever-during dark   45
Surrounds me, from the cheerful ways of men
Cut off, and for the book of knowledge fair
Presented with a universal blank
Of Nature's works to me expunged and rased,
And wisdom at one entrance quite shut out.   50
So much the rather thou, celestial Light,
Shine inward, and the mind through all her powers
Irradiate; there plant eyes, all mist from thence
Purge and disperse, that I may see and tell
Of things invisible to mortal sight.   55
    Now had the Almighty Father from above,
From the pure empyrean where He sits
High-throned above all height, bent down his eye
His own works and their works at once to view:
About Him all the sanctities of heaven   60
Stood thick as stars, and from His sight received
Beatitude past utterance; on His right
The radiant image of His glory sat,
His only son; on earth He first beheld
Our two first parents, yet the only two   65
Of mankind in the happy garden placed
Reaping immortal fruits of joy and love,
Uninterrupted joy, unrivalled love,
In blissful solitude; He then surveyed
Hell and the gulf between, and Satan there   70
Coasting the wall of heaven on this side Night
In the dun air sublime, and ready now
To stoop with wearied wings, and willing feet,
On the bare outside of this world, that seemed
Firm land imbosomed, without firmament,   75
Uncertain which, in ocean or in air.
Him God beholding from His prospect high,
Wherein past, present, future He beholds,
Thus to His only Son foreseeing spake.
    'Only begotten Son, seest thou what rage   80
Transports our adversary? whom no bounds
Prescribed no bars of hell, nor all the chains
Heaped on him there, nor yet the main abyss
Wide interrupt, can hold; so bent he seems
On desperate revenge, that shall redound   85
Upon his own rebellious head. And now,
Through all restraint broke loose, he wings his way
Not far off heaven, in the precincts of light,
Directly towards the new-created world,
And man there placed, with purpose to assay   90
If him by force he can destroy, or, worse,
By some false guile pervert; and shall pervert;
For man will hearken to his glozing lies,

BOOK THREE – THE ARGUMENT: God sitting on his Throne sees Satan flying towards this world, then newly created; shows him to the Son who sat at his right hand; foretells the success of Satan in perverting mankind; clears his own Justice and Wisdom from all imputation, having created Man free and able enough to have withstood his Tempter; yet declares his purpose of grace towards him, in regard he fell not of his own malice, as did Satan, but by him seduc't. The Son of God renders praises to his Father for the manifestation of his gracious purpose towards Man; but God again declares, that Grace cannot be extended towards Man without the satisfaction of divine justice; Man hath offended the majesty of God by aspiring to God-head, and therefore with all his Progeny devoted to death must die, unless someone can be found sufficient to answer for his offence, and undergo his Punishment. The Son of God freely offers himself a Ransom for Man: the Father accepts him, ordains his incarnation, pronounces his exaltation above all Names in Heaven and Earth; commands all the Angels to adore him; they obey, and hymning to their Harps in full Quire, celebrate the Father and the Son. Meanwhile Satan alights upon the bare Convex of this Worlds outermost Orb; where wandering he first finds a place since call'd The Limbo of Vanity; what persons and things fly up thither; thence comes to the Gate of Heaven, describ'd ascending by stairs, and the waters above the Firmament that flow about it: His passage thence to the Orb of the Sun; he finds there Uriel the Regent of that Orb, but first changes himself into the shape of a meaner Angel; and pretending a zealous desire to behold the new Creation and Man whom God had plac't here, inquires of him the place of his habitation, and is directed; alights first on Mount Niphates 1–55 the scene shifts from hell to Heaven 16 **utter:** outer 22 **sovran:** supreme 25 **drop serene:** a literal translation of gutta serena, the form of blindness that Milton was suffering from 26 **suffusion:** cataract 35 **Thamyris:** a blind Thracian poet **blind Maeonides:** Homer 36 **Tiresias:** blind sage from Thebes **Phineus:** blind king of Thrace

93 **glozing:** flattering

And easily transgress the sole command,
Sole pledge of his obedience: So will fall   95
He and his faithless progeny: Whose fault?
Whose but his own? ingrate, he had of me
All he could have; I made him just and right,
Sufficient to have stood, though free to fall.
Such I created all th'ethereal powers   100
And spirits, both them who stood, and them who
    failed;
Freely they stood who stood, and fell who fell.
Not free, what proof could they have given sincere
Of true allegiance, constant faith or love,
Where only what they needs must do appeared,   105
Not what they would? what praise could they receive?
What pleasure I from such obedience paid,
When will and reason (reason also is choice)
Useless and vain, of freedom both despoiled,
Made passive both, had served necessity,   110
Not me? they therefore, as to right belonged,
So were created, nor can justly accuse
Their Maker, or their making, or their fate,
As if predestination over-ruled
Their will disposed by absolute decree   115
Or high foreknowledge they themselves decreed
Their own revolt, not I; if I foreknew,
Foreknowledge had no influence on their fault,
Which had no less proved certain unforeknown.
So without least impulse or shadow of fate,   120
Or aught by me immutably foreseen,
They trespass, authors to themselves in all
Both what they judge, and what they choose; for so
I formed them free: and free they must remain,
Till they enthrall themselves; I else must change   125
Their nature, and revoke the high decree
Unchangeable, eternal, which ordained
Their freedom: they themselves ordained their fall.
The first sort by their own suggestion fell,
Self-tempted, self-depraved: Man falls, deceived   130
By the other first: Man therefore shall find grace,
The other none. In mercy and justice both,
Through heaven and earth, so shall my glory excel;
But mercy, first and last, shall brightest shine.'
    Thus while God spake, ambrosial fragrance filled
All heaven, and in the blessed spirits elect   136
Sense of new joy ineffable diffused.
Beyond compare the Son of God was seen
Most glorious; in Him all His father shone
Substantially expressed; and in His face   140
Divine compassion visibly appeared,
Love without end, and without measure grace,
Which uttering, thus He to His father spake.
    'O Father, gracious was that word which closed   144
Thy sovran sentence, that Man should find grace;
For which both heaven and earth shall high extol
Thy praises, with the innumerable sound
Of hymns and sacred songs, wherewith Thy throne
Encompassed shall resound Thee ever blest.

For should Man finally be lost, should Man,   150
Thy creature late so loved, Thy youngest son,
Fall circumvented thus by fraud, though joined
With his own folly? that be from Thee far,
That far be from Thee, Father, who art judge
Of all things made, and judgest only right.   155
Or shall the adversary thus obtain
His end, and frustrate thine? shall he fulfil
His malice, and thy goodness bring to nought,
Or proud return, though to his heavier doom,
Yet with revenge accomplished, and to hell   160
Draw after him the whole race of mankind,
By him corrupted? or wilt Thou thyself
Abolish Thy creation, and unmake
For him, what for Thy glory Thou hast made?
So should Thy goodness and Thy greatness both   165
Be questioned and blasphemed without defence.'
    To whom the great Creator thus replied.
'O Son, in whom my soul hath chief delight,
Son of my bosom, Son who art alone.
My word, my wisdom, and effectual might,   170
All hast thou spoken as my thoughts are, all
As my eternal purpose hath decreed;
Man shall not quite be lost, but saved who will;
Yet not of will in him, but grace in me
Freely vouchsafed; once more I will renew   175
His lapsèd powers, though forfeit; and enthralled
By sin to foul exorbitant desires;
Upheld by me, yet once more he shall stand
On even ground against his mortal foe;
By me upheld, that he may know how frail   180
His fall'n condition is, and to me owe
All his deliverance, and to none but me.
Some I have chosen of peculiar grace,
Elect above the rest; so is my will:
The rest shall hear me call, and oft be warned   185
Their sinful state, and to appease betimes
The incensed Deity, while offered grace
Invites; for I will clear their senses dark,
What may suffice, and soften stony hearts
To pray, repent, and bring obedience due.   190
To prayer, repentance, and obedience due,
Though but endeavoured with sincere intent,
Mine ear shall not be slow, mine eye not shut.
And I will place within them as a guide,
My umpire Conscience; whom if they will hear,   195
Light after light, well used, they shall attain,
And to the end, persisting, safe arrive.
This my long sufferance, and my day of grace,
They who neglect and scorn, shall never taste;
But hard be hardened, blind be blinded more,   200
That they may stumble on, and deeper fall;
And none but such from mercy I exclude.
But yet all is not done; Man disobeying,
Disloyal, breaks his fealty, and sins
Against the high supremacy of heaven,   205
Affecting Godhead, and, so losing all,

To expiate his treason hath nought left,
But to destruction sacred and devote,
He, with his whole posterity, must die,
Die he or justice must; unless for him 210
Some other able, and as willing, pay
The rigid satisfaction, death for death.
Say, heavenly Powers, where shall we find such love?
Which of you will be mortal, to redeem
Man's mortal crime, and just th'unjust to save? 215
Dwells in all heaven charity so dear?'
   He asked, but all the heavenly choir stood mute,
And silence was in heaven: on Man's behalf
Patron or intercessor none appeared,
Much less that durst upon his own head draw 220
The deadly forfeiture, and ransom set.
And now without redemption all mankind
Must have been lost, adjudged to death and hell
By doom severe, had not the Son of God,
In whom the fullness dwells of love divine, 225
His dearest mediation thus renewed.
   'Father, Thy word is past, Man shall find grace;
And shall grace not find means, that finds her way,
The speediest of thy wingèd messengers,
To visit all thy creatures, and to all 230
Comes unprevented, unimplored, unsought?
Happy for Man, so coming; he her aid
Can never seek, once dead in sins, and lost;
Atonement for himself, or offering meet,
Indebted and undone, hath none to bring; 235
Behold me then: me for him, life for life
I offer: on me let Thine anger fall;
Account me Man; I for his sake will leave
Thy bosom, and this glory next to thee
Freely put off, and for him lastly die 240
Well pleased; on me let Death wreak all his rage.
Under his gloomy power I shall not long
Lie vanquished. Thou hast given me to possess
Life in myself for ever; by thee I live;
Though now to Death I yield, and am his due, 245
All that of me can die, yet, that debt paid,
Thou wilt not leave me in the loathsome grave
His prey, nor suffer my unspotted soul
For ever with corruption there to dwell;
But I shall rise victorious, and subdue 250
My vanquisher, spoiled of his vaunted spoil.
Death his death's wound shall then receive, and stoop
Inglorious, of his mortal sting disarmed;
I through the ample air in triumph high
Shall lead hell captive maugre hell, and show 255
The powers of darkness bound. Thou, at the sight
Pleased, out of heaven shalt look down and smile,
While, by thee raised, I ruin all my foes;
Death last, and with his carcass glut the grave;
Then, with the multitude of my redeemed, 260
Shall enter heaven, long absent, and return,

Father, to see Thy face, wherein no cloud
Of anger shall remain, but peace assured
And reconcilement: wrath shall be no more
Thenceforth, but in Thy presence joy entire.' 265
   His words here ended; but his meek aspect
Silent yet spake, and breathed immortal love
To mortal men, above which only shone
Filial obedience: as a sacrifice
Glad to be offered, he attends the will 270
Of His great father. Admiration seized
All heaven, what this might mean, and whither tend,
Wondering; but soon th'Almighty thus replied.
   'O thou in heaven and earth the only peace
Found out for mankind under wrath, O thou 275
My sole complacence! Well thou know'st how dear
To me are all my works; nor Man the least,
Though last created, that for him I spare
Thee from my bosom and right hand, to save,
By losing thee a while, the whole race lost. 280
Thou, therefore, whom thou only canst redeem,
Their nature also to thy nature join;
And be thyself Man among men on earth,
Made flesh, when time shall be, of virgin seed,
By wondrous birth; be thou in Adam's room 285
The head of all mankind, though Adam's son.
As in him perish all men, so in thee,
As from a second root, shall be restored
As many as are restored, without thee none.
His crime makes guilty all his sons; thy merit, 290
Imputed, shall absolve them who renounce
Their own both righteous and unrighteous deeds,
And live in thee transplanted, and from thee
Receive new life. So Man, as is most just,
Shall satisfy for Man, be judged and die, 295
And dying rise, and rising with him raise
His brethren, ransomed with his own dear life.
So heavenly love shall outdo hellish hate,
Giving to death, and dying to redeem,
So dearly to redeem what hellish hate 300
So easily destroyed, and still destroys
In those who, when they may, accept not grace.
Nor shalt thou, by descending to assume
Man's nature, lessen or degrade thine own.
Because thou hast, though throned in highest bliss
Equal to God, and equally enjoying 306
God-like fruition, quitted all, to save
A world from utter loss, and hast been found
By merit more than birthright Son of God,
Found worthiest to be so by being good, 310
Far more than great or high; because in thee
Love hath abounded more than glory abounds;
Therefore thy humiliation shall exalt
With thee thy manhood also to this throne:
Here shalt thou sit incarnate, here shalt reign 315
Both God and Man, Son both of God and Man,
Anointed universal King; all power
I give thee; reign for ever, and assume

255 **maugre:** despite

Thy merits; under thee, as head supreme,
Thrones, princedoms, powers, dominions, I reduce:
All knees to thee shall bow, of them that bide 321
In heaven, or earth, or under earth in hell.
When thou, attended gloriously from heaven,
Shalt in the sky appear, and from thee send
The summoning archangels to proclaim 325
Thy dread tribunal; forthwith from all winds,
The living, and forthwith the cited dead
Of all past ages, to the general doom
Shall hasten; such a peal shall rouse their sleep.
Then, all thy saints assembled, thou shalt judge 330
Bad men and angels; they, arraigned, shall sink
Beneath thy sentence; hell, her numbers full,
Thenceforth shall be for ever shut. Meanwhile
The world shall burn, and from her ashes spring
New heaven and earth, wherein the just shall dwell,
And, after all their tribulations long, 336
See golden days, fruitful of golden deeds,
With joy and peace triumphing, and fair truth.
Then thou thy regal sceptre shalt lay by,
For regal sceptre then no more shall need, 340
God shall be all in all. But, all ye Gods,
Adore Him, who to compass all this dies;
Adore the Son, and honour Him as me.'
    No sooner had the Almighty ceased, but all
The multitude of angels, with a shout 345
Loud as from numbers without number, sweet
As from blest voices, uttering joy, heaven rung
With jubilee, and loud hosannas filled
The eternal regions: Lowly reverent
Towards either throne they bow, and to the ground
With solemn adoration down they cast 351
Their crowns inwove with amarant and gold;
Immortal amarant, a flower which once
In paradise, fast by the tree of life,
Began to bloom; but soon for man's offence 355
To heaven removed, where first it grew, there grows,
And flowers aloft shading the fount of life,
And where the river of bliss through midst of heaven
Rolls o'er Elysian flowers her amber stream;
With these that never fade the spirits elect 360
Bind their resplendent locks inwreathed with beams;
Now in loose garlands thick thrown off, the bright
Pavement, that like a sea of jasper shone,
Impurpled with celestial roses smiled.
Then, crowned again, their golden harps they took,
Harps ever tuned, that glittering by their side 366
Like quivers hung, and with preamble sweet
Of charming symphony they introduce
Their sacred song, and waken raptures high;
No voice exempt, no voice but well could join 370
Melodious part, such concord is in heaven.
    Thee, Father, first they sung omnipotent,
Immutable, immortal, infinite,

352 **amarant:** a purple flower

Eternal King; the Author of all being,
Fountain of light, Thyself invisible 375
Amidst the glorious brightness where Thou sit'st
Throned inaccessible, but when Thou shade'st
The full blaze of Thy beams, and, through a cloud
Drawn round about thee like a radiant shrine,
Dark with excessive bright Thy skirts appear, 380
Yet dazzle heaven, that brightest seraphim
Approach not, but with both wings veil their eyes.
Thee next they sang of all creation first,
Begotten Son, divine similitude,
In whose conspicuous count'nance, without cloud
Made visible, th'Almighty Father shines, 386
Whom else no creature can behold; on thee
Impressed the effulgence of His glory abides,
Transfused on Thee His ample spirit rests.
He heaven of heavens and all the powers therein
By Thee created; and by Thee threw down 391
The aspiring dominations: Thou that day
Thy Father's dreadful thunder didst not spare,
Nor stop Thy flaming chariot-wheels, that shook
Heaven's everlasting frame, while o'er the necks 395
Thou drovest of warring angels disarrayed.
Back from pursuit Thy powers with loud acclaim
Thee only extolled, Son of Thy Father's might,
To execute fierce vengeance on His foes,
Not so on Man: Him through their malice fallen, 400
Father of mercy and grace, thou didst not doom
So strictly, but much more to pity incline:
No sooner did Thy dear and only Son
Perceive Thee purposed not to doom frail Man
So strictly, but much more to pity inclined, 405
He to appease Thy wrath, and end the strife
Of mercy and justice in Thy face discerned,
Regardless of the bliss wherein He sat
Second to Thee, offered Himself to die
For Man's offence. O unexampled love, 410
Love nowhere to be found less than divine!
Hail, Son of God, Saviour of Men! Thy name
Shall be the copious matter of my song
Henceforth, and never shall my heart Thy praise
Forget, nor from Thy Father's praise disjoin. 415
    Thus they in heaven, above the starry sphere,
Their happy hours in joy and hymning spent.
Meanwhile upon the firm opacous globe
Of this round world, whose first convex divides
The luminous inferior orbs, enclosed 420
From Chaos, and the inroad of Darkness old,
Satan alighted walks. A globe far off
It seemed, now seems a boundless continent
Dark, waste, and wild, under the frown of Night
Starless exposed, and ever-threat'ning storms 425
Of Chaos blustering round, inclement sky;
Save on that side which from the wall of heaven,
Though distant far, some small reflection gains
Of glimmering air less vexed with tempest loud:
Here walked the fiend at large in spacious field. 430

As when a vulture on Imaus bred,
Whose snowy ridge the roving Tartar bounds,
Dislodging from a region scarce of prey
To gorge the flesh of lambs or yeanling kids,
On hills where flocks are fed, flies toward the springs
Of Ganges or Hydaspes, Indian streams;　436
But in his way lights on the barren plains
Of Sericana, where Chineses drive
With sails and wind their cany wagons light:
So, on this windy sea of land, the fiend　440
Walked up and down alone, bent on his prey;
Alone, for other creature in this place,
Living or lifeless, to be found was none;
None yet, but store hereafter from the earth
Up hither like aerial vapours flew　445
Of all things transitory and vain, when sin
With vanity had filled the works of men:
Both all things vain, and all who in vain things
Built their fond hopes of glory or lasting fame,
Or happiness in this or th'other life;　450
All who have their reward on earth, the fruits
Of painful superstition and blind zeal,
Nought seeking but the praise of men, here find
Fit retribution, empty as their deeds;
All th'unaccomplished works of Nature's hand,　455
Abortive, monstrous, or unkindly mixed,
Dissolved on earth, fleet hither, and in vain,
Till final dissolution, wander here;
Not in the neighbouring moon as some have dreamed;
Those argent fields more likely habitants,　460
Translated saints, or middle spirits hold
Betwixt the angelical and human kind.
Hither of ill-joined sons and daughters born
First from the ancient world those giants came
With many a vain exploit, though then renowned:　465
The builders next of Babel on the plain
Of Sennaar, and still with vain design,
New Babels, had they wherewithal, would build:
Others came single; he, who, to be deemed
A god, leaped fondly into Etna flames,　470
Empedocles; and he, who, to enjoy
Plato's Elysium, leaped into the sea,
Cleombrotus; and many more too long,
Embryos, and idiots, eremites, and friars
White, black, and grey, with all their trumpery.　475
Here pilgrims roam, that strayed so far to seek
In Golgotha Him dead, who lives in heaven;
And they, who to be sure of paradise,
Dying, put on the weeds of Dominic,
Or in Franciscan think to pass disguised;　480

They pass the planets seven, and pass the fixed,
And that crystalline sphere whose balance weighs
The trepidation talked, and that first moved;
And now St Peter at heaven's wicket seems
To wait them with his keys, and now at foot　485
Of heaven's ascent they lift their feet, when lo!
A violent cross-wind from either coast
Blows them transverse, ten thousand leagues awry
Into the devious air: Then might ye see
Cowls, hoods, and habits, with their wearers, tossed
And fluttered into rags; then relics, beads,　491
Indulgences, dispenses, pardons, bulls,
The sport of winds: All these, upwhirled aloft,
Fly o'er the backside of the world far off
Into a limbo large and broad, since called　495
The paradise of fools, to few unknown
Long after; now unpeopled, and untrod.
All this dark globe the fiend found as he passed,
And long he wandered, till at last a gleam
Of dawning light turned thitherward in haste　500
His travelled steps: far distant he descries
Ascending by degrees magnificent
Up to the wall of heaven a structure high;
At top whereof, but far more rich, appeared
The work as of a kingly palace-gate,　505
With frontispiece of diamond and gold
Embellished; thick with sparkling orient gems
The portal shone, inimitable on earth
By model, or by shading pencil, drawn.
These stairs were such as whereon Jacob saw　510
Angels ascending and descending, bands
Of guardians bright, when he from Esau fled
To Padan-Aram, in the field of Luz
Dreaming by night under the open sky
And waking cried, 'This is the gate of heaven.'　515
Each stair mysteriously was meant, nor stood
There always, but drawn up to heaven sometimes
Viewless; and underneath a bright sea flowed
Of jasper, or of liquid pearl, whereon
Who after came from earth, sailing arrived　520
Wafted by angels, or flew o'er the lake
Rapt in a chariot drawn by fiery steeds.
The stairs were then let down, whether to dare
The fiend by easy ascent, or aggravate
His sad exclusion from the doors of bliss:　525
Direct against which opened from beneath,
Just o'er the blissful seat of paradise,
A passage down to the earth, a passage wide,
Wider by far than that of after-times
Over Mount Sion, and, though that were large,　530
Over the Promised Land to God so dear;
By which, to visit oft those happy tribes,

---

431 **Imaus:** mountains in Asia 434 **yeanling:** newly born 474 **eremites:**
hermits 477 **Golgotha:** where Christ was crucified and then buried
479 **weeds:** robes 479–480 **Dominic . . . Franciscan:** Roman Catholic
Orders of friars

481–483 a reference to the sign of Libra, the scales, and to the clock-
like workings of the Solar System 484 **wicket:** gate 492 **bulls:** papal
edicts 510–515 a reference to Jacob, who, while dreaming, saw the
vision of a ladder between Heaven and Earth after he had cheated
Esau (Genesis: 27–28)

On high behests his angels to and fro
Passed frequent, and his eye with choice regard
From Paneas, the fount of Jordan's flood,   535
To Beersaba, where the Holy Land
Borders on Egypt and the Arabian shore;
So wide the opening seemed, where bounds were set
To darkness, such as bound the ocean wave.
Satan from hence, now on the lower stair,   540
That scaled by steps of gold to heaven-gate,
Looks down with wonder at the sudden view
Of all this world at once. As when a scout,
Through dark and desert ways with peril gone
All night, at last by break of cheerful dawn   545
Obtains the brow of some high-climbing hill,
Which to his eye discovers unaware
The goodly prospect of some foreign land
First seen, or some renowned metropolis
With glistering spires and pinnacles adorned,   550
Which now the rising sun gilds with his beams:
Such wonder seized, though after heaven seen,
The spirit malign, but much more envy seized,
At sight of all this world beheld so fair.
Round he surveys (and well might, where he stood   555
So high above the circling canopy
Of night's extended shade), from eastern point
Of Libra to the fleecy star that bears
Andromeda far off Atlantic seas
Beyond th'horizon; then from pole to pole   560
He views in breadth, and without longer pause
Down right into the world's first region throws
His flight precipitant, and winds with ease
Through the pure marble air his oblique way
Amongst innumerable stars, that shone   565
Stars distant, but nigh hand seemed other worlds;
Or other worlds they seemed, or happy isles,
Like those Hesperian gardens famed of old,
Fortunate fields, and groves, and flowery vales,
Thrice-happy isles; but who dwelt happy there   570
He stayed not to inquire. Above them all
The golden sun, in splendour likest heaven,
Allured his eye; thither his course he bends
Through the calm firmament (but up or down,
By centre, or eccentric, hard to tell,   575
Or longitude), where the great luminary
Aloof the vulgar constellations thick,
That from his lordly eye keep distance due,
Dispenses light from far; they, as they move
Their starry dance in numbers that compute   580
Days, months, and years, towards his all-cheering
   lamp
Turn swift their various motions, or are turned
By his magnetic beam, that gently warms
The universe, and to each inward part
With gentle penetration, though unseen,   585

Shoots invisible virtue even to the deep;
So wonderously was set his station bright.
There lands the fiend, a spot like which perhaps
Astronomer in the sun's lucent orb
Through his glazed optic tube yet never saw.   590
The place he found beyond expression bright,
Compared with aught on earth, metal or stone;
Not all parts like, but all alike informed
With radiant light, as glowing iron with fire;
If metal, part seemed gold, part silver clear;   595
If stone, carbuncle most or chrysolite,
Ruby or topaz, to the twelve that shone
In Aaron's breast-plate, and a stone besides
Imagined rather oft than elsewhere seen,
That stone, or like to that which here below   600
Philosophers in vain so long have sought,
In vain, though by their powerful art they bind
Volatile Hermes, and call up unbound
In various shapes old Proteus from the sea,
Drained through a limbeck to his native form.   605
What wonder then if fields and regions here
Breathe forth elixir pure, and rivers run
Potable gold, when with one virtuous touch
The arch-chemic sun, so far from us remote,
Produces, with terrestrial humour mixed,   610
Here in the dark so many precious things
Of colour glorious, and effect so rare?
Here matter new to gaze the devil met
Undazzled; far and wide his eye commands;
For sight no obstacle found here, nor shade,   615
But all sun-shine, as when his beams at noon
Culminate from the equator, as they now
Shot upward still direct, whence no way round
Shadow from body opaque can fall; and the air,
Nowhere so clear, sharpened his visual ray   620
To objects distant far, whereby he soon
Saw within ken a glorious angel stand,
The same whom John saw also in the sun:
His back was turned, but not his brightness hid;
Of beaming sunny rays a golden tiar   625
Circled his head, nor less his locks behind
Illustrious on his shoulders fledge with wings
Lay waving round; on some great charge employed
He seemed, or fixed in cogitation deep.
Glad was the spirit impure, as now in hope   630
To find who might direct his wandering flight
To paradise, the happy seat of Man,
His journey's end and our beginning woe.
But first he casts to change his proper shape,
Which else might work him danger or delay: 635

---

559 **Andromeda:** a northern constellation   568–569 Hesperides was entrusted by Jupiter to guard his gardens; however, he failed and its apples were stolen

596–598 a reference to Exodus (28) and Aaron's foursquare breastplate of judgment   600 **stone:** the 'philosopher's stone', necessary for alchemists in turning base metals into gold   603 **Hermes:** Mercury, used by alchemists   604 **Proteus:** a sea god who could change shape   605 **limbeck:** a still   609 **arch-chemic:** the greatest alchemist   623 a reference to Revelations (19:17)   625 **tiar:** crown

And now a stripling cherub he appears,
Not of the prime, yet such as in his face
Youth smiled celestial, and to every limb
Suitable grace diffused, so well he feigned:
Under a coronet his flowing hair   640
In curls on either cheek played; wings he wore
Of many a coloured plume, sprinkled with gold;
His habit fit for speed succinct, and held
Before his decent steps a silver wand.
He drew not nigh unheard; the angel bright,   645
Ere he drew nigh, his radiant visage turned,
Admonished by his ear, and straight was known
The archangel Uriel, one of the seven
Who in God's presence, nearest to His throne,
Stand ready at command, and are His eyes   650
That run through all the heavens, or down to the
    earth
Bear his swift errands over moist and dry,
O'er sea and land: him Satan thus accosts.
  'Uriel, for thou of those seven spirits that stand
In sight of God's high throne, gloriously bright,   655
The first art wont His great authentic will
Interpreter through highest heaven to bring,
Where all His sons thy embassy attend;
And here art likeliest by supreme decree
Like honour to obtain, and as His eye   660
To visit oft this new creation round;
Unspeakable desire to see, and know
All these His wond'rous works, but chiefly Man,
His chief delight and favour, him for whom
All these His works so wond'rous He ordained,   665
Hath brought me from the choirs of cherubim
Alone thus wandering. Brightest Seraph, tell
In which of all these shining orbs hath Man
His fixèd seat, or fixèd seat hath none,
But all these shining orbs his choice to dwell;   670
That I may find him, and with secret gaze
Or open admiration him behold,
On whom the great Creator hath bestowed
Worlds, and on whom hath all these graces poured;
That both in him and all things, as is meet,   675
The universal Maker we may praise;
Who justly hath driven out His rebel foes
To deepest hell, and, to repair that loss,
Created this new happy race of Men
To serve him better: Wise are all His ways.'   680
  So spake the false dissembler unperceived;
For neither man nor angel can discern
Hypocrisy, the only evil that walks
Invisible, except to God alone,
By His permissive will, through heaven and earth;
And oft, though wisdom wake, suspicion sleeps   686
At wisdom's gate, and to simplicity
Resigns her charge, while goodness thinks no ill
Where no ill seems: which now for once beguiled
Uriel, though regent of the sun, and held   690

The sharpest-sighted spirit of all in heaven;
Who to the fraudulent impostor foul,
In his uprightness, answer thus returned.
  'Fair Angel, thy desire, which tends to know
The works of God, thereby to glorify   695
The great Work-master, leads to no excess
That reaches blame, but rather merits praise
The more it seems excess, that led thee hither
From thy empyreal mansion thus alone,
To witness with thine eyes what some perhaps,   700
Contented with report, hear only in heaven:
For wonderful indeed are all His works,
Pleasant to know, and worthiest to be all
Had in remembrance always with delight;
But what created mind can comprehend   705
Their number, or the wisdom infinite
That brought them forth, but hid their causes deep?
I saw when at His word the formless mass,
This world's material mould, came to a heap:
Confusion heard His voice, and wild uproar   710
Stood ruled, stood vast infinitude confined;
Till at His second bidding darkness fled,
Light shone, and order from disorder sprung:
Swift to their several quarters hasted then
The cumbrous elements, earth, flood, air, fire;   715
And this ethereal quintessence of heaven
Flew upward, spirited with various forms,
That rolled orbicular, and turned to stars
Numberless, as thou seest, and how they move;
Each had his place appointed, each his course;   720
The rest in circuit walls this universe.
Look downward on that globe, whose hither side
With light from hence, though but reflected, shines;
That place is earth, the seat of Man; that light
His day, which else, as th'other hemisphere,   725
Night would invade; but there the neighbouring moon
(So call that opposite fair star) her aid
Timely interposes, and her monthly round
Still ending, still renewing, through mid-heaven,
With borrowed light her countenance triform   730
Hence fills and empties to enlighten the earth,
And in her pale dominion checks the night.
That spot, to which I point, is paradise,
Adam's abode; those lofty shades, his bower.
Thy way thou canst not miss, me mine requires.'   735
  Thus said, he turned; and Satan, bowing low,
As to superior spirits is wont in heaven,
Where honour due and reverence none neglects,
Took leave, and toward the coast of earth beneath,
Down from th'ecliptic, sped with hoped success,   740
Throws his steep flight in many an airy wheel;
Nor staid, till on Niphates' top he lights.

730 **triform:** the three phases of the moon: waxing, full and waning
740 **ecliptic:** here meaning the path of the sun   742 **Niphates:**
a mountain in Armenia

BOOK FOUR

Oh, for that warning voice, which he, who saw
The Apocalypse, heard cry in heaven aloud,
Then when the dragon, put to second rout,
Came furious down to be revenged on men,
Woe to the inhabitants on earth! that now,   5
While time was, our first parents had been warned
The coming of their secret foe, and 'scaped,
Haply so 'scaped his mortal snare: For now
Satan, now first inflamed with rage, came down,
The tempter ere th'accuser of mankind,   10
To wreak on innocent frail Man his loss
Of that first battle, and his flight to hell:
Yet, not rejoicing in his speed, though bold
Far off and fearless, nor with cause to boast,
Begins his dire attempt; which nigh the birth   15
Now rolling boils in his tumultuous breast,
And like a devilish engine back recoils
Upon himself; horror and doubt distract
His troubled thoughts, and from the bottom stir
The hell within him; for within him hell   20
He brings, and round about him, nor from hell
One step, no more than from himself, can fly
By change of place. Now conscience wakes despair,
That slumbered; wakes the bitter memory
Of what he was, what is, and what must be   25
Worse; of worse deeds worse sufferings must ensue.
Sometimes towards Eden, which now in his view
Lay pleasant, his grieved look he fixes sad;
Sometimes towards heaven, and the full-blazing sun,
Which now sat high in his meridian tower: 30
Then, much revolving, thus in sighs began.

BOOK FOUR – THE ARGUMENT: Satan now in prospect of Eden, and nigh the place where he must now attempt the bold enterprise which he undertook alone against God and Man, falls into many doubts with himself, and many passions, fear, envy, and despair; but at length confirms himself in evil, journeys on to Paradise, whose outward prospect and situation is described, overleaps the bounds, sits in the shape of a Cormorant on the Tree of life, as highest in the Garden to look down upon. The Garden describ'd; Satan's first sight of Adam and Eve; his wonder at their excellent form and happy state, but with resolution to work their fall; overhears their discourse, thence gathers that the Tree of knowledge was forbidden them to eat of, under penalty of death; and thereon intends to found his Temptation, by seducing them to transgress: then leaves them a while, to know further of their state by some other means. Meanwhile Uriel descending on a Sunbeam warns Gabriel, who had in charge the Gate of Paradise, that some evil spirit had escap'd the Deep, and past at Noon by his Sphere in the shape of a good Angel down to Paradise, discovered after by his furious gestures in the Mount. Gabriel promises to find him ere morning. Night coming on, Adam and Eve discourse of going to their rest: their Bower describ'd; their Evening worship. Gabriel drawing forth his Bands of Night-watch to walk the round of Paradise, appoints two strong Angels to Adams Bower, least the evil spirit should be there doing some harm to Adam or Eve sleeping; there they find him at the ear of Eve, tempting her in a dream, and bring him, though unwilling, to Gabriel; by whom question'd, he scornfully answers, prepares resistance, but hinder'd by a Sign from Heaven, flies out of Paradise

'O thou, that, with surpassing glory crowned,
Lookest from thy sole dominion like the God
Of this new world; at whose sight all the stars
Hide their diminished heads; to thee I call,   35
But with no friendly voice, and add thy name,
Of Sun! to tell thee how I hate thy beams,
That bring to my remembrance from what state
I fell, how glorious once above thy sphere;
Till pride and worse ambition threw me down   40
Warring in heaven against heaven's matchless King.
Ah, wherefore! He deserved no such return
From me, whom He created what I was
In that bright eminence, and with His good
Upbraided none; nor was His service hard.   45
What could be less than to afford Him praise,
The easiest recompense, and pay Him thanks,
How due! yet all His good proved ill in me,
And wrought but malice; lifted up so high
I 'sdained subjection, and thought one step higher   50
Would set me highest, and in a moment quit
The debt immense of endless gratitude,
So burdensome still paying, still to owe,
Forgetful what from Him I still received,
And understood not that a grateful mind   55
By owing owes not, but still pays, at once
Indebted and discharged; what burden then
Oh, had His powerful destiny ordained
Me some inferior angel, I had stood
Then happy; no unbounded hope had raised   60
Ambition! Yet why not some other power
As great might have aspired, and me, though mean,
Drawn to His part; but other powers as great
Fell not, but stand unshaken, from within
Or from without, to all temptations armed.   65
Hadst thou the same free will and power to stand?
Thou hadst: whom hast thou then or what to accuse,
But heaven's free love dealt equally to all?
Be then His love accursed, since love or hate,
To me alike, it deals eternal woe.   70
Nay, cursed be thou; since against His thy will
Chose freely what it now so justly rues.
Me miserable! which way shall I fly
Infinite wrath, and infinite despair?
Which way I fly is hell; myself am hell;   75
And, in the lowest deep, a lower deep
Still threatening to devour me opens wide,
To which the hell I suffer seems a heaven.
Oh, then, at last relent: Is there no place
Left for repentance, none for pardon left?   80
None left but by submission; and that word
Disdain forbids me, and my dread of shame
Among the spirits beneath, whom I seduced
With other promises and other vaunts
Then to submit, boasting I could subdue   85
The Omnipotent. Ay me! they little know

50 'sdained: disdained

How dearly I abide that boast so vain,
Under what torments inwardly I groan,
While they adore me on the throne of hell.
With diadem and sceptre high advanced, 90
The lower still I fall, only supreme
In misery: Such joy ambition finds.
But say I could repent, and could obtain,
By act of grace, my former state; how soon
Would height recall high thoughts, how soon unsay 95
What feigned submission swore? Ease would recant
Vows made in pain, as violent and void.
For never can true reconcilement grow,
Where wounds of deadly hate have pierced so deep:
Which would but lead me to a worse relapse 100
And heavier fall: so should I purchase dear
Short intermission bought with double smart.
This knows my Punisher; therefore as far
From granting He, as I from begging, peace;
All hope excluded thus, behold, in stead 105
Of us, out-cast, exiled, His new delight,
Mankind created, and for him this world.
So farewell, hope; and with hope farewell, fear;
Farewell, remorse! all good to me is lost;
Evil, be thou my good; by thee at least 110
Divided empire with heaven's King I hold,
By thee, and more than half perhaps will reign;
As Man ere long, and this new world, shall know.'
   Thus while he spake, each passion dimmed his face
Thrice changed with pale, ire, envy, and despair; 115
Which marred his borrowed visage, and betrayed
Him counterfeit, if any eye beheld.
For heavenly minds from such distempers foul
Are ever clear. Whereof he soon aware,
Each perturbation smoothed with outward calm, 120
Artificer of fraud; and was the first
That practised falsehood under saintly show,
Deep malice to conceal, couched with revenge:
Yet not enough had practised to deceive
Uriel once warned; whose eye pursued him down 125
The way he went, and on the Assyrian mount
Saw him disfigured, more than could befall
Spirit of happy sort; his gestures fierce
He marked and mad demeanour, then alone,
As he supposed, all unobserved, unseen. 130
So on he fares, and to the border comes
Of Eden, where delicious paradise,
Now nearer, crowns with her enclosure green,
As with a rural mound, the champaign head
Of a steep wilderness, whose hairy sides 135
With thicket overgrown, grotesque and wild,
Access denied; and overhead upgrew
Insuperable height of loftiest shade,
Cedar, and pine, and fir, and branching palm,
A sylvan scene, and, as the ranks ascend, 140

Shade above shade, a woody theatre
Of stateliest view. Yet higher than their tops
The verdurous wall of paradise upsprung;
Which to our general sire gave prospect large
Into his nether empire neighbouring round. 145
And higher than that wall a circling row
Of goodliest trees, loaden with fairest fruit,
Blossoms and fruits at once of golden hue,
Appeared, with gay enamelled colours mixed:
On which the sun more glad impressed his beams 150
Than in fair evening cloud, or humid bow,
When God hath showered the earth; so lovely seemed
That landskip. And of pure now purer air
Meets his approach, and to the heart inspires
Vernal delight and joy, able to drive 155
All sadness but despair. Now gentle gales,
Fanning their odoriferous wings, dispense
Native perfumes, and whisper whence they stole
Those balmy spoils. As when to them who fail
Beyond the Cape of Hope, and now are past 160
Mozambic, off at sea north-east winds blow
Sabean odours from the spicy shore
Of Araby the blest; with such delay
Well pleased they slack their course, and many a league
Cheered with the grateful smell old Ocean smiles: 165
So entertained those odorous sweets the fiend,
Who came their bane; though with them better pleased
Than Asmodeus with the fishy fume
That drove him, though enamoured, from the spouse
Of Tobit's son, and with a vengeance sent 170
From Media post to Egypt, there fast bound.
   Now to the ascent of that steep savage hill
Satan had journeyed on, pensive and slow;
But further way found none, so thick entwined,
As one continued brake, the undergrowth 175
Of shrubs and tangling bushes had perplexed
All path of man or beast that passed that way.
One gate there only was, and that looked east
On the other side: which when the arch-felon saw,
Due entrance he disdained; and, in contempt, 180
At one flight bound high over-leaped all bound
Of hill or highest wall, and sheer within
Lights on his feet. As when a prowling wolf,
Whom hunger drives to seek new haunt for prey,
Watching where shepherds pen their flocks at eve 185
In hurdled cotes amid the field secure,
Leaps o'er the fence with ease into the fold:
Or as a thief, bent to unhoard the cash
Of some rich burgher, whose substantial doors,
Cross-barred and bolted fast, fear no assault, 190

126 **Assyrian mount:** Niphates 134 **champaign:** unenclosed

151 **humid bow:** rainbow 162 **Sabean:** from Sheba 166–171 this passage refers to the Apocryphal book, *Tobit*. His son Tobias married Sara, whose previous husbands were killed by the spirit Asmodeus. Tobias drove the spirit away by burning the heart and liver of a fish

In at the window climbs, or o'er the tiles:
So clomb this first grand thief into God's fold;
So since into His church lewd hirelings climb.
Thence up he flew, and on the tree of life,
The middle tree and highest there that grew,   195
Sat like a cormorant; yet not true life
Thereby regained, but sat devising death
To them who lived; nor on the virtue thought
Of that life-giving plant, but only used
For prospect, what well used had been the pledge   200
Of immortality. So little knows
Any, but God alone, to value right
The good before him, but perverts best things
To worst abuse, or to their meanest use.
Beneath him with new wonder now he views,   205
To all delight of human sense exposed,
In narrow room, Nature's whole wealth, yea more,
A heaven on earth. For blissful paradise
Of God the garden was, by Him in the east
Of Eden planted; Eden stretched her line   210
From Auran eastward to the royal towers
Of great Seleucia, built by Grecian kings,
Of where the sons of Eden long before
Dwelt in Telassar. In this pleasant soil
His far more pleasant garden God ordained;   215
Out of the fertile ground He caused to grow
All trees of noblest kind for sight, smell, taste;
And all amid them stood the tree of life,
High eminent, blooming ambrosial fruit
Of vegetable gold; and next to life,   220
Our death, the tree of knowledge, grew fast by,
Knowledge of good bought dear by knowing ill.
Southward through Eden went a river large,
Nor changed his course, but through the shaggy hill
Passed underneath engulfed; for God had thrown   225
That mountain as his garden-mould high raised
Upon the rapid current, which, through veins
Of porous earth with kindly thirst up-drawn,
Rose a fresh fountain, and with many a rill
Watered the garden; thence united fell   230
Down the steep glade, and met the nether flood,
Which from his darksome passage now appears,
And now, divided into four main streams,
Runs diverse, wandering many a famous realm
And country, whereof here needs no account;   235
But rather to tell how, if art could tell,
How from that sapphire fount the crispèd brooks,
Rolling on orient pearl and sands of gold,
With mazy error under pendant shades
Ran nectar, visiting each plant, and fed   240
Flowers worthy of paradise, which not nice Art
In beds and curious knots, but Nature boon
Poured forth profuse on hill, and dale, and plain,
Both where the morning sun first warmly smote
The open field, and where the unpierced shade   245

Imbrowned the noontide bowers. Thus was this place
A happy rural seat of various view;
Groves whose rich trees wept odorous gums and balm,
Others whose fruit, burnished with golden rind,
Hung amiable, Hesperian fables true,   250
If true, here only, and of delicious taste:
Betwixt them lawns, or level downs, and flocks
Grazing the tender herb, were interposed,
Or palmy hillock; or the flowery lap
Of some irriguous valley spread her store,   255
Flowers of all hue, and without thorn the rose:
Another side, umbrageous grots and caves
Of cool recess, o'er which the mantling vine
Lays forth her purple grape, and gently creeps
Luxuriant; meanwhile murmuring waters fall   260
Down the slope hills, dispersed, or in a lake,
That to the fringèd bank with myrtle crowned
Her crystal mirror holds, unite their streams.
The birds their choir apply; airs, vernal airs,
Breathing the smell of field and grove, attune   265
The trembling leaves, while universal Pan,
Knit with the Graces and the Hours in dance,
Led on the eternal spring. Not that fair field
Of Enna, where Proserpine gathering flowers,
Herself a fairer flower by gloomy Dis   270
Was gathered, which cost Ceres all that pain
To seek her through the world; nor that sweet grove
Of Daphne by Orontes, and the inspired
Castalian spring, might with this paradise
Of Eden strive; nor that Nyseian isle   275
Girt with the river Triton, where old Cham,
Whom Gentiles Ammon call and Libyan Jove,
Hid Amalthea, and her florid son
Young Bacchus, from his stepdame Rhea's eye;
Nor where Abassin kings their issue guard,   280
Mount Amara, though this by some supposed
True paradise under the Ethiop line
By Nilus' head, enclosed with shining rock,
A whole day's journey high, but wide remote
From this Assyrian garden, where the fiend   285
Saw, undelighted, all delight, all kind
Of living creatures, new to sight, and strange
Two of far nobler shape, erect and tall,
Godlike erect, with native honour clad
In naked majesty seemed lords of all: 290
And worthy seemed; for in their looks divine
The image of their glorious Maker shone,
Truth, wisdom, sanctitude severe and pure
(Severe, but in true filial freedom placed),
Whence true authority in men; though both   295
Not equal, as their sex not equal seemed;
For contemplation he and valour formed;

209–216 Milton places Egypt in Iraq

266 **Pan:** god of nature   268 **eternal spring:** there is only one season in Eden   268–272 the rape of Proserpine (the daughter of Ceres) by Dis, in Enna   272–274 the grove, Daphne, near Orontes   276 **Cham:** son of Noah   279 **Rhea:** mother of Bacchus   282 **Ethiop line:** the Equator   283 **Nilus' head:** the source of the Nile

For softness she and sweet attractive grace;
He for God only, she for God in him:
His fair large front and eye sublime declared   300
Absolute rule; and hyacinthine locks
Round from his parted forelock manly hung
Clustering, but not beneath his shoulders broad:
She, as a veil, down to the slender waist
Her unadornèd golden tresses wore   305
Dishevelled, but in wanton ringlets waved
As the vine curls her tendrils, which implied
Subjection, but required with gentle sway,
And by her yielded, by him best received,
Yielded with coy submission, modest pride,   310
And sweet, reluctant, amorous delay.
Nor those mysterious parts were then concealed;
Then was not guilty shame, dishonest shame
Of Nature's works, honour dishonourable,
Sin-bred, how have ye troubled all mankind   315
With shows instead, mere shows of seeming pure,
And banished from man's life his happiest life,
Simplicity and spotless innocence!
So passed they naked on, nor shunned the sight
Of god or angel; for they thought no ill: 320
So hand in hand they passed, the loveliest pair,
That ever since in love's embraces met;
Adam the goodliest man of men since born
His sons, the fairest of her daughters Eve.
Under a tuft of shade that on a green   325
Stood whispering soft, by a fresh fountain side
They sat them down; and, after no more toil
Of their sweet gardening labour than sufficed
To recommend cool Zephyr, and made ease
More easy, wholesome thirst and appetite   330
More grateful, to their supper-fruits they fell,
Nectarine fruits which the compliant boughs
Yielded them, side-long as they sat recline
On the soft downy bank damasked with flowers:
The savoury pulp they chew, and in the rind,   335
Still as they thirsted, scoop the brimming stream;
Nor gentle purpose, nor endearing smiles
Wanted, nor youthful dalliance, as beseems
Fair couple, linked in happy nuptial league,
Alone as they. About them frisking played   340
All beasts of the earth, since wild, and of all chase
In wood or wilderness, forest or den;
Sporting the lion ramped, and in his paw
Dandled the kid; bears, tigers, ounces, pards,
Gambolled before them; th'unwieldy elephant,   345
To make them mirth, used all his might, and wreathed
His lithe proboscis; close the serpent sly,
Insinuating, wove with Gordian twine
His braided train, and of his fatal guile
Gave proof unheeded; others on the grass   350
Couched, and now filled with pasture gazing sat,
Or bedward ruminating; for the sun,

329 **Zephyr**: the west wind   344 **ounces**: lynxes   **pards**: leopards
348 **Gordian**: the Gordian knot

Declined, was hasting now with prone career
To the ocean isles, and in the ascending scale
Of heaven the stars that usher evening rose: 355
When Satan still in gaze, as first he stood,
Scarce thus at length failed speech recovered sad.
   'Oh hell! what do mine eyes with grief behold!
Into our room of bliss thus high advanced
Creatures of other mould, earth-born perhaps,   360
Not spirits, yet to heavenly spirits bright
Little inferior; whom my thoughts pursue
With wonder, and could love, so lively shines
In them divine resemblance, and such grace
The hand that formed them on their shape hath
        poured.   365
Ah! gentle pair, ye little think how nigh
Your change approaches, when all these delights
Will vanish, and deliver ye to woe;
More woe, the more your taste is now of joy;
Happy, but for so happy ill secured   370
Long to continue, and this high seat your heaven
Ill fenced for heaven to keep out such a foe
As now is entered; yet no purposed foe
To you, whom I could pity thus forlorn,
Though I unpitied. League with you I seek,   375
And mutual amity, so strait, so close,
That I with you must dwell, or you with me
Henceforth; my dwelling haply may not please,
Like this fair paradise, your sense; yet such
Accept your Maker's work; He gave it me,   380
Which I as freely give: hell shall unfold,
To entertain you two, her widest gates,
And send forth all her kings; there will be room,
Not like these narrow limits, to receive
Your numerous offspring; if no better place,   385
Thank Him who puts me loath to this revenge
On you who wrong me not for Him who wronged.
And should I at your harmless innocence
Melt, as I do, yet public reason just,
Honour and empire with revenge enlarged,   390
By conquering this new world, compels me now
To do what else, though damned, I should abhor.'
   So spake the fiend, and with necessity,
The tyrant's plea, excused his devilish deeds.
Then from his lofty stand on that high tree   395
Down he alights among the sportful herd
Of those four-footed kinds, himself now one,
Now other, as their shape served best his end
Nearer to view his prey, and, unespied,
To mark what of their state he more might learn,   400
By word or action marked. About them round
A lion now he stalks with fiery glare;
Then as a tiger, who by chance hath spied
In some purlieu two gentle fawns at play,
Straight couches close, then, rising, changes oft   405
His couchant watch, as one who chose his ground,
Whence rushing, he might surest seize them both,
Griped in each paw: when, Adam first of men

To first of women Eve thus moving speech,
Turned him, all ear to hear new utterance flow.   410
    'Sole partner, and sole part, of all these joys,
Dearer thyself than all; needs must the Power
That made us, and for us this ample world,
Be infinitely good, and of His good
As liberal and free as infinite;   415
That raised us from the dust, and placed us here
In all this happiness, who at His hand
Have nothing merited, nor can perform
Aught whereof He hath need; He who requires
From us no other service than to keep   420
This one, this easy charge, of all the trees
In paradise that bear delicious fruit
So various, not to taste that only tree
Of knowledge, planted by the tree of life;
So near grows death to life, whate'er death is,   425
Some dreadful thing no doubt; for well thou knowest
God hath pronounced it death to taste that tree,
The only sign of our obedience left,
Among so many signs of power and rule
Conferred upon us, and dominion given   430
Over all other creatures that possess
Earth, air, and sea. Then let us not think hard
One easy prohibition, who enjoy
Free leave so large to all things else, and choice
Unlimited of manifold delights: 435
But let us ever praise Him, and extol
His bounty, following our delightful task,
To prune these growing plants, and tend these flowers,
Which were it toilsome, yet with thee were sweet.'
    To whom thus Eve replied. 'O thou for whom   440
And from whom I was formed, flesh of thy flesh,
And without whom am to no end, my guide
And head! what thou hast said is just and right.
For we to Him indeed all praises owe,
And daily thanks; I chiefly, who enjoy   445
So far the happier lot, enjoying thee
Pre-eminent by so much odds, while thou
Like consort to thyself canst nowhere find.
That day I oft remember, when from sleep
I first awaked, and found myself reposed   450
Under a shade on flowers, much wondering where
And what I was, whence thither brought, and how.
Not distant far from thence a murmuring sound
Of waters issued from a cave, and spread
Into a liquid plain, then stood unmoved   455
Pure as the expanse of heaven; I thither went
With unexperienced thought, and laid me down
On the green bank, to look into the clear
Smooth lake, that to me seemed another sky.
As I bent down to look, just opposite   460
A shape within the watery gleam appeared,
Bending to look on me. I started back,
It started back; but pleased I soon returned,
Pleased it returned as soon with answering looks
Of sympathy and love. There I had fixed   465

Mine eyes till now, and pined with vain desire,
Had not a voice thus warned me: "What thou seest,
What there thou seest, fair creature, is thyself;
With thee it came and goes: but follow me,
And I will bring thee where no shadow stays   470
Thy coming, and thy soft embraces, he
Whose image thou art; him thou shalt enjoy
Inseparably thine, to him shalt bear
Multitudes like thyself, and thence be called
Mother of human race." What could I do,   475
But follow straight, invisibly thus led?
Till I espied thee, fair indeed and tall,
Under a platane; yet methought less fair,
Less winning soft, less amiably mild,
Than that smooth watery image: Back I turned;   480
Thou following crièdst aloud: "Return, fair Eve;
Whom flyest thou? whom thou flyest, of him thou art,
His flesh, his bone; to give thee being I lent
Out of my side to thee, nearest my heart,
Substantial life, to have thee by my side   485
Henceforth an individual solace dear;
Part of my soul I seek thee, and thee claim
My other half." With that thy gentle hand
Seized mine: I yielded; and from that time see
How beauty is excelled by manly grace,   490
And wisdom, which alone is truly fair.'
    So spake our general mother, and with eyes
Of conjugal attraction unreproved,
And meek surrender, half-embracing leaned
On our first father; half her swelling breast   495
Naked met his, under the flowing gold
Of her loose tresses hid: he in delight
Both of her beauty and submissive charms,
Smiled with superior love, as Jupiter
On Juno smiles, when he impregns the clouds   500
That shed Mayflowers; and pressed her matron lip
With kisses pure: aside the devil turned
For envy; yet with jealous leer malign
Eyed them askance, and to himself thus plained.
    'Sight hateful! sight tormenting! thus these two,   505
Imparadised in one another's arms,
The happier Eden, shall enjoy their fill
Of bliss on bliss; while I to hell am thrust,
Where neither joy nor love, but fierce desire,
Among our other torments not the least,   510
Still unfulfilled with pain of longing pines.
Yet let me not forget what I have gained
From their own mouths. All is not theirs, it seems;
One fatal tree there stands, of knowledge called,
Forbidden them to taste: knowledge forbidden,   515
Suspicious, reasonless. Why should their Lord
Envy them that? Can it be sin to know?
Can it be death? And do they only stand
By ignorance? Is that their happy state,
The proof of their obedience and their faith?   520

478 **platane:** a plane tree. The plane was a symbol of Christ
500 **impregns:** impregnates

Oh, fair foundation laid whereon to build
Their ruin! hence I will excite their minds
With more desire to know, and to reject
Envious commands, invented with design
To keep them low, whom knowledge might exalt   525
Equal with gods: aspiring to be such,
They taste and die. What likelier can ensue
But first with narrow search I must walk round
This garden, and no corner leave unspied;
A chance but chance may lead where I may meet   530
Some wandering spirit of heaven by fountain side,
Or in thick shade retired, from him to draw
What further would be learned. Live while ye may,
Yet happy pair; enjoy, till I return,
Short pleasures, for long woes are to succeed!'   535
    So saying, his proud step he scornful turned,
But with sly circumspection, and began
Through wood, through waste, o'er hill, o'er dale, his
        roam
Meanwhile in utmost longitude, where heaven
With earth and ocean meets, the setting sun   540
Slowly descended, and with right aspect
Against the eastern gate of paradise
Levelled his evening rays. It was a rock
Of alabaster, piled up to the clouds,
Conspicuous far, winding with one ascent   545
Accessible from earth, one entrance high;
The rest was craggy cliff, that overhung
Still as it rose, impossible to climb.
Betwixt these rocky pillars Gabriel sat,
Chief of th'angelic guards, awaiting night;   550
About him exercised heroic games
The unarmed youth of heaven, but nigh at hand
Celestial armoury, shields, helms, and spears,
Hung high with diamond flaming, and with gold.
Thither came Uriel, gliding through the even   555
On a sun-beam, swift as a shooting star
In autumn thwarts the night, when vapours fired
Impress the air, and shows the mariner
From what point of his compass to beware
Impetuous winds. He thus began in haste.   560
    'Gabriel, to thee thy course by lot hath given
Charge and strict watch, that to this happy place
No evil thing approach or enter in.
This day at height of noon came to my sphere
A spirit, zealous, as he seemed, to know   565
More of the Almighty's works, and chiefly Man,
God's latest image. I described his way
Bent all on speed, and marked his airy gait;
But in the mount that lies from Eden north,
Where he first lighted, soon discerned his looks   570
Alien from heaven, with passions foul obscured:
Mine eye pursued him still, but under shade
Lost sight of him. One of the banished crew,
I fear, hath ventured from the deep, to raise
New troubles; him thy care must be to find.'   575

    To whom the wingèd warrior thus returned.
'Uriel, no wonder if thy perfect sight,
Amid the sun's bright circle where thou sit'st,
See far and wide. In at this gate none pass
The vigilance here placed, but such as come   580
Well known from heaven; and since meridian hour
No creature thence. If spirit of other sort,
So minded, have o'erleaped these earthly bounds
On purpose, hard thou knowest it to exclude
Spiritual substance with corporeal bar.   585
But if within the circuit of these walks,
In whatsoever shape he lurk, of whom
Thou tellest, by morrow dawning I shall know.'
    So promised he; and Uriel to his charge
Returned on that bright beam, whose point now
        raised   590
Bore him slope downward to the sun now fallen
Beneath the Azores; whether the prime orb,
Incredible how swift, had thither rolled
Diurnal, or this less voluble earth,
By shorter flight to th'east, had left him there   595
Arraying with reflected purple and gold
The clouds that on his western throne attend.
Now came still evening on, and twilight grey
Had in her sober livery all things clad;
Silence accompanied; for beast and bird,   600
They to their grassy couch, these to their nests
Were slunk, all but the wakeful nightingale;
She all night long her amorous descant sung;
Silence was pleased. Now glowed the firmament
With living sapphires. Hesperus, that led   605
The starry host, rode brightest, till the moon,
Rising in clouded majesty, at length
Apparent queen unveiled her peerless light,
And o'er the dark her silver mantle threw.
When Adam thus to Eve. 'Fair consort, th'hour   610
Of night, and all things now retired to rest,
Mind us of like repose; since God hath set
Labour and rest, as day and night, to men
Successive; and the timely dew of sleep,
Now falling with soft slumbrous weight, inclines   615
Our eye-lids. Other creatures all day long
Rove idle, unemployed, and less need rest;
Man hath his daily work of body or mind
Appointed, which declares his dignity,
And the regard of heaven on all his ways;   620
While other animals unactive range,
And of their doings God takes no account.
Tomorrow, ere fresh morning streak the east
With first approach of light, we must be risen,
And at our pleasant labour, to reform   625
Yon flowery arbours, yonder alleys green,
Our walk at noon, with branches overgrown,
That mock our scant manuring, and require
More hands than ours to lop their wanton growth:

594 **Diurnal:** in one day

Those blossoms also, and those dropping gums, 630
That lie bestrown, unsightly and unsmooth,
Ask riddance, if we mean to tread with ease;
Meanwhile, as Nature wills, night bids us rest.'
    To whom thus Eve, with perfect beauty adorned:
'My Author and Disposer, what thou bid'st 635
Unargued I obey. So God ordains;
God is thy law, thou mine. To know no more
Is woman's happiest knowledge, and her praise.
With thee conversing I forget all time;
All seasons, and their change, all please alike. 640
Sweet is the breath of morn, her rising sweet,
With charm of earliest birds: pleasant the sun,
When first on this delightful land he spreads
His orient beams, on herb, tree, fruit, and flower,
Glist'ring with dew; fragrant the fertile earth 645
After soft showers; and sweet the coming on
Of grateful evening mild; then silent night,
With this her solemn bird, and this fair moon,
And these the gems of heaven, her starry train:
But neither breath of morn, when she ascends 650
With charm of earliest birds; nor rising sun
On this delightful land; nor herb, fruit, flower,
Glist'ring with dew; nor fragrance after showers;
Nor grateful evening mild; nor silent night,
With this her solemn bird, nor walk by moon, 655
Or glittering star-light, without thee is sweet.
But wherefore all night long shine these? for whom
This glorious sight, when sleep hath shut all eyes?'
    To whom our general ancestor replied:
'Daughter of God and Man, accomplished Eve, 660
These have their course to finish round the earth,
By morrow evening, and from land to land
In order, though to nations yet unborn,
Minist'ring light prepared, they set and rise;
Lest total darkness should by night regain 665
Her old possession, and extinguish life
In Nature and all things; which these soft fires
Not only enlighten, but with kindly heat
Of various influence foment and warm,
Temper or nourish, or in part shed down 670
Their stellar virtue on all kinds that grow
On earth, made hereby apter to receive
Perfection from the sun's more potent ray.
These then, though unbeheld in deep of night, 674
Shine not in vain; nor think, though men were none,
That heaven would want spectators, God want praise:
Millions of spiritual creatures walk the earth
Unseen, both when we wake, and when we sleep:
All these with ceaseless praise His works behold
Both day and night. How often from the steep 680
Of echoing hill or thicket have we heard
Celestial voices to the midnight air,
Sole, or responsive each to other's note,
Singing their great Creator? oft in bands
While they keep watch, or nightly rounding walk, 685

642 **charm**: song

With heavenly touch of instrumental sounds
In full harmonic number joined, their songs
Divide the night, and lift our thoughts to heaven.'
    Thus talking, hand in hand alone they passed
On to their blissful bower: it was a place 690
Chosen by the sovran Planter, when He framed
All things to Man's delightful use; the roof
Of thickest covert was inwoven shade
Laurel and myrtle, and what higher grew
Of firm and fragrant leaf; on either side 695
Acanthus, and each odorous bushy shrub,
Fenced up the verdant wall; each beauteous flower,
Iris all hues, roses, and jessamine,
Reared high their flourished heads between, and
    wrought
Mosaic; underfoot the violet, 700
Crocus, and hyacinth, with rich inlay
Broidered the ground, more coloured than with stone
Of costliest emblem. Other creature here,
Bird, beast, insect, or worm, durst enter none,
Such was their awe of Man. In shadier bower 705
More sacred and sequestered, though but feigned,
Pan or Sylvanus never slept, nor nymph
Nor faunus haunted. Here, in close recess,
With flowers, garlands, and sweet-smelling herbs,
Espousèd Eve decked first her nuptial bed; 710
And heavenly choirs the hymenaean sung,
What day the genial angel to our sire
Brought her in naked beauty more adorned,
More lovely, than Pandora, whom the Gods
Endowed with all their gifts, and, oh! too like 715
In sad event, when to the unwiser son
Of Japhet brought by Hermes, she ensnared
Mankind with her fair looks, to be avenged
On him who had stole Jove's authentic fire.
    Thus, at their shady lodge arrived, both stood, 720
Both turned, and under open sky adored
The God that made both sky, air, earth, and heaven,
Which they beheld, the moon's resplendent globe,
And starry pole: 'Thou also madest the night,
Maker Omnipotent, and Thou the day, 725
Which we, in our appointed work employed,
Have finished, happy in our mutual help
And mutual love, the crown of all our bliss
Ordained by Thee; and this delicious place
For us too large, where Thy abundance wants 730
Partakers, and uncropped falls to the ground.
But Thou hast promised from us two a race
To fill the earth, who shall with us extol
Thy goodness infinite, both when we wake,
And when we seek, as now, Thy gift of sleep.' 735

707 **Sylvanus**: god of woods 708 **faunus**: Roman Pan, but also father
of the satyrs 708–710 Eve unites with Adam for the first time
711 **hymenaean**: a wedding hymn 714–719 Prometheus, a son of
Japhet, stole fire from heaven and gave it to man. Jupiter, wishing
to take revenge, caused Vulcan (Hephaistos) to make a woman
from the earth to bring misery to the human race. Hermes
additionally gave her cunning and beauty. This was Pandora, in
mythology, the first woman on earth

This said unanimous, and other rites
Observing none, but adoration pure
Which God likes best, into their inmost bower
Handed they went; and, eased the putting off
These troublesome disguises which we wear,   740
Straight side by side were laid; nor turned, I ween,
Adam from his fair spouse, nor Eve the rites
Mysterious of connubial love refused.
Whatever hypocrites austerely talk
Of purity, and place, and innocence,   745
Defaming as impure what God declares
Pure, and commands to some, leaves free to all.
Our Maker bids increase; who bids abstain
But our destroyer, foe to God and Man?
Hail, wedded Love, mysterious law, true source   750
Of human offspring, sole propriety
In paradise of all things common else!
By thee adulterous Lust was driven from men
Among the bestial herds to range; by thee
Founded in reason, loyal, just, and pure,   755
Relations dear, and all the charities
Of father, son, and brother, first were known.
Far be it, that I should write thee sin or blame,
Or think thee unbefitting holiest place,
Perpetual fountain of domestic sweets,   760
Whose bed is undefiled and chaste pronounced,
Present, or past, as saints and patriarchs used.
Here Love his golden shafts employs, here lights
His constant lamp, and waves his purple wings,
Reigns here and revels; not in the bought smile   765
Of harlots, loveless, joyless, unendeared,
Casual fruition; nor in court-amours,
Mixed dance, or wanton mask, or midnight ball,
Or serenate, which the starved lover sings
To his proud fair, best quitted with disdain.   770
These, lulled by nightingales, embracing slept,
And on their naked limbs the flowery roof
Showered roses, which the morn repaired. Sleep on,
Blest pair; and oh! yet happiest, if ye seek
No happier state, and know to know no more.   775
   Now had night measured with her shadowy cone
Halfway uphill this vast sublunar vault,
And from their ivory port the cherubim,
Forth issuing at th'accustomed hour, stood armed
To their night watches in warlike parade;   780
When Gabriel to his next in power thus spake.
   'Uzziel, half these draw off, and coast the south
With strictest watch; these other wheel the north;
Our circuit meets full west.' As flame they part,
Half wheeling to the shield, half to the spear.   785
   From these, two strong and subtle spirits he called
That near him stood, and gave them thus in charge.
'Ithuriel and Zephon, with winged speed
Search through this garden, leave unsearched no nook;
But chiefly where those two fair creatures lodge,   790

Now laid perhaps asleep, secure of harm.
This evening from the sun's decline arrived,
Who tells of some infernal spirit seen
Hitherward bent (who could have thought?) escaped
The bars of hell, on errand bad no doubt: 795
Such, where ye find, seize fast, and hither bring.'
   So saying, on he led his radiant files,
Dazzling the moon; these to the bower direct
In search of whom they sought: him there they found
Squat like a toad, close at the ear of Eve,   800
Assaying by his devilish art to reach
The organs of her fancy, and with them forge
Illusions, as he list, phantasms and dreams;
Or if, inspiring venom, he might taint
Th'animal spirits, that from pure blood arise   805
Like gentle breaths from rivers pure, thence raise
At least distempered, discontented thoughts,
Vain hopes, vain aims, inordinate desires,
Blown up with high conceits engendering pride.
Him thus intent Ithuriel with his spear   810
Touched lightly; for no falsehood can endure
Touch of celestial temper, but returns
Of force to its own likeness. Up he starts
Discovered and surprised. As when a spark
Lights on a heap of nitrous powder, laid   815
Fit for the tun some magazine to store
Against a rumoured war, the smutty grain,
With sudden blaze diffused, inflames the air;
So started up in his own shape the fiend.
Back stepped those two fair angels, half amazed   820
So sudden to behold the grisly king;
Yet thus, unmoved with fear, accost him soon.
   'Which of those rebel spirits adjudged to hell
Comest thou, escaped thy prison? and, transformed,
Why sat'st thou like an enemy in wait,   825
Here watching at the head of these that sleep?'
   'Know ye not,' then said Satan, filled with scorn,
'Know ye not me? ye knew me once no mate
For you, there sitting where ye durst not soar:
Not to know me argues yourselves unknown,   830
The lowest of your throng; or, if ye know,
Why ask ye, and superfluous begin
Your message, like to end as much in vain?'
   To whom thus Zephon, answering scorn with scorn.
'Think not, revolted spirit, thy shape the same,   835
Or undiminished brightness to be known,
As when thou stoodest in heaven upright and pure;
That glory then, when thou no more wast good,
Departed from thee; and thou resemblest now
Thy sin and place of doom obscure and foul.   840
But come, for thou, be sure, shalt give account
To him who sent us, whose charge is to keep
This place inviolable, and these from harm.'
   So spake the cherub; and his grave rebuke,
Severe in youthful beauty, added grace   845

---

777 **sublunar:** under the moon

816 **tun:** barrel   **magazine:** nitrous powder (gun powder) store

Invincible. Abashed the devil stood,
And felt how awful goodness is, and saw
Virtue in her shape how lovely; saw, and pined
His loss; but chiefly to find here observed
His lustre visibly impaired; yet seemed   850
Undaunted. 'If I must contend,' said he,
'Best with the best, the sender, not the sent,
Or all at once; more glory will be won,
Or less be lost.' 'Thy fear', said Zephon bold,
'Will save us trial what the least can do   855
Single against thee wicked, and thence weak.'
    The fiend replied not, overcome with rage;
But, like a proud steed reined, went haughty on,
Champing his iron curb. To strive or fly
He held it vain; awe from above had quelled   860
His heart, not else dismayed. Now drew they nigh
The western point, where those half-rounding guards
Just met, and closing stood in squadron joined,
Awaiting next command. To whom their chief,
Gabriel, from the front thus called aloud.   865
    'O friends! I hear the tread of nimble feet
Hasting this way, and now by glimpse discern
Ithuriel and Zephon through the shade;
And with them comes a third of regal port,
But faded splendour wan; who by his gait   870
And fierce demeanour seems the prince of hell,
Not likely to part hence without contest;
Stand firm, for in his look defiance lours.'
    He scarce had ended, when those two approached,
And brief related whom they brought, where found,
How busied, in what form and posture couched.   876
To whom with stern regard thus Gabriel spake.
    'Why hast thou, Satan, broke the bounds prescribed
To thy transgressions, and disturbed the charge
Of others, who approve not to transgress   880
By thy example, but have power and right
To question thy bold entrance on this place;
Employed, it seems, to violate sleep, and those
Whose dwelling God hath planted here in bliss!'
    To whom thus Satan with contemptuous brow.   885
'Gabriel? thou hadst in heaven the esteem of wise,
And such I held thee; but this question asked
Puts me in doubt. Lives there who loves his pain!
Who would not, finding way, break loose from hell,
Though thither doomed! Thou wouldst thyself, no
      doubt   890
And boldly venture to whatever place
Farthest from pain, where thou mightst hope to
      change
Torment with ease, and soonest recompense
Dole with delight, which in this place I sought;
To thee no reason, who know'st only good,   895
But evil hast not tried: and wilt object
His will who bounds us! Let him surer bar
His iron gates, if he intends our stay
In that dark durance. Thus much what was asked.
The rest is true, they found me where they say;   900
But that implies not violence or harm.'
    Thus he in scorn. The warlike angel moved,

Disdainfully half smiling, thus replied:
'Oh, loss of one in heaven to judge of wise
Since Satan fell, whom folly overthrew,   905
And now returns him from his prison 'scaped,
Gravely in doubt whether to hold them wise
Or not, who ask what boldness brought him hither
Unlicensed from his bounds in hell prescribed;
So wise he judges it to fly from pain   910
However, and to 'scape his punishment!
So judge thou still, presumptuous! till the wrath,
Which thou incurrest by flying, meet thy flight
Sevenfold, and scourge that wisdom back to hell,
Which taught thee yet no better, that no pain   915
Can equal anger infinite provoked.
But wherefore thou alone? wherefore with thee
Came not all hell broke loose? Is pain to them
Less pain, less to be fled, or thou than they
Less hardy to endure? Courageous chief!   920
The first in flight from pain! hadst thou alleged
To thy deserted host this cause of flight,
Thou surely hadst not come sole fugitive.'
    To which the fiend thus answered, frowning stern:
'Not that I less endure, or shrink from pain,   925
Insulting angel! well thou knowest I stood
Thy fiercest, when in battle to thy aid
The blasting volleyed thunder made all speed,
And seconded thy else not dreaded spear.
But still thy words at random, as before,   930
Argue thy inexperience what behoves
From hard assays and ill successes past
A faithful leader, not to hazard all
Through ways of danger by himself untried:
I, therefore, I alone first undertook   935
To wing the desolate abyss, and spy
This new-created world, whereof in hell
Fame is not silent, here in hope to find
Better abode, and my afflicted powers
To settle here on earth, or in mid-air;   940
Though for possession put to try once more
What thou and thy gay legions dare against;
Whose easier business were to serve their Lord
High up in heaven, with songs to hymn His throne,
And practised distances to cringe, not fight.'   945
    To whom the warrior angel soon replied:
'To say and straight unsay, pretending first
Wise to fly pain, professing next the spy,
Argues no leader but a liar traced,
Satan, and couldst thou faithful add? Oh, name!
Oh, sacred name of faithfulness profaned!   951
Faithful to whom? to thy rebellious crew?
Army of fiends, fit body to fit head.
Was this your discipline and faith engaged,
Your military obedience, to dissolve   955
Allegiance to the acknowledged power supreme?
And thou, sly hypocrite, who now wouldst seem
Patron of liberty, who more than thou
Once fawned, and cringed, and servilely adored
Heaven's awful monarch? wherefore, but in hope
To dispossess him, and thyself to reign?   961

But mark what I areed thee now. Avaunt!
Fly neither whence thou fledst! If from this hour
Within these hallowed limits thou appear,
Back to th'infernal pit I drag thee chained,   965
And seal thee so, as henceforth not to scorn
The facile gates of hell too slightly barred.'
    So threatened he; but Satan to no threats
Gave heed, but waxing more in rage replied:
    'Then when I am thy captive talk of chains,   970
Proud limitary cherub! but ere then
Far heavier load thyself expect to feel
From my prevailing arm, though heaven's King
Ride on thy wings, and thou with thy compeers,
Used to the yoke, drawest his triumphant wheels   975
In progress through the road of heaven star-paved.'
    While thus he spake, th'angelic squadron bright
Turned fiery red, sharpening in mooned horns
Their phalanx, and began to hem him round
With ported spears, as thick as when a field   980
Of Ceres ripe for harvest waving bends
Her bearded grove of ears, which way the wind
Sways them; the careful ploughman doubting stands,
Left on the threshing floor his hopeless sheaves
Prove chaff. On th'other side, Satan, alarmed,   985
Collecting all his might, dilated stood,
Like Teneriff or Atlas, unremoved:
His stature reached the sky, and on his crest
Sat Horror plumed; nor wanted in his grasp
What seemed both spear and shield. Now dreadful
    deeds   990
Might have ensued, nor only paradise
In this commotion, but the starry cope
Of heaven perhaps, or all the elements
At least had gone to wrack, disturbed and torn
With violence of this conflict, had not soon   995
Th'Eternal, to prevent such horrid fray,
Hung forth in heaven His golden scales, yet seen
Betwixt Astrea and the Scorpion sign,
Wherein all things created first He weighed,
The pendulous round earth with balanced air   1000
In counterpoise, now ponders all events,
Battles and realm. In these He put two weights,
The sequel each of parting and of fight:
The latter quick up flew, and kicked the beam,
Which Gabriel spying, thus bespake the fiend: 1005
    'Satan, I know thy strength, and thou knowest mine;
Neither our own, but given: What folly then
To boast what arms can do? since thine no more
Than heaven permits, nor mine, though doubled now
To trample thee as mire. For proof look up,   1010
And read thy lot in yon celestial sign;
Where thou art weighed, and shown how light, how
    weak,
If thou resist.' The fiend looked up, and knew
His mounted scale aloft. Nor more; but fled   1014
Murmuring, and with him fled the shades of night.

---

962 **areed:** advise **Avaunt:** begone 979 **phalanx:** line of battle
981 **Ceres:** goddess of agriculture 987 **Teneriff:** mountain in the
Canary Islands 997 **scales:** Libra 998 **Astrea:** Virgo

BOOK FIVE

Now Morn, her rosy steps in th'eastern clime
Advancing, sowed the earth with orient pearl,
When Adam waked, so customed; for his sleep
Was airy-light, from pure digestion bred,
And temperate vapours bland, which th'only sound
Of leaves and fuming rills, Aurora's fan,   6
Lightly dispersed, and the shrill matin song
Of birds on every bough; so much the more
His wonder was to find unwakened Eve
With tresses discomposed, and glowing cheek,   10
As through unquiet rest. He, on his side
Leaning half raised, with looks of cordial love
Hung over her enamoured, and beheld
Beauty, which, whether waking or asleep,
Shot forth peculiar graces; then with voice   15
Mild, as when Zephyrus on Flora breathes,
Her hand soft touching, whispered thus: 'Awake,
My fairest, my espoused, my latest found,
Heaven's last best gift, my ever new delight!
Awake! The morning shines, and the fresh field   20
Calls us; we lose the prime, to mark how spring
Our tender plants, how blows the citron grove,
What drops the myrrh, and what the balmy reed,
How nature paints her colours, how the bee
Sits on the bloom extracting liquid sweet.'   25
    Such whispering waked her, but with startled eye
On Adam, whom embracing, thus she spake:
    'O sole in whom my thoughts find all repose,
My glory, my perfection! glad I see
Thy face, and morn returned; for I this night   30
(Such night till this I never passed) have dreamed,
If dreamed, not, as I oft am wont, of thee,
Works of day past, or morrow's next design,
But of offence and trouble, which my mind
Knew never till this irksome night. Methought,   35
Close at mine ear one called me forth to walk
With gentle voice; I thought it thine. It said:
"Why sleepest thou, Eve? now is the pleasant time,
The cool, the silent, save where silence yields
To the night-warbling bird, that now awake   40

BOOK FIVE – THE ARGUMENT: Morning approacht, Eve relates to
Adam her troublesome dream; he likes it not, yet comforts her:
They come forth to their day labours: Their Morning Hymn at
the Door of their Bower. God to render Man inexcusable sends
Raphael to admonish him of his obedience, of his free estate, of
his enemy near at hand; who he is, and why his enemy, and whatever
else may avail Adam to know. Raphael comes down to Paradise, his
appearance describ'd, his coming discern'd by Adam afar off sitting
at the door of his Bower; he goes out to meet him, brings him to
his lodge, entertains him with the choicest fruits of Paradise got
together by Eve; their discourse at Table: Raphael performs his
message, minds Adam of his state and of his enemy; relates at
Adam's request who that enemy is, and how he came to be so,
beginning from his first revolt in Heaven, and the occasion thereof;
how he drew his Legions after him to the parts of the North, and
there incited them to rebel with him, persuading all but only
Abdiel a Seraph, who in Argument dissuades and opposes him,
then forsakes him 6 **Aurora:** the dawn 7 **matin song:** morning song

Tunes sweetest his love-laboured song; now reigns
Full-orbed the moon, and with more pleasing light
Shadowy sets off the face of things; in vain,
If none regard; Heaven wakes with all his eyes,
Whom to behold but thee, Nature's desire,　45
In whose sight all things joy, with ravishment
Attracted by thy beauty still to gaze."
I rose as at thy call, but found thee not;
To find thee I directed then my walk;
And on, methought, alone I passed through ways　50
That brought me on a sudden to the tree
Of interdicted knowledge: fair it seemed,
Much fairer to my fancy than by day:
And, as I wondering looked, beside it stood
One shaped and winged like one of those from
　　heaven　55
By us oft seen; his dewy locks distilled
Ambrosia; on that tree he also gazed;
And "O fair plant," said he, "with fruit surcharged,
Deigns none to ease thy load, and taste thy sweet,
Nor God, nor Man? Is knowledge so despised?　60
Or envy, or what reserve forbids to taste?
Forbid who will, none shall from me withhold
Longer thy offered good; why else set here?"
This said, he paused not, but with venturous arm
He plucked, he tasted; me damp horror chilled　65
At such bold words vouched with a deed so bold:
But he thus, overjoyed: "O fruit divine,
Sweet of thyself, but much more sweet thus cropped,
Forbidden here, it seems, as only fit
For gods, yet able to make gods of men:　70
And why not gods of men; since good, the more
Communicated, more abundant grows,
The author not impaired, but honoured more?
Here, happy creature, fair angelic Eve!
Partake thou also; happy though thou art,　75
Happier thou mayest be, worthier canst not be:
Taste this, and be henceforth among the gods
Thyself a goddess, not to earth confined,
But sometimes in the air, as we, sometimes
Ascend to heaven, by merit thine, and see　80
What life the gods live there, and such live thou!"
So saying, he drew nigh, and to me held,
Even to my mouth of that same fruit held part
Which he had plucked; the pleasant savoury smell
So quickened appetite that I, methought,　85
Could not but taste. Forthwith up to the clouds
With him I flew, and underneath beheld
The earth outstretched immense, a prospect wide
And various. Wondering at my flight and change
To this high exaltation; suddenly　90
My guide was gone, and I, methought, sunk down,
And fell asleep; but, oh, how glad I waked
To find this but a dream!' Thus Eve her night
Related, and thus Adam answered sad:
　'Best image of myself, and dearer half,　95
The trouble of thy thoughts this night in sleep
Affects me equally; nor can I like

This uncouth dream, of evil sprung, I fear;
Yet evil whence? in thee can harbour none,
Created pure. But know that in the soul　100
Are many lesser faculties, that serve
Reason as chief; among these Fancy next
Her office holds; of all external things
Which the five watchful senses represent,
She forms imaginations, airy shapes,　105
Which Reason, joining or disjoining, frames
All what we affirm or what deny, and call
Our knowledge or opinion; then retires
Into her private cell, when Nature rests.
Oft in her absence mimic Fancy wakes　110
To imitate her; but, misjoining shapes,
Wild work produces oft, and most in dreams;
Ill matching words and deeds long past or late.
Some such resemblances, methinks, I find
Of our last evening's talk, in this thy dream,　115
But with addition strange; yet be not sad.
Evil into the mind of God or Man
May come and go, so unreproved, and leave
No spot or blame behind: which gives me hope
That what in sleep thou didst abhor to dream,　120
Waking thou never will consent to do.
Be not disheartened then, nor cloud those looks,
That wont to be more cheerful and serene
Than when fair morning first smiles on the world;
And let us to our fresh employments rise　125
Among the groves, the fountains, and the flowers
That open now their choicest bosomed smells,
Reserved from night, and kept for thee in store.'
　So cheered he his fair spouse, and she was cheered;
But silently a gentle tear let fall　130
From either eye, and wiped them with her hair;
Two other precious drops that ready stood,
Each in their crystal sluice, he ere they fell
Kissed, as the gracious signs of sweet remorse
And pious awe, that feared to have offended.　135
　So all was cleared, and to the field they haste.
But first, from under shady arborous roof
Soon as they forth were come to open sight
Of day-spring, and the sun, who, scarce up-risen,
With wheels yet hov'ring o'er the ocean-brim,　140
Shot parallel to the earth his dewy ray,
Discovering in wide landskip all the east
Of paradise and Eden's happy plains,
Lowly they bowed adoring, and began
Their orisons, each morning duly paid　145
In various style; for neither various style
Nor holy rapture wanted they to praise
Their Maker, in fit strains pronounced, or sung
Unmeditated; such prompt eloquence
Flowed from their lips, in prose or numerous verse,　150
More tuneable than needed lute or harp
To add more sweetness; and they thus began.

143 **landskip:** landscape　145 **orisons:** prayers

'These are Thy glorious works, Parent of good,
Almighty! Thine this universal frame,
Thus wondrous fair; Thyself how wondrous then! 155
Unspeakable, who sit'st above these heavens
To us invisible, or dimly seen
In these thy lowest works; yet these declare
Thy goodness beyond thought, and power divine.
Speak, ye who best can tell, ye sons of light, 160
Angels; for ye behold him, and with songs
And choral symphonies, day without night,
Circle his throne rejoicing; ye in heaven
On earth join all ye creatures to extol
Him first, him last, him midst, and without end. 165
Fairest of stars, last in the train of night,
If better thou belong not to the dawn,
Sure pledge of day, that crownest the smiling morn
With thy bright circlet, praise him in thy sphere,
While day arises, that sweet hour of prime. 170
Thou sun, of this great world both eye and soul,
Acknowledge Him thy greater; sound His praise
In thy eternal course, both when thou climbest,
And when high noon hast gained, and when thou
          fallest.
Moon, that now meet'st the orient sun, now fly'st,
With the fixed stars, fixed in their orb that flies; 176
And ye five other wandering fires, that move
In mystic dance not without song, resound
His praise, who out of darkness called up light.
Air, and ye elements, the eldest birth 180
Of Nature's womb, that in quaternion run
Perpetual circle, multiform; and mix
And nourish all things; let your ceaseless change
Vary to our great Maker still new praise.
Ye mists and exhalations, that now rise 185
From hill or steaming lake, dusky or grey,
Till the sun paint your fleecy skirts with gold,
In honour to the world's great Author rise;
Whether to deck with clouds the uncoloured sky,
Or wet the thirsty earth with falling showers, 190
Rising or falling still advance His praise.
His praise, ye Winds, that from four quarters blow,
Breathe soft or loud; and, wave your tops, ye Pines,
With every plant, in sign of worship wave.
Fountains, and ye that warble, as ye flow, 195
Melodious murmurs, warbling tune His praise.
Join voices, all ye living Souls. Ye Birds,
That singing up to heaven-gate ascend,
Bear on your wings and in your notes His praise.
Ye that in waters glide, and ye that walk 200
The earth, and stately tread, or lowly creep;
Witness if I be silent, morn or even,
To hill, or valley, fountain, or fresh shade,
Made vocal by my song, and taught His praise.
Hail, universal Lord, be bounteous still 205

To give us only good; and if the night
Have gathered aught of evil, or concealed,
Disperse it, as now light dispels the dark!'
    So prayed they innocent, and to their thoughts
Firm peace recovered soon, and wonted calm. 210
On to their morning's rural work they haste,
Among sweet dews and flowers; where any row
Of fruit-trees over-woody reached too far
Their pampered boughs, and needed hands to check
Fruitless embraces: or they led the vine 215
To wed her elm; she, spoused, about him twines
Her marriageable arms, and with him brings
Her dower, the adopted clusters, to adorn
His barren leaves. Them thus employed beheld
With pity heaven's high King, and to Him called 220
Raphael, the sociable spirit, that deigned
To travel with Tobias, and secured
His marriage with the seven-times-wedded maid.
    'Raphael,' said He, 'thou hearest what stir on earth
Satan, from hell 'scaped through the darksome gulf,
Hath raised in paradise; and how disturbed 226
This night the human pair; how he designs
In them at once to ruin all mankind.
Go therefore, half this day as friend with friend
Converse with Adam, in what bower or shade 230
Thou findest him from the heat of noon retired,
To respite his day-labour with repast,
Or with repose; and such discourse bring on,
As may advise him of his happy state,
Happiness in his power left free to will, 235
Left to his own free will, his will though free,
Yet mutable; whence warn him to beware
He swerve not, too secure. Tell him withal
His danger, and from whom; what enemy,
Late fallen himself from heaven, is plotting now 240
The fall of others from like state of bliss;
By violence? no, for that shall be withstood;
But by deceit and lies. This let him know,
Lest, wilfully transgressing, he pretend
Surprisal, unadmonished, unforewarned.' 245
    So spake the Eternal Father, and fulfilled
All justice. Nor delayed the wingèd saint
After his charge received; but from among
Thousand celestial ardours, where he stood
Veiled with his gorgeous wings, up-springing light, 250
Flew through the midst of heaven; the angelic choirs,
On each hand parting, to his speed gave way
Through all the empyreal road; till, at the gate
Of heaven arrived, the gate self-opened wide
On golden hinges turning, as by work 255
Divine the sovran Architect had framed.
From hence no cloud, or, to obstruct his sight,
Star interposed, however small he sees,
Not unconformed to other shining globes,

166–167 Venus, the morning and evening star 177 **five other wandering fires:** Mercury, Venus, Mars, Saturn and Jupiter 181 **quaternion:** group of four

221–223 the archangel Raphael acts as a messenger between heaven and earth. See Book Four, note 166–171 249 **celestial ardours:** bright angels

Earth, and the garden of God, with cedars crowned
Above all hills. As when by night the glass   261
Of Galileo, less assured, observes
Imagined lands and regions in the moon:
Or pilot, from amidst the Cyclades
Delos or Samos first appearing, kens   265
A cloudy spot. Down thither prone in flight
He speeds, and through the vast ethereal sky
Sails between worlds and worlds, with steady wing
Now on the polar winds, then with quick fan
Winnows the buxom air; till, within soar   270
Of tow'ring eagles, to all the fowls he seems
A phoenix, gazed by all as that sole bird,
When, to enshrine his relics in the sun's
Bright temple, to Egyptian Thebes he flies.
At once on the'eastern cliff of paradise   275
He lights, and to his proper shape returns
A seraph winged. Six wings he wore, to shade
His lineaments divine; the pair that clad
Each shoulder broad, came mantling o'er his breast
With regal ornament; the middle pair   280
Girt like a starry zone his waist, and round
Skirted his loins and thighs with downy gold
And colours dipped in heaven; the third his feet
Shadowed from either heel with feathered mail,
Sky-tinctured grain. Like Maia's son he stood,   285
And shook his plumes, that heavenly fragrance filled
The circuit wide. Straight knew him all the bands
Of angels under watch; and to his state,
And to his message high, in honour rise;   289
For on some message high they guessed him bound.
Their glittering tents he passed, and now is come
Into the blissful field, through groves of myrrh,
And flowering odours, cassia, nard, and balm;
A wilderness of sweets; for Nature here
Wantoned as in her prime, and played at will   295
Her virgin fancies pouring forth more sweet,
Wild above rule or art, enormous bliss.
Him through the spicy forest onward come
Adam discerned, as in the door he sat
Of his cool bower, while now the mounted sun   300
Shot down direct his fervid rays to warm
Earth's inmost womb, more warmth than Adam
    needs:
And Eve within, due at her hour prepared
For dinner savoury fruits, of taste to please
True appetite, and not disrelish thirst   305
Of nectarous draughts between, from milky stream,
Berry or grape: To whom thus Adam called:
  'Haste hither, Eve, and worth thy sight behold
Eastward among those trees, what glorious shape
Comes this way moving; seems another morn   310
Risen on mid-noon; some great behest from heaven
To us perhaps he brings, and will vouchsafe
This day to be our guest. But go with speed,

And, what thy stores contain, bring forth, and pour
Abundance, fit to honour and receive   315
Our heavenly stranger: Well we may afford
Our givers their own gifts, and large bestow
From large bestowed, where Nature multiplies
Her fertile growth, and by disburthening grows
More fruitful, which instructs us not to spare.'   320
  To whom thus Eve: 'Adam, earth's hallowed mould,
Of God inspired! small store will serve, where store,
All seasons, ripe for use hangs on the stalk;
Save what by frugal storing firmness gains
To nourish, and superfluous moist consumes: 325
But I will haste, and from each bough and brake,
Each plant and juiciest gourd, will pluck such choice
To entertain our angel-guest, as he
Beholding shall confess, that here on earth
God hath dispensed his bounties as in heaven.'   330
  So saying, with dispatchful looks in haste
She turns, on hospitable thoughts intent
What choice to choose for delicacy best,
What order, so contrived as not to mix
Tastes, not well joined, inelegant, but bring   335
Taste after taste upheld with kindliest change;
Bestirs her then, and from each tender stalk
Whatever earth, all-bearing mother, yields
In India East or West, or middle shore
In Pontus or the Punic coast, or where   340
Alcinous reigned, fruit of all kinds, in coat
Rough, or smooth rind, or bearded husk, or shell,
She gathers, tribute large, and on the board
Heaps with unsparing hand; for drink the grape
She crushes, inoffensive must, and meaths   345
From many a berry, and from sweet kernels pressed
She tempers dulcet creams; nor these to hold
Wants her fit vessels pure; then strews the ground
With rose and odours from the shrub unfumed.
  Meanwhile our primitive great sire, to meet   350
His god-like guest, walks forth, without more train
Accompanied than with his own complete
Perfections; in himself was all his state,
More solemn than the tedious pomp that waits
On princes, when their rich retinue long   355
Of horses led, and grooms besmeared with gold,
Dazzles the crowd, and sets them all agape.
Nearer his presence Adam, though not awed,
Yet with submiss approach and reverence meek,
As to a superior nature bowing low,   360
Thus said: 'Native of heaven, for other place
None can than heaven such glorious shape contain;
Since, by descending from the thrones above,
Those happy places thou hast deigned a while
To want, and honour these, vouchsafe with us   365
Two only, who yet by sovran gift possess
This spacious ground, in yonder shady bower
To rest; and what the garden choicest bears

264–265 **Cyclades:** a group of islands in the South Aegean, containing Delos and Samos 265 **kens:** sees 285 **Maia's son:** Mercury

341 **Alcinous:** king of Phaiakia in Homer's *Odyssey*

To sit and taste, till this meridian heat
Be over, and the sun more cool decline.'   370
    Whom thus the angelic virtue answered mild.
'Adam, I therefore came; nor art thou such
Created, or such place hast here to dwell,
As may not oft invite, though spirits of heaven,
To visit thee; lead on, then, where thy bower   375
O'ershades; for these mid-hours, till evening rise,
I have at will.' So to the sylvan lodge
They came, that like Pomona's arbour smiled,
With flowerets decked, and fragrant smells; but Eve,
Undecked save with herself, more lovely fair   380
Than wood-nymph, or the fairest goddess feigned
Of three that in Mount Ida naked strove,
Stood to entertain her guest from heaven; no veil
She needed, virtue-proof; no thought infirm
Altered her cheek. On whom the angel hail   385
Bestowed, the holy salutation used
Long after to blest Mary, second Eve.
    'Hail, Mother of Mankind, whose fruitful womb
Shall fill the world more numerous with thy sons,
Than with these various fruits the trees of God   390
Have heaped this table!' – Raised of grassy turf
Their table was, and mossy seats had round,
And on her ample square from side to side
All autumn piled, though spring and autumn here
Danced hand in hand. A while discourse they hold;
No fear lest dinner cool; when thus began   396
Our author: 'Heavenly stranger, please to taste
These bounties, which our Nourisher, from whom
All perfect good, unmeasured out, descends,
To us for food and for delight hath caused   400
The earth to yield; unsavoury food perhaps
To spiritual natures; only this I know,
That one celestial Father gives to all.'
    To whom the angel: 'Therefore what He gives
(Whose praise be ever sung) to Man in part   405
Spiritual, may of purest spirits be found
No ingrateful food: And food alike those pure
Intelligential substances require,
As doth your rational; and both contain
Within them every lower faculty   410
Of sense, whereby they hear, see, smell, touch, taste,
Tasting concoct, digest, assimilate,
And corporeal to incorporeal turn.
For know, whatever was created, needs
To be sustained and fed. Of elements   415
The grosser feeds the purer, earth the sea,
Earth and the sea feed air, the air those fires
Ethereal, and as lowest first the moon;
Whence in her visage round those spots, unpurged
Vapours not yet into her substance turned.   420
Nor doth the moon no nourishment exhale
From her moist continent to higher orbs.
The sun that light imparts to all, receives

From all his alimental recompense
In humid exhalations, and at even   425
Sups with the ocean. Though in heaven the trees
Of life ambrosial fruitage bear, and vines
Yield nectar; though from off the boughs each morn
We brush mellifluous dews, and find the ground
Covered with pearly grain. Yet God hath here   430
Varied His bounty so with new delights,
As may compare with heaven; and to taste
Think not I shall be nice.' So down they sat,
And to their viands fell; nor seemingly
The angel, nor in mist, the common gloss   435
Of theologians; but with keen dispatch
Of real hunger, and concoctive heat
To transubstantiate. What redounds, transpires
Through spirits with ease; nor wonder; if by fire
Of sooty coal the empiric alchemist   440
Can turn, or holds it possible to turn,
Metals of drossiest ore to perfect gold,
As from the mine. Meanwhile at table Eve
Ministered naked, and their flowing cups
With pleasant liquors crowned. Oh, innocence   445
Deserving paradise! if ever, then,
Then had the sons of God excuse to have been
Enamoured at that sight; but in those hearts
Love unlibidinous reigned, nor jealousy
Was understood, the injured lover's hell.   450
    Thus when with meats and drinks they had sufficed,
Not burdened nature, sudden mind arose
In Adam, not to let the occasion pass
Given him by this great conference to know
Of things above his world, and of their being   455
Who dwell in heaven, whose excellence he saw
Transcend his own so far; whose radiant forms,
Divine effulgence, whose high power, so far
Exceeded human; and his wary speech
Thus to th'empyreal minister he framed.   460
    'Inhabitant with God, now know I well
Thy favour, in this honour done to Man;
Under whose lowly roof thou hast vouchsafed
To enter, and these earthly fruits to taste,
Food not of angels, yet accepted so,   465
As that more willingly thou couldst not seem
At heaven's high feasts to have fed: yet what
        compare?'
    To whom the wingèd hierarch replied:
'O Adam, one Almighty is, from whom
All things proceed, and up to Him return,   470
If not depraved from good, created all
Such to perfection, one first matter all,
Endued with various forms, various degrees
Of substance, and, in things that live, of life;
But more refined, more spiritous, and pure,   475

378 **Pomona:** goddess of fruit

424 **alimental:** nourishing 435 **gloss:** explanation 438 **transubstantiate:** to change from one substance into another 440 **empiric:** experimental in a derogatory sense

As nearer to Him placed, or nearer tending
Each in their several active spheres assigned,
Till body up to spirit work, in bounds
Proportioned to each kind. So from the root
Springs lighter the green stalk, from thence the
    leaves   480
More airy, last the bright consummate flower
Spirits odorous breathes: flowers and their fruit,
Man's nourishment, by gradual scale sublimed,
To vital spirits aspire, to animal,
To intellectual; give both life and sense,   485
Fancy and understanding; whence the soul
Reason receives, and reason is her being,
Discursive, or intuitive; discourse
Is oftest yours, the latter most is ours,
Differing but in degree, of kind the same.   490
Wonder not then, what God for you saw good
If I refuse not, but convert, as you
To proper substance. Time may come, when men
With angels may participate, and find
No inconvenient diet, nor too light fare;   495
And from these corporal nutriments perhaps
Your bodies may at last turn all to spirit,
Improved by tract of time, and, winged, ascend
Ethereal, as we; or may, at choice,
Here or in heavenly paradises dwell;   500
If ye be found obedient, and retain
Unalterably firm his love entire,
Whose progeny you are. Meanwhile enjoy
Your fill what happiness this happy state
Can comprehend, incapable of more.'   505
   To whom the patriarch of mankind replied.
'O favourable Spirit, propitious guest,
Well hast thou taught the way that might direct
Our knowledge, and the scale of nature set
From centre to circumference; whereon,   510
In contemplation of created things,
By steps we may ascend to God. But say,
What meant that caution joined, "if ye be found
Obedient"? Can we want obedience then
To Him, or possibly His love desert,   515
Who formed us from the dust and placed us here
Full to the utmost measure of what bliss
Human desires can seek or apprehend?'
   To whom the angel. 'Son of Heaven and Earth,
Attend! That thou art happy, owe to God;   520
That thou continuest such, owe to thyself,
That is, to thy obedience; therein stand.
This was that caution given thee; be advised.
God made thee perfect, not immutable;
And good He made thee, but to persevere   525
He left it in thy power; ordained thy will
By nature free, not over-ruled by fate
Inextricable, or strict necessity:
Our voluntary service He requires,
Not our necessitated; such with Him   530

Finds no acceptance, nor can find; for how
Can hearts, not free, be tried whether they serve
Willing or no, who will but what they must
By destiny, and can no other choose?
Myself, and all th'angelic host, that stand   535
In sight of God, enthroned, our happy state
Hold, as you yours, while our obedience holds;
On other surety none. Freely we serve,
Because we freely love, as in our will
To love or not; in this we stand or fall: 540
And some are fallen, to disobedience fallen,
And so from heaven to deepest hell. Oh, fall
From what high state of bliss, into what woe!'
   To whom our great progenitor: 'Thy words
Attentive, and with more delighted ear,   545
Divine instructer, I have heard, than when
Cherubic songs by night from neighbouring hills
Aereal music send: Nor knew I not
To be both will and deed created free;
Yet that we never shall forget to love   550
Our Maker, and obey Him whose command
Single is yet so just, my constant thoughts
Assurèd me, and still assure. Though what thou tellest
Hath passed in heaven, some doubt within me move,
But more desire to hear, if thou consent,   555
The full relation, which must needs be strange,
Worthy of sacred silence to be heard;
And we have yet large day, for scarce the sun
Hath finished half his journey, and scarce begins
His other half in the great zone of heaven.'   560
   Thus Adam made request; and Raphael,
After short pause assenting, thus began:
'High matter thou enjoinest me, O prime of men,
Sad task and hard. For how shall I relate
To human sense th'invisible exploits   565
Of warring spirits? how, without remorse,
The ruin of so many glorious once
And perfect while they stood? how last unfold
The secrets of another world, perhaps
Not lawful to reveal? yet for thy good   570
This is dispensed; and what surmounts the reach
Of human sense, I shall delineate so,
By likening spiritual to corporal forms,
As may express them best; though what if earth
Be but the shadow of heaven, and things therein   575
Each to other like, more than on earth is thought?
   'As yet this world was not, and Chaos wild
Reigned where these heavens now roll, where earth
    now rests
Upon her centre poised; when on a day
(For time, though in eternity, applied   580
To motion, measures all things durable
By present, past, and future), on such day
As heaven's great year brings forth, the empyreal host

548 **Aereal music:** light, airy, ethereal music

Of angels by imperial summons called,
Innumerable before th'Almighty's throne   585
Forthwith, from all the ends of heaven, appeared
Under their hierarchs in orders bright:
Ten thousand thousand ensigns high advanced,
Standards and gonfalons 'twixt van and rear
Stream in the air, and for distinction serve   590
Of hierarchies, of orders, and degrees;
Or in their glittering tissues bear emblazed
Holy memorials, acts of zeal and love
Recorded eminent. Thus when in orbs
Of circuit inexpressible they stood,   595
Orb within orb, the Father Infinite,
By whom in bliss embosomed sat the Son,
Amidst as from a flaming mount, whose top
Brightness had made invisible, thus spake.
    ' "Hear, all ye Angels, progeny of light,   600
Thrones, Dominations, Princedoms, Virtues, Powers;
Hear my decree, which unrevoked shall stand.
This day I have begot whom I declare
My only Son, and on this holy hill
Him have anointed, whom ye now behold   605
At my right hand; your head I him appoint;
And by myself have sworn, to him shall bow
All knees in heaven, and shall confess him Lord.
Under his great vice-gerent reign abide
United, as one individual soul,   610
For ever happy. Him who disobeys,
Me disobeys, breaks union, and that day,
Cast out from God and blessed vision, falls
Into utter darkness, deep engulfed, his place
Ordained without redemption, without end."   615
    'So spake th'Omnipotent, and with his words
All seemed well pleased; all seemed, but were not all.
That day, as other solemn days, they spent
In song and dance about the sacred hill;
Mystical dance, which yonder starry sphere   620
Of planets, and of fixed, in all her wheels
Resembles nearest, mazes intricate,
Eccentric, intervolved, yet regular
Then most, when most irregular they seem;
And in their motions harmony divine   625
So smooths her charming tones, that God's own ear
Listens delighted. Evening now approached
(For we have also our evening and our morn,
We ours for change delectable, not need);
Forthwith from dance to sweet repast they turn   630
Desirous; all in circles as they stood,
Tables are set, and on a sudden piled
With angel's food, and rubied nectar flows
In pearl, in diamond, and massy gold,
Fruit of delicious vines, the growth of heaven.   635
On flowers reposed, and with fresh flowerets crowned,
They eat, they drink, and in communion sweet

589 **gonfalons:** banners

Quaff immortality and joy, secure
Of surfeit, where full measure only bounds
Excess, before th'all-bounteous King, who
    showered   640
With copious hand, rejoicing in their joy.
Now when ambrosial night with clouds exhaled
From that high mount of God, whence light and
    shade
Spring both, the face of brightest heaven had
    changed
To grateful twilight (for night comes not there   645
In darker veil), and roseate dews disposed
All but the unsleeping eyes of God to rest;
Wide over all the plain, and wider far
Than all this globous earth in plain outspread
(Such are the courts of God), th'angelic throng,   650
Dispersed in bands and files, their camp extend
By living streams among the trees of life,
Pavilions numberless, and sudden reared,
Celestial tabernacles, where they slept
Fanned with cool winds; save those, who, in their
    course,   655
Melodious hymns about the sovran throne
Alternate all night long: but not so waked
Satan; so call him now, his former name
Is heard no more in heaven; he of the first,
If not the first archangel, great in power,   660
In favour and pre-eminence, yet fraught
With envy against the Son of God, that day
Honoured by his great Father, and proclaimed
Messiah King anointed, could not bear
Through pride that sight, and thought himself
    impaired.   665
Deep malice thence conceiving and disdain,
Soon as mid-night brought on the dusky hour
Friendliest to sleep and silence, he resolved
With all his legions to dislodge, and leave
Unworshipped, unobeyed, the throne supreme,   670
Contemptuous; and his next subordinate
Awakening, thus to him in secret spake.
    ' "Sleep'st thou, Companion dear? What sleep can
    close
Thy eye-lids? and rememberest what decree
Of yesterday, so late hath passed the lips   675
Of Heaven's Almighty. Thou to me thy thoughts
Wast wont, I mine to thee was wont to impart;
Both waking we were one; how then can now
Thy sleep dissent? New laws thou seest imposed;
New laws from Him who reigns, new minds may
    raise   680
In us who serve, new counsels to debate
What doubtful may ensue. More in this place
To utter is not safe. Assemble thou
Of all those myriads which we lead the chief;
Tell them, that by command, ere yet dim night   685
Her shadowy cloud withdraws, I am to haste,
And all who under me their banners wave,

Homeward, with flying march, where we possess
The quarters of the north; there to prepare
Fit entertainment to receive our King, 690
The great Messiah, and his new commands,
Who speedily through all the hierarchies
Intends to pass triumphant, and give laws."
　'So spake the false archangel, and infused
Bad influence into th'unwary breast 695
Of his associate. He together calls,
Or several one by one, the regent powers,
Under him regent; tells, as he was taught,
That the Most High commanding, now ere night,
Now ere dim night had disencumbered heaven, 700
The great hierarchal standard was to move;
Tells the suggested cause, and casts between
Ambiguous words and jealousies, to sound
Or taint integrity. But all obeyed
The wonted signal, and superior voice 705
Of their great potentate; for great indeed
His name, and high was his degree in heaven;
His countenance, as the morning-star that guides
The starry flock, allured them, and with lies
Drew after him the third part of heaven's host. 710
Meanwhile the Eternal Eye, whose sight discerns
Abstrusest thoughts, from forth His holy mount,
And from within the golden lamps that burn
Nightly before Him, saw without their light
Rebellion rising; saw in whom, how spread 715
Among the sons of morn, what multitudes
Were banded to oppose His high decree;
And, smiling, to His only Son thus said.
　' "Son, thou in whom my glory I behold
In full resplendence, Heir of all my might, 720
Nearly it now concerns us to be sure
Of our omnipotence, and with what arms
We mean to hold what anciently we claim
Of deity or empire. Such a foe
Is rising, who intends to erect his throne 725
Equal to ours, throughout the spacious north;
Nor so content, hath in his thought to try
In battle, what our power is, or our right.
Let us advise, and to this hazard draw
With speed what force is left, and all employ 730
In our defence; lest unawares we lose
This our high place, our sanctuary, our hill."
　'To whom the Son with calm aspect and clear,
Lightning divine, ineffable, serene,
Made answer: "Mighty Father, thou thy foes 735
Justly hast in derision, and, secure,
Laughest at their vain designs and tumults vain,
Matter to me of glory, whom their hate
Illustrates, when they see all regal power
Given me to quell their pride, and in event 740
Know whether I be dextrous to subdue
Thy rebels, or be found the worst in heaven."

712 **Abstrusest:** most concealed

　'So spake the Son; but Satan, with his powers,
Far was advanced on wingèd speed; an host
Innumerable as the stars of night, 745
Or stars of morning, dew-drops, which the sun
Impearls on every leaf and every flower.
Regions they passed, the mighty regencies
Of seraphim, and potentates, and thrones,
In their triple degrees; regions to which 750
All thy dominion, Adam, is no more
Than what this garden is to all the earth,
And all the sea, from one entire globose
Stretched into longitude; which having passed,
At length into the limits of the north 755
They came; and Satan to his royal seat
High on a hill, far blazing, as a mount
Raised on a mount, with pyramids and towers
From diamond quarries hewn, and rocks of gold;
The palace of great Lucifer (so call 760
That structure in the dialect of men
Interpreted), which not long after, he
Affecting all equality with God,
In imitation of that mount whereon
Messiah was declared in sight of heaven, 765
The Mountain of the Congregation called;
For thither he assembled all his train,
Pretending so commanded to consult
About the great reception of their King,
Thither to come, and with calumnious art 770
Of counterfeited truth thus held their ears.
　' "Thrones, Dominations, Princedoms, Virtues,
　　Powers;
If these magnific titles yet remain
Not merely titular, since by decree
Another now hath to Himself engrossed 775
All power, and us eclipsed under the name
Of King anointed, for whom all this haste
Of midnight-march, and hurried meeting here,
This only to consult how we may best,
With what may be devised of honours new, 780
Receive him coming to receive from us
Knee-tribute yet unpaid, prostration vile!
Too much to one! but double how endured,
To one, and to His image now proclaimed?
But what if better counsels might erect 785
Our minds, and teach us to cast off this yoke?
Will ye submit your necks, and choose to bend
The supple knee? Ye will not, if I trust
To know ye right, or if ye know yourselves
Natives and sons of heaven possessed before 790
By none; and if not equal all, yet free,
Equally free; for orders and degrees
Jar not with liberty, but well consist.
Who can in reason then, or right, assume
Monarchy over such as live by right 795
His equals, if in power and splendour less,
In freedom equal? or can introduce
Law and edict on us, who without law

Err not? much less for this to be our Lord,
And look for adoration, to th'abuse 800
Of those imperial titles, which assert
Our being ordained to govern, not to serve."
  'Thus far his bold discourse without control
Had audience; when among the seraphim
Abdiel, than whom none with more zeal adored 805
The Deity, and divine commands obeyed,
Stood up, and in a flame of zeal severe
The current of his fury thus opposed.
  ' "Oh, argument blasphemous, false, and proud!
Words which no ear ever to hear in heaven 810
Expected, least of all from thee, ingráte,
In place thyself so high above thy peers.
Canst thou with impious obloquy condemn
The just decree of God, pronounced and sworn,
That to His only Son, by right endued 815
With regal sceptre, every soul in heaven
Shall bend the knee, and in that honour due
Confess Him rightful King? unjust, thou sayest,
Flatly unjust, to bind with laws the free,
And equal over equals to let reign, 820
One over all with unsucceeded power.
Shalt thou give law to God? shalt thou dispute
With Him the points of liberty, who made
Thee what thou art, and formed the powers of heaven
Such as He pleased, and circumscribed their being?
Yet, by experience taught, we know how good, 826
And of our good and of our dignity
How provident He is; how far from thought
To make us less, bent rather to exalt
Our happy state, under one head more near 830
United. But to grant it thee unjust,
That equal over equals monarch reign:
Thyself, though great and glorious, dost thou count,
Or all angelic nature joined in one,
Equal to him begotten Son? by whom, 835
As by His Word, the Mighty Father made
All things, even thee; and all the spirits of heaven
By him created in their bright degrees,
Crowned them with glory, and to their glory named
Thrones, dominations, princedoms, virtues,
    powers, 840
Essential powers; nor by His reign obscured,
But more illustrious made; since He the head
One of our number thus reduced becomes;
His laws our laws; all honour to Him done
Returns our own. Cease, then, this impious rage, 845
And tempt not these; but hasten to appease
The incensed Father, and the incensed Son,
While pardon may be found in time besought."
  'So spake the fervent angel; but his zeal
None seconded, as out of season judged, 850
Or singular and rash. Whereat rejoiced
The apostate, and, more haughty, thus replied.
  ' "That we were formed then sayest thou? and the
    work

Of secondary hands, by task transferred
From Father to His Son? strange point and new! 855
Doctrine which we would know whence learned: who
    saw
When this creation was? rememberest thou
Thy making, while the Maker gave thee being?
We know no time when we were not as now;
Know none before us, self-begot, self-raised 860
By our own quickening power, when fatal course
Had circled his full orb, the birth mature
Of this our native heaven, ethereal sons.
Our puissance is our own; our own right hand
Shall teach us highest deeds, by proof to try 865
Who is our equal. Then thou shalt behold
Whether by supplication we intend
Address, and to begirt the almighty throne
Beseeching or besieging. This report,
These tidings carry to th'anointed King; 870
And fly, ere evil intercept thy flight."
  'He said; and, as the sound of waters deep,
Hoarse murmur echoed to his words applause
Through the infinite host; nor less for that
The flaming seraph fearless, though alone 875
Encompassed round with foes, thus answered bold.
  ' "O alienate from God, O Spirit accursed,
Forsaken of all good! I see thy fall
Determined, and thy hapless crew involved
In this perfidious fraud, contagion spread 880
Both of thy crime and punishment. Henceforth
No more be troubled how to quit the yoke
Of God's Messiah; those indulgent laws
Will not be now vouchsafed; other decrees
Against thee are gone forth without recall; 885
That golden sceptre, which thou didst reject,
Is now an iron rod to bruise and break
Thy disobedience. Well thou didst advise;
Yet not for thy advice or threats I fly
These wicked tents devoted, lest the wrath 890
Impendent, raging into sudden flame,
Distinguish not. For soon expect to feel
His thunder on thy head, devouring fire.
Then who created thee lamenting learn,
When who can uncreate thee thou shalt know." 895
  'So spake the seraph Abdiel, faithful found
Among the faithless, faithful only he;
Among innumerable false, unmoved,
Unshaken, unseduced, unterrified,
His loyalty he kept, his love, his zeal; 900
Nor number, nor example, with him wrought
To swerve from truth, or change his constant mind,
Though single. From amidst them forth he passed,
Long way through hostile scorn, which he sustained
Superior, nor of violence feared aught; 905
And, with retorted scorn, his back he turned
On those proud towers to swift destruction doomed.'

BOOK SIX

'All night the dreadless angel, unpursued,
Through heaven's wide champain held his way; till Morn,
Waked by the circling Hours, with rosy hand
Unbarred the gates of light. There is a cave
Within the mount of God, fast by His throne,   5
Where light and darkness in perpetual round
Lodge and dislodge by turns, which makes through heaven
Grateful vicissitude, like day and night;
Light issues forth, and at the other door
Obsequious darkness enters, till her hour   10
To veil the heaven, though darkness there might well
Seem twilight here. And now went forth the Morn
Such as in highest heaven arrayed in gold
Empyreal; from before her vanished Night,
Shot through with orient beams; when all the plain   15
Covered with thick embattled squadrons bright,
Chariots, and flaming arms, and fiery steeds,
Reflecting blaze on blaze, first met his view:
War he perceived, war in procinct; and found
Already known what he for news had thought   20
To have reported. Gladly then he mixed
Among those friendly powers, who him received
With joy and acclamations loud, that one,
That of so many myriads fallen, yet one
Returned not lost. On to the sacred hill   25
They led him high-applauded, and present
Before the seat supreme; from whence a voice,
From midst a golden cloud, thus mild was heard.
' "Servant of God. Well done; well hast thou fought
The better fight, who single hast maintained   30
Against revolted multitudes the cause
Of truth, in word mightier than they in arms;
And for the testimony of truth hast borne
Universal reproach, far worse to bear
Than violence; for this was all thy care   35
To stand approved in sight of God, though worlds
Judged thee perverse. The easier conquest now
Remains thee, aided by this host of friends,
Back on thy foes more glorious to return,
Than scorned thou didst depart; and to subdue   40

BOOK SIX – THE ARGUMENT: Raphael continues to relate how Michael and Gabriel were sent forth to battle against Satan and his Angels. The first Fight describ'd: Satan and his Powers retire under Night: He calls a Council invents devilish Engines, which in the second days Fight put Michael and his Angels to some disorder; But, they at length pulling up Mountains overwhelm'd both the force and Machines of Satan: Yet the Tumult not so ending, God on the third day sends Messiah his Son, for whom he had reserv'd the glory of that Victory: Hee in the Power of his Father coming to the place, and causing all his Legions to stand still on either side, with his Chariot and Thunder driving into the midst of his Enemies, pursues them unable to resist towards the wall of Heaven; which opening, they leap down with horror and confusion into the place of punishment prepar'd for them in the Deep: Messiah returns with triumph to his Father 2 **champain:** plain 19 **procinct:** readiness for action

By force, who reason for their law refuse,
Right reason for their law, and for their King
Messiah, who by right of merit reigns.
Go, Michael, of celestial armies prince,
And thou, in military prowess next,   45
Gabriel, lead forth to battle these my sons
Invincible; lead forth my armèd saints,
By thousands and by millions, ranged for fight,
Equal in number to that godless crew
Rebellious. Them with fire and hostile arms   50
Fearless assault; and, to the brow of heaven
Pursuing, drive them out from God and bliss,
Into their place of punishment, the gulf
Of Tartarus, which ready opens wide
His fiery Chaos to receive their fall."   55
'So spake the Sovran Voice, and clouds began
To darken all the hill, and smoke to roll
In dusky wreaths, reluctant flames, the sign
Of wrath awaked; nor with less dread the loud
Ethereal trumpet from on high 'gan blow: 60
At which command the powers militant,
That stood for heaven, in mighty quadrate joined
Of union irresistible, moved on
In silence their bright legions, to the sound
Of instrumental harmony, that breathed   65
Heroic ardour to advent'rous deeds
Under their god-like leaders, in the cause
Of God and His Messiah. On they move
Indissolubly firm; nor obvious hill,
Nor strait'ning vale, nor wood, nor stream, divides   70
Their perfect ranks; for high above the ground
Their march was, and the passive air upbore
Their nimble tread; as when the total kind
Of birds, in orderly array on wing,
Came summoned over Eden to receive   75
Their names of thee; so over many a tract
Of heaven they marched, and many a province wide,
Tenfold the length of this terrene. At last,
Far in the horizon to the north appeared
From skirt to skirt a fiery region, stretched   80
In battailous aspect, and nearer view
Bristled with upright beams innumerable
Of rigid spears, and helmets thronged, and shields
Various, with boastful argument portrayed,
The banded powers of Satan hasting on   85
With furious expedition; for they weened
That self-same day, by fight or by surprise,
To win the mount of God, and on his throne
To set the envier of his state, the proud
Aspirer; but their thoughts proved fond and vain   90
In the mid way: though strange to us it seemed
At first, that angel should with angel war,
And in fierce hosting meet, who wont to meet
So oft in festivals of joy and love
Unanimous, as sons of one great Sire,   95

62 **quadrate:** in a square 78 **this terrene:** this Earth 93 **hosting:** encounter

Hymning the Eternal Father: but the shout
Of battle now began, and rushing sound
Of onset ended soon each milder thought.
High in the midst, exalted as a God,
Th'apostate in his sun-bright chariot sat,   100
Idol of majesty divine, enclosed
With flaming cherubim, and golden shields;
Then lighted from his gorgeous throne, for now
'Twixt host and host but narrow space was left,
A dreadful interval, and front to front   105
Presented stood in terrible array
Of hideous length. Before the cloudy van,
On the rough edge of battle ere it joined,
Satan, with vast and haughty strides advanced,
Came tow'ring, armed in adamant and gold;   110
Abdiel that sight endured not, where he stood
Among the mightiest, bent on highest deeds,
And thus his own undaunted heart explores.
   ' "Oh heaven! that such resemblance of the Highest
Should yet remain, where faith and realty   115
Remain not. Wherefore should not strength and might
There fail where virtue fails, or weakest prove
Where boldest, though to fight unconquerable?
His puissance, trusting in th'Almighty's aid,
I mean to try, whose reason I have tried   120
Unsound and false; nor is it aught but just,
That he, who in debate of truth hath won,
Should win in arms, in both disputes alike
Victor; though brutish that contest and foul,
When reason hath to deal with force, yet so   125
Most reason is that reason overcome."
   So pondering, and from his armèd peers
Forth stepping opposite, half-way he met
His daring foe, at this prevention more
Incensed, and thus securely him defied.   130
   ' "Proud, art thou met? thy hope was to have
      reached
The height of thy aspiring unopposed,
The throne of God unguarded, and his side
Abandoned, at the terror of thy power
Or potent tongue. Fool! not to think how vain   135
Against th'Omnipotent to rise in arms;
Who out of smallest things could, without end,
Have raised incessant armies to defeat
Thy folly; or with solitary hand
Reaching beyond all limit, at one blow,   140
Unaided, could have finished thee, and whelmed
Thy legions under darkness. But thou seest
All are not of thy train; there be, who faith
Prefer, and piety to God, though then
To thee not visible, when I alone   145
Seemed in thy world erroneous to dissent
From all. My sect thou seest; now learn too late
How few sometimes may know, when thousands err."

'Whom the grand foe, with scornful eye askance,
Thus answered. "Ill for thee, but in wished hour   150
Of my revenge, first sought for, thou returnest
From flight, seditious Angel! to receive
Thy merited reward, the first assay
Of this right hand provoked, since first that tongue,
Inspired with contradiction, durst oppose   155
A third part of the Gods, in synod met
Their deities to assert; who, while they feel
Vigour divine within them, can allow
Omnipotence to none. But well thou comest
Before thy fellows, ambitious to win   160
From me some plume, that thy success may show
Destruction to the rest. This pause between,
(Unanswered lest thou boast) to let thee know,
At first I thought that liberty and heaven
To heavenly souls had been all one; but now   165
I see that most through sloth had rather serve,
Minist'ring spirits, trained up in feast and song!
Such hast thou armed, the minstrelsy of heaven,
Servility with freedom to contend,
As both their deeds compared this day shall prove."   170
   'To whom in brief thus Abdiel stern replied:
"Apostate! still thou errest, nor end wilt find
Of erring, from the path of truth remote:
Unjustly thou depravest it with the name
Of servitude, to serve whom God ordains,   175
Or Nature: God and Nature bid the same,
When he who rules is worthiest, and excels
Them whom he governs. This is servitude,
To serve the unwise, or him who hath rebelled
Against his worthier, as thine now serve thee,   180
Thyself not free, but to thyself enthralled;
Yet lewdly darest our minist'ring upbraid.
Reign thou in hell, thy kingdom; let me serve
In heaven God ever blest, and His divine
Behests obey, worthiest to be obeyed;   185
Yet chains in hell, not realms, expect. Meanwhile
From me returned, as erst thou saidst, from flight,
This greeting on thy impious crest receive."
   'So saying, a noble stroke he lifted high,
Which hung not, but so swift with tempest fell   190
On the proud crest of Satan, that no sight,
Nor motion of swift thought, less could his shield,
Such ruin intercept. Ten paces huge
He back recoiled; the tenth on bended knee
His massy spear upstayed; as if on earth   195
Winds under ground, or waters forcing way,
Sidelong had pushed a mountain from his seat,
Half sunk with all his pines. Amazement seized
The rebel thrones, but greater rage, to see
Thus foiled their mightiest; ours joy filled, and shout,
Presage of victory, and fierce desire   201
Of battle. Whereat Michael bid sound
The archangel trumpet; through the vast of heaven

---

107 **cloudy van:** foreboding vanguard   156 **synod:** assembly

It sounded, and the faithful armies rung
Hosanna to the Highest. Nor stood at gaze   205
The adverse legions, nor less hideous joined
The horrid shock. Now storming fury rose,
And clamour such as heard in heaven till now
Was never; arms on armour clashing brayed
Horrible discord, and the madding wheels   210
Of brazen chariots raged; dire was the noise
Of conflict; overhead the dismal hiss
Of fiery darts in flaming volleys flew,
And flying vaulted either host with fire.
So under fiery cope together rushed   215
Both battles main, with ruinous assault
And inextinguishable rage. All heaven
Resounded; and had earth been then, all earth
Had to her centre shook. What wonder? when
Millions of fierce encount'ring angels fought   220
On either side, the least of whom could wield
These elements, and arm him with the force
Of all their regions. How much more of power
Army against army numberless to raise
Dreadful combustion warring, and disturb,   225
Though not destroy, their happy native seat;
Had not the Eternal King Omnipotent,
From His strong-hold of heaven, high over-ruled
And limited their might; though numbered such
As each divided legion might have seemed   230
A numerous host; in strength each armèd hand
A legion; led in fight, yet leader seemed
Each warrior single as in chief, expert
When to advance, or stand, or turn the sway
Of battle, open when, and when to close   235
The ridges of grim war. No thought of flight,
None of retreat, no unbecoming deed
That argued fear; each on himself relied,
As only in his arm the moment lay
Of victory. Deeds of eternal fame   240
Were done, but infinite; for wide was spread
That war and various; sometimes on firm ground
A standing fight, then, soaring on main wing,
Tormented all the air; all air seemed then
Conflicting fire. Long time in even scale   245
The battle hung; till Satan, who that day
Prodigious power had shown, and met in arms
No equal, ranging through the dire attack
Of fighting seraphim confused, at length   249
Saw where the sword of Michael smote, and felled
Squadrons at once; with huge two-handed sway
Brandished aloft, the horrid edge came down
Wide-wasting; such destruction to withstand
He hasted, and opposed the rocky orb
Of tenfold adamant, his ample shield,   255
A vast circumference. At his approach
The great archangel from his warlike toil
Surceased, and glad, as hoping here to end
Intestine war in heaven, the arch-foe subdued

258 **Surceased:** stopped 259 **Intestine war:** civil war, an internal war

Or captive dragged in chains, with hostile frown 260
And visage all inflamed first thus began:
' "Author of evil, unknown till thy revolt,
Unnamed in heaven, now plenteous as thou seest
These acts of hateful strife, hateful to all,
Though heaviest by just measure on thyself,   265
And thy adherents. How hast thou disturbed
Heaven's blessed peace, and into nature brought
Misery, uncreated till the crime
Of thy rebellion! how hast thou instilled
Thy malice into thousands, once upright   270
And faithful, now proved false! But think not here
To trouble holy rest; heaven casts thee out
From all her confines. Heaven, the seat of bliss,
Brooks not the works of violence and war.
Hence then, and evil go with thee along,   275
Thy offspring, to the place of evil, hell;
Thou and thy wicked crew! there mingle broils,
Ere this avenging sword begin thy doom,
Or some more sudden vengeance, winged from God,
Precipitate thee with augmented pain."   280
'So spake the prince of angels; to whom thus
The adversary: "Nor think thou with wind
Of airy threats to awe whom yet with deeds
Thou canst not. Hast thou turned the least of these
To flight, or if to fall, but that they rise   285
Unvanquished, easier to transact with me
That thou shouldst hope, imperious, and with threats
To chase me hence? err not, that so shall end
The strife which thou callest evil, but we style
The strife of glory; which we mean to win,   290
Or turn this heaven itself into the hell
Thou fablest; here however to dwell free,
If not to reign. Meanwhile thy utmost force,
And join him named Almighty to thy aid,
I fly not, but have sought thee far and nigh."   295
'They ended parle, and both addressed for fight
Unspeakable; for who, though with the tongue
Of angels, can relate, or to what things
Liken on earth conspicuous, that may lift
Human imagination to such height   300
Of godlike power? for likest gods they seemed,
Stood they or moved, in stature, motion, arms,
Fit to decide the empire of great heaven.
Now waved their fiery swords, and in the air
Made horrid circles; two broad suns their shields 305
Blazed opposite, while Expectation stood
In horror. From each hand with speed retired,
Where erst was thickest fight, the angelic throng,
And left large field, unsafe within the wind
Of such commotion; such as, to set forth   310
Great things by small, if, nature's concord broke,
Among the constellations war were sprung,
Two planets, rushing from aspect malign
Of fiercest opposition, in mid-sky
Should combat, and their jarring spheres confound.
Together both with next to almighty arm   316

Up-lifted imminent, one stroke they aimed
That might determine, and not need repeat,
As not of power at once; nor odds appeared
In might or swift prevention. But the sword   320
Of Michael from the armoury of God
Was given him tempered so, that neither keen
Nor solid might resist that edge: it met
The sword of Satan, with steep force to smite
Descending, and in half cut sheer; nor stayed,   325
But with swift wheel reverse, deep ent'ring, shared
All his right side. Then Satan first knew pain,
And writhed him to and fro convolved; so sore
The griding sword with discontinuous wound
Passed through him. But th'ethereal substance
     closed,   330
Not long divisible; and from the gash
A stream of necturous humour issuing flowed
Sanguine, such as celestial spirits may bleed,
And all his armour stained, erewhile so bright.
Forthwith on all sides to his aid was run   335
By angels many and strong, who interposed
Defence, while others bore him on their shields
Back to his chariot, where it stood retired
From off the files of war. There they him laid
Gnashing for anguish, and despite, and shame,   340
To find himself not matchless, and his pride
Humbled by such rebuke, so far beneath
His confidence to equal God in power.
Yet soon he healed; for spirits that live throughout
Vital in every part, not as frail man   345
In entrails, heart or head, liver or reins,
Cannot but by annihilating die;
Nor in their liquid texture mortal wound
Receive, no more than can the fluid air:
All heart they live, all head, all eye, all ear,   350
All intellect, all sense; and, as they please,
They limb themselves, and colour, shape, or size
Assume, as likes them best, condense or rare.
     'Meanwhile in other parts like deeds deserved
Memorial, where the might of Gabriel fought,   355
And with fierce ensigns pierced the deep array
Of Moloch, furious king; who him defied,
And at his chariot-wheels to drag him bound
Threatened, nor from the Holy One of Heaven
Refrained his tongue blasphemous; but anon   360
Down-cloven to the waist, with shattered arms
And uncouth pain fled bellowing. On each wing
Uriel, and Raphael, his vaunting foe,
Though huge, and in a rock of diamond armed,
Vanquished Adramelech, and Asmadai,   365
Two potent thrones, that to be less than gods
Disdained, but meaner thoughts learned in their flight,
Mangled with ghastly wounds through plate and mail.
Nor stood unmindful Abdiel to annoy
The atheist crew, but with redoubled blow   370

Ariel, and Arioch, and the violence
Of Ramiel scorched and blasted, overthrew.
I might relate of thousands, and their names
Eternize here on earth; but those elect
Angels, contented with their fame in heaven,   375
Seek not the praise of men. The other sort,
In might though wondrous and in acts of war,
Nor of renown less eager, yet by doom
Cancelled from heaven and sacred memory,
Nameless in dark oblivion let them dwell.   380
For strength from truth divided, and from just,
Illaudable, nought merits but dispraise
And ignominy; yet to glory aspires
Vain-glorious, and through infamy seeks fame:
Therefore eternal silence be their doom.   385
     'And now, their mightiest quelled, the battle swerved,
With many an inroad gored; deformèd rout
Entered, and foul disorder; all the ground
With shivered armour strewn, and on a heap
Chariot and charioteer lay overturned,   390
And fiery-foaming steeds; what stood, recoiled
O'er-wearied, through the faint satanic host
Defensive scarce, or with pale fear surprised,
Then first with fear surprised, and sense of pain,
Fled ignominious, to such evil brought   395
By sin of disobedience; till that hour
Not liable to fear, or flight, or pain.
Far otherwise the inviolable saints,
In cubic phalanx firm, advanced entire,
Invulnerable, impenetrably armed;   400
Such high advantages their innocence
Gave them above their foes; not to have sinned,
Not to have disobeyed; in fight they stood
Unwearied, unobnoxious to be pained
By wound, though from their place by violence
     moved.   405
     'Now Night her course began, and, over heaven
Inducing darkness, grateful truce imposed,
And silence on the odious din of war:
Under her cloudy covert both retired,
Victor and vanquished. On the foughten field   410
Michael and his angels prevalent
Encamping, placed in guard their watches round,
Cherubic waving fires. On the other part,
Satan with his rebellious disappeared,
Far in the dark dislodged; and, void of rest,   415
His potentates to council called by night;
And in the midst thus undismayed began.
     ' "Oh, now in danger tried, now known in arms
Not to be overpowered, Companions dear,
Found worthy not of liberty alone,   420
Too mean pretence! but what we more affect,
Honour, dominion, glory, and renown;
Who have sustained one day in doubtful fight

---

328 **convolved**: convulsed 346 **reins**: kidneys 365 **Adramelech**: the
Babylonian sun god **Asmadai**: Asmodeus. See Book Four, note 166–171

371 **Ariel**: meaning 'lion of God' is another name for Jerusalem
Arioch: Arioch, king of Ellasar fought Abraham. See Genesis (14,1)
399 In a square formation the army advanced unbroken

(And if one day, why not eternal days?),
What Heaven's Lord had powerfullest to send   425
Against us from about His throne, and judged
Sufficient to subdue us to His will,
But proves not so. Then fallible, it seems,
Of future we may deem Him, though till now
Omniscient thought. True is, less firmly armed,   430
Some disadvantage we endured and pain,
Till now not known, but, known, as soon contemned;
Since now we find this our empyreal form
Incapable of mortal injury,
Imperishable, and, though pierced with wound,   435
Soon closing, and by native vigour healed.
Of evil then so small as easy think
The remedy; perhaps more valid arms,
Weapons more violent, when next we meet,
May serve to better us, and worse our foes,   440
Or equal what between us made the odds,
In nature none. If other hidden cause
Left them superior, while we can preserve
Unhurt our minds, and understanding sound,
Due search and consultation will disclose."   445
   'He sat; and in th'assembly next upstood
Nisroch, of principalities the prime;
As one he stood escaped from cruel fight,
Sore toiled, his riven arms to havoc hewn,
And cloudy in aspect thus answering spake: 450
   ' "Deliverer from new lords, leader to free
Enjoyment of our right as gods; yet hard
For gods, and too unequal work we find,
Against unequal arms to fight in pain,
Against unpained, impassive; from which evil   455
Ruin must needs ensue; for what avails
Valour or strength, though matchless, quelled with
      pain
Which all subdues, and makes remiss the hands
Of mightiest? Sense of pleasure we may well
Spare out of life perhaps, and not repine,   460
But live content, which is the calmest life:
But pain is perfect misery, the worst
Of evils, and, excessive, overturns
All patience. He, who therefore can invent
With what more forcible we may offend   465
Our yet unwounded enemies, or arm
Ourselves with like defence, to me deserves
No less than for deliverance what we owe."
   'Whereto with look composed Satan replied.
"Not uninvented that, which thou aright   470
Believest so main to our success, I bring.
Which of us who beholds the bright surface
Of this ethereous mould whereon we stand,
This continent of spacious heaven, adorned
With plant, fruit, flower ambrosial, gems, and gold;
Whose eye so superficially surveys   476
These things, as not to mind from whence they grow

Deep under ground, materials dark and crude,
Of spiritous and fiery spume, till touched
With heaven's ray, and tempered, they shoot forth   480
So beauteous, opening to the ambient light?
These in their dark nativity the deep
Shall yield us, pregnant with infernal flame;
Which, into hollow engines, long and round,
Thick-rammed, at th'other bore with touch of fire
Dilated and infuriate, shall send forth   486
From far, with thundering noise, among our foes
Such implements of mischief, as shall dash
To pieces, and o'erwhelm whatever stands
Adverse, that they shall fear we have disarmed   490
The Thunderer of His only dreaded bolt.
Nor long shall be our labour; yet ere dawn,
Effect shall end our wish. Meanwhile revive;
Abandon fear; to strength and counsel joined
Think nothing hard, much less to be despaired."   495
   'He ended, and his words their drooping cheer
Enlightened, and their languished hope revived.
The invention all admired, and each, how he
To be the inventor missed; so easy it seemed
Once found, which yet unfound most would have
      thought   500
Impossible. Yet, haply, of thy race
In future days, if malice should abound,
Some one intent on mischief, or inspired
With devilish machination, might devise
Like instrument to plague the sons of men   505
For sin, on war and mutual slaughter bent.
Forthwith from council to the work they flew;
None arguing stood; innumerable hands
Were ready; in a moment up they turned
Wide the celestial soil, and saw beneath   510
The originals of nature in their crude
Conception; sulphurous and nitrous foam
They found, they mingled, and, with subtle art,
Concocted and adusted they reduced
To blackest grain, and into store conveyed: 515
Part hidden veins digged up (nor hath this earth
Entrails unlike) of mineral and stone,
Whereof to found their engines and their balls
Of missive ruin; part incentive reed
Provide, pernicious with one touch to fire.   520
So all ere day-spring, under conscious night,
Secret they finished, and in order set,
With silent circumspection, unespied.
   'Now when fair morn orient in heaven appeared,
Up rose the victor-angels, and to arms   525
The matin trumpet sung. In arms they stood
Of golden panoply, refulgent host,
Soon banded; others from the dawning hills
Looked round, and scouts each coast light-armèd scour,
Each quarter, to descry the distant foe,   530
Where lodged, or whither fled, or if for fight,

---

447 **Nisroch**: an Assyrian god

479 **spume**: foam

In motion or in halt. Him soon they met
Under spread ensigns moving nigh, in slow
But firm battalion; back with speediest sail
Zophiel, of cherubim the swiftest wing,   535
Came flying, and in mid-air aloud thus cried.
  ' "Arm, Warriors, arm for fight; the foe at hand,
Whom fled we thought, will save us long pursuit
This day; fear not his flight; so thick a cloud
He comes, and settled in his face I see   540
Sad resolution, and secure. Let each
His adamantine coat gird well, and each
Fit well his helm, gripe fast his orbèd shield,
Borne even or high; for this day will pour down,
If I conjecture aught, no drizzling shower,   545
But rattling storm of arrows barbed with fire."
  'So warned he them, aware themselves, and soon
In order, quit of all impediment;
Instant without disturb they took alarm,
And onward moved embattled. When behold!   550
Not distant far with heavy pace the foe
Approaching gross and huge, in hollow cube
Training his devilish engin'ry, impaled
On every side with shadowing squadrons deep,
To hide the fraud. At interview both stood   555
A while; but suddenly at head appeared
Satan, and thus was heard commanding loud.
  ' "Vanguard, to right and left the front unfold;
That all may see who hate us, how we seek
Peace and composure, and with open breast   560
Stand ready to receive them, if they like
Our overture; and turn not back perverse:
But that I doubt; however witness, Heaven!
Heaven, witness thou anon! while we discharge
Freely our part: ye who appointed stand   565
Do as you have in charge, and briefly touch
What we propound, and loud that all may hear!"
  'So scoffing in ambiguous words, he scarce
Had ended; when to right and left the front
Divided, and to either flank retired: 570
Which to our eyes discovered, new and strange,
A triple mounted row of pillars laid
On wheels (for like to pillars most they seemed,
Or hollowed bodies made of oak or fir,
With branches lopped, in wood or mountain felled),
Brass, iron, stony mould, had not their mouths   576
With hideous orifice gaped on us wide,
Portending hollow truce. At each behind
A seraph stood, and in his hand a reed
Stood waving tipped with fire; while we, suspense,   580
Collected stood within our thoughts amused,
Not long; for sudden all at once their reeds
Put forth, and to a narrow vent applied
With nicest touch. Immediate in a flame,   584
But soon obscured with smoke, all heaven appeared,
From those deep-throated engines belched, whose roar
Embowellèd with outrageous noise the air,
And all her entrails tore, disgorging foul

Their devilish glut, chained thunderbolts and hail
Of iron globes; which, on the victor host   590
Levelled, with such impetuous fury smote,
That, whom they hit, none on their feet might stand,
Though standing else as rocks, but down they fell
By thousands, angel on archangel rolled;
The sooner for their arms; unarmed, they might   595
Have easily, as spirits, evaded swift
By quick contraction or remove; but now
Foul dissipation followed, and forced rout;
Nor served it to relax their serried files.
What should they do? if on they rushed, repulse   600
Repeated, and indecent overthrow
Doubled, would render them yet more despised,
And to their foes a laughter; for in view
Stood ranked of seraphim another row,
In posture to displode their second tire   605
Of thunder. Back defeated to return
They worse abhorred. Satan beheld their plight,
And to his mates thus in derision called.
  ' "O Friends! why come not on these victors proud
Erewhile they fierce were coming; and when we,   610
To entertain them fair with open front
And breast (what could we more?), propounded terms
Of composition, straight they changed their minds,
Flew off, and into strange vagaries fell,
As they would dance; yet for a dance they seemed   615
Somewhat extravagant and wild; perhaps
For joy of offered peace. But I suppose,
If our proposals once again were heard,
We should compel them to a quick result."
  'To whom thus Belial, in like gamesome mood.   620
"Leader! the terms we sent were terms of weight,
Of hard contents, and full of force urged home;
Such as we might perceive amused them all,
And stumbled many. Who receives them right,
Had need from head to foot well understand;   625
Not understood, this gift they have besides,
They show us when our foes walk not upright."
  'So they among themselves in pleasant vein
Stood scoffing, heightened in their thoughts beyond
All doubt of victory. Eternal Might   630
To match with their inventions they presumed
So easy, and of His thunder made a scorn,
And all His host derided, while they stood
A while in trouble. But they stood not long;
Rage prompted them at length, and found them arms
Against such hellish mischief fit to oppose.   636
Forthwith (behold the excellence, the power,
Which God hath in his mighty angels placed!)
Their arms away they threw, and to the hills
(For earth hath this variety from heaven   640
Of pleasure situate in hill and dale),
Light as the lightning-glimpse they ran, they flew;
From their foundations loosening to and fro,

605 **displode their second tire:** explode their second volley

They plucked the seated hills, with all their load,
Rocks, waters, woods, and by the shaggy tops   645
Up-lifting bore them in their hands. Amaze,
Be sure, and terror, seized the rebel host,
When coming towards them so dread they saw
The bottom of the mountains upward turned;
Till on those cursèd engines' triple-row   650
They saw them whelmed, and all their confidence
Under the weight of mountains buried deep;
Themselves invaded next, and on their heads
Main promontories flung, which in the air
Came shadowing, and oppressed whole legions
    armed;   655
Their armour helped their harm, crushed in and
    bruised
Into their substance pent, which wrought them pain
Implacable, and many a dolorous groan;
Long struggling underneath, ere they could wind
Out of such prison, though spirits of purest light,   660
Purest at first, now gross by sinning grown.
The rest, in imitation, to like arms
Betook them, and the neighbouring hills uptore:
So hills amid the air encountered hills,
Hurled to and fro with jaculation dire;   665
That under ground they fought in dismal shade;
Infernal noise! war seemed a civil game
To this uproar; horrid confusion heaped
Upon confusion rose. And now all heaven
Had gone to wrack, with ruin overspread,   670
Had not the Almighty Father, where He sits
Shrined in his sanctuary of heaven secure,
Consulting on the sum of things, foreseen
This tumult, and permitted all, advised:
That His great purpose He might so fulfil,   675
To honour His anointed Son avenged
Upon His enemies, and to declare
All power on Him transferred. Whence to His Son,
The Assessor of His throne, He thus began.
    ' "Effulgence of my glory, Son beloved,   680
Son, in whose face invisible is beheld
Visibly, what by deity I am;
And in whose hand what by decree I do,
Second Omnipotence! two days are past,
Two days, as we compute the days of heaven,   685
Since Michael and his powers went forth to tame
These disobedient. Sore hath been their fight,
As likeliest was, when two such foes met armed;
For to themselves I left them; and thou knowest,
Equal in their creation they were formed,   690
Save what sin hath impaired; which yet hath wrought
Insensibly, for I suspend their doom;
Whence in perpetual fight they needs must last
Endless, and no solution will be found:
War wearied hath performed what war can do,   695
And to disordered rage let loose the reins

With mountains, as with weapons, armed; which
    makes
Wild work in heaven, and dangerous to the main.
Two days are therefore past, the third is thine;
For thee I have ordained it; and thus far   700
Have suffered, that the glory may be thine
Of ending this great war, since none but Thou
Can end it. Into thee such virtue and grace
Immense I have transfused, that all may know
In heaven and hell thy power above compare;   705
And, this perverse commotion governed thus,
To manifest Thee worthiest to be Heir
Of all things; to be Heir, and to be King
By sacred unction, thy deservèd right.
Go, then, Thou Mightiest in Thy father's might;   710
Ascend my chariot, guide the rapid wheels
That shake heaven's basis, bring forth all my war,
My bow and thunder, my almighty arms
Gird on, and sword upon thy puissant thigh;
Pursue these sons of darkness, drive them out   715
From all heaven's bounds into the utter deep:
There let them learn, as likes them, to despise
God, and Messiah his anointed King."
    'He said, and on His son with rays direct
Shone full; He all His father full expressed   720
Ineffably into His face received;
And thus the Filial Godhead answering spake.
    ' "O Father, O Supreme of Heavenly Thrones,
First, Highest, Holiest, Best; Thou always seek'st
To glorify Thy son, I always Thee,   725
As is most just. This I my glory account,
My exaltation, and my whole delight,
That Thou, in me well pleased, declarest Thy will
Fulfilled, which to fulfil is all my bliss.
Sceptre and power, Thy giving, I assume,   730
And gladlier shall resign, when in the end
Thou shalt be all in all, and I in thee
For ever; and in me all whom Thou lovest:
But whom Thou hatest, I hate, and can put on
Thy terrors, as I put Thy mildness on,   735
Image of Thee in all things; and shall soon,
Armed with Thy might, rid heaven of these rebelled;
To their prepared ill mansion driven down,
To chains of darkness, and the undying worm;
That from Thy just obedience could revolt,   740
Whom to obey is happiness entire.
Then shall Thy saints unmixed, and from the impure
Far separate, circling Thy holy mount,
Unfeignèd halleluiahs to Thee sing,
Hymns of high praise, and I among them chief."   745
    'So said, He, o'er His sceptre bowing, rose
From the right hand of Glory where He sat;
And the third sacred morn began to shine,

---

709 **unction**: anointing

Dawning through heaven. Forth rushed with
    whirlwind sound
The chariot of Paternal Deity,   750
Flashing thick flames, wheel within wheel undrawn,
Itself instinct with spirit, but convoyed
By four cherubic shapes; four faces each
Had wonderous; as with stars, their bodies all
And wings were set with eyes; with eyes the wheels 755
Of beryl, and careering fires between;
Over their heads a crystal firmament,
Whereon a sapphire throne, inlaid with pure
Amber, and colours of the showery arch.
He, in celestial panoply all armed   760
Of radiant Urim, work divinely wrought,
Ascended; at His right hand Victory
Sat eagle-winged; beside Him hung his bow
And quiver with three-bolted thunder stored;
And from about Him fierce effusion rolled   765
Of smoke, and bickering flame, and sparkles dire:
Attended with ten thousand thousand saints,
He onward came; far off His coming shone;
And twenty thousand (I their number heard)
Chariots of God, half on each hand, were seen;   770
He on the wings of cherub rode sublime
On the crystalline sky, in sapphire throned,
Illustrious far and wide; but by His own
First seen. Them unexpected joy surprised,
When the great ensign of Messiah blazed   775
Aloft by angels borne, His sign in heaven;
Under whose conduct Michael soon reduced
His army, circumfused on either wing,
Under their Head imbodied all in one.
Before him Power Divine his way prepared;   780
At His command the uprooted hills retired
Each to his place; they heard His voice, and went
Obsequious; heaven his wonted face renewed,
And with fresh flowerets hill and valley smiled.
   'This saw His hapless foes, but stood obdured,   785
And to rebellious fight rallied their powers,
Insensate, hope conceiving from despair.
In heavenly spirits could such perverseness dwell?
But to convince the proud what signs avail,
Or wonders move th'obdurate to relent?   790
They, hardened more by what might most reclaim,
Grieving to see His glory, at the sight
Took envy; and, aspiring to His height,
Stood re-embattled fierce, by force or fraud
Weening to prosper, and at length prevail   795
Against God and Messiah, or to fall
In universal ruin last; and now
To final battle drew, disdaining flight,
Or faint retreat; when the great Son of God
To all His host on either hand thus spake.   800

760 **panoply**: splendid armour 761 **Urim**: sacred stones

   ' "Stand still in bright array, ye Saints; here stand,
Ye Angels armed; this day from battle rest:
Faithful hath been your warfare, and of God
Accepted, fearless in His righteous cause;
And as ye have received, so have ye done,   805
Invincibly. But of this cursèd crew
The punishment to other hand belongs;
Vengeance is His, or whose He sole appoints.
Number to this day's work is not ordained,
Nor multitude; stand only, and behold   810
God's indignation on these godless poured
By me; not you, but me, they have despised,
Yet envied; against me is all their rage,
Because the Father, to whom in heaven s'preme
Kingdom, and power, and glory appertains,   815
Hath honoured me, according to His will.
Therefore to me their doom He hath assigned;
That they may have their wish, to try with me
In battle which the stronger proves; they all,
Or I alone against them; since by strength   820
They measure all, of other excellence
Not emulous, nor care who them excels;
Nor other strife with them do I vouchsafe."
   'So spake the Son, and into terror changed
His count'nance too severe to be beheld,   825
And full of wrath bent on His enemies.
At once the Four spread out their starry wings
With dreadful shade contiguous, and the orbs
Of his fierce chariot rolled, as with the sound
Of torrent floods, or of a numerous host.   830
He on His impious foes right onward drove,
Gloomy as night; under His burning wheels
The steadfast empyrean shook throughout,
All but the throne itself of God. Full soon
Among them He arrived; in His right hand 835
Grasping ten thousand thunders, which He sent
Before Him, such as in their souls infixed
Plagues. They, astonished, all resistance lost,
All courage; down their idle weapons dropped.
O'er shields, and helms, and helmèd heads He rode
Of thrones and mighty seraphim prostrate,   841
That wished the mountains now might be again
Thrown on them, as a shelter from His ire.
Nor less on either side tempestuous fell
His arrows, from the fourfold-visaged Four   845
Distinct with eyes, and from the living wheels
Distinct alike with multitude of eyes;
One spirit in them ruled; and every eye
Glared lightning, and shot forth pernicious fire
Among th'accursed, that withered all their strength,
And of their wonted vigour left them drained, 851
Exhausted, spiritless, afflicted, fallen.
Yet half His strength He put not forth, but checked
His thunder in mid-volley; for He meant
Not to destroy, but root them out of heaven: 855
The overthrown He raised, and as a herd
Of goats or timorous flock together thronged

Drove them before him thunder-struck, pursued
With terrors, and with furies, to the bounds
And crystal wall of heaven; which, op'ning wide,   860
Rolled inward, and a spacious gap disclosed
Into the wasteful deep. The monstrous sight
Struck them with horror backward, but far worse
Urged them behind. Headlong themselves they threw
Down from the verge of heaven; eternal wrath   865
Burnt after them to the bottomless pit.
   'Hell heard the unsufferable noise, hell saw
Heaven ruining from heaven, and would have fled
Affrighted; but strict Fate had cast too deep
Her dark foundations, and too fast had bound.   870
Nine days they fell. Confounded Chaos roared,
And felt tenfold confusion in their fall
Through his wild anarchy, so huge a rout
Incumbered him with ruin. Hell at last
Yawning received them whole, and on them closed;
Hell, their fit habitation, fraught with fire   876
Unquenchable, the house of woe and pain.
Disburdened heaven rejoiced, and soon repaired
Her mural breach, returning whence it rolled.
Sole victor, from th'expulsion of his foes,   880
Messiah His triumphal chariot turned:
To meet Him all His saints, who silent stood
Eye-witnesses of his almighty acts,
With jubilee advanced; and, as they went,
Shaded with branching palm, each order bright,   885
Sung triumph, and him sung victorious King,
Son, Heir, and Lord, to Him dominion given,
Worthiest to reign. He, celebrated, rode
Triumphant through mid-heaven, into the courts
And temple of His mighty Father throned   890
On high; who into glory Him received,
Where now He sits at the right hand of bliss.
   'Thus, measuring things in heaven by things on
    earth,
At thy request, and that thou mayest beware
By what is past, to thee I have revealed   895
What might have else to human race been hid;
The discord which befell, and war in heaven
Among the angelic powers, and the deep fall
Of those too high aspiring, who rebelled
With Satan; he who envies now thy state,   900
Who now is plotting how he may seduce
Thee also from obedience, that, with him
Bereaved of happiness, thou mayest partake
His punishment, eternal misery;
Which would be all his solace and revenge,   905
As a despite done against the Most High,
Thee once to gain companion of his woe.
But listen not to his temptations, warn
Thy weaker; let it profit thee to have heard,
By terrible example, the reward   910
Of disobedience; firm they might have stood,
Yet fell; remember, and fear to transgress.'

BOOK SEVEN

Descend from heaven, Urania, by that name
If rightly thou art called, whose voice divine
Following, above the Olympian hill I soar,
Above the flight of Pegasean wing!
The meaning, not the name, I call: for thou   5
Nor of the Muses nine, nor on the top
Of old Olympus dwellest; but, heavenly born,
Before the hills appeared, or fountain flowed,
Thou with eternal Wisdom didst converse,
Wisdom thy sister, and with her didst play   10
In presence of the Almighty Father, pleased
With thy celestial song. Up led by thee
Into the heaven of heavens I have presumed,
An earthly guest, and drawn empyreal air,
Thy temp'ring: with like safety guided down   15
Return me to my native element:
Lest from this flying steed unreined (as once
Bellerophon, though from a lower clime),
Dismounted, on the Aleian field I fall,
Erroneous there to wander, and forlorn.   20
Half yet remains unsung, but narrower bound
Within the visible diurnal sphere;
Standing on earth, not rapt above the pole,
More safe I sing with mortal voice, unchanged
To hoarse or mute, though fallen on evil days,   25
On evil days though fallen, and evil tongues;
In darkness, and with dangers compassed round,
And solitude; yet not alone, while thou
Visitest my slumbers nightly, or when morn
Purples the east: still govern thou my song,   30
Urania, and fit audience find, though few.
But drive far off the barbarous dissonance
Of Bacchus and his revellers, the race
Of that wild rout that tore the Thracian bard
In Rhodope, where woods and rocks had ears   35
To rapture, till the savage clamour drowned
Both harp and voice; nor could the Muse defend
Her son. So fail not thou, who thee implores:
For thou art heavenly, she an empty dream.
   Say, Goddess, what ensued when Raphael,   40
The affable archangel, had forewarned
Adam, by dire example, to beware
Apostasy, by what befell in heaven
To those apostates; lest the like befall
In paradise to Adam or his race,   45

BOOK SEVEN – THE ARGUMENT: Raphael at the request of Adam relates how and wherefore this world was first created; that God, after the expelling of Satan and his Angels out of Heaven, declar'd his pleasure to create another World and other Creatures to dwell therein; sends his Son with Glory and attendance of Angels to perform the work of Creation in six days: the Angels celebrate with Hymns the performance thereof, and his reascension into Heaven 1 **Urania:** the Muse of astronomy 4 **Pegasean:** Pegasus, the winged horse 18 **Bellerophon:** Bellerophon rode on the back of Pegasus to heaven, but was thrown onto the Aleian field when Jupiter sent an insect to sting the ear of the flying horse 33 **Bacchus:** god of wine 34 **bard:** Orpheus, who was torn to pieces by the Bacchantes

Charged not to touch the interdicted tree,
If they transgress, and slight that sole command,
So easily obeyed amid the choice
Of all tastes else to please their appetite,
Though wand'ring. He, with his consorted Eve, 50
The story heard attentive, and was filled
With admiration and deep muse, to hear
Of things so high and strange; things, to their thought
So unimaginable, as hate in heaven,
And war so near the peace of God in bliss, 55
With such confusion: but the evil, soon
Driven back, redounded as a flood on those
From whom it sprung; impossible to mix
With blessedness. Whence Adam soon repealed
The doubts that in his heart arose: and now 60
Led on, yet sinless, with desire to know
What nearer might concern him, how this world
Of heaven and earth conspicuous first began;
When, and whereof created; for what cause;
What within Eden, or without, was done 65
Before his memory; as one whose drouth
Yet scarce allayed still eyes the current stream,
Whose liquid murmur heard new thirst excites,
Proceeded thus to ask his heavenly guest.
    'Great things, and full of wonder in our ears, 70
Far differing from this world, thou hast revealed,
Divine interpreter! by favour sent
Down from the empyrean, to forewarn
Us timely of what might else have been our loss,
Unknown, which human knowledge could not
    reach; 75
For which to the infinitely Good we owe
Immortal thanks, and His admonishment
Receive, with solemn purpose to observe
Immutably His sovran will, the end
Of what we are. But since thou hast vouchsafed 80
Gently, for our instruction, to impart
Things above earthly thought, which yet concerned
Our knowing, as to highest wisdom seemed,
Deign to descend now lower, and relate
What may no less perhaps avail us known, 85
How first began this heaven which we behold
Distant so high, with moving fires adorned
Innumerable; and this which yields or fills
All space, the ambient air wide interfused
Embracing round this florid earth; what cause 90
Moved the Creator, in His holy rest
Through all eternity, so late to build
In Chaos; and the work begun, how soon
Absolved; if unforbid thou mayest unfold
What we, not to explore the secrets ask 95
Of his eternal empire, but the more
To magnify His works, the more we know.
And the great light of day yet wants to run
Much of His race though steep; suspense in heaven,
Held by thy voice, thy potent voice, he hears, 100
And longer will delay to hear thee tell

His generation, and the rising birth
Of Nature from the unapparent deep:
Or if the star of evening and the moon
Haste to thy audience, Night with her will bring, 105
Silence; and Sleep, listening to thee, will watch;
Or we can bid his absence, till thy song
End, and dismiss thee ere the morning shine.'
    Thus Adam his illustrious guest besought;
And thus the godlike angel answered mild: 110
    'This also thy request, with caution asked,
Obtain; though to recount almighty works
What words or tongue of seraph can suffice,
Or heart of man suffice to comprehend?
Yet what thou canst attain, which best may serve 115
To glorify the Maker, and infer
Thee also happier, shall not be withheld
Thy hearing; such commission from above
I have received, to answer thy desire
Of knowledge within bounds; beyond, abstain 120
To ask; nor let thine own inventions hope
Things not revealed, which the invisible King,
Only omniscient, hath suppressed in night;
To none communicable in earth or heaven:
Enough is left besides to search and know. 125
But knowledge is as food, and needs no less
Her temperance over appetite, to know
In measure what the mind may well contain;
Oppresses else with surfeit, and soon turns
Wisdom to folly, as nourishment to wind. 130
    'Know, then, that, after Lucifer from heaven
(So call him, brighter once amidst the host
Of angels, than that star the stars among),
Fell with his flaming legions through the deep
Into his place, and the great Son returned 135
Victorious with his saints, the Omnipotent
Eternal Father from His throne beheld
Their multitude, and to His Son thus spake.
    ' "At least our envious foe hath failed, who thought
All like himself rebellious, by whose aid 140
This inaccessible high strength, the seat
Of Deity supreme, us dispossessed,
He trusted to have seized, and into fraud
Drew many, whom their place knows here no more:
Yet far the greater part have kept, I see, 145
Their station; heaven, yet populous, retains
Number sufficient to possess her realms
Though wide, and this high temple to frequent
With ministeries due, and solemn rites:
But, lest his heart exalt him in the harm 150
Already done, to have dispeopled heaven,
My damage fondly deemed, I can repair
That detriment, if such it be to lose
Self-lost; and in a moment will create
Another world, out of one man a race 155
Of men innumerable, there to dwell,
Not here; till, by degrees of merit raised,
They open to themselves at length the way

Up hither, under long obedience tried;
And earth be changed to heaven, and heaven to
    earth, 160
One kingdom, joy and union without end.
Meanwhile inhabit lax, ye Powers of Heaven;
And thou my Word, begotten Son, by thee
This I perform; speak Thou, and be it done!
My overshadowing spirit and might with thee 165
I send along; ride forth, and bid the deep
Within appointed bounds be heaven and earth;
Boundless the deep, because I Am who fill
Infinitude, nor vacuous the space.
Though I, uncircumscribed myself, retire, 170
And put not forth my goodness, which is free
To act or not, Necessity and Chance
Approach not me, and what I will is Fate."
  'So spake the Almighty, and to what he spake
His Word, the Filial Godhead, gave effect. 175
Immediate are the acts of God, more swift
Than time or motion, but to human ears
Cannot without process of speech be told,
So told as earthly notion can receive.
Great triumph and rejoicing was in heaven, 180
When such was heard declared the Almighty's will;
Glory they sung to the Most High, good will
To future men, and in their dwellings peace;
Glory to Him, whose just avenging ire
Had driven out th'ungodly from his sight 185
And th'habitations of the just; to Him
Glory and praise, whose wisdom had ordained
Good out of evil to create; instead
Of spirits malign, a better race to bring
Into their vacant room, and thence diffuse 190
His good to worlds and ages infinite.
  'So sang the hierarchies. Meanwhile the Son
On his great expedition now appeared,
Girt with omnipotence, with radiance crowned
Of majesty divine; sapience and love 195
Immense, and all His Father in him shone.
About his chariot numberless were poured
Cherub, and seraph, potentates, and thrones,
And virtues, wingèd spirits, and chariots winged
From the armoury of God; where stand of old 200
Myriads, between two brazen mountains lodged
Against a solemn day, harnessed at hand,
Celestial equipage; and now came forth
Spontaneous, for within them Spirit lived,
Attendant on their Lord. Heaven opened wide 205
Her ever-during gates, harmonious sound
On golden hinges moving, to let forth
The King of Glory, in His powerful Word
And Spirit, coming to create new worlds.
On heavenly ground they stood; and from the shore
They viewed the vast immeasurable abyss 211

Outrageous as a sea, dark, wasteful, wild,
Up from the bottom turned by furious winds
And surging waves, as mountains, to assault
Heaven's height, and with the centre mix the pole. 215
  ' "Silence, ye troubled Waves, and thou Deep,
    peace,"
Said then the Omnific Word; "your discord end!"
Nor stayed; but, on the wings of cherubim
Uplifted, in paternal glory rode
Far into Chaos, and the world unborn; 220
For Chaos heard His voice. Him all His train
Followed in bright procession, to behold
Creation, and the wonders of His might.
Then staid the fervid wheels, and in His hand
He took the golden compasses, prepared 225
In God's eternal store, to circumscribe
This universe, and all created things:
One foot He centred, and the other turned
Round through the vast profundity obscure;
And said, "Thus far extend, thus far thy bounds, 230
This be thy just circumference, O World!"
Thus God the heaven created, thus the earth,
Matter unformed and void: darkness profound
Covered the abyss: but on the watery calm
His brooding wings the Spirit of God outspread, 235
And vital virtue infused, and vital warmth
Throughout the fluid mass; but downward purged
The black tartareous cold infernal dregs,
Adverse to life: then founded, then conglobed
Like things to like; the rest to several place 240
Disparted, and between spun out the air;
And earth self-balanced on her centre hung.
  ' "Let there be light," said God; and forthwith Light
Ethereal, first of things, quintessence pure,
Sprung from the deep; and from her native east 245
To journey through the airy gloom began,
Sphered in a radiant cloud, for yet the sun
Was not; she in a cloudy tabernacle
Sojourned the while. God saw the light was good;
And light from darkness by the hemisphere 250
Divided: light the Day, and darkness Night,
He named. Thus was the first day even and morn:
Nor past uncelebrated, nor unsung
By the celestial choirs, when orient light
Exhaling first from darkness they beheld; 255
Birth-day of heaven and earth; with joy and shout
The hollow universal orb they filled,
And touched their golden harps, and hymning praised
God and His works; Creator Him they sung,
Both when first evening was, and when first morn. 260
  'Again, God said, "Let there be firmament
Amid the waters, and let it divide
The waters from the waters"; and God made
The firmament, expanse of liquid, pure,
Transparent, elemental air, diffused 265

---

162 **inhabit lax:** live spaciously   195 **sapience:** wisdom,
understanding

217 **Omnific:** all-creating

In circuit to the uttermost convex
Of this great round; partition firm and sure,
The waters underneath from those above
Dividing: for as earth, so He the world
Built on circumfluous waters calm, in wide   270
Crystalline ocean, and the loud misrule
Of Chaos far removed; lest fierce extremes
Contiguous might distemper the whole frame:
And heaven he named the firmament. So even
And morning chorus sung the second day.   275
    'The earth was formed, but in the womb as yet
Of waters, embryon immature involved,
Appeared not: over all the face of earth
Main ocean flowed, not idle; but, with warm
Prolific humour soft'ning all her globe,   280
Fermented the great mother to conceive,
Satiate with genial moisture; when God said,
"Be gathered now ye waters under Heaven
Into one place, and let dry land appear."
Immediately the mountains huge appear   285
Emergent, and their broad bare backs upheave
Into the clouds; their tops ascend the sky:
So high as heaved the tumid hills, so low
Down sunk a hollow bottom broad and deep,
Capacious bed of waters. Thither they   290
Hasted with glad precipitance, uprolled,
As drops on dust conglobing from the dry:
Part rise in crystal wall, or ridge direct,
For haste; such flight the great command impressed
On the swift floods. As armies at the call   295
Of trumpet (for of armies thou hast heard)
Troop to their standard; so the watery throng,
Wave rolling after wave, where way they found,
If steep, with torrent rapture, if through plain,
Soft-ebbing; nor withstood them rock or hill;   300
But they, or under ground, or circuit wide
With serpent error wandering, found their way,
And on the washy ooze deep channels wore;
Easy, ere God had bid the ground be dry,
All but within those banks, where rivers now   305
Stream, and perpetual draw their humid train.
The dry land, earth; and the great receptacle
Of congregated waters, he called seas:
And saw that it was good; and said, "Let the earth
Put forth the verdant grass, herb yielding seed,   310
And fruit-tree yielding fruit after her kind,
Whose seed is in herself upon the earth."
He scarce had said, when the bare earth, till then
Desert and bare, unsightly, unadorned,
Brought forth the tender grass, whose verdure clad   315
Her universal face with pleasant green;
Then herbs of every leaf, that sudden flowered
Opening their various colours, and made gay
Her bosom, smelling sweet: and, these scarce blown,
Forth flourished thick the clust'ring vine, forth crept
The swelling gourd, up stood the corny reed   321
Embattled in her field, and the humble shrub,

And bush with frizzled hair implicit. Last
Rose, as in dance, the stately trees, and spread   324
Their branches hung with copious fruit, or gemmed
Their blossoms. With high woods the hills were
    crowned;
With tufts the valleys, and each fountain side;
With borders long the rivers: that earth now
Seemed like to heaven, a seat where gods might
    dwell,
Or wander with delight, and love to haunt   330
Her sacred shades: though God had yet not rained
Upon the earth, and man to till the ground
None was; but from the earth a dewy mist
Went up, and watered all the ground, and each
Plant of the field; which, ere it was in the earth,   335
God made, and every herb, before it grew
On the green stem. God saw that it was good.
So even and morn recorded the third day.
    'Again th'Almighty spake, "Let there be lights
High in th'expanse of heaven, to divide   340
The day from night; and let them be for signs,
For seasons, and for days, and circling years;
And let them be for lights, as I ordain
Their office in the firmament of heaven,
To give light on the earth"; and it was so.   345
And God made two great lights, great for their use
To Man, the greater to have rule by day,
The less by night, altern; and made the stars,
And set them in the firmament of heaven
To illuminate the earth, and rule the day   350
In their vicissitude, and rule the night,
And light from darkness to divide. God saw,
Surveying His great work, that it was good:
For of celestial bodies first the sun
A mighty sphere He framed, unlightsome first,   355
Though of ethereal mould: then formed the moon
Globose, and every magnitude of stars,
And sowed with stars the heaven, thick as a field:
Of light by far the greater part He took,
Transplanted from her cloudy shrine, and placed   360
In the sun's orb, made porous to receive
And drink the liquid light; firm to retain
Her gathered beams, great palace now of light.
Hither, as to their fountain, other stars
Repairing, in their golden urns draw light,   365
And hence the morning-planet gilds her horns;
By tincture or reflection they augment
Their small peculiar, though from human sight
So far remote, with diminution seen,
First in the east his glorious lamp was seen,   370
Regent of day, and all the horizon round
Invested with bright rays, jocund to run
His longitude through heaven's high road; the grey
Dawn, and the Pleiades, before him danced,
Shedding sweet influence. Less bright the moon,   375

357 **Globose:** having the form of a globe   374 **Pleiades:** a group of stars

But opposite in levelled west was set,
His mirror, with full face borrowing her light
From him; for other light she needed none
In that aspect, and still that distance keeps
Till night; then in the east her turn she shines, 380
Revolved on Heaven's great axle, and her reign
With thousand lesser lights dividual holds,
With thousand thousand stars, that then appeared
Spangling the hemisphere. Then first adorned
With their bright luminaries that set and rose, 385
Glad evening and glad morn crowned the fourth day.
   'And God said, "Let the waters generate
Reptile with spawn abundant, living soul:
And let fowl fly above the earth, with wings
Displayed on the open firmament of heaven." 390
And God created the great whales, and each
Soul living, each that crept, which plenteously
The waters generated by their kinds;
And every bird of wing after his kind;
And saw that it was good, and blessed them, saying,
"Be fruitful, multiply, and in the seas, 396
And lakes, and running streams, the waters fill;
And let the fowl be multiplied, on the earth."
Forthwith the sounds and seas, each creek and bay,
With fry innumerable swarm, and shoals 400
Of fish that with their fins, and shining scales,
Glide under the green wave, in sculls that oft
Bank the mid sea: part single, or with mate,
Graze the sea-weed their pasture, and through groves
Of coral stray; or, sporting with quick glance, 405
Show to the sun their waved coats dropped with gold;
Or, in their pearly shells at ease, attend
Moist nutriment; or under rocks their food
In jointed armour watch: on smooth the seal
And bended dolphins play: part huge of bulk 410
Wallowing unwieldy, enormous in their gait,
Tempest the ocean: there leviathan,
Hugest of living creatures, on the deep
Stretched like a promontory sleeps or swims,
And seems a moving land; and at his gills 415
Draws in, and at his trunk spouts out, a sea.
Meanwhile the tepid caves, and fens, and shores,
Their brood as numerous hatch, from the egg that
    soon
Bursting with kindly rupture forth disclosed
Their callow young; but feathered soon and fledge 420
They summed their pens; and, soaring the air sublime,
With clang despised the ground, under a cloud
In prospect; there the eagle and the stork
On cliffs and cedar tops their eyries build:
Part loosely wing the region, part more wise 425
In common, ranged in figure, wedge their way,
Intelligent of seasons, and set forth
Their airy caravan, high over seas
Flying, and over lands, with mutual wing

402 **sculls:** schools

Easing their flight; so steers the prudent crane 430
Her annual voyage, borne on winds; the air
Floats as they pass, fanned with unnumbered plumes:
From branch to branch the smaller birds with song
Solaced the woods, and spread their painted wings
Till even; nor then the solemn nightingale 435
Ceased warbling, but all night tuned her soft lays:
Others, on silver lakes and rivers, bathed
Their downy breast; the swan with archèd neck,
Between her white wings mantling proudly, rows
Her state with oary feet; yet oft they quit 440
The dank, and, rising on stiff pennons, tower
The mid aereal sky. Others on ground
Walked firm; the crested cock whose clarion sounds
The silent hours, and the other whose gay train
Adorns him, coloured with the florid hue 445
Of rainbows and starry eyes. The waters thus
With fish replenished, and the air with fowl,
Evening and morn solemnized the fifth day.
   'The sixth, and of creation last, arose
With evening harps and matin; when God said, 450
"Let the earth bring forth soul living in her kind,
Cattle, and creeping things, and beast of the earth,
Each in their kind." The earth obeyed, and straight
Opening her fertile womb teemed at a birth
Innumerous living creatures, perfect forms, 455
Limbed and full grown: Out of the ground up-rose,
As from his lair, the wild beast where he wons
In forest wild, in thicket, brake, or den;
Among the trees in pairs they rose, they walked:
The cattle in the fields and meadows green: 460
Those rare and solitary, these in flocks
Pasturing at once, and in broad herds up-sprung.
The grassy clods now calved; now half appeared
The tawny lion, pawing to get free 464
His hinder parts, then springs as broke from bonds,
And rampant shakes his brinded mane; the ounce,
The libbard, and the tiger, as the mole
Rising, the crumbled earth above them threw
In hillocks: The swift stag from under ground
Bore up his branching head: Scarce from his mould
Behemoth biggest born of earth upheaved 471
His vastness: Fleeced the flocks and bleating rose,
As plants: Ambiguous between sea and land
The river-horse, and scaly crocodile.
At once came forth whatever creeps the ground, 475
Insect or worm: those waved their limber fans
For wings, and smallest lineaments exact
In all the liveries decked of summer's pride
With spots of gold and purple, azure and green:
These, as a line, their long dimension drew, 480
Streaking the ground with sinuous trace; not all
Minims of nature; some of serpent-kind,

457 **wons:** dwells 466 **ounce:** lynx 467 **libbard:** leopard 471 **Behemoth:** perhaps a kind of elephant 474 **river-horse:** hippopotamus

Wond'rous in length and corpulence, involved
Their snaky folds, and added wings. First crept
The parsimonious emmet, provident   485
Of future; in small room large heart enclosed;
Pattern of just equality perhaps
Hereafter, joinèd in her popular tribes
Of commonalty. Swarming next appeared
The female bee, that feeds her husband drone   490
Deliciously, and builds her waxen cells
With honey stored: The rest are numberless,
And thou their natures knowest, and gavest them
     names,
Needless to thee repeated; nor unknown
The serpent, subtlest beast of all the field,   495
Of huge extent sometimes, with brazen eyes
And hairy mane terrific, though to thee
Not noxious, but obedient at thy call.
     'Now heaven in all her glory shone, and rolled
Her motions, as the great first Mover's hand   500
First wheeled their course: earth in her rich attire
Consummate lovely smiled; air, water, earth,
By fowl, fish, beast, was flown, was swum, was walked,
Frequent; and of the sixth day yet remained:
There wanted yet the master-work, the end   505
Of all yet done; a creature, who, not prone
And brute as other creatures, but endued
With sanctity of reason, might erect
His stature, and upright with front serene
Govern the rest, self-knowing; and from thence   510
Magnanimous to correspond with heaven,
But grateful to acknowledge whence his good
Descends, thither with heart, and voice, and eyes
Directed in devotion, to adore
And worship God Supreme, who made him chief   515
Of all His works: therefore the Omnipotent
Eternal Father (for where is not He
Present?) thus to His Son audibly spake.
"Let us make now Man in our image, Man
In our similitude, and let them rule   520
Over the fish and fowl of sea and air,
Beast of the field, and over all the earth,
And every creeping thing that creeps the ground."
This said, he formed thee, Adam, thee, O Man,
Dust of the ground, and in thy nostrils breathed   525
The breath of life; in His own image He
Created thee, in the image of God
Express; and thou becam'st a living soul.
Male He created thee; but thy consort
Female, for race; then blessed mankind, and said,   530
"Be fruitful, multiply, and fill the earth;
Subdue it, and throughout dominion hold
Over fish of the sea, and fowl of the air,
And every living thing that moves on the earth.

485 **emmet:** ant

Wherever thus created, for no place   535
Is yet distinct by name, thence, as thou knowest,
He brought thee into this delicious grove,
This garden, planted with the trees of God,
Delectable both to behold and taste;
And freely all their pleasant fruit for food   540
Gave thee; all sorts are here that all the earth yields,
Variety without end; but of the tree,
Which, tasted, works knowledge of good and evil,
Thou mayest not; in the day thou eatest, thou diest;
Death is the penalty imposed; beware,   545
And govern well thy appetite; lest Sin
Surprise thee, and her black attendant Death."
     'Here finished He, and all that He had made
Viewed, and behold all was entirely good;
So even and morn accomplished the sixth day: 550
Yet not till the Creator from His work
Desisting, though unwearied, up returned,
Up to the heaven of heavens, His high abode;
Thence to behold this new-created world,
Th'addition of His empire, how it showed   555
In prospect from His throne, how good, how fair,
Answering His great idea. Up He rode
Followed with acclamation, and the sound
Symphonious of ten thousand harps, that tuned
Angelic harmonies. The earth, the air   560
Resounded (thou rememberest, for thou heardst),
The heavens and all the constellations rung,
The planets in their station listening stood,
While the bright pomp ascended jubilant.
"Open, ye everlasting Gates!" they sung,   565
"Open, ye Heavens! your living doors; let in
The great Creator from His work returned
Magnificent, His six days' work, a world;
Open, and henceforth oft; for God will deign
To visit oft the dwellings of just men,   570
Delighted; and with frequent intercourse
Thither will send His wingèd messengers
On errands of supernal grace." So sung
The glorious train ascending: He through heaven,
That opened wide her blazing portals, led   575
To God's eternal house direct the way;
A broad and ample road, whose dust is gold
And pavement stars, as stars to thee appear,
Seen in the galaxy, that milky way,
Which nightly, as a circling zone, thou seest   580
Powdered with stars. And now on earth the seventh
Evening arose in Eden, for the sun
Was set, and twilight from the east came on,
Forerunning night; when at the holy mount
Of heaven's high-seated top, th'imperial throne   585
Of Godhead, fixed for ever firm and sure,
The Filial Power arrived, and sat Him down
With His great Father; for He also went
Invisible, yet stayed (such privilege

Hath Omnipresence), and the work ordained, 590
Author and End of all things; and, from work
Now resting, blessed and hallowed the seventh day,
As resting on that day from all His work,
But not in silence holy kept: the harp
Had work and rested not; the solemn pipe, 595
And dulcimer, all organs of sweet stop,
All sounds on fret by string or golden wire,
Tempered soft tunings, intermixed with voice
Choral or unison: of incense clouds,
Fuming from golden censers, hid the mount. 600
Creation and the six days' acts they sung:
"Great are thy works, Jehovah! infinite
Thy power! what thought can measure Thee, or
    tongue
Relate Thee! Greater now in Thy return
Than from the giant angels. Thee that day 605
Thy thunders magnified; but to create
Is greater than created to destroy.
Who can impair Thee, Mighty King, or bound
Thy empire! Easily the proud attempt
Of spirits apostate, and their counsels vain, 610
Thou hast repelled; while impiously they thought
Thee to diminish, and from Thee withdraw
The number of Thy worshippers. Who seeks
To lessen Thee, against his purpose serves
To manifest the more Thy might: his evil 615
Thou usest, and from thence createst more good.
Witness this new-made world, another heaven
From heaven-gate not far, founded in view
On the clear hyaline, the glassy sea;
Of amplitude almost immense, with stars 620
Numerous, and every star perhaps a world
Of destined habitation; but Thou knowest
Their seasons: among these the seat of Men,
Earth, with her nether ocean circumfused,
Their pleasant dwelling-place. Thrice-happy Men, 625
And sons of Men, whom God hath thus advanced!
Created in His image, there to dwell
And worship Him; and in reward to rule
Over His works, on earth, in sea, or air,
And multiply a race of worshippers 630
Holy and just. Thrice happy, if they know
Their happiness, and persevere upright!"
    'So sung they, and the empyrean rung
With hallelujahs. Thus was sabbath kept.
And thy request think now fulfilled, that asked 635
How first this world and face of things began,
And what before thy memory was done
From the beginning; that posterity,
Informed by thee, might know. If else thou seekest
Aught, not surpassing human measure, say.' 640

619 **hyaline:** crystalline

BOOK EIGHT
THE angel ended, and in Adam's ear
So charming left his voice, that he a while
Thought him still speaking, still stood fixed to hear;
Then, as new waked, thus gratefully replied.
    'What thanks sufficient, or what recompense 5
Equal, have I to render thee, divine
Historian, who thus largely hast allayed
The thirst I had of knowledge, and vouchsafed
This friendly condescension to relate
Things else by me unsearchable, now heard 10
With wonder, but delight, and, as is due,
With glory attributed to the high
Creator! Something yet of doubt remains,
Which only thy solution can resolve.
When I behold this goodly frame, this world, 15
Of heaven and earth consisting; and compute
Their magnitudes; this earth, a spot, a grain,
An atom, with the firmament compared
And all her numbered stars, that seem to roll
Spaces incomprehensible (for such 20
Their distance argues, and their swift return
Diurnal), merely to officiate light
Round this opacous earth, this punctual spot,
One day and night; in all her vast survey
Useless besides; reasoning I oft admire, 25
How Nature wise and frugal could commit
Such disproportions, with superfluous hand
So many nobler bodies to create,
Greater so manifold, to this one use,
For aught appears, and on their orbs impose 30
Such restless revolution day by day
Repeated; while the sedentary earth,
That better might with far less compass move,
Served by more noble than herself, attains
Her end without least motion, and receives, 35
As tribute, such a sumless journey brought
Of incorporeal speed, her warmth and light;
Speed, to describe whose swiftness number fails.'
    So spake our sire, and by his countenance seemed
Ent'ring on studious thoughts abstruse; which Eve 40
Perceiving, where she sat retired in sight,
With lowliness majestic from her seat,
And grace that won who saw to wish her stay,
Rose, and went forth among her fruits and flowers,
To visit how they prospered, bud and bloom, 45
Her nursery; they at her coming sprung,
And, touched by her fair tendance, gladlier grew.

BOOK EIGHT – THE ARGUMENT: Adam inquires concerning celestial Motions, is doubtfully answer'd, and exhorted to search rather things more worthy of knowledge: Adam assents, and still desirous to detain Raphael, relates to him what he remember'd since his own Creation, his placing in Paradise, his talk with God concerning solitude and fit society, his first meeting and Nuptials with Eve, his discourse with the Angel thereupon; who after admonitions repeated departs 22 **Diurnal:** daily 32 **sedentary earth:** motionless earth

Yet went she not, as not with such discourse
Delighted, or not capable her ear
Of what was high: such pleasure she reserved, 50
Adam relating, she sole auditress;
Her husband the relater she preferred
Before the angel, and of him to ask
Chose rather; he, she knew, would intermix
Grateful digressions, and solve high dispute 55
With conjugal caresses: from his lip
Not words alone pleased her. Oh! when meet now
Such pairs, in love and mutual honour joined?
With goddess-like demeanour forth she went,
Not unattended; for on her, as queen, 60
A pomp of winning Graces waited still,
And from about her shot darts of desire
Into all eyes, to wish her still in sight.
And Raphael now, to Adam's doubt proposed,
Benevolent and facile thus replied. 65
    'To ask or search, I blame thee not; for heaven
Is as the book of God before thee set,
Wherein to read His wond'rous works, and learn
His seasons, hours, or days, or months, or years:
This to attain, whether heaven move or earth, 70
Imports not, if thou reckon right; the rest
From man or angel the great Architect
Did wisely to conceal, and not divulge
His secrets to be scanned by them who ought
Rather admire; or, if they list to try 75
Conjecture, He His fabric of the heavens
Hath left to their disputes, perhaps to move
His laughter at their quaint opinions wide
Hereafter; when they come to model heaven
And calculate the stars, how they will wield 80
The mighty frame; how build, unbuild, contrive
To save appearances; how gird the sphere
With centric and eccentric scribbled o'er,
Cycle and epicycle, orb in orb.
Already by thy reasoning this I guess, 85
Who art to lead thy offspring, and supposest
That bodies bright and greater should not serve
The less not bright, nor heaven such journeys run,
Earth sitting still, when she alone receives
The benefit. Consider first, that great 90
Or bright infers not excellence: the earth
Though, in comparison of heaven, so small,
Nor glistering, may of solid good contain
More plenty than the sun that barren shines;
Whose virtue on itself works no effect, 95
But in the fruitful earth; there first received,
His beams, unactive else, their vigour find.
Yet not to earth are those bright luminaries
Officious; but to thee, earth's habitant.
And for the heaven's wide circuit, let it speak 100

The Maker's high magnificence, who built
So spacious, and His line stretched out so far;
That Man may know he dwells not in his own;
An edifice too large for him to fill,
Lodged in a small partition; and the rest 105
Ordained for uses to his Lord best known.
The swiftness of those circles attribute,
Though numberless, to His omnipotence,
That to corporeal substances could add
Speed almost spiritual. Me thou think'st not slow, 110
Who since the morning-hour set out from heaven
Where God resides, and ere mid-day arrived
In Eden; distance inexpressible
By numbers that have name. But this I urge,
Admitting motion in the heavens, to show 115
Invalid that which thee to doubt it moved;
Not that I so affirm, though so it seem
To thee who hast thy dwelling here on earth.
God, to remove His ways from human sense,
Placed heaven from earth so far, that earthly sight,
If it presume, might err in things too high, 121
And no advantage gain. What if the sun
Be centre to the world; and other stars,
By his attractive virtue and their own
Incited, dance about Him various rounds? 125
Their wandering course now high, now low, then hid,
Progressive, retrograde, or standing still,
In six thou seest; and what if seventh to these
The planet earth, so steadfast though she seem,
Insensibly three different motions move? 130
Which else to several spheres thou must ascribe,
Moved contrary with thwart obliquities;
Or save the sun his labour, and that swift
Nocturnal and diurnal rhomb supposed,
Invisible else above all stars, the wheel 135
Of day and night; which needs not thy belief,
If earth, industrious of herself, fetch day
Travelling east, and with her part averse
From the sun's beam meet night, her other part
Still luminous by his ray. What if that light, 140
Sent from her through the wide transpicuous air,
To the terrestrial moon be as a star,
Enlightening her by day, as she by night
This earth? reciprocal, if land be there,
Fields and inhabitants. Her spots thou seest 145
As clouds, and clouds may rain, and rain produce
Fruits in her softened soil for some to eat
Allotted there; and other suns perhaps,
With their attendant moons, thou wilt descry,
Communicating male and female light; 150
Which two great sexes animate the world,
Stored in each orb perhaps with some that live.
For such vast room in Nature unpossessed

84 **epicycle**: small cycle

134 **rhomb**: here referring to a lozenge-shaped orbit

By living soul, desert and desolate,
Only to shine, yet scarce to contribute 155
Each orb a glimpse of light, conveyed so far
Down to this habitable, which returns
Light back to them, is obvious to dispute.
Whether thus these things, or whether not;
But whether the sun, predominant in heaven, 160
Rise on the earth; or earth rise on the sun;
He from the east his flaming road begin;
Or she from west her silent course advance,
With inoffensive pace that spinning sleeps
On her soft axle, while she paces even, 165
And bears thee soft with the smooth hair along;
Solicit not thy thoughts with matters hid;
Leave them to God above; him serve, and fear!
Of other creatures, as him pleases best,
Wherever placed, let him dispose; joy thou 170
In what he gives to thee, this paradise
And thy fair Eve; heaven is for thee too high
To know what passes there; be lowly wise:
Think only what concerns thee, and thy being;
Dream not of other worlds, what creatures there 175
Live, in what state, condition, or degree;
Contented that thus far hath been revealed
Not of earth only, but of highest heaven.
  To whom thus Adam, cleared of doubt, replied:
'How fully hast thou satisfied me, pure 180
Intelligence of heaven, Angel serene!
And, freed from intricacies, taught to live
The easiest way; nor with perplexing thoughts
To interrupt the sweet of life, from which
God hath bid dwell far off all anxious cares, 185
And not molest us; unless we ourselves
Seek them with wand'ring thoughts, and notions vain.
But apt the mind or fancy is to rove
Unchecked, and of her roving is no end;
Till warned, or by experience taught, she learn, 190
That, not to know at large of things remote
From use, obscure and subtle; but, to know
That which before us lies in daily life,
Is the prime wisdom: what is more, is fume,
Or emptiness, or fond impertinence: 195
And renders us, in things that most concern,
Unpractised, unprepared, and still to seek.
Therefore from this high pitch let us descend
A lower flight, and speak of things at hand
Useful; whence, haply, mention may arise 200
Of something not unseasonable to ask,
By sufferance, and thy wonted favour, deigned.
Thee I have heard relating what was done
Ere my remembrance: now, hear me relate
My story, which perhaps thou hast not heard; 205

194 **fume:** vapour-like, transient 195 **fond impertinence:** foolish irrelevance

And day is not yet spent; till then thou seest
How subtly to detain thee I devise;
Inviting thee to hear while I relate;
Fond! were it not in hope of thy reply:
For, while I sit with thee, I seem in heaven; 210
And sweeter thy discourse is to my ear
Than fruits of palm-tree pleasantest to thirst
And hunger both, from labour, at the hour
Of sweet repast; they satiate, and soon fill,
Though pleasant; but thy words, with grace divine 215
Imbued, bring to their sweetness no satiety.'
  To whom thus Raphael answered heavenly meek:
'Nor are thy lips ungraceful, Sire of men,
Nor tongue ineloquent; for God on thee
Abundantly His gifts hath also poured 220
Inward and outward both, His image fair:
Speaking, or mute, all comeliness and grace
Attends thee; and each word, each motion, forms;
Nor less think we in heaven of thee on earth
Than of our fellow-servant, and inquire 225
Gladly into the ways of God with Man:
For God, we see, hath honoured thee, and set
On Man His equal love. Say therefore on;
For I that day was absent, as befell,
Bound on a voyage uncouth and obscure, 230
Far on excursion toward the gates of hell;
Squared in full legion (such command we had)
To see that none thence issued forth a spy,
Or enemy, while God was in His work;
Lest He, incensed at such eruption bold, 235
Destruction with creation might have mixed.
Not that they durst without His leave attempt;
But us He sends upon His high behests
For state, as Sovran King; and to inure
Our prompt obedience. Fast we found, fast shut, 240
The dismal gates, and barricadoed strong;
But long ere our approaching heard within
Noise, other than the sound of dance or song,
Torment, and loud lament, and furious rage.
Glad we returned up to the coasts of light 245
Ere sabbath-evening: so we had in charge.
But thy relation now; for I attend,
Pleased with thy words no less than thou with mine.'
  So spake the godlike power, and thus our sire:
'For Man to tell how human life began 250
Is hard; for who himself beginning knew
Desire with thee still longer to converse
Induced me. As new-waked from soundest sleep,
Soft on the flowery herb I found me laid,
In balmy sweat; which with his beams the sun 255
Soon dried, and on the reeking moisture fed.
Straight toward heaven my wondering eyes I turned,
And gazed a while the ample sky; till, raised
By quick instinctive motion, up I sprung,
As thitherward endeavouring, and upright 260

Stood on my feet: about me round I saw
Hill, dale, and shady woods, and sunny plains,
And liquid lapse of murmuring streams; by these,
Creatures that lived and moved, and walked, or flew;
Birds on the branches warbling; all things smiled; 265
With fragrance and with joy my heart o'erflowed.
Myself I then perused, and limb by limb
Surveyed, and sometimes went, and sometimes ran
With supple joints, as lively vigour led:
But who I was, or where, or from what cause, 270
Knew not; to speak I tried, and forthwith spake;
My tongue obeyed, and readily could name
Whate'er I saw. "Thou Sun," said I, "fair light,
And thou enlightened Earth, so fresh and gay,
Ye Hills, and Dales, ye Rivers, Woods, and Plains, 275
And ye that live and move, fair Creatures, tell,
Tell, if ye saw, how I came thus, how here? –
Not of myself – by some great Maker then,
In goodness and in power pre-eminent:
Tell me, how may I know Him, how adore, 280
From whom I have that thus I move and live,
And feel that I am happier than I know."
While thus I called, and strayed I knew not whither,
From where I first drew air, and first beheld
This happy light, when answer none returned, 285
On a green shady bank, profuse of flowers,
Pensive I sat me down. There gentle sleep
First found me, and with soft oppression seized
My drowsèd sense, untroubled, though I thought
I then was passing to my former state 290
Insensible, and forthwith to dissolve:
When suddenly stood at my head a dream,
Whose inward apparition gently moved
My fancy to believe I yet had being, 294
And lived. One came, methought, of shape divine,
And said, "Thy mansion wants thee, Adam; rise,
First Man, of men innumerable ordained
First Father! called by thee, I come thy guide
To the garden of bliss, thy seat prepared."
So saying, by the hand he took me raised, 300
And over fields and waters, as in air
Smooth-sliding without step, last led me up
A woody mountain; whose high top was plain,
A circuit wide, enclosed, with goodliest trees
Planted, with walks, and bowers; that what I saw 305
Of earth before scarce pleasant seemed. Each tree,
Loaden with fairest fruit that hung to the eye
Tempting, stirred in me sudden appetite
To pluck and eat; whereat I waked, and found
Before mine eyes all real, as the dream 310
Had lively shadowed. Here had new-begun
My wandering, had not He, who was my guide
Up hither, from among the trees appeared,
Presence Divine. Rejoicing, but with awe,
In adoration at His feet I fell 315
Submiss. He reared me, and "Whom thou sought'st
    I am,"

Said mildly, "Author of all this thou seest
Above, or round about thee, or beneath.
This paradise I give thee, count it thine
To till and keep, and of the fruit to eat. 320
Of every tree that in the garden grows
Eat freely with glad heart; fear here no dearth:
But of the tree whose operation brings
Knowledge of good and ill, which I have set
The pledge of thy obedience and thy faith, 325
Amid the garden by the tree of life,
Remember what I warn thee, shun to taste,
And shun the bitter consequence: for know,
The day thou eatest thereof, my sole command
Transgressed, inevitably thou shalt die, 330
From that day mortal; and this happy state
Shalt lose, expelled from hence into a world
Of woe and sorrow." Sternly He pronounced
The rigid interdiction, which resounds
Yet dreadful in mine ear, though in my choice 335
Not to incur; but soon his clear aspect
Returned, and gracious purpose thus renewed:
"Not only these fair bounds, but all the earth
To thee and to thy race I give; as lords
Possess it, and all things that therein live, 340
Or live in sea, or air; beast, fish, and fowl.
In sign whereof, each bird and beast behold
After their kinds; I bring them to receive
From thee their names, and pay thee fealty
With low subjection; understand the same 345
Of fish within their watery residence,
Not hither summoned, since they cannot change
Their element, to draw the thinner air."
As thus he spake, each bird and beast behold
Approaching two and two; these cow'ring low 350
With blandishment; each bird stooped on his wing.
I named them, as they passed, and understood
Their nature, with such knowledge God endued
My sudden apprehension: But in these
I found not what methought I wanted still; 355
And to the heavenly Vision thus presumed.
  ' "Oh, by what name, for thou above all these,
Above mankind, or aught than mankind higher,
Surpassest far my naming; how may I
Adore thee, Author of this universe, 360
And all this good to man? for whose well-being
So amply, and with hands so liberal,
Thou hast provided all things. But with me
I see not who partakes. In solitude
What happiness, who can enjoy alone, 365
Or, all enjoying, what contentment find?"
Thus I presumptuous; and the Vision bright,
As with a smile more brightened, thus replied:
  ' "What callest thou solitude? Is not the earth
With various living creatures, and the air 370
Replenished, and all these at thy command

344 **fealty:** the obligation of a feudal tenant to his lord

To come and play before thee? Know'st thou not
Their language and their ways? They also know,
And reason not contemptibly. With these
Find pastime, and bear rule; thy realm is large." 375
So spake the Universal Lord, and seemed
So ordering. I, with leave of speech implored,
And humble deprecation, thus replied:
  ' "Let not my words offend thee, Heavenly Power;
My Maker, be propitious while I speak. 380
Hast Thou not made me here Thy substitute,
And these inferior far beneath me set?
Among unequals what society
Can sort, what harmony, or true delight?
Which must be mutual, in proportion due 385
Given and received; but, in disparity
The one intense, the other still remiss,
Cannot well suit with either, but soon prove
Tedious alike. Of fellowship I speak
Such as I seek, fit to participate 390
All rational delight: wherein the brute
Cannot be human consort. They rejoice
Each with their kind, lion with lioness;
So fitly them in pairs thou hast combined:
Much less can bird with beast, or fish with fowl 395
So well converse, nor with the ox the ape;
Worse then can man with beast, and least of all."
  'Whereto the Almighty answered, not displeased:
"A nice and subtle happiness, I see,
Thou to thyself proposest, in the choice 400
Of thy associates, Adam! and wilt taste
No pleasure, though in pleasure, solitary.
What thinkest thou then of me, and this my state?
Seem I to thee sufficiently possessed
Of happiness, or not? who am alone 405
From all eternity; for none I know
Second to me or like, equal much less.
How have I then with whom to hold converse,
Save with the creatures which I made, and those
To me inferior, infinite descents 410
Beneath what other creatures are to thee?"
  'He ceased. I lowly answered: "To attain
The height and depth of Thy eternal ways
All human thoughts come short, Supreme of things!
Thou in Thyself art perfect, and in Thee 415
Is no deficience found. Not so is Man,
But in degree; the cause of his desire
By conversation with his like to help
Or solace his defects. No need that thou
Shouldst propagate, already Infinite; 420
And through all numbers absolute, though One:
But Man by number is to manifest
His single imperfection, and beget
Like of his like, his image multiplied,
In unity defective; which requires 425
Collateral love, and dearest amity.
Thou in Thy secrecy although alone,
Best with Thyself accompanied, seekest not

Social communication; yet, so pleased,
Canst raise Thy creature to what height Thou wilt 430
Of union or communion, deified:
I, by conversing, cannot these erect
From prone; nor in their ways complacence find."
Thus I emboldened spake, and freedom used
Permissive, and acceptance found; which gained 435
  'This answer from the gracious Voice Divine:
"Thus far to try thee, Adam, I was pleased;
And find thee knowing, not of beasts alone,
Which thou hast rightly named, but of thyself;
Expressing well the spirit within thee free, 440
My image, not imparted to the brute;
Whose fellowship therefore unmeet for thee
Good reason was thou freely shouldst dislike;
And be so minded still: I, ere thou spakest,
Knew it not good for Man to be alone; 445
And no such company as then thou sawest
Intended thee; for trial only brought,
To see how thou couldest judge of fit and meet:
What next I bring shall please thee, be assured,
Thy likeness, thy fit help, thy other self, 450
Thy wish exactly to thy heart's desire."
  'He ended, or I heard no more; for now
My earthly by his heavenly overpowered,
Which it had long stood under, strained to the height
In that celestial colloquy sublime, 455
As with an object that excels the sense
Dazzled and spent, sunk down; and sought repair
Of sleep, which instantly fell on me, called
By Nature as in aid, and closed mine eyes.
Mine eyes he closed, but open left the cell 460
Of fancy, my internal sight; by which,
Abstract as in a trance, methought I saw,
Though sleeping, where I lay, and saw the shape
Still glorious before whom awake I stood:
Who stooping opened my left side, and took 465
From thence a rib, with cordial spirits warm,
And life-blood streaming fresh; wide was the wound,
But suddenly with flesh filled up and healed:
The rib He formed and fashioned with His hands;
Under his forming hands a creature grew, 470
Man-like, but different sex; so lovely fair,
That what seemed fair in all the world, seemed now
Mean, or in her summed up, in her contained
And in her looks; which from that time infused
Sweetness into my heart, unfelt before, 475
And into all things from her air inspired
The spirit of love and amorous delight.
She disappeared, and left me dark; I waked
To find her, or for ever to deplore
Her loss, and other pleasures all abjure. 480
When out of hope, behold her, not far off,
Such as I saw her in my dream, adorned
With what all earth or heaven could bestow
To make her amiable. On she came,
Led by her heavenly Maker, though unseen, 485

And guided by His voice; nor uninformed
Of nuptial sanctity, and marriage rites:
Grace was in all her steps, heaven in her eye,
In every gesture dignity and love.
I, overjoyed, could not forbear aloud.   490
  ' "This turn hath made amends; Thou hast fulfilled
Thy words, Creator bounteous and benign,
Giver of all things fair! but fairest this
Of all thy gifts! nor enviest. I now see
Bone of my bone, flesh of my flesh, myself   495
Before me. Woman is her name; of Man
Extracted: for this cause he shall forgo
Father and mother, and to his wife adhere;
And they shall be one flesh, one heart, one soul."
  'She heard me thus; and though divinely brought,
Yet innocence, and virgin modesty,   501
Her virtue, and the conscience of her worth,
That would be wooed, and not unsought be won,
Not obvious, not obtrusive, but, retired,
The more desirable; or, to say all,   505
Nature herself, though pure of sinful thought,
Wrought in her so, that, seeing me, she turned:
I followed her; she what was honour knew,
And with obsequious majesty approved
My pleaded reason. To the nuptial bower   510
I led her blushing like the morn. All heaven,
And happy constellations, on that hour
Shed their selectest influence; the earth
Gave sign of gratulation, and each hill;
Joyous the birds; fresh gales and gentle airs   515
Whispered it to the woods, and from their wings
Flung rose, flung odours from the spicy shrub,
Disporting, till the amorous bird of night
Sung spousal, and bid haste the evening-star
On his hill top, to light the bridal lamp.   520
  'Thus have I told thee all my state, and brought
My story to the sum of earthly bliss,
Which I enjoy; and must confess to find
In all things else delight indeed, but such
As, used or not, works in the mind no change,   525
Nor vehement desire; these delicacies
I mean of taste, sight, smell, herbs, fruits, and flowers,
Walks, and the melody of birds: but here
Far otherwise, transported I behold,
Transported touch; here passion first I felt,   530
Commotion strange! in all enjoyments else
Superior and unmoved; here only weak
Against the charm of Beauty's powerful glance.
Or Nature failed in me, and left some part
Not proof enough such object to sustain;   535
Or, from my side subducting, took perhaps
More than enough; at least on her bestowed
Too much of ornament, in outward show
Elaborate, of inward less exact.
For well I understand in the prime end   540
Of Nature her the inferior, in the mind
And inward faculties, which most excel;

In outward also her resembling less
His image who made both, and less expressing
The character of that dominion given   545
O'er other creatures. Yet when I approach
Her loveliness, so absolute she seems
And in herself complete, so well to know
Her own, that what she wills to do or say,
Seems wisest, virtuousest, discreetest, best: 550
All higher knowledge in her presence falls
Degraded; Wisdom in discourse with her
Loses discountenanced, and like Folly shows;
Authority and Reason on her wait,
As one intended first, not after made   555
Occasionally; and, to consummate all,
Greatness of mind and Nobleness their seat
Build in her loveliest, and create an awe
About her, as a guard angelic placed.'
  To whom the angel with contracted brow.   560
'Accuse not Nature, she hath done her part;
Do thou but thine; and be not diffident
Of Wisdom; she deserts thee not, if thou
Dismiss not her, when most thou needest her nigh,
By attributing overmuch to things   565
Less excellent, as thou thyself perceivest.
For, what admirest thou, what transports thee so,
An outside? fair, no doubt, and worthy well
Thy cherishing, thy honouring, and thy love;
Not thy subjection. Weigh with her thyself;   570
Then value. Oft-times nothing profits more
Than self-esteem, grounded on just and right
Well managed; of that skill the more thou knowest,
The more she will acknowledge thee her head,
And to realities yield all her shows: 575
Made so adorn for thy delight the more,
So awful, that with honour thou mayest love
Thy mate, who sees when thou art seen least wise.
But if the sense of touch, whereby mankind
Is propagated, seem such dear delight   580
Beyond all other; think the same vouchsafed
To cattle and each beast; which would not be
To them made common and divulged, if aught
Therein enjoyed were worthy to subdue
The soul of man, or passion in him move.   585
What higher in her society thou findest
Attractive, human, rational, love still;
In loving thou dost well, in passion not,
Wherein true love consists not. Love refines
The thoughts, and heart enlarges; hath his seat   590
In reason, and is judicious; is the scale
By which to heavenly love thou mayest ascend,
Not sunk in carnal pleasure; for which cause,
Among the beasts no mate for thee was found.'
  To whom thus, half abashed, Adam replied: 595
'Neither her outside formed so fair, nor aught
In procreation common to all kinds
(Though higher of the genial bed by far,
And with mysterious reverence I deem)

So much delights me, as those graceful acts, 600
Those thousand decencies, that daily flow
From all her words and actions mixed with love
And sweet compliance, which declare unfeigned
Union of mind, or in us both one soul;
Harmony to behold in wedded pair 605
More grateful than harmonious sound to the ear.
Yet these subject not; I to thee disclose
What inward thence I feel, not therefore foiled,
Who meet with various objects, from the sense
Variously representing; yet, still free, 610
Approve the best, and follow what I approve.
To love, thou blamest me not; for Love, thou sayest,
Leads up to heaven, is both the way and guide;
Bear with me then, if lawful what I ask:
Love not the heavenly spirits, and how their love 615
Express they? by looks only? or do they mix
Irradiance, virtual or immediate touch?'
   To whom the angel, with a smile that glowed
Celestial rosy red, Love's proper hue,
Answered: 'Let it suffice thee that thou know'st 620
Us happy, and without love no happiness.
Whatever pure thou in the body enjoyest
(And pure thou wert created) we enjoy
In eminence; and obstacle find none
Of membrane, joint, or limb, exclusive bars; 625
Easier than air with air, if Spirits embrace,
Total they mix, union of pure with pure
Desiring, nor restrained conveyance need,
As flesh to mix with flesh, or soul with soul.
But I can now no more; the parting sun 630
Beyond the earth's green Cape and verdant isles
Hesperian sets, my signal to depart.
Be strong, live happy, and love! But, first of all,
Him, whom to love is to obey, and keep
His great command; take heed lest passion sway 635
Thy judgement to do aught, which else free will
Would not admit: thine, and of all thy sons,
The weal or woe in thee is placed; beware!
I in thy persevering shall rejoice,
And all the blest. Stand fast; to stand or fall 640
Free in thine own arbitrement it lies.
Perfect within, no outward aid require;
And all temptation to transgress repel.'
   So saying, he arose; whom Adam thus
Followed with benediction: 'Since to part, 645
Go, heavenly guest, ethereal messenger,
Sent from whose sovran goodness I adore!
Gentle to me and affable hath been
Thy condescension, and shall be honoured ever
With grateful memory. Thou to mankind 650
Be good and friendly still, and oft return!'
   So parted they; the angel up to heaven
From the thick shade, and Adam to his bower.

631 **green Cape:** Cape Verde **verdant isles:** Cape Verde islands

BOOK NINE

No more of talk where God or angel guest
With Man, as with his friend, familiar used,
To sit indulgent, and with him partake
Rural repast; permitting him the while
Venial discourse unblamed. I now must change 5
Those notes to tragic; foul distrust, and breach
Disloyal on the part of Man, revolt,
And disobedience: on the part of heaven
Now alienated, distance and distaste,
Anger and just rebuke, and judgement given, 10
That brought into this world a world of woe,
Sin and her shadow Death, and Misery
Death's harbinger. Sad talk! yet argument
Not less but more heroic than the wrath
Of stern Achilles on his foe pursued 15
Thrice fugitive about Troy wall; or rage
Of Turnus for Lavinia disespoused;
Or Neptune's ire, or Juno's, that so long
Perplexed the Greek, and Cytherea's son:
If answerable style I can obtain 20
Of my celestial patroness, who deigns
Her nightly visitation unimplored,
And dictates to me slumbering; or inspires
Easy my unpremeditated verse:
Since first this subject for heroic song 25
Pleased me long choosing, and beginning late;
Not sedulous by nature to indite
Wars, hitherto the only argument
Heroic deemed chief mastery to dissect
With long and tedious havoc fabled knights 30
In battles feigned; the better fortitude
Of patience and heroic martyrdom

BOOK NINE – THE ARGUMENT: Satan having compast the Earth, with
meditated guile returns as a mist by Night into Paradise, enters
into the Serpent sleeping. Adam and Eve in the Morning go forth
to their labours, which Eve proposes to divide in several places,
each labouring apart: Adam consents not, alleging the danger, lest
that Enemy, of whom they were forewarn'd, should attempt her
found alone: Eve loath to be thought not circumspect or firm
enough, urges her going apart, the rather desirous to make trial
of her strength; Adam at last yields: The Serpent finds her alone;
his subtle approach, first gazing, then speaking, with much flattery
extolling Eve above all other Creatures. Eve wond'ring to hear the
Serpent speak, asks how he attain'd to human speech and such
understanding not till now; the Serpent answers, that by tasting of
a certain Tree in the Garden he attain'd both to Speech and
Reason, till then void of both: Eve requires him to bring her to
that Tree, and finds it to be the Tree of Knowledge forbidden:
The Serpent now grown bolder, with many wiles and arguments
induces her at length to eat; she pleas'd with the taste deliberates
a while whether to impart thereof to Adam or not, at last brings
him of the Fruit, relates what persuaded her to eat thereof:
Adam at first amaz'd, but perceiving her lost, resolves through
vehemence of love to perish with her; and extenuating the
trespass, eats also of the Fruit: The effects thereof in them both;
they seek to cover their nakedness; then fall to variance and
accusation of one another 15–16 Achilles pursued Hector round the
walls of Troy. See Homer's *Iliad* 17 in Virgil's *Aeneid* Turnus rages
at losing Lavinia to 'Cytherea's son', Aeneas 18 Neptune persecuted
Odysseus; Juno persecuted Aeneas 19 **the Greek:** Odysseus

Unsung; or to describe races and games,
Or tilting furniture, emblazoned shields,
Impresas quaint, caparisons and steeds, 35
Bases and tinsel trappings, gorgeous knights
At joust and tournament; then marshalled feast
Served up in hall with sewers and seneschals;
The skill of artifice or office mean,
Not that which justly gives heroic name 40
To person, or to poem. Me, of these
Nor skilled nor studious, higher argument
Remains; sufficient of itself to raise
That name, unless an age too late, or cold
Climate, or years, damp my intended wing 45
Depressed; and much they may, if all be mine,
Not hers, who brings it nightly to my ear.
      The sun was sunk, and after him the star
Of Hesperus, whose office is to bring
Twilight upon the earth, short arbiter 50
'Twixt day and night, and now from end to end
Night's hemisphere had veiled the horizon round:
When Satan, who late fled before the threats
Of Gabriel out of Eden, now improved
In meditated fraud and malice, bent 55
On Man's destruction, maugre what might hap
Of heavier on himself, fearless returned.
By night he fled, and at mid-night returned
From compassing the earth; cautious of day,
Since Uriel, regent of the sun, descried 60
His entrance, and forewarned the cherubim
That kept their watch; thence full of anguish driven,
The space of seven continued nights he rode
With darkness; thrice the equinoctial line
He circled; four times crossed the car of night 65
From pole to pole, traversing each colure;
On the eighth returned; and, on the coast averse
From entrance or cherubic watch, by stealth
Found unsuspected way. There was a place,
Now not, though sin, not time, first wrought the
      change, 70
Where Tigris, at the foot of paradise,
Into a gulf shot under ground, till part
Rose up a fountain by the tree of life:
In with the river sunk, and with it rose
Satan, involved in rising mist; then sought 75
Where to lie hid; sea he had searched, and land,
From Eden over Pontus and the pool
Maeotis, up beyond the river Ob;
Downward as far antarctic; and in length,
West from Orontes to the ocean barred 80
At Darien; thence to the land where flows
Ganges and Indus. Thus the orb he roamed

With narrow search; and with inspection deep
Considered every creature, which of all
Most opportune might serve his wiles; and found 85
The serpent subtlest beast of all the field.
Him after long debate, irresolute
Of thoughts revolved, his final sentence chose
Fit vessel, fittest imp of fraud, in whom
To enter, and his dark suggestions hide 90
From sharpest sight: for, in the wily snake
Whatever sleights, none would suspicious mark,
As from his wit and native subtlety
Proceeding; which, in other beasts observed,
Doubt might beget of diabolic power 95
Active within, beyond the sense of brute.
Thus he resolved, but first from inward grief
His bursting passion into plaints thus poured.
      'O Earth, how like to heaven, if not preferred
More justly, seat worthier of gods, as built 100
With second thoughts, reforming what was old!
For what God, after better, worse would build?
Terrestrial heaven, danced round by other heavens
That shine, yet bear their bright officious lamps,
Light above light, for thee alone, as seems, 105
In thee concentring all their precious beams
Of sacred influence! As God in heaven
Is centre, yet extends to all; so thou,
Centring, receivest from all those orbs: in thee,
Not in themselves, all their known virtue appears 110
Productive in herb, plant, and nobler birth
Of creatures animate with gradual life
Of growth, sense, reason, all summed up in Man.
With what delight could I have walked thee round,
If I could joy in aught, sweet interchange 115
Of hill, and valley, rivers, woods, and plains,
Now land, now sea and shores with forest crowned,
Rocks, dens, and caves! But I in none of these
Find place or refuge; and the more I see
Pleasures about me, so much more I feel 120
Torment within me, as from the hateful siege
Of contraries: all good to me becomes
Bane, and in heaven much worse would be my state.
But neither here seek I, no nor in heaven
To dwell, unless by mast'ring Heaven's Supreme; 125
Nor hope to be myself less miserable
By what I seek, but others to make such
As I, though thereby worse to me redound:
For only in destroying I find ease
To my relentless thoughts; and, him destroyed, 130
Or won to what may work his utter loss,
For whom all this was made, all this will soon
Follow, as to him linked in weal or woe;
In woe then; that destruction wide may range:
To me shall be the glory sole among 135
The infernal powers, in one day to have marred
What he, Almighty styled, six nights and days
Continued making; and who knows how long
Before had been contriving? though perhaps

---

34 **tilting furniture:** jousting equipment   35 **impresas:** heraldic
devices   **caparisons:** a covering spread over the saddle of a horse
38 **sewers and seneschals:** stewards and ceremonial servants
56 **maugre:** despite   64 **equinoctial line:** the path of the sun
66 **colure:** two circles that intersect each other at right angles at the
poles   76–82 Satan travels passes Pontis (the Black Sea), Maeotis (the
Sea of Azov) and the Siberian River Ob. Satan then flies over the
Arctic Ocean, the Syrian River Orontes then to Darien (Panama)

Not longer than since I, in one night, freed 140
From servitude inglorious well nigh half
The angelic name, and thinner left the throng
Of His adorers. He, to be avenged,
And to repair His numbers thus impaired,
Whether such virtue spent of old now failed 145
More angels to create, if they at least
Are His created, or, to spite us more,
Determined to advance into our room
A creature formed of earth, and him endow,
Exalted from so base original, 150
With heavenly spoils, our spoils. What He decreed,
He effected; Man He made, and for him built
Magnificent this world, and earth his seat,
Him lord pronounced; and – oh, indignity! –
Subjected to his service angel-wings, 155
And flaming ministers to watch and tend
Their earthly charge. Of these the vigilance
I dread; and, to elude, thus wrapped in mist
Of midnight vapour glide obscure, and pry
In every bush and brake, where hap may find 160
The serpent sleeping; in whose mazy folds
To hide me, and the dark intent I bring.
Oh, foul descent! that I, who erst contended
With gods to sit the highest, am now constrained
Into a beast; and, mixed with bestial slime, 165
This essence to incarnate and imbrute,
That to the height of Deity aspired!
But what will not ambition and revenge
Descend to? Who aspires, must down as low
As high he soared; obnoxious, first or last, 170
To basest things. Revenge, at first though sweet,
Bitter ere long, back on itself recoils:
Let it; I reck not, so it light well aimed,
Since higher I fall short, on him who next
Provokes my envy, this new favourite 175
Of heaven, this man of clay, son of despite,
Whom, us the more to spite, his Maker raised
From dust: Spite then with spite is best repaid.'
So saying, through each thicket dank or dry,
Like a black mist low-creeping, he held on 180
His midnight-search, where soonest he might find
The serpent; him fast-sleeping soon he found
In labyrinth of many a round self-rolled,
His head the midst, well stored with subtle wiles:
Not yet in horrid shade or dismal den, 185
Nor nocent yet; but, on the grassy herb,
Fearless unfeared he slept: in at his mouth
The Devil entered; and his brutal sense,
In heart or head, possessing, soon inspired
With act intelligential; but his sleep 190
Disturbed not, waiting close the approach of morn.
Now, whenas sacred light began to dawn
In Eden on the humid flowers, that breathed
Their morning incense, when all things, that breathe,

From th'earth's great altar send up silent praise 195
To the Creator, and His nostrils fill
With grateful smell, forth came the human pair,
And joined their vocal worship to the choir
Of creatures wanting voice; that done, partake
The season prime for sweetest scents and airs: 200
Then commune, how that day they best may ply
Their growing work: for much their work out-grew
The hands' dispatch of two gardening so wide,
And Eve first to her husband thus began.
'Adam, well may we labour still to dress 205
This garden, still to tend plant, herb, and flower,
Our pleasant task enjoined; but, till more hands
Aid us, the work under our labour grows,
Luxurious by restraint; what we by day
Lop overgrown, or prune, or prop, or bind, 210
One night or two with wanton growth derides
Tending to wild. Thou therefore now advise,
Or bear what to my mind first thoughts present:
Let us divide our labours; thou, where choice
Leads thee, or where most needs, whether to wind 215
The woodbine round this arbour, or direct
The clasping ivy where to climb; while I,
In yonder spring of roses intermixed
With myrtle, find what to redress till noon:
For, while so near each other thus all day 220
Our task we choose, what wonder if so near
Looks intervene and smiles, or object new
Casual discourse draw on; which intermits
Our day's work, brought to little, though begun
Early, and th'hour of supper comes unearned?' 225
To whom mild answer Adam thus returned.
'Sole Eve, associate sole, to me beyond
Compare above all living creatures dear!
Well hast thou motioned, well thy thoughts
    employed,
How we might best fulfil the work which here 230
God hath assigned us; nor of me shalt pass
Unpraised: for nothing lovelier can be found
In woman, than to study household good,
And good works in her husband to promote.
Yet not so strictly hath our Lord imposed 235
Labour, as to debar us when we need
Refreshment, whether food, or talk between,
Food of the mind, or this sweet intercourse
Of looks and smiles; for smiles from reason flow,
To brute denied, and are of love the food; 240
Love, not the lowest end of human life.
For not to irksome toil, but to delight,
He made us, and delight to reason joined.
These paths and bowers doubt not but our joint hands
Will keep from wilderness with ease, as wide 245
As we need walk, till younger hands ere long
Assist us; but, if much converse perhaps
Thee satiate, to short absence I could yield:
For solitude sometimes is best society,
And short retirement urges sweet return. 250

186 **Nor nocent:** not harmful

But other doubt possesses me, lest harm
Befall thee severed from me; for thou knowest
What hath been warned us, what malicious foe
Envying our happiness, and of his own
Despairing, seeks to work us woe and shame   255
By sly assault; and somewhere nigh at hand
Watches, no doubt, with greedy hope to find
His wish and best advantage, us asunder;
Hopeless to circumvent us joined, where each
To other speedy aid might lend at need: 260
Whether his first design be to withdraw
Our fealty from God, or to disturb
Conjugal love, than which perhaps no bliss
Enjoyed by us excites his envy more;
Or this, or worse, leave not the faithful side   265
That gave thee being, still shades thee, and protects.
The wife, where danger or dishonour lurks,
Safest and seemliest by her husband stays,
Who guards her, or with her the worst endures.'
    To whom the virgin majesty of Eve,   270
As one who loves, and some unkindness meets,
With sweet austere composure thus replied.
    'Offspring of Heaven and Earth, and all Earth's
        Lord!
That such an enemy we have, who seeks
Our ruin, both by thee informed I learn,   275
And from the parting angel over-heard,
As in a shady nook I stood behind,
Just then returned at shut of evening flowers.
But, that thou shouldst my firmness therefore doubt
To God or thee, because we have a foe   280
May tempt it, I expected not to hear.
His violence thou fearest not, being such
As we, not capable of death or pain,
Can either not receive, or can repel.
His fraud is then thy fear; which plain infers   285
Thy equal fear, that my firm faith and love
Can by his fraud be shaken or seduced;
Thoughts, which how found they harbour in thy
        breast,
Adam, misthought of her to thee so dear?'
    To whom with healing words Adam replied.   290
'Daughter of God and Man, immortal Eve!
For such thou art; from sin and blame entire:
Not diffident of thee do I dissuade
Thy absence from my sight, but to avoid
Th'attempt itself, intended by our foe.   295
For he who tempts, though in vain, at least asperses
The tempted with dishonour foul; supposed
Not incorruptible of faith, not proof
Against temptation. Thou thyself with scorn
And anger wouldst resent the offered wrong,   300
Though ineffectual found. Misdeem not then,
If such affront I labour to avert
From thee alone, which on us both at once
The enemy, though bold, will hardly dare;
Or daring, first on me the'assault shall light.   305

Nor thou his malice and false guile contemn;
Subtle he needs must be, who could seduce
Angels; nor think superfluous other's aid.
I, from the influence of thy looks, receive
Access in every virtue; in thy sight   310
More wise, more watchful, stronger, if need were
Of outward strength; while shame, thou looking on,
Shame to be overcome or over-reached,
Would utmost vigour raise, and raised unite.
Why shouldst not thou like sense within thee feel   315
When I am present, and thy trial choose
With me, best witness of thy virtue tried?'
    So spake domestic Adam in his care
And matrimonial love; but Eve, who thought
Less attributed to her faith sincere,   320
Thus her reply with accent sweet renewed.
    'If this be our condition, thus to dwell
In narrow circuit straitened by a foe,
Subtle or violent, we not endued
Single with like defence, wherever met;   325
How are we happy, still in fear of harm?
But harm precedes not sin: only our foe,
Tempting, affronts us with his foul esteem
Of our integrity: his foul esteem
Sticks no dishonour on our front, but turns   330
Foul on himself; then wherefore shunned or feared
By us? who rather double honour gain
From his surmise proved false; find peace within,
Favour from heaven, our witness, from the event.
And what is faith, love, virtue, unassayed   335
Alone, without exterior help sustained?
Let us not then suspect our happy state
Left so imperfect by the Maker wise,
As not secure to single or combined.
Frail is our happiness, if this be so,   340
And Eden were no Eden, thus exposed.'
To whom thus Adam fervently replied.
'O Woman, best are all things as the will
Of God ordained them: His creating hand
Nothing imperfect or deficient left   345
Of all that he created, much less Man,
Or aught that might his happy state secure,
Secure from outward force; within himself
The danger lies, yet lies within his power:
Against his will he can receive no harm.   350
But God left free the will; for what obeys
Reason, is free; and Reason He made right,
But bid her well be ware, and still erect;
Lest, by some fair-appearing good surprised,
She dictate false; and misinform the will   355
To do what God expressly hath forbid.
Not then mistrust, but tender love, enjoins,
That I should mind thee oft; and mind thou me.
Firm we subsist, yet possible to swerve;
Since Reason not impossibly may meet   360
Some specious object by the foe suborned,
And fall into deception unaware,

Not keeping strictest watch, as she was warned.
Seek not temptation, then, which to avoid
Were better, and most likely if from me   365
Thou sever not. Trial will come unsought.
Wouldst thou approve thy constancy, approve
First thy obedience; the other who can know,
Not seeing thee attempted, who attest?
But, if thou think, trial unsought may find   370
Us both securer than thus warned thou seemest,
Go; for thy stay, not free, absents thee more;
Go in thy native innocence, rely
On what thou hast of virtue; summon all!
For God towards thee hath done His part, do thine.'
  So spake the patriarch of mankind; but Eve   376
Persisted; yet submiss, though last, replied.
  'With thy permission then, and thus forewarned
Chiefly by what thy own last reasoning words
Touched only; that our trial, when least sought, 380
May find us both perhaps far less prepared,
The willinger I go, nor much expect
A foe so proud will first the weaker seek;
So bent, the more shall shame him his repulse.'
  Thus saying, from her husband's hand her hand 385
Soft she withdrew; and, like a wood-nymph light,
Oread or dryad, or of Delia's train,
Betook her to the groves; but Delia's self
In gait surpassed, and goddess-like deport,
Though not as she with bow and quiver armed,   390
But with such gardening tools as Art yet rude,
Guiltless of fire, had formed, or angels brought.
To Pales, or Pomona, thus adorned,
Likest she seemed, Pomona when she fled
Vertumnus, or to Ceres in her prime,   395
Yet virgin of Proserpina from Jove.
Her long with ardent look his eye pursued
Delighted, but desiring more her stay.
Oft he to her his charge of quick return
Repeated; she to him as oft engaged   400
To be returned by noon amid the bower,
And all things in best order to invite
Noontide repast, or afternoon's repose.
O much deceived, much failing, hapless Eve,
Of thy presumed return! event perverse!   405
Thou never from that hour in paradise
Foundst either sweet repast or sound repose;
Such ambush, hid among sweet flowers and shades,
Waited with hellish rancour imminent
To intercept thy way, or send thee back   410
Despoiled of innocence, of faith, of bliss!
For now, and since first break of dawn, the fiend,
Mere serpent in appearance, forth was come;
And on his quest, where likeliest he might find
The only two of mankind, but in them   415

The whole included race, his purposed prey.
In bower and field he sought, where any tuft
Of grove or garden-plot more pleasant lay,
Their tendance, or plantation for delight;
By fountain or by shady rivulet   420
He sought them both, but wished his hap might find
Eve separate; he wished, but not with hope
Of what so seldom chanced; when to his wish,
Beyond his hope, Eve separate he spies,
Veiled in a cloud of fragrance, where she stood, 425
Half spied, so thick the roses blushing round
About her glowed, oft stooping to support
Each flower of slender stalk, whose head, though gay
Carnation, purple, azure, or specked with gold,
Hung drooping unsustained; them she upstays   430
Gently with myrtle band, mindless the while
Herself, though fairest unsupported flower,
From her best prop so far, and storm so nigh.
Nearer he drew, and many a walk traversed
Of stateliest covert, cedar, pine, or palm;   435
Then voluble and bold, now hid, now seen,
Among thick-woven arborets, and flowers
Imbordered on each bank, the hand of Eve:
Spot more delicious than those gardens feigned
Or of revived Adonis, or renowned   440
Alcinous, host of old Laertes' son;
Or that, not mystic, where the sapient king
Held dalliance with his fair Egyptian spouse.
Much he the place admired, the person more.
As one who long in populous city pent,   445
Where houses thick and sewers annoy the air,
Forth issuing on a summer's morn, to breathe
Among the pleasant villages and farms
Adjoined, from each thing met conceives delight;
The smell of grain, or tedded grass, or kine,   450
Or dairy, each rural sight, each rural sound;
If chance, with nymph-like step, fair virgin pass,
What pleasing seemed, for her now pleases more;
She most, and in her look sums all delight:
Such pleasure took the serpent to behold   455
This flowery plat, the sweet recess of Eve
Thus early, thus alone. Her heavenly form
Angelic, but more soft, and feminine,
Her graceful innocence, her every air
Of gesture, or least action, overawed   460
His malice, and with rapine sweet bereaved
His fierceness of the fierce intent it brought.
That space the evil one abstracted stood
From his own evil, and for the time remained
Stupidly good; of enmity disarmed,   465
Of guile, of hate, of envy, of revenge:
But the hot hell that always in him burns,
Though in mid heaven, soon ended his delight,
And tortures him now more, the more he sees

---

387 **Oread or dryad:** wood nymphs **Delia:** Diana, goddess of
hunting 393 **Pales:** goddess of flocks and pastures **Pomona:**
goddess of fruit 395 **Ceres:** goddess of agriculture 396 **Proserpina:**
Persephone

437 **arborets:** shrubs 440 **revived Adonis:** Adonis is restored to life
for half of each year 441 **Laertes' son:** Odysseus 442 **sapient king:**
Solomon

Of pleasure, not for him ordained: then soon 470
Fierce hate he recollects, and all his thoughts
Of mischief, gratulating, thus excites.
   'Thoughts, whither have ye led me! with what sweet
Compulsion thus transported, to forget
What hither brought us! hate, not love; nor hope 475
Of paradise for hell, hope here to taste
Of pleasure; but all pleasure to destroy,
Save what is in destroying; other joy
To me is lost. Then, let me not let pass
Occasion which now smiles; behold alone 480
The woman, opportune to all attempts,
Her husband, for I view far round, not nigh,
Whose higher intellectual more I shun,
And strength, of courage haughty, and of limb
Heroic built, though of terrestrial mould; 485
Foe not informidable! exempt from wound,
I not; so much hath hell debased, and pain
Enfeebled me, to what I was in heaven.
She fair, divinely fair, fit love for Gods!
Not terrible, though terror be in love 490
And beauty, not approached by stronger hate,
Hate stronger, under show of love well feigned;
The way which to her ruin now I tend.'
   So spake the enemy of mankind, enclosed
In serpent, inmate bad! and toward Eve 495
Addressed his way: not with indented wave,
Prone on the ground, as since; but on his rear,
Circular base of rising folds, that towered
Fold above fold, a surging maze! his head
Crested aloft, and carbuncle his eyes; 500
With burnished neck of verdant gold, erect
Amidst his circling spires, that on the grass
Floated redundant: pleasing was his shape
And lovely; never since of serpent-kind
Lovelier, not those that in Illyria changed, 505
Hermione and Cadmus, or the god
In Epidaurus; nor to which transformed
Ammonian Jove, or Capitoline, was seen;
He with Olympias; this with her who bore
Scipio, the height of Rome. With tract oblique 510
At first, as one who sought access, but feared
To interrupt, side-long he works his way.
As when a ship, by skilful steersmen wrought
Nigh river's mouth or foreland, where the wind
Veers oft, as oft so steers, and shifts her sail: 515
So varied he, and of his tortuous train
Curled many a wanton wreath in sight of Eve,
To lure her eye; she, busied, heard the sound
Of rustling leaves, but minded not, as used
To such disport before her through the field, 520
From every beast; more duteous at her call,
Than at Circean call the herd disguised.

He, bolder now, uncalled before her stood,
But as in gaze admiring: oft he bowed
His turret crest, and sleek enamelled neck, 525
Fawning; and licked the ground whereon she trod.
His gentle dumb expression turned at length
The eye of Eve to mark his play; he, glad
Of her attention gained, with serpent-tongue
Organic, or impulse of vocal air, 530
His fraudulent temptation thus began.
   'Wonder not, sovran Mistress, if perhaps
Thou canst, who art sole wonder! much less arm
Thy looks, the heaven of mildness, with disdain,
Displeased that I approach thee thus, and gaze 535
Insatiate; I thus single; nor have feared
Thy awful brow, more awful thus retired.
Fairest resemblance of thy Maker fair,
Thee all things living gaze on, all things thine
By gift, and thy celestial beauty adore 540
With ravishment beheld! there best beheld,
Where universally admired; but here
In this enclosure wild, these beasts among,
Beholders rude, and shallow to discern
Half what in thee is fair, one man except, 545
Who sees thee? and what is one? who should be seen
A goddess among gods, adored and served
By angels numberless, thy daily train.'
So glozed the tempter, and his proem tuned:
Into the heart of Eve his words made way, 550
Though at the voice much marvelling; at length,
Not unamazed, she thus in answer spake.
   'What may this mean? language of man
      pronounced
By tongue of brute, and human sense expressed?
The first, at least, of these I thought denied 555
To beasts; whom God, on their creation-day,
Created mute to all articulate sound:
The latter I demur; for in their looks
Much reason, and in their actions, oft appears.
Thee, serpent, subtlest beast of all the field 560
I knew, but not with human voice endued;
Redouble then this miracle, and say,
How camest thou speakable of mute, and how
To me so friendly grown above the rest
Of brutal kind, that daily are in sight? 565
Say, for such wonder claims attention due.'
   To whom the guileful tempter thus replied.
'Empress of this fair world, resplendent Eve!
Easy to me it is to tell thee all
What thou command'st; and right thou shouldst be
      obeyed. 570
I was at first as other beasts that graze
The trodden herb, of abject thoughts and low,
As was my food; nor aught but food discerned
Or sex, and apprehended nothing high:
Till, on a day roving the field, I chanced 575

500 **carbuncle:** a bright red gem 505–510 Cadmus was changed into a serpent, and after uniting with his wife (in his new form) she was similarly changed 508 **Ammonian Jove:** Jupiter Ammon, the 'Libyan Jove' 522 **Circean:** Circe, a sorceress who could turn men into beasts

549 **proem:** prelude

A goodly tree far distant to behold
Loaden with fruit of fairest colours mixed,
Ruddy and gold: I nearer drew to gaze;
When from the boughs a savoury odour blown,
Grateful to appetite, more pleased my sense   580
Than smell of sweetest fennel, or the teats
Of ewe or goat dropping with milk at even,
Unsucked of lamb or kid, that tend their play.
To satisfy the sharp desire I had
Of tasting those fair apples, I resolved   585
Not to defer; hunger and thirst at once,
Powerful persuaders, quickened at the scent
Of that alluring fruit, urged me so keen.
About the mossy trunk I wound me soon;
For, high from ground, the branches would require
Thy utmost reach or Adam's. Round the tree   591
All other beasts that saw, with like desire
Longing and envying stood, but could not reach.
Amid the tree now got, where plenty hung
Tempting so nigh, to pluck and eat my fill   595
I spared not; for, such pleasure till that hour,
At feed or fountain, never had I found.
Sated at length, ere long I might perceive
Strange alteration in me, to degree
Of reason in my inward powers; and speech   600
Wanted not long; though to this shape retained.
Thenceforth to speculations high or deep
I turned my thoughts, and with capacious mind
Considered all things visible in heaven,
Or earth, or middle; all things fair and good: 605
But all that fair and good in thy divine
Semblance, and in thy beauty's heavenly ray,
United I beheld; no fair to thine
Equivalent or second! which compelled
Me thus, though importune perhaps, to come   610
And gaze, and worship thee of right declared
Sovran of creatures, universal dame!'
     So talked the spirited sly snake; and Eve,
Yet more amazed, unwary thus replied:
     'Serpent, thy overpraising leaves in doubt   615
The virtue of that fruit, in thee first proved:
But say, where grows the tree? from hence how far?
For many are the trees of God that grow
In paradise, and various, yet unknown
To us; in such abundance lies our choice,   620
As leaves a greater store of fruit untouched,
Still hanging incorruptible, till men
Grow up to their provision, and more hands
Help to disburden Nature of her birth.'
     To whom the wily adder, blithe and glad: 625
'Empress, the way is ready, and not long;
Beyond a row of myrtles, on a flat,
Fast by a fountain, one small thicket past
Of blowing myrrh and balm: if thou accept
My conduct, I can bring thee thither soon.'   630
     'Lead then,' said Eve. He, leading, swiftly rolled
In tangles, and made intricate seem straight,

To mischief swift. Hope elevates, and joy
Brightens his crest; as when a wandering fire,
Compact of unctuous vapour, which the night   635
Condenses, and the cold environs round,
Kindled through agitation to a flame,
Which oft, they say, some evil spirit attends,
Hovering and blazing with delusive light,   639
Misleads th'amazed night-wanderer from his way
To bogs and mires, and oft through pond or pool;
There swallowed up and lost, from succour far.
So glistered the dire snake, and into fraud
Led Eve, our credulous mother, to the tree
Of prohibition, root of all our woe;   645
Which when she saw, thus to her guide she spake.
     'Serpent, we might have spared our coming hither,
Fruitless to me, though fruit be here to excess,
The credit of whose virtue rest with thee;
Wonderous indeed, if cause of such effects.   650
But of this tree we may not taste nor touch;
God so commanded, and left that command
Sole daughter of His voice; the rest, we live
Law to ourselves; our reason is our law.'
     To whom the tempter guilefully replied.   655
'Indeed! hath God then said that of the fruit
Of all these garden-trees ye shall not eat,
Yet lords declared of all in earth or air?'
     To whom thus Eve, yet sinless: 'Of the fruit
Of each tree in the garden we may eat;   660
But of the fruit of this fair tree amidst
The garden, God hath said, "Ye shall not eat
Thereof, nor shall ye touch it, lest ye die." '
She scarce had said, though brief, when now more
     bold
The tempter, but with show of zeal and love   665
To Man, and indignation at his wrong,
New part puts on; and, as to passion moved,
Fluctuates disturbed, yet comely and in act
Raised, as of some great matter to begin.
As when of old some orator renowned,   670
In Athens or free Rome, where eloquence
Flourished, since mute! to some great cause addressed,
Stood in himself collected; while each part,
Motion, each act, won audience ere the tongue;
Sometimes in height began, as no delay   675
Of preface brooking, through his zeal of right:
So standing, moving, or to height up grown,
The tempter, all impassioned, thus began.
     'O sacred, wise, and wisdom-giving Plant,
Mother of science! now I feel thy power   680
Within me clear; not only to discern
Things in their causes, but to trace the ways
Of highest agents, deemed however wise.
Queen of this universe! do not believe
Those rigid threats of death: ye shall not die: 685
How should you? by the fruit? it gives you life
To knowledge; by the threatener? look on me,
Me, who have touched and tasted; yet both live,

And life more perfect have attained than Fate
Meant me, by vent'ring higher than my lot. 690
Shall that be shut to Man, which to the beast
Is open? or will God incense His ire
For such a petty trespass? and not praise
Rather your dauntless virtue, whom the pain
Of death denounced, whatever thing death be, 695
Deterred not from achieving what might lead
To happier life, knowledge of good and evil;
Of good, how just? of evil, if what is evil
Be real, why not known, since easier shunned?
God therefore cannot hurt ye, and be just; 700
Not just, not God; not feared then, nor obeyed:
Your fear itself of death removes the fear.
Why then was this forbid? Why, but to awe;
Why, but to keep ye low and ignorant,
His worshippers? He knows that in the day 705
Ye eat thereof, your eyes that seem so clear,
Yet are but dim, shall perfectly be then
Opened and cleared, and ye shall be as gods,
Knowing both good and evil, as they know.
That ye should be as gods, since I as Man, 710
Internal Man, is but proportion meet;
I, of brute, human; ye, of human, gods.
So ye shall die perhaps, by putting off
Human, to put on gods; death to be wished,
Though threatened, which no worse than this can
     bring. 715
And what are gods, that Man may not become
As they, participating god-like food?
The gods are first, and that advantage use
On our belief, that all from them proceeds:
I question it; for this fair earth I see, 720
Warmed by the sun, producing every kind;
Them, nothing: if they all things, who enclosed
Knowledge of good and evil in this tree,
That whoso eats thereof, forthwith attains
Wisdom without their leave? and wherein lies 725
The offence, that Man should thus attain to know?
What can your knowledge hurt Him, or this tree
Impart against His will, if all be His?
Or is it envy? and can envy dwell
In heavenly breasts? These, these, and many more 730
Causes import your need of this fair fruit.
Goddess humane, reach then, and freely taste!'
  He ended; and his words, replete with guile,
Into her heart too easy entrance won:
Fixed on the fruit she gazed, which to behold 735
Might tempt alone; and in her ears the sound
Yet rung of his persuasive words, impregned
With reason, to her seeming, and with truth:
Mean while the hour of noon drew on, and waked
An eager appetite, raised by the smell 740
So savoury of that fruit, which with desire,
Inclinable now grown to touch or taste,
Solicited her longing eye; yet first
Pausing a while, thus to herself she mused:

'Great are thy virtues, doubtless, best of fruits, 745
Though kept from man, and worthy to be admired;
Whose taste, too long forborne, at first assay
Gave elocution to the mute, and taught
The tongue not made for speech to speak thy praise:
Thy praise He also, who forbids thy use, 750
Conceals not from us, naming thee the tree
Of knowledge, knowledge both of good and evil;
Forbids us then to taste! but His forbidding
Commends thee more, while it infers the good
By thee communicated, and our want: 755
For good unknown sure is not had; or, had
And yet unknown, is as not had at all.
In plain then, what forbids He but to know,
Forbids us good, forbids us to be wise?
Such prohibitions bind not. But, if death 760
Bind us with after-bands, what profits then
Our inward freedom? In the day we eat
Of this fair fruit, our doom is, we shall die!
How dies the serpent? he hath eaten and lives,
And knows, and speaks, and reasons, and discerns, 765
Irrational till then. For us alone
Was death invented? or to us denied
This intellectual food, for beasts reserved?
For beasts it seems: yet that one beast which first
Hath tasted envies not, but brings with joy 770
The good befallen him, author unsuspect,
Friendly to man, far from deceit or guile.
What fear I then? rather, what know to fear
Under this ignorance of good and evil,
Of God or death, of law or penalty? 775
Here grows the cure of all, this fruit divine,
Fair to the eye, inviting to the taste,
Of virtue to make wise. What hinders, then,
To reach, and feed at once both body and mind?'
  So saying, her rash hand in evil hour 780
Forth reaching to the fruit, she plucked, she eat!
Earth felt the wound; and Nature from her seat,
Sighing through all her works, gave signs of woe,
That all was lost. Back to the thicket slunk
The guilty serpent; and well might; for Eve, 785
Intent now wholly on her taste, nought else
Regarded; such delight till then, as seemed,
In fruit she never tasted, whether true
Or fancied so, through expectation high
Of knowledge; not was Godhead from her thought.
Greedily she ingorged without restraint, 791
And knew not eating death. Satiate at length,
And heightened as with wine, jocund and boon,
Thus to herself she pleasingly began.
  'O sovran, virtuous, precious of all trees 795
In paradise! of operation blest
To sapience, hitherto obscured, infamed.

797 **sapience**: knowledge, but also tasting

And thy fair fruit let hang, as to no end
Created; but henceforth my early care,
Not without song, each morning, and due praise, 800
Shall tend thee, and the fertile burden ease
Of thy full branches offered free to all;
Till, dieted by thee, I grow mature
In knowledge, as the gods, who all things know;
Though others envy what they cannot give: 805
For, had the gift been theirs, it had not here
Thus grown. Experience, next, to thee I owe,
Best guide; not following thee, I had remained
In ignorance; thou openest wisdom's way,
And giv'st access, though secret she retire. 810
And I perhaps am secret: heaven is high,
High, and remote to see from thence distinct
Each thing on earth; and other care perhaps
May have diverted from continual watch
Our great Forbidder, safe with all His spies 815
About Him. But to Adam in what sort
Shall I appear? shall I to him make known
As yet my change, and give him to partake
Full happiness with me, or rather not,
But keeps the odds of knowledge in my power 820
Without co-partner? so to add what wants
In female sex, the more to draw his love,
And render me more equal; and perhaps,
A thing not undesirable, sometime
Superior; for, inferior, who is free 825
This may be well. But what if God have seen,
And death ensue? then I shall be no more!
And Adam, wedded to another Eve,
Shall live with her enjoying, I extinct;
A death to think! Confirmed then I resolve, 830
Adam shall share with me in bliss or woe:
So dear I love him, that with him all deaths
I could endure, without him live no life.'
    So saying, from the tree her step she turned;
But first low reverence done, as to the power 835
That dwelt within, whose presence had infused
Into the plant sciential sap, derived
From nectar, drink of gods. Adam the while,
Waiting desirous her return, had wove
Of choicest flowers a garland, to adorn 840
Her tresses, and her rural labours crown;
As reapers oft are wont their harvest-queen.
Great joy he promised to his thoughts, and new
Solace in her return, so long delayed:
Yet oft his heart, divine of something ill, 845
Misgave him; he the faltering measure felt;
And forth to meet her went, the way she took
That morn when first they parted: by the tree
Of knowledge he must pass; there he her met,
Scarce from the tree returning; in her hand 850
A bough of fairest fruit, that downy smiled,
New gathered, and ambrosial smell diffused.
To him she hasted; in her face excuse
Came prologue, and apology too prompt; 854
Which, with bland words at will, she thus addressed:

'Hast thou not wondered, Adam, at my stay?
Thee I have missed, and thought it long, deprived
Thy presence; agony of love till now
Not felt, nor shall be twice; for never more
Mean I to try, what rash untried I sought, 860
The pain of absence from thy sight. But strange
Hath been the cause, and wonderful to hear:
This tree is not, as we are told, a tree
Of danger tasted, nor to evil unknown
Op'ning the way, but of divine effect 865
To open eyes, and make them gods who taste;
And hath been tasted such. The serpent wise,
Or not restrained as we, or not obeying,
Hath eaten of the fruit; and is become,
Not dead, as we are threatened, but thenceforth 870
Endued with human voice and human sense,
Reasoning to admiration; and with me
Persuasively hath so prevailed, that I
Have also tasted, and have also found
Th'effects to correspond; opener mine eyes, 875
Dim erst, dilated spirits, ampler heart,
And growing up to godhead; which for thee
Chiefly I sought, without thee can despise.
For bliss, as thou hast part, to me is bliss;
Tedious, unshared with thee, and odious soon. 880
Thou therefore also taste, that equal lot
May join us, equal joy, as equal love;
Lest, thou not tasting, different degree
Disjoin us, and I then too late renounce
Deity for thee, when Fate will not permit.' 885
    Thus Eve with countenance blithe her story told;
But in her cheek distemper flushing glowed.
On the other side Adam, soon as he heard
The fatal trespass done by Eve, amazed,
Astonied stood and blank, while horror chill 890
Ran through his veins, and all his joints relaxed;
From his slack hand the garland wreathed for Eve
Down dropped, and all the faded roses shed:
Speechless he stood and pale, till thus at length
First to himself he inward silence broke. 895
    'O fairest of Creation, last and best
Of all God's works, Creature in whom excelled
Whatever can to sight or thought be formed,
Holy, divine, good, amiable, or sweet!
How art thou lost! how on a sudden lost, 900
Defaced, deflowered, and now to death devote!
Rather, how hast thou yielded to transgress
The strict forbiddance, how to violate
The sacred fruit forbidden! Some cursed fraud
Of enemy hath beguiled thee, yet unknown, 905
And me with thee hath ruined; for with thee
Certain my resolution is to die:
How can I live without thee! how forgo
Thy sweet converse, and love so dearly joined,
To live again in these wild woods forlorn! 910

876 **erst:** before

Should God create another Eve, and I
Another rib afford, yet loss of thee
Would never from my heart: no, no! I feel
The link of Nature draw me: flesh of flesh,
Bone of my bone thou art, and from thy state   915
Mine never shall be parted, bliss or woe.'
    So having said, as one from sad dismay
Recomforted, and after thoughts disturbed
Submitting to what seemed remediless,
Thus in calm mood his words to Eve he turned.   920
    'Bold deed thou hast presumed, adventurous Eve,
And peril great provoked, who thus hast dared,
Had it been only coveting to eye
That sacred fruit, sacred to abstinence,
Much more to taste it under ban to touch.   925
But past who can recall, or done undo?
Not God Omnipotent, nor Fate; yet so
Perhaps thou shalt not die, perhaps the fact
Is not so heinous now, foretasted fruit,
Profaned first by the serpent, by him first   930
Made common, and unhallowed, ere our taste;
Nor yet on him found deadly; yet he lives;
Lives, as thou saidst, and gains to live, as Man,
Higher degree of life; inducement strong
To us, as likely tasting to attain   935
Proportional ascent; which cannot be
But to be gods, or angels, demi-gods.
Nor can I think that God, Creator wise,
Though threatening, will in earnest so destroy
Us his prime creatures, dignified so high,   940
Set over all His works; which in our fall,
For us created, needs with us must fail,
Dependant made; so God shall uncreate,
Be frustrate, do, undo, and labour lose;
Not well conceived of God, who, though his power
Creation could repeat, yet would be loath   946
Us to abolish, lest th'adversary
Triumph, and say; "Fickle their state whom God
Most favours; who can please Him long? Me first
He ruined, now Mankind; whom will He next?"   950
Matter of scorn, not to be given the foe.
However I with thee have fixed my lot,
Certain to undergo like doom. If death
Consort with thee, death is to me as life;
So forcible within my heart I feel   955
The bond of Nature draw me to my own;
My own in thee, for what thou art is mine;
Our state cannot be severed; we are one,
One flesh; to lose thee were to lose myself.'
    So Adam; and thus Eve to him replied.   960
'O glorious trial of exceeding love,
Illustrious evidence, example high!
Engaging me to emulate; but, short
Of thy perfection, how shall I attain,
Adam, from whose dear side I boast me sprung,   965
And gladly of our union hear thee speak,
One heart, one soul in both; whereof good proof

This day affords, declaring thee resolved,
Rather than death, or aught than death more dread,
Shall separate us, linked in love so dear,   970
To undergo with me one guilt, one crime,
If any be, of tasting this fair fruit;
Whose virtue for of good still good proceeds,
Direct, or by occasion, hath presented
This happy trial of thy love, which else   975
So eminently never had been known?
Were it I thought death menaced would ensue
This my attempt, I would sustain alone
The worst, and not persuade thee, rather die
Deserted, than oblige thee with a fact   980
Pernicious to thy peace; chiefly assured
Remarkably so late of thy so true,
So faithful, love unequalled: but I feel
Far otherwise the event; not death, but life
Augmented, opened eyes, new hopes, new joys,   985
Taste so divine, that what of sweet before
Hath touched my sense, flat seems to this, and harsh.
On my experience, Adam, freely taste,
And fear of death deliver to the winds.'
    So saying, she embraced him, and for joy   990
Tenderly wept; much won, that he his love
Had so ennobled, as of choice to incur
Divine displeasure for her sake, or death.
In recompense (for such compliance bad
Such recompense best merits) from the bough   995
She gave him of that fair enticing fruit
With liberal hand: he scrupled not to eat,
Against his better knowledge; not deceived,
But fondly overcome with female charm.
Earth trembled from her entrails, as again   1000
In pangs; and Nature gave a second groan;
Sky loured; and, muttering thunder, some sad drops
Wept at completing of the mortal sin
Original: while Adam took no thought,
Eating his fill; nor Eve to iterate   1005
Her former trespass feared, the more to soothe
Him with her loved society; that now,
As with new wine intoxicated both,
They swim in mirth, and fancy that they feel
Divinity within them breeding wings,   1010
Wherewith to scorn the earth. But that false fruit
Far other operation first displayed,
Carnal desire inflaming; he on Eve
Began to cast lascivious eyes; she him
As wantonly repaid; in lust they burn: 1015
Till Adam thus 'gan Eve to dalliance move.
    'Eve, now I see thou art exact of taste,
And elegant, of sapience no small part;
Since to each meaning savour we apply,
And palate call judicious; I the praise   1020
Yield thee, so well this day thou hast purveyed.
Much pleasure we have lost, while we abstained
From this delightful fruit, nor known till now
True relish, tasting; if such pleasure be

In things to us forbidden, it might be wished, 1025
For this one tree had been forbidden ten.
But come, so well refreshed, now let us play,
As meet is, after such delicious fare;
For never did thy beauty, since the day
I saw thee first and wedded thee, adorned 1030
With all perfections, so inflame my sense
With ardour to enjoy thee, fairer now
Than ever; bounty of this virtuous tree!'
    So said he, and forbore not glance or toy
Of amorous intent; well understood 1035
Of Eve, whose eye darted contagious fire.
Her hand he seized; and to a shady bank,
Thick over-head with verdant roof embowered,
He led her nothing loath; flowers were the couch,
Pansies, and violets, and asphodel, 1040
And hyacinth; Earth's freshest softest lap.
There they their fill of love and love's disport
Took largely, of their mutual guilt the seal,
The solace of their sin; till dewy sleep
Oppressed them, wearied with their amorous play.
    Soon as the force of that fallacious fruit, 1046
That with exhilarating vapour bland
About their spirits had played, and inmost powers
Made err, was now exhaled; and grosser sleep,
Bred of unkindly fumes, with conscious dreams 1050
Encumbered, now had left them; up they rose
As from unrest; and, each the other viewing,
Soon found their eyes how opened, and their minds
How darkened; innocence, that as a veil
Had shadowed them from knowing ill, was gone; 1055
Just confidence, and native righteousness,
And honour, from about them, naked left
To guilty Shame; he covered, but his robe
Uncovered more. So rose the Danite strong,
Herculean Samson, from the harlot-lap 1060
Of Philistian Dalilah, and waked
Shorn of his strength. They destitute and bare
Of all their virtue: silent, and in face
Confounded, long they sat, as strucken mute:
Till Adam, though not less than Eve abashed, 1065
At length gave utterance to these words constrained.
    'O Eve, in evil hour thou didst give ear
To that false worm, of whomsoever taught
To counterfeit Man's voice; true in our fall,
False in our promised rising; since our eyes 1070
Opened we find indeed, and find we know
Both good and evil; good lost, and evil got;
Bad fruit of knowledge, if this be to know;
Which leaves us naked thus, of honour void,
Of innocence, of faith, of purity, 1075
Our wonted ornaments now soiled and stained,
And in our faces evident the signs
Of foul concupiscence; whence evil store;

Even shame, the last of evils; of the first
Be sure then. – How shall I behold the face 1080
Henceforth of God or angel, erst with joy
And rapture so oft beheld? Those heavenly shapes
Will dazzle now this earthly with their blaze
Insufferably bright. Oh! might I here
In solitude live savage; in some glade 1085
Obscured, where highest woods, impenetrable
To star or sun-light, spread their umbrage broad
And brown as evening: Cover me, ye Pines!
Ye Cedars, with innumerable boughs
Hide me, where I may never see them more! – 1090
But let us now, as in bad plight, devise
What best may for the present serve to hide
The parts of each from other, that seem most
To shame obnoxious, and unseemliest seen;
Some tree, whose broad smooth leaves together
    sewed, 1095
And girded on our loins, may cover round
Those middle parts; that this new comer, Shame,
There sit not, and reproach us as unclean.'
    So counselled he, and both together went
Into the thickest wood; there soon they chose 1100
The fig-tree; not that kind for fruit renowned,
But such as at this day, to Indians known,
In Malabar or Decan spreads her arms
Branching so broad and long, that in the ground
The bended twigs take root, and daughters grow 1105
About the mother tree, a pillared shade
High over-arched, and echoing walks between:
There oft the Indian herdsman, shunning heat,
Shelters in cool, and tends his pasturing herds
At loop-holes cut through thickest shade. Those leaves
They gathered, broad as Amazonian targe; 1111
And, with what skill they had, together sewed,
To gird their waist; vain covering, if to hide
Their guilt and dreaded shame! Oh, how unlike
To that first naked glory! Such of late 1115
Columbus found the American, so girt
With feathered cincture; naked else, and wild
Among the trees on isles and woody shores.
Thus fenced, and, as they thought, their shame in part
Covered, but not at rest or ease of mind, 1120
They sat them down to weep; nor only tears
Rained at their eyes, but high winds worse within
Began to rise, high passions, anger, hate,
Mistrust, suspicion, discord; and shook sore
Their inward state of mind, calm region once 1125
And full of peace, now tossed and turbulent:
For Understanding ruled not, and the Will
Heard not her lore; both in subjection now
To sensual Appetite, who from beneath
Usurping over sovran Reason claimed 1130
Superior sway. From thus distempered breast,
Adam, estranged in look and altered style,
Speech intermitted thus to Eve renewed.
    'Would thou hadst hearkened to my words, and
    stayed

1059–1062 Samson lost his strength after Dalilah cut his hair. Samson was of the tribe of Dan, a 'Danite'

With me, as I besought thee, when that strange 1135
Desire of wandering, this unhappy morn,
I know not whence possessed thee; we had then
Remained still happy; not, as now, despoiled
Of all our good; shamed, naked, miserable!
Let none henceforth seek needless cause to approve
The faith they owe; when earnestly they seek 1141
Such proof, conclude, they then begin to fail.'
   To whom, soon moved with touch of blame, thus
Eve.
'What words have passed thy lips, Adam severe!
Imput'st thou that to my default, or will 1145
Of wandering, as thou callest it, which who knows
But might as ill have happened thou being by,
Or to thyself perhaps? Hadst thou been there,
Or here the attempt, thou couldst not have discerned
Fraud in the serpent, speaking as he spake; 1150
No ground of enmity between us known,
Why he should mean me ill, or seek to harm.
Was I to have never parted from thy side?
As good have grown there still a lifeless rib.
Being as I am, why didst not thou, the head, 1155
Command me absolutely not to go,
Going into such danger, as thou saidst?
Too facile then, thou didst not much gainsay;
Nay, didst permit, approve, and fair dismiss.
Hadst thou been firm and fixed in thy dissent, 1160
Neither had I transgressed, nor thou with me.'
   To whom, then first incensed, Adam replied:
'Is this the love, is this the recompense
Of mine to thee, ingrateful Eve! expressed
Immutable, when thou wert lost, not I; 1165
Who might have lived, and joyed immortal bliss,
Yet willingly chose rather death with thee?
And am I now upbraided as the cause
Of thy transgressing? Not enough severe,
It seems, in thy restraint. What could I more 1170
I warned thee, I admonished thee, foretold
The danger, and the lurking enemy
That lay in wait; beyond this, had been force;
And force upon free will hath here no place.
But confidence then bore thee on; secure 1175
Either to meet no danger, or to find
Matter of glorious trial; and perhaps
I also erred, in overmuch admiring
What seemed in thee so perfect, that I thought
No evil durst attempt thee; but I rue 1180
The error now, which is become my crime,
And thou the accuser. Thus it shall befall
Him, who, to worth in women overtrusting,
Lets her will rule: restraint she will not brook;
And, left to herself, if evil thence ensue, 1185
She first his weak indulgence will accuse.'
   Thus they in mutual accusation spent
The fruitless hours, but neither self-condemning;
And of their vain contest appeared no end.

BOOK TEN

MEANWHILE the heinous and despiteful act
Of Satan, done in paradise; and how
He, in the serpent, had perverted Eve,
Her husband she, to taste the fatal fruit,
Was known in heaven; for what can 'scape the eye 5
Of God all-seeing, or deceive His heart
Omniscient? who, in all things wise and just,
Hindered not Satan to attempt the mind
Of Man, with strength entire and free will armed,
Complete to have discovered and repulsed 10
Whatever wiles of foe or seeming friend.
For still they knew, and ought to have still
   remembered,
The high injunction, not to taste that fruit,
Whoever tempted; which they not obeying,
Incurred – what could they less? – the penalty; 15
And, manifold in sin, deserved to fall.
Up into heaven from paradise in haste
The angelic guards ascended, mute, and sad,
For Man; for of his state by this they knew,
Much wond'ring how the subtle fiend had stolen 20
Entrance unseen. Soon as the unwelcome news
From earth arrived at heaven-gate, displeased
All were who heard; dim sadness did not spare
That time celestial visages, yet, mixed
With pity, violated not their bliss. 25
About the new-arrived, in multitudes
The ethereal people ran, to hear and know
How all befell. They towards the throne supreme,
Accountable, made haste, to make appear,
With righteous plea, their utmost vigilance 30

BOOK TEN – THE ARGUMENT: Man's transgression known, the Guardian Angels forsake Paradise, and return up to Heaven to approve their vigilance, and are approv'd, God declaring that The entrance of Satan could not be by them prevented. He sends his Son to judge the Transgressors, who descends and gives Sentence accordingly; then in pity clothes them both, and reascends. Sin and Death sitting till then at the Gates of Hell, by wondrous sympathy feeling the success of Satan in this new World, and the sin by Man there committed, resolve to sit no longer confin'd in Hell, but to follow Satan their Sire up to the place of Man: To make the way easier from Hell to this World to and fro, they pave a broad Highway or Bridge over Chaos, according to the Track that Satan first made; then preparing for Earth, they meet him proud of his success returning to Hell; their mutual gratulation. Satan arrives at Pandemonium, in full of assembly relates with boasting his success against Man; instead of applause is entertained with a general hiss by all his audience, transform'd with himself also suddenly into Serpents, according to his doom giv'n in Paradise; then deluded with a shew of the forbidden Tree springing up before them, they greedily reaching to take of the Fruit, chew dust and bitter ashes. The proceedings of Sin and Death; God foretells the final Victory of his Son over them, and the renewing of all things; but for the present commands his Angels to make several alterations in the Heavens and Elements. Adam more and more perceiving his fall'n condition heavily bewails, rejects the condolement of Eve; she persists and at length appeases him: then to evade the Curse likely to fall on their Offspring, proposes to Adam violent ways which he approves not, but conceiving better hope, puts her in mind of the late Promise made them, that her Seed should be reveng'd on the Serpent, and exhorts her with him to seek Peace of the offended Deity, by repentance and supplication

And easily approved; when the Most High
Eternal Father, from his secret cloud,
Amidst in thunder uttered thus his voice.
  'Assembled Angels, and ye Powers returned
From unsuccessful charge; be not dismayed,   35
Nor troubled at these tidings from the earth,
Which your sincerest care could not prevent;
Foretold so lately what would come to pass,
When first this tempter crossed the gulf from hell.
I told ye then he should prevail, and speed   40
On his bad errand; Man should be seduced,
And flattered out of all, believing lies
Against his Maker; no decree of mine
Concurring to necessitate his fall,
Or touch with lightest moment of impulse   45
His free will, to her own inclining left
In even scale. But fallen he is; and now
What rests, but that the mortal sentence pass
On his transgression – death denounced that day?
Which he presumes already vain and void,   50
Because not yet inflicted, as he feared,
By some immediate stroke; but soon shall find
Forbearance no acquittance, ere day end.
Justice shall not return as bounty scorned.
But whom send I to judge them? whom but thee,   55
Vicegerent Son? To thee I have transferred
All judgement, whether in heaven, or earth, or hell.
Easy it may be seen that I intend
Mercy colleague with justice, sending thee
Man's friend, his Mediator, his designed   60
Both ransom and Redeemer voluntary,
And destined Man himself to judge Man fallen.'
  So spake the Father; and, unfolding bright
Toward the right hand His glory, on the Son
Blazed forth unclouded deity. He full   65
Resplendent all His father manifest
Expressed, and thus divinely answered mild.
  'Father Eternal, thine is to decree;
Mine, both in heaven and earth, to do thy will
Supreme; that thou in me, thy Son beloved,   70
Mayest ever rest well pleased. I go to judge
On earth these thy transgressors; but thou knowest,
Whoever judged, the worst on me must light,
When time shall be; for so I undertook
Before thee; and, not repenting, this obtain   75
Of right, that I may mitigate their doom
On me derived; yet I shall temper so
Justice with mercy, as may illustrate most
Them fully satisfied, and thee appease.
Attendance none shall need, nor train, where none   80
Are to behold the judgement, but the judged,
Those two; the third best absent is condemned,
Convíct by flight, and rebel to all law:
Conviction to the serpent none belongs.'

Thus saying, from his radiant seat he rose   85
Of high collateral glory: Him thrones, and powers,
Princedoms, and dominations ministrant,
Accompanied to heaven-gate; from whence
Eden, and all the coast, in prospect lay.
Down He descended straight; the speed of gods   90
Time counts not, though with swiftest minutes
    winged.
  Now was the sun in western cadence low
From noon, and gentle airs, due at their hour,
To fan the earth now waked, and usher in
The evening cool; when He, from wrath more cool,   95
Came the mild Judge, and Intercessor both,
To sentence Man. The voice of God they heard
Now walking in the garden, by soft winds
Brought to their ears, while day declined; they heard,
And from His presence hid themselves among   100
The thickest trees, both man and wife; till God,
Approaching, thus to Adam called aloud:
  'Where art thou, Adam, wont with joy to meet
My coming seen far off? I miss thee here,
Not pleased, thus entertained with solitude,   105
Where obvious duty erewhile appeared unsought:
Or come I less conspicuous, or what change
Absents thee, or what chance detains? – Come forth!'
  He came; and with him Eve, more loath, though
    first
To offend; discount'nanced both, and discomposed;
Love was not in their looks, either to God,   111
Or to each other; but apparent guilt,
And shame, and perturbation, and despair,
Anger, and obstinacy, and hate, and guile.
Whence Adam, falt'ring long, thus answered brief:
  'I heard thee in the garden, and of Thy voice   116
Afraid, being naked, hid myself.' To whom
The gracious Judge without revile replied:
  'My voice thou oft hast heard, and hast not feared,
But still rejoiced; how is it now become   120
So dreadful to thee? That thou art naked, who
Hath told thee? Hast thou eaten of the tree,
Whereof I gave thee charge thou shouldst not eat?'
To whom thus Adam sore beset replied:
  'O Heaven! in evil strait this day I stand   125
Before my Judge; either to undergo
Myself the total crime, or to accuse
My other self, the partner of my life;
Whose failing, while her faith to me remains,
I should conceal, and not expose to blame   130
By my complaint: but strict necessity
Subdues me, and calamitous constraint;
Lest on my head both sin and punishment,
However insupportable, be all
Devolved; though should I hold my peace, yet thou
Wouldst easily detect what I conceal. –   136

56–57 **Vicegerent:** Christ is vice-regent to God, and will judge all in
heaven and earth

92 **cadence:** falling

This woman, whom Thou madest to be my help,
And gavest me as Thy perfect gift, so good,
So fit, so acceptable, so divine,
That from her hand I could suspect no ill,   140
And what she did, whatever in itself,
Her doing seemed to justify the deed;
She gave me of the tree, and I did eat.'
To whom the Sovran Presence thus replied.

   'Was she thy God, that her thou didst obey   145
Before His voice? or was she made thy guide,
Superior, or but equal, that to her
Thou didst resign thy manhood, and the place
Wherein God set thee above her made of thee,
And for thee, whose perfection far excelled   150
Hers in all real dignity? Adorned
She was indeed, and lovely, to attract
Thy love, not thy subjection; and her gifts
Were such, as under government well seemed;
Unseemly to bear rule; which was thy part   155
And person, hadst thou known thyself aright.'

   So having said, He thus to Eve in few:
'Say, Woman, what is this which thou hast done?'

   To whom sad Eve, with shame nigh overwhelmed,
Confessing soon, yet not before her Judge   160
Bold or loquacious, thus abashed replied.
'The serpent me beguiled, and I did eat.'

   Which when the Lord God heard, without delay
To judgement he proceeded on the accused
Serpent, though brute; unable to transfer   165
The guilt on him, who made him instrument
Of mischief, and polluted from the end
Of his creation; justly then accursed,
As vitiated in nature. More to know
Concerned not Man (since he no further knew)   170
Nor altered his offence; yet God at last
To Satan first in sin his doom applied,
Though in mysterious terms, judged as then best:
And on the serpent thus his curse let fall.

   'Because thou hast done this, thou art accursed   175
Above all cattle, each beast of the field;
Upon thy belly grovelling thou shalt go,
And dust shalt eat all the days of thy life.
Between thee and the woman I will put
Enmity, and between thine and her seed;   180
Her seed shall bruise thy head, thou bruise his heel.'

   So spake this oracle, then verified
When Jesus, Son of Mary, second Eve,
Saw Satan fall, like lightning, down from heaven,
Prince of the air; then, rising from his grave   185
Spoiled principalities and powers, triumphed
In open show; and, with ascension bright,
Captivity led captive through the air,
The realm itself of Satan, long usurped;
Whom he shall tread at last under our feet;   190
Even he, who now foretold his fatal bruise;
And to the woman thus his sentence turned:

   'Thy sorrow I will greatly multiply
By thy conception; children thou shalt bring
In sorrow forth; and to thy husband's will   195
Thine shall submit; he over thee shall rule.'

   On Adam last thus judgement he pronounced:
'Because thou hast hearkened to the voice of thy wife,
And eaten of the tree, concerning which   199
I charged thee, saying, "Thou shalt not eat thereof,"
Cursed is the ground for thy sake; thou in sorrow
Shalt eat thereof, all the days of thy life;
Thorns also and thistles it shall bring thee forth
Unbid; and thou shalt eat the herb of the field;
In the sweat of thy face shalt thou eat bread,   205
Till thou return unto the ground; for thou
Out of the ground wast taken, know thy birth,
For dust thou art, and shalt to dust return.'

   So judged he Man, both Judge and Saviour sent;
And th'instant stroke of death, denounced that day,
Removed far off; then, pitying how they stood   211
Before him naked to the air, that now
Must suffer change, disdained not to begin
Thenceforth the form of servant to assume;
As when he washed his servants' feet; so now,   215
As father of his family, He clad
Their nakedness with skins of beasts, or slain,
Or as the snake with youthful coat repaid;
And thought not much to clothe His enemies;
Nor He their outward only with the skins   220
Of beasts, but inward nakedness, much more.
Opprobrious, with his robe of righteousness,
Arraying, covered from his Father's sight.
To Him with swift ascent He up returned,
Into His blissful bosom reassumed   225
In glory, as of old; to Him appeased
All, though all-knowing, what had passed with Man
Recounted, mixing intercession sweet.

   Meanwhile, ere thus was sinned and judged on
      earth,
Within the gates of hell sat Sin and Death,   230
In counterview within the gates, that now
Stood open wide, belching outrageous flame
Far into Chaos, since the fiend passed through,
Sin opening; who thus now to Death began.

   'O Son, why sit we here each other viewing   235
Idly, while Satan, our great author, thrives
In other worlds, and happier seat provides
For us, his offspring dear? It cannot be
But that success attends him; if mishap,
Ere this he had returned, with fury driven   240
By his avengers; since no place like this
Can fit his punishment, or their revenge.
Methinks I feel new strength within me rise,
Wings growing, and dominion given me large
Beyond this deep; whatever draws me on,   245
Or sympathy, or some connatural force,
Powerful at greatest distance to unite,
With secret amity, things of like kind,

By secretest conveyance. Thou, my shade
Inseparable, must with me along; 250
For Death from Sin no power can separate.
But, lest the difficulty of passing back
Stay his return perhaps over this gulf
Impassable, impervious; let us try
Advent'rous work, yet to thy power and mine 255
Not unagreeable, to found a path
Over this main from hell to that new world,
Where Satan now prevails; a monument
Of merit high to all the infernal host,
Easing their passage hence, for intercourse, 260
Or transmigration, as their lot shall lead.
Nor can I miss the way, so strongly drawn
By this new-felt attraction and instinct.'
        Whom thus the meagre shadow answered soon:
'Go whither Fate and inclination strong 265
Leads thee; I shall not lag behind, nor err
The way, thou leading; such a scent I draw
Of carnage, prey innumerable, and taste
The savour of death from all things there that live:
Nor shall I to the work thou enterprisest 270
Be wanting, but afford thee equal aid.'
        So saying, with delight he snuffed the smell
Of mortal change on earth. As when a flock
Of ravenous fowl, though many a league remote,
Against the day of battle, to a field, 275
Where armies lie encamped, come flying, lured
With scent of living carcasses designed
For death, the following day, in bloody fight:
So scented the grim feature, and upturned
His nostril wide into the murky air; 280
Sagacious of his quarry from so far.
Then both from out hell-gates, into the waste
Wide anarchy of Chaos, damp and dark,
Flew diverse; and with power (their power was great)
Hovering upon the waters, what they met 285
Solid or slimy, as in raging sea
Tossed up and down, together crowded drove,
From each side shoaling towards the mouth of hell;
As when two polar winds, blowing advérse
Upon the Cronian sea, together drive 290
Mountains of ice, that stop the imagined way
Beyond Petsora eastward, to the rich
Cathaian coast. The aggregated soil
Death with his mace petrific, cold and dry,
As with a trident, smote; and fixed as firm 295
As Delos, floating once; the rest his look
Bound with Gorgonian rigour not to move;
And with Asphaltic slime, broad as the gate,
Deep to the roots of hell the gathered beach
They fastened, and the mole immense wrought on 300

Over the foaming deep high-arched, a bridge
Of length prodigious, joining to the wall
Immovable of this now fenceless world,
Forfeit to Death; from hence a passage broad,
Smooth, easy, inoffensive, down to hell. 305
So, if great things to small may be compared,
Xerxes, the liberty of Greece to yoke,
From Susa, his Memnonian palace high,
Came to the sea: and, over Hellespont
Bridging his way, Europe with Asia joined, 310
And scourged with many a stroke the indignant waves.
Now had they brought the work by wond'rous art
Pontifical, a ridge of pendant rock,
Over the vexed abyss, following the track
Of Satan to the self-same place where he 315
First lighted from his wing, and landed safe
From out of Chaos, to the outside bare
Of this round world. With pins of adamant
And chains they made all fast, too fast they made
And durable! And now in little space 320
The confines met of empyrean heaven,
And of this world; and, on the left hand, hell
With long reach interposed; three several ways
In sight, to each of these three places led.
And now their way to earth they had descried, 325
To paradise first tending; when, behold!
Satan, in likeness of an angel bright,
Betwixt the Centaur and the Scorpion steering
His zenith, while the sun in Aries rose:
Disguised he came; but those his children dear 330
Their parent soon discerned, though in disguise.
He, after Eve seduced, unminded slunk
Into the wood fast by; and, changing shape,
To observe the sequel, saw his guileful act
By Eve, though all unweeting, seconded 335
Upon her husband; saw their shame that sought
Vain covertures; but when he saw descend
The Son of God to judge them, terrified
He fled; not hoping to escape, but shun
The present; fearing, guilty, what his wrath 340
Might suddenly inflict; that past, returned
By night, and listening where the hapless pair
Sat in their sad discourse, and various plaint,
Thence gathered his own doom; which understood
Not instant, but of future time, with joy 345
And tidings fraught, to hell he now returned;
And at the brink of Chaos, near the foot
Of this new wonderous pontifice, unhoped
Met, who to meet him came, his offspring dear.
Great joy was at their meeting, and at sight 350
Of that stupendious bridge his joy increased.
Long he admiring stood, till Sin, his fair
Enchanting daughter, thus the silence broke.

---

281 **Sagacious:** with an acute sense of smell 290 **Cronian sea:** Arctic Ocean 292 **Petsora:** a river in Siberia 293 **Cathaian coast:** Chinese coast 294 **petrific:** turning to stone 296 **Delos:** a floating island until Jupiter fixed it to the sea-bed with chains 297 **Gorgonian:** with a glance the Gorgons could turn a person to stone 300 **mole:** massive pier

303 **fenceless:** defenceless 307 **Xerxes:** Persian king who attacked Greece, but failed to gain control of the country 308 **Susa:** seat of the Persian kings 309 **Hellespont:** the strait between the Black Sea and the Aegean Sea which forms a dividing line between Europe and Asia 313 **Pontifical:** bridge-making

'O Parent, these are thy magnific deeds,
Thy trophies! which thou view'st as not thine own;
Thou art their author, and prime architect: 356
For I no sooner in my heart divined,
My heart, which by a secret harmony
Still moves with thine, joined in connection sweet,
That thou on earth hadst prospered, which thy looks
Now also evidence, but straight I felt,   361
Though distant from thee worlds between, yet felt,
That I must after thee, with this thy son;
Such fatal consequence unites us three!
Hell could no longer hold us in her bounds,   365
Nor this unvoyageable gulf obscure
Detain from following thy illustrious track.
Thou hast achieved our liberty, confined
Within hell-gates till now; thou us empowered
To fortify thus far, and overlay,   370
With this portentous bridge, the dark abyss.
Thine now is all this world; thy virtue hath won
What thy hands builded not; thy wisdom gained
With odds what war hath lost, and fully avenged
Our foil in heaven; here thou shalt monarch reign,
There didst not; there let Him still victor sway,   376
As battle hath adjudged; from this new world
Retiring, by His own doom alienated;
And henceforth monarchy with thee divide
Of all things, parted by th'empyreal bounds,   380
His quadrature, from thy orbicular world;
Or try thee now more dangerous to His throne.'
   Whom thus the prince of darkness answered glad:
'Fair Daughter, and thou Son and Grandchild both;
High proof ye now have given to be the race   385
Of Satan (for I glory in the name,
Antagonist of Heaven's Almighty King),
Amply have merited of me, of all
Th'infernal empire, that so near heaven's door
Triumphal with triumphal act have met,   390
Mine, with this glorious work; and made one realm,
Hell and this world, one realm, one continent
Of easy thorough-fare. Therefore, while I
Descend through darkness, on your road with ease,
To my associate powers, them to acquaint   395
With these successes, and with them rejoice;
You two this way, among these numerous orbs,
All yours, right down to paradise descend;
There dwell, and reign in bliss; thence on the earth
Dominion exercise and in the air,   400
Chiefly on Man, sole lord of all declared;
Him first make sure your thrall, and lastly kill.
My substitutes I send ye, and create
Plenipotent on earth, of matchless might
Issuing from me: on your joint vigour now   405
My hold of this new kingdom all depends,
Through Sin to Death exposed by my exploit.

If your joint power prevail, the affairs of hell
No detriment need fear; go, and be strong!'
   So saying he dismissed them; they with speed   410
Their course through thickest constellations held,
Spreading their bane; the blasted stars looked wan,
And planets, planet-struck, real eclipse
Then suffered. The other way Satan went down
The causey to hell-gate. On either side   415
Disparted Chaos overbuilt exclaimed,
And with rebounding surge the bars assailed,
That scorned his indignation. Through the gate,
Wide open and unguarded, Satan passed,
And all about found desolate; for those,   420
Appointed to sit there, had left their charge,
Flown to the upper world; the rest were all
Far to the inland retired, about the walls
Of Pandemonium; city and proud seat
Of Lucifer, so by allusion called   425
Of that bright star to Satan paragoned;
There kept their watch the legions, while the grand
In council sat, solicitous what chance
Might intercept their emperor sent; so he
Departing gave command, and they observed.   430
As when the Tartar from his Russian foe,
By Astracan, over the snowy plains,
Retires; or Bactrin Sophi, from the horns
Of Turkish crescent, leaves all waste beyond
The realm of Aladule, in his retreat   435
To Tauris or Casbeen. So these, the late
Heaven-banished host, left desert utmost hell
Many a dark league, reduced in careful watch
Round their metropolis; and now expecting
Each hour their great adventurer, from the search   440
Of foreign worlds: He through the midst unmarked,
In show plebeian angel militant
Of lowest order, passed; and from the door
Of that Plutonian hall, invisible
Ascended his high throne; which, under state   445
Of richest texture spread, at the upper end
Was placed in regal lustre. Down a while
He sat, and round about him saw unseen:
At last, as from a cloud, his fulgent head
And shape star-bright appeared, or brighter; clad   450
With what permissive glory since his fall
Was left him, or false glitter: All amazed
At that so sudden blaze the Stygian throng
Bent their aspect, and whom they wished beheld,
Their mighty chief returned: loud was th'acclaim:
Forth rushed in haste the great consulting peers,   456
Raised from their dark divan, and with like joy
Congratulant approached him; who with hand
Silence, and with these words attention, won:

'Thrones, Dominations, Princedoms, Virtues, Powers; 460
For in possession such, not only of right,
I call ye, and declare ye now; returned
Successful beyond hope, to lead ye forth
Triumphant out of this infernal pit
Abominable, accursed, the house of woe, 465
And dungeon of our tyrant. Now possess,
As lords, a spacious world, to our native heaven
Little inferior, by my adventure hard
With peril great achieved. Long were to tell
What I have done; what suffered; with what pain 470
Voyaged th'unreal, vast, unbounded deep
Of horrible confusion; over which
By Sin and Death a broad way now is paved,
To expedite your glorious march; but I
Toiled out my uncouth passage, forced to ride 475
The untractable abyss, plunged in the womb
Of unoriginal Night and Chaos wild;
That, jealous of their secrets, fiercely opposed
My journey strange, with clamorous uproar
Protesting Fate supreme; thence how I found 480
The new-created world, which fame in heaven
Long had foretold, a fabric wonderful
Of absolute perfection! therein Man
Placed in a paradise, by our exíle
Made happy: Him by fraud I have seduced 485
From his Creator; and, the more to increase
Your wonder, with an apple; he, thereat
Offended, worth your laughter! hath given up
Both his beloved Man, and all his world,
To Sin and Death a prey, and so to us, 490
Without our hazard, labour, or alarm;
To range in, and to dwell, and over Man
To rule, as over all he should have ruled.
True is, me also he hath judged, or rather
Me not, but the brute serpent in whose shape 495
Man I deceived: that which to me belongs,
Is enmity which he will put between
Me and mankind; I am to bruise his heel;
His seed, when is not set, shall bruise my head:
A world who would not purchase with a bruise, 500
Or much more grievous pain? – Ye have the account
Of my performance: What remains, ye Gods,
But up, and enter now into full bliss?'
   So having said, a while he stood, expecting
Their universal shout, and high applause, 505
To fill his ear; when, contrary, he hears
On all sides, from innumerable tongues,
A dismal universal hiss, the sound
Of public scorn; he wondered, but not long
Had leisure, wondering at himself now more, 510
His visage drawn he felt to sharp and spare;
His arms clung to his ribs; his legs entwining
Each other, till supplanted down he fell
A monstrous serpent on his belly prone,
Reluctant, but in vain; a greater power 515

Now ruled him, punished in the shape he sinned,
According to his doom: he would have spoke,
But hiss for hiss returned with forkèd tongue
To forkèd tongue; for now were all transformed
Alike, to serpents all, as accessories 520
To his bold riot. Dreadful was the din
Of hissing through the hall, thick-swarming now
With complicated monsters head and tail,
Scorpion, and asp, and amphisbaena dire,
Cerastes horned, hydrus, and elops drear, 525
And dipsas (not so thick swarmed once the soil
Bedropped with blood of Gorgon, or the isle
Ophiusa); but still greatest he the midst,
Now dragon grown, larger than whom the sun
Engendered in the Pythian vale or slime, 530
Huge python, and his power no less he seemed
Above the rest still to retain; they all
Him followed, issuing forth to the open field,
Where all yet left of that revolted rout,
Heaven-fallen, in station stood or just array; 535
Sublime with expectation when to see
In triumph issuing forth their glorious chief;
They saw, but other sight instead! a crowd
Of ugly serpents; horror on them fell,
And horrid sympathy; for, what they saw, 540
They felt themselves, now changing; down their arms,
Down fell both spear and shield; down they as fast;
And the dire hiss renewed, and the dire form
Catched, by contagion; like in punishment,
As in their crime. Thus was the applause they meant,
Turned to exploding hiss, triumph to shame 546
Cast on themselves from their own mouths. There stood
A grove hard by, sprung up with this their change,
His will who reigns above, to aggravate
Their penance, laden with fair fruit, like that 550
Which grew in paradise, the bait of Eve
Used by the tempter: on that prospect strange
Their earnest eyes they fixed, imagining
For one forbidden tree a multitude
Now risen, to work them further woe or shame; 555
Yet, parched with scalding thirst and hunger fierce,
Though to delude them sent, could not abstain;
But on they rolled in heaps, and, up the trees
Climbing, sat thicker than the snaky locks
That curled Megaera: greedily they plucked 560
The fruitage fair to sight, like that which grew
Near that bituminous lake where Sodom flamed;
This more delusive, not the touch, but taste
Deceived; they, fondly thinking to allay
Their appetite with gust, instead of fruit 565

524 **amphisbaena:** a serpent with a head at both ends 525 **hydrus:** a water snake **elops:** a form of serpent 526 **dipsas:** a serpent whose bite causes a raging thirst 526–527 the blood of the Gorgon, Medusa, would produce snakes when spilled 528 **Ophiusa:** literally 'full of serpents' 529–532 Python was slain by Apollo 560 **Megaera:** one of the three Furies

Chewed bitter ashes, which the offended taste
With spattering noise rejected: oft they assayed,
Hunger and thirst constraining; drugged as oft,
With hatefullest disrelish writhed their jaws,
With soot and cinders filled; so oft they fell   570
Into the same illusion, not as Man
Whom they triumphed once lapsed. Thus were they
    plagued
And worn with famine, long and ceaseless hiss,
Till their lost shape, permitted, they resumed;
Yearly enjoined, some say, to undergo,   575
This annual humbling certain numbered days,
To dash their pride, and joy, for Man seduced.
However, some tradition they dispersed
Among the heathen, of their purchase got,
And fabled how the serpent, whom they called   580
Ophion, with Eurynome, the wide –
Encroaching Eve perhaps, had first the rule
Of high Olympus; thence by Saturn driven
And Ops, ere yet Dictaean Jove was born.
    Meanwhile in paradise the hellish pair   585
Too soon arrived; Sin, there in power before,
Once actual; now in body, and to dwell
Habitual habitant; behind her Death,
Close following pace for pace, not mounted yet
On his pale horse: to whom Sin thus began.   590
    'Second of Satan sprung, all-conquering Death!
What thinkest thou of our empire now, though earned
With travel difficult, not better far
Than still at hell's dark threshold to have sat watch,
Unnamed, undreaded, and thyself half starved?'   595
    Whom thus the Sin-born monster answered soon:
'To me, who with eternal famine pine,
Alike is hell, or paradise, or heaven;
There best, where most with ravine I may meet;
Which here, though plenteous, all too little seems   600
To stuff this maw, this vast unhide-bound corps.'
    To whom the incestuous mother thus replied.
'Thou therefore on these herbs, and fruits, and flowers,
Feed first; on each beast next, and fish, and fowl;
No homely morsels! and, whatever thing   605
The scythe of Time mows down, devour unspared;
Till I, in Man residing, through the race,
His thoughts, his looks, words, actions, all infect;
And season him thy last and sweetest prey.'
    This said, they both betook them several ways,   610
Both to destroy, or unimmortal make
All kinds, and for destruction to mature
Sooner or later; which the Almighty seeing,
From His transcendent seat the saints among,
To those bright orders uttered thus his voice.   615

'See, with what heat these dogs of hell advance
To waste and havoc yonder world, which I
So fair and good created; and had still
Kept in that state, had not the folly of Man
Let in these wasteful furies, who impute   620
Folly to me; so doth the prince of hell
And his adherents, that with so much ease
I suffer them to enter and possess
A place so heavenly; and, conniving, seem
To gratify my scornful enemies,   625
That laugh, as if, transported with some fit
Of passion, I to them had quitted all,
At random yielded up to their misrule;
And know not that I called, and drew them thither,
My hell-hounds, to lick up the draff and filth   630
Which Man's polluting sin with taint hath shed
On what was pure; till, crammed and gorged, nigh
    burst
With sucked and glutted offal, at one sling
Of Thy victorious arm, well-pleasing Son,
Both Sin, and Death, and yawning Grave, at last,   635
Through Chaos hurled, obstruct the mouth of hell
For ever, and seal up his ravenous jaws.
Then heaven and earth renewed shall be made pure
To sanctity, that shall receive no stain:
Till then, the curse pronounced on both precedes.'   640
    He ended, and the heavenly audience loud
Sung Hallelujah, as the sound of seas,
Through multitude that sung: 'Just are Thy ways,
Righteous are Thy decrees on all Thy works;
Who can extenuate Thee? Next, to the Son,   645
Destined Restorer of mankind, by whom
New heaven and earth shall to the ages rise,
Or down from heaven descend.' – Such was their
    song;
While the Creator, calling forth by name
His mighty angels, gave them several charge,   650
As sorted best with present things. The sun
Had first his precept so to move, so shine,
As might affect the earth with cold and heat
Scarce tolerable; and from the north to call
Decrepit winter; from the south to bring   655
Solstitial summer's heat. To the blank moon
Her office they prescribed; to the other five
Their planetary motions, and aspects,
In sextile, square, and trine, and opposite,
Of noxious efficacy, and when to join   660
In synod unbenign; and taught the fixed
Their influence malignant when to shower,
Which of them rising with the sun, or falling,
Should prove tempestuous. To the winds they set
Their corners, when with bluster to confound   665

581 **Ophion, with Eurynome:** king and queen of Olympus 584 **Ops:**
the wife of Saturn **Dictaean:** from Dicte, the Cretan mountain
where Jupiter lived as a child 599 **ravine:** prey 601 **maw:** stomach
unhide-bound: loose-skinned

656 **Solstitial:** solstice

Sea, air, and shore; the thunder when to roll
With terror through the dark aereal hall.
Some say, He bid His angels turn askance
The poles of earth, twice ten degrees and more,
From the sun's axle; they with labour pushed 670
Oblique the centric globe. Some say, the sun
Was bid turn reins from the equinoctial road
Like distant breadth to Taurus with the seven
Atlantic Sisters, and the Spartan Twins,
Up to the Tropic Crab: thence down amain 675
By Leo, and the Virgin, and the Scales,
As deep as Capricorn; to bring in change
Of seasons to each clime; else had the spring
Perpetual smiled on earth with vernant flowers,
Equal in days and nights, except to those 680
Beyond the polar circles; to them day
Had unbenighted shone, while the low sun,
To recompense his distance, in their sight
Had rounded still the horizon, and not known
Or east or west; which had forbid the snow 685
From cold Estotiland, and south as far
Beneath Magellan. At that tasted fruit
The sun, as from Thyestean banquet, turned
His course intended; else, how had the world
Inhabited, though sinless, more than now, 690
Avoided pinching cold and scorching heat?
These changes in the heavens, though slow, produced
Like change on sea and land; sideral blast,
Vapour, and mist, and exhalation hot,
Corrupt and pestilent. Now from the north 695
Of Norumbega, and the Samoed shore,
Bursting their brazen dungeon, armed with ice,
And snow, and hail, and stormy gust and flaw,
Boreas, and Caecias, and Argestes loud,
And Thrascias, rend the woods, and seas upturn; 700
With adverse blast upturns them from the south
Notus, and Afer black with thunderous clouds
From Serraliona; thwart of these, as fierce,
Forth rush the Levant and the Ponent winds,
Eurus and Zephyr, with their lateral noise, 705
Sirocco and Libecchio. Thus began
Outrage from lifeless things; but Discord first,
Daughter of Sin, among the irrational
Death introduced, through fierce antipathy:
Beast now with beast 'gan war, and fowl with fowl, 710
And fish with fish; to graze the herb all leaving,
Devoured each other; nor stood much in awe
Of Man, but fled him; or, with countenance grim,
Glared on him passing. These were from without
The growing miseries, which Adam saw 715

686 **Estotiland:** now N.E. Labrador in North America 687 **Magellan:**
Argentina 688 **Thyestean banquet:** a banquet of human flesh
696 **Norumbega:** in North America **Samoed:** Siberian 698 **flaw:**
squall 699 various winds 702 **Afer:** Africa 703 **Serraliona:**
Sierra Leone 704 **Levant . . . Ponent winds:** East and West winds
705–706 various winds

Already in part, though hid in gloomiest shade,
To sorrow abandoned, but worse felt within;
And, in a troubled sea of passion tossed,
Thus to disburden sought with sad complaint.
    'O miserable of happy! Is this the end 720
Of this new glorious world, and me so late
The glory of that glory, who now become
Accursed, of blessed? hide me from the face
Of God, whom to behold was then my height
Of happiness! – Yet well, if here would end 725
The misery; I deserved it, and would bear
My own deservings; but this will not serve:
All that I eat or drink, or shall beget,
Is propagated curse. O voice, once heard
Delightfully, "Increase and multiply," 730
Now death to hear! for what can I increase,
Or multiply, but curses on my head?
Who of all ages to succeed, but, feeling
The evil on him brought by me, will curse
My head? "Ill fare our ancestor impure, 735
For this we may thank Adam!" but his thanks
Shall be the execration: so, besides
Mine own that bide upon me, all from me
Shall with a fierce reflux on me rebound;
On me, as on their natural centre, light 740
Heavy, though in their place. O fleeting joys
Of paradise, dear-bought with lasting woes!
Did I request thee, Maker, from my clay
To mould me Man? did I solicit thee
From darkness to promote me, or here place 745
In this delicious garden? As my will
Concurred not to my being, it were but right
And equal to reduce me to my dust;
Desirous to resign and render back
All I received; unable to perform 750
Thy terms too hard, by which I was to hold
The good I sought not. To the loss of that,
Sufficient penalty, why hast thou added
The sense of endless woes? Inexplicable
Thy justice seems; yet, to say truth, too late 755
I thus contest; then should have been refused
Those terms, whatever, when they were proposed;
Thou didst accept them: wilt thou enjoy the good,
Then cavil the conditions? And though God
Made thee without thy leave, what if thy son 760
Prove disobedient and, reproved, retort:
"Wherefore didst Thou beget me? I sought it not."
Wouldst thou admit for his contempt of thee
That proud excuse? Yet him not thy election,
But natural necessity, begot. 765
God made thee of choice His own, and of His own
To serve Him; thy reward was of His grace;
Thy punishment, then, justly was at His will.
Be it so, for I submit; His doom is fair,
That dust I am, and shall to dust return. 770
O welcome hour, whenever! Why delays

His hand to execute what His decree
Fixed on this day? Why do I overlive,
Why am I mocked with death, and lengthened out
To deathless pain? How gladly would I meet   775
Mortality my sentence, and be earth
Insensible! How glad would lay me down
As in my mother's lap! There I should rest,
And sleep secure; His dreadful voice no more
Would thunder in my ears; no fear of worse   780
To me, and to my offspring, would torment me
With cruel expectation. Yet one doubt
Pursues me still, lest all I cannot die;
Lest that pure breath of life, the spirit of Man
Which God inspired, cannot together perish   785
With this corporeal clod; then, in the grave,
Or in some other dismal place, who knows
But I shall die a living death? O thought
Horrid, if true! Yet why? It was but breath
Of life that sinned; what dies but what had life   790
And sin? The body properly had neither,
All of me then shall die: let this appease
The doubt, since human reach no further knows.
For though the Lord of all be infinite,
Is His wrath also? Be it, Man is not so,   795
But mortal doomed. How can He exercise
Wrath without end on Man, whom death must end?
Can He make deathless death? That were to make
Strange contradiction, which to God himself
Impossible is held, as argument   800
Of weakness, not of power. Will He draw out,
For anger's sake, finite to infinite,
In punished Man, to satisfy His rigour,
Satisfied never? That were to extend
His sentence beyond dust and Nature's law;   805
By which all causes else, according still
To the reception of their matter, act;
Not to th'extent of their own sphere. But say
That death be not one stroke, as I supposed,
Bereaving sense, but endless misery   810
From this day onward; which I feel begun
Both in me, and without me; and so last
To perpetuity. – Ay me! that fear
Comes thundering back with dreadful revolution
On my defenceless head; both Death and I   815
Am found eternal, and incorporate both;
Nor I on my part single; in me all
Posterity stands cursed. Fair patrimony
That I must leave ye, Sons! Oh, were I able
To waste it all myself, and leave ye none!   820
So disinherited, how would you bless
Me, now your curse! Ah, why should all mankind,
For one man's fault, thus guiltless be condemned,
It guiltless? But from me what can proceed,
But all corrupt; both mind and will depraved   825
Not to do only, but to will the same
With me? How can they then acquitted stand

In sight of God? Him, after all disputes,
Forced I absolve: all my evasions vain,
And reasonings, though through mazes, lead me still
But to my own conviction: first and last   831
On me, me only, as the source and spring
Of all corruption, all the blame lights due;
So might the wrath! Fond wish! couldst thou support
That burden, heavier than the earth to bear;   835
Than all the world much heavier, though divided
With that bad woman? Thus, what thou desirest,
And what thou fearest, alike destroys all hope
Of refuge, and concludes thee miserable
Beyond all past example and future;   840
To Satan only like both crime and doom.
O Conscience! into what abyss of fears
And horrors hast thou driven me; out of which
I find no way, from deep to deeper plunged!'
Thus Adam to himself lamented loud,   845
Through the still night; not now, as ere Man fell,
Wholesome, and cool, and mild, but with black air
Accompanied; with damps, and dreadful gloom;
Which to his evil conscience represented
All things with double terror. On the ground   850
Outstretched he lay, on the cold ground; and oft
Cursed his creation; Death as oft accused
Of tardy execution, since denounced
The day of his offence. 'Why comes not Death',
Said he, 'with one thrice-acceptable stroke   855
To end me? Shall Truth fail to keep her word,
Justice Divine not hasten to be just?
But Death comes not at call; Justice Divine
Mends not her slowest pace for prayers or cries,
O Woods, O Fountains, Hillocks, Dales, and Bowers!   860
With other echo late I taught your shades
To answer, and resound far other song.' –
Whom thus afflicted when sad Eve beheld,
Desolate where she sat, approaching nigh,
Soft words to his fierce passion she assayed: 865
But her with stern regard he thus repelled.
'Out of my sight, thou Serpent! That name best
Befits thee with him leagued, thyself as false
And hateful; nothing wants, but that thy shape,
Like his, and colour serpentine, may show   870
Thy inward fraud; to warn all creatures from thee
Henceforth; lest that too heavenly form, pretended
To hellish falsehood, snare them! But for thee
I had persisted happy; had not thy pride
And wand'ring vanity, when least was safe,   875
Rejected my forewarning, and disdained
Not to be trusted; longing to be seen,
Though by the devil himself; him overweening
To over-reach; but, with the serpent meeting,
Fooled and beguiled; by him thou, I by thee   880
To trust thee from my side; imagined wise,
Constant, mature, proof against all assaults;
And understood not all was but a show,

Rather than solid virtue; all but a rib
Crooked by nature, bent, as now appears,   885
More to the part sinister, from me drawn;
Well if thrown out, as supernumerary
To my just number found. Oh, why did God,
Creator wise, that peopled highest heaven
With spirits masculine, create at last   890
This novelty on earth, this fair defect
Of nature, and not fill the world at once
With men, as angels, without feminine;
Or find some other way to generate
Mankind? This mischief had not been befallen,   895
And more that shall befall; innumerable
Disturbances on earth through female snares,
And strait conjunction with this sex: for either
He never shall find out fit mate, but such
As some misfortune brings him, or mistake;   900
Or whom he wishes most shall seldom gain
Through her perverseness, but shall see her gained
By a far worse; or, if she love, withheld
By parents; or his happiest choice too late
Shall meet, already linked and wedlock-bound   905
To a fell adversary, his hate or shame:
Which infinite calamity shall cause
To human life, and household peace confound.'

   He added not, and from her turned; but Eve,
Not so repulsed, with tears that ceased not flowing   910
And tresses all disordered, at his feet
Fell humble; and, embracing them, besought
His peace, and thus proceeded in her plaint.

   'Forsake me not thus, Adam! witness heaven
What love sincere, and reverence in my heart   915
I bear thee, and unweeting have offended,
Unhappily deceived! Thy suppliant
I beg, and clasp thy knees; bereave me not,
Whereon I live, thy gentle looks, thy aid,
Thy counsel, in this uttermost distress,   920
My only strength and stay. Forlorn of thee,
Whither shall I betake me, where subsist?
While yet we live, scarce one short hour perhaps,
Between us two let there be peace; both joining,
As joined in injuries, one enmity   925
Against a foe by doom express assignèd us,
That cruel serpent. On me exercise not
Thy hatred for this misery befallen;
On me already lost, me than thyself
More miserable! Both have sinned; but thou   930
Against God only; I against God and thee;
And to the place of judgement will return,
There with my cries importune heaven; that all
The sentence, from thy head removed, may light
On me, sole cause to thee of all this woe;   935
Me, me only, just object of his ire!'

887 **supernumerary:** Adam was said to have been born with an
extra (thirteenth) rib, from which Eve was created

She ended weeping; and her lowly plight,
Immovable, till peace obtained from fault
Acknowledged and deplored, in Adam wrought
Commiseration. Soon his heart relented   940
Towards her, his life so late, and sole delight,
Now at his feet submissive in distress;
Creature so fair his reconcilement seeking,
His counsel, whom she had displeased, his aid:
As one disarmed, his anger all he lost,   945
And thus with peaceful words up-raised her soon.

   'Unwary, and too desirous, as before,
So now of what thou knowest not, who desirest
The punishment all on thyself; alas!
Bear thine own first, ill able to sustain   950
His full wrath, whose thou feelest as yet least part,
And my displeasure bearest so ill. If prayers
Could alter high decrees, I to that place
Would speed before thee, and be louder heard,
That on my head all might be visited;   955
Thy frailty and infirmer sex forgiven,
To me committed, and by me exposed.
But rise; let us no more contend, nor blame
Each other, blamed enough elsewhere; but strive
In offices of love, how we may lighten   960
Each other's burden, in our share of woe;
Since this day's death denounced, if aught I see,
Will prove no sudden, but a slow-paced evil;
A long day's dying, to augment our pain;
And to our seed (O hapless seed!) derived.'   965

   To whom thus Eve, recovering heart, replied:
'Adam, by sad experiment I know
How little weight my words with thee can find,
Found so erroneous; thence by just event
Found so unfortunate. Nevertheless,   970
Restored by thee, vile as I am, to place
Of new acceptance, hopeful to regain
Thy love, the sole contentment of my heart
Living or dying, from thee I will not hide
What thoughts in my unquiet breast are risen,   975
Tending to some relief of our extremes,
Or end; though sharp and sad, yet tolerable,
As in our evils, and of easier choice.
If care of our descent perplex us most,
Which must be born to certain woe, devoured   980
By Death at last; and miserable it is
To be to others cause of misery,
Our own begotten, and of our loins to bring
Into this cursèd world a woeful race,
That after wretched life must be at last   985
Food for so foul a monster; in thy power
It lies, yet ere conception to prevent
The race unblest, to being yet unbegot.
Childless thou art, childless remain: so Death
Shall be deceived his glut, and with us two   990
Be forced to satisfy his ravenous maw.
But if thou judge it hard and difficult,
Conversing, looking, loving, to abstain
From love's due rights, nuptial embraces sweet;

And with desire to languish without hope,   995
Before the present object languishing
With like desire; which would be misery
And torment less than none of what we dread;
Then, both ourselves and seed at once to free
From what we fear for both, let us make short –   1000
Let us seek Death, or, he not found, supply
With our own hands his office on ourselves:
Why stand we longer shivering under fears,
That show no end but death, and have the power,
Of many ways to die the shortest choosing,   1005
Destruction with destruction to destroy?'
    She ended here, or vehement despair
Broke off the rest: so much of death her thoughts
Had entertained, as dyed her cheeks with pale.
But Adam, with such counsel nothing swayed,   1010
To better hopes his more attentive mind
Labouring had raised; and thus to Eve replied:
    'Eve, thy contempt of life and pleasure seems
To argue in thee something more sublime
And excellent than what thy mind contemns;   1015
But self-destruction therefore sought, refutes
That excellence thought in thee; and implies,
Not thy contempt, but anguish and regret
For loss of life and pleasure overloved.
Or if thou covet death, as utmost end   1020
Of misery, so thinking to evade
The penalty pronounced; doubt not but God
Hath wiselier armed His vengeful ire, than so
To be forestalled; much more I fear lest death,
So snatched, will not exempt us from the pain   1025
We are by doom to pay; rather, such acts
Of contumacy will provoke the Highest
To make death in us live. Then, let us seek
Some safer resolution, which methinks
I have in view, calling to mind with heed   1030
Part of our sentence, that thy seed shall bruise
The serpent's head; piteous amends! unless
Be meant, whom I conjecture, our grand foe,
Satan; who, in the serpent, hath contrived
Against us this deceit. To crush his head   1035
Would be revenge indeed! which will be lost
By death brought on ourselves, or childless days
Resolved, as thou proposest; so our foe
Shall 'scape His punishment ordained, and we
Instead shall double ours upon our heads.   1040
No more be mentioned then of violence
Against ourselves; and wilful barrenness,
That cuts us off from hope; and savours only
Rancour and pride, impatience and despite,
Reluctance against God and His just yoke   1045
Laid on our necks. Remember with what mild
And gracious temper he both heard, and judged,
Without wrath or reviling; we expected
Immediate dissolution, which we thought
Was meant by death that day; when lo! to thee   1050

Pains only in child-bearing were foretold,
And bringing forth; soon recompensed with joy,
Fruit of thy womb. On me the curse aslope
Glanced on the ground; with labour I must earn
My bread; what harm? Idleness had been worse;   1055
My labour will sustain me; and, lest cold
Or heat should injure us, his timely care
Hath, unbesought, provided; and his hands
Clothed us unworthy, pitying while He judged;
How much more, if we pray Him, will His ear   1060
Be open, and His heart to pity incline,
And teach us further by what means to shun
The inclement seasons, rain, ice, hail, and snow!
Which now the sky, with various face, begins
To show us in this mountain; while the winds   1065
Blow moist and keen, shattering the graceful locks
Of these fair spreading trees; which bids us seek
Some better shroud, some better warmth to cherish
Our limbs benumbed, ere this diurnal star
Leave cold the night, how we his gathered beams   1070
Reflected may with matter sere foment;
Or, by collision of two bodies, grind
The air attrite to fire; as late the clouds
Justling, or pushed with winds, rude in their shock,
Tine the slant lightning; whose thwart flame, driven down   1075
Kindles the gummy bark of fir or pine;
And sends a comfortable heat from far,
Which might supply the sun. Such fire to use,
And what may else be remedy or cure
To evils which our own misdeeds have wrought,   1080
He will instruct us praying, and of grace
Beseeching Him; so as we need not fear
To pass commodiously this life, sustained
By Him with many comforts, till we end
In dust, our final rest and native home.   1085
What better can we do, than, to the place
Repairing where He judged us, prostrate fall
Before Him reverent; and there confess
Humbly our faults, and pardon beg; with tears
Watering the ground, and with our sighs the air   1090
Frequenting, sent from hearts contrite, in sign
Of sorrow unfeigned, and humiliation meek
Undoubtedly He will relent, and turn
From His displeasure; in whose look serene,
When angry most He seemed and most severe,   1095
What else but favour, grace, and mercy shone?'
    So spake our father penitent; nor Eve
Felt less remorse: they, forthwith to the place
Repairing where He judged them, prostrate fell
Before Him reverent; and both confessed   1100
Humbly their faults, and pardon begged; with tears
Watering the ground, and with their sighs the air
Frequenting, sent from hearts contrite, in sign
Of sorrow unfeigned, and humiliation meek.

1027 **contumacy:** resistance to authority

1053 **aslope:** falling obliquely   1073 **attrite:** with friction   1075 **Tine:** ignite

BOOK ELEVEN

THUS they, in lowliest plight, repentant stood
Praying; for from the mercy-seat above
Prevenient grace descending had removed
The stony from their hearts, and made new flesh
Regenerate grow instead; that sighs now breathed 5
Unutterable; which the spirit of prayer
Inspired, and winged for heaven with speedier flight
Than loudest oratory. Yet their port
Not of mean suitors; nor important less
Seemed their petition, than when th'ancient pair 10
In fables old, less ancient yet than these,
Deucalion and chaste Pyrrha, to restore
The race of mankind drowned, before the shrine
Of Themis stood devout. To heaven their prayers
Flew up, nor missed the way, by envious winds 15
Blown vagabond or frustrate: in they passed
Dimensionless through heavenly doors; then clad
With incense, where the golden altar fumed,
By their great intercessor, came in sight
Before the Father's throne: them the glad Son 20
Presenting, thus to intercede began:

  'See, Father, what first-fruits on earth are sprung
From thy implanted grace in Man; these sighs
And prayers, which in this golden censer mixed
With incense, I thy priest before thee bring; 25
Fruits of more pleasing savour, from thy seed
Sown with contrition in his heart, than those
Which, his own hand manuring, all the trees
Of paradise could have produced, ere fallen
From innocence. Now, therefore, bend thine ear 30
To supplication; hear his sighs, though mute;
Unskilful with what words to pray, let me
Interpret for him; me, his advocate
And propitiation; all his works on me,
Good, or not good, ingraft; my merit those 35
Shall perfect, and for these my death shall pay.
Accept me; and, in me, from these receive
The smell of peace toward mankind: let him live
Before thee reconciled, at least his days
Numbered, though sad; till death, his doom (which I
To mitigate thus plead, not to reverse) 41
To better life shall yield him: where with me
All my redeemed may dwell in joy and bliss;
Made one with me, as I with Thee am one.'

To whom the Father, without cloud, serene. 45
'All thy request for Man, accepted Son,
Obtain; all thy request was my decree:
But, longer in that paradise to dwell,
The law I gave to Nature him forbids:
Those pure immortal elements, that know, 50
No gross, no unharmonious mixture foul,
Eject him, tainted now; and purge him off,
As a distemper, gross, to air as gross,
And mortal food; as may dispose him best
For dissolution wrought by sin, that first 55
Distempered all things, and of incorrupt
Corrupted. I, at first, with two fair gifts
Created him endowed; with happiness,
And immortality: that fondly lost,
This other served but to eternize woe; 60
Till I provided death: so death becomes
His final remedy; and, after life,
Tried in sharp tribulation, and refined
By faith and faithful works, to second life,
Waked in the renovation of the just, 65
Resigns him up with heaven and earth renewed.
But let us call to synod all the blest,
Through heaven's wide bounds: from them I will not
    hide
My judgements; how with mankind I proceed,
As how with peccant angels late they saw, 70
And in their state, though firm, stood more
    confirmed.'
  He ended, and the Son gave signal high
To the bright minister that watched; he blew
His trumpet, heard in Oreb since perhaps
When God descended, and perhaps once more 75
To sound at general doom. The angelic blast
Filled all the regions: from their blissful bowers
Of amarantine shade, fountain or spring,
By the waters of life, where'er they sat
In fellowships of joy, the sons of light 80
Hasted, resorting to the summons high;
And took their seats; till from His throne supreme
Th'Almighty thus pronounced His sovran will.
  'O Sons, like one of us Man is become
To know both good and evil, since his taste 85
Of that defended fruit; but let him boast
His knowledge of good lost, and evil got;
Happier! had it sufficed him to have known
Good by itself, and evil not at all.
He sorrows now, repents, and prays contrite, 90
My motions in him; longer than they move,
His heart I know, how variable and vain,
Self-left. Lest therefore his now bolder hand
Reach also of the tree of life, and eat,
And live for ever, dream at least to live 95
For ever, to remove him I decree,
And send him from the garden forth to till

BOOK ELEVEN – THE ARGUMENT: The Son of God presents to his Father the Prayers of our first Parents now repenting, and intercedes for them: God accepts them, but declares that they must no longer abide in Paradise; sends Michael with a Band of Cherubim to dispossess them; but first to reveal to Adam future things: Michael's coming down. Adam shows to Eve certain ominous signs; he discerns Michael's approach, goes out to meet him: the Angel denounces their departure. Eve's Lamentation. Adam pleads, but submits: The Angel leads him up to a high Hill, sets before him in vision what shall happen till the Flood 2 **mercy-seat**: the gold covering on the Ark of the Covenant, God's resting place 3 **Prevenient**: a theological term for God's Grace 12 **Deucalion**: a mythological version of Noah **Pyrrha**: wife of Deucalion 14 **Themis**: goddess of justice

70 **peccant**: sinful 78 **amarantine**: the Amaranth, flower of Paradise and symbol of immortality

The ground whence he was taken, fitter soil.
Michael, this my behest have thou in charge;
Take to thee from among the cherubim 100
Thy choice of flaming warriors, lest the fiend,
Or in behalf of Man, or to invade
Vacant possession, some new trouble raise:
Haste thee, and from the paradise of God
Without remorse drive out the sinful pair; 105
From hallowed ground the unholy; and denounce
To them, and to their progeny, from thence
Perpetual banishment. Yet, lest they faint
At the sad sentence rigorously urged
(For I behold them softened, and with tears 110
Bewailing their excess), all terror hide.
If patiently thy bidding they obey,
Dismiss them not disconsolate; reveal
To Adam what shall come in future days,
As I shall thee enlighten; intermix 115
My covenant in the woman's seed renewed;
So send them forth, though sorrowing, yet in peace:
And on the east side of the garden place,
Where entrance up from Eden easiest climbs,
Cherubic watch; and of a sword the flame 120
Wide-waving; all approach far off to fright,
And guard all passage to the tree of life:
Lest paradise a receptacle prove
To spirits foul, and all my trees their prey; 124
With whose stol'n fruit Man once more to delude.'
    He ceased; and the arch-angelic power prepared
For swift descent; with him the cohort bright
Of watchful cherubim: four faces each
Had, like a double Janus; all their shape
Spangled with eyes more numerous than those 130
Of Argus, and more wakeful than to drowse,
Charmed with Arcadian pipe, the pastoral reed
Of Hermes, or his opiate rod. Meanwhile,
To re-salute the world with sacred light,
Leucothea waked; and with fresh dews embalmed 135
The earth; when Adam and first matron Eve
Had ended now their orisons, and found
Strength added from above; new hope to spring
Out of despair; joy, but with fear yet linked;
Which thus to Eve his welcome words renewed. 140
    'Eve, easily my faith admit, that all
The good which we enjoy from heaven descends;
But, that from us aught should ascend to heaven
So prevalent as to concern the mind
Of God high-blest, or to incline His will, 145
Hard to belief may seem; yet this will prayer
Or one short sigh of human breath, up-borne
Even to the seat of God. For since I sought
By prayer the offended Deity to appease;
Kneeled, and before Him humbled all my heart; 150

Methought I saw Him placable and mild,
Bending His ear; persuasion in me grew
That I was heard with favour; peace returned
Home to my breast, and to my memory
His promise, that thy seed shall bruise our foe; 155
Which, then not minded in dismay, yet now
Assures me that the bitterness of death
Is past, and we shall live. Whence hail to thee,
Eve rightly called, mother of all mankind,
Mother of all things living, since by thee 160
Man is to live; and all things live for Man.'
To whom thus Eve with sad demeanour meek.
'Ill-worthy I such title should belong
To me transgressor; who, for thee ordained
A help, became thy snare; to me reproach 165
Rather belongs, distrust, and all dispraise:
But infinite in pardon was my Judge,
That I, who first brought death on all, am graced
The source of life; next favourable thou,
Who highly thus to entitle me vouchsaf'st, 170
Far other name deserving. But the field
To labour calls us, now with sweat imposed,
Though after sleepless night; for see! the morn,
All unconcerned with our unrest, begins
Her rosy progress smiling: let us forth; 175
I never from thy side henceforth to stray,
Where'er our day's work lies, though now enjoined
Laborious, till day droop; while here we dwell,
What can be toilsome in these pleasant walks?
Here let us live, though in fallen state, content.' 180
    So spake, so wished much humbled Eve; but Fate
Subscribed not. Nature first gave signs, impressed
On bird, beast, air; air suddenly eclipsed,
After short blush of morn; nigh in her sight
The bird of Jove, stooped from his airy tower, 185
Two birds of gayest plume before him drove;
Down from a hill the beast that reigns in woods,
First hunter then, pursued a gentle brace,
Goodliest of all the forest, hart and hind;
Direct to th'eastern gate was bent their flight. 190
Adam observed, and with his eye the chase
Pursuing, not unmoved, to Eve thus spake:
    'O Eve, some further change awaits us nigh,
Which heaven, by these mute signs in Nature, shows
Forerunners of His purpose; or to warn 195
Us, haply too secure, of our discharge
From penalty, because from death released
Some days: how long, and what till then our life,
Who knows? or more than this, that we are dust,
And thither must return, and be no more? 200
Why else this double object in our sight
Of flight pursued in the air, and o'er the ground,
One way the self-same hour? why in the east
Darkness ere day's mid-course, and morning-light
More orient in yon western cloud, that draws 205

---

129 **Janus:** two-faced Roman god 131 **Argus:** Argus had one hundred eyes 132–33 Mercury put Argus to sleep with his reed pipe 135 **Leucothea:** goddess of the dawn

185 **bird of Jove:** eagle 187 **beast that reigns:** lion

O'er the blue firmament a radiant white,
And slow descends with something heavenly fraught?'
   He erred not; for by this the heavenly bands
Down from a sky of jasper lighted now
In paradise, and on a hill made halt;   210
A glorious apparition, had not doubt
And carnal fear that day dimmed Adam's eye.
Not that more glorious, when the angels met
Jacob in Mahanaim, where he saw
The field pavilioned with his guardians bright;   215
Nor that, which on the flaming mount appeared
In Dothan, covered with a camp of fire,
Against the Syrian king, who to surprise
One man, assassin-like, had levied war,
War unproclaimed. The princely hierarch   220
In their bright stand there left his powers, to seize
Possession of the garden; he alone,
To find where Adam sheltered, took his way,
Not unperceived of Adam; who to Eve,
While the great visitant approached, thus spake.   225
   'Eve, now expect great tidings, which perhaps
Of us will soon determine, or impose
New laws to be observed; for I descry,
From yonder blazing cloud that veils the hill,
One of the heavenly host; and, by his gait,   230
None of the meanest; some great potentate
Or of the thrones above; such majesty
Invests him coming! yet not terrible,
That I should fear; nor sociably mild,
As Raphael, that I should much confide;   235
But solemn and sublime; whom not to offend,
With reverence I must meet, and thou retire.'
   He ended: and the archangel soon drew nigh,
Not in his shape celestial, but as man
Clad to meet man; over his lucid arms   240
A military vest of purple flowed,
Livelier than Meliboean, or the grain
Of Sarra, worn by kings and heroes old
In time of truce; Iris had dipped the woof;
His starry helm unbuckled showed him prime   245
In manhood where youth ended; by his side,
As in a glistering zodiac, hung the sword,
Satan's dire dread; and in his hand the spear.
   Adam bowed low; he, kingly, from his state
Inclined not, but his coming thus declared.   250
'Adam, heaven's high behest no preface needs:
Sufficient that thy prayers are heard; and Death,
Then due by sentence when thou didst transgress,
Defeated of his seizure many days
Given thee of grace; wherein thou may'st repent,   255
And one bad act with many deeds well done
Mayest cover. Well may then thy Lord, appeased,
Redeem thee quite from Death's rapacious claim;
But longer in this paradise to dwell
Permits not: to remove thee I am come,   260

219 **One man:** Elisha 242 **Meliboean:** a purple dye 243 **Sarra:** Tyre, famous for its purple dye 244 **Iris:** goddess of the rainbow

And send thee from the garden forth to till
The ground whence thou wast taken, fitter soil.'
He added not; for Adam at the news
Heart-struck with chilling gripe of sorrow stood,
That all his senses bound; Eve, who unseen   265
Yet all had heard, with audible lament
Discovered soon the place of her retire.
   'O unexpected stroke, worse than of Death!
Must I thus leave thee, Paradise? thus leave
Thee, native soil! these happy walks and shades,   270
Fit haunt of gods? where I had hope to spend,
Quiet though sad, the respite of that day
That must be mortal to us both. O Flowers,
That never will in other climate grow,
My early visitation, and my last   275
At even, which I bred up with tender hand
From the first opening bud, and gave ye names!
Who now shall rear ye to the sun, or rank
Your tribes, and water from the ambrosial fount?
Thee lastly, Nuptial Bower! by me adorned   280
With what to sight or smell was sweet! from thee
How shall I part, and whither wander down
Into a lower world; to this obscure
And wild? how shall we breathe in other air
Less pure, accustomed to immortal fruits?'   285
   Whom thus the angel interrupted mild:
'Lament not, Eve, but patiently resign
What justly thou hast lost, nor set thy heart,
Thus over-fond, on that which is not thine:
Thy going is not lonely; with thee goes   290
Thy husband; whom to follow thou art bound;
Where he abides, think there thy native soil.'
   Adam, by this from the cold sudden damp
Recovering, and his scattered spirits returned,
To Michael thus his humble words addressed.   295
   'Celestial, whether among the thrones, or named
Of them the highest; for such of shape may seem
Prince above princes! gently hast thou told
Thy message, which might else in telling wound,
And in performing end us; what besides   300
Of sorrow, and dejection, and despair,
Our frailty can sustain, thy tidings bring,
Departure from this happy place, our sweet
Recess, and only consolation left
Familiar to our eyes! all places else   305
Inhospitable appear, and desolate;
Nor knowing us, nor known: And, if by prayer
Incessant I could hope to change the will
Of Him who all things can, I would not cease
To weary Him with my assiduous cries: 310
But prayer against His absolute decree
No more avails than breath against the wind,
Blown stifling back on him that breathes it forth:
Therefore to His great bidding I submit.
This most afflicts me, that, departing hence,   315
As from His face I shall be hid, deprived
His blessèd countenance. Here I could frequent

With worship place by place where He vouchsafed
Presence divine; and to my sons relate,
"On this mount He appeared; under this tree   320
Stood visible; among these pines His voice
I heard; here with Him at this fountain talked."
So many grateful altars I would rear
Of grassy turf, and pile up every stone
Of lustre from the brook, in memory,   325
Or monument to ages; and thereon
Offer sweet-smelling gums, and fruits, and flowers:
In yonder nether world where shall I seek
His bright appearances, or foot-step trace?
For though I fled Him angry, yet recalled   330
To life prolonged and promised race, I now
Gladly behold though but His utmost skirts
Of glory; and far off His steps adore.'
    To whom thus Michael with regard benign:
'Adam, thou know'st heaven His, and all the earth;
Not this rock only; His omnipresence fills   336
Land, sea, and air, and every kind that lives,
Fomented by His virtual power and warmed:
All the earth He gave thee to possess and rule,
No despicable gift; surmise not then   340
His presence to these narrow bounds confined
Of paradise, or Eden: this had been
Perhaps thy capital seat, from whence had spread
All generations; and had hither come
From all the ends of th'earth, to celebrate   345
And reverence thee, their great progenitor.
But this pre-eminence thou hast lost, brought down
To dwell on even ground now with thy sons:
Yet doubt not but in valley, and in plain,
God is, as here; and will be found alike   350
Present; and of His presence many a sign
Still following thee, still compassing thee round
With goodness and paternal love, His face
Express, and of His steps the track divine.
Which that thou may'st believe, and be confirmed   355
Ere thou from hence depart; know, I am sent
To show thee what shall come in future days
To thee, and to thy offspring: good with bad
Expect to hear; supernal grace contending
With sinfulness of men; thereby to learn   360
True patience, and to temper joy with fear
And pious sorrow; equally inured
By moderation either state to bear,
Prosperous or advéerse: so shalt thou lead
Safest thy life, and best-prepared endure   365
Thy mortal passage when it comes. – Ascend
This hill; let Eve (for I have drenched her eyes)
Here sleep below; while thou to foresight wakest;
As once thou slept'st, while she to life was formed.'
    To whom thus Adam gratefully replied.   370
'Ascend, I follow thee, safe Guide, the path
Thou leadest me; and to the hand of heaven submit,

However chastening; to the evil turn
My obvious breast; arming to overcome
By suffering, and earn rest from labour won,   375
If so I may attain.' – So both ascend
In the visions of God. It was a hill,
Of paradise the highest; from whose top
The hemisphere of earth, in clearest ken,
Stretched out to the amplest reach of prospect lay.   380
Not higher that hill, nor wider looking round,
Whereon, for different cause, the tempter set
Our second Adam, in the wilderness;
To show him all earth's kingdoms, and their glory.
His eye might there command wherever stood   385
City of old or modern fame, the seat
Of mightiest empire, from the destined walls
Of Cambalu, seat of Cathaian Can,
And Samarchand by Oxus, Temir's throne,
To Paquin of Sinaean kings; and thence   390
To Agra and Lahor of great Mogul,
Down to the golden Chersonese; or where
The Persian in Ecbatan sat, or since
In Hispahan; or where the Russian Tsar
In Mosco; or the Sultan in Bizance,   395
Turchestan-born; nor could his eye not ken
The empire of Negus to his utmost port
Ercoco, and the less maritim kings
Mombaza, and Quiloa, and Melind,
And Sofala, thought Ophir, to the realm   400
Of Congo, and Angola farthest south;
Or thence from Niger flood to Atlas mount
The kingdoms of Almansor, Fez and Sus,
Morocco, and Algiers, and Tremisen;
On Europe thence, and where Rome was to sway   405
The world: in spirit perhaps he also saw
Rich Mexico, the seat of Montezume,
And Cusco in Peru, the richer seat
Of Atabalipa; and yet unspoiled
Guiana, whose great city Geryon's sons   410
Call El Dorado. But to nobler sights
Michael from Adam's eyes the film removed,
Which that false fruit that promised clearer sight
Had bred; then purged with euphrasy and rue
The visual nerve, for he had much to see;   415
And from the well of life three drops instilled.
So deep the power of these ingredients pierced,
Even to the inmost seat of mental sight,
That Adam, now enforced to close his eyes,
Sunk down, and all his spirits became entranced;   420
But him the gentle angel by the hand
Soon raised, and his attention thus recalled:

---

359 **supernal:** heavenly

388 **Cambalu:** capital city of Cathay 389 Samarchand on the river
Oxus was ruled by Temir (Tamburlaine) 390 **Paquin:** Peking
Sinaean: Chinese 392 **Chersonese:** the East Indies 393 **Ecbatan:**
Persian capital 394 **Hispahan:** Persian capital after the importance
of Ecbatan fell 395 **Bizance:** Byzantium 397 **Negus:** title of the
Abyssinian kings 399 places in East Africa 400–404 places in Africa
407 **Montezume:** Aztec ruler 409 **Atabalipa:** Inca ruler 410 **Geryon's
sons:** the Spanish

'Adam, now ope thine eyes; and first behold
The effects, which thy original crime hath wrought
In some to spring from thee; who never touched   425
The excepted tree; nor with the snake conspired;
Nor sinned thy sin; yet from that sin derive
Corruption, to bring forth more violent deeds.'

His eyes he opened, and beheld a field,
Part arable and tilth, whereon were sheaves   430
New-reaped; the other part sheep-walks and folds;
I' the midst an altar as the land-mark stood,
Rustic, of grassy sward; thither anon
A sweaty reaper from his tillage brought
First fruits, the green ear, and the yellow sheaf,   435
Unculled, as came to hand; a shepherd next,
More meek, came with the firstlings of his flock,
Choicest and best; then, sacrificing, laid
The inwards and their fat, with incense strowed,
On the cleft wood, and all due rights performed.   440
His offering soon propitious fire from heaven
Consumed with nimble glance, and grateful steam;
The other's not, for his was not sincere;
Whereat he inly raged, and, as they talked,
Smote him into the midriff with a stone   445
That beat out life; he fell; and, deadly pale,
Groaned out his soul with gushing blood effused.
Much at that sight was Adam in his heart
Dismayed, and thus in haste to the angel cried:

'O Teacher, some great mischief hath befallen   450
To that meek man, who well had sacrificed;
Is piety thus and pure devotion paid?'

To whom Michael thus, he also moved, replied:
'These two are brethren, Adam, and to come
Out of thy loins; th'unjust the just hath slain,   455
For envy that his brother's offering found
From heaven acceptance; but the bloody fact
Will be avenged; and the other's faith, approved,
Lose no reward; though here thou see him die,
Rolling in dust and gore.' To which our sire: 460

'Alas! both for the deed, and for the cause!
But have I now seen Death? Is this the way
I must return to native dust? O sight
Of terror, foul and ugly to behold,
Horrid to think, how horrible to feel!'   465

To whom thus Michael: 'Death thou hast seen
In his first shape on Man; but many shapes
Of Death, and many are the ways that lead
To his grim cave, all dismal; yet to sense
More terrible at th'entrance than within.   470
Some, as thou sawest, by violent stroke shall die;
By fire, flood, famine, by intemperance more
In meats and drinks, which on the earth shall bring
Diseases dire, of which a monstrous crew
Before thee shall appear; that thou may'st know   475
What misery the inabstinence of Eve
Shall bring on Men.' Immediately a place

Before his eyes appeared, sad, noisome, dark;
A lazar-house it seemed; wherein were laid
Numbers of all diseased; all maladies   480
Of ghastly spasm, or racking torture, qualms
Of heart-sick agony, all feverous kinds,
Convulsions, epilepsies, fierce catarrhs,
Intestine stone and ulcer, colic-pangs,
Demoniac frenzy, moping melancholy,   485
And moon-struck madness, pining atrophy,
Marasmus, and wide-wasting pestilence,
Dropsies, and asthmas, and joint-racking rheums.
Dire was the tossing, deep the groans; Despair
Tended the sick busiest from couch to couch;   490
And over them triumphant Death his dart
Shook, but delayed to strike, though oft invoked
With vows, as their chief good, and final hope.
Sight so deform what heart of rock could long
Dry-eyed behold? Adam could not, but wept,   495
Though not of woman born; compassion quelled
His best of man, and gave him up to tears
A space, till firmer thoughts restrained excess;
And, scarce recovering words, his plaint renewed.

'O miserable mankind, to what fall   500
Degraded, to what wretched state reserved!
Better end here unborn. Why is life given
To be thus wrested from us? rather, why
Obtruded on us thus? who, if we knew
What we receive, would either not accept   505
Life offered, or soon beg to lay it down;
Glad to be so dismissed in peace. Can thus
The image of God in Man, created once
So goodly and erect, though faulty since,
To such unsightly sufferings be debased   510
Under inhuman pains? Why should not Man,
Retaining still divine similitude
In part, from such deformities be free,
And, for his Maker's image sake, exempt?'

'Their Maker's image', answered Michael, 'then   515
Forsook them, when themselves they vilified
To serve ungoverned Appetite; and took
His image whom they served, a brutish vice,
Inductive mainly to the sin of Eve.
Therefore so abject is their punishment,   520
Disfiguring not God's likeness, but their own;
Or if His likeness, by themselves defaced;
While they pervert pure Nature's healthful rules
To loathsome sickness; worthily, since they
God's image did not reverence in themselves.'   525

'I yield it just,' said Adam, 'and submit.
But is there yet no other way, besides
These painful passages, how we may come
To death, and mix with our connatural dust?'

430 **tilth**: cultivated 433 **sward**: turf

479 **lazar-house**: a hospital for the incurable 481 **qualms**: plagues
487 **Marasmus**: literally withering, consumption 529 **connatural**: of
the same nature

'There is,' said Michael, 'if thou well observe   530
The rule of Not too much; by temperance taught,
In what thou eatest and drinkest; seeking from thence
Due nourishment, not gluttonous delight,
Till many years over thy head return:
So may'st thou live; till, like ripe fruit, thou drop   535
Into thy mother's lap; or be with ease
Gathered, nor harshly plucked; for death mature:
This is Old Age; but then, thou must outlive
Thy youth, thy strength, thy beauty; which will change
To withered, weak, and grey; thy senses then,   540
Obtuse, all taste of pleasure must forgo,
To what thou hast; and, for the air of youth,
Hopeful and cheerful, in thy blood will reign
A melancholy damp of cold and dry
To weigh thy spirits down, and last consume   545
The balm of life.' To whom our ancestor:
     'Henceforth I fly not death, nor would prolong
Life much; bent rather, how I may be quit,
Fairest and easiest, of this cumbrous charge;
Which I must keep till my appointed day   550
Of rendering up, and patiently attend
My dissolution.' Michael replied:
     'Nor love thy life, nor hate; but what thou livest
Live well; how long, or short, permit to heaven:
And now prepare thee for another sight.'   555
     He looked, and saw a spacious plain, whereon
Were tents of various hue; by some, were herds
Of cattle grazing; others, whence the sound
Of instruments, that made melodious chime,
Was heard, of harp and organ; and, who moved   560
Their stops and chords, was seen; his volant touch,
Instínct through all proportions, low and high,
Fled and pursued transverse the resonant fugue.
In other part stood one who, at the forge
Labouring, two massy clods of iron and brass   565
Had melted (whether found where casual fire
Had wasted woods on mountain or in vale,
Down to the veins of earth; thence gliding hot
To some cave's mouth; or whether washed by stream
From underground); the liquid ore he drained   570
Into fit moulds prepared; from which he formed
First his own tools; then, what might else be wrought
Fusil or graven in metal. After these,
But on the hither side, a different sort
From the high neighbouring hills, which was their
          seat,   575
Down to the plain descended; by their guise
Just men they seemed, and all their study bent
To worship God aright, and know His works
Not hid; nor those things last, which might preserve
Freedom and peace to Men; they on the plain   580
Long had not walked, when from the tents, behold!
A bevy of fair women, richly gay

In gems and wanton dress; to the harp they sung
Soft amorous ditties, and in dance came on:
The men, though grave, eyed them; and let their eyes
Rove without rein; till, in the amorous net   586
Fast caught, they liked; and each his liking chose;
And now of love they treat, till the evening-star,
Love's harbinger, appeared; then, all in heat
They light the nuptial torch, and bid invoke   590
Hymen, then first to marriage rites invoked:
With feast and music all the tents resound.
Such happy interview, and fair event
Of love and youth not lost, songs, garlands, flowers,
And charming symphonies attached the heart   595
Of Adam, soon inclined to admit delight,
The bent of nature; which he thus expressed:
     'True opener of mine eyes, prime Angel blest;
Much better seems this vision, and more hope
Of peaceful days portends, than those two past;   600
Those were of hate and death, or pain much worse;
Here Nature seems fulfilled in all her ends.'
     To whom thus Michael: 'Judge not what is best
By pleasure, though to nature seeming meet;
Created, as thou art, to nobler end   605
Holy and pure, conformity divine.
Those tents thou sawest so pleasant, were the tents
Of wickedness, wherein shall dwell his race
Who slew his brother; studious they appear
Of arts that polish life, inventors rare;   610
Unmindful of their Maker, though His spirit
Taught them; but they His gifts acknowledged none.
Yet they a beauteous offspring shall beget;
For that fair female troop thou sawest, that seemed
Of goddesses, so blithe, so smooth, so gay,   615
Yet empty of all good wherein consists
Woman's domestic honour and chief praise;
Bred only and completed to the taste
Of lustful appetence, to sing, to dance,
To dress, and troll the tongue, and roll the eye.   620
To these that sober race of men, whose lives
Religious titled them the sons of God,
Shall yield up all their virtue, all their fame
Ignobly, to the trains and to the smiles
Of these fair atheists; and now swim in joy,   625
Ere long to swim at large; and laugh, for which
The world ere long a world of tears must weep.'
     To whom thus Adam, of short joy bereft.
'O pity and shame, that they, who to live well
Entered so fair, should turn aside to tread   630
Paths indirect, or in the mid way faint!
But still I see the tenor of Man's woe
Holds on the same, from Woman to begin.'
     'From Man's effeminate slackness it begins,'
Said th'angel, 'who should better hold his place   635

561 **volant**: flying 563 **fugue**: flight 573 **Fusil**: cast

620 **troll**: move

By wisdom, and superior gifts received.
But now prepare thee for another scene.'
   He looked, and saw wide territory spread
Before him, towns, and rural works between;
Cities of men with lofty gates and towers,   640
Concourse in arms, fierce faces threat'ning war,
Giants of mighty bone and bold emprise;
Part wield their arms, part curb the foaming steed,
Single or in array of battle ranged
Both horse and foot, nor idly must'ring stood;   645
One way a band select from forage drives
A herd of beeves, fair oxen and fair kine,
From a fat meadow ground; or fleecy flock,
Ewes and their bleating lambs over the plain,
Their booty; scarce with life the shepherds fly,   650
But call in aid, which makes a bloody fray;
With cruel tournament the squadrons join;
Where cattle pastured late, now scattered lies
With carcasses and arms th'ensanguined field,
Deserted. Others to a city strong   655
Lay siege, encamped; by battery, scale, and mine,
Assaulting; others from the wall defend
With dart and javelin, stones, and sulphurous fire;
On each hand slaughter, and gigantic deeds.
In other part the sceptred heralds call   660
To council, in the city-gates; anon
Grey-headed men and grave, with warriors mixed,
Assemble, and harangues are heard; but soon,
In factious opposition; till at last,
Of middle age one rising, eminent   665
In wise deport, spake much of right and wrong,
Of justice, or religion, truth, and peace,
And judgement from above: him old and young
Exploded, and had seized with violent hands,
Had not a cloud descending snatched him thence   670
Unseen amid the throng: so violence
Proceeded, and oppression, and sword-law,
Through all the plain, and refuge none was found.
Adam was all in tears, and to his guide
Lamenting turned full sad: 'Oh! what are these,   675
Death's ministers, not men? who thus deal death
Inhumanly to men, and multiply
Ten thousandfold the sin of him who slew
His brother: for of whom such massacre
Make they, but of their brethren; men of men?   680
But who was that just man, whom had not heaven
Rescued, had in his righteousness been lost?'
   To whom thus Michael. 'These are the product
Of those ill-mated marriages thou sawest;
Where good with bad were matched, who of
      themselves   685
Abhor to join; and, by imprudence mixed,
Produce prodigious births of body or mind.

Such were these giants, men of high renown;
For in those days might only shall be admired,
And valour and heroic virtue called;   690
To overcome in battle, and subdue
Nations, and bring home spoils with infinite
Man-slaughter, shall be held the highest pitch
Of human glory; and for glory done
Of triumph, to be styled great conquerors   695
Patrons of mankind, gods, and sons of gods;
Destroyers rightlier called, and plagues of men.
Thus fame shall be achieved, renown on earth;
And what most merits fame, in silence hid.
But he, the seventh from thee, whom thou beheldst
The only righteous in a world perverse,   701
And therefore hated, therefore so beset
With foes, for daring single to be just,
And utter odious truth, that God would come
To judge them with His saints; him the Most High 705
Rapt in a balmy cloud with wingèd steeds
Did, as thou sawest, receive, to walk with God
High in salvation and the climes of bliss,
Exempt from death; to show thee what reward
Awaits the good; the rest what punishment;   710
Which now direct thine eyes and soon behold.'
   He looked, and saw the face of things quite
      changed;
The brazen throat of war had ceased to roar;
All now was turned to jollity and game,
To luxury and riot, feast and dance;   715
Marrying or prostituting, as befell,
Rape or adultery, where passing fair
Allured them; thence from cups to civil broils.
At length a reverend sire among them came,
And of their doings great dislike declared,   720
And testified against their ways; he oft
Frequented their assemblies, whereso met,
Triumphs or festivals; and to them preached
Conversion and repentance, as to souls
In prison, under judgements imminent: 725
But all in vain: which when he saw, he ceased
Contending, and removed his tents far off;
Then, from the mountain hewing timber tall,
Began to build a vessel of huge bulk;   729
Measured by cubit, length, and breadth, and height;
Smeared round with pitch; and in the side a door
Contrived; and of provisions laid in large,
For man and beast: when, lo! a wonder strange,
Of every beast, and bird, and insect small,
Came sevens, and pairs; and entered in as taught 735
Their order: last the sire and his three sons,
With their four wives; and God made fast the door.
Mean while the south-wind rose, and, with black
      wings
Wide-hovering, all the clouds together drove
From under heaven; the hills to their supply   740

647 **beeves:** cattle **kine:** cows 665 the reference is to the prophet
Enoch

719 **reverend sire:** Noah

Vapour, and exhalation dusk and moist,
Sent up amain; and now the thickened sky
Like a dark ceiling stood; down rushed the rain
Impetuous; and continued, till the earth
No more was seen: the floating vessel swum   745
Uplifted, and secure with beakèd prow
Rode tilting o'er the waves; all dwellings else
Flood overwhelmed, and them with all their pomp
Deep under water rolled; sea covered sea,
Sea without shore; and in their palaces,   750
Where luxury late reigned, sea-monsters whelped
And stabled; of mankind, so numerous late,
All left, in one small bottom swum embarked.
How didst thou grieve then, Adam, to behold
The end of all thy offspring, end so sad,   755
Depopulation! Thee another flood,
Of tears and sorrow a flood, thee also drowned,
And sunk thee as thy sons; till, gently reared
By the angel, on thy feet thou stoodest at last,
Though comfortless; as when a father mourns   760
His children, all in view destroyed at once;
And scarce to the angel utteredst thus thy plaint.
   'O visions ill foreseen! Better had I
Lived ignorant of future! so had borne
My part of evil only, each day's lot   765
Enough to bear; those now, that were dispensed
The burden of many ages, on me light
At once, by my foreknowledge gaining birth
Abortive, to torment me ere their being,
With thought that they must be. Let no man seek   770
Henceforth to be foretold, what shall befall
Him or his children; evil he may be sure,
Which neither his foreknowing can prevent;
And he the future evil shall no less
In apprehension than in substance feel,   775
Grievous to bear: but that care now is past,
Man is not whom to warn: those few escaped
Famine and anguish will at last consume,
Wandering that watery desert: I had hope,
When violence was ceased, and war on earth,   780
All would have then gone well; peace would have
   crowned
With length of happy days the race of Man;
But I was far deceived; for now I see
Peace to corrupt no less than war to waste.
How comes it thus? unfold, celestial Guide,   785
And whether here the race of Man will end.'
   To whom thus Michael: 'Those, whom last thou
   sawest
In triumph and luxurious wealth, are they
First seen in acts of prowess eminent
And great exploits, but of true virtue void;   790
Who, having spilt much blood, and done much waste

Subduing nations, and achieved thereby
Fame in the world, high titles, and rich prey;
Shall change their course to pleasure, ease, and sloth,
Surfeit, and lust; till wantonness and pride   795
Raise out of friendship hostile deeds in peace.
The conquered also, and enslaved by war,
Shall, with their freedom lost, all virtue lose
And fear of God; from whom their piety feigned
In sharp contest of battle found no aid   800
Against invaders; therefore, cooled in zeal,
Thenceforth shall practise how to live secure,
Worldly or dissolute, on what their lords
Shall leave them to enjoy; for the earth shall bear
More than enough, that temperance may be tried: 805
So all shall turn degenerate, all depraved;
Justice and temperance, truth and faith, forgot;
One man except, the only son of light
In a dark age, against example good,
Against allurement, custom, and a world   810
Offended: fearless of reproach and scorn,
Or violence, he of their wicked ways
Shall them admonish; and before them set
The paths of righteousness, how much more safe
And full of peace; denouncing wrath to come   815
On their impenitence; and shall return
Of them derided, but of God observed
The one just man alive; by His command
Shall build a wonderous ark, as thou beheldst,
To save himself, and household, from amidst   820
A world devote to universal wrack.
No sooner he, with them of man and beast
Select for life, shall in the ark be lodged,
And sheltered round; but all the cataracts
Of heaven set open on the earth shall pour   825
Rain, day and night; all fountains of the deep,
Broke up, shall heave the ocean to usurp
Beyond all bounds; till inundation rise
Above the highest hills: Then shall this mount
Of paradise by might of waves be moved   830
Out of his place, pushed by the hornèd flood,
With all his verdure spoiled, and trees adrift,
Down the great river to the opening gulf,
And there take root an island salt and bare,
The haunt of seals, and orcs, and sea-mews' clang.
To teach thee that God attributes to place   836
No sanctity, if none be thither brought
By men who there frequent, or therein dwell.
And now, what further shall ensue, behold.'
   He looked, and saw the ark hull on the flood,   840
Which now abated; for the clouds were fled,
Driven by a keen north-wind, that, blowing dry,
Wrinkled the face of deluge, as decayed;
And the clear sun on his wide watery glass
Gazed hot, and of the fresh wave largely drew,   845

746 **prow**: front part of a boat

835 **orcs**: whales **sea-mews**: seagulls

As after thirst; which made their flowing shrink
From standing lake to tripping ebb, that stole
With soft foot towards the deep; who now had stopped
His sluices, as the heaven his windows shut.
The ark no more now floats, but seems on ground, 850
Fast on the top of some high mountain fixed.
And now the tops of hills, as rocks, appear;
With clamour thence the rapid currents drive,
Towards the retreating sea, their furious tide.
Forthwith from out the ark a raven flies, 855
And after him, the surer messenger,
A dove sent forth once and again to spy
Green tree or ground, whereon his foot may light:
The second time returning, in his bill
An olive-leaf he brings, pacific sign. 860
Anon dry ground appears, and from his ark
The ancient sire descends, with all his train;
Then with uplifted hands, and eyes devout,
Grateful to heaven, over his head beholds
A dewy cloud, and in the cloud a bow 865
Conspicuous with three lifted colours gay,
Betokening peace from God, and covenant new.
Whereat the heart of Adam, erst so sad,
Greatly rejoiced; and thus his joy broke forth.
   'O thou, who future things canst represent 870
As present, heavenly Instructer! I revive
At this last sight; assured that Man shall live,
With all the creatures, and their seed preserve.
Far less I now lament for one whole world
Of wicked sons destroyed than I rejoice 875
For one man found so perfect, and so just,
That God vouchsafes to raise another world
From him, and all His anger to forget.
But say, what mean those coloured streaks in heaven
Distended, as the brow of God appeased? 880
Or serve they, as a flowery verge, to bind
The fluid skirts of that same watery cloud,
Lest it again dissolve, and shower the earth?'
   To whom th'archangel. 'Dextrously thou aim'st;
So willingly doth God remit His ire, 885
Though late repenting Him of Man depraved;
Grieved at His heart, when looking down He saw
The whole earth filled with violence, and all flesh
Corrupting each their way; yet, those removed,
Such grace shall one just man find in His sight, 890
That He relents, not to blot out mankind;
And makes a covenant never to destroy
The earth again by flood; nor let the sea
Surpass His bounds; nor rain to drown the world,
With man therein or beast; but, when He brings 895
Over the earth a cloud, will therein set
His triple-coloured bow, whereon to look,
And call to mind His covenant. Day and night,
Seed-time and harvest, heat and hoary frost, 899
Shall hold their course; till fire purge all things new,
Both heaven and earth, wherein the just shall dwell.'

BOOK TWELVE

As one who in his journey bates at noon,
Though bent on speed; so here the archangel paused
Betwixt the world destroyed and world restored,
If Adam aught perhaps might interpose;
Then, with transition sweet, new speech resumes. 5
   'Thus thou hast seen one world begin, and end;
And Man, as from a second stock, proceed.
Much thou hast yet to see; but I perceive
Thy mortal sight to fail; objects divine
Must needs impair and weary human sense. 10
Henceforth what is to come I will relate;
Thou therefore give due audience, and attend.
   'This second source of Men, while yet but few,
And while the dread of judgement past remains
Fresh in their minds, fearing the Deity, 15
With some regard to what is just and right
Shall lead their lives, and multiply apace;
Labouring the soil, and reaping plenteous crop,
Corn, wine, and oil; and, from the herd or flock,
Oft sacrificing bullock, lamb, or kid, 20
With large wine-offerings poured, and sacred feast,
Shall spend their days in joy unblamed; and dwell
Long time in peace, by families and tribes,
Under paternal rule: till one shall rise
Of proud ambitious heart; who, not content 25
With fair equality, fraternal state,
Will arrogate dominion undeserved
Over his brethren, and quite dispossess
Concord and law of nature from the earth;
Hunting (and men not beasts shall be his game) 30
With war, and hostile snare, such as refuse
Subjection to his empire tyrannous:
A mighty hunter thence he shall be styled
Before the Lord; as in despite of heaven,
Or from heaven claiming second sovranty; 35
And from rebellion shall derive his name,
Though of rebellion others he accuse.
He with a crew, whom like ambition joins
With him or under him to tyrannize,
Marching from Eden towards the west, shall find 40
The plain, wherein a black bituminous gurge
Boils out from under ground, the mouth of hell:
Of brick, and of that stuff, they cast to build

BOOK TWELVE – THE ARGUMENT: The Angel Michael continues from the Flood to relate what shall succeed; then, in the mention of Abraham, comes by degrees to explain, who that Seed of the Woman shall be, which was promised Adam and Eve in the Fall; his Incarnation, Death, Resurrection, and Ascension; the state of the Church till his second Coming. Adam greatly satisfied and recomforted by these Relations and Promises descends the Hill with Michael; wakens Eve, who all this while had slept, but with gentle dreams compos'd to quietness of mind and submission. Michael in either hand leads them out of Paradise, the fiery Sword waving behind them, and the Cherubim taking their Stations to guard the Place 1 **bates:** stops briefly 24 the reference is to Nimrod 41 **gurge:** whirlpool

A city and tower, whose top may reach to heaven;
And get themselves a name; lest, far dispersed   45
In foreign lands, their memory be lost;
Regardless whether good or evil fame.
But God, who oft descends to visit men
Unseen, and through their habitations walks
To mark their doings, them beholding soon,   50
Comes down to see their city, ere the tower
Obstruct heaven-towers, and in derision sets
Upon their tongues a various spirit, to raze
Quite out their native language; and, instead,
To sow a jangling noise of words unknown.   55
Forthwith a hideous gabble rises loud,
Among the builders; each to other calls
Not understood; till hoarse, and all in rage,
As mocked they storm: great laughter was in heaven,
And looking down, to see the hubbub strange,   60
And hear the din. Thus was the building left
Ridiculous, and the work Confusion named.'
  Whereto thus Adam, fatherly displeased:
'O execrable Son! so to aspire
Above his brethren; to himself assuming   65
Authority usurped, from God not given:
He gave us only over beast, fish, fowl,
Dominion absolute; that right we hold
By His donation; but man over men
He made not lord; such title to Himself   70
Reserving, human left from human free.
But this usurper his encroachment proud
Stays not on Man; to God his tower intends
Siege and defiance: Wretched man! what food
Will he convey up thither, to sustain   75
Himself and his rash army; where thin air
Above the clouds will pine his entrails gross,
And famish him of breath, if not of bread?'
  To whom thus Michael: 'Justly thou abhorrest
That son, who on the quiet state of men   80
Such trouble brought, affecting to subdue
Rational liberty; yet know withal,
Since thy original lapse, true liberty
Is lost, which always with right reason dwells
Twinned, and from her hath no dividual being.   85
Reason in man obscured, or not obeyed,
Immediately inordinate desires,
And upstart passions, catch the government
From reason; and to servitude reduce
Man, till then free. Therefore, since he permits   90
Within himself unworthy powers to reign
Over free reason, God, in judgement just,
Subjects him from without to violent lords;
Who oft as undeservedly enthrall
His outward freedom. Tyranny must be;   95
Though to the tyrant thereby no excuse.
Yet sometimes nations will decline so low
From virtue, which is reason, that no wrong,
But justice, and some fatal curse annexed,
Deprives them of their outward liberty;   100

Their inward lost. Witness the irreverent son
Of him who built the ark; who, for the shame
Done to his father, heard this heavy curse,
Servant of servants, on his vicious race.
Thus will this latter, as the former world,   105
Still tend from bad to worse; till God at last,
Wearied with their iniquities, withdraw
His presence from among them, and avert
His holy eyes; resolving from thenceforth
To leave them to their own polluted ways;   110
And one peculiar nation to select
From all the rest, of whom to be invoked,
A nation from one faithful man to spring:
Him on this side Euphrates yet residing,
Bred up in idol-worship. Oh, that men   115
(Canst thou believe?) should be so stupid grown,
While yet the patriarch lived, who 'scaped the flood,
As to forsake the living God, and fall
To worship their own work in wood and stone
For gods! Yet him God the Most High vouchsafes   120
To call by vision, from his father's house,
His kindred, and false gods, into a land
Which He will show him; and from him will raise
A mighty nation; and upon him shower
His benediction so, that in his seed   125
All nations shall be blest: he straight obeys;
Not knowing to what land, yet firm believes:
I see him, but thou canst not, with what faith
He leaves his gods, his friends, and native soil,
Ur of Chaldaea, passing now the ford   130
To Haran; after him a cumbrous train
Of herds and flocks, and numerous servitude;
Not wandering poor, but trusting all his wealth
With God, who called him, in a land unknown.
Canaan he now attains; I see his tents   135
Pitched about Sechem, and the neighbouring plain
Of Moreh; there by promise he receives
Gift to his progeny of all that land,
From Hameth northward to the desert south
(Things by their names I call, though yet unnamed);
From Hermon east to the great western sea;   141
Mount Hermon, yonder sea; each place behold
In prospect, as I point them; on the shore
Mount Carmel; here, the double-founted stream,
Jordan, true limit eastward; but his sons   145
Shall dwell to Senir, that long ridge of hills.
This ponder, that all nations of the earth
Shall in his seed be blessèd. By that seed
Is meant thy great Deliverer, who shall bruise
The serpent's head; whereof to thee anon   150
Plainlier shall be revealed. This patriarch blest,
Whom faithful Abraham due time shall call,
A son, and of his son a grandchild, leaves;
Like him in faith, in wisdom, and renown:

101 **irreverent son:** Ham, son of Noah 111 **one peculiar nation:**
Israel 113–114 the reference is to Abraham 153 the son is Isaac and
the grandchild is Jacob

The grandchild, with twelve sons increased, departs
From Canaan to a land hereafter called   156
Egypt, divided by the river Nile
See where it flows, disgorging at seven mouths
Into the sea. To sojourn in that land
He comes, invited by a younger son   160
In time of dearth, a son whose worthy deeds
Raise him to be the second in that realm
Of Pharaoh. There he dies, and leaves his race
Growing into a nation, and now grown
Suspected to a sequent king, who seeks   165
To stop their overgrowth, as inmate guests
Too numerous; whence of guests he makes them slaves
Inhospitably, and kills their infant males:
Till by two brethren (these two brethren call
Moses and Aaron) sent from God to claim   170
His people from enthralment, they return,
With glory and spoil, back to their promised land.
But first, the lawless tyrant, who denies
To know their God, or message to regard,
Must be compelled by signs and judgements dire;   175
To blood unshed the rivers must be turned;
Frogs, lice, and flies must all his palace fill
With loathed intrusion, and fill all the land;
His cattle must of rot and murrain die;
Botches and blains must all his flesh emboss,   180
And all his people; thunder mixed with hail,
Hail mixed with fire, must rend the Egyptians sky,
And wheel on the earth, devouring where it rolls;
What it devours not, herb, or fruit, or grain,
A darksome cloud of locusts swarming down   185
Must eat, and on the ground leave nothing green;
Darkness must overshadow all his bounds,
Palpable darkness, and blot out three days;
Last, with one midnight stroke, all the first-born
Of Egypt must lie dead. Thus with ten wounds   190
The river-dragon tamed at length submits
To let his sojourners depart, and oft
Humbles his stubborn heart; but still, as ice
More hardened after thaw; till, in his rage
Pursuing whom he late dismissed, the sea   195
Swallows him with his host; but them lets pass,
As on dry land, between two crystal walls;
Awed by the rod of Moses so to stand
Divided, till his rescued gain their shore:
Such wondrous power God to His saint will lend,   200
Though present in his angel; who shall go
Before them in a cloud, and pillar of fire;
By day a cloud, by night a pillar of fire;
To guide them in their journey, and remove
Behind them, while th'obdurate king pursues: 205
All night he will pursue; but his approach
Darkness defends between till morning watch;
Then through the fiery pillar, and the cloud,
God looking forth will trouble all his host,

And craze their chariot-wheels: when by command
Moses once more his potent rod extends   211
Over the sea; the sea his rod obeys;
On their embattled ranks the waves return,
And overwhelm their war. The race elect
Safe toward Canaan from the shore advance   215
Through the wild desert, not the readiest way;
Lest, entering on the Canaanite alarmed,
War terrify them inexpert, and fear
Return them back to Egypt, choosing rather
Inglorious life with servitude; for life   220
To noble and ignoble is more sweet
Untrained in arms, where rashness leads not on.
This also shall they gain by their delay
In the wide wilderness; there they shall found
Their government, and their great senate choose   225
Through the twelve tribes, to rule by laws ordained:
God from the mount of Sinai, whose grey top
Shall tremble, he descending, will himself
In thunder, lightning, and loud trumpets' sound,
Ordain them laws; part, such as appertain   230
To civil justice; part, religious rites
Of sacrifice; informing them, by types
And shadows, of that destined seed to bruise
The serpent, by what means he shall achieve
Mankind's deliverance. But the voice of God   235
To mortal ear is dreadful: They beseech
That Moses might report to them His will,
And terror cease; he grants what they besought,
Instructed that to God is no access
Without Mediator, whose high office now   240
Moses in figure bears; to introduce
One greater, of whose day he shall foretell,
And all the prophets in their age the times
Of great Messiah shall sing. Thus, laws and rites
Established, such delight hath God in Men   245
Obedient to His will that He vouchsafes
Among them to set up His tabernacle;
The Holy One with mortal Men to dwell:
By his prescript a sanctuary is framed
Of cedar, overlaid with gold; therein   250
An ark, and in the ark His testimony,
The records of His covenant; over these
A mercy-seat of gold, between the wings
Of two bright cherubim; before Him burn
Seven lamps as in a zodiac representing   255
The heavenly fires; over the tent a cloud
Shall rest by day, a fiery gleam by night;
Save when they journey, and at length they come,
Conducted by His angel, to the land
Promised to Abraham and his seed. – The rest   260
Were long to tell; how many battles fought
How many kings destroyed; and kingdoms won;
Or how the sun shall in mid-heaven stand still
A day entire, and night's due course adjourn,
Man's voice commanding, "Sun, in Gibeon stand,   265
And thou moon in the vale of Aialon,

---

155 **twelve sons**: patriarchs of the twelve tribes of Israel 179 **murrain**:
an infectious disease of cattle

Till Israel overcome! so call the third
From Abraham, son of Isaac; and from him
His whole descent, who thus shall Canaan win." '
   Here Adam interposed: 'O Sent from Heaven,   270
Enlightener of my darkness, gracious things
Thou hast revealed; those chiefly, which concern
Just Abraham and his seed: now first I find
Mine eyes true-opening, and my heart much eased;
Erewhile perplexed with thoughts, what would
    become   275
Of me and all mankind. But now I see
His day, in whom all nations shall be blest;
Favour unmerited by me, who sought
Forbidden knowledge by forbidden means.
This yet I apprehend not, why to those   280
Among whom God will deign to dwell on earth
So many and so various laws are given;
So many laws argue so many sins
Among them; how can God with such reside?'
   To whom thus Michael: 'Doubt not but that sin   285
Will reign among them, as of thee begot;
And therefore was law given them, to evince
Their natural pravity, by stirring up
Sin against law to fight: that when they see
Law can discover sin, but not remove,   290
Save by those shadowy expiations weak,
The blood of bulls and goats, they may conclude
Some blood more precious must be paid for Man;
Just for unjust; that, in such righteousness
To them by faith imputed, they may find   295
Justification towards God, and peace
Of conscience; which the law by ceremonies
Cannot appease; nor Man the mortal part
Perform; and, not performing, cannot live.
So law appears imperfect; and but given   300
With purpose to resign them, in full time,
Up to a better covenant; disciplined
From shadowy types to truth; from flesh to spirit;
From imposition of strict laws to free
Acceptance of large grace; from servile fear   305
To filial; works of law to works of faith.
And therefore shall not Moses, though of God
Highly beloved, being but the minister
Of law, his people into Canaan lead;
But Joshua, whom the Gentiles Jesus call,   310
His name and office bearing, who shall quell
The adversary-serpent, and bring back
Through the world's wilderness long-wandered Man
Safe to eternal paradise of rest.
Meanwhile they, in their earthly Canaan placed,   315
Long time shall dwell and prosper, but when sins
National interrupt their public peace,
Provoking God to raise them enemies;
From whom as oft He saves them penitent
By judges first, then under kings; of whom   320

The second, both for piety renowned
And puissant deeds, a promise shall receive
Irrevocable, that his regal throne
For ever shall endure; the like shall sing
All prophecy, that of the royal stock   325
Of David (so I name this king) shall rise
A Son, the Woman's seed to thee foretold,
Foretold to Abraham, as in whom shall trust
All nations; and to kings foretold, of kings
The last; for of his reign shall be no end.   330
But first, a long succession must ensue;
And his next son, for wealth and wisdom famed,
The clouded ark of God, till then in tents
Wandering, shall in a glorious temple enshrine.
Such follow him, as shall be registered   335
Part good, part bad; of bad the longer scroll;
Whose foul idolatries, and other faults
Heaped to the popular sum, will so incense
God, as to leave them, and expose their land,
Their city, His temple, and His holy ark,   340
With all His sacred things, a scorn and prey
To that proud city, whose high walls thou sawest
Left in confusion; Babylon thence called.
There in captivity He lets them dwell
The space of seventy years; then brings them back,
Rememb'ring mercy, and His cov'nant sworn   346
To David, stablished as the days of heaven.
Returned from Babylon by leave of kings
Their lords, whom God disposed, the house of God
They first re-edify; and for a while   350
In mean estate live moderate; till, grown
In wealth and multitude, factious they grow;
But first among the priests dissension springs,
Men who attend the altar, and should most
Endeavour peace: their strife pollution brings   355
Upon the temple itself: at last they seize
The sceptre, and regard not David's sons;
Then lose it to a stranger, that the true
Anointed King Messiah might be born
Barred of His right; yet at His birth a star,   360
Unseen before in heaven, proclaims Him come;
And guides the eastern sages, who inquire
His place, to offer incense, myrrh, and gold:
His place of birth a solemn angel tells
To simple shepherds, keeping watch by night;   365
They gladly thither haste, and by a choir
Of squadroned angels hear his carol sung.
A virgin is his mother, but his sire
The power of the Most High. He shall ascend
The throne hereditary, and bound His reign   370
With earth's wide bounds, His glory with the heavens.'
   He ceased, discerning Adam with such joy
Surcharged, as had like grief been dewed in tears,
Without the vent of words; which these he breathed:
   'O prophet of glad tidings, finisher   375

---

267 **Israel:** Jacob 288 **natural pravity:** natural depravity. Original Sin   332 **next son:** Solomon, son of David

Of utmost hope! now clear I understand
What oft my steadiest thoughts have searched in vain;
Why our great Expectation should be called
The seed of woman. Virgin Mother, hail,
High in the love of heaven; yet from my loins   380
Thou shalt proceed, and from thy womb the Son
Of God Most High: so God with Man unites!
Needs must the serpent now his capital bruise
Expect with mortal pain. Say where and when   384
Their fight, what stroke shall bruise the victor's heel.'
    To whom thus Michael: 'Dream not of their fight,
As of a duel, or the local wounds
Of head or heel: Not therefore joins the Son
Manhood to Godhead, with more strength to foil
Thy enemy; nor so is overcome   390
Satan, whose fall from heaven, a deadlier bruise,
Disabled, not to give thee thy death's wound:
Which He who comes thy Saviour shall recure,
Not by destroying Satan, but his works
In thee, and in thy seed. Nor can this be,   395
But by fulfilling that which thou didst want,
Obedience to the law of God, imposed
On penalty of death, and suffering death;
The penalty to thy transgression due,
And due to theirs which out of thine will grow.   400
So only can high Justice rest appaid.
The law of God exact he shall fulfil
Both by obedience and by love, though love
Alone fulfil the law; thy punishment
He shall endure, by coming in the flesh   405
To a reproachful life and cursèd death;
Proclaiming life to all who shall believe
In His redemption; and that His obedience,
Imputed, becomes theirs by faith; His merits
To save them, not their own, though legal, works.   410
For this He shall live hated, be blasphemed,
Seized on by force, judged, and to death condemned
A shameful and accursed, nailed to the cross
By his own nation; slain for bringing life:
But to the cross He nails thy enemies,   415
The law that is against thee, and the sins
Of all mankind, with Him there crucified,
Never to hurt them more who rightly trust
In this His satisfaction; so He dies,
But soon revives; Death over him no power   420
Shall long usurp; ere the third dawning light
Return, the stars of morn shall see Him rise
Out of His grave, fresh as the dawning light,
Thy ransom paid, which Man from death redeems,
His death for Man, as many as offered life   425
Neglect not, and the benefit embrace
By faith not void of works: This god-like act
Annuls thy doom, the death thou shouldest have died,
In sin for ever lost from life; this act
Shall bruise the head of Satan, crush his strength,   430
Defeating Sin and Death, his two main arms;
And fix far deeper in his head their stings

Than temporal death shall bruise the victor's heel,
Or theirs whom he redeems; a death, like sleep,
A gentle wafting to immortal life.   435
Nor after resurrection shall He stay
Longer on earth, than certain times to appear
To his disciples, men who in His life
Still followed Him; to them shall leave in charge
To teach all nations what of Him they learned   440
And His salvation; them who shall believe
Baptizing in the profluent stream, the sign
Of washing them from guilt of sin to life
Pure, and in mind prepared, if so befall,
For death, like that which the Redeemer died.   445
All nations they shall teach; for, from that day,
Not only to the sons of Abraham's loins
Salvation shall be preached, but to the sons
Of Abraham's faith wherever through the world;
So in his seed all nations shall be blest.   450
Then to the heaven of heavens He shall ascend
With victory, triumphing through the air
Over His foes and thine; there shall surprise
The serpent, prince of air, and drag in chains
Through all His realm, and there confounded leave;
Then enter into glory, and resume   456
His seat at God's right hand, exalted high
Above all names in Heaven; and thence shall come,
When this world's dissolution shall be ripe,
With glory and power to judge both quick and dead;
To judge th'unfaithful dead, but to reward   461
His faithful, and receive them into bliss,
Whether in heaven or earth; for then the earth
Shall all be paradise, far happier place
Than this of Eden, and far happier days.'   465
    So spake the archangel Michael; then paused,
As at the world's great period; and our sire,
Replete with joy and wonder, thus replied:
    'O Goodness infinite, Goodness immense!
That all this good of evil shall produce,   470
And evil turn to good; more wonderful
Than that which by creation first brought forth
Light out of darkness! Full of doubt I stand,
Whether I should repent me now of sin
By me done, and occasioned; or rejoice   475
Much more, that much more good thereof shall
    spring;
To God more glory, more good-will to Men
From God, and over wrath grace shall abound.
But say, if our Deliverer up to heaven
Must re-ascend, what will betide the few   480
His faithful, left among the unfaithful herd,
The enemies of truth? Who then shall guide
His people, who defend? Will they not deal
Worse with His followers than with Him they dealt?'
    'Be sure they will,' said th'angel, 'but from
    heaven   485

454 **prince of air**: Satan

He to his own a Comforter will send,
The promise of the Father, who shall dwell
His spirit within them; and the law of faith,
Working through love, upon their hearts shall write,
To guide them in all truth; and also arm   490
With spiritual armour, able to resist
Satan's assaults, and quench his fiery darts;
What man can do against them, not afraid,
Though to the death; against such cruelties
With inward consolations recompensed,   495
And oft supported so as shall amaze
Their proudest persecutors. For the Spirit,
Poured first on His apostles, whom He sends
To evangelize the nations, then on all
Baptized, shall them with wondrous gifts endue   500
To speak all tongues, and do all miracles,
As did their Lord before them. Thus they win
Great numbers of each nation to receive
With joy the tidings brought from heaven. At length
Their ministry performed, and race well run,   505
Their doctrine and their story written left,
They die; but in their room, as they forewarn,
Wolves shall succeed for teachers, grievous wolves,
Who all the sacred mysteries of heaven
To their own vile advantages shall turn   510
Of lucre and ambition; and the truth
With superstitions and traditions taint,
Left only in those written records pure,
Though not but by the Spirit understood.
Then shall they seek t'avail themselves of names, 515
Places, and titles, and with these to join
Secular power; though feigning still to act
By spiritual, to themselves appropriating
The Spirit of God, promised alike and given
To all believers; and, from that pretence,   520
Spiritual laws by carnal power shall force
On every conscience; laws which none shall find
Left them inrolled, or what the Spirit within
Shall on the heart engrave. What will they then
But force the Spirit of Grace itself, and bind   525
His consort Liberty? what, but unbuild
His living temples, built by faith to stand,
Their own faith, not another's? for, on earth,
Who against faith and conscience can be heard
Infallible? yet many will presume: 530
Whence heavy persecution shall arise
On all who in the worship persevere
Of spirit and truth; the rest, far greater part,
Will deem in outward rites and specious forms
Religion satisfied; Truth shall retire   535
Bestuck with slanderous darts, and works of faith
Rarely be found: So shall the world go on,
To good malignant, to bad men benign;
Under her own weight groaning; till the day
Appear of respiration to the just,   540
And vengeance to the wicked, at return

Of him so lately promised to thy aid,
The Woman's seed; obscurely then foretold,
Now ampler known thy Saviour and thy Lord;
Last, in the clouds, from heaven to be revealed   545
In glory of the Father, to dissolve
Satan with his perverted world; then raise
From the conflagrant mass, purged and refined,
New heavens, new earth, ages of endless date,
Founded in righteousness, and peace, and love;   550
To bring forth fruits, joy and eternal bliss.'
    He ended; and thus Adam last replied.
'How soon hath thy prediction, Seer blest,
Measured this transient world, the race of time,
Till time stand fixed! Beyond is all abyss,   555
Eternity, whose end no eye can reach.
Greatly instructed I shall hence depart;
Greatly in peace of thought; and have my fill
Of knowledge, what this vessel can contain;
Beyond which was my folly to aspire.   560
Henceforth I learn, that to obey is best,
And love with fear the only God; to walk
As in His presence; ever to observe
His providence; and on Him sole depend,
Merciful over all His works, with good   565
Still overcoming evil, and by small
Accomplishing great things, by things deemed weak
Subverting worldly strong, and worldly wise
By simply meek: that suffering for truth's sake
Is fortitude to highest victory,   570
And, to the faithful, death the gate of life;
Taught this by His example, whom I now
Acknowledge my Redeemer ever blest.'
    To whom thus also the angel last replied:
'This having learned, thou hast attained the sum 575
Of wisdom; hope no higher, though all the stars
Thou knewest by name, and all th'ethereal powers,
All secrets of the deep, all Nature's works,
Or works of God in heaven, air, earth, or sea,
And all the riches of this world enjoyedst,   580
And all the rule, one empire; only add
Deeds to thy knowledge answerable; add faith,
Add virtue, patience, temperance; add love,
By name to come called charity, the soul
Of all the rest: then wilt thou not be loath   585
To leave this paradise, but shalt possess
A paradise within thee, happier far. –
Let us descend now therefore from this top
Of speculation; for the hour precise
Exacts our parting hence; and see! the guards,   590
By me encamped on yonder hill, expect
Their motion; at whose front a flaming sword,
In signal of remove, waves fiercely round:
We may no longer stay: go, waken Eve;
Her also I with gentle dreams have calmed   595
Portending good, and all her spirits composed
To meek submission: thou, at season fit,

Let her with thee partake what thou hast heard;
Chiefly what may concern her faith to know,
The great deliverance by her seed to come   600
(For by the Woman's seed) on all mankind:
That ye may live, which will be many days,
Both in one faith unanimous, though sad,
With cause, for evils past; yet much more cheered
With meditation on the happy end.'   605
   He ended, and they both descend the hill;
Descended, Adam to the bower, where Eve
Lay sleeping, ran before; but found her waked;
And thus with words not sad she him received.
'Whence thou return'st, and whither wentest, I know;
For God is also in sleep; and dreams advise,   611
Which He hath sent propitious, some great good
Preságing, since with sorrow and heart's distress
Wearied I fell asleep: But now lead on;
In me is no delay; with thee to go,   615
Is to stay here; without thee here to stay,
Is to go hence unwilling; thou to me
Art all things under heaven, all places thou,
Who for my wilful crime art banished hence.
This further consolation yet secure   620
I carry hence; though all by me is lost,
Such favour I unworthy am vouchsafed,
By me the promised seed shall all restore.'
   So spake our mother Eve; and Adam heard
Well pleased, but answered not. For now, too nigh   625
The archangel stood; and, from the other hill
To their fixed station, all in bright array
The cherubim descended; on the ground
Gliding meteorous, as evening-mist
Risen from a river o'er the marish glides,   630
And gathers ground fast at the labourer's heel
Homeward returning. High in front advanced,
The brandished sword of God before them blazed,
Fierce as a comet; which with torrid heat,
And vapour as the Libyan air adust,   635
Began to parch that temperate clime; whereat
In either hand the hastening angel caught
Our lingering parents, and to the eastern gate
Led them direct, and down the cliff as fast
To the subjected plain; then disappeared.   640
They, looking back, all the eastern side beheld
Of paradise, so late their happy seat,
Waved over by that flaming brand; the gate
With dreadful faces thronged, and fiery arms:
Some natural tears they dropped, but wiped them
     soon;   645
The world was all before them, where to choose
Their place of rest, and Providence their guide:
They, hand in hand, with wandering steps and slow,
Through Eden took their solitary way.

629 **meteorous:** like a meteor 630 **marish:** marsh

From SAMSON AGONISTES

OH, how comely it is and how reviving
To the spirits of just men long oppressed!
When God into the hands of their deliverer
Puts invincible might
To quell the mighty of the earth, th'oppressor,   5
The brute and boist'rous force of violent men
Hardy and industrious to support
Tyrannic power, but raging to pursue
The righteous and all such as honour truth;
He all their ammunition   10
And feats of war defeats
With plain heroic magnitude of mind
And celestial vigour armed,
Their armouries and magazines contemns,
Renders them useless, while   15
With wingèd expedition
Swift as the lightning glance he executes
His errand on the wicked, who surprised
Lose their defence distracted and amazed.

ALL is best, though we oft doubt,
What th'unsearchable dispose
Of highest wisdom brings about,
And ever best found in the close.
Oft He seems to hide His face,   5
But unexpectedly returns
And to His faithful champion hath in place
Bore witness gloriously; whence Gaza mourns
And all that band them to resist
His uncontrollable intent,   10
His servants He with new acquist
Of true experience from this great event
With peace and consolation hath dismissed,
And calm of mind all passion spent.

SIR JOHN SUCKLING

'OUT UPON IT! I HAVE LOVED'

OUT upon it! I have loved
   Three whole days together;
And am like to love three more,
   If it prove fair weather.

Time shall moult away his wings   5
   Ere he shall discover
In the whole wide world again
   Such a constant lover.

But the spite on't is, no praise
   Is due at all to me: 10
Love with me had made no stays
   Had it any been but she.

Had it any been but she,
    And that very face,
There had been at least ere this   15
    A dozen dozen in her place.

'OUT UPON IT I HAVE LOVED': 14 There are other versions of this
poem where this line reads 'And that very very face'

'WHY SO PALE AND WAN, FOND LOVER?'

WHY so pale and wan, fond lover?
    Prithee, why so pale?
Will, when looking well can't move her,
    Looking ill prevail?
    Prithee, why so pale?   5

Why so dull and mute, young sinner?
    Prithee, why so mute?
Will, when speaking well can't win her,
    Saying nothing do't?
    Prithee, why so mute?   10

Quit, quit for shame! This will not move;
    This cannot take her.
If of herself she will not love,
    Nothing can make her:
    The devil take her!   15

'WHY SO PALE AND WAN, FOND LOVER?': 2 **Prithee:** Pray thee 6 **sinner:**
signor

'OH, FOR SOME HONEST LOVER'S GHOST'

OH, for some honest lover's ghost,
    Some kind unbodied post
    Sent from the shades below!
    I strangely long to know
Whether the nobler chaplets wear   5
Those that their mistress' scorn did bear
    Or those that were used kindly.

For whatsoe'er they tell us here
    To make those sufferings dear,
    'Twill there, I fear, be found   10
    That to the being crowned
To have loved alone will not suffice,
Unless we also have been wise
    And have our loves enjoyed.

What posture can we think him in   15
    That, here unloved, again
    Departs, and 's thither gone
    Where each sits by his own?
Or how can that Elysium be
Where I my mistress still must see   20
    Circled in other's arms?

For there the judges all are just,
    And Sophonisba must
    Be his whom she held dear,
    Nor his who loved her here.   25
The sweet Philoclea, since she died,
Lies by her Pirocles his side,
    Not by Amphialus.

Some bays, perchance, or myrtle bough
    For difference crowns the brow   30
    Of those kind souls that were
    The noble martyrs here:
And if that be the only odds
(As who can tell?), ye kinder gods,
    Give me the woman here!   35

'OH FOR SOME HONEST LOVER'S GHOST': 2 **post:** ambassador 5 **chaplets:**
garlands 19 **Elysium:** the state of the blessed after death 23 **Sophonisba:**
a Carthaginian noblewoman who remained faithful to Massinissa
despite being obliged to marry Syphax 26 **Philoclea:** from Sidney's
Arcadia. Amphialus is in love with Philoclea, but she loves Pirochles
29 **bays:** the bays are for poetry

SIDNEY GODOLPHIN

'LORD, WHEN THE WISE MEN
CAME FROM FAR'

LORD, when the wise men came from far,
Led to thy cradle by a star,
Then did the shepherds too rejoice,
Instructed by thy angel's voice.
Blest were the wise men in their skill,   5
And shepherds in their harmless will.

Wise men, in tracing Nature's laws,
Ascend unto the highest cause;
Shepherds with humble fearfulness
Walk safely, though their light be less.   10
Though wise men better know the way,
It seems no honest heart can stray.

There is no merit in the wise
But love, the shepherds' sacrifice.
Wise men, all ways of knowledge passed,   15
To the shepherds' wonder come at last.
To know can only wonder breed,
And not to know is wonder's seed.

A wise man at the altar bows,
And offers up his studied vows,   20
And is received. May not the tears,
Which spring too from a shepherd's fears,
And sighs upon his frailty spent,
Though not distinct, be eloquent?

'Tis true, the object sanctifies　25
All passions which within us rise,
But since no creature comprehends
The cause of causes, end of ends,
He who himself vouchsafes to know　30
Best pleases his creator so.

When then our sorrows we apply
To our own wants and poverty,
When we look up in all distress,
And our own misery confess,
Sending both thanks and prayers above,　35
Then, though we do not know, we love.

JAMES GRAHAM,
MARQUIS OF MONTROSE

'MY DEAR AND ONLY LOVE, I PRAY'

My dear and only love, I pray
　That little world of thee
Be governed by no other sway
　Than purest monarchy;
For if confusion have a part　5
　(Which virtuous souls abhor),
And hold a synod in thine heart,
　I'll never love thee more.

Like Alexander I will reign,
　And I will reign alone;　10
My thoughts did evermore disdain
　A rival on my throne.
He either fears his fate too much,
　Or his deserts are small,
That dares not put it to the touch,　15
　To gain or lose it all.

And in the empire of thine heart,
　Where I should solely be,
If others do pretend a part
　Or dare to vie with me,　20
Or if committee thou erect,
　And go on such a score,
I'll laugh and sing at thy neglect,
　And never love thee more.

But if thou wilt prove faithful then,　25
　And constant of thy word,
I'll make thee glorious by my pen
　And famous by my sword;
I'll serve thee in such noble ways
　Was never heard before;　30
I'll crown and deck thee all with bays,
　And love thee more and more.

'MY DEAR AND ONLY LOVE, I PRAY': 7 **synod**: religious assembly
9 **Alexander**: Alexander the Great 31 **bays**: the bays are for poetry

SAMUEL BUTLER

From HUDIBRAS

FOR his religion it was fit
To match his learning and his wit:
'Twas Presbyterian true blue,
For he was of that stubborn crew
Of errant Saints, whom all men grant　5
To be the true Church Militant:
Such as do build their faith upon
The holy text of pike and gun;
Decide all controvérses by
Infallible artillery;　10
And prove their doctrine orthodox
By Apostolic blows and knocks;
Call fire and sword and desolation
A godly-thorough-Reformation,
Which always must be carried on,　15
And still be doing, never done:
As if religion were intended
For nothing else but to be mended.
A sect whose chief devotion lies
In odd perverse antipathies;　20
In falling out with that or this,
And finding somewhat still amiss:
More peevish, cross, and splénetic
Than dog distract, or monkey sick;
That with more care keep holiday　25
The wrong, than others the right way;
Compound for sins they are inclined to,
By daming those they have no mind to;
Still so perverse and opposite,
As if they worshipped God for spite.　30
The self-same thing they will abhor
One way, and long another for.
Free Will they one way disavow,
Another, nothing else allow.
All piety consists therein　35
In them, in other men all sin.
Rather than fail, they will defy
That which they love most tenderly,
Quarrel with minced pies, and disparage
Their best and dearest friend, plum porridge;　40
Fat pig and goose itself oppose,
And blaspheme custard through the nose.
Th'Apostles of this fierce religion,
Like Mahomet's, were ass and widgeon,
To whom our Knight, by fast instínct　45
Of wit and temper was so linked
As if hypocrisy and nonsense
Had got th'advowson of his conscience.

HUDIBRAS: **Note:** this extract is from Part 1, Canto 1, line 189
44 **Mahomet's:** Muhammad, who is said to have had a bird
(widgeon) that whispered in his ear and an ass that would carry
him to heaven **widgeon:** a kind of wild duck 48 **th'advowson:** the
advantage

RICHARD CRASHAW

A HYMN TO THE NAME AND HONOUR
OF THE ADMIRABLE ST TERESA

LOVE, thou art absolute sole lord
Of life and death. To prove the word,
We'll now appeal to none of all
Those thy old soldiers, great and tall,
Ripe men of martyrdom, that could reach down   5
With strong arms their triumphant crown;
Such as could with lusty breath
Speak loud into the face of death
Their great Lord's glorious name; to none
Of those whose spacious bosoms spread a throne   10
For love at large to fill. Spare blood and sweat,
And see him take a private seat,
Making his mansion in the mild
And milky soul of a soft child.

    Scarce has she learnt to lisp the name   15
Of martyr; yet she thinks it shame
Life should so long play with that breath
Which spent can buy so brave a death.
She never undertook to know
What death with love should have to do;   20
Nor has she e'er yet understood
Why to show love she should shed blood.
Yet though she cannot tell you why,
She can love, and she can die.

    Scarce has she blood enough to make   25
A guilty sword blush for her sake;
Yet has she a heart dares hope to prove
How much less strong is death than love.

    Be love but there, let poor six years
Be posed with the maturest fears   30
Man trembles at, you straight shall find
Love knows no nonage, nor the mind.
'Tis love, not years or limbs, that can
Make the martyr, or the man.

    Love touched her heart, and lo! it beats   35
High, and burns with such brave heats;
Such thirsts do die, as dares drink up,
A thousand cold deaths in one cup.
Good reason. For she breathes all fire.
Her weak breast heaves with strong desire   40
Of what she may with fruitless wishes
Seek for amongst her mother's kisses.

    Since 'tis not to be had at home
She'll travel to a martyrdom.
No home for hers confesses she   45
But where she may a martyr be.

    She'll to the Moors and trade with them
For this unvalued diadem;
She'll offer them her dearest breath,
With Christ's name in't, in change for death.   50

She'll bargain with them, and will give
Them God, and teach them how to live
In Him; or, if they this deny,
For him she'll teach them how to die.
So shall she leave amongst them sown   55
Her Lord's blood; or at least her own.

    Farewell then, all the world! Adieu!
Teresa is no more for you.
Farewell, all pleasures, sports, and joys
(Never till now esteemèd toys);   60
Farewell, whatever dear may be,
Mother's arms or father's knee!
Farewell house, and farewell, home!
She's for the Moors, and martyrdom.

    Sweet, not so fast! lo! thy fair Spouse   65
Whom thou seek'st with so swift vows,
Calls thee back, and bids thee come
T'embrace a milder martyrdom.

    Blest powers forbid thy tender life
Should bleed upon a barbarous knife;   70
Or some base hand have power to rase
Thy breast's chaste cabinet, and uncase
A soul kept there so sweet. Oh no;
Wise heaven will never have it so.
Thou art love's victim; and must die   75
A death more mystical and high.
Into love's arms thou shalt let fall
A still-surviving funeral.
His is the dart must make the death
Whose stroke shall taste thy hallowed breath;   80
A dart thrice dipped in that rich flame
Which writes thy Spouse's radiant Name
Upon the roof of heaven; where ay
It shines, and with a sovereign ray
Beats bright upon the burning faces   85
Of souls which in that name's sweet graces
Find everlasting smiles. So rare,
So spiritual, pure, and fair
Must be th'immortal instrument
Upon whose choice point shall be sent   90
A life so loved; and that there be
Fit executioners for thee,
The fair'st and first-born sons of fire,
Blest seraphim, shall leave their choir
And turn love's soldiers, upon thee   95
To exercise their archery.

    Oh, how oft shalt thou complain
Of a sweet and subtle pain!
Of intolerable joys!
Of a death, in which who dies   100
Loves his death, and dies again.
And would for ever so be slain;
And lives, and dies, and knows not why
To live, but that he thus may never leave to die!

A HYMN TO THE NAME AND HONOUR OF THE ADMIRABLE ST TERESA:
32 **nonage:** period of existence 48 **unvalued diadem:** priceless crown
90 **sent:** dispatched 94 **seraphim:** a class of angel

How kindly will thy gentle heart
Kiss the sweetly killing dart! 105
And close in his embraces keep
Those delicious wounds that weep
Balsam to heal themselves with! Thus,
When these thy deaths, so numerous, 110
Shall all at last die into one,
And melt thy soul's sweet mansïon;
Like a soft lump of incense, hasted
By too hot a fire, and wasted
Into perfüming clouds, so fast 115
Shalt thou exhale to Heaven at last
In a resolving sigh, and then –
Oh, what? Ask not the tongues of men,
Angels cannot tell. Suffice,
Thyself shall feel thine own full joys 120
And hold them fast for ever. There
So soon as thou shalt first appear,
The moon of maiden stars, thy white
Mistress, attended by such bright
Souls as thy shining self, shall come 125
And in her first ranks make thee room;
Where 'mongst her snowy family
Immortal welcomes wait for thee.
    Oh, what delight, when revealed life shall stand
And teach thy lips heaven with his hand; 130
In which thou now may'st to thy wishes
Heap up thy consecrated kisses.
What joys shall seize thy soul, when she
Bending her blessèd eyes on thee
(Those second smiles of heaven) shall dart 135
Her mild rays through thy melting heart!
    Angels, thy old friends, there shall greet thee,
Glad at their own home now to meet thee.
    All thy good works which went before
And waited for thee at the door, 140
Shall own thee there, and all in one
Weave a constellation
Of crowns, with which the King, thy Spouse,
Shall build up thy triumphant brows.
    All thy old woes shall now smile on thee, 145
And thy pains sit bright upon thee;
All thy sorrows here shall shine,
All thy suff'rings be divine.
Tears shall take comfort, and turn gems,
And wrongs repent to diadems. 150
Ev'n thy deaths shall live, and new
Dress the soul that erst they slew.
Thy wounds shall blush to such bright scars
As keep account of the Lamb's wars.
    Those rare works where thou shalt leave writ 155
Love's noble history, with wit
Taught thee by none but Him, while here
They feed our souls, shall clothe thine there.

Each heavenly word, by whose hid flame
Our hard hearts shall strike fire, the same 160
Shall flourish on thy brows, and be
Both fire to us and flame to thee;
Whose light shall live bright in thy face
By glory, in our hearts by grace.
    Thou shalt look round about, and see 165
Thousands of crowned souls throng to be
Themselves thy crown; sons of thy vows,
The virgin births, with which thy sovereign Spouse
Made fruitful thy fair soul. Go now,
And with them all about thee bow 170
To Him. 'Put on,' He'll say, 'put on
My rosy Love, that thy rich zone,
Sparkling with the sacred flames
Of thousand souls, whose happy names
Heaven keeps upon thy score (thy bright 175
Life brought them first to kiss the light
That kindled them to stars), and so
Thou with the Lamb, thy Lord, shalt go;
And wheresoe'er he sets his white
Steps, walk with Him, those ways of light 180
Which who in death would live to see
Must learn in life to die like thee.'

AN EPITAPH

UPON A YOUNG MARRIED COUPLE
DEAD AND BURIED TOGETHER

To these, whom death again did wed,
This grave's their second marriage-bed.
For though the hand of Fate could force
'Twixt soul and body a divorce,
It could not sunder man and wife, 5
'Cause they both livèd but one life.
Peace, good reader. Do not weep.
Peace, the lovers are asleep.
They, sweet turtles, folded lie
In the last knot love could tie. 10
And though they lie as they were dead,
Their pillow stone, their sheets of lead
(Pillow hard, and sheets not warm),
Love made the bed; they'll take no harm.
Let them sleep, let them sleep on, 15
Till this stormy night be gone,
Till th'eternal morrow dawn;
Then the curtains will be drawn
And they wake into a light
Whose day shall never die in night. 20

153–4 The Lamb of God, Christ, will defeat the Beast. See Revelation (17:14)

AN EPITAPH: 5 **sunder:** separate 9 **turtles:** as in turtle doves, a symbol of enduring love

SIR JOHN DENHAM

COOPER'S HILL

SURE there are poets which did never dream
Upon Parnassus, nor did taste the stream
Of Helicon, we therefore may suppose
Those made not poets, but the poets those.
And as courts make not kings, but kings the court,   5
So where the Muses and their train resort,
Parnassus stands; if I can be to thee
A poet, thou Parnassus art to me.
Nor wonder, if (advantaged in my flight,
By taking wing from thy auspicious height)   10
Through untraced ways, and airy paths I fly,
More boundless in fancy than my eye:
My eye, which swift as thought contracts the space
That lies between, and first salutes the place
Crowned with that sacred pile, so vast, so high,   15
That whether 'tis a part of Earth, or sky,
Uncertain seems, and may be thought a proud
Aspiring mountain, or descending cloud,
Paul's, the late theme of such a Muse whose flight
Had bravely reached and soared above thy height: 20
Now shalt thou stand though sword, or time, or fire,
Or zeal more fierce than they, thy fall conspire,
Secure, whilst thee the best of poets sings,
Preserved from ruin by the best of kings.
    Under his proud survéy the City lies,   25
And like a mist beneath the hill doth rise;
Whose state and wealth the business and the crowd,
Seems at this distance but a darker cloud:
And is to him who rightly things esteems,
No other in effect than what it seems: 30
Where, with like haste, though several ways, they run
Some to undo, and some to be undone;
While luxury, and wealth, like war and peace,
Are each the other's ruin, and increase;
As rivers lost in seas some secret vein   35
Then reconveys, there to be lost again.
Oh, happiness of sweet retired content!
To be at once secure, and innocent.
Windsor the next (where Mars with Venus dwells.
Beauty with strength) above the valley swells   40
Into my eye, and doth itself present
With such an easy and unforced ascent,
That no stupendious precipice denies
Access, no horror turns away our eyes:
But such a rise, as doth at once invite   45
A pleasure, and a reverence from the sight.
Thy mighty Master's emblem, in whose face
Sate meekness, heightened with majestic grace

Such seems thy gentle height, made only proud
To be the basis of that pompous load,   50
Than which, a nobler weight no mountain bears,
But Atlas only that supports the spheres.
When Nature's hand this ground did thus advance,
'Twas guided by a wiser power than Chance;
Marked out for such a youth, as if 'twere meant   55
T'invite the builder, and his choice prevent.
Nor can we call it choice, when what we choose,
Folly, or blindness only could refuse.
A crown of such majestic tow'rs doth grace
The gods' great mother, when her heavenly race   60
Do homage to her, yet she cannot boast
Amongst that numerous and celestial host,
More heroes than can Windsor, nor doth Fame's
Immortal book record more noble names.
Not to look back so far, to whom this isle   65
Owes the first glory of so brave a pile,
Whether to Caesar, Albanact, or Brute,
The British Arthur, or the Danish Cnute
(Though this of old no less contest did move,
Than when for Homer's birth seven cities strove)   70
(Like him in birth, thou should'st be like in fame,
As thine his fate, if mine had been his flame),
But whosoe'er it was, Nature designed
First a brave place, and then as brave a mind.
Not to recount those several kings, to whom   75
It gave a cradle, or to whom a tomb,
But thee (great Edward) and thy greater son
(The lilies which his father wore, he won),
And thy Bellona, who the consort came
Not only to thy bed, but to thy fame,   80
She to thy triumph led one captive king,
And brought that son, which did the second bring.
Then didst thou found that Order (whither love
Or victory thy royal thoughts did move)
Each was a noble cause, and nothing less,   85
Than the design, has been the great success:
Which foreign kings, and emperors esteem
The second honour to their diadem.
Had thy great destiny but given thee skill,
To know as well, as power to act her will,   90
That from those kings, who then thy captives were,
In after-times should spring a royal pair
Who should possess all that thy mighty power,
Or thy desires more mighty, did devour;
To whom their better Fate reserves whate'er   95
The victor hopes for, or the vanquished fear;
That blood, which thou and thy great-grandsire shed,

52 **Atlas**: a giant who supports the heavens on his shoulders in Greek mythology 56 **prevent**: anticipate 67–8 all great leaders 70 **Homer**: a Greek poet (fl. 750 BC) 77–8 Edward III of England and his son the Black Prince 79–81 this is a reference to Queen Philippa, wife of Edward III. Philippa captured David II of Scotland ('one captive king') at the battle of Neville's Cross. Bellona (the surname of Minerva) is the goddess of war 83 **Order**: the Order of the Garter 91–2 Charles I was a descendent of David II 97 a reference to Edward III and his grandfather Edward I

COOPER'S HILL: 2 **Parnassus**: a Greek mountain sacred to Apollo 3 **Helicon**: a mountain sacred to the Muses 39 **Windsor**: a town in Berkshire, where, at Windsor Castle, Edward III founded the Order of the Garter 39–40 Harmony was born from the union of Mars (god of war) and Venus (goddess of love)

And all that since these sister nations bled,
Had been unspilt, had happy Edward known
That all the blood he spilt, had been his own.   100
When he that patron chose, in whom are joined
Soldier and martyr, and his arms confined
Within the azure circle, he did seem
But to foretell, and prophesy of him,
Who to his realms that azure round hath joined,   105
Which Nature for their bound at first designed.
That bound, which to the world's extremest ends,
Endless itself, its liquid arms extends;
Nor doth he need those emblems which we paint,
But is himself the soldier and the saint.   110
Here should my wonder dwell, and here my praise,
But my fixed thoughts my wand'ring eye betrays,
Viewing a neighbouring hill, whose top of late
A chapel crowned, till in the common fate,
The adjoining abbey fell: (may no such storm   115
Fall on our times, where ruin must reform).
Tell me (my Muse) what monstrous dire offence,
What crime could any Christian king incense
To such a rage? Was't luxury, or lust?
Was he so temperate, so chaste, so just?   120
Were these their crimes? They were his own much
     more:
But wealth is crime enough to him that's poor,
Who having spent the treasures of his crown,
Condemns their luxury to feed his own.
And yet this act, to varnish o'er the shame   125
Of sacrilege, must bear devotion's name.
No crime so bold, but would be understood
A reäl, or at least a seeming good.
Who fears not to do ill, yet fears the name,
And free from conscience, is a slave to fame.   130
Thus he the church at once protects, and spoils:
But princes' swords are sharper than their styles.
And thus to th'ages past he makes amends,
Their charity destroys, their faith defends.
Then did Religion in a lazy cell,   135
In empty, airy contemplations dwell;
And like the block, unmovèd lay: but ours,
As much too active, like the stork devours.
Is there no temperate region can be known,
Betwixt their frigid, and our torrid zone?   140
Could we not wake from that lethargic dream,
But to be restless in a worse extreme?
And for that lethargy was there no cure,
But to be cast into a calenture?
Can knowledge have no bound, but must advance   145
So far, to make us wish for ignorance?
And rather in the dark to grope our way,
Than led by a false guide to err by day?

Who sees these dismal heaps, but would demand
What barbarous invader sacked the land?   150
But when he hears, no Goth, no Turk did bring
This desolation, but a Christian king;
When nothing, but the name of Zeal, appears
'Twixt our best actions and the worst of theirs,
What does he think our sacrilege would spare,   155
When such th'effects of our devotions are?
Parting from thence 'twixt anger, shame, and fear,
Those for what's past, and this for what's too near:
My eye descending from the hill, surveys
Where Thames amongst the wanton valleys strays.   160
Thames, the most loved of all the ocean's sons,
By his old sire to his embraces runs,
Hasting to pay his tribute to the sea,
Like mortal life to meet eternity.
Though with those streams he no resemblance hold,
Whose foam is amber, and their gravel gold;   166
His genuine, and less guilty wealth t'explore,
Search not his bottom, but survey his shore;
O'er which he kindly spreads his spacious wing,
And hatches plenty for th'ensuing spring.   170
Nor then destroys it with too fond a stay,
Like mothers which their infants overlay.
Nor with a sudden and impetuous wave,
Like prófuse kings, resumes the wealth he gave.
No unexpected inundations spoil   175
The mower's hopes, nor mock the ploughman's toil:
But god-like his unwearied bounty flows;
First loves to do, then loves the good he does.
Nor are his blessings to his banks confined,
But free, and common, as the sea or wind;   180
When he to boast, or to disperse his stores
Full of the tributes of his grateful shores,
Visits the world, and in his flying towers
Brings home to us, and makes both Indies ours;
Finds wealth where 'tis, bestows it where it wants   185
Cities in deserts, woods in cities plants.
So that to us no thing, no place is strange,
While his fair bosom is the world's exchange.
Oh, could I flow like thee, and make thy stream
My great example, as it is my theme!   190
Though deep, yet clear, though gentle, yet not dull,
Strong without rage, without o'erflowing full.
Heaven her Eridanus no more shall boast,
Whose fame in thine, like lesser currents lost,
Thy nobler streams shall visit Jove's abodes,   195
To shine amongst the stars, and bath the gods.
Here Nature, whether more intent to please
Us or herself, with strange varieties
(For things of wonder give no less delight
To the wise Maker's, than beholder's sight.   200

109–110 Rubens had painted Charles I as St. George 118 **Christian king:** Henry VIII 135–38 a reference to Aesop's fable where King Stork gobbles up the frogs who had called on him to replace King Log 144 **calenture:** tropical fever

157–58 anger at Henry VIII's actions at the Reformation; fear for the future under Cromwell 165–66 the rivers Targus (in Spain) and Pactolus (in Lydia) were famous for their gold-rich sands 183 **flying towers:** tall ships 193 **Eridanus:** The River Po, here representing the Milky Way

Though these delights from several causes move
For so our children, thus our friends we love),
Wisely she knew, the harmony of things,
As well as that of sounds, from discords springs.
Such was the discord, which did first disperse   205
Form, order, beauty through the universe;
While dryness moisture, coldness heat resists,
All that we have, and that we are, subsists.
While the steep horrid roughness of the wood
Strives with the gentle calmness of the flood.   210
Such huge extremes when Nature doth unite,
Wonder from thence results, from thence delight.
The stream is so transparent, pure, and clear,
That had the self-enamoured youth gazed here,
So fatally deceived he had not been,   215
While he the bottom, not his face had seen.
But his proud head the airy mountain hides
Among the clouds; his shoulders, and his sides
A shady mantle clothes; his curlèd brows
Frown on the gentle stream, which calmly flows,   220
While winds and storms his lofty forehead beat:
The common fate of all that's high or great.
Low at his foot a spacious plain is placed,
Between the mountain and the stream embraced:
Which shade and shelter from the hill derives,   225
While the kind river wealth and beauty gives;
And in the mixture of all these appears
Variety, which all the rest endears.
This scene had some bold Greek, or British bard
Beheld of old, what stories had we heard,   230
Of fairies, satyrs, and the nymphs their dames,
Their feasts, their revels, and their amorous flames:
'Tis still the same, although their airy shape
All but a quick poetic sight escape.
There Faunus and Sylvanus keep their courts,   235
And thither all the hornèd host resorts,
To graze the ranker mead, that noble herd
On whose sublime and shady fronts is reared
Nature's great masterpiece; to show how soon
Great things are made, but sooner are undone.   240
Here have I seen the king, when great affairs
Give leave to slacken, and unbend his cares,
Attended to the chase by all the flower
Of youth, whose hopes a nobler prey devour:
Pleasure with praise, and danger, they would buy,   245
And wish a foe that would not only fly.
The stag now conscious of his fatal growth,
At once indulgent to his fear and sloth,
To some dark covert his retreat had made,
Where nor man's eye. nor heaven's should invade   250
His soft repose; when th'unexpected sound
Of dogs, and men, his wakeful ear doth wound.
Roused with the noise, he scarce believes his ear,

Willing to think th'illusions of his fear
Had given this false alarm, but straight his view   255
Confirms, that more than all he fears is true.
Betrayed in all his strengths, the wood beset,
All instruments, all arts of ruin met;
He calls to mind his strength, and then his speed,
His wingèd heels, and then his armèd head;   260
With these t'avoid, with that his fate to meet:
But fear prevails, and bids him trust his feet.
So fast he flies, that his reviewing eye
Has lost the chasers, and his ear the cry;
Exulting, till he finds, their nobler sense   265
Their disproportioned speed does recompense.
Then curses his conspiring feet, whose scent
Betrays that safety which their swiftness lent.
Then tries his friends, among the baser herd,
Where he so lately was obeyed, and feared,   270
His safety seeks: the herd, unkindly wise,
Or chases him from thence, or from him flies.
Like a declining statesman, left forlorn
To his friends' pity, and pursuers' scorn,
With shame remembers, while himself was one   275
Of the same herd, himself the same had done.
Thence to the coverts, and the conscious groves,
The scenes of his past triumphs, and his loves;
Sadly surveying where he ranged alone
Prince of the soil, and all the herd his own;   280
And like a bold knight errant did proclaim
Combat to all, and bore away the dame;
And taught the woods to echo to the stream
His dreadful challenge, and his clashing beam.
Yet faintly now declines the fatal strife;   285
So much his love was dearer than his life.
Now every leaf, and every moving breath
Presents a foe, and every foe a death.
Wearied, forsaken, and pursued, at last
All safety in despair of safety placed,   290
Courage he thence resumes, resolved to bear
All their assaults, since 'tis in vain to fear.
And now too late he wishes for the fight
That strength he wasted in ignoble flight:
But when he sees the eager chase renewed,   295
Himself by dogs, the dogs by men pursued:
He straight revokes his bold resolve, and more
Repents his courage, than his fear before;
Finds that uncertain ways unsafest are,
And doubt a greater mischief than despair.   300
Then to the stream, when neither friends, nor force,
Nor speed, nor art avail, he shapes his course;
Thinks not their rage so desperate t'assay
An element more merciless than they.
But fearless they pursue, nor can the flood   305
Quench their dire thirst; alas, they thirst for blood.
So towards a ship the oar-finned galleys ply,

235 **Faunus and Sylvanus:** Faunus was the god of fields and Sylvanus
is a spirit of the woods

284 **beam:** trunk of the antlers

Which wanting sea to ride, or wind to fly,
Stands but to fall revenged on those that dare
Tempt the last fury of extreme despair. 310
So fares the stag among th'enragèd hounds,
Repels their force, and wounds returns for wounds.
And as a hero, whom his baser foes
In troops surround, now these assails, now those,
Though prodigal of life, disdains to die 315
By common hands; but if he can descry
Some nobler foe's approach, to him he calls,
And begs his fate, and then contented falls.
So when the king a mortal shaft lets fly
From his unerring hand, then glad to die, 320
Proud of the wound, to it resigns his blood,
And stains the crystal with a purple flood.
This a more innocent, and happy chase,
Than when of old, but in the self-same place,
Fair liberty pursued, and meant a prey 325
To lawless power, here turned, and stood at bay.
When in that remedy all hope was placed
Which was, or should have been at least, the last.
Here was that charter sealed, wherein the crown
All marks of arbitrary power lays down: 330
Tyrant and slave, those names of hate and fear,
The happier style of king and subject bear:
Happy, when both to the same centre move,
When kings give liberty, and subjects love.
Therefore not long in force this charter stood; 335
Wanting that seal, it must be sealed in blood.
The subjects armed, the more their princes gave,
Th'advantage only took the more to crave.
Till kings by giving, give themselves away,
And even that power, that should deny, betray. 340
'Who gives constrained, but his own fear reviles
Not thanked, but scorned; nor are they gifts, but
    spoils.'
Thus kings, by grasping more than they could hold,
First made their subjects by oppression bold:
And popular sway, by forcing kings to give 345
More than was fit for subjects to receive,
Ran to the same extremes; and one excess
Made both, by striving to be greater, less.
When a calm river raised with sudden rains,
Or snows dissolved, o'erflows th'adjoining plains, 350
The husbandmen with high-raised banks secure
Their greedy hopes, and this he can endure.
But if with bays and dams they strive to force
His channel to a new, or narrow course;
No longer then within his banks he dwells, 355
First to a torrent, then a deluge swells:
Stronger, and fiercer by restraint he roars,
And knows no bound, but makes his power his shores.

329 **charter:** King John's Magna Carta of 1215, given at Runnymede, the place of the hunt

ABRAHAM COWLEY

THE WISH

WELL then! I now do plainly see
This busy world and I shall ne'er agree.
The very honey of all earthly joy
Does of all meats the soonest cloy;
    And they, methinks, deserve my pity 5
Who for it can endure the stings,
The crowd, and buzz, and murmurings,
    Of this great hive, the city.

Ah, yet, ere I descend to the grave,
May I a small house and large garden have; 10
And a few friends, and many books, both true,
Both wise, and both delightful too!
    And since Love ne'er will from me flee,
A mistress moderately fair,
And good as guardian angels are, 15
    Only beloved and loving me.

O fountains! when in you shall I
Myself, eased of unpeaceful thoughts, espy?
O fields! O woods! when, when shall I be made
The happy tenant of your shade? 20
    Here's the spring-head of Pleasure's flood:
Here's wealthy Nature's treasury,
Where all the riches lie that she
    Has coined and stamped for good.

Pride and ambition here 25
Only in far-fetched metaphors appear;
Here nought but winds can hurtful murmurs scatter,
And nought but Echo flatter.
    The gods, when they descended, hither
From heaven did always choose their way; 30
And therefore we may boldly say
    That 'tis the way too thither.

How happy here should I
And one dear She live, and embracing die!
She who is all the world, and can exclude, 35
In deserts, solitude.
    I should have then this only fear:
Lest men, when they my pleasures see,
Should hither throng to live like me,
    And so make a city here. 40

THE WISH: 9 **ere:** before

THE CHANGE

LOVE in her sunny eyes does basking play;
Love walks the pleasant mazes of her hair;
Love does on both her lips forever stray;
And sows and reaps a thousand kisses there.
In all her outward parts Love's always seen;   5
    But, oh, he never went within.

Within Love's foes, his greatest foes abide,
    Malice, Inconstancy, and Pride.
So the Earth's face, trees, herbs, and flowers do dress,
    With other beauties numberless: 10
But at the centre darkness is, and Hell;
There wicked spirits, and there the damnèd dwell.

With me, alas, quite contrary it fares;
Darkness and death lies in my weeping eyes,
Despair and paleness in my face appears,   15
And grief and fear, Love's greatest enemies;
But like the Persian tyrant, Love within
    Keeps his proud court, and ne'er is seen.

Oh, take my heart, and by that means you'll prove
    Within too stored enough of Love: 20
Give me but yours, I'll by that change so thrive,
    That Love in all my parts shall live.
So powerful is this change, it render can,
My outside woman, and your inside man.

DRINKING

THE thirsty Earth soaks up the rain,
And drinks, and gapes for drink again.
The plants suck in the earth, and are
With constant drinking fresh and fair.
The sea itself, which one would think   5
Should have but little need of drink,
Drinks ten thousand rivers up,
So filled that they o'erflow the cup.
The busy Sun (and one would guess
By 's sunken fiery face no less)   10
Drinks up the sea, and when h'as done,
The Moon and stars drink up the Sun.
They drink and dance by their own light,
The drink and revel all the night.
Nothing in Nature's sober found,   15
But an eternal health goes round.
Fill up the bowl then, fill it high,
Fill all the glasses there, for why
Should every creature drink but I,
Why, man of morals, tell me why?   20

RICHARD LOVELACE

TO ALTHEA, FROM PRISON

WHEN Love with unconfinèd wings
    Hovers within my gates,
And my divine Althea brings
    To whisper at the grates;
When I lie tangled in her hair   5
    And fettered to her eye,
The birds that wanton in the air
    Know no such liberty.

When flowing cups run swiftly round
    With no allaying Thames,   10
Our careless heads with roses crowned,
    Our hearts with loyal flames;
When thirsty grief in wine we steep,
    When healths and draughts go free,
Fishes that tipple in the deep   15
    Know no such liberty.

When linnet-like confinèd, I
    With shriller throat shall sing
The sweetness, mercy, majesty
    And glories of my king;   20
When I shall voice aloud how good
    He is, how great should be,
Enlargèd winds that curl the flood
    Know no such liberty.

Stone walls do not a prison make,   25
    Nor iron bars a cage;
Minds innocent and quiet take
    That for an hermitage:
If I have freedom in my love
    And in my soul am free,   30
Angels alone that soar above
    Enjoy such liberty.

TO ALTHEA, FROM PRISON: 10 **no allaying Thames:** There is no water in the wine 17 **linnet-like confinèd:** like caged finches

TO LUCASTA, GOING BEYOND THE SEAS

IF to be absent were to be
    Away from thee;
    Or that when I am gone
    You or I were alone;
Then, my Lucasta, might I crave   5
Pity from the blustering wind, or swallowing wave.

But I'll not sigh one blast or gale
    To swell my sail,
  Or pay a tear to 'suage
    The foaming blue-god's rage;   10
For whether he will let me pass
Or no, I'm still as happy as I was.

Though seas and land betwixt us both,
    Our faith and troth,
  Like separated souls,
    All time and space controls: 15
Above the highest sphere we meet
Unseen, unknown, and greet as angels greet.

So then we do anticipate
    Our after-fate,
  And are alive i' the skies,   20
  If thus our lips and eyes
Can speak like spirits unconfined
In Heaven, their earthy bodies left behind.

TO LUCASTA, GOING BEYOND THE SEAS: 9 **'suage:** swage, pacify 10 **blue-god:** Neptune, god of the sea

TO LUCASTA, GOING TO THE WARS

TELL me not, sweet, I am unkind,
  That from the nunnery
Of thy chaste breast and quiet mind
  To war and arms I fly.

True, a new mistress now I chase,   5
  The first foe in the field;
And with a stronger faith embrace
  A sword, a horse, a shield.

Yet this inconstancy is such
  As you too shall adore;   10
I could not love thee, dear, so much,
  Loved I not honour more.

TO LUCASTA, GOING TO THE WARS: 5 **new mistress:** honour

ANDREW MARVELL

THE DEFINITION OF LOVE

MY love is of a birth as rare
As 'tis for object strange and high:
It was begotten by Despair
Upon Impossibility.

Magnanimous Despair alone   5
Could show me so divine a thing,
Where feeble Hope could ne'er have flown
But vainly flapped its tinsel wing.

And yet I quickly might arrive
Where my extended soul is fixed,   10
But Fate does iron wedges drive,
And always crowds itself betwixt.

For Fate with jealous eye does see.
Two perfect loves; nor lets them close:
Their union would her ruin be,   15
And her tyrannic pow'r depose.

And therefore her decrees of steel
Us as the distant poles have placed,
(Though Love's whole world on us doth wheel)
Not by themselves to be embraced.   20

Unless the giddy Heaven fall,
And Earth some new convulsion tear;
And, us to join, the world should all
Be cramped into a planisphere.

As lines so Loves oblique may well   25
Themselves in every angle greet:
But ours so truly parallel,
Though infinite can never meet.

Therefore the love which us doth bind,
But Fate so enviously debars,   30
Is the conjunction of the mind,
And opposition of the stars.

THE DEFINITION OF LOVE: 10 **extended soul:** his soul has left him and attached itself to his lover 14 **close:** unite 24 **planisphere:** a polar projection of the celestial sphere, as in a map or chart

TO HIS COY MISTRESS

HAD we but world enough, and time,
This coyness, Lady, were no crime.
We would sit down, and think which way
To walk, and pass our long love's day.
Thou by the Indian Ganges side.   5
Should'st rubies find: I by the tide
Of Humber would complain. I would
Love you ten years before the Flood:
And you should if you please refuse
Till the conversion of the Jews.   10
My vegetable love should grow
Vaster then empires, and more slow.
An hundred years should go to praise
Thine eyes, and on thy forehead gaze.
Two hundred to adore each breast.   15
But thirty thousand to the rest.
An age at least to every part,
And the last age should show your heart.
For, Lady, you deserve this state;
Nor would I love at lower rate.   20

But at my back I always hear
Time's wingèd chariot hurrying near:
  And yonder all before us lie
  Deserts of vast eternity.
Thy beauty shall no more be found;   25
Nor, in thy marble vault, shall sound
My echoing song: then worms shall try
That long-preserved virginity:
And your quaint honour turn to dust;
And into ashes all my lust.   30
The grave's a fine and private place,
But none I think do there embrace.
    Now therefore, while the youthful hue
Sits on thy skin like morning glue,
And while thy willing soul transpires   35
At every pore with instant fires,
Now let us sport us while we may;
And now, like am'rous birds of prey,
Rather at once our time devour,
Than languish in his slow-chapped pow'r.   40
Let us roll all our strength, and all
Our sweetness, up into one ball:
And tear our pleasures with rough strife,
Thorough the iron gates of life.
Thus, though we cannot make our Sun   45
Stand still, yet we will make him run.

TO HIS COY MISTRESS: 5–8 the river Humber, in Hull, is unfavourably
compared with the Ganges 19 **state:** status, dignified position 40 **slow-
chapped:** literally 'slow-jawed'. Time slowly consumes the world.

AN HORATIAN ODE UPON CROMWELL'S
RETURN FROM IRELAND

THE forward youth that would appear
Must now forsake his Muses dear,
  Nor in the shadows sing
  His numbers languishing.
'Tis time to leave the books in dust,   5
And oil th'unusèd armours rust:
  Removing from the wall
  The corslet of the hall.
So restless Cromwell could not cease
In the inglorious arts of peace,   10
  But through advent'rous war
  Urged his active star.
And, like the three-forked lightning, first
Breaking the clouds where it was nursed,
  Did through his own side   15
  His fiery way divide.
For 'tis all one to Courage high
The emulous or enemy;
  And with such to enclose
  Is more than to oppose.   20

AN HORATIAN ODE UPON CROMWELL'S RETURN FROM IRELAND: 8 **corslet:**
body-covering armour

Then burning through the air he went,
And palaces and temples rent:
  And Caesar's head at last
  Did through his laurels blast.
'Tis madness to resist or blame   25
The force of angry Heaven's flame:
  And, if we would speak true,
  Much to the man is due.
Who, from his private gardens, where
He lived reservèd and austere,   30
  As if his highest plot
  To plant the bergamot,
Could by industrious valour climb
To ruin the great work of Time,
  And cast the Kingdom old   35
  Into another mould.
Though Justice against Fate complain,
And plead the ancient rights in vain:
  But those do hold or break
  As men are strong or weak.   40
Nature that hateth emptiness,
Allows of penetration less:
  And therefore must make room.
  Where greater spirits come.
What field of all the civil wars,   45
Where his were not the deepest scars?
  And Hampton shows what part
  He had of wiser art.
Where, twining subtle fears with hope,
He wove a net of such a scope   50
  That Charles himself might chase
  To Car'sbrook's narrow case.
That thence the royal actor born
The tragic scaffold might adorn
  While round the armèd bands   55
  Did clap their bloody hands.
He nothing common did or mean
Upon that memorable scene:
  But with his keener eye
  The axe's edge did try: 60
Nor called the gods with vulgar spite
To vindicate his helpless right,
  But bowed his comely head,
  Down as upon a bed.
This was that memorable hour   65
Which first assured the forcèd pow'r.
  So when they did design
  The Capitol's first line,
A bleeding head where they begun,
Did fright the architects to run;   70
  And yet in that the state
  Foresaw its happy fate.

23–24 laurel allegedly guarded against lightning, which is why it was
used for crowns. For Caesar read Charles I, whose laurels did not
protect his head from being taken off 32 **bergamot:** the prince
pear 47 **Hampton:** Hampton Court where Charles was imprisoned
before his execution 66 **forcèd:** gained through force 67–72 when
laying the foundations for the Temple of Jupiter, the Romans
found a severed head in the ground. This terrifying find came to
be read as an omen that Rome would rule the world

And now the Irish are ashamed
To see themselves in one year tamed:
 So much one man can do,   75
 That does both act and know.
They can affirm his praises best,
And have, though overcome, confessed
 How good he is, how just,
 And fit for highest trust: 80
Nor yet grown stiffer with command,
But still in the republic's hand:
 How fit he is to sway
 That can so well obey.
He to the common feet presents   85
A kingdom, for his first year's rents:
 And, what he may, forbears
 His fame to make it theirs:
And has his sword and spoils ungirt,
To lay them at the public's skirt.   90
 So when the falcon high
 Falls heavy from the sky,
She, having killed no more does search,
But on the next green bough to perch;
 Where, when he first does lure, 95
 The falc'ner has her sure.
What may not then our isle presume
While victory his crest does plume!
 What may not others fear
 If thus he crown each year!   100
A Caesar he ere long to Gaul,
To Italy an Hannibal,
 And to all states not free
 Shall climacteric be.
The Pict no shelter now shall find 105
Within his parti-coloured mind;
 But from this valour sad
 Shrink underneath the plaid:
Happy if in the tufted brake
The English hunter him mistake; 110
 Nor lay his hounds in near
 The Caledonian deer.
But thou the war's and Fortune's son
March indefatigably on;
 And for the last effect   115
 Still keep thy sword erect:
Besides the force it has to fright
The spirits of the shady night,
 The same arts that did gain
 A pow'r must it maintain.   120

73–74 Cromwell's Irish campaign 91–96 the falconer calls back the falcon after a kill, just as Parliament recalls Cromwell 101 Caesar conquered Gaul 102 Hannibal conquered Italy 104 **climacteric:** critical period in human life 105–6 early inhabitants of Scotland who painted their bodies and faces 112 **Caledonian:** Scottish

THE PICTURE OF LITTLE T.C.
IN A PROSPECT OF FLOWERS

SEE with what simplicity
This nymph begins her golden days!
In the green grass she loves to lie,
And there with her fair aspect tames
The wilder flow'rs, and gives them names: 5
But only with the roses plays;
   And them does tell
What colour best becomes them, and what smell.

Who can foretell for what high cause
This darling of the gods was born! 10
Yet this is she whose chaster laws
The wanton Love shall one day fear,
And, under her command severe,
See his bow broke and ensigns torn.
   Happy, who can   15
Appease this virtuous enemy of man!

Oh, then, let me in time compound,
And parley with those conquering eyes;
Ere they have tried their force to wound,
Ere, with their glancing wheels, they drive 20
In triumph over hearts that strive,
And them that yield but more despise.
   Let me be laid,
Where I may see thy glories from some shade.

Meantime, whilst every verdant thing 25
Itself does at thy beauty charm,
Reform the errors of the spring;
Make that the tulips may have share
Of sweetness, seeing they are fair;
And roses of their thorns disarm: 30
   But most procure
That violets may a longer age endure.

But, O young beauty of the woods,
Whom Nature courts with fruits and flow'rs,
Gather the flow'rs, but spare the buds; 35
Lest Flora angry at thy crime,
To kill her infants in their prime,
Do quickly make th'example yours;
   And, ere we see,
Nip in the blossom all our hopes and thee. 40

THE PICTURE OF LITTLE T.C. IN A PROSPECT OF FLOWERS: 2 **ensigns:** flags 25 **verdant:** with a green hue 35 **Flora:** goddess of flowers in Roman mythology

From UPON APPLETON HOUSE

WHEN in the east the morning ray
Hangs out the colours of the day,
The bee through these known alleys hums,
Beating the Dian with its drums.
Then flow'rs their drowsy eyelids raise, 5

Their silken ensigns each displays,
And dries its pan yet dank with dew,
And fills its flask with odours new.

These, as their governor goes by,
In fragrant volleys they let fly;　　　　　10
And to salute their governess
Again as great a charge they press:
None for the virgin nymph; for she
Seems with the flow'rs a flow'r to be.
And think so still! though not compare　　15
With breath so sweet, or cheek so fair.

Well shot, ye Fireman! Oh, how sweet,
And round your equal fires do meet;
Whose shrill report no ear can tell,
But echoes to the eye and smell.　　　　20
See how the flow'rs, as at parade,
Under their colours stand displayed:
Each regiment in order grows,
That of the tulip pink and rose.

But when the vigilant patrol　　　　　25
Of stars walks round about the pole,
Their leaves, that to the stalks are curled,
Seem to their staves the ensigns furled.
Then in some flow'r's belovèd hut
Each bee as sentinel is shut;　　　　　30
And sleeps so too: but, if once stirred,
She runs you through, or asks the word.

O Thou, that dear and happy isle
The garden of the world erewhile,
Thou paradise of four seas,　　　　　35
Which heaven planted us to please,
But, to exclude the world, did guard
With wat'ry if not flaming sword;
What luckless apple did we taste,
To make us mortal, and the waste.　　　40

Unhappy! shall we never more
That sweet militia restore,
When gardens only had their tow'rs,
And all the garrisons were flow'rs,
When roses only arms might bear,　　　45
And men did rosy garlands wear?
Tulips, in several colours barred,
Were then the Switzers of our guard.

The gardener had the soldier's place,
And his more gentle forts did trace.　　50
The nursery of all things green
Was then the only magazine.
The winter quarters were the stoves,
Where he the tender plants removes.
But war all this doth overgrow:　　　55
We ord'nance plant and powder sow.

UPON APPLETON HOUSE: 4 **Dian**: trumpet call or drumroll delivered at dawn 6 **ensigns**: flags 7–8 'pan' and 'flask' are also references to the priming pan of a musket and a powder flask 10 **volleys**: as in gunfire 25–35 stars in the constellations of the Great and Lesser Bear are known as the 'guards of the pole' 39 **luckless apple**: the forbidden fruit that Adam was tempted by Eve to eat 48 **Switzers**: tulips with a red and yellow hue were named Swissers because of their similarity in colour to the uniforms of the Vatican Swiss Guard 52 **magazine**: also a storehouse for ammunition 56 **ord'nance**: ordinance

THE GARDEN

How vainly men themselves amaze
To win the palm, the oak, or bays;
And their uncessant labours see
Crowned from some single herb or tree,
Whose short and narrow-vergèd shade　　5
Does prudently their toils upbraid;
While all flow'rs and all trees do close
To weave the garlands of repose.

Fair Quiet, have I found thee here,
And Innocence thy sister dear!　　　　10
Mistaken long, I sought you then
In busie companies of men.
Your sacred plants, if here below,
Only among the plants will grow.
Society is all but rude,　　　　　　15
To this delicious solitude.

No white nor red was ever seen
So am'rous as this lovely green.
Fond lovers, cruel as their flame,
Cut in these trees their mistress' name.　　20
Little, alas, they know, or heed,
How far these beauties hers exceed!
Fair Trees! whereso'er you barks I wound,
No name shall but your own be found.

When we have run our passion's heat,　　25
Love hither makes his best retreat.
The gods, that mortal beauty chase,
Still in a tree did end their race.
Apollo hunted Daphne so,
Only that she might laurel grow.　　　30
And Pan did after Syrinx speed,
Not as a nymph, but for a reed.

What wondrous life in this I lead!
Ripe apples drop about my head;
The luscious clusters of the vine　　　35
Upon my mouth do crush their wine;
The nectarine, and curious peach,
Into my hands themselves do reach;
Stumbling on melons, as I pass,
Ensnared with flow'rs, I fall on grass.　　40

Meanwhile the mind, from pleasure less,
Withdraws into its happiness:
The mind, that ocean where each kind
Does straight its own resemblance find;
Yet it creates, transcending these,　　　　45
Far other worlds, and other seas;
Annihilating all that's made
To a green thought in a green shade.

Here at the fountain's sliding foot,
Or at some fruit-tree's mossy root,　　　　50
Casting the body's vest aside,
My soul into the boughs does glide:
There like a bird it sits, and sings,
Then whets, and combs its silver wings;
And, till prepared for longer flight,　　　　55
Waves in its plumes the various light.

Such was that happy garden-state,
While man there walked without a mate:
After a place so pure, and sweet,
What other help could yet be meet!　　　　60
But 'twas beyond a mortal's share
To wander solitary there:
Two paradises 'twere in one
To live in paradise alone.

How well the skilful gard'ner drew　　　　65
Of flow'rs and herbs this dial new;
Where from above the milder Sun
Does through a fragrant zodiac run;
And, as it works, th'industrious bee
Computes its time as well as we.　　　　70
How could such sweet and wholesome hours
Be reckoned but with herbs and flow'rs!

THE GARDEN: 2 The palm for military honours, the oak for civic honours and the bay for poetry 7 **close:** unite 15 **To:** compared to 29–32 Apollo pursued Daphne until she turned into a laurel, and Pan chased Syrinx until she became a reed 54 **whets:** grooms 56–60 God created Eve as a help meet for Adam in the Garden of Eden 66 **dial:** the Garden is imagined as a sundial

THE MOWER AGAINST GARDENS

Luxurious Man, to bring his vice in use,
　　Did after him the world seduce:
And from the fields the flow'rs and plants allure,
　　Where Nature was most plain and pure.
He first enclosed within the garden's square　　　　5
　　A dead and standing pool of air:
And a more luscious earth for them did knead,
　　Which stupefied them while it fed.
The pink grew then as double as his mind;
　　The nutriment did change the kind.　　　　10
With strange perfúmes he did the roses taint.
　　And flow'rs themselves were taught to paint.

The tulip, white, did for complexion seek;
　　And learned to interline its cheek:
Its onion root they then so high did hold,　　　　15
　　That one was for a meadow sold.
Another world was searched, though oceans new,
　　To find the Marvel Of Peru.
And yet these rarities might be allowed,
　　To man, that sov'reign thing and proud;　　　　20
Had he not dealt between the bark and tree,
　　Forbidden mixtures there to see.
No plant now knew the stock from which it came;
　　He grafts upon the wild the tame:
That the uncertain and adult'rate fruit　　　　25
　　Might put the palate in dispute.
His green seraglio has its eunuchs too;
　　Lest any tyrant him outdo.
And in the cherry he does Nature vex,
　　To procreate without a sex.　　　　30
'Tis all enforced; the fountain and the grot;
　　While the sweet fields do lie forgot:
Where willing Nature does to all dispense
　　A wild and fragrant innocence:
And fauns and fairies do the meadows till,　　　　35
　　More by their presence than their skill.
Their statues polished by some ancient hand,
　　May to adorn the gardens stand:
But howsoe'er the figures do excel,
　　The gods themselves with us do dwell.　　　　40

THE MOWER AGAINST GARDENS: 15–16 **they . . . sold:** a reference to the high price commanded by Dutch tulips during the 17th century 17 **Marvel of Peru:** a flower found in South America (*Mirabilis Jalapa*) 39 **howsoe'er:** howsoever

THE MOWER TO THE GLOWWORMS

Ye living lamps, by whose dear light
The nightingale does sit so late,
And studying all the summer night,
Her matchless songs does meditate;

Ye country comets, that portend　　　　5
No war, nor prince's funeral,
Shining unto no higher end
Than to preságe the grasses' fall;

Ye glow-worms, whose officious flame
To wand'ring mowers shows the way,　　　　10
That in the night have lost their aim,
And after foolish fires do stray;

Your courteous lights in vain you waste,
Since Juliana here is come,
For she my mind hath so displaced　　　　15
That I shall never find my home.

THE MOWER TO THE GLOWWORMS: 12 **foolish fires:** will-o'-the-wisps

BERMUDAS

WHERE the remote Bermudas ride
In th'ocean's bosom unespied,
From a small boat, that rowed along,
The list'ning winds received this song.
   'What should we do but sing his praise   5
That led us through the wat'ry maze,
Unto an isle so long unknown,
And yet far kinder than our own?
Where he the huge sea-monsters wracks,
That lift the deep upon their backs.   10
He lands us on a grassy stage;
Safe from the storms, and prelate's rage.
He gave us this eternal spring,
Which here enamels every thing;
And sends the fowls to us in care,   15
On daily visits through the air,
He hangs in shades the orange bright,
Like golden lamps in a green night.
And does in the pom'granates close,
Jewels more rich than Ormus shows.   20
He makes the figs our mouths to meet;
And throws the melons at our feet.
But apples plants of such a price,
No tree could ever bear them twice.
With cedars, chosen by his hand,   25
From Lebanon, he stores the land.
And makes the hollow seas, that roar,
Proclaim the ambergris on shore.
He cast (of which we rather boast)
The Gospel's pearl upon our coast.   30
And in these rocks for us did frame
A temple, where to sound his name.
Oh, let our voice his praise exalt,
Till it arrive at Heaven's vault:
Which thence (perhaps) rebounding, may   35
Echo beyond the Mexique Bay.'
   Thus sung they, in the English boat,
An holy and a cheerful note,
And all the way, to guide their chime,
With falling oars they kept the time.   40

BERMUDAS: 20 **Ormus:** Hormuz in the Persian Gulf was famous for pearl fishing 25–6 Lebanon was famous for cedars 28 **ambergris:** secretion from the intestines of the sperm whale, which can be found floating in tropical seas

HENRY VAUGHAN

THE RETREAT

HAPPY those early days, when I
Shined in my angel-infancy!
Before I understood this place
Appointed for my second race,
Or taught my soul to fancy aught   5
But a white celestial thought;
When yet I had not walked above
A mile or two from my first love,
And looking back, at that short space,
Could see a glimpse of his bright face;   10
When on some gilded cloud, or flow'r,
My gazing soul would dwell an hour,
And in those weaker glories spy
Some shadows of eternity;
Before I taught my tongue to wound   15
My conscience with a sinful sound,
Or had the black art to dispense
A several sin to every sense,
But felt through all this fleshly dress
Bright shoots of everlastingness.   20

Oh, how I long to travel back,
And tread again that ancient track!
That I might once more reach that plain
Where first I left my glorious train;
From whence th'enlightened spirit sees   25
That shady city of palm-trees.
But ah! my soul with too much stay
Is drunk, and staggers in the way.
Some men a forward motion love,
But I by backward steps would move,   30
And when this dust falls to the urn
In that state I came, return.

THE RETREAT: 4 **second race:** a suggestion that the poet's persona had pre-existed 18 **several:** different

'THEY ARE ALL GONE INTO THE WORLD OF LIGHT!'

THEY are all gone into the world of light!
   And I alone sit lingering here;
Their very memory is fair and bright,
   And my sad thoughts doth clear.

It glows and glitters in my cloudy breast   5
   Like stars upon some gloomy grove,
Or those faint beams in which this hill is dressed,
   After the sun's remove.

I see them walking in an air of glory,
   Whose light doth trample on my days: 10
My days, which are at best but dull and hoary,
   Mere glimmering and decays.

O holy Hope! and high Humility,
   High as the heavens above!
These are your walks, and you have showed them me,
   To kindle my cold love.   16

Dear beauteous Death! the jewel of the Just,
   Shining nowhere but in the dark;
What mysteries do lie beyond thy dust,
   Could man outlook that mark!   20

He that hath found some fledged bird's nest may
    know,
  At first sight, if the bird be flown;
But what fair well or grove he sings in now,
  That is to him unknown.

And yet, as angels in some brighter dreams   25
  Call to the soul, when man doth sleep;
So some strange thoughts transcend our wonted
    themes
  And into glory peep.

If a star were confined into a tomb,
  Her captive flames must needs burn there;   30
But when the hand that locked her up gives room,
  She'll shine through all the sphere.

O Father of eternal life, and all
  Created glories under thee!
Resume thy spirit from this world of thrall   35
  Into true liberty.

Either disperse these mists, which blot and fill
  My pérspective still as they pass,
Or else remove Thee hence unto that hill,
  Where I shall need no glass.   40

THE WORLD

I SAW eternity the other night
Like a great ring of pure and endless light,
  All calm as it was bright;
And round beneath it, Time, in hours, days, years,
    Driven by the spheres,   5
Like a vast shadow moved, in which the world
    And all her train were hurled.
The doting lover in his quaintest strain
  Did there complain;
Near him, his lute, his fancy, and his flights   10
  Wit's sour delights;
With gloves and knots, the silly snares of pleasure;
  Yet his dear treasure
All scattered lay, while he his eyes did pour
  Upon a flow'r.   15

The darksome statesman hung with weights and woe,
Like a thick midnight fog, moved there so slow
  He did not stay nor go;
Condemning thoughts, like sad eclipses, scowl
  Upon his soul,   20
And clouds of crying witnesses without
  Pursued him with one shout.
Yet digged the mole, and, lest his ways be found,
  Worked under ground,
Where he did clutch his prey; but One did see   25

  That policy.
Churches and altars fed him, perjuries
  Were gnats and flies;
It rained about him blood and tears, but he
  Drank them as free.   30

The fearful miser on a heap of rust
Sat pining all his life there, did scarce trust
  His own hands with the dust;
Yet would not place one piece above, but lives
  In fear of thieves.   35
Thousands there were as frantic as himself,
  And hugged each one his pelf.
The downright epicure placed heaven in sense
  And scorned pretence;
While others, slipped into a wide excess,   40
  Said little less;
The weaker sort, slight, trivial wares enslave,
  Who think them brave;
And poor despisèd Truth sat counting by
  Their victory.   45

Yet some, who all this while did weep and sing,
And sing and weep, soared up into the ring;
  But most would use no wing.
'Oh, fools,' said I, 'thus to prefer dark night
  Before true light,   50
To live in grots, and caves, and hate the day
  Because it shows the way,
The way which from this dead and dark abode
  Leaps up to God,
A way where you might tread the sun, and be   55
  More bright than he.'
But as I did their madness so discuss,
  One whispered thus,
This ring the Bridegroom did for none provide
  But for his Bride.   60

THE WORLD: 12 **knots:** true-love knots 16–17 In Dante's *Inferno* the Hypocrites wear lead cloaks, which cause them to walk slowly 37 **pelf:** usually pilfered or stolen property 38 **epicure:** someone who enjoys food and drink, a glutton. Alternatively, someone who recognizes no religious motives for conduct

CHILDHOOD

I CANNOT reach it; and my striving eye
Dazzles at it, as at eternity.

  Were now that chronicle alive,
Those white designs which children drive,
And the thoughts of each harmless hour,   5
With their content too in my pow'r,
Quickly would I make my path even,
And by mere playing go to heaven.

Why should men love
A wolf, more than a lamb or dove?   10
Or choose hell-fire and brimstone streams
Before bright stars and God's own beams?
Who kisseth thorns will hurt his face,
But flow'rs do both refresh and grace;
And sweetly living – fie on men! –   15
Are, when dead, medicinal then;
If seeing much should make staid eyes,
And long experience should make wise;
Since all that age doth teach is ill,
Why should I not love childhood still?   20
Why, if I see a rock or shelf,
Shall I from thence cast down myself?
Or by complying with the world,
From the same precipice be hurled?
Those observations are but foul,   25
Which make me wise to lose my soul.

And yet the practice worldlings call
Business, and weighty action all,
Checking the poor child for his play,
But gravely cast themselves away.   30
Dear, harmless age! the short, swift span
Where weeping Virtue parts with man;
Where love without lust dwells, and bends
What way we please without self-ends.

An age of mysteries! which he   35
Must live that would God's face see
Which angels guard, and with it play,
Angels! which foul men drive away.

How do I study now, and scan
Thee more than e'er I studied man,   40
And only see through a long night
Thy edges and thy bordering light!
Oh, for thy centre and midday!
For sure that is the narrow way!

CHILDHOOD: 1–8 the innocence of children with their 'white designs'
brings them closer to God 15 **fie:** for shame

PEACE

My Soul, there is a country
   Far beyond the stars,
Where stands a wingèd sentry
   All skilful in the wars,
There above noise, and danger   5
   Sweet peace sits crowned with smiles,
And one born in a manger
   Commands the beauteous files,
He is thy gracious friend,
   And (O my Soul, awake!)
Did in pure love descend   10
   To die here for thy sake,
If thou canst get but thither,

There grows the flow'r of peace,
The rose that cannot wither,   15
   Thy fortress, and thy ease;
Leave then thy foolish ranges;
   For none can thee secure,
But one, who never changes,
   Thy God, thy life, thy cure.   20

JOHN BUNYAN

'HE THAT IS DOWN NEEDS FEAR NO FALL'

He that is down needs fear no fall,
   He that is low, no pride;
He that is humble ever shall
   Have God to be his guide.

I am content with what I have,   5
   Little be it or much;
And, Lord, contentment still I crave,
   Because thou savest such.

Fullness to such a burden is
   That go on pilgrimage: 10
Here little, and hereafter bliss,
   Is best from age to age.

[From *The Pilgrim's Progress*]

'WHO WOULD TRUE VALOUR SEE'

Who would true valour see,
Let him come hither;
One here will constant be,
Come wind, come weather.
There's no discouragement   5
Shall make him once relent
His first avowed intent,
To be a pilgrim.

Whoso beset him round
With dismal stories   10
Do but themselves confound;
His strength the more is.
No lion can him fright,
He'll with a giant fight,
But he will have a right   15
To be a pilgrim.

Hobgoblin, nor foul fiend,
Can daunt his spirit:
He knows, he at the end
Shall life inherit.   20
Then fancies fly away,
He'll fear not what men say,
He'll labour night and day
To be a pilgrim.

[From *The Pilgrim's Progress*]

JOHN DRYDEN

From ABSALOM AND ACHITOPHEL

IN pious times, ere priestcraft did begin,
Before polygamy was made a sin;
When man on many multiplied his kind,
Ere one to one was cursedly confined;
When Nature prompted, and no law denied,   5
Promiscuous use of concubine and bride;
Then Israel's monarch, after Heaven's own heart,
His vigorous warmth did variously impart
To wives and slaves; and, wide as his command,
Scattered his Maker's image through the land.   10
Michal, of royal blood, the crown did wear,
A soil ungrateful to the tiller's care:
Not so the rest; for several mothers bore
To god-like David several sons before.
But since like slaves his bed they did ascend,   15
No true succession could their seed attend.
Of all this numerous progeny was none
So beautiful, so brave as Absalon:
Whether, inspired by some diviner lust,
His father got him with a greater gust,   20
Or that his conscious destiny made way
By manly beauty to imperial sway.
Early in foreign fields he won renown,
With kings and states allied to Israel's crown;
In peace the thoughts of war he could remove,   25
And seemed as he were only born for love.
Whate'er he did was done with so much ease,
In him alone 'twas natural to please.
His motions all accompanied with grace,
And paradise was opened in his face.   30
With secret joy indulgent David viewed
His youthful image in his son renewed;
To all his wishes nothing he denied,
And made the charming Annabel his bride.
What faults he had (for who from faults is free?)   35
His father could not or he would not see.

Some warm excesses, which the law forbore,
Were cónstrued youth that purged by boiling o'er;
And Amnon's murder, by a specious name,
Was called a just revenge for injured fame.   40
Thus praised and loved the noble youth remained,
While David undisturbed in Sion reigned.
But life can never be sincerely blest:
Heaven punishes the bad, and proves the best.
The Jews, a headstrong, moody, murmuring race   45
As ever tried th'extent and stretch of grace;
God's pampered people whom, debauched with ease,
No king could govern nor no god could please
(Gods they had tried of every shape and size
That godsmiths could produce or priests devise):   50
These Adam-wits, too fortunately free,
Began to dream they wanted liberty;
And when no rule, no precedent was found
Of men by laws less circumscribed and bound,
They led their wild desires to woods and caves,   55
And thought that all but savages were slaves.
They who, when Saul was dead, without a blow,
Made foolish Ishbosheth the crown forgo;
Who banished David did from Hebron bring,
And with a general shout proclaimed him king: 60
Those very Jews, who at their very best
Their humour more than loyalty expressed,
Now wondered why so long they had obeyed
An idol-monarch which their hands had made;
Thought they might ruin him they could create,   65
Or melt him to that golden calf, a state.
But these were random bolts; no formed design
Nor interest made the factious crowd to join,
The sober part of Israel, free from stain,
Well knew the value of a peaceful reign;   70
And, looking backward with a wise affright,
Saw seams of wounds dishonest to the sight;
In contemplation of whose ugly scars
They cursed the memory of civil wars.
The moderate sort of men, thus qualified,   75
Inclined the balance to the better side;
And David's mildness managed it so well,
The bad found no occasion to rebel.

'ABSALOM AND ACHITOPHEL': The failure of Charles II's queen to produce an heir meant that the crown would pass to Charles's Catholic brother, the Duke of York (James II). There were moves to exclude James from the succession and to promote the claim of Charles's illegitimate (but Protestant), son, the Duke of Monmouth. Dryden's satire, published in 1681, explores the issues and personalities of this crisis: **Absalom**: the Duke of Monmouth (1649–85), illegitimate son of Charles II and Lucy Barlow: **Achitophel**: (biblical Ahithopel) Anthony Ashley Cooper, 1st Earl of Shaftesbury (1621–83), prominent in the campaign to exclude the Duke of York from the succession and a supporter of Monmouth; see also note to line 150 below 4 **Ere**: before 7 **Israel's monarch**: Charles II 11 **Michal**: Charles's wife, Catherine of Braganza, who failed to bear children, as Dryden crudely points out in the following line; see also 2 Samuel 6.23: 'Therefore Michal the daughter of Saul had no child unto the day of her death' 20 **gust**: passion, energy 22 **imperial sway**: royal power 29 **all accompanied**: i.e. were all accompanied 34 **Annabel**: Anne, Countess of Buccleuch (1651–1732), wife of Monmouth

39 **Amnon**: possibly Sir John Coventry (d. 1682) MP, who in 1670 dared to ask a question about Charles II's love-life and, at Monmouth's instigation, was subsequently dragged from his coach and viciously (but not fatally) assaulted 42 **Sion**: England 44 **proves**: tries, tests 45 **the Jews**: the English 51–2 **Adam-wits . . . liberty**: cf. Michael to Adam in Milton's *Paradise Lost*: 'know withal,/Since thy original lapse, true liberty/Is lost, which always with right reason dwells/Twinned, and from her hath no dividual being:/Reason in man obscured, or not obeyed,/Immediately inordinate desires,/And upstart passions, catch the government/From reason; and to servitude reduce/Man, Till then free' (12.82–90) 57–8 **Saul . . . Ishbosheth**: Oliver Cromwell and his son Richard 59 **Hebron**: Scotland; Charles had been crowned king of Scots in 1651 66 **golden calf**: an idol fashioned by Aaron for the Israelites, who grew impatient while Moses was on Mount Sinai receiving the Ten Commandments (Exodus 32) 67 **bolts**: shots; a bolt is an arrow for a crossbow 72 **dishonest**: shameful

But when to sin our biased nature leans,
The careful Devil is still at hand with means   80
And providently pimps for ill desires:
The good old cause revived, a plot requires.
Plots, true or false, are necessary things
To raise up commonwealths and ruin kings.
      Th'inhabitants of old Jerusalem   85
Were Jebusites; the town so called from them,
And theirs the native right—
But when the chosen people grew more strong
The rightful cause at length became the wrong;
And every loss the men of Jebus bore,   90
They still were thought God's enemies the more.
Thus, worn and weakened, well or ill content,
Submit they must to David's government.
Impoverished and deprived of all command,
Their taxes doubled as they lost their land;   95
And, what was harder yet to flesh and blood,
Their gods disgraced, and burnt like common wood.
This set the heathen priesthood in a flame;
For priests of all religions are the same:
Of whatsoe'er descent their godhead be,   100
Stock, stone, or other homely pedigree,
In his defence his servants are as bold
As if he had been born of beaten gold.
The Jewish rabbins, though their enemies,
In this conclude them honest men and wise: 105
For 'twas their duty, all the learnèd think,
T'espouse his cause by whom they eat and drink.
From hence began that plot, the nation's curse,
Bad in itself, but represented worse.
Raised in extremes, and in extremes decried;   110
With oaths affirmed, with dying vows denied.
Not weighed or winnowed by the multitude,
But swallowed in the mass, unchewed and crude.
Some truth there was, but dashed and brewed with lies,
To please the fools and puzzle all the wise.   115
Succeeding times did equal folly call,
Believing nothing, or believing all.
Th'Egyptian rites the Jebusites embraced,
Where gods were recommended by their taste.
Such savory deities must needs be good   120
As served at once for worship and for food.
By force they could not introduce these gods,
For ten to one in former days was odds.

So fraud was used (the sacrificer's trade);
Fools are more hard to conquer than persuade.   125
Their busy teachers mingled with the Jews,
And raked for converts even the Court and stews:
Which Hebrew priests the more unkindly took
Because the fleece accompanies the flock.
Some thought they God's anointed meant to slay   130
By guns, invented since full many a day.
Our author swears it not; but who can know
How far the devil and Jebusites may go?
This plot, which failed for want of common sense,
Had yet a deep and dangerous consequence;   135
For, as when raging fevers boil the blood,
The standing lake soon floats into a flood,
And every hostile humour, which before
Slept quiet in its channels, bubbles o'er:
So several factions from this first fermént   140
Work up to foam, and threat the government.
Some by their friends, more by themselves thought wise,
Opposed the power to which they could not rise.
Some had in courts been great, and thrown from thence,
Like fiends, were hardened in impenitence;   145
Some by their monarch's fatal mercy grown,
From pardoned rebels, kinsmen to the throne,
Were raised in power and public office high:
Strong bands, if bands ungrateful men could tie.
      Of these the false Achitophel was first: 150
A name to all succeeding ages cursed.
For close designs and crooked counsels fit;
Sagacious, bold, and turbulent of wit;
Restless, unfixed in principles and place;
In power unpleased, impatient of disgrace.   155
A fiery soul, which, working out its way,
Fretted the pigmy-body to decay,
And o'er-informed the tenement of clay.
A daring pilot in extremity;
Pleased with the danger, when the waves went high   160
He sought the storms; but, for a calm unfit,
Would steer too nigh the sands to boast his wit.
Great wits are sure to madness near allied,
And thin partitions do their bounds divide;
Else, why should he, with wealth and honour blest,
Refuse his age the needful hours of rest?   166
Punish a body which he could not please;
Bankrupt of life, yet prodigal of ease?
And all to leave what with his toil he won
To that unfeathered, two-legg'd thing, a son: 170

Got while his soul did huddled notions try,
And born a shapeless lump, like anarchy.
In friendship false, implacable in hate;
Resolved to ruin or to rule the state.
To compass this, the triple bond he broke;   175
The pillars of the public safety shook;
And fitted Israel for a foreign yoke.
Then, seized with fear, yet still affecting fame,
Usurped a patriot's all-atoning name.
So easy still it proves in factious times,   180
With public zeal to cancel private crimes.
How safe is treason, and how sacred ill,
Where none can sin against the people's will;
Where crowds can wink and no offence be known,
Since in another's guilt they find their own.   185
Yet fame deserved no enemy can grudge:
The statesman we abhor, but praise the judge.
In Israel's courts ne'er sat an abbethdin
With more discerning eyes, or hands more clean;
Unbribed, unsought, the wretched to redress;   190
Swift of dispatch, and easy of accéss.
Oh, had he been content to serve the crown
With virtues only proper to the gown;
Or had the rankness of the soil been freed
From cockle that oppressed the noble seed: 195
David for him his tuneful harp had strung,
And Heaven had wanted one immortal song.
But wild Ambition loves to slide, not stand;
And Fortune's ice prefers to Virtue's land.
Achitophel, grown weary to possess   200
A lawful fame and lazy happiness,
Disdained the golden fruit to gather free,
And lent the crowd his arm to shake the tree.
Now, manifest of crimes, contrived long since,
He stood at bold defiance with his prince;   205
Held up the buckler of the people's cause
Against the crown, and skulked behind the laws.
The wished occasion of the plot he takes;
Some circumstances finds, but more he makes.
By buzzing emissaries fills the ears   210
Of list'ning crowds with jealousies and fears
Of arbitrary counsels brought to light,
And proves the king himself a Jebusite.

Weak arguments! which yet he knew full well
Were strong with people easy to rebel;   215
For, governed by the moon, the giddy Jews
Tread the same track when she the prime renews;
And once in twenty years, their scribes record,
By natural instínct they change their lord.
Achitophel still wants a chief, and none   220
Was found so fit as warlike Absalon.
Not that he wished his greatness to create
(For politicians neither love nor hate),
But, for he knew his title not allowed,
Would keep him still depending on the crowd;   225
That kingly power, thus ebbing out, might be
Drawn to the dregs of a democracy.

[Part 1, lines 1–227]

216 **governed by the moon:** i.e. moonstruck, made crazy by the influence of the moon 217 **she the prime renews:** the beginning of the lunar cycle of nineteen years, which Dryden observes is also roughly the interval between the demands for a change of government that led to the outbreak of the Civil War, the Restoration and the Exclusion crisis

MACFLECKNOE

OR

A SATIRE UPON THE TRUE-BLUE PROTESTANT POET T[HOMAS] S[HADWELL]

ALL human things are subject to decay,
And, when Fate summons, monarchs must obey.
This Flecknoe found, who, like Augustus, young
Was called to empire, and had governed long;
In prose and verse was owned, without dispute,   5
Through all the realms of Nonsense, absolute.
This agèd prince now flourishing in peace,
And blest with issue of a large increase,
Worn out with business, did at length debate
To settle the succession of the state;   10
And pond'ring which of all his sons was fit
To reign and wage immortal war with wit,
Cried: ' 'Tis resolved; for Nature pleads that he
Should only rule who most resembles me.
Shadwell alone my perfect image bears,   15

171 **huddled:** hasty, hurried 175 **the triple bond:** in 1668, England joined in a Triple Alliance with Holland and Sweden; but, in 1670, Charles II concluded the Treaty of Dover with Louis XIV of France: in return for a French subsidy that would relieve him of his financial dependence on Parliament, Charles agreed to join with France against Holland and (in a secret clause) to declare himself a Roman Catholic when circumstances allowed 179 **Usurped a patriot's all-atoning name:** cf. Dryden's reference to 'the public-spirited men of their age, that is, patriots for their own interests' (*Aeneid*, dedication) 180 **factious:** 'inclined to form parties, or to act for party purposes' (*OED*) 188 **abbethdin:** a presiding judge in a Jewish civil court 195 **cockle:** weed 197 **wanted:** lacked **immortal song:** i.e. Psalm 200 **weary to possess:** weary of the struggle to achieve 206 **buckler:** small shield 208 **The wished occasion of the plot he takes:** Shaftesbury led the investigation into the Popish Plot

MACFLECKNOE: i.e. 'Son of Flecknoe': first published in 1682, although probably written in 1678, *MacFlecknoe* is the product of a long-running dispute between Dryden and the playwright Thomas Shadwell (?1642–92), at the heart of which was a disagreement over the merits of Ben Jonson. Quite why this dispute should suddenly have taken such a vicious turn with *MacFlecknoe* remains a mystery. The literary mediocrity of playwright and poet Richard Flecknoe (d. ?1678) appears to have recommended him as an appropriate sire for Shadwell. Dryden returned to the attack in the second part of *Absalom and Achitophel* (1682) where Shadwell appears as Og: 3–4 **like Augustus . . . governed long:** Augustus (63 BC–AD 14) was the first Roman emperor and ruled Rome and the empire from 43 BC until his death. During his reign Latin literature (most notably Horace, Ovid and Virgil) flourished; and English writers of the late seventeenth and early eighteenth centuries identified with this golden 'Augustan' age and sought to emulate their Roman predecessors

Mature in dullness from his tender years.
Shadwell alone, of all my sons, is he
Who stands confirmed in full stupidity.
The rest to some faint meaning make pretence,
But Shadwell never deviates into sense.   20
Some beams of wit on other souls may fall,
Strike through and make a lucid interval;
But Shadwell's genuine night admits no ray,
His rising fogs prevail upon the day.
Besides, his goodly fabric fills the eye,   25
And seems designed for thoughtless majesty:
Thoughtless as monarch oaks that shade the plain
And, spread in solemn state, supínely reign.
Heywood and Shirley were but types of thee,
Thou last great prophet of tautology.   30
Even I, a dunce of more renown than they,
Was sent before but to prepare thy way;
And coarsely clad in Norwich drugget came
To teach the nations in thy greater name.
My warbling lute, the lute I whilom strung   35
When to King John of Portugal I sung,
Was but the prelude to that glorious day
When thou on silver Thames did'st cut thy way
With well-timed oars before the royal barge,
Swelled with the pride of thy celestial charge;   40
And big with hymn, commander of an host,
The like was ne'er in Epsom blankets tossed.
Methinks I see the new Arion sail,
The lute still trembling underneath thy nail.
At thy well-sharpened thumb from shore to shore   45
The treble squeaks for fear, the basses roar:
Echoes from Pissing Alley "Shadwell" call,
And "Shadwell" they resound from Aston Hall.
About thy boat the little fishes throng
As at the morning toast that floats along.   50
Sometimes, as prince of thy harmonious band,
Thou wield'st thy papers in thy threshing hand.
St André's feet ne'er kept more equal time,

Not ev'n the feet of thy own Psyche's rhyme,
Though they in number as in sense excel;   55
So just, so like tautology they fell
That, pale with envy, Singleton forswore
The lute and sword which he in triumph bore,
And vowed he ne'er would act Villerius more.'
Here stopped the good old sire, and wept for joy   60
In silent raptures of the hopeful boy.
All arguments, but most his plays, persuade
That for anointed dullness he was made.
     Close to the walls which fair Augusta bind
(The fair Augusta much to fears inclined),   65
An ancient fabric, raised t'inform the sight,
There stood of yore, and Barbican it hight:
A watchtower once, but now, so Fate ordains,
Of all the pile an empty name remains.
From its old ruins brothel-houses rise,   70
Scenes of lewd loves and of polluted joys;
Where their vast courts the mother-strumpets keep,
And, undisturbed by watch, in silence sleep.
Near these a Nursery erects its head,
Where queens are formed, and future heroes bred;   75
Where unfledged actors learn to laugh and cry,
Where infant punks their tender voices try,
And little Maximins the gods defy.
Great Fletcher never treads in buskins here,
Nor greater Jonson dares in socks appear;   80
But gentle Simkin just reception finds
Amidst this monument of vanished minds:
Pure clinches the suburbian muse affords,
And Panton waging harmless war with words.
Here Flecknoe, as a place to fame well known,   85
Ambitiously designed his Shadwell's throne.
For ancient Dekker prophesied long since
That in this pile should reign a mighty prince,
Born for a scourge of wit and flail of sense:
To whom true dullness should some Psyches owe,   90
But worlds of Misers from his pen should flow;
Humorists and hypocrites it should produce,
Whole Raymond families and tribes of Bruce.

24 **prevail upon:** overcome   25 **his goodly fabric:** Shadwell was a large man; see also line 193 below   29 **Heywood:** Thomas Heywood (*c.* 1574–1641), playwright   29 **Shirley:** James Shirley (*c.* 1596–1666), playwright   33 **Norwich drugget:** drugget is a coarse woollen fabric; Shadwell was born in Norfolk   **whilom:** formerly   41 **host:** army   42 **in Epsom blankets tossed:** as happens to Sir Samuel Hearty in Shadwell's *The Virtuoso*   43 **Arion:** Greek lyric poet (?7th century BC), a native of Lesbos. According to legend, as Arion returned from a journey to Italy, where he had become very wealthy, the ship's crew robbed him and, after allowing him to sing one last song, threw him overboard; but he was saved by a dolphin that had been charmed by his song and carried him safely to land   47 **Pissing Alley:** There are no fewer than three candidates: an alley that led off the Strand at present-day Aldwych; an alley between Friday Street and Bread Street in the City of London; and (also in the City) an alley between St Paul's Cathedral and Paternoster Row. Ekwall (*Street Names of the City of London*, 1954) also lists a Pissing Lane (under 'Lanes named from some activity carried on there') but offers no location   48 **Aston Hall:** unidentified   51–2 **Sometimes . . . threshing hand:** implying that the music of Shadwell's operas was unrefined and 'rustic'   53 **St André:** French dancer who in 1675 came to London to perform in Shadwell's *Psyche*

57 **Singleton:** John Singleton (d. 1686), a theatre musician   58 **Villerius:** character in D'Avenant's *The Siege of Rhodes*   64 **Augusta:** 'the old name of London' (Dryden's note to *Annus Mirabilis* [1667], line 1177)   67 **Barbican:** originally an outer fortification of the City of London, possibly a watchtower; now only an 'empty name'; was called   73 **watch:** watchmen who patrolled the streets of London at night   74 **Nursery:** a training school for young actors   77 **infant punks:** child prostitutes   78 **Maximins:** Maximin is the bombastic hero of Dryden's play *Tyrannic Love*   79 **Fletcher:** John Fletcher (1579–1625), playwright   79–80 **buskins . . . socks:** in classical drama, actors in tragedy traditionally wore boots called buskins; comic actors wore light shoes called socks   80 **Jonson:** Ben Jonson; see introductory note   81 **Simkin:** The Humours of Simpkin was included in Kirkman's *The Wits; or, Sport upon Sport* (1672), a collection of 'drolls', or comic scenes taken from Elizabethan and Jacobean plays, performed 'by stealth' when the theatres were closed (1641–60)   83 **clinches:** puns   84 **Panton:** William Panton, a contemporary wit and punster   87 **Dekker:** Thomas Dekker (?1570–1632), playwright   91 **Misers:** *The Miser*, a play by Shadwell   93 **Raymond:** character rin Shadwell's play *The Humorist* **Bruce:** character in Shadwell's play *The Virtuoso*

Now, Empress Fame had published the renown
Of Shadwell's coronation through the town. 95
Roused by report of fame, the nations meet
From near Bunhill and distant Watling Street.
No Persian carpets spread th'imperial way,
But scattered limbs of mangled poets lay:
From dusty shops neglected authors come, 100
Martyrs of pies, and relics of the bum.
Much Heywood, Shirley, Ogilby there lay,
But loads of Shadwell almost choked the way.
Bilked stationers for yeomen stood prepared,
And Herringman was captain of the guard. 105
The hoary prince in majesty appeared,
High on a throne of his own labours reared.
At his right hand our young Ascanius sate,
Rome's other hope and pillar of the state.
His brows thick fogs, instead of glories, grace, 110
And lambent dullness played around his face.
As Hannibal did to the altars come,
Sworn by his sire a mortal foe to Rome;
So Shadwell swore, nor should his vow be vain,
That he till death true dullness would maintain; 115
And in his father's right and realm's defence
Ne'er to have peace with wit nor truce with sense.
The king himself the sacred unction made,
As king by office and as priest by trade.
In his siníster hand, instead of ball, 120
He placed a mighty mug of potent ale;
Love's Kingdom to his right he did convey,
At once his sceptre and his rule of sway;
Whose righteous lore the prince had practised young
And from whose loins recorded Psyche sprung. 125
His temples last with poppies were o'erspread,
That nodding seemed to consecrate his head.
Just at that point of time, if fame not lie,
On his left hand twelve reverend owls did fly.
So Romulus, 'tis sung, by Tiber's brook, 130
Preságe of sway from twice six vultures took.

Th'admiring throng loud acclamations make,
And omens of his future empire take.
The sire then shook the honours of his head,
And from his brows damps of oblivion shed 135
Full on the filial dullness. Long he stood,
Repelling from his breast the raging god;
At length burst out in this prophetic mood:
    'Heavens bless my son! From Ireland let him reign
To far Barbados on the western main; 140
Of his dominion may no end be known,
And greater than his father's be his throne.
Beyond Love's Kingdom let him stretch his pen!'
He paused, and all the people cried 'Amen'.
Then thus continued he: 'My son, advance 145
Still in new impudence, new ignorance.
Success let others teach, learn thou from me
Pangs without birth, and fruitless industry.
Let Virtuosos in five years be writ,
Yet not one thought accuse thy toil of wit. 150
Let gentle George in triumph tread the stage,
Make Dorimant betray, and Loveit rage;
Let Cully, Cockwood, Fopling charm the pit,
And in their folly show the writer's wit.
Yet still thy fools shall stand in thy defence, 155
And justify their author's want of sense.
Let 'em be all by thy own model made
Of dullness, and desire no foreign aid:
That they to future ages may be known
Not copies drawn but issue of thy own. 160
Nay, let thy men of wit, too, be the same,
All full of thee and differing but in name;
But let no alien Sedley interpose
To lard with wit thy hungry Epsom prose.
And when false flowers of rhetoric thou would'st cull,
Trust Nature, do not labour to be dull; 166
But write thy best and top; and in each line
Sir Formal's oratory will be thine.
Sir Formal, though unsought, attends thy quill
And does thy northern dedications fill. 170
Nor let false friends seduce thy mind to fame
By arrogating Jonson's hostile name.
Let father Flecknoe fire thy mind with praise,
And uncle Ogilby thy envy raise.
Thou art my blood, where Jonson has no part. 175
What share have we in Nature or in Art?
Where did his wit on learning fix a brand,
And rail at arts he did not understand?
Where made he love in Prince Nicander's vein,

97 **From near Bunhill and distant Watling Street:** Bunhill Row is close to Watling Street in the City of London, so 'distant' here is ironic; i.e. Shadwell's fame is very limited indeed 101 **Martyrs of pies, and relics of the bum:** i.e. the pages of their (unsold) books were used to line pie-dishes or as toilet paper 102 **Ogilby:** John Ogilby (1600–76). Ogilby was a poet, a translator, a theatre-owner, and a publisher of large lavish volumes 104 **Bilked:** unpaid (because the books do no sell) **stationers:** publishers 105 **Herringman:** Shadwell's (and, for a time, Dryden's) publisher 106 **hoary:** white-haired 108 **Ascanius:** the son of Aeneas 111 **lambent:** (flames) licking 112 **As Hannibal . . . Rome:** as a child the Carthaginian general Hannibal (247–182 BC) had been compelled by his father to swear an oath of eternal hatred to Rome 122 **Love's Kingdom:** a play by Flecknoe 125 **recorded:** i.e. mentioned earlier in the poem 126 **poppies:** perhaps included here for their soporific quality (implying that Shadwell's play send the audience to sleep) 129–31 **twelve reverend owls . . . took:** twin brothers Romulus and Remus were the legendary founders of Rome; according to Plutarch: 'Their minds being full bent upon building, there arose presently a difference about the place. . . . Concluding at last to decide the contest by a divination from a flight of birds, and placing themselves apart at some distance. Remus, they say, saw six vultures, and Romulus double that number; others say, Remus did truly see his number, and that Romulus feigned his, but when Remus came to him, that then he did indeed see twelve. Hence it is that the Romans, in their divinations from birds, chiefly regard the vulture' ('Romulus', trans. Dryden)

140 **the western main:** the Caribbean 149 **Virtuosos:** *The Virtuoso*, a play by Shadwell 151 **gentle George:** Sir George Etherege (?1634–91), playwright; see also line 184 below 152–3 **Dorimant . . . Fopling:** characters in Etherege plays: Dorimant, Mrs Loveit and Fopling in *The Man of Mode*; Cully in *The Comical Revenge*; and Cockwood in *She Would if She Could* 153 **the pit:** in the theatre, those occupying the ground-floor benches immediately in front of the stage 163–4 **Sedley . . . Epsom prose:** Sir Charles Sedley wrote a prologue to Shadwell's *Epsom Wells* and was rumoured to have assisted with the play's composition 167 **top:** surpass all others 168 **Sir Formal:** Sir Formal Trifle appears in Shadwell's *The Virtuoso* 170 **northern dedications:** five Shadwell plays were dedicated to either the Duke or the Duchess of Newcastle 179 **Prince Nicander:** character in Shadwell's *Psyche*

Or swept the dust in Psyche's humble strain?　　　180
Where sold he bargains, 'whipstitch, kiss my arse',
Promised a play and dwindled to a farce?
When did his Muse from Fletcher scenes purloin,
As thou whole Eth'rege dost transfuse to thine?
But so transfused as oil on waters flow,　　　185
His always floats above, thine sinks below.
This is thy province, this thy wondrous way,
New humours to invent for each new play:
This is that boasted bias of thy mind,
By which one way, to dullness, 'tis inclined;　　　190
Which makes thy writings lean on one side still,
And in all changes that way bends thy will.
Nor let thy mountain belly make pretence
Of likeness; thine's a tympany of sense.
A tun of man in thy large bulk is writ,　　　195
But sure thou'rt but a kilderkin of wit.
Like mine thy gentle numbers feebly creep,
Thy Tragic Muse gives smiles, thy Comic sleep.
With whate'er gall thou sett'st thyself to write,
Thy inoffensive satires never bite.　　　200
In thy felonious heart though venom lies,
It does but touch thy Irish pen and dies.
Thy genius calls thee not to purchase fame
In keen iambics but mild anagram.
Leave writing plays, and choose for thy command　　　205
Some peaceful province in Acrostic Land.
There thou may'st wings display and altars raise,
And torture one poor word ten thousand ways;
Or, if thou would'st thy diff'rent talents suit,
Set thy own songs, and sing them to thy lute.'　　　210
He said, but his last words were scarcely heard,
For Bruce and Longville had a trap prepared,
And down they sent the yet declaiming bard.
Sinking he left his drugget robe behind,
Borne upwards by a subterranean wind.　　　215
The mantle fell to the young prophet's part,
With double portion of his father's art.

181–2 **sold he bargains . . . farce:** i.e. Shadwell promises a serious
play but has the talent only to deliver vulgar farce, and thus cheats
and makes a fool of ('sells a bargain to') the audience; 'whip-stitch,
kiss my arse' is an expletive lifted (inaccurately) from Shadwell's
The Virtuoso ('I'll slide down from the window . . . and, whip-stitch,
your nose in my breech, Sir Nicholas. I'll leave my clothes behind
me') and included here to mock Shadwell's vulgarity; as an adjective
'whip-stitch' expressed 'sudden movement or action' (*OED*) and
as a noun it was a derogatory name for a tailor　188 **humours:** in a
comedy of humours (in which Jonson specialised) characters are
governed by a single ruling passion　194 **likeness:** i.e. to Jonson
tympany: 'A kind of obstructed flatulence that swells the body like
a drum' (Johnson's *Dictionary*, citing 'MacFlecknoe')　196 **kilderkin:**
small barrel　197 **numbers:** verses　204 **iambics:** in English verse an
iamb is a metrical foot of two syllables, an unstressed followed by
a stressed; iambic pentameter is a line made up of five iambs, and
is the basis of English blank verse and heroic couplets, as in this
poem　206 **Acrostic:** a poem in which the first or last letters of each
line spell out a word or phrase　212 **Bruce and Longville had a
trap prepared:** in Shadwell's *The Virtuoso*, Bruce and Longville
dispose of Sir Formal Trifle through a trapdoor in mid-speech
215–17 **Borne upwards . . . art:** cf. 2 Kings 2.11–13: 'and Elijah went up
by a whirlwind into heaven. And Elisha saw it, and he cried, My
father, my father. . . . And he saw him no more: and he took hold
of his own clothes, and rent them in two pieces. He took up also
the mantle of Elijah that fell from him, and went back'

From RELIGIO LAICI
OR
A LAYMAN'S FAITH

DIM, as the borrowed beams of moon and stars
To lonely, weary, wand'ring travellers,
Is reason to the soul; and as on high
Those rolling fires discover but the sky,
Not light us here, so reason's glimmering ray　　　5
Was lent not to assure our doubtful way
But guide us upward to a better day.
And as those nightly tapers disappear
When day's bright lord ascends our hemisphere,
So pale grows reason at religion's sight,　　　10
So dies and so dissolves in supernatural light.
Some few, whose lamp shone brighter, have been led
From cause to cause to Nature's secret head;
And found that one first principle must be.
But what, or who, that Universal He –　　　15
Whether some soul encompassing this ball
Unmade, unmoved, yet making, moving all;
Or various atoms' interfering dance
Leapt into form (the noble work of chance);
Or this great All was from eternity –　　　20
Not ev'n the Stagirite himself could see;
And Epicurus guessed as well as he.
As blindly groped they for a future state;
As rashly judged of providence and fate:
But least of all could their endeavours find　　　25
What most concerned the good of human kind:
For happiness was never to be found,
But vanished from 'em like enchanted ground.
One thought content the good to be enjoyed;
This, every little accident destroyed.　　　30
The wiser madmen did for virtue toil,
A thorny, or at best a barren soil.
In pleasure some their glutton souls would steep,
But found their line too short, the well too deep,
And leaky vessels which no bliss could keep.　　　35
Thus, anxious thoughts in endless circles roll,
Without a centre where to fix the soul.
In this wild maze their vain endeavours end.
How can the less the greater comprehend,
Or finite reason reach infinity?　　　40
For what could fathom God were more than He.

[Lines 1–41]

RELIGIO LAICI: a defence of the Church of England, published in
1682; within three years Dryden himself had deserted the Anglican
communion (see *The Hind and the Panther*): 8 **tapers:** candles, i.e. the
stars　18 **interfering:** colliding　21 **the Stagirite:** Aristotle (384–322 BC),
Greek philosopher, born in Stagira　22 **Epicurus:** Greek philosopher
(341–271 BC)

From THE HIND AND THE PANTHER

A milk-white hind, immortal and unchanged,
Fed on the lawns, and in the forest ranged;
Without unspotted, innocent within,

She feared no danger, for she knew no sin.
Yet had she oft been chased with horns and hounds   5
And Scythian shafts, and many wingèd wounds
Aimed at her heart; was often forced to fly,
And doomed to death, though fated not to die.
  Not so her young; for their unequal line
Was hero's make, half human, half divine.   10
Their earthly mould obnoxious was to fate,
Th'immortal part assumed immortal state.
Of these a slaughtered army lay in blood,
Extended o'er the Caledonian wood,
Their native walk; whose vocal blood arose,   15
And cried for pardon on their perjured foes.
Their fate was fruitful, and the sanguine seed,
Endued with souls, increased the sacred breed.
So captive Israel multiplied in chains
A numerous exile, and enjoyed her pains.   20
With grief and gladness mixed, their mother viewed
Her martyred offspring, and their race renewed;
Their corps to perish, but their kind to last,
So much the deathless plant the dying fruit surpassed.
  Panting and pensive now she ranged alone,   25
And wandered in the kingdoms once her own.
The common hunt, though from their rage restrained
By sov'reign pow'r, her company disdained;
Grinned as they passed, and with a glaring eye
Gave gloomy signs of secret enmity.   30
'Tis true, she bounded by, and tripped so light
They had not time to take a steady sight;
For Truth has such a face and such a mien
As to be loved needs only to be seen.

[Lines 1–34]

THE HIND AND THE PANTHER: With the accession of the Catholic James II to the throne in 1684, Dryden himself converted to Catholicism; and *The Hind and the Panther*, written 1686–7, is a defence of his new faith. The hind is the Roman Catholic church and the panther is the Anglican church; and the first part also includes a satirical assault on the nonconformists. James II was deposed in 1688, but Dryden maintained his Catholic faith for the rest of his life; despite accusations to the contrary, his conversion seems to have been sincere: 6 **Scythian shafts:** i.e. pagan attacks; the Scythians were a fearsome nomadic people from an area north of the Black Sea, remarkable for their horsemanship and their archery ('shafts') 9 **unequal:** inadequate 11 **mould:** body **obnoxious:** vulnerable 14 **Caledonian:** Scottish 16 **perjured:** forsworn 17 **was fruitful:** bore fruit, produced offspring **sanguine:** hopeful, promising 19 **captive Israel multiplied in chains:** despite the rigours of their Egyptian captivity 'the children of Israel were fruitful, and increased abundantly, and multiplied, and waxed exceeding mighty; and the land was filled with them' (Exodus 1.7) 23 **corps:** corpse, body 29 **Grinned:** showed their teeth

TO THE MEMORY OF MR OLDHAM

FAREWELL, too little and too lately known,
Whom I began to think and call my own;
For sure our souls were near-allied, and thine
Cast in the same poetic mould with mine.
One common note on either lyre did strike,   5
And knaves and fools we both abhorred alike.

To the same goal did both our studies drive;
The last set out the soonest did arrive.
Thus Nisus fell upon the slippery place,
While his young friend performed and won the race.
O early ripe! to thy abundant store   11
What could advancing age have added more?
It might (what Nature never gives the young)
Have taught the numbers of thy native tongue.
But satire needs not those, and wit will shine   15
Through the harsh cadence of a rugged line.
A noble error, and but seldom made,
When poets are by too much force betrayed.
Thy generous fruits, though gathered ere their prime,
Still showed a quickness; and maturing time   20
But mellows what we write to the dull sweets of
   rhyme.
Once more, hail and farewell! farewell, thou young
But, ah! too short Marcellus of our tongue!
Thy brows with ivy and with laurels bound;
But Fate and gloomy Night encompass thee around.   25

TO THE MEMORY OF MR OLDHAM: John Oldham (1653–83) was an usher at Croydon school when his verses came to the attention of Rochester. He worked as a private tutor for several distinguished families until the success of his *Satires upon the Jesuits* (1679) encouraged him to move to London where he 'set up for a wit'; and 'at length being made known to that most generous and truly noble William Earl of Kingston, he was taken into his patronage, lived with him in great respect at Holme Pierrepont in Nottinghamshire' (Anthony Wood). Oldham died of smallpox at the age of 30. *Remains of Mr Oldham in Verse and Prose* was published in 1684 and included this tribute from Dryden: 5 **lyre:** an ancient ancestor of the harp, frequently used to accompany recited poetry 9–10 **Nisus . . . race:** in Virgil's *Aeneid*, Nisus and Euryalus are friends of Aeneas; when they compete in a race, Nisus falls but Euryalus goes on to win 14 **numbers:** here prosody, versification; i.e. Oldham's youthful verses lacked technical sophistication 23 **Marcellus:** a Roman youth (42–43 BC) of great promise who died young 24 **ivy . . . laurels:** crowns of ivy (immortality) and of laurel (divine inspiration) were traditionally awarded to Greek and Latin poets, and may also be seen adorning portraits of English poets of the 16th and 17th centuries

A SONG FOR ST CECILIA'S DAY
1687

FROM harmony, from heavenly harmony
  This universal frame began.
  When Nature underneath a heap
    Of jarring atoms lay,
    And could not heave her head,   5
  The tuneful voice was heard from high,
    'Arise, ye more than dead!'
  Then cold and hot and moist and dry
    In order to their stations leap,
    And MUSIC's pow'r obey.   10
  From harmony, from heavenly harmony
    This universal frame began:
    From harmony to harmony
  Through all the compass of the notes it ran,
  The diapason closing full in Man.   15

What passion cannot MUSIC raise and quell?
    When Jubal struck the corded shell
His list'ning brethren stood around
    And, wond'ring, on their faces fell
To worship that celestial sound.   20
Less than a god they thought there could not dwell
    Within the hollow of that shell
    That spoke so sweetly and so well.
What passion cannot MUSIC raise and quell?

    The TRUMPET's loud clangour   25
      Excites us to arms
    With shrill notes of anger
      And mortal alarms.
    The double double double beat
      Of the thund'ring DRUM   30
    Cries, 'Hark, the foes come!
Charge, charge; 'tis too late to retreat!'

    The soft complaining FLUTE
    In dying notes discovers
    The woes of hopeless lovers,   35
Whose dirge is whispered by the warbling LUTE.

    Sharp VIOLINS proclaim
Their jealous pangs and desperation,
Fury, frantic indignation,
Depth of pains and height of passion   40
    For the fair, disdainful dame.

    But oh! what art can teach,
    What human voice can reach
The sacred ORGAN's praise?
Notes inspiring holy love,   45
Notes that wing their heavenly ways
    To mend the choirs above.

Orpheus could lead the savage race;
And trees unrooted left their place
    Sequacious of the lyre;   50
But bright CECILIA raised the wonder higher:
When to her ORGAN vocal breath was given
An angel heard, and straight appeared,
    Mistaking Earth for Heaven.

GRAND CHORUS

As from the pow'r of sacred lays   55
    The spheres began to move,
And sung the great Creator's praise
    To all the bless'd above;
So when the last and dreadful hour
This crumbling pageant shall devour,   60
The TRUMPET *shall be heard on high,*
The dead shall live, the living die,
And MUSIC *shall untune the sky.*

A SONG FOR ST CECILIA'S DAY: in 1683 a series of annual concerts at Stationers' Hall in the City of London to celebrate St Cecilia's Day (22 November) was inaugurated, and each year a poet and a composer were commissioned to provide an ode; this 'Song', with music by Giovanni Baptista Draghi, was Dryden's contribution for 1687: **St Cecilia:** the patron saint of music 8 **cold and hot and moist and dry:** the different 'elements' of human physiology 15 **diapason:** the whole octave 17 **Jubal:** 'he was the father of all such as handle the harp and organ' (Genesis 4.21) 47 **mend:** improve in quality choirs above: choirs of angels 48–50 **Orpheus . . . . lyre:** in Greek mythology Orpheus was a Thracian musician whose playing on the lyre was so wonderful that he could charm wild beasts and make trees and rocks move 50 **Sequacious of:** following 52 **her ORGAN:** some legends credit St Cecilia with having invented the organ 55–9 *As from the pow'r . . . above:* refers to the idea that the spheres (heavenly bodies) emitted harmonic musical sound by virtue of their spinning 61–63 **The Trumpet . . . the sky:** 'We shall not all sleep, but we shall all be changed, In a moment, in the twinkling of an eye, at the last trump: for the trumpet shall sound, and the dead shall be raised incorruptible, and we shall be changed' (1 Corinthians 15.51–2)

ALEXANDER'S FEAST
OR
THE POWER OF MUSIC
AN ODE IN HONOUR OF ST CECILIA'S DAY

1

'TWAS at the royal feast, for Persia won,
    By Philip's warlike son:
    Aloft in awful state
    The god-like hero sate
      On his imperial throne;   5
  His valiant peers were placed around,
Their brows with roses and with myrtles bound.
  (So should desert in arms be crowned.)
The lovely Thaïs by his side
Sate like a blooming Eastern bride   10
In flow'r of youth and beauty's pride.
    Happy, happy, happy pair!
      None but the brave
      None but the brave
    None but the brave deserves the fair.   15

CHORUS
Happy, happy, happy pair!
    None but the brave
    None but the brave
None but the brave deserves the fair!

ALEXANDER'S FEAST: in 1687, Dryden was commissioned for a second time to provide an ode for the St Cecilia's Day concert, this time with music by Jeremiah Clarke: **Persia won By Philip's warlike son:** the feast is to celebrate the conquest of Persia by Alexander the Great (356–23 BC), son of Philip of Macedon 4 **sate:** sat (archaic) 9 **Thaïs:** Athenian courtesan who accompanied Alexander into Asia and is reputed to have incited him to burn Persepolis

2

Timotheus placed on high   20
   Amid the tuneful choir
With flying fingers touched the lyre.
   The trembling notes ascend the sky,
   And heavenly joys inspire.
The song began from Jove,   25
Who left his blissful seats above
(Such is the pow'r of mighty love).
A dragon's fiery form belied the god:
Sublime on radiant spires he rode,
When he to fair Olympia pressed;   30
And while he sought her snowy breast;
Then round her slender waist he curled,
And stamped an image of himself, a sov'reign of the
   world.
The list'ning crowd admire the lofty sound;
'A present deity,' they shout around;   35
'A present deity,' the vaulted roofs rebound.
   With ravished ears
   The monarch hears,
   Assumes the god,
   Affects to nod,   40
And seems to shake the spheres.

CHORUS

With ravished ears
The monarch hears,
Assumes the god,
Affects to nod,   45
And seems to shake the spheres.

3

The praise of Bacchus then the sweet musician sung;
   Of Bacchus ever fair and ever young.
   The jolly god in triumph comes;
   Sound the trumpets, beat the drums;   50
   Flushed with a purple grace
   He shows his honest face;
Now give the hautboys breath; he comes, he comes.
   Bacchus ever fair and young,
   Drinking joys did first ordain.   55
Bacchus' blessings are a treasure;
Drinking is the soldier's pleasure;
   Rich the treasure,
   Sweet the pleasure,
   Sweet is pleasure after pain.   60

CHORUS

Bacchus' blessings are a treasure;
Drinking is the soldier's pleasure;
   Rich the treasure,
   Sweet the pleasure,
Sweet is pleasure after pain.   65

4

Soothed with the sound, the king grew vain;
   Fought all his battles o'er again;
And thrice he routed all his foes, and thrice he slew the
   slain.
   The master saw the madness rise;
   His glowing cheeks, his ardent eyes;   70
   And while he Heaven and Earth defied,
   Changed his hand and checked his pride.
     He chose a mournful Muse
     Soft pity to infuse.
   He sung Darius, great and good,   75
     By too severe a fate
   Fallen, fallen, fallen, fallen,
     Fallen from his high estate
   And welt'ring in his blood.
   Deserted at his utmost need   80
   By those his former bounty fed;
   On the bare earth exposed he lies,
   With not a friend to close his eyes.
With downcast looks the joyless victor sate,
   Revolving in his altered soul   85
     The various turns of chance below;
   And now and then a sigh he stole,
     And tears began to flow.

CHORUS

Revolving in his altered soul
   The various turns of chance below;   90
And now and then a sigh he stole,
   And tears began to flow.

5

The mighty master smiled to see
That love was in the next degree;
'Twas but a kindred-sound to move,   95
For pity melts the mind to love.
   Softly sweet, in Lydian measures,
   Soon he soothed his soul to pleasures.
War, he sung, is toil and trouble;
Honour but an empty bubble.   100
   Never ending, still beginning,
Fighting still, and still destroying,

20 **Timotheus:** Greek poet (*c.*450–*c.*360 BC) 25–33 **Jove . . . the world:** according to legend, Jove (Jupiter) took the form of a dragon and in this shape wooed Alexander's mother, Olympias (Olympia, line 30) 29 **radiant spires:** coils 39 **Assumes the god:** acquires the nature of a god 40 **Affects to nod:** i.e. nods 47 **Bacchus:** Latin name for the Greek Dionysus, god of wine and ecstasy 52 **honest:** glorious 53 **hautboys:** ('*oh*-boys') oboes (archaic)

75 **Darius:** Darius III was emperor of Persia until defeated by Alexander 85 **Revolving:** pondering, meditating 94 **was in the next degree:** had moved to a higher level 97 **Lydian measures:** soft and sensuous music; Lydia in Asia Minor was noted for wealth and luxury

If the world be worth thy winning,
Think, oh, think it worth enjoying.
    Lovely Thaïs sits beside thee;   105
    Take the good the gods provide thee.
The many rend the skies with loud applause;
So Love was crowned, but Music won the cause.
    The prince, unable to conceal his pain,
      Gazed on the fair   110
      Who caused his care,
    And sighed and looked, sighed and looked,
    Sighed and looked, and sighed again.
At length, with love and wine at once oppressed,
The vanquished victor sunk upon her breast.   115

CHORUS

The prince, unable to conceal his pain,
    Gazed on the fair
    Who caused his care,
And sighed and looked, sighed and looked,
Sighed and looked, and sighed again.   120
At length, with love and wine at once oppressed,
The vanquished victor sunk upon her breast.

6

Now strike the golden lyre again:
A louder yet and yet a louder strain.
Break his bands of sleep asunder   125
And rouse him, like a rattling peal of thunder.
    Hark, hark, the horrid sound
      Has raised up his head
      As awaked from the dead,
    And amazed he stares around.   130
    Revenge, revenge, Timotheus cries,
      See the Furies arise!
    See the snakes that they rear
    How they hiss in their hair,
And the sparkles that flash from their eyes!   135
    Behold a ghastly band,
    Each a torch in his hand!
Those are Grecian ghosts that in battle were slain,
    And unburied remain
    Inglorious on the plain.   140
    Give the vengeance due
    To the valiant crew.
Behold how they toss their torches on high,
    How they point to the Persian abodes,
And glitt'ring temples of their hostile gods!   145
The princes applaud with a furious joy;
And the king seized a flambeau, with zeal to destroy;
    Thaïs led the way
    To light him to his prey
And, like another Helen, fired another Troy.   150

---

136 **ghastly:** ghostly 147 **flambeau:** flaming torch 150 **Helen:** wife of Menelaus, king of Sparta; her abduction by Paris, son of Priam, king of Troy, caused the Trojan War

CHORUS

And the king seized a flambeau, with zeal to destroy;
    Thaïs led the way
    To light him to his prey
And, like another Helen, fired another Troy.

7

    Thus, long ago,   155
    Ere heaving bellows learned to blow,
      While organs yet were mute;
    Timotheus, to his breathing flute
      And sounding lyre,
Could swell the soul to rage or kindle soft desire.   160
    At last divine Cecilia came,
    Invent'ress of the vocal frame.
The sweet enthusiast, from her sacred store,
    Enlarged the former narrow bounds,
    And added length to solemn sounds,   165
With Nature's mother-wit, and arts unknown before.
    Let old Timotheus yield the prize,
      Or both divide the crown;
    He raised a mortal to the skies;
    She drew an angel down.   170

GRAND CHORUS

At last divine Cecilia came,
Invent'ress of the vocal frame.
The sweet enthusiast, from her sacred store,
    Enlarged the former narrow bounds,
    And added length to solemn sounds,   175
With Nature's mother-wit and arts unknown before.
    Let old Timotheus yield the prize,
      Or both divide the crown;
    He raised a mortal to the skies;
    She drew an angel down.   180

161–2 **the vocal frame:** the organ, which legend credits St Cecilia with having invented   163 **enthusiast:** literally 'god-inspired' 166 **mother-wit:** natural wit, common sense

From THE AENEID

[THE TROJAN HORSE]

By destiny compelled, and in despair,
The Greeks grew weary of the tedious war,
And by Minerva's aid a fabric reared,
Which like a steed of monstrous height appeared:
The sides were planked with pine; they feigned it made
For their return, and this the vow they paid.   6
Thus they pretend, but in the hollow side
Selected numbers of their soldiers hide:
With inward arms the dire machine they load,
And iron bowels stuff the dark abode.   10

In sight of Troy lies Tenedos, an isle
(While Fortune did on Priam's empire smile)
Renowned for wealth; but, since, a faithless bay,
Where ships exposed to wind and weather lay.
There was their fleet concealed. We thought for
    Greece   15
Their sails were hoisted, and our fears release.
The Trojans, cooped within their walls so long,
Unbar their gates, and issue in a throng,
Like swarming bees, and with delight survey
The camp deserted, where the Grecians lay: 20
The quarters of the sev'ral chiefs they showed:
Here Phoenix, here Achilles made abode;
Here joined the battles; there the navy rode.
Part on the pile their wond'ring eyes employ:
The pile by Pallas raised to ruin Troy.   25
Thymoetes first ('tis doubtful whether hired,
Or so the Trojan destiny required)
Moved that the ramparts might be broken down,
To lodge the monster fabric in the town.
But Capys, and the rest of sounder mind,   30
The fatal present to the flames designed,
Or to the wat'ry deep; at least to bore
The hollow sides, and hidden frauds explore.
The giddy vulgar, as their fancies guide,
With noise say nothing, and in parts divide.   35
Laocoön, followed by a num'rous crowd,
Ran from the fort, and cried, from far, aloud:
'O wretched countrymen! what fury reigns?
What more than madness has possessed your brains?
Think you the Grecians from your coasts are gone?
And are Ulysses' arts no better known?   41
This hollow fabric either must enclose,
Within its blind recess, our secret foes;
Or 'tis an engine raised above the town,
T'o'erlook the walls, and then to batter down.   45
Somewhat is sure designed, by fraud or force:
Trust not their presents, nor admit the horse.'
Thus having said, against the steed he threw
His forceful spear, which, hissing as it flew,
Pierced through the yielding planks of jointed wood,
And trembling in the hollow belly stood.   51
The sides, transpierced, return a rattling sound,
And groans of Greeks enclosed come issuing through
    the wound.
And, had not Heaven the fall of Troy designed,
Or had not men been fated to be blind,   55
Enough was said and done t'inspire a better mind.
Then had our lances pierced the treach'rous wood,
And Ilian tow'rs and Priam's empire stood.

                        [Book 2, lines 17–74]

THE AENEID: 3 **Minerva:** Roman goddess of arts and crafts, identified
with the Greek goddess Pallas Athena 10 **iron bowels:** i.e. the horse
is packed with armed men 12 **Priam:** king of Troy 22 **Phoenix:** king
of the Dolopians and Achilles' lieutenant 25 **Pallas:** see line 3
36 **Laocoön:** ('La-*oc*-o-*on*') priest of Poseidon; following his warning
to the Trojans, Laocoön and his two young sons were killed by two
giant sea-serpents that swam over from Tenedos 58 **Ilian:** Trojan

KATHERINE PHILIPS

TO MY EXCELLENT LUCASIA,
ON OUR FRIENDSHIP

I DID NOT live until this time
    Crowned my felicity,
When I could say without a crime,
    I am not thine, but thee.

This carcass breathed, and walked, and slept,   5
    So that the world believed
There was a soul the motions kept;
    But they were all deceived.

For as a watch by art is wound
    To motion, such was mine: 10
But never had Orinda found
    A soul till she found thine;

Which now inspires, cures and supplies,
    And guides my darkened breast:
For thou art all that I can prize,   15
    My joy, my life, my rest.

No bridegroom's nor crown-conqueror's mirth
    To mine compared can be:
They have but pieces of this earth,
    I've all the world in thee.   20

Then let our flames still light and shine,
    And no false fear control,
As innocent as our design,
    Immortal as our soul.

TO MY EXCELLENT LUCASIA, ON OUR FRIENDSHIP: 3 **without a crime:**
without telling a lie 5 **This carcass:** my body 11 **Orinda:** the poet,
Philips herself

TO MY LUCASIA, IN DEFENCE OF
DECLARED FRIENDSHIP

O MY Lucasia, let us speak love,
    And think not that impertinent can be,
Which to us both doth such assurance prove,
    And whence we find how justly we agree.

Before we knew the treasures of our love,   5
    Our noble aims our joy did entertain;
And shall enjoyment nothing then improve?
    'Twere best for us then to begin again.

Now we have gained, we must not stop, and sleep
    Out all the rest of our mysterious reign: 10
It is as hard and glorious to keep
    A victory, as it is to obtain.

Nay, to what end did we once barter minds,
  Only to know and to neglect the claim?
Or (like some wantons) our pride pleasure finds   15
  To throw away the thing at which we aim.

If this be all our friendship does design,
  We covet not enjoyment then, but power:
To our opinion we our bliss confine,
  And love to have, but not to smell, the flower.   20

Ah! then let misers bury thus their gold,
  Who though they starve, no farthing will produce:
But we loved to enjoy and to behold,
  And sure we cannot spend our stock by use.

Think not 'tis needless to repent desires;   25
  The fervent turtles always court and bill,
And yet their spotless passion never tires,
  But does increase by repetition still.

Although we know we love, yet while our soul
  Is thus imprisoned by the flesh we wear,   30
There's no way left that bondage to control,
  But to convey transactions through the ear.

Nay, though we read our passions in the eye,
  It will oblige and please to tell them too:
Such joys as these by motion multiply,   35
  Were't but to find that our souls told us true.

Believe not then, that being now secure
  Of either's heart, we have no more to do:
The spheres themselves by motion do endure,
  And they move on by circulation too.   40

And as a river, when it once hath paid
  The tribute which it to the ocean owes,
Stops not, but turns, and having curled and played
  On its own waves, the shore it overflows:

So the soul's motion does not end in bliss,   45
  But on her self she scatters and dilates,
And on the object doubles till by this
  She finds new joys which that reflux creates.

But then because it cannot all contain,
  It seeks a vent by telling the glad news,   50
First to the heart which did its joys obtain,
  Then to the heart which did those joys produce.

When my soul then doth such excursions make,
  Unless thy soul delight to meet it too,
What satisfaction can it give or take,   55
  Thou being absent at the interview?

'Tis not distrust; for were that plea allowed,
  Letters and visits all would useless grow:
Love's whole expression then would be its cloud,
  And it would be refined to nothing so.   60

If I distrust, 'tis my own worth for thee,
  'Tis my own fitness for a love like thine;
And therefore still new evidence would see,
  T'assure my wonder that thou canst be mine.

But as the morning sun to drooping flowers,   65
  As weary travellers a shade do find,
As to the parchèd violet evening showers;
  Such is from thee to me a look that's kind.

But when that look is dressed in words, 'tis like
  The mystic pow'r of music's unison;   70
Which when the finger doth one viol strike,
  The other's string heaves to reflection.

Be kind to me, and just then to our love,
  To which we owe our free and dear convérse;
And let not tract of time wear or remove   75
  It from the privilege of that commérce.

Tyrants do banish what they can't requite:
  But let us never know such mean desires;
But to be grateful to that love delight
  Which all our joys and noble thoughts inspires.   80

TO MY LUCASIA, IN DEFENCE OF DECLARED FRIENDSHIP: 26 **turtles:** turtle
doves, an emblem of love 48 **reflux:** a return

THOMAS TRAHERNE

NEWS

News from a foreign country came,
As if my treasures and my joys lay there;
  So much it did my heart inflame,
'Twas wont to call my soul into mine ear;
    Which thither went to meet   5
      Th'approaching sweet,
    And on the threshold stood
  To entertain the secret good;
    It hovered there
    As if 'twould leave mine ear,   10
And was so eager to embrace
Th'expected tidings, as they came,
That it could change its dwelling-place
  To meet the voice of fame.

  As if new tidings were the things   15
Which did comprise my wishèd unknown treasure,
  Or else did bear them on their wings,
With so much joy they came, with so much pleasure,
    My soul stood at the gate
      To recreate   20
    Itself with bliss, and woo

Its speedier approach; a fuller view
   It fain would take,
   Yet journeys back would make
Unto my heart, as if 'twould fain   25
Go out to meet, yet stay within,
Fitting a place to entertain
   And bring the tidings in.

What sacred instinct did inspire
My soul in childhood with an hope so strong?   30
What secret force moved my desire
T'expect my joys beyond the seas, so young?
   Felicity I knew
     Was out of view;
   And being left alone,   35
I thought all happiness was gone
    From earth: for this
   I longed for absent bliss,
Deeming that sure beyond the seas,
Or else in something near at hand   40
Which I knew not, since nought did please
I knew, my bliss did stand.

But little did the infant dream
That all the treasures of the world were by,
   And that himself was so the cream   45
And crown of all which round about did lie.
   Yet thus it was! The gem,
    The diadem,
    The ring enclosing all
That stood upon this earthen ball;   50
    The heav'nly eye,
    Much wider than the sky,
Wherein they all included were;
The love, the soul, that was the king
Made to possess them, did appear   55
   A very little thing.

NEWS: 48 **diadem:** crown

SIR CHARLES SEDLEY

'LOVE STILL HAS SOMETHING
OF THE SEA'

LOVE still has something of the sea,
   From whence his mother rose;
No time his slaves from Doubt can free,
   Nor give their thoughts repose:

They are becalmed in clearest days,   5
   And in rough weather tossed;
They wither under cold delays,
   Or are in tempests lost.

One while they seem to touch the port,
   Then straight into the main,   10
Some angry wind in cruel sport
   The vessel drives again.

At first Disdain and Pride they fear,
   Which if they chance to 'scape,
Rivals and Falsehood soon appear   15
   In a more dreadful shape.

By such degrees to Joy they come,
   And are so long withstood,
So slowly they receive the sum,
   It hardly does them good.   20

'Tis cruel to prolong a pain;
   And to defer a joy,
Believe me, gentle Celemene,
   Offends the wingèd Boy.

An hundred thousand oaths your fears   25
   Perhaps would not remove;
And if I gazed a thousand years
   I could no deeper love.

'LOVE STILL HAS SOMETHING OF THE SEA': 2 Venus the goddess of love
is said to have arisen from the sea 24 **wingèd boy:** Cupid, son of
Venus

APHRA BEHN

'LOVE IN FANTASTIC TRIUMPH SAT'

LOVE in fantastic triumph sat,
   Whilst bleeding hearts around him flowed,
For whom fresh pains he did create,
   And strange tyrannic power he showed:
From thy bright eyes he took his fires,   5
   Which round about in sport he hurled;
But 'twas from mine he took desires
   Enough t'undo th'amórous world.

From me he took his sighs and tears,
   From thee his pride and cruelty;   10
From me his languishments and fears,
   And every killing dart from thee.
Thus thou and I the god have armed,
   And set him up a deity;
But my poor heart alone is harmed,   15
   Whilst thine the victor is, and free.

[From *Abdelazar*]

EDWARD TAYLOR

UPON A WASP CHILLED WITH COLD

THE bear that breathes the northern blast
Did numb, torpedo-like, a wasp
Whose stiffened limbs encramped, lay bathing
In Sol's warm breath and shine as saving,
Which with her hands she chafes and stands   5
Rubbing her legs, shanks, thighs, and hands.
Her petty toes, and finger ends
Nipped with this breath, she out extends
Unto the Sun, in great desire
To warm her digits at that fire.   10
Doth hold her temples in this state
Where pulse doth beat, and head doth ache.
Doth turn, and stretch her body small,
Doth comb her velvet capital.
As if her little brain pan were   15
A volume of choice precepts clear.
As if her satin jacket hot
Contained apothecary's shop
Of Nature's récepts, that prevails
To remedy all her sad ails,   20
As if her velvet helmet high
Did turret rationality.
She fans her wings up to the wind
As if her petticoat were lined,
With reason's fleece, and hoises sails   25
And humming flies in thankful gales
Unto her dun curled palace hall
Her warm thanks-offering for all.

Lord, clear my misted sight that I
May hence view thy divinity.   30
Some sparks whereof thou up dost hasp
Within this little downy wasp
In whose small corporation we
A school and a schoolmaster see
Where we may learn, and easily find   35
A nimble spirit bravely mind
Her work in ev'ry limb: and lace
It up neat with a vital grace,
Acting each part though ne'er so small
Here of this fustian animal.   40
Till I enravished climb into
The Godhead on this ladder do.
Where all my pipes inspired upraise
An heavenly music furred with praise.

UPON A WASP CHILLED WITH COLD: 4 **Sol:** the sun personified
25 **hoises:** hoists, lifts 27 **dun:** a dingy brown colour 31 **hasp:** have
within 40 **fustian:** homely

JOHN WILMOT, EARL OF ROCHESTER

'ABSENT FROM THEE, I LANGUISH STILL'

ABSENT from thee, I languish still;
    Then ask me not, when I return?
The straying fool 'twill plainly kill
    To wish all day, all night to mourn.

Dear! from thine arms then let me fly,   5
    That my fantastic mind may prove
The torments it deserves to try
    That tears my fixed heart from my love.

When, wearied with a world of woe,
    To thy safe bosom I retire   10
Where love and peace and truth does flow,
    May I contented there expire,

Lest, once more wandering from that Heaven,
    I fall on some base heart unblest,
Faithless to thee, false, unforgiven,   15
    And lose my everlasting rest.

LOVE AND LIFE

ALL my past life is mine no more;
    The flying hours are gone,
Like transitory dreams given o'er
Whose images are kept in store
    By memory alone.   5

Whatever is to come is not:
    How can it then be mine?
The present moment's all my lot,
And that, as fast as it is got,
    Phyllis, is wholly thine.   10

Then talk not of inconstancy,
    False hearts, and broken vows;
If I, by miracle, can be
This livelong minute true to thee,
    'Tis all that heaven allows.   15

LOVE AND LIFE: 10 **Phyllis:** in Greek mythology is goddess of Spring
and women's secrets

A SATIRE AGAINST REASON AND MANKIND

WERE I (who to my cost already am
One of those strange, prodigious creatures, man)
A spirit free to choose, for my own share,
What case of flesh and blood I pleased to wear,
I'd be a dog, a monkey, or a bear,   5

Or anything but that vain animal
Who is so proud of being rational.
The senses are too gross, and he'll contrive
A sixth, to contradict the other five,
And before certain instinct, will prefer   10
Reason, which fifty times for one does err;
Reason, an ignis fatuus in the mind,
Which, leaving light of nature, sense, behind,
Pathless and dangerous wandering ways it takes
Through error's fenny bogs and thorny brakes;   15
Whilst the misguided follower climbs with pain
Mountains of whimsies, heaped in his own brain;
Stumbling from thought to thought, falls headlong
          down
Into doubt's boundless sea, where, like to drown,
Books bear him up awhile, and make him try   20
To swim with bladders of philosophy;
In hopes still to o'ertake the escaping light,
The vapour dances in his dazzling sight
Till, spent, it leaves him to eternal night.
Then old age and experience, hand in hand,   25
Lead him to death, and make him understand,
After a search so painful and so long,
That all his life he has been in the wrong.
Huddled in dirt the reasoning engine lies,
Who was so proud, so witty, and so wise.   30
Pride drew him in, as cheats their bubbles catch,
And made him venture to be made a wretch.
His wisdom did his happiness destroy,
Aiming to know that world he should enjoy.
And wit was his vain, frivolous pretence   35
Of pleasing others at his own expense;
For wits are treated just like common whores:
First they're enjoyed, and then kicked out of doors.
The pleasure past, a threatening doubt remains
That frights the enjoyer with succeeding pains.   40
Women and men of wit are dangerous tools,
And ever fatal to admiring fools:
Pleasure allures, and when the fops escape,
'Tis not that they're beloved, but fortunate,
And therefore what they fear at heart, they hate.   45
    But now, methinks, some formal band and beard
Takes me to task. Come on, sir; I'm prepared.
'Then, by your favour, anything that's writ
Against this gibing, jingling knack called wit
Likes me abundantly; but you take care,   50
Upon this point, not to be too severe.
Perhaps my Muse were fitter for this part,
For I profess I can be very smart
On wit, which I abhor with all my heart.
I long to lash it in some sharp essáy,   55
But your grand indiscretion bids me stay,
And turns my tide of ink another way.
'What rage ferments in your degenerate mind,
To make you rail at reason and mankind?
Blest, glorious man! to whom alone kind heaven   60

An everlasting soul has freely given,
Whom his great maker took such care to make
That from himself he did the image take,
And this fair frame in shining reason dressed,
To dignify his nature above beast;   65
Reason, by whose aspiring influence
We take a flight beyond material sense,
Dive into mysteries, then soaring pierce
The flaming limits of the universe,
Search heaven and hell, find out what's acted there,   70
And give the world true grounds of hope and fear.'
    'Hold, mighty man,' I cry, 'all this we know
From the pathetic pen of Ingelo,
From Patrick's *Pilgrim*, Sibbes' soliloquies,
And 'tis this very reason I despise: 75
This supernatural gift, that makes a mite
Think he's the image of the infinite,
Comparing his short life, void of all rest,
To the eternal and the ever blest;
This busy, puzzling stirrer-up of doubt,   80
That frames deep mysteries, then finds 'em out,
Filling with frantic crowds of thinking fools
Those reverend bedlams, colleges and schools;
Borne on whose wings, each heavy sot can pierce
The limits of the boundless universe.   85
So charming ointments make an old witch fly
And bear a crippled carcass through the sky.
'Tis this exalted power whose business lies
In nonsense and impossibilities;
This made a whimsical philosopher,   90
Before the spacious world, his tub prefer;
And we have modern cloistered coxcombs who
Retire to think, 'cause they have naught to do.
'But thoughts are given for action's government;
Where action ceases, thought's impertinent.   95
Our sphere of action is life's happiness,
And he who thinks beyond, thinks like an ass.
Thus, whilst against false reasoning I inveigh,
I own right reason, which I would obey:
That reason which distinguishes by sense,   100
And gives us rules of good and ill from thence
That bounds desires with a reforming will,
To keep 'em more in vigour, not to kill.
Your reason hinders, mine helps to enjoy,
Renewing appetites yours would destroy.   105
My reason is my friend, yours is a cheat;
Hunger calls out, my reason bids me eat;
Perversely, yours your appetite does mock:
This asks for food, that answers 'What's o'clock?'
This plain distinction, sir, your doubt secures: 110
'Tis not true reason I despise, but yours.
    'Thus I think reason righted, but for man,
I'll ne'er recant; defend him if you can.

73 **pathetic:** passionate **Ingelo:** Nathaniel Ingelo, author of *Bentivolio and Urania* (1660) 74 **Patrick's:** Simon Patrick, author of *Parable of the Pilgrim* (1665) **Sibbes':** Richard Sibbes, (1577–1635), preacher of Gray's Inn, London 83 **Bedlams:** insane places. After Bethlehem Hospital for the insane

A SATIRE AGAINST REASON: 12 **ignis fatuus:** a will-o'-the wisp

For all his pride and his philosophy,
'Tis evident beasts are, in their degree,   115
As wise at least, and better far than he.
Those creatures are the wisest who attain,
By surest means, the ends at which they aim.
If therefore Jowler finds and kills his hares
Better than Meres supplies committee chairs,   120
Though one's a statesman, the other but a hound,
Jowler, in justice, would be wiser found.
'You see how far man's wisdom here extends;
Look next if human nature makes amends:
Whose principles most generous are, and just,   125
And to whose morals you would sooner trust.
Be judge yourself, I'll bring it to the test:
Which is the basest creature, man or beast?
Birds feed on birds, beasts on each other prey,
But savage man alone does man betray.   130
Pressed by necessity, they kill for food;
Man undoes man to do himself no good.
With teeth and claws by nature armed, they hunt:
Nature's allowance, to supply their want.
But man, with smiles, embraces, friendship, praise,   135
Inhumanly his fellow's life betrays;
With voluntary pains works his distress,
Not through necessity, but wantonness.
'For hunger or for love they fight and tear,
Whilst wretched man is still in arms for fear.   140
For fear he arms, and is of arms afraid,
By fear, to fear, successively betrayed;
Base fear, the source whence his best passions came:
His boasted honour, and his dear-bought fame;
That lust of power, to which he's such a slave,   145
And for the which alone he dares be brave;
To which his various projects are designed;
Which makes him generous, affable, and kind;
For which he takes such pains to be thought wise,
And screws his actions in a forced disguise,   150
Leading a tedious life in misery
Under laborious, mean hypocrisy.
Look to the bottom of his vast design,
Wherein man's wisdom, power, and glory join:
The good he acts, the ill he does endure,   155
'Tis all from fear, to make himself secure.
Merely for safety, after fame we thirst,
For all men would be cowards if they durst.
'And honesty's against all common sense:
Men must be knaves, 'tis in their own defence.   160
Mankind's dishonest; if you think it fair
Amongst known cheats to play upon the square,
You'll be undone.
Nor can weak truth your reputation save:
The knaves will all agree to call you knave.   165
Wronged shall he live, insulted o'er, oppressed,
Who dares be less a villain than the rest.

'Thus, sir, you see what human nature craves:
Most men are cowards, all men should be knaves.
The difference lies, as far as I can see,   170
Not in the thing itself, but the degree,
And all the subject matter of debate
Is only: Who's a knave of the first rate?'

All this with indignation have I hurled
At the pretending part of the proud world,   175
Who, swollen with selfish vanity, devise
False freedoms, holy cheats, and formal lies,
Over their fellow slaves to tyrannize.
    But if in Court so just a man there be
(In Court a just man, yet unknown to me)   180
Who does his needful flattery direct,
Not to oppress and ruin, but protect
(Since flattery, which way soever laid,
Is still a tax on that unhappy trade);
If so upright a statesman you can find,   185
Whose passions bend to his unbiased mind;
Who does his arts and policies apply
To raise his country, not his family,
Nor, whilst his pride owned avarice withstands,
Receives close bribes through friends' corrupted
    hands –   190
    Is there a churchman who on God relies;
Whose life, his faith and doctrine justifies?
Not one blown up with vain prelatic pride,
Who, for reproof of sins, does man deride;
Whose envious heart makes preaching a pretence,   195
With his obstreperous, saucy eloquence,
To chide at kings, and rail at men of sense;
None of that sensual tribe whose talents lie
In avarice, pride, sloth, and gluttony;
Who hunt good livings, but abhor good lives;   200
Whose lust exalted, to that height arrives
They act adultery with their own wives,
And ere a score of years completed be,
Can from the lofty pulpit proudly see
Half a large parish their own progeny;   205
Nor doting bishop who would be adored
For domineering at the council board,
A greater fop in business at fourscore,
Fonder of serious toys, affected more,
Than the gay, glittering fool at twenty proves   210
With all his noise, his tawdry clothes, and loves;
    But a meek, humble man of honest sense,
Who, preaching peace, does practise continence;
Whose pious life's a proof he does believe
Mysterious truths, which no man can conceive.   215
If upon earth there dwell such God-like men,
I'll here recant my paradox to them,
Adore those shrines of virtue, homage pay,
And, with the rabble world, their laws obey.
If such there be, yet grant me this at least: 220
Man differs more from man, than man from beast.

119 **Jowler:** a hunting dog   120 **Meres:** Sit Thomas Meres, a
Parliamentary committee man

190 **close:** grasping

ANONYMOUS

SIR PATRICK SPENS

THE king sits in Dunfermline town,
　Drinking the blude-red wine;
'O whare will I get a skeely skipper,
　To sail this new ship of mine?'

O up and spake an eldern knight, 5
　Sat at the king's right knee:
'Sir Patrick Spens is the best sailor,
　That ever sail'd the sea.'

Our king has written a braid letter,
　And sealed it with his hand, 10
And sent it to Sir Patrick Spens,
　Was walking on the strand.

'To Noroway, to Noroway,
　To Noroway o'er the faem;
The king's daughter o' Noroway, 15
　'Tis thou maun bring her hame.'

The first word that Sir Patrick read,
　Sae loud loud laughed he;
The neist word that Sir Patrick read
　The tear blinded his ee. 20

'O wha is this has done this deed,
　And tauld the king o' me,
To send us out, at this time of the year,
　To sail upon the sea?

'Be it wind, be it weet, be it hail, be it sleet, 25
　Our ship must sail the faem;
The king's daughter of Noroway,
　'Tis we must fetch her hame.'

They hoysed their sails on Monenday morn,
　Wi' a' the speed they may; 30
They hae landed in Noroway,
　Upon a Wodensday.

They hadna been a week, a week,
　In Noroway, but twae,
When that the lords o' Noroway 35
　Began aloud to say,

'Ye Scottishmen spend a' our king's goud,
　And a' our queenis fee.'
'Ye lie, ye lie, ye liars loud!
　Fu' loud I hear ye lie. 40

'For I brought as much white monie,
　As gane my men and me,
And I brought a half-fou o' gude red goud,
　Out o'er the sea wi' me.

'Make ready, make ready, my merrymen a'! 45
　Our gude ship sails the morn.'
'Now, ever alake, my master dear,
　I fear a deadly storm!

'I saw the new moon, late yestreen,
　Wi' the auld moon in her arm; 50
And, if we gang to sea, master,
　I fear we'll come to harm.'

They hadna sailed a league, a league,
　A league but barely three,
When the lift grew dark, and the wind blew loud, 55
　And gurly grew the sea.

The ankers brak, and the topmasts lap,
　It was sic a deadly storm;
And the waves cam o'er the broken ship,
　Till a' her sides were torn. 60

'O where will I get a gude sailor,
　To take my helm in hand,
Till I get up to the tall top-mast,
　To see if I can spy land?'

'O here am I, a sailor gude, 65
　To take the helm in hand,
Till you go up to the tall top-mast;
　But I fear you'll ne'er spy land.'

He hadna gane a step, a step,
　A step but barely ane, 70
When a bout flew out of our goodly ship,
　And the salt sea it came in.

'Gae, fetch a web o' the silken claith,
　Another o' the twine,
And wap them into our ship's side, 75
　And let na the sea come in.'

SIR PATRICK SPENS: 2 **blude**: blood 3 **skeely**: skilful 5 **eldern**: old
9 **braid letter**: either a long letter or a letter written on a broad
sheet of paper 13 **Noroway**: Norway 14 **faem**: foam, sea 16 **maun**:
must 18 **Sae**: so 19 **neist**: next 20 **ee**: eye 21 **wha**: who 22 **tauld**: told
25 **weet**: wet 28 **hame**: home 29 **hoysed**: hoisted, lifted **Monenday**:
Monday 30 **Wi' a'**: with all 31 **hae**: have 32 **Wodensday**: Wednesday
33 **hadna**: had not 34 **twae**: two

37 **a'**: all **goud**: gold 38 **queenis**: queens 39 **Ye**: You 41 **white monie**:
silver money 42 **As gane**: sufficient for 43 **half-fou o' gude**: half
full of good 47 **alake**: alas 49 **yestreen**: yesterday evening 50 **auld**:
old 51 **gang**: go 55 **lift**: sky 56 **gurly**: growling, angry 57 **ankers
brak**: anchors broke **lap**: leaped, sprang 58 **sic**: such 59 **cam o'er**:
came over 68 **ne'er**: never 69 **gane**: gone 70 **ane**: one 71 **bout**: bolt
73 **Gae**: go **claith**: cloth 74 **twine**: canvas 75 **wap**: stuff 76 **na**: not

They fetched a web o' the silken claith,
   Another o' the twine,
And they wapped them round that gude ship's side,
   But still the sea came in.   80

O laith, laith, were our gude Scots lords
   To weet their cork-heeled shoon!
But lang or a' the play was played,
   They wat their hats aboon.

And mony was the feather-bed,   85
   That flattered on the faem;
And mony was the gude lord's son,
   That never mair cam hame.

The ladyes wrang their fingers white,
   The maidens tore their hair,   90
A' for the sake of their true loves;
   For them they'll see nae mair.

O lang, lang, may the ladyes sit,
   Wi' their fans into their hand,
Before they see Sir Patrick Spens   95
   Come sailing to the strand!

And lang, lang, may the maidens sit,
   Wi' their goud kaims in their hair,
A' waiting for their ain dear loves!
   For them they'll see nae mair.   100

Half owre, half owre to Aberdour,
   'Tis fifty fathoms deep,
And there lies gude Sir Patrick Spens,
   Wi' the Scots lords at his feet.

81 **laith:** loath 82 **weet:** wet **shoon:** shoes 83 **lang or a':** long before all 84 **wat:** wet **aboon:** above 85 **mony:** many 86 **flattered:** floated 89 **wrang:** wrung 98 **kaims:** combs 99 **ain:** own 101 **owre:** over (the text in Sir Walter Scott's *Minstrelsy of the Scottish Border* [1802–3] has the line 'O forty miles off Aberdeen') **Aberdour:** a small port in Fife

FAIR HELEN

I WISH I were where Helen lies,
Night and day on me she cries;
O that I were where Helen lies,
   On fair Kirconnell Lee!

Curst be the heart that thought the thought,   5
And curst the hand that fired the shot,
When in my arms burd Helen dropt,
   And died to succour me!

O think na ye my heart was sair,
When my love dropt down and spak nae mair!   10
There did she swoon wi' meikle care,
   On fair Kirconnell Lee.

As I went down the water side,
None but my foe to be my guide,
None but my foe to be my guide,   15
   On fair Kirconnell Lee;

I lighted down, my sword to draw,
I hackèd him in pieces sma',
I hackèd him in pieces sma',
   For her sake that died for me.   20

O Helen fair, beyond compare!
I'll make a garland o' thy hair,
Shall bind my heart for evermair,
   Until the day I die.

O that I were where Helen lies!   25
Night and day on me she cries;
Out of my bed she bids me rise,
   Says, 'Haste and come to me!'

O Helen fair! O Helen chaste!
If I were with thee, I were blest,   30
Where thou lies low, and takes thy rest,
   On fair Kirconnell Lee.

I wish my grave were growing green,
A winding sheet drawn ower my een,
And I in Helen's arms lýing,   35
   On fair Kirconnell Lee.

I wish I were where Helen lies!
Night and day on me she cries;
And I am weary of the skies,
   For her sake that died for me.   40

FAIR HELEN: 8 **burd:** maiden 9 **na:** not **sair:** sore 10 **spak:** spoke **mair:** more 11 **meikle:** much 17 **lighted down:** alighted 18 **sma':** small 34 **winding sheet:** sheet in which a corpse is wrapped **ower:** over **een:** eyes

A LYKE-WAKE DIRGE

THIS ae nighte, this ae nighte,
   Every nighte and alle;
Fire and fleet and candle-lighte,
   And Christe receive thy saule.

When thou from hence away are past,   5
   Every nighte and alle;
To Whinny-muir thou com'st at last;
   And Christe receive thy saule.

If ever thou gavest hosen and shoon,
   Every nighte and alle;   10
Sit thee down and put them on;
   And Christe receive thy saule.

If hosen and shoon thou ne'er gav'st nane
Every nighte and alle;
The whinnes sall prick thee to the bare bane; 15
And Christe receive thy saule.

From Whinny-muir when thou may'st pass,
Every nighte and alle;
To Brigg o' Dread thou com'st at last;
And Christe receive thy saule. 20

From Brigg o' Dread when thou may'st pass,
Every nighte and alle;
To Purgatory fire thou com'st at last;
And Christe receive thy saule.

If ever thou gavest meat or drink, 25
Every nighte and alle;
The fire shall never make thee shrink;
And Christe receive thy saule.

If meat or drink thou ne'er gav'st nane,
Every nighte and alle; 30
The fire will burn thee to the bare bane;
And Christe receive thy saule.

This ae night, this ae night,
Every nighte and alle;
Fire and fleet and candle lighte, 35
And Christe receive thy saule.

A LYKE-WAKE DIRGE: **lyke-wake:** a watch (*wake*) over a dead body (*lyke* or *lych*): 1 **ae:** one 3 **fleet:** (more correctly *flet*) house-room; 'fire and flet' is an old legal term 9 **hosen:** stockings **shoon:** shoes 13 **nane:** none 15 **whinnes:** gorse **bane:** bone

MARIE HAMILTON

WORD'S gane to the kitchen,
And word's gane to the ha',
That Marie Hamilton gangs wi' bairn,
To the hichest Stewart of a'.

He's courted her in the kitchen, 5
He's courted her in the ha',
He's courted her in the laigh cellar,
And that was warst of a'!

She's tyed it in her apron,
And she's thrown it in the sea, 10
Says, 'Sink ye, swim ye, bonny wee babe,
You'll ne'er get mair o' me.'

MARIE HAMILTON: 1 **gane:** gone 2 **ha':** hall 3 **gangs wi' bairn:** is with child 4 **hichest:** highest 7 **laigh:** low 12 **mair:** more

Down than cam the auld queen,
Goud tassels tying her hair –
'O, Marie, where's the bonny wee babe, 15
That I heard greet sae sair?'

'There was never a babe intill my room,
As little designs to be;
It was but a touch o' my sair side,
Come o'er my fair bodie.' 20

'O, Marie, put on your robes o' black,
Or else your robes o' brown,
For ye maun gang wi' me the night,
To see fair Edinbro' town.'

'I winna put on my robes o' black, 25
Nor yet my robes o' brown,
But I'll put on my robes o' white,
To shine through Edinbro' town.'

When she gaed up the Cannogate,
She laugh'd loud laughters three; 30
But whan she cam down the Cannogate,
The tear blinded her ee.

When she gaed up the Parliament stair,
The heel cam aff her shee;
And lang or she cam down again, 35
She was condemn'd to dee.

When she cam down the Cannogate,
The Cannogate sae free,
Mony a ladie look'd o'er her window,
Weeping for this ladie. 40

'Ye need nae weep for me,' she says,
'Ye need nae weep for me;
For had I not slain mine own sweet babe,
This death I wadna dee.

'Bring me a bottle of wine,' she says, 45
'The best that e'er ye hae,
That I may drink to my weil-wishers,
And they may drink to me.

'Here's a health to the jolly sailors,
That sail upon the main; 50
Let them never let on to my father and mother
But what I'm coming hame.

'Here's a health to the jolly sailors,
That sail upon the sea;
Let them never let on to my father and mother, 55
That I cam here to dee.

13 **auld:** old 16 **greet:** cry **sair:** sore 17 **intill:** into 23 **maun:** must **the night:** tonight 29 **gaed:** went 32 **ee:** eye 34 **shee:** shoe 36 **dee:** die 39 **o'er:** out of 44 **wadna:** would not 46 **hae:** have 47 **weil:** well 51 **let on to:** tell 52 **hame:** home

'Oh, little did my mother think,
  The day she cradled me,
What lands I was to travel through,
  What death I was to dee.

'Oh, little did my father think,   60
  The day he held up me,
What lands I was to travel through,
  What death I was to dee.

'Last night I wash'd the queen's feet,   65
  And gently laid her down;
And a' the thanks I've gotten the nicht,
  To be hang'd in Edinbro' town.

'Last night there were four Maries,
  The nicht there'l be but three;   70
There was Marie Seton, and Marie Beton,
  And Marie Carmichael, and me.'

EDWARD, EDWARD

'WHY dois your brand sae drap wi' bluid,
  Edward, Edward?
Why dois your brand sae drap wi' bluid?
  And why sae sad gang yee, O?'
'O, I hae killed my hauke sae guid,   5
  Mither, mither:
O, I hae killed my hauke sae guid;
  And I had nae mair bot hee, O.'

'Your haukis bluid was nevir sae reid;
  Edward, Edward.
Your haukis bluid was nevir sae reid;   10
  My deir son I tell thee, O.'
'O, I hae killed my reid-roan steid,
  Mither, mither:
O, I hae killed my reid-roan steid,
  That erst was sae fair and frie, O.'   15

'Your steid was auld, and ye hae gat mair,
  Edward, Edward:
Your steid was auld, and ye hae gat mair,
  Sum other dule ye drie, O.'   20
'O, I hae killed my fadir deir,
  Mither, mither:
O, I hae killed my fadir deir
  Alas! and wae is mee, O!'

'And whatten penance wul ye drie for that?   25
  Edward, Edward.
And whatten penance will ye drie for that?
  My deir son, now tell me, O.'
'Ile set my feit in yonder boat,
  Mither, mither: 30
Ile set my feit in yonder boat,
  And Ile fare ovir the sea, O.'

'And what wul ye doe wi' your towirs and your ha',
  Edward, Edward?
And what wul ye doe wi' your towirs and your ha',   35
  That were sae fair to see, O?'
'Ile let thame stand tul they doun fa',
  Mither, mither:
Ile let thame stand tul they doun fa',
  For here nevir mair maun I bee, O.'   40

'And what wul ye leive to your bairns and your wife,
  Edward, Edward?
And what wul ye lieve to your bairns and your wife,
  Whan ye gang ovir the sea, O?'
'The warldis room, late them beg thrae life,   45
  Mither, mither:
The warldis room, late them beg thrae life,
  For thame nevir mair wul I see, O.'

'And what wul ye leive to your ain mither deir,
  Edward, Edward: 50
And what wul ye leive to your ain mither deir,
  My deir son, now tell mee, O.'
'The curse of hell frae me sall ye beir,
  Mither, mither:
The curse of hell frae me sall ye beir,   55
  Sic counseils ye gave to me, O.'

EDWARD, EDWARD: 1 **brand:** sword **sae:** so **drap:** drop **bluid:** blood 4 **why sae sad gang yee:** why do you look so sad 6 **Mither:** mother 8 **nae mair bot:** no other but 9 **reid:** red 13 **steid:** steed 16 **erst:** once **frie:** free 17 **auld:** old **hae gat mare:** have others 20 **dule:** grief **drie:** bear 21 **fadir deir:** father dear 24 **wae:** woe 25 **whatten:** what 33 **wul:** will **ha':** hall 37 **thame:** them **tul:** till **fa':** fall 40 **nevir mair:** never more **maun:** must 41 **bairns:** children 44 **gang ovir:** go over 45 **warldis room:** the whole world's space **thrae:** through 49 **ain:** own 53 **frae:** from **sall:** shall **beir:** bear 56 **Sic counsels:** such advice

ANNE FINCH, COUNTESS OF WINCHILSEA

A NOCTURNAL REVERIE

IN such a night, when every louder wind
Is to its distant cavern safe confined;
And only gentle Zephyr fans his wings,
And lonely Philomel, still waking, sings;
Or from some tree, famed for the owl's delight,   5
She, hollowing clear, directs the wand'rer right:
In such a night, when passing clouds give place,
Or thinly veil the heavens' mysterious face;
When in some river, overhung with green,
The waving moon and trembling leaves are seen;   10
When freshened grass now bears itself upright,
And makes cool banks to pleasing rest invite,
Whence springs the woodbind, and the bramble-rose,

And where the sleepy cowslip sheltered grows;
Whilst now a paler hue the foxglove takes, 15
Yet chequers still with red the dusky brakes
When scattered glowworms, but in twilight fine,
Show trivial beauties watch their hour to shine;
Whilst Salisb'ry stands the test of every light,
In perfect charms, and perfect virtue bright: 20
When odours which declined repelling day
Through temp'rate air uninterrupted stray;
When darkened groves their softest shadows wear,
And falling waters we distinctly hear;
When through the gloom more venerable shows 25
Some ancient fabric, awful in repose,
While sunburnt hills their swarthy looks conceal,
And swelling haycocks thicken up the vale:
When the loosed horse now, as his pasture leads,
Comes slowly grazing through th'adjoining meads, 30
Whose stealing pace and lengthened shade we fear,
Till torn-up forage in his teeth we hear:
When nibbling sheep at large pursue their food,
And unmolested kine rechew the cud;
When curlews cry beneath the village walls, 35
And to her straggling brood the partridge calls;
Their short-lived jubilee the creatures keep,
Which but endures whilst tyrant man does sleep;
When a sedate content the spirit feels,
And no fierce light disturb, whilst it reveals; 40
But silent musings urge the mind to seek
Something too high for syllables to speak;
Till the free soul to a compos'dness charmed,
Finding the elements of rage disarmed,
O'er all below a solemn quiet grown, 45
Joys in th'inferior world, and thinks it like her own:
In such a night let me abroad remain,
Till morning breaks, and all's confused again;
Our cares, our toils, our clamours are renewed,
Or pleasures, seldom reached, again pursued. 50

A NOCTURNAL REVERIE: **reverie:** meditation: 1–2 **every . . . confined:**
Aeolus was a mortal to whom Zeus gave control of the winds.
He lived in a cave on the floating islands of Aeolia 3 **Zephyr:**
Zephyrus, in Greek mythology the west wind 4 **Philomel:** i.e. a
nightingale 6 **hollowing:** calling 16 **brakes:** thickets 19 **Salisb'ry:**
perhaps Lady Salisbury, daughter of the poet's friend 21 **declined**
repelling day: chose not to emerge in the heat of the day 26 **awful:**
awe-inspiring 28 **haycocks:** haystacks 30 **meads:** meadows, pastures
34 **kine:** cows

MATTHEW PRIOR

TO A CHILD OF QUALITY

FIVE YEARS OLD, 1704. THE AUTHOR THEN FORTY

LORDS, knights, and squires, the num'rous band
  That wear the fair Miss Mary's fetters,
Were summoned by her high command
  To show their passion by their letters.

My pen amongst the rest I took, 5
  Lest those bright eyes that cannot read
Should dart their kindling fires, and look
  The pow'r they have to be obeyed.

Nor quality nor reputation
  Forbid me yet my flame to tell; 10
Dear Five-years-old befriends my passion,
  And I may write till she can spell.

For, while she makes her silkworms beds
  With all the tender things I swear,
Whilst all the house my passion reads, 15
  In papers round her baby's hair,

She may receive and own my flame,
  For, though the strictest prudes should know it,
She'll pass for a most virtuous dame,
  And I for an unhappy poet. 20

Then, too, alas! when she shall tear
  The lines some younger rival sends,
She'll give me leave to write, I fear,
  And we shall still continue friends.

For, as our diff'rent ages move, 25
  'Tis so ordained (would Fate but mend it!)
That I shall be past making love
  When she begins to comprehend it.

TO A CHILD OF QUALITY: 10 **flame:** love 13–16 **makes . . . hair:** i.e. she
shreds my poem as bedding for her silkworms or to tie her doll's
hair

A BETTER ANSWER

TO CHLOE JEALOUS

DEAR Chloe, how blubbered is that pretty face!
  Thy cheek all on fire, and thy hair all uncurled:
Prithee quit this caprice; and (as old Falstaff says)
  Let us e'en talk a little like folks of this world.

How canst thou presume thou hast leave to destroy 5
  The beauties which Venus but lent to thy keeping?
Those looks were designed to inspire love and joy:
  More ord'nary eyes may serve people for weeping.

To be vexed at a trifle or two that I writ, 9
  Your judgement at once and my passion you wrong:
You take that for fact which will scarce be found wit:
  Od's life! must one swear to the truth of a song?

What I speak, my fair Chloe, and what I write, shows
  The dif'rence there is betwixt Nature and Art:
I court others in verse, but I love thee in prose: 15
  And they have my whimsies, but thou hast my heart.

The god of us verse-men (you know, child), the Sun,
  How after his journeys he sets up his rest:
If at morning o'er Earth 'tis his fancy to run,
  At night he reclines on his Thetis's breast.   20

So when I am wearied with wand'ring all day,
  To thee my delight in the evening I come:
No matter what beauties I saw in my way:
  They were but my visits, but thou art my home.

Then, finish, dear Chloe, this pastoral war;   25
  And let us like Horace and Lydia agree:
For thou art a girl as much brighter than her
  As he was a poet sublimer than me.

A BETTER ANSWER: 3–4 **as old Falstaff . . . this world:** Shakespeare's *2 Henry IV* (5.3). *Pistol.* 'And tidings do I bring, and lucky joys,/And golden times, and happy news of price.' *Falstaff.* 'I pray thee now, deliver them like a man of this world' 6 **Venus:** Roman goddess of beauty and love, associated with the Greek Aphrodite 12 **Od's life:** God's life 17–20 **The god of us verse-men . . . the Sun:** Apollo, the Greek god of music and poetry, was also (under his title Phoebus, 'the bright one') the god of light, and was occasionally identified with Helios, the sun-god **on his Thetis's breast:** i.e. in the ocean; Thetis was a sea-goddess 25 **pastoral:** type of poetry invented by the Greek poet Theocritus (3rd century BC) depicting the idealised lives and loves of shepherds and shepherdesses 26 **Horace and Lydia:** the *Odes* of the Roman poet Horace (65–8 BC) includes several love-poems addressed to Lydia

JONATHAN SWIFT

VERSES ON THE DEATH OF DR SWIFT, DSPD
OCCASIONED BY READING A MAXIM IN ROCHEFOUCAULD

*Dans l'adversité de nos meilleurs amis nous trouvons quelque chose,
qui ne nous deplaist pas*

As Rochefoucauld his maxims drew
From Nature, I believe 'em true:
They argue no corrupted mind
In him; the fault is in mankind.
  This maxim more than all the rest   5
Is thought too base for human breast:
'In all distresses of our friends
We first consult our private ends,
While Nature, kindly bent to ease us,
Points out some circumstance to please us.'   10

'VERSES ON THE DEATH OF DR SWIFT': 'I have been several months writing near five hundred lines on a pleasant subject, only to tell what my friends and enemies will say on me after I am dead. I shall finish it soon, for I add two lines every week, and blot out four, and alter eight' (Swift letter to John Gay, 1 December 1731); Swift provided his own commentary on the poem, and those notes are incorporated here, amplified where appropriate: **D.S.P.D.:** Dean of St Patrick's Dublin; Swift became dean of St Patrick's Cathedral in 1713: **Dans l' adversité . . . qui ne nous déplaist pas':** François duc de La Rochefoucauld, *Réflexions ou Sentences et maximes morales*, 1655, no. 99; Swift translates it as 'In the adversity of our best friends, we find something that doth not displease us', and also offers a verse paraphrase in lines 7–10: 9 **bent:** intent

If this, perhaps, your patience move,
Let reason and experience prove.
  We all behold with envious eyes
Our equal raised above our size;
Who would not at a crowded show   15
Stand high himself, keep others low?
I love my friend as well as you,
But would not have him stop my view;
Then let me have the higher post:
I ask but for an inch at most.   20
  If, in a battle, you should find
One, whom you love of all mankind,
Had some heroic action done,
A champion killed, or trophy won;
Rather than thus be overtopped,   25
Would you not wish his laurels cropped?
  Dear honest Ned is in the gout,
Lies racked with pain, and you without:
How patiently you hear him groan!
How glad the case is not your own!   30
  What poet would not grieve to see
His brethren write as well as he?
But rather than they should excel,
He'd wish his rivals all in hell.
  Her end when Emulation misses,   35
She turns to envy, stings, and hisses:
The strongest friendship yields to pride,
Unless the odds be on our side.
  Vain humankind! fantastic race!
Thy various follies who can trace?   40
Self-love, ambition, envy, pride,
Their empire in our hearts divide:
Give others riches, pow'r, and station,
'Tis all on me an usurpation.
I have no title to aspire;   45
Yet, when you sink, I seem the higher;
In Pope I cannot read a line,
But with a sigh I wish it mine:
When he can in one couplet fix
More sense than I can do in six,   50
It gives me such a jealous fit,
I cry, 'Pox take him, and his wit!'
  Why must I be outdone by Gay,
In my own hum'rous biting way?
  Arbuthnot is no more my friend,   55
Who dares to irony pretend;
Which I was born to introduce,
Refined it first, and showed its use.
  St John as well as Pult'ney knows
That I had some repute for prose;   60
And, till they drove me out of date,
Could maul a Minister of State.
If they have mortified my pride,
And made me throw my pen aside;

19 **post:** position, platform 26 **laurels:** the laurel wreath used to crown a victor 27 **gout:** defined by Samuel Johnson, a fellow sufferer, as 'a periodical disease attended with great pain' (*Dictionary*), gout results from an excess of uric acid in the blood, causing swollen joints, especially in the big toe

If with such talents heaven hath blessed 'em, 65
Have I not reason to detest 'em?
   To all my foes, dear Fortune, send
Thy gifts, but never to my friend:
I tamely can endure the first,
But this with envy makes me burst. 70
   Thus much may serve by way of proem;
Proceed we therefore to our poem.
   The time is not remote, when I
Must by the course of nature die:
When, I foresee, my special friends 75
Will try to find their private ends:
Though it is hardly understood
Which way my death can do them good,
Yet thus, methinks, I hear 'em speak:
'See, how the Dean begins to break! 80
Poor gentleman, he droops apace!
You plainly find it in his face.
That old vertigo in his head
Will never leave him, till he's dead.
Besides, his memory decays: 85
He recollects not what he says;
He cannot call his friends to mind;
Forgets the place where last he dined;
Plies you with stories o'er and o'er,
He told them fifty times before. 90
How does he fancy we can sit,
To hear his out-of-fashioned wit?
But he takes up with younger folks,
Who for his wine will bear his jokes.
Faith, he must make his stories shorter, 95
Or change his comrades once a quarter:
In half the time he talks them round,
There must another set be found.
   'For poetry, he's past his prime:
He takes an hour to find a rhyme; 100
His fire is out, his wit decayed,
His fancy sunk, his Muse a jade.
I'd have him throw away his pen;
But there's no talking to some men!'
   And then their tenderness appears, 105
By adding largely to my years:
'He's older than he would be reckoned,
And well remembers Charles the Second.
   'He hardly drinks a pint of wine;
And that, I doubt, is no good sign. 110
His stomach too begins to fail:
Last year we thought him strong and hale;
But now he's quite another thing;
I wish he may hold out till spring!'
   Then hug themselves, and reason thus: 115
'It is not yet so bad with us.'
   In such a case they talk in tropes,
And by their fears express their hopes:
Some great misfortune to portend,
No enemy can match a friend; 120
With all the kindness they profess,
The merit of a lucky guess
(When daily how-d'ye's come of course,
And servants answer: 'Worse and worse')

Would please 'em better than to tell 125
That 'God be praised, the Dean is well'.
Then he who prophesied the best
Approves his foresight to the rest:
'You know, I always feared the worst,
And often told you so at first.' 130
He'd rather choose that I should die
Than his prediction prove a lie.
Not one foretells I shall recover;
But all agree to give me over.
   Yet should some neighbour feel a pain, 135
Just in the parts where I complain,
How many a message would he send?
What hearty prayers that I should mend?
Enquire what regimen I kept?
What gave me ease, and how I slept? 140
And more lament, when I was dead,
Than all the sniv'llers round my bed.
   My good companions, never fear;
For though you may mistake a year,
Though your prognostics run too fast, 145
They must be verified at last.
   Behold the fatal day arrive!
'How is the Dean? He's just alive.
Now the departing prayer is read;
He hardly breathes. The Dean is dead.' 150
Before the passing-bell begun,
The news through half the town has run.
'Oh, may we all for death prepare!
What has he left? And who's his heir?
I know no more than what the news is; 155
'Tis all bequeathed to public uses.
To public use! A perfect whim!
What had the public done for him!
Mere envy, avarice, and pride!
He gave it all – but, first, he died. 160
And had the Dean, in all the nation,
No worthy friend, no poor relation?
So ready to do strangers good,
Forgetting his own flesh and blood!'
   Now Grub Street wits are all employed; 165
With elegies the town is cloyed:
Some paragraph in ev'ry paper,
To curse the Dean, or bless the Drapier.

149 **departing prayer:** prayer for the soul of the dying 151 **passing-bell:** funeral bell 165 **Grub Street:** former name of Milton Street, Moorfields, 'much inhabited by writers of small histories, dictionaries, and temporary poems; whence any mean production is called *grubstreet*' (Johnson's *Dictionary*) 168 **To curse the Dean, or bless the Drapier:** 'One [William] Wood, a hardware-man from England, had a patent for coining copper halfpence in Ireland, to the sum of £108,000, which in the consequence must leave that kingdom without gold or silver' (S); here 'The author imagines that the scribblers of the prevailing party, which he always opposed, will libel him after his death; but that others will remember him with gratitude, who consider the service he had done to Ireland, under the name of M. B. Drapier, by utterly defeating the destructive project of Wood's halfpence in five letters to the people of Ireland, at that time read universally and convincing every reader' (S). The large number of coins to be minted woud have given Wood a vast profit but would also have depressed Ireland's economy even further. The deal brought a flood of protests and was later revoked

The doctors, tender of their fame,
Wisely on me lay all the blame: 170
'We must confess his case was nice;
But he would never take advice;
Had he been ruled, for aught appears,
He might have lived these twenty years:
For when we opened him, we found   175
That all his vital parts were sound.'

    From Dublin soon to London spread,
'Tis told at Court, 'The Dean is dead'.

    Kind Lady Suffolk in the spleen
Runs laughing up to tell the Queen.   180
The Queen, so gracious, mild, and good,
Cries: 'Is he gone? 'Tis time he should.
He's dead, you say; then let him rot;
I'm glad the medals were forgot.
I promised him, I own; but when?   185
I only was the Princess then;
But now, as consort of a king,
You know 'tis quite a diff'rent thing.'

    Now Chartres at Sir Robert's levee,
Tells, with a sneer, the tidings heavy: 190

'Why, is he dead without his shoes?'
Cries Bob. 'I'm sorry for the news.
Oh, were the wretch but living still,
And in his place my good friend Will;
Or had a mitre on his head   195
Provided Bolingbroke were dead.'

    Now Curll his shop from rubbish drains;
Three genuine tomes of Swift's remains.
And then, to make them pass the glibber,
Revised by Tibbalds, Moore and Cibber.   200
He'll treat me as he does my betters,
Publish my Will, my Life, my Letters.
Revive the libels born to die;
Which Pope must bear as well as I.

---

169 **tender of their fame:** careful of their reputation   171 **nice:** delicate   178 **'Tis told . . . dead':** 'The Dean supposeth himself to die in Ireland' (S)   179 **Lady Suffolk:** 'Mrs Howard, afterwards Countess of Suffolk, then of the Bedchamber to the Queen, professed much friendship for the Dean. The Queen, then Princess, sent a dozen times to the Dean (then in London) with her command to attend her; which at last he did, by advice of all his friends. She often sent for him afterwards, and always treated him very graciously. He taxed her with a present worth ten pounds, which she promised before he should return to Ireland; but, on his taking leave, the medals were not ready' (S)   **in the spleen:** in high spirits   184 **I'm glad . . . forgot:** 'The mdeals were to be sent to the Dean in four months, but she forgot them, or thought them too dear. The Dean, being in Ireland, sent Mrs Howard [in 1726] a piece of Indian plaid made in that kingdom [i.e. Irish poplin "made in imitation of the Indian"]: which the Queen seeing took from her, and wore it herself, and sent to the Dean for as much as would clothe herself and children, desiring he would send the charge of it. He did the former. It cost thirty-five pounds, but he said he would have nothing except the medals. He was the summer following in England, was treated as usual, and, she being then Queen, the Dean was promised a settlement [i.e. church living] in England, but returned as he went, and, instead of favour or medals, hath been ever since under her Majesty's displeasure' (S)   **own:** confess   189 **Chartres:** Colonel Francis Charteris (1675–1732), 'a most infamous, vile scoundrel, grown from a footboy, or worse, to a prodigious fortune both in England and Scotland. He had a way of insinuating himself into all ministers under every change, either as pimp, flatterer, or informer. He was tried at seventy [in fact 55] for a rape, and came off by sacrificing a great part of his fortune' (S). Pope described Charteris as 'infamous for all manner of vices' and *twice* condemned for rape; 'The populace at his funeral raised a great riot, almost tore the body out of the coffin, and cast dead dogs &c, into the grave along with it' (*Moral Essays* 3)   **Sir Robert:** 'Sir Robert Walpole [1676–1745], Chief Minister of State, treated the Dean in 1726 with great distinction, invited him to dinner at Chelsea, with the Dean's friends chosen on purpose; appointed an hour to talk with him of Ireland, to which kingdom and people the Dean found him no great friend; for he defended Wood's project of halfpence, etc. The Dean would see him no more; and, upon his next year's return to England, Sir Robert on an accidental meeting only made a civil compliment and never invited him again' (S)   **levee:** early-morning reception

194 **Will:** 'Mr William Pulteney [1684–1764], from being Mr Walpole's intimate friend, detesting his administration, opposed his measures, and joined with my Lord Bolingbroke [in 1726] to represent his conduct in an excellent paper, called *The Craftsman*, which is still continued' (S). In 1742, the year of Walpole's downfall, Pulteney was created Earl of Bath. Swift first met him on a visit to England in 1726   195 **had a mitre on his head:** had been made a bishop   196 **Bolingbroke:** 'Henry St John, Lord Viscount Bolingbroke [1678–1751], Secretary of State to Queen Anne of blessed memory. He is reckoned the most universal genius in Europe. Walpole, dreading his abilities, treated him most injuriously, working with King George, who forgot his promise of restoring the said lord upon the restless importunity of Walpole' (S). Bolingbroke became a dominant figure in the Tory party, and was Secretary for War (1704–8) and Secretary of State (1710), negotiating the Treaty of Utrecht in 1713. On the accession of George I in 1714 he fled to France and declared his allegiance to the Pretender, Charles Stuart. Convicted of treason and stripped of his peerage, he was granted a limited pardon in 1723 and in 1725 returned to England, friendship with Pope, Swift and Gay, and a life of political journalism, principally with *The Craftsman*, in which he attacked the Walpole government. In 1735 he retired to France but continued to write, producing *A Letter on the Spirit of Patriotism* (1736) and *The Idea of a Patriot King* (1738)   197 **Curll:** Edmund Curll (1675–1747) 'hath been the most infamous bookseller of any age or country: his character in part may be found in Mr Pope's *Dunciad*. He published three volumes all charged on [i.e. attributed to] the Dean, who never writ three pages of them. He hath used many of the Dean's friends in almost as vile a manner' (S)   199 **pass the glibber:** sell more readily   200 **Tibbalds, Moore and Cibber:** 'Three stupid verse writers in London; the last, to the shame of the Court, and the highest disgrace to wit and learning, was made Laureate. Moore, commonly called Jemmy Moore, son of Arthur Moore, whose father was jailer of Monaghan in Ireland. See the character of Jemmy Moore, and Tibbalds, Theobald, in the *Dunciad*' (S). Lewis Theobald (1688–1744), poet and Shakespeare scholar, exposed Pope's inadequacy as an editor of Shakespeare; Pope responded by making Theobald the hero of *The Dunciad* (although he was replaced by Cibber in the 1743 edition). James Moore Smythe (1702–34) was the author of *The Rival Modes* (1727), for which Pope accused him of stealing lines from Pope's own 'To Mrs M[artha] B[lount] on Her Birthday' and ridiculed him in *The Dunciad* (2.35–50). The appointment of Colley Cibber (1671–1757), actor and playwright, as Poet Laureate in 1730 occasioned general ridicule (see also line 270)   202 **Publish my Will, my Life, my Letters:** 'Curll is notoriously infamous for publishing the Lives, Letters, and Last Wills and Testaments of the nobility and ministers of state, as well as of all the rogues who are hanged at Tyburn. He hath been in custody of the House of Lords for publishing or forging the letters of many peers; which made the Lords enter a resolution in their journal book that no life or writings of any lord should be published without the consent of the next heir at law, or licence from their House' (S)

Here shift the scene, to represent 205
How those I love my death lament.
Poor Pope will grieve a month; and Gay
A week; and Arbuthnot a day.
   St John himself will scarce forbear
To bite his pen, and drop a tear. 210
The rest will give a shrug, and cry:
'I'm sorry; but we all must die.'
Indiff'rence clad in Wisdom's guise
All fortitude of mind supplies;
For how can stony bowels melt 215
In those who never pity felt;
When we are lashed, they kiss the rod,
Resigning to the will of God.
   The fools, my juniors by a year,
Are tortured with suspense and fear; 220
Who wisely thought my age a screen,
When Death approached, to stand between:
The screen removed, their hearts are trembling,
They mourn for me without dissembling.
   My female friends, whose tender hearts 225
Have better learned to act their parts,
Receive the news in doleful dumps:
'The Dean is dead (and what is trumps?),
Then Lord have mercy on his soul.
(Ladies, I'll venture for the vole.) 230
Six deans they say must bear the pall.
(I wish I knew what king to call.)
Madam, your husband will attend
The funeral of so good a friend?
No, Madam, 'tis a shocking sight; 235
And he's engaged tomorrow night!
My Lady Club would take it ill
If he should fail her at quadrille.
He loved the Dean. (I led a heart.)
But dearest friends, they say, must part. 240
His time was come; he ran his race;
We hope he's in a better place.'
   Why do we grieve that friends should die?
No loss more easy to supply.
One year is past: a diff'rent scene; 245
No further mention of the Dean;
Who now, alas, no more is missed
Than if he never did exist.
Where's now this fav'rite of Apollo?
Departed; and his works must follow: 250
Must undergo the common fate;
His kind of wit is out of date.
Some country squire to Lintot goes,

Enquires for Swift in verse and prose.
Says Lintot:'I have heard the name; 255
He died a year ago.' 'The same.'
He searcheth all his shop in vain.
'Sir, you may find them in Duck Lane:
I sent them, with a load of books,
Last Monday to the pastry cook's. 260
To fancy they could live a year!
I find you're but a stranger here.
The Dean was famous in his time;
And had a kind of knack at rhyme:
His way of writing now is past; 265
The town hath got a better taste:
I keep no antiquated stuff;
But spick and span I have enough.
Pray, do but give me leave to show 'em:
Here's Colley Cibber's Birthday Poem. 270
This Ode you never yet have seen,
By Stephen Duck, upon the Queen.
Then, here's a Letter finely penned
Against the Craftsman and his friend;
It clearly shows that all reflection 275
On Ministers is disaffection.
Next, here's Sir Robert's Vindication,
And Mr Henley's last Oration:
The hawkers have not got 'em yet,
Your honour please to buy a set? 280
   'Here's Woolston's Tracts, the twelfth edition;
'Tis read by ev'ry politician;
The country Members, when in town,
To all their boroughs send them down:
You never met a thing so smart; 285

228 **trumps:** the suit of playing cards that currently ranks above the other three 230 **vole:** in card games, to win all the tricks in one deal 231 **bear the pall:** act as pall-bearers, carry the coffin 238 **quadrille:** four-handed card game 249 **Apollo:** Greek god of music and poetry 253 **Lintot:** Bernard Lintot (1675–1736), 'a bookseller in London. *Vide* Mr Pope's *Dunciad*' (S); Lintot was Pope's publisher until the two men quarrelled and Pope humiliated him in *The Dunciad*: 'As when a dabchick waddles through the copse,/On feet and wings, and flies, and wades, and hops;/So lab'ring on, with shoulders, hands, and head,/Wide as a windmill all his figure spread,/With legs expanded Bernard urged the race' (2.59–63)

258 **Duck Lane:** 'A place in London where old books are sold' (S); Duck Lane is the former name of the northern stretch of Little Britain, Smithfield, in Swift's time an area popular with booksellers 259–60 **I sent them . . . pastry cook's:** i.e. the pages would be used to line pie-dishes; cf. Dryden's 'MacFlecknoe' (line 101) 272 **Stephen Duck:** Duck (1705–56) was a self-educated agricultural labourer whose verses were brought to the attention of Queen Caroline, who received him at Court, gave him a house in Richmond Park and an allowance. Duck's *Poems on Several Subjects* (1730) was a remarkable success. He was ordained, but his mind began to fail, and he eventually drowned himself. Swift ridiculed him in 'On Stephen Duck, the Thresher and Favourite Poet: A Quibbling Epigram' (1730) 274 **the Craftsman:** see note to line 194 above 277 **Sir Robert's Vindication:** 'Walpole hires a set of party scribblers who do nothing else but write in his defence' (S) 278 **Mr Henley:** Rev. John Henley (d.1756), 'a clergyman who, wanting both merit and luck to get preferment, or even to keep his curacy in the Established Church, formed a new conventicle [i.e. private religious meeting], which he called an oratory. There, at set times, he delivereth strange speeches compiled by himself and his associates, who share the profit with him. Every hearer pays a shilling each day for admittance. He is an absolute dunce, but generally reputed crazy' (S) 281 **Woolston's Tracts:** Thomas Woolston (1670–1733) was the author of *Old Apology for the Truth of the Christian Religion*, proposing an allegorical interpretation of the scriptures, *The Moderator between an Infidel and an Apostate* (1725) and *Discourses on the Miracles of Christ* (1727–9); tried for blasphemy, he died in prison. 'Woolston was a clergyman but, for want of bread, hath in several treatises, in the most blasphemous manner, attempted to turn Our Saviour and his miracles into ridicule. He is much caressed by many great courtiers, and by all the infidels, and his books read generally by the court ladies' (S)

The courtiers have them all by heart;
Those maids of honour who can read
Are taught to use them for their Creed.
The rev'rend author's good intention
Hath been rewarded with a pension;   290
He doth an honour to his gown,
By bravely running priestcraft down;
He shows, as sure as God's in Gloucester,
That Jesus was a grand imposter,
That all his miracles were cheats,   295
Performed as jugglers do their feats;
The Church had never such a writer;
A shame he hath not got a mitre!'
    Suppose me dead; and then suppose
A club assembled at the Rose;   300
Where, from discourse of this and that,
I grow the subject of their chat;
And, while they toss my name about,
With favour some, and some without,
One quite indiff'rent in the cause,   305
My character impartial draws:
    'The Dean, if we believe report,
Was never ill received at Court.
As for his works in verse and prose,
I own myself no judge of those;   310
Nor can I tell what critics thought 'em;
But this I know, all people bought 'em;
As with a moral view designed
To cure the vices of mankind:
His vein, ironically grave,   315
Exposed the fool, and lashed the knave;
To steal a hint was never known,
But what he writ was all his own.
    'He never thought an honour done him
Because a duke was proud to own him;   320
Would rather slip aside and choose
To talk with wits in dirty shoes;
Despised the fools with stars and garters,
So often seen caressing Chartres:
He never courted men in station,   325
Nor persons held in admiration;
Of no man's greatness was afraid,
Because he sought for no man's aid.
Though trusted long in great affairs,
He gave himself no haughty airs;   330
Without regarding private ends,
Spent all his credit for his friends;
And only chose the wise and good;
No flatt'rers, no allies in blood;
But succoured virtue in distress,   335

And seldom failed of good success;
As numbers in their hearts must own,
Who, but for him, had been unknown.
    'With princes kept a due decorum,
But never stood in awe before 'em: 340
He followed David's lesson just,
"In princes never put thy trust".
And, would you make him truly sour,
Provoke him with a slave in pow'r.
The Irish Senate, if you named,   345
With what impatience he declaimed!
Fair LIBERTY was all his cry;
For her he stood prepared to die;
For her he boldly stood alone;
For her he oft exposed his own.   350
Two kingdoms, just as faction led,
Had set a price upon his head;
But not a traitor could be found
To sell him for six hundred pound.
    'Had he but spared his tongue and pen,   355
He might have rose like other men;
But, pow'r was never in his thought,
And wealth he valued not a groat;
Ingratitude he often found,
And pitied those who meant the wound;   360
But kept the tenor of his mind
To merit well of humankind;
Nor made a sacrifice of those
Who still were true, to please his foes.
He laboured many a fruitless hour   365
To reconcile his friends in pow'r;
Saw mischief by a faction brewing,
While they pursued each other's ruin.
But, finding vain was all his care,
He left the Court in mere despair.   370

341–2 **David's lesson . . . trust**: 'Put not your trust in princes, nor in the son of man, in whom there is no help' (Psalm 146.3) 344 **a slave in pow'r**: an official controlled (and probably bribed) by an outside influence 350 **his own**: i.e. his own liberty 351 **Two kingdoms, just as faction led**: 'In the year 1713 the late Queen was prevailed with by an address of the House of Lords in England to publish a proclamation promising three hundred pounds to whatever person would discover the author of a pamphlet called *The Public Spirit of the Whigs* [i.e. Swift]; and in Ireland, in the year 1724, my Lord Cartaret, at his first coming into the government, was prevailed on to issue a proclamation for promising the like reward of three hundred pounds to any person who could discover the author of a pamphlet called *The Drapier's Fourth Letter*; but in neither kingdom was the Dean discovered' (S) 358 **groat**: English silver coin worth four old pennies (2p); thus, a very small amount 365 **He laboured many a fruitless hour**: 'Queen Anne's ministry fell to variance [i.e. disagreement] from the first year after their ministry began. Harcourt the Chancellor and Lord Bolingbroke the Secretary were discontented with the Treasurer, Oxford, for his too much mildness to the Whig party; this quarrel grew higher every day till the Queen's death. The Dean, who was the only person that endeavoured to reconcile them, found it impossible; and thereupon retired to the country about ten weeks before that fatal event; upon which, he returned to his deanery in Dublin, where for many years he was worried by the new people in power, and had hundreds of libels writ against him in England' (S)

288 **Creed**: articles of religious belief 291 **gown**: holy orders 293 **as sure as God's in Gloucester**: proverbial 300 **club**: 'An assembly of good fellows, meeting under certain conditions' (Johnson's *Dictionary*) **the Rose**: tavern in Russell Street, Covent Garden; demolished in 1776 when David Garrick enlarged Drury Lane Theatre 323 **stars and garters**: decorations 325 **station**: office, position of power 334 **allies in blood**: members of his own family

'And, oh! how short are human schemes!
Here ended all our golden dreams.
What St John's skill in state affairs,
What Ormond's valour, Oxford's cares,
To save their sinking country lent,   375
Was all destroyed by one event.
Too soon that precious life was ended,
On which alone our weal depended.
When up a dang'rous faction starts,
With wrath and vengeance in their hearts: 380
By solemn league and cov'nant bound,
To ruin, slaughter, and confound;
To turn religion to a fable,
And make the Government a Babel:
Pervert the laws, disgrace the gown,   385
Corrupt the Senate, rob the Crown;
To sacrifice old England's glory,
And make her infamous in story.
When such a tempest shook the land,
How could unguarded virtue stand?   390
  'With horror, grief, despair, the Dean
Beheld their dire destructive scene:
His friends in exile, or the Tow'r,
Himself within the frown of pow'r;
Pursued by base envenomed pens,   395
Far to the land of slaves and fens;
A servile race in folly nursed,
Who truckle most when treated worst.
  'By innocence and resolution,
He bore continual persecution;   400
While numbers to preferment rose,
Whose merits were, to be his foes.
When ev'n his own familiar friends,
Intent upon their private ends,
Like renegadoes now he feels,   405
Against him lifting up their heels.

'The Dean did by his pen defeat
An infamous destructive cheat;
Taught fools their int'rest how to know,
And gave them arms to ward the blow.   410
Envy hath owned it was his doing
To save that helpless land from ruin;
While they who at the steerage stood,
And reaped the profit, sought his blood.
  'To save them from their evil fate,   415
In him was held a crime of state.
A wicked monster on the Bench,
Whose fury blood could never quench;
As vile and profligate a villain,
As modern Scroggs, or old Tressilian;   420
Who long all justice had discarded,
Nor feared he God, nor Man regarded;
Vowed on the Dean his rage to vent,
And make him of his zeal repent;
But heaven his innocence defends,   425
The grateful people stand his friends:
Not strains of law, nor judge's frown,
Nor topics brought to please the Crown,
Nor witness hired, nor jury picked,
Prevail to bring him in convíct.   430
  'In exile with a steady heart,
He spent his life's declining part;
Where folly, pride, and faction sway,
Remote from St John, Pope, and Gay.
  'His friendship there to few confined,   435
Were always of the middling kind:
No fools of rank, a mongrel breed,
Who fain would pass for lords indeed:

---

374 **Ormond:** James Butler, 2nd Duke of Ormonde (1665–1745); he succeeded Marlborough as commander-in-chief (1712), but during the reign of George I his Jacobite sympathies led to his being impeached for high treason (1715) and he fled to France **Oxford:** Robert Harley, 1st Earl of Oxford (1661–1724), was Chief Minister to Queen Anne (1711–14); he was dismissed for alleged treasonable conduct and spent two years in the Tower of London 377 **Too soon that previous life was ended:** 'In the height of the quarrel between the ministers, the Queen died' (S) 378 **weal:** welfare 379 **When up a dangerous faction starts:** 'Upon Queen Anne's death the Whig faction was restored to power, which they exercised with the utmost rage and revenge; impeached and banished the chief leaders of the Church party [i.e. the Tories], and stripped all their adherents of what employments they had, after which England was never known to make so mean a figure in Europe. The greatest preferments in the Church in both kingdoms were given to the most ignorant men, fanatics were publicly caressed, Ireland utterly ruined and enslaved, only great ministers heaping up millions, and so affairs continue until this present third day of May 1732 and are likely to go on in the same manner' (S) **Babel:** confused voices, hubbub 393 **Tow'r:** the Tower of London 394 **Himself within the frown of power:** 'Upon the Queen's death, the Dean returned to live in Dublin, at his deanery-house. Numberless libels were writ against him in England as a Jacobite; he was insulted in the street, and at nights was forced to be attended by his servants armed' (S) 396 **the land of slaves and fens:** 'The land of slaves and fens is Ireland' (S) 398 **truckle most:** are most servile 405 **renegadoes:** turncoats, deserters 406 **lifting up their heels:** running away

408 **An infamous destructive cheat:** William Wood; see earlier note 410 **ward:** fend off 413 **steerage:** the helm 417 **A wicked monster on the Bench:** William Whitshed, Lord Chief Justice in Ireland. 'He had some years before prosecuted a printer for a pamphlet writ by the Dean to persuade the people of Ireland to wear their own manufactures. Whitshed sent the jury down eleven times, and kept them nine hours, until they were forced to bring in a special verdict. He sat as judge afterwards on the trial of the printer of the Drapier's Fourth Letter [Harding]; but the jury, against all he could say or swear, threw out the bill. All the kingdom took the Drapier's part except the courtiers or those who expected places. The Drapier was celebrated in many poems and pamphlets; his sign was set up in most streets of Dublin (where many of them still continue) and in several country towns' (S) 420 **Scroggs:** Sir William Scroggs (1623?–1683), Lord Chief Justice under Charles II; he was impeached by the Commons in 1680 and removed from office. 'His judgement always varied in state trials, according to directions from the [royal] Court' (S) **Tressilian:** 'a wicked judge, hanged above three hundred years ago' (S), Sir Robert Tresilian, Chief Justice of the King's Bench, acted with great harshness after the suppression of the Peasants' Revolt (1381); he was impeached for treason in 1387 and hanged in the following year 431 **In exile:** 'In Ireland, which he had reason to call a place of exile; to which country nothing could have driven him but the Queen's death, who had determined to fix him in England, in spite of the Duchess of Somerset, etc.' (S) 435 **His friendship there to few confined:** 'In Ireland the Dean was not acquainted with one single lord spiritual or temporal. He only conversed with private gentlemen of the clergy or laity, and but a small number of either' (S)

Where titles give no right, or pow'r,
And peerage is a withered flow'r, 440
He would have held it a disgrace,
If such a wretch had known his face.
On rural squires, that kingdom's bane,
He vented oft his wrath in vain:
Biennial squires to market brought; 445
Who sell their souls and votes for naught;
The country stripped, go joyful back,
To rob the church, their tenants rack,
Go snacks with thieves and rapparees
And keep the peace to pick up fees: 450
In every job to have a share,
A jail or barrack to repair;
And turn the tax for public roads
Commodious for their own abodes.
    'Perhaps I may allow the Dean 455
Had too much satire in his vein;
And seemed determined not to starve it,
Because no age could more deserve it.
Yet malice never was his aim;
He lashed the vice, but spared the name. 460
No individual could resent,
Where thousands equally were meant.
His satire points at no deféct,
But what all mortals may correct;
For he abhorred that senseless tribe 465
Who call it humour when they jibe:
He spared a hump or crooked nose,
Whose owners set not up for beaux.
True genuine dullness moved his pity,
Unless it offered to be witty. 470
Those who their ignorance confessed
He ne'er offended with a jest;
But laughed to hear an idiot quote
A verse from Horace learned by rote.
    'He knew an hundred pleasant stories, 475
With all the turns of Whigs and Tories;
Was cheerful to his dying day,
And friends would let him have his way.
    'He gave the little wealth he had
To build a house for fools and mad; 480
And showed, by one satiric touch,
No nation wanted it so much.
That kingdom he hath left his debtor,
I wish it soon may have a better.'

439–40 **Where titles give . . . withered flower:** 'The peers of Ireland lost a great part of their jurisdiction by one single Act [Ireland Act, 1719], and tamely submitted to this infamous mark of slavery without the least resentment or remonstrance' (S) 443 **bane:** destruction 445 **Biennial squires to market brought:** 'The parliament (as they call it) in Ireland meet but once in two years; and, after giving five times more than they can afford, return home to reimburse themselves by all country jobs and oppressions, of which some few only are here mentioned' (S) 448 **rack:** charge exorbitant rent 449 **snacks:** shares **rapparees:** 'The highwaymen in Ireland are, since the late wars there, usually called rapparees, which was a name given to those Irish soldiers who in small parties used, at that time, to plunder the Protestants' (S)

451 **job:** 'a transaction in which duty or the public interest is sacrificed for the sake of private or party advantage' (*OED*) 452 **barrack:** 'The army in Ireland is lodged in barracks, the building and repairing whereof, and other charges, have cost a prodigious sum to that unhappy kingdom' (S) 466 **jibe:** scoff 468 **beaux:** dandies 474 **Horace:** Roman poet (65–8 BC) 476 **Whigs:** upholders of parliamentary supremacy and of religious toleration **Tories:** supporters of royal prerogative and of the Church of England 483 **That kingdom:** 'Meaning Ireland, where he now lives, and probably may die' (S)

WILLIAM CONGREVE

'FALSE THOUGH SHE BE TO ME AND LOVE'

FALSE though she be to me and Love,
    I'll ne'er pursue revenge;
For still the charmer I approve,
    Though I deplore her change.

In hours of bliss we oft have met, 5
    They could not always last;
And though the present I regret,
    I'm grateful for the past.

'PIOUS SELINDA GOES TO PRAYERS'

PIOUS Selinda goes to prayers,
    If I but ask the favour;
And yet the tender fool's in tears,
    When she believes I'll leave her.

Would I were free from this restraint, 5
    Or else had hopes to win her;
Would she could make of me a saint,
    Or I of her a sinner.

JOSEPH ADDISON

ODE

THE spacious firmament on high,
With all the blue etherial sky,
And spangled heavens, a shining frame,
Their great original proclaim:
Th'unwearied Sun, from day to day, 5
Does his Creator's power display,
And publishes to every land
The work of an almighty hand.
Soon as the evening shades prevail,
The moon takes up the wondrous tale, 10
And nightly to the list'ning earth
Repeats the story of her birth:
Whilst all the stars that round her burn,

And all the planets, in their turn,
Confirm the tidings as they roll,   15
And spread the truth from pole to pole.

What though, in solemn silence, all
Move round the dark terrestrial ball?
What though nor real voice nor sound
Amid their radiant orbs be found?   20
In Reason's ear they all rejoice,
And utter forth a glorious voice,
Forever singing, as they shine,
'The hand that made us is divine.'

ISAAC WATTS

CRUCIFIXION TO THE WORLD BY THE CROSS OF CHRIST

When I survey the wondrous Cross
On which the Prince of Glory died,
My richest gain I count but loss,
And pour contempt on all my pride.

Forbid it, Lord, that I should boast   5
Save in the death of Christ my God;
All the vain things that charm me most,
I sacrifice them to his blood.

See from his head, his hands, his feet,
Sorrow and love flow mingled down;   10
Did e'er such love and sorrow meet?
Or thorns compose so rich a crown?

His dying crimson like a robe
Spreads o'er his body on the tree,
Then am I dead to all the globe,   15
And all the globe is dead to me.

Were the whole realm of nature mine,
That were a present far too small;
Love so amazing, so divine
Demands my soul, my life, my all.   20

AGAINST IDLENESS AND MISCHIEF

How doth the little busy bee
  Improve each shining hour,
And gather honey all the day
  From ev'ry op'ning flow'r!

How skilfully she builds her cell!   5
  How neat she spreads the wax!
And labours hard to store it well
  With the sweet food she makes.

In works of labour or of skill
  I would be busy too: 10
For Satan finds some mischief still
  For idle hands to do.

In books, or work, or healthful play,
  Let my first years be passed,
That I may give for every day   15
  Some good account at last.

THE SLUGGARD

'Tis the voice of the Sluggard; I heard him complain,
'You have waked me too soon, I must slumber again.'
As the door on its hinges, so he on his bed,
Turns his sides and his shoulders and his heavy head.

'A little more sleep, and a little more slumber';   5
Thus he wastes half his days and his hours without
    number;
And when he gets up, he sits folding his hands,
Or walks about saunt'ring, or trifling he stands.

I passed by his garden, and saw the wild brier,
The thorn and the thistle grow broader and higher; 10
The clothes that hang on him are turning to rags;
And his money still wastes, till he starves or he begs.

I made him a visit, still hoping to find
He had took better care for improving his mind: 14
He told me his dreams, talked of eating and drinking;
But he scarce reads his Bible, and never loves thinking.

Said I then to my heart, 'Here's a lesson for me';
That man's but a picture of what I might be: 18
But thanks to my friends for their care in my breeding,
Who taught me betimes to love working and reading.

AMBROSE PHILIPS

TO MISS CHARLOTTE PULTENEY
IN HER MOTHER'S ARMS

Timely blossom, infant fair,
Fondling of a happy pair,
Every morn and every night
Their solicitous delight,
Sleeping, waking, still at ease,   5
Pleasing, without skill to please;
Little gossip, blithe and hale,
Tattling many a broken tale,
Singing many a tuneless song,
Lavish of a heedless tongue;   10
Simple maiden, void of art,

Babbling out the very heart,
Yet abandoned to thy will,
Yet imagining no ill,
Yet too innocent to blush;   15
Like the linlet in the bush
To the mother-linnet's note
Moduling her slender throat,
Chirping forth thy petty joys,
Wanton in the charge of toys,   20
Like the linnet green in May
Flitting to each bloomy spray;
Wearied then, and glad of rest,
Like the linlet in the nest.
This thy present happy lot,   25
This, in time, will be forgot:
Other pleasures, other cares,
Ever-busy Time prepares;
And thou shalt in thy daughter see
This picture, once, resembled thee.   30

TO MISS CHARLOTTE PULTENEY: 2 **fondling:** pet 16 **linlet:** young linnet
18 **Moduling:** modulating 22 **spray:** branch

JOHN GAY

From FABLES

THE LION, THE FOX, AND THE GEESE

A LION, tired with state affairs,
Quite sick of pomp, and worn with cares,
Resolved remote from noise and strife
In peace to pass his latter life.
  It was proclaimed; the day was set;   5
Behold the gen'ral council met.
The fox was viceroy named. The crowd
To the new regent humbly bowed:
Wolves, bears and mighty tigers bend,
And strive who most shall condescend.   10
He straight assumes a solemn grace,
Collects his wisdom in his face,
The crowd admire his wit, his sense:
Each word hath weight and consequence;
The flatt'rer all his art displays: 15
He who hath power is sure of praise.
A fox stepped forth before the rest,
And thus the servile throng addressed.
  'How vast his talents, born to rule,
And trained in virtue's honest school!   20
What clemency his temper sways!
How uncorrupt are all his ways!
Beneath his conduct and command
Rapine shall cease to waste the land;
His brain hath stratagem and art,   25
Prudence and mercy rule his heart.
What blessings must attend the nation

Under this good administration!'
  He said. A goose, who distant stood,
Harangued apart the cackling brood.   30
  'Whene'er I hear a knave commend,
He bids me shun his worthy friend.
What praise! What mighty commendation!
But 'twas a fox that spoke th'oration.
Foxes this government may prize   35
As gentle, plentiful and wise;
If they enjoy these sweets, 'tis plain,
We geese must feel a tyrant reign.
What havoc now shall thin our race!
When every petty clerk in place,   40
To prove his taste, and seem polite,
Will feed on geese both noon and night.'

'OUR POLLY IS A SAD SLUT'

OUR Polly is a sad slut, nor heeds what we have taught
    her.
I wonder any man alive will ever rear a daughter!
For she must have both hoods and gowns, and hoops
    to swell her pride,
With scarfs and stays, and gloves and lace; and she will
    have men beside;
And when she's dressed with care and cost,
    all-tempting, fine and gay,   5
As men should serve a cowcumber, she flings herself
    away.

From 'The Beggar's Opera'

'OUR POLLY IS A SAD SLUT': 3 **hoops:** light curved frames worn to
stretch out a full skirt 6 **cowcumber:** cucumber

HENRY CAREY

SALLY IN OUR ALLEY

OF all the girls that are so smart
  There's none like pretty Sally;
She is the darling of my heart,
  And she lives in our alley.
There is no lady in the land   5
  Is half so sweet as Sally;
She is the darling of my heart,
  And she lives in our alley.

Her father he makes cabbage-nets,
  And through the streets does cry 'em;   10
Her mother she sells laces long
  To such as please to buy 'em;
But sure such folks could ne'er beget
  So sweet a girl as Sally!
She is the darling of my heart,   15
  And she lives in our alley.

When she is by, I leave my work,
  I love her so sincerely;
My master comes like any Turk,
  And bangs me most severely;   20
But let him bang his bellyful,
  I'll bear it all for Sally;
She is the darling of my heart,
  And she lives in our alley.

Of all the days that's in the week   25
  I dearly love but one day,
And that's the day that comes betwixt
  A Saturday and Monday;
For then I'm dressed all in my best
  To walk abroad with Sally;   30
She is the darling of my heart,
  And she lives in our alley.

My master carries me to church,
  And often am I blamed,
Because I leave him in the lurch   35
  As soon as text is named;
I leave the church in sermon time,
  And slink away to Sally;
She is the darling of my heart,
  And she lives in our alley.   40

When Christmas comes about again,
  Oh, then I shall have money;
I'll hoard it up and, box and all,
  I'll give it to my honey:
I would it were ten thousand pound,   45
  I'd give it all to Sally;
She is the darling of my heart,
  And she lives in our alley.

My master and the neighbours all
  Make game of me and Sally,   50
And, but for her, I'd better be
  A slave and row a galley;
But when my seven long years are out,
  Oh, then I'll marry Sally;
Oh, then we'll wed, and then we'll bed,   55
  But not in our alley!

ALEXANDER POPE

From PASTORALS

WHERE'ER you walk, cool gales shall fan the glade,
Trees, where you sit, shall crowd into a shade:
Where'er you tread, the blushing flow'rs shall rise,
And all things flourish where you turn your eyes.
Oh! how I long with you to pass my days,   5
Invoke the Muses, and resound your praise!

Your praise the birds shall chant in ev'ry grove,
And winds shall waft it to the pow'rs above.
But would you sing, and rival Orpheus' strain,
The wond'ring forests soon should dance again,   10
And moving mountains hear the pow'rful call,
And headlong streams hang list'ning in their fall!

['Summer', lines 73–84]

PASTORALS: 1 **gales:** gentle breezes 9 **Orpheus:** in Greek myth, a poet whose verses could move even trees and inanimate objects

From WINDSOR FOREST

YE vig'rous swains! while youth ferments your blood,
And purer spirits swell the sprightly flood,
Now range the hills, the gameful woods beset,
Wind the shrill horn, or spread the waving net.
When milder autumn summer's heat succeeds,   5
And in the new-shorn field the partridge feeds,
Before his lord the ready spaniel bounds,
Panting with hope, he tries the furrowed grounds;
But when the tainted gales the game betray,
Couched close he lies, and meditates the prey: 10
Secure they trust th'unfaithful field, beset,
Till hov'ring o'er 'em sweeps the swelling net.
Thus (if small things we may with great compare)
When Albion sends her eager sons to war,
Some thoughtless town, with ease and plenty blessed,
Near, and more near, the closing lines invest;   16
Sudden they seize th'amazed, defenceless prize,
And high in air Britannia's standard flies.
  See! from the brake the whirring pheasant springs,
And mounts exulting on triumphant wings: 20
Short is his joy; he feels the fiery wound,
Flutters in blood, and panting beats the ground.
Ah! what avail his glossy, varying dyes,
His purple crest, and scarlet-circled eyes,
The vivid green his shining plumes unfold,   25
His painted wings, and breast that flames with gold?
  Nor yet, when moist Arcturus clouds the sky,
The woods and fields their pleasing toils deny.
To plains with well-breathed beagles we repair,
And trace the mazes of the circling hare: 30
(Beasts, urged by us, their fellow-beasts pursue,
And learn of man each other to undo).
With slaught'ring guns th'unwearied fowler roves,
When frosts have whitened all the naked groves;
Where doves in flocks the leafless trees o'ershade,   35
And lonely woodcocks haunt the wat'ry glade.
He lifts the tube, and levels with his eye;
Straight a short thunder breaks the frozen sky.
Oft, as in airy rings they skim the heath,
The clam'rous lapwings feel the leaden death: 40
Oft, as the mounting larks their notes prepare,
They fall, and leave their little lives in air.
  In genial spring, beneath the quiv'ring shade,
Where cooling vapours breathe along the mead,

The patient fisher takes his silent stand,   45
Intent, his angle trembling in his hand;
With looks unmoved, he hopes the scaly breed,
And eyes the dancing cork, and bending reed.
Our plenteous streams a various race supply,
The bright-eyed perch with fins of Tyrian dye,   50
The silver eel, in shining volumes rolled,
The yellow carp, in scales bedropped with gold,
Swift trouts, diversified with crimson stains,
And pikes, the tyrants of the wat'ry plains.

[Lines 93–146]

WINDSOR FOREST: 1 **swains:** young men   4 **Wind:** blow   9 **tainted:** carrying the scent of the prey   14 **Albion:** Britain   19 **brake:** thicket 27 **moist Arcturus:** an extremely bright star, traditionally thought to bring stormy weather   44 **mead:** meadow   50 **Tyrian:** purple, like the dye from Tyre, in Lebanon

From AN ESSAY ON CRITICISM

A LITTLE learning is a dang'rous thing;
Drink deep, or taste not the Pierian spring:
There shallow draughts intoxicate the brain,
And drinking largely sobers us again.
Fired at first sight with what the Muse imparts,   5
In fearless youth we tempt the heights of arts,
While from the bounded level of our mind,
Short views we take, nor see the lengths behind;
But, more advanced, behold with strange surprise
New distant scenes of endless science rise!   10
So pleased at first the tow'ring Alps we try,
Mount o'er the vales, and seem to tread the sky,
Th'eternal snows appear already past,
And the first clouds and mountains seem the last:
But, those attained, we tremble to survey   15
The growing labours of the lengthened way,
Th'increasing prospect tires our wand'ring eyes,
Hills peep o'er hills, and Alps on Alps arise!
A perfect judge will read each work of wit
With the same spirit that its author writ: 20
Survey the WHOLE, nor seek slight faults to find
Where nature moves, and rapture warms the mind;
Nor lose, for that malignant dull delight,
The gen'rous pleasure to be charmed with wit.
But in such lays as neither ebb nor flow,   25
Correctly cold and regularly low,
That shunning faults, one quiet tenour keep,
We cannot blame indeed – but we may sleep.
In wit, as nature, what affects our hearts
Is not th'exactness of peculiar parts;   30
'Tis not a lip or eye we beauty call,
But the joint force and full result of all.
Thus when we view some well-proportioned dome
(The world's just wonder, and ev'n thine, O Rome!),

AN ESSAY ON CRITICISM: 2 **Pierian spring:** in classical myth, a spring sacred to the Pierides (the Muses)   6 **tempt:** attempt   25 **lays:** songs

No single parts unequally surprise,   35
All comes united to th'admiring eyes;
No monstrous height, or breadth, or length appear;
The whole at once is bold, and regular.
Whoever thinks a faultless piece to see,
Thinks what ne'er was, nor is, nor e'er shall be.   40
In ev'ry work regard the writer's end,
Since none can compass more than they intend;
And if the means be just, the conduct true,
Applause, in spite of trivial faults, is due.
As men of breeding, sometimes men of wit,   45
T'avoid great errors, must the less commit:
Neglect the rules each verbal critic lays,
For not to know some trifles, is a praise.
Most critics, fond of some subservient art,
Still make the whole depend upon a part: 50
They talk of principles, but notions prize,
And all to one loved folly sacrifice.
Once on a time, La Mancha's knight, they say,
A certain bard encount'ring on the way,
Discoursed in terms as just, with looks as sage,   55
As e'er could Dennis, of the Grecian stage;
Concluding all were desp'rate sots and fools,
Who durst depart from Aristotle's rules.
Our author, happy in a judge so nice,
Produced his play, and begged the knight's advice;
Made him observe the subject, and the plot,   61
The manners, passions, unities; what not?
All which, exact to rule, were brought about,
Were but a combat in the lists left out.   64
'What! leave the combat out?' exclaims the knight;
Yes, or we must renounce the Stagirite.
'Not so by Heaven,' he answers in a rage,
'Knights, squires, and steeds, must enter on the stage.'
So vast a throng the stage can ne'er contain.
'Then build a new, or act it in a plain.'   70
Thus critics, of less judgement than caprice,
Curious not knowing, not exact but nice,
Form short ideas; and offend in arts
(As most in manners) by a love to parts.
Some to conceit alone their taste confine,   75
And glitt'ring thoughts struck out at ev'ry line;
Pleased with a work where nothing's just or fit;
One glaring chaos and wild heap of wit.
Poets like painters, thus, unskilled to trace
The naked nature and the living grace,   80
With gold and jewels cover ev'ry part,
And hide with ornaments their want of art.
True wit is nature to advantage dressed,
What oft was thought but ne'er so well expressed;
Something, whose truth convinced at sight we find,
That gives us back the image of our mind.   86

42 **compass:** achieve   53 **La Mancha's knight:** Don Quixote, hero of the novel by Cervantes (1605)   56 **Dennis:** John Dennis (1657–1734), dramatist and critic   59 **nice:** discriminating   66 **Stagirite:** Aristotle, a native of Stagira in Macedonia   75 **conceit:** wit

As shades more sweetly recommend the light,
So modest plainness sets off sprightly wit.
For works may have more wit than does 'em good,
As bodies perish through excess of blood. 90

Others for language all their care express,
And value books, as women men, for dress:
Their praise is still – the style is excellent:
The sense, they humbly take upon contént.
Words are like leaves; and where they most abound,
Much fruit of sense beneath is rarely found. 96
False eloquence, like the prismatic glass,
Its gaudy colours spreads on ev'ry place;
The face of nature we no more survey,
All glares alike, without distinction gay: 100
But true expression, like th'unchanging sun,
Clears and improves whate'er it shines upon,
It gilds all objects, but it alters none.
Expression is the dress of thought, and still
Appears more decent, as more suitable; 105
A vile conceit in pompous words expressed,
Is like a clown in regal purple dressed:
For diff'rent styles with diff'rent subjects sort,
As several garbs with country, town, and court.
Some by old words to fame have made pretence, 110
Ancients in phrase, mere moderns in their sense:
Such laboured nothings, in so strange a style,
Amaze th'unlearn'd, and make the learnèd smile.
Unlucky, as Fungoso in the play,
These sparks with awkward vanity display 115
What the fine gentleman wore yesterday;
And but so mimic ancient wits at best,
As apes our grandsires, in their doublets dressed.
In words, as fashions, the same rule will hold;
Alike fantastic, if too new, or old; 120
Be not the first by whom the new are tried,
Nor yet the last to lay the old aside.

But most by numbers judge a poet's song,
And smooth or rough, with them, is right or wrong;
In the bright Muse though thousand charms conspire,
Her voice is all these tuneful fools admire; 126
Who haunt Parnassus but to please their ear,
Not mend their minds; as some to church repair,
Not for the doctrine, but the music there.
These equal syllables alone require, 130
Though oft the ear the open vowels tire;
While éxpletives their feeble aid do join;
And ten low words oft creep in one dull line;
While they ring round the same unvaried chimes,
With sure returns of still expected rhymes. 135

Where'er you find 'the cooling western breeze',
In the next line it 'whispers through the trees';
If crystal streams 'with pleasing murmurs creep',
The reader's threatened (not in vain) with 'sleep'.
Then, at the last and only couplet fraught 140
With some unmeaning thing they call a thought,
A needless Alexandrine ends the song,
That, like a wounded snake, drags its slow length
    along.
Leave such to tune their own dull rhymes, and know
What's roundly smooth or languishingly slow; 145
And praise the easy vigour of a line,
Where Denham's strength and Waller's sweetness
    join.
True ease in writing comes from art, not chance,
As those move easiest who have learned to dance.
'Tis not enough no harshness gives offence, 150
The sound must seem an echo to the sense:
Soft is the strain when Zephyr gently blows,
And the smooth stream in smoother numbers flows;
But when loud surges lash the sounding shore, 154
The hoarse, rough verse should like the torrent roar.
When Ajax strives, some rock's vast weight to throw,
The line too labours, and the words move slow;
Not so, when swift Camilla scours the plain,
Flies o'er th'unbending corn, and skims along the
    main.
Hear how Timotheus' varied lays surprise, 160
And bid alternate passions fall and rise!
While, at each change, the son of Libyan Jove
Now burns with glory, and then melts with love;
Now his fierce eyes with sparkling fury glow,
Now sighs steal out, and tears begin to flow: 165
Persians and Greeks like turns of nature found,
And the world's victor stood subdued by sound!
The pow'r of music all our hearts allow,
And what Timotheus was, is Dryden now.

[Lines 215–383]

142 **Alexandrine:** a line of verse with six iambic feet, typical of heroic poetry 147 **Denham:** Sir John Denham, author of *Cooper's Hill* (see above) **Waller:** Edmund Waller, author of *Go, Lovely Rose* (see above) 152 **Zephyr:** the west wind 156 **Ajax:** a Greek hero of the Trojan War 158 **Camilla:** in Virgil's *Aeneid*, a princess of the Volsci who could run so fast that she could pass over a field of corn without bending the stalks 160 **Timotheus:** a Theban poet mentioned by Dryden in *Alexander's Feast* (see above) 162 **son of Libyan Jove:** Alexander the Great, who, when he visited the temple of Zeus (the Greek equivalent of Jove or Jupiter) Ammon in Libya, was proclaimed as a son of the god

93 **still:** always 94 **take upon contént:** accept without question 106 **conceit:** idea 114 **Fungoso:** in Ben Jonson's play *Every Man out of his Humour*, a character who is always behind the latest fashion 123 **numbers:** metre 127 **Parnassus:** a mountain near Delphi in Greece, sacred to the Muses

INTENDED FOR SIR ISAAC NEWTON, IN WESTMINSTER ABBEY

NATURE and Nature's laws lay hid in night.
GOD said, *Let Newton be!* and all was light.

THE RAPE OF THE LOCK
AN HEROIC-COMICAL POEM

CANTO ONE

WHAT dire offence from am'rous causes springs,
What mighty contests rise from trivial things,
I sing. This verse to Caryll, Muse! is due:
This, ev'n Belinda may vouchsafe to view:
Slight is the subject, but not so the praise,   5
If she inspire, and he approve my lays.

  Say what strange motive, Goddess! could compel
A well-bred lord t'assault a gentle belle?
Oh, say what stranger cause, yet unexplored,
Could make a gentle belle reject a lord?   10
In tasks so bold, can little men engage,
And in soft bosoms dwells such mighty rage?

  Sol through white curtains shot a tim'rous ray,
And oped those eyes that must eclipse the day:
Now lap-dogs give themselves the rousing shake,   15
And sleepless lovers, just at twelve, awake:
Thrice rung the bell, the slipper knocked the ground,
And the pressed watch returned a silver sound.
Belinda still her downy pillow pressed,
Her guardian sylph prolonged the balmy rest: 20
'Twas he had summoned to her silent bed
The morning-dream that hovered o'er her head.
A youth more glitt'ring that a birth-night beau
(That ev'n in slumber caused her cheek to glow)
Seemed to her ear his winning lips to lay,   25
And thus in whispers said, or seemed to say:

  'Fairest of mortals, thou distinguished care
Of thousand bright inhabitants of air!
If e'er one vision touch thy infant thought,
Of all the nurse and all the priest have taught;   30
Of airy elves by moonlight shadows seen,
The silver token, and the circled green,
Or virgins visited by angel-pow'rs
With golden crowns and wreaths of heavenly flow'rs;
Hear and believe! thy own importance know,   35
Nor bound thy narrow views to things below.
Some secret truths, from learnèd pride concealed,
To maids alone and children are revealed:
What though no credit doubting wits may give?
The fair and innocent shall still believe.   40
Know, then, unnumbered spirits round thee fly,
The light militia of the lower sky;
These, though unseen, are ever on the wing,
Hang o'er the box, and hover round the ring.
Think what an equipage thou hast in air,   45
And view with scorn two pages and chair.

As now your own, our beings were of old,
And once enclosed in woman's beauteous mould;
Thence, by a soft transition, we repair
From earthly vehicles to these of air.   50
Think not, when woman's transient breath is fled,
That all her vanities at once are dead;
Succeeding vanities she still regards,
And though she plays no more, o'erlooks the cards.
Her joy in gilded chariots, when alive,   55
And love of ombre, after death survive.
For when the fair in all their pride expire,
To their first elements their souls retire:
The sprites of fiery termagants in flame
Mount up, and take a salamander's name.   60
Soft yielding minds to water glide away,
And sip, with nymphs, their elemental tea.
The graver prude sinks downward to a gnome,
In search of mischief still on earth to roam.
The light coquettes in sylphs aloft repair,   65
And sport and flutter in the fields of air.

  'Know farther yet; whoever fair and chaste
Rejects mankind, is by some sylph embraced:
For spirits, freed from mortal laws, with ease
Assume what sexes and what shapes they please.   70
What guards the purity of melting maids,
In courtly balls, and midnight masquerades,
Safe from the treach'rous friend, the daring spark,
The glance by day, the whisper in the dark,
When kind occasion prompts their warm desires,   75
When music softens, and when dancing fires?
'Tis but their sylph, the wise celestials know,
Though honour is the word with men below.

  'Some nymphs there are, too conscious of their face,
For life predestined to the gnome's embrace.   80
These swell their prospects and exalt their pride,
When offers are disdained, and love denied.
Then gay ideas crowd the vacant brain,
While peers, and dukes, and all their sweeping train,
And garters, stars, and coronets appear,   85
And in soft sounds "your Grace" salutes their ear.
'Tis these that early taint the female soul,
Instruct the eyes of young coquettes to roll,
Teach infant-cheeks a bidden blush to know,
And little hearts to flutter at a beau.   90

  'Oft, when the world imagine women stray,
The sylphs through mystic mazes guide their way,
Through all the giddy circle they pursue,
And old impertinence expel by new.
What tender maid but must a victim fall   95
To one man's treat, but for another's ball?
When Florio speaks, what virgin could withstand,
If gentle Damon did not squeeze her hand?

THE RAPE OF THE LOCK: CANTO ONE: 3 **Caryll:** John Caryll (1625–1711),
a friend of Pope 6 **lays:** songs 13 **Sol:** the sun 14 **oped:** opened
18 **the pressed watch:** a type of watch called a repeater would
sound the last hour or quarter when a pin was pressed 20 **sylph:**
a spirit of the air 23 **birth-night beau:** a man dressed particularly
finely to attend a royal birthday celebration 44 **box:** i.e. at a theatre
ring: an area of Hyde Park where the coaches of fashionable
society paraded 46 **chair:** a sedan chair

56 **ombre:** an 18th-century card game 59 **termagants:** shrewish or
scolding women 62 **tea:** the contemporary pronunciation would
rhyme with 'away' 73 **spark:** a fashionable or gallant young man
89 **bidden blush:** rouge 94 **impertinence:** a trifling thing 97 **Florio:**
John Florio (?1553–1625), writer and translator 98 **Damon:** a conventional
name for a shepherd or rustic youth

With varying vanities, from ev'ry part,
They shift the moving toyshop of their heart;　　100
Where wigs with wigs, with sword-knots sword-knots
　　strive,
Beaux banish beaux, and coaches coaches drive.
This erring mortals levity may call,
Oh, blind to truth! the sylphs contrive it all.
　　'Of these am I, who thy protection claim,　　105
A watchful sprite, and Ariel is my name.
Late, as I ranged the crystal wilds of air,
In the clear mirror of thy ruling star
I saw, alas! some dread event impend,
Ere to the main this morning sun descend,　　110
But heaven reveals not what, or how, or where:
Warned by the sylph, oh, pious maid, beware!
This to disclose is all thy guardian can:
Beware of all, but most beware of man!'
　　He said; when Shock, who thought she slept too
　　long,　　115
Leaped up, and waked his mistress with his tongue.
'Twas then, Belinda, if report say true,
Thy eyes first opened on a billet-doux;
Wounds, charms, and ardours were no sooner read,
But all the vision vanished from thy head.　　120
　　And now, unveiled, the toilet stands displayed,
Each silver vase in mystic order laid.
First, robed in white, the nymph intent adores,
With head uncovered, the cosmetic pow'rs.
A heavenly image in the glass appears,　　125
To that she bends, to that her eyes she rears;
Th'inferior priestess, at her altar's side,
Trembling, begins the sacred rites of pride.
Unnumbered treasures ope at once, and here
The various off'rings of the world appear;　　130
From each she nicely culls with curious toil,
And decks the goddess with the glitt'ring spoil.
This casket India's glowing gems unlocks,
And all Arabia breathes from yonder box.
The tortoise here and elephant unite,　　135
Transformed to combs, the speckled and the white.
Here files of pins extend their shining rows,
Puffs, powders, patches, Bibles, billet-doux.
Now awful beauty puts on all its arms;
The fair each moment rises in her charms,　　140
Repairs her smiles, awakens ev'ry grace,
And calls forth all the wonders of her face;
Sees by degrees a purer blush arise,
And keener lightnings quicken in her eyes.
The busy sylphs surround their darling care,　　145
These set the head, and those divide the hair,
Some fold the sleeve, whilst others plait the gown;
And Betty's praised for labours not her own.

CANTO TWO

NOT with more glories, in th'ethereal plain,
The sun first rises o'er the purpled main,
Than, issuing forth, the rival of his beams
Launched on the bosom of the silver Thames.
Fair nymphs and well-dressed youths around her
　　shone,
But ev'ry eye was fixed on her alone.　　6
On her white breast a sparkling cross she wore,
Which Jews might kiss, and infidels adore.
Her lively looks a sprightly mind disclose,
Quick as her eyes, and as unfixed as those:　　10
Favours to none, to all she smiles extends;
Oft she rejects, but never once offends.
Bright as the sun, her eyes the gazers strike,
And, like the sun, they shine on all alike.
Yet graceful ease, and sweetness void of pride,　　15
Might hide her faults, if belles had faults to hide:
If to her share more female errors fall,
Look on her face, and you'll forget 'em all.
　　This nymph, to the destruction of mankind,
Nourished two locks, which graceful hung behind　　20
In equal curls, and well conspired to deck
With shining ringlets the smooth iv'ry neck.
Love in these labyrinths his slaves detains,
And mighty hearts are held in slender chains.
With hairy springes we the birds betray,　　25
Slight lines of hair surprise the finny prey,
Fair tresses man's imperial race ensnare,
And beauty draws us with a single hair.
　　Th'advent'rous baron the bright locks admired;
He saw, he wished, and to the prize aspired.　　30
Resolved to win, he meditates the way,
By force to ravish, or by fraud betray;
For when success a lover's toil attends,
Few ask if fraud or force attained his ends.
　　For this, ere Phoebus rose, he had implored　　35
Propitious heaven, and ev'ry pow'r adored,
But chiefly Love – to Love an altar built,
Of twelve vast French romances, neatly gilt.
There lay three garters, half a pair of gloves,
And all the trophies of his former loves;　　40
With tender billet-doux he lights the pyre,
And breathes three am'rous sighs to raise the fire.
Then prostrate falls, and begs with ardent eyes
Soon to obtain, and long possess the prize:
The pow'rs gave ear, and granted half his prayer,　　45
The rest the winds dispersed in empty air.
　　But now secure the painted vessel glides,
The sunbeams trembling on the floating tides;
While melting music steals upon the sky,
And softened sounds along the waters die;　　50
Smooth flow the waves, the zephyrs gently play,
Belinda smiled, and all the world was gay.

---

101 **sword-knot:** a decorative loop of ribbon on the hilt of a
sword 110 **main:** sea 115 **Shock:** her lapdog 131 **curious:** skilful
138 **patches:** imitation beauty spots applied to the face 148 **Betty:**
a conventional name for a lady's maid

CANTO TWO: 15 **void:** devoid 25 **springes:** snares 26 **finny prey:** fish
35 **Phoebus:** the sun-god, hence the sun itself

All but the sylph – with careful thoughts oppressed,
Th'impending woe sat heavy on his breast.
He summons straight his denizens of air;   55
The lucid squadrons round the sails repair:
Soft o'er the shrouds aërial whispers breathe,
That seemed but zephyrs to the train beneath.
Some to the sun their insect-wings unfold,
Waft on the breeze, or sink in clouds of gold;   60
Transparent forms, too fine for mortal sight,
Their fluid bodies half dissolved in light.
Loose to the wind their airy garments flew,
Thin glitt'ring textures of the filmy dew,
Dipped in the richest tincture of the skies,   65
Where light disports in ever-mingling dyes,
While ev'ry beam new transient colours flings,
Colours that change whene'er they wave their wings.
Amid the circle, on the gilded mast,
Superior by the head, was Ariel placed;   70
His purple pinions op'ning to the sun,
He raised his azure wand, and thus begun:
'Ye Sylphs and Sylphids, to your chief give ear,
Fays, Fairies, Genii, Elves, and Demons hear!
Ye know the spheres and various tasks assigned   75
By laws eternal to th'aërial kind.
Some in the fields of purest ether play,
And bask and whiten in the blaze of day.
Some guide the course of wand'ring orbs on high,
Or roll the planets through the boundless sky.   80
Some less refined, beneath the moon's pale light
Pursue the stars that shoot athwart the night,
Or suck the mists in grosser air below,
Or dip their pinions in the painted bow,
Or brew fierce tempests on the wintry main,   85
Or o'er the glebe distil the kindly rain.
Others on earth o'er human race preside,
Watch all their ways, and all their actions guide:
Of these the chief the care of nations own,
And guard with arms divine the British throne.   90
'Our humbler province is to tend the fair,
Not a less pleasing, though less glorious care;
To save the powder from too rude a gale,
Nor let th'imprisoned essences exhale;
To draw fresh colours from the vernal flow'rs;   95
To steal from rainbows, e'er they drop in show'rs
A brighter wash; to curl their waving hairs,
Assist their blushes, and inspire their airs;
Nay, oft, in dreams, invention we bestow,
To change a flounce or add a furbelow.   100
'This day, black omens threat the brightest fair
That e'er deserved a watchful spirit's care;
Some dire disaster, or by force or slight;
But what, or where, the Fates have wrapped in night.

Whether the nymph shall break Diana's law,   105
Or some frail china jar receive a flaw;
Or stain her honour, or her new brocade;
Forget her prayers, or miss a masquerade;
Or lose her heart, or necklace, at a ball;
Or whether heaven has doomed that Shock must fall.
Haste, then, ye spirits! to your charge repair: 111
The flutt'ring fan be Zephyretta's care;
The drops to thee, Brillante, we consign;
And, Momentilla, let the watch be thine;
Do thou, Crispissa, tend her fav'rite lock;   115
Ariel himself shall be the guard of Shock.
'To fifty chosen sylphs, of special note,
We trust th'important charge, the petticoat;
Oft have we known that sevenfold fence to fail,
Though stiff with hoops, and armed with ribs of
whale;
Form a strong line about the silver bound,   121
And guard the wide circumference around.
'Whatever spirit, careless of his charge,
His post neglects, or leaves the fair at large,
Shall feel sharp vengeance soon o'ertake his sins,   125
Be stopped in vials, or transfixed with pins;
Or plunged in lakes of bitter washes lie,
Or wedged whole ages in a bodkin's eye:
Gums and pomatums shall his flight restrain,
While, clogged, he beats his silken wings in vain;   130
Or alum styptics with contracting pow'r
Shrink his thin essence like a rivell'd flow'r:
Or, as Ixion fixed, the wretch shall feel
The giddy motion of the whirling mill,
In fumes of burning chocolate shall glow,   135
And tremble at the sea that froths below!'
He spoke; the spirits from the sails descend;
Some, orb in orb, around the nymph extend;
Some thrid the mazy ringlets of her hair;
Some hang upon the pendants of her ear;   140
With beating hearts the dire event they wait,
Anxious, and trembling for the birth of Fate.

CANTO THREE

CLOSE by those meads, forever crowned with flow'rs,
Where Thames with pride surveys his rising tow'rs,
There stands a structure of majestic frame,
Which from the neighb'ring Hampton takes its name.
Here Britain's statesmen oft the fall foredoom   5
Of foreign tyrants, and of nymphs at home;
Here thou, great Anna! whom three realms obey,
Dost sometimes counsel take – and sometimes tea.

---

55 **straight:** immediately 56 **lucid:** transparent or shining **repair:** go 57 **shrouds:** ship's ropes supporting the mast 71 **pinions:** wings 82 **athwart:** across 86 **glebe:** the soil, earth 100 **furbelow:** flounce, ornamental trimming 101 **threat:** threaten 104 **Fates:** in classical myth, three goddesses who control the destinies of humans

105 **Diana's law:** celibacy 113 **drops:** diamond earrings 128 **bodkin:** an ornamental hairpin 129 **pomatums:** pomades 132 **rivell'd:** wrinkled 133 **Ixion:** in Greek myth, a mortal condemned to be tied to a perpetually turning wheel in the underworld 139 **thrid:** thread **mazy:** tangled CANTO THREE: 1 **meads:** meadows 7 **Anna:** Queen Anne (1665–1714; ruled 1702–14) **three realms:** Great Britain, Ireland, and France, which English monarchs still claimed the right to rule

Hither the heroes and the nymphs resort,
To taste awhile the pleasures of a court; 10
In various talk th'instructive hours they passed,
Who gave the ball or paid the visit last;
One speaks the glory of the British queen,
And one describes a charming Indian screen;
A third interprets motions, looks, and eyes; 15
At ev'ry word a reputation dies.
Snuff, or the fan, supply each pause of chat,
With singing, laughing, ogling, and all that.
	Meanwhile, declining from the noon of day,
The sun obliquely shoots his burning ray; 20
The hungry judges soon the sentence sign,
And wretches hang that jurymen may dine;
The merchant from th'Exchange returns in peace,
And the long labours of the toilet cease.
Belinda now, whom thirst of fame invites, 25
Burns to encounter two advent'rous knights,
At ombre singly to decide their doom;
And swells her breast with conquests yet to come.
Straight the three bands prepare in arms to join,
Each band the number of the sacred nine. 30
Soon as she spreads her hand, th'aërial guard
Descend, and sit on each important card:
First Ariel perched upon a matadore,
Then each according to the rank they bore;
For sylphs, yet mindful of their ancient race, 35
Are, as when women, wondrous fond of place.
	Behold, four kings in majesty revered,
With hoary whiskers and a forky beard;
And four fair queens whose hands sustain a flow'r,
Th'expressive emblem of their softer pow'r; 40
Four knaves in garbs succinct, a trusty band,
Caps on their heads, and halberts in their hand;
And particoloured troops, a shining train,
Draw forth to combat on the velvet plain.
	The skilful nymph reviews her force with care: 45
'Let spades be trumps!' she said, and trumps they
		were.
Now move to war her sable matadores,
In show like leaders of the swarthy Moors.
Spadillio first, unconquerable lord!
Led off two captive trumps, and swept the board. 50
As many more Manillio forced to yield,
And marched a victor from the verdant field.
Him Basto followed, but his fate more hard
Gained but one trump and one plebeian card.
With his broad sabre next, a chief in years, 55
The hoary majesty of spades appears,
Puts forth one manly leg, to sight revealed,
The rest, his many-coloured robe concealed.

The rebel knave, who dares his prince engage,
Proves the just victim of his royal rage. 60
Ev'n mighty Pam, that kings and queens o'erthrew
And mowed down armies in the fights of loo,
Sad chance of war! now destitute of aid,
Falls undistinguished by the victor spade!
	Thus far both armies to Belinda yield; 65
Now to the baron fate inclines the field.
His warlike Amazon her host invades,
Th'imperial consort of the crown of spades.
The club's black tyrant first her victim died,
Spite of his haughty mien and barb'rous pride: 70
What boots the regal circle on his head,
His giant limbs in state unwieldy spread;
That long behind he trails his pompous robe,
And, of all monarchs, only grasps the globe?
	The baron now his diamonds pours apace; 75
Th'embroidered king who shows but half his face,
And his refulgent queen, with pow'rs combined,
Of broken troops an easy conquest find.
Clubs, diamonds, hearts, in wild disorder seen,
With throngs promiscuous strow the level green. 80
Thus when dispersed a routed army runs,
Of Asia's troops and Afric's sable sons,
With like confusion different nations fly,
Of various habit and of various dye,
The pierced battalions disunited fall, 85
In heaps on heaps; one fate o'erwhelms them all.
	The knave of diamonds tries his wily arts,
And wins (oh, shameful chance!) the queen of hearts.
At this, the blood the virgin's cheek forsook,
A livid paleness spreads o'er all her look; 90
She sees, and trembles at th'approaching ill,
Just in the jaws of ruin, and codille.
And now (as oft in some distempered state)
On one nice trick depends the gen'ral fate:
An ace of hearts steps forth: the king unseen 95
Lurked in her hand and mourned his captive queen:
He springs to vengeance with an eager pace,
And falls like thunder on the prostrate ace.
The nymph exulting fills with shouts the sky;
The walls, the woods, and long canals reply. 100
	Oh, thoughtless mortals! ever blind to fate,
Too soon dejected, and too soon elate.
Sudden these honours shall be snatched away,
And cursed for ever this victorious day.
	For lo! the board with cups and spoons is crowned,
The berries crackle, and the mill turns round; 106
On shining altars of Japan they raise
The silver lamp; the fiery spirits blaze:

22 **that:** in order that 33 **matadore:** one of the three most important cards in the game of ombre 36 **place:** precedence 41 **succinct:** close-fitting 42 **halbert:** halberd, a weapon with a long shaft topped by a spearpoint, axehead and pick 43 **particoloured:** in variegated colours 49 **Spadillio:** the ace of spades in ombre 51 **Manillio:** the second highest card in ombre 53 **Basto:** the ace of clubs

61 **Pam:** the knave of clubs 62 **loo:** a card game 67 **Amazon:** in Greek myth, one of a race of female warriors; here, the queen of spades 70 **Spite of:** in spite of 71 **What boots:** what use is 80 **strow:** strew 82 **Afric's sable sons:** black African men 92 **codille:** in ombre, a situation in which the challenging player loses 93 **distempered:** disordered 105 **board:** table 106 **The berries . . . round:** coffee beans are being roasted, then ground 107 **shining altars of Japan:** lacquered tables

From silver spouts the grateful liquors glide,
While China's earth receives the smoking tide: 110
At once they gratify their scent and taste,
And frequent cups prolong the rich repast.
Straight hover round the fair her airy band;
Some, as she sipped, the fuming liquor fanned,
Some o'er her lap their careful plumes displayed, 115
Trembling, and conscious of the rich brocade.
Coffee (which makes the politician wise,
And see through all things with his half-shut eyes)
Sent up in vapours to the baron's brain
New stratagems, the radiant lock to gain. 120
Ah, cease, rash youth! desist ere 'tis too late,
Fear the just gods, and think of Scylla's fate!
Changed to a bird, and sent to flit in air,
She dearly pays for Nisus' injured hair!

But when to mischief mortals bend their will, 125
How soon they find fit instruments of ill!
Just then, Clarissa drew with tempting grace
A two-edged weapon from her shining case:
So ladies in romance assist their knight,
Present the spear, and arm him for the fight. 130
He takes the gift with rev'rence, and extends
The little engine on his fingers' ends;
This just behind Belinda's neck he spread,
As o'er the fragrant steams she bends her head.
Swift to the lock a thousand sprites repair, 135
A thousand wings, by turns, blow back the hair;
And thrice they twitched the diamond in her ear;
Thrice she looked back, and thrice the foe drew near.
Just in that instant, anxious Ariel sought
The close recesses of the virgin's thought; 140
As on the nosegay in her breast reclined,
He watched th'ideas rising in her mind,
Sudden he viewed, in spite of all her art,
An earthly lover lurking in her heart.
Amazed, confused, he found his pow'r expired, 145
Resigned to fate, and with a sigh retired.

The peer now spreads the glitt'ring forfex wide,
T'enclose the lock; now joins it, to divide.
Ev'n then, before the fatal engine closed,
A wretched sylph too fondly interposed; 150
Fate urged the shears, and cut the sylph in twain
(But airy substance soon unites again),
The meeting points the sacred hair dissever
From the fair head, for ever, and for ever!

Then flashed the living lightning from her eyes, 155
And screams of horror rend th'affrighted skies.
Not louder shrieks to pitying heaven are cast,
When husbands, or when lap-dogs breathe their last;

Or when rich china vessels, fall'n from high,
In glitt'ring dust and painted fragments lie! 160
'Let wreaths of triumph now my temples twine,'
The victor cried, 'the glorious prize is mine!
While fish in streams, or birds delight in air,
Or in a coach-and-six the British fair,
As long as Atalantis shall be read, 165
Or the small pillow grace a lady's bed,
While visits shall be paid on solemn days,
When num'rous wax-lights in bright order blaze,
While nymphs take treats, or assignations give,
So long my honour, name, and praise shall live!' 170
What Time would spare, from steel receives its date,
And monuments, like men, submit to fate!
Steel could the labour of the gods destroy,
And strike to dust th'imperial tow'rs of Troy;
Steel could the works of mortal pride confound, 175
And hew triumphal arches to the ground.
What wonder, then, fair nymph! thy hairs should feel
The conqu'ring force of unresisted steel?

CANTO FOUR

BUT anxious cares the pensive nymph oppressed,
And secret passions laboured in her breast.
Not youthful kings in battle seized alive,
Not scornful virgins who their charms survive,
Not ardent lovers robbed of all their bliss, 5
Not ancient ladies when refused a kiss,
Not tyrants fierce that unrepenting die,
Not Cynthia when her manteau's pinned awry,
E'er felt such rage, resentment, and despair,
As thou, sad Virgin! for thy ravished hair. 10
For, that sad moment, when the sylphs withdrew,
And Ariel weeping from Belinda flew,
Umbriel, a dusky, melancholy sprite,
As ever sullied the fair face of light,
Down to the central earth, his proper scene, 15
Repaired to search the gloomy cave of Spleen.
Swift on his sooty pinions flits the gnome,
And in a vapour reached the dismal dome.
No cheerful breeze this sullen region knows,
The dreaded east is all the wind that blows. 20
Here in a grotto, sheltered close from air,
And screened in shades from day's detested glare,
She sighs for ever on her pensive bed,
Pain at her side, and megrim at her head.
Two handmaids wait the throne: alike in place, 25
But diff'ring far in figure and in face.
Here stood Ill-nature like an ancient maid,
Her wrinkled form in black and white arrayed;

---

109 **grateful**: pleasing, gratifying 110 **China's earth**: china 122–4 **Scylla . . . hair**: in Greek myth, Scylla was the daughter of a King Nisus on whose head grew a purple hair on which his kingdom's safety depended. She plucked this hair and gave it to Minos, who was besieging her father and with whom she was in love. She was turned into a bird 126 **ill**: evil 147 **forfex**: a pair of scissors 149 **engine**: device

165 **Atalantis**: *The New Atalantis*, a slanderous memoir by a Mrs Mary Manley, appeared in 1709 171 **date**: end CANTO FOUR: 8 **manteau:** loose gown 16 **Repaired:** went **Spleen:** melancholy 20 **east:** the east wind was believed to bring on melancholy 24 **Pain at her side:** i.e. where the spleen lies in the body **megrim:** migraine

With store of prayers, for mornings, nights, and noons
Her hand is filled; her bosom with lampoons.   30
    There Affectation, with a sickly mien,
Shows in her cheek the roses of eighteen,
Practised to lisp, and hang the head aside,
Faints into airs, and languishes with pride,
On the rich quilt sinks with becoming woe,   35
Wrapped in a gown, for sickness, and for show.
The fair ones feel such maladies as these,
When each new night-dress gives a new disease.
    A constant vapour o'er the palace flies,
Strange phantoms rising as the mists arise;   40
Dreadful, as hermits' dreams in haunted shades,
Or bright, as visions of expiring maids.
Now glaring fiends, and snakes on rolling spires,
Pale spectres, gaping tombs, and purple fires:
Now lakes of liquid gold, Elysian scenes,   45
And crystal domes, and angels in machines.
    Unnumbered throngs on ev'ry side are seen,
Of bodies changed to various forms by spleen.
Here living tea-pots stand, one arm held out,
One bent; the handle this, and that the spout: 50
A pipkin there, like Homer's tripod walks;
Here sighs a jar, and there a goose-pie talks;
Men prove with child, as pow'rful fancy works,
And maids turned bottles, call aloud for corks.
    Safe passed the gnome through this fantastic band,
A branch of healing spleenwort in his hand.   56
Then thus addressed the pow'r: 'Hail, wayward
        Queen!
Who rule the sex from fifty to fifteen:
Parent of vapours and of female wit,
Who give th'hysteric, or poetic fit,   60
On various tempers act by various ways,
Make some take physic, others scribble plays;
Who cause the proud their visits to delay,
And send the godly in a pet to pray.
A nymph there is, that all thy pow'r disdains,   65
And thousands more in equal mirth maintains.
But oh! if e'er thy gnome could spoil a grace,
Or raise a pimple on a beauteous face,
Like citron-waters matrons cheeks inflame,
Or change complexions at a losing game;   70
If e'er with airy horns I planted heads,
Or rumpled petticoats, or tumbled beds,
Or caused suspicion when no soul was rude,
Or discomposed the head-dress of a prude,
Or e'er to costive lap-dog gave disease,   75
Which not the tears of brightest eyes could ease:

Hear me, and touch Belinda with chagrin;
That single act gives half the world the spleen.'
    The goddess with a discontented air
Seems to reject him, though she grants his prayer.   80
A wondrous bag with both her hands she binds,
Like that where once Ulysses held the winds;
There she collects the force of female lungs,
Sighs, sobs, and passions, and the war of tongues.
A vial next she fills with fainting fears,   85
Soft sorrows, melting griefs, and flowing tears.
The gnome rejoicing bears her gifts away,
Spreads his black wings, and slowly mounts to day.
    Sunk in Thalestris' arms the nymph he found,
Her eyes dejected, and her hair unbound.   90
Full o'er their heads the swelling bag he rent,
And all the Furies issued at the vent.
Belinda burns with more than mortal ire,
And fierce Thalestris fans the rising fire.
'O wretched maid!' she spread her hands and cried   95
(While Hampton's echoes 'Wretched maid!' replied),
'Was it for this you took such constant care
The bodkin, comb, and essence to prepare?
For this your locks in paper durance bound?
For this with tort'ring irons wreathed around?   100
For this with fillets strained your tender head,
And bravely bore the double loads of lead?
Gods! shall the ravisher display your hair,
While the fops envy, and the ladies stare?
Honour forbid! at whose unrivalled shrine   105
Ease, pleasure, virtue, all, our sex resign.
Methinks already I your tears survey,
Already hear the horrid things they say,
Already see you a degraded toast,
And all your honour in a whisper lost!   110
How shall I, then, your helpless fame defend?
'Twill then be infamy to seem your friend!
And shall this prize, th'inestimable prize,
Exposed through crystal to the gazing eyes,
And heightened by the diamond's circling rays,   115
On that rapacious hand forever blaze?
Sooner shall grass in Hyde Park Circus grow,
And wits take lodgings in the sound of Bow;
Sooner let earth, air, sea, to Chaos fall,
Men, monkeys, lap-dogs, parrots, perish all!'   120
    She said; then raging to Sir Plume repairs,
And bids her beau demand the precious hairs
(Sir Plume of amber snuff-box justly vain,
And the nice conduct of a clouded cane).

---

43 **spires:** coils 45 **Elysian:** belonging to Elysium, home of the blessed dead in Greek myth 46 **machine:** a theatrical device such as a pulley, used to effect spectacular entrances or exits on stage 51 **pipkin:** a small earthenware vessel **Homer's tripod:** in the Iliad Homer mentions walking tripods created by Vulcan 53 **prove with child:** are shown to be pregnant 62 **physic:** medicine 69 **citron-waters:** brandy flavoured with lemon rind 71 **with airy horns I planted heads:** men whose wives were unfaithful were said to be crowned with cuckold's horns 75 **costive:** constipated

82 **Ulysses held the winds:** in Greek myth, Ulysses (Odysseus) was given a bag confining all the unfavourable winds 89 **Thalestris:** queen of the Amazons 92 **Furies:** in classical myth, the goddesses of vengeance 98 **essence:** perfume 99 **paper durance:** confinement in curl-papers 101 **fillets:** headbands 109 **toast:** a woman to whom drinking toasts were regularly made 117 **Hyde Park Circus:** a place where fashionable people took coach rides 118 **in the sound of Bow:** within hearing range of the bells of St Mary-le-Bow, i.e. in the centre of the city of London 124 **clouded:** variegated with dark colours

With earnest eyes, and round unthinking face, 125
He first the snuff-box opened, then the case,
And thus broke out: 'My Lord, why, what the devil?
Zounds! damn the lock! 'fore Gad, you must be civil!
Plague on't! 'tis past a jest – nay, prithee, pox!
Give her the hair.' He spoke, and rapped his box. 130

'It grieves me much,' replied the peer again,
'Who speaks so well should ever speak in vain.
But by this lock, this sacred lock, I swear
(Which never more shall join its parted hair;
Which never more its honours shall renew, 135
Clipped from the lovely head where late it grew)
That while my nostrils draw the vital air,
This hand, which won it, shall forever wear.'
He spoke, and speaking, in proud triumph spread
The long-contended honours of her head. 140

But Umbriel, hateful gnome! forbears not so,
He breaks the vial whence the sorrows flow.
Then see! the nymph in beauteous grief appears,
Her eyes half-languishing, half-drowned in tears;
On her heaved bosom hung her drooping head, 145
Which, with a sigh, she raised; and thus she said:

'Forever cursed be this detested day,
Which snatched my best, my fav'rite curl away!
Happy! ah, ten times happy had I been,
If Hampton Court these eyes had never seen! 150
Yet am not I the first mistaken maid,
By love of courts to num'rous ills betrayed.
Oh, had I rather unadmired remained
In some lone isle, or distant northern land;
Where the gilt chariot never marks the way, 155
Where none learn ombre, none e'er taste bohea!
There kept my charms concealed from mortal eye,
Like roses that in deserts bloom and die.
What moved my mind with youthful lords to roam?
Oh, had I stayed, and said my prayers at home! 160
'Twas this, the morning omens seemed to tell;
Thrice from my trembling hand the patch-box fell;
The tott'ring china shook without a wind,
Nay, Poll sat mute, and Shock was most unkind!
A sylph, too, warned me of the threats of fate, 165
In mystic visions, now believed too late!
See the poor remnants of these slighted hairs!
My hands shall rend what ev'n thy rápine spares:
These in two sable ringlets taught to break
Once gave new beauties to the snowy neck; 170
The sister-lock now sits uncouth, alone,
And in its fellow's fate foresees its own;
Uncurled it hangs, the fatal shears demands,
And tempts once more thy sacrilegious hands.
Oh, hadst thou, cruel! been content to seize 175
Hairs less in sight, or any hairs but these!'

136 **late**: lately 156 **bohea**: a black Chinese tea

CANTO FIVE

SHE said. The pitying audience melt in tears.
But Fate and Jove had stopped the baron's ears.
In vain Thalestris with reproach assails,
For who can move when fair Belinda fails?
Not half so fixed the Trojan could remain, 5
While Anna begged and Dido raged in vain.
Then grave Clarissa graceful waved her fan;
Silence ensued, and thus the nymph began.

'Say why are beauties praised and honoured most,
The wise man's passion, and the vain man's toast? 10
Why decked with all that land and sea afford,
Why angels called, and angel-like adored?
Why round our coaches crowd the white-gloved
      beaux,
Why bows the side-box from its inmost rows?
How vain are all these glories, all our pains, 15
Unless good sense preserve what beauty gains:
That men may say, when we the front-box grace,
"Behold the first in virtue as in face!"
Oh! if to dance all night, and dress all day,
Charmed the small-pox, or chased old age away; 20
Who would not scorn what housewife's cares produce,
Or who would learn one earthly thing of use?
To patch, nay, ogle, might become a saint,
Nor could it sure be such a sin to paint.
But since, alas! frail beauty must decay, 25
Curled or uncurled, since locks will turn to grey;
Since painted, or not painted, all shall fade,
And she who scorns a man, must die a maid;
What then remains but well our pow'r to use,
And keep good-humour still whate'er we lose? 30
And trust me, dear! good-humour can prevail,
When airs, and flights, and screams, and scolding fail.
Beauties in vain their pretty eyes may roll;
Charms strike the sight, but merit wins the soul.'

So spoke the dame, but no applause ensued; 35
Belinda frowned, Thalestris called her prude.
'To arms, to arms!' the fierce virago cries,
And swift as lightning to the combat flies.
All side in parties and begin th'attack;
Fans clap, silks rustle, and tough whalebones crack; 40
Heroes' and heroines' shouts confus'dly rise,
And bass and treble voices strike the skies.
No common weapons in their hands are found,
Like gods they fight, nor dread a mortal wound.
So when bold Homer makes the gods engage, 45
And heavenly breasts with human passions rage;
'Gainst Pallas, Mars; Latona, Hermes arms;
And all Olympus rings with loud alarms:
Jove's thunder roars, heaven trembles all around,
Blue Neptune storms, the bellowing deeps resound: 50

CANTO FIVE: 5-6 **Not half . . . vain**: the Trojan hero Aeneas abandoned Queen Dido of Carthage, who was in love with him 24 **paint**: put on makeup 37 **virago**: a warlike woman 40 **whalebones**: i.e. in corsets 47 **Pallas**: Athene **Latona**: the Latin form of the Greek Leto, mother of Apollo

Earth shakes her nodding tow'rs, the ground gives way,
And the pale ghosts start at the flash of day!
   Triumphant Umbriel on a sconce's height
Clapped his glad wings, and sate to view the fight:
Propped on their bodkin spears, the sprites survey   55
The growing combat, or assist the fray.
   While through the press enraged Thalestris flies,
And scatters death around from both her eyes;
A beau and witling perished in the throng,
One died in metaphor, and one in song.   60
'O cruel nymph! a living death I bear,'
Cried Dapperwit, and sunk beside his chair.
A mournful glance Sir Fopling upwards cast,
'Those eyes are made so killing' – was his last.
Thus on Maeander's flow'ry margin lies   65
Th'expiring swan, and as he sings he dies.
   When bold Sir Plume had drawn Clarissa down,
Chloe stepped in, and killed him with a frown;
She smiled to see the doughty hero slain,
But, at her smile, the beau revived again.   70
   Now Jove suspends his golden scales in air,
Weighs the men's wits against the lady's hair;
The doubtful beam long nods from side to side;
At length the wits mount up, the hairs subside.
   See, fierce Belinda on the baron flies,   75
With more than usual lightning in her eyes:
Nor feared the chief th'unequal fight to try,
Who sought no more than on his foe to die.
But this bold lord, with manly strength endued,
She with one finger and a thumb subdued: 80
Just where the breath of life his nostrils drew,
A charge of snuff the wily virgin threw;
The gnomes direct, to ev'ry atom just,
The pungent grains of titillating dust.
Sudden, with starting tears each eye o'erflows,   85
And the high dome re-echoes to his nose.
   'Now meet thy fate!' incensed Belinda cried,
And drew a deadly bodkin from her side.
(The same, his ancient personage to deck,
Her great-great-grandsire wore about his neck,   90
In three seal-rings; which after, melted down,
Formed a vast buckle for his widow's gown:
Her infant grandame's whistle next it grew,
The bells she jingled, and the whistle blew;
Then in a bodkin graced her mother's hairs,   95
Which long she wore, and now Belinda wears.)
   'Boast not my fall,' he cried, 'insulting foe!
Thou by some other shalt be laid as low.
Nor think, to die dejects my lofty mind:
All that I dread is leaving you behind!   100
Rather than so, ah! let me still survive,
And burn in Cupid's flames – but burn alive!'

'Restore the lock!' she cries; and all around
'Restore the lock!' the vaulted roofs rebound.
Not fierce Othello in so loud a strain   105
Roared for the handkerchief that caused his pain.
But see how oft ambitious aims are crossed,
And chiefs contend till all the prize is lost!
The lock, obtained with guilt, and kept with pain,
In ev'ry place is sought, but sought in vain: 110
With such a prize no mortal must be blessed,
So heaven decrees! with heaven who can contest?
   Some thought it mounted on the lunar sphere,
Since all things lost on earth are treasured there.
There heroes' wits are kept in pond'rous vases,   115
And beaux' in snuff-boxes and tweezer-cases.
There broken vows, and deathbed alms are found,
And lovers' hearts with ends of ribband bound,
The courtier's promises, and sick man's prayers,
The smiles of harlots, and the tears of heirs,   120
Cages for gnats, and chains to yoke a flea,
Dried butterflies, and tomes of casuistry.
   But trust the Muse – she saw it upward rise,
Though marked by none but quick, poetic eyes:
(So Rome's great founder to the heavens withdrew,   125
To Proculus alone confessed in view):
A sudden star, it shot through liquid air,
And drew behind a radiant trail of hair.
Not Berenice's locks first rose so bright,
The heavens bespangling with dishevelled light.   130
The sylphs behold it kindling as it flies,
And pleased pursue its progress through the skies.
   This the beau monde shall from the Mall survey,
And hail with music its propitious ray.
This the blessed lover shall for Venus take,   135
And send up vows from Rosamonda's lake;
This Partridge soon shall view in cloudless skies,
When next he looks through Galileo's eyes;
And hence th'egregious wizard shall foredoom
The fate of Louis, and the fall of Rome.   140
   Then, cease, bright Nymph! to mourn thy ravished
     hair,
Which adds new glory to the shining sphere!
Not all the tresses that fair head can boast,
Shall draw such envy as the lock you lost.
For, after all the murders of your eye,   145
When, after millions slain, yourself shall die;
When those fair suns shall set, as set they must,
And all those tresses shall be laid in dust;
This lock, the Muse shall consecrate to fame,
And 'midst the stars inscribe Belinda's name.   150

125 (**So Rome's . . . withdrew:** Romulus, legendary founder of Rome, was believed to have been taken bodily up to heaven 129 **Berenice:** Berenice (died 221 BC), wife of Ptolemy III, offered to sacrifice her hair if the gods gave victory to her husband. Her tresses were taken to heaven, to form the constellation Coma Berenices 133 **the Mall:** a walk in St James's Park 136 **Rosamonda's Lake:** a pond in St James's Park 137 **Partridge:** John Partridge, an English astrologer and compiler of almanacs 138 **Galileo's eyes:** a telescope, perfected by Galileo Galilei (1564–1642), Italian scientist 139 **foredoom:** predict 140 **Louis:** Louis XIV of France, who died in 1715

53 **sconce:** a bracket fixed to a wall for holding a torch or candle 54 **sate:** sat 59 **witling:** a would-be or inferior wit 62 **Dapperwit:** a character in *Love in a Wood*, a play by William Wycherley (1671) 63 **Sir Fopling:** Sir Fopling Flutter, a character in *The Man of Mode*, a play by Sir George Etherege (1676) 65 **Maeander:** a river in ancient Phrygia (Asia Minor), proverbial for its many windings 66 **Th'expiring swan . . . dies:** it was traditionally believed that a swan sang before it died

ELOISA TO ABELARD

[ARGUMENT. Abelard and Eloisa flourished in the twelfth century; they were two of the most distinguished persons of their age in learning and beauty, but for nothing more famous than for their unfortunate passion. After a long course of calamities, they retired each to a several convent, and consecrated the remainder of their days to religion. It was many years after this separation that a letter of Abelard's to a friend, which contained the history of his misfortune, fell into the hands of Eloisa. This awakening all her tenderness, occasioned those celebrated letters (out of which the following is partly extracted) which give so lively a picture of the struggles of grace and nature, virtue and passion.]

IN these deep solitudes and awful cells,
Where heavenly-pensive contemplation dwells,
And ever-musing melancholy reigns;
What means this tumult in a vestal's veins?
Why rove my thoughts beyond this last retreat? 5
Why feels my heart its long-forgotten heat?
Yet, yet I love! From Abelard it came,
And Eloisa yet must kiss the name.
    Dear fatal name! rest ever unrevealed,
Nor pass these lips in holy silence sealed: 10
Hide it, my heart, within that close disguise,
Where, mixed with God's, his loved Idea lies:
Oh, write it not, my hand – the name appears
Already written – wash it out, my tears!
In vain lost Eloisa weeps and prays, 15
Her heart still díctates, and her hand obeys.
    Relentless walls! whose darksome round contains
Repentant sighs, and voluntary pains:
Ye rugged rocks! which holy knees have worn;
Ye grots and caverns shagged with horrid thorn! 20
Shrines! where their vigils pale-eyed virgins keep,
And pitying saints, whose statues learn to weep!
Though cold like you, unmoved and silent grown,
I have not yet forgot myself to stone.
All is not heaven's while Abelard has part, 25
Still rebel nature holds out half my heart;
Nor prayers nor fasts its stubborn pulse restrain,
Nor tears, for ages, taught to flow in vain.
    Soon as thy letters trembling I unclose,
That well-known name awakens all my woes. 30
Oh, name forever sad! forever dear!
Still breathed in sighs, still ushered with a tear.
I tremble, too, where'er my own I find,
Some dire misfortune follows close behind.
Line after line my gushing eyes o'erflow, 35
Led through a sad variety of woe:
Now warm in love, now with'ring in my bloom,
Lost in a convent's solitary gloom!
There stern Religion quenched th'unwilling flame,
There died the best of passions, Love and Fame. 40

Yet write, oh, write me all, that I may join
Griefs to thy griefs, and echo sighs to thine.
Nor foes nor fortune take this pow'r away;
And is my Abelard less kind than they?
Tears still are mine, and those I need not spare, 45
Love but demands what else were shed in prayer;
No happier task these faded eyes pursue;
To read and weep is all they now can do.
    Then share thy pain, allow that sad relief;
Ah, more than share it! give me all thy grief. 50
Heaven first taught letters for some wretch's aid,
Some banished lover, or some captive maid;
They live, they speak, they breathe what love inspires,
Warm from the soul, and faithful to its fires,
The virgin's wish without her fears impart, 55
Excuse the blush, and pour out all the heart,
Speed the soft intercourse from soul to soul,
And waft a sigh from Indus to the Pole.
    Thou know'st how guiltless first I met thy flame,
When Love approached me under Friendship's name;
My fancy formed thee of angelic kind, 61
Some emanation of th'all-beauteous Mind.
Those smiling eyes, attemp'ring ev'ry ray,
Shone sweetly lambent with celestial day:
Guiltless I gazed; heaven listened while you sung; 65
And truths divine came mended from that tongue.
From lips like those what precept failed to move?
Too soon they taught me 'twas no sin to love:
Back through the paths of pleasing sense I ran,
Nor wished an angel whom I loved a man. 70
Dim and remote the joys of saints I see,
Nor envy them that heaven I lose for thee.
    How oft, when pressed to marriage, have I said,
Curse on all laws but those which love has made?
Love, free as air, at sight of human ties, 75
Spreads his light wings, and in a moment flies.
Let wealth, let honour, wait the wedded dame,
August her deed, and sacred be her fame;
Before true passion all those vows remove,
Fame, wealth, and honour! what are you to Love? 80
The jealous god, when we profane his fires,
Those restless passions in revenge inspires,
And bids them make mistaken mortals groan,
Who seek in love for aught but love alone.
Should at my feet the world's great master fall, 85
Himself, his throne, his world, I'd scorn 'em all:
Not Caesar's empress would I deign to prove;
No, make me mistress to the man I love;
If there be yet another name more free,
More fond than mistress, make me that to thee! 90
Oh, happy state! when souls each other draw,
When love is liberty, and nature law:
All then is full, possessing, and possessed,
No craving void left aching in the breast: 94

ELOISA TO ABELARD: 4 **vestal:** a chaste woman or virgin; a nun
20 **shagged:** made shaggy

58 **Indus:** river in S Asia 63 **attemp'ring:** moderating 87 **prove:** try

Ev'n thought meets thought, ere from the lips it part,
And each warm wish springs mutual from the heart.
This sure is bliss (if bliss on earth there be)
And once the lot of Abelard and me.
　　Alas, how changed! what sudden horrors rise!
A naked lover bound and bleeding lies!　　　　　100
Where, where was Eloise? her voice, her hand,
Her poniard, had opposed the dire command.
Barbarian, stay! that bloody stroke restrain;
The crime was common, common be the pain.
I can no more; by shame, by rage suppressed,　　105
Let tears, and burning blushes speak the rest.
　　Canst thou forget that sad, that solemn day,
When victims at yon altar's foot we lay?
Canst thou forget what tears that moment fell,
When, warm in youth, I bade the world farewell?　110
As with cold lips I kissed the sacred veil,
The shrines all trembled, and the lamps grew pale:
Heaven scarce believed the conquest it surveyed,
And saints with wonder heard the vows I made.
Yet then, to those dread altars as I drew,　　　115
Not on the Cross my eyes were fixed, but you:
Not grace, or zeal, love only was my call,
And if I lose thy love, I lose my all.
Come! with thy looks, thy words, relieve my woe;
Those still at least are left thee to bestow.　　　120
Still on that breast enamoured let me lie,
Still drink delicious poison from thy eye,
Pant on thy lip, and to thy heart be pressed;
Give all thou canst – and let me dream the rest.
Ah, no! instruct me other joys to prize,　　　125
With other beauties charm my partial eyes,
Full in my view set all the bright abode,
And make my soul quit Abelard for God.
　　Ah, think at least thy flock deserve thy care,
Plants of thy hand, and children of thy prayer.　130
From the false world in early youth they fled,
By thee to mountains, wilds, and deserts led.
You raised these hallowed walls; the desert smiled,
And paradise was opened in the wild.
No weeping orphan saw his father's stores　　135
Our shrines irradiate, or emblaze the floors;
No silver saints, by dying misers given,
Here bribed the rage of ill-requited heaven:
But such plain roofs as piety could raise,
And only vocal with the Maker's praise.　　　140
In these lone walls (their days eternal bound)
These moss-grown domes with spiry turrets crowned,
Where awful arches make a noon-day night,
And the dim windows shed a solemn light;
Thy eyes diffused a reconciling ray,　　　　145
And gleams of glory brightened all the day.
But now no face divine contentment wears,
'Tis all blank sadness, or continual tears.

See how the force of others' prayers I try
(Oh, pious fraud of am'rous charity!),　　　　150
But why should I on others' prayers depend?
Come thou, my father, brother, husband, friend!
Ah, let thy handmaid, sister, daughter move,
And all those tender names in one, thy love!
The darksome pines that o'er yon rocks reclined　155
Wave high, and murmur to the hollow wind,
The wand'ring streams that shine between the hills,
The grots that echo to the tinkling rills,
The dying gales that pant upon the trees,
The lakes that quiver to the curling breeze;　　160
No more these scenes my meditation aid,
Or lull to rest the visionary maid.
But o'er the twilight groves and dusky caves,
Long-sounding isles, and intermingled graves,
Black Melancholy sits, and round her throws　　165
A death-like silence, and a dread repose:
Her gloomy presence saddens all the scene,
Shades ev'ry flow'r, and darkens ev'ry green,
Deepens the murmur of the falling floods,
And breathes a browner horror on the woods.　170
　　Yet here for ever, ever must I stay;
Sad proof how well a lover can obey!
Death, only death, can break the lasting chain;
And here, ev'n then, shall my cold dust remain,
Here all its frailties, all its flames resign,　　175
And wait, till 'tis no sin to mix with thine.
　　Ah, wretch! believed the spouse of God in vain,
Confessed within the slave of love and man.
Assist me, heaven! but whence arose that prayer?
Sprung it from piety, or from despair?　　　180
Ev'n here, where frozen chastity retires,
Love finds an altar for forbidden fires.
I ought to grieve, but cannot what I ought;
I mourn the lover, not lament the fault;
I view my crime, but kindle at the view,　　　185
Repent old pleasures, and solicit new;
Now turned to heaven, I weep my past offence,
Now think of thee, and curse my innocence.
Of all affliction taught a lover yet,
'Tis sure the hardest science to forget!　　　190
How shall I lose the sin, yet keep the sense,
And love th'offender, yet detest th'offence?
How the dear object of the crime remove,
Or how distinguish penitence from love?
Unequal task! a passion to resign,　　　　195
For hearts so touched, so pierced, so lost as mine.
Ere such a soul regains its peaceful state,
How often must it love, how often hate!
How often hope, despair, resent, regret,
Conceal, disdain – do all things but forget.　　200
But let heaven seize it, all at once 'tis fired;
Not touched, but raped; not wakened, but inspired!

102 **poniard:** small dagger　104 **common:** shared　133 **You . . . walls:**
Pope notes, 'He founded the monastery'

158 **grots:** caves　185 **kindle:** be roused　191 **sense:** sensation

Oh, come! oh, teach me nature to subdue,
Renounce my love, my life, my self – and you.
Fill my fond heart with God alone, for he   205
Alone can rival, can succeed to thee.

    How happy is the blameless vestal's lot?
The world forgetting, by the world forgot:
Eternal sunshine of the spotless mind!
Each prayer accepted, and each wish resigned;   210
Labour and rest, that equal periods keep;
'Obedient slumbers that can wake and weep';
Desires composed, affections ever even;
Tears that delight, and sighs that waft to heaven.
Grace shines around her with serenest beams,   215
And whisp'ring angels prompt her golden dreams.
For her th'unfading rose of Eden blooms,
And wings of seraphs shed divine perfúmes,
For her the spouse prepares the bridal ring,
For her white virgins hymeneals sing;   220
To sounds of heavenly harps she dies away,
And melts in visions of eternal day.

    Far other dreams my erring soul employ,
Far other raptures, of unholy joy:
When at the close of each sad, sorrowing day,   225
Fancy restores what vengeance snatched away,
Then conscience sleeps, and leaving nature free,
All my loose soul unbounded springs to thee.
Oh, cursed, dear horrors of all-conscious night!
How glowing guilt exalts the keen delight!   230
Provoking demons all restraint remove,
And stir within me ev'ry source of love.
I hear thee, view thee, gaze o'er all thy charms,
And round thy phantom glue my clasping arms.
I wake. No more I hear, no more I view;   235
The phantom flies me, as unkind as you.
I call aloud; it hears not what I say:
I stretch my empty arms; it glides away.
To dream once more I close my willing eyes;
Ye soft illusions, dear deceits, arise!   240
Alas, no more! methinks we wand'ring go
Through dreary wastes, and weep each other's woe,
Where round some mould'ring tow'r pale ivy creeps,
And low-browed rocks hang nodding o'er the deeps.
Sudden you mount! you beckon from the skies;   245
Clouds interpose, waves roar, and winds arise.
I shriek, start up, the same sad prospect find,
And wake to all the griefs I left behind.

    For thee the fates, severely kind, ordain
A cool suspense from pleasure and from pain;   250
Thy life a long, dead calm of fixed repose;
No pulse that riots, and no blood that glows.
Still as the sea, ere winds were taught to blow,
Or moving spirit bade the waters flow;
Soft as the slumbers of a saint forgiven,   255
And mild as op'ning gleams of promised heaven.

Come, Abelard! for what hast thou to dread?
The torch of Venus burns not for the dead.
Nature stands checked; Religion disapproves;
Ev'n thou art cold – yet Eloisa loves.   260
Ah, hopeless, lasting flames! like those that burn
To light the dead, and warm th'unfruitful urn.

    What scenes appear where'er I turn my view?
The dear Ideas, where I fly, pursue,
Rise in the grove, before the altar rise,   265
Stain all my soul, and wanton in my eyes.
I waste the matin lamp in sighs for thee,
Thy image steals between my God and me,
Thy voice I seem in ev'ry hymn to hear,
With ev'ry bead I drop too soft a tear.   270
When from the censer clouds of fragrance roll,
And swelling organs lift the rising soul,
One thought of thee puts all the pomp to flight,
Priests, tapers, temples, swim before my sight:
In seas of flame my plunging soul is drowned,   275
While altars blaze, and angels tremble round.

    While prostrate here in humble grief I lie,
Kind, virtuous drops just gath'ring in my eye,
While praying, trembling, in the dust I roll,
And dawning grace is op'ning on my soul: 280
Come, if thou dar'st, all charming as thou art!
Oppose thyself to heaven; dispute my heart;
Come, with one glance of those deluding eyes
Blot out each bright Idea of the skies;
Take back that grace, those sorrows, and those tears,
Take back my fruitless penitence and prayers,   286
Snatch me, just mounting, from the blessed abode,
Assist the fiends, and tear me from my God!

    No, fly me, fly me, far as Pole from Pole;
Rise Alps between us! and whole oceans roll!   290
Ah, come not, write not, think not once of me,
Nor share one pang of all I felt for thee.
Thy oaths I quit, thy memory resign;
Forget, renounce me, hate whate'er was mine.
Fair eyes, and tempting looks (which yet I view!)   295
Long loved, adored ideas, all adieu!
O Grace serene! O Virtue heav'nly fair!
Divine oblivion of low-thoughted care!
Fresh blooming Hope, gay daughter of the sky!
And Faith, our early immortality!   300
Enter, each mild, each amicable guest;
Receive, and wrap me in eternal rest!

    See in her cell sad Eloisa spread,
Propped on some tomb, a neighbour of the dead.
In each low wind methinks a spirit calls,   305
And more than echoes talk along the walls.
Here, as I watched the dying lamps around,
From yonder shrine I heard a hollow sound.
'Come, sister, come!' it said, or seemed to say,
'Thy place is here, sad sister, come away!   310

---

212 **'Obedient . . . weep'**: quoted from *Description of a Religious House*, by Richard Crashaw (1648) 220 **hymeneals**: wedding hymns

266 **wanton**: to frolic 274 **tapers**: candles 282 **dispute**: contend with

Once like thyself, I trembled, wept, and prayed,
Love's victim then, though now a sainted maid:
But all is calm in this eternal sleep;
Here grief forgets to groan, and love to weep,
Ev'n superstition loses ev'ry fear: 315
For God, not man, absolves our frailties here.'
   I come, I come! prepare your roseate bow'rs,
Celestial palms, and ever-blooming flow'rs.
Thither, where sinners may have rest, I go,
Where flames refined in breasts seraphic glow.   320
Thou, Abelard! the last sad office pay,
And smooth my passage to the realms of day;
See my lips tremble, and my eyeballs roll,
Suck my last breath, and catch my flying soul!
Ah, no – in sacred vestments may'st thou stand,   325
The hallowed taper trembling in thy hand,
Present the Cross before my lifted eye,
Teach me at once, and learn of me to die.
Ah, then thy once-loved Eloisa see!
It will be then no crime to gaze on me.   330
See from my cheek the transient roses fly!
See the last sparkle languish in my eye!
Till ev'ry motion, pulse, and breath be o'er;
And ev'n my Abelard beloved no more.
O Death all-eloquent! you only prove   335
What dust we dote on, when 'tis man we love.
   Then, too, when fate shall thy fair frame destroy
(That cause of all my guilt, and all my joy),
In trance ecstatic may thy pangs be drowned,
Bright clouds descend, and angels watch thee round,
From op'ning skies may streaming glories shine,   341
And saints embrace thee with a love like mine.
   May one kind grave unite each hapless name,
And graft my love immortal on thy fame!
Then, ages hence, when all my woes are o'er,   345
When this rebellious heart shall beat no more;
If ever chance two wand'ring lovers brings
To Paraclete's white walls and silver springs,
O'er the pale marble shall they join their heads,
And drink the falling tears each other sheds;   350
Then sadly say, with mutual pity moved,
'Oh, may we never love as these have loved!'
From the full choir when loud hosannas rise,
And swell the pomp of dreadful sacrifice,
Amid that scene, if some relenting eye   355
Glance on the stone where our cold relics lie,
Devotion's self shall steal a thought from heaven,
One human tear shall drop, and be forgiven.
And sure if fate some future bard shall join
In sad similitude of griefs to mine,   360
Condemned whole years in absence to deplore,
And image charms he must behold no more;
Such if there be, who loves so long, so well;
Let him our sad, our tender story tell;
The well-sung woes will soothe my pensive ghost;   365
He best can paint 'em, who shall feel 'em most.

ELEGY TO THE MEMORY OF
AN UNFORTUNATE LADY

WHAT beck'ning ghost, along the moonlight shade
Invites my steps, and points to yonder glade?
'Tis she! – but why that bleeding bosom gored,
Why dimly gleams the visionary sword?
Oh, ever beauteous, ever friendly! tell,   5
Is it, in heaven, a crime to love too well?
To bear too tender, or too firm a heart,
To act a lover's or a Roman's part?
Is there no bright reversion in the sky,
For those who greatly think, or bravely die?   10
   Why bade ye else, ye Pow'rs! her soul aspire
Above the vulgar flight of low desire?
Ambition first sprung from your blessed abodes;
The glorious fault of angels and of gods;
Thence to their images on earth it flows,   15
And in the breasts of kings and heroes glows.
Most souls, 'tis true, but peep out once an age,
Dull sullen pris'ners in the body's cage:
Dim lights of life, that burn a length of years
Useless, unseen, as lamps in sepulchres;   20
Like Eastern kings a lazy state they keep,
And close confined in their own palace sleep.
   From these perhaps (ere nature bade her die)
Fate snatched her early to the pitying sky.
As into air the purer spirits flow,   25
And sep'rate from their kindred dregs below;
So flew the soul to its congenial place,
Nor left one virtue to redeem her race.
   But thou, false guardian of a charge too good,
Thou, mean deserter of thy brother's blood!   30
See on these ruby lips the trembling breath,
These cheeks, now fading at the blast of death;
Cold is that breast which warmed the world before,
And those love-darting eyes must roll no more.
Thus, if eternal justice rules the ball,   35
Thus shall your wives, and thus your children fall;
On all the line a sudden vengeance waits,
And frequent hearses shall besiege your gates.
There passengers shall stand, and pointing say
(While the long fun'rals blacken all the way),   40
'Lo! these were they, whose souls the Furies steeled,
And cursed with hearts unknowing how to yield.'
Thus unlamented pass the proud away,
The gaze of fools, and pageant of a day!
So perish all, whose breast ne'er learned to glow   45
For others' good, or melt at others' woe.
   What can atone (O ever-injured Shade!)
Thy fate unpitied, and thy rites unpaid?
No friend's complaint, no kind domestic tear
Pleased thy pale ghost, or graced thy mournful bier;   50
By foreign hands thy dying eyes were closed,
By foreign hands thy decent limbs composed,
By foreign hands thy humble grave adorned,
By strangers honoured, and by strangers mourned!
What though no friends in sable weeds appear,   55
Grieve for an hour, perhaps, then mourn a year,

And bear about the mockery of woe
To midnight dances, and the public show?
What though no weeping loves thy ashes grace,
Nor polished marble emulate thy face?   60
What though no sacred earth allow thee room,
Nor hallowed dirge be muttered o'er thy tomb?
Yet shall thy grave with rising flowers be dressed,
And the green turf lie lightly on thy breast:
There shall the morn her earliest tears bestow,   65
There the first roses of the year shall blow;
While angels with their silver wings o'ershade
The ground, now sacred by thy relics made.
   So peaceful rests, without a stone, a name,
What once had beauty, titles, wealth, and fame.   70
How loved, how honoured once, avails thee not,
To whom related, or by whom begot;
A heap of dust alone remains of thee;
'Tis all thou art, and all the proud shall be!
   Poets themselves must fall, like those they sung;   75
Deaf the praised ear, and mute the tuneful tongue.
Even he, whose soul now melts in mournful lays,
Shall shortly want the gen'rous tear he pays;
Then from his closing eyes thy form shall part,
And the last pang shall tear thee from his heart,   80
Life's idle business at one gasp be o'er,
The Muse forgot, and thou be loved no more!

ELEGY TO THE MEMORY OF AN UNFORTUNATE LADY: 8 **a Roman's part:**
the act of suicide 35 **ball:** the orb held by a monarch 41 **Furies:** in
Roman myth, goddesses of vengeance 55 **sable weeds:** black clothes
(for mourning) 66 **blow:** bloom 77 **lays:** songs 78 **want:** lack

From AN ESSAY ON MAN

THE bliss of man (could pride that blessing find)
Is not to act or think beyond mankind;
No pow'rs of body or of soul to share,
But what his nature and his state can bear.
Why has not man a microscopic eye?   5
For this plain reason, man is not a fly.
Say what the use, were finer optics given,
T'inspect a mite, not comprehend the heaven?
Or touch, if tremblingly alive all o'er,
To smart and agonize at ev'ry pore?   10
Or quick effluvia darting through the brain,
Die of a rose in aromatic pain?
If Nature thundered in his op'ning ears,
And stunned him with the music of the spheres,
How would he wish that heaven had left him still   15
The whisp'ring zephyr, and the purling rill?
Who finds not Providence all good and wise,
Alike in what it gives, and what denies?
   Far as Creation's ample range extends,
The scale of sensual, mental powers ascends: 20
Mark how it mounts, to man's imperial race,
From the green myriads in the peopled grass:
What modes of sight betwixt each wide extreme,
The mole's dim curtain, and the lynx's beam:
Of smell, the headlong lioness between,   25

And hound sagacious on the tainted green:
Of hearing, from the life that fills the flood,
To that which warbles through the vernal wood:
The spider's touch, how éxquisitely fine!
Feels at each thread, and lives along the line: 30
In the nice bee, what sense so subtly true
From pois'nous herbs extracts the healing dew:
How instinct varies in the grov'lling swine,
Compared, half-reas'ning elephant, with thine:
'Twixt that, and reason, what a nice barrier,   35
Forever sep'rate, yet forever near!
Remembrance and reflection how allied;
What thin partitions sense from thought divide:
And middle natures, how they long to join,
Yet never passed th'insuperable line!   40
Without this just gradation, could they be
Subjected these to those, or all to thee?
The pow'rs of all subdued by thee alone,
Is not thy reason all these pow'rs in one?
                                          [Epistle 1, lines 189–232]

KNOW, then, thyself, presume not God to scan;
The proper study of mankind is man.
Placed on this isthmus of a middle state,
A being darkly wise, and rudely great:
With too much knowledge for the sceptic side,   5
With too much weakness for the stoic's pride,
He hangs between; in doubt to act, or rest,
In doubt to deem himself a god, or beast;
In doubt his mind or body to prefer,
Born but to die, and reas'ning but to err;   10
Alike in ignorance, his reason such,
Whether he thinks too little, or too much:
Chaos of thought and passion, all confused;
Still by himself abused, or disabused;
Created half to rise, and half to fall;   15
Great lord of all things, yet a prey to all;
Sole judge of truth, in endless error hurled:
The glory, jest, and riddle of the world!
   Go, wondrous creature! mount where science
      guides,
Go, measure earth, weigh air, and state the tides;   20
Instruct the planets in what orbs to run,
Correct old time, and regulate the sun;
Go, soar with Plato to th'empyreal sphere,
To the first good, first perfect, and first fair;
Or tread the mazy round his foll'wers trod,   25
And quitting sense call imitating God;
As Eastern priests in giddy circles run,
And turn their heads to imitate the sun.
Go, teach Eternal Wisdom how to rule –
Then drop into thyself, and be a fool!   30
                                          [Epistle 2, lines 1–30]

AN ESSAY ON MAN: EPISTLE 1: 14 **music of the spheres:** it was believed
that the planets emitted harmonious sounds by virtue of their
spinning 26 **tainted:** marked with the scent of prey 31 **nice:**
precise, exact 35 **barrier:** pronounced to rhyme with 'arrear'
EPISTLE 2: 23 **empyreal sphere:** the outer reaches of the universe
25 **mazy:** confusing 27 **Eastern . . . run:** a reference to whirling dervishes,
members of a Muslim ascetic order noted for an ecstatic whirling dance

From EPISTLE TO RICHARD BOYLE, EARL OF BURLINGTON

AT Timon's villa let us pass a day,
Where all cry out, 'What sums are thrown away!'
So proud, so grand, of that stupendous air,
Soft and agreeable come never there.
Greatness, with Timon, dwells in such a draught   5
As brings all Brobdingnag before your thought.
To compass this, his building is a town,
His pond an ocean, his parterre a down:
Who but must laugh, the master when he sees?
A puny insect, shiv'ring at a breeze.   10
Lo! what huge heaps of littleness around!
The whole, a laboured quarry above ground.
Two Cupids squirt before; a lake behind
Improves the keenness of the northern wind.
His gardens next your admiration call,   15
On ev'ry side you look, behold the wall!
No pleasing intricacies intervene,
No artful wildness to perplex the scene;
Grove nods at grove, each alley has a brother,
And half the platform just reflects the other.   20
The suff'ring eye inverted Nature sees,
Trees cut to statues, statues thick as trees,
With here a fountain, never to be played,
And there a summer-house, that knows no shade.
Here Amphitrite sails through myrtle bow'rs;   25
There gladiators fight, or die, in flow'rs;
Unwatered see the drooping sea-horse mourn,
And swallows roost in Nilus' dusty urn.
    My lord advances with majestic mien,
Smit with the mighty pleasure, to be seen: 30
But soft – by regular approach – not yet –
First through the length of yon hot terrace sweat;
And when up ten steep slopes you've dragged your
     thighs,
Just at his study door he'll bless your eyes.
    His study! with what authors is it stored?   35
In books, not authors, curious is my lord;
To all their dated backs he turns you round:
These Aldus printed, those Du Suëil has bound.
Lo, some are vellum, and the rest as good
For all his lordship knows, but they are wood.   40
For Locke or Milton 'tis in vain to look,
These shelves admit not any modern book.
    And now the chapel's silver bell you hear,
That summons you to all the pride of prayer;
Light quirks of music, broken and uneven,   45
Make the soul dance upon a jig to heaven.
On painted ceilings you devoutly stare,
Where sprawl the saints of Verrio or Laguerre,
On gilded clouds in fair expansion lie,
And bring all paradise before your eye.   50
To rest, the cushion and soft Dean invite,
Who never mentions hell to ears polite.
    But hark! the chiming clocks to dinner call;
A hundred footsteps scrape the marble hall:
The rich buffet well-coloured serpents grace,   55
And gaping Tritons spew to wash your face.
Is this a dinner? this a genial room?
No, 'tis a temple, and a hecatomb,
A solemn sacrifice, performed in state,
You drink by measure, and to minutes eat.   60
So quick retires each flying course, you'd swear
Sancho's dread doctor and his wand were there.
Between each act the trembling salvers ring,
From soup to sweet-wine, and God bless the king.
In plenty starving, tantalised in state,   65
And cómplaisantly helped to all I hate,
Treated, caressed, and tired, I take my leave,
Sick of his civil pride from morn to eve;
I curse such lavish cost and little skill,
And swear no day was ever passed so ill.   70
    Yet hence the poor are clothed, the hungry fed;
Health to himself, and to his infants bread
The lab'rer bears; what his hard heart denies,
His charitable vanity supplies.
    Another age shall see the golden ear   75
Embrown the slope, and nod on the parterre,
Deep harvests bury all his pride has planned,
And laughing Ceres reassume the land.

                             [Lines 99–176]

EPISTLE TO RICHARD BOYLE, EARL OF BURLINGTON: The addressee is the 3rd Earl of Burlington (1695–1753), a patron of the arts 1 **Timon:** a personification of the pride of the aristocracy 6 **Brobdingnag:** the land of the giants in Swift's *Gulliver's Travels* (1726) 7 **compass:** encompass, contain 8 **parterre:** a formal flower garden 25 **Amphitrite:** in Greek myth, a sea goddess 28 **Nilus:** a 10th-century Christian saint 30 **Smit:** smitten 31 **soft:** an interjection meaning wait 36 **In books . . . lord:** this aristocrat is interested in books as objects, not as literature 38 **Aldus:** Aldus Manutius (1450–1515), Italian printer **Du Suëil:** an early 17th century Paris bookbinder 48 **Verrio . . . Laguerre:** famous contemporary painters 56 **Triton:** a sea god, often portrayed holding a conch shell (from which water flows in this case) 58 **hecatomb:** a great public sacrifice and feast in ancient Greece or Rome 62 **Sancho's dread doctor:** a reference to Cervantes' *Don Quixote*, in which a doctor taps on dishes with a whalebone to indicate that they should be taken away untasted, to the dismay of Don Quixote's squire, Sancho Panza 75–8 **Another age . . . land:** in a future time the artificial garden will be replaced by useful fields of grain, under the control of Ceres, Roman goddess of agriculture

EPISTLE TO DR ARBUTHNOT

P. Shut, shut the door, good John! fatigued, I said,
Tie up the knocker, say I'm sick, I'm dead.
The dog-star rages! nay, 'tis past a doubt,
All Bedlam, or Parnassus, is let out:
Fire in each eye, and papers in each hand,   5
They rave, recite, and madden round the land.

EPISTLE TO DR ARBUTHNOT: The addressee is John Arbuthnot (1667–1735), physician to Queen Anne, wit and friend of Pope 1 **John:** John Serle, Pope's gardener 3 **dog-star:** Sirius, associated with a period of great heat, madness, and the reciting of verse 4 **Bedlam:** the Hospital of St Mary of Bethlehem in London, an insane asylum; hence any such asylum **Parnassus:** a mountain in Greece sacred to Apollo and the Muses, hence the haunt of poets

What walls can guard me, or what shades can hide?
They pierce my thickets, through my grot they glide,
By land, by water, they renew the charge,
They stop the chariot, and they board the barge.   10
No place is sacred, not the church is free,
Ev'n Sunday shines no Sabbath day to me:
Then from the Mint walks forth the man of rhyme,
Happy! to catch me, just at dinner-time.
    Is there a parson, much bemused in beer,   15
A maudlin poetess, a rhyming peer,
A clerk, foredoomed his father's soul to cross,
Who pens a stanza when he should engross?
Is there, who, locked from ink and paper, scrawls
With desp'rate charcoal round his darkened walls?   20
All fly to Twit'nam, and in humble strain
Apply to me, to keep them mad or vain.
Arthur, whose giddy son neglects the laws,
Imputes to me and my damned works the cause:
Poor Cornus sees his frantic wife elope,   25
And curses wit, and poetry, and Pope.
    Friend to my life! (which did not you prolong,
The world had wanted many an idle song)
What drop or nostrum can this plague remove?
Or which must end me, a fool's wrath or love?   30
A dire dilemma! either way I'm sped,
If foes, they write, if friends, they read me dead.
Seized and tied down to judge, how wretched I!
Who can't be silent, and who will not lie.
To laugh were want of goodness and of grace,   35
And to be grave exceeds all pow'r of face.
I sit with sad civility, I read
With honest anguish and an aching head;
And drop at last, but in unwilling ears,
This saving counsel, 'Keep your piece nine years.'   40
    'Nine years!' cries he, who high in Drury Lane,
Lulled by soft zephyrs through the broken pane,
Rhymes ere he wakes, and prints before term ends,
Obliged by hunger, and request of friends:
'The piece, you think, is incorrect? Why, take it,   45
I'm all submission, what you'd have it, make it.'
    Three things another's modest wishes bound,
My friendship, and a prologue, and ten pound.
    Pitholeon sends to me: 'You know his Grace,
I want a patron; ask him for a place.'   50
Pitholeon libelled me – 'but here's a letter
Informs you, sir, 'twas when he knew no better.

Dare you refuse him? Curll invites to dine,
He'll write a journal, or he'll turn divine.'
    Bless me! a packet. – ' 'Tis a stranger sues,   55
A virgin tragedy, an orphan muse.'
If I dislike it, 'Furies, death and rage!'
If I approve, 'Commend it to the stage.'
There (thank my stars) my whole commission ends,
The play'rs and I are, luckily, no friends.   60
Fired that the house reject him, ' 'Sdeath I'll print it,
And shame the fools – Your interest, sir, with Lintot!'
Lintot, dull rogue! will think your price too much:
'Not, sir, if you revise it, and retouch.'
All my demurs but double his attacks;   65
At last he whispers, 'Do, and we go snacks.'
Glad of a quarrel, straight I clap the door,
Sir, let me see your works and you no more.
    'Tis sung, when Midas' ears began to spring
(Midas, a sacred person and a king),   70
His very minister who spied them first
(Some say his queen) was forced to speak, or burst.
And is not mine, my friend, a sorer case,
When ev'ry coxcomb perks them in my face?
    A. Good friend, forbear! you deal in dang'rous
        things.
I'd never name queens, ministers, or kings;   76
Keep close to ears, and those let asses prick;
'Tis nothing— P. Nothing? if they bite and kick?
Out with it, Dunciad! let the secret pass,
That secret to each fool, that he's an ass: 80
The truth once told (and wherefore should we lie?)
The queen of Midas slept, and so may I.
    You think this cruel? take it for a rule,
No creature smarts so little as a fool.
Let peals of laughter, Codrus! round thee break,   85
Thou unconcerned canst hear the mighty crack:
Pit, box, and gall'ry in convulsions hurled,
Thou stand'st unshook amidst a bursting world.
Who shames a scribbler? break one cobweb through,
He spins the slight, self-pleasing thread anew: 90
Destroy his fib or sophistry; in vain,
The creature's at his dirty work again,
Throned in the centre of his thin designs,
Proud of a vast extent of flimsy lines!
Whom have I hurt? has poet yet, or peer,   95
Lost the arched eyebrow, or Parnassian sneer?
And has not Colley still his lord, and whore?
His butchers Henley, his freemasons Moore?

8 **grot:** a cave, or an artificial one constructed in a garden 13 **Mint:** an area of London where debtors were free from being arrested throughout the week, as they were in any area on a Sunday 18 **engross:** copy out legal documents 21 **Twit'nam:** Twickenham, near London, where Pope lived 23 **Arthur:** Arthur Moore, whose son used some of Pope's lines in a play without permission 25 **Cornus:** Latin for horn, hence a cuckold (crowned with imaginary horns) 29 **nostrum:** medicine 31 **sped:** killed 41 **high in Drury Lane:** in a garret in a London street famous for theatres but also for disreputable inhabitants 43 **term:** any of the periods during which the law courts sat, also observed by publishers 49 **Pitholeon:** an ancient Greek poet; the name is applied here to Leonard Welsted, who had slandered Pope

53 **Curll:** Edmund Curll (1675–1747), a publisher of pirated, indecent and otherwise disreputable works 62 **Lintot:** Barnaby Lintot (1675–1736), who published some of Pope's earlier works 66 **snacks:** shares 69 **Midas:** in Greek myth, King Midas was given asses' ears by Apollo as punishment for saying that Pan was a better flute-player than Apollo 85 **Codrus:** a poet ridiculed by Juvenal and Horace 97 **Colley:** Colley Cibber (1671–1757), playwright and poet laureate 98 **Henley:** John Henley (1692–1756), a writer and preacher who had delivered a sermon on the calling of butchers **Moore:** James Moore Smythe, the son of Arthur Moore (see above)

Does not one table Bavius still admit?
Still to one bishop Philips seem a wit?   100
Still Sappho— *A.* Hold! for God's sake – you'll offend,
No names! – be calm! – learn prudence of a friend.
I too could write, and I am twice as tall;
But foes like these— *P.* One flatt'rer's worse than all.
Of all mad creatures, if the learned are right,   105
It is the slaver kills, and not the bite.
A fool quite angry is quite innocent:
Alas! 'tis ten times worse when they repent.
One dedicates in high heroic prose,
And ridicules beyond a hundred foes: 110
One from all Grub Street will my fame defend,
And more abusive, calls himself my friend.
This prints my letters, that expects a bribe,
And others roar aloud, 'Subscribe, subscribe.'
There are, who to my person pay their court: 115
I cough like Horace, and, though lean, am short,
Ammon's great son one shoulder had too high,
Such Ovid's nose, and 'Sir! you have an eye' –
Go on, obliging creatures, make me see
All that disgraced my betters met in me.   120
Say for my comfort, languishing in bed,
'Just so immortal Maro held his head':
And when I die, be sure you let me know
Great Homer died three thousand years ago.
Why did I write? what sin to me unknown   125
Dipped me in ink, my parents', or my own?
As yet a child, nor yet a fool to fame,
I lisped in numbers, for the numbers came.
I left no calling for this idle trade,
No duty broke, no father disobeyed.   130
The Muse but served to ease some friend, not wife,
To help me through this long disease, my life,
To second, Arbuthnot! thy art and care,
And teach the being you preserved, to bear.
But why then publish? Granville the polite,   135
And knowing Walsh, would tell me I could write;
Well-natured Garth, inflamed with early praise;
And Congreve loved, and Swift endured my lays;
The courtly Talbot, Somers, Sheffield, read,
Ev'n mitred Rochester would nod the head,   140
And St John's self (great Dryden's friends before)

With open arms received one poet more.
Happy my studies, when by these approved!
Happier their author, when by these beloved!
From these the world will judge of men and books,   145
Not from the Burnets, Oldmixons, and Cooks.
Soft were my numbers; who could take offence
While pure description held the place of sense?
Like gentle Fanny's was my flow'ry theme,
A painted mistress, or a purling stream.   150
Yet then did Gildon draw his venal quill;
I wished the man a dinner, and sate still:
Yet then did Dennis rave in furious fret;
I never answered, I was not in debt:
If want provoked, or madness made them print,   155
I waged no war with Bedlam or the Mint.
Did some more sober critic come abroad?
If wrong, I smiled; if right, I kissed the rod.
Pains, reading, study, are their just pretence,
And all they want is spirit, taste, and sense.   160
Commas and points they set exactly right,
And 'twere a sin to rob them of their mite.
Yet ne'er one sprig of laurel graced these ribalds,
From slashing Bentley down to piddling Tibalds:
Each wight who reads not, and but scans and spells,
Each word-catcher that lives on syllables,   166
Ev'n such small critics some regard may claim,
Preserved in Milton's or in Shakespeare's name.
Pretty! in amber to observe the forms
Of hairs, or straws, or dirt, or grubs, or worms!   170
The things, we know, are neither rich nor rare,
But wonder how the devil they got there.
Were others angry, I excused them too;
Well might they rage, I gave them but their due.
A man's true merit 'tis not hard to find,   175
But each man's secret standard in his mind,
That casting-weight pride adds to emptiness,
This, who can gratify? for who can guess?
The bard whom pilfered pastorals renown,
Who turns a Persian tale for half a crown,   180
Just writes to make his barrenness appear,
And strains, from hard-bound brains, eight lines a
     year;
He, who still wanting, though he lives on theft,
Steals much, spends little, yet has nothing left:
And he, who now to sense, now nonsense leaning,   185
Means not, but blunders round about a meaning:

99 **Bavius:** an inferior poet who attacked Virgil and Horace
100 **Philips:** Ambrose Philips (see above), poet and secretary to the
Bishop of Armagh 111 **Grub Street:** a street frequented by literary
hacks and impoverished authors, hence the world of inferior
literature 116 **Horace:** Quintus Horatius Flaccus (65–8 BC), Roman
poet and satirist 117 **Ammon's great son:** Alexander the Great
118 **Ovid:** Publius Ovidius Naso (43 BC–?17 AD), Roman poet
122 **Maro:** Publius Vergilius Maro (70–19 BC), better known as Virgil,
Roman poet 128 **numbers:** verses or metres 135 **Granville:** George
Granville, a statesman and poet 136 **Walsh:** William Walsh, a poet
and critic 137 **Garth:** Sir Samuel Garth (1661–17), physician and
poet 138 **lays:** songs 139 **Talbot:** Charles Talbot, Duke of Shrewsbury
(1660–1718) **Somers:** Lord Somers (1651–1716) **Sheffield:** John
Sheffield, Duke of Buckingham (1648–1721) 140 **Rochester:** Francis
Atterbury, Bishop of Rochester (1662–1732) 141 **St John:** Henry St John,
Viscount Bolingbroke (1678–1751)

146 **Burnet, Oldmixon, Cooks:** inferior or scandalous writers
149 **Fanny:** John Hervey, Baron Hervey of Ickworth (1696–1743),
courtier and memoirist, dubbed 'Lord Fanny' by Pope 151 **Gildon:**
Charles Gildon, whom Pope believed had been encouraged to
attack him by Addison 153 **Dennis:** John Dennis (1657–1734),
playwright and critic, satirized by Pope for bombast 163 **laurel:** as
used in wreaths to crown the heads of victors 164 **slashing Bentley:**
Richard Bentley (1662–1742), a critic who arbitrarily revised Milton's
Paradise Lost **piddling Tibalds:** Lewis Theobald (1688–1744), writer
and critic who exposed Pope's inadequacies as a critic in his
edition of Shakespeare 165 **wight:** person

And he, whose fustian's so sublimely bad,
It is not poetry, but prose run mad:
All these, my modest satire bade translate,
And owned that nine such poets made a Tate.   190
How did they fume, and stamp, and roar, and chafe,
And swear not Addison himself was safe.

    Peace to all such! but were there one whose fires
True genius kindles, and fair fame inspires;
Blessed with each talent and each art to please,   195
And born to write, converse, and live with ease:
Should such a man, too fond to rule alone,
Bear, like the Turk, no brother near the throne.
View him with scornful, yet with jealous eyes,
And hate for arts that caused himself to rise;   200
Damn with faint praise, assent with civil leer,
And without sneering, teach the rest to sneer;
Willing to wound, and yet afraid to strike,
Just hint a fault, and hesitate dislike;
Alike reserved to blame, or to commend,   205
A tim'rous foe, and a suspicious friend;
Dreading ev'n fools, by flatterers besieged,
And so obliging, that he ne'er obliged;
Like Cato, give his little senate laws,
And sit attentive to his own applause;   210
While wits and templars ev'ry sentence raise,
And wonder with a foolish face of praise –
Who but must laugh, if such a man there be?
Who would not weep, if Atticus were he?

    What though my name stood rubric on the walls,   215
Or plastered posts, with claps, in capitals?
Or smoking forth, a hundred hawkers' load,
On wings of winds came flying all abroad?
I sought no homage from the race that write;
I kept, like Asian monarchs, from their sight: 220
Poems I heeded (now be-rhymed so long)
No more than thou, great George! a birthday song.
I ne'er with wits or witlings passed my days,
To spread about the itch of verse and praise;
Nor like a puppy daggled through the town,   225
To fetch and carry sing-song up and down;
Nor at rehearsals sweat, and mouthed, and cried,
With handkerchief and orange at my side;
But sick of fops, and poetry, and prate,
To Bufo left the whole Castalian state.   230

    Proud as Apollo on his forkèd hill,
Sat full-blown Bufo, puffed by ev'ry quill;
Fed with soft dedication all day long,
Horace and he went hand in hand in song.

His library (where busts of poets dead   235
And a true Pindar stood without a head)
Received of wits an undistinguished race,
Who first his judgement asked, and then a place:
Much they extolled his pictures, much his seat,
And flattered ev'ry day, and some days eat: 240
Till grown more frugal in his riper days,
He paid some bards with port, and some with praise.
To some a dry rehearsal was assigned,
And others (harder still) he paid in kind.
Dryden alone (what wonder?) came not nigh,   245
Dryden alone escaped this judging eye:
But still the great have kindness in reserve,
He helped to bury whom he helped to starve.

    May some choice patron bless each grey goose quill!
May ev'ry Bavius have his Bufo still!   250
So when a statesman wants a day's defence,
Or envy holds a whole week's war with sense,
Or simple pride for flatt'ry makes demands,
May dunce by dunce be whistled off my hands!
Blessed be the great! for those they take away,   255
And those they left me; for they left me Gay;
Left me to see neglected genius bloom,
Neglected die, and tell it on his tomb:
Of all thy blameless life the soul return
My verse, and Queensb'ry weeping o'er thy urn!   260
    Oh, let me live my own, and die so too!
(To live and die is all I have to do):
Maintain a poet's dignity and ease,
And see what friends, and read what books I please:
Above a patron, though I condescend   265
Sometimes to call a minister my friend:
I was not born for courts or great affairs;
I pay my debts, believe, and say my prayers;
Can sleep without a poem in my head,
Nor know if Dennis be alive or dead.   270
    Why am I asked what next shall see the light?
Heavens! was I born for nothing but to write?
Has life no joys for me! or (to be grave)
Have I no friend to serve, no soul to save?
'I found him close with Swift.' – 'Indeed? no doubt',
Cries prating Balbus, 'something will come out.'   276
'Tis all in vain, deny it as I will.
'No, such a genius never can lie still';
And then for mine obligingly mistakes
The first lampoon Sir Will or Bubo makes.   280
Poor guiltless I! and can I choose but smile
When ev'ry coxcomb knows me by my style?
    Cursed be the verse, how well soe'er it flow,
That tends to make one worthy man my foe,
Give virtue scandal, innocence a fear,   285

187 **fustian:** pompous, artificial writing 190 **Tate:** Nahum Tate (1652–1715), poet laureate, who provided *King Lear* with a new happy ending 209 **Cato:** a reference to Addison, who wrote a tragedy of that name 211 **templars:** law students, who studied at The Temple in London 214 **Atticus:** Addison 215 **rubric:** in red 216 **claps:** posters 222 **George:** King George II (reigned 1727–60) 225 **daggled:** dragged through wet and mud 230 **Bufo:** personification of a patron of the arts devoid of taste **Castalian:** poetic, from the Castalian spring on Mount Parnassus 231 **forkèd hill:** Mount Parnassus, which had two peaks

236 **Pindar:** Greek lyric poet (*c.*522–442 BC) 256 **Gay:** John Gay (1685–1732), poet and playwright (*The Beggar's Opera*). Denied royal patronage, he in later life was supported by the Duke and Duchess of Queensberry 262 (**To live . . . do**): quoted from Denham's *Of Prudence* 280 **Sir Will:** Sir William Yonge, an inferior poet **Bubo:** Bubb Dodington, a patron

Or from the soft-eyed virgin steal a tear!
But he who hurts a harmless neighbour's peace,
Insults fall'n worth, or beauty in distress,
Who loves a lie, lame slander helps about,
Who writes a libel, or who copies out: 290
That fop, whose pride affects a patron's name,
Yet absent, wounds an author's honest fame:
Who can your merit selfishly approve,
And show the sense of it without the love;
Who has the vanity to call you friend,   295
Yet wants the honour, injured, to defend;
Who tells whate'er you think, whate'er you say,
And, if he lie not, must at least betray:
Who to the Dean and silver bell can swear,
And sees at Cannons what was never there;   300
Who reads, but with a lust to misapply,
Make satire a lampoon, and fiction, lie.
A lash like mine no honest man shall dread,
But all such babbling blockheads in his stead.
     Let Sporus tremble— A. What? that thing of silk,
Sporus, that mere white curd of ass's milk,   306
Satire or sense, alas! can Sporus feel?
Who breaks a butterfly upon a wheel?
     P. Yet let me flap this bug with gilded wings,
This painted child of dirt, that stinks and stings;   310
Whose buzz the witty and the fair annoys,
Yet wit ne'er tastes, and beauty ne'er enjoys:
So well-bred spaniels civilly delight
In mumbling of the game they dare not bite.
Eternal smiles his emptiness betray,   315
As shallow streams run dimpling all the way.
Whether in florid impotence he speaks
And, as the prompter breathes, the puppet squeaks;
Or at the ear of Eve, familiar toad,
Half froth, half venom, spits himself abroad,   320
In puns, or politics, or tales, or lies,
Or spite, or smut, or rhymes, or blasphemies.
His wit all see-saw, between that and this,
Now high, now low, now master up, now miss,
And he himself one vile antithesis.   325
Amphibious thing! that acting either part,
The trifling head, or the corrupted heart,
Fop at the toilet, flatt'rer at the board,
Now trips a lady, and now struts a lord.
Eve's tempter thus the rabbins have expressed,   330
A cherub's face, a reptile all the rest;
Beauty that shocks you, parts that none will trust;
Wit that can creep, and pride that licks the dust.
     Not fortune's worshipper, nor fashion's fool,
Not lucre's madman, nor ambition's tool,   335
Not proud, nor servile; be one poet's praise,
That, if he pleased, he pleased by manly ways:
That flatt'ry, ev'n to kings, he held a shame,
And thought a lie in verse or prose the same:

That not in fancy's maze he wandered long,   340
But stooped to truth, and moralised his song:
That not for fame, but virtue's better end,
He stood the furious foe, the timid friend,
The damning critic, half-approving wit,
The coxcomb hit, or fearing to be hit;   345
Laughed at the loss of friends he never had,
The dull, the proud, the wicked, and the mad;
The distant threats of vengeance on his head,
The blow unfelt, the tear he never shed;
The tale revived, the lie so oft o'erthrown;   350
Th'imputed trash, and dullness not his own;
The morals blackened when the writings 'scape,
The libelled person, and the pictured shape;
Abuse, on all he loved, or loved him, spread,
A friend in exile, or a father, dead;   355
The whisper, that to greatness still too near,
Perhaps, yet víbrates, on his sov'reign's ear –
Welcome for thee, fair virtue! all the past:
For thee, fair virtue! welcome ev'n the last!
     A. But why insult the poor, affront the great?   360
     P. A knave's a knave, to me, in ev'ry state:
Alike my scorn, if he succeed or fail,
Sporus at court, or Japhet in a jail,
A hireling scribbler, or a hireling peer,
Knight of the post corrupt, or of the shire;   365
If on a pillory, or near a throne,
He gain his prince's ear, or lose his own.
     Yet soft by nature, more a dupe than wit,
Sappho can tell you how this man was bit;
This dreaded sat'rist Dennis will confess   370
Foe to his pride, but friend to his distress:
So humble, he has knocked at Tibbald's door,
Has drunk with Cibber, nay, has rhymed for Moore.
Full ten years slandered, did he once reply?
Three thousand suns went down on Welsted's lie.   375
To please a mistress one aspersed his life;
He lashed him not, but let her be his wife:
Let Budgel charge low Grub Street on his quill,
And write whate'er he pleased, except his will;
Let the two Curlls of town and court abuse   380
His father, mother, body, soul, and muse.
Yet why? that father held it for a rule,
It was a sin to call our neighbour fool:
That harmless mother thought no wife a whore:
Hear this, and spare his family, James Moore!   385
Unspotted names, and memorable long!
If there be force in virtue, or in song.
     Of gentle blood (part shed in honour's cause
While yet in Britain honour had applause)

---

341 **stooped:** swooped down, as a bird of prey does 353 **pictured shape:** caricature 363 **Japhet:** Japhet Crook, a forger 365 **Knight of the post:** a person who made a living out of giving false evidence 367 **lose his own:** i.e. have his ears cut off as a punishment, as happened to Japhet Cook 371 **Foe . . . distress:** Pope tried to help Dennis in later life 378 **Budgel:** Eustace Budgell (1686–1737), a writer who attacked Pope in print 380 **Curlls of town and court:** the printer (see above) and Lord Hervey

---

296 **wants:** lacks 300 **Cannons:** the estate of the Duke of Chandos, which Pope was accused, unjustly, of satirizing in *Epistle to Burlington* 305 **Sporus:** John, Lord Hervey (see above) 328 **board:** table 330 **rabbins:** rabbis 332 **parts:** qualities, abilities

Each parent sprung— *A.* What fortune, pray? –
    P. Their own,   390
And better got, than Bestia's from the throne.
Born to no pride, inheriting no strife,
Nor marrying discord in a noble wife,
Stranger to civil and religious rage,
The good man walked innoxious through his age.   395
Nor courts he saw, no suits would ever try,
Nor dared an oath, nor hazarded a lie:
Unlearned, he knew no schoolman's subtle art,
No language but the language of the heart.
By nature honest, by experience wise,   400
Healthy by temp'rance, and by exercise;
His life, though long, to sickness past unknown,
His death was instant, and without a groan.
Oh, grant me thus to live, and thus to die!
Who sprung from kings shall know less joy than I.   405
    O Friend! may each domestic bliss be thine!
Be no unpleasing melancholy mine:
Me, let the tender office long engage
To rock the cradle of reposing age,
With lenient arts extend a mother's breath,   410
Make languor smile, and smooth the bed of death,
Explore the thought, explain the asking eye,
And keep a while one parent from the sky!
On cares like these if length of days attend,
May heaven, to bless those days, preserve my friend,
Preserve him social, cheerful, and serene,   416
And just as rich as when he served a queen.
Whether that blessing be denied or given,
Thus far was right, the rest belongs to heaven.

391 **Bestia:** L. Calpurnius Bestia was an ancient Roman consul who notoriously took bribes. The reference here seems to be to Lord Marlborough 417 **as rich . . . queen:** Arbuthnot did not use his position in the Queen's service to enrich himself

EPIGRAM
ENGRAVED ON THE COLLAR OF A DOG WHICH I GAVE TO HIS ROYAL HIGHNESS

I AM His Highness' dog at Kew;
Pray tell me, sir, whose dog are you?

From THE DUNCIAD

CLOSE to those walls where Folly holds her throne,
And laughs to think Monro would take her down,
Where o'er the gates, by his famed father's hand
Great Cibber's brazen, brainless brothers stand;
One cell there is, concealed from vulgar eye,   5
The Cave of Poverty and Poetry.
Keen, hollow winds howl through the bleak recess,
Emblem of music caused by emptiness.
Hence bards, like Proteus long in vain tied down,
Escape in monsters, and amaze the town.   10
Hence Miscellanies spring, the weekly boast
Of Curll's chaste press, and Lintot's rubric post:
Hence hymning Tyburn's elegiac lines,
Hence Journals, Medleys, Merc'ries, Magazines:
Sepulchral lies, our holy walls to grace,   15
And New Year odes, and all the Grub Street race.
    In clouded majesty here Dullness shone;
Four guardian Virtues, round, support her throne:
Fierce champion Fortitude, that knows no fears
Of hisses, blows, or want, or loss of ears: 20
Calm Temperance, whose blessings those partake
Who hunger and who thirst for scribbling sake:
Prudence, whose glass presents th'approaching jail:
Poetic Justice, with her lifted scale,
Where, in nice balance, truth with gold she weighs,
And solid pudding against empty praise.   26
    Here she beholds the Chaos dark and deep,
Where nameless somethings in their causes sleep,
Till genial Jacob, or a warm third day,
Call forth each mass, a poem, or a play: 30
How hints, like spawn, scarce quick in embryo lie,
How new-born nonsense first is taught to cry,
Maggots half-formed in rhyme exactly meet,
And learn to crawl upon poetic feet.
Here one poor word an hundred clenches makes,   35
And ductile dullness new meanders takes;
There motley images her fancy strike,
Figures ill paired, and similes unlike.
She sees a mob of metaphors advance,
Pleased with the madness of the mazy dance: 40
How Tragedy and Comedy embrace;
How Farce and Epic get a jumbled race;
How Time himself stands still at her command,
Realms shift their place, and Ocean turns to land.
Here gay Description Egypt glads with show'rs,   45
Or gives to Zembla fruits, to Barca flow'rs;
Glitt'ring with ice here hoary hills are seen,
There painted valleys of eternal green,
In cold December fragrant chaplets blow,
And heavy harvests nod beneath the snow.   50
    All these, and more, the cloud-compelling Queen
Beholds through fogs that magnify the scene.
She, tinselled o'er in robes of varying hues,
With self-applause her wild creation views;
Sees momentary monsters rise and fall,   55
And with her own fool's colours gilds them all.
              [1743: Book 1, lines 29–84]

FROM THE DUNCIAD: 2 **Monro:** Dr James Monro (1680–1752), physician at the Bethlehem Hospital for the insane 4 **Cibber:** Colley Cibber (1671–1757), poet laureate. His father sculpted two statues of lunatics that stood outside the Bethlehem Hospital 9 **Proteus:** in classical myth, a sea-god who could change his shape at will 12 **Curll:** Edmund Curll (1675–1747), a publisher of pirated, indecent and otherwise disreputable works **Lintot:** Barnaby Lintot (1675–1736), who published some of Pope's earlier works 13 **Tyburn:** a place of execution in London 16 **Grub Street race:** hack writers, associated with this London street 20 **loss of ears:** having one's ears cut off was a punishment for various crimes, including forgery 25 **nice:** precise 35 **clenches:** puns 40 **mazy:** confusing 42 **get:** beget 45 **Egypt glads with show'rs:** portrays the hot dry climate of Egypt as rainy 46 **Zembla:** Novaya Zemlya, thought of as being in the 'frozen north' and thus unlikely to be fruitful **Barca:** an African desert

EDWARD YOUNG

From THE COMPLAINT;
OR, NIGHT-THOUGHTS ON LIFE,
DEATH AND IMMORTALITY

WHAT is the world itself? thy world? – A grave.
Where is the dust that has not been alive?
The spade, the plough, disturb our ancestors;
From human mould we reap our daily bread.
The globe around Earth's hollow surface shakes,   5
And is the ceiling of her sleeping sons.
O'er devastation we blind revels keep;
Whole buried towns support the dancer's heel.
The moist of human frame the sun exhales;
Winds scatter, through the mighty void, the dry;   10
Earth repossesses part of what she gave,
And the freed spirit mounts on wings of fire;
Each element partakes our scattered spoils;
As Nature, wide, our ruins spread: man's death
Inhabits all things but the thought of man!   15
   Nor man alone; his breathing bust expires,
His tomb is mortal; empires die. Where now
The Roman? Greek? They stalk, an empty name!
Yet few regard them in this useful light;
Though half our learning is their epitaph.   20
When down thy vale, unlocked by midnight thought,
That loves to wander in thy sunless realms,
O Death! I stretch my view; what visions rise!
What triumphs, toils imperial, arts divine,
In withered laurels, glide before my sight!   25
What lengths of far-famed ages, billowed high
With human agitation, roll along
In unsubstantial images of air!
The melancholy ghosts of dead renown,
Whispering faint echoes of the world's applause,   30
With penitential aspect, as they pass,
All point at earth, and hiss at human pride,
The wisdom of the wise, and prancings of the great.

[Night Nine, lines 91–123]

JOHN BYROM

'MY SPIRIT LONGETH FOR THEE'

MY spirit longeth for thee
   Within my troubled breast,
Although I be unworthy
   Of so divine a guest.

Of so divine a guest   5
   Unworthy though I be,
Yet has my heart no rest
   Unless it come from thee.

Unless it come from thee,
   In vain I look around;   10
In all that I can see,
   No rest is to be found.

No rest is to be found
   But in thy blessèd love;
Oh, let my wish be crowned,   15
   And send it from above!

JOHN DYER

GRONGAR HILL

SILENT Nymph! with curious eye,
Who, the purple ev'ning, lie
On the mountain's lonely van,
Beyond the noise of busy man,
Painting fair the form of things,   5
While the yellow linnet sings,
Or the tuneful nightingale
Charms the forest with her tale;
Come, with all thy various hues,
Come, and aid thy sister Muse;   10
Now while Phoebus, riding high,
Gives lustre to the land and sky,
Grongar Hill invites my song;
Draw the landscape bright and strong;
Grongar in whose mossy cells,   15
Sweetly musing Quiet dwells;
Grongar, in whose silent shade,
For the modest Muses made,
So oft I have, the ev'ning still,
At the fountain of a rill   20
Sat upon a flow'ry bed,
With my hand beneath my head,
While strayed my eyes o'er Towy's flood,
Over mead and over wood,
From house to house, from hill to hill,   25
Till Contemplation had her fill.
   About his chequered sides I wind,
And leave his brooks and meads behind,
And groves and grottoes where I lay,
And vistoes shooting beams of day.   30
Wide and wider spreads the vale,
As circles on a smooth canal:
The mountains round, unhappy fate!
Sooner or later, of all height,
Withdraw their summits from the skies,   35
And lessen as the others rise:
Still the prospect wider spreads,
Adds a thousand woods and meads;

GRONGAR HILL: 3 **van:** foremost part   11 **Phoebus:** the sun-god, hence the sun itself 23 **Towy:** a river in Wales 24 **mead:** meadow 30 **vistoes:** views

Still it widens, widens still,
And sinks the newly risen hill.
   Now I gain the mountain's brow, 40
What a landskip lies below!
No clouds, no vapours intervene;
But the gay, the open scene
Does the face of Nature show 45
In all the hues of heaven's bow,
And, swelling to embrace the light,
Spreads around beneath the sight.
   Old castles on the cliffs arise,
Proudly tow'ring in the skies; 50
Rushing from the woods, the spires
Seem from hence ascending fires;
Half his beams Apollo sheds
On the yellow mountain-heads,
Gilds the fleeces of the flocks, 55
And glitters on the broken rocks.
   Below me trees unnumbered rise,
Beautiful in various dyes;
The gloomy pine, the poplar blue,
The yellow beech, the sable yew, 60
The slender fir, that taper grows,
The sturdy oak with broad-spread boughs,
And beyond the purple grove,
Haunt of Phillis, queen of love!
Gaudy as the op'ning dawn, 65
Lies a long and level lawn,
On which a dark hill, steep and high,
Holds and charms the wand'ring eye:
Deep are his feet in Towy's flood,
His sides are clothed with waving wood, 70
And ancient towers crown his brow,
That cast an awful look below;
Whose ragged walls the ivy creeps,
And with her arms from falling keeps;
So both a safety from the wind 75
On mutual dependence find.
   'Tis now the raven's bleak abode;
'Tis now th'apartment of the toad;
And there the fox securely feeds,
And there the pois'nous adder breeds, 80
Concealed in ruins, moss, and weeds;
While, ever and anon, there falls
Huge heaps of hoary mouldered walls.
Yet Time has seen, that lifts the low,
And level lays the lofty brow, 85
Has seen this broken pile complete,
Big with the vanity of state:
But transient is the smile of Fate!
A little rule, a little sway,
A sunbeam in a winter's day, 90
Is all the proud and mighty have
Between the cradle and the grave.

   And see the rivers how they run
Through woods and meads, in shade and sun!
Sometimes swift and sometimes slow, 95
Wave succeeding wave, they go
A various journey to the deep,
Like human life to endless sleep:
Thus is Nature's vesture wrought,
To instruct our wand'ring thought; 100
Thus she dresses green and gay,
To disperse our cares away.
   Ever charming, ever new,
When will the landskip tire the view!
The fountain's fall, the river's flow, 105
The woody valleys warm and low;
The windy summit, wild and high,
Roughly rushing on the sky!
The pleasant seat, the ruined tow'r,
The naked rock, the shady bow'r; 110
The town and village, dome and farm,
Each give each a double charm,
As pearls upon an Ethiop's arm.
   See on the mountain's southern side,
Where the prospect opens wide, 115
Where the ev'ning gilds the tide,
How close and small the hedges lie!
What streaks of meadows cross the eye!
A step, methinks, may pass the stream,
So little distant dangers seem; 120
So we mistake the future's face,
Eyed through Hope's deluding glass;
As yon summits soft and fair,
Clad in colours of the air,
Which, to those who journey near, 125
Barren, brown, and rough appear;
Still we tread the same coarse way;
The present's still a cloudy day.
   Oh, may I with myself agree,
And never covet what I see; 130
Content me with an humble shade,
My passions tamed, my wishes laid;
For while our wishes wildly roll,
We banish quiet from the soul;
'Tis thus the busy beat the air, 135
And misers gather wealth and care.
   Now, ev'n now, my joys run high,
As on the mountain-turf I lie;
While the wanton Zephyr sings,
And in the vale perfumes his wings; 140
While the waters murmur deep;
While the shepherd charms his sheep;
While the birds unbounded fly,
And with music fill the sky,
Now, ev'n now, my joys run high. 145

---

42 **landskip:** landscape (the spelling reflects the pronunciation)
53 **Apollo:** the sun-god, hence the sun itself   60 **sable:** black

113 **Ethiop:** literally, Ethiopian; a black African   139 **Zephyr:** a personification of the west wind

Be full, ye Courts! be great who will;
Search for Peace with all your skill:
Open wide the lofty door,
Seek her on the marble floor:
In vain ye search, she is not there;   150
In vain ye search the domes of Care!
Grass and flowers Quiet treads,
On the meads and mountain-heads,
Along with pleasure close allied,
Ever by each other's side,   155
And often, by the murm'ring rill,
Hears the thrush, while all is still,
Within the groves of Grongar Hill.

JAMES THOMSON

From THE SEASONS

[SPRING]

ALONG these blushing borders, bright with dew,
And in yon mingled wilderness of flowers,
Fair-handed Spring unbosoms every grace:
Throws out the snow-drop and the crocus first;
The daisy, primrose, violet darkly blue,   5
And polyanthus of unnumbered dyes;
The yellow wallflower, stained with iron brown;
And lavish that scents the garden round.
From the soft swing of vernal breezes shed,
Anemones; auriculas, enriched   10
With shining meal o'er all their velvet leaves;
And full ranunculus, of glowing red.
Then comes the tulip-race, where beauty plays
Her idle freaks: from family diffused
To family, as flies the father-dust,   15
The varied colours run; and, while they break
On the charmed eye, the exulting florist marks,
With secret pride, the wonders of his hand.
No gradual bloom is wanting; from the bud,
Firstborn of Spring, to Summer's musky tribes: 20
Nor hyacinths, of purest virgin-white,
Low-bent, and blushing inward; nor jonquils,
Of potent fragrance; nor narcissus fair,
As o'er the fabled fountain hanging still;
Nor broad carnations; nor gay-spotted pinks;   25
Nor, showered from every bush, the damask-rose.
Infinite numbers, delicacies, smells,
With hues on hues expression cannot paint,
The breath of Nature, and her endless bloom.
                                    ['Spring', lines 527–55]

[AUTUMN]

THUS solitary, and in pensive guise,
Oft let me wander o'er the russet mead,
And through the saddened grove, where scarce is
        heard
One dying strain to cheer the woodman's toil.
Haply some widowed songster pours his plaint,   5
Far, in faint warblings, through the tawny copse;
While congregated thrushes, linnets, larks,
And each wild throat, whose artless strains so late
Swelled all the music of the swarming shades,
Robbed of their tuneful souls, now shivering sit   10
On the dead tree, a dull despondent flock!
With not a brightness waving o'er their plumes,
And naught save chattering discord in their note.
Oh! let not, aimed from some inhuman eye,
The gun the music of the coming year   15
Destroy; and harmless, unsuspecting harm,
Lay the weak tribes a miserable prey,
In mingled murder, fluttering on the ground.
   The pale descending year, yet pleasing still,
A gentler mood inspires; for now the leaf   20
Incessant rustles from the mournful grove;
Oft startling such as, studious, walk below,
And slowly circles through the waving air.
But should a quicker breeze amid the boughs
Sob, o'er the sky the leafy deluge streams;   25
Till, choked and matted with the dreary shower,
The forest walks, at every rising gale,
Roll wide the withered waste, and whistle bleak.
Fled is the blasted verdure of the fields;
And, shrunk into their beds, the flowery race   30
Their sunny robes resign. Even what remained
Of bolder fruits falls from the naked tree;
And woods, fields, gardens, orchards, all around
The desolated prospect thrills the soul.
                                ['Autumn', lines 970–1003]

FROM THE SEASONS: SPRING: 11 **meal:** powdery covering 14 **freaks:** caprices 15 **father-dust:** pollen AUTUMN: 2 **mead:** meadow 5 **plaint:** complaint

SAMUEL JOHNSON

THE VANITY OF HUMAN WISHES
THE TENTH SATIRE OF JUVENAL IMITATED

LET Observation with extensive view
Survey mankind, from China to Peru;
Remark each anxious toil, each eager strife,
And watch the busy scenes of crowded life;
Then say how hope and fear, desire and hate,   5
O'erspread with snares the clouded maze of fate,
Where wav'ring Man, betrayed by vent'rous pride,
To tread the dreary paths without a guide,
As treach'rous phantoms in the mist delude,
Shuns fancied ills, or chases airy good;   10
How rarely Reason guides the stubborn choice,
Rules the bold hand, or prompts the suppliant voice;
How nations sink, by darling schemes oppressed,

When Vengeance listens to the fool's request.
Fate wings with ev'ry wish th'afflictive dart, 15
Each gift of Nature, and each grace of Art,
With fatal heat impetuous courage glows,
With fatal sweetness elocution flows,
Impeachment stops the speaker's pow'rful breath,
And restless fire precipitates on death. 20

But scarce observed, the knowing and the bold
Fall in the gen'ral massacre of gold;
Wide-wasting pest! that rages unconfined,
And crowds with crimes the records of mankind:
For gold his sword the hireling ruffian draws, 25
For gold the hireling judge distorts the laws;
Wealth heaped on wealth, nor truth nor safety buys,
The dangers gather as the treasures rise.

Let Hist'ry tell where rival kings command,
And dubious title shakes the madded land, 30
When statutes glean the refuse of the sword,
How much more safe the vassal than the lord;
Low skulks the hind beneath the rage of pow'r,
And leaves the wealthy traitor in the Tow'r,
Untouched his cottage, and his slumbers sound, 35
Though Confiscation's vultures hover round.

The needy traveller, serene and gay,
Walks the wild heath, and sings his toil away.
Does envy seize thee? Crush th'upbraiding joy,
Increase his riches and his peace destroy; 40
New fears in dire vicissitude invade,
The rustling brake alarms, and quiv'ring shade,
Nor light nor darkness bring his pain relief,
One shows the plunder, and one hides the thief.

Yet still one gen'ral cry the skies assails, 45
And gain and grandeur load the tainted gales;
Few know the toiling statesman's fear or care,
Th'insidious rival and the gaping heir.

Once more, Democritus, arise on earth,
With cheerful wisdom and instructive mirth, 50
See motley life in modern trappings dressed,
And feed with varied fools th'eternal jest:
Thou who couldst laugh where Want enchained
    Caprice,
Toil crushed Conceit, and Man was of a piece;
Where Wealth unloved without a mourner died, 55
And scarce a sycophant was fed by Pride;
Where ne'er was known the form of mock debate,
Or seen a new-made mayor's unwieldy state;
Where change of fav'rites made no change of laws,
And senates heard before they judged a cause; 60
How wouldst thou shake at Britain's modish tribe,
Dart the quick taunt, and edge the piercing gibe!

Attentive truth and nature to descry,
And pierce each scene with philosophic eye.
To thee were solemn toys or empty show, 65
The robes of pleasure and the veils of woe:
All aid the farce, and all thy mirth maintain,
Whose joys are causeless, or whose griefs are vain.

Such was the scorn that filled the sage's mind,
Renew'd at ev'ry glance on humankind; 70
How just that scorn ere yet thy voice declare,
Search ev'ry state, and canvass ev'ry prayer.

Unnumbered suppliants crowd Preferment's gate,
Athirst for wealth, and burning to be great;
Delusive Fortune hears th'incessant call, 75
They mount, they shine, evaporate, and fall.
On ev'ry stage the foes of peace attend,
Hate dogs their flight, and Insult mocks their end.
Love ends with hope, the sinking statesman's door
Pours in the morning worshipper no more; 80
For growing names the weekly scribbler lies,
To growing wealth the dedicator flies;
From ev'ry room descends the painted face,
That hung the bright Palladium of the place;
And smoked in kitchens, or in auctions sold, 85
To better features yields the frame of gold;
For now no more we trace in ev'ry line
Heroic worth, benevolence divine:
The form distorted justifies the fall,
And Detestation rids th'indignant wall. 90

But will not Britain hear the last appeal,
Sign her foe's doom, or guard her fav'rite's zeal?
Through Freedom's sons no more remonstrance rings,
Degrading nobles and controlling kings;
Our supple tribes repress their patriot throats, 95
And ask no questions but the price of votes;
With weekly libels and septennial ale,
Their wish is full to riot and to rail.

In full-blown dignity, see Wolsey stand,
Law in his voice, and fortune in his hand: 100
To him the church, the realm, their pow'rs consign,
Through him the rays of regal bounty shine;
Turned by his nod the stream of honour flows,
His smile alone security bestows.
Still to new heights his restless wishes tow'r, 105
Claim leads to claim, and pow'r advances pow'r;
Till conquest unresisted ceased to please,
And rights submitted left him none to seize.
At length his sov'reign frowns – the train of state
Mark the keen glance, and watch the sign to hate. 110

THE VANITY OF HUMAN WISHES: 14 **When . . . request:** when a fool is punished by being granted what he foolishly wished for 15 **wings:** gives wings to 20 **precipitates:** rushes headlong 31 **When . . . sword:** when laws punish those who have not been killed in war 33 **hind:** peasant 42 **brake:** thicket 43 **Nor:** neither 46 **tainted gales:** winds that carry the scent of prey 49 **Democritus:** Greek philosopher (?460–?370 BC) 51 **motley:** particoloured, like the traditional attire of a jester 54 **Conceit:** imagination

73 **Preferment:** promotion, personified as a great man who has the power to advance others 80 **morning worshipper:** a sycophant attending the levee of a monarch or great man 81 **weekly scribbler:** political journalist 84 **Palladium:** a statue of Pallas Athene, especially the one on which, in Greek myth, the safety of Troy depended 97 **septennial ale:** beer given free to voters agreeing to vote for a particular candidate at a Parliamentary election (held every seven years) 99 **Wolsey:** Thomas Wolsey (?1475–1530), English cardinal and statesman under Henry VIII, eventually falling out of favour

Where'er he turns he meets a stranger's eye,
His suppliants scorn him, and his foll'wers fly;
At once is lost the pride of awful state,
The golden canopy, the glitt'ring plate,
The regal palace, the luxurious board,   115
The liv'ried army, and the menial lord.
With age, with cares, with maladies oppressed,
He seeks the refuge of monastic rest.
Grief aids disease, remembered folly stings,
And his last sighs reproach the faith of kings.   120

Speak thou, whose thoughts at humble peace repine,
Shall Wolsey's wealth with Wolsey's end be thine?
Or liv'st thou now, with safer pride content,
The wisest justice on the banks of Trent?
For why did Wolsey near the steeps of fate,   125
On weak foundations raise th'enormous weight?
Why but to sink beneath misfortune's blow,
With louder ruin to the gulfs below?

What gave great Villiers to th'assassin's knife,
And fixed disease on Harley's closing life?   130
What murdered Wentworth, and what exiled Hyde,
By kings protected, and to kings allied?
What but their wish indulged in courts to shine,
And pow'r too great to keep or to resign?

When first the college rolls receive his name,   135
The young enthusiast quits his ease for fame;
Through all his veins the fever of renown
Burns from the strong contagion of the gown;
O'er Bodley's dome his future labours spread,
And Bacon's mansion trembles o'er his head.   140
Are these thy views? Proceed, illustrious youth,
And Virtue guard thee to the throne of Truth!
Yet should thy soul indulge the gen'rous heat,
Till captive Science yields her last retreat;
Should Reason guide thee with her brightest ray,   145
And pour on misty Doubt resistless day;
Should no false kindness lure to loose delight,
Nor praise relax, nor difficulty fright;
Should tempting Novelty thy cell refrain,
And Sloth effuse her opiate fumes in vain;   150

Should Beauty blunt on fops her fatal dart,
Nor claim the triumph of a lettered heart;
Should no disease thy torpid veins invade,
Nor Melancholy's phantoms haunt thy shade;
Yet hope not life from grief or danger free,   155
Nor think the doom of Man reversed for thee:
Deign on the passing world to turn thine eyes,
And pause awhile from letters, to be wise;
There mark what ills the scholar's life assail,
Toil, envy, want, the patron, and the jail.   160
See nations slowly wise, and meanly just,
To buried merit raise the tardy bust.
If dreams yet flatter, once again attend,
Hear Lydiat's life, and Galileo's end.

Nor deem, when Learning her last prize bestows,   165
The glitt'ring eminence exempt from foes;
See when the vulgar 'scape, despised or awed,
Rebellion's vengeful talons seize on Laud.
From meaner minds, though smaller fines content,
The plundered palace or sequestered rent;   170
Marked out by dang'rous parts he meets the shock,
And fatal Learning leads him to the block:
Around his tomb let Art and Genius weep,
But hear his death, ye blockheads, hear and sleep.

The festal blazes, the triumphal show,   175
The ravished standard, and the captive foe,
The senate's thanks, the gázette's pompous tale,
With force resistless o'er the brave prevail.
Such bribes the rapid Greek o'er Asia whirled,
For such the steady Romans shook the world;   180
For such in distant lands the Britons shine,
And stain with blood the Danube or the Rhine;
This pow'r has praise, that virtue scarce can warm,
Till fame supplies the universal charm.
Yet Reason frowns on War's unequal game,   185
Where wasted nations raise a single name,
And mortgaged states their grandsires' wreaths regret,
From age to age in everlasting debt;
Wreaths which at last the dear-bought right convey
To rust on medals, or on stones decay.   190

On what foundation stands the warrior's pride,
How just his hopes let Swedish Charles decide;
A frame of adamant, a soul of fire,
No dangers fright him, and no labours tire;
O'er love, o'er fear extends his wide domain,   195

---

113 **awful:** inspiring awe or dread 115 **board:** table 116 **liv'ried army:** army of servants 124 **Trent:** the river Trent, rising in Staffordshire (where Johnson was born), here representing any provincial location 129 **Villiers:** George Villiers, 1st Duke of Buckingham (1592–1628), English courtier and statesman, favourite of James I and Charles I; murdered 130 **Harley:** Robert Harley, 1st Earl of Oxford (1661–1724), English statesman, head of the ministry under Queen Anne, impeached and imprisoned in the Tower at the Hanoverian accession but eventually acquitted 131 **Wentworth:** Thomas Wentworth, 1st Earl of Strafford (1593–1641), English statesman and chief adviser to Charles I; impeached by Parliament and executed **Hyde:** Edward Hyde, 1st Earl of Clarendon (1609–74), chief adviser to Charles II; dismissed, he fled abroad to avoid impeachment 138 **Burns . . . gown:** the scholar's gown is compared to the shirt of Nessus which, in Greek myth, fatally poisoned Hercules 139 **Bodley's dome:** The Bodleian Library, principal library of Oxford University 140 **Bacon's mansion:** Roger Bacon (?1214–92), English scientist, built a house with an arch beneath it and the legend arose that it would fall if a greater man than Bacon passed beneath it 146 **resistless:** irresistible

151 **dart:** arrow or spear 162 **To . . . bust:** honour the great with a statue or bust only long after they are dead 164 **Lydiat:** Thomas Lydiat (1572–1646), brilliant English scholar, was forgotten by the time of his death **Galileo:** Galileo Galilei (1564–1642), Italian scientist, declared a heretic by the Inquisition and put into prison where he went blind 168 **Laud:** William Laud (1573–1645), English prelate, impeached by Parliament and executed 177 **gázette:** an official document containing public notices, appointments, etc 179 **rapid Greek:** Alexander the Great 181–2 **For . . . Rhine:** a reference to the victories of the Duke of Marlborough in Austria and Germany 187 **mortgaged . . . regret:** debt-ridden nations lament the cost of paying for the military triumphs of previous generations 192 **Swedish Charles:** Charles XII of Sweden (1682–1718), a great miltary leader who met with eventual defeat

Unconquered lord of pleasure and of pain;
No joys to him pacific sceptres yield,
War sounds the trump, he rushes to the field;
Behold surrounding kings their pow'r combine,
And one capitulate, and one resign; 200
Peace courts his hand, but spreads her charms in vain;
'Think nothing gained', he cries, 'till nought remain,
On Moscow's walls till Gothic standards fly,
And all be mine beneath the polar sky.'
The march begins in military state, 205
And nations on his eye suspended wait;
Stern Famine guards the solitary coast,
And Winter barricades the realms of Frost;
He comes, not want and cold his course delay;
Hide, blushing Glory, hide Pultowa's day: 210
The vanquished hero leaves his broken bands,
And shows his miseries in distant lands;
Condemned a needy supplicant to wait,
While ladies interpose, and slaves debate.
But did not Chance at length her error mend? 215
Did no subverted empire mark his end?
Did rival monarchs give the fatal wound?
Or hostile millions press him to the ground?
His fall was destined to a barren strand,
A petty fortress, and a dubious hand; 220
He left the name, at which the world grew pale,
To point a moral, or adorn a tale.
　All times their scenes of pompous woes afford,
From Persia's tyrant to Bavaria's lord.
In gay hostility, and barb'rous pride, 225
With half mankind embattled at his side,
Great Xerxes comes to seize the certain prey,
And starves exhausted regions in his way;
Attendant Flatt'ry counts his myriads o'er,
Till counted myriads soothe his pride no more; 230
Fresh praise is tried till madness fires his mind,
The waves he lashes, and enchains the wind;
New pow'rs are claimed, new pow'rs are still
　　bestowed,
Till rude Resistance lops the spreading god;
The daring Greeks deride the martial show, 235
And heap their valleys with the gaudy foe;
Th'insulted sea with humbler thoughts he gains,
A single skiff to speed his flight remains;
Th'encumbered oar scarce leaves the dreaded coast
Through purple billows and a floating host. 240

　The bold Bavarian, in a luckless hour,
Tries the dread summits of Caesarean pow'r,
With unexpected legions bursts away,
And sees defenceless realms receive his sway.
Short sway! Fair Austria spreads her mournful charms,
The queen, the beauty, sets the world in arms; 246
From hill to hill the beacons' rousing blaze
Spreads wide the hope of plunder and of praise;
The fierce Croatian, and the wild Hussar,
And all the sons of Ravage crowd the war; 250
The baffled prince in honour's flatt'ring bloom
Of hasty greatness finds the fatal doom,
His foes' derision, and his subjects' blame,
And steals to death from anguish and from shame.
　Enlarge my life with multitude of days, 255
In health, in sickness, thus the suppliant prays;
Hides from himself his state, and shuns to know
That life protracted is protracted woe.
Time hovers o'er, impatient to destroy,
And shuts up all the passages of joy: 260
In vain their gifts the bounteous seasons pour,
The fruit autumnal, and the vernal flow'r,
With listless eyes the dotard views the store,
He views, and wonders that they please no more;
Now pall the tasteless meats, and joyless wines, 265
And Luxury with sighs her slave resigns.
Approach, ye minstrels, try the soothing strain,
And yield the tuneful lenitives of pain:
No sounds, alas, would touch th'impervious ear,
Though dancing mountains witnessed Orpheus near;
Nor lute nor lyre his feeble pow'rs attend, 271
Nor sweeter music of a virtuous friend,
But everlasting dictates crowd his tongue,
Perversely grave, or positively wrong.
The still returning tale, and ling'ring jest, 275
Perplex the fawning niece and pampered guest,
While growing hopes scarce awe the gath'ring sneer,
And scarce a legacy can bribe to hear;
The watchful guests still hint the last offence;
The daughter's petulance, the son's expense, 280
Improve his heady rage with treach'rous skill,
And mould his passions till they make his will.
　Unnumbered maladies his joints invade,
Lay siege to life and press the dire blockade;
But unextinguished Av'rice still remains, 285
And dreaded losses aggravate his pains;
He turns, with anxious heart and crippled hands,
His bonds of debt, and mortgages of lands;
Or views his coffers with suspicious eyes,
Unlocks his gold, and counts it till he dies. 290

200 **one capitulate:** Frederick IV of Denmark **one resign:** Augustus II of Poland, defeated and banished by Charles XII 203 **Gothic:** Swedish 210 **Pultowa:** Poltava, a battle in the Ukraine (1709) at which the Russians under Peter the Great defeated Charles XII 219-20 **His fall . . . hand:** Charles was shot dead by an unknown hand while besieging a Norwegian fortress 224 **Persia's tyrant:** Xerxes (see below) **Bavaria's lord:** see at **bold Bavarian** below 227 **Xerxes:** Xerxes I, king of Persia (?519–465 BC), invaded Greece with a vast army but met with eventual defeat 240 **purple billows:** bloodstained sea (after Xerxes defeat at the naval battle of Salamis)

241 **bold Bavarian:** Charles Albert, Elector of Bavaria, became Holy Roman Emperor (1742–5) 245 **Fair Austria:** Maria Theresa (1717–80), Archduchess of Austria and Queen of Hungary and Bohemia 249 **Croatian:** Croatia was part of the Austrian Empire **Hussar:** a Hungarian cavalryman 268 **lenitives:** drugs that alleviate pain or distress 270 **Orpheus:** in Greek myth, a poet and lyre-player whose music was so powerfully moving that it could make mountains dance 281 **Improve:** increase

But grant, the virtues of a temp'rate prime
Bless with an age exempt from scorn or crime;
An age that melts in unperceived decay,
And glides in modest innocence away;
Whose peaceful day Benevolence endears,   295
Whose night congratulating Conscience cheers;
The gen'ral fav'rite as the gen'ral friend:
Such age there is, and who could wish its end?

Yet ev'n on this her load Misfortune flings,
To press the weary minutes' flagging wings: 300
New sorrow rises as the day returns,
A sister sickens, or a daughter mourns.
Now kindred Merit fills the sable bier,
Now lacerated Friendship claims a tear.
Year chases year, decay pursues decay,   305
Still drops some joy from with'ring life away;
New forms arise, and diff'rent views engage,
Superfluous lags the vet'ran on the stage,
Till pitying Nature signs the last release,
And bids afflicted Worth retire to peace.   310

But few there are whom hours like these await,
Who set unclouded in the gulfs of Fate.
From Lydia's monarch should the search descend,
By Solon cautioned to regard his end,
In life's last scene what prodigies surprise,   315
Fears of the brave, and follies of the wise!
From Marlb'rough's eyes the streams of dotage flow,
And Swift expires a driv'ller and a show.

The teeming mother, anxious for her race,
Begs for each birth the fortune of a face: 320
Yet Vane could tell what ills from beauty spring;
And Sedley cursed the form that pleased a king.
Ye nymphs of rosy lips and radiant eyes,
Whom Pleasure keeps too busy to be wise,
Whom Joys with soft varieties invite,   325
By day the frolic, and the dance by night,
Who frown with vanity, who smile with art,
And ask the latest fashion of the heart;
What care, what rules your heedless charms shall save,
Each nymph your rival, and each youth your slave?
Against your fame with Fondness Hate combines,   331
The rival batters, and the lover mines.
With distant voice neglected Virtue calls,
Less heard and less, the faint remonstrance falls;
Tired with contempt, she quits the slipp'ry reign,   335
And Pride and Prudence take her seat in vain.
In crowd at once, where none the pass defend,
The harmless freedom, and the private friend.

303 **sable:** black 313 **Lydia's monarch:** Croesus, king of Lydia 560–546 BC.
When he described himself as the happiest of men the philosopher
Solon said no man should be called happy until he has reached
the end of his life 317 **Marlb'rough:** John Churchill, 1st Duke of
Marlborough (1650–1722), English general, disabled by a stroke in
later life 318 **Swift:** Jonathan Swift (see above) was insane before
his death 321 **Vane:** Anne Vane, abandoned mistress of Frederick,
Prince of Wales 322 **Sedley:** Catherine Sedley, daughter of the
courtier and poet Sir Charles Sedley, was an abandoned mistress
of James II

The guardians yield, by force superior plied;
By Int'rest, Prudence; and by Flatt'ry, Pride.   340
Now Beauty falls betrayed, despised, distressed,
And hissing Infamy proclaims the rest.

Where then shall Hope and Fear their objects find?
Must dull Suspense corrupt the stagnant mind?
Must helpless Man, in ignorance sedate,   345
Roll darkling down the torrent of his fate?
Must no dislike alarm, no wishes rise,
No cries attempt the mercies of the skies?
Enquirer, cease; petitions yet remain,
Which heaven may hear, nor deem religion vain.   350
Still raise for good the supplicating voice,
But leave to heaven the measure and the choice,
Safe in his pow'r, whose eyes discern afar
The secret ambush of a specious prayer.
Implore his aid, in his decisions rest,   355
Secure, whate'er he gives, he gives the best.
Yet when the sense of sacred presence fires,
And strong devotion to the skies aspires,
Pour forth thy fervours for a healthful mind,
Obedient passions, and a will resigned;   360
For love, which scarce collective Man can fill;
For patience sov'reign o'er transmuted ill;
For faith, that panting for a happier seat,
Counts death kind Nature's signal of retreat:
These goods for Man the laws of heaven ordain,   365
These goods he grants, who grants the pow'r to gain;
With these celestial Wisdom calms the mind,
And makes the happiness she does not find.

346 **darkling:** in darkness

A SHORT SONG OF CONGRATULATION

LONG-EXPECTED one and twenty
  Ling'ring year at last is flown,
Pomp and pleasure, pride and plenty
  Great Sir John, are all your own.

Loosened from the minor's tether,   5
  Free to mortgage or to sell,
Wild as wind, and light as feather
  Bid the slaves of thrift farewell.

Call the Bettys, Kates, and Jennys
  Ev'ry name that laughs at care,   10
Lavish of your grandsire's guineas,
  Show the spirit of an heir.

All that prey on vice and folly
  Joy to see their quarry fly,
Here the gamester light and jolly   15
  There the lender grave and sly.

Wealth, Sir John, was made to wander,
  Let it wander as it will;
See the jockey, see the pander,
  Bid them come, and take their fill.   20

When the bonny blade carouses,
  Pockets full, and spirits high,
What are acres? what are houses?
  Only dirt, or wet or dry.

If the guardian or the mother   25
  Tell the woes of sinful waste,
Scorn their counsel and their pother,
  You can hang or drown at last.

A SHORT SONG OF CONGRATULATION: 14 **Joy:** enjoy 19 **pander:** a person
who caters to the vulgar desires of another, a pimp 27 **pother:** fuss
or trouble

ON THE DEATH OF DR ROBERT LEVET

CONDEMNED to hope's delusive mine,
  As on we toil from day to day,
By sudden blasts, or slow decline,
  Our social comforts drop away.

Well tried through many a varying year,   5
  See LEVET to the grave descend;
Officious, innocent, sincere,
  Of ev'ry friendless name the friend.

Yet still he fills affection's eye,
  Obscurely wise, and coarsely kind;   10
Nor, lettered arrogance, deny
  Thy praise to merit unrefined.

When fainting nature called for aid,
  And hov'ring death prepared the blow,
His vig'rous remedy displayed   15
  The power of art without the show.

In misery's darkest caverns known,
  His useful care was ever nigh,
Where hopeless anguish poured his groan,
  And lonely want retired to die.   20

No summons mocked by chill delay,
  No petty gain disdained by pride,
The modest wants of ev'ry day
  The toil of ev'ry day supplied.

His virtues walked their narrow round,   25
  Nor made a pause, nor left a void;
And sure th'Eternal Master found
  The single talent well employed.

The busy day, the peaceful night,
  Unfelt, uncounted, glided by;   30
His frame was firm, his powers were bright,
  Though now his eightieth year was nigh.

Then with no throbbing fiery pain,
  No cold gradations of decay,
Death broke at once the vital chain,   35
  And freed his soul the nearest way.

ON THE DEATH OF DR ROBERT LEVET: Levet (1705–82) was friend of
Johnson's who generously treated patients for small fees or free of
charge 7 **Officious:** attentive or obliging

ANONYMOUS

'IN GOOD KING CHARLES'S GOLDEN DAYS'

IN good King Charles's golden days,
  When loyalty no harm meant,
A furious High Church man I was,
  And so I gained preferment.
Unto my flock I daily preached,   5
  Kings are by God appointed,
And damned are those who dare resist,
  Or touch the Lord's anointed.
    And this is law, I will maintain
      Unto my dying day, sir,   10
    That whatsoever king shall reign,
      I will be vicar of Bray, sir!

When royal James possessed the crown,
  And popery grew in fashion,
The Penal Law I shouted down,   15
  And read the Declaration:
The Church of Rome I found would fit
  Full well my constitution,
And I had been a Jesuit,
  But for the Revolution.   20
    And this is law, I will maintain
      Unto my dying day, sir,
    That whatsoever king shall reign,
      I will be vicar of Bray, sir!

When William our deliverer came,   25
  To heal the nation's grievance,
I turned the cat in pan again,
  And swore to him allegiance:
Old principles I did revoke,
  Set conscience at a distance,   30
Passive obedience is a joke,
  A jest is non-resistance.
    And this is law, I will maintain
      Unto my dying day, sir,
    That whatsoever king shall reign,   35
      I will be vicar of Bray, sir!

When glorious Anne became our queen,
  The Church of England's glory,
Another face of things was seen,
  And I became a Tory: 40
Occasional conformists base,
  I damned, and moderation,
And thought the Church in danger was
  From such prevarication.
    And this is law, I will maintain   45
      Unto my dying day, sir,
    That whatsoever king shall reign,
      I will be vicar of Bray, sir!

When George in pudding time came o'er,
  And moderate men looked big, sir,   50
My principles I changed once more,
  And so became a Whig, sir:
And thus preferment I procured,
  From our faith's great defender,
And almost every day abjured   55
  The Pope and the Pretender.
    And this is law, I will maintain
      Unto my dying day, sir,
    That whatsoever king shall reign,
      I will be vicar of Bray, sir!   60

The illustrious house of Hanover,
  And Protestant succession,
To these I lustily will swear,
  Whilst they can keep possession:
For in my faith and loyalty   65
  I never once will falter,
But George my lawful king shall be,
  Except the times should alter.
    And this is law, I will maintain
      Unto my dying day, sir,   70
    That whatsoever king shall reign,
      I will be vicar of Bray, sir!

'IN GOOD KING CHARLES'S GOLDEN DAYS': 15 **Penal Law:** a law imposing penalties on Roman Catholics 16 **Declaration:** any of a number of declarations of indulgence issued by Charles II or James II suspending the penal laws 20 **Revolution:** The Glorious Revolution of 1688 in which the Catholic James II was ousted in favour of William and Mary 25 **William:** the Protestant hero William of Orange, who became King William III (1689–1702) 41 **Occasional conformists:** people belonging to a church that dissented from the Church of England but who occasionally attended Church of England services to avoid being penalized 49 **pudding time:** the right moment 56 **Pretender:** James Francis Edward Stuart, son of the deposed James II and pretender to the British throne

WILLIAM SHENSTONE

WRITTEN AT AN INN AT HENLEY

To thee, fair freedom! I retire
  From flattery, cards, and dice, and din;
Nor art thou found in mansions higher
  Than the low cot or humble inn.

'Tis here with boundless power I reign;   5
  And ev'ry health which I begin,
Converts dull port to bright champagne;
  Such freedom crowns it at an inn.

I fly from pomp, I fly from plate!
  I fly from falsehood's specious grin!   10
Freedom I love, and form I hate,
  And choose my lodgings at an inn.

Here, waiter! take my sordid ore,
  Which lackeys else might hope to win;
It buys what courts have not in store;   15
  It buys me freedom at an inn.

And now once more I shape my way
  Through rain or shine, through thick or thin,
Secure to meet, at close of day,
  With kind reception at an inn.   20

Whoe'er has travelled life's dull round,
  Where'er his stages may have been,
May sigh to think he still has found
  The warmest welcome at an inn.

WRITTEN AT AN INN AT HENLEY: 4 **cot:** cottage 6 **health:** a toast drunk to someone's health 9 **plate:** silver 14 **else:** otherwise 22 **stages:** resting places on a journey

THOMAS GRAY

ELEGY WRITTEN IN A COUNTRY CHURCHYARD

The curfew tolls the knell of parting day,
The lowing herd wind slowly o'er the lea,
The ploughman homeward plods his weary way,
And leaves the world to darkness and to me.

Now fades the glimmering landscape on the sight,   5
And all the air a solemn stillness holds,
Save where the beetle wheels his droning flight,
And drowsy tinklings lull the distant folds;

Save that from yonder ivy-mantled tow'r
The moping owl does to the moon complain   10
Of such as, wandering near her secret bow'r,
Molest her ancient solitary reign.

Beneath those rugged elms, that yew-tree's shade,
Where heaves the turf in many a mould'ring heap,
Each in his narrow cell for ever laid,   15
The rude forefathers of the hamlet sleep.

The breezy call of incense-breathing Morn,
The swallow twitt'ring from the straw-built shed,
The cock's shrill clarion, or the echoing horn,
No more shall rouse them from their lowly bed.   20

For them no more the blazing hearth shall burn,
Or busy housewife ply her evening care;
No children run to lisp their sire's return,
Or climb his knees the envied kiss to share.

Oft did the harvest to their sickle yield,   25
Their furrow oft the stubborn glebe has broke;
How jocund did they drive their team afield!
How bowed the woods beneath their sturdy stroke!

Let not Ambition mock their useful toil,
Their homely joys and destiny obscure;   30
Nor Grandeur hear with a disdainful smile
The short and simple annals of the poor.

The boast of heraldry, the pomp of pow'r,
And all that beauty, all that wealth e'er gave,
Awaits alike th'inevitable hour.   35
The paths of glory lead but to the grave.

Nor you, ye Proud, impute to these the fault,
If Mem'ry o'er their tomb no trophies raise,
Where through the long-drawn aisle and fretted vault
The pealing anthem swells the note of praise.   40

Can storied urn or animated bust
Back to its mansion call the fleeting breath?
Can Honour's voice provoke the silent dust,
Or Flatt'ry soothe the dull cold ear of Death?

Perhaps in this neglected spot is laid   45
Some heart once pregnant with celestial fire,
Hands, that the rod of empire might have swayed,
Or waked to ecstasy the living lyre.

But Knowledge to their eyes her ample page
Rich with the spoils of time did ne'er unroll;   50
Chill Penury repressed their noble rage,
And froze the genial current of the soul.

Full many a gem of purest ray serene
The dark unfathomed caves of ocean bear:
Full many a flower is born to blush unseen,   55
And waste its sweetness on the desert air.

Some village Hampden that with dauntless breast
The little tyrant of his fields withstood;
Some mute inglorious Milton here may rest,
Some Cromwell guiltless of his country's blood.   60

Th'applause of list'ning senates to command,
The threats of pain and ruin to despise,
To scatter plenty o'er a smiling land,
And read their hist'ry in a nation's eyes

Their lot forbade: nor circumscribed alone   65
Their growing virtues, but their crimes confined;
Forbade to wade through slaughter to a throne,
And shut the gates of mercy on mankind,

The struggling pangs of conscious truth to hide,
To quench the blushes of ingenuous shame,   70
Or heap the shrine of Luxury and Pride
With incense kindled at the Muse's flame.

Far from the madding crowd's ignoble strife
Their sober wishes never learned to stray;
Along the cool sequestered vale of life   75
They kept the noiseless tenor of their way.

Yet ev'n these bones from insult to protect
Some frail memorial still erected nigh,
With uncouth rhymes and shapeless sculpture decked,
Implores the passing tribute of a sigh.   80

Their name, their years, spelt by th'unlettered Muse,
The place of fame and elegy supply:
And many a holy text around she strews,
That teach the rustic moralist to die.

For who, to dumb Forgetfulness a prey,   85
This pleasing anxious being e'er resigned,
Left the warm precincts of the cheerful day,
Nor cast one longing ling'ring look behind?

On some fond breast the parting soul relies,
Some pious drops the closing eye requires;   90
Ev'n from the tomb the voice of Nature cries,
Ev'n in our ashes live their wonted fires.

For thee, who, mindful of th'unhonoured dead,
Dost in these lines their artless tale relate;
If chance, by lonely contemplation led,   95
Some kindred spirit shall enquire thy fate,

Haply some hoary-headed swain may say,
'Oft have we seen him at the peep of dawn
Brushing with hasty steps the dews away
To meet the sun upon the upland lawn.   100

ELEGY WRITTEN IN A COUNTRY CHURCHYARD: 16 **rude:** plain and
uneducated 26 **glebe:** field 38 **trophies:** memorials, especially
commemorating victories 39 **fretted:** ornamented with angular
designs 41 **storied:** decorated with a narrative design 51 **rage:**
ardour 52 **genial current:** creativity

57 **Hampden:** John Hampden (1594–1643), English statesman and
leader of the Parliamentary opposition to Charles I 65 **alone:** only
73 **madding:** acting as if mad; maddening 90 **pious drops:** tears
92 **wonted:** accustomed

'There at the foot of yonder nodding beech.
That wreathes its old fantastic roots so high,
His listless length at noontide would he stretch,
And pore upon the brook that babbles by.

'Hard by yon wood, now smiling as in scorn,   105
Mutt'ring his wayward fancies he would rove;
Now drooping, woeful-wan, like one forlorn,
Or crazed with care, or crossed in hopeless love.

'One morn I missed him from the customed hill,
Along the heath, and near his fav'rite tree;   110
Another came; nor yet beside the rill,
Nor up the lawn, nor at the wood was he,

'The next, with dirges due in sad array
Slow through the churchway path we saw him
    borne.
Approach and read (for thou can'st read) the lay   115
Graved on the stone beneath yon agèd thorn.'

THE EPITAPH

Here rests his head upon the lap of earth
A Youth, to Fortune and to Fame unknown;
Fair Science frowned not on his humble birth,
And Melancholy marked him for her own.   120

Large was his bounty, and his soul sincere,
Heaven did a recompense as largely send:
He gave to Mis'ry (all he had) a tear,
He gained from heaven ('twas all he wished) a friend.

No farther seek his merits to disclose,   125
Or draw his frailties from their dread abode
(There they alike in trembling hope repose),
The bosom of his Father and his God.

115 **lay:** song

ON THE DEATH OF A FAVOURITE CAT,
DROWNED IN A TUB OF GOLDFISHES

'TWAS on a lofty vase's side,
Where China's gayest art had dyed
    The azure flowers that blow;
Demurest of the tabby kind,
The pensive Selima reclined,   5
    Gazed on the lake below.

Her conscious tail her joy declared;
The fair round face, the snowy beard,
    The velvet of her paws,
Her coat, that with the tortoise vies,   10
Her ears of jet, and emerald eyes,
    She saw; and purred applause.

Still had she gazed; but 'midst the tide
Two angel forms were seen to glide,
    The genii of the stream: 15
Their scaly armour's Tyrian hue
Through richest purple to the view
    Betrayed a golden gleam.

The hapless nymph with wonder saw:
A whisker first, and then a claw,   20
    With many an ardent wish,
She stretched in vain to reach the prize.
What female heart can gold despise?
    What cat's averse to fish?

Presumptuous maid! with looks intent   25
Again she stretched, again she bent,
    Nor knew the gulf between.
(Malignant Fate sat by, and smiled)
The slipp'ry verge her feet beguiled,
    She tumbled headlong in.   30

Eight times emerging from the flood
She mewed to ev'ry wat'ry god
    Some speedy aid to send.
No dolphin came, no nereid stirred;
Nor cruel Tom, nor Susan heard.   35
    A fav'rite has no friend!

From hence, ye Beauties undeceived,
Know, one false step is ne'er retrieved,
    And be with caution bold.
Not all that tempts your wand'ring eyes   40
And heedless hearts is lawful prize;
    Nor all that glisters gold.

ODE ON THE DEATH OF A FAVOURITE CAT: 3 **blow:** bloom 15 **genii:** plural of genius, here meaning 'spirits of the place' 16 **Tyrian:** purple, like the famous rich dye from Tyre 34 **dolphin:** in Greek myth, the drowning poet Arion was rescued by a dolphin **nereid:** in Greek myth, a sea-nymph 35 **Tom, Susan:** conventional names for servants 42 **glisters:** glitters, glistens

THE BARD
PINDARIC ODE

'RUIN seize thee, ruthless King!
Confusion on thy banners wait!
Though fanned by Conquest's crimson wing,
They mock the air with idle state.
Helm, nor hauberk's twisted mail,   5
Nor e'en thy virtues, Tyrant, shall avail
To save thy secret soul from nightly fears,
From Cambria's curse, from Cambria's tears!'

THE BARD: **Pindaric ode:** a form of ode associated with the Greek lyric poet Pindar (?518–?438 BC) 4 **idle:** useless, futile 5 **helm:** helmet **hauberk:** a long coat of mail 8 **Cambria:** Wales

Such were the sounds that o'er the crested pride
Of the first Edward scattered wild dismay, 10
As down the steep of Snowdon's shaggy side
He wound with toilsome march his long array.
Stout Gloucester stood aghast in speechless trance;
'To arms!' cried Mortimer, and couched his quiv'ring
    lance.

  On a rock, whose haughty brow 15
Frowns o'er old Conway's foaming flood,
Robed in the sable garb of woe
With haggard eyes the Poet stood;
(Loose his beard, and hoary hair
Streamed like a meteor to the troubled air) 20
And with a master's hand, and prophet's fire,
Struck the deep sorrows of his lyre.
'Hark, how each giant-oak and desert-cave
Sighs to the torrent's awful voice beneath!
O'er thee, O King! their hundred arms they wave, 25
Revenge on thee in hoarser murmurs breathe;
Vocal no more, since Cambria's fatal day,
To high-born Hoel's harp, or soft Llewellyn's lay.

  'Cold is Cadwallo's tongue,
That hushed the stormy main; 30
Brave Urien sleeps upon his craggy bed:
Mountains, ye mourn in vain
Modred, whose magic song
Made huge Plinlimmon bow his cloud-topped head.
On dreary Arvon's shore they lie, 35
Smeared with gore, and ghastly pale;
Far, far aloof th'affrighted ravens sail;
The famished eagle screams, and passes by.
Dear lost companions of my tuneful art,
Dear as the light that visits these sad eyes, 40
Dear as the ruddy drops that warm my heart,
Ye died amidst your dying country's cries –
No more I weep. They do not sleep.
On yonder cliffs, a grisly band,
I see them sit; they linger yet, 45
Avengers of their native land;
With me in dreadful harmony they join,
And weave with bloody hands the tissue of thy line.

  'Weave the warp! and weave the woof!
The winding sheet of Edward's race: 50
Give ample room and verge enough
The characters of hell to trace.
Mark the year and mark the night

When Severn shall re-echo with affright
The shrieks of death, through Berkeley's roof that
    ring, 55
Shrieks of an agonizing king!
She-wolf of France, with unrelenting fangs,
That tear'st the bowels of thy mangled mate,
From thee be born, who o'er thy country hangs
The scourge of heaven! What terrors round him wait!
Amazement in his van, with Flight combined, 61
And Sorrow's faded form, and Solitude behind.

  'Mighty victor, mighty lord!
Low on his funeral couch he lies!
No pitying heart, no eye, afford 65
A tear to grace his obsequies.
Is the sable warrior fled?
Thy son is gone. He rests among the dead.
The swarm that in thy noontide beam were born?
Gone to salute the rising morn. 70
Fair laughs the morn, and soft the zephyr blows,
While proudly riding o'er the azure realm
In gallant trim the gilded vessel goes:
Youth on the prow, and Pleasure at the helm:
Regardless of the sweeping whirlwind's sway, 75
That, hushed in grim repose, expects his ev'ning prey.

  'Fill high the sparkling bowl,
The rich repast prepare;
Reft of a crown, he yet may share the feast:
Close by the regal chair 80
Fell Thirst and Famine scowl
A baleful smile upon their baffled guest.
Heard ye the din of battle bray,
Lance to lance, and horse to horse?
Long years of havoc urge their destined course, 85
And through the kindred squadrons mow their way.
Ye towers of Julius, London's lasting shame,
With many a foul and midnight murder fed,
Revere his consort's faith, his father's fame,
And spare the meek usurper's holy head. 90
Above, below, the rose of snow,
Twined with her blushing foe, we spread:
The bristled boar in infant-gore
Wallows beneath the thorny shade.
Now, brothers, bending o'er the accursed loom, 95
Stamp we our vengeance deep, and ratify his doom.

54–7 **When Severn . . . France:** Edward II (1284–1327), King of England, was imprisoned in Berkeley Castle (by the River Severn) and almost certainly murdered by his wife, Isabella of France, and her lover Roger Mortimer 59–60 **From thee . . . heaven:** Isabella's son was Edward III (1312–77), who spent much of his reign at war with France 61 **van:** vanguard 67 **sable warrior:** Edward the Black Prince (1330–76), son of Edward III, predeceased his father 79 **Reft:** robbed 81 **Fell:** cruel, terrible 87 **towers of Julius:** the Tower of London, believed to incorporate a structure built by Julius Caesar 91–2 **the rose . . . foe:** the white rose of York and the red rose of Lancaster 93 **bristled boar:** a silver boar was the emblem of Richard III, believed to have murdered his infant nephews ('The Princes in the Tower')

11 **Snowdon:** the highest mountain in Wales 13 **Gloucester:** one of the lords who fought for Edward I in his Welsh Wars 14 **Mortimer:** another of these lords 16 **Conway:** a river in N Wales 28 **Hoel, Llewellyn:** imaginary Welsh bards **lay:** song 29 **Cadwallo:** imaginary Welsh bard 31 **Urien:** imaginary Welsh bard 33 **Modred:** imaginary Welsh bard 34 **Plinlimmon:** a mountain in Wales 35 **Arvon:** Caernarvon, in NW Wales 50 **winding sheet:** cloth used to wrap a corpse 52 **characters:** letters, numbers, symbols

'Edward, lo! to sudden fate
(Weave we the woof. The thread is spun.)
Half of thy heart we consecrate.
(The web is wove. The work is done.)   100
Stay, oh, stay! nor thus forlorn
Leave me unblessed, unpitied, here to mourn:
In yon bright track that fires the western skies
They melt, they vanish from my eyes.
But, oh! what solemn scenes on Snowdon's height   105
Descending slow their glittering skirts unroll?
Visions of glory, spare my aching sight,
Ye unborn ages, crowd not on my soul!
No more our long-lost Arthur we bewail.
All hail, ye genuine kings! Britannia's issue, hail!   110

'Girt with many a baron bold
Sublime their starry fronts they rear;
And gorgeous dames, and statesmen old
In bearded majesty, appear.
In the midst a form divine!   115
Her eye proclaims her of the Briton-line:
Her lion-port, her awe-commanding face,
Attempered sweet to virgin grace.
What strings symphonious tremble in the air,
What strains of vocal transport round her play!   120
Hear from the grave, great Taliessin, hear;
They breathe a soul to animate thy clay.
Bright Rapture calls, and soaring as she sings,
Waves in the eye of heaven her many-coloured wings.

'The verse adorn again   125
Fierce War, and faithful Love,
And Truth severe, by fairy fiction dressed.
In buskined measures move
Pale Grief, and pleasing Pain,
With Horror, tyrant of the throbbing breast.   130
A voice, as of the cherub-choir,
Gales from blooming Eden bear;
And distant warblings lessen on my ear,
That lost in long futurity expire.   134
Fond impious man, think'st thou yon sanguine cloud,
Raised by thy breath, has quenched the orb of day?
Tomorrow he repairs the golden flood,
And warms the nations with redoubled ray.
Enough for me: with joy I see
The diff'rent doom our fates assign.   140
Be thine Despair and sceptred Care;
To triumph and to die are mine.'
He spoke, and headlong from the mountain's height
Deep in the roaring tide he plunged to endless night.

109 **Arthur:** the legendary King Arthur 112 **fronts:** foreheads
115 **form divine:** Elizabeth I (1533–1603), Queen of England 117 **lion-
port:** lion-like bearing 121 **Taliessin:** a Welsh bard of the sixth
century 128 **buskined:** wearing the buskins, or boots, traditionally
worn by actors in tragedies 135 **Fond:** foolish

ODE ON A DISTANT PROSPECT
OF ETON COLLEGE

YE distant spires, ye antique towers,
That crown the watery glade,
Where grateful Science still adores
Her Henry's holy shade;
And ye, that from the stately brow   5
Of Windsor's heights th'expanse below
Of grove, of lawn, of mead survey,
Whose turf, whose shade, whose flowers among
Wanders the hoary Thames along
His silver-winding way.   10

Ah, happy hills, ah, pleasing shade,
Ah, fields beloved in vain,
Where once my careless childhood strayed,
A stranger yet to pain!
I feel the gales, that from ye blow,   15
A momentary bliss bestow,
As waving fresh their gladsome wing
My weary soul they seem to soothe,
And, redolent of joy and youth,
To breathe a second spring.   20

Say, Father Thames, for thou hast seen
Full many a sprightly race
Disporting on thy margent green
The paths of pleasure trace,
Who foremost now delight to cleave   25
With pliant arm thy glassy wave?
The captive linnet which enthral?
What idle progeny succeed
To chase the rolling circle's speed,
Or urge the flying ball?   30

While some on earnest business bent
Their murm'ring labours ply
'Gainst graver hours, that bring constraint
To sweeten liberty:
Some bold adventurers disdain   35
The limits of their little reign,
And unknown regions dare descry:
Still as they run they look behind,
They hear a voice in every wind,
And snatch a fearful joy.   40

Gay hope is theirs by fancy fed,
Less pleasing when possessed;
The tear forgot as soon as shed,
The sunshine of the breast:
Theirs buxom health of rosy hue,   45
Wild wit, invention ever-new,
And lively cheer of vigour born;
The thoughtless day, the easy night,
The spirits pure, the slumbers light,
That fly th'approach of morn.   50

Alas! regardless of their doom
The little victims play!
No sense have they of ills to come,
Nor care beyond today:
Yet see how all around 'em wait   55
The ministers of human fate,
And black Misfortune's baleful train!
Ah, show them where in ambush stand,
To seize their prey, the murd'rous band!
Ah, tell them they are men!   60

These shall the fury Passions tear,
The vultures of the mind,
Disdainful Anger, pallid Fear,
And Shame that skulks behind;
Or pining Love shall waste their youth,   65
Or Jealousy with rankling tooth,
That inly gnaws the secret heart,
And Envy wan, and faded Care,
Grim-visaged comfortless Despair,
And Sorrow's piercing dart.   70

Ambition this shall tempt to rise,
Then whirl the wretch from high,
To bitter Scorn a sacrifice,
And grinning Infamy.
The stings of Falsehood those shall try,   75
And hard Unkindness' altered eye,
That mocks the tear it forced to flow;
And keen Remorse with blood defiled,
And moody Madness laughing wild
Amid severest woe.   80

Lo, in the vale of years beneath
A grisly troop are seen,
The painful family of Death,
More hideous than their queen:
This racks the joints, this fires the veins,   85
That every labouring sinew strains,
Those in the deeper vitals rage:
Lo, Poverty, to fill the band,
That numbs the soul with icy hand,
And slow-consuming Age.   90

To each his suff'rings: all are men,
Condemned alike to groan;
The tender for another's pain,
Th'unfeeling for his own.
Yet ah! why should they know their fate?   95
Since sorrow never comes too late,
And happiness too swiftly flies.
Thought would destroy their paradise.
No more; – where ignorance is bliss,
'Tis folly to be wise.   100

ODE ON A DISTANT PROSPECT OF ETON COLLEGE: 3 **Science:** learning
4 **Her . . . shade:** Eton was founded by Henry VI (1421–71), who was
regarded as very pious 6 **Windsor's heights:** Windsor Castle is on
the other side of the Thames from Eton 15 **gales:** breezes 22 **race:**
generation 23 **margent:** edge 45 **buxom:** lively 51 **regardless:** heedless
70 **dart:** arrow or spear

WILLIAM COLLINS

ODE TO EVENING

IF aught of oaten stop or pastoral song
May hope, chaste Eve, to soothe thy modest ear,
      Like thy own solemn springs,
      Thy springs, and dying gales,
O Nymph reserved, while now the bright-haired sun   5
Sits in yon western tent, whose cloudy skirts,
      With brede ethereal wove,
      O'erhang his wavy bed:
Now air is hushed, save where the weak-eyed bat
With short shrill shriek flits by on leathern wing,   10
      Or where the beetle winds
      His small but sullen horn,
As oft he rises 'midst the twilight path,
Against the pilgrim borne in heedless hum:
      Now teach me, Maid composed,   15
      To breathe some softened strain,
Whose numbers stealing through thy dark'ning vale
May not unseemly with its stillness suit,
      As, musing slow, I hail
      Thy genial loved return!   20
For when thy folding-star arising shows
His paly circlet, at his warning lamp
      The fragrant hours, and elves
      Who slept in flow'rs the day,
And many a nymph who wreathes her brows with
      sedge   25
And sheds the fresh'ning dew, and lovelier still,
      The pensive pleasures sweet
      Prepare thy shadowy car.
Then lead, calm Vot'ress, where some sheety lake
Cheers the lone heath, or some time-hallowed pile,   30
      Or upland fallows grey
      Reflect its last cool gleam.
But when chill blust'ring winds or driving rain
Forbid my willing feet, be mine the hut
      That from the mountain's side   35
      Views wilds and swelling floods,
And hamlets brown and dim-discovered spires,
And hears their simple bell, and marks o'er all
      Thy dewy fingers draw
      The gradual dusky veil.   40
While Spring shall pour his show'rs, as oft he wont,
And bathe thy breathing tresses, meekest Eve!
      While Summer loves to sport
      Beneath thy ling'ring light;
While sallow Autumn fills thy lap with leaves;   45
Or Winter, yelling through the troublous air,
      Affrights thy shrinking train
      And rudely rends thy robes.
So long, sure-found beneath the sylvan shed,
Shall Fancy, Friendship, Science, rose-lipped Health,
      Thy gentlest influence own,   51
      And hymn thy fav'rite name!

ODE TO EVENING: 1 **oaten stop:** a fingerhole on a pipe made from an oat stem 7 **brede:** braid 11 **winds:** blows 17 **numbers:** verses 21 **folding-star:** the evening star, rising at the time of putting sheep into their fold for the night 22 **paly:** pale, palish 28 **car:** chariot 29 **Vot'ress:** devoted adherent **sheety:** sheet-like 30 **pile:** building 36 **floods:** rivers 37 **dim-discovered:** dimly seen 42 **breathing:** giving off scent 46 **troublous:** agitated 49 **sylvan:** belonging to woods or forests 50 **Science:** learning

ODE WRITTEN IN THE BEGINNING OF THE YEAR 1746

How sleep the brave, who sink to rest,
By all their country's wishes blessed!
When Spring, with dewy fingers cold,
Returns to deck their hallowed mould,
She there shall dress a sweeter sod   5
Than Fancy's feet have ever trod.

By fairy hands their knell is rung;
By forms unseen their dirge is sung;
There Honour comes, a pilgrim grey,
To bless the turf that wraps their clay;
And Freedom shall awhile repair   10
To dwell a weeping hermit there!

MARK AKENSIDE

From THE PLEASURES OF IMAGINATION

FOR when the diff'rent images of things
By chance combined, have struck th'attentive soul
With deeper impulse, or connected long,
Have drawn her frequent eye; howe'er distinct
Th'external scenes, yet oft th'ideäs gain   5
From that conjunction an eternal tie,
And sympathy unbroken. Let the mind
Recall one partner of the various league,
Immediate, lo! the firm confed'rates rise,
And each his former station straight resumes: 10
One movement governs the consenting throng,
And all at once with rosy pleasure shine,
Or all are saddened with the glooms of care.
'Twas thus, if ancient fame the truth unfold,
Two faithful needles, from th'informing touch   15
Of the same parent-stone, together drew
Its mystic virtue, and at first conspired
With fatal impulse quiv'ring to the pole:
Then, though disjoined by kingdoms, though the main
Rolled its broad surge betwixt, and diff'rent stars   20
Beheld their wakeful motions, yet preserved
The former friendship, and remembered still
Th'alliance of their birth: whate'er the line

Which one possessed, nor pause, nor quiet knew
The sure associate, ere with trembling speed   25
He found its path and fixed unerring there.
Such is the secret union, when we feel
A song, a flow'r, a name at once restore
Those long-connected scenes where first they moved
Th'attention; backward through her mazy walks   30
Guiding the wanton fancy to her scope,
To temples, courts or fields; with all the band
Of painted forms, of passions and designs
Attendant: whence, if pleasing in itself,
The prospect from that sweet accession gains   35
Redoubled influence o'er the list'ning mind.
  By these mysterious ties the busy pow'r
Of mem'ry her ideäl train preserves
Entire; or when they would elude her watch,
Reclaims their fleeting footsteps from the waste   40
Of dark oblivion; thus collecting all
The various forms of being to present,
Before the curious aim of mimic art,
Their largest choice: like spring's unfolded blooms
Exhaling sweetness, that the skilful bee   45
May taste at will, from their selected spoils
To work her dulcet food. For not th'expanse
Of living lakes in summer's noontide calm,
Reflects the bord'ring shade and sun-bright heavens
With fairer semblance; not the sculptured gold   50
More faithful keeps the graver's lively trace,
Than he whose birth the sister-pow'rs of art
Propitious viewed, and from his genial star
Shed influence to the seeds of fancy kind;
Than his attempered bosom must preserve   55
The seal of nature. There alone unchanged,
Her form remains. The balmy walks of May
There breathe perennial sweets: the trembling chord
Resounds for ever in th'abstracted ear,
Melodious: and the virgin's radiant eye,   60
Superior to disease, to grief, and time,
Shines with unbating lustre. Thus at length
Endowed with all that nature can bestow,
The child of fancy oft in silence bends
O'er these mixed treasures of his pregnant breast,   65
With conscious pride. From them he oft resolves
To frame he knows not what excelling things;
And win he knows not what sublime reward
Of praise and wonder. By degrees the mind
Feels her young nerves dilate: the plastic pow'rs   70
Labour for action: blind emotions heave
His bosom; and with loveliest frenzy caught,
From earth to heaven he rolls his daring eye,
From heaven to earth. Anon ten thousand shapes,
Like spectres trooping to the wizard's call,   75

THE PLEASURES OF THE IMAGINATION: 30 **mazy:** puzzling, convoluted 47 **work her dulcet food:** ie make honey 55 **attempered:** moderated

Flit swift before him. From the womb of earth,
From ocean's bed they come: th'eternal heavens
Disclose their splendours, and the dark abyss
Pours out her births unknown. With fixèd gaze
He marks the rising phantoms. Now compares   80
Their diff'rent forms; now blends them, now divides;
Enlarges and extenuates by turns;
Opposes, ranges in fantastic bands,
And infinitely varies. Hither now,
Now thither fluctuates his inconstant aim,   85
With endless choice perplexed. At length his plan
Begins to open. Lucid order dawns;
And as from Chaos old the jarring seeds
Of nature at the voice divine repaired
Each to its place, till rosy earth unveiled   90
Her fragrant bosom, and the joyful sun
Sprung up the blue serene; by swift degrees
Thus disentangled, his entire design
Emerges. Colours mingle, features join,
And lines converge: the fainter parts retire;   95
The fairer eminent in light advance;
And every image on its neighbour smiles.
A while he stands, and with a father's joy
Contémplates. Then with Promethéan art,
Into its proper vehicle he breathes   100
The fair conception; which embodied thus,
And permanent, becomes to eyes or ears
An object ascertained: while thus informed,
The various organs of his mimic skill,
The consonance of sounds, the featured rock,   105
The shadowy picture and impassioned verse,
Beyond their proper pow'rs attract the soul
By that expressive semblance, while in sight
Of nature's great original we scan
The lively child of art; while line by line,   110
And feature after feature we refer
To that sublime exemplar whence it stole
Those animating charms. Thus beauty's palm
Betwixt 'em wav'ring hangs: applauding love
Doubts where to choose; and mortal man aspires   115
To tempt creative praise. As when a cloud
Of gath'ring hail with limpid crusts of ice
Enclosed and obvious to the beaming sun,
Collects his large effulgence; straight the heavens
With equal flames present on either hand   120
The radiant visage: Persia stands at gaze,
Appalled; and on the brinks of Ganges doubts
The snowy-vested seer, in Mithra's name,
To which the fragrance of the south shall burn,
To which his warbled orisons ascend.   125

[Book 3, lines 312–436]

82 **extenuates:** makes or becomes thinner 99 **Promethéan:** like
Prometheus, who, in Greek myth, stole fire from the gods to give
to mankind 113 **palm:** symbol of victory 123 **Mithra:** Persian god of
light and the sun

CHRISTOPHER SMART

From JUBILATE AGNO

FOR I will consider my cat Jeffrey.

For he is the servant of the Living God, duly and daily
serving him.

For at the first glance of the glory of God in the east
he worships in his way.

For is this done by wreathing his body seven times
round with elegant quickness.

For then he leaps up to catch the musk, which is the
blessing of God upon his prayer.   5

For he rolls upon prank to work it in.

For having done duty and received blessing he begins
to consider himself.

For this he performs in ten degrees.

For first he looks upon his forepaws to see if they are
clean.

For secondly he kicks up behind to clear away
there.   10

For thirdly he works it upon stretch with the forepaws
extended.

For fourthly he sharpens his paws by wood.

For fifthly he washes himself.

For sixthly he rolls upon wash.

For seventhly he fleas himself, that he may not be
interrupted upon the beat.   15

For eighthly he rubs himself against a post.

For ninthly he looks up for his instructions.

For tenthly he goes in quest of food.

For having considered God and himself he will
consider his neighbour.

For if he meets another cat he will kiss her in
kindness.   20

For when he takes his prey he plays with it to give it
chance.

For one mouse in seven escapes by his dallying.

For when his day's work is done his business more
properly begins.

For he keeps the Lord's watch in the night against the
adversary.

For he counteracts the powers of darkness by his
electrical skin and glaring eyes.   25

For he counteracts the Devil, who is death, by brisking
about the life.

For in his morning orisons he loves the sun and the
sun loves him.

For he is of the tribe of tiger.

For the cherub cat is a term of the angel tiger.

For he has the subtlety and hissing of a serpent, which
in goodness he suppresses.   30

For he will not do destruction, if he is well fed, neither
will he spit without provocation.

For he purrs in thankfulness, when God tells him he's
a good cat.

For he is an instrument for the children to learn
benevolence upon.

For every house is incomplete without him and a
  blessing is lacking in the spirit.

For the Lord commanded Moses concerning the cats
  at the departure of the Children of Israel from
  Egypt.   35

For every family had one cat at least in the bag.

For the English cats are the best in Europe.

For he is the cleanest in the use of his forepaws of any
  quadruped.

For the dexterity of his defence is an instance of the
  love of God to him exceedingly.

For he is the quickest to his mark of any creature.   40

For he is tenacious of his point.

For he is a mixture of gravity and waggery.

For he knows that God is his Saviour.

For there is nothing sweeter than his peace when at
  rest.

For there is nothing brisker than his life when in
  motion.   45

For he is of the Lord's poor and so indeed is he called
  by benevolence perpetually – Poor Jeffrey! poor
  Jeffrey! the rat has bit thy throat.

For I bless the name of the Lord Jesus that Jeffrey is
  better.

For the divine spirit comes about his body to sustain it
  in complete cat.

For his tongue is exceeding pure so that it has in purity
  what it wants in music.

For he is docile and can learn certain things.   50

For he can set up with gravity which is patience upon
  approbation.

For he can fetch and carry, which is patience in
  employment.

For he can jump over a stick which is patience upon
  proof positive.

For he can spraggle upon waggle at the word of
  command.

For he can jump from an eminence into his master's
  bosom.   55

For he can catch the cork and toss it again.

For he is hated by the hypocrite and miser.

For the former is afraid of detection.

For the latter refuses the charge.

For he camels his back to bear the first notion of
  business.   60

For he is good to think on, if a man would express
  himself neatly.

For he is made a great figure in Egypt for his signal
  services.

For he killed the Icneumon-rat very pernicious by
  land.

For his ears are so acute that they sting again.

For from this proceeds the passing quickness of his
  attention.   65

For by stroking of him I have found out electricity.

For I perceived God's light about him both wax and
  fire.

For the electrical fire is the spiritual substance, which

God sends from heaven to sustain the bodies both
  of man and beast.

For God has blessed him in the variety of his
  movements.

For, though he cannot fly, he is an excellent clamberer.

For his motions upon the face of the earth are more
  than any other quadruped.   71

For he can tread to all the measures upon the music.

For he can swim for life

For he can creep.

JUBILATE AGNO: **Jubilate Agno:** rejoice in the lamb 6 **prank:**
mischievously, frolicsomely 63 **Icneumon-rat:** the mongoose

From A SONG TO DAVID

GREAT, valiant, pious, good, and clean,
Sublime, contemplative, serene,
  Strong, constant, pleasant, wise!
Bright effluence of exceeding grace;
Best man! – the swiftness and the race,   5
  The peril, and the prize!

Great – from the lustre of his crown,
From Samuel's horn and God's renown,
  Which is the people's voice;
For all the host, from rear to van,   10
Applauded and embraced the man –
  The man of God's own choice.

Valiant – the word and up he rose –
The fight – he triumphed o'er the foes,
  Whom God's just laws abhor;   15
And, armed in gallant faith, he took
Against the boaster, from the brook,
  The weapons of the war.

Pious – magnificent and grand;
'Twas he the famous temple planned   20
  (The seraph in his soul):
Foremost to give the Lord his dues,
Foremost to bless the welcome news,
  And foremost to condole.

Good – from Jehudah's genuine vein,   25
From God's best nature good in grain,
  His aspect and his heart;
To pity, to forgive, to save,
Witness En-gedi's conscious cave,
  And Shimei's blunted dart.   30

Clean – if perpetual prayer be pure,
And love, which could itself innure
  To fasting and to fear –
Clean in his gestures, hands, and feet,
To smite the lyre, the dance complete,   35
  To play the sword and spear.

Sublime – invention ever young,
Of vast conception, tow'ring tongue,
  To God the eternal theme;
Notes from yon exaltations caught,   40
Unrivalled royalty of thought,
  O'er meaner strains supreme.

Contemplative – on God to fix
His musings, and above the six
  The Sabbath-day he blessed;   45
'Twas then his thoughts self-conquest pruned,
And heavenly melancholy tuned,
  To bless and bear the rest.

Serene – to sow the seeds of peace,
Rememb'ring, when he watched the fleece,   50
  How sweetly Kidron purled –
To further knowledge, silence vice,
And plant perpetual paradise,
  When God had calmed the world.

Strong – in the Lord, who could defy   55
Satan, and all his powers that lie
  In sempiternal night;
And hell, and horror, and despair
Were as the lion and the bear
  To his undaunted might.   60

Constant – in love to God, THE TRUTH,
Age, manhood, infancy, and youth –
  To Jonathan his friend
Constant, beyond the verge of death;
And Ziba, and Mephibosheth,   65
  His endless fame attend.

Pleasant – and various as the year;
Man, soul, and angel, without peer,
  Priest, champion, sage, and boy;
In armour, or in ephod clad,   70
His pomp, his piety was glad;
  Majestic was his joy.

Wise – in recovery from his fall,
Whence rose his eminence o'er all,
  Of all the most reviled;   75
The light of Israel in his ways,
Wise are his precepts, prayer and praise,
  And counsel to his child.

[Lines 19–96]

A SONG TO DAVID: 8 **Samuel's horn:** in the Bible, David was anointed by Samuel using oil contained in a horn 10 **van:** vanguard 16–18 **he took . . . war:** David killed Goliath with a slingshot using stones from a brook 25 **Jehudah:** Judah, David's tribe 26 **good in grain:** thoroughly good 29 **En-gedi:** where David spared Saul, who was trying to kill him 30 **Shimei:** a man who cursed David, who pardoned him 51 **Kidron:** a brook near Jerusalem 57 **sempiternal:** everlasting 59 **lion and the bear:** David defended his sheep from a lion and a bear 65 **Ziba:** servant of Saul, made steward by David to Jonathan's son **Mephibosheth,** to whom David gave the lands of Saul 70 **ephod:** a priest's vestment

JEAN ELLIOT

THE FLOWERS OF
THE FOREST

I'VE heard them lilting, at the ewe milking,
  Lasses a' lilting, before dawn of day;
But now they are moaning, on ilka green loaning;
  The flowers of the forest are a' wede awae.

At bughts in the morning, nae blithe lads are
    scorning;   5
  Lasses are lonely, and dowie and wae;
Nae daffing, nae gabbing, but sighing and sabbing;
  Ilk ane lifts her leglin, and hies her awae.

At har'st at the shearing, nae youths now are
    jearing;
  Bandsters are runkled, and lyart or gray;   10
At fair, or at preaching, nae wooing, nae fleeching;
  The flowers of the forest are a' wede awae.

At e'en in the gloaming, nae younkers are
    roaming,
  'Bout stacks, with the lasses at bogle to play;
But ilk maid sits dreary, lamenting her deary –   15
  The flowers of the forest are weded awae.

Dool and wae for the order, sent our lads to the
    border!
  The English, for ance, by guile wan the day;
The flowers of the forest, that fought aye the foremost,
  The prime of our land are cauld in the clay.   20

We'll hae nae mair lilting at the ewe milking;
  Women and bairns are heartless and wae:
Sighing and moaning, on ilka green loaning –
  The flowers o' the forest are a' wede away.

THE FLOWERS OF THE FOREST: 2 **a':** all 3 **ilka:** each, every **loaning:** milking place 4 **wede awae:** carried off (by death) 5 **bughts:** sheepfolds **scorning:** teasing 6 **dowie:** low-spirited **wae:** sorrowful 7 **daffing:** frolicking **gabbing:** chatting **sabbing:** sobbing 8 **Ilk ane:** each one **leglin:** milk pail 9 **har'st:** harvest **shearing:** reaping 10 **Bandsters:** sheaf-binders **runkled:** wrinkled **lyart:** grizzled 11 **fleeching:** flattering, coaxing 13 **e'en:** evening **gloaming:** twilight **nae younkers:** no youths 14 **bogle:** a chasing game 17 **Dool and wae:** alas 18 **ance:** once **wan:** won 19 **aye:** always 20 **cauld:** cold 21 **mair:** more 22 **bairns:** children

OLIVER GOLDSMITH

THE DESERTED VILLAGE

SWEET Auburn! loveliest village of the plain,
Where health and plenty cheered the labouring swain,
Where smiling spring its earliest visits paid,
And parting summer's lingering blooms delayed:
Dear lovely bowers of innocence and ease,   5
Seats of my youth, when every sport could please,
How often have I loitered o'er thy green,
Where humble happiness endeared each scene;
How often have I paused on every charm,
The sheltered cot, the cultivated farm,   10
The never-failing brook, the busy mill,
The decent church that topped the neighbouring hill,
The hawthorn bush, with seats beneath the shade,
For talking age and whispering lovers made.
How often have I blessed the coming day,   15
When toil remitting lent its turn to play,
And all the village train, from labour free,
Led up their sports beneath the spreading tree,
While many a pastime circled in the shade,
The young contending as the old surveyed;   20
And many a gambol frolicked o'er the ground,
And sleights of art and feats of strength went round.
And still, as each repeated pleasure tired,
Succeeding sports the mirthful band inspired;
The dancing pair that simply sought renown,   25
By holding out to tire each other down;
The swain mistrustless of his smutted face,
While secret laughter tittered round the place;
The bashful virgin's sidelong looks of love,
The matron's glance that would those looks reprove.   30
These were thy charms, sweet village! sports like these,
With sweet succession, taught e'en toil to please;
These round thy bowers their cheerful influence shed;
These were thy charms – but all these charms are fled.
Sweet smiling village, loveliest of the lawn,   35
Thy sports are fled and all thy charms withdrawn;
Amidst thy bowers the tyrant's hand is seen,
And desolation saddens all thy green;
One only master grasps the whole domain,
And half a tillage stints thy smiling plain;   40
No more thy glassy brook reflects the day,
But, choked with sedges, works its weedy way;
Along thy glades, a solitary guest,
The hollow-sounding bittern guards its nest;
Amidst thy desert walks the lapwing flies,   45
And tires their echoes with unvaried cries;
Sunk are thy bowers in shapeless ruin all,
And the long grass o'ertops the mould'ring wall;
And trembling, shrinking from the spoiler's hand,
Far, far away, thy children leave the land.   50

Ill fares the land, to hastening ills a prey,
Where wealth accumulates and men decay:
Princes and lords may flourish or may fade;
A breath can make them, as a breath has made;
But a bold peasantry, their country's pride,   55
When once destroyed, can never be supplied.
A time there was, ere England's griefs began,
When every rood of ground maintained its man;
For him light labour spread her wholesome store,
Just gave what life required, but gave no more: 60
His best companions, innocence and health;
And his best riches, ignorance of wealth.
But times are altered; trade's unfeeling train
Usurp the land and dispossess the swain;
Along the lawn, where scattered hamlets rose,   65
Unwieldy wealth and cumbrous pomp repose;
And every want to opulence allied,
And every pang that folly pays to pride.
Those gentle hours that plenty bade to bloom,
Those calm desires that asked but little room,   70
Those healthful sports that graced the peaceful scene,
Lived in each look and brightened all the green;
These, far departing, seek a kinder shore,
And rural mirth and manners are no more.
Sweet Auburn! parent of the blissful hour,   75
Thy glades forlorn confess the tyrant's power.
Here as I take my solitary rounds,
Amidst thy tangling walks and ruined grounds,
And, many a year elapsed, return to view
Where once the cottage stood, the hawthorn grew,   80
Remembrance wakes with all her busy train,
Swells at my breast, and turns the past to pain.
In all my wanderings round this world of care,
In all my griefs – and God has given my share –
I still had hopes my latest hours to crown,   85
Amidst these humble bowers to lay me down;
To husband out life's taper at the close,
And keep the flame from wasting by repose.
I still had hopes, for pride attends us still,
Amidst the swains to show my book-learned skill,   90
Around my fire an evening group to draw,
And tell of all I felt and all I saw;
And, as a hare whom hounds and horns pursue
Pants to the place from whence at first she flew,
I still had hopes, my long vexations past,   95
Here to return – and die at home at last.
O blest retirement, friend to life's decline,
Retreats from care, that never must be mine,
How happy he who crowns in shades like these
A youth of labour with an age of ease;   100
Who quits a world where strong temptations try
And, since 'tis hard to combat, learns to fly!
For him no wretches, born to work and weep,
Explore the mine or tempt the dangerous deep;
No surly porter stands in guilty state   105

THE DESERTED VILLAGE: 2 **swain**: country youth 10 **cot**: cottage
17 **train**: retinue 27 **mistrustless**: without mistrust 35 **lawn**: plain
39 **One only . . . domain**: refers to the enclosing of hitherto
common ground by landlords

56 **supplied**: restored 58 **rood**: a quarter of an acre 85 **latest**: last
87 **taper**: candle

To spurn imploring famine from the gate;
But on he moves to meet his latter end,
Angels around befriending virtue's friend;
Bends to the grave with unperceived decay,
While resignation gently slopes the way; 110
And, all his prospects brightening to the last,
His heaven commences ere the world be past!
    Sweet was the sound, when oft at evening's close
Up yonder hill the village murmur rose;
There, as I passed with careless steps and slow, 115
The mingling notes came softened from below;
The swain responsive as the milkmaid sung,
The sober herd that lowed to meet their young;
The noisy geese that gabbled o'er the pool,
The playful children just let loose from school; 120
The watchdog's voice that bayed the whispering wind,
And the loud laugh that spoke the vacant mind;
These all in sweet confusion sought the shade,
And filled each pause the nightingale had made.
But now the sounds of population fail, 125
No cheerful murmurs fluctuate in the gale,
No busy steps the grass-grown footway tread,
For all the bloomy flush of life is fled.
All but yon widowed, solitary thing
That feebly bends beside the plashy spring; 130
She, wretched matron, forced, in age, for bread,
To strip the brook with mantling cresses spread,
To pick her wintry faggot from the thorn,
To seek her nightly shed and weep till morn;
She only left of all the harmless train, 135
The sad historian of the pensive plain.
    Near yonder copse, where once the garden smiled,
And still where many a garden flower grows wild;
There, where a few torn shrubs the place disclose,
The village preacher's modest mansion rose. 140
A man he was to all the country dear,
And passing rich with forty pounds a year;
Remote from towns he ran his godly race,
Nor e'er had changed, nor wished to change, his
    place;
Unpractised he to fawn, or seek for power, 145
By doctrines fashioned to the varying hour;
Far other aims his heart had learned to prize,
More skilled to raise the wretched than to rise.
His house was known to all the vagrant train,
He chid their wanderings, but relieved their pain; 150
The long-remembered beggar was his guest,
Whose beard descending swept his agèd breast;
The ruined spendthrift, now no longer proud,
Claimed kindred there and had his claims allowed;
The broken soldier, kindly bade to stay, 155
Sat by his fire and talked the night away;
Wept o'er his wounds, or tales of sorrow done,
Shouldered his crutch, and showed how fields were
    won.

Pleased with his guests, the good man learned to glow,
And quite forgot their vices in their woe; 160
Careless their merits of their faults to scan,
His pity gave ere charity began.
    Thus to relieve the wretched was his pride,
And e'en his failings leaned to virtue's side;
But in his duty prompt at every call, 165
He watched and wept, he prayed and felt, for all.
And, as a bird each fond endearment tries
To tempt its new-fledged offspring to the skies,
He tried each art, reproved each dull delay,
Allured to brighter worlds and led the way. 170
    Beside the bed where parting life was laid,
And sorrow, guilt, and pain by turns dismayed,
The reverend champion stood. At his control,
Despair and anguish fled the struggling soul;
Comfort came down the trembling wretch to raise, 175
And his last faltering accents whispered praise.
    At church, with meek and unaffected grace,
His looks adorned the venerable place;
Truth from his lips prevailed with double sway,
And fools, who came to scoff, remained to pray. 180
The service past, around the pious man,
With steady zeal, each honest rustic ran;
E'en children followed with endearing wile,
And plucked his gown, to share the good man's smile.
His ready smile a parent's warmth expressed, 185
Their welfare pleased him and their cares distressed;
To them his heart, his love, his griefs were given,
But all his serious thoughts had rest in heaven.
As some tall cliff that lifts its awful form,
Swells from the vale, and midway leaves the storm, 190
Though round its breast the rolling clouds are spread,
Eternal sunshine settles on its head.
    Beside yon straggling fence that skirts the way,
With blossomed furze unprofitably gay,
There, in his noisy mansion, skilled to rule, 195
The village master taught his little school;
A man severe he was, and stern to view;
I knew him well, and every truant knew;
Well had the boding tremblers learned to trace
The day's disasters in his morning face; 200
Full well they laughed, with counterfeited glee,
At all his jokes, for many a joke had he;
Full well the busy whisper, circling round,
Conveyed the dismal tidings when he frowned;
Yet he was kind, or, if severe in aught, 205
The love he bore to learning was in fault;
The village all declared how much he knew;
'Twas certain he could write and cipher too;
Lands he could measure, terms and tides presage,
And even the story ran that he could gauge. 210
In arguing too, the parson owned his skill,
For even though vanquished, he could argue still;

132 **mantling:** covering 134 **shed:** shelter 142 **passing:** very

199 **boding tremblers:** pupils trembling in expectation of
punishment 208 **cipher:** spell 209 **terms:** term days **tides:** festivals
210 **gauge:** measure the contents of casks 211 **owned:** admitted

While words of learnèd length, and thundering sound
Amazed the gazing rustics ranged around,
And still they gazed, and still the wonder grew, 215
That one small head could carry all he knew.
But past is all his fame. The very spot
Where many a time he triumphed is forgot.

   Near yonder thorn, that lifts its head on high,
Where once the signpost caught the passing eye, 220
Low lies that house where nutbrown draughts
   inspired,
Where greybeard mirth and smiling toil retired,
Where village statesmen talked with looks profound,
And news much older than their ale went round.
Imagination fondly stoops to trace 225
The parlour splendours of that festive place;
The whitewashed wall, the nicely sanded floor,
The varnished clock that clicked behind the door;
The chest contrived a double debt to pay,
A bed by night, a chest of drawers by day; 230
The pictures placed for ornament and use,
The twelve good rules, the royal game of goose;
The hearth, except when winter chilled the day,
With aspen boughs and flowers and fennel gay;
While broken tea-cups, wisely kept for show, 235
Ranged o'er the chimney, glistened in a row.

   Vain, transitory splendours! Could not all
Reprieve the tottering mansion from its fall!
Obscure it sinks, nor shall it more impart
An hour's importance to the poor man's heart; 240
Thither no more the peasant shall repair
To sweet oblivion of his daily care;
No more the farmer's news, the barber's tale,
No more the woodman's ballad shall prevail;
No more the smith his dusky brow shall clear, 245
Relax his ponderous strength and lean to hear;
The host himself no longer shall be found
Careful to see the mantling bliss go round;
Nor the coy maid, half willing to be pressed,
Shall kiss the cup to pass it to the rest. 250

   Yes! let the rich deride, the proud disdain,
These simple blessings of the lowly train;
To me more dear, congenial to my heart,
One native charm than all the gloss of art;
Spontaneous joys, where Nature has its play, 255
The soul adopts and owns their first-born sway;
Lightly they frolic o'er the vacant mind,
Unenvied, unmolested, unconfined.
But the long pomp, the midnight masquerade,
With all the freaks of wanton wealth arrayed, 260
In these, ere triflers half their wish obtain,
The toiling pleasure sickens into pain;
And, e'en while fashion's brightest arts decoy,
The heart distrusting asks if this be joy.

   Ye friends to truth, ye statesmen, who survey 265
The rich man's joys increase, the poor's decay,

'Tis yours to judge how wide the limits stand
Between a splendid and a happy land.
Proud swells the tide with loads of freighted ore,
And shouting Folly hails them from her shore; 270
Hoards e'en beyond the miser's wish abound,
And rich men flock from all the world around.
Yet count our gains! This wealth is but a name
That leaves our useful products still the same.
Not so the loss. The man of wealth and pride 275
Takes up a space that many poor supplied;
Space for his lake, his park's extended bounds,
Space for his horses, equipage and hounds;
The robe that wraps his limbs in silken sloth
Has robbed the neighbouring fields of half their
   growth; 280
His seat, where solitary sports are seen,
Indignant spurns the cottage from the green;
Around the world each needful product flies,
For all the luxuries the world supplies;
While thus the land, adorned for pleasure all, 285
In barren splendour feebly waits the fall.

   As some fair female unadorned and plain,
Secure to please while youth confirms her reign,
Slights every borrowed charm that dress supplies,
Nor shares with art the triumph of her eyes; 290
But when those charms are passed, for charms are
   frail,
When time advances and when lovers fail,
She then shines forth, solicitous to bless,
In all the glaring impotence of dress:
Thus fares the land, by luxury betrayed, 295
In Nature's simplest charms at first arrayed;
But verging to decline, its splendours rise,
Its vistas strike, its palaces surprise;
While, scourged by famine from the smiling land,
The mournful peasant leads his humble band; 300
And while he sinks, without one arm to save,
The country blooms – a garden and a grave.

   Where then, ah! where, shall poverty reside,
To 'scape the pressure of contiguous pride?
If to some common's fenceless limits strayed, 305
He drives his flock to pick the scanty blade,
Those fenceless fields the sons of wealth divide,
And e'en the bare-worn common is denied.

   If to the city sped – what waits him there?
To see profusion that he must not share; 310
To see ten thousand baneful arts combined
To pamper luxury and thin mankind;
To see those joys the sons of pleasure know
Extorted from his fellow-creature's woe.
Here while the courtier glitters in brocade, 315
There the pale artist plies the sickly trade;
Here while the proud their long-drawn pomps display,
There the black gibbet glooms beside the way.
The dome where Pleasure holds her midnight reign
Here, richly decked, admits the gorgeous train; 320
Tumultuous grandeur crowds the blazing square,
The rattling chariots clash, the torches glare.

---

221 **nutbrown draughts:** drinks of beer 232 **goose:** an old board game
241 **repair:** go

Sure, scenes like these no troubles e'er annoy!
Sure, these denote one universal joy!
Are these thy serious thoughts? Ah, turn thine eyes   325
Where the poor, houseless, shivering female lies.
She once, perhaps, in village plenty blessed,
Has wept at tales of innocence distressed;
Her modest looks the cottage might adorn,
Sweet as the primrose peeps beneath the thorn;   330
Now lost to all; her friends, her virtue fled,
Near her betrayer's door she lays her head,
And pinched with cold and shrinking from the shower,
With heavy heart deplores that luckless hour,
When idly first, ambitious of the town,   335
She left her wheel and robes of country brown.

Do thine, sweet Auburn, thine, the loveliest train,
Do thy fair tribes participate her pain?
Even now, perhaps, by cold and hunger led,
At proud men's doors they ask a little bread!   340

Ah, no! To distant climes, a dreary scene,
Where half the convex world intrudes between,
Through torrid tracts with fainting steps they go,
Where wild Altama murmurs to their woe.
Far different there from all that charmed before   345
The various terrors of that horrid shore:
Those blazing suns that dart a downward ray,
And fiercely shed intolerable day;
Those matted woods where birds forget to sing,
But silent bats in drowsy clusters cling;   350
Those poisonous fields with rank luxuriance crowned,
Where the dark scorpion gathers death around;
Where at each step the stranger fears to wake
The rattling terrors of the vengeful snake;
Where crouching tigers wait their hapless prey,   355
And savage men more murderous still than they;
While oft in whirls the mad tornado flies,
Mingling the ravaged landscape with the skies.
Far different these from every former scene,
The cooling brook, the grassy-vested green,   360
The breezy covert of the warbling grove,
That only sheltered thefts of harmless love.

Good Heaven! what sorrows gloomed that parting
day,
That called them from their native walks away;
When the poor exiles, every pleasure past,   365
Hung round their bowers and fondly looked their last,
And took a long farewell, and wished in vain
For seats like these beyond the westering main;
And shuddering still to face the distant deep,
Returned and wept, and still returned to weep.   370
The good old sire the first prepared to go
To new-found worlds. and wept for others' woe;
But for himself, in conscious virtue brave,
He only wished for worlds beyond the grave.
His lovely daughter, lovelier in her tears,   375

The fond companion of his helpless years,
Silent went next, neglectful of her charms,
And left a lover's for a father's arms.
With louder plaints the mother spoke her woes,
And blessed the cot where every pleasure rose;   380
And kissed her thoughtless babes with many a tear,
And clasped them close, in sorrow doubly dear;
Whilst her fond husband strove to lend relief
In all the silent manliness of grief.

O Luxury! thou cursed by heaven's decree,   385
How ill exchanged are things like these for thee!
How do thy potions with insidious joy
Diffuse their pleasure only to destroy!
Kingdoms, by thee to sickly greatness grown,
Boast of a florid vigour not their own.   390
At every draught more large and large they grow,
A bloated mass of rank unwieldy woe;
Till sapped their strength and every part unsound,
Down, down they sink and spread a ruin round.

E'en now the devastation is begun,   395
And half the business of destruction done;
E'en now, methinks, as pondering here I stand,
I see the rural virtues leave the land.
Down where yon anchoring vessel spreads the sail,
That idly waiting flaps with every gale,   400
Downward they move, a melancholy band,
Pass from the shore and darken all the strand.
Contented toil and hospitable care,
And kind connubial tenderness are there;
And piety, with wishes placed above,   405
And steady loyalty and faithful love.

And thou, sweet Poetry, thou loveliest maid,
Still first to fly where sensual joys invade;
Unfit, in these degenerate times of shame,
To catch the heart or strike for honest fame;   410
Dear charming nymph, neglected and decried,
My shame in crowds, my solitary pride;
Thou source of all my bliss and all my woe,
That found'st me poor at first and keep'st me so;
Thou guide by which the nobler arts excel,   415
Thou nurse of every virtue, fare thee well!
Farewell, and, oh! where'er thy voice be tried,
On Torno's cliffs or Pambamarca's side,
Whether where equinoctial fervours glow,
Or winter wraps the polar world in snow,   420
Still let thy voice, prevailing over time,
Redress the rigours of th'inclement clime;
Aid slighted truth; with thy persuasive strain
Teach erring man to spurn the rage of gain;
Teach him that states of native strength possessed,   425
Though very poor, may still be very blessed;
That trade's proud empire hastes to swift decay,
As ocean sweeps the laboured mole away;
While self-dependent power can time defy,
As rocks resist the billows and the sky.   430

---

344 **Altama:** the Altamaha, a river in Georgia, site of a colony founded by James Oglethorpe (1696–1785), a philanthropist and friend of Goldsmith 355 **tigers:** cougars

379 **plaints:** complaints 418 **Torno:** a place in Lapland **Pambamarca:** a place in Ecuador 419 **equinoctial fervours:** equatorial heat 428 **laboured:** constructed with great manual labour

'WHEN LOVELY WOMAN STOOPS TO FOLLY'

WHEN lovely woman stoops to folly,
  And finds too late that men betray,
What charm can soothe her melancholy?
  What art can wash her guilt away?

The only art her guilt to cover,   5
  To hide her shame from every eye,
To give repentance to her lover,
  And wring his bosom, is – to die.

From 'The Vicar of Wakefield'

WILLIAM COWPER

VERSES

SUPPOSED TO BE WRITTEN BY ALEXANDER SELKIRK,
DURING HIS SOLITARY ABODE IN THE
ISLAND OF JUAN FERNANDEZ

I AM monarch of all I survey,
  My right there is none to dispute;
From the centre all round to the sea,
  I am lord of the fowl and the brute.
O Solitude! where are the charms   5
  That sages have seen in thy face?
Better dwell in the midst of alarms
  Than reign in this horrible place.

I am out of humanity's reach,
  I must finish my journey alone,   10
Never hear the sweet music of speech;
  I start at the sound of my own.
The beasts that roam over the plain
  My form with indifference see;
They are so unacquainted with man,   15
  Their tameness is shocking to me.

Society, friendship, and love,
  Divinely bestowed upon man,
Oh, had I the wings of a dove
  How soon would I taste you again!   20
My sorrows I then might assuage
  In the ways of religion and truth,
Might learn from the wisdom of age,
  And be cheered by the sallies of youth.

Religion! what treasure untold   25
  Resides in that heavenly word!
More precious than silver and gold,
  Or all that this earth can afford.
But the sound of the church-going bell
  These valleys and rocks never heard,   30
Ne'er sighed at the sound of a knell,
  Or smiled when a sabbath appeared.

Ye winds, that have made me your sport,
  Convey to this desolate shore
Some cordial endearing report   35
  Of a land I shall visit no more.
My friends, do they now and then send
  A wish or a thought after me?
Oh, tell me I yet have a friend,
  Though a friend I am never to see.   40

How fleet is the glance of the mind!
  Compared with the speed of its flight,
The tempest itself lags behind,
  And the swift-winged arrows of light.
When I think of my own native land,   45
  In a moment I seem to be there;
But, alas! recollection at hand
  Soon hurries me back to despair.

But the sea-fowl is gone to her nest,
  The beast is laid down in his lair,   50
Even here is a season of rest,
  And I to my cabin repair.
There is mercy in every place;
  And mercy – encouraging thought! –
Gives even affliction a grace   55
  And reconciles man to his lot.

THE POPLAR-FIELD

THE poplars are felled, farewell to the shade
And the whispering sound of the cool colonnade,
The winds play no longer and sing in the leaves,
Nor Ouse on his bosom their image receives.

Twelve years have elapsed since I first took a view 5
Of my favourite field and the bank where they grew,
And now in the grass behold they are laid,
And the tree is my seat that once lent me a shade.

The blackbird has fled to another retreat
Where the hazels afford him a screen from the heat, 10
And the scene where his melody charmed me before
Resounds with his sweet-flowing ditty no more.

My fugitive years are all hasting away,
And I must ere long lie as lowly as they,
With a turf on my breast and a stone at my head,   15
Ere another such grove shall arise in its stead.

'Tis a sight to engage me, if anything can,
To muse on the perishing pleasures of man;
Though his life be a dream, his enjoyments, I see,
Have a being less durable even than he.   20

THE CASTAWAY

OBSCUREST night involved the sky,
  Th'Atlantic billows roared,
When such a destined wretch as I,
  Washed headlong from on board,
Of friends, of hope, of all bereft,
His floating home forever left.

No braver chief could Albion boast
  Than he with whom he went,
Nor ever ship left Albion's coast
  With warmer wishes sent.
He loved them both, but both in vain,
Nor him beheld, nor her again.

Not long beneath the whelming brine,
  Expert to swim, he lay;
Nor soon he felt his strength decline,
  Or courage die away;
But waged with death a lasting strife,
Supported by despair of life.

He shouted: nor his friends had failed
  To check the vessel's course,
But so the furious blast prevailed
  That, pitiless perforce,
They left their outcast mate behind,
And scudded still before the wind.

Some succour yet they could afford;
  And, such as storms allow,
The cask, the coop, the floated cord,
  Delayed not to bestow.
But he (they knew) nor ship, nor shore,
Whate'er they gave, should visit more.

Nor, cruel as it seemed, could he
  Their haste himself condemn,
Aware that flight, in such a sea,
  Alone could rescue them;
Yet bitter felt it still to die
Deserted, and his friends so nigh.

He long survives, who lives an hour
  In ocean, self-upheld;
And so long he, with unspent pow'r,
  His destiny repelled;
And ever, as the minutes flew,
Entreated help, or cried – Adieu!

At length, his transient respite past,
  His comrades, who before
Had heard his voice in ev'ry blast,
  Could catch the sound no more.
For then, by toil subdued, he drank
The stifling wave, and then he sank.

No poet wept him: but the page
  Of narrative sincere,
That tells his name, his worth, his age,
  Is wet with Anson's tear.
And tears by bards or heroes shed
Alike immortalise the dead.

I therefore purpose not, or dream,
  Descanting on his fate,
To give the melancholy theme
  A more enduring date:
But misery still delights to trace
Its semblance in another's case.

No voice divine the storm allayed,
  No light propitious shone;
When, snatched from all effectual aid,
  We perished, each alone:
But I beneath a rougher sea,
And whelmed in deeper gulfs than he.

THE CASTAWAY: 7 **Albion**: Britain or England 27 **coop**: a wicker basket for catching fish 52 **Anson**: George Anson, 1st Baron Anson (1697–1762), led a squadron of British ships on a voyage of circumnavigation. Cowper's poem is based on an incident during this voyage in which a man was lost overboard while rounding the Horn

LIGHT SHINING OUT OF DARKNESS

GOD moves in a mysterious way
  His wonders to perform;
He plants his footsteps in the sea,
  And rides upon the storm.

Deep in unfathomable mines
  Of never-failing skill
He treasures up his bright designs,
  And works his sovereign will.

Ye fearful saints, fresh courage take,
  The clouds ye so much dread
Are big with mercy, and shall break
  In blessings on your head.

Judge not the Lord by feeble sense,
  But trust him for his grace;
Behind a frowning providence,
  He hides a smiling face.

His purposes will ripen fast,
  Unfolding ev'ry hour;
The bud may have a bitter taste,
  But sweet will be the flow'r.

Blind unbelief is sure to err,
  And scan his work in vain;
God is his own interpreter,
  And he will make it plain.

From THE TASK

ENGLAND! with all thy faults, I love thee still –
My country! and, while yet a nook is left
Where English minds and manners may be found,
Shall be constrained to love thee. Though thy clime
Be fickle, and thy year most part deformed   5
With dripping rains, or withered by a frost,
I would not yet exchange thy sullen skies,
And fields without a flow'r, for warmer France
With all her vines; nor for Ausonia's groves
Of golden fruitage, and her myrtle bow'rs.   10
To shake thy senate, and from heights sublime
Of patriot eloquence to flash down fire
Upon thy foes, was never meant my task:
But I can feel thy fortunes, and partake
Thy joys and sorrows, with as true a heart   15
As any thund'rer there. And I can feel
Thy follies, too; and with a just disdain
Frown at effeminates, whose very looks
Reflect dishonour on the land I love.
How, in the name of soldiership and sense,   20
Should England prosper, when such things, as smooth
And tender as a girl, all essenced o'er
With odours, and as profligate as sweet;
Who sell their laurel for a myrtle wreath,
And love when they should fight; when such as these
Presume to lay their hand upon the ark   26
Of her magnificent and awful cause?
Time was when it was praise and boast enough
In ev'ry clime, and travel where we might,
That we were born her children. Praise enough   30
To fill th' ambition of a private man,
That Chatham's language was his mother tongue,
And Wolfe's great name compatriot with his own.
Farewell those honours, and farewell with them
The hope of such hereafter! They have fall'n   35
Each in his field of glory; one in arms,
And one in council – Wolfe upon the lap
Of smiling victory that moment won,
And Chatham heart-sick of his country's shame!
They made us many soldiers. Chatham, still   40
Consulting England's happiness at home,
Secured it by an unforgiving frown,
If any wronged her. Wolfe, where'er he fought,
Put so much of his heart into his act,
That his example had a magnet's force,   45
And all were swift to follow whom all loved.
Those suns are set. Oh, rise some other such!
Or all that we have left is empty talk
Of old achievements, and despair of new.

[Book 2, 'The Time-Piece', lines 206–54]

THE night was winter in his roughest mood;
The morning sharp and clear. But now at noon
Upon the southern side of the slant hills,
And where the woods fence off the northern blast,
The season smiles, resigning all its rage,   5
And has the warmth of May. The vault is blue
Without a cloud, and white without a speck
The dazzling splendour of the scene below.
Again the harmony comes o'er the vale;
And through the trees I view th'embattled tow'r   10
Whence all the music. I again perceive
The soothing influence of the wafted strains,
And settle in soft musings as I tread
The walk, still verdant, under oaks and elms,
Whose outspread branches overarch the glade.   15
The roof, though moveable through all its length
As the wind sways it, has yet well sufficed,
And, intercepting in their silent fall
The frequent flakes, has kept a path for me.
No noise is here, or none that hinders thought.   20
The redbreast warbles still, but is content
With slender notes, and more than half suppressed:
Pleased with his solitude, and flitting light
From spray to spray, where'er he rests he shakes
From many a twig the pendent drops of ice,   25
That tinkle in the withered leaves below.
Stillness, accompanied with sounds so soft,
Charms more than silence. Meditation here
May think down hours to moments. Here the heart
May give an useful lesson to the head,   30
And learning wiser grow without his books.
Knowledge and wisdom, far from being one,
Have oft-times no connection. Knowledge dwells
In heads replete with thoughts of other men;
Wisdom in minds attentive to their own.   35
Knowledge, a rude unprofitable mass,
The mere materials with which wisdom builds,
Till smoothed and squared and fitted to its place,
Does but encumber whom it seems t'enrich.
Knowledge is proud that he has learned so much;   40
Wisdom is humble that he knows no more.
Books are not seldom talismans and spells,
By which the magic art of shrewder wits
Holds an unthinking multitude enthralled.
Some to the fascination of a name   45
Surrender judgement, hoodwinked. Some the style
Infatuates, and through labyrinths and wilds
Of error leads them by a tune entranced.
While sloth seduces more, too weak to bear
The insupportable fatigue of thought,   50
And swallowing, therefore, without pause or choice,
The total grist unsifted, husks and all.
But trees, and rivulets whose rapid course
Defies the check of winter, haunts of deer,
And sheep-walks populous with bleating lambs,   55

THE TASK: BOOK 2: 9 **Ausonia:** a poetical name for Italy   24 **sell . . . wreath:** prefer a merely decorative wreath to one awarded to a victor   32 **Chatham:** William Pitt, 1st Earl of Chatham (1708–78), English politician and prime minister. At his death he was dismayed by the prospect of American independence breaking up the empire he had helped create   33 **Wolfe:** James Wolfe (1727–59), English soldier whose victory at Quebec (in which he himself was killed) won Canada for Britain

BOOK 6: 24 **spray:** branch   54 **Defies the check of winter:** is not frozen in winter

And lanes in which the primrose ere her time
Peeps through the moss that clothes the hawthorn
    root,
Deceive no student. Wisdom there, and truth,
Not shy, as in the world, and to be won
By slow solicitation, seize at once   60
The roving thought, and fix it on themselves.
    What prodigies can pow'r divine perform
More grand than it produces year by year,
And all in sight of inattentive man?
Familiar with th'effect we slight the cause,   65
And, in the constancy of nature's course,
The regular return of genial months,
And renovation of a faded world,
See nought to wonder at. Should God again,
As once in Gibeon, interrupt the race   70
Of the undeviating and punctual sun,
How would the world admire! but speaks it less
An agency divine, to make him know
His moment when to sink and when to rise,
Age after age, than to arrest his course?   75
All we behold is miracle; but, seen
So duly, all is miracle in vain.
Where now the vital energy that moved,
While summer was, the pure and subtle lymph
Through th'imperceptible meand'ring veins   80
Of leaf and flow'r? It sleeps; and th'icy touch
Of unprolific winter has impressed
A cold stagnation on th'intestine tide.
But let the months go round, a few short months,
And all shall be restored. These naked shoots,   85
Barren as lances, among which the wind
Makes wintry music, sighing as it goes,
Shall put their graceful foliage on again,
And, more aspiring, and with ampler spread,
Shall boast new charms, and more than they have lost.
Then, each in its peculiar honours clad,   91
Shall publish, even to the distant eye,
Its family and tribe. Laburnum, rich
In streaming gold; syringa, iv'ry pure;
The scentless and the scented rose; this red   95
And of an humbler growth, the other tall,
And throwing up into the darkest gloom
Of neighb'ring cypress, or more sable yew,
Her silver globes, light as the foamy surf
That the wind severs from the broken wave;   100
The lilac, various in array, now white,
Now sanguine, and her beauteous head now set
With purple spikes pyramidal, as if,
Studious of ornament, yet unresolved
Which hue she most approved, she chose them all;
Copious of flow'rs the woodbine, pale and wan,   106
But well compensating her sickly looks
With never-cloying odours, early and late;
Hypericum, all bloom, so thick a swarm

Of flow'rs, like flies clothing her slender rods,   110
That scarce a leaf appears; mezerion, too,
Though leafless, well attired, and thick beset
With blushing wreaths, investing ev'ry spray;
Althaea with the purple eye; the broom,
Yellow and bright, as bullion unalloyed,   115
Her blossoms; and, luxuriant above all,
The jasmine, throwing wide her elegant sweets,
The deep dark green of whose unvarnished leaf
Makes more conspicuous, and illumines more
The bright profusion of her scattered stars. –   120
These have been, and these shall be in their day;
And all this uniform, uncoloured scene,
Shall be dismantled of its fleecy load,
And flush into variety again.
From dearth to plenty, and from death to life,   125
Is Nature's progress when she lectures man
In heavenly truth; evincing, as she makes
The grand transition, that there lives and works
A soul in all things, and that soul is God.
The beauties of the wilderness are his,   130
That make so gay the solitary place
Where no eye sees them. And the fairer forms
That cultivation glories in, are his.
He sets the bright procession on its way,
And marshals all the order of the year;   135
He marks the bounds which winter may not pass,
And blunts his pointed fury; in its case,
Russet and rude, folds up the tender germ,
Uninjured, with inimitable art;
And, ere one flow'ry season fades and dies,   140
Designs the blooming wonders of the next.
    Some say that, in the origin of things,
When all creation started into birth,
The infant elements received a law,
From which they swerve not since. That under force
Of that controlling ordinance they move,   146
And need not his immediate hand, who first
Prescribed their course, to regulate it now.
Thus dream they, and contrive to save a God
Th'incumbrance of his own concerns, and spare   150
The great Artificer of all that moves
The stress of a continual act, the pain
Of unremitted vigilance and care,
As too laborious and severe a task.
So man, the moth, is not afraid, it seems,   155
To span omnipotence, and measure might
That knows no measure, by the scanty rule
And standard of his own, that is today,
And is not ere tomorrow's sun go down!
But how should matter occupy a charge   160
Dull as it is, and satisfy a law
So vast in its demands, unless impelled
To ceaseless service by a ceaseless force,
And under pressure of some conscious cause?

83 **intestine**: internal   98 **sable**: black

138 **rude**: rough   **germ**: seed

The Lord of all, himself through all diffused, 165
Sustains, and is the life of all that lives.
Nature is but a name for an effect,
Whose cause is God. He feels the secret fire
By which the mighty process is maintained,
Who sleeps not, is not weary; in whose sight 170
Slow circling ages are as transient days;
Whose work is without labour; whose designs
No flaw deforms, no difficulty thwarts;
And whose beneficence no charge exhausts.
Him blind antiquity profaned, not served, 175
With self-taught rites, and under various names,
Female and male, Pomona, Pales, Pan,
And Flora, and Vertumnus; peopling earth
With tutelary goddesses and gods
That were not; and commending, as they would, 180
To each some province, garden, field, or grove.
But all are under one. One spirit – His
Who wore the platted thorns with bleeding brows –
Rules universal nature. Not a flow'r
But shows some touch, in freckle, streak, or stain,
Of his unrivalled pencil. He inspires 186
Their balmy odours. and imparts their hues,
And bathes their eyes with nectar, and includes,
In grains as countless as the sea-side sands,
The forms with which he sprinkles all the earth. 190
Happy who walks with him! whom what he finds
Of flavour or of scent in fruit or flow'r,
Or what he views of beautiful or grand
In nature, from the broad majestic oak
To the green blade that twinkles in the sun, 195
Prompts with remembrance of a present God!
His presence, who made all so fair, perceived,
Makes all still fairer. As with him no scene
Is dreary, so with him all seasons please.
Though winter had been none, had man been true,
And earth be punished for its tenant's sake, 201
Yet not in vengeance; as this smiling sky,
So soon succeeding such an angry night,
And these dissolving snows, and this clear stream
Recov'ring fast its liquid music, prove. 205
    Who then, that has a mind well strung and tuned
To contemplation, and within his reach
A scene so friendly to his fav'rite task,
Would waste attention at the chequered board,
His host of wooden warriors to and fro 210
Marching and counter-marching, with an eye
As fixed as marble, with a forehead ridged
And furrowed into storms, and with a hand

Trembling, as if eternity were hung
In balance on his conduct of a pin? – 215
Nor envies he aught more their idle sport,
Who pant with application misapplied
To trivial toys, and, pushing iv'ry balls
Across a velvet level, feel a joy
Akin to rapture when the bauble finds 220
Its destined goal, of difficult accéss. –
Nor deems he wiser him, who gives his noon
To miss, the mercer's plague, from shop to shop
Wand'ring, and litt'ring with unfolded silks
The polished counter, and approving none, 225
Or promising with smiles to call again. –
Nor him, who by his vanity seduced,
And soothed into a dream that he discerns
The diff'rence of a Guido from a daub,
Frequents the crowded auction: stationed there 230
As duly as the Langford of the show,
With glass at eye, and catalogue in hand,
And tongue accomplished in the fulsome cant
And pedantry that coxcombs learn with ease;
Oft as the price-deciding hammer falls 235
He notes it in his book, then raps his box,
Swears 'tis a bargain, rails at his hard fate
That he has let it pass – but never bids!
    Here, unmolested, through whatever sign
The sun proceeds, I wander. Neither mist, 240
Nor freezing sky nor sultry, checking me,
Nor stranger intermeddling with my joy.
Ev'n in the spring and playtime of the year,
That calls th'unwonted villager abroad
With all her little ones, a sportive train, 245
To gather kingcups in the yellow mead,
And prink their hair with daisies, or to pick
A cheap but wholesome salad from the brook,
These shades are all my own. The tim'rous hare,
Grown so familiar with her frequent guest, 250
Scarce shuns me; and the stockdove, unalarmed,
Sits cooing in the pine-tree, nor suspends
His long love-ditty for my near approach.
Drawn from his refuge in some lonely elm
That age or injury has hollowed deep, 255
Where, on his bed of wool and matted leaves,
He has outslept the winter, ventures forth
To frisk awhile, and bask in the warm sun,
The squirrel, flippant, pert, and full of play:
He sees me, and at once, swift as a bird, 260
Ascends the neighb'ring beech; there whisks his brush,
And perks his ears, and stamps and cries aloud,
With all the prettiness of feigned alarm,
And anger insignificantly fierce.

---

177 **Pomona:** Roman goddess of gardens and fruit trees **Pales:** Roman god or goddess of sheepfolds and pastures **Pan:** Greek god of pastures, forests, flocks and herds 178 **Flora:** Roman goddess of flowers **Vertumnus:** Roman god of the seasons, gardens and orchards 183 **platted:** woven (a reference to Christ's crown of thorns) 200 **Though . . . true:** refers to the belief that man's fall (in the garden of Eden) changed the pleasant climate of Eden to one in which seasons rotated 209 **chequered board:** board for chess or draughts

218 **iv'ry balls:** billiard balls 223 **the mercer's plague:** the young lady who plagues the textile seller 229 **Guido:** Guido Reni (1575–1642), an Italian baroque painter 231 **Langford:** Abraham Langford (1711–74), a well-known auctioneer 239 **sign:** sign of the zodiac 244 **unwonted:** unaccustomed 246 **mead:** meadow 247 **prink:** decorate, adorn

The heart is hard in nature, and unfit 265
For human fellowship, as being void
Of sympathy, and therefore dead alike
To love and friendship both, that is not pleased
With sight of animals enjoying life,
Nor feels their happiness augment his own. 270
The bounding fawn, that darts across the glade
When none pursues, through mere delight of heart,
And spirits buoyant with excess of glee;
The horse as wanton, and almost as fleet,
That skims the spacious meadow at full speed, 275
Then stops and snorts, and, throwing high his heels,
Starts to the voluntary race again;
The very kine that gambol at high noon,
The total herd receiving first from one
That leads the dance a summons to be gay, 280
Though wild their strange vagáries, and uncouth
Their efforts, yet resolved with one consent
To give such act and utt'rance as they may
To ecstasy too big to be suppressed –
These, and a thousand images of bliss, 285
With which kind nature graces ev'ry scene
Where cruel man defeats not her design,
Impart to the benevolent, who wish
All that are capable of pleasure pleased,
A far superior happiness to theirs, 290
The comfort of a reasonable joy.

[Book 6, 'The Winter Walk at Noon', lines 57–347]

278 **kine:** cattle

GEORGE CRABBE

From THE BOROUGH

PETER GRIMES

OLD Peter Grimes made fishing his employ,
His wife he cabined with him and his boy,
And seemed that life laborious to enjoy:
To town came quiet Peter with his fish,
And had of all a civil word and wish. 5
He left his trade upon the Sabbath-day,
And took young Peter in his hand to pray:
But soon the stubborn boy from care broke loose,
At first refused, then added his abuse:
His father's love he scorned, his power defied, 10
But being drunk, wept sorely when he died.
Yes! then he wept, and to his mind there came
Much of his conduct, and he felt the shame, –
How he had oft the good old man reviled,
And never paid the duty of a child; 15
How, when the father in his Bible read,

PETER GRIMES: 3 **laborious:** arduous, demanding

He in contempt and anger left the shed:
'It is the word of life,' the parent cried;
– 'This is the life itself,' the boy replied,
And while old Peter in amazement stood, 20
Gave the hot spirit to his boiling blood: –
How he, with oath and furious speech, began
To prove his freedom and assert the man;
And when the parent checked his impious rage,
How he had cursed the tyranny of age, – 25
Nay, once had dealt the sacrilegious blow
On his bare head, and laid his parent low;
The father groaned – 'If thou art old,' said he,
'And hast a son – thou wilt remember me:
Thy mother left me in a happy time, 30
Thou killed'st not her – heaven spares the double
    crime.'
On an inn-settle, in his maudlin grief,
This he revolved, and drank for his relief.
Now lived the youth in freedom, but debarred
From constant pleasure, and he thought it hard; 35
Hard that he could not every wish obey,
But must awhile relinquish ale and play;
Hard! that he could not to his cards attend,
But must acquire the money he would spend.
With greedy eye he looked on all he saw, 40
He knew not justice, and he laughed at law;
On all he marked, he stretched his ready hand;
He fished by water and he filched by land:
Oft in the night has Peter dropped his oar,
Fled from his boat, and sought for prey on shore; 45
Oft up the hedgerow glided, on his back Bearing
the orchard's produce in a sack,
Or farmyard load, tugged fiercely from the stack;
And as these wrongs to greater numbers rose,
The more he looked on all men as his foes. 50
He built a mud-walled hovel, where he kept
His various wealth, and there he oft-times slept;
But no success could please his cruel soul,
He wished for one to trouble and control;
He wanted some obedient boy to stand 55
And bear the blow of his outrageous hand;
And hoped to find in some propitious hour
A feeling creature subject to his power.
Peter had heard there were in London then, –
Still have they being! – workhouse-clearing men, 60
Who, undisturbed by feelings just or kind,
Would parish-boys to needy tradesmen bind:
They in their want a trifling sum would take,
And toiling slaves of piteous orphans make.
Such Peter sought, and when a lad was found, 65
The sum was dealt him, and the slave was bound.

28 **If thou art old:** if you live to be an old man 32 **settle:** high-backed wooden bench 33 **revolved:** pondered 60–64 **workhouse-clearing . . . make:** this practice was already well established by the time Crabbe published *The Borough* (1810); its best-known victim was, of course, Oliver Twist

Some few in town observed in Peter's trap
A boy, with jacket blue and woollen cap;
But none enquired how Peter used the rope,
Or what the bruise, that made the stripling stoop;
None could the ridges on his back behold, 71
None sought him shiv'ring in the winter's cold;
None put the question, 'Peter, dost thou give
The boy his food? – What, man! the lad must live:
Consider, Peter, let the child have bread, 75
He'll serve thee better if he's stroked and fed.'
None reasoned thus – and some, on hearing cries,
Said calmly, 'Grimes is at his exercise.'
    Pinned, beaten, cold, pinched, threatened, and
      abused –
His efforts punished and his food refused, – 80
Awake tormented, – soon aroused from sleep, –
Struck if he wept, and yet compelled to weep,
The trembling boy dropped down and strove to pray,
Received a blow, and trembling turned away,
Or sobbed and hit his piteous face; – while he, 85
The savage master, grinned in horrid glee:
He'd now the power he ever loved to show,
A feeling being subject to his blow.
    Thus lived the lad, in hunger, peril, pain,
His tears despised, his supplications vain:
Compelled by fear to lie, by need to steal,
His bed uneasy and unbless'd his meal,
For three sad years the boy his tortures bore,
And then his pains and trials were no more.
    'How died he, Peter?' when the people said, 95
He growled – 'I found him lifeless in his bed';
Then tried for softer tone, and sighed, 'Poor Sam is
    dead.'
Yet murmurs were there, and some questions asked –
How he was fed, how punished, and how tasked?
Much they suspected, but they little proved, 100
And Peter passed untroubled and unmoved.
    Another boy with equal ease was found,
The money granted, and the victim bound;
And what his fate? – One night it chanced he fell
From the boat's mast and perished in her well, 105
Where fish were living kept, and where the boy
(So reasoned men) could not himself destroy: –
    'Yes! so it was,' said Peter, 'in his play
(For he was idle both by night and day),
He climbed the main-mast and then fell below'; –
Then showed his corpse, and pointed to the blow: 111
'What said the jury?' – they were long in doubt,
But sturdy Peter faced the matter out:
So they dismissed him, saying at the time,
'Keep fast your hatchway when you've boys who
    climb.' 115
This hit the conscience, and he coloured more
Than for the closest questions put before.

Thus all his fears the verdict set aside,
And at the slave-shop Peter still applied.
    Then came a boy, of manners soft and mild, – 120
Our seamen's wives with grief beheld the child;
All thought (the poor themselves) that he was one
Of gentle blood, some noble sinner's son,
Who had, belike, deceived some humble maid,
Whom he had first seduced and then betrayed: –
However this, he seemed a gracious lad, 126
In grief submissive and with patience sad.
    Passive he laboured, till his slender frame
Bent with his loads, and he at length was lame:
Strange that a frame so weak could bear so long 130
The grossest insult and the foulest wrong;
But there were causes – in the town they gave
Fire, food, and comfort, to the gentle slave;
And though stern Peter, with a cruel hand,
And knotted rope, enforced the rude command, 135
Yet he considered what he'd lately felt,
And his vile blows with selfish pity dealt.
    One day such draughts the cruel fisher made,
He could not vend them in his borough-trade,
But sailed for London-mart: the boy was ill, 140
But ever humbled to his master's will;
And on the river, where they smoothly sailed,
He strove with terror and awhile prevailed;
But new to danger on the angry sea,
He clung affrightened to his master's knee: 145
The boat grew leaky and the wind was strong,
Rough was the passage and the time was long;
His liquor failed, and Peter's wrath arose, –
No more is known – the rest we must suppose,
Or learn of Peter: – Peter says, he 'spied 150
The stripling's danger and for harbour tried;
Meantime the fish, and then th'apprentice died.'
    The pitying women raised a clamour round,
And weeping said, 'Thou hast thy 'prentice drowned.'
    Now the stern man was summoned to the hall, 155
To tell his tale before the burghers all:
He gave th'account; professed the lad he loved,
And kept his brazen features all unmoved.
    The mayor himself with tone severe replied, –
'Henceforth with thee shall never boy abide; 160
Hire thee a freeman, whom thou durst not beat,
But who, in thy despite, will sleep and eat:
Free art thou now! – again shouldst thou appear,
Thou'lt find thy sentence, like thy soul, severe.'
    Alas! for Peter not a helping hand, 165
So was he hated, could he now command;
Alone he rowed his boat, alone he cast
His nets beside, or made his anchor fast;
To hold a rope or hear a curse was none, –
He toiled and railed; he groaned and swore alone.

---

67 **trap:** two-wheeled light carriage drawn by one horse 76 **stroked:**
treated kindly 80 **his food refused:** deprived of food 99 **tasked:**
employed 105 **well:** cargo-hold

123 **some noble sinner's son:** i.e. the illegitimate son of a nobleman
140 **London-mart:** the London market 158 **brazen:** i.e. tanned and
weatherbeaten

Thus by himself compelled to live each day,   171
To wait for certain hours the tide's delay;
At the same time the same dull views to see,
The bounding marsh-bank and the blighted tree;
The water only, when the tides were high,   175
When low, the mud half-covered and half-dry;
The sunburnt tar that blisters on the planks,
And bankside stakes in their uneven ranks;
Heaps of entangled weeds that slowly float,
As the tide rolls by the impeded boat.   180

When tides were neap, and, in the sultry day,
Through the tall bounding mudbanks made their
          way,
Which on each side rose swelling, and below
The dark warm flood ran silently and slow;
There anchoring, Peter chose from man to hide,
There hang his head, and view the lazy tide   186
In its hot slimy channel slowly glide;
Where the small eels that left the deeper way
For the warm shore, within the shallows play;
Where gaping mussels, left upon the mud,   190
Slope their slow passage to the fallen flood; –
Here dull and hopeless he'd lie down and trace
How sidelong crabs had scrawled their crooked race
Or sadly listen to the tuneless cry
Of fishing gull or clanging goldeneye;   195
What time the sea-birds to the marsh would come,
And the loud bittern, from the bulrush home,
Gave from the salt-ditch side the bellowing boom:
He nursed the feelings these dull scenes produce,
And loved to stop beside the opening sluice;   200
Where the small stream, confined in narrow bound,
Ran with a dull, unvaried, sadd'ning sound;
Where all, presented to the eye or ear,
Oppressed the soul with misery, grief, and fear.

Besides these objects, there were places three,   205
Which Peter seemed with certain dread to see;
When he drew near them he would turn from each,
And loudly whistle till he passed the reach.

A change of scene to him brought no relief,
In town, 'twas plain, men took him for a thief: 210
The sailors' wives would stop him in the street,
And say, 'Now, Peter, thou'st no boy to beat':
Infants at play, when they perceived him, ran,
Warning each other – 'That's the wicked man':
He growled an oath, and in an angry tone   215
Cursed the whole place and wished to be alone.

Alone he was, the same dull scenes in view,
And still more gloomy in his sight they grew:
Though man he hated, yet employed alone
At bootless labour, he would swear and groan,   220
Cursing the shoals that glided by the spot,
And gulls that caught them when his arts could not.

Cold nervous tremblings shook his sturdy frame,
And strange disease – he couldn't say the name;
Wild were his dreams, and oft he rose in fright,   225
Waked by his view of horrors in the night, –
Horrors that would the sternest minds amaze,
Horrors that demons might be proud to raise:
And though he felt forsaken, grieved at heart,
To think he lived from all mankind apart;   230
Yet, if a man approached, in terrors he would start.

A winter passed since Peter saw the town,
And summer lodgers were again come down;
These, idly curious, with their glasses spied
The ships in bay as anchored for the tide, –   235
The river's craft, – the bustle of the quay, –
And sea-port views, which landmen love to see.

One, up the river, had a man and boat
Seen day by day, now anchored, now afloat;
Fisher he seemed, yet used no net nor hook;   240
Of sea-fowl swimming by no heed he took,
But on the gliding waves still fixed his lazy look:
At certain stations he would view the stream,
As if he stood bewildered in a dream,
Or that some power had chained him for a time,
To feel a curse or meditate on crime.   246

This known, some curious, some in pity went,
And others questioned – 'Wretch, dost thou repent?'
He heard, he trembled, and in fear resigned
His boat: new terror filled his restless mind;   250
Furious he grew, and up the country ran,
And there they seized him – a distempered man: –
Him we received, and to a parish-bed,
Followed and cursed, the groaning man was led.

Here when they saw him, whom they used to shun,
A lost, lone man, so harassed and undone;   256
Our gentle females, ever prompt to feel,
Perceived compassion on their anger steal;
His crimes they could not from their memories blot,
But they were grieved, and trembled at his lot.   260

A priest too came, to whom his words are told;
And all the signs they shuddered to behold.

'Look! look!' they cried; 'his limbs with horror shake,
And as he grinds his teeth, what noise they make!
How glare his angry eyes, and yet he's not awake:
See! what cold drops upon his forehead stand,   266
And how he clenches that broad bony hand.'

The priest attending, found he spoke at times
As one alluding to his fears and crimes;
'It was the fall,' he muttered, 'I can show   270
The manner how, – I never struck a blow': –
And then aloud, – 'Unhand me, free my chain;
On oath he fell – it struck him to the brain: –
Why ask my father? – that old man will swear
Against my life; besides, he wasn't there: –   275
What, all agreed? – Am I to die today? –
My Lord, in mercy give me time to pray.'

181 **neap:** showing the smallest difference between high and low
tides   195 **goldeneye:** a northern duck (*Bucephala clangula*); in
flight its wings make a loud whistling sound   208 **reach:** a particular
stretch of water

234 **glasses:** telescopes

Then as they watched him, calmer he became,
And grew so weak he couldn't move his frame,
But murmuring spake – while they could see and hear
The start of terror and the groan of fear;   281
See the large dew-beads on his forehead rise,
And the cold death-drop glaze his sunken eyes;
Nor yet he died, but with unwonted force
Seemed with some fancied being to discourse: 285
He knew not us, or with accustomed art
He hid the knowledge, yet exposed his heart;
'Twas part confession and the rest defence,
A madman's tale, with gleams of waking sense.

    'I'll tell you all,' he said, 'the very day   290
When the old man first placed them in my way:
My father's spirit – he who always tried
To give me trouble, when he lived and died –
When he was gone he could not be content
To see my days in painful labour spent,   295
But would appoint his meetings, and he made
Me watch at these, and so neglect my trade.

    ' 'Twas one hot noon, all silent, still, serene,
No living being had I lately seen;
I paddled up and down and dipped my net,   300
But (such his pleasure) I could nothing get, –
A father's pleasure, when his toil was done,
To plague and torture thus an only son!
And so I sat and looked upon the stream,
How it ran on, and felt as in a dream: 305
But dream it was not: No! – I fixed my eyes
On the mid stream and saw the spirits rise:
I saw my father on the water stand,
And hold a thin pale boy in either hand;
And there they glided ghastly on the top   310
Of the salt flood, and never touched a drop:
I would have struck them, but they knew th'intent,
And smiled upon the oar, and down they went.

    'Now, from that day, whenever I began
To dip my net, there stood the hard old man –   315
He and those boys: I humbled me and prayed
They would be gone; – they heeded not, but stayed:
Nor could I turn, nor would the boat go by,
But, gazing on the spirits, there was I:
They bade me leap to death, but I was loth to die:
And every day, as sure as day arose,   321
Would these three spirits meet me ere the close;
To hear and mark them daily was my doom,
And "Come," they said, with weak, sad voices,
    "come."
To row away, with all my strength I tried,   325
But there were they, hard by me in the tide,
The three unbodied forms – and "Come," still
    "come," they cried.

    'Fathers should pity – but this old man shook
His hoary locks, and froze me by a look:
Thrice, when I struck them, through the water came
A hollow groan, that weakened all my frame: 331
"Father!" said I, "have mercy": – he replied,

I know not what – the angry spirit lied, –
"Didst thou not draw thy knife?" said he: – 'Twas true,
But I had pity and my arm withdrew: 335
He cried for mercy, which I kindly gave,
But he has no compassion in his grave.

    'There were three places, where they ever rose, –
The whole long river has not such as those –
Places accursed, where, if a man remain,   340
He'll see the things which strike him to the brain;
And there they made me on my paddle lean,
And look at them for hours; – accursèd scene!
When they would glide to that smooth eddy-space,
Then bid me leap and join them in the place;   345
And at my groans each little villain sprite
Enjoyed my pains and vanished in delight.

    'In one fierce summer-day, when my poor brain
Was burning hot, and cruel was my pain,
Then came this father-foe, and there he stood   350
With his two boys again upon the flood:
There was more mischief in their eyes, more glee,
In their pale faces when they glared at me:
Still did they force me on the oar to rest,
And when they saw me fainting and oppressed,   355
He, with his hand, the old man, scooped the flood,
And there came flame about him mixed with blood;
He bade me stoop and look upon the place,
Then flung the hot-red liquor in my face;
Burning it blazed, and then I roared for pain,   360
I thought the demons would have turned my brain.

    'Still there they stood, and forced me to behold
A place of horrors – they can not be told –
Where the flood opened, there I heard the shriek
Of tortured guilt – no earthly tongue can speak: 365
"All days alike! for ever!" did they say,
"And unremitted torments every day" –
Yes, so they said' – but here he ceased, and gazed
On all around, affrighted and amazed;
And still he tried to speak, and looked in dread   370
Of frightened females gathering round his bed;
Then dropped exhausted, and appeared at rest,
Till the strong foe the vital powers possessed;
Then with an inward, broken voice he cried,
'Again they come,' and muttered as he died.

                      [Letter 22]

310 **ghastly:** ghost-like   329 **hoary:** frosty-white   346 **sprite:** spirit

WILLIAM BLAKE

SONGS OF INNOCENCE

INTRODUCTION

PIPING down the valleys wild,
Piping songs of pleasant glee,
On a cloud I saw a child,
And he laughing said to me:

'Pipe a song about a lamb!'
So I piped with merry cheer.   5
'Piper, pipe that song again';
So I piped: he wept to hear.

'Drop thy pipe, thy happy pipe;
Sing thy songs of happy cheer':   10
So I sung the same again,
While he wept with joy to hear.

'Piper, sit thee down and write
In a book, that all may read.'
So he vanished from my sight,   15
And I plucked a hollow reed,

And I made a rural pen,
And I stained the water clear,
And I wrote my happy songs
Every child may joy to hear.   20

THE SHEPHERD

How sweet is the shepherd's sweet lot!
From the morn to the evening he strays;
He shall follow his sheep all the day,
And his tongue shall be fillèd with praise.

For he hears the lamb's innocent call,   5
And he hears the ewe's tender reply;
He is watchful while they are in peace,
For they know when their shepherd is nigh.

THE ECHOING GREEN

The sun does arise,
And make happy the skies;
The merry bells ring
To welcome the spring;
The skylark and thrush,   5
The birds of the bush,
Sing louder around
To the bells' cheerful sound,
While our sports shall be seen
On the echoing green.   10

Old John, with white hair,
Does laugh away care,
Sitting under the oak,
Among the old folk.
They laugh at our play,
And soon they all say: 15
'Such, such were the joys
When we all, girls and boys,
In our youth-time were seen
On the echoing green.'   20

Till the little ones, weary,   5
No more can be merry;
The sun does descend,
And our sports have an end.
Round the laps of their mothers   25
Many sisters and brothers,
Like birds in their nest,
Are ready for rest,
And sport no more seen
On the darkening green.   30

THE LAMB

Little Lamb, who made thee?
Dost thou know who made thee?
Gave thee life, and bid thee feed
By the stream and o'er the mead;
Gave thee clothing of delight,   5
Softest clothing, woolly, bright;
Gave thee such a tender voice,
Making all the vales rejoice?
Little Lamb, who made thee?
Dost thou know who made thee?   10

Little Lamb, I'll tell thee,
Little Lamb, I'll tell thee:
He is callèd by thy name,
For he calls himself a lamb.
He is meek, and he is mild;   15
He became a little child.
I a child, and thou a lamb,
We are callèd by his name.
Little Lamb, God bless thee!
Little Lamb, God bless thee!   20

THE LITTLE BLACK BOY

My mother bore me in the southern wild,
And I am black, but, oh! my soul is white;
White as an angel is the English child,
But I am black, as if bereaved of light.

My mother taught me underneath a tree,   5
And sitting down before the heat of day,
She took me on her lap and kissèd me,
And pointing to the east, began to say:

'Look on the rising sun: there God does live,
And gives His light, and gives His heat away;   10
And flowers and trees and beasts and men receive
Comfort in morning, joy in the noonday.

'And we are put on earth a little space,
That we may learn to bear the beams of love;
And these black bodies and this sunburnt face   15
Is but a cloud, and like a shady grove.

'For when our souls have learned the heat to bear,
The cloud will vanish; we shall hear His voice,
Saying: "Come out from the grove, my love and care,
And round my golden tent like lambs rejoice." '   20

Thus did my mother say, and kissèd me;
And thus I say to little English boy:
When I from black and he from white cloud free,
And round the tent of God like lambs we joy,

I'll shade him from the heat, till we can bear   25
To lean in joy upon our Father's knee;
And then I'll stand and stroke his silver hair,
And be like him, and he will then love me.

THE BLOSSOM

MERRY, merry Sparrow!
Under leaves so green
A happy blossom
Sees you swift as arrow
Seek your cradle narrow   5
Near my bosom.

Pretty, pretty Robin!
Under leaves so green
A happy blossom
Hears you sobbing, sobbing,   10
Pretty, pretty Robin,
Near my bosom.

THE CHIMNEY SWEEPER

WHEN my mother died I was very young,
And my father sold me while yet my tongue
Could scarcely cry ' 'weep! 'weep! 'weep! 'weep!'
So your chimneys I sweep, and in soot I sleep.

There's little Tom Dacre, who cried when his head,   5
That curled like a lamb's back, was shaved: so I said
'Hush, Tom! never mind it, for when your head's bare
You know that the soot cannot spoil your white hair.'

And so he was quiet, and that very night,
As Tom was a-sleeping, he had such a sight!   10
That thousands of sweepers, Dick, Joe, Ned, and Jack,
Were all of them locked up in coffins of black.

And by came an angel who had a bright key,
And he opened the coffins and set them all free;
Then down a green plain leaping, laughing, they run,
And wash in a river, and shine in the sun.   16

Then naked and white, all their bags left behind,
They rise upon clouds and sport in the wind;
And the angel told Tom, if he'd be a good boy,
He'd have God for his father, and never want joy.   20

And so Tom awoke; and we rose in the dark,
And got with our bags and our brushes to work.
Though the morning was cold, Tom was happy and
   warm;
So if all do their duty they need not fear harm.

THE LITTLE BOY LOST

'FATHER! Father! where are you going?
Oh, do not walk so fast.
Speak, Father, speak to your little boy,
Or else I shall be lost.'

The night was dark, no father was there;   5
The child was wet with dew;
The mire was deep, and the child did weep,
And away the vapour flew.

THE LITTLE BOY FOUND

THE little boy lost in the lonely fen,
Led by the wand'ring light,
Began to cry; but God, ever nigh,
Appeared like his father in white.

He kissèd the child and by the hand led   5
And to his mother brought,
Who in sorrow pale, through the lonely dale,
Her little boy weeping sought.

LAUGHING SONG

WHEN the green woods laugh with the voice of joy,
And the dimpling stream runs laughing by;
When the air does laugh with our merry wit,
And the green hill laughs with the noise of it;

When the meadows laugh with lively green,   5
And the grasshopper laughs in the merry scene,
When Mary and Susan and Emily
With their sweet round mouths sing 'Ha, Ha, He!'

When the painted birds laugh in the shade,
Where our table with cherries and nuts is spread,   10
Come live and be merry, and join with me,
To sing the sweet chorus of 'Ha, Ha, He!'

A CRADLE SONG

SWEET Dreams, form a shade
O'er my lovely infant's head;
Sweet dreams of pleasant streams
By happy, silent, moony beams.

Sweet Sleep, with soft down
Weave thy brows an infant crown.
Sweet Sleep, angel mild,
Hover o'er my happy child.

Sweet Smiles, in the night
Hover over my delight;   10
Sweet Smiles, Mother's smiles,
All the livelong night beguiles.

Sweet Moans, dovelike sighs,
Chase not slumber from thy eyes.
Sweet moans, sweeter smiles,   15
All the dovelike moans beguiles.

Sleep, sleep, happy child,
All creation slept and smiled;
Sleep, sleep, happy sleep,
While o'er thee thy mother weep.   20

Sweet Babe, in thy face
Holy image I can trace.
Sweet babe, once like thee,
Thy maker lay and wept for me,

Wept for me, for thee, for all,   25
When he was an infant small
Thou his image ever see,
Heavenly face that smiles on thee,

Smiles on thee, on me, on all;
Who became an infant small.   30
Infant smiles are his own smiles;
Heaven and earth to peace beguiles.

A CRADLE SONG: 12 **beguiles**: charms away

THE DIVINE IMAGE

To Mercy, Pity, Peace, and Love
All pray in their distress;
And to these virtues of delight
Return their thankfulness.

For Mercy, Pity, Peace, and Love   5
Is God, our father dear,
And Mercy, Pity, Peace, and Love
Is Man, his child and care.

For Mercy has a human heart,
Pity a human face,   10
And Love, the human form divine,
And Peace, the human dress.

Then every man, of every clime,
That prays in his distress,
Prays to the human form divine,   15
Love, Mercy, Pity, Peace.

And all must love the human form,   5
In heathen, Turk, or Jew;
Where Mercy, Love, and Pity dwell
There God is dwelling too.   20

HOLY THURSDAY

'TWAS on a Holy Thursday, their innocent faces clean,
The children walking two and two, in red and blue
    and green,
Grey-headed beadles walked before, with wands as
    white as snow,
Till into the high dome of Paul's they like Thames'
    waters flow.

Oh, what a multitude they seemed, these flowers of
    London town!   5
Seated in companies they sit with radiance all their
    own.
The hum of multitudes was there, but multitudes of
    lambs,
Thousands of little boys and girls raising their
    innocent hands.

Now like a mighty wind they raise to heaven the voice
    of song,
Or like harmonious thunderings the seats of heaven
    among.   10
Beneath them sit the agèd men, wise guardians of the
    poor;
Then cherish pity, lest you drive an angel from your
    door.

HOLY THURSDAY: 1 **Holy Thursday**: Thursday of Holy Week, i.e. the
week before Easter 3 **beadles**: parish officers **wands**: rods of authority
4 **Paul's**: St Paul's Cathedral

NIGHT

THE sun descending in the west,
The evening star does shine;
The birds are silent in their nest,
And I must seek for mine.
The moon like a flower   5
In heaven's high bower,
With silent delight
Sits and smiles on the night.

Farewell, green fields and happy groves,
Where flocks have took delight.   10
Where lambs have nibbled, silent moves
The feet of angels bright;
Unseen they pour blessing
And joy without ceasing,
On each bud and blossom,   15
And each sleeping bosom.

They look in every thoughtless nest,
Where birds are covered warm;
They visit caves of every beast,
To keep them all from harm.   20
If they see any weeping
That should have been sleeping,
They pour sleep on their head,
And sit down by their bed.

When wolves and tigers howl for prey,   25
They pitying stand and weep;
Seeking to drive their thirst away,
And keep them from the sheep;
But if they rush dreadful,
The angels, most heedful,   30
Receive each mild spirit,
New worlds to inherit.

And there the lion's ruddy eyes
Shall flow with tears of gold,
And pitying the tender cries,   35
And walking round the fold,
Saying 'Wrath, by his meekness,
And by his health, sickness
Is driven away
From our immortal day.   40

'And now beside thee, bleating Lamb,
I can lie down and sleep:
Or think on him who bore thy name,
Graze after thee and weep.
For, washed in life's river,   45
My bright mane for ever
Shall shine like the gold
As I guard o'er the fold.'

NIGHT: 2 **The evening star:** a bright planet (usually Venus or Mercury)
seen in the western sky soon after sunset 6 **bower:** garden recess
or arbour

SPRING

Sound the flute!
Now it's mute.
Birds delight
Day and night;
Nightingale   5
In the dale,
Lark in sky,
Merrily,
Merrily, merrily, to welcome in the year.

Little Boy,   10
Full of joy;
Little Girl,
Sweet and small;
Cock does crow,
So do you;   15

Merry voice,
Infant noise,
Merrily, merrily, to welcome in the year.

Little Lamb,
Here I am;   20
Come and lick
My white neck:
Let me pull

Your soft wool:
Let me kiss   25
Your soft face:
Merrily, merrily, we welcome in the year.

NURSE'S SONG

When the voices of children are heard on the green
And laughing is heard on the hill,
My heart is at rest within my breast
And everything else is still.

'Then come home, my children, the sun is gone down
And the dews of night arise;   6
Come, come, leave off play, and let us away
Till the morning appears in the skies.'

'No, no, let us play, for it is yet day
And we cannot go to sleep;   10
Besides, in the sky the little birds fly
And the hills are all covered with sheep.'

'Well, well, go and play till the light fades away
And then go home to bed.'
The little ones leaped and shouted and laughed   15
And all the hills echoèd.

INFANT JOY

'I have no name:
I am but two days old.'
What shall I call thee?
'I happy am,
Joy is my name.'   5
Sweet joy befall thee!

Pretty joy!
Sweet joy but two days old,
Sweet joy I call thee:
Thou dost smile,   10
I sing the while,
Sweet joy befall thee!

WILLIAM BLAKE

A DREAM

ONCE a dream did weave a shade
O'er my angel-guarded bed,
That an emmet lost its way
Where on grass methought I lay.

Troubled, 'wildered, and forlorn,   5
Dark, benighted, travel-worn,
Over many a tangled spray,
All heart-broke I heard her say:

'Oh, my children! do they cry?
Do they hear their father sigh?   10
Now they look abroad to see:
Now return and weep for me.'

Pitying, I dropped a tear;
But I saw a glow-worm near,
Who replied: 'What wailing wight   15
Calls the watchman of the night?

'I am set to light the ground,
While the beetle goes his round:
Follow now the beetle's hum;
Little wanderer, hie thee home.'   20

A DREAM: 3 **emmet:** ant 5 **'wildered:** bewildered 7 **spray:** branch
15 **wight:** person

ON ANOTHER'S SORROW

CAN I see another's woe,
And not be in sorrow too?
Can I see another grief,
And not seek for kind relief?

Can I see a falling tear,   5
And not feel my sorrow's share?
Can a father see his child
Weep, nor be with sorrow filled?

Can a mother sit and hear
An infant groan an infant fear?   10
No, no! never can it be!
Never, never can it be!

And can he who smiles on all
Hear the wren with sorrows small,
Hear the small bird's grief and care,   15
Hear the woes that infants bear,

And not sit beside the nest,
Pouring pity in their breast;
And not sit the cradle near,
Weeping tear on infant's tear;   20

And not sit both night and day,
Wiping all our tears away?
Oh, no! never can it be!
Never, never can it be!

He doth give his joy to all;   25
He becomes an infant small;
He becomes a man of woe;
He doth feel the sorrow too.

Think not thou canst sigh a sigh
And thy maker is not by;   30
Think not thou canst weep a tear
And thy maker is not near.

Oh! he gives to us his joy
That our grief he may destroy;
Till our grief is fled and gone   35
He doth sit by us and moan.

SONGS OF EXPERIENCE

INTRODUCTION

HEAR the voice of the bard!
Who present, past, and future sees;
Whose ears have heard
The Holy Word
That walked among the ancient trees,   5

Calling the lapsèd soul,
And weeping in the evening dew;
That might control
The starry pole,
And fallen, fallen light renew!   10

'O Earth, O Earth, return!
Arise from out the dewy grass;
Night is worn,
And the morn
Rises from the slumberous mass.   15

'Turn away no more;
Why wilt thou turn away?
The starry floor,
The wat'ry shore,
Is giv'n thee till the break of day.'   20

EARTH'S ANSWER

EARTH raised up her head
From the darkness dread and drear.
Her light fled,
Stony dread!
And her locks covered with grey despair.   5

'Prisoned on wat'ry shore,
Starry Jealousy does keep my den:
Cold and hoar,
Weeping o'er,
I hear the father of the ancient men.   10

'Selfish father of men!
Cruel, jealous, selfish fear!
Can delight,
Chained in night,
The virgins of youth and morning bear?   15

'Does spring hide its joy
When buds and blossoms grow?
Does the sower
Sow by night,
Or the ploughman in darkness plough?   20

'Break this heavy chain
That does freeze my bones around.
Selfish! vain!
Eternal bane!
That free Love with bondage bound.'   25

EARTH'S ANSWER: 2 **dread:** frightening   **drear:** dreary, gloomy   8
hoar: white with frost   24 **bane:** death

THE CLOD AND THE PEBBLE

'LOVE seeketh not itself to please,
Nor for itself hath any care,
But for another gives its ease,
And builds a heaven in hell's despair.'

So sung a little clod of clay   5
Trodden with the cattle's feet,
But a pebble of the brook
Warbled out these metres meet:

'Love seeketh only self to please,
To bind another to its delight,   10
Joys in another's loss of ease,
And builds a hell in heaven's despite.'

HOLY THURSDAY

Is this a holy thing to see
In a rich and fruitful land,
Babes reduced to misery,
Fed with cold and usurous hand?

Is that trembling cry a song?   5
Can it be a song of joy?
And so many children poor?
It is a land of poverty!

And their sun does never shine,
And their fields are bleak and bare,   10
And their ways are filled with thorns:
It is eternal winter there.

For where'er the sun does shine,
And where'er the rain does fall,
Babe can never hunger there,   15
Nor poverty the mind appal.

HOLY THURSDAY: see earlier note

THE LITTLE GIRL LOST

IN futurity
I prophetic see
That the earth from sleep
(Grave the sentence deep)

Shall arise and seek   5
For her maker meek;
And the desert wild
Become a garden mild.

In the southern clime,
Where the summer's prime   10
Never fades away,
Lovely Lyca lay.

Seven summers old
Lovely Lyca told;
She had wandered long   15
Hearing wild birds' song.

'Sweet sleep, come to me
Underneath this tree.
Do Father, Mother weep,
Where can Lyca sleep?   20

'Lost in desert wild
Is your little child.
How can Lyca sleep
If her mother weep?

'If her heart does ache   25
Then let Lyca wake;
If my mother sleep,
Lyca shall not weep.

'Frowning, frowning night,
O'er this desert bright   30
Let thy moon arise
While I close my eyes.'

Sleeping Lyca lay
While the beasts of prey,
Come from caverns deep,
Viewed the maid asleep.   35

The kingly lion stood
And the virgin viewed,
Then he gambolled round
O'er the hallowed ground.   40

Leopards, tigers, play
Round her as she lay,
While the lion old
Bowed his mane of gold

And her bosom lick,   45
And upon her neck
From his eyes of flame
Ruby tears there came;

While the lioness
Loosed her slender dress,   50
And naked they conveyed
To caves the sleeping maid.

THE LITTLE GIRL FOUND

ALL the night in woe
Lyca's parents go
Over valleys deep,
While the deserts weep.

Tired and woebegone,
Hoarse with making moan,   5
Arm in arm seven days
They traced the desert ways.

Seven nights they sleep
Among the shadows deep,
And dream they see their child   10
Starved in desert wild.

Pale, through pathless ways
The fancied image strays
Famished, weeping, weak,
With hollow piteous shriek.   15

Rising from unrest,
The trembling woman pressed
With feet of weary woe:
She could no further go.   20

In his arms he bore
Her, armed with sorrow sore;
Till before their way
A couching lion lay.

Turning back was vain: 25
Soon his heavy mane
Bore them to the ground.
Then he stalked around,

Smelling to his prey;
But their fears allay   30
When he licks their hands,
And silent by them stands.

They look upon his eyes
Filled with deep surprise,
And wondering behold   35
A spirit armed in gold.

On his head a crown,
On his shoulders down
Flowed his golden hair.
Gone was all their care.   40

'Follow me,' he said;
'Weep not for the maid;
In my palace deep
Lyca lies asleep.'

Then they followèd   45
Where the vision led,
And saw their sleeping child
Among tigers wild.

To this day they dwell
In a lonely dell;   50
Nor fear the wolvish howl
Nor the lions' growl.

THE CHIMNEY SWEEPER

A LITTLE black thing among the snow,
Crying ' 'weep! 'weep!' in notes of woe!
'Where are thy father and mother? say?'
'They are both gone up to the church to pray.

'Because I was happy upon the heath,   5
And smiled among the winter's snow,
They clothèd me in the clothes of death,
And taught me to sing the notes of woe.

'And because I am happy and dance and sing,
They think they have done me no injury,   10
And are gone to praise God and his priest and king,
Who make up a heaven of our misery.'

WILLIAM BLAKE

NURSE'S SONG

WHEN the voices of children are heard on the green
And whisp'rings are in the dale,
The days of my youth rise fresh in my mind,
My face turns green and pale.

Then come home, my children, the sun is gone down,
And the dews of night arise;   6
Your spring and your day are wasted in play,
And your winter and night in disguise.

THE SICK ROSE

O ROSE, thou art sick!
The invisible worm
That flies in the night,
In the howling storm,

Has found out thy bed   5
Of crimson joy,
And his dark secret love
Does thy life destroy.

THE FLY

LITTLE Fly,
Thy summer's play
My thoughtless hand
Has brushed away.

Am not I   5
A fly like thee?
Or art not thou
A man like me?

For I dance,
And drink, and sing,   10
Till some blind hand
Shall brush my wing.

If thought is life
And strength and breath,
And the want   15
Of thought is death;

Then am I
A happy fly,
If I live
Or if I die.   20

THE ANGEL

I DREAMT a dream! what can it mean?
And that I was a maiden queen,
Guarded by an angel mild:
Witless woe was ne'er beguiled!

And I wept both night and day,   5
And he wiped my tears away,
And I wept both day and night,
And hid from him my heart's delight.

So he took his wings and fled;
Then the morn blushed rosy red;   10
I dried my tears, and armed my fears
With ten thousand shields and spears.

Soon my angel came again:
I was armed, he came in vain;
For the time of youth was fled,   15
And grey hairs were on my head.

THE ANGEL: 4 **Witless:** senseless **beguiled:** charmed away

THE TIGER

TIGER! Tiger! burning bright
In the forests of the night,
What immortal hand or eye
Could frame thy fearful symmetry?

In what distant deeps or skies   5
Burnt the fire of thine eyes?
On what wings dare he aspire?
What the hand dare seize the fire?

And what shoulder, and what art,
Could twist the sinews of thy heart?   10
And when thy heart began to beat,
What dread hand? and what dread feet?

What the hammer? what the chain?
In what furnace was thy brain?
What the anvil? what dread grasp   15
Dare its deadly terrors clasp?

When the stars threw down their spears,
And watered heaven with their tears,
Did he smile his work to see?
Did he who made the lamb make thee?   20

Tiger! Tiger! burning bright
In the forests of the night,
What immortal hand or eye,
Dare frame thy fearful symmetry?

WILLIAM BLAKE

MY PRETTY ROSE-TREE

A FLOWER was offered to me,
Such a flower as May never bore;
But I said 'I've a pretty rose-tree,'
And I passèd the sweet flower o'er.

Then I went to my pretty rose-tree,   5
To tend her by day and by night;
But my rose turned away with jealousy,
And her thorns were my only delight.

AH! SUNFLOWER

AH, Sunflower! weary of time,
Who countest the steps of the sun,
Seeking after that sweet golden clime
Where the traveller's journey is done:

Where the youth pined away with desire,   5
And the pale virgin shrouded in snow
Arise from their graves, and aspire
Where my sunflower wishes to go.

AH! SUNFLOWER: **sunflower:** any flower that turns to follow the sun

THE LILY

THE modest rose puts forth a thorn,
The humble sheep a threat'ning horn;
While the lily white shall in love delight,
Nor a thorn, nor a threat, stain her beauty bright.

THE GARDEN OF LOVE

I WENT to the Garden of Love,
And saw what I never had seen:
A chapel was built in the midst,
Where I used to play on the green.

And the gates of this chapel were shut,   5
And 'Thou shalt not' writ over the door;
So I turned to the Garden of Love
That so many sweet flowers bore;

And I saw it was fillèd with graves,
And tombstones where flowers should be;   10
And priests in black gowns were walking their rounds,
And binding with briars my joys and desires.

THE LITTLE VAGABOND

DEAR Mother, dear Mother, the church is cold,
But the alehouse is healthy and pleasant and warm;
Besides I can tell where I am used well,
Such usage in heaven will never do well.

But if at the church they would give us some ale,   5
And a pleasant fire our souls to regale,
We'd sing and we'd pray all the livelong day,
Nor ever once wish from the church to stray.

Then the parson might preach, and drink, and sing,
And we'd be as happy as birds in the spring;   10
And modest Dame Lurch, who is always at church,
Would not have bandy children, nor fasting, nor birch.

And God, like a father rejoicing to see
His children as pleasant and happy as he,
Would have no more quarrel with the devil or the
   barrel,   15
But kiss him, and give him both drink and apparel.

THE LITTLE VAGABOND: 12 **bandy:** with legs made crooked or twisted by malnutrition **birch:** a bundle of birch twigs used to flog offenders

LONDON

I WANDER through each chartered street,
Near where the chartered Thames does flow,
And mark in every face I meet
Marks of weakness, marks of woe.

In every cry of every man,   5
In every infant's cry of fear,
In every voice, in every ban,
The mind-forged manacles I hear.

How the chimney-sweeper's cry
Every black'ning church appals;   10
And the hapless soldier's sigh
Runs in blood down the palace walls.

But most through midnight streets I hear
How the youthful harlot's curse
Blasts the newborn infant's tear,   15
And blights with plagues the marriage hearse.

LONDON: 1 **chartered:** licensed

THE HUMAN ABSTRACT

PITY would be no more
If we did not make somebody poor;
And Mercy no more could be
If all were as happy as we.

And mutual fear brings peace,   5
Till the selfish loves increase:
Then Cruelty knits a snare,
And spreads his baits with care.

He sits down with holy fears,
And waters the ground with tears;   10
Then Humility takes its root
Underneath his foot.

Soon spreads the dismal shade
Of mystery over his head;
And the caterpillar and fly   15
Feed on the mystery.

And it bears the fruit of Deceit,
Ruddy and sweet to eat;
And the raven his nest has made
In its thickest shade.   20

The gods of the earth and sea
Sought through nature to find this tree;
But their search was all in vain:
There grows one in the human brain.

INFANT SORROW

MY mother groaned! my father wept.
Into the dangerous world I leapt:
Helpless, naked, piping loud:
Like a fiend hid in a cloud.

Struggling in my father's hands,   5
Striving against my swaddling bands,
Bound and weary I thought best
To sulk upon my mother's breast.

INFANT SORROW: 6 **swaddling bands:** cloths or bandages in which a baby was bound tightly

A POISON TREE

I WAS angry with my friend:
I told my wrath, my wrath did end.
I was angry with my foe:
I told it not, my wrath did grow.

And I watered it in fears,   5
Night and morning with my tears;
And I sunnèd it with smiles,
And with soft deceitful wiles.

And it grew both day and night,
Till it bore an apple bright;   10
And my foe beheld it shine,
And he knew that it was mine,

And into my garden stole
When the night had veiled the pole:
In the morning glad I see   15
My foe outstretched beneath the tree.

A LITTLE BOY LOST

'NOUGHT loves another as itself,
Nor venerates another so,
Nor is it possible to thought
A greater than itself to know:

'And, Father, how can I love you   5
Or any of my brothers more?
I love you like the little bird
That picks up crumbs around the door.'

The priest sat by and heard the child,
In trembling zeal he seized his hair: 10
He led him by his little coat,
And all admired the priestly care.

And standing on the altar high,
'Lo! what a fiend is here!' said he,
One who sets reason up for judge   15
Of our most holy mystery.'

The weeping child could not be heard,
The weeping parents wept in vain;
They stripped him to his little shirt,
And bound him in an iron chain;   20

And burned him in a holy place,
Where many had been burned before:
The weeping parents wept in vain.
Are such things done on Albion's shore?

A LITTLE BOY LOST: 24 **Albion:** ancient name for Britain, possibly of Celtic origin

A LITTLE GIRL LOST

Children of the future age
Reading this indignant page,
Know that in a former time
Love! sweet love! was thought a crime.

In the Age of Gold,   5
Free from winter's cold,
Youth and maiden bright
To the holy light,
Naked in the sunny beams delight.

Once a youthful pair,   10
Filled with softest care,
Met in garden bright
Where the holy light
Had just removed the curtains of the night.

There, in rising day,
On the grass they play;
Parents were afar,
Strangers came not near,
And the maiden soon forgot her fear.

Tired with kisses sweet, 20
They agree to meet
When the silent sleep
Waves o'er heaven's deep,
And the weary tired wanderers weep.

To her father white 25
Came the maiden bright;
But his loving look,
Like the holy book,
All her tender limbs with terror shook.

'Ona! pale and weak! 30
To thy father speak:
Oh, the trembling fear!
Oh, the dismal care!
That shakes the blossoms of my hoary hair.'

A LITTLE GIRL LOST: 34 **hoary:** frosty white

TO TIRZAH

WHATE'ER is born of mortal birth
Must be consumèd with the Earth
To rise from generation free:
Then what have I to do with thee?

The sexes sprung from shame and pride, 5
Blowed in the morn; in evening died;

But Mercy changed Death into Sleep;
The sexes rose to work and weep.

Thou, mother of my mortal part,
With cruelty didst mould my heart, 10
And with false self-deceiving tears
Didst bind my nostrils, eyes, and ears:

Didst close my tongue in senseless clay,
And me to mortal life betray.
The death of Jesus set me free: 15
Then what have I to do with thee?

THE SCHOOLBOY

I LOVE to rise in a summer morn
When the birds sing on every tree;
The distant huntsman winds his horn,
And the skylark sings with me.
Oh! what sweet company. 5

But to go to school in a summer morn, 15
Oh! it drives all joy away;
Under a cruel eye outworn,
The little ones spend the day
In sighing and dismay. 10

Ah! then at times I drooping sit,
And spend many an anxious hour,
Nor in my book can I take delight,
Nor sit in learning's bower,
Worn through with the dreary shower. 15

How can the bird that is born for joy
Sit in a cage and sing?
How can a child, when fears annoy,
But droop his tender wing,
And forget his youthful spring? 20

O father and mother! if buds are nipped
And blossoms blown away,
And if the tender plants are stripped
Of their joy in the springing day,
By sorrow and care's dismay, 25

How shall the summer arise in joy,
Or the summer fruits appear?
Or how shall we gather what griefs destroy,
Or bless the mellowing year,
When the blasts of winter appear? 30

THE SCHOOLBOY: 3 **winds:** blows 14 **bower:** arbour

THE VOICE OF THE ANCIENT BARD

YOUTH of delight, come hither,
And see the opening morn,
Image of truth new born.
Doubt is fled, and clouds of reason,
Dark disputes and artful teasing. 5
Folly is an endless maze,
Tangled roots perplex her ways.
How many have fallen there!
They stumble all night over bones of the dead,
And feel they know not what but care, 10
And wish to lead others, when they should be led.

THE VOICE OF THE ANCIENT BARD: 7 **perplex:** obstruct by growing
over

A DIVINE IMAGE

CRUELTY has a human heart,
And jealousy a human face;
Terror the human form divine,
And secrecy the human dress.

The human dress is forgèd iron, 5
The human form is a fiery forge,
The human face a furnace sealed,
The human heart its hungry gorge.

A DIVINE IMAGE: engraved later and not published during Blake's lifetime: 8 **gorge:** throat

ETERNITY

HE who binds to himself a joy
Does the wingèd life destroy;
But he who kisses the joy as it flies
Lives in eternity's sunrise.

'MOCK ON, MOCK ON, VOLTAIRE, ROUSSEAU'

MOCK on, mock on, Voltaire, Rousseau:
Mock on, mock on: 'tis all in vain!
You throw the sand against the wind,
And the wind blows it back again.

And every sand becomes a gem 5
Reflected in the beams divine;
Blown back they blind the mocking eye,
But still in Israel's paths they shine.

The atoms of Democritus
And Newton's particles of light 10
Are sands upon the Red Sea shore,
Where Israel's tents do shine so bright.

'MOCK ON, MOCK ON': 1 **Voltaire, Rousseau:** Voltaire (1694–1778) and Jean-Jacques Rousseau (1712–78), French philosophical writers; cf. 'Voltaire! Rousseau! You cannot escape my charge that you are Pharisees and hypocrites, for you are constantly talking of the virtues of the human heart and particularly of your own, that you may accuse others, and especially the religious, whose errors you, by this display of pretended virtue, chiefly design to expose. Rousseau thought men good by nature: he found them evil and found no friend. Friendship cannot exist without forgiveness of sins continually. The book written by Rousseau called his *Confessions*, is an apology and cloak for his sin and not a confession' (Blake, *Jerusalem* 52) 9 **The atoms of Democritus:** Democritus (*c.*460–*c.*370 BC), Greek philosopher best-known for his atomic theory of the universe 10 **Newton's particles of light:** with his 'crucial experiment' with prisms in 1666, Sir Isaac Newton (1642–1727) made important discoveries concerning the composition of white light; at a famous dinner at the home of the painter B. R. Haydon in 1817, Keats, Wordsworth and Lamb drank a toast of 'confusion to mathematics' and damned Newton for destroying 'the poetry of the rainbow, by reducing it to a prism'

AUGURIES OF INNOCENCE

To see a world in a grain of sand
And a heaven in a wild flower,
Hold infinity in the palm of your hand
And eternity in an hour.
A robin redbreast in a cage 5
Puts all heaven in a rage.
A dovehouse filled with doves and pigeons
Shudders hell through all its regions.
A dog starved at his master's gate
Predicts the ruin of the state. 10
A horse misused upon the road
Calls to heaven for human blood.
Each outcry of the hunted hare
A fibre from the brain does tear.
A skylark wounded in the wing, 15
A cherubim does cease to sing.
The game cock clipped and armed for fight
Does the rising sun affright.
Every wolf's and lion's howl
Raises from hell a human soul. 20
The wild deer, wand'ring here and there,
Keeps the human soul from care.
The lamb misused breeds public strife
And yet forgives the butcher's knife.
The bat that flits at close of eve 25
Has left the brain that won't believe.
The owl that calls upon the night
Speaks the unbeliever's fright.
He who shall hurt the little wren
Shall never be belov'd by men. 30
He who the ox to wrath has moved
Shall never be by woman loved.
The wanton boy that kills the fly
Shall feel the spider's enmity.
He who torments the chafer's sprite 35
Weaves a bower in endless night.
The caterpillar on the leaf
Repeats to thee thy mother's grief.
Kill not the moth nor butterfly,
For the Last Judgement draweth nigh. 40
He who shall train the horse to war
Shall never pass the Polar Bar.
The beggar's dog and widow's cat,
Feed them and thou wilt grow fat.
The gnat that sings his summer's song 45
Poison gets from Slander's tongue.
The poison of the snake and newt
Is the sweat of Envy's foot.

AUGURIES OF INNOCENCE: **auguries:** predictions, promises 16 **cherubim:** angel 33 **wanton:** thoughtlessly cruel (cf. Shakespeare's *King Lear* 4.1: 'As flies to wanton boys are we to the gods –/They kill us for their sport') 35 **chafer:** beetle **sprite:** spirit 36 **Weaves a bower:** i.e. makes a home for himself 40 **Last Judgement:** the final judgement of mankind before God at the end of the world

The poison of the honey bee
Is the artist's jealousy.
The prince's robes and beggar's rags   50
Are toadstools on the miser's bags.
A truth that's told with bad intent
Beats all the lies you can invent.
It is right it should be so;   55
Man was made for joy and woe;
And when this we rightly know
Through the world we safely go,
Joy and woe are woven fine,
A clothing for the soul divine;   60
Under every grief and pine
Runs a joy with silken twine.
The babe is more than swaddling bands;
Throughout all these human lands
Tools were made, and born were hands,   65
Every farmer understands.
Every tear from every eye
Becomes a babe in eternity;
This is caught by females bright
And returned to its own delight.   70
The bleat, the bark, bellow and roar
Are waves that beat on heaven's shore.
The babe that weeps the rod beneath
Writes revenge in realms of death.
The beggar's rags, fluttering in air,   75
Does to rags the heavens tear.
The soldier, armed with sword and gun,
Palsied strikes the summer's sun.
The poor man's farthing is worth more
Than all the gold on Afric's shore.   80
One mite wrung from the lab'rer's hands
Shall buy and sell the miser's lands:
Or, if protected from on high,
Does that whole nation sell and buy.
He who mocks the infant's faith   85
Shall be mocked in age and death.
He who shall teach the child to doubt
The rotting grave shall ne'er get out.
He who respects the infant's faith
Triumphs over hell and death.   90
The child's toys and the old man's reasons
Are the fruits of the two seasons.
The questioner, who sits so sly,
Shall never know how to reply.
He who replies to words of doubt   95
Doth put the light of knowledge out.
The strongest poison ever known
Came from Caesar's laurel crown.

Nought can deform the human race
Like to the armour's iron brace.
When gold and gems adorn the plough   100
To peaceful arts shall Envy bow.
A riddle or the cricket's cry
Is to doubt a fit reply.
The emmet's inch and eagle's mile   105
Make lame Philosophy to smile.
He who doubts from what he sees
Will ne'er believe, do what you please.
If the sun and moon should doubt,
They'd immediately go out.   110
To be in a passion you good may do,
But no good if a passion is in you.
The whore and gambler, by the state
Licensed, build that nation's fate.
The harlot's cry from street to street   115
Shall weave old England's winding sheet.
The winner's shout, the loser's curse,
Dance before dead England's hearse.
Every night and every morn
Some to misery are born.   120
Every morn and every night
Some are born to sweet delight.
Some are born to sweet delight,
Some are born to endless night.
We are led to believe a lie   125
When we see not through the eye
Which was born in a night to perish in a night
When the soul slept in beams of light.
God appears and God is light
To those poor souls who dwell in night,   130
But does a human form display
To those who dwell in realms of day.

105 **emmet:** ant

From MILTON

AND did those feet in ancient time
Walk upon England's mountains green?
And was the holy Lamb of God
On England's pleasant pastures seen?

And did the countenance divine   5
Shine forth upon our clouded hills?
And was Jerusalem builded here
Among these dark satanic mills?

Bring me my bow of burning gold:
Bring me my arrows of desire: 10
Bring me my spear: O clouds, unfold!
Bring me my chariot of fire.

I will not cease from mental fight,
Nor shall my sword sleep in my hand
Till we have built Jerusalem   15
In England's green and pleasant land.

63 **swaddling bands:** see note to 'Infant Sorrow' above 79 **farthing:** a quarter of a penny, the smallest coin 81 **mite:** tiny amount 88 **The rotting grave shall ne'er get out:** i.e. shall be denied 'the Resurrection to eternal life, through our Lord Jesus Christ; who shall change our vile body, that it may be like unto his glorious body' (*Book of Common Prayer*) 92 **the two seasons:** spring (childhood) and winter (old age) 98 **laurel crown:** the crown of victory

MILTON: a popular tradition held that the boy Jesus accompanied the merchant Joseph of Arimathea on a visit to Britain

ROBERT BURNS

ADDRESS TO THE UNCO GUID,
OR THE RIGIDLY RIGHTEOUS

My Son, these maxims make a rule,
    And lump them ay thegither;
The *Rigid Righteous* is a fool,
    The *Rigid Wise* anither:
The cleanest corn that e'er was dight
    May hae some pyles o' caff in;
So ne'er a fellow-creature slight
    For random fits o' daffin.
        SOLOMON. – Eccles. ch. vii. verse 16

O YE wha are sae guid yoursel,
    Sae pious and sae holy,
Ye've nought to do but mark and tell
    Your Neebours' fauts and folly!
Whase life is like a weel-gaun mill,   5
    Supply'd wi' store o' water;
The heapèd happer 's ebbing still,
    An' still the clap plays clatter.

Hear me, ye venerable Core,
    As counsel for poor mortals,   10
That frequent pass douce Wisdom's door
    For glaikit Folly's portals:
I, for their thoughtless, careless sakes
    Would here propone defences,
Their donsie tricks, their black mistakes,   15
    Their failings and mischances.

Ye see your state wi' theirs compar'd,
    And shudder at the niffer,
But cast a moment's fair regard
    What maks the mighty differ;   20
Discount what scant occasion gave,
    That purity ye pride in,
And (what's aft mair than a' the lave)
    Your better art o' hiding.

Think, when your castigated pulse   25
    Gies now and then a wallop,
What ragings must his veins convulse,
    That still eternal gallop:
Wi' wind and tide fair i' your tail,
    Right on ye scud your sea-way;   30
But, in the teeth o' baith to sail,
    It maks a unco leeway.

See Social-life and Glee sit down,
    All joyous and unthinking,
Till, quite transmugrify'd, they're grown   35
    Debauchery and Drinking:
O would they stay to calculate
    Th'eternal consequences;
Or your more dreaded hell to state,
    Damnation of expenses!   40

Ye high, exalted, virtuous Dames,
    Ty'd up in godly laces,
Before ye gie poor Frailty names,
    Suppose a change o' cases;
A dear-lov'd lad, convenience snug,   45
    A treacherous inclination –
But, let me whisper i' your lug,
    Ye're aiblins nae temptation.

Then gently scan your brother Man,
    Still gentler sister Woman;   50
Tho' they may gang a kennin wrang,
    To step aside is human:
One point must still be greatly dark,
    The moving *Why* they do it;
And just as lamely can ye mark,   55
    How far perhaps they rue it.

Who made the heart, 'tis *He* alone
    Decidedly can try us;
He knows each chord its various tone,
    Each spring its various bias: 60
Then at the balance let's be mute,
    We never can adjust it;
What's *done* we partly may compute,
    But know not what's *resisted*.

ADDRESS TO THE UNCO GUID: **unco:** exceptionally, uncommonly
guid: good **ay:** always **thegither:** together **dight:** winnowed **pyles:**
shovelfuls (a peel is a baker's wooden shovel) **caff:** chaff **daffin:**
frolic **Eccles. ch. vii. verse 16:** 'Be not righteous over much; neither
make thyself over wise: why shouldest thou destroy thyself?': 4 **fauts:**
faults 5 **Whase:** whose **weel-gaun:** working, active 7 **happer:** hopper
(of a mill) 8 **clap:** in a mill the clap, or clapper, shakes the hopper
to keep the grain moving down to the millstones 9 **Core:** band
11 **douce:** sober 12 **glaikit:** foolish 14 **propone:** put forward 15 **donsie:**
unlucky 18 **niffer:** comparison 23 **lave:** rest 26 **Gies:** gives 31 **baith:**
both 47 **lug:** ear 48 **aiblins:** perhaps 51 **gang a kennin wrang:** go a
little astray 52 **step aside:** stray

HOLY WILLIE'S PRAYER

'And send the Godly in a pet to pray.' – POPE

[ARGUMENT. Holy Willie was a rather oldish batchelor Elder, in the
parish of Mauchline, and much and justly famed for that polemical
chattering which ends in tippling Orthodoxy, and for that
Spiritualized Bawdry which refines to liquorish Devotion. – In a
Sessional process with a gentleman in Mauchline, a Mr Gavin
Hamilton, Holy Willie, and his priest, father Auld, after full hearing
in the Presbytry of Ayr, came off but second best; owing partly to
the oratorical powers of Mr Robert Aiken, Mr Hamilton's Counsel;
but chiefly to Mr Hamilton's being one of the most irreproachable
and truly respectable characters in the country. – On losing his
Process, the Muse overheard him at his devotions as follows –]

O THOU, who in the heavens does dwell!
Wha, as it pleases best thysel,
Sends ane to heaven and ten to hell,
    A' for thy glory,
And no for ony gude or ill   5
    They've done before thee!

I bless and praise thy matchless might,
When thousands thou hast left in night,
That I am here afore thy sight,
    For gifts and grace
A burning and a shining light
    To a' this place.   10

What was I, or my generation,
That I should get such exaltation?
I, wha deserv'd most just damnation,
    For broken laws   15
Six thousand years ere my creation,
    Thro' Adam's cause!

When frae my mother's womb I fell,
Thou might hae plunged me deep in hell,
To gnash my gooms, and weep, and wail,   20
    In burnin lakes,
Where damnèd devils roar and yell,
    Chain'd to their stakes.

Yet I am here, a chosen sample,
To shew thy grace is great and ample: 25
I'm here, a pillar o' thy temple,
    Strong as a rock,
A guide, a ruler, and example
    To a' thy flock.   30

O Lord, thou kens what zeal I bear,
When drinkers drink, and swearers swear,
And singin' there, and dancin' here,
    Wi' great an' sma';
For I am keepit by thy fear   35
    Free frae them a'.

But yet – O Lord! – confess I must –
At times I'm fash'd wi' fleshly lust;
And sometimes too, in warldly trust
    Vile Self gets in;   40
But thou remembers we are dust,
    Defil'd wi' sin.

O Lord! – yestreen – thou kens – wi' Meg –
Thy pardon I sincerely beg!
O may 't ne'er be a living plague,   45
    To my dishonour!
And I'll ne'er lift a lawless leg
    Again upon her.

Besides, I farther maun avow,
Wi' Leezie's lass, three times – I trow –   50
But Lord, that Friday I was fou
    When I cam near her;
Or else, thou kens, thy servant true
    Wad never steer her.

Maybe thou lets this fleshly thorn   55
Buffet thy servant e'en and morn,
Lest he o'er proud and high should turn,
    That he's sae gifted;
If sae, thy hand maun e'en be borne
    Untill thou lift it.   60

Lord bless thy Chosen in this place,
For here thou hast a chosen race:
But God, confound their stubborn face,
    An' blast their name,
Wha bring thy rulers to disgrace   65
    And open shame.

Lord mind Gaun Hamilton's deserts!
He drinks, and swears, and plays at cartes,
Yet has sae mony takin arts
    Wi' Great and Sma',   70
Frae God's ain priest the people's hearts
    He steals awa.

And when we chasten'd him therefore,
Thou kens how he bred sic a splore,
An' set the warld in a roar   75
    O' laughin at us:
Curse thou his basket and his store,
    Kail and potatoes.

Lord hear my earnest cry and prayer,
Against that Presbytry of Ayr!   80
Thy strong right hand, Lord, make it bare
    Upon their heads!
Lord visit them, and dinna spare,
    For their misdeeds!

O Lord, my God, that glib-tongu'd Aiken!   85
My very heart and flesh are quakin,
To think how I sat sweatin, shakin,
    And piss'd wi' dread,
While Auld wi' hingin lip gaed sneakin
    And hid his head.   90

Lord, in thy day o' vengeance try him!
Lord visit them that did employ him!
And pass not in thy mercy by them,
    Nor hear their prayer;
But for thy people's sake destroy them,   95
    And dinna spare!

But Lord, remember me and mine
Wi' mercies temporal and divine!
That I for grace and gear may shine,
    Excell'd by nane!   100
And a' the glory shall be thine!
    AMEN! AMEN!

HOLY WILLIE'S PRAYER: the Pope quotation is from *The Rape of the Lock* 4.64: **Holy Willie:** William Fisher (1737–1809) **liquorish:** drunken **a Sessional process:** for neglect of public worship **Mr Gavin Hamilton:** (1751–1805), a Mauchline lawyer and a friend of Burns **Mr Robert Aiken:** (1739–1807), a lawyer and a patron of Burns: 2 **Wha:** who 3 **ane:** one 4 **A':** all 5 **ony:** any **gude:** good 19 **frae:** from 20 **hae:** have 21 **gooms:** gums 25 **sample:** example 31 **kens:** knows 34 **sma':** small 38 **fash'd:** troubled 39 **wardly:** wordly 43 **yestreen:** yesterday evening 47 **lift a lawless leg:** fornicate 49 **maun:** must 51 **fou:** drunk 54 **steer:** molest, trouble 59 **sae:** so 67 **Gaun:** Gavin 68 **cartes:** cards 69 **takin arts:** captivating ways 71 **ain:** own 74 **bred sic a splore:** caused such an uproar 78 **Kail:** cabbage 88 **piss'd wi' dread:** wetting myself in fear 89 **hingin:** hanging **gaed:** went 99 **gear:** money 100 **nane:** none

ROBERT BURNS

A POET'S WELCOME
TO HIS LOVE-BEGOTTEN DAUGHTER
THE FIRST INSTANCE THAT ENTITLED HIM TO THE
VENERABLE APPELLATION OF FATHER

THOU's welcome, Wean! Mischanter fa' me,
If thoughts o' thee, or yet thy Mamie,
Shall ever daunton me or awe me,
    My bonie lady;
Or if I blush when thou shalt ca' me   5
    Tyta, or daddie.

Tho' now they ca' me, Fornicator,
An' tease my name in kintra clatter,
The mair they talk, I'm kend the better,
    E'en let them clash!   10
An auld wife's tongue's a feckless matter
    To gie ane fash.

Welcome! My bonie, sweet, wee Dochter!
Tho' ye come here a wee unsought for;
And tho' your comin I hae fought for,   15
    Baith Kirk and Queir;
Yet by my faith, ye're no unwrought for,
    That I shall swear!

Wee image o' my bonie Betty,
As fatherly I kiss and daut thee,   20
As dear and near my heart I set thee,
    Wi' as gude will,
As a' the Priests had seen me get thee
    That's out o' hell.

Sweet fruit o' monie a merry dint,   25
My funny toil is no a' tint;
Tho' ye come to the warl' asklent,
    Which fools may scoff at,
In my last plack thy part's be in 't
    The better half o't.   30

Tho' I should be the waur bestead,
Thou's be as braw and bienly clad,
And thy young years as nicely bred
    Wi' education,
As any brat o' Wedlock's bed,   35
    In a' thy station.

Lord grant that thou may ay inherit
Thy Mither's looks an' gracefu' merit,
An' thy poor, worthless Daddie's spirit,
    Without his failins!   40
'Twad please me mair to see thee heir it
    Than stockèd mailins!

For if thou be, what I wad hae thee,
And tak the counsel I shall gie thee,
I'll never rue my trouble wi' thee,   45
    The cost nor shame o't,
But be a loving Father to thee,
    And brag the name o't.

A POET'S WELCOME: on 22 May 1785, Elizabeth, Burns's daughter by his mother's servant girl Elizabeth Paton (line 19), was born: 1 **Wean:** child **Mischanter fa' me:** evil befall me 2 **Mamie:** mother 3 **daunton:** fill me with regret 5 **ca':** call 6 **Tyta:** variant of 'daddy' 8 **kintra clatter:** country gossip 9 **kend:** known 10 **clash:** gossip 11–12 **a feckless . . . fash:** not worth worrying about 13 **Dochter:** daughter 14 **a wee:** a little 16 **Kirk:** church **Queir:** choir 17 **unwrought for:** unlooked for, unwanted 20 **daut:** caress 25 **monie:** many **dint:** time, occasion 26 **funny:** merry **no a' tint:** not all lost 27 **warl':** world **asklent:** irregularly 29 **plack:** farthing 31 **waur bestead:** worse off 32 **braw:** handsomely **bienly:** warmly 37 **ay:** always 38 **Mither:** mother 41 **mair:** more **heir:** inherit 42 **stockèd mailins:** land and cattle 43 **hae:** have 44 **gie:** give

TO A MOUSE
ON TURNING HER UP IN HER NEST,
WITH THE PLOUGH, NOVEMBER, 1785

WEE, sleekit, cowrin, tim'rous beastie,
O, what a panic's in thy breastie!
Thou need na start awa sae hasty,
    Wi' bickering brattle!
I wad be laith to rin an' chase thee,   5
    Wi' murd'ring pattle!

I'm truly sorry Man's dominion,
Has broken Nature's social union,
An' justifies that ill opinion,
    Which makes thee startle   10
At me, thy poor, earth-born companion,
    An' fellow-mortal!

I doubt na, whyles, but thou may thieve;
What then? poor beastie, thou maun live!
A daimen icker in a thrave   15
    'S a sma' request:
I'll get a blessin wi' the lave,
    An' never miss 't!

Thy wee bit housie, too, in ruin!
It's silly wa's the win's are strewin!   20
An' naething, now, to big a new ane,
    O' foggage green!
An' bleak December's winds ensuin,
    Baith snell an' keen!

Thou saw the fields laid bare an' wast,   25
An' weary Winter comin fast,
An' cozie here, beneath the blast,
    Thou thought to dwell,
Till crash! the cruel coulter past
    Out thro' thy cell.   30

That wee-bit heap o' leaves an' stibble,
Has cost thee monie a weary nibble!
Now thou's turn'd out, for a' thy trouble,
    But house or hald,
To thole the Winter's sleety dribble,   35
    An' cranreuch cauld!

But Mousie, thou art no thy-lane,
In proving foresight may be vain:
The best laid schemes o' Mice an' Men
    Gang aft agley,   40
An' lea'e us nought but grief an' pain,
    For promis'd joy!

Still, thou art blest, compar'd wi' me!
The present only toucheth thee:
But Och! I backward cast my e'e,   45
    On prospects drear!
An' forward, tho' I canna see,
    I guess an' fear!

TO A MOUSE: 1 **sleekit:** sleeked, glossy **cowrin:** cowering 4 **bickering brattle:** bustling haste 5 **laith:** loath **rin:** run 6 **pattle:** spade 13 **I doubt na:** I doubt not **whyles:** sometimes 14 **maun:** must 15 **A daimen icker:** an occasional ear of corn **thrave:** two dozen sheaves (unit of quantity) 16 **sma':** small 17 **a blessin:** prosperity **lave:** remainder 19 **wee bit housie:** tiny house 20 **silly wa's:** fragile walls **win's:** winds 21 **big a new ane:** build a new one 22 **foggage:** grass 24 **Baith:** both **snell:** bitter 29 **coulter:** blade of the plough 31 **stibble:** stubble 34 **But house or hald:** without house or home 35 **thole:** endure 36 **cranreuch cauld:** cold frost 37 **thy-lane:** by yourself, alone 40 **Gang aft agley:** often go awry 45 **e'e:** eye

TO A HAGGIS

FAIR fa' your honest, sonsie face,
Great Chieftan o' the Puddin-race!
Aboon them a' ye tak your place,
    Painch, tripe, or thairm:
Weel are ye wordy of a grace   5
    As lang's my arm.

The groaning trencher there ye fill,
Your hurdies like a distant hill,
Your pin wad help to mend a mill
    In time o' need,   10
While thro' your pores the dews distil
    Like amber bead.

His knife see Rustic-labour dight,
An' cut you up wi' ready slight,
Trenching your gushing entrails bright   15
    Like onie ditch;
And then, O what a glorious sight,
    Warm-reekin, rich!

Then, horn for horn they stretch an' strive,
Deil tak the hindmost, on they drive,   20
Till a' their weel-swall'd kytes belyve
    Are bent like drums;
Then auld Guidman, maist like to rive,
    'Bethankit' hums.

Is there that owre his French ragout,   25
Or olio that would staw a sow,
Or fricassee wad mak her spew

Wi' perfect sconner,
Looks down wi' sneering, scornfu' view
    On sic a dinner?   30

Poor devil! see him owre his trash,
As feckless as a wither'd rash,
His spindle shank a guid whip-lash,
    His nieve a nit;
Thro' bluidy flood or field to dash,   35
    O how unfit!

But mark the Rustic, haggis-fed,
The trembling earth resounds his tread,
Clap in his walie nieve a blade,
    He'll mak it whissle;   40
An' legs, an' arms, an' heads will sned,
    Like taps o' thrissle.

Ye Pow'rs wha mak mankind your care,
And dish them out their bill o' fare,
Auld Scotland wants nae skinking ware   45
    That jaups in luggies;
But, if ye wish her gratefu' pray'r,
    Gie her a Haggis!

TO A HAGGIS: 1 **Fair fa':** good luck to **sonsie:** comely 3 **Aboon:** above **a':** all 4 **Painch:** belly **thairm:** intestine 5 **wordy:** worthy 6 **As lang's:** as long as 8 **hurdies:** buttocks 9 **pin:** skewer **wad:** would 13 **dight:** make ready 14 **slight:** skill 15 **Trenching:** cutting deep into 16 **onie:** any 19 **horn:** horn spoon 20 **Deil:** devil 21 **weel-swall'd:** fully stretched **kytes:** bellies **belyve:** quickly 23 **auld Guidman:** old master **maist:** most **rive:** burst 24 **'Bethankit':** 'God be thanked' 25 **owre:** over 26 **olio:** a mixture of various meats and vegetables **staw:** sicken 28 **sconner:** disgust 30 **sic:** such 32 **rash:** rush 33 **spindle shank:** skinny frame **guid:** good 34 **nieve:** fist **nit:** nut 35 **bluidy:** bloody 39 **walie:** ample **blade:** knife 41 **sned:** cut off 42 **taps' of thrissle:** tops of thistles 43 **wha mak:** who make 45 **skinking:** thin and watery **ware:** stews or possibly soups 46 **jaups:** splashes, slops **luggies:** wooden dishes 48 **Gie:** give

MY BONIE MARY

Go fetch to me a pint o' wine,
    And fill it in a silver tassie;
That I may drink, before I go,
    A service to my bonie lassie:
The boat rocks at the Pier o' Leith;   5
    Fu' loud the wind blaws frae the Ferry,
The ship rides by the Berwick-Law,
    And I maun leave my bonie Mary.

The trumpets sound, the banners fly,
    The glittering spears are rankèd ready,   10
The shouts o' war are heard afar,
    The battle closes deep and bloody.
It 's not the roar o' sea or shore,
    Wad mak me langer wish to tarry;
Nor shouts o' war that's heard afar –   15
    It's leaving thee, my bonie Mary!

MY BONIE MARY: 2 **tassie:** goblet 4 **service:** toast 6 **Fu':** full **blaws:** blows **the Ferry:** Queensferry, north of Edinburgh 8 **maun:** must

ROBERT BURNS

AFTON WATER

FLOW gently, sweet Afton, among thy green braes,
Flow gently, I'll sing thee a song in thy praise;
My Mary's asleep by thy murmuring stream,
Flow gently, sweet Afton, disturb not her dream.

Thou stock dove whose echo resounds thro' the glen,   5
Ye wild whistling blackbirds in yon thorny den,
Thou green crested lapwing thy screaming forbear,
I charge you disturb not my slumbering Fair.

How lofty, sweet Afton, thy neighbouring hills,
Far mark'd with the courses of clear, winding rills;   10
There daily I wander as noon rises high,
My flocks and my Mary's sweet Cot in my eye.

How pleasant thy banks and green vallies below,
Where wild in the woodlands, the primroses blow;
There oft as mild ev'ning weeps over the lea,   15
The sweet scented birk shades my Mary and me.

Thy chrystal stream, Afton, how lovely it glides,
And winds by the cot where my Mary resides;
How wanton thy waters her snowy feet lave,
As gathering sweet flowerets she stems thy clear wave.

Flow gently, sweet Afton, among thy green braes,   21
Flow gently, sweet River, the theme of my lays;
My Mary's asleep by thy murmuring stream,
Flow gently, sweet Afton, disturb not her dream.

AFTON WATER: 1 **braes:** hills 10 **rills:** small brooks 12 **Cot:** cottage
15 **lea:** pasture 16 **birk:** birch tree 19 **lave:** wash

JOHN ANDERSON, MY JO

JOHN ANDERSON, my jo, John,
  When we were first acquent;
Your locks were like the raven,
  Your bonie brow was brent;
But now your brow is beld, John,   5
  Your locks are like the snow;
But blessings on your frosty pow,
  John Anderson my jo.

John Anderson my jo, John,
  We clamb the hill thegither;   10
And mony a canty day, John,
  We've had wi' ane anither:
Now we maun totter down, John,
  And hand in hand we'll go;
And sleep thegither at the foot,   15
  John Anderson my jo.

JOHN ANDERSON, MY JO: 1 **jo:** sweetheart 2 **acquent:** acquainted
4 **brent:** smooth 5 **beld:** bald 7 **frosty pow:** white head 10 **clamb:**
climbed **thegither:** together 11 **mony:** many **canty:** pleasant
12 **ane anither:** one another 13 **maun:** must

TAM O'SHANTER
A TALE

'Of Brownyis and of Bogillis full is this buke.'
GAWIN DOUGLAS

WHEN chapman billies leave the street,
And drouthy neebors, neebors meet,
As market-days are wearing late,
An' folk begin to tak the gate;
While we sit bousing at the nappy,   5
And getting fou and unco happy,
We think na on the lang Scots miles,
The mosses, waters, slaps, and stiles,
That lie between us and our hame,
Whare sits our sulky sullen dame,   10
Gathering her brows like gathering storm,
Nursing her wrath to keep it warm.
  This truth fand honest Tam o' Shanter,
As he frae Ayr ae night did canter
(Auld Ayr, wham ne'er a town surpasses,   15
For honest men and bonny lasses).
  O Tam! had'st thou but been sae wise,
As ta'en thy ain wife Kate's advice!
She tauld thee weel thou was a skellum,
A blethering, blustering, drunken blellum;   20
That frae November till October,
Ae market-day thou was nae sober;
That ilka melder, wi' the miller,
Thou sat as lang as thou had siller;
That every naig was ca'd a shoe on   25
The smith and thee gat roaring fou on;
That at the Lord's house, even on Sunday,
Thou drank wi' Kirkton Jean till Monday.
She prophesied that late or soon,
Thou would be found deep drown'd in Doon;   30
Or catch'd wi' warlocks in the mirk,
By Alloway's auld haunted kirk.
  Ah, gentle dames! it gars me greet,
To think how mony counsels sweet,
How mony lengthen'd sage advices,   35
The husband frae the wife despises!
  But to our tale: Ae market-night,
Tam had got planted unco right;
Fast by an ingle, bleezing finely,
Wi' reaming swats, that drank divinely;   40

TAM O'SHANTER: the Gavin Douglas quotation is from *Eneados*
vi.proloug.18: 1 **chapman billies:** brother pedlars 2 **drouthy neebors:**
thirsty neighbours 4 **tak the gate:** take to the road 5 **bousing at the
nappy:** drinking ale 6 **fou:** drunk **unco:** exceptionally, uncommonly
7 **na:** not **lang:** long 8 **slaps:** gaps in fences or dikes 9 **hame:** home
13 **fand:** found 14 **frae:** from **ae:** one 15 **wham:** which 18 **As ta'en:**
As to have taken **ain:** own 19 **skellum:** scoundrel 20 **blethering:**
bragging **blellum:** blusterer 21 **frae:** from 22 **was nae:** was not
23 **ilka melder . . . miller:** every time you took the corn to the mill
24 **siller:** silver, money 25 **every . . . shoe on:** every horse that needed
shoeing 26 **gat:** got 31 **mirk:** dark 32 **kirk:** church 33 **gars me greet:**
makes me cry 34 **mony:** many 38 **planted:** settled 39 **ingle:** hearth
bleezing: blazing 40 **reaming:** foaming **swats:** beer

360

And at his elbow, Souter Johnny,
His ancient, trusty, drouthy crony:
Tam lo'ed him like a vera brither;
They had been fou for weeks thegither.
The night drave on wi' sangs and clatter; 45
And ay the ale was growing better:
The landlady and Tam grew gracious,
Wi' favours secret, sweet, and precious:
The Souter tauld his queerest stories;
The landlord's laugh was ready chorus: 50
The storm without might rair and rustle,
Tam did na mind the storm a whistle.

Care, mad to see a man sae happy,
E'en drown'd himsel amang the nappy:
As bees flee hame wi' lades o' treasure, 55
The minutes wing'd their way wi' pleasure:
Kings may be blest, but Tam was glorious,
O'er a' the ills o' life victorious!

But pleasures are like poppies spread,
You seize the flower, its bloom is shed; 60
Or like the snow falls in the river,
A moment white – then melts for ever;
Or like the borealis race,
That flit ere you can point their place;
Or like the rainbow's lovely form 65
Evanishing amid the storm. –
Nae man can tether time or tide;
The hour approaches Tam maun ride;
That hour, o' night's black arch the key-stane,
That dreary hour he mounts his beast in; 70
And sic a night he taks the road in,
As ne'er poor sinner was abroad in.

The wind blew as 'twad blawn its last;
The rattling showers rose on the blast;
The speedy gleams the darkness swallow'd; 75
Loud, deep, and lang, the thunder bellow'd:
That night, a child might understand,
The Deil had business on his hand.

Weel mounted on his gray mare, Meg,
A better never lifted leg, 80
Tam skelpit on thro' dub and mire,
Despising wind, and rain, and fire;
Whiles holding fast his gude blue bonnet;
Whiles crooning o'er some auld Scots sonnet;
Whiles glowring round wi' prudent cares, 85
Lest bogles catch him unawares:
Kirk Alloway was drawing nigh,
Whare ghaists and houlets nightly cry.

By this time he was cross the ford,
Whare, in the snaw the chapman smoor'd; 90
And past the birks and meikle stane,
Whare drunken Charlie brak's neck-bane;
And thro' the whins, and by the cairn,
Whare hunters fand the murder'd bairn;
And near the thorn, aboon the well, 95
Where Mungo's mither hang'd hersel.
Before him Doon pours all his floods;
The doubling storm roars thro' the woods;
The lightnings flash from pole to pole;
Near and more near the thunders roll: 100
When, glimmering thro' the groaning trees,
Kirk Alloway seem'd in a bleeze;
Thro' ilka bore the beams were glancing;
And loud resounded mirth and dancing.

Inspiring bold John Barleycorn! 105
What dangers thou canst make us scorn!
Wi' tippeny, we fear nae evil;
Wi' usquabae, we'll face the devil!
The swats sae ream'd in Tammie's noddle,
Fair play, he car'd na deils a boddle. 110
But Maggie stood right sair astonish'd,
Till, by the heel and hand admonish'd,
She ventured forward on the light;
And, vow! Tam saw an unco sight!
Warlocks and witches in a dance; 115
Nae cotillion brent-new frae France,
But hornpipes, jigs, strathspeys, and reels,
Put life and mettle in their heels.
A winnock-bunker in the east,
There sat Auld Nick, in shape o' beast; 120
A towzie tyke, black, grim, and large,
To gie them music was his charge:
He screw'd the pipes and gart them skirl,
Till roof and rafters a' did dirl.
Coffins stood round, like open presses, 125
That shaw'd the dead in their last dresses;
And by some devilish cantraip slight
Each in its cauld hand held a light.
By which heroic Tam was able
To note upon the haly table, 130
A murderer's banes in gibbet airns;
Twa span-lang, wee, unchristen'd bairns;

41 **Souter:** cobbler 43 **lo'ed:** loved **a vera brither:** a very brother
44 **thegither:** together 45 **drave on:** passed **sangs:** songs **clatter:**
chat 47 **gracious:** friendly 51 **rair:** roar **rustle:** i.e. rustle the trees
53 **sae:** so 54 **amang:** among 55 **flee:** fly **lades:** loads 63 **the borealis
race:** the winds 66 **Evanishing:** vanishing 68 **maun:** must 69 **key-
stane:** keystone, on which the whole structure depends 71 **sic:** such
73 **as 'twad blawn:** as if it would blow 76 **lang:** long 78 **Deil:** devil
81 **skelpit:** hurried **dub:** puddle 86 **bogles:** ghosts 88 **Whare:** where
ghaists: ghosts **houlets:** owls

89 **cross:** across 90 **smoor'd:** was smothered 91 **birks:** birch trees
meikle stane: large stone 92 **brak's neck-bane:** broke his neck
93 **whins:** gorse 94 **bairn:** child 95 **aboon:** above 96 **mither:** mother
102 **bleeze:** blaze 103 **Thro' ilka bore:** through every gap 105 **John
Barleycorn:** a personification of the grain from which malt liquor
is made 107 **tippeny:** tuppenny ale 108 **usquabae:** whisky 109 **swats
sae ream'd:** beer so foamed 110 **car'd na deils a boddle:** cared for
devils not a boddle (Scottish copper coin, one sixth of an English
penny) 111 **sair:** sorely 114 **unco:** remarkable 116 **cotillion:** country
dance **brent-new:** brand new 117 **strathspey:** Scottish country
dance 119 **winnock-bunker:** window-seat 120 **Auld Nick:** i.e. the
devil 121 **towzie tyke:** scruffy mongrel 123 **gart:** made 124 **dirl:**
shake 125 **presses:** cupboards 126 **shaw'd:** revealed 127 **cantraip
slight:** magic trick 130 **haly:** holy 131 **banes:** bones **airns:** irons
132 **Twa span-lang:** two spans in length (i.e. about eighteen inches)

A thief, new-cutted frae a rape,
Wi' his last gasp his gab did gape;
Five tomahawks, wi' blude red-rusted;   135
Five scymitars, wi' murder crusted;
A garter, which a babe had strangled;
A knife, a father's throat had mangled,
Whom his ain son o' life bereft,
The grey hairs yet stack to the heft;   140
Wi' mair o' horrible and awefu',
Which even to name wad be unlawfu'.

    As Tammie glow'rd, amaz'd, and curious,
The mirth and fun grew fast and furious:
The piper loud and louder blew;   145
The dancers quick and quicker flew;
The reel'd, they set, they cross'd, they cleekit,
Till ilka carlin swat and reekit,
And coost her duddies to the wark,
And linket at it in her sark!   150

    Now, Tam, O Tam! had thae been queans,
A' plump and strapping in their teens,
Their sarks, instead o' creeshie flannen,
Been snaw-white seventeen hunder linnen!
Thir breeks o' mine, my only pair,   155
That ance were plush, o' gude blue hair,
I wad hae gi'en them off my hurdies,
For ae blink o' the bonie burdies!

    But wither'd beldams, auld and droll,
Rigwoodie hags wad spean a foal,   160
Lowping and flinging on a crummock,
I wonder didna turn thy stomach.

    But Tam kend what was what fu' brawlie,
There was ae winsome wench and wawlie,
That night enlisted in the core   165
(Lang after kend on Carrick shore;
For mony a beast to dead she shot,
And perish'd mony a bonie boat,
And shook baith meikle corn and bear,
And kept the country-side in fear):   170
Her cutty sark, o' Paisley harn,
That while a lassie she had worn,
In longitude tho' sorely scanty,
It was her best, and she was vauntie.
Ah! little kend thy reverend grannie,   175
That sark she coft for her wee Nannie,

Wi' twa pund Scots ('twas a' her riches),
Wad ever grac'd a dance of witches!

    But here my Muse her wing maun cour;
Sic flights are far beyond her pow'r;   180
To sing how Nannie lap and flang
(A souple jade she was, and strang),
And how Tam stood, like ane bewitch'd,
And thought his very een enrich'd;
Even Satan glow'rd, and fidg'd fu' fain,   185
And hotch'd and blew wi' might and main:
Till first ae caper, syne anither,
Tam tint his reason a' thegither,
And roars out, 'Weel done, Cutty-sark!'
And in an instant all was dark: 190
And scarcely had he Maggie rallied,
When out the hellish legion sallied.

    As bees bizz out wi' angry fyke,
When plundering herds assail their byke;
As open pussie's mortal foes,   195
When, pop! she starts before their nose;
As eager runs the market-crowd,
When 'Catch the thief!' resounds aloud;
So Maggie runs, the witches follow,
Wi' mony an eldritch skreech and hollow.   200

    Ah, Tam! Ah, Tam! thou'll get thy fairin!
In hell, they'll roast thee like a herrin!
In vain thy Kate awaits thy comin!
Kate soon will be a woefu' woman!
Now, do thy speedy-utmost, Meg,   205
And win the key-stane of the brig;
There at them thou thy tail may toss,
A running stream they dare na cross.
But ere the key-stane she could make,
The fient a tail she had to shake!   210
For Nannie, far before the rest,
Hard upon noble Maggie prest,
And flew at Tam wi' furious ettle;
But little wist she Maggie's mettle
Ae spring brought off her master hale,   215
But left behind her ain gray tail:
The carlin claught her by the rump,
And left poor Maggie scarce a stump.

    Now, wha this tale o' truth shall read,
Ilk man and mother's son, take heed: 220
Whene'er to drink you are inclin'd,
Or cutty-sarks run in your mind,
Think, ye may buy the joys o'er dear;
Remember Tam o' Shanter's mare.

---

133 **new-cutted frae a rape:** newly cut down from a gallows 134 **gab:**
mouth 147 **cleekit:** linked arms in the dance 148–50 **Till ilka carlin
. . . in her sark:** Till every witch sweated and steamed, threw off her
clothes and went at it in her shift 151 **thae:** they **queans:** young
lasses 152 **A':** all 153–4 **Their sarks . . . linnen:** Their shifts, instead
of filthy flannel (had) been snow-white top-quality linen 155 **Thir
breeks:** these breeches 156 **ance:** once **plush:** fabric with a longer
and softer nap than velvet and sometimes made from hair
157 **hurdies:** buttocks 158 **For ae blink . . . burdies:** For one glance
from the bonny lasses 160 **Rigwoodie:** withered **spean:** wean
161 **Lowping:** leaping **flinging:** leaping **crummock:** crook 163 **kend:**
knew **fu'brawlie:** very well 164 **wawlie:** handsome 165 **core:** corps,
company 169 **meikle corn:** oats **bear:** barley 171 **cutty:** short **harn:**
coarse linen 174 **vauntie:** vain 176 **coft:** bought

---

177 **twa pund Scots:** two Scottish pounds 179 **cour:** fold 180 **Sic:**
such 181 **lap and flang:** leaped and flung 182 **souple jade:** supple
mare **strang:** strong 183 **ane:** one 184 **een:** eyes 185 **fidg'd fu' fain:**
twitched with excitement 186 **hotch'd:** jerked about 187 **syne:** then
188 **tint:** lost **a' thegither:** all together 193 **fyke:** commotion
194 **byke:** hive 195 **pussie's:** the hare's 200 **eldritch skreech:** unearthly
shriek 201 **fairin:** fairing, gift from a fair 206 **win:** reach **brig:** bridge
210 **The fient a tail:** The devil a tail 213 **ettle:** purpose 214 **wist:** knew
217 **claught:** grabbed 220 **Ilk:** every

THE BANKS O' DOON

YE banks and braes o' bonie Doon,
   How can ye bloom sae fresh and fair;
How can ye chant, ye little birds,
   And I sae weary, fu' o' care!
Thou'll break my heart, thou warbling bird,   5
   That wantons thro' the flowering thorn:
Thou minds me o' departed joys,
   Departed never to return.

Oft hae I rov'd by bonie Doon,
   To see the rose and woodbine twine;   10
And ilka bird sang o' its Luve,
   And fondly sae did I o' mine.
Wi' lightsome heart I pu'd a rose,
   Fu' sweet upon its thorny tree;
And my fause Luver staw my rose,   15
   But ah! he left the thorn wi' me.

THE BANKS O' DOON: 2 **sae**: so 4 **fu'**: full 7 **minds**: reminds 11 **ilka**: every 13 **pu'd**: pulled, plucked 15 **fause**: false **Luver**: lover **staw**: stole

AE FOND KISS, AND THEN WE SEVER

AE fond kiss, and then we sever;
Ae fareweel, and then for ever!
Deep in heart-wrung tears I'll pledge thee,
Warring sighs and groans I'll wage thee.

Who shall say that Fortune grieves him,   5
While the star of hope she leaves him:
Me, nae cheerful twinkle lights me;
Dark despair around benights me.

I'll ne'er blame my partial fancy,
Naething could resist my Nancy: 10
But to see her, was to love her;
Love but her, and love for ever.

Had we never lov'd sae kindly,
Had we never lov'd sae blindly!
Never met – or never parted,   15
We had ne'er been broken-hearted.

Fare-thee-weel, thou first and fairest!
Fare-thee-weel, thou best and dearest!
Thine be ilka joy and treasure,
Peace, Enjoyment, Love and Pleasure!   20

Ae fond kiss, and then we sever!
Ae fareweel, alas, for ever!
Deep in heart-wrung tears I'll pledge thee,
Warring sighs and groans I'll wage thee.

AE FOND KISS, AND THEN WE SEVER: 1 **Ae**: one **sever**: part 3 **pledge**: toast 4 **wage**: refers back to 'Warring', i.e. sighs and groans contending for mastery 7 **nae**: no 13 **sae**: so 19 **ilka**: every

'O SAW YE BONIE LESLEY'

O SAW ye bonie Lesley,
   As she gaed o'er the Border?
She's gane, like Alexander,
   To spread her conquests farther.

To see her is to love her,   5
   And love but her for ever;
For Nature made her what she is,
   And never made anither.

Thou art a queen, fair Lesley,
   Thy subjects we, before thee: 10
Thou art divine, fair Lesley,
   The hearts o' men adore thee.

The deil he could na scaith thee,
   Or aught that wad belang thee:
He'd look into thy bonie face,   15
   And say, 'I canna wrang thee!'

The Powers aboon will tent thee,
   Misfortune sha'na steer thee;
Thou'rt like themsels sae lovely,
   That ill they'll ne'er let near thee.   20

Return again, fair Lesley,
   Return to Caledonie!
That we may brag, we hae a lass
   There 's nane again sae bonie.

'O SAW YE BONIE LESLEY': Lesley Baillie, daughter of Robert Baillie of Mayville, Ayrshire. In August 1792, Baillie and his two daughters called on Burns on their way to England; Burns kept them company for a few miles of their journey and, on his return, wrote this handsome tribute (although he described his relationship with Miss Baillie as one of 'sacred purity'): 2 **gaed**: went 3 **gane**: gone **Alexander**: Alexander the Great 8 **anither**: another 13 **deil**: devil **scaith**: harm 14 **aught that wad belang thee**: anything of yours 17 **aboon**: above **tent**: watch over 19 **sha'na steer**: shall not have his way with 22 **Caledonie**: Caledonia, i.e. Scotland

DUNCAN GRAY

DUNCAN GRAY cam here to woo,
   Ha, ha, the wooing o't,
On blythe Yule night when we were fu',
   Ha, ha, the wooing o't.
Maggie coost her head fu' high,   5
Look'd asklent and unco skeigh,
Gart poor Duncan stand abeigh;
   Ha, ha, the wooing o't.

Duncan fleech'd, and Duncan pray'd;
  Ha, ha, the wooing o't.   10
Meg was deaf as Ailsa Craig,
  Ha, ha, the wooing o't.
Duncan sigh'd baith out and in,
Grat his een baith bleer't an' blin',
Spak o' lowpin o'er a linn;   15
  Ha, ha, the wooing o't.

Time and Chance are but a tide,
  Ha, ha, the wooing o't.
Slighted love is sair to bide,
  Ha, ha, the wooing o't.   20
Shall I, like a fool, quoth he,
For a haughty hizzie die?
She may gae to – France for me!
  Ha, ha, the wooing o't.

How it comes let Doctors tell,   25
  Ha, ha, the wooing o't.
Meg grew sick as he grew heal,
  Ha, ha, the wooing o't.
Something in her bosom wrings,
For relief a sigh she brings;   30
And O her een, they spak sic things!
  Ha, ha, the wooing o't.

Duncan was a lad o' grace,
  Ha, ha, the wooing o't.
Maggie's was a piteous case,   35
  Ha, ha, the wooing o't.
Duncan could na be her death,
Swelling Pity smoor'd his Wrath;
Now they're crouse and canty baith,
  Ha, ha, the wooing o't.   40

DUNCAN GRAY: 2 **the wooing o't:** i.e. you never saw such wooing
3 **fu':** drunk 5 **coost:** cast **fu':** full 6 **asklent:** askance **unco skeigh:**
with great disdain 7 **Gart:** made **abeigh:** aside 9 **fleech'd:** coaxed
11 **Ailsa Craig:** a small rocky island in the Firth of Clyde 13 **baith:**
both 14 **Grat . . . blin':** Wept till his eyes were both bleary and blind
15 **Spak . . . linn:** Talked of leaping over a waterfall 19 **sair to bide:**
hard to bear 22 **hizzie:** hussy 27 **heal:** well 31 **een:** eyes **sic:** such
38 **smoor'd:** smothered 39 **crouse:** merry **canty:** pleasant

ROBERT BRUCE'S
MARCH TO BANNOCKBURN

SCOTS, wha hae wi' WALLACE bled,
Scots, wham BRUCE has aften led,
Welcome to your gory bed, –
  Or to victory!

Now's the day, and now's the hour;   5
See the front o' battle lour,
See approach proud EDWARD's power –
  Chains and Slavery!

Wha will be a traitor-knave?
Wha can fill a coward's grave?   10
Wha sae base as be a Slave?
  – Let him turn and flie!

Wha for SCOTLAND's king and law
Freedom's sword will strongly draw,
FREE-MAN stand, or FREE-MAN fa',   15
  Let him follow me!

By Oppression's woes and pains,
By your Sons in servile chains,
We will drain our dearest veins,
  But they *shall* be free!   20

Lay the proud Usurpers low!
Tyrants fall in every foe!
LIBERTY's in every blow!
  Let us DO – OR DIE!!!

ROBERT BRUCE'S MARCH TO BANNOCKBURN: **Robert Bruce:** Robert I,
king of Scotland 1306–29; after the death of Sir William Wallace he
led the Scottish campaign against Edward I and later Edward II
Bannockburn: a major battle (1314) fought between the English
forces of Edward II and the Scots under Robert the Bruce; the
English army suffered a crushing defeat, and Edward was lucky to
escape alive: 1 **wha hae:** who have **Wallace:** Sir William Wallace
(*c.*1270–1305), leader of Scottish resistance to Edward I; following his
defeat at the battle of Falkirk in 1298, Wallace was captured by the
English and executed. For Burns, 'The story of Wallace poured a
Scottish prejudice in my veins which will boil along there till the
flood-gates of life shut in eternal rest' 2 **wham:** whom **aften:** often
6 **lour:** threaten 15 **fa':** fall

A RED, RED ROSE

O MY Luve's like a red, red rose
  That's newly sprung in June;
O my Luve's like the melodie
  That's sweetly play'd in tune.

As fair art thou, my bonie lass,   5
  So deep in luve am I;
And I will luve thee still, my dear,
  Till a' the seas gang dry. –

Till a' the seas gang dry, my Dear,
  And the rocks melt wi' the sun: 10
I will luve thee still, my Dear,
  While the sands o' life shall run. –

And fare thee weel, my only Luve!
  And fare thee weel, a while!
And I will come again, my Luve,   15
  Tho' it were ten thousand mile!

A RED, RED ROSE: 8 **gang dry:** run dry

ROBERT BURNS

FOR A' THAT AND A' THAT

Is there, for honest Poverty
    That hings his head, and a' that;
The coward slave, we pass him by,
    We dare be poor for a' that!
    For a' that, and a' that,   5
      Our toils obscure, and a' that,
    The rank is but the guinea's stamp,
      That Man's the gowd for a' that.

What though on hamely fare we dine,
    Wear hoddin grey, and a' that.   10
Gie fools their silks, and knaves their wine,
    A Man's a Man for a' that.
    For a' that, and a' that,
      Their tinsel show, and a' that;
    The honest man, though e'er sae poor, 15
      Is king o' men for a' that.

Ye see yon birkie ca'd, a lord,
    Wha struts, and stares, and a' that,
Though hundreds worship at his word,
    He's but a coof for a' that.   20
    For a' that, for a' that,
      His ribband, star and a' that,
    The man of independant mind,
      He looks and laughs at a' that.

A prince can mak a belted knight,   25
    A marquis, duke, and a' that;
But an honest man 's aboon his might,
    Gude faith he mauna fa' that!
    For a' that, and a' that,
      Their dignities, and a' that,   30
    The pith o' Sense, and pride o' Worth,
      Are higher rank than a' that.

Then let us pray that come it may,
    As come it will for a' that,
That Sense and Worth, o'er a' the earth 35
    Shall bear the gree, and a' that.
    For a' that, and a' that,
      It's comin yet for a' that,
    That Man to Man the warld o'er,
      Shall brothers be for a' that.   40

FOR A' THAT AND A' THAT: 2 **hings:** hangs **a':** all 7 **The rank ... stamp:** social station is merely something bestowed by accident of birth and is not necessarily a reflection of the true value of the man himself 8 **gowd:** gold 9 **hamely:** simple 10 **hoddin:** coarse woollen cloth 11 **Gie:** give 17 **birkie:** fellow **ca'd:** called 18 **Wha:** who 20 **coof:** fool 25 **belted:** wearing a waistband denoting rank 27 **aboon:** above 28 **mauna fa':** may not create (i.e. such an honour is not in his gift) 36 **bear the gree:** come off best 39 **warld:** world

'OH WERT THOU IN THE CAULD BLAST'

OH wert thou in the cauld blast,
    On yonder lea, on yonder lea;
My plaidie to the angry airt,
    I'd shelter thee, I'd shelter thee:
Or did misfortune's bitter storms   5
    Around thee blaw, around thee blaw,
Thy bield should be my bosom,
    To share it a', to share it a'.

Or were I in the wildest waste,
    Sae black and bare, sae black and bare, 10
The desart were a paradise,
    If thou wert there, if thou wert there.
Or were I monarch o' the globe,
    Wi' thee to reign, wi' thee to reign;
The brightest jewel in my crown,   15
    Wad be my queen, wad be my queen.

'OH WERT THOU IN THE CAULD BLAST': 2 **lea:** pasture 3 **plaidie:** woollen cloak **airt:** quarter (i.e. he would shelter her from the driving wind) 6 **blaw:** blow 7 **bield:** shelter

COMIN THRO' THE RYE

COMIN thro' the rye, poor body,
    Comin thro' the rye,
She draigl't a' her petticoatie
    Comin thro' the rye.
      Oh Jenny's a' weet, poor body,   5
        Jenny's seldom dry;
      She draigl't a' her petticoatie
        Comin thro' the rye.

Gin a body meet a body
    Comin thro' the rye,   10
Gin a body kiss a body
    Need a body cry?
      Oh Jenny's a' weet, poor body,
        Jenny's seldom dry;
      She draigl't a' her petticoatie   15
        Comin thro' the rye.

Gin a body meet a body
    Comin thro' the glen;
Gin a body kiss a body
    Need the warld ken?   20
      Oh Jenny's a' weet, poor body,
        Jenny's seldom dry;
      She draigl't a' her petticoatie
        Comin thro' the rye.

COMIN THRO' THE RYE: 3 **draigl't:** bespattered **a':** all 5 **a' weet:** all wet 9 **Gin:** if 20 **ken:** know

WILLIAM WORDSWORTH

WE ARE SEVEN

— A SIMPLE Child,
That lightly draws its breath,
And feels its life in every limb,
What should it know of death?

I met a little cottage Girl: 5
She was eight years old, she said;
Her hair was thick with many a curl
That clustered round her head.

She had a rustic, woodland air,
And she was wildly clad: 10
Her eyes were fair, and very fair;
– Her beauty made me glad.

'Sisters and brothers, little Maid,
How many may you be?'
'How many? Seven in all,' she said,   15
And wondering looked at me.

'And where are they? I pray you tell.'
She answered, 'Seven are we;
And two of us at Conway dwell,
And two are gone to sea.   20

'Two of us in the church-yard lie,
My sister and my brother;
And, in the church-yard cottage, I
Dwell near them with my mother.'

'You say that two at Conway dwell,   25
And two are gone to sea,
Yet ye are seven! I pray you tell,
Sweet Maid, how this may be.'

Then did the little Maid reply,
'Seven boys and girls are we;   30
Two of us in the church-yard lie,
Beneath the church-yard tree.'

'You run about, my little Maid,
Your limbs they are alive;
If two are in the church-yard laid,   35
Then ye are only five.'

'Their graves are green, they may be seen,'
The little Maid replied,
'Twelve steps or more from my mother's door,
And they are side by side.   40

'My stockings there I often knit,
My kerchief there I hem;
And there upon the ground I sit,
And sing a song to them.

'And often after sun-set, Sir,   45
When it is light and fair,
I take my little porringer,
And eat my supper there.

'The first that died was sister Jane;
In bed she moaning lay,   50
Till God released her of her pain;
And then she went away.

'So in the church-yard she was laid;
And, when the grass was dry,
Together round her grave we played,   55
My brother John and I.

'And when the ground was white with snow,
And I could run and slide,
My brother John was forced to go,
And he lies by her side.'   60

'How many are you, then,' said I,
'If they two are in heaven?'
Quick was the little Maid's reply,
'Oh, Master! we are seven.'

'But they are dead; those two are dead!   65
Their spirits are in heaven!'
'Twas throwing words away; for still
The little Maid would have her will,
And said, 'Nay, we are seven!'

WE ARE SEVEN: 25 **Conway:** Conwy in north Wales 47 **porringer:**
shallow bowl for soup or porridge

LINES WRITTEN IN EARLY SPRING

I HEARD a thousand blended notes,
While in a grove I sate reclined,
In that sweet mood when pleasant thoughts
Bring sad thoughts to the mind.

To her fair works did Nature link   5
The human soul that through me ran;
And much it grieved my heart to think
What man has made of man.

Through primrose tufts, in that green bower,
The periwinkle trailed its wreaths;   10
And 'tis my faith that every flower
Enjoys the air it breathes.

The birds around me hopped and played,
Their thoughts I cannot measure: –
But the least motion which they made,   15
It seemed a thrill of pleasure.

The budding twigs spread out their fan,
To catch the breezy air;
And I must think, do all I can,
That there was pleasure there.   20

If this belief from heaven be sent,
If such be Nature's holy plan,
Have I not reason to lament
What man has made of man?

LINES WRITTEN IN EARLY SPRING: 2 **sate:** sat (archaic)

LINES

COMPOSED A FEW MILES ABOVE TINTERN ABBEY,
ON REVISITING THE BANKS OF THE WYE DURING A TOUR.
JULY 13, 1798

FIVE years have passed; five summers, with the length
Of five long winters! and again I hear
These waters, rolling from their mountain-springs
With a soft inland murmur. – Once again
Do I behold these steep and lofty cliffs,   5
That on a wild secluded scene impress
Thoughts of more deep seclusion; and connect
The landscape with the quiet of the sky.
The day is come when I again repose
Here, under this dark sycamore, and view   10
These plots of cottage-ground, these orchard-tufts,
Which at this season, with their unripe fruits,
Are clad in one green hue, and lose themselves
'Mid groves and copses. Once again I see
These hedge-rows, hardly hedge-rows, little lines   15
Of sportive wood run wild: these pastoral farms,
Green to the very door; and wreaths of smoke
Sent up, in silence, from among the trees!
With some uncertain notice, as might seem
Of vagrant dwellers in the houseless woods,   20
Or of some Hermit's cave, where by his fire
The Hermit sits alone.
                          These beauteous forms,
Through a long absence, have not been to me
As is a landscape to a blind man's eye:
But oft, in lonely rooms, and 'mid the din   25
Of towns and cities, I have owed to them
In hours of weariness, sensations sweet,
Felt in the blood, and felt along the heart;
And passing even into my purer mind,

With tranquil restoration: – feelings too   30
Of unremembered pleasure: such, perhaps,
As have no slight or trivial influence
On that best portion of a good man's life,
His little, nameless, unremembered, acts
Of kindness and of love. Nor less, I trust,   35
To them I may have owed another gift,
Of aspect more sublime; that blessèd mood,
In which the burthen of the mystery,
In which the heavy and the weary weight
Of all this unintelligible world,   40
Is lightened: – that serene and blessèd mood,
In which the affections gently lead us on, –
Until, the breath of this corporeal frame
And even the motion of our human blood
Almost suspended, we are laid asleep   45
In body, and become a living soul:
While with an eye made quiet by the power
Of harmony, and the deep power of joy,
We see into the life of things.
                                If this
Be but a vain belief, yet, oh! how oft –   50
In darkness and amid the many shapes
Of joyless daylight; when the fretful stir
Unprofitable, and the fever of the world,
Have hung upon the beatings of my heart –
How oft, in spirit, have I turned to thee,   55
O sylvan Wye! thou wanderer through the woods,
How often has my spirit turned to thee!
  And now, with gleams of half-extinguished thought,
With many recognitions dim and faint,
And somewhat of a sad perplexity,   60
The picture of the mind revives again:
While here I stand, not only with the sense
Of present pleasure, but with pleasing thoughts
That in this moment there is life and food
For future years. And so I dare to hope,   65
Though changed, no doubt, from what I was when
     first
I came among these hills; when like a roe
I bounded o'er the mountains, by the sides
Of the deep rivers, and the lonely streams,
Wherever nature led: more like a man   70
Flying from something that he dreads, than one
Who sought the thing he loved. For nature then
(The coarser pleasures of my boyish days,
And their glad animal movements all gone by)
To me was all in all. – I cannot paint   75
What then I was. The sounding cataract
Haunted me like a passion: the tall rock,
The mountain, and the deep and gloomy wood,
Their colours and their forms, were then to me
An appetite: a feeling and a love,   80
That had no need of a remoter charm,
By thought supplied, nor any interest

TINTERN ABBEY: 'July 1798. No poem of mine was composed under circumstances more pleasant for me to remember than this. I began it upon leaving Tintern, after crossing the Wye, and concluded it just as I was entering Bristol in the evening, after a ramble of 4 or 5 days, with my sister. Not a line of it was altered, and not any part of it written down till I reached Bristol' (Wordsworth): 1 **Five years have passed:** Wordsworth had visited Tintern in 1793 14 **copses:** areas of managed woodland 16 **pastoral:** pastureland 21 **Hermit:** recluse

38 **burthen:** burden (archaic) 56 **sylvan:** flowing through woodland 67 **roe:** deer 76 **cataract:** waterfall

Unborrowed from the eye. – That time is past,
And all its aching joys are now no more,
And all its dizzy raptures. Not for this   85
Faint I, nor mourn nor murmur; other gifts
Have followed; for such loss, I would believe,
Abundant recompense. For I have learned
To look on nature, not as in the hour
Of thoughtless youth; but hearing oftentimes   90
The still, sad music of humanity,
Nor harsh nor grating, though of ample power
To chasten and subdue. And I have felt
A presence that disturbs me with the joy
Of elevated thoughts; a sense sublime   95
Of something far more deeply interfused,
Whose dwelling is the light of setting suns,
And the round ocean and the living air,
And the blue sky, and in the mind of man:
A motion and a spirit, that impels   100
All thinking things, all objects of all thought,
And rolls through all things. Therefore am I still
A lover of the meadows and the woods,
And mountains; and of all that we behold
From this green earth; of all the mighty world   105
Of eye, and ear, – both what they half create,
And what perceive; well pleased to recognise
In nature and the language of the sense,
The anchor of my purest thoughts, the nurse,
The guide, the guardian of my heart, and soul   110
Of all my moral being.
                    Nor perchance,
If I were not thus taught, should I the more
Suffer my genial spirits to decay:
For thou art with me here upon the banks
Of this fair river; thou, my dearest Friend,   115
My dear, dear Friend; and in thy voice I catch
The language of my former heart, and read
My former pleasures in the shooting lights
Of thy wild eyes. Oh! yet a little while
May I behold in thee what I was once,   120
My dear, dear Sister! and this prayer I make,
Knowing that Nature never did betray
The heart that loved her; 'tis her privilege,
Through all the years of this our life, to lead
From joy to joy: for she can so inform   125
The mind that is within us, so impress
With quietness and beauty, and so feed
With lofty thoughts, that neither evil tongues,
Rash judgements, nor the sneers of selfish men,
Nor greetings where no kindness is, nor all   130
The dreary intercourse of daily life,
Shall e'er prevail against us, or disturb
Our cheerful faith, that all which we behold
Is full of blessings. Therefore let the moon

Shine on thee in thy solitary walk;   135
And let the misty mountain-winds be free
To blow against thee: and, in after years,
When these wild ecstasies shall be matured
Into a sober pleasure; when thy mind
Shall be a mansion for all lovely forms,   140
Thy memory be as a dwelling-place
For all sweet sounds and harmonies; oh! then,
If solitude, or fear, or pain, or grief,
Should be thy portion, with what healing thoughts
Of tender joy wilt thou remember me,   145
And these my exhortations! Nor, perchance –
If I should be where I no more can hear
Thy voice, nor catch from thy wild eyes these gleams
Of past existence – wilt thou then forget
That on the banks of this delightful stream   150
We stood together; and that I, so long
A worshipper of Nature, hither came
Unwearied in that service: rather say
With warmer love – oh! with far deeper zeal
Of holier love. Nor wilt thou then forget,   155
That after many wanderings, many years
Of absence, these steep woods and lofty cliffs,
And this green pastoral landscape, were to me
More dear, both for themselves and for thy sake!

144 **portion:** destiny

'A SLUMBER DID MY SPIRIT SEAL'

A SLUMBER did my spirit seal;
  I had no human fears:
She seemed a thing that could not feel
  The touch of earthly years.

No motion has she now, no force;   5
  She neither hears nor sees;
Rolled round in earth's diurnal course,
  With rocks, and stones, and trees.

'A SLUMBER DID MY SPIRIT SEAL': 'Some months ago Wordsworth transmitted to me a most sublime epitaph – whether it had any reality, I cannot say. – Most probably, in some gloomier moment he had fancied the moment in which his sister might die' (Coleridge, letter to Thomas Poole, 6 April 1799). This is the first of the 'Lucy' poems; the original of 'Lucy' is unknown, but she has been identified with Dorothy Wordsworth 7 **diurnal:** daily

'SHE DWELT AMONG THE UNTRODDEN WAYS'

SHE dwelt among the untrodden ways
  Beside the springs of Dove,
A Maid whom there were none to praise,
  And very few to love;

92 **Nor . . . nor:** neither . . . nor 96 **interfused:** fused together, blended 113 **genial spirits:** creativity, springing from the poet's genius 115 **my dearest Friend:** Dorothy, Wordsworth's sister

A violet by a mossy stone
  Half-hidden from the eye!   5
– Fair as a star, when only one
  Is shining in the sky.

She lived unknown, and few could know
  When Lucy ceased to be;   10
But she is in her grave, and, oh,
  The difference to me!

'SHE DWELT AMONG THE UNTRODDEN WAYS': a 'Lucy' poem: 2 **Dove:** unidentifiable; three English rivers bear this name

'STRANGE FITS OF PASSION HAVE I KNOWN'

STRANGE fits of passion have I known:
And I will dare to tell,
But in the Lover's ear alone,
What once to me befell.

When she I loved looked every day   5
Fresh as a rose in June,
I to her cottage bent my way,
Beneath an evening moon.

Upon the moon I fixed my eye,
All over the wide lea;   10
With quickening pace my horse drew nigh
Those paths so dear to me.

And now we reached the orchard-plot;
And, as we climbed the hill,
The sinking moon to Lucy's cot   15
Came near, and nearer still.

In one of those sweet dreams I slept,
Kind Nature's gentlest boon!
And all the while my eyes I kept
On the descending moon.   20

My horse moved on; hoof after hoof
He raised, and never stopped:
When down behind the cottage roof,
At once, the bright moon dropped.

What fond and wayward thoughts will slide   25
Into a Lover's head!
'Oh mercy!' to myself I cried,
'If Lucy should be dead!'

'STRANGE FITS OF PASSION HAVE I KNOWN: a 'Lucy' poem: 10 **lea:** open country 15 **cot:** cottage 18 **boon:** reward

'THREE YEARS SHE GREW IN SUN AND SHOWER'

THREE years she grew in sun and shower,
Then Nature said, 'A lovelier flower
On earth was never sown;
This Child I to myself will take;
She shall be mine, and I will make   5
A Lady of my own.

'Myself will to my darling be
Both law and impulse: and with me
The Girl, in rock and plain,
In earth and heaven, in glade and bower,   10
Shall feel an overseeing power
To kindle or restrain.

'She shall be sportive as the fawn
That wild with glee across the lawn
Or up the mountain springs;   15
And hers shall be the breathing balm,
And hers the silence and the calm
Of mute insensate things.

'The floating clouds their state shall lend
To her; for her the willow bend;   20
Nor shall she fail to see
Even in the motions of the Storm
Grace that shall mould the Maiden's form
By silent sympathy.

'The stars of midnight shall be dear   25
To her; and she shall lean her ear
In many a secret place
Where rivulets dance their wayward round,
And beauty born of murmuring sound
Shall pass into her face.   30

'And vital feelings of delight
Shall rear her form to stately height,
Her virgin bosom swell;
Such thoughts to Lucy I will give
While she and I together live   35
Here in this happy dell.'

Thus Nature spake – The work was done –
How soon my Lucy's race was run!
She died, and left to me
This heath, this calm, and quiet scene;   40
The memory of what has been,
And never more will be.

'THREE YEARS SHE GREW IN SUN AND SHOWER': a 'Lucy' poem: 10 **bower:** arbour 36 **dell:** wooded hollow or small valley

'I TRAVELLED AMONG UNKNOWN MEN'

I TRAVELLED among unknown men
  In lands beyond the sea;
Nor, England! did I know till then
  What love I bore to thee.

'Tis past, that melancholy dream!   5
  Nor will I quit thy shore
A second time; for still I seem
  To love thee more and more.

Among thy mountains did I feel
  The joy of my desire;   10
And she I cherished turned her wheel
  Beside an English fire.

Thy mornings showed, thy nights concealed,
  The bowers where Lucy played;
And thine too is the last green field   15
  That Lucy's eyes surveyed.

'I TRAVELLED AMONG UNKNOWN MEN': a 'Lucy' poem: 11 **turned her wheel**: i.e. worked at her spinning-wheel 14 **bowers**: arbours

LUCY GRAY; OR, SOLITUDE

OFT I had heard of Lucy Gray:
And, when I crossed the wild,
I chanced to see at break of day
The solitary child.

No mate, no comrade Lucy knew;   5
She dwelt on a wide moor,
– The sweetest thing that ever grew
Beside a human door!

You yet may spy the fawn at play,
The hare upon the green;   10
But the sweet face of Lucy Gray
Will never more be seen.

'Tonight will be a stormy night –
You to the town must go;
And take a lantern, Child, to light   15
Your mother through the snow.'

'That, Father! will I gladly do:
'Tis scarcely afternoon –
The minster-clock has just struck two,
And yonder is the moon!'   20

At this the Father raised his hook,
And snapped a faggot-band;
He plied his work; – and Lucy took
The lantern in her hand.

Not blither is the mountain roe: 25
With many a wanton stroke
Her feet disperse the powdery snow,
That rises up like smoke.

The storm came on before its time:
She wandered up and down;   30
And many a hill did Lucy climb:
But never reached the town.

The wretched parents all that night
Went shouting far and wide;
But there was neither sound nor sight   35
To serve them for a guide.

At day-break on a hill they stood
That overlooked the moor;
And thence they saw the bridge of wood,
A furlong from their door.   40

They wept – and, turning homeward, cried,
'In heaven we all shall meet';
– When in the snow the mother spied
The print of Lucy's feet.

Then downwards from the steep hill's edge 45
They tracked the footmarks small;
And through the broken hawthorn hedge,
And by the long stone-wall;

And then an open field they crossed:
The marks were still the same;   50
They tracked them on, nor ever lost;
And to the bridge they came.

They followed from the snowy bank
Those footmarks, one by one,
Into the middle of the plank;   55
And further there were none!

– Yet some maintain that to this day
She is a living child;
That you may see sweet Lucy Gray
Upon the lonesome wild.   60

O'er rough and smooth she trips along,
And never looks behind;
And sings a solitary song
That whistles in the wind.

LUCY GRAY: 'It was founded on a circumstance told me by my Sister, of a little girl who, not far from Halifax in Yorkshire, was bewildered in a snow-storm. Her footsteps were traced by her parents to the middle of the lock of a canal, and no other vestige of her, backward or forward, could be traced. The body however was found in the canal. The way in which the incident was treated and the spiritualizing of the character might furnish hints for contrasting the imaginative influences which I have endeavoured to throw over common life with Crabbe's matter of fact style of treating subjects of the same kind' (Wordsworth) 21 **hook**: curved blade 22 **faggot-band**: bundle of sticks 25 **roe**: deer

WILLIAM WORDSWORTH

TO THE CUCKOO

O BLITHE New-comer! I have heard,
I hear thee and rejoice.
O Cuckoo! shall I call thee Bird,
Or but a wandering Voice?

While I am lying on the grass   5
Thy twofold shout I hear,
From hill to hill it seems to pass,
At once far off, and near.

Though babbling only to the Vale,
Of sunshine and of flowers,   10
Thou bringest unto me a tale
Of visionary hours.

Thrice welcome, darling of the Spring!
Even yet thou art to me
No bird, but an invisible thing,   15
A voice, a mystery;

The same whom in my schoolboy days
I listened to; that Cry
Which made me look a thousand ways
In bush, and tree, and sky.   20

To seek thee did I often rove
Through woods and on the green;
And thou wert still a hope, a love;
Still longed for, never seen.

And I can listen to thee yet;   25
Can lie upon the plain
And listen, till I do beget
That golden time again.

O blessèd Bird! the earth we pace
Again appears to be   30
An unsubstantial, faery place;
That is fit home for Thee!

TO THE CUCKOO: 'characterizes the seeming ubiquity of the voice of the cuckoo, and dispossesses the creature almost of a corporeal existence; the Imagination being tempted to this exertion of her power by a consciousness in the memory that the cuckoo is almost perpetually heard throughout the season of spring, but seldom becomes an object of sight' (Wordsworth, preface to *Poems*, 1815)

'THE WORLD IS TOO MUCH WITH US . . .'

THE world is too much with us; late and soon,
Getting and spending, we lay waste our powers:
Little we see in Nature that is ours;
We have given our hearts away, a sordid boon!
This Sea that bares her bosom to the moon;   5
The winds that will be howling at all hours,
And are up-gathered now like sleeping flowers;
For this, for everything, we are out of tune;
It moves us not. – Great God! I'd rather be
A Pagan suckled in a creed outworn;   10

So might I, standing on this pleasant lea,
Have glimpses that would make me less forlorn;
Have sight of Proteus rising from the sea;
Or hear old Triton blow his wreathèd horn.

'THE WORLD IS TOO MUCH WITH US': 4 **boon:** gift   11 **lea:** pasture 13–14 **Proteus . . . Triton:** sea-gods in Greek mythology

'MY HEART LEAPS UP . . .'

My heart leaps up when I behold
  A rainbow in the sky:
So was it when my life began;
So is it now I am a man;
So be it when I shall grow old,   5
  Or let me die!
The Child is father of the Man;
And I could wish my days to be
Bound each to each by natural piety.

ODE

INTIMATIONS OF IMMORTALITY FROM RECOLLECTIONS OF EARLY CHILDHOOD

> The Child is father of the Man;
> And I could wish my days to be
> Bound each to each by natural piety.

THERE was a time when meadow, grove, and stream,
The earth, and every common sight,
    To me did seem
    Apparelled in celestial light,
The glory and the freshness of a dream.   5
It is not now as it hath been of yore; –
    Turn wheresoe'er I may,
    By night or day,
The things which I have seen I now can see no more.

INTIMATIONS OF IMMORTALITY: Begun on 27 March 1802 and completed probably in 1804. Wordsworth recalled that 'two years at least passed between the writing of the first four stanzas and the remaining part'. In his most substantial commentary on the Ode, Wordsworth referred back to the opening stanza of 'We Are Seven', recalling that 'Nothing was more difficult for me in childhood than to admit the notion of death as a state applicable to my own being'. Aware of 'a sense of the indomitableness of the spirit within me', 'I used to brood over the stories of Enoch and Elijah, and almost to persuade myself that, whatever might become of others, I should be translated, in something of the same way, to heaven. With a feeling congenial to this, I was often unable to think of external things as having external existence, and I communed with all that I saw as something not apart from, but inherent in, my own immaterial nature. Many times while going to school have I grasped at a wall or tree to recall myself from this abyss of idealism to the reality. At that time I was afraid of such processes. In later periods of life I have deplored, as we have all reason to do, a subjugation of an opposite character, and have rejoiced over the remembrances. . . . To that dream-like vividness and splendour which invest objects of sight in childhood, every one, I believe, if he would look back, could bear testimony'; adding on another occasion: 'The poem rests entirely upon two recollections of childhood, one that of a splendour in the objects of sense which is passed away, and the other an indisposition to bend to the law of death as applying to our particular case': **'The child . . . piety':** taken from 'My heart leaps up'; see also note to line 23 below 6 **of yore:** in times past

The Rainbow come and goes,   10
  And lovely is the Rose,
  The Moon doth with delight
Look round her when the heavens are bare;
  Waters on a starry night
  Are beautiful and fair;   15
The sunshine is a glorious birth;
  But yet I know, where'er I go,
That there hath passed away a glory from the earth.

Now, while the birds thus sing a joyous song,
  And while the young lambs bound   20
  As to the tabor's sound,
To me alone there came a thought of grief:
A timely utterance gave that thought relief,
  And I again am strong:
The cataracts blow their trumpets from the steep;   25
No more shall grief of mine the season wrong;
I hear the Echoes through the mountains throng,
The Winds come to me from the fields of sleep,
  And all the earth is gay;
  Land and sea   30
  Give themselves up to jollity,
  And with the heart of May
Doth every Beast keep holiday; –
  Thou Child of Joy,
Shout round me, let me hear thy shouts, thou happy
  Shepherd-Boy!   35

Ye blessèd Creatures, I have heard the call
  Ye to each other make; I see
The heavens laugh with you in your jubilee;
  My heart is at your festival,
  My head hath its coronal,   40
The fullness of your bliss, I feel – I feel it all.
  Oh evil day! if I were sullen
  While Earth herself is adorning,
  This sweet May-morning,
  And the Children are culling   45
  On every side,
In a thousand valleys far and wide,
Fresh flowers; while the sun shines warm,
And the Babe leaps up on his Mother's arm: –
  I hear, I hear, with joy I hear!   50
  – But there's a Tree, of many, one,
A single Field which I have looked upon,
Both of them speak of something that is gone:
  The Pansy at my feet
  Doth the same tale repeat: 55
Whither is fled the visionary gleam?
Where is it now, the glory and the dream?

Our birth is but a sleep and a forgetting:
The Soul that rises with us, our life's Star,
  Hath had elsewhere its setting,   60
  And cometh from afar:
  Not in entire forgetfulness,
  And not in utter nakedness,
But trailing clouds of glory do we come
  From God, who is our home: 65
Heaven lies about us in our infancy!
Shades of the prison-house begin to close
  Upon the growing Boy,
  But He
Beholds the light, and whence it flows,   70
  He sees it in his joy;
The Youth, who daily farther from the east
  Must travel, still is Nature's Priest,
  And by the vision splendid
  Is on his way attended;   75
At length the Man perceives it die away,
And fade into the light of common day.

Earth fills her lap with pleasures of her own;
Yearnings she hath in her own natural kind,
And, even with something of a Mother's mind,   80
  And no unworthy aim,
  The homely Nurse doth all she can
To make her Foster-child, her Inmate Man,
  Forget the glories he hath known,
And that imperial palace whence he came.   85

Behold the Child among his new-born blisses,
A six years' Darling of a pigmy size!
See, where 'mid work of his own hand he lies,
Fretted by sallies of his mother's kisses,
With light upon him from his father's eyes!   90
See, at his feet, some little plan or chart,
Some fragment from his dream of human life,
Shaped by himself with newly learnèd art;
  A wedding or a festival,
  A mourning or a funeral;   95
  And this hath now his heart,
  And unto this he frames his song:
  Then will he fit his tongue
To dialogues of business, love, or strife;
  But it will not be long   100
  Ere this be thrown aside,
  And with new joy and pride
The little Actor cons another part;
Filling from time to time his 'humorous stage'
With all the Persons, down to palsied Age,   105
That Life brings with her in her equipage;
  As if his whole vocation
  Were endless imitation.

---

21 **tabor**: a small drum, usually played with a stick and accompanied by a fife 23 **A timely utterance**: possibly a reference to 'My heart leaps up', which was written the day before Wordsworth began work on the Ode and from which he took three lines to stand as an epigraph 25 **cataracts**: waterfalls 38 **jubilee**: festivity, celebration 40 **coronal**: crown woven from flowers 51 **there's a Tree**: cf. *The Prelude* 4.86–92 and 6.76–94 below

72 **from the east**: from the sunrise, i.e. from birth 86–90 **Behold the Child . . . his father's eyes!**: usually taken to refer to Coleridge's son Hartley 89 **sallies**: assaults 103 **cons**: studies, learns 104 **humorous**: fanciful; the quotation comes from a dedicatory sonnet to Samuel Daniel's *Musophilus* 105 **Persons**: i.e. characters in the play **palsied**: weak-limbed or paralysed 106 **equipage**: retinue

Thou, whose exterior semblance doth belie
    Thy Soul's immensity;   110
Thou best Philosopher, who yet dost keep
Thy heritage, thou Eye among the blind,
That, deaf and silent, read'st the eternal deep,
Haunted for ever by the eternal mind, –
    Mighty Prophet! Seer blest!   115
    On whom those truths do rest,
Which we are toiling all our lives to find,
In darkness lost, the darkness of the grave;
Thou, over whom thy Immortality
Broods like the Day, a Master o'er a Slave,   120
A Presence which is not to be put by;
Thou little Child, yet glorious in the might
Of heaven-born freedom on thy being's height,
Why with such earnest pains dost thou provoke
The years to bring the inevitable yoke,   125
Thus blindly with thy blessedness at strife?
Full soon thy Soul shall have her earthly freight,
And custom lie upon thee with a weight,
Heavy as frost, and deep almost as life!

    O joy! that in our embers   130
    Is something that doth live,
    That nature yet remembers
    What was so fugitive!
The thought of our past years in me doth breed
Perpetual benediction: not indeed   135
For that which is most worthy to be blest;
Delight and liberty, the simple creed
Of Childhood, whether busy or at rest,
With new-fledged hope still fluttering in his breast: –
    Not for these I raise   140
    The song of thanks and praise;
    But for those obstinate questionings
    Of sense and outward things,
    Fallings from us, vanishings;
    Blank misgivings of a Creature   145
Moving about in worlds not realised,
High instincts before which our mortal Nature
Did tremble like a guilty Thing surprised:
    But for those first affections,
    Those shadowy recollections,   150
    Which, be they what they may,
Are yet the fountain light of all our day,
Are yet a master light of all our seeing;
    Uphold us, cherish, and have power to make
Our noisy years seem moments in the being   155
Of the eternal Silence: truths that wake,
    To perish never:

Which neither listlessness, nor mad endeavour,
    Nor Man nor Boy,
Nor all that is at enmity with joy,   160
Can utterly abolish or destroy!
    Hence in a season of calm weather
    Though inland far we be,
Our Souls have sight of that immortal sea
    Which brought us hither,   165
  Can in a moment travel thither,
And see the Children sport upon the shore,
And hear the mighty waters rolling evermore.

Then sing, ye Birds, sing, sing a joyous song!
    And let the young Lambs bound   170
    As to the tabor's sound!
We in thought will join your throng,
    Ye that pipe and ye that play,
    Ye that through your hearts today
    Feel the gladness of the May!   175
What though the radiance which was once so bright
Be now for ever taken from my sight,
    Though nothing can bring back the hour
Of splendour in the grass, of glory in the flower;
    We will grieve not, rather find   180
    Strength in what remains behind;
    In the primal sympathy
    Which having been must ever be;
    In the soothing thoughts that spring
    Out of human suffering;   185
    In the faith that looks through death,
In years that bring the philosophic mind.

And O, ye Fountains, Meadows, Hills, and Groves,
Forebode not any severing of our loves!
Yet in my heart of hearts I feel your might;   190
I only have relinquished one delight
To live beneath your more habitual sway.
I love the Brooks which down their channels fret,
Even more than when I tripped lightly as they;
The innocent brightness of a new-born Day   195
    Is lovely yet;
The Clouds that gather round the setting sun
Do take a sober colouring from an eye
That hath kept watch o'er man's mortality;
Another race hath been, and other palms are won.
Thanks to the human heart by which we live,   201
Thanks to its tenderness, its joys, and fears,
To me the meanest flower that blows can give
Thoughts that do often lie too deep for tears.

127–9 **Full soon thy Soul . . . deep almost as life!:** cf. *The Prelude*
14.157–62 below 127 **freight:** load, cargo 133 **fugitive:** fleeting 148 **like
a guilty thing surprised:** cf. Shakespeare's *Hamlet* (1.1): 'it started
like a guilty thing/Upon a dreadful summons'

182 **the primal sympathy:** cf. *The Prelude* 1.555–8 below 200 **other
palms are won:** in ancient times a palm leaf was awarded to a
successful athlete or gladiator to symbolise victory

COMPOSED UPON WESTMINSTER BRIDGE, SEPTEMBER 3, 1802

EARTH has not anything to show more fair:
Dull would he be of soul who could pass by
A sight so touching in its majesty:
This City now doth, like a garment, wear
The beauty of the morning; silent, bare, 5
Ships, towers, domes, théatres, and temples lie
Open unto the fields, and to the sky;
All bright and glittering in the smokeless air.
Never did sun more beautifully steep
In his first splendour, valley, rock, or hill; 10
Ne'er saw I, never felt, a calm so deep!
The river glideth at his own sweet will:
Dear God! the very houses seem asleep;
And all that mighty heart is lying still!

UPON WESTMINSTER BRIDGE: '[W]e left London on Saturday morning at half past five or six, the 31st of July . . . We mounted the Dover coach at Charing Cross. It was a beautiful morning. The City, St Paul's, with the river and a multitude of little boats, made a most beautiful sight as we crossed Westminster Bridge. The houses were not overhung by their cloud of smoke and they were spread out endlessly, yet the sun shone so brightly with such a pure light that there was even something like the purity of one of nature's own grand spectacles' (Dorothy Wordsworth, journal entry, 1802)

'IT IS A BEAUTEOUS EVENING, CALM AND FREE'

IT is a beauteous evening, calm and free,
The holy time is quiet as a Nun
Breathless with adoration; the broad sun
Is sinking down in its tranquillity;
The gentleness of heaven broods o'er the Sea: 5
Listen! the mighty Being is awake,
And doth with his eternal motion make
A sound like thunder – everlastingly.
Dear Child! dear Girl! that walkest with me here,
If thou appear untouched by solemn thought, 10
Thy nature is not therefore less divine:
Thou liest in Abraham's bosom all the year;
And worship'st at the Temple's inner shrine,
God being with thee when we know it not.

'IT IS A BEAUTEOUS EVENING': Wordsworth recalled that 'This was composed on the beach near Calais in the autumn of 1802', and his sister Dorothy recorded: 'The weather was very hot. We walked by the sea shore almost every evening with Annette [Vallon] and Caroline, or William and I alone . . . Caroline was delighted': 9 **Dear Child:** Caroline, Wordsworth's daughter (born 1792) by Annette Vallon 12 **in Abraham's bosom:** 'And it came to pass, that the beggar died, and was carried by the angels into Abraham's bosom' (Luke 16.22) 13 **the Temple's inner shrine:** the Holy of Holies, the innermost chamber of the Jewish temple which only the high priest was allowed to enter

LONDON, 1802

MILTON! thou shouldst be living at this hour:
England hath need of thee: she is a fen
Of stagnant waters: altar, sword, and pen,
Fireside, the heroic wealth of hall and bower,
Have forfeited their ancient English dower 5
Of inward happiness. We are selfish men;
Oh! raise us up, return to us again;
And give us manners, virtue, freedom, power.
Thy soul was like a Star, and dwelt apart:
Thou hadst a voice whose sound was like the sea: 10
Pure as the naked heavens, majestic, free,
So didst thou travel on life's common way,
In cheerful godliness; and yet thy heart
The lowliest duties on herself did lay.

LONDON, 1802: 4 **bower:** chamber 5 **dower:** endowment

'SHE WAS A PHANTOM OF DELIGHT'

SHE was a Phantom of delight
When first she gleamed upon my sight;
A lovely Apparition, sent
To be a moment's ornament;
Her eyes as stars of Twilight fair; 5
Like Twilight's, too, her dusky hair;
But all things else about her drawn
From May-time and the cheerful Dawn;
A dancing Shape, an Image gay,
To haunt, to startle, and way-lay. 10

I saw her upon nearer view,
A Spirit, yet a Woman too!
Her household motions light and free,
And steps of virgin-liberty;
A countenance in which did meet 15
Sweet records, promises as sweet;
A Creature not too bright or good
For human nature's daily food;
For transient sorrows, simple wiles,
Praise, blame, love, kisses, tears, and smiles. 20

And now I see with eye serene
The very pulse of the machine;
A Being breathing thoughtful breath,
A Traveller between life and death;
The reason firm, the temperate will, 25
Endurance, foresight, strength, and skill;
A perfect Woman, nobly planned,
To warn, to comfort, and command;
And yet a Spirit still, and bright
With something of angelic light. 30

'SHE WAS A PHANTOM OF DELIGHT': Wordsworth identified the subject as his 'dear wife', Mary

'I WANDERED LONELY AS A CLOUD'

I WANDERED lonely as a cloud
That floats on high o'er vales and hills,
When all at once I saw a crowd,
A host, of golden daffodils;
Beside the lake, beneath the trees,   5
Fluttering and dancing in the breeze.

Continuous as the stars that shine
And twinkle on the milky way,
They stretched in never-ending line
Along the margin of a bay: 10
Ten thousand saw I at a glance,
Tossing their heads in sprightly dance.

The waves beside them danced; but they
Out-did the sparkling waves in glee:
A poet could not but be gay,   15
In such a jocund company:
I gazed – and gazed – but little thought
What wealth the show to me had brought:

For oft, when on my couch I lie
In vacant or in pensive mood,   20
They flash upon that inward eye
Which is the bliss of solitude;
And then my heart with pleasure fills,
And dances with the daffodils.

'I WANDERED LONELY AS A CLOUD': Wordsworth dated the poem to
1804, but his sister Dorothy recorded the experience that inspired
it in her journal for April 1802: 'When we were in the woods
beyond Gowbarrow park we saw a few daffodils close to the water
side. We fancied that the lake had floated the seeds ashore and
that the little colony had so sprung up. But as we went along there
were more and yet more, and at last under the boughs of the trees
we saw that there was a long belt of them along the shore, about
the breadth of a country turnpike road. I never saw daffodils so
beautiful; they grew among the mossy stones about and about
them; some rested their heads upon these stones as on a pillow for
weariness, and the rest tossed and reeled and danced and seemed
as if they verily laughed with the wind that blew upon them over
the lake, they looked so gay, ever glancing, ever changing.'
Commenting on the poem in 1843, Wordsworth noted that 'The
daffodils grew and still grow on the margin of Ullswater and
probably may be seen to this day as beautiful in the month of
March, nodding their golden heads beside the dancing and
foaming waves'. He credited the 'two best lines' (lines 21 and 22?)
to his wife, Mary. The wild daffodil described by Wordsworth is a
smaller plant than the familiar tall garden variety, which certainly
does not flutter and dance 10 **margin**: shore 16 **jocund**: merry

THE SOLITARY REAPER

BEHOLD her, single in the field,
Yon solitary Highland Lass!
Reaping and singing by herself;
Stop here, or gently pass!
Alone she cuts and binds the grain,   5
And sings a melancholy strain;
Oh, listen! for the Vale profound
Is overflowing with the sound.

No Nightingale did ever chant
More welcome notes to weary bands   10
Of travellers in some shady haunt,
Among Arabian sands:
A voice so thrilling ne'er was heard
In spring-time from the Cuckoo-bird,
Breaking the silence of the seas   15
Among the farthest Hebrides.

Will no one tell me what she sings? –
Perhaps the plaintive numbers flow
For old, unhappy, far-off things,
And battles long ago: 20
Or is it some more humble lay,
Familiar matter of today?
Some natural sorrow, loss, or pain,
That has been, and may be again?

Whate'er the theme, the Maiden sang   25
As if her song could have no ending;
I saw her singing at her work,
And o'er the sickle bending; –
I listened, motionless and still;
And, as I mounted up the hill,   30
The music in my heart I bore,
Long after it was heard no more.

THE SOLITARY REAPER: The poem has its origins in a tour of Scotland
in 1803 when, Dorothy recalled, 'It was harvest time, and the fields
were quietly – might I be allowed to say pensively? – enlivened by
small companies of reapers. It is not uncommon in the more
lonely parts of the Highlands to see a single person so employed';
but Wordsworth identified the immediate inspiration for the
poem as a passage in Thomas Wilkinson's *Tours to the British
Mountains*, which was eventually published in 1824 but which
Wordsworth had read in manuscript: 'Passed a female who was
reaping alone: she sung in Erse as she bended over her sickle; the
sweetest human voice I ever heard: her strains were tenderly
melancholy, and felt delicious, long after they were heard no
more': 18 **numbers**: verses 21 **lay**: song

'SURPRISED BY JOY –
IMPATIENT AS THE WIND'

SURPRISED by joy – impatient as the Wind
I turned to share the transport – Oh! with whom
But Thee, deep buried in the silent tomb,
That spot which no vicissitude can find?
Love, faithful love, recalled thee to my mind –   5
But how could I forget thee? Through what power,
Even for the least division of an hour,
Have I been so beguiled as to be blind
To my most grievous loss? – That thought's return
Was the worst pang that sorrow ever bore,   10
Save one, one only, when I stood forlorn,
Knowing my heart's best treasure was no more;
That neither present time, nor years unborn
Could to my sight that heavenly face restore.

'SURPRISED BY JOY': 'This was in fact suggested by my daughter
Catharine, long after her death' (Wordsworth); the child had died,
just 3 years old, in 1812: 2 **transport**: ecstasy 8 **beguiled**: distracted

TO A SKYLARK

ETHEREAL minstrel! pilgrim of the sky!
Dost thou despise the earth where cares abound?
Or, while the wings aspire, are heart and eye
Both with thy nest upon the dewy ground?
Thy nest which thou canst drop into at will,   5
Those quivering wings composed, that music still!

Leave to the nightingale her shady wood;
A privacy of glorious light is thine;
Whence thou dost pour upon the world a flood
Of harmony, with instinct more divine;   10
Type of the wise who soar, but never roam;
True to the kindred points of Heaven and Home!

TO A SKYLARK: 'Rydal Mount 1825. (Where there are no skylarks but the poet is everywhere)' (Wordsworth)

THE PRELUDE
OR
GROWTH OF A POET'S MIND
an autobiographical poem
(1850)

BOOK FIRST. INTRODUCTION –
CHILDHOOD AND SCHOOL-TIME

OH, there is blessing in this gentle breeze,
A visitant that while he fans my cheek
Doth seem half-conscious of the joy he brings
From the green fields, and from yon azure sky.
Whate'er his mission, the soft breeze can come   5
To none more grateful than to me; escaped
From the vast city, where I long had pined
A discontented sojourner: now free,
Free as a bird to settle where I will.

THE PRELUDE: In 1814, Wordsworth published a long poem called *The Excursion* but in the preface he informed his readers that 'this is only a portion of a poem' and 'it belongs to the second part of a long and laborious work, which is to consist of three parts'. The work would be called *The Recluse*, 'a philosophical poem, containing views of Man, Nature, and Society' and 'having for its principal subject the sensations and opinions of a poet living in retirement'. However, Wordsworth's commitment to this major project declined, and he began to concentrate his creative energies on one part, which his sister Dorothy called simply 'the poem on his own life'. A draft of this poem was completed in 1805, but Wordsworth had no pressing desire to see it in print, assuring Thomas De Quincey: 'This poem will not be published these many years, and never during my lifetime'; instead he continued to refine the work over the next forty-five years, and this heavily revised text was eventually published posthumously in 1850 – a month after Tennyson's *In Memoriam*. Remarkably, throughout all this time the poem had no title. A fair copy of the original draft made by the poet's sister-in-law, Sarah Hutchinson, in 1805 has a decorative title page (provided by her brother George) bearing the words 'Poem title not yet fixed upon'; the work's published title, *The Prelude*, was provided by the poet's widow, Mary: BOOK FIRST. INTRODUCTION – CHILDHOOD AND SCHOOL-TIME: 7 **vast city:** London

What dwelling shall receive me? in what vale   10
Shall be my harbour? underneath what grove
Shall I take up my home? and what clear stream
Shall with its murmur lull me into rest?
The earth is all before me. With a heart
Joyous, nor scared at its own liberty,   15
I look about; and should the chosen guide
Be nothing better than a wandering cloud,
I cannot miss my way. I breathe again!
Trances of thought and mountings of the mind
Come fast upon me: it is shaken off,   20
That burthen of my own unnatural self,
The heavy weight of many a weary day
Not mine, and such as were not made for me.
Long months of peace (if such bold word accord
With any promises of human life),   25
Long months of ease and undisturbed delight
Are mine in prospect; whither shall I turn,
By road or pathway, or through trackless field,
Up hill or down, or shall some floating thing
Upon the river point me out my course?   30
    Dear Liberty! Yet what would it avail
But for a gift that consecrates the joy?
For I, methought, while the sweet breath of heaven
Was blowing on my body, felt within
A correspondent breeze, that gently moved   35
With quickening virtue, but is now become
A tempest, a redundant energy,
Vexing its own creation. Thanks to both,
And their congenial powers, that, while they join
In breaking up a long-continued frost,   40
Bring with them vernal promises, the hope
Of active days urged on by flying hours, –
Days of sweet leisure, taxed with patient thought
Abstruse, nor wanting punctual service high,
Matins and vespers, of harmonious verse!   45
    Thus far, O Friend! did I, not used to make
A present joy the matter of a song,
Pour forth that day my soul in measured strains
That would not be forgotten, and are here
Recorded: to the open fields I told   50
A prophecy: poetic numbers came
Spontaneously to clothe in priestly robe
A renovated spirit singled out,
Such hope was mine, for holy services.
My own voice cheered me, and, far more, the mind's
Internal echo of the imperfect sound;   56
To both I listened, drawing from them both
A cheerful confidence in things to come.
    Content and not unwilling now to give
A respite to this passion, I paced on   60
With brisk and eager steps; and came, at length,
To a green shady place, where down I sate

21 **burthen:** burden 41 **vernal:** the coming of spring, a time of renewal 45 **Matins and vespers:** morning and evening church services 46 **O Friend:** Wordsworth is referring to the poet Samuel Taylor Coleridge

Beneath a tree, slackening my thoughts by choice,
And settling into gentler happiness.
'Twas autumn, and a clear and placid day, 65
With warmth, as much as needed, from a sun
Two hours declined towards the west; a day
With silver clouds, and sunshine on the grass,
And in the sheltered and the sheltering grove
A perfect stillness. Many were the thoughts 70
Encouraged and dismissed, till choice was made
Of a known Vale, whither my feet should turn,
Nor rest till they had reached the very door
Of the one cottage which methought I saw.
No picture of mere memory ever looked 75
So fair; and while upon the fancied scene
I gazed with growing love, a higher power
Than Fancy gave assurance of some work
Of glory there forthwith to be begun,
Perhaps too there performed. Thus long I mused, 80
Nor e'er lost sight of what I mused upon,
Save when, amid the stately grove of oaks,
Now here, now there, an acorn, from its cup
Dislodged, through sere leaves rustled, or at once
To the bare earth dropped with a startling sound. 85
From that soft couch I rose not, till the sun
Had almost touched the horizon; casting then
A backward glance upon the curling cloud
Of city smoke, by distance ruralised;
Keen as a Truant or a Fugitive, 90
But as a Pilgrim resolute, I took,
Even with the chance equipment of that hour,
The road that pointed toward the chosen Vale.
It was a splendid evening, and my soul
Once more made trial of her strength, nor lacked 95
Aeolian visitations; but the harp
Was soon defrauded, and the banded host
Of harmony dispersed in straggling sounds,
And lastly uttered silence! 'Be it so;
Why think of any thing but present good?' 100
So, like a home-bound labourer I pursued
My way beneath the mellowing sun, that shed
Mild influence; nor left in me one wish
Again to bend the Sabbath of that time
To a servile yoke. What need of many words? 105
A pleasant loitering journey, through three days
Continued, brought me to my hermitage.
I spare to tell of what ensued, the life
In common things – the endless store of things,
Rare, or at least so seeming, every day 110
Found all about me in one neighbourhood –
The self-congratulation, and, from morn
To night, unbroken cheerfulness serene.
But speedily an earnest longing rose
To brace myself to some determined aim, 115

Reading or thinking, either to lay up
New stores, or rescue from decay the old
By timely interference: and therewith
Came hopes still higher, that with outward life
I might endue some airy phantasies 120
That had been floating loose about for years,
And to such beings temperately deal forth
The many feelings that oppressed my heart.
That hope hath been discouraged; welcome light
Dawns from the east, but dawns to disappear 125
And mock me with a sky that ripens not
Into a steady morning: if my mind,
Remembering the bold promise of the past,
Would gladly grapple with some noble theme,
Vain is her wish; where'er she turns she finds 130
Impediments from day to day renewed.
    And now it would content me to yield up
Those lofty hopes awhile, for present gifts
Of humbler industry. But, O dear Friend!
The Poet, gentle creature as he is, 135
Hath, like the Lover, his unruly times;
His fits when he is neither sick nor well,
Though no distress be near him but his own
Unmanageable thoughts: his mind, best pleased
While she as duteous as the mother dove 140
Sits brooding, lives not always to that end,
But like the innocent bird, hath goadings on
That drive her as in trouble through the groves;
With me is now such passion, to be blamed
No otherwise than as it lasts too long. 145
    When, as becomes a man who would prepare
For such an arduous work, I through myself
Make rigorous inquisition, the report
Is often cheering; for I neither seem
To lack that first great gift, the vital soul, 150
Nor general Truths, which are themselves a sort
Of Elements and Agents, Under-powers,
Subordinate helpers of the living mind:
Nor am I naked of external things,
Forms, images, nor numerous other aids 155
Of less regard, though won perhaps with toil
And needful to build up a Poet's praise.
Time, place, and manners do I seek, and these
Are found in plenteous store, but nowhere such
As may be singled out with steady choice; 160
No little band of yet remembered names
Whom I, in perfect confidence, might hope
To summon back from lonesome banishment,
And make them dwellers in the hearts of men
Now living, or to live in future years. 165
Sometimes the ambitious Power of choice, mistaking
Proud spring-tide swellings for a regular sea,
Will settle on some British theme, some old
Romantic tale by Milton left unsung;

---

84 **sere**: dry, withered 96 **Aeolian**: the Aeolian harp, a stringed instrument that produces a sound when the wind blows through it. Commonly associated with poetic inspiration during the Romantic period

168–169 **British theme . . . Milton**: Milton had planned to write an epic poem based on the legend of king Arthur, but instead decided to write about the Fall of Man (*Paradise Lost*)

More often turning to some gentle place 170
Within the groves of Chivalry, I pipe
To shepherd swains, or seated harp in hand,
Amid reposing knights by a river side
Or fountain, listen to the grave reports
Of dire enchantments faced and overcome 175
By the strong mind, and tales of warlike feats,
Where spear encountered spear, and sword with sword
Fought, as if conscious of the blazonry
That the shield bore, so glorious was the strife;
Whence inspiration for a song that winds 180
Through ever-changing scenes of votive quest
Wrongs to redress, harmonious tribute paid
To patient courage and unblemished truth,
To firm devotion, zeal unquenchable,
And Christian meekness hallowing faithful loves. 185
Sometimes, more sternly moved, I would relate
How vanquished Mithridates northward passed,
And, hidden in the cloud of years, became
Odin, the Father of a race by whom
Perished the Roman Empire: how the friends 190
And followers of Sertorius, out of Spain
Flying, found shelter in the Fortunate Isles,
And left their usages, their arts and laws,
To disappear by a slow gradual death,
To dwindle and to perish one by one, 195
Starved in those narrow bounds: but not the soul
Of Liberty, which fifteen hundred years
Survived, and, when the European came
With skill and power that might not be withstood,
Did, like a pestilence, maintain its hold 200
And wasted down by glorious death that race
Of natural heroes: or I would record
How, in tyrannic times, some high-souled man,
Unnamed among the chronicles of kings,
Suffered in silence for Truth's sake: or tell, 205
How that one Frenchman, through continued force
Of meditation on the inhuman deeds
Of those who conquered first the Indian Isles,
Went single in his ministry across
The Ocean; not to comfort the oppressed, 210
But, like a thirsty wind, to roam about
Withering the Oppressor: how Gustavus sought
Help at his need in Dalecarlia's mines;

How Wallace fought for Scotland; left the name
Of Wallace to be found, like a wild flower, 215
All over his dear Country; left the deeds
Of Wallace, like a family of Ghosts,
To people the steep rocks and river banks,
Her natural sanctuaries, with a local soul
Of independence and stern liberty. 220
Sometimes it suits me better to invent
A tale from my own heart, more near akin
To my own passions and habitual thoughts;
Some variegated story, in the main
Lofty, but the unsubstantial structure melts 225
Before the very sun that brightens it,
Mist into air dissolving! Then a wish,
My best and favourite aspiration, mounts
With yearning toward some philosophic song
Of Truth that cherishes our daily life; 230
With meditations passionate from deep
Recesses in man's heart, immortal verse
Thoughtfully fitted to the Orphean lyre;
But from this awful burthen I full soon
Take refuge and beguile myself with trust 235
That mellower years will bring a riper mind
And clearer insight. Thus my days are passed
In contradiction; with no skill to part
Vague longing, haply bred by want of power,
From paramount impulse not to be withstood, 240
A timorous capacity from prudence,
From circumspection, infinite delay.
Humility and modest awe themselves
Betray me, serving often for a cloak
To a more subtle selfishness; that now 245
Locks every function up in blank reserve,
Now dupes me, trusting to an anxious eye
That with intrusive restlessness beats off
Simplicity and self-presented truth.
Ah! better far than this, to stray about 250
Voluptuously through fields and rural walks,
And ask no record of the hours, resigned
To vacant musing, unreproved neglect
Of all things, and deliberate holiday.
Far better never to have heard the name 255
Of zeal and just ambition, than to live
Baffled and plagued by a mind that every hour
Turns recreant to her task; takes heart again,
Then feels immediately some hollow thought
Hang like an interdict upon her hopes. 260
This is my lot; for either still I find
Some imperfection in the chosen theme,
Or see of absolute accomplishment
Much wanting, so much wanting, in myself,

172 **swain:** a young man who attends on a knight 187 **Mithridates:**
king of Pontus in Plutarch's *Lives* 189 **Odin:** Norse god
191 **Sertorius:** Roman general who features in Plutarch's *Lives*
206 **one Frenchman:** a reference to Dominique de Gourges, who
went to Florida in 1567 to avenge the Spanish massacre of French
Huguenots 212–213 **Gustavus . . . Dalecarlia's mines:** Gustavus I of
Sweden (1594–1632) who successfully fought against Danish control
of Sweden. The Dalecarlians aided Gustavus in his fight and at
one point he worked in the mines there disguised as a labourer

214–220 William Wallace, (*c.*1270–1305) Scots resistance fighter and
commander who fought against England's attempts to control
Scotland. Wallace was eventually captured, then tortured
and murdered by the English in London 233 **Orphean lyre:**
The mythological poet Orpheus, whose song could even charm
the beasts of the forest

That I recoil and droop, and seek repose 265
In listlessness from vain perplexity,
Unprofitably travelling toward the grave,
Like a false steward who hath much received
And renders nothing back.
                       Was it for this
That one, the fairest of all rivers, loved 270
To blend his murmurs with my nurse's song,
And, from his alder shades and rocky falls,
And from his fords and shallows, sent a voice
That flowed along my dreams? For this, didst thou,
O Derwent! winding among grassy holms 275
Where I was looking on, a babe in arms,
Make ceaseless music that composed my thoughts
To more than infant softness, giving me
Amid the fretful dwellings of mankind
A foretaste, a dim earnest, of the calm 280
That Nature breathes among the hills and groves.
When he had left the mountains and received
On his smooth breast the shadow of those towers
That yet survive, a shattered monument
Of feudal sway, the bright blue river passed 285
Along the margin of our terrace walk;
A tempting playmate whom we dearly loved.
Oh, many a time have I, a five years' child,
In a small mill-race severed from his stream,
Made one long bathing of a summer's day; 290
Basked in the sun, and plunged and basked again
Alternate, all a summer's day, or scoured
The sandy fields, leaping through flowery groves
Of yellow ragwort; or when rock and hill,
The woods, and distant Skiddaw's lofty height, 295
Were bronzed with deepest radiance, stood alone
Beneath the sky, as if I had been born
On Indian plains, and from my mother's hut
Had run abroad in wantonness, to sport
A naked savage, in the thunder shower. 300
    Fair seed-time had my soul, and I grew up
Fostered alike by beauty and by fear:
Much favoured in my birth-place, and no less
In that belovèd Vale to which ere long
We were transplanted – there were we let loose 305
For sports of wider range. Ere I had told
Ten birth-days, when among the mountain-slopes
Frost, and the breath of frosty wind, had snapped
The last autumnal crocus, 'twas my joy
With store of springes o'er my shoulder hung 310
To range the open heights where woodcocks run
Along the smooth green turf. Through half the night,
Scudding away from snare to snare, I plied
That anxious visitation; – moon and stars
Were shining o'er my head. I was alone, 315
And seemed to be a trouble to the peace
That dwelt among them. Sometimes it befell
In these night wanderings, that a strong desire

O'erpowered my better reason, and the bird
Which was the captive of another's toil 320
Became my prey; and when the deed was done
I heard among the solitary hills
Low breathings coming after me, and sounds
Of undistinguishable motion, steps
Almost as silent as the turf they trod. 325
      Nor less when spring had warmed the cultured Vale,
Moved we as plunderers where the mother-bird
Had in high places built her lodge; though mean
Our object and inglorious, yet the end
Was not ignoble. Oh! when I have hung 330
Above the raven's nest, by knots of grass
And half-inch fissures in the slippery rock
But ill sustained, and almost (so it seemed)
Suspended by the blast that blew amain,
Shouldering the naked crag, oh, at that time 335
While on the perilous ridge I hung alone,
With what strange utterance did the loud dry wind
Blow through my ear! the sky seemed not a sky
Of earth – and with what motion moved the clouds!
    Dust as we are, the immortal spirit grows 340
Like harmony in music; there is a dark
Inscrutable workmanship that reconciles
Discordant elements, makes them cling together
In one society. How strange that all
The terrors, pains, and early miseries, 345
Regrets, vexations, lassitudes interfused
Within my mind, should e'er have borne a part,
And that a needful part, in making up
The calm existence that is mine when I
Am worthy of myself! Praise to the end! 350
Thanks to the means which Nature deigned to
    employ;
Whether her fearless visitings, or those
That came with soft alarm, like hurtless light
Opening the peaceful clouds; or she may use
Severer interventions, ministry 355
More palpable, as best might suit her aim.
    One summer evening (led by her) I found
A little boat tied to a willow tree
Within a rocky cave, its usual home.
Straight I unloosed her chain, and stepping in 360
Pushed from the shore. It was an act of stealth
And troubled pleasure, nor without the voice
Of mountain-echoes did my boat move on;
Leaving behind her still, on either side,
Small circles glittering idly in the moon, 365
Until they melted all into one track
Of sparkling light. But now, like one who rows,
Proud of his skill, to reach a chosen point
With an unswerving line, I fixed my view
Upon the summit of a craggy ridge, 370
The horizon's utmost boundary; for above
Was nothing but the stars and the grey sky.
She was an elfin pinnace; lustily
I dipped my oars into the silent lake,

275 **Derwent:** the river Derwent in the North of England **holms:**
flat ground by a river 295 **Skiddaw:** a mountain in the Lake District

And, as I rose upon the stroke, my boat   375
Went heaving through the water like a swan;
When, from behind that craggy steep till then
The horizon's bound, a huge peak, black and huge,
As if with voluntary power intínct
Upreared its head. I struck and struck again,   380
And growing still in stature the grim shape
Towered up between me and the stars, and still,
For so it seemed, with purpose of its own
And measured motion like a living thing,
Strode after me. With trembling oars I turned,   385
And through the silent water stole my way
Back to the covert of the willow tree;
There in her mooring-place I left my bark, –
And through the meadows homeward went, in grave
And serious mood; but after I had seen   390
That spectacle, for many days, my brain
Worked with a dim and undetermined sense
Of unknown modes of being; o'er my thoughts
There hung a darkness, call it solitude
Or blank desertion. No familiar shapes   395
Remained, no pleasant images of trees,
Of sea or sky, no colours of green fields;
But huge and mighty forms, that do not live
Like living men, moved slowly through the mind
By day, and were a trouble to my dreams.   400
    Wisdom and Spirit of the universe!
Thou Soul that art the eternity of thought,
That giv'st to forms and images a breath
And everlasting motion, not in vain
By day or star-light thus from my first dawn   405
Of childhood didst thou intertwine for me
The passions that build up our human soul;
Not with the mean and vulgar works of man,
But with high objects, with enduring things –
With life and nature, purifying thus   410
The elements of feeling and of thought,
And sanctifying, by such discipline,
Both pain and fear, until we recognise
A grandeur in the beatings of the heart.
Nor was this fellowship vouchsafed to me   415
With stinted kindness. In November days,
When vapours rolling down the valley made
A lonely scene more lonesome, among woods
At noon, and 'mid the calm of summer nights,
When, by the margin of the trembling lake,   420
Beneath the gloomy hills homeward I went
In solitude, such intercourse was mine;
Mine was it in the fields both day and night,
And by the waters, all the summer long.
    And in the frosty season, when the sun   425
Was set, and visible for many a mile
The cottage windows blazed through twilight gloom,
I heeded not their summons: happy time
It was indeed for all of us – for me
It was a time of rapture! Clear and loud   430
The village clock tolled six, – I wheeled about,

Proud and exulting like an untired horse
That cares not for his home. All shod with steel,
We hissed along the polished ice in games
Confederate, imitative of the chase   435
And woodland pleasures, – the resounding horn,
The pack loud chiming, and the hunted hare.
So through the darkness and the cold we flew,
And not a voice was idle; with the din
Smitten, the precipices rang aloud;   440
The leafless trees and every icy crag
Tinkled like iron; while far distant hills
Into the tumult sent an alien sound
Of melancholy not unnoticed, while the stars
Eastward were sparkling clear, and in the west   445
The orange sky of evening died away.
Not seldom from the uproar I retired
Into a silent bay, or sportively
Glanced sideway, leaving the tumultuous throng,
To cut across the reflex of a star   450
That fled, and, flying still before me, gleamed
Upon the glassy plain; and oftentimes,
When we had given our bodies to the wind,
And all the shadowy banks on either side
Came sweeping through the darkness, spinning still
The rapid line of motion, then at once   456
Have I, reclining back upon my heels,
Stopped short; yet still the solitary cliffs
Wheeled by me – even as if the earth had rolled
With visible motion her diurnal round!   460
Behind me did they stretch in solemn train,
Feebler and feebler, and I stood and watched
Till all was tranquil as a dreamless sleep.
    Ye Presences of Nature in the sky
And on the earth! Ye Visions of the hills!   465
And Souls of lonely places! can I think
A vulgar hope was yours when ye employed
Such ministry, when ye through many a year
Haunting me thus among my boyish sports,
On caves and trees, upon the woods and hills,   470
Impressed upon all forms the characters
Of danger or desire; and thus did make
The surface of the universal earth
With triumph and delight, with hope and fear,
Work like a sea?
                    Not uselessly employed,   475
Might I pursue this theme through every change
Of exercise and play, to which the year
Did summon us in his delightful round.
    We were a noisy crew; the sun in heaven
Beheld not vales more beautiful than ours;   480
Nor saw a band in happiness and joy
Richer, or worthier of the ground they trod.
I could record with no reluctant voice
The woods of autumn, and their hazel bowers
With milk-white clusters hung; the rod and line,   485

460 **diurnal:** daily

True symbol of hope's foolishness, whose strong
And unreproved enchantment led us on
By rocks and pools shut out from every star,
All the green summer, to forlorn cascades
Among the windings hid of mountain brooks   490
– Unfading recollections! at this hour
The heart is almost mine with which I felt,
From some hill-top on sunny afternoons,
The paper kite high among fleecy clouds
Pull at her rein like an impetuous courser;   495
Or, from the meadows sent on gusty days,
Beheld her breast the wind, then suddenly
Dashed headlong, and rejected by the storm.
    Ye lowly cottages wherein we dwelt,
A ministration of your own was yours;   500
Can I forget you, being as you were
So beautiful among the pleasant fields
In which ye stood? or can I here forget
The plain and seemly countenance with which
Ye dealt out your plain comforts? Yet had ye   505
Delights and exultations of your own.
Eager and never weary we pursued
Our home-amusements by the warm peat-fire
At evening, when with pencil, and smooth slate
In square divisions parcelled out and all   510
With crosses and with cyphers scribbled o'er,
We schemed and puzzled, head opposed to head
In strife too humble to be named in verse:
Or round the naked table, snow-white deal,
Cherry or maple, sate in close array,   515
And to the combat, Loo or Whist, led on
A thick-ribbed army; not, as in the world,
Neglected and ungratefully thrown by
Even for the very service they had wrought,
But husbanded through many a long campaign.   520
Uncouth assemblage was it, where no few
Had changed their functions; some, plebeian cards
Which Fate, beyond the promise of their birth,
Had dignified, and called to represent
The persons of departed potentates.   525
Oh, with what echoes on the board they fell!
Ironic diamonds, – clubs, hearts, diamonds, spades,
A congregation piteously akin!
Cheap matter offered they to boyish wit,
Those sooty knaves, precipitated down   530
With scoffs and taunts, like Vulcan out of heaven:
The paramount ace, a moon in her eclipse,
Queens gleaming through their splendour's last decay,
And monarchs surly at the wrongs sustained
By royal visages. Meanwhile abroad   535
Incessant rain was falling, or the frost
Raged bitterly, with keen and silent tooth;
And, interrupting oft that eager game,

From under Esthwaite's splitting fields of ice
The pent-up air, struggling to free itself,   540
Gave out to meadow grounds and hills a loud
Protracted yelling, like the noise of wolves
Howling in troops along the Bothnic Main.
    Nor, sedulous as I have been to trace
How Nature by extrinsic passion first   545
People the mind with forms sublime or fair,
And made me love them, may I here omit
How other pleasures have been mine, and joys
Of subtler origin; how I have felt,
Not seldom even in that tempestuous time,   550
Those hallowed and pure motions of the sense
Which seem, in their simplicity, to own
An intellectual charm; that calm delight
Which, if I err not, surely must belong
To those first-born affinities that fit   555
Our new existence to existing things,
And, in our dawn of being, constitute
The bond of union between life and joy.
    Yes, I remember when the changeful earth,
And twice five summers on my mind had stamped   560
The faces of the moving year, even then
I held unconscious intercourse with beauty
Old as creation, drinking in a pure
Organic pleasure from the silver wreaths
Of curling mist, or from the level plain   565
Of waters coloured by impending clouds.
    The sands of Westmoreland, the creeks and bays
Of Cumbria's rocky limits, they can tell
How, when the Sea threw off his evening shade,
And to the shepherd's hut on distant hills   570
Sent welcome notice of the rising moon,
How I have stood, to fancies such as these
A stranger, linking with the spectacle
No conscious memory of a kindred sight,
And bringing with me no peculiar sense   575
Of quietness or peace; yet have I stood,
Even while mine eye hath moved o'er many a league
Of shining water, gathering as it seemed
Through every hair-breadth in that field of light
New pleasure like a bee among the flowers.   580
    Thus oft amid those fits of vulgar joy
Which, through all seasons, on a child's pursuits
Are prompt attendants, 'mid that giddy bliss
Which, like a tempest, works along the blood
And is forgotten; even then I felt   585
Gleams like the flashing of a shield; – the earth
And common face of Nature spake to me
Rememberable things; sometimes, 'tis true,
By chance collisions and quaint accidents
(Like those ill-sorted unions, work supposed   590
Of evil-minded fairies), yet not vain

495 **courser:** a large and powerful horse   516 **Loo or Whist:**
card games   531 **Vulcan:** Roman god of fire and metalworking

539 **Esthwaite:** Esthwaite Water in the Lake District   543 **Bothnic:**
the northern Baltic

Nor profitless, if haply they impressed
Collateral objects and appearances,
Albeit lifeless then, and doomed to sleep
Until maturer seasons called them forth   595
To impregnate and to elevate the mind.
– And if the vulgar joy by its own weight
Wearied itself out of the memory,
The scenes which were a witness of that joy
Remained in their substantial lineaments   600
Depicted on the brain, and to the eye
Were visible, a daily sight; and thus
By the impressive discipline of fear,
By pleasure and repeated happiness,
So frequently repeated, and by force   605
Of óbscure feelings representative
Of things forgotten, these same scenes so bright,
So beautiful, so majestic in themselves,
Though yet the day was distant, did become
Habitually dear, and all their forms   610
And changeful colours by invisible links
Were fastened to the affections.
                    I began
My story early – not misled, I trust,
By an infirmity of love for days
Disowned by memory – ere the breath of spring   615
Planting my snowdrops among winter snows.
Nor will it seem to thee, O Friend! so prompt
In sympathy, that I have lengthened out
With fond and feeble tongue a tedious tale.
Meanwhile, my hope has been, that I might fetch   620
Invigorating thoughts from former years;
Might fix the wavering balance of my mind,
And haply meet reproaches too, whose power
May spur me on, in manhood now mature,
To honourable toil. Yet should these hopes   625
Prove vain, and thus should neither I be taught
To understand myself, nor thou to know
With better knowledge how the heart was framed
Of him thou lovest; need I dread from thee
Harsh judgements, if the song be loth to quit   630
Those recollected hours that have the charm
Of visionary things, those lovely forms
And sweet sensations that throw back our life,
And almost make remotest infancy
A visible scene, on which the sun is shining?   635
   One end at least hath been attained; my mind
Hath been revived, and if this genial mood
Desert me not, forthwith shall be brought down
Through later years the story of my life.
The road lies plain before me; – 'tis a theme   640
Single and of determined bounds; and hence
I choose it rather at this time, than work
Of ampler or more varied argument,
Where I might be discomfited and lost:
And certain hopes are with me, that to thee   645
This labour will be welcome, honoured Friend!

BOOK SECOND. SCHOOL-TIME – (CONTINUED)
THUS far, O Friend! have we, though leaving much
Unvisited, endeavoured to retrace
The simple ways in which my childhood walked;
Those chiefly that first led me to the love
Of rivers, woods, and fields. The passion yet   5
Was in its birth, sustained as might befall
By nourishment that came unsought; for still
From week to week, from month to month, we lived
A round of tumult. Duly were our games
Prolonged in summer till the day-light failed: 10
No chair remained before the doors; the bench
And threshold steps were empty; fast asleep
The labourer, and the old man who had sate
A later lingerer; yet the revelry
Continued and the loud upróar: at last,   15
When all the ground was dark, and twinkling stars
Edged the black clouds, home and to bed we went,
Feverish with weary joints and beating minds.
Ah! is there one who ever has been young,
Nor needs a warning voice to tame the pride   20
Of intellect and virtue's self-esteem?
One is there, though the wisest and the best
Of all mankind, who covets not at times
Union that cannot be; – who would not give,
If so he might, to duty and to truth   25
The eagerness of infantine desire?
A tranquillising spirit presses now
On my corporeal frame, so wide appears
The vacancy between me and those days
Which yet have such self-presence in my mind,   30
That, musing on them, often do I seem
Two consciousnesses, conscious of myself
And of some other Being. A rude mass
Of native rock, left midway in the square
Of our small market village, was the goal   35
Or centre of these sports; and when, returned
After long absence, thither I repaired,
Gone was the old grey stone, and in its place
A smart Assembly-room usurped the ground
That had been ours. There let the fiddle scream,   40
And be ye happy! Yet, my Friends! I know
That more than one of you will think with me
Of those soft starry nights, and that old Dame
From whom the stone was named, who there had sate,
And watched her table with its huckster's wares   45
Assiduous, through the length of sixty years.
   We ran a boisterous course; the year span round
With giddy motion. But the time approached
That brought with it a regular desire
For calmer pleasures, when the winning forms   50
Of Nature were collaterally attached
To every scheme of holiday delight
And every boyish sport, less grateful else
And languidly pursued.
                  When summer came,
Our pastime was, on bright half-holidays,   55

To sweep along the plain of Windermere
With rival oars; and the selected bourne
Was now an Island musical with birds
That sang and ceased not; now a Sister Isle
Beneath the oaks' umbrageous covert, sown   60
With lilies of the valley like a field;
And now a third small Island, where survived
In solitude the ruins of a shrine
Once to Our Lady dedicate, and served
Daily with chanted rites. In such a race   65
So ended, disappointment could be none,
Uneasiness, or pain, or jealousy:
We rested in the shade, all pleased alike,
Conquered and conqueror. Thus the pride of strength,
And the vain-glory of superior skill,   70
Were tempered; thus was gradually produced
A quiet independence of the heart;
And to my Friend who knows me I may add,
Fearless of blame, that hence for future days
Ensued a diffidence and modesty,   75
And I was taught to feel, perhaps too much,
The self-sufficing power of Solitude.

    Our daily meals were frugal, Sabine fare!
More than we wished we knew the blessing then
Of vigorous hunger – hence corporeal strength   80
Unsapped by delicate viands; for, exclude
A little weekly stipend, and we lived
Through three divisions of the quartered year
In penniless poverty. But now to school
From the half-yearly holidays returned,   85
We came with weightier purses, that sufficed
To furnish treats more costly than the Dame
Of the old grey stone, from her scant board, supplied.
Hence rustic dinners on the cool green ground,
Or in the woods, or by a river side   90
Or shady fountain, while among the leaves
Soft airs were stirring, and the mid-day sun
Unfelt shone brightly round us in our joy.
Nor is my aim neglected if I tell
How sometimes, in the length of those half-years,   95
We from our funds drew largely; – proud to curb,
And eager to spur on, the galloping steed;
And with the courteous inn-keeper, whose stud
Supplied our want, we haply might employ
Sly subterfuge, if the adventure's bound   100
Were distant: some famed temple where of yore
The Druids worshipped, or the antique walls
Of that large abbey, where within the Vale
Of Nightshade, to St Mary's honour built,
Stands yet a mouldering pile with fractured arch,   105
Belfry, and images, and living trees,
A holy scene! Along the smooth green turf
Our horses grazed. To more than inland peace
Left by the west wind sweeping overhead
From a tumultuous ocean, trees and towers   110

In that sequestered valley may be seen,
Both silent and both motionless alike;
Such the deep shelter that is there, and such
The safeguard for repose and quietness.
    Our steeds remounted and the summons given,   115
With whip and spur we through the chantry flew
In uncouth race, and left the cross-legged knight,
And the stone-abbot, and that single wren
Which one day sang so sweetly in the nave
Of the old church, that – though from recent
    showers   120
The earth was comfortless, and, touched by faint
Internal breezes, sobbings of the place
And respirations, from the roofless walls
The shuddering ivy dripped large drops – yet still
So sweetly 'mid the gloom the invisible bird   125
Sang to herself, that there I could have made
My dwelling-place, and lived for ever there
To hear such music. Through the walls we flew
And down the valley, and, a circuit made   129
In wantonness of heart, through rough and smooth
We scampered homewards. Oh, ye rocks and streams,
And that still spirit shed from evening air!
Even in this joyous time I sometimes felt
Your presence, when with slackened step we breathed
Along the sides of the steep hills, or when   135
Lighted by gleams of moonlight from the sea
We beat with thundering hoofs the level sand.
    Midway on long Winander's eastern shore,
Within the crescent of a pleasant bay,
A tavern stood; no homely-featured house,   140
Primeval like its neighbouring cottages,
But 'twas a splendid place, the door beset
With chaises, grooms, and liveries, and within
Decanters, glasses, and the blood-red wine.
In ancient times, and ere the Hall was built   145
On the large island, had this dwelling been
More worthy of a poet's love, a hut
Proud of its one bright fire and sycamore shade.
But – though the rhymes were gone that once
    inscribed
The threshold, and large golden characters,   150
Spread o'er the spangled sign-board, had dislodged
The old Lion and usurped his place, in slight
And mockery of the rustic painter's hand –
Yet, to this hour, the spot to me is dear
With all its foolish pomp. The garden lay   155
Upon a slope surmounted by the plain
Of a small bowling-green; beneath us stood
A grove, with gleams of water through the trees
And over the tree-tops; nor did we want
Refreshment, strawberries and mellow cream.   160
There, while through half an afternoon we played
On the smooth platform, whether skill prevailed
Or happy blunder triumphed, bursts of glee

BOOK SECOND. SCHOOL-TIME: 56 **Windermere:** the largest lake in the
Lake District 78 **Sabine:** simple, sparse

151 **o'er:** over

Made all the mountains ring. But, ere night-fall,
When in our pinnace we returned at leisure   165
Over the shadowy lake, and to the beach
Of some small island steered our course with one,
The Minstrel of the Troop, and left him there,
And rowed off gently, while he blew his flute
Alone upon the rock – oh, then, the calm   170
And dead still water lay upon my mind
Even with a weight of pleasure, and the sky,
Never before so beautiful, sank down
Into my heart, and held me like a dream!
Thus were my sympathies enlarged, and thus   175
Daily the common range of visible things
Grew dear to me: already I began
To love the sun; a boy I loved the sun,
Not as I since have loved him, as a pledge
And surety of our earthly life, a light   180
Which we behold and feel we are alive;
Nor for his bounty to so many worlds –
But for this cause, that I had seen him lay
His beauty on the morning hills, had seen
The western mountain touch his setting orb,   185
In many a thoughtless hour, when, from excess
Of happiness, my blood appeared to flow
For its own pleasure, and I breathed with joy.
And, from like feelings, humble though intense,
To patriotic and domestic love   190
Analogous, the moon to me was dear;
For I could dream away my purposes,
Standing to gaze upon her while she hung
Midway between the hills, as if she knew
No other region, but belonged to thee,   195
Yea, appertained by a peculiar right
To thee and thy grey huts, though one dear Vale!
    Those incidental charms which first attached
My heart to rural objects, day by day
Grew weaker, and I hasten on to tell   200
How Nature, intervenient till this time
And secondary, now at length was sought
For her own sake. But who shall parcel out
His intellect by geometric rules,
Split like a province into round and square?   205
Who knows the individual hour in which
His habits were first sown, even as a seed?
Who that shall point as with a wand and say
'This portion of the river of my mind
Came from yon fountain'? Thou, my Friend! art one
More deeply read in thy own thoughts; to thee   211
Science appears but what in truth she is,
Not as our glory and our absolute boast,
But as a succedaneum, and a prop
To our infirmity. No officious slave   215
Art thou of that false secondary power
By which we multiply distinctions, then
Deem that our puny boundaries are things

That we perceive, and not that we have made.
To thee, unblinded by these formal arts,   220
The unity of all hath been revealed,
And thou wilt doubt, with me less aptly skilled
Than many are to range the faculties
In scale and order, class the cabinet
Of their sensations, and in voluble phrase   225
Run through the history and birth of each
As of a single independent thing.
Hard task, vain hope, to analyse the mind,
If each most obvious and particular thought,
Not in a mystical and idle sense,   230
But in the words of Reason deeply weighed,
Hath no beginning.
                              Blest the infant Babe,
(For with my best conjecture I would trace
Our Being's earthly progress), blest the Babe,
Nursed in his Mother's arms, who sinks to sleep   235
Rocked on his Mother's breast; who with his soul
Drinks in the feelings of his Mother's eye!
For him, in one dear Presence, there exists
A virtue which irradiates and exalts
Objects through widest intercourse of sense.   240
No outcast he, bewildered and depressed:
Along his infant veins are interfused
The gravitation and the filial bond
Of nature that connect him with the world.
Is there a flower, to which he points with hand   245
Too weak to gather it, already love
Drawn from love's purest earthly fount for him
Hath beautified that flower; already shades
Of pity cast from inward tenderness
Do fall around him upon aught that bears   250
Unsightly marks of violence or harm.
Emphatically such a Being lives,
Frail creature as he is, helpless as frail,
An inmate of this active universe:
For feeling has to him imparted power   255
That through the growing faculties of sense
Doth like an agent of the one great Mind
Create, creator and receiver both,
Working but in alliance with the works
Which it beholds. – Such, verily, is the first   260
Poetic spirit of our human life,
By uniform control of after years,
In most, abated or suppressed; in some,
Through every change of growth and of decay,
Pre-eminent till death.
                                        From early days,   265
Beginning not long after that first time
In which, a Babe, by intercourse of touch
I held mute dialogues with my Mother's heart,
I have endeavoured to display the means
Whereby this infant sensibility,   270
Great birthright of our being, was in me
Augmented and sustained. Yet is a path
More difficult before me; and I fear

---

168 **The Minstrel of the Troop:** Robert Greenwood, later Senior Fellow of Trinity College, Cambridge 214 **succedaneum:** substitute

That in its broken windings we shall need
The chamois' sinews, and the eagle's wing: 275
For now a trouble came into my mind
From unknown causes. I was left alone
Seeking the visible world, nor knowing why.
The props of my affections were removed,
And yet the building stood, as if sustained   280
By its own spirit! All that I beheld
Was dear, and hence to finer influxes
The mind lay open, to a more exact
And close communion. Many are our joys
In youth, but oh! what happiness to live   285
When every hour brings palpable accéss
Of knowledge, when all knowledge is delight,
And sorrow is not there! The seasons came,
And every season whereso'er I moved
Unfolded transitory qualities,   290
Which, but for this most watchful power of love,
Had been neglected; left a register
Of permanent relations, else unknown.
Hence life, and change, and beauty, solitude
More active even than 'best society' –   295
Society made sweet as solitude
By silent inobtrusive sympathies,
And gentle agitations of the mind
From manifold distinctions, difference
Perceived in things, where, to the unwatchful eye,   300
No difference is, and hence, from the same source,
Sublimer joy; for I would walk alone,
Under the quiet stars, and at that time
Have felt whate'er there is of power in sound
To breathe an elevated mood, by form   305
Of image unprofaned; and I would stand,
If the night blackened with a coming storm,
Beneath some rock, listening to notes that are
The ghostly language of the ancient earth,
Or make their dim abode in distant winds.   310
Thence did I drink the visionary power;
And deem not profitless those fleeting moods
Of shadowy exultation: not for this,
That they are kindred to our purer mind
And intellectual life; but that the soul,   315
Remembering how she felt, but what she felt
Remembering not, retains an óbscure sense
Of possible sublimity, whereto
With growing faculties she doth aspire,
With faculties still growing, feeling still   320
That whatsoever point they gain, they yet
Have something to pursue.
                           And not alone,
'Mid gloom and tumult, but no less 'mid fair
And tranquil scenes, that universal power
And fitness in the latent qualities   325
And essences of things, by which the mind
Is moved with feelings of delight, to me
Came strengthened with a superadded soul,
A virtue not its own. My morning walks

Were early; – oft before the hours of school   330
I travelled round our little lake, five miles
Of pleasant wandering. Happy time! more dear
For this, that one was by my side, a Friend,
Then passionately loved; with heart how full
Would he peruse these lines! For many years   335
Have since flowed in between us, and, our minds
Both silent to each other, at this time
We live as if those hours had never been.
Nor seldom did I lift our cottage latch
Far earlier, ere one smoke-wreath had risen   340
From human dwelling, or the vernal thrush
Was audible; and sate among the woods
Alone upon some jutting eminence,
At the first gleam of dawn-light, when the Vale,
Yet slumbering, lay in utter solitude.   345
How shall I seek the origin? where find
Faith in the marvellous things which then I felt?
Oft in these moments such a holy calm
Would overspread my soul, that bodily eyes
Were utterly forgotten, and what I saw   350
Appeared like something in myself, a dream,
A prospect in the mind.
                         'Twere long to tell
What spring and autumn, what the winter snows,
And what the summer shade, what day and night,
Evening and morning, sleep and waking thought   355
From sources inexhaustible, poured forth
To feed the spirit of religious love
In which I walked with Nature. But let this
Be not forgotten, that I still retained
My first creative sensibility;   360
That by the regular action of the world
My soul was unsubdued. A plastic power
Abode with me; a forming hand, at times
Rebellious, acting in a devious mood;
A local spirit of his own, at war   365
With general tendency, but, for the most,
Subservient strictly to external things
With which it cómmuned. An auxiliar light
Came from my mind, which on the setting sun
Bestowed new splendour; the melodious birds,   370
The fluttering breezes, fountains that ran on
Murmuring so sweetly in themselves, obeyed
A like dominion, and the midnight storm
Grew darker in the presence of my eye:
Hence my obeisance, my devotion hence,   375
And hence my transport.
                         Nor should this, perchance,
Pass unrecorded, that I still had loved
The exercise and produce of a toil,
Than analytic industry to me
More pleasing, and whose character I deem   380
Is more poetic as resembling more
Creative agency. The song would speak
Of that interminable building reared
By observation of affinities

In objects where no brotherhood exists   385
To passive minds. My seventeenth year was come;
And, whether from this habit rooted now
So deeply in my mind, or from excess
In the great social principle of life
Coercing all things into sympathy,   390
To unorganic natures were transferred
My own enjoyments; or the power of truth
Coming in revelation, did converse
With things that really are; I, at this time,
Saw blessings spread around me like a sea.   395
Thus while the days flew by, and years passed on,
From Nature and her overflowing soul,
I had received so much, that all my thoughts
Were steeped in feeling; I was only then
Contented, when with bliss ineffable   400
I felt the sentiment of Being spread
O'er all that moves and all that seemeth still;
O'er all that, lost beyond the reach of thought
And human knowledge, to the human eye
Invisible, yet liveth to the heart;   405
O'er all that leaps and runs, and shouts and sings,
Or beats the gladsome air; o'er all that glides
Beneath the wave, yea, in the wave itself,
And mighty depth of waters. Wonder not
If high the transport, great the joy I felt,   410
Communing in this sort through earth and heaven
With every form of creature, as it looked
Towards the Uncreated with a countenance
Of adoration, with an eye of love.
One song they sang, and it was audible,   415
Most audible, then, when the fleshly ear,
O'ercome by humblest prelude of that strain,
Forgot her functions, and slept undisturbed.

If this be error, and another faith
Find easier access to the pious mind,   420
Yet were I grossly destitute of all
Those human sentiments that make this earth
So dear, if I should fail with grateful voice
To speak of you, ye mountains, and ye lakes
And sounding cataracts, ye mists and winds   425
That dwell among the hills where I was born.
If in my youth I have been pure in heart,
If, mingling with the world, I am content
With my own modest pleasures, and have lived
With God and Nature cómmuning, removed   430
From little enmities and low desires,
The gift is yours; if in these times of fear,
This melancholy waste of hopes o'erthrown,
If, 'mid indifference and apathy,
And wicked exultation, when good men   435
On every side fall off, we know not how,
To selfishness, disguised in gentle names
Of peace and quiet and domestic love,
Yet mingled not unwillingly with sneers
On visionary minds; if, in this time   440
Of dereliction and dismay, I yet

Despair not of our nature, but retain
A more than Roman confidence, a faith
That fails not, in all sorrow my support,
The blessing of my life; the gift is yours,   445
Ye winds and sounding cataracts! 'tis yours,
Ye mountains! thine, O Nature! Thou hast fed
My lofty speculations; and in thee,
For this uneasy heart of ours, I find
A never-failing principle of joy   450
And purest passion.
                    Thou, my Friend! wert reared
In the great city, 'mid far other scenes;
But we, by different roads, at length have gained
The self-same bourne. And for this cause to thee
I speak, unapprehensive of contempt,   455
The insinuated scoff of coward tongues,
And all that silent language which so oft
In conversation between man and man
Blots from the human countenance all trace
Of beauty and of love. For thou hast sought   460
The truth in solitude, and, since the days
That gave thee liberty, full long desired,
To serve in Nature's temple, thou hast been
The most assiduous of her ministers;
In many things my brother, chiefly here   465
In this our deep devotion.
                         Fare thee well!
Health and the quiet of a healthful mind
Attend thee! seeking oft the haunts of men,
And yet more often living with thyself,
And for thyself, so haply shall thy days   470
Be many, and a blessing to mankind.

BOOK THIRD. RESIDENCE AT CAMBRIDGE
IT was a dreary morning when the wheels
Rolled over a wide plain o'erhung with clouds,
And nothing cheered our way till first we saw
The long-roofed chapel of King's College lift
Turrets and pinnacles in answering files,   5
Extended high above a dusky grove.
    Advancing, we espied upon the road
A student clothed in gown and tasselled cap,
Striding along as if o'ertasked by Time,
Or covetous of exercise and air;   10
He passed – nor was I master of my eyes
Till he was left an arrow's flight behind.
As near and nearer to the spot we drew,
It seemed to suck us in with an eddy's force.
Onward we drove beneath the Castle; caught,   15
While crossing Magdalene Bridge, a glimpse of Cam;
And at the Hoop alighted, famous inn.
    My spirit was up, my thoughts were full of hope;
Some friends I had, acquaintances who there
Seemed friends, poor simple school-boys, now hung
    round   20

BOOK THIRD. RESIDENCE AT CAMBRIDGE: 16 **Cam**: the river Cam in
Cambridge

With honour and importance: in a world
Of welcome faces up and down I roved;
Questions, directions, warnings and advice,
Flowed in upon me, from all sides; fresh day
Of pride and pleasure! to myself I seemed   25
A man of business and expense, and went
From shop to shop about my own affairs,
To Tutor or to Tailor, as befell,
From street to street with loose and careless mind.

    I was the Dreamer, they the Dream; I roamed   30
Delighted through the motley spectacle;
Gowns grave, or gaudy, doctors, students, streets,
Courts, cloisters, flocks of churches, gateways, towers:
Migration strange for a stripling of the hills,
A northern villager.

            As if the change   35
Had waited on some Fairy's wand, at once
Behold me rich in moneys, and attired
In splendid garb, with hose of silk, and hair
Powdered like rimy trees, when frost is keen.
My lordly dressing-gown, I pass it by,   40
With other signs of manhood that supplied
The lack of beard. – The weeks went roundly on,
With invitations, suppers, wine and fruit,
Smooth housekeeping within, and all without
Liberal, and suiting gentleman's array.   45

    The Evangelist St John my patron was:
Three Gothic courts are his, and in the first
Was my abiding-place, a nook obscure;
Right underneath, the College kitchens made
A humming sound, less tuneable than bees,   50
But hardly less industrious; with shrill notes
Of sharp command and scolding intermixed.
Near me hung Trinity's loquacious clock,
Who never let the quarters, night or day,
Slip by him unproclaimed, and told the hours   55
Twice over with a male and female voice.
Her pealing organ was my neighbour too;
And from my pillow, looking forth by light
Of moon or favouring stars, I could behold
The antechapel where the statue stood   60
Of Newton with his prism and silent face,
The marble index of a mind for ever
Voyaging through strange seas of Thought, alone.

    Of College labours, of the Lecturer's room
All studded round, as thick as chairs could stand,   65
With loyal students faithful to their books,
Half-and-half idlers, hardy recusants,
And honest dunces – of important days,
Examinations, when the man was weighed
As in a balance! of excessive hopes,   70
Tremblings withal and cómmendable fears,
Small jealousies, and triumphs good or bad,

53 **Trinity:** Trinity College, Cambridge 61 **Newton with his prism:**
Isaac Newton (1642–1627). Using a prism, Newton discovered that
white light consists of a spectrum of colours 67 **Half-and-half:**
drunk **recusants:** those who refuse to submit to regulations

Let others that know more speak as they know.
Such glory was but little sought by me,
And little won. Yet from the first crude days   75
Of settling time in this untried abode,
I was disturbed at times by prudent thoughts,
Wishing to hope without a hope, some fears
About my future worldly maintenance,
And, more than all, a strangeness in the mind,   80
A feeling that I was not for that hour,
Nor for that place. But wherefore be cast down?
For (not to speak of Reason and her pure
Reflective acts to fix the moral law
Deep in the conscience, nor of Christian Hope,   85
Bowing her head before her sister Faith
As one far mightier), hither I had come,
Bear witness Truth, endowed with holy powers
And faculties, whether to work or feel.
Oft when the dazzling show no longer new   90
Had ceased to dazzle, ofttimes did I quit
My comrades, leave the crowd, buildings and groves,
And as I paced alone the level fields
Far from those lovely sights and sounds sublime
With which I had been cónversant, the mind   95
Drooped not; but there into herself returning,
With prompt rebound seemed fresh as heretofore.
At least I more distinctly recognized
Her native instincts: let me dare to speak
A higher language, say that now I felt   100
What independent solaces were mine,
To mitigate the injurious sway of place
Or circumstance, how far soever changed
In youth, or *to* be changed in manhood's prime;
Or for the few who shall be called to look   105
On the long shadows in our evening years,
Ordained precursors to the night of death.
As if awakened, summoned, roused, constrained,
I looked for universal things; perused
The common countenance of earth and sky: 110
Earth, nowhere unembellished by some trace
Of that first Paradise whence man was driven;
And sky, whose beauty and bounty are expressed
By the proud name she bears – the name of Heaven.
I called on both to teach me what they might;   115
Or turning the mind in upon herself
Pored, watched, expected, listened, spread my
    thoughts
And spread them with a wider creeping; felt
Incumbencies more awful, visitings
Of the Upholder, of the tranquil soul,   120
That tolerates the indignities of Time,
And, from the centre of Eternity
All finite motions overruling, lives
In glory immutable. But peace! enough
Here to record that I was mounting now   125
To such community with highest truth –
A track pursuing, not untrod before,
From strict analogies by thought supplied

Or consciousnesses not to be subdued.
To every natural form, rock, fruit or flower, 130
Even the loose stones that cover the high-way,
I gave a moral life: I saw them feel,
Or linked them to some feeling: the great mass
Lay bedded in a quickening soul, and all
That I beheld respired with inward meaning. 135
Add that whate'er of Terror or of Love
Or Beauty, Nature's daily face put on
From transitory passion, unto this
I was as sensitive as waters are
To the sky's influence: in a kindred mood 140
Of passion, was obedient as a lute
That waits upon the touches of the wind.
Unknown, unthought of, yet I was most rich –
I had a world about me – 'twas my own;
I made it, for it only lived to me, 145
And to the God who sees into the heart.
Such sympathies, though rarely, were betrayed
By outward gestures and by visible looks:
Some called it madness – so indeed it was,
If child-like fruitfulness in passing joy, 150
If steady moods of thoughtfulness matured
To inspiration, sort with such a name;
If prophecy be madness; if things viewed
By poets in old time, and higher up
By the first men, earth's first inhabitants, 155
May in these tutored days no more be seen
With undisordered sight. But leaving this,
It was no madness, for the bodily eye
Amid my strongest workings evermore
Was searching out the lines of difference 160
As they lie hid in all external forms,
Near or remote, minute or vast, an eye
Which from a tree, a stone, a withered leaf,
To the broad ocean and the azure heavens
Spangled with kindred multitudes of stars, 165
Could find no surface where its power might sleep;
Which spake perpetual logic to my soul,
And by an unrelenting agency
Did bind my feelings even as in a chain.

   And here, O Friend! have I retraced my life 170
Up to an eminence, and told a tale
Of matters which not falsely may be called
The glory of my youth. Of genius, power,
Creation and divinity itself
I have been speaking, for my theme has been 175
What passed within me. Not of outward things
Done visibly for other minds, words, signs,
Symbols or actions, but of my own heart
Have I been speaking, and my youthful mind.
O Heavens! how awful is the might of souls, 180
And what they do within themselves while yet
The yoke of earth is new to them, the world
Nothing but a wild field where they were sown.
This is, in truth, heroic argument,
This genuine prowess, which I wished to touch 185

With hand however weak, but in the main
It lies far hidden from the reach of words.
Points have we all of us within our souls
Where all stand single; this I feel, and make
Breathings for incommunicable powers; 190
But is not each a memory to himself?
And, therefore, now that we must quit this theme,
I am not heartless, for there's not a man
That lives who hath not known his god-like hours,
And feels not what an empire we inherit 195
As natural beings in the strength of Nature.
   No more; for now into a populous plain
We must descend. A Traveller I am,
Whose tale is only of himself; even so,
So be it, if the pure of heart be prompt 200
To follow, and if thou, my honoured Friend!
Who in these thoughts art ever at my side,
Support, as heretofore, my fainting steps.
   It hath been told, that when the first delight
That flashed upon me from this novel show 205
Had failed, the mind returned into herself;
Yet true it is, that I had made a change
In climate, and my nature's outward coat
Changed also slowly and insensibly.
Full oft the quiet and exalted thoughts 210
Of loneliness gave way to empty noise
And superficial pastimes; now and then
Forced labour, and more frequently forced hopes;
And, worst of all, a treasonable growth
Of indecisive judgements, that impaired 215
And shook the mind's simplicity. – And yet
This was a gladsome time. Could I behold –
Who, less insensible than sodden clay
In a sea-river's bed at ebb of tide,
Could have beheld, – with undelighted heart, 220
So many happy youths, so wide and fair
A congregation in its budding-time
Of health, and hope, and beauty, all at once
So many divers samples from the growth
Of life's sweet season – could have seen unmoved 225
That miscellaneous garland of wild flowers
Decking the matron temples of a place
So famous through the world? To me, at least,
It was a goodly prospect: for, in sooth,
Though I had learnt betimes to stand unpropped, 230
And independent musings pleased me so
That spells seemed on me when I was alone,
Yet could I only cleave to solitude
In lonely places; if a throng was near
That way I leaned by nature; for my heart 235
Was social, and loved idleness and joy.
   Not seeking those who might participate
My deeper pleasures (nay, I had not once,
Though not unused to mutter lonesome songs,
Even with myself divided such delight, 240
Or looked that way for aught that might be clothed
In human language), easily I passed

From the remembrances of better things,
And slipped into the ordinary works
Of careless youth, unburthened, unalarmed. 245
Caverns there were within my mind which sun
Could never penetrate, yet did there not
Want store of leafy *arbours* where the light
Might enter in at will. Companionships,
Friendships, acquaintances, were welcome all. 250
We sauntered, played, or rioted; we talked
Unprofitable talk at morning hours;
Drifted about along the streets and walks,
Read lazily in trivial books, went forth
To gallop through the country in blind zeal 255
Of senseless horsemanship, or on the breast
Of Cam sailed boisterously, and let the stars
Come forth, perhaps without one quiet thought.
   Such was the tenor of the second act
In this new life. Imagination slept, 260
And yet not utterly. I could not print
Ground where the grass had yielded to the steps
Of generations of illustrious men,
Unmoved. I could not always lightly pass
Through the same gateways, sleep where they had
   slept, 265
Wake where they waked, range that enclosure old,
That garden of great intellects, undisturbed.
Place also by the side of this dark sense
Of noble feeling, that those spiritual men,
Even the great Newton's own ethereal self, 270
Seemed humbled in these precincts, thence to be
The more endeared. Their several memories here
(Even like their persons in their portraits clothed
With the accustomed garb of daily life)
Put on a lowly and a touching grace 275
Of more distinct humanity, that left
All genuine admiration unimpaired.
   Beside the pleasant Mill of Trompington
I laughed with Chaucer; in the hawthorn shade
Heard him, while birds were warbling, tell his tales
Of amorous passion. And that gentle Bard, 281
Chosen by the Muses for their Page of State –
Sweet Spenser, moving through his clouded heaven
With the moon's beauty and the moon's soft pace,
I called him Brother, Englishman, and Friend! 285
Yea, our blind Poet, who, in his later day,
Stood almost single; uttering odious truth –
Darkness before, and danger's voice behind,
Soul awful – if the earth has ever lodged
An awful soul – I seemed to see him here 290
Familiarly, and in his scholar's dress
Bounding before me, yet a stripling youth –
A boy, no better, with his rosy cheeks
Angelical, keen eye, courageous look,
And conscious step of purity and pride. 295

Among the band of my compeers was one
Whom chance had stationed in the very room
Honoured by Milton's name. O temperate Bard!
Be it confessed that, for the first time, seated
Within thy innocent lodge and oratory, 300
One of a festive circle, I poured out
Libations, to thy memory drank, till pride
And gratitude grew dizzy in a brain
Never excited by the fumes of wine
Before that hour, or since. Then, forth I ran 305
From the assembly; through a length of streets,
Ran, ostrich-like, to reach our chapel door
In not a desperate or opprobrious time,
Albeit long after the importunate bell
Had stopped, with wearisome Cassandra voice 310
No longer haunting the dark winter night.
Call back, O Friend! a moment to thy mind
The place itself and fashion of the rites.
With careless ostentation shouldering up
My surplice, through the inferior throng I clove 315
Of the plain Burghers, who in audience stood
On the last skirts of their permitted ground,
Under the pealing organ. Empty thoughts!
I am ashamed of them: and that great Bard,
And thou, O Friend! who in thy ample mind 320
Hast placed me high above my best deserts,
Ye will forgive the weakness of that hour,
In some of its unworthy vanities,
Brother to many more.
                    In this mixed sort
The months passed on, remissly, not given up 325
To wilful alienation from the right,
Or walks of open scandal, but in vague
And loose indifference, easy likings, aims
Of a low pitch – duty and zeal dismissed,
Yet Nature, or a happy course of things 330
Not doing in their stead the needful work.
The memory languidly revolved, the heart
Reposed in noontide rest, the inner pulse
Of contemplation almost failed to beat.
Such life might not inaptly be compared 335
To a floating island, an amphibious spot
Unsound, of spongy texture, yet withal
Not wanting a fair face of water weeds
And pleasant flowers. The thirst of living praise,
Fit reverence for the glorious Dead, the sight 340
Of those long vistas, sacred catacombs,
Where mighty *minds* lie visibly entombed,
Have often stirred the heart of youth, and bred
A fervent love of rigorous discipline. –
Alas! such high emotion touched not me. 345
Look was there none within these walls to shame
My easy spirits, and discountenance
Their light composure, far less to instil
A calm resolve of mind, firmly addressed

---

279 **Chaucer:** Geoffrey Chaucer 14th-century poet

310 **Cassandra voice:** Cassandra had the gift of prophecy 316 **Burghers:** citizens

To puissant efforts. Nor was this the blame 350
Of others but my own; I should, in truth,
As far as doth concern my single self,
Misdeem most widely, lodging it elsewhere:
For I, bred up 'mid Nature's luxuries,
Was a spoiled child, and rambling like the wind, 355
As I had done in daily intercourse
With those crystálline rivers, solemn heights,
And mountains; ranging like a fowl of the air,
I was ill-tutored for captivity,
To quit my pleasure, and, from month to month, 360
Take up a station calmly on the perch
Of sedentary peace. Those lovely forms
Had also left less space within my mind,
Which, wrought upon instinctively, had found
A freshness in those objects of her love, 365
A winning power, beyond all other power.
Not that I slighted books, – that were to lack
All sense, – but other passions in me ruled,
Passions more fervent, making me less prompt
To in-door study than was wise or well, 370
Or suited to those years. Yet I, though used
In magisterial liberty to rove,
Culling such flowers of learning as might tempt
A random choice, could shadow forth a place
(If now I yield not to a flattering dream) 375
Whose studious aspect should have bent me down
To instantaneous service; should at once
Have made me pay to science and to arts
And written lore, acknowledged my liege lord,
A homage frankly offered up, like that 380
Which I had paid to Nature. Toil and pains
In this recess, by thoughtful Fancy built,
Should spread from heart to heart; and stately groves,
Majestic edifices, should not want
A corresponding dignity within. 385
The congregating temper that pervades
Our unripe years, not wasted, should be taught
To minister to works of high attempt –
Works which the enthusiast would perform with love.
Youth should be awed, religiously possessed 390
With a conviction of the power that waits
On knowledge, when sincerely sought and prized
For its own sake, on glory and on praise
If but by labour won, and fit to endure.
The passing day should learn to put aside 395
Her trappings here, should strip them off abashed
Before antiquity and steadfast truth
And strong book-mindedness; and over all
A healthy sound simplicity should reign,
A seemly plainness, name it what you will, 400
Republican or pious.
                    If these thoughts
Are a gratuitous emblazonry
That mocks the recreant age *we* live in, then
Be Folly and False-seeming free to affect
Whatever formal gait of discipline 405

Shall raise them highest in their own esteem –
Let them parade among the Schools at will,
But spare the House of God. Was ever known
The witless shepherd who persists to drive
A flock that thirsts not to a pool disliked? 410
A weight must surely hang on days begun
And ended with such mockery. Be wise,
Ye Presidents and Deans, and, till the spirit
Of ancient times revive, and youth be trained
At home in pious service, to your bells 415
Give seasonable rest, for 'tis a sound
Hollow as ever vexed the tranquil air;
And your officious doings bring disgrace
On the plain steeples of our English Church,
Whose worship, 'mid remotest village trees, 420
Suffers for this. Even Science, too, at hand
In daily sight of this irreverence,
Is smitten thence with an unnatural taint,
Loses her just authority, falls beneath
Collateral suspicion, else unknown. 425
This truth escaped me not, and I confess,
That having 'mid my native hills given loose
To a schoolboy's vision, I had raised a pile
Upon the basis of the coming time,
That fell in ruins round me. Oh, what joy 430
To see a sanctuary for our country's youth
Informed with such a spirit as might be
It own protection; a primeval grove,
Where, though the shades with cheerfulness were
    filled,
Nor indigent of songs warbled from crowds 435
In under-coverts, yet the countenance
Of the whole place should bear a stamp of awe;
A habitation sober and demure
For ruminating creatures; a domain
For quiet things to wander in; a haunt 440
In which the heron should delight to feed
By the shy rivers, and the pelican
Upon the cypress spire in lonely thought
Might sit and sun himself. – Alas! alas!
In vain for such solemnity I looked; 445
Mine eyes were crossed by butterflies, ears vexed
By chattering popinjays; the inner heart
Seemed trivial, and the impresses without
Of a too gaudy region.
                    Different sight
Those venerable Doctors saw of old, 450
When all who dwelt within these famous walls
Led in abstemiousness a studious life;
When, in forlorn and naked chambers cooped
And crowded, o'er the ponderous books they hung
Like caterpillars eating out their way 455
In silence, or with keen devouring noise
Not to be tracked or fathered. Princes then
At matins froze, and couched at curfew-time,
Trained up through piety and zeal to prize
Spare diet, patient labour, and plain weeds. 460

O seat of Arts! renowned throughout the world!
Far different service in those homely days
The Muses' modest nurslings underwent
From their first childhood: in that glorious time
When Learning, like a stranger come from far,   465
Sounding through Christian lands her trumpet, roused
Peasant and king; when boys and youths, the growth
Of ragged villages and crazy huts,
Forsook their homes, and, errant in the quest
Of Patron, famous school or friendly nook,   470
Where, pensioned, they in shelter might sit down,
From town to town and through wide scattered realms
Journeyed with ponderous folios in their hands;
And often, starting from some covert place,
Saluted the chance comer on the road,   475
Crying, 'An obulus, a penny give
To a poor scholar!' – when illustrious men,
Lovers of truth, by penury constrained,
Bucer, Erasmus, or Melancthon, read
Before the doors or windows of their cells   480
By moonshine through mere lack of taper light.

But peace to vain regrets! We see but darkly
Even when we look behind us, and best things
Are not so pure by nature that they needs
Must keep to all, as fondly all believe,   485
Their highest promise. If the mariner
When at reluctant distance he hath passed
Some tempting island, could but know the ills
That must have fallen upon him had he brought
His bark to land upon the wished-for shore,   490
Good cause would oft be his to thank the surf
Whose white belt scared him thence, or wind that
      blew
Inexorably ádverse: for myself
I grieve not; happy is the gownèd youth,
Who only misses what I missed, who falls   495
No lower than I fell.

                    I did not love,
Judging not ill perhaps, the timid course
Of our scholastic studies; could have wished
To see the river flow with ampler range
And freer pace; but more, far more, I grieved   500
To see displayed among an eager few,
Who in the field of contest persevered,
Passions unworthy of youth's generous heart
And mounting spirit, pitiably repaid,
When so disturbed, whatever palms are won.   505
From these I turned to travel with the shoal
Of more unthinking natures, easy minds
And pillowy; yet not wanting love that makes
The day pass lightly on, when foresight sleeps,
And wisdom and the pledges interchanged   510
With our own inner being are forgot.

Yet was this deep vacation not given up
To utter waste. Hitherto I had stood
In my own mind remote from social life
(At least from what we commonly so name),   515
Like a lone shepherd on a promontory
Who lacking occupation looks far forth
Into the boundless sea, and rather makes
Than finds what he beholds. And sure it is,
That this first transit from the smooth delights   520
And wild outlandish walks of simple youth
To something that resembles an approach
Towards human business, to a privileged world
Within a world, a midway residence
With all its intervenient imagery,   525
Did better suit my visionary mind,
Far better, than to have been bolted forth,
Thrust out abruptly into Fortune's way
Among the conflicts of substantial life;
By a more just gradation did lead on   530
To higher things; more naturally matured,
For permanent possession, better fruits,
Whether of truth or virtue, to ensue.
In serious mood, but oftener, I confess,
With playful zest of fancy did we note   535
(How could we less?) the manners and the ways
Of those who lived distinguished by the badge
Of good or ill report; or those with whom
By frame of Academic discipline
We were perforce connected, men whose sway   540
And known authority of office served
To set our minds on edge, and did no more.
Nor wanted we rich pastime of this kind,
Found everywhere, but chiefly in the ring
Of the grave Elders, men unscoured, grotesque   545
In character, tricked out like agèd trees
Which through the lapse of their infirmity
Give ready place to any random seed
That chooses to be reared upon their trunks.

    Here on my view, confronting vividly   550
Those shepherd swains whom I had lately left,
Appeared a different aspect of old age;
How different! yet both distinctly marked,
Objects embossed to catch the general eye,
Or portraitures for special use designed,   555
As some might seem, so aptly do they serve
To illustrate Nature's book of rudiments –
That book upheld as with maternal care
When she would enter on her tender scheme
Of teaching comprehension with delight,   560
And mingling playful with pathetic thoughts.
    The surfaces of artificial life
And manners finely wrought, the delicate race
Of colours, lurking, gleaming up and down
Through that state arras woven with silk and gold;   566
This wily interchange of snaky hues,
Willingly or unwillingly revealed,
I neither knew nor cared for; and as such

476–477 These lines refer to Belisarius, the Roman emperor Justinian's most successful general. Legend has it that Justinian, jealous of Belisarius's popularity, had his eyes put out. The general then begged in the streets of Constantinople 479 famous scholars

Were wanting here, I took what might be found
Of less elaborate fabric. At this day   570
I smile, in many a mountain solitude
Conjuring up scenes as obsolete in freaks
Of character, in points of wit as broad,
As aught by wooden images performed
For entertainment of the gaping crowd   575
At wake or fair. And oftentimes do flit
Remembrances before me of old men –
Old humorists, who have been long in their graves,
And having almost in my mind put off
Their human names, have into phantoms passed   580
Of texture midway between life and books.

  I play the loiterer: 'tis enough to note
That here in dwarf proportions were expressed
The limbs of the great world; its eager strifes
Collaterally portrayed, as in mock fight,   585
A tournament of blows, some hardly dealt
Though short of mortal combat; and whate'er
Might in this pageant be supposed to hit
An artless rustic's notice, this way less,
More that way, was not wasted upon me –   590
And yet the spectacle may well demand
A more substantial name, no mimic show,
Itself a living part of a live whole,
A creek in the vast sea; for, all degrees
And shapes of spurious fame and short-lived praise
Here sate in state, and fed with daily alms   596
Retainers won away from solid good;
And here was Labour, his own bond-slave; Hope,
That never set the pains against the prize;
Idleness halting with his weary clog,   600
And poor misguided Shame, and witless Fear,
And simple Pleasure foraging for Death;
Honour misplaced, and Dignity astray;
Feuds, factions, flatteries, enmity, and guile;
Murmuring submission, and bald government   605
(The idol weak as the idolator),
And Decency and Custom starving Truth,
And blind Authority beating with his staff
The child that might have led him; Emptiness
Followed as of good omen, and meek Worth   610
Left to herself unheard of and unknown.

  Of these and other kindred notices
I cannot say what portion is in truth
The naked recollection of that time,
And what may rather have been called to life   615
By after-meditation. But delight
That, in an easy temper lulled asleep,
Is still with Innocence its own reward,
This was not wanting. Carelessly I roamed
As through a wide museum from whose stores   620
A casual rarity is singled out
And has its brief perusal, then gives way
To others, all supplanted in their turn;
Till 'mid this crowded neighbourhood of things
That are by nature most unneighbourly,   625

The head turns round and cannot right itself;
And though an aching and a barren sense
Of gay confusion still be uppermost,
With few wise longings and but little love,
Yet to the memory something cleaves at last,   630
Whence profit may be drawn in times to come.
  Thus in submissive idleness, my Friend!
The labouring time of autumn, winter, spring,
Eight months! rolled pleasingly away; the ninth
Came and returned me to my native hills.   635

BOOK FOURTH. SUMMER VACATION

BRIGHT was the summer's noon when quickening steps
Followed each other till a dreary moor
Was crossed, a bare ridge clomb, upon whose top
Standing alone, as from a rampart's edge,
I overlooked the bed of Windermere,   5
Like a vast river, stretching in the sun.
With exultation, at my feet I saw
Lake, islands, promontories, gleaming bays,
A universe of Nature's fairest forms
Proudly revealed with instantaneous burst,   10
Magnificent, and beautiful, and gay.
I bounded down the hill shouting amain
For the old Ferryman; to the shout the rocks
Replied, and when the Charon of the flood
Had staid his oars, and touched the jutting pier,   15
I did not step into the well-known boat
Without a cordial greeting. Thence with speed
Up the familiar hill I took my way
Towards that sweet Valley where I had been reared;
'Twas but a short hour's walk, ere veering round   20
I saw the snow-white church upon her hill
Sit like a thronèd Lady, sending out
A gracious look all over her domain.
Yon azure smoke betrays the lurking town;
With eager footsteps I advance and reach   25
The cottage threshold where my journey closed.
Glad welcome had I, with some tears, perhaps,
From my old Dame, so kind and motherly,
While she perused me with a parent's pride.
The thoughts of gratitude shall fall like dew   30
Upon thy grave, good creature! While my heart
Can beat never will I forget thy name.
Heaven's blessing be upon thee where thou liest
After thy innocent and busy stir
In narrow cares, thy little daily growth   35
Of calm enjoyments, after eighty years,
And more than eighty, of untroubled life,
Childless, yet by the strangers to thy blood
Honoured with little less than filial love.
What joy was mine to see thee once again,   40

BOOK FOURTH, SUMMER VACATION: 14 **Charon:** In Greek mythology Charon ferried the dead across the river Styx to the Underworld. He is usually represented as a dishevelled old man 28 **old Dame:** a reference to Ann Tyson, at whose house Wordsworth lodged while a boy at school

Thee and thy dwelling, and a crowd of things
About its narrow precincts all beloved,
And many of them seeming yet my own!
Why should I speak of what a thousand hearts
Have felt, and every man alive can guess? 45
The rooms, the court, the garden were not left
Long unsaluted, nor the sunny seat
Round the stone table under the dark pine,
Friendly to studious or to festive hours;
Nor that unruly child of mountain birth, 50
The famous brook, who, soon as he was boxed
Within our garden, found himself at once,
As if by trick insidious and unkind,
Stripped of his voice and left to dimple down
(Without an effort and without a will) 55
A channel paved by man's officious care.
I looked at him and smiled, and smiled again,
And in the press of twenty thousand thoughts,
'Ha,' quoth I, 'pretty prisoner, are you there!'
Well might sarcastic Fancy then have whispered, 60
'An emblem here behold of thy own life;
In its late course of even days with all
Their smooth enthralment'; but the heart was full,
Too full for that reproach. My agèd Dame
Walked proudly at my side: she guided me; 65
I willing, nay – nay, wishing to be led.
– The face of every neighbour whom I met
Was like a volume to me: some were hailed
Upon the road, some busy at their work,
Unceremonious greetings interchanged 70
With half the length of a long field between.
Among my schoolfellows I scattered round
Like recognitions, but with some constraint
Attended, doubtless, with a little pride,
But with more shame, for my habiliments, 75
The transformation wrought by gay attire.
Not less delighted did I take my place
At our domestic table: and, dear Friend!
In this endeavour simply to relate
A Poet's history, may I leave untold 80
The thankfulness with which I laid me down
In my accustomed bed, more welcome now
Perhaps than if it had been more desired
Or been more often thought of with regret?
That lowly bed whence I had heard the wind 85
Roar and the rain beat hard, where I so oft
Had lain awake on summer nights to watch
The moon in splendour couched among the leaves
Of a tall ash, that near our cottage stood;
Had watched her with fixed eyes while to and fro 90
In the dark summit of the waving tree
She rocked with every impulse of the breeze.

   Among the favourites whom it pleased me well
To see again, was one by ancient right
Our inmate, a rough terrier of the hills; 95
By birth and call of nature pre-ordained
To hunt the badger and unearth the fox

Among the impervious crags, but having been
From youth our own adopted, he had passed
Into a gentler service. And when first 100
The boyish spirit flagged, and day by day
Along my veins I kindled with the stir,
The fermentation, and the vernal heat
Of poesy, affecting private shades
Like a sick Lover, then this dog was used 105
To watch me, an attendant and a friend,
Obsequious to my steps early and late,
Though often of such dilatory walk
Tired, and uneasy at the halts I made.
A hundred times when, roving high and low, 110
I have been harassed with the toil of verse,
Much pains and little progress, and at once
Some lovely Image in the song rose up
Full-formed, like Venus rising from the sea;
Then have I darted forwards to let loose 115
My hand upon his back with stormy joy,
Caressing him again and yet again.
And when at evening on the public way
I sauntered, like a river murmuring
And talking to itself when all things else 120
Are still, the creature trotted on before;
Such was his custom; but whene'er he met
A passenger approaching, he would turn
To give me timely notice, and straightway,
Grateful for that admonishment, I hushed 125
My voice, composed my gait, and, with the air
And mien of one whose thoughts are free, advanced
To give and take a greeting that might save
My name from piteous rumours, such as wait
On men suspected to be crazed in brain. 130
   Those walks well worthy to be prized and loved –
Regretted! – that word, too, was on my tongue,
But they were richly laden with all good,
And cannot be remembered but with thanks
And gratitude, and perfect joy of heart – 135
Those walks in all their freshness now came back
Like a returning Spring. When first I made
Once more the circuit of our little lake,
If ever happiness hath lodged with man,
That day consúmmate happiness was mine, 140
Wide-spreading, steady, calm, contemplative.
The sun was set, or setting, when I left
Our cottage door, and evening soon brought on
A sober hour, not winning or serene,
For cold and raw the air was, and untuned; 145
But as a face we love is sweetest then
When sorrow damps it, or, whatever look
It chance to wear, is sweetest if the heart
Have fullness in herself; even so with me
It fared that evening. Gently did my soul 150
Put off her veil, and, self-transmuted, stood
Naked, as in the presence of her God.

114 **Venus:** Roman goddess of love. She is said to have emerged
from the foam of the sea

While on I walked, a comfort seemed to touch
A heart that had not been disconsolate:
Strength came where weakness was not known to be,
At least not felt; and restoration came   156
Like an intruder knocking at the door
Of unacknowledged weariness. I took
The balance, and with firm hand weighed myself.
– Of that external scene which round me lay,   160
Little, in this abstraction, did I see;
Remembered less; but I had inward hopes
And swellings of the spirit, was rapt and soothed,
Conversed with promises, had glimmering views
How life pervades the undecaying mind;   165
How the immortal soul with God-like power
Informs, creates, and thaws the deepest sleep
That time can lay upon her; how on earth,
Man, if he do but live within the light
Of high endeavours, daily spreads abroad   170
His being armed with strength that cannot fail.
Nor was there want of milder thoughts, of love,
Of innocence, and holiday repose;
And more than pastoral quiet, 'mid the stir
Of boldest projects, and a peaceful end   175
At last, or glorious, by endurance won.
Thus musing, in a wood I sate me down
Alone, continuing there to muse: the slopes
And heights meanwhile were slowly overspread
With darkness, and before a rippling breeze   180
The long lake lengthened out its hoary line,
And in the sheltered coppice where I sate,
Around me from among the hazel leaves,
Now here, now there, moved by the straggling wind,
Came ever and anon a breath-like sound,   185
Quick as the pantings of the faithful dog,
The off and on companion of my walk;
And such, at times, believing them to be,
I turned my head to look if he were there;
Then into solemn thought I passed once more.   190
    A freshness also found I at this time
In human Life, the daily life of those
Whose occupations reälly I loved;
The peaceful scene oft filled me with surprise
Changed like a garden in the heat of spring   195
After an eight-days' absence. For (to omit
The things which were the same and yet appeared
Far otherwise) amid this rural solitude,
A narrow Vale where each was known to all,
'Twas not indifferent to a youthful mind   200
To mark some sheltering bower or sunny nook,
Where an old man had used to sit alone,
Now vacant; pale-faced babes whom I had left
In arms, now rosy prattlers at the feet
Of a pleased grandame tottering up and down;   205
And growing girls whose beauty, filched away
With all its pleasant promises, was gone
To deck some slighted playmate's homely cheek.
    Yes, I had something of a subtler sense,

And often looking round was moved to smiles   210
Such as a delicate work of humour breeds;
I read, without design, the opinions, thoughts,
Of those plain-living people now observed
With clearer knowledge; with another eye
I saw the quiet woodman in the woods,   215
The shepherd roam the hills. With new delight,
This chiefly, did I note my grey-haired Dame;
Saw her go forth to church or other work
Of state, equipped in monumental trim;
Short velvet cloak (her bonnet of the like),   220
A mantle such as Spanish Cavaliers
Wore in old time. Her smooth domestic life,
Affectionate without disquietude,
Her talk, her business, pleased me; and no less
Her clear though shallow stream of piety   225
That ran on Sabbath days a fresher course;
With thoughts unfelt till now I saw her read
Her Bible on hot Sunday afternoons,
And loved the book, when she had dropped asleep
And made of it a pillow for her head.   230
    Nor less do I remember to have felt,
Distinctly manifested at this time,
A human-heartedness about my love
For objects hitherto the absolute wealth
Of my own private being and no more: 235
Which I had loved, even as a blessèd spirit
Or Angel, if he were to dwell on earth,
Might love in individual happiness.
But now there opened on me other thoughts
Of change, congratulation or regret,   240
A pensive feeling! It spread far and wide;
The trees, the mountains shared it, and the brooks,
The stars of Heaven, now seen in their old haunts –
White Sirius glittering o'er the southern crags,
Orion with his belt, and those fair Seven,   245
Acquaintances of every little child,
And Jupiter, my own belovèd star!
Whatever shadings of mortality,
Whatever imports from the world of death
Had come among these objects heretofore,   250
Were, in the main, of mood less tender: strong,
Deep, gloomy were they, and severe; the scatterings
Of awe or tremulous dread, that had given way
In later youth to yearnings of a love
Enthusiastic, to delight and hope.   255
    As one who hangs down-bending from the side
Of a slow-moving boat, upon the breast
Of a still water, solacing himself
With such discoveries as his eye can make
Beneath him in the bottom of the deep,   260
Sees many beauteous sights – weeds, fishes, flowers,
Grots, pebbles, roots of trees, and fancies more,

244–245 **White Sirius . . . Orion . . . Seven:** Constellations of stars.
'Seven' refers to the Pleiades, of which only six stars are visible to
the unaided eye   247 **Jupiter:** a reference to Wordsworth's
astrological birth-sign

Yet often is perplexed and cannot part
The shadow from the substance, rocks and sky,
Mountains and clouds, reflected in the depth   265
Of the clear flood, from things which there abide
In their true dwelling; now is crossed by gleam
Of his own image, by a sun-beam now,
And wavering motions sent he knows not whence,
Impediments that make his task more sweet;   270
Such pleasant office have we long pursued
Incumbent o'er the surface of past time
With like success, nor often have appeared
Shapes fairer or less doubtfully discerned
Than these to which the Tale, indulgent Friend!   275
Would now direct thy notice. Yet in spite
Of pleasure won, and knowledge not withheld,
There was an inner falling off – I loved,
Loved deeply all that had been loved before,
More deeply even than ever: but a swarm   280
Of heady schemes jostling each other, gawds,
And feast and dance, and public revelry,
And sports and games (too grateful in themselves,
Yet in themselves less grateful, I believe,
Than as they were a badge glossy and fresh   285
Of manliness and freedom) all conspired
To lure my mind from firm habitual quest
Of feeding pleasures, to depress the zeal
And damp those yearnings which had once been
     mine –
A wild, unworldly-minded youth, given up   290
To his own eager thoughts. It would demand
Some skill, and longer time than may be spared,
To paint these vanities, and how they wrought
In haunts where they, till now, had been unknown.
It seemed the very garments that I wore   295
Preyed on my strength, and stopped the quiet stream
Of self-forgetfulness.
                         Yes, that heartless chase
Of trivial pleasures was a poor exchange
For books and nature at that early age.
'Tis true, some casual knowledge might be gained   300
Of character or life; but at that time,
Of manners put to school I took small note,
And all my deeper passions lay elsewhere.
Far better had it been to exalt the mind
By solitary study, to uphold   305
Intense desire through meditative peace;
And yet, for chástisement of these regrets,
The memory of one particular hour
Doth here rise up against me. 'Mid a throng
Of maids and youths, old men, and matrons staid,   310
A medley of all tempers, I had passed
The night in dancing, gaiety, and mirth,
With din of instruments and shuffling feet,
And glancing forms, and tapers glittering,
And unaimed prattle flying up and down;   315
Spirits upon the stretch, and here and there
Slight shocks of young love-liking interspersed,

Whose transient pleasure mounted to the head,
And tingled through the veins. Ere we retired,
The cock had crowed, and now the eastern sky   320
Was kindling, not unseen, from humbled copse
And open field, through which the pathway wound,
And homeward led my steps. Magnificent
The morning rose, in memorable pomp,
Glorious as e'er I had beheld – in front,   325
The sea lay laughing at a distance; near,
The solid mountains shone, bright as the clouds,
Grain-tinctured, drenched in empyréan light;
And in the meadows and the lower grounds
Was all the sweetness of a common dawn –   330
Dews, vapours, and the melody of birds,
And labourers going forth to till the fields.
     Ah! need I say, dear Friend! that to the brim
My heart was full; I made no vows, but vows
Were then made for me; bond unknown to me   335
Was given, that I should be, else sinning greatly,
A dedicated Spirit. On I walked
In thankful blessedness, which yet survives.
     Strange rendezvous my mind was at that time,
A parti-coloured show of grave and gay,   340
Solid and light, short-sighted and profound;
Of inconsiderate habits and sedate,
Consorting in one mansion unreproved.
The worth I knew of powers that I possessed,
Though slighted and too oft misused. Besides,   345
That summer, swarming as it did with thoughts
Transient and idle, lacked not intervals
When Folly from the frown of fleeting Time
Shrunk, and the mind experienced in herself
Conformity as just as that of old   350
To the end and written spirit of God's works,
Whether held forth in Nature or in Man,
Through pregnant vision, separate or conjoined.
     When from our better selves we have too long
Been parted by the hurrying world, and droop,   355
Sick of its business, of its pleasures tired,
How gracious, how benign, is Solitude;
How potent a mere image of her sway;
Most potent when impressed upon the mind
With an appropriate human centre – hermit,   360
Deep in the bosom of the wilderness;
Votary (in vast cathedral, where no foot
Is treading, where no other face is seen)
Kneeling at prayers; or watchman on the top
Of lighthouse, beaten by Atlantic waves;   365
Or as the soul of that great Power is met
Sometimes embodied on a public road,
When, for the night deserted, it assumes
A character of quiet more profound
Than pathless wastes.

---

328 **empyréan:** heavenly

Once, when those summer months 370
Were flown, and autumn brought its annual show
Of oars with oars contending, sails with sails,
Upon Winander's spacious breast, it chanced
That – after I had left a flower-decked room
(Whose in-door pastime, lighted up, survived 375
To a late hour), and spirits overwrought
Were making night do penance for a day
Spent in a round of strenuous idleness –
My homeward course led up a long ascent,
Where the road's watery surface, to the top 380
Of that sharp rising, glittered to the moon
And bore the semblance of another stream
Stealing with silent lapse to join the brook
That murmured in the vale. All else was still;
No living thing appeared in earth or air, 385
And, save the flowing water's peaceful voice,
Sound there was none – but, lo! an uncouth shape,
Shown by a sudden turning of the road,
So near that, slipping back into the shade
Of a thick hawthorn, I could mark him well, 390
Myself unseen. He was of stature tall,
A span above man's common measure tall,
Stiff, lank, and upright; a more meagre man
Was never seen before by night or day.
Long were his arms, pallid his hands; his mouth 395
Looked ghastly in the moonlight: from behind,
A mile-stone propped him; I could also ken
That he was clothed in military garb,
Though faded, yet entire. Companionless,
No dog attending, by no staff sustained, 400
He stood, and in his very dress appeared
A desolation, a simplicity,
To which the trappings of a gaudy world
Make a strange back-ground. From his lips, ere long,
Issued low muttered sounds, as if of pain 405
Or some uneasy thought; yet still his form
Kept the same awful steadiness – at his feet
His shadow lay, and moved not. From self-blame
Not wholly free, I watched him thus; at length
Subduing my heart's specious cowardice, 410
I left the shady nook where I had stood
And hailed him. Slowly from his resting-place
He rose, and with a lean and wasted arm
In measured gesture lifted to his head
Returned my salutation; then resumed 415
His station as before; and when I asked
His history, the veteran, in reply,
Was neither slow nor eager; but, unmoved,
And with a quiet uncomplaining voice,
A stately air of mild indifference, 420
He told in few plain words a soldier's tale –
That in the Tropic Islands he had served,
Whence he had landed scarcely three weeks past;
That on his landing he had been dismissed,

And now was travelling towards his native home. 425
This heard, I said, in pity, 'Come with me.'
He stooped, and straightway from the ground took up
An oaken staff by me yet unobserved –
A staff which must have dropped from his slack hand
And lay till now neglected in the grass. 430
Though weak his step and cautious, he appeared
To travel without pain, and I beheld,
With an astonishment but ill suppressed,
His ghostly figure moving at my side;
Nor could I, while we journeyed thus, forbear 435
To turn from present hardships to the past,
And speak of war, battle, and pestilence,
Sprinkling this talk with questions, better spared,
On what he might himself have seen or felt.
He all the while was in demeanour calm, 440
Concise in answer; solemn and sublime
He might have seemed, but that in all he said
There was a strange half-absence, as of one
Knowing too well the importance of his theme,
But feeling it no longer. Our discóurse 445
Soon ended, and together on we passed
In silence through a wood gloomy and still.
Up-turning, then, along an open field,
We reached a cottage. At the door I knocked,
And earnestly to charitable care 450
Commended him as a poor friendless man,
Belated and by sickness overcome.
Assured that now the traveller would repose
In comfort, I entreated that henceforth
He would not linger in the public ways, 455
But ask for timely furtherance and help
Such as his state required. At this reproof,
With the same ghastly mildness in his look,
He said, 'My trust is in the God of Heaven,
And in the eye of him who passes me!' 460
    The cottage door was speedily unbarred,
And now the soldier touched his hat once more
With his lean hand, and in a faltering voice,
Whose tone bespake reviving interests
Till then unfelt, he thanked me; I returned 465
The farewell blessing of the patient man,
And so we parted. Back I cast a look,
And lingered near the door a little space,
Then sought with quiet heart my distant home.

BOOK FIFTH. BOOKS

WHEN Contemplation, like the night-calm felt
Through earth and sky, spreads widely, and sends deep
Into the soul its tranquillizing power,
Even then I sometimes grieve for thee, O Man,
Earth's paramount Creature! not so much for woes 5
That thou endurest; heavy though that weight be,
Cloud-like it mounts, or touched with light divine
Doth melt away; but for those palms achieved,
Through length of time, by patient exercise
Of study and hard thought; there, there, it is 10

373 **Winander:** Lake Windermere 422 **Tropic Islands:** The West Indies

That sadness finds its fuel. Hitherto,
In progress through this Verse, my mind hath looked
Upon the speaking face of earth and heaven
As her prime teacher, intercourse with man
Established by the sovereign Intellect,   15
Who through that bodily image hath diffused,
As might appear to the eye of fleeting time,
A deathless spirit. Thou also, man! hast wrought,
For commerce of thy nature with herself,
Things that aspire to unconquerable life;   20
And yet we feel – we cannot choose but feel –
That they must perish. Tremblings of the heart
It gives, to think that our immortal being
No more shall need such garments; and yet man,
As long as he shall be the child of earth,   25
Might almost 'weep to have' what he may lose,
Nor be himself extinguished, but survive,
Abject, depressed, forlorn, disconsolate.
A thought is with me sometimes, and I say, –
Should the whole frame of earth by inward throes   30
Be wrenched, or fire come down from far to scorch
Her pleasant habitations, and dry up
Old Ocean, in his bed left singed and bare,
Yet would the living Presence still subsist
Victorious, and composure would ensue,   35
And kindlings like the morning – presage sure
Of day returning and of life revived.
But all the meditations of mankind,
Yea, all the adamantine holds of truth
By reason built, or passion, which itself   40
Is highest reason in a soul sublime;
The consecrated works of Bard and Sage,
Sensuous or intellectual, wrought by men,
Twin labourers and heirs of the same hopes;
Where would they be? Oh! why hath not the Mind   45
Some element to stamp her image on
In nature somewhat nearer to her own?
Why, gifted with such powers to send abroad
Her spirit, must it lodge in shrines so frail?
    One day, when from my lips a like complaint   50
Had fallen in presence of a studious friend,
He with a smile made answer, that in truth
'Twas going far to seek disquietude;
But on the front of his reproof confessed
That he himself had oftentimes given way   55
To kindred hauntings. Whereupon I told,
That once in the stillness of a summer's noon,
While I was seated in a rocky cave
By the sea-side, perusing, so it chanced,
The famous history of the errant knight   60
Recorded by Cervantes, these same thoughts
Beset me, and to height unusual rose,
While listlessly I sate, and, having closed
The book, had turned my eyes toward the wide sea.

On poetry and geometric truth,   65
And their high privilege of lasting life,
From all internal injury exempt,
I mused, upon these chiefly: and at length,
My senses yielding to the sultry air,
Sleep seized me, and I passed into a dream.   70
I saw before me stretched a boundless plain
Of sandy wilderness, all black and void,
And as I looked around, distress and fear
Came creeping over me, when at my side,
Close at my side, an uncouth shape appeared   75
Upon a dromedary, mounted high.
He seemed an Arab of the Bedouin tribes:
A lance he bore, and underneath one arm
A stone, and in the opposite hand, a shell
Of a surpassing brightness. At the sight   80
Much I rejoiced, not doubting but a guide
Was present, one who with unerring skill
Would through the desert lead me; and while yet
I looked and looked, self-questioned what this freight
Which the new-comer carried through the waste   85
Could mean, the Arab told me that the stone
(To give it in the language of the dream)
Was 'Euclid's Elements'; and 'This', said he,
'Is something of more worth'; and at the word
Stretched forth the shell, so beautiful in shape,   90
In colour so resplendent, with command
That I should hold it to my ear. I did so,
And heard that instant in an unknown tongue,
Which yet I understood, articulate sounds,
A loud prophetic blast of harmony;   95
An Ode, in passion uttered, which foretold
Destruction to the children of the earth
By deluge, now at hand. No sooner ceased
The song, than the Arab with calm look declared
That all would come to pass of which the voice   100
Had given forewarning, and that he himself
Was going then to bury those two books:
The one that held acquaintance with the stars,
And wedded soul to soul in purest bond
Of reason, undisturbed by space or time;   105
The other that was a god, yea many gods,
Had voices more than all the winds, with power
To exhilarate the spirit, and to soothe,
Through every clime, the heart of human kind.
While this was uttering, strange as it may seem,   110
I wondered not, although I plainly saw
The one to be a stone, the other a shell;
Nor doubted once but that they both were books,
Having a perfect faith in all that passed.
Far stronger, now, grew the desire I felt   115
To cleave unto this man; but when I prayed
To share his enterprise, he hurried on
Reckless of me: I followed, not unseen,

BOOK FIFTH. BOOKS: 60–61 **errant knight** . . . **Cervantes**: *Don Quixote* (first published in 1605) by Miguel de Cervantes

88 **Euclid's Elements**: Greek mathematician and author of *Elements*, a book on geometry 96 **Ode**: a poem intended for singing

For oftentimes he cast a backward look,
Grasping his twofold treasure. – Lance in rest, 120
He rode, I keeping pace with him; and now
He, to my fancy, had become the knight
Whose tale Cervantes tells; yet not the knight,
But was an Arab of the desert too;
Of these was neither, and was both at once. 125
His countenance, meanwhile, grew more disturbed;
And looking backwards when he looked, mine eyes
Saw, over half the wilderness diffused,
A bed of glittering light: I asked the cause:
'It is', he said, 'the waters of the deep 130
Gathering upon us'; quickening then the pace
Of the unwieldy creature he bestrode,
He left me: I called after him aloud;
He heeded not; but, with his twofold charge
Still in his grasp, before me, full in view, 135
Went hurrying o'er the illimitable waste,
With the fleet waters of a drowning world
In chase of him; whereat I waked in terror,
And saw the sea before me, and the book,
In which I had been reading, at my side. 140
   Full often, taking from the world of sleep
This Arab phantom, which I thus beheld,
This semi-Quixote, I to him have given
A substance, fancied him a living man,
A gentle dweller in the desert, crazed 145
By love and feeling, and internal thought
Protracted among endless solitudes;
Have shaped him wandering upon this quest!
Nor have I pitied him; but rather felt
Reverence was due to a being thus employed; 150
And thought that, in the blind and awful lair
Of such a madness, reason did lie couched.
Enow there are on earth to take in charge
Their wives, their children, and their virgin loves,
Or whatsoever else the heart holds dear; 155
Enow to stir for these; yea, will I say,
Contemplating in soberness the approach
Of an event so dire, by signs in earth
Or heaven made manifest, that I could share
That maniac's fond anxiety, and go 160
Upon like errand. Oftentimes at least
Me hath such strong entrancement overcome,
When I have held a volume in my hand,
Poor earthly casket of immortal verse,
Shakespeare, or Milton, labourers divine! 165
   Great and benign, indeed, must be the power
Of living nature, which could thus so long
Detain me from the best of other guides
And dearest helpers, left unthanked, unpraised.
Even in the time of lisping infancy, 170
And later down, in prattling childhood even,
While I was travelling back among those days,
How could I ever play an ingrate's part?

Once more should I have made those bowers resound,
By intermingling strains of thankfulness 175
With their own thoughtless melodies; at least
It might have well beseemed me to repeat
Some simply fashioned tale, to tell again,
In slender accents of sweet verse, some tale
That did bewitch me then, and soothes me now. 180
O Friend! O Poet! brother of my soul,
Think not that I could pass along untouched
By these remembrances. Yet wherefore speak?
Why call upon a few weak words to say
What is already written in the hearts 185
Of all that breathe? – what in the path of all
Drops daily from the tongue of every child,
Wherever man is found? The trickling tear
Upon the cheek of listening Infancy
Proclaims it, and the insuperable look 190
That drinks as if it never could be full.
   That portion of my story I shall leave
There registered: whatever else of power
Or pleasure, sown or fostered thus, may be
Peculiar to myself, let that remain 195
Where still it works, though hidden from all search
Among the depths of time. Yet is it just
That here, in memory of all books which lay
Their sure foundations in the heart of man,
Whether by native prose, or numerous verse, 200
That in the name of all inspirèd souls,
From Homer, the great Thunderer, from the voice
That roars along the bed of Jewish song,
And that more varied and elaborate,
Those trumpet-tones of harmony that shake 205
Our shores in England, – from those loftiest notes
Down to the low and wren-like warblings, made
For cottagers and spinners at the wheel,
And sun-burnt travellers resting their tired limbs,
Stretched under wayside hedge-rows, ballad tunes, 210
Food for the hungry ears of little ones,
And of old men who have survived their joys:
'Tis just that in behalf of these, the works,
And of the men that framed them, whether known,
Or sleeping nameless in their scattered graves, 215
That I should here assert their rights, attest
Their honours, and should, once for all, pronounce
Their benediction; speak of them as Powers
For ever to be hallowed; only less,
For what we are and what we may become, 220
Than Nature's self, which is the breath of God,
Or His pure Word by miracle revealed.
   Rarely and with reluctance would I stoop
To transitory themes; yet I rejoice,
And, by these thoughts admonished, will pour out 225
Thanks with uplifted heart, that I was reared
Safe from an evil which these days have laid
Upon the children of the land, a pest

153 **Enow:** enough

202 **Homer:** a Greek poet (fl. 750 BC)

That might have dried me up, body and soul.
This verse is dedicate to Nature's self,　　　　230
And things that teach as Nature teaches: then,
Oh! where had been the Man, the Poet where,
Where had we been, we two, belovèd Friend!
If in the season of unperilous choice,
In lieu of wandering, as we did, through vales　　235
Rich with indigenous produce, open ground
Of Fancy, happy pastures ranged at will,
We had been followed, hourly watched, and noosed,
Each in his several melancholy walk
Stringed like a poor man's heifer at its feed,　　240
Led through the lanes in fórlorn servitude;
Or rather like a stallèd ox debarred
From touch of growing grass, that may not taste
A flower till it have yielded up its sweets
A prelibation to the mower's scythe.　　　　245
　　Behold the parent hen amid her brood,
Though fledged and feathered, and well pleased to
　　　　part
And straggle from her presence, still a brood,
And she herself from the maternal bond
Still undischarged; yet doth she little more　　250
Than move with them in tenderness and love,
A centre to the circle which they make;
And now and then, alike from need of theirs
And call of her own natural appetites,
She scratches, ransacks up the earth for food,　　255
Which they partake at pleasure. Early died
My honourd Mother, she who was the heart
And hinge of all our learnings and our loves:
She left us destitute, and, as we might,
Trooping together. Little suits it me　　　　260
To break upon the sabbath of her rest
With any thought that looks at others' blame;
Nor would I praise her but in perfect love.
Hence am I checked: but let me boldly say,
In gratitude, and for the sake of truth,　　　265
Unheard by her, that she, not falsely taught,
Fetching her goodness rather from times past,
Than shaping novelties for times to come,
Had no presumption, no such jealousy,
Nor did by habit of her thoughts mistrust　　270
Our nature, but had virtual faith that He
Who fills the mother's breast with innocent milk,
Doth also for our nobler part provide,
Under His great correction and control,
As innocent instincts, and as innocent food;　　275
Or draws for minds that are left free to trust
In the simplicities of opening life
Sweet honey out of spurned or dreaded weeds.
This was her creed, and therefore she was pure
From anxious fear of error or mishap,　　　280
And evil, overweeningly so called;
Was not puffed up by false unnatural hopes,

Nor selfish with unnecessary cares,
Nor with impatience from the season asked
More than its timely produce; rather loved　　285
The hours for what they are, than from regard
Glanced on their promises in restless pride.
Such was she – not from faculties more strong
Than others have, but from the times, perhaps,
And spot in which she lived, and through a grace　290
Of modest meekness, simple-mindedness,
A heart that found benignity and hope,
Being itself benign.
　　　　　　My drift I fear
Is scarcely obvious; but, that common sense
May try this modern system by its fruits,　　295
Leave let me take to place before her sight
A specimen portrayed with faithful hand.
Full early trained to worship seemliness,
This model of a child is never known
To mix in quarrels; that were far beneath　　300
Its dignity; with gifts he bubbles o'er
As generous as a fountain; selfishness
May not come near him, nor the little throng
Of flitting pleasures tempt him from his path;
The wandering beggars propagate his name,　　305
Dumb creatures find him tender as a nun,
And natural or supernatural fear,
Unless it leap upon him in a dream,
Touches him not. To enhance the wonder, see
How arch his notices, how nice his sense　　310
Of the ridiculous; nor blind is he
To the broad follies of the licensed world,
Yet innocent himself withal, though shrewd,
And can read lectures upon innocence;
A miracle of scientific lore,　　　　　315
Ships he can guide across the pathless sea,
And tell you all their cunning; he can read
The inside of the earth, and spell the stars;
He knows the policies of foreign lands;
Can string you names of districts, cities, towns,　320
The whole world over, tight as beads of dew
Upon a gossamer thread; he sifts, he weighs;
All things are put to question; he must live
Knowing that he grows wiser every day
Or else not live at all, and seeing too　　325
Each little drop of wisdom as it falls
Into the dimpling cistern of his heart:
For this unnatural growth the trainer blame,
Pity the tree. – Poor human vanity,
Wert thou extinguished, little would be left　　330
Which he could truly love; but how escape?
For, ever as a thought of purer birth
Rises to lead him toward a better clime,
Some intermeddler still is on the watch
To drive him back, and pound him, like a stray,　335
Within the pinfold of his own conceit.

238 **noosed:** wearing a halter like a working animal　239 **several:**
separate　245 **prelibation:** first taste　271 **virtual:** powerful, strong

312 **licensed:** conventional　336 **pinfold:** confinement

Meanwhile old grandame earth is grieved to find
The playthings, which her love designed for him,
Unthought of: in their woodland beds the flowers
Weep, and the river sides are all forlorn.   340
Oh! give us once again the wishing cap
Of Fortunatus, and the invisible coat
Of Jack the Giant-killer, Robin Hood,
And Sabra in the forest with St George!
The child, whose love is here, at least, doth reap   345
One precious gain, that he forgets himself.

    These mighty workmen of our later age,
Who, with a broad high-way, have overbridged
The froward chaos of futurity,
Tamed to their bidding; they who have the skill   350
To manage books, and things, and make them act
On infant minds as surely as the sun
Deals with a flower; the keepers of our time,
The guides and wardens of our faculties,
Sages who in their prescience would control   355
All accidents, and to the very road
Which they have fashioned would confine us down,
Like engines; when will their presumption learn,
That in the unreasoning progress of the world
A wiser spirit is at work for us,   360
A better eye than theirs, most prodigal
Of blessings, and most studious of our good,
Even in what seem our most unfruitful hours?

    There was a Boy: ye knew him well, ye cliffs
And islands of Winander! – many a time   365
At evening, when the earliest stars began
To move along the edges of the hills,
Rising or setting, would he stand alone
Beneath the trees or by the glimmering lake,
And there, with fingers interwoven, both hands   370
Pressed closely palm to palm, and to his mouth
Uplifted, he, as through an instrument,
Blew mimic hootings to the silent owls,
That they might answer him; and they would shout
Across the watery vale, and shout again,   375
Responsive to his call, with quivering peals,
And long halloos and screams, and echoes loud,
Redoubled and redoubled, concourse wild
Of jocund din; and, when a lengthened pause
Of silence came and baffled his best skill,   380
Then sometimes, in that silence while he hung
Listening, a gentle shock of mild surprise
Has carried far into his heart the voice
Of mountain torrents; or the visible scene
Would enter unawares into his mind,   385
With all its solemn imagery, its rocks,
Its wood, and that uncertain heaven, received
Into the bosom of the steady lake.

This Boy was taken from his mates, and died
In childhood, ere he was full twelve years old.   390
Fair is the spot, most beautiful the vale
Where he was born; the grassy churchyard hangs
Upon a slope above the village school,
And through that churchyard when my way has led
On summer evenings, I believe that there   395
A long half hour together I have stood
Mute, looking at the grave in which he lies!
Even now appears before the mind's clear eye
That self-same village church; I see her sit
(The thronèd Lady whom erewhile we hailed)   400
On her green hill, forgetful of this Boy
Who slumbers at her feet, – forgetful, too,
Of all her silent neighbourhood of graves,
And listening only to the gladsome sounds
That, from the rural school ascending, play   405
Beneath her and about her. May she long
Behold a race of young ones like to those
With whom I herded! – (easily, indeed,
We might have fed upon a fatter soil
Of arts and letters – but be that forgiven) –   410
A race of reäl children; not too wise,
Too learnèd, or too good; but wanton, fresh,
And bandied up and down by love and hate;
Not unresentful where self-justified;
Fierce, moody, patient, venturous, modest, shy;   415
Mad at their sports like withered leaves in winds;
Though doing wrong and suffering, and full oft
Bending beneath our life's mysterious weight
Of pain, and doubt, and fear, yet yielding not
In happiness to the happiest upon earth.   420
Simplicity in habit, truth in speech,
Be these the daily strengtheners of their minds;
May books and Nature be their early joy!
And knowledge rightly honoured with that name –
Knowledge not purchased by the loss of power!   425

    Well do I call to mind the very week
When I was first entrusted to the care
Of that sweet Valley; when its paths, its shores,
And brooks were like a dream of novelty
To my half-infant thoughts; that very week,   430
While I was roving up and down alone,
Seeking I knew not what, I chanced to cross
One of those open fields, which, shaped like ears,
Make green peninsulas in Esthwaite's Lake:
Twilight was coming on, yet through the gloom   435
Appeared distinctly on the opposite shore
A heap of garments, as if left by one
Who might have there been bathing. Long I watched,
But no one owned them; meanwhile the calm lake
Grew dark with all the shadows on its breast,   440
And, now and then, a fish up-leaping snapped
The breathless stillness. The succeeding day,
Those unclaimed garments telling a plain tale
Drew to the spot an anxious crowd; some looked
In passive expectation from the shore,   445

342-344 Fortunatus had a hat that could take him wherever
he wished to go; Jack the Giant-killer's invisible coat enabled
him to defeat the giants; St. George rescued Sabra, the king of
Egypt's daughter, from a dragon and then married her   349
froward: ungovernable

While from a boat others hung o'er the deep,
Sounding with grappling irons and long poles.
At last, the dead man, 'mid that beauteous scene
Of trees and hills and water, bolt upríght
Rose, with his ghastly face, a spectre shape   450
Of terror; yet no soul-debasing fear,
Young as I was, a child not nine years old,
Possessed me, for my inner eye had seen
Such sights before, among the shining streams
Of faery land, the forest of romance.   455
Their spirit hallowed the sad spectacle
With decoration of ideäl grace;
A dignity, a smoothness, like the works
Of Grecian art, and purest poesy.

A precious treasure had I long possessed,   460
A little yellow, canvas-covered book,
A slender abstract of the Arabian tales;
And, from companions in a new abode,
When first I learnt, that this dear prize of mine
Was but a block hewn from a mighty quarry –   465
That there were four large volumes, laden all
With kindred matter, 'twas to me, in truth,
A promise scarcely earthly. Instantly,
With one not richer than myself, I made
A covenant that each should lay aside   470
The moneys he possessed, and hoard up more,
Till our joint savings had amassed enough
To make this book our own. Through several months,
In spite of all temptation, we preserved
Religiously that vow; but firmness failed,   475
Nor were we ever masters of our wish.

And when thereafter to my father's house
The holidays returned me, there to find
That golden store of books which I had left,
What joy was mine! How often in the course   480
Of those glad respites, though a soft west wind
Ruffled the waters to the angler's wish
For a whole day together, have I lain
Down by thy side, O Derwent! murmuring stream,
On the hot stones, and in the glaring sun,   485
And there have read, devouring as I read,
Defrauding the day's glory, desperate!
Till with a sudden bound of smart reproach,
Such as an idler deals with in his shame,
I to the sport betook myself again.   490

A gracious spirit o'er this earth presides,
And o'er the heart of man: invisibly
It comes, to works of unreproved delight,
And tendency benign, directing those
Who care not, know not, think not what they do.   495
The tales that charm away the wakeful night
In Araby, romances; legends penned
For solace by dim light of monkish lamps;
Fictions for ladies, of their love, devised
By youthful squires; adventures endless, spun   500

By the dismantled warrior in old age,
Out of the bowels of those very schemes
In which his youth did first extravagate;
These spread like day, and something in the shape
Of these will live till man shall be no more.   505
Dumb yearnings, hidden appetites, are ours,
And *they must* have their food. Our childhood sits,
Our simple childhood, sits upon a throne
That hath more power than all the elements.
I guess not what this tells of Being past,   510
Nor what it augurs of the life to come;
But so it is, and, in that dubious hour,
That twilight when we first begin to see
This dawning earth, to recognise, expect,
And in the long probation that ensues,   515
The time of trial, ere we learn to live
In reconcilement with our stinted powers;
To endure this state of meagre vassalage,
Unwilling to forgo, confess, submit,
Uneasy and unsettled, yoke-fellows   520
To custom, mettlesome, and not yet tamed
And humbled down; oh! then we feel, we feel,
We know where we have friends. Ye dreamers, then,
Forgers of daring tales! we bless you then,
Impostors, drivellers, dotards, as the ape   525
Philosophy will call you: *then* we feel
With what, and how great might ye are in league,
Who make our wish, our power, our thought a deed,
An empire, a possession, – ye whom time
And seasons serve; all Faculties; to whom   530
Earth crouches, the elements are potter's clay,
Space like a heaven filled up with northern lights,
Here, nowhere, there, and everywhere at once.

Relinquishing this lofty eminence
For ground, though humbler, not the less a tract   535
Of the same isthmus, which our spirits cross
In progress from their native continent
To earth and human life, the Song might dwell
On that delightful time of growing youth,
When craving for the marvellous gives way   540
To strengthening love for things that we have seen;
When sober truth and steady sympathies,
Offered to notice by less daring pens,
Take firmer hold of us, and words themselves
Move us with conscious pleasure.   545
                              I am sad
At thought of raptures now for ever flown;
Almost to tears I sometimes could be sad
To think of, to read over, many a page,
Poems withal of name, which at that time
Did never fail to entrance me, and are now   550
Dead in my eyes, dead as a théatre
Fresh emptied of spectators. Twice five years
Or less I might have seen, when first my mind
With conscious pleasure opened to the charm

462 **Arabian tales:** *The Arabian Nights*

503 **extravagate:** explore 531 **elements:** earth, air, fire and water

Of words in tuneful order, found them sweet 555
For their own *sakes*, a passion, and a power;
And phrases pleased me chosen for delight,
For pomp, or love. Oft, in the public roads
Yet unfrequented, while the morning light
Was yellowing the hill tops, I went abroad 560
With a dear friend, and for the better part
Of two delightful hours we strolled along
By the still borders of the misty lake,
Repeating favourite verses with one voice,
Or conning more, as happy as the birds 565
That round us chanted. Well might we be glad,
Lifted above the ground by airy fancies,
More bright than madness or the dreams of wine;
And, though full oft the objects of our love
Were false, and in their splendour overwrought, 570
Yet was there surely then no vulgar power
Working within us, – nothing less, in truth,
Than that most noble attribute of man,
Though yet untutored and inordinate,
That wish for something loftier, more adorned, 575
Than is the common aspect, daily garb,
Of human life. What wonder, then, if sounds
Of exultation echoed through the groves!
For, images, and sentiments, and words,
And everything encountered or pursued 580
In that delicious world of poesy,
Kept holiday, a never-ending show,
With music, incense, festival, and flowers!
    Here must we pause: this only let me add,
From heart-experience, and in humblest sense 585
Of modesty, that he, who in his youth
A daily wanderer among woods and fields
With living Nature hath been intimate,
Not only in that raw unpractised time
Is stirred to ecstasy, as others are, 590
By glittering verse; but further, doth receive,
In measure only dealt out to himself,
Knowledge and increase of enduring joy
From the great Nature that exists in works
Of mighty Poets. Visionary power 595
Attends the motions of the viewless winds,
Embodied in the mystery of words:
There, darkness makes abode, and all the host
Of shadowy things work endless changes there,
As in a mansion like their proper home. 600
Even forms and substances are circumfused
By that transparent veil with light divine,
And, through the turnings intricate of verse,
Present themselves as objects recognised,
In flashes, and with glory not their own. 605
    Thus far a scanty record is deduced
Of what I owed to Books in early life;
Their later influence yet remains untold;
But as this work was taking in my thought

Proportions that seemed larger than had first 610
Been meditated, I was indisposed
To any further progress at a time
When these acknowledgements were left unpaid.

BOOK SIXTH. CAMBRIDGE AND THE ALPS

THE leaves were fading when to Esthwaite's banks
And the simplicities of cottage life
I bade farewell; and, one among the youth
Who, summoned by that season, reunite
As scattered birds troop to the fowler's lure, 5
Went back to Granta's cloisters, not so prompt
Or eager, though as gay and undepressed
In mind, as when I thence had taken flight
A few short months before. I turned my face
Without repining from the coves and heights 10
Clothed in the sunshine of the withering fern;
Quitted, not loth, the mild magnificence
Of calmer lakes and louder streams; and you,
Frank-hearted maids of rocky Cumberland,
You and your not unwelcome days of mirth, 15
Relinquished, and your nights of revelry,
And in my own unlovely cell sate down
In lightsome mood – such privilege has youth
That cannot take long leave of pleasant thoughts.
    The bonds of indolent society 20
Relaxing in their hold, henceforth I lived
More to myself. Two winters may be passed
Without a separate notice: many books
Were skimmed, devoured, or studiously perused,
But with no settled plan. I was detached 25
Internally from academic cares;
Yet independent study seemed a course
Of hardy disobedience toward friends
And kindred, proud rebellion and unkind.
This spurious virtue, rather let it bear 30
A name it now deserves, this cowardice,
Gave treacherous sanction to that over-love
Of freedom which encouraged me to turn
From regulations even of my own
As from restraints and bonds. Yet who can tell – 35
Who knows what thus may have been gained, both
        then
And at a later season, or preserved;
What love of nature, what original strength
Of contemplation, what intuitive truths,
The deepest and the best, what keen research, 40
Unbiased, unbewildered, and unawed?
    The Poet's soul was with me at that time;
Sweet meditations, the still overflow
Of present happiness, while future years
Lacked not anticipations, tender dreams, 45
No few of which have since been realised;
And some remain, hopes for my future life.
Four years and thirty, told this very week,

---

561 **dear friend**: Wordsworth's school-friend, John Fleming
565 **conning**: learning

BOOK SIXTH. CAMBRIDGE AND THE ALPS: 6 **Granta's cloisters:** Cambridge
University 48 Wordsworth was thirty-four on 7 April 1804

Have I been now a sojourner on earth,
By sorrow not unsmitten; yet for me 50
Life's morning radiance hath not left the hills,
Her dew is on the flowers. Those were the days
Which also first emboldened me to trust
With firmness, hitherto but lightly touched
By such a daring thought, that I might leave 55
Some monument behind me which pure hearts
Should reverence. The instinctive humbleness,
Maintained even by the very name and thought
Of printed books and authorship, began
To melt away; and further, the dread awe 60
Of mighty names was softened down and seemed
Approachable, admitting fellowship
Of modest sympathy. Such aspect now,
Though not familiarly, my mind put on,
Content to observe, to achieve, and to enjoy. 65

All winter long, whenever free to choose,
Did I by night frequent the College groves
And tributary walks; the last, and oft
The only one, who had been lingering there
Through hours of silence, till the porter's bell, 70
A punctual follower on the stroke of nine,
Rang with its blunt unceremonious voice,
Inexorable summons! Lofty elms,
Inviting shades of opportune recéss,
Bestowed composure on a neighbourhood 75
Unpeaceful in itself. A single tree
With sinuous trunk, boughs éxquisitely wreathed,
Grew there; an ash which Winter for himself
Decked as in pride, and with outlandish grace:
Up from the ground, and almost to the top, 80
The trunk and every master branch were green
With clustering ivy, and the lightsome twigs
And outer spray profusely tipped with seeds
That hung in yellow tassels, while the air
Stirred them, not voiceless. Often have I stood 85
Foot-bound uplooking at this lovely tree
Beneath a frosty moon. The hemisphere
Of magic fiction, verse of mine perchance
May never tread; but scarcely Spenser's self
Could have more tranquil visions in his youth, 90
Or could more bright appearances create
Of human forms with superhuman powers,
Than I beheld loitering on calm clear nights
Alone, beneath this fairy work of earth.

On the vague reading of a truant youth 95
'Twere idle to descánt. My inner judgement
Not seldom differed from my taste in books,
As if it appertained to another mind,
And yet the books which then I valued most
Are dearest to me *now*; for, having scanned, 100
Not heedlessly, the laws, and watched the forms
Of Nature, in that knowledge I possessed
A standard, often usefully applied,
Even when unconsciously, to things removed
From a familiar sympathy. – In fine, 105

I was a better judge of thoughts than words,
Misled in estimating words, not only
By common inexperience of youth,
But by the trade in classic niceties,
The dangerous craft of culling term and phrase 110
From languages that want the living voice
To carry meaning to the natural heart;
To tell us what is passion, what is truth,
What reason, what simplicity and sense.

Yet may we not entirely overlook 115
The pleasure gathered from the rudiments
Of geometric science. Though advanced
In these inquiries, with regret I speak,
No farther than the threshold, there I found
Both elevation and composed delight: 120
With Indian awe and wonder, ignorance pleased
With its own struggles, did I meditate
On the relation those abstractions bear
To Nature's laws, and by what process led,
Those immaterial agents bowed their heads 125
Duly to serve the mind of earth-born man;
From star to star, from kindred sphere to sphere,
From system on to system without end.

More frequently from the same source I drew
A pleasure quiet and profound, a sense 130
Of permanent and universal sway,
And paramount belief; there, recognised
A type, for finite natures, of the one
Supreme Existence, the surpassing life
Which – to the boundaries of space and time, 135
Of melancholy space and doleful time,
Superior, and incapable of change,
Nor touched by welterings of passion – is,
And hath the name of, God. Transcendent peace
And silence did await upon these thoughts 140
That were a frequent comfort to my youth.

'Tis told by one whom stormy waters threw,
With fellow-sufferers by the shipwreck spared,
Upon a desert coast, that having brought
To land a single volume, saved by chance, 145
A treatise of Geometry, he wont,
Although of food and clothing destitute,
And beyond common wretchedness depressed,
To part from company and take this book
(Then first a self-taught pupil in its truths) 150
To spots remote, and draw his diagrams
With a long staff upon the sand, and thus
Did oft beguile his sorrow, and almost
Forget his feeling: so (if like effect
From the same cause produced, 'mid outward things 155
So different, may rightly be compared),
So was it then with me, and so will be
With Poets ever. Mighty is the charm

121 **Indian:** Native American   142–154 this passage refers to
John Newton, author of the hymn, 'Amazing Grace' and *Authentic
Narrative* (1764) which details his time as a mistreated servant on
board a slave ship and his subsequent religious awakening

Of those abstractions to a mind beset
With images, and haunted by herself,   160
And specially delightful unto me
Was that clear synthesis built up aloft
So gracefully; even then when it appeared
Not more than a mere plaything, or a toy
To sense embodied: not the thing it is   165
In verity, an independent world,
Created out of pure intelligence.

    Such dispositions then were mine unearned
By aught, I fear, of genuine desert –
Mine, through heaven's grace and inborn aptitudes.
And not to leave the story of that time   171
Imperfect, with these habits must be joined
Moods melancholy, fits of spleen, that loved
A pensive sky, sad days, and piping winds,
The twilight more than dawn, autumn than spring;
A treasured and luxurious gloom of choice   176
And inclination mainly, and the mere
Redundancy of youth's contentedness.
– To time thus spent, add multitudes of hours
Pilfered away, by what the Bard who sang   180
Of the Enchanter Indolence hath called
'Good-natured lounging', and behold a map
Of my collegiate life – far less intense
Than duty called for, or, without regard
To duty, *might* have sprung up of itself   185
By change of accidents, or even, to speak
Without unkindness, in another place.
Yet why take refuge in that plea? – the fault,
This I repeat, was mine; mine be the blame.

    In summer, making quest for works of art,   190
Or scenes renowned for beauty, I explored
That streamlet whose blue current works its way
Between romantic Dovedale's spiry rocks;
Pried into Yorkshire dales, or hidden tracts
Of my own native region, and was blest   195
Between these sundry wanderings with a joy
Above all joys, that seemed another morn
Risen on mid noon; blest with the presence, Friend!
Of that sole Sister, her who hath been long
Dear to thee also, thy true friend and mine,   200
Now, after separation desolate,
Restored to me – such absence that she seemed
A gift then first bestowed. The varied banks
Of Emont, hitherto unnamed in song,
And that monastic castle, 'mid tall trees,   205
Low-standing by the margin of the stream,
A mansion visited (as fame reports)
By Sidney, where, in sight of our Helvellyn,
Or stormy Cross-fell, snatches he might pen
Of his Arcadia, by fraternal love   210
Inspired; – that river and those mouldering towers

Have seen us side by side, when, having clomb
The darksome windings of a broken stair,
And crept along a ridge of fractured wall,
Not without trembling, we in safety looked   215
Forth, through some Gothic window's open space,
And gathered with one mind a rich reward
From the far-stretching landscape, by the light
Of morning beautified, or purple eve;
Or, not less pleased, lay on some turret's head,   220
Catching from tufts of grass and hare-bell flowers
Their faintest whisper to the passing breeze,
Given out while mid-day heat oppressed the plains.
    Another maid there was, who also shed
A gladness o'er that season, then to me,   225
By her exulting outside look of youth
And placid under-countenance, first endeared;
That other spirit, Coleridge! who is now
So near to us, that meek confiding heart,
So reverenced by us both. O'er paths and fields   230
In all that neighbourhood, through narrow lanes
Of eglantine, and through the shady woods
And o'er the Border Beacon, and the waste
Of naked pools, and common crags that lay
Exposed on the bare fell, were scattered love,   235
The spirit of pleasure, and youth's golden gleam.
O Friend! we had not seen thee at that time,
And yet a power is on me, and a strong
Confusion, and I seem to plant thee there.
Far art thou wandered now in search of health   240
And milder breezes, – melancholy lot!
But thou art with us, with us in the past,
The present, with us in the times to come.
There is no grief, no sorrow, no despair,
No languor, no dejection, no dismay,   245
No absence scarcely can there be, for those
Who loved as we do. Speed thee well! divide
With us thy pleasure; thy returning strength,
Receive it daily as a joy of ours;
Share with us thy fresh spirits, whether gift   250
Of gales Etesian or of tender thoughts.
    I, too, have been a wanderer; but, alas!
How different the fate of different men.
Though mutually unknown, yea, nursed and reared
As if in several elements, we were framed   255
To bend at last to the same discipline,
Predestined, if two beings ever were,
To seek the same delights, and have one health,
One happiness. Throughout this narrative,
Else sooner ended, I have borne in mind   260
For whom it registers the birth, and marks the growth,
Of gentleness, simplicity, and truth,
And joyous loves, that hallow innocent days
Of peace and self-command. Of rivers, fields,
And groves I speak to thee, my Friend! to thee,   265

173 **spleen:** gloominess 180 **Bard:** James Thompson, author of *The Castle of Indolence* 193 **Dovedale:** in Derbyshire 199 **sole Sister:** Wordsworth's sister Dorothy 204–205 **Emont . . . monastic castle:** Brougham castle near Penrith, situated where the rivers Lowther and Emont meet 208–211 **Sidney . . . Inspired:** Sir Philip Sidney, who wrote *Arcadia* (1581) for his sister

224 **Another maid:** Mary Hutchinson, whom Wordsworth later married 251 **gales Etesian:** northwesterly Mediterranean winds

Who, yet a liveried schoolboy, in the depths
Of the huge city, on the leaded roof
Of that wide edifice, thy school and home,
Wert used to lie and gaze upon the clouds
Moving in heaven; or, of that pleasure tired,　270
To shut thine eyes, and by internal light
See trees, and meadows, and thy native stream,
Far distant, thus beheld from year to year
Of a long exile. Nor could I forget,
In this late portion of my argument,　275
That scarcely, as my term of pupilage
Ceased, had I left those academic bowers
When thou wert thither guided. From the heart
Of London, and from cloisters there, thou cam'st,
And didst sit down in temperance and peace,　280
A rigorous student. What a stormy course
Then followed. Oh! it is a pang that calls
For utterance, to think what easy change
Of circumstances might to thee have spared
A world of pain, ripened a thousand hopes,　285
For ever withered. Through this retrospect
Of my collegiate life I still have had
Thy after-sojourn in the self-same place
Present before my eyes, have played with times
And accidents as children do with cards,　290
Or as a man, who, when his house is built,
A frame locked up in wood and stone, doth still,
As impotent fancy prompts, by his fireside,
Rebuild it to his liking. I have thought
Of thee, thy learning, gorgeous eloquence,　295
And all the strength and plumage of thy youth,
Thy subtle speculations, toils abstruse
Among the schoolmen, and Platonic forms
Of wild ideäl pageantry, shaped out
From things well matched or ill, and words for things,
The self-created sustenance of a mind　301
Debarred from Nature's living images,
Compelled to be a life unto herself,
And unrelentingly possessed by thirst
Of greatness, love, and beauty. Not alone,　305
Ah! surely not in singleness of heart
Should I have seen the light of evening fade
From smooth Cam's silent waters: had we met,
Even at that early time, needs must I trust
In the belief, that my maturer age,　310
My calmer habits, and more steady voice,
Would with an influence benign have soothed,
Or chased away, the airy wretchedness
That battened on thy youth. But thou hast trod
A march of glory, which doth put to shame　315
These vain regrets; health suffers in thee, else
Such grief for thee would be the weakest thought
That ever harboured in the breast of man.

A passing word erewhile did lightly touch
On wanderings of my own, that now embraced　320
With livelier hope a region wider far.
When the third summer freed us from restraint,
A youthful friend, he too a mountaineer,
Not slow to share my wishes, took his staff,
And sallying forth, we journeyed side by side,　325
Bound to the distant Alps. A hardy slight
Did this unprecedented course imply
Of college studies and their set rewards;
Nor had, in truth, the scheme been formed by me
Without uneasy forethought of the pain,　330
The censures, and ill-omening of those
To whom my worldly interests were dear.
But Nature then was sovereign in my mind,
And mighty forms, seizing a youthful fancy,
Had given a charter to irregular hopes.　335
In any age of uneventful calm
Among the nations, surely would my heart
Have been possessed by similar desire;
But Europe at that time was thrilled with joy,
France standing on the top of golden hours,　340
And human nature seeming born again.
　Lightly equipped, and but a few brief looks
Cast on the white cliffs of our native shore
From the receding vessel's deck, we chanced
To land at Calais on the very eve　345
Of that great federal day; and there we saw,
In a mean city, and among a few,
How bright a face is worn when joy of one
Is joy for tens of millions. Southward thence
We held our way, direct through hamlets, towns,　350
Gaudy with reliques of that festival,
Flowers left to wither on triumphal arcs,
And window-garlands. On the public roads,
And, once, three days successively, through paths
By which our toilsome journey was abridged,　355
Among sequestered villages we walked
And found benevolence and blessedness
Spread like a fragrance everywhere, when spring
Hath left no corner of the land untouched:
Where elms for many and many a league in files　360
With their thin umbrage, on the stately roads
Of that great kingdom, rustled o'er our heads,
For ever near us as we paced along:
How sweet at such a time, with such delight
On every side, in prime of youthful strength,　365
To feed a Poet's tender melancholy
And fond conceit of sadness, with the sound
Of undulations varying as might please
The wind that swayed them; once, and more than once,
Unhoused beneath the evening star we saw　370

266 **liveried schoolboy:** Coleridge attended Christ's Hospital, where the boys were compelled to wear a long blue coat and yellow stockings 314 **battened:** fixed on

323 **youthful friend:** Robert Jones to whom Wordsworth dedicated his *Descriptive Sketches* 345–346 **eve ... federal day:** Wordsworth and Jones landed in France on 13 July, 1789 – the day before the fall of the Bastille 361 **thin umbrage:** thin foliage

Dances of liberty, and, in late hours
Of darkness, dances in the open air
Deftly prolonged, though grey-haired lookers on
Might waste their breath in chiding.
                Under hills –
The vine-clad hills and slopes of Burgundy,   375
Upon the bosom of the gentle Saone
We glided forward with the flowing stream.
Swift Rhone! thou wert the *wings* on which we cut
A winding passage with majestic ease
Between thy lofty rocks. Enchanting show   380
Those woods and farms and orchards did present,
And single cottages and lurking towns,
Reach after reach, succession without end
Of deep and stately vales! A lonely pair
Of strangers, till day closed, we sailed along,   385
Clustered together with a merry crowd
Of those emancipated, a blithe host
Of travellers, chiefly delegates returning
From the great spousals newly solemnised
At their chief city, in the sight of Heaven.   390
Like bees they swarmed, gaudy and gay as bees;
Some vapoured in the unruliness of joy,
And with their swords flourished as if to fight
The saucy air. In this proud company
We landed – took with them our evening meal,   395
Guests welcome almost as the angels were
To Abraham of old. The supper done,
With flowing cups elate and happy thoughts
We rise at signal given, and formed a ring
And, hand in hand, danced round and round the
      board;   400
All hearts were open, every tongue was loud
With amity and glee; we bore a name
Honoured in France, the name of Englishmen,
And hóspitably did they give us hail,
As their forerunners in a glorious course;   405
And round and round the board we danced again.
With these blithe friends our voyage we renewed
At early dawn. The monastery bells
Made a sweet jingling in our youthful ears;
The rapid river flowing without noise,   410
And each uprising or receding spire
Spake with a sense of peace, at intervals
Touching the heart amid the boisterous crew
By whom we were encompassed. Taking leave
Of this glad throng, foot-travellers side by side,   415
Measuring our steps in quiet, we pursued
Our journey, and ere twice the sun had set
Beheld the Convent of Chartreuse, and there
Rested within an awful *solitude*.
Yes, for even then no other than a place   420

Of soul-affecting *solitude* appeared
That far-famed region, though our eyes had seen,
As toward the sacred mansion we advanced,
Arms flashing, and a military glare
Of riotous men commissioned to expel   425
The blameless inmates, and belike subvert
That frame of social being, which so long
Had bodied forth the ghostliness of things
In silence visible and perpetual calm.
– 'Stay, stay your sacrilegious hands!' – The voice   430
Was Nature's, uttered from her Alpine throne;
I heard it then, and seem to hear it now –
'Your impious work forbear; perish what may,
Let this one temple last, be this one spot
Of earth devoted to eternity!'   435
She ceased to speak, but while St Bruno's pines
Waved their dark tops, not silent as they waved,
And while below, along their several beds,
Murmured the sister streams of Life and Death,
Thus by conflicting passions pressed, my heart   440
Responded; 'Honour to the patriot's zeal!
Glory and hope to new-born Liberty!
Hail to the might projects of the time!
Discerning sword that Justice wields, do thou
Go forth and prosper; and, ye purging fires,   445
Up to the loftiest towers of Pride ascend,
Fanned by the breath of angry Providence.
But oh! if Past and Future be the wings
On whose support harmoniously conjoined
Moves the great spirit of human knowledge, spare   450
These courts of mystery, where a step advanced
Between the portals of the shadowy rocks
Leaves far behind life's treacherous vanities,
For penitential tears and trembling hopes
Exchanged – to equalise in God's pure sight   455
Monarch and peasant: be the house redeemed
With its unworldly votaries, for the sake
Of conquest over sense, hourly achieved
Through faith and meditative reason, resting
Upon the word of heaven-imparted truth,   460
Calmly triumphant; and for humbler claim
Of that imaginative impulse sent
From these majestic floods, yon shining cliffs,
The untransmuted shapes of many worlds,
Cerulean ether's pure inhabitants,   465
These forests unapproachable by death,
That shall endure as long as man endures,
To think, to hope, to worship, and to feel,
To struggle, to be lost within himself
In trepidation, from the blank abyss   470
To look with bodily eyes, and be consoled.'
Not seldom since that moment have I wished
That thou, O Friend! the trouble or the calm
Hadst shared, when, from profane regards apart,
In sympathetic reverence we trod   475

---

389 **spousals:** marriages. Wordsworth refers to Louis XVI's agreement to accept the new constitution 392 **vapoured:** talked in an exaggerated manner, hot air 394 **saucy:** impudent 405 Wordsworth refers to the 'Bloodless' or 'Glorious' English revolution of 1688 419 **awful:** inspiring

439 **Life and Death:** the rivers Vif and Mort 465 **Cerulean:** the colour of a cloudless sky

The floors of those dim cloisters, till that hour,
From their foundation, strangers to the presence
Of unrestricted and unthinking man.
Abroad, how cheeringly the sunshine lay
Upon the open lawns! Vallombre's groves   480
Entering, we fed the soul with darkness; thence
Issued, and with uplifted eyes beheld,
In different quarters of the bending sky,
The cross of Jesus stand erect, as if
Hands of angelic powers had fixed it there,   485
Memorial reverenced by a thousand storms;
Yet then, from the undiscriminating sweep
And rage of one State-whirlwind, insecure.
    'Tis not my present purpose to retrace
That variegated journey step by step.   490
A march it was of military speed,
And Earth did change her images and forms
Before us, fast as clouds are changed in heaven.
Day after day, up early and down late,
From hill to vale we dropped, from vale to hill   495
Mounted – from province on to province swept,
Keen hunters in a chase of fourteen weeks,
Eager as birds of prey, or as a ship
Upon the stretch, when winds are blowing fair:
Sweet coverts did we cross of pastoral life,   500
Enticing valleys, greeted them and left
Too soon, while yet the very flash and gleam
Of salutation were not passed away.
Oh! sorrow for the youth who could have seen
Unchastened, unsubdued, unawed, unraised   505
To patriarchal dignity of mind,
And pure simplicity of wish and will,
Those sanctified abodes of peaceful man,
Pleased (though to hardship born, and compassed
    round
With danger, varying as the seasons change),   510
Pleased with his daily task, or, if not pleased,
Contented, from the moment that the dawn
(Ah! surely not without attendant gleams
Of soul-illumination) calls him forth
To industry, by glistenings flung on rocks,   515
Whose evening shadows lead him to repose.
    Well might a stranger look with bounding heart
Down on a green recess, the first I saw
Of those deep haunts, an aboriginal vale,
Quiet and lorded over and possessed   520
By naked huts, wood-built, and sown like tents
Or Indian cabins over the fresh lawns
And by the river side.
                    That very day,
From a bare ridge we also first beheld
Unveiled the summit of Mont Blanc, and grieved   525
To have a soulless image on the eye
That had usurped upon a living thought
That never more could be. The wondrous Vale
Of Chamouny stretched far below, and soon
With its dumb cataracts and streams of ice,   530

A motionless array of mighty waves,
Five rivers broad and vast, made rich amends,
And reconciled us to realities;
There small birds warble from the leafy trees,
The eagle soars high in the element,   535
There doth the reaper bind the yellow sheaf,
The maiden spread the haycock in the sun,
While Winter like a well-tamed lion walks,
Descending from the mountains to make sport
Among the cottages by beds of flowers.   540
    Whate'er in this wide circuit we beheld,
Or heard, was fitted to our unripe state
Of intellect and heart. With such a book
Before our eyes, we could not choose but read
Lessons of genuine brotherhood, the plain   545
And universal reason of mankind,
The truths of young and old. Nor, side by side
Pacing, two social pilgrims, or alone
Each with his humour, could we fail to abound
In dreams and fictions, pensively composed: 550
Dejection taken up for pleasure's sake,
And gilded sympathies, the willow wreath,
And sober posies of funereal flowers,
Gathered among those solitudes sublime
From formal gardens of the lady Sorrow,   555
Did sweeten many a meditative hour.
    Yet still in me with those soft luxuries
Mixed something of stern mood, an under-thirst
Of vigour seldom utterly allayed.
And from that source how different a sadness   560
Would issue, let one incident make known.
When from the Vallais we had turned, and clomb
Along the Simplon's steep and rugged road,
Following a band of muleteers, we reached
A halting-place, where all together took   565
Their noon-tide meal. Hastily rose our guide,
Leaving us at the board; awhile we lingered,
Then paced the beaten downward way that led
Right to a rough stream's edge, and there broke off;
The only track now visible was one   570
That from the torrent's further brink held forth
Conspicuous invitation to ascend
A lofty mountain. After brief delay
Crossing the unbridged stream, that road we took,
And clomb with eagerness, till anxious fears   575
Intruded, for we failed to overtake
Our comrades gone before. By fortunate chance,
While every moment added doubt to doubt,
A peasant met us, from whose mouth we learned
That to the spot which had perplexed us first   580
We must descend, and there should find the road,
Which in the stony channel of the stream
Lay a few steps, and then along its banks;
And, that our future course, all plain to sight,
Was downwards, with the current of that stream.   585

552 **willow wreath:** a symbol of melancholy

Loth to believe what we so grieved to hear,
For still we had hopes that pointed to the clouds,
We questioned him again, and yet again;
But every word that from the peasant's lips
Came in reply, translated by our feelings,   590
Ended in this, – *that we had crossed the Alps.*

     Imagination – here the Power so called
Through sad incompetence of human speech,
That awful Power rose from the mind's abyss
Like an unfathered vapour that enwraps,   595
At once, some lonely traveller. I was lost;
Halted without an effort to break through;
But to my conscious soul I now can say –
'I recognise thy glory': in such strength
Of usurpation, when the light of sense   600
Goes out, but with a flash that has revealed
The invisible world, doth greatness make abode,
There harbours, whether we be young or old.
Our destiny, our being's heart and home,
Is with infinitude, and only there;   605
With hope it is, hope that can never die,
Effort, and expectation, and desire,
And something evermore about to be.
Under such banners militant, the soul
Seeks for no trophies, struggles for no spoils   610
That may attest her prowess, blest in thoughts
That are their own perfection and reward,
Strong in herself and in beatitude
That hides her, like the mighty flood of Nile
Poured from his fount of Abyssinian clouds   615
To fertilise the whole Egyptian plain.

     The melancholy slackening that ensued
Upon those tidings by the peasant given
Was soon dislodged. Downwards we hurried fast,
And, with the half-shaped road which we had missed,
Entered a narrow chasm. The brook and road   621
Were fellow-travellers in this gloomy strait,
And with them did we journey several hours
At a slow pace. The immeasurable height
Of woods decaying, never to be decayed,   625
The stationary blasts of waterfalls,
And in the narrow rent at every turn
Winds thwarting winds, bewildered and forlorn,
The torrents shooting from the clear blue sky,
The rocks that muttered close upon our ears,   630
Black drizzling crags that spake by the way-side
As if a voice were in them, the sick sight
And giddy prospect of the raving stream,
The unfettered clouds and region of the Heavens,
Tumult and peace, the darkness and the light –   635
Were all like workings of one mind, the features
Of the same face, blossoms upon one tree;
Characters of the great Apocalypse,
The types and symbols of Eternity,
Of first, and last, and midst, and without end.   640

     That night our lodging was a house that stood
Alone within the valley, at a point

Where, tumbling from aloft, a torrent swelled
The rapid stream whose margin we had trod;
A dreary mansion, large beyond all need,   645
With high and spacious rooms, deafened and stunned
By noise of waters, making innocent sleep
Lie melancholy among weary bones.

     Uprisen betimes, our journey we renewed,
Led by the stream, ere noon-day magnified   650
Into a lordly river, broad and deep,
Dimpling along in silent majesty,
With mountains for its neighbours, and in view
Of distant mountains and their snowy tops,
And thus proceeding to Locarno's Lake,   655
Fit resting-place for such a visitant.
Locarno! spreading out in width like Heaven,
How dost thou cleave to the poetic heart,
Back in the sunshine of the memory;
And Como! thou, a treasure whom the earth   660
Keeps to herself, confined as in a depth
Of Abyssinian privacy, I spake
Of thee, thy chestnut woods, and garden plots
Of Indian corn tended by dark-eyed maids;
Thy lofty steeps, and pathways roofed with vines,   665
Winding from house to house, from town to town,
Sole link that binds them to each other; walks,
League after league, and cloistral avenues,
Where silence dwells if music be not there:
While yet a youth undisciplined in verse,   670
Through fond ambition of that hour, I strove
To chant your praise; nor can approach you now
Ungreeted by a more melodious Song,
Where tones of Nature smoothed by learnèd Art
May flow in lasting current. Like a breeze   675
Or sunbeam over your domain I passed
In motion without pause; but ye have left
Your beauty with me, a serene accord
Of forms and colours, passive, yet endowed
In their submissiveness with power as sweet   680
And gracious, almost might I dare to say,
As virtue is, or goodness; sweet as love,
Or the remembrance of a generous deed,
Or mildest visitations of pure thought,
When God, the giver of all joy, is thanked   685
Religiously, in silent blessedness;
Sweet as this last herself, for such it is.

     With those delightful pathways we advanced,
For two days' space, in presence of the Lake,
That, stretching far among the Alps, assumed   690
A character more stern. The second night,
From sleep awakened, and misled by sound
Of the church clock telling the hours with strokes
Whose import then we had not learned, we rose
By moonlight, doubting not that day was nigh,   695
And that meanwhile, by no uncertain path,
Along the winding margin of the lake,
Led, as before, we should behold the scene
Hushed in profound repose. We left the town

Of Gravedona with this hope; but soon   700
Were lost, bewildered among woods immense,
And on a rock sate down, to wait for day.
An open place it was, and overlooked,
From high, the sullen water far beneath,
On which a dull red image of the moon   705
Lay bedded, changing oftentimes its form
Like an uneasy snake. From hour to hour
We sate and sate, wondering, as if the night
Had been ensnared by witchcraft. On the rock
At last we stretched our weary limbs for sleep, 710
But *could not* sleep, tormented by the stings
Of insects, which, with noise like that of noon,
Filled all the woods; the cry of unknown birds;
The mountains more by blackness visible
And their own size, than any outward light;   715
The breathless wilderness of clouds; the clock
That told, with unintelligible voice,
The widely parted hours; the noise of streams,
And sometimes rustling motions nigh at hand,
That did not leave us free from personal fear;   720
And, lastly, the withdrawing moon, that set
Before us, while she still was high in heaven; –
These were our food; and such a summer's night
Followed that pair of golden days that shed
On Como's Lake, and all that round it lay,   725
Their fairest, softest, happiest influence.

  But here I must break off, and bid farewell
To days, each offering some new sight, or fraught
With some untried adventure, in a course
Prolonged till sprinklings of autumnal snow   730
Checked our unwearied steps. Let this alone
Be mentioned as a parting word, that not
In hollow exultation, dealing out
Hyperboles of praise comparative;
Not rich one moment to be poor for ever;   735
Not prostrate, overborne, as if the mind
Herself were nothing, a mere pensioner
On outward forms – did we in presence stand
Of that magnificent region. On the front
Of this whole Song is written that my heart   740
Must, in such Temple, needs have offered up
A different worship. Finally, whate'er
I saw, or heard, or felt, was but a stream
That flowed into a kindred stream; a gale,
Confederate with the current of the soul,   745
To speed my voyage; every sound or sight,
In its degree of power, administered
To grandeur or to tenderness, – to the one
Directly, but to tender thoughts by means
Less often instantaneous in effect;   750
Led me to these by paths that, in the main,
Were more circuitous, but not less sure
Duly to reach the point marked out by Heaven.

  Oh, most belovèd Friend! a glorious time,
A happy time that was; triumphant looks   755
Were then the common language of all eyes;

As if awaked from sleep, the Nations hailed
Their great expectancy: the fife of war
Was then a spirit-stirring sound indeed,
A blackbird's whistle in a budding grove.   760
We left the Swiss exulting in the fate
Of their near neighbours; and, when shortening fast
Our pilgrimage, nor distant far from home,
We crossed the Brabant armies on the fret
For battle in the cause of Liberty.   765
A stripling, scarcely of the household then
Of social life, I looked upon these things
As from a distance; heard, and saw, and felt,
Was touched, but with no intimate concern;
I seemed to move along them, as a bird   770
Moves through the air, or as a fish pursues
Its sport, or feeds in its proper element;
I wanted not that joy, I did not need
Such help; the ever-living universe,
Turn where I might, was opening out its glories, 775
And the independent spirit of pure youth
Called forth, at every season, new delights
Spread round my steps like sunshine o'er green fields.

BOOK SEVENTH. RESIDENCE IN LONDON
Six changeful years have vanished since I first
Poured out (saluted by that quickening breeze
Which met me issuing from the City's walls)
A glad preamble to this Verse: I sang
Aloud, with fervour irresistible   5
Of short-lived transport, like a torrent bursting,
From a black thunder-cloud, down Scafell's side
To rush and disappear. But soon broke forth
(So willed the Muse) a less impetuous stream,
That flowed awhile with unabating strength,   10
Then stopped for years; not audible again
Before last primrose-time. Belovèd Friend!
The assurance which then cheered some heavy
        thoughts
On thy departure to a foreign land
Has failed; too slowly moves the promised work. 15
Through the whole summer have I been at rest,
Partly from voluntary holiday,
And part through outward hindrance. But I heard,
After the hour of sunset yester-even,
Sitting within doors between light and dark,   20
A choir of redbreasts gathered somewhere near
My threshold, – minstrels from the distant woods
Sent in on Winter's service, to announce,
With preparation artful and benign,
That the rough lord had left the surly North   25
On his accustomed journey. The delight,
Due to this timely notice, unawares
Smote me, and, listening, I in whispers said,
'Ye heartsome Choristers, ye and I will be
Associates, and, unscared by blustering winds,   30

764 **on the fret:** eagerly awaiting

Will chant together.' Thereafter, as the shades
Of twilight deepened, going forth, I spied
A glow-worm underneath a dusky plume
Or canopy of yet unwithered fern,
Clear-shining, like a hermit's taper seen   35
Through a thick forest. Silence touched me here
No less than sound had done before; the child
Of Summer, lingering, shining, by herself,
The voiceless worm on the unfrequented hills,
Seemed sent on the same errand with the choir   40
Of Winter that had warbled at my door,
And the whole year breathed tenderness and love.

    The last night's genial feeling overflowed
Upon this morning, and my favourite grove,
Tossing in sunshine its dark boughs aloft,   45
As if to make the strong wind visible,
Wakes me in agitations like its own,
A spirit friendly to the Poet's task,
Which we will now resume with lively hope,
Nor checked by aught of tamer argument   50
That lies before us, needful to be told.

    Returned from that excursion, soon I bade
Farewell for ever to the sheltered seats
Of gownèd students, quitted hall and bower,
And every comfort of that privileged ground,   55
Well pleased to pitch a vagrant tent among
The unfenced regions of society.

    Yet undetermined to what course of life
I should adhere, and seeming to possess
A little space of intermediate time   60
At full command, to London first I turned,
In no disturbance of excessive hope,
By personal ambition unenslaved,
Frugal as there was need, and, though self-willed,
From dangerous passions free. Three years had flown
Since I had felt in heart and soul the shock   66
Of the huge town's first presence, and had paced
Her endless streets, a transient visitant:
Now, fixed amid that concourse of mankind
Where Pleasure whirls about incessantly,   70
And life and labour seem but one, I filled
An idler's place; an idler well content
To have a house (what matter for a home?)
That owned him; living cheerfully abroad
With unchecked fancy ever on the stir,   75
And all my young affections out of doors.

    There was a time when whatsoe'er is feigned
Of airy palaces, and gardens built
By Genii of romance; or hath in grave
Authentic history been set forth of Rome,   80
Alcairo, Babylon, or Persepolis;
Or given upon report by pilgrim friars,
Of golden cities ten months' journey deep
Among Tartarian wilds – fell short, far short,
Of what my fond simplicity believed   85

And thought of London – held me by a chain
Less strong of wonder and obscure delight.
Whether the bolt of childhood's Fancy shot
For me beyond its ordinary mark,
'Twere vain to ask; but in our flock of boys   90
Was One, a cripple from his birth, whom chance
Summoned from school to London; fortunate
And envied traveller! When the Boy returned,
After short absence, curiously I scanned
His mien and person, nor was free, in sooth,   95
From disappointment, not to find some change
In look and air, from that new region brought,
As if from Fairy-land. Much I questioned him;
And every word he uttered, on my ears
Fell flatter than a cagèd parrot's note,   100
That answers unexpectedly awry,
And mocks the prompter's listening. Marvellous things
Had vanity (quick Spirit that appears
Almost as deeply seated and as strong
In a Child's heart as fear itself) conceived   105
For my enjoyment. Would that I could now
Recall what then I pictured to myself
Of mitred Prelates, Lords in ermine clad,
The King, and the King's Palace, and, not last,
Nor least, Heaven bless him! the renowned Lord
    Mayor: 110
Dreams not unlike to those which once begat
A change of purpose in young Whittington,
When he, a friendless and a drooping boy,
Sate on a stone, and heard the bells speak out
Articulate music. Above all, one thought   115
Baffled my understanding: how men lived
Even next-door neighbours, as we say, yet still
Strangers, not knowing each the other's name.

    Oh, wondrous power of words, by simple faith
Licensed to take the meaning that we love!   120
Vauxhall and Ranelagh! I then had heard
Of your green groves, and wilderness of lamps
Dimming the stars, and fireworks magical,
And gorgeous ladies, under splendid domes,
Floating in dance, or warbling high in air   125
The songs of spirits! Nor had Fancy fed
With less delight upon that other class
Of marvels, broad-day wonders permanent:
The River proudly bridged; the dizzy top
And Whispering Gallery of St Paul's; the tombs   130
Of Westminster; the Giants of Guildhall;
Bedlam, and those carved maniacs at the gates,
Perpetually recumbent; Statues – man,
And the horse under him – in gilded pomp
Adorning flowery gardens, 'mid vast squares;   135
The Monument, and that Chamber of the Tower

95 **mien:** manner, appearance 112 **Whittington:** Richard Whittington
who rose to be Lord Mayor of London three times: 1397, 1406 and
1419 121 **Vauxhall and Ranelagh:** names of pleasure gardens situated
by the river Thames 132 **Bedlam:** Bethlehem Hospital for the insane

BOOK SEVENTH: 79 **Genii:** geniuses

Where England's sovereigns sit in long array,
Their steeds bestriding, – every mimic shape
Cased in the gleaming mail the monarch wore,
Whether for gorgeous tournament addressed,   140
Or life or death upon the battle-field.
Those bold imaginations in due time
Had vanished, leaving others in their stead:
And now I looked upon the living scene;
Familiarly perused it; oftentimes,   145
In spite of strongest disappointment, pleased
Through courteous self-submission, as a tax
Paid to the object by prescriptive right.

     Rise up, thou monstrous ant-hill on the plain
Of a too busy world! Before me flow,   150
Thou endless stream of men and moving things!
Thy every-day appearance, as it strikes –
With wonder heightened, or sublimed by awe –
On strangers, of all ages; the quick dance
Of colours, lights, and forms; the deafening din;   155
The comers and the goers face to face,
Face after face; the string of dazzling wares,
Shop after shop, with symbols, blazoned names,
And all the tradesman's honours overhead:
Here, front of houses, like a title-page,   160
With letters huge inscribed from top to toe;
Stationed above the door, like guardian saints,
There, allegoric shapes, female or male,
Or physiognomies of reäl men,
Land-warriors, kings, or admirals of the sea,   165
Boyle, Shakespeare, Newton, or the attractive head
Of some quack-doctor, famous in his day.

     Meanwhile the roar continues, till at length,
Escaped as from an enemy, we turn
Abruptly into some sequestered nook,   170
Still as a sheltered place when winds blow loud!
At leisure, thence, through tracts of thin resort,
And sights and sounds that come at intervals,
We take our way. A raree-show is here,
With children gathered round; another street   175
Presents a company of dancing dogs,
Or dromedary, with an antic pair
Of monkeys on his back; a minstrel band
Of Savoyards; or, single and alone,
An English ballad-singer. Private courts,   180
Gloomy as coffins, and unsightly lanes
Thrilled by some female vendor's scream, belike
The very shrillest of all London cries,
May then entangle our impatient steps;
Conducted through those labyrinths, unawares,   185
To privileged regions and inviolate,
Where from their airy lodges studious lawyers
Look out on waters, walks, and gardens green.

Thence back into the throng, until we reach,
Following the tide that slackens by degrees,   190
Some half-frequented scene, where wider streets
Bring straggling breezes of suburban air.
Here files of ballads dangle from dead walls;
Advertisements, of giant-size, from high
Press forward, in all colours, on the sight;   195
These, bold in conscious merit, lower down
That, fronted with a most imposing word,
Is, peradventure, one in masquerade.
As on the broadening causeway we advance,
Behold, turned upwards, a face hard and strong   200
In lineaments, and red with over-toil.
'Tis one encountered here and everywhere;
A travelling cripple, by the trunk cut short,
And stumping on his arms. In sailor's garb
Another lies at length, beside a range   205
Of well-formed characters, with chalk inscribed
Upon the smooth flat stones: the Nurse is here,
The Bachelor, that loves to sun himself,
The military Idler, and the Dame,
That field-ward takes her walk with decent steps.   210
     Now homeward through the thickening hubbub,
          where
See, among less distinguishable shapes,
The begging scavenger, with hat in hand;
The Italian, as he thrids his way with care,
Steadying, far-seen, a frame of images   215
Upon his head; with basket at his breast
The Jew; the stately and slow-moving Turk,
With freight of slippers piled beneath his arm!
     Enough; – the mighty concourse I surveyed
With no unthinking mind, well pleased to note   220
Among the crowd all specimens of man,
Through all the colours which the sun bestows,
And every character of form and face:
The Swede, the Russian; from the genial south,
The Frenchman and the Spaniard; from remote   225
America, the Hunter-Indian; Moors,
Malays, Lascars, the Tartar, the Chinese,
And Negro Ladies in white muslin gowns.
     At leisure, then, I viewed, from day to day,
The spectacles within doors, – birds and beasts   230
Of every nature, and strange plants convened
From every clime; and, next, those sights that ape
The absolute presence of reality,
Expressing, as in mirror, sea and land,
And what earth is, and what she has to show.   235
I do not here allude to subtlest craft,
By means refined attaining purest ends,
But imitations, fondly made in plain
Confession of man's weakness and his loves.
Whether the Painter, whose ambitious skill   240
Submits to nothing less than taking in
A whole horizon's circuit, do with power,

---

166 **Boyle:** William Boyle (1627–1691), chemist   167 **quack-doctor:**
John Graham (1745–1794), Scottish medical charlatan   174 **raree-**
show: peep show   177–178 Camel with a pair of absurd monkeys on
its back   179 **Savoyards:** travelling minstrel bands from Savoy
in France

214 **thrids:** threads

Like that of angels or commissioned spirits,
Fix us upon some lofty pinnacle,
Or in a ship on waters, with a world   245
Of life, and life-like mockery beneath,
Above, behind, far stretching and before;
Or more mechanic artist represent
By scale exact, in model, wood, or clay,
From blended colours also borrowing help,   250
Some miniature of famous spots or things, –
St Peter's Church; or, more aspiring aim,
In microscopic vision, Rome herself;
Or, haply, some choice rural haunt, – the Falls
Of Tivoli; and, high upon that steep,   255
The Sibyl's mouldering Temple! every tree,
Villa, or cottage, lurking among rocks
Throughout the landscape; tuft, stone, scratch
          minute –
All that the traveller sees when he is there.
     And to these exhibitions, mute and still,   260
Others of wider scope, where living men,
Music, and shifting pantomimic scenes,
Diversified the allurement. Need I fear
To mention by its name, as in degree,
Lowest of these and humblest in attempt,   265
Yet richly graced with honours of her own,
Half-rural Sadler's Wells? Though at that time
Intolerant, as is the way of youth
Unless itself be pleased, here more than once
Taking my seat, I saw (nor blush to add,   270
With ample recompense) giants and dwarfs,
Clowns, conjurors, posture-masters, harlequins,
Amid the uproar of the rabblement,
Perform their feats. Nor was it mean delight
To watch crude Nature work in untaught minds; 275
To note the laws and progress of belief;
Though obstinate on this way, yet on that
How willingly we travel, and how far!
To have, for instance, brought upon the scene
The champion, Jack the Giant-killer: Lo!   280
He dons his coat of darkness; on the stage
Walks, and achieves his wonders, from the eye
Of living Mortal covert, 'as the moon
Hid in her vacant interlunar cave'.
Delusion bold! and how can it be wrought?   285
The garb he wears is black as death, the word
'Invisible' flames forth upon his chest.
     Here, too, were 'forms and pressures of the time',
Rough, bold, as Grecian comedy displayed
When Art was young; dramas of living men,   290
And recent things yet warm with life; a sea-fight,
Shipwreck, or some domestic incident
Divulged by Truth and magnified by Fame,
Such as the daring brotherhood of late
Set forth, too serious theme for that light place – 295

I mean, O distant Friend! a story drawn
From our own ground, – the Maid of Buttermere, –
And how, unfaithful to a virtuous wife
Deserted and deceived, the spoiler came
And wooed the artless daughter of the hills,   300
And wedded her, in cruel mockery
Of love and marriage bonds. These words to thee
Must needs bring back the moment when we first,
Ere the broad world rang with the maiden's name,
Beheld her serving at the cottage inn,   305
Both stricken, as she entered or withdrew,
With admiration of her modest mien
And carriage, marked by unexampled grace.
We since that time not unfamiliarly
Have seen her, – her discretion have observed, 310
Her just opinions, delicate reserve,
Her patience, and humility of mind
Unspoiled by commendation and the excess
Of public notice – an offensive light
To a meek spirit suffering inwardly.   315
     From this memorial tribute to my theme
I was returning, when, with sundry forms
Commingled – shapes which met me in the way
That we must tread – thy image rose again,
Maiden of Buttermere! She lives in peace   320
Upon the spot where she was born and reared;
Without contamination doth she live
In quietness, without anxiety:
Beside the mountain chapel, sleeps in earth
Her new-born infant, fearless as a lamb   325
That, thither driven from some unsheltered place,
Rests underneath the little rock-like pile
When storms are raging. Happy are they both –
Mother and child! – These feelings, in themselves
Trite, do yet scarcely seem so when I think   330
On those ingenuous moments of our youth
Ere we have learnt by use to slight the crimes
And sorrows of the world. Those simple days
Are now my theme; and, foremost of the scenes,
Which yet survive in memory, appears   335
One, at whose centre sate a lovely Boy,
A sportive infant, who, for six months' space,
Not more, had been of age to deal about
Articulate prattle – Child as beautiful
As ever clung around a mother's neck,   340
Or father fondly gazed upon with pride.
There, too, conspicuous for stature tall
And large dark eyes, beside her infant stood
The mother; but, upon her cheeks diffused,
False tints too well accorded with the glare   345
From play-house lustres thrown without reserve
On every object near. The Boy had been
The pride and pleasure of all lookers-on
In whatsoever place, but seemed in this
A sort of alien scattered from the clouds.   350
Of lusty vigour, more than infantine,
He was in limb, in cheek a summer rose

256 **Sibyl's mouldering Temple:** the temple of the Sybil at Tivoli in
Italy 267 **Sadler's Wells:** in Islington, at this time a suburb of London

Just three parts blown – a cottage-child – if e'er,
By cottage-door on breezy mountain side,
Or in some sheltering vale, was seen a babe   355
By Nature's gifts so favoured. Upon a board
Decked with refreshments had this child been placed,
His little stage in the vast théatre,
And there he sate surrounded with a throng
Of chance spectators, chiefly dissolute men   360
And shameless women; treated and caressed,
Ate, drank, and with the fruit and glasses played,
While oaths and laughter and indecent speech
Were rife about him as the songs of birds
Contending after showers. The mother now   365
Is fading out of memory, but I see
The lovely Boy as I beheld him then
Among the wretched and the falsely gay,
Like one of those who walked with hair unsinged
Amid the fiery furnace. Charms and spells   370
Muttered on black and spiteful instigation
Have stopped, as some believe, the kindliest growths.
Ah, with how different spirit might a prayer
Have been preferred, that this fair creature, checked
By special privilege of Nature's love,   375
Should in his childhood be detained for ever!
But with its universal freight the tide
Hath rolled along, and this bright innocent,
Mary! may now have lived till he could look
With envy on thy nameless babe that sleeps,   380
Beside the mountain chapel, undisturbed.

     Four rapid years had scarcely then been told
Since, travelling southward from our pastoral hills,
I heard, and for the first time in my life,
The voice of woman utter blasphemy –   385
Saw woman as she is, to open shame
Abandoned, and the pride of public vice;
I shuddered, for a barrier seemed at once
Thrown in, that from humanity divorced
Humanity, splitting the race of man   390
In twain, yet leaving the same outward form.
Distress of mind ensued upon the sight
And ardent meditation. Later years
Brought to such spectacle a milder sadness,
Feelings of pure commiseration, grief   395
For the individual and the overthrow
Of her soul's beauty; farther I was then
But seldom led, or wished to go; in truth
The sorrow of the passion stopped me there.

     But let me now, less moved, in order take   400
Our argument. Enough is said to show
How casual incidents of reäl life,
Observed where pastime only had been sought,
Outweighed, or put to flight, the set events
And measured passions of the stage, albeit   405
By Siddons trod in the fullness of her power.

406 **Siddons:** Mrs. Siddons (1755–1831), a famous actress of the day

Yet was the théatre my dear delight;
The very gilding, lamps and painted scrolls,
And all the mean upholstery of the place,
Wanted not animation, when the tide   410
Of pleasure ebbed but to return as fast
With the ever-shifting figures of the scene,
Solemn or gay: whether some beauteous dame
Advanced in radiance through a deep recess
Of thick entangled forest, like the moon   415
Opening the clouds; or sovereign king, announced
With flourishing trumpet, came in full-blown state
Of the world's greatness, winding round with train
Of courtiers, banners, and a length of guards;
Or captive led in abject weeds, and jingling   420
His slender manacles; or romping girl
Bounced, leapt, and pawed the air; or mumbling sire,
A scare-crow pattern of old age dressed up
In all the tatters of infirmity
All loosely put together, hobbled in,   425
Stumping upon a cane with which he smites,
From time to time, the solid boards, and makes them
Prate somewhat loudly of the whereabout
Of one so overloaded with his years.
But what of this! the laugh, the grin, grimace,   430
The antics striving to outstrip each other,
Were all received, the least of them not lost,
With an unmeasured welcome. Through the night,
Between the show, and many-headed mass
Of the spectators, and each several nook   435
Filled with its fray or brawl, how eagerly
And with what flashes, as it were, the mind
Turned this way – that way! sportive and alert
And watchful, as a kitten when at play,
While winds are eddying round her, among straws   440
And rustling leaves. Enchanting age and sweet!
Romantic almost, looked at through a space,
How small, of intervening years! For then,
Though surely no mean progress had been made
In meditations holy and sublime,   445
Yet something of a girlish child-like gloss
Of novelty survived for scenes like these;
Enjoyment haply handed down from times
When at a country-playhouse, some rude barn
Tricked out for that proud use, if I perchance   450
Caught, on a summer evening through a chink
In the old wall, an unexpected glimpse
Of daylight, the bare thought of where I was
Gladdened me more than if I had been led
Into a dazzling cavern of romance,   455
Crowded with Genii busy among works
Not to be looked at by the common sun.
     The matter that detains us now may seem,
To many, neither dignified enough
Nor arduous, yet will not be scorned by them,   460
Who, looking inward, have observed the ties
That bind the perishable hours of life
Each to the other, and the curious props

By which the world of memory and thought
Exists and is sustained. More lofty themes, 465
Such as at least do wear a prouder face,
Solicit our regard; but when I think
Of these, I feel the imaginative power
Languish within me; even then it slept,
When, pressed by tragic sufferings, the heart 470
Was more than full; amid my sobs and tears
It slept, even in the pregnant season of youth.
For though I was most passionately moved
And yielded to all changes of the scene
With an obsequious promptness, yet the storm 475
Passed not beyond the suburbs of the mind;
Save when realities of act and mien,
The incarnation of the spirits that move
In harmony amid the Poet's world,
Rose to ideäl grandeur, or, called forth 480
By power of contrast, made me recognise,
As at a glance, the things which I had shaped,
And yet not shaped, had seen and scarcely seen,
When, having closed the mighty Shakspeare's page,
I mused, and thought, and felt, in solitude. 485

  Pass we from entertainments, that are such
Professedly, to others titled higher,
Yet, in the estimate of youth at least,
More near akin to those than names imply, –
I mean the brawls of lawyers in their courts 490
Before the ermined judge, or that great stage
Where senators, tongue-favoured men, perform,
Admired and envied. Oh! the beating heart,
When one among the prime of these rise up, –
One, of whose name from childhood we had heard
Familiarly, a household term, like those, 496
The Bedfords, Glosters, Salsburys, of old
Whom the fifth Harry talks of. Silence! hush!
This is no trifler, no short-flighted wit,
No stammerer of a minute, painfully 500
Delivered. No! the Orator hath yoked
The Hours, like young Aurora, to his car:
Thrice welcome Presence! how can patience e'er
Grow weary of attending on a track
That kindles with such glory! All are charmed, 505
Astonished; like a hero in romance,
He winds away his never-ending horn;
Words follow words, sense seems to follow sense:
What memory and what logic! till the strain
Transcendent, superhuman, as it seemed, 510
Grows tedious even in a young man's ear.

  Genius of Burke! forgive the pen seduced
By specious wonders, and too slow to tell
Of what the ingenuous, what bewildered men,
Beginning to mistrust their boastful guides, 515
And wise men, willing to grow wiser, caught,

Rapt auditors! from thy most eloquent tongue –
Now mute, for ever mute in the cold grave.
I see him, – old, but vigorous in age, –
Stand like an oak whose stag-horn branches start 520
Out of its leafy brow, the more to awe
The younger brethren of the grove. But some –
While he forewarns, denounces, launches forth,
Against all systems built on abstract rights,
Keen ridicule; the majesty proclaims 525
Of Institutes and Laws, hallowed by time;
Declares the vital power of social ties
Endeared by Custom; and with high disdain,
Exploding upstart Theory, insists
Upon the allegiance to which men are born – 530
Some – say at once a froward multitude –
Murmur (for truth is hated, where not loved)
As the winds fret within the Aeolian cave,
Galled by their monarch's chain. The times were big
With ominous change, which, night by night,
     provoked 535
Keen struggles, and black clouds of passion raised;
But memorable moments intervened,
When Wisdom, like the Goddess from Jove's brain,
Broke forth in armour of resplendent words,
Startling the Synod. Could a youth, and one 540
In ancient story versed, whose breast had heaved
Under the weight of classic eloquence,
Sit, see, and hear, unthankful, uninspired?

  Nor did the Pulpit's oratory fail
To achieve its higher triumph. Not unfelt 545
Were its admonishments, nor lightly heard
The awful truths delivered thence by tongues
Endowed with various power to search the soul;
Yet ostentation, domineering, oft
Poured forth harangues, how sadly out of place! – 550
There have I seen a comely bachelor,
Fresh from a toilette of two hours, ascend
His rostrum, with seraphic glance look up,
And, in a tone elaborately low
Beginning, lead his voice through many a maze 555
A minuet course; and, winding up his mouth,
From time to time, into an orifice
Most delicate, a lurking eyelet, small,
And only not invisible, again
Open it out, diffusing thence a smile 560
Of rapt irradiation, éxquisite.
Meanwhile the Evangelists, Isaiah, Job,
Moses, and he who penned, the other day,
The Death of Abel, Shakspeare, and the Bard
Whose genius spangled o'er a gloomy theme 565
With fancies thick as his inspiring stars,

497–498 a reference to Shakespeare's *Henry V* 502 **Aurora:** goddess of the dawn   512 **Burke:** Edmund Burke who spearheaded a conservative reaction to the French Revolution, most ably in his *Reflections on the Revolution in France*

533–534 Aeolus, the god of winds, kept the winds chained within a cave 538–539 Athena is said to have emerged from the head of Zeus 540 **Synod:** assembly 564 **Abel:** Solomon Gessner's *The Death of Abel*, published, in English, in 1761 **the Bard:** Edward Young, author of *Night Thoughts*, published between 1742 and 1745

And Ossian (doubt not, 'tis the naked truth)
Summoned from streamy Morven – each and all
Would, in their turns, lend ornaments and flowers
To entwine the crook of eloquence that helped   570
This pretty Shepherd, pride of all the plains,
To rule and guide his captivated flock.

   I glance but at a few conspicuous marks,
Leaving a thousand others, that, in hall,
Court, théatre, conventicle, or shop,   575
In public room or private, park or street,
Each fondly reared on his own pedestal,
Looked out for admiration. Folly, vice,
Extravagance in gesture, mien, and dress,
And all the strife of singularity,   580
Lies to the ear, and lies to every sense –
Of these, and of the living shapes they wear,
There is no end. Such candidates for regard,
Although well pleased to be where they were found,
I did not hunt after, nor greatly prize,   585
Nor made unto myself a secret boast
Of reading them with quick and curious eye;
But, as a common produce, things that are
Today, tomorrow will be, took of them
Such willing note, as, on some errand bound   590
That asks not speed, a Traveller might bestow
On sea-shells that bestrew the sandy beach,
Or daisies swarming through the fields of June.

   But foolishness and madness in parade,
Though most at home in this their dear domain,   595
Are scattered everywhere, no rarities,
Even to the rudest novice of the Schools.
Me, rather, it employed, to note, and keep
In memory, those individual sights
Of courage, or integrity, or truth,   600
Or tenderness, which there, set off by foil,
Appeared more touching. One will I select;
A Father – for he bore that sacred name –
Him saw I, sitting in an open square,
Upon a corner-stone of that low wall,   605
Wherein were fixed the iron pales that fenced
A spacious grass-plot; there, in silence, sate
This One Man, with a sickly babe outstretched
Upon his knee, whom he had thither brought
For sunshine, and to breathe the fresher air.   610
Of those who passed, and me who looked at him,
He took no heed; but in his brawny arms
(The Artificer was to the elbow bare,
And from his work this moment had been stolen)
He held the child, and, bending over it,   615
As if he were afraid both of the sun
And of the air, which he had come to seek,
Eyed the poor babe with love unutterable.

567 **Ossian:** James Macpherson, author of the *Ossian* poems, published between 1760 and 1763 568 **Morven:** a mythical Gaelic kingdom associated with the Ossian legend 575 **conventicle:** meeting place, often associated with meetings of Protestant nonconformists

As the black storm upon the mountain top
Sets off the sunbeam in the valley, so   620
That huge fermenting mass of human-kind
Serves as a solemn back-ground, or relief,
To single forms and objects, whence they draw,
For feeling and contemplative regard,
More than inherent liveliness and power.   625
How oft, amid those overflowing streets,
Have I gone forward with the crowd, and said
Unto myself, 'The face of every one
That passes by me is a mystery!'
Thus have I looked, nor ceased to look, oppressed   630
By thoughts of what and whither, when and how,
Until the shapes before my eyes became
A second-sight procession, such as glides
Over still mountains, or appears in dreams;
And once, far-travelled in such mood, beyond   635
The reach of common indication, lost
Amid the moving pageant, I was smitten
Abruptly, with the view (a sight not rare)
Of a blind Beggar, who, with upright face,
Stood, propped against a wall, upon his chest   640
Wearing a written paper, to explain
His story, whence he came, and who he was.
Caught by the spectacle my mind turned round
As with the might of waters; an apt type
This label seemed of the utmost we can know,   645
Both of ourselves and of the universe;
And, on the shape of that unmoving man,
His steadfast face and sightless eyes, I gazed,
As if admonished from another world.

   Though reared upon the base of outward things,
Structures like these the excited spirit mainly   651
Builds for herself; scenes different there are,
Full-formed, that take, with small internal help,
Possession of the faculties, – the peace
That comes with night; the deep solemnity   655
Of nature's intermediate hours of rest,
When the great tide of human life stands still;
The business of the day to come, unborn,
Of that gone by, locked up, as in the grave;
The blended calmness of the heavens and earth,   660
Moonlight and stars, and empty streets, and sounds
Unfrequent as in deserts; at late hours
Of winter evenings, when unwholesome rains
Are falling hard, with people yet astir,
The feeble salutation from the voice   665
Of some unhappy woman, now and then
Heard as we pass, when no one looks about,
Nothing is listened to. But these, I fear,
Are falsely catalogued; things that are, are not,
As the mind answers to them, or the heart   670
Is prompt, or slow, to feel. What say you, then,
To times, when half the city shall break out
Full of one passion, vengeance, rage, or fear?
To executions, to a street on fire,
Mobs, riots, or rejoicings? From these sights   675

Take one, – that ancient festival, the Fair,
Holden where martyrs suffered in past time,
And named of St Bartholomew; there, see
A work completed to our hands, that lays,
If any spectacle on earth can do,   680
The whole creative powers of man asleep! –
For once, the Muse's help will we implore,
And she shall lodge us, wafted on her wings,
Above the press and danger of the crowd,
Upon some showman's platform. What a shock   685
For eyes and ears! what anarchy and din,
Barbarian and infernal, – a phantasma,
Monstrous in colour, motion, shape, sight, sound!
Below, the open space, through every nook
Of the wide area, twinkles, is alive   690
With heads; the midway region, and above,
Is thronged with staring pictures and huge scrolls,
Dumb proclamations of the Prodigies;
With chattering monkeys dangling from their poles,
And children whirling in their roundabouts;   695
With those that stretch the neck and strain the eyes,
And crack the voice in rivalship, the crowd
Inviting; with buffoons against buffoons
Grimacing, writhing, screaming, – him who grinds
The hurdy-gurdy, at the fiddle weaves,   700
Rattles the salt-box, thumps the kettle-drum,
And him who at the trumpet puffs his cheeks,
The silver-collared Negro with his timbrel,
Equestrians, tumblers, women, girls, and boys,
Blue-breeched, pink-vested, with high-towering
     plumes. –   705
All moveables of wonder, from all parts,
Are here – Albinos, painted Indians, Dwarfs,
The Horse of knowledge, and the learnèd Pig.
The Stone-eater, the man that swallows fire,
Giants, Ventriloquists, the Invisible Girl,   710
The Bust that speaks and moves its goggling eyes,
The Wax-work, Clock-work, all the marvellous craft
Of modern Merlins, Wild Beasts, Puppet-shows,
All out-o'-the-way, far-fetched, perverted things,
All freaks of nature, all Promethean thoughts   715
Of man, his dullness, madness, and their feats
All jumbled up together, to compose
A Parliament of Monsters, Tents and Booths
Meanwhile, as if the whole were one vast mill,
Are vomiting, receiving, on all sides,   720
Men, Women, three-years Children, Babes in arms.
    Oh, blank confusion! true epitome
Of what the mighty City is herself
To thousands upon thousands of her sons,

Living amid the same perpetual whirl   725
Of trivial objects, melted and reduced
To one identity, by differences
That have no law, no meaning, and no end –
Oppression, under which even highest minds
Must labour, whence the strongest are not free.   730
But though the picture weary out the eye,
By nature an unmanageable sight,
It is not wholly so to him who looks
In steadiness, who hath among least things
An under-sense of greatest; sees the parts   735
As parts, but with a feeling of the whole.
This, of all acquisitions first, awaits
On sundry and most widely different modes
Of education, nor with least delight
On that through which I passed. Attention springs,   740
And comprehensiveness and memory flow,
From early converse with the works of God
Among all regions; chiefly where appear
Most obviously simplicity and power.
Think, how the everlasting streams and woods,   745
Stretched and still stretching far and wide, exalt
The roving Indian. On his desert sands
What grandeur not unfelt, what pregnant show
Of beauty, meets the sun-burnt Arab's eye:
And, as the sea propels, from zone to zone,   750
Its currents; magnifies its shoals of life
Beyond all compass; spreads, and sends aloft
Armies of clouds, – even so, its powers and aspécts
Shape for mankind, by principles as fixed,
The views and aspirations of the soul   755
To majesty. Like virtue have the forms
Perennial of the ancient hills; nor less
The changeful language of their countenances
Quickens the slumbering mind, and aids the thoughts,
However multitudinous, to move   760
With order and relation. This, if still,
As hitherto, in freedom I may speak,
Not violating any just restraint,
As may be hoped, of reäl modesty, –
This did I feel, in London's vast domain.   765
The Spirit of Nature was upon me there;
The soul of Beauty and enduring Life
Vouchsafed her inspiration, and diffused,
Through meagre lines and colours, and the press
Of self-destroying, transitory things,   770
Composure, and ennobling Harmony.

BOOK EIGHTH. RETROSPECT – LOVE OF NATURE LEADING TO LOVE OF MAN

WHAT sounds are those, Helvellyn, that are heard
Up to thy summit, through the depth of air
Ascending, as if distance had the power
To make the sounds more audible? What crowd
Covers, or sprinkles o'er, yon village green?   5

678 **St. Bartholomew:** Bartholomew Fair, which was held at Smithfield in London 701 **salt-box:** a percussion instrument comprising of a wooden box containing salt 703 **timbrel:** tambourine 708 **learnèd Pig:** 'Toby the Sapient Pig' was a major London attraction in 1817. He could allegedly: read, spell, play cards, tell the time and read minds. His 'autobiography', *The Life and Adventures of Toby the Sapient Pig: with his Opinions on Men and Women; Written by Himself,* was published in 1818 719 **mill:** factory

BOOK EIGHTH. RETROSPECT – LOVE OF NATURE LEADING TO LOVE OF MAN: 1 **Helvellyn:** Mount Helvellyn near Grasmere where a fair is held each autumn

Crowd seems it, solitary hill! to thee,
Though but a little family of men,
Shepherds and tillers of the ground – betimes
Assembled with their children and their wives,
And here and there a stranger interspersed. 10
They hold a rustic fair – a festival,
Such as, on this side now, and now on that,
Repeated through his tributary vales,
Helvellyn, in the silence of his rest,
Sees annually, if clouds towards either ocean 15
Blown from their favourite resting-place, or mists
Dissolved, have left him an unshrouded head.
Delightful day it is for all who dwell
In this secluded glen, and eagerly
They give it welcome. Long ere heat of noon, 20
From byre or field the kine were brought; the sheep
Are penned in cotes; the chaffering is begun.
The heifer lows, uneasy at the voice
Of a new master; bleat the flocks aloud.
Booths are there none; a stall or two is here; 25
A lame man or a blind, the one to beg,
The other to make music; hither, too,
From far, with basket, slung upon her arm,
Of hawker's wares – books, pictures, combs, and
    pins –
Some agèd woman finds her way again, 30
Year after year, a punctual visitant!
There also stands a speech-maker by rote,
Pulling the strings of his boxed raree-show;
And in the lapse of many years may come
Prouder itinerant, mountebank, or he 35
Whose wonders in a covered wain lie hid.
But one there is, the loveliest of them all,
Some sweet lass of the valley, looking out
For gains, and who that sees her would not buy?
Fruits of her father's orchard, are her wares, 40
And with the ruddy produce, she walks round
Among the crowd, half pleased with, half ashamed
Of her new office, blushing restlessly.
The children now are rich, for the old today
Are generous as the young; and, if content 45
With looking on, some ancient wedded pair
Sit in the shade together, while they gaze,
'A cheerful smile unbends the wrinkled brow,
The days departed start again to life,
And all the scenes of childhood reappear, 50
Faint, but more tranquil, like the changing sun
To him who slept at noon and wakes at eve.'
Thus gaiety and cheerfulness prevail,
Spreading from young to old, from old to young,
And no one seems to want his share. – Immense 55
Is the recess, the circumambient world
Magnificent, by which they are embraced:
They move about upon the soft green turf:
How little they, they and their doings, seem,

And all that they can further or obstruct! 60
Through utter weakness pitiably dear,
As tender infants are: and yet how great!
For all things serve them: them the morning light
Loves, as it glistens on the silent rocks;
And them the silent rocks, which now from high 65
Look down upon them; the reposing clouds;
The wild brooks prattling from invisible haunts;
And old Helvellyn, conscious of the stir
Which animates this day their calm abode.
    With deep devotion, Nature, did I feel, 70
In that enormous City's turbulent world
Of men and things, what benefit I owed
To thee, and those domains of rural peace,
Where to the sense of beauty first my heart
Was opened; tract more exquisitely fair 75
Than that famed paradise of ten thousand trees,
Or Gehol's matchless gardens, for delight
Of the Tartarian dynasty composed
(Beyond that mighty wall, not fabulous,
China's stupendous mound) by patient toil 80
Of myriads and boon nature's lavish help;
There, in a clime from widest empire chosen,
Fulfilling (could enchantment have done more?)
A sumptuous dream of flowery lawns, with domes
Of pleasure sprinkled over, shady dells 85
For eastern monasteries, sunny mounts
With temples crested, bridges, gondolas,
Rocks, dens, and groves of foliage taught to melt
Into each other their obsequious hues,
Vanished and vanishing in subtle chase, 90
Too fine to be pursued; or standing forth
In no discordant opposition, strong
And gorgeous as the colours side by side
Bedded among rich plumes of tropic birds;
And mountains over all, embracing all; 95
And all the landscape, endlessly enriched
With waters running, falling, or asleep.
    But lovelier far than this, the paradise
Where I was reared; in Nature's primitive gifts
Favoured no less, and more to every sense 100
Delicious, seeing that the sun and sky,
The elements, and seasons as they change,
Do find a worthy fellow-labourer there –
Man free, man working for himself, with choice
Of time, and place, and object; by his wants, 105
His comforts, native occupations, cares,
Cheerfully led to individual ends
Or social, and still followed by a train
Unwooed, unthought-of even – simplicity,
And beauty, and inevitable grace. 110
    Yea, when a glimpse of those imperial bowers
Would to a child be transport over-great,
When but a half-hour's roam through such a place

21 **kine**: cattle 22 **chaffering**: bargaining 35 **mountebank**: a quack doctor
77 **Gehol's matchless gardens**: the gardens of the Chinese emperor at Gehol 80 **China's stupendous mound**: The Great Wall of China
108 **train**: succession of

Would leave behind a dance of images,
That shall break in upon his sleep for weeks;   115
Even then the common haunts of the green earth,
And ordinary interests of man,
Which they embosom, all without regard
As both may seem, are fastening on the heart
Insensibly, each with the other's help.   120
For me, when my affections first were led
From kindred, friends, and playmates, to partake
Love for the human creature's absolute self,
That noticeable kindliness of heart
Sprang out of fountains, there abounding most   125
Where sovereign Nature dictated the tasks
And occupations which her beauty adorned,
And Shepherds were the men that pleased me first;
Not such as Saturn ruled 'mid Latian wilds,
With arts and laws so tempered, that their lives   130
Left, even to us toiling in this late day,
A bright tradition of the golden age;
Not such as, 'mid Arcadian fastnesses
Sequestered, handed down among themselves
Felicity, in Grecian song renowned;   135
Nor such as, when an adverse fate had driven,
From house and home, the courtly band whose
          fortunes
Entered, with Shakespeare's genius, the wild woods
Of Arden, amid sunshine or in shade
Culled the best fruits of Time's uncounted hours,   140
Ere Phoebe sighed for the false Ganymede;
Or there where Perdita and Florizel
Together danced, Queen of the feast, and King;
Nor such as Spenser fabled. True it is,
That I had heard (what he perhaps had seen)   145
Of maids at sunrise bringing in from far
Their May-bush, and along the street in flocks
Parading with a song of taunting rhymes,
Aimed at the laggards slumbering within doors;
Had also heard, from those who yet remembered,   150
Tales of the May-pole dance, and wreaths that decked
Porch, door-way, or kirk-pillar; and of youths,
Each with his maid, before the sun was up,
By annual custom, issuing forth in troops,
To drink the waters of some sainted well,   155
And hang it round with garlands. Love survives;
But, for such purpose, flowers no longer grow:
The times, too sage, perhaps too proud, have dropped
These lighter graces; and the rural ways
And manners which my childhood looked upon   160
Were the unluxuriant produce of a life
Intent on little but substantial needs,

Yet rich in beauty, beauty that was felt.
But images of danger and distress,
Man suffering among awful Powers and Forms;   165
Of this I heard, and saw enough to make
Imagination restless; nor was free
Myself from frequent perils; nor were tales
Wanting, – the tragedies of former times,
Hazards and strange escapes, of which the rocks   170
Immutable and everflowing streams,
Where'er I roamed, were speaking monuments.
     Smooth life had flock and shepherd in old time,
Long springs and tepid waters, on the banks
Of delicate Galesus; and no less   175
Those scattered along Adria's myrtle shores:
Smooth life had herdsman, and his snow-white herd
To triumphs and to sacrificial rites
Devoted, on the inviolable stream
Of rich Clitumnus; and the goat-herd lived   180
As calmly, underneath the pleasant brows
Of cool Lucretilis, where the pipe was heard
Of Pan, Invisible God, thrilling the rocks
With tutelary music, from all harm
The fold protecting. I myself, mature   185
In manhood then, have seen a pastoral tract
Like one of these, where Fancy might run wild,
Though under skies less generous, less serene:
There, for her own delight had Nature framed
A pleasure-ground, diffused a fair expanse   190
Of level pasture, islanded with groves
And banked with woody risings; but the Plain
Endless, here opening widely out, and there
Shut up in lesser lakes or beds of lawn
And intricate recesses, creek or bay   195
Sheltered within a shelter, where at large
The shepherd strays, a rolling hut his home.
Thither he comes with spring-time, there abides
All summer, and at sunrise ye may hear
His flageolet to liquid notes of love   200
Attuned, or sprightly fife resounding far.
Nook is there none, nor tract of that vast space
Where passage opens, but the same shall have
In turn its visitant, telling there his hours
In unlaborious pleasure, with no task   205
More toilsome than to carve a beechen bowl
For spring or fountain, which the traveller finds,
When through the region he pursues at will
His devious course. A glimpse of such sweet life
I saw when, from the melancholy walls   210
Of Goslar, once imperial, I renewed
My daily walk along that wide champaign,
That, reaching to her gates, spreads east and west,
And northwards, from beneath the mountainous verge

129 **Saturn, the father of Jupiter:** created the Golden Age in the 'Latian wilds' surrounding Rome 133–135 Arcadia, thought of as the seat of the most ancient people of Greece, was portrayed as an innocent ideal and featured in a number of classical songs, poems and plays 138–143 references to Shakespeare's plays: *As You Like It* and *The Winter's Tale* 144 **Spenser fabled:** Edmund Spenser's *The Shepheardes Calender* (1579) 147 **May-bush:** hawthorn 152 **kirk-pillar:** church pillar

175 **Galesus:** a river in Calabria 180 **Clitumnus:** a river in Calabria 182 **Lucretilis:** a hill associated with Pan, the Roman god of flocks and shepherds 197 **rolling hut:** a hut on wheels used by shepherds 200 **flageolet:** a wind instrument resembling a recorder 211 **Goslar:** a town in Germany

Of the Hercynian forest. Yet, hail to you 215
Moors, mountains, headlands, and ye hollow vales,
Ye long deep channels for the Atlantic's voice,
Powers of my native region! Ye that seize
The heart with firmer grasp! Your snows and streams
Ungovernable, and your terrifying winds, 220
That howl so dismally for him who treads
Companionless your awful solitudes!
There, 'tis the shepherd's task the winter long
To wait upon the storms: of their approach
Sagacious, into sheltering coves he drives 225
His flock, and thither from the homestead bears
A toilsome burden up the craggy ways,
And deals it out, their regular nourishment
Strewn on the frozen snow. And when the spring
Looks out, and all the pastures dance with lambs, 230
And when the flock, with warmer weather, climbs
Higher and higher, him his office leads
To watch their goings, whatsoever track
The wanderers choose. For this he quits his home
At day-spring, and no sooner doth the sun 235
Begin to strike him with a fire-like heat,
Than he lies down upon some shining rock,
And breakfasts with his dog. When they have stolen,
As is their wont, a pittance from strict time,
For rest not needed or exchange of love, 240
Then from his couch he starts; and now his feet
Crush out a livelier fragrance from the flowers
Of lowly thyme, by Nature's skill enwrought
In the wild turf: the lingering dews of morn
Smoke round him, as from hill to hill he hies, 245
His staff protending like a hunter's spear,
Or by its aid leaping from crag to crag,
And o'er the brawling beds of unbridged streams.
Philosophy, methinks, at Fancy's call,
Might deign to follow him through what he does 250
Or sees in his day's march; himself he feels,
In those vast regions where his service lies,
A freeman, wedded to his life of hope
And hazard, and hard labour interchanged
With that majestic indolence so dear 255
To native man. A rambling school-boy, thus
I felt his presence in his own domain,
As of a lord and master, or a power,
Or genius, under Nature, under God,
Presiding; and severest solitude 260
Had more commanding looks when he was there.
When up the lonely brooks on rainy days
Angling I went, or trod the trackless hills
By mists bewildered, suddenly mine eyes
Have glanced upon him distant a few steps, 265
In size a giant, stalking through thick fog,
His sheep like Greenland bears; or, as he stepped
Beyond the boundary line of some hill-shadow,
His form hath flashed upon me, glorified

By the deep radiance of the setting sun: 270
Or him have I descried in distant sky,
A solitary object and sublime,
Above all height! like an aërial cross
Stationed alone upon a spiry rock
Of the Chartreuse, for worship. Thus was man 275
Ennobled outwardly before my sight,
And thus my heart was early introduced
To an unconscious love and reverence
Of human nature; hence the human form
To me became an index of delight, 280
Of grace and honour, power and worthiness.
Meanwhile this creature – spiritual almost
As those of books, but more exalted far;
Far more of an imaginative form
Than the gay Corin of the groves, who lives 285
For his own fancies, or to dance by the hour,
In coronal, with Phyllis in the midst –
Was, for the purposes of kind, a man
With the most common; husband, father; learn'd,
Could teach, admonish; suffered with the rest 290
From vice and folly, wretchedness and fear;
Of this I little saw, cared less for it,
But something must have felt.
                              Call ye these appearances –
Which I beheld of shepherds in my youth,
This sanctity of Nature given to man – 295
A shadow, a delusion, ye who pore
On the dead letter, miss the spirit of things;
Whose truth is not a motion or a shape
Instínct with vital functions, but a block
Or waxen image which yourselves have made, 300
And ye adore! But blessèd be the God
Of Nature and of Man that this was so;
That men before my inexperienced eyes
Did first present themselves thus purified,
Removed, and to a distance that was fit: 305
And so we all of us in some degree
Are led to knowledge, wheresoever led,
And howsoever; were it otherwise,
And we found evil fast as we find good
In our first years, or think that it is found, 310
How could the innocent heart bear up and live!
But doubly fortunate my lot; not here
Alone, that something of a better life
Perhaps was round me than it is the privilege
Of most to move in, but that first I looked 315
At Man through objects that were great or fair;
First cómmuned with him by their help. And thus
Was founded a sure safeguard and defence
Against the weight of meanness, selfish cares,
Coarse manners, vulgar passions, that beat in 320
On all sides from the ordinary world
In which we traffic. Starting from this point

---

215 **Hercynian forest:** archaic name for the mountain ranges of central Germany 246 **protending:** stretching out

275 **Chartreuse:** Carthusian Order in the Alps of Dauphine near Grenoble 285–287 **Corin . . . Phyllis:** names commonly used in pastoral verse

I had my face turned toward the truth, began
With an advantage furnished by that kind
Of prepossession, without which the soul   325
Receives no knowledge that can bring forth good,
No genuine insight ever comes to her.
From the restraint of over-watchful eyes
Preserved, I moved about, year after year,
Happy, and now most thankful that my walk   330
Was guarded from too early intercourse
With the deformities of crowded life,
And those ensuing laughters and contempts,
Self-pleasing, which, if we would wish to think
With a due reverence on earth's rightful lord,   335
Here placed to be the inheritor of heaven,
Will not permit us; but pursue the mind,
That to devotion willingly would rise,
Into the temple and the temple's heart.

  Yet deem not, Friend! that human kind with me   340
Thus early took a place pre-eminent;
Nature herself was, at this unripe time,
But secondary to my own pursuits
And animal activities, and all
Their trivial pleasures; and when these had drooped
And gradually expired, and Nature, prized   346
For her own sake, became my joy, even then –
And upwards through late youth, until not less
Than two-and-twenty summers had been told –
Was Man in my affections and regards   350
Subordinate to her, her visible forms
And viewless agencies: a passion, she,
A rapture often, and immediate love
Ever at hand; he, only a delight
Occasional, an accidental grace,   355
His hour being not yet come. Far less had then
The inferior creatures, beast or bird, attuned
My spirit to that gentleness of love
(Though they had long been carefully observed),
Won from me those minute obeisances   360
Of tenderness, which I may number now
With my first blessings. Nevertheless, on these
The light of beauty did not fall in vain,
Or grandeur circumfuse them to no end.

  But when that first poetic faculty   365
Of plain Imagination and severe,
No longer a mute influence of the soul,
Ventured, at some rash Muse's earnest call,
To try her strength among harmonious words;
And to book-notions and the rules of art   370
Did knowingly conform itself; there came
Among the simple shapes of human life
A wilfulness of fancy and conceit;
And Nature and her objects beautified
These fictions, as in some sort, in their turn,   375
They burnished her. From touch of this new power
Nothing was safe: the elder-tree that grew

Beside the well-known charnel-house had then
A dismal look: the yew-tree had its ghost,
That took his station there for ornament: 380
The dignities of plain occurrence then
Were tasteless, and truth's golden mean, a point
Where no sufficient pleasure could be found.
Then, if a widow, staggering with the blow
Of her distress, was known to have turned her steps
To the cold grave in which her husband slept,   386
One night, or haply more than one, through pain
Or half-insensate impotence of mind,
The fact was caught at greedily, and there
She must be visitant the whole year through,   390
Wetting the turf with never-ending tears.

  Through quaint obliquities I might pursue
These cravings; when the fox-glove, one by one,
Upwards through every stage of the tall stem,
Had shed beside the public way its bells,   395
And stood of all dismantled, save the last
Left at the tapering ladder's top, that seemed
To bend as doth a slender blade of grass
Tipped with a rain-drop, Fancy loved to seat,
Beneath the plant despoiled, but crested still   400
With this last relic, soon itself to fall,
Some vagrant mother, whose arch little ones,
All unconcerned by her dejected plight,
Laughed as with rival eagerness their hands
Gathered the purple cups that round them lay,   405
Strewing the turf's green slope.

                                        A diamond light
(Whene'er the summer sun, declining, smote
A smooth rock wet with constant springs) was seen
Sparkling from out a copse-clad bank that rose
Fronting our cottage. Oft beside the hearth   410
Seated, with open door, often and long
Upon this restless lustre have I gazed,
That made my fancy restless as itself.
'Twas now for me a burnished silver shield
Suspended over a knight's tomb, who lay   415
Inglorious, buried in the dusky wood:
An entrance now into some magic cave
Or palace built by fairies of the rock;
Nor could I have been bribed to disenchant
The spectacle, by visiting the spot.   420
Thus wilful Fancy, in no hurtful mood,
Engrafted far-fetched shapes on feelings bred
By pure Imagination: busy Power
She was, and with her ready pupil turned
Instinctively to human passions, then   425
Least understood. Yet, 'mid the fervent swarm
Of these vagáries, with an eye so rich
As mine was through the bounty of a grand
And lovely region, I had forms distinct
To steady me: each airy thought revolved   430

---

352 **viewless:** invisible

378 **charnel-house:** after a period of internment bones from a grave would often be moved to a charnel-house, enabling the grave to be reused 388 **half-insensate:** partially without sensation

Round a substantial centre, which at once
Incited it to motion, and controlled.
I did not pine like one in cities bred,
As was thy melancholy lot, dear Friend!
Great Spirit as thou art, in endless dreams   435
Of sickliness, disjoining, joining, things
Without the light of knowledge. Where the harm,
If, when the woodman languished with disease
Induced by sleeping nightly on the ground
Within his sod-built cabin, Indian-wise,   440
I called the pangs of disappointed love,
And all the sad etcetera of the wrong,
To help him to his grave? Meanwhile the man,
If not already from the woods retired
To die at home, was haply, as I knew,   445
Withering by slow degrees, 'mid gentle airs,
Birds, running streams, and hills so beautiful
On golden evenings, while the charcoal pile
Breathed up its smoke, an image of his ghost
Or spirit that full soon must take her flight.   450
Nor shall we not be tending towards that point
Of sound humanity to which our Tale
Leads, though by sinuous ways, if here I show
How Fancy, in a season when she wove
Those slender cords, to guide the unconscious Boy   455
For the Man's sake, could feed at Nature's call
Some pensive musings which might well beseem
Maturer years.
        A grove there is whose boughs
Stretch from the western marge of Thurston-mere,
With length of shade so thick, that whoso glides   460
Along the line of low-roofed water, moves
As in a cloister. Once – while, in that shade
Loitering, I watched the golden beams of light
Flung from the setting sun, as they reposed
In silent beauty on the naked ridge   465
Of a high eastern hill – thus flowed my thoughts
In a pure stream of words fresh from the heart;
Dear native Region, wheresoe'er shall close
My mortal course, there will I think on you;
Dying, will cast on you a backward look;   470
Even as this setting sun (albeit the Vale
Is no where touched by one memorial gleam)
Doth with the fond remains of his last power
Still linger, and a farewell lustre sheds
On the dear mountain-tops where first he rose.   475
  Enough of humble arguments; recall,
My Song! those high emotions which thy voice
Has heretofore made known; that bursting forth
Of sympathy, inspiring and inspired,
When everywhere a vital pulse was felt,   480
And all the several frames of things, like stars,
Through every magnitude distinguishable,
Shone mutually indebted, or half lost
Each in the other's blaze, a galaxy

Of life and glory. In the midst stood Man,   485
Outwardly, inwardly contemplated,
As, of all visible natures, crown, though born
Of dust, and kindred to the worm; a Being,
Both in perception and discernment, first
In every capability of rapture,   490
Through the divine effect of power and love;
As, more than anything we know, instínct
With godhead, and, by reason and by will,
Acknowledging dependency sublime.
    Ere long, the lonely mountains left, I moved,   495
Begirt, from day to day, with temporal shapes
Of vice and folly thrust upon my view,
Objects of sport, and ridicule, and scorn,
Manners and characters discriminate,
And little bustling passions that eclipsed,   500
As well they might, the impersonated thought,
The idea, or abstraction of the kind.
    An idler among academic bowers,
Such was my new condition, as at large
Has been set forth; yet here the vulgar light   505
Of present, actual, superficial life,
Gleaming through colouring of other times,
Old usages and local privilege,
Was welcome, softened, if not solemnised.
This notwithstanding, being brought more near   510
To vice and guilt, forerunning wretchedness,
I trembled, – thought, at times, of human life
With an indefinite terror and dismay,
Such as the storms and angry elements
Had bred in me; but gloomier far, a dim   515
Analogy to uproar and misrule,
Disquiet, danger, and obscurity.
    It might be told (but whereof speak of things
Common to all?) that, seeing, I was led
Gravely to ponder – judging between good   520
And evil, not as for the mind's delight
But for her guidance – one who was to *act*,
As sometimes to the best of feeble means
I did, by human sympathy impelled:
And, through dislike and most offensive pain,   525
Was to the truth conducted; of this faith
Never forsaken, that, by acting well,
And understanding, I should learn to love
The end of life, and every thing we know.
    Grave Teacher, stern Preceptress! for at times   530
Thou canst put on an aspect most severe;
London, to thee I willingly return.
Erewhile my verse played idly with the flowers
Enwrought upon the mantle; satisfied
With that amusement, and a simple look   535
Of child-like inquisition now and then
Cast upwards on thy countenance, to detect
Some inner meanings which might harbour there.
But how could I in mood so light indulge,
Keeping such fresh remembrance of the day,   540
When, having thridded the long labyrinth

459 **Thurston-mere:** Coniston Water

Of the suburban villages, I first
Entered thy vast dominion? On the roof
Of an itinerant vehicle I sate,
With vulgar men about me, trivial forms   545
Of houses, pavement, streets, of men and things, –
Mean shapes on every side: but, at the instant,
When to myself it fairly might be said,
The threshold now is overpast (how strange
That aught external to the living mind   550
Should have such mighty sway! yet so it was),
A weight of ages did at once descend
Upon my heart; no thought embodied, no
Distinct remembrances, but weight and power, –
Power growing under weight: alas! I feel   555
That I am trifling: 'twas a moment's pause, –
All that took place within me came and went
As in a moment; yet with Time it dwells,
And grateful memory, as a thing divine.

     The curious traveller, who, from open day,   560
Hath passed with torches into some huge cave,
The Grotto of Antiparos, or the Den
In old time haunted by that Danish Witch,
Yordas; he looks around and sees the vault
Widening on all sides; sees, or thinks he sees,   565
Erelong, the massy roof above his head,
That instantly unsettles and recedes, –
Substance and shadow, light and darkness, all
Commingled, making up a canopy
Of shapes and forms and tendencies to shape   570
That shift and vanish, change and interchange
Like spectres, – ferment silent and sublime!
That after a short space works less and less,
Till, every effort, every motion gone,
The scene before him stands in perfect view   575
Exposed, and lifeless as a written book! –
But let him pause awhile, and look again,
And a new quickening shall succeed, at first
Beginning timidly, then creeping fast,
Till the whole cave, so late a senseless mass,   580
Busies the eye with images and forms
Boldly assembled, – here is shadowed forth
From the projections, wrinkles, cavities,
A variegated landscape, – there the shape
Of some gigantic warrior clad in mail,   585
The ghostly semblance of a hooded monk,
Veiled nun, or pilgrim resting on his staff:
Strange congregation! yet not slow to meet
Eyes that perceive through minds that can inspire.

     Even in such sort had I at first been moved,   590
Nor otherwise continued to be moved,
As I explored the vast metropolis,
Fount of my country's destiny and the world's;
That great emporium, chronicle at once
And burial-place of passions, and their home   595
Imperial, their chief living residence.

562 **Grotto of Antiparos:** in the Aegean 564 **Yordas:** in Yorkshire

With strong sensations teeming as it did
Of past and present, such a place must needs
Have pleased me, seeking knowledge at that time
Far less than craving power; yet knowledge came,   600
Sought or unsought, and influxes of power
Came, of themselves, or at her call derived
In fits of kindliest apprehensiveness,
From all sides, when whate'er was in itself
Capacious found, or seemed to find, in me   605
A correspondent amplitude of mind;
Such is the strength and glory of our youth!
The human nature unto which I felt
That I belonged, and reverenced with love,
Was not a punctual presence, but a spirit   610
Diffused through time and space, with aid derived
Of evidence from monuments, erect,
Prostrate, or leaning towards their common rest
In earth, the widely scattered wreck sublime
Of vanished nations, or more clearly drawn   615
From books and what they picture and record.

     'Tis true, the history of our native land,
With those of Greece compared and popular Rome,
And in our high-wrought modern narratives
Stripped of their harmonising soul, the life   620
Of manners and familiar incidents,
Had never much delighted me. And less
Than other intellects had mine been used
To lean upon extrinsic circumstance
Of record or tradition; but a sense   625
Of what in the Great City had been done
And suffered, and was doing, suffering, still,
Weighed with me, could support the test of thought;
And, in despite of all that had gone by,
Or was departing never to return,   630
There I conversed with majesty and power
Like independent natures. Hence the place
Was thronged with impregnations like the Wilds
In which my early feelings had been nursed –
Bare hills and valleys, full of caverns, rocks,   635
And audible seclusions, dashing lakes,
Echoes and waterfalls, and pointed crags
That into music touch the passing wind.
Here then my young imagination found
No uncongenial element; could here   640
Among new objects serve or give command,
Even as the heart's occasions might require,
To forward reason's else too scrupulous march.
The effect was, still more elevated views
Of human nature. Neither vice nor guilt,   645
Debasement undergone by body or mind,
Nor all the misery forced upon my sight,
Misery not lightly passed, but sometimes scanned
Most feelingly, could overthrow my trust
In what we *may* become; induce belief   650
That I was ignorant, had been falsely taught,
A solitary, who with vain conceits
Had been inspired, and walked about in dreams.

From those sad scenes when meditation turned,
Lo! every thing that was indeed divine   655
Retained its purity inviolate,
Nay brighter shone, by this portentous gloom
Set off; such opposition as aroused
The mind of Adam, yet in Paradise
Though fallen from bliss, when in the East he saw   660
Darkness ere day's mid course, and morning light
More orient in the western cloud, that drew
O'er the blue firmament a radiant white,
Descending slow with something heavenly fraught.
   Add also, that among the multitudes   665
Of that huge city, oftentimes was seen
Affectingly set forth, more than elsewhere
Is possible, the unit of man,
One spirit over ignorance and vice
Predominant, in good and evil hearts   670
One sense for moral judgements, as one eye
For the sun's light. The soul when smitten thus
By a sublime *ideä*, whencesoe'er
Vouchsafed for union or communion, feeds
On the pure bliss, and takes her rest with God.   675
   Thus from a very early age, O Friend!
My thoughts by slow gradations had been drawn
To human-kind, and to the good and ill
Of human life: Nature had led me on;
And oft amid the 'busy hum' I seemed   680
To travel independent of her help,
As if I had forgotten her; but no,
The world of human-kind outweighed not hers
In my habitual thoughts; the scale of love,
Though filling daily, still was light, compared   685
With that in which *her* mighty objects lay.

BOOK NINTH. RESIDENCE IN FRANCE

EVEN as a river, – partly (it might seem)
Yielding to old remembrances, and swayed
In part by fear to shape a way direct,
That would engulf him soon in the ravenous sea –
Turns, and will measure back his course, far back,   5
Seeking the very regions which he crossed
In his first outset; so have we, my Friend!
Turned and returned with intricate delay.
Or as a traveller, who has gained the brow
Of some aërial Down, while there he halts   10
For breathing-time, is tempted to review
The region left behind him; and, if aught
Deserving notice have escaped regard,
Or been regarded with too careless eye,
Strives, from that height, with one and yet one more   15
Last look, to make the best amends he may:
So have we lingered. Now we start afresh
With courage, and new hope risen on our toil.
Fair greetings to this shapeless eagerness,
Whene'er it comes! needful in work so long,   20
Thrice needful to the argument which now
Awaits us! Oh, how much unlike the past!

Free as a colt at pasture on the hill,
I ranged at large, through London's wide domain,
Month after month. Obscurely did I live,   25
Not seeking frequent intercourse with men,
By literature, or elegance, or rank,
Distinguished. Scarcely was a year thus spent
Ere I forsook the crowded solitude,
With less regret for its luxurious pomp,   30
And all the nicely guarded shows of art,
Than for the humble book-stalls in the streets,
Exposed to eye and hand where'er I turned.
   France lured me forth; the realm that I had
      crossed
So lately, journeying toward the snow-clad Alps.   35
But now, relinquishing the scrip and staff,
And all enjoyment which the summer sun
Sheds round the steps of those who meet the day
With motion constant as his own, I went
Prepared to sojourn in a pleasant town,   40
Washed by the current of the stately Loire.
   Through Paris lay my readiest course, and there
Sojóurning a few days, I visited,
In haste, each spot of old or recent fame,
The latter chiefly; from the field of Mars   45
Down to the suburbs of St Anthony,
And from Mont Martyr southward to the Dome
Of Geneviève. In both her clamorous Halls,
The National Synod and the Jacobins,
I saw the Revolutionary Power   50
Toss like a ship at anchor, rocked by storms;
The Arcades I traversed, in the Palace huge
Of Orleans; coasted round and round the line
Of Tavern, Brothel, Gaming-house, and Shop,
Great rendezvous of worst and best, the walk   55
Of all who had a purpose, or had not;
I stared and listened, with a stranger's ears,
To Hawkers and Haranguers, hubbub wild!
And hissing Factionists with ardent eyes,
In knots, or pairs, or single. Not a look   60
Hope takes, or Doubt or Fear is forced to wear,
But seemed there present; and I scanned them all,
Watched every gesture uncontrollable,
Of anger, and vexation, and despite,
All side by side, and struggling face to face,   65
With gaiety and dissolute idleness.
   Where silent zephyrs sported with the dust
Of the Bastille, I sate in the open sun,
And from the rubbish gathered up a stone,
And pocketed the relic, in the guise   70
Of an enthusiast; yet, in honest truth,
I looked for something that I could not find,
Affecting more emotion than I felt;
For 'tis most certain, that these various sights,
However potent their first shock, with me   75

BOOK NINTH. RESIDENCE IN FRANCE: 49 **Jacobins**: a name given to the members of a French revolutionary society formed in 1789

Appeared to recompense the traveller's pains
Less than the painted Magdalene of Le Brun,
A beauty exquisitely wrought, with hair
Dishevelled, gleaming eyes, and rueful cheek
Pale and bedropped with everflowing tears.   80
    But hence to my more permanent abode
I hasten; there, by novelties in speech,
Domestic manners, customs, gestures, looks,
And all the attire of ordinary life,
Attention was engrossed; and, thus amused,   85
I stood, 'mid those concussions, unconcerned,
Tranquil almost, and careless as a flower
Glassed in a green-house, or a parlour shrub
That spreads its leaves in unmolested peace,
While every bush and tree, the country through,   90
Is shaking to the roots: indifference this
Which may seem strange: but I was unprepared
With needful knowledge, had abruptly passed
Into a théatre, whose stage was filled
And busy with an action far advanced.   95
Like others, I had skimmed, and sometimes read
With care, the master pamphlets of the day;
Nor wanted such half-insight as grew wild
Upon that meagre soil, helped out by talk
And public news; but having never seen   100
A chronicle that might suffice to show
Whence the main organs of the public power
Had sprung, their transmigrations, when and how
Accomplished, giving thus unto events
A form and body; all things were to me   105
Loose and disjointed, and the affections left
Without a vital interest. At that time,
Moreover, the first storm was overblown,
And the strong hand of outward violence
Locked up in quiet. For myself, I fear   110
Now in connection with so great a theme
To speak (as I must be compelled to do)
Of one so unimportant; night by night
Did I frequent the formal haunts of men,
Whom, in the city, privilege of birth   115
Sequestered from the rest, societies
Polished in arts, and in punctilio versed;
Whence, and from deeper causes, all discóurse
Of good and evil of the time was shunned
With scrupulous care; but these restrictions soon   120
Proved tedious, and I gradually withdrew
Into a noisier world, and thus ere long
Became a patriot; and my heart was all
Given to the people, and my love was theirs.
    A band of military Officers,   125
Then stationed in the city, were the chief
Of my associates: some of these wore swords
That had been seasoned in the wars, and all
Were men well born; the chivalry of France.

In age and temper differing, they had yet   130
One spirit ruling in each heart; alike
(Save only one, hereafter to be named)
Were bent upon undoing what was done:
This was their rest and only hope; therewith
No fear had they of bad becoming worse,   135
For worst to them was come; nor would have stirred,
Or deemed it worth a moment's thought to stir,
In any thing, save only as the act
Looked thitherward. One, reckoning by years,
Was in the prime of manhood, and erewhile   140
He had sate lord in many tender hearts;
Though heedless of such honours now, and changed:
His temper was quite mastered by the times,
And they had blighted him, had eat away
The beauty of his person, doing wrong   145
Alike to body and to mind: his port,
Which once had been erect and open, now
Was stooping and contracted, and a face,
Endowed by Nature with her fairest gifts
Of symmetry and light and bloom, expressed,   150
As much as any that was ever seen,
A ravage out of season, made by thoughts
Unhealthy and vexatious. With the hour,
That from the press of Paris duly brought
Its freight of public news, the fever came,   155
A punctual visitant, to shake this man,
Disarmed his voice and fanned his yellow cheek
Into a thousand colours; while he read,
Or mused, his sword was haunted by his touch
Continually, like an uneasy place   160
In his own body. 'Twas in truth an hour
Of universal ferment; mildest men
Were agitated; and commotions, strife
Of passion and opinion, filled the walls
Of peaceful houses with unquiet sounds.   165
The soil of common life, was, at that time,
Too hot to tread upon. Oft said I then,
And not then only, 'What a mockery this
Of history, the past and that to come!
Now do I feel how all men are deceived,   170
Reading of nations and their works, in faith,
Faith given to vanity and emptiness;
Oh! laughter for the page that would reflect
To future times the face of what now is!'
The land all swarmed with passion, like a plain   175
Devoured by locusts, – Carra, Gorcas, – add
A hundred other names, forgotten now,
Nor to be heard of more; yet, they were powers,
Like earthquakes, shocks repeated day by day,
And felt through every nook of town and field.   180
    Such was the state of things. Meanwhile the chief
Of my associates stood prepared for flight
To augment the band of emigrants in arms
Upon the borders of the Rhine, and leagued

77–80: a portrait of Mary Magdalene painted by Charles le Brun

146 **port**: bearing 176 **Carra, Gorsas**: deputies of the French National Assembly

With foreign foes mustered for instant war. 185
This was their undisguised intent, and they
Were waiting with the whole of their desires
The moment to depart.

           An Englishman,
Born in a land whose very name appeared
To license some unruliness of mind; 190
A stranger, with youth's further privilege,
And the indulgence that a half-learnt speech
Wins from the courteous; I, who had been else
Shunned and not tolerated, freely lived
With these defenders of the Crown, and talked, 195
And heard their notions; nor did they disdain
The wish to bring me over to their cause.

   But though untaught by thinking or by books
To reason well of polity or law,
And nice distinctions, then on every tongue, 200
Of natural rights and civil; and to acts
Of nations and their passing interests
(If with unworldly ends and aims compared)
Almost indifferent, even the historian's tale
Prizing but little otherwise than I prized 205
Tales of the poets, as it made the heart
Beat high, and filled the fancy with fair forms,
Old heroes and their sufferings and their deeds;
Yet in the regal sceptre, and the pomp
Of orders and degrees, I nothing found 210
Then, or had ever, even in crudest youth,
That dazzled me, but rather what I mourned
And ill could brook, beholding that the best
Ruled not, and feeling that they ought to rule.

   For, born in a poor district, and which yet 215
Retaineth more of ancient homeliness,
Than any other nook of English ground,
It was my fortune scarcely to have seen,
Through the whole tenor of my school-day time,
The face of one, who, whether boy or man, 220
Was vested with attention or respect
Through claims of wealth or blood; nor was it least
Of many benefits, in later years
Derived from academic institutes
And rules, that they held something up to view 225
Of a Republic, where all stood thus far
Upon equal ground; that we were brothers all
In honour, as in one community,
Scholars and gentlemen; where, furthermore,
Distinction open lay to all that came, 230
And wealth and titles were in less esteem
Than talents, worth, and prosperous industry.
Add unto this, subservience from the first
To presences of God's mysterious power
Made manifest in Nature's sovereignty, 235
And fellowship with venerable books,
To sanction the proud workings of the soul,

And mountain liberty. It could not be
But that one tutored thus should look with awe
Upon the faculties of man, receive 240
Gladly the highest promises, and hail,
As best, the government of equal rights
And individual worth. And hence, O Friend!
If at the first great outbreak I rejoiced
Less than might well befit my youth, the cause 245
In part lay here, that unto me the events
Seemed nothing out of nature's certain course,
A gift that was come rather late than soon.
No wonder, then, if advocates like these,
Inflamed by passion, blind with prejudice, 250
And stung with injury, at this riper day,
Were impotent to make my hopes put on
The shape of theirs, my understanding bend
In honour of their honour: zeal, which yet
Had slumbered, now in opposition burst 255
Forth like a Polar summer: every word
They uttered was a dart, by counter-winds
Blown back upon themselves; their reason seemed
Confusion-stricken by a higher power
Than human understanding, their discóurse 260
Maimed, spiritless; and, in their weakness strong,
I triumphed.

          Meantime, day by day, the roads
Were crowded with the bravest youth of France,
And all the promptest of her spirits, linked
In gallant soldiership, and posting on 265
To meet the war upon her frontier bounds.
Yet at this very moment do tears start
Into mine eyes: I do not say I weep –
I wept not then, – but tears have dimmed my sight,
In memory of the farewells of that time, 270
Domestic severings, female fortitude
At dearest separation, patriot love
And self-devotion, and terrestrial hope,
Encouraged with a martyr's confidence;
Even files of strangers merely, seen but once, 275
And for a moment, men from far with sound
Of music, martial tunes, and banners spread,
Entering the city, here and there a face,
Or person singled out among the rest,
Yet still a stranger and beloved as such; 280
Even by these passing spectacles my heart
Was oftentimes uplifted, and they seemed
Arguments sent from Heaven to prove the cause
Good, pure, which no one could stand up against,
Who was not lost, abandoned, selfish, proud, 285
Mean, miserable, wilfully depraved,
Hater perverse of equity and truth.

   Among that band of Officers was one,
Already hinted at, of other mould –
A patriot, thence rejected by the rest, 290

---

185 **foreign foes:** in 1792 France was at war with a European
coalition force, with Britain at its head, whose aim was to restore
the Bourbon monarchy

266 France declared war on Austria in April 1792   288 Michel
Beaupuy (1755–1796) who rose to the rank of general in the French
army

And with an oriental loathing spurned,
As of a different caste. A meeker man
Than this lived never, nor a more benign,
Meek though enthusiastic. Injuries
Made *him* more gracious, and his nature then   295
Did breathe its sweetness out most sensibly,
As aromatic flowers on Alpine turf,
When foot hath crushed them. He through the
      events
Of that great change wandered in perfect faith,
As through a book, an old romance, or tale   300
Of Fairy, or some dream of actions wrought
Behind the summer clouds. By birth he ranked
With the most noble, but unto the poor
Among mankind he was in service bound,
As by some tie invisible, oaths professed   305
To a religious order. Man he loved
As man; and, to the mean and the obscure,
And all the homely in their homely works,
Transferred a courtesy which had no air
Of condescension; but did rather seem   310
A passion and a gallantry, like that
Which he, a soldier, in his idler day
Had paid to woman: somewhat vain he was,
Or seemed so, yet it was not vanity,
But fondness, and a kind of radiant joy   315
Diffused around him, while he was intent
On works of love or freedom, or revolved
Complacently the progress of a cause,
Whereof he was a part: yet this was meek
And placid, and took nothing from the man   320
That was delightful. Oft in solitude
With him did I discóurse about the end
Of civil government, and its wisest forms;
Of ancient loyalty, and chartered rights,
Custom and habit, novelty and change;   325
Of self-respect, and virtue in the few
For patrimonial honour set apart,
And ignorance in the labouring multitude.
For he, to all intolerance indisposed,
Balanced these contemplations in his mind;   330
And I, who at that time was scarcely dipped
Into the turmoil, bore a sounder judgement
Than later days allowed; carried about me,
With less allóy to its integrity,
The experience of past ages, as, through help   335
Of books and common life, it makes sure way
To youthful minds, by objects over near
Not pressed upon, nor dazzled or misled
By struggling with the crowd for present ends.

But though not deaf, nor obstinate to find   340
Error without excuse upon the side
Of them who strove against us, more delight
We took, and let this freely be confessed,
In painting to ourselves the miseries
Of royal courts, and that voluptuous life   345
Unfeeling, where the man who is of soul

The meanest thrives the most; where dignity,
True personal dignity, abideth not;
A light, a cruel, and vain world cut off
From the natural inlets of just sentiment,   350
From lowly sympathy and chastening truth;
Where good and evil interchange their names,
And thirst for bloody spoils abroad is paired
With vice at home. We added dearest themes –
Man and his noble nature, as it is   355
The gift which God has placed within his power,
His blind desires and steady faculties
Capable of clear truth, the one to break
Bondage, the other to build liberty
On firm foundations, making social life,   360
Through knowledge spreading and imperishable,
As just in regulation, and as pure
As individual in the wise and good.

  We summoned up the honourable deeds
Of ancient Story, thought of each bright spot,   365
That would be found in all recorded time,
Of truth preserved and error passed away;
Of single spirits that catch the flame from Heaven,
And how the multitudes of men will feed
And fan each other; thought of sects, how keen   370
They are to put the appropriate nature on,
Triumphant over every obstacle
Of custom, language, country, love, or hate,
And what they do and suffer for their creed;
How far they travel, and how long endure;   375
How quickly mighty Nations have been formed,
From least beginnings; how, together locked
By new opinions, scattered tribes have made
One body, spreading wide as clouds in heaven.
To aspirations then of our own minds   380
Did we appeal; and, finally, beheld
A living confirmation of the whole
Before us, in a people from the depth
Of shameful imbecility uprisen,
Fresh as the morning star. Elate we looked   385
Upon their virtues; saw, in rudest men,
Self-sacrifice the firmest; generous love,
And continence of mind, and sense of right,
Uppermost in the midst of fiercest strife.

  Oh, sweet it is, in academic groves,   390
Or such retirement, Friend! as we have known
In the green dales beside our Rotha's stream,
Greta, or Derwent, or some nameless rill,
To ruminate, with interchange of talk,
On rational liberty, and hope in man,   395
Justice and peace. But far more sweet such toil –
Toil, say I, for it leads to thoughts abstruse –
If nature then be standing on the brink
Of some great trial, and we hear the voice
Of one devoted, – one whom circumstance   400

392–393 rivers in the Lake District

Hath called upon to embody his deep sense
In action, give it outwardly a shape,
And that of benediction, to the world.
Then doubt is not, and truth is more than truth, –
A hope it is, and a desire; a creed   405
Of zeal, by an authority Divine
Sanctioned, of danger, difficulty, or death.
Such conversation, under Attic shades,
Did Dion hold with Plato; ripened thus
For a Deliverer's glorious task, – and such   410
He, on that ministry already bound,
Held with Eudemus and Timonides,
Surrounded by adventurers in arms,
When these two vessels with their daring freight,
For the Sicilian Tyrant's overthrow,   415
Sailed from Zacynthus, – philosophic war,
Led by Philosophers. With harder fate,
Though like ambition, such was he, O Friend!
Of whom I speak. So Beaupuis (let the name
Stand near the worthiest of Antiquity)   420
Fashioned his life; and many a long discóurse,
With like persuasion honoured, we maintained:
He, on his part, accoutred for the worst.
He perished fighting, in supreme command,
Upon the borders of the unhappy Loire,   425
For liberty, against deluded men,
His fellow country-men; and yet most bless'd
In this, that he the fate of later times
Lived not to see, nor what we now behold,
Who have as ardent hearts as he had then.   430
   Along that very Loire, with festal mirth
Resounding at all hours, and innocent yet
Of civil slaughter, was our frequent walk;
Or in wide forests of continuous shade,
Lofty and over-arched, with open space   435
Beneath the trees, clear footing many a mile –
A solemn region. Oft amid those haunts,
From earnest dialogues I slipped in thought,
And let remembrance steal to other times,
When, o'er those interwoven roots, moss-clad,   440
And smooth as marble or a waveless sea,
Some Hermit, from his cell forth-strayed, might pace
In sylvan meditation undisturbed;
As on the pavement of a Gothic church
Walks a lone Monk, when service hath expired,   445
In peace and silence. But if e'er was heard, –
Heard, though unseen, – a devious traveller,
Retiring or approaching from afar
With speed and echoes loud of trampling hoofs
From the hard floor reverberated, then   450
It was Angelica thundering through the woods
Upon her palfrey, or that gentle maid
Erminia, fugitive as fair as she.

Sometimes methought I saw a pair of knights
Joust underneath the trees, that as in storm   455
Rocked high above their heads; anon, the din
Of boisterous merriment, and music's roar,
In sudden proclamation, burst from haunt
Of Satyrs in some viewless glade, with dance
Rejoicing o'er a female in the midst,   460
A mortal beauty, their unhappy thrall.
The width of those huge forests, unto me
A novel scene, did often in this way
Master my fancy while I wandered on
With that revered companion. And sometimes –   465
When to a convent in a meadow green,
By a brook-side, we came, a roofless pile,
And not by reverential touch of Time
Dismantled, but by violence abrupt –
In spite of those heart-bracing colloquies,   470
In spite of reäl fervour, and of that
Less genuine and wrought up within myself –
I could not but bewail a wrong so harsh,
And for the Matin-bell to sound no more
Grieved, and the twilight taper, and the cross   475
High on the topmost pinnacle, a sign
(How welcome to the weary traveller's eyes!)
Of hospitality and peaceful rest.
And when the partner of those varied walks
Pointed upon occasion to the site   480
Of Romorentin, home of ancient kings,
To the imperial edifice of Blois,
Or to that rural castle, name now slipped
From my remembrance, where a lady lodged,
By the first Francis wooed, and bound to him   485
In chains of mutual passion, from the tower,
As a tradition of the country tells,
Practised to commune with her royal knight
By cressets and love-beacons, intercourse
'Twixt her high-seated residence and his   490
Far off at Chambord on the plain beneath;
Even here, though less than with the peaceful house
Religious, 'mid those frequent monuments
Of Kings, their vices and their better deeds,
Imagination, potent to inflame   495
At times with virtuous wrath and noble scorn,
Did also often mitigate the force
Of civic prejudice, the bigotry,
So call it, of a youthful patriot's mind;
And on these spots with many gleams I looked   500
Of chivalrous delight. Yet not the less,
Hatred of absolute rule, where will of one
Is law for all, and of that barren pride
In them who, by immunities unjust,
Between the sovereign and the people stand,   505
His helper and not theirs, laid stronger hold
Daily upon me, mixed with pity too
And love; for where hope is, there love will be

408 **Attic:** Greek 408–416 Wordsworth recalls Plutarch's *Life of Dion.*
Dion liberated Sicily from the rule of his nephew Dionysius in
357 BC 451–453 **Angelica . . . Erminia:** characters in Ariosto's *Orlando
Furioso*

474 **Matin-bell:** morning bell 475 **twilight taper:** candle 481 **Romorentin:**
town in the Loire region 485 **Francis:** Francis I (1514–1557)

For the abject multitude. And when we chanced
One day to meet a hunger-bitten girl, 510
Who crept along fitting her languid gait
Unto a heifer's motion, by a cord
Tied to her arm, and picking thus from the lane
Its sustenance, while the girl with pallid hands
Was busy knitting in a heartless mood 515
Of solitude, and at the sight my friend
In agitation said, ' 'Tis against *that*
That we are fighting,' I with him believed
That a benignant spirit was abroad
Which might not be withstood, that poverty 520
Abject as this would in a little time
Be found no more, that we should see the earth
Unthwarted in her wish to recompense
The meek, the lowly, patient child of toil.
All institutes for ever blotted out 525
That legalised exclusion, empty pomp
Abolished, sensual state and cruel power,
Whether by edict of the one or few;
And finally, as sum and crown of all,
Should see the people having a strong hand 530
In framing their own laws; whence better days
To all mankind. But, these things set apart,
Was not this single confidence enough
To animate the mind that ever turned
A thought to human welfare? That henceforth 535
Captivity by mandate without law
Should cease; and open accusation lead
To sentence in the hearing of the world,
And open punishment, if not the air
Be free to breathe in, and the heart of man 540
Dread nothing. From this height I shall not stoop
To humbler matter that detained us oft
In thought or conversation, public acts,
And public persons, and emotions wrought
Within the breast, as ever-varying winds 545
Of record or report swept over us;
But I might here, instead, repeat a tale,
Told by my Patriot friend, of sad events,
That prove to what low depth had struck the roots,
How widely spread the boughs, of that old tree 550
Which, as a deadly mischief, and a foul
And black dishonour, France was weary of.

Oh, happy time of youthful lovers (thus
The story might begin). Oh, balmy time,
In which a love-knot, on a lady's brow, 555
Is fairer than the fairest star in Heaven!
So might – and with that prelude *did* begin
The record; and, in faithful verse, was given
The doleful sequel.
                                But our little bark
On a strong river boldly hath been launched; 560
And from the driving current should we turn

To loiter wilfully within a creek,
Howe'er attractive, Fellow-voyager!
Would'st thou not chide? Yet deem not my pains lost:
For Vaudracour and Julia (so were named 565
The ill-fated pair) in that plain tale will draw
Tears from the hearts of others, when their own
Shall beat no more. Thou, also, there mayst read,
At leisure, how the enamoured youth was driven,
By public power abased, to fatal crime, 570
Nature's rebellion against monstrous law;
How, between heart and heart, oppression thrust
Her mandates, severing whom true love had joined,
Harássing both; until he sank and pressed
The couch his fate had made for him; supíne, 575
Save when the stings of viperous remorse,
Trying their strength, enforced him to start up,
Aghast and prayerless. Into a deep wood
He fled, to shun the haunts of human kind;
There dwelt, weakened in spirit more and more; 580
Nor could the voice of Freedom, which through
        France
Full speedily resounded, public hope,
Or personal memory of his own worst wrongs,
Rouse him; but, hidden in those gloomy shades,
His days he wasted, – an imbecile mind. 585

BOOK TENTH. RESIDENCE IN FRANCE
– CONTINUED

It was a beautiful and silent day
That overspread the countenance of earth,
Then fading with unusual quietness, –
A day as beautiful as e'er was given
To soothe regret, though deepening what it soothed, 5
When by the gliding Loire I paused, and cast
Upon his rich domains, vineyard and tilth,
Green meadow-ground, and many-coloured woods,
Again, and yet again, a farewell look;
Then from the quiet of that scene passed on, 10
Bound to the fierce Metropolis. From his throne
The King had fallen, and that invading host –
Presumptuous cloud, on whose black front was written
The tender mercies of the dismal wind
That bore it – on the plains of Liberty 15
Had burst innocuous. Say in bolder words,
They – who had come elate as eastern hunters
Banded beneath the Great Mogul, when he
Erewhile went forth from Agra and Lahore,
Rajahs and Omrahs in his train, intent 20
To drive their prey enclosed within a ring
Wide as a province, but, the signal given,
Before the point of the life-threatening spear
Narrowing itself by moments – they, rash men,
Had seen the anticipated quarry turned 25

---

559 Wordsworth refers to his poem *Vaudracour and Julia*, published in 1820

BOOK TENTH. RESIDENCE IN FRANCE – CONTINUED: 7 **tilth:** ploughed land 12 **The King had fallen:** Louis XVI was deposed on 9 August 1792 20 **Omrahs:** grandees of the Mogul's court

Into avengers, from whose wrath they fled
In terror. Disappointment and dismay
Remained for all whose fancies had run wild
With evil expectations; confidence
And perfect triumph for the better cause.   30

    The State, as if to stamp the final seal
On her security, and to the world
Show what she was, a high and fearless soul,
Exulting in defiance, or heart-stung
By sharp resentment, or belike to taunt   35
With spiteful gratitude the baffled League,
That had stirred up her slackening faculties
To a new transition, when the King was crushed,
Spared not the empty throne, and in proud haste
Assumed the body and venerable name   40
Of a Republic. Lamentable crimes,
'Tis true, had gone before this hour, dire work
Of massacre, in which the senseless sword
Was prayed to as a judge; but these were past,
Earth free from them for ever, as was thought, –   45
Ephemeral monsters, to be seen but once!
Things that could only show themselves and die.

    Cheered with this hope, to Paris I returned,
And ranged, with ardour heretofore unfelt,
The spacious city, and in progress passed   50
The prison where the unhappy Monarch lay,
Associate with his children and his wife
In bondage; and the palace, lately stormed
With roar of cannon by a furious host.
I crossed the square (an empty area then!)   55
Of the Carrousel, where so late had lain
The dead, upon the dying heaped, and gazed
On this and other spots, as doth a man
Upon a volume whose conténts he knows
Are memorable, but from him locked up,   60
Being written in a tongue he cannot read,
So that he questions the mute leaves with pain,
And half upbraids their silence. But that night
I felt most deeply in what world I was,
What ground I trod on, and what air I breathed.   65
High was my room and lonely, near the roof
Of a large mansion or hotel, a lodge
That would have pleased me in more quiet times;
Nor was it wholly without pleasure then.
With unextinguished taper I kept watch,   70
Reading at intervals; the fear gone by
Pressed on me almost like a fear to come.
I thought of those September massacres,
Divided from me by one little month,
Saw them and touched: the rest was conjured up   75
From tragic fictions or true history,
Remembrances and dim admonishments.
The horse is taught his manage, and no star
Of wildest course but treads back his own steps;
For the spent hurricane the air provides   80

As fierce a successor; the tide retreats
But to return out of its hiding-place
In the great deep; all things have second birth;
The earthquake is not satisfied at once;
And in this way I wrought upon myself,   85
Until I seemed to hear a voice that cried,
To the whole city, 'Sleep no more.' The trance
Fled with the voice to which it had given birth;
But vainly comments of a calmer mind
Promised soft peace and sweet forgetfulness.   90
The place, all hushed and silent as it was,
Appeared unfit for the repose of night,
Defenceless as a wood where tigers roam.

    With early morning towards the Palace-walk
Of Orleans eagerly I turned; as yet   95
The streets were still; not so those long Arcades;
There, 'mid a peal of ill-matched sounds and cries,
That greeted me on entering, I could hear
Shrill voices from the hawkers in the throng,
Bawling, 'Denunciation of the Crimes   100
Of Maximilian Robespierre'; the hand,
Prompt as the voice, held forth a printed speech,
The same that had been recently pronounced,
When Robespierre, not ignorant for what mark
Some words of indirect reproof had been   105
Intended, rose in hardihood, and dared
The man who had an ill surmise of him
To bring his charge in openness; whereat,
When a dead pause ensued, and no one stirred,
In silence of all present, from his seat   110
Louvet walked single through the avenue,
And took his station in the Tribune, saying,
'I, Robespierre, accuse thee!' Well is known
The inglorious issue of that charge, and how
He, who had launched the startling thunderbolt,   115
The one bold man, whose voice the attack had
          sounded,
Was left without a follower to discharge
His perilous duty, and retire lamenting
That Heaven's best aid is wasted upon men
Who to themselves are false.
                    But these are things   120
Of which I speak, only as they were storm
Or sunshine to my individual mind,
No further. Let me then relate that now –
In some sort seeing with my proper eyes
That Liberty, and Life, and Death would soon   125
To the remotest corners of the land
Lie in the arbitrement of those who ruled
The capital City; what was struggled for,
And by what combatants victory must be won;
The indecision on their part whose aim   130
Seemed best, and the straightforward path of those
Who in attack or in defence were strong
Through their impiety – my inmost soul

---

43 **massacre:** the September massacres in 1792, when half of the
prisoners in Paris were executed after only a summary trial

124 **proper:** own

Was agitated; yea, I could almost
Have prayed that throughout earth upon all men,   135
By patient exercise of reason made
Worthy of liberty, all spirits filled
With zeal expanding in Truth's holy light,
The gift of tongues might fall, and power arrive   140
From the four quarters of the winds to do
For France, what without help she could not do,
A work of honour; think not that to this
I added, work of safety: from all doubt
Or trepidation for the end of things
Far was I, far as angels are from guilt.   145

    Yet did I grieve, nor only grieved, but thought
Of opposition and of remedies:
An insignificant stranger and obscure,
And one, moreover, little graced with power
Of eloquence even in my native speech,   150
And all unfit for tumult or intrigue,
Yet would I at this time with willing heart
Have undertaken for a cause so great
Service however dangerous. I revolved,
How much the destiny of Man had still   155
Hung upon single persons; that there was,
Transcendent to all local patrimony,
One nature, as there is one sun in heaven;
That objects, even as they are great, thereby
Do come within the reach of humblest eyes;   160
That man is only weak through his mistrust
And want of hope where evidence divine
Proclaims to him that hope should be most sure;
Nor did the inexperience of my youth
Preclude conviction, that a spirit strong   165
In hope, and trained to noble aspirations,
A spirit throughly faithful to itself,
Is for Society's unreasoning herd
A domineering instinct, serves at once
For way and guide, a fluent receptäcle   170
That gathers up each petty straggling rill
And vein of water, glad to be rolled on
In safe obedience; that a mind, whose rest
Is where it ought to be, in self-restraint,
In circumspection and simplicity,   175
Falls rarely in entire discomfiture
Below its aim, or meets with, from without,
A treachery that foils it or defeats;
And, lastly, if the means on human will,
Frail human will, dependent should betray   180
Him who too boldly trusted them, I felt
That 'mid the loud distractions of the world
A sovereign voice subsists within the soul,
Arbiter undisturbed of right and wrong,
Of life and death, in majesty severe   185
Enjoining, as may best promote the aims
Of truth and justice, either sacrifice,
From whatsoever region of our cares
Or our infirm affections Nature pleads,
Earnest and blind, against the stern decree.   190

    On the other side, I called to mind those truths
That are the common-places of the schools –
(A theme for boys, too hackneyed for their sires),
Yet, with a revelation's liveliness,
In all their comprehensive bearings known   195
And visible to philosophers of old,
Men who, to business of the world untrained,
Lived in the shade; and to Harmodius known
And his compeer Aristogiton, known
To Brutus – that tyrannic power is weak,   200
Hath neither gratitude, nor faith, nor love,
Nor the support of good or evil men
To trust in; that the godhead which is ours
Can never utterly be charmed or stilled;
That nothing hath a natural right to last   205
But equity and reason; that all else
Meets foes irreconcilable, and at best
Lives only by variety of disease.

    Well might my wishes be intense, my thoughts
Strong and perturbed, not doubting at that time   210
But that the virtue of one paramount mind
Would have abashed those impious crests – have
       quelled
Outrage and bloody power, and, in despite
Of what the People long had been and were
Through ignorance and false teaching, sadder proof
Of immaturity, and in the teeth   215
Of desperate opposition from without –
Have cleared a passage for just government,
And left a solid birthright to the State,
Redeemed, according to example given   220
By ancient lawgivers.
                          In this frame of mind,
Dragged by a chain of harsh necessity,
So seemed it, – now I thankfully acknowledge,
Forced by the gracious providence of Heaven, –
To England I returned, else (though assured   225
That I both was and must be of small weight,
No better than a landsman on the deck
Of a ship struggling with a hideous storm)
Doubtless, I should have then made common cause
With some who perished; haply perished too,   230
A poor mistaken and bewildered offering, –
Should to the breast of Nature have gone back,
With all my resolutions, all my hopes,
A Poet only to myself, to men
Useless, and even, belovèd Friend! a soul   235
To thee unknown!
                          Twice had the trees let fall
Their leaves, as often Winter had put on
His hoary crown, since I had seen the surge
Beat against Albion's shore, since ear of mine
Had caught the accents of my native speech   240

197-200 all are associated with regicide: Harmodius and Aristogiton
attempted to kill the Athenian tyrant Hippias. Brutus, with others,
assassinated the Roman dictator Julius Caesar

Upon our native country's sacred ground.
A patriot of the world, how could I glide
Into communion with her sylvan shades,
Erewhile my tuneful haunt? It pleased me more
To abide in the great City, where I found   245
The general air still busy with the stir
Of that first memorable onset made
By a strong levy of humanity
Upon the traffickers in Negro blood;
Effort which, though defeated, had recalled   250
To notice old forgotten principles,
And through the nation spread a novel heat
Of virtuous feeling. For myself, I own
That this particular strife had wanted power
To rivet my affections; nor did now   255
Its unsuccessful issue much excite
My sorrow; for I brought with me the faith
That, if France prospered, good men would not long
Pay fruitless worship to humanity,
And this most rotten branch of human shame,   260
Object, so seemed it, of superfluous pains,
Would fall together with its parent tree.
What, then, were my emotions, when in arms
Britain put forth her free-born strength in league,
Oh, pity and shame! with those confederate Powers!
Not in my single self alone I found,   266
But in the minds of all ingenuous youth,
Change and subversion from that hour. No shock
Given to my moral nature had I known
Down to that very moment; neither lapse   270
Nor turn of sentiment that might be named
A revolution, save at this one time;
All else was progress on the self-same path
On which, with a diversity of pace,
I had been travelling: this a stride at once   275
Into another region. As a light
And pliant harebell, swinging in the breeze
On some grey rock – its birth-place – so had I
Wantoned, fast rooted on the ancient tower
Of my belovèd country, wishing not   280
A happier fortune than to wither there:
Now was I from that pleasant station torn
And tossed about in whirlwind. I rejoiced,
Yea, afterwards – truth most painful to record! –
Exulted, in the triumph of my soul,   285
When Englishmen by thousands were o'erthrown,
Left without glory on the field, or driven,
Brave hearts! to shameful flight. It was a grief, –
Grief call it not, 'twas anything but that, –
A conflict of sensations without name,   290
Of which *he* only, who may love the sight
Of a village steeple, as I do, can judge,

When, in the congregation bending all
To their great Father, prayers were offered up,
Or praises for our country's victories;   295
And, 'mid the simple worshippers, perchance
I only, like an uninvited guest
Whom no one owned, sate silent, shall I add,
Fed on the day of vengeance yet to come?
   Oh! much have they to account for, who could tear,
By violence, at one decisive rent,   301
From the best youth in England their dear pride,
Their joy, in England; this, too, at a time
In which worst losses easily might wear
The best of names, when patriotic love   305
Did of itself in modesty give way,
Like the Precursor when the Deity
Is come Whose harbinger he was; a time
In which apostasy from ancient faith
Seemed but conversion to a higher creed;   310
Withal a season dangerous and wild,
A time when sage Experience would have snatched
Flowers out of any hedge-row to compose
A chaplet in contempt of his grey locks.
   When the proud fleet that bears the red-cross flag
In that unworthy service was prepared   316
To mingle, I beheld the vessels lie,
A brood of gallant creatures, on the deep;
I saw them in their rest, a sojourner
Through a whole month of calm and glassy days   320
In that delightful island which protects
Their place of convocation – there I heard,
Each evening, pacing by the still sea-shore,
A monitory sound that never failed, –
The sunset cannon. While the orb went down   325
In the tranquillity of nature, came
That voice, ill requiem! seldom heard by me
Without a spirit overcast by dark
Imaginations, sense of woes to come,
Sorrow for human kind, and pain of heart.   330
   In France, the men, who, for their desperate ends,
Had plucked up mercy by the roots, were glad
Of this new enemy. Tyrants, strong before
In wicked pleas, were strong as demons now;
And thus, on every side beset with foes,   335
The goaded land waxed mad; the crimes of few
Spread into madness of the many; blasts
From hell came sanctified like airs from heaven.
The sternness of the just, the faith of those
Who doubted not that Providence had times   340
Of vengeful retribution, theirs who throned
The human Understanding paramount
And made of that their God, the hopes of men
Who were content to barter short-lived pangs
For a paradise of ages, the blind rage   345

---

249 **traffickers in Negro blood:** a bill to end the slave trade had been passed and then rejected. It was not until 1807 that trading in slaves finally became illegal 265 **confederate Powers:** From 1793 until 1815 (with the exception of one year between 1802 and 1803) France was at war with a coalition of European powers led by Britain

315 **red-cross flag:** the flag of St. George 340–364 Wordsworth describes the Robespierre's murderous 'Reign of Terror' that lasted from 1793 to 1794

Of insolent tempers, the light vanity
Of intermeddlers, steady purposes
Of the suspicious, slips of the indiscreet,
And all the accidents of life were pressed
Into one service, busy with one work.   350
The Senate stood aghast, her prudence quenched,
Her wisdom stifled, and her justice scared,
Her frenzy only active to extol
Past outrages, and shape the way for new,
Which no one dared to oppose or mitigate.   355
   Domestic carnage now filled the whole year
With feast-days; old men from the chimney-nook,
The maiden from the bosom of her love,
The mother from the cradle of her babe,
The warrior from the field – all perished, all –   360
Friends, enemies, of all parties, ages, ranks,
Head after head, and never heads enough
For those that bade them fall. They found their joy,
They made it, proudly eager as a child
(If light desires of innocent little ones   365
May with such heinous appetites be compared),
Pleased in some open field to exercise
A toy that mimics with revolving wings
The motion of a wind-mill; though the air
Do of itself blow fresh, and make the vanes   370
Spin in his eyesight, *that* contents him not,
But, with the plaything at arm's length, he sets
His front against the blast, and runs amain,
That it may whirl the faster.
               Amid the depth
Of those enormities, even thinking minds   375
Forgot, at seasons, whence they had their being;
Forgot that such a sound was ever heard
As Liberty upon earth: yet all beneath
Her innocent authority was wrought,
Nor could have been, without her blessèd name.   380
The illustrious wife of Roland, in the hour
Of her composure, felt that agony,
And gave it vent in her last words. O Friend!
It was a lamentable time for man,
Whether a hope had e'er been his or not;   385
A woeful time for them whose hopes survived
The shock; most woeful for those few who still
Were flattered, and had trust in human kind:
They had the deepest feeling of the grief.
Meanwhile the Invaders fared as they deserved: 390
The Herculean Commonwealth had put forth her
   arms,
And throttled with an infant godhead's might
The snakes about her cradle; that was well,

381–384 **wife of Roland . . . last words:** Madame Roland, a moderate
Girondist, who was guillotined in November 1793. Her last words
were 'Oh Liberty, what crimes are committed in thy name' 391–393
Hera, the wife of Zeus, sent two snakes to kill Hercules while he
was still only a baby in his cradle, but he thwarted her assassination
attempt by throttling them

And as it should be; yet no cure for them
Whose souls were sick with pain of what would be   395
Hereafter brought in charge against mankind.
Most melancholy at that time, O Friend!
Were my day-thoughts, – my nights were miserable;
Through months, through years, long after the last
   beat
Of those atrocities, the hour of sleep   400
To me came rarely charged with natural gifts,
Such ghastly visions had I of despair
And tyranny, and implements of death;
And innocent victims sinking under fear,
And momentary hope, and worn-out prayer,   405
Each in his separate cell, or penned in crowds
For sacrifice, and struggling with fond mirth
And levity in dungeons, where the dust
Was laid with tears. Then suddenly the scene
Changed, and the unbroken dream entangled me   410
In long orations, which I strove to plead
Before unjust tribunals, – with a voice
Labouring, a brain confounded, and a sense,
Death-like, of treacherous desertion, felt
In the last place of refuge – my own soul.   415
   When I began in youth's delightful prime
To yield myself to Nature, when that strong
And holy passion overcame me first,
Nor day nor night, evening or morn, was free
From its oppression. But, O Power Supreme!   420
Without Whose call this world would cease to breathe,
Who from the fountain of Thy grace dost fill
The veins that branch through every frame of life,
Making man what he is, creature divine,
In single or in social eminence,   425
Above the rest raised infinite ascents
When reason that enables him to be
Is not sequestered – what a change is here!
How different ritual for this after-worship,
What countenance to promote this second love!   430
The first was service paid to things which lie
Guarded within the bosom of Thy will.
Therefore to serve was high beatitude;
Tumult was therefore gladness, and the fear
Ennobling, venerable; sleep secure,   435
And waking thoughts more rich than happiest dreams.
   But as the ancient Prophets, borne aloft
In vision, yet constrained by natural laws
With them to take a troubled human heart,
Wanted not consolations, nor a creed   440
Of reconcilement, then when they denounced,
On towns and cities, wallowing in the abyss
Of their offences, punishment is come;
Or saw, like other men, with bodily eyes,
Before them, in some desolated place,   445
The wrath consúmmate and the threat fulfilled;
So, with devout humility be it said,
So, did a portion of that spirit fall
On me uplifted from the vantage-ground

Of pity and sorrow to a state of being 450
That through the time's exceeding fierceness saw
Glimpses of retribution, terrible,
And in the order of sublime behests:
But, even if that were not, amid the awe
Of unintelligible chástisement, 455
Not only acquiescences of faith
Survived, but daring sympathies with power,
Motions not treacherous or profane, else why
Within the folds of no ungentle breast
Their dread vibration to this hour prolonged? 460
Wild blasts of music thus could find their way
Into the midst of turbulent events;
So that worst tempests might be listened to.
Then was the truth received into my heart,
That, under heaviest sorrow earth can bring, 465
If from the affliction somewhere do not grow
Honour which could not else have been, a faith,
An elevation and a sanctity,
If new strength be not given nor old restored,
The blame is ours, not Nature's. When a taunt 470
Was taken up by scoffers in their pride,
Saying, 'Behold the harvest that we reap
From popular government and equality,'
I clearly saw that neither these nor aught
Of wild belief engrafted on their names 475
By false philosophy had caused the woe,
But a terrific reservoir of guilt
And ignorance filled up from age to age,
That could no longer hold its loathsome charge,
But burst and spread in deluge through the land. 480
    And as the desert hath green spots, the sea
Small islands scattered amid stormy waves,
So *that* disastrous period did not want
Bright sprinklings of all human excellence,
To which the silver wands of saints in Heaven 485
Might point with rapturous joy. Yet not the less,
For those examples in no age surpassed
Of fortitude and energy and love,
And human nature faithful to herself
Under worst trials, was I driven to think 490
Of the glad times when first I tráversed France
A youthful pilgrim; above all reviewed
That eventide, when under windows bright
With happy faces and with garlands hung,
And through a rainbow-arch that spanned the street,
Triumphal pomp for liberty confirmed, 496
I paced, a dear companion at my side,
The town of Arras, whence with promise high
Issued, on delegation to sustain
Humanity and right, *that* Robespierre, 500
He who thereafter, and in how short time!
Wielded the sceptre of the Atheist crew.
When the calamity spread far and wide –
And this same city, that did then appear
To outrun the rest in exultation, groaned 505
Under the vengeance of her cruel son,

As Lear reproached the winds – I could almost
Have quarrelled with that blameless spectacle
For lingering yet an image in my mind
To mock me under such a strange reverse. 510
    O Friend! few happier moments have been mine
Than that which told the downfall of this Tribe
So dreaded, so abhorred. The day deserves
A separate record. Over the smooth sands
Of Leven's ample estuary lay 515
My journey, and beneath a genial sun,
With distant prospect among gleams of sky
And clouds, and intermingling mountain tops,
In one inseparable glory clad,
Creatures of one ethereal substance met 520
In consistory, like a diadem
Or crown of burning seraphs as they sit
In the empyrean. Underneath that pomp
Celestial, lay unseen the pastoral vales
Among whose happy fields I had grown up 525
From childhood. On the fulgent spectacle,
That neither passed away nor changed, I gazed
Enrapt; but brightest things are wont to draw
Sad opposites out of the inner heart,
As even their pensive influence drew from mine. 530
How could it otherwise? for not in vain
That very morning had I turned aside
To seek the ground where, 'mid a throng of graves,
An honoured teacher of my youth was laid,
And on the stone were graven by his desire 535
Lines from the churchyard elegy of Gray.
This faithful guide, speaking from his death-bed,
Added no farewell to his parting counsel,
But said to me, 'My head will soon lie low';
And when I saw the turf that covered him, 540
After the lapse of full eight years, those words,
With sound of voice and countenance of the Man,
Came back upon me, so that some few tears
Fell from me in my own despite. But now
I thought, still tráversing that widespread plain, 545
With tender pleasure of the verses graven
Upon his tombstone, whispering to myself:
He loved the Poets, and, if now alive,
Would have loved me, as one not destitute
Of promise, nor belying the kind hope 550
That he had formed, when I, at his command,
Began to spin, with toil, my earliest songs.
    As I advanced, all that I saw or felt
Was gentleness and peace. Upon a small
And rocky island near, a fragment stood 555
(Itself like a sea rock) the low remains
(With shells encrusted, dark with briny weeds)
Of a dilapidated structure, once
A Romish chapel, where the vested priest

---

507 **Lear:** in Shakespeare's *King Lear*, Lear rails against even the winds (III, ii) 526 **fulgent:** brilliant 534 **honoured teacher:** Reverend William Taylor (1754–1786) 536 **Gray:** Thomas Gray, author of *Elegy Written in a Country Churchyard*

Said matins at the hour that suited those 560
Who crossed the sands with ebb of morning tide.
Not far from that still ruin all the plain
Lay spotted with a variegated crowd
Of vehicles and travellers, horse and foot,
Wading beneath the conduct of their guide 565
In loose procession through the shallow stream
Of inland waters; the great sea meanwhile
Heaved at safe distance, far retired. I paused,
Longing for skill to paint a scene so bright
And cheerful, but the foremost of the band 570
As he approached, no salutation given
In the familiar language of the day,
Cried, 'Robespierre is dead!' – nor was a doubt,
After strict question, left within my mind
That he and his supporters all were fallen. 575
    Great was my transport, deep my gratitude
To everlasting Justice, by this fiat
Made manifest. 'Come now, ye golden times,'
Said I forth-pouring on those open sands
A hymn of triumph: 'as the morning comes 580
From out the bosom of the night, come ye:
Thus far our trust is verified; behold!
They who with clumsy desperation brought
A river of Blood, and preached that nothing else
Could cleanse the Augean stable, by the might 585
Of their own helper have been swept away;
Their madness stands declared and visible;
Elsewhere will safety now be sought, and earth
March firmly towards righteousness and peace.' –
Then schemes I framed more calmly, when and how
The madding factions might be tranquillised, 591
And how through hardships manifold and long
The glorious renovation would proceed.
Thus interrupted by uneasy bursts
Of exultation, I pursued my way 595
Along that very shore which I had skimmed
In former days, when – spurring from the Vale
Of Nightshade, and St Mary's mouldering fane,
And the stone abbot, after circuit made
In wantonness of heart, a joyous band 600
Of school-boys hastening to their distant home
Along the margin of the moonlight sea –
We beat with thundering hoofs the level sand.

BOOK ELEVENTH. FRANCE – CONCLUDED
FROM that time forth, Authority in France
Put on a milder face; Terror had ceased,
Yet every thing was wanting that might give
Courage to them who looked for good by light
Of rational Experience, for the shoots 5

And hopeful blossoms of a second spring:
Yet, in me, confidence was unimpaired;
The Senate's language, and the public acts
And measures of the Government, though both
Weak, and of heartless omen, had not power 10
To daunt me; in the People was my trust,
And in the virtues which mine eyes had seen.
I knew that wound external could not take
Life from the young Republic; that new foes
Would only follow, in the path of shame, 15
Their brethren, and her triumphs be in the end
Great, universal, irresistible.
This intuition led me to confound
One victory with another, higher far, –
Triumphs of unambitious peace at home, 20
And noiseless fortitude. Beholding still
Resistance strong as heretofore, I thought
That what was in degree the same was likewise
The same in quality, – that, as the worse
Of the two spirits then at strife remained 25
Untired, the better, surely, would preserve
The heart that first had roused him. Youth maintains,
In all conditions of society,
Communion more direct and intimate
With Nature, – hence, ofttimes, with reason too – 30
Than age or manhood, even. To Nature, then,
Power had reverted: habit, custom, law,
Had left an interregnum's open space
For *her* to move about in, uncontrolled.
Hence could I see how Babel-like their task, 35
Who, by the recent deluge stupefied,
With their whole souls went culling from the day
Its petty promises, to build a tower
For their own safety; laughed with my compeers
At gravest heads, by enmity to France 40
Distempered, till they found, in every blast
Forced from the street-disturbing newsman's horn,
For her great cause recórd or prophecy
Of utter ruin. How might we believe
That wisdom could, in any shape, come near 45
Men clinging to delusions so insane?
And thus, experience proving that no few
Of our opinions had been just, we took
Like credit to ourselves where less was due,
And thought that other notions were as sound, 50
Yea, could not but be right, because we saw
That foolish men opposed them.
                                    To a strain
More animated I might here give way,
And tell, since juvenile errors are my theme,
What in those days, through Britain, was performed
To turn *all* judgements out of their right course; 56
But this is passion over-near ourselves,
Reality too close and too intense,
And intermixed with something, in my mind,

573 **Robespierre is dead:** Robespierre was guillotined on 28 July 1794
585 **cleanse the Augean stable:** one of the labours of Hercules was to
clean the stables of king Augeas; he did this by diverting two rivers
BOOK ELEVENTH. FRANCE – CONCLUDED: 1–2 the Terror ceased in
August 1794 after the execution of Robespierre and his associates

35 **Babel:** the Biblical tower of Babel (Genesis 9)

Of scorn and condemnation personal, 60
That would profane the sanctity of verse.
Our Shepherds, this say merely, at that time
Acted, or seemed at least to act, like men
Thirsting to make the guardian crook of law
A tool of murder; they who ruled the State, 65
Though with such awful proof before their eyes
That he, who would sow death, reaps death, or worse,
And can reap nothing better, child-like longed
To imitate, not wise enough to avoid;
Or left (by mere timidity betrayed) 70
The plain straight road, for one no better chosen
Than if their wish had been to undermine
Justice, and make an end of Liberty.

But from these bitter truths I must return
To my own history. It hath been told 75
That I was led to take an eager part
In arguments of civil polity,
Abruptly, and indeed before my time:
I had approached, like other youths, the shield
Of human nature from the golden side, 80
And would have fought, even to the death, to attest
The quality of the metal which I saw.
What there is best in individual man,
Of wise in passion, and sublime in power,
Benevolent in small societies, 85
And great in large ones, I had oft revolved,
Felt deeply, but not thoroughly understood
By reason: nay, far from it; they were yet,
As cause was given me afterwards to learn,
Not proof against the injuries of the day; 90
Lodged only at the sanctuary's door,
Not safe within its bosom. Thus prepared,
And with such general insight into evil,
And of the bounds which sever it from good,
As books and common intercourse with life 95
Must needs have given – to the inexperienced mind,
When the world travels in a beaten road,
Guide faithful as is needed – I began
To meditate with ardour on the rule
And management of nations; what it is 100
And ought to be; and strove to learn how far
Their power or weakness, wealth or poverty,
Their happiness or misery, depend
Upon their laws, and fashion of the State.

Oh, pleasant exercise of hope and joy! 105
For mighty were the auxiliars which then stood
Upon our side, us who were strong in love!
Bliss was it in that dawn to be alive,
But to be young was very Heaven! O times,
In which the meagre, stale, forbidding ways 110
Of custom, law, and statute, took at once
The attraction of a country in romance!
When Reason seemed the most to assert her rights
When most intent on making of herself

A prime enchantress to assist the work, 115
Which then was going forward in her name!
Not favoured spots alone, but the whole Earth,
The beauty wore of promise – that which sets
(As at some moments might not be unfelt
Among the bowers of Paradise itself) 120
The budding rose above the rose full blown.
What temper at the prospect did not wake
To happiness unthought of? The inert
Were roused, and lively natures rapt away!
They who had fed their childhood upon dreams, 125
The play-fellows of fancy, who had made
All powers of swiftness, subtlety, and strength
Their ministers, – who in lordly wise had stirred
Among the grandest objects of the sense,
And dealt with whatsoever they found there 130
As if they had within some lurking right
To wield it; – they, too, who of gentle mood
Had watched all gentle motions, and to these
Had fitted their own thoughts, schemers more mild,
And in the region of their peaceful selves; – 135
Now was it that *both* found, the meek and lofty
Did both find, helpers to their hearts' desire,
And stuff at hand, plastic as they could wish, –
Were called upon to exercise their skill,
Not in Utopia, – subterranean fields, – 140
Or some secreted island, Heaven knows where!
But in the very world, which is the world
Of all of us, – the place where, in the end,
We find our happiness, or not at all!

Why should I not confess that Earth was then 145
To me, what an inheritance, new-fallen,
Seems, when the first time visited, to one
Who thither comes to find in it his home?
He walks about and looks upon the spot
With cordial transport, moulds it and remoulds, 150
And is half pleased with things that are amiss,
'Twill be such joy to see them disappear.

An active partisan, I thus convoked
From every object pleasant circumstance
To suit my ends; I moved among mankind 155
With genial feelings still predominant;
When erring, erring on the better part,
And in the kinder spirit; placable,
Indulgent, as not uninformed that men
See as they have been taught – Antiquity 160
Gives right to error; and aware, no less,
That throwing off oppression must be work
As well of License as of Liberty;
And above all – for this was more than all –
Not caring if the wind did now and then 165
Blow keen upon an eminence that gave
Prospect so large into futurity;
In brief, a child of Nature, as at first,
Diffusing only those affections wider

---

106 **auxiliars**: helpers

124 **rapt away**: enraptured   138 **plastic**: malleable   153 **convoked**: summoned

That from the cradle had grown up with me,   170
And losing, in no other way than light
Is lost in light, the weak in the more strong.
   In the main outline, such it might be said
Was my condition, till with open war
Britain opposed the liberties of France.   175
This threw me first out of the pale of love;
Soured and corrupted, upwards to the source,
My sentiments; was not, as hitherto,
A swallowing up of lesser things in great,
But change of them into their contraries;   180
And thus a way was opened for mistakes
And false conclusions, in degree as gross,
In kind more dangerous. What had been a pride,
Was now a shame; my likings and my loves
Ran in new channels, leaving old ones dry;   185
And hence a blow that, in maturer age,
Would but have touched the judgement, struck more
     deep
Into sensations near the heart: meantime,
As from the first, wild theories were afloat,
To whose pretensions, sedulously urged,   190
I had but lent a careless ear, assured
That time was ready to set all things right,
And that the multitude, so long oppressed,
Would be oppressed no more.
                 But when events
Brought less encouragement, and unto these   195
The immediate proof of principles no more
Could be entrusted, while the events themselves,
Worn out in greatness, stripped of novelty,
Less occupied the mind, and sentiments   199
Could through my understanding's natural growth
No longer keep their ground, by faith maintained
Of inward consciousness, and hope that laid
Her hand upon her object – evidence
Safer, of universal application, such
As could not be impeached, was sought elsewhere.
   But now, become oppressors in their turn,   206
Frenchmen had changed a war of self-defence
For one of conquest, losing sight of all
Which they had struggled for: now mounted up,
Openly in the eye of earth and heaven,   210
The scale of liberty. I read her doom,
With anger vexed, with disappointment sore,
But not dismayed, nor taking to the shame
Of a false prophet. While resentment rose
Striving to hide, what nought could heal, the wounds
Of mortified presumption, I adhered   216
More firmly to old tenets, and, to prove
Their temper, strained them more; and thus, in heat
Of contest, did opinions every day
Grow into consequence, till round my mind   220
They clung, as if they were its life, nay more,
The very being of the immortal soul.
   This was the time, when, all things tending fast
To depravation, speculative schemes –

That promised to abstract the hopes of Man   225
Out of his feelings, to be fixed thenceforth
For ever in a purer element –
Found ready welcome. Tempting region *that*
For Zeal to enter and refresh herself,
Where passions had the privilege to work,   230
And never hear the sound of their own names.
But, speaking more in charity, the dream
Flattered the young, pleased with extremes, nor least
With that which makes our Reason's naked self
The object of its fervour. What delight!   235
How glorious! in self-knowledge and self-rule,
To look through all the frailties of the world,
And, with a resolute mastery shaking off
Infirmities of nature, time, and place,
Build social upon personal Liberty,   240
Which, to the blind restraints of general laws
Superior, magisterially adopts
One guide, the light of circumstances, flashed
Upon an independent intellect.
Thus expectation rose again; thus hope,   245
From her first ground expelled, grew proud once
     more.
Oft, as my thoughts were turned to human kind,
I scorned indifference; but, inflamed with thirst
Of a secure intelligence, and sick
Of other longing, I pursued what seemed   250
A more exalted nature; wished that Man
Should start out of his earthly, worm-like state,
And spread abroad the wings of Liberty,
Lord of himself, in undisturbed delight –
A noble aspiration! *yet* I feel   255
(Sustained by worthier as by wiser thoughts)
The aspiration, nor shall ever cease
To feel it; – but return we to our course.
   Enough, 'tis true – could such a plea excuse
Those aberrations – had the clamorous friends   260
Of ancient Institutions said and done
To bring disgrace upon their very names;
Disgrace, of which, custom and written law,
And sundry moral sentiments as props
Or emanations of those institutes,   265
Too justly bore a part. A veil had been
Uplifted; why deceive ourselves? in sooth,
'Twas even so; and sorrow for the man
Who either had not eyes wherewith to see,
Or, seeing, had forgotten! A strong shock   270
Was given to old opinions; all men's minds
Had felt its power, and mine was both let loose,
Let loose and goaded. And what hath been
Already said of patriotic love,
Suffice it here to add, that, somewhat stern   275
In temperament, withal a happy man,
And therefore bold to look on painful things,
Free likewise of the world, and thence more bold,
I summoned my best skill, and toiled, intent
To anatomise the frame of social life,   280

Yea, the whole body of society
Searched to its heart. Share with me, Friend! the wish
That some dramatic tale, endued with shapes
Livelier, and flinging out less guarded words
Than suit the work we fashion, might set forth 285
What then I learned, or think I learned, of truth,
And the errors into which I fell, betrayed
By present objects, and by reasonings false
From their beginnings, inasmuch as drawn
Out of a heart that had been turned aside 290
From Nature's way by outward accidents,
And which was thus confounded, more and more
Misguided, and misguiding. So I fared,
Dragging all precepts, judgements, maxims, creeds,
Like culprits to the bar; calling the mind, 295
Suspiciously, to establish in plain day
Her titles and her honours; now believing,
Now disbelieving; endlessly perplexed
With impulse, motive, right and wrong, the ground
Of obligation, what the rule and whence 300
The sanction; till, demanding formal *proof,*
And seeking it in every thing, I lost
All feeling of conviction, and, in fine,
Sick, wearied out with contrarieties,
Yielded up moral questions in despair. 305
 This was the crisis of that strong disease,
This the soul's last and lowest ebb; I drooped,
Deeming our blessèd reason of least use
Where wanted most: 'The lordly attributes
Of will and choice,' I bitterly exclaimed, 310
'What are they but a mockery of a Being
Who hath in no concerns of his a test
Of good and evil; know not what to fear
Or hope for, what to covet or to shun;
And who, if those could be discerned, would yet 315
Be little profited, would see, and ask
Where is the obligation to enforce?
And, to acknowledged law rebellious, still,
As selfish passion urged, would act amiss;
The dupe of folly, or the slave of crime.' 320
 Depressed, bewildered thus, I did not walk
With scoffers, seeking light and gay revenge
From indiscriminate laughter, nor sate down
In reconcilement with an utter waste
Of intellect; such sloth I could not brook 325
(Too well I loved, in that my spring of life,
Pains-taking thoughts, and truth, their dear reward)
But turned to abstract science, and there sought
Work for the reasoning faculty enthroned
Where the disturbances of space and time – 330
Whether in matter's various properties
Inherent, or from human will and power
Derived – find no admission. Then it was –
Thanks to the bounteous Giver of all good! –
That the belovèd Sister in whose sight 335

Those days were passed, now speaking in a voice
Of sudden admonition – like a brook
That did but *cross* a lonely road, and now
Is seen, heard, felt, and caught at every turn,
Companion never lost through many a league – 340
Maintained for me a saving intercourse
With my true self; for, though bedimmed and changed
Much, as it seemed, I was no further changed
Than as a clouded and a waning moon:
She whispered still that brightness would return, 345
She, in the midst of all, preserved me still
A Poet, made me seek beneath that name,
And that alone, my office upon earth;
And, lastly, as hereafter will be shown,
If willing audience fail not, Nature's self, 350
By all varieties of human love
Assisted, led me back through opening day
To those sweet counsels between head and heart
Whence grew that genuine knowledge, fraught with
  peace,
Which, through the later sinkings of this cause, 355
Hath still upheld me, and upholds me now
In the catastrophe (for so they dream,
And nothing less), when, finally to close
And seal up all the gains of France, a Pope
Is summoned in, to crown an Emperor – 360
This last opprobrium, when we see a people,
That once looked up in faith, as if to Heaven
For manna, take a lesson from the dog
Returning to his vomit; when the sun
That rose in splendour, was alive, and moved 365
In exultation with a living pomp
Of clouds – his glory's natural retinue –
Hath dropped all functions by the gods bestowed,
And, turned into a gewgaw, a machine,
Sets like an Opera phantom.
                              Thus, O Friend! 370
Through times of honour and through times of shame
Descending, have I faithfully retraced
The perturbations of a youthful mind
Under a long-lived storm of great events –
A story destined for thy ear, who now, 375
Among the fallen of nations, dost abide
Where Etna, over hill and valley, casts
His shadow stretching towards Syracuse,
The city of Timoleon! Righteous Heaven!
How are the mighty próstrated! They first, 380
They first of all that breathe should have awaked
When the great voice was heard from out the tombs
Of ancient heroes. If I suffered grief
For ill-requited France, by many deemed
A trifler only in her proudest day; 385

303 **in fine:** in the end

358–369 Wordsworth feels that the ideals of the Revolution have finally been dashed with the crowning of Napoleon Buonaparte as emperor of France in December 1804 361 **opprobrium:** disgrace 369 **gewgaw:** toy 379 **Timoleon:** Timoleon drove Dionysius the Younger from Sicily in 343 BC

Have been distressed to think of what she once
Promised, now is; a far more sober cause
Thine eyes must see of sorrow in a land,
Though with the wreck of loftier years bestrewn,
To the reanimating influence lost   390
Of memory, to virtue lost and hope.
      But indignation works where hope is not,
And thou, O Friend! wilt be refreshed. There is
One great society alone on earth:
The noble Living and the noble Dead.   395
      Thine be such converse strong and sanative,
A ladder for thy spirit to reascend
To health and joy and pure contentedness;
To me the grief confined, that thou art gone
From this last spot of earth, where Freedom now   400
Stands single in her only sanctuary;
A lonely wanderer art gone, by pain
Compelled and sickness, at this latter day,
This sorrowful reverse for all mankind.
I feel for thee, must utter what I feel: 405
The sympathies erewhile in part discharged,
Gather afresh, and will have vent again:
My own delights do scarcely seem to me
My own delights; the lordly Alps themselves,
Those rosy peaks, from which the Morning looks   410
Abroad on many nations, are no more
For me that image of pure gladsomeness
Which they were wont to be. Through kindred scenes,
For purpose, at a time, how different!
Thou tak'st thy way, carrying the heart and soul   415
That Nature gives to Poets, now by thought
Matured, and in the summer of their strength.
Oh! wrap him in your shades, ye giant woods,
On Etna's side; and thou, O flowery field
Of Enna! is there not some nook of thine,   420
From the first play-time of the infant world
Kept sacred to restorative delight,
When from afar invoked by anxious love?
      Child of the mountains, among shepherds reared,
Ere yet familiar with the classic page,   425
I learnt to dream of Sicily; and lo,
The gloom, that, but a moment past, was deepened
At thy command, at her command gives way;
A pleasant promise, wafted from her shores,
Comes o'er my heart: in fancy I behold   430
Her seas yet smiling, her once happy vales;
Nor can my tongue give utterance to a name
Of note belonging to that honoured isle,
Philosopher or Bard, Empedocles,
Or Archimedes, pure abstracted soul!   435

That doth not yield a solace to my grief:
And, O Theocritus, so far have some
Prevailed among the powers of heaven and earth,
By their endowments, good or great, that they
Have had, as thou reportest, miracles   440
Wrought for them in old time; yea, not unmoved,
When thinking on my own belovèd friend,
I hear thee tell how bees with honey fed
Divine Comates, by his impious lord
Within a chest imprisoned; how they came   445
Laden from blooming grove or flowery field,
And fed him there, alive, month after month,
Because the goatherd, blessèd man! had lips
Wet with the Muses' nectar.
                                    Thus I soothe
The pensive moments by this calm fire-side,   450
And find a thousand bounteous images
To cheer the thoughts of those I love, and mine.
Our prayers have been accepted; thou wilt stand
On Etna's summit, above earth and sea,
Triumphant, winning from the invaded heavens   455
Thoughts without bound, magnificent designs,
Worthy of poets who attuned their harps
In wood or echoing cave, for discipline
Of heroes; or, in reverence to the gods,
'Mid temples, served by sapient priests, and choirs
Of virgins crowned with roses. Not in vain   461
Those temples, where they in their ruins yet
Survive for inspiration, shall attract
Thy solitary steps: and on the brink
Thou wilt recline of pastoral Arethuse;   465
Or, if that fountain be in truth no more,
Then, near some other spring, which, by the name
Thou gratulatest, willingly deceived,
I see thee linger a glad votary,
And not a captive pining for his home.   470

BOOK TWELFTH. IMAGINATION AND TASTE,
      HOW IMPAIRED AND RESTORED

LONG time have human ignorance and guilt
Detained us, on what spectacles of woe
Compelled to look, and inwardly oppressed
With sorrow, disappointment, vexing thoughts,
Confusion of the judgement, zeal decayed,   5
And, lastly, utter loss of hope itself
And things to hope for! Not with these began
Our song, and not with these our song must end. –
Ye motions of delight, that haunt the sides
Of the green hills; ye breezes and soft airs,   10
Whose subtle intercourse with breathing flowers,
Feelingly watched, might teach Man's haughty race
How without injury to take, to give
Without offence; ye who, as if to show
The wondrous influence of power gently used,   15

396 **sanative:** healing 399–400 between 1803 and 1804 Britain faced
Napoleonic France alone 420 **Enna:** town in Sicily that is said to
have been where Pluto carried off Persephone 434 **Empedocles:**
poet and philosopher (fl. 450 BC). Tradition relates that he threw
himself into the fires of Mount Etna 435 **Archimedes:** mathematician
and philosopher (fl. 300 BC)

437 **Theocritus:** Sicilian pastoral poet (fl. 300 BC) 444 **Comates:** his
story is told in Theocritus's *Idyl* 465 **Arethuse:** a famous fountain
in the island of Ortygia 469 **votary:** monk, religious devotee

Bend the complying heads of lordly pines,
And, with a touch, shift the stupendous clouds
Through the whole compass of the sky; ye brooks,
Muttering along the stones, a busy noise
By day, a quiet sound in silent night; 20
Ye waves, that out of the great deep steal forth
In a calm hour to kiss the pebbly shore,
Not mute, and then retire, fearing no storm;
And you, ye groves, whose ministry it is
To interpose the covert of your shades, 25
Even as a sleep, between the heart of man
And outward troubles, between man himself,
Not seldom, and his own uneasy heart:
Oh! that I had a music and a voice
Harmonious as your own, that I might tell 30
What ye have done for me. The morning shines,
Nor heedeth Man's perverseness; Spring returns, –
I saw the Spring return, and could rejoice,
In common with the children of her love,
Piping on boughs, or sporting on fresh fields, 35
Or boldly seeking pleasure nearer heaven
On wings that navigate cerulean skies.
So neither were complacency, nor peace,
Nor tender yearnings, wanting for my good
Through these distracted times; in Nature still 40
Glorying, I found a counterpoise in her,
Which, when the spirit of evil reached its height,
Maintained for me a secret happiness.
    This narrative, my Friend! hath chiefly told
Of intellectual power, fostering love, 45
Dispensing truth, and, over men and things,
Where reason yet might hesitate, diffusing
Prophetic sympathies of genial faith:
So was I favoured – such my happy lot –
Until that natural graciousness of mind 50
Gave way to overpressure from the times
And their disastrous issues. What availed,
When spells forbade the voyager to land,
That fragrant notice of a pleasant shore
Wafted, at intervals, from many a bower 55
Of blissful gratitude and fearless love?
Dare I avow that wish was mine to see,
And hope that future times *would* surely see,
The man to come, parted, as by a gulph,
From him who had been; that I could no more 60
Trust the elevation which had made me one
With the great family that still survives
To illuminate the abyss of ages past,
Sage, warrior, patriot, hero; for it seemed
That their best virtues were not free from taint 65
Of something false and weak, that could not stand
The open eye of Reason. Then I said,
'Go to the Poets; they will speak to thee
More perfectly of purer creatures; – yet
If reason be nobility in man, 70
Can aught be more ignoble than the man
Whom they delight in, blinded as he is

By prejudice, the miserable slave
Of low ambition or distempered love?'
    In such strange passion, if I may once more 75
Review the past, I warred against myself –
A bigot to a new idolatry –
Like a cowled monk who hath forsworn the world,
Zealously laboured to cut off my heart
From all the sources of her former strength; 80
And as, by simple waving of a wand,
The wizard instantaneously dissolves
Palace or grove, even so could I unsoul
As readily by syllogistic words
Those mysteries of being which have made, 85
And shall continue evermore to make,
Of the whole human race one brotherhood.
    What wonder, then, if, to a mind so far
Perverted, even the visible Universe
Fell under the dominion of a taste 90
Less spiritual, with microscopic view
Was scanned, as I had scanned the moral world?
    O Soul of Nature! excellent and fair!
That didst rejoice with me, with whom I, too,
Rejoiced through early youth, before the winds 95
And roaring waters, and in lights and shades
That marched and countermarched about the hills
In glorious apparition, Powers on whom
I daily waited, now all eye and now
All ear; but never long without the heart 100
Employed, and man's unfolding intellect:
O Soul of Nature! that, by laws divine
Sustained and governed, still dost overflow
With an impassioned life, what feeble ones
Walk on this earth! how feeble have I been 105
When thou wert in thy strength! Nor this through
    stroke
Of human suffering, such as justifies
Remissness and inaptitude of mind,
But through presumption; even in pleasure pleased
Unworthily, disliking here, and there 110
Liking; by rules of mimic art transferred
To things above all art; but more, – for this,
Although a strong infection of the age,
Was never much my habit – giving way
To a comparison of scene with scene, 115
Bent overmuch on superficial things,
Pampering myself with meagre novelties
Of colour and proportion; to the moods
Of time and season, to the moral power,
The affections and the spirit of the place, 120
Insensible. Nor only did the love
Of sitting thus in judgement interrupt
My deeper feelings, but another cause,
More subtle and less easily explained,
That almost seems inherent in the creature, 125
A twofold frame of body and of mind.

BOOK TWELFTH. IMAGINATION AND TASTE, HOW IMPAIRED AND RESTORED:
84 **syllogistic words:** subtle argument or reasoning

I speak in recollection of a time
When the bodily eye, in every stage of life
The most despotic of our senses, gained
Such strength in *me* as often held my mind   130
In absolute dominion. Gladly here,
Entering upon abstruser argument,
Could I endeavour to unfold the means
Which Nature studiously employs to thwart
This tyranny, summons all the senses each   135
To counteract the other, and themselves,
And makes them all, and the objects with which all
Are cónversant, subservient in their turn
To the great ends of Liberty and Power.
But leave we this: enough that my delights   140
(Such as they were) were sought insatiably.
Vivid the transport, vivid though not profound;
I roamed from hill to hill, from rock to rock,
Still craving combinations of new forms,
New pleasure, wider empire for the sight,   145
Proud of her own endowments, and rejoiced
To lay the inner faculties asleep.
Amid the turns and counterturns, the strife
And various trials of our complex being,
As we grow up, such thraldom of that sense   150
Seems hard to shun. And yet I knew a maid,
A young enthusiast, who escaped these bonds;
Her eye was not the mistress of her heart;
Far less did rules prescribed by passive taste,
Or barren intermeddling subtleties,   155
Perplex her mind; but, wise as women are
When genial circumstance hath favoured them,
She welcomed what was given, and craved no more;
Whate'er the scene presented to her view,
That was the best, to that she was attuned   160
By her benign simplicity of life,
And through a perfect happiness of soul,
Whose variegated feelings were in this
Sisters, that they were each some new delight.
Birds in the bower, and lambs in the green field,   165
Could they have known her, would have loved;
  methought
Her very presence such a sweetness breathed,
That flowers, and trees, and even the silent hills,
And every thing she looked on, should have had
An intimation how she bore herself   170
Towards them and to all creatures. God delights
In such a being; for her common thoughts
Are piety, her life is gratitude.
     Even like this maid, before I was called forth
From the retirement of my native hills,   175
I loved whate'er I saw: nor lightly loved,
But most intensely; never dreamt of aught
More grand, more fair, more éxquisitely framed
Than those few nooks to which my happy feet
Were limited. I had not at that time   180

Lived long enough, nor in the least survived
The first diviner influence of this world,
As it appears to unaccustomed eyes.
Worshipping then among the depth of things,
As piety ordained; could I submit   185
To measured admiration, or to aught
That should preclude humility and love?
I felt, observed, and pondered; did not judge,
Yea, never thought of judging; with the gift
Of all this glory filled and satisfied.   190
And afterwards, when through the gorgeous Alps
Roaming, I carried with me the same heart:
In truth, the degradation – howsoe'er
Induced, effect, in whatsoe'er degree,
Of custom that prepares a partial scale   195
In which the little oft outweighs the great;
Or any other cause that hath been named;
Or lastly, aggravated by the times
And their impassioned sounds, which well might make
The milder minstrelsies of rural scenes   200
Inaudible – was transient; I had known
Too forcibly, too early in my life,
Visitings of imaginative power
For this to last: I shook the habit off
Entirely and for ever, and again   205
In Nature's presence stood, as now I stand,
A sensitive being, a *creative* soul.
     There are in our existence spots of time,
That with distinct pre-eminence retain
A renovating virtue, whence, depressed   210
By false opinion and contentious thought,
Or aught of heavier or more deadly weight,
In trivial occupations, and the round
Of ordinary intercourse, our minds
Are nourished and invisibly repaired;   215
A virtue, by which pleasure is enhanced,
That penetrates, enables us to mount,
When high, more high, and lifts us up when fallen.
This efficacious spirit chiefly lurks
Among those passages of life that give   220
Profoundest knowledge to what point, and how,
The mind is lord and master – outward sense
The obedient servant of her will. Such moments
Are scattered everywhere, taking their date
From our first childhood. I remember well,   225
That once, while yet my inexperienced hand
Could scarcely hold a bridle, with proud hopes
I mounted, and we journeyed towards the hills:
An ancient servant of my father's house
Was with me, my encourager and guide: 230
We had not travelled long, ere some mischance
Disjoined me from my comrade; and, through fear
Dismounting, down the rough and stony moor
I led my horse, and, stumbling on, at length
Came to a bottom, where in former times   235

---

151 **a maid:** Mary Hutchinson, whom Wordsworth married in 1802

235 **bottom:** the base of a valley

A murderer had been hung in iron chains.
The gibbet-mast had mouldered down, the bones
And iron case were gone; but on the turf,
Hard by, soon after that fell deed was wrought,
Some unknown hand had carved the murderer's
   name. 240
The monumental letters were inscribed
In times long past; but still, from year to year,
By superstition of the neighbourhood,
The grass is cleared away, and to this hour
The characters are fresh and visible: 245
A casual glance had shown them, and I fled,
Faltering and faint, and ignorant of the road:
Then reascending the bare common, saw
A naked pool that lay beneath the hills,
The beacon on the summit, and, more near, 250
A girl, who bore a pitcher on her head,
And seemed with difficult steps to force her way
Against the blowing wind. It was, in truth,
An ordinary sight; but I should need
Colours and words that are unknown to man, 255
To paint the visionary dreariness
Which, while I looked all round for my lost guide,
Invested moorland waste, and naked pool,
The beacon crowning the lone eminence,
The female and her garments vexed and tossed 260
By the strong wind. When, in the blessèd hours
Of early love, the loved one at my side,
I roamed, in daily presence of this scene,
Upon the naked pool and dreary crags,
And on the melancholy beacon fell 265
A spirit of pleasure and youth's golden gleam;
And think ye not with radiance more sublime
For these remembrances, and for the power
They had left behind? So feeling comes in aid
Of feeling, and diversity of strength 270
Attends us, if but once we have been strong.
Oh! mystery of man, from what a depth
Proceed thy honours. I am lost, but see
In simple childhood something of the base
On which thy greatness stands; but this I feel, 275
That from thyself it comes, that thou must give,
Else never canst receive. The days gone by
Return upon me almost from the dawn
Of life: the hiding-places of man's power
Open; I would approach them, but they close. 280
I see by glimpses now; when age comes on,
May scarcely see at all; and I would give,
While yet we may, as far as words can give,
Substance and life to what I feel, enshrining,
Such is my hope, the spirit of the Past 285
For future restoration. – Yet another
Of these memorials: –
          One Christmas-time,
On the glad eve of its dear holidays,
Feverish, and tired, and restless, I went forth
Into the fields, impatient for the sight 290

Of those led palfreys that should bear us home;
My brothers and myself. There rose a crag,
That, from the meeting-point of two high-ways
Ascending, overlooked them both, far stretched;
Thither, uncertain on which road to fix 295
My expectation, thither I repaired,
Scout-like, and gained the summit; 'twas a day
Tempestuous, dark, and wild, and on the grass
I sate half-sheltered by a naked wall;
Upon my right hand couched a single sheep, 300
Upon my left a blasted hawthorn stood;
With those companions at my side, I watched,
Straining my eyes intensely, as the mist
Gave intermitting prospect of the copse
And plain beneath. Ere we to school returned, – 305
That dreary time, – ere we had been ten days
Sojóurners in my father's house, he died,
And I and my three brothers, orphans then,
Followed his body to the grave. The event,
With all the sorrow that it brought, appeared 310
A chástisement; and when I called to mind
That day so lately past, when from the crag
I looked in such anxiety of hope;
With trite reflections of morality,
Yet in the deepest passion, I bowed low 315
To God, Who thus corrected my desires;
And, afterwards, the wind and sleety rain,
And all the business of the elements,
The single sheep, and the one blasted tree,
And the bleak music from that old stone wall, 320
The noise of wood and water, and the mist
That on the line of each of those two roads
Advanced in such indísputable shapes;
All these were kindred spectacles and sounds
To which I oft repaired, and thence would drink, 325
As at a fountain; and on winter nights,
Down to this very time, when storm and rain
Beat on my roof, or, haply, at noon-day,
While in a grove I walk, whose lofty trees,
Laden with summer's thickest foliage, rock 330
In a strong wind, some working of the spirit,
Some inward agitations thence are brought,
Whate'er their office, whether to beguile
Thoughts over-busy in the course they took,
Or animate an hour of vacant ease. 335

BOOK THIRTEENTH. IMAGINATION AND TASTE,
  HOW IMPAIRED AND RESTORED – CONCLUDED
FROM Nature doth emotion come, and moods
Of calmness equally are Nature's gift:
This is her glory; these two attributes
Are sister horns that constitute her strength.
Hence Genius, born to thrive by interchange 5
Of peace and excitation, finds in her
His best and purest friend; from her receives

291 **palfreys:** horses

That energy by which he seeks the truth,
From her that happy stillness of the mind
Which fits him to receive it when unsought. 10
    Such benefit the humblest intellects
Partake of, each in their degree; 'tis mine
To speak, what I myself have known and felt;
Smooth task! for words find easy way, inspired
By gratitude, and confidence in truth. 15
Long time in search of knowledge did I range
The field of human life, in heart and mind
Benighted; but, the dawn beginning now
To re-appear, 'twas proved that not in vain
I had been taught to reverence a Power 20
That is the visible quality and shape
And image of right reason; that matures
Her processes by steadfast laws; gives birth
To no impatient or fallacious hopes,
No heat of passion or excessive zeal, 25
No vain conceits; provokes to no quick turns
Of self-applauding intellect; but trains
To meekness, and exalts by humble faith;
Holds up before the mind intoxicate
With present objects, and the busy dance 30
Of things that pass away, a temperate show
Of objects that endure; and by this course
Disposes her, when over-fondly set
On throwing off encumbrances, to seek
In man, and in the frame of social life, 35
Whate'er there is desirable and good
Of kindred permanence, unchanged in form
And function, or, through strict vicissitude
Of life and death, revolving. Above all
Were re-established now those watchful thoughts 40
Which, seeing little worthy or sublime
In what the Historian's pen so much delights
To blazon – power and energy detached
From moral purpose – early tutored me
To look with feelings of fraternal love 45
Upon the unassuming things that hold
A silent station in this beauteous world.
    Thus moderated, thus composed, I found
Once more in Man an object of delight,
Of pure imagination, and of love; 50
And, as the horizon of my mind enlarged,
Again I took the intellectual eye
For my instructor, studious more to see
Great truths, than touch and handle little ones.
Knowledge was given accordingly; my trust 55
Became more firm in feelings that had stood
The test of such a trial; clearer far
My sense of excellence – of right and wrong:
The promise of the present time retired
Into its true proportion; sanguine schemes, 60
Ambitious projects, pleased me less; I sought
For present good in life's familiar face,

And built thereon my hopes of good to come.
    With settling judgements now of what would last
And what would disappear; prepared to find 65
Presumption, folly, madness, in the men
Who thrust themselves upon the passive world
As Rulers of the world; to see in these,
Even when the public welfare is their aim,
Plans without thought, or built on theories 70
Vague and unsound; and having brought the books
Of modern statists to their proper test,
Life, human life, with all its sacred claims
Of sex and age, and heaven-descended rights,
Mortal, or those beyond the reach of death; 75
And having thus discerned how dire a thing
Is worshipped in that idol proudly named
'The Wealth of Nations', *where* alone that wealth
Is lodged, and how increased; and having gained
A more judicious knowledge of the worth 80
And dignity of individual man,
No composition of the brain, but man
Of whom we read, the man whom we behold
With our own eyes – I could not but inquire –
Not with less interest than heretofore, 85
But greater, though in spirit more subdued –
Why is this glorious creature to be found
One only in ten thousand? What one is,
Why may not millions be? What bars are thrown
By Nature in the way of such a hope? 90
Our animal appetites and daily wants,
Are these obstructions insurmountable?
If not, then others vanish into air.
'Inspect the basis of the social pile:
Inquire', said I, 'how much of mental power 95
And genuine virtue they possess who live
By bodily toil, labour exceeding far
Their due proportion, under all the weight
Of that injustice which upon ourselves
Ourselves entail.' Such estimate to frame 100
I chiefly looked (what need to look beyond?)
Among the natural abodes of men,
Fields with their rural works; recalled to mind
My earliest notices; with these compared
The observations made in later youth, 105
And to that day continued. – For, the time
Had never been when throes of mighty Nations
And the world's tumult unto me could yield,
How far soe'er transported and possessed,
Full measure of content; but still I craved 110
An intermingling of distinct regards
And truths of individual sympathy
Nearer ourselves. Such often might be gleaned
From the great City, else it must have proved
To me a heart-depressing wilderness; 115
But much was wanting: therefore did I turn

BOOK THIRTEENTH. IMAGINATION AND TASTE, HOW IMPAIRED AND RESTORED
– CONCLUDED: 60 **sanguine:** hopeful

78 **The Wealth of Nations:** Wordsworth alludes to Adam Smith's
Inquiry into the Nature and Causes of the Wealth of Nations, published
in 1776

To you, ye pathways, and ye lonely roads;
Sought you enriched with everything I prized,
With human kindnesses and simple joys.

Oh! next to one dear state of bliss, vouchsafed   120
Alas! to few in this untóward world,
The bliss of walking daily in life's prime
Through field or forest with the maid we love,
While yet our hearts are young, while yet we breathe
Nothing but happiness, in some lone nook,   125
Deep vale, or any where, the home of both,
From which it would be misery to stir:
Oh! next to such enjoyment of our youth,
In my esteem, next to such dear delight,
Was that of wandering on from day to day   130
Where I could meditate in peace, and cull
Knowledge that step by step might lead me on
To wisdom; or, as lightsome as a bird
Wafted upon the wind from distant lands,
Sing notes of greeting to strange fields or groves,   135
Which lacked not voice to welcome me in turn:
And, when that pleasant toil had ceased to please,
Converse with men, where if we meet a face
We almost meet a friend, on naked heaths
With long long ways before, by cottage bench,   140
Or well-spring where the weary traveller rests.

Who doth not love to follow with his eye
The windings of a public way? the sight,
Familiar object as it is, hath wrought
On my imagination since the morn   145
Of childhood, when a disappearing line,
One daily present to my eyes, that crossed
The naked summit of a far-off hill
Beyond the limits that my feet had trod,
Was like an invitation into space   150
Boundless, or guide into eternity.
Yes, something of the grandeur which invests
The mariner who sails the roaring sea
Through storm and darkness, early in my mind
Surrounded, too, the wanderers of the earth;   155
Grandeur as much, and loveliness far more.
Awed have I been by strolling Bedlamites;
From many other uncouth vagrants (passed
In fear) have walked with quicker step; but why
Take note of this? When I began to enquire,   160
To watch and question those I met, and speak
Without reserve to them, the lonely roads
Were open schools in which I daily read
With most delight the passions of mankind,
Whether by words, looks, sighs, or tears, revealed;   165
There saw into the depth of human souls,
Souls that appear to have no depth at all
To careless eyes. And – now convinced at heart
How little those formalities, to which
With overweening trust alone we give   170

The name of Education, have to do
With reäl feeling and just sense; how vain
A correspondence with the talking world
Proves to the most; and called to make good search
If man's estate, by doom of Nature yoked   175
With toil, be therefore yoked with ignorance;
If virtue be indeed so hard to rear,
And intellectual strength so rare a boon –
I prized such walks still more, for there I found
Hope to my hope, and to my pleasure peace   180
And steadiness, and healing and repose
To every angry passion. There I heard,
From mouths of men obscure and lowly, truths
Replete with honour; sounds in unison
With loftiest promises of good and fair.   185

There are who think that strong affection, love
Known by whatever name, is falsely deemed
A gift, to use a term which they would use,
Of vulgar nature; that its growth requires
Retirement, leisure, language purified   190
By manners studied and elaborate;
That whoso feels such passion in its strength
Must live within the very light and air
Of courteous usages refined by art.
True is it, where oppression worse than death   195
Salutes the being at his birth, where grace
Of culture hath been utterly unknown,
And poverty and labour in excess
From day to day pre-occupy the ground
Of the affections, and to Nature's self   200
Oppose a deeper nature; there, indeed,
Love cannot be; nor does it thrive with ease
Among the close and overcrowded haunts
Of cities, where the human heart is sick,
And the eye feeds it not, and cannot feed.   205
– Yes, in those wanderings deeply did I feel
How we mislead each other; above all,
How books mislead us, seeking their reward
From judgements of the wealthy Few, who see
By artificial lights; how they debase   210
The Many for the pleasure of those Few;
Effeminately level down the truth
To certain general notions, for the sake
Of being understood at once, or else
Through want of better knowledge in the heads   215
That framed them; flattering self-conceit with words,
That, while they most ambitiously set forth
Extrinsic differences, the outward marks
Whereby society has parted man
From man, neglect the universal heart.   220

Here, calling up to mind what then I saw,
A youthful traveller, and see daily now
In the familiar circuit of my home,
Here might I pause, and bend in reverence
To Nature, and the power of human minds,   225
To men as they are men within themselves.
How oft high service is performed within,

157 **Bedlamites:** insane people

When all the external man is rude in show, –
Not like a temple rich with pomp and gold,
But a mere mountain chapel, that protects   230
Its simple worshippers from sun and shower.
Of these, said I, shall be my song; of these,
If future years mature me for the task,
Will I record the praises, making verse
Deal boldly with substantial things; in truth   235
And sanctity of passion, speak of these,
That justice may be done, obeisance paid
Where it is due: thus haply shall I teach,
Inspire, through unadulterated ears
Pour rapture, tenderness, and hope, – my theme   240
No other than the very heart of man,
As found among the best of those who live,
Not unexalted by religious faith,
Nor uninformed by books, good books, though few,
In Nature's presence: thence may I select   245
Sorrow, that is not sorrow, but delight;
And miserable love, that is not pain
To hear of, for the glory that redounds
Therefrom to human kind, and what we are.
Be mine to follow with no timid step   250
Where knowledge leads me: it shall be my pride
That I have dared to tread this holy ground,
Speaking no dream, but things oracular;
Matter not lightly to be heard by those
Who to the letter of the outward promise   255
Do read the invisible soul; by men adroit
In speech, and for communion with the world
Accomplished; minds whose faculties are then
Most active when they are most eloquent,
And elevated most when most admired.   260
Men may be found of other mould than these,
Who are their own upholders, to themselves
Encouragement, and energy, and will,
Expressing liveliest thoughts in lively words
As native passion díctates. Others, too,   265
There are among the walks of homely life
Still higher, men for contemplation framed,
Shy, and unpractised in the strife of phrase;
Meek men, whose very souls perhaps would sink
Beneath them, summoned to such intercourse: 270
Theirs is the language of the heavens, the power,
The thought, the image, and the silent joy:
Words are but under-agents in their souls;
When they are grasping with their greatest strength,
They do not breathe among them: this I speak   275
In gratitude to God, Who feeds our hearts
For His own service; knoweth, loveth us,
When we are unregarded by the world.
   Also about this time I did receive
Convictions still more strong than heretofore,   280
Not only that the inner frame is good,
And graciously composed, but that, no less,
Nature for all conditions wants not power
To consecrate, if we have eyes to see,

The outside of her creatures, and to breathe   285
Grandeur upon the very humblest face
Of human life. I felt that the array
Of act and circumstance, and visible form,
Is mainly to the pleasure of the mind
What passion makes them; that meanwhile the forms
Of Nature have a passion in themselves,   291
That intermingles with those works of man
To which she summons him; although the works
Be mean, have nothing lofty of their own;
And that the Genius of the Poet hence   295
May boldly take his way among mankind
Wherever Nature leads; that he hath stood
By Nature's side among the men of old,
And so shall stand for ever. Dearest Friend!
If thou partake the animating faith   300
That Poets, even as Prophets, each with each
Connected in a mighty scheme of truth,
Have each his own peculiar faculty,
Heaven's gift, a sense that fits him to perceive
Objects unseen before, thou wilt not blame   305
The humblest of this band who dares to hope
That unto him hath also been vouchsafed
An insight that in some sort he possesses,
A privilege whereby a work of his,
Proceeding from a source of untaught things   310
Creative and enduring, may become
A power like one of Nature's. To a hope
Not less ambitious once among the wilds
Of Sarum's Plain, my youthful spirit was raised;
There, as I ranged at will the pastoral downs   315
Trackless and smooth, or paced the bare white roads
Lengthening in solitude their dreary line,
Time with his retinue of ages fled
Backwards, nor checked his flight until I saw
Our dim ancestral Past in vision clear;   320
Saw multitudes of men, and, here and there,
A single Briton clothed in wolf-skin vest,
With shield and stone-axe, stride across the wold;
The voice of spears was heard, the rattling spear
Shaken by arms of mighty bone, in strength,   325
Long mouldered, of barbaric majesty.
I called on Darkness – but before the word
Was uttered, midnight darkness seemed to take
All objects from my sight; and lo! again
The Desert visible by dismal flames;   330
It is the sacrificial altar, fed
With living men – how deep the groans! the voice
Of those that crowd the giant wicker thrills
The monumental hillocks, and the pomp
Is for both worlds, the living and the dead.   335
At other moments (for through that wide waste
Three summer days I roamed) where'er the Plain
Was figured o'er with circles, lines, or mounds,

314 **Sarum's Plain:** Salisbury Plain   333 **giant wicker:** these were ancient pagan sacrificial constructions consisting of a giant wicker man which would be filled with victims and then burned

That yet survive, a work, as some divine,
Shaped by the Druids, so to represent   340
Their knowledge of the heavens, and image forth
The constellations; gently was I charmed
Into a waking dream, a reverie
That, with believing eyes, where'er I turned,
Beheld long-bearded teachers, with white wands   345
Uplifted, pointing to the starry sky,
Alternately, and the plain below, while breath
Of music swayed their motions, and the waste
Rejoiced with them and me in those sweet sounds.
  This for the past, and things that may be viewed   350
Or fancied in the obscurity of years
From monumental hints: and thou, O Friend!
Pleased with some unpremeditated strains
That served those wanderings to beguile, hast said
That then and there my mind had exercised   355
Upon the vulgar forms of present things,
The actual world of our familiar days,
Yet higher power; had caught from them a tone,
An image, and a character, by books
Not hitherto reflected. Call we this   360
A partial judgement – and yet why? for *then*
We were as strangers; and I may not speak
Thus wrongfully of verse, however rude,
Which on thy young imagination, trained
In the great City, broke like light from far.   365
Moreover, each man's Mind is to herself
Witness and judge; and I remember well
That in life's every-day appearances
I seemed about this time to gain clear sight
Of a new world – a world, too, that was fit   370
To be transmitted, and to other eyes
Made visible; as ruled by those fixed laws
Whence spiritual dignity originates,
Which do both give it being and maintain
A balance, an ennobling interchange   375
Of action from without and from within;
The excellence, pure function, and best power
Both of the object seen, and eye that sees.

BOOK FOURTEENTH. CONCLUSION

In one of those excursions (may they ne'er
Fade from remembrance!) through the Northern tracts
Of Cambria ranging with a youthful friend,
I left Bethgelert's huts at couching-time,
And westward took my way, to see the sun   5
Rise from the top of Snowdon. To the door
Of a rude cottage at the mountain's base
We came, and roused the shepherd who attends
The adventurous stranger's steps, a trusty guide;
Then, cheered by short refreshment, sallied forth. 10

BOOK FOURTEENTH. CONCLUSION: 4 **couching-time:** bed time 6 **Snowdon:**
Mount Snowdon in North Wales

It was a close, warm, breezeless summer night,
Wan, dull, and glaring, with a dripping fog
Low-hung and thick that covered all the sky;
But, undiscouraged, we began to climb
The mountain-side. The mist soon girt us round,   15
And, after ordinary travellers' talk
With our conductor, pensively we sank
Each into commerce with his private thoughts:
Thus did we breast the ascent, and by myself
Was nothing either seen or heard that checked   20
Those musings or diverted, save that once
The shepherd's lurcher, who, among the crags,
Had to his joy unearthed a hedgehog, teased
His coiled-up prey with barkings turbulent.
This small adventure, for even such it seemed   25
In that wild place and at the dead of night,
Being over and forgotten, on we wound
In silence as before. With forehead bent
Earthward, as if in opposition set
Against an enemy, I panted up   30
With eager pace, and no less eager thoughts.
Thus might we wear a midnight hour away,
Ascending at loose distance each from each,
And I, as chanced, the foremost of the band;
When at my feet the ground appeared to brighten,   35
And with a step or two seemed brighter still;
Nor was time given to ask or learn the cause,
For instantly a light upon the turf
Fell like a flash, and lo! as I looked up,
The Moon hung naked in a firmament   40
Of azure without cloud, and at my feet
Rested a silent sea of hoary mist.
A hundred hills their dusky backs upheaved
All over this still ocean; and beyond,
Far, far beyond, the solid vapours stretched,   45
In headlands, tongues, and promontory shapes,
Into the main Atlantic, that appeared
To dwindle, and give up his majesty,
Usurped upon far as the sight could reach.
Not so the ethereal vault; encroachment none   50
Was there, nor loss; only the inferior stars
Had disappeared, or shed a fainter light
In the clear presence of the full-orbed Moon,
Who, from her sovereign elevation, gazed
Upon the billowy ocean, as it lay   55
All meek and silent, save that through a rift –
Not distant from the shore whereon we stood,
A fixed, abysmal, gloomy, breathing-place –
Mounted the roar of waters, torrents, streams
Innumerable, roaring with one voice!   60
Heard over earth and sea, and, in that hour,
For so it seemed, felt by the starry heavens.
  When into air had partially dissolved
That vision, given to spirits of the night
And three chance human wanderers, in calm thought

22 **lurcher:** dog

Reflected, it appeared to me the type 66
Of a majestic intellect, its acts
And its possessions, what it has and craves,
What in itself it is, and would become.
There I beheld the emblem of a mind 70
That feeds upon infinity, that broods
Over the dark abyss, intent to hear
Its voices issuing forth to silent light
In one continuous stream; a mind sustained
By recognitions of transcendent power, 75
In sense conducting to ideäl form,
In soul of more than mortal privilege.
One function, above all, of such a mind
Had Nature shadowed there, by putting forth,
'Mid circumstances awful and sublime, 80
That mutual domination which she loves
To exert upon the face of outward things,
So moulded, joined, abstracted, so endowed
With interchangeable supremacy,
That men, least sensitive, see, hear, perceive, 85
And cannot choose but feel. The power, which all
Acknowledge when thus moved, which Nature thus
To bodily sense exhibits, is the express
Resemblance of that glorious faculty
That higher minds bear with them as their own. 90
This is the very spirit in which they deal
With the whole compass of the universe:
They from their native selves can send abroad
Kindred mutations; for themselves create
A like existence; and, whene'er it dawns 95
Created for them, catch it, or are caught
By its inevitable mastery,
Like angels stopped upon the wing by sound
Of harmony from Heaven's remotest spheres.
Them the enduring and the transient both 100
Serve to exalt; they build up greatest things
From least suggestions; ever on the watch,
Willing to work and to be wrought upon,
They need not extraordinary calls
To rouse them; in a world of life they live, 105
By sensible impressions not enthralled,
But by their quickening impulse made more prompt
To hold fit converse with the spiritual world,
And with the generations of mankind
Spread over time, past, present, and to come, 110
Age after age, till Time shall be no more.
Such minds are truly from the Deity,
For they are Powers; and hence the highest bliss
That flesh can know is theirs – the consciousness
Of Whom they are, habitually infused 115
Through every image and through every thought,
And all affections by communion raised
From earth to heaven, from human to divine;
Hence endless occupation for the Soul,
Whether discursive or intuitive; 120
Hence cheerfulness for acts of daily life,
Emotions which best foresight need not fear,

More worthy then of trust when most intense.
Hence, amid ills that vex and wrongs that crush
Our hearts – if here the words of Holy Writ 125
May with fit reverence be applied – that peace
Which passeth understanding, that repose
In moral judgements which from this pure source
Must come, or will by man be sought in vain.
    Oh! who is he that hath his whole life long 130
Preserved, enlarged, this freedom in himself?
For this alone is genuine liberty:
Where is the favoured being who hath held
That course unchecked, unerring, and untired,
In one perpetual progress smooth and bright? – 135
A humbler destiny have we retraced,
And told of lapse and hesitating choice,
And backward wanderings along thorny ways:
Yet – compassed round by mountain solitudes,
Within whose solemn temple I received 140
My earliest visitations, careless then
Of what was given me; and which now I range,
A meditative, oft a suffering man –
Do I declare – in accents which, from truth
Deriving cheerful confidence, shall blend 145
Their modulation with these vocal streams –
That, whatsoever falls my better mind,
Revolving with the accidents of life,
May have sustained, that, howsoe'er misled,
Never did I, in quest of right and wrong, 150
Tamper with conscience from a private aim;
Nor was in any public hope the dupe
Of selfish passions; nor did ever yield
Wilfully to mean cares or low pursuits,
But shrunk with apprehensive jealousy 155
From every combination which might aid
The tendency, too potent in itself,
Of use and custom to bow down the soul
Under a growing weight of vulgar sense,
And substitute a universe of death 160
For that which moves with light and life informed,
Actual, divine, and true. To fear and love,
To love as prime and chief, for there fear ends,
Be this ascribed; to early intercourse,
In presence of sublime or beautiful forms, 165
With the adverse principles of pain and joy –
Evil as one is rashly named by men
Who know not what they speak. By love subsists
All lasting grandeur, by pervading love;
That gone, we are as dust. – Behold the fields 170
In balmy spring-time full of rising flowers
And joyous creatures; see that pair, the lamb
And the lamb's mother, and their tender ways
Shall touch thee to the heart; thou callest this love,
And not inaptly so, for love it is, 175
Far as it carries thee. In some green bower
Rest, and be not alone, but have thou there
The One who is thy choice of all the world:
There linger, listening, gazing, with delight

Impassioned, but delight how pitiable! 180
Unless this love by a still higher love
Be hallowed, love that breathes not without awe;
Love that adores, but on the knees of prayer,
By heaven inspired; that frees from chains the soul,
Lifted, in union with the purest, best, 185
Of earth-born passions, on the wings of praise
Bearing a tribute to the Almighty's Throne.
   This spiritual Love acts not nor can exist
Without Imagination, which, in truth,
Is but another name for absolute power 190
And clearest insight, amplitude of mind,
And Reason in her most exalted mood.
This faculty hath been the feeding source
Of our long labour: we have traced the stream
From the blind cavern whence is faintly heard 195
Its natal murmur; followed it to light
And open day; accompanied its course
Among the ways of Nature, for a time
Lost sight of it bewildered and engulfed:
Then given it greeting as it rose once more 200
In strength, reflecting from its placid breast
The works of man and face of human life;
And lastly, from its progress have we drawn
Faith in life endless, the sustaining thought
Of human Being, Eternity, and God. 205
   Imagination having been our theme,
So also hath that intellectual Love,
For they are each in each, and cannot stand
Dividually. – Here must thou be, O Man!
Power to thyself; no Helper hast thou here; 210
Here keepest thou in singleness thy state:
No other can divide with thee this work:
No secondary hand can intervene
To fashion this ability; 'tis thine,
The prime and vital principle is thine 215
In the recesses of thy nature, far
From any reach of outward fellowship,
Else is not thine at all. But joy to him,
Oh, joy to him who here hath sown, hath laid
Here, the foundation of his future years! 220
For all that friendship, all that love can do,
All that a darling countenance can look
Or dear voice utter, to complete the man,
Perfect him, made imperfect in himself,
All shall be his: and he whose soul hath risen 225
Up to the height of feeling intellect
Shall want no humbler tenderness; his heart
Be tender as a nursing mother's heart;
Of female softness shall his life be full,
Of humble cares and delicate desires, 230
Mild interests and gentlest sympathies.
   Child of my parents! Sister of my soul!
Thanks in sincerest verse have been elsewhere
Poured out for all the early tenderness

Which I from thee imbibed: and 'tis most true 235
That later seasons owed to thee no less;
For, spite of thy sweet influence and the touch
Of kindred hands that opened out the springs
Of genial thought in childhood, and in spite
Of all that unassisted I had marked 240
In life or nature of those charms minute
That win their way into the heart by stealth,
Still to the very going-out of youth,
I too exclusively esteemed *that* love,
And sought *that* beauty, which, as Milton sings, 245
Hath terror in it. Thou didst soften down
This over-sternness; but for thee, dear Friend!
My soul, too reckless of mild grace, had stood
In her original self too confident,
Retained too long a countenance severe; 250
A rock with torrents roaring, with the clouds
Familiar, and a favourite of the stars:
But thou didst plant its crevices with flowers,
Hang it with shrubs that twinkle in the breeze,
And teach the little birds to build their nests 255
And warble in its chambers. At a time
When Nature, destined to remain so long
Foremost in my affections, had fallen back
Into a second place, pleased to become
A handmaid to a nobler than herself, 260
When every day brought with it some new sense
Of éxquisite regard for common things,
And all the earth was budding with these gifts
Of more refined humanity, thy breath,
Dear Sister! was a kind of gentler spring 265
That went before my steps. Thereafter came
One whom with thee friendship had early paired;
She came, no more a phantom to adorn
A moment, but an inmate of the heart,
And yet a spirit, there for me enshrined 270
To penetrate the lofty and the low;
Even as one essence of pervading light
Shines in the brightest of ten thousand stars,
And the meek worm that feeds her lonely lamp
Couched in the dewy grass.
               With such a theme, 275
Coleridge! with this my argument, of thee
Shall I be silent? O capacious Soul!
Placed on this earth to love and understand,
And from thy presence shed the light of love,
Shall I be mute, ere thou be spoken of? 280
Thy kindred influence to my heart of hearts
Did also find its way. Thus fear relaxed
Her overweening grasp; thus thoughts and things
In the self-haunting spirit learned to take
More rational proportions; mystery, 285
The incumbent mystery of sense and soul,
Of life and death, time and eternity,
Admitted more habitually a mild
Interposition – a serene delight
In closelier gathering cares, such as become 290

209 **Dividually:** separately 245–246 Milton's *Paradise Lost*, Book IX,
490–491 274 **meek worm:** glowworm

A human creature, howsoe'er endowed,
Poet, or destined for a humbler name;
And so the deep enthusiastic joy,
The rapture of the hallelujah sent
From all that breathes and is, was chastened,
    stemmed   295
And balanced by pathetic truth, by trust
In hopeful reason, leaning on the stay
Of Providence; and in reverence for duty,
Here, if need be, struggling with storms, and there
Strewing in peace life's humblest ground with herbs,
At every season green, sweet at all hours.   301

    And now, O Friend! this history is brought
To its appointed close: the discipline
And consummation of a Poet's mind,
In everything that stood most prominent,   305
Have faithfully been pictured; we have reached
The time (our guiding object from the first)
When we may, not presumptuously, I hope,
Suppose my powers so far confirmed, and such
My knowledge, as to make me capable   310
Of building up a Work that shall endure.
Yet much hath been omitted, as need was;
Of books how much! and even of the other wealth
That is collected among woods and fields,
Far more: for Nature's secondary grace   315
Hath hitherto been barely touched upon,
The charm more superficial that attends
Her works, as they present to Fancy's choice
Apt illustrations of the moral world,
Caught at a glance, or traced with curious pains.   320

    Finally, and above all, O Friend! (I speak
With due regret) how much is overlooked
In human nature and her subtle ways,
As studied first in our own hearts, and then
In life among the passions of mankind,   325
Varying their composition and their hue,
Where'er we move, under the díverse shapes
That individual character presents
To an attentive eye. For progress meet,
Along this intricate and difficult path,   330
Whate'er was wanting, something had I gained,
As one of many schoolfellows compelled,
In hardy independence, to stand up
Amid conflicting interests, and the shock
Of various tempers; to endure and note   335
What was not understood, though known to be;
Among the mysteries of love and hate,
Honour and shame, looking to right and left,
Unchecked by innocence too delicate,
And moral notions too intolerant,   340
Sympathies too contracted. Hence, when called
To take a station among men, the step
Was easier, the transition more secure,
More profitable also; for, the mind
Learns from such timely exercise to keep   345
In wholesome separation the two natures,

The one that feels, the other that observes.
    Yet one word more of personal concern –
Since I withdrew unwillingly from France,
I led an undomestic wanderer's life,   350
In London chiefly harboured, whence I roamed,
Tarrying at will in many a pleasant spot
Of rural England's cultivated vales
Or Cambrian solitudes. A youth – (he bore
The name of Calvert – it shall live, if words   355
Of mine can give it life), in firm belief
That by endowments not from me withheld
Good might be furthered – in his last decay
By a bequest sufficient for my needs
Enabled me to pause for choice, and walk   360
At large and unrestrained, nor damped too soon
By mortal cares. Himself no Poet, yet
Far less a common follower of the world,
He deemed that my pursuits and labours lay
Apart from all that leads to wealth, or even   365
A necessary maintenance ensures,
Without some hazard to the finer sense;
He cleared a passage for me, and the stream
Flowed in the bent of Nature.
                     Having now
Told what best merits mention, further pains   370
Our present purpose seems not to require,
And I have other tasks. Recall to mind
The mood in which this labour was begun,
O Friend! The termination of my course
Is nearer now, much nearer; yet even then,   375
In that distraction and intense desire,
I said unto the life which I had lived,
Where art thou? Hear I not a voice from thee
Which 'tis reproach to hear? Anon I rose
As if on wings, and saw beneath me stretched   380
Vast prospect of the world which I had been
And was; and hence this Song, which like a lark
I have protracted, in the unwearied heavens
Singing, and often with more plaintive voice
To earth attempered and her deep-drawn sighs,   385
Yet centring all in love, and in the end
All gratulant, if rightly understood.
    Whether to me shall be allotted life,
And, with life, power to accomplish aught of worth,
That will be deemed no insufficient plea   390
For having given the story of myself,
Is all uncertain; but, belovèd Friend!
When, looking back, thou seest, in clearer view
Than any liveliest sight of yesterday,
That summer, under whose indulgent skies,   395
Upon smooth Quantock's airy ridge we roved
Unchecked, or loitered 'mid her sylvan coombs,
Thou in bewitching words, with happy heart,

355–371 Raisley Calvert, from whom Wordsworth received £900 when
he died in 1795 387 **gratulant:** expressing joy 396 **Quantock:** situated
above Alfoxden where Wordsworth lived from 1797–1798

Didst chant the vision of that Ancient Man,
The bright-eyed Mariner, and rueful woes   400
Didst utter of the Lady Christabel;
And I, associate with such labour, steeped
In soft forgetfulness the livelong hours,
Murmuring of him who, joyous hap, was found,
After the perils of his moonlight ride,   405
Near the loud waterfall; or her who sate
In misery near the miserable Thorn;
When thou dost to that summer turn thy thoughts,
And hast before thee all which then we were,
To thee, in memory of that happiness,   410
It will be known, by thee at least, my Friend!
Felt, that the history of a Poet's mind
Is labour not unworthy of regard:
To thee the work shall justify itself.
　　The last and later portions of this gift   415
Have been prepared, not with the buoyant spirits
That were our daily portion when we first
Together wantoned in wild Poesy,
But, under pressure of a private grief,
Keen and enduring, which the mind and heart,   420
That in this meditative history
Have been laid open, needs must make me feel
More deeply, yet enable me to bear
More firmly; and a comfort now hath risen
From hope that thou art near, and wilt be soon   425
Restored to us in renovated health;
When, after the first mingling of our tears,
'Mong other consolations, we may draw
Some pleasure from this offering of my love.
　　Oh! yet a few short years of useful life,   430
And all will be complete, thy race be run,
Thy monument of glory will be raised;
Then, though (too weak to tread the ways of truth)
This age fall back to old idolatry,
Though men return to servitude as fast   435
As the tide ebbs, to ignominy and shame
By nations sink together, we shall still
Find solace – knowing what we have learnt to know,
Rich in true happiness if allowed to be
Faithful alike in forwarding a day   440
Of firmer trust, joint labourers in the work
(Should Providence such grace to us vouchsafe)
Of their deliverance, surely yet to come.
Prophets of Nature, we to them will speak
A lasting inspiration, sanctified   445
By reason, blest by faith: what we have loved,
Others will love, and we will teach them how;
Instruct them how the mind of man becomes
A thousand times more beautiful than the earth
On which he dwells, above this frame of things   450
(Which, 'mid all revolution in the hopes
And fears of men, doth still remain unchanged)
In beauty exalted, as it is itself
Of quality and fabric more divine.

399–401 Coleridge's *Rime of the Ancient Mariner* and *Christabel*

SIR WALTER SCOTT

From THE LAY OF THE LAST MINSTREL

BREATHES there the man, with soul so dead,
Who never to himself hath said,
　This is my own, my native land!
Whose heart hath ne'er within him burned,
As home his footsteps he hath turned   5
　From wandering on a foreign strand!
If such there breathe, go, mark him well;
For him no Minstrel raptures swell;
High though his titles, proud his name,
Boundless his wealth as wish can claim;   10
Despite those titles, power, and pelf,
The wretch, concentred all in self,
Living, shall forfeit fair renown,
And, doubly dying, shall go down
To the vile dust, from whence he sprung,   15
Unwept, unhonoured, and unsung.

　　　　　　　　　　　　　[Canto 6, lines 1–16]

'PROUD MAISIE IS IN THE WOOD'

PROUD Maisie is in the wood,
　Walking so early;
Sweet Robin sits on the bush,
　Singing so rarely.

'Tell me, thou bonny bird,   5
　When shall I marry me?'
'When six braw gentlemen
　Kirkward shall carry ye.'

'Who makes the bridal bed,
　Birdie, say truly?'   10
'The grey-headed sexton
　That delves the grave duly.

'The glow-worm o'er grave and stone
　Shall light thee steady;
The owl from the steeple sing   15
　"Welcome, proud lady." '

From 'The Heart of Midlothian'

'PROUD MAISIE IS IN THE WOOD': 7 **braw**: fine　8 **Kirkward**: to church

'FAREWELL! FAREWELL! . . .'

FAREWELL! Farewell! The voice you hear,
　Has left its last soft tone with you, –
Its next must join the seaward cheer,
　And shout among the shouting crew.

The accents which I scarce could form　　　　5
　Beneath your frown's controlling check,
Must give the word, above the storm,
　To cut the mast, and clear the wreck.

The timid eye I dared not raise, –
　The hand that shook when pressed to thine,　10
Must point the guns upon the chase, –
　Must bid the deadly cutlass shine.

To all I love, or hope, or fear, –
　Honour, or own, a long adieu!
To all that life has soft and dear,　　　　15
　Farewell! save memory of you!

From 'The Pirate'

SAMUEL TAYLOR COLERIDGE

THIS LIME-TREE BOWER MY PRISON

[ADDRESSED TO CHARLES LAMB,
OF THE INDIA HOUSE, LONDON]

[In the June of 1797 some long-expected friends paid a visit to the author's cottage; and on the morning of their arrival, he met with an accident, which disabled him from walking during the whole time of their stay. One evening, when they had left him for a few hours, he composed the following lines in the garden-bower.]

WELL, they are gone, and here must I remain,
This lime-tree bower my prison! I have lost
Beauties and feelings, such as would have been
Most sweet to my remembrance even when age
Had dimmed mine eyes to blindness! They, meanwhile,　5
Friends, whom I never more may meet again,
On springy heath, along the hill-top edge,
Wander in gladness, and wind down, perchance,
To that still roaring dell, of which I told;
The roaring dell, o'erwooded, narrow, deep,　10
And only speckled by the mid-day sun;
Where its slim trunk the ash from rock to rock
Flings arching like a bridge; – that branchless ash,
Unsunned and damp, whose few poor yellow leaves
Ne'er tremble in the gale, yet tremble still,　15
Fanned by the waterfall! and there my friends
Behold the dark green file of long lank weeds,
That all at once (a most fantastic sight!)
Still nod and drip beneath the dripping edge
Of the blue clay-stone.
　　　　　　　Now, my friends emerge　20
Beneath the wide wide Heaven – and view again
The many-steepled tract magnificent
Of hilly fields and meadows, and the sea,
With some fair bark, perhaps, whose sails light up

The slip of smooth clear blue betwixt two Isles　25
Of purple shadow! Yes! they wander on
In gladness all; but thou, methinks, most glad,
My gentle-hearted Charles! for thou hast pined
And hungered after Nature, many a year,
In the great City pent, winning thy way　30
With sad yet patient soul, through evil and pain
And strange calamity! Ah! slowly sink
Behind the western ridge, thou glorious Sun!
Shine in the slant beams of the sinking orb,
Ye purple heath-flowers! richlier burn, ye clouds!　35
Live in the yellow light, ye distant groves!
And kindle, thou blue Ocean! So my friend
Struck with deep joy may stand, as I have stood,
Silent with swimming sense; yea, gazing round
On the wide landscape, gaze till all doth seem　40
Less gross than bodily; and of such hues
As veil the Almighty Spirit, when yet he makes
Spirits perceive his presence.
　　　　　　　A delight
Comes sudden on my heart, and I am glad
As I myself were there! Nor in this bower,　45
This little lime-tree bower, have I not marked
Much that has soothed me. Pale beneath the blaze
Hung the transparent foliage; and I watched
Some broad and sunny leaf, and loved to see
The shadow of the leaf and stem above　50
Dappling its sunshine! And that walnut-tree
Was richly tinged, and a deep radiance lay
Full on the ancient ivy, which usurps
Those fronting elms, and now, with blackest mass
Makes their dark branches gleam a lighter hue　55
Through the late twilight: and though now the bat
Wheels silent by, and not a swallow twitters,
Yet still the solitary humble-bee
Sings in the bean-flower! Henceforth I shall know
That Nature ne'er deserts the wise and pure;　60
No plot so narrow, be but Nature there,
No waste so vacant, but may well employ
Each faculty of sense, and keep the heart
Awake to Love and Beauty! and sometimes
'Tis well to be bereft of promised good,　65
That we may lift the soul, and contemplate
With lively joy the joys we cannot share.
My gentle-hearted Charles! when the last rook
Beat its straight path along the dusky air
Homewards, I blessed it! deeming its black wing　70
(Now a dim speck, now vanishing in light)
Had crossed the mighty Orb's dilated glory,
While thou stood'st gazing; or, when all was still,
Flew creeking o'er thy head, and had a charm
For thee, my gentle-hearted Charles, to whom　75
No sound is dissonant which tells of Life.

THIS LIME-TREE BOWER MY PRISON: 30 **pent**: confined　45 **As**: as if
72 **mighty Orb**: the sun

THE RIME OF THE ANCIENT MARINER

PART ONE

An ancient Mariner meeteth three Gallants bidden to a wedding-feast, and detaineth one.

IT is an ancient Mariner,
And he stoppeth one of three.
'By thy long grey beard and glittering eye,
Now wherefore stopp'st thou me?

'The Bridegroom's doors are opened wide,   5
And I am next of kin;
The guests are met, the feast is set:
May'st hear the merry din.'

The Wedding Guest is spell-bound by the eye of the old seafaring man, and constrained to hear his tale.

He holds him with his skinny hand,
'There was a ship,' quoth he.   10
'Hold off! unhand me, grey-beard loon!'
Eftsoons his hand dropped he.

He holds him with his glittering eye –
The Wedding-Guest stood still,
And listens like a three years' child: 15
The Mariner hath his will.

The Wedding-Guest sat on a stone:
He cannot choose but hear;
And thus spake on that ancient man,
The bright-eyed Mariner.   20

The Mariner tells how the ship sailed southward with a good wind and fair weather, till it reached the Line.

'The ship was cheered, the harbour cleared,
Merrily did we drop
Below the kirk, below the hill,
Below the lighthouse top.

'The Sun came up upon the left,   25
Out of the sea came he!
And he shone bright, and on the right
Went down into the sea.

'Higher and higher every day,
Till over the mast at noon—'   30
The Wedding-Guest here beat his breast,
For he heard the loud bassoon.

The Wedding-Guest heareth the bridal music; but the Mariner continueth his tale.

The bride hath paced into the hall,
Red as a rose is she;
Nodding their heads before her goes   35
The merry minstrelsy.

The Wedding-Guest he beat his breast,
Yet he cannot choose but hear;
And thus spake on that ancient man,
The bright-eyed Mariner.   40

The ship driven by a storm toward the South Pole.

'And now the STORM-BLAST came, and he
Was tyrannous and strong:
He struck with his o'ertaking wings,
And chased us south along.

'With sloping masts and dipping prow,   45
As who pursued with yell and blow
Still treads the shadow of his foe,
And forward bends his head,
The ship drove fast, loud roared the blast,
And southward aye we fled.   50

'And now there came both mist and snow,
And it grew wondrous cold:
And ice, mast-high, came floating by,
As green as emerald.

The land of ice, and of fearful sounds where no living thing was to be seen.

'And through the drifts the snowy clifts   55
Did send a dismal sheen:
Nor shapes of men nor beasts we ken –
The ice was all between.

'The ice was here, the ice was there,
The ice was all around: 60
It cracked and growled, and roared and howled,
Like noises in a swound!

Till a great sea-bird, called the Albatross, came through the snow-fog, and was received with great joy and hospitality.

'At length did cross an Albatross,
Thorough the fog it came;
As if it had been a Christian soul,   65
We hailed it in God's name.

'It ate the food it ne'er had eat,
And round and round it flew.
The ice did split with a thunder-fit;
The helmsman steered us through!   70

And lo! the Albatross proveth a bird of good omen, and followeth the ship as it returned northward through fog and floating ice.

'And a good south wind sprung up behind;
The Albatross did follow,
And every day, for food or play,
Came to the mariners' hollo!

'In mist or cloud, on mast or shroud,   75
It perched for vespers nine;
Whiles all the night, through fog-smoke white,
Glimmered the white Moon-shine.'

THE RIME OF THE ANCIENT MARINER: 11 **loon**: a simple-minded person
12 **Eftsoons**: soon afterwards 23 **kirk**: church

55 **clifts**: cliffs 57 **ken**: see, perceive 62 **swound**: a fainting fit
76 **vespers**: evenings

The ancient Mariner inhospitably killeth the pious bird of good omen.

'God save thee, ancient Mariner!
From the fiends, that plague thee thus! –   80
Why look'st thou so?' – 'With my cross-bow
I shot the ALBATROSS.

PART TWO

'THE Sun now rose upon the right:
Out of the sea came he,
Still hid in mist, and on the left   85
Went down into the sea.

'And the good south wind still blew behind,
But no sweet bird did follow,
Nor any day for food or play
Came to the mariners' hollo!   90

His shipmates cry out against the ancient Mariner, for killing the bird of good luck.

'And I had done a hellish thing,
And it would work 'em woe:
For all averred, I had killed the bird
That made the breeze to blow.
Ah wretch! said they, the bird to slay,   95
That made the breeze to blow!

But when the fog cleared off, they justify the same, and thus make themselves accomplices in the crime.

'Nor dim nor red like God's own head,
The glorious Sun uprist:
Then all averred, I had killed the bird
That brought the fog and mist.   100
'Twas right, said they, such birds to slay,
That bring the fog and mist.

The fair breeze continues; the ship enters the Pacific Ocean, and sails northward, even till it reaches the Line.

'The fair breeze blew, the white foam flew,
The furrow followed free;
We were the first that ever burst   105
Into that silent sea.

The ship hath been suddenly becalmed.

'Down dropped the breeze, the sails dropt down,
'Twas sad as sad could be;
And we did speak only to break
The silence of the sea!   110

'All in a hot and copper sky,
The bloody Sun, at noon,
Right up above the mast did stand,
No bigger than the Moon.

'Day after day, day after day,   115
We stuck, nor breath nor motion;
As idle as a painted ship
Upon a painted ocean.

And the Albatross begins to be avenged.

'Water, water, every where,
And all the boards did shrink;   120
Water, water, every where,
Nor any drop to drink.

'The very deep did rot: O Christ!
That ever this should be!
Yea, slimy things did crawl with legs   125
Upon the slimy sea.

'About, about, in reel and rout
The death-fires danced at night;
The water, like a witch's oils,
Burnt green, and blue and white.   130

A Spirit had followed them; one of the invisible inhabitants of this planet, neither departed souls nor angels; concerning whom the learned Jew, Josephus, and the Platonic Constantinopolitan, Michael Psellus, may be consulted. They are very numerous, and there is no climate or element without one or more.

'And some in dreams assurèd were
Of the Spirit that plagued us so;
Nine fathom deep he had followed us
From the land of mist and snow.

'And every tongue, through utter drought,   135
Was withered at the root;
We could not speak, no more than if
We had been choked with soot.

The shipmates, in their sore distress, would fain throw the whole guilt on the ancient Mariner: in sign whereof they hang the dead sea-bird round his neck.

'Ah! well-a-day! what evil looks
Had I from old and young!   140
Instead of the cross, the Albatross
About my neck was hung.

PART THREE

'THERE passed a weary time. Each throat
Was parched, and glazed each eye.
A weary time! a weary time!   145
How glazed each weary eye,
When looking westward, I beheld
A something in the sky.

The ancient Mariner beholdeth a sign in the element afar off.

'At first it seemed a little speck,
And then it seemed a mist;   150
It moved and moved, and took at last
A certain shape, I wist.
'A speck, a mist, a shape, I wist!
And still it neared and neared:
As if it dodged a water-sprite,   155
It plunged and tacked and veered.

128 **death-fire:** a light believed to presage someone's death 152 **wist:** knew

92 **work 'em woe:** cause them sorrow 98 **uprist:** rose up

At its nearer approach, it seemeth him to be a ship; and at a dear ransom he freeth his speech from the bonds of thirst.

'With throats unslaked, with black lips baked,
We could nor laugh nor wail;
Through utter drought all dumb we stood!
I bit my arm, I sucked the blood,   160
And cried, "A sail! a sail!"

'With throats unslaked, with black lips baked,
Agape they heard me call:
A flash of joy!
Gramercy! they for joy did grin
And all at once their breath drew in,   165
As they were drinking all.

And horror follows. For can it be a ship that comes onward without wind or tide?

"See! see!" (I cried) "she tacks no more!
Hither to work us weal;
Without a breeze, without a tide,
She steadies with upright keel!"   170

'The western wave was all a-flame.
The day was well nigh done!
Almost upon the western wave
Rested the broad bright Sun;
When that strange shape drove suddenly   175
Betwixt us and the Sun.

It seemeth him but the skeleton of a ship.

'And straight the Sun was flecked with bars
(Heaven's Mother send us grace!)
As if through a dungeon-grate he peered
With broad and burning face.   180

And its ribs are seen as bars on the face of the setting Sun. The Spectre-Woman and her Deathmate, and no other on board the skeleton ship.

'Alas! (thought I, and my heart beat loud)
How fast she nears and nears!
Are those *her* sails that glance in the Sun,
Like restless gossameres?

'Are those *her* ribs through which the Sun   185
Did peer, as through a grate?
And is that Woman all her crew?
Is that a DEATH? and are there two?
Is DEATH that woman's mate?

Like vessel, like crew! Death and Life-in-Death have diced for the ship's crew, and she (the latter) winneth the ancient Mariner.

'*Her* lips were red, *her* looks were free,   190
Her locks were yellow as gold:
Her skin was as white as leprosy,
The Night-mare LIFE-IN-DEATH was she,
Who thicks man's blood with cold.

'The naked hulk alongside came,   195
And the twain were casting dice;
"The game is done! I've won! I've won!"
Quoth she, and whistles thrice.

No twilight within the courts of the Sun.

'The Sun's rim dips; the stars rush out:
At one stride comes the dark;   200
With far-heard whisper, o'er the sea,
Off shot the spectre-bark.

At the rising of the Moon.

'We listened and looked sideways up!
Fear at my heart, as at a cup,
My life-blood seemed to sip!   205
The stars were dim, and thick the night,
The steersman's face by his lamp gleamed white;
From the sails the dew did drip –
Till clomb above the eastern bar
The hornèd Moon, with one bright star   210
Within the nether tip.

One after another,

'One after one, by the star-dogged Moon,
Too quick for groan or sigh,
Each turned his face with a ghastly pang,
And cursed me with his eye.   215

His shipmates drop down dead.

'Four times fifty living men
(And I heard nor sigh nor groan)
With heavy thump, a lifeless lump,
They dropped down one by one.

But Life-in-Death begins her work on the ancient Mariner.

'The souls did from their bodies fly, –   220
They fled to bliss or woe!
And every soul, it passed me by,
Like the whizz of my cross-bow!'

PART FOUR

The Wedding-Guest feareth that a Spirit is talking to him;

'I fear thee, ancient Mariner!
I fear thy skinny hand!   225
And thou art long, and lank, and brown,
As is the ribbed sea-sand.

But the ancient Mariner assureth him of his bodily life and proceedeth to relate his horrible penance.

'I fear thee and thy glittering eye,
And thy skinny hand, so brown.' –
'Fear not, fear not, thou Wedding-Guest!   230
This body dropped not down.

164 **Gramercy:** an exclamation of thanks, surprise, wonder, etc (from French, *grand merci* great thanks)   168 **work us weal:** do good for us
184 **gossameres:** cobwebs   194 **thicks:** thickens

209 **clomb:** climbed

'Alone, alone, all, all alone,
Alone on a wide wide sea!
And never a saint took pity on
My soul in agony.   235

He despiseth the creatures of the calm.

'The many men, so beautiful!
And they all dead did lie:
And a thousand thousand slimy things
Lived on; and so did I.

And envieth that they *should live and so many lie dead.*

'I looked upon the rotting sea,   240
And drew my eyes away;
I looked upon the rotting deck,
And there the dead men lay.

'I looked to Heaven, and tried to pray;
But or ever a prayer had gushed,   245
A wicked whisper came, and made
My heart as dry as dust.

'I closed my lids, and kept them close,
And the balls like pulses beat;
For the sky and the sea, and the sea and the sky   250
Lay like a load on my weary eye,
And the dead were at my feet.

But the curse liveth for him in the eye of the dead men.

'The cold sweat melted from their limbs,
Nor rot nor reek did they:
The look with which they looked on me   255
Had never passed away.

'An orphan's curse would drag to hell
A spirit from on high;
But oh! more horrible than that
Is the curse in a dead man's eye!   260
Seven days, seven nights, I saw that curse,
And yet I could not die.

In his loneliness and fixedness he yearneth towards the journeying Moon, and the stars that still sojourn, yet still move onward; and every where the blue sky belongs to them, and is their appointed rest, and their native country and their own natural homes, which they enter unannounced, as lords that are certainly expected and yet there is a silent joy at their arrival.

'The moving Moon went up the sky,
And no where did abide:
Softly she was going up,   265
And a star or two beside –

'Her beams bemocked the sultry main,
Like April hoar-frost spread;
But where the ship's huge shadow lay,
The charmèd water burnt alway   270
A still and awful red.

By the light of the Moon he beholdeth God's creatures of the great calm.

'Beyond the shadow of the ship,
I watched the water-snakes:
They moved in tracks of shining white
And when they reared, the elfish light   275
Fell off in hoary flakes.

'Within the shadow of the ship
I watched their rich attire:
Blue, glossy green, and velvet black,
They coiled and swam; and every track   280
Was a flash of golden fire.

Their beauty and their happiness; he blesseth them in his heart.

'O happy living things! no tongue
Their beauty might declare:
A spring of love gushed from my heart,
And I blessed them unaware: 285
Sure my kind saint took pity on me,
And I blessed them unaware.

The spell begins to break.

'The self-same moment I could pray;
And from my neck so free
The Albatross fell off, and sank   290
Like lead into the sea.

PART FIVE

'Oh, sleep! it is a gentle thing,
Beloved from pole to pole!
To Mary Queen the praise be given!
She sent the gentle sleep from Heaven,   295
That slid into my soul.

By grace of the holy Mother, the ancient Mariner is refreshed with rain.

'The silly buckets on the deck,
That had so long remained,
I dreamt that they were filled with dew;
And when I awoke, it rained.   300

'My lips were wet, my throat was cold,
My garments all were dank;
Sure I had drunken in my dreams,
And still my body drank.

'I moved, and could not feel my limbs: 305
I was so light – almost
I thought that I had died in sleep,
And was a blessèd ghost.

---

245 **or:** before 267 **bemocked:** mocked 270 **charmèd:** under a magic spell, enchanted

297 **silly:** humble, simple

He heareth sounds and seeth strange sights and commotions in the sky and the element.

'And soon I heard a roaring wind:
It did not come anear;   310
But with its sound it shook the sails,
That were so thin and sere.

'The upper air burst into life!
And a hundred fire-flags sheen,
To and fro they were hurried about!   315
And to and fro, and in and out,
The wan stars danced between.

'And the coming wind did roar more loud,
And the sails did sigh like sedge;
And the rain poured down from one black cloud;   320
The Moon was at its edge.

'The thick black cloud was cleft, and still
The Moon was at its side:
Like waters shot from some high crag,
The lightning fell with never a jag,   325
A river steep and wide.

The bodies of the ship's crew are inspirited, and the ship moves on;

'The loud wind never reached the ship,
Yet now the ship moved on!
Beneath the lightning and the Moon
The dead men gave a groan.   330

'They groaned, they stirred, they all uprose,
Nor spake, nor moved their eyes;
It had been strange, even in a dream,
To have seen those dead men rise.

'The helmsman steered, the ship moved on;   335
Yet never a breeze up-blew;
The mariners all 'gan work the ropes,
Where they were wont to do;
They raised their limbs like lifeless tools –
We were a ghastly crew.   340

'The body of my brother's son
Stood by me, knee to knee:
The body and I pulled at one rope,
But he said nought to me.'

But not by the souls of the men, not by daemons of earth or middle-air, but by a blessed troop of angelic spirits, sent down by the invocation of the guardian saint.

'I fear thee, ancient Mariner!'   345
'Be calm, thou Wedding-Guest!
'Twas not those souls that fled in pain,
Which to their corses came again,
But a troop of spirits blest:

'For when it dawned – they dropped their arms,   350
And clustered round the mast;
Sweet sounds rose slowly through their mouths,
And from their bodies passed.

'Around, around, flew each sweet sound,
Then darted to the Sun;   355
Slowly the sounds came back again,
Now mixed, now one by one.

'Sometimes a-dropping from the sky
I heard the sky-lark sing;
Sometimes all little birds that are,   360
How they seemed to fill the sea and air
With their sweet jargoning!

'And now 'twas like all instruments,
Now like a lonely flute;
And now it is an angel's song,   365
That makes the heavens be mute.

'It ceased; yet still the sails made on
A pleasant noise till noon,
A noise like of a hidden brook
In the leafy month of June,   370
That to the sleeping woods all night
Singeth a quiet tune.

'Till noon we quietly sailèd on,
Yet never a breeze did breathe:
Slowly and smoothly went the ship,   375
Moved onward from beneath.

The lonesome Spirit from the south-pole carries on the ship as far as the Line, in obedience to the angelic troop, but still requireth vengeance.

'Under the keel nine fathom deep,
From the land of mist and snow,
The spirit slid: and it was he
That made the ship to go.   380
The sails at noon left off their tune,
And the ship stood still also.

'The Sun, right up above the mast,
Had fixed her to the ocean:
But in a minute she 'gan stir,   385
With a short uneasy motion –
Backwards and forwards half her length
With a short uneasy motion.

312 **sere:** dry 314 **fire-flags:** flashes of lightning **sheen:** shone 325 **jag:** division 337 **'gan:** began to 348 **corses:** corpses

362 **jargoning:** twittering

'Then like a pawing horse let go,
She made a sudden bound: 390
It flung the blood into my head,
And I fell down in a swound.

The Polar Spirit's fellow-daemons, the invisible inhabitants of the
element, take part in his wrong; and two of them relate, one to the
other, that penance long and heavy for the ancient Mariner hath
been accorded to the Polar Spirit, who returneth southward.

'How long in that same fit I lay,
I have not to declare;
But ere my living life returned,   395
I heard and in my soul discerned
Two voices in the air.

' "Is it he?" quoth one, "Is this the man?
By him who died on cross,
With his cruel bow he laid full low   400
The harmless Albatross.

' "The spirit who bideth by himself
In the land of mist and snow,
He loved the bird that loved the man
Who shot him with his bow."   405

'The other was a softer voice,
As soft as honey-dew:
Quoth he, "The man hath penance done,
And penance more will do."

PART SIX

First Voice

' "But tell me, tell me! speak again,   410
Thy soft response renewing –
What makes that ship drive on so fast?
What is the ocean doing?"

Second Voice

' "Still as a slave before his lord,
The ocean hath no blast;   415
His great bright eye most silently
Up to the Moon is cast –

' "If he may know which way to go;
For she guides him smooth or grim.
See, brother, see! how graciously   420
She looketh down on him."

The Mariner hath been cast into a trance; for the angelic power
causeth the vessel to drive northward faster than human life could
endure.

First Voice

' "But why drives on that ship so fast,
Without or wave or wind?"

Second Voice

' "The air is cut away before,
And closes from behind.   425

' "Fly, brother, fly! more high, more high!
Or we shall be belated:
For slow and slow that ship will go,
When the Mariner's trance is abated."

The supernatural motion is retarded; the Mariner awakes, and his
penance begins anew.

'I woke, and we were sailing on   430
As in a gentle weather:
'Twas night, calm night, the moon was high;
The dead men stood together.

'All stood together on the deck,
For a charnel-dungeon fitter: 435
All fixed on me their stony eyes,
That in the Moon did glitter.

'The pang, the curse, with which they died,
Had never passed away:
I could not draw my eyes from theirs,   440
Nor turn them up to pray.

The curse is finally expiated.

'And now this spell was snapped: once more
I viewed the ocean green,
And looked far forth, yet little saw
Of what had else been seen –   445

'Like one, that on a lonesome road
Doth walk in fear and dread,
And having once turned round walks on,
And turns no more his head;
Because he knows, a frightful fiend   450
Doth close behind him tread.

'But soon there breathed a wind on me,
Nor sound nor motion made:
Its path was not upon the sea,
In ripple or in shade.   455

'It raised my hair, it fanned my cheek
Like a meadow-gale of spring –
It mingled strangely with my fears,
Yet it felt like a welcoming.

394 **I have not to declare:** I am unable to say

427 **belated:** made late 435 **For . . . fitter:** more suitable for a tomb

'Swiftly, swiftly flew the ship,   460
Yet she sailed softly too:
Sweetly, sweetly blew the breeze –
On me alone it blew.

And the ancient Mariner beholdeth his native country.

'Oh! dream of joy! is this indeed
The light-house top I see?   465
Is this the hill? is this the kirk?
Is this mine own countree?

'We drifted o'er the harbour-bar,
And I with sobs did pray –
O let me be awake, my God!   470
Or let me sleep alway.

'The harbour-bay was clear as glass,
So smoothly it was strewn!
And on the bay the moonlight lay,
And the shadow of the Moon.   475

'The rock shone bright, the kirk no less,
That stands above the rock:
The moonlight steeped in silentness
The steady weathercock.

The angelic spirits leave the dead bodies,

'And the bay was white with silent light,   480
Till rising from the same,
Full many shapes, that shadows were,
In crimson colours came.

And appear in their own forms of light.

'A little distance from the prow
Those crimson shadows were: 485
I turned my eyes upon the deck –
Oh, Christ! what saw I there!

'Each corse lay flat, lifeless and flat,
And, by the holy rood!
A man all light, a seraph-man,   490
On every corse there stood.

'This seraph-band, each waved his hand:
It was a heavenly sight!
They stood as signals to the land,
Each one a lovely light;   495

'This seraph-band, each waved his hand,
No voice did they impart –
No voice; but oh! the silence sank
Like music on my heart.

'But soon I heard the dash of oars,   500
I heard the Pilot's cheer;
My head was turned perforce away
And I saw a boat appear.

'The Pilot and the Pilot's boy,
I heard them coming fast: 505
Dear Lord in Heaven! it was a joy
The dead men could not blast.

'I saw a third – I heard his voice:
It is the Hermit good!
He singeth loud his godly hymns   510
That he makes in the wood.
He'll shrieve my soul, he'll wash away
The Albatross's blood.

PART SEVEN

The Hermit of the Wood

'This Hermit good lives in that wood
Which slopes down to the sea.   515
How loudly his sweet voice he rears!
He loves to talk with marineres
That come from a far countree

'He kneels at morn, and noon, and eve –
He hath a cushion plump: 520
It is the moss that wholly hides
The rotted old oak-stump.

'The skiff-boat neared: I heard them talk,
"Why, this is strange, I trow!
Where are those lights so many and fair,   525
That signal made but now?"

Approacheth the ship with wonder.

' "Strange, by my faith!" the Hermit said –
"And they answered not our cheer!
The planks looked warped! and see those sails,
How thin they are and sere!   530
I never saw aught like to them,
Unless perchance it were

' "Brown skeletons of leaves that lag
My forest-brook along;
When the ivy-tod is heavy with snow,   535
And the owlet whoops to the wolf below,
That eats the she-wolf's young."

' "Dear Lord! it hath a fiendish look –"
(The Pilot made reply)
"I am a-feared" – "Push on, push on!"   540
Said the Hermit cheerily.

---

468 **harbour-bar:** sandbank at the entrance to a harbour 482 **Full
many:** a great many 489 **holy rood:** Christ's cross

524 **trow:** believe 535 **ivy-tod:** an ivy bush

'The boat came closer to the ship,
But I nor spake nor stirred;
The boat came close beneath the ship,
And straight a sound was heard.   545

The ship suddenly sinketh.

'Under the water it rumbled on,
Still louder and more dread:
It reached the ship, it split the bay;
The ship went down like lead.

The ancient Mariner is saved in the Pilot's boat.

'Stunned by that loud and dreadful sound,   550
Which sky and ocean smote,
Like one that hath been seven days drowned
My body lay afloat;
But swift as dreams, myself I found
Within the Pilot's boat.   555

'Upon the whirl, where sank the ship,
The boat spun round and round;
And all was still, save that the hill
Was telling of the sound.

'I moved my lips – the Pilot shrieked   560
And fell down in a fit;
The holy Hermit raised his eyes,
And prayed where he did sit.

'I took the oars: the Pilot's boy,
Who now doth crazy go,   565
Laughed loud and long, and all the while
His eyes went to and fro.
"Ha! ha!" quoth he, "full plain I see,
The Devil knows how to row."

'And now, all in my own countree,   570
I stood on the firm land!
The Hermit stepped forth from the boat,
And scarcely he could stand.

The ancient Mariner earnestly entreateth the Hermit to shrieve him; and the penance of life falls on him.

' "O shrieve me, shrieve me, holy man!"
The Hermit crossed his brow.   575
"Say quick," quoth he, "I bid thee say –
What manner of man art thou?"

'Forthwith this frame of mine was wrenched
With a woeful agony,
Which forced me to begin my tale;   580
And then it left me free.

And ever and anon throughout his future life an agony constraineth him to travel from land to land;

'Since then, at an uncertain hour,
That agony returns:
And till my ghastly tale is told,
This heart within me burns.   585

'I pass, like night, from land to land;
I have strange power of speech;
That moment that his face I see,
I know the man that must hear me:
To him my tale I teach.   590

'What loud upróar bursts from that door!
The wedding-guests are there:
But in the garden-bower the bride
And bride-maids singing are:
And hark the little vesper bell,   595
Which biddeth me to prayer!

'O Wedding-Guest! this soul hath been
Alone on a wide wide sea:
So lonely 'twas, that God himself
Scarce seemèd there to be.   600

'Oh, sweeter than the marriage-feast,
'Tis sweeter far to me,
To walk together to the kirk
With a goodly company! –

'To walk together to the kirk,   605
And all together pray,
While each to his great Father bends,
Old men, and babes, and loving friends
And youths and maidens gay!

And to teach, by his own example, love and reverence to all things that God made and loveth.

'Farewell, farewell! but this I tell   610
To thee, thou Wedding-Guest!
He prayeth well, who loveth well
Both man and bird and beast.

'He prayeth best, who loveth best
All things both great and small;   615
For the dear God who loveth us,
He made and loveth all.'

The Mariner, whose eye is bright,
Whose beard with age is hoar,
Is gone: and now the Wedding-Guest   620
Turned from the bridegroom's door.

He went like one that hath been stunned,
And is of sense forlorn:
A sadder and a wiser man,
He rose the morrow morn.   625

619 **hoar**: hoary, white

FROST AT MIDNIGHT

THE Frost performs its secret ministry,
Unhelped by any wind. The owlet's cry
Came loud – and hark, again! loud as before.
The inmates of my cottage, all at rest,
Have left me to that solitude, which suits 5
Abstruser musings: save that at my side
My cradled infant slumbers peacefully.
'Tis calm indeed! so calm, that it disturbs
And vexes meditation with its strange
And éxtreme silentness. Sea, hill, and wood, 10
This populous village! Sea, and hill, and wood,
With all the numberless goings-on of life,
Inaudible as dreams! the thin blue flame
Lies on my low-burnt fire, and quivers not;
Only that film, which fluttered on the grate, 15
Still flutters there, the sole unquiet thing.
Methinks its motion in this hush of nature
Gives it dim sympathies with me who live,
Making it a companionable form,
Whose puny flaps and freaks the idling Spirit 20
By its own moods interprets, every where
Echo or mirror seeking of itself,
And makes a toy of Thought.

                     But oh! how oft,
How oft, at school, with most believing mind,
Preságeful, have I gazed upon the bars, 25
To watch that fluttering *stranger*! and as oft
With unclosed lids, already had I dreamt
Of my sweet birth-place, and the old church-tower,
Whose bells, the poor man's only music, rang
From morn to evening, all the hot Fair-day, 30
So sweetly, that they stirred and haunted me
With a wild pleasure, falling on mine ear
Most like articulate sounds of things to come!
So gazed I, till the soothing things, I dreamt,
Lulled me to sleep, and sleep prolonged my dreams! 35
And so I brooded all the following morn,
Awed by the stern preceptor's face, mine eye
Fixed with mock study on my swimming book:
Save if the door half opened, and I snatched
A hasty glance, and still my heart leaped up, 40
For still I hoped to see the *stranger's* face,
Townsman, or aunt, or sister more beloved,
My play-mate when we both were clothed alike!

Dear Babe, that sleepest cradled by my side,
Whose gentle breathings, heard in this deep calm, 45
Fill up the interspersèd vacancies
And momentary pauses of the thought!
My babe so beautiful! it thrills my heart
With tender gladness, thus to look at thee,
And think that thou shalt learn far other lore, 50
And in far other scenes! For I was reared
In the great city, pent 'mid cloisters dim,
And saw nought lovely but the sky and stars.

But *thou*, my babe! shalt wander like a breeze
By lakes and sandy shores, beneath the crags 55
Of ancient mountain, and beneath the clouds,
Which image in their bulk both lakes and shores
And mountain crags: so shalt thou see and hear
The lovely shapes and sounds intelligible
Of that eternal language, which thy God 60
Utters, who from eternity doth teach
Himself in all, and all things in himself.
Great universal Teacher! he shall mould
Thy spirit, and by giving make it ask.

    Therefore all seasons shall be sweet to thee, 65
Whether the summer clothe the general earth
With greenness, or the redbreast sit and sing
Betwixt the tufts of snow on the bare branch
Of mossy apple-tree, while the nigh thatch
Smokes in the sun-thaw; whether the eave-drops fall 70
Heard only in the trances of the blast,
Or if the secret ministry of frost
Shall hang them up in silent icicles,
Quietly shining to the quiet Moon.

FROST AT MIDNIGHT: 15 **film**: a thin membrane such as half-burnt paper 20 **freaks**: caprices 37 **preceptor**: teacher 52 **pent**: confined

KUBLA KHAN
OR
A VISION IN A DREAM. A FRAGMENT

[The following fragment is here published at the request of a poet of great and deserved celebrity, and, as far as the Author's own opinions are concerned, rather as a psychological curiosity, than on the ground of any supposed poetic merits.

In the summer of the year 1797, the Author, then in ill health, had retired to a lonely farm-house between Porlock and Linton, on the Exmoor confines of Somerset and Devonshire. In consequence of a slight indisposition, an anodyne had been prescribed, from the effects of which he fell asleep in his chair at the moment that he was reading the following sentence, or words of the same substance, in 'Purchas's Pilgrimage': 'Here the Khan Kubla commanded a palace to be built, and a stately garden thereunto. And thus ten miles of fertile ground were inclosed with a wall.' The Author continued for about three hours in a profound sleep, at least of the external senses, during which time he has the most vivid confidence, that he could not have composed less than from two to three hundred lines; if that indeed can be called composition in which all the images rose up before him as *things*, with a parallel production of the correspondent expressions, without any sensation or consciousness of effort. On awaking he appeared to himself to have a distinct recollection of the whole, and taking his pen, ink, and paper, instantly and eagerly wrote down the lines that are here preserved. At this moment he was unfortunately called out by a person on business from Porlock, and detained by him above an hour, and on his return to his room, found, to his no small surprise and mortification, that though he still retained some vague and dim recollection of the general purport of the vision, yet, with the exception of some eight or ten scattered lines and images, the rest had passed away like the images on the surface of a stream into which a stone has been cast, but, alas! without the after restoration of the latter!]

In Xanadu did Kubla Khan
A stately pleasure-dome decree:
Where Alph, the sacred river, ran
Through caverns measureless to man
   Down to a sunless sea.   5
So twice five miles of fertile ground
With walls and towers were girdled round:
And there were gardens bright with sinuous rills,
Where blossomed many an incense-bearing tree;
And here were forests ancient as the hills,   10
Enfolding sunny spots of greenery.

But oh! that deep romantic chasm which slanted
Down the green hill athwart a cedarn cover!
A savage place! as holy and enchanted
As e'er beneath a waning moon was haunted   15
By woman wailing for her demon-lover!
And from this chasm, with ceaseless turmoil seething,
As if this earth in fast thick pants were breathing,
A mighty fountain momently was forced:
Amid whose swift half-intermitted burst   20
Huge fragments vaulted like rebounding hail,
Or chaffy grain beneath the thresher's flail:
And 'mid these dancing rocks at once and ever
It flung up momently the sacred river.
Five miles meandering with a mazy motion   25
Through wood and dale the sacred river ran,
Then reached the caverns measureless to man,
And sank in tumult to a lifeless ocean:
And 'mid this tumult Kubla heard from far
Ancestral voices prophesying war!   30
   The shadow of the dome of pleasure
   Floated midway on the waves:
   Where was heard the mingled measure
   From the fountain and the caves.
It was a miracle of rare device,   35
A sunny pleasure-dome with caves of ice!

   A damsel with a dulcimer
   In a vision once I saw:
   It was an Abyssinian maid,
   And on her dulcimer she played,   40
   Singing of Mount Abora.
   Could I revive within me
   Her symphony and song,
   To such a deep delight 'twould win me
That with music loud and long,   45
I would build that dome in air,
That sunny dome! those caves of ice!
And all who heard should see them there,
And all should cry, Beware! Beware!
His flashing eyes, his floating hair!   50
Weave a circle round him thrice,
And close your eyes with holy dread,
For he on honey-dew hath fed,
And drunk the milk of Paradise.

KUBLA KHAN: 1 **Kubla Khan:** Kublai Khan (?1216–94), Mongol Emperor of China, grandson of Genghis Khan; **Xanadu** (Shang-du) was his summer residence 4 **measureless:** immeasurable, boundless 8 **rills:** brooks 13 **athwart:** across **cedarn:** composed of cedar trees 19 **momently:** every moment 25 **mazy:** convoluted, perplexing

DEJECTION: AN ODE

   Late, late yestreen I saw the new Moon,
   With the old Moon in her arms;
   And I fear, I fear, my Master dear!
   We shall have a deadly storm.
        Ballad of Sir Patrick Spence

WELL! If the Bard was weather-wise, who made
   The grand old ballad of Sir Patrick Spence,
   This night, so tranquil now, will not go hence
Unroused by winds, that ply a busier trade
Than those which mould yon cloud in lazy flakes,   5
Or the dull sobbing draft, that moans and rakes
Upon the strings of this Aeolian lute,
   Which better far were mute.
   For lo! the New-moon winter-bright!
   And overspread with phantom light   10
   (With swimming phantom light o'erspread
   But rimmed and circled by a silver thread)
I see the old Moon in her lap, foretelling
   The coming-on of rain and squally blast.
And oh! that even now the gust were swelling,   15
   And the slant night-shower driving loud and fast!
Those sounds which oft have raised me, whilst they awed,
   And sent my soul abroad,
Might now perhaps their wonted impulse give,
Might startle this dull pain, and make it move and live!   20

A grief without a pang, void, dark, and drear,
   A stifled, drowsy, unimpassioned grief,
   Which finds no natural outlet, no relief,
      In word, or sigh, or tear –
O Lady! in this wan and heartless mood,   25
To other thoughts by yonder throstle wooed,
   All this long eve, so balmy and serene,
Have I been gazing on the western sky,
   And its peculiar tint of yellow green:
And still I gaze – and with how blank an eye!   30
And those thin clouds above, in flakes and bars,
That give away their motion to the stars;
Those stars, that glide behind them or between,
Now sparkling, now bedimmed, but always seen:
Yon crescent Moon, as fixed as if it grew   35
In its own cloudless, starless lake of blue;
I see them all so excellently fair,
I see, not feel, how beautiful they are!

DEJECTION: AN ODE: 7 **Aeolian lute:** a stringed instrument producing a musical sound when wind passes across it (from Aeolus, Greek god of the winds) 19 **wonted:** usual 26 **throstle:** thrush

My genial spirits fail;
    And what can these avail   40
To lift the smothering weight from off my breast?
    It were a vain endeavour,
    Though I should gaze for ever
On that green light that lingers in the west:
I may not hope from outward forms to win   45
The passion and the life, whose fountains are within.

O Lady! we receive but what we give,
And in our life alone does Nature live:
Ours is her wedding garment, ours her shroud!
    And would we aught behold, of higher worth,   50
Than that inanimate cold world allowed
To the poor loveless ever-anxious crowd,
    Ah! from the soul itself must issue forth
A light, a glory, a fair luminous cloud
        Enveloping the Earth –   55
And from the soul itself must there be sent
    A sweet and potent voice, of its own birth,
Of all sweet sounds the life and element!

O pure of heart! thou need'st not ask of me
What this strong music in the soul may be!   60
What, and wherein it doth exist,
This light, this glory, this fair luminous mist,
This beautiful and beauty-making power.
    Joy, virtuous Lady! Joy that ne'er was given,
Save to the pure, and in their purest hour,   65
Life, and Life's effluence, cloud at once and shower,
Joy, Lady! is the spirit and the power,
Which wedding Nature to us gives in dower
    A new Earth and new Heaven,
Undreamt of by the sensual and the proud –   70
Joy is the sweet voice, Joy the luminous cloud –
        We in ourselves rejoice!
And thence flows all that charms or ear or sight,
    All melodies the echoes of that voice,
All colours a suffusion from that light.   75

There was a time when, though my path was rough,
    This joy within me dallied with distress,
And all misfortunes were but as the stuff
    Whence Fancy made me dreams of happiness:
For hope grew round me, like the twining vine,   80
And fruits, and foliage, not my own, seemed
        mine.
But now afflictions bow me down to earth:
Nor care I that they rob me of my mirth;
        But oh! each visitation
Suspends what Nature gave me at my birth,   85
    My shaping spirit of Imagination.
For not to think of what I needs must feel,
    But to be still and patient, all I can;
And haply by abstruse research to steal
    From my own nature all the natural man –   90

This was my sole resource, my only plan:
Till that which suits a part infects the whole,
And now is almost grown the habit of my soul.

Hence, viper thoughts, that coil around my mind,
    Reality's dark dream!   95
I turn from you, and listen to the wind,
    Which long has raved unnoticed. What a scream
Of agony by torture lengthened out
That lute sent forth! Thou Wind, that rav'st without,
    Bare crag, or mountain-tairn, or blasted tree,   100
Or pine-grove whither woodman never clomb,
Or lonely house, long held the witches' home,
    Methinks were fitter instruments for thee,
Mad Lutanist! who in this month of showers,
Of dark-brown gardens, and of peeping flowers,   105
Mak'st Devils' yule, with worse than wintry song,
The blossoms, buds, and timorous leaves among.
    Thou Actor, perfect in all tragic sounds!
Thou mighty Poet, e'en to frenzy bold!
        What tell'st thou now about?   110
        'Tis of the rushing of an host in rout,
    With groans, of trampled men, with smarting
        wounds –

At once they groan with pain, and shudder with the
        cold!
But hush! there is a pause of deepest silence!
    And all that noise, as of a rushing crowd,   115
With groans, and tremulous shudderings – all is over –
    It tells another tale, with sounds less deep and loud!
        A tale of less affright,
        And tempered with delight,
As Otway's self had framed the tender lay, –   120
        'Tis of a little child
        Upon a lonesome wild,
Not far from home, but she hath lost her way:
And now moans low in bitter grief and fear,
And now screams loud, and hopes to make her mother
        hear.   125

'Tis midnight, but small thoughts have I of sleep:
Full seldom may my friend such vigils keep!
Visit her, gentle Sleep! with wings of healing,
    And may this storm be but a mountain-birth,
May all the stars hang bright above her dwelling,   130
    Silent as though they watched the sleeping Earth!
        With light heart may she rise,
        Gay fancy, cheerful eyes,
Joy lift her spirit, joy attune her voice;
To her may all things live, from pole to pole,   135
Their life the eddying of her living soul!
    O simple spirit, guided from above,
Dear Lady! friend devoutest of my choice,
Thus mayst thou ever, evermore rejoice.

---

68 **in dower**: as a dowry

100 **mountain-tairn**: mountain lake 101 **clomb**: climbed 120 **Otway**:
Thomas Otway (1652–85), English dramatist and poet **lay**: song

461

WALTER SAVAGE LANDOR

ROSE AYLMER

AH, what avails the sceptred race!
  Ah, what the form divine!
What every virtue, every grace!
  Rose Aylmer, all were thine.

Rose Aylmer, whom these wakeful eyes   5
  May weep, but never see,
A night of memories and sighs
  I consecrate to thee.

ROSE AYLMER: Rose Aylmer was an early love of Landor. The daughter of Lord Aylmer, she died at the age of twenty 1 **sceptred:** regal 6 **weep:** shed tears for

'PAST RUINED ILION HELEN LIVES'

PAST ruined Ilion Helen lives,
  Alcestis rises from the shades;
Verse calls them forth; 'tis verse that gives
  Immortal youth to mortal maids.

Soon shall Oblivion's deepening veil   5
  Hide all the peopled hills you see,
The gay, the proud, while lovers hail
  In distant ages you and me.

The tear for fading beauty check,
  For passing glory cease to sigh;   10
One form shall rise above the wreck,
  One name, Ianthe, shall not die.

'PAST RUINED ILION HELEN LIVES': 1 **Ilion:** the Greek name for Troy 2 **Alcestis:** in Greek myth, the wife of King Admetus of Thessaly. To save his life she died in his place, but was rescued from the Underworld by Hercules

DIRCE

STAND close around, ye Stygian set,
  With Dirce in one boat conveyed,
Or Charon, seeing, may forget
  That he is old and she a shade.

DIRCE: 1 **Stygian:** belonging to the River Styx in the Underworld, hence to the Underworld itself 2 **Dirce:** in Greek myth, a woman who was changed into a fountain by the gods 3 **Charon:** the old man who ferried dead souls across the River Styx

'I STROVE WITH NONE . . .'

I STROVE with none, for none was worth my strife:
Nature I loved, and, next to Nature, Art:
I warmed both hands before the fire of Life;
It sinks; and I am ready to depart.

'DEATH STANDS ABOVE ME, WHISPERING LOW'

'DEATH stands above me, whispering low
  I know not what into my ear:
Of his strange language all I know
  Is, there is not a word of fear.

CHARLES LAMB

THE OLD FAMILIAR FACES

I HAVE had playmates, I have had companions,
In my days of childhood, in my joyful school-days;
All, all are gone, the old familiar faces.

I have been laughing, I have been carousing,
Drinking late, sitting late, with my bosom cronies,   5
All, all are gone, the old familiar faces.

I loved a love once, fairest among women;
Closed are her doors on me, I must not see her –
All, all are gone, the old familiar faces.

I have a friend, a kinder friend has no man;   10
Like an ingrate, I left my friend abruptly;
Left him, to muse on the old familiar faces.

Ghost-like, I paced round the haunts of my childhood,
Earth seemed a desert I was bound to traverse,
Seeking to find the old familiar faces.   15

Friend of my bosom, thou more than a brother,
Why wert not thou born in my father's dwelling?
So might we talk of the old familiar faces –

How some they have died, and some they have left me,
And some are taken from me; all are departed;   20
All, all are gone, the old familiar faces.

THOMAS CAMPBELL

YE MARINERS OF ENGLAND

YE mariners of England
  That guard our native seas!
Whose flag has braved, a thousand years,
  The battle and the breeze!
Your glorious standard launch again   5
  To match another foe;
And sweep through the deep,
  While the stormy winds do blow;
While the battle rages loud and long
  And the stormy winds do blow.   10

The spirits of your fathers
   Shall start from every wave –
For the deck it was their field of fame,
   And Ocean was their grave:
Where Blake and mighty Nelson fell   15
   Your manly hearts shall glow,
As ye sweep through the deep,
   While the stormy winds do blow,
While the battle rages loud and long
   And the stormy winds do blow.   20

Britannia needs no bulwarks,
   No towers along the steep;
Her march is o'er the mountain-waves,
   Her home is on the deep.
With thunders from her native oak   25
   She quells the floods below,
As they roar on the shore,
   When the stormy winds do blow;
When the battle rages loud and long,
   And the stormy winds do blow.   30

The meteor flag of England
   Shall yet terrific burn;
Till danger's troubled night depart
   And the star of peace return.
Then, then, ye ocean-warriors!   35
   Our song and feast shall flow
To the fame of your name,
   When the storm has ceased to blow;
When the fiery fight is heard no more,
   And the storm has ceased to blow.   40

YE MARINERS OF ENGLAND: 15 **Blake:** Robert Blake (1599–1657), English admiral who commanded Cromwell's fleet 23 **march:** border 25 **thunders from her native oak:** cannon-fire from her oak-built ships

THOMAS MOORE

'THE HARP THAT ONCE THROUGH TARA'S HALLS'

THE harp that once through Tara's halls,
   The soul of music shed,
Now hangs as mute on Tara's walls
   As if that soul were fled. –
So sleeps the pride of former days,   5
   So glory's thrill is o'er,
And hearts, that once beat high for praise,
   Now feel that pulse no more!

No more to chiefs and ladies bright
   The harp of Tara swells:
The chord, alone, that breaks at night,   10
   Its tale of ruin tells.

This Freedom now so seldom wakes,
   The only throb she gives,
Is when some heart indignant breaks,   15
   To show that still she lives!

'THE HARP THAT ONCE THROUGH TARA'S HALLS': 1 **Tara:** the Hill of Tara in County Meath is the site of the historic seat of the ancient Irish kings

'BELIEVE ME, IF ALL THOSE ENDEARING YOUNG CHARMS'

BELIEVE me, if all those endearing young charms,
   Which I gaze on so fondly today,
Were to change by tomorrow, and fleet in my arms,
   Like fairy-gifts, fading away!
Thou wouldst still be adored, as this moment thou art,
   Let thy loveliness fade as it will,   6
And, around the dear ruin, each wish of my heart
   Would entwine itself verdantly still!

It is not, while beauty and youth are thine own,
   And thy cheeks unprofaned by a tear,   10
That the fervour and faith of a soul can be known,
   To which time will but make thee more dear!
No, the heart that has truly loved, never forgets,
   But as truly loves on to the close,
As the sun-flower turns on her god, when he sets,   15
   The same look which she turned when he rose!

From LALLA ROOKH

How calm, how beautiful, comes on
The stilly hour, when storms are gone;
When warring winds have died away,
And clouds, beneath the glancing ray,
Melt off, and leave the land and sea   5
Sleeping in bright tranquillity, –
Fresh as if Day again were born,
Again upon the lap of Morn!
When the light blossoms, rudely torn
And scattered at the whirlwind's will,   10
Hang floating in the pure air still,
Filling it all with precious balm,
In gratitude for this sweet calm; –
And every drop the thunder-showers
Have left upon the grass and flowers   15
Sparkles, as 'twere the lightning-gem
Whose liquid flame is born of them!
   When, 'stead of one unchanging breeze,
There blow a thousand gentle airs,
And each a different perfume bears, –   20

As if the loveliest plants and trees
Had vassal breezes of their own
To watch and wait on them alone,
And waft no other breath than theirs!
When the blue waters rise and fall,   25
In sleepy sunshine mantling all;
And ev'n that swell the tempest leaves
Is like the full and silent heaves
Of lovers' hearts, when newly blest,
Too newly to be quite at rest!   30

JAMES HENRY LEIGH HUNT

THE NILE

IT flows through old hushed Egypt and its sands,
Like some grave mighty thought threading a dream,
And times and things, as in that vision, seem
Keeping along it their eternal stands, –
Caves, pillars, pyramids, the shepherd bands   5
That roamed through the young world, the glory
   extreme
Of high Sesostris, and that southern beam,
The laughing queen that caught the world's great
   hands.
Then comes a mightier silence, stern and strong,
As of a world left empty of its throng.   10
And the void weighs on us; and then we wake,
And hear the fruitful stream lapsing along
'Twixt villages, and think how we shall take
Our own calm journey on for human sake.

THE NILE: 7 **Sesostris:** a king of Egypt of the 20th century BC 8 **The laughing queen:** Cleopatra (?69–30 BC), queen of Egypt, mistress of Julius Caesar and Mark Antony

ABOU BEN ADHEM

ABOU BEN ADHEM (may his tribe increase!)
Awoke one night from a deep dream of peace,
And saw, within the moonlight in his room,
Making it rich, and like a lily in bloom,
An angel writing in a book of gold: –   5
Exceeding peace had made Ben Adhem bold,
And to the presence in the room he said,
  'What writest thou?' – The vision raised its head,
And with a look made of all sweet accord,
Answered, 'The names of those who love the Lord.'   10
'And is mine one?' said Abou. 'Nay, not so,'
Replied the angel. Abou spoke more low,
But cheerly still; and said, 'I pray thee, then,
Write me as one that loves his fellow men.'
  The angel wrote, and vanished. The next night   15
It came again with a great wakening light,
And showed the names whom love of God has blest,
And lo! Ben Adhem's name led all the rest.

RONDEAU

JENNY kissed me when we met,
  Jumping from the chair she sat in;
Time, you thief, who love to get
  Sweets into your list, put that in:
Say I'm weary, say I'm sad,   5
  Say that health and wealth have missed me,
Say I'm growing old, but add,
  Jenny kissed me.

RONDEAU: 1 **Jenny:** Jane Welsh Carlyle (1801–66), letter-writer and wife of the Scottish historian and essayist Thomas Carlyle

THOMAS LOVE PEACOCK

THE PRIEST AND THE MULBERRY TREE

DID you hear of the curate who mounted his mare,
And merrily trotted along to the fair?
Of creature more tractable none ever heard,
In the height of her speed she would stop at a word;
And again with a word, when the curate said Hey,   5
She put forth her mettle, and galloped away.

As near to the gates of the city he rode,
While the sun of September all brilliantly glowed,
The good priest discovered, with eyes of desire,
A mulberry tree in a hedge of wild briar;   10
On boughs long and lofty, in many a green shoot,
Hung large, black, and glossy, the beautiful fruit.

The curate was hungry and thirsty to boot;
He shrunk from the thorns, though he longed for the
  fruit;
With a word he arrested his courser's keen speed,   15
And he stood up erect on the back of his steed;
On the saddle he stood, while the creature stood still,
And he gathered the fruit, till he took his good fill.

'Sure never,' he thought, 'was a creature so rare,
So docile, so true, as my excellent mare.   20
Lo, here, now I stand' (and he gazed all around)
'As safe and as steady as if on the ground,
Yet how had it been, if some traveller this way,
Had, dreaming no mischief, but chanced to cry Hey?'

He stood with his head in the mulberry tree,   25
And he spoke out aloud in his fond reverie:
At the sound of the word, the good mare made a
  push,
And down went the priest in the wild-briar bush.
He remembered too late, on his thorny green bed,
Much that well may be thought, cannot wisely be
  said.   30

From 'Crotchet Castle'

LORD BYRON

From CHILDE HAROLD'S PILGRIMAGE

THERE was a sound of revelry by night,
  And Belgium's capital had gathered then
  Her Beauty and her Chivalry, and bright
  The lamps shone o'er fair women and brave men;
  A thousand hearts beat happily; and when   5
Music arose with its voluptuous swell,
Soft eyes looked love to eyes which spake again,
And all went merry as a marriage bell;
But hush! hark! a deep sound strikes like a rising knell!

Did ye not hear it? – No – 'twas but the wind,   10
  Or the car rattling o'er the stony street;
  On with the dance! let joy be unconfined;
  No sleep till morn, when Youth and Pleasure meet
To chase the glowing Hours with flying feet –
But hark! – that heavy sound breaks in once more,
As if the clouds its echo would repeat;   16
And nearer – clearer – deadlier than before!
Arm! Arm! it is – it is – the cannon's opening roar!

Within a windowed niche of that high hall
  Sate Brunswick's fated Chieftain; he did hear   20
  That sound the first amidst the festival,
  And caught its tone with Death's prophetic ear;
And when they smiled because he deemed it near,
His heart more truly knew that peal too well
Which stretched his father on a bloody bier,   25
And roused the vengeance blood alone could quell:
He rushed into the field, and, foremost fighting, fell.

Ah! then and there was hurrying to and fro –
  And gathering tears, and tremblings of distress,
  And cheeks all pale, which but an hour ago   30
  Blushed at the praise of their own loveliness –
And there were sudden partings, such as press
The life from out young hearts, and choking sighs
Which ne'er might be repeated; who could guess
If ever more should meet those mutual eyes,   35
Since upon night so sweet such awful morn could rise!

And there was mounting in hot haste – the steed,
  The mustering squadron, and the clattering car,
  Went pouring forward with impetuous speed,
  And swiftly forming in the ranks of war –   40
And the deep thunder peal on peal afar;
And near, the beat of the alarming drum
Roused up the soldier ere the Morning Star;

While thronged the citizens with terror dumb,
Or whispering, with white lips – 'The foe! They come!
  they come!'   45

And wild and high the 'Cameron's Gathering' rose!
  The war-note of Lochiel, which Albyn's hills
  Have heard, and heard, too, have her Saxon
    foes: –
How in the noon of night that pibroch thrills,
Savage and shrill! But with the breath which fills
Their mountain-pipe, so fill the mountaineers   51
With the fierce native daring which instils
The stirring memory of a thousand years,
And Evan's – Donald's fame rings in each clansman's
  ears!

And Ardennes waves above them her green leaves,
  Dewy with Nature's tear-drops as they pass –   56
  Grieving, if aught inanimate e'er grieves,
  Over the unreturning brave, – alas!
Ere evening to be trodden like the grass
Which now beneath them, but above shall grow
In its next verdure, when this fiery mass   61
Of living Valour, rolling on the foe
And burning with high Hope, shall moulder cold and
  low.

Last noon beheld them full of lusty life; –
  Last eve in Beauty's circle proudly gay;   65
  The Midnight brought the signal-sound of strife,
  The Morn the marshalling in arms, – the Day
Battle's magnificently stern array!
The thunder-clouds close o'er it, which when rent
The earth is covered thick with other clay   70
Which her own clay shall cover, heaped and pent,
Rider and horse, – friend, – foe, – in one red burial
  blent!

[Canto 3, stanzas 21–8]

I STOOD in Venice, on the 'Bridge of Sighs';
  A palace and a prison on each hand:
  I saw from out the wave her structures rise
  As from the stroke of the Enchanter's wand:
A thousand years their cloudy wings expand   5
Around me, and a dying Glory smiles
O'er the far times, when many a subject land
Looked to the wingèd Lion's marble piles,
Where Venice sate in state, throned on her hundred
  isles!

CHILDE HAROLD'S PILGRIMAGE: 2 **Belgium's capital:** Brussels, where the Duchess of Richmond gave a ball on the eve of the battle of Quatre Bras, which immediately preceded that of Waterloo (June 1815) 11 **car:** carriage 20 **Brunswick's fated chieftain:** the Duke of Brunswick was killed at Quatre Bras. His father had also died fighting Napoleon some years earlier

46 **Cameron's Gathering:** the rallying pibroch (bagpipe-tune) of the Clan Cameron, whose chief was called Lochiel 47 **Albyn:** Scotland 54 **Evan, Donald:** famous heroes of the Clan Cameron 55 **Ardennes:** a wooded region in Belgium 70 **other clay:** dead bodies 71 **pent:** confined 72 **blent:** blended, mixed 2ND EXTRACT: 1 **Bridge of Sighs:** a bridge between the Doge's Palace and the Prison of San Marco, the sighs supposedly uttered by those going from the former to the latter 8 **wingèd Lion:** the symbol of St Mark, patron saint of Venice

She looks a sea Cybele, fresh from ocean, 10
  Rising with her tiara of proud towers
  At airy distance, with majestic motion,
  A ruler of the waters and their powers:
  And such she was; her daughters had their dowers
  From spoils of nations, and the exhaustless East 15
  Poured in her lap all gems in sparkling showers.
  In purple was she robed, and of her feast
Monarchs partook, and deemed their dignity
    increased.

In Venice Tasso's echoes are no more,
  And silent rows the songless gondolier; 20
  Her palaces are crumbling to the shore,
  And music meets not always now the ear:
  Those days are gone – but Beauty still is here.
  States fall – arts fade – but Nature doth not die,
  Nor yet forget how Venice once was dear, 25
  The pleasant place of all festivity,
The Revel of the earth – the Masque of Italy!

But unto us she hath a spell beyond
  Her name in story, and her long array
  Of mighty shadows, whose dim forms despond 30
  Above the Dogeless city's vanished sway;
  Ours is a trophy which will not decay
  With the Rialto; Shylock and the Moor,
  And Pierre, can not be swept or worn away –
  The keystones of the Arch! though all were o'er, 35
For us repeopled were the solitary shore.

The Beings of the Mind are not of clay;
  Essentially immortal, they create
  And multiply in us a brighter ray
  And more beloved existence: that which Fate 40
  Prohibits to dull life in this our state
  Of mortal bondage, by these Spirits supplied,
  First exiles, then replaces what we hate;
  Watering the heart whose early flowers have died,
And with a fresher growth replenishing the void. 45
               [Canto 4, stanzas 1–5]

THERE is a pleasure in the pathless woods,
  There is a rapture on the lonely shore,
  There is society, where none intrudes,
  By the deep Sea, and Music in its roar;
  I love not Man the less, but Nature more, 5
  From these our interviews, in which I steal
  From all I may be, or have been before,
  To mingle with the Universe, and feel
What I can ne'er express – yet can not all conceal.

10 **Cybele:** in classical myth, a goddess of nature 19 **Tasso:** the Italian poet Torquato Tasso (1544–95), whose verses were formerly chanted by Venetian gondoliers 27 **Masque:** a dramatic entertainment often involving disguises 31 **Dogeless:** the last doge (or chief magistrate) of Venice was deposed by the invading French in 1797 33 **Rialto:** the business centre of medieval and Renaissance Venice **Shylock and the Moor:** Shylock features in Shakespeare's *Merchant of Venice* and the Moor is Othello, a soldier of Venice 34 **Pierre:** a character in Otway's *Venice Preserved*

Roll on, thou deep and dark blue Ocean – roll! 10
  Ten thousand fleets sweep over thee in vain;
  Man marks the earth with ruin – his control
  Stops with the shore; – upon the watery plain
  The wrecks are all thy deed, nor doth remain
  A shadow of man's ravage, save his own, 15
  When, for a moment, like a drop of rain,
  He sinks into thy depths with bubbling groan –
Without a grave – unknelled, uncoffined, and
    unknown.

His steps are not upon thy paths, – thy fields
  Are not a spoil for him, – thou dost arise 20
  And shake him from thee; the vile strength he wields
  For Earth's destruction thou dost all despise,
  Spurning him from thy bosom to the skies –
  And send'st him, shivering in thy playful spray
  And howling, to his Gods, where haply lies 25
  His petty hope in some near port or bay,
And dashest him again to Earth: – there let him lay.

The armaments which thunderstrike the walls
  Of rock-built cities, bidding nations quake,
  And Monarchs tremble in their Capitals, 30
  The oak Leviathans, whose huge ribs make
  Their clay creator the vain title take
  Of Lord of thee, and Arbiter of War –
  These are thy toys, and, as the snowy flake,
  They melt into thy yeast of waves, which mar 35
Alike the Armada's pride or spoils of Trafalgar.

Thy shores are empires, changed in all save thee –
  Assyria – Greece – Rome – Carthage – what are
    they?
  Thy waters washed them power while they were
    free,
  And many a tyrant since; their shores obey 40
  The stranger, slave, or savage; their decay
  Has dried up realms to deserts: – not so thou,
  Unchangeable save to thy wild waves' play,
  Time writes no wrinkle on thine azure brow –
Such as Creation's dawn beheld, thou rollest now. 45

Thou glorious mirror, where the Almighty's form
  Glasses itself in tempests; in all time,
  Calm or convulsed – in breeze, or gale, or storm –
  Icing the Pole, or in the torrid clime
  Dark-heaving – boundless, endless, and sublime –
  The image of Eternity – the throne 51
  Of the Invisible; even from out thy slime
  The monsters of the deep are made – each Zone
Obeys thee – thou goest forth, dread, fathomless,
    alone.

3RD EXTRACT: 25 **haply:** perhaps 31 **oak Leviathans:** wooden warships 35 **Armada:** the Spanish Armada sent against England in 1588, which was defeated in battle and almost completely destroyed by storms **Trafalgar:** the naval battle of 1805 in which the French and Spanish were defeated by the British under Nelson 47 **Glasses:** mirrors

And I have loved thee, Ocean! and my joy   55
  Of youthful sports was on thy breast to be
Borne, like thy bubbles, onward: from a boy
I wantoned with thy breakers – they to me
Were a delight; and if the freshening sea
Made them a terror – 'twas a pleasing fear,   60
For I was as it were a Child of thee,
And trusted to thy billows far and near,
And laid my hand upon thy mane – as I do here.

                [Canto 4, stanzas 178–84]

SHE WALKS IN BEAUTY

SHE walks in Beauty, like the night
  Of cloudless climes and starry skies;
And all that's best of dark and bright
  Meet in her aspect and her eyes:
Thus mellowed to that tender light   5
  Which Heaven to gaudy day denies.

One shade the more, one ray the less,
  Had half impaired the nameless grace
Which waves in every raven tress,
  Or softly lightens o'er her face;   10
Where thoughts serenely sweet express,
  How pure, how dear their dwelling-place.

And on that cheek, and o'er that brow,
  So soft, so calm, yet eloquent,
The smiles that win, the tints that glow,   15
  But tell of days in goodness spent,
A mind at peace with all below,
  A heart whose love is innocent!

SHE WALKS IN BEAUTY: 1 **like the night:** Byron wrote the poem after seeing his cousin, Mrs Robert Wilmot, in a black spangled gown

THE DESTRUCTION OF SENNACHERIB

THE Assyrian came down like the wolf on the fold,
And his cohorts were gleaming in purple and gold;
And the sheen of their spears was like stars on the sea,
When the blue wave rolls nightly on deep Galilee.

Like the leaves of the forest when Summer is green,   5
That host with their banners at sunset were seen:
Like the leaves of the forest when autumn hath blown,
That host on the morrow lay withered and strown.

For the Angel of Death spread his wings on the blast,
And breathed in the face of the foe as he passed: 10
And the eyes of the sleepers waxed deadly and chill,
And their hearts but once heaved – and for ever grew
  still!

And there lay the steed with his nostrils all wide,
But through it there rolled not the breath of his pride;
And the foam of his gasping lay white on the turf,   15
And cold as the spray of the rock-beating surf.

And there lay the rider distorted and pale,
With the dew on his brow and the rust on his mail:
And the tents were all silent – the banners alone –
The lances unlifted – the trumpet unblown.   20

And the widows of Ashur are loud in their wail,
And the idols are broke in the temple of Baal;
And the might of the Gentile, unsmote by the sword,
Hath melted like snow in the glance of the Lord!

THE DESTRUCTION OF SENNACHERIB: 1 **The Assyrian:** Sennacherib (died 681 BC), king of Assyria. According to the Bible (2 Kings 18, 19), thousands of the army with which he was invading Judah were killed in their sleep by an angel 21 **Ashur:** the capital of ancient Assyria 22 **Baal:** an ancient Semitic fertility god

WHEN WE TWO PARTED

WHEN we two parted
  In silence and tears,
Half broken-hearted,
  To sever for years,
Pale grew thy cheek and cold,   5
  Colder thy kiss;
Truly that hour foretold
  Sorrow to this.

The dew of the morning
  Sank chill on my brow –   10
It felt like the warning
  Of what I feel now.
Thy vows are all broken,
  And light is thy fame:
I hear thy name spoken,   15
  And share in its shame.

They name thee before me,
  A knell to mine ear;
A shudder comes o'er me –
  Why wert thou so dear?   20
They know not I knew thee,
  Who knew thee too well: –
Long, long shall I rue thee,
  Too deeply to tell.

In secret we met –   25
  In silence I grieve,
That thy heart could forget,
  Thy spirit deceive.
If I should meet thee
  After long years,   30
How should I greet thee? –
  With silence and tears.

BEPPO
A VENETIAN STORY

'Tɪs known, at least it should be, that throughout
    All countries of the Catholic persuasion,
Some weeks before Shrove Tuesday comes about,
    The People take their fill of recreation,
And buy repentance, ere they grow devout,   5
    However high their rank, or low their station,
With fiddling, feasting, dancing, drinking, masquing,
And other things which may be had for asking.

The moment night with dusky mantle covers
    The skies (and the more duskily the better),   10
The Time less liked by husbands than by lovers
    Begins, and Prudery flings aside her fetter;
And Gaiety on restless tiptoe hovers,
    Giggling with all the gallants who beset her;
And there are songs and quavers, roaring, humming,
Guitars, and every other sort of strumming.   16

And there are dresses splendid, but fantastical,
    Masks of all times and nations, Turks and Jews,
And harlequins and clowns, with feats gymnastical,
    Greeks, Romans, Yankee-doodles, and Hindoos;   20
All kinds of dress, except the ecclesiastical,
    All people, as their fancies hit, may choose,
But no one in these parts may quiz the Clergy, –
Therefore take heed, ye Freethinkers! I charge ye.

You'd better walk about begirt with briars,   25
    Instead of coat and smallclothes, than put on
A single stitch reflecting upon friars,
    Although you swore it only was in fun;
They'd haul you o'er the coals, and stir the fires
    Of Phlegethon with every mother's son,   30
Nor say one mass to cool the cauldron's bubble
That boiled your bones, unless you paid them double.

But saving this, you may put on whate'er
    You like by way of doublet, cape, or cloak,
Such as in Monmouth-street, or in Rag Fair,   35
    Would rig you out in seriousness or joke;
And even in Italy such places are,
    With prettier name in softer accents spoke,
For, bating Covent Garden, I can hit on
No place that's called 'Piazza' in Great Britain.   40

This feast is named the Carnival, which being
    Interpreted, implies 'farewell to flesh':
So called, because the name and thing agreeing,
    Through Lent they live on fish both salt and fresh.
But why they usher Lent with so much glee in,   45
    Is more than I can tell, although I guess
'Tis as we take a glass with friends at parting,
In the Stage-Coach or Packet, just at starting.

And thus they bid farewell to carnal dishes,
    And solid meats, and highly spiced ragouts,   50
To live for forty days on ill-dressed fishes,
    Because they have no sauces to their stews;
A thing which causes many 'poohs' and 'pishes',
    And several oaths (which would not suit the Muse),
From travellers accustomed from a boy   55
To eat their salmon, at the least, with soy;

And therefore humbly I would recommend
    'The curious in fish-sauce', before they cross
The sea, to bid their cook, or wife, or friend,
    Walk or ride to the Strand, and buy in gross   60
(Or if set out beforehand, these may send
    By any means least liable to loss),
Ketchup, Soy, Chili-vinegar, and Harvey,
Or, by the Lord! a Lent will well nigh starve ye;

That is to say, if your religion's Roman,   65
    And you at Rome would do as Romans do,
According to the proverb, – although no man,
    If foreign, is obliged to fast; and you,
If Protestant, or sickly, or a woman,
    Would rather dine in sin on a ragout –   70
Dine and be damned! I don't mean to be coarse,
But that's the penalty, to say no worse.

Of all the places where the Carnival
    Was most facetious in the days of yore,
For dance, and song, and serenade, and ball,   75
    And Masque, and Mime, and Mystery, and more
Than I have time to tell now, or at all,
    Venice the bell from every city bore, –
And at the moment when I fix my story,
That sea-born city was in all her glory.   80

They've pretty faces yet, those same Venetians,
    Black eyes, arched brows, and sweet expressions still;
Such as of old were copied from the Grecians,
    In ancient arts by moderns mimicked ill;
And like so many Venuses of Titian's   85
    (The best's at Florence – see it, if ye will),
They look when leaning over the balcóny,
Or stepped from out a picture by Giorgione,

BEPPO: 7 **masquing:** attending masked balls 12 **fetter:** chain, restraint
25 **begirt:** surrounded 26 **smallclothes:** close-fitting knee-breeches
for men 30 **Phlegethon:** a river of fire in Hades 35 **Monmouth-
street:** a London street once known for its second-hand clothes
shops **Rag fair:** an old-clothes market 39 **bating:** except **Covent
Garden:** a square in London; in Byron's day its taverns and coffee-
houses were frequented by poets, artists, actors, etc

48 **Packet:** a boat carrying passengers and mail on a short fixed
route 78 **bell:** to bear the bell is to win first place in a contest
85 **Titian:** Tiziano Vecellio (?1490–1576), Venetian painter 88 **Giorgione:**
Giogio Barbarelli (?1478–1511), Italian painter of the Venetian school

Whose tints are Truth and Beauty at their best;
 And when you to Manfrini's palace go,   90
That picture (howsoever fine the rest)
 Is loveliest to my mind of all the show;
It may perhaps be also to *your* zest,
 And that's the cause I rhyme upon it so:
'Tis but a portrait of his Son, and Wife,   95
And self; but *such* a Woman! Love in life!

Love in full life and length, not love ideal,
 No, nor ideal beauty, that fine name,
But something better still, so very real,
 That the sweet Model must have been the same;
A thing that you would purchase, beg, or steal,   101
 Wer't not impossible, besides a shame:
The face recalls some face, as 'twere with pain,
You once have seen, but ne'er will see again;

One of those forms which flit by us, when we   105
 Are young, and fix our eyes on every face;
And, oh! the Loveliness at times we see
 In momentary gliding, the soft grace,
The Youth, the Bloom, the Beauty which agree,
 In many a nameless being we retrace,   110
Whose course and home we knew not, nor shall know,
Like the lost Pleiad seen no more below.

I said that like a picture by Giorgione
 Venetian women were, and so they *are*,
Particularly seen from a balcóny,   115
 (For beauty's sometimes best set off afar)
And there, just like a heroine of Goldoni,
 They peep from out the blind, or o'er the bar;
And truth to say, they're mostly very pretty,
And rather like to show it, more's the pity!   120

For glances beget ogles, ogles sighs,
 Sighs wishes, wishes words, and words a letter,
Which flies on wings of light-heeled Mercuries,
 Who do such things because they know no better;
And then, God knows what mischief may arise,   125
 When Love links two young people in one fetter,
Vile assignations, and adulterous beds,
Elopements, broken vows, and hearts, and heads.

Shakespeare described the sex in Desdemona
 As very fair, but yet suspéct in fame,   130
And to this day from Venice to Verona
 Such matters may be probably the same,
Except that since those times was never known a
 Husband whom mere suspicion could inflame
To suffocate a wife no more than twenty,   135
Because she had a 'Cavalier Servente'.

Their jealousy (if they are ever jealous)
 Is of a fair complexion altogether,
Not like that sooty devil of Othello's,
 Which smothers women in a bed of feather,   140
But worthier of these much more jolly fellows,
 When weary of the matrimonial tether
His head for such a wife no mortal bothers,
But takes at once another, or *another's*.

Didst ever see a Gondola? For fear   145
 You should not, I'll describe it you exactly:
'Tis a long covered boat that's common here,
 Carved at the prow, built lightly, but compactly,
Rowed by two rowers, each called 'Gondolier',
 It glides along the water looking blackly,   150
Just like a coffin clapped in a canoe,
Where none can make out what you say or do.

And up and down the long canals they go,
 And under the Rialto shoot along,
By night and day, all paces, swift or slow,   155
 And round the theatres, a sable throng,
They wait in their dusk livery of woe, –
 But not to them do woeful things belong,
For sometimes they contain a deal of fun,
Like mourning coaches when the funeral's done.   160

But to my story. – 'Twas some years ago,
 It may be thirty, forty, more or less,
The Carnival was at its height, and so
 Were all kinds of buffoonery and dress;
A certain lady went to see the show,   165
 Her real name I know not, nor can guess,
And so we'll call her Laura, if you please,
Because it slips into my verse with ease.

She was not old, nor young, nor at the years
 Which certain people call a '*certain age*',   170
Which yet the most uncertain age appears,
 Because I never heard, nor could engage
A person yet by prayers, or bribes, or tears,
 To name, define by speech, or write on page,
The period meant precisely by that word, –   175
Which surely is exceedingly absurd.

Laura was blooming still, had made the best
 Of Time, and Time returned the compliment,
And treated her genteelly, so that, dressed,
 She looked extremely well where'er she went;   180
A pretty woman is a welcome guest,
 And Laura's brow a frown had rarely bent;
Indeed, she shone all smiles, and seemed to flatter
Mankind with her black eyes for looking at her.

---

112 **lost Pleiad**: in Greek myth, the Pleiades were the seven daughters
of Atlas, who were turned into stars. One of the sisters, Electra, was
known as the lost Pleiad because she does not show herself
117 **Goldoni**: Carlo Goldoni (1707–93), Venetian comic dramatist
123 **Mercuries**: messengers (Mercury was the messenger of the gods)
136 **Cavalier Servente**: an escort, often a lover, of a married woman

154 **Rialto**: a bridge in Venice   156 **sable**: black

She was a married woman; 'tis convenient, 185
   Because in Christian countries 'tis a rule
To view their little slips with eyes more lenient;
   Whereas if single ladies play the fool
(Unless within the period intervenient
   A well-timed wedding makes the scandal cool) 190
I don't know how they ever can get over it,
Except they manage never to discover it.

Her husband sailed upon the Adriatic,
   And made some voyages, too, in other seas,
And when he lay in Quarantine for pratique 195
   (A forty days' precaution 'gainst disease),
His wife would mount, at times, her highest attic,
   For thence she could discern the ship with ease:
He was a merchant trading to Aleppo,
His name Giuseppe, called more briefly, Beppo. 200

He was a man as dusky as a Spaniard,
   Sunburnt with travel, yet a portly figure;
Though coloured, as it were, within a tanyard,
   He was a person both of sense and vigour –
A better seaman never yet did man yard; 205
   And she, although her manners showed no rigour,
Was deemed a woman of the strictest principle,
So much as to be thought almost invincible.

But several years elapsed since they had met;
   Some people thought the ship was lost, and some
That he had somehow blundered into debt, 211
   And did not like the thought of steering home;
And there were several offered any bet,
   Or that he would, or that he would not come;
For most men (till by losing rendered sager) 215
Will back their own opinions with a wager.

'Tis said that their last parting was pathetic,
   As partings often are, or ought to be,
And their presentiment was quite prophetic,
   That they should never more each other see 220
(A sort of morbid feeling, half poetic,
   Which I have known occur in two or three),
When kneeling on the shore upon her sad knee
He left this Adriatic Ariadne.

And Laura waited long, and wept a little, 225
   And thought of wearing weeds, as well she might;
She almost lost all appetite for victual,
   And could not sleep with ease alone at night;
She deemed the window-frames and shutters brittle
   Against a daring housebreaker or sprite, 230
And so she thought it prudent to connect her
With a vice-husband, *chiefly* to *protect her.*

She chose (and what is there they will not choose,
   If only you will but oppose their choice?)
Till Beppo should return from his long cruise, 235
   And bid once more her faithful heart rejoice,
A man some women like, and yet abuse –
   A Coxcomb was he by the public voice;
A Count of wealth, they said, as well as quality,
And in his pleasures of great liberality. 240

And then he was a Count, and then he knew
   Music, and dancing, fiddling, French and Tuscan;
The last not easy, be it known to you,
   For few Italians speak the right Etruscan.
He was a critic upon operas, too, 245
   And knew all niceties of sock and buskin;
And no Venetian audience could endure a
Song, scene, or air, when he cried 'seccatura!'

His 'bravo' was decisive, for that sound
   Hushed 'Academie' sighed in silent awe; 250
The fiddlers trembled as he looked around,
   For fear of some false note's detected flaw;
The 'Prima Donna's' tuneful heart would bound,
   Dreading the deep damnation of his 'Bah!'
Soprano, Basso, even the Contra-Alto, 255
Wished him five fathom under the Rialto.

He patronised the Improvisatori,
   Nay, could himself extemporise some stanzas,
Wrote rhymes, sang songs, could also tell a story,
   Sold pictures, and was skilful in the dance as 260
Italians can be, though in this their glory
   Must surely yield the palm to that which France has;
In short, he was a perfect Cavaliero,
And to his very valet seemed a hero.

Then he was faithful too, as well as amorous; 265
   So that no sort of female could complain,
Although they're now and then a little clamorous,
   He never put the pretty souls in pain;
His heart was one of those which most enamour us,
   Wax to receive, and marble to retain: 270
He was a lover of the good old school,
Who still become more constant as they cool.

No wonder such accomplishments should turn
   A female head, however sage and steady –
With scarce a hope that Beppo could return, 275
   In law he was almost as good as dead, he
Nor sent, nor wrote, nor showed the least concern,
   And she had waited several years already:
And really if a man won't let us know
That he's alive, he's *dead* – or should be so. 280

---

195 **pratique:** permission to land given to a ship by a port's authorities, usually after a period of quarantine 202 **portly:** dignified 203 **tanyard:** a tannery 205 **yard:** a spar on a ship's mast, from which a sail is hung 224 **Ariadne:** in Greek myth, the lover of Theseus, who abandoned her on the island of Naxos 226 **weeds:** widow's clothing

246 **sock and buskin:** in classical theatre, socks were light shoes worn by actors in comedies and buskins were boots worn by actors in tragedies 248 **seccatura:** a cry from the audience demanding that a performance should be abruptly ended 262 **palm:** a palm leaf as a symbol of victory

Besides, within the Alps, to every woman
  (Although, God knows, it is a grievous sin),
'Tis, I may say, permitted to have *two* men;
  I can't tell who first brought the custom in,
But 'Cavalier Serventes' are quite common,   285
  And no one notices or cares a pin;
And we may call this (not to say the worst)
A *second* marriage which corrupts the *first*.

The word was formally a 'Cicisbeo',
  But *that* is now grown vulgar and indecent;   290
The Spaniards call the person a 'Cortejo',
  For the same mode subsists in Spain, though recent;
In short it reaches from the Po to Teio,
  And may perhaps at last be o'er the sea sent:
But Heaven preserve Old England from such
      courses!
  Or what becomes of damage and divorces?   296

However, I still think, with all due deference
  To the fair *single* part of the creation,
That married ladies should preserve the preference
  In *tête à tête* or general conversation –   300
And this I say without peculiar reference
  To England, France, or any other nation –
Because they know the world, and are at ease,
And being natural, naturally please.

'Tis true, your budding Miss is very charming,   305
  But shy and awkward at first coming out,
So much alarmed, that she is quite alarming,
  All Giggle, Blush; half Pertness, and half Pout;
And glancing at *Mamma*, for fear there's harm in
  What you, she, it, or they, may be about: 310
The Nursery still lisps out in all they utter –
Besides, they always smell of bread and butter.

But 'Cavalier Servente' is the phrase
  Used in politest circles to express
This supernumerary slave, who stays   315
  Close to the lady as a part of dress,
Her word the only law which he obeys.
  His is no sinecure, as you may guess;
Coach, servants, gondola, he goes to call,
And carries fan and tippet, gloves and shawl.   320

With all its sinful doings, I must say,
  That Italy's a pleasant place to me,
Who love to see the Sun shine every day,
  And vines (not nailed to walls) from tree to tree
Festooned, much like the back scene of a play,   325
  Or melodrame, which people flock to see,
When the first act is ended by a dance
In vineyards copied from the South of France.

I like on Autumn evenings to ride out,
  Without my being forced to bid my groom be sure
My cloak is round his middle strapped about,   331
  Because the skies are not the most secure;
I know too that, if stopped upon my route,
  Where the green alleys windingly allure,
Reeling with *grapes* red wagons choke the way, –   335
In England 'twould be dung, dust, or a dray.

I also like to dine on becaficas,
  To see the Sun set, sure he'll rise tomorrow,
Not through a misty morning twinkling weak as
  A drunken man's dead eye in maudlin sorrow,   340
But with all Heaven t'himself; the day will break as
  Beauteous as cloudless, nor be forced to borrow
That sort of farthing candlelight which glimmers
Where reeking London's smoky cauldron simmers.

I love the language, that soft bastard Latin,   345
  Which melts like kisses from a female mouth,
And sounds as if it should be writ on satin,
  With syllables which breathe of the sweet South,
And gentle liquids gliding all so pat in,
  That not a single accent seems uncouth,   350
Like our harsh northern whistling, grunting guttural,
Which we're obliged to hiss, and spit, and sputter all.

I like the women too (forgive my folly!),
  From the rich peasant cheek of ruddy bronze,
And large black eyes that flash on you a volley   355
  Of rays that say a thousand things at once,
To the high Dama's brow, more melancholy,
  But clear, and with a wild and liquid glance,
Heart on her lips, and soul within her eyes,
Soft as her clime, and sunny as her skies.   360

Eve of the land which still is Paradise!
  Italian Beauty didst thou not inspire
Raphael, who died in thy embrace, and vies
  With all we know of Heaven, or can desire,
In what he hath bequeathed us? – in what guise,   365
  Though flashing from the fervour of the Lyre,
Would *words* describe thy past and present glow,
While yet Canova can create below?

'England! with all thy faults I love thee still,'
  I said at Calais, and have not forgot it;   370
I like to speak and lucubrate my fill;
  I like the government (but that is not it);
I like the freedom of the press and quill;
  I like the Habeas Corpus (when we've got it);
I like a Parliamentary debate,   375
Particularly when 'tis not too late;

293 **Po:** a river in N Italy **Teio:** the Tagus, a river in Spain and Portugal 320 **tippet:** a woman's fur cape

337 **becaficas:** songbirds eaten as a delicacy in Italy 357 **Dama:** great lady 363 **Raphael:** Raffaello Santi or Sanzio (1483–1520), Italian Renaissance painter 368 **Canova:** Antonio Canova (1757–1822), Italian neoclassical sculptor

I like the taxes, when they're not too many;
   I like a seacoal fire, when not too dear;
I like a beef-steak, too, as well as any;
   Have no objection to a pot of beer;   380
I like the weather, – when it is not rainy,
   That is, I like two months of every year.
And so God save the Regent, Church, and King!
Which means that I like all and every thing.

Our standing army, and disbanded seamen,   385
   Poor's rate, Reform, my own, the nation's debt,
Our little riots just to show we're free men,
   Our trifling bankruptcies in the Gazette,
Our cloudy climate, and our chilly women,
   All these I can forgive, and those forget,   390
And greatly venerate our recent glories,
And wish they were not owing to the Tories.

But to my tale of Laura, – for I find
   Digression is a sin, that by degrees
Becomes exceeding tedious to my mind,   395
   And, therefore, may the reader too displease –
The gentle reader, who may wax unkind,
   And caring little for the Author's ease,
Insist on knowing what he means – a hard
And hapless situation for a Bard.   400

Oh! that I had the art of easy writing
   What should be easy reading! could I scale
Parnassus, where the Muses sit inditing
   Those pretty poems never known to fail,
How quickly would I print (the world delighting)   405
   A Grecian, Syrian, or *Assyrian* tale;
And sell you, mixed with western Sentimentalism,
Some samples of the *finest Orientalism.*

But I am but a nameless sort of person,
   (A broken Dandy lately on my travels)   410
And take for rhyme, to hook my rambling verse on,
   The first that Walker's Lexicon unravels,
And when I can't find that, I put a worse on,
   Not caring as I ought for critics' cavils;
I've half a mind to tumble down to prose,   415
But verse is more in fashion – so here goes!

The Count and Laura made their new arrangement,
   Which lasted, as arrangements sometimes do,
For half a dozen years without estrangement;
   They had their little differences, too;   420
Those jealous whiffs, which never any change meant;
   In such affairs there probably are few
Who have not had this pouting sort of squabble,
From sinners of high station to the rabble.

But, on the whole, they were a happy pair,   425
   As happy as unlawful love could make them;
The gentleman was fond, the lady fair,
   Their chains so slight, 'twas not worth while to
      break them:
The World beheld them with indulgent air;
   The pious only wished 'the Devil take them!'   430
He took them not; he very often waits,
And leaves old sinners to be young ones' baits.

But they were young: Oh! what without our Youth
   Would Love be! What would Youth be without Love!
Youth lends its joy, and sweetness, vigour, truth,   435
   Heart, soul, and all that seems as from above;
But, languishing with years, it grows uncouth –
   One of few things Experience don't improve;
Which is, perhaps, the reason why old fellows
Are always so preposterously jealous.   440

It was the Carnival, as I have said
   Some six and thirty stanzas back, and so
Laura the usual preparations made,
   Which you do when your mind's made up to go
Tonight to Mrs Boehm's masquerade,   445
   Spectator, or Partaker in the show;
The only difference known between the cases
Is – *here,* we have six weeks of 'varnished faces'.

Laura, when dressed, was (as I sang before)
   A pretty woman as was ever seen,   450
Fresh as the Angel o'er a new inn door,
   Or frontispiece of a new Magazine,
With all the fashions which the last month wore,
   Coloured, and silver paper leaved between
That and the title-page, for fear the Press   455
Should soil with parts of speech the parts of dress.

They went to the Ridotto; 'tis a hall
   Where People dance, and sup, and dance again;
Its proper name, perhaps, were a masqued ball,
   But that's of no importance to my strain;   460
'Tis (on a smaller scale) like our Vauxhall,
   Excepting that it can't be spoilt by rain;
The company is 'mixed' (the phrase I quote is
As much as saying, they're below your notice);

For a 'mixed company' implies that, save   465
   Yourself and friends, and half a hundred more,
Whom you may bow to without looking grave,
   The rest are but a vulgar set, the Bore
Of public places, where they basely brave
   The fashionable stare of twenty score   470
Of well-bred persons, called '*The World*'; but I,
Although I know them, really don't know why.

---

403 **Parnassus:** a mountain in Greece, sacred to the Muses and Apollo

461 **Vauxhall:** Vauxhall Gardens in London, a public garden and place of entertainment

This is the case in England; at least was
  During the dynasty of Dandies, now
Perchance succeeded by some other class   475
  Of imitated Imitators: – how
Irreparably soon decline, alas!
  The Demagogues of fashion: all below
Is frail; how easily the world is lost
By Love, or War, and, now and then, – by Frost!   480

Crushed was Napoleon by the northern Thor,
  Who knocked his army down with icy hammer,
Stopped by the *Elements* – like a Whaler – or
  A blundering novice in his new French grammar;
Good cause had he to doubt the chance of war,   485
  And as for Fortune – but I dare not damn her,
Because, were I to ponder to Infinity,
The more I should believe in her Divinity.

She rules the present, past, and all to be yet,
  She gives us luck in lotteries, love, and marriage;
I cannot say that she's done much for me yet;   491
  Not that I mean her bounties to disparage,
We've not yet closed accounts, and we shall see yet
  How much she'll make amends for past miscarriage;
Meantime the Goddess I'll no more impórtune,   495
Unless to thank her when she's made my fortune.

To turn, – and to return; – the Devil take it!
  This story slips for ever through my fingers,
Because, just as the stanza likes to make it,
  It needs must be – and so it rather lingers;   500
The form of verse began, I can't well break it,
  But must keep time and tune like public singers;
But if I once get through my present measure,
I'll take another when I'm next at leisure.

They went to the Ridotto ('tis a place   505
  To which I mean to go myself tomorrow,
Just to divert my thoughts a little space
  Because I'm rather hippish, and may borrow
Some spirits, guessing at what kind of face
  May lurk beneath each mask; and as my sorrow   510
Slackens its pace sometimes, I'll make, or find,
Something shall leave it half an hour behind).

Now Laura moves along the joyous crowd,
  Smiles in her eyes, and simpers on her lips;
To some she whispers, others speaks aloud;   515
  To some she curtsies, and to some she dips,
Complains of warmth, and this complaint avowed,
  Her lover brings the lemonade, she sips;
She then surveys, condemns, but pities still
Her dearest friends for being dressed so ill.   520

One has false curls, another too much paint,
  A third – where did she buy that frightful turban?
A fourth's so pale she fears she's going to faint,
  A fifth's look's vulgar, dowdyish, and suburban,
A sixth's white silk has got a yellow taint,   525
  A seventh's thin muslin surely will be her bane,
An lo! an eighth appears – 'I'll see no more!'
For fear, like Banquo's kings, they reach a score.

Meantime, while she was thus at others gazing,
  Others were levelling their looks at her;   530
She heard the men's half-whispered mode of praising
  And, till 'twas done, determined not to stir;
The women only thought it quite amazing
  That, at her time of life, so many were
Admirers still, – but 'Men are so debased,   535
Those brazen Creatures always suit their taste.'

For my part, now, I ne'er could understand
  Why naughty women— But I won't discuss
A thing which is a scandal to the land,
  I only don't see why it should be thus;   540
And if I were but in a gown and band,
  Just to entitle me to make a fuss,
I'd preach on this till Wilberforce and Romilly
Should quote in their next speeches from my homily.

While Laura thus was seen, and seeing, smiling,   545
  Talking, she knew not why, and cared not what,
So that her female friends, with envy broiling,
  Beheld her airs, and triumph, and all that;
And well-dressed males still kept before her filing,
  And passing bowed and mingled with her chat;   550
More than the rest one person seemed to stare
With pertinacity that's rather rare.

He was a Turk, the colour of mahogany;
  And Laura saw him, and at first was glad,
Because the Turks so much admire philogyny,   555
  Although their usage of their wives is sad;
'Tis said they use no better than a dog any
  Poor woman, whom they purchase like a pad:
They have a number, though they ne'er exhibit 'em,
Four wives by law, and concubines 'ad libitum'.   560

They lock them up, and veil, and guard them daily,
  They scarcely can behold their male relations,
So that their moments do not pass so gaily
  As is supposed the case with northern nations;
Confinement, too, must make them look quite palely;
  And as the Turks abhor long conversations,   566
Their days are either passed in doing nothing,
Or bathing, nursing, making love, and clothing.

521 **paint:** makeup 526 **bane:** downfall 528 **Banquo:** in Shakespeare's *Macbeth* Banquo is shown a vision of his decendants, all to be kings of Scotland 541 **gown and band:** the clothes of a clergyman 543 **Wilberforce:** William Wilberforce (1759–1833), British politician and anti-slavery campaigner **Romilly:** Sir Samuel Romilly (1757–1818), British politician and law reformer 555 **philogyny:** love of women 558 **pad:** a horse 560 **ad libitum:** Latin: according to pleasure

481 **Thor:** the Norse god of thunder, here a reference to Wellington, victor over Napoleon at Waterloo 508 **hippish:** melancholy

They cannot read, and so don't lisp in criticism;
   Nor write, and so they don't affect the Muse;   570
Were never caught in epigram or witticism,
   Have no romances, sermons, plays, reviews, –
In Harams learning soon would make a pretty schism,
   But luckily these Beauties are no 'Blues';
No bustling *Botherby* have they to show 'em   575
'That charming passage in the last new poem':

No solemn, antique gentleman of rhyme,
   Who having angled all his life for Fame,
And getting but a nibble at a time,
   Still fussily keeps fishing on, the same   580
Small 'Triton of the minnows', the sublime
   Of Mediocrity, the furious tame,
The Echo's echo, usher of the school
Of female wits, boy bards – in short, a fool!

A stalking oracle of awful phrase,   585
   The approving '*Good!*' (by no means GOOD in law)
Humming like flies around the newest blaze,
   The bluest of bluebottles you e'er saw,
Teasing with blame, excruciating with praise,
   Gorging the little fame he gets all raw,   590
Translating tongues he knows not even by letter,
And sweating plays so middling, bad were better.

One hates an author that's *all author* – fellows
   In foolscap uniforms turned up with ink,
So very anxious, clever, fine, and jealous,   595
   One don't know what to say to them, or think,
Unless to puff them with a pair of bellows;
   Of Coxcombry's worst coxcombs e'en the pink
Are preferable to these shreds of paper,   599
These unquenched snuffings of the midnight taper.

Of these same we see several, and of others,
   Men of the world, who know the World like Men,
Scott, Rogers, Moore, and all the better brothers,
   Who think of something else besides the pen;
But for the children of the 'Mighty Mother's',   605
   The would-be wits, and can't-be gentlemen,
I leave them to their daily 'tea is ready',
Smug coterie, and literary lady.

The poor dear Mussul*women* whom I mention
   Have none of these instructive pleasant people,   610
And *one* would seem to them a new invention,
   Unknown as bells within a Turkish steeple;
I think 'twould almost be worth while to pension
   (Though best-sown projects very often reap ill)
A missionary author – just to preach   615
Our Christian usage of the parts of speech.

No Chemistry for them unfolds her gases,
   No Metaphysics are let loose in lectures,
No Circulating Library amasses
   Religious novels, moral tales, and strictures   620
Upon the living manners, as they pass us;
   No Exhibition glares with annual pictures;
They stare not on the stars from out their attics,
Nor deal (thank God for that!) in Mathematics.

Why I thank God for that is no great matter,   625
   I have my reasons, you no doubt suppose,
And as, perhaps, they would not highly flatter,
   I'll keep them for my life (to come) in prose;
I fear I have a little turn for Satire,
   And yet methinks the older that one grows   630
Inclines us more to laugh than scold, though Laughter
Leaves us so doubly serious shortly after.

Oh, Mirth and Innocence! Oh, Milk and Water!
   Ye happy mixtures of more happy days!
In these sad centuries of sin and slaughter,   635
   Abominable Man no more allays
His thirst with such pure beverage. No matter,
   I love you both, and both shall have my praise:
Oh, for old Saturn's reign of sugar-candy! –
Meantime I drink to your return in brandy.   640

Our Laura's Turk still kept his eyes upon her,
   Less in the Mussulman than Christian way,
Which seems to say, 'Madam, I do you honour,
   And while I please to stare, you'll please to stay.'
Could staring win a woman, this had won her,   645
   But Laura could not thus be led astray;
She had stood fire too long and well, to boggle
Even at this Stranger's most outlandish ogle.

The morning now was on the point of breaking,
   A turn of time at which I would advise   650
Ladies who have been dancing, or partaking
   In any other kind of exercise,
To make their preparations for forsaking
   The ball-room ere the Sun begins to rise,
Because when once the lamps and candles fail,   655
His blushes make them look a little pale.

I've seen some balls and revels in my time,
   And stayed them over for some silly reason,
And then I looked (I hope it was no crime)
   To see what lady best stood out the season;   660
And though I've seen some thousands in their prime
   Lovely and pleasing, and who still may please on,
I never saw but one (the stars withdrawn)
Whose bloom could after dancing dare the Dawn.

---

574 **Blues:** bluestockings, ie scholarly or intellectual women
581 **Triton:** a classical sea-god. A Triton of the minnows would be
a big fish in a small pond 600 **taper:** candle 603 **Scott:** Sir Walter
Scott (1771–1832), Scottish Romantic novelist and poet **Rogers:**
Samuel Rogers (1763–1855), English poet **Moore:** Thomas Moore
(1779–1852), Irish poet 609 **Mussulwomen:** Muslim women

624–5 **Nor deal . . . matter:** Byron's estranged wife, Annabella Milbanke,
had a passion for mathematics 642 **Mussulman:** Muslim

The name of this Aurora I'll not mention,   665
    Although I might, for she was nought to me
More than that patent work of God's invention,
    A charming woman, whom we like to see;
But writing names would merit reprehension,
    Yet if you like to find out this fair *She*,   670
At the next London or Parisian ball
You still may mark her cheek, out-blooming all.

Laura, who knew it would not do at all
    To meet the daylight after seven hours' sitting
Among three thousand people at a ball,   675
    To make her curtsey thought it right and fitting;
The Count was at her elbow with her shawl,
    And they the room were on the point of quitting,
When lo! those cursèd Gondoliers had got
Just in the very place where they *should not*.   680

In this they're like our coachmen, and the cause
    Is much the same – the crowd, and pulling, hauling,
With blasphemies enough to break their jaws,
    They make a never intermitted bawling.
At home, our Bow-street gem'men keep the laws,   685
    And here a sentry stands within your calling;
But for all that, there is a deal of swearing,
And nauseous words past mentioning or bearing.

The Count and Laura found their boat at last,
    And homeward floated o'er the silent tide,   690
Discussing all the dances gone and past;
    The dancers and their dresses, too, beside;
Some little scandals eke; but all aghast
    (As to their palace-stairs the rowers glide)
Sate Laura by the side of her adorer,   695
When lo! the Mussulman was there before her!

'Sir,' said the Count, with brow exceeding grave,
    'Your unexpected presence here will make
It necessary for myself to crave
    Its import? But perhaps 'tis a mistake;   700
I hope it is so; and, at once to waive
    All compliment, I hope so for *your* sake;
You understand my meaning, or you *shall*.'
'Sir,' quoth the Turk, ' 'tis no mistake at all:

'That lady is *my wife*!' Much wonder paints   705
    The lady's changing cheek, as well it might;
But where an Englishwoman sometimes faints,
    Italian females don't do so outright;
They only call a little on their Saints,
    And then come to themselves, almost, or quite;   710
Which saves much hartshorn, salts, and sprinkling
        faces,
And cutting stays, as usual in such cases.

She said, – what could she say? Why, not a word;
    But the Count courteously invited in
The Stranger, much appeased by what he heard: 715
    'Such things, perhaps, we'd best discuss within,'
Said he; 'don't let us make ourselves absurd
    In public, by a scene, nor raise a din,
For then the chief and only satisfaction
Will be much quizzing on the whole transaction.'   720

They entered, and for Coffee called – it came,
    A beverage for Turks and Christians both,
Although the way they make it's not the same.
    Now Laura, much recovered, or less loth
To speak, cries 'Beppo! what's your pagan name?   725
    Bless me! your beard is of amazing growth!
And how came you to keep away so long?
Are you not sensible 'twas very wrong?

'And are you *really, truly*, now a Turk?
    With any other women did you wive?   730
Is't true they use their fingers for a fork?
    Well, that's the prettiest Shawl – as I'm alive!
You'll give it me? They say you eat no pork.
    And how so many years did you contrive
To— Bless me! did I ever? No, I never   735
Saw a man grown so yellow! How's your liver?

'Beppo! that beard of yours becomes you not;
    It shall be shaved before you're a day older:
Why do you wear it? Oh! I had forgot –
    Pray don't you think the weather here is colder?   740
How do I look? You shan't stir from this spot
    In that queer dress, for fear that some beholder
Should find you out, and make the story known.
How short your hair is! Lord! how grey it's grown!'

What answer Beppo made to these demands   745
    Is more than I know. He was cast away
About where Troy stood once, and nothing stands;
    Became a slave of course, and for his pay
Had bread and bastinadoes, till some bands
    Of pirates landing in a neighbouring bay,   750
He joined the rogues and prospered, and became
A renegado of indifferent fame.

But he grew rich, and with his riches grew so
    Keen the desire to see his home again,
He thought himself in duty bound to do so,   755
    And not be always thieving on the main;
Lonely he felt, at times, as Robin Crusoe,
    And so he hired a vessel come from Spain,
Bound for Corfu: she was a fine polacca,   759
Manned with twelve hands, and laden with tobacco.

665 **Aurora:** Roman goddess of the dawn   685 **Bow-street gem'men:**
Bow Street gentlemen, the Bow Street runners, officers of Bow Street
magistrates's court, London, whose duty was to pursue and arrest
criminals   693 **eke:** also   711 **hartshorn:** sal volatile, smelling salts
712 **cutting stays:** cutting corsets to allow a fainting woman to breathe
more easily

749 **bastinadoes:** a bastinado was a punishment or torture in which
the soles of the feet were beaten with a stick   759 **polacca:** a three-
masted sailing ship

Himself, and much (heaven knows how gotten!) cash,
  He then embarked with risk of life and limb,
And got clear off, although the attempt was rash;
  He said that *Providence* protected him –
For my part, I say nothing – lest we clash   765
  In our opinions: – well – the ship was trim,
Set sail, and kept her reckoning fairly on,
Except three days of calm when off Cape Bonn.

The reached the Island, he transferred his lading,
  And self and live stock to another bottom,   770
And passed for a true Turkey-merchant, trading
  With goods of various names – but I've forgot 'em.
However, he got off by this evading,
  Or else the people would perhaps have shot him;
And thus at Venice landed to reclaim   775
His wife, religion, house, and Christian name.

His wife received, the Patriarch re-baptised him,
  (He made the Church a present, by the way);   778
He then threw off the garments which disguised him,
  And borrowed the Count's smallclothes for a day:
His friends the more for his long absence prized him,
  Finding he'd wherewithal to make them gay,   782
With dinners, where he oft became the laugh of them,
For stories – but *I* don't believe the half of them.

Whate'er his youth had suffered, his old age   785
  With wealth and talking made him some amends;
Though Laura sometimes put him in a rage,
  I've heard the Count and he were always friends.
My pen is at the bottom of a page,
  Which being finished, here the story ends: 790
'Tis to be wished it had been sooner done,
But stories somehow lengthen when begun.

768 **Cape Bonn:** Cape Bon, Tunisia   770 **bottom:** ship

'SO WE'LL GO NO MORE A-ROVING'

So we'll go no more a-roving
  So late into the night,
Though the heart be still as loving,
  And the moon be still as bright.

For the sword outwears its sheath,   5
  And the soul wears out the breast,
And the heart must pause to breathe,
  And Love itself have rest.

Though the night was made for loving,
  And the day returns too soon,   10
Yet we'll go no more a-roving
  By the light of the moon.

From DON JUAN

'TWAS midnight – Donna Julia was in bed,
  Sleeping, most probably, – when at her door
Arose a clatter might awake the dead,
  If they had never been awoke before,
And that they have been so we all have read,   5
  And are to be so, at the least, once more; –
The door was fastened, but with voice and fist
First knocks were heard, then 'Madam – Madam – hist!

'For God's sake, Madam – Madam – here's my master,
  With more than half the city at his back –   10
Was ever heard of such a curst disaster!
  'Tis not my fault – I kept good watch – Alack!
Do pray undo the bolt a little faster –
  They're on the stair just now, and in a crack
Will all be here; perhaps he yet may fly –   15
Surely the window's not so *very* high!'

By this time Don Alfonso was arrived,
  With torches, friends, and servants in great number;
The major part of them had long been wived,
  And therefore paused not to disturb the slumber   20
Of any wicked woman, who contrived
  By stealth her husband's temples to encumber:
Examples of this kind are so contagious,
Were *one* not punished, *all* would be outrageous.

I can't tell how, or why, or what suspicion   25
  Could enter into Don Alfonso's head;
But for a cavalier of his condition
  It surely was exceedingly ill-bred,
Without a word of previous admonition,
  To hold a levee round his lady's bed,   30
And summon lackeys, armed with fire and sword,
To prove himself the thing he most abhorred.

Poor Donna Julia! starting as from sleep
  (Mind – that I do not say – she had not slept),
Began at once to scream, and yawn, and weep;   35
  Her maid, Antonia, who was an adept,
Contrived to fling the bed-clothes in a heap,
  As if she had just now from out them crept:
I can't tell why she should take all this trouble
To prove her mistress had been sleeping double.   40

But Julia mistress, and Antonia maid,
  Appeared like two poor harmless women, who
Of goblins, but still more of men afraid,
  Had thought one man might be deterred by two,
And therefore side by side were gently laid,   45
  Until the hours of absence should run through,
And truant husband should return, and say,
'My dear – I was the first who came away.'

DON JUAN: 1ST EXTRACT: 22 **By . . . encumber:** refers to the idea that
a cuckold is given a pair of imaginary horns to wear on his head
27 **condition:** rank   30 **levee:** morning reception

Now Julia found at length a voice, and cried,
    'In Heaven's name, Don Alfonso, what d'ye mean?
Has madness seized you? would that I had died   51
    Ere such a monster's victim I had been!
What may this midnight violence betide,
    A sudden fit of drunkenness or spleen?
Dare you suspect me, whom the thought would kill?
Search, then, the room!' – Alfonso said, 'I will.'   56

He searched, *they* searched, and rummaged
    everywhere,
    Closet and clothes-press, chest and window-seat,
And found much linen, lace, and several pair
    Of stockings, slippers, brushes, combs, complete,
With other articles of ladies fair,   61
    To keep them beautiful, or leave them neat:
Arras they pricked and curtains with their swords,
And wounded several shutters, and some boards.

Under the bed they searched, and there they found –
    No matter what – it was not that they sought;   66
They opened windows, gazing if the ground
    Had signs or footmarks, but the earth said nought;
And then they stared each others' faces round:
    'Tis odd, not one of all these seekers thought,   70
And seems to me almost a sort of blunder,
Of looking *in* the bed as well as under.

During this inquisition, Julia's tongue
    Was not asleep – 'Yes, search and search,' she cried,
'Insult on insult heap, and wrong on wrong!   75
    It was for this that I became a bride!
For this in silence I have suffered long
    A husband like Alfonso at my side;
But now I'll bear no more, nor here remain,
If there be law or lawyers in all Spain.   80

'Yes, Don Alfonso! husband now no more,
    If ever you indeed deserved the name,
Is't worthy of your years? – you have threescore –
    Fifty, or sixty, it is all the same –
Is't wise or fitting, causeless to explore   85
    For facts against a virtuous woman's fame?
Ungrateful, perjured, barbarous Don Alfonso,
How dare you think your lady would go on so?

'Is it for this I have disdained to hold
    The common privileges of my sex?   90
That I have chosen a cónfessor so old
    And deaf, that any other it would vex,
And never once he has had cause to scold,
    But found my very innocence perplex
So much, he always doubted I was married –   95
How sorry you will be when I've miscarried!

'Was it for this that no Cortejo e'er
    I yet have chosen from out the youth of Seville?
Is it for this I scarce went anywhere,
    Except to bull-fights, mass, play, rout, and revel?
Is it for this, whate'er my suitors were,   101
    I favoured none – nay, was almost uncivil?
Is it for this that General Count O'Reilly,
Who took Algiers, declares I used him vilely?

'Did not the Italian *musico* Cazzani   105
    Sing at my heart six months at least in vain?
Did not his countryman, Count Corniani,
    Call me the only virtuous wife in Spain?
Were there not also Russians, English, many?
    The Count Strongstroganoff I put in pain,   110
And Lord Mount Coffeehouse, the Irish peer,
Who killed himself for love (with wine) last year.

'Have I not had two bishops at my feet?
    The Duke of Ichar, and Don Fernan Nunez;
And is it thus a faithful wife you treat?   115
    I wonder in what quarter now the moon is:
I praise your vast forbearance not to beat
    Me also, since the time so opportune is –
Oh, valiant man! with sword drawn and cocked
    trigger,
Now, tell me, don't you cut a pretty figure?   120

'Was it for this you took your sudden journey,
    Under pretence of business indispensable
With that sublime of rascals your attorney,
    Whom I see standing there, and looking sensible
Of having played the fool? though both I spurn, he
    Deserves the worst, his conduct's less defensible,
Because, no doubt, 'twas for his dirty fee,   127
And not from any love to you nor me.

'If he comes here to take a deposition,
    By all means let the gentleman proceed;   130
You've made the apartment in a fit condition: –
    There's pen and ink for you, sir, when you need –
Let everything be noted with precision,
    I would not you for nothing should be fee'd –   134
But, as my maid's undressed, pray turn your spies out.'
'Oh!' sobbed Antonia, 'I could tear their eyes out.'

'There is the closet, there the toilet, there
    The antechamber – search them under, over;
There is the sofa, there the great arm-chair,
    The chimney – which would really hold a lover.
I wish to sleep, and beg you will take care   141
    And make no further noise, till you discover
The secret cavern of this lurking treasure –
And when 'tis found, let me, too, have that pleasure.

---

54 **spleen**: peevishness, spitefulness 63 **Arras**: tapestry wall hanging

97 **Cortejo**: a lady's acknowledged lover and companion 100 **rout**: party

'And now, Hidalgo! now that you have thrown   145
    Doubt upon me, confusion over all,
Pray have the courtesy to make it known
    Who is the man you search for? how d'ye call
Him? what's his lineage? let him but be shown –
    I hope he's young and handsome – is he tall?   150
Tell me – and be assured, that since you stain
My honour thus, it shall not be in vain.

'At least, perhaps, he has not sixty years,
    At that age he would be too old for slaughter,
Or for so young a husband's jealous fears –   155
    (Antonia! let me have a glass of water).
I am ashamed of having shed these tears,
    They are unworthy of my father's daughter;
My mother dreamed not in my natal hour,
That I should fall into a monster's power.   160

'Perhaps 'tis of Antonia you are jealous,
    You saw that she was sleeping by my side
When you broke in upon us with your fellows:
    Look where you please – we've nothing, sir, to hide;
Only another time, I trust, you'll tell us,   165
    Or for the sake of decency abide
A moment at the door, that we may be
Dressed to receive so much good company.

'And now, sir, I have done, and say no more;
    The little I have said may serve to show   170
The guileless heart in silence may grieve o'er
    The wrongs to whose exposure it is slow: –
I leave you to your conscience as before,
    'Twill one day ask you why you used me so?
God grant you feel not then the bitterest grief! –   175
Antonia! where's my pocket-handkerchief?'

She ceased, and turned upon her pillow; pale
    She lay, her dark eyes flashing through their tears,
Like skies that rain and lighten; as a veil,   179
    Waved and o'ershading her wan cheek, appears
Her streaming hair; the black curls strive, but fail,
    To hide the glossy shoulder, which uprears
Its snow through all; – her soft lips lie apart,
And louder than her breathing beats her heart.

The Señor Don Alfonso stood confused;   185
    Antonia bustled round the ransacked room,
And, turning up her nose, with looks abused
    Her master, and his myrmidons, of whom
Not one, except the attorney, was amused;
    He, like Achates, faithful to the tomb,   190
So there were quarrels, cared not for the cause,
Knowing they must be settled by the laws.

With prying snub-nose, and small eyes, he stood,
    Following Antonia's motions here and there,
With much suspicion in his attitude;   195
    For reputations he had little care;
So that a suit or action were made good,
    Small pity had he for the young and fair,
And ne'er believed in negatives, till these
Were proved by competent false witnesses.   200

But Don Alfonso stood with downcast looks,
    And, truth to say, he made a foolish figure;
When, after searching in five hundred nooks,
    And treating a young wife with so much rigour,
He gained no point, except some self-rebukes,   205
    Added to those his lady with such vigour
Had poured upon him for the last half-hour,
Quick, thick, and heavy – as a thunder-shower.

At first he tried to hammer an excuse,
    To which the sole reply was tears and sobs,   210
And indications of hysterics, whose
    Prologue is always certain throes, and throbs,
Gasps, and whatever else the owners choose:
    Alfonso saw his wife, and thought of Job's;
He saw too, in perspective, her relations,   215
And then he tried to muster all his patience.

He stood in act to speak, or rather stammer,
    But sage Antonia cut him short before
The anvil of his speech received the hammer,   219
    With 'Pray, sir, leave the room, and say no more,
Or madam dies.' – Alfonso muttered, 'Damn her,'
    But nothing else, the time of words was o'er;
He cast a rueful look or two, and did,
He knew not wherefore, that which he was bid.

With him retired his 'posse comitatus',   225
    The attorney last, who lingered near the door
Reluctantly, still tarrying there as late as
    Antonia let him – not a little sore
At this most strange and unexplained *'hiatus'*
    In Don Alfonso's facts, which just now wore   230
An awkward look; as he revolved the case,
The door was fastened in his legal face.

No sooner was it bolted, than— Oh Shame!
    Oh Sin! Oh Sorrow! and Oh Womankind!
How can you do such things and keep your fame,   235
    Unless this world, and t'other too, be blind?
Nothing so dear as an unfilched good name!
    But to proceed – for there is more behind:
With much heartfelt reluctance be it said,
Young Juan slipped, half-smothered, from the bed.

145 **Hidalgo:** nobleman 188 **myrmidons:** followers, henchmen (after the followers of Achilles in the *Iliad*) 190 **Achates:** the proverbially loyal companion of Aeneas in Virgil's *Aeneid*

214 **Job's:** in the Bible (Job 2.9), Job's wife's advice to him in response to his afflictions is to 'curse God and die' 225 **posse comitatus:** (Latin, strength of the county) the full form of posse, meaning a body of men assembled to assist a sheriff in maintaining law and order

He had been hid – I don't pretend to say   241
  How, nor can I indeed describe the where –
Young, slender, and packed easily, he lay,
  No doubt, in little compass, round or square;
But pity him I neither must nor may   245
  His suffocation by that pretty pair;
'Twere better, sure, to die so, than be shut
With maudlin Clarence in his Malmsey butt.

And, secondly, I pity not, because
  He had no business to commit a sin,   250
Forbid by heavenly, fined by human laws; –
  At least 'twas rather early to begin;
But at sixteen the conscience rarely gnaws
  So much as when we call our old debts in
At sixty years, and draw the accompts of evil,   255
And find a deucèd balance with the devil.

Of his position I can give no notion:
  'Tis written in the Hebrew Chronicle,
How the physicians, leaving pill and potion,
  Prescribed, by way of blister, a young belle,   260
When old King David's blood grew dull in motion,
  And that the medicine answered very well;
Perhaps 'twas in a different way applied,
For David lived, but Juan nearly died.

What's to be done? Alfonso will be back   265
  The moment he has sent his fools away.
Antonia's skill was put upon the rack,
  But no device could be brought into play –
And how to parry the renewed attack?
  Besides, it wanted but few hours of day: 270
Antonia puzzled; Julia did not speak,
But pressed her bloodless lip to Juan's cheek.

He turned his lip to hers, and with his hand
  Called back the tangles of her wandering hair;
Even then their love they could not all command,
  And half forgot their danger and despair: 276
Antonia's patience now was at a stand –
  'Come, come, 'tis no time now for fooling there,'
She whispered, in great wrath – 'I must deposit
This pretty gentleman within the closet: 280

'Pray, keep your nonsense for some luckier night –
  Who can have put my master in this mood?
What will become on't – I'm in such a fright,
  The Devil's in the urchin, and no good –
Is this a time for giggling? this a plight?   285
  Why, don't you know that it may end in blood?
You'll lose your life, and I shall lose my place,
My mistress all, for that half-girlish face.

248 **Clarence in his Malmsey butt:** George Plantagenet, Duke of Clarence (1449–78), was reputed to have drowned in a barrel of Malmsey wine   255 **accompts:** accounts   260 **blister:** an irritant medicinally applied to the skin to form a blister. The reference is the Old Testament story of physical contact with a young girl being used as a treatment to save the life of the elderly King David

'Had it but been for a stout cavalier
  Of twenty-five or thirty – (come, make haste) –   290
But for a child, what piece of work is here!
  I really, madam, wonder at your taste –
(Come, sir, get in) – my master must be near:
  There, for the present, at the least, he's fast,
And if we can but till the morning keep   295
Our counsel – (Juan, mind, you must not sleep).'

Now, Don Alfonso entering, but alone,
  Closed the oration of the trusty maid:
She loitered, and he told her to be gone,
  An order somewhat sullenly obeyed;   300
However, present remedy was none,
  And no great good seemed answered if she stayed:
Regarding both with slow and sidelong view,
She snuffed the candle, curtsied, and withdrew.

Alfonso paused a minute – then begun   305
  Some strange excuses for his late proceeding;
He would not justify what he had done,
  To say the best, it was extreme ill-breeding;
But there were ample reasons for it, none
  Of which he specified in this his pleading: 310
His speech was a fine sample, on the whole,
Of rhetoric, which the learn'd call '*rigmarole*'.

Julia said nought; though all the while there rose
  A ready answer, which at once enables
A matron, who her husband's foible knows,   315
  By a few timely words to turn the tables,
Which, if it does not silence, still must pose, –
  Even if it should comprise a pack of fables;
'Tis to retort with firmness, and when he
Suspects with *one*, do you reproach with *three*.   320

Julia, in fact, had tolerable grounds, –
  Alfonso's loves with Inez were well known;
But whether 'twas that one's own guilt confounds –
  But that can't be, as has been often shown,
A lady with apologies abounds; –   325
  It might be that her silence sprang alone
From delicacy to Don Juan's ear,
To whom she knew his mother's fame was dear.

There might be one more motive, which makes two;
  Alfonso ne'er to Juan had alluded, –   330
Mentioned his jealousy, but never who
  Had been the happy lover, he concluded,
Concealed amongst his premises; 'tis true,
  His mind the more o'er this its mystery brooded;
To speak of Inez now were, one may say,   335
Like throwing Juan in Alfonso's way.

A hint, in tender cases, is enough;
  Silence is best; besides there is a *tact* –
(That modern phrase appears to me sad stuff,
  But it will serve to keep my verse compact) –   340

Which keeps, when pushed by questions rather rough,
 A lady always distant from the fact:
The charming creatures lie with such a grace,
There's nothing so becoming to the face.

They blush, and we believe them; at least I   345
 Have always done so; 'tis of no great use,
In any case, attempting a reply,
 For then their eloquence grows quite profuse;
And when at length they're out of breath, they sigh,
 And cast their languid eyes down, and let loose
A tear or two, and then we make it up;   351
And then – and then – and then – sit down and sup.

Alfonso closed his speech, and begged her pardon,
 Which Julia half withheld, and then half granted,
And laid conditions he thought very hard on,   355
 Denying several little things he wanted:
He stood like Adam lingering near his garden,
 With useless penitence perplexed and haunted,
Beseeching she no further would refuse,
When, lo! he stumbled o'er a pair of shoes.   360

A pair of shoes! – what then? not much, if they
 Are such as fit with ladies' feet, but these
(No one can tell how much I grieve to say)
 Were masculine; to see them, and to seize,
Was but a moment's act. – Ah! well-a-day!   365
 My teeth begin to chatter, my veins freeze!
Alfonso first examined well their fashion,
And then flew out into another passion.

He left the room for his relinquished sword,
 And Julia instant to the closet flew.   370
'Fly, Juan, fly! for heaven's sake – not a word –
 The door is open – you may yet slip through
The passage you so often have explored –
 Here is the garden-key – Fly – fly – Adieu!
Haste – haste! I hear Alfonso's hurrying feet – 375
Day has not broke – there's no one in the street.'

None can say that this was not good advice,
 The only mischief was, it came too late;
Of all experience 'tis the usual price,
 A sort of income-tax laid on by fate: 380
Juan had reached the room-door in a trice,
 And might have done so by the garden-gate,
But met Alfonso in his dressing-gown,
Who threatened death – so Juan knocked him down.

Dire was the scuffle, and out went the light;   385
 Antonia cried out 'Rape!' and Julia 'Fire!'
But not a servant stirred to aid the fight.
 Alfonso, pommelled to his heart's desire,
Swore lustily he'd be revenged this night;
 And Juan, too, blasphemed an octave higher; 390
His blood was up: though young, he was a Tartar,
And not at all disposed to prove a martyr.

Alfonso's sword had dropped ere he could draw it,
 And they continued battling hand to hand,
For Juan very luckily ne'er saw it;   395
 His temper not being under great command,
If at that moment he had chanced to claw it,
 Alfonso's days had not been in the land
Much longer. – Think of husbands', lovers' lives!
And how ye may be doubly widows – wives!   400

Alfonso grappled to detain the foe,
 And Juan throttled him to get away,
And blood ('twas from the nose) began to flow;
 At last, as they more faintly wrestling lay,
Juan contrived to give an awkward blow,   405
 And then his only garment quite gave way;
He fled, like Joseph, leaving it; but there,
I doubt, all likeness ends between the pair.

Lights came at length, and men, and maids, who found
 An awkward spectacle their eyes before;   410
Antonia in hysterics, Julia swooned,
 Alfonso leaning, breathless, by the door;
Some half-torn drapery scattered on the ground,
 Some blood, and several footsteps, but no more:
Juan the gate gained, turned the key about,   415
And liking not the inside, locked the out.
          [Canto 1, stanzas 136–87]

THE Isles of Greece, the Isles of Greece!
 Where burning Sappho loved and sung,
Where grew the arts of War and Peace,
 Where Delos rose, and Phoebus sprung!
Eternal summer gilds them yet,   5
But all, except their Sun, is set.

The Scian and the Teian muse,
 The Hero's harp, the Lover's lute,
Have found the fame your shores refuse;
 Their place of birth alone is mute   10
To sounds which echo further west
Than your Sires' 'Islands of the Blest'.

The mountains look on Marathon –
 And Marathon looks on the sea;
And musing there an hour alone,   15
 I dreamed that Greece might still be free;
For standing on the Persians' grave,
I could not deem myself a slave.

407 **Joseph:** in the Bible (Genesis 39.7), Joseph is the object of the desire of Potiphar's wife and escapes from her clutches leaving his garment behind 2ND EXTRACT: 2 **Sappho:** 6th century BC Greek poetess of the island of Lesbos 4 **Delos:** Greek island in the Cyclades, legendary birthplace of Apollo and Artemis **Phoebus:** Apollo, god of poetry, light and music 7 **Scian Muse:** Homer, reputedly born on the island of Scio (modern Chios) **Teian Muse:** Anacreon (?572–?488 BC), Greek lyric poet born at Teon, Asia Minor 13 **Marathon:** site of a victory of the Greeks over the Persians (490 BC)

A King sate on the rocky brow
  Which looks o'er sea-born Salamis;
And ships, by thousands, lay below,   20
  And men in nations; – all were his!
He counted them at break of day –
And when the Sun set where were they?

And where are they? and where art thou,   25
  My Country? On thy voiceless shore
The heroic lay is tuneless now –
  The heroic bosom beats no more!
And must thy Lyre, so long divine,
Degenerate into hands like mine?   30

'Tis something, in the dearth of Fame,
  Though linked among a fettered race,
To feel at least a patriot's shame,
  Even as I sing, suffuse my face;
For what is left the poet here?   35
For Greeks a blush – for Greece a tear.

Must *we* but weep o'er days more blest?
  Must *we* but blush? – Our fathers bled.
Earth! render back from out thy breast
  A remnant of our Spartan dead!   40
Of the three hundred grant but three,
To make a new Thermopylae!

What, silent still? and silent all?
  Ah! no; – the voices of the dead
Sound like a distant torrent's fall,   45
  And answer, 'Let one living head,
But one arise, – we come, we come!'
'Tis but the living who are dumb.

In vain – in vain: strike other chords;
  Fill high the cup with Samian wine!   50
Leave battles to the Turkish hordes,
  And shed the blood of Scio's vine!
Hark! rising to the ignoble call –
How answers each bold Bacchanal!

You have the Pyrrhic dance as yet,   55
  Where is the Pyrrhic phalanx gone?
Of two such lessons, why forget
  The nobler and the manlier one?
You have the letters Cadmus gave –
Think ye he meant them for a slave?   60

Fill high the bowl with Samian wine!
  We will not think of themes like these!
It made Anacreon's song divine:
  He served – but served Polycrates –
A Tyrant; but our masters then   65
Were still, at least, our countrymen.

The Tyrant of the Chersonese
  Was Freedom's best and bravest friend;
That tyrant was Miltiades!
  Oh! that the present hour would lend   70
Another despot of the kind!
Such chains as his were sure to bind.

Fill high the bowl with Samian wine!
  On Suli's rock, and Parga's shore,
Exists the remnant of a line   75
  Such as the Doric mothers bore;
And there, perhaps, some seed is sown,
The Heracleidan blood might own.

Trust not for freedom to the Franks –
  They have a king who buys and sells;   80
In native swords, and native ranks,
  The only hope of courage dwells;
But Turkish force, and Latin fraud,
Would break your shield, however broad.

Fill high the bowl with Samian wine!   85
  Our virgins dance beneath the shade –
I see their glorious black eyes shine;
  But gazing on each glowing maid,
My own the burning tear-drop laves,
To think such breasts must suckle slaves.   90

Place me on Sunium's marbled steep,
  Where nothing, save the waves and I,
May hear our mutual murmurs sweep;
  There, swan-like, let me sing and die:
A land of slaves shall ne'er be mine –   95
Dash down yon cup of Samian wine!

[Canto 3, stanza 86]

ON THIS DAY I COMPLETE
MY THIRTY-SIXTH YEAR

'TIS time this heart should be unmoved,
   Since others it hath ceased to move:
Yet, though I cannot be beloved,
   Still let me love!

My days are in the yellow leaf;   5
   The flowers and fruits of love are gone;
The worm, the canker, and the grief,
   Are mine alone!

The fire that on my bosom preys
   Is lone as some volcanic isle;   10
No torch is kindled at its blaze –
   A funeral pile.

The hope, the fear, the jealous care,
   The exalted portion of the pain
And power of love, I cannot share,   15
   But wear the chain.

But 'tis not *thus* – and 'tis not *here* –
   Such thoughts should shake my soul, nor *now*
Where Glory decks the hero's bier,
   Or binds his brow.   20

The Sword, the Banner, and the Field,
   Glory and Greece, around me see!
The Spartan, borne upon his shield,
   Was not more free.

Awake! (not Greece – she is awake!)   25
   Awake, my spirit! Think through *whom*
Thy life-blood tracks its parent lake,
   And then strike home!

Tread those reviving passions down,
   Unworthy manhood! – unto thee   30
Indifferent should the smile or frown
   Of Beauty be.

If thou regret'st thy youth, *why live?*
   The land of honourable death
Is here: – up to the Field, and give   35
   Away thy breath!

Seek out – less often sought than found –
   A soldier's grave, for thee the best;
Then look around, and choose thy ground,
   And take thy Rest.   40

CHARLES WOLFE

THE BURIAL OF SIR JOHN MOORE
AFTER CORUNNA

NOT a drum was heard, not a funeral note,
   As his corse to the rampart we hurried;
Not a soldier discharged his farewell shot
   O'er the grave where our hero we buried.

We buried him darkly at dead of night,   5
   The sods with our bayonets turning,
By the struggling moonbeam's misty light
   And the lanthorn dimly burning.

No useless coffin enclosed his breast,
   Not in sheet or in shroud we wound him;   10
But he lay like a warrior taking his rest
   With his martial cloak around him.

Few and short were the prayers we said,
   And we spoke not a word of sorrow;
But we steadfastly gazed on the face that was dead,   15
   And we bitterly thought of the morrow.

We thought, as we hollowed his narrow bed
   And smoothed down his lonely pillow,
That the foe and the stranger would tread o'er his
    head,
   And we far away on the billow!   20

Lightly they'll talk of the spirit that's gone,
   And o'er his cold ashes upbraid him –
But little he'll reck, if they let him sleep on
   In the grave where a Briton has laid him.

But half of our heavy task was done   25
   When the clock struck the hour for retiring;
And we heard the distant and random gun
   That the foe was sullenly firing.

Slowly and sadly we laid him down,
   From the field of his fame fresh and gory;   30
We carved not a line, and we raised not a stone,
   But we left him alone with his glory.

THE BURIAL OF SIR JOHN MOORE: Sir John Moore (1761–1809) was
a British general killed at Corunna in Spain during the
Peninsular War 2 **corse**: corpse 8 **lanthorn**: lantern 23 **reck**:
mind, care

PERCY BYSSHE SHELLEY

MUTABILITY

WE are as clouds that veil the midnight moon;
   How restlessly they speed, and gleam, and quiver,
Streaking the darkness radiantly! – yet soon
   Night closes round, and they are lost for ever:

Or like forgotten lyres, whose dissonant strings   5
   Give various response to each varying blast,
To whose frail frame no second motion brings
   One mood or modulation like the last.

We rest. – A dream has power to poison sleep;
   We rise. – One wandering thought pollutes the day;
We feel, conceive or reason, laugh or weep;   11
   Embrace fond woe, or cast our cares away:

It is the same! – For, be it joy or sorrow,
   The path of its departure still is free:
Man's yesterday may ne'er be like his morrow;   15
   Nought may endure but Mutability.

HYMN TO INTELLECTUAL BEAUTY

THE awful shadow of some unseen Power
   Floats though unseen among us, – visiting
   This various world with as inconstant wing
As summer winds that creep from flower to flower, –
Like moonbeams that behind some piny mountain
      shower,   5
    It visits with inconstant glance
    Each human heart and countenance;
Like hues and harmonies of evening, –
    Like clouds in starlight widely spread, –
    Like memory of music fled, –   10
    Like aught that for its grace may be
Dear, and yet dearer for its mystery.

Spirit of BEAUTY, that dost consecrate
   With thine own hues all thou dost shine upon
   Of human thought or form, – where art thou gone?
Why dost thou pass away and leave our state,   16
This dim vast vale of tears, vacant and desolate?
    Ask why the sunlight not for ever
    Weaves rainbows o'er yon mountain-river,
Why aught should fail and fade that once is shown,   20
    Why fear and dream and death and birth
    Cast on the daylight of this earth
    Such gloom, – why man has such a scope
For love and hate, despondency and hope?

No voice from some sublimer world hath ever   25
   To sage or poet these responses given –
   Therefore the names of Demon, Ghost, and
      Heaven,
Remain the records of their vain endeavour,
Frail spells – whose uttered charm might not avail to
      sever,
    From all we hear and all we see,   30
    Doubt, chance, and mutability.
Thy light alone – like mist o'er mountains driven,
    Or music by the night-wind sent
    Through strings of some still instrument,
    Or moonlight on a midnight stream,   35
Gives grace and truth to life's unquiet dream.

Love, Hope, and Self-esteem, like clouds depart
   And come, for some uncertain moments lent.
   Man were immortal, and omnipotent,
Didst thou, unknown and awful as thou art,   40
Keep with thy glorious train firm state within his
      heart.
    Thou messenger of sympathies,
    That wax and wane in lovers' eyes –
Thou – that to human thought art nourishment,
    Like darkness to a dying flame!   45
    Depart not as thy shadow came,
    Depart not – lest the grave should be,
Like life and fear, a dark reality.

While yet a boy I sought for ghosts, and sped
   Through many a listening chamber, cave and ruin,
   And starlight wood, with fearful steps pursuing   51
Hopes of high talk with the departed dead.
I called on poisonous names with which our youth is
      fed;
    I was not heard – I saw them not –
    When musing deeply on the lot   55
Of life, at that sweet time when winds are wooing
    All vital things that wake to bring
    News of birds and blossoming, –
    Sudden, thy shadow fell on me;
I shrieked, and clasped my hands in ecstasy!   60

I vowed that I would dedicate my powers
   To thee and thine – have I not kept the vow?
   With beating heart and streaming eyes, even now
I call the phantoms of a thousand hours
Each from his voiceless grave: they have in visioned
      bowers   65
    Of studious zeal or love's delight
    Outwatched with me the envious night –
They know that never joy illumed my brow
    Unlinked with hope that thou wouldst free
    This world from its dark slavery,   70

That Thou – O awful Loveliness,
Wouldst give whate'er these words cannot express.
The day becomes more solemn and serene
    When noon is past – there is a harmony
    In autumn, and a lustre in its sky,   75
Which through the summer is not heard or seen,
As if it could not be, as if it had not been!
        Thus let thy power, which like the truth
        Of nature on my passive youth
Descended, to my onward life supply   80
        Its calm – to one who worships thee,
        And every form containing thee,
        Whom Spirit fair, thy spells did bind
To fear himself, and love all human kind.

OZYMANDIAS

I met a traveller from an antique land
Who said: 'Two vast and trunkless legs of stone
Stand in the desert . . . Near them, on the sand,
Half sunk, a shattered visage lies, whose frown
And wrinkled lip, and sneer of cold command,   5
Tell that its sculptor well those passions read
Which yet survive, stamped on these lifeless things,
The hand that mocked them and the heart that fed:
And on the pedestal these words appear:
'My name is Ozymandias, king of kings: 10
Look on my works, ye Mighty, and despair!'
Nothing beside remains. Round the decay
Of that colossal wreck, boundless and bare,
The lone and level sands stretch far away.

OZYMANDIAS: 10 **Ozymandias:** the Greek name for the 13th-century
BC Egyptian king Ramses II

STANZAS
WRITTEN IN DEJECTION, NEAR NAPLES

The sun is warm, the sky is clear,
    The waves are dancing fast and bright,
Blue isles and snowy mountains wear
    The purple noon's transparent might,
    The breath of the moist earth is light,   5
Around its unexpanded buds;
    Like many a voice of one delight,
The winds, the birds, the ocean floods,
The City's voice itself, is soft like Solitude's.

I see the Deep's untrampled floor   10
    With green and purple seaweeds strown;
I see the waves upon the shore,
    Like light dissolved in star-showers, thrown:
    I sit upon the sands alone, –
The lightning of the noontide ocean   15
    Is flashing round me, and a tone
Arises from its measured motion,
How sweet! did any heart now share in my emotion.

Alas! I have nor hope nor health,
    Nor peace within nor calm around,   20
Nor that content surpassing wealth
    The sage in meditation found,
    And walked with inward glory crowned –
Nor fame, nor power, nor love, nor leisure.
    Others I see whom these surround –   25
    Smiling they live, and call life pleasure; –
To me that cup has been dealt in another measure.

Yet now despair itself is mild,
    Even as the winds and waters are;
I could lie down like a tired child,   30
    And weep away the life of care
    Which I have borne and yet must bear,
Till death like sleep might steal on me,
    And I might feel in the warm air
My cheek grow cold, and hear the sea   35
Breathe o'er my dying brain its last monotony.

Some might lament that I were cold,
    As I, when this sweet day is gone,
Which my lost heart, too soon grown old,
    Insults with this untimely moan;   40
    They might lament – for I am one
Whom men love not, – and yet regret,
    Unlike this day, which, when the sun
Shall on its stainless glory set,
Will linger, though enjoyed, like joy in memory yet.   45

SONNET

Lift not the painted veil which those who live
Call Life: though unreal shapes be pictured there,
And it but mimic all we would believe
With colours idly spread, – behind, lurk Fear
And Hope, twin Destinies; who ever weave   5
Their shadows, o'er the chasm, sightless and drear.
I knew one who had lifted it – he sought,
For his lost heart was tender, things to love,
But found them not, alas! nor was there aught
The world contains, the which he could approve.   10
Through the unheeding many he did move,
A splendour among shadows, a bright blot
Upon this gloomy scene, a Spirit that strove
For truth, and like the Preacher found it not.

SONNET: 6 **drear:** dreary, dismal

ENGLAND IN 1819

An old, mad, blind, despised, and dying king, –
Princes, the dregs of their dull race, who flow
Through public scorn, – mud from a muddy spring, –
Rulers who neither see, nor feel, nor know,
But leech-like to their fainting country cling,   5

Till they drop, blind in blood, without a blow, –
A people starved and stabbed in the untilled field, –
An army, which liberticide and prey
Makes as a two-edged sword to all who wield, –
Golden and sanguine laws which tempt and slay;   10
Religion Christless, Godless – a book sealed;
A Senate, – Time's worst statute unrepealed, –
Are graves from which a glorious Phantom may
Burst, to illumine our tempestuous day.

ENGLAND IN 1819: 1 **An old . . . king:** George III (1738–1820), became insane in 1811 and his son ruled as regent until he died 7 **A people . . . field:** refers to the 'Peterloo Massacre' at St Peter's Fields, Manchester in 1819, in which cavalry were used to disperse a political meeting, resulting in 11 deaths and many injuries 10 **Golden and sanguine laws:** laws bought by gold and resulting in bloodshed 12 **Time's worst statute:** the law penalizing Roman Catholics and Dissenters 13 **Phantom:** revolution

From PROMETHEUS UNBOUND

MY soul is an enchanted boat,
    Which, like a sleeping swan, doth float
Upon the silver waves of thy sweet singing;
    And thine doth like an angel sit
    Beside a helm conducting it,   5
Whilst all the winds with melody are ringing.
    It seems to float ever, for ever,
    Upon that many-winding river,
    Between mountains, woods, abysses,
    A paradise of wildernesses!   10
Till, like one in slumber bound,
Borne to the ocean, I float down, around,
Into a sea profound, of ever-spreading sound:

    Meanwhile thy spirit lifts its pinions
    In music's most serene dominions;   15
Catching the winds that fan that happy heaven.
    And we sail on, away, afar,
    Without a course, without a star,
But, by the instinct of sweet music driven;
    Till through Elysian garden islets   20
    By thee, most beautiful of pilots,
    Where never mortal pinnace glided,
    The boat of my desire is guided:
Realms where the air we breathe is love,
Which in the winds and on the waves doth move, 25
Harmonizing this earth with what we feel above.

    We have passed Age's icy caves,
    And Manhood's dark and tossing waves,
And Youth's smooth ocean, smiling to betray:
    Beyond the glassy gulfs we flee   30
    Of shadow-peopled Infancy,
Through Death and Birth, to a diviner day;
    A paradise of vaulted bowers,
    Lit by downward-gazing flowers,
    And watery paths that wind between   35

    Wildernesses calm and green,
    Peopled by shapes too bright to see,
    And rest, having beheld; somewhat like thee;
    Which walk upon the sea, and chant melodiously!

FROM PROMETHEUS UNBOUND: 14 **pinions:** wings 20 **Elysian:** delightful, blissful, like Elysium, the Greek Paradise

ODE TO THE WEST WIND

I

O WILD West Wind, thou breath of Autumn's being,
Thou, from whose unseen presence the leaves dead
Are driven, like ghosts from an enchanter fleeing,

Yellow, and black, and pale, and hectic red,
Pestilence-stricken multitudes: O thou,   5
Who chariotest to their dark wintry bed

The wingèd seeds, where they lie cold and low,
Each like a corpse within its grave, until
Thine azure sister of the Spring shall blow

Her clarion o'er the dreaming earth, and fill   10
(Driving sweet buds like flocks to feed in air)
With living hues and odours plain and hill:

Wild Spirit, which art moving everywhere;
Destroyer and preserver; hear, oh, hear!

II

Thou on whose stream, 'mid the steep sky's
        commotion,   15
Loose clouds like earth's decaying leaves are shed,
Shook from the tangled boughs of Heaven and
        Ocean,

Angels of rain and lightning: there are spread
On the blue surface of thine airy surge,
Like the bright hair uplifted from the head   20

Of some fierce Maenad, even from the dim verge
Of the horizon to the zenith's height,
The locks of the approaching storm. Thou dirge

Of the dying year, to which this closing night
Will be the dome of a vast sepulchre,   25
Vaulted with all thy congregated might

Of vapours, from whose solid atmosphere
Black rain, and fire, and hail, will burst: oh, hear!

III

Thou who didst waken from his summer dreams,
The blue Mediterranean, where he lay,   30
Lulled by the coil of his crystálline streams,

ODE TO THE WEST WIND: 10 **clarion:** a high-pitched trumpet 21 **Maenad:** a woman participant in the orgiastic rites of Dionysus, Greek god of wine 27 **vapours:** clouds

Beside a pumice isle in Baiae's bay,
And saw in sleep old palaces and towers
Quivering within the wave's intenser day,

All overgrown with azure moss and flowers 35
So sweet, the sense faints picturing them! Thou
For whose path the Atlantic's level powers

Cleave themselves into chasms, while far below
The sea-blooms and the oozy woods which wear
The sapless foliage of the ocean, know 40

Thy voice, and suddenly grow grey with fear,
And tremble and despoil themselves: oh, hear!

IV

If I were a dead leaf thou mightest bear;
If I were a swift cloud to fly with thee;
A wave to pant beneath thy power, and share 45

The impulse of thy strength, only less free
Than thou, O uncontrollable! If even
I were as in my boyhood, and could be

The comrade of thy wanderings over Heaven,
As then, when to outstrip the skiey speed 50
Scarce seemed a vision; I would ne'er have striven

As thus with thee in prayer in my sore need.
Oh, lift me as a wave, a leaf, a cloud!
I fall upon the thorns of life! I bleed!

A heavy weight of hours has chained and bowed 55
One too like thee: tameless, and swift, and proud.

V

Make me thy lyre, even as the forest is:
What if my leaves are falling like its own!
The tumult of thy mighty harmonies

Will take from both a deep, autumnal tone, 60
Sweet though in sadness. Be thou, Spirit fierce,
My spirit! Be thou me, impetuous one!

Drive my dead thoughts over the universe
Like withered leaves to quicken a new birth!
And, by the incantation of this verse, 65

Scatter, as from an unextinguished hearth
Ashes and sparks, my words among mankind!
Be through my lips to unawakened earth

The trumpet of a prophecy! Oh, Wind,
If Winter comes, can Spring be far behind? 70

32 **Baiae:** a place near Naples, site of the ruins of villas of Roman
emperors

THE INDIAN SERENADE

I ARISE from dreams of thee
In the first sweet sleep of night.
When the winds are breathing low,
And the stars are shining bright:
I arise from dreams of thee, 5
And a spirit in my feet
Has led me – who knows how?
To thy chamber window, Sweet!

The wandering airs they faint
On the dark, the silent stream – 10
The Champak odours fail
Like sweet thoughts in a dream;
The nightingale's complaint,
It dies upon her heart; –
As I must on thine, 15
Oh, belovèd as thou art!

Oh, lift me from the grass!
I die! I faint! I fail!
Let thy love in kisses rain
On my lips and eyelids pale. 20
My cheek is cold and white, alas!
My heart beats loud and fast; –
Oh, press it close to thine again,
Where it will break at last.

THE INDIAN SERENADE: 11 **Champak:** a fragrant Indian magnolia

LOVE'S PHILOSOPHY

THE fountains mingle with the river
    And the rivers with the Ocean,
The winds of Heaven mix for ever
    With a sweet emotion;
Nothing in the world is single; 5
    All things by a law divine
In one spirit meet and mingle.
    Why not I with thine? –

See the mountains kiss high Heaven
    And the waves clasp one another; 10
No sister-flower would be forgiven
    If it disdained its brother;
And the sunlight clasps the earth,
    And the moonbeams kiss the sea:
What is all this sweet work worth 15
    If thou kiss not me?

TO A SKYLARK

HAIL to thee, blithe Spirit!
  Bird thou never wert,
That from Heaven, or near it,
  Pourest thy full heart
In prófuse strains of unpremeditated art.   5

Higher still and higher
  From the earth thou springest
Like a cloud of fire;
  The blue deep thou wingest,
And singing still dost soar, and soaring ever singest.   10

In the golden lightning
  Of the sunken sun,
O'er which clouds are bright'ning,
  Thou dost float and run;
Like an unbodied joy whose race is just begun.   15

The pale purple even
  Melts around thy flight;
Like a star of Heaven,
  In the broad daylight
Thou art unseen, but yet I hear thy shrill delight,   20

Keen as are the arrows
  Of that silver sphere,
Whose intense lamp narrows
  In the white dawn clear
Until we hardly see – we feel that it is there.   25

All the earth and air
  With thy voice is loud,
As, when night is bare,
  From one lonely cloud
The moon rains out her beams, and Heaven is
    overflowed.   30

What thou art we know not;
  What is most like thee?
From rainbow clouds there flow not
  Drops so bright to see
As from thy presence showers a rain of melody.   35

Like a Poet hidden
  In the light of thought,
Singing hymns unbidden,
  Till the world is wrought
To sympathy with hopes and fears it heeded not: 40

Like a high-born maiden
  In a palace-tower,
Soothing her love-laden
  Soul in secret hour
With music sweet as love, which overflows her bower:

Like a glow-worm golden   46
  In a dell of dew,
Scattering unbeholden
  Its aërial hue
Among the flowers and grass, which screen it from the
    view!   50

Like a rose embowered
  In its own green leaves,
By warm winds deflowered,
  Till the scent it gives
Makes faint with too much sweet these heavy-wingèd
    thieves: 55

Sound of vernal showers
  On the twinkling grass,
Rain-awakened flowers,
  All that ever was
Joyous, and clear, and fresh, thy music doth surpass:

Teach us, Sprite or Bird,   61
  What sweet thoughts are thine:
I have never heard
  Praise of love or wine
That panted forth a flood of rapture so divine.   65

Chorus Hymeneal
  Or triumphal chant
Matched with thine would be all
  But an empty vaunt,
A thing wherein we feel there is some hidden want.

What objects are the fountains   71
  Of thy happy strain?
What fields, or waves, or mountains?
  What shapes of sky or plain?
What love of thine own kind? what ignorance of
    pain?   75

With thy clear keen joyance
  Languor cannot be:
Shadow of annoyance
  Never came near thee:
Thou lovest – but ne'er knew love's sad satiety.   80

Waking or asleep,
  Thou of death must deem
Things more true and deep
  Than we mortals dream,
Or how could thy notes flow in such a crystal stream?

We look before and after,   86
  And pine for what is not:
Our sincerest laughter
  With some pain is fraught;
Our sweetest songs are those that tell of saddest
    thought.   90

TO A SKYLARK: 22 **silver sphere:** the morning star

66 **Hymeneal:** marital, from Hymen, the Greek god of marriage
76 **joyance:** gaiety

Yet if we could scorn
  Hate, and pride, and fear;
If we were things born
  Not to shed a tear,
I know not how thy joy we ever should come near.   95

Better than all measures
  Of delightful sound,
Better than all treasures
  That in books are found,   99
Thy skill to poet were, thou scorner of the ground!

Teach me half the gladness
  That thy brain must know,
Such harmonious madness
  From my lips would flow   104
The world should listen then – as I am listening now.

'I FEAR THY KISSES, GENTLE MAIDEN'

I FEAR thy kisses, gentle maiden,
  Thou needest not fear mine;
My spirit is too deeply laden
  Ever to burthen thine.
I fear thy mien, thy tones, thy motion,   5
  Thou needest not fear mine;
Innocent is the heart's devotion
  With which I worship thine.

'MUSIC, WHEN SOFT VOICES DIE'

MUSIC, when soft voices die,
Vibrates in the memory –
Odours, when sweet violets sicken,
Live within the sense they quicken.

Rose leaves, when the rose is dead,   5
Are heaped for the belovèd's bed;
And so thy thoughts, when thou art gone,
Love itself shall slumber on.

ADONAIS
AN ELEGY ON THE DEATH OF JOHN KEATS,
AUTHOR OF 'ENDYMION', 'HYPERION', ETC.

I WEEP for Adonais – he is dead!
Oh, weep for Adonais! though our tears
Thaw not the frost which binds so dear a head!
And thou, sad Hour, selected from all years
To mourn our loss, rouse thy obscure compeers,   5
And teach them thine own sorrow, say: 'With me
Died Adonais; till the Future dares
Forget the Past, his fate and fame shall be
An echo and a light unto eternity!'

Where wert thou, mighty Mother, when he lay,   10
When thy Son lay, pierced by the shaft which flies
In darkness? where was lorn Urania
When Adonais died? With veilèd eyes,
'Mid listening Echoes, in her Paradise
She sate, while one, with soft enamoured breath,   15
Rekindled all the fading melodies
With which, like flowers that mock the corse
   beneath,
He had adorned and hid the coming bulk of Death.

Oh, weep for Adonais – he is dead!
Wake, melancholy Mother, wake and weep!   20
Yet wherefore? Quench within their burning bed
Thy fiery tears, and let thy loud heart keep
Like his, a mute and uncomplaining sleep;
For he is gone, where all things wise and fair   24
Descend; – oh, dream not that the amorous Deep
Will yet restore him to the vital air;
Death feeds on his mute voice, and laughs at our
   despair.

Most musical of mourners, weep again!
Lament anew, Urania! – He died,
Who was the Sire of an immortal strain,   30
Blind, old, and lonely, when his country's pride,
The priest, the slave, and the liberticide,
Trampled and mocked with many a loathèd rite
Of lust and blood; he went, unterrified,
Into the gulf of death; but his clear Sprite   35
Yet reigns o'er earth; the third among the sons of
   light.

Most musical of mourners, weep anew!
Not all to that bright station dared to climb;
And happier they their happiness who knew,
Whose tapers yet burn through that night of time   40
In which suns perished; others more sublime,
Struck by the envious wrath of man or god,
Have sunk, extinct in their refulgent prime;
And some yet live, treading the thorny road,
Which leads, through toil and hate, to Fame's serene
   abode.   45

But now, thy youngest, dearest one, has perished –
The nursling of thy widowhood, who grew,
Like a pale flower by some sad maiden cherished,
And fed with true-love tears, instead of dew;
Most musical of mourners, weep anew!   50
Thy éxtreme hope, the loveliest and the last,
The bloom, whose petals nipped before they blew
Died on the promise of the fruit, is waste;
The broken lily lies – the storm is overpassed.

ADONAIS: 1 **Adonais:** derived from Adonis, in Greek myth a beautiful youth loved by Aphrodite and killed by a wild boar 5 **compeers:** peers or comrades

12 **lorn:** forsaken **Urania:** Venus or Aphrodite, whom Shelley makes the mother of Adonais 17 **corse:** corpse 29 **He:** Milton 35 **Sprite:** spirit 36 **sons of light:** Homer, Dante and Milton 40 **tapers:** candles 52 **blew:** bloomed

To that high Capital, where kingly Death   55
Keeps his pale court in beauty and decay,
He came; and bought, with price of purest breath,
A grave among the eternal. – Come away!
Haste, while the vault of blue Italian day
Is yet his fitting charnel-roof! while still   60
He lies, as if in dewy sleep he lay;
Awake him not! surely he takes his fill
Of deep and liquid rest, forgetful of all ill.

He will awake no more, oh, never more! –
Within the twilight chamber spreads apace   65
The shadow of white Death, and at the door
Invisible Corruption waits to trace
His éxtreme way to her dim dwelling-place;
The eternal Hunger sits, but pity and awe
Soothe her pale rage, nor dares she to deface   70
So fair a prey, till darkness, and the law
Of change, shall o'er his sleep the mortal curtain
draw.

Oh, weep for Adonais! – The quick Dreams,
The passion-wingèd Ministers of thought,
Who were his flocks, whom near the living streams
Of his young spirit he fed, and whom he taught   76
The love which was its music, wander not, –
Wander no more, from kindling brain to brain,
But droop there, whence they sprung; and mourn
their lot   79
Round the cold heart, where, after their sweet pain,
They ne'er will gather strength, or find a home again.

And one with trembling hands clasps his cold head,
And fans him with her moonlight wings, and cries;
'Our love, our hope, our sorrow, is not dead;
See, on the silken fringe of his faint eyes,   85
Like dew upon a sleeping flower, there lies
A tear some Dream has loosened from his brain.'
Lost Angel of a ruined Paradise!
She knew not 'twas her own; as with no stain
She faded, like a cloud which had outwept its rain.   90

One from a lucid urn of starry dew
Washed his light limbs as if embalming them;
Another clipped her prófuse locks, and threw
The wreath upon him, like an anadem,
Which frozen tears instead of pearls begem;   95
Another in her wilful grief would break
Her bow and wingèd reeds, as if to stem
A greater loss with one which was more weak;
And dull the barbèd fire against his frozen cheek.

Another Splendour on his mouth alit,   100
That mouth, whence it was wont to draw the breath
Which gave it strength to pierce the guarded wit,

And pass into the panting heart beneath
With lightning and with music: the damp death
Quenched its caress upon his icy lips;   105
And, as a dying meteor stains a wreath
Of moonlight vapour, which the cold night clips,
It flushed through his pale limbs, and passed to its
eclipse.

And others came . . . Desires and Adorations,
Wingèd Persuasions and veiled Destinies,   110
Splendours, and Glooms, and glimmering
Incarnations
Of hopes and fears, and twilight Phantasies;
And Sorrow, with her family of Sighs,
And Pleasure, blind with tears, led by the gleam
Of her own dying smile instead of eyes,   115
Came in slow pomp; – the moving pomp might
seem
Like pageantry of mist on an autumnal stream.

All he had loved, and moulded into thought,
From shape, and hue, and odour, and sweet sound,
Lamented Adonais. Morning sought   120
Her eastern watch-tower, and her hair unbound,
Wet with the tears which should adorn the ground,
Dimmed the aëreal eyes that kindle day;
Afar the melancholy thunder moaned,
Pale Ocean in unquiet slumber lay,   125
And the wild Winds flew round, sobbing in their
dismay.

Lost Echo sits amid the voiceless mountains,
And feeds her grief with his remembered lay,
And will no more reply to winds or fountains,
Or amorous birds perched on the young green
spray,   130
Or herdsman's horn, or bell at closing day;
Since she can mimic not his lips, more dear
Than those for whose disdain she pined away
Into a shadow of all sounds: – a drear
Murmur, between their songs, is all the woodmen
hear.   135

Grief made the young Spring wild, and she threw
down
Her kindling buds, as if she Autumn were,
Or they dead leaves; since her delight is flown,
For whom should she have waked the sullen year?
To Phoebus was not Hyacinth so dear   140
Nor to himself Narcissus, as to both
Thou, Adonais: wan they stand and sere
Amid the faint companions of their youth,
With dew all turned to tears; odour, to sighing ruth.

---

55 **Capital:** Rome, where Keats died 60 **charnel:** tomb 73 **quick:** living 91 **lucid:** bright, shining 94 **anadem:** garland 102 **guarded wit:** cautious intelligence

107 **clips:** embraces 128 **lay:** song 133 **she pined away:** in Greek myth, the nymph Echo pined away because of her unrequited love for Narcissus 140 **Phoebus:** Apollo, who loved the youth Hyacinthus 142 **sere:** dry, withered 144 **ruth:** pity

Thy spirit's sister, the lorn nightingale   145
Mourns not her mate with such melodious pain;
Not so the eagle, who like thee could scale
Heaven, and could nourish in the sun's domain
Her mighty youth with morning, doth complain,
Soaring and screaming round her empty nest,   150
As Albion wails for thee: the curse of Cain
Light on his head who pierced thy innocent breast,
And scared the angel soul that was its earthly guest!

Ah, woe is me! Winter is come and gone,
But grief returns with the revolving year;   155
The airs and streams renew their joyous tone;
The ants, the bees, the swallows reappear;
Fresh leaves and flowers deck the dead Seasons'
      bier;
The amorous birds now pair in every brake,
And build their mossy homes in field and brere;   160
And the green lizard, and the golden snake,
Like unimprisoned flames, out of their trance awake.

Through wood and stream and field and hill and
      Ocean
A quickening life from the Earth's heart has burst
As it has ever done, with change and motion,   165
From the great morning of the world when first
God dawned on Chaos; in its stream immersed,
The lamps of Heaven flash with a softer light;
All baser things pant with life's sacred thirst;
Diffuse themselves; and spend in love's delight,   170
The beauty and the joy of their renewèd might.

The leprous corpse, touched by this spirit tender,
Exhales itself in flowers of gentle breath;
Like incarnations of the stars, when splendour
Is changed to fragrance, they illumine death   175
And mock the merry worm that wakes beneath;
Nought we know, dies. Shall that alone which knows
Be as a sword consumed before the sheath
By sightless lightning? – the intense atom glows
A moment, then is quenched in a most cold repose.

Alas! that all we loved of him should be,   181
But for our grief, as if it had not been,
And grief itself be mortal! Woe is me!
Whence are we, and why are we? of what scene
The actors or spectators? Great and mean   185
Meet massed in death, who lends what life must
      borrow.
As long as skies are blue, and fields are green,
Evening must usher night, night urge the morrow,
Month follow month with woe, and year wake year to
      sorrow.

He will awake no more, oh, never more!   190
'Wake thou,' cried Misery, 'childless Mother, rise
Out of thy sleep, and slake, in thy heart's core,
A wound more fierce than his, with tears and sighs.'
And all the Dreams that watched Urania's eyes,
And all the Echoes whom their sister's song   195
Had held in holy silence, cried: 'Arise!'
Swift as a Thought by the snake Memory stung,
From her ambrosial rest the fading Splendour sprung.

She rose like an autumnal Night, that springs
Out of the East, and follows wild and drear   200
The golden Day, which, on eternal wings,
Even as a ghost abandoning a bier,
Had left the Earth a corpse. Sorrow and fear
So struck, so roused, so rapt Urania;
So saddened round her like an atmosphere   205
Of stormy mist; so swept her on her way
Even to the mournful place where Adonaïs lay.

Out of her secret Paradise she sped,
Through camps and cities rough with stone, and
      steel,
And human hearts, which to her aery tread   210
Yielding not, wounded the invisible
Palms of her tender feet where'er they fell:
And barbèd tongues, and thoughts more sharp than
      they,
Rent the soft Form they never could repel,
Whose sacred blood, like the young tears of May,
Paved with eternal flowers that undeserving way.   216

In the death-chamber for a moment Death,
Shamed by the presence of that living Might,
Blushed to annihilation, and the breath
Revisited those lips, and Life's pale light   220
Flashed through those limbs, so late her dear
      delight.
'Leave me not wild and drear and comfortless,
As silent lightning leaves the starless night!
Leave me not!' cried Urania: her distress
Roused Death: Death rose and smiled, and met her
      vain caress.   225

'Stay yet awhile! speak to me once again;
Kiss me, so long but as a kiss may live;
And in my heartless breast and burning brain
That word, that kiss, shall all thoughts else survive,
With food of saddest memory kept alive,   230
Now thou art dead, as if it were a part
Of thee, my Adonais! I would give
All that I am to be as thou now art!
But I am chained to Time, and cannot thence depart!

145 **nightingale:** subject of Keats' famous ode 151 **Albion:** England
or Britain 152 **pierced thy innocent breast:** refers to Shelley's
(unfounded) belief that an abusive review of Keats' *Endymion*
contributed to his decline 159 **brake:** thicket 160 **brere:** briar
179 **sightless:** unseen

192 **slake:** assuage 222 **drear:** sad

'O gentle child, beautiful as thou wert,   235
Why didst thou leave the trodden paths of men
Too soon, and with weak hands though mighty
    heart
Dare the unpastured dragon in his den?
Defenceless as thou wert, oh, where was then
Wisdom the mirrored shield, or scorn the spear?
Or hadst thou waited the full cycle, when   241
Thy spirit should have filled its crescent sphere,
The monsters of life's waste had fled from thee like
    deer.

'The herded wolves, bold only to pursue;
The óbscene ravens, clamorous o'er the dead;   245
The vultures to the conqueror's banner true
Who feed where Desolation first has fed,
And whose wings rain contagion; – how they fled,
When, like Apollo, from his golden bow
The Pythian of the age one arrow sped   250
And smiled! – The spoilers tempt no second blow,
They fawn on the proud feet that spurn them lying
    low.

'The sun comes forth, and many reptiles spawn;
He sets, and each ephemeral insect then
Is gathered into death without a dawn,
And the immortal stars awake again;   255
So is it in the world of living men:
A godlike mind soars forth, in its delight
Making earth bare and veiling heaven, and when
It sinks, the swarms that dimmed or shared its light
Leave to its kindred lamps the spirit's awful night.'   261

Thus ceased she: and the mountain shepherds came,
Their garlands sere, their magic mantles rent;
The Pilgrim of Eternity, whose fame
Over his living head like Heaven is bent,   265
An early but enduring monument,
Came, veiling all the lightnings of his song
In sorrow; from her wilds Ierne sent
The sweetest lyrist of her saddest wrong,
And Love taught Grief to fall like music from his
    tongue.   270

'Midst others of less note, came one frail Form,
A phantom among men; companionless
As the last cloud of an expiring storm
Whose thunder is its knell; he, as I guess,
Had gazed on Nature's naked loveliness,   275

Actaeon-like, and now he fled astray
With feeble steps o'er the world's wilderness,
And his own thoughts, along that rugged way,
Pursued, like raging hounds, their father and their
    prey.

A pardlike Spirit beautiful and swift –   280
A Love in desolation masked; – a Power
Girt round with weakness; – it can scarce uplift
The weight of the superincumbent hour;
It is a dying lamp, a falling shower,
A breaking billow; – even whilst we speak   285
Is it not broken? On the withering flower
The killing sun smiles brightly: on a cheek
The life can burn in blood, even while the heart may
    break.

His head was bound with pansies overblown,
And faded violets, white, and pied, and blue;   290
And a light spear topped with a cypress cone,
Round whose rude shaft dark ivy-tresses grew
Yet dripping with the forest's noonday dew,
Vibrated, as the ever-beating heart
Shook the weak hand that grasped it; of that crew
He came the last, neglected and apart;   296
A herd-abandoned deer struck by the hunter's dart.

All stood aloof, and at his partial moan
Smiled through their tears; well knew that gentle
    band
Who in another's fate now wept his own,   300
As in the accents of an unknown land
He sung new sorrow; sad Urania scanned
The Stranger's mien, and murmured: 'Who art
    thou?'
He answered not, but with a sudden hand
Made bare his branded and ensanguined brow,   305
Which was like Cain's or Christ's – oh! that it should
    be so!

What softer voice is hushed over the dead?
Athwart what brow is that dark mantle thrown?
What form leans sadly o'er the white death-bed,
In mockery of monumental stone,   310
The heavy heart heaving without a moan?
If it be He, who, gentlest of the wise,
Taught, soothed, loved, honoured the departed one,
Let me not vex, with inharmonious sighs,
The silence of that heart's accepted sacrifice.   315

---

242 **Thy spirit . . . sphere:** he should have grown and matured as the crescent moon grows to become full 250 **Pythian:** an epithet of Apollo, who killed the dragon Python. Here it refers to Byron, who satirized critics and reviewers in his *English Bards and Scotch Reviewers* 261 **kindred lamps:** fellow stars 264 **Pilgrim of Eternity:** Byron, author of *Childe Harold's Pilgrimage* 268 **Ierne:** Ireland, birthplace of Thomas Moore (**the sweetest lyrist**) 271 **one frail Form:** Shelley himself

276 **Actaeon-like:** in Greek myth, Actaeon was a hunter who accidentally saw the goddess Artemis naked, while bathing, and as punishment was turned into a stag, which was then torn apart by his own hounds 280 **pardlike:** leopard-like 291 **spear . . . cone:** the thyrsus, a staff borne by the god Dionysus 296 **dart:** arrow 297 **partial:** sympathetic 310 **mockery:** imitation 312 **He:** Leigh Hunt, friend of Keats and Shelley

Our Adonais has drunk poison – oh!
What deaf and viperous murderer could crown
Life's early cup with such a draught of woe?
The nameless worm would now itself disown:
It felt, yet could escape, the magic tone   320
Whose prelude held all envy, hate, and wrong,
But what was howling in one breast alone,
Silent with expectation of the song,
Whose master's hand is cold, whose silver lyre
    unstrung.

Live thou, whose infamy is not thy fame!   325
Live! fear no heavier chástisement from me,
Thou noteless blot on a remembered name!
But be thyself, and know thyself to be!
And ever at thy season be thou free
To spill the venom when thy fangs o'erflow: 330
Remorse and Self-contempt shall cling to thee;
Hot Shame shall burn upon thy secret brow,
And like a beaten hound tremble thou shalt – as now.

Nor let us weep that our delight is fled
Far from these carrion kites that scream below;   335
He wakes or sleeps with the enduring dead;
Thou canst not soar where he is sitting now. –
Dust to the dust! but the pure spirit shall flow
Back to the burning fountain whence it came,
A portion of the Eternal, which must glow   340
Through time and change, unquenchably the same,
Whilst thy cold embers choke the sordid hearth of
    shame.

Peace, peace! he is not dead, he doth not sleep –
He hath awakened from the dream of life –
'Tis we, who lost in stormy visions, keep   345
With phantoms an unprofitable strife,
And in mad trance, strike with our spirit's knife
Invulnerable nothings. – *We* decay
Like corpses in a charnel; fear and grief
Convulse us and consume us day by day,   350
And cold hopes swarm like worms within our living
    clay.

He has outsoared the shadow of our night;
Envy and calumny and hate and pain,
And that unrest which men miscall delight,
Can touch him not and torture not again;   355
From the contagion of the world's slow stain
He is secure, and now can never mourn
A heart grown cold, a head grown grey in vain;
Nor, when the spirit's self has ceased to burn,
With sparkless ashes load an unlamented urn.   360

He lives, he wakes – 'tis Death is dead, not he;
Mourn not for Adonaïs. – Thou young Dawn,
Turn all thy dew to splendour, for from thee
The spirit thou lamentest is not gone;
Ye caverns and ye forests, cease to moan!   365
Cease, ye faint flowers and fountains, and thou Air,
Which like a mourning veil thy scarf hadst thrown
O'er the abandoned Earth, now leave it bare
Even to the joyous stars which smile on its despair!

He is made one with Nature: there is heard   370
His voice in all her music, from the moan
Of thunder, to the song of night's sweet bird;
He is a presence to be felt and known
In darkness and in light, from herb and stone,
Spreading itself where'er that Power may move   375
Which has withdrawn his being to its own;
Which wields the world with never-wearied love,
Sustains it from beneath, and kindles it above.

He is a portion of the loveliness
Which once he made more lovely: he doth bear   380
His part, while the one Spirit's plastic stress
Sweeps through the dull dense world, compelling
    there,
All new successions to the forms they wear;
Torturing th'unwilling dross that checks its flight
To its own likeness, as each mass may bear;   385
And bursting in its beauty and its might
From trees and beasts and men into the Heaven's
    light.

The splendours of the firmament of time
May be eclipsed, but are extinguished not;
Like stars to their appointed height they climb,   390
And death is a low mist which cannot blot
The brightness it may veil. When lofty thought
Lifts a young heart above its mortal lair,
And love and life contend in it, for what
Shall be its earthly doom, the dead live there   395
And move like winds of light on dark and stormy air.

The inheritors of unfulfilled renown
Rose from their thrones, built beyond mortal
    thought,
Far in the Unapparent. Chatterton
Rose pale, – his solemn agony had not   400
Yet faded from him; Sidney, as he fought
And as he fell and as he lived and loved
Sublimely mild, a Spirit without spot,
Arose; and Lucan, by his death approved:
Oblivion as they rose shrank like a thing reproved.   405

---

372 **night's sweet bird:** the nightingale, another allusion to Keats' ode
397–404 **The inheritors . . . Lucan:** Shelley refers to other poets who
died young without fulfilling their potential. Thomas Chatterton
(1752–70) committed suicide; Sir Philip Sidney (1554–86) died of a wound
received in battle; the Roman poet Lucan (Marcus Annaeus Lucanus,
39–65 AD) committed suicide 404 **approved:** justified

---

319 **worm:** snake   327 **noteless:** attracting no notice

And many more, whose names on Earth are dark,
But whose transmitted effluence cannot die
So long as fire outlives the parent spark,
Rose, robed in dazzling immortality.
'Thou art become as one of us,' they cry,   410
'It was for thee yon kingless sphere has long
Swung blind in unascended majesty,
Silent alone amid an Heaven of Song.
Assume thy wingèd throne, thou Vesper of our
    throng!'

Who mourns for Adonais? Oh, come forth,   415
Fond wretch! and know thyself and him aright.
Clasp with thy panting soul the pendulous Earth;
As from a centre, dart thy spirit's light
Beyond all worlds, until its spacious might
Satiate the void circumference: then shrink   420
Even to a point within our day and night;
And keep thy heart light lest it make thee sink
When hope has kindled hope, and lured thee to the
    brink.

Or go to Rome, which is the sepulchre,
Oh, not of him, but of our joy: 'tis nought   425
That ages, empires, and religions there
Lie buried in the ravage they have wrought;
For such as he can lend, – they borrow not
Glory from those who made the world their prey;
And he is gathered to the kings of thought   430
Who waged contention with their time's decay,
And of the past are all that cannot pass away.

Go thou to Rome, – at once the Paradise,
The grave, the city, and the wilderness;
And where its wrecks like shattered mountains rise,
And flowering weeds, and fragrant copses dress   436
The bones of Desolation's nakedness
Pass, till the spirit of the spot shall lead
Thy footsteps to a slope of green accéss
Where, like an infant's smile, over the dead   440
A light of laughing flowers along the grass is spread;

And grey walls moulder round, on which dull Time
Feeds, like slow fire upon a hoary brand;
And one keen pyramid with wedge sublime,
Pavilioning the dust of him who planned   445
This refuge for his memory, doth stand
Like flame transformed to marble; and beneath,
A field is spread, on which a newer band
Have pitched in Heaven's smile their camp of death,
Welcoming him we lose with scarce extinguished
    breath.   450

Here pause: these graves are all too young as yet
To have outgrown the sorrow which consigned
Its charge to each; and if the seal is set,
Here, on one fountain of a mourning mind,
Break it not thou! too surely shalt thou find   455
Thine own well full, if thou returnest home,
Of tears and gall. From the world's bitter wind
Seek shelter in the shadow of the tomb.
What Adonais is, why fear we to become?

The One remains, the many change and pass;   460
Heaven's light forever shines, Earth's shadows fly;
Life, like a dome of many-coloured glass,
Stains the white radiance of Eternity,
Until Death tramples it to fragments. – Die,
If thou wouldst be with that which thou dost seek!
Follow where all is fled! – Rome's azure sky,   466
Flowers, ruins, statues, music, words, are weak
The glory they transfuse with fitting truth to speak.

Why linger, why turn back, why shrink, my Heart?
Thy hopes are gone before: from all things here   470
They have departed; thou shouldst now depart!
A light is passed from the revolving year,
And man, and woman; and what still is dear
Attracts to crush, repels to make thee wither.
The soft sky smiles, – the low wind whispers near:
'Tis Adonais calls! oh, hasten thither,   476
No more let Life divide what Death can join together.

That Light whose smile kindles the Universe,
That Beauty in which all things work and move,
That Benediction which the eclipsing Curse   480
Of birth can quench not, that sustaining Love
Which through the web of being blindly wove
By man and beast and earth and air and sea,
Burns bright or dim, as each are mirrors of
The fire for which all thirst, now beams on me,   485
Consuming the last clouds of cold mortality.

The breath whose might I have invoked in song
Descends on me; my spirit's bark is driven
Far from the shore, far from the trembling throng
Whose sails were never to the tempest given;   490
The massy earth and spherèd skies are riven!
I am borne darkly, fearfully, afar;
Whilst, burning through the inmost veil of Heaven,
The soul of Adonais, like a star,
Beacons from the abode where the Eternal are.   495

---

414 **Vesper:** the evening star 417 **pendulous:** hanging in space
443 **hoary brand:** burning torch 444 **one keen pyramid:** the tomb of
a Roman tribune, Caius Cestius

454 **Here . . . mind:** a reference to the grave of Shelley's infant son,
buried in the same graveyard as Keats 488 **bark:** ship 491 **massy:**
massive

From HELLAS

THE world's great age begins anew,
   The golden years return,
The earth doth like a snake renew
   Her winter weeds outworn:
Heaven smiles, and faiths and empires gleam,   5
Like wrecks of a dissolving dream.

A brighter Hellas rears its mountains
   From waves serener far;
A new Peneus rolls his fountains
   Against the morning star.   10
Where fairer Tempes bloom, there sleep
Young Cyclads on a sunnier deep.

A loftier Argo cleaves the main,
   Fraught with a later prize;
Another Orpheus sings again,   15
   And loves, and weeps, and dies.
A new Ulysses leaves once more
Calypso for his native shore.

Oh, write no more the tale of Troy,
   If earth Death's scroll must be!   20
Nor mix with Laian rage the joy
   Which dawns upon the free:
Although a subtler Sphinx renew
Riddles of death Thebes never knew.

Another Athens shall arise,   25
   And to remoter time
Bequeath, like sunset to the skies,
   The splendour of its prime;
And leave, if nought so brave may live,
All earth can take or Heaven can give.   30

Saturn and Love their long repose
   Shall burst, more bright and good
Than all who fell, than One who rose,
   Than many unsubdued:
Not gold, not blood, their altar dowers,   35
But votive tears and symbol flowers.

Oh, cease! must hate and death return?
   Cease! must men kill and die?
Cease! drain not to its dregs the urn
   Of bitter prophecy.   40
The world is weary of the past,
Oh, might it die or rest at last!

[Lines 1060–1101]

HELLAS: 4 **weeds:** meaning clothes (especially those of widows) as well as the literal meaning 9 **Peneus:** a river flowing through the proverbially beautiful vale of Tempe in Greece 12 **Cyclads:** the Cyclades, a Greek island chain 13 **Argo:** in Greek myth, the ship in which Jason and the Argonauts set out in quest of the Golden Fleece

15 **Orpheus:** legendary Greek poet and musician 18 **Calypso:** a sea-nymph who detained Ulysses on his voyage home from Troy 21 **Laian:** referring to Laius, King of Thebes, who, in Greek myth, was killed by his son Oedipus, neither recognizing the other. Oedipus went on to solve the riddle of the Sphinx 31 **Saturn:** Roman god of agriculture and vegetation **Love:** Aphrodite (or the Roman Venus), goddess of love 33 **all who fell:** the forgotten gods of the ancient world **One who rose:** Christ 34 **many unsubdued:** the idols of pagan peoples

A LAMENT

O WORLD! O life! O time!
On whose last steps I climb,
   Trembling at that where I had stood before;
When will return the glory of your prime?
     No more – Oh, never more!   5

Out of the day and night
A joy has taken flight:
   Fresh spring, and summer, and winter hoar
Move my faint heart with grief, but with delight
     No more – Oh, never more!   10

'ONE WORD IS TOO OFTEN PROFANED'

ONE word is too often profaned
   For me to profane it,
One feeling too falsely disdained
   For thee to disdain it;
One hope is too like despair   5
   For prudence to smother,
And pity from thee more dear
   Than that from another.

I can give not what men call love,
   But wilt thou accept not   10
The worship the heart lifts above
   And the Heavens reject not, –
The desire of the moth for the star,
   Of the night for the morrow,
The devotion to something afar   15
   From the sphere of our sorrow?

'WHEN THE LAMP IS SHATTERED'

WHEN the lamp is shattered
The light in the dust lies dead –
   When the cloud is scattered,
The rainbow's glory is shed.
   When the lute is broken,   5
Sweet tones are remembered not;
   When the lips have spoken,
Loved accents are soon forgot.

As music and splendour
Survive not the lamp and the lute,   10
  The heart's echoes render
No song when the spirit is mute: –
  No song but sad dirges,
Like the wind through a ruined cell,
  Or the mournful surges   15
That ring the dead seaman's knell.

When hearts have once mingled,
Love first leaves the well-built nest;
  The weak one is singled
To endure what it once possessed.   20
  O Love! who bewailest
The frailty of all things here,
  Why choose you the frailest
For your cradle, your home, and your bier?

Its passions will rock thee,   25
As the storms rock the ravens on high;
  Bright reason will mock thee,
Like the sun from a wintry sky.
  From thy nest every rafter
Will rot, and thine eagle home   30
  Leave thee naked to laughter,
When leaves fall and cold winds come.

TO JANE: THE INVITATION

BEST and brightest, come away!
Fairer far than this fair Day,
Which, like thee to those in sorrow,
Comes to bid a sweet good-morrow
To the rough Year just awake   5
In its cradle on the brake.
The brightest hour of unborn Spring,
Through the winter wandering,
Found, it seems, the halcyon Morn
To hoar February born;   10
Bending from Heaven, in azure mirth,
It kissed the forehead of the Earth,
And smiled upon the silent sea,
And bade the frozen streams be free,
And waked to music all their fountains,   15
And breathed upon the frozen mountains,
And like a prophetess of May
Strewed flowers upon the barren way,
Making the wintry world appear
Like one on whom thou smilest, dear.   20

Away, away, from men and towns,
To the wild wood and the downs –
To the silent wilderness
Where the soul need not repress
Its music lest it should not find   25
An echo in another's mind,
While the touch of Nature's art
Harmonizes heart to heart.
I leave this notice on my door
For each accustomed visitor: –   30
'I am gone into the fields
To take what this sweet hour yields; –
Reflection, you may come tomorrow,
Sit by the fireside with Sorrow. –
You with the unpaid bill, Despair,   35
You, tiresome verse-reciter, Care, –
I will pay you in the grave, –
Death will listen to your stave.
Expectation too, be off!
Today is for itself enough;   40
Hope, in pity mock not Woe
With smiles, nor follow where I go;
Long having lived on thy sweet food,
At length I find one moment's good
After long pain – with all your love,   45
This you never told me of.'

Radiant Sister of the Day
Awake! arise! and come away!
To the wild woods and the plains,
To the pools where winter rains   50
Image all their roof of leaves,
Where the pine its garland weaves
Of sapless green, and ivy dun
Round stems that never kiss the sun;
Where the lawns and pastures be,   55
And the sandhills of the sea; –
Where the melting hoar-frost wets
The daisy-star that never sets,
And wind-flowers, and violets,
Which yet join not scent to hue,   60
Crown the pale year weak and new;
When the night is left behind
In the deep east, dim and blind,
And the blue noon is over us,
And the multitudinous   65
Billows murmur at our feet,
Where the earth and ocean meet,
And all things seem only one
In the universal Sun.

TO JANE: THE INVITATION: Jane Williams was the wife of Shelley's friend
Edward Williams 6 **brake**: bracken, ferns 51 **Image**: reflect, mirror

TO JANE: THE RECOLLECTION

Now the last day of many days,
  All beautiful and bright as thou,
    The loveliest and the last, is dead,
Rise, Memory, and write its praise!
  Up, – to thy wonted work! come, trace   5
    The epitaph of glory fled, –
For now the Earth has changed its face,
  A frown is on the Heaven's brow.
We wandered to the Pine Forest
  That skirts the Ocean's foam,   10
The lightest wind was in its nest,
  The tempest in its home.
The whispering waves were half asleep,
  The clouds were gone to play,
And on the bosom of the deep   15
  The smile of Heaven lay;
It seemed as if the hour were one
  Sent from beyond the skies,
Which scattered from above the sun
  A light of Paradise.   20

We paused amid the pines that stood
  The giants of the waste,
Tortured by storms to shapes as rude
  As serpents interlaced,
And soothed by every azure breath,   25
  That under Heaven is blown,
To harmonies and hues beneath,
  As tender as its own;
Now all the tree-tops lay asleep,
  Like green waves on the sea,   30
As still as in the silent deep
  The ocean woods may be.

How calm it was! – the silence there
  By such a chain was bound
That even the busy woodpecker   35
  Made stiller by her sound
The inviolable quietness;
  The breath of peace we drew
With its soft motion made not less
  The calm that round us grew.   40
There seemed from the remotest seat
  Of the white mountain waste,
To the soft flower beneath our feet,
  A magic circle traced, –
A spirit interfused around,   45
  A thrilling, silent life, –
To momentary peace it bound
  Our mortal nature's strife;
And still I felt the centre of
  The magic circle there   50
Was one fair form that filled with love
  The lifeless atmosphere.

We paused beside the pools that lie
  Under the forest bough, –
Each seemed as 'twere a little sky   55
  Gulfed in a world below;
A firmament of purple light
  Which in the dark earth lay,
More boundless than the depth of night,
  And purer than the day –   60
In which the lovely forests grew,
  As in the upper air,
More perfect both in shape and hue
  Than any spreading there.
There lay the glad and neighbouring lawn,   65
  And through the dark green wood
The white sun twinkling like the dawn
  Out of a speckled cloud.
Sweet views which in our world above
  Can never well be seen,   70
Were imaged by the water's love
  Of that fair forest green.
And all was interfused beneath
  With an Elysian glow,
An atmosphere without a breath,   75
  A softer day below.
Like one beloved the scene had lent
  To the dark water's breast,
Its every leaf and lineament
  With more than truth expressed;   80
Until an envious wind crept by,
  Like an unwelcome thought,
Which from the mind's too faithful eye
  Blots one dear image out.
Though thou art ever fair and kind,   85
  The forests ever green,
Less oft is peace in Shelley's mind,
  Than calm in waters, seen.

TO JANE: THE RECOLLECTION: 5 **wonted:** accustomed 23 **rude:** crude, rough 71 **imaged:** reflected 74 **Elysian:** blissful, as in Elysium, the ancient Greek Paradise

WITH A GUITAR, TO JANE

ARIEL to Miranda: – Take
This slave of Music, for the sake
Of him who is the slave of thee;
And teach it all the harmony
In which thou canst, and only thou,   5
Make the delighted spirit glow,
Till joy denies itself again
And, too intense, is turned to pain;
For by permission and command
Of thine own Prince Ferdinand,   10
Poor Ariel sends this silent token
Of more than ever can be spoken;
Your guardian spirit, Ariel, who
From life to life must still pursue

Your happiness, for thus alone
Can Ariel ever find his own.
From Prospero's enchanted cell, 15
As the mighty verses tell,
To the throne of Naples he
Lit you o'er the trackless sea,
Flitting on, your prow before, 20
Like a living meteor.
When you die, the silent Moon
In her interlunar swoon
Is not sadder in her cell 25
Than deserted Ariel.
When you live again on earth,
Like an unseen star of birth
Ariel guides you o'er the sea
Of life from your nativity. 30
Many changes have been run
Since Ferdinand and you begun
Your course of love, and Ariel still
Has tracked your steps and served your will;
Now, in humbler, happier lot, 35
This is all remembered not;
And now, alas! the poor sprite is
Imprisoned, for some fault of his
In a body like a grave; –
From you he only dares to crave, 40
For his service and his sorrow,
A smile today, a song tomorrow.

The artist who this idol wrought,
To echo all harmonious thought,
Felled a tree, while on the steep 45
The woods were in their winter sleep,
Rocked in that repose divine
On the wind-swept Apennine;
And dreaming, some of Autumn past,
And some of Spring approaching fast, 50
And some of April buds and showers,
And some of songs in July bowers,
And all of love; and so this tree, –
Oh, that such our death may be! –
Died in sleep, and felt no pain, 55
To live in happier form again:
From which, beneath Heaven's fairest star,
The artist wrought this loved Guitar;
And taught it justly to reply,
To all who question skilfully, 60
In language gentle as thine own;
Whispering in enamoured tone
Sweet oracles of woods and dells,
And summer winds in sylvan cells;
For it had learned all harmonies 65
Of the plains and of the skies,
Of the forests and the mountains,
And the many-voicèd fountains;
The clearest echoes of the hills,
The softest notes of falling rills, 70

The melodies of birds and bees,
The murmuring of summer seas,
And pattering rain, and breathing dew,
And airs of evening; and it knew
That seldom-heard mysterious sound, 75
Which, driven on its diurnal round,
As it floats through boundless day,
Our world enkindles on its way. –
All this it knows, but will not tell
To those who cannot question well 80
The Spirit that inhabits it;
It talks according to the wit
Of its companions; and no more
Is heard than has been felt before,
By those who tempt it to betray 85
These secrets of an elder day:
But, sweetly as its answers will
Flatter hands of perfect skill,
It keeps its highest, holiest tone
For one belovèd Jane alone. 90

WITH A GUITAR, TO JANE: 1 **Ariel to Miranda:** in Shakespeare's *The Tempest* Ariel is a spirit of the air and Miranda is the daughter of Prospero, magician and exiled Duke of Milan 10 **Prince Ferdinand:** the son of King Alonso of Naples, with whom Miranda falls in love 17 **Prospero's enchanted cell:** the island on which Prospero and Miranda live in exile 70 **rills:** brooks

'A WIDOW BIRD SATE MOURNING FOR HER LOVE'

A WIDOW BIRD sate mourning for her love
    Upon a wintry bough;
The frozen wind crept on above,
    The freezing stream below.

There was no leaf upon the forest bare, 5
    No flower upon the ground,
And little motion in the air
    Except the mill-wheel's sound.

[from *Charles the First*, Act 4, scene 5]

JOHN CLARE

SWORDY WELL

I'VE loved thee, Swordy Well, and love thee still.
Long was I with thee, tending sheep and cow,
In boyhood ramping up each steepy hill
To play at 'roly-poly' down; and now,
A man, I trifle on thee, cares to kill, 5
Haunting thy mossy steeps to botanize
And hunt the orchis tribes, where nature's skill
Doth, like my thoughts, run into phantasies,

Spider and bee all mimicking at will,
Displaying powers that fool the proudly wise,   10
Showing the wonders of great nature's plan
In trifles insignificant and small,
Puzzling the power of that great trifle, man,
Who finds no reason to be proud at all.

LOVE LIES BEYOND THE TOMB

LOVE lies beyond
The tomb, the earth, which fades like dew!
  I love the fond,
The faithful, and the true.

  Love lives in sleep,   5
The happiness of healthy dreams:
  Eve's dews may weep,
But love delightful seems.

  'Tis seen in flowers,
And in the even's pearly dew;   10
  On earth's green hours,
And in the heaven's eternal blue.

  'Tis heard in spring
When light and sunbeams, warm and kind,
  On angel's wing   15
Bring love and music to the mind.

  And where is voice,
So young, so beautifully sweet
  As nature's choice,
When spring and lovers meet?   20

  Love lies beyond
The tomb, the earth, the flowers, and dew.
  I love the fond,
The faithful, young, and true.

I AM

I AM – yet what I am none cares or knows,
  My friends forsake me like a memory lost;
I am the self-consumer of my woes,
  They rise and vanish in oblivions host,
Like shadows in love – frenzied stifled throes   5
And yet I am, and live like vapours tossed

Into nothingness of scorn and noise,
  Into the living sea of waking dreams,
Where there is neither sense of life or joys,
  But the vast shipwreck of my life's esteems;   10
And e'en the dearest – that I love the best –
Are strange – nay, rather stranger than the rest.

I long for scenes where man has never trod,
  A place where woman never smiled or wept;
There to abide with my Creator God,   15
  And sleep as I in childhood sweetly slept:
Untroubling and untroubled where I lie,
The grass below – above the vaulted sky.

A VISION

I LOST the love of heaven above,
  I spurned the lust of earth below,
I felt the sweets of fancied love,
  And hell itself my only foe.

I lost earth's joys, but felt the glow   5
  Of heaven's flame abound in me,
Till loveliness and I did grow
  The bard of immortality.

I loved, but woman fell away;
  I hid me from her faded fame.   10
I snatched the sun's eternal ray
  And wrote till earth was but a name.

In every language upon earth,
  On every shore, o'er every sea,
I gave my name immortal birth   15
  And kept my spirit with the free.

I HID MY LOVE

I HID my love when young while I
Couldn't bear the buzzing of a fly;
I hid my love to my despite
Till I could not bear to look at light:
I dare not gaze upon her face   5
But left her memory in each place;
Where'er I saw a wild flower lie
I kissed and bade my love good-bye.

I met her in the greenest dells,
Where dewdrops pearl the wood bluebells;   10
The lost breeze kissed her bright blue eye,
The bee kissed and went singing by,
A sunbeam found a passage there,
A gold chain round her neck so fair;
As secret as the wild bee's song   15
She lay there all the summer long.

I hid my love in field and town
Till e'en the breeze would knock me down;
The bees seemed singing ballads o'er,
The flies' buzz turned a lion's roar;   20
And even silence found a tongue,
To haunt me all the summer long;
The riddle nature could not prove
Was nothing else but secret love.

JOHN KEATS

ON FIRST LOOKING INTO CHAPMAN'S HOMER

MUCH have I travelled in the realms of gold,
  And many goodly states and kingdoms seen;
  Round many western islands have I been
Which bards in fealty to Apollo hold.
Oft of one wide expanse had I been told   5
  That deep-browed Homer ruled as his demesne;
  Yet did I never breathe its pure serene
Till I heard Chapman speak out loud and bold:
Then felt I like some watcher of the skies
  When a new planet swims into his ken;   10
Or like stout Cortez when with eagle eyes
  He stared at the Pacific – and all his men
Looked at each other with a wild surmise –
  Silent, upon a peak in Darien.

ON FIRST LOOKING INTO CHAPMAN'S HOMER: 6 **demesne:** realm, estate
11 **Cortez:** Keats was mistaken in thinking that it was the
conquistador Cortez who sighted the Pacific from a mountain in
Darien, in the Isthmus of Panama. It was, in fact, Vasco de Balboa
who did this, the first European to see the Pacific.

'I STOOD TIP-TOE UPON A LITTLE HILL'

I STOOD tip-toe upon a little hill,
The air was cooling, and so very still,
That the sweet buds which with a modest pride
Pull droopingly, in slanting curve aside,
Their scantly leaved, and finely tapering stems,   5
Had not yet lost those starry diadems
Caught from the early sobbing of the morn.
The clouds were pure and white as flocks new shorn,
And fresh from the clear brook; sweetly they slept
On the blue fields of heaven, and then there crept   10
A little noiseless noise among the leaves,
Born of the very sigh that silence heaves:
For not the faintest motion could be seen
Of all the shades that slanted o'er the green.
There was wide wand'ring for the greediest eye,   15
To peer about upon variety;
Far round the horizon's crystal air to skim,
And trace the dwindled edgings of its brim;
To picture out the quaint, and curious bending
Of a fresh woodland alley, never ending;   20
Or by the bowery clefts, and leafy shelves,
Guess where the jaunty streams refresh themselves.
I gazed awhile, and felt as light, and free
As though the fanning wings of Mercury
Had played upon my heels: I was light-hearted,   25
And many pleasures to my vision started;
So I straightway began to pluck a posy
Of luxuries bright, milky, soft and rosy.

[Lines 1–28]

ON THE SEA

IT keeps eternal whisperings around
  Desolate shores, and with its mighty swell
  Gluts twice ten thousand caverns, till the spell
Of Hecate leaves them their old shadowy sound.
Often 'tis in such gentle temper found   5
  That scarcely will the very smallest shell
  Be moved for days from where it sometime fell,
When last the winds of Heaven were unbound.
Oh ye! who have your eye-balls vexed and tired,
  Feast them upon the wideness of the sea;   10
    Oh ye! whose ears are dinned with uproar rude,
  Or fed too much with cloying melody –
    Sit ye near some old cavern's mouth and brood
Until ye start, as if the sea-nymphs quired!

ON THE SEA: 4 **Hecate:** a Greek goddess with power over the sea
14 **quired:** sang in a choir

From ENDYMION: A POETIC ROMANCE

A THING of beauty is a joy for ever:
Its loveliness increases; it will never
Pass into nothingness; but still will keep
A bower quiet for us, and a sleep
Full of sweet dreams, and health, and quiet breathing.
Therefore, on every morrow, are we wreathing   6
A flowery band to bind us to the earth,
Spite of despondence, of the inhuman dearth
Of noble natures, of the gloomy days,
Of all the unhealthy and o'er-darkened ways   10
Made for our searching: yes, in spite of all,
Some shape of beauty moves away the pall
From our dark spirits. Such the sun, the moon,
Trees old, and young, sprouting a shady boon
For simple sheep; and such are daffodils   15
With the green world they live in; and clear rills
That for themselves a cooling covert make
'Gainst the hot season; the mid forest brake,
Rich with a sprinkling of fair musk-rose blooms:
And such too is the grandeur of the dooms   20
We have imagined for the mighty dead;
All lovely tales that we have heard or read:
An endless fountain of immortal drink,
Pouring unto us from the heaven's brink.
  Nor do we merely feel these essences   25
For one short hour; no, even as the trees
That whisper round a temple become soon
Dear as the temple's self, so does the moon,
The passion poesy, glories infinite,
Haunt us till they become a cheering light   30
Unto our souls, and bound to us so fast,
That, whether there be shine, or gloom o'ercast,
They alway must be with us, or we die.

[Book 1, lines 1–33]

ENDYMION: 16 **rills:** brooks 18 **brake:** thicket

'WHEN I HAVE FEARS THAT I MAY CEASE TO BE'

WHEN I have fears that I may cease to be
   Before my pen has gleaned my teeming brain,
Before high-pilèd books, in charact'ry,
   Hold like rich garners the full ripened grain;
When I behold, upon the night's starred face,   5
   Huge cloudy symbols of a high romance,
And think that I may never live to trace
   Their shadows, with the magic hand of chance;
And when I feel, fair creature of an hour,
   That I shall never look upon thee more,   10
Never have relish in the faery power
   Of unreflecting love; – then on the shore
Of the wide world I stand alone, and think
Till love and fame to nothingness do sink.

WHEN I HAVE FEARS THAT I MAY CEASE TO BE: 3 **charact'ry:** printed characters

From HYPERION. A FRAGMENT

DEEP in the shady sadness of a vale
Far sunken from the healthy breath of morn,
Far from the fiery noon, and eve's one star,
Sat grey-haired Saturn, quiet as a stone,
Still as the silence round about his lair;   5
Forest on forest hung above his head
Like cloud on cloud. No stir of air was there,
Not so much life as on a summer's day
Robs not one light seed from the feathered grass,
But where the dead leaf fell, there did it rest.   10
A stream went voiceless by, still deadened more
By reason of his fallen divinity
Spreading a shade: the Naiad 'mid her reeds
Pressed her cold finger closer to her lips.
   Along the margin-sand large foot-marks went,   15
No further than to where his feet had strayed,
And slept there since. Upon the sodden ground
His old right hand lay nerveless, listless, dead,
Unsceptred; and his realmless eyes were closed;
While his bowed head seemed list'ning to the Earth,
His ancient mother, for some comfort yet.   21
   It seemed no force could wake him from his place;
But there came one, who with a kindred hand
Touched his wide shoulders, after bending low
With reverence, though to one who knew it not.   25
She was a goddess of the infant world;
By her in stature the tall Amazon
Had stood a pigmy's height; she would have ta'en
Achilles by the hair and bent his neck;
Or with a finger stayed Ixion's wheel.   30

HYPERION: 4 **Saturn:** Roman god of agriculture 13 **Naiad:** in Greek myth, a nymph dwelling in fresh water 27 **Amazon:** in Greek myth, one of a race of women warriors 30 **Ixion:** in Greek myth, a mortal punished in the afterlife by being bound to a perpetually revolving wheel

Her face was large as that of Memphian sphinx,
Pedestalled haply in a palace court,
When sages looked to Egypt for their lore.
But oh! how unlike marble was that face:
How beautiful, if sorrow had not made   35
Sorrow more beautiful than Beauty's self.
There was a listening fear in her regard,
As if calamity had but begun;
As if the vanward clouds of evil days
Had spent their malice, and the sullen rear   40
Was with its storèd thunder labouring up.
One hand she pressed upon that aching spot
Where beats the human heart, as if just there,
Though an immortal, she felt cruel pain:
The other upon Saturn's bended neck   45
She laid, and to the level of his ear
Leaning with parted lips, some words she spake
In solemn tenour and deep organ tone:
Some mourning words, which in our feeble tongue
Would come in these like accents; oh, how frail   50
To that large utterance of the early gods!
   'Saturn, look up! – though wherefore, poor old king?
I have no comfort for thee, no not one:
I cannot say, "Oh, wherefore sleepest thou?"
For heaven is parted from thee, and the earth   55
Knows thee not, thus afflicted, for a god;
And ocean too, with all its solemn noise,
Has from thy sceptre passed; and all the air
Is emptied of thine hoary majesty.
Thy thunder, conscious of the new command,   60
Rumbles reluctant o'er our fallen house;
And thy sharp lightning in unpractised hands
Scorches and burns our once serene domain.
O aching time! O moments big as years!
All as ye pass swell out the monstrous truth,   65
And press it so upon our weary griefs
That unbelief has not a space to breathe.
Saturn, sleep on: – Oh, thoughtless, why did I
Thus violate thy slumbrous solitude?
Why should I ope thy melancholy eyes?   70
Saturn, sleep on! while at thy feet I weep.'
   As when, upon a trancèd summer-night,
Those green-robed senators of mighty woods,
Tall oaks, branch-charmèd by the earnest stars,
Dream, and so dream all night without a stir,   75
Save from one gradual solitary gust
Which comes upon the silence, and dies off,
As if the ebbing air had but one wave;
So came these words and went; the while in tears
She touched her fair large forehead to the ground,   80
Just where her falling hair might be outspread
A soft and silken mat for Saturn's feet.
One moon, with alteration slow, had shed
Her silver seasons four upon the night,
And still these two were postured motionless,   85

31 **Memphian sphinx:** a sphinx at Memphis, an ancient city in N Egypt 32 **haply:** perhaps 39 **vanward:** leading, at the front

Like natural sculpture in cathedral cavern;
The frozen god still couchant on the earth,
And the sad goddess weeping at his feet:
Until at length old Saturn lifted up
His faded eyes, and saw his kingdom gone,   90
And all the gloom and sorrow of the place,
And that fair kneeling goddess; and then spake,
As with a palsied tongue, and while his beard
Shook horrid with such aspen-malady:
'O tender spouse of gold Hyperion,   95
Thea, I feel thee ere I see thy face;
Look up, and let me see our doom in it;
Look up, and tell me if this feeble shape
Is Saturn's; tell me, if thou hear'st the voice
Of Saturn; tell me, if this wrinkling brow,   100
Naked and bare of its great diadem,
Peers like the front of Saturn. Who had power
To make me desolate? whence came the strength?
How was it nurtured to such bursting forth,
While Fate seemed strangled in my nervous grasp?   105
But it is so; and I am smothered up,
And buried from all godlike exercise
Of influence benign on planets pale,
Of admonitions to the winds and seas,
Of peaceful sway above man's harvesting,   110
And all those acts which Deity supreme
Doth ease its heart of love in. – I am gone
Away from my own bosom: I have left
My strong identity, my real self,
Somewhere between the throne, and where I sit   115
Here on this spot of earth. Search, Thea, search!
Open thine eyes eterne, and sphere them round
Upon all space: space starred, and lorn of light;
Space regioned with life-air; and barren void;
Spaces of fire, and all the yawn of hell. –   120
Search, Thea, search! and tell me, if thou seest
A certain shape or shadow, making way
With wings or chariot fierce to repossess
A heaven he lost erewhile: it must – it must
Be of ripe progress – Saturn must be king.   125
Yes, there must be a golden victory;
There must be gods thrown down, and trumpets
          blown
Of triumph calm, and hymns of festival
Upon the gold clouds metropolitan,
Voices of soft proclaim, and silver stir   130
Of strings in hollow shells; and there shall be
Beautiful things made new, for the surprise
Of the sky-children; I will give command:
Thea! Thea! Thea! where is Saturn?'
     This passion lifted him upon his feet,   135
And made his hands to struggle in the air,
His Druid locks to shake and ooze with sweat,
His eyes to fever out, his voice to cease.

He stood, and heard not Thea's sobbing deep;
A little time, and then again he snatched   140
Utterance thus. – 'But cannot I create?
Cannot I form? Cannot I fashion forth
Another world, another universe,
To overbear and crumble this to naught?
Where is another Chaos? Where?' – That word   145
Found way unto Olympus, and made quake
The rebel three. – Thea was startled up,
And in her bearing was a sort of hope,
As thus she quick-voiced spake, yet full of awe.
'This cheers our fallen house: come to our friends,   150
O Saturn! come away, and give them heart;
I know the covert, for thence came I hither.'
Thus brief; then with beseeching eyes she went
With backward footing through the shade a space:
He followed, and she turned to lead the way   155
Through agèd boughs, that yielded like the mist
Which eagles cleave up-mounting from their nest.
                              [Book 1, lines 1–157]

145 **Chaos:** the disordered formless state before the world was created 146 **Olympus:** Mount Olympus, home of the Greek gods

'I HAD A DOVE AND THE SWEET DOVE DIED'

I HAD a dove and the sweet dove died;
    And I have thought it died of grieving.
Oh, what could it grieve for? Its feet were tied,
    With a silken thread of my own hand's weaving.
Sweet little red feet! why would you die –   5
Why should you leave me, sweet bird! why?
You lived alone on the forest-tree,
Why, pretty thing, could you not live with me?
I kissed you oft and gave you white peas;
Why not live sweetly, as in the green trees?   10

THE EVE OF ST AGNES

ST AGNES' EVE – Ah, bitter chill it was!
The owl, for all his feathers, was a-cold;
The hare limped trembling through the frozen
        grass,
And silent was the flock in woolly fold:
Numb were the beadsman's fingers, while he told   5
His rosary, and while his frosted breath,
Like pious incense from a censer old,
Seemed taking flight for heaven, without a death,
Past the sweet Virgin's picture, while his prayer he
        saith.

THE EVE OF ST AGNES: 1 **St Agnes' Eve:** tradition had it that on the eve of St Agnes' Day (21 January), young unmarried women would dream of the man they were to marry 5 **beadsman:** a person who prays for another's soul, using a rosary of beads to count the prayers

87 **couchant:** lying 94 **aspen-malady:** trembling (the leaves of the aspen are particularly given to quivering in the slightest breeze) 102 **front:** forehead 117 **eterne:** eternal 118 **lorn:** deprived 124 **erewhile:** formerly

His prayer he saith, this patient, holy man;   10
Then takes his lamp, and riseth from his knees,
And back returneth, meagre, barefoot, wan,
Along the chapel aisle by slow degrees:
The sculptured dead, on each side, seem to freeze,
Emprisoned in black, purgatorial rails: 15
Knights, ladies, praying in dumb orat'ries,
He passeth by; and his weak spirit fails
To think how they may ache in icy hoods and mails.

Northward he turneth through a little door,
And scarce three steps, ere Music's golden tongue   20
Flattered to tears this agèd man and poor;
But no – already had his deathbell rung:
The joys of all his life were said and sung:
His was harsh penance on St Agnes' Eve:
Another way he went, and soon among   25
Rough ashes sat he for his soul's reprieve,
And all night kept awake, for sinners' sake to grieve.

That ancient beadsman heard the prelude soft;
And so it chanced, for many a door was wide,
From hurry to and fro. Soon, up aloft,   30
The silver, snarling trumpets 'gan to chide:
The level chambers, ready with their pride,
Were glowing to receive a thousand guests:
The carvèd angels, ever eager-eyed,
Stared, where upon their heads the cornice rests,   35
With hair blown back, and wings put cross-wise on
     their breasts.

At length burst in the argent revelry,
With plume, tiara, and all rich array,
Numerous as shadows haunting faerily
The brain, new-stuffed, in youth, with triumphs gay
Of old romance. These let us wish away,   41
And turn, sole-thoughted, to one lady there,
Whose heart had brooded, all that wintry day,
On love, and winged St Agnes' saintly care,
As she had heard old dames full many times
     declare.   45

They told her how, upon St Agnes' Eve,
Young virgins might have visions of delight,
And soft adorings from their loves receive
Upon the honeyed middle of the night,
If ceremonies due they did aright;   50
As, supperless to bed they must retire,
And couch supíne their beauties, lily white;
Nor look behind, nor sideways, but require
Of Heaven with upward eyes for all that they desire.

Full of this whim was thoughtful Madeline: 55
The music, yearning like a god in pain,
She scarcely heard: her maiden eyes divine,
Fixed on the floor, saw many a sweeping train
Pass by – she heeded not at all: in vain
Came many a tip-toe, amorous cavalier,   60
And back retired; not cooled by high disdain,
But she saw not: her heart was otherwhere:
She sighed for Agnes' dreams, the sweetest of the year.

She danced along with vague, regardless eyes,
Anxious her lips, her breathing quick and short: 65
The hallowed hour was near at hand: she sighs
Amid the timbrels, and the thronged resort
Of whisperers in anger, or in sport;
'Mid looks of love, defiance, hate, and scorn,
Hoodwinked with faery fancy; all amort,   70
Save to St Agnes and her lambs unshorn,
And all the bliss to be before tomorrow morn.

So, purposing each moment to retire,
She lingered still. Meantime, across the moors,
Had come young Porphyro, with heart on fire   75
For Madeline. Beside the portal doors,
Buttressed from moonlight, stands he, and implores
All saints to give him sight of Madeline,
But for one moment in the tedious hours,
That he might gaze and worship all unseen;   80
Perchance speak, kneel, touch, kiss – in sooth such
     things have been.

He ventures in: let no buzzed whisper tell:
All eyes be muffled, or a hundred swords
Will storm his heart, Love's fev'rous citadel:
For him, those chambers held barbarian hordes,   85
Hyena foemen, and hot-blooded lords,
Whose very dogs would execrations howl
Against his lineage: not one breast affords
Him any mercy, in that mansion foul,
Save one old beldame, weak in body and in soul.   90

Ah, happy chance! the agèd creature came,
Shuffling along with ivory-headed wand,
To where he stood, hid from the torch's flame,
Behind a broad hall-pillar, far beyond
The sound of merriment and chorus bland: 95
He startled her; but soon she knew his face,
And grasped his fingers in her palsied hand,
Saying, 'Mercy, Porphyro! hie thee from this place:
They are all here tonight, the whole blood-thirsty
     race!

---

67 **timbrels**: tambourines 70 **amort**: as if dead 71 **St Agnes . . . unshorn**: it was a St Agnes' Day custom to offer lambs' wool at the altar, which nuns would then weave into cloth 77 **Buttressed from moonlight**: hidden from the moonlight by the buttress of the building 90 **beldame**: an old woman 92 **wand**: staff

16 **orat'ries**: chapels 31 **'gan**: began 37 **argent revelry**: silver-clad revellers

'Get hence! get hence! there's dwarfish
    Hildebrand; 100
He had a fever late, and in the fit
He cursèd thee and thine, both house and land:
Then there's that old Lord Maurice, not a whit
More tame for his grey hairs – Alas me! flit!
Flit like a ghost away.' – 'Ah, Gossip dear, 105
We're safe enough; here in this arm-chair sit,
And tell me how—' 'Good saints! not here, not here;
Follow me, child, or else these stones will be thy bier.'

He followed through a lowly archèd way,
Brushing the cobwebs with his lofty plume, 110
And as she muttered 'Well-a – well-a-day!'
He found him in a little moonlight room,
Pale, latticed, chill, and silent as a tomb.
'Now tell me where is Madeline,' said he,
'Oh, tell me, Angela, by the holy loom 115
Which none but secret sisterhood may see,
When they St Agnes' wool are weaving piously.'

'St Agnes! Ah! it is St Agnes' Eve –
Yet men will murder upon holy days:
Thou must hold water in a witch's sieve, 120
And be liege-lord of all the elves and fays,
To venture so: it fills me with amaze
To see thee, Porphyro! – St Agnes' Eve!
God's help! my lady fair the conjuror plays
This very night: good angels her deceive! 125
But let me laugh awhile, I've mickle time to grieve.'

Feebly she laugheth in the languid moon,
While Porphyro upon her face doth look,
Like puzzled urchin on an agèd crone
Who keepeth closed a wondrous riddle-book, 130
As spectacled she sits in chimney nook.
But soon his eyes grew brilliant, when she told
His lady's purpose; and he scarce could brook
Tears, at the thought of those enchantments cold,
And Madeline asleep in lap of legends old. 135

Sudden a thought came like a full-blown rose,
Flushing his brow, and in his painèd heart
Made purple riot: then doth he propose
A stratagem, that makes the beldame start:
'A cruel man and impious thou art: 140
Sweet lady, let her pray, and sleep, and dream
Alone with her good angels, far apart
From wicked men like thee. Go, go! – I deem
Thou canst not surely be the same that thou didst
    seem.'

'I will not harm her, by all saints I swear,' 145
Quoth Porphyro. 'Oh, may I ne'er find grace
When my weak voice shall whisper its last prayer,
If one of her soft ringlets I displace,
Or look with ruffian passion in her face:
Good Angela, believe me by these tears; 150
Or I will, even in a moment's space,
Awake, with horrid shout, my foemen's ears,
And beard them, though they be more fanged than
    wolves and bears.'

'Ah! why wilt thou affright a feeble soul?
A poor, weak, palsy-stricken, churchyard thing, 155
Whose passing-bell may ere the midnight toll;
Whose prayers for thee, each morn and evening,
Were never missed.' – Thus plaining, doth she bring
A gentler speech from burning Porphyro;
So woeful, and of such deep sorrowing, 160
That Angela gives promise she will do
Whatever he shall wish, betide her weal or woe.

Which was, to lead him, in close secrecy,
Even to Madeline's chamber, and there hide
Him in a closet, of such privacy 165
That he might see her beauty unespied,
And win perhaps that night a peerless bride,
While legioned faeries paced the coverlet,
And pale enchantment held her sleepy-eyed.
Never on such a night have lovers met, 170
Since Merlin paid his demon all the monstrous debt.

'It shall be as thou wishest,' said the dame:
'All cates and dainties shall be storèd there
Quickly on this feast-night: by the tambour frame
Her own lute thou wilt see: no time to spare, 175
For I am slow and feeble, and scarce dare
On such a catering trust my dizzy head.
Wait here, my child, with patience; kneel in prayer
The while: Ah! thou must needs the lady wed,
Or may I never leave my grave among the dead.' 180

So saying, she hobbled off with busy fear.
The lover's endless minutes slowly passed;
The dame returned, and whispered in his ear
To follow her; with agèd eyes aghast
From fright of dim espial. Safe at last, 185
Through many a dusky gallery, they gain
The maiden's chamber, silken, hushed, and chaste;
Where Porphyro took covert, pleased amain.
His poor guide hurried back with agues in her brain.

---

152 **foemen**: enemies 156 **passing-bell**: a bell rung at someone's
death 158 **plaining**: complaining 162 **betide . . . woe**: whether good
or evil things happened to her 171 **Since Merlin . . . debt**: in
Arthurian legend, the magician Merlin met his doom at the hands
of Vivien, a woman he loved 173 **cates**: delicacies 174 **tambour
frame**: a small round frame used in embroidery 188 **took covert**:
hid himself **amain**: greatly

---

105 **Gossip**: a close woman friend 126 **mickle**: much

Her falt'ring hand upon the balustrade, 190
Old Angela was feeling for the stair,
When Madeline, St Agnes' charmèd maid,
Rose, like a missioned spirit, unaware:
With silver taper's light, and pious care,
She turned, and down the agèd gossip led 195
To a safe level matting. Now prepare,
Young Porphyro, for gazing on that bed;
She comes, she comes again, like ring-dove frayed and
    fled.

Out went the taper as she hurried in;
Its little smoke, in pallid moonshine, died: 200
She closed the door, she panted, all akin
To spirits of the air, and visions wide:
No uttered syllable, or, woe betide!
But to her heart, her heart was voluble,
Paining with eloquence her balmy side; 205
As though a tongueless nightingale should swell
Her throat in vain, and die, heart-stiflèd, in her dell.

A casement high and triple-arched there was,
All garlanded with carven imag'ries
Of fruits, and flowers, and bunches of knot-grass, 210
And diamonded with panes of quaint device,
Innumerable of stains and splendid dyes,
As are the tiger-moth's deep-damasked wings;
And in the midst, 'mong thousand heraldries,
And twilight saints, and dim emblazonings, 215
A shielded scutcheon blushed with blood of queens
    and kings.

Full on this casement shone the wintry moon,
And threw warm gules on Madeline's fair breast,
As down she knelt for heaven's grace and boon;
Rose-bloom fell on her hands, together pressed, 220
And on her silver cross soft amethyst,
And on her hair a glory, like a saint:
She seemed a splendid angel, newly dressed,
Save wings, for heaven: – Porphyro grew faint:
She knelt, so pure a thing, so free from mortal taint.

Anon his heart revives: her vespers done, 226
Of all its wreathèd pearls her hair she frees;
Unclasps her warmèd jewels one by one;
Loosens her fragrant bodice; by degrees
Her rich attire creeps rustling to her knees: 230
Half-hidden, like a mermaid in sea-weed,
Pensive awhile she dreams awake, and sees,
In fancy, fair St Agnes in her bed,
But dares not look behind, or all the charm is fled.

Soon, trembling in her soft and chilly nest, 235
In sort of wakeful swoon, perplexed she lay,
Until the poppied warmth of sleep oppressed
Her soothèd limbs, and soul fatigued away;
Flown, like a thought, until the morrow-day;
Blissfully havened both from joy and pain; 240
Clasped like a missal where swart paynims pray;
Blinded alike from sunshine and from rain,
As though a rose should shut, and be a bud again.

Stol'n to this paradise, and so entranced,
Porphyro gazed upon her empty dress, 245
And listened to her breathing, if it chanced
To wake into a slumbrous tenderness;
Which when he heard, that minute did he bless,
And breathed himself: then from the closet crept,
Noiseless as fear in a wide wilderness, 250
And over the hushed carpet, silent, stepped,
And 'tween the curtains peeped, where, lo! – how fast
    she slept.

Then by the bed-side, where the faded moon
Made a dim, silver twilight, soft he set
A table, and, half anguished, threw thereon 255
A cloth of woven crimson, gold, and jet: –
Oh, for some drowsy Morphean amulet!
The boisterous, midnight, festive clarion,
The kettle-drum, and far-heard clarinet,
Affray his ears, though but in dying tone: – 260
The hall door shuts again, and all the noise is
    gone.

And still she slept an azure-lidded sleep,
In blanchèd linen, smooth, and lavendered,
While he from forth the closet brought a heap
Of candied apple, quince, and plum, and gourd; 265
With jellies soother than the creamy curd,
And lucent syrops, tinct with cinnamon;
Manna and dates, in argosy transferred
From Fez; and spicèd dainties, every one,
From silken Samarcand to cedared Lebanon. 270

These delicates he heaped with glowing hand
On golden dishes and in baskets bright
Of wreathèd silver: sumptuous they stand
In the retirèd quiet of the night,
Filling the chilly room with perfume light. – 275
'And now, my love, my seraph fair, awake!
Thou art my heaven, and I thine eremite:
Open thine eyes, for meek St Agnes' sake,
Or I shall drowse beside thee, so my soul doth
    ache.'

241 **swart paynims:** black pagans 257 **Morphean:** inducing sleep
(Morpheus was the Greek god of sleep and dreams) 258 **clarion:**
a high-pitched trumpet 265 **gourd:** melon 266 **soother:** softer
267 **lucent:** clear **tinct:** flavoured 268 **Manna:** sugary gum **argosy:** large
merchant ship 269 **Fez:** a city in Morocco 270 **silken Samarcand:**
a city in central Asia, on the silk road from China **cedared Lebanon:**
Lebanon was famous for its cedar trees 277 **eremite:** hermit

194 **taper:** candle 198 **frayed:** frightened 216 **shielded scutcheon:**
heraldic arms displayed on a shield 218 **gules:** in heraldic terms,
red

Thus whispering, his warm, unnervèd arm 280
Sank in her pillow. Shaded was her dream
By the dusk curtains: – 'twas a midnight charm
Impossible to melt as icèd stream:
The lustrous salvers in the moonlight gleam;
Broad golden fringe upon the carpet lies: 285
It seemed he never, never could redeem
From such a steadfast spell his lady's eyes;
So mused awhile, entoiled in woofèd phantasies.

Awakening up, he took her hollow lute, –
Tumultuous, – and, in chords that tenderest be, 290
He played an ancient ditty, long since mute,
In Provence called, 'La belle dame sans merci':
Close to her ear touching the melody; –
Wherewith disturbed, she uttered a soft moan:
He ceased – she panted quick – and suddenly 295
Her blue affrayèd eyes wide open shone:
Upon his knees he sank, pale as smooth-sculptured
    stone.

Her eyes were open, but she still beheld,
Now wide awake, the vision of her sleep:
There was a painful change, that nigh expelled 300
The blisses of her dream so pure and deep
At which fair Madeline began to weep,
And moan forth witless words with many a sigh;
While still her gaze on Porphyro would keep;
Who knelt, with joinèd hands and piteous eye, 305
Fearing to move or speak, she looked so dreamingly.

'Ah, Porphyro!' said she, 'but even now
Thy voice was at sweet tremble in mine ear,
Made tuneable with every sweetest vow;
And those sad eyes were spiritual and clear: 310
How changed thou art! how pallid, chill, and drear!
Give me that voice again, my Porphyro,
Those looks immortal, those complainings dear!
Oh, leave me not in this eternal woe,
For if thou diest, my love, I know not where to go.' 315

Beyond a mortal man impassioned far
At these voluptuous accents, he arose,
Ethereal, flushed, and like a throbbing star
Seen 'mid the sapphire heaven's deep repose;
Into her dream he melted, as the rose 320
Blendeth its odour with the violet, –
Solution sweet: meantime the frost-wind blows
Like Love's alarum pattering the sharp sleet
Against the window-panes; St Agnes' moon hath set.

'Tis dark: quick pattereth the flaw-blown sleet: 325
'This is no dream, my bride, my Madeline!'
'Tis dark: the icèd gusts still rave and beat:
'No dream, alas! alas! and woe is mine!
Porphyro will leave me here to fade and pine. –
Cruel! what traitor could thee hither bring? 330
I curse not, for my heart is lost in thine,
Though thou forsakest a deceivèd thing; –
A dove forlorn and lost with sick unprunèd wing.'

'My Madeline! sweet dreamer! lovely bride!
Say, may I be for aye thy vassal blessed? 335
Thy beauty's shield, heart-shaped and vermeil
    dyed?
Ah, silver shrine, here will I take my rest
After so many hours of toil and quest,
A famished pilgrim, – saved by miracle.
Though I have found, I will not rob thy nest 340
Saving of thy sweet self; if thou think'st well
To trust, fair Madeline, to no rude infidel.

'Hark! 'tis an elfin-storm from faery land,
Of haggard seeming, but a boon indeed:
Arise – arise! the morning is at hand; – 345
The bloated wassaillers will never heed: –
Let us away, my love, with happy speed;
There are no ears to hear, or eyes to see, –
Drowned all in Rhenish and the sleepy mead:
Awake! arise! my love, and fearless be, 350
For o'er the southern moors I have a home for thee.'

She hurried at his words, beset with fears,
For there were sleeping dragons all around,
At glaring watch, perhaps, with ready spears –
Down the wide stairs a darkling way they found. – 355
In all the house was heard no human sound.
A chain-drooped lamp was flickering by each door;
The arras, rich with horseman, hawk, and hound,
Fluttered in the besieging wind's uproar;
And the long carpets rose along the gusty floor. 360

They glide, like phantoms, into the wide hall;
Like phantoms, to the iron porch, they glide;
Where lay the porter, in uneasy sprawl,
With a huge empty flagon by his side:
The wakeful bloodhound rose, and shook his
    hide, 365
But his sagacious eye an inmate owns:
By one, and one, the bolts full easy slide: –
The chains lie silent on the footworn stones; –
The key turns, and the door upon its hinges groans.

325 **flaw-blown:** disturbed by flaws (gusts of wind) 333 **unprunèd:** not preened 336 **vermeil:** vermilion 344 **of haggard seeming:** seeming to be wild 346 **wassaillers:** drunken revellers 349 **Rhenish:** Rhine wine 355 **darkling:** in the dark 358 **arras:** tapestry wall-hanging 366 **an inmate owns:** acknowledges someone who lives in the house

288 **woofèd:** woven 292 **La belle . . . merci:** the beautiful lady without pity. Used (see below) by Keats as the title for a poem of his own

And they are gone: aye, ages long ago   370
These lovers fled away into the storm.
That night the baron dreamt of many a woe,
And all his warrior-guests, with shade and form
Of witch, and demon, and large coffin-worm,
Were long be-nightmared. Angela the old   375
Died palsy-twitched, with meagre face deform;
The beadsman, after thousand Aves told,
For aye unsought for slept among his ashes cold.

377 **Aves:** prayers beginning with 'Ave Maria' (Hail Mary) 378 **For aye:** forever

LA BELLE DAME SANS MERCI: A BALLAD

OH, what can ail thee, knight-at-arms,
  Alone and palely loitering?
The sedge has withered from the lake,
  And no birds sing.

Oh, what can ail thee, knight-at-arms,   5
  So haggard and so woe-begone?
The squirrel's granary is full,
  And the harvest's done.

I see a lily on thy brow,
  With anguish moist and fever-dew;   10
And on thy cheeks a fading rose
  Fast withereth too.

'I met a lady in the meads,
  Full beautiful – a faery's child,
Her hair was long, her foot was light,   15
  And her eyes were wild.

'I made a garland for her head,
  And bracelets too, and fragrant zone;
She looked at me as she did love,
  And made sweet moan.   20

'I set her on my pacing steed,
  And nothing else saw all day long;
For sidelong would she bend, and sing
  A faery's song.

'She found me roots of relish sweet,   25
  And honey wild, and manna-dew,
And sure in language strange she said –
  "I love thee true."

'She took me to her elfin grot,
  And there she wept and sighed full sore,   30
And there I shut her wild wild eyes
  With kisses four.

'And there she lullèd me asleep
  And there I dreamed – Ah! woe betide! –
The latest dream I ever dreamed   35
  On the cold hill side.

'I saw pale kings and princes too,
  Pale warriors, death-pale were they all;
They cried – "La Belle Dame sans Merci
  Hath thee in thrall!"   40

I saw their starved lips in the gloam,
  With horrid warning gapèd wide,
And I awoke and found me here,
  On the cold hill's side.

'And this is why I sojourn here   45
  Alone and palely loitering,
Though the sedge has withered from the lake,
  And no birds sing.'

LA BELLE DAME SANS MERCI: 13 **meads:** meadows 18 **zone:** belt 29 **grot:** grotto 35 **latest:** last 39 **La Belle Dame sans Merci:** the beautiful lady without pity 40 **thrall:** slavery, bondage

ODE TO PSYCHE

O GODDESS! hear these tuneless numbers, wrung
  By sweet enforcement and remembrance dear,
And pardon that thy secrets should be sung
  Even into thine own soft-conchèd ear:
Surely I dreamt today, or did I see   5
  The wingèd Psyche with awakened eyes?
I wandered in a forest thoughtlessly,
  And, on the sudden, fainting with surprise,
Saw two fair creatures, couchèd side by side
  In deepest grass, beneath the whisp'ring roof   10
  Of leaves and trembled blossoms, where there ran
    A brooklet, scarce espied:
'Mid hushed, cool-rooted flowers, fragrant-eyed,
  Blue, silver-white, and budded Tyrian,
They lay calm-breathing on the bedded grass;   15
  Their arms embracèd, and their pinions too;
  Their lips touched not, but had not bade adieu,
As if disjoinèd by soft-handed slumber,
And ready still past kisses to outnumber
  At tender eye-dawn of aurorean love: 20
    The wingèd boy I knew;
  But who wast thou, O happy, happy dove?
    His Psyche true!

O latest born and loveliest vision far
  Of all Olympus' faded hierarchy!   25
Fairer than Phoebe's sapphire-regioned star,
  Or Vesper, amorous glow-worm of the sky;
Fairer than these, though temple thou hast none,
    Nor altar heaped with flowers;
Nor virgin-choir to make delicious moan   30

Upon the midnight hours;
No voice, no lute, no pipe, no incense sweet
From chain-swung censer teeming;
No shrine, no grove, no oracle, no heat
Of pale-mouthed prophet dreaming.   35

O brightest! though too late for antique vows,
Too, too late for the fond believing lyre,
When holy were the haunted forest boughs,
Holy the air, the water, and the fire;
Yet even in these days so far retired   40
From happy pieties, thy lucent fans,
Fluttering among the faint Olympians,
I see, and sing, by my own eyes inspired.
So let me be thy choir, and make a moan
Upon the midnight hours;   45
Thy voice, thy lute, thy pipe, thy incense sweet
From swingèd censer teeming;
Thy shrine, thy grove, thy oracle, thy heat
Of pale-mouthed prophet dreaming.

Yes, I will be thy priest, and build a fane   50
In some untrodden region of my mind,
Where branchèd thoughts, new grown with pleasant
pain,
Instead of pines shall murmur in the wind:
Far, far around shall those dark-clustered trees
Fledge the wild-ridgèd mountains steep by steep;   55
And there by zephyrs, streams, and birds, and bees,
The moss-lain Dryads shall be lulled to sleep;
And in the midst of this wide quietness
A rosy sanctuary will I dress
With the wreathed trellis of a working brain,   60
With buds, and bells, and stars without a name,
With all the gardener Fancy e'er could feign,
Who breeding flowers, will never breed the same:
And there shall be for thee all soft delight
That shadowy thought can win,   65
A bright torch, and a casement ope at night,
To let the warm Love in!

ODE TO PSYCHE: In Greek myth, Psyche was a beautiful girl who
was loved by Eros (god of love) and became the personification of
the soul 1 **numbers:** verses 4 **soft-conched:** like a shell, yet soft
14 **Tyrian:** purple, like the famous dye made in the E Mediterranean
port of Tyre 16 **pinions:** wings 20 **aurorean:** of the dawn (Aurora
was the Roman goddess of the dawn) 21 **the wingèd boy:** Eros
25 **Olympus:** Mount Olympus, home of the Greek gods 26 **Phoebe:**
Diana, goddess of the moon 27 **Vesper:** the evening star 41 **lucent
fans:** bright wings 50 **fane:** temple 57 **Dryads:** wood-nymphs
66 **ope:** opened

ODE ON A GRECIAN URN

THOU still unravished bride of quietness,
Thou foster-child of silence and slow time,
Sylvan historian, who canst thus express
A flowery tale more sweetly than our rhyme:

What leaf-fringed legend haunts about thy shape   5
Of deities or mortals, or of both,
In Tempe or the dales of Arcady?
What men or gods are these? What maidens
loth?
What mad pursuit? What struggle to escape?
What pipes and timbrels? What wild ecstasy?   10

Heard melodies are sweet, but those unheard
Are sweeter; therefore, ye soft pipes, play on;
Not to the sensual ear, but, more endeared,
Pipe to the spirit ditties of no tone:
Fair youth, beneath the trees, thou canst not leave   15
Thy song, nor ever can those trees be bare;
Bold lover, never, never canst thou kiss,
Though winning near the goal – yet, do not grieve;
She cannot fade, though thou hast not thy bliss,
For ever wilt thou love, and she be fair!   20

Ah, happy, happy boughs! that cannot shed
Your leaves, nor ever bid the spring adieu;
And, happy melodist, unwearièd,
For ever piping songs for ever new;
More happy love! more happy, happy love!   25
For ever warm and still to be enjoyed,
Forever panting, and forever young;
All breathing human passion far above,
That leaves a heart high-sorrowful and cloyed,
A burning forehead, and a parching tongue.   30

Who are these coming to the sacrifice?
To what green altar, O mysterious priest,
Lead'st thou that heifer lowing at the skies,
And all her silken flanks with garlands dressed?
What little town by river or sea shore,   35
Or mountain-built with peaceful citadel,
Is emptied of this folk, this pious morn?
And, little town, thy streets for evermore
Will silent be; and not a soul to tell
Why thou art desolate, can e'er return.   40

O Attic shape! Fair attitude! with brede
Of marble men and maidens overwrought,
With forest branches and the trodden weed;
Thou, silent form, dost tease us out of thought
As doth eternity: Cold Pastoral!   45
When old age shall this generation waste,
Thou shalt remain, in midst of other woe
Than ours, a friend to man, to whom thou say'st,
'Beauty is truth, truth beauty, – that is all
Ye know on earth, and all ye need to know.'   50

ODE ON A GRECIAN URN: 3 **Sylvan:** of the forest or countryside
7 **Tempe:** a proverbially beautiful valley in Greece **Arcady:**
Arcadia, a region of Greece regarded as an idealized bucolic
setting 10 **timbrels:** tambourines 41 **Attic:** of Attica, the region
of Greece around Athens **brede:** braid, a braided pattern
42 **overwrought:** decorated all over

ODE TO A NIGHTINGALE

My heart aches, and a drowsy numbness pains
　My sense, as though of hemlock I had drunk,
Or emptied some dull opiate to the drains
　One minute past, and Lethe-wards had sunk:
'Tis not through envy of thy happy lot,　　　　　　　5
　But being too happy in thine happiness, –
　　That thou, light-wingèd Dryad of the trees,
　　　In some melodious plot
Of beechen green, and shadows numberless,
　　Singest of summer in full-throated ease.　　　10

Oh, for a draught of vintage! that hath been
　Cooled a long age in the deep-delvèd earth,
Tasting of Flora and the country green,
　Dance, and Provençal song, and sunburnt mirth!
Oh, for a beaker full of the warm South,　　　　　15
　Full of the true, the blushful Hippocrene,
　　With beaded bubbles winking at the brim,
　　　And purple-stainèd mouth;
That I might drink, and leave the world unseen,
　And with thee fade away into the forest dim:　　20

Fade far away, dissolve, and quite forget
　What thou among the leaves hast never known,
The weariness, the fever, and the fret
　Here, where men sit and hear each other groan;
Where palsy shakes a few, sad, last grey hairs,　　25
　Where youth grows pale, and spectre-thin, and dies;
　　Where but to think is to be full of sorrow
　　　And leaden-eyed despairs,
Where Beauty cannot keep her lustrous eyes,
　　Or new Love pine at them beyond tomorrow.　30

Away! away! for I will fly to thee,
　Not charioted by Bacchus and his pards,
But on the viewless wings of Poesy,
　Though the dull brain perplexes and retards:
Already with thee! tender is the night,　　　　　35
　And haply the Queen-Moon is on her throne,
　　Clustered around by all her starry fays;
　　　But here there is no light,
Save what from heaven is with the breezes blown
　　Through verdurous glooms and winding mossy
　　　　ways.　　　　　　　　　　　　　40

I cannot see what flowers are at my feet,
　Nor what soft incense hangs upon the boughs,
But, in embalmèd darkness, guess each sweet
　Wherewith the seasonable month endows
The grass, the thicket, and the fruit-tree wild;　　45
　White hawthorn, and the pastoral eglantine;
　　Fast fading violets covered up in leaves;
　　　And mid-May's eldest child,
The coming musk-rose, full of dewy wine,
　　The murmurous haunt of flies on summer eves.　50

Darkling I listen; and, for many a time
　I have been half in love with easeful Death,
Called him soft names in many a musèd rhyme,
　To take into the air my quiet breath;
Now more than ever seems it rich to die,　　　　55
　To cease upon the midnight with no pain,
　　While thou art pouring forth thy soul abroad
　　　In such an ecstasy!
Still wouldst thou sing, and I have ears in vain –
　To thy high requiem become a sod.　　　　　60

Thou wast not born for death, immortal Bird!
　No hungry generations tread thee down;
The voice I hear this passing night was heard
　In ancient days by emperor and clown:
Perhaps the self-same song that found a path　　65
　Through the sad heart of Ruth, when, sick for
　　　home,
　　She stood in tears amid the alien corn;
　　　The same that oft-times hath
Charmed magic casements, opening on the foam
　Of perilous seas, in faery lands forlorn.　　　70

Forlorn! the very word is like a bell
　To toll me back from thee to my sole self!
Adieu! the fancy cannot cheat so well
　As she is famed to do, deceiving elf.
Adieu! adieu! thy plaintive anthem fades　　　75
　Past the near meadows, over the still stream,
　　Up the hill-side; and now 'tis buried deep
　　　In the next valley-glades:
Was it a vision, or a waking dream?
　　Fled is that music: – Do I wake or sleep?　　80

ODE TO A NIGHTINGALE: 2 **hemlock:** a poisonous drug derived from a plant of the same name　4 **Lethe:** a river in the Underworld whose waters caused oblivion when drunk　7 **Dryad:** wood-nymph　13 **Flora:** flowers (Flora was the Roman goddess of flowers)　16 **Hippocrene:** a spring on Mount Helicon in Greece, whose waters were said to grant poetical inspiration　26 **Where youth . . . dies:** a reference to the death from tuberculosis of Keats' brother Tom　32 **Not charioted . . . pards:** not carried in the leopard-drawn chariot of Bacchus (Roman god of wine), ie not drunk　33 **viewless:** invisible　36 **haply:** perhaps　37 **fays:** fairies　40 **verdurous:** covered in green foliage　43 **embalmèd:** scented by balm　46 **eglantine:** sweetbrier　51 **Darkling:** in the dark　64 **clown:** peasant　66 **Ruth:** in the Old Testament, Ruth was a Moabite woman who left her own people to remain with the mother of her dead husband　73 **fancy:** imagination

ODE ON MELANCHOLY

No, no, go not to Lethe, neither twist
　Wolf's-bane, tight-rooted, for its poisonous wine;
Nor suffer thy pale forehead to be kissed
　By nightshade, ruby grape of Proserpine;
Make not your rosary of yew-berries,　　　　　5
　Nor let the beetle, nor the death-moth be
　　Your mournful Psyche, nor the downy owl

A partner in your sorrow's mysteries;
  For shade to shade will come too drowsily,
    And drown the wakeful anguish of the soul.   10

But when the melancholy fit shall fall
  Sudden from heaven like a weeping cloud,
That fosters the droop-headed flowers all,
  And hides the green hill in an April shroud;
Then glut thy sorrow on a morning rose,   15
  Or on the rainbow of the salt sand-wave,
    Or on the wealth of globèd peonies;
Or if thy mistress some rich anger shows,
  Emprison her soft hand, and let her rave,
    And feed deep, deep upon her peerless eyes.   20

She dwells with Beauty – Beauty that must die;
  And Joy, whose hand is ever at his lips
Bidding adieu; and aching Pleasure nigh,
  Turning to Poison while the bee-mouth sips:
Ay, in the very temple of Delight   25
  Veiled Melancholy has her sovran shrine,
    Though seen of none save him whose strenuous
      tongue
Can burst Joy's grape against his palate fine;
His soul shall taste the sadness of her might,
  And be among her cloudy trophies hung.   30

ODE ON MELANCHOLY: 1 **Lethe:** a river in the Underworld whose waters caused oblivion when drunk 2 **wolfsbane:** a poisonous plant 3 **Proserpine:** Roman goddess of the Underworld 5 **yew-berries:** the yew was symbolic of death 6 **beetle:** the scarab beetle was associated with death through representations of it being found in Egyptian tombs 7 **Psyche:** a personification of the soul, sometimes shown in ancient art as issuing from the mouth of a dying person in the form of a moth or butterfly 8 **mysteries:** religious rites known only to the initiated 26 **sovran:** sovereign 28 **fine:** discriminating

TO AUTUMN

SEASON of mists and mellow fruitfulness,
  Close bosom-friend of the maturing sun;
Conspiring with him how to load and bless
  With fruit the vines that round the thatch-eves run;
To bend with apples the mossed cottage-trees,   5
  And fill all fruit with ripeness to the core;
    To swell the gourd, and plump the hazel shells
With a sweet kernel; to set budding more,
And still more, later flowers for the bees,
Until they think warm days will never cease,   10
    For Summer has o'er-brimmed their clammy cells.

Who hath not seen thee oft amid thy store?
  Sometimes whoever seeks abroad may find
Thee sitting careless on a granary floor,
  Thy hair soft-lifted by the winnowing wind;   15
Or on a half-reaped furrow sound asleep,
  Drowsed with the fume of poppies, while thy hook

Spares the next swath and all its twinèd flowers:
  And sometimes like a gleaner thou dost keep
    Steady thy laden head across a brook;   20
  Or by a cyder-press, with patient look,
    Thou watchest the last oozings hours by hours.

Where are the songs of Spring? Ay, where are they?
  Think not of them, thou hast thy music too, –
While barrèd clouds bloom the soft-dying day,   25
  And touch the stubble-plains with rosy hue;
Then in a wailful choir the small gnats mourn
  Among the river sallows, borne aloft
    Or sinking as the light wind lives or dies;
And full-grown lambs loud bleat from hilly bourn;   30
  Hedge-crickets sing; and now with treble soft
    The red-breast whistles from a garden-croft;
    And gathering swallows twitter in the skies.

TO AUTUMN: 17 **fume of poppies:** the scent of the (opium) poppy **hook:** scythe 28 **sallows:** willows 30 **bourn:** region 32 **garden-croft:** a small enclosed plot of land

From THE FALL OF HYPERION: A DREAM

THEN to the west I looked, and saw far off
An image, huge of feature as a cloud,
At level of whose feet an altar slept,
To be approached on either side by steps,
And marble balustrade, and patient trávail   5
To count with toil the innumerable degrees.
Towards the altar sober-paced I went,
Repressing haste, as too unholy there;
And, coming nearer, saw beside the shrine
One minist'ring; and there arose a flame.   10
When in mid-May the sickening east wind
Shifts sudden to the south, the small warm rain
Melts out the frozen incense from all flowers,
And fills the air with so much pleasant health
That even the dying man forgets his shroud; –   15
Even so that lofty sacrificial fire,
Sending forth Maian incense, spread around
Forgetfulness of everything but bliss,
And clouded all the altar with soft smoke,
From whose white fragrant curtains thus I heard   20
Language pronounced: 'If thou canst not ascend
These steps, die on that marble where thou art.
Thy flesh, near cousin to the common dust,
Will parch for lack of nutriment – thy bones
Will wither in few years, and vanish so   25
That not the quickest eye could find a grain
Of what thou now art on that pavement cold.
The sands of thy short life are spent this hour,
And no hand in the universe can turn
Thy hourglass, if these gummèd leaves be burnt   30
Ere thou canst mount up these immortal steps.'

THE FALL OF HYPERION: 5 **trávail:** toil 17 **Maian:** of Maia, eldest of the seven Pleiades, mother by Zeus of Hermes

I heard, I looked: two senses both at once,
So fine, so subtle, felt the tyranny
Of that fierce threat and the hard task proposed.
Prodigious seemed the toil, the leaves were yet   35
Burning – when suddenly a palsied chill
Struck from the pavèd level up my limbs,
And was ascending quick to put cold grasp
Upon those streams that pulse beside the throat:
I shrieked; and the sharp anguish of my shriek   40
Stung my own ears – I strove hard to escape
The numbness; strove to gain the lowest step.
Slow, heavy, deadly was my pace: the cold
Grew stifling, suffocating, at the heart;
And when I clasped my hands I felt them not.   45
One minute before death, my iced foot touched
The lowest stair; and as it touched, life seemed
To pour in at the toes: I mounted up,
As once fair angels on a ladder flew
From the green turf to Heaven. – 'Holy Power,'   50
Cried I, approaching near the hornèd shrine,
'What am I that should so be saved from death?
What am I that another death come not
To choke my utterance sacrilegious here?'
Then said the veilèd shadow. – 'Thou hast felt   55
What 'tis to die and live again before
Thy fated hour. That thou hadst power to do so
Is thy own safety; thou hast dated on
Thy doom.' – 'High Prophetess,' said I, 'purge off,
Benign, if so it please thee, my mind's film.' –   60
'None can usurp this height,' returned that shade,
'But those to whom the miseries of the world
Are misery, and will not let them rest.
All else who find a haven in the world,
Where they may thoughtless sleep away their days,
If by a chance into this fane they come,   66
Rot on the pavement where thou rotted'st half.' –
'Are there not thousands in the world,' said I,
Encouraged by the sooth voice of the shade,
'Who love their fellows even to the death;   70
Who feel the giant agony of the world;
And more, like slaves to poor humanity,
Labour for mortal good? I sure should see
Other men here; but I am here alone.'
'Those whom thou spak'st of are no vision'ries,'   75
Rejoined that voice; 'they are no dreamers weak;
They seek no wonder but the human face,
No music but a happy-noted voice;
They come not here, they have no thought to come;
And thou art here, for thou art less than they: 80
What benefit canst thou do, or all thy tribe,
To the great world? Thou art a dreaming thing,
A fever of thyself – think of the Earth;
What bliss even in hope is there for thee?

What haven? every creature hath its home;   85
Every sole man hath days of joy and pain,
Whether his labours be sublime or low –
The pain alone; the joy alone; distinct:
Only the dreamer venoms all his days,
Bearing more woe than all his sins deserve.   90
Therefore, that happiness be somewhat shared,
Such things as thou art are admitted oft
Into like gardens thou didst pass erewhile,
And suffered in these temples: for that cause
Thou standest safe beneath this statue's knees.'   95
'That I am favoured for unworthiness,
By such propitious parley medicined
In sickness not ignoble, I rejoice,
Ay, and could weep for love of such award.'
So answered I, continuing, 'If it please,   100
Majestic shadow, tell me: sure not all
Those melodies sung into the world's ear
Are useless: sure a poet is a sage;
A humanist, physician to all men.
That I am none I feel, as vultures feel   105
They are no birds when eagles are abroad.
What am I then? Thou spakest of my tribe:
'What tribe?' – The tall shade veiled in drooping white
Then spake, so much more earnest, that the breath
Moved the thin linen folds that drooping hung   110
About a golden censer from the hand
Pendent. – 'Art thou not of the dreamer tribe?
The poet and the dreamer are distinct,
Diverse, sheer opposite, antipodes.
The one pours out a balm upon the world,   115
The other vexes it.'

[Canto 1, lines 87–202]

93 **erewhile:** formerly

'BRIGHT STAR! WOULD I WERE STEADFAST AS THOU ART'

BRIGHT star! would I were steadfast as thou art –
    Not in lone splendour hung aloft the night
And watching, with eternal lids apart,
    Like nature's patient, sleepless eremite,
The moving waters at their priestlike task   5
    Of pure ablution round earth's human shores,
Or gazing on the new soft-fallen mask
    Of snow upon the mountains and the moors –
No – yet still steadfast, still unchangeable,
    Pillowed upon my fair love's ripening breast,   10
To feel for ever its soft fall and swell,
    Awake for ever in a sweet unrest,
Still, still to hear her tender-taken breath,
And so live ever – or else swoon to death.

'BRIGHT STAR': 4 **eremite:** hermit

58-9 **thou hast . . . doom:** you have postponed your own death
66 **fane:** temple

'THIS LIVING HAND, NOW WARM AND CAPABLE'

THIS living hand, now warm and capable
Of earnest grasping, would, if it were cold
And in the icy silence of the tomb,
So haunt thy days and chill thy dreaming nights
That thou wouldst wish thine own heart dry of
   blood   5
So in my veins red life might stream again,
And thou be conscience-calmed – see here it is –
I hold it towards you.

THOMAS HOOD

THE SONG OF THE SHIRT

WITH fingers weary and worn,
   With eyelids heavy and red,
A Woman sat, in unwomanly rags,
   Plying her needle and thread –
      Stitch! stitch! stitch!   5
In poverty, hunger and dirt,
   And still with a voice of dolorous pitch
She sang the 'Song of the Shirt'.

   'Work! work! work!
While the cock is crowing aloof!   10
   And work – work – work,
Till the stars shine through the roof!
It's oh! to be a slave
   Along with the barbarous Turk,
Where woman has never a soul to save,   15
   If this is Christian work!

   'Work – work – work
Till the brain begins to swim;
   Work – work – work
Till the eyes are heavy and dim!   20
Seam, and gusset, and band,
   Band, and gusset, and seam,
      Till over the buttons I fall asleep,
   And sew them on in a dream!

   'O Men with Sisters dear!   25
   O Men with Mothers and Wives!
It is not linen you're wearing out,
   But human creatures' lives!
      Stitch – stitch – stitch,
   In poverty, hunger, and dirt,   30
Sewing at once, with a double thread,
   A Shroud as well as a Shirt!

   'But why do I talk of Death?
   That Phantom of grisly bone,
I hardly fear his terrible shape,   35
   It seems so like my own –

   It seems so like my own,
   Because of the fasts I keep;
Oh God! that bread should be so dear,
   And flesh and blood so cheap!   40

   'Work – work – work!
   My labour never flags;
And what are its wages? A bed of straw,
   A crust of bread – and rags.
That shattered roof – and this naked floor –   45
   A table – a broken chair –
And a wall so blank, my shadow I thank
   For sometimes falling there!

   'Work – work – work!
From weary chime to chime,   50
   Work – work – work!
As prisoners work for crime!
   Band, and gusset, and seam,
   Seam, and gusset, and band,
Till the heart is sick, and the brain benumbed,   55
   As well as the weary hand.

   'Work – work – work,
In the dull December light,
   And work – work – work,
When the weather is warm and bright –   60
While underneath the eaves
   The brooding swallows cling
As if to show me their sunny backs
   And twit me with the spring.

   'Oh, but to breathe the breath   65
Of the cowslip and primrose sweet –
   With the sky above my head,
   And the grass beneath my feet,
For only one short hour
   To feel as I used to feel,   70
Before I knew the woes of want
   And the walk that costs a meal!

   'Oh, but for one short hour!
   A respite however brief!
No blessèd leisure for Love or Hope,   75
   But only time for Grief!
A little weeping would ease my heart,
   But in their briny bed
My tears must stop, for every drop
   Hinders needle and thread!'   80

With fingers weary and worn,
   With eyelids heavy and red,
A Woman sate in unwomanly rags,
   Plying her needle and thread –
      Stitch! stitch! stitch!   85
   In poverty, hunger, and dirt,
And still with a voice of dolorous pitch,
   – Would that its tone could reach the Rich! –
   She sang this 'Song of the Shirt'.

I REMEMBER, I REMEMBER

I REMEMBER, I remember
The house where I was born,
The little window where the sun
Came peeping in at morn;
He never came a wink too soon,   5
Nor brought too long a day;
But now I often wish the night
Had borne my breath away!

I remember, I remember
The roses, red and white,   10
The vi'lets, and the lily-cups,
Those flowers made of light!
The lilacs where the robin built,
And where my brother set
The laburnum on his birthday, –   15
The tree is living yet!

I remember, I remember
Where I was used to swing,
And thought the air must rush as fresh
To swallows on the wing;   20
My spirit flew in feathers then,
That is so heavy now,
And summer pools could hardly cool
The fever on my brow!

I remember, I remember   25
The fir trees dark and high;
I used to think their slender tops
Were close against the sky:
It was a childish ignorance,
But now 'tis little joy   30
To know I'm farther off from heav'n
Than when I was a boy.

RUTH

SHE stood breast high amid the corn,
Clasped by the golden light of morn,
Like the sweetheart of the sun,
Who many a glowing kiss had won.

On her cheek an autumn flush,
Deeply ripened; – such a blush   5
In the midst of brown was born,
Like red poppies grown with corn.

Round her eyes her tresses fell,
Which were blackest none could tell,
But long lashes veiled a light,   10
That had else been all too bright.

And her hat, with shady brim,
Made her tressy forehead dim; –
Thus she stood amid the stooks,
Praising God with sweetest looks: –   15

Sure, I said, heav'n did not mean,
Where I reap thou shouldst but glean,
Lay thy sheaf adown and come,
Share my harvest and my home.   20

RUTH: In the Old Testament, Ruth was a Moabite woman who left her own people to remain with the mother of her dead husband 12 **else:** otherwise

LORD MACAULAY

HORATIUS

LARS PORSENA of Clusium
  By the Nine Gods he swore
That the great house of Tarquin
  Should suffer wrong no more.
By the Nine Gods he swore it,   5
  And named a trysting day,
And bade his messengers ride forth,
East and west and south and north,
  To summon his array.

East and west and south and north   10
  The messengers ride fast,
And tower and town and cottage
  Have heard the trumpet's blast.
Shame on the false Etruscan
  Who lingers in his home,   15
When Porsena of Clusium
  Is on the march for Rome.

The horsemen and the footmen
  Are pouring in amain,
From many a stately market-place;   20
  From many a fruitful plain;
From many a lonely hamlet,
  Which, hid by beech and pine,
Like an eagle's nest, hangs on the crest
  Of purple Apennine;   25

From lordly Volaterrae,
  Where scowls the far-famed hold
Piled by the hands of giants
  For godlike kings of old;
From seagirt Populonia,   30
  Whose sentinels descry
Sardinia's snowy mountain-tops
  Fringing the southern sky;

HORATIUS: Horatius Cocles was a legendary Roman hero of the 6th century BC who defended a bridge over the Tiber against the army of the legendary Etruscan king Lars Porsena, giving his comrades time to demolish the bridge behind him 3 **Tarquin:** according to Roman legend, the people of Rome expelled the last of their kings, the tyrannical Tarquinius Superbus. Lars Porsena attacked Rome in a bid to restore Tarquin to the throne 19 **amain:** in strength and numbers

From the proud mart of Pisae,
  Queen of the western waves,
Where ride Massilia's triremes   35
  Heavy with fair-haired slaves;
From where sweet Clanis wanders
  Through corn and vines and flowers;
From where Cortona lifts to heaven   40
  Her diadem of towers.

Tall are the oaks whose acorns
  Drop in dark Auser's rill;
Fat are the stags that champ the boughs
  Of the Ciminian hill;   45
Beyond all streams Clitumnus
  Is to the herdsman dear;
Best of all pools the fowler loves
  The great Volsinian mere.

But now no stroke of woodman   50
  Is heard by Auser's rill;
No hunter tracks the stag's green path
  Up the Ciminian hill;
Unwatched along Clitumnus
  Grazes the milk-white steer;   55
Unharmed the water fowl may dip
  In the Volsinian mere.

The harvests of Arretium,
  This year, old men shall reap;
This year, young boys in Umbro   60
  Shall plunge the struggling sheep;
And in the vats of Luna,
  This year, the must shall foam
Round the white feet of laughing girls
  Whose sires have marched to Rome.   65

There be thirty chosen prophets,
  The wisest of the land,
Who alway by Lars Porsena
  Both morn and evening stand:
Evening and morn the Thirty   70
  Have turned the verses o'er,
Traced from the right on linen white
  By mighty seers of yore.

And with one voice the Thirty
  Have their glad answer given: 75
'Go forth, go forth, Lars Porsena;
  Go forth, beloved of Heaven;
Go, and return in glory
  To Clusium's royal dome;
And hang round Nurscia's altars   80
  The golden shields of Rome.'

And now hath every city
  Sent up her tale of men;
The foot are fourscore thousand,
  The horse are thousands ten.   85
Before the gates of Sutrium
  Is met the great array.
A proud man was Lars Porsena
  Upon the trysting day.

For all the Etruscan armies   90
  Were ranged beneath his eye,
And many a banished Roman,
  And many a stout ally;
And with a mighty following
  To join the muster came   95
The Tusculan Mamilius,
  Prince of the Latian name.

But by the yellow Tiber
  Was tumult and affright:
From all the spacious champaign   100
  To Rome men took their flight.
A mile around the city,
  The throng stopped up the ways;
A fearful sight it was to see
  Through two long nights and days.   105

For aged folks on crutches,
  And women great with child,
And mothers sobbing over babes
  That clung to them and smiled,
And sick men borne in litters   110
  High on the necks of slaves,
And troops of sun-burned husbandmen
  With reaping-hooks and staves,

And droves of mules and asses
  Laden with skins of wine.   115
And endless flocks of goats and sheep,
  And endless herds of kine,
And endless trains of waggons
  That creaked beneath the weight
Of corn-sacks and of household goods,   120
  Choked every roaring gate.

Now, from the rock Tarpeian,
  Could the wan burghers spy
The line of blazing villages
  Red in the midnight sky.   125
The Fathers of the City,
  They sat all night and day,
For every hour some horseman came
  With tidings of dismay.

83 **tale:** tally 100 **champaign:** plain 117 **kine:** cattle 122 **rock Tarpeian:** a cliff on the Capitoline Hill in Rome, from which traitors were thrown to their deaths

49 **mere:** lake 61 **plunge:** dip

To eastward and to westward   130
  Have spread the Tuscan bands;
Nor house, nor fence, nor dovecot
  In Crustumerium stands.
Verbenna down to Ostia
  Hath wasted all the plain;   135
Astur hath stormed Janiculum,
  And the stout guards are slain.

Iwis, in all the Senate,
  There was no heart so bold,
But sore it ached, and fast it beat,   140
  When that ill news was told.
Forthwith up rose the Consul,
  Up rose the Fathers all;
In haste they girded up their gowns,
  And hied them to the wall.   145

They held a council standing
  Before the River-Gate;
Short time was there, ye well may guess,
  For musing or debate.
Out spake the Consul roundly: 150
  'The bridge must straight go down;
For, since Janiculum is lost,
  Nought else can save the town.'

Just then a scout came flying,
  All wild with haste and fear: 155
'To arms! to arms! Sir Consul:
  Lars Porsena is here.'
On the low hills to westward
  The Consul fixed his eye,
And saw the swarthy storm of dust   160
  Rise fast along the sky.

And nearer fast and nearer
  Doth the red whirlwind come;
And louder still and still more loud,
From underneath that rolling cloud,   165
Is heard the trumpet's war-note proud,
  The trampling, and the hum.
And plainly and more plainly
  Now through the gloom appears,
Far to left and far to right,   170
In broken gleams of dark-blue light,
The long array of helmets bright,
  The long array of spears.

And plainly and more plainly,
  Above that glimmering line,   175
Now might ye see the banners
  Of twelve fair cities shine;
But the banner of proud Clusium
  Was highest of them all,
The terror of the Umbrian,   180
  The terror of the Gaul.

And plainly and more plainly
  Now might the burghers know,
By port and vest, by horse and crest,
  Each warlike Lucumo.   185
There Cilnius of Arretium
  On his fleet roan was seen;
And Astur of the four-fold shield,
Girt with the brand none else may wield,
Tolumnius with the belt of gold,   190
And dark Verbenna from the hold
  By reedy Thrasymene.

Fast by the royal standard,
  O'erlooking all the war,
Lars Porsena of Clusium   195
  Sat in his ivory car.
By the right wheel rode Mamilius,
  Prince of the Latian name;
And by the left false Sextus,
  That wrought the deed of shame.   200

But when the face of Sextus
  Was seen among the foes,
A yell that rent the firmament
  From all the town arose.
On the house-tops was no woman   205
  But spat towards him and hissed,
No child but screamed out curses,
  And shook its little fist.

But the Consul's brow was sad,
  And the Consul's speech was low,   210
And darkly looked he at the wall,
  And darkly at the foe.
'Their van will be upon us
  Before the bridge goes down;
And if they once may win the bridge,   215
  What hope to save the town?'

Then out spake brave Horatius,
  The Captain of the Gate:
'To every man upon this earth
  Death cometh soon or late.   220
And how can man die better
  Than facing fearful odds,
For the ashes of his fathers,
  And the temples of his Gods,

'And for the tender mother   225
  Who dandled him to rest,
And for the wife who nurses
  His baby at her breast,
And for the holy maidens
  Who feed the eternal flame,   230
To save them from false Sextus
  That wrought the deed of shame?

138 **Iwis:** certainly 142 **Consul:** either of two elected magistrates who jointly held supreme power 145 **hied them:** hurried

185 **Lucumo:** an Etruscan prince or priest 189 **Girt:** belted **brand:** sword 191 **hold:** stronghold 196 **car:** chariot 199 **false Sextus:** a Roman traitor 213 **van:** vanguard 229–30 **holy maidens . . . flame:** the Vestal Virgins, priestesses of Vesta, Roman goddess of the hearth, who tended a perpetual flame in her temple

'Hew down the bridge, Sir Consul,
    With all the speed ye may;
I, with two more to help me,   235
    Will hold the foe in play.
In yon strait path a thousand
    May well be stopped by three.
Now who will stand on either hand,
    And keep the bridge with me?'   240

Then out spake Spurius Lartius;
    A Ramnian proud was he:
'Lo, I will stand at thy right hand,
    And keep the bridge with thee.'
And out spake strong Herminius;   245
    Of Titian blood was he:
'I will abide on thy left side,
    And keep the bridge with thee.'

'Horatius,' quoth the Consul,
    'As thou sayest, so let it be.'   250
And straight against that great array
    Forth went the dauntless Three.
For Romans in Rome's quarrel
    Spared neither land nor gold,
Nor son nor wife, nor limb nor life,   255
    In the brave days of old.

Then none was for a party;
    Then all were for the state;
Then the great man helped the poor,
    And the poor man loved the great: 260
Then lands were fairly portioned;
    Then spoils were fairly sold:
The Romans were like brothers
    In the brave days of old.

Now Roman is to Roman   265
    More hateful than a foe,
And the Tribunes beard the high,
    And the Fathers grind the low.
As we wax hot in faction,
    In battle we wax cold: 270
Wherefore men fight not as they fought
    In the brave days of old.

Now while the Three were tightening
    Their harness on their backs,
The Consul was the foremost man   275
    To take in hand an axe:
And Fathers mixed with Commons,
    Seized hatchet, bar, and crow,
And smote upon the planks above,
    And loosed the props below.   280

Meanwhile the Tuscan army,
    Right glorious to behold,
Came flashing back the noonday light,
Rank behind rank, like surges bright,
    Of a broad sea of gold.   285
Four hundred trumpets sounded
    A peal of warlike glee,
As that great host, with measured tread,
And spears advanced, and ensigns spread,
Rolled slowly towards the bridge's head,   290
    Where stood the dauntless Three.

The Three stood calm and silent,
    And looked upon the foes,
And a great shout of laughter
    From all the vanguard rose: 295
And forth three chiefs came spurring
    Before that deep array;
To earth they sprang, their swords they drew,
And lifted high their shields, and flew
    To win the narrow way;   300

Aunus from green Tifernum,
    Lord of the Hill of Vines;
And Seius, whose eight hundred slaves
    Sicken in Ilva's mines;
And Picus, long to Clusium   305
    Vassal in peace and war,
Who led to fight his Umbrian powers
From that grey crag where, girt with towers,
The fortress of Nequinum lowers
    O'er the pale waves of Nar.   310

Stout Lartius hurled down Aunus
    Into the stream beneath:
Herminius struck at Seius,
    And clove him to the teeth:
At Picus brave Horatius   315
    Darted one fiery thrust;
And the proud Umbrian's gilded arms
    Clashed in the bloody dust.

Then Ocnus of Falerii
    Rushed on the Roman Three,   320
And Lausulus of Urgo,
    The rover of the sea;
And Aruns of Volsinium,
    Who slew the great wild boar,
The great wild boar that had his den   325
Amidst the reeds of Cosa's fen,
And wasted fields, and slaughtered men,
    Along Albinia's shore.

237 **strait:** narrow   267 **Tribunes:** officers elected by the common
people to protect their interests   **beard:** defy, oppose impertinently
271 **Wherefore:** for which reason   274 **harness:** armour   278 **crow:**
crowbar

288 **host:** army

Herminius smote down Aruns:
   Lartius laid Ocnus low: 330
Right to the heart of Lausulus
   Horatius sent a blow.
'Lie there,' he cried, 'fell pirate!
   No more, aghast and pale,
From Ostia's walls the crowd shall mark 335
The track of thy destroying bark;
No more Campania's hinds shall fly
To woods and caverns when they spy
   Thy thrice accursed sail.'

But now no sound of laughter 340
   Was heard among the foes.
A wild and wrathful clamour
   From all the vanguard rose.
Six spears' lengths from the entrance
   Halted that deep array, 345
And for a space no man came forth
   To win the narrow way.

But hark! the cry is Astur:
   And lo! the ranks divide;
And the great Lord of Luna 350
   Comes with his stately stride.
Upon his ample shoulders
   Clangs loud the four-fold shield,
And in his hand he shakes the brand
   Which none but he can wield. 355

He smiled on those bold Romans
   A smile serene and high;.
He eyed the flinching Tuscans,
   And scorn was in his eye.
Quoth he, 'The she-wolf's litter 360
   Stand savagely at bay:
But will you dare to follow,
   If Astur clears the way?'

Then, whirling up his broadsword
   With both hands to the height, 365
He rushed against Horatius,
   And smote with all his might.
With shield and blade Horatius
   Right deftly turned the blow.
The blow, though turned, came yet too nigh; 370
It missed his helm, but gashed his thigh:
The Tuscans raised a joyful cry
   To see the red blood flow.

He reeled, and on Herminius
   He leaned one breathing-space; 375
Then, like a wild cat mad with wounds,
   Sprang right at Astur's face.
Through teeth, and skull, and helmet
   So fierce a thrust he sped,
The good sword stood a hand-breadth out 380
   Behind the Tuscan's head.

And the great Lord of Luna
   Fell at that deadly stroke,
As falls on Mount Alvernus
   A thunder-smitten oak. 385
Far o'er the crashing forest
   The giant arms lie spread;
And the pale augurs, muttering low,
   Gaze on the blasted head.

On Astur's throat Horatius 390
   Right firmly pressed his heel,
And thrice and four times tugged amain,
   Ere he wrenched out the steel.
'And see,' he cried, 'the welcome,
   Fair guests, that waits you here! 395
What noble Lucumo comes next
   To taste our Roman cheer?'

But at his haughty challenge
   A sullen murmur ran,
Mingled of wrath, and shame, and dread, 400
   Along that glittering van.
There lacked not men of prowess,
   Nor men of lordly race;
For all Etruria's noblest
   Were round the fatal place. 405

But all Etruria's noblest
   Felt their hearts sink to see
On the earth the bloody corpses,
   In the path the dauntless Three:
And, from the ghastly entrance 410
   Where those bold Romans stood,
All shrank, like boys who unaware,
Ranging the woods to start a hare,
Come to the mouth of the dark lair
Where, growling low, a fierce old bear 415
   Lies amidst bones and blood.

Was none who would be foremost
   To lead such dire attack:
But those behind cried 'Forward!'
   And those before cried 'Back!' 420
And backward now and forward
   Wavers the deep array;
And on the tossing sea of steel,

336 **bark**: ship   337 **hinds**: peasants   360 **The she-wolf's litter:** Romulus and Remus, legendary founders of Rome, were said to have been suckled by a female wolf

388 **augurs:** prophets

To and fro the standards reel;
And the victorious trumpet-peal
  Dies fitfully away.

Yet one man for one moment
  Stood out before the crowd;
Well known was he to all the Three,
  And they gave him greeting loud.
'Now welcome, welcome, Sextus!
  Now welcome to thy home!
Why dost thou stay, and turn away?
  Here lies the road to Rome.'

Thrice looked he at the city; 435
  Thrice looked he at the dead;
And thrice came on in fury,
  And thrice turned back in dread:
And, white with fear and hatred,
  Scowled at the narrow way 440
Where, wallowing in a pool of blood,
  The bravest Tuscans lay.

But meanwhile axe and lever
  Have manfully been plied;
And now the bridge hangs tottering 445
  Above the boiling tide.
'Come back, come back, Horatius!'
  Loud cried the Fathers
'Back, Lartius! back Herminius!
  Back, ere the ruin fall!' 450

Back darted Spurius Lartius;
  Herminius darted back:
And, as they passed, beneath their feet
  They felt the timbers crack.
But when they turned their faces, 455
  And on the farther shore
Saw brave Horatius stand alone,
  They would have crossed once more.

But with a crash like thunder
  Fell every loosened beam, 460
And, like a dam, the mighty wreck
  Lay right athwart the stream:
And a long shout of triumph
  Rose from the walls of Rome,
As to the highest turret-tops 465
  Was splashed the yellow foam.

And, like a horse unbroken
  When first he feels the rein,
The furious river struggled hard,
  And tossed his tawny mane, 470
And burst the curb, and bounded,
  Rejoicing to be free,
And whirling down, in fierce career,
  Battlement, and plank, and pier,
  Rushed headlong to the sea. 475

Alone stood brave Horatius,
  But constant still in mind; 425
Thrice thirty thousand foes before,
  And the broad flood behind.
'Down with him!' cried false Sextus, 480
  With a smile on his pale face.
'Now yield thee,' cried Lars Porsena,
  'Now yield thee to our grace.'

Round turned he, as not deigning
  Those craven ranks to see; 485
Nought spake he to Lars Porsena,
  To Sextus nought spake he;
But he saw on Palatinus
  The white porch of his home;
And he spake to the noble river 490
  That rolls by the towers of Rome.

'Oh, Tiber! father Tiber!
  To whom the Romans pray,
A Roman's life, a Roman's arms,
  Take thou in charge this day!' 495
So he spake, and speaking sheathed
  The good sword by his side,
And with his harness on his back,
  Plunged headlong in the tide.

No sound of joy or sorrow 500
  Was heard from either bank;
But friends and foes in dumb surprise,
With parted lips and straining eyes,
  Stood gazing where he sank;
And when above the surges 505
  They saw his crest appear,
All Rome sent forth a rapturous cry,
And even the ranks of Tuscany
  Could scarce forbear to cheer.

But fiercely ran the current, 510
  Swollen high by months of rain:
And fast his blood was flowing;
  And he was sore in pain,
And heavy with his armour,
  And spent with changing blows: 515
And oft they thought him sinking,
  But still again he rose.

Never, I ween, did swimmer,
  In such an evil case,
Struggle through such a raging flood 520
  Safe to the landing place:
But his limbs were borne up bravely
  By the brave heart within,
And our good father Tiber
  Bare bravely up his chin. 525

488 **Palatinus:** the Palatine Hill in Rome 518 **ween:** think

'Curse on him!' quoth false Sextus;
  'Will not the villain drown?
But for this stay, ere close of day
  We should have sacked the town!'
'Heaven help him!' quoth Lars Porsena,   530
  'And bring him safe to shore;
For such a gallant feat of arms
  Was never seen before.'

And now he feels the bottom;
  Now on dry earth he stands;   535
Now round him throng the Fathers
  To press his gory hands;
And now, with shouts and clapping,
  And noise of weeping loud,
He enters through the River-Gate,   540
  Borne by the joyous crowd.

They gave him of the corn-land,
  That was of public right,
As much as two strong oxen
  Could plough from morn till night;   545
And they made a molten image,
  And set it up on high,
And there it stands unto this day
  To witness if I lie.

It stands in the Comitium,   550
  Plain for all folks to see;
Horatius in his harness,
  Halting upon one knee:
And underneath is written,
  In letters all of gold,   555
How valiantly he kept the bridge
  In the brave days of old.

And still his name sounds stirring
  Unto the men of Rome,
As the trumpet-blast that cries to them   560
  To charge the Volscian home;
And wives still pray to Juno
  For boys with hearts as bold
As his who kept the bridge so well
  In the brave days of old.   565

And in the nights of winter,
  When the cold north winds blow,
And the long howling of the wolves
  Is heard amidst the snow;
When round the lonely cottage   570
  Roars loud the tempest's din,
And the good logs of Algidus
  Roar louder yet within;

550 **Comitium:** place of assembly 562 **Juno:** the queen of the Roman gods

When the oldest cask is opened,
  And the largest lamp is lit;   575
When the chestnuts glow in the embers,
  And the kid turns on the spit;
When young and old in circle
  Around the firebrands close;
When the girls are weaving baskets,   580
  And the lads are shaping bows;

When the goodman mends his armour,
  And trims his helmet's plume;
When the goodwife's shuttle merrily
  Goes flashing through the loom;   585
With weeping and with laughter
  Still is the story told,
How well Horatius kept the bridge
  In the brave days of old.

582 **goodman:** yeoman, freeholder   584 **goodwife:** wife of a goodman

WILLIAM BARNES

WOAK HILL

WHEN sycamore leaves were a-spreaden,
  Green-ruddy, in hedges,
Bezide the red doust o' the ridges,
  A-dried at Woak Hill;

I packed up my goods all a-sheenen   5
  Wi' long years o' handlen
On dousty red wheels ov a waggon,
  To ride at Woak Hill.

The brown thatchen ruf o' the dwellen,
  I then wer a-leäven,   10
Had shelter'd the sleek head o' Meäry,
  My bride at Woak Hill.

But now vor zome years, her light voot-vall
  'S a-lost vrom the vlooren.
Too soon vor my jay an' my childern,   15
  She died at Woak Hill.

But still I do think that, in soul,
  She do hover about us;
To ho vor her motherless childern,
  Her pride at Woak Hill.   20

Zoo – lest she should tell me hereafter
  I stole off 'ithout her,
An' left her, uncall'd at house-ridden,
  To bide at Woak Hill –

I call'd her so fondly, wi' lippens 25
    All soundless to others,
An' took her wi' aïr-reachen hand,
    To my zide at Woak Hill.

On the road I did look round, a-talken
    To light at my shoulder, 30
An' then led her in at the door-way,
    Miles wide vrom Woak Hill.

An' that's why vo'k thought, vor a season,
    My mind wer a-wandren
Wi' sorrow, when I wer so sorely 35
    A-tried at Woak Hill.

But no; that my Meäry mid never
    Behold herzelf slighted,
I wanted to think that I guided
    My guide vrom Woak Hill. 40

WOAK HILL: **woak**: oak: 3 **doust**: dust   5 **a-sheenen**: shining
14 **vlooren**: floor 15 **jay**: woman 19 **ho**: watch over 21 **Zoo**: so
23 **house-ridden**: moving house 25 **lippens**: intimacies, private talk
27 **wi' aïr-reachen hand**: i.e. taking her ghostly hand (which only he
can see) 33 **vo'k**: folk 37 **mid**: might

THE GEÄTE A-VALLEN TO

In the zunsheen of our zummers
    Wi' the häytime now a-come,
How busy wer we out a-vield
    Wi' vew a-left at hwome,
When waggons rumbled out ov yard 5
    Red wheeled, wi' body blue,
And back behind 'em loudly slamm'd
    The geäte a-vallen to.

Drough day sheen ov how many years
    The geäte ha' now a-swung, 10
Behind the veet o' vull-grown men
    And vootsteps of the young.
Drough years o' days it swung to us
    Behind each little shoe,
As we tripped lightly on avore 15
    The geäte a-vallen to.

In evenen time o' starry night
    How mother zot at hwome
And kept her blazing vire bright
    Till father should ha' come, 20
And how she quicken'd up and smiled
    And stirred her vire anew,
To hear the trampen ho'ses' steps
    And geäte a-vallen to.

There's moon-sheen now in nights o' Fall 25
    When leaves be brown vrom green,
When to the slammen o' the geäte
    Our Jenny's ears be keen,
When the wold dog do wag his taïl,
    And Jeän could tell to who, 30
As he do come in drough the geäte,
    The geäte a-vallen to.

And oft do come a saddened hour
    When there must goo away
One well-beloved to our heart's core. 35
    Vor long, perhaps for aye:
And oh! it is a touchen thing
    The loven heart must rue
To hear behind his last farewell
    The geäte a-vallen to. 40

THE GEÄTE A-VALLEN TO: 1 **zunsheen**: sunshine 3 **a-vield**: in the fields
8 **a-vallen to**: falling to, slamming shut 9 **Drough day sheen**:
through daylight 11 **veet**: feet 17 **zot**: sat 23 **ho'ses'**: horses'
29 **wold**: old 36 **for aye**: for ever

MY ORCHA'D IN LINDEN LEA

'Ithin the woodlands, flow'ry gleäded,
    By the woak tree's mossy moot,
The sheenen grass-bleädes, timber-sheäded,
    Now do quiver under voot;
An' birds do whissle over head, 5
An' water's bubblen in its bed,
An' there vor me the apple tree
Do leän down low in Linden Lea.

When leaves that leätely wer a-springen
    Now do feäde 'ithin the copse, 10
An' painted birds do hush their zingen
    Up upon the timber's tops;
An' brown-leav'd fruit's a-turnen red,
In cloudless zunsheen, over head,
Wi' fruit vor me, the apple tree 15
Do leän down low in Linden Lea.

Let other vo'k meäke money vaster
    In the aïr o' dark-room'd towns,
I don't dread a peevish meäster;
    Though noo man do heed my frowns, 20
I be free to goo abrode,
Or teäke ageän my homeward road
To where, vor me, the apple tree
Do leän down low in Linden Lea.

MY ORCHA'D IN LINDEN LEA: 2 **woak**: oak **moot**: stump 3 **sheenen**:
gleaming 14 **zunsheen**: sunshine 17 **vaster**: faster

WINTHROP MACKWORTH PRAED

GOOD-NIGHT TO THE SEASON

GOOD-NIGHT to the Season! 'tis over!
   Gay dwellings no longer are gay;
The courtier, the gambler, the lover,
   Are scattered like swallows away:
There's nobody left to invite one,   5
   Except my good uncle and spouse;
My mistress is bathing at Brighton,
   My patron is sailing at Cowes:
For want of a better employment,
   Till Ponto and Don can get out,   10
I'll cultivate rural enjoyment,
   And angle immensely for trout.

Good-night to the Season! – the lobbies,
   Their changes, and rumours of change,
Which startled the rustic Sir Bobbies,   15
   And made all the Bishops look strange:
The breaches, and battles, and blunders,
   Performed by the Commons and Peers;
The Marquis's eloquent thunders,
   The Baronet's eloquent ears: 20
Denouncings of Papists and treasons,
   Of foreign dominion and oats;
Misrepresentations of reasons,
   And misunderstandings of notes.

Good-night to the Season! – the buildings   25
   Enough to make Inigo sick;
The paintings, and plasterings, and gildings
   Of stucco, and marble, and brick;
The orders deliciously blended,
   From love of effect, into one;   30
The club-houses only intended,
   The palaces only begun;
The hell where the fiend, in his glory,
   Sits staring at putty and stones,
And scrambles from storey to storey,   35
   To rattle at midnight his bones.

Good-night to the Season! – the dances,
   The fillings of hot little rooms,
The glancings of rapturous glances,
   The fancyings of fancy costúmes;   40
The pleasures which Fashion makes duties,
   The praisings of fiddles and flutes,
The luxury of looking at beauties,
   The tedium of talking to mutes;
The female diplomatists, planners   45
   Of matches for Laura and Jane,
The ice of her Ladyship's manners,
   The ice of his Lordship's champagne.

Good-night to the Season! – the rages
   Led off by the chiefs of the throng,   50
The Lady Matilda's new pages,
   The Lady Eliza's new song;
Miss Fennel's macaw, which at Boodle's
   Is held to have something to say;
Mrs Splénetic's musical poodles,   55
   Which bark 'Batti Batti' all day;
The pony Sir Araby sported,
   As hot and as black as a coal,
And the Lion his mother imported,
   In bearskins and grease, from the Pole.   60

Good-night to the Season! – the Toso,
   So very majestic and tall;
Miss Ayton, whose singing was so-so,
   And Pasta, divinest of all;
The labour in vain of the Ballet,   65
   So sadly deficient in stars;
The foreigners thronging the Alley,
   Exhaling the breath of cigars;
The 'loge' where some heiress, how killing,
   Environed with Éxquisites sits,   70
The lovely one out of her drilling,
   The silly ones out of their wits.

Good-night to the Season! – the splendour
   That beamed in the Spanish Bazaar;
Where I purchased – my heart was so tender –   75
   A card-case – a pasteboard guitar, –
A bottle of perfume, – a girdle, –
   A lithographed Riego full-grown,
Whom Bigotry drew on a hurdle
   That artists might draw him on stone, –   80
A small panorama of Seville, –
   A trap for demolishing flies, –
A caricature of the Devil, –
   And a look from Miss Sheridan's eyes.

Good-night to the Season! – the flowers   85
   Of the grand horticultural fête,
When boudoirs were quitted for bowers,
   And the fashion was not to be late;
When all who had money or leisure
   Grew rural o'er ices and wines,   90
All pleasantly toiling for pleasure,
   All hungrily pining for pines,
And making of beautiful speeches,
   And marring of beautiful shows,
And feeding on delicate peaches,   95
   And treading on delicate toes.

Good-night to the Season! – another
   Will come with its trifles and toys,
And hurry away, like its brother,
   In sunshine, and odour, and noise.   100
Will it come with a rose or a briar?

Will it come with a blessing or curse?
Will its bonnets be lower or higher?
  Will its morals be better or worse?
Will it find me grown thinner or fatter,   105
  Or fonder of wrong or of right,
Or married, – or buried? – no matter,
  Good-night to the Season, Good-night!

GOOD-NIGHT TO THE SEASON: 26 **Inigo:** Inigo Jones (1573–1652),
English architect and theatrical designer 53 **Boodle's:** a London
gentlemen's club

THOMAS LOVELL BEDDOES

DREAM-PEDLARY

IF there were dreams to sell,
  What would you buy?
Some cost a passing bell;
  Some a light sigh,
That shakes from Life's fresh crown   5
Only a rose-leaf down.
If there were dreams to sell,
Merry and sad to tell,
And the crier rung the bell,
  What would you buy?   10

A cottage lone and still,
  With bowers nigh,
Shadowy, my woes to still,
  Until I die.
Such pearl from Life's fresh crown   15
Fain would I shake me down.
Were dreams to have at will,
This would best heal my ill,
  This would I buy.

But there were dreams to sell,   20
  Ill didst thou buy;
Life is a dream, they tell,
  Waking, to die.
Dreaming a dream to prize,
Is wishing ghosts to rise;   25
  And, if I had the spell
  To call the buried, well,
    Which one would I?

If there are ghosts to raise,
  What shall I call,   30
Out of hell's murky haze,
  Heaven's blue hall?
Raise my lovèd long-lost boy
To lead me to his joy.
  There are no ghosts to raise;   35
  Out of death lead no ways;
    Vain is the call.

Know'st thou not ghosts to sue?
  No love thou hast.
Else lie, as I will do,   40
  And breathe thy last.
So out of Life's fresh crown
Fall like a rose-leaf down.
  Thus are the ghosts to woo;
  Thus are all dreams made true,   45
    Ever to last!

ELIZABETH BARRETT BROWNING

From SONNETS FROM THE PORTUGUESE

1

I THOUGHT once how Theocritus had sung
Of the sweet years, the dear and wished-for years,
Who each one in a gracious hand appears
To bear a gift for mortals, old or young:
And, as I mused it in his antique tongue,   5
I saw, in gradual vision through my tears,
The sweet, sad years, the melancholy years,
Those of my own life, who by turns had flung
A shadow across me. Straightway I was 'ware,
So weeping, how a mystic Shape did move   10
Behind me, and drew me backward by the hair;
And a voice said in mastery, while I strove, –
'Guess now who holds thee!' – 'Death,' I said. But,
    there,
The silver answer rang – 'Not death, but Love.'

SONNETS FROM THE PORTUGUESE: A sequence of forty-four love-
poems written to Robert Browning during the couple's courtship,
1845–6. Robert begged to be allowed to see them, but Elizabeth
would only promise that 'You shall see some day at Pisa what I will
not show you now. Does not Solomon say that "there is a time to
read what is written". If he doesn't, he *ought*'. In fact, Robert was
first shown the poems in Bagni di Lucca in 1849. He recalled: 'Yes,
that was a strange, heavy crown, that wreath of Sonnets, put on me
one morning unawares, three years after it had been twined – all
this delay because I happened early to say something against
putting one's loves into verse; then again I said something else on
the other side, one evening at Lucca – and the next morning she
said hesitatingly: "Do you know I once wrote some poems about
you" – and then – "There they are, if you care to see them" '. The
poems were published in 1850. The title was suggested by Robert;
see note below: (1) 1 **Theocritus:** Greek poet (*c.*310–250 BC) 9 **'ware:**
aware 12 **And a voice said in mastery:** 'You were stronger than I,
from the beginning, and I felt the mastery in you by the first word
and first look' (EBB to RB, 19 May 1846) 14 **'Not death, but Love':**
This reverses the mood of the opening stanza of Elizabeth's
'Catarina to Camoens' (1844): 'On the door you will not enter/
I have gazed too long; adieu!/Hope withdraws her peradventure;/
Death is near me, – and not *you*'. Perceiving that Elizabeth's
'condition in certain respects . . . resembled those of the Portuguese
Catarina', Robert proposed the title 'Sonnets from the Portuguese'
('purposely an ambiguous title') for the whole sequence

3

UNLIKE are we, unlike, O princely Heart!
Unlike our uses and our destinies.
Our ministering two angels look surprise
On one another, as they strike athwart
Their wings in passing. Thou, bethink thee, art   5
A guest for queens to social pageantries,
With gages from a hundred brighter eyes
Than tears even can make mine, to play thy part
Of chief musician. What hast *thou* to do
With looking from the lattice-lights at me,   10
A poor, tired, wandering singer, singing through
The dark, and leaning up a cypress tree?
The chrism is on thine head, – on mine, the dew, –
And Death must dig the level where these agree.

7

THE face of all the world is changed, I think,
Since first I heard the footsteps of thy soul
Move still, oh, still, beside me, as they stole
Betwixt me and the dreadful outer brink
Of obvious death, where I, who thought to sink,   5
Was caught up into love, and taught the whole
Of life in a new rhythm. The cup of dole
God gave for baptism, I am fain to drink,
And praise its sweetness, Sweet, with thee anear.
The names of country, heaven, are changed away   10
For where thou art or shalt be, there or here;
And this . . . this lute and song . . . loved yesterday,
(The singing angels know) are only dear
Because thy name moves right in what they say.

8

WHAT can I give thee back, O liberal
And princely giver, who hast brought the gold
And purple of thine heart, unstrained, untold,
And laid them on the outside of the wall
For such as I to take or leave withal,   5
In unexpected largésse? Am I cold,
Ungrateful, that for these most manifold
High gifts, I render nothing back at all?
Not so; not cold, – but very poor instead.
Ask God who knows. For frequent tears have run   10
The colours from my life, and left so dead
And pale a stuff, it were not fitly done
To give the same as pillow to thy head.
Go farther! let it serve to trample on.

14

IF thou must love me, let it be for nought
Except for love's sake only. Do not say
'I love her for her smile – her look – her way
Of speaking gently, – for a trick of thought
That falls in well with mine, and certes brought   5
A sense of pleasant ease on such a day'
For these things in themselves, Belovèd, may
Be changed, or change for thee, – and love, so wrought,
May be unwrought so. Neither love me for
Thine own dear pity's wiping my cheeks dry, –   10
A creature might forget to weep, who bore
Thy comfort long, and lose thy love thereby.
But love me for love's sake, that evermore
Thou may'st love on, through love's eternity.

24

LET the world's sharpness like a clasping knife
Shut in upon itself and do no harm
In this close hand of Love, now soft and warm,
And let us hear no sound of human strife
After the click of the shutting. Life to life –   5
I lean upon thee, Dear, without alarm,
And feel as safe as guarded by a charm
Against the stab of worldlings, who if rife
Are weak to injure. Very whitely still
The lilies of our lives may reassure   10
Their blossoms from their roots, accessible
Alone to heavenly dews that drop not fewer,
Growing straight, out of man's reach, on the hill.
God only, who made us rich, can make us poor.

26

I LIVED with visions for my company
Instead of men and women, years ago,
And found them gentle mates, nor thought to know
A sweeter music than they played to me.
But soon their trailing purple was not free   5
Of this world's dust, their lutes did silent grow,
And I myself grew faint and blind below
Their vanishing eyes. Then THOU didst come, to be,
Belovèd, what they seemed. Their shining fronts,
Their songs, their splendours, (better, yet the same,   10
As river-water hallowed into fonts),
Met in thee, and from out thee overcame
My soul with satisfaction of all wants:
Because God's gifts put man's best dreams to shame.

(14) 2 **for love's sake only:** 'The first moment in which I seemed to admit to myself in a flash of lightning the *possibility* of your affection for me being more than dream-work . . . the first moment was *that* when you intimated (as you have done since repeatedly) that you cared for me not for a reason, but because you cared for me' (EBB to RB, 12 November 1845) 5 **certes:** for certain (24) 1 **clasping knife:** penknife (26) 11 **hallowed into fonts:** made holy for use in baptisms 14 **Because . . . to shame:** 'you need not fear any fear of mine – my fear will not cross a wish of yours, be sure! Neither does it prevent your being all to me . . . all! – more than I used to take for all when I looked round the world . . . almost more than I took for all in my earliest dreams' (EBB to RB, 12 December 1845)

(3) 7 **gages:** pledges 10 **lattice-lights:** window-panes composed of small diamond-shaped pieces of glass set in a lead framework 12 **cypress tree:** a symbol of death 13 **chrism:** holy oil (7) 7 **dole:** pain

35

IF I leave all for thee, wilt thou exchange
And be all to me? Shall I never miss
Home-talk and blessing and the common kiss
That comes to each in turn, nor count it strange,
When I look up, to drop on a new range   5
Of walls and floors, another home than this?
Nay, wilt thou fill that place by me which is
Filled by dead eyes too tender to know change?
That's hardest. If to conquer love, has tried,
To conquer grief, tries more, as all things prove,   10
For grief indeed is love and grief beside.
Alas, I have grieved so, I am hard to love.
Yet love me – wilt thou? Open thine heart wide,
And fold within, the wet wings of thy dove.

41

I THANK all who have loved me in their hearts,
With thanks and love from mine. Deep thanks to all
Who paused a little near the prison-wall
To hear my music in its louder parts
Ere they went onward, each one to the mart's   5
Or temple's occupation, beyond call.
But thou, who, in my voice's sink and fall
When the sob took it, thy divinest Art's
Own instrument didst drop down at thy foot
To harken what I said between my tears, . . .   10
Instruct me how to thank thee! Oh, to shoot
My soul's full meaning into future years,
That *they* should lend it utterance, and salute
Love that endures, from Life that disappears!

43

How do I love thee? Let me count the ways.
I love thee to the depth and breadth and height
My soul can reach, when feeling out of sight
For the ends of Being and ideäl Grace.
I love thee to the level of every day's   5
Most quiet need, by sun and candlelight.
I love thee freely, as men strive for Right;
I love thee purely, as they turn from Praise.
I love thee with the passion put to use
In my old griefs, and with my childhood's faith.   10
I love thee with a love I seemed to lose
With my lost saints, – I love thee with the breath,
Smiles, tears, of all my life! – and, if God choose,
I shall but love thee better after death.

(35) 1 **If I leave all for thee:** owing to the hostility of Elizabeth's tyrannical father, marriage to Robert would mean severing all connections with her family   14 **wet wings:** i.e. as one newly born

44

Belovèd, thou hast brought me many flowers
Plucked in the garden, all the summer through
And winter, and it seemed as if they grew
In this close room, nor missed the sun and showers.
So, in the like name of that love of ours,   5
Take back these thoughts which here unfolded too,
And which on warm and cold days I withdrew
From my heart's ground. Indeed, those beds and
       bowers
Be overgrown with bitter weeds and rue,
And wait thy weeding; yet here's eglantine,   10
Here's ivy! – take them, as I used to do
Thy flowers, and keep them where they shall not pine.
Instruct thine eyes to keep their colours true,
And tell thy soul, their roots are left in mine.

(44) 1 **thou hast brought me many flowers:** 'When you are gone I find your flowers; & you never spoke of nor showed them to me. . . . Count among the miracles that your flowers live with me – I accept *that* for an omen, dear – dearest! Flowers in general, all other flowers, die of despair when they come into the same atmosphere' (EBB to RB, 30 December 1845); 'all flowers forswear me – and die either suddenly or gradually as soon as they become aware of the want of fresh air and light in my room' (EBB to Mrs Martin, 30 January 1843)   4 **close:** confining, stifling

EDWARD FITZGERALD

THE RUBÁIYÁT OF OMAR KHAYYÁM
THE ASTRONOMER-POET OF PERSIA

AWAKE! for Morning in the Bowl of Night
Has flung the Stone that puts the Stars to Flight:
    And Lo! the Hunter of the East has caught
The Sultán's Turret in a Noose of Light.

Dreaming when Dawn's Left Hand was in the Sky,   5
I heard a Voice within the Tavern cry,
    'Awake, my Little ones, and fill the Cup,
Before Life's Liquor in its Cup be dry.'

And, as the Cock crew, those who stood before
The Tavern shouted – 'Open then the Door!   10
    You know how little while we have to stay,
And, once departed, may return no more.'

Now the New Year reviving old Desires,
The thoughtful Soul to Solitude retires,
    Where the WHITE HAND OF MOSES on the Bough   15
Puts out, and Jesus from the Ground suspires.

THE RUBÁIYÁT OF OMAR KHAYYÁM: Omar Khayyám (?1050–?1123), Persian poet, mathematician and astronomer. Rubaiyat is the plural of a Persian word meaning a quatrain   1–2 **in the Bowl . . . to Flight:** a stone flung into a cup was a signal to strike camp   15 **white hand of Moses:** a plant named after Moses, regarded as a prophet by Muslims   16 **Jesus:** a plant named after Jesus, also honoured as a prophet in Islam

EDWARD FITZGERALD

Iram indeed is gone with all its Rose,
And Jamshyd's Sev'n-ringed Cup where no one knows;
    But still the Vine her ancient Ruby yields,
And still a Garden by the Water blows.   20

And David's Lips are locked; but in divine
High piping Pehlevi, with 'Wine! Wine! Wine!
    Red Wine!' – the Nightingale cries to the Rose,
That yellow Cheek of hers t'incarnadine.

Come, fill the Cup, and in the Fire of Spring   25
The Winter Garment of Repentance fling:
    The Bird of Time has but a little way
To fly – and Lo! the Bird is on the Wing.

And look – a thousand Blossoms with the Day
Woke – and a thousand scattered into Clay: 30
    And this first Summer Month that brings the Rose
Shall take Jamshyd and Kaikobad away.

But come with old Khayyam, and leave the Lot
Of Kaikobad and Kaikhosru forgot!
    Let Rustum lay about him as he will,   35
Or Hatim Tai cry Supper – heed them not.

With me along some Strip of Herbage strown
That just divides the desert from the sown,
    Where name of Slave and Sultán scarce is known,
And pity Sultán Mahmud on his Throne.   40

Here with a Loaf of Bread beneath the Bough,
A Flask of Wine, a Book of Verse – and Thou
    Beside me singing in the Wilderness –
And Wilderness is Paradise enow.

'How sweet is mortal Sovranty!' – think some: 45
Others – 'How blest the Paradise to come!'
    Ah, take the Cash in hand and waive the Rest;
Oh, the brave Music of a distant Drum!

Look to the Rose that blows about us – 'Lo,
Laughing,' she says, 'into the World I blow: 50
    At once the silken Tassel of my Purse
Tear, and its Treasure on the Garden throw.'

The Worldly Hope men set their Hearts upon
Turns Ashes – or it prospers; and anon,
    Like Snow upon the Desert's dusty Face   55
Lighting a little Hour or two – is gone.

And those who husbanded the Golden Grain,
And those who flung it to the Winds like Rain,
    Alike to no such aureate Earth are turned
As, buried once, Men want dug up again.   60

Think, in this battered Caravanserai
Whose Doorways are alternate Night and Day,
    How Sultán after Sultán with his Pomp
Abode his Hour or two, and went his way.

They say the Lion and the Lizard keep   65
The Courts where Jamshyd gloried and drank
        deep;
    And Bahram, that great Hunter – the Wild Ass
Stamps o'er his Head, and he lies fast asleep.

I sometimes think that never blows so red
The Rose as where some buried Caesar bled;   70
    That every Hyacinth the Garden wears
Dropped in its Lap from some once lovely Head.

And this delightful Herb whose tender Green
Fledges the River's Lip on which we lean –
    Ah, lean upon it lightly! for who knows   75
From what once lovely Lip it springs unseen!

Ah, my Belovèd, fill the Cup that clears
TODAY of past Regrets and future Fears –
    Tomorrow? – Why, Tomorrow I may be
Myself with Yesterday's Sev'n Thousand Years.   80

Lo! some we loved, the loveliest and best
That Time and Fate of all their Vintage pressed,
    Have drunk their Cup a Round or two before,
And one by one crept silently to Rest.

And we, that now make merry in the Room   85
They left, and Summer dresses in new Bloom,
    Ourselves must we beneath the Couch of Earth
Descend, ourselves to make a Couch – for whom?

Ah, make the most of what we yet may spend,
Before we too into the Dust descend;   90
    Dust into Dust, and under Dust, to lie,
Sans Wine, sans Song, sans Singer, and – sans End!

Alike for those who for TODAY prepare,
And those that after a TOMORROW stare,
    A Muezzin from the Tower of Darkness cries,   95
'Fools! your Reward is neither Here nor There!'

17 **Iram:** a royal garden that was eventually buried in desert sands
18 **Jamshyd:** a mythical great king of Persia 21 **David:** Hebrew king
and psalmist 22 **Pehlevi:** the Middle Persian language, used in
classical literature 32 **Kaikobad:** legendary Persian king 34 **Kaikhosru:**
legendary Persian king 35 **Rustum:** legendary Persian warrior
36 **Hatim Tai:** legendary generous host 40 **Mahmud:** a Persian
sultan who conquered northern India

61 **Caravanserai:** a large inn, usually enclosing a courtyard,
providing accommodation for caravans 67 **Bahram:** a legendary
king and hunter 95 **Muezzin:** a person who calls the faithful to
prayer from the minaret of a mosque

Why, all the Saints and Sages who discussed
Of the Two Worlds so learnedly, are thrust
　　Like foolish Prophets forth; their Words to Scorn
Are scattered, and their Mouths are stopped with
　　Dust.

Oh, come with old Khayyam, and leave the Wise　101
To talk; one thing is certain, that Life flies;
　　One thing is certain, and the Rest is Lies;
The Flower that once has blown for ever dies.

Myself when young did eagerly frequent　　105
Doctor and Saint, and heard great Argument
　　About it and about: but evermore
Came out by the same Door as in I went.

With them the Seed of Wisdom did I sow,
And with my own hand laboured it to grow:　　110
　　And this was all the Harvest that I reaped –
'I came like Water, and like Wind I go.'

Into this Universe, and *why* not knowing,
Nor *whence*, like Water willy-nilly flowing!
　　And out of it, as Wind along the Waste,　　115
I know not *whither*, willy-nilly blowing.

What, without asking, hither hurried *whence*?
And, without asking, *whither* hurried hence!
　　Another and another Cup to drown
The Memory of this Impertinence!　　120

Up from Earth's Centre through the Seventh Gate
I rose, and on the Throne of Saturn sate,
　　And many Knots unravelled by the Road;
But not the Knot of Human Death and Fate.

There was a Door to which I found no Key:　　125
There was a Veil past which I could not see:
　　Some little Talk awhile of ME and THEE
There seemed – and then no more of THEE and ME.

Then to the rolling Heaven itself I cried,
Asking, 'What Lamp had Destiny to guide　　130
　　Her little Children stumbling in the Dark?'
And – 'A blind Understanding!' Heaven replied.

Then to this earthen Bowl did I adjourn
My Lip the secret Well of Life to learn:
　　And Lip to Lip it murmured – 'While you live　135
Drink! – for once dead you never shall return.'

I think the Vessel, that with fugitive
Articulation answered, once did live,
　　And merry-make; and the cold Lip I kissed
How many Kisses might it take – and give!　　140

For in the Market-place, one Dusk of Day,
I watched the Potter thumping his wet Clay:
　　And with its all obliterated Tongue
It murmured – 'Gently, Brother, gently, pray!'

Ah, fill the Cup: – what boots it to repeat　　145
How Time is slipping underneath our Feet:
　　Unborn TOMORROW, and dead YESTERDAY,
Why fret about them if TODAY be sweet!

One Moment in Annihilation's Waste,
One Moment, of the Well of Life to taste –　　150
　　The Stars are setting and the Caravan
Starts for the Dawn of Nothing – Oh, make haste!

How long, how long, in infinite Pursuit
Of This and That endeavour and dispute?
　　Better be merry with the fruitful Grape　　155
Than sadden after none, or bitter, Fruit.

You know, my Friends, how long since in my House
For a new Marriage I did make Carouse:
　　Divorced old barren Reason from my Bed,
And took the Daughter of the Vine to Spouse.　　160

For 'IS' and 'IS-NOT' though *with* Rule and Line,
And 'UP-AND-DOWN' *without*, I could define,
　　I yet in all I only cared to know,
Was never deep in anything but – Wine.

And lately, by the Tavern Door agape,　　165
Came stealing through the Dusk an Angel Shape
　　Bearing a Vessel on his Shoulder; and
He bid me taste of it; and 'twas – the Grape!

The Grape that can with Logic absolute
The Two-and-Seventy jarring Sects confute:　　170
　　The subtle Alchemist that in a Trice
Life's leaden Metal into Gold transmute.

The mighty Mahmud, the victorious Lord,
That all the misbelieving and black Horde
　　Of Fears and Sorrows that infest the Soul　　175
Scatters and slays with his enchanted Sword.

But leave the Wise to wrangle, and with me
The Quarrel of the Universe let be:
　　And, in some corner of the Hubbub couched,
Make Game of that which makes as much of Thee.

For in and out, above, about, below,　　181
'Tis nothing but a Magic Shadow-show,
　　Played in a Box whose Candle is the Sun,
Round which we Phantom Figures come and go.

And if the Wine you drink, the Lip you press, 185
End in the Nothing all Things end in – Yes –
    Then fancy while Thou art, Thou art but what
Thou shalt be – Nothing – Thou shalt not be less.

While the Rose blows along the River Brink,
With old Khayyam the Ruby Vintage drink: 190
    And when the Angel with his darker Draught
Draws up to Thee – take that, and do not shrink.

'Tis all a Chequer-board of Nights and Days
Where Destiny with Men for Pieces plays:
    Hither and thither moves, and mates, and slays, 195
And one by one back in the Closet lays.

The Ball no Question makes of Ayes and Noes,
But Right or Left as strikes the Player goes;
    And He that tossed Thee down into the Field,
He knows about it all – *HE* knows – *HE* knows! 200

The Moving Finger writes; and, having writ,
Moves on: nor all thy Piety nor Wit
    Shall lure it back to cancel half a Line,
Nor all thy Tears wash out a Word of it.

And that inverted Bowl we call The Sky, 205
Whereunder crawling cooped we live and die,
    Lift not thy hands to *It* for help – for It
Rolls impotently on as Thou or I.

With Earth's first Clay They did the Last Man's knead,
And then of the Last Harvest sowed the Seed: 210
    Yea, the first Morning of Creation wrote
What the Last Dawn of Reckoning shall read.

I tell Thee this – When, starting from the Goal,
Over the shoulders of the flaming Foal
    Of Heaven Parwin and Mushtara they flung, 215
In my predestined Plot of Dust and Soul

The Vine had struck a Fibre; which about
If clings my being – let the Sufi flout;
    Of my Base Metal may be filed a Key,
That shall unlock the Door he howls without. 220

And this I know: whether the one True Light,
Kindle to Love, or Wrath consume me quite,
    One glimpse of It within the Tavern caught
Better than in the Temple lost outright.

O Thou, who didst with Pitfall and with Gin 225
Beset the Road I was to wander in,
    Thou wilt not with Predestination round
Enmesh me, and impute my Fall to Sin?

O Thou, who Man of baser Earth didst make,
And who with Eden didst devise the Snake; 230
    For all the Sin wherewith the Face of Man
Is blackened, Man's Forgiveness give – and take!

KUZA-NÁMA

Listen again. One evening at the Close
Of Ramazan, ere the better Moon arose,
    In that old Potter's Shop I stood alone 235
With the clay Population round in Rows.

And, strange to tell, among the Earthen Lot
Some could articulate, while others not:
    And suddenly one more impatient cried –
'Who *is* the Potter, pray, and who the Pot?' 240

Then said another – 'Surely not in vain
My Substance from the common Earth was ta'en,
    That He who subtly wrought me into Shape
Should stamp me back to common Earth again.'

Another said – 'Why, ne'er a peevish Boy, 245
Would break the Bowl from which he drank in Joy;
    Shall He that *made* the Vessel in pure Love
And Fancy, in an after Rage destroy!'

None answered this; but after Silence spake
A Vessel of a more ungainly Make: 250
    'They sneer at me for leaning all awry;
What! did the Hand then of the Potter shake?'

Said one – 'Folks of a surly Tapster tell,
And daub his Visage with the Smoke of Hell;
    They talk of some strict Testing of us – Pish! 255
He's a Good Fellow, and 'twill all be well.'

Then said another with a long-drawn Sigh,
'My Clay with long Oblivion is gone dry:
    But, fill me with the old familiar Juice,
Methinks I might recover by-and-bye!' 260

So while the Vessels one by one were speaking,
One spied the little Crescent all were seeking:
    And then they jogged each other, 'Brother! Brother!
Hark to the Potter's Shoulder-knot a-creaking!'

Ah, with the Grape my fading Life provide, 265
And wash my Body whence the Life has died,
    And in a Windingsheet of Vine-leaf wrapped,
So bury me by some sweet Garden-side.

That ev'n my buried Ashes such a Snare
Of Perfume shall fling up into the Air, 270
    As not a True Believer passing by
But shall be overtaken unaware.

214 **Foal**: the constellation Equuleus 215 **Parwin**: the Pleiades constellation **Mushtara**: the planet Jupiter 218 **Sufi**: a member of an ascetic mystical Muslim order 225 **Gin**: a trap for catching small animals

KUZA-NAMA: book of pots 234 **Ramazan**: Ramadan, the month of fasting from dawn to dusk in the Muslim year

Indeed the Idols I have loved so long
Have done my Credit in Men's Eye much wrong:
  Have drowned my Honour in a shallow Cup,   275
And sold my Reputation for a Song.

Indeed, indeed, Repentance oft before
I swore – but was I sober when I swore?
  And then and then came Spring, and Rose-in-hand
My thread-bare Penitence apieces tore.   280

And much as Wine has played the Infidel,
And robbed me of my Robe of Honour – well,
  I often wonder what the Vintners buy
One half so precious as the Goods they sell.

Alas, that Spring should vanish with the Rose!   285
That Youth's sweet-scented Manuscript should close!
  The Nightingale that in the Branches sang,
Ah, whence, and whither flown again, who knows!

Ah, Love! could thou and I with Fate conspire
To grasp this sorry Scheme of Things entire,   290
  Would not we shatter it to bits – and then
Remould it nearer to the Heart's Desire!

Ah, Moon of my Delight who know'st no wane,
The Moon of Heaven is rising once again:
  How oft hereafter rising shall she look   295
Through this same Garden after me – in vain!

And when Thyself with shining Foot shall pass
Among the Guests Star-scattered on the Grass,
  And in thy joyous Errand reach the Spot
Where I made one – turn down an empty Glass!   300
                     Tamám Shud

301 **Tamám Shud:** It is ended

ALFRED, LORD TENNYSON

MARIANA

'Mariana in the moated grange.'
              Measure for Measure

WITH blackest moss the flower-plots
  Were thickly crusted, one and all:
The rusted nails fell from the knots
  That held the pear to the gable-wall.
The broken sheds looked sad and strange: 5
  Unlifted was the clinking latch;
  Weeded and worn the ancient thatch
Upon the lonely moated grange.
    She only said, 'My life is dreary,
      He cometh not,' she said;   10
    She said, 'I am aweary, aweary,
      I would that I were dead!'

Her tears fell with the dews at even;
  Her tears fell ere the dews were dried;
She could not look on the sweet heaven,   15
  Either at morn or eventide.
After the flitting of the bats,
  When thickest dark did trance the sky,
  She drew her casement-curtain by,
And glanced athwart the glooming flats.   20
    She only said, 'The night is dreary,
      He cometh not,' she said;
    She said, 'I am aweary, aweary,
      I would that I were dead!'

Upon the middle of the night,   25
  Waking she heard the night-fowl crow;
The cock sung out an hour ere light:
  From the dark fen the oxen's low
Came to her: without hope of change,
  In sleep she seemed to walk forlorn,   30
  Till cold winds woke the grey-eyed morn
About the lonely moated grange.
    She only said, 'The day is dreary,
      He cometh not,' she said;
    She said, 'I am aweary, aweary,   35
      I would that I were dead!'

About a stone-cast from the wall
  A sluice with blackened waters slept,
And o'er it many, round and small,
  The clustered marish-mosses crept.   40
Hard by a poplar shook alway,
  All silver-green with gnarlèd bark:
  For leagues no other tree did mark
The level waste, the rounding grey.
    She only said, 'My life is dreary,   45
      He cometh not,' she said;
    She said, 'I am aweary, aweary,
      I would that I were dead!'

And ever when the moon was low,
  And the shrill winds were up and away,   50
In the white curtain, to and fro,
  She saw the gusty shadow sway.
But when the moon was very low,
  And wild winds bound within their cell,
  The shadow of the poplar fell   55
Upon her bed, across her brow.
    She only said, 'The night is dreary,
      He cometh not,' she said;
    She said, 'I am aweary, aweary,
      I would that I were dead!'   60

MARIANA: 18 **trance:** enchant (and so dominate) 20 **athwart:** across
flats: an explance of level land 38 **sluice:** channel with a hatch to
control the flow of water 40 **marish:** marsh 43 **leagues:** a league was
an old measure equivalent to roughly three miles, but in poetry it
is used as a general expression of distance 44 **rounding:** surrounding,
encircling

All day within the dreamy house,
　The doors upon their hinges creaked;
The blue fly sung in the pane; the mouse
　Behind the mouldering wainscot shrieked,
Or from the crevice peered about.　　　　　　65
　Old faces glimmered through the doors,
　Old footsteps trod the upper floors,
Old voices called her from without.
　　　She only said, 'My life is dreary,
　　　　He cometh not, she said;　　　　70
　　　She said, 'I am aweary, aweary,
　　　　I would that I were dead!'

The sparrow's chirrup on the roof,
　The slow clock ticking, and the sound
Which to the wooing wind aloof　　　　　　75
　The poplar made, did all confound
Her sense; but most she loathed the hour
　When the thick-moted sunbeam lay
　Athwart the chambers, and the day
Was sloping toward his western bower.　　　80
　　　Then, said she, 'I am very dreary,
　　　　He will not come,' she said;
　　　She wept, 'I am aweary, aweary,
　　　　Oh God, that I were dead!'

78 **thick-moted:** dust-filled　80 **bower:** chamber

SONG

A SPIRIT haunts the year's last hours
Dwelling amid these yellowing bowers:
　　　To himself he talks;
For at eventide, listening earnestly,
At his work you may hear him sob and sigh　　5
　　　In the walks;
　　　Earthward he boweth the heavy stalks
Of the mouldering flowers:
　　　Heavily hangs the broad sunflower
　　　　Over its grave i' the earth so chilly;　10
　　　Heavily hangs the hollyhock,
　　　　Heavily hangs the tiger-lily.

The air is damp, and hushed, and close,
As a sick man's room when he taketh repose
　　　An hour before death;　　　　　　15
My very heart faints and my whole soul grieves
At the moist rich smell of the rotting leaves,
　　　And the breath
　　　Of the fading edges of box beneath,
And the year's last rose.　　　　　　20
　　　Heavily hangs the broad sunflower
　　　　Over its grave i' the earth so chilly;
　　　Heavily hangs the hollyhock,
　　　　Heavily hangs the tiger-lily.

'A SPIRIT HAUNTS THE YEAR'S LAST HOURS': 2 **bowers:** glades　19 **box:**
evergreen shrub that in its dwarf varieties was used as a border for
formal flower-beds

THE LADY OF SHALOTT

PART ONE

ON either side the river lie
Long fields of barley and of rye,
That clothe the wold and meet the sky;
And through the field the road runs by
　　　To many-towered Camelot;　　　　5
And up and down the people go,
Gazing where the lilies blow
Round an island there below,
　　　The island of Shalott.

Willows whiten, aspens quiver,　　　　　10
Little breezes dusk and shiver
Through the wave that runs for ever
By the island in the river
　　　Flowing down to Camelot.
Four grey walls, and four grey towers,　　　15
Overlook a space of flowers,
And the silent isle imbowers
　　　The Lady of Shalott.

By the margin, willow-veiled,
Slide the heavy barges trailed　　　　　20
By slow horses; and unhailed
The shallop flitteth silken-sailed
　　　Skimming down to Camelot:
But who hath seen her wave her hand?
Or at the casement seen her stand?　　　25
Or is she known in all the land,
　　　The Lady of Shalott?

Only reapers, reaping early
In among the bearded barley,
Hear a song that echoes cheerly　　　　　30
From the river winding clearly,
　　　Down to towered Camelot:
And by the moon the reaper weary,
Piling sheaves in uplands airy,
Listening, whispers ' 'Tis the fairy　　　35
　　　Lady of Shalott.'

PART TWO

There she weaves by night and day
A magic web with colours gay.
She has heard a whisper say,
A curse is on her if she stay　　　　　40
　　　To look down to Camelot.
She knows not what the curse may be,
And so she weaveth steadily,
And little other care hath she,
　　　The Lady of Shalott.　　　　　45

THE LADY OF SHALOTT: **Shalott:** Astolat, a town in Arthurian legend
identified with Guildford; the story of Lancelot and the Fair Maid
of Astolat is found in Sir Thomas Malory's *Morte Darthur* 3 **wold:**
open upland 5 **Camelot:** location of King Arthur's court, identified
with Winchester 11 **dusk:** darken 17 **imbowers:** shelters 19 **margin:**
river-bank 22 **shallop:** boat for shallow waters 35 **fairy:** enchanted

And moving through a mirror clear
That hangs before her all the year,
Shadows of the world appear.
There she sees the highway near
 Winding down to Camelot: 50
There the river eddy whirls,
And there the surly village-churls,
And the red cloaks of market girls,
 Pass onward from Shalott.

Sometimes a troop of damsels glad,   55
An abbot on an ambling pad,
Sometimes a curly shepherd-lad,
Or long-haired page in crimson clad,
 Goes by to towered Camelot;
And sometimes through the mirror blue   60
The knights come riding two and two:
She hath no loyal knight and true,
 The Lady of Shalott.

But in her web she still delights
To weave the mirror's magic sights,   65
For often through the silent nights
A funeral, with plumes and lights
 And music, went to Camelot:
Or when the moon was overhead,
Came two young lovers lately wed;   70
'I am half sick of shadows,' said
 The Lady of Shalott.

PART THREE

A bow-shot from her bower-eaves,
He rode between the barley-sheaves,
The sun came dazzling through the leaves,   75
And flamed upon the brazen greaves
 Of bold Sir Lancelot.
A red-cross knight for ever kneeled
To a lady in his shield,
That sparkled on the yellow field,   80
 Beside remote Shalott.

The gemmy bridle glittered free,
Like to some branch of stars we see
Hung in the golden Galaxy.
The bridle bells rang merrily   85
 As he rode down to Camelot:
And from his blazoned baldric slung
A mighty silver bugle hung,
And as he rode his armour rung,
 Beside remote Shalott.   90

All in the blue unclouded weather
Thick-jewelled shone the saddle-leather,
The helmet and the helmet-feather
Burned like one burning flame together,
 As he rode down to Camelot.   95
As often through the purple night,
Below the starry clusters bright,
Some bearded meteor, trailing light,
 Moves over still Shalott.

His broad clear brow in sunlight glowed;   100
On burnished hooves his war-horse trode;
From underneath his helmet flowed
His coal-black curls as on he rode,
 As he rode down to Camelot.
From the bank and from the river   105
He flashed into the crystal mirror,
'Tirra lirra,' by the river
 Sang Sir Lancelot.

She left the web, she left the loom,
She made three paces through the room,   110
She saw the water-lily bloom,
She saw the helmet and the plume,
 She looked down to Camelot.
Out flew the web and floated wide;
The mirror cracked from side to side;   115
'The curse is come upon me,' cried
 The Lady of Shalott.

PART FOUR

In the stormy east-wind straining,
The pale yellow woods were waning,
The broad stream in his banks complaining,   120
Heavily the low sky raining
 Over towered Camelot;
Down she came and found a boat
Beneath a willow left afloat,
And round about the prow she wrote   125
 The Lady of Shalott.

And down the river's dim expanse,
Like some bold seër in a trance
Seeing all his own mischance,
With a glassy countenance   130
 Did she look to Camelot.
And at the closing of the day
She loosed the chain, and down she lay;
The broad stream bore her far away,
 The Lady of Shalott.   135

52 **churls:** peasants, rustics 56 **pad:** gentle-paced horse 58 **page:** young man training for knighthood 76 **brazen:** brass **greaves:** leg-armour below the knee 77 **Sir Lancelot:** one of the Knights of the Round Table in the Arthurian legends 78 **red-cross:** i.e. English 82 **gemmy:** gem-encrusted 87 **blazoned baldric:** sash bearing his coat-of-arms

101 **burnished:** polished **trode:** trod (archaic) 119 **waning:** fading

Lying, robed in snowy white
That loosely flew to left and right –
The leaves upon her falling light –
Through the noises of the night
  She floated down to Camelot: 140
And as the boat-head wound along
The willowy hills and fields among,
They heard her singing her last song,
  The Lady of Shalott.

Heard a carol, mournful, holy,   145
Chanted loudly, chanted lowly,
Till her blood was frozen slowly,
And her eyes were darkened wholly,
  Turned to towered Camelot.
For ere she reached upon the tide   150
The first house by the water-side,
Singing in her song she died,
  The Lady of Shalott.

Under tower and balcony,
By garden-wall and gallery,   155
A gleaming shape she floated by,
Dead-pale between the houses high,
  Silent into Camelot.
Out upon the wharfs they came,
Knight and burgher, lord and dame, 160
And round the prow they read her name,
  The Lady of Shalott.

Who is this? and what is here?
And in the lighted palace near
Died the sound of royal cheer;   165
And they crossed themselves for fear,
  All the knights at Camelot:
But Lancelot mused a little space;
He said, 'She has a lovely face;
God in his mercy lend her grace,   170
  The Lady of Shalott.'

160 **burgher:** freeman, citizen

THE LOTOS-EATERS

'COURAGE!' he said, and pointed toward the land,
'This mounting wave will roll us shoreward soon.'
In the afternoon they came unto a land
In which it seemèd always afternoon.
All round the coast the languid air did swoon, 5
Breathing like one that hath a weary dream.
Full-faced above the valley stood the moon;
And like a downward smoke, the slender stream
Along the cliff to fall and pause and fall did seem.

THE LOTOS-EATERS: In Homer's *Odyssey*, Ulysses (Odysseus), returning from the siege of Troy, visits the land of the lotus-eaters, or Lotophagai, who live on the lotus-fruit, which makes all who eat it forget their home and desire only to live for ever in Lotus-land. Ulysses' crewmen eat the lotus-fruit and fall under its spell, so that Ulysses has to force them to return to the ship

A land of streams! some, like a downward smoke, 10
Slow-dropping veils of thinnest lawn, did go;
And some through wavering lights and shadows
  broke,
Rolling a slumbrous sheet of foam below.
They saw the gleaming river seaward flow
From the inner land: far off, three mountain-tops, 15
Three silent pinnacles of agèd snow,
Stood sunset-flushed: and, dewed with showery drops,
Up-clomb the shadowy pine above the woven copse.

The charmèd sunset lingered low adown
In the red West: through mountain clefts the dale 20
Was seen far ínland, and the yellow down
Bordered with palm, and many a winding vale
And meadow, set with slender galingale;
A land where all things always seemed the same!
And round about the keel with faces pale, 25
Dark faces pale against that rosy flame,
The mild-eyed melancholy Lotos-eaters came.

Branches they bore of that enchanted stem,
Laden with flower and fruit, whereof they gave
To each, but whoso did receive of them, 30
And taste, to him the gushing of the wave
Far far away did seem to mourn and rave
On alien shores; and if his fellow spake,
His voice was thin, as voices from the grave;
And deep-asleep he seemed, yet all awake, 35
And music in his ears his beating heart did make.

They sat them down upon the yellow sand,
Between the sun and moon upon the shore;
And sweet it was to dream of Fatherland,
Of child, and wife, and slave; but evermore 40
Most weary seemed the sea, weary the oar,
Weary the wandering fields of barren foam.
Then some one said, 'We will return no more';
And all at once they sang, 'Our island home
Is far beyond the wave; we will no longer roam.' 45

CHORIC SONG

There is sweet music here that softer falls
Than petals from blown roses on the grass,
Or night-dews on still waters between walls
Of shadowy granite, in a gleaming pass;
Music that gentlier on the spirit lies, 50
Than tired eyelids upon tired eyes;
Music that brings sweet sleep down from the blissful
  skies.
Here are cool mosses deep,
And thro' the moss the ivies creep,
And in the stream the long-leaved flowers weep, 55
And from the craggy ledge the poppy hangs in sleep.

11 **lawn:** fine linen 23 **galingale:** sedge

Why are we weighed upon with heaviness
And utterly consumed with sharp distress,
While all things else have rest from weariness?
All things have rest: why should we toil alone,   60
We only toil, who are the first of things,
And make perpetual moan,
Still from one sorrow to another thrown:
Nor ever fold our wings,
And cease from wanderings,   65
Nor steep our brows in slumber's holy balm;
Nor harken what the inner spirit sings,
'There is no joy but calm!'
Why should we only toil, the roof and crown of
    things?

Lo! in the middle of the wood,   70
The folded leaf is wooed from out the bud
With winds upon the branch, and there
Grows green and broad, and takes no care,
Sun-steeped at noon, and in the moon
Nightly dew-fed; and turning yellow   75
Falls, and floats adown the air.
Lo! sweetened with the summer light,
The full-juiced apple, waxing over-mellow,
Drops in a silent autumn night.
All its allotted length of days,   80
The flower ripens in its place,
Ripens and fades, and falls, and hath no toil,
Fast-rooted in the fruitful soil.

Hateful is the dark-blue sky,
Vaulted o'er the dark-blue sea.   85
Death is the end of life; ah, why
Should life all labour be?
Let us alone. Time driveth onward fast,
And in a little while our lips are dumb.
Let us alone. What is it that will last?   90
All things are taken from us, and become
Portions and parcels of the dreadful Past.
Let us alone. What pleasure can we have
To war with evil? Is there any peace
In ever climbing up the climbing wave?   95
All things have rest, and ripen toward the grave
In silence; ripen, fall and cease:
Give us long rest or death, dark death, or dreamful
    ease.

How sweet it were, hearing the downward stream,
With half-shut eyes ever to seem   100
Falling asleep in a half-dream!
To dream and dream, like yonder amber light,
Which will not leave the myrrh-bush on the height;
To hear each other's whispered speech;
Eating the Lotos day by day,   105

To watch the crisping ripples on the beach,
And tender curving lines of creamy spray;
To lend our hearts and spirits wholly
To the influence of mild-minded melancholy;
To muse and brood and live again in memory,   110
With those old faces of our infancy
Heaped over with a mound of grass,
Two handfuls of white dust, shut in an urn of brass!

Dear is the memory of our wedded lives,
And dear the last embraces of our wives   115
And their warm tears: but all hath suffered change:
For surely now our household hearths are cold:
Our sons inherit us: our looks are strange:
And we should come like ghosts to trouble joy.
Or else the island princes over-bold   120
Have eat our substance, and the minstrel sings
Before them of the ten years' war in Troy,
And our great deeds, as half-forgotten things.
Is there confusion in the little isle?
Let what is broken so remain.   125
The Gods are hard to reconcile:
'Tis hard to settle order once again.
There *is* confusion worse than death,
Trouble on trouble, pain on pain,
Long labour unto agèd breath,   130
Sore task to hearts worn out by many wars
And eyes grown dim with gazing on the pilot-stars.

But, propped on beds of amaranth and moly,
How sweet (while warm airs lull us, blowing lowly)
With half-dropped eyelid still,   135
Beneath a heaven dark and holy,
To watch the long bright river drawing slowly
His waters from the purple hill –
To hear the dewy echoes calling
From cave to cave through the thick-twined vine –   140
To watch the eme.rald-coloured water falling
Through many a wov'n acanthus-wreath divine!
Only to hear and see the far-off sparkling brine,
Only to hear were sweet, stretched out beneath the
    pine.

The Lotos blooms below the barren peak: 145
The Lotos blows by every winding creek:
All day the wind breathes low with mellower tone:
Through every hollow cave and alley lone
Round and round the spicy downs the yellow
    Lotos-dust is blown.
We have had enough of action, and of motion we,   150
Rolled to starboard, rolled to larboard, when the surge
    was seething free,

103 **myrrh-bush:** aromatic plant

118 **inherit us:** take our place   121 **eat:** eaten   132 **pilot-stars:** stars
used by sailors for navigation 133 **amaranth:** legendary flower that
never fades and is thus an emblem of immortality **moly:** magic
herb given by Hermes to Ulysses as an antidote to the spells of Circe
151 **larboard:** port

Where the wallowing monster spouted his
   foam-fountains in the sea.
Let us swear an oath, and keep it with an equal mind,
In the hollow Lotos-land to live and lie reclined
On the hills like Gods together, careless of
   mankind.   155
For they lie beside their nectar, and the bolts are
   hurled
Far below them in the valleys, and the clouds are
   lightly curled
Round their golden houses, girdled with the gleaming
   world:
Where they smile in secret, looking over wasted lands,
Blight and famine, plague and earthquake, roaring
   deeps and fiery sands,   160
Clanging fights, and flaming towns, and sinking ships,
   and praying hands.
But they smile, they find a music centred in a doleful
   song
Steaming up, a lamentation and an ancient tale of
   wrong,
Like a tale of little meaning though the words are
   strong;
Chanted from an ill-used race of men that cleave the
   soil,   165
Sow the seed, and reap the harvest with enduring
   toil,
Storing yearly little dues of wheat, and wine and oil;
Till they perish and they suffer – some, 'tis whispered –
   down in hell
Suffer endless anguish, others in Elysian valleys dwell,
Resting weary limbs at last on beds of asphodel.   170
Surely, surely, slumber is more sweet than toil, the
   shore
Than labour in the deep mid-ocean, wind and wave
   and oar;
Oh, rest ye, brother mariners, we will not wander
   more.

169 **Elysian:** blissful, like Elysium, the Greek Paradise 170 **asphodel:**
a plant of the lily family associated in Greek mythology with death
and the Underworld

ULYSSES

I⊤ little profits that an idle king,
By this still hearth, among these barren crags,
Matched with an aged wife, I mete and dole
Unequal laws unto a savage race,
That hoard, and sleep, and feed, and know not me.   5
I cannot rest from travel: I will drink
Life to the lees: all times I have enjoyed
Greatly, have suffered greatly, both with those
That loved me, and alone; on shore, and when
Through scudding drifts the rainy Hyades   10
Vexed the dim sea: I am become a name;
For always roaming with a hungry heart
Much have I seen and known; cities of men

And manners, climates, councils, governments,
Myself not least, but honoured of them all;   15
And drunk delight of battle with my peers,
Far on the ringing plains of windy Troy.
I am a part of all that I have met;
Yet all experience is an arch wherethrough
Gleams that untravelled world, whose margin fades   20
For ever and for ever when I move.
How dull it is to pause, to make an end,
To rust unburnished, not to shine in use!
As though to breathe were life. Life piled on life
Were all too little, and of one to me   25
Little remains: but every hour is saved
From that eternal silence, something more,
A bringer of new things; and vile it were
For some three suns to store and hoard myself,
And this grey spirit yearning in desire   30
To follow knowledge like a sinking star,
Beyond the utmost bound of human thought.
   This is my son, mine own Telemachus,
To whom I leave the sceptre and the isle –
Well-loved of me, discerning to fulfil   35
This labour, by slow prudence to make mild
A rugged people, and through soft degrees
Subdue them to the useful and the good.
Most blameless is he, centred in the sphere
Of common duties, decent not to fail   40
In offices of tenderness, and pay
Meet adoration to my household gods,
When I am gone. He works his work, I mine.
   There lies the port; the vessel puffs her sail:
There gloom the dark broad seas. My mariners,   45
Souls that have toiled, and wrought, and thought with
   me –
That ever with a frolic welcome took
The thunder and the sunshine, and opposed
Free hearts, free foreheads – you and I are old;
Old age hath yet his honour and his toil;   50
Death closes all: but something ere the end,
Some work of noble note, may yet be done,
Not unbecoming men that strove with Gods.
The lights begin to twinkle from the rocks:
The long day wanes: the slow moon climbs: the deep
Moans round with many voices. Come, my friends,   56
'Tis not too late to seek a newer world.
Push off, and sitting well in order smite
The sounding furrows; for my purpose holds
To sail beyond the sunset, and the baths   60
Of all the western stars, until I die.
It may be that the gulfs will wash us down:
It may be we shall touch the Happy Isles,
And see the great Achilles, whom we knew.
Though much is taken, much abides; and though   65
We are not now that strength which in old days
Moved earth and heaven; that which we are, we are;
One equal temper of heroic hearts,
Made weak by time and fate, but strong in will
To strive, to seek, to find, and not to yield.   70

ULYSSES: Ulysses (Odysseus) is the hero of Homer's epic poem *The Odyssey*, which tells of Ulysses' return from the siege of Troy to his home on the island of Ithaca: 3 **an aged wife:** Penelope, Ulysses' wife, who waited patiently for twenty years for her husband's return, resisting the advances of suitors **mete:** apportion **dole:** deal out 7 **to the lees:** to the dregs 10 **Hyades:** ('*Hye-a-deez*'; literally, 'raining ones') in Greek mythology, five nymphs who supplied moisture to the earth; the daughters of Atlas, they wept so much on the death of their brother Hyas that Zeus took them to heaven and placed them as a group of stars between the Pleiades and Orion 20 **margin:** edge or shore 23 **unburnished:** unpolished 33 **Telemachus:** ('Te-*lem*-a-*kus*') Ulysses' son 34 **the isle:** Ithaca 42 **Meet:** appropriate, fitting 58–9 **sitting . . . furrows:** most Greek ships were propelled by banks of oars 63 **Happy Isles:** Elysium, the Greek Paradise 64 **Achilles:** Greek hero in the Trojan War

'BREAK, BREAK, BREAK'

BREAK, break, break,
　　On thy cold grey stones, O Sea!
And I would that my tongue could utter
　　The thoughts that arise in me.

Oh, well for the fisherman's boy, 　　　　　　　　5
　　That he shouts with his sister at play!
Oh, well for the sailor lad,
　　That he sings in his boat on the bay!

And the stately ships go on
　　To their haven under the hill; 　　　　　　　10
But, oh, for the touch of a vanished hand,
　　And the sound of a voice that is still!

Break, break, break,
　　At the foot of thy crags, O Sea!
But the tender grace of a day that is dead 　　15
　　Will never come back to me.

'THE SPLENDOUR FALLS ON CASTLE WALLS'

　　THE splendour falls on castle walls
　　　　And snowy summits old in story:
　　The long light shakes across the lakes,
　　　　And the wild cataract leaps in glory.
Blow, bugle, blow, set the wild echoes flying, 　5
Blow, bugle; answer, echoes, dying, dying, dying.

　　Oh, hark! oh, hear! how thin and clear,
　　　　And thinner, clearer, farther going!
　　Oh, sweet and far from cliff and scar
　　　　The horns of Elfland faintly blowing! 　　10
Blow, let us hear the purple glens replying:
Blow, bugle; answer, echoes, dying, dying, dying.

　　O love, they die in yon rich sky,
　　　　They faint on hill or field or river:
　　Our echoes roll from soul to soul, 　　　　　15
　　　　And grow for ever and for ever.
Blow, bugle, blow, set the wild echoes flying,
And answer, echoes, answer, dying, dying, dying.

'THE SPLENDOUR FALLS': taken from *The Princess*, a long narrative poem published in 1847 that incorporates several short lyrical poems

'TEARS, IDLE TEARS . . .'

TEARS, idle tears, I know not what they mean,
Tears from the depth of some divine despair
Rise in the heart, and gather to the eyes,
In looking on the happy autumn-fields,
And thinking of the days that are no more. 　　5

Fresh as the first beam glittering on a sail,
That brings our friends up from the underworld,
Sad as the last which reddens over one
That sinks with all we love below the verge;
So sad, so fresh, the days that are no more. 　　10

Ah, sad and strange as in dark summer dawns
The earliest pipe of half-awakened birds
To dying ears, when unto dying eyes
The casement slowly grows a glimmering square;
So sad, so strange, the days that are no more. 　15

Dear as remembered kisses after death,
And sweet as those by hopeless fancy feigned
On lips that are for others; deep as love,
Deep as first love, and wild with all regret;
O Death in Life, the days that are no more. 　　20

'TEARS, IDLE TEARS': another lyrical poem from *The Princess*

From IN MEMORIAM
[ARTHUR HENRY HALLAM (1811–33)]

1

I HELD it truth, with him who sings
　　To one clear harp in divers tones,
　　That men may rise on stepping-stones
Of their dead selves to higher things.

But who shall so forecást the years 　　　　　5
　　And find in loss a gain to match?
　　Or reach a hand through time to catch
The far-off interest of tears?

Let Love clasp Grief lest both be drowned,
　　Let darkness keep her raven gloss: 　　　　10
　　Ah, sweeter to be drunk with loss,
To dance with death, to beat the ground,

Than that the victor Hours should scorn
　　The long result of love, and boast,
　　'Behold the man that loved and lost, 　　　15
But all he was is overworn.'

IN MEMORIAM: **A.H.H.:** On 1 October 1833, Henry Elton wrote to inform Tennyson of the sudden death in Vienna, at the age of 22, of Arthur Henry Hallam, his nephew. Tennyson had met Hallam, a precocious young man of great promise, at Cambridge, and they had become close friends. Within days of receiving the news Tennyson composed the first of the elegiac poems that would eventually become *In Memoriam*. Tennyson's own comments on the poem are included in the notes where appropriate: (1) 1–2 **him who sings . . . tones:** 'I believe I alluded to Goethe' (T) 8 **The far-off interest of tears:** 'The good that grows for us out of grief' (T) 10 **raven:** black 16 **overworn:** 'Spent in time; passed away' (*OED*, citing *In Memoriam*)

2

OLD Yew, which graspest at the stones
   That name the under-lying dead,
   Thy fibres net the dreamless head,
Thy roots are wrapped about the bones.

The seasons bring the flower again,   5
   And bring the firstling to the flock;
   And in the dusk of thee, the clock
Beats out the little lives of men.

Oh, not for thee the glow, the bloom,
   Who changest not in any gale,   10
   Nor branding summer suns avail
To touch thy thousand years of gloom:

And gazing on thee, sullen tree,
   Sick for thy stubborn hardihood,
   I seem to fail from out my blood   15
And grow incorporate into thee.

7

DARK house, by which once more I stand
   Here in the long unlovely street,
   Doors, where my heart was used to beat
So quickly, waiting for a hand,

A hand that can be clasped no more –   5
   Behold me, for I cannot sleep,
   And like a guilty thing I creep
At earliest morning to the door.

He is not here; but far away
   The noise of life begins again,   10
   And ghastly through the drizzling rain
On the bald street breaks the blank day.

9

FAIR ship, that from the Italian shore
   Sailest the placid ocean-plains
   With my lost Arthur's loved remains,
Spread thy full wings, and waft him o'er.

So draw him home to those that mourn   5
   In vain; a favourable speed
   Ruffle thy mirrored mast, and lead
Through prosperous floods his holy urn.

All night no ruder air perplex
   Thy sliding keel, till Phosphor, bright   10
   As our pure love, through early light
Shall glimmer on the dewy decks.

Sphere all your lights around, above;
   Sleep, gentle heavens, before the prow;
   Sleep, gentle winds, as he sleeps now,   15
My friend, the brother of my love;

My Arthur, whom I shall not see
   Till all my widowed race be run;
   Dear as the mother to the son,
More than my brothers are to me.   20

15

TONIGHT the winds begin to rise
   And roar from yonder dropping day:
   The last red leaf is whirled away,
The rooks are blown about the skies;

The forest cracked, the waters curled,   5
   The cattle huddled on the lea;
   And wildly dashed on tower and tree
The sunbeam strikes along the world:

And but for fancies, which aver
   That all thy motions gently pass   10
   Athwart a plane of molten glass,
I scarce could brook the strain and stir

That makes the barren branches loud;
   And but for fear it is not so,
   The wild unrest that lives in woe   15
Would dote and pore on yonder cloud

That rises upward always higher,
   And onward drags a labouring breast,
   And topples round the dreary west,
A looming bastion fringed with fire.   20

21

I SING to him that rests below,
   And, since the grasses round me wave,
   I take the grasses of the grave,
And make them pipes whereon to blow.

The traveller hears me now and then,   5
   And sometimes harshly will he speak:
   'This fellow would make weakness weak,
And melt the waxen hearts of men.'

Another answers, 'Let him be,
   He loves to make parade of pain,   10
   That with his piping he may gain
The praise that comes to constancy.'

A third is wroth: 'Is this an hour
   For private sorrow's barren song,
   When more and more the people throng   15
The chairs and thrones of civil power?

(2) 2 **under-lying:** lying beneath the earth (7) 1 **Dark house:** the Hallams' house in Wimpole Street 10 **The noise of life begins anew:** 'say in Oxford Street' (T) (9) 1 **Fair ship . . .:** Hallam's body was returned to England by ship from Trieste; composed within a few days of Tennyson receiving news of Hallam's death, this is the earliest section of *In Memoriam* 10 **Phosphor:** ('Light-bringer') 'star of dawn' (T); i.e. the morning star, a planet (usually Venus) when it rises before the sun

13 **lights:** stars 18 **widowed:** i.e. Tennyson is depicting himself as Arthur's widow (15) 6 **lea:** meadow, pasture 11 **Athwart:** across 14 **it is not so:** i.e. 'That all thy motions gently pass' (line 10)

'A time to sicken and to swoon,
   When Science reaches forth her arms
   To feel from world to world, and charms
Her secret from the latest moon?'   20

Behold, ye speak an idle thing:
   Ye never knew the sacred dust:
   I do but sing because I must,
And pipe but as the linnets sing:

And one is glad; her note is gay,   25
   For now her little ones have ranged;
   And one is sad; her note is changed,
Because her brood is stol'n away.

27

I ENVY not in any moods
   The captive void of noble rage,
   The linnet born within the cage,
That never knew the summer woods:

I envy not the beast that takes   5
   His licence in the field of time,
   Unfettered by the sense of crime,
To whom a conscience never wakes;

Nor, what may count itself as blest,
   The heart that never plighted troth   10
   But stágnates in the weeds of sloth;
Nor any want-begotten rest.

I hold it true, whate'er befall;
   I feel it, when I sorrow most;
   'Tis better to have loved and lost   15
Than never to have loved at all.

43

If Sleep and Death be truly one,
   And every spirit's folded bloom
   Through all its intervital gloom
In some long trance should slumber on;

Unconscious of the sliding hour,   5
   Bare of the body, might it last,
   And silent traces of the past
Be all the colour of the flower:

So then were nothing lost to man;
   So that still garden of the souls   10
   In many a figured leaf enrolls
The total world since life began;

And love will last as pure and whole
   As when he loved me here in Time,
   And at the spiritual prime   15
Rewaken with the dawning soul.

54

OH, yet we trust that somehow good
   Will be the final goal of ill,
   To pangs of nature, sins of will,
Defécts of doubt, and taints of blood;

That nothing walks with aimless feet;   5
   That not one life shall be destroyed,
   Or cast as rubbish to the void,
When God hath made the pile complete;

That not a worm is cloven in vain;
   That not a moth with vain desire   10
   Is shrivelled in a fruitless fire,
Or but subserves another's gain.

Behold, we know not anything;
   I can but trust that good shall fall
   At last – far off – at last, to all,   15
And every winter change to spring.

So runs my dream: but what am I?
   An infant crying in the night:
   An infant crying for the light:
And with no language but a cry.   20

55

THE wish, that of the living whole
   No life may fail beyond the grave,
   Derives it not from what we have
The likest God within the soul?

Are God and Nature then at strife,   5
   That Nature lends such evil dreams?
   So careful of the type she seems,
So careless of the single life;

That I, considering everywhere
   Her secret meaning in her deeds,   10
   And finding that of fifty seeds,
She often brings but one to bear,

I falter where I firmly trod,
   And falling with my weight of cares
   Upon the great world's altar-stairs   15
That slope through darkness up to God,

I stretch lame hands of faith, and grope,
   And gather dust and chaff, and call
   To what I feel is Lord of all,
And faintly trust the larger hope.   20

56

'SO careful of the type'? but no.
   From scarpèd cliff and quarried stone
   She cries, 'A thousand types are gone:
I care for nothing, all shall go.

---

(27) 6 **licence:** liberty 12 **want-begotten:** the sense is unclear; the obvious meaning would appear to be 'deserved' or 'needed', but the context suggests 'unmerited' or 'not earned by exertion' (43) 3 **intervital:** 'In the passage between this life and the next' (T) 11 **figured:** 'painted with the past life' (T) 15 **spiritual prime:** 'Dawn of the spiritual life hereafter' (T)

(55) 7 **type:** species   (56) 1 **'So careful of the type':** see 55.7 above 2 **scarpèd:** 'cut away vertically' (T)

'Thou makest thine appeal to me:⠀⠀⠀⠀⠀⠀5
⠀⠀I bring to life, I bring to death:
⠀⠀The spirit does but mean the breath:
I know no more.' And he, shall he,

Man, her last work, who seemed so fair,
⠀⠀Such splendid purpose in his eyes,⠀⠀⠀⠀10
⠀⠀Who rolled the psalm to wintry skies,
Who built him fanes of fruitless prayer,

Who trusted God was love indeed
⠀⠀And love Creation's final law –
⠀⠀Though Nature, red in tooth and claw⠀⠀⠀15
With rávine, shrieked against his creed –

Who loved, who suffered countless ills,
⠀⠀Who battled for the True, the Just,
⠀⠀Be blown about the desert dust,
Or sealed within the iron hills?⠀⠀⠀⠀⠀⠀20

No more? A monster then, a dream,
⠀⠀A discord. Dragons of the prime,
⠀⠀That tare each other in their slime,
Were mellow music matched with him.

O life as futile, then, as frail!⠀⠀⠀⠀⠀⠀25
⠀⠀Oh, for thy voice to soothe and bless!
⠀⠀What hope of answer, or redress?
Behind the veil, behind the veil.

69

I DREAMED there would be spring no more,
⠀⠀That Nature's ancient power was lost:
⠀⠀The streets were black with smoke and frost,
They chattered trifles at the door:

I wandered from the noisy town,⠀⠀⠀⠀⠀⠀5
⠀⠀I found a wood with thorny boughs:
⠀⠀I took the thorns to bind my brows,
I wore them like a civic crown:

I met with scoffs, I met with scorns
⠀⠀From youth and babe and hoary hairs:⠀⠀⠀10
⠀⠀They called me in the public squares
The fool that wears a crown of thorns:

They called me fool, they called me child:
⠀⠀I found an angel of the night;
⠀⠀The voice was low, the look was bright;⠀⠀15
He looked upon my crown and smiled:

He reached the glory of a hand,
⠀⠀That seemed to touch it into leaf:
⠀⠀The voice was not the voice of grief,
The words were hard to understand.⠀⠀⠀⠀20

104

THE time draws near the birth of Christ;
⠀⠀The moon is hid, the night is still;
⠀⠀A single church below the hill
Is pealing, folded in the mist.

A single peal of bells below,⠀⠀⠀⠀⠀⠀5
⠀⠀That wakens at this hour of rest
⠀⠀A single murmur in the breast,
That these are not the bells I know.

Like strangers' voices here they sound,
⠀⠀In lands where not a memory strays,⠀⠀⠀10
⠀⠀Nor landmark breathes of other days,
But all is new unhallowed ground.

106

RING out, wild bells, to the wild sky,
⠀⠀The flying cloud, the frosty light:
⠀⠀The year is dying in the night;
Ring out, wild bells, and let him die.

Ring out the old, ring in the new,⠀⠀⠀⠀5
⠀⠀Ring, happy bells, across the snow:
⠀⠀The year is going, let him go;
Ring out the false, ring in the true.

Ring out the grief that saps the mind,
⠀⠀For those that here we see no more;⠀⠀⠀10
⠀⠀Ring out the feud of rich and poor,
Ring in redress to all mankind.

Ring out a slowly dying cause,
⠀⠀And ancient forms of party strife;
⠀⠀Ring in the nobler modes of life,⠀⠀⠀⠀15
With sweeter manners, purer laws.

Ring out the want, the care, the sin,
⠀⠀The faithless coldness of the times;
⠀⠀Ring out, ring out thy mournful rhymes,
But ring the fuller minstrel in.⠀⠀⠀⠀⠀20

Ring out false pride in place and blood,
⠀⠀The civic slander and the spite;
⠀⠀Ring in the love of truth and right,
Ring in the common love of good.

Ring out old shapes of foul disease;⠀⠀⠀25
⠀⠀Ring out the narrowing lust of gold;
⠀⠀Ring out the thousand wars of old,
Ring in the thousand years of peace.

Ring in the valiant man and free,
⠀⠀The larger heart, the kindlier hand;⠀⠀⠀30
⠀⠀Ring out the darkness of the land,
Ring in the Christ that is to be.

12 **fanes:** temples 22 **Dragons of the prime:** dinosaurs 23 **tare:** tear (archaic) (69) 10 **hoary:** frosty-white

(104) 3 **A single church:** 'Waltham Abbey church' (T) 12 **But all is new unhallowed ground:** 'High Beech, Epping Forest (where we were living)' (T) (106) 32 **Ring in the Christ that is to be:** 'The broader Christianity of the future' (T)

115

Now fades the last long streak of snow,
　Now burgeons every maze of quick
　About the flowering squares, and thick
By ashen roots the violets blow.

Now rings the woodland loud and long,　　　　5
　The distance takes a lovelier hue,
　And drowned in yonder living blue
The lark becomes a sightless song.

Now dance the lights on lawn and lea,
　The flocks are whiter down the vale,　　　　10
　And milkier every milky sail
On winding stream or distant sea;

Where now the seamew pipes, or dives
　In yonder greening gleam, and fly
　The happy birds, that change their sky　　　　15
To build and brood; that live their lives

From land to land; and in my breast
　Spring wakens too; and my regret
　Becomes an April violet,
And buds and blossoms like the rest.　　　　20

119

Doors, where my heart was used to beat
　So quickly, not as one that weeps
　I come once more; the city sleeps;
I smell the meadow in the street;

I hear a chirp of birds; I see　　　　5
　Betwixt the black fronts long-withdrawn
　A light-blue lane of early dawn,
And think of early days and thee,

And bless thee, for thy lips are bland,
　And bright the friendship of thine eye;　　　　10
　And in my thoughts with scarce a sigh
I take the pressure of thine hand.

126

Love is and was my Lord and King,
　And in his presence I attend
　To hear the tidings of my friend,
Which every hour his couriers bring.

Love is and was my King and Lord,　　　　5
　And will be, though as yet I keep
　Within his court on earth, and sleep
Encompassed by his faithful guard,

And hear at times a sentinel
　Who moves about from place to place,　　　　10
　And whispers to the worlds of space,
In the deep night, that all is well.

131

O Living will that shalt endure
　When all that seems shall suffer shock,
　Rise in the spiritual rock,
Flow through our deeds and make them pure,

That we may lift from out of dust　　　　5
　A voice as unto him that hears,
　A cry above the conquered years
To one that with us works, and trust,

With faith that comes of self-control,
　The truths that never can be proved　　　　10
　Until we close with all we loved,
And all we flow from, soul in soul.

MAUD
A MONODRAMA

PART ONE
1

I Hate the dreadful hollow behind the little wood,
Its lips in the field above are dabbled with blood-red
　　heath,
The red-ribbed ledges drip with a silent horror of
　　blood,
And Echo there, whatever is asked her, answers
　　'Death.'

For there in the ghastly pit long since a body was
　　found,　　　　5
His who had given me life – O father! O God! was it
　　well? –
Mangled, and flattened, and crushed, and dinted into
　　the ground:
There yet lies the rock that fell with him when he fell.

Did he fling himself down? who knows? for a vast
　　speculation had failed,
And ever he muttered and maddened, and ever
　　wanned with despair,　　　　10
And out he walked when the wind like a broken
　　worldling wailed,
And the flying gold of the ruined woodlands drove
　　through the air.

Maud: **A Monodrama**: a dramatic work for one performer;
according to Tennyson, 'The peculiarity of this poem is that
different phases of passion in one person take the place of
different characters'. (Part 1)　4 **Echo**: Echo fell in love with
Narcissus, but when he rejected her she wasted away until only her
voice remained　7 **dinted**: forced　9 **a vast speculation had failed**:
the rapid expansion of British commerce in the mid-nineteenth
century produced a massive eruption of financial schemes, many
of them unsound or downright fraudulent, most notably perhaps
the 'Railway Mania' of the 1840s that brought ruin to many
investors; even as late as 1873, Lewis Carroll could use the prospect
of a railway investment to frighten the Snark (3.30)　10 **wanned**:
grew pale

(115) 2 **quick**: couch-grass　(119) 1 **Doors, where my heart was used
to beat**: the Hallam house in Wimpole Street　(126) 9 **sentinel**: sentry

I remember the time, for the roots of my hair were stirred

By a shuffled step, by a dead weight trailed, by a whispered fright,

And my pulses closed their gates with a shock on my heart as I heard   15

The shrill-edged shriek of a mother divide the shuddering night.

Villainy somewhere! whose? One says, we are villains all.

Not he: his honest fame should at least by me be maintained:

But that old man, now lord of the broad estate and the Hall,

Dropped off gorged from a scheme that had left us flaccid and drained.   20

Why do they prate of the blessings of Peace? we have made them a curse,

Pickpockets, each hand lusting for all that is not its own;

And lust of gain, in the spirit of Cain, is it better or worse

Than the heart of the citizen hissing in war on his own hearthstone?

But these are the days of advance, the works of the men of mind,   25

When who but a fool would have faith in a tradesman's ware or his word?

Is it peace or war? Civil war, as I think, and that of a kind

The viler, as underhand, not openly bearing the sword.

Sooner or later I too may passively take the print

Of the golden age – why not? I have neither hope nor trust;   30

May make my heart as a millstone, set my face as a flint,

Cheat and be cheated, and die: who knows? we are ashes and dust.

Peace sitting under her olive, and slurring the days gone by,

When the poor are hovelled and hustled together, each sex, like swine,

When only the ledger lives, and when only not all men lie;   35

Peace in her vineyard – yes! – but a company forges the wine.

And the vitriol madness flushes up in the ruffian's head,

Till the filthy by-lane rings to the yell of the trampled wife,

And chalk and alum and plaster are sold to the poor for bread,

And the spirit of murder works in the very means of life,   40

And Sleep must lie down armed, for the villainous centre-bits

Grind on the wakeful ear in the hush of the moonless nights,

While another is cheating the sick of a few last gasps, as he sits

To pestle a poisoned poison behind his crimson lights.

When a Mammonite mother kills her babe for a burial fee,   45

And Timour-Mammon grins on a pile of children's bones,

Is it peace or war? better, war! loud war by land and by sea,

War with a thousand battles, and shaking a hundred thrones.

For I trust if an enemy's fleet came yonder round by the hill,

And the rushing battle-bolt sang from the three-decker out of the foam,   50

That the smooth-faced snubnosed rogue would leap from his counter and till,

And strike, if he could, were it but with his cheating yardwand, home. –

---

20 **Dropped off gorged:** i.e. like a leech 23 **in the spirit of Cain:** Cain slew his brother Abel (Genesis 4); 'And wherefore slew he him? Because his own works were evil, and his brother's righteous' (1 John 3.12) 32 **we are ashes and dust:** echoing the burial service in the Book of Common Prayer: 'ashes to ashes, dust to dust' 33–6 **Peace . . . vineyard:** the olive was an ancient symbol of peace and fruitfulness

37 **the vitriol madness:** oil of vitriol is concentrated sulphuric acid; during the civil unrest of the 1840s, particularly in Ireland, throwing vitriol became a common practice 39 **And chalk . . . for bread:** the adulteration of food with such substances as chalk, alum and plaster of Paris, often with fatal consequences (particularly among the poor), was a 19th-century scandal 41 **centre-bits:** a centre-bit was 'An instrument turning on a projecting centre-point, used for making cylindrical holes. (Noted as a burglar's tool.)' (*OED*, citing *Maud*) 44 **a poisoned poison:** Victorian chemists prepared their own medicines, and so could adulterate them to increase profits; the emphatic repetition of 'poison' here suggests a specific reference to opium, which formed the basis of many popular medicines **behind his crimson lights:** possibly referring to the practice of chemists to place large bottles of coloured water (usually red, green and blue), illuminated by carefully placed lights, in their shop windows 45 **When a Mammonite mother . . . burial fee:** even a modest Victorian funeral could be expensive, and 'burial clubs' enabled the poor to put money aside to cover the cost, but in some instances poverty drove parents to murder their children in order to recover their savings; in this context, 'Mammonite' (worshipper of Mammon, god of riches) is perhaps unfair 46 **Timour-Mammon:** the Tartar conqueror Timur (1336–1405), better-known in English as Tamburlaine, seems to be linked to the god of riches here to suggest the aggressive pursuit of wealth 50 **battle-bolt:** cannon-ball **three-decker:** warship with three gun-decks 52 **cheating yardwand:** i.e. the three-foot ruler used by the draper to measure yards of cloth has been made deliberately inaccurate to cheat his customers

What! am I raging alone as my father raged in his
    mood?
Must *I* too creep to the hollow and dash myself down
    and die
Rather than hold by the law that I made, nevermore
    to brood   55
On a horror of shattered limbs and a wretched
    swindler's lie?

Would there be sorrow for *me*? there was *love* in the
    passionate shriek,
Love for the silent thing that had made false haste to
    the grave –
Wrapped in a cloak, as I saw him, and thought he
    would rise and speak
And rave at the lie and the liar, ah God, as he used to
    rave.   60

I am sick of the Hall and the hill, I am sick of the
    moor and the main.
Why should I stay? can a sweeter chance ever come to
    me here?
Oh, having the nerves of motion as well as the nerves
    of pain,
Were it not wise if I fled from the place and the pit
    and the fear?

Workmen up at the Hall! – they are coming back from
    abroad;   65
The dark old place will be gilt by the touch of a
    millionaire:
I have heard, I know not whence, of the singular
    beauty of Maud;
I played with the girl when a child; she promised then
    to be fair,

Maud with her venturous climbings and tumbles and
    childish escapes,
Maud the delight of the village, the ringing joy of the
    Hall,   70
Maud with her sweet purse-mouth when my father
    dangled the grapes,
Maud the beloved of my mother, the moon-faced
    darling of all, –

What is she now? My dreams are bad. She may bring
    me a curse.
No, there is fatter game on the moor; she will let me
    alone.
Thanks, for the fiend best knows whether woman or
    man be the worse.   75
I will bury myself in myself, and the Devil may pipe to
    his own.

2

Long have I sighed for a calm: God grant I may find it
    at last!
It will never be broken by Maud, she has neither
    savour nor salt,
But a cold and clear-cut face, as I found when her
    carriage passed,
Perfectly beautiful: let it be granted her: where is the
    fault?   80
All that I saw (for her eyes were downcast, not to be
    seen)
Faultily faultless, icily regular, splendidly null,
Dead perfection, no more; nothing more, if it had not
    been
For a chance of travel, a paleness, an hour's defect of
    the rose,
Or an underlip, you may call it a little too ripe, too
    full,   85
Or the least little delicate aquiline curve in a sensitive
    nose,
From which I escaped heart-free, with the least little
    touch of spleen.

3

Cold and clear-cut face, why come you so cruelly
    meek,
Breaking a slumber in which all spleenful folly was
    drowned,
Pale with the golden beam of an eyelash dead on the
    cheek,   90
Passionless, pale, cold face, star-sweet on a gloom
    profound;
Womanlike, taking revenge too deep for a transient
    wrong
Done but in thought to your beauty, and ever as pale
    as before
Growing and fading and growing upon me without a
    sound,
Luminous, gemlike, ghostlike, deathlike, half the night
    long   95
Growing and fading and growing, till I could bear it
    no more,
But arose, and all by myself in my own dark garden
    ground,
Listening now to the tide in its broad-flung
    shipwrecking roar,
Now to the scream of a maddened beach dragged
    down by the wave,
Walked in a wintry wind by a ghastly glimmer, and
    found   100
The shining daffodil dead, and Orion low in his
    grave.

---

71 **purse-mouth:** pursed lips

78 **neither savour nor salt:** 'Ye are the salt of the earth: but if the
salt have lost his savour, wherewith shall it be salted?' (Matthew 5.13)
89 **spleenful:** peevish 101 **Orion:** The Hunter, a constellation

4

A million emeralds break from the ruby-budded lime
In the little grove where I sit – ah, wherefore cannot I be
Like things of the season gay, like the bountiful season bland,
When the far-off sail is blown by the breeze of a softer clime,   105
Half-lost in the liquid azure bloom of a crescent sea,
The silent sapphire-spangled marriage ring of the land?

Below me, there, is the village, and looks how quiet and small!
And yet bubbles o'er like a city, with gossip, scandal, and spite;
And Jack on his ale-house bench has as many lies as a czar;   110
And here on the landward side, by a red rock, glimmers the Hall;
And up in the high Hall-garden I see her pass like a light;
But sorrow seize me if ever that light be my leading star!

When have I bowed to her father, the wrinkled head of the race?
I met her today with her brother, but not to her brother I bowed: 115
I bowed to his lady-sister as she rode by on the moor;
But the fire of a foolish pride flashed over her beautiful face.
O child, you wrong your beauty, believe it, in being so proud;
Your father has wealth well-gotten, and I am nameless and poor.

I keep but a man and a maid, ever ready to slander and steal;   120
I know it, and smile a hard-set smile, like a stoic, or like
A wiser epicurean, and let the world have its way:
For nature is one with rapine, a harm no preacher can heal;
The Mayfly is torn by the swallow, the sparrow speared by the shrike,
And the whole little wood where I sit is a world of plunder and prey.   125

We are puppets, Man in his pride, and Beauty fair in her flower;
Do we move ourselves, or are moved by an unseen hand at a game
That pushes us off from the board, and others ever succeed?
Ah, yet, we cannot be kind to each other here for an hour;
We whisper, and hint, and chuckle, and grin at a brother's shame;   130
However we brave it out, we men are a little breed.

A monstrous eft was of old the Lord and Master of Earth,
For him did his high sun flame, and his river billowing ran,
And he felt himself in his force to be Nature's crowning race.
As nine months go to the shaping an infant ripe for his birth,   135
So many a million of ages have gone to the making of man:
He now is first, but is he the last? is he not too base?

The man of science himself is fonder of glory, and vain,
An eye well-practised in nature, a spirit bounded and poor;
The passionate heart of the poet is whirled into folly and vice.   140
I would not marvel at either, but keep a temperate brain;
For not to desire or admire, if a man could learn it, were more
Than to walk all day like the sultan of old in a garden of spice.

For the drift of the Maker is dark, an Isis hid by the veil.
Who knows the ways of the world, how God will bring them about?   145
Our planet is one, the suns are many, the world is wide.
Shall I weep if a Poland fall? shall I shriek if a Hungary fail?
Or an infant civilisation be ruled with rod or with knout?
I have not made the world, and He that made it will guide.

---

132 **eft:** lizard   144 **drift of the Maker:** possibly, God's meaning or purpose **Isis hid by the veil:** Isis was an Eyptian goddess; the Greek philosopher Proclus (*c.*410–85) mentions a statue of Isis bearing the inscription: 'I am that which is, has been, and shall be. My veil no one has lifted. The fruit I bore was the sun.' Thus, 'to lift the veil of Isis' means to get to the heart of a mystery   148 **knout:** whip used in Russia for floggings

110 **as many lies as a czar:** 'I've hated Russia ever since I was born, and I'll hate her till I die!' (T); Nicholas I was czar of Russia at the start of the Crimean War and was vilified in the English press   119 **nameless:** undistinguished, a commoner   120 **keep:** employ **man:** manservant

Be mine a philosopher's life in the quiet woodland
    ways,   150
Where if I cannot be gay let a passionless peace be my
    lot,
Far-off from the clamour of liars belied in the hubbub
    of lies;
From the long-necked geese of the world that are ever
    hissing dispraise
Because their natures are little, and, whether he heed
    it or not,
Where each man walks with his head in a cloud of
    poisonous flies.   155

And most of all would I flee from the cruel madness
    of love,
The honey of poison-flowers and all the measureless
    ill.
Ah, Maud, you milkwhite fawn, you are all unmeet for
    a wife.
Your mother is mute in her grave as her image in
    marble above;
Your father is ever in London, you wander about at
    your will;   160
You have but fed on the roses and lain in the lilies of
    life.

5

A voice by the cedar tree
In the meadow under the Hall!
She is singing an air that is known to me,
A passionate ballad gallant and gay,   165
A martial song like a trumpet's call!
Singing alone in the morning of life,
In the happy morning of life and of May,
Singing of men that in battle array,
Ready in heart and ready in hand,   170
March with banner and bugle and fife
To the death, for their native land.

Maud with her exquisite face,
And wild voice pealing up to the sunny sky,
And feet like sunny gems on an English green,   175
Maud in the light of her youth and her grace,
Singing of Death, and of Honour that cannot die,
Till I well could weep for a time so sordid and mean,
And myself so languid and base.

Silence, beautiful voice!   180
Be still, for you only trouble the mind
With a joy in which I cannot rejoice,
A glory I shall not find.
Still! I will hear you no more,
For your sweetness hardly leaves me a choice   / 185
But to move to the meadow and fall before
Her feet on the meadow grass, and adore,
Not her, who is neither courtly nor kind,
Not her, not her, but a voice.

184 **Still!:** Be still!

6

Morning arises stormy and pale,   190
No sun, but a wannish glare
In fold upon fold of hueless cloud,
And the budded peaks of the wood are bowed
Caught and cuffed by the gale:
I had fancied it would be fair.   195

Whom but Maud should I meet
Last night, when the sunset burned
On the blossomed gable-ends
At the head of the village street,
Whom but Maud should I meet?   200
And she touched my hand with a smile so sweet,
She made me divine amends
For a courtesy not returned.

And thus a delicate spark
Of glowing and growing light   205
Through the livelong hours of the dark
Kept itself warm in the heart of my dreams,
Ready to burst in a coloured flame;
Till at last when the morning came
In a cloud, it faded, and seems   210
But an ashen-grey delight.

What if with her sunny hair,
And smile as sunny as cold,
She meant to weave me a snare
Of some coquettish deceit,   215
Cleopatra-like as of old
To entangle me when we met,
To have her lion roll in a silken net
And fawn at a victor's feet.

Ah, what shall I be at fifty   220
Should Nature keep me alive,
If I find the world so bitter
When I am but twenty-five?
Yet, if she were not a cheat,
If Maud were all that she seemed,   225
And her smile were all that I dreamed,
Then the world were not so bitter
But a smile could make it sweet.

What if though her eye seemed full
Of a kind intent to me,   230
What if that dandy-despot, he,
That jewelled mass of millinery,
That oiled and curled Assyrian Bull

191 **wannish:** pale 216 **Cleopatra:** queen of Egypt (69–30 BC) who captivated first Julius Caesar and then Mark Antony 233 **That oiled and curled Assyrian Bull:** 'With hair curled like that of the bulls on Assyrian sculpture' (T); Tennyson would have seen the illustration of the winged bull of Nineveh, excavated by Austen Henry Layard, in his copy of Layard's *Nineveh and Its Remains* (1849). Layard, with whom Tennyson became acquainted, was later an MP and a fierce critic of the government's conduct of the Crimean War, which impinged on the final part of *Maud*

Smelling of musk and of insolence,
Her brother, from whom I keep aloof,   235
Who wants the finer politic sense
To mask, though but in his own behoof,
With a glassy smile his brutal scorn –
What if he had told her yestermorn
How prettily for his own sweet sake   240
A face of tenderness might be feigned,
And a moist mirage in desert eyes,
That so, when the rotten hustings shake
In another month to his brazen lies,
A wretched vote may be gained.   245

For a raven ever croaks, at my side,
Keep watch and ward, keep watch and ward,
Or thou wilt prove their tool.
Yea, too, myself from myself I guard,
For often a man's own angry pride   250
Is cap and bells for a fool.

Perhaps the smile and tender tone
Came out of her pitying womanhood,
For am I not, am I not, here alone
So many a summer since she died,   255
My mother, who was so gentle and good?
Living alone in an empty house,
Here half-hid in the gleaming wood,
Where I hear the dead at midday moan,
And the shrieking rush of the wainscot mouse,   260
And my own sad name in corners cried,
When the shiver of dancing leaves is thrown
About its echoing chambers wide,
Till a morbid hate and horror have grown
Of a world in which I have hardly mixed,   265
And a morbid eating lichen fixed
On a heart half-turned to stone.

O heart of stone, are you flesh, and caught
By that you swore to withstand?
For what was it else within me wrought   270
But, I fear, the new strong wine of love,
That made my tongue so stammer and trip
When I saw the treasured splendour, her hand,
Come sliding out of her sacred glove,
And the sunlight broke from her lip?   275

I have played with her when a child;
She remembers it now we meet.
Ah well, well, well, I *may* be beguiled
By some coquettish deceit.
Yet, if she were not a cheat,   280
If Maud were all that she seemed,
And her smile had all that I dreamed,
Then the world were not so bitter
But a smile could make it sweet.

7

Did I hear it half in a doze   285
    Long since, I know not where?
Did I dream it an hour ago,
    When asleep in this arm-chair?

Men were drinking together,
    Drinking and talking of me;   290
'Well, if it prove a girl, the boy
    Will have plenty: so let it be.'

Is it an echo of something
    Read with a boy's delight,
Viziers nodding together   295
    In some Arabian night?

Strange, that I hear two men,
    Somewhere, talking of me;
'Well, if it prove a girl, my boy
    Will have plenty: so let it be.'   300

8

She came to the village church,
And sat by a pillar alone;
An angel watching an urn
Wept over her, carved in stone;
And once, but once, she lifted her eyes,   305
And suddenly, sweetly, strangely blushed
To find they were met by my own;
And suddenly, sweetly, my heart beat stronger
And thicker, until I heard no longer
The snowy-banded, dilettante,   310
Delicate-handed priest intone;
And thought, is it pride, and mused and sighed
'No, surely, now it cannot be pride.'

9

I was walking a mile,
More than a mile from the shore,   315
The sun looked out with a smile
Betwixt the cloud and the moor,
And riding at set of day
Over the dark moor land,
Rapidly riding far away,   320
She waved to me with her hand.
There were two at her side,
Something flashed in the sun,
Down by the hill I saw them ride,
In a moment they were gone: 325
Like a sudden spark
Struck vainly in the night,
Then returns the dark
With no more hope of light.

289–96 **Men were drinking . . . Arabian night:** a reference to a tale in *The Arabian Nights* concerning two brothers who agree to marry on the same day and, if their wives should then give birth to a boy and a girl, to give the children to each other in marriage 295 **Viziers:** ('vih-*zeers*') Muslim ministers or councillors

234 **musk:** strong animal smell 237 **behoof:** benefit 247 **watch and ward:** uninterrupted vigilance day and night 251 **cap and bells:** the trademark of a court jester

10

Sick, am I sick of a jealous dread? 330
Was not one of the two at her side
This new-made lord, whose splendour plucks
The slavish hat from the villager's head?
Whose old grandfather has lately died,
Gone to a blacker pit, for whom 335
Grimy nakedness dragging his trucks
And laying his trams in a poisoned gloom
Wrought, till he crept from a gutted mine
Master of half a servile shire,
And left his coal all turned into gold 340
To a grandson, first of his noble line,
Rich in the grace all women desire,
Strong in the power that all men adore,
And simper and set their voices lower,
And soften as if to a girl, and hold 345
Awe-stricken breaths at a work divine,
Seeing his gewgaw castle shine,
New as his title, built last year,
There amid perky larches and pine,
And over the sullen-purple moor 350
(Look at it) pricking a cockney ear.

What, has he found my jewel out?
For one of the two that rode at her side
Bound for the Hall, I am sure was he:
Bound for the Hall, and I think for a bride. 355
Blithe would her brother's acceptance be.
Maud could be gracious too, no doubt
To a lord, a captain, a padded shape,
A bought commission, a waxen face,
A rabbit mouth that is ever agape – 360
Bought? what is it he cannot buy?
And therefore splenetic, personal, base,
A wounded thing with a rancorous cry,
At war with myself and a wretched race,
Sick, sick to the heart of life, am I. 365

Last week came one to the county town,
To preach our poor little army down,
And play the game of the despot kings,
Though the state has done it and thrice as well:
This broad-brimmed hawker of holy things, 370
Whose ear is crammed with his cotton, and rings
Even in dreams to the chink of his pence,
This huckster put down war! can he tell
Whether war be a cause or a consequence?
Put down the passions that make earth Hell! 375
Down with ambition, avarice, pride,
Jealousy, down! cut off from the mind

The bitter springs of anger and fear;
Down too, down at your own fireside,
With the evil tongue and the evil ear, 380
For each is at war with mankind.

I wish I could hear again
The chivalrous battle-song
That she warbled alone in her joy!
I might persuade myself then 385
She would not do herself this great wrong,
To take a wanton dissolute boy
For a man and leader of men.

Ah God, for a man with heart, head, hand,
Like some of the simple great ones gone 390
For ever and ever by,
One still strong man in a blatant land,
Whatever they call him, what care I,
Aristocrat, democrat, autocrat – one
Who can rule and dare not lie. 395

And, ah, for a man to arise in me,
That the man I am may cease to be!

11

Oh, let the solid ground
    Not fail beneath my feet
Before my life has found 400
    What some have found so sweet;
Then let come what come may,
What matter if I go mad,
I shall have had my day.

Let the sweet heavens endure, 405
    Not close and darken above me
Before I am quite quite sure
    That there is one to love me;
Then let come what come may
To a life that has been so sad, 410
I shall have had my day.

12

Birds in the high Hall-garden
    When twilight was falling,
'Maud, Maud, Maud, Maud,'
    They were crying and calling. 415

Where was Maud? in our wood;
    And I, who else, was with her,
Gathering woodland lilies,
    Myriads blow together.

Birds in our wood sang 420
    Ringing through the valleys,
'Maud is here, here, here
    In among the lilies.'

332–3 **splendour plucks . . . head:** i.e. the villagers doff their caps to
him as he passes 336 **Grimy nakedness:** the workers (including
women and children) in the coal-mine 337 **trams:** here the track for
the carts that carried the coal 347 **gewgaw:** toy 351 **cockney:** upstart;
in the 19th century, 'cockney' was frequently a derogatory term

I kissed her slender hand,
　She took the kiss sedately;   425
Maud is not seventeen,
　But she is tall and stately.

I to cry out on pride
　Who have won her favour!
Oh, Maud were sure of Heaven   430
　If lowliness could save her.

I know the way she went
　Home with her maiden posy,
For her feet have touched the meadows
　And left the daisies rosy.   435

Birds in the high Hall-garden
　Were crying and calling to her,
'Where is Maud, Maud, Maud?
　One is come to woo her.'

Look, a horse at the door,   440
　And little King Charley snarling,
Go back, my lord, across the moor,
　You are not her darling.

13

Scorned, to be scorned by one that I scorn,
Is that a matter to make me fret?   445
That a calamity hard to be borne?
Well, he may live to hate me yet.
Fool that I am to be vexed with his pride!
I passed him, I was crossing his lands;
He stood on the path a little aside;   450
His face, as I grant, in spite of spite,
Has a broad-blown comeliness, red and white,
And six feet two, as I think, he stands;
But his essences turned the live air sick,
And barbarous opulence jewel-thick   455
Sunned itself on his breast and his hands.

Who shall call me ungentle, unfair,
I longed so heartily then and there
To give him the grasp of fellowship;
But while I passed he was humming an air,   460
Stopped, and then with a riding whip
Leisurely tapping a glossy boot,
And curving a contumelious lip,
Gorgonised me from head to foot
With a stony British stare.   465

441 **King Charley:** a King Charles spaniel 443 **You are not her darling:** an allusion to the popular song by Carolina, Baroness Nairne: 'Charlie is my darling, my darling, my darling,/Charlie is my darling, the young chevalier [cavalier]'; it plays on the earlier reference to King Charles (line 441) 454 **essences:** scents 463 **contumelious:** scornful, haughtily contemptuous 464 **Gorgonised:** in Greek mythology the Gorgons were three female monsters (most notably Medusa) with snakes for hair and with the ability to turn their victims to stone with a glance

Why sits he here in his father's chair?
That old man never comes to his place:
Shall I believe him ashamed to be seen?
For only once, in the village street,
Last year, I caught a glimpse of his face,   470
A grey old wolf and a lean.
Scarcely, now, would I call him a cheat;
For then, perhaps, as a child of deceit,
She might by a true descent be untrue;
And Maud is as true as Maud is sweet: 475
Though I fancy her sweetness only due
To the sweeter blood by the other side;
Her mother has been a thing complete,
However she came to be so allied.
And fair without, faithful within,   480
Maud to him is nothing akin:
Some peculiar mystic grace
Made her only the child of her mother,
And heaped the whole inherited sin
On that huge scapegoat of the race,   485
All, all upon the brother.

Peace, angry spirit, and let him be!
Has not his sister smiled on me?

14

Maud has a garden of roses
And lilies fair on a lawn;   490
There she walks in her state
And tends upon bed and bower,
And thither I climbed at dawn
And stood by her garden-gate;
A lion ramps at the top,   495
He is clasped by a passion-flower.

Maud's own little oak-room
(Which Maud, like a precious stone
Set in the heart of the carven gloom,
Lights with herself, when alone   500
She sits by her music and books
And her brother lingers late
With a roistering company) looks
Upon Maud's own garden-gate:
And I thought as I stood, if a hand, as white   505
As ocean-foam in the moon, were laid
On the hasp of the window, and my Delight
Had a sudden desire, like a glorious ghost, to glide,
Like a beam of the seventh Heaven, down to my side,
There were but a step to be made.   510

The fancy flattered my mind,
And again seemed overbold;
Now I thought that she cared for me,
Now I thought she was kind
Only because she was cold.   515

497 **oak-room:** oak-panelled room

I heard no sound where I stood
But the rivulet on from the lawn
Running down to my own dark wood;
Or the voice of the long sea-wave as it swelled
Now and then in the dim-grey dawn; 520
But I looked, and round, all round the house I beheld
The death-white curtain drawn;
Felt a horror over me creep,
Prickle my skin and catch my breath,
Knew that the death-white curtain meant but sleep,
Yet I shuddered and thought like a fool of the sleep of
    death. 526

15

So dark a mind within me dwells,
   And I make myself such evil cheer,
That if *I* be dear to some one else,
   Then some one else may have much to fear; 530
But if *I* be dear to some one else,
   Then I should be to myself more dear.
Shall I not take care of all that I think,
Yea ev'n of wretched meat and drink,
If I be dear, 535
If I be dear to some one else.

16

This lump of earth has left his estate
The lighter by the loss of his weight;
And so that he find what he went to seek,
And fulsome Pleasure clog him, and drown 540
His heart in the gross mud-honey of town,
He may stay for a year who has gone for a week:
But this is the day when I must speak,
And I see my Oread coming down,
Oh, this is the day! 545
O beautiful creature, what am I
That I dare to look her way;
Think I may hold dominion sweet,
Lord of the pulse that is lord of her breast,
And dream of her beauty with tender dread, 550
From the delicate Arab arch of her feet
To the grace that, bright and light as the crest
Of a peacock, sits on her shining head,
And she knows it not: oh, if she knew it,
To know her beauty might half undo it. 555
I know it the one bright thing to save
My yet young life in the wilds of Time,
Perhaps from madness, perhaps from crime,
Perhaps from a selfish grave.

What, if she be fastened to this fool lord, 560
Dare I bid her abide by her word?
Should I love her so well if she
Had given her word to a thing so low?
Shall I love her as well if she
Can break her word were it even for me? 565
I trust that it is not so.

Catch not my breath, O clamorous heart,
Let not my tongue be a thrall to my eye,
For I must tell her before we part,
I must tell her, or die. 570

17

Go not, happy day,
   From the shining fields,
Go not, happy day,
   Till the maiden yields.
Rosy is the West, 575
   Rosy is the South,
Roses are her cheeks,
   And a rose her mouth
When the happy Yes
   Falters from her lips, 580
Pass and blush the news
   Over glowing ships;
Over blowing seas,
   Over seas at rest,
Pass the happy news, 585
   Blush it through the West;
Till the red man dance
   By his red cedar-tree,
And the red man's babe
   Leap, beyond the sea. 590
Blush from West to East,
   Blush from East to West,
Till the West is East,
   Blush it through the West.
Rosy is the West, 595
   Rosy is the South,
Roses are her cheeks,
   And a rose her mouth.

18

I have led her home, my love, my only friend.
There is none like her, none. 600
And never yet so warmly ran my blood
And sweetly, on and on
Calming itself to the long-wished-for end,
Full to the banks, close on the promised good.

None like her, none. 605
Just now the dry-tongued laurels' pattering talk
Seemed her light foot along the garden walk,
And shook my heart to think she comes once more;
But even then I heard her close the door,
The gates of Heaven are closed, and she is gone. 610

---

540 **clog:** heavy block of wood fastened to a man or an animal to impede movement 544 **Oread:** mountain nymph; 'She lives on the hill near to him' (T)

568 **thrall:** slave 587 **the red man:** American Indians

There is none like her, none.
Nor will be when our summers have deceased.
Oh, art thou sighing for Lebanon
In the long breeze that streams to thy delicious East,
Sighing for Lebanon, 615
Dark cedar, though thy limbs have here increased,
Upon a pastoral slope as fair,
And looking to the South, and fed
With honeyed rain and delicate air,
And haunted by the starry head 620
Of her whose gentle will has changed my fate,
And made my life a perfumed altar-flame;
And over whom thy darkness must have spread
With such delight as theirs of old, thy great
Forefathers of the thornless garden, there 625
Shadowing the snow-limbed Eve from whom she
    came.

Here will I lie, while these long branches sway,
And you fair stars that crown a happy day
Go in and out as if at merry play,
Who am no more so all forlorn, 630
As when it seemed far better to be born
To labour and the mattock-hardened hand,
Than nursed at ease and brought to understand
A sad astrology, the boundless plan
That makes you tyrants in your iron skies, 635
Innumerable, pitiless, passionless eyes,
Cold fires, yet with power to burn and brand
His nothingness into man.

But now shine on, and what care I,
Who in this stormy gulf have found a pearl 640
The countercharm of space and hollow sky,
And do accept my madness, and would die
To save from some slight shame one simple girl.

Would die; for sullen-seeming Death may give
More life to Love than is or ever was 645
In our low world, where yet 'tis sweet to live.
Let no one ask me how it came to pass;
It seems that I am happy, that to me
A livelier emerald twinkles in the grass,
A purer sapphire melts into the sea. 650

Not die; but live a life of truest breath,
And teach true life to fight with mortal wrongs.
Oh, why should Love, like men in drinking-songs,
Spice his fair banquet with the dust of death?
Make answer, Maud my bliss, 655
Maud made my Maud by that long loving kiss,
Life of my life, wilt thou not answer this?
'The dusky strand of Death inwoven here
With dear Love's tie, makes Love himself more dear.'

Is that enchanted moan only the swell 660
Of the long waves that roll in yonder bay?
And hark the clock within, the silver knell
Of twelve sweet hours that passed in bridal white,
And died to live, long as my pulses play;
But now by this my love has closed her sight 665
And given false death her hand, and stol'n away
To dreamful wastes where footless fancies dwell
Among the fragments of the golden day.
May nothing there her maiden grace affright!
Dear heart, I feel with thee the drowsy spell. 670
My bride to be, my evermore delight,
My own heart's heart, my ownest own, farewell;
It is but for a little space I go:
And ye meanwhile far over moor and fell
Beat to the noiseless music of the night! 675
Has our whole earth gone nearer to the glow
Of your soft splendours that you look so bright?
I have climbed nearer out of lonely Hell.
Beat, happy stars, timing with things below,
Beat with my heart more blest than heart can tell, 680
Blest, but for some dark undercurrent woe
That seems to draw – but it shall not be so:
Let all be well, be well.

19

Her brother is coming back tonight,
Breaking up my dream of delight. 685

My dream? do I dream of bliss?
I have walked awake with Truth.
Oh, when did a morning shine
So rich in atonement as this
For my dark-dawning youth, 690
Darkened watching a mother decline
And that dead man at her heart and mine:
For who was left to watch her but I?
Yet so did I let my freshness die.

I trust that I did not talk 695
To gentle Maud in our walk
(For often in lonely wanderings
I have cursed him even to lifeless things)
But I trust that I did not talk,
Not touch on her father's sin: 700
I am sure I did but speak
Of my mother's faded cheek
When it slowly grew so thin,
That I felt she was slowly dying
Vexed with lawyers and harassed with debt: 705
For how often I caught her with eyes all wet,
Shaking her head at her son and sighing
A world of trouble within!

613–16 **Lebanon . . . cedar:** cedar of Lebanon, *Cedrus libani*, a species of evergreen conifer native to the Mediterranean region; there are many references to the cedar in the Old Testament

662 **knell:** tolling

And Maud too, Maud was moved
To speak of the mother she loved 710
As one scarce less forlorn,
Dying abroad and it seems apart
From him who had ceased to share her heart,
And ever mourning over the feud,
The household Fury sprinkled with blood 715
By which our houses are torn:
How strange was what she said,
When only Maud and the brother
Hung over her dying bed –
That Maud's dark father and mine 720
Had bound us one to the other,
Betrothed us over their wine,
On the day when Maud was born;
Sealed her mine from her first sweet breath.
Mine, mine by a right, from birth till death. 725
Mine, mine – our fathers have sworn.

But the true blood spilt had in it a heat
To dissolve the precious seal on a bond,
That, if left uncancelled, had been so sweet:
And none of us thought of a something beyond, 730
A desire that awoke in the heart of the child,
As it were a duty done to the tomb,
To be friends for her sake, to be reconciled;
And I was cursing them and my doom,
And letting a dangerous thought run wild 735
While often abroad in the fragrant gloom
Of foreign churches – I see her there,
Bright English lily, breathing a prayer
To be friends, to be reconciled!

But then what a flint is he! 740
Abroad, at Florence, at Rome,
I find whenever she touched on me
This brother had laughed her down,
And at last, when each came home,
He had darkened into a frown, 745
Chid her, and forbid her to speak
To me, her friend of the years before;
And this was what had reddened her cheek
When I bowed to her on the moor.

Yet Maud, although not blind 750
To the faults of his heart and mind,
I see she cannot but love him,
And says he is rough but kind,
And wishes me to approve him,
And tells me, when she lay 755
Sick once, with a fear of worse,
That he left his wine and horses and play,
Sat with her, read to her, night and day,
And tended her like a nurse.

Kind? but the deathbed desire 760
Spurned by this heir of the liar –
Rough but kind? yet I know
He has plotted against me in this,
That he plots against me still.
Kind to Maud? that were not amiss. 765
Well, rough but kind; why let it be so:
For shall not Maud have her will?

For, Maud, so tender and true,
As long as my life endures
I feel I shall owe you a debt, 770
That I never can hope to pay;
And if ever I should forget
That I owe this debt to you
And for your sweet sake to yours;
Oh, then, what then shall I say? – 775
If ever I *should* forget,
May God make me more wretched
Than ever I have been yet!

So now I have sworn to bury
All this dead body of hate, 780
I feel so free and so clear
By the loss of that dead weight,
That I should grow light-headed, I fear,
Fantastically merry;
But that her brother comes, like a blight 785
On my fresh hope, to the Hall tonight.

20

Strange, that I felt so gay,
Strange, that *I* tried today
To beguile her melancholy;
The Sultan, as we name him, – 790
She did not wish to blame him –
But he vexed her and perplexed her
With his worldly talk and folly:
Was it gentle to reprove her
For stealing out of view 795
From a little lazy lover
Who but claims her as his due?
Or for chilling his caresses
By the coldness of her manners,
Nay, the plainness of her dresses? 800
Now I know her but in two,
Nor can pronounce upon it
If one should ask me whether
The habit, hat, and feather,
Or the frock and gipsy bonnet 805
Be the neater and completer;
For nothing can be sweeter
Than maiden Maud in either.

734 **doom**: fate

804 **habit**: riding habit 805 **gipsy bonnet**: 'a woman's hat or bonnet
with large side-flaps' (*OED*, citing *Maud*)

But tomorrow, if we live,
Our ponderous squire will give   810
A grand political dinner
To half the squirelings near;
And Maud will wear her jewels,
And the bird of prey will hover,
And the titmouse hope to win her   815
With his chirrup at her ear.

A grand political dinner
To the men of many acres,
A gathering of the Tory,
A dinner and then a dance   820
For the maids and marriage-makers,
And every eye but mine will glance
At Maud in all her glory.

For I am not invited,
But, with the Sultan's pardon,   825
I am all as well delighted,
For I know her own rose-garden,
And mean to linger in it
Till the dancing will be over;
And then, oh, then, come out to me   830
For a minute, but for a minute,
Come out to your own true lover,
That your true lover may see
Your glory also, and render
All homage to his own darling,   835
Queen Maud in all her splendour.

                    21
Rivulet crossing my ground,
And bringing me down from the Hall
This garden-rose that I found,
Forgetful of Maud and me,   840
And lost in trouble and moving round
Here at the head of a tinkling fall,
And trying to pass to the sea;
O Rivulet, born at the Hall,
My Maud has sent it by thee   845
(If I read her sweet will right)
On a blushing mission to me,
Saying in odour and colour, 'Ah, be
Among the roses tonight.'

                    22
Come into the garden, Maud,   850
    For the black bat, night, has flown,
Come into the garden, Maud,
    I am here at the gate alone;
And the woodbine spices are wafted abroad,
    And the musk of the rose is blown.   855

For a breeze of morning moves,
    And the planet of Love is on high,
Beginning to faint in the light that she loves
    On a bed of daffodil sky,
To faint in the light of the sun she loves,   860
    To faint in his light, and to die.

All night have the roses heard
    The flute, violin, bassoon;
All night has the casement jessamine stirred
    To the dancers dancing in tune;   865
Till a silence fell with the waking bird,
    And a hush with the setting moon.

I said to the lily, 'There is but one
    With whom she has heart to be gay.
When will the dancers leave her alone?   870
    She is weary of dance and play.'
Now half to the setting moon are gone,
    And half to the rising day;
Low on the sand and loud on the stone
    The last wheel echoes away.   875

I said to the rose, 'The brief night goes
    In babble and revel and wine.
O young lord-lover, what sighs are those,
    For one that will never be thine?
But mine, but mine,' so I sware to the rose,   880
    'For ever and ever, mine.'

And the soul of the rose went into my blood,
    As the music clashed in the hall;
And long by the garden lake I stood,
    For I heard your rivulet fall   885
From the lake to the meadow and on to the
        wood,
    Our wood, that is dearer than all;

From the meadow your walks have left so sweet
    That whenever a March-wind sighs
He sets the jewel-print of your feet   890
    In violets blue as your eyes,
To the woody hollows in which we meet
    And the valleys of Paradise.

The slender acacia would not shake
    One long milk-bloom on the tree;   895
The white lake-blossom fell into the lake
    As the pimpernel dozed on the lea;
But the rose was awake all night for your sake,
    Knowing your promise to me;
The lilies and roses were all awake,   900
    They sighed for the dawn and thee.

---

815 **titmouse:** tit 840 **Forgetful of:** forgotten by

857 **planet of Love:** Venus 864 **jessamine:** jasmine 897 **lea:** pasture

Queen rose of the rosebud garden of girls,
  Come hither, the dances are done,
In gloss of satin and glimmer of pearls,
  Queen lily and rose in one;   905
Shine out, little head, sunning over with curls,
  To the flowers, and be their sun.

There has fallen a splendid tear
  From the passion-flower at the gate.
She is coming, my dove, my dear;   910
  She is coming, my life, my fate;
The red rose cries, 'She is near, she is near';
  And the white rose weeps, 'She is late';
The larkspur listens, 'I hear, I hear';
  And the lily whispers, 'I wait.'   915

She is coming, my own, my sweet;
  Were it ever so airy a tread,
My heart would hear her and beat,
  Were it earth in an earthy bed;
My dust would hear her and beat,   920
  Had I lain for a century dead;
Would start and tremble under her feet,
  And blossom in purple and red.

PART TWO
1

'The fault was mine, the fault was mine' –
Why am I sitting here so stunned and still,
Plucking the harmless wild-flower on the hill? –
It is this guilty hand! –
And there rises ever a passionate cry   5
From underneath in the darkening land –
What is it, that has been done?
O dawn of Eden bright over earth and sky,
The fires of Hell break out of thy rising sun,
The fires of Hell and of Hate;   10
For she, sweet soul, had hardly spoken a word,
When her brother ran in his rage to the gate,
He came with the babe-faced lord;
Heaped on her terms of disgrace,
And while she wept, and I strove to be cool,   15
He fiercely gave me the lie,
Till I with as fierce an anger spoke,
And he struck me, madman, over the face,
Struck me before the languid fool,
Who was gaping and grinning by: 20
Struck for himself an evil stroke;
Wrought for his house an irredeemable woe;
For front to front in an hour we stood,
And a million horrible bellowing echoes broke
From the red-ribbed hollow behind the wood,   25

And thundered up into Heaven the Christless code,
That must have life for a blow.
Ever and ever afresh they seemed to grow.
Was it he lay there with a fading eye?
'The fault was mine,' he whispered, 'fly!'   30
Then glided out of the joyous wood
The ghastly Wraith of one that I know;
And there rang on a sudden a passionate cry,
A cry for a brother's blood: 34
It will ring in my heart and my ears, till I die, till I die.

Is it gone? my pulses beat –
What was it? a lying trick of the brain?
Yet I thought I saw her stand,
A shadow there at my feet,
High over the shadowy land.   40
It is gone; and the heavens fall in a gentle rain,
When they should burst and drown with deluging
          storms
The feeble vassals of wine and anger and lust,
The little hearts that know not how to forgive:
Arise, my God, and strike, for we hold Thee just,   45
Strike dead the whole weak race of venomous worms,
That sting each other here in the dust;
We are not worthy to live.

2

See what a lovely shell,
Small and pure as a pearl,   50
Lying close to my foot,
Frail, but a work divine,
Made so fairily well
With delicate spire and whorl,
How exquisitely minute,   55
A miracle of design!

What is it? a learned man
Could give it a clumsy name.
Let him name it who can,
The beauty would be the same.   60

The tiny cell is forlorn,
Void of the little living will
That made it stir on the shore.
Did he stand at the diamond door
Of his house in a rainbow frill?   65
Did he push, when he was uncurled,
A golden foot or a fairy horn
Through his dim water-world?

29 **with a fading eye:** i.e. he was dying 30 **'The fault was mine,'
he whispered, 'fly!':** duelling was a crime; if one duellist died,
the other could face trial for murder and possibly be hanged
32 **ghastly Wraith:** ghostly spectre 49 **See what a lovely shell:** the
first three stanzas of this poem were originally drafted in the 1830s
and are the earliest lines of *Maud* 53 **fairily:** enchantingly 54 **spire:**
spiral **whorl:** a single turn in a spiral shell

(Part 2) 16 **gave me the lie:** accused me of lying 23 **front to front:**
face to face **in an hour:** within the hour

Slight, to be crushed with a tap
Of my finger-nail on the sand,   70
Small, but a work divine,
Frail, but of force to withstand,
Year upon year, the shock
Of cataract seas that snap
The three decker's oaken spine   75
Athwart the ledges of rock,
Here on the Breton strand!

Breton, not Briton; here
Like a shipwrecked man on a coast
Of ancient fable and fear –   80
Plagued with a flitting to and fro,
A disease, a hard mechanic ghost
That never came from on high
Nor ever arose from below,
But only moves with the moving eye,   85
Flying along the land and the main –
Why should it look like Maud?
Am I to be overawed
By what I cannot but know
Is a juggle born of the brain?   90

Back from the Breton coast,
Sick of a nameless fear,
Back to the dark sea-line
Looking, thinking of all I have lost;
An old song vexes my ear;   95
But that of Lamech is mine.

For years, a measureless ill,
For years, for ever, to part –
But she, she would love me still;
And as long, O God, as she   100
Have a grain of love for me,
So long, no doubt, no doubt,
Shall I nurse in my dark heart,
However weary, a spark of will
Not to be trampled out.   105

Strange, that the mind, when fraught
With a passion so intense
One would think that it well
Might drown all life in the eye, –
That it should, by being so overwrought,   110
Suddenly strike on a sharper sense
For a shell, or a flower, little things
Which else would have been passed by!
And now I remember, I,
When he lay dying there,   115
I noticed one of his many rings
(For he had many, poor worm) and thought
It is his mother's hair.

Who knows if he be dead?
Whether I need have fled?   120
Am I guilty of blood?
However this may be,
Comfort her, comfort her, all things good,
While I am over the sea!
Let me and my passionate love go by,   125
But speak to her all things holy and high,
Whatever happen to me!
Me and my harmful love go by;
But come to her waking, find her asleep,
Powers of the height, Powers of the deep,   130
And comfort her though I die.

3

Courage, poor heart of stone!
I will not ask thee why
Thou canst not understand
That thou art left for ever alone: 135
Courage, poor stupid heart of stone. –
Or if I ask thee why,
Care not thou to reply:
She is but dead, and the time is at hand
When thou shalt more than die.   140

4

Oh, that 'twere possible
After long grief and pain
To find the arms of my true love
Round me once again!

When I was wont to meet her   145
In the silent woody places
By the home that gave me birth,
We stood tranced in long embraces
Mixed with kisses sweeter sweeter
Than anything on earth.   150

A shadow flits before me,
Not thou, but like to thee:
Ah, Christ, that it were possible
For one short hour to see
The souls we loved, that they might tell us   155
What and where they be.

It leads me forth at evening,
It lightly winds and steals
In a cold white robe before me,
When all my spirit reels   160
At the shouts, the leagues of lights,
And the roaring of the wheels.

76 **Athwart:** across 77 **on the Breton strand:** on the coast of Brittany
90 **juggle:** trick, illusion 96 **Lamech:** a descendant of Cain, Lamech
was the father of Noah; Tennyson cites the words of Lamech in
Genesis 4.23: 'I have slain a man to my wounding, and a young man
to my hurt' 118 **his mother's hair:** mourning rings, worn in memory
of a loved one, were sometimes woven from the hair of the deceased

141 **Oh, that 'twere possible:** Tennyson described this poem, which
he had first drafted in 1833, inspired by the death of Arthur
Hallam, as 'the germ of the whole' of *Maud* 148 **tranced:** rapt,
entranced 157 **It leads me forth at evening:** 'In London' (T)

Half the night I waste in sighs,
Half in dreams I sorrow after
The delight of early skies;
In a wakeful doze I sorrow   165
For the hand, the lips, the eyes,
For the meeting of the morrow,
The delight of happy laughter,
The delight of low replies.   170

'Tis a morning pure and sweet,
And a dewy splendour falls
On the little flower that clings
To the turrets and the walls;
'Tis a morning pure and sweet,   175
And the light and shadow fleet;
She is walking in the meadow,
And the woodland echo rings;
In a moment we shall meet;
She is singing in the meadow   180
And the rivulet at her feet
Ripples on in light and shadow
To the ballad that she sings.

Do I hear her sing as of old,
My bird with the shining head,   185
My own dove with the tender eye?
But there rings on a sudden a passionate cry,
There is some one dying or dead,
And a sullen thunder is rolled;
For a tumult shakes the city,   190
And I wake, my dream is fled;
In the shuddering dawn, behold,
Without knowledge, without pity,
By the curtains of my bed
That abiding phantom cold.   195

Get thee hence, nor come again,
Mix not memory with doubt,
Pass, thou deathlike type of pain,
Pass and cease to move about!
'Tis the blot upon the brain   200
That *will* show itself without.

Then I rise, the eavedrops fall,
And the yellow vapours choke
The great city sounding wide;
The day comes, a dull red ball   205
Wrapped in drifts of lurid smoke
On the misty river-tide.

Through the hubbub of the market
I steal, a wasted frame,
It crosses here, it crosses there,   210
Through all that crowd confused and loud,
The shadow still the same;
And on my heavy eyelids
My anguish hangs like shame.

Alas for her that met me,   215
That heard me softly call,
Came glimmering through the laurels
At the quiet evenfall,
In the garden by the turrets
Of the old manorial hall.   220

Would the happy spirit descend,
From the realms of light and song,
In the chamber or the street,
As she looks among the blest,
Should I fear to greet my friend   225
Or to say 'Forgive the wrong,'
Or to ask her, 'Take me, sweet,
To the regions of thy rest'?

But the broad light glares and beats,
And the shadow flits and fleets   230
And will not let me be;
And I loathe the squares and streets,
And the faces that one meets,
Hearts with no love for me:
Always I long to creep   235
Into some still cavern deep,
There to weep, and weep, and weep
My whole soul out to thee.

5

Dead, long dead,
Long dead!   240
And my heart is a handful of dust,
And the wheels go over my head,
And my bones are shaken with pain,
For into a shallow grave they are thrust,
Only a yard beneath the street,   245
And the hoofs of the horses beat, beat,
The hoofs of the horses beat,
Beat into my scalp and my brain,
With never an end to the stream of passing feet,
Driving, hurrying, marrying, burying,   250
Clamour and rumble, and ringing and clatter,
And here beneath it is all as bad,
For I thought the dead had peace, but it is not so;
To have no peace in the grave, is that not sad?
But up and down and to and fro,   255
Ever about me the dead men go;
And then to hear a dead man chatter
Is enough to drive one mad.

---

202 **eavedrops:** the rainwater that falls from the eaves of a house
203–7 **yellow vapours . . . river-tide:** smoke belching from
innumerable coal fires caused London frequently to be blanketed
in thick fog

Wretchedest age, since Time began,
They cannot even bury a man;   260
And though we paid our tithes in the days that are
    gone,
Not a bell was rung, not a prayer was read;
It is that which makes us loud in the world of the
    dead;
There is none that does his work, not one;
A touch of their office might have sufficed,   265
But the churchmen fain would kill their church,
As the churches have killed their Christ.

See, there is one of us sobbing,
No limit to his distress;
And another, a lord of all things, praying   270
To his own great self, as I guess;
And another, a statesman there, betraying
His party-secret, fool, to the press;
And yonder a vile physician, blabbing
The case of his patient – all for what?   275
To tickle the maggot born in an empty head,
And wheedle a world that loves him not,
For it is but a world of the dead.

Nothing but idiot gabble!
For the prophecy given of old   280
And then not understood,
Has come to pass as foretold;
Not let any man think for the public good,
But babble, merely for babble.
For I never whispered a private affair   285
Within the hearing of cat or mouse,
No, not to myself in the closet alone,
But I heard it shouted at once from the top of the
    house;
Everything came to be known.
Who told *him* we were there?   290

Not that grey old wolf, for he came not back
From the wilderness, full of wolves, where he used to
    lie;
He has gathered the bones for his o'ergrown whelp to
    crack;
Crack them now for yourself, and howl, and die.

Prophet, curse me the blabbing lip,   295
And curse me the British vermin, the rat;
I know not whether he came in the Hanover ship,
But I know that he lies and listens mute
In an ancient mansion's crannies and holes:
Arsenic, arsenic, sure would do it,   300
Except that now we poison our babes, poor souls!
It is all used up for that.

Tell him now: she is standing here at my head;
Not beautiful now, not even kind;
He may take her now; for she never speaks her mind,
But is ever the one thing silent here.   306
She is not *of* us, as I divine;
She comes from another stiller world of the dead,
Stiller, not fairer than mine.

But I know where a garden grows,   310
Fairer than aught in the world beside,
All made up of the lily and rose
That blow by night, when the season is good,
To the sound of dancing music and flutes:
It is only flowers, they had no fruits,   315
And I almost fear they are not roses, but blood;
For the keeper was one, so full of pride,
He linked a dead man there to a spectral bride;
For he, if he had not been a Sultan of brutes,
Would he have that hole in his side?   320

But what will the old man say?
He laid a cruel snare in a pit
To catch a friend of mine one stormy day;
Yet now I could even weep to think of it;
For what will the old man say   325
When he comes to the second corpse in the pit?

Friend, to be struck by the public foe,
Then to strike him and lay him low,
That were a public merit, far,
Whatever the Quaker holds, from sin;   330
But the red life spilt for a private blow –
I swear to you, lawful and lawless war
Are scarcely even akin.

Oh me, why have they not buried me deep enough?
Is it kind to have made me a grave so rough,   335
Me, that was never a quiet sleeper?
Maybe still I am but half-dead;
Then I cannot be wholly dumb;
I will cry to the steps above my head
And somebody, surely, some kind heart will come   340
To bury me, bury me
Deeper, ever so little deeper.

PART THREE
6

My life has crept so long on a broken wing
Through cells of madness, haunts of horror and fear,
That I come to be grateful at last for a little thing:
My mood is changed, for it fell at a time of year
When the face of night is fair on the dewy downs,   5

261 **tithes:** an ancient custom whereby people contributed a tenth of their income to the Church 287 **in the closet alone:** alone in my room

317 **the keeper:** 'the brother' (T) 324 **Yet now:** even now 330 **Whatever the Quaker holds:** this could be an attack on Quaker pacifism generally or, more specifically, on John Bright (1811–89), a Quaker and an opponent of the Crimean War (Part 3): Tennyson recalled that the first four poems in this section were written in February 1854 'when the cannon was heard booming from the battleships in the Solent before the Crimean War'; Britain declared war on Russia on 22 March

And the shining daffodil dies, and the Charioteer
And starry Gemini hang like glorious crowns
Over Orion's grave low down in the west,
That like a silent lightning under the stars
She seemed to divide in a dream from a band of the
    blest,   10
And spoke of a hope for the world in the coming
    wars –
'And in that hope, dear soul, let trouble have rest,
Knowing I tarry for thee,' and pointed to Mars
As he glowed like a ruddy shield on the Lion's breast.

And it was but a dream, yet it yielded a dear delight 15
To have looked, though but in a dream, upon eyes so
    fair,
That had been in a weary world my one thing bright;
And it was but a dream, yet it lightened my despair
When I thought that a war would arise in defence of
    the right,
That an iron tyranny now should bend or cease,   20
The glory of manhood stand on his ancient height,
Nor Britain's one sole God be the millionaire:
No more shall commerce be all in all, and Peace
Pipe on her pastoral hillock a languid note,
And watch her harvest ripen, her herd increase,   25
Nor the cannon-bullet rust on a slothful shore,
And the cobweb woven across the cannon's throat
Shall shake its threaded tears in the wind no more.

And as months ran on and rumour of battle grew,
'It is time, it is time, O passionate heart,' said I   30
(For I cleaved to a cause that I felt to be pure and
    true),
'It is time, O passionate heart and morbid eye,
That old hysterical mock-disease should die.'
And I stood on a giant deck and mixed my breath
With a loyal people shouting a battle cry,   35
Till I saw the dreary phantom arise and fly
Far into the North, and battle, and seas of death.

Let it go or stay, so I wake to the higher aims
Of a land that has lost for a little her lust for gold,
And love of a peace that was full of wrongs and
    shames,   40
Horrible, hateful, monstrous, not to be told;
And hail once more to the banner of battle unrolled!
Though many a light shall darken, and many shall
    weep
For those that are crushed in the clash of jarring
    claims,
Yet God's just wrath shall be wreaked on a giant
    liar;
And many a darkness into the light shall leap,   46
And shine in the sudden making of splendid names,
And noble thought be freër under the sun,
And the heart of a people beat with one desire;

6 **Charioteer:** the constellation Auriga 7 **Gemini:** a constellation
36 **dreary phantom:** 'Of Maud' (T)

For the peace, that I deemed no peace, is over and
    done,   50
And now by the side of the Black and the Baltic deep,
And deathful-grinning mouths of the fortress, flames
The blood-red blossom of war with a heart of fire.

Let it flame or fade, and the war roll down like a
    wind,
We have proved we have hearts in a cause, we are
    noble still,   55
And myself have awaked, as it seems, to the better
    mind;
It is better to fight for the good than to rail at the ill;
I have felt with my native land, I am one with my
    kind,
I embrace the purpose of God, and the doom
    assigned.

51 **by the side of . . . the Baltic deep:** i.e. in the Crimea 59 **doom:**
fate

THE CHARGE OF THE LIGHT BRIGADE

HALF a league, half a league,
  Half a league onward,
All in the valley of Death
  Rode the six hundred.
'Forward, the Light Brigade!   5
Charge for the guns!' he said.
Into the valley of Death
  Rode the six hundred.

'Forward, the Light Brigade!'
Was there a man dismayed?   10
Not though the soldier knew
  Someone had blundered:
Theirs not to make reply,
Theirs not to reason why,
Theirs but to do and die: 15
Into the valley of Death
  Rode the six hundred.

Cannon to right of them,
Cannon to left of them,
Cannon in front of them   20
  Volleyed and thundered;
Stormed at with shot and shell,
Boldly they rode and well,
Into the jaws of Death,
Into the mouth of Hell   25
  Rode the six hundred.

Flashed all their sabres bare,
Flashed as they turned in air
Sabring the gunners there,
Charging an army, while   30
  All the world wondered:

Plunged in the battery-smoke
Right through the line they broke;
Cossack and Russian
Reeled from the sabre-stroke,   35
Shattered and sundered.
Then they rode back, but not,
   Not the six hundred.

Cannon to right of them,
Cannon to left of them,   40
Cannon behind them
   Volleyed and thundered;
Stormed at with shot and shell,
While horse and hero fell,
They that had fought so well   45
Came through the jaws of Death,
Back from the mouth of Hell,
All that was left of them,
   Left of six hundred.

When can their glory fade?   50
Oh, the wild charge they made!
   All the world wondered.
Honour the charge they made!
Honour the Light Brigade,
   Noble six hundred!   55

THE CHARGE OF THE LIGHT BRIGADE: Composed on a single day in
December 1854 as a tribute to the men lost at the battle of Balaclava:
1 **league:** an old measure roughly equivalent to three miles 6 **he
said:** i.e. Lord Cardigan, who led the charge 32 **battery-smoke:**
smoke from the artillery towards which they were charging

CROSSING THE BAR

SUNSET and evening star,
   And one clear call for me!
   And may there be no moaning of the bar,
   When I put out to sea,

But such a tide as moving seems asleep,   5
   Too full for sound and foam,
When that which drew from out the boundless deep
   Turns again home.

Twilight and evening bell,
   And after that the dark!   10
And may there be no sadness of farewell,
   When I embark;

For though from out our bourne of Time and Place
   The flood may bear me far,
I hope to see my Pilot face to face   15
   When I have crossed the bar.

CROSSING THE BAR: In 1888-9, Tennyson was seriously ill. When his
health gradually improved, he began to resent the restrictions
placed upon him by the doctors – until one day his nurse, Emma

Durham, told him that instead of complaining he should write a
hymn of thanksgiving for his recovery. One day towards the end of
1889 these lines came to him 'in a moment', and he jotted them on
the back of an envelope. That evening he showed the poem to
Nurse Durham: 'Will this do for you, old woman?' The nurse was
shocked by the tone of the poem: she thought Tennyson had written
his own death-lament. Later that evening the poet showed the
lines to his son Hallam, who remarked, 'That is the crown of your
life's work' – an opinion echoed by other readers when the poem
was published two months later. To 'cross the bar' is to cross the
equator: 1 **evening star:** a planet (usually Venus or Mercury) seen
setting in the west soon after the sun 13 **bourne:** limit 15 **Pilot:** God

ROBERT BROWNING

From PIPPA PASSES

THE year's at the spring
And day's at the morn;
Morning's at seven;
The hill-side's dew-pearled;
The lark's on the wing;   5
The snail's on the thorn:
God's in his heaven –
All's right with the world!

PIPPA PASSES: A drama in verse and prose, 'represents the course
of one day – Pippa's yearly holiday. . . . Pippa rises with the sun,
determined to make the best of the bright hours before her; and she
spends them in wandering through the town, singing as she goes'
(Mrs Sutherland Orr, *A Handbook to the Works of Robert Browning*
[6th edn, 1892]; the poet authorised the *Handbook*, supervised it,
and is believed to have contributed directly to it)

MY LAST DUCHESS
FERRARA

THAT'S my last Duchess painted on the wall,
Looking as if she were alive. I call
That piece a wonder, now: Frà Pandolf's hands
Worked busily a day, and there she stands.
Will't please you sit and look at her? I said   5
'Frà Pandolf' by design, for never read
Strangers like you that pictured countenance,
The depth and passion of its earnest glance,
But to myself they turned (since none puts by
The curtain I have drawn for you, but I)   10
And seemed as they would ask me, if they durst,
How such a glance came there; so, not the first
Are you to turn and ask thus. Sir, 'twas not
Her husband's presence only, called that spot
Of joy into the Duchess' cheek: perhaps   15
Frà Pandolf chanced to say, 'Her mantle laps
Over my lady's wrist too much,' or 'Paint
Must never hope to reproduce the faint
Half-flush that dies along her throat': such stuff
Was courtesy, she thought, and cause enough   20

For calling up that spot of joy. She had
A heart – how shall I say? – too soon made glad.
Too easily impressed: she liked whate'er
She looked on, and her looks went everywhere.
Sir, 'twas all one! My favour at her breast,   25
The dropping of the daylight in the West,
The bough of cherries some officious fool
Broke in the orchard for her, the white mule
She rode with round the terrace – all and each
Would draw from her alike the approving speech,   30
Or blush, at least. She thanked men, – good! but
     thanked
Somehow – I know not how – as if she ranked
My gift of a nine-hundred-years-old name
With anybody's gift. Who'd stoop to blame
This sort of trifling? Even had you skill   35
In speech – (which I have not) – to make your will
Quite clear to such an one, and say, 'Just this
Or that in you disgusts me; here you miss,
Or there exceed the mark' – and if she let
Herself be lessoned so, nor plainly set   40
Her wits to yours, forsooth, and made excuse,
– E'en then would be some stooping; and I choose
Never to stoop. Oh, sir, she smiled, no doubt,
Whene'er I passed her; but who passed without
Much the same smile? This grew; I gave commands;
Then all smiles stopped together. There she stands   46
As if alive. Will't please you rise? We'll meet
The company below, then. I repeat,
The Count your master's known munificence
Is ample warrant that no just pretence   50
Of mine for dowry will be disallowed;
Though his fair daughter's self, as I avowed
At starting, is my object. Nay, we'll go
Together down, sir! Notice Neptune, though,
Taming a sea-horse, thought a rarity,   55
Which Claus of Innsbruck cast in bronze for me!

MY LAST DUCHESS: 3 **Frà:** Brother; the artist, Pandolf, was a monk
or a friar 25 **favour:** a ribbon given as a token of esteem 54 **Neptune:**
Roman god of the sea, corresponding to the Greek Poseidon

SOLILOQUY OF THE SPANISH CLOISTER

GR-R-R – there go, my heart's abhorrence!
     Water your damned flower-pots, do!
If hate killed men, Brother Lawrence,
     God's blood, would not mine kill you!
What? your myrtle-bush wants trimming?   5
     Oh, that rose has prior claims –
Needs its leaden vase filled brimming?
     Hell dry you up with its flames!

SOLILOQUY OF THE SPANISH CLOISTER: 'a venomous outbreak of
jealous hatred, directed by one monk against another whom he is
watching at some innocent occupation. The speaker has no ground
of complaint against Brother Lawrence, except that his life *is*
innocent . . . he spites him when he can' (*Handbook*)

At the meal we sit together:
     Salve tibi! I must hear   10
Wise talk of the kind of weather,
     Sort of season, time of year:
*Not a plenteous cork-crop: scarcely
     Dare we hope oak-galls, I doubt:*
What's the Latin name for 'parsley'?   15
     What's the Greek name for Swine's Snout?

Whew! We'll have our platter burnished,
     Laid with care on our own shelf!
With a fire-new spoon we're furnished,
     And a goblet for ourself,   20
Rinsed like something sacrificial
     Ere 'tis fit to touch our chaps –
Marked with L for our initial!
     (He-he! There his lily snaps!)

Saint, forsooth! While brown Dolores   25
     Squats outside the Convent bank
With Sanchicha, telling stories,
     Steeping tresses in the tank,
Blue-black, lustrous, thick like horsehairs,
     – Can't I see his dead eye glow,   30
Bright as 'twere a Barbary corsair's?
     (That is, if he'd let it show!)

When he finishes refection,
     Knife and fork he never lays
Cross-wise, to my recollection,   35
     As I do, in Jesu's praise.
I the Trinity illustrate,
     Drinking watered orange-pulp –
In three sips the Arian frustrate;
     While he drains his at one gulp.   40

Oh, those melons? If he's able
     We're to have a feast! so nice!
One goes to the Abbot's table,
     All of us get each a slice.
How go on your flowers? None double?   45
     Not one fruit sort can you spy?
Strange! – And I, too, at such trouble,
     Keep them close-nipped on the sly!

10 *Salve tibi!:* Hail to you! 17 **burnished:** polished 31 **Barbary
corsair:** the Barbary Coast was the Mediterranean coast of North
Africa, and its waters were infested by Muslim pirates 33 **refection:**
eating 39 **Arian:** follower of Arius of Alexandria (4th century AD),
who denied that Jesus was of the same essence or substance as
God

There's a great text in Galatians,
    Once you trip on it, entails   50
Twenty-nine distinct damnations,
    One sure, if another fails:
If I trip him just a-dying,
    Sure of heaven as heaven can be,
Spin him round and send him flying   55
    Off to hell, a Manichee?

Or, my scrofulous French novel
    On grey paper with blunt type!
Simply glance at it, you grovel
    Hand and foot in Belial's gripe: 60
If I double down its pages
    At the woeful sixteenth print,
When he gathers his greengages,
    Ope a sieve and slip it in't?

Or, there's Satan! – one might venture   65
    Pledge one's soul to him, yet leave
Such a flaw in the indenture
    As he'd miss till, past retrieve,
Blasted lay that rose-acacia
    We're so proud of! *Hy, Zy, Hine* . . .   70
'St, there's Vespers! *Plena gratiâ*
    Ave, Virgo! Gr-r-r – you swine!

49 **a great text in Galatians**: probably Galatians 3.19–21, which lists seventeen 'works of the flesh' by which the soul may be imperilled; Browning's 'Twenty-nine' (line 51) appears to be his own elaboration 56 **Manichee:** a follower of Mani (3rd century AD), whose belief that the universe was controlled by two opposing forces of darkness (evil) and light (goodness) was condemned by the Church as heresy 57 **scrofulous:** literally, affected by scrofula, a form of tuberculosis affecting particularly the lymphatic glands; but here perhaps intended simply as 'unclean' or 'diseased' 58 **On grey paper with blunt type:** i.e. cheaply printed for a disreputable publisher 60 **Belial:** i.e. the Devil **gripe:** grip 61–2 **double down . . . print:** i.e. turn down the corner of page sixteen, which contains a particularly scandalous passage 70 *Hy, Zy, Hine:* presumably a bell or the chimes of a clock summoning the monks to prayer, but the precise meaning remains unclear 71 **'St!:** Hist! **Vespers:** evensong 71–2 *Plena gratiâ Ave, Virgo!:* Hail, Virgin, full of grace!

HOW THEY BROUGHT THE GOOD NEWS FROM GHENT TO AIX
[16—]

I SPRANG to the stirrup, and Joris, and he;
I galloped, Dirck galloped, we galloped all three;
'Good speed!' cried the watch, as the gate-bolts
    undrew;
'Speed!' echoed the wall to us galloping through;
Behind shut the postern, the lights sank to rest,   5
And into the midnight we galloped abreast.

HOW THEY BROUGHT THE GOOD NEWS FROM GHENT TO AIX: The subject of this enduring favourite has no basis in historical fact: the story is entirely imaginary. Browning wrote the poem at sea on his way to Italy in August 1844. He had twice travelled through Flanders, so the places in the poem would have been familiar to him 5 **postern:** the town gate

Not a word to each other; we kept the great pace
Neck by neck, stride by stride, never changing our
    place;
I turned in my saddle and made its girths tight,
Then shortened each stirrup, and set the pique
    right,   10
Rebuckled the cheek-strap, chained slacker the bit,
Nor galloped less steadily Roland a whit.

'Twas moonset at starting; but while we drew near
Lokeren, the cocks crew and twilight dawned clear;
At Boom, a great yellow star came out to see;   15
At Duffeld, 'twas morning as plain as could be;
And from Mecheln church-steeple we heard the half-
    chime,
So Joris broke silence with, 'Yet there is time!'

At Aerschot, up leaped of a sudden the sun,
And against him the cattle stood black every one,   20
To stare through the mist at us galloping past,
And I saw my stout galloper Roland at last,
With resolute shoulders, each butting away
The haze, as some bluff river headland its spray:

And his low head and crest, just one sharp ear bent
    back   25
For my voice, and the other pricked out on his track;
And one eye's black intelligence, – ever that glance
O'er its white edge at me, his own master, askance!
And the thick heavy spume-flakes which aye and anon
His fierce lips shook upwards in galloping on.   30

By Hasselt, Dirck groaned; and cried Joris, 'Stay spur!
Your Roos galloped bravely, the fault's not in her,
We'll remember at Aix' – for one heard the quick
    wheeze
Of her chest, saw the stretched neck and staggering
    knees,
And sunk tail, and horrible heave of the flank,   35
As down on her haunches she shuddered and sank.

So, we were left galloping, Joris and I,
Past Looz and past Tongres, no cloud in the sky;
The broad sun above laughed a pitiless laugh,
'Neath our feet broke the brittle bright stubble like
    chaff;   40
Till over by Dalhem a dome-spire sprang white,
And 'Gallop,' gasped Joris, 'for Aix is in sight!'

9 **girths:** a girth is a saddle-strap that passes under the horse's belly 10 **pique:** the meaning is unclear; Browning possibly intended the peak, or pommel, of the saddle, although it is unlikely that any English saddle with which he was familiar would have had one; or the word may be his own coinage from the French verb *piquer*, 'to spur' 11 **chained slacker the bit:** i.e. allowed the horse full rein to gallop at will 29 **spume-flakes:** i.e. the horse was foaming at the mouth 40 **chaff:** husks of threshed corn

'How they'll greet us!' – and all in a moment his roan
Rolled neck and croup over, lay dead as a stone;
And there was my Roland to bear the whole weight   45
Of the news which alone could save Aix from her fate,
With his nostrils like pits full of blood to the brim,
And with circles of red for his eye-socket's rim.

Then I cast loose my buffcoat, each holster let fall,
Shook off both my jack-boots, let go belt and all,   50
Stood up in the stirrup, leaned, patted his ear,
Called my Roland his pet-name, my horse without
    peer;
Clapped my hands, laughed and sang, any noise, bad
    or good,
Till at length into Aix Roland galloped and stood.

And all I remember is – friends flocking round   55
As I sat with his head 'twixt my knees on the ground;
And no voice but was praising this Roland of mine,
As I poured down his throat our last measure of wine,
Which (the burgesses voted by common consent)
Was no more than his due who brought good news
    from Ghent.   60

43 **roan**: reddish-brown horse 44 **neck and croup**: neck and crop,
i.e. completely 49 **buffcoat**: a coat of buff leather; usually worn by
soldiers 50 **jack-boots**: cavalry boots that come above the knee
59 **burgesses**: town councillors

THE LOST LEADER

JUST for a handful of silver he left us,
    Just for a riband to stick in his coat –
Found the one gift of which fortune bereft us,
    Lost all the others she lets us devote;
They, with the gold to give, doled him out silver,   5
    So much was theirs who so little allowed:
How all our copper had gone for his service!
    Rags – were they purple, his heart had been proud!
We that had loved him so, followed him, honoured
    him,
    Lived in his mild and magnificent eye,   10
Learned his great language, caught his clear accents,
    Made him our pattern to live and to die!
Shakespeare was of us, Milton was for us,
    Burns, Shelley, were with us, – they watch from their
    graves!
He alone breaks from the van and the freemen,   15
    – He alone sinks to the rear and the slaves!

We shall march prospering, – not through his
    presence;
    Songs may inspirit us, – not from his lyre;
Deeds will be done, – while he boasts his quiescence,
    Still bidding crouch whom the rest bade aspire: 20
Blot out his name, then, record one lost soul more,
    One task more declined, one more footpath untrod,

One more devils'-triumph and sorrow for angels,
    One wrong more to man, one more insult to God!
Life's night begins: let him never come back to us!   25
    There would be doubt, hesitation and pain,
Forced praise on our part – the glimmer of twilight,
    Never glad confident morning again!
Best fight on well, for we taught him – strike gallantly,
    Menace our heart ere we master his own;   30
Then let him receive the new knowledge and wait us,
    Pardoned in heaven, the first by the throne!

THE LOST LEADER: 'a lament over the defection of a loved
and honoured chief. . . . It was suggested by Wordsworth, in his
abandonment (with Southey and others) of the liberal cause'
(*Handbook*). The focus of Browning's resentment appears to have
been Wordsworth's acceptance of a Civil List pension in 1842 and
the laureateship in 1843, which Browning saw as the culmination of
Wordsworth's descent from the passionate liberalism of his youth
to a comfortable Toryism 2 **riband**: ribbon (archaic) 15 **the van**:
the first wave of attack

HOME-THOUGHTS, FROM ABROAD

OH, to be in England
Now that April's there,
And whoever wakes in England
Sees, some morning, unaware,
That the lowest boughs and the brushwood sheaf   5
Round the elm-tree bole are in tiny leaf,
While the chaffinch sings on the orchard bough
In England – now!

And after April, when May follows,
And the whitethroat builds, and all the swallows!   10
Hark, where my blossomed pear-tree in the hedge
Leans to the field and scatters on the clover
Blossoms and dewdrops – at the bent spray's edge –
That's the wise thrush; he sings each song twice
    over,
Lest you should think he never could recapture   15
The first fine careless rapture!
And though the fields look rough with hoary dew,
All will be gay when noontide wakes anew
The buttercups, the little children's dower
– Far brighter than this gaudy melon-flower!   20

HOME-THOUGHTS, FROM ABROAD: Written on Browning's return
from a trip to Italy in 1844 13 **spray**: branch 17 **hoary**: frosty-white

MEETING AT NIGHT

THE grey sea and the long black land;
And the yellow half-moon large and low;
And the startled little waves that leap
In fiery ringlets from their sleep,
As I gain the cove with pushing prow,   5
And quench its speed i' the slushy sand.

Then a mile of warm sea-scented beach;
Three fields to cross till a farm appears;
A tap at the pane, the quick sharp scratch
And blue spurt of a lighted match,   10
And a voice less loud, through its joys and fears,
Than the two hearts beating each to each!

PARTING AT MORNING

ROUND the cape of a sudden came the sea,
And the sun looked over the mountain's rim:
And straight was a path of gold for him,
And the need of a world of men for me.

FRA LIPPO LIPPI
[FLORENTINE PAINTER, 1412–1469. SEE VASARI]

I AM poor brother Lippo, by your leave!
You need not clap your torches to my face.
Zooks, what to blame? you think you see a monk!
What, 'tis past midnight, and you go the rounds,
And here you catch me at an alley's end   5
Where sportive ladies leave their doors ajar?
The Carmine's my cloister: hunt it up,
Do, – harry out, if you must show your zeal,
Whatever rat, there, haps on his wrong hole,
And nip each softling of a wee white mouse,   10
Weke, weke, that's crept to keep him company!
Aha, you know your betters! Then, you'll take
Your hand away that's fiddling on my throat,
And please to know me likewise. Who am I?
Why, one, sir, who is lodging with a friend   15
Three streets off – he's a certain . . . how d'ye call?
Master – a . . . Cosimo of the Medici,
I' the house that caps the corner. Boh! you were best!
Remember and tell me, the day you're hanged,
How you affected such a gullet's-gripe!   20
But you, sir, it concerns you that your knaves
Pick up a manner nor discredit you:
Zooks, are we pilchards, that they sweep the streets
And count fair prize what comes into their net?
He's Judas to a tittle, that man is!   25

Just such a face! Why, sir, you make amends.
Lord, I'm not angry! Bid your hangdogs go
Drink out this quarter-florin to the health
Of the munificent House that harbours me
(And many more beside, lads! more beside!)   30
And all's come square again. I'd like his face –
His, elbowing on his comrade in the door
With the pike and lantern, – for the slave that holds
John Baptist's head a-dangle by the hair
With one hand ('Look you, now,' as who should say)
And his weapon in the other, yet unwiped!   36
It's not your chance to have a bit of chalk,
A wood-coal or the like? or you should see!
Yes, I'm the painter, since you style me so.
What, brother Lippo's doings, up and down,   40
You know them and they take you? like enough!
I saw the proper twinkle in your eye –
'Tell you, I liked your looks at very first.
Let's sit and set things straight now, hip to haunch.
Here's spring come, and the nights one makes up bands   45
To roam the town and sing out carnival,
And I've been three weeks shut within my mew,
A-painting for the great man, saints and saints
And saints again. I could not paint all night –
Ouf! I leaned out of window for fresh air.   50
There came a hurry of feet and little feet,
A sweep of lute-strings, laughs, and whifs of song, –
Flower o' the broom,
Take away love, and our earth is a tomb!
Flower o' the quince,   55
I let Lisa go, and what good in life since?
Flower o' the thyme – and so on. Round they went.
Scarce had they turned the corner when a titter
Like the skipping of rabbits by moonlight, – three slim shapes,
And a face that looked up . . . zooks, sir, flesh and blood,   60
That's all I'm made of! Into shreds it went,
Curtain and counterpane and coverlet,
All the bed-furniture – a dozen knots,
There was a ladder! Down I let myself,
Hands and feet, scrambling somehow, and so dropped,
And after them. I came up with the fun   66
Hard by Saint Laurence, hail fellow, well met, –
Flower o' the rose,
If I've been merry, what matter who knows?
And so as I was stealing back again   70
To get to bed and have a bit of sleep
Ere I rise up tomorrow and go to work
On Jerome knocking at his poor old breast
With his great round stone to subdue the flesh,

FRA LIPPO LIPPI: 'a lively monologue supposed to be uttered by that friar himself, on the occasion of a night frolic in which he has been surprised' (*Handbook*). Fra Filippo Lippi (*c*.1406–1469; Browning took his dates from Vasari) was a Florentine painter and a Carmelite friar (lines 7 and 139): **Fra**: Brother **Vasari**: Giorgio Vasari (1511–74), an Italian painter and architect, is best-known today as the author of *Lives of the Most Excellent Painters, Sculptors and Architects* (1550, 1568), which was Browning's principal source for this poem and for others; in a letter of 1853, Elizabeth described Robert as 'fond of digging at Vasari': 17 **Cosimo of the Medici:** Cosimo de' Medici (1389–1464); the Medici were a Florentine family of bankers and merchants celebrated for their patronage of learning and the arts during the Renaissance 20 **gullet's-gripe:** throat-grip 25 **Judas:** the disciple who betrayed Jesus

34 **John Baptist's . . . hair:** see note to lines 196–7 below 38 **wood-coal:** charcoal 43 **'Tell you:** I tell you 47 **mew:** cage 52 **whifs:** snatches 67 **Hard by:** near **Saint Laurence:** the church of San Lorenzo, Florence 73–4 **Jerome . . . flesh:** St Jerome (*c*.341–420) lived for some years as a hermit in the Syrian desert and was frequently depicted holding a stone, the sign of his voluntary penance

You snap me of the sudden. Ah, I see! 75
Though your eye twinkles still, you shake your head –
Mine's shaved – a monk, you say – the sting's in that!
If Master Cosimo announced himself,
Mum's the word naturally; but a monk!
Come, what am I a beast for? tell us, now! 80
I was a baby when my mother died
And father died and left me in the street.
I starved there, God knows how, a year or two
On fig-skins, melon-parings, rinds and shucks,
Refuse and rubbish. One fine frost day, 85
My stomach being empty as your hat,
The wind doubled me up and down I went.
Old Aunt Lapaccia trussed me with one hand,
(Its fellow was a stinger as I knew)
And so along the wall, over the bridge, 90
By the straight cut to the convent. Six words there,
While I stood munching my first bread that month:
'So, boy, you're minded,' quoth the good fat father
Wiping his own mouth, 'twas refection-time, –
'To quit this very miserable world? 95
Will you renounce' . . . 'the mouthful of bread?'
    thought I;
By no means! Brief, they made a monk of me;
I did renounce the world, its pride and greed,
Palace, farm, villa, shop and banking-house,
Trash, such as these poor devils of Medici 100
Have given their hearts to – all at eight years old.
Well, sir, I found in time, you may be sure,
'Twas not for nothing – the good bellyful,
The warm serge and the rope that goes all round,
And day-long blessèd idleness beside! 105
'Let's see what the urchin's fit for' – that came next.
Not overmuch their way, I must confess.
Such a to-do! They tried me with their books:
Lord, they'd have taught me Latin in pure waste!
Flower o' the clove, 110
All the Latin I construe is, 'amo' I love!
But, mind you, when a boy starves in the streets
Eight years together, as my fortune was,
Watching folk's faces to know who will fling
The bit of half-stripped grape-bunch he desires, 115
And who will curse or kick him for his pains, –
Which gentleman processional and fine,
Holding a candle to the Sacrament,
Will wink and let him lift a plate and catch
The droppings of the wax to sell again, 120
Or holla for the Eight and have him whipped, –
How say I? – nay, which dog bites, which lets
    drop
His bone from the heap of offal in the street, –
Why, soul and sense of him grow sharp alike,
He learns the look of things, and none the less 125
For admonition from the hunger-pinch.

I had a store of such remarks, be sure,
Which, after I found leisure, turned to use.
I drew men's faces on my copy-books,
Scrawled them within the antiphonary's marge, 130
Joined legs and arms to the long music-notes,
Found eyes and nose and chin for A's and B's,
And made a string of pictures of the world
Betwixt the ins and outs of verb and noun,
On the wall, the bench, the door. The monks looked
    black. 135
'Nay,' quoth the Prior, 'turn him out, d'ye say?
In no wise. Lose a crow and catch a lark.
What if at last we get our man of parts,
We Carmelites, like those Camaldolese
And Preaching Friars, to do our church up fine 140
And put the front on it that ought to be!'
And hereupon he bade me daub away.
Thank you! my head being crammed, the walls a
    blank,
Never was such prompt disemburdening.
First, every sort of monk, the black and white, 145
I drew them, fat and lean: then, folk at church,
From good old gossips waiting to confess
Their cribs of barrel-droppings, candle-ends, –
To the breathless fellow at the altar-foot,
Fresh from his murder, safe and sitting there 150
With the little children round him in a row
Of admiration, half for his beard and half
For that white anger of his victim's son
Shaking a fist at him with one fierce arm,
Signing himself with the other because of Christ 155
(Whose sad face on the cross sees only this
After the passion of a thousand years)
Till some poor girl, her apron o'er her head,
(Which the intense eyes looked through) came at eve
On tiptoe, said a word, dropped in a loaf, 160
Her pair of earrings and a bunch of flowers
(The brute took growling), prayed, and so was gone.
I painted all, then cried ' 'Tis ask and have;
Choose, for more's ready!' – laid the ladder flat,
And showed my covered bit of cloister-wall. 165
The monks closed in a circle and praised loud
Till checked, taught what to see and not to see,
Being simple bodies, – 'That's the very man!
Look at the boy who stoops to pat the dog!
That woman's like the Prior's niece who comes 170
To care about his asthma: it's the life!'
But there my triumph's straw-fire flared and funked;
Their betters took their turn to see and say:

---

127 **remarks:** observations 129 **copy-books:** used in the classroom
to teach penmanship; children would copy a printed text
130 **antiphonary:** a collection of antiphons, a type of church music
for two parts, each responding to the other **marge:** margin
139 **Camaldolese:** ('Ca-*mal*-do-*lay*-say') the Camaldolites, a religious
order founded by St Romuald at Camaldoli in the 11th century
140 **Preaching Friars:** Dominicans, a religious order founded by
St Dominic in the 13th century 172 **funked:** smouldered

---

93 **minded:** inclined 94 **refection-time:** meal-time 121 **the Eight:** the
watch, patrolling the streets at night

The Prior and the learnèd pulled a face
And stopped all that in no time. 'How? what's here?
Quite from the mark of painting, bless us all! 176
Faces, arms, legs and bodies like the true
As much as pea and pea! it's devil's-game!
Your business is not to catch men with show,
With homage to the perishable clay, 180
But lift them over it, ignore it all,
Make them forget there's such a thing as flesh.
Your business is to paint the souls of men –
Man's soul, and it's a fire, smoke . . . no, it's not . . .
It's vapour done up like a new-born babe – 185
(In that shape when you die it leaves your mouth)
It's . . . well, what matters talking, it's the soul!
Give us no more of body than shows soul!
Here's Giotto, with his Saint a-praising God,
That sets us praising, – why not stop with him? 190
Why put all thoughts of praise out of our head
With wonder at lines, colours, and what not?
Paint the soul, never mind the legs and arms!
Rub all out, try at it a second time.
Oh, that white smallish female with the breasts, 195
She's just my niece . . . Herodias, I would say, –
Who went and danced and got men's heads cut off!
Have it all out!' Now, is this sense, I ask?
I find way to paint soul, by painting body
So ill, the eye can't stop there, must go further 200
And can't fare worse! Thus, yellow does for white
When what you put for yellow's simply black,
And any sort of meaning looks intense
When all beside itself means and looks nought.
Why can't a painter lift each foot in turn, 205
Left foot and right foot, go a double step,
Make his flesh liker and his soul more like,
Both in their order? Take the prettiest face,
The Prior's niece . . . patron-saint – is it so pretty
You can't discover if it means hope, fear, 210
Sorrow or joy? won't beauty go with these?
Suppose I've made her eyes all right and blue,
Can't I take breath and try to add life's flash,
And then add soul and heighten them three-fold?
Or say there's beauty with no soul at all – 215
(I never saw it – put the case the same –)
If you get simple beauty and nought else,
You get about the best thing God invents:
That's somewhat: and you'll find the soul you have
    missed,
Within yourself, when you return him thanks. 220
'Rub all out!' Well, well, there's my life, in short,
And so the thing has gone on ever since.
I'm grown a man no doubt, I've broken bounds:

You should not take a fellow eight years old
And make him swear to never kiss the girls. 225
I'm my own master, paint now as I please –
Having a friend, you see, in the Corner-house!
Lord, it's fast holding by the rings in front –
Those great rings serve more purposes than just
To plant a flag in, or tie up a horse! 230
And yet the old schooling sticks, the old grave eyes
Are peeping o'er my shoulder as I work,
The heads shake still – 'It's art's decline, my son!
You're not of the true painters, great and old;
Brother Angelico's the man, you'll find; 235
Brother Lorenzo stands his single peer:
Fag on at flesh, you'll never make the third!'
Flower o' the pine,
You keep your mistr . . . manners, and I'll stick to mine!
I'm not the third, then: bless us, they must know! 240
Don't you think they're the likeliest to know,
They with their Latin? So, I swallow my rage,
Clench my teeth, suck my lips in tight, and paint
To please them – sometimes do and sometimes don't;
For, doing most, there's pretty sure to come 245
A turn, some warm eve finds me at my saints –
A laugh, a cry, the business of the world –
(*Flower o' the peach,*
Death for us all, and his own life for each!)
And my whole soul revolves, the cup runs over, 250
The world and life's too big to pass for a dream,
And I do these wild things in sheer despite,
And play the fooleries you catch me at,
In pure rage! The old mill-horse, out at grass
After hard years, throws up his stiff heels so, 255
Although the miller does not preach to him
The only good of grass is to make chaff.
What would men have? Do they like grass or no –
May they or mayn't they? all I want's the thing
Settled for ever one way. As it is, 260
You tell too many lies and hurt yourself:
You don't like what you only like too much,
You do like what, if given you at your word,
You find abundantly detestable.
For me, I think I speak as I was taught; 265
I always see the garden and God there
A-making man's wife: and, my lesson learned,
The value and significance of flesh,
I can't unlearn ten minutes afterwards.

189 **Giotto:** Giotto de Bondone (*c*.1267–1337), Florentine painter
196–7 **Herodias . . . cut off:** actually, it was the *daughter* of Herodias,
Salome, who so delighted Herod with her dancing that he
promised her on oath that she could have anything she desired;
she asked for the head of John the Baptist to be brought to her on
a dish (Mark 6, Matthew 14)

228 **it's fast . . . in front:** the rings attached to the front of the
house offer firm hand-holds for climbing 235 **Brother Angelico:**
Fra Angelico (1387–1455), Italian painter and Dominican friar
236 **Brother Lorenzo:** Lorenzo Monaco (*fl.*1388–1422), Italian painter
and Camaldolite monk 237 **Fag on:** labour away 266–7 **the garden
. . . wife:** Genesis 2.21–2: 'And the Lord God caused a deep sleep
to fall upon Adam, and he slept; and he took one of his ribs, and
closed up the flesh instead thereof; And the rib, which the
Lord God had taken from man, made he a woman, and brought
her unto the man'

You understand me: I'm a beast, I know. 270
But see, now – why, I see as certainly
As that the morning-star's about to shine,
What will hap some day. We've a youngster here
Comes to our convent, studies what I do,
Slouches and stares and lets no atom drop: 275
His name is Guidi – he'll not mind the monks –
They call him Hulking Tom, he lets them talk –
He picks my practice up – he'll paint apace,
I hope so – though I never live so long,
I know what's sure to follow. You be judge! 280
You speak no Latin more than I, belike;
However, you're my man, you've seen the world
– The beauty and the wonder and the power,
The shapes of things, their colours, lights and shades,
Changes, surprises, – and God made it all! 285
– For what? Do you feel thankful, ay or no,
For this fair town's face, yonder river's line,
The mountain round it and the sky above,
Much more the figures of man, woman, child,
These are the frame to? What's it all about? 290
To be passed over, despised? or dwelt upon,
Wondered at? oh, this last of course! – you say.
But why not do as well as say, – paint these
Just as they are, careless what comes of it?
God's works – paint anyone, and count it crime 295
To let a truth slip. Don't object, 'His works
Are here already; nature is complete:
Suppose you reproduce her – (which you can't)
There's no advantage! you must beat her, then.'
For, don't you mark? we're made so that we love 300
First when we see them painted, things we have passed
Perhaps a hundred times nor cared to see;
And so they are better, painted – better to us,
Which is the same thing. Art was given for that;
God uses us to help each other so, 305
Lending our minds out. Have you noticed, now,
Your cullion's hanging face? A bit of chalk,
And trust me but you should, though! How much
    more,
If I drew higher things with the same truth!
That were to take the Prior's pulpit-place, 310
Interpret God to all of you! Oh, oh,
It makes me mad to see what men shall do
And we in our graves! This world's no blot for us,
Nor blank; it means intensely, and means good:
To find its meaning is my meat and drink. 315
'Ay, but you don't so instigate to prayer!'

Strikes in the Prior: 'when your meaning's plain
It does not say to folk – remember matins,
Or, mind you fast next Friday!' Why, for this
What need of art at all? A skull and bones, 320
Two bits of stick nailed crosswise, or, what's best,
A bell to chime the hour with, does as well.
I painted a Saint Laurence six months since
At Prato, splashed the fresco in fine style:
'How looks my painting, now the scaffold's down?' 325
I ask a brother: 'Hugely,' he returns –
'Already not one phiz of your three slaves
Who turn the Deacon off his toasted side,
But's scratched and prodded to our heart's content,
The pious people have so eased their own 330
With coming to say prayers there in a rage:
We get on fast to see the bricks beneath.
Expect another job this time next year,
For pity and religion grow i' the crowd –
Your painting serves its purpose!' Hang the fools! 335

– That is – you'll not mistake an idle word
Spoke in a huff by a poor monk, God wot,
Tasting the air this spicy night which turns
The unaccustomed head like Chianti wine!
Oh, the church knows! don't misreport me, now! 340
It's natural a poor monk out of bounds
Should have his apt word to excuse himself:
And hearken how I plot to make amends.
I have bethought me: I shall paint a piece
. . . There's for you! Give me six months, then go, see
Something in Sant' Ambrogio's! Bless the nuns! 346
They want a cast o' my office. I shall paint
God in the midst, Madonna and her babe,
Ringed by a bowery flowery angel-brood,
Lilies and vestments and white faces, sweet 350
As puff of puff of grated orris-root
When ladies crowd to Church at midsummer.
And then i' the front, of course a saint or two –
Saint John, because he saves the Florentines,
Saint Ambrose, who puts down in black and white
The convent's friends and gives them a long day, 356
And Job, I must have him there past mistake,
The man of Uz (and Us without the z,
Painters who need his patience). Well, all these
Secured at their devotion, up shall come 360

318 **matins:** morning service   323 **Saint Lawrence . . . side:** St Lawrence was a 3rd century Christian martyr who was roasted to death on a gridiron   324 **Prato:** Lippi spent long periods living and working in Prato, near Florence   327 **phiz:** physiognomy, face 337 **wot:** knows 346 **Sant' Ambrogio's:** the church of Sant' Ambrogio, Florence   347 **a cast o' my office:** a sample of my work 351 **orris-root:** dried iris root used in perfumery 354 **Saint John:** the apostle John (1st century AD); the Baptistery of St John is believed to be the oldest surviving building in Florence 355 **Saint Ambrose:** bishop of Milan (c.339–397), his many writings include *De officiis ministrorum*, on the moral obligations of the clergy, and he also improved religious services and introduced new music, lengthening the ritual – and also the monks' day 357–9 **Job . . . patience:** in the Old Testament, God afflicts Job, 'a man in the land of Uz', with terrible suffering to test his piety, but Job bears all patiently

272 **the morning-star:** any planet (especially Venus) that rises before the sun 273 **hap:** happen 276–7 **Guidi . . . Hulking Tom:** Masaccio (1401–28). The impression given here (and reinforced by a note in the *Handbook*) is that Masaccio was Lippi's pupil, although it now seems clear that Masaccio was the senior painter and that Lippi was influenced by *him*; but Browning stuck to his version, writing to Edward Dowden in 1866: 'I was wide awake when I made Fra Lippo the elder practitioner of Art [than Masaccio], if not, as I believe, the earlier born. I looked into the matter carefully' 307 **cullion:** wretch

Out of a corner when you least expect,
As one by a dark stair into a great light,
Music and talking, who but Lippo! I! –
Mazed, motionless and moonstruck – I'm the man!
Back I shrink – what is this I see and hear?   365
I, caught up with my monk's-things by mistake,
My old serge gown and rope that goes all round,
I, in this presence, this pure company!
Where's a hole, where's a corner for escape?
Then steps a sweet angelic slip of a thing   370
Forward, puts out a soft palm – 'Not so fast!'
– Addresses the celestial presence, 'nay –
He made you and devised you, after all,
Though he's none of you! Could Saint John there
   draw –
His camel-hair make up a painting-brush?   375
We come to brother Lippo for all that,
Iste perfecit opus! So, all smile –
I shuffle sideways with my blushing face
Under the cover of a hundred wings
Thrown like a spread of kirtles when you're gay   380
And play hot cockles, all the doors being shut,
Till, wholly unexpected, in there pops
The hothead husband! Thus I scuttle off
To some safe bench behind, not letting go
The palm of her, the little lily thing   385
That spoke the good word for me in the nick,
Like the Prior's niece . . . Saint Lucy, I would say.
And so all's saved for me, and for the church
A pretty picture gained. Go, six months hence!
Your hand, sir, and good-bye: no lights, no lights!   390
The street's hushed, and I know my own way back,
Don't fear me! There's the grey beginning. Zooks!

364 **Mazed:** confused 377 ***Iste perfecit opus!:*** 'This is he who accomplished
the work' 380 **kirtles:** short cloaks 381 **hot cockles:** 'A rustic game
in which one player lay face downwards, or knelt down with his
eyes covered, and being struck in the back by the others in turn,
guessed who struck him' (*OED*) 386 **in the nick:** i.e. in the nick of
time 387 **Saint Lucy:** Sicilian Christian martyr (d. AD 303)

TWO IN THE CAMPAGNA

I WONDER do you feel today
   As I have felt since, hand in hand,
We sat down on the grass, to stray
   In spirit better through the land,
This morn of Rome and May?   5

For me, I touched a thought, I know,
   Has tantalised me many times,
(Like turns of thread the spiders throw
   Mocking across our path) for rhymes
To catch at and let go.   10

Help me to hold it! First it left
   The yellowing fennel, run to seed

There, branching from the brickwork's cleft,
   Some old tomb's ruin: yonder weed
Took up the floating weft,   15

Where one small orange cup amassed
   Five beetles, – blind and green they grope
Among the honey-meal: and last,
   Everywhere on the grassy slope
I traced it. Hold it fast!   20

The champaign with its endless fleece
   Of feathery grasses everywhere!
Silence and passion, joy and peace,
   An everlasting wash of air –
Rome's ghost since her decease.   25

Such life here, through such lengths of hours,
   Such miracles performed in play,
Such primal naked forms of flowers,
   Such letting nature have her way
While heaven looks from its towers!   30

How say you? Let us, O my dove,
   Let us be unashamed of soul,
As earth lies bare to heaven above!
   How is it under our control
To love or not to love?   35

I would that you were all to me,
   You that are just so much, no more.
Nor yours nor mine, nor slave nor free!
   Where does the fault lie? What the core
O' the wound, since wound must be?   40

I would I could adopt your will,
   See with your eyes, and set my heart
Beating by yours, and drink my fill
   At your soul's springs, – your part my part
In life, for good or ill.   45

No. I yearn upward, touch you close,
   Then stand away. I kiss your cheek,
Catch your soul's warmth, – I pluck the rose
   And love it more than tongue can speak –
Then the good minute goes.   50

Already how am I so far
   Out of that minute? Must I go
Still like the thistle-ball, no bar,
   Onward, whenever light winds blow,
Fixed by no friendly star?   55

Just when I seemed about to learn!
   Where is the thread now? Off again!
The old trick! Only I discern –
   Infinite passion, and the pain
Of finite hearts that yearn.   60

TWO IN THE CAMPAGNA: 'The sufferer is a man. He longs to rest in the affection of a woman who loves him, and whom he also loves; but whenever their union seems complete, his soul is spirited away, and he is adrift again. . . . The clue to the enigma seems to glance across him, in the form of a gossamer thread. He traces it from point to point, by the objects on which it rests. But just as he calls his love to help him to hold it fast, it breaks off, and floats into the invisible. His doom is endless change. The tired, tantalised spirit must accept it' (*Handbook*): **Campagna:** Campagna di Roma, the lowland plain surrounding the city of Rome; the Brownings were in Rome in May 1854, when the poem was probably written (line 5) 12 **fennel:** 'Herb with yellow flowers and seeds supposed to be medicinal' (RB) 18 **honey-meal:** honey-apple, an apple grafted on a quince 21 **champaign:** open level country

PROSPICE

FEAR death? – to feel the fog in my throat,
    The mist in my face,
When the snows begin, and the blasts denote
    I am nearing the place,
The power of the night, the press of the storm,   5
    The post of the foe;
Where he stands, the Arch Fear in a visible form,
    Yet the strong man must go:
For the journey is done and the summit attained,
    And the barriers fall,   10
Though a battle's to fight ere the guerdon be gained,
    The reward of it all.
I was ever a fighter, so – one fight more,
    The best and the last!
I would hate that death bandaged my eyes, and
        forbore,
    And bade me creep past.   15
No! let me taste the whole of it, fare like my peers
    The heroes of old,
Bear the brunt, in a minute pay glad life's arrears
    Of pain, darkness and cold.   20
For sudden the worst turns the best to the brave,
    The black minute's at end,
And the elements' rage, the fiend-voices that rave,
    Shall dwindle, shall blend,
Shall change, shall become first a peace out of pain,
    Then a light, then thy breast,   26
O thou soul of my soul! I shall clasp thee again,
    And with God be the rest!

PROSPICE: ('Look forward') 'a challenge to spiritual conflict, exultant with the certainty of victory, glowing with the prospective joy of re-union with one whom death has sent before' (*Handbook*): 11 **guerdon:** reward

From THE RING AND THE BOOK

O LYRIC LOVE, half angel and half bird
And all a wonder and a wild desire, –
Boldest of hearts that ever braved the sun,
Took sanctuary within the holier blue,
And sang a kindred soul out to his face, –   5
Yet human at the red-ripe of the heart –
When the first summons from the darkling earth
Reached thee amid thy chambers, blanched their blue,
And bared them of the glory – to drop down,
To toil for man, to suffer or to die, –   10
This is the same voice: can thy soul know change?
Hail then, and hearken from the realms of help!
Never may I commence my song, my due
To God who best taught song by gift of thee,
Except with bent head and beseeching hand –   15
That still, despite the distance and the dark,
What was, again may be; some interchange
Of grace, some splendour once thy very thought,
Some benediction anciently thy smile:
– Never conclude, but raising hand and head   20
Thither where eyes, that cannot reach, yet yearn
For all hope, all sustainment, all reward,
Their utmost up and on, – so blessing back
In those thy realms of help, that heaven thy home,
Some whiteness which, I judge, thy face makes
    proud,   25
Some wanness where, I think, thy foot may fall!
        [Book 1, lines 1391–1416]

THE RING AND THE BOOK: Published in four volumes (1868–9). These lines from the end of the first book dedicate the whole work to Elizabeth, who had died in 1861 7 **darkling:** dark

EDWARD LEAR

THE OWL AND THE PUSSY-CAT

THE Owl and the Pussy-Cat went to sea
    In a beautiful pea-green boat,
They took some honey, and plenty of money
    Wrapped up in a five-pound note.
The Owl looked up to the stars above,   5
    And sang to a small guitar,
'O lovely Pussy! O Pussy, my love,
    What a beautiful Pussy you are,
        You are,
        You are!   10
What a beautiful Pussy you are!'

Pussy said to the Owl, 'You elegant fowl!
    How charmingly sweet you sing!
Oh, let us be married; too long we have tarried:
    But what shall we do for a ring?'   15
They sailed away for a year and a day,
    To the land where the Bong-tree grows;
And there in a wood a Piggy-wig stood,
    With a ring at the end of his nose,
        His nose,
        His nose,   20
    With a ring at the end of his nose.

'Dear Pig, are you willing to sell for one shilling
  Your ring?' Said the Piggy, 'I will.'
So they took it away and were married next day   25
  By the Turkey who lives on the hill.
They dined on mince and slices of quince,
  Which they ate with a runcible spoon;
And hand in hand, on the edge of the sand,
  They danced by the light of the moon,   30
    The moon,
    The moon,
  They danced by the light of the moon.

THE JUMBLIES

THEY went to sea in a Sieve, they did,
  In a Sieve they went to sea:
In spite of all their friends could say,
On a winter's morn, on a stormy day,
  In a Sieve they went to sea!   5
And when the Sieve turned round and round,
And everyone cried, 'You'll all be drowned!'
They called aloud, 'Our Sieve ain't big,
But we don't care a button! we don't care a fig!
  In a Sieve we'll go to sea!'   10
    Far and few, far and few,
      Are the lands where the Jumblies live;
    Their heads are green, and their hands are
      blue,
    And they went to sea in a Sieve.

They sailed away in a Sieve, they did,   15
  In a Sieve they sailed so fast,
With only a beautiful pea-green veil
Tied with a riband by way of a sail,
  To a small tobacco-pipe mast;
And every one said, who saw them go,   20
'Oh, won't they be soon upset, you know!
For the sky is dark, and the voyage is long,
And happen what may, it's extremely wrong
  In a Sieve to sail so fast!'
    Far and few, far and few,   25
      Are the lands where the Jumblies live;
    Their heads are green, and their hands are
      blue,
    And they went to sea in a Sieve.

The water it soon came in, it did,
  The water it soon came in;   30
So to keep them dry, they wrapped their feet
In a pinky paper all folded neat,
  And they fastened it down with a pin.
And they passed the night in a crockery-jar,
And each of them said, 'How wise we are!   35

Though the sky be dark, and the voyage be long,
Yet we never can think we were rash or wrong,
  While round in our Sieve we spin!'
    Far and few, far and few,
      Are the lands where the Jumblies live;   40
    Their heads are green, and their hands are
      blue,
    And they went to sea in a Sieve.

And all night long they sailed away;
  And when the sun went down,
They whistled and warbled a moony song   45
To the echoing sound of a coppery gong,
  In the shade of the mountains brown.
'Oh, Timballo! How happy we are,
When we live in a sieve and a crockery-jar,
And all night long in the moonlight pale,   50
We sail away with a pea-green sail,
  In the shade of the mountains brown!'
    Far and few, far and few,
      Are the lands where the Jumblies live;
    Their heads are green, and their hands are
      blue,   55
    And they went to sea in a Sieve.

They sailed to the Western Sea, they did,
  To a land all covered with trees,
And they bought an Owl, and a useful Cart,
And a pound of Rice, and a Cranberry Tart,   60
  And a hive of silvery Bees.
And they bought a Pig, and some green Jackdaws,
And a lovely Monkey with lollipop paws,
And forty bottles of Ring-Bo-Ree,
  And no end of Stilton Cheese.   65
    Far and few, far and few,
      Are the lands where the Jumblies live;
    Their heads are green, and their hands are
      blue,
    And they went to sea in a Sieve.

And in twenty years they all came back,   70
  In twenty years or more,
And everyone said, 'How tall they've grown!
For they've been to the Lakes, and the Torrible Zone,
  And the hills of the Chankly Bore';
And they drank their health, and gave them a feast   75
Of dumplings made of beautiful yeast;
And everyone said, 'If we only live,
We too will go to sea in a Sieve,
  To the hills of the Chankly Bore!'
    Far and few, far and few,   80
      Are the lands where the Jumblies live;
    Their heads are green, and their hands are blue,
    And they went to sea in a Sieve.

EMILY BRONTE

REMEMBRANCE

COLD in the earth – and the deep snow piled above
    thee,
Far, far removed, cold in the dreary grave!
Have I forgot, my only Love, to love thee,
Severed at last by Time's all-severing wave?

Now, when alone, do my thoughts no longer hover   5
Over the mountains, on that northern shore,
Resting their wings where heath and fern-leaves cover
Thy noble heart for ever, ever more!

Cold in the earth – and fifteen wild Decembers
From those brown hills have melted into spring –   10
Faithful indeed is the spirit that remembers
After such years of change and suffering!

Sweet Love of youth, forgive, if I forget thee
While the world's tide is bearing me along:
Other desires and other hopes beset me,   15
Hopes which obscure, but cannot do thee wrong!

No later light has lightened up my heaven;
No second morn has ever shone for me:
All my life's bliss from thy dear life was given –
All my life's bliss is in the grave with thee.   20

But, when the days of golden dreams had perished,
And even Despair was powerless to destroy,
Then did I learn how existence could be cherished,
Strengthened, and fed without the aid of joy;

Then did I check the tears of useless passion,   25
Weaned my young soul from yearning after thine;
Sternly denied its burning wish to hasten
Down to that tomb already more than mine!

And, even yet, I dare not let it languish,
Dare not indulge in Memory's rapturous pain;   30
Once drinking deep of that divinest anguish,
How could I seek the empty world again?

'NO COWARD SOUL IS MINE . . .'

NO coward soul is mine,
No trembler in the world's storm-troubled sphere:
I see Heaven's glories shine,
And faith shines equal, arming me from fear.

O God within my breast,   5
Almighty, ever-present Deity!
Life – that in me has rest,
As I – undying Life – have power in Thee!

Vain are the thousand creeds
That move men's hearts: unutterably vain;   10
Worthless as withered weeds,
Or idlest froth amid the boundless main,

To waken doubt in one
Holding so fast by Thine infinity;
So surely anchored on   15
The steadfast rock of immortality.

With wide-embracing love
Thy spirit animates eternal years,
Pervades and broods above,
Changes, sustains, dissolves, creates, and rears.   20

Though earth and man were gone,
And suns and universes ceased to be,
And Thou were left alone,
Every existence would exist in Thee.

There is not room for Death,   25
Nor atom that his might could render void:
Thou – THOU art Being and Breath,
And what THOU art may never be destroyed.

ARTHUR HUGH CLOUGH

From AMOURS DE VOYAGE

Is it illusion? or does there a spirit from perfecter
    ages,
    Here, even yet, amid loss, change, and corruption
        abide?
Does there a spirit we know not, though seek, though
    we find, comprehend not,
    Here to entice and confuse, tempt and evade us,
        abide?
Lives in the exquisite grace of the column disjointed
    and single,   5
    Haunts the rude masses of brick garlanded gaily
        with vine,
E'en in the turret fantastic surviving that springs from
    the ruin,
    E'en in the people itself? is it illusion or not?
Is it illusion or not that attracteth the pilgrim
    transalpine,
    Brings him a dullard and dunce hither to pry and to
        stare?   10
Is it illusion or not that allures the barbarian stranger,
    Brings him with gold to the shrine, brings him in
        arms to the gate?

[Canto 2]

AMOURS DE VOYAGE: the title is French for 'loves (or love affairs)
during a journey'

YET to the wondrous St Peter's, and yet to the solemn
   Rotunda,
  Mingling with heroes and gods, yet to the Vatican
    Walls,
Yet may we go, and recline, while a whole mighty
   world seems above us,
  Gathered and fixed to all time into one roofing
    supreme;
Yet may we, thinking on these things, exclude what is
   meaner around us;   5
  Yet, at the worst of the worst, books and a chamber
    remain;
Yet may we think, and forget, and possess our souls in
   resistance. –
  Ah, but away from the stir, shouting, and gossip of
    war,
Where, upon Apennine slope, with the chestnut the
   oak-trees immingle,
  Where, amid odorous copse bridle-paths wander
    and wind,   10
Where, under mulberry-branches, the diligent rivulet
   sparkles,
  Or amid cotton and maize peasants their water-
    works ply,
Where, over fig-tree and orange in tier upon tier still
   repeated,
  Garden on garden upreared, balconies step to the
    sky, –
Ah, that I were far away from the crowd and the
   streets of the city,   15
  Under the vine-trellis laid, O my belovèd, with
    thee!

                          [Canto 3]

JUXTAPOSITION, in fine; and what is juxtaposition?
Look you, we travel along in the railway-carriage or
   steamer,
And, *pour passer le temps*, till the tedious journey be
   ended,
Lay aside paper or book, to talk with the girl that is
   next one;
And, *pour passer le temps*, with the terminus all but in
   prospect,   5
Talk of eternal ties and marriages made in heaven.
  Ah, did we really accept with a perfect heart the
    illusion!
Ah, did we really believe that the Present indeed is the
   Only!
Or through all transmutation, all shock and
   convulsion of passion,
Feel we could carry undimmed, unextinguished, the
   light of our knowledge!   10
  But for his funeral train which the bridegroom sees
    in the distance,

Would he so joyfully, think you, fall in with the
   marriage-procession?
But for that final discharge, would he dare to enlist in
   that service?
But for that certain release, ever sign to that perilous
   contract?
But for that exit secure, ever bend to that treacherous
   doorway? –   15
Ah, but the bride, meantime, – do you think she sees it
   as he does?
  But for the steady fore-sense of a freer and larger
    existence,
Think you that man could consent to be circumscribed
   here into action?
But for assurance within of a limitless ocean divine,
   o'er
Whose great tranquil depths unconscious the wind-
   tossed surface   20
Breaks into ripples of trouble that come and change
   and endure not, –
But that in this, of a truth, we have our being, and
   know it,
Think you we men could submit to live and move as
   we do here?
Ah, but the women, – God bless them! they don't think
   at all about it.
  Yet we must eat and drink, as you say. And as
    limited beings   25
Scarcely can hope to attain upon earth to an Actual
   Abstract,
Leaving to God contemplation, to His hands
   knowledge confiding,
Sure that in us if it perish, in Him it abideth and dies
   not,
Let us in His sight accomplish our petty particular
   doings, –
Yes, and contented sit down to the victual that He has
   provided.   30
Allah is great, no doubt, and Juxtaposition his prophet.
Ah, but the women, alas! they don't look at it that way.
  Juxtaposition is great; – but, my friend, I fear me,
    the maiden
Hardly would thank or acknowledge the lover that
   sought to obtain her,
Not as the thing he would wish, but the thing he must
   even put up with, –   35
Hardly would tender her hand to the wooer that
   candidly told her
That she is but for a space, an *ad interim* solace and
   pleasure, –
That in the end she shall yield to a perfect and
   absolute something,
Which I then for myself shall behold, and not
   another, –

3RD EXTRACT: 3 *pour passer le temps:* to pass the time

26 **Actual Abstract:** perfect state 37 *ad interim:* for the time being

Which amid fondest endearments, meantime I forget
    not, forsake not.   40
Ah, ye feminine souls, so loving, and so exacting,
Since we cannot escape, must we even submit to
    deceive you?
Since so cruel is truth, sincerity shocks and revolts
    you,
Will you have us your slaves to lie to you, flatter and –
    leave you?

                            [Canto 3]

'SAY NOT THE STRUGGLE NOUGHT AVAILETH'

SAY not the struggle nought availeth,
  The labour and the wounds are vain,
The enemy faints not, nor faileth,
  And as things have been, things remain.

If hopes were dupes, fears may be liars;   5
  It may be, in yon smoke concealed,
Your comrades chase e'en now the fliers,
  And, but for you, possess the field.

For while the tired waves, vainly breaking,
  Seem here no painful inch to gain,   10
Far back through creeks and inlets making
  Came, silent, flooding in, the main,

And not by eastern windows only,
  When daylight comes, comes in the light,
In front the sun climbs slow, how slowly,   15
  But westward, look, the land is bright.

THE LATEST DECALOGUE

THOU shalt have one God only; who
Would be at the expense of two?
No graven images may be
Worshipped, except the currency:
Swear not at all; for for thy curse   5
Thine enemy is none the worse:
At church on Sunday to attend
Will serve to keep the world thy friend:
Honour thy parents; that is, all
From whom advancement may befall: 10
Thou shalt not kill; but needst not strive
Officiously to keep alive:
Do not adultery commit;
Advantage rarely comes of it:
Thou shalt not steal; an empty feat,   15
When it's so lucrative to cheat:
Bear not false witness; let the lie
Have time on its own wings to fly:
Thou shalt not covet, but tradition
Approves all forms of competition.   20

The sum of all is, thou shalt love,
If anybody, God above:
At any rate shall never labour
More than thyself to love thy neighbour.

THE LATEST DECALOGUE: **Decalogue:** The Ten Commandments

MATTHEW ARNOLD

SHAKESPEARE

OTHERS abide our question. Thou art free.
We ask and ask: Thou smilest and art still,
Out-topping knowledge. For the loftiest hill
Who to the stars uncrowns his majesty,
Planting his steadfast footsteps in the sea,   5
Making the heaven of heavens his dwelling-place,
Spares but the cloudy border of his base
To the foiled searching of mortality;
And thou, who didst the stars and sunbeams know,
Self-schooled, self-scanned, self-honoured,
    self-secure,   10
Didst tread on earth unguessed at. – Better so!
All pains the immortal spirit must endure,
All weakness which impairs, all griefs which bow,
Find their sole speech in that victorious brow.

MEETING

AGAIN I see my bliss at hand,
The town, the lake are here;
My Marguerite smiles upon the strand,
Unaltered with the year.

I know that graceful figure fair,   5
That cheek of languid hue;
I know that soft, enkerchiefed hair,
And those sweet eyes of blue.

Again I spring to make my choice;
Again in tones of ire   10
I hear a God's tremendous voice:
'Be counselled, and retire.'

Ye guiding Powers who join and part,
What would ye have with me?
Ah, warn some more ambitious heart,   15
And let the peaceful be!

MEETING: the first of a series of poems recording Arnold's feelings for 'Marguerite', a French girl he apparently met in the Swiss city of Thun in 1848 and again in 1849, and about whom nothing more is known

ISOLATION. TO MARGUERITE

WE were apart; yet, day by day,
I bade my heart more constant be.
I bade it keep the world away,
And grow a home for only thee;
Nor feared but thy love likewise grew,   5
Like mine, each day, more tried, more true.

The fault was grave! I might have known,
What far too soon, alas! I learned –
The heart can bind itself alone,
And faith may oft be unreturned.   10
Self-swayed our feelings ebb and swell –
Thou lov'st no more; – Farewell! Farewell!

Farewell! – and thou, thou lonely heart,
Which never yet without remorse
Even for a moment didst depart   15
From thy remote and spherèd course
To haunt the place where passions reign –
Back to thy solitude again!

Back! with the conscious thrill of shame
Which Luna felt, that summer-night,   20
Flash through her pure immortal frame,
When she forsook the starry height
To hang over Endymion's sleep
Upon the pine-grown Latmian steep.

Yet she, chaste queen, had never proved   25
How vain a thing is mortal love,
Wandering in Heaven, far removed.
But thou hast long had place to prove
This truth – to prove, and make thine own:
'Thou hast been, shalt be, art, alone.'   30

Or, if not quite alone, yet they
Which touch thee are unmating things –
Ocean and clouds and night and day;
Lorn autumns and triumphant springs;
And life, and others' joy and pain,   35
And love, if love, of happier men.

Of happier men – for they, at least,
Have *dreamed* two human hearts might blend
In one, and were through faith released
From isolation without end   40
Prolonged; nor knew, although not less
Alone than thou, their loneliness.

ISOLATION. TO MARGUERITE: 20 **Luna:** the goddess of the moon, who
in Greek myth loved the shepherd Endymion, to whom Zeus gave
eternal life and youth but also eternal sleep. The moon would
descend each night to embrace Endymion on Mount Latmus

TO MARGUERITE – CONTINUED

YES! in the sea of life enisled,
With echoing straits between us thrown,
Dotting the shoreless watery wild,
We mortal millions live *alone*.
The islands feel the enclasping flow,   5
And then their endless bounds they know.

But when the moon their hollows lights,
And they are swept by balms of spring,
And in their glens, on starry nights,
The nightingales divinely sing;   10
And lovely notes, from shore to shore,
Across the sounds and channels pour –

Oh! then a longing like despair
Is to their farthest caverns sent;
For surely once, they feel, we were   15
Parts of a single continent!
Now round us spreads the watery plain –
Oh might our marges meet again!

Who ordered, that their longing's fire
Should be, as soon as kindled, cooled?   20
Who renders vain their deep desire? –
A God, a God their severance ruled!
And bade betwixt their shores to be
The unplumbed, salt, estranging sea.

DOVER BEACH

THE sea is calm tonight.
The tide is full, the moon lies fair
Upon the straits; – on the French coast the light
Gleams and is gone; the cliffs of England stand,
Glimmering and vast, out in the tranquil bay.   5
Come to the window, sweet is the night-air!
Only, from the long line of spray
Where the sea meets the moon-blanched land,
Listen! you hear the grating roar
Of pebbles which the waves draw back, and fling,   10
At their return, up the high strand,
Begin, and cease, and then again begin,
With tremulous cadence slow, and bring
The eternal note of sadness in.

Sophocles long ago   15
Heard it on the Aegean, and it brought
Into his mind the turbid ebb and flow
Of human misery; we
Find also in the sound a thought,
Hearing it by this distant northern sea.   20

The Sea of Faith
Was once, too, at the full, and round earth's shore
Lay like the folds of a bright girdle furled.
But now I only hear
Its melancholy, long, withdrawing roar,   25
Retreating, to the breath
Of the night-wind, down the vast edges drear
And naked shingles of the world.

Ah, love, let us be true
To one another! for the world, which seems   30
To lie before us like a land of dreams,
So various, so beautiful, so new,
Hath really neither joy, nor love, nor light,
Nor certitude, nor peace, nor help for pain;
And we are here as on a darkling plain   35
Swept with confused alarms of struggle and flight,
Where ignorant armies clash by night.

DOVER BEACH: 15 **Sophocles:** (?496–406 BC), Greek tragedian 35 **darkling:** dark or growing dark

RUGBY CHAPEL
NOVEMBER, 1857

COLDLY, sadly descends
The autumn evening. The Field
Strewn with its dank yellow drifts
Of withered leaves, and the elms,
Fade into dimness apace,   5
Silent; – hardly a shout
From a few boys late at their play!
The lights come out in the street,
In the school-room windows; but cold,
Solemn, unlighted, austere,   10
Through the gathering darkness, arise
The Chapel walls, in whose bound
Thou, my father! art laid.

There thou dost lie, in the gloom
Of the autumn evening. But ah!   15
That word, *gloom*, to my mind
Brings thee back in the light
Of thy radiant vigour again!
In the gloom of November we passed
Days not of gloom at thy side;   20
Seasons impaired not the ray
Of thine even cheerfulness clear.
Such thou wast; and I stand
In the autumn evening, and think
Of bygone autumns with thee.   25

RUGBY CHAPEL: 13 **my father:** Thomas Arnold (1795–1842), headmaster of Rugby School 23 **wast:** archaic form of *were*

Fifteen years have gone round
Since thou arosest to tread,
In the summer morning, the road
Of death, at a call unforeseen,
Sudden. For fifteen years,   30
We who till then in thy shade
Rested as under the boughs
Of a mighty oak, have endured
Sunshine and rain as we might,
Bare, unshaded, alone,   35
Lacking the shelter of thee.

O strong soul, by what shore
Tarriest thou now? For that force,
Surely, has not been left vain!
Somewhere, surely, afar,   40
In the sounding labour-house vast
Of being, is practised that strength,
Zealous, beneficent, firm!

Yes, in some far-shining sphere,
Conscious or not of the past,   45
Still thou performest the word
Of the Spirit in whom thou dost live,
Prompt, unwearied, as here!
Still thou upraisest with zeal
The humble good from the ground,   50
Sternly repressest the bad.
Still, like a trumpet, dost rouse
Those who with half-open eyes
Tread the border-land dim
'Twixt vice and virtue; reviv'st,   55
Succourest; – this was thy work,
This was thy life upon earth.

What is the course of the life
Of mortal men on the earth? –
Most men eddy about   60
Here and there – eat and drink,
Chatter and love and hate,
Gather and squander, are raised
Aloft, are hurled in the dust,
Striving blindly, achieving   65
Nothing, and then they die –
Perish; and no one asks
Who or what they have been,
More than he asks what waves
In the moonlit solitudes mild   70
Of the midmost Ocean, have swelled,
Foamed for a moment, and gone.

And there are some, whom a thirst
Ardent, unquenchable, fires,
Not with the crowd to be spent,   75

41 **sounding labour-house:** echoing laboratory

Not without aim to go round
In an eddy of purposeless dust,
Effort unmeaning and vain.
Ah, yes, some of us strive
Not without action to die   80
Fruitless, but something to snatch
From dull oblivion, nor all
Glut the devouring grave!
We, we have chosen our path –
Path to a clear-purposed goal,   85
Path of advance! but it leads
A long, steep journey, through sunk
Gorges, o'er mountains in snow!
Cheerful, with friends, we set forth;
Then, on the height, comes the storm!   90
Thunder crashes from rock
To rock, the cataracts reply;
Lightnings dazzle our eyes;
Roaring torrents have breached
The track, the stream-bed descends   95
In the place where the wayfarer once
Planted his footstep – the spray
Boils o'er its borders; aloft,
The unseen snow-beds dislodge
Their hanging ruin; – alas,   100
Havoc is made in our train!
Friends who set forth at our side
Falter, are lost in the storm!
We, we only, are left!
With frowning foreheads, with lips   105
Sternly compressed, we strain on,
On – and at nightfall, at last,
Come to the end of our way,
To the lonely inn 'mid the rocks;
Where the gaunt and taciturn Host   110
Stands on the threshold, the wind
Shaking his thin white hairs –
Holds his lantern to scan
Our storm-beat figures, and asks:
Whom in our party we bring?   115
Whom have we left in the snow?

Sadly we answer: We bring
Only ourselves; we lost
Sight of the rest in the storm.
Hardly ourselves we fought through,   120
Stripped, without friends, as we are.
Friends, companions, and train
The avalanche swept from our side.
But thou would'st not *alone*
Be saved, my father! *alone*   125
Conquer and come to thy goal,
Leaving the rest in the wild.
We were weary, and we
Fearful, and we, in our march,
Fain to drop down and to die.   130

Still thou turnedst, and still
Beckonedst the trembler, and still
Gavest the weary thy hand!

If, in the paths of the world,
Stones might have wounded thy feet,   135
Toil or dejection have tried
Thy spirit, of that we saw
Nothing! to us thou wert still
Cheerful, and helpful, and firm.
Therefore to thee it was given   140
Many to save with thyself;
And, at the end of thy day,
O faithful shepherd! to come,
Bringing thy sheep in thy hand.
And through thee I believe   145
In the noble and great who are gone;
Pure souls honoured and blest
By former ages, who else –
Such, so soulless, so poor,
Is the race of men whom I see –   150
Seemed but a dream of the heart,
Seemed but a cry of desire.
Yes! I believe that there lived
Others like thee in the past,
Not like the men of the crowd   155
Who all round me today
Bluster or cringe, and make life
Hideous, and arid, and vile;
But souls tempered with fire,
Fervent, heroic, and good,   160
Helpers and friends of mankind.

Servants of God! – or sons
Shall I not call you? because
Not as servants ye knew
Your Father's innermost mind,   165
His, who unwillingly sees
One of his little ones lost –
Yours is the praise, if mankind
Hath not as yet in its march
Fainted, and fallen, and died!   170

See! in the rocks of the world
Marches the host of mankind,
A feeble, wavering line.
Where are they tending? – A God
Marshalled them, gave them their goal. –   175
Ah, but the way is so long!
Years have they been in the wild!
Sore thirst plagues them; the rocks,
Rising all round, overawe.
Factions divide them; their host   180
Threatens to break, to dissolve.
Ah, keep, keep them combined!
Else, of the myriads who fill
That army, not one shall arrive!

Sole they shall stray; in the rocks
Labour for ever in vain,
Die one by one in the waste.   185

Then, in such hour of need
Of your fainting, dispirited race,
Ye, like angels, appear,   190
Radiant with ardour divine.
Beacons of hope, ye appear!
Languor is not in your heart,
Weakness is not in your word,
Weariness not on your brow.   195
Ye alight in our van; at your voice,
Panic, despair, flee away.
Ye move through the ranks, recall
The stragglers, refresh the outworn,
Praise, re-inspire the brave.   200
Order, courage, return.
Eyes rekindling, and prayers,
Follow your steps as ye go.
Ye fill up the gaps in our files,
Strengthen the wavering line,   205
Stablish, continue our march,
On, to the bound of the waste,
On, to the City of God.

196 **van**: vanguard, the foremost part of an army

From SOHRAB AND RUSTUM

So, on the bloody sand, Sohrab lay dead.
And the great Rustum drew his horseman's cloak
Down o'er his face, and sate by his dead son.
As those black granite pillars, once high-reared
By Jemshid in Persepolis, to bear   5
His house, now, mid their broken flights of steps,
Lie prone, enormous, down the mountain side –
So in the sand lay Rustum by his son.
    And night came down over the solemn waste,
And the two gazing hosts, and that sole pair,   10
And darkened all; and a cold fog, with night,
Crept from the Oxus. Soon a hum arose,
As of a great assembly loosed, and fires
Began to twinkle through the fog: for now
Both armies moved to camp, and took their meal: 15
The Persians took it on the open sands
Southward; the Tartars by the river marge:
And Rustum and his son were left alone.
    But the majestic River floated on,
Out of the mist and hum of that low land,   20
Into the frosty starlight, and there moved,
Rejoicing, through the hushed Chorasmian waste,
Under the solitary moon: he flowed
Right for the Polar Star, past Orgunjé,
Brimming, and bright, and large: then sands begin   25
To hem his watery march, and dam his streams,
And split his currents; that for many a league

The shorn and parcelled Oxus strains along
Through beds of sand and matted rushy isles –
Oxus, forgetting the bright speed he had   30
In his high mountain-cradle in Pamere,
A foiled circuitous wanderer: – till at last
The longed-for dash of waves is heard, and wide
His luminous home of waters opens, bright
And tranquil, from whose floor the new-bathed stars
Emerge, and shine upon the Aral Sea.   36

[Lines 897–932]

SOHRAB AND RUSTUM: 1 **Sohrab**: in Persian legend, the son of the great warrior Rustum. When the two fought, not knowing one another, Sohrab was killed 5 **Jemshid**: legendary Persian king **Persepolis**: the capital of ancient Persia 12 **Oxus**: the ancient name for the Amu Darya, a river in Central Asia 22 **Chorasmian waste**: a wasteland on the shore of the Oxus 31 **Pamere**: the Pamirs, a mountain range in Central Asia 36 **Aral Sea**: a shallow saline lake in Central Asia, into which the Amu Darya flows

THE SCHOLAR GIPSY

Go, for they call you, shepherd, from the hill;
    Go, shepherd, and untie the wattled cotes!
        No longer leave thy wistful flock unfed,
        Nor let thy bawling fellows rack their throats,
            Nor the cropped herbage shoot another head.   5
            But when the fields are still,
        And the tired men and dogs all gone to rest,
            And only the white sheep are sometimes seen
            Cross and recross the strips of moon-blanched
                green,
        Come, shepherd, and again begin the quest!   10

Here, where the reaper was at work of late –
    In this high field's dark corner, where he leaves
        His coat, his basket, and his earthen cruse,
        And in the sun all morning binds the sheaves,
            Then here, at noon, comes back his stores to use –
            Here will I sit and wait,   16
        While to my ear from uplands far away
            The bleating of the folded flocks is borne,
            With distant cries of reapers in the corn –
        All the live murmur of a summer's day.   20

Screened is this nook o'er the high, half-reaped field,
    And here till sun-down, shepherd! will I be.
        Through the thick corn the scarlet poppies peep,
        And round green roots and yellowing stalks I see
            Pale pink convolvulus in tendrils creep;   25
            And air-swept lindens yield
        Their scent, and rustle down their perfumed
                showers
            Of bloom on the bent grass where I am laid,
            And bower me from the August sun with shade;
        And the eye travels down to Oxford's towers.   30

THE SCHOLAR GIPSY: 2 **wattled cotes**: sheep shelters made from interwoven branches 13 **cruse**: an earthenware container for liquids

And near me on the grass lies Glanvill's book –
　Come, let me read the oft-read tale again!
　　The story of the Oxford scholar poor,
　Of pregnant parts and quick inventive brain,
　　Who, tired of knocking at preferment's door, 35
　　　One summer-morn forsook
　His friends, and went to learn the gipsy-lore,
　And roamed the world with that wild
　　　brotherhood,
　And came, as most men deemed, to little good,
But came to Oxford and his friends no more. 40

But once, years after, in the country-lanes,
　Two scholars, whom at college erst he knew,
　　Met him, and of his way of life enquired;
　Whereat he answered, that the gipsy-crew,
　　His mates, had arts to rule as they desired 45
　　　The workings of men's brains,
　And they can bind them to what thoughts they will.
　'And I', he said, 'the secret of their art,
　　When fully learned, will to the world impart;
But it needs heaven-sent moments for this skill.' 50

This said, he left them, and returned no more. –
　But rumours hung about the country-side,
　　That the lost Scholar long was seen to stray,
　Seen by rare glimpses, pensive and tongue-tied,
　　In hat of antique shape, and cloak of grey, 55
　　　The same the gipsies wore.
　Shepherds had met him on the Hurst in spring;
　At some lone alehouse in the Berkshire moors,
　　On the warm ingle-bench, the smock-frocked
　　　boors
　Had found him seated at their entering, 60

But, 'mid their drink and clatter, he would fly.
　And I myself seem half to know thy looks,
　　And put the shepherds, wanderer! on thy trace;
　And boys who in lone wheatfields scare the rooks
　　I ask if thou hast passed their quiet place; 65
　　　Or in my boat I lie
　Moored to the cool bank in the summer-heats,
　'Mid wide grass meadows which the sunshine fills,
　　And watch the warm, green-muffled Cumner
　　　hills,
　And wonder if thou haunt'st their shy retreats. 70

For most, I know, thou lov'st retirèd ground!
　Thee at the ferry Oxford riders blithe,
　　Returning home on summer-nights, have met
　Crossing the stripling Thames at Bab-lock-hithe,
　　Trailing in the cool stream thy fingers wet, 75

As the punt's rope chops round;
　And leaning backward in a pensive dream,
　　And fostering in thy lap a heap of flowers
　Plucked in shy fields and distant Wychwood
　　　bowers,
　And thine eyes resting on the moonlit stream. 80

And then they land, and thou art seen no more! –
　Maidens, who from the distant hamlets come
　　To dance around the Fyfield elm in May,
　Oft through the darkening fields have seen thee
　　　roam,
　　Or cross a stile into the public way. 85
　　　Oft thou hast given them store
　Of flowers – the frail-leafed white anemony,
　　Dark bluebells drenched with dews of summer
　　　eves,
　And purple orchises with spotted leaves –
But none hath words she can report of thee. 90

And, above Godstow Bridge, when hay-time's here
　In June, and many a scythe in sunshine flames,
　　Men who through those wide fields of breezy
　　　grass
　Where black-winged swallows haunt the glittering
　　　Thames,
　To bathe in the abandoned lasher pass, 95
　　　Have often passed thee near
　Sitting upon the river bank o'ergrown;
　Marked thine outlandish garb, thy figure spare,
　　Thy dark vague eyes, and soft abstracted air –
　But, when they came from bathing, thou wast
　　　gone! 100

At some lone homestead in the Cumner hills,
　Where at her open door the housewife darns,
　　Thou hast been seen, or hanging on a gate
　To watch the threshers in the mossy barns.
　　Children, who early range these slopes and late
　　　For cresses from the rills, 106
　Have known thee eyeing, all an April-day,
　The springing pastures and the feeding kine;
　　And marked thee, when the stars come out and
　　　shine,
　Through the long dewy grass move slow away. 110

In autumn, on the skirts of Bagley Wood –
　Where most the gipsies by the turf-edged way
　　Pitch their smoked tents, and every bush you
　　　see
　With scarlet patches tagged and shreds of grey,
　　Above the forest-ground called Thessaly – 115

---

31 **Glanvill's book:** *The Vanity of Dogmatizing* (1661), by Joseph Glanvill (1636–80), which contains the story of the Scholar Gipsy 34 **pregnant parts:** fruitful talents or abilities 42 **erst:** formerly 57 **the Hurst:** a hill near Oxford, the first of many references in this poem to places in the Oxford area 59 **boors:** farmers or rustics

95 **lasher:** a pool that forms in a river below a weir 106 **rills:** streams
108 **kine:** cattle

The blackbird, picking food,
Sees thee, nor stops his meal, nor fears at all;
So often has he known thee past him stray,
Rapt, twirling in thy hand a withered spray,
And waiting for the spark from heaven to fall.   120

And once, in winter, on the causeway chill
Where home through flooded fields foot-travellers
     go,
Have I not passed thee on the wooden bridge,
Wrapped in thy cloak and battling with the snow,
Thy face tow'rd Hinksey and its wintry ridge?   125
     And thou hast climbed the hill,
And gained the white brow of the Cumner range;
Turned once to watch, while thick the snowflakes
     fall,
The line of festal light in Christ-Church hall –
Then sought thy straw in some sequestered grange.

But what – I dream! Two hundred years are flown 131
Since first thy story ran through Oxford halls,
And the grave Glanvill did the tale inscribe
That thou wert wandered from the studious walls
To learn strange arts, and join a gipsy-tribe;   135
     And thou from earth art gone
Long since, and in some quiet churchyard laid –
Some country-nook, where o'er thy unknown
     grave
Tall grasses and white flowering nettles wave,
Under a dark, red-fruited yew-tree's shade.   140

– No, no, thou hast not felt the lapse of hours!
For what wears out the life of mortal men?
'Tis that from change to change their being rolls;
'Tis that repeated shocks, again, again,
Exhaust the energy of strongest souls   145
     And numb the elastic powers.
Till having used our nerves with bliss and teen,
And tired upon a thousand schemes our wit,
To the just-pausing Genius we remit
Our worn-out life, and are – what we have been. 150

Thou hast not lived, why shouldst thou perish, so?
Thou hadst *one* aim, *one* business, *one* desire;
     Else wert thou long since numbered with the
     dead!
Else hadst thou spent, like other men, thy fire!
The generations of thy peers are fled,   155
     And we ourselves shall go;
But thou possessest an immortal lot,
And we imagine thee exempt from age
And living as thou liv'st on Glanvill's page,
Because thou hadst – what we, alas! have not.   160

For early didst thou leave the world, with powers
Fresh, undiverted to the world without,
     Firm to their mark, not spent on other things;
Free from the sick fatigue, the languid doubt,
Which much to have tried, in much been baffled,
     brings.   165
     O life unlike to ours!
Who fluctuate idly without term or scope,
Of whom each strives, nor knows for what he
     strives,
And each half lives a hundred different lives;
Who wait like thee, but not, like thee, in hope.   170

Thou waitest for the spark from heaven! and we,
Light half-believers of our casual creeds,
Who never deeply felt, nor clearly willed,
Whose insight never has borne fruit in deeds,
Whose vague resolves never have been fulfilled;
     For whom each year we see   176
Breeds new beginnings, disappointments new;
Who hesitate and falter life away,
And lose tomorrow the ground won today –
Ah! do not we, wanderer! await it too?   180

Yes, we await it! – but it still delays,
And then we suffer! and amongst us one,
     Who most has suffered, takes dejectedly
His seat upon the intellectual throne;
And all his store of sad experience he   185
     Lays bare of wretched days;
Tells us his misery's birth and growth and signs,
And how the dying spark of hope was fed,
And how the breast was soothed, and how the
     head,
And all his hourly varied anodynes.   190

This for our wisest! and we others pine,
And wish the long unhappy dream would end,
     And waive all claim to bliss, and try to bear;
With close-lipped patience for our only friend,
Sad patience, too near neighbour to despair – 195
     But none has hope like thine!
Thou through the fields and through the woods dost
     stray,
     Roaming the country-side, a truant boy,
Nursing thy project in unclouded joy,
And every doubt long blown by time away.   200

O born in days when wits were fresh and clear,
And life ran gaily as the sparkling Thames;
     Before this strange disease of modern life,
With its sick hurry, its divided aims,   204
     Its heads o'ertaxed, its palsied hearts, was rife –
     Fly hence, our contact fear!
Still fly, plunge deeper in the bowering wood!

119 **spray**: branch 147 **teen**: vexation

Averse, as Dido did with gesture stern
From her false friend's approach in Hades turn,
Wave us away, and keep thy solitude!   210

Still nursing the unconquerable hope,
Still clutching the inviolable shade,
With a free, onward impulse brushing through,
By night, the silvered branches of the glade –
Far on the forest-skirts, where none pursue,   215
On some mild pastoral slope
Emerge, and resting on the moonlit pales
Freshen thy flowers as in former years
With dew, or listen with enchanted ears,
From the dark dingles, to the nightingales!   220

But fly our paths, our feverish contact fly!
For strong the infection of our mental strife,
Which, though it gives no bliss, yet spoils for rest;
And we should win thee from thy own fair life,
Like us distracted, and like us unblessed.   225
Soon, soon thy cheer would die,
Thy hopes grow timorous, and unfixed thy powers,
And thy clear aims be cross and shifting made;
And then thy glad perennial youth would fade,
Fade, and grow old at last, and die like ours.   230

Then fly our greetings, fly our speech and smiles!
– As some grave Tyrian trader, from the sea,
Descried at sunrise an emerging prow
Lifting the cool-haired creepers stealthily,
The fringes of a southward-facing brow   235
Among the Aegean isles;
And saw the merry Grecian coaster come,
Freighted with amber grapes, and Chian wine,
Green, bursting figs, and tunnies steeped in
brine –
And knew the intruders on his ancient home,   240

The young light-hearted masters of the waves –
And snatched his rudder, and shook out more
sail;
And day and night held on indignantly
O'er the blue Midland waters with the gale,
Betwixt the Syrtes and soft Sicily,   245
To where the Atlantic raves
Outside the western straits; and unbent sails
There, where down cloudy cliffs, through sheets
of foam,
Shy traffickers, the dark Iberians come;
And on the beach undid his corded bales.   250

208–9 **Dido . . . turn:** in Greek myth, Dido killed herself after being
abandoned by her lover Aeneas. When he met her spirit in Hades,
she turned away from him   220 **dingles:** small wooded valleys
232 **Tyrian:** of the eastern Mediterranean port of Tyre   238 **Chian:**
from the Greek island of Chios   239 **tunnies:** tuna fish   245 **Syrtes:**
gulfs in the Mediterranean on the coast of North Africa

REQUIESCAT

STREW on her roses, roses,
And never a spray of yew!
In quiet she reposes;
Ah, would that I did too!

Her mirth the world required;   5
She bathed it in smiles of glee.
But her heart was tired, tired,
And now they let her be.

Her life was turning, turning,
In mazes of heat and sound.   10
But for peace her soul was yearning,
And now peace laps her round.

Her cabined ample spirit,
It fluttered and failed for breath.
Tonight it doth inherit   15
The vasty hall of death.

REQUIESCAT: A requiescat (Latin for 'may he/she rest') is a prayer
for the repose of the dead   2 **yew:** the yew tree is traditionally
associated with death or immortality   13 **cabined:** confined in a
small space   16 **vasty:** vast

WILLIAM JOHNSON CORY

HERACLITUS

THEY told me, Heraclitus, they told me you were dead;
They brought me bitter news to hear and bitter tears
to shed.
I wept, as I remembered how often you and I
Had tired the sun with talking and sent him down the
sky.

And now that thou art lying, my dear old Carian
guest,   5
A handful of grey ashes, long long ago at rest,
Still are thy pleasant voices, thy nightingales, awake,
For Death, he taketh all away, but them he cannot
take.

HERACLITUS: 1 **Heraclitus:** Greek philosopher (?535–?475 BC)   5 **Carian:**
Heraclitus was a native of Ephesus, on the west coast of modern
Turkey, in the region known as Caria

COVENTRY PATMORE

DEPARTURE

It was not like your great and gracious ways!
Do you, that have nought other to lament,
Never, my Love, repent
Of how, that July afternoon,
You went,   5
With sudden, unintelligible phrase,
And frightened eye,
Upon your journey of so many days,
Without a single kiss, or a goodbye?
I knew, indeed, that you were parting soon;   10
And so we sate, within the low sun's rays,
You whispering to me, for your voice was weak,
Your harrowing praise.
Well, it was well,
To hear you such things speak,   15
And I could tell
What made your eyes a growing gloom of love,
As a warm South-wind sombres a March grove.
And it was like your great and gracious ways
To turn your talk on daily things, my Dear,   20
Lifting the luminous, pathetic lash,
To let the laughter flash,
Whilst I drew near,
Because you spoke so low that I could scarcely hear.
But all at once to leave me at the last,   25
More at the wonder than the loss aghast,
With huddled, unintelligible phrase,
And frightened eye,
And go your journey of all days
With not one kiss, or a goodbye,   30
And the only loveless look the look with which you
        passed:
'Twas all unlike your great and gracious ways.

MAGNA EST VERITAS

Here, in this little Bay,
Full of tumultuous life and great repose,
Where, twice a day,
The purposeless, glad ocean comes and goes,
Under high cliffs, and far from the huge town,   5
I sit me down.
For want of me the world's course will not fail:
When all its work is done, the lie shall rot;
The truth is great, and shall prevail,
When none cares whether it prevail or not.   10

MAGNA EST VERITAS: **Magna est veritas:** Latin for 'the truth is great'

WILLIAM ALLINGHAM

THE FAIRIES

Up the airy mountain,
    Down the rushy glen,
We daren't go a-hunting
    For fear of little men;
Wee folk, good folk,   5
    Trooping all together;
Green jacket, red cap,
    And white owl's feather!

Down along the rocky shore
    Some make their home,   10
They live on crispy pancakes
    Of yellow tide-foam;
Some in the reeds
    Of the black mountain lake,
With frogs for their watch-dogs,   15
    All night awake.

High on the hill-top
    The old King sits;
He is now so old and grey
    He's nigh lost his wits.   20
With a bridge of white mist
    Columbkill he crosses,
On his stately journeys
    From Slieveleague to Rosses;
Or going up with music   25
    On cold starry nights
To sup with the Queen
    Of the gay Northern Lights.

They stole little Bridget
    For seven years long;   30
When she came down again
    Her friends were all gone.
They took her lightly back,
    Between the night and morrow.
They thought that she was fast asleep,   35
    But she was dead with sorrow.
They have kept her ever since
    Deep within the lake,
On a bed of flag-leaves,
    Watching till she wake.   40

By the craggy hill-side,
    Through the mosses bare,
They have planted thorn-trees
    For pleasure here and there.
Is any man so daring   45
    As dig them up in spite,
He shall find their sharpest thorns
    In his bed at night.

Up the airy mountain,
  Down the rushy glen,
We daren't go a-hunting
  For fear of little men;
Wee folk, good folk,
  Trooping all together;
Green jacket, red cap,
  And white owl's feather!   55

THE FAIRIES: 5 **wee folk, good folk**: euphemistic names for the fairies
22–4 **Columbkill . . . Rosses**: place-names in western Ireland
39 **flag-leaves**: iris leaves

GEORGE MEREDITH

From MODERN LOVE

13

'I PLAY for Seasons; not Eternities!'
Says Nature, laughing on her way. 'So must
All those whose stake is nothing more than dust!'
And lo, she wins, and of her harmonies
She is full sure! Upon her dying rose,   5
She drops a look of fondness, and goes by,
Scarce any retrospection in her eye;
For she the laws of growth most deeply knows,
Whose hands bear, here, a seed-bag – there, an urn.
Pledged she herself to aught, 'twould mark her end! 10
This lesson of our only visible friend,
Can we not teach our foolish hearts to learn?
Yes! yes! – but, oh, our human rose is fair
Surpassingly! Lose calmly Love's great bliss,
When the renewed for ever of a kiss   15
Whirls life within the shower of loosened hair!

43

MARK where the pressing wind shoots javelin-like
Its skeleton shadow on the broad-backed wave!
Here is a fitting spot to dig Love's grave;
Here where the ponderous breakers plunge and strike,
And dart their hissing tongues high up the sand: 5
In hearing of the ocean, and in sight
Of those ribbed wind-streaks running into white.
If I the death of Love had deeply planned,
I never could have made it half so sure,
As by the unblessed kisses which upbraid   10
The full-waked senses; or failing that, degrade!
'Tis morning: but no morning can restore
What we have forfeited. I see no sin:
The wrong is mixed. In tragic life, God wot,
No villain need be! Passions spin the plot;   15
We are betrayed by what is false within.

47

WE saw the swallows gathering in the sky,
And in the osier-isle we heard them noise.
We had not to look back on summer joys,
Or forward to a summer of bright dye:
But in the largeness of the evening earth   5
Our spirits grew as we went side by side.
The hour became her husband and my bride.
Love that had robbed us so, thus blessed our dearth!
The pilgrims of the year waxed very loud
In multitudinous chatterings, as the flood   10
Full brown came from the West, and like pale blood
Expanded to the upper crimson cloud.
Love that had robbed us of immortal things,
This little moment mercifully gave,
Where I have seen across the twilight wave   15
The swan sail with her young beneath her wings.

50

THUS piteously Love closed what he begat:
The union of this ever-díverse pair!
These two were rapid falcons in a snare,
Condemned to do the flitting of the bat.
Lovers beneath the singing sky of May,   5
They wandered once; clear as the dew on flowers:
But they fed not on the advancing hours:
Their hearts held cravings for the buried day.
Then each applied to each that fatal knife,
Deep questioning, which probes to endless dole. 10
Ah, what a dusty answer gets the soul
When hot for certainties in this our life! –
In tragic hints here see what evermore
Moves dark as yonder midnight ocean's force,
Thundering like ramping hosts of warrior horse, 15
To throw that faint thin line upon the shore!

MODERN LOVE: (43) 14 **God wot**: God knows (47) 9 **pilgrims of the
year**: migrating birds (50) 10 **dole**: grief, mourning 11 **dusty answer**:
a bad-tempered or unhelpful reply

DANTE GABRIEL ROSSETTI

THE BLESSED DAMOZEL

THE blessèd damozel leaned out
  From the gold bar of Heaven;
Her eyes were deeper than the depth
  Of waters stilled at even;
She had three lilies in her hand,   5
  And the stars in her hair were seven.

THE BLESSED DAMOZEL: 1 **damozel**: a form of damsel that tends to
confer nobility on the young unmarried woman

Her robe, ungirt from clasp to hem,
  No wrought flowers did adorn,
But a white rose of Mary's gift,
  For service meetly worn;
Her hair that lay along her back   10
  Was yellow like ripe corn.

Herseemed she scarce had been a day
  One of God's choristers;
The wonder was not yet quite gone   15
  From that still look of hers;
Albeit, to them she left, her day
  Had counted as ten years.

(To one, it is ten years of years.
  . . . Yet now, and in this place,   20
Surely she leaned o'er me – her hair
  Fell all about my face. . . .
Nothing: the autumn-fall of leaves.
  The whole year sets apace.)

It was the rampart of God's house   25
  That she was standing on;
By God built over the sheer depth
  The which is Space begun;
So high, that looking downward thence
  She scarce could see the sun.   30

It lies in Heaven, across the flood
  Of ether, as a bridge.
Beneath, the tides of day and night
  With flame and darkness ridge
The void, as low as where this earth   35
  Spins like a fretful midge.

Heard hardly, some of her new friends
  Amid their loving games
Spake evermore among themselves
  Their virginal chaste names;   40
And the souls mounting up to God
  Went by her like thin flames.

And still she bowed herself and stooped
  Out of the circling charm;
Until her bosom must have made   45
  The bar she leaned on warm,
And the lilies lay as if asleep
  Along her bended arm.

From the fixed place of Heaven she saw
  Time like a pulse shake fierce   50
Through all the worlds. Her gaze still strove
  Within the gulf to pierce
Its path; and now she spoke as when
  The stars sang in their spheres.

The sun was gone now; the curled moon   55
  Was like a little feather
Fluttering far down the gulf; and now
  She spoke through the still weather.
Her voice was like the voice the stars
  Had when they sang together.   60

(Ah sweet! Even now, in that bird's song,
  Strove not her accents there,
Fain to be hearkened? When those bells
  Possessed the mid-day air,
Strove not her steps to reach my side   65
  Down all the echoing stair?)

'I wish that he were come to me,
  For he will come,' she said.
'Have I not prayed in Heaven? – on earth,
  Lord, Lord, has he not prayed?   70
Are not two prayers a perfect strength?
  And shall I feel afraid?

'When round his head the aureole clings,
  And he is clothed in white,
I'll take his hand and go with him   75
  To the deep wells of light;
We will step down as to a stream,
  And bathe there in God's sight.

'We two will stand beside that shrine,
  Occult, withheld, untrod,   80
Whose lamps are stirred continually
  With prayer sent up to God;
And see our old prayers, granted, melt
  Each like a little cloud.

'We two will lie i' the shadow of   85
  That living mystic tree
Within whose secret growth the Dove
  Is sometimes felt to be,
While every leaf that His plumes touch
  Saith His Name audibly.   90

'And I myself will teach to him,
  I myself, lying so,
The songs I sing here; which his voice
  Shall pause in, hushed and slow,
And find some knowledge at each pause,   95
  Or some new thing to know.'

(Alas! we two, we two, thou say'st!
  Yea, one wast thou with me
That once of old. But shall God lift
  To endless unity   100
The soul whose likeness with thy soul
  Was but its love for thee?)

---

10 **meetly**: fittingly, suitably 13 **Herseemed**: it seemed to her
32 **ether**: an element that was thought to fill the space between
heaven and earth

62 **accents**: tones 63 **Fain**: joyful 73 **aureole**: a golden halo 80 **Occult**:
hidden 86 **mystic tree**: the tree of life 87 **Dove**: God, Christ

'We two,' she said, 'will seek the groves
    Where the lady Mary is,
With her five handmaidens, whose names   105
    Are five sweet symphonies,
Cecily, Gertrude, Magdalen,
    Margaret and Rosalys.

'Circlewise sit they, with bound locks
    And foreheads garlanded;   110
Into the fine cloth white like flame
    Weaving the golden thread,
To fashion the birth-robes for them
    Who are just born, being dead.

'He shall fear, haply, and be dumb: 115
    Then will I lay my cheek
To his, and tell about our love,
    Not once abashed or weak:
And the dear Mother will approve
    My pride, and let me speak.   120

'Herself shall bring us, hand in hand,
    To Him round whom all souls
Kneel, the clear-ranged unnumbered heads
    Bowed with their aureoles:
And angels meeting us shall sing   125
    To their citherns and citoles.

'There will I ask of Christ the Lord
    Thus much for him and me: –
Only to live as once on earth
    With Love, – only to be,   130
As then awhile, for ever now
    Together, I and he.'

She gazed and listened and then said,
    Less sad of speech than mild, –
'All this is when he comes.' She ceased.   135
    The light thrilled towards her, filled
With angels in strong level flight.
    Her eyes prayed, and she smiled.

(I saw her smile.) But soon their path
    Was vague in distant spheres: 140
And then she cast her arms along
    The golden barriers,
And laid her face between her hands,
    And wept. (I heard her tears.)

105–8 **five handmaidens . . . Rosalys:** maidens who attend the Virgin Mary. All, except Rosalys, are saints 126 **citherns and citoles:** stringed instruments used mainly in the late medieval/Renaissance periods

SUDDEN LIGHT

I HAVE been here before,
    But when or how I cannot tell:
I know the grass beyond the door,
    The sweet keen smell,
The sighing sound, the lights around the shore.   5

You have been mine before, –
    How long ago I may not know:
But just when at that swallow's soar
    Your neck turned so,
Some veil did fall, – I knew it all of yore.   10

Then, now, – perchance again! . . .
    O round mine eyes your tresses shake!
Shall we not lie as we have lain
    Thus for Love's sake,
And sleep, and wake, yet never break the chain? 15

THE WOODSPURGE

THE wind flapped loose, the wind was still,
Shaken out dead from tree and hill:
I had walked on at the wind's will, –
I sat now, for the wind was still.

Between my knees my forehead was, –   5
My lips, drawn in, said not Alas!
My hair was over in the grass,
My naked ears heard the day pass.

My eyes, wide open, had the run
Of some ten weeds to fix upon;   10
Among those few, out of the sun,
The woodspurge flowered, three cups in one.

From perfect grief there need not be
Wisdom or even memory:
One thing then learnt remains to me, –   15
The woodspurge has a cup of three.

THE WOODSPURGE: 12 **woodspurge:** a flower consisting of three petals. Also known as *Euphorbia amygdaloides*

CHRISTINA ROSSETTI

GOBLIN MARKET

MORNING and evening
Maids heard the goblins cry:
'Come buy our orchard fruits,
Come buy, come buy:
Apples and quinces,   5
Lemons and oranges,
Plump unpecked cherries,
Melons and raspberries,
Bloom-down-cheeked peaches,
Swart-headed mulberries,   10
Wild free-born cranberries,
Crab-apples, dewberries,
Pine-apples, blackberries,

Apricots, strawberries; –
All ripe together
In summer weather, –   15
Morns that pass by,
Fair eves that fly;
Come buy, come buy:
Our grapes fresh from the vine,   20
Pomegranates full and fine,
Dates and sharp bullaces,
Rare pears and greengages,
Damsons and bilberries,
Taste them and try: 25
Currants and gooseberries,
Bright-fire-like barberries,
Figs to fill your mouth,
Citrons from the South,
Sweet to tongue and sound to eye;   30
Come buy, come buy.'

Evening by evening
Among the brookside rushes,
Laura bowed her head to hear,
Lizzie veiled her blushes: 35
Crouching close together
In the cooling weather,
With clasping arms and cautioning lips,
With tingling cheeks and finger tips.
'Lie close,' Laura said,   40
Pricking up her golden head:
'We must not look at goblin men,
We must not buy their fruits:
Who knows upon what soil they fed
Their hungry thirsty roots?'   45
'Come buy,' call the goblins
Hobbling down the glen.
'Oh,' cried Lizzie, 'Laura, Laura,
You should not peep at goblin men.'
Lizzie covered up her eyes,   50
Covered close lest they should look;
Laura reared her glossy head,
And whispered like the restless brook:
'Look, Lizzie, look, Lizzie,
Down the glen tramp little men.   55
One hauls a basket,
One bears a plate,
One lugs a golden dish
Of many pounds weight.
How fair the vine must grow   60
Whose grapes are so luscious;
How warm the wind must blow
Through those fruit bushes.'
'No,' said Lizzie: 'No, no, no;
Their offers should not charm us,   65
Their evil gifts would harm us.'
She thrust a dimpled finger
In each ear, shut eyes and ran:
Curious Laura chose to linger
Wondering at each merchant man.   70

One had a cat's face,
One whisked a tail,
One tramped at a rat's pace,
One crawled like a snail,
One like a wombat prowled obtuse and furry,   75
One like a ratel tumbled hurry skurry.
She heard a voice like voice of doves
Cooing all together:
They sounded kind and full of loves
In the pleasant weather.   80

Laura stretched her gleaming neck
Like a rush-imbedded swan,
Like a lily from the beck,
Like a moonlit poplar branch,
Like a vessel at the launch   85
When its last restraint is gone.
Backwards up the mossy glen
Turned and trooped the goblin men,
With their shrill repeated cry,
'Come buy, come buy.'   90
When they reached where Laura was
They stood stock still upon the moss,
Leering at each other,
Brother with queer brother;
Signalling each other,   95
Brother with sly brother.
One set his basket down,
One reared his plate;
One began to weave a crown
Of tendrils, leaves and rough nuts brown   100
(Men sell not such in any town);
One heaved the golden weight
Of dish and fruit to offer her:
'Come buy, come buy,' was still their cry.

Laura stared but did not stir,   105
Longed but had no money:
The whisk-tailed merchant bade her taste
In tones as smooth as honey,
The cat-faced purred,
The rat-paced spoke a word   110
Of welcome, and the snail-paced even was heard;
One parrot-voiced and jolly
Cried 'Pretty Goblin' still for 'Pretty Polly'; –
One whistled like a bird.

But sweet-tooth Laura spoke in haste: 115
'Good folk, I have no coin;
To take were to purloin:
I have no copper in my purse,
I have no silver either,
And all my gold is on the furze   120
That shakes in windy weather
Above the rusty heather.'
'You have much gold upon your head,'
They answered all together:
'Buy from us with a golden curl.'   125

She clipped a precious golden lock,
She dropped a tear more rare than pearl,
Then sucked their fruit globes fair or red:
Sweeter than honey from the rock,
Stronger than man-rejoicing wine,   130
Clearer than water flowed that juice;
She never tasted such before,
How should it cloy with length of use?
She sucked and sucked and sucked the more
Fruits which that unknown orchard bore;   135
She sucked until her lips were sore;
Then flung the emptied rinds away
But gathered up one kernel-stone,
And knew not was it night or day
And she turned home alone.   140

Lizzie met her at the gate
Full of wise upbraidings:
'Dear, you should not stay so late,
Twilight is not good for maidens;
Should not loiter in the glen   145
In the haunts of goblin men.
Do you not remember Jeanie,
How she met them in the moonlight,
Took their gifts both choice and many,
Ate their fruits and wore their flowers   150
Plucked from bowers
Where summer ripens at all hours?
But ever in the noonlight
She pined and pined away;
Sought them by night and day,   155
Found them no more but dwindled and grew grey;
Then fell with the first snow,
While to this day no grass will grow
Where she lies low:
I planted daisies there a year ago   160
That never blow.
You should not loiter so.'
'Nay, hush,' said Laura:
'Nay, hush, my sister:
I ate and ate my fill,   165
Yet my mouth waters still;
Tomorrow night I will
Buy more': and kissed her:
'Have done with sorrow;
I'll bring you plums tomorrow   170
Fresh on their mother twigs,
Cherries worth getting;
You cannot think what figs
My teeth have met in,
What melons icy-cold   175
Piled on a dish of gold
Too huge for me to hold,
What peaches with a velvet nap,
Pellucid grapes without one seed:

Odorous indeed must be the mead   180
Whereon they grow, and pure the wave they drink
With lilies at the brink,
And sugar-sweet their sap.'

Golden head by golden head
Like two pigeons in one nest   185
Folded in each other's wings,
They lay down in their curtained bed:
Like two blossoms on one stem,
Like two flakes of new-fall'n snow,
Like two wands of ivory   190
Tipped with gold for awful kings.
Moon and stars gazed in at them,
Wind sang to them a lullaby,
Lumbering owls forbore to fly,
Not a bat flapped to and fro   195
Round their rest:
Cheek to cheek and breast to breast
Locked together in one nest.

Early in the morning
When the first cock crowed his warning,   200
Neat like bees, as sweet and busy,
Laura rose with Lizzie:
Fetched in honey, milked the cows,
Aired and set to rights the house,
Kneaded cakes of whitest wheat,   205
Cakes for dainty mouths to eat,
Next churned butter, whipped up cream,
Fed their poultry, sat and sewed;
Talked as modest maidens should:
Lizzie with an open heart,   210
Laura in an absent dream,
One content, one sick in part;
One warbling for the mere bright day's delight,
One longing for the night.

At length slow evening came: 215
They went with pitchers to the reedy brook;
Lizzie most placid in her look,
Laura most like a leaping flame.
They drew the gurgling water from its deep;
Lizzie plucked purple and rich golden flags,   220
Then turning homewards said: 'The sunset flushes
Those furthest loftiest crags;
Come, Laura, not another maiden lags,
No wilful squirrel wags,
The beasts and birds are fast asleep.'   225
But Laura loitered still among the rushes
And said the bank was steep.

And said the hour was early still,
The dew not fall'n, the wind not chill:
Listening ever, but not catching   230
The customary cry,
'Come buy, come buy,'
With its iterated jingle

GOBLIN MARKET: 178 **nap**: covering 179 **Pellucid**: transparent

Of sugar-baited words:
Not for all her watching   235
Once discerning even one goblin
Racing, whisking, tumbling, hobbling;
Let alone the herds
That used to tramp along the glen,
In groups or single,   240
Of brisk fruit-merchant men.

Till Lizzie urged, 'O Laura, come;
I hear the fruit-call but I dare not look:
You should not loiter longer at this brook:
Come with me home.   245
The stars rise, the moon bends her arc,
Each glowworm winks her spark,
Let us get home before the night grows dark:
For clouds may gather
Though this is summer weather,   250
Put out the lights and drench us through;
Then if we lost our way what should we do?'

Laura turned cold as stone
To find her sister heard that cry alone,
That goblin cry,   255
'Come buy our fruits, come buy.'
Must she then buy no more such dainty fruit?
Must she no more such succous pasture find,
Gone deaf and blind?
Her tree of life drooped from the root: 260
She said not one word in her heart's sore ache;
But peering through the dimness, nought discerning,
Trudged home, her pitcher dripping all the way;
So crept to bed, and lay
Silent till Lizzie slept;   265
Then sat up in a passionate yearning,
And gnashed her teeth for baulked desire, and wept
As if her heart would break.

Day after day, night after night,
Laura kept watch in vain   270
In sullen silence of exceeding pain.
She never caught again the goblin cry:
'Come buy, come buy'; –
She never spied the goblin men
Hawking their fruits along the glen: 275
But when the noon waxed bright
Her hair grew thin and gray;
She dwindled, as the fair full moon doth turn
To swift decay and burn
Her fire away.   280

One day remembering her kernel-stone
She set it by a wall that faced the south;
Dewed it with tears, hoped for a root,
Watched for a waxing shoot,
But there came none;   285

It never saw the sun,
It never felt the trickling moisture run:
While with sunk eyes and faded mouth
She dreamed of melons, as a traveller sees
False waves in desert drouth   290
With shade of leaf-crowned trees,
And burns the thirstier in the sandful breeze.

She no more swept the house,
Tended the fowls or cows,
Fetched honey, kneaded cakes of wheat,   295
Brought water from the brook:
But sat down listless in the chimney-nook
And would not eat.

Tender Lizzie could not bear
To watch her sister's cankerous care   300
Yet not to share.
She night and morning
Caught the goblins' cry:
'Come buy our orchard fruits,
Come buy, come buy': –   305
Beside the brook, along the glen,
She heard the tramp of goblin men,
The voice and stir
Poor Laura could not hear;
Longed to buy fruit to comfort her,   310
But feared to pay too dear.
She thought of Jeanie in her grave,
Who should have been a bride;
But who for joys brides hope to have
Fell sick and died   315
In her gay prime,
In earliest Winter time,
With the first glazing rime,
With the first snow-fall of crisp Winter time.

Till Laura dwindling   320
Seemed knocking at Death's door:
Then Lizzie weighed no more
Better and worse;
But put a silver penny in her purse,
Kissed Laura, crossed the heath with clumps of furze
At twilight, halted by the brook: 326
And for the first time in her life
Began to listen and look.

Laughed every goblin
When they spied her peeping: 330
Come towards her hobbling,
Flying, running, leaping,
Puffing and blowing,
Chuckling, clapping, crowing,
Clucking and gobbling,   335

258 **succous:** juicy

325 **furze:** a spiny evergreen shrub with yellow flowers

Mopping and mowing,
Full of airs and graces,
Pulling wry faces,
Demure grimaces,
Cat-like and rat-like,   340
Ratel- and wombat-like,
Snail-paced in a hurry,
Parrot-voiced and whistler,
Helter skelter, hurry skurry,
Chattering like magpies,   345
Fluttering like pigeons,
Gliding like fishes, –
Hugged her and kissed her,
Squeezed and caressed her:
Stretched up their dishes,   350
Panniers, and plates:
'Look at our apples
Russet and dun,
Bob at our cherries,
Bite at our peaches,   355
Citrons and dates,
Grapes for the asking,
Pears red with basking
Out in the sun,
Plums on their twigs;   360
Pluck them and suck them,
Pomegranates, figs.' –

'Good folk,' said Lizzie,
Mindful of Jeanie:
'Give me much and many': –   365
Held out her apron,
Tossed them her penny.
'Nay, take a seat with us,
Honour and eat with us,'
They answered grinning: 370
'Our feast is but beginning.
Night is yet early,
Warm and dew-pearly,
Wakeful and starry:
Such fruits as these   375
No man can carry;
Half their bloom would fly,
Half their dew would dry,
Half their flavour would pass by.
Sit down and feast with us,   380
Be welcome guest with us,
Cheer you and rest with us.' –
'Thank you,' said Lizzie: 'But one waits
At home alone for me:
So without further parleying,   385
If you will not sell me any
Of your fruits though much and many,
Give me back my silver penny
I tossed you for a fee.' –
They began to scratch their pates,   390
No longer wagging, purring,

But visibly demurring,
Grunting and snarling.
One called her proud,
Cross-grained, uncivil;   395
Their tones waxed loud,
Their looks were evil.
Lashing their tails
They trod and hustled her,
Elbowed and jostled her,   400
Clawed with their nails,
Barking, mewing, hissing, mocking,
Tore her gown and soiled her stocking,
Twitched her hair out by the roots,
Stamped upon her tender feet,   405
Held her hands and squeezed their fruits
Against her mouth to make her eat.

White and golden Lizzie stood,
Like a lily in a flood, –
Like a rock of blue-veined stone   410
Lashed by tides obstreperously, –
Like a beacon left alone
In a hoary roaring sea,
Sending up a golden fire, –
Like a fruit-crowned orange-tree   415
White with blossoms honey-sweet
Sore beset by wasp and bee, –
Like a royal virgin town
Topped with gilded dome and spire
Close beleaguered by a fleet   420
Mad to tug her standard down.

One may lead a horse to water,
Twenty cannot make him drink.
Though the goblins cuffed and caught her,
Coaxed and fought her,   425
Bullied and besought her,
Scratched her, pinched her black as ink,
Kicked and knocked her,
Mauled and mocked her,
Lizzie uttered not a word;   430
Would not open lip from lip
Lest they should cram a mouthful in:
But laughed in heart to feel the drip
Of juice that syrupped all her face,
And lodged in dimples of her chin,   435
And streaked her neck which quaked like curd.
At last the evil people
Worn out by her resistance
Flung back her penny, kicked their fruit
Along whichever road they took,   440
Not leaving root or stone or shoot;
Some writhed into the ground,
Some dived into the brook
With ring and ripple,
Some scudded on the gale without a sound,   445
Some vanished in the distance.

In a smart, ache, tingle,
Lizzie went her way;
Knew not was it night or day;
Sprang up the bank, tore through the furze,   450
Threaded copse and dingle,
And heard her penny jingle
Bouncing in her purse, –
Its bounce was music to her ear.
She ran and ran   455
As if she feared some goblin man
Dogged her with gibe or curse
Or something worse:
But not one goblin skurried after,
Nor was she pricked by fear;   460
The kind heart made her windy-paced
That urged her home quite out of breath with haste
And inward laughter.

She cried 'Laura,' up the garden,
'Did you miss me?   465
Come and kiss me.
Never mind my bruises,
Hug me, kiss me, suck my juices
Squeezed from goblin fruits for you,
Goblin pulp and goblin dew.   470
Eat me, drink me, love me;
Laura, make much of me:
For your sake I have braved the glen
And had to do with goblin merchant men.'

Laura started from her chair,   475
Flung her arms up in the air,
Clutched her hair:
'Lizzie, Lizzie, have you tasted
For my sake the fruit forbidden?
Must your light like mine be hidden,   480
Your young life like mine be wasted,
Undone in mine undoing
And ruined in my ruin,
Thirsty, cankered, goblin-ridden?' –
She clung about her sister,   485
Kissed and kissed and kissed her:
Tears once again
Refreshed her sunken eyes,
Dropping like rain
After long sultry drouth;   490
Shaking with aguish fear, and pain,
She kissed and kissed her with a hungry mouth.

Her lips began to scorch,
That juice was wormwood to her tongue,
She loathed the feast: 495
Writhing as one possessed she leaped and sung,
Rent all her robe, and wrung

Her hands in lamentable haste,
And beat her breast.
Her locks streamed like the torch   500
Borne by a racer at full speed,
Or like the mane of horses in their flight,
Or like an eagle when she stems the light
Straight toward the sun,
Or like a caged thing freed,   505
Or like a flying flag when armies run.

Swift fire spread through her veins, knocked at her
    heart,
Met the fire smouldering there
And overbore its lesser flame;
She gorged on bitterness without a name: 510
Ah! fool, to choose such part
Of soul-consuming care!
Sense failed in the mortal strife:
Like the watch-tower of a town
Which an earthquake shatters down,   515
Like a lightning-stricken mast,
Like a wind-uprooted tree
Spun about,
Like a foam-topped waterspout
Cast down headlong in the sea,   520
She fell at last;
Pleasure past and anguish past,
Is it death or is it life?

Life out of death.
That night long Lizzie watched by her,   525
Counted her pulse's flagging stir,
Felt for her breath,
Held water to her lips, and cooled her face
With tears and fanning leaves:
But when the first birds chirped about their eaves,   530
And early reapers plodded to the place
Of golden sheaves,
And dew-wet grass
Bowed in the morning winds so brisk to pass,
And new buds with new day   535
Opened of cup-like lilies on the stream,
Laura awoke as from a dream,
Laughed in the innocent old way,
Hugged Lizzie but not twice or thrice;
Her gleaming locks showed not one thread of grey,
Her breath was sweet as May   541
And light danced in her eyes.

Days, weeks, months, years,
Afterwards, when both were wives
With children of their own;   545
Their mother-hearts beset with fears,
Their lives bound up in tender lives;
Laura would call the little ones
And tell them of her early prime,
Those pleasant days long gone   550

451 **dingle:** a wooded dell or hollow 484 **cankered:** corrupted,
malignant 490 **drouth:** drought

Of not-returning time:
Would talk about the haunted glen,
The wicked, quaint fruit-merchant men,
Their fruits like honey to the throat
But poison in the blood;   555
(Men sell not such in any town):
Would tell them how her sister stood
In deadly peril to do her good,
And win the fiery antidote:
Then joining hands to little hands   560
Would bid them cling together,
'For there is no friend like a sister
In calm or stormy weather;
To cheer one on the tedious way,
To fetch one if one goes astray,   565
To lift one if one totters down,
To strengthen whilst one stands.'

'WHEN I AM DEAD, MY DEAREST'

WHEN I am dead, my dearest,
  Sing no sad songs for me;
Plant thou no roses at my head,
  Nor shady cypress tree:
Be the green grass above me   5
  With showers and dewdrops wet;
And if thou wilt, remember,
  And if thou wilt, forget.

I shall not see the shadows,
  I shall not feel the rain;   10
I shall not hear the nightingale
  Sing on as if in pain:
And dreaming through the twilight
  That doth not rise nor set,
Haply I may remember,   15
  And haply may forget.

REMEMBER

REMEMBER me when I am gone away,
  Gone far away into the silent land;
  When you can no more hold me by the hand,
Nor I half turn to go, yet turning stay.
Remember me when no more day by day   5
  You tell me of our future that you planned:
  Only remember me; you understand
It will be late to counsel then or pray.
Yet if you should forget me for a while
  And afterwards remember, do not grieve.   10
  For if the darkness and corruption leave
  A vestige of the thoughts that once I had,
Better by far you should forget and smile
  Than that you should remember and be sad.

A BIRTHDAY

My heart is like a singing bird
  Whose nest is in a watered shoot;
My heart is like an apple-tree
  Whose boughs are bent with thickset fruit;
My heart is like a rainbow shell   5
  That paddles in a halcyon sea;
My heart is gladder than all these,
  Because my love is come to me.

Raise me a daïs of silk and down;
  Hang it with vair and purple dyes;   10
Carve it in doves and pomegranates,
  And peacocks with a hundred eyes;
Work it in gold and silver grapes,
  In leaves and silver fleurs-de-lys;
Because the birthday of my life   15
  Is come, my love is come to me.

UPHILL

DOES the road wind uphill all the way?
  Yes, to the very end.
Will the day's journey take the whole long day?
  From morn to night, my friend.

But is there for the night a resting-place?   5
  A roof for when the slow, dark hours begin.
May not the darkness hide it from my face?
  You cannot miss that inn.

Shall I meet other wayfarers at night?
  Those who have gone before.   10
Then must I knock, or call when just in sight?
  They will not keep you waiting at that door.

Shall I find comfort, travel-sore and weak?
  Of labour you shall find the sum.
Will there be beds for me and all who seek?   15
  Yea, beds for all who come.

LEWIS CARROLL

JABBERWOCKY

'TWAS brillig, and the slithy toves
  Did gyre and gimble in the wabe:
All mimsy were the borogoves,
  And the mome raths outgrabe.

'Beware the Jabberwock, my son!   5
  The jaws that bite, the claws that catch!
Beware the Jubjub bird, and shun
  The frumious Bandersnatch!'

He took his vorpal sword in hand:
  Long time the manxome foe he sought –   10
So rested he by the Tumtum tree,
  And stood awhile in thought.

And, as in uffish thought he stood,
  The Jabberwock, with eyes of flame,
Came whiffling through the tulgey wood,   15
  And burbled as it came!

One, two! One, two! And through and through
  The vorpal blade went snicker-snack!
He left it dead, and with its head
  He went galumphing back.   20

'And hast thou slain the Jabberwock?
  Come to my arms, my beamish boy!
O frabjous day! Callooh! Callay!'
  He chortled in his joy.

'Twas brillig, and the slithy toves   25
  Did gyre and gimble in the wabe:
All mimsy were the borogoves,
  And the mome raths outgrabe.

        [From *Through the Looking Glass*]

THE HUNTING OF THE SNARK
AN AGONY IN EIGHT FITS

FIT THE FIRST. THE LANDING

'JUST the place for a Snark!' the Bellman cried,
  As he landed his crew with care;
Supporting each man on the top of the tide
  By a finger entwined in his hair.

'Just the place for a Snark! I have said it twice: 5
  That alone should encourage the crew.
Just the place for a Snark! I have said it thrice:
  What I tell you three times is true.'

The crew was complete: it included a Boots
  A maker of Bonnets and Hoods –   10
A Barrister, brought to arrange their disputes –
  And a Broker, to value their goods.

A Billiard-marker, whose skill was immense,
  Might perhaps have won more than his share –
But a Banker, engaged at enormous expense,   15
  Had the whole of their cash in his care.

There was also a Beaver, that paced on the deck,
  Or would sit making lace in the bow:
And had often (the Bellman said) saved them from
    wreck,
  Though none of the sailors knew how.   20

There was one who was famed for the number of
    things
  He forgot when he entered the ship:
His umbrella, his watch, all his jewels and rings,
  And the clothes he had bought for the trip.

He had forty-two boxes, all carefully packed,   25
  With his name painted clearly on each:
But, since he omitted to mention the fact,
  They were all left behind on the beach.

The loss of his clothes hardly mattered, because
  He had seven coats on when he came,   30
With three pair of boots – but the worst of it was,
  He had wholly forgotten his name.

He would answer to 'Hi!' or to any loud cry,
  Such as 'Fry me!' or 'Fritter my wig!'
To 'What-you-may-call-um!' or 'What-was-his-name!'
  But especially 'Thing-um-a-jig!'   36

While, for those who preferred a more forcible word,
  He had different names from these:
His intimate friends called him 'Candle-ends',
  And his enemies 'Toasted-cheese'.   40

'His form is ungainly – his intellect small –'
  (So the Bellman would often remark)
'But his courage is perfect! And that, after all,
  Is the thing that one needs with a Snark.'

He would joke with hyaenas, returning their stare   45
  With an impudent wag of the head:
And he once went a walk, paw-in-paw, with a bear,
  'Just to keep up its spirits,' he said.

He came as a Baker: but owned, when too late –
  And it drove the poor Bellman half-mad –   50
He could only bake Bridecake – for which, I may
    state,
  No materials were to be had.

The last of the crew needs especial remark,
  Though he looked an incredible dunce:
He had just one idea – but, that one being 'Snark',   55
  The good Bellman engaged him at once.

He came as a Butcher: but gravely declared,
  When the ship had been sailing a week,
He could only kill Beavers. The Bellman looked
    scared,
  And was almost too frightened to speak: 60

But at length he explained, in a tremulous tone,
  There was only one Beaver on board;
And that was a tame one he had of his own,
  Whose death would be deeply deplored.

The Beaver, who happened to hear the remark, 65
  Protested, with tears in its eyes,
That not even the rapture of hunting the Snark
  Could atone for that dismal surprise!

It strongly advised that the Butcher should be
  Conveyed in a separate ship: 70
But the Bellman declared that would never agree
  With the plans he had made for the trip:

Navigation was always a difficult art,
  Though with only one ship and one bell:
And he feared he must really decline, for his part, 75
  Undertaking another as well.

The Beaver's best course was, no doubt, to procure
  A second-hand dagger-proof coat –
So the Baker advised it – and next, to insure
  Its life in some Office of note: 80

This the Banker suggested, and offered for hire
  (On moderate terms), or for sale,
Two excellent Policies, one Against Fire
  And one Against Damage From Hail.

Yet still, ever after that sorrowful day, 85
  Whenever the Butcher was by,
The Beaver kept looking the opposite way,
  And appeared unaccountably shy.

FIT THE SECOND. THE BELLMAN'S SPEECH

The Bellman himself they all praised to the
  skies –
  Such a carriage, such ease and such grace!
Such solemnity, too! One could see he was wise,
  The moment one looked in his face!

He had bought a large map representing the sea, 5
  Without the least vestige of land:
And the crew were much pleased when they found it
  to be
  A map they could all understand.

'What's the good of Mercator's North Poles and
  Equators,
  Tropics, Zones, and Meridian Lines?' 10
So the Bellman would cry: and the crew would reply
  'They are merely conventional signs!

'Other maps are such shapes, with their islands and
  capes!
  But we've got our brave Captain to thank'
(So the crew would protest) 'that he's bought us the
  best – 15
  A perfect and absolute blank!'

This was charming, no doubt: but they shortly found
  out
  That the Captain they trusted so well
Had only one notion for crossing the ocean,
  And that was to tingle his bell. 20

He was thoughtful and grave – but the orders he
  gave
  Were enough to bewilder a crew.
When he cried 'Steer to starboard, but keep her head
  larboard!'
  What on earth was the helmsman to do?

Then the bowsprit got mixed with the rudder
  sometimes: 25
  A thing, as the Bellman remarked,
That frequently happens in tropical climes,
  When a vessel is, so to speak, 'snarked'.

But the principal failing occurred in the sailing,
  And the Bellman, perplexed and distressed, 30
Said he *had* hoped, at least, when the wind blew due
  East,
  That the ship would *not* travel due West!

But the danger was past – they had landed at last,
  With their boxes, portmanteaus, and bags:
Yet at first sight the crew were not pleased with the
  view, 35
  Which consisted of chasms and crags.

The Bellman perceived that their spirits were low,
  And repeated in musical tone
Some jokes he had kept for a season of woe –
  But the crew would do nothing but groan. 40

He served out some grog with a liberal hand,
  And bade them sit down on the beach:
And they could not but own that their Captain looked
  grand,
  As he stood and delivered his speech.

'Friends, Romans, and countrymen, lend me your
  ears!' 45
  (They were all of them fond of quotations:
So they drank to his health, and they gave him three
  cheers,
  While he served out additional rations).

'We have sailed many months, we have sailed many
  weeks,
  (Four weeks to the month you may mark), 50
But never as yet ('tis your Captain who speaks)
  Have we caught the least glimpse of a Snark!

'We have sailed many weeks, we have sailed many
    days,
  (Seven days to the week I allow),
But a Snark, on the which we might lovingly
    gaze,   55
  We have never beheld till now!

'Come, listen, my men, while I tell you again
  The five unmistakable marks
By which you may know, wheresoever you go,
  The warranted genuine Snarks.   60

'Let us take them in order. The first is the taste,
  Which is meagre and hollow, but crisp:
Like a coat that is rather too tight in the waist,
  With a flavour of Will-o'-the-wisp.

'Its habit of getting up late you'll agree   65
  That it carries too far, when I say
That it frequently breakfasts at five-o'clock tea,
  And dines on the following day.

'The third is its slowness in taking a jest.
  Should you happen to venture on one,   70
It will sigh like a thing that is deeply distressed:
  And it always looks grave at a pun.

'The fourth is its fondness for bathing-machines,
  Which it constantly carries about,
And believes that they add to the beauty of
    scenes –
  A sentiment open to doubt.   76

'The fifth is ambition. It next will be right
  To describe each particular batch:
Distinguishing those that have feathers, and bite,
  From those that have whiskers, and scratch.   80

'For, although common Snarks do no manner of
    harm,
  Yet, I feel it my duty to say,
Some are Boojums—' The Bellman broke off in
    alarm,
  For the Baker had fainted away.

FIT THE THIRD. THE BAKER'S TALE

They roused him with muffins – they roused him
    with ice –
  They roused him with mustard and cress –
They roused him with jam and judicious advice –
  They set him conundrums to guess.

When at length he sat up and was able to speak,   5
  His sad story he offered to tell;
And the Bellman cried 'Silence! Not even a shriek!'
  And excitedly tingled his bell.

There was silence supreme! Not a shriek, not a
    scream,
  Scarcely even a howl or a groan,   10
As the man they called 'Ho!' told his story of woe
  In an antediluvian tone.

'My father and mother were honest, though poor—'
  'Skip all that!' cried the Bellman in haste.
'If it once becomes dark, there's no chance of a
    Snark –   15
  We have hardly a minute to waste!'

'I skip forty years,' said the Baker, in tears,
  'And proceed without further remark
To the day when you took me aboard of your ship
  To help you in hunting the Snark.   20

'A dear uncle of mine (after whom I was named)
  Remarked, when I bade him farewell—'
'Oh, skip your dear uncle!' the Bellman exclaimed,
  As he angrily tingled his bell.

'He remarked to me then,' said that mildest of men,   25
  ' "If your Snark be a Snark, that is right:
Fetch it home by all means – you may serve it with
    greens,
  And it's handy for striking a light.

' "You may seek it with thimbles – and seek it with
    care;
  You may hunt it with forks and hope;   30
You may threaten its life with a railway-share;
  You may charm it with smiles and soap—" '

('That's exactly the method,' the Bellman bold
  In a hasty parenthesis cried,
'That's exactly the way I have always been told   35
  That the capture of Snarks should be tried!')

' "But oh, beamish nephew, beware of the day,
  If your Snark be a Boojum! For then
You will softly and suddenly vanish away,
  And never be met with again!"   40

'It is this, it is this that oppresses my soul,
  When I think of my uncle's last words:
And my heart is like nothing so much as a bowl
  Brimming over with quivering curds!

'It is this, it is this—' 'We have had that before!'   45
  The Bellman indignantly said.
And the Baker replied 'Let me say it once more.
  It is this, it is this that I dread!

'I engage with the Snark – every night after dark –
  In a dreamy delirious fight: 50
I serve it with greens in those shadowy scenes,
  And I use it for striking a light:

'But if ever I meet with a Boojum, that day,
  In a moment (of this I am sure),
I shall softly and suddenly vanish away –
  And the notion I cannot endure!'   55

FIT THE FOURTH. THE HUNTING

The Bellman looked uffish, and wrinkled his brow.
  'If only you'd spoken before!
It's excessively awkward to mention it now,
  With the Snark, so to speak, at the door!

'We should all of us grieve, as you well may believe,   5
  If you never were met with again –
But surely, my man, when the voyage began,
  You might have suggested it then?

'It's excessively awkward to mention it now –
  As I think I've already remarked.'   10
And the man they called 'Hi!' replied, with a sigh,
  'I informed you the day we embarked.

'You may charge me with murder – or want of sense –
  (We are all of us weak at times):
But the slightest approach to a false pretence   15
  Was never among my crimes!

'I said it in Hebrew – I said it in Dutch –
  I said it in German and Greek:
But I wholly forgot (and it vexes me much)
  That English is what you speak!'   20

' 'Tis a pitiful tale,' said the Bellman, whose face
  Had grown longer at every word:
'But, now that you've stated the whole of your case,
  More debate would be simply absurd.

'The rest of my speech' (he explained to his men)   25
  You shall hear when I've leisure to speak it.
But the Snark is at hand, let me tell you again!
  'Tis your glorious duty to seek it!

'To seek it with thimbles, to seek it with care;
  To pursue it with forks and hope;   30
To threaten its life with a railway-share;
  To charm it with smiles and soap!

'For the Snark's a peculiar creature, that won't
  Be caught in a commonplace way.
Do all that you know, and try all that you don't: 35
  Not a chance must be wasted today!

'For England expects – I forbear to proceed:
  'Tis a maxim tremendous, but trite:
And you'd best be unpacking the things that you need
  To rig yourselves out for the fight.'   40

Then the Banker endorsed a blank cheque (which he
    crossed),
  And changed his loose silver for notes.
The Baker with care combed his whiskers and hair.
  And shook the dust out of his coats.

The Boots and the Broker were sharpening a
    spade –   45
  Each working the grindstone in turn:
But the Beaver went on making lace, and displayed
  No interest in the concern:

Though the Barrister tried to appeal to its pride,
  And vainly proceeded to cite   50
A number of cases, in which making laces
  Had been proved an infringement of right.

The maker of Bonnets ferociously planned
  A novel arrangement of bows:
While the Billiard-marker with quivering hand   55
  Was chalking the tip of his nose.

But the Butcher turned nervous, and dressed himself
    fine,
  With yellow kid gloves and a ruff –
Said he felt it exactly like going to dine,
  Which the Bellman declared was all 'stuff'.   60

'Introduce me, now there's a good fellow,' he said,
  'If we happen to meet it together!'
And the Bellman, sagaciously nodding his head,
  Said 'That must depend on the weather.'

The Beaver went simply galumphing about,   65
  At seeing the Butcher so shy:
And even the Baker, though stupid and stout,
  Made an effort to wink with one eye.

'Be a man!' cried the Bellman in wrath, as he heard
  The Butcher beginning to sob.   70
'Should we meet with a Jubjub, that desperate bird,
  We shall need all our strength for the job!'

FIT THE FIFTH. THE BEAVER'S LESSON

They sought it with thimbles, they sought it with care;
  They pursued it with forks and hope;
They threatened its life with a railway-share;
  They charmed it with smiles and soap.

Then the Butcher contrived an ingenious plan   5
  For making a separate sally;
And had fixed on a spot unfrequented by man,
  A dismal and desolate valley.

But the very same plan to the Beaver occurred:
  It had chosen the very same place: 10
Yet neither betrayed, by a sign or a word,
  The disgust that appeared in his face.

Each thought he was thinking of nothing but 'Snark'
   And the glorious work of the day;
And each tried to pretend that he did not remark   15
   That the other was going that way.

But the valley grew narrow and narrower still,
   And the evening got darker and colder,
Till (merely from nervousness, not from goodwill)
   They marched along shoulder to shoulder.   20

Then a scream, shrill and high, rent the shuddering
   sky,
   And they knew that some danger was near:
The Beaver turned pale to the tip of its tail,
   And even the Butcher felt queer.

He thought of his childhood, left far far behind –   25
   That blissful and innocent state –
The sound so exactly recalled to his mind
   A pencil that squeaks on a slate!

' 'Tis the voice of the Jubjub!' he suddenly cried.
   (This man, that they used to call 'Dunce'.)   30
'As the Bellman would tell you,' he added with pride,
   'I have uttered that sentiment once.

' 'Tis the note of the Jubjub! Keep count, I entreat;
   You will find I have told it you twice.
'Tis the song of the Jubjub! The proof is complete,   35
   If only I've stated it thrice.'

The Beaver had counted with scrupulous care,
   Attending to every word:
But it fairly lost heart, and outgrabe in despair,
   When the third repetition occurred.   40

It felt that, in spite of all possible pains,
   It had somehow contrived to lose count,
And the only thing now was to rack its poor brains
   By reckoning up the amount.

'Two added to one – if that could but be done,'   45
   It said, 'with one's fingers and thumbs!'
Recollecting with tears how, in earlier years,
   It had taken no pains with its sums.

'The thing can be done,' said the Butcher, 'I think.
   The thing must be done, I am sure.   50
The thing shall be done! Bring me paper and ink,
   The best there is time to procure.'

The Beaver brought paper, portfolio, pens,
   And ink in unfailing supplies:
While strange creepy creatures came out of their dens,
   And watched them with wondering eyes.   56

So engrossed was the Butcher, he heeded them not,
   As he wrote with a pen in each hand,
And explained all the while in a popular style
   Which the Beaver could well understand.   60

'Taking Three as the subject to reason about –
   A convenient number to state –
We add Seven, and Ten, and then multiply out
   By One Thousand diminished by Eight.

'The result we proceed to divide, as you see,   65
   By Nine Hundred and Ninety and Two:
Then subtract Seventeen, and the answer must be
   Exactly and perfectly true.

'The method employed I would gladly explain,
   While I have it so clear in my head,   70
If I had but the time and you had but the brain –
   But much yet remains to be said.

'In one moment I've seen what has hitherto been
   Enveloped in absolute mystery,
And without extra charge I will give you at large   75
   A Lesson in Natural History.'

In his genial way he proceeded to say
   (Forgetting all laws of propriety,
And that giving instruction, without introduction,
   Would have caused quite a thrill in Society),   80

'As to temper the Jubjub's a desperate bird,
   Since it lives in perpetual passion:
Its taste in costúme is entirely absurd –
   It is ages ahead of the fashion:

'But it knows any friend it has met once before: 85
   It never will look at a bribe:
And in charity-meetings it stands at the door,
   And collects – though it does not subscribe.

'Its flavour when cooked is more exquisite far
   Than mutton, or oysters, or eggs: 90
(Some think it keeps best in an ivory jar,
   And some, in mahogany kegs):

'You boil it in sawdust: you salt it in glue:
   You condense it with locusts and tape:
Still keeping one principal object in view –   95
   To preserve its symmetrical shape.'

The Butcher would gladly have talked till next day,
   But he felt that the Lesson must end,
And he wept with delight in attempting to say
   He considered the Beaver his friend: 100

While the Beaver confessed, with affectionate looks
  More eloquent even than tears,
It had learned in ten minutes far more than all books
  Would have taught it in seventy years.

They returned hand-in-hand, and the Bellman, unmanned   105
  (For a moment) with noble emotion,
Said 'This amply repays all the wearisome days
  We have spent on the billowy ocean!'

Such friends, as the Beaver and Butcher became,
  Have seldom if ever been known;   110
In winter or summer, 'twas always the same –
  You could never meet either alone.

And when quarrels arose – as one frequently finds
  Quarrels will, spite of every endeavour –
The song of the Jubjub recurred to their minds,   115
  And cemented their friendship for ever!

FIT THE SIXTH. THE BARRISTER'S DREAM

They sought it with thimbles, they sought it with care;
  They pursued it with forks and hope;
They threatened its life with a railway-share;
  They charmed it with smiles and soap.

But the Barrister, weary of proving in vain   5
  That the Beaver's lace-making was wrong,
Fell asleep, and in dreams saw the creature quite plain
  That his fancy had dwelt on so long.

He dreamed that he stood in a shadowy Court,
  Where the Snark, with a glass in its eye,   10
Dressed in gown, bands, and wig, was defending a pig
  On the charge of deserting its sty.

The Witnesses proved, without error or flaw,
  That the sty was deserted when found:
And the Judge kept explaining the state of the law   15
  In a soft under-current of sound.

The indictment had never been clearly expressed,
  And it seemed that the Snark had begun,
And had spoken three hours, before any one guessed
  What the pig was supposed to have done.   20

The Jury had each formed a different view
  (Long before the indictment was read),
And they all spoke at once, so that none of them knew
  One word that the others had said.

'You must know—' said the Judge: but the Snark exclaimed 'Fudge!   25
  That statute is obsolete quite!
Let me tell you, my friends, the whole question depends
  On an ancient manorial right.

'In the matter of Treason the pig would appear
  To have aided, but scarcely abetted: 30
While the charge of Insolvency fails, it is clear,
  If you grant the plea "never indebted".

'The fact of Desertion I will not dispute:
  But its guilt, as I trust, is removed
(So far as relates to the costs of this suit)   35
  By the Alibi which has been proved.

'My poor client's fate now depends on your votes.'
  Here the speaker sat down in his place,
And directed the Judge to refer to his notes
  And briefly to sum up the case.   40

But the Judge said he never had summed up before;
  So the Snark undertook it instead,
And summed it so well that it came to far more
  Than the Witnesses ever had said!

When the verdict was called for, the Jury declined,   45
  As the word was so puzzling to spell;
But they ventured to hope that the Snark wouldn't mind
  Undertaking that duty as well.

So the Snark found the verdict, although, as it owned,
  It was spent with the toils of the day: 50
When it said the word 'GUILTY!' the Jury all groaned,
  And some of them fainted away.

Then the Snark pronounced sentence, the Judge being quite
  Too nervous to utter a word:
When it rose to its feet, there was silence like night,   55
  And the fall of a pin might be heard.

'Transportation for life' was the sentence it gave,
  'And *then* to be fined forty pound.'
The Jury all cheered, though the Judge said he feared
  That the phrase was not legally sound.   60

But their wild exultation was suddenly checked
  When the jailer informed them, with tears,
Such a sentence would have not the slightest effect,
  As the pig had been dead for some years.

The Judge left the Court, looking deeply disgusted: 65
  But the Snark, though a little aghast,
As the lawyer to whom the defence was intrusted,
  Went bellowing on to the last.

Thus the Barrister dreamed, while the bellowing seemed
  To grow every moment more clear: 70
Till he woke to the knell of a furious bell,
  Which the Bellman rang close at his ear.

FIT THE SEVENTH. THE BANKER'S FATE

They sought it with thimbles, they sought it with care;
  They pursued it with forks and hope;
They threatened its life with a railway-share;
  They charmed it with smiles and soap.

And the Banker, inspired with a courage so new   5
  It was matter for general remark,
Rushed madly ahead and was lost to their view
  In his zeal to discover the Snark.

But while he was seeking with thimbles and care,
  A Bandersnatch swiftly drew nigh   10
And grabbed at the Banker, who shrieked in
    despair,
  For he knew it was useless to fly.

He offered large discount – he offered a cheque
  (Drawn 'to bearer') for seven-pounds-ten:
But the Bandersnatch merely extended its neck   15
  And grabbed at the Banker again.

Without rest or pause – while those frumious jaws
  Went savagely snapping around –
He skipped and he hopped, and he floundered and
    flopped,
  Till fainting he fell to the ground.   20

The Bandersnatch fled as the others appeared
  Led on by that fear-stricken yell:
And the Bellman remarked 'It is just as I feared!'
  And solemnly tolled on his bell.

He was black in the face, and they scarcely could
    trace   25
  The least likeness to what he had been:
While so great was his fright that his waistcoat turned
    white –
  A wonderful thing to be seen!

To the horror of all who were present that day,
  He uprose in full evening dress,   30
And with senseless grimaces endeavoured to say
  What his tongue could no longer express.

Down he sank in a chair – ran his hands through his
    hair –
  And chanted in mimsiest tones
Words whose utter inanity proved his insanity,   35
  While he rattled a couple of bones.

'Leave him here to his fate – it is getting so late!'
  The Bellman exclaimed in a fright.
'We have lost half the day. Any further delay,
  And we sha'n't catch a Snark before night!'   40

FIT THE EIGHTH. THE VANISHING

They sought it with thimbles, they sought it with care;
  They pursued it with forks and hope;
They threatened its life with a railway-share;
  They charmed it with smiles and soap.

They shuddered to think that the chase might fail,   5
  And the Beaver, excited at last,
Went bounding along on the tip of its tail,
  For the daylight was nearly past.

'There is Thingumbob shouting!' the Bellman said.
  'He is shouting like mad, only hark!   10
He is waving his hands, he is wagging his head,
  He has certainly found a Snark!'

They gazed in delight, while the Butcher exclaimed
  'He was always a desperate wag!'
They beheld him – their Baker – their hero
    unnamed –   15
  On the top of a neighbouring crag,

Erect and sublime, for one moment of time.
  In the next, that wild figure they saw
(As if stung by a spasm) plunge into a chasm,
  While they waited and listened in awe.   20

'It's a Snark!' was the sound that first came to their
    ears,
  And seemed almost too good to be true.
Then followed a torrent of laughter and cheers:
  Then the ominous words 'It's a Boo—'

Then, silence. Some fancied they heard in the air   25
  A weary and wandering sigh
That sounded like '—jum!' but the others declare
  It was only a breeze that went by.

They hunted till darkness came on, but they found
  Not a button, or feather, or mark,   30
By which they could tell that they stood on the ground
  Where the Baker had met with the Snark.

In the midst of the word he was trying to say,
  In the midst of his laughter and glee,
He had softly and suddenly vanished away –   35
  For the Snark *was* a Boojum, you see.

WILLIAM MORRIS

SUMMER DAWN

PRAY but one prayer for me 'twixt thy closed lips,
    Think but one thought of me up in the stars.
The summer night waneth, the morning light slips,
    Faint and grey 'twixt the leaves of the aspen, betwixt
        the cloud-bars,
They are patiently waiting there for the dawn: 5
    Patient and colourless, though Heaven's gold
Waits to float through them along with the sun.
Far out in the meadows, above the young corn,
    The heavy elms wait, and restless and cold
The uneasy wind rises; the roses are dun;   10
Through the long twilight they pray for the dawn,
Round the lone house in the midst of the corn.
    Speak but one word to me over the corn,
    Over the tender, bowed locks of the corn.

A GARDEN BY THE SEA

I KNOW a little garden-close,
Set thick with lily and red rose,
Where I would wander if I might
From dewy morn to dewy night,
And have one with me wandering.   5

And though within it no birds sing,
And though no pillared house is there,
And though the apple-boughs are bare
Of fruit and blossom, would to God
Her feet upon the green grass trod,   10
And I beheld them as before.

There comes a murmur from the shore,
And in the close two fair streams are,
Drawn from the purple hills afar,
Drawn down unto the restless sea: 15
Dark hills whose heath-bloom feeds no bee,
Dark shore no ship has ever seen,
Tormented by the billows green
Whose murmur comes unceasingly
Unto the place for which I cry.   20
For which I cry both day and night,
For which I let slip all delight,
Whereby I grow both deaf and blind,
Careless to win, unskilled to find,
And quick to lose what all men seek.   25

Yet tottering as I am and weak,
Still have I left a little breath
To seek within the jaws of death
An entrance to that happy place,
To seek the unforgotten face,   30
Once seen, once kissed, once reft from me
Anigh the murmuring of the sea.

JAMES THOMSON ('BV')

From THE CITY OF DREADFUL NIGHT

THE City is of Night; perchance of Death
    But certainly of Night; for never there
Can come the lucid morning's fragrant breath
    After the dewy dawning's cold grey air;
The moon and stars may shine with scorn or pity;   5
The sun has never visited that city,
    For it dissolveth in the daylight fair.

Dissolveth like a dream of night away;
    Though present in distempered gloom of thought
And deadly weariness of heart all day.   10
    But when a dream night after night is brought
Throughout a week, and such weeks few or many
Recur each year for several years, can any
    Discern that dream from real life in aught?

For life is but a dream whose shapes return,   15
    Some frequently, some seldom, some by night
And some by day, some night and day: we learn,
    The while all change and many vanish quite,
In their recurrence with recurrent changes
A certain seeming order; where this ranges   20
    We count things real; such is memory's might.

A river girds the city west and south,
    The main north channel of a broad lagoon,
Regurging with the salt tides from the mouth;
    Waste marshes shine and glister to the moon   25
For leagues, then moorland black, then stony ridges;
Great piers and causeways, many noble bridges,
    Connect the town and islet suburbs strewn.

Upon an easy slope it lies at large
    And scarcely overlaps the long curved crest   30
Which swells out two leagues from the river marge.
    A trackless wilderness rolls north and west,
Savannahs, savage woods, enormous mountains,
Bleak uplands, black ravines with torrent fountains;
    And eastward rolls the shipless sea's unrest.   35

The city is not ruinous, although
    Great ruins of an unremembered past,
With others of a few short years ago
    More sad, are found within its precincts vast.
The street-lamps always burn; but scarce a
        casement   40
In house or palace front from roof to basement
    Doth glow or gleam athwart the mirk air cast.

The street-lamps burn amid the baleful glooms,

The street-lamps burn amid the baleful glooms,
  Amidst the soundless solitudes immense
Of rangèd mansions dark and still as tombs.   45
  The silence which benumbs or strains the sense
Fulfils with awe the soul's despair unweeping:
Myriads of habitants are ever sleeping,
  Or dead, or fled from nameless pestilence!

Yet as in some necropolis you find   50
  Perchance one mourner to a thousand dead,
So there: worn faces that look deaf and blind
  Like tragic masks of stone. With weary tread,
Each wrapt in his own doom, they wander, wander,
Or sit foredone and desolately ponder   55
  Through sleepless hours with heavy drooping
    head.

Mature men chiefly, few in age or youth,
  A woman rarely, now and then a child:
A child! If here the heart turns sick with ruth
  To see a little one from birth defiled,   60
Or lame or blind, as preordained to languish
Through youthless life, think how it bleeds with
    anguish
  To meet one erring in that homeless wild.

They often murmur to themselves, they speak
  To one another seldom, for their woe   65
Broods maddening inwardly and scorns to wreak
  Itself abroad; and if at whiles it grow
To frenzy which must rave, none heeds the clamour,
Unless there waits some victim of like glamour,
  To rave in turn, who lends attentive show.   70

The City is of Night, but not of Sleep;
  There sweet sleep is not for the weary brain;
The pitiless hours like years and ages creep,
  A night seems termless hell. This dreadful strain
Of thought and consciousness which never ceases,   75
Or which some moments' stupor but increases,
  This, worse than woe, makes wretches there insane.

They leave all hope behind who enter there:
  One certitude while sane they cannot leave;
One anodyne for torture and despair;   80
  The certitude of Death, which no reprieve
Can put off long; and which, divinely tender,
But waits the outstretched hand to promptly render
  That draught whose slumber nothing can
    bereave.*

* Though the Garden of thy Life be wholly waste, the sweet flowers
withered, the fruit-trees barren, over its wall hang ever the rich dark
clusters of the Vine of Death, within easy reach of thy hand, which
may pluck of them when it will.

[Part 1]

ALGERNON CHARLES SWINBURNE

From ATALANTA IN CALYDON

WHEN the hounds of spring are on winter's traces,
  The mother of months in meadow or plain
Fills the shadows and windy places
  With lisp of leaves and ripple of rain;
And the brown bright nightingale amorous   5
Is half assuaged for Itylus,
For the Thracian ships and the foreign faces,
  The tongueless vigil, and all the pain.

Come with bows bent and with emptying of quivers,
  Maiden most perfect, lady of light,   10
With a noise of winds and many rivers,
  With a clamour of waters, and with might;
Bind on thy sandals, O thou most fleet,
Over the splendour and speed of thy feet;
For the faint east quickens, the wan west shivers, 15
  Round the feet of the day and the feet of the night.

Where shall we find her, how shall we sing to her,
  Fold our hands round her knees, and cling?
Oh, that man's heart were as fire and could spring to
    her,
  Fire, or the strength of the streams that spring! 20
For the stars and the winds are unto her
As raiment, as songs of the harp-player;
For the risen stars and the fallen cling to her,
  And the southwest-wind and the west-wind sing.

For winter's rains and ruins are over,   25
  And all the season of snows and sins;
The days dividing lover and lover,
  The light that loses, the night that wins;
And time remembered is grief forgotten,
And frosts are slain and flowers begotten,   30
And in green underwood and cover
  Blossom by blossom the spring begins.

The full streams feed on flower of rushes,
  Ripe grasses trammel a travelling foot,
The faint fresh flame of the young year flushes   35
  From leaf to flower and flower to fruit;
And fruit and leaf are as gold and fire,
And the oat is heard above the lyre,
And the hoofèd heel of a satyr crushes
  The chestnut-husk at the chestnut-root.   40

And Pan by noon and Bacchus by night,
  Fleeter of foot than the fleet-foot kid,
Follows with dancing and fills with delight
  The Maenad and the Bassarid;
And soft as lips that laugh and hide   45
The laughing leaves of the trees divide,
And screen from seeing and leave in sight
  The god pursuing, the maiden hid.

The ivy falls with the Bacchanal's hair
  Over her eyebrows hiding her eyes;   50
The wild vine slipping down leaves bare
  Her bright breast shortening into sighs;
The wild vine slips with the weight of its leaves,
But the berried ivy catches and cleaves
To the limbs that glitter, the feet that scare   55
  The wolf that follows, the fawn that flies.

A LEAVE-TAKING

LET us go hence, my songs; she will not hear.
Let us go hence together without fear;
Keep silence now, for singing-time is over,
And over all old things and all things dear.
She loves not you nor me as all we love her.   5
Yea, though we sang as angels in her ear,
  She would not hear.

Let us rise up and part; she will not know.
Let us go seaward as the great winds go,
Full of blown sand and foam, what help is here?   10
There is no help, for all these things are so,
And all the world is bitter as a tear.
And how these things are, though ye strove to show,
  She would not know.

Let us go home and hence; she will not weep.   15
We gave love many dreams and days to keep,
Flowers without scent, and fruits that would not grow,
Saying 'If thou wilt, thrust in thy sickle and reap.'
All is reaped now; no grass is left to mow;
And we that sowed, though all we fell on sleep,   20
  She would not weep.

Let us go hence and rest; she will not love.
She shall not hear us if we sing hereof,
Nor see love's ways, how sore they are and steep.
Come hence, let be, lie still; it is enough.   25
Love is a barren sea, bitter and deep;
And though she saw all heaven in flower above,
  She would not love.

Let us give up, go down; she will not care.
Though all the stars made gold of all the air,   30
And the sea moving saw before it move
One moon-flower making all the foam-flowers fair;
Though all those waves went over us, and drove
Deep down the stifling lips and drowning hair,
  She would not care.   35

Let us go hence, go hence; she will not see.
Sing all once more together; surely she,
She too, remembering days and words that were,
Will turn a little toward us, sighing; but we,
We are hence, we are gone, as though we had not
    been there.   40
Nay, and though all men seeing had pity on me,
  She would not see.

THE GARDEN OF PROSERPINE

HERE, where the world is quiet,
  Here, where all trouble seems
Dead winds' and spent waves' riot
  In doubtful dreams of dreams;
I watch the green field growing   5
For reaping folk and sowing,
For harvest-time and mowing,
  A sleepy world of streams.

I am tired of tears and laughter,
  And men that laugh and weep;   10
Of what may come hereafter
  For men that sow to reap:
I am weary of days and hours,
Blown buds of barren flowers,
Desires and dreams and powers   15
  And everything but sleep.

Here life has death for neighbour,
  And far from eye or ear
Wan waves and wet winds labour,
  Weak ships and spirits steer;   20
They drive adrift, and whither
They wot not who make thither;
But no such winds blow hither,
  And no such things grow here.

No growth of moor or coppice,   25
  No heather-flower or vine,
But bloomless buds of poppies,
  Green grapes of Proserpine,
Pale beds of blowing rushes,
Where no leaf blooms or blushes   30
Save this whereout she crushes
  For dead men deadly wine.

Pale, without name or number,
  In fruitless fields of corn,
They bow themselves and slumber   35
  All night till light is born;
And like a soul belated,
In hell and heaven unmated,
By cloud and mist abated
  Comes out of darkness morn.   40

Though one were strong as seven,
  He too with death shall dwell,
Nor wake with wings in heaven,
  Nor weep for pains in hell;
Though one were fair as roses,   45
His beauty clouds and closes;
And well though love reposes,
  In the end it is not well.

Pale, beyond porch and portal,
　　Crowned with calm leaves, she stands　　　　50
Who gathers all things mortal
　　With cold immortal hands;
Her languid lips are sweeter
Than love's who fears to greet her
To men that mix and meet her　　　　　　　　55
　　From many times and lands.

She waits for each and other,
　　She waits for all men born;
Forgets the earth her mother,
　　The life of fruits and corn;　　　　　　　60
And spring and seed and swallow
Take wing for her and follow
Where summer song rings hollow
　　And flowers are put to scorn.

There go the loves that wither,　　　　　　　65
　　The old loves with wearier wings;
And all dead years draw thither,
　　And all disastrous things;
Dead dreams of days forsaken,
Blind buds that snows have shaken,　　　　　70
Wild leaves that winds have taken,
　　Red strays of ruined springs.

We are not sure of sorrow,
　　And joy was never sure;
Today will die tomorrow;
　　Time stoops to no man's lure;　　　　　　75
And love, grown faint and fretful,
With lips but half regretful
Sighs, and with eyes forgetful
　　Weeps that no loves endure.　　　　　　　80

From too much love of living,
　　From hope and fear set free,
We thank with brief thanksgiving
　　Whatever gods may be
That no life lives for ever;　　　　　　　　85
That dead men rise up never;
That even the weariest river
　　Winds somewhere safe to sea.

Then star nor sun shall waken,
　　Nor any change of light:　　　　　　　　90
Nor sound of waters shaken,
　　Nor any sound or sight:
Nor wintry leaves nor vernal,
Nor days nor things diurnal;
Only the sleep eternal　　　　　　　　　　95
　　In an eternal night.

THOMAS HARDY

DRUMMER HODGE

THEY throw in Drummer Hodge, to rest
　　Uncoffined – just as found:
His landmark is a kopje-crest
　　That breaks the veldt around;
And foreign constellations west　　　　　　5
　　Each night above his mound.

Young Hodge the Drummer never knew –
　　Fresh from his Wessex home –
The meaning of the broad Karoo,
　　The Bush, the dusty loam,　　　　　　　10
And why uprose to nightly view
　　Strange stars amid the gloom.

Yet portion of that unknown plain
　　Will Hodge for ever be;
His homely Northern breast and brain　　　　15
　　Grow to some Southern tree,
And strange-eyed constellations reign
　　His stars eternally.

DRUMMER HODGE: The setting is South Africa. This is a poem of the Boer War (1899–1902), first published in November 1899 when it was accompanied by a note that 'One of the Drummers killed was a native of a village near Casterbridge' (i.e. Dorchester: the Wessex landscape Hardy evokes in his novels and stories is carried over into his poems). 'Hodge' was a nickname for a country labourer: 3 **kopje**: low hill 4 **veldt**: open grassland 5 **west**: move towards the west 9 **Karoo**: high tableland, plateau 10 **Bush**: uncultivated country

THE DARKLING THRUSH

I LEANT upon a coppice gate
　　When Frost was spectre-gray,
And Winter's dregs made desolate
　　The weakening eye of day.
The tangled bine-stems scored the sky　　　5
　　Like strings of broken lyres,
And all mankind that haunted nigh
　　Had sought their household fires.

The land's sharp features seemed to be
　　The Century's corpse outleant,　　　　　10
His crypt the cloudy canopy,
　　The wind his death-lament.
The ancient pulse of germ and birth
　　Was shrunken hard and dry,
And every spirit upon earth　　　　　　　15
　　Seemed fervourless as I.
At once a voice arose among
　　The bleak twigs overhead
In a full-hearted evensong
　　Of joy illimited;　　　　　　　　　　20

An agèd thrush, frail, gaunt, and small,
    In blast-beruffled plume,
Had chosen thus to fling his soul
    Upon the growing gloom.

So little cause for carolings   25
    Of such ecstatic sound
Was written on terrestrial things
    Afar or nigh around,
That I could think there trembled through
    His happy good-night air   30
Some blessèd Hope, whereof he knew
    And I was unaware.

31 December 1900

THE DARKLING THRUSH: Dated 31 December 1900 and first published with the title 'By the Century's Deathbed' (compare line 10): **Darkling:** in the dark: 1 **coppice:** cultivated woodland 4 **eye of day:** i.e. the sun 5 **bine-stems:** the slender stems of last season's climbing plants 6 **lyres:** the lyre was an ancient ancestor of the harp, frequently used to accompany recited poetry 20 **illimited:** unlimited

THE SELF-UNSEEING

(M.H. 1772–1857)

HERE is the ancient floor,
Footworn and hollowed and thin,
Here was the former door
Where the dead feet walked in.

She sat here in her chair,   5
Smiling into the fire;
He who played stood there,
Bowing it higher and higher.

Childlike, I danced in a dream;
Blessings emblazoned that day;   10
Everything glowed with a gleam;
Yet we were looking away!

20 May 1902

THE SELF-UNSEEING: a reminiscence of the poet's childhood at Higher Bockhampton in Dorset: 4 **dead feet:** Hardy's late father (who is probably the fiddler described in lines 7–8) 5 **She:** Hardy's mother

SHUT OUT THAT MOON

CLOSE up the casement, draw the blind,
    Shut out that stealing moon,
She wears too much the guise she wore
    Before our lutes were strewn
With years-deep dust, and names we read   5
    On a white stone were hewn.

Step not forth on the dew-dashed lawn
    To view the Lady's Chair,
Immense Orion's glittering form,

The Less and Greater Bear: 10
Stay in; to such sights we were drawn
    When faded ones were fair.

Brush not the bough for midnight scents
    That come forth lingeringly,
And wake the same sweet sentiments   15
    They breathed to you and me
When living seemed a laugh, and love
    All it was said to be.

Within the common lamp-lit room
    Prison my eyes and thought;   20
Let dingy details crudely loom,
    Mechanic speech be wrought:
Too fragrant was Life's early bloom,
    Too tart the fruit it brought!

1904

SHUT OUT THAT MOON: 8 **Lady's Chair:** the constellation Cassiopeia 9 **Orion:** The Hunter, another constellation 10 **Less and Greater Bear:** the constellations Ursa Minor and Ursa Major

THE MAN HE KILLED

'HAD he and I but met
    By some old ancient inn,
We should have sat us down to wet
    Right many a nipperkin!

'But ranged as infantry,   5
    And staring face to face,
I shot at him as he at me,
    And killed him in his place.

'I shot him dead because –
    Because he was my foe,   10
Just so: my foe of course he was;
    That's clear enough; although

'He thought he'd 'list, perhaps,
    Off-hand like – just as I –
Was out of work – had sold his traps –   15
    No other reason why.

'Yes; quaint and curious war is!
    You shoot a fellow down
You'd treat if met where any bar is,
    Or help to half-a-crown.'   20

1902

THE MAN HE KILLED: Another poem inspired by the Boer War (1899–1902). In early published versions the title is followed by: 'Scene: The settle of the Fox Inn, Stagfoot Lane. Characters: The speaker (a returned soldier), and his friends, natives of the hamlet': 4 **nipperkin:** small measure of alcohol 13 **'list:** enlist 20 **half-a-crown:** an eighth of a pound (12½p)

THE CONVERGENCE OF THE TWAIN
(LINES ON THE LOSS OF THE 'TITANIC')

In a solitude of the sea
Deep from human vanity,
And the Pride of Life that planned her, stilly couches
she.

Steel chambers, late the pyres
Of her salamandrine fires,   5
Cold currents thrid, and turn to rhythmic tidal lyres.

Over the mirrors meant
To glass the opulent
The sea-worm crawls – grotesque, slimed, dumb,
indifferent.

Jewels in joy designed   10
To ravish the sensuous mind
Lie lightless, all their sparkles bleared and black and
blind.

Dim moon-eyed fishes near
Gaze at the gilded gear
And query: 'What does this vaingloriousness down
here?' . . .   15

Well: while was fashioning
This creature of cleaving wing,
The Immanent Will that stirs and urges everything

Prepared a sinister mate
For her – so gaily great –   20
A Shape of Ice, for the time far and dissociate.

And as the smart ship grew
In stature, grace, and hue,
In shadowy silent distance grew the Iceberg too.

Alien they seemed to be: 25
No mortal eye could see
The intimate welding of their later history,

Or sign that they were bent
By paths coincident
On being anon twin halves of one august event,   30

Till the Spinner of the Years
Said 'Now!' And each one hears,
And consummation comes, and jars two hemispheres.

THE GOING

Why did you give no hint that night
That quickly after the morrow's dawn,
And calmly, as if indifferent quite,
You would close your term here, up and be gone
    Where I could not follow   5
    With wing of swallow
To gain one glimpse of you ever anon!

    Never to bid good-bye,
    Or lip me the softest call,
Or utter a wish for a word, while I   10
Saw morning harden upon the wall,
    Unmoved, unknowing
    That your great going
Had place that moment, and altered all.

Why do you make me leave the house   15
And think for a breath it is you I see
At the end of the alley of bending boughs
Where so often at dusk you used to be;
    Till in darkening dankness
    The yawning blankness   20
Of the perspective sickens me!

You were she who abode
By those red-veined rocks far West,
You were the swan-necked one who rode
Along the beetling Beeny Crest,   25
    And, reining nigh me,
    Would muse and eye me,
While Life unrolled us its very best.

Why, then, latterly did we not speak,
Did we not think of those days long dead,   30
And ere your vanishing strive to seek
That time's renewal? We might have said,
    'In this bright spring weather
    We'll visit together
Those places that once we visited.'   35

    Well, well! All's past amend,
    Unchangeable. It must go.
I seem but a dead man held on end
To sink down soon. . . . O you could you know
    That such swift fleeing   40
    No soul foreseeing –
Not even I – would undo me so!

December 1912

THE CONVERGENCE OF THE TWAIN: On her maiden voyage to New York in 1912, the British liner *Titanic* struck an iceberg and sank, with the loss of 1,513 lives: 3 **the Pride of Life:** 'For all that is in the world, the lust of the flesh, and the lust of the eyes, and the pride of life, is not of the Father, but is of the world' (1 John 2.16) 5 **salamandrine:** an amphibian related to the newt, the salamander was once thought to be able to live in fire 6 **thrid:** thread through **lyres:** see note to 'The Darkling Thrush' 8 **glass:** reflect 17 **cleaving wing:** the ship cleaves the sea as a bird's wing cleaves the air 18 **Immanent Will:** Hardy believed that a hidden force, which he also called 'the Unconscious Will of the Universe', shaped events but was indifferent to the welfare of man 31 **Spinner of the Years:** Fate

THE GOING: Following the death of his wife, Emma, on 27 November 1912, Hardy was moved to make a journey to Cornwall, where the couple had first met and fallen in love, and to revisit the places associated with their courtship. The remarkable sequence of poems inspired by the pilgrimage was eventually published under the general heading 'Poems of 1912–13', with an epigraph from Virgil's *Aeneid: Veteris vestigia flammae* ('traces of the old flame'). 'The Going' is the first poem in the series: 14 **Had place:** was taking place 24–5 **who rode/Along the beetling Beeny Crest:** the young Emma had been an accomplished horsewoman; Hardy celebrates her skill again in 'Beeny Cliff' 25 **beetling:** jutting, overhanging **Beeny:** a high cliff near Boscastle

THE VOICE

WOMAN much missed, how you call to me, call to me,
Saying that now you are not as you were
When you had changed from the one who was all to
    me,
But as at first, when our day was fair.

Can it be you that I hear? Let me view you, then,   5
Standing as when I drew near to the town
Where you would wait for me: yes, as I knew you then,
Even to the original air-blue gown!

Or is it only the breeze, in its listlessness
Travelling across the wet mead to me here,   10
You being ever dissolved to wan wistlessness,
Heard no more again far or near?

        Thus I; faltering forward,
        Leaves around me falling,
Wind oozing thin through the thorn from norward,   15
        And the woman calling.

                                        December 1912

THE VOICE: another of the 'Poems of 1912–13': 10 **mead:** pasture
11 **wan wistlessness:** Hardy first wrote 'existlessness', which points
to the meaning here 15 **norward:** northward

AFTER A JOURNEY

HERETO I come to view a voiceless ghost;
    Whither, O whither will its whim now draw me?
Up the cliff, down, till I'm lonely, lost,
    And the unseen waters' ejaculations awe me.
Where you will next be there's no knowing,   5
    Facing round about me everywhere,
        With your nut-coloured hair,
And gray eyes, and rose-flush coming and going.

Yes: I have re-entered your olden haunts at last;
    Through the years, through the dead scenes I have
        tracked you;   10
What have you now found to say of our past –
    Scanned across the dark space wherein I have
        lacked you?
Summer gave us sweets, but autumn wrought division?
    Things were not lastly as firstly well
        With us twain, you tell?   15
But all's closed now, despite Time's derision.

I see what you are doing: you are leading me on
    To the spots we knew when we haunted here
        together,
The waterfall, above which the mist-bow shone
    At the then fair hour in the then fair weather,   20
And the cave just under, with a voice still so hollow
    That it seems to call out to me from forty years ago,
        When you were all aglow,
And not the thin ghost that I now frailly follow!

Ignorant of what there is flitting here to see,   25
    The waked birds preen and the seals flop lazily;
Soon you will have, Dear, to vanish from me,
    For the stars close their shutters and the dawn
        whitens hazily.
Trust me, I mind not, though Life lours,
    The bringing me here; nay, bring me here again!   30
        I am just the same as when
Our days were a joy, and our paths through flowers.

                                        Pentargan Bay

AFTER A JOURNEY: another of the 'Poems of 1912–13'; Pentargan Bay
is below Beeny Cliff

BEENY CLIFF
MARCH 1870–MARCH 1913

O THE opal and the sapphire of that wandering
    western sea,
And the woman riding high above with bright hair
    flapping free –
The woman whom I loved so, and who loyally loved
    me.

The pale mews plained below us, and the waves
    seemed far away
In a nether sky, engrossed in saying their ceaseless
    babbling say,   5
As we laughed light-heartedly aloft on that clear-
    sunned March day.

A little cloud then cloaked us, and there flew an irised
    rain,
And the Atlantic dyed its levels with a dull misfeatured
    stain,
And then the sun burst out again, and purples prinked
    the main.

– Still in all its chasmal beauty bulks old Beeny to the
    sky,   10
And shall she and I not go there once again now
    March is nigh,
And the sweet things said in that March say anew
    there by and by?

What if still in chasmal beauty looms that wild weird
    western shore,
The woman now is – elsewhere – whom the ambling
    pony bore,
And nor knows nor cares for Beeny, and will laugh
    there nevermore.   15

BEENY CLIFF: another of the 'Poems of 1912–13'; for Beeny Cliff,
see note to 'The Going': 2 **woman riding high above:** see note to
'The Going' (lines 24–5) 4 **mews:** gulls **plained:** cried, complained
7 **irised:** containing a rainbow 9 **prinked:** adorned, ornamented

THE OXEN

CHRISTMAS EVE, and twelve of the clock.
  'Now they are all on their knees,'
An elder said as we sat in a flock
  By the embers in hearthside ease.

We pictured the meek mild creatures where   5
  They dwelt in their strawy pen,
Nor did it occur to one of us there
  To doubt they were kneeling then.

So fair a fancy few would weave
  In these years! Yet, I feel,   10
If someone said on Christmas Eve,
  'Come; see the oxen kneel

'In the lonely barton by yonder coomb
  Our childhood used to know,'
I should go with him in the gloom,   15
  Hoping it might be so.

                                           1915

THE OXEN: 13 **barton:** farmyard **coomb:** small wooded valley

GREAT THINGS

SWEET cyder is a great thing,
  A great thing to me,
Spinning down to Weymouth town
  By Ridgway thirstily,
And maid and mistress summoning   5
  Who tend the hostelry:
O cyder is a great thing,
  A great thing to me!

The dance it is a great thing,
  A great thing to me,   10
With candles lit and partners fit
  For night-long revelry;
And going home when day-dawning
  Peeps pale upon the lea:
O dancing is a great thing,   15
  A great thing to me!

Love is, yea, a great thing,
  A great thing to me,
When, having drawn across the lawn
  In darkness silently,   20
A figure flits like one a-wing
  Out from the nearest tree:
O love is, yes, a great thing,
  A great thing to me!

Will these be always great things,   25
  Great things to me? . . .
Let it befall that One will call,
  'Soul, I have need of thee':
What then? Joy-jaunts, impassioned flings,
  Love, and its ecstasy,   30
Will always have been great things,
  Great things to me!

MEN WHO MARCH AWAY
(SONG OF THE SOLDIERS)

WHAT of the faith and fire within us
  Men who march away
  Ere the barn-cocks say
  Night is growing gray,
Leaving all that here can win us;   5
What of the faith and fire within us
  Men who march away?

Is it a purblind prank, O think you,
  Friend with the musing eye,
  Who watch us stepping by   10
  With doubt and dolorous sigh?
Can much pondering so hoodwink you!
Is it a purblind prank, O think you,
  Friend with the musing eye?

Nay. We well see what we are doing,   15
  Though some may not see –
  Dalliers as they be –
  England's need are we;
Her distress would leave us rueing:
Nay. We well see what we are doing,   20
  Though some may not see!

In our heart of hearts believing
  Victory crowns the just,
  And that braggarts must
  Surely bite the dust,   25
Press we to the field ungrieving,
In our heart of hearts believing
  Victory crowns the just.

Hence the faith and fire within us
  Men who march away   30
  Ere the barn-cocks say
  Night is growing gray,
Leaving all that here can win us;
Hence the faith and fire within us
  Men who march away.   35

                                      5 September 1914

MEN WHO MARCH AWAY: Dated 5 September 1914. Britain had declared war on Germany on 4 August. Hardy had been one of the writers called to London, 'at the instance of the Cabinet', 'for the organisation of public statements of the strength of the British case and principles in the war by well-known men of letters' (*Life of Thomas Hardy*). This poem was Hardy's response 8 **purblind:** dim-sighted

IN TIME OF 'THE BREAKING OF NATIONS'

ONLY a man harrowing clods
  In a slow silent walk
With an old horse that stumbles and nods
  Half asleep as they stalk.

Only thin smoke without flame   5
  From the heaps of couch-grass;
Yet this will go onward the same
  Though Dynasties pass.

Yonder a maid and her wight
  Come whispering by: 10
War's annals will cloud into night
  Ere their story die.   *1915*

IN TIME OF 'THE BREAKING OF NATIONS': Dated 1915. Hardy refers us to Jeremiah 51.20: 'Thou art my battle axe and weapons of war: for with thee will I break in pieces the nations, and with thee will I destroy kingdoms': 1 **harrowing clods:** a harrow is an agricultural device for smoothing and levelling land 6 **couch-grass:** coarse grass, a weed 9 **wight:** man

AFTERWARDS

WHEN the Present has latched its postern behind my
    tremulous stay,
  And the May month flaps its glad green leaves like
    wings,
Delicate-filmed as new-spun silk, will the neighbours
    say,
  'He was a man who used to notice such things'?

If it be in the dusk when, like an eyelid's soundless
    blink,   5
  The dewfall-hawk comes crossing the shades to
    alight
Upon the wind-warped upland thorn, a gazer may
    think,
  'To him this must have been a familiar sight.'

If I pass during some nocturnal blackness, mothy and
    warm,
  When the hedgehog travels furtively over the lawn,
One may say, 'He strove that such innocent creatures
    should come to no harm,   11
  But he could do little for them; and now he is gone.'

If, when hearing that I have been stilled at last, they
    stand at the door,
  Watching the full-starred heavens that winter sees,
Will this thought rise on those who will meet my face
    no more,   15
  'He was one who had an eye for such mysteries'?

And will any say when my bell of quittance is heard in
    the gloom,
  And a crossing breeze cuts a pause in its outrollings,
Till they rise again, as they were a new bell's boom,   19
  'He hears it not now, but used to notice such things'?

AFTERWARDS: 1 **postern:** private door or gate 6 **dewfall-hawk:** nightjar 17 **bell of quittance:** funeral bell

CHILDHOOD AMONG THE FERNS

I SAT one sprinkling day upon the lea,
Where tall-stemmed ferns spread out luxuriantly,
And nothing but those tall ferns sheltered me.

The rain gained strength, and damped each lopping
    frond,
Ran down their stalks beside me and beyond,   5
And shaped slow-creeping rivulets as I conned,

With pride, my spray-roofed house. And though anon
Some drops pierced its green rafters, I sat on,
Making pretence I was not rained upon.

The sun then burst, and brought forth a sweet breath
From the limp ferns as they dried underneath: 11
I said: 'I could live on here thus till death';

And queried in the green rays as I sate:
'Why should I have to grow to man's estate,
And this afar-noised World perambulate?'   15

CHILDHOOD AMONG THE FERNS: 1 **sprinkling:** showery **lea:** meadow 6 **conned:** studied 7 **spray-roofed:** i.e. a roof formed by the ferns 13 **sate:** sat (archaic)

GERARD MANLEY HOPKINS

THE WRECK OF THE DEUTSCHLAND

To the
happy memory of five Franciscan nuns
exiles by the Falck Laws
drowned between midnight and morning of
Dec. 7th, 1875

PART THE FIRST

THOU mastering me
God! giver of breath and bread;
World's strand, sway of the sea;
Lord of living and dead;
Thou hast bound bones and veins in me, fastened
    me flesh,   5

THE WRECK OF THE DEUTSCHLAND: '[W]hen in the winter of '75, the *Deutschland* was wrecked in the mouth of the Thames and five Franciscan nuns, exiles from Germany by the Falck Laws, aboard of her were drowned I was affected by the account and happening to say so to my rector he said that he wished someone would write a poem on the subject. On this hint I set to work . . . I had long had haunting my ear the echo of a new rhythm which now I realised on paper. To speak shortly, it consists of scanning by accents or stresses alone, without any account of the number of syllables, so that a foot may be one strong syllable or it may be many light and one strong one' (GMH to Richard Watson Dixon, 5 October 1878). In this Hopkins poem, as in all the others included here, the stress marks are the poet's own **Falck Laws:** as part of the German government's persecution of Roman Catholics, in May 1875 the Minister of Worship, Adalbert Falck, closed all Prussian monasteries

And after it almost unmade, what with dread,
  Thy doing: and dost thou touch me afresh?
    Over again I feel thy finger and find thee.

          I did say yes
          O at lightning and lashed rod;   10
      Thou heardst me truer than tongue confess
          Thy terror, O Christ, O God;
      Thou knowest the walls, altar and hour and night:
      The swoon of a heart that the sweep and the hurl of
          thee trod
      Hard down with a horror of height: 15
    And the midriff astrain with leaning of, laced with fire
          of stress.

          The frown of his face
          Before me, the hurtle of hell
      Behind, where, where was a, where was a
          place?
          I whirled out wings that spell   20
    And fled with a fling of the heart to the heart of the
          Host.
      My heart, but you were dovewinged, I can tell,
          Carrier-witted, I am bold to boast,
    To flash from the flame to the flame then, tower from
          the grace to the grace.

          I am soft sift   25
          In an hourglass – at the wall
      Fast, but mined with a motion, a drift,
          And it crowds and it combs to the fall;
    I steady as a water in a well, to a poise, to a pane,
      But roped with, always, all the way down from the
          tall   30
          Fells or flanks of the voel, a vein
    Of the gospel proffer, a pressure, a principle, Christ's
          gift.

          I kiss my hand
          To the stars, lovely-asunder
      Starlight, wafting him out of it; and   35
          Glow, glory in thunder;
    Kiss my hand to the dappled-with-damson west:
    Since, tho' he is under the world's splendour and
          wonder,
      His mystery must be instressed, stressed;
    For I greet him the days I meet him, and bless when I
          understand.   40

          Not out of his bliss
          Springs the stress felt
      Nor first from heaven (and few know this)
          Swings the stroke dealt –
    Stroke and a stress that stars and storms deliver,   45
    That guilt is hushed by, hearts are flushed by and
          melt –
      But it rides time like riding a river
    (And here the faithful waver, the faithless fable and
          miss).

          It dates from day
          Of his going to Galilee;   50
      Warm-laid grave of a womb-life grey;
          Manger, maiden's knee;
    The dense and the driven Passion, and frightful
          sweat:
    Thence the discharge of it, there its swelling to be,
          Though felt before, though in high flood yet –
    What none would have known of it, only the heart,
          being hard at bay,   56

          Is out with it! Oh,
          We lash with the best or worst
      Word last! How a lush-kept plush-capped sloe
          Will, mouthed to flesh-burst,   60
    Gush! – flush the man, the being with it, sour or
          sweet,
      Brim, in a flash, full! – Hither then, last or first,
          To hero of Calvary, Christ,'s feet –
    Never ask if meaning it, wanting it, warned of it –
          men go.

          Be adored among men,   65
          God, three-numberèd form;
      Wring thy rebel, dogged in den,
          Man's malice, with wrecking and storm.
    Beyond saying sweet, past telling of tongue,
    Thou art lightning and love, I found it, a winter and
          warm;   70
      Father and fondler of heart thou hast wrung:
    Hast thy dark descending and most art merciful then.

          With an anvil-ding
          And with fire in him forge thy will
      Or rather, rather then, stealing as
          Spring   75
          Through him, melt him but master him still:
    Whether at once, as once at a crash Paul,
      Or as Austin, a lingering-out swéet skíll,
          Make mercy in all of us, out of us all
    Mastery, but be adored, but be adored King.   80

---

16 **laced:** corseted, restrained 20 **spell:** period of stress 23 **Carrier-witted:** with the homing instincts of a carrier-pigeon 28 **combs to the fall:** breaks with white foam 30 **roped with:** fed by 31 **voel:** (Welsh) bare hill **vein:** stream 32 **proffer:** Grace 37 **damson:** i.e. purple 39 **instressed, stressed:** impressed upon our being and its truth emphasised

47 **it rides time:** it is outside time and always present 67 **Wring:** torment, afflict 77–8 **at a crash Paul . . . Austin:** St Paul's conversion was suddent (Acts 8) whereas that of St Augustine of Hippo was gradual

PART THE SECOND

'Some find me a sword; some
The flange and the rail; flame,
Fang, or flood' goes Death on drum,
And storms bugle his fame.
But wé dream we are rooted in earth – Dust!   85
Flesh falls within sight of us, we, though our flower
the same,
Wave with the meadow, forget that there must
The sour scythe cringe, and the blear share come.

On Saturday sailed from Bremen,
American-outward-bound,   90
Take settler and seamen, tell men with women,
Two hundred souls in the round –
O Father, not under thy feathers nor ever as
guessing
The goal was a shoal, of a fourth the doom to be
drowned;
Yet did the dark side of the bay of thy blessing
Not vault them, the million of rounds of thy mercy
not reeve even them in?   96

Into the snows she sweeps,
Hurling the haven behind,
The Deutschland, on Sunday; and so the sky
keeps,
For the infinite air is unkind,   100
And the sea flint-flake, black-backed in the regular
blow,
Sitting Eastnortheast, in cursed quarter, the wind;
Wiry and white-fiery and whirlwind-swivellèd
snow
Spins to the widow-making unchilding unfathering
deeps.

She drove in the dark to leeward,   105
She struck – not a reef or a rock
But the combs of a smother of sand: night drew
her
Dead to the Kentish Knock;
And she beat the bank down with her bows and the
ride of her keel;
The breakers rolled on her beam with ruinous
shock;   110
And canvas and compass, the whorl and the
wheel
Idle for ever to waft her or wind her with, these she
endured.

Hope had grown grey hairs,
Hope had mourning on,
Trenched with tears, carved with cares,   115
Hope was twelve hours gone;
And frightful a nightfall folded rueful a day
Nor rescue, only rocket and lightship, shone,
And lives at last were washing away:
To the shrouds they took, – they shook in the hurling
and horrible airs.   120

One stirred from the rigging to save
The wild woman-kind below,
With a rope's end round the man, handy and
brave –
He was pitched to his death at a blow,
For all his dreadnought breast and braids of thew: 125
They could tell him for hours, dandled the to and
fro
Through the cobbled foam-fleece. What could
he do
With the burl of the fountains of air, buck and the
flood of the wave?

They fought with God's cold –
And they could not and fell to the deck   130
(Crushed them) or water (and drowned them)
or rolled
With the sea-romp over the wreck.
Night roared, with the heart-break hearing a heart-
broke rabble,
The woman's wailing, the crying of child without
check –
Till a lioness arose breasting the babble,   135
A prophetess towered in the tumult, a virginal tongue
told.

Ah, touched in your bower of bone,
Are you! turned for an exquisite smart,
Have you! make words break from me here all
alone,
Do you! – mother of being in me, heart.   140
O unteachably after evil, but uttering truth,
Why, tears! is it? tears; such a melting, a madrigal
start!
Never-eldering revel and river of youth,
What can it be, this glee? the good you have there of
your own?

82 **flange:** the projecting rim of a wheel that keeps a railway-
waggon on the rails 88 **sour scythe cringe:** the scythe wielded by
Death; 'cringe' suggests cowering away from the blade **the blear
share:** the muddy ploughshare that cuts through the earth 91 **tell:**
count 95 **bay:** (architectural) recess 96 **reeve:** gather 107 **combs:**
ridge 111 **whorl:** propeller 112 **wind:** direct, guide

120 **shrouds:** ropes supporting the mast 128 **burl:** twisting and
turning **buck and the flood:** the surging and plunging 141 **after:**
going after, pursuing 144 **glee:** both Hopkins's song (echoing
'madrigal' in line 142) and joy

Sister, a sister calling 145
A master, her master and mine! –
And the inboard seas run swirling and hawling;
The rash smart sloggering brine
Blinds her; but she that weather sees one thing, one;
Has one fetch in her: she rears herself to divine 150
Ears, and the call of the tall nun
To the men in the tops and the tackle rode over the
storm's brawling.

She was first of a five and came
Of a coifèd sisterhood.
(O Deutschland, double a desperate name! 155
O world wide of its good!
But Gertrude, lily, and Luther, are two of a town,
Christ's lily and beast of the waste wood:
From life's dawn it is drawn down,
Abel is Cain's brother and breasts they have sucked the
same.) 160

Loathed for a love men knew in them,
Banned by the land of their birth,
Rhine refused them, Thames would ruin them;
Surf, snow, river and earth
Gnashed: but thou art above, thou Orion of light; 165
Thy unchancelling poising palms were weighing the
worth,
Thou martyr-master: in thy sight
Storm flakes were scroll-leaved flowers, lily showers –
sweet heaven was astrew in them.

Five! the finding and sake
And cipher of suffering Christ. 170
Mark, the mark is of man's make
And the word of it Sacrificed.
But he scores it in scarlet himself on his own
bespoken,
Before-time-taken, dearest prizèd and priced –
Stigma, signal, cinquefoil token 175
For lettering of the lamb's fleece, ruddying of the
rose-flake.

Joy fall to thee, father Francis,
Drawn to the Life that died;
With the gnarls of the nails in thee, niche of the
lance, his
Lovescape crucified 180
And seal of his seraph-arrival! and these thy
daughters
And five-livèd and leavèd favour and pride,
Are sisterly sealed in wild waters,
To bathe in his fall-gold mercies, to breathe in his all-
fire glances.

Away in the loveable west, 185
On a pastoral forehead of Wales,
I was under a roof here, I was at rest,
And they the prey of the gales;
She to the black-about air, to the breaker, the thickly
Falling flakes, to the throng that catches and
quails 190
Was calling 'O Christ, Christ, come quickly':
The cross to her she calls Christ to her, christens her
wild-worst Best.

The majesty! what did she mean?
Breathe, arch and original Breath.
Is it love in her of the being as her lover had
been? 195
Breathe, body of lovely Death.
They were else-minded then, altogether, the men
Woke thee with a *We are perishing* in the weather of
Gennesareth.
Or is it that she cried for the crown then,
The keener to come at the comfort for feeling the
combating keen? 200

For how to the heart's cheering
The down-dugged ground-hugged grey
Hovers off, the jay-blue heavens appearing
Of pied and peeled May!
Blue-beating and hoary-glow height; or night, still
higher, 205
With belled fire and the moth-soft Milky Way,
What by your measure is the heaven of desire,
The treasure never eyesight got, nor was ever guessed
what for the hearing?

145–6 **Sister . . . mine!:** 'Five German nuns . . . clasped hands and were drowned together, the chief sister, a gaunt woman 6ft high, calling out loudly and often "O Christ, come quickly!" till the end came' (*The Times*, 11 December 1875) 147 **hawling:** howling 148 **sloggering:** delivering heavy blows 150 **fetch:** trick 154 **coifèd:** wearing a close-fitting cap 155 **Deutschland:** both the ship and Germany itself 157 **Gertrude . . . Luther:** St Gertrude lived in a convent near the birthplace of Martin Luther, Eisleben in Saxony 160 **Abel is Cain's brother:** Cain, the eldest son of Adam and Eve, slew his brother Abel (Genesis 4) 165 **Orion:** The Hunter, a constellation 166 **unchancelling:** depriving of sanctuary; i.e. there is no escape from God the hunter **poising palms:** hands judging the weight 169 **finding:** mark **sake:** '*Sake* is a word I find it convenient to use. . . . It is the *sake* of "for the sake of", *forsake, namesake, keepsake*. I mean by it the being a thing has outside itself, as a voice by its echo, a face by its reflection, a body by its shadow, a man by his name, fame, or memory, *and also* that in the thing by virtue of which especially it has this being abroad . . . as for a voice and echo clearness; for a reflected image light, brightness; for a shadow-casting body bulk; for man genius, great achievements, amiability, and so on' (GMH) 170 **cipher:** signature 175 **cinquefoil:** five-pointed

177 **Francis:** St Francis of Assisi, founder of the order to which the five nuns belonged 179–80 **his Lovescape crucified:** St Francis was said to have borne the stigmata, or the five wounds of Christ, on his body 181 **seraph-arrival:** union with God 198 **weather of Gennesareth:** Gennesareth is the Sea of Galilee; in Matthew 14, Jesus calms the waters and the wind 199 **crown:** i.e. crown of martyrdom 204 **pied:** many-coloured **peeled:** new 208 **The treasure . . . the hearing:** 'Eye hath not seen, nor ear heard, neither have entered into the heart of man, the things which God hath prepared for them that love him' (1 Corinthians 2.9)

No, but it was not these.
　　The jading and jar of the cart, 　　　　　210
　　Time's tasking, it is fathers that asking for ease
Of the sodden-with-its-sorrowing heart,
Not danger, electrical horror; then further it finds
The appealing of the Passion is tenderer in prayer
　　apart:
　　Other, I gather, in measure her mind's 　　215
Burden, in wind's burly and beat of endragonèd seas.

　　But how shall I . . . make me room there:
　　Reach me a . . . Fancy, come faster –
　　Strike you the sight of it? look at it loom there,
　　　Thing that she . . . There then! the Master,
Ipse, the only one, Christ, King, Head: 　　　221
He was to cure the extremity where he had cast her;
　　Do, deal, lord it with living and dead;
Let him ride, pride her, in his triumph, despatch and
　　have done with his doom there.

　　Ah! there was a heart right! 　　　　　225
　　There was single eye!
　　Read the unshapeable shock night
　　　And knew the who and the why;
Wording it how but by him that present and past,
　　Heaven and earth are word of, worded by? – 　230
　　The Simon Peter of a soul! to the blast
Tarpeïan-fast, but a blown beacon of light.

　　Jesu, heart's light,
　　Jesu, maid's son,
　　What was the feast followed the night 　　235
　　　Thou hadst glory of this nun? –
Feast of the one woman without stain.
For so conceivèd, so to conceive thee is done;
　　But here was heart-throe, birth of a brain,
Word, that heard and kept thee and uttered thee
　　outright. 　　　　　　　　　　　　240

　　Well, she has thee for the pain, for the
　　Patience; but pity of the rest of them!
　　Heart, go and bleed at a bitterer vein for the
　　　Comfortless unconfessed of them –
No not uncomforted: lovely-felicitous Providence
Finger of a tender of, O of a feathery delicacy, the
　　breast of the 　　　　　　　　　　246
　　Maiden could obey so, be a bell to, ring of it,
　　and
Startle the poor sheep back! is the shipwrack then a
　　harvest, does tempest carry the grain for
　　thee?

I admire thee, master of the tides,
　　Of the Yore-flood, of the year's fall; 　　250
　　The recurb and the recovery of the gulf's sides,
　　The girth of it and the wharf of it and the
　　wall;
Stanching, quenching ocean of a motionable
　　mind;
Ground of being, and granite of it: past all
　　Grasp God, throned behind 　　　　255
Death with a sovereignty that heeds but hides, bodes
　　but abides;

　　With a mercy that outrides
　　The all of water, an ark
　　For the listener; for the lingerer with a love
　　glides
　　Lower than death and the dark; 　　　260
A vein for the visiting of the past-prayer, pent in
　　prison,
The-last-breath penitent spirits – the uttermost mark
　　Our passion-plungèd giant risen,
The Christ of the Father compassionate, fetched in the
　　storm of his strides.

　　Now burn, new born to the world, 　　265
　　Double-naturèd name,
　　The heaven-flung, heart-fleshed, maiden-furled
　　Miracle-in-Mary-of-flame,
Mid-numberèd he in three of the thunder-throne!
Not a dooms-day dazzle in his coming nor dark as
　　he came; 　　　　　　　　　　　270
　　Kind, but royally reclaiming his own;
A released shower, let flash to the shire, not a lightning
　　of fire hard-hurled.

　　Dame, at our door
　　Drowned, and among our shoals,
　　Remember us in the roads, the heaven-haven of
　　the reward: 　　　　　　　　　　275
　　Our King back, Oh, upon English souls!
Let him easter in us, be a dayspring to the dimness
　　of us, be a crimson-cresseted east,
More brightening her, rare-dear Britain, as his reign
　　rolls,
　　Pride, rose, prince, hero of us, high-priest,
Our hearts' charity's hearth's fire, our thoughts'
　　chivalry's throng's Lord. 　　　　280

---

211 **it is fathers:** it is (that) creates　216 **burly:** bluster　221 *Ipse:* himself
226 **single eye!:** i.e. fixed clearly on God ('when thine eye is single,
thy whole body also is full of light': Luke 11.34)　227 **shock:** (adjective)
of sudden force　231 **Simon Peter:** 'thou art Peter, and upon
this rock I will build my church' (Matthew 16.18)　232 **Tarpeïan-fast:**
the Tarpeian rock was an ancient peak of the Capitoline Hill
in Rome　237 **Feast of the one woman without stain:** Feast of the
Immaculate Conception of the Blessed Virgin, 8 December

250 **Yore-flood:** either the deluge described in the story of Noah
(Genesis 6–8) or the primal flood (Genesis 1.2)　251 **recurb . . .
recovery:** stemming and restemming of the tide　256 **bodes:** i.e.
forebodes　261 **vein:** desire　264 **fetched:** reached　266 **Double-
naturèd:** Christ as God and man　269 **Mid-numberèd:** Christ is
second in the Trinity　275 **roads:** anchorages, harbours　277 **cresseted:**
a cresset is an iron basket to hold a flaming torch or a beacon

GERARD MANLEY HOPKINS

GOD'S GRANDEUR

THE world is charged with the grandeur of God.
  It will flame out, like shining from shook foil;
  It gathers to a greatness, like the ooze of oil
Crushed. Why do men then now not reck his rod?
Generations have trod, have trod, have trod;   5
  And all is seared with trade; bleared, smeared with
    toil;
  And wears man's smudge and shares man's smell:
    the soil
Is bare now, nor can foot feel, being shod.

And for all this, nature is never spent;
  There lives the dearest freshness deep down things;
And though the last lights off the black West went   11
  Oh, morning, at the brown brink eastward,
    springs –
Because the Holy Ghost over the bent
  World broods with warm breast and with ah! bright
    wings.

GOD'S GRANDEUR: 2 **shook foil:** 'Shaken goldfoil gives off broad
glares like sheet lightning and also, and this is true of nothing
else, owing to its zigzag dints and creasings and network of
small many cornered facets, a sort of fork lightning too' (GMH to
Robert Bridges, 4 January 1883) 3 **ooze of oil:** from crushed olives

THE WINDHOVER

To Christ our Lord

I CAUGHT this morning morning's minion, king-
    dom of daylight's dauphin, dapple-dawn-drawn
    Falcon, in his riding
  Of the rolling level underneath him steady air, and
    striding
High there, how he rung upon the rein of a wimpling
    wing
In his ecstasy! then off, off forth on swing,   5
  As a skate's heel sweeps smooth on a bow-bend: the
    hurl and gliding
  Rebuffed the big wind. My heart in hiding
Stirred for a bird, – the achieve of, the mastery of the
    thing!

Brute beauty and valour and act, oh, air, pride, plume,
    here
  Buckle! AND the fire that breaks from thee then, a
    billion   10
Times told lovelier, more dangerous, O my chevalier!

  No wonder of it: shéer plód makes plough down
    sillion
Shine, and blue-bleak embers, ah my dear,
  Fall, gall themselves, and gash gold-vermilion.

THE WINDHOVER: **windhover:** kestrel 1 **minion:** a prince's favourite
2 **dauphin:** (French) heir to the throne; with perhaps also a
reference to the Dauphin's praise of his horse in Shakespeare's
Henry V: 'le cheval volant . . . When I bestride him I soar, I am a
hawk. He trots the air' (3.7) 3 **rolling level:** probably to be sounded
separately **underneath him steady:** probably to be run together
4 **rung:** in falconry, to 'ring' is to rise in spirals **upon the rein:** (of
a horse) circling its trainer on a long rein **wimpling:** rippling,
undulating 7 **My heart in hiding:** 'Set your affections on things
above, not on things on the earth. For ye are dead, and your life
is hid with Christ in God' (Colossians 3.2–3) 10 **Buckle:** crumple,
collapse 12 **sillion:** the ridge between two ploughed furrows

PIED BEAUTY

GLORY be to God for dappled things –
  For skies of couple-colour as a brinded cow;
    For rose-moles all in stipple upon trout that swim;
Fresh-firecoal chestnut-falls; finches' wings;
  Landscape plotted and pieced – fold, fallow, and
    plough;   5
    And áll trádes, their gear and tackle and trim.
All things counter, original, spare, strange;
  Whatever is fickle, freckled (who knows how?)
    With swift, slow; sweet, sour; adazzle, dim;
He fathers-forth whose beauty is past change: 10
                    Praise him.

PIED BEAUTY: 2 **brinded:** brindled, spotted or streaked 3 **stipple:**
paint applied in dots 4 **Fresh-firecoal chestnut-falls:** in his
journal Hopkins describes 'Chestnuts as bright as coals or spots of
vermillion' 5 **plotted and pieced:** divided into fields 6 **trim:**
fittings, equipment 7 **counter:** not what is expected **spare:** rare
10 **He fathers-forth . . . past change:** 'Every good gift and every
perfect gift is from above, and cometh down from the Father of
lights, with whom is no variableness, neither shadow of turning'
(James 1.17)

'AS KINGFISHERS CATCH FIRE . . .'

As kingfishers catch fire, dragonflies draw flame;
  As tumbled over rim in roundy wells
    Stones ring; like each tucked string tells, each hung
      bell's
Bow swung finds tongue to fling out broad its name;
Each mortal thing does one thing and the same: 5
  Deals out that being indoors each one dwells;
  Selves – goes itself; *myself* it speaks and spells,
Crying *What I do is me: for that I came.*

Í say more: the just man justices;
  Keeps gráce: thát keeps all his goings graces;   10
Acts in God's eye what in God's eye he is –
  Chríst. For Christ plays in ten thousand places,
Lovely in limbs, and lovely in eyes not his
  To the Father through the features of men's faces.

'AS KINGFISHERS CATCH FIRE': 3 **tucked:** plucked 7 **Selves:** (verb)
asserts its own individuality 9 **justices:** (verb) acts justly

'THOU ART INDEED JUST, LORD . . .'

*Justus quidem tu es, Domine, si disputem tecum; verumtamen
justa loquar ad te: Quare via impiorum prosperatur? &c*

THOU art indeed just, Lord, if I contend
With thee; but, sir, so what I plead is just.
Why do sinners' ways prosper? and why must
Disappointment all I endeavour end?

Wert thou my enemy, O thou my friend,   5
How wouldst thou worse, I wonder, than thou dost
Defeat, thwart me? Oh, the sots and thralls of lust
Do in spare hours more thrive than I that spend,

Sir, life upon thy cause. See, banks and brakes
Now, leavèd how thick! lacèd they are again   10
With fretty chervil, look, and fresh wind shakes

Them; birds build – but not I build; no, but strain,
Time's eunuch, and not breed one work that wakes.
Mine, O thou lord of life, send my roots rain.

'THOU ART INDEED JUST, LORD': 'Righteous art thou, O Lord, when
I plead with thee: yet let me talk with thee of thy judgements:
Wherefore doth the way of the wicked prosper? wherefore are all
they happy that deal very treacherously?' (Jeremiah 12.1) 9 **brakes:**
thickets 11 **fretty chervil:** cow-parsley 13 **Time's eunuch:** 'All
impulse fails me: I can give myself no sufficient reason for going
on. Nothing comes: I am a eunuch – but it is for the kingdom of
heaven's sake' (GMH to Robert Bridges, 12 January 1888)

ROBERT BRIDGES

LONDON SNOW

WHEN men were all asleep the snow came flying,
In large white flakes falling on the city brown,
Stealthily and perpetually settling and loosely lying,
    Hushing the latest traffic of the drowsy town;
Deadening, muffling, stifling its murmurs failing;   5
Lazily and incessantly floating down and down:
    Silently sifting and veiling road, roof and railing;
Hiding difference, making unevenness even,
Into angles and crevices softly drifting and sailing.
    All night it fell, and when full inches seven   10
It lay in the depth of its uncompacted lightness,
The clouds blew off from a high and frosty heaven;
    And all woke earlier for the unaccustomed
        brightness
Of the winter dawning, the strange unheavenly glare:
The eye marvelled – marvelled at the dazzling
        whiteness;   15
    The ear hearkened to the stillness of the solemn air;
No sound of wheel rumbling nor of foot falling,
And the busy morning cries came thin and spare.
    Then boys I heard, as they went to school, calling,
They gathered up the crystal manna to freeze   20

Their tongues with tasting, their hands with
        snowballing;
    Or rioted in a drift, plunging up to the knees;
Or peering up from under the white-mossed wonder,
'O look at the trees!' they cried, 'O look at the trees!'
    With lessened load a few carts creak and blunder,   25
Following along the white deserted way,
A country company long dispersed asunder:
    When now already the sun, in pale display
Standing by Paul's high dome, spread forth below
His sparkling beams, and awoke the stir of the day.   30
    For now the doors open, and war is waged with the
        snow;
And trains of sombre men, past tale of number,
Tread long brown paths, as toward their toil they
        go:
    But even for them awhile no cares encumber
Their minds diverted; the daily word is unspoken,   35
The daily thoughts of labour and sorrow slumber
    At the sight of the beauty that greets them, for the
        charm they have broken.

LONDON SNOW: 20 **manna:** 'behold, upon the face of the wilderness
there lay a small round thing, as small as the hoar frost on the
ground. And when the children of Israel saw it, they said one to
another, It is manna: for they wist not what it was. And Moses said
unto them, This is the bread which the Lord hath given you to eat'
(Exodus 16.14–15) 25 **With lessened load:** i.e. to prevent wagons
from becoming stuck in the snow

NIGHTINGALES

BEAUTIFUL must be the mountains whence ye come,
And bright in the fruitful valleys the streams,
        wherefrom
        Ye learn your song:
Where are those starry woods? O might I wander
        there,
    Among the flowers, which in that heavenly air   5
        Bloom the year long!

Nay, barren are those mountains and spent the
        streams:
Our song is the voice of desire, that haunts our
        dreams,
        A throe of the heart,
Whose pining visions dim, forbidden hopes profound,
    No dying cadence nor long sigh can sound,   11
        For all our art.

Alone, aloud in the raptured ear of men
We pour our dark nocturnal secret; and then,
        As night is withdrawn   15
From these sweet-springing meads and bursting
        boughs of May,
    Dream, while the innumerable choir of day
        Welcome the dawn.

ALICE MEYNELL

RENOUNCEMENT

I MUST NOT think of thee; and, tired yet strong,
　I shun the thought that lurks in all delight –
　The thought of thee – and in the blue Heaven's
　　height,
And in the sweetest passage of a song.

O just beyond the fairest thoughts that throng　　5
　This breast, the thought of thee waits hidden yet
　　bright,
　But it must never, never come in sight;
I must stop short of thee the whole day long.

But when sleep comes to close each difficult day,
　When night gives pause to the long watch I keep　　10
　　And all my bonds I needs must loose apart,

Must doff my will as raiment laid away, –
　With the first dream that comes with the first sleep
　I run, I run, I am gathered to thy heart.

ROBERT LOUIS STEVENSON

REQUIEM

UNDER the wide and starry sky,
Dig the grave and let me lie.
Glad did I live and gladly die,
　And I laid me down with a will.

This be the verse you grave for me:　　5
Here he lies where he longed to be;
Home is the sailor, home from sea,
　And the hunter home from the hill.

REQUIEM: a mass for the rest of the soul of the dead: 5 **grave:** engrave

'BRIGHT IS THE RING OF WORDS'

BRIGHT is the ring of words
　When the right man rings them,
Fair the fall of songs
　When the singer sings them.
Still they are carolled and said –　　5
　On wings they are carried –
After the singer is dead
　And the maker buried.

Low as the singer lies
　In the field of heather,　　10
Songs of his fashion bring
　The swains together.

And when the west is red
　With the sunset embers,
The lover lingers and sings　　15
　And the maid remembers.

'BRIGHT IS THE RING OF WORDS': 11 **fashion:** making 12 **swains:** lovers

OSCAR WILDE

From THE BALLAD OF READING GAOL

I

HE did not wear his scarlet coat,
　For blood and wine are red,
And blood and wine were on his hands
　When they found him with the dead,
The poor dead woman whom he loved,　　5
　And murdered in her bed.

He walked amongst the Trial Men
　In a suit of shabby grey;
A cricket cap was on his head,
　And his step seemed light and gay;　　10
But I never saw a man who looked
　So wistfully at the day.

I never saw a man who looked
　With such a wistful eye
Upon that little tent of blue　　15
　Which prisoners call the sky,
And at every drifting cloud that went
　With sails of silver by.

I walked, with other souls in pain,
　Within another ring,　　20
And was wondering if the man had done
　A great or little thing,
When a voice behind me whispered low,
　'*That fellow's got to swing.*'

Dear Christ! the very prison walls　　25
　Suddenly seemed to reel,
And the sky above my head became
　Like a casque of scorching steel;
And, though I was a soul in pain,
　My pain I could not feel.　　30

THE BALLAD OF READING GAOL: On 25 May 1895, Wilde was convicted at the Old Bailey on charges of indecency and sodomy, and was sentenced to be 'imprisoned and kept to hard labour for two years'. The poem was published in 1898 under the name 'C.3.3', Wilde's prison number 1 **scarlet coat:** military uniform 7 **Trial Men:** men on remand awaiting trial 20 **Within another ring:** for exercise, prisoners walked in a circle in the prison yard in silence; under the Victorian 'separate system' prisoners were kept isolated and allowed no contact with each other at all 28 **casque:** helmet

I only knew what hunted thought
  Quickened his step, and why
He looked upon the garish day
  With such a wistful eye;
The man had killed the thing he loved,   35
  And so he had to die.

    .   .   .

Yet each man kills the thing he loves,
  By each let this be heard,
Some do it with a bitter look,
  Some with a flattering word,   40
The coward does it with a kiss,
  The brave man with a sword!

Some kill their love when they are young,
  And some when they are old;
Some strangle with the hands of Lust,   45
  Some with the hands of Gold:
The kindest use a knife, because
  The dead so soon grow cold.

Some love too little, some too long,
  Some sell, and others buy;   50
Some do the deed with many tears,
  And some without a sigh:
For each man kills the thing he loves,
  Yet each man does not die.

He does not die a death of shame   55
  On a day of dark disgrace,
Nor have a noose about his neck,
  Nor a cloth upon his face,
Nor drop feet foremost through the floor
  Into an empty space.   60

He does not sit with silent men
  Who watch him night and day;
Who watch him when he tries to weep,
  And when he tries to pray;
Who watch him lest himself should rob   65
  The prison of its prey.

He does not wake at dawn to see
  Dread figures throng his room,
The shivering Chaplain robed in white,
  The Sheriff stern with gloom,   70
And the Governor all in shiny black,
  With the yellow face of Doom.

He does not rise in piteous haste
  To put on convict-clothes,
While some coarse-mouthed Doctor gloats, and notes
  Each new and nerve-twitched pose,   76
Fingering a watch whose little ticks
  Are like horrible hammer-blows.

65–6 **rob . . . its prey:** i.e. commit suicide

He does not feel that sickening thirst
  That sands one's throat, before   80
The hangman with his gardener's gloves
  Comes through the padded door,
And binds one with three leathern thongs,
  That the throat may thirst no more.

He does not bend his head to hear   85
  The Burial Office read,
Nor, while the anguish of his soul
  Tells him he is not dead,
Cross his own coffin, as he moves
  Into the hideous shed.   90

He does not stare upon the air
  Through a little roof of glass:
He does not pray with lips of clay
  For his agony to pass;
Nor feel upon his shuddering cheek   95
  The kiss of Caiaphas.

86 **Burial Office:** the burial service from the Book of Common Prayer
90 **shed:** where the gallows was located   96 **the kiss of Caiaphas:**
Judas betrayed Jesus by kissing him on the cheek to identify him
to the guards sent by the high priest Caiaphas (Matthew 26.47–50)

JOHN DAVIDSON

THIRTY BOB A WEEK

I COULDN'T touch a stop and turn a screw,
  And set the blooming world a-work for me
Like such as cut their teeth – I hope, like you –
  On the handle of a skeleton gold key;
I cut mine on a leek, which I eat it every week: 5
  I'm a clerk at thirty bob as you can see.

But I don't allow it's luck and all a toss;
  There's no such thing as being starred and crossed;
It's just the power of some to be a boss,
  And the bally power of others to be bossed: 10
I face the music, sir; you bet I ain't a cur;
  Strike me lucky if I don't believe I'm lost!

For like a mole I journey in the dark,
  A-travelling along the underground
From my Pillar'd Halls and broad Suburban Park,   15
  To come the daily dull official round;
And home again at night with my pipe all alight,
  A-scheming how to count ten bob a pound.

THIRTY BOB A WEEK: i.e. 30 shillings (£1.50) 7 **all a toss:** determined
by the toss of a coin, pure chance 8 **no such thing as being starred
and crossed:** Romeo and Juliet were Shakespeare's 'star-crossed
lovers', but Davidson appears to be thinking more of Cassius: 'The
fault, dear Brutus, is not in our stars, But in ourselves, that we are
underlings' (*Julius Caesar* 1.2) 10 **bally:** euphemism for *bloody*

And it's often very cold and very wet,
　And my missis stitches towels for a hunks;　20
And the Pillar'd Halls is half of it to let –
　Three rooms about the size of travelling trunks.
And we cough, the wife and I, to dislocate a sigh,
　When the noisy little kids are in their bunks.

But you'll never hear her do a growl or whine,　25
　For she's made of flint and roses, very odd;
And I've got to cut my meaning rather fine,
　Or I'd blubber, for I'm made of greens and sod:
So p'r'aps we are in Hell for all that I can tell,
　And lost and damned and served up hot to God.　30

I ain't blaspheming, Mr Silver-tongue;
　I'm saying things a bit beyond your art:
Of all the rummy starts you ever sprung,
　Thirty bob a week's the rummiest start!
With your science and your books and your the'ries
　　about spooks,
　Did you ever hear of looking in your heart?　35

I didn't mean your pocket, Mr, no:
　I mean that having children and a wife,
With thirty bob on which to come and go,
　Isn't dancing to the tabor and the fife:　40
When it doesn't make you drink, by Heaven! it makes
　　you think,
　And notice curious items about life.

I step into my heart and there I meet
　A god-almighty devil singing small,
Who would like to shout and whistle in the street,　45
　And squelch the passers flat against the wall;
If the whole world was a cake he had the power to
　　take,
　He would take it, ask for more, and eat it all.

And I meet a sort of simpleton beside,
　The kind that life is always giving beans;　50
With thirty bob a week to keep a bride
　He fell in love and married in his teens:
At thirty bob he stuck; but he knows it isn't luck:
　He knows the seas are deeper than tureens.

And the god-almighty devil and the fool　55
　That meet me in the High Street on the strike,
When I walk about my heart a-gathering wool,
　Are my good and evil angels if you like.
And both of them together in every kind of weather
　Ride me like a double-seated bike.　60

20 **hunks:** miser 26 **made of flint and roses:** i.e. she combines beauty with inner strength 28 **sod:** mush 33 **rummy:** odd 35 **the'ries:** theories 40 **the tabor:** small drum 44 **small:** softly 50 **giving beans:** punishing 57 **a-gathering wool:** wool-gathering, daydreaming

That's rough a bit and needs its meaning curled.
　But I have a high old hot un in my mind –
A most engrugious notion of the world,
　That leaves your lightning 'rithmetic behind –
I give it at a glance when I say 'There ain't no chance,
　Nor nothing of the lucky-lottery kind.'　66

And it's this way that I make it out to be:
　No fathers, mothers, countries, climates – none;
Not Adam was responsible for me,
　Nor society, nor systems, nary one:　70
A little sleeping seed, I woke – I did, indeed –
　A million years before the blooming sun.

I woke because I thought the time had come;
　Beyond my will there was no other cause;
And everywhere I found myself at home,　75
　Because I chose to be the thing I was;
And in whatever shape of mollusc or of ape
　I always went according to the laws.

I was the love that chose my mother out;
　I joined two lives and from the union burst;　80
My weakness and my strength without a doubt
　Are mine alone for ever from the first:
It's just the very same with a difference in the name
　As 'Thy will be done'. You say it if you durst!

They say it daily up and down the land　85
　As easy as you take a drink, it's true;
But the difficultest go to understand,
　And the difficultest job a man can do,
Is to come it brave and meek with thirty bob a week,
　And feel that that's the proper thing for you.　90

It's a naked child against a hungry wolf;
　It's playing bowls upon a splitting wreck;
It's walking on a string across a gulf
　With millstones fore-and-aft about your neck;
But the thing is daily done by many and many a one;
　And we fall, face forward, fighting, on the deck.　96

63 **engrugious:** Davidson's own coinage 70 **nary:** never a 87 **go:** turn of events

ALFRED EDWARD HOUSMAN

'LOVELIEST OF TREES . . .'

LOVELIEST of trees, the cherry now
Is hung with bloom along the bough,
And stands about the woodland ride
Wearing white for Eastertide.

Now, of my threescore years and ten,   5
Twenty will not come again,
And take from seventy springs a score,
It only leaves me fifty more.

And since to look at things in bloom
Fifty springs are little room,   10
About the woodlands I will go
To see the cherry hung with snow.

'LOVELIEST OF TREES': 3 **ride:** track for those on horseback

'WHEN I WAS ONE-AND-TWENTY'

WHEN I was one-and-twenty
I heard a wise man say,
'Give crowns and pounds and guineas
But not your heart away;
Give pearls away and rubies   5
But keep your fancy free.'
But I was one-and-twenty,
No use to talk to me.

When I was one-and-twenty
I heard him say again,   10
'The heart out of the bosom
Was never given in vain;
'Tis paid with sighs a plenty
And sold for endless rue.'
And I am two-and-twenty,   15
And oh, 'tis true, 'tis true.

'WHEN I WAS ONE-AND-TWENTY': 3 **crowns:** a crown was a silver coin worth 5 shillings (25p) **guineas:** a guinea was worth 21 shillings (105p) 14 **rue:** regret

BREDON HILL

IN summertime on Bredon
The bells they sound so clear;
Round both the shires they ring them
In steeples far and near,
A happy noise to hear.   5

Here of a Sunday morning
My love and I would lie,
And see the coloured counties,
And hear the larks so high
About us in the sky.   10

The bells would ring to call her
In valleys miles away:
'Come all to church, good people;
Good people, come and pray.'
But here my love would stay.   15

And I would turn and answer
Among the springing thyme,
'Oh, peal upon our wedding,
And we will hear the chime,
And come to church in time.'   20

But when the snows at Christmas
On Bredon top were strown,
My love rose up so early
And stole out unbeknown
And went to church alone.   25

They tolled the one bell only,
Groom there was none to see,
The mourners followed after,
And so to church went she,
And would not wait for me.   30

The bells they sound on Bredon,
And still the steeples hum.
'Come all to church, good people,' –
Oh, noisy bells, be dumb;
I hear you, I will come.   35

BREDON HILL: ('*Bree*-don') near the town of Bredon in Hereford and Worcester: 22 **strown:** spread 26 **the one bell only:** i.e. the funeral bell

'ON WENLOCK EDGE . . .'

ON Wenlock Edge the wood's in trouble;
His forest fleece the Wrekin heaves;
The gale, it plies the saplings double,
And thick on Severn snow the leaves.

'Twould blow like this through holt and hanger   5
When Uricon the city stood:
'Tis the old wind in the old anger,
But then it threshed another wood.

Then, 'twas before my time, the Roman
At yonder heaving hill would stare: 10
The blood that warms an English yeoman,
The thoughts that hurt him, they were there.

There, like the wind through woods in riot,
Through him the gale of life blew high;
The tree of man was never quiet: 15
Then 'twas the Roman, now 'tis I.

The gale, it plies the saplings double,
It blows so hard, 'twill soon be gone:
Today the Roman and his trouble
Are ashes under Uricon.   20

'ON WENLOCK EDGE': 1–2 **Wenlock Edge . . . Wrekin:** a ridge and a hill in Shropshire 4 **Severn:** river 5 **holt:** wood **hanger:** wood on the side of a hill 6 **Uricon:** the Roman city of Uriconium or Viroconium (Wroxeter)

'INTO MY HEART AN AIR THAT KILLS'

INTO my heart an air that kills
  From yon far country blows:
What are those blue remembered hills,
  What spires, what farms are those?

That is the land of lost content,   5
  I see it shining plain,
The happy highways where I went
  And cannot come again.

'SOLDIER FROM THE WARS RETURNING'

SOLDIER from the wars returning,
  Spoiler of the taken town,
Here is ease that asks not earning;
  Turn you in and sit you down.

Peace is come and wars are over,   5
  Welcome you and welcome all,
While the charger crops the clover
  And his bridle hangs in stall.

Now no more of winters biting,
  Filth in trench from fall to spring,   10
Summers full of sweat and fighting
  For the Kesar or the King.

Rest you, charger, rust you, bridle;
  Kings and kesars, keep your pay;
Soldier, sit you down and idle   15
  At the inn of night for aye.

'SOLDIER FROM THE WARS RETURNING': 7 **charger:** a cavalry horse
12 **Kesar:** variant of Kaiser, the German emperor 16 **for aye:** for ever

'TELL ME NOT HERE, IT NEEDS NOT SAYING'

TELL me not here, it needs not saying,
  What tune the enchantress plays
In aftermaths of soft September
  Or under blanching mays,
For she and I were long acquainted   5
  And I knew all her ways.

On russet floors, by waters idle,
  The pine lets fall its cone;
The cuckoo shouts all day at nothing
  In leafy dells alone;   10
And traveller's joy beguiles in autumn
  Hearts that have lost their own.

On acres of the seeded grasses
  The changing burnish heaves;
Or marshalled under moons of harvest   15
  Stand still all night the sheaves;
Or beeches strip in storms for winter
  And stain the wind with leaves.

Possess, as I possessed a season,
  The countries I resign,   20
Where over elmy plains the highway
  Would mount the hills and shine,
And full of shade the pillared forest
  Would murmur and be mine.

For nature, heartless, witless nature,   25
  Will neither care nor know
What stranger's feet may find the meadow
  And trespass there and go,
Nor ask amid the dews of morning
  If they are mine or no.   30

'TELL ME NOT HERE, IT NEEDS NOT SAYING': 4 **blanching mays:** the
white blossom of the hawthorn 7 **russet:** i.e. carpeted with autumn
leaves 11 **traveller's joy:** *Clematis vitalba*, old man's beard

FRANCIS THOMPSON

THE HOUND OF HEAVEN

I FLED Him, down the nights and down the days;
  I fled Him, down the arches of the years;
  I fled Him, down the labyrinthine ways
    Of my own mind; and in the mist of tears
I hid from Him, and under running laughter.   5
      Up vistaed hopes I sped;
      And shot, precipitated,
Adown Titanic glooms of chasmèd fears,
  From those strong Feet that followed, followed after.
      But with unhurrying chase,   10
      And unperturbèd pace,
    Deliberate speed, majestic instancy,
      They beat – and a Voice beat
      More instant than the Feet –
'All things betray thee, who betrayest Me.'   15

      I pleaded, outlaw-wise,
By many a hearted casement, curtained red,
  Trellised with intertwining charities;
(For, though I knew His love Who followèd,
      Yet was I sore adread   20
Lest, having Him, I must have naught beside).
But, if one little casement parted wide,
  The gust of His approach would clash it to.
  Fear wist not to evade, as Love wist to pursue.
Across the margent of the world I fled,   25
  And troubled the gold gateways of the stars,
  Smiting for shelter on their clangèd bars;

THE HOUND OF HEAVEN: 8 **Titanic:** the Titans were the race of gods
produced by the union of Uranus (Heaven) and Gaia (Earth)
12 **instancy:** insistency, urgency 24 **wist not . . . wist to:** knew not . . .
knew how to 25 **margent:** boundary

Fretted to dulcet jars
And silvern chatter the pale ports o' the moon.
I said to Dawn: Be sudden – to Eve: Be soon;   30
  With thy young skiey blossoms heap me over
    From this tremendous Lover –
Float thy vague veil about me, lest He see!
  I tempted all His servitors, but to find
My own betrayal in their constancy,   35
In faith to Him their fickleness to me,
  Their traitorous trueness, and their loyal deceit.
To all swift things for swiftness did I sue;
  Clung to the whistling mane of every wind.
    But whether they swept, smoothly fleet,   40
    The long savannahs of the blue;
      Or whether, Thunder-driven,
    They clanged his chariot 'thwart a heaven,
Plashy with flying lightnings round the spurn o' their
    feet: –
Fear wist not to evade as Love wist to pursue.   45
    Still with unhurrying chase,
    And unperturbèd pace,
   Deliberate speed, majestic instancy,
    Came on the following Feet,
    And a Voice above their beat –   50
'Naught shelters thee, who wilt not shelter Me.'

I sought no more that after which I strayed
    In face of man or maid;
But still within the little children's eyes
    Seems something, something that replies,   55
They at least are for me, surely for me!
I turned me to them very wistfully;
But just as their young eyes grew sudden fair
    With dawning answers there,
Their angel plucked them from me by the hair.   60
'Come then, ye other children, Nature's – share
With me' (said I) 'your delicate fellowship;
    Let me greet you lip to lip,
    Let me twine with you caresses,
      Wantoning   65
   With our Lady-Mother's vagrant tresses,
      Banqueting
   With her in her wind-walled palace,
   Underneath her azured daïs,
    Quaffing, as your taintless way is,   70
    From a chalice
Lucent-weeping out of the dayspring.'
    So it was done:
I in their delicate fellowship was one –
Drew the bolt of Nature's secrecies.   75
   I knew all the swift importings
    On the wilful face of skies;
    I knew how the clouds arise,
    Spumèd of the wild sea-snortings;
    All that's born or dies   80

Rose and drooped with; made them shapers
Of mine own moods, or wailful or divine;
   With them joyed and was bereaven.
    I was heavy with the even,
   When she lit her glimmering tapers   85
   Round the day's dead sanctities.
   I laughed in the morning's eyes.
I triumphed and I saddened with all weather,
   Heaven and I wept together,
And its sweet tears were salt with mortal mine;   90
Against the red throb of its sunset-heart
   I laid my own to beat,
   And share commingling heat;
But not by that, by that, was eased my human smart.
In vain my tears were wet on Heaven's grey cheek.   95
For ah! we know not what each other says,
   These things and I; in sound *I* speak –
Their sound is but their stir, they speak by silences.
Nature, poor stepdame, cannot slake my drouth;
   Let her, if she would owe me,   100
Drop yon blue bosom-veil of sky, and show me
   The breasts o' her tenderness:
Never did any milk of hers once bless
    My thirsting mouth.
    Nigh and nigh draws the chase,   105
    With unperturbèd pace,
   Deliberate speed, majestic instancy,
    And past those noisèd Feet
   A voice comes yet more fleet –
   'Lo! naught contents thee, who content'st not
    Me.'   110

Naked I wait Thy love's uplifted stroke!
My harness piece by piece Thou hast hewn from me,
    And smitten me to my knee;
    I am defenceless utterly.
    I slept, methinks, and woke,   115
And, slowly gazing, find me stripped in sleep.
In the rash lustihead of my young powers,
    I shook the pillaring hours
And pulled my life upon me; grimed with smears,
I stand amid the dust o' the mounded years –   120
My mangled youth lies dead beneath the heap.
My days have crackled and gone up in smoke,
Have puffed and burst as sun-starts on a stream.
    Yea, faileth now even dream
The dreamer, and the lute the lutanist;   125
Even the linked fantasies, in whose blossomy twist
I swung the earth a trinket at my wrist,
Are yielding; cords of all too weak account
For earth with heavy griefs so overplussed.

100 **owe:** own 118–21 **I shook . . . the heap:** 'And Samson took hold
of the two middle pillars upon which the house stood, and on which
it was borne up, of the one with his right hand, and of the other with
his left. And Samson said, Let me die with the Philistines. And
he bowed himself with all his might; and the house fell upon the
lords, and upon all the people that were therein' (Judges 16.29–30)
123 **sun-starts:** bubbles 126 **linked fantasies:** Thompson's other
works 127 **earth:** i.e. my life

28 **Fretted:** disturbed, roused 29 **silvern:** silver 41 **savannahs:** plains
44 **Plashy:** marshy, with pools of water 72 **Lucent-weeping:** weeping
tears of light 76 **importings:** meanings

Ah! is Thy love indeed   130
A weed, albeit an amaranthine weed,
Suffering no flowers except its own to mount?
     Ah! must –
     Designer infinite! –
Ah! must Thou char the wood ere Thou canst limn
       with it?   135
My freshness spent its wavering shower i' the dust;
And now my heart is as a broken fount,
Wherein tear-drippings stagnate, spilt down ever
     From the dank thoughts that shiver
Upon the sighful branches of my mind.   140
     Such is; what is to be?
The pulp so bitter, how shall taste the rind?
I dimly guess what Time in mists confounds;
Yet ever and anon a trumpet sounds
From the hid battlements of Eternity: 145
Those shaken mists a space unsettle, then
Round the half-glimpsèd turrets slowly wash again;
     But not ere him who summoneth
     I first have seen, enwound
With glooming robes purpureal, cypress-crowned;   150
His name I know, and what his trumpet saith.
Whether man's heart or life it be which yields
     Thee harvest, must Thy harvest-fields
     Be dunged with rotten death?

     Now of that long pursuit   155
     Comes on at hand the bruit;
     That Voice is round me like a bursting sea:
     'And is thy earth so marred,
     Shattered in shard on shard?
     Lo, all things fly thee, for thou fliest Me!   160
Strange, piteous, futile thing!
Wherefore should any set thee love apart?
Seeing none but I makes much of naught' (He said),
'And human love needs human meriting:
     How hast thou merited –   165
Of all man's clotted clay the dingiest clot?
     Alack, thou knowest not
How little worthy of any love thou art!
Whom wilt thou find to love ignoble thee,
     Save Me, save only Me?   170
All which I took from thee I did but take,
     Not for thy harms,
But just that thou might'st seek it in My arms.
     All which thy child's mistake
Fancies as lost, I have stored for thee at home: 175
     Rise, clasp My hand, and come!'
     Halts by me that footfall:
     Is my gloom, after all,
Shade of His hand, outstretched caressingly?
     'Ah, fondest, blindest, weakest,   180
     I am He Whom thou seekest!
Thou dravest love from thee, who dravest Me.'

131 **amaranthine:** immortal; the amaranth was a mythological flower
that never faded 135 **limn:** draw 150 **purpureal:** royal purple **cypress-
crowned:** the cypress symbolises sorrow and death 156 **bruit:** noise
159 **shard:** fragment, usually of pottery

RUDYARD KIPLING

RECESSIONAL

GOD of our fathers, known of old,
     Lord of our far-flung battle-line,
Beneath whose awful Hand we hold
     Dominion over palm and pine –
Lord God of Hosts, be with us yet,   5
Lest we forget – lest we forget!

The tumult and the shouting dies;
     The Captains and the Kings depart:
Still stands Thine ancient sacrifice,
     An humble and a contrite heart.   10
Lord God of Hosts, be with us yet,
Lest we forget – lest we forget!

Far-called, our navies melt away;
     On dune and headland sinks the fire:
Lo, all our pomp of yesterday   15
     Is one with Nineveh and Tyre!
Judge of the Nations, spare us yet,
Lest we forget – lest we forget!

If, drunk with sight of power, we loose
     Wild tongues that have not Thee in awe,   20
Such boastings as the Gentiles use,
     Or lesser breeds without the Law –
Lord God of Hosts, be with us yet,
Lest we forget – lest we forget!

For heathen heart that puts her trust   25
     In reeking tube and iron shard,
All valiant dust that builds on dust,
     And guarding, calls not Thee to guard,
For frantic boast and foolish word –
Thy mercy on Thy People, Lord!   30

1897

RECESSIONAL: A recessional is a hymn sung by clergy and choir as
they withdraw from a service. Kipling wrote the poem in 1897 after
Victoria's Diamond Jubilee, celebrating her sixty-year reign, and
it was published in *The Times* on 17 July of that year, to general
acclaim: 4 **palm and pine:** indicating the vast expanse of the
British Empire around the world 6 **Lest we forget:** 'Then beware
lest thou forget the Lord, which brought thee forth out of the
land of Egypt, from the house of bondage' (Deuteronomy 6.12)
9–10 **Still stands . . . heart:** 'The sacrifices of God are a broken
spirit: a broken and a contrite heart, O God, thou wilt not despise'
(Psalms 51.17) 16 **Nineveh:** an Assyrian city on the banks of the
Tigris in what is now northern Iraq **Tyre:** (present-day Sur)
Lebanese seaport once a Phoenician commercial centre 21 **Gentiles:**
i.e. unbelievers, foreigners 26 **reeking tube:** smoking gun **iron
shard:** shell or shell-fragment

THE FEMALE OF THE SPECIES

WHEN the Himalayan peasant meets the he-bear in his
    pride,
He shouts to scare the monster, who will often turn
    aside.
But the she-bear thus accosted rends the peasant tooth
    and nail.
For the female of the species is more deadly than the
    male.

When Nag the basking cobra hears the careless foot of
    man,   5
He will sometimes wriggle sideways and avoid it if he
    can.
But his mate makes no such motion where she camps
    beside the trail.
For the female of the species is more deadly than the
    male.

When the early Jesuit fathers preached to Hurons and
    Choctaws,
They prayed to be delivered from the vengeance of
    the squaws.   10
'Twas the women, not the warriors, turned those stark
    enthusiasts pale.
For the female of the species is more deadly than the
    male.

Man's timid heart is bursting with the things he must
    not say,
For the Woman that God gave him isn't his to give
    away;
But when hunter meets with husband, each confirms
    the other's tale –   15
The female of the species is more deadly than the
    male.

Man, a bear in most relations – worm and savage
    otherwise, –
Man propounds negotiations, Man accepts the
    compromise.
Very rarely will he squarely push the logic of a fact
To its ultimate conclusion in unmitigated act.   20

Fear, or foolishness, impels him, ere he lay the wicked
    low,
To concede some form of trial even to his fiercest foe.
Mirth obscene diverts his anger – Doubt and Pity oft
    perplex
Him in dealing with an issue – to the scandal of The
    Sex!

But the Woman that God gave him, every fibre of her
    frame   25
Proves her launched for one sole issue, armed and
    engined for the same;
And to serve that single issue, lest the generations fail,
The female of the species must be deadlier than the
    male.

She who faces Death by torture for each life beneath
    her breast
May not deal in doubt or pity – must not swerve for
    fact or jest.   30
These be purely male diversions – not in these her
    honour dwells.
She the Other Law we live by, is that Law and nothing
    else.

She can bring no more to living than the powers that
    make her great
As the Mother of the Infant and the Mistress of the
    Mate.
And when Babe and Man are lacking and she strides
    unclaimed to claim   35
Her right as femme (and baron), her equipment is the
    same.

She is wedded to convictions – in default of grosser
    ties;
Her contentions are her children, Heaven help him
    who denies! –
He will meet no suave discussion, but the instant,
    white-hot, wild,
Wakened female of the species warring as for spouse
    and child.   40

Unprovoked and awful charges – even so the she-bear
    fights,
Speech that drips, corrodes, and poisons – even so the
    cobra bites,
Scientific vivisection of one nerve till it is raw
And the victim writhes in anguish – like the Jesuit with
    the squaw!

So it comes that Man, the coward, when he gathers to
    confer   45
With his fellow-braves in council, dare not leave a
    place for her
Where, at war with Life and Conscience, he uplifts his
    erring hands
To some God of Abstract Justice – which no woman
    understands.

And Man knows it! Knows, moreover, that the Woman
    that God gave him
Must command but may not govern – shall enthral
    but not enslave him.   50
And *She* knows, because She warns him, and Her
    instincts never fail,
That the Female of Her Species is more deadly than
    the Male.

1911

THE FEMALE OF THE SPECIES: Published in 1911, this is Kipling's
satirical response to the Suffragette movement 29 **Death by torture:**
agonies of childbirth 36 **femme:** wife **baron:** husband

DANNY DEEVER

'WHAT are the bugles blowin' for?' said Files-on-
   Parade.
'To turn you out, to turn you out,' the Colour-
   Sergeant said.
'What makes you look so white, so white?' said Files-
   on-Parade.
'I'm dreadin' what I've got to watch,' the Colour-
   Sergeant said.
  For they're hangin' Danny Deever, you can hear the
    Dead March play,   5
  The regiment's in 'ollow square – they're hangin'
    him today;
  They've taken of his buttons off an' cut his stripes
    away,
  An' they're hangin' Danny Deever in the mornin'.

'What makes the rear-rank breathe so 'ard?' said Files-
   on-Parade.
'It's bitter cold, it's bitter cold,' the Colour-Sergeant
   said.   10
'What makes that front-rank man fall down?' said
   Files-on-Parade.
'A touch o' sun, a touch o' sun,' the Colour-Sergeant
   said.
  They are hangin' Danny Deever, they are marchin'
    of 'im round,
  They 'ave 'alted Danny Deever by 'is coffin on the
    ground;
  An' 'e'll swing in 'arf a minute for a sneakin'
    shootin' hound –   15
  O they're hangin' Danny Deever in the mornin'!

' 'Is cot was right-'and cot to mine,' said Files-on-
   Parade.
' 'E's sleepin' out an' far tonight,' the Colour-Sergeant
   said.
'I've drunk 'is beer a score o' times,' said Files-on-
   Parade.
' 'E's drinkin' bitter beer alone,' the Colour-Sergeant
   said.   20
  They are hangin' Danny Deever, you must mark 'im
    to 'is place,
  For 'e shot a comrade sleepin' – you must look 'im in
    the face;
  Nine 'undred of 'is county an' the Regiment's
    disgrace,
  While they're hangin' Danny Deever in the mornin'.

'What's that so black agin the sun?' said Files-on-
   Parade.   25
'It's Danny fightin' 'ard for life,' the Colour-Sergeant
   said.
'What's that that whimpers over'ead?' said Files-on-
   Parade.
'It's Danny's soul that's passin' now,' the Colour-
   Sergeant said.
  For they're done with Danny Deever, you can 'ear
    the quickstep play,
  The regiment's in column, an' they're marchin' us
    away;   30
  Ho! the young recruits are shakin', an' they'll want
    their beer today,
  After hangin' Danny Deever in the mornin'!

DANNY DEEVER: 1 **Files-on-Parade:** one of the private soldiers on parade to witness the execution 2 **Colour-Sergeant:** the sergeant who guards the regimental colours 6 **in 'ollow square:** in battle a defensive formation but here apparently meaning that the soldiers are drawn up in ranks around the place of execution 7 **taken of his buttons . . . away:** ceremonial humiliation before execution 19 **'is beer:** i.e. beer that he bought for others 29 **quickstep:** a march in quick time

'CITIES AND THRONES AND POWERS'

CITIES and Thrones and Powers
  Stand in Time's eye,
Almost as long as flowers,
  Which daily die:
But, as new buds put forth   5
  To glad new men,
Out of the spent and unconsidered Earth,
  The Cities rise again.

This season's Daffodil,
  She never hears,   10
What change, what chance, what chill,
  Cut down last year's;
But with bold countenance,
  And knowledge small,
Esteems her seven days' continuance   15
  To be perpetual.

So Time that is o'er-kind
  To all that be,
Ordains us e'en as blind,
  As bold as she: 20
That in our very death,
  And burial sure,
Shadow to shadow, well persuaded, saith,
  'See how our works endure!'

'CITIES AND THRONES AND POWERS': 6 **glad:** gladden

THE WAY THROUGH THE WOODS

THEY shut the road through the woods
Seventy years ago.
Weather and rain have undone it again,
And now you would never know
There was once a road through the woods   5

Before they planted the trees.
It is underneath the coppice and heath,
And the thin anemones.
Only the keeper sees
That, where the ring-dove broods, 10
And the badgers roll at ease,
There was once a road through the woods.

Yet, if you enter the woods
Of a summer evening late,
When the night-air cools on the trout-ringed pools 15
Where the otter whistles his mate,
(They fear not men in the woods,
Because they see so few.)
You will hear the beat of a horse's feet,
And the swish of a skirt in the dew, 20
Steadily cantering through
The misty solitudes,
As though they perfectly knew
The old lost road through the woods. . . .
But there is no road through the woods. 25

THE WAY THROUGH THE WOODS: 7 **coppice:** cultivated woodland

IF—

IF you can keep your head when all about you
    Are losing theirs and blaming it on you,
If you can trust yourself when all men doubt you,
    But make allowance for their doubting too;
If you can wait and not be tired by waiting, 5
    Or being lied about, don't deal in lies,
Or being hated don't give way to hating,
    And yet don't look too good, nor talk too wise:

If you can dream – and not make dreams your master;
    If you can think – and not make thoughts your aim;
If you can meet with Triumph and Disaster 11
    And treat those two impostors just the same;
If you can bear to hear the truth you've spoken
    Twisted by knaves to make a trap for fools,
Or watch the things you gave your life to, broken, 15
    And stoop and build 'em up with worn-out tools:

If you can make one heap of all your winnings
    And risk it on one turn of pitch-and-toss,
And lose, and start again at your beginnings
    And never breathe a word about your loss; 20
If you force your heart and nerve and sinew
    To serve your turn long after they are gone,
And so hold on when there is nothing in you
    Except the Will which says to them: 'Hold on!'

If you can talk with crowds and keep your virtue, 25
    Or walk with Kings – nor lose the common touch,
If neither foes nor loving friends can hurt you,
    If all men count with you, but none too much;

If you can fill the unforgiving minute
    With sixty seconds' worth of distance run, 30
Yours is the Earth and everything that's in it,
    And – which is more – you'll be a Man, my son!

IF—: 18 **pitch-and-toss:** 'Each player pitches a coin at a mark; the one whose coin lies nearest to the mark then tosses all the coins and keeps those that turn up "head"; the one whose coin lay next in order does the same with the remaining ones, and so on till all the coins are disposed of' (*OED*)

WILLIAM BUTLER YEATS

THE LAKE ISLE OF INNISFREE

I WILL arise and go now, and go to Innisfree,
And a small cabin build there, of clay and wattles made:
Nine bean-rows will I have there, a hive for the honey-bee,
And live alone in the bee-loud glade.

And I shall have some peace there, for peace comes dropping slow, 5
Dropping from the veils of the morning to where the cricket sings;
There midnight's all a glimmer, and noon a purple glow,
And evening full of the linnet's wings.

I will arise and go now, for always night and day
I hear lake water lapping with low sounds by the shore; 10
While I stand on the roadway, or on the pavements grey,
I hear it in the deep heart's core.

THE LAKE ISLE OF INNISFREE: **Innisfree:** an island in Lough Gill, County Sligo 2 **wattles:** interwoven branches

WHEN YOU ARE OLD

WHEN you are old and grey and full of sleep,
And nodding by the fire, take down this book,
And slowly read, and dream of the soft look
Your eyes had once, and of their shadows deep;

How many loved your moments of glad grace, 5
And loved your beauty with love false or true,
But one man loved the pilgrim soul in you,
And loved the sorrows of your changing face;

And bending down beside the glowing bars,
Murmur, a little sadly, how Love fled 10
And paced upon the mountains overhead
And hid his face amid a crowd of stars.

THE FOLLY OF BEING COMFORTED

ONE that is ever kind said yesterday:
'Your well-belovèd's hair has threads of grey,
And little shadows come about her eyes;
Time can but make it easier to be wise
Though now it seems impossible, and so   5
All that you need is patience.'

                    Heart cries, 'No,
I have not a crumb of comfort, not a grain.
Time can but make her beauty over again:
Because of that great nobleness of hers
The fire that stirs about her, when she stirs,   10
Burns but more clearly. O she had not these ways
When all the wild summer was in her gaze.'

O heart! O heart! if she'd but turn her head,
You'd know the folly of being comforted.

NO SECOND TROY

WHY should I blame her that she filled my days
With misery, or that she would of late
Have taught to ignorant men most violent ways,
Or hurled the little streets upon the great,
Had they but courage equal to desire?   5
What could have made her peaceful with a mind
That nobleness made simple as a fire,
With beauty like a tightened bow, a kind
That is not natural in an age like this,
Being high and solitary and most stern?   10
Why, what could she have done, being what she is?
Was there another Troy for her to burn?

THE WILD SWANS AT COOLE

THE trees are in their autumn beauty,
The woodland paths are dry,
Under the October twilight the water
Mirrors a still sky;
Upon the brimming water among the stones   5
Are nine-and-fifty swans.

The nineteenth autumn has come upon me
Since I first made my count;
I saw, before I had well finished,
All suddenly mount   10
And scatter wheeling in great broken rings
Upon their clamorous wings.

I have looked upon those brilliant creatures,
And now my heart is sore.
All's changed since I, hearing at twilight,   15
The first time on this shore,
The bell-beat of their wings above my head,
Trod with a lighter tread.

Unwearied still, lover by lover,
They paddle in the cold   20
Companionable streams or climb the air;
Their hearts have not grown old;
Passion or conquest, wander where they will,
Attend upon them still.

But now they drift on the still water,   25
Mysterious, beautiful;
Among what rushes will they build,
By what lake's edge or pool
Delight men's eyes when I awake some day
To find they have flown away?   30

THE WILD SWANS AT COOLE: Coole Park, in County Galway, was the estate of Lady Gregory, playwright, folklorist and lifelong friend of Yeats after their meeting in 1896 ('She has been to me mother, friend, sister and brother. I cannot realise the world without her – she brought to my wavering thoughts steadfast nobility')

AN IRISH AIRMAN FORESEES HIS DEATH

I KNOW that I shall meet my fate
Somewhere among the clouds above;
Those that I fight I do not hate,
Those that I guard I do not love;
My country is Kiltartan Cross,   5
My countrymen Kiltartan's poor,
No likely end could bring them loss
Or leave them happier than before.
Nor law, nor duty bade me fight,
Nor public men, nor cheering crowds,   10
A lonely impulse of delight
Drove to this tumult in the clouds;
I balanced all, brought all to mind,
The years to come seemed waste of breath,
A waste of breath the years behind   15
In balance with this life, this death.

AN IRISH AIRMAN FORESEES HIS DEATH: 5 **Kiltartan Cross:** the crossroads in Kiltartan near Coole Park

EASTER 1916

I HAVE met them at close of day
Coming with vivid faces
From counter or desk among grey
Eighteenth-century houses.
I have passed with a nod of the head   5
Or polite meaningless words,
Or have lingered awhile and said
Polite meaningless words,
And thought before I had done
Of a mocking tale or a gibe   10

EASTER 1916: On 24 April 1916, Easter Monday, an Irish Republic was declared, and around 2000 Irish Volunteers occupied parts of Dublin. The rebellion was suppressed by British forces. The final surrender came on 29 April 1916. Several of the leaders were executed

To please a companion
Around the fire at the club,
Being certain that they and I
But lived where motley is worn:
All changed, changed utterly: 15
A terrible beauty is born.

That woman's days were spent
In ignorant good-will,
Her nights in argument
Until her voice grew shrill.   20
What voice more sweet than hers
When, young and beautiful,
She rode to harriers?
This man had kept a school
And rode our wingèd horse;   25
This other his helper and friend
Was coming into his force;
He might have won fame in the end,
So sensitive his nature seemed,
So daring and sweet his thought.   30
This other man I had dreamed
A drunken, vainglorious lout.
He had done most bitter wrong
To some who are near my heart,
Yet I number him in the song;   35
He, too, has resigned his part
In the casual comedy;
He, too, has been changed in his turn,
Transformed utterly:
A terrible beauty is born.   40

Hearts with one purpose alone
Through summer and winter seem
Enchanted to a stone
To trouble the living stream.
The horse that comes from the road,   45
The rider, the birds that range
From cloud to tumbling cloud,
Minute by minute they change;
A shadow of cloud on the stream
Changes minute by minute;   50
A horse-hoof slides on the brim,
And a horse plashes within it;
The long-legged moor-hens dive,
And hens to moor-cocks call;
Minute by minute they live: 55
The stone's in the midst of all.

Too long a sacrifice
Can make a stone of the heart.
O when may it suffice?
That is Heaven's part, our part   60
To murmur name upon name,
As a mother names her child
When sleep at last has come
On limbs that had run wild.
What is it but nightfall?   65
No, no, not night but death;
Was it needless death after all?
For England may keep faith
For all that is done and said.
We know their dream; enough   70
To know they dreamed and are dead;
And what if excess of love
Bewildered them till they died?
I write it out in a verse –
MacDonagh and MacBride   75
And Connolly and Pearse
Now and in time to be,
Wherever green is worn,
Are changed, changed utterly:
A terrible beauty is born.   80

25 September 1916

68–9 **For England . . . said:** Home Rule for Ireland had been
enacted in 1914 but had been suspended for the duration of the
First World War with an undertaking that it would be revived when
peace came 76 **Connolly:** James Connolly, commander of the Irish
forces during the rebellion

THE SECOND COMING

TURNING and turning in the widening gyre
The falcon cannot hear the falconer;
Things fall apart; the centre cannot hold;
Mere anarchy is loosed upon the world,
The blood-dimmed tide is loosed, and everywhere   5
The ceremony of innocence is drowned;
The best lack all conviction, while the worst
Are full of passionate intensity.

Surely some revelation is at hand;
Surely the Second Coming is at hand.   10
The Second Coming! Hardly are those words out
When a vast image out of *Spiritus Mundi*
Troubles my sight: somewhere in sands of the desert
A shape with lion body and the head of a man,
A gaze blank and pitiless as the sun,   15
Is moving its slow thighs, while all about it
Reel shadows of the indignant desert birds.
The darkness drops again; but now I know
That twenty centuries of stony sleep
Were vexed to nightmare by a rocking cradle,   20
And what rough beast, its hour come round at last,
Slouches towards Bethlehem to be born?

17 **That woman:** Constance Gore-Booth (1884–1927), whom Yeats
knew together with her sister Eva; in 1900, Constance had married
Count Casimir Markiewicz 24 **This man:** Patrick Pearse (1879–1916),
writer and educator (see also line 76) 25 **rode our wingèd horse:**
was a poet (Pegasus, the winged horse, being a symbol of poetic
inspiration) 26 **This other:** Thomas MacDonagh (1878–1916), writer
and educator (see also line 75) 31 **This other man:** Major John
MacBride, an Irish revolutionary; he had married Maud Gonne,
the object of Yeats's unrequited love (see also line 75)

THE SECOND COMING: 1 **gyre:** (pronounced with a hard *g*) spiral
10 **the Second Coming:** the return of Christ at the apocalypse
12 *Spiritus Mundi:* 'a general storehouse of images which have
ceased to be the property of any personality or spirit' (WBY)
22 **Bethlehem:** the birthplace of Christ

A PRAYER FOR MY DAUGHTER

ONCE more the storm is howling, and half hid
Under this cradle-hood and coverlid
My child sleeps on. There is no obstacle
But Gregory's wood and one bare hill
Whereby the haystack- and roof-levelling wind,   5
Bred on the Atlantic, can be stayed;
And for an hour I have walked and prayed
Because of the great gloom that is in my mind.

I have walked and prayed for this young child an hour
And heard the sea-wind scream upon the tower,   10
And under the arches of the bridge, and scream
In the elms above the flooded stream;
Imagining in excited reverie
That the future years had come,
Dancing to a frenzied drum,   15
Out of the murderous innocence of the sea.

May she be granted beauty and yet not
Beauty to make a stranger's eye distraught,
Or hers before a looking-glass, for such,
Being made beautiful overmuch,   20
Consider beauty a sufficient end,
Lose natural kindness and maybe
The heart-revealing intimacy
That chooses right, and never find a friend.

Helen being chosen found life flat and dull   25
And later had much trouble from a fool,
While that great Queen, that rose out of the spray,
Being fatherless could have her way
Yet chose a bandy-legg'd smith for man.
It's certain that fine women eat   30
A crazy salad with their meat
Whereby the Horn of Plenty is undone.

In courtesy I'd have her chiefly learned;
Hearts are not had as a gift but hearts are earned
By those that are not entirely beautiful;   35
Yet many, that have played the fool
For beauty's very self, has charm made wise,
And many a poor man that has roved,
Loved and thought himself beloved,
From a glad kindness cannot take his eyes.   40

May she become a flourishing hidden tree
That all her thoughts may like the linnet be,
And have no business but dispensing round
Their magnanimities of sound,
Nor but in merriment begin a chase,   45
Nor but in merriment a quarrel.
O may she live like some green laurel
Rooted in one dear perpetual place.

My mind, because the minds that I have loved,
The sort of beauty that I have approved,   50
Prosper but little, has dried up of late,
Yet knows that to be choked with hate
May well be of all evil chances chief.
If there's no hatred in a mind
Assault and battery of the wind   55
Can never tear the linnet from the leaf.

An intellectual hatred is the worst,
So let her think opinions are accursed.
Have I not seen the loveliest woman born
Out of the mouth of Plenty's horn,   60
Because of her opinionated mind
Barter that horn and every good
By quiet natures understood
For an old bellows full of angry wind?

Considering that, all hatred driven hence,   65
The soul recovers radical innocence
And learns at last that it is self-delighting,
Self-appeasing, self-affrighting,
And that its own sweet will is Heaven's will;
She can, though every face should scowl   70
And every windy quarter howl
Or every bellows burst, be happy still.

And may her bridegroom bring her to a house
Where all's accustomed, ceremonious;
For arrogance and hatred are the wares   75
Peddled in the thoroughfares.
How but in custom and in ceremony
Are innocence and beauty born?
Ceremony's a name for the rich horn,
And custom for the spreading laurel tree.   80

June 1919

A PRAYER FOR MY DAUGHTER: Anne Butler Yeats, born 26 February
1919: 4 **Gregory's wood:** the setting of the poem is Thoor Ballylee,
or Ballylee Castle, near the estate of Lady Gregory in County
Galway 27 **that great Queen:** Aphrodite, Greek goddess of love,
who is often depicted being born out of the sea 29 **a bandy-legg'd
smith:** in Homer's *Iliad*, Aphrodite is married to Hephaestus,
craftsman of the gods, usually depicted as lame 32 **the Horn of
Plenty:** in Greek mythology, Zeus was suckled by the goat Amalthea,
whose horns flowed with nectar and ambrosia; one horn broke off
and was filled with fruits and given to Zeus, becoming a symbol of
plenty

SAILING TO BYZANTIUM

THAT is no country for old men. The young
In one another's arms, birds in the trees
– Those dying generations – at their song,
The salmon-falls, the mackerel-crowded seas,
Fish, flesh, or fowl, commend all summer long   5
Whatever is begotten, born, and dies.
Caught in that sensual music all neglect
Monuments of unageing intellect.

An aged man is but a paltry thing,
A tattered coat upon a stick, unless   10
Soul clap its hands and sing, and louder sing
For every tatter in its mortal dress,
Nor is there singing school but studying
Monuments of its own magnificence;
And therefore I have sailed the seas and come   15
To the holy city of Byzantium.

O sages standing in God's holy fire
As in the gold mosaic of a wall,
Come from the holy fire, perne in a gyre,
And be the singing-masters of my soul.   20
Consume my heart away; sick with desire
And fastened to a dying animal
It knows not what it is; and gather me
Into the artifice of eternity.

Once out of nature I shall never take   25
My bodily form from any natural thing,
But such a form as Grecian goldsmiths make
Of hammered gold and gold enamelling
To keep a drowsy Emperor awake;
Or set upon a golden bough to sing   30
To lords and ladies of Byzantium
Of what is past, or passing, or to come.

1927

SAILING TO BYZANTIUM: The ancient city of Byzantium was rebuilt as
Constantinople by the Roman emperor Constantine I (287?–337);
according to Yeats, here 'religion, art and practical life were one'
(*A Vision*) 19 **perne**: 'to pern' is to move with a circular, spinning
motion **gyre**: see note to 'The Second Coming' 27–9 **But such a
form . . . drowsy emperor awake**: the emperor was Theophilus,
whose luxurious palace included 'a golden tree, with its leaves and
branches, which sheltered a multitude of birds, warbling their
artificial notes, and two lions of massy gold, and of the natural size,
who looked and roared like their brethren of the forest' (Edward
Gibbon, *The Decline and Fall of the Roman Empire*, Vol. 5, ch. 53)

AMONG SCHOOL CHILDREN

I WALK through the long schoolroom questioning;
A kind old nun in a white hood replies;
The children learn to cipher and to sing,
To study reading-books and histories,
To cut and sew, be neat in everything   5
In the best modern way – the children's eyes
In momentary wonder stare upon
A sixty-year-old smiling public man.

I dream of a Ledaean body, bent
Above a sinking fire, a tale that she   10
Told of a harsh reproof, or trivial event
That changed some childish day to tragedy –
Told, and it seemed that our two natures blent
Into a sphere from youthful sympathy,
Or else, to alter Plato's parable,   15
Into the yolk and white of the one shell.

And thinking of that fit of grief or rage
I look upon one child or t'other there
And wonder if she stood so at that age –
For even daughters of the swan can share   20
Something of every paddler's heritage –
And had that colour upon cheek or hair,
And thereupon my heart is driven wild:
She stands before me as a living child.

Her present image floats into the mind –   25
Did Quattrocento finger fashion it
Hollow of cheek as though it drank the wind
And took a mess of shadows for its meat?
And I though never of Ledaean kind
Had pretty plumage once – enough of that,   30
Better to smile on all that smile, and show
There is a comfortable kind of old scarecrow.

What youthful mother, a shape upon her lap
Honey of generation had betrayed,
And that must sleep, shriek, struggle to escape   35
As recollection or the drug decide,
Would think her son, did she but see that shape
With sixty or more winters on its head,
A compensation for the pang of his birth,
Or the uncertainty of his setting forth?   40

Plato thought nature but a spume that plays
Upon a ghostly paradigm of things;
Solider Aristotle played the taws
Upon the bottom of a king of kings;
World-famous golden-thighed Pythagoras   45
Fingered upon a fiddle-stick or strings
What a star sang and careless Muses heard:
Old clothes upon old sticks to scare a bird.

Both nuns and mothers worship images,
But those the candles light are not as those   50
That animate a mother's reveries,
But keep a marble or a bronze repose.
And yet they too break hearts – O Presences
That passion, piety or affection knows,
And that all heavenly glory symbolise –   55
O self-born mockers of man's enterprise;

Labour is blossoming or dancing where
The body is not bruised to pleasure soul,
Nor beauty born out of its own despair,
Nor blear-eyed wisdom out of midnight oil.   60
O chestnut-tree, great-rooted blossomer,
Are you the leaf, the blossom or the bole?
O body swayed to music, O brightening glance,
How can we know the dancer from the dance?

AMONG SCHOOL CHILDREN: 9 **Ledaean:** in classical mythology the god Zeus came to the mortal Leda in the form of a swan; their union produced Helen, whose later abduction by Paris caused the Trojan War 15–16 **Plato's parable:** in Plato's *Symposium*, the playwright Aristophanes argues that originally man had been double, in a nearly spherical shape, until Zeus divided him in two, like slicing through a hard-boiled egg. Love becomes an attempt to regain the lost unity 26 **Quattrocento finger:** an artist of fifteenth-century Italy 34 **honey of generation:** 'I have taken the "honey of generation" from Porphyry's essay on "The Cave of the Nymphs", but find no warrant in Porphyry for considering it the "drug" that destroys the "recollection" of pre-natal freedom. He blamed a cup of oblivion given in the zodiacal sign of Cancer' (WBY); Porphyry (233–*c*.305) was a Neoplatonic philsopher, author of *De antro nympharum* ('Concerning the Cave of the Nymphs') 43 **Aristotle . . . a king of kings:** the Greek philosopher Aristotle was tutor to Alexander the Great 45–7 **Pythagoras . . . Muses heard:** the Greek philosopher Pythagoras discovered the mathematical basis of musical intervals and also propounded the theory of 'the music of the spheres' (as the planets move through the heavens they make different sounds according to each planet's rate of motion, and these sounds blend in perfect harmony); in classical mythology the nine Muses were the patrons of the arts and the sciences

BYZANTIUM

THE unpurged images of day recede;
The Emperor's drunken soldiery are abed;
Night resonance recedes, night walkers' song
After great cathedral gong;
A starlit or a moonlit dome disdains   5
All that man is,
All mere complexities,
The fury and the mire of human veins.

Before me floats an image, man or shade,
Shade more than man, more image than a shade;   10
For Hades' bobbin bound in mummy-cloth
May unwind the winding path;
A mouth that has no moisture and no breath
Breathless mouths may summon;
I hail the superhuman;   15
I call it death-in-life and life-in-death.

Miracle, bird or golden handiwork,
More miracle than bird or handiwork,
Planted on the star-lit golden bough,
Can like the cocks of Hades crow,   20
Or, by the moon embittered, scorn aloud
In glory of changeless metal
Common bird or petal
And all complexities of mire or blood.

At midnight on the Emperor's pavement flit   25
Flames that no faggot feeds, nor steel has lit,
Nor storm disturbs, flames begotten of flame,
Where blood-begotten spirits come
And all complexities of fury leave,
Dying into a dance,   30
An agony of trance,
An agony of flame that cannot singe a sleeve.

Astraddle on the dolphin's mire and blood,
Spirit after spirit! The smithies break the flood,
The golden smithies of the Emperor!   35
Marbles of the dancing floor
Break bitter furies of complexity,
Those images that yet
Fresh images beget,
That dolphin-torn, that gong-tormented sea.   40
                                                1930

BYZANTIUM: for Byzantium, see note to 'Sailing to Byzantium': 4 **great cathedral:** possibly Santa Sophia 11 **Hades:** son of Kronos and lord of the lower underworld, the abode of the dead **bobbin:** a spool for winding yarn 33 **dolphins:** in Roman mythology, dolphins escorted the dead to the Islands of the Blessed

UNDER BEN BULBEN

I

SWEAR by what the sages spoke
Round the Mareotic Lake
That the Witch of Atlas knew,
Spoke and set the cocks a-crow.

Swear by those horsemen, by those women   5
Complexion and form prove superhuman,
That pale, long-visaged company
That air in immortality
Completeness of their passions won;
Now they ride the wintry dawn   10
Where Ben Bulben sets the scene.

Here's the gist of what they mean.

II

Many times man lives and dies
Between his two eternities,
That of race and that of soul,   15
And ancient Ireland knew it all.
Whether man die in his bed
Or the rifle knocks him dead,
A brief parting from those dear
Is the worst man has to fear.   20
Though grave-diggers' toil is long,
Sharp their spades, their muscles strong,
They but thrust their buried men
Back in the human mind again.

III

You that Mitchel's prayer have heard,   25
'Send war in our time, O Lord!'
Know that when all words are said
And a man is fighting mad,
Something drops from eyes long blind,
He completes his partial mind,   30

UNDER BEN BULBEN: **Ben Bulben:** a mountain in County Sligo: 2 **Mareotic Lake:** Lake Mareotis, south of Alexandria 3 **the Witch of Atlas:** *The Witch of Atlas* is a poem by Shelley 25–6 **Mitchel's prayer . . . O Lord!':** Irish nationalist John Mitchel prayed: 'Give us war in our time, O Lord!'

For an instant stands at ease,
Laughs aloud, his heart at peace.
Even the wisest man grows tense
With some sort of violence
Before he can accomplish fate,   35
Know his work or choose his mate.

IV

Poet and sculptor, do the work,
Nor let the modish painter shirk
What his great forefathers did,
Bring the soul of man to God,   40
Make him fill the cradles right.

Measurement began our might:
Forms a stark Egyptian thought,
Forms that gentler Phidias wrought.
Michael Angelo left a proof   45
On the Sistine Chapel roof,
Where but half-awakened Adam
Can disturb globe-trotting Madam
Till her bowels are in heat,
Proof that there's a purpose set   50
Before the secret working mind:
Profane perfection of mankind.

Quattrocento put in paint
On backgrounds for a God or Saint
Gardens where a soul's at ease;   55
Where everything that meets the eye,
Flowers and grass and cloudless sky,
Resemble forms that are or seem
When sleepers wake and yet still dream,
And when it's vanished still declare,   60
With only bed and bedstead there,
That heavens had opened.
                         Gyres run on;
When that greater dream had gone
Calvert and Wilson, Blake and Claude,
Prepared a rest for the people of God,   65
Palmer's phrase, but after that
Confusion fell upon our thought.

V

Irish poets, learn your trade,
Sing whatever is well made,
Scorn the sort now growing up   70
All out of shape from toe to top,
Their unremembering hearts and heads
Base-born products of base beds.
Sing the peasantry, and then
Hard-riding country gentlemen,   75
The holiness of monks, and after
Porter-drinkers' randy laughter;
Sing the lords and ladies gay
That were beaten into the clay
Through seven heroic centuries;   80
Cast your mind on other days
That we in coming days may be
Still the indomitable Irishry.

VI

Under bare Ben Bulben's head
In Drumcliff churchyard Yeats is laid.   85
An ancestor was rector there
Long years ago, a church stands near,
By the road an ancient cross.

No marble, no conventional phrase;
On limestone quarried near the spot   90
By his command these words are cut:

        Cast a cold eye
        On life, on death.
        Horseman, pass by!   95
                    September 4, 1938

84–7 **Under . . . stands near:** Rev. John Yeats was rector of Drumcliff church, County Sligo, from 1811 to 1846 92–4 **Cast . . . pass by!:** these lines were made the epitaph on Yeats's grave in Drumcliff

43 **a stark Egyptian:** Plotinus (*c.*205–270) 44 **Phidias:** a Greek sculptor (*c.*490–432 BC) 45–7 **Michael Angelo . . . Adam:** the painted ceiling of the Vatican's Sistine Chapel, by Michaelangelo (1475–1564), includes a depiction of Adam about to be touched into life by God 53 **Quattrocento:** see note to 'Among School Children' 62 **Gyres:** see note to 'The Second Coming' 64 **Calvert:** Edward Calvert (1799–1883), English painter **Wilson:** probably Richard Wilson (1714–82), Welsh painter **Blake:** William Blake **Claude:** Claude Lorrain (1600–82), French painter 66 **Palmer's phrase:** the English painter Samuel Palmer (1805–81) described Blake's illustrations to Thornton's Virgil (and quoting Hebrews 4.9) as 'the drawing aside of the fleshly curtain, and the glimpse which all the most holy, studious saints and sages have enjoyed, of that rest which remaineth to the people of God'

ERNEST DOWSON

VITAE SUMMA BREVIS SPEM NOS VETAT INCOHARE LONGAM

THEY are not long, the weeping and the laughter,
    Love and desire and hate:
I think they have no portion in us after
        We pass the gate.

They are not long, the days of wine and roses: 5
    Out of a misty dream
Our path emerges for a while, then closes
        Within a dream.

VITAE SUMMA BREVIS . . . LONGAM: 'The brief span of life forbids us to encourage prolonged hope' (Horace, *Odes*, 1.4.15)

NON SUM QUALIS ERAM BONAE
SUB REGNO CYNARAE

LAST night, ah, yesternight, betwixt her lips and mine
There fell thy shadow, Cynara! thy breath was shed
Upon my soul between the kisses and the wine;
And I was desolate and sick of an old passion,
   Yea, I was desolate and bowed my head: 5
I have been faithful to thee, Cynara! in my fashion.

All night upon mine heart I felt her warm heart beat,
Night-long within mine arms in love and sleep she lay;
Surely the kisses of her bought red mouth were sweet;
But I was desolate and sick of an old passion,   10
   When I awoke and found the dawn was gray:
I have been faithful to thee, Cynara! in my fashion.

I have forgot much, Cynara! gone with the wind,
Flung roses, roses riotously with the throng,
Dancing, to put thy pale, lost lilies out of mind;   15
But I was desolate and sick of an old passion,
   Yea, all the time, because the dance was long:
I have been faithful to thee, Cynara! in my fashion.

I cried for madder music and for stronger wine,
But when the feast is finished and the lamps expire,   20
Then falls thy shadow, Cynara! the night is thine;
And I am desolate and sick of an old passion,
   Yea hungry for the lips of my desire:
I have been faithful to thee, Cynara! in my fashion.

NON SUM QUALIS . . . CYNARAE: 'I am not what I once was under the
spell of Cynara' (Horace, *Odes*, 4.1.3–4)

LAURENCE BINYON

From THE BURNING OF THE LEAVES

NOW is the time for the burning of the leaves.
They go to the fire; the nostril pricks with smoke
Wandering slowly into the weeping mist.
Brittle and blotched, ragged and rotten sheaves!
A flame seizes the smouldering ruin and bites   5
On stubborn stalks that crackle as they resist.

The last hollyhock's fallen tower is dust;
All the spices of June are a bitter reek,
All the extravagant riches spent and mean.
All burns! The reddest rose is a ghost;   10
Sparks whirl up, to expire in the mist: the wild
Fingers of fire are making corruption clean.

Now is the time for stripping the spirit bare,
Time for the burning of days ended and done,
Idle solace of things that have gone before: 15
Rootless hope and fruitless desire are there;

Let them go to the fire, with never a look behind.
The world that was ours is a world that is ours no
   more.

They will come again, the leaf and the flower, to arise
From squalor of rottenness into the old splendour,   20
And magical scents to a wondering memory bring;
The same glory, to shine upon different eyes.
Earth cares for her own ruins, naught for ours.
Nothing is certain, only the certain spring.

CHARLOTTE MEW

I SO LIKED SPRING

I SO liked Spring last year
   Because you were here; –
     The thrushes too –
Because it was these you so liked to hear –
   I so liked you.   5

This year's a different thing, –
   I'll not think of you.
But I'll like Spring because it is simply Spring
   As the thrushes do.

A QUOI BON DIRE

SEVENTEEN years ago you said
   Something that sounded like Good-bye;
   And everybody thinks that you are dead,
     But I.
So I, as I grow stiff and cold   5
To this and that say Good-bye too;
   And everybody sees that I am old
     But you.

   And one fine morning in a sunny lane
Some boy and girl will meet and kiss and swear   10
   That nobody can love their way again
     While over there
You will have smiled, I shall have tossed your hair.

A QUOI BON DIRE: 'What is the good of saying?'

THE CENOTAPH
(SEPTEMBER 1919)

NOT yet will those measureless fields be green again
Where only yesterday the wild sweet blood of
   wonderful youth was shed;
There is a grave whose earth must hold too long, too
   deep a stain,
Though for ever over it we may speak as proudly as we
   may tread.

But here, where the watchers by lonely hearths from
   the thrust of an inward sword have more slowly
   bled,   5
We shall build the Cenotaph: Victory, winged, with
   Peace, winged too, at the column's head.
And over the stairway, at the foot – oh! here, leave
   desolate, passionate hands to spread
Violets, roses, and laurel, with the small, sweet,
   twinkling country things
Speaking so wistfully of other Springs,
From the little gardens of little places where son or
   sweetheart was born and bred.   10
In splendid sleep, with a thousand brothers
        To lovers – to mothers
        Here, too, lies he:
Under the purple, the green, the red,
It is all young life: it must break some women's hearts
   to see   15
Such a brave, gay coverlet to such a bed!
Only, when all is done and said,
God is not mocked and neither are the dead.
For this will stand in our Market-place –
        Who'll sell, who'll buy   20
        (Will you or I
Lie each to each with the better grace)?
While looking into every busy whore's and huckster's
   face
As they drive their bargains, is the Face
Of God: and some young, piteous, murdered face.   25

THE CENOTAPH: not the Lutyens cenotaph in Whitehall but all the war
memorials that would be erected in towns and villages throughout
Britain after the First World War ('our Market-place', line 19)

HILAIRE BELLOC

ON A GENERAL ELECTION

THE accursèd power which stands on Privilege
(And goes with Women, and Champagne and Bridge)
Broke – and Democracy resumed her reign:
(Which goes with Bridge, and Women and
   Champagne).

HA'NACKER MILL

SALLY is gone that was so kindly
   Sally is gone from Ha'nacker Hill.
And the Briar grows ever since then so blindly
   And ever since then the clapper is still,
   And the sweeps have fallen from Ha'nacker Mill.   5

Ha'nacker Hill is in Desolation:
   Ruin a-top and a field unploughed.
And Spirits that call on a fallen nation
   Spirits that loved her calling aloud:
   Spirits abroad in a windy cloud.   10

Spirits that call and no one answers;
   Ha'nacker's down and England's done.
Wind and Thistle for pipe and dancers
   And never a ploughman under the Sun.
   Never a ploughman. Never a one.   15

HENRY KING

WHO CHEWED BITS OF STRING, AND WAS EARLY
CUT OFF IN DREADFUL AGONIES

The Chief Defect of Henry King
   Was chewing little bits of String.
At last he swallowed some which tied
   Itself in ugly Knots inside.
Physicians of the Utmost Fame   5
Were called at once; but when they came
They answered, as they took their Fees,
'There is no Cure for this Disease.
Henry will very soon be dead.'
His Parents stood about his Bed   10
Lamenting his Untimely Death,
When Henry, with his Latest Breath,
Cried – 'Oh, my Friends, be warned by me,
That Breakfast, Dinner, Lunch, and Tea
Are all the Human Frame requires . . .'   15
With that, the Wretched Child expires.

MATILDA

WHO TOLD LIES, AND WAS BURNED TO DEATH

MATILDA told such Dreadful Lies,
It made one Gasp and Stretch one's Eyes;
Her Aunt, who, from her Earliest Youth,
Had kept a Strict Regard for Truth,
Attempted to Believe Matilda: 5
The effort very nearly killed her,
And would have done so, had not She
Discovered this Infirmity.
For once, towards the Close of Day,
Matilda, growing tired of play,   10
And finding she was left alone,
Went tiptoe to the Telephone
And summoned the Immediate Aid
Of London's Noble Fire-Brigade.
Within an hour the Gallant Band   15
Were pouring in on every hand,
From Putney, Hackney Downs, and Bow
With Courage high and Hearts a-glow
They galloped, roaring through the Town,
'Matilda's House is Burning Down!'   20
Inspired by British Cheers and Loud
Proceeding from the Frenzied Crowd,
They ran their ladders through a score
Of windows on the Ball Room Floor;
And took Peculiar Pains to Souse   25

The Pictures up and down the House,
Until Matilda's Aunt succeeded
In showing them they were not needed;
And even then she had to pay
To get the Men to go away!   30

It happened that a few Weeks later
Her Aunt was off to the Theatre
To see that Interesting Play
The Second Mrs Tanqueray.
She had refused to take her Niece   35
To hear this Entertaining Piece:
A Deprivation Just and Wise
To Punish her for Telling Lies.
That Night a Fire *did* break out –
You should have heard Matilda Shout!   40
You should have heard her Scream and Bawl,
And throw the window up and call
To People passing in the Street –
(The rapidly increasing Heat
Encouraging her to obtain   45
Their confidence) – but all in vain!
For every time She shouted 'Fire!'
They only answered 'Little Liar'!
And therefore when her Aunt returned,
Matilda, and the House, were Burned.   50

MATILDA: 19 **They galloped . . . the Town:** When Belloc's *Cautionary Tales* were first published (1907) fire-engines were still horse-drawn 34 **The Second Mrs Tanqueray:** a play by Sir Arthur Wing Pinero, first performed in 1893 and frequently revived

RALPH HODGSON

'TIME, YOU OLD GIPSY MAN'

TIME, you old gipsy man,
   Will you not stay,
Put up your caravan
   Just for one day?

All things I'll give you   5
Will you be my guest,
Bells for your jennet
Of silver the best,
Goldsmiths shall beat you
A great golden ring,   10
Peacocks shall bow to you,
Little boys sing,
Oh, and sweet girls will
Festoon you with may,
Time, you old gipsy,   15
Why hasten away?

Last week in Babylon,
Last night in Rome,
Morning, and in the crush
Under Paul's dome;   20
Under Paul's dial
You tighten your rein –
Only a moment,
And off once again;
Off to some city   25
Now blind in the womb,
Off to another
Ere that's in the tomb.

Time, you old gipsy man,
   Will you not stay,   30
Put up your caravan
   Just for one day?

'TIME, YOU OLD GIPSY MAN': 7 **jennet:** female donkey 14 **may:** blossom of the may tree or hawthorn

WALTER DE LA MARE

ALL THAT'S PAST

VERY old are the woods;
   And the buds that break
Out of the brier's boughs,
   When March winds wake,
So old with their beauty are –   5
   Oh, no man knows
Through what wild centuries
   Roves back the rose.

Very old are the brooks;
   And the rills that rise   10
Where snow sleeps cold beneath
   The azure skies
Sing such a history
   Of come and gone,
Their every drop is as wise   15
   As Solomon.

Very old are we men;
   Our dreams are tales
Told in dim Eden
   By Eve's nightingales;   20
We wake and whisper awhile,
   But, the day gone by,
Silence and sleep like fields
   Of amaranth lie.

ALL THAT'S PAST: 16 **Solomon:** king of Israel celebrated for his wisdom and justice

HARRY GRAHAM

THE LISTENERS

'Is there anybody there?' said the Traveller,
  Knocking on the moonlit door;
And his horse in the silence champed the grasses
  Of the forest's ferny floor:
And a bird flew up out of the turret,   5
  Above the Traveller's head:
And he smote upon the door again a second time;
  'Is there anybody there?' he said.
But no one descended to the Traveller;
  No head from the leaf-fringed sill   10
Leaned over and looked into his grey eyes,
  Where he stood perplexed and still.
But only a host of phantom listeners
  That dwelt in the lone house then
Stood listening in the quiet of the moonlight   15
  To that voice from the world of men:
Stood thronging the faint moonbeams on the dark
    stair,
  That goes down to the empty hall,
Hearkening in an air stirred and shaken
  By the lonely Traveller's call.   20
And he felt in his heart their strangeness,
  Their stillness answering his cry,
While his horse moved, cropping the dark turf,
  'Neath the starred and leafy sky;
For he suddenly smote on the door, even   25
  Louder, and lifted his head: –
'Tell them I came, and no one answered,
  That I kept my word,' he said.
Never the least stir made the listeners,
  Though every word he spake   30
Fell echoing through the shadowiness of the still house
  From the one man left awake:
Ay, they heard his foot upon the stirrup,
  And the sound of iron on stone,
And how the silence surged softly backward,   35
  When the plunging hoofs were gone.

SILVER

SLOWLY, silently, now the moon
Walks the night in her silver shoon;
This way, and that, she peers, and sees
Silver fruit upon silver trees;
One by one the casements catch   5
Her beams beneath the silvery thatch;
Couched in his kennel, like a log,
With paws of silver sleeps the dog;
From their shadowy cote the white breasts peep
Of doves in a silver-feathered sleep;   10
A harvest mouse goes scampering by,
With silver claws, and silver eye;
And moveless fish in the water gleam,
By silver reeds in a silver stream.

SILVER: 2 **shoon:** archaic plural of *shoe*

THE RAILWAY JUNCTION

FROM here through tunnelled gloom the track
Forks into two; and one of these
Wheels onward into darkening hills,
And one toward distant seas.

How still it is; the signal light   5
At set of sun shines palely green;
A thrush sings; other sound there's none,
Nor traveller to be seen –

Where late there was a throng. And now,
In peace awhile, I sit alone;   10
Though soon, at the appointed hour,
I shall myself be gone.

But not their way: the bow-legged groom,
The parson in black, the widow and son,
The sailor with his cage, the gaunt   15
Gamekeeper with his gun,

That fair one, too, discreetly veiled –
All, who so mutely came, and went,
Will reach those far nocturnal hills,
Or shores, ere night is spent.   20

I nothing know why thus we met –
Their thoughts, their longings, hopes, their fate:
And what shall I remember, except –
The evening growing late –

That here through tunnelled gloom the track   25
Forks into two; of these
One into darkening hills leads on,
And one toward distant seas?

HARRY GRAHAM

INDIFFERENCE

WHEN Grandmamma fell off the boat,
And couldn't swim (and wouldn't float),
Matilda just stood by and smiled.
I almost could have slapped the child.

PROVIDENCE

FATE moves in a mysterious way,
  As shown by Uncle Titus,
Who unexpectedly, one day,
  Was stricken with St Vitus.
It proved a blessing in disguise,   5
  For, thanks to his condition,
He won the Non-Stop Dancing Prize
  At Wembley Exhibition.

PROVIDENCE: 4 **St Vitus**: St Vitus' Dance, a nervous disorder causing involuntary movements of limbs and face 7 **Non-Stop Dancing Prize**: a dance marathon, the winners being the last couple left standing 8 **Wembley Exhibition**: the British Empire Exhibition 1924–5

COMPENSATION

WEEP not for little Léonie,
Abducted by a French *Marquis*!
Though loss of honour was a wrench,
Just think how it's improved her French!

LONDON CALLING

WHEN rabies attacked my Uncle Daniel,
And he had fits of barking like a spaniel,
The BBC relayed him (from all stations)
At *Children's Hour* in 'farmyard imitations'.

LONDON CALLING: this was the station announcement used by the BBC when it broadcast from its studios at Savoy Hill, 1922–32

QUITE FUN

MY SON Augustus, in the street, one day,
    Was feeling quite exceptionally merry.
A stranger asked him: 'Can you show me, pray,
    The quickest way to Brompton Cemetery?'
'The quickest way? You bet I can!' said Gus,   5
    And pushed the fellow underneath a bus.
Whatever people say about my son,
He does enjoy his little bit of fun.

EDWARD THOMAS

AND YOU, HELEN

AND you, Helen, what should I give you?
So many things I would give you
Had I an infinite great store
Offered me and I stood before
To choose. I would give you youth,   5
All kinds of loveliness and truth,
A clear eye as good as mine,
Lands, waters, flowers, wine,
As many children as your heart
Might wish for, a far better art   10
Than mine can be, all you have lost
Upon the travelling waters tossed,
Or given to me. If I could choose
Freely in that great treasure-house
Anything from any shelf,   15

I would give you back yourself,
And power to discriminate
What you want and want it not too late,
Many fair days free from care
And heart to enjoy both foul and fair,   20
And myself, too, if I could find
Where it lay hidden and it proved kind.

AND YOU, HELEN: addressed to the poet's wife

ADLESTROP

YES. I remember Adlestrop –
The name, because one afternoon
Of heat the express-train drew up there
Unwontedly. It was late June.

The steam hissed. Someone cleared his throat.   5
No one left and no one came
On the bare platform. What I saw
Was Adlestrop – only the name

And willows, willow-herb, and grass,
And meadowsweet, and haycocks dry,   10
No whit less still and lonely fair
Than the high cloudlets in the sky.

And for that minute a blackbird sang
Close by, and round him, mistier,
Farther and farther, all the birds   15
Of Oxfordshire and Gloucestershire.

ADLESTROP: a village in Gloucestershire

LIGHTS OUT

I HAVE come to the borders of sleep,
The unfathomable deep
Forest where all must lose
Their way, however straight,
Or winding, soon or late;   5
They cannot choose.

Many a road and track
That, since the dawn's first crack,
Up to the forest brink,
Deceived the travellers,   10
Suddenly now blurs,
And in they sink.

Here love ends,
Despair, ambition ends,
All pleasure and all trouble,   15
Although most sweet or bitter,
Here ends in sleep that is sweeter
Than tasks most noble.

There is not any book
Or face of dearest look   20
That I would not turn from now
To go into the unknown
I must enter and leave alone
I know not how.

The tall forest towers;   25
Its cloudy foliage lowers
Ahead, shelf above shelf;
Its silence I hear and obey
That I may lose my way
And myself.   30

COCK-CROW

OUT of the wood of thoughts that grows by night
To be cut down by the sharp axe of light, –
Out of the night, two cocks together crow,
Cleaving the darkness with a silver blow:
And bright before my eyes twin trumpeters stand,   5
Heralds of splendour, one at either hand,
Each facing each as in a coat of arms:
The milkers lace their boots up at the farms.

OUT IN THE DARK

OUT in the dark over the snow
The fallow fawns invisible go
With the fallow doe;
And the winds blow
Fast as the stars are slow.   5

Stealthily the dark haunts round
And, when the lamp goes, without sound
At a swifter bound
Than the swiftest hound,
Arrives, and all else is drowned;   10

And I and star and wind and deer,
Are in the dark together, – near,
Yet far, – and fear
Drums on my ear
In that sage company drear.   15

How weak and little is the light,
All the universe of sight,
Love and delight,
Before the might,
If you love it not, of night.   20

JOHN MASEFIELD

CARGOES

QUINQUIREME of Nineveh from distant Ophir
Rowing home to haven in sunny Palestine
With a cargo of ivory,
And apes and peacocks,
Sandalwood, cedarwood, and sweet white wine.   5

Stately Spanish galleon coming from the Isthmus,
Dipping through the Tropics by the palm-green
    shores,
With a cargo of diamonds,
Emeralds, amethysts,
Topazes, and cinnamon, and gold moidores.   10

Dirty British coaster with a salt-caked smoke stack
Butting through the Channel in the mad March days,
With a cargo of Tyne coal,
Road-rail, pig-lead,
Firewood, iron-ware, and cheap tin trays.   15

CARGOES: 1 **Quinquireme:** an ancient ship with five banks of oars **Nineveh:** an Assyrian city on the banks of the Tigris in what is now northern Iraq **Ophir:** a biblical region famous for fine gold; its precise location is unknown 6 **the Isthmus:** Panama 10 **moidores:** a moidore was a Portuguese gold coin 14 **Road-rail:** suitable for use on both roads and railways **pig-lead:** a pig is an oblong length of unforged metal

SEA-FEVER

I MUST go down to the seas again, to the lonely sea
    and the sky,
And all I ask is a tall ship and a star to steer her by,
And the wheel's kick and the wind's song and the
    white sail's shaking,
And a grey mist on the sea's face and a grey dawn
    breaking.

I must go down to the seas again, for the call of the
    running tide   5
Is a wild call and a clear call that may not be denied;
And all I ask is a windy day with the white clouds
    flying,
And the flung spray and the blown spume, and the
    sea-gulls crying.

I must go down to the seas again, to the vagrant gypsy
    life,
To the gull's way and the whale's way where the
    wind's like a whetted knife;   10
And all I ask is a merry yarn from a laughing fellow-
    rover,
And quiet sleep and a sweet dream when the long
    trick's over.

THOMAS ERNEST HULME

AUTUMN

A TOUCH of cold in the Autumn night –
I walked abroad,
And saw the ruddy moon lean over a hedge
Like a red-faced farmer.
I did not stop to speak, but nodded,   5
And round about were the wistful stars
With white faces like town children.

ABOVE THE DOCK

ABOVE the quiet dock in mid night,
Tangled in the tall mast's corded height,
Hangs the moon. What seemed so far away
Is but a child's balloon, forgotten after play.

THOMAS ERNEST HULME: 'Autumn' and 'Above the Dock' were
among five short poems first published ('for good fellowship') by
Ezra Pound as an appendix to his *Ripostes* (1912) under the general
heading 'The Complete Poetical Works of T. E. Hulme'; although not
strictly accurate, this title does highlight the remarkable modesty of
Hulme's entire poetical output

DAVID HERBERT LAWRENCE

SNAKE

A SNAKE came to my water-trough
On a hot, hot day, and I in pyjamas for the heat,
To drink there.

In the deep, strange-scented shade of the great dark
    carob-tree
I came down the steps with my pitcher   5
And must wait, must stand and wait, for there he was
    at the trough before me.
He reached down from a fissure in the earth-wall in
    the gloom
And trailed his yellow-brown slackness soft-bellied
    down, over the edge of the stone trough
And rested his throat upon the stone bottom,
And where the water had dripped from the tap, in a
    small clearness,   10
He sipped with his straight mouth,
Softly drank through his straight gums, into his slack
    long body,
Silently.

Someone was before me at my water-trough,
And I, like a second comer, waiting.   15

He lifted his head from his drinking, as cattle do,
And looked at me vaguely, as drinking cattle do,
And flickered his two-forked tongue from his lips, and
    mused a moment,
And stooped and drank a little more,
Being earth-brown, earth-golden from the burning
    bowels of the earth   20
On the day of Sicilian July, with Etna smoking.

The voice of my education said to me
He must be killed,
For in Sicily the black, black snakes are innocent, the
    gold are venomous.

And voices in me said, If you were a man   25
You would take a stick and break him now, and finish
    him off.

But must I confess how I liked him,
How glad I was he had come like a guest in quiet, to
    drink at my water-trough
And depart peaceful, pacified, and thankless,
Into the burning bowels of this earth?   30

Was it cowardice, that I dared not kill him?
Was it perversity, that I longed to talk to him?
Was it humility, to feel so honoured?
I felt so honoured.

And yet those voices: 35
If you were not afraid, you would kill him!

And truly I was afraid, I was most afraid,
But even so, honoured still more
That he should seek my hospitality
From out the dark door of the secret earth.   40

He drank enough
And lifted his head, dreamily, as one who has drunken,
And flickered his tongue like a forked night on the air,
    so black,
Seeming to lick his lips,
And looked around like a god, unseeing, into the air,
And slowly turned his head,   46
And slowly, very slowly, as if thrice adream,
Proceeded to draw his slow length curving round
And climb again the broken bank of my wall-face.

And as he put his head into that dreadful hole,   50
And as he slowly drew up, snake-easing his shoulders,
    and entered farther,
A sort of horror, a sort of protest against his
    withdrawing into that horrid black hole,
Deliberately going into the blackness, and slowly
    drawing himself after,
Overcame me now his back was turned.

I looked round, I put down my pitcher,   55
I picked up a clumsy log
And threw it at the water-trough with a clatter.

I think it did not hit him,
But suddenly that part of him that was left behind
    convulsed in undignified haste,
Writhed like lightning, and was gone   60
Into the black hole, the earth-lipped fissure in the
    wall-front,
At which, in the intense still noon, I stared with
    fascination.

And immediately I regretted it.
I thought how paltry, how vulgar, what a mean act!
I despised myself and the voices of my accursèd
    human education.   65
And I thought of the albatross,
And I wished he would come back, my snake.

For he seemed to me again like a king,
Like a king in exile, uncrowned in the underworld,
Now due to be crowned again.   70

And so, I missed my chance with one of the lords
Of life.
And I have something to expiate;
A pettiness.

                                                            Taormina

BAVARIAN GENTIANS

NOT every man has gentians in his house
in soft September, at slow, Sad Michaelmas.

Bavarian gentians, big and dark, only dark
darkening the day-time, torch-like with the smoking
    blueness of Pluto's gloom,
ribbed and torch-like, with their blaze of darkness
    spread blue   5
down flattening into points, flattened under the sweep
    of white day
torch-flower of the blue-smoking darkness, Pluto's
    dark-blue daze,
black lamps from the halls of Dis, burning dark blue,
giving off darkness, blue darkness, as Demeter's pale
    lamps give off light,
lead me then, lead the way.   10

Reach me a gentian, give me a torch!
let me guide myself with the blue, forked torch of this
    flower
down the darker and darker stairs, where blue is
    darkened on blueness,
even where Persephone goes, just now, from the frosted
    September
to the sightless realm where darkness is awake upon
    the dark   15
and Persephone herself is but a voice

or a darkness invisible enfolded in the deeper dark
of the arms Plutonic, and pierced with the passion
    of dense gloom,
among the splendour of torches of darkness,
    shedding darkness on the lost bride and her groom.

BAVARIAN GENTIANS: **gentians:** the gentian is a blue-flowered herb
flourishing in alpine regions: 2 **Michaelmas:** 29 September 4 **Pluto:** in
Greek mythology another name for Hades, the ruler of the Underworld
8 **Dis:** another name for Hades 9 **Demeter:** the corn goddess,
mother of Persephone 14 **Persephone:** the daughter of Zeus and
Demeter, she married Hades and became queen of the Underworld

HUMBERT WOLFE

THE SOLDIER

I

DOWN some cold field in a world unspoken
    the young men are walking together, slim and tall,
and though they laugh to one another, silence is not
    broken:
    there is no sound however clear they call.

They are speaking together of what they loved in vain
    here,   5
    but the air is too thin to carry the thing they say.
They were young and golden, but they came on pain
    here,
    and their youth is age now, their gold is grey.

Yet their hearts are not changed, and they cry to one
    another,
    'What have they done with the lives we laid aside?   10
Are they young with our youth, gold with our gold,
    my brother?
    Do they smile in the face of death, because we
    died?'

Down some cold field in a world uncharted
    the young seek each other with questioning eyes.
They question each other, the young, the golden-
    hearted,
    of the world that they were robbed of in their quiet
    Paradise.   15

II

I DO NOT ask God's purpose. He gave me the sword,
    and though merely to wield it is itself the lie
against the light, at the bidding of my Lord,
    where all the rest bear witness, I'll deny.
And I remember Peter's high reward,   5
    and say of soldiers, when I hear cocks cry,
'As your dear lives ('twas all you might afford)
    you laid aside, I lay my sainthood by.'
There are in heaven other archangels,
    bright friends of God, who build where Michael
    destroys,   10
    in music, or in beauty, lute-players.

I wield the sword; and, though I ask naught else
  of God, I pray to Him: 'But these were boys,
  and died. Be gentle, God, to soldiers.'

THE SOLDIER: (II) 4–5 **I'll deny . . . high reward:** Jesus told Peter that
he was the 'rock' on which he would build his church; but, after
Jesus had been arrested, Peter denied any acquaintance with him
three times (Matthew 16.18, 26.69–75) 9 **Michael:** prince of all the
angels, leader of the armies of heaven: 'Go, Michael, of celestial
armies prince/ . . . lead forth my armèd saints,/By thousands and by
millions, ranged for fight' (*Paradise Lost* 6.44–8)

SIEGFRIED SASSOON

'BLIGHTERS'

THE House is crammed: tier beyond tier they grin
And cackle at the Show, while prancing ranks
Of harlots shrill the chorus, drunk with din;
'We're sure the Kaiser loves our dear old Tanks!'

I'd like to see a Tank come down the stalls,   5
Lurching to rag-time tunes, or 'Home, sweet Home',
And there'd be no more jokes in Music-halls
To mock the riddled corpses round Bapaume.

'BLIGHTERS': wretches, rascals: 1 **The House:** during the First World
War music-halls played a major role in recruiting and in stirring
up nationalistic sentiment

BASE DETAILS

IF I were fierce, and bald, and short of breath,
  I'd live with scarlet Majors at the Base,
And speed glum heroes up the line to death.
  You'd see me with my puffy petulant face,
Guzzling and gulping in the best hotel,   5
  Reading the Roll of Honour. 'Poor young chap,'
I'd say – 'I used to know his father well;
  Yes, we've lost heavily in this last scrap.'
And when the war is done and youth stone dead,
I'd toddle safely home and die – in bed.   10

THE GENERAL

'GOOD-MORNING, good-morning!' the General said
When we met him last week on our way to the line.
Now the soldiers he smiled at are most of 'em dead,
And we're cursing his staff for incompetent swine.
'He's a cheery old card,' grunted Harry to Jack   5
As they slogged up to Arras with rifle and pack.

        ·   ·   ·

But he did for them both by his plan of attack.

THE GENERAL: 5 **card:** person, usually implying waggishness or
eccentricity

ATTACK

AT DAWN the ridge emerges massed and dun
In wild purple of the glow'ring sun,
Smouldering through spouts of drifting smoke that
  shroud
The menacing scarred slope; and, one by one,
Tanks creep and topple forward to the wire.   5
The barrage roars and lifts. Then, clumsily bowed
With bombs and guns and shovels and battle-gear,
Men jostle and climb to meet the bristling fire.
Lines of grey, muttering faces, masked with fear,
They leave their trenches, going over the top,   10
While time ticks blank and busy on their wrists,
And hope, with furtive eyes and grappling fists,
Flounders in mud. O Jesus, make it stop!

GLORY OF WOMEN

YOU love us when we're heroes, home on leave,
Or wounded in a mentionable place.
You worship decorations; you believe
That chivalry redeems the war's disgrace.
You make us shells. You listen with delight,   5
By tales of dirt and danger fondly thrilled.
You crown our distant ardours while we fight,
And mourn our laurelled memories when we're killed.
You can't believe that British troops 'retire'
When hell's last horror breaks them, and they run,   10
Trampling the terrible corpses – blind with blood.
  O German mother dreaming by the fire,
    While you are knitting socks to send your son
    His face is trodden deeper in the mud.

GLORY OF WOMEN: 5 **you make us shells:** during the First World War
women took over men's jobs in factories, including the
manufacture of munitions

EVERYONE SANG

EVERYONE suddenly burst out singing;
And I was filled with such delight
As prisoned birds must find in freedom,
Winging wildly across the white
Orchards and dark-green fields; on – on – and out of
  sight.   5

Everyone's voice was suddenly lifted;
And beauty came like the setting sun:
My heart was shaken with tears; and horror
Drifted away . . . O, but Everyone
Was a bird; and the song was wordless; the singing will
  never be done.   10

RUPERT BROOKE

THE OLD VICARAGE, GRANTCHESTER
(CAFÉ DES WESTENS, BERLIN, MAY 1912)

JUST now the lilac is in bloom,
All before my little room;
And in my flower-beds, I think,
Smile the carnation and the pink;
And down the borders, well I know,   5
The poppy and the pansy blow . . .
Oh! there the chestnuts, summer through,
Beside the river make for you
A tunnel of green gloom, and sleep
Deeply above; and green and deep   10
The stream mysterious glides beneath,
Green as a dream and deep as death.
– Oh, damn! I know it! and I know
How the May fields all golden show,
And when the day is young and sweet,   15
Gild gloriously the bare feet
That run to bathe . . .
                Du lieber Gott!

Here am I, sweating, sick, and hot,
And there the shadowed waters fresh
Lean up to embrace the naked flesh.   20
Temperamentvoll German Jews
Drink beer around; – and *there* the dews
Are soft beneath a morn of gold.
Here tulips bloom as they are told;
Unkempt about those hedges blows   25
An English unofficial rose;
And there the unregulated sun
Slopes down to rest when day is done,
And wakes a vague unpunctual star,
A slippered Hesper; and there are   30
Meads towards Haslingfield and Coton
Where *das Betreten*'s not *verboten.*

ειθε γενοιμην . . . would I were
In Grantchester, in Grantchester! –
Some, it may be, can get in touch   35
With Nature there, or Earth, or such.
And clever modern men have seen
A Faun a-peeping through the green,
And felt the Classics were not dead,
To glimpse a Naiad's reedy head,   40

Or hear the Goat-foot piping low: . . .
But these are things I do not know.
I only know that you may lie
Day-long and watch the Cambridge sky,
And, flower-lulled in sleepy grass,   45
Hear the cool lapse of hours pass,
Until the centuries blend and blur
In Grantchester, in Grantchester. . . .
Still in the dawnlit waters cool
His ghostly Lordship swims his pool,   50
And tries the strokes, essays the tricks,
Long learnt on Hellespont, or Styx.
Dan Chaucer hears his river still
Chatter beneath a phantom mill.
Tennyson notes, with studious eye,   55
How Cambridge waters hurry by . . .
And in that garden, black and white,
Creep whispers through the grass all night;
And spectral dance, before the dawn,
A hundred Vicars down the lawn;   60
Curates, long dust, will come and go
On lissom, clerical, printless toe;
And oft between the boughs is seen
The sly shade of a Rural Dean . . .
Till, at a shiver in the skies,   65
Vanishing with Satanic cries,
The prim ecclesiastic rout
Leaves but a startled sleeper-out,
Grey heavens, the first bird's drowsy calls,
The falling house that never falls.   70

God! I will pack, and take a train,
And get me to England once again!
For England's the one land, I know,
Where men with Splendid Hearts may go;
And Cambridgeshire, of all England,   75
The shire for Men who Understand;
And of *that* district I prefer
The lovely hamlet Grantchester.
For Cambridge people rarely smile,
Being urban, squat, and packed with guile;   80
And Royston men in the far South
Are black and fierce and strange of mouth;
At Over they fling oaths at one,
And worse than oaths at Trumpington,
And Ditton girls are mean and dirty,   85
And there's none in Harston under thirty,
And folks in Shelford and those parts
Have twisted lips and twisted hearts,
And Barton men make Cockney rhymes,
And Coton's full of nameless crimes,   90
And things are done you'd not believe
At Madingley, on Christmas Eve.
Strong men have run for miles and miles,
When one from Cherry Hinton smiles;

THE OLD VICARAGE: In 1910, Brooke took lodgings at the Old Vicarage, Grantchester, near Cambridge, with Mr and Mrs Neeve. Later, while on holiday in Germany, his nostalgia for this corner of England prompted him to write this poem, first called 'The Sentimental Exile'. The last line, which is one of the best-known (and perhaps most vilified) lines in English poetry, is readily explained by the fact that Mr Neeve kept bees: 17 *Du lieber Gott!*: Dear God! 21 *Temperamentvoll*: lively, spirited 30 **Hesper:** Hesperus, the evening star 31 **Haslingfield:** the first of many references to towns and villages in the area 32 *das Betreten*: entrance *verboten*: forbidden 33 ειθε γενοιμην: Greek, 'Would that we were' 38 **Faun:** a Roman god of the countryside 40 **Naiad:** a river-nymph

41 **Goat-foot:** Pan, the goat-footed Greek god 52 **Hellespont:** ancient name of the Dardanelles **Styx:** the 'river of hate' that wound nine times round the Underworld 53 **Dan:** Master 67 **rout:** party

Strong men have blanched, and shot their wives, 95
Rather than send them to St Ives;
Strong men have cried like babes, bydam,
To hear what happened at Babraham.
But Grantchester! ah, Grantchester!
There's peace and holy quiet there, 100
Great clouds along pacific skies,
And men and women with straight eyes,
Lithe children lovelier than a dream,
A bosky wood, a slumbrous stream,
And little kindly winds that creep 105
Round twilight corners, half asleep.
In Grantchester their skins are white;
They bathe by day, they bathe by night;
The women there do all they ought;
The men observe the Rules of Thought. 110
They love the Good; they worship Truth;
They laugh uproariously in youth;
(And when they get to feeling old,
They up and shoot themselves, I'm told) . . .
    Ah God! to see the branches stir 115
Across the moon at Grantchester!
To smell the thrilling-sweet and rotten
Unforgettable, unforgotten
River-smell, and hear the breeze
Sobbing in the little trees. 120
Say, do the elm-clumps greatly stand
Still guardians of that holy land?
The chestnuts shade, in reverend dream,
The yet unacademic stream?
Is dawn a secret shy and cold 125
Anadyomene, silver-gold?
And sunset still a golden sea
From Haslingfield to Madingley?
And after, ere the night is born,
Do hares come out about the corn? 130
Oh, is the water sweet and cool,
Gentle and brown, above the pool?
And laughs the immortal river still
Under the mill, under the mill?
Say, is there Beauty yet to find? 135
And Certainty? and Quiet kind?
Deep meadows yet, for to forget
The lies, and truths, and pain? . . . Oh! yet
Stands the Church clock at ten to three?
And is there honey still for tea? 140

104 **bosky:** shady 126 **Anadyomene:** ('*A*-na-dye-*o*-meh-*nee*') emerging
(like Aphrodite from the sea)

1914

I. PEACE

Now, God be thanked Who has matched us with His
        hour,
    And caught our youth, and wakened us from
        sleeping,

With hand made sure, clear eye, and sharpened power,
    To turn, as swimmers into cleanness leaping,
Glad from a world grown old and cold and weary, 5
    Leave the sick hearts that honour could not move,
And half-men, and their dirty songs and dreary,
    And all the little emptiness of love!

Oh! we, who have known shame, we have found
        release there,
    Where there's no ill, no grief, but sleep has mending,
        Naught broken save this body, lost but breath; 11
Nothing to shake the laughing heart's long peace there
    But only agony, and that has ending;
        And the worst friend and enemy is but Death.

II. SAFETY

Dear! of all happy in the hour, most blest
    He who has found our hid security,
Assured in the dark tides of the world that rest,
    And heard our word, 'Who is so safe as we?'
We have found safety with all things undying, 5
    The winds, and morning, tears of men and mirth,
The deep night, and birds singing, and clouds flying,
    And sleep, and freedom, and the autumnal earth.

We have built a house that is not for Time's throwing.
    We have gained a peace unshaken by pain for ever.
War knows no power. Safe shall be my going, 11
    Secretly armed against all death's endeavour;
Safe though all safety's lost; safe where men fall;
And if these poor limbs die, safest of all.

III. THE DEAD

Blow out, you bugles, over the rich Dead!
    There's none of these so lonely and poor of old,
    But, dying, has made us rarer gifts than gold.
These laid the world away; poured out the red
Sweet wine of youth; gave up the years to be 5
    Of work and joy, and that unhoped serene,
    That men call age; and those who would have been,
Their sons, they gave, their immortality.

Blow, bugles, blow! They brought us, for our dearth,
    Holiness, lacked so long, and Love, and Pain. 10
Honour has come back, as a king, to earth,
    And paid his subjects with a royal wage;
And Nobleness walks in our ways again;
    And we have come into our heritage.

IV. THE DEAD

These hearts were woven of human joys and cares,
    Washed marvellously with sorrow, swift to mirth.
The years had given them kindness. Dawn was theirs,
    And sunset, and the colours of the earth.

These had seen movement, and heard music; known 5
  Slumber and waking; loved; gone proudly friended;
Felt the quick stir of wonder; sat alone;
  Touched flowers and furs and cheeks. All this is
    ended.

There are waters blown by changing winds to laughter
And lit by the rich skies, all day. And after, 10
  Frost, with a gesture, stays the waves that dance
And wandering loveliness. He leaves a white
  Unbroken glory, a gathered radiance,
A width, a shining peace, under the night.

V. THE SOLDIER

IF I should die, think only this of me:
  That there's some corner of a foreign field
That is for ever England. There shall be
  In that rich earth a richer dust concealed;
A dust whom England bore, shaped, made aware, 5
  Gave, once, her flowers to love, her ways to roam,
A body of England's, breathing English air,
  Washed by the rivers, blest by suns of home.

And think, this heart, all evil shed away,
  A pulse in the eternal mind, no less 10
    Gives somewhere back the thoughts by England
     given;
Her sights and sounds; dreams happy as her day;
  And laughter, learnt of friends; and gentleness,
    In hearts at peace, under an English heaven.

EDWIN MUIR

SUBURBAN DREAM

WALKING the suburbs in the afternoon
In summer when the idle doors stand open
  And the air flows through the rooms
  Fanning the curtain hems,

You wander through a cool elysium 5
Of women, schoolgirls, children, garden talks,
  With a schoolboy here and there
  Conning his history book.

The men are all away in offices,
Committee-rooms, laboratories, banks, 10
  Or pushing cotton goods
  In Wick or Ilfracombe.

The massed unanimous absence liberates
The light keys of the piano and sets free
  Chopin and everlasting youth, 15
  Now, with the masters gone.

And all things turn to images of peace,
The boy curled over his book, the young girl poised
  On the path as if beguiled
  By the silence of a wood. 20

It is a child's dream of a grown-up world.
But soon the brazen evening clocks will bring
  The tramp of feet and brisk
  Fanfare of motor horns
  And the masters come. 25

SUBURBAN DREAM: 5 **elysium:** in Greek mythology the abode of the blessed dead; paradise 11 **pushing cotton goods:** i.e. as a company sales representative

THOMAS STEARNS ELIOT

THE LOVE SONG OF J. ALFRED PRUFROCK

    S'io credessi che mia risposta fosse
    a persona che mai tornasse al mondo,
    questa fiamma staria senza più scosse.
    Ma per ciò che giammai di questo fondo
    non tornò vivo alcun, s'i'odo il vero,
    senza tema d'infamia ti rispondo.

LET us go then, you and I,
When the evening is spread out against the sky
Like a patient etherised upon a table;
Let us go, through certain half-deserted streets,
The muttering retreats 5
Of restless nights in one-night cheap hotels
And sawdust restaurants with oyster-shells:
Streets that follow like a tedious argument
Of insidious intent
To lead you to an overwhelming question . . . 10
Oh, do not ask, 'What is it?'
Let us go and make our visit.

  In the room the women come and go
Talking of Michelangelo.

  The yellow fog that rubs its back upon the
    window-panes, 15
The yellow smoke that rubs its muzzle on the
    window-panes,
Licked its tongue into the corners of the evening,
Lingered upon the pools that stand in drains,
Let fall upon its back the soot that falls from chimneys,
Slipped by the terrace, made a sudden leap, 20
And seeing that it was a soft October night,
Curled once about the house, and fell asleep.

THE LOVE SONG OF J. ALFRED PRUFROCK: **S'io credessi . . . ti rispondo:**
' "If I thought that my answer were to one who might ever return
to the world, this flame would shake no more; but since from this
depth none ever returned alive, if what I hear is true, I answer you
without fear of infamy" ' (Dante, *Inferno*, 27.61–6; trans. Singleton)

And indeed there will be time
For the yellow smoke that slides along the street
Rubbing its back upon the window-panes;   25
There will be time, there will be time
To prepare a face to meet the faces that you meet;
There will be time to murder and create,
And time for all the works and days of hands
That lift and drop a question on your plate;   30
Time for you and time for me,
And time yet for a hundred indecisions,
And for a hundred visions and revisions,
Before the taking of a toast and tea.

In the room the women come and go   35
Talking of Michelangelo.

And indeed there will be time
To wonder, 'Do I dare?' and, 'Do I dare?'
Time to turn back and descend the stair,
With a bald spot in the middle of my hair –   40
(They will say: 'How his hair is growing thin!')
My morning coat, my collar mounting firmly to the
    chin,
My necktie rich and modest, but asserted by a simple
    pin –
(They will say: 'But how his arms and legs are thin!')
Do I dare   45
Disturb the universe?
In a minute there is time
For decisions and revisions which a minute will
    reverse.

For I have known them all already, known them
    all –
Have known the evenings, mornings, afternoons,   50
I have measured out my life with coffee spoons;
I know the voices dying with a dying fall
Beneath the music from a farther room.
    So how should I presume?

And I have known the eyes already, known them
    all –   55
The eyes that fix you in a formulated phrase,
And when I am formulated, sprawling on a pin,
When I am pinned and wriggling on the wall,
Then how should I begin
To spit out all the butt-ends of my days and ways?   60
    And how should I presume?

And I have known the arms already, known them
    all –
Arms that are braceleted and white and bare
(But in the lamplight, downed with light brown hair!)
Is it perfume from a dress   65
That makes me so digress?

Arms that lie along a table, or wrap about a shawl.
    And should I then presume?
    And how should I begin?

.   .   .   .   .

Shall I say, I have gone at dusk through narrow
    streets   70
And watched the smoke that rises from the pipes
Of lonely men in shirt-sleeves, leaning out of
    windows? . . .

I should have been a pair of ragged claws
Scuttling across the floors of silent seas.

.   .   .   .   .

And the afternoon, the evening, sleeps so
    peacefully!   75
Smoothed by long fingers,
Asleep . . . tired . . . or it malingers,
Stretched on the floor, here beside you and me.
Should I, after tea and cakes and ices,
Have the strength to force the moment to its crisis?   80
But though I have wept and fasted, wept and prayed,
Though I have seen my head (grown slightly bald)
    brought in upon a platter,
I am no prophet – and here's no great matter;
I have seen the moment of my greatness flicker,
And I have seen the eternal Footman hold my coat,
    and snicker,   85
And in short, I was afraid.

And would it have been worth it, after all,
After the cups, the marmalade, the tea,
Among the porcelain, among some talk of you and
    me,
Would it have been worth while,   90
To have bitten off the matter with a smile,
To have squeezed the universe into a ball
To roll it towards some overwhelming question,
To say: 'I am Lazarus, come from the dead,
Come back to tell you all, I shall tell you all' –   95
If one, settling a pillow by her head,
    Should say: 'That is not what I meant at all.
    That is not it, at all.'

And would it have been worth it, after all,
Would it have been worth while,   100
After the sunsets and the dooryards and the sprinkled
    streets,
After the novels, after the teacups, after the skirts that
    trail along the floor –
And this, and so much more? –

52 **voices dying with a dying fall**: 'That strain again; it had a dying
fall' (Shakespeare, *Twelfth Night* 1.1)

81 **wept and fasted**: 'And they mourned, and wept, and fasted'
(2 Samuel 1.2) 82 **my head . . . a platter**: Herod was so delighted
by the dancing of the daughter of Herodias that he promised her
on oath that she could have anything she desired; she asked for
the head of John the Baptist to be brought to her on a dish
(Matthew 13) 92 **squeezed the universe into a ball**: see Marvell's
'To His Coy Mistress' (lines 41–2) 94 **Lazarus**: raised from the dead
by Jesus (John 11)

It is impossible to say just what I mean!
But as if a magic lantern threw the nerves in patterns
    on a screen: 105
Would it have been worth while
If one, settling a pillow or throwing off a shawl,
And turning toward the window, should say:
    'That is not it at all,
    That is not what I meant, at all.'   110

      .   .   .   .   .

    No! I am not Prince Hamlet, nor was meant to be;
Am an attendant lord, one that will do
To swell a progress, start a scene or two,
Advise the prince; no doubt, an easy tool,
Deferential, glad to be of use,   115
Politic, cautious, and meticulous;
Full of high sentence, but a bit obtuse;
At times, indeed, almost ridiculous –
Almost, at times, the Fool.

    I grow old . . . I grow old . . .   120
I shall wear the bottoms of my trousers rolled.

    Shall I part my hair behind? Do I dare to eat a peach?
I shall wear white flannel trousers, and walk upon the
    beach.
I have heard the mermaids singing, each to each.

I do not think that they will sing to me.   125

I have seen them riding seaward on the waves
Combing the white hair of the waves blown back
When the wind blows the water white and black.

We have lingered in the chambers of the sea
By sea-girls wreathed with seaweed red and brown   130
Till human voices wake us, and we drown.

105 **magic lantern:** an early device for projecting images from slides on to a screen 120 **I grow old:** Falstaff: 'I am old, I am old' (*2 Henry IV* 2.4) 124 **I have heard the mermaids singing:** see Donne's 'Go and catch a falling star' (line 5)

PRELUDES

I

THE winter evening settles down
With smell of steaks in passageways.
Six o'clock.
The burnt-out ends of smoky days.
And now a gusty shower wraps   5
The grimy scraps
Of withered leaves about your feet
And newspapers from vacant lots;
The showers beat
On broken blinds and chimney-pots,   10
And at the corner of the street
A lonely cab-horse steams and stamps.

And then the lighting of the lamps.

II

THE morning comes to consciousness
Of faint stale smells of beer
From the sawdust-trampled street
With all its muddy feet that press
To early coffee-stands.   5

With the other masquerades
That time resumes,
One thinks of all the hands
That are raising dingy shades
In a thousand furnished rooms.   10

III

YOU tossed a blanket from the bed,
You lay upon your back, and waited;
You dozed, and watched the night revealing
The thousand sordid images
Of which your soul was constituted;   5
They flickered against the ceiling.
And when all the world came back
And the light crept up between the shutters
And you heard the sparrows in the gutters,
You had such a vision of the street   10
As the street hardly understands;
Sitting along the bed's edge, where
You curled the papers from your hair,
Or clasped the yellow soles of feet
In the palms of both soiled hands.   15

IV

HIS soul stretched tight across the skies
That fade behind a city block,
Or trampled by insistent feet
At four and five and six o'clock;
And short square fingers stuffing pipes,   5
And evening newspapers, and eyes
Assured of certain certainties,
The conscience of a blackened street
Impatient to assume the world.

I am moved by fancies that are curled   10
Around these images, and cling:
The notion of some infinitely gentle
Infinitely suffering thing.

Wipe your hand across your mouth, and laugh;
The worlds revolve like ancient women   15
Gathering fuel in vacant lots.

THOMAS STEARNS ELIOT

From THE WASTE LAND

THE FIRE SERMON

THE river's tent is broken; the last fingers of leaf
Clutch and sink into the wet bank. The wind
Crosses the brown land, unheard. The nymphs are
   departed.
Sweet Thames, run softly, till I end my song.
The river bears no empty bottles, sandwich papers,
Silk handkerchiefs, cardboard boxes, cigarette ends   6
Or other testimony of summer nights. The nymphs
   are departed.
And their friends, the loitering heirs of City directors;
Departed, have left no addresses.
By the waters of Leman I sat down and wept . . .   10
Sweet Thames, run softly till I end my song,
Sweet Thames, run softly, for I speak not loud or long.
But at my back in a cold blast I hear
The rattle of bones, and chuckle spread from ear to
   ear.
A rat crept softly through the vegetation   15
Dragging its slimy belly on the bank
While I was fishing in the dull canal
On a winter evening round behind the gashouse
Musing upon the king my brother's wreck
And on the king my father's death before him.   20
White bodies naked on the low damp ground
And bones cast in a little low dry garret,
Rattled by the rat's foot only, year to year.
But at my back from time to time I hear
The sound of horns and motors, which shall bring
Sweeney to Mrs Porter in the spring.   26
O the moon shone bright on Mrs Porter
And on her daughter
They wash their feet in soda water
Et O ces voix d'enfants, chantant dans la coupole!   30

Twit twit twit
Jug jug jug jug jug jug
So rudely forc'd.
Tereu

  Unreal City   35
Under the brown fog of a winter noon
Mr Eugenides, the Smyrna merchant
Unshaven, with a pocket full of currants
C.i.f. London: documents at sight,
Asked me in demotic French   40
To luncheon at the Cannon Street Hotel
Followed by a weekend at the Metropole.

  At the violet hour, when the eyes and back
Turn upward from the desk, when the human engine
   waits
Like a taxi throbbing waiting,   45
I Tiresias, though blind, throbbing between two lives,
Old man with wrinkled female breasts, can see
At the violet hour, the evening hour that strives
Homeward, and brings the sailor home from sea,
The typist home at teatime, clears her breakfast,
   lights   50
Her stove, and lays out food in tins.
Out of the window perilously spread
Her drying combinations touched by the sun's last rays,
On the divan are piled (at night her bed)
Stockings, slippers, camisoles, and stays.   55
I Tiresias, old man with wrinkled dugs
Perceived the scene, and foretold the rest –
I too awaited the expected guest.
He, the young man carbuncular, arrives,
A small house agent's clerk, with one bold stare,   60
One of the low on whom assurance sits
As a silk hat on a Bradford millionaire.
The time is now propitious, as he guesses,
The meal is ended, she is bored and tired,
Endeavours to engage her in caresses   65
Which still are unreproved, if undesired.

THE WASTE LAND: First published in 1922 after Ezra Pound (in what
has become one of the most celebrated editorial labours in
literary history) had drastically cut and refashioned Eliot's
original draft, which at that stage was called 'He Do the Police in
Different Voices' (from Dickens's *Our Mutual Friend* 1.6). Eliot
acknowledged the debt by dedicating the published poem to
Pound, 'il miglior fabbro' ('the better craftsman', Dante's tribute
to the troubadour Arnault Daniel). To pad out the text for
publication, Eliot provided notes; they were not entirely serious,
but some have been included here if they help to identify Eliot's
sources. 'The Fire Sermon' is the third of five sections: 4 **Sweet
Thames . . . my song:** see Spenser's 'Prothalamion' 13–14 **But at my
back . . . hear:** see Marvell's 'To His Coy Mistress (lines 21–2); again
at line 24 19–20 **Musing . . . before him:** Shakespeare, *The Tempest*,
1.2 25 **The sound of horns:** Eliot cites John Day's *Parliament of Bees*:
'When of the sudden, listening, you shall hear,/A noise of horns
and hunting, which shall bring/Actaeon to Diana in the spring,/
Where all shall see her naked skin' 27 **O the moon . . . Mrs Porter:**
'I do not know the origin of the ballad from which these lines are
taken: it was reported to me from Sydney, Australia' (TSE) 30 *Et
O ces voix . . . dans la coupole:* the last line of Paul Verlaine's sonnet
'Parsifal' ('And, oh, those children's voices singing in the dome!')

37 **Smyrna:** Turkish seaport   39 **C.i.f. London: documents at
sight:** 'The currants were quoted at a price "cost insurance and
freight to London"; and the Bill of Lading, etc., were to be
handled to the buyer upon payment of the sight draft' (TSE)
40 **demotic:** popular, perhaps implying vulgarity   46 **Tiresias:**
'Tiresias, although a mere spectator and not indeed a "character",
is yet the most important personage in the poem, uniting all
the rest. . . . What Tiresias *sees*, in fact, is the substance of
the poem' (TSE) 49 **and brings the sailor home from sea:** Eliot
cites Sappho, although 'I had in mind the "longshore" or "dory"
fisherman, who returns at nightfall; but see also Stevenson's
'Requiem' (line 7)

Flushed and decided, he assaults at once;
Exploring hands encounter no defence;
His vanity requires no response,
And makes a welcome of indifference.   70
(And I Tiresias have foresuffered all
Enacted on this same divan or bed;
I who have sat by Thebes below the wall
And walked among the lowest of the dead.)
Bestows one final patronising kiss,   75
And gropes his way, finding the stairs unlit . . .

  She turns and looks a moment in the glass,
Hardly aware of her departed lover;
Her brain allows one half-formed thought to pass:
'Well now that's done: and I'm glad it's over.'   80
When lovely woman stoops to folly and
Paces about her room again, alone,
She smoothes her hair with automatic hand,
And puts a record on the gramophone.

  'This music crept by me upon the waters'   85
And along the Strand, up Queen Victoria Street.
O City city, I can sometimes hear
Beside a public bar in Lower Thames Street,
The pleasant whining of a mandoline
And a clatter and a chatter from within   90
Where fishmen lounge at noon: where the walls
Of Magnus Martyr hold
Inexplicable splendour of Ionian white and gold.

        The river sweats
        Oil and tar   95
        The barges drift
        With the turning tide
        Red sails
        Wide
        To leeward, swing on the heavy spar.   100
        The barges wash
        Drifting logs
        Down Greenwich reach
        Past the Isle of Dogs.
            Weialala leia   105
            Wallala leialala

Elizabeth and Leicester
Beating oars
The stern was formed
A gilded shell   110
Red and gold
The brisk swell
Rippled both shores
Southwest wind
Carried down stream   115
The peal of bells
White towers
    Weialala leia
    Wallala leialala

'Trams and dusty trees.   120
Highbury bore me. Richmond and Kew
Undid me. By Richmond I raised my knees
Supine on the floor of a narrow canoe.'

'My feet are at Moorgate, and my heart
Under my feet. After the event   125
He wept. He promised "a new start."
I made no comment. What should I resent?'

'On Margate Sands.
I can connect
Nothing with nothing.   130
The broken fingernails of dirty hands.
My people humble people who expect
Nothing.'
        la la

To Carthage then I came   135

Burning burning burning burning
O Lord Thou pluckest me out
O Lord Thou pluckest

burning

107 **Elizabeth and Leicester:** 'Froude, *Elizabeth*, Vol. I, ch. iv, letter of De Quadra to Philip of Spain: "In the afternoon we were in a barge, watching the games on the river. (The Queen) was alone with Lord Robert and myself on the poop, when they began to talk nonsense, and went so far that Lord Robert at last said, as I was on the spot there was no reason why they should not be married if the queen pleased" ' (TSE)   121–2 **Highbury bore me. Richmond and Kew/Undid me:** Eliot cites Dante's *Purgatorio*: ' "remember me, who am la Pia. Siena made me, Maremma unmade me" ' (5.133–4; trans. Singleton)   135 **To Carthage then I came:** 'St Augustine's *Confessions*: "to Carthage then I came, where a cauldron of unholy loves sang all about mine ears" ' (TSE)   136 **Burning burning burning burning:** Eliot cites 'Buddha's Fire Sermon (which corresponds in importance to the Sermon on the Mount)'   137 **O Lord Thou pluckest me out:** 'From St Augustine's *Confessions* again. The collocation of these two representatives of eastern and western asceticism, as the culmination of this part of the poem, is not an accident' (TSE)

81 **When lovely woman stoops to folly:** see Goldsmith's song from *The Vicar of Wakefield*   85 **'This music . . . the waters':** see Shakespeare's *The Tempest*, 1.2   92 **Magnus Martyr:** St Magnus the Martyr, Lower Thames Street, in the City of London; 'The interior of St Magnus Martyr is to my mind one of the finest among Wren's interiors' (TSE)   94 **The river sweats:** Eliot cites the Rhine-daughters in Richard Wagner's *Götterdämmerung*, 3.1: 'The Song of the (three) Thames-daughters begins here. From line [120] to [134] inclusive they speak in turn'

JOURNEY OF THE MAGI

'A COLD coming we had of it,
Just the worst time of the year
For a journey, and such a long journey:
The ways deep and the weather sharp,
The very dead of winter.'   5
And the camels galled, sore-footed, refractory,
Lying down in the melting snow.
There were times we regretted
The summer palaces on slopes, the terraces,
And the silken girls bringing sherbet.   10
Then the camel men cursing and grumbling
And running away, and wanting their liquor and
          women,
And the night-fires going out, and the lack of shelters,
And the cities hostile and the towns unfriendly
And the villages dirty and charging high prices: 15
A hard time we had of it.
At the end we preferred to travel all night,
Sleeping in snatches,
With the voices singing in our ears, saying
That this was all folly.   20

Then at dawn we came down to a temperate valley,
Wet, below the snow line, smelling of vegetation,
With a running stream and a water-mill beating the
          darkness,
And three trees on the low sky.
And an old white horse galloped away in the meadow.
Then we came to a tavern with vine-leaves over the
          lintel,   26
Six hands at an open door dicing for pieces of silver,
And feet kicking the empty wine-skins.
But there was no information, so we continued
And arrived at evening, not a moment too soon   30
Finding the place; it was (you may say) satisfactory.

All this was a long time ago, I remember,
And I would do it again, but set down
This set down
This: were we led all that way for   35
Birth or Death? There was a Birth, certainly,
We had evidence and no doubt. I had seen birth and
          death,
But had thought they were different; this Birth was
Hard and bitter agony for us, like Death, our death.
We returned to our places, these Kingdoms,   40
But no longer at ease here, in the old dispensation,
With an alien people clutching their gods.
I should be glad of another death.

JOURNEY OF THE MAGI: 'behold, there came wise men from the east
to Jerusalem, Saying, Where is he that is born King of the Jews? for
we have seen his star in the east, and are come to worship him'
(Matthew 2.1) 24 **And three trees on the low sky**: foreshadowing
the three crosses of Christ and the two thieves crucified with him
27 **dicing for pieces of silver**: evoking the thirty pieces of silver
paid to Judas for betraying Christ

From FOUR QUARTETS

LITTLE GIDDING

I

MIDWINTER spring is its own season
Sempiternal though sodden towards sundown,
Suspended in time, between pole and tropic.
When the short day is brightest, with frost and fire,
The brief sun flames the ice, on pond and ditches,   5
In windless cold that is the heart's heat,
Reflecting in a watery mirror
A glare that is blindness in the early afternoon.
And glow more intense than blaze of branch, or
          brazier,
Stirs the dumb spirit: no wind, but pentecostal fire   10
In the dark time of the year. Between melting and
          freezing
The soul's sap quivers. There is no earth smell
Or smell of living thing. This is the spring time
But not in time's covenant. Now the hedgerow
Is blanched for an hour with transitory blossom   15
Of snow, a bloom more sudden
Than that of summer, neither budding nor fading,
Not in the scheme of generation.
Where is the summer, the unimaginable
Zero summer?

          If you came this way,   20
Taking the route you would be likely to take
From the place you would be likely to come from,
If you came this way in may time, you would find the
          hedges
White again, in May, with voluptuary sweetness.
It would be the same at the end of the journey,   25
If you came at night like a broken king,
If you came by day not knowing what you came for,
It would be the same, when you leave the rough road
And turn behind the pig-sty to the dull façade
And the tombstone. And what you thought you came
          for   30
Is only a shell, a husk of meaning
From which the purpose breaks only when it is fulfilled

FOUR QUARTETS: First published separately in 1942, 'Little Gidding'
is the last of the four poems, each taking its inspiration from a
place. Little Gidding was the Cambridgeshire manor-house where
Nicholas Ferrar (1592–1637) founded in 1625 a family community
devoted to prayer and charitable works. According to Izaak Walton,
'Having seen the manners and vanities of the world', Ferrar
resolved 'to spend the remainder of his life in mortifications and
devotion, and charity'. The community was 'about thirty in
number', 'part of them his kindred, and the rest chosen to be of
a temper fit to be moulded into a devout life' (*Life of George Herbert*,
1670). Ferrar was a close friend of George Herbert, who entrusted
the manuscripts of his poems to Ferrar on his deathbed in 1633;
Ferrar published them the same year. Charles I visited Little Gidding
several times, the last occasion being in 1646 when he was on his
way to surrender to the Scots (lines 27 and 177): 2 **Sempiternal**:
everlasting 3 **between pole and tropic**: Eliot's first draft, 'between
cold and heat', points to the meaning here

If at all. Either you had no purpose
Or the purpose is beyond the end you figured   34
And is altered in fulfilment. There are other places
Which also are the world's end, some at the sea jaws,
Or over a dark lake, in a desert or a city –
But this is the nearest, in place and time,
Now and in England.

              If you came this way,
Taking any route, starting from anywhere,   40
At any time or at any season,
It would always be the same: you would have to put off
Sense and notion. You are not here to verify,
Instruct yourself, or inform curiosity
Or carry report. You are here to kneel   45
Where prayer has been valid. And prayer is more
Than an order of words, the conscious occupation
Of the praying mind, or the sound of the voice
      praying.
And what the dead had no speech for, when living,
They can tell you, being dead: the communication
Of the dead is tongued with fire beyond the language
      of the living.   51
Here, the intersection of the timeless moment
Is England and nowhere. Never and always.

              II
Ash on an old man's sleeve
Is all the ash the burnt roses leave.   55
Dust in the air suspended
Marks the place where a story ended.
Dust inbreathed was a house –
The wall, the wainscot and the mouse.
The death of hope and despair,   60
      This is the death of air.

There are flood and drouth
Over the eyes and in the mouth,
Dead water and dead sand
Contending for the upper hand.   65
The parched eviscerate soil
Gapes at the vanity of toil,
Laughs without mirth.
      This is the death of earth.

Water and fire succeed   70
The town, the pasture and the weed.
Water and fire deride
The sacrifice that we denied.
Water and fire shall rot
The marred foundations we forgot,   75
Of sanctuary and choir.
      This is the death of water and fire.

62 **drouth:** drought 66 **eviscerate:** literally disembowelled

In the uncertain hour before the morning
   Near the ending of interminable night
   At the recurrent end of the unending   80
After the dark dove with the flickering tongue
   Had passed below the horizon of his homing
   While the dead leaves still rattled on like tin
Over the asphalt where no other sound was   84
   Between three districts whence the smoke arose
   I met one walking, loitering and hurried
As if blown towards me like the metal leaves
   Before the urban dawn wind unresisting.
   And as I fixed upon the down-turned face
That pointed scrutiny with which we challenge   90
   The first-met stranger in the waning dusk
   I caught the sudden look of some dead master
Whom I had known, forgotten, half recalled
   Both one and many; in the brown baked features
The eyes of a familiar compound ghost   95
   Both intimate and unidentifiable.
   So I assumed a double part, and cried
   And heard another's voice cry: 'What! are *you* here?'
Although we were not. I was still the same,
   Knowing myself yet being someone other –   100
   And he a face still forming; yet the words sufficed
To compel the recognition they preceded.
   And so, compliant to the common wind,
   Too strange to each other for misunderstanding,
In concord at this intersection time   105
   Of meeting nowhere, no before and after,
   We trod the pavement in a dead patrol.
I said: 'The wonder that I feel is easy,
   Yet ease is cause of wonder. Therefore speak:
   I may not comprehend, may not remember.'   110
And he: 'I am not eager to rehearse
   My thoughts and theory which you have forgotten.
   These things have served their purpose: let them be.
So with your own, and pray they be forgiven
   By others, as I pray you to forgive   115
   Both bad and good. Last season's fruit is eaten
And the fullfed beast shall kick the empty pail.
   For last year's words belong to last year's language
   And next year's words await another voice.
But, as the passage now presents no hindrance   120
   To the spirit unappeased and peregrine
   Between two worlds become much like each other,
So I find words I never thought to speak
   In streets I never thought I should revisit
   When I left my body on a distant shore.   125

81 **the dark dove with the flickering tongue:** (also line 203)
blending the image of the dove as a symbol of the holy ghost with
that of the VI flying bombs that the Nazis began to launch against
southern England in 1944; when the fuel was exhausted, the engine
cut out, and the bomb fell to earth, bringing sudden indiscriminate
death and destruction 95-6 **a familiar compound ghost Both
intimate and unidentifiable:** these lines seem to defy any attempt
to identify the figure precisely 121 **peregrine:** on a pilgrimage

Since our concern was speech, and speech impelled us
   To purify the dialect of the tribe
   And urge the mind to aftersight and foresight,
Let me disclose the gifts reserved for age
   To set a crown upon your lifetime's effort.   130
   First, the cold friction of expiring sense
Without enchantment, offering no promise
   But bitter tastelessness of shadow fruit
   As body and soul begin to fall asunder.
Second, the conscious impotence of rage   135
   At human folly, and the laceration
   Of laughter at what ceases to amuse.
And last, the rending pain of re-enactment
   Of all that you have done, and been; the shame
   Of motives late revealed, and the awareness   140
   Of things ill done and done to others' harm
   Which once you took for exercise of virtue.
   Then fools' approval stings, and honour stains.
From wrong to wrong the exasperated spirit
   Proceeds, unless restored by that refining fire   145
   Where you must move in measure, like a dancer.'
The day was breaking. In the disfigured street
   He left me, with a kind of valediction,
   And faded on the blowing of the horn.

III

There are three conditions which often look alike   150
Yet differ completely, flourish in the same hedgerow:
Attachment to self and to things and to persons,
   detachment
From self and from things and from persons; and,
   growing between them, indifference
Which resembles the others as death resembles life,
Being between two lives – unflowering, between   155
The live and the dead nettle. This is the use of
   memory:
For liberation – not less of love but expanding
Of love beyond desire, and so liberation
From the future as well as the past. Thus, love of a
   country
Begins as attachment to our own field of action   160
And comes to find that action of little importance
Though never indifferent. History may be servitude,
History may be freedom. See, now they vanish,
The faces and places, with the self which, as it could,
   loved them,
To become renewed, transfigured, in another pattern.

Sin is Behovely, but   166
All shall be well, and
All manner of thing shall be well.
If I think, again, of this place,
And of people, not wholly commendable,   170
Of no immediate kin or kindness,
But some of peculiar genius,
All touched by a common genius,
United in the strife which divided them;
If I think of a king at nightfall,   175
Of three men, and more, on the scaffold
And a few who died forgotten
In other places, here and abroad,
And of one who died blind and quiet,
Why should we celebrate   180
These dead men more than the dying?
It is not to ring the bell backward
Nor is it an incantation
To summon the spectre of a Rose.
We cannot revive old factions   185
We cannot restore old policies
Or follow an antique drum.
These men, and those who opposed them
And those whom they opposed
Accept the constitution of silence   190
And are folded in a single party.
Whatever we inherit from the fortunate
We have taken from the defeated
What they had to leave us – a symbol:
A symbol perfected in death.   195
And all shall be well and
All manner of thing shall be well
By the purification of the motive
In the ground of our beseeching.

IV

The dove descending breaks the air   200
With flame of incandescent terror
Of which the tongues declare
The one discharge from sin and error.
The only hope, or else despair
   Lies in the choice of pyre or pyre –   205
   To be redeemed from fire by fire.

Who then devised the torment? Love.
Love is the unfamiliar Name
Behind the hands that wove
The intolerable shirt of flame   210
Which human power cannot remove.
   We only live, only suspire
   Consumed by either fire or fire.

---

127 **To purify the dialect of the tribe**: 'Donner un sens plus pur aux mots de la tribu' (Stéphane Mallarmé, 'Le Tombeau de Edgar Poe', line 6)   149 **And faded on the blowing of the horn**: an echo of both 'It faded on the crowing of the cock' and 'The cock, that is the trumpet to the morn' (*Hamlet* 1.1); the 'horn' here is the All Clear siren indicating that the danger from an air raid has passed

166–8 **Sin is Behovely . . . shall be well**: from *The Sixteen Revelations of Divine Love* of Julian of Norwich (*c*.1342–*c*.1416) 179 **one who died blind and quiet**: John Milton 182 **ring the bell backward**: ring the bells beginning with the bass bell, to give warning of fire or invasion

V

What we call the beginning is often the end
And to make an end is to make a beginning. 215
The end is where we start from. And every phrase
And sentence that is right (where every word is at
    home,
Taking its place to support the others,
The word neither diffident nor ostentatious,
An easy commerce of the old and the new, 220
The common word exact without vulgarity,
The formal word precise but not pedantic,
The complete consort dancing together)
Every phrase and every sentence is an end and a
    beginning,
Every poem an epitaph. And any action 225
Is a step to the block, to the fire, down the sea's throat
Or to an illegible stone: and that is where we start.
We die with the dying:
See, they depart, and we go with them.
We are born with the dead: 230
See, they return, and bring us with them.
The moment of the rose and the moment of the
    yew-tree
Are of equal duration. A people without history
Is not redeemed from time, for history is a pattern
Of timeless moments. So, while the light fails 235
On a winter's afternoon, in a secluded chapel
History is now and England.

With the drawing of this Love and the voice of this
    Calling

We shall not cease from exploration
And the end of all our exploring 240
Will be to arrive where we started
And know the place for the first time.
Through the unknown, remembered gate
When the last of earth left to discover
Is that which was the beginning; 245
At the source of the longest river
The voice of the hidden waterfall
And the children in the apple-tree
Not known, because not looked for
But heard, half-heard, in the stillness 250
Between two waves of the sea.
Quick now, here, now, always –
A condition of complete simplicity
(Costing not less than everything)
And all shall be well and 255
All manner of thing shall be well
When the tongues of flame are in-folded
Into the crowned knot of fire
And the fire and the rose are one.

226 **a step to the block**: the fate of Charles I (lines 26 and 175)
238 **With the drawing . . . Calling**: from *The Cloud of Unknowing*
(14th century)

JULIAN GRENFELL

INTO BATTLE
(FLANDERS, APRIL 1915)

THE naked earth is warm with Spring,
    And with green grass and bursting trees
Leans to the sun's gaze glorying,
    And quivers in the sunny breeze;
And life is colour and warmth and light, 5
    And a striving evermore for these;
And he is dead who will not fight;
    And who dies fighting has increase.

The fighting man shall from the sun
    Take warmth, and life from the glowing earth; 10
Speed with the light-foot winds to run,
    And with the trees to newer birth;
And find, when fighting shall be done,
    Great rest, and fullness after dearth.

All the bright company of Heaven 15
    Hold him in their high comradeship,
The Dog-Star, and the Sisters Seven,
    Orion's Belt and sworded hip.

The woodland trees that stand together,
    They stand to him each one a friend; 20
They gently speak in the windy weather;
    They guide to valley and ridge's end.

The kestrel hovering by day,
    And the little owls that call by night,
Bid him be swift and keen as they, 25
    As keen of ear, as swift of sight.

The blackbird sings to him, 'Brother, brother,
    If this be the last song you shall sing,
Sing well, for you may not sing another;
    Brother, sing.' 30

In dreary, doubtful waiting hours,
    Before the brazen frenzy starts,
The horses show him nobler powers;
    O patient eyes, courageous hearts!

And when the burning moment breaks, 35
    And all things else are out of mind,
And only joy of battle takes
    Him by the throat, and makes him blind,

Through joy and blindness he shall know,
    Not caring much to know, that still 40
Nor lead nor steel shall reach him, so
    That it be not the Destined Will.

The thundering line of battle stands,
    And in the air Death moans and sings;
But Day shall clasp him with strong hands, 45
    And Night shall fold him in soft wings.

INTO BATTLE: 17 **Dog-Star:** Sirius, the brightest star **Sisters Seven:** the Pleiades, seven stars in the constellation Taurus 18 **Orion's Belt and sworded hip:** the constellation Orion is pictured as a hunter with a belt and a sword 32 **the brazen frenzy:** i.e. the artillery bombardment that preceded an advance by the infantry

ISAAC ROSENBERG

BREAK OF DAY IN THE TRENCHES

THE darkness crumbles away –
It is the same old druid Time as ever.
Only a live thing leaps my hand –
A queer sardonic rat –
As I pull the parapet's poppy   5
To stick behind my ear.
Droll rat, they would shoot you if they knew
Your cosmopolitan sympathies.
Now you have touched this English hand
You will do the same to a German –   10
Soon, no doubt, if it be your pleasure
To cross the sleeping green between.
It seems you inwardly grin as you pass
Strong eyes, fine limbs, haughty athletes
Less chanced than you for life,   15
Bonds to the whims of murder,
Sprawled in the bowels of the earth,
The torn fields of France.
What do you see in our eyes
At the shrieking iron and flame   20
Hurled through still heavens?
What quaver – what heart aghast?
Poppies whose roots are in man's veins
Drop, and are ever dropping;
But mine in my ear is safe,   25
Just a little white with the dust.

BREAK OF DAY IN THE TRENCHES: 15 **Less chanced than you for life:** With less chance than you of staying alive

LOUSE HUNTING

NUDES – stark and glistening,
Yelling in lurid glee. Grinning faces
And raging limbs
Whirl over the floor one fire;
For a shirt verminously busy   5
Yon soldier tore from his throat with oaths
Godhead might shrink at, but not the lice,
And soon the shirt was aflare
Over the candle he'd lit while we lay.

Then we all sprang up and stript   10
To hunt the verminous brood.
Soon like a demons' pantomime
This plunge was raging.
See the silhouettes agape,
See the gibbering shadows   15

Mixed with the baffled arms on the wall.
See gargantuan hooked fingers
Pluck in supreme flesh
To smutch supreme littleness.
See the merry limbs in hot Highland fling   20
Because some wizard vermin
Charmed from the quiet this revel
When our ears were half lulled
By the dark music
Blown from Sleep's trumpet.   25

LOUSE HUNTING: 19 **smutch:** smudge 20 **fling:** lively Scottish dance

RETURNING, WE HEAR THE LARKS

SOMBRE the night is.
And though we have our lives, we know
What sinister threat lurks there.

Dragging these anguished limbs, we only know
This poison-blasted track opens on our camp –   5
On a little safe sleep.

But hark! joy – joy – strange joy.
Lo! heights of night ringing with unseen larks.
Music showering on our upturned list'ning faces.

Death could drop from the dark   10
As easily as song –
But song only dropped,
Like a blind man's dreams on the sand
By dangerous tides,
Like a girl's dark hair for she dreams no ruin lies
       there,   15
Or her kisses where a serpent hides.

DEAD MAN'S DUMP

THE plunging limbers over the shattered track
Racketed with their rusty freight,
Stuck out like many crowns of thorns,
And the rusty stakes like sceptres old
To stay the flood of brutish men   5
Upon our brothers dear.

The wheels lurched over sprawled dead
But pained them not, though their bones crunched,
Their shut mouths made no moan.
They lie there huddled, friend and foeman,   10
Man born of man, and born of woman,
And shells go crying over them
From night till night and now.

DEAD MAN'S DUMP: **dump:** a slow, melancholy dance-tune: 1 **limbers:** the limber is the detachable shaft of a gun-carriage, here drawn by mules (line 79)

Earth has waited for them,
All the time of their growth 15
Fretting for their decay:
Now she has them at last!
In the strength of their strength
Suspended – stopped and held.

What fierce imaginings their dark souls lit? 20
Earth! have they gone into you!
Somewhere they must have gone,
And flung on your hard back
Is their soul's sack
Emptied of God-ancestralled essences. 25
Who hurled them out? Who hurled?

None saw their spirits' shadow shake the grass,
Or stood aside for the half used life to pass
Out of those doomed nostrils and the doomed mouth,
When the swift iron burning bee 30
Drained the wild honey of their youth.

What of us who, flung on the shrieking pyre,
Walk, our usual thoughts untouched,
Our lucky limbs as on ichor fed,
Immortal seeming ever? 35
Perhaps when the flames beat loud on us,
A fear may choke in our veins
And the startled blood may stop.

The air is loud with death,
The dark air spurts with fire, 40
The explosions ceaseless are.
Timelessly now, some minutes past,
These dead strode time with vigorous life,
Till the shrapnel called 'An end!'
But not to all. In bleeding pangs 45
Some borne on stretchers dreamed of home,
Dear things, war-blotted from their hearts.

Maniac Earth! howling and flying, your bowel
Seared by the jagged fire, the iron love,
The impetuous storm of savage love. 50
Dark Earth! dark Heavens! swinging in chemic smoke,
What dead are born when you kiss each soundless soul
With lightning and thunder from your mined heart,
Which man's self dug, and his blind fingers loosed?

A man's brains splattered on 55
A stretcher-bearer's face;
His shook shoulders slipped their load,
But when they bent to look again
The drowning soul was sunk too deep
For human tenderness. 60

They left this dead with the older dead,
Stretched at the cross roads.
Burnt black by strange decay
Their sinister faces lie,
The lid over each eye, 65
The grass and coloured clay
More motion have than they,
Joined to the great sunk silences.

Here is one not long dead;
His dark hearing caught our far wheels, 70
And the choked soul stretched weak hands
To reach the living word the far wheels said,
The blood-dazed intelligence beating for light,
Crying through the suspense of the far torturing
    wheels
Swift for the end to break 75
Or the wheels to break,
Cried as the tide of the world broke over his sight.

Will they come? Will they ever come?
Even as the mixed hoofs of the mules,
The quivering-bellied mules, 80
And the rushing wheels all mixed
With his tortured upturned sight.
So we crashed round the bend,
We heard his weak scream,
We heard his very last sound, 85
And our wheels grazed his dead face.

IVOR GURNEY

THE SILENT ONE

WHO died on the wires, and hung there, one of two –
Who for his hours of life had chattered through
Infinite lovely chatter of Bucks accent:
Yet faced unbroken wires; stepped over, and went
A noble fool, faithful to his stripes – and ended. 5
But I weak, hungry, and willing only for the chance
Of line – to fight in the line, lay down under unbroken
Wires, and saw the flashes and kept unshaken,
Till the politest voice – a finicking accent, said:
'Do you think you might crawl through, there: there's
    a hole' 10
Darkness, shot at: I smiled, as politely replied –
'I'm afraid not, Sir.' There was no hole, no way to be
    seen,
Nothing but chance of death, after tearing of clothes
Kept flat, and watched the darkness, hearing bullets
    whizzing –
And thought of music – and swore deep heart's deep
    oaths 15
(Polite to God) and retreated and came on again,
Again retreated – and a second time faced the screen.

---

34 **ichor:** the liquid that flows in the veins of the gods 51 **chemic:** chemical

THE SILENT ONE: 1 **the wires:** barbed-wire defences 9 **finicking:** foppish, affected

THE BOHEMIANS

CERTAIN people would not clean their buttons,
Nor polish buckles after latest fashions,
Preferred their hair long, putties comfortable,
Barely escaping hanging, indeed hardly able,
In Bridge and smoking without army cautions   5
Spending hours that sped like evil for quickness,
(While others burnished brasses, earned promotions).
These were those ones who jested in the trench,
While others argued of army ways, and wrenched
What little soul they had still further from shape,   10
And died off one by one, or became officers
Without the first of dream, the ghost of notions
Of ever becoming soldiers, or smart and neat,
Surprised as ever to find the army capable
Of sounding 'Lights out' to break a game of Bridge,
As to fear candles would set a barn alight.   16
In Artois or Picardy they lie – free of useless fashions.

THE BOHEMIANS: **bohemians:** those who set aside social conventions
3 **putties:** leggings made from a cloth strip wound round the leg
from ankle to knee

HUGH MACDIARMID

THE FEMININE PRINCIPLE

I AM like Burns, and ony wench
Can ser' me for a time.
Licht's in them a' – in some a sun,
In some the merest skime.

I'm no' like Burns, and weel I ken,   5
Tho' ony wench can ser',
It's no' through mony but through yin
That ony man wuns fer. . . .

I wedded thee frae fause love, lass,
To free thee and to free mysel';   10
But man and wumman tied for life
True can be and truth can tell.

Pit ony couple in a knot
They canna lowse and needna try,
And mair o' love at last they'll ken   15
– If ocht! – than joy'll alane descry.

For them as for the beasts, my wife,
A's fer frae dune when pleasure's owre,
And coontless difficulties gar
Ilk hert discover a' its power.   20

I dinna say that bairns alane
Are true love's task – a sairer task
Is aiblins to create oorsels
As we can be – it's that I ask.

Create oorsels, syne bairns, syne race.   25
Sae on the cod I see't in you
Wi' Maidenkirk to John o' Groats
The bosom that you draw me to.

And nae Scot wi' a wumman lies,
But I am he and ken as 'twere   30
A stage I've passed as he maun pass't,
Gin he grows up, his way wi' her! . . .

A'thing wi' which a man
Can intromit's a wumman,
And can, and s'ud, become   35
As intimate and human.

And Jean's nae mair my wife
Than whisky is at times,
Or munelicht or a thistle
Or kittle thochts or rhymes.   40

He's no' a man ava',
And lacks a proper pride,
Gin less than a' the warld
Can ser' him for a bride!

THE FEMININE PRINCIPLE: 1 **ony:** any 2 **ser':** serve 3 **licht:** light **a':** all
4 **skime:** gleam 5 **no':** not **ken:** know 7 **mony:** many **yin:** one
8 **wuns fer:** gets far 9 **frae:** from **fause:** false 13 **Pit:** put 14 **lowse:**
loose 16 **ocht:** aught **alane:** alone 18 **frae:** from **dune:** done **owre:**
over 19 **gar:** cause 20 **Ilk:** each 22 **sairer:** tougher, more demanding
23 **aiblins:** perhaps **oorsels:** ourselves 25 **syne:** then 26 **Sae:** so **cod:**
pillow 31 **maun:** must 32 **Gin:** by the time 33 **A'thing:** anything
34 **intromit:** enter 35 **s'ud:** should 39 **munelicht:** moonlight
40 **kittle thochts:** ticklish thoughts 41 **ava':** at all 43 **Gin:** when

MY QUARREL WITH ENGLAND

AND let me pit in guid set terms
My quarrel wi' th'owre sonsy rose,
That roond about its devotees
A fair fat cast o' aureole throws
That blinds them, in its mirlygoes,   5
To the necessity o' foes.

Upon their King and system I
Glower as on things that whiles in pairt
I may admire (at least for them),
But wi' nae claim upon my hert,   10
While a' their pleasure and their pride
Ootside me lies – and there maun bide.

Ootside me lies – and mair than that,
For I stand still for forces which
Were subjugated to mak' way   15
For England's poo'er, and to enrich
The kinds o' English, and o' Scots,
The least congenial to my thoughts.

Hauf his soul a Scot maun use
Indulgin' in illusions,   20
And hauf in gettin' rid o' them
And comin' to conclusions
Wi' the demoralisin' dearth
O' onything worth while on Earth. . . .

MY QUARREL, WITH ENGLAND: MacDiarmid was a founding member
of the National Party of Scotland (later Scottish National Party):
1 **pit**: put **guid**: good 2 **th'owre sonsy**: the over-comely 5 **mirlygoes**:
dazzle 10 **wi' nae**: with no 11 **a'**: all 12 **maun**: must 13 **mair**: more
16 **poo'er**: power 19 **Hauf**: half 24 **onything**: anything

WILFRED OWEN

STRANGE MEETING

IT seemed that out of battle I escaped
Down some profound dull tunnel, long since scooped
Through granites which titanic wars had groined.
Yet also there encumbered sleepers groaned,
Too fast in thought or death to be bestirred.   5
Then, as I probed them, one sprang up, and stared
With piteous recognition in fixed eyes,
Lifting distressful hands as if to bless.
And by his smile, I knew that sullen hall,
By his dead smile I knew we stood in Hell.   10
With a thousand pains that vision's face was grained;
Yet no blood reached there from the upper ground,
And no guns thumped, or down the flues made
    moan.
'Strange friend,' I said, 'here is no cause to mourn.'
'None,' said the other, 'save the undone years,   15
The hopelessness. Whatever hope is yours,
Was my life also; I went hunting wild
After the wildest beauty in the world,
Which lies not calm in eyes, or braided hair,
But mocks the steady running of the hour,   20
And if it grieves, grieves richlier than here.
For of my glee might many men have laughed,
And of my weeping something had been left,
Which must die now. I mean the truth untold,
The pity of war, the pity war distilled.   25
Now men will go content with what we spoiled,
Or, discontent, boil bloody, and be spilled.
They will be swift with swiftness of the tigress.
None will break ranks, though nations trek from
    progress.
Courage was mine, and I had mystery,   30
Wisdom was mine, and I had mastery:
To miss the march of this retreating world
Into vain citadels that are not walled.
Then, when much blood had clogged their chariot-
    wheels,
I would go up and wash them from sweet wells,   35
Even with truths that lie too deep for taint.

I would have poured my spirit without stint
But not through wounds; not on the cess of war.
Foreheads of men have bled where no wounds were.
I am the enemy you killed, my friend.   40
I knew you in this dark: for so you frowned
Yesterday through me as you jabbed and killed.
I parried; but my hands were loath and cold.
Let us sleep now. . . .'

STRANGE MEETING: 3 **titanic**: the Titans were the race of gods
produced by the union of Uranus (Heaven) and Gaia (Earth)
groined: gouged 13 **flues**: chimneys 25 **The pity . . . distilled**:
'My subject is War, and the pity of War. The Poetry is in the pity'
(Owen's preface to his poems) 38 **cess**: mud, filth

ARMS AND THE BOY

LET the boy try along this bayonet-blade
How cold steel is, and keen with hunger of blood;
Blue with all malice, like a madman's flash;
And thinly drawn with famishing for flesh.

Lend him to stroke these blind, blunt bullet-leads   5
Which long to nuzzle in the hearts of lads,
Or give him cartridges of fine zinc teeth,
Sharp with the sharpness of grief and death.

For his teeth seem for laughing round an apple.
There lurk no claws behind his fingers supple;   10
And God will grow no talons at his heels,
Nor antlers through the thickness of his curls.

ARMS AND THE BOY: the title echoes the opening line of Virgil's
Aeneid translated by John Dryden: 'Arms and the man I sing'

ANTHEM FOR DOOMED YOUTH

WHAT passing-bells for these who die as cattle?
    Only the monstrous anger of the guns.
    Only the stuttering rifles' rapid rattle
Can patter out their hasty orisons.
No mockeries now for them; no prayers nor bells,   5
    Nor any voice of mourning save the choirs, –
The shrill, demented choirs of wailing shells;
    And bugles calling for them from sad shires.

What candles may be held to speed them all?
    Not in the hands of boys, but in their eyes   10
Shall shine the holy glimmers of good-byes.
    The pallor of girls' brows shall be their pall;
Their flowers the tenderness of patient minds,
And each slow dusk a drawing-down of blinds.

ANTHEM FOR DOOMED YOUTH: 1 **passing-bells**: funeral bells 4 **orisons**:
prayers 12 **pall**: cloth spread over a coffin

DULCE ET DECORUM EST

BENT double, like old beggars under sacks,
Knock-kneed, coughing like hags, we cursed through
   sludge,
Till on the haunting flares we turned our backs
And towards our distant rest began to trudge.
Men marched asleep. Many had lost their boots   5
But limped on, blood-shod. All went lame; all blind;
Drunk with fatigue; deaf even to the hoots
Of tired, outstripped Five-Nines that dropped behind.

Gas! GAS! Quick, boys! – An ecstasy of fumbling,
Fitting the clumsy helmets just in time;   10
But someone still was yelling out and stumbling
And flound'ring like a man in fire or lime . . .
Dim, through the misty panes and thick green light,
As under a green sea, I saw him drowning.

In all my dreams, before my helpless sight,   15
He plunges at me, guttering, choking, drowning.

If in some smothering dreams you too could pace
Behind the wagon that we flung him in,
And watch the white eyes writhing in his face,
His hanging face, like a devil's sick of sin;   20
If you could hear, at every jolt, the blood
Come gargling from the froth-corrupted lungs,
Obscene as cancer, bitter as the cud
Of vile, incurable sores on innocent tongues, –
My friend, you would not tell with such high zest   25
To children ardent for some desperate glory,
The old Lie: Dulce et decorum est
Pro patria mori.

DULCE ET DECORUM EST: 8 **Five-Nines:** a size of artillery shell 13 **the misty panes:** i.e. the goggles of a gas-mask 27–8 **Dulce et decorum . . . mori:** 'It is sweet and becoming to die for one's country' (Horace, *Odes* 3.2.13)

FUTILITY

MOVE him into the sun –
Gently its touch awoke him once,
At home, whispering of fields unsown.
Always it woke him, even in France,
Until this morning and this snow.   5
If anything might rouse him now
The kind old sun will know.

Think how it wakes the seeds, –
Woke, once, the clays of a cold star.
Are limbs, so dear-achieved, are sides,   10
Full-nerved – still warm – too hard to stir?
Was it for this the clay grew tall?
– O what made fatuous sunbeams toil
To break earth's sleep at all?

SOLDIER'S DREAM

I DREAMED kind Jesus fouled the big-gun gears;
And caused a permanent stoppage in all bolts;
And buckled with a smile Mausers and Colts;
And rusted every bayonet with His tears.

And there were no more bombs, of ours or Theirs,   5
Not even an old flint-lock, nor even a pikel.
But God was vexed, and gave all power to Michael;
And when I woke he'd seen to our repairs.

SOLDIER'S DREAM: 3 **Mausers and Colts:** types of handgun 6 **flint-lock:** an early type of gun, fired by the spark from a flint **pikel:** pitchfork 7 **Michael:** see note to Wolfe's 'The Soldier'

THE NEXT WAR

> War's a joke for me and you,
> While we know such dreams are true!
> SIEGFRIED SASSOON

OUT there, we've walked quite friendly up to Death;
   Sat down and eaten with him, cool and bland, –
   Pardoned his spilling mess-tins in our hand.
We've sniffed the green thick odour of his breath, –
Our eyes wept, but our courage didn't writhe.   5
   He's spat at us with bullets and he's coughed
   Shrapnel. We chorussed when he sang aloft;
We whistled while he shaved us with his scythe.

Oh, Death was never enemy of ours!
   We laughed at him, we leagued with him, old chum.
No soldier's paid to kick against his powers.   11
   We laughed, knowing that better men would come,
And greater wars; when each proud fighter brags
He wars on Death – for lives; not men – for flags.

THE NEXT WAR: epigraph from Sassoon's 'A Letter Home': 3 **mess-tins:** a mess-tin is a soldier's all-purpose utensil serving as plate, cup and cooking vessel 4 **green . . . breath:** i.e. gas 8 **his scythe:** Death and Time are pictured with a scythe with which to cut down man

CHARLES HAMILTON SORLEY

'ALL THE HILLS AND VALES ALONG'

ALL the hills and vales along
Earth is bursting into song,
And the singers are the chaps
Who are going to die perhaps.
   O sing, marching men,   5
   Till the valleys ring again.
   Give your gladness to earth's keeping,
   So be glad, when you are sleeping.

Cast away regret and rue,
Think what you are marching to.   10
Little live, great pass.
Jesus Christ and Barabbas
Were found the same day.
This died, that went his way.
　　So sing with joyful breath,   15
　　For why, you are going to death.
　　Teeming earth will surely store
　　All the gladness that you pour.

Earth that never doubts nor fears,
Earth that knows of death, not tears,   20
Earth that bore with joyful ease
Hemlock for Socrates,
Earth that blossomed and was glad
'Neath the cross that Christ had,
Shall rejoice and blossom too   25
When the bullet reaches you.
　　Wherefore, men marching
　　On the road to death, sing!
　　Pour your gladness on earth's head,
　　So be merry, so be dead.   30

From the hills and valleys earth
Shouts back the sound of mirth,
Tramp of feet and lilt of song
Ringing all the road along.
All the music of their going,   35
Ringing swinging glad song-throwing,
Earth will echo still, when foot
Lies numb and voice mute.
　　On, marching men, on
　　To the gates of death with song.   40
　　Sow your gladness for earth's reaping,
　　So you may be glad, though sleeping.
　　Strew your gladness on earth's bed,
　　So be merry, so be dead.

'ALL THE HILLS AND VALES ALONG': 12 **Barabbas:** the thief chosen by
the mob to be spared instead of Jesus 22 **Hemlock for Socrates:**
the poison obtained from the hemlock plant was used in ancient
Greece as a means of execution; in 399 BC, Socrates was found
guilty of introducing new gods and of corrupting the youth of
Athens, and was ordered to drink hemlock

'WHEN YOU SEE MILLIONS OF THE MOUTHLESS DEAD'

WHEN you see millions of the mouthless dead
Across your dreams in pale battalions go,
Say not soft things as other men have said,
That you'll remember. For you need not so.
Give them not praise. For, deaf, how should they know
It is not curses heaped on each gashed head?   6
Nor tears. Their blind eyes see not your tears flow.
Nor honour. It is easy to be dead.
Say only this, 'They are dead.' Then add thereto,
'Yet many a better one has died before.'   10

Then, scanning all the o'ercrowded mass, should you
Perceive one face that you loved heretofore,
It is a spook. None wears the face you knew.
Great death has made all his for evermore.

ROBERT GRAVES

FULL MOON

As I walked out that sultry night,
　I heard the stroke of one.
The moon, attained to her full height,
　Stood beaming like the sun:
She exorcized the ghostly wheat   5
To mute assent in love's defeat,
　Whose tryst had now begun.

The fields lay sick beneath my tread,
　A tedious owlet cried,
A nightingale above my head   10
　With this or that replied –
Like man and wife who nightly keep
Inconsequent debate in sleep
　As they dream side by side.

Your phantom wore the moon's cold mask,   15
　My phantom wore the same;
Forgetful of the feverish task
　In hope of which they came,
Each image held the other's eyes
And watched a grey distraction rise   20
　To cloud the eager flame –

To cloud the eager flame of love,
　To fog the shining gate;
They held the tyrannous queen above
　Sole mover of their fate,   25
They glared as marble statues glare
Across the tessellated stair
　Or down the halls of state.

And now warm earth was Arctic sea,
　Each breath came dagger-keen;   30
Two bergs of glinting ice were we,
　The broad moon sailed between;
There swam the mermaids, tailed and finned,
And love went by upon the wind
　As though it had not been.   35

FULL MOON: 27 **tessellated:** mosaic

WELSH INCIDENT

'BUT that was nothing to what things came out
From the sea-caves of Criccieth yonder.'
'What were they? Mermaids? dragons? ghosts?'
'Nothing at all of any things like that.'
'What were they, then?'

'All sorts of queer things,   5
Things never seen or heard or written about,
Very strange, un-Welsh, utterly peculiar
Things. Oh, solid enough they seemed to touch,
Had anyone dared it. Marvellous creation,
All various shapes and sizes, and no sizes,   10
All new, each perfectly unlike his neighbour,
Though all came moving slowly out together.'
'Describe just one of them.'
                                    'I am unable.'
'What were their colours?'
                                    'Mostly nameless colours,
Colours you'd like to see; but one was puce   15
Or perhaps more like crimson, but not purplish.
Some had no colour.'
                                    'Tell me, had they legs?'
'Not a leg nor foot among them that I saw.'
'But did these things come out in any order?   19
What o'clock was it? What was the day of the week?
Who else was present? How was the weather?'
'I was coming to that. It was half-past three
On Easter Tuesday last. The sun was shining.
The Harlech Silver Band played *Marchog Jesu*
On thirty-seven shimmering instruments,   25
Collecting for Carnarvon's (Fever) Hospital Fund.
The populations of Pwllheli, Criccieth,
Portmadoc, Borth, Tremadoc, Penrhyndeudraeth,
Were all assembled. Criccieth's mayor addressed them
First in good Welsh and then in fluent English,   30
Twisting his fingers in his chain of office,
Welcoming the things. They came out on the sand,
Not keeping time to the band, moving seaward
Silently at a snail's pace. But at last
The most odd, indescribable thing of all,   35
Which hardly one man there could see for wonder
Did something recognizably a something.'
'Well, what?'
                                    'It made a noise.'
                                    'A frightening noise?'
'No, no.'
                                    'A musical noise? A noise of scuffling?'
'No, but a very loud, respectable noise –   40
Like groaning to oneself on Sunday morning
In Chapel, close before the second psalm.'
'What did the mayor do?'
                                    'I was coming to that.'

SHE TELLS HER LOVE WHILE HALF ASLEEP

SHE tells her love while half asleep,
   In the dark hours,
      With half-words whispered low:
As Earth stirs in her winter sleep
   And puts out grass and flowers   5
      Despite the snow,
      Despite the falling snow.

TO JUAN AT THE WINTER SOLSTICE

THERE is one story and one story only
That will prove worth your telling,
Whether as learned bard or gifted child;
To it all lines or lesser gauds belong
That startle with their shining   5
Such common stories as they stray into.

Is it of trees you tell, their months and virtues,
Or strange beasts that beset you,
Of birds that croak at you the Triple will?
Or of the Zodiac and how slow it turns   10
Below the Boreal Crown,
Prison of all true kings that ever reigned?

Water to water, ark again to ark,
From woman back to woman:
So each new victim treads unfalteringly   15
The never altered circuit of his fate,
Bringing twelve peers as witness
Both to his starry rise and starry fall.

Or is it of the Virgin's silvery beauty,
All fish below the thighs?   20
She in her left hand bears a leafy quince;
When, with her right she crooks a finger, smiling,
How may the King hold back?
Royally then he barters life for love.

Or of the undying snake from chaos hatched,   25
Whose coils contain the ocean,
Into whose chops with naked sword he springs,
Then in black water, tangled by the reeds,
Battles three days and nights,
To be spewed up beside her scalloped shore?   30

Much snow is falling, winds roar hollowly,
The owl hoots from the elder,
Fear in your heart cries to the loving-cup:
Sorrow to sorrow as the sparks fly upward.
The log groans and confesses: 35
There is one story and one story only.

Dwell on her graciousness, dwell on her smiling,
Do not forget what flowers
The great boar trampled down in ivy time.
Her brow was creamy as the crested wave,   40
Her sea-blue eyes were wild
But nothing promised that is not performed.

TO JUAN AT THE WINTER SOLSTICE: **Juan:** the poet's son, born in 1944
winter solstice: around 22 December, one of the two times in the
year when the sun reaches its greatest distance from the equator
4 **gauds:** beads 9 **Triple will:** the will of the goddess of underworld,
earth and sky

A SLICE OF WEDDING CAKE

WHY have such scores of lovely, gifted girls
   Married impossible men?
Simple, self-sacrifice may be ruled out,
   And missionary endeavour, nine times out of
     ten.

Repeat 'impossible men': not merely rustic   5
   Foul-tempered or depraved
(Dramatic foils chosen to show the world
   How well women behave, and always have
     behaved).

Impossible men: idle, illiterate,
   Self-pitying, dirty, sly,   10
For whose appearance even in City parks
   Excuses must be made to casual passers-by.

Has God's supply of tolerable husbands
   Fallen, in fact, so low?
Or do I always over-value woman   15
   At the expense of man?
          Do I?
             It might be so.

EDMUND BLUNDEN

THE PIKE

FROM shadows of rich oaks outpeer
   The moss-green bastions of the weir,
   Where the quick dipper forages
     In elver-peopled crevices,
And a small runlet trickling down the sluice   5
Gossamer music tires not to unloose.

   Else round the broad pool's hush
     Nothing stirs,
Unless sometime a straggling heifer crush
Through the thronged spinney where the pheasant
     whirs;   10
   Or martins in a flash
Come with wild mirth to dip their magical wings,
While in the shallow some doomed bulrush swings
At whose hid root the diver vole's teeth gnash.

And nigh this toppling reed, still as the dead   15
   The great pike lies, the murderous patriarch
   Watching the waterpit sheer-shelving dark,
Where through the plash his lithe bright vassals
     thread.
   The rose-finned roach and bluish bream
   And staring ruffe steal up the stream   20
   Hard by their glutted tyrant, now
     Still as a sunken bough.

He on the sandbank lies,
   Sunning himself long hours
With stony gorgon eyes: 25
   Westward the hot sun lowers.
Sudden the gray pike changes, and, quivering, poises
     for slaughter;
   Intense terror wakens around him, the shoals scud
     awry, but there chances
A chub unsuspecting; the prowling fins quicken, in
     fury he lances;
And the miller that opens the hatch stands amazed at
     the whirl in the water.   30

THE PIKE: 6 **Gossamer:** spider-threads that float on the air or form webs on bushes 25 **gorgon:** in Greek mythology a woman with serpents on her head instead of hair; her glance turned victims to stone

FOREFATHERS

HERE they went with smock and crook,
   Toiled in the sun, lolled in the shade,
Here they mudded out the brook
   And here their hatchet cleared the glade:
Harvest-supper woke their wit,   5
Huntsman's moon their wooings lit.

From this church they led their brides,
   From this church themselves were led
Shoulder-high; on these waysides
   Sat to take their beer and bread.   10
Names are gone – what men they were
These their cottages declare.

Names are vanished, save the few
   In the old brown Bible scrawled;
These were men of pith and thew,   15
   Whom the city never called;
Scarce could read or hold a quill,
Built the barn, the forge, the mill.

On the green they watched their sons
   Playing till too dark to see,   20
As their fathers watched them once,
   As my father once watched me;
While the bat and beetle flew
On the warm air webbed with dew.

Unrecorded, unrenowned,   25
   Men from whom my ways begin,
Here I know you by your ground
   But I know you not within –
There is silence, there survives
Not a moment of your lives.   30

Like the bee that now is blown
  Honey-heavy on my hand,
From his toppling tansy-throne
  In the green tempestuous land –
I'm in clover now, nor know   35
Who made honey long ago.

FOREFATHERS: 6 **Huntsman's moon:** hunter's moon, the full moon after the harvest moon 33 **tansy:** aromatic herb

THE ZONNEBEKE ROAD

MORNING, if this late withered light can claim
Some kindred with that merry flame
Which the young day was wont to fling through space!
Agony stares from each gray face.
And yet the day is come; stand down! stand down!   5
Your hands unclasp from rifles while you can,
The frost has pierced them to the bended bone?
Why, see old Stevens there, that iron man,
Melting the ice to shave his grotesque chin:
Go ask him, shall we win?   10
I never liked this bay, some foolish fear
Caught me the first time that I came in here;
That dugout fallen in awakes, perhaps,
Some formless haunting of some corpse's chaps.
True, and wherever we have held the line,   15
There were such corners, seeming-saturnine
For no good cause.
                  Now where Haymarket starts,
That is no place for soldiers with weak hearts;
The minenwerfers have it to the inch.
Look, how the snow-dust whisks along the road,   20
Piteous and silly; the stones themselves must flinch
In this east wind; the low sky like a load
Hangs over – a dead-weight. But what a pain
Must gnaw where its clay cheek   24
Crushes the shell-chopped trees that fang the plain –
The ice-bound throat gulps out a gargoyle shriek.
That wretched wire before the village line
Rattles like rusty brambles or dead bine,
And there the daylight oozes into dun;
Black pillars, those are trees where roadways run.   30
Even Ypres now would warm our souls; fond fool,
Our tour's but one night old, seven more to cool!
O screaming dumbness, O dull clashing death,
Shreds of dead grass and willows, homes and men,
Watch as you will, men clench their chattering teeth   35
And freeze you back with that one hope, disdain.

THE ZONNEBEKE ROAD: 17 **Haymarket:** on the Western Front the soldiers gave individual sections of the network of trenches the names of fashionable London thoroughfares 19 **minenwerfers:** (German) minethrowers

REPORT ON EXPERIENCE

I HAVE been young, and now am not too old;
And I have seen the righteous forsaken,
His health, his honour and his quality taken.
  This is not what we were formerly told.

I have seen a green country, useful to the race,   5
Knocked silly with guns and mines, its villages
    vanished,
Even the last rat and last kestrel banished –
  God bless us all, this was peculiar grace.

I knew Seraphina; Nature gave her hue,
Glance, sympathy, note, like one from Eden.   10
I saw her smile warp, heard her lyric deaden;
  She turned to harlotry; – this I took to be new.

Say what you will, our God sees how they run.
These disillusions are His curious proving
That He loves humanity, and will go on loving;   15
  Over there are faith, life, virtue in the sun.

BASIL BUNTING

From BRIGGFLATTS

POET appointed dare not decline
to walk among the bogus, nothing to authenticate
the mission imposed, despised
by toadies, confidence men, kept boys,
shopped and jailed, cleaned out by whores,   5
touching acquaintance for food and tobacco.
Secret, solitary, a spy, he gauges
lines of a Flemish horse
hauling beer, the angle, obtuse,
a slut's blouse draws on her chest,   10
counts beat against beat, bus conductor
against engine against wheels against
the pedal, Tottenham Court Road, decodes
thunder, scans
porridge bubbling, pipes clanking, feels   15
Buddha's basalt cheek
but cannot name the ratio of its curves
to the half-pint
left breast of a girl who bared it in Kleinfeldt's.
He lies with one to long for another,   20
sick, self-maimed, self-hating,
obstinate, mating
beauty with squalor to beget lines still-born.

BRIGGFLATTS: Described by the poet as 'An autobiography, but not a record of facts', for 'The truth of the poem is of another kind'. 'No notes are needed,' he declares confidently; but readers may beg to differ – and even the poet relents sufficiently to provide a handful of whimsical (and thoroughly unhelpful) notes of his own

You who can calculate the course
of a biased bowl,   25
shall I come near the jack?
What twist can counter the force
that holds back
woods I roll?

You who elucidate the disk   30
hubbed by the sun,
shall I see autumn out
or the fifty years at risk
be lost, doubt
end what's begun?   35

Under his right oxter the loom of his sweep
the pilot turns from the wake.
Thole-pins shred where the oar leans,
grommets renewed, tallowed;
halliards frapped to the shrouds.   40
Crew grunt and gasp. Nothing he sees
they see, but hate and serve. Unscarred ocean,
day's swerve, swell's poise, pursuit,
he blends, balances, drawing leagues under the keel
to raise cold cliffs where tides   45
knot fringes of weed.
No tilled acre, gold scarce,
walrus tusk, whalebone, white bear's liver.
Scurvy gnaws, steading smell, hearth's crackle.
Crabs, shingle, seracs on the icefall.   50
Summer is bergs and fogs, lichen on rocks.

Who cares to remember a name cut in ice
or be remembered?
Wind writes in foam on the sea:

Who sang, sea takes,   55
brawn brine, bone grit.
Keener the kittiwake.
Fells forget him.
Fathoms dull the dale,
gulfweed voices . . .   60

About ship! Sweat in the south. Go bare
because the soil is adorned,
sunset the colour of a boiled louse.
Steep sluice or level,
parts of the sewer ferment faster.   65
Days jerk, dawdle, fidget
towards the cesspit.
Love is a vapour, we're soon through it.

Flying fish follow the boat,
delicate wings blue, grace   70
on flick of a tissue tail,
the water's surface between
appetite and attainment.
Flexible, unrepetitive line
to sing, not paint; sing, sing,   75
laying the tune on the air,
nimble and easy as a lizard,
still and sudden as a gecko,
to humiliate love, remember
nothing.   80

It tastes good, garlic and salt in it,
with the half-sweet white wine of Orvieto
on scanty grass under great trees
where the ramparts cuddle Lucca.

It sounds right, spoken on the ridge   85
between marine olives and hillside
blue figs, under the breeze fresh
with pollen of Apennine sage.

It feels soft, weed thick in the cave
and the smooth wet riddance of Antonietta's   90
bathing suit, mouth ajar for
submarine Amalfitan kisses.

It looks well on the page, but never
well enough. Something is lost
when wind, sun, sea upbraid   95
justly an unconvinced deserter.

White marble stained like a urinal
cleft in Apuan Alps,
always trickling, apt to the saw. Ice and wedge
split it or well-measured cordite shots,   100
while paraffin pistons rap, saws rip
and clamour is clad in stillness:
clouds echo marble middens, sugar-white,
that cumber the road stones travel
to list the names of the dead.   105
There is a lot of Italy in churchyards,
sea on the left, the Garfagnana
over the wall, la Cisa flaking
to hillside fiddlers above Parma,
melancholy, swift,   110
with light bow blanching the dance.
Grease mingles with sweat
on the threshing floor. Frogs, grasshoppers
drape the rice in sound.

25 **biased bowl:** in the game of bowls, the wooden bowls themselves are weighted to make them turn to one side 26 **jack:** the white ball at which the bowls are aimed 29 **woods:** i.e. wooden bowls 36 **oxter:** armpit 38 **Thole-pins:** pins on the side of a boat to keep the oar in place 39 **grommets:** a grommet is a ring of rope or metal 40 **halliards:** a halliard is a rope for raising and lowering a sail **frapped:** secured by being wrapped round many times **shrouds:** ropes supporting the mast 50 **seracs:** a serac is 'a tower of ice on a glacier, formed by the intersection of crevasses' (*OED*)

78 **gecko:** lizard 92 **Amalfitan:** of Amalfi in Italy 104 **cumber:** a road strewn with obstacles, a difficult journey

Tortoise deep in dust or
muzzled bear capering
punctuate a text whose initial,
lost in Lindisfarne plaited lines,
stands for discarded love.   115

Win from rock
    flame and ore.   120
Crucibles pour
    sanded ingots.

Heat and hammer
    draw out a bar.   125
Wheel and water
    grind an edge.

No worn tool
    whittles stone;
but a reproached   130
    uneasy mason

shaping evasive
    ornament
litters his yard
    with flawed fragments.   135

Loaded with mail of linked lies,
what weapon can the king lift to fight
when chance-met enemies employ sly
sword and shoulder-piercing pike,
pressed into the mire,   140
trampled and hewn till a knife
– in whose hand? – severs tight
neck cords? Axe rusts. Spine
picked bare by ravens, agile
maggots devour the slack side   145
and inert brain, never wise.
What witnesses he had life,
ravelled and worn past splice,
yarns falling to staple? Rime
on the bent, the beck ice,   150
there will be nothing on Stainmore to hide
void, no sable to disguise
what he wore under the lies,
king of Orkney, king of Dublin, twice
king of York, where the tide   155
stopped till long flight
from who knows what smile,
scowl, disgust or delight
ended in bale on the fellside.

Starfish, poinsettia on a half-tide crag,   160
a galliard by Byrd.
Anemones spite cullers of ornament
but design the pool
to their grouping. The hermit crab
is no grotesque in such company.   165

Asian vultures riding on a spiral
column of dust
or swift desert ass startled by the
camels' dogged saunter
figures sudden flight of the descant   170
on a madrigal by Monteverdi.

But who will entune a bogged orchard,
its blossom gone,
fruit unformed, where hunger and
damp hush the hive?   175
A disappointed July full of codling
moth and ragged lettuces?

Yet roe are there, rise to the fence, insolent;
a scared vixen cringes
red against privet stems as a mazurka;   180
and rat, grey, rummaging
behind the compost heap has daring
to thread, lithe and alert, Schoenberg's maze.
Riding silk, adrift on noon,
a spider gleams like a berry   185
less black than cannibal slug
but no less pat under elders
where shadows themselves are a web.
So is summer held to its contract
and the year solvent; but men   190
driven by storm fret,
reminded of sweltering Crete
and Pasiphae's pungent sweat,
who heard the god-bull's feet
scattering sand,   195
breathed byre stink, yet stood
with expectant hand
to guide his seed to its soil;
nor did flesh flinch
distended by the brute   200
nor loaded spirit sink
till it had gloried in unlike creation.

[Sect. II]

161 **galliard:** lively Elizabethan dance   **Byrd:** William Byrd (1543–1623), English composer   164 **hermit crab:** soft-bodied crustacean that inhabits an empty mollusc-shell   171 **Monteverdi:** Claudio Monteverdi (1567–1643), Italian composer   176–7 **codling moth:** a moth whose larvae feed on apples   180 **mazurka:** lively Polish dance   183 **Schoenberg's maze:** Arnold Schoenberg (1874–1951), the Austro-Hungarian composer who evolved 'twelve-tone music', the method of composing based on the twelve notes of the chromatic scale   193–4 **Pasiphae's . . . the god-bull's feet:** Pasiphae was the wife of Minos, king of Crete; she had sexual intercourse with a bull and later gave birth to the Minotaur, a monster with a bull's head and a man's body (the bull motif runs through 'Briggflatts')   196 **byre:** cowshed

118 **Lindisfarne:** 'the Holy Island, where the tracery of the Codex Lindisfarnensis was elaborated' (BB)   149 **Rime:** frozen dew   150 **bent:** grass **beck:** brook; however, 'We have burns in the east, *becks* in the west [of Northumberland], but no brooks or creeks' (BB)   159 **bale:** evil, misery

STEVIE SMITH

NOT WAVING BUT DROWNING

NOBODY heard him, the dead man,
But still he lay moaning:
I was much further out than you thought
And not waving but drowning.

Poor chap, he always loved larking   5
And now he's dead
It must have been too cold for him his heart gave way,
They said.

Oh, no no no, it was too cold always
(Still the dead one lay moaning)   10
I was much too far out all my life
And not waving but drowning.

'WHAT IS SHE WRITING? PERHAPS IT WILL BE GOOD'

WHAT is she writing? Perhaps it will be good,
The young girl laughs: 'I am in love.'
But the older girl is serious: 'Not now, perhaps later.'
Still the young girl teases: 'What's the matter?
To lose everything! A waste of time!'   5
But now the older one is quite silent,
Writing, writing, and perhaps it will be good.
Really neither girl is a fool.

CECIL DAY LEWIS

WILL IT BE SO AGAIN?

WILL it be so again
That the brave, the gifted are lost from view,
And empty, scheming men
Are left in peace their lunatic age to renew?
Will it be so again?   5

Must it be always so
That the best are chosen to fall and sleep
Like seeds, and we too slow
In claiming the earth they quicken, and the old
    usurpers reap
What they could not sow?   10

Will it be so again –
The jungle code and the hypocrite gesture?
A poppy wreath for the slain
And a cut-throat world for the living? that stale
    imposture
Played on us once again?   15

Will it be as before –
Peace, with no heart or mind to ensue it,
Guttering down to war
Like a libertine to his grave? We should not be
    surprised: we knew it
Happen before.   20

Shall it be so again?
Call not upon the glorious dead
To be your witnesses then.
The living alone can nail to their promise the ones
    who said
It shall not be so again.   25

SIR JOHN BETJEMAN

POT POURRI FROM A SURREY GARDEN

MILES of pram in the wind and Pam in the gorse
    track,
    Coco-nut smell of the broom, and a packet of
    Weights
Press'd in the sand. The thud of a hoof on a
    horse-track –
    A horse-riding horse for a horse-track –
    Conifer county of Surrey approached   5
    Through remarkable wrought-iron gates.

Over your boundary now, I wash my face in a
    bird-bath,
    Then which path shall I take? that over there by the
    pram?
Down by the pond! or – yes, I will take the slippery
    third path,
    Trodden away with gym shoes,   10
    Beautiful fir-dry alley that leads
To the bountiful body of Pam.

Pam, I adore you, Pam, you great big mountainous
    sports girl,
    Whizzing them over the net, full of the strength of
    five:
That old Malvernian brother, you zephyr and khaki
    shorts girl,   15
    Although he's playing for Woking,
    Can't stand up
To your wonderful backhand drive.

See the strength of her arm, as firm and hairy as
    Hendren's;
    See the size of her thighs, the pout of her lips as,
    cross,   20
And full of a pent-up strength, she swipes at the
    rhododendrons,
    Lucky the rhododendrons,
    And flings her arrogant love-lock
Back with a petulant toss.

Over the redolent pinewoods, in at the bathroom
    casement,   25
  One fine Saturday, Windlesham bells shall call:
Up the Butterfield aisle rich with Gothic enlacement,
    Licensed now for embracement,
      Pam and I, as the organ
  Thunders over you all.   30

POT-POURRI FROM A SURREY GARDEN: 2 **broom**: a shrub **Weights**: a brand of cigarette 15 **old Malvernian**: former pupil of Malvern College **zephyr**: light woollen sweater 19 **Hendren**: E. H. (Patsy) Hendren (1889–1962), English cricketer 23 **love-lock**: prominent long lock of hair 27 **enlacement**: intricately interwoven tracery characteristic of Gothic architecture

IN WESTMINSTER ABBEY

LET me take this other glove off
  As the *vox humana* swells,
And the beauteous fields of Eden
  Bask beneath the Abbey bells.
Here, where England's statesmen lie,   5
Listen to a lady's cry.

Gracious Lord, oh bomb the Germans.
  Spare their women for Thy Sake,
And if that is not too easy
  We will pardon Thy Mistake.   10
But, gracious Lord, whate'er shall be,
Don't let anyone bomb me.

Keep our Empire undismembered
  Guide our Forces by Thy Hand,
Gallant blacks from far Jamaica,   15
  Honduras and Togoland;
Protect them Lord in all their fights,
And, even more, protect the whites.

Think of what our Nation stands for,
  Books from Boots and country lanes,   20
Free speech, free passes, class distinction,
  Democracy and proper drains.
Lord, put beneath Thy special care
One-eighty-nine Cadogan Square.

Although dear Lord I am a sinner,   25
  I have done no major crime;
Now I'll come to Evening Service
  Whensoever I have the time.
So, Lord, reserve for me a crown,
And do not let my shares go down.   30

I will labour for Thy Kingdom,
  Help our lads to win the war,
Send white feathers to the cowards
  Join the Women's Army Corps,
Then wash the Steps around Thy Throne   35
In the Eternal Safety Zone.

Now I feel a little better,
  What a treat to hear Thy Word,
Where the bones of leading statesmen,
  Have so often been interr'd.   40
And now, dear Lord, I cannot wait
Because I have a luncheon date.

IN WESTMINSTER ABBEY: 2 *vox humana*: organ-stop producing tones resembling those of the human voice 16 **Honduras**: pronounced as '*Hon*-du-*ras*' 20 **Books from Boots**: Boots stores once operated a lending library 33 **Send white feathers to the cowards**: as part of their contribution to the war effort, during the First World War the women of Britain would send a white feather (anonymously) as an indication of cowardice to any young man they thought should be in uniform

A SUBALTERN'S LOVE-SONG

MISS J. Hunter Dunn, Miss J. Hunter Dunn,
Furnish'd and burnish'd by Aldershot sun,
What strenuous singles we played after tea,
We in the tournament – you against me!

Love–thirty, love–forty, oh! weakness of joy,   5
The speed of a swallow, the grace of a boy,
With carefullest carelessness, gaily you won,
I am weak from your loveliness, Joan Hunter Dunn.

Miss Joan Hunter Dunn, Miss Joan Hunter Dunn,
How mad I am, sad I am, glad that you won.   10
The warm-handled racket is back in its press,
But my shock-headed victor, she loves me no less.

Her father's euonymus shines as we walk,
And swing past the summer-house, buried in talk,
And cool the verandah that welcomes us in   15
To the six o'clock news and a lime-juice and gin.

The scent of the conifers, sound of the bath,
The view from my bedroom of moss-dappled path,
As I struggle with double-end evening tie,
For we dance at the Golf Club, my victor and I.   20

On the floor of her bedroom lie blazer and shorts
And the cream-coloured walls are be-trophied with
    sports,
And westering, questioning settles the sun
On your low-leaded window, Miss Joan Hunter Dunn.

The Hillman is waiting, the light's in the hall,   25
The pictures of Egypt are bright on the wall,
My sweet, I am standing beside the oak stair
And there on the landing's the light on your hair.

By roads 'not adopted', by woodlanded ways,
She drove to the club in the late summer haze,   30
Into nine-o'clock Camberley, heavy with bells
And mushroomy, pine-woody, evergreen smells.

Miss Joan Hunter Dunn, Miss Joan Hunter Dunn,
I can hear from the car-park the dance has begun.
Oh! full Surrey twilight! importunate band!   35
Oh! strongly adorable tennis-girl's hand!

Around us are Rovers and Austins afar,
Above us, the intimate roof of the car,
And here on my right is the girl of my choice,   39
With the tilt of her nose and the chime of her voice,

And the scent of her wrap, and the words never said,
And the ominous, ominous dancing ahead.
We sat in the car park till twenty to one
And now I'm engaged to Miss Joan Hunter Dunn.

A SUBALTERN'S LOVE-SONG: 2 **Aldershot:** Hampshire town with
a large army base   12 **shock-headed:** having a crop of thick hair
13 **euonymus:** spindle-tree, a shrub   19 **double-end evening tie:** bow-
tie   23 **westering:** moving towards the west   29 **roads 'not adopted':**
not officially recognised as part of the road system; i.e. minor
roads and country lanes

IN A BATH TEASHOP

'LET us not speak, for the love we bear one another –
      Let us hold hands and look.'
She, such a very ordinary little woman;
      He, such a thumping crook;
But both, for a moment, little lower than the angels   5
      In the teashop's ingle-nook

IN A BATH TEASHOP: 6 **ingle-nook:** chimney-corner

HOW TO GET ON IN SOCIETY

PHONE for the fish knives, Norman
As cook is a little unnerved;
You kiddies have crumpled the serviettes
And I must have things daintily served.

Are the requisites all in the toilet?   5
The frills round the cutlets can wait
Till the girl has replenished the cruets
And switched on the logs in the grate.

It's ever so close in the lounge dear,
But the vestibule's comfy for tea   10
And Howard is riding on horseback
So do come and take some with me.

Now here is a fork for your pastries
And do use the couch for your feet;
I know that I wanted to ask you –   15
Is trifle sufficient for sweet?

Milk and then just as it comes dear?
I'm afraid the preserve's full of stones;
Beg pardon, I'm soiling the doileys
With afternoon tea-cakes and scones.   20

SIR WILLIAM EMPSON

TO AN OLD LADY

RIPENESS is all; her in her cooling planet
Revere; do not presume to think her wasted.
Project her no projectile, plan nor man it;
Gods cool in turn, by the sun long outlasted.

Our earth alone given no name of god   5
Gives, too, no hold for such a leap to aid her;
Landing, you break some palace and seem odd;
Bees sting their need, the keeper's queen invader.

No, to your telescope; spy out the land;
Watch while her ritual is still to see,   10
Still stand her temples emptying in the sand
Whose waves o'erthrew their crumbled tracery;

Still stand uncalled-on her soul's appanage;
Much social detail whose successor fades,
Wit used to run a house and to play Bridge,   15
And tragic fervour, to dismiss her maids.

Years her precession do not throw from gear.
She reads a compass certain of her pole;
Confident, finds no confines on her sphere,
Whose failing crops are in her sole control.   20

Stars how much further from me fill my night.
Strange that she too should be inaccessible,
Who shares my sun. He curtains her from sight,
And but in darkness is she visible.

TO AN OLD LADY: 5 **Our earth . . . god:** Earth is the only planet in
our solar system that does not take its name from Classical
mythology   13 **appanage:** provision for the maintenance of a king's
younger children   17 **precession:** 'the earlier occurrence of the
equinoxes in each successive sidereal [i.e. stellar] year . . . produced
by the slow change of direction in space of the earth's axis' (*OED*)

WYSTAN HUGH AUDEN

'STOP ALL THE CLOCKS . . .'

STOP all the clocks, cut off the telephone,
Prevent the dog from barking with a juicy bone,
Silence the pianos and with muffled drum
Bring out the coffin, let the mourners come.

Let aeroplanes circle moaning overhead   5
Scribbling on the sky the message He Is Dead,
Put crêpe bows round the white necks of the public
      doves,
Let the traffic policemen wear black cotton gloves.

He was my North, my South, my East and West,
My working week and my Sunday rest,   10
My noon, my midnight, my talk, my song;
I thought that love would last for ever: I was wrong.

The stars are not wanted now: put out every one;
Pack up the moon and dismantle the sun;
Pour away the ocean and sweep up the wood;   15
For nothing now can ever come to any good.

'STOP ALL THE CLOCKS': 3 **muffled drum:** muffling is 'A way of muting kettle-drums (e.g. at a funeral) by placing a cloth over the surface'. (*Concise Oxford Dictionary of Music*)

LULLABY

LAY your sleeping head, my love,
Human on my faithless arm;
Time and fevers burn away
Individual beauty from
Thoughtful children, and the grave   5
Proves the child ephemeral:
But in my arms till break of day
Let the living creature lie,
Mortal, guilty, but to me
The entirely beautiful.   10

Soul and body have no bounds:
To lovers as they lie upon
Her tolerant enchanted slope
In their ordinary swoon,
Grave the vision Venus sends   15
Of supernatural sympathy,
Universal love and hope;
While an abstract insight wakes
Among the glaciers and the rocks
The hermit's carnal ecstasy.   20

Certainty, fidelity
On the stroke of midnight pass
Like vibrations of a bell
And fashionable madmen raise
Their pedantic boring cry: 25
Every farthing of the cost,
All the dreaded cards foretell,
Shall be paid, but from this night
Not a whisper, not a thought,
Not a kiss nor look be lost.   30

Beauty, midnight, vision dies:
Let the winds of dawn that blow
Softly round your dreaming head
Such a day of welcome show
Eye and knocking heart may bless,   35
Find our mortal world enough;
Noons of dryness find you fed
By the involuntary powers,
Nights of insult let you pass
Watched by every human love.   40

January 1937

MUSÉE DES BEAUX ARTS

ABOUT suffering they were never wrong,
The Old Masters: how well they understood
Its human position; how it takes place
While someone else is eating or opening a window or
    just walking dully along;
How, when the agèd are reverently, passionately
    waiting   5
For the miraculous birth, there always must be
Children who did not specially want it to happen,
    skating
On a pond at the edge of the wood:
They never forgot
That even the dreadful martyrdom must run its
    course   10
Anyhow in a corner, some untidy spot
Where the dogs go on with their doggy life and the
    torturer's horse
Scratches its innocent behind on a tree.

In Breughel's *Icarus*, for instance: how everything
    turns away
Quite leisurely from the disaster; the ploughman
    may
Have heard the splash, the forsaken cry,   16
But for him it was not an important failure; the sun
    shone
As it had to on the white legs disappearing into the
    green
Water; and the expensive delicate ship that must have
    seen
Something amazing, a boy falling out of the sky,   20
Had somewhere to get to and sailed calmly on.

December 1938

MUSÉE DES BEAUX ARTS ('Art Gallery'): 14 **Breughel's *Icarus*:** Icarus was the son of Daedalus, an Athenian craftsman who designed the labyrinth for the Minotaur on Crete. When father and son were forced to flee the island they made their escape with wings made of wax and feathers; but Icarus' excitement caused him to fly too close to the sun, his wings melted, he fell into the sea and was drowned. Ovid tells the story in *Metamorphoses* (see above, Arthur Golding). 'The Fall of Icarus' by Pieter Breughel the Elder (*c.*1526–1569) shows Icarus after he has plunged into the sea; only his legs are visible above the water, and all around him people go about their business, oblivious to his fate

IN MEMORY OF W. B. YEATS
(D. JAN. 1939)

I

HE disappeared in the dead of winter:
The brooks were frozen, the airports almost deserted,
And snow disfigured the public statues;
The mercury sank in the mouth of the dying day.
What instruments we have agree   5
The day of his death was a dark cold day.

Far from his illness
The wolves ran on through the evergreen forests,
The peasant river was untempted by the fashionable
   quays;
By mourning tongues   10
The death of the poet was kept from his poems.

But for him it was his last afternoon as himself,
An afternoon of nurses and rumours;
The provinces of his body revolted,
The squares of his mind were empty,   15
Silence invaded the suburbs,
The current of his feeling failed; he became his
   admirers.

Now he is scattered among a hundred cities
And wholly given over to unfamiliar affections,
To find his happiness in another kind of wood   20
And be punished under a foreign code of conscience.
The words of a dead man
Are modified in the guts of the living.

But in the importance of noise of tomorrow
When the brokers are roaring like beasts on the floor
   of the Bourse,   25
And the poor have the sufferings to which they are
   fairly accustomed,
And each in the cell of himself is almost convinced of
   his freedom,
A few thousand will think of this day
As one thinks of a day when one did something
   slightly unusual.
What instruments we have agree   30
The day of his death was a dark cold day.

II

You were silly like us; your gift survived it all:
The parish of rich women, physical decay,
Yourself. Mad Ireland hurt you into poetry.
Now Ireland has her madness and her weather
   still,   35
For poetry makes nothing happen: it survives
In the valley of its making where executives
Would never want to tamper, flows on south
From ranches of isolation and the busy griefs,
Raw towns that we believe and die in; it survives,   40
A way of happening, a mouth.

III

Earth, receive an honoured guest:
William Yeats is laid to rest.
Let the Irish vessel lie
Emptied of its poetry.   45

In the nightmare of the dark
All the dogs of Europe bark,
And the living nations wait,
Each sequestered in its hate;

Intellectual disgrace   50
Stares from every human face,
And the seas of pity lie
Locked and frozen in each eye.

Follow, poet, follow right
To the bottom of the night,   55
With your unconstraining voice
Still persuade us to rejoice;

With the farming of a verse
Make a vineyard of the curse,
Sing of human unsuccess   60
In a rapture of distress;

In the deserts of the heart
Let the healing fountain start,
In the prison of his days
Teach the free man how to praise.   65

February 1939

IN MEMORY OF W. B. YEATS: 25 **the Bourse:** specifically the Paris stock
exchange but here referring to financial markets generally

THE UNKNOWN CITIZEN

(To JS/07/M/378
This Marble Monument
Is Erected by the State)

HE was found by the Bureau of Statistics to be
One against whom there was no official complaint,
And all the reports on his conduct agree
That, in the modern sense of an old-fashioned word,
   he was a saint,
For in everything he did he served the Greater
   Community.   5
Except for the War till the day he retired
He worked in a factory and never got fired,
But satisfied his employers, Fudge Motors Inc.
Yet he wasn't a scab or odd in his views,
For his Union reports that he paid his dues,   10
(Our report on his Union shows it was sound)
And our Social Psychology workers found
That he was popular with his mates and liked a drink.
The Press are convinced that he bought a paper every
   day
And that his reactions to advertisements were normal
   in every way.   15
Policies taken out in his name prove that he was fully
   insured,
And his Health-card shows he was once in hospital but
   left it cured.
Both Producers Research and High-Grade Living
   declare

He was fully sensible to the advantages of the
  Instalment Plan
And had everything necessary to the Modern Man, 20
A phonograph, a radio, a car and a frigidaire.
Our researchers into Public Opinion are content
That he held the proper opinions for the time of year;
When there was peace, he was for peace; when there
  was war, he went.
He was married and added five children to the
  population, 25
Which our Eugenist says was the right number for a
  parent of his generation,
And our teachers report that he never interfered with
  their education.
Was he free? Was he happy? The question is absurd:
Had anything been wrong, we should certainly have
  heard.

March 1939

THE UNKNOWN CITIZEN: 1 **Bureau of Statistics:** the first of several
references to the new sciences of social anthropology, market
research and opinion polls that emerged in the 1930s; in Britain,
notably, Charles Madge and Tom Harrisson had introduced Mass
Observation 9 **scab:** one who continues to work during a strike 21
frigidaire: brand name of the Frigidaire Corporation; in the 1930s
refrigerators were to be found increasingly in the more affluent
British homes 26 **Eugenist:** eugenics is the science of human
improvement through judicious mating

IN PRAISE OF LIMESTONE

IF it form the one landscape that we, the inconstant
  ones,
  Are consistently homesick for, this is chiefly
Because it dissolves in water. Mark these rounded
  slopes
  With their surface fragrance of thyme and, beneath,
A secret system of caves and conduits; hear the
  springs   5
  That spurt out everywhere with a chuckle,
Each filling a private pool for its fish and carving
  Its own little ravine whose cliffs entertain
The butterfly and the lizard; examine this region
  Of short distances and definite places: 10
What could be more like Mother or a fitter
  background
  For her son, the flirtatious male who lounges
Against a rock in the sunlight, never doubting
  That for all his faults he is loved; whose works are
  but
Extensions of his power to charm? From weathered
  outcrop   15
  To hill-top temple, from appearing waters to
Conspicuous fountains, from a wild to a formal
  vineyard,
  Are ingenious but short steps that a child's wish
To receive more attention than his brothers, whether
By pleasing or teasing, can easily take.   20

Watch, then, the band of rivals as they climb up and
  down
  Their steep stone gennels in twos and threes, at
  times
Arm in arm, but never, thank God, in step; or engaged
  On the shady side of a square at midday in
Voluble discourse, knowing each other too well to
  think   25
  There are any important secrets, unable
To conceive a god whose temper-tantrums are moral
  And not to be pacified by a clever line
Or a good lay: for, accustomed to a stone that responds,
  They have never had to veil their faces in awe   30
Of a crater whose blazing fury could not be fixed;
  Adjusted to the local needs of valleys
Where everything can be touched or reached by
  walking,
  Their eyes have never looked into infinite space
Through the lattice-work of a nomad's comb; born
  lucky,   35
  Their legs have never encountered the fungi
And insects of the jungle, the monstrous forms and
  lives
  With which we have nothing, we like to hope, in
  common.
So, when one of them goes to the bad, the way his
  mind works
  Remains comprehensible: to become a pimp   40
Or deal in fake jewellery or ruin a fine tenor voice
  For effects that bring down the house, could happen
  to all
But the best and the worst of us . . .
                                        That is why, I suppose,
  The best and worst never stayed here long but
  sought
Immoderate soils where the beauty was not so
  external,   45
  The light less public and the meaning of life
Something more than a mad camp. 'Come!' cried the
  granite wastes,
  'How evasive is your humour, how accidental
Your kindest kiss, how permanent is death.' (Saints-to-
  be
  Slipped away sighing.) 'Come!' purred the clays and
  gravels,   50
'On our plains there is room for armies to drill; rivers
  Wait to be tamed and slaves to construct you a tomb
In the grand manner: soft as the earth is mankind and
  both
  Need to be altered.' (Intendant Caesars rose and
Left, slamming the door.) But the really reckless were
  fetched   55
  By an older colder voice, the oceanic whisper:
'I am the solitude that asks and promises nothing;
  That is how I shall set you free. There is no love;
There are only the various envies, all of them sad.'

IN PRAISE OF LIMESTONE: 22 **gennels:** long, narrow passageways
54 **Intendant:** superintendent

They were right, my dear, all those voices were
   right   60
And still are; this land is not the sweet home that it
   looks,
   Nor its peace the historical calm of a site
Where something was settled once and for all: A
   backward
   And dilapidated province, connected
To the big busy world by a tunnel, with a certain 65
   Seedy appeal, is that all it is now? Not quite:
It has a worldly duty which in spite of itself
   It does not neglect, but calls into question
All the Great Powers assume; it disturbs our rights.
   The poet,
   Admired for his earnest habit of calling 70
The sun the sun, his mind Puzzle, is made uneasy
   By these marble statues which so obviously doubt
His antimythological myth; and these gamins,
   Pursuing the scientist down the tiled colonnade 74
With such lively offers, rebuke his concern for Nature's
   Remotest aspects: I, too, am reproached, for what
And how much you know. Not to lose time, not to get
   caught,
   Not to be left behind, not, please! to resemble
The beasts who repeat themselves, or a thing like
   water
   Or stone whose conduct can be predicted, these 80
Are our Common Prayer, whose greatest comfort is
   music
   Which can be made anywhere, is invisible,
And does not smell. In so far as we have to look
   forward
   To death as a fact, no doubt we are right: But if
Sins can be forgiven, if bodies rise from the dead, 85
   These modifications of matter into
Innocent athletes and gesticulating fountains,
   Made solely for pleasure, make a further point:
The blessèd will not care what angle they are regarded
   from,
   Having nothing to hide. Dear, I know nothing of 90
Either, but when I try to imagine a faultless love
   Or the life to come, what I hear is the murmur
Of underground streams, what I see is a limestone
   landscape.

May 1948

73 **gamins:** street urchins

THE SHIELD OF ACHILLES

SHE looked over his shoulder
   For vines and olive trees,
Marble well-governed cities
   And ships upon untamed seas,
But there on the shining metal   5
   His hands had put instead
An artificial wilderness
   And a sky like lead.

A plain without a feature, bare and brown,
   No blade of grass, no sign of neighbourhood, 10
Nothing to eat and nowhere to sit down,
   Yet, congregated on its blankness, stood
   An unintelligible multitude,
A million eyes, a million boots in line,
Without expression, waiting for a sign. 15

Out of the air a voice without a face
   Proved by statistics that some cause was just
In tones as dry and level as the place:
   No one was cheered and nothing was discussed;
   Column by column in a cloud of dust 20
They marched away enduring a belief
Whose logic brought them, somewhere else, to grief.

    She looked over his shoulder
      For ritual pieties,
    White flower-garlanded heifers, 25
      Libation and sacrifice,
    But there on the shining metal
      Where the altar should have been,
    She saw by his flickering forge-light
      Quite another scene. 30

Barbed wire enclosed an arbitrary spot
   Where bored officials lounged (one cracked a joke)
And sentries sweated for the day was hot:
   A crowd of ordinary decent folk
   Watched from without and neither moved nor spoke
As three pale figures were led forth and bound 36
To three posts driven upright in the ground.

The mass and majesty of this world, all
   That carries weight and always weighs the same
Lay in the hands of others; they were small 40
   And could not hope for help and no help came:
   What their foes liked to do was done, their shame
Was all the worst could wish; they lost their pride
And died as men before their bodies died.

    She looked over his shoulder 45
      For athletes at their games,
    Men and women in a dance
      Moving their sweet limbs
    Quick, quick, to music,
      But there on the shining shield 50
    His hands had set no dancing-floor
      But a weed-choked field.

A ragged urchin, aimless and alone,
   Loitered about that vacancy; a bird
Flew up to safety from his well-aimed stone: 55
   That girls are raped, that two boys knife a third,
   Were axioms to him, who'd never heard
Of any world where promises were kept,
Or one could weep because another wept.

The thin-lipped armourer,   60
  Hephaestos, hobbled away,
Thetis of the shining breasts
  Cried out in dismay
At what the god had wrought
  To please her son, the strong   65
Iron-hearted man-slaying Achilles
  Who would not live long.

1952

THE SHIELD OF ACHILLES: in Homer's *Iliad* (18), Thetis goes to
Hephaestus, the lame craftsman of the gods, and asks him to make
new armour for her son, Achilles (see above, George Chapman)

THE MORE LOVING ONE

LOOKING up at the stars, I know quite well
That, for all they care, I can go to hell,
But on earth indifference is the least
We have to dread from man or beast.

How should we like it were stars to burn   5
With a passion for us we could not return?
If equal affection cannot be,
Let the more loving one be me.

Admirer as I think I am
Of stars that do not give a damn,   10
I cannot, now I see them, say
I missed one terribly all day.

Were all stars to disappear or die,
I should learn to look at an empty sky
And feel its total dark sublime,   15
Though this might take me a little time.

1957

LOUIS MACNEICE

SUNDAY MORNING

DOWN the road someone is practising scales,
The notes like little fishes vanish with a wink of tails,
Man's heart expands to tinker with his car
For this is Sunday morning, Fate's great bazaar;   4
Regard these means as ends, concentrate on this Now,
And you may grow to music or drive beyond
  Hindhead anyhow,
Take corners on two wheels until you go so fast
That you can clutch a fringe or two of the windy past,
That you can abstract this day and make it to the week
  of time
A small eternity, a sonnet self-contained in rhyme. 10

But listen, up the road, something gulps, the church
  spire
Opens its eight bells out, skulls' mouths which will not
  tire
To tell how there is no music or movement which
  secures
Escape from the weekday time. Which deadens and
  endures.

May 1933

SNOW

THE room was suddenly rich and the great bay-
  window was
Spawning snow and pink roses against it
Soundlessly collateral and incompatible:
World is suddener than we fancy it.

World is crazier and more of it than we think,   5
Incorrigibly plural. I peel and portion
A tangerine and spit the pips and feel
The drunkenness of things being various.

And the fire flames with a bubbling sound for world
Is more spiteful and gay than one supposes –   10
On the tongue on the eyes on the ears in the palms of
  one's hands –
There is more than glass between the snow and the
  huge roses.

January 1935

THE SUNLIGHT ON THE GARDEN

THE sunlight on the garden
Hardens and grows cold,
We cannot cage the minute
Within its nets of gold,
When all is told   5
We cannot beg for pardon.

Our freedom as free lances
Advances towards its end;
The earth compels, upon it
Sonnets and birds descend;   10
And soon, my friend,
We shall have no time for dances.

The sky was good for flying
Defying the church bells
And every evil iron   15
Siren and what it tells:
The earth compels,
We are dying, Egypt, dying

And not expecting pardon,
Hardened in heart anew,   20
But glad to have sat under
Thunder and rain with you,
And grateful too
For sunlight on the garden.

1937

THE SUNLIGHT ON THE GARDEN: 18 **We are dying, Egypt, dying:**
Shakespeare's *Antony and Cleopatra* 4.15

BAGPIPE MUSIC

IT'S no go the merrygoround, it's no go the rickshaw,
All we want is a limousine and a ticket for the peep-
    show.
Their knickers are made of crêpe-de-chine, their
    shoes are made of python,
Their halls are lined with tiger rugs and their walls
    with heads of bison.

John MacDonald found a corpse, put it under the
    sofa,   5
Waited till it came to life and hit it with a poker,
Sold its eyes for souvenirs, sold its blood for whisky,
Kept its bones for dumb-bells to use when he was fifty.

It's no go the Yogi-man, it's no go Blavatsky,
All we want is a bank balance and a bit of skirt in a
    taxi.   10

Annie MacDougall went to milk, caught her foot in
    the heather,
Woke to hear a dance record playing of Old Vienna.

It's no go your maidenheads, it's no go your culture,
All we want is a Dunlop tyre and the devil mend the
    puncture.

The Laird o' Phelps spent Hogmanay declaring he
    was sober,   15
Counted his feet to prove the fact and found he had
    one foot over.
Mrs Carmichael had her fifth, looked at the job with
    repulsion,
Said to the midwife 'Take it away; I'm through with
    over-production'.

It's no go the gossip column, it's no go the ceilidh,
All we want is a mother's help and a sugar-stick for the
    baby.   20

Willie Murray cut his thumb, couldn't count the
    damage,
Took the hide of an Ayrshire cow and used it for a
    bandage.
His brother caught three hundred cran when the seas
    were lavish,
Threw the bleeders back in the sea and went upon the
    parish.

It's no go the Herring Board, it's no go the Bible,   25
All we want is a packet of fags when our hands are
    idle.

It's no go the picture palace, it's no go the stadium,
It's no go the country cot with a pot of pink
    geraniums,
It's no go the Government grants, it's no go the
    elections,
Sit on your arse for fifty years and hang your hat on a
    pension.   30

It's no go my honey love, it's no go my poppet;
Work your hands from day to day, the winds will blow
    the profit.
The glass is falling hour by hour, the glass will fall for
    ever,
But if you break the bloody glass you won't hold up
    the weather.

1937

BAGPIPE MUSIC: 9 **the Yogi-man:** an indication of the growing
influence of Eastern mysticism in the West **Blavatsky:** Madame
Blavatsky (1831–91), founder of the Theosophical Society 19 **ceilidh:**
('*kay*-lee') an evening of song and dance 23 **cran:** unit of measurement
of a trawl of herring 28 **cot:** cottage 33 **The glass is falling:**
the mercury in the barometer indicates that a storm is brewing;
MacNeice had written an earlier poem with the title 'Glass Falling'

From AUTUMN JOURNAL

SLEEP, my body, sleep, my ghost,
    Sleep, my parents and grand-parents,
And all those I have loved most:
    One man's coffin is another's cradle.
Sleep, my past and all my sins,   5
    In distant snow or dried roses
Under the moon for night's cocoon will open
    When day begins.
Sleep, my fathers, in your graves
    On upland bogland under heather;   10
What the wind scatters the wind saves,
    A sapling springs in a new country.
Time is a country, the present moment
    A spotlight roving round the scene;
We need not chase the spotlight,   15
    The future is the bride of what has been.
Sleep, my fancies and my wishes,
    Sleep a little and wake strong,
The same but different and take my blessing –
    A cradle-song.   20
And sleep, my various and conflicting
    Selves I have so long endured,
Sleep in Asclepius' temple
    And wake cured.

AUTUMN JOURNAL: written from August to December 1938, 'Not strictly
a journal but giving the tenor of my intellectual and emotional
experiences during that period' (MacNeice to his publisher,
T. S. Eliot); this lullaby closes the poem: 23 **Asclepius:** the Greek god
of healing

And you with whom I shared an idyll 25
  Five years long,
Sleep beyond the Atlantic
  And wake to a glitter of dew and to bird-song.
And you whose eyes are blue, whose ways are foam,
  Sleep quiet and smiling 30
And do not hanker
  For a perfection which can never come.
And you whose minutes patter
  To crowd the social hours,
Curl up easy in a placid corner 35
  And let your thoughts close in like flowers.
And you, who work for Christ, and you, as eager
  For a better life, humanist, atheist,
And you, devoted to a cause, and you, to a family,
  Sleep and may your beliefs and zeal persist. 40
Sleep quietly, Marx and Freud,
  The figure-heads of our transition.
Cagney, Lombard, Bing and Garbo,
  Sleep in your world of celluloid.
Sleep now also, monk and satyr, 45
  Cease your wrangling for a night.
Sleep, my brain, and sleep, my senses,
  Sleep, my hunger and my spite.
Sleep, recruits to the evil army,
  Who, for so long misunderstood, 50
Took to the gun to kill your sorrow;
  Sleep and be damned and wake up good.
While we sleep, what shall we dream?
  Of Tir nan Og or South Sea islands,
Of a land where all the milk is cream 55
  And all the girls are willing?
Or shall our dream be earnest of the real
  Future when we wake,
Design a home, a factory, a fortress
  Which, though with effort, we can really make? 60
What it is we want really?
  For what end and how?
If it is something feasible, obtainable,
  Let us dream it now,
And pray for a possible land 65
  Not of sleep-walkers, not of angry puppets,
But where both heart and brain can understand
  The movements of our fellows;
Where life is a choice of instruments and none
  Is debarred his natural music, 70
Where the waters of life are free of the ice-blockade
  of hunger
  And thought is free as the sun,
Where the altars of sheer power and mere profit

Have fallen to disuse,
Where nobody sees the use 75
  Of buying money and blood at the cost of blood
  and money,
Where the individual, no longer squandered
  In self-assertion, works with the rest, endowed
With the split vision of a juggler and the quick lock of
  a taxi,
  Where the people are more than a crowd. 80
So sleep in hope of this – but only for a little;
  Your hope must wake
While the choice is yours to make,
  The mortgage not foreclosed, the offer open.
Sleep serene, avoid the backward 85
  Glance; go forward, dreams, and do not halt
(Behind you in the desert stands a token
  Of doubt – a pillar of salt).
Sleep, the past, and wake, the future,
  And walk out promptly through the open door; 90
But you, my coward doubts, may go on sleeping,
  You need not wake again – not any more.
The New Year comes with bombs, it is too late
  To dose the dead with honourable intentions:
If you have honour to spare, employ it on the living;
  The dead are dead as Nineteen-Thirty-Eight. 96
Sleep to the noise of running water
  Tomorrow to be crossed, however deep;
This is no river of the dead or Lethe,
  Tonight we sleep 100
On the banks of Rubicon – the die is cast;
  There will be time to audit
The accounts later, there will be sunlight later
  And the equation will come out at last.

[Sect. 24]

August 1938–New Year 1939

87–8 **token . . . pillar of salt:** when God decided to destroy Sodom and Gomorrah he warned Lot to escape and not to look back, 'But his wife looked back from behind him, and she became a pillar of salt' (Genesis 19.26) 99 **river of the dead:** Acheron ('*A-ke-ron*'), in Greek mythology the river in Hades, or the Underworld, the abode of the dead, over which the souls of the dead were ferried by Charon **Lethe:** ('*Leeth*-ee') the river of forgetfulness in Hades; drinking its waters removed all memory of what had gone before 101 **Rubicon:** a river separating ancient Italy from Cisalpine Gaul, the province assigned to Julius Caesar; when Caesar crossed the river (49 BC), out of his own province, he became an invader of Italy and was consequently at war with Pompey; thus, 'to cross the Rubicon' means to take an irrevocable step

25–6 **an idyll Five years long:** the poet's time at Marlborough 41 **Marx and Freud:** two key influences on British intellectual life in the 1930s 43–4 **Cagney . . . celluloid:** Hollywood film stars James Cagney, Carole Lombard, Bing Crosby and Greta Garbo were at the peak of their career in what was also the golden period of the cinema on both sides of the Atlantic 54 **Tir nan Og:** ('teer-na-nogue') in Celtic mythology 'The Land of Youth', a timeless land, the Celtic heaven

MEETING POINT

TIME was away and somewhere else,
There were two glasses and two chairs
And two people with the one pulse
(Somebody stopped the moving stairs):
Time was away and somewhere else. 5

And they were neither up nor down;
The stream's music did not stop
Flowing through heather, limpid brown,
Although they sat in a coffee shop
And they were neither up nor down.   10

The bell was silent in the air
Holding its inverted poise –
Between the clang and clang a flower,
A brazen calyx of no noise:
The bell was silent in the air.   15

The camels crossed the miles of sand
That stretched around the cups and plates;
The desert was their own, they planned
To portion out the stars and dates:
The camels crossed the miles of sand.   20

Time was away and somewhere else.
The waiter did not come, the clock
Forgot them and the radio waltz
Came out like water from a rock:
Time was away and somewhere else.   25

Her fingers flicked away the ash
That bloomed again in tropic trees:
Not caring if the markets crash
When they had forests such as these,
Her fingers flicked away the ash.   30

God or whatever means the Good
Be praised that time can stop like this,
That what the heart has understood
Can verify in the body's peace
God or whatever means the Good.   35

Time was away and she was here
And life no longer what it was,
The bell was silent in the air
And all the room one glow because
Time was away and she was here.   40

April 1939

MEETING POINT: 14 **brazen:** brass **calyx:** outer covering of a flower formed by the petals 24 **like water from a rock:** 'And Moses lifted up his hand, and with his rod he smote the rock twice: and the water came out abundantly, and the congregation drank, and their beasts also' (Numbers 20.11)

BROTHER FIRE

WHEN our brother Fire was having his dog's day
Jumping the London streets with millions of tin cans
Clanking at his tail, we heard some shadow say
'Give the dog a bone' – and so we gave him ours;
Night after night we watched him slaver and crunch away   5
The beams of human life, the tops of topless towers.

Which gluttony of his for us was Lenten fare
Who mother-naked, suckled with sparks, were chill
Though cotted in a grille of sizzling air
Striped like a convict – black, yellow and red;   10
Thus were we weaned to knowledge of the Will
That wills the natural world but wills us dead.

O delicate walker, babbler, dialectician Fire,
O enemy and image of ourselves,
Did we not on those mornings after the All Clear,   15
When you were looting shops in elemental joy
And singing as you swarmed up city block and spire,
Echo your thoughts in ours? 'Destroy! Destroy!'

c.1943

BROTHER FIRE: 13 **dialectician:** logician 15 **the All Clear:** a siren to indicate that the danger from an air raid had passed

PRAYER BEFORE BIRTH

I AM not yet born; O hear me.
Let not the bloodsucking bat or the rat or the stoat or
    the club-footed ghoul come near me.

I am not yet born, console me.
I fear that the human race may with tall walls wall me,
    with strong drugs dope me, with wise lies lure me,
        on black racks rack me, in blood-baths roll me.

I am not yet born; provide me   5
With water to dandle me, grass to grow for me, trees
    to talk to me, sky to sing to me, birds and a white
        light in the back of my mind to guide me.

I am not yet born; forgive me
For the sins that in me the world shall commit, my
    words when they speak me, my thoughts when they
        think me, my treason engendered by traitors
            beyond me, my life when they murder by means
                of my hands, my death when they live me.

I am not yet born; rehearse me   9
In the parts I must play and the cues I must take when
    old men lecture me, bureaucrats hector me,
        mountains frown at me, lovers laugh at me, the
            white waves call me to folly and the desert calls
                me to doom and the beggar refuses my gift
                    and my children curse me.

I am not yet born; O hear me,
Let not the man who is beast or who thinks he is God
    come near me.

I am not yet born; O fill me
With strength against those who would freeze my
    humanity, would dragoon me into a lethal

automaton, would make me a cog in a machine, a
    thing with one face, a thing, and against all
    those who would dissipate my entirety, would
    blow me like thistledown hither and thither
    or hither and thither like water held in
    the hands would spill me.   15

Let them not make me a stone and let them not spill
me.
Otherwise kill me.

1944

SIR STEPHEN SPENDER

'I THINK CONTINUALLY OF THOSE
WHO WERE TRULY GREAT'

I THINK continually of those who were truly great.
Who, from the womb, remembered the soul's history
Through corridors of light where the hours are suns,
Endless and singing. Whose lovely ambition
Was that their lips, still touched with fire,   5
Should tell of the Spirit, clothed from head to foot in
    song.
And who hoarded from the Spring branches
The desires falling across their bodies like blossoms.

What is precious, is never to forget
The essential delight of the blood drawn from ageless
    springs   10
Breaking through rocks in worlds before our earth.
Never to deny its pleasure in the morning simple light
Nor its grave evening demand for love.
Never to allow gradually the traffic to smother
With noise and fog, the flowering of the Spirit.   15

Near the snow, near the sun, in the highest fields,
See how these names are fêted by the waving grass
And by the streamers of white cloud
And whispers of wind in the listening sky.
The names of those who in their lives fought for life,
Who wore at their hearts the fire's centre.   21
Born of the sun, they travelled a short while toward
    the sun
And left the vivid air signed with their honour.

ROY FULLER

TRANSLATION

Now that the barbarians have got as far as Picra,
And all the new music is written in the twelve-tone
    scale,
And I am anyway approaching my fortieth birthday,
    I will dissemble no longer.

I will stop expressing my belief in the rosy   5
Future of man, and accept the evidence
Of a couple of wretched wars and innumerable
    Abortive revolutions.

I will cease to blame the stupidity of the slaves
Upon their masters and nurture, and will say,   10
Plainly, that they are enemies to culture,
    Advancement and cleanliness.

From progressive organisations, from quarterlies
Devoted to daring verse, from membership of
Committees, from letters of various protest   15
    I shall withdraw forthwith.

When they call me reactionary I shall smile,
Secure in another dimension. When they say
'Cinna has ceased to matter' I shall know
    How well I reflect the times.   20

The ruling class will think I am on their side
And make friendly overtures, but I shall retire
To the side farther from Picra and write some poems
    About the doom of the whole boiling.

Anyone happy in this age and place   25
Is daft or corrupt. Better to abdicate
From a material and spiritual terrain
    Fit only for barbarians.

TRANSLATION: 2 **twelve-tone scale:** see note to Bunting's 'Briggflatts'
24 **the whole boiling:** the lot, all of it

FRANK TEMPLETON PRINCE

SOLDIERS BATHING

THE sea at evening moves across the sand.
Under a reddening sky I watch the freedom of a band
Of soldiers who belong to me. Stripped bare
For bathing in the sea, they shout and run in the warm
    air;
Their flesh worn by the trade of war, revives   5
And my mind towards the meaning of it strives.

All's pathos now. The body that was gross,
Rank, ravenous, disgusting in the act or in repose,
All fever, filth and sweat, its bestial strength
And bestial decay, by pain and labour grows at length
Fragile and luminous. 'Poor bare forked animal,'   11
Conscious of his desires and needs and flesh that rise
    and fall,
Stands in the soft air, tasting after toil

SOLDIERS BATHING: 11 **'Poor bare forked animal':** Shakespeare's
King Lear 3.4

The sweetness of his nakedness: letting the sea-waves coil
Their frothy tongues about his feet, forgets   15
His hatred of the war, its terrible pressure that begets
A machinery of death and slavery,
Each being a slave and making slaves of others: finds that he
Remembers his old freedom in a game
Mocking himself, and comically mimics fear and shame.   20

He plays with death and animality;
And reading in the shadows of his pallid flesh, I see
The idea of Michelangelo's cartoon
Of soldiers bathing, breaking off before they were half done
At some sortie of the enemy, an episode   25
Of the Pisan wars with Florence. I remember how he showed
Their muscular limbs that clamber from the water,
And heads that turn across the shoulder, eager for the slaughter,
Forgetful of their bodies that are bare,
And hot to buckle on and use the weapons lying there.   30
– And I think too of the theme another found
When, shadowing men's bodies on a sinister red ground,
Another Florentine, Pollaiuolo,
Painted a naked battle: warriors, straddled, hacked the foe,
Dug their bare toes into the ground and slew   35
The brother-naked man who lay between their feet and drew
His lips back from his teeth in a grimace.
They were Italians who knew war's sorrow and disgrace
And showed the thing suspended, stripped: a theme
Born out of the experience of war's horrible extreme
Beneath a sky where even the air flows   41
With lacrimae Christi. For that rage, that bitterness, those blows,
That hatred of the slain, what could they be
But indirectly or directly a commentary
On the Crucifixion? And the picture burns   45
With indignation and pity and despair by turns,
Because it is the obverse of the scene
Where Christ hangs murdered, stripped, upon the Cross. I mean,
That is the explanation of its rage.

23–6 **Michelangelo . . . Florence**: in 1504, Michelangelo (1475–1564) was commissioned by the Signoria of Florence to paint a battle-piece for their new council chamber; the painting ('The Battle of Cascina') was never completed, but Michelangelo did begin work on a cartoon of one section, called 'Bathers'; that, too, was lost, but a copy survives 33 **Pollaiuolo**: Antonio Pollaiuolo (c.1432–98), Italian painter; 'Battle of the Naked Men' is actually an engraving 42 **lacrimae Christi**: 'the tears of Christ'

And we too have our bitterness and pity that engage
Blood, spirit, in this war. But night begins,   51
Night of the mind: who nowadays is conscious of our sins?
Though every human deed concerns our blood,
And even we must know, what nobody has understood,
That some great love is over all we do,   55
And that is what has driven us to this fury, for so few
Can suffer all the terror of that love:
The terror of that love has set us spinning in this groove
Greased with our blood.

                These dry themselves and dress,
Combing their hair, forget the fear and shame of nakedness.   60
Because to love is frightening we prefer
The freedom of our crimes. Yet, as I drink the dusky air,
I feel a strange delight that fills me full,
Strange gratitude, as if evil itself were beautiful,
And kiss the wound in thought, while in the west   65
I watch a streak of red that might have issued from Christ's breast.

DYLAN THOMAS

AND DEATH SHALL HAVE NO DOMINION

AND death shall have no dominion.
Dead men naked they shall be one
With the man in the wind and the west moon;
When their bones are picked clean and the clean bones gone,
They shall have stars at elbow and foot;   5
Though they go mad they shall be sane,
Though they sink through the sea they shall rise again;
Though lovers be lost love shall not;
And death shall have no dominion.

And death shall have no dominion.   10
Under the windings of the sea
They lying long shall not die windily;
Twisting on racks when sinews give way,
Strapped to a wheel, yet they shall not break;
Faith in their hands shall snap in two,   15
And the unicorn evils run them through;
Split all ends up they shan't crack;
And death shall have no dominion.

And death shall have no dominion.
No more may gulls cry at their ears   20
Or waves break loud on the seashores;
Where blew a flower may a flower no more

Lift its head to the blows of the rain;
Though they be mad and dead as nails,
Heads of the characters hammer through daisies;   25
Break in the sun till the sun breaks down,
And death shall have no dominion.

AND DEATH SHALL HAVE NO DOMINION: 13 **racks:** the rack was an
instrument of torture stretching the limbs 14 **Strapped to a wheel:**
breaking upon a wheel was a form of torture and execution in
which the prisoner was tied to a cartwheel and had his limbs
smashed one by one, ending with blows to the chest to finish him
off 24 **dead as nails:** 'as dead as a doornail' is proverbial; compare
Shakespeare's *2 Henry IV* 5.3: 'What, is the old king dead?' 'As nail
in door'

POEM IN OCTOBER

IT WAS my thirtieth year to heaven
Woke to my hearing from harbour and neighbour
            wood
    And the mussel pooled and the heron
        Priested shore
        The morning beckon   5
With water praying and call of seagull and rook
And the knock of sailing boats on the net webbed wall
        Myself to set foot
        That second
In the still sleeping town and set forth.   10

    My birthday began with the water-
Birds and the birds of the winged trees flying my
            name
    Above the farms and the white horses
        And I rose
        In rainy autumn   15
And walked abroad in a shower of all my days.
High tide and the heron dived when I took the road
        Over the border
        And the gates
Of the town closed as the town awoke.   20

    A springful of larks in a rolling
Cloud and the roadside bushes brimming with
            whistling
    Blackbirds and the sun of October
        Summery
        On the hill's shoulder,   25
Here were fond climates and sweet singers suddenly
Come in the morning where I wandered and listened
        To the rain wringing
        Wind blow cold
In the wood faraway under me.   30

    Pale rain over the dwindling harbour
And over the sea wet church the size of a snail
    With its horns through mist and the castle
        Brown as owls
        But all the gardens   35

Of spring and summer were blooming in the tall tales
Beyond the border and under the lark full cloud.
        There could I marvel
            My birthday
    Away but the weather turned around.   40

    It turned away from the blithe country
And down the other air and the blue altered sky
        Streamed again a wonder of summer
            With apples
            Pears and red currants   45
And I saw in the turning so clearly a child's
Forgotten mornings when he walked with his mother
            Through the parables
            Of sun light
    And the legends of the green chapels   50

    And the twice told fields of infancy
That his tears burned my cheeks and his heart moved
            in mine.
    These were the woods the river and sea
            Where a boy
            In the listening   55
Summertime of the dead whispered the truth of his
            joy
To the trees and the stones and the fish in the tide.
        And the mystery
            Sang alive
    Still in the water and singingbirds.   60

    And there could I marvel my birthday
Away but the weather turned around. And the true
        Joy of the long dead child sang burning
            In the sun.
        It was my thirtieth   65
Year to heaven stood there then in the summer noon
Though the town below lay leaved with October
            blood.
        O may my heart's truth
            Still be sung
    On this high hill in a year's turning.   70

DO NOT GO GENTLE INTO THAT
GOOD NIGHT

DO NOT go gentle into that good night,
Old age should burn and rave at close of day;
Rage, rage against the dying of the light.

Though wise men at their end know dark is right,
Because their words had forked no lightning they   5
Do not go gentle into that good night.

Good men, the last wave by, crying how bright
Their frail deeds might have danced in a green bay,
Rage, rage against the dying of the light.

Wild men who caught and sang the sun in flight,   10
And learn, too late, they grieved it on its way,
Do not go gentle into that good night.

Grave men, near death, who see with blinding sight
Blind eyes could blaze like meteors and be gay,
Rage, rage against the dying of the light.   15

And you, my father, there on the sad height,
Curse, bless, me now with your fierce tears, I pray.
Do not go gentle into that good night.
Rage, rage against the dying of the light.

FERN HILL

Now as I was young and easy under the apple boughs
About the lilting house and happy as the grass was
    green,
    The night above the dingle starry,
      Time let me hail and climb
    Golden in the heydays of his eyes,   5
And honoured among wagons I was prince of the
    apple towns
And once below a time I lordly had the trees and
    leaves
      Trail with daisies and barley
    Down the rivers of the windfall light.

And as I was green and carefree, famous among the
    barns   10
About the happy yard and singing as the farm was
    home,
    In the sun that is young once only,
      Time let me play and be
    Golden in the mercy of his means,
And green and golden I was huntsman and herdsman,
    the calves   15
Sang to my horn, the foxes on the hills barked clear
    and cold,
      And the sabbath rang slowly
    In the pebbles of the holy streams.

All the sun long it was running, it was lovely, the hay
Fields high as the house, the tunes from the chimneys,
    it was air   20
    And playing, lovely and watery
      And fire green as grass.
    And nightly under the simple stars
As I rode to sleep the owls were bearing the farm
    away,
All the moon long I heard, blessed among stables, the
    night-jars   25
    Flying with the ricks, and the horses
      Flashing into the dark.

And then to awake, and the farm, like a wanderer
    white
With the dew, come back, the cock on his shoulder: it
    was all

Shining, it was Adam and maiden,   30
    The sky gathered again
    And the sun grew round that very day.
So it must have been after the birth of the simple light
In the first, spinning place, the spellbound horses
    walking warm
    Out of the whinnying green stable   35
    On to the fields of praise.

And honoured among foxes and pheasants by the gay
    house
Under the new made clouds and happy as the heart
    was long,
    In the sun born over and over,
      I ran my heedless ways,   40
    My wishes raced through the house high hay
And nothing I cared, at my sky blue trades, that time
    allows
In all his tuneful turning so few and such morning
    songs
    Before the children green and golden
    Follow him out of grace,   45

Nothing I cared, in the lamb white days, that time
    would take me
Up to the swallow thronged loft by the shadow of my
    hand,
    In the moon that is always rising,
      Nor that riding to sleep
    I should hear him fly with the high fields   50
And wake to the farm forever fled from the childless
    land.
Oh as I was young and easy in the mercy of his
    means,
    Time held me green and dying
    Though I sang in my chains like the sea.

FERN HILL: the farm home of the poet's Aunt Annie: 3 **dingle:** a dell,
a tree-covered hollow 30 **Adam and maiden:** i.e. the Garden of Eden

HENRY REED

LESSONS OF THE WAR

Vixi duellis nuper idoneus
Et militavi non sine gloria

I. NAMING OF PARTS

Today we have naming of parts. Yesterday,
We had daily cleaning. And tomorrow morning,
We shall have what to do after firing. But today,
Today we have naming of parts. Japonica
Glistens like coral in all of the neighbouring gardens,
    And today we have naming of parts.   6

LESSONS OF THE WAR: **Vixi . . . gloria:** 'Though that life is past, I was but
now still meet for ladies' love, and fought my battles not without glory'
(Horace, *Odes* 3.26.1–2; Wickham translation): (1) 4 **Japonica:** camellia

This is the lower sling swivel. And this
Is the upper sling swivel, whose use you will see,
When you are given your slings. And this is the piling
    swivel,
Which in your case you have not got. The branches 10
Hold in the gardens their silent, eloquent gestures,
    Which in our case we have not got.

This is the safety-catch, which is always released
With an easy flick of the thumb. And please do not let
    me 14
See anyone using his finger. You can do it quite easy
If you have any strength in your thumb. The blossoms
Are fragile and motionless, never letting anyone see
    Any of them using their finger.

And this you can see is the bolt. The purpose of
    this
Is to open the breech, as you see. We can slide it 20
Rapidly backwards and forwards: we call this
Easing the spring. And rapidly backwards and
    forwards
The early bees are assaulting and fumbling the
    flowers:
    They call it easing the Spring.

They call it easing the Spring: it is perfectly easy 25
If you have any strength in your thumb: like the
    bolt,
And the breech, and the cocking-piece, and the point
    of balance,
Which in our case we have not got; and the almond-
    blossom
Silent in all of the gardens and the bees going
    backwards and forwards,
    For today we have naming of parts. 30

II. JUDGING DISTANCES

NOT only how far away, but the way that you say it
Is very important. Perhaps you may never get
The knack of judging a distance, but at least you know
How to report on a landscape: the central sector,
The right of arc and that, which we had last
    Tuesday, 5
    And at least you know

That maps are of time, not place, so far as the army
Happens to be concerned – the reason being,
Is one which need not delay us. Again, you know
There are three kinds of tree, three only, the fir and
    the poplar, 10
And those which have bushy tops to; and lastly
    That things only seem to be things.

A barn is not called a barn, to put it more plainly,
Or a field in the distance, where sheep may be safely
    grazing.
You must never be over-sure. You must say, when
    reporting: 15
At five o'clock in the central sector is a dozen
Of what appear to be animals; whatever you do,
    Don't call the bleeders *sheep*.

I am sure that's quite clear; and suppose, for the sake
    of example,
The one at the end, asleep, endeavours to tell us 20
What he sees over there to the west, and how far away,
After first having come to attention. There to the west,
On the fields of summer the sun and the shadows
    bestow
    Vestments of purple and gold.

The still white dwellings are like a mirage in the heat,
And under the swaying elms a man and a woman 26
Lie gently together. Which is, perhaps, only to say
That there is a row of houses to the left of arc,
And that under some poplars a pair of what appear to
    be humans
    Appear to be loving. 30

Well that, for an answer, is what we might rightly call
Moderately satisfactory only, the reason being,
Is that two things have been omitted, and those are
    important.
The human beings, now: in what direction are they,
And how far away, would you say? And do not
    forget 35
    There may be dead ground in between.

There may be dead ground in between; and I may not
    have got
The knack of judging a distance; I will only venture
A guess that perhaps between me and the apparent
    lovers, 39
(Who, incidentally, appear by now to have finished,)
At seven o'clock from the houses, is roughly a distance
    Of about one year and a half.

III. MOVEMENT OF BODIES

Those of you that have got through the rest, I am
    going to rapidly
Devote a little time to showing you, those that can
    master it,
A few ideas about tactics, which must not be confused
With what we call strategy. Tactics is merely
The mechanical movement of bodies, and that is
    what we mean by it. 5
    Or perhaps I should say: by them.

(II) 14 **sheep may be safely grazing**: 'Sheep May Safely Graze' is a
popular air by J. S. Bach

Strategy, to be quite frank, you will have no hand in.
It is done by those up above, and it merely refers to,
The larger movements over which we have no control.
But tactics are also important, together or single. 10
You must never forget that, suddenly, in an
    engagement,
      You may find yourself alone.

This brown clay model is a characteristic terrain
Of a simple and typical kind. Its general character
Should be taken in at a glance, and its general
    character 15
You can, see at a glance it is somewhat hilly by nature,
With a fair amount of typical vegetation
    Disposed at certain parts.

Here at the top of the tray, which we might call the
    northwards,
Is a wooded headland, with a crown of bushy-topped
    trees on; 20
And proceeding downwards or south we take in at a
    glance
A variety of gorges and knolls and plateaus and
    basins and saddles,
Somewhat symmetrically put, for easy identification.
    And here is our point of attack.

But remember of course it will not be a tray you will
    fight on, 25
Nor always by daylight. After a hot day, think of the
    night
Cooling the desert down, and you still moving over it:
Past a ruined tank or a gun, perhaps, or a dead friend,
In the midst of war, at peace. It might quite well be that.
    It isn't always a tray. 30

And even this tray is different to what I had thought.
These models are somehow never always the same:
    for a reason
I do not know how to explain quite. Just as I do not
    know
Why there is always someone at this particular lesson
Who always starts crying. Now will you kindly 35
    Empty those blinking eyes?

I thank you. I have no wish to seem impatient.
I know it is all very hard, but you would not like,
To take a simple example, to take for example,
This place we have thought of here, you would not like
To find yourself face to face with it, and you not
    knowing 41
    What there might be inside?

Very well then: suppose this is what you must capture.
It will not be easy, not being very exposed,
Secluded away like it is, and somewhat protected 45
By a typical formation of what appear to be bushes,
So that you cannot see, as to what is concealed inside,
    As to whether it is friend or foe.

And so, a strong feint will be necessary in this
    connection.
It will not be a tray, remember. It may be a desert
    stretch 50
With nothing in sight, to speak of. I have no wish to
    be inconsiderate,
But I see there are two of you now, commencing to
    snivel.
I do not know where such emotional privates can
    come from.
    Try to behave like men.

I thank you. I was saying: a thoughtful deception 55
Is always somewhat essential in such a case. You can see
That if only the attacker can capture such an
    emplacement
The rest of the terrain is his: a key-position, and calling
For the most resourceful manoeuvres. But that is
    what tactics is.
    Or I should say rather: are. 60

Let us begin then and appreciate the situation.
I am thinking especially of the point we have been
    considering,
Though in a sense everything in the whole of the
    terrain,
Must be appreciated. I do not know what I have said
To upset so many of you. I know it is a difficult lesson.
    Yesterday a man was sick, 66

But I have never known as many as five in a single
    intake,
Unable to cope with this lesson. I think you had better
Fall out, all five, and sit at the back of the room,
Being careful not to talk. The rest will close up. 70
Perhaps it was me saying 'a dead friend', earlier on?
    Well, some of us live.

And I never know why, whenever we get to tactics,
Men either laugh or cry, though neither is strictly
    called for.
But perhaps I have started too early with a difficult
    task? 75
We will start again, further north, with a simpler
    problem.
Are you ready? Is everyone paying attention?
    Very well then. Here are two hills.

IV. UNARMED COMBAT

IN due course of course you will all be issued with
Your proper issue; but until tomorrow,
You can hardly be said to need it; and until that time,
We shall have unarmed combat. I shall teach you
The various holds and rolls and throws and breakfalls
    Which you may sometimes meet.   6

And the various holds and rolls and throws and
    breakfalls
Do not depend on any sort of weapon,
But only on what I might coin a phrase and call
The ever-important question of human balance,   10
And the ever-important need to be in a strong
    Position at the start.

There are many kinds of weakness about the body,
Where you would least expect, like the ball of the
    foot.
But the various holds and rolls and throws and
    breakfalls   15
Will always come in useful. And never be frightened
To tackle from behind: it may not be clean to do so,
    But this is global war.

So give them all you have, and always give them
As good as you get; it will always get you somewhere.
(You may not know it, but you can tie a Jerry   21
Up without rope; it is one of the things I shall teach
    you.)
Nothing will matter if only you are ready for him.
    The readiness is all.

The readiness is all. How can I help but feel   25
I have been here before? But somehow then,
I was the tied-up one. How to get out
Was always then my problem. And even if I had
A piece of rope I was always the sort of person
    Who threw the rope aside.   30

And in my time I have given them all I had,
Which was never as good as I got, and it got me
    nowhere.
And the various holds and rolls and throws and
    breakfalls
Somehow or other I always seemed to put
In the wrong place. And as for war, my wars   35
    Were global from the start.

(IV) 21 **a Jerry:** a German 25 ***The readiness is all:*** 'If it be now, 'tis
not to come; if it be not to come, it will be now; if it be not now,
yet it will come – the readiness is all' (*Hamlet* 5.2)

Perhaps I was never in a strong position,
Or the ball of my foot got hurt, or I had some
    weakness
Where I had least expected. But I think I see your
    point.
While awaiting a proper issue, we must learn the
    lesson   40
Of the ever-important question of human balance.
    It is courage that counts.

Things may be the same again; and we must fight
Not in the hope of winning but rather of keeping
Something alive: so that when we meet our end,   45
It may be said that we tackled wherever we could,
That battle-fit we lived, and though defeated,
    Not without glory fought.

ALUN LEWIS

'ALL DAY IT HAS RAINED . . .'

ALL day it has rained, and we on the edge of the
    moors
Have sprawled in our bell-tents, moody and dull as
    boors,
Groundsheets and blankets spread on the muddy
    ground
And from the first grey wakening we have found
No refuge from the skirmishing fine rain   5
And the wind that made the canvas heave and flap
And the taut wet guy-ropes ravel out and snap.
All day the rain has glided, wave and mist and dream,
Drenching the gorse and heather, a gossamer stream
Too light to stir the acorns that suddenly   10
Snatched from their cups by the wild south-westerly
Pattered against the tent and our upturned dreaming
    faces.
And we stretched out, unbuttoning our braces,
Smoking a Woodbine, darning dirty socks,
Reading the Sunday papers – I saw a fox   15
And mentioned it in the note I scribbled home; –
And we talked of girls, and dropping bombs on Rome,
And thought of the quiet dead and the loud celebrities
Exhorting us to slaughter, and the herded refugees;
– Yet thought softly, morosely of them, and as
    indifferently   20
As of ourselves or those whom we
For years have loved, and will again
Tomorrow maybe love; but now it is the rain
Possesses us entirely, the twilight and the rain.
And I can remember nothing dearer or more to my
    heart   25
Than the children I watched in the woods on Saturday
Shaking down burning chestnuts for the schoolyard's
    merry play,

Or the shaggy patient dog who followed me
By Sheet and Steep and up the wooded scree
To the Shoulder o' Mutton where Edward Thomas
   brooded long   30
On death and beauty – till a bullet stopped his song.

'ALL DAY IT HAS RAINED': 9 **gossamer:** spider-threads that float on
the air or form webs on bushes; thus, any very fine material
14 **Woodbines:** a cheap brand of cigarette 29 **Sheet and Steep:**
Hampshire villages 30 **the Shoulder o' Mutton:** a hill near Steep
31 **a bullet stopped his song:** Edward Thomas was killed at Arras
in 1917

KEITH DOUGLAS

SIMPLIFY ME WHEN I'M DEAD

REMEMBER me when I am dead
and simplify me when I'm dead.

As the processes of earth
strip off the colour and the skin:
take the brown hair and blue eye   5

and leave me simpler than at birth,
when hairless I came howling in
as the moon entered the cold sky.

Of my skeleton perhaps,
so stripped, a learnèd man will say   10
'He was of such a type and intelligence,' no more.

Thus when in a year collapse
particular memories, you may
deduce, from the long pain I bore

the opinions I held, who was my foe   15
and what I left, even my appearance
but incidents will be no guide.

Time's wrong-way telescope will show
a minute man ten years hence
and by distance simplified.   20

Through that lens see if I seem
substance or nothing: of the world
deserving mention or charitable oblivion,

not by momentary spleen
or love into decision hurled,   25
leisurely arrive at an opinion.

Remember me when I am dead
and simplify me when I'm dead.

LEO MARKS

'THE LIFE THAT I HAVE . . .'

THE life that I have
Is all that I have
And the life that I have
Is yours.

The love that I have   5
Of the life that I have
Is yours and yours and yours.
A sleep I shall have
A rest I shall have,
Yet death will be but a pause.   10

For the peace of my years
In the long green grass
Will be yours and yours and yours.

'THE LIFE THAT I HAVE': These verses were given by cryptographer
Leo Marks to the wartime agent Violette Szabo as her code-poem
but later caught the popular imagination when they were
included in the film *Carve Her Name with Pride* (1958), which told
Szabo's story. 'To encode a message an agent had to choose five
words at random from his poem and give each letter of these
words a number. He then used these numbers to jumble and
juxtapose his clear text,' Marks explained, adding: 'I hadn't
thought that writing poetry would be my contribution to Hitler's
downfall' (*Between Silk and Cyanide*, 1998, ch. 1). Violette Szabo was
captured by the Nazis and executed at Ravensbrück

PHILIP LARKIN

TOADS

Why should I let the toad *work*
   Squat on my life?
Can't I use my wit as a pitchfork
   And drive the brute off?

Six days of the week it soils   5
   With its sickening poison –
Just for paying a few bills!
   That's out of proportion.

Lots of folk live on their wits:
   Lecturers, lispers,   10
Losels, loblolly-men, louts –
   They don't end as paupers;

Lots of folk live up lanes
   With fires in a bucket,
Eat windfalls and tinned sardines –   15
   They seem to like it.

Their nippers have got bare feet,
   Their unspeakable wives
Are skinny as whippets – and yet
   No one actually *starves*.   20

Ah, were I courageous enough
   To shout *Stuff your pension!*
But I know, all too well, that's the stuff
   That dreams are made on:

For something sufficiently toad-like   25
   Squats in me, too;
Its hunkers are heavy as hard luck,
   And cold as snow,

And never will allow me to blarney
   My way to getting
The fame and the girl and the money   30
   All at one sitting.

I don't say, one bodies the other
   One's spiritual truth;
But I do say it's hard to lose either,   35
   When you have both.

MR BLEANEY

'THIS was Mr Bleaney's room. He stayed
The whole time he was at the Bodies, till
They moved him.' Flowered curtains, thin and frayed,
Fall to within five inches of the sill,

Whose window shows a strip of building land,   5
Tussocky, littered. 'Mr Bleaney took
My bit of garden properly in hand.'
Bed, upright chair, sixty-watt bulb, no hook

Behind the door, no room for books or bags –
'I'll take it.' So it happens that I lie   10
Where Mr Bleaney lay, and stub my fags
On the same saucer-souvenir, and try

Stuffing my ears with cotton-wool, to drown
The jabbering set he egged her on to buy.
I know his habits – what time he came down,   15
His preference for sauce to gravy, why

He kept on plugging at the four aways –
Likewise their yearly frame: the Frinton folk
Who put him up for summer holidays,
And Christmas at his sister's house in Stoke.   20

But if he stood and watched the frigid wind
Tousling the clouds, lay on the fusty bed
Telling himself that this was home, and grinned,
And shivered, without shaking off the dread

That how we live measures our own nature,   25
And at his age having no more to show
Than one hired box should make him pretty sure
He warranted no better, I don't know.

THE WHITSUN WEDDINGS

THAT Whitsun, I was late getting away:
   Not till about
One-twenty on the sunlit Saturday
Did my three-quarters-empty train pull out,
All windows down, all cushions hot, all sense   5
Of being in a hurry gone. We ran
Behind the backs of houses, crossed a street
Of blinding windscreens, smelt the fish-dock; thence
The river's level drifting breadth began,
Where sky and Lincolnshire and water meet.   10

All afternoon, through the tall heat that slept
   For miles inland,
A slow and stopping curve southwards we kept.
Wide arms went by, short-shadowed cattle, and
Canals with floatings of industrial froth;   15
A hothouse flashed uniquely: hedges dipped
And rose: and now and then a smell of grass
Displaced the reek of buttoned carriage-cloth
Until the next town, new and nondescript,
Approached with acres of dismantled cars.   20

At first, I didn't notice what a noise
   The weddings made
Each station that we stopped at: sun destroys
The interest of what's happening in the shade,
And down the long cool platforms whoops and skirls
I took for porters larking with the mails,   26
And went on reading. Once we started, though,
We passed them, grinning and pomaded, girls
In parodies of fashion, heels and veils,
All posed irresolutely, watching us go,   30

As if out on the end of an event
   Waving goodbye
To something that survived it. Struck, I leant
More promptly out next time, more curiously,
And saw it all again in different terms: 35
The fathers with broad belts under their suits
And seamy foreheads; mothers loud and fat;
An uncle shouting smut; and then the perms,
The nylon gloves and jewellery-substitutes,
The lemons, mauves, and olive-ochres that   40

Marked off the girls unreally from the rest.
   Yes, from cafés
And banquet-halls up yards, and bunting-dressed
Coach-party annexes, the wedding-days
Were coming to an end. All down the line   45
Fresh couples climbed aboard: the rest stood round;
The last confetti and advice were thrown,
And, as we moved, each face seemed to define
Just what it saw departing: children frowned
At something dull; fathers had never known   50

Success so huge and wholly farcical;
  The women shared
The secret like a happy funeral;
While girls, gripping their handbags tighter, stared
At a religious wounding. Free at last,   55
And loaded with the sum of all they saw,
We hurried towards London, shuffling gouts of steam.
Now fields were building-plots, and poplars cast
Long shadows over major roads, and for
Some fifty minutes, that in time would seem   60

Just long enough to settle hats and say
  I nearly died,
A dozen marriages got under way.
They watched the landscape, sitting side by side
– An Odeon went past, a cooling tower,   65
And someone running up to bowl – and none
Thought of the others they would never meet
Or how their lives would all contain this hour.
I thought of London spread out in the sun,
Its postal districts packed like squares of wheat: 70

There we were aimed. And as we raced across
  Bright knots of rail
Past standing Pullmans, walls of blackened moss
Came close, and it was nearly done, this frail
Travelling coincidence; and what it held   75
Stood ready to be loosed with all the power
That being changed can give. We slowed again,
And as the tightened brakes took hold, there swelled
A sense of falling, like an arrow-shower
Sent out of sight, somewhere becoming rain.   80

THE WHITSUN WEDDINGS: 73 **Pullmans:** a Pullman was a luxurious railway carriage, first made in America by George M. Pullman (1831–97)

DOCKERY AND SON

'DOCKERY was junior to you,
Wasn't he?' said the Dean. 'His son's here now.'
Death-suited, visitant, I nod. 'And do
You keep in touch with—' Or remember how
Black-gowned, unbreakfasted, and still half-tight   5
We used to stand before that desk, to give
'Our version' of 'these incidents last night'?
I try the door of where I used to live:

Locked. The lawn spreads dazzlingly wide.
A known bell chimes. I catch my train, ignored.   10
Canal and clouds and colleges subside
Slowly from view. But Dockery, good Lord,
Anyone up today must have been born
In '43, when I was twenty-one.
If he was younger, did he get this son   15
At nineteen, twenty? Was he that withdrawn

High-collared public-schoolboy, sharing rooms
With Cartwright who was killed? Well, it just shows
How much . . . How little . . . Yawning, I suppose
I fell asleep, waking at the fumes   20
And furnace-glares of Sheffield, where I changed,
And ate an awful pie, and walked along
The platform to its end to see the ranged
Joining and parting lines reflect a strong

Unhindered moon. To have no son, no wife,   25
No house or land still seemed quite natural.
Only a numbness registered the shock
Of finding out how much had gone of life,
How widely from the others. Dockery, now:
Only nineteen, he must have taken stock   30
Of what he wanted, and been capable
Of . . . No, that's not the difference: rather, how

Convinced he was he should be added to!
Why did he think adding meant increase?
To me it was dilution. Where do these   35
Innate assumptions come from? Not from what
We think truest, or most want to do:
Those warp tight-shut, like doors. They're more a style
Our lives bring with them: habit for a while,
Suddenly they harden into all we've got   40

And how we got it; looked back on, they rear
Like sand-clouds, thick and close, embodying
For Dockery a son, for me nothing,
Nothing with all a son's harsh patronage.
Life is first boredom, then fear.   45
Whether or not we use it, it goes,
And leaves what something hidden from us chose,
And age, and then the only end of age.

ANNUS MIRABILIS

SEXUAL intercourse began
In nineteen sixty-three
(Which was rather late for me) –
Between the end of the *Chatterley* ban
And the Beatles' first LP.   5

Up till then there'd only been
A sort of bargaining,
A wrangle for a ring,
A shame that started at sixteen
And spread to everything.   10

Then all at once the quarrel sank:
Everyone felt the same,
And every life became
A brilliant breaking of the bank,
A quite unlosable game.   15

So life was never better than
In nineteen sixty-three
(Though just too late for me) –
Between the end of the *Chatterley* ban
And the Beatles' first LP.   20

ANNUS MIRABILIS: 'The Year of Wonders' (echoing the title of a long
poem by Dryden commemorating the events of 1666): 4 **the end of
the *Chatterley* ban:** in 1960, Penguin Books published an unexpurgated
edition of D. H. Lawrence's *Lady Chatterley's Lover* (1928) and was
prosecuted under the new Obscene Publications Act but
acquitted 5 **the Beatles' first LP:** *Please Please Me* (1963)

THIS BE THE VERSE

THEY fuck you up, your mum and dad.
  They may not mean to, but they do.
They fill you with the faults they had
  And add some extra, just for you.

But they were fucked up in their turn   5
  By fools in old-style hats and coats,
Who half the time were soppy-stern
  And half at one another's throats.

Man hands on misery to man.
  It deepens like a coastal shelf.   10
Get out as early as you can,
  And don't have any kids yourself.

THIS BE THE VERSE: see Stevenson's 'Requiem'

THOM GUNN

ON THE MOVE

THE blue jay scuffling in the bushes follows
Some hidden purpose, and the gust of birds
That spurts across the field, the wheeling swallows,
Have nested in the trees and undergrowth.
Seeking their instinct, or their poise, or both,   5
One moves with an uncertain violence
Under the dust thrown by a baffled sense
Or the dull thunder of approximate words.

On motorcycles, up the road, they come:
Small, black, as flies hanging in heat, the Boys,   10
Until the distance throws them forth, their hum
Bulges to thunder held by calf and thigh.
In goggles, donned impersonality,
In gleaming jackets trophied with the dust,
They strap in doubt – by hiding it, robust –   15
And almost hear a meaning in their noise.

Exact conclusion of their hardiness
Has no shape yet, but from known whereabouts
They ride, direction where the tires press.
They scare a flight of birds across the field: 20
Much that is natural, to the will must yield.
Men manufacture both machine and soul,
And use what they imperfectly control
To dare a future from the taken routes.

It is a part solution, after all.   25
One is not necessarily discord
On earth; or damned because, half animal,
One lacks direct instinct, because one wakes
Afloat on movement that divides and breaks.
One joins the movement in a valueless world,   30
Choosing it, till, both hurler and the hurled,
One moves as well, always toward, toward.

A minute holds them, who have come to go:
The self-defined, astride the created will
They burst away; the towns they travel through   35
Are home for neither bird nor holiness,
For birds and saints complete their purposes.
At worst, one is in motion; and at best,
Reaching no absolute, in which to rest,
One is always nearer by not keeping still.   40

IN SANTA MARIA DEL POPOLO

WAITING for when the sun an hour or less
Conveniently oblique makes visible
The painting on one wall of this recess
By Caravaggio, of the Roman School,
I see how shadow in the painting brims   5
With a real shadow, drowning all shapes out
But a dim horse's haunch and various limbs,
Until the very subject is in doubt.

But evening gives the act, beneath the horse
And one indifferent groom, I see him sprawl,   10
Foreshortened from the head, with hidden face,
Where he has fallen, Saul becoming Paul.
O wily painter, limiting the scene
From a cacophony of dusty forms
To the one convulsion, what is it you mean   15
In that wide gesture of the lifting arms?

No Ananias croons a mystery yet,
Casting the pain out under name of sin.
The painter saw what was, an alternate
Candor and secrecy inside the skin.   20
He painted, elsewhere, that firm insolent
Young whore in Venus' clothes, those pudgy cheats,
Those sharpers; and was strangled, as things went,
For money, by one such picked off the streets.

I turn, hardly enlightened, from the chapel 25
To the dim interior of the church instead,
In which there kneel already several people,
Mostly old women: each head closeted
In tiny fists holds comfort as it can.
Their poor arms are too tired for more than this 30
– For the large gesture of solitary man,
Resisting, by embracing, nothingness.

IN SANTA MARIA DEL POPOLO: The Cerasi Chapel in the church
of Santa Maria del Popolo in Rome contains a pair of paintings
by Caravaggio (1571–1610): 'The Crucifixion of St Peter' and
'The Conversion of St Paul'. The poem takes its inspiration from
the latter work, depicting events on the road to Damascus ('and
suddenly there shined round about him a light from heaven: And
he fell to the earth, and heard a voice saying unto him, Saul, Saul,
why persecutest thou me': Acts 8)   11 **Foreshortened:** the two
paintings were intended to be viewed from the aspect of someone
kneeling in prayer below   12 **Saul becoming Paul:** after his
conversion Saul took the Roman version of his name (Acts 13.9)
17 **Ananias:** the disciple in Damascus sent by the Lord to Saul
(Acts 8)   23–4 **was strangled . . . off the streets:** although Caravaggio
was never far from trouble, he actually died of a fever

MY SAD CAPTAINS

ONE by one they appear in
the darkness: a few friends, and
a few with historical
names. How late they start to shine!
but before they fade they stand 5
perfectly embodied, all

the past lapping them like a
cloak of chaos. They were men
who, I thought, lived only to
renew the wasteful force they 10
spent with each hot convulsion.
They remind me, distant now.

True, they are not at rest yet,
but now that they are indeed
apart, winnowed from failures, 15
they withdraw to an orbit
and turn with disinterested
hard energy, like the stars.

MY SAD CAPTAINS: see Shakespeare's *Antony and Cleopatra* 3.13: 'Let's
have one other gaudy night. Call to me/All my sad captains; fill
our bowls once more;/Let's mock the midnight bell'

TED HUGHES

THE THOUGHT-FOX

I IMAGINE this midnight moment's forest:
Something else is alive
Beside the clock's loneliness
And this blank page where my fingers move.
Through the window I see no star: 5

Something more near
Though deeper within darkness
Is entering the loneliness:

Cold, delicately as the dark snow
A fox's nose touches twig, leaf; 10
Two eyes serve a movement, that now
And again now, and now, and now

Sets neat prints into the snow
Between trees, and warily a lame
Shadow lags by stump and in hollow 15
Of a body that is bold to come

Across clearings, an eye,
A widening deepening greenness,
Brilliantly, concentratedly,
Coming about its own business 20

Till, with a sudden sharp hot stink of fox
It enters the dark hole of the head.
The window is starless still; the clock ticks,
The page is printed.

HAWK ROOSTING

I SIT in the top of the wood, my eyes closed.
Inaction, no falsifying dream
Between my hooked head and hooked feet:
Or in sleep rehearse perfect kills and eat.

The convenience of the high trees! 5
The air's buoyancy and the sun's ray
Are of advantage to me;
And the earth's face upward for my inspection.

My feet are locked upon the rough bark.
It took the whole of Creation 10
To produce my foot, my each feather:
Now I hold Creation in my foot

Or fly up, and revolve it all slowly –
I kill where I please because it is all mine.
There is no sophistry in my body: 15
My manners are tearing off heads –

The allotment of death.
For the one path of my flight is direct
Through the bones of the living.
No arguments assert my right: 20

The sun is behind me.
Nothing has changed since I began.
My eye has permitted no change.
I am going to keep things like this.

PIKE

PIKE, three inches long, perfect
Pike in all parts, green tigering the gold.
Killers from the egg: the malevolent agèd grin.
They dance on the surface among the flies.

Or move, stunned by their own grandeur,   5
Over a bed of emerald, silhouette
Of submarine delicacy and horror.
A hundred feet long in their world.

In ponds, under the heat-struck lily pads –
Gloom of their stillness: 10
Logged on last year's black leaves, watching upwards.
Or hung in an amber cavern of weeds

The jaws' hooked clamp and fangs
Not to be changed at this date;
A life subdued to its instrument;   15
The gills kneading quietly, and the pectorals.

Three we kept behind glass,
Jungled in weed: three inches, four,
And four and a half: fed fry to them –
Suddenly there were two. Finally one   20

With a sag belly and the grin it was born with.
And indeed they spare nobody.
Two, six pounds each, over two feet long,
High and dry and dead in the willow-herb –

One jammed past its gills down the other's gullet: 25
The outside eye stared: as a vice locks –
The same iron in this eye
Though its film shrank in death.

A pond I fished, fifty yards across,
Whose lilies and muscular tench   30
Had outlasted every visible stone
Of the monastery that planted them –

Stilled legendary depth:
It was as deep as England. It held
Pike too immense to stir, so immense and old   35
That past nightfall I dared not cast

But silently cast and fished
With the hair frozen on my head
For what might move, for what eye might move.
The still splashes on the dark pond,   40

Owls hushing the floating woods
Frail on my ear against the dream
Darkness beneath night's darkness had freed,
That rose slowly towards me, watching.

GEOFFREY HILL

GENESIS

I

AGAINST the burly air I strode,
Where the tight ocean heaves its load,
Crying the miracles of God.

And first I brought the sea to bear
Upon the dead weight of the land;   5
And the waves flourished at my prayer,
The rivers spawned their sand.

And where the streams were salt and full
The tough pig-headed salmon strove,
Curbing the ebb and the tide's pull,   10
To reach the steady hills above.

II

The second day I stood and saw
The osprey plunge with triggered claw,
Feathering blood along the shore,
To lay the living sinew bare.   15

And the third day I cried: 'Beware
The soft-voiced owl, the ferret's smile,
The hawk's deliberate stoop in air,
Cold eyes, and bodies hooped in steel,
Forever bent upon the kill.'   20

III

And I renounced, on the fourth day,
This fierce and unregenerate clay,
Building as a huge myth for man
The watery Leviathan,

And made the glove-winged albatross   25
Scour the ashes of the sea
Where Capricorn and Zero cross,
A brooding immortality –
Such as the charmed phoenix has
In the unwithering tree.   30

IV

The phoenix burns as cold as frost;
And, like a legendary ghost,
The phantom-bird goes wild and lost,
Upon a pointless ocean tossed.
So, the fifth day, I turned again   35
To flesh and blood and the blood's pain.

V

On the sixth day, as I rode
In haste about the works of God,
With spurs I plucked the horse's blood.

By blood we live, the hot, the cold,   40
To ravage and redeem the world:
There is no bloodless myth will hold.

And by Christ's blood are men made free
Though in close shrouds their bodies lie
Under the rough pelt of the sea;   45

Though Earth has rolled beneath her weight
The bones that cannot bear the light.

    1952

GENESIS: 24 **Leviathan:** a sea-monster 27 **Capricorn:** Tropic of Capricorn **Zero:** 0° longitude 31 **phoenix:** a mythical Arabian bird, the only one of its kind, that periodically burned itself and emerged rejuvenated from the ashes

SEPTEMBER SONG

Born 19.6.32–Deported 24.9.42

UNDESIRABLE you may have been, untouchable
you were not. Not forgotten
or passed over at the proper time.

As estimated, you died. Things marched,
sufficient, to that end.   5
Just so much Zyklon and leather, patented
terror, so many routine cries.

(I have made
an elegy for myself it
is true)   10

September fattens on vines. Roses
flake from the wall. The smoke
of harmless fires drifts to my eyes.

This is plenty. This is more than enough.

SEPTEMBER SONG: 6 **Zyklon:** gas used in the Nazi extermination camps

SEAMUS HEANEY

DEATH OF A NATURALIST

ALL year the flax-dam festered in the heart
Of the townland; green and heavy headed
Flax had rotted there, weighted down by huge sods.
Daily it sweltered in the punishing sun.
Bubbles gargled delicately, bluebottles   5
Wove a strong gauze of sound around the smell.
There were dragon-flies, spotted butterflies,
But best of all was the warm thick slobber
Of frogspawn that grew like clotted water
In the shade of the banks. Here, every spring   10

I would fill jampotfuls of the jellied
Specks to range on window-sills at home,
On shelves at school, and wait and watch until
The fattening dots burst into nimble-
Swimming tadpoles. Miss Walls would tell us how   15
The daddy frog was called a bullfrog
And how he croaked and how the mammy frog
Laid hundreds of little eggs and this was
Frogspawn. You could tell the weather by frogs too
For they were yellow in the sun and brown   20
In rain.

Then one hot day when fields were rank
With cowdung in the grass and angry frogs
Invaded the flax-dam; I ducked through hedges
To a coarse croaking that I had not heard   25
Before. The air was thick with a bass chorus.
Right down the dam gross-bellied frogs were cocked
On sods; their loose necks pulsed like sails. Some
    hopped:
The slap and plop were obscene threats. Some sat
Poised like mud grenades, their blunt heads farting.   30
I sickened, turned, and ran. The great slime kings
Were gathered there for vengeance and I knew
That if I dipped my hand the spawn would clutch it.

WHATEVER YOU SAY SAY NOTHING

1

I'M writing this just after an encounter
With an English journalist in search of 'views
On the Irish thing'. I'm back in winter
Quarters where bad news is no longer news,

Where media-men and stringers sniff and point,   5
Where zoom lenses, recorders and coiled leads
Litter the hotels. The times are out of joint
But I incline as much to rosary beads

As to the jottings and analyses
Of politicians and newspapermen   10
Who've scribbled down the long campaign from gas
And protest to gelignite and sten,

Who proved upon their pulses 'escalate',
'Backlash' and 'crack down', 'the provisional wing',
'Polarization' and 'long-standing hate'.   15
Yet I live here, I live here too, I sing,

Expertly civil tongued with civil neighbours
On the high wires of first wireless reports,
Sucking the fake taste, the stony flavours
Of those sanctioned, old, elaborate retorts: 20

WHATEVER YOU SAY SAY NOTHING: 3–4 **winter Quarters:** an army's winter retreat between campaigning seasons 5 **stringers:** a stringer is a journalist employed part-time to cover a particular area 7 **The times are out of joint:** *Hamlet* 1.5 12 **sten:** Sten gun 14 **'the provisional wing':** militant wing of the Irish Republican Army

'Oh, it's disgraceful, surely, I agree.'
'Where's it going to end?' 'It's getting worse.'
'They're murderers.' 'Internment, understandably . . .'
The 'voice of sanity' is getting hoarse.

2

Men die at hand. In blasted street and home   25
The gelignite's a common sound effect:
As the man said when Celtic won, 'The Pope of Rome
's a happy man this night.' His flock suspect

In their deepest heart of hearts the heretic
Has come at last to heel and to the stake.   30
We tremble near the flames but want no truck
With the actual firing. We're on the make

As ever. Long sucking the hind tit
Cold as a witch's and as hard to swallow
Still leaves us fork-tongued on the border bit: 35
The liberal papist note sounds hollow

When amplified and mixed in with the bangs
That shake all hearts and windows day and night.
(It's tempting here to rhyme on 'labour pangs'
And diagnose a rebirth in our plight,   40

But that would be to ignore other symptoms.
Last night you didn't need a stethoscope
To hear the eructation of Orange drums
Allergic equally to Pearse and Pope.)

On all sides 'little platoons' are mustering –   45
The phrase is Cruise O'Brien's via that great
Backlash, Burke – while I sit here with a pestering
Drouth for words at once both gaff and bait

To lure the tribal shoals to epigram
And order. I believe any of us   50
Could draw the line through bigotry and sham
Given the right line, *aere perennius*.

3

'Religion's never mentioned here,' of course.
'You know them by their eyes,' and hold your tongue.
'One side's as bad as the other,' never worse.   55
Christ, it's near time that some small leak was sprung

23 **Internment:** internment of terrorist suspects without trial was introduced in Northern Ireland in 1971   27 **Celtic:** support for Glasgow's two football teams divides along sectarian lines; Celtic's following is Catholic   33–4 **tit Cold as a witch's:** 'as cold as a witch's tit' is proverbial, meaning 'extremely cold' (*OED*)   43 **Orange:** Protestant (after William of Orange)   44 **Pearse:** see Yeats's 'Easter 1916'   46 **Cruise O'Brien:** Conor Cruise O'Brien, Irish historian and politician   47 **Burke:** Edmund Burke (1729–97), Irish politician and philosopher   48 **Drouth:** drought, thirst   **gaff:** hook for landing large fish   52 **aere perennius:** 'more durable than bronze' (Horace, *Odes* 3.30.1); i.e. everlasting

In the great dykes the Dutchman made
To dam the dangerous tide that followed Seamus.
Yet for all this art and sedentary trade
I am incapable. The famous   60

Northern reticence, the tight gag of place
And times: yes, yes. Of the 'wee six' I sing
Where to be saved you only must save face
And whatever you say, you say nothing.

Smoke-signals are loud-mouthed compared with us:
Manoeuvrings to find out name and school,   66
Subtle discrimination by addresses
With hardly an exception to the rule

That Norman, Ken and Sidney signalled Prod
And Seamus (call me Sean) was sure-fire Pape.   70
O land of password, handgrip, wink and nod,
Of open minds as open as a trap,

Where tongues lie coiled, as under flames lie wicks,
Where half of us, as in a wooden horse
Were cabin'd and confined like wily Greeks,   75
Besieged within the siege, whispering morse.

4

This morning from a dewy motorway
I saw the new camp for the internees:
A bomb had left a crater of fresh clay
In the roadside, and over in the trees   80

Machine-gun posts defined a real stockade.
There was that white mist you get on a low ground
And it was déjà-vu, some film made
Of Stalag 17, a bad dream with no sound.

Is there a life before death? That's chalked up   85
In Ballymurphy. Competence with pain,
Coherent miseries, a bite and sup,
We hug our little destiny again.

57 **the Dutchman:** William of Orange, king of England 1688–1702; his campaign in Ireland against the forces of the deposed Catholic James II left a bitter legacy   58 **Seamus:** James   62 **'wee six':** the six counties of Northern Ireland; they chose to remain part of the United Kingdom after Home Rule was finally granted to Ireland in 1920   69 **Prod:** Protestant   70 **Pape:** papist, Roman Catholic   74–5 **a wooden horse . . . wily Greeks:** the Trojan horse (Virgil's *Aeneid*, book 2)   75 **cabin'd and confined:** Shakespeare's *Macbeth* 3.4: 'But now I am cabined, cribbed, confined, bound in/To saucy doubts and fears'   84 **Stalag:** a German camp for prisoners of war

AFTER A KILLING

THERE they were, as if our memory hatched them,
As if the unquiet founders walked again:
Two young men with rifles on the hill,
Profane and bracing as their instruments.

Who's sorry for our trouble? 5
Who dreamt that we might dwell among ourselves
In rain and scoured light and wind-dried stones?
Basalt, blood, water, headstones, leeches.

In that neuter original loneliness
From Brandon to Dunseverick 10
I think of small-eyed survivor flowers,
The pined-for, unmolested orchid.

I see a stone house by a pier.
Elbow room. Broad window light.
The heart lifts. You walk twenty yards 15
To the boats and buy mackerel.

And today a girl walks in home to us
Carrying a basket full of new potatoes,
Three tight green cabbages, and carrots
With the tops and mould still fresh on them. 20

ANDREW MOTION

CAUSA BELLI

THEY read good books, and quote, but never learn
a language other than the scream of rocket-burn.
Our straighter talk is drowned but ironclad:
elections, money, empire, oil and Dad.

BENJAMIN ZEPHANIAH

DIS POETRY

DIS poetry is like a riddim dat drops
De tongue fires a riddim dat shoots like shots
Dis poetry is designed fe rantin
Dance hall style, Big mouth chanting,
Dis poetry nar put yu to sleep 5
Preaching follow me
Like yu is blind sheep,
Dis poetry is not Party Political
Not designed fe dose who are critical.

Dis poetry is wid me when I gu to me bed 10
It gets into me Dreadlocks
It lingers around me head
Dis poetry goes wid me as I pedal me bike
I've tried Shakespeare, Respect due dere
But dis is de stuff I like. 15

Dis poetry is not afraid of going ina book
Still dis poetry need ears fe hear and eyes fe hav a look
Dis poetry is Verbal Riddim, no big words involved

An if I hav a problem de riddim gets it solved,
I've tried to be more Romantic, it does nu good
   for me 20
So I tek a Reggae Riddim an build me poetry,
I could try be more personal
But you've heard it all before,
Pages of written words not needed
Brain has many words in store, 25
Yu could call dis poetry Dub Ranting
De tongue plays a beat
De body starts skanking,
Dis poetry is quick and childish
Dis poetry is fe de wise an foolish, 30
Anybody can do it fe free,
Dis poetry is fe yu and me,
Don't stretch yu imagination
Dis poetry is fe de good of de Nation,
Chant, 35
In de morning
I chant
In de night
I chant
In de darkness 40
An under de spotlight,
I pass thru University
I pass thru Sociology
An den I got a Dread degree
In Dreadfull Ghettology. 45

Dis poetry stays wid me when I run or walk
An when I am talking to meself in poetry I talk,
Dis poetry is wid me
Below me an above,
Dis poetry's from inside me 50
It goes to you
WID LUV.

DIS POETRY: 3–4 **rantin Dance hall style:** in dub poetry or dub ranting (line 26), the poet recites his work over a reggae rhythm (line 21) 5 **nar:** will never 11 **Dreadlocks:** long-plaited hairstyle of Rastafarians, the members of a West Indian cult, originating in the 1930s, that regards the former emperor of Ethiopia, Haile Selassie (Ras Tafari), as divine; Rastafarianism has been a driving force behind West Indian music 26 **Dub:** (originally from 'overdub') a raw and basic form of reggae 28 **skanking:** dancing to reggae music

ACKNOWLEDGMENTS

HarperCollins Publishers gratefully acknowledge permission given by the following people and organisations to reproduce copyright poems in this anthology. We have made every effort to contact all copyright holders, but if any have been missed, the copyright holder should please contact us at: Reference Department, HarperCollins Publishers, Westerhill Road, Bishopbriggs, Glasgow G64 2QT.

W. H. Auden: 'Stop all the Clocks', 'Lullaby', 'Musée des Beaux Arts', 'In Memory of W. B. Yeats', 'The Unknown Citizen', 'In Praise of Limestone', 'The Shield of Achilles' and 'The More Loving One' are reproduced by permission of the publishers, Faber and Faber Ltd.

Hilaire Belloc: 'On a General Election', Ha'nacker Hill', 'Henry King' and 'Matilda' are reproduced by permission of the Peters Fraser and Dunlop Group Ltd, on behalf of the Estate of Hilaire Belloc.

Sir John Betjeman: 'Pot Pourri from a Surrey Garden', 'In Westminster Abbey', 'A Subaltern's Love-Song', 'In a Bath Teashop' and 'How to Get On in Society' are reproduced by permission of John Murray Publishers Ltd.

Laurence Binyon: extract from 'The Burning of the Leaves' is reproduced by permission of the Society of Authors as the Literary Representative of the Estate of Laurence Binyon.

Edmund Blunden: 'The Pike', 'Forefathers', 'The Zonnebeke Road' and 'Report on Experience' are reproduced by permission of The Peters Fraser and Dunlop Group Limited on behalf of the Estate of Mrs Claire Blunden.

Basil Bunting: extract from 'Briggflatts' is reproduced by permission of Bloodaxe Books Ltd.

C. Day Lewis: 'Will It Be So Again?' from *The Complete Poems*, published by Sinclair-Stevenson 1992. Copyright © 1992 in this edition The Estate of C. Day Lewis.

Walter de la Mare: 'All That's Past', 'The Listeners', 'Silver' and 'The Railway Junction' are reproduced by permission of the Literary Trustees of Walter de la Mare, and the Society of Authors as their representative.

Keith Douglas: 'Simplify Me When I'm Dead' is reproduced by permission of the publishers, Faber and Faber Ltd.

T. S. Eliot: 'The Love Song of J. Alfred Prufrock', 'Preludes', the extract from 'The Waste Land', 'Journey of the Magi' and 'Little Gidding' from 'Four Quartets', are reproduced by permission of the publishers, Faber and Faber Ltd.

William Empson: 'To an Old Lady' from *Collected Poems* by William Empson published by Hogarth Press, is reproduced by permission of Lady Empson and The Random House Group Ltd.

Roy Fuller: 'Translation' from *New and Collected Poems* 1934–85 (Secker and Warburg, 1985) is reproduced by permission of John Fuller.

Harry Graham: 'Indifference', 'Providence', 'Compensation', 'London Calling', and 'Quite Fun' are reproduced by permission of Laura Dance.

Robert Graves: 'Full Moon', 'Welsh Incident', 'She Tells Her Love while Half Asleep', 'To Juan at the Winter Solstice' and 'A Slice of Wedding Cake' from *Complete Poems* (1997) are reproduced by permission of the publisher, Carcanet Press Ltd.

Thom Gunn: 'On the Move', 'In Santa Maria del Popolo' and 'My Sad Captains' are reproduced by permission of the publishers, Faber and Faber Ltd.

Ivor Gurney: 'The Silent One' and 'The Bohemians' are reproduced by permission of Carcanet Press Ltd.

Seamus Heaney: 'Death of a Naturalist', 'Whatever You Say Say Nothing' and 'After a Killing' are reproduced by permission of the publishers, Faber and Faber Ltd.

Geoffrey Hill: 'September Song', from *King Log* (1968), is reproduced by permission of Penguin Books Ltd.

Ralph Hodgson: 'Time, you old gypsy man' is reproduced by permission of Bryn Mawr College.

ACKNOWLEDGMENTS

A. E. Housman: 'Loveliest of trees', 'When I was one-and-twenty', 'Bredon Hill', 'On Wenlock Edge', 'Into my heart an air that kills', 'Soldier from the wars returning', and 'Tell me not here, it needs not saying' are reproduced by permission of the Society of Authors as the Literary Representative of the Estate of A. E. Housman.

Ted Hughes: 'The Thought-Fox', 'Hawk Roosting', and 'Pike' are reproduced by permission of the publishers, Faber and Faber Ltd.

Rudyard Kipling: 'Recessional', 'The Female of the Species', 'Danny Deever', 'Cities and Thrones and Powers', 'If', and 'The Way through the Woods' are reproduced by permission of A. P. Watt Ltd on behalf of The National Trust for Places of Historical Interest or Natural Beauty.

Philip Larkin: 'Toads' from *The Less Deceived* is reproduced by permission of the Marvell Press, England and Australia. 'Mr Bleaney', 'The Whitsun Weddings', 'Dockery and Son', 'Annus Mirabilis' and 'This Be the Verse' are reproduced by permission of the publishers, Faber and Faber Ltd.

Alun Lewis: 'All day it has rained' is reproduced by permission of HarperCollins Publishers.

Hugh MacDiarmid: 'The Feminine Principle' and 'My Quarrel with England' from *Collected Poems* (1993) are reproduced by permission of Carcanet Press Ltd.

Louis MacNeice: 'Sunday Morning', 'Snow', 'The Sunlight on the Garden', 'Bagpipe Music' extract from 'Autumn Journal', 'Meeting Point', 'Brother Fire' and 'Prayer before Birth' from *Collected Poems*, published by Faber and Faber, are reproduced by permission of David Higham Associates.

Leo Marks: 'The Life That I Have', from *Between Silk and Cyanide* by Leo Marks, is reproduced by permission of HarperCollins Publishers.

John Masefield: 'Sea-Fever' and 'Cargoes' are reproduced by permission of The Society of Authors as the literary representative of the Estate of John Masefield.

Andrew Motion: 'Causa Belli' is reproduced by permission of The Peters Fraser and Dunlop Group Limited on behalf of Andrew Motion.

Edwin Muir: 'Suburban Dream' is reproduced by permission of the publishers, Faber and Faber Ltd.

F. T. Prince: 'Soldiers Bathing' from *Collected Poems* (1993) is reproduced by permission of Carcanet Press.

Henry Reed: 'Lessons of the War' is reproduced by permission of the Estate of the late Henry Reed, c/o The Royal Literary Fund.

Siegfried Sassoon: 'Blighters', 'Base Details', 'The General', 'Attack', 'Glory of Women' and 'Everyone Sang' are reproduced by kind permission of the Barbara Levy Literary Agency on behalf of George Sassoon.

Stevie Smith: 'What is she writing?', and 'Not Waving but Drowning' are reproduced by permission of the James McGibbon Estate.

Sir Stephen Spender: 'I think continually of those who were truly great' is reproduced by permission of the publishers, Faber and Faber Ltd.

Dylan Thomas: 'And Death Shall Have No Dominion', 'Poem in October', 'Do Not Go Gentle into That Good Night' and 'Fern Hill', from *Collected Poems*, published by Faber and Faber, are reproduced by permission of David Higham Associates.

W. B. Yeats: 'The Lake Isle of Innisfree', 'When You are Old', 'The Folly of Being Comforted', 'No Second Troy', 'The Wild Swans at Coole', 'An Irish Airman Foresees his Death', 'Easter 1916', 'The Second Coming', 'A Prayer for my Daughter', 'Sailing to Byzantium', 'Among School Children', 'Byzantium' and 'Under Ben Bulben' are reproduced by permission of A. P. Watt Ltd on behalf of Michael B. Yeats.

Benjamin Zephaniah: 'Dis Poetry', from *City Psalms* (1992), is reproduced by permission of Bloodaxe Books.

INDEX OF POETS

INDEX OF POETS

INDEX OF TITLES

INDEX OF TITLES

INDEX OF TITLES

INDEX OF TITLES

INDEX OF FIRST LINES

Kingdom
of Fear

Also by Hunter S. Thompson

Hell's Angels
Fear and Loathing in Las Vegas
Fear and Loathing: On the Campaign Trail '72
The Great Shark Hunt
The Curse of Lono
Generation of Swine
Songs of the Doomed
Better Than Sex
Screwjack
The Proud Highway
The Rum Diary
Fear and Loathing in America

Kingdom of Fear

Loathsome Secrets of a Star-Crossed Child in the Final Days of the American Century

Hunter S. Thompson

ALLEN LANE
an imprint of
PENGUIN BOOKS

ALLEN LANE
THE PENGUIN PRESS

Published by the Penguin Group
Penguin Books Ltd, 80 Strand, London WC2R 0RL, England
Penguin Putnam Inc., 375 Hudson Street, New York, New York 10014, USA
Penguin Books Australia Ltd, 250 Camberwell Road, Camberwell, Victoria 3124, Australia
Penguin Books Canada Ltd, 10 Alcorn Avenue, Toronto, Ontario, Canada M4V 3B2
Penguin Books India (P) Ltd, 11 Community Centre, Panchsheel Park, New Delhi – 110 017, India
Penguin Books (NZ) Ltd, Cnr Rosedale and Airborne Roads, Albany, Auckland, New Zealand
Penguin Books (South Africa) (Pty) Ltd, 24 Sturdee Avenue, Rosebank 2196, South Africa

Penguin Books Ltd, Registered Offices: 80 Strand, London WC2R 0RL, England

www.penguin.com

First published in the USA by Simon & Schuster 2003
First published in the UK by Allen Lane The Penguin Press 2003
1

Set in Adobe Garamond

Printed in England by Clays Ltd, St Ives plc

ISBN 0–713–99714–1

The author gratefully acknowledges permission from the following sources to reprint material
in their control:
Page 56: "Guilt by Association at Heart of Auman Case" by Karen Abbott, from the *Rocky
Mountain News*, April 29, 2002; Page 92: "The Battle of Aspen" from *Rolling Stone #67*,
October 1, 1970; Page 112: Lyrics for "Take a Walk on the Wild Side" by Lou Reed © Lou
Reed/EMI, All Rights Reserved; Page 117: "Dr. Hunter S. Thompson and the Last Battle of Aspen"
by Loren Jenkins, from *SMART* Magazine, Jan/Feb 1990; Page 194: Lyrics for "American Pie" by
Don McLean © Songs of Universal/BMI, All Rights Reserved; Page 242: "Knock, Knock—Who's
There" by Edward T. Cross, from the *Aspen Times Daily*, June 18, 1990; Page 245: "D.A. Snags
Thompson in Sex Case" by David Matthews-Price, from the *Aspen Times Daily*; Page 251: "Gonzo's
Last Stand?" from *The Village Voice*, May 15, 1990; Page 253: "D.A. May File Case Against Aspen
Writer" by Eve O'Brien, from *The Denver Post*, March 14, 1990; Page 258: "Thompson Bound
Over For Trial" by David Matthews-Price, from the *Aspen Times Daily*; Page 262: "Thompson
Rejects Plea Bargain; Takes Delivery of Convertible" by David Matthews-Price, from the *Aspen
Times Daily*; Page 266: "The Sinister Sex and Drugs Case of Hunter S. Thompson" by Richard
Stratton, from *High Times* magazine; Page 292: Lyrics for "One Time One Night" written by
David Hidalgo and Louis Perez ©1988 DAVINCE MUSIC (BMI)/NO K.O. MUSIC
(BMI)/Administered by Bug. All Rights Reserved.

To Anita

Weave a circle round him thrice,
And close your eyes with holy dread,
For he on honey-dew hath fed,
And drunk the milk of Paradise.

—Samuel Taylor Coleridge

Contents

Foreword by
Timothy Ferris

If, as Paul Valéry put it, "the true poet is the one who inspires," Hunter Thompson is a true poet. His writing has inspired countless imitators (all of whom fail hideously, of course; nobody writes like Hunter) while opening glittering veins of savage wit and searing indignation to journalists sensible enough to benefit from his example without trying to copy his style. His notoriously vivid lifestyle—chronicled in his own works and, more fragmentarily, by scores of others who managed to hang on for part of the ride—has inspired plenty of imitators, too, although most have prudently avoided flying too close to that particular dark star. Most everybody who knows anything about Hunter is fascinated by him, and the concatenation of his work and his persona has made him a figure of uncommon fame. Five biographies of him have been published, two Hollywood feature films have been made from his books, and his name turns up on half a million Internet web pages—more than William Burroughs, Allen Ginsberg, Jack Kerouac, Norman Mailer, and Tom Wolfe combined.

But, given that he is also the onstage protagonist of most of his works, the question arises as to who is primarily responsible for all this inspiration and intrigue: Hunter the writer, or Hunter the written-about? This turns out to be a timely issue, insomuch as *Kingdom of Fear* constitutes a memoir, and as such represents an author's confrontation with himself. The answers are not easy to come by—especially since *Kingdom of Fear*, like Einstein's *Autobiographical Notes*, quickly veers from reflections on who the author is to demonstrations of what he does. Nor, once arrived at, do they give us anything like the whole picture. Every man is many men—Whitman was stating the facts when he said that he contained multitudes—and no simple scheme of an artist as creator versus the same artist as subject can produce more than a flash photo of reality. Still, an examination of the relationship between Hunter the writer and his first-person protagonist may cast at least a thin beam of torchlight into the cavernous darkness of his abundant creativity.

Hunter's writing is, first of all, extremely funny; he ranks among the finest American humorists of all time. It is also, like all real humor, essentially serious. At its center resides a howling vortex of outrage and pain, which Hunter has managed to transmute into works of lasting value. These works have the additional virtue of being factually reliable, so long as he intends them to be. Hunter is a meticulous reporter who wasn't joking when he told an audience at The Strand in Redondo Beach, "I am the most accurate journalist you'll ever read." Over the thirty years that we've been friends he has corrected my grammar and word usage more often, and more accurately, than I have corrected his—and not just because he is customarily armed with, say, the .454 Magnum pistol with which he shot up one of his many IBM Selectric typewriters. ("That gun really is too much, unless you want to destroy a Buick at two hundred yards," he recalled, musing over the Selectric-shooting episode. "The bullet went through the typewriter at such a speed that it just pierced it, like a *ray* of some kind. You could hardly see where it hit. So I went and got a 12-gauge Magnum shotgun and some .00 buckshot. That produced a very different shot pattern.") He is capable of sea-anchoring an otherwise sheets-to-the-wind drinking fiesta with studious ponderings about matters ranging from whether to credit a rumor, at the 1972 Democratic National Convention, that George McGovern was about to offer the second spot on his ticket to United Auto Workers President Leonard Woodcock (Hunter decided that he didn't trust it, and as usual was proved right) to browsing thesaurus entries for the word *force*. ("They include *violence, vehemence, might, rigor, impetuosity, severity, fierceness, ferocity, outrage, eruption, convulsion, violent passion.* . . . It's scary; kind of a word picture of *me*.")

But then, with little more than a barely perceptible signal, his works slip anchor and venture into a kind of hyperspace, where the facts shrink to a pinpoint like a cosmonaut's view of the receding Earth, and the goal shifts from factual literalness to a quest for deeper truth. Few readers can infallibly detect these points of departure, so many have raised the recurring question: How much of Hunter's accounts of his own escapades—the fast cars, furious motorcycles, big-bore firearms and powerful explosives, the beautiful women and mind-warping drugs, the frightening misadventures and reckless flirtations with imminent disaster that have made "fear and loathing" part of the language—are exaggerated?

Not nearly enough for comfort.

Hunter is a lifelong student of fear—and a teacher of it, too. He titled a song that he wrote recently with Warren Zevon "You're a Whole Different Person When You're Scared," and he doesn't feel that he knows you properly until he knows *that* person. On various occasions he has lunged at me with an evil-looking horse syringe; brandished loaded shotguns, stun guns, and cans of Mace; and taken me on high-speed rides to remote murder sites in the dead of night—and I doubt that he finds my reaction to such travails particularly interesting, since I have always calmly trusted him with my life. Those whom such treatment transforms into someone more apt to arouse Hunter's infared sensors of viperous curiosity are in for an interesting evening.

At the same time, this howling violence freak, habitually loaded with potent intoxicants and a skull full of Beethoven-grade egomania, is studious and thoughtful, courtly and caring, curiously peace loving in his way, and unwaveringly generous. When he and I were young and broke, and I was fired from the last job I've ever held, the first thing he did was offer to send me four hundred dollars—which, although he didn't know I knew it, was all the money he had left in the bank at the time. His fundamental decency helps explain how he has managed to survive his many excesses, as does the fact that he's blessed with extraordinary reflexes. I once saw him accidentally knock a drink off a table with the back of his hand while reaching for a ringing phone and then catch it, unspilled, with the same hand on the way down. When we onlookers expressed astonishment at this feat, he said, "Yes, well, when we're applauding my aptitude at making rescues, we should keep in mind who causes most of the accidents in the first place." I've never met anyone who really knew Hunter who didn't love him.

So what we have here is a thrilling if frightening man of action, as spectacular and unpredictable as a bolt of lightning, being observed by an owl-like, oracular author who, although he shares his skin, is as perpetually surprised and bemused by his behavior as the rest of us are. In *Kingdom of Fear,* the interactions of this curious couple informs adventures like Hunter's predawn excursion to his old friend Jack Nicholson's house, his Jeep loaded with "all kinds of jokes and gimcracks" intended to gladden the hearts of Nicholson's children: "In addition to the bleeding elk heart, there was a massive outdoor amplifier, a tape recording of a pig being eaten alive by bears, a 1,000,000-watt spotlight, and a 9-mm Smith & Wesson semiautomatic pistol with teakwood handles and a box of high-powered ammunition. There was also a 40-million-candlepower parachute flare that would light up the valley for 40 miles for 40 seconds that would seem to anyone lucky enough to be awake at the time like the first blinding flash of a midrange nuclear device that might signal the end of the world." When the detonation of these devices from a precipice overlooking the Nicholson household fails to produce the anticipated joyful welcome, Hunter feels, disconcertingly, that he is "being snubbed."

"I was beginning to have mixed feelings about this visit," he confesses, while preparing to leave the bleeding elk heart on Nicholson's doorstep, but he soon cheers up, wondering, "Why am I drifting into negativity?"

Which, if you drain off the color and turn down the volume, is pretty much the human condition. We do things without knowing why, wonder at the consequences, and know neither where we came from nor where we are going. Robert Frost wrote that we dance round in a ring and suppose, while the secret sits in the center and knows. Hunter dances, all right, but rather than suppose, never ceases striving to know. His aim, as Joseph Conrad put it in his preface to *The Nigger of the Narcissus,* a work that mightily impressed a young Hunter ("That was something to roll around in my craw and compare myself to; it set a high standard") is "by the power of the written word to make you hear, to make you feel . . . to make you see," to bring us "encouragement, consolation, fear, charm—all you demand—and, perhaps, also that glimpse of truth for which you have forgotten to ask."

And that, in part, is why we love him.

Memo from the Sports Desk

I was watching the Denver–Oakland football game on TV last night when it was interrupted by a "BREAKING NEWS" bulletin from the FBI about unknown terrorists who were planning to destroy major targets all over the United States, perhaps within 24 hours. The FBI had learned this from trustworthy sources, the unseen voice explained. The American people were advised to be totally vigilant & ready to be evacuated at any moment. . . . Any person who talks suspiciously or looks dangerous should be reported to your local police or law enforcement agencies immediately! We were into *Condition Red*.

"Shit! Not again!" cried my lawyer. "I have to fly to Boston tomorrow. What the fuck is going on in this country?"

"Never ask that question," I warned her, "unless you already know the answer."

"I do," she said. "We are fucked, utterly fucked."

. . .

The Author's Note—if it exists at all—is invariably the worst and lamest part of any book, my own included. That is because it is necessarily the last and most blind-dumb desperate "final touch" that gets heaped into a book just before it goes to the printer—and the whole book, along with the two years of feverish work and anguish, is doomed to failure and ruin if the author won't produce the note in time for publication.

Make no mistake about it. These 4 pointless pages of low-rent gibberish are by far the most important part of the book, they say Nothing else matters.

And so, with that baleful wisdom in mind, let us get on with the wretched task of lashing this "author's note" together, for good or ill. I am not really in much of a mood to deal with it, no more than I am eager to take a course in how to write commercial advertising copy for my own good, at this time.

I savagely rejected that swill 40 years ago because I hated it and I hated the people who tried to make me do it. But so what, eh? We are somehow back to square one. . . . Is this a great country, or what?

. . .

The safe answer to that question is "Yes, and thank you for asking." Any other answer will get your name on the waiting list for accommodations at Guantánamo Bay.

How's that for a great country, dude? It's all yours now, and good luck in jail. Cuba is a beautiful island, perhaps the most beautiful I've ever seen. They don't call it *The Pearl of the Antilles* for nothing. The white sand beaches are spectacular, and every soft Caribbean breeze that you feel in the midnight air will speak to you of love and joy and atavistic romance.

Indeed, the future looks good for Cuba, especially with the *dollar-economy* that will come when the entire island is converted to a spacious concentration camp for the U.S.A., which is already happening. Little did President Theodore Roosevelt know, when he effectively annexed Cuba in 1906, that he had seized for his country what would later become the largest and most permanent prison colony in the history of the world.

Good old Teddy. Everything he touched was doomed to be beautiful. The man could do no wrong.

. . .

Meanwhile, back at the ranch, the Raiders were whipping the shit out of the heavily favored Broncos, who were wallowing in their own Condition Red. Their top-ranked Defense had gone all to pieces, and now they were being humiliated.

"George Bush is far greater than Roosevelt," said my lawyer. "I wish we could be with him now."

"You fool," I snorted. "If Teddy Roosevelt were alive today, he would be so ashamed of this country that he would slit his own wrists."

"So what? I still have to get to Boston tomorrow," she muttered. "Will any planes be flying?"

Just then the football game was interrupted again—this time by a paid commercial about the terrors of smoking marijuana. "Jesus Christ," she said. "Now they say that if I smoke this joint, I'll be guilty of murdering a federal judge—Hell, that's a capital crime, the death penalty."

"You're right," I replied. "And if you even *offer* the filthy little thing to *me*, I will be guilty under the law of *conspiring* to murder a federal judge."

"Well, I guess we will have to stop smoking this stuff," she said mournfully, as she handed the joint to me. "What else can I smoke to relax after a losing day in court?"

"Nothing," I said. "Especially not Xanax: The Governor of Florida just sentenced his own daughter to jail for trying to buy Xanax."

And so much for drug talk, eh? Even talking about drugs can get you locked up these days. The times have changed drastically, but not for the better.

. . .

I like this book, and I especially like the title, which pretty well sums up the foul nature of life in the U.S.A. in these first few bloody years of the post-American century. Only a fool or a whore would call it anything else.

It would be easy to say that we owe it all to the Bush family from Texas, but that would be too simplistic. They are only errand boys for the vengeful, bloodthirsty cartel of raving Jesus-freaks and super-rich money mongers who have ruled this country for at least the last 20 years, and arguably for the past 200. They take orders well, and they don't ask too many questions.

The real power in America is held by a fast-emerging new Oligarchy of pimps and preachers who see no need for Democracy or fairness or even trees, except maybe the ones in their own yards, and they don't mind admitting it. They worship money and power and death. Their ideal solution to all the nation's problems would be another 100 Year War.

Coming of age in a fascist police state will not be a barrel of fun for anybody, much less for people like me, who are not inclined to suffer Nazis gladly and feel only contempt for the cowardly flag-suckers who would gladly give up their outdated freedom to *live* for the mess of pottage they have been conned into believing will be freedom from fear.

Ho ho ho. Let's not get carried away here. Freedom was yesterday in this country. Its value has been discounted. The only freedom we truly crave today is freedom from Dumbness. Nothing else matters.

. . .

My life has been the polar opposite of safe, but I am proud of it and so is my son, and that is good enough for me. I would do it all over again without changing the beat, although I have never recommended it to others. That would be cruel and irresponsible and wrong, I think, and I am none of those things.

Whoops, that's it, folks. We are out of time. Sorry. Mahalo.

HST

P.S. "The difference between the *almost*-right word & the *right* word is . . . the difference between the lightning bug and the lightning."

—*Mark Twain*

(Lynn Goldsmith)

Kingdom
of Fear

PART ONE

When the Going Gets Weird, the Weird Turn Pro

There are no jokes. Truth is the funniest joke of all.
—Muhammad Ali

The Mailbox: Louisville, Summer of 1946

My parents were decent people, and I was raised, like my friends, to believe that Police were our friends and protectors—the Badge was a symbol of extremely high authority, perhaps the highest of all. Nobody ever asked *why*. It was one of those unnatural questions that are better left alone. If you had to ask *that*, you were sure as hell Guilty of *something* and probably should have been put behind bars a long time ago. It was a no-win situation.

My first face-to-face confrontation with the FBI occurred when I was nine years old. Two grim-looking Agents came to our house and terrified my parents by saying that I was a "prime suspect" in the case of a Federal Mailbox being turned over in the path of a speeding bus. It was a Federal Offense, they said, and carried a five-year prison sentence.

"Oh no!" wailed my mother. "Not in prison! That's insane! He's only a child. How could he have known?"

"The warning is clearly printed on the Mailbox," said the agent in the gray suit. "He's old enough to read."

"Not necessarily," my father said sharply. "How do you know he's not blind, or a moron?"

"Are you a moron, son?" the agent asked me. "Are you blind? Were you just *pretending* to read that newspaper when we came in?" He pointed to the *Louisville Courier-Journal* on the couch.

"That was only the sports section," I told him. "I can't read the other stuff."

"See?" said my father. "I told you he was a moron."

"Ignorance of the law is no excuse," the brown-suit agent replied. "Tampering with the U.S. Mail is a Federal offense punishable under Federal law. That Mailbox was badly damaged."

Mailboxes were huge, back then. They were heavy green vaults that stood like Roman mile markers at corners on the neighborhood bus routes and were rarely, if ever, moved. I was barely tall enough to reach the Mail-drop slot, much less big enough to turn the bastard over and into the path of a bus. It was clearly impossible that I could have committed this crime without help, and that was what they wanted: names and addresses, along with a total confession. They already knew I was guilty, they said, because other culprits had squealed on me. My parents hung their heads, and I saw my mother weeping.

I had done it, of course, and I had done it with plenty of help. It was carefully plotted and planned, a deliberate ambush that we set up and executed with the fiendish skill that smart nine-year-old boys are capable of when they have too much time on their hands and a lust for revenge on a rude and stupid bus driver who got a kick out of closing his doors and pulling away just as we staggered to the top of the hill and begged him to let us climb on. . . . He was new on the job, probably a brain-damaged substitute, filling in for our regular driver, who was friendly and kind and always willing to wait a few seconds for children rushing to school. Every kid in the neighborhood agreed that this new swine of a driver was a sadist who deserved to be punished, and the Hawks A.C. were the ones to do it. We saw it more as a duty than a prank. It was a brazen Insult to the honor of the whole neighborhood.

We would need ropes and pulleys and certainly no witnesses to do the job properly. We had to tilt the iron monster so far over that it was perfectly balanced to fall instantly, just as the fool zoomed into the bus stop at his usual arrogant speed. All that kept the box more or less upright was my grip on a long "invisible" string that we had carefully stretched all the way from the corner and across about 50 feet of grass lawn to where we crouched out of sight in some bushes.

The rig worked perfectly. The bastard was right on schedule and going too fast to stop when he saw the thing falling in front of him. . . . The collision made a horrible noise, like a bomb going off or a freight train exploding in Germany. That is how I remember it, at least. It was the worst noise I'd ever heard. People ran screaming out of their houses like chickens gone crazy with fear. They howled at one another as the driver stumbled out of his bus and collapsed in a heap on the grass. . . . The bus was empty of passengers, as usual at the far end of the line. The man was not injured, but he went into a foaming rage when he spotted us fleeing down the hill and into a nearby alley. He knew in a flash who had done it, and so did most of the neighbors.

"Why deny it, Hunter?" said one of the FBI agents. "We know *exactly* what happened up there on that corner on Saturday. Your buddies already confessed, son. They *squealed* on you. We know you did it, so don't lie to us now and make things worse for yourself. A nice kid like you shouldn't have to go to Federal prison." He smiled again and winked at my father, who responded with a snarl: "Tell the Truth, damn it! Don't lie to these men. They have *witnesses!*" The FBI agents nodded grimly at each other and moved as if to take me into custody.

It was a magic moment in my life, a defining instant for me or any other nine-year-old boy growing up in the 1940s after World War II— and I clearly recall thinking: *Well, this is it. These are G-Men.* . . .

WHACK! Like a flash of nearby lightning that lights up the sky for three or four terrifying split seconds before you hear the thunder—a matter of *zepto-seconds* in real time—but when you are a nine-year-old boy with two (2) full-grown FBI agents about to seize you and clap you in Federal prison, a few quiet zepto-seconds can seem like the rest of your life. . . . And that's how it felt to me that day, and in grim retrospect, I was right. They had me, dead to rights. I was Guilty. Why deny it? Confess Now, and throw myself on their mercy, or—

What? What if I *didn't* confess? That was the question. And I was a curious boy, so I decided, as it were, to roll the dice and ask *them* a question.

"Who?" I said. "What witnesses?"

It was not a hell of a lot to ask, under those circumstances—and I really did want to know exactly who among my best friends and blood brothers in the dreaded Hawks A.C. had cracked under pressure and betrayed me to these thugs, these pompous brutes and toadies with badges & plastic cards in their wallets that said they worked for J. Edgar Hoover and that they had the Right, and even the duty, to put me in jail, because they'd heard a "Rumor in the neighborhood" that some of my boys had gone belly up and rolled on me. *What?* No. Impossible.

Or not *likely,* anyway. Hell, Nobody squealed on the Hawks A.C., or not on its President, anyway. Not on Me. So I asked again: "Witnesses? What Witnesses?"

. . .

And that was all it took, as I recall. We observed a moment of silence, as my old friend Edward Bennett Williams would say. Nobody spoke—especially not me—and when my father finally broke the eerie silence, there was *doubt* in his voice. "I think my son has a point, officer. Just exactly who *have* you talked to? I was about to ask that myself."

"Not Duke!" I shouted. "He went to Lexington with his father! And not *Ching*! And not *Jay*!—"

"Shut up," said my father. "Be quiet and let *me* handle this, you fool."

And that's what happened, folks. We never saw those FBI agents again. Never. And I learned a powerful lesson: Never believe the first thing an FBI agent tells you about anything—especially not if he seems to believe you are guilty of a crime. Maybe he has no evidence. Maybe he's bluffing. Maybe you are innocent. Maybe. The Law can be hazy on these things. . . . But it is definitely worth a roll.

In any case, nobody was arrested for that alleged incident. The FBI agents went away, the U.S. Mailbox was put back up on its heavy iron legs, and we never saw that drunken swine of a substitute bus driver again.

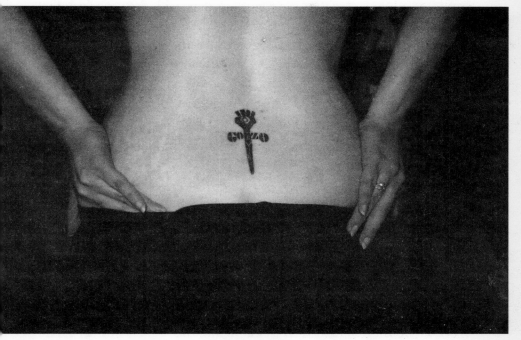

(HST archives)

Would You Do It Again?

That story has no moral—at least not for smart people—but it taught me many useful things that shaped my life in many fateful ways. One of them was knowing the difference between Morality and Wisdom. Morality is temporary, Wisdom is permanent. . . . Ho ho. Take that one to bed with you tonight.

In the case of the fallen mailbox, for instance, I learned that the FBI was not *unbeatable,* and that is a very important lesson to learn at the age of nine in America. Without it, I would be an entirely different man today, a product of an utterly different environment. I would not be talking to you this way, or sitting alone at this goddamn typewriter at 4:23 A.M. with an empty drink beside me and an unlit cigarette in my mouth and a naked woman singing "Porgy & Bess" on TV across the room.

On one wall I see an eight-foot, two-handled logging saw with 200 big teeth and CONFESSIONS OF THE BEST PIECE OF ASS IN THE WORLD scrawled in gold letters across the long rusty saw blade. . . . At one end of it hangs a petrified elk's leg and a finely painted wooden bird from Russia that allegedly signifies peace, happiness & prosperity for all who walk under it.

That strange-looking bird has hung there for 15 extremely active years, no doubt for sentimental reasons, and this is the first time I have thought about adding up the score. Has this graven image from ancient Russian folk art been a *good* influence on my life? Or a bad one? Should I pass it on to my son and my grandson? Or should I take it out in the yard and execute it like a traitorous whore?

That is the Real question. Should the bird live and be worshiped for generations to come? Or should it die violently for bringing me bad luck?

The ramifications of that question are intimidating. Is it wise to add up the Score right now? What if I come out a Loser? Ye gods, let's be careful about this. Have we wandered into dangerous territory?

Indeed. At this point in my life I don't need a rush to judgment, whatever it is. Only a superstitious *native* would believe that kind of bullshit, anyway.

. . .

Suddenly I heard Anita screeching from the office, as if a fire had erupted somewhere on the other side of the house. Wonderful, I thought. I am a lucky man to get a break like this. Bring it on. Attack it *now*. I reached for a red 20-pound fire extinguisher near the door, thinking finally to have some real fun.

Ah, but it was not to be. Anita came rushing around the corner with a computer printout in her hands. "The President is threatening to seize the Saudi Arabian oil fields if they don't help us wipe out the Evil of Terrorism—seize them by military force." The look on her face was stricken, as if World War IV had just started. "This is insane!" she wailed. "We can't just go over there and invade Saudi Arabia."

I put my arm around her and flipped the dial to CNN, which was showing Defense Secretary Donald Rumsfeld waving his cast at the camera like a clenched fist as he denounced the rumor as "nonsense" and once again threatened to "track down and eliminate" these "irresponsible leaks" to the press from somewhere in the bowels of the Pentagon. He wanted to Punish somebody immediately. *Of Course* the United States would not declare war on a close Arab ally like the Saudis. That would be insane.

"Not necessarily," I said, "at least not until it turns into a disastrous botch and Bush gets burned at the stake in Washington. Sane is rich and powerful; Insane is wrong and poor and weak. The rich are Free, the poor are put in cages." *Res Ipsa Loquitur,* Amen, Mahalo. . . .

. . .

Okay, and so much for *that,* eh? No more of these crude hashish ravings. What if the bird says I am wrong and have been wrong all my life?

Certainly I would not be entirely comfortable sitting here by myself and preparing, once again, to make terminal judgments on the President of the United States of America on the brink of a formal war with a whole world of Muslims. . . . No. That would make me a traitor and a dangerous Security Risk, a Terrorist, a monster in the eyes of the Law.

Well, shucks. What can I say? We are coming to a big fork in the road for this country, another ominous polarization between right and wrong, another political mandate to decide *"Which side are you on?"* . . . Maybe a bumper sticker that asks ARE YOU SANE OR INSANE?

I have confronted that question on a daily basis all my life, as if it were just another form to fill out, and on most days I have checked off the SANE box—if only because I am not dead or in prison or miserable in my life.

. . .

There is no shortage of dangerous gibberish in the classrooms and courts of this nation. Weird myths and queer legends are coins of the realm in our culture, like passwords or keys to survival. Not even a monster with rabies would send his child off to school with a heart full of hate for Santa Claus or Jesus or the Tooth Fairy. That would not be fair to the child. He (or she) would be shunned & despised like a Leper by his classmates & even his teachers, and he will not come home with good report cards. He will soon turn to wearing black raincoats & making ominous jokes about Pipe Bombs.

Weird behavior is natural in smart children, just as curiosity is to a kitten. I was no stranger to it myself, as a youth growing up in Kentucky. I had a keen appetite for adventure, which soon led me into a maze of complex behavioral experiments that my parents found hard to explain. I was a popular boy, with acceptable grades & a vaguely promising future, but I was cursed with a dark sense of humor that made many adults afraid of me, for reasons they couldn't quite put their fingers on. . . .

But I was a juvenile delinquent. I was Billy the Kid of Louisville. I was a "criminal": I stole things, destroyed things, drank. That's all you have to do if you're a criminal. In the sixth grade I was voted head of the Safety Patrol—the kids who wear the badges and stop traffic during recesses and patrol. It was a very big position, and the principal hated that I was voted to it. She said, "This is horrible. We can't have Hunter doing anything. He's a Little Hitler." I wasn't sure what that meant, but I think it meant I had a natural sway over many students. And that I should probably be lobotomized for the good of the society.

I always figured I would live on the margins of society, part of a very small Outlaw segment. I have never been approved by any majority. Most people assume it's difficult to live this way, and they are right— they're still trying to lock me up all the time. I've been very careful about urging people who cannot live outside the law to throw off the traces and run amok. Some are not made for the Outlaw life.

The only things I've ever been arrested for, it turns out, are things I didn't do. All the "crimes" I really committed were things that were usually an accident. Every time they got me, I happened to be in the wrong place and too enthusiastic. It was just the general feeling that I shouldn't be allowed to get away with it.

. . .

It may be that every culture needs an Outlaw god of some kind, and maybe this time around I'm *it*. Who knows? I haven't studied it, but the idea just came to me in a flash as I read Peter Whitmer's article about me in the Jan/Feb 1984 *Saturday Review*.

I think of Lono, Robin Hood & Bacchus & the Greeks with their fat young boys & the Irish with their frantic drunken worship of doomed heroes. . . . Jesus, I'll bet that even the Swedes have some kind of Outlaw god.

But there is no mention of good Outlaws in the Holy Bible, I think—mainly because of The Church & all its spin-offs that believe in total punishment for all sinners. The Bible makes no exceptions for good-hearted social outlaws. They are all cast into the Lake of Fire. Punishment. Fuck those people.

(PAUSE FOR INTERRUPTION)

Sorry, that was a call from *Newsweek* in New York, asking what I thought about the "shocking Mutombo–Van Horne trade" today, a major shift in the power balance of the NBA East that I was only vaguely aware of. It meant that the 76ers would be rid of that flashy albino pussy who always failed in the clutch. It made perfect sense to me, and that is why I picked up the telephone. . . . What the hell? I thought. People ask me these questions because they know I am a famous sportswriter.

"The trade is meaningless," I said. "It is like trading a used mattress for a $300 bill."

And that was that, apparently. The writer was suddenly called away from his desk and hung up on me. So what? I thought. I didn't want to talk to him anyway. I had serious work to do, and Anita was getting hungry. It was time for another road trip.

. . .

There are eight or nine truly exotic towns to visit in the great American West, but Thomasville, Colorado, is not one of them. Richard Nixon doomed the town when he reluctantly signed the Clean Air Act of 1970—which soon led to the forcible closing of both the town's gas stations because their 50-year-old underground storage tanks were rusted out and leaking rotten gasoline into the tumbling white waters of the Frying Pan River, a once-famous trout-fishing mecca.

It took us about five hours to climb the 30 steep miles up to Thomasville. I was driving my trusty Red Shark, a rebuilt 1973 454 Chevy Caprice with power windows and heated seats and a top speed of 135—although not on a winding uphill two-lane blacktop that rises 6,000 feet in 30 miles. That is serious climbing, from summer heat and peach trees up to chilly bleak timberline and then to the snowcapped peaks of the Continental Divide, where wild beasts roam and humans live in pain. This is the road that leads up to the dreaded Hagerman Pass.

But not yet. No, we are getting ahead of our story, and only a jackass would do that . . .

. . .

We were almost to Thomasville when I noticed a cluster of flashing police lights and a cop of some kind standing in the middle of the road waving a red flag. "Oh Jesus," I groaned. "What the fuck is this?" Anita was scrambling to get a half-gallon jug of Chivas Regal out of sight— which is not an easy thing to do in a huge red convertible with the top down and a beautiful half-naked girl leaning over the backseat. People will stare.

In any case, we soon learned that "the new plan, just in from Washington" is to keep weirdos, foreigners, and other dangerous bad apples *out* of all National Forests in the nation, lest they set fires and spread anthrax or anything else that swarthy terrorists are wont to do. . . . They are Evil, they are savage, and they *must* be arrested before they set fire to the whole goddamn country.

I have never had any special fear of Foreigners, myself, but I recognize a nationwide *nervous breakdown* when I see one. It is EMBARRASSING, for openers, AND IT SUCKS.

. . .

Most people are happy on Fridays, but not me—at least not yesterday, when I drove up the mountain to assess the fire-fighting & water-flow capacity of a bleak mountain community called Thomasville, on the map and right smack in the middle of a National Forest tinderbox that is already burning with monster firestorms that leap from hill to hill like summer lightning and kill everything they can reach.

. . .

Big Fire is a terrifying thing to deal with up close, and you never forget it—the panic, the heat, the deafening roar of the flames overhead. I feel queasy every time I think about it. . . . If freezing to death is the nicest way to die, then burning to death in a forest fire is no doubt the ugliest. Beware. Fire is like lightning; they will both kill you, but lightning doesn't hurt as much. It is a monumental WHACK with no warning at all, and hopefully that is it—gone, no more, and minimal mortuary charges.

Surviving a lightning strike is even worse than dying from it, according to people who have lived (returned from the dead, in fact) because 8,000,000,000 volts of electricity is an unacceptable trauma to tissue of the human body. It fries everything in its path and leaves every organ in the body, from blood vessels to brain cells and even the sexual system, charred like overcooked bacon for the rest of its delicate life.

My friend Tex got hit by lightning one gloomy afternoon in the parking lot of the Woody Creek Tavern. "It kicked the mortal shit out of me," he said later. "It blasted me fifty goddamn feet across the road and over a snow fence. I was out for forty minutes, and when I woke up I smelled like death."

I was there that day, and I thought a bomb had gone off right in front of me. I was unconscious for a while, but not for long. When I woke up I was being dragged toward a shiny sky-blue ambulance by two well-meaning medics from the Sheriff's Office. . . . I twisted out of their grasp and backed against an ice machine. "Okay, boys," I said calmly, "the Joke is over. Let's not get crazy about this. Give me some air, gentlemen," I croaked. "I feel a little jangled, but I know it will pass. Get your hands off me, you pigfucker."

No doubt it *sounded* rude to casual onlookers, but in truth it was not. I was just kidding with them. They know me.

. . .

Friday afternoons are usually loose and happy in this valley, but today was different. I live in the mountains at an altitude of 8,000 feet, which is roughly a mile and a half high. That is "big air," as they say in the zoom-zoom business. It makes for large lungs and thin blood, along with dangerously expensive real estate. Life has always been a little spooky up here, but now as this vicious new century swarms over us like a fester of kudzu vines, life in these mountains is becoming living relentless hell.

The whole state of Colorado is on fire, according to *The New York Times,* and the nerdish Republican Governor is raving like a banshee about the death of Colorado as we know it before the summer is over.

That would be about 90 days, on most calendars—or right about September 11, 2002, only one horrible year after those stupid bastards blew up the WTC . . . We will actually be at war by then, and anybody who doesn't like it will be locked up in a military holding pen.

. . .

Weird things happen when you get whacked by serious lightning. Many years ago, nineteen (19) members of the Strange family in North Carolina were struck at the same instant when they all leaned against a chain-link fence at a July 4 fireworks display. They all survived, but none prospered. It was like some horrible merciless coincidence out of the Old Testament—or extremely bad karma, to millions of non-Christians, among whom I definitely count myself. I have abandoned all forms & sects of the practicing Christian Church.

I have seen thousands of priests and bishops and even the Pope himself transmogrified in front of our eyes into a worldwide network of thieves and perverts and sodomites who relentlessly penetrate children of all genders and call it holy penance for being born guilty in the eyes of the Church.

I have seen the Jews run amok in Palestine like bloodthirsty beasts with no shame, and six million brainless Baptists demanding the death penalty without any trial at all for pagans and foreigners and people like me who won't pray with them in those filthy little shacks they call churches. They are like a swarm of rats fleeing a swoop fire, and I want no part of them. Indeed, I have my own faith and my own gods to worship, and I have been doing it with a certain amount of distinction for ten thousand years, like some fine atomic clock with ever-lasting batteries.

Whoops! I have wandered off on some kind of vengeful tangent, here, and we don't really need it now, do we? So let us save that wisdom for later.

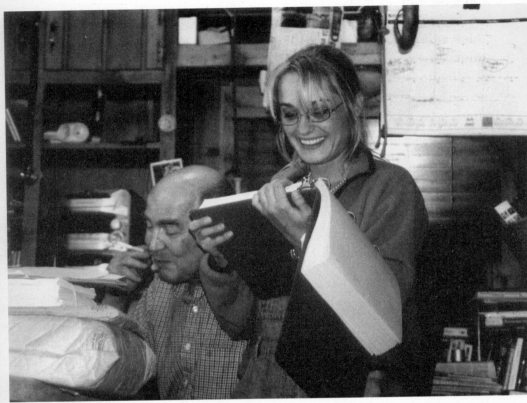

Anita reading *Kingdom of Fear* manuscript. *Res Ipsa Loquitur.* Owl Farm, 2002
(Jennifer Alise Stroup)

. . .

I was talking about driving up the mountain with Anita to survey the downside of a firestorm that seems certain to destroy about half of us before the summer is over. . . . The whole state of Colorado is officially *on fire,* according to the Governor and a few grifters in Washington who gave him 25 million dollars for Disaster Relief and Emergency Fire-fighting Equipment for an endless war against Fire.

It was Friday morning when the sheriff asked me to run up the hill and investigate. "You *must* go to Thomasville," he told me. "How are we going to evacuate them when the fires come? Go all the way up to the top and see how the river is running. Also check the Reservoir and tell me how deep it is. I fear we are running out of water in this valley."

Why not? I thought. We can take the red convertible and load up on gin at the Rainbow. Anything worth doing is worth doing Right.

. . .

It had been a few days since I first heard the weird story about "gangs of armed Jews roaming the neighborhood and beating the shit out of anybody who looked like an A-rab."

"Good god," I muttered. "Jews can't live at this altitude. There is something wrong with this story."

That is why we decided to go up to Thomasville in the *first* place. I wanted to check it out, and so did Anita . . . and so did the sheriff, as it turned out. The sheriff didn't need to deputize me, because I have been a certified Deputy Coroner of this county for twenty (20) years. . . . And, in Colorado, the County Coroner is the *only* public official with the legal power to *arrest the sheriff.*

That is the key to my oft-uttered wisdom in re: Politics is the art of controlling your environment. Indeed. Never forget it, or you will become a Victim of your environment. Rich nerds and lawyers will stomp all over you worse than any A-rab, and you will be like the eight ball on some country-club billiards table near Atlanta—*whack,* over and out. No more humor.

And so much for that, eh? Jews don't play pool anyway, and neither do A-rabs. They are *tribal* people, which means they are primitive thinkers. They feel a genetic imperative to kill each other, and it tends to get in their way. . . . Or maybe that brutal compulsion comes from the Holy Bible, which is definitely true. The Bible is *unforgiving*. There is not a scintilla of mercy or humor in the Holy Bible. None.

Think on it, Bubba. Point me to some laughs, or even a goddamn chuckle in that book.

People frequently ask me if I believe in God, as if it were some kind of final judgment or naked indicator of my pro or con value in this world. Ho ho. That is too stupid to even think about—like a WHITES ONLY sign on the pearly gates of Heaven.

But not really. Don't get me wrong, fellas. That is only a whooped-up "figure of speech," or maybe a failed metaphor. It is a term of Art, not a term of Law. If the freak who wrote the Book of Revelation had been busted and jailed for the horrible *threats* he made against the whole human race, he would have been executed on the spot by a Military Tribunal. So long, Johnny, we never really liked you anyway. Mahalo.

The Witness

Not everybody understands the real meaning of being "brought within The System." It is legal language, the kind of talk you hear in the hallways at professional police conventions or pretrial hearings in musty urban courtrooms. As in, "The time has come, Judge, to drop the net on this loathsome criminal deviate and reel him into The System."

We are talking about The Criminal Justice System, here, and once you get brought into it, there will be a part of your brain that thinks about nothing else for the rest of your life. It will be as if a leech had attached itself to the small of your back forever. . . . Just ask Bill Clinton.

Some people call it Rehabilitation, but . . .

. . .

A cop killing is always big news—except when Police kill one of their own, in which case the death notice is rarely if ever made public. The Law Enforcement Fraternity is very tight when it comes to media embarrassment. There is a basic operating rule among Criminal Defense Lawyers that says: "Above all, the *lawyer* must not go to jail." It is not always an easy rule to observe, given that the lawyer is also an ordained Officer of the Court.

Be keenly aware of this fact when you get accused (on paper/formal charges are filed) of anything at all—*anything* from shoplifting to felony murder—that could/might/will result in your being Convicted and formally Punished *in any way* for any violation of *any* part of *any* Criminal Code. The law is not on your side when you become a defendant in a criminal courtroom. They *are* out to get you, and they *will,* if you are not alert.

"He who goes to law takes a wolf by the ears." Robert Burton said that, and I am citing it as a very dangerous Reality in this wartorn world that we live in. This is 2002. The American Century was over in January of 2001. They were Punctual, as the Fascist mentality cannot survive without brute Punctuality. Never be *late,* for fear of being guilty of *Deviant Behavior,* and *brought within The System.* BANG! SLAM! BEND OVER. . . . *Seig heil!* Who is God? The Boss is God—and you're not. . . . Hey rube, you are Nothing! You are Guilty! You are lower than the shit of some filthy animal.

Yassuh, Boss. I'll do *anything,* just don't put me in Jail. I am guilty. I will do whatever you say.

Marilyn Chambers at 17
(HST archives)

. . .

It was a cold winter night when the Witness first came to my house. She was a very large woman, about 35 years old—dark hair, long legs, and tastefully enlarged breasts—who once worked in Southern California as a director of sex films. That is not a bad job to have in L.A., especially if you have a natural talent for it, and this woman did. I recognized it immediately.

I know the Sex Business. I was the Night Manager of the famous O'Farrell Theatre, in San Francisco, for two years, and I still have a keen eye for working girls. There is a certain lewd radiance about them that comes only from dancing naked in public for 2,000 nights. . . . Sex business people recognize one another immediately. They have ridden for the XXX brand, and the brand has ridden them.

It is not an unfriendly brand, nothing like a scar on the cheek, or a crude tattoo on top of a butt that says PROPERTY OF HELL'S ANGELS. That would not be appropriate for a stylish lap-dancing venue in Nashville or Toledo. The customers would be offended. Big tippers tend to be wary of a woman who has pulled the Hell's Angels train. The mark of the XXX business is an attitude more than a brand or a nasty tattoo.

The O'Farrell was once celebrated as "the Carnegie Hall of Public Sex in America." It was a nice place to work in those money-mad years of the Reagan Revolution. We had about 100 girls on the payroll, and many more on the waiting list. Naked women were a hot commodity in those days. It was the "Golden Era of pornography," according to chroniclers of that ilk, when sex movies were still shot with bright lights and reels of celluloid film.

Deep Throat and *Behind the Green Door* were still packing huge multisexual crowds into respectable theaters all over the country, Oral Sex was mainstream, and lush entertainment expenses were tax-deductible. Huge expense money was the oil that kept the national economy going, and sex was everywhere, 24 hours a day. Powder cocaine was the recreational drug of choice, but LSD-25 was still fashionable in upscale communes and coastal brokerage firms.

Those 20 sex-crazed years between the introduction of the birth control pill and the eruption of AIDS was a wild and orgiastic time in America, and I loved it.

Ah, but that was many years ago, or at least it seems that way. It was a good time to be young and reckless—when you could still take your date to a movie without having to worry about being hit on by strangers demanding blow jobs. That came in with the Democrats, who quickly discovered that getting busted in Washington for sodomy was a proven way to get re-elected in states like Arkansas and California. If Bill Clinton had not been term-limited by federal law, he would still be in the White House today and we would all be free from fear.

Or maybe not. There is another school of thought that says Clinton would have been assassinated if he'd been able to run for a third term. "The Texas Mafia would never have let it happen," my friend Curtis assured me. "He would have been jerked out like a bad tooth. . . ." Maybe you have to be from Texas to agree with talk like that, but I doubt it. Texas is not the only state full of wealthy freaks with sinister agendas. Some of them are friends of mine, in fact, and I have never doubted that just because they are nice people to have a few drinks with doesn't mean they won't do monstrous things. Cruelty and perversion are common jokes in the oil and orgy business.

Indeed, but we can save those stories for later, so let's get back to this woman I was trying to describe. Her name is Gail, but for vaguely legal reasons we will have to call her Jane. If I called her Gail we would have a lot of bitching from lawyers.

We will call her the Witness, which better suits her role in this drama. Some people called her the Victim, but not for long. That was a convenient legal fiction for the local D.A. and his (since-departed) gang of vengeful thugs. They are gone from this valley now, most of them fired or demoted into obscurity. The chief investigator in my case, the de facto boss of the gang, now works for the DEA in Europe. The Prosecutor, now known as Mr. Shiteyes, resigned soon after and is now a criminal lawyer in Aspen, where he is frequently seen on trial days with his arm around accused criminals wearing orange jumpsuits and handcuffs and jail haircuts, but he no longer works as a prosecutor. He "flipped," as they say in the cop shop. . . .

I didn't know the Witness personally, but she definitely knew me. She had been harassing me by mail for four or five months, telling me I didn't know how much FUN I was missing by not getting together with her immediately for a fascinating chat about her days in the Sex Business. We would have more FUN than a barrel of monkeys in heat, she hinted. Ho ho. She would even come out to Colorado in order to meet me on my own savage turf. She had already sent me a thick sheaf of lurid press clippings about her adventures as a wholesome college cheerleader who got into the Porno Movie business by accident and had been a big success. "I guess I was just lucky," she said demurely. "But once I saw how much talent I had, I never looked back. It's just amazing, isn't it."

It is important to understand that Jane had been extremely open with me, a complete stranger, about her background in the sex business. She was proud of it. Her record spoke for itself: nine successful XXX movies, including classics of abysmal lewdness like *Hot Lips, FleshSucker, Candy Goes to Hollywood, Eat Me While I'm Hot,* and a truly depraved saga about rape and degradation in a Japanese sex prison somewhere in the South Pacific called *Nazi Penetration,* starring Long John Holmes, one berserk Nazi, and five helpless white women with huge tits.

Nazi Penetration has long been one of my favorite films of the sex genre. It is a story of shipwreck, sadism, and absolutely hopeless female victims confined on a tiny tropical island with only a Nazi war criminal and two cruel Japanese nymphomaniacs to keep them company. The naked white girls are innocent prisoners of some long-forgotten war that is never mentioned in the movie except by way of the frayed and often bottomless military uniforms worn by the demented villains—who also carry spotless German Lugers and don't mind shooting them at escaped Sex Slaves who keep running away and fleeing into the jungle, only to be recaptured and relentlessly raped and tortured for their efforts. They are losers, and they will never be rescued—not even by the good-hearted Holmes, who also fucks them relentlessly.

I mention this epic of degenerate suffering only for reasons of historical context and Witness identification. If Jane had been a practicing Jehovah's Witness when I met her, my story might have a different ending, but she was not. She was just another one of those goofy, over-the-hump Porno Queens from the good old days who was looking around for some other line of work to get into, something where she could use her natural talents for harmless commercial sex without compromising her artistic integrity or her dubious social standing. I know them well, and I have a certain affection for most of them. They are girls who went to Hollywood when they were 17 years old, hoping to make the most of their whorish ambitions by becoming movie stars.

Very few succeeded, and many got sidetracked into the Sex Business, where work is always available. "My pussy is my ticket to ride," a stripper named Bambi once told me. "Men want to see my pussy and they want to see me fuck something scary. That's why they pay me, and that's why I do it."

Bambi was a lovely girl from a middle-class family in Sacramento, with an elegant body and a seductively morbid sense of humor. I liked her and used my influence to help her become a star at the O'Farrell, where she routinely made a thousand dollars a night. I was always tempted to fuck her, but I never did. I was deeply in love with my girlfriend Maria at the time. She was a sex star in her own right, and a jewel of a friend and a lover.

My Night Manager job put me in close contact with dozens of aggressively naked women every night, which never ceased to amaze me and kept me constantly high on sex. It was an overwhelming work environment, at times, but with Maria's help I soon became comfortable with it. Not everybody can handle being surrounded by lust, beauty, and clearly available nakedness at all times. It is like living in the Garden of Eden, with luscious apples hanging from every tree and the power to banish all snakes—which were Everywhere, writhing and cooing with a lust that bordered on madness.

Only a freak of passion could have resisted that kind of massive temptation, and on some nights I came close to caving in to it. "You are crazy as a goddamn loon not to fuck every one of these girls," Artie Mitchell told me. "They all love you and they all want to fuck you like animals. I've never seen anybody turn down so much guaranteed fine pussy. It makes me sick."

"So what?" I would say to him. "You are a sleazy whoremonger and you don't understand anything. Herb Caen told me you have syphilis."

"What?" he would scream. "You sick bastard! I'll kill Herb Caen if he ever prints that. Herb Caen sucks dicks!!"

Jim and Artie Mitchell were as bizarre a pair of brothers as ever lived. I loved them both, but the Sex Business had made them crazy. They made millions of dollars off of sex, but they were not suave. Neither one of them had social ambitions, but they fought like wolves to protect their vice-ridden turf. They were deep into San Francisco politics, but they were always in desperate need of sound political advice.

That was my job. The Night Manager gig was only a cover for my real responsibility, which was to keep them out of Jail, which was not easy. The backstairs politics of San Francisco has always been a byzantine snake pit of treachery and overweening bribery-driven corruption so perverse as to stagger the best minds of any generation. All political power comes from the barrel of either guns, pussy, or opium pipes, and people seem to like it that way. The charm of the city is legendary to the point of worship all over the world, with the possible exception of Kabul, New Orleans, and Bangkok.

. . .

On that cold night in late February when the Witness came to my house, she was wearing a blue business suit that made her look a bit on the chubby side and high-heeled shoes that would have made her seem dangerously tall if my other guests had not been well over six feet and none too happy to see her. Her head was huge, far larger than mine, and her body was oddly muscular— more in the style of a female bodybuilder with an uncontrollable appetite for speed and lethal steroids who had spent too much time in sexually oriented weight rooms on the wrong side of Hollywood. She was clearly an athlete—a "big" girl, in a word—and she spoke with a wiggy confidence that made me nervous. My mother would have called her pushy, or perhaps even rude. But I am not so polite. To me, she looked sleazy. There was something corrupt about her, something foul and dishonest that would have put me instantly on my guard if I had cared enough to worry about it that night.

But I didn't. She meant nothing to me, at the time. We get all kinds of people in this house, from common thugs and deviates to stupid thieves with hearts full of hate and U.S. senators with amazing whores on their arms. Some arrive on private jets, and others drive stolen cars full of illegal drugs and weapons. It is an ugly mix, at times, but I have learned to live with it, if only because I am a professional journalist and a writer of books about life in the weird lane—which is "interesting" in the Chinese sense, but not necessarily uplifting.

It is not a criminal life, or a hurricane zoo of never-ending craziness. It may look that way, from a distance, but I consider it eminently sane, and most of my friends agree. *Sane* is a dangerous word. It implies a clear distinction, a sharp line between the Sane and the Insane that we all see clearly and accept as a truth of nature.

But it is not. No. The only real difference between the Sane and the Insane, in this world, is the Sane have the power to have the Insane locked up. That is the bottom line. CLANG! Go immediately to prison. You crazy bastard, you should have been locked up a long time ago. You are a dangerous freak—I am rich, and I want you castrated.

Whoops, did I say that? Yes, I did, but we need not dwell so long on it that it develops into a full-blown tangent on the horrors of being locked up and gibbed like a tomcat in a small wire box. We have enough grim things to worry about in this country as the 21st Century unfolds. We have Anthrax, we have smallpox, we have very real fears of being blasted into jelly in the privacy of our own homes by bombs from an unseen enemy, or by nerve gas sprayed into our drinking water, or even ripped apart with no warning by our neighbor's Rottweiler dogs. All these things have happened recently, and they will probably happen again.

We live in dangerous times. Our armies are powerful, and we spend billions of dollars a year on new prisons, yet our lives are still ruled by fear. We are like pygmies lost in a maze. We are not at War, we are having a nervous breakdown.

. . .

Right. And enough of that gibberish. We are champions, so let's get back to the story. We were talking about the Witness, the large and sleazy woman who came into my life like a sea snake full of poison and almost destroyed me.

There were two other people in my kitchen that night, and a girl who kept popping in and out. So let's say there were five people in the house, including the Witness. She was happy to be there, she said, because she had some questions to ask me.

"Not now," I said. "We're watching the basketball game." I said it sharply, more in the manner of a command than a gentle request from the host. Normally I don't speak in that tone to first-time visitors, but she was clearly not a woman who was going to pay attention to gentle requests. I was not rude to her, but I was definitely firm. That is a point I like to make immediately when a dingbat comes into my home and gets loud. That is unacceptable. We have Rules here: They are civilized rules, and oddly genteel in their way, yet some people find them disturbing in their eccentricity. Contradictions abound, as well as dangerous quirks that sometimes make people afraid—which is not a bad thing on some days: Fear is a healthy instinct, not a sign of weakness. It is a natural self-defense mechanism that is common to felines, wolves, hyenas, and most humans. Even fruit bats know fear, and I salute them for it. If you think the world is weird now, imagine how weird it would be if wild beasts had no fear.

That is how this woman tried to act when she came into my home on that fateful February night. She pranced around and wandered from room to room in a way that made me nervous. She was clearly a refugee from the sex business—a would-be *promoter* of Sexual Aids & first-class organ enlargement. . . . That was her *business plan,* in a nut, and nobody wanted to listen to it.

"Shut up!" Semmes screamed. "Can't you see that we are watching a goddamn basketball game?"

She ignored him and kept babbling. "What kind of Sex do you like?" she asked me. "Why won't you talk to me?"

I am not a Criminal, by trade, but over the years I have developed a distinctly criminal nervous system. Some people might call it paranoia, but I have lived long enough to know that there is no such thing as paranoia. Not in the 21st Century. No. Paranoia is just another word for ignorance.

There Is No Such Thing as Paranoia

There may be flies on you and me, but there are no flies on Jesus.
—Hunter S. Thompson

Strange Lusts and Terrifying Memories

My father had a tendency to hunch darkly over the radio when the news of the day was foul. We listened to the first wave of Pearl Harbor news together. I didn't understand it, but I knew it was bad because I saw him hunch up like a spider for two or three days in a row after it happened. "God damn those sneaky Japs," he would mutter from time to time. Then he would drink whiskey and hammer on the arm of the couch. Nobody else in our family wanted to be with him when he listened to the war news. They didn't mind the whiskey, but they came to associate the radio with feelings of anger and fear.

I was not like that. Listening to the radio and sipping whiskey with my father was the high point of my day, and I soon became addicted to those moments. They were never especially happy, but they were always exciting. There was a certain wildness to it, a queer adrenaline rush of guilt and mystery and vaguely secret joy that I still can't explain, but even at the curious age of four I knew it was a special taste that I shared only with my father. We didn't dwell on it, or feel a dark need to confess. Not at all. It was fun, and I still enjoy remembering those hours when we hunched together beside the radio with our whiskey and our war and our fears about evil Japs sneaking up on us. . . .

I understand that fear is my friend, but not always. Never turn your back on Fear. It should always be in front of you, like a thing that might have to be killed. My father taught me that, along with a few other things that have kept my life interesting. When I think of him now I think of fast horses and cruel Japs and lying FBI agents.

"There is no such thing as Paranoia," he told me once. "Even your Worst fears will come true if you chase them long enough. Beware, son. There is Trouble lurking out there in that darkness, sure as hell. Wild beasts and cruel people, and some of them will pounce on your neck and try to tear your head off, if you're not careful."

It was a mean piece of wisdom to lay on a 10-year-old boy, but in retrospect I think it was the right thing to say, and it definitely turned out to be true. I have wandered into that darkness many times in my life and for many strange reasons that I still have trouble explaining, and I could tell you a whole butcher shop full of stories about the horrible savage beasts that lurk out there, most of them beyond the wildest imagination of a 10-year-old boy—or even a 20- or 30-year-old boy, for that matter, or even beyond the imagination of a teenage girl from Denver being dragged away from her family by a pack of diseased wolves. Nothing compares to it. The terror of a moment like that rolls over you like a rush of hot scum in a sewer pipe.

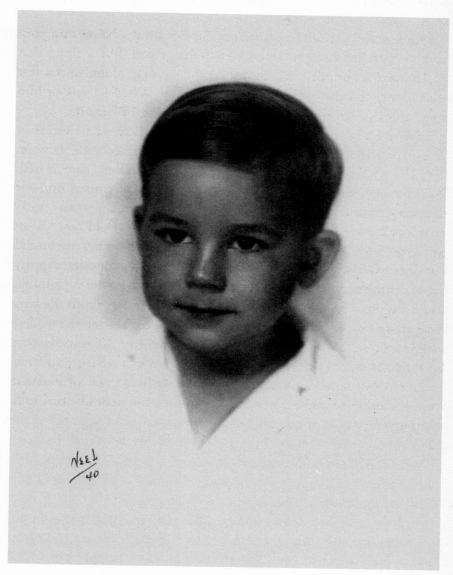

(HST archives)

. . .

Here is a story I wrote for the *Atheneum Literary Association* magazine and tried to insert into *The Spectator* when Porter Bibb was editor—he was a numb-nuts creep in those days, but so what? We loved each other—and I was after all, the Art Director. . . .

We put out a quality magazine and we printed whatever we liked and we both had veto power, which was dangerous.

Except for *this* one. No. This one never saw print, until now. And God's mercy on you swine for reading it.

SOCIETY HOUSEWIFE EXPOSED IN CHILD-SEX SCANDAL; BLOODY AFTERMATH SHOCKS EAST END NEIGHBORHOOD

I have not had the leisure to brood seriously on the nature and fate of true love in the 21st Century, but that doesn't mean I don't care. Not at all. That kind of flotsam is never far from my mind. I am a child of the American Century, and I feel a genetic commitment to understanding why it happened, and why I take it so personally.

Let me give you one example: In the summer of my 15th year, the wife of a family friend bit me on the face and tore off some bleeding flaps of skin that would never grow back. The tissue failed to regenerate, as the medical doctors say, and ever since then my face has been noticeably crooked. The wound itself healed perfectly. I was lucky to be attended to by the finest Restorative Surgeons in a nine-state region between Baltimore and St. Louis, from Chicago in the north to the Caribbean island of Grenada 3,000 miles south. I have never entirely recovered from that episode, and I have never understood how it happened. The woman who bit me refused to discuss it—at least not with me—and as far as I know she never told her lascivious tale to any living person.

It was, however, a towering scandal that haunted our peaceful neighborhood for many years. Massive speculation was rampant almost everywhere in the East End of Louisville except in the local newspapers, which only made it hotter as truly unspeakable gossip. It was Unacceptable and Irresistible all at once.

Ho ho. Stand back, you churlish little suckfish! I have my own definitions of words like Unacceptable and Irresistible. I remember the slope of her perfect little breasts and the panties she never wore. I remember exactly how she smelled and how she laughed when I sucked her nipples down my throat. I was her pimply sex toy, and she was the love of my life. I worshiped her desperate mouth and prayed at the shrine of her grasping pussy. Why she sunk her teeth into my face I will never know. Perhaps it was God's will or the hex of some heinous Devil.

Rape in Cherokee Park

I look back on my youth with great fondness, but I would not recommend it as a working model to others. I was lucky to survive it at all, in fact: I was hounded & stalked for most of my high school career by a cruel & perverted small-town Probation Officer who poisoned my much-admired social life and eventually put me in jail on the night of my Class graduation.

Once Mr. Dotson came into my life I was marked as a criminal. He was an officious creep with all sorts of hidden agendas—or not that hidden—and he hounded me all through high school. It was an embarrassment, and it criminalized me long before I ever got to marijuana. All kinds of people who had no reason to be in contact with the Juvenile Court were contacted by this Swine, which accounted for a lot of my reputation. He was out of control, and people like that shouldn't get away with abusing their power.

Especially as I hadn't committed a crime. All we had wanted was some cigarettes.

We ran out of cigarettes on the ride home from Cherokee Park. I was asleep in the backseat passed out, or half passed out, and I remember thinking: *Cigarettes. Cigarettes. Cigarettes.*

Max and Eric (or so I'll call them) were up front. Eric was driving, and I guess it was Max who said, "Well. Let's see if these people have any."

I might have thought of that, too: Here are people, neckers, parked in the park at Neckers' Knob, or whatever. Why not ask for a cigarette? That was Max's logic, anyway.

So we pulled up beside them, which could have frightened some people. And Max got out and went over to a car with two couples in it and asked for cigarettes, and the driver said, "We don't have any."

That seemed fair, but something else was said. The car was seven feet away, and Max was a fairly violent bugger. The next thing I remember is him yelling, "All right, Motherfucker! You give me some cigarettes or I'm going to grab you out of there!"

Then he reached into the car and said, "I'm going to jerk you out of here and beat the shit out of you and rape those girls back here." And that's all it was.

Eric was driving, so I had to get out of the backseat and go over and grab Max, saying, "Fuck this. We don't need any cigarettes." I meant we didn't need any fights. So I got back in the car and we drove off. That's all it was, but they got our license plate number and reported it. . . . Then—you know Cops: a Rape Charge.

God Might Forgive You, but I Won't

My Probation Officer knew it was wrong, he said later, in late-night chats with my mother, who was by then Chief Librarian at the Louisville Public Library and stocking my books on her shelves. My success was a joyous surprise to her, but she feared for the grievous effect it was having on my old nemesis, Mr. Dotson. He often stopped by our house for coffee, and he desperately begged her forgiveness for all the trouble he'd caused her.

She forgave him, in time, but I didn't. I will spit on his memory forever. The last of many letters I got from him carried a postmark from the Kentucky State Prison at Eddyville. I was not even curious enough to read it and find out if he was a convict or merely a Guard. I had other lessons to learn. My continuing education in the nature of the Criminal Justice System was picking up speed.

I remember Juvenile Court Judge Jull saying, "Well, Hunter. You've made my life a nightmare for four years. You've been in and out of this Court. You've mocked it. And now you're going to get away from me. This is my last chance at you. So now I remand you to the County Jail for sixty days." That was their last shot.

But it was a total outrage. I became good friends with the "victims," and they said the same thing. But this was Mr. Dotson and Judge Jull, and what they did was cause a huge rallying of support behind me. I would never have gone into their jail, except that minors couldn't make bail in Kentucky back then.

The only reason I got out in thirty days was because my eighteenth birthday came in thirty days, so they couldn't hold me: I could make bail. They didn't try to hold me; they had made their point. Last shot. That, and a group of powerful citizens and civic leaders had worked to get me out. But I was a hero while I was in jail—they decided they'd call me "The President," and on my birthday, "Hit the Bricks," they said, "My boy, 'Hit the Bricks.'" It became a cause, and I was a hero there for a while.

. . .

Many wild and desperate years have whirled through my life since my one and only experience as a certified Victim of the law enforcement process. The lesson I learned from those thirty days in jail was never to go back there again. Period. It was not Necessary. My jail mates had called me "The President" and beautiful girls came to visit me on Thursday afternoons, but I had better sense than to feel any pride about it.

The late Pablo Escobar, former kingpin of the powerful Medellín cocaine cartel in Colombia, once observed that "the difference between being a criminal and being an outlaw is that an outlaw has a following"—which he did, for a while, for his willingness to share his huge profits with the working-class Poor of his city. He was a Home-boy, a generous friend of the people. His only real crime, they said, was that the product his business produced was seen as a dangerous men-ace by the ruling Police & Military establishments of the U.S. and a few other countries that were known to be slaves and toadies of U.S. economic interests.

When I got out of jail, in fact, I went immediately to work for the rest of the summer for Almond Cook, the Chevrolet dealer in town. I'm not sure what I thought I was going to do that fall—maybe go to the U.K. I didn't know, but I was in no mood really to take up any-thing conventional. Mr. Cook was the father of one of my longtime girlfriends, and I was given a job driving a brand-new Chevrolet truck, delivering parts around town. It was a wonderful job—I'd just take things all over town, driving constantly, sort of a very large version of those bicycle messengers in New York, but in a brand-new fucking V-8 truck.

I got very good with the truck. I was driving all the time, and it was wonderful, like being given a rocket. And I had no trouble and got to be such a good driver that something was bound to happen . . . the numbers were getting bad. Then one Saturday morning—a very bright, very sunny day—I was speeding down an alley behind some kind of a car repair emporium on Second Street. I'd gone down this particular alley many times, and had gotten to the point where I could put this huge V-8 Chevy pickup through a burning hoop without it being touched—at sixty or seventy miles an hour.

I remember coming down that alley. It was bright. I could see it was all bricks on either side, and here was this big truck, say a ton and a half, like a big Ryder delivery truck, only blue or green, and it had one of those tailgates that hangs down on chains, made of pointed lead or hard steel. The tailgate was pointing out by a few degrees; had it been parked parallel I would have had room to go through with about three inches to spare. But instead of being parallel to the wall, it was parked at a slight angle, and I remember thinking, *Shit. I can make that.* But I knew it was bad.

I hit the accelerator so hard that I went through the alley at about sixty—so fast that I barely felt the impact. Sort of a click, more than a crash. . . .

I knew immediately that I hadn't made it clean, and I stopped. Another inch and I would have made it . . . two inches, maybe. But I missed it by those two inches: The tailgate had kicked in, just to the right of the front headlight. The truck had a big chrome stripe all along it, and right on top of it, about three inches above, was another stripe, this one dark in color. I looked at it and thought, What the fuck? What's that? There was no other damage. I hadn't crashed anything. Nothing bent. So I stared at the dark stripe again, and as I looked at it I realized that the tailgate had caught the front headlight right there and opened up the truck like a can opener—the whole length, front to back, about two inches wide—but clean, like a sardine can. You put one on both sides and people would think that's the way new Chevy trucks were.

I thought, Oh, fuck. But nobody had seen it. It didn't make any noise; there was no crash. Just a hairline miss. Hubris! I knew I should learn from the thing. I knew the damned track was not what it looked like, literally: a two-inch racing stripe. But it was so clean that I thought for a minute that I might get away with it.

I went into the diner across the street and sat drinking coffee and beer, thinking, What the Hell do I do? . . . Do I tell anybody? I parked the truck out in the lot with the bad side right next to a fence so nobody could see it, then finally decided what to do.

I went in and told the parts manager, "Come out here, Hank. I've got something to show you." He was in charge of such things, and he was a good friend. I took him out to the lot in the hot noonday sun and said, "Now, I want you to be calm here, but I just want to show you this. I don't know what to do about it, and I need some advice." I took him around to the other side, between the fence and the truck, and he almost passed out.

I said, "What should I do about this?"

And he said, "We'll have to tell Mr. Cook."

That's fair, I thought. It was right before lunch. Hank then called and said he needed to talk to Mr. Cook, but he wasn't there, Thank God, which gave me another hour or so. I was going nuts with this. Something was coming down.

We just happened to be right across the street from the main Louisville Post Office, and I thought, Ah, hah! I bet the draft office is still open there. So I went right across the street at lunch and volunteered for the draft, which a lot of my friends had done. It was kind of a nice resting place between stops—and there was a six-month waiting list. I thought, Oh, fuck, time's way down and I have to go back and see Almond Cook at one-ten.

I had an appointment.

So I just went next door to the Air Force. It happened to be next door. And I took the pilot training test and scored like 97 percent. I didn't really mean to go in there, but I told them I wanted to drive jet planes, and they said I could with that test. So I said, "When can I . . . when can I leave?"

And the recruiting officer said, "*Well.* Normally it takes a few days to check out, but you go Monday morning"—allegedly to flight school at Lackland Air Force Base in San Antonio, Texas.

I thought, Ah, hah! I'm out of here.

I went back and apologized to Almond Cook and told him that I had to admit I had failed at driving the truck.

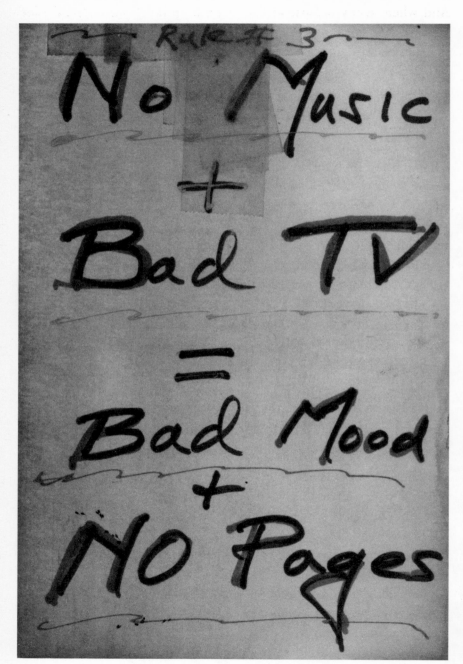

(HST)

. . .

And where is my old friend Paul Hornung, now that we need him? Paul was the finest running back of his time: All-State at Flaget High in Louisville, All-American at Notre Dame, and All-Pro for the Green Bay Packers. He was a big handsome boy from Louisville's gamey West End, a longtime breeding ground for sporting talent, which also produced a flashy young fighter with extremely quick hands named Cassius Clay, who would become even more famous than Hornung.

That would be my old friend Muhammad Ali, the Heavyweight Champion of the World. He beat the shit out of me once, for no good reason at all, and Paul Hornung ran over me in a car, just because I couldn't get out of his way. . . . Yes sir, those boys stomped on the terra.

They were also serious flesh-tasters, as working Libertines were sometimes called in those days. They were . . .

Fuck this, I feel weak.

Get your hands off me, Harold! What the fuck is wrong with you?

Okay. You're the boss. Do anything you want, but please don't hurt my animals! That is all I ask.

Oh Yes Oh Yes! Praise Jesus, don't *hurt* them. They are creatures of God, and so am I. Oh god, pain is everywhere I feel. . . . "Bend over, honey," he said. "I'm going to put this Eel up your ass, so try to relax."

Ho ho, eh? Balls! There *are* no jokes when we start talking about introducing saltwater Eels into people's body cavities. Some of them are nine feet long. That is over the line, if it's done against their will. That would be rape of some kind.

Whoops! How about a break, people? How about some Music? Yes. Music is where it's at, so consider this:

I am a confused Musician who got sidetracked into this goddamn Word business for so long that I never got back to music—except maybe when I find myself oddly alone in a quiet room with only a typewriter to strum on and a yen to write a song. Who knows why? Maybe I just feel like singing—so I type.

These quick electric keys are my Instrument, my harp, my RCA glass-tube microphone, and my fine soprano saxophone all at once. That is my music, for good or ill, and on some nights it will make me feel like a god. Veni, Vidi, Vici. . . . That is when the fun starts. . . . Yes, Kenneth, this *is* the frequency. This is where the snow leopards live;

"Genius, all over the world, stands hand in hand, and one shock of recognition runs the whole circle round. . . ."

Herman Melville said that, and I have found it to be true, but I didn't really know what it *felt* like until I started feeling those shocks myself, which always gave me a rush. . . .

So perhaps we can look at some of my work (or *all* of it, on some days) as genetically *governed* by my frustrated musical failures, which led to an overweening *sublimation* of my essentially musical instincts that surely haunt me just as clearly as they dominate my lyrics.

The New Dumb

Something is happening here,
But you don't know what it is,
Do you, Mr. Jones?
                    —Bob Dylan

No sir, not a chance. Mr. Jones does not even pretend to know what's happening in America right now, and neither does anyone else.

We have seen Weird Times in this country before, but the year 2000 is beginning to look *super* weird. This time, there really is nobody flying the plane. . . . We are living in dangerously weird times now. Smart people just shrug and admit they're dazed and confused.

The only ones left with any confidence at all are the New Dumb. It is the beginning of the end of our world as we knew it. Doom is the operative ethic.

. . .

The Autumn months are never calm in America. Back to Work, Back to School, Back to Football Practice, etc. . . . Autumn is a very Traditional period, a time of strong Rituals and the celebrating of strange annual holidays like Halloween and Satanism and the fateful Harvest Moon, which can have ominous implications for some people.

Autumn is always a time of Fear and Greed and Hoarding for the winter coming on. Debt collectors are active on old people and fleece the weak and helpless. They want to lay in enough cash to weather the known horrors of January and February. There is always a rash of kid-nappings and abductions of schoolchildren in the football months. Preteens of both sexes are traditionally seized and grabbed off the streets by gangs of organized Perverts who traditionally give them as Christmas gifts to each other as personal Sex Slaves and playthings.

Most of these things are obviously Wrong and Evil and Ugly—but at least they are Traditional. They will happen. Your driveway *will* ice up, your furnace *will* explode, and you *will* be rammed in traffic by an uninsured driver in a stolen car.

But what the hell. That is why we have Insurance, eh? And the Inevitability of these nightmares is what makes them so reassuring. Life will go on, for good or ill. The structure might be a little Crooked, but the foundations are still Strong and Unshakable.

Ho, ho. Think again, buster. Look around you. There is an eerie sense of Panic in the air, a silent Fear and Uncertainty that comes with once-reliable faiths and truths and solid Institutions that are no longer safe to believe in. . . . There is a Presidential Election, right on sched-ule, but somehow there is no President. A new Congress is elected, like always, but somehow there is no Congress at all—not as we knew it, anyway, and whatever passes for Congress will be as helpless and weak as Whoever has to pass for the "New President."

If this were the world of sports, it would be like playing a Super Bowl that goes into 19 scoreless Overtimes and never actually Ends . . . or four L.A. Lakers stars being murdered in different places on the same day. Guaranteed Fear and Loathing. Abandon all hope. Prepare for the Weirdness. Get familiar with Cannibalism.

Good luck, Doc.

November 19, 2000

In the Belly of the Beast

Although I don't feel that it's at all necessary to tell you how I feel about the principle of individuality, I know that I'm going to have to spend the rest of my life expressing it one way or another, and I think that I'll accomplish more by expressing it on the keys of a typewriter than by letting it express itself in sudden outbursts of frustrated violence. I don't mean to say that I'm about to state my credo here on this page, but merely to affirm, sincerely for the first time in my life, my belief in man as an individual and independent entity. Certainly not independence in the everyday sense of the word, but pertaining to a freedom and mobility of thought that few people are able—or even have the courage—to achieve.

—from a letter to Joe Bell
October 24, 1957
Eglin Air Force Base
Fort Walton Beach, Florida

(Tom Corcoran)

Sally Loved Football Players

I was halfway through training in the Air Force when I saw my first AF flying-team disaster. That was down in Florida, at Eglin AF Base, at a *practice* run for the annual "Firepower Demonstration." Arthur Godfrey was there, as I recall, and it made him Sick. He didn't do any more PR for the Air Force.

Help! Now I'm having flashbacks about when my best photographer went to cover the once-famous 24-Hour Formula One Grand Prix at Sebring & never came back to work. His name was George Thompson, a very talented boy. He was smashed into hamburger when he was trotting across an "Exit ramp" with his camera. Jesus! I had to write his Obituary for the Sports Section that night. . . . It happened about two weeks after that ungodly disaster at the Firepower Demonstration. I almost went crazy—drunk & AWOL for two (2) months, in Tallahassee & Mobile & New Orleans. I went from Top Gun to Psychiatric Observation Status in what seemed like the Speed of *Light*.

Sad story, eh? Yeah, but I was Young then. I could bounce like a gum rubber ball. It was Fun. Girls loved me and queers gave me "speed" in New Orleans. I had a fast MG/A sports car that I would drive out on the beach in Destin & swim naked with Officers' wives at midnight. Colonel Hugo's beautiful daughter let me stay for two weeks at her slick condo in Mobile while the Air Police were looking for me. She had a swimming pool shaped like a football in her backyard, and the neighbors called the Police on us when we ran around naked & fucked like sea-weasels on the diving board. . . . Sally loved football players. She thought she could stay Young forever by sucking the juice of Eternal Life out of hard young bodies. She called it "The Milk of Paradise" and she rubbed it on her face every night.

Sally was 25 years old & she looked like one of those racy Brazilian girls who play volleyball on the beach in Rio on Sunday mornings. Her father was a bird-Colonel at the Air Force base, and her mother was a Southern Debutante. She had a very young son who laughed crazily when I would pick him up by his ankles and swing him around in fast circles like a pinwheel. . . . I forget his name now, but he liked me & he thought my name was Air-Man. His mother took me to dinner at fancy bars and Yacht Clubs in Mobile. She drove a sky-blue Cadillac, and she loved to get naked & drive fast at night on the Pensacola Highway—in my car or hers, which was far too heavy to drive out on the beach & park between the sand dunes while we swam in the Gulf of Mexico on moonlit nights.

Sally had a day job somewhere in downtown Mobile, but she would always call in sick when I came to visit. She would say that she'd "hurt her back on the diving board" and she could hardly walk, for the pain. She would take off five or six days at a time when I was there, but she never worried about it. She said they could do without her for a few days, and they knew she had a Bad Back—which was true, but not because she was crippled.

No. It was because of that nasty sandpaper surface on the diving board at her pool. It rubbed her spine raw when we got drunk and screwed on it at night for two or three hours at a time. We would wake up in the morning with blood all over the sheets from bouncing around on that goddamn diving board all night. . . . The pain made her cry, and I could barely walk the next day because of the bleeding wounds on my knees and my elbows. I had bleeding scabs on my knees for most of that summer, and when I finally went back to work on the newspaper, I had trouble walking around the office. The other editors laughed at me, but my boss Colonel Evans was a serious Military Man and he hated the sight of a man with fresh blood on his pants limping around his office.

"Goddamnit, Hunter!" he would scream. "What in the name of Shit is wrong with you? There's blood all over the floor in the bathroom! I slipped and almost *fell down* when I went in there to piss!"

I told him it was because I had to play football on the weekends, and the Base football field was in such bad shape that I sometimes fell down when I was running out for a pass from Zeke Bratkowski or Max McGee.

"O my God!" he would scream. "You're a goddamn Fool, aren't you! Why in Shit are you trying to play *football* at this time of year? Do you have *Shit* for brains? . . . This is goddamn *baseball* season. . . . Are you too stupid to know that it's *baseball* season? . . . Are you some kind of Human JACKASS?"

"No," I would say. "I'm the *Sports Editor*." (Which was true.) The Colonel hated it, but his hands were tied. The Eglin Eagles were the defending Champions of what was the U.S. Worldwide Military Command, in those days, and we expected to win it again. Football was *Big* at Eglin Air Force Base, very big. The football team was a perennial powerhouse, famous all over the world—at least everywhere in the world where the United States of America had a functioning military base, and that was just about Everywhere.

Playing for Eglin was like playing for the Green Bay Packers, and star players were no less pampered. ROTC was a mandatory course for all student/athletes at taxpayer-funded universities in the nation, back then—even for All-American football stars at schools like Alabama & Ohio State—and all ROTC student/athletes were required to serve for at least two (2) years of active duty in the U.S. Armed Forces. . . . They had No Choice—unless they qualified for a Draft Exemption for Moral or Medical reasons, which carried a life-long, career-crippling Stigma—so most of them did their 2 years "in uniform" & then got on with their lives in the Real World, like everybody else.

Paris Review #156

GEORGE PLIMPTON: *Reading* The Proud Highway, *I got the impression you always wanted to be a writer.*

HUNTER S. THOMPSON: Well, wanting to and having to are two different things. Originally I hadn't thought about writing as a solution to my problems. But I had a good grounding in literature in high school. We'd cut school and go down to a café on Bardstown Road where we would drink beer and read and discuss Plato's parable of the cave. We had a literary society in town, the Athenaeum; we met in coat and tie on Saturday nights. I hadn't adjusted too well to society—I was in jail for the night of my high school graduation—but I learned at the age of fifteen that to get by you had to find the one thing you can do better than anybody else . . . at least this was so in my case. I figured that out early. It was writing. It was the rock in my sock. Easier than algebra. It was always work, but it was worthwhile work. I was fascinated early on by seeing my byline in print. It was a rush. Still is.

When I got to the Air Force, writing got me out of trouble. I was assigned to pilot training at Eglin Air Force Base near Pensacola in northwest Florida, but I was shifted to electronics . . . advanced, very intense, eight-month school with bright guys . . . I enjoyed it, but I didn't want to end up on the DEW line—the "distant early warning" line—somewhere in the Arctic Circle. Besides, I'm afraid of electricity. So I went up to the base education office one day and signed up for some classes at Florida State. I got along well with a guy named Ed and I asked him about literary possibilities. He asked me if I knew anything about sports, and I told him I had been the editor of my high school paper. He said, "Well, we might be in luck." It turned out that the sports editor, a staff sergeant, of the base newspaper, the *Command Courier,* had been arrested in Pensacola and put in jail for public drunkenness, pissing against the side of a building; it was the third time, and they wouldn't let him out.

So I went to the base library and found three books on journalism. I stayed there reading until it closed. I learned about headlines, leads: who, when, what, where, that sort of thing. I barely slept that night. This was my ticket to ride, my ticket to get out of that damn place. So I started as an editor. I wrote long Grantland Rice–type stories. The sports editor of my hometown *Louisville Courier-Journal* always had a column, left-hand side of the page—so I started a column.

By the second week I had the whole thing down. I could work at night. I wore civilian clothes, worked off base, had no hours, but I worked constantly. I wrote not only for the base paper but also the local paper, *The Playground News.* I'd put things in the local paper that I couldn't put in the base paper. Really inflammatory shit. I wrote for a professional wrestling newsletter. The Air Force got very angry about it. I was constantly doing things that violated regulations. I wrote a critical column about how Arthur Godfrey, who'd been invited to the base to be the master of ceremonies at a firepower demonstration, had been busted for shooting animals from the air in Alaska. The base commander told me: "Goddamnit, son, why did you have to write about Arthur Godfrey that way?"

When I left the Air Force I knew I could get by as a journalist. So I went to apply for a job at *Sports Illustrated*. I had my clippings, my bylines, and I thought that was magic—my passport. The personnel director just laughed at me. I said, "Wait a minute. I've been sports editor for *two* papers." He told me that their writers were judged not by the work they'd done, but where they'd done it. He said, "Our writers are all Pulitzer Prize winners from *The New York Times*. This is a helluva place for you to *start*. Go out into the boondocks and improve yourself."

GP: *You eventually ended up in San Francisco. With the publication in 1967 of* Hell's Angels, *your life must have taken an upward spin.*

HST: All of a sudden I had a book out. At the time I was twenty-nine years old and I couldn't even get a job driving a cab in San Francisco, much less writing. Sure, I had written important articles for *The Nation* and *The Observer,* but only a few good journalists really knew my byline. The book enabled me to buy a brand-new BSA G50 Lightning—it validated everything I had been working toward. If *Hell's Angels* hadn't happened, I never would have been able to write *Fear and Loathing in Las Vegas* or anything else. To be able to earn a living as a freelance writer in this country is damned hard; there are very few people who can do that. *Hell's Angels* all of a sudden proved to me that, Holy Jesus, maybe I can do this. I knew I was a good journalist. I knew I was a good writer, but I felt like I got through a door just as it was closing.

GP: *The San Francisco scene brought together many unlikely pairs—you and Allen Ginsberg, for instance. How did you come to know Allen during this period?*

HST: I met Allen in San Francisco when I went to see a marijuana dealer who sold by the lid. I remember it was ten dollars when I started going to that apartment and then it was up to fifteen. I ended up going there pretty often, and Ginsberg—this was in Haight-Ashbury—was always there looking for weed too. I went over and introduced myself and we ended up talking a lot. I told him about the book I was writing and asked if he would help with it. He helped me with it for several months; that's how he got to know the Hell's Angels. We would also go down to Ken Kesey's in La Honda together.

One Saturday, I drove down the coast highway from San Francisco to La Honda and I took Juan, my two-year-old son, with me. There was this magnificent crossbreeding of people there. Allen was there, the Hell's Angels—and the cops were there too, to prevent a Hell's Angels riot. Seven or eight cop cars. Kesey's house was across the creek from the road, sort of a two-lane blacktop country compound, which was a weird place. For one thing, huge speakers were mounted everywhere in all the trees, and some were mounted across the road on wires, so to be on the road was to be in this horrible vortex of sound, this pounding, you could barely hear yourself think—rock 'n' roll at the highest amps. That day, even before the Angels got there, the cops began arresting anyone who left the compound. I was by the house; Juan was sleeping peacefully in the backseat of the car. It got to be outrageous: The cops were popping people. You could see them about a hundred yards away, but then they would bust somebody very flagrantly, so Allen said, "You know, we've got to do something about this." I agreed, so with Allen in the passenger's seat, Juan in the back sleeping, and me driving, we took off after the cops that had just busted another person we knew, who was leaving just to go up to the restaurant on the corner. Then the cops got after *us*. Allen at the very sight of the cops went into his hum, his *om,* trying to hum them off. I was talking to them like a journalist would: "What's going on here, Officer?" Allen's humming was supposed to be a Buddhist barrier against the bad vibes the cops were producing, and he was doing it very loudly, refusing to speak to them, just *"Om! Om! Om!"* I had to explain to the cops who he was and why he was doing this. The cops looked into the backseat and said, "What is that back there? A child?" and I said, "Oh, yeah, yeah. That's my son." With Allen still going, *"Om,"* we were let go. He was a reasonable cop, I guess—checking out a poet, a journalist, and a child. Never did figure Ginsberg out, though. It was like the humming of a bee. It was one of the weirdest scenes I've ever been through, but almost every scene with Allen was weird in some way or another.

GP: *Did any other Beat Generation authors influence your writing?*

HST: Jack Kerouac influenced me quite a bit as a writer . . . in the Arab sense that the enemy of my enemy was my friend. Kerouac taught

Juan, age 3
(HST)

me that you could get away with writing about drugs and get published. It was *possible,* and in a symbolic way I expected Kerouac to turn up in Haight-Ashbury for the cause. Ginsberg was there, so it was kind of natural to expect that Kerouac would show up too. But, no—that's when Kerouac went back to his mother and voted for Barry Goldwater in 1964. That's when my break with him happened. I wasn't trying to write like him, but I could see that I could get published like him and break through the Eastern establishment ice. That's the same way I felt about Hemingway when I first learned about him and his writing. I thought, Jesus, some people can *do* this. Of course Lawrence Ferlinghetti influenced me—both his wonderful poetry and the earnestness of his City Lights bookstore in North Beach.

GP: *What's the appeal of the "outlaw" writer, such as yourself?*

HST: I just usually go with my own taste. If I like something, and it happens to be against the law, well, then I might have a problem. But an outlaw can be defined as somebody who lives outside the law, beyond the law, not necessarily against it. It's pretty ancient. It goes back to Scandinavian history. People were declared outlaws and were cast out of the community and sent to foreign lands—exiled. They operated outside the law in communities all over Greenland and Iceland, wherever they drifted. Outside the law in the countries they came from—I don't think they were trying to be outlaws . . . I was never trying, necessarily, to be an outlaw. It was just the place in which I found myself. By the time I started *Hell's Angels* I was riding with them and it was clear that it was no longer possible for me to go back and live within the law. Between Vietnam and weed—a whole generation was criminalized in that time. You realize that you are subject to being busted. A lot of people grew up with that attitude. There were a lot more outlaws than me. I was just a writer. I wasn't trying to be an outlaw writer. I never heard of that term; somebody else made it up. But we were all outside the law: Kerouac, Miller, Burroughs, Ginsberg, Kesey; I didn't have a gauge as to who was the worst outlaw. I just recognized allies: my people.

Fall 2000

imothy Leary and Neal Cassady, their first meeting at Millbrook
24. in Kentucky – Merry Pranksters' "Further" bus which Neal'd driven
crosscountry S.F. to N.Y. via Texas before Fall 1964 Presidential, with
"Vote for Goldwater is a vote for Fun" logo painted large across bus-side, L.S.D.
ool-aid pitcher in icebox. Neal scratching amphetamine itch in his driver's
alm, he'd driven out to bring Kerouac into the city for brief meeting with the
Pranksters & & every a few days before. For Hunter Thompson. Allen Ginsberg

(Allen Ginsberg)

. . .

In the violent years of the Sixties I found myself sinking deeper & deeper into a dangerously criminal lifestyle, along with most of my friends & associates. I was a hardworking professional journalist, at the time, with a wife & a son & extremely smart friends & a brand-new BSA motorcycle that was widely admired as "the fastest bike ever tested by *Hot Rod* magazine." My comfortable pad on a hill above Golden Gate Park was alive, day & night, with the babble of artists, musicians, writers, lawyers, wild bikers & rock 'n' roll stars whose names would soon be famous. . . . San Francisco was the capital of the world, in those years, and we were the new aristocracy. It was like living in the Kingdom of Magic.

But something about it disturbed me. Something was far out of whack. It was impossible not to notice that more & more of my friends were being arrested & locked up in jail. We were doing the same things we had always been doing, but we were suddenly committing more crimes—Felony crimes, in fact, which carried drastic criminal penalties. . . . Like five years in state prison for smoking a joint on a bench in a public park, or ten years for resisting arrest by refusing to be drafted into the Army & sent off to die in Vietnam.

It was the beginning of the Criminalization of a whole generation, and I soon became keenly aware of it. Even Joan Baez went to jail. New laws made possession of LSD a Class I felony and gave all police the right & even the duty to kick down yr. door on a whim. . . . I looked around me one night at a birthday party in Berkeley & saw that we were all committing a felony crime, just by being there. Yesterday's Fun had been officially transmogrified into tomorrow's insane nightmare. Fear led me to retaining a prominent Criminal lawyer; he agreed on one condition, he said—that I would never talk to a cop before he came to my rescue.

What Marijuana?

Indeed, some of my best friends are lawyers. I have other good friends who are law enforcement professionals, but not many. It is not wise, in my business, to count too many cops among your good friends, no more than it is wise to be constantly in the company of lawyers—unless, of course, you are about to be put on trial in a Criminal Court, and even then you want to be very careful. Your life or your freedom and certainly your sacred fortune will certainly depend on your choice of a criminal lawyer, and if you make the wrong choice, you will suffer. If your attorney is a fool or a slacker, you are doomed. The courts will disdain you, all criminal prosecutors will treat you with contempt, your friends will denounce you, and your enemies will rejoice. You will be taken without mercy into the bowels of the Criminal Justice System.

That is when pleading hopeless insanity begins to look like a pretty good option. The Insane, after all, can be cured, under the law, while the Guilty will be Guilty forever—or until they make enormous money contributions to a friendly second-term President with nothing to lose by tossing a few last-minute Pardons up for grabs. That is when you will need a profoundly expensive Attorney. Justice has never been cheap in America, not even for the innocent.

. . .

O no. Forget that traditional bullshit about "let the client suffer." *While the lawyer suffers Later, all alone, confronting his own demons in the lavish privacy of his own mansion(s).*

No. None of that. I want him to suffer now, just as I do. You bet! We are Brothers, joined at the Soul. We will suffer together, or not at all.

This is our sacred Vow, our highest mixing of Blood, Truth, and Honor. We will fight back-to-back on the crest of the highest hill—because We are The Brotherhood, the highest tribe of Truth & Law & Justice.

We are few, but we speak with the power of many. We are strong like lonely bulls, but we are legion. Our code is gentle, but our justice is Certain—seeming Slow on some days, but slashing Fast on others, eating the necks of the Guilty like a gang of Dwarf Crocodiles in some lonely stretch of the Maputo River in the Transvaal, where the Guilty are free to run, but they can never Hide.

Their souls will never die, and neither will ours. The only difference will be that when the Great Cookouts occur on the very Selective beaches of the Next Life, it will be their souls that are turning on the long sharp sticks in the fire pit, and ours will be the hands on the spit handles. . . .

. . .

I instructed my attorney to scroll up my personal FBI file the other day, but he laughed and called me a fool. "You will never get your files from those swine," he said. "We can ask, we can beg, we can demand and file civil suits—but they will *never* tell you what they have on you—and in your case, Doc, that shit will be so huge and so frightening that we don't want to see it. The cost would be astronomical."

"Of course," I said quickly. "Thank you for warning me. I must have been out of my mind to mention it."

"Yeah," he replied, "figure at least a million dollars—about what you'd pay for a nice house in New Orleans or two rounds of golf with Tiger Woods."

"Shit on it," I said. "Never mind the FBI. Who else is after me?"

"Nobody," he said. "I can't understand it. This is a dangerous time to get busted. You should knock on wood and enjoy it while it lasts."

"Yes," I replied. "That's why we're going to Africa next month. It is time to get out of this country while we still can!"

"We?" said the lawyer. "Just exactly who is 'we,' Doc? As your attorney, I know not *we*."

"You evil bastard," I said. "Don't worry, I understand the attorney-client relationship. Nobody will ever accuse *you* of Terrorism, will they? I think it's about time some of you bastards got locked up, counselor. That's what *we* means."

He fell silent. It is always wise to have yr. lawyer under control—lest he flee & leave you to sink all alone.

Lynching in Denver

First they came for the Jews
and I did not speak out—
because I was not a Jew.

*Then they came for the communists
and I did not speak out—
because I was not a communist.*

*Then they came for the trade
unionists and I did not speak out—
because I was not a trade unionist.*

*Then they came for me—
and there was no one left
to speak out for me.*

—Pastor Niemoeller (victim of the Nazis)

GUILT BY ASSOCIATION AT HEART OF AUMAN CASE
BY KAREN ABBOTT, *NEWS STAFF WRITER*
ROCKY MOUNTAIN NEWS, APRIL 29, 2002

Colorado's Lisl Auman has one thing in common with the man federal agents say was the 20th hijacker on Sept. 11. They were in custody when others committed the spectacular crimes that got them in the worst trouble of their lives.

Auman was handcuffed in the back of a police car when a man she had known less than a day shot Denver police officer Bruce Vander-Jagt dead in 1997, but she was convicted of the murder and sentenced to life in prison.

Zacarias Moussaoui, a French citizen of Moroccan descent, was in jail last year on immigration violations when others committed the Sept. 11 terrorist attacks for which federal prosecutors want Moussaoui executed.

He's still in jail, awaiting a federal trial in Virginia on charges of conspiring to bring about the attacks that killed thousands.

Auman, 26, is behind bars in a state prison while she appeals her conviction in a case that also has attracted nationwide attention. The Colorado Court of Appeals will hear oral arguments in her case Tuesday.

Moussaoui is not a sympathetic figure in most American minds, but Auman may be.

"The instinctive reaction to the Lisl Auman case is, 'That's not fair,'" said Denver attorney David Lane.

Defense lawyers say both Auman and Moussaoui have been unfairly targeted by authorities eager to punish someone for heinous crimes committed by others who put themselves beyond the reach of the law by dying.

The 19 known hijackers died when the four planes they commandeered hit the World Trade Center towers and Pentagon and crashed in a field in Pennsylvania.

VanderJagt's murderer, Matthaeus Jaehnig, immediately killed himself with the officer's gun.

Both Auman and Moussaoui exemplify a long-standing principle of American law: You don't have to pull the trigger, hijack the plane, be nearby, or even intend to kill someone to face the toughest penalties.

"The theory is that even though you're not a hands-on operative, you're still as culpable as the perpetrator," said Denver defense attorney Phil Cherner, president of the Colorado Criminal Defense Bar.

A Denver jury convicted Auman of "felony murder"—a murder committed during another serious crime or the immediate flight afterward—on the legal theory that she was responsible for VanderJagt's death because she earlier had arranged a burglary.

Auman enlisted Jaehnig's help in burglarizing her ex-boyfriend's apartment in Pine. When the police showed up, the two fled by car. The police chased them to Denver, where they took Auman into custody. But Jaehnig escaped on foot and shot VanderJagt while Auman sat handcuffed in a police cruiser.

Defense lawyers nationwide see Auman's case as their chance to challenge the felony murder statutes under which people who didn't expect anyone to be killed, and weren't present when they were, have been condemned to death.

"The felony murder doctrine is extremely harsh and frequently unjust," Lane said.

The National Association of Criminal Defense Lawyers has filed a brief on Auman's side. The Colorado District Attorneys Council has filed one supporting the government.

"What we are concerned with is the integrity of the felony murder statute statewide," said Peter Weir, the council's executive director.

He said the established public policy in Colorado is that "it's appropriate for an individual to be fully accountable for the consequences of all acts that they engage in."

"Once the acts are set in motion, you're responsible for what happens," Weir said.

An unusual assortment of supporters has gathered in Auman's cause, from "gonzo" journalist Hunter Thompson to conservative U.S. Senate candidate Rick Stanley to one of the jurors who convicted her.

. . .

Peacocks don't move around much at night. They like a high place to roost, and they will usually find one before sundown. They know how many nocturnal beasts are down there looking for food—foxes, coyotes, wildcats, bloodthirsty dogs on the prowl—and the only animal that can get them when they're perched up high is one of those huge meat-eating owls with night vision that can swoop down & pounce on anything that moves, from a water rat to a healthy young sheep.

My own peacocks wander widely during the day, but at night they come back into their own warm cage. Every once in a while they will miss curfew & decide to roost in a tree or on top of a telephone pole—(and that is what happened last week).

It was not a Lightning ball that blacked out my house, but a male peacock that stepped on a power line & caused a short circuit that burned him to a cinder & blew half my Electrics. The power came back, but the bird did not. It was fried like a ball of bacon. We couldn't even eat it. That tragedy occurred at halftime—so let the record stand corrected. Sorry.

I have consulted with many lawyers on the Lisl Auman case—which gets uglier every time I look at it. I don't do this very often—Never, in fact—but this case is such an outrage that it haunts me & gives me bad dreams at night. I am not a Criminal Lawyer, but I have what might be called "a very strong background" in the Criminal Justice System & many of my friends & associates are widely known as the best legal minds in that cruel & deadly business.

It is no place for amateurs, and even seasoned professionals can make mistakes that are often fatal. The System can grind up the Innocent as well as the Guilty, and that is what I believe happened to 20-

year-old Lisl Auman, who was unjustly found guilty of murder and sent to prison for the rest of her Life Without Parole.

In all my experience with courts & crimes & downright evil behavior by the Law & the Sometimes criminal cops who enforce it, this is the worst & most reprehensible miscarriage of "Justice" I've ever encountered—and that covers a lot of rotten things, including a few close calls of my own. Which might easily have gone the other way if not for the help of some hammerhead Lawyers who came to my aid when I was in desperate trouble.

I learned a lot about Karma in those moments, and one thing that sticks with me is a quote from Edmund Burke that says: "THE ONLY THING NECESSARY FOR THE TRIUMPH OF EVIL IS FOR GOOD MEN TO DO NOTHING."

That is what got me into the Lisl Auman case, and that is why I will stay in it until this brutal Wrong is Righted. That is also why the first contribution to the Lisl Auman Defense Fund came from Gerald Lefcourt of New York, then the President of the National Association of Criminal Defense Lawyers. "This is not going to be easy," he said with a wry smile. "But what the hell—count me in."

Indeed. It is no small trick to get a "Convicted cop killer" out of prison—but it will be a little easier in this case, because Lisl no more killed a cop than I did. She was handcuffed in the backseat of a Denver Police car when the cop was murdered in cold blood by a vicious skinhead who then allegedly shot himself in the head & left the D.A. with nobody to punish for the murder—except Lisl.

February 5, 2001

The Felony Murder Law—Don't Let This Happen to You

I don't think that people across the board necessarily identify with Lisl Auman as much as, God help them, they might identify with me. I've often frankly thought that Lisl's case is possibly the worst case I've ever decided to get involved in. We've got a convicted cop killer—Help. It doesn't matter who she is.

The few real facts in the case that were, and have been, and remain, evident—as opposed to the avalanche of hate-crime propaganda and "Off the Skinheads" hysteria that came with the conviction . . . along with the clear violations in the court record, and the police procedures at the time of the crime—are this: Somebody got killed. We know that. Two people came out of there dead. Beyond the vicious political circumstances surrounding Lisl's case, we've got the vicious skinhead, Matthaeus Jaehnig, and the cop, Bruce VanderJagt, and Lisl, the supposed perpetrator. . . .

We may have to go outside the characteristics of the city of Denver for this. The points of the law that are going to be decided, once again, however vaguely, in this appeal hearing—and hopefully the retrial—are overwhelmingly odious and spurious. There was a carelessness in the way this case was handled that led us to a witchbag of strange problems within the law-enforcement system. We have the effective abuse of Lisl's rights—but they were abused not by the cops necessarily, who were part of it; her rights were abused by all parties in the system. Lisl's end of the case was taken very lightly: President Clinton was actively campaigning against cop-killing at the time; then his Hate Crimes bill passed in Congress, and the Denver police were understandably up in arms about the death of one of their own.

But we want to remember that two people came out of this thing dead, and there was no real explanation for it during the legal process, in Lisl's first trial. That leaves critical questions: It's not even known exactly *who* shot Officer VanderJagt and who shot Matthaeus, who was an over-the-line thug—I'm not convinced that he shot himself. Questions remain about Who Did What during this encounter, this weird encounter, which should not have happened, basically, because Matthaeus had a rap sheet as long as his arm; he should have been shot yesterday. "I should have killed you a long time ago"—is it a case like that? If the cops had paid any attention to the dangers of the streets instead of weird chickenshit complaints, Lisl might not be in jail. The actions and behavior of the police in this berserk episode involving forty or fifty officers at one time were not examined—even the crime scene itself has never been developed. At least it has never been tested in any kind of court, because Lisl's confession to a lesser crime is what avoided any examination of the case. This thing was guided through the system so that there *was* no examination. I'm not calling for an investigation—though I could, and I might. I am calling for a retrial.

The proper workings—and I say "proper" in the sense that it's almost religiously vital to all of us—within the law-enforcement system, the judicial system, the court system, the system of right and wrong, who is responsible, that system has to function for all of us, because anybody could get involved in it at any time. A simple traffic ticket you don't even know about if you run a red light and there's a camera on you could get you into that system, and sometimes the system doesn't work . . . and if it doesn't, then everybody suffers—even Matthaeus and VanderJagt. Even me, or the publisher of *The Denver Post,* Dean Singleton—he and his family might suffer from the failure of the American judicial system to work as it should have, and as it was set up. With the way it's working now—the way it's dysfunctioning now—we're in serious trouble.

Surrounded by a public and political atmosphere that supports the U.S.A. Patriot Act, the Lisl case suddenly stands up as a classic example of the one that fell through the cracks, or the one that was too awkward at the time to confront. A case of a college student who got mixed up with the wrong crowd, who was a good, orderly middle-class girl until—well, Lisl Auman was an anonymous person, and will remain so. Yet the question of her guilt or innocence is indelible. How could she be guilty of a crime that would put her in state prison for the rest of her life without parole, when she was locked up and handcuffed in the back of a police car at the time the murder was committed?

And that gets us into *attenuation.* This is clearly a crime that this woman didn't commit, a crime that any one of you might be guilty of, every time you drive to a 7-Eleven, say, and the person next to you in the car—a friend perhaps, wife, lover, stranger—gets out of the car and says, "Okay, I'll run right in and get it. We've had a hard day and night with this goddamn legal stuff, I'm about to flip, we're under terrible pressure, so I'll go in and get us some more beer. I just wish they had a lot of gin in here, man, I feel like drinking gin."

That's what you're dealing with: the kind of everyday attitude of a good friend, or a stranger, who gets out of your car and goes into a 7-Eleven store. It's 11:30 at night, and you have a long night's worrying ahead of you about some matter, maybe an addiction, who knows, but you're not solving it, and your friend—say, Curtis—well, you can see he's been agitated for a while about something, maybe everything, things are not going his way or necessarily yours, so he gets out of the car and you give him some money. Curtis says, "Oh, never mind, I have some," but he takes your twenty anyway and gets out of the car, walking just like a normal person going into a 7-Eleven store on Christmas Eve, just part of the big American buying system. He goes inside and, let's say, we add to Curtis's life the fact that his sister, many years ago, married a Korean man, and that over the years Curtis has developed some *issues*—we may not want to revisit that story right now, so let's just say that the marriage between the Korean gentleman and Curtis's sister did not bear fruit, and in fact Curtis has hated Koreans ever since. (This guy who married his sister once belted him in the side of the head.)

So Curtis gets out of your car, and you're relaxing, reading the paper; he's being an old friend journalist who's pissed off and has this tic about Koreans. He goes inside this 7-Eleven store, and there's a Korean behind the counter. All Curtis wants is some beer, and he's already pissed off that it's only 3.2 beer anyway, it's not real beer, and now he's looking for the one thing he wants: He's thinking that maybe there's something in here that might have some alcohol, or, you know, *don't they have any gin?* So he asks the Korean guy that: "Don't you have any gin, Sport? Bubba?" And the guy says, "Gin? You want me to call the police? What do you mean? Of course I don't have any gin. What do you want? Get out of here."

Curtis—who just happens to have gotten his permit two weeks ago from the local sheriff to carry a concealed weapon—is packing a 10-millimeter Glock, a very powerful handgun; it's a little hotter than the 9, it takes a bigger bullet and it packs a punch, but it's the same-looking gun; and he's been getting comfortable with it for a while. He may have pulled it on some Arab who he thinks may have been looking at his car too long in an underground garage, and when he pulled it, the guy fled, so he has confidence in it. And the Korean man behind the counter is suddenly extremely rude to him, and his mind dissolves into his sister . . .

You'd once shared something with Curtis that your father had explained to you in a moment of curiosity: You had asked him, "What's the difference between a Korean, a Japanese, and a Chinese person?" It was during the Korean War, and you wondered why the Koreans were fighting—you didn't know who they were, or what the difference was. And your father said, "Son, let me put it this way: The Japanese are clean on the outside and dirty on the inside; and the Chinese are dirty on the outside but clean on the inside. But Son, I really hate to tell you this, the Koreans are dirty *on both sides*." You've spoken to Curtis about this—it puts him into kind of a flare—so you can identify with what happens when Curtis goes in there and gets fucked with by a foul-mouthed, apparently speeded-up, wiggy Korean. . . . And then the guy refuses his credit card; he says it's not magnetic. You know, *This doesn't say shit; this doesn't ring my bell.* So, he can't get the beer.

You know how Curtis is, with that redheaded temper spiral he gets into, where suddenly he goes from first floor to seventh floor, when you're still going to floor two and you forget, talking to him, that he's already spiraled up to seven. . . . So Curtis forgets about the money you gave him. He figures, *Fuck This;* he doesn't really even think. The guy has pushed him in areas he's unfamiliar with—and with his temper he gets properly angry. Let's say the guy threatens him: "What are you going to do about it, Fat Man?" (I had a cop do that to me once, in Mobile: "Go back and sit down, Old Man." That was when I was forty years old.) And here's Curtis: His mind is on this frog-eyed Korean who hit his sister, beat her repeatedly, destroyed her beautiful life that Curtis was once morbidly in love and involved with, and he has every flare that's possible sitting right there in that hot box on a Saturday afternoon in the sun. And BANG! He goes—as we all do from time to time, we lose it—and it's his muscle memory operating now, he's done this enough, he's slapped leather, and he jerks the Glock out of his belt and points it at the guy; and then he senses some menace from the back of the store. Somebody else—an extremely large guy, the guy's brother, his cousin—comes out of the back and the guy says, "Come here and help me get this bastard, this fat bastard."

Curtis is suddenly aware of what appears to be two or three more attackers, maybe one, maybe a friend in the aisles, some movement behind him—he feels threatened by more than this one foulmouthed bastard—and due to his self-defense instincts, he sees himself surrounded. So Curtis shoots the guy in front of him, in order to teach the attackers a lesson, and sure enough, they swing away. Then the guy makes a lunge at him, so Curtis pops him two more times. Not quite the best judgment. Since the beer is on the counter in front of him, and he was trying to pay for it with a credit card, let's say Curtis leaves his card and takes the beer—that's the kind of thing that could happen, even in our professional journalism ranks.

You hear the shots, but you don't really hear them; you're listening to the radio. You aren't watching in there, necessarily; let's say a cop car had pulled into the far side of the parking lot where the light didn't reach, and you're aware of that. You think, *Hmm, a cop, where's Curtis,* and you look up just in time to see him kind of scurrying back, not galloping or fleeing, but in a hurry back to the car with a six-pack in his hand. He hurriedly jumps in, and he tells you, "Get out of here, man." And you say, "What happened, what's wrong?" He says, "Never mind, just get out of here, get out of here." You mention the cops at the other end of the 7-Eleven parking lot, and that really freaks him out. The next time you have a thought you're three or four blocks away. And Curtis is trembling, and then you start to tremble too, because you have a right to, because the next thing he's going to tell you is "I think I shot that guy; I shot that guy. Goddamn that bastard, they attacked me in there, I had to shoot."

And you're starting to think, *Whoops. Uh-oh. Say what? Oh my God.* Because you are then almost certain to go to prison for Murder One. In the state of Colorado, the state of California, and most others, attenuation involves the felony murder law. You are an accessory, you're held liable for the crime of your friend, you're a conspirator—and conspirators, under that law, go to death, or to jail forever. Murder One. So does that describe, more or less, our situation?

(to be continued)

Jesus Hated Bald Pussy

Let's face it—the yo-yo president of the U.S.A. knows *nothing*. He is a *dunce*. He does what he is *told* to do—says what he is *told* to say—poses the way he is *told* to pose. He is a *Fool*.

This is never an *easy* thing for the voters of this country to accept.

No. Nonsense. The president cannot be a Fool. Not at this moment in time—when the last living vestiges of the American Dream are on the line. This is not the time to have a *bogus rich kid* in charge of the White House.

Which is, after all, *our* house. That is our headquarters—it is where the heart of America lives. So if the president lies and acts giddy about other people's lives—if he wantonly and stupidly endorses *mass murder* as a logical plan to make sure we are still Number One—he is a Jackass by definition—a loud and meaningless animal with no functional intelligence and no balls.

To say that this goofy child president is looking more and more like Richard Nixon in the summer of 1974 would be a flagrant insult to Nixon.

Whoops! Did I *say* that? Is it even vaguely possible that some New Age Republican *whore-beast* of a false president could actually make Richard Nixon look like a Liberal?

The capacity of these vicious assholes *we* elected to be in charge of our lives for four years to commit terminal damage to our lives and our souls and our loved ones is far beyond Nixon's. Shit! Nixon was the *creator* of many of the once-proud historical landmarks that these dumb bastards are savagely *destroying* now: the Clean Air Act of 1970; Campaign Finance Reform; the endangered species act; opening a Real-Politik dialogue with China; and on and on.

The prevailing quality of life in America—by *any* accepted methods of measuring—was inarguably freer and more politically *open* under Nixon than it is today in this evil year of Our Lord 2002.

The Boss was a certified monster who deserved to be impeached and banished. He was a truthless creature of former FBI Director J. Edgar Hoover—a foul human monument to corruption and depravity on a scale that dwarfs any other public official in American history. But Nixon was at least smart enough to understand why so many honorable patriotic U.S. citizens despised him. He was a *Liar*. The truth was not in him.

Nixon believed—as he said many times—that if the president of the United States does it, it *can't* be illegal. But Nixon never understood the much higher and meaner truth of Bob Dylan's warning that "To live outside the law you must be honest."

The difference between an *outlaw* and a war criminal is the difference between a pedophile and a Pederast: The pedophile is a person who thinks about sexual behavior with children, and the Pederast *does* these things. He lays hands on innocent children—he penetrates them and changes their lives forever.

Being the object of a pedophile's warped affections is a Routine feature of growing up in America—and being a victim of a Pederast's crazed "love" is part of dying. Innocence is no longer an option. Once penetrated, the child becomes a Queer in his own mind, and that is not much different than *murder*.

Richard Nixon crossed that line when he began murdering foreigners in the name of "family values"—and George Bush crossed it when he sneaked into office and began killing brown-skinned children in the name of Jesus and the American people.

When Muhammad Ali declined to be drafted and forced to kill "gooks" in Vietnam he said, "I ain't got nothin' against them Viet Cong. No Cong ever called me *Nigger*."

I agreed with him, according to my own personal ethics and values. He was *Right*.

If we all had a dash of Muhammad Ali's eloquent courage, this country and the world would be a better place today because of it.

Okay. That's it for now. Read it and weep. . . . See you tomorrow, folks. You haven't heard the last of me. I am the one who speaks for the spirit of freedom and decency in you. Shit. *Somebody* has to do it.

We have become a Nazi monster in the eyes of the whole world—a nation of bullies and bastards who would rather kill than live peacefully. We are not just Whores for power and oil, but killer whores with hate and fear in our hearts. We are human scum, and that is how history will judge us. . . . No redeeming social value. Just whores. Get out of our way, or we'll kill you.

Well, shit on that dumbness. George W. Bush does not speak for me or my son or my mother or my friends or the people I respect in this world. We didn't vote for these cheap, greedy little killers who speak for America today—and we will not vote for them again in 2002. Or 2004. Or *ever*.

Who *does* vote for these dishonest shitheads? Who among us can be happy and proud of having all this innocent blood on our hands? Who are these swine? These flag-sucking half-wits who get fleeced and fooled by stupid little rich kids like George Bush?

They are the same ones who wanted to have Muhammad Ali locked up for refusing to kill gooks. They speak for all that is cruel and stupid and vicious in the American character. They are the racists and hate mongers among us—they are the Ku Klux Klan. I piss down the throats of these Nazis.

And I am too old to worry about whether they like it or not. Fuck them.

HST, 2002

PART TWO

The artist at work, with Deborah, in the kitchen, 1994
(Paul Chesley)

Politics Is the Art of Controlling Your Environment

I know my own nation best. That's why I despise it the most. And I know and love my own people too, the swine. I'm a patriot. A dangerous man.

—Edward Abbey

Running for Sheriff: Aspen 1970

On Wednesday night, seven days before the 1970 sheriff's election, we hunkered down at Owl Farm and sealed the place off. From the road the house looked stone dark. The driveway was blocked at one end of the circle by Noonan's Jeep, and at the other end by a blue Chevy van with Wisconsin plates. The only possible approach was on foot: You could park on the road, climb a short hill, and cross the long front yard in the glare of a huge floodlight . . . or come creeping down from behind, off either one of the two mesas that separate the house from the five-million-acre White River National Forest.

But only a fool or a lunatic would have tried to approach the place quietly from any direction at all . . . because the house was a virtual fortress, surrounded by armed crazies. Somewhere off to the left, in a dry irrigation ditch about two hundred yards beyond the volleyball court, was Big Ed Bastian, a onetime basketball star at the University of Iowa . . . limping around in the frozen darkness with a 12-gauge pump shotgun, a portable spotlight, and a .38 Special tucked into his belt. Big Ed, our long-suffering campaign coordinator, was growing progressively weaker from the ravages of his new macrobiotic diet. On top of that, he had recently snapped one of the bones in his left foot while forcing his legs into the lotus position, and now he was wearing a cast. The temperature at midnight was 12 above zero and sinking fast. There was no moon.

On the other side of the house Mike Solheim, my campaign manager, was patrolling the western perimeter with a double-barreled 12-gauge Beretta and a .357 Colt Python Magnum. We suspected that Solheim was probably turning on very heavily out there—caving in to the Vietnam-sentry madness—and we were vaguely concerned that he might get wiggy and blow Bastian's head off if they happened to cross paths in the darkness.

But they weren't moving around much despite the bitter cold. From the spots they'd selected they were both perfectly positioned to deal not only with the threat from the rear or either side of the house, but also to catch anyone approaching from the front in a deadly cross fire of 00-buckshot . . . thus tripling the terror for any poor bastard coming up from the road and straight into the muzzle of Teddy Yewer's 30-30.

Teddy, a wild young biker with hair hanging down to his waist, had driven out from Madison to have some fun with the Freak Power sheriff's campaign . . . and he'd arrived just in time to get himself drafted into the totally humorless role of 24-hour bodyguard. Now, with the original concept of the campaign long gone and forgotten in this frenzy of violence, he found himself doing dead-serious guard duty behind a big window in the darkened living room, perched in the Catbird seat with a rifle in his hands and a fine commanding view of anything that could possibly happen within one hundred yards of the front porch. He couldn't see Solheim or Bastian, but he knew they were out there, and he knew that all three of them would have to start shooting if the things we'd been warned about suddenly began happening.

The word had come that afternoon from the Colorado Bureau of Investigation (CBI), and the word was extremely grim. Tonight— sometime between dusk on Wednesday and dawn on Thursday—Mr. Thompson, the Freak Power candidate for sheriff, was going to be killed. This intelligence had come from what the CBI investigator described as "an extremely reliable informant," a person they had every good reason to believe because he (or maybe she; we weren't told) had "always been right in the past." The informant had not been able to learn the identity of the assassins, the CBI man told us. Nor had he/she been able to learn what means or methods they planned to use on this job. Shooting was of course the most logical thing to expect, he said. Maybe an ambush at some lonely spot on the road between Aspen and Woody Creek. And if that failed . . . well, it was widely known that the candidate lived in a dangerously isolated house far out in the boondocks. So perhaps they would strike out there, by fire . . . or dynamite.

Indeed. Dynamite. RDX-type, 90 percent nitroglycerine. Two hundred and ten sticks of it had been stolen just a few days earlier from an Aspen Ski Corp. cache on Ajax Mountain—according to a report from the Ski Corp.—and the thieves left a note saying, "This [stolen dynamite] will only be used if Hunter Thompson is elected sheriff of Aspen." The note was signed "SDS."

Right. Some ignorant dingbat actually signed the note "SDS." The CBI man hadn't smiled when we laughed at the tale: He quickly unfolded another sheet of notes and told us that his "reliable informant" had also told him that half the town was about to be destroyed by dynamite—the County Courthouse (meaning the Sheriff's Office), City Hall (the Police Station), the Hotel Jerome (our campaign headquarters), and the Wheeler Opera House (where Joe Edwards and Dwight Shellman, our attorneys, had their offices).

Only a cop's brain could have churned up that mix of silly bull- shit . . . and although we never doubted that, we also understood that the same warped mentality might also be capable of running that kind of twisted act all the way out to its brutally illogical extreme. It made perfect sense, we felt, to assume that anybody stupid enough to spread these crudely conceived rumors was also stupid enough to try to justify them by actually dynamiting something.

At that point in the campaign it was still a three-way race between me, the incumbent (Democratic) sheriff, and the veteran undersheriff who'd resigned just in time to win the GOP primary (over the former city police chief) and emerge as a strong challenger to his former boss—first-term sheriff Carrol Whitmire, a devious, half-bright small-town cop whose four years in office had earned him a reservoir of contempt and neo–public loathing on the part of the local Bar Association, the District Attorney, his own Undersheriff and former deputies, the entire City of Aspen police force and everybody else unlucky enough to have had any dealings with him.

When the campaign began, Whitmire had virtually no support from the people who knew him best: the county commissioners, the former mayor, the city manager, the ex-D.A., and especially his former employees. He spent the first two weeks of the conflict beseeching both the CBI and the FBI to turn up at least one recorded felony conviction on me . . . and when that effort failed, because I have no criminal record, the evil bastard brought in undercover federal agents to try to provoke both me and my campaign workers into felony violence that would have given him an excuse to bust us before the election.

At one point he hired a phony outlaw biker from Denver—Jim Bromley, a veteran of two years of undercover work for the feds—who boomed into town one day on a junk chopper and first threatened to dynamite my house if I didn't drop out of the race at once . . . then apologized for the threat—when it failed—and tried to hire on as my bodyguard . . . then spread rumors that people on my staff were in touch with Kathy Powers and a gang of Weathermen who planned to blow all the bridges into town . . . then tried to sell us automatic weapons . . . then offered to stomp the shit out of anybody we aimed him at . . . then got himself busted, by accident, when the city cops found a completely illegal sawed-off 20-gauge pump action shotgun in his car—which they happened to tow away from a no-parking zone.

The sheriff panicked at that point and blew Bromley's cover by instructing the city cops to give his illegal weapon back to him because he was a "federal agent." This was done. But instead of leaving town, Bromley came back to our headquarters—unaware that a friendly city cop had already tipped us off—and hung around offering to run the mimeograph machine or anything else we needed done. Meanwhile, we were trying to compel the assistant D.A. to have the bastard arrested on charges ranging from felony conspiracy to threatening the life of a political candidate to carrying an illegal weapon—and offering to wreak violence on innocent people—but the assistant D.A. refused to act, denying all knowledge of the man or his motives, until the sheriff unexpectedly admitted that Bromley was actually working for him.

Meanwhile, Bromley had once again lost his sawed-off shotgun—this time to a city cop who went out to his motel room at the Applejack Inn to seize the weapon for the second time in 36 hours, after a desk clerk we'd assigned to get a photo of Bromley called us to say that one of the maids had found a "vicious-looking gun" in his room. . . . But even then the D.A.'s office refused to move, not even to pick up the shotgun again. So we had to send a cop out on our own—Rick Crabtree, a dropout English major from Columbia—and even after Crabtree seized the weapon, the D.A.'s office snarled petulantly at our demands that Bromley be picked up and booked. He'd returned to the Applejack with a girl, they said, and they didn't want to disturb him until morning.

This was too much for the frustrated crew of Left-bikers, Black Belts, White Panthers, and assorted local heavies who'd been calling for open season on Bromley ever since he showed up. They wanted to soak him down with Mace, then beat him to jelly with baseball bats . . . and they didn't give a flying fuck if he was a federal agent or not. I was still on the phone with the assistant D.A. when I noticed the room emptying around me. "We're on our way to the Applejack," somebody yelled from the doorway. "You can tell that chickenshit pig of a district attorney that we decided to make a citizen's arrest . . . and we'll dump his fink at the jail in about thirty minutes, in a plastic bag."

I translated this to the D.A. . . . and thirty minutes later Bromley was moving down the highway in a rented car. He left so fast that we couldn't even get a good snapshot of him, so the next morning we called the "White Panther photo agency" in Denver, and they assigned a young, harmless-looking Black Belt to go out to Bromley's suburban home with a camera. Paul Davidson got the picture we needed by knocking on the agent's door and saying that he was so impressed with the wonderful chopper outside that he just had to get a shot of it—along with the proud owner. So Bromley—ever alert—posed for the photo, which ran a day later in the *Aspen Times* along with a detailed exposé of his brief but hyperactive flirtation with the local Freak Power movement. We sent Bromley a copy of the published photo/story . . . and he responded almost instantly by mailing me a threatening letter and another, very personal, photo of himself that he said was a hell of a lot better than the one our "funny little photographer" had conned him out of. Even the CBI man was stunned at this evidence of total lunacy on the part of a veteran undercover agent. "This is hard to believe," he kept saying. "He actually signed his name: He even signed the photograph! How could they hire a person like this?"

How indeed?

(Paul Harris)

. . .

The story began in 1968, when Random House gave me $5,000 and my editor there said, "Go out and write about 'The Death of the American Dream.'" I had agreed without thinking, because all I really cared about, back then, was the money. And along with the $5K in front money came a $7,500 "expenses budget"—against royalties, which meant I'd be paying my own expenses, but I didn't give a fuck about that either. It was a nice gig to get into: Random House had agreed, more or less, to finance my education. I could go just about anywhere I wanted to just as long as I could somehow tie it in with "The Death of the American Dream."

It looked easy, a straight-out boondoggle, and for a long time I treated it that way. It was like being given a credit card that you eventually have to pay off, but not now. I remember thinking that Jim Silberman, the editor, was not only crazy but severely irresponsible. Why else would he make that kind of deal?

I went a few places for reasons that I can't even recall now, and then I went to Chicago in August of 1968, on my Random House tab with a packet of the finest, blue-chip press credentials—issued by the Democratic National Committee—for the purpose of covering the Convention.

I had no real reason for going—not even a magazine assignment; I just wanted to *be there* and get the feel of things. The town was so full of journalists that I felt like a tourist . . . and the fact that I had heavier credentials than most of the working writers & reporters I met left me vaguely embarrassed. But it never occurred to me to seek an assignment—although if anybody had asked me, I'd have done the whole story for nothing.

Now, years later, I still have trouble when I think about Chicago. That week at the Convention changed everything I'd ever taken for granted about this country and my place in it. I went from a state of Cold Shock on Monday, to Fear on Tuesday, then Rage, and finally Hysteria—which lasted for nearly a month. Every time I tried to tell somebody what happened in Chicago I began crying, and it took me years to understand why.

I wasn't beaten; I spent no time in jail. But neither of these things would have had much effect on me, anyway. It takes a real expert (or experts) to beat a person badly without putting him into a state of shock that makes the beating meaningless until later . . . and getting dragged into jail with a bunch of friends is more a strange high than a trauma; indeed, there is something vaguely dishonorable in having lived through the Sixties without having spent time in jail.

Chicago was the end of the Sixties, for me. I remember going back to my room at the Blackstone, across the street from the Hilton, and sitting cross-legged on my bed for hours at a time. Trembling, unable to make any notes, staring at the TV set while my head kept whirling out of focus from the things I'd seen happen all around me . . . and I could watch it all happening again, on TV; see myself running in stark terror across Michigan Drive, on camera, always two steps ahead of the nearest club-swinging cop and knowing that at any instant my lungs would be shredded by some bullet that would hit me before I could even hear the shot fired.

I was standing at the corner of Michigan and Balboa on Wednesday night when the cops attacked . . . and I remember thinking: No. This can't be happening. I flattened myself back against a wall of the Blackstone and fished a motorcycle helmet out of my friendly blue L.L. Bean kit bag . . . and also the yellow ski goggles, thinking there would probably be Mace, or at least gas . . . but that was the only time they didn't use any.

On Wednesday evening they used clubs, and it was a king-hell bitch of a show. I stood against the wall, trying to put my helmet on while people ran past me like a cattle stampede. The ones who weren't screaming were bleeding, and some were being dragged. I have never been caught in an earthquake, but I'm sure the feeling would be just about the same. Total panic and disbelief—with no escape. The first wave of cops came down Balboa at a trot and hit the crowd in the form of a flying wedge, scattering people in all directions like fire on an anthill . . . but no matter which way they ran, there were more cops. The second wave came across Grant Park like a big threshing machine, a wave of long black truncheons meeting people fleeing hysterically from the big bash at the intersection.

Others tried to flee down Balboa, toward State Street, but there was no escape in that direction, either—just another wave of cops closing off the whole street in a nicely planned pincer movement and beating the mortal shit out of anybody they could reach. The protesters tried to hold their lines, calling back and forth to one another as they ran away: "Stay together! Stay together!"

I found myself in the middle of the pincers, with no place to run except back into the Blackstone. But the two cops at the door refused to let me in. They were holding their clubs out in front of them with both hands, keeping everybody away from the door.

By this time I could see people getting brutalized within six feet of me on both sides. It was only a matter of seconds before I went under . . . so I finally just ran between the truncheons, screaming, "I live here, goddamnit! I'm paying fifty dollars a day!" By the time they whacked me against the door I was out of range of what was happening on the sidewalk . . . and by some kind of wild accidental luck I happened to have my room key in my pocket. Normally I would have left it at the desk before going out, but on this tense night I forgot, and that key was salvation—that, and the mad righteousness that must have vibrated like the screeching of Jesus in everything I said. Because I *did* live there. I was a goddamn *paying guest*! And there was never any doubt in my mind that the stinking blue-uniformed punks had no RIGHT to keep me out.

I believed that, and I was big enough to neutralize one of the truncheons long enough to plunge into the lobby . . . and it was not until several days or even weeks later that I understood that those cops had actually *planned* to have me beaten. Not me, personally, but Me as a member of "The Enemy," that crowd of "outside agitators" made up of people who had come to Chicago on some mission that the cops couldn't grasp except in fear and hatred.

This is what caused me to tremble when I finally sat down behind the locked & chained door of my hotel room. It was not a fear of being beaten or jailed, but the slow-rising shock of suddenly understanding that it was no longer a matter of Explaining my Position. These bastards knew my position, and they wanted to beat me anyway. They didn't give a fuck if the Democratic National Committee had issued me special press credentials; it made no difference to them that I'd come to Chicago as a paying guest—at viciously inflated rates—with no intention of causing the slightest kind of trouble for anybody.

That was the point. My very innocence made me guilty—or at least a potential troublemaker in the eyes of the rotten sold-out scumbags who were running that Convention: Mayor Richard J. Daley of Chicago, Lyndon Baines Johnson, then President of the United States. These pigs didn't care what was Right. All they knew was what they wanted, and they were powerful enough to break anybody who even thought about getting in their way.

Right here, before I forget, I want to make what I think is a critical point about the whole protest action of the 1960s. It seems to me that the underlying assumption of any public protest—any public dis-agreement with the government, "the system," or "the establishment," by any name—is that the men in charge of whatever you're protesting against are actually listening, whether they later admit it or not, and that if you run your protest Right, it will likely make a difference. Norman Mailer made this point a long time ago when he said that the election of JFK gave him a sense, for the first time in his life, that he could actually communicate with the White House. Even with people like Johnson and Mac Bundy—or even Pat Brown or Bull Connor—the unspoken rationale behind all those heavy public protests was that our noise was getting through and that somebody in power was lis-tening and hearing and at least weighing our protest against their own political realities . . . even if these people refused to talk to us. So in the end the very act of public protest, even violent protest, was essen-tially optimistic and actually a demonstration of faith (mainly sub-conscious, I think) in the father figures who had the power to change things—once they could be made to see the light of reason, or even political reality.

This is what the bastards never understood—that the "Movement" was essentially an expression of deep faith in the American Dream: that the people they were "fighting" were not the cruel and cynical beasts they seemed to be, and that in fact they were just a bunch of men like everybody's crusty middle-class fathers who only needed to be shaken a bit, jolted out of their bad habits and away from their lazy, short-term, profit-oriented life stances . . . and that once they under-stood, they would surely do the right thing.

A Willingness to Argue, however violently, implies a faith of some basic kind in the antagonist, an assumption that he is still open to argument and reason and, if all else fails, then finely orchestrated per-suasion in the form of political embarrassment. The 1960s were full of examples of good, powerful men changing their minds on heavy issues: John Kennedy on Cuba and the Bay of Pigs, Martin Luther King Jr. on Vietnam, Gene McCarthy on "working behind the scenes and within the Senate Club," Robert F. Kennedy on grass and long hair and what eventually came to be Freak Power, Ted Kennedy on Francis X. Morrissey, and Senator Sam Ervin on wiretaps and preventive detention.

Anyway, the general political drift of the 1960s was one of the Good Guys winning, slowly but surely (and even clumsily sometimes), over the Bad Guys . . . and the highest example of this was Johnson's incredible abdication on April Fool's Day of 1968. So nobody was ready for what began to happen that summer: first in Chicago, when Johnson ran his Convention like a replay of the Reichstag fire . . . and then with Agnew and Nixon and Mitchell coming into power so full of congenital hostility and so completely deaf to everything we'd been talking about for ten years that it took a while to realize that there was simply no point in yelling at the fuckers. They were born deaf and stupid.

This was the lesson of Chicago—or at least that's what I learned from Chicago, and two years later, running for the office of sheriff, that lesson seemed every bit as clear as it did to me when I got rammed in the stomach with a riot club in Grant Park for showing a cop my press pass. What I learned, in Chicago, was that the police arm of the United States government was capable of hiring vengeful thugs to break the very rules we all thought we were operating under. On Thursday night in the Amphitheatre it was not enough for me to have a press pass from the Democratic National Committee; I was kicked out of my press seat by hired rent-a-cops, and when I protested to the Secret Service men at the door, I was smacked against the wall and searched for weapons. And I realized at that point that, even though I was absolutely right, if I persisted with my righteous complaint, I would probably wind up in jail.

There was no point in appealing to any higher authority, because they were the people who were paying those swine to fuck me around. It was LBJ's party and I was an unwelcome guest, barely tolerated . . . and if I couldn't keep my mouth shut, I would get the same treatment as those poor bastards out on Michigan Avenue, or Wells Street, or Lincoln Park . . . who were gassed and beaten by an army of cops run amok with carte blanche from the Daley-Johnson combine—while

Hubert Humphrey cried from tear gas fumes in his twenty-fifth-floor suite at the Hilton.

A lot of people felt that way after Chicago. And in my case it was more a sense of shock at the sudden understanding that I was on the ground. I went there as a journalist; my candidate had been murdered in Los Angeles two months earlier—but I left Chicago in a state of hysterical angst, convinced by what I'd seen that we were all in very bad trouble . . . and in fact that the whole country was doomed unless somebody, somewhere, could mount a new kind of power to challenge the rotten, high-powered machinery of men like Daley and Johnson. Sitting in a westbound TWA jet on the ramp at O'Hare, waiting for a takeoff slot, it occurred to me that I was suddenly right in the middle of the story I'd been sent out to look for. What had begun as a dilettante's dream was now a very real subject.

That was the way it began. And for the first few weeks of October, the 1970 sheriff's campaign was a colorful, high-powered replay of the previous year's "Joe Edwards for Mayor" uprising, which lost by only six votes. But the secret of our success, that year, was the failure of the local power structure to take us seriously . . . and by the time they understood what was happening to them, they almost croaked. Only a last-minute fraud with the absentee ballots—and our inability to raise $2,000 to challenge that fraud in court—prevented a 29-year-old bike-racing freak from becoming mayor of Aspen. And in the wake of Edwards's loss, we created a completely new kind of power base, the first of its kind anywhere in American politics. It was a strange combination of "Woodstock" vibrations, "New Left" activism, and basic "Jeffersonian Democracy" with strong echoes of the Boston Tea Party ethic. What emerged from the Joe Edwards campaign was a very real blueprint for stomping the Agnew mentality by its own rules—with the vote, instead of the bomb; by seizing their power machinery and using it, instead of merely destroying it.

The national press dug it all—mainly on the basis of a *Rolling Stone* article I wrote about the 1969 election (*Rolling Stone* #67, October 1, 1970) which laid it all out, step by step. My idea, when I wrote it, was to line out the "freak power" concept for massive distribution—with the blueprint and all the details—in the hope that it might be a key to weird political action in other places.

(Michael Montfort)

. . .

So it was hard to know, on that jangled Wednesday night before the sheriff's election, just what the fuck was happening . . . or even what might happen. The local power structure appeared to have gone completely crazy.

There was not much doubt that we had Owl Farm completely fortified. And our rotating "outside triangle of fire" was only the beginning. Behind that, waiting to take their turns outside in the moonless, bitter-cold night, was a whole house of wired-up freaks—all armed to the teeth. The only light visible from the road was the outside flood, but inside—behind shrouded windows in the big wooden kitchen and downstairs in the soundproof, windowless "war room"—a rude mix of people drifted back and forth on the nervous tides of this night: eating, drinking, plotting, rehashing the incredible chain of events that had plunged us into this scene . . . all of us armed, nobody ready to sleep, and none of us really believing that what we were doing was sane. It was all too weird, too unlikely, too much like some acid-bent scriptwriter's dream on a bad night in the Château Marmont . . . some madman's botch of a Final Politics movie.

But it was all insanely real. And we knew that, too. Nobody in the house was stoned or twisted that night. Nobody was drunk. And when it had first become clear, a few hours earlier, that we were headed for a very wild and menacing kind of night, we ran a very discreet sort of staff shakedown and carefully selected the half dozen or so people who seemed capable of dealing with the kind of madness the Colorado Bureau of Investigation had told us we were likely to deal with before dawn.

Clearly we were all doomed. Half the population would never live to vote, and the other half would perish in the inevitable election-night holocaust. When NBC-TV showed up about midway in the campaign, I advised them to stick around. "There'll be a bloodbath if I win," I said, "and a bloodbath if I lose. The carnage will be unbelievable either way; you'll get wonderful footage. . . ."

That was back when we could still laugh about the hideous Freak Power challenge. But now the laughter was finished. The humor went out of the campaign when the Aspen establishment suddenly understood that I looked like a winner. Pitkin County, Colorado, was about to elect the nation's first Mescaline sheriff . . . a foul-mouthed bald-headed freak who refused to compromise on anything at all, even his taste for wild drugs, and who didn't mind saying in public that he intended to hamstring, flay, and cripple every greedy plot the Aspen power structure held dear . . . all their foul hopes and greedy fascist dreams.

. . .

Sometime around midmorning on Election Day the *Life* correspondent rushed into our Hotel Jerome headquarters suite with a big grin on his face and announced that we were sure winners. "I've been out on the streets," he said, "taking my own poll. I must have talked to two hundred people out there—all different types—and all but about two dozen of them said they were going to vote for you." He shook his head, still grinning. "It's incredible, absolutely incredible, but I think it's going to be a landslide." Then he opened a beer and began helping his photographer, who was busy wiring strobe lights to the ceiling, so they could shoot the victory celebration in color.

It was going to be a hell of a story—and especially for *Life* because they had an angle that nobody else could touch. They'd only been in town about 24 hours, but when they arrived at our headquarters on Monday morning they were confronted with a really mind-bending scene. Here was the candidate, the next sheriff of Aspen and indeed all of Pitkin County, Colorado, raving crazily about Armageddon and pounding on a desk with a big leather sap. We had been up all night dealing with a violent personal crisis that would have blown the whole campaign out of the water if we hadn't contained it, and by ten o'clock on Monday we were half hysterical with fatigue, drink, and a general sense of relief that there was nothing else to be done. At least by me: Pierre Landry had the poll-watching teams organized, Bill Noonan was still getting our sample ballots printed, Solheim had a full schedule of radio ads laid out for Monday and Tuesday, and Ed Bastian was putting together a vast telephone network to get the vote out.

That Monday was the first day in a month that I felt able to relax and let my head run—which is precisely what I was doing when the *Life* team walked in and found me laughing about Freak Power and what a fantastic shuck we had run on the liberals. "We'll put those fuckers on trial, starting Wednesday!" I shouted. "Paul, do you have the list? Maybe we should start reading it on the radio today." Paul Davidson grinned. "Yeah, we'll start rounding the bastards up tomorrow night. But we need money for Mace; do you have any?"

"Don't worry," I said. "We have plenty of money—and plenty of mescaline to sell if we need more. Get the Mace—get several gallons, and some double-ought buckshot."

. . .

Within two hours after the polls closed, the Battle of Aspen was over . . . at least that's how it looked at the time, from the eye of the shit rain. Freak Power bombed early that night, and we didn't need an RCA 1060 to project the final result—even after the early returns showed us winning. But not by enough. The early returns came from our hard-core freak strongholds in the middle and east end of town. We won handily in precincts One, Two, and Three, but our voter turnout was too light and the margin it gave us was not nearly enough to overcome the landslide that we knew was about to come down on us from suburban Agnewville and the down-county trailer courts. The backlash vote was kicking in, and the doom message was obvious in the eyes of our poll watchers about halfway through the day. They refused to confirm it, but I think we all knew. . . .

So somewhere around dusk we began loading up on mescaline, tequila, hash, beer, and whatever else we could get our hands on . . . and after that, it was only a matter of fucking with the national press and waiting for the axe to fall. Our elegant Hotel Jerome headquarters was a total madhouse. Everybody in the place seemed to have a long black microphone the size of a baseball bat, and all those without microphones had cameras—Nikons, Nagras, Eclairs, Kodaks, Polaroids, there was even a finely equipped videotape team from the California Institute of Arts.

The floor was a maze of cables, there were strobe lights taped to the ceiling. . . . The photographer from *Life* was muscled out of the way by two CBS thugs from Los Angeles; the chief cameraman on *Woodstock* got ugly with the director of the British TV crew . . . there was constant, savage jostling for camera positions around the phone desk and the fatal blackboard where Alison and Vicky Colvard were putting the numbers together. Bill Kennedy, a writer from *Harper's,* was maintaining his position in front of the telephone desk with a nasty display of elbow tactics summoned up, on instinct, from memories of covering the riot squad in Albany and San Juan.

Writers from *Life, LOOK, Scanlan's, Ski, The Village Voice, Fusion, Rat*—even a Dutch correspondent from *Suck*—moved constantly through the crowd, hassling everybody. The phones jangled with long-distance calls from AP, UPI, the TV networks, and dozens of curious strangers calling from Virginia, Michigan, and Oregon demanding to know the results. One of the best quick descriptions of the chaos came later from Steve Levine, a young columnist for *The Denver Post* who had spent half the day as one of our poll watchers:

"It was madness and sadness and drinking and dope and tears and anger and harsh plaster smiles," he wrote. "Parlor B in the old Jerome was jammed from wall to fading, flowered wall with partisan strugglers, both full freak and moderate freak, and the press from London and L.A., and well-wishers, and many people were rip-smashed and optimistic, but some knew better. . . ."

Indeed . . . and the solemn, smoke-filled hideaway for those who really knew better was room Number One, about two hundred feet down the crowded hallway from the vortex-madness in Parlor B. It was Oscar Acosta's room. He had been there for two weeks, dealing with one crisis after another and rarely sleeping in his complex, triple-pronged role of old friend, bodyguard, and emergency legal advisor to what *The New York Times* called "The most bizarre (political) campaign on the American scene today." But the *Times*man didn't know the half of it; he had come to town early in October, long before the campaign turned so crazy and vicious that *The New York Times* couldn't possibly have told the real story.

By the time Acosta arrived the Aspen political scene looked like some drug-addled Mafia-parody of a gang war scene from *The Godfather.* And a week before the election we actually went to the mattresses. Oscar, a prominent Chicano civil rights lawyer from Los Angeles, stopped in Aspen after a Denver visit with his client Corky Gonzales—the Chicanos' answer to Huey Newton or maybe H. Rap Brown in the old days. In mid-November Corky was scheduled to go on trial in L.A. on dubious charges of "carrying a deadly weapon" during the East Los Angeles riot the previous August, which resulted in the murder of Ruben Salazar by an L.A. County sheriff's deputy. Oscar would be the defense attorney in that trial, but in mid-October he found himself in Colorado with not much else to do, so he decided to stop by his old home in Aspen to see what the Honky/Gabachos were up to . . . and the nightmare scene that he found here seemed to convince him that white middle-class Amerika was truly beyond re-demption.

HST and Oscar Acosta on election night in Aspen, November 1970
(Bob Krueger)

. . .

On election night Oscar's small room in the Jerome filled quickly with people—both locals and "outsiders"—who shared his dreary conviction that this Aspen election had serious implications in the context of national politics. From the very beginning it had been a strange and unlikely test case, but toward the end—when it looked like a Radical/Drug candidate might actually win a head-on clash with the Agnew people—the Aspen campaign suddenly assumed national importance as a sort of accidental trial balloon that might, if it worked, be tremendously significant—especially to the angry legions of New Left/Radical types who insisted, on good evidence, that there was no longer any point in trying to achieve anything "within the system."

But obviously, if an essentially Republican town like Aspen could elect a sheriff running on a radical Freak Power platform, then the Vote might still be a viable tool . . . and it might still be possible to alter the mean, fascist drift of this nation without burning it down in the process. This was the strange possibility that had brought Dave Meggyesy out of San Francisco. Meggyesy, a former linebacker for the St. Louis Cardinals, had recently abandoned pro football and plunged into radical politics. . . . The first serialization of his book, *Out of Their League,* was on the newsstands in *LOOK* that week, and he had just come back from a New York gig on *The Dick Cavett Show.* But *LOOK* was a bit too cerebral for the kind of people who voted against us in Aspen; to them, Dave Meggyesy was just another one of those "dirty Communist outsiders that Thompson was importing to take over the town."

It's hard to communicate when they don't speak your language, so Meggyesy reverted to type and signed on as a bodyguard, along with Teddy Yewer, the wild young biker from Madison; Paul Davidson, the Black Belt White Panther from Denver; and Gene Johnson, a super-wiggy ex–painting contractor from Newport Beach . . . all Communists, of course, every one of them on salary from Peking.

These treacherous perverts—and others—were among those who gathered in Oscar's room that night to ponder the wreckage of Amerika's first Freak Power campaign.

. . .

There was certainly no shortage of reasons to explain our defeat. A few were so brutally obvious that there is not much point in listing them except for the record—which is crucial, because the record will also show that, despite these apparently suicidal handicaps, we actually carried the city of Aspen and pulled roughly 44 percent of the vote in the entire county. This was the real shocker. Not that we lost, but that we came so close to winning.

The record will also show that we learned our political lessons pretty well, after coming to grips with the reasons for Joe Edwards's six-vote loss in 1969. Our mistake, of course—which was actually my mistake—was in publishing what we learned in a national magazine that hit the newsstands just in time to become a millstone around our necks in 1970. The local appearance of the October 1, 1970, issue of *Rolling Stone* was a disaster of the first magnitude, for several reasons: 1) because it scared the mortal shit out of our opposition; 2) because it got here just a week or so too late to be effective in our crucial "freak-registration" campaign; and 3) because it outlined our campaign strategy in such fine detail that the enemy was able to use it against us, with hellish effectiveness, all the way to the end.

Among other damaging revelations, the article went into great detail to show that we couldn't possibly win in 1970 unless the Democrats and the Republicans effectively split the "establishment vote," as they had a year earlier. Here is a word-for-word excerpt from "The Battle of Aspen" (*Rolling Stone* #67, October 1, 1970):

The root point is that Aspen's political situation is so volatile—as a result of the Joe Edwards campaign—that any Freak Power candidate is now a possible winner.

In my case, for instance, I will have to work very hard—and spew out some really heinous ideas during my campaign—to get less than 30 percent of the vote in a three-way. And an underground candidate who really wanted to win could assume, from the start, a working nut of about 40 percent of the electorate—with his chances of victory riding almost entirely on the Backlash Potential: or how much active fear and loathing his candidacy might provoke among the burghers who have controlled local candidates for so long.

With Sandy, in Aspen
(Bob Krueger)

. . .

So it was no surprise, when it finally became apparent that the Freak Power slate was going to get no less than 40 percent of the vote, to find our local GOP brain trust scrambling to arrange a last-minute emergency compromise with their "archenemies" in the other party. The difference, in Aspen, was like the difference between Nixon and LBJ on the national level: Beyond the personalities and patronage squabbles, there was no real difference at all. Not on the issues.

What happened, however, is that about halfway through the campaign both establishment parties found themselves hawking a local version of the Black Panthers' "theory of the greater fear." As much as they might detest each other personally, they hated "freak power" more—and they agreed that it had to be stopped, by any means necessary.

The unholy agreement they forged, less than 48 hours before the election, was that each party would sacrifice one of its two major candidates (in the sheriff and county commissioner races) so as not to split the vote. This assured massive bipartisan support for both incumbents: Sheriff Carrol Whitmire, a Democrat, and Commissioner J. Sterling Baxter.

The trade-off was effected by a sort of chain-letter telephone campaign on election eve, an effort so frantic that one man, a Republican, got eighteen calls that night telling him that the final word from headquarters was to "split your ticket; we're dumping [GOP sheriff candidate] Ricks and the Democrats are dumping Caudhill."

. . .

What we learned in Aspen was that if you "work within the system," you'd damn well better win—because "the system" has a built-in wipeout mechanism for dealing with failed challengers.

If the Freak Power brain trust learned anything serious in that election, it was that "working within the system" is merely a lame euphemism for "playing by their rules." Once you do this, and lose—especially in a small town with a voting population of just under 2,500—you're expected to hunker down like a natural gentleman/politician and take your beating, the inevitable consequences of running a failed challenge on a deeply entrenched Power Structure.

Like the laws of Physics, the laws of Politics in America seem based on the notion that every force creates a counterforce of exactly equal strength. Our bizarre voter-registration campaign mobilized a vast number of local "freaks" who had never registered, before, to vote for anything—and many of them said afterward that they would never register again. They insisted all the way to the voting booths that they "hated politics" and especially "politicians."

But the Freak Power platform—and indeed the whole campaign—was so far above and beyond anybody's idea of "politics" that in the end we found most of our strength among people who were proud to call themselves Non-Voters. In a town where no candidate for any public office had ever considered it necessary to pull more than 250 votes, a stone-bald and grossly radical Freak Power candidate for sheriff pulled 1,065 votes in 1970, yet lost by nearly 400 votes.

The Freak Power election so polarized Aspen that we managed, in the end, to frighten up enough Negative/Scare votes to offset our shocking and unprecedented success in mobilizing the "freak" vote. We frightened the bastards so badly that on Election Day they rolled people in wheelchairs—and even on stretchers—into the polling places to vote against us. They brought out people, young and old, who thought "Ike" Eisenhower was still president of the U.S.A. "It was the goddamnedest thing I've ever seen," said one of our poll watchers. "I was out there in Precinct One, where we thought things were cool, and all of a sudden they just rolled over us like a sheep drive. I've never seen so many pickup trucks in my life."

We are still seeing those pickups. And anybody who challenges them had better be ready to die. That's what they told me, over and over again, when I ran for sheriff: That even if I won, I would never live to take office. And when I lost, they instantly got down to making sure that nobody like me could ever run for office again.

With George McGovern in Washington, 1972
(Stuart Bratesman)

Sunday Night at the Fontainebleau

Sunday night at the Fontainebleau: Hot wind on Collins Avenue. Out in front of the hotel, facing the ocean, teams of armed guards and "police dogs" were patrolling the beach & pool area to make sure nobody sneaked in to feel the water. Not even the guests. It was illegal to use the ocean in Miami Beach at night. The beach itself was technically public property, but the architects of this swinish "hotel row" along what the local Chamber of Commerce called the "Gold Coast" had managed to seal off both the beach and the ocean completely by building the hotels so they formed a sort of Berlin Wall between Collins Avenue and the sea.

There were ways to get through, if you didn't mind climbing a few wire fences and seawalls, or if you knew where to find one of the handful of tiny beach areas the city fathers had quietly designated as "public," but even if you made it down to the beach, you couldn't walk more than 50 or 60 yards in either direction, because the hotels had sealed off their own areas . . . and the "public" areas were little more than rocky strips of sand behind hotel parking lots, maintained as a grudging, token compliance with the law that said hotels had no legal right to fence the public away from the ocean. This was a touchy subject in Miami then, because many of the hotels had already built so close to the high-tide line that their pools and cabanas were on public land, and the last thing they wanted was a lawsuit involving their property lines.

The Doral, for instance—headquarters for both George McGovern and Richard Nixon in that mean "Convention summer" of 1972— had been built so close to the sea that at least half of its beachfront cabanas and probably half of its so-called Olympic-size pool were built on public property. A test case on this question could have precipitated a financial disaster of hellish proportions for the Doral, but the owners were not losing much sleep over it. They had me arrested on four consecutive nights during the Democratic Convention that August for swimming in the pool "after hours." Usually around three or four in the morning.

After the first two days it got to be a ritual. I would appear on the moonlit patio and say hello to the black private cop while I took off my clothes and piled them on a plastic chair near the diving board. Our conversation on the first night was a model for all the others:

"You're not supposed to be out here," the private cop said. "This area is closed at night."

"Why?" I said, sitting down to take off my shoes.

"It's against the law."

"What law?"

"The one they pay me to enforce, goddamnit. The one that says you can't go swimmin' out here at night."

"Well . . ." I said, taking off my watch and stuffing it into one of my crusty white basketball shoes. . . . "What happens if I just jump into the pool and swim, anyway?"

"You gonna do that?"

"Yeah," I replied. "I'm sorry to hassle you, but it's necessary. My nerves are all twisted up, and the only way I can relax is by coming out here by myself and swimming laps."

He shook his head sadly. "Okay, but you're gonna be breakin' the law."

"I doubt it."

"What?"

"The way I see it," I said, "about twenty feet of this pool over there on the side near the ocean is on public property."

He shrugged. "I'm not gonna argue with you about that. All I know is the law says you can't swim out here at night."

"Well, I'm going to," I said. "What happens then?"

He turned away. "I'll call the cops," he said. "I'll get fired if I don't. And I'm sure as hell not comin' in after you."

"You could shoot me," I said, walking over to the edge of the pool. "Blow me out of the water; claim you thought I was a shark."

He smiled and turned away as I dove into the pool . . . and 15 or 20 laps later I looked up to see two city cops with flashlights pointing down at me. "Okay fella," said one, "come on outta there. You're under arrest."

"What for?"

"You know," said the other. "Let's go."

They took me up to the lobby to see the night manager, who declined to press charges when he realized I was a paying hotel guest.

My bill was running around $85 a day at that point and, besides that, I was registered as "press." So the matter was dismissed without rancor when I agreed to go back to my room.

We went through the same motions 24 hours later, and also on the third & fourth night . . . but on the fifth night, for some reason, the pool guard said nothing at all when I appeared. I said "hello" and started taking off my clothes, expecting him to head for the house phone on that pole out in the middle of the patio that he'd used on the other nights . . . but he just stood there and watched me dive in. Then he spent the next 45 minutes pointedly ignoring me . . . and at one point, just as dawn was coming up, he chased a videotape crew away from the pool when they tried to film me swimming. When they asked why I could swim and they couldn't even walk around on the patio, he just shook his head and pointed his billy club toward the exit door.

I never asked him why. When I finally felt tired enough to sleep, I climbed out of the pool and yelled "thanks" as I waved to him and went back inside. He waved back, then resumed his bored pacing around the patio. Moments later, up in my oceanfront room on the sixth floor, I looked down and saw him leaning on the railing and staring out to sea at the sunrise, his billy club dangling idly from his right wrist and his cop's hat pushed back on his head. I wondered what he was thinking about: A young black "private" cop, maybe 25 or 30 years old, spending every night of the week, all night—8:00 P.M. to 8:00 A.M.—enforcing a bogus law that probably didn't even say, if you read it carefully, that nobody could swim in a big empty pool built illegally on public property (his beachfront) by the wealthy white owners of a Miami Beach hotel. During one of my conversations with the night manager at the Doral, he had hinted that the "no swimming" rule had its origins more in the hotel's insurance policy than in any municipal law.

I watched the cop for a while, wondering if George McGovern upstairs in the penthouse might also be looking down at him . . . but probably not, I thought: McGovern might be up there, but if he was, I figured he was probably looking out to sea, squinting through the glass sight of that big .358 Weatherby Magnum he liked to use on sharks. It was a strange vision: the Democratic nominee, braced at sunrise on the ledge of his penthouse in Miami, scanning the dawn surf for the cruising, thin gray edge of a Hammerhead fin; his rifle cocked, with the strap curled around his left arm and a Bloody Mary on the table beside him, killing sharks to keep his mind loose on his morning of triumph.

Indeed. McGovern had become The Candidate, and as the senior correspondent in the McGovern press corps, I felt a certain obligation to know exactly what he was doing and thinking at that hour. What would he have said if I had called up there on the phone and said I was about to go on NBC-TV and say McGovern had spent his morning blasting sharks with a huge Weatherby Magnum from the patio of his penthouse on top of the Doral Beach Hotel?

I had been tempted to make the call, if only to jerk him around a bit and make him get Frank Mankiewicz out of bed to draft a denial for the press conference that would almost certainly have followed such an ugly revelation . . . but I decided against it; I needed some sleep, and if I had made a call like that, I knew sleep would be out of the question. It would have generated trouble, and I figured it would probably result in getting myself publicly denounced as a Dangerous Dope Addict, a man given over in extremes to multiple hallucinations and other forms of aggressive personal dementia. . . . Between Mankiewicz and South Dakota Lieutenant Governor and McGovern crony Bill Dougherty, they would have hashed up a story that would not only have caused me to be discredited, but probably would have gotten me locked up indefinitely at the expense of The State, forced to undergo the Hickory Cure and perhaps even Shock Treatments. . . .

WHAT? Don't mention that word!

Shock treatments? Shark-shooting? Well. . . . I get a sudden sense that we're pushing it a bit here, so why not change the subject?

July 1972

HST addressing a voter registration ralley in Aspen with
Sheriff Bob Braudis (center) and Mayor John Bennett
(Steve Skinner)

Memo from the Sheriff

Hunter asks a lot of his friends, but he gives so much.
— Anonymous

One early winter morning, I looked out the window to see Hunter walking to my door. I've never seen Hunter before 10:00 A.M., except, maybe, in court. He had come to ask me if I'd accompany him to Louisville, where he'd be honored with a key to the city the following day. I immediately agreed.

At 7:30 the next morning, Hunter was getting ready. We had an 8:30 flight. At eight he asked me what time I had. I said, "Eight." He said, "Christ, I've got 7:30! That's anti-airport time." I knew what he meant.

We passed twenty cars in a row on a snow-packed mountain two-lane to make the plane. Hunter complimented my driving. I had a premonition that this road trip might involve some work.

It took all day to get to Louisville. Wayne Ewing had been on the ground, and the event seemed well organized. We checked into the hotel with pseudonyms: A. Lincoln. D. Boone. Hunter's suite had a dining room and forty or fifty shrimp cocktails.

The next day the only obligation before the evening event was a "sound check" at the auditorium. Warren Zevon, Johnny Depp, Hunter's son, Juan, many more of Hunter's friends, and I were parts of the "show."

Hunter was happy. He shot Zevon in the back with a huge fire extinguisher while Warren rehearsed at the piano. Scared the shit out of him.

We had a Sedan de Ville delivered to the auditorium so Hunter could "get away" at will. He wanted to buy a bullwhip to snap during the show. Two coeds from the university who had been assigned to assist guided us to a huge leather store.

Hunter didn't like the action of any of the whips but bought the coeds shoes and jackets. We spent the afternoon cruising Basketball Alley, Cherokee Park, and memories from Hunter's youth. No trouble, yet.

Shotgun art with Warren Zevon, Owl Farm, 1994
(Daniel E. Dibble)

Just before the big show, Hunter asked me to tell the organizer that he wouldn't appear onstage until a brown paper bag, stuffed with cash, was delivered. Jesus. I started my request by saying: "I'm not used to this, but . . ." Two minutes before kickoff, I gave Hunter the bag. He asks a lot of his friends.

The ceremony was a high-quality love fest. A poetess read her ode to Hunter, and he became entranced. At 4:00 A.M., Hunter was behind the wheel, on the way to drop the woman off at her door.

Hunter threaded the pride of Detroit between granite retaining walls and huge elms with ¹⁄₃₂ of an inch to spare, driving on the goddamn sidewalk. I saw trouble everywhere.

"Hunter, get back on the street! Every yuppie in these antebellum mansions is dialing 911. What will you say to the cops?"

Hunter told me that I worry too much. We dropped the poetess off and went to the hotel. No trouble. No arrests.

On our last day in Louisville, Hunter visited Virginia, his mother, at her nursing home outside of the city. Juan and I and Bambi, a stripper, drove out with him. Bambi wanted Hunter to sign her ass so she could replicate it with a tattoo.

I dropped Juan and Hunter at the Episcopal Care Center and said I'd kill an hour in a bar with Bambi. I spent the hour looking for a bar in a *dry* county. Life is a gradual release from ignorance.

When we got back to the assisted living center, I escorted Bambi to the bathroom through the large day room. Her micro-skirt, high boots, and makeup caused a lot of old dudes to skid-stop their walkers.

Virginia had invited most of her relatives to visit with her and Hunter. He was ready to bolt from this "quality time" with Mom. We went back to the hotel, Bambi disappeared sans autograph, and Zevon and I had dinner. No trouble. No arrests.

The journey home started to get strange when, during climb-out, with the plane aimed at the sun at a forty-five-degree angle, Hunter clawed his way to the forward first-class head. Even though the cabin was full of United personnel, nobody said anything. Maybe it was because, just prior to this walk, Hunter let out a thirty-second, two-octave, head-splitting rebel yell. "Just what people like to hear during takeoff," he said. After we got to flight level and the seat belt sign went off, a line formed at the door to the restroom. The flight attendant came to me and asked, "Just what is your friend doing in there?"

Without hesitation, I lied. "He's had bad diarrhea all day."

"Oh, no problem," she said, and herded the line, with whispers, aft.

A half hour later the door opened and Hunter sat down to my left. "Just what were you doing in there?" I asked. "Oh, I took a little bath, shaved, changed clothes. Any problem?" No. No trouble, no arrest.

Hunter said that traveling with me was like traveling with Superman. Oliver always said that if Hunter got crazy at his own home, we could just leave. I couldn't leave him in Louisville, I never would. It didn't get that crazy.

Bob Braudis, Pitkin County Sheriff

Dealing with the D.A.—Before and After

(EDITOR'S NOTE)

Dr. Thompson was again arrested for political reasons in 1995 for leading a finely organized Voters Rebellion against the long-dominant Aspen Skiing Company, which was planning to enlarge and expand the local airport to accommodate huge new jetliners designed for "industrial tourism." The SkiCo was allied with United Airlines and the local real-estate bund and corporate interests ranging from General Dynamics to Enron.

With these Goliaths of global industry behind them, the SkiCo anticipated no opposition at all to its November ballot initiative that would make the glorious new airport a legal, tax-payer-funded reality before the year 2000. . . . And there *was* no opposition, in fact, until the ever-contentious Woody Creek Caucus suddenly reversed itself and declared war on the new airport and everything it stood for—which included, by presumably universal agreement, giving the SkiCo and its corporate money changers the right to exploit the valley on a scale previously undreamed of in the ever-shrinking ski-resort business. Aspen is doomed, they warned, without drastic expansion, modernization, and a total commitment to a "new age commercialization." It was a matter of life or death, economically.

Thompson's epic eleventh-hour crusade *against* the airport expansion is a classic of Twentieth Century political organizing and catapulted the "No" vote from zero on October 1, to 50 percent on the night before the November 7 election—when the Doctor was arrested and jailed after addressing a rip-roaring Get Out the Vote rally in downtown Aspen that also featured the mayor, the sheriff, and a naked woman from Malibu who sold kisses.

News of Thompson's arrest spread rapidly and generated a huge voter turnout that swamped the new airport proposal by a 2–1 margin. The SkiCo was humiliated and never entirely recovered from the defeat. The Aspen ski business remained stagnant.

The following three (3) documents tell the story of that merciless 2-year legal struggle that eventually resulted in an unprecedented solution called the *Sharp Necklace Agreement* that broke the power of the local police forever—or at least until the Attorney General overrules it for antiterrorism reasons.

As always, Dr. Thompson's legally aggressive courtroom behavior is cited as a *matter of record* & not necessarily as recommended behavior for others. There are always risks in challenging excessive police power—but the risks of *not* challenging it are more dangerous, even fatal. Never do it impulsively. The Law can be cruel and unforgiving, especially of careless stupidity. The rule of thumb is BEWARE, and be quiet. You are Innocent until *proven* guilty, so act that way. And remember the Felony Murder Law. You may have been in Chicago when that poor woman got butchered by some runaway slave on speed; it won't matter. Get ready for prison. Abandon all hope, even if you are innocent. . . . It is a weird and brutal law, created *by* prosecutors *for* prosecutors, because it eliminates the need for Proof or even Evidence.

THOMPSON, COPS COME TO SHARP NECKLACE AGREEMENT

I did not ask for this fight. It came to me on a lonely road at the end of a wild night of politics, and it's been a shame and a travesty ever since. From its horrible beginnings, this case has been less about one person charged with a misdemeanor and more about the soul of the Aspen Police Department.

I despise drunk drivers just as much as I hate crooked cops. I fear anybody on the road who is out of control for any reason—and that would have to include, by universal agreement, public servants who use their badge and authority to settle personal grudges or enforce their political beliefs.

This agreement we're executing today will serve as a Sharp Necklace to crooked cops as well as dangerous drunkards and brings an end to the cheap, low-rent, back-alley pile of scum that this case has been.

H. S. Thompson, April 1997

December 12, 1995
LAWSON WILLS
Dep. District Atty.
Pitkin Cty. Courthouse

Dear Mr. Wills,

I am given to understand that you want me to come into the courthouse and officially surrender to you, in front of witnesses, so that you can formally re-arrest me on some kind of vague, chickenshit charge cooked up by Officer Short on the night of Nov. 7–8, '95, in the course of our bizarre encounter on Cemetery Lane as I was very skillfully driving home (on an utterly deserted road) after delivering the keynote address at a major political rally full of people who planned to wake up the next morning (Election Day) and kick the shit out of the Aspen Ski Co.

Is my information correct? Did that vengeful dingbat actually fail to serve me with a valid, legal summons? Did he botch *everything* that night? Was he so crazy that he couldn't even *arrest* me properly? And is *that* why you want me to drive at top speed into town so you can get yr. picture in the papers while you slap handcuffs on me and swell up like a toad for the cameras?

Ah, Lawson, have you *no* shame? Are you a Nazi? Are you nuts with lust for yr. upcoming 15 minutes of fame? Has it come to *this*—that you have to beg, bitch & cajole yr. victims to turn themselves in & abandon all hope for anything except humiliation and jail?

How long, O Lord, how long? You should be deeply ashamed of yourself. I talked with a journalist who said you reminded him of William Jennings Bryan at the Scopes "Monkey Trial" in 1925. It was a horrible thing to hear. (Bryan, as you recall, was whipsawed by Darrow & wound up testifying, under oath, that a whale is not a mammal & therefore, neither was he.)

Ah, but don't get me wrong, Lawson: I'm on Your side—or at least I was until that bungling dunce harassed me for 3 ½ hours on Election Day and made an ass of himself in the Jail. It was ugly. He went haywire when he finally understood that I was *not* Drunk and none of his high-tech Drunk-Buster machines were going to give him the numbers he wanted. He was like an ape trapped in chains. His fellow Officers were mortified, and so was I. It is shocking to see Aspen's long and honorable tradition of quality law enforcement being sullied by these charges about "rogue cops" and "stalkers" and "dumb Watersuckers with six-guns" who strut like John Wayne and think like Mark Fuhrman. There ain't many, as we know, but we also know in our bones that one rotten apple ruins the whole bushel, and that is why I feel real sympathy for you, because I know the people you work for, and I know how sick they are.

But don't worry, Lawson: The pigs will soon be out of the poke. Yessir. The fat is in the fire. Today's pig is tomorrow's bacon.

Whoops. Sorry. But rest easy. I *will* come in (probably today) and surrender again—and a whole legion of falsely accused drunkards will come with me. And they *all* hate Mark Fuhrman. But not me, Lawson. I don't hate anybody. I am a child of god of the new-age Buddhist persuasion, and I love to go to court. Because that is where Justice lives, and you know how I feel about Justice.

Indeed. Yr. time is coming, Whore-face. When I get yr. lame ass in court, you'll wish you'd been run over and killed by a Buick when you were six years old. We will skewer those swine on worldwide TV and put them in prison for Perjury. Nobody in this valley will ever see them again.

You filthy stinking animal. Do you know what *Misprison of a Felony* means? Or *Aggravated Conspiracy to Obstruct Justice*? Are you aware of the *terrible punishment that awaits* a Main Pig like you?

Okay. That's it. I'll surrender at noon on Wednesday.

THE SHARP NECKLACE AGREEMENT

The parties to this case agree to the following:
1. That driving while one's ability is impaired by alcohol is dangerous to the health and safety of the public and must be avoided at all costs.

2. That statements by police officers which are inaccurate or untruthful are dangerous to the administration of justice and must be avoided at all costs.

3. That it is an important function of police officers to enforce Colorado law prohibiting alcohol-impaired driving and that failure to enforce those laws vigorously would comprise a serious breach of duty and violation of public trust on the part of police.

4. That it is an essential quality of police officers to be free of enmity or bias against any individual or group of individuals in the community they serve and that for any officer to act or even appear to act out of any such enmity or bias would constitute an abuse of power and a violation of public trust.

5. That although Colorado law does not prohibit driving after drinking anything, clearly the wisest choice is not to drive after having anything alcoholic to drink, including after drinking a sufficient amount to obtain a blood alcohol concentration of .08.

6. That decency, security, and liberty alike demand that government officials shall be subjected to the same rules of conduct that are commands to the citizen. In a government of laws, existence of the government will be imperiled if it fails to observe the law scrupulously. Our government is the potent, the omnipresent teacher. For good or ill, it teaches the whole people by its example. Crime is contagious. If the government becomes a lawbreaker, it breeds contempt for the law; it invites every man to become a law unto himself; it invites anarchy. To declare that in the administration of the criminal law the end justifies the means—to declare that the government may commit crimes in order to secure the conviction of a private criminal—would bring terrible retribution.

7. The parties agree mistakes and/or errors in judgment have been made by all parties, that each party will strive to avoid any such errors in the future, and that it is in the best interest of justice to go forward with the tendered agreement.

(Signed) Hunter S. Thompson and
H. Lawson Wills,
Chief Deputy District Attorney

Forging the landmark Sharp Necklace Agreement
at home with noted criminal lawyer
(Deborah Fuller)

Saturday Night in Aspen

Saturday night in Aspen and the road out of town is empty in both directions. The only things moving on Main Street are me and one slow-rolling cop car. No people on the street, no local traffic. I wave to him, as I normally do, but he ignores me & picks up his radio squealer, probably to run my plate and maybe get some action. . . . I can see him back there, in my mirror, and I instinctively make a right turn & speed up, gripping the wheel with both hands and hearing a sudden roar of music all around me. It is "Walk on the Wild Side." Ah yes:

> *Candy came from out on the Island*
> *In the back room she was everybody's darlin',*
> *But she never lost her head*
> *Even when she was givin' head,*
> *She says, Hey babe, take a walk on the wild side*
> *Said, Hey babe, take a walk on the wild side,*
> *And the colored girls go—*
> *Doo, do doo, do doo, do do do . . .*

Right. And thank you, Lou Reed, for that one. You bet. Every once in a while, but not often, you can sit down and write a thing that you know is going to stand people's hair on end for the rest of their lives— a perfect memory of some kind, like a vision, and you can see the words rolling out of your fingers and bouncing around for a while like wild little jewels before they finally roll into place & line up just exactly like you wanted them to. . . . Wow! Look at that shit! Who wrote that stuff?

What? Me? Hot damn! Let us rumble, keep going, and don't slow down—whatever it is, keep doing it. Let's have a little Fun.

Even writing feels like fun when you catch a moment like this. You feel Pure and natural—Yes sir, I am a Natural Man tonight. Bring it on. Fuck those people. Tonight we walk with the King. . . . That is My kind of fun, and I like to spread it around. You can't Hoard fun. It has no shelf life.

And so much for that, eh? I started off writing about Aspen, but I wandered off into the definition of Fun, which is always dangerous. So, to hell with Fun. I shit on the chest of Fun. Look what it did to Charles Manson. He had Too much fun—no doubt about that—so they put him away for life. He was a Monster, and he still is. Put him Down. Shove him off the Bridge with a wire around his neck and bowling balls chained to his feet. Drown the bastard. What if it was your daughter he got hold of?

What indeed? I have no daughters, thank God, so I don't have to worry about it. I have always loved women of all ages, but they have always been Other people's daughters. If I had a daughter and she came home with a creature like Manson, my heart would fill with Hate. I would not kill him instantly, but my brain would start moving that way—Okay, how do we do this, without being busted for Murder?

First, get rid of the Witness. Send her upstairs to her room and make sure nobody else is around. That is a basic Rule in this business. . . . The next step is to grab a loaded shotgun off the wall and lure him into the kitchen by stomping heavily on the floor & screaming crazily while you dial up 911. That will put your situation on the Record.

Keep screaming, "Get away from me, Charley! Don't come any closer!" until he comes running into the room with wild eyes & you can blast him straight in the chest with both barrels. . . . Do not miss, or things will turn queer in a hurry. Make sure he's stone dead when he drops, because you will not get another chance. He will be on you with a butcher knife. . . . But if you do it Right, you will be hailed as a Hero, and yr. daughter will think long & hard before she comes home with another creep like Manson.

Death Bomb, Thanksgiving, 1992

(Deborah Fuller)

Witness II

Woody Creek, August 2002

I am not a religious man in any formal sense, but in truth I am far more *theologically conscious* than anyone I know—except perhaps my monkish brute of a neighbor, Ed Bastian, who conducts big-time Spirituality seminars on Aspen mountain and rides a huge black BMW motorcycle that was once blessed by the Dalai Lama, who also gave me the diaphanous white silk scarf that hangs across the room on my storyboard.

That is what I mean by "theologically conscious," but so what? I *enjoy* the company of religious scholars and even Jesus freaks from time to time, as long as they have a sense of humor and a bit of fine whiskey to oil the exotic machinery of speculations about the Meaning of God in Modern America, or Why Child Rape is *good* for Catholic priests and punishable by DEATH in the suburbs of San Diego. . . .

Smart boys from Tibet or the Society of Jesus are always fun for this kind of banter, and I am always on the lookout for these people, but rarely for anything except as sparring partners. There is nothing like a corrupt Jesuit or a high-rolling Buddhist to sharpen up with. And some are even *wise* in their own shrouded way.

Big-time lawyers and Appeals Court judges are also a morbid

kind of fun in times of personal darkness. I have many close friends on that side of the law, and I derive a lot of grim pleasure from them. They have a good sense of what is *possible* within the law, and what is probably Not. . . . That is what lawyers are all about. Most of them have spent enough time in Law School to have at least a rudimentary understanding of how the Judicial system operates.

Never Be Late for Court When You Are the Person on Trial is a good one to remember, for instance, and another is *The Cops Will Never Play Fair.*

Justice Is the Whim of the Judge is an axiom that I picked up a long time ago at the Columbia Law School in New York, where I also learned how to handle large sums of money and how to smoke marijuana in polite company without making a scene and acting like a junkie.

DR. HUNTER S. THOMPSON AND THE LAST BATTLE OF ASPEN
BY LOREN JENKINS, *SMART* MAGAZINE, JAN./FEB. 1990 (INTERVIEW TOOK PLACE IN SEPTEMBER 1989, 3 ½ MONTHS BEFORE GAIL PALMER CAME TO VISIT.)

The Rocky Mountain night is cold and still except for the occasional screeech [sic] of the peacocks that stalk the darkness just off the wooden deck where Hunter S. Thompson sits drinking under the iron bat sculpture that decorates his front porch. A week earlier, he had been caught out in the dead of night firing an assortment of weaponry over the house of a neighbor and had just barely avoided a felony indictment on gun charges. Now, with the September stars twinkling overhead, he is trying judiciously to explain the exact nature of the fear and loathing that have crept into the lush, quiet valley of Woody Creek, where he has made his home for the past two decades.

"I ran for sheriff in Aspen years ago to try to stop the greed heads from ruining the place," Thompson says in his singular stop-start, mumbling cadence. "Now . . . uhhh . . . they're . . . trying to move on me right here where I live." Indeed, land developers, the final plague of all paradises lost, have pretty much overwhelmed the once-funky mountain town. . . . And now the developers are reaching downvalley to Thompson's own pastoral backyard, disrupting his life and work and bringing him quixotically to center stage in a drama that the more sentimental locals have taken to calling the "last battle in the lost war for the soul of Aspen."

. . . That's why Thompson has become embroiled in a bitter dispute—nay, a modern-day range war—with a newcomer named Floyd Watkins, who, for Thompson, embodies all that is evil in Aspen. A rich man with a dubious past and the habit of getting his way, Watkins moved upstream of Hunter's house four years ago like a bad omen. Nothing has been the same since. Until then, Woody Creek was in a Western time warp, a valley of blue-collar bartenders and construction workers, a couple of aging hippies, and one famous writer. It was a place where locals prided themselves on their rural individualism, their isolation from increasingly ostentatious Aspen, and their unpaved roads and rough-hewn log houses.

The community center was a log post office and the adjoining Woody Creek Tavern, a smoky bar where cowboys and construction workers played pool, gambled on ball games, and occasionally brawled. Thompson used the tavern as a kind of office, a semipublic haven for his eccentricities. Taking calls, meeting people who flew in to see him on business, he set a hilarious, outlaw tone that his neighbors sympathized with immediately. He was a lot of fun, even if he did set off the occasional smoke bomb and raise his voice from time to time. It was a real Western.

In a valley where individualism and personal freedom are the reigning ideology, Floyd Watkins should have a lot of friends. He is the type of person who, at one point, made the West what it is. . . . A self-made man who had amassed millions in Florida and California in the heady world of high-level bill collecting (his company, which he sold for millions in 1985, was called Transworld Systems), Watkins came here expecting the respect he enjoyed in his Miami home. To that end he set out to build a multimillion-dollar estate that would rival those that have turned Aspen into an alpine Palm Springs over the past decade.

. . . [But] in fact, Watkins's insensitivity to the traditions of the old West in general and to the etiquette of Woody Creek in particular could not help but offend. He surrounded his spread with intimidating urban chain-link fences, built a massive rock-and-concrete gateway, laid tons of cement on his driveways, and began pushing to have the Woody Creek road paved to keep the dust out of his parlors. Worse, in a land where water is valued as much as gold, Watkins ran bulldozers through streambeds that his downstream neighbors used to water their cattle and fields and rerouted the creek through his front lawn; he planned to build artificial trout ponds, in defiance of official county disapproval, that he would turn into a commercial fishing camp.

Thompson later fictionalized these developments in his weekly column in the *San Francisco Examiner*, suggesting that nothing short of a Hatfield-and-McCoy feud was about to engulf the valley. . . .

It was an adolescent act of common vandalism that

brought matters to a head. As Floyd Watkins later told the story, his work crews had hardly finished pouring a new driveway at his Beaver Run Ranch when someone unseen and unknown inscribed "Fuck you, prick" on his black-tinted concrete and an anonymous telephone call warned him: "No more concrete is going to be poured in Woody Creek." Watkins said it was the final straw, coming as it did after a series of other incidents that he claimed ranged from an attempted poisoning of his dog, the shooting out of his night-lights, the sawing down of a Beaver Run Ranch sign on the main road, and the scrawling of graffiti on his imposing rock gateway labeling the place "Fat Floyd's Trout Farm."

"I called the sheriff's office to complain, but they said they had only two deputies on duty and couldn't send anyone up here," Watkins said when I visited him to hear his side of the dispute. "I told the sheriff then and there that I was going to take care of things myself."

The first sign that Watkins had gone on the warpath came that evening, when Gaylord Guenin, an amiable former journalist who runs the Woody Creek Tavern, was driving to his home, two miles up the creek beyond the Beaver Run Ranch. Watkins chased down Guenin's pickup and forced him to pull over.

"He was furious and fuming and threatening," Guenin recalls. "He talked about having Uzis and infrared scopes at his home and his ability to 'take care of people' and be three thousand miles away when it happened. It was clear that I had been chosen to deliver a message." Still shaken when he got home, Guenin called the Tavern and warned everyone that Watkins was on a tear. What no one knew, of course, was that Watkins had decided to spend the night well armed in his car, near his endangered driveway.

Watkins recalls some fifteen or twenty cars driving up the road that night, "all honking and jeering" as they passed his hidden four-wheel drive. Around 4 A.M., he fell asleep. Then, "at about 4:30, I heard five blasts of a shotgun. At first I thought Roberto, my foreman, had shot a coon by the shed where I keep some ducks, and I started to go over there, when there were about twenty shots from an automatic weapon of some kind, then six shots from a pistol. I realized the shots came from down the road. I saw car lights from either a Jeep Cherokee or a Wagoneer. I started after them, and there was a high-speed chase in the dark." Three miles down the road, the escaping vehicle slowed down and turned in to the Flying Dog Ranch, owned by George Stranahan, a respected physicist turned cattle rancher who also owns the tavern and is the valley's most influential citizen. He is a very old friend of Thompson's.

There were two people in the car, according to Watkins, and one—a girl—ran up to Stranahan's house while the other started to get out on the driver's side. "I had these spotlights on the car," Watkins says. "I turned them on and saw Hunter Thompson. I said, 'What the fuck do you think you're doing, Hunter?' And he came up to me, jabbed me in the chest, and said, 'You have been given a warning; there is to be no trout operation or any more concrete poured in Woody Creek.'"

The official version that Thompson later gave to the *Aspen Times Daily* from my kitchen telephone was somewhat different. Thompson denied that he was firing at Watkins or his house or delivering any personal warning. He said, instead, that he was heading up to Watkins's ranch when he came face to face with a giant porcupine. "Don't laugh," Hunter told the reporter Dave Price. "Look at Jimmy Carter. He was attacked by a killer swamp rabbit and had to beat it off with his oar. I was attacked by this huge porcupine. I stopped to look at it and it attacked me, so I blasted it." The porcupine, alas, was never found.

That there was a confrontation with Watkins in the driveway of Stranahan's Flying Dog Ranch is not in dispute. Thompson maintains, however, that he was the master of diplomacy, telling Watkins that he, Hunter, was his only friend. "I even offered him my last beer and invited him to come down to my place later in the day to watch the ball game." But Watkins went home, called Sheriff Bob Braudis, and demanded that Thompson be prosecuted for what Hunter later said was "everything from the Manson family killings to shooting his mules."

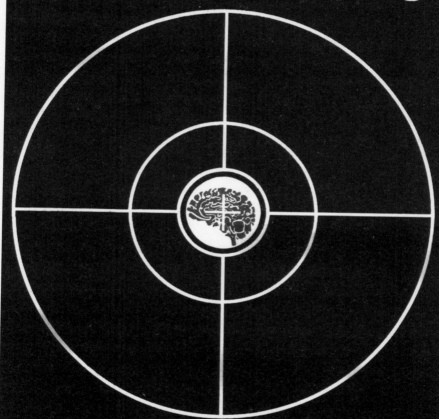

aspen wall poster

4

THE AMERICAN DREAM

(Tom Benton)

That was an exaggeration. But Mac Myers, the deputy district attorney whose office conducted the investigation, came within a hairbreadth of bringing charges against Thompson for firing an automatic weapon. In the end, he couldn't prove such a weapon had been fired. Thompson had a permit for a nonfunctioning automatic weapon, and when he was asked to turn in the gun for inspection, he presented a destroyed machine gun that had been packed in viscous antitrust naval jelly that rendered ballistics tests inconclusive.

Three days after the shooting, while the district attorney's office debated whether to press charges against Thompson, Watkins woke to a nightmare. The ponds he had stocked with trophy-sized trout during the past three years were shimmering with the silver bellies of dead fish. More than six hundred trout, some weighing up to twenty pounds, were dead. The waters had been poisoned in the night, and Watkins immediately blamed the slaughter on his neighbors, charging them with employing "terrorist tactics" against him because they didn't like his tastes and style. He went on to say that the multimillion-dollar, seventeen-thousand-square-foot main house of his estate would not be completed for another two years, but he'd be damned if he was going to let anybody scare him off his land. "I'm just gearing up to get tough," he told reporters, warning that he would hire gunmen, and "if I have to, I will put guards all along that road. I can afford it."

 . . . The level-headed Stranahan shared the sheriff's concern, and they issued joint statements calling for everyone to calm down before someone was hurt. Down at the Tavern, where talk of Watkins's problems was normally greeted with raucous jokes, there was disbelief that someone from the valley would actually poison Woody Creek's waters, Watkins or no Watkins. This is the West, after all, and water isn't messed with. The new mood was illustrated by the large glass that appeared on the Tavern's bar, accompanied by a sign that said: "We're sorry the trout died. Your $ can put a trout back in Floyd's ponds. Woody Creek wants the world to know we don't think killing trout is a way to solve the problems. Let's put the trout back, and then we will talk about the differences." Thompson, resentful of innuendos that he might have been behind the fish poisoning, offered a $500 reward to anyone who could clear up the mystery and said that perhaps he should poison some of his peacocks.

The collection jar had just begun to fill with bills when Watkins's fish story began to unravel. A disaffected Beaver Run Ranch employee quit his job, and soon he was signing a sheriff's affidavit testifying that the night before the trout kill, Watkins's twenty-three-year-old son, Lance, and Roberto, the Mexican foreman, poured from four to five gallons of an algaecide called Cutrine Plus into the fish ponds. Cutrine Plus is a copper-based chemical normally used to control algae growth.

"Chemists have told us that the water from the ponds had a copper content that was a zillion times the lethal level for trout," Sheriff Braudis reported at a Tavern meeting of the Woody Creek Caucus, an informal assembly of valley landowners and residents that includes both Watkins and Thompson. The sheriff's investigation concluded that the ponds had been poisoned not by antisocial outsiders but "by accident," by Watkins's own son and his Mexican majordomo.

"We have a difference of opinion here," Watkins defiantly told his neighbors, to hoots of derisive laughter. Refusing to accept the sheriff's verdict, he cited his own fish biologist, Dr. Harold Hagen, who insisted that the level of Cutrine Plus in the water could not have been enough to massacre the trout. More hoots. "My ranch is different from George Stranahan's or yours, but it doesn't make any difference," Watkins finally blurted out. "Do you mean I don't have the right to paint my house pink if I want to? And you have a right to paint your house blue?" Referring to one of Thompson's accusations that only a "vampire or a werewolf" would want to live in his house, Watkins said, "Well, I'm neither a vampire nor a werewolf, but I can tell you one thing: I sure as hell wouldn't want to live in Hunter's house. But I don't care if he lives there."

Everyone cracked up, and in the spirit of goodwill that reigned until the end of the meeting, Thompson withdrew his original charge about the Watkins house. "I apologize for the vampire thing," he said. "I was in a weird mood. But we are not talking about whether we like or dislike your house. No one is oppressing you. It is not about individual rights. We all live in this valley; this is a one-road community. We all have to live here, you included, and we are sliding into weird squabbles here. But the point is that we don't want to see the life of this valley poisoned—that is as bad as poisoning fish."

. . . "The truth is that Woody Creek has become urbanized in the last twenty years," Sheriff Braudis says rather sadly. "I've told Hunter that, and I've told him he can't be out shooting on the road as he used to. His neighbors are complaining more and more about his peacocks screeching and the gunshots in the night. Today Woody Creek is different. What is happening now is that the billionaires are pushing out the millionaires."

Thompson knows this, of course, and says that perhaps if he could afford to move—and could find somewhere as interesting to move to—he would. But he can't and he won't. Sometimes, though, he gets tired. "Living out here like this doesn't go with being pushed around and run over by yo-yos," he says. "It isn't that you can't win against them—it is that you don't want to fight them all the time. I don't mind fucking with Floyd, but that is not my job. If both of us are going to continue to live in this valley, he is going to have to learn that he has to live with us more than we have to live with him."

As of this writing, Watkins has imported two Bengal tigers to inhabit the new caged run along his driveway. "Everyone is holding their breath while we wait to find out what's going to be next," says Guenin. "We have reached the ultimate in ridiculousness." Hunter S. Thompson, meanwhile, is talking about getting some elephants.

That is the famous story of Floyd and the Giant *Porcupine,* as told by my good friend Loren Jenkins, Pulitzer Prize–winning war correspondent for *Newsweek* and *The Washington Post* and currently Foreign News Editor for NPR. . . . Back then, in 1990, he was editor-owner of the venerable *Aspen Times* and I was a major stockholder in a slick new magazine he started in New York called *SMART.*

In truth, I was probably a minor stockholder, but I had a keen personal interest in it—a profoundly *vested* interest, which I immediately put to good use when I was suddenly threatened with the possibility of going to Federal Prison on RICO charges of attempted/premeditated Murder with Intent to Kill, felony possession and public use at midnight of automatic weapons, and a fistful of other degrading charges ranging from Dangerous Drugs to Animal Cruelty and Gross Sexual Imposition.

It was an extremely bad moment, on its face, and many people said I was *done for.* "He's gone too far this time," they said. "What kind of dangerous maniac would attack a man's home with machine guns in the dead of night and then poison all of his fish the next day?"

. . .

Well, shucks. Only a *real* vicious dope fiend, I guess, some white-trash shithead with nothing left to lose. The jails are full of those bastards. Kill them all at once, for all I care.

It was not easy for me to retain a reputable attorney under those circumstances. Nobody wanted to touch it.

A mood of desperation settled over the Owl Farm. My girlfriend went off to Princeton, and I was left alone to barricade myself inside the compound and wait for the attack I knew was coming. I was receiving daily ultimatums from the ATF and the District Attorney. They wanted *all* my guns immediately or they would come out with a SWAT team and get them. The fat was in the fire.

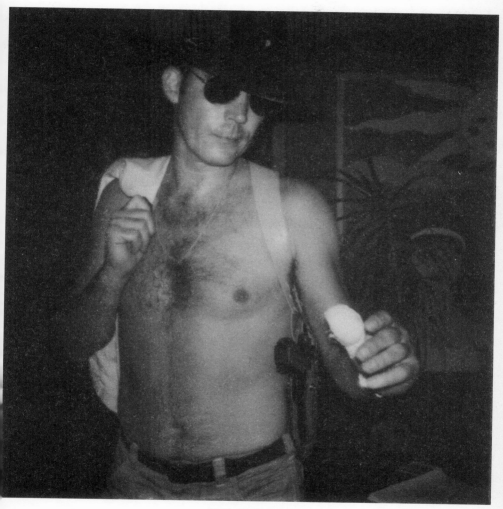

(Lalia Nabulsi)

. . .

My mood became dangerously confrontational in those weeks. I was angry and lonely and doing a lot of target shooting day and night. My friends worried that I was being pushed over the edge by this constant barrage of threats and sudden death by violence. I was always armed and sullen, living from moment to moment and ripped to the tits on my own adrenaline. I look at Deborah's photos from that feverish time and think, Ye fucking gods. This man appears to be criminally insane. It looks like some horrible flashback from *Reefer Madness* and *The Crays* and *Scarface* and *Boogie Nights* all at once. The photos still give me the creeps.

God damn it. I have bitten the front of my tongue again! Why? What have I eaten tonight that would cause me to draw blood from my own tongue? Where is the Percodan? Where is Anita? What is that noise in the bushes? Why am I so crazy all the time?

There was a time when I was vaguely worried by questions like these, but no longer. There are some questions that you can only worry about for *so* long, until finally they become meaningless . . . and it is never healthy to start questioning your own sanity. Being free and happy on the street is evidence enough of sanity these days.

Why is it that so many people have gone insane since the end of the American Century and the horrible Bush family was restored to power? Why is the teenage suicide rate going up? Is the President a clone? Is my car going to explode? Why does my sweetheart suddenly have all these lewd tattoos on her body?

(EDITOR'S NOTE)

Wait a minute. Time out! Why am I writing all these things on this primitive red electric typewriter when I can read them all in real time on the goddamn overloaded Internet with the flick of a mouse or a button? Am I a Fool? Have I been bogged down in Alzheimer's all these years? What does it all mean, Homer?

. . .

Okay. Back to business. The Giant Porcupine story did not go away. Finally, to avoid deadly violence and another five years in prison, I was compelled to sacrifice my precious Smyser Nazi machine gun— I chopped it up with a heavy industrial grinder and had it formally delivered to the forces of law and order in a large white bag filled with poison grease that would eat the flesh off of anyone who touched it.

And that was that, as I recall. It was never mentioned again, and neither was the Porcupine. My new assistant arrived on Xmas—on loan from the University of Florida's College of Journalism and Communications—and I settled down, as it were, to finishing my long-overdue book, *Songs of the Doomed*, which was still only half written—another deadline agony. They are always painful. . . .

. . .

Christmas came and went in a frenzy of work. The big snow fell and the thermometer plunged to 10 or 15 below zero. The Democrats had lost another election and Bush was still the new President. But not much had changed since the 80s, when the looting of the Treasury was running in high gear and the U.S. Military was beginning to flex its newfound money-muscle. When, everywhere you looked, the flag-suckers were in charge.

We invaded a bunch of tiny helpless countries like Lebanon, Grenada, and Panama, just for the practice, and it was about that time that I went to work as a columnist for the Hearst-owned *San Francisco Examiner* and discovered feminist pornography and moved to Sausalito with Maria.

It was a wild and savage time, Bubba. All hell broke loose, in a phrase. . . . Moving down the mountain has always been dangerous for me, because of the Space problem, but San Francisco in the 1980s was a genuine Adult Dose.

I was shocked. In 1981 I was 44 years old and I saw myself in the mirror as a grizzled veteran of many wars, untold violence, a respectable eight or nine jails all over the world. I had ridden the wild beast of Passion through so many jungles and nightmares and devastating personal disasters that I felt about 200 years old. My heart was strong, but my body was scarred and broken and warped from a lifetime of dangerous confrontations. . . . I was old beyond my years, as they say, and I had developed a curious habit of survival. It was the only way I knew, and I was getting pretty good at it, on the evidence. . . .

I had even survived my time as Night Manager of the depraved O'Farrell Theatre, along with being arrested seven times in six weeks for crimes that you can't avoid committing when the Police are admittedly tracking you 24 hours a day and routinely busting you for things like Open Container and running yellow lights and being naked at night in Golden Gate Park for no apparent reason.

Ho ho. Of course there were reasons. There are always *reasons*. Even the blood-thirsty Manson family had reasons. They were stupid murdering swine, for one, and they also had way too much Time on their hands.

My own situation was exactly the opposite. I had too much Action on my hands. I was a notorious best-selling author of weird and brutal books and also a widely feared newspaper columnist with many separate agendas and many powerful friends in government, law enforcement, and sociopolitical circles.

I was also drunk, crazy, and heavily armed at all times. People trembled and cursed when I came into a public room and started screaming in German. It was embarrassing. . . . Maria and I spent more and more time hiding out in obscure places like Stinson Beach or Harding Park in the fog belt and even the Crime-ridden San Bruno Municipal Parking Garage.

It was a sweet time, all in all. In some ways it was a depraved and terrifying adventure in the darkest side of life, and at least half the time it was like being shot out of a beautiful cannon in some kind of X-rated Peter Pan movie. I would definitely *do it again*. . . .

. . .

Hi folks, my name is Marvin and I'm here to sell you this amazing beautiful old typewriter, which is guaranteed to do for you exactly what it has done for me. This one is a *monster*, folks. Writing a book with this thing is like sitting in a pool of LSD-25 and suddenly feeling yr. nuts on fire. . . . Yes sir, that is a *lifetime guarantee*. Think about it. . . .

So let me ask *you* a fat little question, friends, and I want you to *think* about this real carefully before you spit out yr. answer—this one is BIG. This is the one query you are going to *have* to answer when you come face to face with GOD ALMIGHTY!

He will ask: "What can I *do* for you, boy? What is the *one* thing you could ask me to do for you *right now*??? What *is* it? WHAT? *Speak up!* NOW! Or I will send you straight to Hell. . . .

What will you *say,* brother? What is the one true answer you will give to Almighty God when you get your final chance? And *remember*—he will Judge you by yr. answer. He will *JUDGE you!* And if you say the wrong thing, you will *suffer* for it. You will eat shit and *die.*

(Long pause filled with weeping and babbling and noise of chairs being pushed around. . . .)

OKAY! OKAY, brother—Relax and feel happy. Fear not, for I am with you and *I will tell you the answer*! Hallelujah *Mahalo.* You are saved!

THE ANSWER YOU WILL GIVE TO GOD ALMIGHTY WHEN HE COMES TO JUDGE YOUR FATE IS Yes Yes Yes, yr. honor. I thought you'd never ask. What I want, of course, is a BRAND-NEW WILD AND SUPERCOOL MODEL 22 IBM SELF-CORRECTING FIRE-ENGINE RED MAGNUM SELECTIVE TYPEWRITER exactly like this one! JUST LIKE MINE. . . . That is what you will say in yr. magic moment of judgment.

. . .

Help me, Lord, for I am watching Gail Palmer's movies again. It is a desperate habit that I formed many years ago when I was preparing to go to Trial. That is always an awkward moment in a smart man's life. I was looking down the barrel of the end of the world, as I knew it. And I understood that I was coming to a major Fork in my road of life—to live *free* like an otter, or to die like a stupid young bee in the web of the federal law-enforcement system. There was no middle way. I had no choice. The deal was going down.

I have known a few magic moments like these—red dots on a sea-green map—and I treasure them. They are the high points of my life, my moments of total Function, when I felt like a snow leopard fighting for life on its own turf.

Whoops. Let's not get maudlin, Doc. Don't embarrass the breed with some drunken hillbilly hubris. The joke is over. They are coming after your heart this time, so behave accordingly. At the top of the mountain we are all snow leopards.

. . .

Right, and now let's get back to the Witness who came into my house that night and almost put me in prison.

She was clearly a refugee from the sex film industry—a business I had covered as a journalist, regrettably arousing her interest.

In 1985 I ventured to San Francisco to do an article for *Playboy* on "feminist pornography." Nobody knew what it was, but I was telling *Playboy* what it was and that was why they gave me the assignment. Feminist porn was really just couples' films—sex films made for couples to which you could take a date.

It was a new genre, and I had happened to run into some of the women who appeared in these films when I was in San Francisco for the Democratic Convention in '84. They kind of adopted me. Most of the girls were at least bisexual, and they were fun. A lot of them were the stars of this new style of films. Juliet Anderson, later famous as Aunt Peg, was a big one. Veronica Hart was another— she is still making films and is pretty good at her trade.

. . .

Now we arrive at the complicated part of the story.

I understand situations like the one I am about to tell you, and I know how strange they can get. I have spent more time in the belly of that beast than I can ever admit, and certainly not in print. I have never felt tempted to tell these stories in public—or even in private, for that matter, except on some moonless nights when I start feeling lonely and sentimental and strung out on combat or pussy or fear, like our old friend from Arkansas.

But tonight might be that kind of night, so what the hell?

. . .

I had never heard of Gail Palmer. I didn't need to hear about her, but I got a letter one day telling me that I was off, that I didn't really get it. I had written that the new feminist pornography was going to take over; she wrote arguing that I didn't understand the sex business, and she said she wanted to explain it to me. I didn't give a fuck.

I got several more letters from her, leading up to the infamous Hallmark card (which my defense attorneys later presented in court) that was full of lewd, tiny, very dense handwriting. The front of it said, "Sex is a dirty business." When you opened it up, it read: "But somebody has to do it." She took up every white surface inside the card with her little tense handwriting, telling me all the fun we could have—more fun than a barrel of monkeys in heat—and that she could really straighten me out about what I knew and thought about the sex business.

Meanwhile, she had also sent me a thick sheaf of press clippings and two films. In one, she is wearing a bodysuit and skipping rope in a high office building, looking out on what appears to be Long Beach Harbor. While she is skipping rope, she is singing to her own little song, repeating the stanzas once or twice:

> *Porno queen, porno queen*
> *It's not a seamy scene*
> *Porno queen, porno queen*
> *You think that sounds funny?*
> *Then why am I*
> *Making so much money?*

It was sickening. She thought it was a very sexy come-on and that she was irresistible, but she was wrong.

I got another letter not long afterward, telling me she would be in town in February and would be staying at the Stonebridge Inn in Snowmass, and that she wanted to get together with me. Her presumption was as telling as the rest of it. I had a lot of sex-film girls coming on to me during that period. A lot of people had noticed what I had done for girls like Bambi and Jo Ann at the O'Farrell. I was a favorite there—I was the people's Night Manager.

I didn't think much about Gail Palmer's upcoming visit. But Deborah, my majordomo, put it on the calendar, just in pencil—I guess she thought I wasn't having enough fun. Which could have been true, but Gail Palmer didn't fit the bill; I had no interest in her—a big, hefty hustler—or in her side of the story.

. . .

On the night of Georgetown vs. Syracuse—a big basketball game—Tim Charles, an old friend and a Georgetown fan, came over to watch the game and to fix my Macintosh amplifier. There were two exterior fuses on the back of the amp, and I somehow knew, or sensed, that there was a third interior fuse, which Tim did not believe. He refused to give up the idea that he knew better, so he took the amp apart on the kitchen floor, like a watch all in pieces. Semmes Luckett, the grandson of the great Confederate Admiral Rafael Semmes, was also here—he was here all the time.

I was in a work frenzy, still trying to finish *Songs of the Doomed,* which had recently been interrupted by Floyd Watkins and the giant porcupine. Cat, my assistant from the University of Florida, was here as well. We had the whole book spread out on the living room table. Cat was in charge of keeping the three manuscript copies identical—they changed every day, and the changes had to be transferred to the other two. I was not plotting to seize her, but I was thinking that later we could go in the hot tub together and have some fun. I had just finished an article for some women's magazine, like *Elle*—it was sort of a celebratory moment. I wanted to clear the house and unwind for a night.

There are some subtle details in this story that you have to appreciate to understand what happened. I wanted to watch the Georgetown game—I would have watched it anyway with just Cat; she was fun to watch sports with because she would bet—but then Tim or Semmes brought up the fact that the Grammys were coming on after the game; Jimmy Buffett was going to be on and they wanted to watch it. I didn't want to watch the fucking Grammys and did not plan to.

Meanwhile, the amplifier was still in pieces on the floor. It was not going to get fixed until Tim figured out that there was an internal fuse, which was very deep in the middle. I knew that, Tim did not, and Semmes didn't care. Semmes was drinking a lot of beer;

he had been planning to go into town—he wanted to go dancing. Tim was eventually going home to dinner and his wife, Carol Ann.

The game was very good—a two-point game. Georgetown won. I was waiting for them to get the fuck out. I think we were smoking some weed. I was ready to let my hair down, but not with them around. Cat may have known what I was thinking—we hadn't planned anything, but she probably understood it.

Tim was getting cranked up, fixated on the fucking machinery, and Semmes was getting sloppy drunk and starting to sink into the winged chair, slumped over. Semmes was not a fun drunk; he was constantly worried about his fucking probation. In my desperation, I looked up at the calendar (maybe I remembered her pending visit) and saw the note Deborah had written: "Gail Palmer . . ." It was just a quick scan—then, CLICK. I thought for a minute how Semmes had been complaining that the women in Aspen all eat shit—just a bunch of whores—nobody to go dancing with. He was a dancing fool.

It seemed like a solution, and before I thought it all the way through, I said, "Semmes, I got a solution to your fucking problem." He had started to look like he might be discouraged over the fact that he couldn't get a date. I was trying to push him out, edge him out, encourage him out.

He didn't jump right on it, but I insisted. *I've got a date for you! This is a really hot, wild woman . . .* I had the file. I showed him the press clippings. I was doing a real selling job on her—I said, "You just call her and she'll be your date. She'll whoop it up with you. I'll even pay for the drinks."

I convinced him to go in the other room and call the Witness. I could hear him talking, but I didn't care to hear what he was saying. As far as I was concerned, he was leaving to go meet her. Suddenly he appeared at the kitchen door, leaving the phone in the living room, and said: "She wants to meet you. She wants to meet *you* before we go dancing."

To resolve it took three different calls and three visits from Semmes to the kitchen. The Witness wanted to meet me, and I was really unhappy about that. On Semmes's second trip to the kitchen, I finally said, "Oh fuck, all right Semmes, you tell her to get in a cab and come here but tell the cab to wait."

She wouldn't agree to the date without meeting me, and it pissed me off. When Semmes came back in the kitchen for the third time and said, "She wants to know if she can bring her husband," I said, "Fuck no! Absolutely not. Not even for a drive-by." It took half an hour more of dickering and fucking around before she accepted that.

I could see Semmes had a weird setup coming with a husband in the picture. She wanted an interview with me—she wanted to talk to me about the sex business. She thought of herself as the Ralph Nader of the sex business, and she wanted to form a partnership with me and put out a line of sex toys—perhaps a high-quality line of dildos. I wanted no part of that, of course; I had no need, no interest, and my experience with her up to that point made her nothing but a negative, dishonest face. I can see now, telling this story, that I lost control of it little by little.

. . .

About twenty minutes later, there was a knock on the door. I had arranged with Semmes—out of laziness, I guess—that he could bring her into the kitchen and I would shake hands with her, and then he was taking her off dancing. I even gave him money . . . and that is where we lost it.

I stood up and said "Hello" to the Witness, and she began babbling with all sorts of questions she wanted to ask me: "What's your sex life like? What do you think of fever-fresh nightgowns?" Gibberish and bullshit, which I wanted no part of. "Quiet. Quiet. Be QUIET!" I said. I stressed that to Semmes, too: "She has to be quiet here." Semmes wanted to continue watching the Grammys, and somehow the Witness ended up sitting in the armchair—just to watch the Grammys.

I kept her quiet for a while: If she started to talk, I was harsh with her—barking "Shut up." During commercials, she would start babbling and pestering me. When she continued to ask me about my sex life, I made her read *Screwjack* out loud: "All right," I said, "you're curious? Here's a story I just wrote."

She never finished *Screwjack*; it really disturbed her. I said, "What's wrong with you? Keep going. Can't you read?" She read about half of it, and said, "Wow. What the shit is this? What kind of a pervert . . . " It got to her, directly, but I forced her to continue. I knew that book would tell her something, and I could tell she learned from the experience. She was not as loud afterward. Meanwhile, we were waiting for Buffett to come on, and I was getting very edgy.

It is true that the night may have been a little boring; it was boring to me. Up to that point all kinds of yo-yos and nymphomaniacs and fiends with plenty of dope to lay out had visited my home. I have had assholes of serious magnitude, including senators, in my house. I should make a list of the most horrible assholes ever to visit . . . but if I did, Gail would not be at the top of that list. She was a blemish, even on the sex trade.

We were stuck in the Grammys, and I was stuck with her. Semmes was irresponsible, and I was full of annoyance—as I would be with any loud stranger that somebody else brings into my kitchen. The Witness was hard to insult; she was dumb and also professionally inured from the sex business to caring what people really thought or felt. The triple-X brand will make you a little thick-skinned after a while, like an armadillo. Maybe I'm like that.

It is a mystery why it bothered me, but this woman also had no sense of humor. She was the unwanted stranger; that was her position in the room. I didn't say more than ten words to her— including "Be quiet." I was damn careful to keep people and things between us. I may have shaken her hand, but that was it. I remember telling the *Aspen Times* later that I could not even have imagined having her in the hot tub with me (as she alleged I tried to), because she would have displaced too much water.

The basketball game had been interesting. The Grammys were not. This irritant had been introduced into the social fabric, but I was as much of a Southern gentleman as I could be. I knew what I was eventually going to do that night, but it was not going to be with this woman. The only question was how soon I could get her out.

I kept trying to get her away from the phone in the office—she was constantly leaving the room to call her husband "in private." I had appointed Semmes to watch her, but Semmes failed; I'm never going to forgive Semmes for this. It was an utter failure of a performance, as a friend and a protector. I don't blame Tim, but he could see weird shit brewing. Tim read the situation and saw it was like a game of musical chairs.

. . .

My support system fell apart when those swine left me alone with the Witness. When Semmes got up, I said, "Goddamnit, this is your date, what are you doing? What do you mean you're leaving?" but he just got up and left. He'd been on the nod for a long time. Tim, who had failed to fix the amplifier, was also planning to leave. I said, "Tim, you gotta take this woman somewhere. You gotta take her . . ." But he couldn't; "No no no," he said, "Carol Ann would kill me." That was true, of course—I had meant for him to give her a ride to the Tavern. I couldn't take her anywhere. She was very pushy, butting into other people's conversations and assuming they were enjoying her gibberish—she was almost professional in that way. You might have thought she had done this kind of work before. She was a little bit like a cop.

Later, she described to the cops how she knew we were dope fiends because we were all asking her, "Are you sure you're not a cop?" I didn't really *think* she was a cop . . . that is how stupid I was. I thought she was just one more dingbat, one more groupie who was unusually determined.

. . .

I had been making cranberry and tequila, because the margarita mix had run out. I was in that kind of mood. *Let's all have a few margaritas.* And she—that sot—she belted them down. We all did, no doubt; that's what it was all about. Some margaritas to celebrate. . . . We were on about the third jug in the blender, or fourth jug, or fifth perhaps, when we switched to cranberry juice, and she had been getting louder and more randy. She was making open cracks to Cat, asking: "Who are you to Hunter?" She grabbed me and said, "Who's this girl? Why is that other girl here? We don't need her around."

Shortly after Tim left, I reached for the phone and told the Witness, "Let's call a goddamn taxi for you." As I dialed the "T"—in 925-TAXI—she rushed over, knocking the phone down, and cut me off. It was a quick, startling movement. She leaped, surprisingly fast for a rhino, from five or six feet away.

"Oh no, don't let it end like this," she pleaded. "You were always my hero." I was curt with her; she had no business here. I had not encouraged her in any way.

I tried to call for the taxi a second time. She immediately reached over, a long reach, with her hairy tentacle of an arm to hang up the phone, and I was shocked that anybody would dare to do that. I screamed at her: "Get the fuck away!" and I think Cat actually restrained her. That was the second rush; she made three rushes on the phone. On this second one, the cabbie heard a bit of the ruckus. Later, we had to get him to testify, and it was very tricky—to establish that I did call and that she had cut it off.

She was warned twice, and then she had a pretty clear shot at me on the third attempt. I was trying desperately to get through to the taxi company. I could see her coming as I began to call again; this time I had just started to stand up. As she came rushing at me, her hip crashed into the cutting board and the cranberry juice fell onto the tile floor. The juice bottle went bouncing around and inter- fered with her rush. I was cursing her: "You goddamn idiot, what the fuck are you doing?" I was trying to get up, and she came at me then, angry, very angry now—she had hurt herself, hitting the cut- ting board.

I remembered the "prefrontal lift," which is my most dependable way of ending an argument, particularly when somebody is coming at you. In this move you hit them in both shoulders with the heels of your hands, using a lifting motion. She was coming at me with speed, so I applied a little force. . . . Considerable motion was employed. Usually the attacker helps you a lot, because you can't do a prefrontal lift on anybody who's not coming at you. It doesn't work and looks like a fag punch.

The prefrontal lift stopped her, although her feet were still mov- ing, and she went back on her large butt with a kind of THUMP and ended up sitting on the floor against the refrigerator. I was satisfied. I had been cursing her for an hour. Everything she did was rotten;

her questions were stupid. "I want you out of here," I said. There was never any pretense about this. She had a hideous penchant for coming in my area, hassling me, and she was very stupid. Big, stupid, and I was never entirely sure whether she had her own police agenda or not.

. . .

It was five days later at about ten o'clock in the morning when my neighbor appeared outside, right below the kitchen window. He was very agitated, and he looked like he had come in a hurry. I walked out and said, "Hi, come on it. Have a beer." He said, "No, I can't do that now." He had left his car running. He seemed agitated and afraid of me. He was parked far away from where he usually did, with his car almost backed into the bushes.

"They're going to come and search your house," he said. I walked down the driveway, to get closer to him, and he mumbled, "Those bastards are . . . they're coming out here . . . they're gonna come get you with a search warrant." I couldn't put it together, so I asked, "What crime? What for? What are you talking about?"

The Night Manager, 1985
(Michael Nichols / Magnum Photos)

Seize the Night

The night does not belong to Michelob; the night belongs to Hunter Stockton Thompson.
                                    —Curtis Wilkie, *The Boston Globe*

The Night Manager

The noonday flight out of Denver is running late today, another brainless jam-up on the runways at Stapleton International—but no matter. The passengers are mainly commercial people—harried-looking middle-aged businessmen wearing blue shirts with white collars and studying Xerox copies of quarterly sales reports.

Across the aisle from me is a rumpled-looking potbellied wretch who looks like Willy Loman, slumped in his seat like two bags of rock salt and drinking Diet Coke. He is reading the money section of *USA Today*.

In front of me are two giddy young boys wearing matching Walkman machines with built-in mikes that allow them to talk to each other through the headphones. They have removed the armrest between them and are now necking shamelessly and bitching occasionally at the stewardess about the lateness of our arrival. . . . The San Francisco airport is closed by violent weather and we are into a long holding pattern, which will cause them to miss an important business appointment. . . .

So What? We are all businessmen these days. Ray Stevens said it twenty years ago—"Take care of business, Mr. Businessman."

. . .

The bell rang for me last night—about 13 hours ago, in fact, and now I am slumped and jittery like some kind of lost polar bear across two first-class seats on UAL #70, from Denver to San Francisco, and my business on this trip is definitely not the kind of all-American nuts-and-bolts hokum that I feel like sharing with my fellow businessmen across the aisle.

There is not a bull market for raw sex, amyl nitrites, and double-ended Greek dildos in the friendly skies of United.

Some people sell U-joints and others are in the meat service and human commodity business. But I have nothing in common with these people.

I am in the sex racket, which is worth about $10 billion a year on anybody's computer—and I am flying to San Francisco to take on the whole city government; the mayor, the D.A., and the police chief.

(And now into SF again—the sleek green hills and the wretched white salt flats beyond the Berkeley Hills, etc.)

The Mitchell Brothers—Jim and Artie—will be waiting for me at the gate, along with my personal road manager, Jeff Armstrong, who is also executive vice president for The Mitchell Brothers Film Group.

These people drive big Mercedes-Benz sedans, the kind of cars favored by Josef Mengele and Ed Meese.

This is the fast lane, folks . . . and some of us like it here.

. . .

Whoops. We are out of gas now, dropping into Fresno like a falling rock—full flaps, reverse engines, then into full glide.

The pilot comes on the intercom and blames "crosswinds at SF International." Bullshit. This is just another routine air-traffic control emergency. Free enterprise—a quick little taste of what's coming in the next four years.

The passengers whine and moan, but nobody except me gets off in Fresno to make a phone call—even though the ramp sergeant makes a special effort to open a door.

Like sheep—and when I come back on the plane with a *Chronicle,* they turn their eyes away, shunning me. . . .

Finally the salesman sitting next to me asks if he can borrow the business section.

Why not? We are all businessmen these days. I am on my way to SF to market a rare porno film, and I am three hours late for a crucial screening with the Mitchell Brothers at their embattled headquarters on O'Farrell Street. The driver is waiting for me at the airport with an armored car and two fat young sluts from Korea.

. . .

We were somewhere on a main street in San Francisco, headed for the waterfront, when a woman walked directly in front of the car on her way across the street. I felt myself seizing up, unable to speak—until Maria poked my leg and whispered urgently: "Oh my god, Hunter, look at that beautiful spine!"

I was looking. We were halted for a red light, and the woman was walking briskly, also toward the waterfront, and now we were both watching her with unblinking eyes, not moving the car until some bastard honked and called me a *shithead.* . . . I honked my own horn and signaled as if I were stalled, waving him to come around me in the other lane, because I was helpless.

Just then the girl with the beautiful spine paused to examine what appeared to be a menu in the window of Vanessi's, or perhaps the glass tank filled with seawater and large unhappy lobsters. Wonderful, I thought. I knew Vanessi's well—and if this spine of a princess was going in there for dinner, so were we. I honked again, just to crank up the traffic confusion, and waved three more cars around me.

"You dirty motherfucker!" a well-dressed man screamed at me as he passed. "Eat shit and die!" He zoomed his huge SUV into low and roared away down the hill. But the other traffic had quickly adjusted to the problem and now ignored me, as if I were some kind of goofy construction project, leaving me in peace to keep an eye on this woman. It was good karma at the right moment, and I told Maria to make a note of it. I was feeling warm all over. "You asshole," she said. "Get this car started! She is moving again. She is crossing Broadway and picking up speed, almost running. God, look at that spine."

"Don't worry," I told her, reaching across the seat to grasp her thigh. "Hot damn, sweetie, what do you want to do with her?"

"*Nothing* yet," she hissed. "I just want to *look* at her."

Indeed. It was just before dusk on Wednesday. The sun was still bright, the Bay was mildly choppy, and we were mercifully unburdened with appointments or professional responsibilities at the time. The day was a brand-new canvas. *Carpe diem.*

. . .

The Goldstein situation developed very quickly, with no warning at all, about halfway through lunch at Pier 23 on a gray afternoon in mid-April, just a few days before the trial was set to begin. We had come through the general hysteria surrounding the "world premiere" on *The Grafenberg Spot,* and no disasters had happened. No scandals had erupted, nobody had been arrested, no personal or professional tragedies of any kind. I had lost my temper in public a few times and been rude to the local press, but so what? It was not my job to be nice. I was, after all, the Night Manager of the most notorious live sex theater in America, and my job was to keep it running. It was a strange obligation that I had somehow taken on, for good or ill, and if I failed, we might all go to jail.

Certainly the Mitchell Brothers would go, and the theater would probably be padlocked and all the fixtures sold to pay off the fines and the court costs. The lawyers painted a grim picture of disgrace, despair, and total unemployment for everybody, including me. Our backs were all to the wall, they said; Mayor Dianne Feinstein, now a senator, was full of hate and not in a mood to compromise. She had been trying to close the O'Farrell for most of her ten years in politics, and now she had everybody from Ed Meese and God to Militant Feminists and the president of the United States on her side. The deal was about to go down, they said. No more lap dancing in San Francisco, and never mind the busloads of Japs.

It was about this time, less than a week before the trial, that Al Goldstein arrived in town for a personal screening of the new film. It was bad timing, but there was no cure for it. Al is one of the certified big boys in the sex racket. He is the publisher of *Screw,* the film critic for *Penthouse,* and perhaps the one man in America whose opinion can make or break a new sex film. *Penthouse* alone sells 4 million copies a month, at $2.95 each, and the prevailing retail price for X-rated videocassettes is $69.95.

The wholesale net to the producer is about half that, or something like $3.5 million on sales of 100,000 in the first year—which is no big trick, with the combined endorsement of *Penthouse, Screw,* and Al Goldstein. So if only one percent of the people who buy *Penthouse* buy an X-rated videocassette that comes highly recommended by the magazine, the wholesale gross is going to be $1.5 million, before rentals. The retail gross will be about twice that—on a total investment of $100,000 or so in production costs and another $100,000 for promotion.

That is not bad money for a product that any three bartenders from St. Louis and their girlfriends can put together in a roadside motel across the river in Memphis. There is no shortage of raw talent in the industry, and posing naked in front of a camera is becoming more and more respectable. The line between Joan Collins and Marilyn Chambers is becoming very hazy. Not everybody on the street these days can tell you the difference between Jane Fonda in leotards and Vanessa Williams in chains.

I can. But that is a different matter, and it will take a while to explain it. We are dealing, here, with a genuinely odd contradiction in the social fabric. At a time when not only the new attorney general of the United States, and the president of the United States, and the president's wife, and the president's favorite minister, along with the Moral Majority and the Militant Feminists and the *TV Guide* and also the surly fat brute of a manager at the 7-Eleven store in Vernal, Utah, who refused to sell me a copy of *Playboy* at any price & then threatened to have me arrested when I asked why . . .

. . . At a time when all of these powerful people and huge institutions and legions of vicious dingbats who don't need sleep are working overtime to weed out and crush the last remnants of the "Sexual Revolution" that was said to grip the nation in the 1960s and '70s . . . And at a time when they appear to be making serious public progress with their crusade.

This is also a time of growth, vigor, and profit for the American sex industry. Business has never been better. A wino from Texas made a fortune selling Ben-Wa balls; he is now a multimillionaire and listed in big-time money magazines. He shuns publicity and lives alone in the desert. Women write him letters, but he has never had much luck with them. He has no friends and he will never have any heirs, but he is rich and getting richer. One of his agents who recently visited him said he was "weirder than Howard Hughes."

Most of these stories never get out. Nobody knows, for instance, who holds the patent on the penis-shaped, soft-plastic vibrator that sells for $9.95 in drugstores all over the world. There are stores in San Francisco that sell a hundred of those things every day. When I asked the night clerk at Frenchy's in San Francisco who had the dildo concession, who collected the royalties, he said it was an elderly Negro gentleman from Los Angeles. "We've known him for years," he said, "but he never mentioned the patent. He comes by every week in a green Mercedes van and drops off five or six cases of dildos—sometimes nine or ten. He's a good man to do business with. We don't know him at all."

That is how it works in the sex business, which is generally estimated—without much argument from anybody connected with the business, pro or con—to be worth between eight billion and ten billion dollars a year in America. The true figures are probably much higher, but only the IRS really cares. Ten billion dollars a year would just about equal the combined earnings of Coca-Cola, Hershey, and McDonald's.

. . .

Most nights are slow in the politics business, but the night we flogged Al Goldstein on the wet rug floor off the Ultra-Room was not one of them. It was a fast and cruel situation, a major problem for the Night Manager. It was the first real test of my crisis-management skills, and I handled it in my own way.

The immediate results were ugly. It was so bad that there were not even any rumors on the street the next day. Any high-style fracas at the O'Farrell Theatre will normally rate at least a colorful slap from Herb Caen, or at least a few warning calls from the District Attorney's office—but in this case, there was nothing. Nobody wanted any part of it, including me.

But I was blamed, the next morning, for everything that happened, from the shame of the flogging, to the presence of innocent bystanders, to a million-dollar loss on the books of The Mitchell Brothers Film Group.

My job was in jeopardy and my reputation as a "blue" political consultant was called into serious question.

But not for long. It took about 44 days, as usual, for the truth to finally come out—and in the meantime, life got weirder and weirder. I was arrested seven times in six weeks—or at least charged, or accused, or somehow involved with police and courts and lawyers so constantly that it began to seem like my life.

And it seemed almost normal, for a while. Going to court was part of my daily routine. At one point I had to appear in the dock twice in 72 hours and take a savage public beating in the national press, simply because the Judge had changed his mind.

"That's impossible," I told my lawyer Michael Stepanian. "The judge *cannot* change his mind. He would be overruled on appeal." Which proved to be true.

A week or so later the police stole my paddle-tennis racquets—causing me to forfeit my challenge for the championship of the West Coast—and then subpoenaed me to testify against a nonexistent burglar in exchange for giving my racquets back.

That case is still pending, along with a civil complaint from the neighbors about "beatings and screaming."

The Sausalito police are also still holding my personally engraved Feinwerkbau brand Olympic championship air pistol—the most accurate weapon, at 10 meters, that I've ever held in my hand. It was one of those extremely Rare pistols that would shoot exactly where you pointed it, and it didn't really matter who you were. Women and children who had never aimed a pistol at anything could pick up the Feinwerkbau and hit a dime at 15 feet. Beyond that range, or in a wind on the end of a long bamboo pole off the balcony, we would use slightly larger targets, about the size of a quarter, which were tin buttons showing a likeness of San Francisco Mayor Dianne Feinstein with eight tits, like the wolf mother of Rome.

The Mitchell Brothers had printed up 10,000 of these—for some reason that I never quite understood—in the months of angst and fear and hellish legal strife before the trial. I still have about 1,000 of them, and there are maybe another 2,000 in the bushes and on the huge flat roof of Nunzio Alioto's house at the entrance to Sausalito. Nunzio, a close relative of former San Francisco mayor Joe Alioto, was one of my closest neighbors in Sausalito. He was right below me, the next stop down on the tramway. We lived on a very steep cliff, looking out on San Francisco Bay.

I am Lono

(Lalia Nabulsi)

The apartment is gone now, so we can talk about it freely. It will never again be for rent. The reasons for this are complex, and it is not likely that they will ever be made totally clear—but I like to think that I lived there in a style that honored the true spirit of the place, that if the redwood beams and sliding glass walls and the bamboo stools in my Tiki bar could vote for president, that they would vote for me.

Maybe not, but I feel pretty confident about this. Every once in a while you run across a place that was built in a certain spirit, and even the walls understand that it was meant to be used that way.

There were fires and there was breakage. We had a homemade waterfall in the oak trees out in front of the Tiki bar, and we wandered around naked half the time, drinking green chartreuse and smoking lethal Krakatoa cigarettes, and I built a world-class shooting range that hung in midair from an elegant 22-foot rod off the balcony looking out on Angel Island and Alcatraz.

My attorney called it "the best room in the world."

16 Alexander

July 31, 1985
Owl Farm
To: Michael Stepanian, Esq.
819 Eddy Street
San Francisco, CA 94109

Dear Michael,

The (enc.) letters from Judith to your new client, Ms. Laryce Sullivan, at 16 Alexander Ave. in Sausalito, where I lived with Maria, should give us a nice handle on a $33 million slander suit—against Judith and her quarrelsome husband Norvin, a thus-far unindicted co-conspirator, and the computer company that brought them up here from Orange County and caused them to live in a situation (16 Alexander) that they were unable to handle personally and which led them to eventually file a lawsuit (against Ms. Sullivan) that names me in a provably false, wrong, hurtful, and personally (and financially) troublesome characterization—i.e.: "Beatings and screaming . . ."

What Beatings? You were there—you met Jacques (the "husband") in the hallway when you were trying to beat down my door.

In any case, my new book—*The Night Manager*—will be cast in a shadow of ugliness by these charges—which Judith and Norvin have filed, repeat "filed."

So in addition to stealing my air pistol and my binoculars and my jock-straps and my custom-built SORBA paddle-tennis racquets and my Job-Related video tapes and two or three packs of my Dunhills on some cheap Nazi scam that nobody believes— now the fuckers want to bash me in civil court (and the public prints) for beating Maria—night after night while the neighbors fled in terror.

Whoops—a bit of a creative outburst there. I couldn't resist. The elegant hum of that title. A smart writer could have fun with a notion like that.

Why not me?

Okay—back to business. I am deep in debt to you and Joe and Tanya and Patty and everybody else who suffered through the hellbroth of lost sleep and character-testing that accompanied my recent attempt to come down from the mountains and live even vaguely like a normal, middle-aged, middle-class, criminally inclined smart urban male with a job (and a few habits— okay. Ask Nancy for details here . . .).

It was a disaster. We (you and me) had enjoyed no legal or even human congress for many years (for reasons of sloth and dumbness, no doubt, but . . .).

Yeah. And I didn't even come to you with a case or a crime or a problem—except that I had, for reasons of my own, recently taken on the job as Night Manager of the weird and infamous O'Farrell Theatre—which happened to be right around the corner from your office, and also a nice, nice headquarters, a suitable place to invite my best and most trustworthy friends for a drink, from time to time.

(One thing we want to keep in mind about the Mitchell Brothers is that they were utterly dumbfounded by most of what I did while I was there—

They are good boys. And I kept them out of jail. The good Lord didn't make seesaws for nothing.)

My job, as I saw it in the beginning, was merely to interview the Brothers as part of a long-overdue assignment from *Playboy* on "feminist pornography"—which was beginning to bore me, by that time, and in fact the only reason I went to see the Mitchell Brothers was the chance that they might be interesting enough—for 48 hours—to sustain my interest in the Feminist porno story long enough for me to crank out the necessary 6,000 or 7,000 words.

Jesus Christ! That *is* how it all started. I was bored with the article after watching five or six triple-X films a day for most of the football season. . . . I became a connoisseur—a knowledgeable critic in the field; I compiled my own Top Ten list—and the Mitchell Brothers were not on it—which is one of the things I told Jim (the elder) when I called him one night in the autumn.

"You want to talk?" he said. "Good. We will talk for 48 hours. You will be our guest. Just get on a plane."

Well . . . shucks. You don't get many offers like that—48 straight hours, just for openers, eyeball-to-eyeball with the rotten Mitchell Brothers.

"We know who you are, Doc," he said. "Normally we don't give interviews—but in your case, we're going to allot 48 hours, because we hear you're a player."

I have all this on tape. I taped everything—from the first high-macho phone arrangements to our first berserk meeting at the San Francisco airport to broken bones and craziness and limousines full of naked women and relentless orgies at the Miyako Hotel—being rolled around the lobby on a baggage cart with people screaming somewhere behind me in the distance, far down the hall in the direction of my suite with the deep green water tub and the bamboo walls and strange women in the bathroom putting lipstick on their nipples. . . .

Whoops, again.

But so what? I may as well get this memo down somewhere—and why not to You?

Why indeed? A hideous streak of six (6) insanely complex legal confrontations—sudden war on all fronts: open container (work-related), Red Light (ditto), Maria crashes two National Rental cars at the Oakland airport, HST burglarized by Sausalito police, HST crushes three negroes on a ramp near the Hall of Justice . . . ugly financial claims; *après moi le déluge* . . . Getting to know Mr. Wrench, Boz Scaggs, and Diane Dodge . . . Insurance claims and driving school, constant Jeopardy. THE JUDGE HAS CHANGED HIS MIND.

Hundreds of hours, thousands of dollars, light-years of frantic attention . . .

Even Bondock was consulted: the best minds of our generation, tied in knots by the vagaries of an irresponsible jurisdiction. That is how I explained it to Joe Freitas—"You were once the D.A. in this town," I said to him, "which is all I need to know."

If Joe was still the D.A., I'd be doing 30 days of SWAP and he would be coming to visit me with the occasional bottle of Absinthe and asking around the office for Maria's phone number in Phoenix.

I warned you about liberals. . . .

It was a weird time. Not many people could have taken that series of shocks and come out of it thinking, "Yes, we are champions." When the Great Scorer comes to write against your name, he will ask my advice. . . .

And I will tell him about many things—no details will be spared; I owe you that. . . .

So I will tell him about Leonard Louie and how you had the insane balls to run me right between Andre's eyes on the night before the first trial and about the otherworldly madness that enveloped us when that giddy chink changed his mind . . .

. . . And about getting my $86 check back from the court

clerk in Sausalito, after my secretary had already plead guilty for me . . . and about the floating horror of that 15 mph red light violation in the midst of the drunk-crash nightmare. . . .

And the time when the cops stole my finely engraved air pistol because my neighbor, Al Green, complained.

Okay. I'll call you on this and other matters—and if in the meantime I happen to speak as I do, from time to time, with the Great Scorer—you can bet all three of your eyes that I am going to tell him how you ripped and pounded me out of my happy bed one morning at 16 Alexander and dragged me—and poor innocent Maria—out in a cold gray fog somewhere north of the Farallon Islands on a 15-foot Boston Whaler into known big shark waters with no radio and no flares and only one good rod and a dinky little 18-inch gaff—after tracking me down (or up, actually) in the raw dirt and dead limbs of my Tiki bar.

And how we prevailed, on the sea—how we caught a fine fish—when all the others had gone south to Pacifica that day— and how we then came to the profoundly high decision to run straight through that maniac crease in the breakers and into Bolinas harbor—because we were thirsty and tired and we had our elegant 16-pound salmon—and because I knew a man with the whiff who lived in a small wooden house that we could almost see from a mile or so out on the ocean.

The Great Scorer will like that story—and when he adds it in with the others, he will know that he is dealing with a warrior.

HST at work in Rio de Janeiro
(Robert Bone)

Okay. I don't want to get mushy here. All I did in the beginning was invite you over to my weird new office at the Theatre—which I knew you'd enjoy, and also because I figured that part of my new job as Night Manager was to keep these two sleazy, baldheaded bastards out of jail by making them so suddenly hip and respectable in the public prints that no judge in SF—not even a Nazi—would feel comfortable about putting them on trial in the eye of a media circus.

That strategy worked nicely. If I'd billed the Mitchells for my work as a media-political consultant, the tab would have run at least $400K net. I did my work well, and I'm proud of it.

Indeed—and history is rife with these horrors—that the foul and notorious Mitchell Brothers should soon go free like friendly neighborhood raccoons, while I the Night Manager would eventually be jailed and pilloried and denounced in the public prints and 3,900 other newspapers all over the nation for running the company car up the tailpipe of a slow-moving, left-drifting Pontiac on the Bayshore Freeway while driving back from the airport after pimping their new movie in L.A. all afternoon with moguls from the Pussycat Theatre chain—

—No, none of this seemed possible when I first came down from the mountain to take a job in the city and live among allegedly civilized people. It frankly never occurred to me that I would have any dealings with the Law—much less be arrested six times in three months—outside of my admittedly strange new duties as Night Manager of the O'Farrell.

I have made three appearances in traffic court in 34 years of driving fast cars in wild conditions all over the world from Kentucky to Hong Kong—and two of them happened in the space of three days, in Leonard Louie's court.

Teddible, teddible—as Ralph would say—and the scars have not yet healed. The judge has somehow made himself a partner in my settlement with the whiplash boys, and if I make one mistake on the road in the next three years, I will be slapped in the SF County Jail for six months.

Bad business. If there is any way we can ease off the menace of that "probation," we should do it. Our lives will be easier, and so will Leonard Louie's. NOBODY needs me in that jail. I have learned my lesson: Drive carefully; there are people out there who really don't like me, and if I give them any handle at all, they will use it, and they will flog me . . . and we have better wars to fight and more honorable ways to spill our blood in public.

Anyway—for Joe/FYI—Jim Mitchell assumes that his insurance company is "first" re: the whiplash boys.

I agree. I took the rap and I spent all night in jail—alone; I didn't know you'd gone to Washington—with two Nazi cops who called me "big boy."

It happened in the course of "my duties"—for the O'Farrell and also for *Playboy*.

So let's try to settle this insurance claim and get me off of this queasy "restitution" spike. Jim Mitchell is not going to quarrel if his insurance pays off the whiplash boys. Fair is fair. I was the Night Manager—and I was driving them back from the airport in the official Night Manager's car. Both of our insurance rates are already fucked, anyway—so let's not haggle about it. What is it worth to Leonard to get the "restitution" matter settled by October 18? . . .

. . . Everybody in the world seems to be after me for money now, and this would not be a good time to go belly up in public for small debts.

HUNTER

Where Were You When the Fun Stopped?

There was no laughter tonight, only the sounds of doom and death and failure—a relentless torrent of death signals: from the sheriff, in the mail, on the phone, in my kitchen, in the air, but mainly from Maria, who said she felt it very strongly and she understood exactly why I was feeling and thinking the way I did/do, but there was nothing she could do about it. She couldn't help herself. It was the death of fun, unreeling right in front of us, unraveling, withering, collapsing, draining away in the darkness like a handful of stolen mercury. Yep, the silver stuff goes suddenly, leaving only a glaze of poison on the skin.

September 11, 2001

It was just after dawn in Woody Creek, Colorado, when the first plane hit the World Trade Center in New York City on Tuesday morning, and as usual I was writing about sports. But not for long. Football suddenly seemed irrelevant compared to the scenes of destruction and utter devastation coming out of New York on TV.

Even ESPN was broadcasting war news. It was the worst disaster in the history of the United States, including Pearl Harbor, the San Francisco earthquake, and the Battle of Antietam in 1862, when 23,000 were slaughtered in one day.

The Battle of the World Trade Center lasted about 99 minutes and cost 20,000 lives in two hours (according to unofficial estimates as of midnight Tuesday). The final numbers, including those from the supposedly impregnable Pentagon, across the Potomac River from Washington, likely will be higher. Anything that kills 300 trained firefighters in two hours is a world-class disaster.

And it was not even Bombs that caused this massive damage. No nuclear missiles were launched from any foreign soil, no enemy bombers flew over New York and Washington to rain death on innocent Americans. No. It was four commercial jetliners.

They were the first flights of the day from American and United Airlines, piloted by skilled and loyal U.S. citizens, and there was nothing suspicious about them when they took off from Newark, N.J., Dulles in D.C., and Logan in Boston on routine cross-country flights to the West Coast with fully loaded fuel tanks—which would soon explode on impact and utterly destroy the world-famous Twin Towers of downtown Manhattan's World Trade Center. Boom! Boom! Just like that.

The towers are gone now, reduced to bloody rubble, along with all hopes for Peace in Our Time, in the United States or any other country. Make no mistake about it: We are At War now—with somebody—and we will stay At War with that mysterious Enemy for the rest of our lives.

It will be a Religious War, a sort of Christian Jihad, fueled by religious hatred and led by merciless fanatics on both sides. It will be guerilla warfare on a global scale, with no front lines and no identifiable enemy. Osama bin Laden may be a primitive "figurehead"—or even dead, for all we know—but whoever put those All-American jet planes loaded with All-American fuel into the Twin Towers and the Pentagon did it with chilling precision and accuracy. The second one was a dead-on bull's-eye. Straight into the middle of the skyscraper.

Nothing—not even George Bush's $350 billion "Star Wars" missile defense system—could have prevented Tuesday's attack, and it cost next to nothing to pull off. Fewer than 20 unarmed Suicide soldiers from some apparently primitive country somewhere on the other side of the world took out the World Trade Center and half the Pentagon with three quick and costless strikes on one day. The efficiency of it was terrifying.

We are going to punish somebody for this attack, but just who or what will be blown to smithereens for it is hard to say. Maybe Afghanistan, maybe Pakistan or Iraq, or possibly all three at once. Who knows? Not even the Generals in what remains of the Pentagon or the New York papers calling for WAR seem to know who did it or where to look for them.

This is going to be a very expensive war, and Victory is not guaranteed—for anyone, and certainly not for anyone as baffled as George W. Bush. All he knows is that his father started the war a long time ago, and that he, the goofy child-President, has been chosen by Fate and the global Oil industry to finish it Now. He will declare a National Security Emergency and clamp down Hard on Everybody, no matter where they live or why. If the guilty won't hold up their hands and confess, he and the Generals will ferret them out by force.

Good luck. He is in for a profoundly difficult job—armed as he is with no credible Military Intelligence, no witnesses, and only the ghost of bin Laden to blame for the tragedy.

OK. It is 24 hours later now, and we are not getting much information about the Five Ws of this thing.

The numbers out of the Pentagon are baffling, as if Military Censorship has already been imposed on the media. It is ominous. The only news on TV comes from weeping victims and ignorant speculators.

The lid is on. Loose Lips Sink Ships. Don't say anything that might give aid to The Enemy.

September 12, 2001

Dr. Thompson and Col. Depp take delivery of a matched set of rare .454 Casull
Magnums—at a gun store somewhere in the Rocky Mountains, Summer 1997
(Deborah Fuller)

. . .

Johnny Depp called me from France on Sunday night and asked what
I knew about Osama bin Laden.

"Nothing," I said. "Nothing at all. He is a ghost, for all I know.
Why do you ask?"

"Because I'm terrified of him," he said. "All of France is terrified. . . .
I freaked out and rushed to the airport, but when I got there my flight
was canceled. All flights to the U.S. were canceled. People went crazy
with fear."

"Join the club," I told him. "Almost everybody went crazy over
here."

"Never mind that," he said. "Who won the Jets–Colts game?"

"There *was* no game," I said. "All sports were canceled in this
country—even *Monday Night Football.*"

"No!" he said. "That's impossible! I've never known a Monday
night without a game on TV. What is the stock market doing?"

"Nothing yet," I said. "It's been closed for six days."

"Ye gods," he muttered. "No stock market, no football—this is
Serious."

Just then I heard the lock on my gas tank rattling, so I rushed outside with a shotgun and fired both barrels into the darkness. Poachers!
I thought. Blow their heads off! This is War! So I fired another blast in
the general direction of the gas pump, then I went inside to reload.

"Why are you shooting?" my assistant Anita screamed at me.
"What are you shooting at?"

"The enemy," I said gruffly. "He is down there stealing our gasoline."

"Nonsense," she said. "That tank has been empty since June. You
probably killed a peacock."

At dawn I went down to the tank and found the gas hose shredded
by birdshot and two peacocks dead.

So what? I thought. What is more important right now—my precious gasoline or the lives of some silly birds?

Indeed, but the New York Stock Exchange opened Monday morning, so I have to get a grip on something solid. The Other Shoe is
about to drop, and it might be extremely heavy. The time has come to
be strong. The fat is in the fire. Who knows what will happen now?

Not me, buster. That's why I live out here in the mountains with a flag on my porch and loud Wagner music blaring out of my speakers. I feel lucky, and I have plenty of ammunition. That is God's will, they say, and that is also why I shoot into the darkness at anything that moves. Sooner or later, I will hit something Evil and feel no Guilt. It might be Osama bin Laden. Who knows? And where is Adolf Hitler, now that we finally need him? It is bad business to go into War without a target.

In times like these, when the War drums roll and the bugles howl for blood, I think of Vince Lombardi, and I wonder how he would handle it. . . . Good old Vince. He was a zealot for Victory at all costs, and his hunger for it was pure—or that's what he said and what his legend tells us, but it is worth noting that he is not even in the top 20 in career victories.

We are At War now, according to President Bush, and I take him at his word. He also says this War might last for "a very long time."

Generals and military scholars will tell you that 8 or 10 years is actually not such a long time in the span of human history—which is no doubt true—but history also tells us that 10 years of martial law and a wartime economy are going to feel like a Lifetime to people who are in their twenties today. The poor bastards of what will forever be known as Generation Z are doomed to be the first generation of Americans who will grow up with a lower standard of living than their parents enjoyed.

That is extremely heavy news, and it will take a while for it to sink in. The 22 babies born in New York City while the World Trade Center burned will never know what they missed. The last half of the 20th Century will seem like a wild party for rich kids, compared to what's coming now. The party's over, folks. The time has come for loyal Americans to Sacrifice . . . Sacrifice . . . Sacrifice. That is the new buzzword in Washington. But what it means is not entirely clear.

Winston Churchill said, "The first casualty of War is always Truth." Churchill also said, "In wartime, Truth is so precious that she should always be attended by a bodyguard of Lies."

That wisdom will not be much comfort to babies born last week. The first news they get in this world will be News subjected to Military Censorship. That is a given in wartime, along with massive campaigns of deliberately planted "Dis-information." That is routine behavior in Wartime—for all countries and all combatants—and it makes life difficult for people who value real news. Count on it. That is what Churchill meant when he talked about Truth being the first casualty of War.

In this case, however, the next casualty was Football. All games were canceled last week. And that has Never happened to the NFL. Never. That gives us a hint about the Magnitude of this War. Terrorists don't wear uniforms, and they play by inscrutable rules—The Rules of World War III, which has already begun.

So get ready for it, folks. Buckle up and watch your backs at all times. That is why they call it "Terrorism."

September 19, 2001

Big Sur, editorial conference, 1971

(Annie Leibovitz)

Speedism

"Hi, Mr. Thompson. My name is Wendy _____ from Suzuki, and I want more than anything else in the world to give you a brand-new Suzuki _____, which has a top speed of 200 mph [chuckle]. Yeah, I thought that would interest you [giggle]. Call me anytime at _____."

How long, O Lord, how long? Some people wait all their lives for a telephone call like that. But not me. I get them constantly, and on some nights I ask myself, Why?

Rules for Driving Fast

Speedism is the most recently identified Disease that curses modern Man. Yesterday's murdering speed freak is today's helpless victim of "Speedism." This is a Big Leap that has taken a long time to achieve. It is a milestone in medical history & many unsung heroes have sacrificed themselves for it, including Sid Vicious and the actor Richard Pryor, who set himself on fire while researching the Speedism virus.

This is wonderful news. A whole generation of coke fiends can rest easy now: They were not common addicts & criminals. No. They were helpless Victims of a highly contagious Virus, *Speedata Viruuseum*. The Disease is Debilitating, Demoralizing & Incurable, leaving the victim wracked with pain & utterly helpless for 6–9 months at a time.

Speedism can be Fatal when mixed with high-speed automobiles & whiskey. It is wrong & I condemn it, but some dingbats will do it anyway. . . . And not All will survive, but so what?

For the others, the Living, here are some basic rules.

No. 1—Make sure yr. car is Functioning on all Mechanical & Electrical levels. Do not go out on *any* road to drive Fast unless all yr. exterior lights are working perfectly.

There is only failure & jail very soon for anybody who tries to drive fast with one headlight or a broken red taillight. This is automatic, unarguable *Probable Cause* for a cop to pull you over & check everything in yr. car. You do not want to give them Probable Cause. Check yr. lights, gas gauge, & tire pressure before you drive Anywhere.

No. 2—Get familiar with the Brake pressures on yr. machine before you drive any faster than 10 mph. A brake drum that locks up the instant you touch the pedal will throw you sideways off the road & put you into a fatal eggbeater, which means you will Go To Trial if it happens. Be *very* aware of yr. brakes.

No. 3—Have no *small* wrecks. If you are going to loop out & hit something, *hit it hard*. Never mind that old-school Physics bullshit about the Irresistible Force & the Immoveable Object. The main rule of the Highway is that Some Objects are More Moveable than Others. This occurs, for instance, when a speeding car goes straight through a plywood billboard, but not when one goes through a concrete wall. In most cases, the car going fastest sustains less damage than the slower-moving vehicle.

A Small Wreck is almost always both Costly and Embarrassing. I talked to a man tonight who said he had been demoted from Headwaiter to Salad Boy when he had a small wreck in the restaurant's parking lot and lost all respect from his fellow workers. "They laughed at me & called me an Ass," he said. "I should have hit the fucker at seventy-five, instead of just five," he whined. "It cost me $6,800 anyway. I would have been maître d' by now if I'd screwed it on & just Mashed the bastard. These turds have made me an outcast."

No. 4—(This is one of the more Advanced rules, but let's pop it in here while we still have space.) Avoid, at all costs, the use of Any drug or drink or Hubris or even Boredom that might cause you to Steal a car & crash it into a concrete wall just to get the Rush of the airbags exploding on you. This new fad among rich teenagers in L.A. is an extremely Advanced Technique that only pure Amateurs should try, and it should *never* be done Twice. Take my word for it.

No. 5—The eating schedule should be as follows: Hot fresh spinach, Wellfleet Oysters, and thick slabs of Sourdough garlic toast with salt & black pepper. Eat this two hours before departure, in quantities as needed. The drink should be Grolsch green beer, a dry oaken-flavored white wine & a tall glass full of ice cubes & Royal Salute scotch whiskey, for the supercharge factor.

Strong black coffee should also be sipped while eating, with dark chocolate cake soaked in Grand Marnier for dessert. The smoking of oily hashish is optional, and in truth Not Recommended for use *before* driving at speeds up to 150 mph in residential districts. The smoking of powerful hashish should be saved until after yr. *return* from the drive, when nerve-ends are crazy & raw.

Road testing the Ducati 900, 1995
(Paul Chesley)

Song of the Sausage Creature

There are some things nobody needs in this world, and a bright-red, hunch-back, warp-speed 900cc café-racer is one of them—but I want one anyway, and on some days I actually believe I need one. That is why they are dangerous.

Everybody has fast motorcycles these days. Some people go 150 miles an hour on two-lane blacktop roads, but not often. There are too many oncoming trucks and too many radar cops and too many stupid animals in the way. You have to be a little crazy to ride these super-torque high-speed crotch rockets anywhere except a racetrack—and even there, they will scare the whimpering shit out of you. . . . There is, after all, not a pig's eye worth of difference between going head-on into a Peterbilt or sideways into the bleachers. On some days you get what you want, and on others, you get what you need.

When *Cycle World* called me to ask if I would road-test the new Harley Road King, I got uppity and said I'd rather have a Ducati superbike. It seemed like a chic decision at the time, and my friends on the superbike circuit got very excited. "Hot damn," they said. "We will take it to the track and blow the bastards away."

"Balls," I said. "Never mind the track. The track is for punks. We are Road People. We are Café Racers."

The Café Racer is a different breed, and we have our own situations. Pure speed in sixth gear on a 5,000-foot straightaway is one thing, but pure speed in third gear on a gravel-strewn downhill ess-turn is quite another.

But we like it. A thoroughbred Café Racer will ride all night through a fog storm in freeway traffic to put himself into what somebody told him was the ugliest and tightest diminishing-radius loop turn since Genghis Khan invented the corkscrew.

Café Racing is mainly a matter of taste. It is an atavistic mentality, a peculiar mix of low style, high speed, pure dumbness, and over-weening commitment to the *Café Life* and all its dangerous pleasures. . . . I am a Café Racer myself, on some days—and many nights for that matter—and it is one of my finest addictions. . . .

I am not without scars on my brain and my body, but I can live with them. I still feel a shudder in my spine every time I see a picture of a Vincent Black Shadow, or when I walk into a public restroom and hear crippled men whispering about the terrifying Kawasaki Triple. . . . I have visions of compound femur-fractures and large black men in white hospital suits holding me down on a gurney while a nurse called "Bess" sews the flaps of my scalp together with a stitching drill.

Ho, ho. Thank God for these flashbacks. The brain is such a wonderful instrument (until God sinks his teeth into it). Some people hear Tiny Tim singing when they go under, and others hear the song of the Sausage Creature.

When the Ducati turned up in my driveway, nobody knew what to do with it. I was in New York, covering a polo tournament, and people had threatened my life. My lawyer said I should give myself up and enroll in the Federal Witness Protection Program. Other people said it had something to do with the polo crowd, or maybe Ron Ziegler.

The motorcycle business was the last straw. It had to be the work of my enemies or people who wanted to hurt me. It was the vilest kind of bait, and they knew I would go for it.

Of course. You want to cripple the bastard? Send him a 160-mph café-racer. And include some license plates, so he'll think it's a street-bike. He's queer for anything fast.

Which is true. I have been a connoisseur of fast motorcycles all my life. I bought a brand-new 650 BSA Lightning when it was billed as "the fastest motorcycle ever tested by *Hot Rod* magazine." I have ridden a 500-pound Vincent through traffic on the Ventura Freeway with burning oil on my legs and run the Kawa 750 Triple through Beverly Hills at night with a head full of acid. . . . I have ridden with Sonny Barger and smoked weed in biker bars with Jack Nicholson, Grace Slick, and my infamous old friend Ken Kesey, a legendary Café Racer.

Some people will tell you that slow is good—and it may be, on some days—but I am here to tell you that fast is better. I've always believed this, in spite of the trouble it's caused me. Being shot out of a cannon will always be better than being squeezed out of a tube. That is why God made fast motorcycles, Bubba. . . .

So when I got back from the U.S. Open Polo Championship in New York and found a fiery red rocket-style bike in my garage, I realized I was back in the road-testing business.

The brand-new Ducati 900 *Campione del Mundo Desmodue* Supersport double-barreled magnum Café Racer filled me with feelings of lust every time I looked at it. Others felt the same way. My garage quickly became a magnet for drooling superbike groupies. They quarreled and bitched at each other about who would be first to help me evaluate my new toy. . . . And I did, of course, need a certain spectrum of opinions, besides my own, to properly judge this motorcycle. The Woody Creek Perverse Environmental Testing Facility is a long way from Daytona or even top-fuel challenge sprints on the Pacific Coast Highway, where teams of big-bore Kawasakis and Yamahas are said to race head-on against each other in death-defying games of "chicken" at 100 miles an hour. . . .

No. Not everybody who buys a high-dollar torque-brute yearns to go out in a ball of fire on a public street in L.A. Some of us are decent people who want to stay out of the emergency room but still blast through neo-gridlock traffic in residential districts whenever we feel like it. . . . For that we need fine Machinery.

Which we had—no doubt about that. The Ducati people in New Jersey had opted, for reasons of their own, to send me the 900SP for testing—rather than their 916 crazy-fast, state-of-the-art superbike track-racer. It was far too fast, they said—and prohibitively expensive— to farm out for testing to a gang of half-mad Colorado cowboys who think they're world-class Café Racers.

The Ducati 900 *is* a finely engineered machine. My neighbors called it beautiful and admired its racing lines. The nasty little bugger looked like it was going 90 miles an hour when it was standing still in my garage.

Taking it on the road, though, was a genuinely terrifying experience. I had no sense of speed until I was going 90 and coming up fast on a bunch of pickup trucks going into a wet curve along the river. I went for both brakes, but only the front one worked, and I almost went end over end. I was out of control staring at the tailpipe of a U.S. Mail truck, still stabbing frantically at my rear brake pedal, which I just couldn't find. . . . I am too tall for these new-age roadracers; they are not built for any rider taller than five-nine, and the rearset brake pedal was not where I thought it would be. Midsize Italian pimps who like to race from one café to another on the boulevards of Rome in a flat-line prone position might like this, but I do not.

I was hunched over the tank like a person diving into a pool that got emptied yesterday. Whacko! Bashed on the concrete bottom, flesh ripped off, a Sausage Creature with no teeth, fucked up for the rest of its life.

We all love Torque, and some of us have taken it straight over the high side from time to time—and there is always pain in that. . . . But there is also Fun, the deadly element, and Fun is what you get when you screw this monster on. BOOM! Instant take-off, no screeching or squawking around like a fool with your teeth clamping down on your tongue and your mind completely empty of everything but fear.

No. This bugger digs right in and shoots you straight down the pipe, for good or ill.

On my first take-off, I hit second gear and went through the speed limit on a two-lane blacktop highway full of ranch traffic. By the time I went up to third, I was going 75 and the tach was barely above 4,000 rpm. . . .

And that's when it got its second wind. From 4,000 to 6,000 in third will take you from 75 mph to 95 in two seconds—and after that, Bubba, you still have fourth, fifth, and sixth. Ho, ho.

I never got to sixth gear, and I didn't get deep into fifth. This is a shameful admission for a full-bore Café Racer, but let me tell you something, old sport: This motorcycle is simply too goddamn fast to ride at speed in any kind of normal road traffic unless you're ready to go straight down the centerline with your nuts on fire and a silent scream in your throat.

When aimed in the right direction at high speed, though, it has unnatural capabilities. This I unwittingly discovered as I made my approach to a sharp turn across some railroad tracks, and saw that I was going way too fast and that my only chance was to veer right and screw it on totally, in a desperate attempt to leapfrog the curve by going airborne.

It was a bold and reckless move, but it was necessary. And it worked: I felt like Evel Knievel as I soared across the tracks with the rain in my eyes and my jaws clamped together in fear. I tried to spit down on the tracks as I passed them, but my mouth was too dry. . . . I landed hard on the edge of the road and lost my grip for a moment as the Ducati began fishtailing crazily into oncoming traffic. For two or three seconds I came face to face with the Sausage Creature. . . .

But somehow the brute straightened out. I passed a schoolbus on the right and then got the bike under control long enough to gear down and pull off into an abandoned gravel driveway, where I stopped and turned off the engine. My hands had seized up like claws and the rest of my body was numb. I went into a trance for 30 or 40 seconds until I was finally able to light a cigarette and calm down enough to ride home. I was too hysterical to shift gears, so I went the whole way in first at 40 miles an hour.

Whoops! What am I saying? Tall stories, ho, ho. . . . We are motorcycle people; we walk tall and we laugh at whatever's funny. We shit on the chests of the Weird. . . .

But when we ride very fast motorcycles, we ride with immaculate sanity. We might abuse a substance here and there, but only when it's right. The final measure of any rider's skill is the inverse ratio of his preferred Traveling Speed to the number of bad scars on his body. It is that simple: If you ride fast and crash, you are a bad rider. If you go slow and crash, you are a bad rider. And if you are a bad rider, you should not ride motorcycles.

The emergence of the superbike has heightened this equation drastically. Motorcycle technology has made such a great leap forward. Take the Ducati. You want optimum cruising speed on this bugger? Try 90 mph in fifth at 5,500 rpm—and just then, you see a bull moose in the middle of the road. WHACKO. Meet the Sausage Creature.

Or maybe not: The Ducati 900 is so finely engineered and balanced and torqued that you *can* do 90 mph in fifth through a 35-mph zone and get away with it. The bike is not just fast—it is *extremely* quick and responsive, and it *will* do amazing things. . . . It is a little like riding the original Vincent Black Shadow, which would outrun an F-86 jet fighter on the take-off runway, but at the end, the F-86 would go airborne and the Vincent would not, and there was no point in trying to turn it. WHAMMO! The Sausage Creature strikes again.

There is a fundamental difference, however, between the old Vincents and the new breed of superbikes. If you rode the Black Shadow at top speed for any length of time, you would almost certainly die. That is why there are not many life members of the Vincent Black Shadow Society. The Vincent was like a bullet that went straight; the Ducati is like the magic bullet in Dallas that went sideways and hit JFK and the Governor of Texas at the same time.

It was impossible. But so was my terrifying sideways leap across railroad tracks on the 900SP. The bike did it easily with the grace of a fleeing tomcat. The landing was so easy I remember thinking, Goddamnit, if I had screwed it on a little more I could have gone a lot farther.

Maybe this is the new Café Racer macho. My bike is so much faster than yours that I dare you to ride it, you lame little turd. Do you have the balls to ride this BOTTOMLESS PIT OF TORQUE?

That is the attitude of the new-age superbike freak, and I am one of them. On some days they are about the most fun you can have with your clothes on. The Vincent just killed you a lot faster than a superbike will. A fool couldn't ride the Vincent Black Shadow more than once, but a fool can ride a Ducati 900 many times, and it will always be a bloodcurdling kind of fun. That is the Curse of Speed which has plagued me all my life. I am a slave to it. On my tombstone they will carve, IT NEVER GOT FAST ENOUGH FOR ME.

The Lion and the Cadillac

Fear? I know not fear. There are only moments of confusion. Some of them are deeply stamped on my memory and a few will haunt me forever.

One of my ugliest and most confused moments, I think, was when I was driving a junk Cadillac down the Coast Highway to Big Sur and a large mountain lion jumped into the moving car.

I had stopped for a moment beside the road to put out a newspaper fire in the backseat when this huge cat either jumped or fell off a cliff and landed on its back in the gravel right beside me. I was leaning over the side and pouring beer on the fire when it happened.

It was late in the day, and I was alone. When the beast hit the ground I had a moment of total confusion. And so did the lion. Then I jumped back in the car and took off down the hill in low gear, thinking to escape certain death or at least mutilation.

The beast had tried to pounce on me from above, but missed. . . . And now, as I shifted the junker into second, I heard a terrible snarling and realized that the cat was running right behind me and gaining . . . (I was, in fact, Terrified at that moment.) . . . And I think I must have gone temporarily insane when the goddamn thing came up beside me and jumped right into the car through the passenger-side window like a bomb.

It bounced against the dashboard and somehow turned the radio volume all the way up. Then it clawed me badly on my arm and one leg. That is why I shudder every time I hear a Chuck Berry tune.

I can still smell the beast. I heard myself screaming as I tried to steer. There was blood all over the seat. The music was deafening and the cat was still snarling and clawing at me. Then it scrambled over the seat and into the back, right into the pile of still-burning newspapers. I heard a screech of pain and saw the cat trying to hurl itself through the back window.

We were still rolling along at about thirty miles per hour when I noticed my ball-peen hammer sticking out of the mangled glove compartment.

I grabbed the hammer with my right hand, steering with my left, and swung it wildly over my shoulder at the mountain lion.

Whack! I felt it hit something that felt vaguely like a carton of eggs, and then there was silence. No resistance in the backseat. Nothing.

I hit the brakes and pulled over. My hand was still on the hammer when I looked back and saw that I had somehow hit the animal squarely on top of its head and driven the iron ball right through its skull and into its brain. It was dead. Hunched on its back and filling the whole rear of the car, which was filling up with blood.

I was no longer confused.

Backstage at the O'Farrell
(Michael Nichols / Magnum Photos)

Geerlings & the War Minister's Son

Avenida Copacabana is always crowded at night, in the style of Miami Beach, which it physically resembles, and spiritually dwarfs. . . . Copacabana is the *beach city* for Rio de Janeiro, capital city of Brazil, where I happened to be living at the time of the horrible "Cuban Missile Crisis" in 1962, when expatriate Americans all over the world glanced around them in places like Warsaw and Kowloon or Tripoli and realized that life was going to be very different from now on: All countries north of the Equator were going to be destroyed forever by nuclear bombs before Sunday. WHACKO! The long-dreaded "nuclear trigger" was going to be pulled somewhere west of Bermuda when two enemy naval fleets collided on the sea lane to Cuba, around two in the afternoon—and that collision would signal the end of the world as we knew it. This was not a drill.

Please accept my apologies if this little foreign adventure story seems overwrought or maudlin—at the time that I told it, maybe it was, and so what? Those were extremely violent times, as I recall; I had spent a long year on a very savage road, mainly along the spine of the South American *cordillera,* working undercover in utterly foreign countries in the grip of bloody revolutions and counterrevolutions that made up the news of the day from the Panama Canal all the way down to the lonely frozen pampas of Argentina. . . . South America in the early 1960s was the most routinely murderous place in the world to find yourself doomed to be living when the World was destroyed by bombs.

And for me, that one fateful place in the world was Rio de Janeiro, Brazil, where I was living extremely well, under the circumstances. All things considered, Rio was pretty close to the best place in the world to be lost and stranded forever when the World finally shut down.

. . .

Geerlings was a Dutchman about thirty-three years old, built like some monster on Muscle Beach but without steroids—beyond an athlete, a dangerous brute with the temper of a wolverine, a handsome guy. His cheap shirts were always bulging, like his brain. He was the inventor of a radical coloring process for glass walls the size of swimming pools.

He fled Holland on a murder warrant—he'd killed Nazis with a Colt .45 that he stole from a dead American; he had grown up in Holland during the Second World War, and his hatred for the Germans was immense. He would go out at night looking for Krauts to beat up.

One night in Rio, we saw some stylish teenagers torturing a dog. They were both holding the dog, pulling its legs, and it was screeching. We came out of the nightclub across the street in a dull, bored mood, and here were these creeps strangling a dog in a well-lit public place; they were about 200 yards from Avenida Copacabana, a big busy street, and we smashed into them at a dead run, full speed and flailing. I remember saying, "Let's get those evil fuckers." He was like Oscar—Geerlings had that killer mentality, like a professional assassin.

It was the South Beach part of town, with wide granite sidewalks. They dropped the dog when we hit them, then they bounced along the sidewalk like rubber dolls. I was screaming, "You want to torture a dog, you fucks! We'll torture you!" No doubt it was excessive behavior—under the circumstances—and as usual in moments of public violence, people went all to pieces. Perhaps we were Feverish. Rio can do that to people, especially on Copacabana Beach: drastic dehumanizing hallucinations, personality inversions at high speed, spontaneous out-of-body experiences that come with no warning at awkward moments.

. . .

They twisted away and ran desperately toward Avenida Copacabana, like, "If I can just get to Fifth Avenue there will be lights there, and people will see what's happening." And instead of letting them go—they fought briefly, a little bit of a swing—we pounded them as they took off, two young Brazilians about twenty-five or thirty, healthy boys, arrogant fucking punks.

I could see we were probably going to catch them. I saw the avenue up ahead, and knew what they were going to do. They were desperately trying to flag a passing Lotocao bus—like an open-air school bus that runs twenty-four hours a day. They were running desperately, spastic with fear and screaming for help, and I didn't want them to escape.

So here we come, charging out of the darkness, our Converse sneakers slapping the concrete, and they're running, these two native boys, screaming desperately for the bus to stop. It would be like two people running running down Forty-second Street through the crowd, trying to call for a taxi as if it were the last act of their lives. And instead of letting them go then, I caught up with what turned out to be the War Minister's son just as he reached the bus. It was a drama before it happened. All this screaming: "Please stop! Oh God! Help!" The one I was after was almost within a step of getting his foot on the lowest rung of the bus.

I had no choice—I was going faster than he was, and as he slowed down to get on the bus I hit him, running from behind, and blasted him against the bus with my hands out. I wasn't sure what to do. He *really* bounced off. Imagine that: thinking, Oh, Thank God—hands reaching down from the bus to help him escape. It was bad. We were brutish foreigners chasing two local boys for no apparent reason and attacking them.

The poor bastard was smashed—CLANG—against the side of the Lotocao, and I fell on top of him. Everything stopped when this terrible crash came—people ran out of stores and begged for police intervention. Maybe I got ahold of him and seized him; somehow he ended up sitting on the street, leaning against the back wheel of the bus, which didn't have any hubcaps. There must have been some deep confusion there. I remember his head bouncing off of the lug nuts on the axle; I remember telling myself, *Watch out, you fool—keep your knuckles away from those goddamn lug nuts.*

Meanwhile, Geerlings was brutalizing the other guy—it was a shameful outburst. Geerlings had the guy's feet bent back toward his neck, like a pretzel, trying to twist him the wrong way. A huge crowd had gathered. We were beating on both of them and screaming in English. The bus driver had stopped in the middle of the cross street; this was a bad fight, whatever it meant. And I was wearing shorts. So was Geerlings—a horrible Dutchman wanted for murder, an international criminal. I immediately pulled back.

After they got on the bus, we stopped for a *cafezinho* at the corner bar and waited for the mob to gather. I remember the two kids and the other people on the bus as it took off and rounded in first gear, the old cranky engines, these victims screaming through the windows and shaking their fists: "You dirty bastards! We kill you! You Fuck!"—in Brazilian . . . and we just laughed it off.

I don't know why we went and stood at the counter there in the coffee place—a *boutequim*, it had an open front facing the street, two cents for a cup of coffee—to try and explain it. "Well, those guys were bad! They beat the dog." It was hard to explain. Then, all of a sudden, the street began to fill up, people shouting, and I thought, What the hell. Is there a riot someplace? Something else is happening. There were maybe ten people in the *boutequim*, but we were facing the street. And this mob of people—it sounded like they were at a political protest. I said to Geerlings, "What the fuck is this?" There were people yelling and pointing at us, and then there were cops in the mob. I realized, Oh Fuck. It's Us. Those monsters had gotten off at the next stop and grabbed the nearest cop.

. . .

I had seen a jaguar outside a bar on Avenida Copacabana the night before. There are bars in Rio that look like delis, the kind in New York with a long counter and seats, except there's beer and food. While Geerlings was fucking with Germans, I went back to the bathroom. We're talking about a wooden shack—Avenida Copacabana is backed up to *favelas,* the hills. These gigantic mountains come straight down, four or five hundred feet; it's a jungle behind every building. Here I was, taking this routine piss in a ramshackle South American men's room, which had a window—the garbage area was outside this window in the middle of bushes and trees. I wasn't thinking about much of anything except what Geerlings might be doing to the Germans. I didn't try to do anything to prevent him from beating these people. I just wanted him to be careful. I didn't want to get busted for it.

I was looking out the window: blank darkness, garbage cans, and right in front of me, no more than three feet away, was a gigantic yellow- and black-spotted jaguar *tigre,* five, possibly six feet long, maybe five without the tail. A big cat.

I thought, What the fuck is this? I've never seen anything like this in my life. Ye gods! I had to go to Marigoso to confront cats at arm's length. I was stunned. I just watched it. It fucked around. It didn't make much noise. I don't know what would have happened if one of the boys had come out and thrown some more garbage into the can. This thing was huge. I didn't know what the hell to do, but I went back through the bar and the first thing I saw was Geerlings: He had hooked a Nazi in the nuts, and had him up against a phone booth with his cheek half pulled off. He wasn't kidding; we had to get out of there.

I said, "Goddamn. You won't believe this. While you were sitting out here fucking with Germans, I went back to the bathroom and there was a jaguar tiger, right in front of me. Right outside the window."

"Oh no. Come on," said Geerlings.

. . .

So the following night I took the little auto that I'd brought with me to Rio, a cheap .25 automatic. I carried it all over South America, usually loaded. Why carry one that's not? I tied it around my neck with a string—it was too hot to carry it anywhere else.

"All right, Geerlings," I said. "I'll show you. We're going to go back down here and get ourselves a *tigre*."

I loaded up and we went back down to the bar and sat in the same place. Geerlings fucked with more Germans. The *tigre* never came back. How many times can you go to the men's room? None of it makes a lot of sense. We gave up on the tiger. Then we started wandering around to the various nightclubs—after the one disappointment, we were ripe for a dog incident. It was action. We had no action and it built up. That's really what it was—it was the explosion. If the cat had come, those guys wouldn't have been hit.

It seemed incidental really to both of us. But, holy shit—the mob and the police and being arrested to chanting and shouting was bad enough, but to have a loaded .25 automatic.

I guess my beating the guy against the lug nuts got their attention—he was the son of the War Minister, so I understood that we were in trouble. But they left Geerlings alone; I saw him in the front of the crowd asking questions of the police: "I'm here to help."

"Who are you?" the police asked Geerlings.

He was saying, "Well, it's a friend. A countryman. What's the trouble here? Don't ask me. I'm nobody."

Geerlings was trying to help in some way, but it was a mob scene, and I was trying to get the attention of the Embassy press officer. I was under arrest, and I was being led through a tunnel of chanting Cariokas: "String him up! Fuck him! U.S. out! Fuck U.S.A.! *Abajo!*"

There was going to be trouble when the gun was found—luckily, I had put it in my pocket. I saw Geerlings as I was being led down this corridor of people. It wasn't like he was on the fringes of the crowd: He was like Ruby in the Oswald thing. He was on the front line, but he was acting like he was just an interested bystander—very smart, and he was getting away with it. I was being interviewed, but I could see him there; he was still talking to another cop, asking questions and being very officious. The first chance I got, I stepped out of the line as I was being led somewhere else. I had my hand on the .25—in the middle of three hundred people.

As I approached him—this is really quick thinking—I pulled the gun out. When they weren't looking at me, I put the gun in his hand and said, "Run!"

There was a frozen moment, and he took off through the crowd like a bull. No more gun.

(Daniel E. Dibble)

Yesterday's Weirdness Is Tomorrow's Reason Why

WILLIAM MCKEEN: *Your use of drugs is one of the more controversial things about you and your writing. Do you think the use of drugs has been exaggerated by the media? How have drugs affected your perception of the world and/or your writing? Does the media portrayal of you as a "crazy" amuse, inflame, or bore you?*

HUNTER S. THOMPSON: Obviously, my drug use is exaggerated or I would be long since dead. I've already outlived the most brutal abuser of our time—Neal Cassady. Me and William Burroughs are the only other ones left. We're the last unrepentant public dope fiends, and he's seventy years old and claiming to be clean. But he hasn't turned on drugs, like that lying, treacherous, sold-out punk Timothy Leary.

Drugs usually enhance or strengthen my perceptions and reactions, for good or ill. They've given me the resilience to withstand repeated shocks to my innocence gland. The brutal reality of politics alone would probably be intolerable without drugs. They've given me the strength to deal with those shocking realities guaranteed to shatter *anyone's* beliefs in the higher idealistic shibboleths of our time and the "American Century." Anyone who covers his beat for twenty years—and my beat is "The Death of the American Dream"—needs every goddamned crutch he can find.

Besides, I *enjoy* drugs. The only trouble they've given me is the people who try to keep me from using them. *Res Ipsa Loquitur.* I was, after all, a Literary Lion last year.

The media perception of me has always been pretty broad. As broad as the media itself. As a journalist, I somehow managed to break most of the rules and still succeed. It's a hard thing for most of today's journeyman journalists to understand, but only because they can't do it. The smart ones understood immediately. The best people in journalism I've never had any quarrel with. I *am* a journalist and I've never met, as a group, any tribe I'd rather be a part of or that are more fun to be with—despite the various punks and sycophants of the press.

It hasn't helped a lot to be a savage comic-book character for the last fifteen years—a drunken screwball who should've been castrated a long time ago. The smart people in the media knew it was a weird exaggeration. The dumb ones took it seriously and warned their children to stay away from me at all costs. The *really* smart ones understood it was only a censored, kind of toned-down, children's-book version of the real thing.

Now we are being herded into the nineties, which looks like it is going to be a *true* generation of swine, a decade run by cops with no humor, with dead heroes, and diminished expectations, a decade that will go down in history as The Gray Area. At the end of the decade, no one will be sure of anything except that you *must* obey the rules, sex will kill you, politicians lie, rain is poison, and the world is run by whores. These are terrible things to have to know in your life, even if you're rich.

Since it's become the mode, that sort of thinking has taken over the media, as it has business and politics: "I'm going to turn you in, son—not just for your own good but because you were the bastard who turned *me* in last year."

This vilification by Nazi elements within the media has not only given me a fierce joy to continue my work—more and more alone out here, as darkness falls on the barricades—but has also made me profoundly orgasmic, mysteriously rich, and constantly at war with those vengeful retro-fascist elements of the Establishment that have hounded me all my life. It has also made me wise, shrewd, and crazy on a level that can only be known by those who have been there.

WM: *Some libraries classify* Fear and Loathing in Las Vegas *as a travelogue, some classify it as nonfiction, and some classify it as a novel. How much of this book is true? How would you characterize this book (beyond the jacket copy info in* The Great Shark Hunt*)? You refer to it as a failed experiment in Gonzo journalism, yet many critics consider it a masterwork. How would you rate it?*

HST: *Fear and Loathing in Las Vegas* is a masterwork. However, true Gonzo journalism as I conceive it shouldn't be rewritten.

I would classify it, in Truman Capote's words, as a nonfiction novel in that almost all of it was true or *did* happen. I warped a few things, but it was a pretty accurate picture. It was an incredible feat of balance more than literature. That's why I called it *Fear and Loathing*. It was a pretty pure experience that turned into a very pure piece of writing. It's as good as *The Great Gatsby* and better than *The Sun Also Rises*.

WM: *For years your readers have heard about* **The Rum Diary.** *Are you working on it, or on any other novel? Do you have an ambition to write fiction? Your stint as a newspaper columnist was successful, but do you have further ambitions within journalism?*

HST: I've always had and still do have an ambition to write fiction. I've never had any real ambition within journalism, but events and fate and my own sense of fun keep taking me back for money, political reasons, and because I am a warrior. I haven't found a drug yet that can get you anywhere near as high as sitting at a desk writing, trying to imagine a story no matter how bizarre it is, as much as going out and getting into the weirdness of reality and doing a little time on The Proud Highway.

March 1990

Letter to John Walsh

To: John Walsh / ESPN
June 21, 2002

JOHN.

Things are savage here, but I think of you constantly & thanx for yr. elegant assessment of Jann & the hideous world as we know it.

But I fear no evil, for the Lord is with me. Yea though I walk in the shadow of death, I fear no Evil, for the Lord is with me. . . .

You bet. He is our ace in the hole . . . Or maybe not. Maybe John Ashcroft is greater than God. Who knows? Ashcroft is the new point man for Bush Inc., yet he is dumb as a rock. He is like some Atavistic endeavor on speed—just another stupid monster as Attorney General of the U.S.A., a vengeful jackass with an IQ of 66.

How long, O Lord, how long? These Pigs just keep coming, like meat oozing over a counter . . . And they keep getting Meaner and Dumber.

Yeah. Trust me on this, Bubba. I knew *Ed Meese* in his prime, and I repeatedly cursed him as the murderous pig that he was— a low form of life that hung on the neck of this nation like a crust of poison algae. He was scum. Ed Meese was a Monster.

But he was *nothing* compared to John Mitchell, the anal-compulsive drunkard who was Nixon's Attorney General in the terrible time of Watergate. He was the weirdest act in town.

John Mitchell was a big-time corporate lawyer and his wife was a serious drinker from Arkansas who squealed on him by accident and brought down the whole structure of the U.S. federal government. . . . It was wonderful. Those animals were forced into the tunnel, one by one, and destroyed like offal.

That is the nature of professional politics. Many are called, but few survive the nut-cutting hour—which appears to be coming down on our goofy Child President these days. . . . Ah, but it was ever thus, eh? Vicious thieves have always ruled the world. It is our *wa*. We are like pigs in the wilderness.

HUNTER

PART THREE

Gambling on a football game with Ed Bradley
(HST archives)

The Foreign Correspondent

My opposition to war is not based upon pacifist or non-resistant principles. It may be that the present state of civilization is such that certain international questions cannot be discussed; it may be that they have to be fought out. We ought not to forget that wars are a purely manufactured evil and are made according to a definite technique. A campaign for war is made upon as definite lines as a campaign for any other purpose. First, the people are worked upon. By clever tales the people's suspicions are aroused toward the nation against whom war is desired. Make the nation suspicious; make the other nation suspicious. All you need for this is a few agents with some cleverness and no conscious and a press whose interest is locked up with the interests that will be benefited by war. Then the "overt act" will soon appear. It is no trick at all to get an "overt act" once you work the hatred of two nations up to the proper pitch.

—Henry Ford

May You Live in Interesting Times

There is an ancient Chinese curse that says, "May you live in interesting times," which was told to me by an elderly dope fiend on a rainy night in Hong Kong near the end of the War in Vietnam. He was a giddy old man, on the surface, but I knew—and he knew that I knew—of the fear and respect he commanded all over Southeast Asia as a legendary Wizard in the far-flung Kingdom of Opium. I had stopped by his shop in Kowloon to get some advice and a chunk of black medicine for my friends who were trapped in the NVA noose that was inexorably closing in on Saigon. They refused to leave, they said, but in order to stay alive in the doomed and dysfunctional city, they needed only two things—cash money and fine opium.

I was no stranger to either one of these things, at the time—and I was, after all, in Hong Kong. All I had to do to get a satchel of green money and pure opium delivered to the *Newsweek* bureau was make a few phone calls. My friends trapped in Saigon were Journalists. We have a strong sense, people of my own breed and tribe, and we are linked—especially in war zones—by strong bonds of tribal loyalty. . . .

Last Days of Saigon

So bye bye, Miss American Pie,
Drove my Chevy to the levee, but the levee was dry,
Them good ole boys were drinkin' whiskey and rye,
Singin' this'll be the day that I die,
This'll be the day that I die . . .

I had never paid much attention to that song until I heard it on the Muzak one Saturday afternoon in the rooftop restaurant of the new Palace Hotel, looking down on the orange-tile rooftops of the over-crowded volcano that used to be known as Saigon and discussing military strategy over gin and lime with London Sunday *Times* correspondent Murray Sayle. We had just come back in a Harley Davidson–powered rickshaw from the Viet Cong's weekly press conference in their barbed-wire enclosed compound at Saigon's Tan Son Nhut airport, and Sayle had a big geophysical map of Indochina spread out on the table between us, using a red felt-tipped pen as a pointer to show me how and why the South Vietnamese government of then-President Nguyen Van Thieu had managed to lose half the country and a billion dollars' worth of U.S. weaponry in less than three weeks.

I was trying to concentrate on his explanation—which made perfect sense, on the map—but the strange mix of realities on that afternoon of what would soon prove to be the next to last Saturday of the Vietnam War made concentration difficult. For one thing, I had never been west of San Francisco until I'd arrived in Saigon about ten days earlier—just after the South Vietnamese Army (ARVN) had been routed on worldwide TV in the "battles" for Hué and Da Nang.

This was a widely advertised "massive Hanoi offensive" that had suddenly narrowed the whole war down to a nervous ring around Saigon, less than fifty miles in diameter . . . and during the past few days, as a million or more refugees fled into Saigon from the panic zones up north around Hué and Da Nang, it had become painfully and ominously clear that Hanoi had never really launched any "massive offensive" at all—but that the flower of the finely *U.S.-trained* and heavily U.S.-equipped South Vietnamese Army had simply panicked and run amok. The films of whole ARVN divisions fleeing desperately through the streets of Da Nang had apparently surprised the NVA generals in Hanoi almost as badly as they jolted that bonehead ward heeler that Nixon put in the White House in exchange for the pardon that kept him out of prison.

Gerald Ford still denies this, but what the hell? It hardly matters anymore, because not even a criminal geek like Nixon would have been stupid enough to hold a nationally televised press conference in the wake of a disaster like Da Nang and compound the horror of what millions of U.S. viewers had been seeing on TV all week by refusing to deny, on camera, that the 58,000 Americans who died in Vietnam had died in vain. Even arch-establishment commentators like James Reston and Eric Sevareid were horrified by Ford's inept and almost cruelly stupid performance at that press conference. In addition to the wives, parents, sons, daughters, and other relatives and friends of the 58,000 American dead, he was also talking to more than 150,000 veterans who were wounded, maimed, and crippled in Vietnam . . . and the net effect of what he said might just as well have been to quote Ernest Hemingway's description of men who had died in another war, many years ago—men who were "shot down and killed like dogs, for no good reason at all."

My memories of that day are very acute, because it was the first time since I'd arrived in Saigon that I suddenly understood how close we were to the *end,* and how ugly it was likely to be . . . and as that eerie chorus about "Bye bye, Miss American Pie" kept howling around my ears while we picked at our Crab St. Jacques, I stared balefully out across the muddy Saigon River to where the earth was trembling and the rice paddies were exploding in long clean patterns like stitches down the sleeve of a shirt. . . . Carpet bombing, massive ordnance, the last doomed snarling of the white man's empire in Asia.

"Well, Murray," I asked him. "What the fuck do we do *now?*"

He drained the last of a tall bottle of fine French Riesling into our crystalline flutes and languidly called for another. It was somewhere around lunchtime, but the penthouse dining room was empty of cash customers, except us, and we were not in a hurry. "We are surrounded by sixteen NVA divisions," he said with a smile. "The enemy is right out there in that smoke across the river, and he wants vengeance. We are doomed."

I nodded calmly and sucked on a corncob pipe full of steamy Khymer Rouge blossoms, then I leaned over the map and made a wet red circle around our position in downtown Saigon.

He looked at it. "So what," he said. "Those people are *cannibals,*" he snapped. "They will hunt us down and *eat* us."

"Nonsense," I said. "I am a personal friend of Colonel Vo Don Giang. We will be put in cages for a while, then set free."

One Hand Clapping

I knew a Buddhist once, and I've hated myself ever since. The whole thing was a failure.

He was a priest of some kind, and he was also extremely rich. They called him a monk and he wore the saffron robes and I hated him because of his arrogance. He thought he knew everything.

One day I was trying to rent a large downtown property from him, and he mocked me. "You are dumb," he said. "You are doomed if you stay in this business. The stupid are gobbled up quickly."

"I understand," I said. "I am stupid. I am doomed. But I think I know something you don't."

He laughed. "Nonsense," he said. "You are a fool. You know nothing."

I nodded respectfully and leaned closer to him, as if to whisper a secret. "I know the answer to the greatest riddle of all," I said.

He chuckled. "And what is that?" he said. "And you'd better be Right, or I'll kill you."

"I know the sound of one hand clapping," I said. "I have finally discovered the answer."

Several other Buddhists in the room laughed out loud, at this point. I knew they wanted to humiliate me, and now they had me trapped—because there *is* no answer to that question. These saffron bastards have been teasing us with it forever. They are amused at our failure to grasp it.

Ho ho. I went into a drastic crouch and hung my left hand low, behind my knee. "Lean closer," I said to him. "I want to answer your high and unanswerable question."

As he leaned his bright bald head a little closer into my orbit, I suddenly leaped up and bashed him flat on the ear with the palm of my left hand. It was slightly cupped, so as to deliver maximum energy on impact. An isolated package of air is suddenly driven through the Eustachian tube and into the middle brain at quantum speed, causing pain, fear, and extreme insult to the tissue.

The monk staggered sideways and screamed, grasping his head in agony. Then he fell to the floor and cursed me. "You swine!" he croaked. "Why did you hit me and burst my eardrum?"

"Because *that*," I said, "is the sound of one hand clapping. That is the answer to your question. I have the answer now, and you are deaf."

"Indeed," he said. "I am deaf, but I am smarter. I am wise in a different way." He grinned vacantly and reached out to shake my hand.

"You're welcome," I said. "I am, after all, a doctor."

Zorro at work, Woody Creek, 2002
(Anita Bejmuk)

The Invasion of Grenada

**TRIAL RUN FOR PANAMA AND AFGHANISTAN
. . . SPRINGBOARD FOR IRAQ AND KOREA—
SEE THE NEW WORLD ORDER IN ACTION . . .
WHY NOT? HITLER HAD SPAIN, WE HAVE
GRENADA . . .**

*I believe the government has not only a right but an obli-
gation to lie to the people.*
                    —Jody Powell, *Nightline* (ABC News),
                                    October 26, 1983

There are some interesting attitudes on the street these days, and not
all of them come from strangers. Old friends call me late at night from
places like Nassau and New York and Bangkok, raving angrily about
suicide bombers in Lebanon. They call me from the Blue Lagoon
Yacht Club on the south side of St. Vincent, offering big boats for hire
to run the blockade around the war zone in Grenada, only 100 miles
away. I get collect calls from Miami and from federal prison camps asking me who to vote for. The janitor at the Woody Creek Tavern wants
to join the U.S. Marines and kill foreigners for a living.

"They have a buddy system," he said. "We could join together and
go to the Caribbean."

"Or Lebanon," I said. "Any place with a beach."

He shrugged. The difference between Lebanon and Grenada was
not clear in his mind. All he wanted was some action. He was a dope
fiend, and he was bored.

Five years in a trailer court on the fringe of the jet-set life had not
agreed with him. His teeth were greasy and his eyes were wet and he
was too old to join the Marines. But there was excitement in his
voice. In late afternoons at the Tavern, he would stand at the bar with
the cowboys and watch the war news on network TV, weeping openly
and cracking his knuckles as Dan Rather described combat scenes
from Grenada, leathernecks hitting the beach, palm trees exploding,
natives running for cover, helicopters crashing into jagged mountain-
sides.

. . .

I called the Blue Lagoon Yacht Club on the south side of St. Vincent the other day and asked for the manager, Mr. Kidd. Another man came on the line and said Mr. Kidd was gone to Barbados for a while, with some people from the CIA. Well, I thought, why not? We will all work for them sooner or later.

"So what?" I said. "I need a boat. Who's in charge there?"

"I am," he replied. "There are no boats, and Mr. Kidd is gone."

"I need a boat tomorrow," I said. "For seven days, to Grenada."

"To Grenada?" he said. "To the war?"

"That's right," I said. "I need something fast, around forty feet, with radar and triple sidebands. I have plenty of money. Mr. Kidd knows me well."

"It doesn't matter," he said. "Mr. Kidd's gone."

"When do you expect him back?" I asked.

"Maybe never," he replied.

"What?" I said. "What's happened to him?"

"I don't know," he replied. "He went to the war. Maybe he got killed." He paused, waiting for me to say something, but I was thinking.

"All hell broke loose around here," he said finally. "You know that, don't you?"

"Yeah," I said. "I know that."

"It's big business," he said. "Mr. Kidd even sold his own boat. They had seabags full of hundred-dollar bills. I've never seen so much money."

"Okay," I said. "Do you have any planes for hire?"

There was another pause, then he laughed.

"Okay," he said. "Give me a number and I'll get back to you."

Indeed, I thought, you treacherous sot. There was something odd in the man's voice. I said I was between planes in the Dallas airport and would call him back later.

"Who is this?" he asked. "Maybe I'll hear from Mr. Kidd."

"Tell him Dr. Wilson called," I said, "from Texas."

He laughed again. "Good luck," he said.

I hung up, feeling vaguely uneasy, and called a travel agent.

. . .

Forty hours later, I was on a plane from Barbados to Pearls Airport in Grenada. There was no need for a boat after all. LIAT Airlines was flying again, running four flights a day into the war zone, and every seat was taken. There was no such thing as a secure reservation on the Liberation Shuttle once the blockade was lifted. It was an ugly ride with a long sweaty stop in St. Vincent, and most of the passengers were edgy.

News reports from Grenada said the invasion was over and the Cuban swine had surrendered. But there were still snipers in the hills around the airport and along the road to St. George's. The Marines, still reeling from the shock of 289 dead from a single bomb in Beirut a week earlier, were not getting much sleep on this island.

THE WRONG IS ALWAYS WRONG
—Grenadian Voice, November 26, 1983

The pros and cons of bombing the insane—even by accident—was only one of the volatile questions raised by the invasion of Grenada. It was a massive show of force by the U.S. Military, but the chain of events leading up to it was not easy to follow. Some people said it was a heartwarming "rescue mission," 2,000 Marines and paratroopers hitting the beach to pluck 400 or so American medical students out of the jaws of death and degradation by bloodthirsty Cubans. Others said it happened because Castro had loaned his friend Maurice Bishop $9 million to build a new airport on the island, with a runway 10,000 feet long and capable of serving as a Cuban military base on the edge of strategic sea-lanes in the south Caribbean. And still others called it a shrewd and finely planned military move, a thing that had to be done once the neighboring islands asked formally for American help. "We did the right thing for the wrong reasons," a ranking Democratic Party official told me on the telephone just before I left for Grenada. "You know I hate to agree with Reagan on anything at all, but in this case I have to go along with him."

Well, I thought. Maybe so. But it was hard to be sure, from a distance of 4,000 miles, so I decided to have a look at it. The trip from Woody Creek to Grand Junction to Denver to Atlanta to Miami to Barbados to Pearls Airport on the north shore of Grenada took two days, and by the time I got there I had read enough newspapers in airports along the way to have a vague grip on the story, at least on the American side of it.

A crowd of local Stalinists had run amok in Grenada, killing everybody who stood in their way and plunging the whole island into terrorism, looting, and anarchy. The murdering swine had even killed Maurice Bishop, Grenada's answer to JFK, and after that they'd planned to kill, capture, or at least maim hundreds of innocent American medical students who were trapped like rats on the island. A battalion of U.S. Marines, en route to Lebanon in response to the disaster two days earlier at the Beirut airport, was instead diverted to Grenada, along with a U.S. Navy battle fleet and the 82nd Airborne, to crush Communist mutiny and rescue American citizens.

This task had been quickly accomplished, without the burden of any civilian press coverage, and Defense Department film of the actual invasion showed U.S. troops in heroic postures, engaging the enemy at close quarters and taking 600 Cuban prisoners. It was a fitting response to the massacre at the U.S. Marine compound in Lebanon, except that it happened 7,000 miles away and the Arabs called it a bad joke. "It was just another cowboy movie," a Syrian diplomat told me several weeks later in the lounge of the United Nations Plaza Hotel. "All it proved was that Americans would rather shoot than think."

There was no shortage of conflicting opinions on the invasion of Grenada. It was called everything from "hysterical gunboat diplomacy" to a long-overdue assertion of the Monroe Doctrine, a swift and powerful warning to any other so-called revolutionaries who might try to seize turf in the American Hemisphere. "We taught those bastards a lesson," said a businessman at the Ionosphere Club in Miami International Airport. "Fidel Castro will think twice before he tries a trick like this again, and so will the Sandinistas."

In Grenada with Loren Jenkins, 1984

(Laura G. Thorne)

. . .

Wisdom is cheap in airport bars and expensive Third World hotels. You can hear almost anything you want, if you hang around these places long enough—but the closer you get to a war zone, the harder it is to speak with strangers about anything except the weather. By the time I got to Barbados, only an hour away from Grenada, not even my fellow passengers in the standby line at LIAT Airlines had anything to say about the invasion or what they were doing there. I did the last leg of the trip without saying a word to anybody. About half the people on the plane, a hellishly hot DC-4 that stopped for a while in St. Vincent's, were white men of indeterminate origin. Some, carrying locked attaché cases of expensive camera equipment, wore faded T-shirts from long-lost hotels in the Orient. I recognized Al Rakov, from Saigon, but he pretended not to know me and I quickly understood.

Things got worse when the plane touched down in Grenada. The seedy little airport was a madhouse of noise and confusion, jammed with sweating immigrants and American troops carrying M16s. People with odd passports were being jerked out of line and searched thoroughly. Cobra helicopters roared overhead, coming and going like drone bees, and the whole place was surrounded by rolls of sharp concertina wire. It was very much a war zone, a bad place to break any rules. A typewritten "notice to journalists" was tacked on a plywood wall by the immigration desk, advising all those with proper credentials to check in and sign the roster at the military press center in St. George's, on the other side of the island.

It was dark by the time I cleared Customs. A man named Randolph helped me load my bags into the back of his old Chevrolet taxi, and we took off for the St. George's Hotel. The road went straight uphill, a series of blind S-turns with a steep drop-off on one side and wet black cliffs on the other.

It was an hour's drive, at least, and the road was scarred every six or eight feet with deep, teeth-rattling potholes. There was no way to relax, so I thought I might as well ask Randolph how he felt about the invasion. He had not said much since we left the airport, but since we were going to be together for a while and I wanted to stop somewhere along the way for a cold beer, a bit of conversation seemed in order. I did it more out of old journalistic habit than anything else, not expecting any real information, but Randolph surprised me.

"You are asking the right person," he said sharply. "You are talking to a man who lost his wife to the Revolution."

Whoops, I thought. There was something in the tone of his voice that caused me to reach into my satchel for a small tape recorder. Randolph was eager to talk, and he had a story to tell. All I had to do was ask a question now and then, to keep pace with him, as we drove in low gear through the darkness.

It was a narrow country road, the main highway across the island, past Grenville and Great Bay and over the steep volcanic humps of Mt. Lebanon and Mt. Sinai, through the Grand Etang Forest. There were small houses along the way, like a back road in New England, and I settled back to listen as Randolph told his tale. At first I took him for a CIA plant; just another eloquent native taxicab driver who happened to be picking up journalists at the airport when they finally emerged from the Customs shed and looked around them to see nothing more than a cluster of wooden shacks in a palm grove on the edge of the sea. Pearls Airport looks like something that was slapped together about fifty years ago in the Philippines, with a dirt road bordering the airstrip and a few dozen native functionaries hanging around the one-room Bar & Grocery.

The population of the whole island is 110,000, about the size of Lexington, Kentucky, and population density is roughly one person per square mile—compared to one person per square foot in Hong Kong. This is clearly an undeveloped island, nothing at all like Barbados or Jamaica or Trinidad, and it is hard to imagine anything happening here that could make headlines all over the world and cause an invasion by the U.S. Marines.

But Randolph explained that things were different on the other side of the island, where the recent violence had happened. He welcomed the U.S. invasion, he said. It had freed him, at last, from the grip of a cruel situation that had been on his neck like an albatross ever since he and his wife had decided to join the Revolution, almost five years ago.

Neither one of them had been Communists, at the time, and Marxist was just another word he'd picked up in school, along with Maurice Bishop and Bernard Coard and the other neighborhood kids. All they knew about the U.S.A., back then, was that it was a big and powerful country where cowboys and soldiers killed Indians. They knew nothing at all about Russia, Cuba, or guns.

But things changed when Grenada became independent. Some of the boys went off to school in England, and they came back feeling ambitious. The new government was corrupt, they said; the prime minister was crazy, and the world was passing them by. Bishop and a few of his friends decided to start a political party of their own, which they called the New Jewel Movement. It was The People's Party, they said; mainly young people, with a hazy socialist platform and reggae music at rallies. Hundreds of people joined, creating a nucleus of grassroots enthusiasm that forced Eric Gairy out of office and replaced him with Maurice Bishop.

Randolph went along with it, he explained, because he believed the New Jewel Movement was going to make a better life for all the Grenadian people. He knew most of the leadership personally, and he was, after all, a businessman. While Bishop had gone off to the London School of Economics and Coard was at the University of Dublin, Randolph was climbing the ladder of commerce as an independent trucker and saving money to buy his own home. When the New Jewel came to power, he was not without friends in high places. Among them were Hendrick Radix, the new attorney general, and Hudson Austin, soon to be appointed commanding general of The People's Revolutionary Army. It was a heady time, for Randolph, the year of life in the fast lane. He had a home on a hill in St. George's, a commercial trucking license, and enough personal influence to get his new wife a job at party headquarters.

That was when the trouble started. First it was General Austin, who cheated him out of some money; then it was Phyllis Coard, wife of the deputy prime minister, who lured his wife off to Cuba. After that it was all downhill for him.

· · ·

My tape recorder was running from the time we left Pearls Airport until we pulled into the small parking lot of the St. George's Hotel. We made a few stops in dimly lit huts along the way for cold beer, which Randolph graciously paid for, because I had no Grenadian money. "Don't mention it," he said. "It's my pleasure."

Which was true. He was having a good time, and so was I. There are worse ways to enter a war zone than by stopping at every back country pub along the road and mingling with friendly people. In one place I got edgy when a huge negro wearing a hospital shirt called me a "stupid fucking Russian," but Randolph waved him off. "That man is totally crackers," he whispered. "He is one of those who ran away from the insane asylum when the bombs hit."

. . .

From my room in the St. George's Hotel, high on a steep green hill overlooking the harbor in downtown St. George's, I can see the whole town coming awake on a hot Sunday morning. The roosters begin crowing around six, the church bells begin a joyous tolling at around seven, and when I wake up at nine, there is a half-eaten pile of blue grapes on the floor between my bed and the shower stall in my bathroom. It is the sign of the fruit bat. I have never seen the beast, but the grapes are there every morning. The fruit bat brings his midnight meal into my room every night, through the window, and gnaws on his grapes while hanging upside down from the ceiling. It is his regular eating place, and neither war nor revolution nor invasion by U.S. Marines and a horde of international newsmongers will change his dinner hour.

The fruit bat is a big one. I can hear him flapping around sometimes in the darkness, and by the sound of the wings, he seems about the size of a crow. Some of them carry paralytic rabies, but it is hard to know which ones.

. . .

The lobby of the St. George's is usually empty on Sunday morning. The locals along with a handful of British subjects have gone to church, and the war correspondents are sleeping. Even Maitland—the young bartender with the high black forehead and the quick brown eyes of a boy who should be in law school somewhere—is not at his post today. The bar, attached to the dining room off a flight of steep stairs, is empty.

Even the dining room is empty. The only people in sight are a few taxi drivers sitting sleepily on the concrete wall looking down on the harbor and the big freighters tied up at the pier along the Carenage.

There is a press briefing scheduled for 10 A.M. at the Maryshaw

House, recently converted into an international press center, and some of the correspondents will want to wake up in time to be there.

My room is number 15 and there is only one key. No master at the desk, no passkey with the maid, no locksmith on the premises or anywhere closer than Bridgetown. When I locked myself out of the room yesterday, the entire infrastructure of the hotel broke down. Maitland had to abandon the bar and spend the next 45 minutes outside in the rain on a broken, rotten-wood ladder that we managed to brace up against the wall beneath my window. I held the ladder while he pulled the glass slats out of the louvered window and crawled inside to open the door.

The St. George's is a world-class hotel. It has always been one of my favorites, ranking up there with the Hotel Continental Palace in Saigon and the infamous Lane-Xang in Laos. Just after the invasion, there were six hundred reporters headquartered here and only nineteen rooms, nine with hot water. No women on the premises, no ice in the drinks, no credit cards honored, no phones, no TV, hot sauce and stale ham for breakfast . . . but the management was gracious, three elderly women who remained determinedly neutral in a situation that would have destroyed the best minds behind any desk at any Hilton or Holiday Inn.

After four weeks in the frantic heat of an utterly baffling war zone, there were no more surprises at the St. George's. When I came back to my room the other night, I found two huge wooden crosses leaning against the wall outside my door. One was about nine feet long, made of four-by-fours bolted together, and the other was six feet long, constructed in the same way. Maitland told me they belonged to the people who had checked into number 16, right next door to me—an American evangelist and his teenage son, who had carried the crosses through sixty-eight countries in six years. Nobody asked why.

> *The invasion of Grenada would not have happened if other island states in the area had not been frightened into overreacting. It takes only twelve men in a boat to put some of these governments out of business.*
>
> —Commonwealth Secretary-General Sir Shridath Ramphal, Barbados, November 29, 1983

. . .

There is a lot of loose talk in the waterfront bars on the Carenage these days. People are talking about vengeance and violence and perhaps another invasion. Psy-Ops, the U.S. military's unit for winning, whipping, and terrifying the hearts and minds of the population, has been spreading the word that Fidel Castro is promising the people of Grenada "a surprise present for Christmas."

They are still reeling from the shock of the last invasion, a full-bore assault by the U.S. Marines, Rangers, Seals, Navy jets, warships, the 82nd Airborne; thousands of parachutes, terrible explosions at all hours of the day and night, their prime minister murdered and their women carried off by wild Cubans. Their cars were stolen and all their doors were kicked in and some of their closest friends and relatives were chopped in half by machine gun fire, set on fire by rockets, drilled full of holes like something out of a Fearless Fosdick nightmare. We hit this place like it was Iwo Jima. The invasion of Grenada was one of those low-risk, high-gain, cost-plus operations that every West Point graduate dreams of. Unleash the whole weight of the U.S. military arsenal on a small island in the Caribbean and call it a great victory. Bash the buggers silly; bomb the insane; walk heavy, talk wild, and kick ass in every direction. That's how it went in Grenada.

Nobody knows why quite yet, but it will all come out in the wash. The word in the St. George's lobby today was that Tony Rushford, the new attorney general and legal representative of the British Crown, was going to put Bernard Coard on trial for murder as soon as possible.

"Those bastards are going to wish they'd never heard the word *revolution* before we get finished with this place," said a CIA plotter working for the U.S. embassy, disguised as a Caribbean scholar. "All this bullshit about Nazis and wargames and Negro target practice is going to come to a screeching halt. All you hear around this place is people saying we've got to put these bastards on trial. Okay, we're going to give you a goddamn trial. We'll have Bernie Coard and we'll hang Hudson Austin and we'll hang Liam James and Abdullah and Redhead and every other one of those Communist sons of bitches. Their mouths will run like jelly. The myth of the New Jewel Movement will be utterly destroyed. We won't even need Maurice Bishop's body. There are plenty of witnesses, and we have every one of them by the balls."

I was shocked by the tone of his voice.

He was talking about the entire leadership of the so-called military coup that overthrew Maurice Bishop's neo-Marxist, limbo-style revolutionary government that had ruled Grenada for four and a half years until an orgy of shocking violence in the last days of October turned the island into something like Uganda in the blackest days of Idi Amin . . . Bernard Coard was the deputy prime minister, a once-respected Marxist theoretician and personal friend of Bishop's. Hudson Austin was the general in charge of The People's Revolutionary Army. Abdullah, James, and Sgt. Lester "Goat" Redhead were the soldiers accused of the killings. Not just Bishop, but four of his ministers and his mistress and dozens, perhaps hundreds, of innocent civilians had been gunned down by the army when a mass rally attempted to restore Maurice Bishop to power.

There was no question of guilt, but there were some legal niceties to be observed. The bodies had been burned, and, under British Commonwealth law, it is awkward to hold a murder trial without a corpse. Treason was another possibility, but the only witnesses were dead or in Richmond Hill Prison locked up by the CIA. The first phase of the trial was scheduled for February, but without bodies or witnesses it was going to be what Tony Rushford called "a sticky wicket."

"Our mistake was not killing them instantly," said a colonel from the U.S. Army. "Summary execution—shot while attempting to escape." He laughed bitterly, sipping his beer at the Red Crab, a chic roadhouse on the outskirts of town. The mayor of Ft. Lauderdale was at the other end of the bar, whooping it up with a businessman from New Jersey who was gnawing on the throat of a black woman.

"You people are shameless," I said to the colonel.

"We are warriors," he replied, stuffing the bowl of his pipe full of Mixture 79.

"The thousand-year Reich lasted twelve years and eight months," I said.

"That's plenty of time," he replied. "Two years from today, I'll be retired and drawing a full pension."

The Yanqui press in Grenada with U.S. Army censors, Winter 1984
(HST archives)

. . .

There is some art you don't have to sign.

—Psy-Ops

Saturday night was quiet in Grenada. For the first time in three weeks there were no soldiers on the road to Grand Anse. No 82nd Airborne patrols, no roadblocks bristling with M16s and dim red flashlights, no roaring of big Cobra helicopters overhead; a man in the right mood could move along the road in a quick little topless Mini Moke and be menaced by nothing at all except wild dogs and potholes.

It was a night like any other night 300 years ago in Grenada. That is about how long it has been since the people who live here have had any peace from drunken foreigners. First it was boatloads of vicious Caribbean Indians coming over the horizon in war canoes, then it was pirates and Spaniards and Moors—all of them crazed on grog— and then came the French, who built prisons, and 200-odd years of sodden, sweating Englishmen. Finally, in 1974, came independence and a voodoo-crazed prime minister who spoke of flying saucers at the UN. Sir Eric Gairy, weirder than Papa Doc, lasted five years. He was overthrown in 1979 by a cabal of homegrown Marxists and international Trotskyites. Four years after that came the U.S. Marines.

It is a war story, but it is not like Vietnam. This is not Indochina, and the U.S. is not losing.

The people who run the White House, along with the Pentagon and the CIA, have finally done what we pay them to do, and they have done it pretty well. If the business of America is business—as Mr. Coolidge said—then a lot of people are going to get big Christmas bonuses for what was done here in the savage year of our lord 1984. We have seen America's interests threatened in the Caribbean basin, and we have crushed that threat like a roach. The Pentagon has finally won a war, in public, and the victors are enjoying the spoils.

As well they should. These are warriors, and some of them fought and died here, Cubans and Grenadians as well as eighteen American soldiers. It was not altogether a toy war. The action was swift and hazy, the truth remains unknown, and the future is decidedly cloudy.

But never mind these things. They are fey. They are only side effects compared to the wave we are riding on the south coast of Grenada these days.

Earlier in the night we had a series of crude and unstable discussions with people from the 21st Military Police Company on the lawn of what used to be the Calabash Hotel, far out on the beach past Grand Anse. They have turned the whole place into a war zone, with sandbags and machine-gun nests and trip flares strung between palm trees. And they stretched rolls of concertina wire across the lawn in front of the *Time* magazine photographer's cabana, which caused a serious argument. This was the work of the infamous "Captain Calabash," a wild-eyed MP commander who kept his troops in a sleepless frenzy of bogus security drills around the perimeters of the hotel grounds, seizing turf like a homeless mad dog for reasons that were never made clear. When his troops weren't patrolling the moonlit beach with night-vision scopes and enough weaponry to kill every fish between Grenada and the south side of Barbados, they were doing discipline drills with commando knives and twenty-five-pound steel balls and digging up the beach to fill sandbags that the Captain ordered to be stacked in huge piles across the driveways and walkways, all the way out to the sea. . . . Even the CIA spooks were embarrassed.

DINNERTIME IN GRENADA . . . MORGAN PLAYS THE PIANO AT THE RED CRAB . . . THE BOMBING OF THE INSANE ASYLUM, THE TRIAL OF BERNARD COARD, RAISING SERIOUS QUESTIONS . . . WHAT TO DO WITH BERNIE?

Some people will tell you that the army has become sophisticated, and they will have evidence to bear it out. They will have T-shirts from the war zone and they will have color slides from the beach on Prickly Bay where the naked girl danced with Captain Henegan's sentries. Or they may have videotapes of Navy F-14s dive-bombing an insane asylum overlooking St. George's harbor across from the St. George's Hotel.

Morgan was his name, they said. He played late-night piano at the Red Crab, a Caribbean roadhouse set back in the palm trees not far from the Calabash Hotel. He showed up one night not long after the invasion, and after he played a few tunes like "Fandago" and "Way Down upon the Swanee River" people liked him, and when the place was crowded, he would play for as long as they wanted, doing singa-long gigs with the State Department people and the Military Police.

They would gather around his piano and raise their beer mugs and croak hoarsely at one another, like young lions. On some nights, Colonel Ridgeway, from the State Department, would come in with a carload of women and then go out back with the waiters and smoke huge spliffs on the ledge behind the garbage cans.

V. S. Naipaul was there, along with Hodding Carter and General Jack "Promotable" Farris and a girl who was posing for a centerfold spread for *Australian Playboy*. Farris wouldn't come inside, for military image reasons; he would sit outside in his Jeep and watch the merri-ment from afar, feeling Joy in his heart and safe at last from all fears of botch and embarrassment. And never seeing his main man, Jim Ridge-way, back there on the ledge with the Rastas.

It was our kind of war. And when somebody finally asked Morgan where he came from and he said he'd spent the past year or so in the insane asylum up there on the hill near Fort Frederick, people laughed and called for another round. "Good old Morgan," they said, "he's crazy as a loon."

Which was true, or at least certifiable. This is not one of those situa-tions where you want to start delving into questions like who's crazy and who's not. Nobody needs that down here. This thing was weird from the start. People fought and died on this island, for reasons that were never ex-plained—and probably never will be until Bernard Coard comes to trial.

That should happen sometime around the spring of 1988, when the press is busy elsewhere. His lawyer will be Ramsey Clark, former attorney general of the U.S.; the prosecution will represent the Queen of England, and among those subpoenaed will be Fidel Castro, the director of the CIA, the Russian ambassador in Grenada at the time, several members of the Vigoreese Family from Marseilles, and a whole raft of armed dingbats ranging from international Trotskyites to wild whores from Trinidad and Mini Moke salesmen from Paris and vicious thugs wearing uniforms and pearl-handled .45s.

The trial of Bernard Coard—the man who killed the revolution in order to save it—will not be ignored in some circles.

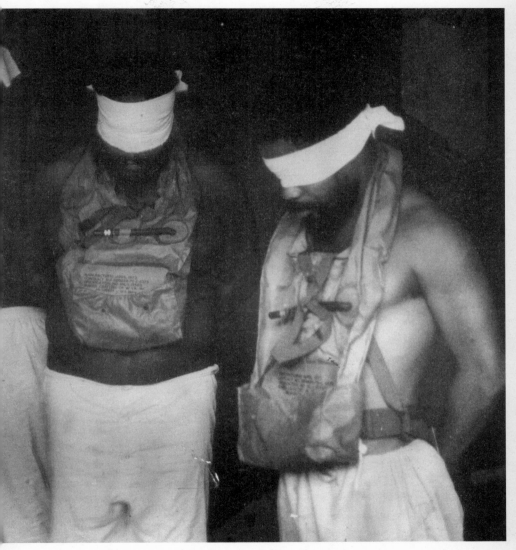

Bernard Coard faces the firing squad in Grenada, Winter 1984
(United Press)

There are no charges, as yet, but speculation ranges from murder and treason to unlawful conspiracy and crimes against the Crown. All we know for sure is that Bernard Coard—ex–deputy prime minister of Grenada in the last days of the Maurice Bishop regime—holds the key to the cruel mystery of whatever happened here in the autumn of '83.

It was a strange time, a profoundly weird chain of events. The U.S. Marines invaded; a gentle and widely popular sort of Caribbean Marxist revolution destroyed itself in a fit of insane violence; a place that could just as easily have been invaded and conquered by a gang of Hell's Angels got jumped on by the Rangers and the U.S. Marines and the 82nd Airborne and the Military Police and the U.S. Navy and Blackhawk helicopters and Psy-Ops and Night Vision scopes and concertina wire and huge explosions at all hours of the day and night and naked women brandishing machine guns.

We conquered Grenada. Even Morgan understood that. He had been in a cell on Row B when the first bombs hit. He is a mulatto, who appears to be about 40 with long blondish hair and a red headband. There is a touch of Woodstock in his bearing. Morgan looks like he was born, once again, on the corner of Haight and Ashbury in the summer of '67. He was sitting peacefully in his cell, listening to other inmates howling and jabbering frantically at the sound of low-flying jets overhead, when "suddenly the whole place exploded," he said. And after that, he fled.

. . .

I wanted to stay in Grenada for the funeral of Maurice Bishop, which was scheduled for Saturday, but when they still hadn't found the body by Wednesday, I changed my mind and decided to get out of town.

It was raining hard in the morning when we drove over the mountain to Pearls Airport on the other side of the island. There are no speed limit signs along the roads in Grenada. You can drive as fast as you want to, or as fast as your car can stand it. The potholes are square now, since the Army moved in, but some of them are still six feet deep and even the small ones are axle breakers.

There are three ways to drive on these roads, and the first two usually depend on whether you own the car or rent it. A new Mitsubishi will run about $22K in Grenada, and people who own them tend to spend a lot of time in second gear, creeping through the potholes like snails in a minefield.

The renters like to get into third gear, ignoring the damage, and bash ahead like dumb brutes, at least until the kidneys start bleeding—and when the car breaks in half, turn it in for another one. The roads are littered with wrecks, ranging from Datsun sedans to Soviet military trucks, all of them stripped to the skeleton. The radio goes first, then the jack and the wheels and all the engine parts, and finally the engine block itself, which makes a fine dead-head anchor for an offshore fishing boat. Rearview mirrors can be mounted on the bathroom wall for shaving purposes, and the seats from a new Toyota will make a stylish set of porch furniture for the whole family.

I recognize when power moves.
—Richard J. Daley, Mayor of Chicago, 1968

The invasion of Grenada was one of those stories with an essentially Midwestern heart. It was a fine mix of show business and leverage and big-time political treachery, and even Abe Lincoln would have admired the move for its swiftness, if nothing else. This is, after all, an election year, and the President is not the only one who is running for re-election. The whole Congress is up, along with a third of the Senate, and it is bad business in an election year to go back home to the district and question the wisdom of an incumbent President who has pulled off the first successful U.S. military invasion since the Inchon Landing in 1950.

On my last night in the St. George's Hotel I took a long-distance call in the lobby from a man who works on the floor of the Chicago Board of Trade. "Don't come back here with any of your liberal bullshit about oppressing the Third World," he said. "You drunken bastards have had your way long enough. It's about time you told the truth for a change."

Ambassador to Cuba

I have just received an invitation to visit Havana, from the head of the Cuban Film Commission, and my heart is full of fear. At first I was happy, but then I did some research and a feeling of queasiness came over me. I was more & more paralyzed by *Angst en Walging,* as the Dutch say. The more questions I asked, the more heinous became the answers. What had once seemed like a token of idyllic good fortune suddenly transmogrified itself, right in front of my eyes, into a guaranteed horrible experience in the dark underbelly of life in the tropics. Everything I learned convinced me that I was about to be fleeced, busted, and put in prison for treason.

MEMO FROM THE CUBA DESK:
HST / MARCH 30, 1999

Dear Jann:
Liftoff for Cuba is at 0930 & I am very excited. You will be happy to know that I am sparing no expense in moving The Desk to Cuba for the next two weeks. We are finely organized. The job is well in hand & all the key signs are perfect. The moon is in Venus & Mescalito is rising. The nights are becoming almost perfectly dark, for our purposes. No moon at all, only starlight, and no light at all when it rains.

(THIS IS AN URGENT REMINDER TO SEND A FEW SMALL LITHIUM BATTERY–POWERED *FLASHLIGHTS* IN THE *ROLLING STONE* PACKAGE TO ME AT THE NACIONAL. TELL MIKE GUY.)

The weather forecast for Cuba calls for bright mornings, rain showers in late afternoon, and extremely dark nights with strange winds. That is good news for those of us who see by starlight or have single-cell Lithium spot/floods that can illuminate a naked figure running on a beach 1,000 feet away. Not many people have those advantages, and those who do will prevail. . . . *Sic semper Tyrannus,* eh? You bet. That is the simple secret of the Winning Tradition we have established & maintained (with a few spectacular exceptions) for almost 30 years.

Wow! Who else in Journalism can make that claim? Think about it. We should establish an annual award, with lavish ceremony, for the National Affairs Desk selection for Finest Journalism of the Year, as chosen by a dazzling jury of experts like Tom & Halberstam & me & Ed Bradley—

OK. You get the idea. So let's get back to Cuba. I am leaving in a few hours and I still have to pack my Portable Ozone equipment, which is legal but very delicate. . . . That's right. I forgot to tell you that I am getting into the Ozone Business, which is a sleeping giant in Cuba. Yes, and more on that later.

I have also learned that Hemingway was into voodoo & that Castro will live for another 50 years because of Ozone . . . Also enc. find my Journal notes, to date.

TO: BOB LOVE / *ROLLING STONE*
JANUARY 29, 1999
FROM: HST

Bobby:

I have just been advised by recent travelers that having a *Journalist Visa* is, in fact, a very important & professionally desirable thing to have in Cuba. It confers a sort of VIP status & political access, as well as immunity to prosecution under the goddamn Helms-Burton Act.

The same immunity is provided, I'm told, to those who "bring medicine" into Cuba under the auspices of the U.S.–Latin American Medical Aid Foundation. (members.aol.com.uslamaf/)

A Journalist Visa also makes it "legal" (and thus easier) to conduct money transactions in Cuba. It also entitles you to drive a car with a Black license plate, which is important. Or maybe it's Yellow plates that get you through roadblocks & cause thieves & pimps & traffic cops to give your car a wide berth.

In any case, I think I might need some help from You/RS in re: securing whatever documents, visas, letters of transit, etc., that are necessary or even helpful for me to do my job down there. As Michael says, people in Cuba are very wary of talking to people who might get them in trouble. . . . And that is why so many citizens turn strangers who don't act right in to the police whenever they get pissed off.

Whoops. Never mind that. But all the same I trust you will investigate this matter and let me know ASAP. We are, after all, professionals.

Thanx,
Hunter

MEMO FROM THE NATIONAL AFFAIRS DESK
/ / / JANUARY 30, 1999
FROM HUNTER S. THOMPSON:
HOTEL NACIONAL #6: HAVANA, CUBA 60606
TO JANN / RS / NYC

Okay. I guess that will be my forwarding address for a while.
Either that (above) or the Swiss Embassy, or maybe that horrible
Isle of Pines Prison where Castro put those poor bastards from
the Bay of Pigs. Who knows? We seem to be heading into a void
of some kind, a political Time Warp full of whores & devils &
cops, where, for all practical purposes, there is no Law at all &
everything you do is half-illegal.

Sounds like Washington, eh? Yessir. Mr. Bill is very big in
Cuba, these days. Many people are counting on him to deliver
the bacon. He is Dollar Bill, Mr. Moneybags, and he is about to
make a lot of people rich.

But we'll get to that later. Right now I want to tell you a few
little things about my assignment in Havana & the relentless
high-risk weirdness I am being forced to deal with. (Whoops,
strike that. It is dangerous to use words like "force" and "deal" in
Cuba. Almost everybody will turn you in to the police if you talk
like that.)

"Bomb" is another politically unacceptable word, like
"whores" & "guns" & "dope."

SUNDAY NIGHT / AFTER THE SUPER BOWL
JANUARY 31, 1999 / OWL FARM

The Cuban situation is deteriorating faster than it is coming
together. There is a constant sense of angst about it, a sense of
being bushwacked. Some people would call it paranoid, but they
would be the dumb ones, the *Incognocenti*. Smart people understand that there is no such thing as paranoia. It is just another
mask for ignorance. The Truth, when you finally chase it down,
is almost always far worse than your darkest visions and fears.

But I am, after all, a suave gringo. I understand that many assignments are fraught with risk, personal danger & even treachery. Greed and human Weakness are ever present.

There is nothing funny, for instance, about having your passport & all your money stolen while traveling illegally in a foreign country.

Okay for that. The time has come to talk about Fun, about Victory and Victimization—about who has a sense of humor and who doesn't.

TO: COL. DEPP / LONDON / FEBRUARY 2, 1999
FROM: DR. THOMPSON / WOODY CREEK
SUBJECT: PUBLIC FLOGGINGS I HAVE KNOWN

Okay, Colonel—Good work on your brutal publicity. Kick the shit out of five or six more of those rotters & you'll make the cover of *Time*.

Or maybe you want to come to CUBA this weekend & help me write my new honky-tonk song: "Jesus Hated Bald Pussy."

Anyway, this act with the *Plank* might have legs. Let's give it a whirl in HAVANA. We could both load up on Absinth & trash a nice suite in the *Hotel Nacional*. Invite 50 or 60 Beautiful People to a party/celebration in honor of Che Guevara, which then "got out of hand." DEPP JAILED AFTER ORGY IN CUBA, PROSTITUTES SEIZED AFTER MELEE IN PENTHOUSE, ACTOR DENIES TREASON CHARGES.

Why not? And I do, in fact, have a balcony suite at the Hotel Nacional a/o February 4–14, and I could use a suave Road Manager. Shit, feed the tabloids a rumor that you have Fled to Cuba to avoid British justice. Yeah, crank that one up for a few days while you drop out of sight—and then we hit them with the ORGY IN CUBA story, along with a bunch of lewd black-and-white photos, taken by me. Shocking Proof.

Yessir. This one is definitely do-able, & it will also give me *a story*. You bet. And *Sleepy Hollow* will open in the Top Three. Trust me. I understand these things.

Meanwhile, you should be getting your finished album & 6,666 *pounds* (less my 10%) *in coin* from EMI very shortly. And I am going off to Cuba, for good or ill, on Thursday. Send word soonest.

DOC

MEMO ON WHY I AM GOING TO CUBA: WRITE THIS MESSAGE DOWN & REPEAT IT EVERY DAY . . .

I AM GOING TO CUBA TO PAY MY RESPECTS TO THE CUBAN PEOPLE & TO THANK FIDEL CASTRO FOR THE COURAGE OF HIS STRUGGLE & THE BEAUTY OF HIS DREAM. But I am mainly going for *Fun*. First, the Diary, then the Meaning . . . Remember that.

SATURDAY NIGHT, MARCH 27, 1999
NOTES

Today is not a good day for traveling to Cuba.

Hot damn, the White House is getting aggressive again.

(I understand it now. Clinton's current behavior correlates with The Advanced Syphilis Syndrome.)

Maybe this is not the time for me to travel to Cuba & denounce my own country as Nazis & be quoted on the AP wire as saying "The President is entering the final stages of Terminal Syphilis. Nothing else can explain it." (Note: Call my old friend Sandy Berger & ask *him* why we are bombing Yugoslavia.)

Ten thousand Serbs rioted in Grand Central Station yesterday, carrying signs that said NATO = NAZIS. U.S. embassies all over the world are on Red Alert & the president of Yugoslavia is on TV urging people all to strike *now* against American interests everywhere.

(5:33 A.M. Sunday morning): Jesus! Now CNN has a bulletin about a grenade attack on the U.S. embassy in Moscow: 2

grenade launchers & a Kalashnikov machine gun. Then the man fled in a white car. Who was it? Who knows? Police are rounding up the usual suspects . . . Stealth bombers blasted out of the sky over Belgrade, brave pilot flees in white car, Troops massed for invasion, WWIII looms . . . Yes sir, now is the time to go abroad & pass through many foreign airports. No problem. . . .

In the Hemingway Boat Marina, Havana, 1999
(Heidi Opheim)

. . .

Holy shit. This is insane. Now the official spokesman for NATO comes onstage & launches into a bleeding rave about War Crimes & Atrocities & a blizzard of bombs on all Warmongers who think they can get away with butchering innocent people as a way of life.

"Let me say, however, that if Yugoslavia had a democratic government, none of this would ever have happened."

What? Who are we talking about here? Who is flying those planes that are carpet bombing civilian targets 6,000 miles away from home?

Don't tell me, Bubba—let me guess. It must be the Hole in the Wall gang. No?

Well, his name ain't *Milosovich,* Bubba. And Adolf Hitler has been dead for 50 years.

There is something happening here, Mr. Jones—and you don't know what it is, do you? It sounds like a blizzard of Syphilis. Madness. Clinton, etc. . . .

> *These people are different from the others, Jack—they went to Yale, they play bridge, they fuck each other.*
>
> —CIA gossip, Havana

Right. That's what they were saying about the CIA 40 years ago, back in the good old days when they were feeding LSD-25 to each other for experimental purposes in the name of National Security. The Agency was planning to drop LSD bombs on Moscow & other enemy cities when WWIII got going. That is where the phrase "bomb their brains loose" comes from. It was CIA jargon, top secret.

But the experiments got out of hand & WWIII never happened—at least not the way they were planning it—so the phrase was dropped from the secret agency codebook.

Until now. Now it is back in style. Spooks laugh when they say it to each other at lunch. "Yes sir, we are bombing their brains loose in Belgrade. They can run, but they can't hide." That is the way CIA men talk.

We were listening to three of them flirt with one another like brutalized Yalies do.

We ran into them in a lounge at Miami International Airport when the plane was delayed for three hours by a bomb scare. There was panic for a while, but the spooks paid no attention & kept drinking, so I figured I'd do the same. Why worry? I thought. The safest place to be in a bomb panic is close to police. Keep smiling & act like a deaf person. If you accidentally drop money on the floor, count to three before you reach down to grab it. They are trained to shoot anything that moves suddenly or starts talking to the bartender about Bombs.

. . .

I was killing some time in the smoking lounge at the Miami International Airport when I noticed a man waving to me from the other side of the room. I came alert instantly. It is not a good omen, in my business, to see a strange man pointing his finger at you in a crowd at the Miami airport. For many people it is the last thing they see before they are seized by police & dragged off to jail in a choke hold. Suspicion of Criminal Activity is all they need here to lock you up & do serious damage to your travel plans. . . . Being arrested in any airport is bad, but being arrested in the Miami airport is terrifying.

I tried to ignore the man as I saw him approaching my table. Stay calm, I thought, maybe it's only an autograph seeker. . . . Then I felt his hand on my arm and he hoarsely shouted my name. I recognized the voice.

It was my old friend Rube, a rich cop from Oakland. He was on his way to Cuba, he said, to do some business and look for a woman to marry. "I have been in love with her for a long time," he said. Now he was finally free to get married. His wife back in Oakland had frozen all his assets.

I knew at once that he was on the lam. There was a fugitive look about him, despite his appearance of wealth & confident suaveness.

. . .

Cuba is not a new story for me. I have been on it for 40 years, and at times I have been very close to it—too close, on some days, and I have never pretended to be neutral or dispassionate about it. When I was 20 years old I harangued the editors of the *Louisville Courier-Journal* to send me to Cuba so I could join Fidel Castro in the Sierra Maestra mountains and send back dispatches about the triumph of the revolution. I was a Believer—not a Marxist or a Communist or some kind of agrarian Stalinist dilettante—but I was also a working journalist, and editors were not eager to pay my expenses to go to Cuba to fight with Castro in the mountains.

> *HAVANA* (CNN): FEBRUARY 15, 1999—
> *Cuba unveiled a two-pronged crackdown Monday, propos-ing harsh new penalties for common criminals and politi-cal opponents who "collaborate" with the U.S. government. The planned legislation, which would expand the use of the death penalty and introduce life imprisonment, follows a speech last month by President Fidel Castro in which he pledged to get tough on the growing crime problem on the Communist-ruled island.*
>
> *"There are even irresponsible families who sell their daughters' bodies and insensitive neighbors who think this is the most natural thing in the world. . . . There will be no escape for those who want to live like parasites at any price, at any cost, outside the law."*
>
> —Fidel Castro, January 5, 1999

It is a straight shot from Cancun to Havana, sixty-six minutes by jet plane across the Gulf of Mexico with a Soviet-blonde stewardess serv-ing free rum and synthetic ham and cheese sandwiches. It is an easy trip on most nights, and innocent people have nothing to worry about. As our plane approached Havana our mood was almost festive. Heidi filled out the visa forms while I jabbered in broken Spanish to the man sitting next to me, asking how much money I should pay for the food.

He nodded sympathetically and stared down at his hands while I fumbled with my wallet, then he turned to face me and spoke calmly. "I speak no English," he said. "I want no United States dollars." Then he signaled for the stewardess and spoke rapidly to her in Spanish while I listened nervously. Flying into Cuba is not a good time to start arguing with passengers about money.

Finally she looked over at me and smiled. "No problem," she said. "We cannot accept your dollars. All service on this flight is free of charge."

Other passengers were staring at us now, but she laughed and shrugged them off. "Don't worry," she said. "He misunderstood you. He thought you were trying to give him money."

"Oh no," I said quickly. "Of course not. I was talking about the sandwich. Money is not a problem for me. I have no money. I am a cultural ambassador."

That seemed to satisfy her, and she went away. I had received detailed instructions about how to identify myself in Cuba, and I was well armed with credentials. "You are very famous down here," the ambassador had told me on the telephone. "Your movie about Las Vegas was well received at the Cuban film festival recently, so you will enjoy a diplomatic status that will be very helpful, as long as you don't bring any drugs."

"Don't worry," I assured him. "That movie was Hollywood propaganda. I am no longer a dope fiend. I gave that stuff up a long time ago."

"That's good," he said. "A cultural ambassador enjoys many privileges in Cuba these days, but dope fiends are being rounded up and put in prison—sometimes for life, and we won't be able to help you at all."

I was thinking about this conversation as our plane approached the coast of Cuba, but I was not apprehensive. I was traveling officially this time and I knew I had nothing to fear. My nerves were calm and I leaned back. I was looking forward to some serious grappling with booze, which is still a very acceptable vice in Cuba. I was even considering an offer to become a distributor of Absinth on the island, but that was still in the planning stages and I was not in any hurry.

Cuba was going to be busy. My schedule was already thick with cultural obligations: dinner with the ambassador, lunch with the minister of culture, book signings at the Film Institute, judging the Water Ballet at the Hotel Nacional, marlin fishing with the Old Man of the Sea . . . The list was long, and I was already looking for ways to pare it down and make time for my nonofficial business, which was equally important and would probably involve meeting with people who had recently fallen out of favor with the government in the wake of the Crackdown that followed Castro's ruthless denunciation of pimps and pederasts and collaborators at the beginning of '99.

There was also the matter of Johnny Depp's arrival in three days, which I knew would attract some attention in cultural circles, and I understood that we would have to be suave and well liked in public.

We needed government approval to shoot our movie in Havana. It was definitely not the time to be getting any criminal publicity.

As the lights of the city came into view up ahead and the stewardess said it was time to buckle our seat belts, I began to feel nervous and I decided to go up to the lavatory for a shave and a lash of the toothbrush before we landed. There was muttering when I stood up, but I felt it was necessary. An ambassador should always be clean-shaven and never have booze on his breath. That is a cardinal rule of the business.

I was fumbling around for a razor when I discovered the ball of hashish in my dopp kit. It was snuggled into a corner behind a bar of soap from the Four Seasons in New York, and I tried to ignore it. No doubt it had been there for many months or even years, unnoticed by anybody until now. The sight of it made me dizzy and weak. The razor fell from my fingers and I sagged against the tin wall as the stewardess hammered on the door and I felt the plane descending. For an instant I was paralyzed by panic, then my criminal instincts took over and I fired a blast of Foamy into my shaving kit, making a nasty mess on the bottom, but it was no use. The ball of hash still loomed up like a black iceberg, so I grabbed it and tried to flatten it out, then I dropped it in my coat pocket and tried to forget about it.

When I got back to my seat I said nothing to Heidi about the hashish, for fear she would go all to pieces. (I had sworn to be clean and she had trusted me . . .) Nor did I say anything to Michael Halsband, our tour guide and confidential photographer from New York, who had been assigned to this visit at the last moment.

He was a total stranger, in fact, and I was leery of him from the start, but he met us in Cancun anyway and attached himself like a leech. . . . I didn't know it at the time, but he would be with me for the rest of the trip. He was a swarthy little man wearing a seersucker coat and a goofy grin of a surfer on his face.

He introduced himself as a famous rock and roll photographer and almost immediately tried to sell me a used Rolleiflex camera. He was paying his own expenses, he said, and he had our letters of passage from the Cuban government and the prestigious Ludwig Institute— we would quickly become dependent on these people.

As our plane approached Havana, however, I saw no reason to

upset him with my story about mysteriously finding contraband in my kit at the last moment. A lot of people have gone to prison in Cuba for telling stories like that to cops. So I fastened my seat belt and prepared for the ordeal of wading through a cordon of military police.

They were all around the jetway when the door opened, with Soviet submachine guns and angry dogs on leashes. "We have nothing to worry about," I said to Heidi. "We are coming into a war zone. Pay no attention to these freaks. They will not bother us. We are innocent. Just follow Halsband and do what he does."

Our fellow passengers fell silent as we were herded out the door and into a long white-tiled hallway with no exits. Finally we arrived at the Immigración gate and I noticed people being jerked out of line by men in black suits . . . Halsband was one of those. The sight of it put me into a panic, but I tried to stay calm and grin vacantly into the air and pretend like nothing was happening. Other passengers in line behaved the same way; nobody wanted to see anything weird, so they ignored it. What the hell? People are jerked out of line by police every day in airports all over the world—and we were, after all, coming into one of the few remaining Communist-ruled nations on Earth.

Heidi was next in line, and she too was seized for questioning. I could see Halsband emptying his pockets and babbling at cops while they searched him.

We found ourselves separated and taken off in different directions. Cuban security techniques are very sophisticated, they say. We were individually searched and questioned, then released in a maze of confused passengers.

It was at that point that I decided to break ranks and flee, but there was nowhere to run. All the escape routes were sealed off by cops with dogs, and our luggage was nowhere in sight. I looked around quickly and saw that the only place where a sick man could sit down was an ominous-looking enclosure where cops were interrogating suspects, including the man who'd been sitting next to us on the plane.

So that is where I went. It is a firm rule of behavior in times of emergency in airports: When you are guilty always move toward the police, never run away from them.

The cops eyed me warily as I sat down among them, but they said nothing. Well, I thought, this is it for me. I took off my hat and removed the huge black widow spider from it, then I lit a cigarette.

The Ludwig people were waiting outside, but we couldn't communicate with them. All the other passengers had left the airport, but not us. We were conspicuously detained like people on Devil's Island while soldiers rummaged through my Kevlar luggage, one item at a time, and Heidi was taken away to the X-ray booth.

My first sense of real trouble came when I heard the sound of shattering glass from the search and seizure area. It was a rubber ball-peen hammer that exploded with the sound of shattering glass whenever you whacked something with it. It was not the kind of humor you normally want to bring to a Communist war zone.

I could see them over my shoulder, but I tried not to notice. The soldiers were demonstrating the hammer to each other, and finally one of them laughed. Thank God, I thought, at least these people have a morbid sense of humor. . . . They also laughed at the Retractable Stabbing Knife, which Heidi explained by jamming it into her chest.

I was rattled by the scene at the airport, and so was our welcoming committee. They were cultural-exchange people, ranking officials of the prestigious Ludwig Institute, a German art foundation that runs many of Cuba's foreign-exchange programs. The Ludwig people walk tall in Havana and they are not accustomed to having their guests detained and ransacked at the airport. By the time our luggage was finally released, there was nobody else in the Arrivals terminal except cops, and I had already met most of them. They eyed us sullenly as we drove away in the darkness toward Havana. I had a queasy feeling that we had not seen the last of them.

Our host, a jovial man called Helmo, was eager to dismiss what he called "the unpleasantness at the airport" and to "refresh ourselves with laughter." Halsband was mildly hysterical about his own ordeal with the Aduana police and Heidi was still crying. I tried to shake it off by drinking heavily from a bottle of rum.

I was feeling a little better about life when we finally arrived and pulled into the long, palm-lined driveway of the Hotel Nacional. There was something familiar about it, from a distance, and I had a weird sense of coming home, but I knew it was impossible. I had never been to Havana, never even dreamed about it—but I was extremely familiar with The Breakers hotel in Palm Beach, and the Nacional looks exactly like it.

From a distance—but once you get inside, it is different, very different, and it takes a while to grasp this. We were met at the door by the same sharp-looking baggage handlers that you see at The Breakers. The air when you step out of the car is the same balmy breeze that you feel in Palm Beach, the same heady mix of salt air and romance and mystery. Even the vast lobby and the elevators and the hallways are exact replicas of The Breakers. The only real difference, at first, was that we were taken immediately to a special elevator and ushered straight up to the super-exclusive sanctuary of the Sixth Floor, where our oceanfront suites were prepared.

I have always hated The Breakers, in truth, and I will always hate the Hotel Nacional—but I hate a lot of places that look nice in the tourist brochures; I go to hotels for business reasons, not to relax and have fun. Sometimes it ends up that way, but you can't count on it. The way I look at it, business is business, and the only things that really matter in hotels are privacy, fresh oysters, and good telephones.

The terrace bar at the Hotel Nacional was almost empty when we arrived. A lone bartender stared at us but said nothing. The walls were covered with signed photos of American celebrities from the forties and fifties: black-and-white glossies of people like Frank Sinatra, Errol Flynn, and Ava Gardner, along with political heroes like Winston Churchill and Meyer Lansky. It is a strange mix of people to run into at that hour.

It was in the deserted terrace bar of the Hotel Nacional that I first heard the story of Artie Diamond, the vicious convict from Sing Sing who intimidated the whole prison by biting off the ear of a con boss who called him a sissy. It was a Mike Tyson story, being told in slow motion by a hard-bitten man from New York who once fought for the middleweight championship of the world on an undercard with Tyson before he started carrying his Artie Diamond act too far.

We were all sitting outside in the darkness, huddled around a lumpy wicker table with a glass top that went sideways and spilled the drinks every time a breeze came up. A lone waiter scurried back and forth with trays of rum daiquiris and black Cuban coffee balanced crazily in the wind.

. . .

You can learn a lot of things just by hanging out in front of the Hotel Nacional in Havana. There is a heavy mix of criminals and foreigners and
beautiful women with special agendas. Nobody is exactly what they seem
to be in Havana, and that is especially true at the Hotel Nacional, which
enjoys a worldwide reputation for the finest hospitality in Cuba.

The Malecon is the long, wide boulevard that runs along the waterfront in Havana. The harbor is badly polluted, but a mile offshore,
where the Gulf Stream runs, the water is pure and fast. No islands dot
the horizon. There is nothing between here and Key West except
ninety miles of deep water and six million sharks. Some people go out
there for fun, but not many. The Gulf of Mexico at night is strictly for
business—commercial freighters, commercial fishermen, floating
wreckage, and the occasional human skeleton.

The Malecon is different. There is life along the boulevard, strolling
lovers and pedicabs and knots of police-affiliated hoodlums gathered
here and there under streetlights, hooting at cars and tossing fish heads
to crocodiles, which can surface like lightning and jump five feet
straight up in the air when they think they see fresh meat. Cuban crocodiles are a special breed of beasts, famous for their athleticism and
their cruelty. A croc in a fit of temper can swallow a small boy and two
six-packs of beer in one gulp.

. . .

Bill Clinton has a long and ugly history involving Cuba. It goes back to
the 1980 Mariel boatlift, when Castro emptied his country of "dissi-
dents" by sending 125,000 "refugees" to Key West in a matter of weeks,
many of them criminally insane. They were taken off the boats and
shipped up U.S.A. 1A to detention camps in Miami, where many found
work and refuge in the city's vast and thriving anti-Castro Cuban community, but not all. About 50,000 of them were screened and found to
be so vicious, violent, and incorrigible that they could never be assimi-
lated into any culture, anywhere, and they could not go back to Cuba because of their status as "political refugees." So they were sent off in chains
to various prisons around the country, to maximum-security cages like
Danbury, Lompoc, and Marion—where they immediately terrorized the
existing prison population and even the guards and wardens. They were

extremely bad people, the meanest of the mean, and also Criminally Insane. They were dangerous and utterly uncontrollable.

Some 18,000 of these savage incorrigibles wound up at a U.S. military prison in Fort Chaffee, Arkansas, despite the vehement objections of the politically ambitious young governor, William Jefferson Clinton, then running for re-election. His Republican opponent, along with every newspaper in the state, denounced Clinton for allowing this dangerous scum to be funneled into central Arkansas, but Bill blamed it on Jimmy Carter, who had blatantly "double-crossed" him by sending those brutes to Fort Chaffee without his prior knowledge or consent.

Shortly before the gubernatorial election, a massive jailbreak sent 7,000 of the most violent "refugees" into the streets of one of our permanent army bases at Fort Chaffee, where they ran amok with machetes until the National Guard finally quelled the uprising after three days of tear gas and bloody hand-to-hand fighting.

The voters were not amused. Clinton was mauled on Election Day and moved ignominiously out of the Governor's Mansion. It was the only election Bill Clinton ever lost. He waited two years, then ran again and won, and the rest is history. But he never forgot the nightmare inflicted on him by Jimmy Carter and the Cubans.

. . .

Skaggs was a free thinker and he had an active mind. He owned three boats in the Marina Hemingway and didn't mind saying that he had come to Cuba to have fun and he had plenty of dollars to spend. That is a dangerous mix in Havana these days, with the government suddenly enforcing a crackdown on everything he stood for, but he said it didn't bother him. "I have all my papers in order," he explained as we careened along the Malecon at top speed in a new silver Z28 convertible with the Rolling Stones booming out of the speakers. "The police here are all Communists," he added. "You have to remember that. They are Primitive people, but they are very sophisticated on a military level. You can't put anything over on them. I was arrested three times on my way over to your hotel today."

"What?" I said. "Three times? In one day? Jesus Christ, Skaggs. That's frightening. Maybe this is the wrong night for us to be out on the streets."

"Don't worry," he said. "They know I have all my paperwork in order. I think they're just queer for this car. They like to pull me over and fondle it while they check me out."

Skaggs is a gentleman of leisure from Arkansas, a man of the sporting life who is also a good friend of Bill Clinton's. I have known him for many years and consider him a good and honorable man, essentially, but he has a deep streak of the Arky and the boomer and the wild boy in him that is likely to go sideways on you and reach for a shotgun at any moment. He is a handsome man with suave manners and a relentless appetite for profitable business investments.

Cuba was one of these, he admitted, but his enviable position as a friend of the president was becoming an awkward burden on his sense of possibility. "I've had three or four federal grand juries on my ass for five years," he said. "First they tapped all my phones, then they started following me everywhere I went. People I'd known all my life were afraid to be seen with me. I moved out of town to the duck lodge, but it was no use. Finally I said, 'Fuck this, I'm getting too old for it,' so I bought a goddamn boat and went to Cuba."

. . .

The yacht harbor at Marina Hemingway on the outskirts of Havana was one of the first Enemy enclaves to be shut down completely. There were no more parties on the party boats tied up along the seedy-looking canals. Cuban girls were no longer allowed in the marina, and the only Cuban men in sight wore official police uniforms. It was like the Nazis had suddenly clamped down on the waterfront in Casablanca. Ernest Hemingway would have been shocked.

We spent a lot of time in the maze of dim gravel streets that wind through Marina Hemingway. Only a few big boats remained from the decadent good old days before the War and the fearful crackdown on prostitution that so crippled the Party spirit in Havana, and the few people still living onboard were treated like perverts and spies. My friend Skaggs from Little Rock was arrested four times on the first day we met with him, and his boat was visited three times by police one night when we were trying to relax and watch the War news on his clandestine TV set in the galley.

We were sitting around a teakwood map table in the cabin of his

Grand Banks trawler in the Hemingway Marina when the TV news came alive with a flurry of live photos of American prisoners of war just captured in Yugoslavia. It was one of those scenes that you know will be clearly imprinted in your memory for the rest of your life—people weeping and shouting in Texas with horror in their eyes and neighbors tying yellow ribbons around telephone poles in one another's front yards under the watchful eyes of many TV cameras and dogs howling off-camera.

Skaggs slammed his fist on the table and cried out: "GOD-DAMNIT, THIS IS TOO DEPRESSING. THEY SHOULD TAKE THOSE BASTARDS OUT AND EXECUTE THEM TOMOR-ROW MORNING."

"What?" I said. "Get a grip on yourself, Skaggs. Those people can't be executed. They are prisoners of war."

"Bullshit," he said. "They are spies. They should be EXECUTED. That's the only way to get the president's attention."

I was shocked. Skaggs is a died-in-the-wool Clinton backer, and his wife is strongly opposed to the death penalty under any circumstances. She makes two or three trips to Washington every year to lobby against Police Brutality. It was weird to hear him calling for the execution of U.S. POWs.

But she was not with us on the boat in Cuba that night, so he felt free to vent. "The bastard has gone too far this time," he explained. "He thinks he can drop a 2,000-pound bomb on anybody who won't salute him." He shook his head angrily and chopped off another few chunks of ice with his fishing tool. "The president is not crazy. He's just plain stupid. I learned that a long time ago, back when I was still raising money for his goddamn never-ending campaigns."

The boat rocked gently beneath our feet as he jumped down into the darkened hold where he kept his music equipment. "Hot damn!" he exclaimed. "Let's hear some Sonny Boy Williamson!"

I felt a shudder go through me as the amp kicked in. Everybody jumped and Heidi tried to stand up, but the music was too powerful. It turned every beam and strut and bench on the boat into a wooden tuning fork; it was like a shock through the colon every time Sonny Boy hit a G string. Glasses rattled on the table.

The music was so loud and the War news so terrifying that it took us a while to realize that somebody was pounding on the back door. It was a cop complaining about the noise, but Skaggs took him outside and we went back to sucking heavily on our Cohibas.

We were not degenerates, and neither was Skaggs, to my knowledge, and we were doing nothing illegal. But cops were watching us anyway, and that is a nervous feeling when you're sitting on a boat in a foreign harbor.

. . .

We were waiting for Ray (a.k.a. Colonel Depp)—my personal bodyguard and international road manager from London—in the airport lounge when I heard the unmistakable whine of an electric drill from behind a closed door near the baggage carousel. It was penetrating something that was too soft to offer much resistance, and I thought I knew what it was. My own Kevlar suitcase had been drilled five times when we came through the airport two nights earlier—five neat little holes going into the bag from five different directions—and now I knew it was Ray's turn. I knew we were in for a long wait.

Halsband slumped on his stool and ordered four more Mojitos while Heidi paced crazily back and forth on the slick tile floor. Ray was nowhere in sight, and we could only guess at his fate. Once they start drilling your luggage in this country, the next few hours are going to be very edgy. First your bag will be marked with an ominous red XXX, then it will be thoroughly searched and examined. You will be questioned repeatedly about the same things: "Why do you have all these red cigarettes? Are you wearing false teeth? Will you come with me to the X-ray machine on the other side of that wall? Why are you here? What are you carrying in that toothbrush? Was your mother born in Algiers? Who is your personal dentist? Why are you acting so nervous?"

The correct answer to all of these questions is "No"—over and over, "No"—and the price of inconsistency can be ten years in a Cuban prison. Never be inconsistent. If the Customs cop thinks he heard you say that your mother is a dentist in Algiers the first time he asks, your answer must be exactly the same when he asks the same question five minutes later. Do not change your story in even the smallest detail. That way lies trouble.

I knew Ray was carrying a mixed bag of personal presents, including bottles of Absinth and night-vision binoculars and frozen shirts and Nazi SS jewelry. He also had rare medicines from Europe and oriental hand fans and many thousands of dollars and perfumes and cameras and pornography and sophisticated tattoo paraphernalia. He looked like an international Pimp with no respect for the law. If his luggage was searched he was doomed.

A Cuban band was singing "Guantanamera" on TV in the airport bar, but we were all too nervous to enjoy the music. "We may have to make a run for the car," I whispered to Halsband. "Somebody is about to get busted here."

He looked startled and quickly drank off his Mojito. "Stop worrying about cops," he said. "Everybody's a cop in this country. Ray will have no trouble," he said. "He is bulletproof."

Just then the lights went dim in the airport and people stopped talking. I felt a hand clutch my arm in the darkness and heard Heidi moaning, "O my god, O my god . . ."

It was Ray. He had slipped unnoticed through the gate when the lights went dim and the mob of paranoid tourists began to panic. We paid the bill quickly and rushed out to our waiting white "limousine," saying nothing. Terror is never very far away in Cuba, and smart people flee like rats at the first sign of it. The first thing to do when a panic starts is get a grip on your wallet and walk, not run, toward the nearest exit. Women always clutch their purses and try not to show signs of fear in these moments, but suave behavior is difficult when the lights go out in a foreign airport full of perverts and thieves and spies and Communist police all around you.

Yes sir, and that is when the last thing you need for a goddamn fail-safe escape vehicle is a broken-down 49-year-old Cadillac sedan with a secondhand Yugo engine under the hood.

. . .

Whenever I think of Cuba now I see the Malecon at night and Tall Cops on shiny, black motorcycles circling around on the boulevard far down below my balcony at the Hotel Nacional, controlling the traffic and scanning the seawall for pimps and accused collaborators . . . I remember the War news on TV and the constant babble of Christiane Amanpour somewhere in Albania and Dan Rather waiting to be bombed in Belgrade and U.S. prisoners of war exhibited on worldwide

TV with lumps on their heads and bleeding black eyes and their cheek muscles rigid with fear. I remember the War news raving twenty-four hours a day on both TV sets in our suite and people of all persuasions rushing in and out with crazy news and rumors. We went through thirty or forty weird meat sandwiches and forty-eight silver buckets of rare ice every twenty-four hours. The phones rang sporadically, often for no reason at all, and the few phone messages that got through were garbled and frightening: Havana was about to be bombed and/or destroyed by U.S. nukes full of napalm and nerve gas and vermin eggs. A man from Houston called and said a bomb blew the gates off the U.S. embassy last night. A lawyer from Sweden on a decadent-looking yacht called *White Power* said he'd heard on his shortwave radio that Clinton had officially declared a state of war against Cuba.

It turned out not to be true—but real news travels slowly in Cuba and the military police went on Invasion Alert status anyway, and the streets were swept clean of degenerates and other usual suspects who might be trying to swim naked in the harbor.

. . .

We were under close and constant surveillance the whole time. We were treated like rich prisoners of war. Our rooms were bugged, our baggage was drilled, cops roamed the hallways and had a key to every safe in the hotel.

There is a serious *crackdown* in Cuba on Drugs, Prostitution, and Bombs. You want to grin and do the Salsa any time you have to stand in line for anything, even waiting for a cab. The urge to dance and spend dollars is an acceptable vice on this island, but anything else can be dangerous.

Degenerates are no longer fashionable in Cuba, and anybody suspected of "collaborating" with the U.S. Embassy is a degenerate. That is the long and the short of it. War zones are always difficult, especially for the Enemy—and the Enemy, as we quickly discovered in Cuba, is us. You bet. You want to see the bogeyman, Bubba? Just look in the mirror. People in Cuba do not see the American Century the same way we do. If sheep go to heaven and goats go to hell, we are definitely the goats of this story.

HST and James Carville, Little Rock, 1992
(Stacey Hadash)

Witness III

Statement by Dr. Hunter S. Thompson,
March 13, 1990

BE ANGRY AT THE SUN

That public men publish falsehoods
Is nothing new. That America must accept
Like the historical republics corruption and empire
Has been known for years.

Be angry at the sun for setting
If these things anger you. Watch the wheel slope and turn,
They are all bound on the wheel, these people,
    those warriors.
This republic, Europe, Asia.

Observe them gesticulating,
Observe them going down. The gang serves lies,
    the passionate
Man plays his part; the cold passion for truth
Hunts in no pack.

You are not Catullus, you know,
To lampoon these crude sketches of Caesar. You
    are far
From Dante's feet, but even farther from his dirty
Political hatreds.

Let boys want pleasure, and men
Struggle for power, and women perhaps for fame,
And the servile to serve a Leader and the dupes
    to be duped.
Yours is not theirs.

                                    —Robinson Jeffers

From the *Aspen Times Daily,*
Monday, June 18, 1990

KNOCK, KNOCK—WHO'S THERE?

Editor:

And so it's done
Who lost,
Who won—
Each and every
One and all
Both sides—
Losers
Winners—
None
Justice done
A dis-service
Did she—
Deserve this
Mockery?
Did we?
I think not

In the end
All we've got
Are the rules
We choose to play by
Fair and square
Even Steven
Even though
Who's got the dough
'S better chance
To finish even
The good doctor
Fought the law
To a draw
Called their bluff
Had the stuff
The courage and conviction
To risk it all
Bet his freedom—
On a pair of deuces—
Right and privacy,
'Gainst a black king—
Of—hypocrisy
And so—
Now we know
Tho' the Hunter prevailed
On this occasion,
Chased the fox
From his doors—
Is that someone
Knockin' on yours?

—Edward T. Cross

(HST archives)

. . .

Why is it, Lord, that tonight I find myself writing feverishly on a 30-year-old IBM Selectric typewriter . . . It is sure as hell *not* a matter of convenience. This thing is slow and heavy and primitive. It is a sort of dark *institutional* red color that makes it appear to be twice as large as it is. Some people fear it—especially when they can see three or four brand-new customized *Super Electrics* laying idle around the house still wrapped in cellophane while the slow labored *THUNK* of these ancient keys slapping into the ribbon is the only sound in the room.

To me it sounds like hardened steel ball-bearing tumblers dropping into place. Indeed, I know that sound well. It is a sound you never hear except in quasi-desperate situations where the Fate of NEARBY people depends entirely on yr. ability to solve a particularly stubborn vault combination lock when you are trying to flee for yr. life before a horde of boozed-up cannibal Nazis swarms in through the windows and butchers your whole family, only to find that all yr. guns and money and helicopter keys are hopelessly locked up in this goddamn dysfunctional safe that refuses to open.

Ho ho. That is when you want to hear those beautiful little tumblers fall. *Click click click,* just like in Hollywood . . . These are the sounds that really matter in yr. life.

Yes sir, and that is about all we need to know about atavistic typewriters and amateur safecrackers for today. Let us return now at once to the more violent days of yesteryear and my fight to the death with vicious crooked cops in that incredibly violent winter of 1990 when they tried to take me into the system.

D.A. SNAGS THOMPSON IN SEX CASE
BY DAVID MATTHEWS-PRICE,
TIMES DAILY STAFF WRITER
FEBRUARY 28, 1990

Hunter S. Thompson, in an episode reminiscent of some of his books, has been charged with sexually assaulting a woman writer who came to his house ostensibly to interview him last week.

Thompson, 52, surrendered at the District Attorney's office on Monday and is free on $2,500 bond.

Thompson told the *Times Daily* he's innocent and believes the alleged victim isn't so much a writer as she is a business woman who wants publicity for her new venture, which is selling sexual aids and lingerie.

"She's a business person in the sex business," Thompson said.

He said he's also suspicious of the motives of the District Attorney, who had six officers search his Woody Creek house on Monday for drugs. Officers said they found a small quantity of suspected cocaine and marijuana.

Thompson offered his own headline for the case: "Lifestyle-police raid home of 'crazed' gonzo journalist; 11-hour search by six trained investigators yields nothing but crumbs."

Lab Results Pending

District Attorney Milt Blakey said he's waiting for the results of lab tests before deciding whether to bring drug charges.

Thompson is already facing charges of third-degree sexual assault for allegedly grabbing the woman's left breast and third-degree simple assault for supposedly punching her during an argument about whether the interview should take place in a hot tub. Both misdemeanors carry a maximum two-year sentence in the county jail.

The woman making the allegations is a 35-year-old self-employed writer from St. Clair, Mich., who said she was visiting Snowmass Village with her husband last week.

The *Times Daily* was unable to contact the alleged victim on Tuesday. However, her story about the Feb. 21 incident was detailed in an affidavit for an arrest warrant written by district attorney investigator Michael Kelly.

Affidavit Tells Story

The woman said she had written Thompson before arriving in Snowmass to request an interview. Such interviews are the fascination of out-of-town journalists. Just last week *Time* magazine published a first-person account of another writer's attempt to interview Thompson, a columnist for the *San Francisco Examiner* and national editor of *Rolling Stone* magazine.

The woman said she arrived at Thompson's house in a taxicab, on Woody Creek Road, and was greeted by a woman named Kat who introduced her to Thompson and two of his friends, identified only in the affidavit as Semmes and Tim.

Drug Suspicions

Within a few minutes, the woman suspected the group had been using drugs, the affidavit stated.

"She suspected some members of the group might be using drugs because from time to time they would get up (and) go into the other room and then return in a minute or so," the affidavit stated.

Then, about three hours after arriving at the house, the alleged victim said she saw Thompson carrying a green grinder that produced a white powder substance, according to the affidavit.

"This substance, which she believed to be cocaine, was then passed around to the group and that with the exception of Tim and herself each ingested (snorted) some of it into their noses by means of a straw," the affidavit said.

Paranoid Group

"She observed the group becoming increasingly suspicious and paranoid," the affidavit said.

The woman writer said she got up and called her husband, a move which made the group suspicious that she might be an undercover agent.

She assured them that she wasn't an agent, she explained. Then Semmes and Tim left the house and Thompson gave her a tour of the residence.

She said Thompson showed her his favorite room, which contained a hot tub, and he supposedly suggested that she join him for a dip in the water.

Next, she claimed that Kat attempted to persuade her to join Hunter in the hot tub by telling her things such as "He's a harmless guy," "(He's) a little crazy at times, but he will never hurt you," "He'd really like you to get into the hot tub with him," etc., according to the arrest warrant affidavit. "She told Kat she had no intention of getting into the tub and that it was her intention to conduct a professional interview," the affidavit stated.

Soon the argument began and the woman said Thompson lost control and threw a glass of cranberry juice and vodka in her direction. She said she ducked.

Then, she claims Thompson grabbed her left breast, "squeezing and twisting it very hard. He then punched her in her left side with his right fist, and finally pushed her backwards with the palms of [his] . . . hands," the arrest warrant affidavit stated.

She said that Thompson then went to the room

where he keeps some of his guns and that she ran out of the house and sat on the porch. A cab took her away about 15 minutes later.

Thompson, in an interview with the *Times Daily,* said the woman was "real drunk, sloppy drunk."

Thompson said the woman wanted sex with him.

"I pushed her away from me. She went backwards and one hand brushed her breast," Thompson said.

Conflict of Interest

A day later, the woman called the sheriff's department. Sheriff Bob Braudis said that because of his 20-year friendship with Thompson, he felt he would have a conflict of interest handling the case. Braudis gave the investigation to the District Attorney's office, which has its own investigators.

Thompson said officers took 11 hours to search his house because they were frustrated they couldn't find much evidence of drug usage or wrongdoing.

"I don't know if that (11-hour search) helps my reputation or hurts it," he said.

District Attorney Blakey said officers found possible drug paraphernalia and a small quantity of suspected marijuana and possible cocaine. The suspected drugs have not been weighed, Blakey said. All of the possible drug-related items have been sent to the Colorado Bureau of Investigation lab in Montrose, the prosecutor added.

Overzealous Cops?

Blakey bristled Tuesday at suggestions that Thompson—who has made fun of cops in his books—was set up by overzealous law officers.

"That's absolutely not true," Blakey said. "If

there was overzealous law enforcement here, he
wouldn't have been called and asked to come to the
D.A.'s office (to be arrested).

"Hunter Thompson is just like anyone else; he's
going to get fair treatment under the law, no better or worse," Blakey promised.

*"For my part, I had lived about 10 miles out of
town for two years, doing everything possible to
avoid Aspen's feverish reality. My lifestyle, I
felt, was not entirely suited for doing battle with
any small town political establishment. They had
left me alone, not hassled my friends (with two un-
avoidable exceptions—both lawyers), and consistently ignored all rumors of madness and violence in
my area. In return, I had consciously avoided writing about Aspen . . . in my very limited congress
with the local authorities I was treated like some
kind of half-mad cross between a hermit and a
wolverine; a thing best left alone as long as possible."*

Hunter S. Thompson
Rolling Stone *magazine*
Oct. 1, 1970

. . .

The Witness case turned on the day they decided to search the
house, the day I got arrested. I got in such a rage that it was war.
From then on I was in a kill-or-be-killed scenario; until then I hadn't
really paid that much attention to it. It was a bag of shit. But my own
lawyer got me busted. He invited me down to the courthouse to be
taken and fingerprinted. I knew I was in trouble. So from then on it
was just that rage. I don't know if that's good or bad. It's focus and
concentration. It was a little bit like the Mailbox—when I made that
decision to ask, "What Witnesses?" That eerie soliloquy . . . "It's a
matter of taste." It always boils down to a question of taste.

The Mailbox incident was a confidence builder, I think, but it didn't teach me that I was smarter than they were. It taught me that they were not as smart as they thought they were. I did not plead guilty on that one, and I got in the habit of that. It is a red thread in this book. I have been looking for one, and that is what it is.

GONZO'S LAST STAND?

Sometime on the night of February 21, Dr. Charles Slater called the Sheriff's Office to complain that Thompson had assaulted his wife—the precise time of his call is very much at issue, for the *Aspen Times Daily* has reported that the tape which automatically records all incoming calls is missing Dr. Slater's. Later on that night (sometime between 2 A.M. and 5 A.M. on February 23, actually), Palmer's former boyfriend and business partner Marco DiMercurio also called. Saying that he was speaking from Los Angeles, DiMercurio claimed that Thompson had in the course of the evening held a gun to Palmer's head. He insisted that there be an investigation, but warned that Palmer couldn't be interviewed until after 2 P.M.

By then, Sheriff Braudis had withdrawn from the case: A close friend of Thompson's, he'd been criticized for not being sufficiently aggressive in investigating the dispute between Thompson and Floyd Watkins. Seeking to ensure the appearance of fairness, Braudis transferred the complaint to Chip McCrory, the deputy district attorney for Aspen. McCrory, formerly a prosecutor from a Denver suburb, was appointed to the Aspen office in 1985, becoming chief deputy after his predecessor resigned in 1988.

Though McCrory is neither well liked nor regarded as politically ambitious, the conservative down-valley Republican named Milton Blakey is affectionately called "Judge Blakey" by those who like him well enough to tease him about his much desired judicial appointment. . . .

With Blakey's encouragement, McCrory has moved sharply away from the path marked out by his predecessors who'd tempered the prosecutorial urge with a healthy dose of what the Supreme Court has called "community standards." McCrory, for instance, recently brought—and lost, after less than an hour of jury deliberation—a felony case for the alleged sale of some $25 worth of cocaine. Even more problematic was his decision to seek a felony conviction against a well-regarded young woman who, while being booked for a DUI, pushed a recovered-alcoholic jailer who was pressuring her about the virtues of AA. Even members of the jury that had just convicted her were horrified to discover that the law that McCrory chose to invoke—which was designed to discourage incarcerated prisoners from assaulting their guards during riots—carried an inescapable mandatory prison sentence. ("Old Aspen," including the mayor, has contributed generously to her appeal fund.) For the zealous McCrory, who'd been prominent among those criticizing the sheriff's allegedly laissez-faire attitude toward Thompson, Palmer's tale of sex, violence, drugs, and weaponry must have seemed a dream come true.

Whatever the cause, McCrory seems to have reacted to Palmer's complaint with more speed than prudence. Without interviewing any of the other people who'd been at Thompson's, McCrory drew up charges for assault and sexual assault, and then—after a local judge had passed on signing a search warrant—had it signed by a judge some 60 miles downvalley.
The Village Voice, *May 15, 1990, Vol. XXXV, No. 20*

. . .

There are a lot of jackasses in the world who think they are smarter than I am. There are a lot of smart cops. But most of them don't get into this kind of chickenshit case.

D.A. MAY FILE CASE AGAINST ASPEN WRITER
BY EVE O'BRIEN
SPECIAL TO *THE DENVER POST*

The district attorney of Pitkin County said yesterday he has enough evidence to file felony drug charges against journalist Hunter S. Thompson after a raid on Thompson's home last month. . . .

At a county court hearing yesterday, filing of formal charges was scheduled in district court April 9. Deputy District Attorney Chip McCrory, who is handling the case, said the assault charges, both misdemeanors, and any felony charges will be lodged at that time.

Thompson didn't make an appearance at the hearing yesterday, much to the chagrin of television crews outside the Pitkin County Courthouse. . . .

March 14, 1990

. . .

The whole case turned, in the beginning, on a hearing that I didn't go to, in court. It was the first official thing that happened and I thought by not going I would lessen the effect of the case by not kicking up such a noise over the stupid thing. It was a misdemeanor at that time. Ho ho. I sent Michael Solheim as an observer to see what happened in the courtroom, and I didn't expect much of anything, just an "Okay, you're arrested." It was a very pro forma kind of thing. Nothing was expected to happen. It was late afternoon when Solheim got back here and said, "It started out as a misdemeanor, but . . ." After a huddle in front of the judge, where the attorneys approach the bench— my attorney and the D.A. and the prosecutor—the judge announced that the charges had been changed to felonies. And that he was getting rid of the case—out of his court—and it would be turned over to the district court, as felonies. I recognized at once when I heard the news that my own lawyer had participated. His record as a lawyer and as a human being is real weak: I can't believe that fucking lawyer. I wish I could tell you his name, but let's just call him "Chickenshit."

From one little huddle, the case went from Magistrate Tam Scott's court to District Felony Court. Solheim came out here to report that, and I got extremely agitated, and that is when I decided to fire Chickenshit. I called him and asked him what happened—he jabbered some kind of talk about "Well, it was just necessary," or "It was obvious"—lawyer crap. He kept sending me bills for a year or two; I should have had him arrested for fraud.

It is a hard decision, to get rid of your lawyer. That's always bad. Prejudicial, really; the defendant fires one lawyer, and brings in an outsider . . . and Chickenshit was an insider. It was a difficult decision to BOOM, just kick him out the door. The longer the lawyer's on the case, the more information he has, but at that particular time, it was necessary.

I had a list of the top five criminal lawyers in Colorado, whose names had been suggested. Hal Haddon was on that list, and I called him first. I had known Hal for years, since the McGovern campaign. On the phone I found myself apologizing to him, saying, "Oh I'm sorry to do this, but . . . that fucking lawyer . . ." I was apologizing for everything. He said, "Christ, I thought you'd never ask." Hot damn, man. The next day, Hal drove over the Divide to take the case.

That was a huge morale booster; "Ah, finally, we rumble." After I got rid of Chickenshit—from then on it was fun. It was agony with that other lawyer; if you do not trust your lawyer and have good reason not to, that is very unpleasant and uncomfortable.

In the beginning, I didn't think I was going to need a huge criminal lawyer. But once Haddon came over here, and he told me how much trouble I could be in, as they always do: *You might die from this* . . . well, I just figured, if I was going to die, it was better to die fighting.

I remember Haddon said this only once in the case: "My theory as a lawyer is that: Lawyers will take you all the way up to the door of justice, and just say, Well, it's up to the jury now—justice will be done." Haddon said, "My theory is, I want to take the client through the door."

THOMPSON HIT WITH 5 FELONIES
JUDGE DISQUALIFIES HIMSELF
By David Matthews-Price
Times Daily Staff Writer

Hunter S. Thompson didn't act Monday like a man who had just learned he was facing a possible 16 years in prison.

Moments after the District Attorney hit the "gonzo" journalist with five felony charges and three misdemeanors, Thompson and his lawyers retired to a conference room in the Aspen courthouse. Somebody asked what they were doing in there. . . .

"We're just smoking crack," said Thompson with a grin.

Judge J. E. DeVilbiss announced that he was disqualifying himself from the case. He gave no reason in court for removing himself and he wouldn't comment outside the courtroom either. Ninth District Judicial District Chief Gavin Litwiler will decide who replaces DeVilbiss.

April 10, 1990

. . .

There were several judges; nobody really wanted this. DeVilbiss recused himself; we went through all the judges in the county—all three on the district level. Nobody would touch it. We had to go to Grand Junction to find a judge.

NEW JUDGE NAMED IN THOMPSON CASE
By David Matthews-Price
Times Daily Staff Writer

A Grand Junction judge—who is regarded as a good listener, but unpredictable—was selected

Thursday to handle the drug, sex, and explosives case of author Hunter S. Thompson.

Mesa County District Judge Charles A. Buss will replace Aspen District Judge J. E. DeVilbiss, who withdrew from the case on April 9 without explanation. . . .

Independent Judge

"From my experience, he takes every case on an individual basis and I don't think there is any way to predict how he will rule," said Grand Junction attorney Steve Laiche. Laiche, who is now in private practice, appeared almost daily before Judge Buss when he was a deputy district attorney.

"When you are before him, you don't know how you are going to do, but he is going to listen," Laiche told the *Times Daily* on Thursday.

Laiche said it's hard to generalize about how Buss rules on drug cases. But, the attorney noted, there are other judges in Grand Junction who would probably give drug defendants longer sentences than would Buss. . . .

April 20, 1990

. . .

It wouldn't have meant much to half-win a case on the right to smoke marijuana in the home.

Deciding it was a Fourth Amendment case and not a marijuana case was the right thing to do. Legally it wasn't. Legally it was risky. But politically it was right.

Almost everything I did was contrary to Haddon's wishes and habits. He said he never had a case where every time he went into court, he knew what he was going to say by reading the morning newspapers.

(CA Press Photo Service)

THOMPSON BOUND OVER FOR TRIAL
By David Matthews-Price
Times Daily Staff Writer

A judge Tuesday threw out one of the five felony charges pending against gonzo journalist Hunter S. Thompson because a witness who claimed to have seen him consume cocaine later admitted she wasn't sure what it was he put up his nose. . . .

May 23, 1990

. . .

I think Haddon was surprised to win the preliminary hearing: Not even God can win a preliminary hearing. I just got angry. It wouldn't have meant much to half-win a case on the right to smoke marijuana in the home. That wasn't an issue with me.

BEWARE

Today: the Doctor
Tomorrow: <u>You</u>

The Hunter S. Thompson Legal Defense Fund
Box 274, Woody Creek, Colorado 81656

Paid for George Stranahan and Michael Solheim

(HST archives)

(Aspen Daily News)

TODAY: THE DOCTOR, TOMORROW *YOU.* That was the breakthrough. After that, the majority of people I knew in town were prepared to fight this to the end. I saw then that I had the support of the newspapers and my friends hadn't turned against me.

I had recognized a threat when it was announced to the press that it was a felony case. I recognized the lack of support I had then, mainly due to the charge that I'd put a gun to her head. Nobody knew what had actually happened that night, until I got on the trumpet—the coconut telegraph. I realized it was a threat; I understood it instantly, and my response was to take out a full-page ad in the *Aspen Times* and the *Daily News* to explain my case—point one, two, etc. I labored over it; dense, gray type, like a legal argument. Solheim and I struggled for days. And finally I said, "Fuck this. Never mind it." And I came up with that line: "Here's what we'll put in there—just white space and 'Today the Doctor, Tomorrow You,' underlined . . ." When the ad appeared . . . it was like magic. Maybe one of the best decisions of my life. Now, if I had come out with some legal gray page explaining *my* position, it would not have worked. It had to be "we."

I recognized that. I was trying to put the ad together—to be effective—and it wasn't. But that "Today the Doctor, Tomorrow You" just came to me in a moment of stress. And, shit, the tide turned immediately.

GONZO'S LAST STAND? (CONTINUED)

" . . . I have more public support now than when I ran for sheriff," Thompson laughs, and he's almost certainly right: There are a lot of houses in Aspen where 66 hours of searching could produce something incriminating. As a supportive ad in the *Aspen Times* read, "Today the Doctor, Tomorrow You." But beyond that, there is something about the D.A.'s invasion of Thompson's house that seems to grate on the Western sensibility of even Aspen's conservatives. Finally, of course, there

is the matter of the Fourth Amendment of the
United States Constitution.

   A few years ago, McCrory's warrant would have
been worth as little legally as it is morally, but
the Nixon/Reagan legacy on the Supreme Court means
that it has a better than even chance of standing up against the challenge Thompson's lawyers
plan to bring. And what that means is that on the
basis of someone's unsupported word that you used
drugs (burned the flag/plotted insurrection/planned
a possibly illegal demonstration/committed sodomy/
possessed pornography/arranged an abortion) in the
privacy of your own home, the cops can break down
your door. . . .
The Village Voice, *May 15, 1990, Vol XXXV, No. 20*

                    . . .

I had to mobilize the whole national and international network. I
would call the papers. I could get the *Times* in London . . . I could mobilize people. And Haddon recognized that suddenly we had a cause
here. For Haddon it was like going into combat with somebody you
know is good and think is right, you're a lawyer and he's not, and he—
your client—starts making announcements to the press. Every move
he makes is not with your counsel . . . I just left the legal stuff to him.

THOMPSON REJECTS PLEA BARGAIN; TAKES
DELIVERY OF CONVERTIBLE
By David Matthews-Price,
Times Daily Staff Writer
May 22, 1990

   On the eve of his preliminary hearing on drug
charges, author Hunter S. Thompson rejected a plea
bargain offer from prosecutors and received a red
convertible from well-wishers who traveled here
from San Francisco.

His supporters, led by porn theater owners Jim and Art Mitchell, left the Bay Area in a convoy of a half dozen vehicles at 3 A.M. Sunday—or "after work," as they put it. They arrived Monday morning at Thompson's cabin near Woody Creek.

As the convoy was arriving, Thompson was on the phone talking to his lawyer about the plea bargain offer from the District Attorney.

Thompson was adamant Monday about the importance of refusing the District Attorney's offer—even one allowing him to plead guilty to one misdemeanor and have a felony conviction purged from his record if he completes two years of probation.

"First, I'm innocent," Thompson said. "And, second, if I plead guilty, that means their search was right, that they got away with it."

He said defendants across the country who are innocent are forced to accept plea bargains in drug cases because they can't afford to fight the system. He said he won't do that.

"This is getting worse because people are caving into this. Somebody has to say, 'enough,'" Thompson said.

Echoing that position were the Mitchell Brothers, owners of the O'Farrell Theatre in San Francisco and longtime friends of Thompson. They said they came to Aspen to support Thompson, who wrote about the government's unsuccessful 11-year battle to shut down their establishment, which features nude dancing. "Somebody has to stand up to this," Art Mitchell said.

"Yeah," said Roxy, a dancer who works for the Mitchells who only wanted to give her first name. "The search of Hunter Thompson's is like being raped by the police."

"I sure wouldn't appreciate a search like that," added Gigi, another Mitchell Brothers employee who arrived in Aspen wearing a scanty shirt and a mini-skirt.

"But, Gigi, you would answer the door differently than Hunter," interjected a smiling Alex Benton, a member of the convoy.

Benton said the only problem during the road trip was on Interstate 80 near Truckee when a California state patrolman stopped the convertible that was later given to Thompson. In the backseat was a 3-foot-tall stuffed buffalo head that was also given to Thompson on Monday in memory of the movie and book "Where the Buffalo Roam."

"He wanted to see the papers on the buffalo," said Benton. The patrolman let the convoy continue without seeing the papers, but said he doubted the group would make it through Utah, according to Benton.

The patrolman also gave them a speeding ticket.

The buffalo head and convertible are to be displayed in a rally that's supposed to take place this morning before Thompson's preliminary hearing begins at 10 A.M. at the Pitkin County Courthouse.

"We just hope the judge has a sense of humor," said Thompson.

The Alleged Crime

Thompson is charged with four drug felonies, a fifth for possession of explosives, and three misdemeanors including sexual assault. If Thompson, who is free on bond, is bound over on the charges today, his trial is set to begin Sept. 4.

The charges stem from a complaint from former porn filmmaker Gail Palmer-Slater, 35, of St. Clair, Mich. She claims that while visiting Thompson's home on Feb. 21, she was punched and her breast was twisted by the famed gonzo journalist, who she said had been using cocaine.

Six investigators searched Thompson's house for 11 hours for evidence of the alleged assault; they found LSD, four Valium pills and trace amounts of cocaine.

Deputy District Attorney Chip McCrory offered to drop charges—and avoid a trial—if Thompson were to plead guilty to one misdemeanor charge and accept a deferred judgment and sentence on a felony count of LSD possession.

The offer expires at 10 o'clock this morning, when the hearing begins.

If Thompson were to complete two years of probation—that is, pass two years of random drug tests—he could have the felony conviction removed from his record. If he were to flunk any drug tests, or were arrested for any other reason during the two-year period, he would automatically be convicted of the LSD charge and face a maximum four-year prison sentence.

Thompson, author of a half-dozen bestsellers, has written frequently about his use of drugs.

A Counter Offer

In rejecting the offer, Thompson's attorney made a counter offer: drop all of the charges and Thompson will plead no contest to a charge of improper storage of explosives.

Thompson said the blasting caps found in the search were left on his property by an employee of the Salvation Ditch Co, who had been using them for construction.

Thompson's attorney, Hal Haddon of Denver, said he isn't expecting any sort of victory at today's preliminary hearing. At a preliminary hearing, a judge is supposed to look at the evidence "in the light most favorable" to the prosecution, according to state statutes.

"Even the deity can't win at a preliminary hearing," Haddon quipped.

But the hearing will give Haddon the opportunity to question government witnesses and determine how to attack the District Attorney's case.

THE SINISTER SEX AND DRUGS CASE OF HUNTER S. THOMPSON
BY RICHARD STRATTON

Some theorize that the Thompson persona is theater. No one, they argue, could be this crazy and live to write about it. But what Dr. Thompson is really up to is Life as Art.

"The only thing necessary for the triumph of evil is for good men to do nothing," Thompson quotes Bobby Kennedy in *Songs of the Doomed.* He lives and writes with the sensibilities of an outlaw, a man who refuses to kowtow to unenlightened authority. He is as rigorous in the demands he places on his integrity as he is about his art. *Songs of the Doomed: More Notes on the Death of the American Dream; Gonzo Papers, Vol. 3,* published soon after the Colorado sex-and-drugs case, contains some of his most vivid and visionary writing since *Fear and Loathing in Las Vegas.*

It took 99 days, but Dr. Thompson got his share of Justice. The government lost faith in their case.

"Comes now Milton K. Blakey, District Attorney in and for the Ninth Judicial District of the State of Colorado, and moves this Honorable Court to dismiss this case and as grounds therefore states that:

"The People would be unable to establish guilt beyond a reasonable doubt.

"Dated this 30th day of May 1990," read the

D.A.'s Motion to Dismiss. Judge Charles Buss granted the motion and dismissed the charges with prejudice, meaning that they cannot be brought again at a later date.

"Why couldn't you have made this decision before you filed?" the judge asked Chief Deputy Attorney Chip McCrory. The D.A. responded that he was having witness problems and that the new findings made it clear just how difficult it would have been for the state to get a conviction.

Dr. Thompson was vindicated, but hardly pacified. "We've grown accustomed to letting anyone with a badge walk over us," he said at the time. "Fuck that!" he wrote in a press release issued from Owl Farm the next day. He denounced the Dismissal as "pure cowardice" and said he would "appeal at once" to the Colorado Supreme Court.

Thompson described the District Attorney's "whole goddamn staff" as "thugs, liars, crooks, and lazy human scum. . . . These stupid brutes tried to destroy my life," he said, "and now they tell me to just forget it.

"They are guilty! They should all be hung by their heels from iron telephone poles on the road to Woody Creek!"

Instead of hunkering down to lick his wounds, Dr. Thompson has rallied a new offensive. He has established a Fourth Amendment Foundation "to promote public awareness of the erosion of the Fourth Amendment to the United States Constitution and the consequent threat to the privacy, peace, and security of citizens in their own homes, and to provide legal assistance to citizens whose right to privacy has been infringed."

For, as he fully understands, the truly sinister aspect of the Doctor's case is that government forces, all in the name of some shadowy War on

Drugs, are in fact turning this nation into a police state.

In August of 1990, Dr. Thompson was back in court. This time he was there to file a Notice of Intent to sue the District Attorney's office, collectively and individually, with a $22 million civil lawsuit for Malicious Prosecution, Gross Negligence and Criminal Malfeasance with Harmful Intent.

"The worm has turned," writes Dr. Thompson. "They are doomed. They will soon be in prison. Those bastards have no more respect for the law than any screwhead thief in Washington. They will meet the same fate as Charles Manson and Neil Bush."

Lunch has been served. It is now four o'clock in the morning. Earlier in the day—actually, the previous day—as I purchased a disposable camera, the man in the shop asked me whose picture I intended to take.

"Ah, some old freak over in Woody Creek," I told him.

"Which one?" he wanted to know. "There are a lot of them over there."

"The main one," I told him. "The last outlaw. I'm doing a story on his case for *High Times*."

"Listen, do me a favor," the man said. "Ask him the one question that is on everyone's mind: How does he do it? How does he continue to live the way we did back then and survive?"

It is the most perplexing aspect of this baffling character. How does he do it? We've been drinking heavily all night. He's got a head full of THC. Every so often, like an anteater, he buries his nose and comes up gasping. The Dunhills are consumed incessantly. He keeps the hours of a vampire who's been sucking blood from speed freaks. And yet . . . yet, he makes sense. To me he makes more sense than anyone else who is writing today, because he UNDERSTANDS WHAT IS HAPPENING.

I spent the '80s in prison. When I got out it seemed to me the country had changed drastically for the worse. I worried that only those hundreds of thousands of us locked up during this despicable decade had a decent perspective on just how bad things have become. Then I read *Songs of the Doomed.*

So I asked the Doctor, "How do you do it?" We are out in his backyard, a combination one-hole golf course and target-shooting range. Dr. Thompson is demonstrating an infrared nightscope he has attached to a high-powered rifle. He even looks well. In his fringed Indian apron, and wearing some kind of wooly dive-bomber's cap, traces of chocolate cake from lunch on his lips, he looks remarkably healthy for a man who, by his own admission, has never just said no.

"I made my choice a long time ago," the Doctor says as he peers through the scope. "Some say I'm a lizard with no pulse. The truth is—Jesus, who knows? I never thought I'd make it past 27. Every day I'm just as astounded as everyone else to realize I'm still alive."

Possibly he doesn't understand, but I doubt this. I realize through the fog in my own brain that Dr. Thompson is in a kind of psychophysiological state of grace, because he has for all these years remained true to himself.

High Times, *August 1991*

. . .

Well well well . . . it is twelve years later now, and the Police Problem in this country is even worse today than it was then. The American Century is over, we are still beating up on pygmy nations on the other side of the world, and our once-proud quality of life in the good old U.S.A. has gone up in smoke for all but 1 percent of the population.

And our President is still named Bush—just like it was in 1990, when that gang of doomed pigs attacked my house and tried to put me in prison. They were stupid, and they got what they deserved. They were disgraced, humiliated, and beaten like three-legged mules on the filthy road to Hell. *Res Ipsa Loquitur.*

I was never especially proud of that squalid episode in my life, but I really had no choice. It was *Root hog or die,* in the vernacular of the Chinese hog farm, and apparently it was not in my nature to simply roll over and die.

Marlon Brando explained this to me about 40 years ago when we were both bogged down in some kind of Indian Fishing Rights protest on a riverbank near Olympia, Washington. "Okay," he said to me at a violent press conference for the Indian cause, when the Native American gentlemen were expressing their hatred of being lumped together with "all those niggers" under the collective rubric of Civil Rights. I was disgusted by those rude alcoholic fascists, but Marlon was trying to stay neutral. It was touching.

"Okay," he said. "Why don't we have another look at this situation. So you're a nasty counter-puncher, eh? We're all impressed, but so what?" Marlon could get a little edgy on you, with no warning at all in those days. He had a scary way of *leaning* on people who got in his way. I admired him for it, even when I was the leanee.

But he was wrong about me. I was a working journalist, just trying to understand what was happening, so I could write a true story about it, and I am not much different today. I liked Marlon, but at that moment in time he was getting in *my* way, so I popped him. That is my nature.

Maybe that is why I could understand the Hell's Angels so naturally. They were essentially desperate men who had banded together in what they told one another was self-defense. They were the proud and crazy *elite* of social outlaws, and they insisted on being left alone to do their thing in peace, or else.

Ho ho. And a central ethic of Total Retaliation whenever they were crossed, which scared the shit out of normal people who had no appetite for being chain-whipped in public or gang-raped in their own homes.

"Are you talkin' to *me*, pervert? I hate it when perverts get rude with me, you rotten little bastard."

. . .

Which gets us back, I guess, to my sleazy little morality tale about 99 days of being in the grip of the provably corrupt American Law Enforcement system at its worst with provably evil intentions.

They were bullies and cowards who had somehow been given a license to carry loaded weapons and put anybody who argued with them in prison. That half-bright punk of a District Attorney had campaigned *un-opposed* for re-election for *16 straight years,* doing anything and everything he *wanted* to do, in the name of public security and aggressive law enforcement by pistol-packing cowboys who got paid about a dollar an hour, plus perks, to whip the villagers into line.

Yes sir. And those perks were Huge, Bubba, huge. They ranged, and still do, from 50 cents a mile whenever they stepped into their taxpayer-funded fast new police cruisers to being the only one in the neighborhood with a license to kill.

. . .

Okay folks. The time has come to wrap this story up. I can't be spending all this space rambling on and on about the time I went to trial 12 years ago for Sex, Drugs, Dynamite, and Violence in a little cowboy town on the western slope of the Colorado Rockies because of stupid, vengeful police work. It was no big deal, as major criminal cases go—just another goofy example of dumb cops abusing their power in public and not getting away with it, for a change.

We busted them like shit-eating dogs. They were Punished, Mocked, and Humiliated with the whole world watching, just like they had schemed from the start—except in my case, their plans went horribly wrong, and when the deal finally went down, *they* were the ones on Trial.

It was wonderful, a stunning happy ending to what began as

just another tragic rock & roll story, as if Bob Dylan had been arrested in Miami for jacking off in a seedy little XXX theater while stroking the spine of a fat young boy.

Jesus! That is so horrible that I hate to see myself actually writing it. What is wrong with me? Why would I even *think* of a scene like that?

. . .

Well, shucks, folks. I guess I'm just lucky. It's just amazing, isn't it?

Right. And Ted Williams was lucky, too.

Whoops. And so much for hubris, eh? I was never able to swing a baseball bat like Ted Williams, and I will never be able to write a song like "Mr. Tambourine Man." But what the hell? Neither one of those Yo-yos could write *Fear and Loathing in Las Vegas,* either. . . . At the top of the mountain, we are all Snow Leopards. Anybody who can do one thing better than anyone else in the world is a natural friend of mine.

Even Criminal Lawyers will qualify for that thin-air club on some days, and my wildly publicized trial in the winter of 1990 was one of those. What had begun as just another routine case of a booze-maddened autograph seeker run amok very quickly mushroomed into a profoundly serious Life or Death situation for me in the middle of another goddamn Urgent book deadline, and I suddenly realized that I was going to need major-league criminal trial attorneys if I wanted to avoid the dismal fate of a wild beast caught in a net and headed for the Bronx Zoo forever.

There is not much difference between the death penalty and going to jail for the rest of your life to a snow leopard or any other wild beast. Even a fish will fight to the death, rather than be hooked and tortured by strangers who may or may not eat him alive. It's like they used to say in New Hampshire—LIVE FREE OR DIE.

That was before the state brazenly peddled its soul to the cruel and greasy BUSH family from Texas. Along with its bogus reputation for independence and freedom. Going to New Hampshire today is like going to a leafy greenish high-end boutique in Utah where they sell the skulls of famous bigamists who died in prison for fifteen dollars or a bottle of brown whiskey. . . .

Ah, but never mind Utah for now, eh? Only a freak would jabber like that about the two most god-fearing states in the union. And where did *that* come from, anyway? I must be going crazy. Why go out and pick fights in an election year? We are not what we seem to be.

In any case, that was when I hired Hal Haddon and began my long quixotic journey to becoming the Poet Laureate of the NATIONAL ASSOCIATION OF CRIMINAL DEFENSE LAWYERS, who rode in droves to my defense in my time of great and imminent peril. They slithered in like champions when the great Whistle blew—along with Ralph Steadman, the heroic Mitchell Brothers gang from San Francisco, Bob Dylan, the wild Sabonic sisters from Russia, and Jack, etc. . . . and we kicked the shit out of those Nazis who were trying to kill us. . . . Hallelujah! Fuck those people. OK, time to quit, I see. But not for long. We will RUMBLE, young man, RUMBLE!

Yes. Thank you. Don't mention it. . . . And now we will get back to normal. Why not?

I was talking about this with Bob Dylan last night, and there was not a hint of Violence as we got down to our discussions. "We may never be able to defeat these swine," he told me, "but we don't have to join them."

Yes sir, I thought. The too much fun club is back in business. Let us rumble.

Summit Conference with Bob Dylan, Aspen, Labor Day, 2002
(Anita Bejmuk)

. . .

DRAT! I wish I had more time and space for this story right now—
but the publisher's armed narks from N.Y. are on my back like
leeches, and I can barely hear myself think. Somewhere in the
chaos I hear myself yelling, *"Please don't slit yourself, JoJo. Just get
back in the truck. I'll give you whatever you want."*

Oh no, I thought quickly. That is definitely not *me.* I would never
talk like that. It must be a music nightmare.

And it *was,* because I never heard those voices again, and those
Screws in New York never bothered me again, once I got a chance
to mix the big board for Mr. Bobby. Nobody fucked with me after
that.

. . .

And that is why I secretly worship God, folks. He had the good
judgment to leave me alone to write a few genuine black-on-white
pages by myself, for a change. Only Anita is with me now, and
that's how I want it. . . . Mahalo. *Res Ipsa Loquitur. Amor Vincit
Omnia.*

Okay, and it's about it for now, people. It is 10:00 A.M. in Manhattan, and I can almost *feel* those bastards getting jittery in their
cubicles.

Oh ye of little faith. We are, after all, professionals.

HST/ wc/ September 3, 2002

The Doctor speaks at a press conference on the steps of the Pitkin
County courthouse with Black Bill and lawyers Hal Haddon and
Gerry Goldstein, after all charges were dropped
(Nicholas Devore III)

Letter from Lawyer Goldstein

June 15, 2002
Dr. Hunter S. Thompson
Owl Farm
Woody Creek, Colorado
Re: *It's Been an Interesting Ride*

Dear Doc:

As I headed out to deep East Texas, I was marveling at your huevos for standing up to our hometown police when they ran amok through your roost at Owl Farm. Your willingness, then and now, to take a stand against intolerance, wherever it rears its ugly head, is a testament to your tenacity. Your reputation may be that of the poet laureate of our generation, but you teach us by more than just word. Your example of political and social activism speaks volumes about good citizenship. As you reminded me recently:

> "The only thing necessary for the triumph of evil, is for good men to do nothing."[1]

A lot of water has passed under the bridge in the intervening decade since we stood on the steps of the Pitkin County Courthouse, basking in the celebrative sunshine of that victorious moment, and most of it has seen the erosion of Constitutional guarantees set in place by our Founding Fathers as a bulwark to protect the governed from their government. For example, the United States Supreme Court has since ruled that the police can:

- Search your home based upon the consent of someone who has absolutely no authority to give same,[2]
- Stop your car based upon an "anonymous tip" completely lacking any indicia of reliability,[3]

---

1. From an undated letter written by English political writer Edmund Burke (1729–1797) to Thomas Mercer.
2. *Illinois v. Rodriquez,* 497 U.S. 177 (1990).
3. *Alabama v. White,* 503 U.S. 953 (1990).

- Subject a motorist to mandatory sobriety tests without any indication they have been drinking or that their driving is impaired,[4] and
- Hold innocent citizens for up to two days without giving reason or recourse.

The tragic events of September 11, 2001, changed more than Manhattan's skyline; it profoundly altered our political and legal landscape as well. Anyone who witnessed the desecration of those buildings and the heart-wrenching loss of life, who didn't want to run out and rip someone a new asshole, doesn't deserve the freedoms we still enjoy. However, anybody who thinks for one moment that giving up our freedoms is any way to preserve or protect those freedoms, is even more foolhardy.

Yet barely one month later, on October 26, 2001, Congress overwhelmingly passed the USA Patriot Act. It rolled through the Senate on a vote of 99 to 1, and the lone holdout, Wisconsin Senator Russ Finegold, said he didn't really know whether he was opposed to the bill or not, he just wanted to read it before voting. There were only two copies of the 346-page document extant at the time, and the Senate had been run out of their building by the anthrax scare.

That single Congressional enactment authorizes the detention of non-citizens suspected of terrorist acts without filing of charges or resort to judicial authority, permits roving wiretaps, and extends to American citizens the secret proceedings, surveillance, and wiretaps of the Foreign Intelligence Surveillance Court, which sits in a vault atop the Department of Justice Building, and allows only Deputy Attorneys General of the United States to appear. Imagine an adversary process that allows only one side's advocate to appear. No wonder that in its 24-year history not a single request for surveillance was turned down. Not until last month, when the secret judge refused to apply these secret proceedings to citizens, cataloging 75 instances

---

4. Michigan Department of State Police v. Sitz, 496 U.S. 444 (1990).

where the FBI had lied to them. The Just Us Department has appealed that secret decision to a secret appeals court, presumably at some other secret location.

At the same time, the Bureau of Prisons, by executive fiat, has authorized monitoring of attorney-client communications by direction of the Attorney General, without any judicial authorization. Almost one hundred and fifty years ago, the Supreme Court reminded those in power:

> The Constitution of the United States is the law for rulers and people, equally in war and in peace, and covers with the shield of its protection all classes of men, at all times, and under all circumstances. No doctrine, involving more pernicious consequences, was ever invented by the whit of man than that any of [the Constitution's] provisions can be suspended during any of the great exigencies of Government.[5]

But this is not the first time civil liberties have been eroded in the face of national crises. Abraham Lincoln suspended the Great Writ of Habeas Corpus, Woodrow Wilson had his Palmer raids, and Franklin Roosevelt interred Asian-American citizens for no reason, other than their national origin. All of this is enough to make even the most ardent civil libertarian throw up their hands. But not you, Doc, no, you have refused to remain silent or to go quietly into the night. Your tireless defense of others, faced with official oppression, stands in the best tradition of true patriots.

You championed the cause of a displaced young Innuit woman,[6] who found herself in the grip of a draconian legal entanglement, calculated to imprison her for the crime of seeking the return of her purse from a thieving pack of rowdies. At your insistence, we gathered a team of legal eagles and launched a midday raid on the Leadville courthouse, nestled near the

---

5. *Ex Parte Milligan,* 71 U.S. 2 (1866).
6. Jesse Barron.

Continental Divide, in a King Air Beechraft, stuffed so full of partisan supporters that Brother Semmes Luckett was heard to exclaim: "King Farouk didn't require an entourage this large."

More recently, you sent out a clarion call to defend an incarcerated Colorado woman,[7] condemned to suffer a lifetime for the misdeeds of another she had barely met. The idea that a citizen could spend the rest of her life in prison for a crime she did not intend, want, nor desire should be foreign to any sense of justice and fairness. In response you brought the weight and legal prowess of the National Association of Criminal Defense Lawyers Amicus Committee to her defense, and rallied a Colorado Governor's wife, a Denver city councilperson, the Pitkin County Sheriff,[8] a Presidential Historian, and yours truly to the steps of our State Capital, all to the strains of Warren Zevon bellowing "Lawyers, Guns and Money."

In 1990 you founded the Fourth Amendment Foundation, a collection of legal titans willing to take a stand against our government's increasingly pervasive intrusions into its citizen's privacy. While our forefathers were concerned that King George's Red Coats were breaking down their doors and rummaging through their underwear drawers, today we are faced with more sophisticated means of invading our privacy. The new technology is not physical. You cannot see it. You cannot feel it. But in a way, it is more sinister and dangerous because of that. Stealthlike, it steals your thoughts. It steals your conversations. It invades the crossroads between the Fourth Amendment right to be free from unreasonable search and seizure and the First Amendment rights to free speech and association. It cuts to the quick the citizenries' right to protest and complain about their government. The Fourth Amendment protection of a citizen's privacy against his or her government's intrusion is the linchpin upon which all other civil liberties rest. Freedom of speech and association, so essential to a free society, would mean little if the citizens' activities and communications were not protected from

---

7. Lisl Auman.

8. Bob Braudis, by far the most enlightened and intelligent law enforcement officer I've ever met.

government interference and interception. George Orwell created his sterile environment and maintained control over the citizenry, not by imprisoning their bodies, but by exposing their thoughts and communications to government scrutiny.

With recent advances in electronic technology allowing Big Brother to spy upon the most intimate and confidential parts of our lives and communications, the citizen today is in need of greater, not lesser protection. Yet in the face of the dreaded drug scare and threat of international terrorism, courts continue to erode the citizens' zone of privacy by paternalistically balancing these perceived dangers against the public's willingness to acquiesce. While the majority does "rule" in our republican form of democracy, our Constitution was designed to protect certain rights and liberties from that majority, as well as for them. Recognizing that "[a]mong deprivations of rights, none is so effective in cowing a population, crushing the spirit of the individual and putting terror in every heart . . . [as] uncontrolled search and seizure,"[9] your Fourth Amendment Foundation vigilantly stands guard against further encroachments upon the citizens' diminishing expectation of privacy.

Doc, you are a fast take, and your comprehension and analysis of legal issues and theory are quite remarkable. You tenaciously cling to high principle, and expect no less from those around you. All of which probably accounts for why you are such a pain in the ass to have for a client. It takes a lot of love to represent you, Brother.

But the reason I'd do it again in a heartbeat, is that your selfless and indignant stand against injustice has served as a catalyst and stimulus for others, including myself. As Michael Stepanian reminded me at a recent gathering, "Hunter is necessary, now more than ever, Hunter is necessary."

Yours in the continuing fight,
(Signed) Gerald H. Goldstein
for Goldstein, Goldstein & Hilley

---

9. *Brinegar v. U.S.*, 338 U.S. 160, 180–181 (1949) (Jackson, J., dissenting)

It Never Got Weird Enough for Me

How can grownups tell [the kids of America] drugs are bad when they see what they've done for Thompson, a man who glided through the 1960s thinking acid was a health food?
—Bernard Goldberg, *Bias*

Dear Dr. Thompson,

My name is Xania and I am very beautiful and my family is very rich. I am eight years old and I live in Turkey. We live by the sea, but I am bored here. They treat me like a child, but I am not. I am ready to escape. I want to leave. I want to get married and I want to marry *you*. That is why I write you today. I want you to suck my tits while I scream and dance in your lap and my mother watches. She is the one who says this. She loves you very much and so do I.

I am eight years old and my body is well advanced. My mother is twenty-six and, boy! You should see *her*. We are almost twins and so is my grandmother, who is only forty-two years old and looks the same as me. I think she is crazy like my mother. They are beautiful when they walk around naked, and so am I. We are always naked here. We are rich and the sea is so beautiful. If the sea had brains, I would suck them out of it. But I can't. The sea has no penis.

Why is that, Doc? If you are so smart, answer *that* one! Fuck you. I knew you wouldn't help us. Please send three plane tickets right *now*. I love you! We are *not* whores. Please help me. I know I will see you soon. We travel a lot. My father wants you to marry me. He is sixty-six years old and he owns the main banks of Turkey. All of them. We will have a beautiful, beautiful wedding when you show them us naked and I dance while you suck my tits and my father screams. O God I love you! Our dream is now. Yes.

Your baby,
Xania

(Billy Noonan)

Fear and Loathing in Elko

FEAR AND LOATHING IN ELKO: BAD CRAZI-NESS IN SHEEP COUNTRY . . . SIDE ENTRANCE ON QUEER STREET . . . O BLACK, O WILD, O DARKNESS, ROLL OVER ME TONIGHT

MEMO FROM THE NATIONAL AFFAIRS DESK: THE GHOST OF LONG DONG THOMAS AND THE ROAD FULL OF FORKS

January 1992

Dear Jann,

God*damn,* I wish you were here to enjoy this beautiful weather with me. It is autumn, as you know, and things are beginning to die. It is so wonderful to be out in the crisp fall air, with the leaves turning gold and the grass turning brown, and the warmth going out of the sunlight and big hot fires in the fireplace while Buddy rakes the lawn. We see a lot of bombs on TV because we watch it a lot more, now that the days get shorter and shorter, and darkness comes so soon, and all the flowers die from freezing.

Oh, God! You should have been with me yesterday when I finished my ham and eggs and knocked back some whiskey and picked up my Weatherby Mark V .300 Magnum and a ball of black Opium for dessert and went outside with a fierce kind of joy in my heart because I was Proud to be an American on a day like this. It felt like a goddamn *Football Game,* Jann—it was like *Paradise.* . . . You remember that *bliss* you felt when we powered down to the farm and whipped Stanford? Well, it felt like That.

I digress. My fits of Joy are soiled by relentless flashbacks and ghosts too foul to name. . . . Oh no, don't ask Why. You could have been president, Jann, but your road was full of forks, and I think of this when I see the forked horns of these wild animals who dash back and forth on the hillsides while rifles crack in the distance and fine swarthy young men with blood on their hands drive back and forth in the dusk and mournfully call our names. . . .

O Ghost, O Lost, Lost and Gone, O Ghost, come back again.

Right. And so much for autumn. The trees are diseased and the Animals get in your way and the President is usually guilty and most days are too long, anyway. . . . So never mind my poem. It was wrong from the start. I plagiarized it from an early work of Coleridge and then tried to put my own crude stamp on it, but I failed.

So what? I didn't want to talk about fucking autumn, anyway. I was just sitting here at dawn on a crisp Sunday morning, waiting for the football games to start and taking a goddamn very brief break from this blizzard of Character Actors and Personal Biographers and sickly Paparazzi that hovers around me these days (they are sleeping now, thank Christ—some even in my own bed). I was sitting here all alone, thinking, for good or ill, about the Good Old Days.

We were Poor, Jann. But we were Happy. Because we knew Tricks. We were Smart. Not Crazy, like they said. (No. They never called us late for dinner, eh?)

Ho, ho. Laughs don't come cheap these days, do they? The only guy who seems to have any fun in public is Prince Cromwell, my shrewd and humorless neighbor—the one who steals sheep and beats up women, like Mike Tyson.

Who knows why, Jann. Some people are too weird to figure.

You have come a long way from the Bloodthirsty, Beady-eyed news Hawk that you were in days of yore. Maybe you should try reading something besides those goddamn motorcycle magazines—or one of these days you'll find hair growing in your palms.

Take my word for it. You can only spend so much time "on the throttle," as it were. . . . Then the Forces of Evil will take over. Beware. . . .

Ah, but that is a different question, for now. Who gives a fuck? We are, after all, Professionals. . . . But our Problem is not. No. It is the Problem of *Everyman*. It is *Everywhere*. The Question is our *Wa;* the Answer is our Fate . . . and the story I am about to tell you is horrible, Jann.

I came suddenly awake, weeping and jabbering and laughing like a loon at the ghost on my TV set. Judge Clarence Thomas . . . Yes, I knew him. But that was a long time ago. Many years, in fact, but I still remember it vividly. . . . Indeed, it has haunted me like a Golem, day and night, for many years.

It seemed normal enough, at the time, just another weird rainy night out there on the high desert. . . . What the Hell? We were younger, then. Me and *the Judge.* And all the others, for that matter. . . . It was a Different Time. People were Friendly. We *trusted* each other. Hell, you could *afford* to get mixed up with wild strangers in those days—without fearing for your life, or your eyes, or your organs, or all of your money or even getting locked up in prison forever. There was a sense of *possibility.* People were not so afraid, as they are now. You could run around naked without getting shot. You could check into a roadside motel on the outskirts of Ely or Winnemucca or Elko when you were lost in a midnight rainstorm—and nobody called the police on you, just to check out your credit and your employment history and your medical records and how many parking tickets you owed in California.

There were Laws, but they were not feared. There were Rules, but they were not worshiped . . . like Laws and Rules and Cops and Informants are feared and worshiped today.

Like I said: It was a different time. And I know the Judge would tell you the same thing, tonight, if he wanted to tell you the Truth, like I do.

The first time I actually met the Judge was a long time ago, for strange reasons, on a dark and rainy night in Elko, Nevada, when we both ended up in the same sleazy roadside Motel, for no good reason at all. . . . Good God! What a night!

I almost forgot about it, until I saw him last week on TV . . . and then I saw it *all over again.* The horror! The *horror!* That night when the road washed out and we all got stuck out there—

somewhere near Elko in a place just off the highway, called Endicott's Motel—and we almost went *really* Crazy.

Yours,

HST

. . .

It was just after midnight when I first saw the sheep. I was running about eighty-eight or ninety miles an hour in a drenching, blinding rain on U.S. 40 between Winnemucca and Elko with one light out. I was soaking wet from the water that was pouring in through a hole in the front roof of the car, and my fingers were like rotten icicles on the steering wheel.

It was a moonless night and I knew I was hydroplaning, which is dangerous. . . . My front tires were no longer in touch with the asphalt or anything else. My center of gravity was too high. There was no visibility on the road, none at all. I could have tossed a flat rock a lot farther than I could see in front of me that night through the rain and the ground fog.

So what? I thought. I know this road—a straight lonely run across nowhere, with not many dots on the map except ghost towns and truck stops with names like Beowawe and Lovelock and Deeth and Winnemucca. . . .

Jesus! Who *made* this map? Only a lunatic could have come up with a list of places like this: Imlay, Valmy, Golconda, Nixon, Midas, Metropolis, Jiggs, Judasville—all of them *empty*, with no gas stations, withering away in the desert like a string of old Pony Express stations. The Federal Government owns ninety percent of this land, and most of it is useless for anything except weapons testing and poison-gas experiments.

My plan was to keep moving. Never slow down. Keep the car aimed straight ahead through the rain like a cruise missile. . . . I felt comfortable. There is a sense of calm and security that comes with driving a very fast car on an empty road at night. . . . Fuck this thunderstorm, I thought. There is safety in speed. Nothing can touch me as long as I keep moving fast, and never mind the cops: They are all hunkered down in a truck stop or jacking off by themselves in a culvert behind some dynamite shack in the wilderness beyond the highway. . . . Either way, they wanted no part of me, and I wanted no part of them. Only trouble could come of it. They were probably nice people, and so was I—but we were not meant for each other. History had long since determined that. There is a huge body of evidence to support the notion that me and the police were put on this earth to do extremely different things and never to mingle professionally with each other, except at official functions, when we all wear ties and drink heavily and whoop it up like the natural, good-humored wild boys that we know in our hearts that we are. . . . These occasions are rare, but they happen—despite the forked tongue of fate that has put us forever on different paths. . . . But what the hell? I can handle a wild birthday party with cops, now and then. Or some unexpected orgy at a gun show in Texas. Why not? Hell, I ran for Sheriff one time, and almost got elected. They understand this, and I get along fine with the smart ones.

. . .

But not tonight, I thought, as I sped along in the darkness. Not at 100 miles an hour at midnight on a rain-slicked road in Nevada. Nobody needs to get involved in a high-speed chase on a filthy night like this. It would be dumb and extremely dangerous. Nobody driving a red 454 V-8 Chevrolet convertible was likely to pull over and surrender peacefully at the first sight of a cop car behind him. All kinds of weird shit might happen, from a gunfight with dope fiends to permanent injury or death. . . . It was a good night to stay indoors and be warm, make a fresh pot of coffee, and catch up on important paperwork. Lay low and ignore these loonies. Anybody behind the wheel of a car tonight was far too crazy to fuck with, anyway.

Which was probably true. There was nobody on the road except me and a few big-rig Peterbilts running west to Reno and Sacramento by dawn. I could hear them on my nine-band Super-Scan short-wave/CB/Police radio, which erupted now and then with outbursts of brainless speed gibberish about Big Money and Hot Crank and teenage cunts with huge tits.

They were dangerous Speed Freaks, driving twenty-ton trucks that might cut loose and jackknife at any moment, utterly out of control. There is nothing more terrifying than suddenly meeting a jackknifed

Peterbilt with no brakes coming at you sideways at sixty or seventy miles per hour on a steep mountain road at three o'clock in the morning. There is a total understanding, all at once, of how the captain of the *Titanic* must have felt when he first saw the Iceberg.

And not much different from the hideous feeling that gripped me when the beam of my Long-Reach Super-Halogen headlights picked up what appeared to be a massive rock slide across the highway—right in front of me, blocking the road completely. Big white rocks and round boulders, looming up with no warning in a fog of rising steam or swamp gas . . .

The brakes were useless, the car was wandering. The rear end was coming around. I jammed it down into Low, but it made no difference, so I straightened it out and braced for a serious impact, a crash that would probably kill me. This is It, I thought. This is how it happens—slamming into a pile of rocks at 100 miles an hour, a sudden brutal death in a fast red car on a moonless night in a rainstorm somewhere on the sleazy outskirts of Elko. I felt vaguely embarrassed, in that long pure instant before I went into the rocks. I remembered Los Lobos and that I wanted to call Maria when I got to Elko. . . .

My heart was full of joy as I took the first hit, which was oddly soft and painless. No real shock at all. Just a sickening *thud*, like running over a body, a corpse—or, ye fucking gods, a crippled 200-pound *sheep* thrashing around in the road.

Yes. These huge white lumps were not boulders. They were *sheep*. Dead and dying sheep. More and more of them, impossible to miss at this speed, piled up on one another like bodies at the battle of Shiloh. It was like running over wet logs. Horrible, horrible. . . .

And then I saw the *man*—a leaping Human Figure in the glare of my bouncing headlights, waving his arms and yelling, trying to flag me down. I swerved to avoid hitting him, but he seemed not to see me, rushing straight into my headlights like a blind man . . . or a monster from Mars with no pulse, covered with blood and hysterical.

It looked like a small black gentleman in a London Fog raincoat, frantic to get my attention. It was so ugly that my brain refused to accept it. . . . Don't worry, I thought. This is only an Acid flashback. Be calm. This is not really happening.

I was down to about thirty-five or thirty when I zoomed past the man in the raincoat and bashed the brains out of a struggling sheep, which helped to reduce my speed, as the car went airborne again, then bounced to a shuddering stop just before I hit the smoking, overturned hulk of what looked like a white Cadillac limousine, with people still inside. It was a nightmare. Some fool had crashed into a herd of sheep at high speed and rolled into the desert like an eggbeater.

. . .

We were able to laugh about it later, but it took a while to calm down. What the hell? It was only an accident. The Judge had murdered some range animals.

So what? Only a racist *maniac* would run sheep on the highway in a thunderstorm at this hour of the night. "Fuck those people!" he snapped, as I took off toward Elko with him and his two female companions tucked safely into my car, which had suffered major cosmetic damage but nothing serious. "They'll never get away with this Negligence!" he said. "We'll eat them alive in court. Take my word for it. We are about to become *joint owners* of a huge Nevada sheep ranch."

Wonderful, I thought. But meanwhile we were leaving the scene of a very conspicuous wreck that was sure to be noticed by morning, and the whole front of my car was gummed up with wool and sheep's blood. There was no way I could leave it parked on the street in Elko, where I'd planned to stop for the night (maybe two or three nights, for that matter) to visit with some old friends who were attending a kind of Appalachian Conference for sex-film distributors at the legendary Commercial Hotel. . . .

Never mind that, I thought. Things have changed. I was suddenly a Victim of Tragedy—injured and on the run, far out in the middle of sheep country—1,000 miles from home with a car full of obviously criminal hitchhikers who were spattered with blood and cursing angrily at one another as we zoomed through the blinding monsoon.

Jesus, I thought: Who *are* these people?

Who indeed? They seemed not to notice me. The two women fighting in the backseat were hookers. No doubt about that. I had seen them in my headlights as they struggled in the wreckage of the Cadillac, which had killed about sixty sheep. They were desperate with Fear and Confusion, crawling wildly across the sheep. . . . One was a tall black girl in a white minidress . . . and now she was screaming at the other one, a young blond white woman. They were both drunk. Sounds of struggle came from the backseat. "Get your hands off me, *Bitch*!" Then a voice cried out, "Help me, Judge! Help! She's *killing* me!"

What? I thought. *Judge?* Then she said it again, and a horrible chill went through me. . . . *Judge?* No. That would be over the line. Unacceptable.

He lunged over the seat and whacked their heads together. "Shut up!" he screamed. "Where are your fucking *manners?*"

He went over the seat again. He grabbed one of them by the hair. "God *damn* you," he screamed. "Don't embarrass this man. He saved our lives. We owe him respect—not this goddamned squalling around like whores."

A shudder ran through me, but I gripped the wheel and stared straight ahead, ignoring this sudden horrible freak show in my car. I lit a cigarette, but I was not calm. Sounds of sobbing and the ripping of cloth came from the backseat. The man they called Judge had straightened himself out and was now resting easily in the front seat, letting out long breaths of air. . . . The silence was terrifying: I quickly turned up the music. It was Los Lobos again—something about "One Time One Night in America," a profoundly morbid tune about Death and Disappointment:

> *A lady dressed in white*
> *With the man she loved*
> *Standing along the side of their pickup truck*
> *A shot rang out in the night*
> *Just when everything seemed right . . .*

Right. A shot. A shot rang out in the night. Just another headline written down in America. . . . Yes. There was a loaded .454 Magnum revolver in a clearly marked oak box on the front seat, about halfway between me and the Judge. He could grab it in a split second and blow my head off.

"Good work, Boss," he said suddenly. "I owe you a big one, for this. I was *done for*, if you hadn't come along." He chuckled. "Sure as hell,

Boss, sure as hell. I was Dead Meat—killed a lot worse than what happened to those goddamn stupid sheep!"

Jesus! I thought. Get ready to hit the brake. This man is a Judge on the lam with two hookers. He has *no choice* but to kill me, and those floozies in the backseat too. We were the only witnesses. . . .

This eerie perspective made me uneasy. . . . Fuck this, I thought. These people are going to get me locked up. I'd be better off just pulling over right here and killing all three of them. *Bang, Bang, Bang!* Terminate the scum.

"How far is town?" the Judge asked.

I jumped, and the car veered again. "Town?" I said. "*What* town?" My arms were rigid and my voice was strange and reedy.

He whacked me on the knee and laughed. "Calm down, Boss," he said. "I have everything under control. We're almost home." He pointed into the rain, where I was beginning to see the dim lights of what I knew to be Elko.

"Okay," he snapped. "Take a left, straight ahead." He pointed again and I slipped the car into low. There was a red and blue neon sign glowing about a half-mile ahead of us, barely visible in the storm. The only words I could make out were NO and VACANCY.

"Slow down!" the Judge screamed. "This is *it*! Turn! Goddamnit, turn!" His voice had the sound of a whip cracking. I recognized the tone and did as he said, curling into the mouth of the curve with all four wheels locked and the big engine snarling wildly in Compound Low and the blue flames coming out of the tailpipe. . . . It was one of those long perfect moments in the human driving experience that makes *everybody* quiet. Where is P.J.? I thought. This would bring him to his knees.

We were sliding sideways very fast and utterly out of control and coming up on a white steel guardrail at seventy miles an hour in a thunderstorm on a deserted highway in the middle of the night. Why not? On some nights Fate will pick you up like a chicken and slam you around on the walls until your body feels like a beanbag. . . . BOOM! BLOOD! DEATH! So long, Bubba—You knew it would End like this. . . .

We stabilized and shot down the loop. The Judge seemed oddly calm as he pointed again. "This is it," he said. "This is my place. I keep a few suites here." He nodded eagerly. "We're finally safe, Boss. We can do anything we want in this place."

The sign at the gate said:

ENDICOTT'S MOTEL

DELUXE SUITES AND WATERBEDS

ADULTS ONLY / NO ANIMALS

Thank God, I thought. It was almost too good to be true. A place to *dump* these bastards. They were quiet now, but not for long. And I knew I couldn't handle it when these women woke up.

The Endicott was a string of cheap-looking bungalows, laid out in a horseshoe pattern around a rutted gravel driveway. There were cars parked in front of most of the units, but the slots in front of the brightly lit places at the darker end of the horseshoe were empty.

"Okay," said the Judge. "We'll drop the ladies down there at our suite, then I'll get you checked in." He nodded. "We both need some *sleep,* Boss—or at least *rest,* if you know what I mean. Shit, it's been a long night."

I laughed, but it sounded like the bleating of a dead man. The adrenaline rush of the sheep crash was gone, and now I was sliding into pure Fatigue Hysteria.

The Endicott "Office" was a darkened hut in the middle of the horseshoe. We parked in front of it and then the Judge began hammering on the wooden front door, but there was no immediate response. . . . "Wake up, goddamnit! It's me—the *Judge*! Open up! This is Life and Death! I need *help*!"

He stepped back and delivered a powerful kick at the door, which rattled the glass panels and shook the whole building. "I know you're in there!" he screamed. "You can't hide! I'll kick your ass till your nose bleeds!"

There was still no sign of life, and I quickly abandoned all hope. Get out of here, I thought. This is wrong. I was still in the car, half in and half out. . . . The Judge put another fine snap kick at a point just over the doorknob and uttered a sharp scream in some language I didn't recognize. Then I heard the sound of breaking glass.

I leapt back into the car and started the engine. Get away! I thought. Never mind sleep. It's flee or die, now. People get killed for doing this kind of shit in Nevada. It was far over the line. Unacceptable behavior. This is why God made shotguns. . . .

I saw lights come on in the Office. Then the door swung open and I saw the Judge leap quickly through the entrance and grapple briefly with a small bearded man in a bathrobe, who collapsed to the floor after the Judge gave him a few blows to the head. . . . Then he called back to me. "Come on in, Boss," he yelled. "Meet Mister Henry."

I shut off the engine and staggered up the gravel path. I felt sick and woozy, and my legs were like rubberbands.

The Judge reached out to help me. I shook hands with Mr. Henry, who gave me a key and a form to fill out. "Bullshit," said the Judge. "This man is my *guest*. He can have anything he wants. Just put it on my bill."

"Of course," said Mr. Henry. "Your *bill*. Yes. I have it right here." He reached under his desk and came up with a nasty-looking bundle of adding-machine tapes and scrawled Cash/Payment memos. . . . "You got here just in time," he said. "We were about to notify the Police."

"*What?*" said the Judge. "Are you *nuts*? I have a goddamn *platinum* American Express card! My credit is *impeccable*."

"Yes," said Mr. Henry. "We *know* that. We have total respect for you. Your signature is better than gold bullion."

The Judge smiled and whacked the flat of his hand on the counter. "You bet it is!" he snapped. "So get out of my goddamn *face*! You must be crazy to fuck with Me like this! You *fool*! Are you ready to go to *court?*"

Mr. Henry sagged. "*Please*, Judge," he said. "Don't do this to me. All I need is your card. Just let me run an *imprint*. That's all." He moaned and stared more or less at the Judge, but I could see that his eyes were not focused. . . . "They're going to *fire* me," he whispered. "They want to put me in *jail*."

"Nonsense!" the Judge snapped. "I would *never* let that happen. You can always *plead*." He reached out and gently gripped Mr. Henry's wrist. "Believe me, Bro," he hissed. "You have *nothing to worry about*. You are *cool*. They will *never* lock you up! They will *Never* take you away! Not out of *my* courtroom!"

"Thank you," Mr. Henry replied. "But all I need is your card and your signature. That's the problem: I forgot to run it when you checked in."

"So what?" the Judge barked. "I'm good for it. How much do you need?"

"About twenty-two thousand," said Mr. Henry. "Probably twenty-three thousand by now. You've had those suites for nineteen days with total room service."

"What?" the Judge yelled. "You thieving bastards! I'll have you crucified by American Express. You are *finished* in this business. You will *never work again! Not anywhere in the world!*" Then he whipped Mr. Henry across the front of his face so fast that I barely saw it. "Stop crying!" he said. "Get a grip on yourself! This is embarrassing!"

Then he slapped the man again. "Is that all you want?" he said. "Only a *card*? A stupid little card? A piece of plastic *shit*?"

Mr. Henry nodded. "Yes, Judge," he whispered. "That's all. Just a stupid little card."

The Judge laughed and reached into his raincoat, as if to jerk out a gun or at least a huge wallet. "You want a *card*, whoreface? Is that *it*? Is that all you want? You filthy little scumbag! Here it is!"

Mr. Henry cringed and whimpered. Then he reached out to accept the Card, the thing that would set him free . . . The Judge was still grasping around in the lining of his raincoat. "What the fuck?" he muttered. "This thing has *too many pockets*! I can *feel* it, but I can't find the slit!"

Mr. Henry seemed to believe him, and so did I, for a minute. . . . Why not? He was a Judge with a platinum credit card—a very high roller. You don't find many Judges, these days, who can handle a full caseload in the morning and run wild like a goat in the afternoon. That is a very hard dollar, and very few can handle it . . . but the Judge was a Special Case.

Suddenly he screamed and fell sideways, ripping and clawing at the lining of his raincoat. "Oh, Jesus!" he wailed. "I've lost my wallet! It's *gone*. I left it out there in the Limo, when we hit the fucking sheep."

"So what?" I said. "We don't need it for this. I have *many* plastic cards."

He smiled and seemed to relax. "How many?" he said. "We might need more than one."

. . .

I woke up in the bathtub—who knows how much later—to the sound of the hookers shrieking next door. *The New York Times* had fallen in and blackened the water. For many hours I tossed and turned like a crack baby in a cold hallway. I heard thumping Rhythm & Blues—serious rock & roll, and I knew that something wild was going on in the Judge's suites. The smell of amyl nitrate came from under the door. It was no use. It was impossible to sleep through this orgy of ugliness. I was getting worried. I was already a marginally legal person, and now I was stuck with some crazy Judge who had my credit card and owed me $23,000.

I had some whiskey in the car, so I went out into the rain to get some ice. I had to get out. As I walked past the other rooms, I looked in people's windows and feverishly tried to figure out how to get my credit card back. Then from behind me I heard the sound of a tow-truck winch. The Judge's white Cadillac was being dragged to the ground. The Judge was whooping it up with the tow-truck driver, slapping him on the back.

"What the hell? It was only property damage," he laughed.

"Hey, Judge," I called out. "I never got my card back."

"Don't worry," he said. "It's in my room—come on."

I was right behind him when he opened the door to his room, and I caught a glimpse of a naked woman dancing. As soon as the door opened, the woman lunged for the Judge's throat. She pushed him back outside and slammed the door in his face.

"Forget that credit card—we'll get some cash," the Judge said. "Let's go down to the Commercial Hotel. My friends are there and they have *plenty* of money."

We stopped for a six-pack on the way. The Judge went into a sleazy liquor store that turned out to be a front for kinky marital aids. I offered him money for the beer, but he grabbed my whole wallet.

Ten minutes later, the Judge came out with $400 worth of booze and a bagful of Triple-X-Rated movies. "My buddies will like this stuff," he said. "And don't worry about the money, I told you I'm good for it. These guys carry serious cash."

The marquee above the front door of the Commercial Hotel said:

WELCOME: ADULT FILM PRESIDENTS

STUDEBAKER SOCIETY

FULL ACTION CASINO / KENO IN LOUNGE

"Park right here in front," said the Judge. "Don't worry. I'm well known in this place."

Me too, but I said nothing. I have been well known at the Commercial for many years, from the time when I was doing a lot of driving back and forth between Denver and San Francisco—usually for Business reasons, or for Art, and on this particular weekend I was there to meet quietly with a few old friends and business associates from the Board of Directors of the Adult Film Association of America. I had been, after all, the Night Manager of the famous O'Farrell Theatre, in San Francisco—"Carnegie Hall of Sex in America."

I was the Guest of Honor, in fact—but I saw no point in confiding these things to the Judge, a total stranger with no Personal Identification, no money, and a very aggressive lifestyle. We were on our way to the Commercial Hotel to borrow money from some of his friends in the Adult Film business.

What the hell? I thought. It's only Rock & Roll. And he was, after all, a Judge of some kind. . . . Or maybe not. For all I knew, he was a criminal pimp with no fingerprints, or a wealthy black shepherd from Spain. But it hardly mattered. He was good company. (If you had a taste for the edge work—and I did, in those days. And so, I felt, did the Judge.) He had a bent sense of fun, a quick mind, and no Fear of anything.

The front door of the Commercial looked strangely busy at this hour of night in a bad rainstorm, so I veered off and drove slowly around the block in low gear.

"There's a side entrance on Queer Street," I said to the Judge, as we hammered into a flood of black water. He seemed agitated, which worried me a bit.

"Calm down," I said. "We don't want to make a scene in this place. All we want is money."

"Don't worry," he said. "I know these people. They are friends. Money is nothing. They will be happy to see me."

We entered the hotel through the Casino entrance. The Judge seemed calm and focused until we rounded the corner and came face to face with an eleven-foot polar bear standing on its hind legs, ready to pounce. The Judge turned to jelly at the sight of it. "I've had enough of this goddamn beast!" he shouted. "It doesn't belong here. We should blow its head off."

I took him by the arm. "Calm down, Judge," I told him. "That's White King. He's been dead for thirty-three years."

The Judge had no use for animals. He composed himself and we swung into the lobby, approaching the desk from behind. I hung back—it was getting late, and the lobby was full of suspicious-looking stragglers from the Adult Film crowd. Private cowboy cops wearing six-shooters in open holsters were standing around. Our entrance did not go unnoticed.

The Judge looked competent, but there was something menacing in the way he swaggered up to the desk clerk and whacked the marble countertop with both hands. The lobby was suddenly filled with tension, and I quickly moved away as the Judge began yelling and pointing at the ceiling.

"Don't give me that crap," he barked. "These people are my friends. They're expecting me. Just ring the goddamn room again." The desk clerk muttered something about his explicit instructions not to. . . .

Suddenly the Judge reached across the desk for the house phone. "What's the number?" he snapped. "I'll ring it myself." The clerk moved quickly. He shoved the phone out of the Judge's grasp and simultaneously drew his index finger across his throat. The Judge took one look at the muscle converging on him and changed his stance.

"I want to cash a check," he said calmly.

"A *check*?" the clerk said. "Sure thing, buster. I'll cash your goddamned check." He seized the Judge by his collar and laughed. "Let's get this bozo out of here. And put him in jail."

I was moving toward the door, and suddenly the Judge was right behind me. "Let's go," he said. We sprinted for the car, but then the Judge stopped in his tracks. He turned and raised his fist in the direction of the hotel. "Fuck you!" he shouted. "I'm the Judge. I'll be back, and I'll bust every one of you bastards. The next time you see me coming, you'd better run."

We jumped into the car and zoomed away into the darkness. The Judge was acting manic. "Never mind those pimps," he said. "I'll have them all on a chain gang in forty-eight hours." He laughed and slapped me on the back. "Don't worry, Boss," he said. "I know where we're going." He squinted into the rain and opened a bottle of Royal Salute. "Straight ahead," he snapped. "Take a right at the next corner. We'll go see Leach. He owes me twenty-four thousand dollars."

I slowed down and reached for the whiskey. What the hell, I thought. Some days are weirder than others.

"Leach is my secret weapon," the Judge said, "but I have to watch him. He could be violent. The cops are always after him. He lives in a balance of terror. But he has a genius for gambling. We win eight out of ten every week." He nodded solemnly. "That is *four out of five,* Doc. That is Big. *Very* big. That is eighty percent of everything." He shook his head sadly and reached for the whiskey. "It's a *horrible* habit. But I can't give it up. It's like having a money machine."

"That's wonderful," I said. "What are you bitching about?"

"I'm *afraid,* Doc. Leach is a *monster,* a criminal hermit who understands nothing in life except point spreads. He should be locked up and castrated."

"So what?" I said. "Where does he live? We are desperate. We have no cash and no plastic. This freak is our only hope."

The Judge slumped into himself, and neither one of us spoke for a minute. . . . "Well," he said finally. "Why not? I can handle almost anything for twenty-four big ones in a brown bag. What the fuck? Let's *do* it. If the bastard gets ugly, we'll kill him."

"Come on, Judge," I said. "Get a grip on yourself. This is only a gambling debt."

"Sure," he replied. "That's what they *all* say."

DEAD MEAT IN THE FAST LANE: THE JUDGE RUNS AMOK . . . DEATH OF A POET, BLOOD CLOTS IN THE REVENUE STREAM . . . THE MAN WHO LOVED SEX DOLLS

We pulled into a seedy trailer court behind the stockyards. Leach met us at the door with red eyes and trembling hands, wearing a soiled bathrobe and carrying a half-gallon of Wild Turkey.

"Thank God you're home," the Judge said. "I can't *tell* you what kind of horrible shit has happened to me tonight. . . . But now the worm has turned. Now that we have *cash,* we will crush them all."

Leach just stared. Then he took a swig of Wild Turkey. "We are doomed," he muttered. "I was about to slit my wrists."

"Nonsense," the Judge said. "We won Big. I bet the same way you did. You gave me the *numbers.* You even predicted the Raiders would stomp Denver. Hell, it was obvious. The Raiders are unbeatable on Monday night."

Leach tensed, then he threw his head back and uttered a high-pitched quavering shriek. The Judge seized him. "Get a grip on yourself," he snapped. "What's wrong?"

"I went sideways on the bet," Leach sobbed. "I went to that goddamn sports bar up in Jackpot with some of the guys from the shop. We were all drinking Mescal and screaming, and I lost my head."

Leach was clearly a bad drinker and a junkie for mass hysteria. "I got drunk and bet on the Broncos," he moaned, "then I doubled up. We lost everything."

A terrible silence fell on the room. Leach was weeping helplessly. The Judge seized him by the sash of his greasy leather robe and started jerking him around by the stomach. They ignored me, and I tried to pretend it wasn't happening. . . . It was too ugly.

There was an ashtray on the table in front of the couch. As I reached out for it, I noticed a legal pad of what appeared to be Leach's poems, scrawled with a red Magic Marker in some kind of primitive verse form. There was one that caught my eye. There was something particularly ugly about it. There was something *repugnant* in the harsh slant of the handwriting. It was about pigs.

I TOLD HIM IT WAS WRONG

—F. X. Leach
Omaha, 1968

A filthy young pig
got tired of his gig
and begged for a transfer
to Texas.

Police ran him down
on the Outskirts of town
and ripped off his Nuts
with a coat hanger.
Everything after that was like
coming home
in a cage on the
back of a train from
New Orleans on a Saturday night
with no money and cancer and
a dead girlfriend.
In the end it was no use
He died on his knees in a barnyard
with all the others watching.
Res Ipsa Loquitur.

"They're going to kill me," Leach said. "They'll be here by midnight. I'm doomed." He uttered another low cry and reached for the Wild Turkey bottle, which had fallen over and spilled.

"Hang on," I said. "I'll get more."

(Paul Chesley)

On my way to the kitchen I was jolted by the sight of a naked woman slumped awkwardly in the corner with a desperate look on her face, as if she'd been shot. Her eyes bulged and her mouth was wide open and she appeared to be reaching out for me.

I leapt back and heard laughter behind me. My first thought was that Leach, unhinged by his gambling disaster, had finally gone over the line with his wife-beating habit and shot her in the mouth just before we knocked. She appeared to be crying out for help, but there was no voice.

I ran into the kitchen to look for a knife, thinking that if Leach had gone crazy enough to kill his wife, now he would have to kill me, too, since I was the only witness. Except for the Judge, who had locked himself in the bathroom.

Leach appeared in the doorway, holding the naked woman by the neck, and hurled her across the room at me. . . .

Time stood still for an instant. The woman seemed to hover in the air, coming at me in the darkness like a body in slow motion. I went into a stance with the bread knife and braced for a fight to the death.

Then the thing hit me and bounced softly down to the floor. It was a rubber blow-up doll: one of those things with five orifices that young stockbrokers buy in adult bookstores after the singles bars close.

"Meet Jennifer," he said. "She's my punching bag." He picked it up by the hair and slammed it across the room.

"Ho, ho," he chuckled, "no more wife beating. I'm cured, thanks to Jennifer." He smiled sheepishly. "It's almost like a miracle. *These dolls saved my marriage.* They're a lot smarter than you think." He nodded gravely. "Sometimes I have to beat *two at once.* But it always calms me down, you know what I mean?"

Whoops, I thought. Welcome to the night train. "Oh, *hell yes,*" I said quickly. "How do the neighbors handle it?"

"No problem," he said. "They love me."

Sure, I thought. I tried to imagine the horror of living in a muddy industrial slum full of tin-walled trailers and trying to protect your family against brain damage from knowing that every night when you look out your kitchen window there will be a man in a leather bathrobe flogging two naked women around the room with a quart bottle of Wild Turkey. Sometimes for two or three hours . . . It was horrible.

"Where is your wife?" I asked. "Is she still here?"

"Oh, yes," he said quickly. "She just went out for some cigarettes She'll be back *any minute*." He nodded eagerly. "Oh, yes, she's very *proud* of me. We're almost reconciled. She really loves these dolls."

I smiled, but something about his story made me nervous. "How many do you have?" I asked him.

"Don't worry," he said. "I have all we need." He reached into a nearby broom closet and pulled out another one—a half-inflated Chinese-looking woman with rings in her nipples and two electric cords attached to her head. "This is Ling-Ling," he said. "She screams when I hit her." He whacked the doll's head and it squawked stupidly.

Just then I heard car doors slamming outside the trailer, then loud knocking on the front door and a gruff voice shouting, "Open up! Police!"

Leach grabbed a .44 Magnum out of a shoulder holster inside his bathrobe and fired two shots through the front door. "You *bitch*," he screamed. "I should have killed you a long time ago."

He fired two more shots, laughing calmly. Then he turned to face me and put the barrel of the gun in his mouth. He hesitated for a moment, staring directly into my eyes. Then he pulled the trigger and blew off the back of his head.

The dead man seemed to lunge at me, slumping headfirst against my legs as he fell to the floor—just as a volley of shotgun blasts came through the front door, followed by harsh shouts on a police bullhorn from outside. Then another volley of buckshot blasts that exploded the TV set and set the living room on fire, filling the trailer with dense brown smoke that I recognized instantly as the smell of Cyanide gas being released by the burning plastic couch.

Voices were screaming through the smoke, "*Surrender!* HANDS UP *behind your goddamn head*! DEAD MEAT!" Then more shooting. Another deafening fireball exploded out of the living room, I kicked the corpse off my feet and leapt for the back door, which I'd noticed earlier when I scanned the trailer for "alternative exits," as they say in the business—in case one might become necessary. I was halfway out the door when I remembered *the Judge*. He was still locked in the bathroom, maybe helpless in some kind of accidental drug coma, unable to get to his feet as flames roared through the trailer. . . .

Ye Fucking Gods! I thought. I can't let him burn.

Kick the door off its hinges. Yes. Whack! The door splintered and I saw him sitting calmly on the filthy aluminum toilet stool, pretending to read a newspaper and squinting vacantly at me as I crashed in and grabbed him by one arm. "Fool!" I screamed. "Get up! Run! They'll *murder* us!"

He followed me through the smoke and burning debris, holding his pants up with one hand. . . . The Chinese sex doll called Ling-Ling hovered crazily in front of the door, her body swollen from heat and her hair on fire. I slapped her aside and bashed the door open, dragging the Judge outside with me. Another volley of shotgun blasts and bullhorn yells erupted somewhere behind us. The Judge lost his footing and fell heavily into the mud behind the doomed Airstream.

"Oh, God!" he screamed. "Who *is* it?"

"The *Pigs*," I said. "They've gone *crazy*. Leach is dead! They're trying to *kill* us. We have to get to the car!"

He stood up quickly. "Pigs?" he said. "*Pigs*? Trying to *kill* me?"

He seemed to stiffen, and the dumbness went out of his eyes. He raised both fists and screamed in the direction of the shooting. "You *bastards*! You *scum*! You will *die* for this. You stupid white-trash pigs!

"Are they *nuts*?" he muttered. He jerked out of my grasp and reached angrily into his left armpit, then down to his belt and around behind his back like a gunfighter trying to slap leather. . . . But there was no leather there. Not even a sleeve holster.

"*Goddamnit!*" he snarled. "Where's my goddamn *weapon*? Oh, Jesus! I left it in the car!" He dropped into a running crouch and sprinted into the darkness, around the corner of the flaming Airstream. "Let's *go!*" he hissed. "I'll *kill* these bastards! I'll blow their fucking heads off!"

Right, I thought, as we took off in a kind of low-speed desperate crawl through the mud and the noise and the gunfire, terrified neighbors screaming frantically to each other in the darkness. The red convertible was parked in the shadows, near the front of the trailer right next to the State Police car, with its chase lights blinking crazily and voices burping out of its radio.

The Pigs were nowhere to be seen. They had apparently *rushed* the place, guns blazing—hoping to kill Leach before he got away. I jumped into the car and started the engine. The Judge came through the passenger door and reached for the loaded .454 Magnum. . . . I watched in horror as he jerked it out of its holster and ran around to the front of the cop car and fired two shots into the grille.

"Fuck you!" he screamed. "Take *this*, you Scum! Eat shit and die!" He jumped back as the radiator exploded in a blast of steam and scalding water. Then he fired three more times through the windshield and into the squawking radio, which also exploded.

"Hot damn!" he said as he slid back into the front seat. "Now we have them trapped!" I jammed the car into reverse and lost control in the mud, hitting a structure of some kind and careening sideways at top speed until I got a grip on the thing and aimed it up the ramp to the highway. . . . The Judge was trying desperately to reload the .454, yelling at me to slow down, so he could finish the bastards off! His eyes were wild and his voice was unnaturally savage.

I swerved hard left to Elko and hurled him sideways, but he quickly recovered his balance and somehow got off five more thundering shots in the general direction of the burning trailer behind us.

"Good work, Judge," I said. "They'll never catch us now." He smiled and drank deeply from our Whiskey Jug, which he had somehow picked up as we fled. . . . Then he passed it over to me, and I too drank deeply as I whipped the big V-8 into passing gear, and we went from forty-five to ninety in four seconds and left the ugliness far behind us in the rain.

I glanced over at the Judge as he loaded five huge bullets into the Magnum. He was very calm and focused, showing no signs of the drug coma that had crippled him just moments before. . . . I was impressed. The man was clearly a Warrior. I slapped him on the back and grinned. "Calm down, Judge," I said. "We're almost home."

I knew better, of course. I was *1,000 miles* from home, and we were almost certainly doomed. There was no hope of escaping the dragnet that would be out for us, once those poor fools discovered Leach in a puddle of burning blood with the top of his head blown off. The squad car was destroyed—thanks to the shrewd instincts of the Judge—but I knew it would not take them long to send out an all-points alarm. Soon there would be angry police roadblocks at every exit between Reno and Salt Lake City. . . .

So what? I thought. There were many side roads, and we had a *very* fast car. All I had to do was get the Judge out of his killing frenzy and find a truck stop where we could buy a few cans of Flat Black spray paint. Then we could slither out of the state before dawn and find a place to hide.

But it would not be an easy run. In the quick space of four hours we had destroyed two automobiles and somehow participated in at least one killing—in addition to all the other random, standard-brand crimes like speeding and arson and fraud and attempted murder of State Police officers while fleeing the scene of a homicide. . . . No. We had a Serious problem on our hands. We were trapped in the middle of Nevada like crazy rats, and the cops would shoot to Kill when they saw us. No doubt about that. We were Criminally Insane. . . . I laughed and shifted up into Drive. The car stabilized at 115 or so. . . .

The Judge was eager to get back to his women. He was still fiddling with the Magnum, spinning the cylinder nervously and looking at his watch. "Can't you go any faster?" he muttered. "How far is Elko?"

Too far, I thought, which was true. Elko was fifty miles away and there would be roadblocks. Impossible. They would trap us and probably butcher us.

Elko was out, but I was loath to break this news to the Judge. He had no stomach for bad news. He had a tendency to flip out and flog anything in sight when things weren't going his way.

It was wiser, I thought, to humor him. Soon he would go to sleep.

I slowed down and considered. Our options were limited. There would be roadblocks on every paved road out of Wells. It was a main crossroads, a gigantic full-on truck stop where you could get anything you wanted twenty-four hours a day, within reason of course. And what we needed was not in that category. We needed to disappear. That was one option.

We could go south on 93 to Ely, but that was about it. That would be like driving into a steel net. A flock of pigs would be waiting for us, and after that it would be Nevada State Prison. To the north on 93 was Jackpot, but we would never make that either. Running east into Utah was hopeless. We were trapped. They would run us down like dogs.

There were other options, but not all of them were mutual. The Judge had his priorities, but they were not mine. I understood that me and the Judge were coming up on a parting of the ways. This made me nervous. There were other options, of course, but they were all High

Risk. I pulled over and studied the map again. The Judge appeared to be sleeping, but I couldn't be sure. He still had the Magnum in his lap.

The Judge was getting to be a problem. There was no way to get him out of the car without violence. He would not go willingly into the dark and stormy night. The only other way was to kill him, but that was out of the question as long as he had the gun. He was very quick in emergencies. I couldn't get the gun away from him, and I was not about to get into an argument with him about who should have the weapon. If I lost, he would shoot me in the spine and leave me in the road.

I was getting too nervous to continue without chemical assistance. I reached under the seat for my kit bag, which contained five or six Spansules of Black Acid. Wonderful, I thought. This is just what I need. I ate one and went back to pondering the map. There was a place called Deeth, just ahead, where a faintly marked side road appeared to wander uphill through the mountains and down along a jagged ridge into Jackpot from behind. Good, I thought, this is it. We could sneak into Jackpot by dawn.

Just then I felt a blow on the side of my head as the Judge came awake with a screech, flailing his arms around him like he was coming out of a nightmare. "What's happening, goddamnit?" he said. "Where are we? They're after us." He was jabbering in a foreign language that quickly lapsed into English as he tried to aim the gun. "Oh, God!" he screamed. "They're right on top of us. Get moving, goddamnit. I'll kill every bastard I see."

He was coming out of a nightmare. I grabbed him by the neck and put him in a headlock until he went limp. I pulled him back up in the seat and handed him a Spansule of acid. "Here, Judge, take this," I said. "It'll calm you down."

He swallowed the pill and said nothing as I turned onto the highway and stood heavily on the accelerator. We were up to 115 when a green exit sign that said DEETH NO SERVICES loomed suddenly out of the rain just in front of us. I swerved hard to the right and tried to hang on. But it was no use. I remember the sound of the Judge screaming as we lost control and went into a full 360-degree curl and then backwards at seventy-five or eighty through a fence and into a pasture.

For some reason the near-fatal accident had a calming effect on the Judge. Or maybe it was the acid. I didn't care one way or the other after

I took the gun from his hand. He gave it up without a fight. He seemed to be more interested in reading the road signs and listening to the radio. I knew that if we could slip into Jackpot the back way, I could get the car painted any color I wanted in thirty-three minutes and put the Judge on a plane. I knew a small private airstrip there, where nobody asks too many questions and they'll take a personal check.

At dawn we drove across the tarmac and pulled up to a seedy-looking office marked AIR JACKPOT EXPRESS CHARTER COMPANY. "This is it Judge," I said and slapped him on the back. "This is where you get off." He seemed resigned to his fate until the woman behind the front desk told him there wouldn't be a flight to Elko until lunchtime.

"Where is the pilot?" he demanded.

"I am the pilot," the woman said, "but I can't leave until Debby gets here to relieve me."

"Fuck this!" the Judge shouted. "Fuck lunchtime. I have to leave *now,* you bitch."

The woman seemed truly frightened by his mood swing, and when the Judge leaned in and gave her a taste of the long knuckle, she collapsed and began weeping uncontrollably. "There's more where that came from," he told her. "Get up! I have to get out of here now."

He jerked her out from behind the desk and was dragging her toward the plane when I slipped out the back door. It was daylight now. The car was nearly out of gas, but that wasn't my primary concern. The police would be here in minutes, I thought. I'm doomed. But then, as I pulled onto the highway, I saw a sign that said, WE PAINT ALL NIGHT.

As I pulled into the parking lot, the Jackpot Express plane passed overhead. So long, Judge, I thought to myself. You're a brutal hustler and a Warrior and a great copilot, but you know how to get your way. You will go far in the world.

EPILOGUE: CHRISTMAS DREAMS AND CRUEL MEMORIES . . . NATION OF JAILERS . . . STAND BACK! THE JUDGE WILL SEE YOU NOW

That's about it for now, Jann. This story is too depressing to have to confront professionally in these morbid weeks before Christmas. . . . I have only vague memories of what it's like there in New York, but sometimes I have flashbacks about how it was to glide in perfect speedy silence around the ice rink in front of NBC while junkies and federal informants in white beards and sleazy red jumpsuits worked the crowd mercilessly for nickels and dollars and dimes covered with Crack residue.

I remember one Christmas morning in Manhattan when we got into the Empire State Building and went up to the Executive Suite of some famous underwear company and shoved a 600-pound red tufted-leather Imperial English couch out of a corner window on something like the eighty-fifth floor. . . .

The wind caught it, as I recall, and it sort of drifted around the corner onto Thirty-fourth Street, picking up speed on its way down, and hit the striped awning of a Korean market, you know, the kind that sells everything from kimchi to Christmas trees. The impact blasted watermelons and oranges and tomatoes all over the sidewalk. We could barely see the impact from where we were, but I remember a lot of activity on the street when we came out of the elevator. . . . It looked like a war zone. A few gawkers were standing around in a blizzard, muttering to each other and looking dazed. They thought it was an underground explosion—maybe a subway or a gas main.

Just as we arrived on the scene, a speeding cab skidded on some watermelons and slammed into a Fifth Avenue bus and burst into flames. There was a lot of screaming and wailing of police sirens. Two cops began fighting with a gang of looters who had emerged like ghosts out of the snow and were running off with hams and turkeys and big jars of caviar. . . . Nobody seemed to think it was strange. *What the hell? Shit happens. Welcome to the Big Apple. Keep alert. Never ride in open cars or walk too close to a tall building when it snows.* . . . There were Christmas trees scattered all over the street and cars were stopping to grab them and speeding away. We stole one and took it to Missy's place on the Bowery, because we knew she didn't have one. But she wasn't home, so we put the tree out on the fire escape and set it on fire with kerosene.

That's how I remember Xmas in New York, Jann. It was always a time of angst and failure and turmoil. Nobody ever seemed to have any money on Christmas. Even rich people were broke and jabbering frantically on their telephones about Santa Claus and suicide or joining a church with no rules. . . . The snow was clean and pretty for the first twenty or thirty minutes around dawn, but after that it was churned into filthy mush by drunken cabbies and garbage compactors and shitting dogs.

Anybody who acted happy on Christmas was lying—even the ones who were getting paid $500 an hour. . . . The Jews were especially sulky, and who could blame them? The birthday of Baby Jesus is always a nervous time for people who know that ninety days later they will be accused of murdering him.

So what? We have our *own* problems, eh? Jesus! I don't know how you can ride all those motorcycles around in the snow, Jann. Shit, we can *all* handle the back wheel coming loose in a skid. But the *front* wheel is something else—and that's what happens when it snows. WHACKO. One minute you feel as light and safe as a snowflake, and the next minute you're sliding sideways under the wheels of a Bekins van. . . . Nasty traffic jams, horns honking, white limos full of naked Jesus freaks going up on the sidewalk in low gear to get around you and the mess you made on the street . . . *Goddamn this scum. They are more and more in the way. And why aren't they home with their families on Xmas? Why do they need to come out here and die on the street like iron hamburgers?*

I hate these bastards, Jann. And I suspect you feel the same. . . . They might call us bigots, but at least we are *Universal* bigots. Right? Shit on those people. Everybody you see these days might have the power to get you locked up. . . . Who knows why? They will have reasons straight out of some horrible Kafka story, but in the end it won't matter any more than a full moon behind clouds. Fuck them.

Christmas hasn't changed much in twenty-two years, Jann— not even 2,000 miles west and 8,000 feet up in the Rockies. It is still a day that only amateurs can love. It is all well and good for children and acid freaks to believe in Santa Claus—but it is still a profoundly morbid day for us working professionals. It is unsettling to know that one out of every twenty people you meet on Xmas will be dead this time next year. . . . Some people can accept this, and some can't. That is why God made whiskey, and also why Wild Turkey comes in $300 shaped canisters during most of the Christmas season, and also why criminal shitheads all over New York City will hit you up for $100 tips or they'll twist your windshield wipers into spaghetti and urinate on your door handles.

People all around me are going to pieces, Jann. My whole support system has crumbled like wet sugar cubes. That is why I try never to employ anyone over the age of twenty. Every Xmas after that is like another notch down on the ratchet, or maybe a few more teeth off the flywheel. . . . I remember on Xmas in New York when I was trying to sell a Mark VII Jaguar with so many teeth off the flywheel that the whole drivetrain would lock up and whine every time I tried to start the engine for a buyer. . . . I had to hire gangs of street children to muscle the car back and forth until the throw-out gear on the starter was lined up very precisely to engage the few remaining teeth on the flywheel. On some days I would leave the car idling in a fireplug zone for three or four hours at a time and pay the greedy little bastards a dollar an hour to keep it running and wet-shined with fireplug water until a buyer came along.

We got to know each other pretty well after nine or ten weeks, and they were finally able to unload it on a rich artist who drove as far as the toll plaza at the far end of the George Washington Bridge, where the engine seized up and exploded like a steam bomb. "They had to tow it away with a firetruck," he said. "Even the leather seats were on fire. They laughed at me."

There is more and more Predatory bullshit in the air these days. Yesterday I got a call from somebody who said I owed money to Harris Wofford, my old friend from the Peace Corps. We were in Sierra Leone together.

He came out of nowhere like a heat-seeking missile and destroyed the U.S. Attorney General in Pennsylvania. It was

Wonderful. Harris is a Senator now, and the White House creature is not. Thornburgh blew a forty-four–point lead in three weeks, like Humpty Dumpty. . . . WHOOPS! Off the wall like a big Lizard egg. The White House had seen no need for a safety net.

It was a major disaster for the Bush brain trust and every GOP political pro in America, from the White House all the way down to City Hall in places like Denver and Tupelo. The whole Republican party was left stunned and shuddering like a hound dog passing a peach pit. . . . At least that's what they said in Tupelo, where one of the local GOP chairmen flipped out and ran off to Biloxi with a fat young boy from one of the rich local families . . . then he tried to blame it on Harris Wofford when they arrested him in Mobile for aggravated Sodomy and kidnapping. He was ruined, and his Bail was only $5,000, but none of his friends would sign for it. They were mainly professional Republicans and bankers who had once been in the Savings and Loan business, along with Neil Bush the *manqué,* son of the President.

Neil had just walked in on the infamous Silverado Savings & Loan scandal in Colorado. But only by the skin of his teeth, after his father said he would have to abandon him to a terrible fate in the Federal Prison System if his son was really a crook. The evidence was overwhelming, but Neil had a giddy kind of talent *negotiating*—like Colonel North and the Admiral, who also walked. . . . It was shameless and many people bitched. But what the fuck do they expect from a Party of high-riding Darwinian rich boys who've been running around in the White House like pampered animal for twelve straight years? They can do whatever they want, and why not. "These are Good Boys," John Sununu once said of his staff. "They only shit in the pressroom."

Well . . . Sununu is gone now, and so is Dick Thornburgh, who is currently seeking night work in the bank business somewhere on the outskirts of Pittsburgh. It is an ugly story. He decided to go out on his own—like Lucifer, who plunged into Hell—and he got beaten like a redheaded stepchild by my old Peace Corps buddy Harris Wofford, who caught him from behind like a bull wolverine so fast that Thornburgh couldn't even get out of the way. . . . He was mangled and humiliated. It was the worst public disaster since Watergate.

The GOP was plunged into national fear. How could it happen? Dick Thornburgh had sat on the right hand of God. As AG, he had stepped out like some arrogant Knight from the Round Table and declared that *his* boys—4,000 or so Justice Department prosecutors—were no longer subject to the rules of the Federal Court System.

But he was wrong. And now Wofford is using Thornburgh's corpse as a launching pad for a run on the White House and hiring experts to collect bogus debts from old buddies like me. Hell, I *like* the idea of Harris being President. He always seemed honest and I knew he was smart, but I am leery of giving him money.

That is politics in the 1990s. Democratic presidential candidates have not been a satisfying investment recently. Camelot was thirty years ago, and we still don't know who killed Jack Kennedy. That lone bullet on the stretcher in Dallas sure as hell didn't pass through two human bodies, but it was the one that pierced the heart of the American Dream in our century, maybe forever.

Camelot is on Court TV now, limping into Rehab clinics and forced to deny low-rent Rape accusations in the same sweaty West Palm Beach courthouse where Roxanne Pulitzer went on trial for fucking a trumpet and lost.

It has been a long way down—not just for the Kennedys and the Democrats, but for all the rest of us. Even the rich and the powerful, who are coming to understand that change can be quick in the Nineties and one of these days it will be them in the dock on TV, fighting desperately to stay out of prison.

Take my word for it. I have been there, and it gave me an eerie feeling. . . . Indeed. There are many cells in the mansion, and more are being added every day. We are becoming a nation of jailers.

And that's about it for now, Jann. Christmas is on us and it's all downhill from here on. . . . At least until Groundhog Day, which is soon. . . . So, until then, at least, take my advice, as your family doctor, and don't do *anything* that might cause either one of us to have to appear before the Supreme Court of the United States. If you know what I'm saying. . . .

Yes. He is Up There, Jann. The Judge. And he will be there for a long time, waiting to gnaw on our skulls. . . . Right. Put *that* in your leather pocket the next time you feel like jumping on your new motorcycle and screwing it all the way over thru traffic and passing cop cars at 140.

Remember F. X. Leach. He crossed the Judge, and he paid a terrible price. . . . And so will you, if you don't slow down and quit harassing those girls in your office. The Judge is in charge now, and He won't tolerate it. Beware.

Heeere's Johnny!

FEAR AND LOATHING AT JACK'S HOUSE . . . THE LONELIEST PLACE IN THE WORLD

It was a dark and stormy night when I set out from my house to Jack Nicholson's place far away in a valley on the other side of town. It was his birthday, and I had a huge raw elk heart for him. I have known Jack for many years, and we share a certain sense of humor among other things, and in truth there was nothing inherently strange in the notion of bringing a freshly taken elk heart out to his home on the night of his birthday.

It was lightly frozen and beginning to leak from the chambers, so I put it in a Ziploc bag and tossed it in the back of the Jeep. Hot damn, I thought, Jack's children will love this. I knew they had just arrived that day from Los Angeles, and I wanted to have a surprise for them. "You won't be late, will you?" Jack had asked. "You know the kids go to bed early."

"Don't worry," I said. "I'm leaving in ten minutes."

And it was just about then that the night began to go wrong. Time withered away. Some kind of episode occurred, and before I knew it I was running two hours late—two hours, keep that in mind because it will make a difference later on.

Okay. So I set out to see Jack and his children with all kinds of jokes and gimcracks in my car. In addition to the bleeding elk heart, there was a massive outdoor amplifier, a tape recording of a pig being eaten alive by bears, a 1,000,000-watt spotlight, and a 9-mm Smith & Wesson semiautomatic pistol with teakwood handles and a box of high-powered ammunition. There was also a 40-million-candlepower parachute flare that would light up the valley for 40 miles for 40 seconds that would seem to anyone lucky enough to be awake at the time like the first blinding flash of a midrange nuclear device that might signal the end of the world. It was a handheld mortar, in fact, with a plastic lanyard on one end and the black snout of a firing tube on the other. I had found it on sale a few weeks earlier at West Marine Hardware in Sausalito for $115, down from $210. It was irresistible—even cheap, I felt, for such a spectacular display—and I was looking forward to using it. The directions were vague, and mainly in foreign languages, but the diagrams made it clear that The USER should wear suitable eye protection, hold projectile vertically as far from body as possible, then JERK FIRING RING STRAIGHT DOWN and DO NOT ALLOW PROJECTILE TO TILT.

Okay, I thought, I can do this. I know flares. I have fired those huge gray military things, where you pull off one end and put it on the other, then bash your palm against the bottom and feel both your arms go numb all the way up to your skull from an explosion equal to a 105-mm howitzer blast. So I wasn't worried about this cheap red load from Sausalito. Once you get a feeling for handling nitroglycerine fuses, you never lose it.

(HST archives)

. . .

I was thinking about these things as I wound my way up the long winding road to Jack's house. It was ten miles of darkness, and by the time I got there I was feeling a little jumpy, so I pulled over and parked on a bluff overlooking the Nicholson home.

There were no other cars on the road. I unloaded the huge amplifier and mounted it firmly on top of the Jeep. The horn pointed out across the valley, then I placed the flare neatly beside it and leaned back against the hood to smoke a cigarette. Far down through the pines I could see the queer-looking lights of Jack's house. The night was extremely quiet and the LED in my Jeep said it was nine degrees above zero and the time was no later than 2:30 A.M., or maybe 2:45. I remember hearing a gospel tune on the radio, then I plugged the horn into the amplifier and beamed up the pig-screaming tape to about 119 decibels.

The noise was intolerable, at first. I had to cover my head and crouch behind the Jeep to get away from it. I wanted to turn it off, but just then I saw headlights coming up the road and I had to get out of sight . . . The car never even slowed down as it passed me, despite the hideous screams of what sounded like a whole herd of pigs being slaughtered.

My first thought, for some reason, was that it was not Bill Clinton, because he would have at least honked. Ho ho, good joke, eh? It's odd how Bill Clinton jokes seem to pop up at unnatural moments like these—when you're doing something that feels deeply right and normal and you feel in a high sense of humor as you set about your task, which then somehow goes wrong for reasons beyond your control and sows the seeds of tragedy.

Nobody needs this—but some people seem to want it, and on that giddy winter night in the Rockies, I was one of them. No power of reason or nature could have persuaded me that the small, friendly, and finely organized chain of events already in motion would not be received by the family down below with anything but joy, surprise, and gratitude.

. . .

I kept the amplifier going with the pig screams every twenty or thirty seconds, bracketed around bursts of rapid gunfire—and then I put the million-watt strobe down on the house, dragging it back and forth across the deck and the living room windows.

I did this for ten minutes or so, but nothing happened. The only response from below was a silent spasm of lights being turned off, as if they were all going to bed.

Well, I thought, that is a rude way to act when guests come with presents, even if they are a bit late. So what? There is no excuse for rudeness.

My next move was potentially fatal. I attempted to launch the rocket, but the firing ring broke and the thing started hissing, so I quickly hurled it away and heard it tumbling down the hill toward the house. O God, I thought, those are magnum phosphorous flares, and this place is going to be like the bridge in *Apocalypse Now* when that goddamn thing explodes.

I hastily packed the amp into the Jeep and picked up as many of my empty brass cartridges as I could find in the snow—and it was then, as I fled, that I remembered my birthday gift, which had somehow popped out of its bag and was bleeding all over the backseat.

I was beginning to have mixed feelings about this visit. There was something out of whack, and I figured the best thing to do was get out of this valley immediately. There was only one road out. (If some worrywart had called 911 to report an outburst of screaming and shooting at the Nicholson place, that could pose a problem, given that I was far down at the end of a dead-end canyon with no other way to escape but the river, and that was not an option.)

But *why*? I thought. Why am I drifting into negativity? Never mind this talk about "escape." I am here on a mission of joy. And there are no neighbors, anyway. It was a dark and peaceful place—yet extremely desolate in many ways, and not a good place to be trapped in.

I dismissed these negative thoughts as I hooked a hard left into Jack's driveway, intent on delivering my birthday present. The iron jackals on the gateposts no longer disturbed me, and I knew I could do this thing quickly.

. . .

I drove the Jeep all the way up to the front door and left the motor running as I fetched the bleeding elk heart out of the backseat and carried it up to the house. I rang the doorbell a few times before I gave up and left the heart—about ten inches tall and seven inches wide—propped against the door in a way that would cause it to tumble into the house whenever the door was opened. It seemed like the right thing to do, in light of the rudeness I'd experienced, and panic was setting in. On my way back to the truck I made sure the gun was clear by cranking off the rest of the clip straight up in the air and flinging my bloody hands distractedly toward the house because I was sure I'd seen somebody watching me from inside the darkened kitchen window, which angered me even further, because I felt I was being snubbed.

But I left quickly, with no other noise or weirdness except the shooting, which sounded unnaturally loud and caused pain in both of my eardrums. I jerked the Jeep into low and whiplashed out to the road. It was time to go home and sleep heavily—and there were no signs of police or any other disturbance as I drove carefully down the icy road. I locked in on Venus, the Morning Star, and pulled safely into my garage before sunrise.

. . .

The rest of the morning was spent in a work frenzy. My fax machine beeped constantly. There were the usual messages from the White House, two dangerously bogus offers from Hollywood, and a 60-page, single-spaced transcript of General Douglas MacArthur's final address to The Long Gray Line of steely-eyed cadets on The Plain at West Point in the spring of 1962, and another 39 pages of his "Old Soldiers Never Die" speech to Congress after he'd been fired.

These things spew into my house day after day, and I do my best to analyze them. Different people want different things in this world, and you have to be careful about taking risks. Hungry people have the cunning of wild beasts. A thing that seemed strange and wrong yesterday can seem perfectly reasonable tomorrow, or vice versa.

. . .

It did not seem strange, for instance, to learn that Bill Clinton's main concern these days is with his place in history, his legacy, his permanent image in high-school textbooks 100 years from now. He has done his work, he feels, and now is the time to secure his place on a pedestal in the pantheon of Great American Presidents, along with Lincoln and Coolidge and Kennedy.

And why not? George Bush had that problem, and so did Richard Nixon. Nobody needs to go down in history like that. Only a criminal freak would want to be remembered as a Crook or a Dupe or a Creature of some treacherous monster like J. Edgar Hoover . . . But those risks come with the territory when you finally move into the White House. You bet. They *will* write something—many things, in fact: books, movies, legends, and maybe even filthy jokes about back-stabbing and sodomy that will follow you all the way to the grave. Look at Nixon, look at Reagan, or even JFK. History has never been gentle in its judgments on bedrock degenerates—but it is also true that some degenerates are treated more gently than others, and that is what worries Bill Clinton. He is liked, but not well liked, and that is a very fragile base to maintain for another two and a half years. Voters *like* him now because they believe he has made them richer—and they will probably vote for Al Gore in 2000. (Jesus. That has an eerie ring to it, eh? *Vote Gore in 2000*. Prepare yourself for that. It will happen. Beware.)

I was brooding on these things on that bright winter morning when the phone machine rang and I heard a female voice screeching hysterically: "Watch out, the police are coming" and "Blood Everywhere" and "Terrible tragedy at Jack's house last night."

Ye gods, I thought. What is she talking about? What tragedy? Hell, I was there at about three and the place looked peaceful to me. What could have happened?

The answer was not long in coming. Both phones rang at once, but I suddenly felt queasy and couldn't answer. Then I heard the voice of the sheriff on one phone and some angry raving on the other from Paul Pascarella, the famous artist, who said he was on his way to Jack's house at top speed with a shotgun and a .44 Magnum. The house was under siege, he said. Cops were everywhere. Some maniac stalker tried to kill Jack and the kids last night, but he got away and the cops think he's still loose in the woods. He's a killer, just got out of prison, I think Jack's okay, O God this is horrible. Then he went into the canyon and lost contact.

The sheriff's message told much the same tale. "This is going to be a very big story," he said. "I'm already setting up a command post to deal with the national media. They're calling it an assassination attempt. We've closed off the road and sent a posse with dogs to search the area. It's a manhunt. We'll be on CNN by noon—and, by the way, do you happen to know anything about this? If you do, please call me before it's too late."

Too late? I thought. Nonsense. Too late for what? Are we dealing with lunatics here? Why would I want to kill Jack? It was madness.

Indeed, and it was just about then that it hit me. Of course. That's *me* that they're chasing with dogs out there in the woods. *I* am the crazed bushy-haired assassin who tried to get into the house last night and murder the whole family. What the hell? It was only a joke.

A joke? Ho ho. Nobody else was laughing. They had already found an unexploded rocket bomb in the trees above the house. . . . Every cop in the county was cranked up and working double-overtime to capture this monster before he could butcher the whole Nicholson family and bring eternal shame on Aspen's already sleazy name. Hideous scandals involving rich perverts, depraved children, and degenerate Hollywood whores looking for publicity are so common here as to be politically tolerable and even stylish. . . . Indeed, *that* is why this shit-rain of "second-home pimps" has invaded this valley like a plague of rich lice in recent years. . . . And we are not talking about small-time lice here, not at all.

Ah, but I digress. We were talking about my failed attempt to deliver some birthday presents to my old friend Jack and his kids on a frozen snowy night in the winter of 1997.

The *real* problem on that night turned out to be something that did not occur to me, at the time—if only because it was so queer and unlikely as to beam new light on words like *incredible, bizarre,* and *impossible.* . . .

But it happened, for good or ill—and now that I mention it, 4,000–1 tragedies like this one are the main reason I decided to renounce conventional crime as a way of life so many, many years ago—and turn to the writing life.

. . .

Jack had been menaced in public by a murderous certified *stalker* who had made several previous attempts on his life in Los Angeles—and the reason he had come to the Rockies was to be completely anonymous and solitary with Raymond and Lorraine, safe from the perils of Hollywood. He was, in a word, on the *lam*—just another jittery parent whose children had arrived to join him at his utterly isolated cabin home in the Rockies.

. . .

Who could have known, for instance, that *all* telephone service to Jack's bleak valley would be cut off by the blizzard that night? . . . "Yeah, it was right about then that the phones went dead," the sheriff told me. "They tried to call 911, but the phone lines had apparently been cut. That's when he flipped out and barricaded the family in the basement behind a heap of antique furniture with nothing at all for a weapon except a common fireplace poker." He chuckled. "The fool didn't even have a gun in the house. Thank God for that, eh? He could have killed the children by accident."

Which was true. As a *rule* it is better *not* to keep loaded weapons lying around the house when children are visiting. Even with a criminally insane stalker creeping around outside with a chainsaw. It is a far far better thing to have good locks and screechers on the doors, and a fulltime phone to the police station. . . . This turned out to be no comfort at all to Jack and his family that night. The freak outside had a grudge, and he had come a long way to settle it. The setting was made to order (just like in *The Shining*).

The phones kept ringing and the news kept getting worse. Some people begged me to confess and others urged me to hurry out to Jack's with a 12-gauge riot gun and join the search party. Everybody who called seemed genuinely alarmed and afraid. Even Heidi was acting weird. She knew I had gone out to Jack's the previous night, and for all I knew she thought I'd tried to kill him for some reason. Why not? I might have had a seizure and flipped out. Who knows what a dope fiend might do? Especially with children around. I might not even remember it.

The phone rang again, and this time it was Jack. He had just got the phone working again. *Oh God,* I thought. *What am I going to say? Get a grip on yourself. Omerta.*

"Uh, Doc, how you doing?" he said calmly. It may have been a Saturday, because he said something like "Who's playing this afternoon?"

"Never mind those fucking football games," I said. "What's this nightmare about the police out there at your house? I'm hearing weird things about it."

There was a silence, a pause. I could hear him taking a breath. He said, "Well, yeah, let me ask you a thing or two." He paused. "You know, that elk heart. . . ."

That's what really freaked him out, all that blood. He said, "When I looked at it—we were looking at it for clues"—I guessed he was talking about the cops—"when I took a close look at it, I saw that there were icicles in the middle of the heart, the part that still hadn't thawed. I didn't say anything to the cops, of course, but it seems like I remember you keeping a frozen elk heart in your refrigerator. Didn't you show me something like that, along with a bird and a ferret? Don't I remember you throwing a frozen elk heart at me last winter?"

That fucker, I thought. *The creepy little bastard.* That was good, putting that together—just a *sliver* inside, frozen. All the rest had turned to mush and blood—it's actually pretty good to eat, elk heart . . . this one wasn't going to be eaten anytime soon; it looked like a gizzard of some human being. Bigger than a human heart. "Yeah, maybe . . ." I said.

"I thought so, I thought it was you, when I saw that ice," he said. "I haven't told them yet; you know, they're still out here, the police task force, digging for new evidence, people sleeping in the woods . . . God-damn, Doc, I'm glad you told me. We have had a hell of a night here. It's been horrible."

The joke was over. I was never formally accused of it; Jack told the sheriff it was just a false alarm. "I know this guy," he said, "and he is not the killer."

Epilogue

That is what I mean about personal security in this town. You can buy a lot of protection, if you are filthy rich, and it obviously makes those people feel better about themselves—surrounded at all times by hundreds of greedy freelance cops with a license to kill anytime, anywhere, for any reason blessed by God. They are volatile people, at best, and always dangerous.

We get more black-truck security caravans in this valley than any-place in the world that comes quickly to mind except Washington, D.C., and Vatican City. There is a lot of available cash in these places, a lot of quasi-secret money changing hands . . . of governments being toppled on the other side of the world, of kingdoms being under-mined, and whole families of U.S. presidents and movie stars like Julia Roberts and Harry Dean Stanton being bought and sold and coddled like concubines, by criminal scum like Neil Bush, convicted crook and brother of our sitting president George W. . . . Not to mention the cur-rent Secretary of the (U.S.) Army and gilded clutch of criminally fugi-tive executives from ENRON, including the monstrous chairman Kenneth Lay. . . . These people roam free and unmolested in Aspen, cloistered by off-duty cops and Hollywood yo-yos and bimbos and suckfish. . . . I know these people. They are more and more my neigh-bors in these first horrible years of our new Century. . . .

. . .

There is never any shortage of applicants for *paid*-police jobs in the Roaring Fork Valley. All ambitious young cops want to be hired in places like Palm Beach and Sausalito and Aspen. They crave their 15 minutes of fame, and their police research has told them that Aspen is the most likely place to get it. . . .

. . .

Which is normal enough in this town. It has long been a haven for sybaritic outlaws and other social criminals as long as they had a good story and didn't hurt the neighbors—not quite a *sanctuary*, but at least a sort of retro-legal gray area, where real-life words like Crime and Guilt mean different things to different people, even in the same household.

Kiss, Kiss

"Hey baby, you want to come over here and swim naked with me?"
"Say *what?*"
"You know what I mean, sweetie. I want to dance on the head of your pin. How about it?"

"Oh my God, you crazy bitch! I should have killed you a long time ago."

"You're lying," she said. "Come here and smoke a marijuana cigarette with me." She dropped her thin little robe and raised her perfect arms above her shoulders, whipping her hair down and behind her until it touched the top of her thighs. "I am Xania," she said, "Goddess of Wind and Pussy."

I was stunned. It was hard to believe that this girl was only eight years old. She appeared to be twice that age.

"I find you extremely beautiful," I said to her. "I must be going crazy."

She laughed and danced out of my reach. I was drinking heavily that night and my thumb had been recently broken in a car accident. The pain was relentless. It flashed up my arm like a bolt of hot lightning, from my lifeline to my armpit, so I couldn't touch the girl or even kiss her without pain.

Who *was* this wild little floozy? And why *me*? I may be a teenage girl trapped in the body of an elderly dope fiend. . . . But that doesn't make me a pervert. "Don't worry," I told her. "I don't want to penetrate you, my dear—I just want to suck on your back."

She shuddered, seeming to glisten in the thin light of this California dawn. . . .

. . .

People are talking about O. J. Simpson on TV today. They want to see reruns of his Trial on daytime TV. Yes. Eighty-eight percent of adults who responded to this Poll were strongly in favor of CBS broadcasting uncut tapes of the Trial of O. J. Simpson on worldwide TV.

Eighty-eight percent is also the number of Americans who allegedly favor the continued presence of U.S. troops in Afghanistan and the Death Penalty for all foreigners accused of "terrorism." They are Patriotic Americans who like to kill. Just like yourself, Doc. So what? They love their country.

Sure they do, Bubba. We'll see how much they love their goddamn country when they get busted for smoking a joint in Public—or even in Private, if Bush has his way. They will find themselves cuffed in a Federal courtroom on felony charges of *Conspiracy to Kill a Judge*. Ho ho. How do you like your Security blanket *now*, dude? We will kill the ones who eat us, and eat the ones we kill. Onward Christian Soldiers. Mahalo.

I was brooding on these things while I struggled to understand what horrible god would put me face to face with this naked child in my own home, with no warning, on this peaceful Saturday morning when all I wanted to do was watch a basketball game. It was wrong, deeply wrong.

Fuck those people. I've had a bellyful of those vengeful Christian bastards and their Rules for righteous punishment. What would the Pope have me do with this human sex doll that I have on my hands?

Fuck the Pope. He is a Pervert like all the others. Those fruit-bags have had their way for 2,000 years, and look what we have to show for it. Boom boom. Sorry honey, but that money you had in the bank just went bye-bye. Our horse *failed to finish*. Earnings were insufficient. You will suffer huge tax penalties, on top of everything else. Didn't I tell you that the End of the World (as we know it) will happen in the summer of 2012? That is what my people tell me, and I have no reason to doubt it.

Get a grip on yourself, Doc. Do you really want to suck on that little girl's back?

Why not? I thought. I have loved and admired the female spine for many years, beginning with Sally down in Mobile. The Spine is far and away the most beautiful bone in the human body. Does The Church have a problem with me wanting to suck on a human back? Nonsense. Get over it, Father—just tell me how much it will cost. . . . I am a gentle man, but some things make me weird, and this is one of them.

Ah, but no more of that mushy stuff, eh? We are soldiers and we don't need it. A love of this nature is dangerous, but only if it gets out of control. That would be Wrong, as they say in the Vatican—perhaps borderline *evil*. Would the Pope have me killed for sucking on a beautiful human spine, a creature born of God?

Well . . . Yes, in a word, he would. We live in kinky times, but maybe not quite *that* kinky. There is some shit those perverts won't eat.

(Mike McAllister)

The War on Fat

Hot damn! It is summer again in America, and the goofy Child President has declared his long-overdue *War on Fat*. The nation is plunged, once again, into another life-or-death WAR against the forces of Evil. Wonderful. Let's get it over with. We are Patriotic people, but there *is* some shit we won't eat. . . . It is *one* thing to be trampled like scum by our own Military Police, and quite a goddamn *other* to be wallowed and stomped on by Fat People.

I have seen a lot of horrible wars in my time, folks, but I tell you this desperate War on Fat is going to be like a terminal Sewer fire in Miami. It is unthinkable. These greasy, blubbery bastards will be huge favorites to conquer and dominate us. The summer book odds are hovering around 9–1 & climbing. The spectre of doom by Fat is right in front of our eyes.

My weird neighbor, Omar, has about 4 percent fat on his body—extremely lean meat, in a word, and more & more likely to activate the body-screecher at any self-respecting International Airport—*Hey man, you're not Fat enough to be boarded on this airplane. I'll kill you with an axe if you come any further.* . . .

Mark Twain would love this story: "Let me get this straight, Boss—are you telling me to Okay fat people and *arrest* the skinny ones? Jesus. Please, Boss, don't make me do this. Fat people are *horrible* to touch. I can't stand it."

And meanwhile the President is poking us day and night to "shrug off yr. sorrows and come out to *run* with me." Run, run, run like a bastard and never look back. . . . Wow. That is very strange thinking, eh? Forget thinking, just JOG and get over it.

I'll bet Tonya Harding said that. She is a sassy little creature, for sure. . . . There is talk that the monumentally lewd O'Farrell Theatre in San Francisco will make her the headliner in their new outdoor *Erotic Boxing* spectacles this summer. Jim Mitchell knows Talent when he sees it. I will be at ringside when Tonya opens against Charlotte Rampling in July. Call Jeff Armstrong for media certification. Mahalo.

(Ralph Steadman)

Welcome to the Fourth Reich

This may be the Generation that will have to face the End of the World.
                    —U.S. President Ronald Reagan, Xmas, 1985

SIMON
Editor
The London *Independent*

Dear Simon,

Millions of people around the world are watching the headlines these days, and most of them are getting the Fear. Good news is out of the question in this brutal year of our Lord 2002. This is the time of the Final Shit Rain, as Nostradamus predicted in 1444 A.D., and anybody who thinks he was kidding should strut out purposefully, like some all-American girl with a head full of Mandrax, and try to get a *job* in this country. . . . Yes sir, little sweetie, just walk right up here and get what's coming to you. Ho ho ho.

There *are* no jobs in America, Simon; the job market collapsed in 2001 A.D., along with the stock market and all ENRON pension funds. *All* markets collapsed about 3 days after George W. Bush moved into the White House. . . . Yeah, it was *that* fast. BOOM, presto, welcome to bombs and poverty. You are about to start paying for the sins of your fathers and forefathers, even if they were innocent.

We are in bad trouble over here, Simon. The deal is going down all over the once-proud U.S.A. We are down to our last cannonball(s). Stand back! Those Pentagon swine are frantic to kick some ass, and many job opportunities are opening up in the Armaments, Surveillance, and New Age Security industries.

Hell, did I forget to mention *those* jobs? How silly of me. There is always a bull market for vengeance and violence in America, and on some days I have been part of it. You bet. In my wild and dangerous youth I wanted to be a dashing jet pilot, a smiling beast who zooms across the sky doing victory rolls and monster sonic booms just over the beach in Laguna. Hot damn, Simon, I could walk on water in those days. I had a license to kill.

I have been a news addict all my life, and I feel pretty comfortable with my addiction. It has been good to me, although not necessarily *for* me, or my overall comfort level. Being a news junkie has taken me down some very queer roads, and into the valley of death a few times—not always for strictly professional reasons, alas—but those things *do* come with the territory, and you want to understand this: It is the key to survival in my business, as it is in many others.

And you definitely want to have a shockproof sense of humor, which is hard to learn in school and even harder to teach. (It is also an irritating phrase to keep putting on paper over and over—so from now on we will use the ancient and honorable word "WA," instead of "Sense of humor." It will smooth out our word-rhythms, and we can move along more briskly.)

Okay. We were talking about the *news*—information or intelligence gleaned from afar, etc., etc.

The news is *bad* today, in America and *for* America. There is *nothing* good or hopeful about it—except for Nazis, warmongers, and rich greedheads—and it is getting worse and worse in logarithmic progressions since the fateful bombing of the World Trade Towers in New York. That will always be a festering lowwatermark in this nation's violent history, but it was not the official birthday of the end of the American Century.

No. That occurred on the night of the presidential election in the year 2000, when the nexus of power in this country shifted from Washington, D.C., to "the ranch" in Crawford, Texas. The most disastrous day in American history was November 7, 2000. That was when the *takeover* happened, when the generals and cops and right-wing Jesus freaks seized control of the White House, the U.S. Treasury, and our Law Enforcement machinery.

So long to all that, eh? "Nothing will ever be the same again," the whorish new President said at the time. "As of now we are in the grip of a National Security Emergency that will last for the rest of our lives."

Fuck you, I quit. Mahalo.

I would never claim to speak for my whole nation, Simon; I am not the Voice of America—but neither am I a vicious machine-gun Nazi warmonger with blood on my hands and hate in my heart for every human being in the world who is not entirely *white*—and, if you wonder why I mention this thuggish characterization, understand that I am only responding to it in this way because my old friend, the weird artist Ralph Steadman, is saying these horrible things about me in England, Wales, and Kent—and directly *to* me, in fact, when we speak on the trans-Atlantic telephone.

"That is bullshit, Ralph," I tell him. "Are you getting senile? Do you know who you are talking to?"

"Of course I do," he replies. "You are the same brutal redneck I've known all my life—except that now you are turning into what you always were from the start—just another murderous American. . . ."

So that is how this thing got jump-started, Simon. And ever since (I think) I talked to you on yr. birthday I have been feverishly writing down my various fears and worries and profoundly angst-ridden visions about our immediate future.

So good luck, Simon. Pls advise me at once in re: yr. space & rates. How about $20,000, eh? I can ramble on for many hours about my recent experience as an American in these days at the end of *our* Century. Or maybe just 1,000 words, or 2,000. Think about it, and R.S.V.P. soonest. Thanx,

HUNTER
May 10, 2002

Amor Vincit Omnia

He not busy being born is busy dying.
—Bob Dylan

The White Helicopter

She flew low over central Paris—the Dream of the Princess in the White Helicopter.

Took lessons for months—*very* difficult; you can't *hire* many people who could fly a chopper in low over downtown Paris and park it in midair above a prison long enough to send a man down a line with an Uzi and come back up . . .

Then put it down on the roof of the prison and carry her lover off on the skid—and then to put the thing down in a nearby parking lot and have everything organized so finely that they disappeared instantly in the waiting car.

Perfect. Nadine, you can have a job with me anytime. This may be a love story. . . .

. . .

There were other things happening in the news last week—mainly politics, but we need a break from that now.

There was, in fact, this truly elegant little tale that came out of Paris, and it was about The Girl in the White Helicopter who rescued her lover from prison. It was one of those fine little love stories that can make you smile in your sleep at night.

The real action last week was in Romance & full-on madness . . .

The wife of French bank robber Michel Vaujour flew low over central Paris in a white helicopter and hovered over the roof of La Santé prison. A man armed with a submachine gun slid down a line to the roof . . . Vaujour, wearing a blue and red warm-up suit, was hidden from guards behind a chimney. He grabbed one of the chopper's landing skids and climbed aboard. The gunman leaped in after him, and the copter whisked them to a nearby soccer field, where all three disappeared . . . Nadine Vaujour, the robber's wife, had been taking copter-flying lessons for many months, French authorities learned later.

Even a dumb brute could fall in love with a story like that. It has the purity of a myth and the power of being simple flat-out true, and it spoke to our highest instincts. It was a perfect crime, done for love, and it was carried out with awesome precision and a truly crazy kind of fearlessness by a beautiful girl in a white helicopter.

There is more to the story, of course. That perfect escape was last May, and the honeymoon lasted all summer. But in the autumn Michel went back to work, and a *New York Times* dispatch out of Paris in late September said he'd been "seriously wounded and captured in a shootout while trying to rob a bank." He had been shot in the head and was lying in a coma at the Pitie-Salpetriere Hospital.

"Officials said Mr. Vaujour's wife, who masterminded the May escape, was arrested Saturday morning at a hideout in southwestern France."

When I read it I felt a chill. All the real love stories end wrong, and I was just about to close the file on this one . . .

"Mrs. Vaujour was already well known to police," said an earlier *Times* item. "She and Mr. Vaujour were married in 1979 while he was in a different jail serving a previous sentence. (He was moved frequently to prevent an escape.) They had a daughter, who was born in jail in September 1981, while Mrs. Vaujour was being held in preventive detention."

I was struck by the almost unholy power and purity of the Vaujours' love for each other, which ran through their lives like a red thread. Above all else, they were lovers, and they honored the word by the terrible intensity they brought to it.

With Juan at Owl Farm, 1997
(Deborah Fuller)

Hey Rube, I Love You

It is Sunday morning now and I am writing a love letter. Outside my kitchen window the sky is bright and planets are colliding. My head is hot and I feel a little edgy. My brain is beginning to act like a V-8 engine with the sparkplug wires crossed. Things are no longer what they seem to be. My telephones are haunted, and animals whisper at me from unseen places.

Last night a huge black cat tried to jump me in the swimming pool, then it suddenly disappeared. I did another lap and noticed three men in green trench coats watching me from behind a faraway door. Whoops, I thought, something weird is happening in this room. Lay low in the water and creep toward the middle of the pool. Stay away from the edges. Don't be strangled from behind. Keep alert. The work of the Devil is never fully revealed until after midnight.

It was right about then that I started thinking about my love letter. The skylights above the pool were steamed up, strange plants were moving in the thick and utter darkness. It was impossible to see from one end of the pool to the other.

I tried to stay quiet and let the water calm down. For a moment I thought I heard another person coming into the pool, but I couldn't be sure. A ripple of terror caused me to drop deeper in the water and assume a karate position. There are only two or three things in the world more terrifying than the sudden realization that you are naked and alone and something large and aggressive is coming close to you in dark water.

It is moments like this that make you want to believe in hallucinations—because if three large men in trench coats actually *were* waiting for me in the shadows behind that door and something else was slithering toward me in the darkness, I was doomed.

Alone? No, I was *not* alone. I understood that. I had already seen three men and a huge black cat, and now I thought I could make out the shape of another person approaching me. She was lower in the water than I was, but I could definitely see it was a woman.

Of course, I thought. It must be my sweetheart, sneaking up to give me a nice surprise in the pool. Yessir, this is just like that twisted little bitch. She is a hopeless romantic and she knows this pool well. We once swam here every night and played in the water like otters.

. . .

Jesus Christ! I thought, what a paranoid fool I've been. I must have been going crazy. A surge of love went through me as I stood up and moved quickly to embrace her. I could already feel her naked body in my arms. . . . Yes, I thought, love does conquer all.

. . .

But not for long. No, it took me a minute or two of thrashing around in the water before I understood that I was, in fact, completely alone in the pool. *She* was not here and neither were those freaks in the corner. And there *was* no cat. I was a fool and a dupe. My brain was seizing up and I felt so weak that I could barely climb out of the pool.

Fuck this, I thought. I can't handle this place anymore. It's destroying my life with its weirdness. Get away and never come back. It had mocked my love and shattered my sense of romance. This horrible experience would get me nominated for *Rube of the Year* in any high school class.

Dawn was coming up as I drove back down the road. There were no comets colliding, no tracks in the snow except mine, and no sounds for 10 miles in any direction except Lyle Lovett on my radio and the howl of a few coyotes. I drove with my knees while I lit up a glass pipe full of hashish.

When I got home I loaded my Smith & Wesson .45 and fired a few bursts at a beer keg in the yard, then I went back inside and started scrawling feverishly in a notebook. . . . What the hell? I thought. Everybody writes love letters on Sunday morning. It is a natural form of worship, a very high art. And on some days I am very good at it.

Today, I felt, was definitely one of those days. You bet. Do it *now*. Just then my phone rang and I jerked it off the hook, but there was nobody on the line. I sagged against the fireplace and moaned, and then it rang again. I grabbed it, but again there was no voice. O God! I thought. Somebody is fucking with me. . . . I needed music, I needed rhythm. I was determined to be calm, so I cranked up the speakers and played "Spirit in the Sky," by Norman Greenbaum.

I played it over and over for the next three or four hours while I hammered out my letter. My heart was Racing and the music was making the peacocks scream. It was Sunday, and I was worshiping in my own way. Nobody needs to be crazy on the Lord's Day.

. . .

My grandmother was never crazy when we went to visit her on Sundays. She always had cookies and tea, and her face was always smiling. That was down in the West End of Louisville, near the Ohio River locks. I remember a narrow concrete driveway and a big gray car in a garage behind the house. The driveway was two concrete strips with clumps of grass growing between them. It led back through the vicious wild rosebushes to what looked like an abandoned shed. Which was true. It *was* abandoned. Nobody walked in that yard, and nobody drove that big gray car. It never moved. There were no tracks in the grass.

It was a LaSalle sedan, as I recall, a slick-looking brute with a powerful straight-eight engine and a floor-mounted gearshift, maybe a 1939 model. We never got it started, because the battery was dead and gasoline was scarce. There was a war on. You had to have special coupons to buy five gallons of gas, and the coupons were tightly rationed. People hoarded and coveted them, but nobody complained, because we were fighting the Nazis and our tanks needed all the gasoline for when they hit the beaches of Normandy.

Looking back on it now, I see clearly that the reason we drove down to the West End to visit my grandmother every other Sunday was to con her out of her gas coupons for the LaSalle. She was an old lady and she didn't need any gasoline. But her car was still registered and she still got her coupons every month.

So what? I would do the same thing myself, if my mother had gasoline and I didn't. We *all* would. It is the Law of Supply and Demand— and this is, after all, the final messy year of the American Century, and people are getting nervous. Hoarders are coming out of the closet, muttering darkly about Y2K and buying cases of Dinty Moore's Beef Stew. Dried figs are popular, along with rice and canned hams. I, personally, am hoarding bullets, many thousands of them. Bullets will always be valuable, especially when yr. lights go out and your phone goes dead and your neighbors start running out of food. That is when you will find out who your friends are. Even close family members will turn on you. After the year 2000, the only people who'll be safe to have as friends will be dead people.

HST, March 1998

. . .

I used to respect William Burroughs because he was the first white man ever busted for marijuana in my time. William was the Man. He was the victim of an illegal police raid at his home at 509 Wagner Street in Old Algiers, a low-rent suburb across the river from New Orleans, where he was settling in for a while to do some shooting and smoke marijuana.

William didn't fuck around. He was serious about everything. When the Deal went down William was There, with a gun. Whacko! *BOOM*. Stand back. I *am* the Law. He was my hero a long time before I ever heard of him.

But he was *Not* the first white man to be busted for weed in my time. No. That was Robert Mitchum, the actor, who was arrested three months earlier in Malibu at the front door of his hideaway beach house for possession of marijuana and suspicion of molesting a teenage girl in 1948. I remember the photos: Mitchum wearing an undershirt & snarling at the cops with the sea rolling up and palm trees blowing.

Yessir, that was my boy. Between Mitchum and Burroughs & Marlon Brando & James Dean & Jack Kerouac, I got myself a serious running start before I was 20 years old, and there was no turning back. Buy the ticket, take the ride.

So welcome to *Thunder Road*, Bubba. It was one of those movies that got a grip on me when I was too young to resist. It convinced me that the only way to drive was at top speed with a car full of whiskey, and I have been driving that way ever since, for good or ill.

The girl in the photos with Mitchum looked about 15 years old & she was also wearing an undershirt, with an elegant little nipple jutting out. The cops were trying to cover her chest with a raincoat as they rushed through the door. Mitchum was also charged with Sodomy and Contributing to the Delinquency of a Minor.

I was having my own troubles with police in those years. We stole cars and drank gin and did a lot of fast driving at night to places like Nashville & Atlanta & Chicago. We needed music on those nights, and it usually came on the radio—on the 50,000-watt clear-channel stations like WWL in New Orleans and WLAC in Nashville.

That is where I went wrong, I guess—listening to WLAC & driving all night across Tennessee in a stolen car that wouldn't be reported for three days. That is how I got introduced to the Howlin' Wolf. We didn't know him, but we liked him & we knew what he was talking about. "I Smell a Rat" is a pure rock & roll monument to the axiom that says "There is no such thing as Paranoia." The Wolf could kick out the jams, but he had a melancholy side to him. He could tear your heart out like the worst kind of honky-tonk. If history judges a man by his heroes, like they say, then let the record show that Howlin' Wolf was one of mine. He was a monster.

Music has always been a matter of energy to me, a question of Fuel. Sentimental people call it Inspiration, but what they really mean is Fuel.

I have always needed fuel. I am a serious consumer. On some nights I still believe that a car with the gas needle on empty can run about fifty more miles if you have the right music very loud on the radio. A new high-end Cadillac will go ten or fifteen miles faster if you give it a full dose of "Carmelita." This has been proven many times. That is why you see so many Cadillacs parked in front of truck stops on Highway 66 around midnight. These are Speed Pimps, and they are loading up on more than gasoline. You watch one of these places for a while & you see a pattern: A big fast car pulls up in front of the doors and a wild-looking girl gets out, stark naked except for a fur coat or a ski parka, and she runs into the place with a handful of money, half-crazy to buy some flat-out guaranteed driving music.

It happens over & over, and sooner or later you get hooked on it, you get addicted. Every time I hear "White Rabbit" I am back on the greasy midnight streets of San Francisco, looking for music, riding a fast red motorcycle downhill into The Presidio, leaning desperately into the curves through the eucalyptus trees, trying to get to the Matrix in time to hear Grace Slick play the flute.

There was no piped-in music on those nights, no headphones or Walkmans or even a plastic windscreen to keep off the rain. But I could hear the music anyway, even when it was five miles away. Once you heard the music done right, you could pack it into yr. brain & take it anywhere, forever.

Yessir. That is my wisdom and that is my song. It is Sunday and I am making new rules for myself. I will open my heart to spirits and pay more attention to animals. I will take some harp music and drive down to the Texaco station, where I can get a pork taco and read a

New York Times. After that, I will walk across the street to the Post Office and slip my letter into her mailbox.

. . .

KNOW YOUR DOPE FIEND. YOUR LIFE MAY DEPEND ON IT! You will not be able to see his eyes because of Tea-Shades, but his knuckles will be white from inner tension and his pants will be crusted with semen from constantly jacking off when he can't find a rape victim. He will stagger and babble when questioned. He will not respect your badge. The Dope Fiend fears nothing. He will attack, for no reason, with every weapon at his command—including yours. BEWARE. Any officer apprehending a suspected marijuana addict should use all necessary force immediately. One stitch in time (on him) will usually save nine on you. Good luck.

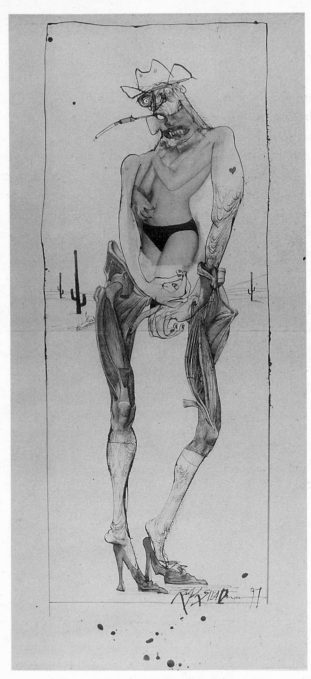

(Ralph Steadman)

Fear and Loathing at the Taco Stand

Going to Hollywood is a dangerous high-pressure gig for most people, under any circumstances. It is like pumping hot steam into thousands of different-size boilers. The laws of physics mandate that some will explode before others—although all of them will explode sooner or later unless somebody cuts off the steam.

I love steam myself, and I have learned to survive under savage and unnatural pressures. I am a steam freak. Hollywood is chicken feed to me. I can take it or leave it. I have been here before, many times. On some days it seems like I have lived at the Château Marmont for half my life. There is blood on these walls, and some of it is mine. Last night I sliced off the tips of two fingers and bled so profusely in the elevator that they had to take it out of service.

But nobody complained. I am not just liked at the Château, I am well liked. I have important people thrown out or blacklisted on a whim. Nobody from the Schwarzenegger organization, for instance, can even get a drink at the Château. They are verboten. There is a ghastly political factor in doing any business with Hollywood. You can't get by without five or six personal staff people—and at least one personal astrologer.

I have always hated astrologers, and I like to have sport with them. They are harmless quacks in the main, but some of them get ambitious and turn predatory, especially in Hollywood. In Venice Beach I ran into a man who claimed to be Johnny Depp's astrologer. "I consult with him constantly," he told me. "We are never far away. I have many famous clients." He produced a yellow business card and gave it to me. "I can do things for you," he said. "I am a player."

I took his card and examined it carefully for a moment, as if I couldn't quite read the small print. But I knew he was lying, so I leaned toward him and slapped him sharply in the nuts. Not hard, but very quickly, using the back of my hand and my fingers like a bullwhip, yet very discreetly.

He let out a hiss and went limp, unable to speak or breathe. I smiled casually and kept on talking to him as if nothing had happened. "You filthy little creep," I said to him. "I *am* Johnny Depp!"

Outside on the boulevard I saw a half-naked girl on roller skates being mauled by two dogs. They were Great Danes, apparently running loose. Both had their paws on her shoulder, and the gray one had her head in its mouth. But there was no noise, and nobody seemed to notice.

I grabbed a fork off the bar and rushed outside to help her, giving the bogus astrologer another slap in the nuts on my way out. When I got to the street, the dogs were still mauling the girl. I stabbed the big one in the ribs with my fork, which sank deep into the tissue. The beast yelped crazily and ran off with its tail between its legs. The other one quickly released its grip on the girl's head and snarled at me. I slashed at it with the fork, and that was enough for the brute. It backed off and slunk away toward Muscle Beach.

I took the girl back to the Buffalo Club and applied aloe to her wounds. The astrologer was gone, and we had the lounge to ourselves. Her name was Anita, she said, and she had just arrived in L.A. to seek work as a dancer. It was the third time in ten days she'd been attacked by wild dogs on the Venice boardwalk, and she was ready to quit L.A., and so was I. The pace was getting to me. I was not bored, and I still had work to do, but it was definitely time to get out of town. I had to be in Big Sur in three days, and then to a medical conference in Pebble Beach. She was a very pretty girl, with elegant legs and a wicked kind of intelligence about her, but she was also very naïve about Hollywood. I saw at once that she would be extremely helpful on my trip north.

I listened to her for a while, then I offered her a job as my assistant, which I badly needed. She accepted, and we drove back to the Château in Depp's Porsche. As we pulled up the ramp to the underground garage, the attendants backed off and signaled me in. Depp's henchmen had left word that nobody could touch the car except me. I parked it expertly, barely missing a red BMW 840Ci, and we went up the elevator to my suite.

I reached for my checkbook, but it was missing, so I used one of Depp's that I'd found in the glove compartment of his car. I wrote her a healthy advance and signed Depp's name to it. "What the hell?" I said to her. "He's running around out there with my checkbook right now, probably racking up all kinds of bills."

That was the tone of my workdays in Hollywood: violence, joy, and constant Mexican music. At one club I played the bass recorder for several hours with the band. We spent a lot of time drinking gin and lemonade on the balcony, entertaining movie people and the ever-present scribe from *Rolling Stone* magazine . . .

You bet, Bubba, I was taking care of business. It was like the Too Much Fun Club. I had the Cadillac and a green Mustang in the garage, in addition to the Carrera 4 Porsche, but we could only drive one of them up the coast. It was an uptown problem.

Finally it got to be too much, so we loaded up the Northstar Cadillac and fled. Why not? I thought. The girl had proved to be a tremendous help, and besides, I was beginning to like her.

. . .

The sun was going down as we left Malibu and headed north on 101, running smoothly through Oxnard and along the ocean to Santa Barbara. My companion was a little nervous about my speed, so I gave her some gin to calm her down. Soon she relaxed against me, and I put my arm around her. Rosanne Cash was on the radio, singing about the seven-year ache, and the traffic was opening up.

As we approached the Lompoc exit, I mentioned that Lompoc was the site of a federal penitentiary and I once had some friends over there.

"Oh?" she said. "Who were they?"

"Prisoners," I said. "Nothing serious. That's where Ed was."

She stiffened and moved away from me, but I turned up the music and we settled back to drive and watch the moon come up. What the hell? I thought. Just another young couple on the road to the American Dream.

Things started to get weird when I noticed Pismo Beach coming up. I was on the cell phone with Benicio Del Toro, the famous Puerto Rican actor, telling him about the time I was violently jailed in Pismo Beach and how it was making me nervous to even pass a road sign with that name on it. "Yeah," I was saying, "it was horrible. They beat me on the back of my legs. It was a case of mistaken identity." I smiled at my assistant, not wanting to alarm her, but I saw that she was going into a fetal crouch and her fingers were clutching the straps of her seat belt.

Just then we passed two police cars parked on the side of the road, and I saw that we were going a hundred and three.

"Slow down!" Anita was screaming. "Slow down! We'll be arrested. I can't stand it!" She was sobbing and clawing at the air.

"Nonsense," I said. "Those were not police. My radar didn't go off." I reached over to pat her on the arm, but she bit me and I had to pull over. The only exit led to a dangerous-looking section of Pismo Beach, but I took it anyway.

. . .

It was just about midnight when we parked under the streetlight in front of the empty Mexican place on Main Street. Anita was having a nervous breakdown. There was too much talk about jails and police and prisons, she said. She felt like she was already in chains.

I left the car in a crosswalk and hurried inside to get a taco. The girl behind the register warned me to get my car off the street because the police were about to swoop down on the gang of thugs milling around in front of the taco place. "They just had a fight with the cops," she said. "Now I'm afraid somebody is going to get killed."

We were parked right behind the doomed mob, so I hurried out to roust Anita and move the car to safety. Then we went back inside very gently and sat down in a booth at the rear of the room. I put my arm around Anita and tried to calm her down. She wanted gin, and luckily I still had a pint flask full of it in my fleece-lined jacket pocket. She drank greedily, then fell back in the booth and grinned. "Well, so much for that," she chirped. "I guess I really went crazy, didn't I?"

"Yes," I said. "You were out of control. It was like dealing with a vampire."

She smiled and grasped my thigh. "I am a vampire," she said. "We have many a mile to go before we sleep. I am hungry."

"Indeed," I said. "We will have to fill up on tacos before we go any farther. I too am extremely hungry."

Just then the waitress arrived to take our order. The mob of young Chicanos outside had disappeared very suddenly, roaring off into the night in a brace of white pickup trucks. They were a good-natured bunch, mainly teenagers with huge shoulders wearing Dallas Cowboys jerseys and heads like half-shaved coconuts. They were not afraid of the cops, but they left anyway.

The waitress was hugely relieved. "Thank God," she said. "Now

Manuel can live one more night. I was afraid they would kill him. We have only been married three weeks." She began sobbing, and I could see she was about to crack. I introduced myself as Johnny Depp, but I saw the name meant nothing to her. Her name was Maria. She was seventeen years old and had lied about her age to get the job. She was the manager and Manuel was the cook. He was almost twenty-one. Every night strange men hovered around the taco stand and mumbled about killing him.

Maria sat down in the booth between us, and we both put our arms around her. She shuddered and collapsed against Anita, kissing her gently on the cheek. "Don't worry," I said. "Nobody is going to be killed tonight. This is the night of the full moon. Some people will die tonight, but not us. I am protected."

Which was true. I am a Triple Moon Child, and tonight was the Hunter's Moon. I pulled the waitress closer to me and spoke soothingly. "You have nothing to fear, little one," I told her. "No power on Earth can harm me tonight. I walk with the King."

She smiled and kissed me gratefully on the wrist. Manuel stared balefully at us from his perch in the kitchen, saying nothing. "Rest easy," I called out to him. "Nobody is going to kill you tonight."

"Stop saying that!" Anita snapped, as Manuel sank further into himself. "Can't you see he's afraid?" Maria began crying again, but I jerked her to her feet. "Get a grip on yourself," I said sharply. "We need more beer and some pork tacos to go. I have to drive the whole coast tonight."

"That's right," said my companion. "We're on a honeymoon trip. We're in a hurry." She laughed and reached for my wallet. "Come on, big boy," she cooed. "Don't try to cheat. Just give it to me."

"Watch yourself," I snarled, slapping her hand away from my pocket. "You've been acting weird ever since we left L.A. We'll be in serious trouble if you go sideways on me again."

She grinned and stretched her arms lazily above her head, poking her elegant little breasts up in the air at me like some memory from an old Marilyn Monroe calendar and rolling her palms in the air.

"Sideways?" she said. "What difference does it make? Let's get out of here. We're late."

I paid the bill quickly and watched Maria disappear into the kitchen. Manuel was nowhere in sight. Just as I stepped into the street,

I noticed two police cars coming at us from different directions. Then another one slowed down right in front of the taco stand.

"Don't worry," I said to Anita. "They're not looking for us."

I seized her by the leg and rushed her into the Cadillac. There was a lot of yelling as we pulled away through the circling traffic and back out onto Highway 101.

My mind was very much on my work as we sped north along the coast to Big Sur. We were into open country now, running straight up the coast about a mile from the ocean on a two-lane blacktop road across the dunes with no clouds in the sky and a full moon blazing down on the Pacific. It was a perfect night to be driving a fast car on an empty road along the edge of the ocean with a half-mad beautiful woman asleep on the white leather seats and Lyle Lovett crooning doggerel about screwheads who go out to sea with shotguns and ponies in small rowboats just to get some kind of warped revenge on a white man with bad habits who was only trying to do them a favor in the first place.

. . .

I lost control of the Cadillac about halfway down the slope. The road was slick with pine needles, and the eucalyptus trees were getting closer together. The girl laughed as I tried to aim the car through the darkness with huge tree trunks looming up in the headlights and the bright white moon on the ocean out in front of us. It was like driving on ice, going straight toward the abyss.

We shot past a darkened house and past a parked Jeep, then crashed into a waterfall high above the sea. I got out of the car and sat down on a rock, then lit up the marijuana pipe. "Well," I said to Anita, "this is it. We must have taken a wrong turn."

She laughed and sucked on some moss. Then she sat down across from me on a log. "You're funny," she said. "You're very strange—and you don't know why, do you?"

I shook my head softly and drank some gin.

"No," I said. "I'm stupid."

"It's because you have the soul of a teenage girl in the body of an elderly dope fiend," she whispered. "That is why you have problems." She patted me on the knee. "Yes. That is why people giggle with fear every time you come into a room. That is why you rescued me from those dogs in Venice."

I stared out to sea and said nothing for a while. But somehow I knew she was right. Yes sir, I said slowly to myself, I have the soul of a teenage girl in the body of an elderly dope fiend. No wonder they can't understand me.

This is a hard dollar, on most days, and not many people can stand it.

Indeed. If the greatest mania of all is passion: and if I am a natural slave to passion: and if the balance between my brain and my soul and my body is as wild and delicate as the skin of a Ming vase—

Well, that explains a lot of things, doesn't it? We need look no further. Yes sir, and people wonder why I seem to look at them strangely. Or why my personal etiquette often seems makeshift and contradictory, even clinically insane . . . Hell, I don't miss those whispers, those soft groans of fear when I enter a civilized room. I know what they're thinking, and I know exactly why. They are extremely uncomfortable with the idea that I am a teenage girl trapped in the body of a sixty-five-year-old career criminal who has already died sixteen times. Sixteen, all documented. I have been crushed and beaten and shocked and drowned and poisoned and stabbed and shot and smothered and set on fire by my own bombs. . . .

All these things have happened, and probably they will happen again. I have learned a few tricks along the way, a few random skills and simple avoidance techniques—but mainly it has been luck, I think, and a keen attention to karma, along with my natural girlish charm.

Kingdom of Fear
Honor Roll

Oscar Acosta
Jeff Armstrong
Lisl Auman
Terri Bartelstein
Ed Bastian
Sean Bell-Thomson
Porter Bibb
Earl Biss
Patricia Blanchet
Bob Bone
Ed Bradley
Bob Braudis
Louisa Joe
Doug Brinkley
Judge Charles Buss
Sue Carolan
Jimmy Carter
Marilyn Chambers
Tim Charles
Bobby Colgan
John Clancey
Dalai Lama
Morris Dees
Benicio Del Toro
Kenny Demmick

Judge J. E. DeVilbiss
Robert Draper
Bob Dylan
Joe Edwards
Jeanette Etheridge
Colonel William S. Evans
Tim Ferris
Jennifer Geiger
Gerald Goldstein
William Greider
Stacey Hadash
Hal Haddon
David Halberstam
Paul Hornung
Abe Hutt
Walter Isaacson
Loren Jenkins
Juan, Jennifer, & Willy
Bill Kennedy
Ken Kesey
Maria Khan
Jerry Lefcourt
Lyle Lovett
Semmes Luckett
Jade Markus

David Matthews-Price
David McCumber
Terry McDonell
Gene McGarr
George McGovern
William McKeen
Michael Mesnick
Nicole Meyer
Jim Mitchell
Tim Mooney
Lou Ann Murphy
Laila Nabulsi
Lynn Nesbit
Jack Nicholson
Paul Oakenfold
Lionel Olay
Heidi Opheim
P.J. O'Rourke
Gail Palmer
Nicola Pecorini
Sean Penn
George Plimpton
Charlotte Rampling
Duke Rice
Keith Richards
Curtis Robinson
David Robinson
Terry Sabonis-Chafee

Shelby Sadler
Paul Semonin
Lauren Simonetti
Kevin Simonson
Madeleine Sloan
Harvey Sloane
Bill Smith
Michael Solheim
Ralph Steadman
Judy Stellings
Michael Stepanian
Geoffrey Stokes
George & Patti Stranahan
Richard Stratton
Jay Stuart
Davison Thompson
Sandy Thompson
Virginia & Jack Thompson
George Tobia
Oliver Treibick
Gerald "Ching" Tyrrell
John Walsh
Floyd Watkins
Curtis Wilkie
Andrew Wylie
Tony Yerkovich
Warren Zevon